BASEBALL PROSPECTUS 2023

The Essential Guide to the 2023 Season

Edited by Ben Carsley, Robert O'Connell and Ginny Searle

Michael Ajeto, Maitreyi Anantharaman, Lucas Apostoleris, Darius Austin, Michael Baumann, Demetrius Bell, Grant Brisbee, Russell A. Carleton, Ben Carsley, Alex Chamberlain, Justin Choi, Michael Clair, Zach Crizer, Patrick Dubuque, Daniel R. Epstein, Noah Frank, Ken Funck, Megan Gailey, Mike Gianella, Steven Goldman, Craig Goldstein, Nathan Graham, Bryan Grosnick, Jon Hegglund, Tim Jackson, Sarah James, Jonathan Judge, Justin Klugh, Kennedi Landry, Rob Mains, Tim Marchman, Allison McCague, Whitney McIntosh, Kelsey McKinney, Sam Miller, Dan Moore, Leo Morgenstern, Blake Murphy, Santul Nerkar, Marc Normandin, Dustin Nosler, Robert O'Connell, Robert Orr, Jeffrey Paternostro, Kate Preusser, Jeff Quinton, Tommy Rancel, David Roth, Shaker Samman, Ginny Searle, Jarrett Seidler, Ben Spanier, Alex Speier, Tyler Stafford, Matt Sussman, Jon Tayler, Lauren Theisen, Ted Walker, Eli Walsh, Collin Whitchurch, Tony Wolfe

Craig Brown, Patrick Dubuque, Craig Goldstein and Andrew Mearns, Associate Editors
Robert Au, Harry Pavlidis and Amy Pircher, Statistics Editors

Library of Congress Cataloging-in-Publication Data:
paperback
ISBN-10: 195071697X
ISBN-13: 978-1950716975

Project Credits
Cover Design: Ginny Searle
Interior Design and Production: Amy Pircher, Robert Au
Layout: Amy Pircher, Robert Au

Cover Photos
Front Cover: Julio Rodríguez. © Lindsey Wasson-USA TODAY Sports

Baseball icon courtesy of Uberux, from https://www.shareicon.net/author/uberux

Manufactured in the United States of America
10 9 8 7 6 5 4 3 2 1

Table of Contents

Foreword

by Tony Clark

If you're reading this 28th edition of Baseball Prospectus, you are in all likelihood not a casual fan. You're immersed in the game we love, revel in its intricacies and are fascinated by the strategy and nuances that make baseball a thinking person's game.

This might come as a surprise, but you have a lot of company in clubhouses across the major and minor leagues.

Players are fans at their core because so many of them grew up emulating their favorite icons on Little League fields and in neighborhood pickup games. They've spent a lifetime honing their skills and preparing for that life-altering call to "The Show." And when it comes, they do their best to navigate the competition, the injuries, the grind of a 162-game season and the constant scrutiny that comes with performing at the highest level.

Players are passionate about baseball's long-term direction and the way the game is played because they spend so much time striving and sacrificing to reach the highest level—and stay there. They accept and embrace their role as caretakers of the game, because they want baseball to be the best version of itself for this and future generations.

In fact, today's Players are as engaged and involved as they have ever been, working in unity to leave the game better for the next generation of Players and fans. Just in the past year, they withstood an unprecedented 99-day lockout by owners and yet were able to make significant improvements in support of their objectives in collective bargaining. They opened satellite offices in both Arizona and the Dominican Republic designed to build on Player involvement and engagement and providing programming to support the active and inactive Player Fraternity. In a historic and legacy-building move, they organized minor-league Players, welcoming about 5,500 new members into their union. They committed to and realized historic gains and improvements within their Group Licensing Program, while also deciding to join the AFL-CIO, where they can become a more powerful voice for all unionized workers.

Now, more than ever, an emotional and intellectual tug-of-war is playing out between the influx of information and its balance with, and against, the "human" element of the game. The debate can be polarizing, exhausting at times and too long on social media "hot takes" that lack context. But intelligent and thoughtful discourse is beneficial to us all because it spurs conversation and a level of interest that allows baseball to flourish, grow and resonate with a new generation of fans.

In recent years, there has been no better source of thoughtful discourse than Baseball Prospectus, which has become a leader in its efforts to capture the human side of our game as well as the analytical by examining baseball from every conceivable angle.

Despite being someone who has played the game since childhood and was blessed to play 15 years and more than 1,500 games in the majors, I never assume I have seen it all or experienced everything our game has to offer. I'll never lose the sense of wonder that I felt growing up in San Diego and watching Tony Gwynn shooting balls through the 5.5 hole at Jack Murphy Stadium, or the sense of awe I felt as a young Player in Detroit sharing a clubhouse with Cecil Fielder, Alan Trammell, Lou Whitaker and other veterans who would have such an indelible impact on my career.

I remain a fan at heart, and I share the sense of passion and curiosity that the talented contributors display in this BP annual and on their thought-provoking website every day. Their efforts help educate and enlighten us and remind us that baseball is special because it touches our imaginations and provides a new surprise around every corner.

We've gleaned an abundance of insight from their extraordinary research and analysis. As you know, during the last round of bargaining, the Players Association proposed and eventually agreed to co-create with Major League Baseball our own version of WAR as a fair way to reward pre-arbitration Players who produce exceptional on-field value for their clubs. After decades of increasingly sophisticated analysis, we've all come to realize that what we really have is a number of tools to help us appreciate what happens on the field, and even perhaps why.

As front offices across the league increasingly employ teams of analysts (many of whom began their careers with this publication) to help with Player development and evaluate on-field performance, baseball continues to try and strike a balance between entertainment and efficiency. There have been plenty of examples of clubs trying to quantify Players' values with tidy, algorithm-based figures. At the same time, and has always been the case, we can find numerous examples of Players using analytics to refine a pitch, alter their approach at the plate and find a way to elevate their games. While the reams of empirical data can be daunting, they can also be synthesized to help a Player on both sides of the ball.

In the big picture, we need to be cautious about the ways we use all of this new information. We don't want to see our games orchestrated by executives in a luxury suite, moving Players around the field like pieces in a board game. In-game overreliance on advanced metrics shouldn't detract from or inhibit the unbridled joy, instinct and athleticism of Players competing on the field. After all, exciting performances by elite athletes are the very reason fans come to the ballpark, watch on television or stream games and highlights on their mobile devices.

As we join together in anticipation of the 2023 season, I want to emphasize how much our fraternity of Players is and always will be protective of baseball. Players love and live the game. We practice it. We study it. We often devote our lives to it. And as custodians of the game, we love that the writers and readers of Baseball Prospectus share our passion for baseball and marvel at their skill, commitment and level of engagement. We may not always agree with every conclusion drawn, but we recognize and applaud the value they provide. ■

—Tony Clark, MLBPA Executive Director

Statistical Introduction

by Bryan Grosnick

The history of baseball is a history of numbers. What started on the scoreboard moved through the advent of the box score, to the backs of baseball cards, to *Moneyball* and well beyond. Statistics have long helped so many people better understand the history, the personalities and the stories of baseball in so many ways. While the study of statistics is not the only way to enjoy America's pastime, it is one of the central ways that we here at Baseball Prospectus have engaged with baseball and shared our love of the game over 26 editions of this very Annual and nearly 30 years online.

This section of the book is designed to help you get familiar with some of the metrics that we think help tell the story of baseball. Our hope is that these give you a new way to engage with the game we all care so much about, or at least give you something else to think about or discuss during your next conversation. *"Who's better, Carlos Correa or Corey Seager?" "How many games do you think the Rays will win next season?" "Why is Jacob deGrom so good?"* Our statistics might help you think differently about these questions, or a million others.

This section is intended as a high-level overview but, as always, if you have any questions about how a metric is developed, what it's trying to measure, or what an acronym stands for, stop by the Baseball Prospectus website and check out our Glossary, search for an article or engage directly with our team. Our goal is to share our love of the game—and its statistics—with you.

Offense

If you're interested in learning how good a hitter was in a given year, or over their career, start with our proprietary metric Deserved Runs Created Plus (**DRC+**). Built by Jonathan Judge in concert with our stats team, this metric measures everything that a hitter can do at the dish. Not only does this measure whether the player got a hit, reached base via some other means, or made an out, it also integrates hitting for power and moving runners over. It's also scaled so that **a DRC+ of 100 is roughly equivalent to league-average performance.** In short, a DRC+ of 150 is outstanding, a DRC+ of 100 is average, and a DRC+ of 75 means that you're probably not an everyday player, no matter how fantastic your defense is.

What makes DRC+ special is how it accounts not just for the events that take place (hits, strikeouts, homers, etc.), but how it takes *context* into account. The model behind DRC+ adjusts for how the ballpark affects play, the skill of the opposing pitcher, temperature, and other factors. Not only does it tell us how successful a player was, it has traditionally also done a better job of predicting how that same player *will do in the future* than other batting statistics. (We'll talk more about predicting the future later.)

DRC+ does not account for baserunning, so we use Baserunning Runs (**BRR**) to give runners credit for what they do between the bags. That certainly includes the value gained or lost during an attempted stolen base, but also includes things like going first to third on a single or advancing on an outfield fly.

Defense

Our traditional defensive metric has been Fielding Runs Above Average (**FRAA**), which measured the positive or negative value offered by a player's actions in run prevention. Defining defensive value is trickier than offensive value; instead of the relatively straightforward, one-on-one, batter-versus-pitcher dynamic, fielding can involve a lot more subjectivity depending on how balls are hit, fielder positioning and plenty of other factors. Many "advanced" defensive metrics are based at least in part on "zone" data: stringers record batted ball type and estimated landing location, and this data is fed into models that generate expected outs compared to actual outs.

Beginning with the 2023 season, we will be moving to a new defensive system we call Deserved Runs Prevented (**DRP**). The largest component of DRP, as with any defensive system, is a fielder's so-called "range outs," or outs made on balls put into play and fielded by the player. Our new measurement of a fielder's range contributions on batted balls will be called "Range Defense Added," and if you want to know more about its philosophy, you are in luck, as Jonathan Judge has written an overview of the new system at the front of this Annual. An even-more-detailed description of the methodology and process will appear on BaseballProspectus.com ahead of the 2023 season.

The toughest and most critical defensive position on the field requires a different methodology than the one we've just outlined. Catchers not only have to "field their position" like everyone else on the diamond, they also have to prevent pitches from sailing through to the backstop, baserunners from stealing and "frame" pitches to make them more (or less) likely to be called strikes.

This last part, typically called "pitch framing" or "presentation," is the trickiest to quantify and one of the major sabermetric innovations of the last dozen years. Our multilevel-model approach takes pitch-tracking data (for the seasons that data exists) and adjusts for factors including pitcher, umpire, batter and home-field advantage. That gives us a number of strikes that the catcher is adding to a pitcher's performance, which we convert to runs added or lost using linear weights.

These framing runs have a significant effect on a catcher's overall defensive value (though a bit less this year than in some previous years, as framing skill appears to have improved across the game, as has the resistance of umpires to framing). When they are combined with the runs added or lost from pitch blocking, stolen base prevention, and fielding balls in play, we get our final DRP number for catchers.

Pitching

Here at Baseball Prospectus, we do our best to separate the effects of pitching from the effects of other participants, in order to better isolate each pitcher's contribution to run prevention. As a community, we've come a long way from the initial sabermetric theory that pitchers have little control over balls in play, and we've created a detailed "defense-independent" pitching metric that also includes some measure of how pitchers influence balls in play.

Deserved Run Average (**DRA**) is our core pitching metric that evaluates a pitcher's performance in a way that *looks a lot like earned run average (ERA), but is actually very different under the hood.* For starters, DRA is set to the scale of runs allowed per nine innings (RA9), instead of *earned* runs, so DRA numbers tend to be a touch higher than what you'd normally expect from ERA.

When creating DRA, we start with an event-by-event look at everything the pitcher does on the mound, and then we adjust the value of each event based on environmental factors including park, batter, catcher, home-field advantage, pitcher role and temperature. We use a multilevel-model approach including all these factors that is similar to our DRC+ and deserved baserunning models (which include the pitcher's effect on stolen bases and passed balls/wild pitches) in order to get our final DRA number.

In addition to the DRA number (that looks a lot like ERA), we also produce **DRA-**, which is very similar to our DRC+ number for hitters. It is a simple way to compare performance to "average," with a DRA- of 100 indicating middle-of-the-road performance. Since we're used to pitcher statistics like ERA for which lower numbers are better, good performance is represented as lower than 100; a DRA- of 75 tells you that a pitcher is about 25% better than league-average. On the other side, a DRA- of 150 tells you that things are going very, very poorly for the pitcher in question.

Projections

For those of you who wish to go beyond what a player *did* and want to explore what they *will do*, we have our **PECOTA** projections. These days, PECOTA bears very little resemblance to the original product created by Nate Silver in the early 2000s, uses none of Silver's spreadsheets or code, nor any of Clay Davenport's venerable translations. Today, using a completely new system, PECOTA builds a 10-year forecast of a player's projected future performance based on that player's past, the tendencies of professional ballplayers in the major, minor, and overseas leagues, and factors like the effects of age and the parks where players take the field.

PECOTA is unique among public projection systems because it provides a probability distribution in addition to a point estimate for each player. The point estimate you see in this book is the median forecast, but, on our website, we publish a much more detailed range of possible outcomes. Please keep in mind that all forecasts have uncertainty, and our goal with PECOTA, beyond simple accuracy, is to make clear both how uncertain our forecasts are, as well as what the rest of that probability distribution can look like.

Now that the basics are out of the way, it's time to break down everything we're including in the book this year.

Team Prospectus

The heart of this book is the team chapter; you'll find one for each of the 30 major-league franchises ... rest assured that we did not forget the Cardinals this year. The first page of each chapter includes a box that includes a stadium diagram as well as key statistics for the team in question. (On this page, you can see an example for the Los Angeles Angels.)

Beneath the team name, you'll find the team's 2022 win-loss record and its divisional standing. Then it's on to 12 important statistics that give you a picture of how the team performed, holistically, over the course of the previous season. Each of those statistics gives you the value for the team, as well as the ordinal ranking among the 30 MLB teams (with 1st always "best" and 30th "worst").

Pythag (short for "Pythagenpat") is an adjusted version of the team's 2022 winning percentage calculated based on runs scored per game (**RS/G**) and runs allowed per game (**RA/G**). Those numbers are run through a version of Bill James' Pythagorean formula that has been refined and improved by David Smyth and Brandon Heipp. We also include Deserved Winning Percentage (**dWin%**), which uses the frameworks that underpin DRC+ and DRA (along with depth charts) to estimate team runs scored and allowed in 2021 as the inputs for the same Pythagenpat formula used above. Then we have **Payroll**, which is the combined salary of all of the team's on-field players, as well as Marginal Dollars per Marginal Win

(**M$/MW**). The latter metric, developed by Doug Pappas, tells us how much money the team spent for each win above the replacement level.

In the right-hand column, we start with Defensive Efficiency Rating (**DER**), which indicates the percentage of balls in play converted to outs for the team and serves as a quick shorthand for team fielding skill. Then there's **DRC+** to indicate the overall offensive ability of the team as compared to league-average, and **DRA-** to indicate the overall pitching ability of the team, as well. Beneath DRA- is another pitching metric: Fielding Independent Pitching (**FIP**), which resembles ERA but is based only on strikeouts, walks and home runs recorded by the team's pitchers. Finally, we have **B-Age** to tell us the average age of a team's batters (weighted by plate appearances), and **P-Age** to do the same for the team's pitchers (weighted by innings pitched), with the corresponding rankings going from youngest (1st) to oldest (30th).

After the stats, we focus on the home ballpark for each franchise. First, there's a lovely diagram of the park's dimensions including distances to the outfield wall. After a couple of bullet points about the playing surface and history of the park, there's a graphic that indicates the height of the wall from left field pole to right field pole. Then we offer a table with the single-season park factors for the stadium. Like DRC+ and DRA-, these factors are displayed as indexes: 100 is average, 110 means that the park inflates the relevant statistic by 10%, and 90 means that the park deflates the relevant statistic by 10%. On this table, we show **Runs** (runs scored), **Runs/RH** (runs produced by right-handed hitters), **Runs/LH** (runs produced by left-handed hitters), **HR/RH** (home runs by right-handed hitters) and **HR/LH** (home runs by left-handed hitters).

Lastly, we indicate the team's top hitter and pitcher by our Wins Above Replacement Player (**WARP**) metric (which we'll explain a little later in this section), as well as the player we've identified as the team's top prospect.

The second page of each team chapter features three graphs. **Payroll History** compares the team payroll to MLB average and the average for the team's division over time.

Graph number two is **Future Commitments** and displays the team's future payroll outlays, if any exist. Due in part to the time of printing of this book, these figures (current as of January 1, 2023) will ultimately change before Opening Day. (Check Baseball Prospectus' Cot's Baseball Contracts page for the most current data.)

Farm System Ranking, the third and final graph, shows how the Baseball Prospectus prospect team has ranked this organization's farm system each year, going back 10 years.

After that, we have a **Personnel** section that lists some of the important decision-makers and upper-level field or operations staff members for the franchise. We also like to share the names of any former Baseball Prospectus staff members who are currently part of the organization, and occasionally someone shows up on both of those lists!

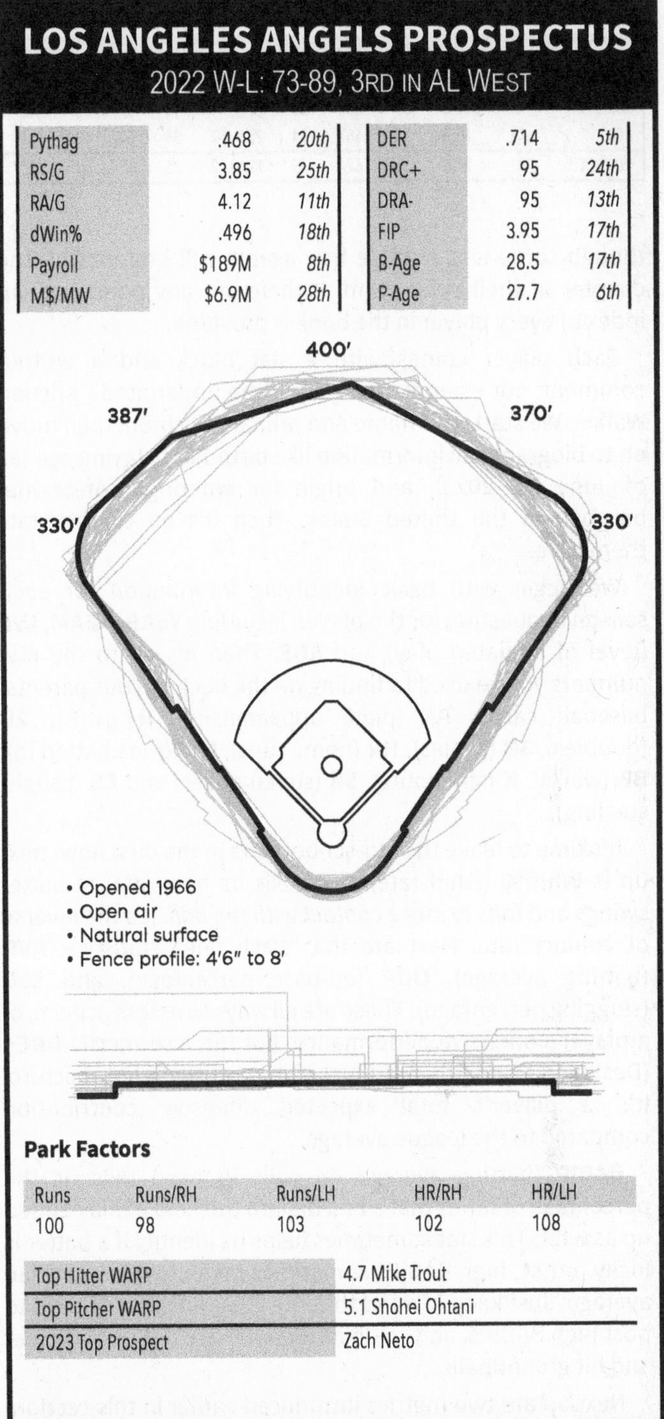

LOS ANGELES ANGELS PROSPECTUS

2022 W-L: 73-89, 3RD IN AL WEST

Pythag	.468	20th	DER	.714	5th
RS/G	3.85	25th	DRC+	95	24th
RA/G	4.12	11th	DRA-	95	13th
dWin%	.496	18th	FIP	3.95	17th
Payroll	$189M	8th	B-Age	28.5	17th
M$/MW	$6.9M	28th	P-Age	27.7	6th

- Opened 1966
- Open air
- Natural surface
- Fence profile: 4'6" to 8'

Park Factors

Runs	Runs/RH	Runs/LH	HR/RH	HR/LH
100	98	103	102	108

Top Hitter WARP	4.7 Mike Trout
Top Pitcher WARP	5.1 Shohei Ohtani
2023 Top Prospect	Zach Neto

Position Players

After all the franchise-centric information and a carefully crafted essay on the team, it's time for the player comments. (The player comments come with a byline or two, but that's a rough guide; due to player movement, each comment is not guaranteed to match the franchise byline.)

Players are listed with the franchise that employed them in early January 2023. If the player changed teams after early January, you'll likely find them in the chapter for their previous squad. We include a free agent chapter for notable free agents who were unsigned as of press time for the book,

Christian Walker 1B Born: 03/28/91 Age: 32 Bats: R Throws: R Height: 6'0" Weight: 208 lb. Origin: Round 4, 2012 Draft (#132 overall)

YEAR	TEAM	LVL	AGE	PA	R	2B	3B	HR	RBI	BB	K	SB	CS	Whiff%	AVG/OBP/SLG	DRC+	BABIP	BRR	DRP	WARP
2020	AZ	MLB	29	243	35	18	1	7	34	19	50	1	1	27.1%	.271/.333/.459	101	.317	0.7	1B(43): 0	0.6
2021	AZ	MLB	30	445	55	23	1	10	46	38	106	0	0	27.4%	.244/.315/.382	92	.307	2.9	1B(107): -4.2	0.4
2022	AZ	MLB	31	667	84	25	2	36	94	69	131	2	2	24.6%	.242/.327/.477	131	.248	-0.1	1B(150): 2.9	4.1
2023 DC	*AZ*	*MLB*	*32*	*622*	*73*	*27*	*2*	*25*	*81*	*61*	*125*	*0*	*1*	*25.0%*	*.248/.331/.444*	*115*	*.279*	*-2.4*	*1B 1*	*1.9*

Comparables: David Segui (74), Babe Dahlgren (71), Justin Smoak (69)

though some less notable free agents will be found in the chapter of their prior team. If there are any questions, an index of every player in the book is provided.

Each player comes with a stat block and a written comment: our example this year is the underrated Christian Walker. We start with name and primary position, then move on to biographical information like birthdate, playing age (as of June 30, 2023), and origin for entering professional baseball in the United States. Then it's on to the stats themselves.

We begin with basic identifying information for each season in question for the player, including **YEAR, TEAM, LVL** (level of affiliated play) and **AGE**. Then it's on to the raw numbers you're used to finding on the back of your parents' baseball cards: **PA** (plate appearances), **R** (runs), **2B** (doubles), **3B** (triples), **HR** (home runs), **RBI** (runs batted in), **BB** (walks), **K** (strikeouts), **SB** (stolen bases) and **CS** (caught stealing).

It's time to leave the old-school stats in the dust now: next up is **Whiff%** (whiff rate). This tells us how often a batter swings and *fails to make contact with the ball*. It's the inverse of contact rate. Next are the "slash line" statistics: **AVG** (batting average), **OBP** (on-base percentage), and **SLG** (slugging percentage). These are all ways to assess aspects of a player's offensive performance, but the next metric **DRC+** (Deserved Runs Created Plus) gives you the whole picture. It's a player's total expected offensive contribution compared to the league average.

BABIP (batting average on balls in play) tells us the percentage of times that a ball hit into the field of play ended up as a hit. This stat sometimes helps us identify if a batter is lucky or not; high BABIPs sometimes mean better luck than average. Just keep in mind that the great hitters also tend to post high BABIPs, and so do hitters who are fast on their feet and hit groundballs.

Next up are two metrics introduced earlier in this section. **BRR** (Baserunning Runs) accounts for all baserunning events, including swiped bags and failed attempts, as well as other things. **DRP** (Deserved Runs Prevented) is a defensive metric that not only has the player's positive or negative value at each of the three positions they played most frequently, but also the number of games they appeared at those positions in parentheses.

The final column is **WARP** (Wins Above Replacement Player), a holistic metric for total player value. For our position players, this means that it takes into account deserved runs above average (an output used in DRC+), BRR, and FRAA, then adjusts for positions played. WARP is a cumulative statistic that credits a player for their value above "replacement level"—think the quality of players that are freely available after the start of the season.

Just below the player's most recent season, you'll find future data: that's the PECOTA projection and comparables. We'll talk about those a bit more in an upcoming section.

Catchers

As mentioned earlier in this introduction, catchers have defensive responsibilities that exceed those of fielders at other positions. For that reason, we create a special, separate box just for their unique catching stats. Let's check out Phillies catcher J.T. Realmuto as an example.

J.T. Realmuto

YEAR	TEAM	P. COUNT	FRM RUNS	BLK RUNS	THRW RUNS	TOT RUNS
2020	PHI	5047	3.1	0.0	0.2	3.3
2021	PHI	16465	15.4	0.8	0.3	16.6
2022	PHI	18477	10.2	0.8	0.3	11.3
2023	*PHI*	*16835*	*7.4*	*0.7*	*0.9*	*9.0*

You should be familiar with the **YEAR** and **TEAM** columns by now; they match the stat boxes for position players and pitchers. **P. COUNT** (pitch count) tells us the number of pitches thrown to that catcher, including swinging strikes, fouls and balls in play. **FRM RUNS** (framing runs) is the total value in runs that the catcher provided or lost by receiving the pitch in a way that influenced the umpire to call a strike. **BLK RUNS** (blocking runs) is the total value in runs above or below average for the catcher's ability to prevent wild pitches and passed balls. **THRW RUNS** (throwing runs) is the total value in runs that the catcher provided or lost from throwing out basestealers, deterring stolen base attempts and picking off runners while avoiding errant throws. (Don't worry, this takes into account factors such as pitcher delivery and speed of the baserunner.) **TOT RUNS** (total runs) is the sum of the previous three statistics, a total run value for the catcher's framing, blocking and throwing.

Pitchers

Rays lefty Shane McClanahan is our example for the pitcher stat block. Much like the position player version, this block includes biographical information up at the top, followed by the same **YEAR**, **TEAM**, **LVL**, and **AGE** columns found for the position players.

Next are the pitcher versions of those "baseball card" statistics by season: **W** (wins), **L** (losses), **SV** (saves), **G** (games pitched), **GS** (games started), **IP** (innings pitched), **H** (hits allowed) and **HR** (home runs allowed). Then we feature two rate statistics, **BB/9** (walks per nine innings) and **K/9** (strikeouts per nine innings), before offering the total **K** (strikeouts).

GB% (ground-ball percentage) is, as you might guess, the percentage of all batted balls in play hit on the ground, including both outs and hits. Please note that, since this is based on the same observational data we talked about in the fielding section, it is subject to occasional human error and bias but still pretty useful.

BABIP (batting average on balls in play) is created the same way that it is for hitters, but it is a bit more useful a metric when trying to predict future performance in pitchers. League-average BABIP for pitchers is typically in the .290–.300 range; BABIP higher than that in pitchers can often be attributed to a leaky defense or bad luck (but not always!) and can indicate potential improved performance in the future. Of course, low BABIP may mean that future performance might not be as sharp as the season that BABIP was posted.

Most long-time baseball fans will recognize **WHIP** (walks plus hits per inning pitched) and especially **ERA** (earned run average), as these are common metrics to measure pitching skill. ERA measures earned runs—*not total runs*—allowed per nine innings of pitching. **DRA-** (Deserved Run Average Minus) was explained earlier; it's a measure of how effective a pitcher's performance was compared to league-average.

WARP (Wins Above Replacement Player) is on the same scale as it is for hitters, though it is calculated specifically for pitching performance, with DRA as the primary input. You might see that relief pitchers have a lower WARP than you might expect; this is due to their limited innings and the fact that WARP does not take leverage into account. For this reason, you may choose to judge high-leverage relievers differently than WARP does.

A pitcher's median fastball velocity (50th percentile) is listed as **MPH**, in order to give you an example of what their typical fastball looks like. Note that this is only available for major-league pitchers, as the data for minor-league pitchers is not publicly available.

The last metrics for each pitcher are additional rates that help describe how they pitch. **FB%** (fastball percentage) is the percentage of fastballs thrown out of all pitches. **Whiff%** (whiff rate) is the percentage of swinging strikes induced on all pitches. Finally, **CSP** (called strike probability) shows the likelihood of any pitch by the hurler resulting in a called strike. This metric is adjusted and controls for factors including handedness, umpire, pitch type, count and location.

PECOTA

We're finally to the point in this intro where we get to talk in depth about PECOTA, Baseball Prospectus' signature projection system. Each player comment includes a PECOTA projection, and all projections for 2023 are for the player as of the date we went to press in early January. They are projected into the park context indicated by the team abbreviation; all PECOTA-projected statistics represent a player's projected major-league performance.

Our PECOTA projections have two major inputs into that final stat line you see: how the player is expected to perform, and how much playing time they'll have available to record that performance. We work to estimate playing time for each player based on team rosters and depth charts, and any projections based on that are noted as **2023 DC**. However, many players aren't projected to receive major-league playing time. Maybe the player in question is a prospect or a minor-league depth option. These players will get a different projection, labeled **2023 non-DC**. This is what we would project the player to provide in 251 plate appearances or 50 innings pitched.

Comparables

The final piece of the puzzle is the comparables. At the bottom of the stat box, you'll see three names after the word "Comparables." These are a player's "targets," or three highest-scoring comparable players, as determined through a modeling process developed by the BP Stats team. A player's targets (or "comps") are examples of people who followed very similar career paths, up to the player's age and in the context of their era. Next to each target, you will find a number. That number is meant to indicate the strength of a match, with 100 being a perfect match and 60 being an average match. Finally, keep in mind that comparables are meant to be backward-facing and match the age of the player in question. If a 23-year-old hitter like Vladimir Guerrero Jr. lists Adrián Beltré as a comparable, his career is being compared to the career of a 23-year-old Beltré, not the late-career Rangers version.

Shane McClanahan LHP Born: 04/28/97 Age: 26 Bats: L Throws: L Height: 6'1" Weight: 200 lb. Origin: Round 1, 2018 Draft (#31 overall)

YEAR	TEAM	LVL	AGE	W	L	SV	G	GS	IP	H	HR	BB/9	K/9	K	GB%	BABIP	WHIP	ERA	DRA-	WARP	MPH	FB%	Whiff%	CSP
2021	TB	MLB	24	10	6	0	25	25	123^{1}	120	14	2.7	10.3	141	45.7%	.330	1.27	3.43	89	1.9	96.8	40.9%	32.1%	56.8%
2022	TB	MLB	25	12	8	0	28	28	166^{1}	116	19	2.1	10.5	194	49.9%	.252	0.93	2.54	70	4.2	97.0	35.7%	34.3%	55.4%
2023 DC	*TB*	*MLB*	*26*	*10*	*7*	*0*	*27*	*27*	*162.3*	*139*	*17*	*2.7*	*11.2*	*201*	*47.9%*	*.308*	*1.16*	*2.82*	*74*	*3.5*	*96.9*	*37.6%*	*32.3%*	*55.9%*

Comparables: Steven Matz (77), Sean Newcomb (75), Jordan Montgomery (75)

Managers

Near the back of the book, you'll find a chapter containing statistics for each major-league manager. For each manager, you'll find a block including a number of statistics pulled from their last five years on the bench. For more information on the statistics back there and what they mean, please visit the Glossary at www.baseballprospectus.com.

The managers are organized by the metric you'll find next to each manager's name: **wRM+** (weighted reliever management plus). Developed by Rob Arthur and Rian Watt, this statistic measures how well a manager aligns their best relievers to the moments of highest leverage. To do this, we use both our DRA metric and a scale called Leverage Index. Like DRC+ and DRA-, wRM+ is scaled to league-average; a wRM+ of 105 indicates that the manager used his relievers about five percent better than average. Conversely, a wRM+ of 95 indicates that the relievers were used about five percent worse than average.

The wRM+ stat does not have a strong correlation with each manager, but it is statistically significant. In other words, a manager isn't *entirely* responsible for their team's wRM+, but the skipper does have an effect on that number. ■

Introducing Range Defense Added

by Jonathan Judge

Today we announce an exciting development in the way we measure baseball defense here at Baseball Prospectus. The range portion of our fielding metric, Fielder Runs Above Average ("FRAA"), which comprises the vast majority of (non-catcher) value we assign to defenders, is being retired for leagues in which we have access to Statcast data. We have decided to name the updated metric Range Defense Added ("RDA").

The current fielder measurement landscape is dominated by Sports Information System's Defensive Runs Saved, which relies on in-house video review of each play, and MLB's Outs Above Average, which uses both Statcast batted ball data and fielder positioning coordinates not available to the general public. Range Defense Added seeks to provide comparable (and possibly greater) accuracy in measuring fielder success, without the use of proprietary sources. RDA will also offer novel information to readers, such as a measure unique to shortstop measuring those defenders' "attempt range," and a "range out score" that provides an easy summary of fielder quality on a rate basis.

Because it relies on Statcast data, RDA will primarily focus on major-league fielders, and will only be available for seasons beginning in 2015. For other seasons and levels, the existing FRAA formula will continue to be used to calculate defensive range, at least publicly. As Statcast data becomes publicly available at other levels, RDA will cover them, too. Other aspects of fielder defense, such as outfield assists, will continue to use our traditional formulas at all levels, which seem to work fine, and which constitute a far smaller portion of overall fielder value.

The Effects of Adopting RDA

As a counting stat, RDA will be expressed in **Range Outs Added**, and a runs-based analogue, **Range Runs Added**, which are the number of outs and runs, respectively, that RDA deems a fielder to have prevented above or below what an average fielder at that position would contribute.

Here are the top fielders for 2022 according to RDA, by **Range Outs Added** and position:

Table 1: Top 2022 Fielders by RDA

Name	Pos	Plays	Range Outs Added
Dansby Swanson	SS	448	15.2
Willy Adames	SS	361	13.7
Steven Kwan	LF	353	10.6
Mookie Betts	RF	430	9.5
Myles Straw	CF	573	9.2
Ke'Bryan Hayes	3B	447	8.9
Michael A. Taylor	CF	445	8.9
Yoán Moncada	3B	252	8.6
Jose Siri	CF	343	8.2
Ha-Seong Kim	SS	367	8.1

And here are RDA's least-favorite fielders, by name and position:

Table 2: Bottom 2022 Fielders by RDA

Name	Pos	Plays	Range Outs Added
Aaron Judge	CF	250	-7.2
Tommy Pham	LF	430	-7.3
Bryan Reynolds	CF	437	-7.4
Bo Bichette	SS	425	-8.1
Jurickson Profar	LF	453	-8.6
Anthony Santander	RF	300	-8.7
Yonathan Daza	CF	350	-8.8
Luis García	SS	187	-9.9
Eduardo Escobar	3B	322	-10.0
Bobby Witt Jr.	SS	336	-17.8

One consequence of the changeover will also be a change in our views of the defense provided by certain defenders over the years. By rank, here are the players whose career estimates of plays/outs made on fielding plays (2015 to the present) go up the most, based on our current estimates:

Table 3: Biggest Career Improvement, 2015—present
(minimum 1,000 fielded balls)

Name	Pos	FRAA Plays Made	RDA Range Outs Added	Delta
Dansby Swanson	SS	-14.2	30.0	44.2
Billy Hamilton	CF	-3.6	38.5	42.1
Anthony Rendon	3B	-26.2	12.8	39.0
Corey Seager	SS	-11.1	17.3	28.4
Eddie Rosario	LF	-19.0	9.0	28.0
Trevor Story	SS	-5.9	21.9	27.8
Freddy Galvis	SS	-8.3	19.4	27.7
Christian Yelich	LF	-18.2	8.0	26.2
Andrew Benintendi	LF	-20.4	5.2	25.6
Robinson Canó	2B	-13.9	6.8	20.7

And here are the fielders who are seen in the most negative light relative to before:

Table 4: Biggest Career Decline, 2015—present
(minimum 1,000 fielded balls)

Name	Pos	FRAA Plays Made	RDA Range Outs Added	Delta
Victor Robles	CF	12.1	-11.5	-23.6
Rougned Odor	2B	9.4	-14.4	-23.8
Giancarlo Stanton	RF	11.4	-12.7	-24.1
Ramón Laureano	CF	12.4	-14.9	-27.3
Rafael Devers	3B	9.5	-19.3	-28.8
Whit Merrifield	2B	19.5	-9.7	-29.2
Anthony Rizzo	1B	39.4	-3.8	-43.2
Justin Upton	LF	40.1	-7.3	-47.4
Joey Votto	1B	48.2	-0.1	-48.3
Marcus Semien	SS	38.4	-14.8	-53.2

The shortstop position is special in that the job is not just to turn fielded balls into outs, but to actually create more fielded plays. Although somewhat true of all infield positions, a talented shortstop has the most ability to affect both the numerator *and* denominator of their success rate. Derek Jeter's high fielding percentage, for example, was criticized by the baseball analysis community as inflated by his poor range. This is because one way to keep a high ratio of outs to attempts is to minimize difficult attempts. Aside from gaming a player's fielding percentage, this lack of range turns infield singles into outfield singles, which have a higher run value and hurt the fielder's pitching staff.

RDA, however, tries to detect this behavior. Groundballs that RDA believes should have been, at a minimum, fielded by the shortstop are charged to the shortstop even if they ended up in the outfield, so that all shortstops are graded on a common denominator. The **Attempt Range** is a counting stat that tells you how many groundballs relative to average the shortstop managed to field, at least according to RDA. Even among top shortstops, you will see the difference between players who convert opportunities to outs, players who create more opportunities and players who manage to do both. Virtually all of the top shortstops are average or better in attempt range according to RDA, but not all of them. Dansby Swanson, for example, is seen as having at-best average range, but terrific execution on the balls he does get to; Willy Adames is good at both.

Table 5: Best Shortstops by RDA, 2022 season

Name	Range Outs Made	Range Out Score	Attempt Range
Dansby Swanson	15.2	4.2	0
Willy Adames	13.7	4.7	9
Ha-Seong Kim	8.1	2.7	8
Isiah Kiner-Falefa	8.0	2.6	12
Trea Turner	7.6	2.5	3
Geraldo Perdomo	7.6	2.6	9
Taylor Walls	5.3	2.4	2
Andrew Velazquez	4.5	1.9	11
Nick Allen	2.6	1.5	4
Nicky Lopez	2.6	2.0	5

Finally, we are introducing the **Range Out Score**, which we hope readers will see as a useful rate stat to evaluate fielding. The Range Out Score is the percent above- or below-average that the player successfully converts a charged play to an out, relative to others at their same position. Different positions have wider ranges. Pitchers and catchers are unlikely to exceed 1 -2% either way, infielders typically range between 3-4% above- or below-average, and outfielders can exceed plus or minus 5% or more, given their unique opportunity to combine fielding acumen with running speed—two distinct skills that can be additive. Across the board, an average player at each position receives a 0, an above- or below-average fielder will be a point or two in either direction, and a great or terrible fielder will go a few points beyond that. Just be sure to compare players only to other players at the same position. Per the chart above, the best-fielding shortstop on a rate basis last year was the aforementioned Adames, combining terrific execution with above-average range.

By contrast, here are the shortstops at the bottom of RDA's list last year:

Table 6: Worst Shortstops by RDA, 2022 season

Name	Range Outs Made	Range Out Score	Attempt Range
Jeremy Peña	-2.9	-0.9	0
Jose Barrero	-3.0	-3.0	-1
Tim Anderson	-3.9	-2.0	4
Oneil Cruz	-4.0	-2.0	-8
Xander Bogaerts	-4.6	-1.2	-5
Brandon Crawford	-5.0	-1.9	-1
Bryson Stott	-5.7	-3.1	-6
Bo Bichette	-8.1	-2.4	0
Luis García	-9.9	-6.6	-3
Bobby Witt Jr.	-17.8	-6.6	-8

This group spans a range of below-average fielding, but again RDA offers subtleties, not just criticism. Jeremy Peña and Bo Bichette have decent range but below-average execution.

Luis García and Bobby Witt Jr. have some of the worst range out scores you will see for a shortstop, although García at least is viewed as having some attempt range at the position.

The Need for Change

FRAA has been our defensive metric at BP for quite some time. It is also the last of BP's Big Three measurements—hitting, pitching, and fielding—to be overhauled to methods we consider to be current best practice. The time for that changeover has come.

Why do we need to update the range portion of FRAA? As of two years ago, in a test of same-season descriptive power, it did well. The answer is that we are also interested in repeatable player skill, not just our ability to calibrate current events. And by this alternative measure, FRAA is not performing well enough, in part because resources like Statcast did not exist when FRAA's range calculation methods were last updated.

How does one measure player skill at fielding? In our view, it requires you to account for confounding factors like batted ball quality, batted ball opportunity, the quality of surrounding teammates and positioning schemes and the effects of different parks. We have decided that the benchmark most likely to serve as a severe test in this regard is the (1) year-to-year reliability (aka "stickiness") of (2) individual ratings for (3) players who changed teams.

Between 2016 and 2022, we identified over 1,000 fielders who fit this category, excluding pitchers and catchers, providing a robust sample. Using Spearman correlations to compare the consistency of their ratings of different fielders on a rate basis, weighted by number of fielded plays we credit to each fielder, here is how the existing range portion of FRAA stacked up to OAA and the range portions of DRS and UZR[1]:

Table 7: Year-to-Year Metric Reliability, Team-Changers by Position, 2016—2022
(higher is better)

Position	OAA	DRS	UZR	FRAA	Players
1B	**0.21**	0.06	0.14	0.16	192
2B	**0.28**	0.24	0.08	0.14	230
3B	0.15	**0.25**	0.11	0.07	229
SS	0.24	**0.26**	0.14	0.23	146
LF	**0.44**	0.31	0.22	0.12	282
CF	**0.35**	0.19	0.11	0.26	195
RF	**0.40**	0.25	0.19	-0.05	248

By this measuring stick, FRAA's performance is not terrible, but it is not great either. A difference of a few points doesn't matter, as these measurements all have a standard deviation of about 0.1 over bootstrap resampling. (Hence the bold text.) But the gap between FRAA and OAA/DRS is consistent. On average, FRAA certainly performs worse:

Table 8: Overall Year-to-Year Reliability, Team-Changers, 2016—2022
(higher is better)

OAA	DRS	UZR	FRAA
0.31	0.23	0.15	0.12

There is no shame in this: the competing metrics (even UZR) have access to resources that FRAA does not, so it is not surprising that they perform better. But there is no need to be satisfied with this state of affairs either. And we are not.

The Improved Performance

RDA incorporates advanced resources like Statcast batted ball data. It also incorporates the foundations of our Deserved metrics, especially the concept of principled skepticism. But it also benefits from original analysis, experimentation, and our willingness to think broadly about the driving causes of good defense. The extra work is unfortunately required, because we still have a significant asymmetry of information: We do not have access to MLB's fielder coordinates, nor do we have a staff of video analysts who study every play. And our goal is to create the best metric we can while relying entirely on data in the public domain.

Fortunately, we seem to have succeeded. Let's show the two previous tables again, and this time we will add RDA into the comparison, with the numbers we have so far:

Table 9: Year-to-Year Metric Reliability, Team-Changers by Position, 2016—2022
(higher is better)

Position	OAA	DRS	UZR	FRAA	RDA	Players
1B	0.21	0.06	0.14	0.16	**0.27**	192
2B	**0.28**	0.24	0.08	0.14	0.27	230
3B	0.15	0.25	0.11	0.07	**0.27**	229
SS	0.24	**0.26**	0.14	0.23	0.21	146
LF	0.44	0.31	0.22	0.12	**0.54**	282
CF	0.35	0.19	0.11	0.26	**0.57**	195
RF	0.40	0.25	0.19	-0.05	**0.49**	248

As you can see, RDA holds its own across the infield, and runs away with it at the outfield positions. The overall average correlations across all of these positions tell a similar story:

Table 10: Overall Year-to-Year Reliability, Team-Changers, 2016—2022
(higher is better)

OAA	DRS	UZR	FRAA	RDA
0.31	0.23	0.15	0.12	**0.39**

RDA also seems to be particularly strong at resisting "house effects" of particular teams, whether due to better positioning or the effects of neighboring fielders. Consider the net difference between the values in Table 10 and Table 11 (below), when we look at all fielders, not just those who changed teams. For this comparison, we want the penalty to be as close to zero as possible:

Table 11: Overall Year-to-Year Reliability Penalty, By Team Status, 2016—2022
(closer to zero is better)

Cohort	OAA	DRS	RDA
Team Changers	+0.31	+0.23	+0.39
Everyone	+0.32	+0.30	+0.36
Net Penalty	-0.01	-0.07	+0.03

RDA and OAA show little difference overall, with DRS demonstrating a much larger penalty. The overall hierarchy between metrics is also maintained when all players are considered, which supports the validity of using the team-changer subset. In defense of DRS, there is something to be said for recording how well a player performs on a particular team. But from our standpoint, the team-independent skill demonstrated by the fielder is of greater interest and better reflects their likely contribution.

RDA also seems to perform well in evaluating pitcher and catcher range. We will elaborate on this more before the season starts.

Last but not least, RDA seems poised to function well going forward. New restrictions on fielder positioning can only make its job easier. Moreover, while RDA seems to work fine with both Trackman and Hawk-Eye-based systems, its performance in the first (full) seasons of the Hawk-Eye system is eye-opening. Again, the weighted Spearman correlations with team-changers:

Table 12: Overall Year-to-Year Reliability, Team-Changers, 2021—2022
(higher is better)

OAA	DRS	UZR	FRAA	RDA
0.22	0.21	0.15	0.10	**0.54**

Perhaps 2021 and 2022 were just randomly good years for RDA, but if Hawk-Eye is truly adding more accuracy to batted ball measurement, it is not surprising to see RDA benefit from it.

With all this said, please remember that evaluating defensive accuracy remains tricky. Although reliability is arguably the most important benchmark by which to grade a metric, at least when you don't know the "right" answer, the fact that you are measuring something consistently does not automatically mean you are measuring it correctly, a point we have made previously. Unlike with batters or pitchers, we cannot simply take next year's OPS or RA9 and see how well it has been "predicted," because fielders do not have an obvious equivalent metric. Without a consensus ground truth, it's difficult to agree upon what is "right" and what is not. With that said, we can't think of a single good metric that doesn't start by being incredibly reliable, nor can we think of a baseball metric that is highly reliable and doesn't also provide useful information.

Why Does RDA Work?

How are we able to provide a credible alternative to DRS and OAA without access to their additional resources?

Fortunately, the outcome of most balls in play is predetermined by the nature of the batted ball itself. As such, we don't need to lose sleep over most of these events: On average, they will be an out or hit of some kind regardless of who fields the position and where their team orders them to field it.

That leaves, however, the plays where additional factors *do* matter. DRS and OAA focus on the fielder's perceived location during each play. Our approach is the opposite: to zoom out, and consider how fielder positioning is part of a larger process.

We begin by noting that every fieldable ball has an outcome driven by (at least) three factors relevant to this discussion: (1) batted ball characteristics, (2) fielder skill and (3) fielder positioning. We know the outcome of the play, and we know most of the relevant batted ball characteristics: they include launch speed, launch angle, and the estimated bearing.[2] That leaves fielder skill and fielder positioning, and in order to solve for the former we need to have some sense of the latter. If fielder positioning is consistent across baseball in its out-generating effects—at least on average—then we can treat individual deviations from it as random and we can solve for fielder skill, as it is the only remaining unknown (at least in this discussion). But if fielder positioning is dynamic and truly unknown from play to play, we could have issues.

Thus, ideally we find some surrogate for fielder positioning on each play. To do this, we consider fielder positioning as a part of an overall *process* rather than a mere set of coordinates for each play. To be more specific, we consider team positioning of fielders as driven by (at least) two sub-factors: (1) shared team goals and (2) batter outcomes by fielding position.

Sub-factor one recognizes that opposing teams share the goal of getting the batter out. If all opposing teams are trying to get the batter out, and they all have access to enhanced fielder data and can watch each other's strategies to see what works best, it is reasonable to assume they will gravitate toward an optimal fielding strategy or strategies for each batter—whether it be a similar set of fielding positions or some other approach that provides the most comparable result. If so, whatever the particular fielding alignment turns out to be for a batter, we can assume that it will have similar overall results on average, conditional on the skills of each team's fielders. In other words, if teams are consistently optimizing for the best outcome, then we can assume that differences between teams in fielder positioning are minimal, random, or a bit of both. The benchmarks cited above suggest that these assumptions do in fact hold, at least on average.

The second sub-factor complements the first: Different batters tend to have different results when their balls in play are fielded by different positions, because few hitters hit with the same power and authority to all locations. Thus, teams know not only what strategies are considered best practice for a given batter (the first component, above), but they (and we as analysts) know which fielded positions typically bode well or poorly for each batter's balls in play. Bound up in this factor is the team's ability to position fielders optimally, and the ability of a batter to generate spin and other factors that affect the success of a struck ball beyond those currently disclosed by MLB.

Because fielder positioning is a function of (at least) these two other factors, it can be recharacterized as a mediator of a larger process, driven by shared team goals and typical batted ball results to each fielding position. If so, actual fielder positioning becomes ignorable in the larger picture for the same reasons that the pathways above it are themselves ignorable or accounted for in our system. ***If*** our stated assumptions hold on average about the drivers of fielder positioning in general, then the precise location of each fielder on each play is no longer necessary to know, at least with respect to our ability to paint an *overall* picture of fielding skill. (It would be *nice* to have the additional information, but that is not the same thing as it being *necessary*). Without that additional information, we cannot grade each individual play with the precision we would like, and the values could be a smidge more volatile, but we also are not trying to grade individual plays. Rather, we are trying to objectively measure the displayed fielding skill over a sample of plays, and ultimately a full season. Plus, from Savant data we at least have the baseline knowledge of whether fielders are in a shifted or standard configuration.

As a result, RDA arguably is trying to answer a slightly different question than DRS and OAA do. DRS and OAA seem to be asking whether a particular play was above- or below-average for that fielder under each system's assumptions about the challenges of that particular play. RDA, on the other hand, asks whether a fielder's overall play was consistently above- or below-average in light of the extent to which an out should have been made by *somebody* on that play.

The OAA/DRS approach has the potential to give you more detail, sometimes, about what a particular fielder actually did on a given play. But the RDA approach arguably tells you more about how a fielder would be expected to perform under typical circumstances, and at the very least establishes an informed prior for how well a fielder is performing. Answers to both questions offer value, and the more answers readers have, the better.

Conclusion

Consider this to be a "soft launch" of RDA. Within the next month, you should be able to review the new proposed defensive values on our website. As we roll out the new metric, we would appreciate hearing feedback from you on the numbers you are seeing, particularly if you notice any persistent biases that are concerning. Our goal is to get this right, or at least as right as reasonably possible, and our eagle-eyed readers are some of our best testers.

—Jonathan Judge is an author of Baseball Prospectus.

---

1. All DRS, UZR, and OAA values were provided courtesy of our friends at FanGraphs.

2. The actual bearing of each ball off the bat, despite being measured, is not made publicly available by MLB. It can be partially estimated from the stringer estimates of where the ball was actually fielded. We would appreciate the actual bearing measurement being published in the public domain.

ATLANTA BRAVES

Essay by Russell A. Carleton
Player comments by Demetrius Bell and BP staff

I had the distinct feeling that I was being winked at. With a 1-0 lead in the fourth inning on October 4, Atlanta hitters William Contreras and Orlando Arcia both singled to open the inning, putting runners on first and second. Michael Harris II stepped to the plate and bunted. It "worked" in the sense that Harris was thrown out and Contreras and Arcia each scampered 90 feet ahead, although the rally fizzled out when Robbie Grossman and Dansby Swanson subsequently struck out.

In years past, Harris' bunt would not have been worth noting. Bunting was part of baseball. If you're reading Baseball Prospectus, you likely already know that the sacrifice bunt is a questionable (and by "questionable," I mean demonstrably bad) baseball play in that it usually lowers a team's run expectancy. But this one was downright cheeky: It took place in Atlanta's 161st game of the season, and was the first (and only) sacrifice bunt that the team laid down the entire year. There are more Michael Harrises than there were sacrifice bunts in Atlanta in 2022, and the timing of that one, right before the bell rang to let school out, makes me think someone said, "Yeah, we should probably do one of those."

To be fair, it wasn't the first time that Atlanta had *tried* to sacrifice in 2022. On May 15, in the 10th inning, Arcia tried to bunt "automatic runner" Contreras over to third to start the inning, but the Padres nabbed Contreras, and so Arcia's sacrifice was in vain. On July 2, Matt Olson bunted into an inning-ending double play that looked to be an attempt to beat the shift. Atlanta had three other "beat the shift" bunts (including a successful one by Harris) with no one on. And that's the entire catalog of the team's bunts for the season. It was the sort of thing that was whispered about as 2022 went on among baseball minutiae aficionados. Could the Braves make trivia ("making history" is reserved for things that people will still care about in two weeks) by not dropping one down? Perhaps Brian Snitker was in on the joke.

Technically, Atlanta wouldn't have been the first team to never square around to move a runner. In 2020, a season shortened by the COVID-19 pandemic to 60 games, three teams (the Reds, Brewers and Rays) didn't have a sac bunt, and Atlanta only had one that year. But in a 162-game

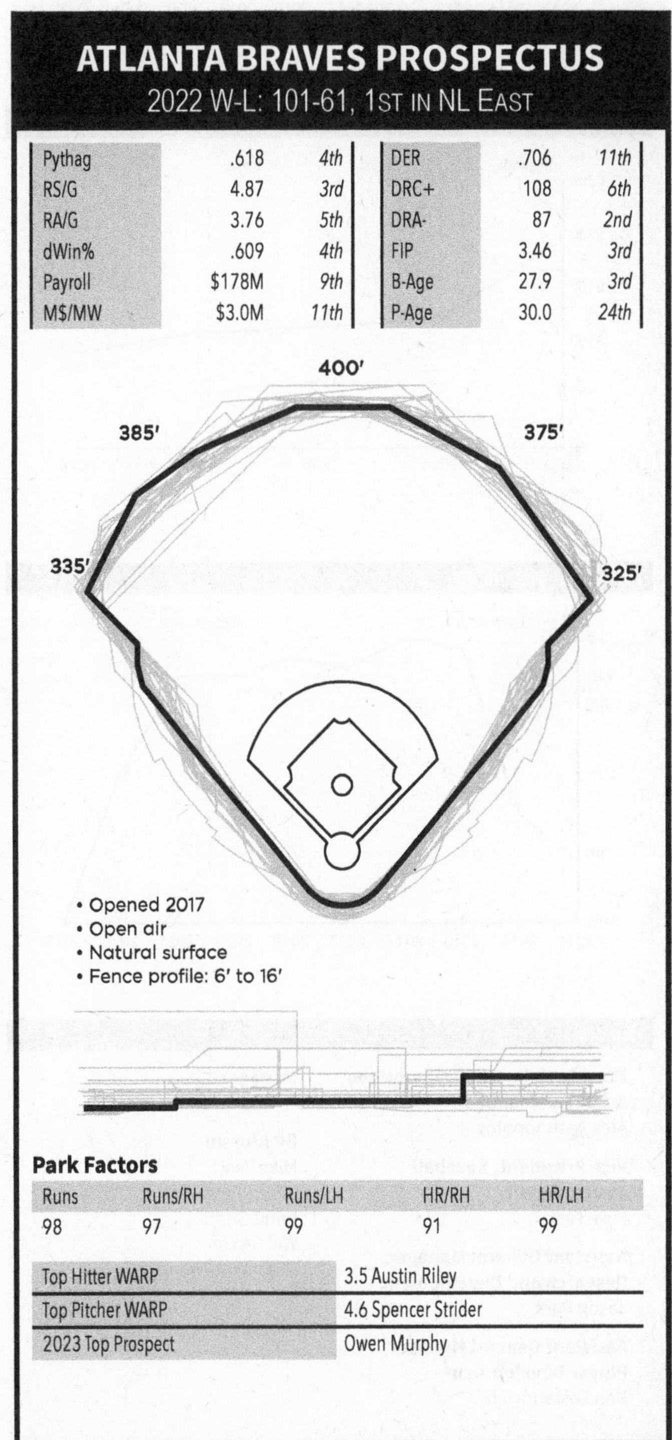

ATLANTA BRAVES PROSPECTUS

2022 W-L: 101-61, 1st in NL East

Pythag	.618	*4th*	DER	.706	*11th*
RS/G	4.87	*3rd*	DRC+	108	*6th*
RA/G	3.76	*5th*	DRA-	87	*2nd*
dWin%	.609	*4th*	FIP	3.46	*3rd*
Payroll	$178M	*9th*	B-Age	27.9	*3rd*
M$/MW	$3.0M	*11th*	P-Age	30.0	*24th*

Park Factors

Runs	Runs/RH	Runs/LH	HR/RH	HR/LH
98	97	99	91	99

Top Hitter WARP	3.5 Austin Riley
Top Pitcher WARP	4.6 Spencer Strider
2023 Top Prospect	Owen Murphy

Payroll History (in millions)

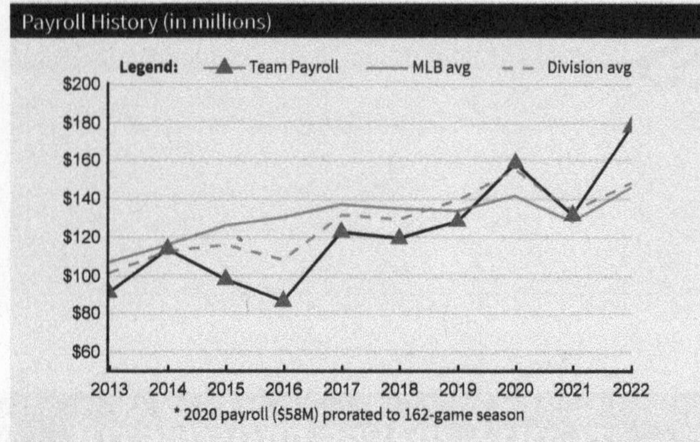

Future Commitments (in millions)

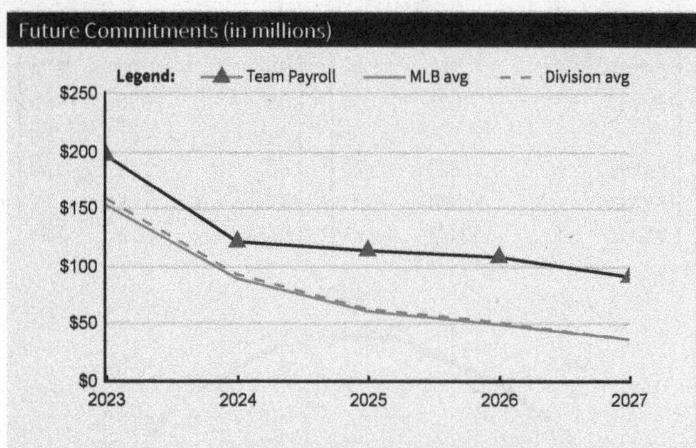

Farm System Ranking

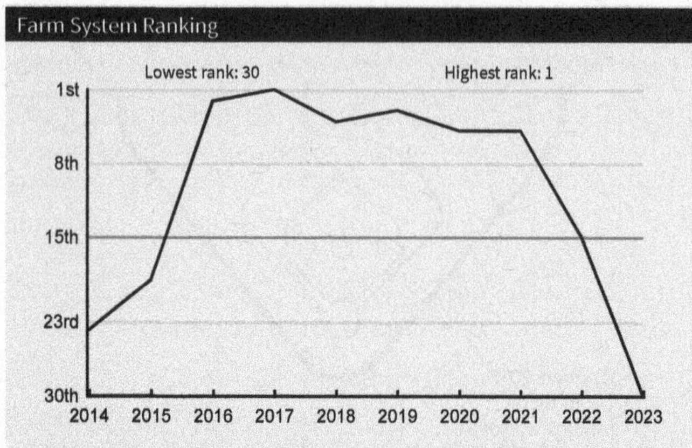

Personnel

President, Baseball Operations & General Manager
Alex Anthopoulos

Vice President, Baseball Development
Mike Fast

Assistant General Manager, Research and Development
Jason Paré

Assistant General Manager, Player Development
Ben Sestanovich

Manager
Brian Snitker

BP Alumni
Mike Fast
Jason Paré
Ronit Shah
Will Siskel
Noah Woodward
Colin Wyers

season, the previous low watermark had been set by the 2019 Angels with four. With the elimination of pitchers batting (and bunting) before the 2022 season, there were now twice as many teams in contention to break the zero-bunt barrier over a full season. But Atlanta didn't seem likely to be *that* team. You see, Snitker is an "old-school" manager. What does it mean when an "old-school" manager doesn't bunt? After all, aren't "old-school" managers supposed to stick to the old strategies, or at least stick it to the new ones? Should we confiscate Snit's student ID from Macon High School?

In the afterglow of Atlanta's 2021 World Series win, *Sports Illustrated* ran a story about how Snitker and the rest of the team's coaching staff, in particular infield coach Ron Washington, were initially reluctant to use the infield shift in the beginning of the season. I guess we now need to point out that, at the time, shifting was fully legal. But after a May meeting, the team turned into one of the shiftiest in the league. There were surely some graphs in that meeting, but *Sports Illustrated* reports that most of what was shared in the room were people's *feelings* on the matter. (Feelings?!) It was after—and only after—Snitker gave the go-ahead that the infielders started wandering to unfamiliar spaces during games. Hold on to that thought.

"Old school" often gets used by members of the Domestic Horticultural Anti-Trespassing Brigade as a badge of honor. Some people are proud of the fact that they don't want to hear new ideas. I guess that's a thing, but it's clear that Snitker isn't in that camp. Reasonable people will listen to reasonable evidence. That's called being an adult.

So, what actually makes Snitker "old school?" I think the first clue came in 2018. At the beginning of an August game against the Marlins, Miami starter José Ureña hit Ronald Acuña Jr. on the elbow (Acuña had to leave the game). Believing the pitch to be intentional, Acuña's teammates streamed out of the dugout and onto the field, led by a visibly irate Snitker. Had no one stepped between Snit and Ureña, Snit might have done some retaliatory damage to Ureña's elbow. Don't think the players didn't notice: Snitker had their backs.

Some people lead. Some people want to be in control. There's a difference, and it's whether you actually care about the people you're working with. If your goal is to make them better in whatever way you can, then you're a leader. When most people think of managing a baseball team, they think about having control over the levers of the game. And sure, pinch-hitting and calling for a bunt are things that managers do, but that's not all they do. Snitker has a responsibility to his players not just to think of them as pawns to be positioned in a game, but as people. It doesn't normally come to the point of running after someone on the other team half your age, but Snitker was the gatekeeper, and he was going to be there for the players.

Managing a baseball team is a massive job. You have to think about what happens both on and off the field. Often, those responsibilities intersect. When someone gets demoted because the results just aren't there, you've got to deliver the news; every line in the transaction column hides a broken heart. A deft hand is required even in less dramatic circumstances. What happens when you have to move someone down in the lineup? That demotion is obvious to the public the moment the night's lineup card gets published. What happens to the player who took pride in hitting fifth? Maybe moving them down was the right decision on paper, but do you now have someone hitting in your eight-spot who is moping? There are 26 players (at least) in that clubhouse. The manager is responsible for all of them on so many levels.

In 2022, Joe Maddon was "relieved of duty" by the Los Angeles Angels. Maddon, never one to mince words, publicly complained afterward about how top brass from the Angels front office would come down to the clubhouse before games and dictate how the game should be played that day. Certain relievers, for example, might be "down" for the night because of their recent workloads. Maddon was quick to say that it wasn't a matter of the information being wrong or useless. It might have even been insightful. Maddon's complaint was that the way in which front office personnel conveyed the information bypassed the manager's job as gatekeeper, even just by physically being in that space. Maybe it is a good idea to sit that reliever tonight, but the front office folks weren't the ones delivering the news to the player or dealing with the aftermath upon hearing, "But my arm feels good, skip."

It's not that managers are infallible. They don't always get the balance right. No one does. A manager has to consider all the available data, and in the modern ballgame, that means understanding analytical thought. Part of taking care of the team is putting it in the best position to win every night. If you don't, based on either laziness or pride around keeping things the same as they were in the 1980s, then you're not doing the job. But you also have to think about the players and how they might react to an unorthodox suggestion. It's telling that when someone suggests a change, the standard response is "Are you sure?" It's not, "Is the expected value positive?" People crave certainty. It's not a logical standard, but it's a human one. You could say, "That unorthodox recommendation was based on a risk-benefit analysis that figures how things will work in the long run. I'm sure that the math is correct," but that's unlikely to resonate. It's not how humans make decisions on an emotional level.

The point of being "old school" isn't that you reject anything that's modern. That's just being stubborn. The point is that you assert that you have the right to review things because you are the gatekeeper. It was Snit who had to bless all the defensive shifting before the team did it. It turns out that if you talk *and* listen to a reasonable person, and make the case that you are *also* concerned about those 26 players, and then hear *them* out in return, they might just end up agreeing with you. At least for 161 games out of the year.

Atlanta walks into 2023 employing what has become an old, but still quite effective, trick: The team has locked up almost all its young, core players to extended contracts. We will likely still be writing about Acuña, Harris, Olson, Austin Riley, Ozzie Albies, Spencer Strider and the newly acquired Sean Murphy in the Atlanta section of Baseball Prospectus *2027*. This is the group of players, for better or worse, that will write the history of the 2020s for the franchise. Given how formidable it looked heading into last season, only to then have Harris and Strider finish first and second, respectively, in NL Rookie of the Year voting, betting on "better" seems prudent.

It's a young group that will be playing under the guidance of the third-oldest manager in MLB, but this is where Snitker's "old-school" approach might come in handy. There's been a trend in MLB toward hiring managers who are younger; occasionally younger than some of the players whom they are managing. One thought is that the new managers are more likely to be "new school," but also that they are going to be more able to relate to the players. (Something about the Domestic Horticultural Anti-Trespassing Brigade.) Maybe some of those new, younger managers really are able to connect better with their players, and that's a very valuable thing. But youth in and of itself isn't what people respond to. It's whether they believe that the manager will be there for them, and everything on Brian Snitker's résumé says he will be.

So Atlanta is as analytical an organization as any in baseball. They employ two Baseball Prospectus alumni (Mike Fast, Colin Wyers) in their Stat Cave. They have an "old-school" manager. They don't have a bunt sign. And this is all perfectly normal in the new ballgame. ■

—Russell A. Carleton is an author of Baseball Prospectus.

Hitters

Ronald Acuña Jr. RF

Born: 12/18/97 Age: 25 Bats: R Throws: R Height: 6'0" Weight: 205 lb. Origin: International Free Agent, 2014

YEAR	TEAM	LVL	AGE	PA	R	2B	3B	HR	RBI	BB	K	SB	CS	Whiff%	AVG/OBP/SLG	DRC+	BABIP	BRR	DRP	WARP
2020	ATL	MLB	22	202	46	11	0	14	29	38	60	8	1	29.9%	.250/.406/.581	128	.302	2.5	CF(34): -1.5, RF(28): -0.4	1.4
2021	ATL	MLB	23	360	72	19	1	24	52	49	85	17	6	27.6%	.283/.394/.596	137	.311	3.4	RF(80): 5.8, CF(2): 0.1	3.7
2022	ATL	MLB	24	533	71	24	0	15	50	53	126	29	11	25.0%	.266/.351/.413	110	.331	3.2	RF(92): 2.9	2.8
2023 DC	*ATL*	*MLB*	*25*	*637*	*102*	*26*	*2*	*31*	*74*	*74*	*146*	*40*	*14*	*25.4%*	*.280/.377/.507*	*148*	*.329*	*2.3*	*RF 7, CF 0*	*6.1*

Comparables: Justin Upton (72), Mickey Mantle (70), Mike Trout (69)

In his return from a devastating knee injury that robbed him of participating in Atlanta's run to the 2021 World Series title, Acuña made sure to remind the (few remaining) detractors that he's still got the goods. Tape-measure throws from the outfield? You got it. Entertaining aggressiveness on the basepaths? Here's 29 stolen bases for ya. Home runs reaching the light towers? Acuña's still got the pop in his bat for that—though they were fewer and farther in between than you'd like to see. His ground-ball rate was astronomical compared to his pre-injury rate, and his fly-ball rate correspondingly cratered. As a result, we only got flashes of the superstar at the height of his powers. The clear hope is that Acuña's power returns, along with the overall confidence in his own game. It's scarcely believable to think that you could describe anything about Acuña as "tepid," but that was the overall vibe as he eased his way back into the fold. The Braves, and baseball as a whole, are better when this absolute dynamo is firing on all cylinders.

Ozzie Albies 2B

Born: 01/07/97 Age: 26 Bats: S Throws: R Height: 5'8" Weight: 165 lb. Origin: International Free Agent, 2013

YEAR	TEAM	LVL	AGE	PA	R	2B	3B	HR	RBI	BB	K	SB	CS	Whiff%	AVG/OBP/SLG	DRC+	BABIP	BRR	DRP	WARP
2020	ATL	MLB	23	124	21	5	0	6	19	5	30	3	1	24.8%	.271/.306/.466	97	.317	0.1	2B(29): 0.3	0.4
2021	ATL	MLB	24	686	103	40	7	30	106	47	128	20	4	25.0%	.259/.310/.488	107	.278	3.0	2B(156): 2.6	3.7
2022	ATL	MLB	25	269	36	16	0	8	35	16	47	3	5	22.9%	.247/.294/.409	102	.270	0.5	2B(64): -0.8	0.9
2023 DC	*ATL*	*MLB*	*26*	*596*	*68*	*28*	*4*	*19*	*67*	*38*	*102*	*13*	*6*	*22.7%*	*.258/.311/.436*	*107*	*.285*	*0.5*	*2B 1*	*2.3*

Comparables: Roberto Alomar (84), Bobby Doerr (82), Bill Mazeroski (82)

If you were to write a book about Albies' season, it would look something like a sequel to *Alexander and the Terrible, Horrible, No Good, Very Bad Day.* The second baseman was snake-bitten: Instead of building upon a campaign that saw him unexpectedly become a reliable source of power, he never even got going. A foot fracture took out a huge chunk of his season, then a fractured pinky finger just two days after his return snuffed out the rest. When he was on the field, he continued to provide valuable defense, though his power production fell off a cliff. It's a shame that injury robbed him of another season sending moonshots into orbit, appearing to defy physics with his small frame (for Major League Baseball). Here's hoping that he'll pick up where he left off.

Orlando Arcia 2B

Born: 08/04/94 Age: 28 Bats: R Throws: R Height: 6'0" Weight: 187 lb. Origin: International Free Agent, 2010

YEAR	TEAM	LVL	AGE	PA	R	2B	3B	HR	RBI	BB	K	SB	CS	Whiff%	AVG/OBP/SLG	DRC+	BABIP	BRR	DRP	WARP
2020	MIL	MLB	25	189	22	10	1	5	20	14	32	2	0	23.2%	.260/.317/.416	107	.292	0.5	SS(57): -0.6	0.7
2021	GWN	AAA	26	322	54	16	0	17	37	31	38	5	3		.282/.351/.516	133	.272	1.2	SS(65): 4.2, LF(4): -0.2, 3B(3): 0.3	2.7
2021	ATL	MLB	26	78	9	3	0	2	13	7	16	1	0	26.4%	.214/.282/.343	93	.245	0.3	LF(14): -0.4, SS(3): 0.1, 2B(1): 0	0.2
2021	MIL	MLB	26	11	0	0	0	0	1	0	3	0	0	26.1%	.091/.091/.091	84	.125		3B(3): 0, SS(2): 0	
2022	ATL	MLB	27	234	25	9	0	9	30	21	51	0	0	27.2%	.244/.316/.416	106	.278	0.3	2B(50): 0.9, LF(6): -0.3, 3B(4): 0	1.0
2023 DC	*ATL*	*MLB*	*28*	*190*	*20*	*7*	*0*	*5*	*18*	*15*	*38*	*1*	*0*	*26.2%*	*.237/.304/.378*	*92*	*.274*	*0.2*	*SS 0, 3B 0*	*0.3*

Comparables: Ed Brinkman (64), Rick Auerbach (62), Roy McMillan (61)

Just when you were thinking it's about time to write off Arcia as a defensive substitute, the former top prospect showed he's got a larger role to play. While it's a far cry from where he broke onto baseball's radar as a youngster, it's still a solid landing given the widespread concerns his bat would never make it. Arcia has morphed into that unheralded middle infielder who you think is there solely as an injury replacement until you look up and see that his DRC+ is north of 100. He's not going to achieve superstar status any time soon, but possesses the critical tool of any backup: He's there when needed, as more than a weak link.

Robinson Canó 2B/DH

Born: 10/22/82 Age: 40 Bats: L Throws: R Height: 6'0" Weight: 212 lb. Origin: International Free Agent, 2001

YEAR	TEAM	LVL	AGE	PA	R	2B	3B	HR	RBI	BB	K	SB	CS	Whiff%	AVG/OBP/SLG	DRC+	BABIP	BRR	DRP	WARP
2020	NYM	MLB	37	182	23	9	0	10	30	9	24	0	0	19.8%	.316/.352/.544	120	.319	-1.9	2B(34): 0.6	0.9
2022	ELP	AAA	39	104	20	5	0	3	20	7	22	0	0	19.0%	.333/.375/.479	96	.403	-2.1	2B(9): -0.2	0.0
2022	ATL	MLB	39	27	1	1	0	0	0	1	4	0	0	23.6%	.154/.185/.192	91	.182	-0.6	2B(8): -0.3	0.0
2022	NYM	MLB	39	43	3	0	0	1	3	2	11	0	0	28.1%	.195/.233/.268	80	.241	-2.0	2B(7): 0.3	-0.2
2022	SD	MLB	39	34	1	0	0	0	1	1	10	0	0	21.9%	.091/.118/.091	70	.130	0.0	2B(5): -0.2	0.0
2023 non-DC	*ATL*	*MLB*	*40*	*251*	*24*	*11*	*0*	*6*	*27*	*13*	*47*	*0*	*0*	*22.7%*	*.246/.293/.380*	*86*	*.283*	*-0.7*	*2B 1*	*0.3*

Comparables: Charlie Gehringer (77), Frankie Frisch (75), Eddie Collins (75)

Going into the postseason, there wasn't a bigger fan of the Mets, Braves and Padres than Canó. Each of those playoff clubs fielded the 17-year-veteran this season—and all three removed him from the roster. But he probably wasn't feeling that sting by the fall, having earned three chances for another World Series ring from the comfort of home. Even with the group's elimination ahead of the Fall Classic, there was little reason for bitterness—he was on and off three rosters by mid-August, for good reason. He had eight hits in 43 plate appearances with the Mets, three in 34 with the Padres and four in 27 with the Braves. Looking ahead, the disappearing hit tool is the most troubling sign—Canó's bat has been the only thing keeping him around big-league clubhouses. Without that, he's been relegated to a fleeting specter on an eternal quest for championship jewelry.

Cal Conley SS Born: 07/17/99 Age: 23 Bats: S Throws: R Height: 5'10" Weight: 185 lb. Origin: Round 4, 2021 Draft (#126 overall)

YEAR	TEAM	LVL	AGE	PA	R	2B	3B	HR	RBI	BB	K	SB	CS	Whiff%	AVG/OBP/SLG	DRC+	BABIP	BRR	DRP	WARP
2021	AUG	A	21	161	21	5	1	2	9	14	33	8	3		.214/.304/.307	98	.262	1.7	SS(20): -1.6, 2B(15): -1.4	0.3
2022	AUG	A	22	349	62	10	6	10	40	25	59	23	7		.246/.307/.414	108	.268	3.9	SS(67): -0.9, 2B(4): -0.9	1.6
2022	ROM	A+	22	199	32	10	1	6	25	19	50	13	1		.260/.337/.429	95	.328	3.0	SS(42): -2.9, 2B(2): 0.2	0.6
2023 non-DC	*ATL*	*MLB*	*23*	*251*	*20*	*9*	*2*	*4*	*22*	*14*	*65*	*10*	*3*	*30.1%*	*.210/.263/.321*	*60*	*.273*	*3.6*	*2B 0, SS 0*	*-0.2*

Comparables: Joseph Rosa (69), Luis Gonzalez (69), Javier Castillo (68)

There are certain descriptions that will cause a moment of pause, and one of those is "switch hitter with power." You can put that descriptor on Conley, who also showed off some surprisingly good baserunning during his first full season as a pro. It was a roller-coaster campaign, but it ended with an exciting showing in the Arizona Fall League, where the 2021 fourth-rounder's newfound focus on pulling the ball less with a toned-down plate approach paid off. Building on that step moving forward is critical, as there's no way Conley can get to his promising switch-hit power unless he can truly tap into his hit tool. His fielding and throwing might necessitate a move to the outfield if he's to really fixate on the hitting side. Either way, he's going to keep on getting opportunities to deliver on his rare promise.

Travis d'Arnaud C Born: 02/10/89 Age: 34 Bats: R Throws: R Height: 6'2" Weight: 210 lb. Origin: Round 1, 2007 Draft (#37 overall)

YEAR	TEAM	LVL	AGE	PA	R	2B	3B	HR	RBI	BB	K	SB	CS	Whiff%	AVG/OBP/SLG	DRC+	BABIP	BRR	DRP	WARP
2020	ATL	MLB	31	184	19	8	0	9	34	16	50	1	0	30.9%	.321/.386/.533	109	.411	-0.8	C(35): 5.4	1.3
2021	ATL	MLB	32	229	21	14	0	7	26	17	53	0	0	24.4%	.220/.284/.388	89	.260	-0.3	C(57): 6.4	1.3
2022	ATL	MLB	33	426	61	25	1	18	60	19	90	0	0	26.9%	.268/.319/.472	117	.306	-1.2	C(99): 11.2	3.5
2023 DC	*ATL*	*MLB*	*34*	*469*	*48*	*21*	*0*	*13*	*50*	*29*	*100*	*0*	*0*	*26.6%*	*.242/.299/.390*	*91*	*.285*	*-2.9*	*C 3, 1B 0*	*0.7*

Comparables: Terry Steinbach (77), Mike Lieberthal (76), Don Slaught (75)

YEAR	TEAM	P. COUNT	FRM RUNS	BLK RUNS	THRW RUNS	TOT RUNS
2020	ATL	5251	4.8	0.0	0.7	5.4
2021	ATL	7703	5.0	0.2	0.0	5.2
2022	ATL	14462	10.7	0.2	0.2	11.1
2023	*ATL*	*7215*	*2.9*	*0.1*	*0.0*	*3.0*

The 2021 championship season saw the Braves succeed in spite of their various backstops, with d'Arnaud's performance when available no better than his battery of replacements during a lengthy recuperation from thumb surgery. His glorious return to full-season action accompanied a drastic shift in the club's fortunes behind the plate; Atlanta ended up with one of the top catching duos in all of baseball. The larger star in that orbit provided his highest DRC+ in a 162-game season since 2015, with plenty of pop to boot. The more surprising turnaround was that d'Arnaud delivered his best defensive season behind the plate since his days in Queens, finishing with a caught stealing percentage of 25% and his FRAA at heights unseen in half a decade. He's one of the best-hitting catchers in baseball right now and, especially after posting a career high in plate appearances, is showing very few signs of slowing down.

Vaughn Grissom MI Born: 01/05/01 Age: 22 Bats: R Throws: R Height: 6'3" Weight: 210 lb. Origin: Round 11, 2019 Draft (#337 overall)

YEAR	TEAM	LVL	AGE	PA	R	2B	3B	HR	RBI	BB	K	SB	CS	Whiff%	AVG/OBP/SLG	DRC+	BABIP	BRR	DRP	WARP
2021	AUG	A	20	328	52	15	4	5	33	34	49	13	3		.311/.402/.446	127	.360	1.6	SS(35): -3.2, 3B(23): 1.8, 2B(10): 3.0	2.3
2021	ROM	A+	20	52	12	2	0	2	10	11	5	3	0		.378/.519/.595	139	.375	0.9	SS(8): -0.8, 2B(2): 0.1	0.4
2022	ROM	A+	21	344	62	17	1	11	55	32	40	20	4		.312/.404/.487	142	.332	0.7	SS(55): -0.6, 2B(6): 0.9, 3B(6): 0.6	3.0
2022	MIS	AA	21	98	10	3	1	3	12	4	14	7	1		.363/.408/.516	122	.405	0.8	SS(21): 0.6, 2B(1): 0.4	0.7
2022	ATL	MLB	21	156	24	6	0	5	18	11	34	5	2	25.7%	.291/.353/.440	108	.350	0.8	2B(40): -2, SS(2): 0	0.5
2023 DC	*ATL*	*MLB*	*22*	*504*	*55*	*20*	*2*	*9*	*48*	*34*	*92*	*15*	*5*	*24.8%*	*.271/.336/.393*	*108*	*.321*	*2.8*	*SS -3, 2B 0*	*1.8*

Comparables: Mookie Betts (64), Jose Altuve (60), Pablo Sandoval (59)

Grissom made his major-league debut on August 10 at Fenway Park, and immediately made sure it would be a memorable debut. His first career hit was a homer that easily cleared the Green Monster; it was at this point Grissom could've retired, taken his made-for-Hollywood moment and rode into the sunset. Naturally, he kept on going, getting plenty of time on a division-winning team. Grissom, mostly playing second base (instead of his usual shortstop) because Ozzie Albies missed most of the season, had a bit of a challenge adjusting to the new position—as his FRAA suggests. His bat was still very much worth fitting in the lineup—while he wasn't the team's highest-profile rookie (or second-highest), it was a very encouraging debut for the man who is not related to Marquis at all.

Michael Harris II CF Born: 03/07/01 Age: 22 Bats: L Throws: L Height: 6'0" Weight: 195 lb. Origin: Round 3, 2019 Draft (#98 overall)

YEAR	TEAM	LVL	AGE	PA	R	2B	3B	HR	RBI	BB	K	SB	CS	Whiff%	AVG/OBP/SLG	DRC+	BABIP	BRR	DRP	WARP
2021	ROM	A+	20	420	55	26	3	7	64	35	76	27	4		.294/.362/.436	116	.349	1.9	CF(76): 5.5, RF(9): -0.3, LF(7): 6.2	3.5
2022	MIS	AA	21	196	33	16	2	5	33	17	39	11	3		.305/.372/.506	118	.364	0.5	CF(41): 0.2, RF(2): 0.2, LF(1): 0.3	1.2
2022	ATL	MLB	21	441	75	27	3	19	64	21	107	20	2	28.2%	.297/.339/.514	107	.361	3.7	CF(114): 2	2.6
2023 DC	*ATL*	*MLB*	*22*	*530*	*55*	*27*	*4*	*9*	*49*	*31*	*124*	*21*	*6*	*27.1%*	*.255/.308/.385*	*92*	*.325*	*5.7*	*CF -4*	*1.2*

Comparables: Victor Robles (62), Carlos Beltrán (58), Mookie Betts (57)

Baseball is supposed to be difficult, and Major League Baseball in particular is known as the hardest level of them all. So you can imagine that Harris' effortless success as a rookie produced shock, to go along with the awe of him consistently making difficult defensive plays look routine. Every time he crushed a home run, it became easier to forget that this was a guy with all of 196 plate appearances in Double-A at the time of his call-up—seemingly to be a defensive stopgap in the outfield. Instead, Harris was electric both in the field and at the plate, and had fans seeing spaceships on Bankhead when it came to visions of his future. After signing a long-term contract to stay in Atlanta and taking home the NL Rookie of the Year award, it's possible Harris himself could be piloting one of those spaceships by the time he's done.

Sam Hilliard OF Born: 02/21/94 Age: 29 Bats: L Throws: L Height: 6'5" Weight: 236 lb. Origin: Round 15, 2015 Draft (#437 overall)

YEAR	TEAM	LVL	AGE	PA	R	2B	3B	HR	RBI	BB	K	SB	CS	Whiff%	AVG/OBP/SLG	DRC+	BABIP	BRR	DRP	WARP
2020	COL	MLB	26	114	13	2	2	6	10	9	42	3	0	38.9%	.210/.272/.438	75	.281	1.1	LF(14): 0.2, RF(13): 0.5, CF(10): 1.6	0.3
2021	ABQ	AAA	27	213	31	12	2	14	37	23	61	6	1		.239/.324/.548	105	.272	1.0	CF(35): 7.2, RF(9): 3.1, LF(7): 0.7	2.0
2021	COL	MLB	27	238	32	7	2	14	34	23	87	5	0	41.8%	.215/.294/.463	87	.283	3.1	CF(46): 0.3, LF(17): 0.4, RF(11): 0.6	1.0
2022	ABQ	AAA	28	158	27	5	2	13	32	21	39	4	1	26.9%	.308/.405/.669	124	.337	1.0	CF(17): 0.0, RF(11): 0.8, LF(3): 0.2	1.2
2022	COL	MLB	28	200	26	6	1	2	14	23	57	5	1	35.0%	.184/.280/.264	71	.256	1.1	LF(59): 3.2, CF(14): 0.2, RF(3): 0	0.4
2023 DC	*ATL*	*MLB*	*29*	*222*	*24*	*7*	*1*	*7*	*22*	*22*	*65*	*5*	*2*	*33.5%*	*.216/.300/.392*	*89*	*.278*	*3.0*	*RF -1, LF 1*	*0.4*

Comparables: Casper Wells (53), Keon Broxton (51), Mike Carp (49)

When is the exact moment when a player goes from prospect to bust? It's tough to say, but it's happened to Hilliard, who struggled through a second straight dismal year of limited playing time and too many strikeouts. To be fair, the risk was always high here, given his propensity for swinging and missing and inability to hit anything with a modicum of break or fade. It's telling, too, that he was MIA in Colorado, then lashed Triple-A pitching for a month after being demoted in mid-July, only to come back up and hit .226/.351/.228 with a 31% strikeout rate for the rest of the season. Maybe he just likes the chili in Albuquerque better than Denver. Now out of options, Hilliard has seen his last of either city for the time being—he'll have a shot to fill out Atlanta's bench. Unless he retires to his spiritual power center in New Mexico to open a turquoise jewelry store, that is.

Jordan Luplow OF Born: 09/26/93 Age: 29 Bats: R Throws: R Height: 6'1" Weight: 195 lb. Origin: Round 3, 2014 Draft (#100 overall)

YEAR	TEAM	LVL	AGE	PA	R	2B	3B	HR	RBI	BB	K	SB	CS	Whiff%	AVG/OBP/SLG	DRC+	BABIP	BRR	DRP	WARP
2020	CLE	MLB	26	92	8	5	1	2	8	12	19	0	1	19.9%	.192/.304/.359	99	.224	0.5	LF(21): -0.1, RF(9): 0.7	0.4
2021	DUR	AAA	27	27	2	1	0	0	2	5	6	0	1		.182/.333/.227	96	.250	-0.1	1B(5): -0.2, LF(1): -0.1	0.0
2021	COL	AAA	27	28	6	4	0	2	7	5	4	0	0		.261/.393/.696	123	.235	0.2	LF(5): -0.1, CF(1): 0.1, RF(1): 0.2	0.2
2021	CLE	MLB	27	121	12	5	0	7	20	21	31	0	2	29.4%	.173/.331/.439	119	.167	-1.0	CF(22): -1.5, RF(11): 0.3, LF(3): 1.7	0.7
2021	TB	MLB	27	72	11	3	0	4	8	7	26	1	0	33.3%	.246/.319/.477	85	.343	-0.4	1B(17): -0.6, LF(3): -0.3	-0.1
2022	RNO	AAA	28	48	10	3	0	6	14	2	9	0	0	26.1%	.289/.333/.756	128	.233	0.3	RF(6): 0.1, CF(3): -0.4	0.3
2022	AZ	MLB	28	234	26	5	0	11	28	25	60	5	1	30.1%	.176/.274/.361	102	.185	-0.8	RF(41): 1, LF(22): 0.4, CF(5): -0.4	0.8
2023 DC	*ATL*	*MLB*	*29*	*207*	*25*	*8*	*0*	*8*	*21*	*22*	*51*	*4*	*1*	*28.5%*	*.221/.316/.409*	*103*	*.262*	*1.2*	*LF 0*	*0.6*

Comparables: Desmond Jennings (48), Stephen Piscotty (46), Corey Hart (46)

Luplow had a bad season. And not bad like good, but like that sandwich you just had for lunch: "What's that smell?" bad. For the second year in a row, he failed to mash lefties, leaving him without a calling card. For the first year in a row, he didn't hit righties. The verdict is still out on how he'd do against pitchers with no arms but, suffice to say, ending a season in historical company with the likes of Heinie Smith (career .276 OBP) isn't how you want to be remembered.

Sean Murphy C Born: 10/04/94 Age: 28 Bats: R Throws: R Height: 6'3" Weight: 228 lb. Origin: Round 3, 2016 Draft (#83 overall)

YEAR	TEAM	LVL	AGE	PA	R	2B	3B	HR	RBI	BB	K	SB	CS	Whiff%	AVG/OBP/SLG	DRC+	BABIP	BRR	DRP	WARP
2020	OAK	MLB	25	140	21	5	0	7	14	24	37	0	0	25.0%	.233/.364/.457	112	.278	-0.7	C(43): 0.5	0.7
2021	OAK	MLB	26	448	47	23	0	17	59	40	114	0	0	27.8%	.216/.306/.405	96	.257	-2.0	C(112): 11.5	2.6
2022	OAK	MLB	27	612	67	37	2	18	66	56	124	1	0	24.0%	.250/.332/.426	114	.290	-0.3	C(101): 7.6	3.9
2023 DC	*ATL*	*MLB*	*28*	*467*	*57*	*22*	*1*	*18*	*55*	*44*	*103*	*0*	*0*	*24.2%*	*.247/.331/.445*	*117*	*.284*	*-0.4*	*C 3*	*3.0*

Comparables: Carlos Santana (73), J.P. Arencibia (73), Chris Iannetta (70)

YEAR	TEAM	P. COUNT	FRM RUNS	BLK RUNS	THRW RUNS	TOT RUNS
2020	OAK	5458	0.6	0.0	0.0	0.6
2021	OAK	14783	11.6	0.2	0.1	11.9
2022	OAK	16561	7.0	0.4	0.4	7.8
2023	*ATL*	*15632*	*2.5*	*0.3*	*0.2*	*3.0*

It seemed inevitable that the Athletics would shed their best (remaining) player during the 2022 season, but the team waited until the offseason to move their backstop. A great defender with a dynamite arm, Murphy's offensive abilities are also well-above average, which is likely why the Braves chose him to upgrade what was already a position of strength. They extended him out for another six seasons; there may not be a better non-Rutschman bet for consistent performance from a catcher through the rest of the 2020s. He'll give Atlanta a fulcrum to guide their lineup, defense and rotation for a good, long time.

Matt Olson 1B Born: 03/29/94 Age: 29 Bats: L Throws: R Height: 6'5" Weight: 225 lb. Origin: Round 1, 2012 Draft (#47 overall)

YEAR	TEAM	LVL	AGE	PA	R	2B	3B	HR	RBI	BB	K	SB	CS	Whiff%	AVG/OBP/SLG	DRC+	BABIP	BRR	DRP	WARP
2020	OAK	MLB	26	245	28	4	1	14	42	34	77	1	0	35.0%	.195/.310/.424	94	.227	-0.7	1B(60): 1.7	0.5
2021	OAK	MLB	27	673	101	35	0	39	111	88	113	4	1	23.0%	.271/.371/.540	136	.269	5.3	1B(152): -0.3	5.0
2022	ATL	MLB	28	699	86	44	0	34	103	75	170	0	0	28.9%	.240/.325/.477	117	.274	-1.8	1B(162): 0.4	2.7
2023 DC	*ATL*	*MLB*	*29*	*636*	*83*	*30*	*1*	*33*	*86*	*72*	*149*	*1*	*0*	*27.8%*	*.247/.341/.484*	*127*	*.279*	*-1.2*	*1B 1*	*3.0*

Comparables: John Mayberry (74), Prince Fielder (74), Boog Powell (73)

Olson spent the better part of five seasons in Oakland, playing well without much attention. Suddenly, his hometown team came calling. Not only did they want him to come home, but they were offering a big extension. It all sounded great; the catch was that he was replacing a guy who'd become the king of his hometown, and Olson arrived just after the king got done conquering the baseball kingdom. Not the smoothest road home. It took more than half of the season for Olson to go from hitting doubles to routinely clearing the fences again, and his defensive work could be best described as "enigmatic." On top of that, the career-low strikeout rate from his final Athletics season ended up being a bit of a mirage. Things weren't bad, as adjustment periods go, but the locals in Cobb County aren't used to change at first base. Olson's still got some huge shoes to fill, but at least he's doing it in his old stomping grounds.

Marcell Ozuna DH/LF Born: 11/12/90 Age: 32 Bats: R Throws: R Height: 6'1" Weight: 225 lb. Origin: International Free Agent, 2008

YEAR	TEAM	LVL	AGE	PA	R	2B	3B	HR	RBI	BB	K	SB	CS	Whiff%	AVG/OBP/SLG	DRC+	BABIP	BRR	DRP	WARP
2020	ATL	MLB	29	267	38	14	0	18	56	38	60	0	0	31.4%	.338/.431/.636	149	.391	-0.8	LF(19): -1.3, RF(2): -0.3	2.1
2021	GIG	WIN	30	90	10	4	0	4	13	10	13	0	0		.316/.389/.519		.333			
2021	ATL	MLB	30	208	21	6	0	7	26	19	46	0	0	27.5%	.213/.288/.356	95	.244	0.3	LF(48): -2.3	0.4
2022	ATL	MLB	31	507	56	19	0	23	56	31	122	2	1	28.7%	.226/.274/.413	100	.252	-0.2	LF(52): -2.8	1.1
2023 DC	*ATL*	*MLB*	*32*	*275*	*35*	*10*	*0*	*14*	*36*	*21*	*61*	*1*	*0*	*28.3%*	*.258/.318/.470*	*118*	*.287*	*-0.1*	*LF 0*	*1.1*

Comparables: Rondell White (75), Shannon Stewart (71), Cleon Jones (70)

Another odious season off the field for Ozuna was compounded by the fact that things continued to go poorly for him on the field. While his power, consistent hard contact and knack for finding barrels made him an acceptable performer as the DH, it was clear that his days as an important part of the Braves lineup were over. It also became evident that he was no longer suited for consistent outfield work, rendered a liability by a precipitous drop in sprint speed that was just as apparent by the eye test. Much of Atlanta's fanbase is waiting intently on Ozuna's contract to come to an end; regardless of his aggravated assault charges being dropped, circumstances have grown increasingly dour with each passing year.

Austin Riley 3B Born: 04/02/97 Age: 26 Bats: R Throws: R Height: 6'3" Weight: 240 lb. Origin: Round 1, 2015 Draft (#41 overall)

YEAR	TEAM	LVL	AGE	PA	R	2B	3B	HR	RBI	BB	K	SB	CS	Whiff%	AVG/OBP/SLG	DRC+	BABIP	BRR	DRP	WARP
2020	ATL	MLB	23	206	24	7	1	8	27	16	49	0	0	30.1%	.239/.301/.415	94	.280	0.5	3B(46): 1.3, 1B(4): 0.2, LF(4): -0.5	0.5
2021	ATL	MLB	24	662	91	33	1	33	107	52	168	0	1	28.1%	.303/.367/.531	121	.368	-0.3	3B(156): -0.1, 1B(10): -0.4, RF(1): 0.1	3.9
2022	ATL	MLB	25	693	90	39	2	38	93	57	168	2	0	27.6%	.273/.349/.528	135	.315	-3.0	3B(159): -1.6, 1B(1): 0	4.2
2023 DC	*ATL*	*MLB*	*26*	*623*	*84*	*28*	*1*	*34*	*93*	*51*	*145*	*1*	*1*	*27.2%*	*.276/.348/.518*	*141*	*.314*	*0.0*	*3B 3*	*4.7*

Comparables: Javier Báez (61), Wilmer Flores (60), Nick Castellanos (60)

If Riley's 2021 was comparable to a Stone Cold Stunner, in that it came out of nowhere and was an extreme crowd pleaser, then the best thing for Riley to do is what Stone Cold himself would do in that situation. That is: Simply give the crowd what they wanted by hitting the Stunner again. Riley did just that, delivering a repeat of his breakout season at the plate. The main difference was that Riley became a barrel machine: If he made contact with the ball—and he was making plenty of contact—it was usually right on the button, and sent flying through the air. Riley's dropoff at third base may be a tiny bit concerning, but it's hard to focus on that when he's hitting at the level he has for the past couple of years. Riley has developed into an incredibly tough competitor at the plate, and that's the bottom line. Yet another extension should keep the focus on that bottom line for the next decade.

Eddie Rosario OF Born: 09/28/91 Age: 31 Bats: L Throws: R Height: 6'1" Weight: 180 lb. Origin: Round 4, 2010 Draft (#135 overall)

YEAR	TEAM	LVL	AGE	PA	R	2B	3B	HR	RBI	BB	K	SB	CS	Whiff%	AVG/OBP/SLG	DRC+	BABIP	BRR	DRP	WARP
2020	MIN	MLB	28	231	31	7	0	13	42	19	34	3	1	22.7%	.257/.316/.476	119	.248	0.7	LF(51): 3.1	1.6
2021	GWN	AAA	29	53	7	2	0	4	16	2	6	0	0		.196/.226/.471	124	.146	0.3	CF(6): 1.8, LF(3): 0.7, RF(2): 0.1	0.6
2021	ATL	MLB	29	106	13	4	2	7	16	9	14	2	1	18.4%	.271/.330/.573	120	.250	0.1	LF(28): -0.7	0.6
2021	CLE	MLB	29	306	29	15	1	7	46	17	47	9	2	19.6%	.254/.296/.389	88	.280	-0.7	LF(72): 2.3	0.8
2022	GWN	AAA	30	37	4	2	0	0	5	4	11	0	0		.273/.351/.333	91	.409	-1.1	LF(3): 0.3	0.0
2022	ATL	MLB	30	270	27	12	1	5	24	17	68	3	0	32.2%	.212/.259/.328	74	.267	0.5	LF(54): 1.1, RF(15): 0	0.2
2023 DC	*ATL*	*MLB*	*31*	*494*	*50*	*20*	*1*	*16*	*52*	*31*	*111*	*7*	*2*	*28.7%*	*.234/.285/.398*	*85*	*.273*	*2.8*	*LF 2, RF 0*	*0.6*

Comparables: Carl Crawford (77), Mike Greenwell (72), Tim Raines (72)

After going on the heater to end all heaters during the 2021 NLCS, it would've been truly astonishing to see Rosario keep it going, especially given his career DRC+ floating around 100. Unfortunately, the good times came to a screeching halt in 2022—though much of that was just rotten injury luck. Rosario got off to a dreadful start before realizing that playing baseball with blurry vision is a terrible idea: Swelling behind his right eye ultimately required laser surgery and ended up costing him May and June. Once recovered from the injury, Rosario was ineffective at the plate and also struggled in the field at times. Not everybody can stay on a heater forever—everybody has to roll snake eyes eventually.

Braden Shewmake SS Born: 11/19/97 Age: 25 Bats: L Throws: R Height: 6'4" Weight: 190 lb. Origin: Round 1, 2019 Draft (#21 overall)

YEAR	TEAM	LVL	AGE	PA	R	2B	3B	HR	RBI	BB	K	SB	CS	Whiff%	AVG/OBP/SLG	DRC+	BABIP	BRR	DRP	WARP
2021	MIS	AA	23	344	40	14	3	12	40	17	75	4	2		.228/.271/.401	100	.262	-0.4	SS(79): 5.3	1.5
2022	GWN	AAA	24	307	37	14	2	7	25	23	57	9	0	21.4%	.259/.316/.399	95	.298	1.5	SS(65): 1.9, 2B(9): -0.1	1.0
2023 DC	*ATL*	*MLB*	*25*	*97*	*9*	*4*	*0*	*1*	*8*	*5*	*21*	*2*	*0*	*26.6%*	*.233/.282/.357*	*75*	*.285*	*1.1*	*2B 0, SS 0*	*0.1*

Comparables: Luis Marté (66), Luis Alfonso Cruz (63), Tzu-Wei Lin (62)

Sometimes a potential trip to The Show is all about being in the right place at the right time. In Shewmake's case, he probably needed to be anywhere last August 6 other than shallow left field in Triple-A Charlotte. That was when he sustained a nasty collision with Travis Demeritte while chasing to field a pop fly, in the process tearing the PCL in his left knee. The injury ended Shewmake's season; instead of calling him up when in need of an infielder, Atlanta turned to Vaughn Grissom. Fortunately, Shewmake recovered in time for a normal offseason, and this season he's positioned to be in the right place at the right time—or at least not the wrong one. Wherever Shewmake is, his duties are likely to include shortstop, where he's appeared exclusively, in efforts to convert fine defense and aggressively average hitting into a big-league role.

Ambioris Tavarez SS Born: 11/12/03 Age: 19 Bats: R Throws: R Height: 6'0" Weight: 168 lb. Origin: International Free Agent, 2021

YEAR	TEAM	LVL	AGE	PA	R	2B	3B	HR	RBI	BB	K	SB	CS	Whiff%	AVG/OBP/SLG	DRC+	BABIP	BRR	DRP	WARP
2022	BRA	ROK	18	69	12	4	0	1	8	3	28	3	1		.277/.304/.385		.459			
2023															*No projection*					

Once the face of Atlanta's return to the International Free Agency market, it almost seemed as if Tavarez would fade into mythology. After all, he didn't play in 2021 and then was largely absent from the public eye following a brief bout of action in major-league spring-training games. Fortunately, Tavarez was eventually able to take the field in the Florida Complex League, getting 17 games under his belt. Those games may not have featured the most impressive showing in the world, but given they constituted his first professional line, it was encouraging that the then-18-year-old shortstop didn't look completely overwhelmed. He's got the chance to stick at third base, with power on several fronts—he's got a big arm, which helps make up for the likelihood that he slows down a bit as he matures into a (potential) power hitter. It's still a long road to the top, but at least now Taveras is on his way.

Luke Waddell SS Born: 07/13/98 Age: 24 Bats: L Throws: R Height: 5'9" Weight: 180 lb. Origin: Round 5, 2021 Draft (#157 overall)

YEAR	TEAM	LVL	AGE	PA	R	2B	3B	HR	RBI	BB	K	SB	CS	Whiff%	AVG/OBP/SLG	DRC+	BABIP	BRR	DRP	WARP
2021	PEJ	WIN	22	71	11	5	0	0	9	9	8	3	0		.311/.394/.393		.352			
2021	ROM	A+	22	78	15	1	0	6	13	7	13	1	1		.304/.372/.580	134	.294	-0.1	SS(8): -0.5, 3B(5): 1.1, 2B(4): 0.2	0.6
2021	MIS	AA	22	33	3	0	0	0	2	2	4	1	1		.161/.212/.161	98	.185	0.2	2B(5): 0.0, SS(2): 0.1, 3B(1): -0.1	0.1
2022	MIS	AA	23	187	20	10	0	2	29	23	22	3	2		.272/.364/.370	120	.302	-0.7	SS(29): -0.2, 2B(9): 0.1	0.9
2023 non-DC	*ATL*	*MLB*	*24*	*251*	*23*	*9*	*1*	*4*	*23*	*19*	*33*	*3*	*1*	*15.7%*	*.244/.308/.350*	*87*	*.270*	*-0.3*	*2B 0, 3B 0*	*0.3*

Comparables: Nicky Lopez (72), Ernie Clement (68), Kevin Newman (67)

Atlanta drafted Waddell to hit now and figure out the rest at some point in the future. The hitting part is going just fine—the Georgia Tech alum has batted at an effective clip at every level, and he's also walking more than he's striking out. Getting on base is quite literally the name of the game, and he's got that part down. The biggest question is if he can run and field; the next-biggest is whether he'll develop some power. Hitting papers over a lot of holes, and as long as Waddell can do that, it doesn't really matter if he runs or waddles out there. There will be a big-league spot waiting—as long as he keeps on hitting.

PITCHERS

Kolby Allard LHP Born: 08/13/97 Age: 25 Bats: L Throws: L Height: 6'1" Weight: 195 lb. Origin: Round 1, 2015 Draft (#14 overall)

YEAR	TEAM	LVL	AGE	W	L	SV	G	GS	IP	H	HR	BB/9	K/9	K	GB%	BABIP	WHIP	ERA	DRA-	WARP	MPH	FB%	Whiff%	CSP
2020	TEX	MLB	22	0	6	0	11	8	33^{2}	31	4	5.3	8.6	32	34.3%	.284	1.51	7.75	121	0.0	90.9	77.2%	23.2%	53.3%
2021	TEX	MLB	23	3	12	0	32	17	124^{2}	128	29	2.2	7.5	104	39.5%	.270	1.28	5.41	117	0.0	91.1	72.1%	19.9%	57.1%
2022	RR	AAA	24	3	3	0	20	20	89	81	21	3.8	11.4	113	37.4%	.287	1.34	4.65	87	1.2	90.8	46.6%	28.6%	
2022	TEX	MLB	24	1	2	1	10	0	21	21	9	2.6	8.1	19	27.9%	.231	1.29	7.29	122	0.0	91.2	53.2%	27.5%	57.1%
2023 DC	*ATL*	*MLB*	*25*	*1*	*1*	*0*	*25*	*0*	*22.3*	*22*	*3*	*3.4*	*8.0*	*19*	*37.6%*	*.293*	*1.39*	*4.49*	*115*	*0.0*	*91.1*	*71.1%*	*23.8%*	*56.2%*

Comparables: Jacob Turner (61), Jordan Lyles (59), Tyler Skaggs (57)

It's never a good sign when metrics like FIP say you pitched worse than your ERA suggests. It's particularly troubling when said ERA begins with a seven. To be fair to Allard, his time in the majors in 2022 was quite brief before he was banished to Round Rock. It was there that he continued allowing too many homers, as he has during virtually every stint he's had in the majors. A former first-round pick, Allard was a prospect of note at one time and is still just 25, but the promise that once defined his career has all but faded. Whatever development Allard needs to succeed was unlikely to occur in Texas, as the team appeared to acknowledge in trading him back to Atlanta in exchange for Jake Odorizzi (and much of the remaining money on his contract).

Ian Anderson RHP Born: 05/02/98 Age: 25 Bats: R Throws: R Height: 6'3" Weight: 170 lb. Origin: Round 1, 2016 Draft (#3 overall)

YEAR	TEAM	LVL	AGE	W	L	SV	G	GS	IP	H	HR	BB/9	K/9	K	GB%	BABIP	WHIP	ERA	DRA-	WARP	MPH	FB%	Whiff%	CSP
2020	ATL	MLB	22	3	2	0	6	6	32^{1}	21	1	3.9	11.4	41	53.1%	.250	1.08	1.95	68	0.9	94.3	48.5%	29.0%	46.6%
2021	GWN	AAA	23	0	0	0	4	4	14^{2}	12	0	5.5	12.3	20	51.4%	.343	1.43	3.68	84	0.3				
2021	ATL	MLB	23	9	5	0	24	24	128^{1}	105	16	3.7	8.7	124	48.2%	.265	1.23	3.58	88	2.0	94.7	47.4%	28.9%	55.1%
2022	GWN	AAA	24	1	2	0	4	4	21^{2}	25	2	4.2	9.6	23	56.9%	.365	1.62	5.40	83	0.5				
2022	ATL	MLB	24	10	6	0	22	22	111^{2}	115	12	4.4	7.8	97	48.1%	.313	1.51	5.00	117	0.1	94.0	48.0%	28.4%	52.6%
2023 DC	*ATL*	*MLB*	*25*	*5*	*6*	*0*	*19*	*19*	*93*	*94*	*8*	*4.4*	*8.9*	*92*	*49.1%*	*.321*	*1.50*	*4.28*	*105*	*0.5*	*94.3*	*47.8%*	*28.4%*	*53.2%*

Comparables: Jhoulys Chacín (69), Shelby Miller (69), Jack Flaherty (68)

Not even 12 months after Anderson became the talk of the town with five no-hit innings in Game 3 of the 2021 World Series, he finished the season in Triple-A. So what happened? Was October 2021 just a collective delusion shared by all of humanity? How did a pitcher on the inside track to a rotation slot find himself demoted on merit not even a full season afterwards? It may be as simple as Anderson's fastball losing a tick of velocity while both his heater and curveball shed a ton of movement—a heater with life at 95 mph can become meaty and hittable at 94 and with less movement. Anderson's changeup became his only reliable pitch, which is not what you want to see. Maybe 2021 was overperformance, and hopefully 2022 was underperformance. The search for the happy medium is on.

Jesse Chavez RHP Born: 08/21/83 Age: 39 Bats: R Throws: R Height: 6'1" Weight: 175 lb. Origin: Round 42, 2002 Draft (#1252 overall)

YEAR	TEAM	LVL	AGE	W	L	SV	G	GS	IP	H	HR	BB/9	K/9	K	GB%	BABIP	WHIP	ERA	DRA-	WARP	MPH	FB%	Whiff%	CSP
2020	TEX	MLB	36	0	0	0	18	0	17	20	6	3.7	6.9	13	39.3%	.280	1.59	6.88	123	0.0	90.6	78.7%	15.4%	50.5%
2021	GWN	AAA	37	1	0	2	13	0	20	12	1	3.6	12.2	27	57.1%	.275	1.00	2.25	84	0.4				
2021	ATL	MLB	37	3	2	0	30	4	33^2	22	0	2.9	9.6	36	43.0%	.256	0.98	2.14	92	0.5	90.1	79.9%	17.7%	55.3%
2022	ATL	MLB	38	3	3	0	46	1	53	49	5	2.4	10.4	61	41.5%	.324	1.19	2.72	78	1.1	89.6	84.0%	26.4%	53.1%
2022	CHC	MLB	38	0	0	0	3	0	5^2	7	1	3.2	4.8	3	26.3%	.333	1.59	6.35	115	0.0	88.8	89.4%	17.6%	54.9%
2022	LAA	MLB	38	1	0	0	11	0	10^2	15	2	3.4	8.4	10	36.1%	.382	1.78	7.59	107	0.1	89.9	89.0%	19.8%	55.7%
2023 DC	*ATL*	*MLB*	*39*	*2*	*2*	*0*	*51*	*0*	*44.7*	*46*	*7*	*3.1*	*8.1*	*40*	*40.8%*	*.304*	*1.38*	*4.45*	*114*	*-0.1*	*89.9*	*81.7%*	*22.2%*	*53.1%*

Comparables: Elmer Dessens (63), Chad Qualls (61), Sergio Romo (59)

Chavez is used to being a rolling stone, and wherever he placed any of his extremely expensive hats was his home. The journeyman reliever actually made four returns to former clubs in 2022: He put on a Cubs hat for a second time, an Angels hat for a third time and was acquired by the Braves on two separate occasions. With that being said, Chavez may have found something resembling an actual home in Atlanta, as his DRA and cFIP for his stints in Cobb County were significantly lower than they were elsewhere. He signed a one-year deal to return to the Braves, so it appears that he has found somewhere to lay his fashionable hat down. It's anybody's guess as to how much Chavez has left in the tank but, judging by how he fared for the past couple seasons, his mileage varies wildly by the zip code.

Bryce Elder RHP Born: 05/19/99 Age: 24 Bats: R Throws: R Height: 6'2" Weight: 220 lb. Origin: Round 5, 2020 Draft (#156 overall)

YEAR	TEAM	LVL	AGE	W	L	SV	G	GS	IP	H	HR	BB/9	K/9	K	GB%	BABIP	WHIP	ERA	DRA-	WARP	MPH	FB%	Whiff%	CSP
2021	ROM	A+	22	2	1	0	9	9	45	38	2	4.0	11.0	55	58.6%	.316	1.29	2.60	79	1.0				
2021	MIS	AA	22	7	1	0	9	9	56	39	7	2.7	9.6	60	58.7%	.244	1.00	3.21	86	1.0				
2021	GWN	AAA	22	2	3	0	7	7	36^2	18	1	4.9	9.8	40	53.5%	.200	1.04	2.21	81	1.0				
2022	GWN	AAA	23	6	5	0	18	17	105	93	14	2.7	8.3	97	55.6%	.275	1.19	4.46	81	2.4				
2022	ATL	MLB	23	2	4	0	10	9	54	44	4	3.8	7.8	47	48.7%	.268	1.24	3.17	107	0.3	90.8	61.4%	23.9%	50.6%
2023 DC	*ATL*	*MLB*	*24*	*3*	*3*	*0*	*20*	*8*	*46*	*46*	*5*	*3.9*	*7.6*	*38*	*52.3%*	*.299*	*1.44*	*4.38*	*110*	*0.1*	*90.8*	*61.4%*	*25.5%*	*50.6%*

Comparables: Dan Straily (78), T.J. Zeuch (76), Matt Harvey (76)

It was a tale of two splits in Elder's first go-around in the majors. He got his first chance in April, and the four starts didn't go particularly well. He wasn't going deep into games, was having an extremely hard time keeping the basepaths empty and routinely had outings with more walks than strikeouts. After spending the summer in Gwinnett, things changed significantly when Elder returned to Atlanta in August. He suddenly started racking up strikeouts, barely walking anybody and getting deep into games. This culminated with him throwing Atlanta's only complete-game shutout of the summer, which would've been inconceivable at the start of the season. While Elder may have flown way under the radar due to incredible performances from rookie teammates, he'll be far more conspicuous if what he figured out sticks.

Max Fried LHP Born: 01/18/94 Age: 29 Bats: L Throws: L Height: 6'4" Weight: 190 lb. Origin: Round 1, 2012 Draft (#7 overall)

YEAR	TEAM	LVL	AGE	W	L	SV	G	GS	IP	H	HR	BB/9	K/9	K	GB%	BABIP	WHIP	ERA	DRA-	WARP	MPH	FB%	Whiff%	CSP
2020	ATL	MLB	26	7	0	0	11	11	56	42	2	3.1	8.0	50	52.3%	.268	1.09	2.25	85	1.1	93.2	51.9%	25.6%	46.7%
2021	ATL	MLB	27	14	7	0	28	28	165^2	139	15	2.2	8.6	158	51.0%	.281	1.09	3.04	81	3.2	94.0	50.4%	24.7%	57.2%
2022	ATL	MLB	28	14	7	0	30	30	185^1	156	12	1.6	8.3	170	50.3%	.280	1.01	2.48	82	3.5	93.9	46.1%	25.9%	51.3%
2023 DC	*ATL*	*MLB*	*29*	*11*	*9*	*0*	*29*	*29*	*183.7*	*180*	*16*	*2.2*	*8.6*	*175*	*50.7%*	*.312*	*1.22*	*3.22*	*86*	*2.8*	*93.9*	*49.2%*	*26.0%*	*52.5%*

Comparables: Atlee Hammaker (76), Dock Ellis (72), Tom Glavine (71)

If there were any lingering questions about Fried's status as a high-end starter following the 2021 season, then the majority of those questions should be answered. It was a year of establishment for Fried—he established himself as the top hurler for the Braves, as a frontline starter in the National League in general and as a reliable and steadying presence in the rotation over a full season. He cut the walk rate and home run rate down considerably while keeping strikeouts, DRA and cFIP in the same lovely neighborhood as before. The whiff machine that is his curveball was as effective as ever, dropping like an anchor in the ocean. Fried even started working in his bat-missing changeup more often. While his 2022 ended on a sour note in the postseason, the bad days on the mound are looking more and more like outliers than anything else.

Raisel Iglesias RHP Born: 01/04/90 Age: 33 Bats: R Throws: R Height: 6'2" Weight: 190 lb. Origin: International Free Agent, 2014

YEAR	TEAM	LVL	AGE	W	L	SV	G	GS	IP	H	HR	BB/9	K/9	K	GB%	BABIP	WHIP	ERA	DRA-	WARP	MPH	FB%	Whiff%	CSP
2020	CIN	MLB	30	4	3	8	22	0	23	16	1	2.0	12.1	31	38.9%	.288	0.91	2.74	80	0.5	96.3	46.3%	39.0%	49.5%
2021	LAA	MLB	31	7	5	34	65	0	70	53	11	1.5	13.2	103	39.5%	.290	0.93	2.57	61	2.1	96.5	44.8%	40.9%	54.6%
2022	ATL	MLB	32	0	0	1	28	0	26^1	17	0	1.7	10.3	30	40.6%	.270	0.84	0.34	84	0.5	94.9	52.3%	35.7%	48.0%
2022	LAA	MLB	32	2	6	16	39	0	35^2	29	5	2.3	12.1	48	29.9%	.296	1.07	4.04	73	0.8	95.3	48.4%	32.7%	55.3%
2023 DC	*ATL*	*MLB*	*33*	*3*	*2*	*33*	*58*	*0*	*50.3*	*41*	*5*	*2.3*	*10.6*	*59*	*36.7%*	*.285*	*1.07*	*2.53*	*70*	*1.0*	*95.8*	*47.6%*	*34.2%*	*52.2%*

Comparables: Jim Gott (81), Kevin Gregg (78), Jonathan Papelbon (78)

On June 12, 2022, Iglesias surrendered a home run to Pete Alonso. There's no shame in that, that's kind of Pete Alonso's thing. With that being said, it was a pivotal day for Iglesias—that was the final time in the season he surrendered a dinger. The closer turned as homer-averse as you can get midway through his second season with the Angels, and when they decided they'd rather not pay the next three years of his contract, Iglesias didn't allow a single dinger as Atlanta's set-up man on his way to a near-nil ERA. While the overall season wasn't quite up there with the incredible campaign preceding it, he's firmly established himself as a reliable high-leverage arm in the back of any bullpen.

Joe Jiménez RHP
Born: 01/17/95 Age: 28 Bats: R Throws: R Height: 6'3" Weight: 277 lb. Origin: Undrafted Free Agent, 2013

YEAR	TEAM	LVL	AGE	W	L	SV	G	GS	IP	H	HR	BB/9	K/9	K	GB%	BABIP	WHIP	ERA	DRA-	WARP	MPH	FB%	Whiff%	CSP
2020	DET	MLB	25	1	3	5	25	0	22^2	25	7	2.4	8.7	22	30.9%	.295	1.37	7.15	142	-0.2	94.3	62.2%	26.4%	48.6%
2021	DET	MLB	26	6	1	1	52	0	45^1	34	6	6.9	11.3	57	34.5%	.269	1.52	5.96	106	0.3	94.8	54.2%	31.2%	54.4%
2022	DET	MLB	27	3	2	2	62	0	56^2	49	4	2.1	12.2	77	32.6%	.328	1.09	3.49	67	1.5	95.9	63.7%	30.4%	58.2%
2023 DC	*ATL*	*MLB*	*28*	*2*	*2*	*6*	*58*	*0*	*50.3*	*42*	*7*	*3.5*	*11.0*	*61*	*34.0%*	*.292*	*1.24*	*3.60*	*92*	*0.4*	*95.3*	*61.1%*	*29.9%*	*55.2%*

Comparables: Bruce Rondón (71), Kelvin Herrera (68), Trevor Gott (63)

Sixth time lucky? We shouldn't attribute too much of Jiménez's success to luck, even if his home run rate was a touch lower than you might expect given his fly-ball tendencies. Instead, this was more the long-touted arrival of the high-leverage reliever once promised, minus the saves. His sixth season saw retooled mechanics return Jiménez to sitting 96 with wicked arm-side run and, for a change, good command on his high-spin four-seam, while also locating his slider far more effectively, keeping it low in the zone for hitters to swing over. Of course, since it's Jiménez, there was still a hiccup: A lumbar strain ended his season prematurely after he allowed multiple earned runs in each of his final two outings. Even that was minor compared to his prior struggles and isn't expected to affect his availability for spring training. Jiménez may not have ascended to the closer role but, in all the aspects that matter, the Tigers finally got the reliever they'd been hoping for—and immediately dealt him to Atlanta.

Dylan Lee LHP
Born: 08/01/94 Age: 28 Bats: L Throws: L Height: 6'3" Weight: 214 lb. Origin: Round 10, 2016 Draft (#293 overall)

YEAR	TEAM	LVL	AGE	W	L	SV	G	GS	IP	H	HR	BB/9	K/9	K	GB%	BABIP	WHIP	ERA	DRA-	WARP	MPH	FB%	Whiff%	CSP
2021	GWN	AAA	26	5	1	1	35	0	46^2	29	4	1.2	10.4	54	35.1%	.231	0.75	1.54	77	1.2				
2021	ATL	MLB	26	0	0	0	2	0	2	3	1	0.0	13.5	3	33.3%	.400	1.50	9.00	103	0.0	93.0	41.4%	27.8%	63.7%
2022	GWN	AAA	27	1	1	2	14	0	15^2	14	2	1.1	13.2	23	27.8%	.353	1.02	2.30	76	0.4				
2022	ATL	MLB	27	5	1	0	46	0	50^2	40	5	1.8	10.5	59	35.6%	.276	0.99	2.13	75	1.1	92.0	45.5%	35.8%	55.0%
2023 DC	*ATL*	*MLB*	*28*	*3*	*2*	*0*	*58*	*0*	*50.3*	*44*	*7*	*2.3*	*9.0*	*50*	*36.9%*	*.277*	*1.13*	*3.06*	*85*	*0.6*	*92.1*	*45.4%*	*31.8%*	*55.2%*

Comparables: Paul Fry (67), Danny Farquhar (64), Steve Geltz (63)

It's pretty difficult to put on a good encore after becoming an instant trivia answer during your first major-league stint. That's the position Lee was in entering 2022: He's the only pitcher in MLB history to make his first career start in the World Series. As it turned out, Lee was up to the task, proving himself to be a more-than-capable reliever in his rookie campaign. With a slider and a four-seamer making a potent one-two punch, Lee hit the sweet spot of striking out a lot of batters without walking many at all. The slider was his primary offering, and got whiffs on almost half of swings. It's not easy being a walking answer to a trivia question, but Lee has already ensured that's not all he's known for.

Lucas Luetge LHP
Born: 03/24/87 Age: 36 Bats: L Throws: L Height: 6'4" Weight: 205 lb. Origin: Round 21, 2008 Draft (#638 overall)

YEAR	TEAM	LVL	AGE	W	L	SV	G	GS	IP	H	HR	BB/9	K/9	K	GB%	BABIP	WHIP	ERA	DRA-	WARP	MPH	FB%	Whiff%	CSP
2021	NYY	MLB	34	4	2	1	57	1	72^1	67	6	1.9	9.7	78	42.6%	.308	1.13	2.74	88	1.1	88.4	62.1%	27.5%	48.9%
2022	NYY	MLB	35	4	4	2	50	0	57^1	63	4	2.7	9.4	60	35.9%	.355	1.40	2.67	98	0.6	87.6	54.6%	27.4%	50.2%
2023 DC	*ATL*	*MLB*	*36*	*2*	*2*	*0*	*45*	*0*	*39*	*39*	*5*	*2.7*	*8.7*	*37*	*39.8%*	*.311*	*1.32*	*4.04*	*104*	*0.1*	*88.0*	*58.3%*	*26.3%*	*49.6%*

Comparables: Javy Guerra (54), Tony Sipp (53), Javier López (50)

In a relief world filled with flamethrowers, Luetge's approach looks out of place. You'll only see him crack 90 once in a blue moon, but that lack of velocity didn't stop him from producing another excellent season. His arsenal of a cutting fastball, sweeping slider (added prior to 2022, like so many others) and looping curveball has been one of the best at suppressing hard contact since joining the Yankees two years ago. He's also been flexible, being utilized in a variety of different roles from lefty specialist to long man—even picking up a 3⅓ inning save at Fenway Park in July. He'll look to bring that same flexibility and above-average production to Atlanta.

Tyler Matzek LHP
Born: 10/19/90 Age: 32 Bats: L Throws: L Height: 6'3" Weight: 230 lb. Origin: Round 1, 2009 Draft (#11 overall)

YEAR	TEAM	LVL	AGE	W	L	SV	G	GS	IP	H	HR	BB/9	K/9	K	GB%	BABIP	WHIP	ERA	DRA-	WARP	MPH	FB%	Whiff%	CSP
2020	ATL	MLB	29	4	3	0	21	0	29	23	1	3.1	13.3	43	45.5%	.338	1.14	2.79	65	0.9	94.3	70.8%	27.6%	47.8%
2021	ATL	MLB	30	0	4	0	69	0	63	40	3	5.3	11.0	77	37.8%	.262	1.22	2.57	85	1.1	96.1	70.6%	30.0%	54.4%
2022	ATL	MLB	31	4	2	1	42	0	43^2	26	3	6.0	7.4	36	33.3%	.202	1.26	3.50	119	0.0	94.1	76.7%	26.1%	52.2%
2023 non-DC	*ATL*	*MLB*	*32*	*2*	*2*	*0*	*57*	*0*	*50*	*44*	*7*	*5.2*	*9.8*	*54*	*38.1%*	*.287*	*1.46*	*4.43*	*108*	*0.0*	*95.0*	*73.1%*	*26.3%*	*52.6%*

Comparables: Zack Britton (59), Liam Hendriks (51), Arthur Rhodes (48)

It was a season of precipitous decline for Matzek. One of Atlanta's 2021 NLCS heroes, who etched himself into the memories of countless fans by striking out Mookie Betts with three straight heaters in the exact same spot, last year he lost a ton of velocity on that same pitch. Consequently, Matzek's DRA and ERA ballooned and his role diminished. As it turned out, this was for good reason: After the regular season ended, he needed Tommy John surgery. Suddenly, three inches of lost break on his curveball and a significantly flatter fastball made a lot of sense, instead of just being some sort of sudden drop-off. If anybody can get all the way back, it's Matzek: He already won the battle against the yips, so this should be a comparative breeze.

Collin McHugh RHP

Born: 06/19/87 Age: 36 Bats: R Throws: R Height: 6'2" Weight: 191 lb. Origin: Round 18, 2008 Draft (#554 overall)

YEAR	TEAM	LVL	AGE	W	L	SV	G	GS	IP	H	HR	BB/9	K/9	K	GB%	BABIP	WHIP	ERA	DRA-	WARP	MPH	FB%	Whiff%	CSP
2021	TB	MLB	34	6	1	1	37	7	64	48	3	1.7	10.4	74	42.8%	.290	0.94	1.55	78	1.3	90.8	10.9%	31.8%	56.4%
2022	ATL	MLB	35	3	2	0	58	0	69^{1}	51	5	1.8	9.7	75	40.4%	.266	0.94	2.60	78	1.5	88.9	48.3%	27.3%	52.3%
2023 DC	*ATL*	*MLB*	*36*	*2*	*2*	*0*	*58*	*0*	*50.3*	*47*	*6*	*2.5*	*9.0*	*50*	*40.4%*	*.296*	*1.21*	*3.51*	*93*	*0.4*	*89.9*	*33.3%*	*27.6%*	*53.0%*

Comparables: Danny Cox (64), Stan Bahnsen (63), Dave Giusti (61)

If you thought McHugh's journey away from his fastball in 2021 following a year off was some sort of outlier, then he had another thing coming for you. Perhaps realizing that a 90-mph fastball wasn't going to play in this era, McHugh proceeded to nearly abandon the four-seamer altogether while focusing on his cutter and slider. It paid off in yet another season where opposing hitters chased McHugh's pitches and made weak contact whenever they did put bat to ball. Maybe you don't need a high velocity to succeed as a pitcher right now—as long as you have a crazy-high spin rate, that is.

A.J. Minter LHP

Born: 09/02/93 Age: 29 Bats: L Throws: L Height: 6'0" Weight: 215 lb. Origin: Round 2, 2015 Draft (#75 overall)

YEAR	TEAM	LVL	AGE	W	L	SV	G	GS	IP	H	HR	BB/9	K/9	K	GB%	BABIP	WHIP	ERA	DRA-	WARP	MPH	FB%	Whiff%	CSP
2020	ATL	MLB	26	1	1	0	22	0	21^{2}	15	1	3.7	10.0	24	48.1%	.280	1.11	0.83	86	0.4	90.9	81.4%	29.1%	47.1%
2021	GWN	AAA	27	0	0	6	7	0	7^{1}	0	0	3.7	12.3	10	41.7%	.000	0.41	0.00	90	0.1				
2021	ATL	MLB	27	3	6	0	61	0	52^{1}	44	2	3.4	9.8	57	46.5%	.300	1.22	3.78	80	1.1	91.2	86.6%	31.5%	53.5%
2022	ATL	MLB	28	5	4	5	75	0	70	49	5	1.9	12.1	94	38.4%	.289	0.91	2.06	66	1.9	96.7	49.8%	33.1%	51.9%
2023 DC	*ATL*	*MLB*	*29*	*3*	*2*	*4*	*58*	*0*	*50.3*	*41*	*5*	*3.0*	*10.5*	*58*	*41.6%*	*.287*	*1.16*	*2.82*	*76*	*0.8*	*94.2*	*66.4%*	*31.9%*	*51.5%*

Comparables: Ken Giles (68), B.J. Ryan (67), Rex Brothers (66)

If 2021 was Minter's grand return to top-tier relief pitching, then last year was proof that he had what it took to stay on that stage. The only blemish on his record: Whenever he did get hit, it was usually when his cutter met an opposing bat's barrel. Otherwise, Minter's four-seamer was imposing and his changeup proved too tough of a puzzle for most hitters to solve. With his role as one of top high-leverage relievers in baseball fully minted, it wouldn't be surprising if Minter held onto it for a while.

Charlie Morton RHP

Born: 11/12/83 Age: 39 Bats: R Throws: R Height: 6'5" Weight: 215 lb. Origin: Round 3, 2002 Draft (#95 overall)

YEAR	TEAM	LVL	AGE	W	L	SV	G	GS	IP	H	HR	BB/9	K/9	K	GB%	BABIP	WHIP	ERA	DRA-	WARP	MPH	FB%	Whiff%	CSP
2020	TB	MLB	36	2	2	0	9	9	38	43	4	2.4	9.9	42	42.1%	.355	1.39	4.74	83	0.8	93.6	56.4%	25.0%	52.4%
2021	ATL	MLB	37	14	6	0	33	33	185^{2}	136	16	2.8	10.5	216	47.5%	.271	1.04	3.34	72	4.5	95.4	49.5%	29.1%	54.0%
2022	ATL	MLB	38	9	6	0	31	31	172	149	28	3.3	10.7	205	39.4%	.293	1.23	4.34	84	3.1	94.9	44.0%	29.2%	52.7%
2023 DC	*ATL*	*MLB*	*39*	*9*	*8*	*0*	*27*	*27*	*154*	*134*	*17*	*3.1*	*9.7*	*166*	*42.1%*	*.291*	*1.22*	*3.44*	*89*	*2.1*	*95.0*	*47.2%*	*27.9%*	*52.8%*

Comparables: Kevin Brown (73), Dennis Martinez (70), Justin Verlander (70)

Some things are just inevitable: Death, taxes, Disney pumping out three to six Marvel projects per calendar year, and Morton persevering as a dependable starting pitcher even as he pushes 40 years old. WARP indicated there might be something amiss, as Morton lost about a third of his 2021 contributions despite his peripherals remaining relatively similar. The main problem was that when he got hit, he got hit hard and for distance, surrendering 28 home runs—a career high by 10. Though Morton's velocity remained stable, batters posted the highest slugging percentage against his four-seamer since 2016. That wasn't the worst of it, though—batters teed off against his fourth option, his cutter, logging a staggering .559 ISO and leaving his curve his only above-average option. The Braves likely think that the homer binge is an outlier, as they brought him back on another $20 million extension inked near the season's end. It just might be, and maybe we'll see Morton and that formidable curveball continue to defy Father Time.

Owen Murphy RHP

Born: 09/27/03 Age: 19 Bats: R Throws: R Height: 6'1" Weight: 190 lb. Origin: Round 1, 2022 Draft (#20 overall)

YEAR	TEAM	LVL	AGE	W	L	SV	G	GS	IP	H	HR	BB/9	K/9	K	GB%	BABIP	WHIP	ERA	DRA-	WARP	MPH	FB%	Whiff%	CSP
2022	AUG	A	18	0	1	0	3	3	7	5	0	7.7	12.9	10	62.5%	.313	1.57	7.71	119	0.0				
2023 non-DC	*ATL*	*MLB*	*19*	*2*	*3*	*0*	*57*	*0*	*50*	*54*	*8*	*7.4*	*7.1*	*39*	*44.9%*	*.302*	*1.91*	*6.77*	*148*	*-1.0*			*21.5%*	

Comparables: Charlie Neuweiler (26), Jake Woodford (26), Robert Gsellman (26)

Here's Murphy! Ready for another two-way player who could potentially take the baseball world by storm? Well, we regret to inform you that the Braves are only going to use him as a pitcher. The dream lived for Murphy's first several hours as a Braves draftee, when it was reported that the high school third baseman was going to be given a shot to play in the field while also training as a pitcher. Though that hope was quickly squashed, it's nevertheless easy to see why Atlanta drafted him 20th overall. He's got a promising fastball and curveball already, and his cutter and changeup, too, could prove to be plus pitches. The fastball velocity isn't dominant, but he possesses uncommon command for a high school arm; maintaining that advantage will be critical. Murphy's still got a long way to go before entering into a big-league rotation, but he'll be able to devote his attention to that craft exclusively, since the two-way dream has already been dead so much longer than it was alive.

Darren O'Day RHP

Born: 10/22/82 Age: 40 Bats: R Throws: R Height: 6'4" Weight: 220 lb. Origin: Undrafted Free Agent, 2006

YEAR	TEAM	LVL	AGE	W	L	SV	G	GS	IP	H	HR	BB/9	K/9	K	GB%	BABIP	WHIP	ERA	DRA-	WARP	MPH	FB%	Whiff%	CSP
2020	ATL	MLB	37	4	0	0	19	0	16^1	8	1	2.8	12.1	22	27.0%	.194	0.80	1.10	92	0.2	86.1	57.1%	31.9%	44.8%
2021	NYY	MLB	38	0	0	0	12	0	10^2	9	2	3.4	9.3	11	26.7%	.250	1.22	3.38	101	0.1	85.7	51.3%	28.1%	46.9%
2022	ATL	MLB	39	2	2	0	28	0	21^2	19	3	4.2	10.8	26	38.6%	.296	1.34	4.15	88	0.3	86.0	52.2%	28.1%	48.5%
2023 DC	*FA*	*MLB*	*40*	*2*	*2*	*0*	*43*	*0*	*37.3*	*34*	*6*	*3.5*	*9.9*	*41*	*35.3%*	*.289*	*1.30*	*4.21*	*107*	*0.0*	*86.0*	*53.0%*	*27.3%*	*47.4%*

Comparables: Rudy Seanez (80), Troy Percival (79), Al Reyes (79)

This is 40, and the ol' submariner is still chugging along. When on the mound, O'Day has remained capable of getting outs in relief. It's still extremely flattering to call his fastball a "heater" and his walk percentage hit double digits for the first time in a few years, so it's more than possible he's running on fumes. It doesn't help that he had yet another unfortunate trip to the 60-O'Day IL, this time a calf strain that prematurely ended his season. Every season feels like it could be the last, but when your 86-mph fastball is somehow still leaving opposing batters with a .132 xBA, there's no reason to stop now. Welcome to 40.

Cole Phillips RHP

Born: 05/26/03 Age: 20 Bats: R Throws: R Height: 6'3" Weight: 200 lb. Origin: Round 2, 2022 Draft (#57 overall)

The Braves went on a bit of a high school run in the 2022 draft, selecting three prep pitchers with their first three draft picks. Phillips is the most intriguing of those pitchers, if you like watching guys too young to drink pumping fastballs in the high-90s range and even touching triple-digits. He also owns a breaking ball that could very well turn into a reliable slider if he can figure out a way to consistently command it. It's an enticing repertoire, which made it understandable that he went in the second round despite already having lost the rest of the year to Tommy John surgery. Assuming all goes well with his recovery, it's going to be exciting to follow Phillips and his high-powered arm as he begins his professional career.

JR Ritchie RHP

Born: 06/26/03 Age: 20 Bats: R Throws: R Height: 6'2" Weight: 185 lb. Origin: Round 1, 2022 Draft (#35 overall)

YEAR	TEAM	LVL	AGE	W	L	SV	G	GS	IP	H	HR	BB/9	K/9	K	GB%	BABIP	WHIP	ERA	DRA-	WARP	MPH	FB%	Whiff%	CSP
2022	AUG	A	19	0	0	0	3	3	10	7	1	3.6	9.0	10	47.8%	.273	1.10	2.70	103	0.1				
2023 non-DC	*ATL*	*MLB*	*20*	*2*	*3*	*0*	*57*	*0*	*50*	*55*	*8*	*6.1*	*7.2*	*39*	*42.1%*	*.310*	*1.79*	*6.45*	*145*	*-0.9*			*23.5%*	

Comparables: Yoendrys Gómez (26), Roansy Contreras (26), José Soriano (26)

Thanks to MLB spinning their draft night into a made-for-television event, Ritchie had the opportunity to promise Braves fans in the audience that he would be "the hardest worker in this draft" and guarantee another championship in the future. He's going to have plenty of time to deliver on both halves of the pact, since the high school hurler from Washington will have to spend a lot of time developing on the farm. While Ritchie has shown he can reach 99 mph, he's been sitting at 93–95 mph with the heater as a professional—99 was fleeting, and he's yet to get back to it. It's not just the heater in need of attention: his curveball, changeup and slider will all need to be refined or remade in order to live up to Ritchie's lofty promises. With that being said, his smooth delivery is a great starting point to reach the higher end of his velocity range. Check back in a couple years.

Dennis Santana RHP

Born: 04/12/96 Age: 27 Bats: R Throws: R Height: 6'2" Weight: 190 lb. Origin: International Free Agent, 2013

YEAR	TEAM	LVL	AGE	W	L	SV	G	GS	IP	H	HR	BB/9	K/9	K	GB%	BABIP	WHIP	ERA	DRA-	WARP	MPH	FB%	Whiff%	CSP
2020	LAD	MLB	24	1	2	0	12	0	17	15	4	3.7	9.5	18	32.6%	.262	1.29	5.29	112	0.1	94.3	38.7%	28.3%	51.7%
2021	TEX	MLB	25	2	4	0	39	0	39^2	30	4	4.8	8.6	38	47.1%	.263	1.29	3.63	108	0.2	95.8	46.7%	29.6%	49.9%
2021	LAD	MLB	25	0	0	0	16	0	15	18	0	6.6	4.8	8	53.8%	.346	1.93	6.00	140	-0.2	95.1	52.0%	21.1%	49.5%
2022	TEX	MLB	26	3	8	1	63	1	58^2	50	2	4.3	8.3	54	47.9%	.287	1.33	5.22	99	0.6	97.0	46.5%	27.4%	49.3%
2023 DC	*ATL*	*MLB*	*27*	*2*	*2*	*0*	*45*	*0*	*39*	*40*	*4*	*4.8*	*8.9*	*38*	*46.9%*	*.324*	*1.57*	*5.01*	*118*	*-0.2*	*96.2*	*46.7%*	*28.3%*	*49.5%*

Comparables: Arodys Vizcaíno (55), Lucas Sims (54), Luke Jackson (53)

A midseason trade to the Rangers in 2021 led Santana to **D**emonstrate Value as a sinker-slider arm with poor command but a knack for keeping the ball in the park. He's been able to **E**ngage Physically over the last three seasons, increasing the average velocity of his fastball to nearly 98 mph. Santana would go on to **N**urture Dependence in Arlington, appearing in more games than any pitcher other than Matt Moore, with whom he tied for the team lead. But pitching in that many games led him to **N**eglect Emotionally the needs of Rangers fans, as he tied for the second-most losses on the club. The difference between his ERA and FIP may **I**nspire Hope in some, but the more likely outcome is that the walks he issues will get out of hand, leading Santana and the Rangers to **S**eparate Entirely. It's only Sunny in Arlington so often, ya know? Maybe skies will be clear in Atlanta.

Jared Shuster LHP

Born: 08/03/98 Age: 24 Bats: L Throws: L Height: 6'3" Weight: 210 lb. Origin: Round 1, 2020 Draft (#25 overall)

YEAR	TEAM	LVL	AGE	W	L	SV	G	GS	IP	H	HR	BB/9	K/9	K	GB%	BABIP	WHIP	ERA	DRA-	WARP	MPH	FB%	Whiff%	CSP
2021	ROM	A+	22	2	0	0	15	14	58^1	47	10	2.3	11.3	73	34.7%	.272	1.06	3.70	95	0.6				
2021	MIS	AA	22	0	0	0	3	3	14^2	19	5	3.1	10.4	17	36.2%	.341	1.64	7.36	90	0.2				
2022	MIS	AA	23	6	7	0	17	16	90^2	65	8	2.2	10.5	106	46.2%	.263	0.96	2.78	81	1.9				
2022	GWN	AAA	23	1	3	0	10	9	48^2	43	10	3.0	7.2	39	45.1%	.246	1.21	4.25	100	0.6	91.3	44.6%	20.9%	
2023 non-DC	*ATL*	*MLB*	*24*	*2*	*2*	*0*	*57*	*0*	*50*	*51*	*7*	*3.2*	*8.3*	*46*	*43.0%*	*.308*	*1.39*	*4.45*	*112*	*-0.1*			*28.3%*	

Comparables: Domingo Acevedo (75), Andrew Heaney (75), Marco Gonzales (74)

Shuster's first full season as a professional went about as well as anyone could ask. While his fastball isn't the most imposing pitch in the world, he added enough strength to move it into the 91–93-mph range. The heater's ultimately just a set-up for his best offering, a changeup; plenty also hinges on Shuster proving he can consistently get lefty hitters out with the slider. Following an excellent run in Double-A, he did run into some homer troubles in Triple-A, though he appeared to have them contained by season's end. As long as his command stays solid, it shouldn't be too long before the onetime Wake Forest star will be asked to test that changeup against major-league hitters, particularly if he can find a touch more velocity. He may not be a diamond of a prospect, but you could do a lot worse than going to Jared.

AJ Smith-Shawver RHP

Born: 11/20/02 Age: 20 Bats: R Throws: R Height: 6'3" Weight: 205 lb. Origin: Round 7, 2021 Draft (#217 overall)

YEAR	TEAM	LVL	AGE	W	L	SV	G	GS	IP	H	HR	BB/9	K/9	K	GB%	BABIP	WHIP	ERA	DRA-	WARP	MPH	FB%	Whiff%	CSP
2021	BRA	ROK	18	0	1	0	4	4	8^{1}	4	2	10.8	17.3	16	33.3%	.200	1.68	8.64						
2022	AUG	A	19	3	4	0	17	17	68^{2}	54	4	5.1	13.5	103	32.9%	.338	1.35	5.11	86	1.3				
2023 non-DC	*ATL*	*MLB*	*20*	*2*	*3*	*0*	*57*	*0*	*50*	*48*	*8*	*6.2*	*8.9*	*49*	*34.2%*	*.290*	*1.65*	*5.66*	*130*	*-0.6*			*26.9%*	

Comparables: Luis Patiño (87), Carlos Martinez (85), Jake Thompson (85)

It's not every day that you see a bona fide Texas high school football prospect turn down a chance to go from Friday night lights to Saturday afternoon showdowns in the Big XII. However, that's what happened when Smith-Shawver chose an over-slot deal with the Braves over the dual-sport dream at Texas Tech. The vision is clear when it comes to his upside: A fastball that can reach the upper 90s will always be appealing. Adding to the intrigue is that Smith-Shawver didn't become a regular pitcher until his senior year of high school. He's been working on a slider that could be just as electric as the fastball, and a changeup that could perfectly complement the other two pitches. He's very raw, but Smith-Shawver's upside could make this decision a definite touchdown.

Mike Soroka RHP

Born: 08/04/97 Age: 25 Bats: R Throws: R Height: 6'5" Weight: 225 lb. Origin: Round 1, 2015 Draft (#28 overall)

YEAR	TEAM	LVL	AGE	W	L	SV	G	GS	IP	H	HR	BB/9	K/9	K	GB%	BABIP	WHIP	ERA	DRA-	WARP	MPH	FB%	Whiff%	CSP
2020	ATL	MLB	22	0	1	0	3	3	13^{2}	11	0	4.6	5.3	8	61.0%	.268	1.32	3.95	93	0.2	92.4	59.3%	22.6%	46.9%
2022	GWN	AAA	24	0	2	0	5	5	21	20	3	3.0	7.3	17	58.7%	.283	1.29	6.43	95	0.3				
2023 DC	*ATL*	*MLB*	*25*	*5*	*6*	*0*	*19*	*19*	*91.3*	*94*	*9*	*3.2*	*8.1*	*81*	*52.9%*	*.314*	*1.38*	*4.06*	*103*	*0.6*	*92.4*	*62.9%*	*24.7%*	*47.7%*

Comparables: Jordan Lyles (59), Jerome Williams (58), Tyler Skaggs (57)

For a while there, it was actually looking like Soroka would finally return to a big-league mound for the first time since he initially tore his right Achilles tendon on that fateful night in August 2020. The Calgarian hurler did make it back to the mound in competitive action, embarking on what figured to be a lengthy rehab stint en route to a major-league return. Any hope of that comeback in 2022 was suddenly defenestrated in late September, when he was shut down with elbow soreness. Fortunately, Soroka appears to have caught a break for a change—there was no structural damage to his elbow. That should finally allow Soroka to finally have something resembling a normal offseason rather than focusing on recovery. Assuming the injury nightmare has finally ended, this campaign should be the light at the end of a dark, dark tunnel of lost seasons.

Jackson Stephens RHP

Born: 05/11/94 Age: 29 Bats: R Throws: R Height: 6'2" Weight: 220 lb. Origin: Round 18, 2012 Draft (#562 overall)

YEAR	TEAM	LVL	AGE	W	L	SV	G	GS	IP	H	HR	BB/9	K/9	K	GB%	BABIP	WHIP	ERA	DRA-	WARP	MPH	FB%	Whiff%	CSP
2021	LAR	WIN	27	6	3	0	14	9	49^{1}	51	3	1.8	8.0	44	58.7%	.327	1.24	1.82						
2022	GWN	AAA	28	1	0	0	1	1	6	4	0	0.0	10.5	7	50.0%	.286	0.67	3.00	90	0.1				
2022	ATL	MLB	28	3	3	2	39	1	53^{2}	49	3	3.9	7.9	47	46.3%	.293	1.34	3.69	104	0.4	94.2	58.1%	22.2%	56.9%
2023 DC	*ATL*	*MLB*	*29*	*0*	*0*	*0*	*19*	*0*	*16.7*	*17*	*1*	*3.8*	*8.1*	*15*	*45.0%*	*.309*	*1.44*	*4.31*	*107*	*0.0*	*94.2*	*58.1%*	*23.5%*	*56.9%*

Comparables: Rafael Montero (59), Kyle Ryan (58), Michael Lorenzen (58)

Stephens spent the entirety of the 2019 season in Triple-A, went uncontacted by big-league teams in the pandemic year, and in 2021 pitched for the only team that called: Tecolotes de los Dos Laredos of the Mexican League. His performance there got him an opportunity with Cardenales de Lara in the Venezuelan Winter League, where he became Pitcher of the Year and earned a call from the Braves. Presumed as minors depth, by April 12, Stephens found himself on the mound in Cobb County, notching a three-inning save in a blowout victory. He stuck in the bullpen for the entirety of the season. While Stephens isn't the most exciting reliever in the world, the curveball plays and he consistently avoided hard contact. Besides, he had more than his share of excitement on the long road back to the big leagues—staying in the same place doesn't have to be boring.

Spencer Strider RHP

Born: 10/28/98 Age: 24 Bats: R Throws: R Height: 6'0" Weight: 195 lb. Origin: Round 4, 2020 Draft (#126 overall)

YEAR	TEAM	LVL	AGE	W	L	SV	G	GS	IP	H	HR	BB/9	K/9	K	GB%	BABIP	WHIP	ERA	DRA-	WARP	MPH	FB%	Whiff%	CSP
2021	AUG	A	22	0	0	0	4	4	15^{1}	6	0	2.9	18.8	32	25.0%	.300	0.72	0.59	53	0.5				
2021	ROM	A+	22	0	0	0	3	3	14^{2}	9	1	3.7	14.7	24	43.3%	.276	1.02	2.45	82	0.3				
2021	MIS	AA	22	3	7	0	14	14	63	48	6	4.1	13.4	94	30.7%	.321	1.22	4.71	80	1.3				
2021	ATL	MLB	22	1	0	0	2	0	2^{1}	2	1	3.9	0.0	0	25.0%	.143	1.29	3.86	145	0.0	97.8	78.9%	18.2%	55.0%
2022	ATL	MLB	23	11	5	0	31	20	131^{2}	86	7	3.1	13.8	202	40.3%	.292	0.99	2.67	51	4.6	98.2	67.0%	34.9%	54.6%
2023 DC	*ATL*	*MLB*	*24*	*9*	*7*	*0*	*27*	*27*	*143*	*112*	*16*	*3.8*	*12.8*	*203*	*39.0%*	*.306*	*1.21*	*3.10*	*79*	*2.5*	*98.2*	*67.1%*	*34.5%*	*54.6%*

Comparables: Matt Harvey (63), Walker Buehler (62), Danny Salazar (62)

"Let him throw in short bursts," we said! "Put him in the bullpen," we clamored! The Braves listened to the fans for nearly 25 innings before deciding to give Strider a shot as a starter, and it was like unleashing the entirety of the Clemson football team past Howard's Rock and down The Hill. Strider finished the season with the lowest DRA- and cFIP among starters, in part due to tallying the group's highest strikeout percentage and second-highest whiff percentage. Those rankings were not among rookie starting pitchers—those were among all pitchers with at least 100 innings under their belt. Strider had a mind-bogglingly excellent rookie season; it's only a testament to Michael Harris II's performance that the NL Rookie of the Year voting was even a debate. It's going to take one hell of an effort for Strider to top his 2022; if he does, his starts might soon be accompanied by stadiums full of mustachioed fans.

Victor Vodnik RHP

Born: 10/09/99 Age: 23 Bats: R Throws: R Height: 6'0" Weight: 200 lb. Origin: Round 14, 2018 Draft (#412 overall)

YEAR	TEAM	LVL	AGE	W	L	SV	G	GS	IP	H	HR	BB/9	K/9	K	GB%	BABIP	WHIP	ERA	DRA-	WARP	MPH	FB%	Whiff%	CSP
2021	MIS	AA	21	1	4	0	11	11	33^{2}	32	5	5.9	11.0	41	52.9%	.333	1.60	5.35	93	0.5				
2022	MIS	AA	22	0	0	1	7	0	7	4	0	3.9	18.0	14	63.6%	.364	1.00	0.00	83	0.1				
2022	GWN	AAA	22	2	0	2	24	0	27^{2}	26	2	5.2	10.7	33	52.9%	.353	1.52	2.93	86	0.6				
2023 non-DC	*ATL*	*MLB*	*23*	*2*	*2*	*0*	*57*	*0*	*50*	*47*	*5*	*5.5*	*9.4*	*52*	*51.4%*	*.308*	*1.56*	*4.63*	*110*	*0.0*			*26.1%*	

Comparables: José Leclerc (55), Phillippe Aumont (54), Jeremy Jeffress (49)

A 2021 experiment placed Vodnik in the Double-A rotation, but 11 starts were enough for the Braves to send him right back to the bullpen. The return to relief paid off in spades—Vodnik was basically unhittable in a second assignment to Mississippi, striking out two batters per inning in a brief stint. That earned Vodnik a call-up to the next level, where he proceeded to post a strong season, albeit one that failed to distinguish him from the Triple-A competition. The velocity on his fastball actually went down a little, but he's continued missing bats. The changeup remained a good option, and he's starting to go to his slider every now and then. On top of everything, it remains an 80-grade name, with alliteration through the roof.

Kyle Wright RHP

Born: 10/02/95 Age: 27 Bats: R Throws: R Height: 6'4" Weight: 215 lb. Origin: Round 1, 2017 Draft (#5 overall)

YEAR	TEAM	LVL	AGE	W	L	SV	G	GS	IP	H	HR	BB/9	K/9	K	GB%	BABIP	WHIP	ERA	DRA-	WARP	MPH	FB%	Whiff%	CSP
2020	ATL	MLB	24	2	4	0	8	8	38	35	7	5.7	7.1	30	44.7%	.262	1.55	5.21	123	0.0	94.4	48.4%	24.0%	43.5%
2021	GWN	AAA	25	10*	5	0	24	24	137	117	9	3.0	9.0	137	51.6%	.293	1.18	3.02	88	2.7				
2021	ATL	MLB	25	0	1	0	2	2	6^{1}	7	2	7.1	8.5	6	40.0%	.294	1.89	9.95	120	0.0	93.4	51.1%	29.4%	55.5%
2022	ATL	MLB	26	21	5	0	30	30	180^{1}	156	19	2.6	8.7	174	55.1%	.284	1.16	3.19	84	3.3	94.8	43.4%	26.5%	56.2%
2023 DC	*ATL*	*MLB*	*27*	*10*	*9*	*0*	*27*	*27*	*162.3*	*154*	*15*	*3.3*	*8.7*	*156*	*52.6%*	*.303*	*1.31*	*3.58*	*92*	*2.0*	*94.7*	*44.4%*	*26.2%*	*54.5%*

Comparables: José Ureña (67), Erik Johnson (65), Andrew Heaney (64)

A standout performance in a victorious World Series bid would do wonders for anybody's confidence. Armed with evidence that his stuff can work on the biggest stage of the game and the knowledge gleaned from years of experience in Triple-A, Wright finally put it together for a full season in a big-league rotation. He leaned more heavily on his curveball, sinker and changeup, and the change to his pitch mix paid dividends. Less of the fastball went a long way—especially since Wright was able to add velocity and movement. It was a winning combination: He kept the walks and homers at a premium while most batted balls went straight into the ground. Wright will never be the most imposing figure on any given mound, but he's proven that he's got some of the right stuff.

Kirby Yates RHP

Born: 03/25/87 Age: 36 Bats: L Throws: R Height: 5'10" Weight: 205 lb. Origin: Round 26, 2005 Draft (#798 overall)

YEAR	TEAM	LVL	AGE	W	L	SV	G	GS	IP	H	HR	BB/9	K/9	K	GB%	BABIP	WHIP	ERA	DRA-	WARP	MPH	FB%	Whiff%	CSP
2020	SD	MLB	33	0	1	2	6	0	4^{1}	7	1	8.3	16.6	8	38.5%	.500	2.54	12.46	83	0.1	93.6	64.4%	41.3%	46.0%
2022	GWN	AAA	35	0	0	0	5	0	5^{1}	2	0	3.4	6.8	4	64.3%	.143	0.75	1.69	93	0.1	93.4	54.8%	20.0%	
2022	ATL	MLB	35	0	0	0	9	0	7	6	2	6.4	7.7	6	36.4%	.200	1.57	5.14	109	0.0	93.4	50.4%	29.8%	50.4%
2023 DC	*ATL*	*MLB*	*36*	*2*	*2*	*0*	*51*	*0*	*44.7*	*39*	*5*	*3.5*	*10.8*	*53*	*42.7%*	*.301*	*1.26*	*3.65*	*93*	*0.4*	*93.5*	*55.8%*	*30.0%*	*46.9%*

Comparables: Brad Brach (58), Shawn Kelley (55), Mike Adams (54)

For the first time since 2020, Yates finally made his return to a major-league mound on a low-risk, multi-year deal with the Braves. The contract was backloaded; Atlanta knew the old-timer probably wasn't going to give them much in 2022, and that ended up being the case. He only made nine appearances, though six saw him keep the other team off the board, so there could still be something there in spite of a career-worst DRA-. The injury bug still persistently buzzed—Yates' regular season came to an end due to elbow inflammation in his throwing arm, so his return felt done and dusted in the blink of an eye. Fortunately, he should finally have a normal offseason to prepare—and just as importantly, not to have to rehab from injury.

Huascar Ynoa RHP

Born: 05/28/98 Age: 25 Bats: R Throws: R Height: 6'2" Weight: 220 lb. Origin: International Free Agent, 2014

YEAR	TEAM	LVL	AGE	W	L	SV	G	GS	IP	H	HR	BB/9	K/9	K	GB%	BABIP	WHIP	ERA	DRA-	WARP	MPH	FB%	Whiff%	CSP
2020	ATL	MLB	22	0	0	0	9	5	21^{2}	23	2	5.4	7.1	17	55.9%	.318	1.66	5.82	99	0.3	95.0	44.3%	25.5%	45.9%
2021	GWN	AAA	23	0	0	0	2	2	8^{1}	8	1	4.3	11.9	11	45.5%	.333	1.44	4.32	102	0.1				
2021	ATL	MLB	23	4	6	0	18	17	91	76	14	2.5	9.9	100	47.3%	.272	1.11	4.05	79	1.9	96.8	44.9%	28.3%	54.3%
2022	GWN	AAA	24	5	6	0	18	17	77^{2}	73	14	4.1	10.1	87	47.7%	.295	1.39	5.68	87	1.6				
2022	ATL	MLB	24	0	2	0	2	2	6^{2}	11	2	8.1	10.8	8	52.2%	.429	2.55	13.50	103	0.1	96.8	53.1%	21.9%	55.2%
2023 non-DC	*ATL*	*MLB*	*25*	*2*	*2*	*0*	*57*	*0*	*50*	*50*	*6*	*4.0*	*9.2*	*50*	*49.0%*	*.316*	*1.46*	*4.44*	*109*	*0.0*	*96.5*	*45.8%*	*26.4%*	*53.2%*

Comparables: Drew Hutchison (40), Luis Severino (40), Aaron Sanchez (37)

Let's start with the positives: Ynoa didn't punch any hard objects with no give, so there's that. Other than that trap, last year Ynoa succumbed to basically every pitfall imaginable. He made a pair of starts for the Braves in April, gave up five runs in both (seeing his fastball absolutely crushed in the season's most anemic month) and was sent down to Gwinnett. He stayed there for the rest of the season; in early September, his season ended with a torn UCL. Tommy John surgery will likely cost him the entirety of this season. It's a tough scene for Ynoa, especially after a promising 2021 campaign. Sometimes life gives you lemons, and Ynoa got enough to start a lemonade company.

Lineouts

Hitters

HITTER	POS	TEAM	LVL	AGE	PA	R	2B	3B	HR	RBI	BB	K	SB	CS	AVG/OBP/SLG	DRC+	BABIP	BRR	DRP	WARP
Ehire Adrianza	3B	ATL	MLB	32	16	3	1	0	0	0	3	3	0	0	.154/.313/.231	97	.200	-0.9	2B(4): 0.3, 3B(1): 0.1	0.0
	3B	WAS	MLB	32	94	5	2	0	0	7	8	22	1	0	.179/.255/.202	86	.238	0.3	3B(18): 0, LF(9): -0.1, 2B(4): -0.1	0.1
Diego Benitez	SS	DSL BRA	ROK	17	182	25	6	0	2	27	29	37	3	2	.196/.363/.283		.240			
Travis Demeritte	OF	GWN	AAA	27	158	14	11	2	2	13	17	54	6	0	.207/.291/.357	76	.318	-0.2	RF(16): 1.1, LF(15): 1.7	0.2
	OF	ATL	MLB	27	96	9	2	0	3	6	6	32	0	0	.213/.260/.337	80	.291	-0.4	RF(20): -0.1, LF(6): 0	0.0
Delino DeShields	OF	GWN	AAA	29	426	61	12	0	1	26	76	116	35	11	.220/.367/.264	90	.326	6.5	CF(76): -6.1, LF(31): -1.2, 2B(1): -0.3	0.3
Alex Dickerson	RF/DH	GWN	AAA	32	357	36	20	2	12	43	29	76	1	0	.239/.305/.425	99	.274	-2.9	RF(40): -1.3, LF(20): 0.3	0.5
	RF/DH	ATL	MLB	32	36	3	0	0	1	2	3	9	0	0	.121/.194/.212	90	.130	0.0	RF(1): -0.0	0.0
Joe Dunand	3B	GWN	AAA	26	260	28	12	1	4	15	27	78	4	1	.205/.300/.319	70	.293	0.4	3B(55): 5.0, 1B(11): -0.7	0.3
	3B	JAX	AAA	26	80	15	6	0	2	9	10	27	2	0	.242/.354/.424	78	.368	-0.9	3B(14): 2.0, 1B(3): 0.0	0.1
	3B	MIA	MLB	26	11	2	1	0	1	1	0	3	0	0	.300/.364/.700	100	.333	0.0	2B(2): -0.2, 3B(1): 0.1	0.0
Guillermo Heredia	OF	ATL	MLB	31	82	12	3	1	3	8	6	32	0	0	.158/.220/.342	72	.220	1.6	LF(35): 0.1, RF(23): 1, CF(6): 0	0.3
Jake Marisnick	OF	GWN	AAA	31	74	8	1	1	1	3	3	18	7	1	.235/.297/.324	89	.306	1.2	CF(12): 0.5, RF(1): 0.1	0.3
	OF	IND	AAA	31	31	2	2	0	0	0	2	13	0	0	.250/.323/.321	67	.467	-0.7	RF(3): -0.4, CF(2): -0.5, LF(1): 0.2	0.1
	OF	PIT	MLB	31	82	9	6	0	2	6	4	24	2	1	.234/.272/.390	86	.314	1.6	CF(14): -0.4, LF(12): -0.1, RF(4): 0.3	0.3
David McCabe	3B	AUG	A	22	118	14	6	0	1	23	15	27	0	2	.260/.347/.350	100	.333	-2.3	3B(21): -1.0	0.1
Hoy Park	IF	IND	AAA	26	375	48	11	0	10	37	52	99	14	0	.225/.332/.354	93	.292	1.5	3B(36): -0.1, 2B(23): 1.4, SS(15): 0.3	1.0
	IF	PIT	MLB	26	60	7	2	0	2	6	4	15	1	0	.216/.276/.373	81	.250	0.8	2B(11): -1.1, 3B(6): -0.3, SS(3): -0.3	-0.1
Geraldo Quintero	3B/2B	AUG	A	20	419	61	22	9	6	47	48	69	26	8	.262/.358/.423	112	.308	0.9	3B(58): -0.7, 2B(30): -0.9	1.8
	3B/2B	ROM	A+	20	96	12	4	0	2	12	10	22	8	3	.238/.347/.363	94	.298	0.4	2B(11): -1.4, 3B(6): 0.5	0.1
Eli White	OF	TEX	MLB	28	117	16	2	0	3	10	11	41	12	1	.200/.274/.305	72	.290	1.8	CF(22): 1.6, LF(21): 0.9, RF(1): 0.1	0.5

After years of floating above the median, **Ehire Adrianza** finally returned to the ground in the promised land of 0 WARP. Perfectly balanced, as all replacement-level players should be. ⚾ The Braves made their full return to the international free agent landscape in a major way, signing **Diego Benitez** for a $2.5 million signing bonus. While there are questions about whether he'll stick at shortstop or shift to third base, there's no questions about why his bat produced such a lofty bonus. ⚾ The highlight of **Travis Demeritte's** 2022 campaign was an inside-the-park homer that pushed the Braves to victory in Texas. Once the hitting well went dry for him, it went bone-dry; he was wearing green uniforms in Gwinnett just a month after that electric roundtripper in Arlington. ⚾ The good news for **Delino DeShields** is that he was able to spend the vast majority of the 2022 season with just one organization instead of being bounced around, like he was in 2021. The bad news is that he was unable to get any major-league action, despite the organizational stability. You win some, you lose some. ⚾ Gwinnett is a long way from San Francisco, literally and figuratively: **Alex Dickerson** found himself again unable to gain a solid foothold at the plate, going 4-for-33 with one homer in 13 games before being designated for assignment and spending the rest of the season in Triple-A. ⚾ **Joe Dunand** one-upped his uncle Alex Rodriguez when he joined the wonderful club of players who hit a home run in their first career major-league plate appearance. Who cares if that was his only homer of a debut that only lasted three games? Joe did something A-Rod didn't do. ⚾ At this stage in his career, **Guillermo Heredia** has firmly established himself as a fourth outfielder and late-game defensive substitution. That has not stopped him from absolutely relishing his secondary role—as an incredibly enthusiastic clubhouse director of good vibes. He'll take those vibes to the KBO. ⚾ If you're still in need of highlight reel-caliber defense, then **Jake Marisnick** is your man with a plan. When it comes to his bat, it's a completely different story, which explains why he's drifted into Quad-A territory. ⚾ Atlanta went searching for gold at UNC-Charlotte, and ended up selecting former 49er **David McCabe** with their fourth-round draft pick. They just might strike it rich with the third base prospect if he can continue to hit for light-tower power as a professional. ⚾ **Hoy Park** was unable to build on his modest success from 2021; his career is looking stuck in park, too, as it looks more and more like he peaked as a Triple-A power-speed bat. ⚾ If recent history has taught us anything, it's that switch-hitting middle infielders under six feet tall who have a knack for barreling up baseballs while also speeding across the basepaths should not be ignored. It just so happens that **Geraldo Quintero** manages to tick all of those aforementioned boxes. ⚾ **Eli White** used his elite speed to make one of the better outfield catches of the season in May, robbing Ji-Man Choi of a home run. That speed didn't help him reach base at a satisfying clip, and his season was cut short by a wrist injury in mid-June. He later became the third Ranger to be traded to Atlanta between Halloween and New Year's.

Pitchers

PITCHER	TEAM	LVL	AGE	W	L	SV	G	GS	IP	H	HR	BB/9	K/9	K	GB%	BABIP	WHIP	ERA	DRA-	WARP	MPH	FB%	WHF	CSP
Nick Anderson	DUR	AAA	31	1	0	1	17	0	16	20	5	1.7	6.7	12	43.4%	.313	1.44	5.62	99	0.2	93.0	51.3%	17.4%	
Brad Brach	GWN	AAA	36	3	1	3	21	0	24	27	3	3.8	9.7	26	42.0%	.364	1.54	4.87	98	0.3				
Alan Rangel	MIS	AA	24	5	8	0	26	26	114^2	122	15	3.9	10.9	139	32.2%	.354	1.50	5.26	108	0.7				
Darius Vines	MIS	AA	24	7	4	0	20	20	107	100	16	2.5	10.7	127	43.5%	.312	1.21	3.95	86	1.9				
	GWN	AAA	24	1	0	0	7	5	33^2	29	1	3.7	7.8	29	42.0%	.283	1.28	3.21	98	0.5				

The formerly dominant **Nick Anderson** appeared in 19 games in 2022, but none in the majors, as he worked to regain the elbow strength and stuff that once made him among the game's best relievers. Though he didn't survive Tampa's offseason roster crunch, the Braves thought him worth a low-cost flier, inking him to a split deal in November. ⚾ **Brad Brach** returned to the Atlanta Braves on a minor-league deal, and Triple-A was where he stayed for the entirety of the 2022 season. He was placed on the Restricted List in June for an undisclosed reason and didn't appear again; you have to start wondering if he's pondering the dusty ol' trail pointing home. ⚾ After getting signed in 2014 and having his contract selected to the 40-man roster in 2021, **Alan Rangel** finally made it to the bigs in 2022. He had a solid full season in Double-A, got a taste of Triple-A and even got called up to The Show. He didn't make an appearance, but he got there! ⚾ **Spencer Schwellenbach** spent the season recovering from Tommy John surgery. He's expected to finally begin his professional journey as a starter: The sooner we get to see him toss that mid-90s heater and dangerous slider, the better. ⚾ Every spring training, there's a player or two per team who wind up making the Opening Day squad and eliciting a reaction of "Wow, good for them!" **Darius Vines** appears a prime candidate to capture that laurel, but his slow curve could be the weapon that allows him to stick around all season. ⚾ With a nasty splitter, a fastball that shot up a tick in velocity and a perfectly capable curveball, **Brooks Wilson** broke out in 2021 and seemed like he was on track to possibly get a taste of life in the bigs. Tommy John surgery scuttled those plans last year, though he could be in the mix again this year.

MIAMI MARLINS

Essay by Santul Nerkar

Player comments by Michael Ajeto and BP staff

The most iconic American sports franchises—like most countries, nations and trade unions—tend to hold uniting, defining and evolving myths, a *modus operandi* based on collective experiences that help grant a sense of identity and belonging to their members and supporters. The New York Yankees are the Bronx Bombers, a perpetually big and mighty team of mashers who embody their city's tough and bruising reputation—but they also strike out a lot and have boo-bird fans. The Chicago Cubs went from being the Lovable Losers whose most memorable moments were on the silver screen, to a World Series winner and back to losers—but not as lovable.

It's a little bit different for the teams that either are too new to have forged an identity, or just lack the juice to develop one—and the Miami Marlins fall somewhere in between. Throughout their 30-year existence, the Marlins have never been able to enter the echelon of teams with a widely known ethos—to the point where even their highest highs are defined by randomness, and until last year, their biggest headlines of the last decade involved a) a name change, presumably because the state of Florida had gotten too embarrassing for even them to be associated with; and b) trading away a reigning, 59-homer-hitting MVP as a cost-cutting measure by a newly installed (and since dissolved) ownership group.

But even a stopped clock is right twice a day—or in the case of Miami, twice in its entire existence.

To this day, the 1997 World Series is better known for the bullpen collapse of its loser, Cleveland, than for the grit and resolve of its anonymous newcomer winner, the Marlins. With an exciting young slugger in Gary Sheffield, a rising star in Charles Johnson and a lights-out starter in Kevin Brown, the Marlins nabbed a Wild Card spot and rode the magic to the World Series, improbably winning and thereby kicking off baseball's era of chaotic postseasons. But rather than riding the post-title glow that many teams enjoy, the Fish were soon back out of water. Instead of going all-in on the squad that had put his franchise on the map in just its fifth year of existence—smack dab in the middle of baseball's late-'90s revival—owner Wayne Huizenga was out on the team. Specifically, he had called it quits on the team earlier that year, before they scaled the mountaintop. Citing losses of

MIAMI MARLINS PROSPECTUS

2022 W-L: 69-93, 4TH IN NL EAST

Pythag	.436	*23rd*	DER	.696	*20th*
RS/G	3.62	*28th*	DRC+	90	*29th*
RA/G	4.17	*12th*	DRA-	94	*11th*
dWin%	.472	*20th*	FIP	3.92	*14th*
Payroll	$79M	*26th*	B-Age	29.3	*19th*
M$/MW	$2.9M	*9th*	P-Age	27.7	*2nd*

400′
386′
387′
344′
335′

- Opened 2012
- Retractable roof
- Synthetic surface
- Fence profile: 7′ to 11′6″

Park Factors

Runs	Runs/RH	Runs/LH	HR/RH	HR/LH
98	97	100	90	96

Top Hitter WARP	1.5 Nick Fortes
Top Pitcher WARP	5.1 Sandy Alcantara
2023 Top Prospect	Eury Pérez

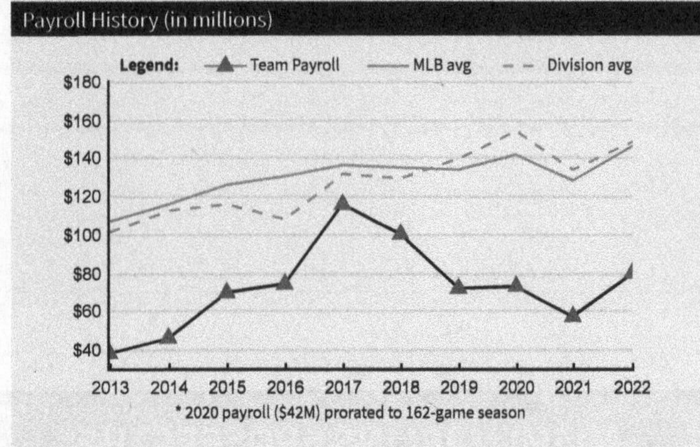

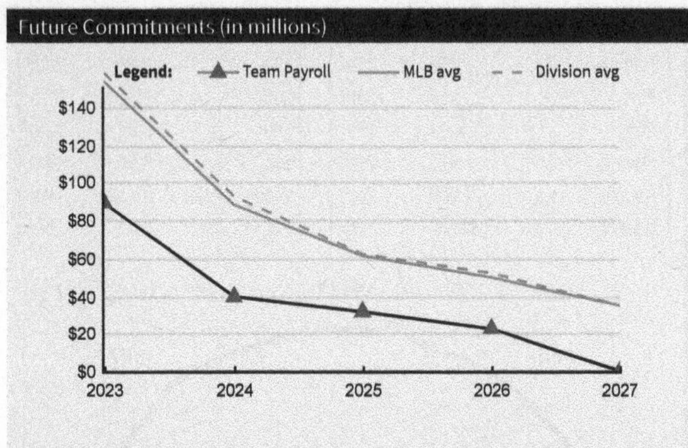

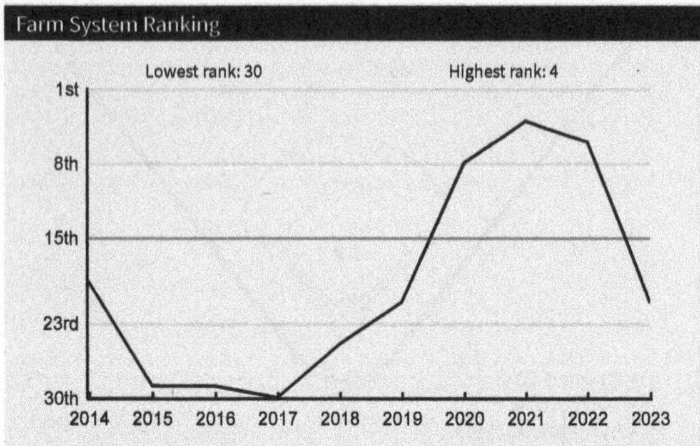

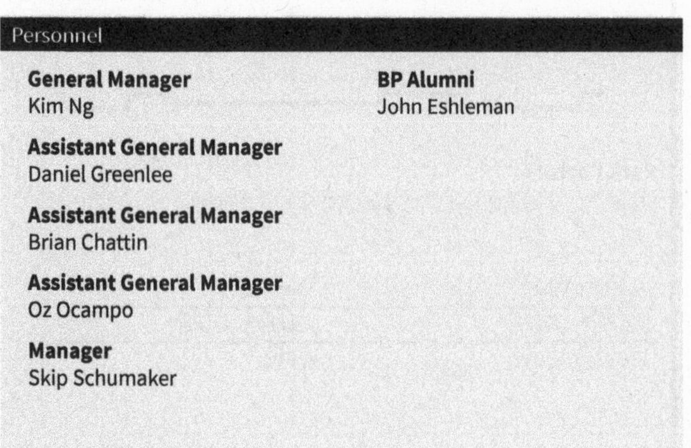
Personnel

General Manager
Kim Ng

Assistant General Manager
Daniel Greenlee

Assistant General Manager
Brian Chattin

Assistant General Manager
Oz Ocampo

Manager
Skip Schumaker

BP Alumni
John Eshleman

tens of millions of dollars, a dubious claim, Huizenga stripped the team of its beloved stars, who had just seemingly brought Miami baseball immortality. The effect of the mass exodus was immediate. The Marlins lost 108 games the next year in one of the biggest roster cleanses of all time, and the culprit was singular and identifiable.

The 2003 Marlins, meanwhile, caught lightning in a bottle while tripping ass-backwards. As the documentarians at Secret Base have chronicled, the Marlins weren't supposed to be good enough to contend for .500—let alone build back better all the way to a bizarro dynasty. They hit on their young talent in a major way, with whippersnappers Josh Beckett, Juan Pierre and Dontrelle Willis combining for more than 11 WARP, and a 20-year-old Miguel Cabrera just scratching the surface of his potential. After firing manager Jeff Torborg 38 games in the season, Florida found its charm, completing the now-trendy midseason turnaround to claw to 91 wins and—you guessed it—another Wild Card spot. This time, the Marlins gave new meaning to iconoclasm, smashing the title dreams of three of the most identifiable franchises in baseball history: the San Francisco Giants, the Cubs and the Yankees. The latter two series victories were a microcosm of the Marlins' franchise experience: In the historical retelling of the 2003 NLCS, Florida is a mere spectator as another spectator—Steve Bartman—assists the Cubs in an epic collapse that helped prolong Chicago's postseason misery. Meanwhile, the Yankees entered yet another chapter into their playoff scrapbook, as then-defensive sub (and now New York Public Enemy No. 1) Aaron Boone prolonged another team's long-lasting playoff misery, the Boston Red Sox. The again-improbable Marlins barely rate a mention.

In both cases, the losers wrote the history, and the Marlins may have come to believe it themselves. Despite prevailing against the Yankees in six games to capture their second World Series in seven years, with Beckett pitching a closeout game for the ages in the decisive matchup, the Marlins again gutted a championship-winning team, losing Ivan Rodríguez and Derrek Lee in the offseason before the slow trickle of departures came for Beckett, Pierre, Brad Penny and Carl Pavano. The on-field drop off was sudden and swift: Miami missed the playoffs the following season, then the next, and the next ... until the tale of the tape for more than a decade and a half of Miami baseball was littered with 80-, 90- and even 100-loss seasons. The fanbase, which had long been cynical of self-sabotaging team owners, lost the interest that it had remaining; Miami's existence transitioned to one of empty orange seats and the occasional star who departed for better times up North.

So what is the myth of the Marlins? If the franchise is a stopped clock, there's no question that right-hander Sandy Alcantara—his club re-branded and re-re-branded, umpteen rebuilds away now from the glory days—would be critical to arriving at the third correct reading in its history. Alcantara, the homegrown phenom who captured the franchise's first Cy Young Award in 2022, may offer a palate cleanser from that history, both a throwback and a welcome sight for a franchise looking to plot a new future. At 6-foot-5 and with flames coming out of his fingertips, Alcantara has the goods all teams want in pitchers in 2023—plus something extra. He has a high-velocity fastball, a prerequisite for most of the game's top aces, but he eschews much of the modern pitching wisdom. Alcantara isn't an especially elite spinner of the ball—he ranked just within the top quartile of spin rate on four-seam fastballs in 2022, according to Baseball Savant—nor is he a prolific strikeout pitcher. But what he is, a gamer, is vanishingly rare in this pitching environment, where aces are yanked after five innings of two-hit ball with even the whiff of a baserunner. Alcantara was the ultimate workhorse. He won the award largely on the back of a 228⅔-inning season—going against the grain for a franchise that's no stranger to it. The gap between Alcantara and the second-place finisher by innings pitched, Aaron Nola, was as large as the gap between the Phils workhorse and the pitchers with the 24th-most innings, the Oakland Athletics' Cole Irvin and the San Diego Padres' Joe Musgrove. It's only fitting that his remarkable season just edged out Brown, a hero for those '97 Fish, for the best single-season rWAR mark in franchise history.

But if the story of the Marlins is something other than baseball's pure randomness coming home to roost for two delightfully weird teams, it has to be its willingness to part ways with stars—many of them homegrown. For all the joy and optimism that Alcantara has provided Marlins fans during his rapid ascent, they've seen this movie before. Sheffield, Brown, Beckett and Cabrera are well-known departures from those title-winning Marlin teams, but fans have also recently endured a front office that's sent away J.T. Realmuto, Marcell Ozuna, Christian Yelich and Giancarlo Stanton. There's only so much you can invest in a franchise that, though it hasn't physically left its fans behind, has sent a bit of itself packing with every jettisoned player. Every time it seemed like Miami had the nucleus of a contender—a unicorn catcher and the game's most feared slugger, for one—it was back to square one before you could blink.

Perhaps the most frustrating part of the Marlins experience isn't the mere fact that the people in charge seem unwilling to spend the dollars to field a contender. It's that *they already have*—twice!—achieved baseball immortality, and the adults in the room didn't taste what was so special about winning. Plenty of regimes in professional sports are bad for no reason other than lovable ineptitude—not an aversion to improving the product they ostensibly oversee. The Marlins were blessed with two of the biggest gift horses in recent sports history, enjoyed their fruits and decided they'd had enough winning for a lifetime. Unless, that is, there's something brewing behind years and years of sub-.500 ball—with a single pandemic-year playoff appearance thrown in there. It wasn't just that you had to tear the thing down, Marlins, it's that the thing you tore down was really special—and you didn't even give it a proper farewell tour.

Though the current squad hasn't yet shown the inklings of a true contender—save that brief pulse in 2020—there are signs of life on 501 Marlins Way. Jazz Chisholm, who earned his first All-Star nod in 2022, is one of the most exciting young position players in baseball. Led by Alcantara, the starting rotation is one of the youngest in baseball and posted 11.1 WARP and a collective 95 DRA-, which placed 11th in MLB. And the team appears to have landed a bargain in infielder Jean Segura, a wily veteran with the postseason pedigree to infuse an immature group with the promise of better days. (That said, the Marlins' general indifference to one of the best free-agent classes in recent history was its own sort of instructive—at printing, 13 teams had signed players to contracts of at least three years over the offseason, and Segura's total contract value might wind up outside the winter's top 50.) Current reports also back up our Miami history lesson: Pretty much everyone is expendable to the front office brass, including top performers from 2022 like Pablo López, Edward Cabrera and even Chisholm. Perhaps the only reason Alcantara is a relatively safe bet to stay in South Florida is his team-friendly deal. Forget the story that Bruce Sherman and company are trying to sell Miami fans on—besides Alcantara, which players on the current roster will be around in mid-August?

For all of the mythmaking associated with baseball teams, perhaps the biggest myth of all is in how they're marketed as public goods despite being private. That is modern sports' foundational lie—that what is theirs is really ours, and the team we have defines who we are. Sure, these identities have nonetheless persisted. But when the avaricious nature of team management starts to take precedence, it can chip away at the facade of collective ownership by fans of the team. Marlins fans got their taste of success 25 years ago, then came back for another swig six years later. Twenty years after that encore, a third act has never felt so far away—and it seems naive to yet dream about it. For now, all that Marlins fans have are some memories, young faces and a whole lot of room to stretch out their legs in loanDepot Park. ■

—Santul Nerkar is an editor and reporter at FiveThirtyEight.

Hitters

Jon Berti IF
Born: 01/22/90 Age: 33 Bats: R Throws: R Height: 5'10" Weight: 190 lb. Origin: Round 18, 2011 Draft (#559 overall)

YEAR	TEAM	LVL	AGE	PA	R	2B	3B	HR	RBI	BB	K	SB	CS	Whiff%	AVG/OBP/SLG	DRC+	BABIP	BRR	DRP	WARP
2020	MIA	MLB	30	149	21	5	0	2	14	23	37	9	2	19.6%	.258/.388/.350	97	.354	1.5	2B(21): 0.3, CF(9): 0.3, RF(7): 1.8	0.8
2021	MIA	MLB	31	271	35	10	1	4	19	32	61	8	4	21.7%	.210/.311/.313	84	.265	2.9	3B(46): 0.3, 2B(27): -0.4, LF(7): 0.1	0.7
2022	MIA	MLB	32	404	47	17	3	4	28	42	89	41	5	24.5%	.240/.324/.338	92	.308	3.7	2B(47): -0.2, 3B(37): 1.8, LF(16): 0.5	1.4
2023 DC	*MIA*	*MLB*	*33*	*395*	*40*	*14*	*2*	*7*	*33*	*40*	*91*	*32*	*5*	*24.1%*	*.238/.326/.360*	*96*	*.301*	*16.2*	*LF 0, SS 0*	*2.6*

Comparables: Jamey Carroll (44), Logan Forsythe (44), Craig Gentry (43)

In celebration of the 20th anniversary of *White Men Can't Jump,* Berti hustled his way into a league-leading 41 stolen bases in his age-32 season. But true to form, he didn't do much in the way of driving the ball, with a .093 ISO mark which didn't even crack the top-15 of Marlins batters. Despite his lack of pop, Berti proved his worth by leveraging his elite speed into strong defensive grades—he mostly plays second and third base, but also fakes it at shortstop and in the outfield. It's not sexy—he's pretty much average across the board aside from his speed, fielding and eye—but on a more competitive team, Berti is probably a beloved utility man.

JJ Bleday OF
Born: 11/10/97 Age: 25 Bats: L Throws: L Height: 6'3" Weight: 205 lb. Origin: Round 1, 2019 Draft (#4 overall)

YEAR	TEAM	LVL	AGE	PA	R	2B	3B	HR	RBI	BB	K	SB	CS	Whiff%	AVG/OBP/SLG	DRC+	BABIP	BRR	DRP	WARP
2021	MSS	WIN	23	115	20	8	2	5	24	20	23	2	0		.316/.435/.600		.373			
2021	PNS	AA	23	468	52	22	3	12	54	64	101	5	3		.212/.323/.373	103	.250	0.0	RF(38): 5.8, LF(28): 5.2, CF(23): 1.1	2.8
2022	JAX	AAA	24	367	54	13	0	20	52	60	99	1	1	20.8%	.228/.365/.470	104	.268	-1.5	CF(39): -0.8, RF(29): 0.5, LF(17): -0.2	0.9
2022	MIA	MLB	24	238	21	10	2	5	16	30	67	4	1	28.0%	.167/.277/.309	76	.216	0.3	CF(38): -0.7, LF(22): -0.1, RF(4): 0	0.1
2023 DC	*MIA*	*MLB*	*25*	*227*	*22*	*9*	*1*	*7*	*22*	*26*	*59*	*2*	*0*	*27.6%*	*.202/.301/.376*	*86*	*.249*	*1.2*	*CF 0, LF 0*	*0.4*

Comparables: Roger Bernadina (68), Brett Phillips (68), Jordan Schafer (65)

Blessed be the day when we see dingers from Bleday. As with many younger prospects, the former fourth-overall pick likely suffered from cancellation of the 2020 minor-league season. After he got up to speed in 2022 and posted more robust numbers in Triple-A, the Marlins gave him the call. Aside from a discerning eye at the plate, he proved to be overmatched against fastballs, so pitchers didn't have much of a problem challenging him in the zone. Bleday hit more high fly balls and pop-ups than almost any player in MLB—especially in the last month or so of the season—and he completely neglected the left side of the field, hitting to the opposite field less than Carlos Santana, and about as much as Joey Gallo. It's difficult to imagine any success with such a narrow approach; given that he's getting under the ball nearly half the time, it's clear that the bat path needs tweaking. There's a reason he was taken so high in the draft, so a sluggish debut is hardly an indictment of Bleday's future, but it was a sobering take on his current reality.

Peyton Burdick OF
Born: 02/26/97 Age: 26 Bats: R Throws: R Height: 6'0" Weight: 205 lb. Origin: Round 3, 2019 Draft (#82 overall)

YEAR	TEAM	LVL	AGE	PA	R	2B	3B	HR	RBI	BB	K	SB	CS	Whiff%	AVG/OBP/SLG	DRC+	BABIP	BRR	DRP	WARP
2021	PNS	AA	24	460	71	17	2	23	52	76	135	9	5		.231/.376/.472	133	.293	0.3	CF(50): -5.1, LF(25): 0.9, RF(15): -1.2	2.7
2021	JAX	AAA	24	31	5	3	0	0	1	3	11	0	0		.143/.226/.250	77	.235	0.1	LF(3): -0.5, CF(3): -0.8, RF(1): -0.1	-0.1
2022	JAX	AAA	25	430	74	16	5	15	58	53	120	13	3	40.8%	.214/.326/.409	89	.272	2.0	CF(42): 0.3, LF(23): -1.0, RF(22): 0.0	1.3
2022	MIA	MLB	25	102	8	4	0	4	11	8	35	1	0	33.6%	.207/.284/.380	81	.283	0.0	LF(14): 0, CF(13): -0.9, RF(4): -0.3	0.0
2023 DC	*MIA*	*MLB*	*26*	*89*	*9*	*3*	*0*	*2*	*8*	*8*	*28*	*1*	*1*	*35.1%*	*.205/.293/.371*	*84*	*.277*	*0.8*	*CF 0, RF 0*	*0.1*

Comparables: Brandon Boggs (68), Chris Heisey (55), Peter O'Brien (54)

There's an understanding that, if burdened by a high strikeout rate, a hitter can buoy their overall line by walking a lot and hitting dingers. We've seen the proliferation of the three true outcomes hitter in the past decade, which is to say that Adam Dunn walked (and hit dingers, and struck out) so Burdick could run. The issue is that Burdick struck out 34% of the time while running a league-average isolated slugging percentage and walk rate. He has plenty of raw power, but he swings through a huge number of fastballs upstairs, and he can't seem to cover the plate away—especially against breaking pitches. Perhaps the Marlins should have seen this coming with the uptick in whiffs in Triple-A; either way, it would probably be judicious to let him work out the kinks down there.

Jazz Chisholm Jr. 2B
Born: 02/01/98 Age: 25 Bats: L Throws: R Height: 5'11" Weight: 184 lb. Origin: International Free Agent, 2015

YEAR	TEAM	LVL	AGE	PA	R	2B	3B	HR	RBI	BB	K	SB	CS	Whiff%	AVG/OBP/SLG	DRC+	BABIP	BRR	DRP	WARP
2020	MIA	MLB	22	62	8	1	1	2	6	5	19	2	2	25.7%	.161/.242/.321	82	.200	-0.1	2B(13): 0.3, SS(9): 0.1	0.1
2021	MIA	MLB	23	507	70	20	4	18	53	34	145	23	8	30.1%	.248/.303/.425	86	.319	2.1	2B(91): 0.2, SS(37): -2.5	0.9
2022	MIA	MLB	24	241	39	10	4	14	45	21	66	12	5	32.5%	.254/.325/.535	114	.294	0.8	2B(60): -0.4	1.2
2023 DC	*MIA*	*MLB*	*25*	*571*	*69*	*21*	*8*	*21*	*58*	*46*	*165*	*35*	*12*	*30.8%*	*.240/.312/.441*	*103*	*.313*	*8.4*	*2B 0*	*2.6*

Comparables: Yoán Moncada (61), Javier Báez (60), Luis Valbuena (59)

He didn't quite make it to the All-Star break thanks to a lower back injury, but before Chisholm found himself on the IL, he was careening toward what very well could have been an all-time campaign for a second baseman. It could be that his numbers were inflated in the shortened sample, but it's equally believable that he's fashioned himself into something resembling a star—and arguably the best player on the Marlins. Stationed solely at second base for the first time, Chisholm shaved his strikeout percentage slightly and raised his walk percentage. Most of his gains, however, came via an improved ability to maximize his batted ball outcomes, limiting weakly hit balls while elevating to his pull side more. Few other players pair an 80-grade personality with this blend of skills, and none with an elite Euro step to boot.

Garrett Cooper 1B/DH Born: 12/25/90 Age: 32 Bats: R Throws: R Height: 6'5" Weight: 235 lb. Origin: Round 6, 2013 Draft (#182 overall)

YEAR	TEAM	LVL	AGE	PA	R	2B	3B	HR	RBI	BB	K	SB	CS	Whiff%	AVG/OBP/SLG	DRC+	BABIP	BRR	DRP	WARP
2020	MIA	MLB	29	133	20	8	0	6	20	11	31	0	0	22.2%	.283/.353/.500	114	.337	-0.9	1B(15): -0.1	0.4
2021	MIA	MLB	30	250	30	10	1	9	33	30	68	1	1	27.2%	.284/.380/.465	104	.374	-2.1	RF(41): -4, 1B(19): -0.8	0.1
2022	MIA	MLB	31	469	37	33	2	9	50	40	119	0	0	25.1%	.261/.337/.415	94	.340	0.1	1B(59): -0.6	0.7
2023 DC	*MIA*	*MLB*	*32*	*519*	*57*	*26*	*1*	*16*	*57*	*48*	*125*	*1*	*0*	*25.1%*	*.258/.338/.426*	*115*	*.321*	*-0.1*	*1B 0*	*1.7*

Comparables: Nelson Cruz (54), Matt Diaz (54), Angel Echevarria (53)

For years, Joey Votto was the poster boy for never giving away the freest out of all: the pop-up. Now that Votto has regressed, Cooper is making a case for the title, even if he's probably (definitely) bested by Tim Anderson. So few pop-ups speaks to elite barrel control, which Cooper harnesses to consistently hit the ball hard. Statcast categorized only about half of his batted balls as weakly hit, which means only 16 hitters squared up the ball as consistently as Cooper. The overall contribution to the team is limited, but that didn't stop him from earning his first All-Star selection as Bryce Harper's replacement.

Bryan De La Cruz OF Born: 12/16/96 Age: 26 Bats: R Throws: R Height: 6'2" Weight: 175 lb. Origin: International Free Agent, 2013

YEAR	TEAM	LVL	AGE	PA	R	2B	3B	HR	RBI	BB	K	SB	CS	Whiff%	AVG/OBP/SLG	DRC+	BABIP	BRR	DRP	WARP
2021	TOR	WIN	24	69	6	4	0	1	12	5	12	0	0		.226/.290/.339		.260			
2021	SUG	AAA	24	293	48	17	0	12	50	17	59	2	4		.324/.362/.518	111	.373	1.9	RF(22): -1.3, LF(19): -0.3, CF(16): -1.5	1.3
2021	MIA	MLB	24	219	17	7	2	5	19	18	53	1	1	25.3%	.296/.356/.427	99	.380	0.2	CF(24): 0, RF(23): -0.3, LF(16): -0.2	0.7
2022	JAX	AAA	25	54	10	3	0	4	10	4	13	1	0		.320/.370/.620	112	.364	0.6	LF(5): -0.2, CF(4): -0.3, RF(3): 0.1	0.6
2022	MIA	MLB	25	355	38	20	0	13	43	19	90	4	0	28.8%	.252/.294/.432	98	.304	-0.8	CF(42): -2.4, RF(41): -0.5, LF(39): 0.2	0.7
2023 DC	*MIA*	*MLB*	*26*	*452*	*43*	*20*	*2*	*10*	*43*	*27*	*116*	*3*	*2*	*28.0%*	*.255/.305/.390*	*91*	*.330*	*0.6*	*CF -3, RF 0*	*0.5*

Comparables: Lorenzo Cain (61), Dexter Fowler (58), Juan Lagares (57)

If there's one player on the Marlins who looks to be on the verge of a breakout, it's De La Cruz. He has had a solid bat path since his major-league debut, limiting his number of mis-hit balls. If there's a critique to be made of his 2021, it's that he made *too* much contact and probably needed to sacrifice contact for power. He did so last year, folding in a little more swing and miss, and the power came. After an August demotion, De La Cruz returned having quieted his leg kick into more of a toe tap, improving his timing: Following his recall, he slashed .388/.419/.719 while flexing higher exit velos and cutting down on the strikeouts. It's tempting to point to his .443 BABIP over that span, but De La Cruz boasts the highest sweet-spot percentage in MLB and one of the lowest standard deviations of launch angle—both indicators of a player who can run a high BABIP. Outside of Chisholm Jr., it's hard to argue that there's a more exciting hitter on the Marlins.

Xavier Edwards IF Born: 08/09/99 Age: 23 Bats: S Throws: R Height: 5'10" Weight: 175 lb. Origin: Round 1, 2018 Draft (#38 overall)

YEAR	TEAM	LVL	AGE	PA	R	2B	3B	HR	RBI	BB	K	SB	CS	Whiff%	AVG/OBP/SLG	DRC+	BABIP	BRR	DRP	WARP
2021	MTG	AA	21	337	40	13	3	0	27	36	42	19	11		.302/.377/.368	110	.348	-1.2	2B(55): -1.1, 3B(22): 1.7	1.3
2022	DUR	AAA	22	400	48	19	1	5	33	43	75	7	4	15.8%	.246/.328/.350	91	.300	-0.7	2B(49): -1.5, 3B(20): 0.1, SS(20): -0.5	0.5
2023 DC	*MIA*	*MLB*	*23*	*27*	*2*	*0*	*0*	*0*	*1*	*2*	*4*	*0*	*0*	*19.1%*	*.241/.306/.322*	*76*	*.293*	*0.1*	*2B 0*	*0.0*

Comparables: Ronald Torreyes (55), Luis Arraez (53), Reegie Corona (53)

Edwards had been mentioned often alongside the Francos and Bruján s of the Rays' system since being acquired by Tampa via trade in late 2019. He possesses top-level speed with good bat-to-ball skills and the glove to play up the middle. That said, he has almost no power, and defensively he's trending toward second base. Although his stint in Triple-A Durham marked the first time in his pro career he failed to hit .300, Edwards will continue to profile as little more than a down-the-order slap-hitter until he can convince scouts the bat won't get knocked out of his hands. Basically, Blake Snell might've had a point. Nonetheless, the Marlins proved willing to gamble on his speed, contact ability and pedigree as the Rays—rich in middle infielders—pared down their 40-man roster.

Jerar Encarnacion OF Born: 10/22/97 Age: 25 Bats: R Throws: R Height: 6'4" Weight: 250 lb. Origin: International Free Agent, 2015

YEAR	TEAM	LVL	AGE	PA	R	2B	3B	HR	RBI	BB	K	SB	CS	Whiff%	AVG/OBP/SLG	DRC+	BABIP	BRR	DRP	WARP
2021	PNS	AA	23	260	24	12	1	9	28	24	99	5	5		.222/.308/.400	78	.341	-1.4	RF(27): 1.2, 1B(16): 0.5, LF(12): -0.4	0.1
2022	PNS	AA	24	136	26	3	0	8	18	13	35	4	2		.358/.426/.583	122	.449	0.0	RF(21): 0.6, LF(6): 1.1, 1B(4): 0.6	1.3
2022	JAX	AAA	24	297	43	12	0	14	40	29	87	0	1	28.6%	.265/.333/.470	96	.335	-1.4	RF(40): 0.7, 1B(13): -1.9, LF(12): 0.5	0.5
2022	MIA	MLB	24	81	7	3	0	3	14	3	32	2	0	42.7%	.182/.210/.338	67	.256	-0.2	LF(10): 0.2, RF(10): 0.5	0.0
2023 DC	*MIA*	*MLB*	*25*	*151*	*15*	*5*	*0*	*4*	*14*	*10*	*53*	*2*	*0*	*37.5%*	*.228/.284/.378*	*80*	*.332*	*-0.3*	*RF 0, LF 0*	*-0.2*

Comparables: Alfredo Marte (59), Aaron Altherr (59), Jason Botts (53)

Pretty much every step of the way, Encarnacion has struggled as he's reached the next level of the minors—but he also has a pattern of addressing those issues the following year and settling into that level. Aside from in Double-A in 2021, his strikeout rates haven't been particularly concerning, but that doesn't mean that his swinging-strike percentages haven't been. Encarnacion has freely swung through fastballs in the zone, especially upstairs, and off-speed pitches out of the zone. With no defensive home, he's going to have to rake: While he's deserving of some time to work through things, whether in Triple-A or MLB, it's not clear that's going to happen.

Nick Fortes C

Born: 11/11/96 Age: 26 Bats: R Throws: R Height: 5'11" Weight: 198 lb. Origin: Round 4, 2018 Draft (#117 overall)

YEAR	TEAM	LVL	AGE	PA	R	2B	3B	HR	RBI	BB	K	SB	CS	Whiff%	AVG/OBP/SLG	DRC+	BABIP	BRR	DRP	WARP
2021	PNS	AA	24	226	21	10	1	3	23	22	36	5	2		.251/.338/.359	114	.289	0.3	C(48): 5.8	1.8
2021	JAX	AAA	24	152	16	7	0	4	21	10	18	0	0		.237/.322/.378	118	.248	-1.9	C(27): -0.9	0.6
2021	MIA	MLB	24	34	6	0	0	4	7	3	8	1	0	19.3%	.290/.353/.677	115	.263	0.6	C(7): -0.9	0.2
2022	JAX	AAA	25	120	13	4	0	3	13	11	17	1	0	19.2%	.257/.342/.381	113	.279	0.5	C(24): 2.6	0.8
2022	MIA	MLB	25	240	41	6	1	9	24	18	45	5	3	22.9%	.230/.304/.392	109	.252	1.4	C(59): 2.9	1.5
2023 DC	*MIA*	*MLB*	*26*	*251*	*23*	*8*	*1*	*5*	*23*	*18*	*47*	*5*	*1*	*22.3%*	*.231/.301/.357*	*86*	*.266*	*1.4*	*C-3*	*0.3*

Comparables: Travis d'Arnaud (69), Martín Maldonado (64), Tony Sanchez (56)

YEAR	TEAM	P. COUNT	FRM RUNS	BLK RUNS	THRW RUNS	TOT RUNS
2021	PNS	6615	5.9	0.1	-0.1	6.0
2021	JAX	3741	0.0	0.1	-0.1	-0.1
2021	MIA	744	-0.7	-0.1	0.0	-0.8
2022	JAX	3480	2.5	0.2	0.0	2.7
2022	MIA	7565	2.5	0.1	0.0	2.6
2023	*MIA*	*9620*	*-3.3*	*-0.1*	*0.1*	*-3.3*

Winner of the superlative *Least Likely to Lead Marlins Batters in WARP*, Fortes forged his way into the top spot by posting the team's second-best DRC+ and offering strong work behind the plate. He makes the most out of limited power: All but one of Fortes' nine home runs were pulled to left and left-center field. He pops the ball up much more than league-average, and doesn't do so with the power that typically accompanies such an elevated pop-up rate. When he's come so far, though, why look for warning signs? Everything else is gravy.

Avisaíl García RF

Born: 06/12/91 Age: 32 Bats: R Throws: R Height: 6'4" Weight: 250 lb. Origin: International Free Agent, 2007

YEAR	TEAM	LVL	AGE	PA	R	2B	3B	HR	RBI	BB	K	SB	CS	Whiff%	AVG/OBP/SLG	DRC+	BABIP	BRR	DRP	WARP
2020	MIL	MLB	29	207	20	10	0	2	15	20	49	1	3	34.7%	.238/.333/.326	91	.315	-1.2	CF(44): -1.1, RF(5): 0.1	0.2
2021	MIL	MLB	30	515	68	18	0	29	86	38	121	8	4	33.6%	.262/.330/.490	114	.291	0.0	RF(121): 3.4, CF(1): -0.1	2.8
2022	JAX	AAA	31	34	3	2	0	0	2	5	11	2	0		.250/.353/.321	85	.389	-0.4	RF(5): 0.2	0.1
2022	MIA	MLB	31	380	31	9	0	8	35	17	109	4	0	36.6%	.224/.266/.317	73	.298	-1.3	RF(86): -4.1	-0.7
2023 DC	*MIA*	*MLB*	*32*	*462*	*45*	*16*	*1*	*14*	*49*	*29*	*124*	*6*	*1*	*35.7%*	*.241/.300/.387*	*91*	*.306*	*1.7*	*RF 0*	*0.5*

Comparables: Jose Guillen (63), Ollie Brown (62), Roberto Clemente (60)

With a plus arm, straightline speed and elite exit velocities, García is the archetypal Statcast darling. The problem, shared by many hitters with his skill set, is that he's had trouble consistently translating his raw power into game power. Last season he saw his greatest power outage yet, resulting in a 73 DRC+. That could've been influenced by lingering injury issues, or it could be that he saw a career-high 39.4% breaking ball percentage. Probably both. It's likely that García puts the ball on the ground at an above-average clip for the rest of his career, but it's hard to imagine him struggling as much as he did in 2022. And there's always the off chance he finally taps into that raw power for good.

Jordan Groshans IF

Born: 11/10/99 Age: 23 Bats: R Throws: R Height: 6'3" Weight: 200 lb. Origin: Round 1, 2018 Draft (#12 overall)

YEAR	TEAM	LVL	AGE	PA	R	2B	3B	HR	RBI	BB	K	SB	CS	Whiff%	AVG/OBP/SLG	DRC+	BABIP	BRR	DRP	WARP
2021	NH	AA	21	316	46	23	0	7	40	34	61	0	0		.291/.367/.450	118	.347	-1.2	SS(43): -1.9, 3B(21): -0.6, 1B(1): -0.1	1.3
2022	BUF	AAA	22	279	30	8	0	1	24	35	46	2	0		.250/.348/.296	98	.303	-0.4	SS(39): -0.8, 3B(14): -0.2, 1B(4): -0.2	0.8
2022	JAX	AAA	22	133	14	7	0	2	10	19	19	1	0		.301/.398/.416	116	.344	-0.4	3B(12): -0.5, SS(10): 0.1, 2B(9): -0.7	0.4
2022	MIA	MLB	22	65	9	0	0	1	2	4	13	0	0	17.9%	.262/.308/.311	96	.319	-1.5	3B(17): 0	0.0
2023 DC	*MIA*	*MLB*	*23*	*29*	*2*	*1*	*0*	*0*	*2*	*2*	*5*	*0*	*0*	*22.1%*	*.251/.319/.345*	*88*	*.304*	*0.0*	*3B 0*	*0.0*

Comparables: Richard Urena (60), Erick Aybar (59), Cristhian Adames (59)

With Bo Bichette and Matt Chapman entrenched at shortstop and third base in Toronto, there wasn't much of a home for Groshans in the first place—but the logistics of finding him playing time were made much easier by him completely forgetting how to hit the ball with authority. That may have to do with a lingering oblique issue, from early on in the season—and he's dealt with his fair share of injuries since he debuted in 2019—but he's also showed limited power as a professional. As a player with good feel for contact who makes strong swing decisions, it wouldn't be surprising if he's a swing change away from producing. Regardless, he's gonna need to trade some contact for power to stick in Miami.

Garrett Hampson UT

Born: 10/10/94 Age: 28 Bats: R Throws: R Height: 5'11" Weight: 196 lb. Origin: Round 3, 2016 Draft (#81 overall)

YEAR	TEAM	LVL	AGE	PA	R	2B	3B	HR	RBI	BB	K	SB	CS	Whiff%	AVG/OBP/SLG	DRC+	BABIP	BRR	DRP	WARP
2020	COL	MLB	25	184	25	4	3	5	11	13	60	6	1	29.6%	.234/.287/.383	75	.330	2.5	2B(26): 2.1, CF(20): 0.3, LF(7): 0.1	0.5
2021	COL	MLB	26	494	69	21	6	11	33	33	118	17	7	24.3%	.234/.289/.380	81	.291	2.5	CF(91): 1.1, 2B(47): 0, SS(5): -0.6	1.1
2022	COL	MLB	27	226	29	7	3	2	15	21	63	12	2	26.2%	.211/.287/.307	76	.294	1.2	CF(36): -0.9, SS(32): -0.1, 2B(10): -0.5	0.0
2023 DC	*FA*	*MLB*	*28*	*202*	*18*	*7*	*1*	*4*	*20*	*16*	*49*	*10*	*3*	*24.9%*	*.229/.295/.357*	*80*	*.290*	*2.5*	*CF -1, 2B 0*	*0.2*

Comparables: Darwin Barney (56), Ronny Cedeno (53), Johnny Giavotella (52)

The book in Colorado has closed on Hampson, who barely got off the bench last year behind Brendan Rodgers and José Iglesias and forgot his bat there every time he stepped to the plate. The former top prospect simply doesn't make enough quality contact, and while it's strange in retrospect that Colorado gave more playing time to a 32-year-old journeyman in Iglesias than a homegrown product, it's not as if Hampson did anything to earn more reps. He brings nothing to the table save prospect pedigree and plus-plus speed, and at this point, it's really only on display when he runs back to the dugout after another fruitless at-bat. Now in Miami on a minor-league deal, his path to playing time is no clearer than in Colorado.

Charles Leblanc 3B Born: 06/03/96 Age: 27 Bats: R Throws: R Height: 6'3" Weight: 195 lb. Origin: Round 4, 2016 Draft (#129 overall)

YEAR	TEAM	LVL	AGE	PA	R	2B	3B	HR	RBI	BB	K	SB	CS	Whiff%	AVG/OBP/SLG	DRC+	BABIP	BRR	DRP	WARP
2021	RR	AAA	25	374	49	16	4	17	57	40	131	5	3		.229/.313/.455	81	.319	2.6	3B(34): -1.3, 1B(21): -0.7, 2B(21): 1.2	0.4
2022	JAX	AAA	26	360	47	20	1	14	45	35	98	6	0	28.7%	.302/.381/.503	99	.396	-1.3	3B(38): 0.2, LF(25): 0.9, 2B(17): 2.8	1.2
2022	MIA	MLB	26	169	18	10	0	4	11	12	53	4	2	25.9%	.263/.320/.404	81	.374	1.5	2B(26): -0.2, 3B(13): 1.4, 1B(8): 0	0.4
2023 DC	*MIA*	*MLB*	*27*	*62*	*5*	*2*	*0*	*1*	*5*	*4*	*17*	*1*	*0*	*27.1%*	*.232/.294/.370*	*82*	*.310*	*0.5*	*1B 0*	*0.0*

Comparables: Chris Johnson (60), Jordy Mercer (59), Phil Gosselin (58)

Selected in the minor-league portion of the 2021 Rule 5 Draft, Leblanc debuted in the middle of last season, boasting skills to prove he could hack it as a major-league bench player. Moving around the infield—much like several other Marlins players—Leblanc flashed strong glovework at second base, but didn't have the arm strength to play a serviceable third. His aggressive first-pitch approach contrasted with an ultra-passive approach on the whole: Despite relatively average swing-and-miss numbers, he ran a high strikeout percentage. He was designated for assignment in early January.

Ian Lewis IF Born: 02/04/03 Age: 20 Bats: S Throws: R Height: 5'10" Weight: 177 lb. Origin: International Free Agent, 2019

YEAR	TEAM	LVL	AGE	PA	R	2B	3B	HR	RBI	BB	K	SB	CS	Whiff%	AVG/OBP/SLG	DRC+	BABIP	BRR	DRP	WARP
2021	MRL	ROK	18	161	24	10	5	3	27	11	24	9	4		.302/.354/.497		.344			
2022	JUP	A	19	213	21	7	3	2	21	22	45	16	1	30.7%	.265/.347/.368	108	.333	0.7	2B(29): -2.1, 3B(14): 0.4, SS(2): -1.1	0.6
2023 non-DC	*MIA*	*MLB*	*20*	*251*	*18*	*9*	*2*	*1*	*19*	*16*	*75*	*10*	*2*	*34.5%*	*.214/.273/.300*	*58*	*.310*	*6.3*	*2B 0, 3B 0*	*0.0*

Comparables: L.J. Hoes (65), Brett Lawrie (64), Carlos Sanchez (63)

It's reasonable to think that we're only a year or so away from Lewis ascending toward the top of prospect lists. Despite his smaller frame, he has plenty of bat speed, and leverages it to make frequent contact. Lately, he can even punish offerings to his pull-side. He doesn't have glaring holes in his game, although it remains to be seen how much the switch hitter can contribute from the right side. There's a good shot that he joins Jazz Chisholm as the second Bahamian on the Marlins.

Miguel Rojas SS Born: 02/24/89 Age: 34 Bats: R Throws: R Height: 6'0" Weight: 188 lb. Origin: International Free Agent, 2005

YEAR	TEAM	LVL	AGE	PA	R	2B	3B	HR	RBI	BB	K	SB	CS	Whiff%	AVG/OBP/SLG	DRC+	BABIP	BRR	DRP	WARP
2020	MIA	MLB	31	143	20	10	1	4	20	16	18	5	1	17.3%	.304/.392/.496	121	.330	-0.4	SS(39): 3.2, 3B(1): 0	1.1
2021	MIA	MLB	32	539	66	30	3	9	48	37	74	13	3	19.3%	.265/.322/.392	97	.295	0.4	SS(128): -1.2	1.6
2022	MIA	MLB	33	507	34	19	2	6	36	26	61	9	3	15.7%	.236/.283/.323	93	.258	-0.2	SS(136): 1, 1B(10): -0.1	1.2
2023 DC	*MIA*	*MLB*	*34*	*539*	*54*	*24*	*1*	*9*	*47*	*33*	*66*	*12*	*3*	*16.7%*	*.256/.309/.367*	*92*	*.279*	*2.5*	*SS 2, 1B 0*	*1.4*

Comparables: Ozzie Smith (68), Rey Sanchez (68), Jose Vizcaino (68)

As time has passed, we've watched the league move away from glove-first shortstops with little feel for hitting—perhaps because teams have improved their ability to judiciously position defenders. Rojas represents one of the few holdovers, having posted an OPS of barely .600 on the year while playing some of the best defense of his life at shortstop. His peripherals suggest that he hasn't changed much as a hitter, despite significantly worse outcomes, but it's probably fair to say that he's reached the end of the line as a starting shortstop.

★ ★ ★ *2023 Top 101 Prospect* **#93** ★ ★ ★

Jose Salas IF Born: 04/26/03 Age: 20 Bats: S Throws: R Height: 6'2" Weight: 191 lb. Origin: International Free Agent, 2019

YEAR	TEAM	LVL	AGE	PA	R	2B	3B	HR	RBI	BB	K	SB	CS	Whiff%	AVG/OBP/SLG	DRC+	BABIP	BRR	DRP	WARP
2021	MRL	ROK	18	107	14	10	0	1	11	11	23	8	5		.370/.458/.511		.485			
2021	JUP	A	18	123	12	4	0	1	8	11	28	6	0		.250/.333/.315	99	.325	2.1	SS(25): -2.6	0.3
2022	JUP	A	19	257	40	13	3	5	24	23	54	15	1	22.1%	.267/.355/.421	119	.327	-2.3	SS(25): -0.3, 3B(16): 1.3, 2B(12): -0.8	1.1
2022	BEL	A+	19	217	29	7	1	4	17	20	41	18	0		.230/.319/.340	99	.274	2.8	SS(16): 0.7, 2B(14): -1.3, 3B(11): 0.2	0.8
2023 non-DC	*MIA*	*MLB*	*20*	*251*	*20*	*9*	*1*	*3*	*21*	*15*	*60*	*10*	*1*	*27.2%*	*.218/.278/.317*	*64*	*.283*	*7.4*	*2B 0, 3B 0*	*0.3*

Comparables: Ketel Marte (76), Jonathan Araúz (68), Cole Tucker (68)

Despite being two or three years younger than average at each level he's played, Salas has already torn it up in complex league and A-ball and continues to hold up against higher-level competition. While his power has waned upon each promotion, it's not peculiar for young hitters to require an adjustment period. He's already addressed some of the question marks regarding his swing, and his sound defense and feel for contact will only help his prospect buzz grow.

Jesús Sánchez OF Born: 10/07/97 Age: 25 Bats: L Throws: R Height: 6'3" Weight: 222 lb. Origin: International Free Agent, 2014

YEAR	TEAM	LVL	AGE	PA	R	2B	3B	HR	RBI	BB	K	SB	CS	Whiff%	AVG/OBP/SLG	DRC+	BABIP	BRR	DRP	WARP
2020	MIA	MLB	22	29	1	1	0	0	2	4	11	0	0	25.0%	.040/.172/.080	68	.071	0.0	RF(10): -0.7	-0.1
2021	TOR	WIN	23	84	11	10	0	0	8	12	15	1	0		.324/.429/.465		.411			
2021	JAX	AAA	23	155	23	5	4	10	31	12	29	1	0		.348/.406/.652	140	.382	0.6	RF(21): 6.7, LF(11): -0.7	1.8
2021	MIA	MLB	23	251	27	8	2	14	36	20	78	0	1	29.4%	.251/.319/.489	94	.316	-2.5	RF(41): 1.6, LF(21): -0.6	0.4
2022	JAX	AAA	24	183	30	7	0	6	27	21	39	4	1		.308/.399/.465	119	.377	1.1	RF(32): 0.2, CF(4): -0.1, LF(2): -0.6	1.0
2022	MIA	MLB	24	343	38	14	3	13	36	26	92	1	0	29.7%	.214/.280/.403	90	.258	-1.6	CF(78): -2.8, LF(12): 0.4	0.4
2023 DC	*MIA*	*MLB*	*25*	*332*	*34*	*13*	*3*	*11*	*37*	*25*	*86*	*3*	*0*	*29.4%*	*.241/.308/.419*	*98*	*.300*	*3.1*	*CF -1, RF 0*	*0.9*

Comparables: Phil Plantier (54), Randal Grichuk (54), Colby Rasmus (52)

When Sánchez got his bat on the ball in 2021, good things happened. He still scorched the ball at times in 2022—he flexed a 114.7-mph exit velocity—but with much less consistency, and a disproportionate decline to his production against fastballs. The result was a nearly 10% increase in the percentage of his batted balls categorized as poorly hit. He already struggles with putting the ball into play, so Sánchez can't afford not to make the most of his batted balls—especially given that he doesn't add much in the way of baserunning or fielding.

Jean Segura 2B

Born: 03/17/90 Age: 33 Bats: R Throws: R Height: 5'10" Weight: 220 lb. Origin: International Free Agent, 2007

YEAR	TEAM	LVL	AGE	PA	R	2B	3B	HR	RBI	BB	K	SB	CS	Whiff%	AVG/OBP/SLG	DRC+	BABIP	BRR	DRP	WARP
2020	PHI	MLB	30	217	28	5	2	7	25	23	45	2	2	22.4%	.266/.347/.422	107	.314	1.3	2B(32): -0.4, 3B(24): 0.1, SS(4): -0.7	0.9
2021	PHI	MLB	31	567	76	27	3	14	58	39	78	9	3	17.3%	.290/.348/.436	110	.317	1.7	2B(128): 1.9	3.1
2022	LHV	AAA	32	36	3	0	0	0	3	6	6	2	0		.200/.333/.200	103	.250	0.1	2B(5): -1.0	0.0
2022	PHI	MLB	32	387	45	9	0	10	33	25	58	13	6	18.6%	.277/.336/.387	117	.307	1.3	2B(97): 0.6, SS(1): 0	2.2
2023 DC	*MIA*	*MLB*	*33*	*371*	*39*	*14*	*1*	*7*	*32*	*26*	*57*	*14*	*3*	*18.7%*	*.269/.330/.385*	*104*	*.306*	*7.1*	*2B 0, 3B 0*	*1.7*

Comparables: José Reyes (76), Howie Kendrick (71), Leo Cardenas (71)

Segura spent the 2022 season as the answer to one of baseball's more depressing trivia questions: which active player has the most games under his belt without a playoff appearance? Fortunately, he shed that distinction in October, tilting back his head and feeling the cool drops of rain on his face as his 1,328-game postseason drought finally came to a close. Up until that exciting ending, it was another typical Segura campaign. His biggest skill continues to be putting the ball in play, which he did enough to post a fair OBP despite a low walk rate. He was also a capable defender and a smart baserunner, making him an above-average all-around player for yet another season. In fact, he might have finished with his highest WARP in years had a broken finger not kept him out for June and July. When he returned, his average exit velocity and launch angle took a nosedive, and his slugging percentage faced the consequences. Segura made it work—drawing more walks and slapping extra ground-ball singles to make up for the missing extra-base hits—but it was a worrisome trend nonetheless—one that is now the Marlins' concern after they inked him to a free-agent contract.

Jorge Soler LF

Born: 02/25/92 Age: 31 Bats: R Throws: R Height: 6'4" Weight: 235 lb. Origin: International Free Agent, 2012

YEAR	TEAM	LVL	AGE	PA	R	2B	3B	HR	RBI	BB	K	SB	CS	Whiff%	AVG/OBP/SLG	DRC+	BABIP	BRR	DRP	WARP
2020	KC	MLB	28	174	17	8	0	8	24	19	60	0	0	37.2%	.228/.326/.443	87	.317	-0.4	RF(8): -0.9	0.0
2021	KC	MLB	29	360	38	16	0	13	37	38	97	0	0	31.6%	.192/.288/.370	93	.229	-0.3	RF(46): -6.5	-0.1
2021	ATL	MLB	29	242	36	11	0	14	33	29	45	0	0	25.5%	.269/.358/.524	124	.278	-0.7	RF(50): -3	1.1
2022	MIA	MLB	30	306	32	13	0	13	34	31	90	0	2	31.5%	.207/.295/.400	98	.256	-0.2	LF(57): -1.1	0.7
2023 DC	*MIA*	*MLB*	*31*	*550*	*66*	*23*	*0*	*26*	*70*	*58*	*136*	*1*	*0*	*30.7%*	*.229/.320/.443*	*113*	*.262*	*-1.0*	*LF 0*	*1.8*

Comparables: Jeff Burroughs (64), Jesse Barfield (61), Mark Whiten (58)

Two years removed from a 48-home run season in 2019, Soler landed a three-year, $36 million contract, a deal likely informed by his strong 2021 playoff performance which helped propel Atlanta to a championship. Soler missed more than half of the season with a collection of injuries, including pelvic inflammation and lower back spasms that bothered him throughout the first half and ended up sidelining him indefinitely in July. Soler will require less time on the field in 2023 in the hopes he finds better health.

Jacob Stallings C

Born: 12/22/89 Age: 33 Bats: R Throws: R Height: 6'5" Weight: 225 lb. Origin: Round 7, 2012 Draft (#226 overall)

YEAR	TEAM	LVL	AGE	PA	R	2B	3B	HR	RBI	BB	K	SB	CS	Whiff%	AVG/OBP/SLG	DRC+	BABIP	BRR	DRP	WARP
2020	PIT	MLB	30	143	13	7	0	3	18	15	40	0	0	26.1%	.248/.326/.376	91	.337	-0.6	C(42): 4.7	0.8
2021	PIT	MLB	31	427	38	20	1	8	53	49	85	0	0	23.4%	.246/.335/.369	97	.297	-2.5	C(104): 3.4	1.7
2022	MIA	MLB	32	384	25	12	0	4	34	29	83	0	1	22.7%	.223/.292/.292	85	.280	-2.5	C(110): -0.8	0.4
2023 DC	*MIA*	*MLB*	*33*	*375*	*35*	*15*	*0*	*7*	*33*	*32*	*73*	*0*	*0*	*23.0%*	*.240/.315/.360*	*91*	*.286*	*-2.6*	*C 0*	*0.7*

Comparables: Ryan Hanigan (66), Gary Bennett (63), Vance Wilson (59)

YEAR	TEAM	P. COUNT	FRM RUNS	BLK RUNS	THRW RUNS	TOT RUNS
2020	PIT	6186	4.2	0.0	0.5	4.7
2021	PIT	15291	4.8	1.4	0.3	6.5
2022	MIA	14818	-2.3	0.5	1.1	-0.7
2023	*MIA*	*14430*	*0.0*	*0.5*	*-0.2*	*0.3*

After looking like he might be a serviceable, late-blooming catcher, Stallings lost the gains he made—both behind the plate and in the batter's box. In hindsight, this outcome probably should have been obvious, given that there weren't any gains made in his skills or peripherals, just in his results. Perhaps this is a Hosmerian thing, where he hits every other year. But it seems more likely that Stallings had a one-off strong season as a result of hard work and statistical noise.

Kahlil Watson IF

Born: 04/16/03 Age: 20 Bats: L Throws: R Height: 5'9" Weight: 178 lb. Origin: Round 1, 2021 Draft (#16 overall)

YEAR	TEAM	LVL	AGE	PA	R	2B	3B	HR	RBI	BB	K	SB	CS	Whiff%	AVG/OBP/SLG	DRC+	BABIP	BRR	DRP	WARP
2021	MRL	ROK	18	42	13	3	2	0	5	8	7	4	1		.394/.524/.606		.500			
2022	JUP	A	19	358	50	16	5	9	44	27	127	16	3	37.6%	.231/.296/.395	80	.346	3.7	SS(46): -1.1, 2B(23): 0.7	0.6
2023 non-DC	*MIA*	*MLB*	*20*	*251*	*19*	*10*	*2*	*4*	*22*	*13*	*101*	*7*	*2*	*40.5%*	*.198/.246/.320*	*49*	*.326*	*4.1*	*2B 0, SS 0*	*-0.5*

Comparables: Anderson Tejeda (84), Jonathan Araúz (81), Reid Brignac (79)

Unlike Jose Salas, Watson has always had success *in spite of* his aggressive approach, rather than because of it. His 43.2% strikeout rate in April was obscured by five dingers and the .941 OPS he ran on the month—but it didn't take long for pitchers to adjust. Without his power to prop up his overall line, Watson posted an OPS of .645 the rest of the season, anchored by an 18.5% swinging-strike percentage. While that degree of swing-and-miss is untenable, it would hardly be the first time a 19-year-old struggled during his first passthrough of Low-A, and the former 16th overall pick is deserving of some time to unlearn bad habits.

Joey Wendle IF Born: 04/26/90 Age: 33 Bats: L Throws: R Height: 6'1" Weight: 195 lb. Origin: Round 6, 2012 Draft (#203 overall)

YEAR	TEAM	LVL	AGE	PA	R	2B	3B	HR	RBI	BB	K	SB	CS	Whiff%	AVG/OBP/SLG	DRC+	BABIP	BRR	DRP	WARP
2020	TB	MLB	30	184	24	9	2	4	17	10	35	8	2	18.9%	.286/.342/.435	92	.338	-1.3	3B(28): 0.1, 2B(20): 0.3, SS(10): 0.4	0.3
2021	TB	MLB	31	501	73	31	4	11	54	28	113	8	6	25.1%	.265/.319/.422	90	.327	1.1	3B(107): -0.5, SS(25): 2.2, 2B(16): 0	1.4
2022	MIA	MLB	32	371	27	24	1	3	32	15	50	12	3	16.9%	.259/.297/.360	89	.293	1.9	3B(43): -1.9, SS(34): 0.2, 2B(33): 0.1	0.6
2023 DC	*MIA*	*MLB*	*33*	*463*	*44*	*25*	*4*	*7*	*43*	*23*	*75*	*11*	*4*	*19.4%*	*.264/.314/.393*	*96*	*.307*	*1.9*	*SS 1, 3B 0*	*1.3*

Comparables: Billy Goodman (58), Mike Aviles (55), Jerry Lumpe (54)

Doing his best Jon Berti impression, Wendle spread himself across the infield, playing even-ish amounts at shortstop, second and third base. He hung his hat on a career-low strikeout rate—swinging more than ever while cutting down on whiffs—and also registered a career-low walk rate, which meant he put the ball in play more than ever. For some, that's a good thing. But for Wendle, it meant a home run total identical to his average launch angle: three. Wendle is a player who could help any team, but he's probably not someone you want entrenched in the leadoff spot.

PITCHERS

Sandy Alcantara RHP Born: 09/07/95 Age: 27 Bats: R Throws: R Height: 6'5" Weight: 200 lb. Origin: International Free Agent, 2013

YEAR	TEAM	LVL	AGE	W	L	SV	G	GS	IP	H	HR	BB/9	K/9	K	GB%	BABIP	WHIP	ERA	DRA-	WARP	MPH	FB%	Whiff%	CSP
2020	MIA	MLB	24	3	2	0	7	7	42	35	4	3.2	8.4	39	49.6%	.277	1.19	3.00	86	0.8	96.7	60.0%	24.1%	51.1%
2021	MIA	MLB	25	9	15	0	33	33	205^2	171	21	2.2	8.8	201	52.8%	.273	1.07	3.19	81	4.0	98.0	50.1%	27.5%	54.6%
2022	MIA	MLB	26	14	9	0	32	32	228^2	174	16	2.0	8.1	207	53.2%	.262	0.98	2.28	76	5.1	98.0	50.0%	25.6%	55.8%
2023 DC	*MIA*	*MLB*	*27*	*13*	*9*	*0*	*29*	*29*	*209.7*	*185*	*18*	*2.4*	*8.5*	*198*	*52.1%*	*.287*	*1.15*	*2.84*	*78*	*4.2*	*97.6*	*51.3%*	*26.2%*	*54.2%*

Comparables: Matt Cain (71), Dave Stieb (69), Félix Hernández (68)

Over the past five seasons, only Gerrit Cole, Aaron Nola and Alcantara have thrown more than 200 innings three times. Last year, in tossing 228⅔ innings—23⅔ more than any starting pitcher—Alcantara compiled more frames than any starting pitcher since David Price in 2016. He's a bona fide workhorse. His 23.7% strikeout percentage isn't what you generally see from a modern ace, but it's also what allows him to pitch deeper into games. At 3.67 pitches per plate appearance, just 18 pitchers amassed fewer pitches per PA last year—and none of them sat 98 mph with four-seam and two-seam fastballs.

Alcantara's increased emphasis on his 92-mph changeup has made it one of the most valuable pitches in MLB. He's able to create the depth of a mid-80s changeup while managing well above-average arm-side run, despite the pitch's firmness. He also throws a 90-mph slider to counter his primary offering's arm-side movement; what it lacks in raw horizontal movement it makes up for with synthetic sweep via a low arm slot and wide position on the rubber. If you weren't counting, that makes for four pitches ranging from 90–98 mph, three of which get a significant amount of seam-shifted wake. He might not rack up the monster strikeout totals, but few create weak contact like Alcantara. Even fewer can work as many innings.

Richard Bleier LHP Born: 04/16/87 Age: 36 Bats: L Throws: L Height: 6'3" Weight: 215 lb. Origin: Round 6, 2008 Draft (#183 overall)

YEAR	TEAM	LVL	AGE	W	L	SV	G	GS	IP	H	HR	BB/9	K/9	K	GB%	BABIP	WHIP	ERA	DRA-	WARP	MPH	FB%	Whiff%	CSP
2020	MIA	MLB	33	1	1	0	19	0	13^2	13	0	2.6	4.6	7	68.9%	.289	1.24	2.63	88	0.2	89.0	55.3%	11.5%	48.9%
2020	BAL	MLB	33	0	0	0	2	0	3	1	0	0.0	12.0	4	83.3%	.167	0.33	0.00	69	0.1	89.5	43.6%	42.1%	46.4%
2021	MIA	MLB	34	3	2	0	68	0	58	51	4	0.9	6.8	44	65.7%	.281	0.98	2.95	91	0.8	90.2	62.8%	19.9%	62.3%
2022	MIA	MLB	35	2	2	1	55	1	50^2	63	3	1.8	5.7	32	53.1%	.343	1.44	3.55	115	0.1	90.1	53.9%	18.5%	58.3%
2023 DC	*MIA*	*MLB*	*36*	*2*	*3*	*0*	*60*	*0*	*51.7*	*62*	*5*	*2.1*	*5.1*	*29*	*57.0%*	*.317*	*1.43*	*4.60*	*118*	*-0.3*	*89.9*	*58.0%*	*18.9%*	*58.3%*

Comparables: Javy Guerra (51), Joe Beimel (51), Brandon Kintzler (50)

Despite strikeout numbers that belong in 1980, Bleier has made a career by not walking anyone and keeping the ball in the yard. He leans on one of the league's steepest sinkers about half the time, pounding it toward the bottom of the zone to produce grounders straight out of grainy 80s footage (missing only the turf infields). Last year, though, hitters started to lift Bleier's offerings—if his days of posting outlier ground-ball rates are behind him, he might soon be a thing of the past, too.

Huascar Brazoban RHP Born: 10/15/89 Age: 33 Bats: R Throws: R Height: 6'3" Weight: 155 lb. Origin: International Free Agent, 2012

YEAR	TEAM	LVL	AGE	W	L	SV	G	GS	IP	H	HR	BB/9	K/9	K	GB%	BABIP	WHIP	ERA	DRA-	WARP	MPH	FB%	Whiff%	CSP
2022	JAX	AAA	32	2	0	0	27	0	45^1	32	6	3.2	11.7	59	43.8%	.263	1.06	3.18	65	1.4	97.1	47.2%	43.5%	
2022	MIA	MLB	32	1	1	0	27	0	32	26	3	5.9	11.2	40	48.7%	.311	1.47	3.09	82	0.6	97.3	33.1%	40.2%	50.2%
2023 DC	*MIA*	*MLB*	*33*	*3*	*2*	*0*	*60*	*0*	*51.7*	*43*	*5*	*4.4*	*10.7*	*61*	*43.8%*	*.292*	*1.32*	*3.59*	*90*	*0.5*	*97.3*	*33.1%*	*33.2%*	*50.2%*

Comparables: James Hoyt (67), Jumbo Díaz (64), Pat Venditte (64)

Brazoban is fascinating. There's zero effort in his delivery. He gets almost no extension down the mound. His arm slot is as generic three-quarters as we've ever seen. And yet…it could work. It's not hard to imagine him using his cutter to suppress barrels. It *is* difficult to see it all coming together if he repeats his 58.2% strike percentage, third-worst of 505 pitchers who logged at least 25 innings. Either way, the guy is 33 years old, and at this time last year he'd just been signed out of indy ball. How can you not root for him?

Edward Cabrera RHP Born: 04/13/98 Age: 25 Bats: R Throws: R Height: 6'5" Weight: 217 lb. Origin: International Free Agent, 2015

YEAR	TEAM	LVL	AGE	W	L	SV	G	GS	IP	H	HR	BB/9	K/9	K	GB%	BABIP	WHIP	ERA	DRA-	WARP	MPH	FB%	Whiff%	CSP
2021	JUP	A	23	0	0	0	2	2	6	4	0	0.0	16.5	11	36.4%	.364	0.67	0.00	89	0.1				
2021	PNS	AA	23	2	1	0	5	5	26	19	3	2.1	11.4	33	48.3%	.296	0.96	2.77	85	0.5				
2021	JAX	AAA	23	1	3	0	6	6	29^1	22	4	5.8	14.7	48	37.7%	.316	1.40	3.68	77	0.8				
2021	MIA	MLB	23	0	3	0	7	7	26^1	24	6	6.5	9.6	28	40.6%	.286	1.63	5.81	107	0.2	96.8	38.5%	28.1%	52.7%
2022	PNS	AA	24	0	0	0	2	2	6	0	0	1.5	12.0	8	54.5%	.000	0.17	0.00	98	0.1				
2022	JAX	AAA	24	2	2	0	6	6	28^2	21	2	3.8	12.2	39	44.6%	.302	1.15	3.77	76	0.7				
2022	MIA	MLB	24	6	4	0	14	14	71^2	44	10	4.1	9.4	75	44.8%	.207	1.07	3.01	94	0.9	96.0	31.8%	31.3%	49.3%
2023 DC	*MIA*	*MLB*	*25*	*6*	*6*	*0*	*22*	*22*	*99.7*	*85*	*12*	*4.5*	*10.4*	*115*	*44.7%*	*.293*	*1.36*	*3.97*	*98*	*0.9*	*96.2*	*33.3%*	*31.4%*	*50.1%*

Comparables: Chris Archer (63), Joe Ross (60), Robert Stephenson (59)

The only reason Sandy Alcantara can't say he throws the hardest changeup of any starter is because, at 92.6 mph, Cabrera holds the distinction. Between his changeup, curveball and slider, he's proven he can throw his secondaries for strikes. His career will come down to whether he can use his harder pitches, four-seam and two-seam fastballs, to keep hitters honest. Last year, he was unable to control the four-seamer, throwing nearly half of them for balls and a handful of others for home runs. In short, Cabrera throws more non-competitive pitches than most starting pitchers, and the list of players who waste pitches so consistently doesn't bode well.

Paul Campbell RHP Born: 07/26/95 Age: 27 Bats: L Throws: R Height: 6'0" Weight: 210 lb. Origin: Round 21, 2017 Draft (#619 overall)

YEAR	TEAM	LVL	AGE	W	L	SV	G	GS	IP	H	HR	BB/9	K/9	K	GB%	BABIP	WHIP	ERA	DRA-	WARP	MPH	FB%	Whiff%	CSP
2021	JAX	AAA	25	0	0	0	3	3	10^2	3	1	5.1	7.6	9	30.8%	.080	0.84	0.84	104	0.1				
2021	MIA	MLB	25	2	3	0	16	1	26^2	32	5	3.4	8.8	26	41.9%	.338	1.58	6.41	97	0.3	92.6	59.2%	24.7%	54.1%
2022	JAX	AAA	26	0	2	0	2	1	8	9	2	5.6	10.1	9	17.4%	.333	1.75	11.25	125	0.0				
2023 non-DC	*MIA*	*MLB*	*27*	*2*	*3*	*0*	*57*	*0*	*50*	*50*	*7*	*3.9*	*7.3*	*40*	*38.2%*	*.293*	*1.45*	*4.73*	*118*	*-0.3*	*92.6*	*59.2%*	*23.7%*	*54.1%*

Comparables: Paul Clemens (60), Donn Roach (59), Jake Buchanan (58)

Campbell has long shown strong feel for supination, which helps him spin his curveball better than just about anyone. And while his fastball's raw spin grades out just as well relative to his peers, he isn't able to weaponize that spin because his fastball is so inefficient. That makes for a straighter, steeper fastball than is ideal, which probably makes him ripe for incorporating a sinker. A 6.41 ERA in his 2021 MLB debut was ugly—but Campbell doesn't lack for intrigue, though he'll need to re-establish his bona fides when he returns from being one of five Marlins with recent big-league experience who underwent Tommy John last season.

Daniel Castano LHP Born: 09/17/94 Age: 28 Bats: L Throws: L Height: 6'3" Weight: 231 lb. Origin: Round 19, 2016 Draft (#586 overall)

YEAR	TEAM	LVL	AGE	W	L	SV	G	GS	IP	H	HR	BB/9	K/9	K	GB%	BABIP	WHIP	ERA	DRA-	WARP	MPH	FB%	Whiff%	CSP
2020	MIA	MLB	25	1	2	0	7	6	29^2	30	3	3.3	3.6	12	46.6%	.270	1.38	3.03	129	-0.1	89.2	50.2%	19.7%	49.9%
2021	JAX	AAA	26	7	2	0	14	14	78^1	69	16	1.8	6.2	54	48.3%	.237	1.09	3.91	110	0.6				
2021	MIA	MLB	26	0	2	0	5	4	20^1	22	3	3.5	5.8	13	37.1%	.288	1.48	4.87	114	0.0	90.4	51.7%	17.1%	60.4%
2022	JAX	AAA	27	3	0	0	7	6	34	33	10	2.9	10.1	38	42.6%	.274	1.29	4.24	86	0.7	89.0	50.0%	42.9%	
2022	MIA	MLB	27	1	3	0	10	7	35^2	42	5	2.3	5.0	20	46.4%	.311	1.43	4.04	123	-0.1	87.3	59.3%	17.5%	59.3%
2023 DC	*MIA*	*MLB*	*28*	*4*	*4*	*0*	*44*	*4*	*49*	*55*	*7*	*2.8*	*5.3*	*29*	*45.9%*	*.295*	*1.44*	*4.86*	*124*	*-0.3*	*88.4*	*55.5%*	*20.6%*	*57.5%*

Comparables: Dillon Peters (72), Tyler Cloyd (68), Vidal Nuño (67)

If you're looking for a precedent for Castano—a reliever with a 7.0% strikeout minus walk percentage—perhaps look to teammate Richard Bleier. The difference between the two is that Bleier flexes more of an outlier release point and has expertly limited home runs over his career, while Castano has struggled to limit dingers and coax hitters into putting the ball on the ground. If nothing else (and there might be nothing else), Castano is fascinating: The gyro-heavy nature of his repertoire means that—in terms of pitch movement—where one pitch ends, another begins.

JT Chargois RHP Born: 12/03/90 Age: 32 Bats: S Throws: R Height: 6'3" Weight: 200 lb. Origin: Round 2, 2012 Draft (#72 overall)

YEAR	TEAM	LVL	AGE	W	L	SV	G	GS	IP	H	HR	BB/9	K/9	K	GB%	BABIP	WHIP	ERA	DRA-	WARP	MPH	FB%	Whiff%	CSP
2021	SEA	MLB	30	1	0	0	31	0	30	23	2	1.8	8.7	29	44.9%	.276	0.97	3.00	95	0.4	95.8	31.0%	29.8%	55.0%
2021	TB	MLB	30	5	1	0	25	0	23^2	15	3	5.3	9.1	24	44.1%	.214	1.23	1.90	103	0.2	96.9	50.7%	24.6%	48.4%
2022	DUR	AAA	31	1	2	0	10	0	5^2	10	1	11.1	6.4	4	27.3%	.429	3.00	20.65	137	0.0				
2022	TB	MLB	31	2	0	0	21	3	22^1	16	3	2.0	6.9	17	59.7%	.220	0.94	2.42	98	0.2	96.6	61.7%	23.2%	55.4%
2023 DC	*MIA*	*MLB*	*32*	*2*	*2*	*0*	*53*	*0*	*46*	*45*	*4*	*3.9*	*7.6*	*38*	*49.0%*	*.296*	*1.40*	*4.26*	*106*	*0.1*	*96.5*	*47.2%*	*24.0%*	*52.8%*

Comparables: Darren O'Day (73), Louis Coleman (73), Nick Vincent (72)

Chargois spent most of last season dealing with an oblique injury suffered in early April that he re-aggravated while on rehab assignment in May. After a four-month layoff he returned to Tampa in late August and once more served as a valuable contributor. Perhaps as a byproduct of injury, he flipped his two-pitch approach on its head. After leading with the slider in previous years, he leaned heavily on his upper-90s sinker, throwing it about 60% of the time. As a result, he notched fewer strikeouts but also issued fewer walks and, as you'd expect from a sinker-steady diet, he saw a noticeable spike in ground-ball rate: it jumped to around 60% after coming in just under 45% in 2021. Despite his continued success, the Rays dealt Chargois to the Marlins in November, sending the 32-year-old righty to his third team in as many years just as he enters arbitration eligibility.

Jake Eder LHP Born: 10/09/98 Age: 24 Bats: L Throws: L Height: 6'4" Weight: 215 lb. Origin: Round 4, 2020 Draft (#104 overall)

YEAR	TEAM	LVL	AGE	W	L	SV	G	GS	IP	H	HR	BB/9	K/9	K	GB%	BABIP	WHIP	ERA	DRA-	WARP	MPH	FB%	Whiff%	CSP
2021	PNS	AA	22	3	5	0	15	15	71^1	43	3	3.4	12.5	99	50.3%	.261	0.98	1.77	82	1.5				
2023 non-DC	*MIA*	*MLB*	*24*	*2*	*2*	*0*	*57*	*0*	*50*	*44*	*5*	*4.5*	*9.2*	*50*	*48.4%*	*.290*	*1.39*	*3.96*	*98*	*0.2*			*27.8%*	

Comparables: Drew Smyly (94), Matt Moore (90), Blake Snell (89)

Between command and velocity, inconsistency has been the name of the game dating back to Eder's high school years. After drafting him in the fourth round, the Marlins aggressively assigned him to Double-A. There, he started 15 games, posting a 1.77 ERA supported by a 25.1% strikeout-minus-walk rate that bested the 2021 Double-A figures of Spencer Strider and teammate Max Meyer. Eder was diagnosed with a torn UCL that August and underwent Tommy John surgery within a month, missing all of the 2022 season. So long as he returns with his command and velo at least somewhere in the proximity of where they last showed, it's hard to think he's not at least a back-end starter—changeup be damned. If his fate is the bullpen, he'll immediately become one of the hardest-throwing lefties in baseball, with an elite slider to boot.

Dylan Floro RHP Born: 12/27/90 Age: 32 Bats: L Throws: R Height: 6'2" Weight: 203 lb. Origin: Round 13, 2012 Draft (#422 overall)

YEAR	TEAM	LVL	AGE	W	L	SV	G	GS	IP	H	HR	BB/9	K/9	K	GB%	BABIP	WHIP	ERA	DRA-	WARP	MPH	FB%	Whiff%	CSP
2020	LAD	MLB	29	3	0	0	25	0	24^1	23	1	1.5	7.0	19	57.3%	.297	1.11	2.59	88	0.4	93.5	46.9%	23.3%	45.7%
2021	MIA	MLB	30	6	6	15	68	0	64	53	2	3.5	8.7	62	49.2%	.282	1.22	2.81	93	0.8	93.8	62.8%	23.0%	51.8%
2022	MIA	MLB	31	1	3	10	56	0	53^2	48	4	2.5	8.0	48	43.9%	.288	1.17	3.02	96	0.6	92.6	63.5%	22.3%	52.9%
2023 DC	*MIA*	*MLB*	*32*	*3*	*3*	*25*	*60*	*0*	*51.7*	*54*	*6*	*3.1*	*7.5*	*43*	*48.4%*	*.308*	*1.39*	*4.11*	*105*	*0.1*	*93.3*	*62.1%*	*22.2%*	*51.7%*

Comparables: Ryan Pressly (59), Tommy Hunter (58), Nick Vincent (57)

It's not often that you see a reliever liberally and successfully deploy four pitches. In two years with the Marlins, that's exactly what Floro has done, avoiding the gopher ball with all four offerings. None of the other skills stands out—but they don't have to. Since 2018, only Tyler Rogers has limited home runs more effectively; between the longball suppression and a perfectly solid K-BB%, Floro has blossomed into a quietly effective reliever.

Braxton Garrett LHP Born: 08/05/97 Age: 25 Bats: R Throws: L Height: 6'2" Weight: 202 lb. Origin: Round 1, 2016 Draft (#7 overall)

YEAR	TEAM	LVL	AGE	W	L	SV	G	GS	IP	H	HR	BB/9	K/9	K	GB%	BABIP	WHIP	ERA	DRA-	WARP	MPH	FB%	Whiff%	CSP
2020	MIA	MLB	22	1	1	0	2	2	7^2	8	3	5.9	9.4	8	61.9%	.278	1.70	5.87	104	0.1	90.0	48.9%	23.1%	38.3%
2021	JAX	AAA	23	5	4	0	18	18	85^2	73	10	3.4	9.0	86	45.3%	.281	1.23	3.89	112	0.7				
2021	MIA	MLB	23	1	2	0	8	7	34	42	3	5.3	8.5	32	36.2%	.398	1.82	5.03	118	0.0	90.1	49.2%	21.8%	53.2%
2022	JAX	AAA	24	2	3	0	7	7	34^1	28	3	2.4	7.6	29	52.0%	.253	1.08	3.15	96	0.5	91.6	46.8%	31.2%	
2022	MIA	MLB	24	3	7	0	17	17	88	86	9	2.5	9.2	90	47.4%	.322	1.25	3.58	99	0.9	91.2	47.6%	26.6%	55.7%
2023 DC	*MIA*	*MLB*	*25*	*8*	*7*	*0*	*52*	*12*	*103.3*	*103*	*13*	*3.5*	*8.4*	*96*	*46.7%*	*.303*	*1.38*	*4.27*	*108*	*0.4*	*90.9*	*48.0%*	*25.5%*	*54.5%*

Comparables: Robbie Erlin (67), Homer Bailey (66), Zach Eflin (66)

The Garrett you saw in 2021 was nothing like the one you saw in 2022—he boosted his sinker and slider usage by about 10% each, at the expense of his curveball and four-seam fastball. Those changes were dictated by an altered release: He lowered his arm slot by about three inches and shifted a foot toward the first-base side of the rubber. In doing so, he found a more natural arm slot, tightened up his command and added at least a tick to all of his pitches. Perhaps more importantly, Garrett lowered his release point, helping to add both depth and run to his sinker while increasing his slider's sweep across the zone—both in terms of raw movement and horizontal approach angle. It all makes for one of the stronger sinker-slider combinations around and, despite the Marlins' abundance of options, is certainly deserving of a rotation spot.

Pablo López RHP Born: 03/07/96 Age: 27 Bats: L Throws: R Height: 6'4" Weight: 225 lb. Origin: International Free Agent, 2012

YEAR	TEAM	LVL	AGE	W	L	SV	G	GS	IP	H	HR	BB/9	K/9	K	GB%	BABIP	WHIP	ERA	DRA-	WARP	MPH	FB%	Whiff%	CSP
2020	MIA	MLB	24	6	4	0	11	11	57^1	50	4	2.8	9.3	59	52.8%	.293	1.19	3.61	70	1.6	93.7	63.1%	26.5%	47.2%
2021	MIA	MLB	25	5	5	0	20	20	102^2	89	11	2.3	10.1	115	46.3%	.302	1.12	3.07	74	2.3	93.7	58.0%	25.8%	52.4%
2022	MIA	MLB	26	10	10	0	32	32	180	157	21	2.7	8.7	174	46.7%	.283	1.17	3.75	91	2.6	93.6	47.0%	28.2%	52.3%
2023 DC	*MIA*	*MLB*	*27*	*11*	*9*	*0*	*29*	*29*	*174.7*	*159*	*18*	*2.6*	*8.6*	*166*	*47.3%*	*.291*	*1.20*	*3.27*	*87*	*2.6*	*93.6*	*52.2%*	*27.5%*	*51.5%*

Comparables: Bret Saberhagen (81), Erik Hanson (80), Alex Fernandez (80)

There are several paths to a good changeup, most of which involve differentiation from the fastball. One approach is velocity differential: The average difference in fastball-changeup velocity is 7.7 mph, whereas López's is 6.0 mph. So that's not it. Another is induced vertical break differential: Again, López is a touch below average. Vertical approach angle differential: average separation. So what gives? López generates more depth and arm-side run on his changeup than you'd expect based on its release, and it's one of the firmest changeups offered by any starter. The cherry on top: He commands it expertly to the bottom corner of the zone. Everything just harmonizes. Much like Kevin Gausman's splitter, the potency of López's changeup helps his four-seam fastball play up, which helps his changeup play up, which...you get the point. López has been one of the most effective starting pitchers in MLB for years now. The only thing that changed is he got 180 innings to demonstrate it.

Jesús Luzardo LHP Born: 09/30/97 Age: 25 Bats: L Throws: L Height: 6'0" Weight: 218 lb. Origin: Round 3, 2016 Draft (#94 overall)

YEAR	TEAM	LVL	AGE	W	L	SV	G	GS	IP	H	HR	BB/9	K/9	K	GB%	BABIP	WHIP	ERA	DRA-	WARP	MPH	FB%	Whiff%	CSP
2020	OAK	MLB	22	3	2	0	12	9	59	58	9	2.6	9.0	59	46.2%	.308	1.27	4.12	89	1.0	95.8	53.3%	29.7%	46.2%
2021	LV	AAA	23	2	2	0	8	8	29	33	3	4.7	8.1	26	47.2%	.349	1.66	6.52	99	0.1				
2021	MIA	MLB	23	4	5	0	12	12	57^1	60	9	5.0	9.1	58	36.5%	.319	1.60	6.44	120	-0.1	95.6	46.4%	30.2%	49.8%
2021	OAK	MLB	23	2	4	0	13	6	38	46	11	3.8	9.5	40	38.5%	.333	1.63	6.87	110	0.2	95.9	59.2%	28.6%	54.5%
2022	JAX	AAA	24	0	0	0	2	2	8^2	3	0	4.2	9.3	9	47.6%	.143	0.81	2.08	91	0.2				
2022	MIA	MLB	24	4	7	0	18	18	100^1	69	10	3.1	10.8	120	40.7%	.254	1.04	3.32	84	1.8	96.2	47.4%	32.0%	54.7%
2023 DC	*MIA*	*MLB*	*25*	*7*	*6*	*0*	*22*	*22*	*111*	*92*	*11*	*3.5*	*9.7*	*119*	*41.6%*	*.284*	*1.22*	*3.14*	*83*	*1.9*	*95.9*	*49.7%*	*31.0%*	*52.3%*

Comparables: Lucas Giolito (51), Luis Severino (50), Martín Pérez (50)

It became fairly apparent after his first few seasons that Luzardo was in fastball purgatory. His four-seam fastball was too steep, running like a two-seamer; his two-seamer failed to create divergence from his four-seamer, separating itself by just inches. That was a problem, in particular, against right-handed hitters, so Luzardo adjusted by fading his four-seamer against righties and remixing his pitch locations. As a result, his changeup took a step forward, helping hide a flawed four-seamer. The secondaries-as-primaries approach works for Luzardo, who now boasts a top-15 strikeout percentage among starting pitchers.

★ ★ ★ *2023 Top 101 Prospect* **#72** ★ ★ ★

Max Meyer RHP Born: 03/12/99 Age: 24 Bats: L Throws: R Height: 6'0" Weight: 196 lb. Origin: Round 1, 2020 Draft (#3 overall)

YEAR	TEAM	LVL	AGE	W	L	SV	G	GS	IP	H	HR	BB/9	K/9	K	GB%	BABIP	WHIP	ERA	DRA-	WARP	MPH	FB%	Whiff%	CSP
2021	PNS	AA	22	6	3	0	20	20	101	84	7	3.6	10.1	113	52.7%	.304	1.23	2.41	91	1.5				
2021	JAX	AAA	22	0	1	0	2	2	10	6	1	1.8	15.3	17	47.4%	.278	0.80	0.90	72	0.3				
2022	JAX	AAA	23	3	4	0	12	12	58	39	5	2.9	10.1	65	51.0%	.246	1.00	3.72	67	1.8	96.0	55.4%	24.5%	
2022	MIA	MLB	23	0	1	0	2	2	6	7	2	3.0	9.0	6	44.4%	.313	1.50	7.50	106	0.0	95.1	39.3%	25.0%	63.6%
2023 DC	*MIA*	*MLB*	*24*	*0*	*0*	*0*	*3*	*3*	*12.7*	*12*	*1*	*3.8*	*8.5*	*12*	*50.7%*	*.296*	*1.36*	*3.84*	*98*	*0.1*	*95.1*	*39.3%*	*27.4%*	*63.6%*

Comparables: Shane Bieber (46), Erik Johnson (46), Daniel Mengden (45)

Now that Meyer has debuted, we have more public data, which means a stronger understanding of what he actually offers. There have been concerns about his fastball shape; we can now say that there might not be another big-league starting pitcher with less transverse (or active) spin on their fastball. The result is a heater that's relatively unbothered by upward Magnus effect, caught halfway between acting like a fastball and gyroball—it sinks like a sinker, but lacks the run of a four-seam fastball or traditional sinker. Suffice to say, it didn't work. The cure-all for pitchers whose fastballs cut is to lean in and starting throwing a cutter, so perhaps that's what Meyer will do—but it'll have to wait. He left the third at-bat of his second MLB start with elbow discomfort, ultimately necessitating Tommy John surgery. Meyer figures to be on the shelf until 2024—if he retains the 95-mph heat and devastating slider, everything else could work itself out.

Tommy Nance RHP Born: 03/19/91 Age: 32 Bats: R Throws: R Height: 6'6" Weight: 235 lb. Origin: Undrafted Free Agent, 2016

YEAR	TEAM	LVL	AGE	W	L	SV	G	GS	IP	H	HR	BB/9	K/9	K	GB%	BABIP	WHIP	ERA	DRA-	WARP	MPH	FB%	Whiff%	CSP
2021	IOW	AAA	30	1	0	0	10	0	15^1	7	1	1.8	10.6	18	58.3%	.171	0.65	2.35	82	0.4				
2021	CHC	MLB	30	1	1	0	27	0	28^2	25	5	4.1	9.4	30	56.8%	.263	1.33	7.22	95	0.3	95.5	62.1%	23.0%	59.3%
2022	MIA	MLB	31	2	3	0	35	2	43^2	45	5	4.3	11.7	57	45.6%	.370	1.51	4.33	77	0.9	94.1	42.3%	29.7%	58.2%
2023 DC	*MIA*	*MLB*	*32*	*3*	*2*	*0*	*60*	*0*	*51.7*	*44*	*5*	*3.8*	*9.1*	*52*	*49.7%*	*.284*	*1.29*	*3.49*	*90*	*0.5*	*94.6*	*48.5%*	*27.4%*	*58.5%*

Comparables: Pat Venditte (57), Rafael Martín (54), Grant Dayton (51)

Nance throws one of seven big-league curveballs that average 85 mph or harder, but none of the rest get nearly as much drop. Because of its big shape, hitters often give up on the bender, giving it a coin flip's chance of a called strike or whiff when he throws it in the zone. Now if only he could throw one of his fastballs for more strikes, we'd really be cooking. With better batted-ball luck, he might not even need to improve the heaters to succeed.

Andrew Nardi LHP Born: 08/18/98 Age: 24 Bats: L Throws: L Height: 6'3" Weight: 215 lb. Origin: Round 16, 2019 Draft (#471 overall)

YEAR	TEAM	LVL	AGE	W	L	SV	G	GS	IP	H	HR	BB/9	K/9	K	GB%	BABIP	WHIP	ERA	DRA-	WARP	MPH	FB%	Whiff%	CSP
2021	JUP	A	22	1	1	2	8	0	15^2	14	0	1.7	13.2	23	54.3%	.400	1.09	3.45	85	0.3				
2021	BEL	A+	22	2	1	0	10	0	19^1	21	4	1.9	12.6	27	44.0%	.370	1.29	4.66	93	0.3				
2021	PNS	AA	22	1	1	0	11	0	17^1	10	2	4.7	9.9	19	45.2%	.200	1.10	2.60	92	0.3				
2022	PNS	AA	23	2	2	2	13	0	19^1	15	1	1.9	14.4	31	46.2%	.368	0.98	1.40	69	0.5				
2022	JAX	AAA	23	3	0	7	24	0	31^2	14	3	4.0	12.8	45	31.7%	.183	0.88	2.84	73	0.9	94.4	72.2%	28.6%	
2022	MIA	MLB	23	1	1	0	13	0	14^2	25	5	8.6	14.7	24	22.2%	.500	2.66	9.82	94	0.2	94.6	62.3%	29.7%	56.2%
2023 DC	*MIA*	*MLB*	*24*	*3*	*2*	*0*	*60*	*0*	*51.7*	*43*	*7*	*4.3*	*10.7*	*61*	*38.1%*	*.285*	*1.32*	*3.91*	*98*	*0.3*	*94.6*	*62.3%*	*31.7%*	*56.2%*

Comparables: José Quijada (72), Greg Mahle (68), Junior Fernández (68)

Perhaps because he was able to blow it past minor-league hitters, Nardi chose to throw his four-seam fastball north of 63% of the time in his first stint as a big leaguer, which led to him getting shellacked several times. That was in part because of its middling shape, but also because he located it most often to his glove-side, whereas it plays best to his arm-side—especially since that's where it tunnels with his slider. Speaking of his slider, it's peculiar that he didn't choose to throw it more: At 84 mph with plus sweep, it's easily his best pitch.

Nick Neidert RHP Born: 11/20/96 Age: 26 Bats: R Throws: R Height: 6'1" Weight: 202 lb. Origin: Round 2, 2015 Draft (#60 overall)

YEAR	TEAM	LVL	AGE	W	L	SV	G	GS	IP	H	HR	BB/9	K/9	K	GB%	BABIP	WHIP	ERA	DRA-	WARP	MPH	FB%	Whiff%	CSP
2020	MIA	MLB	23	0	0	0	4	0	8^{1}	10	1	2.2	4.3	4	60.7%	.333	1.44	5.40	105	0.1	91.8	59.8%	12.9%	52.5%
2021	JAX	AAA	24	6	4	0	14	13	68^{2}	71	8	2.8	6.8	52	43.0%	.296	1.34	3.67	121	0.2				
2021	MIA	MLB	24	1	2	0	8	7	35^{2}	31	4	5.8	5.3	21	35.2%	.262	1.51	4.54	145	-0.5	91.8	47.0%	18.5%	57.4%
2022	JAX	AAA	25	4	0	1	14	8	46	39	6	1.8	9.4	48	43.5%	.280	1.04	1.96	85	1.0	92.5	66.7%	11.1%	
2022	MIA	MLB	25	0	1	0	1	1	5	5	1	0.0	5.4	3	41.2%	.250	1.00	3.60	106	0.0	92.0	48.8%	15.0%	59.1%
2023 DC	*FA*	*MLB*	*26*	*1*	*1*	*0*	*28*	*0*	*25*	*26*	*3*	*3.4*	*6.8*	*18*	*42.3%*	*.300*	*1.42*	*4.51*	*113*	*-0.1*	*91.8*	*48.7%*	*20.4%*	*57.1%*

Comparables: Zach Eflin (54), Alex Sanabia (53), A.J. Cole (53)

For a guy with supposedly plus command, there existed little evidence over Neidert's first two big-league stints that was actually the case. During that time, he threw as many non-competitive pitches as the average pitcher, was well below-average throwing to the edges of the zone and posted a strike percentage in the bottom fifth of pitchers. In 2022 he returned for one start, dotting the outer edges of the plate with his fastball and keeping hitters off-balance with his secondaries. That might the truest version we've seen of Neidert as a major leaguer, given he's entirely mastered the minors at this point.

Steven Okert LHP Born: 07/09/91 Age: 31 Bats: L Throws: L Height: 6'2" Weight: 202 lb. Origin: Round 4, 2012 Draft (#148 overall)

YEAR	TEAM	LVL	AGE	W	L	SV	G	GS	IP	H	HR	BB/9	K/9	K	GB%	BABIP	WHIP	ERA	DRA-	WARP	MPH	FB%	Whiff%	CSP
2021	JAX	AAA	29	2	0	4	15	0	20	13	1	1.8	13.1	29	24.4%	.308	0.85	1.80	81	0.5				
2021	MIA	MLB	29	3	1	0	34	0	36	22	5	3.8	10.0	40	32.5%	.221	1.03	2.75	88	0.5	92.4	40.4%	30.4%	51.2%
2022	MIA	MLB	30	5	5	0	60	0	51^{1}	34	7	4.6	11.0	63	34.4%	.237	1.17	2.98	86	0.9	93.8	31.9%	30.0%	52.9%
2023 DC	*MIA*	*MLB*	*31*	*3*	*2*	*0*	*60*	*0*	*51.7*	*41*	*7*	*3.8*	*10.5*	*60*	*33.1%*	*.272*	*1.22*	*3.61*	*93*	*0.4*	*93.4*	*34.6%*	*28.5%*	*52.3%*

Comparables: Sam Freeman (62), Jerry Blevins (61), Jake Diekman (59)

There might be no more representative example than Okert that sweepers don't always result in a bunch of whiffs, but they do induce weak contact. Of Okert's batted sliders, 74.4% are mishits, which he's used to generate a pitcher-friendly .287 slugging percentage on contact since his return to the major leagues in 2021. He's no Matt Wisler, throwing his slider 92% of the time, but with a 68% slider usage rate, he's the closest thing to it. Okert may well be the most underappreciated member of the Marlins' bullpen.

★ ★ ★ *2023 Top 101 Prospect* **#11** ★ ★ ★

Eury Pérez RHP Born: 04/15/03 Age: 20 Bats: R Throws: R Height: 6'8" Weight: 220 lb. Origin: International Free Agent, 2019

YEAR	TEAM	LVL	AGE	W	L	SV	G	GS	IP	H	HR	BB/9	K/9	K	GB%	BABIP	WHIP	ERA	DRA-	WARP	MPH	FB%	Whiff%	CSP
2021	JUP	A	18	2	3	0	15	15	56	32	2	3.4	13.2	82	36.0%	.268	0.95	1.61	78	1.5				
2021	BEL	A+	18	1	2	0	5	5	22	11	5	2.0	10.6	26	37.7%	.133	0.73	2.86	92	0.3				
2022	PNS	AA	19	3	3	0	17	17	75	62	9	3.0	12.7	106	41.7%	.319	1.16	4.08	79	1.6				
2023 non-DC	*MIA*	*MLB*	*20*	*2*	*2*	*0*	*57*	*0*	*50*	*46*	*7*	*4.0*	*9.4*	*52*	*39.2%*	*.293*	*1.37*	*4.37*	*108*	*0.0*			*29.6%*	

Comparables: Dylan Bundy (73), Julio Teheran (73), Francis Martes (71)

One might imagine any number of flaws in a pitcher who's 6-foot-8 and just 19 years old, but Pérez...doesn't really have them. The relative gentleness with which he goes through his motion and releases the ball makes it all the more remarkable to see the fastball pop out of his hand and routinely hit mid- to upper-90s on the radar gun, and with location. That, plus a changeup that has been described as (prime) Syndergaardian and a hard, complementing breaking ball made him impossible to hit in Double-A, where his 19.0% swinging-strike percentage was one of the highest in the past decade. It's way too early to feel certain about what Pérez is going to be, but his major-league debut is approaching, and he should dazzle in some role sooner than later.

Trevor Rogers LHP Born: 11/13/97 Age: 25 Bats: L Throws: L Height: 6'5" Weight: 217 lb. Origin: Round 1, 2017 Draft (#13 overall)

YEAR	TEAM	LVL	AGE	W	L	SV	G	GS	IP	H	HR	BB/9	K/9	K	GB%	BABIP	WHIP	ERA	DRA-	WARP	MPH	FB%	Whiff%	CSP
2020	MIA	MLB	22	1	2	0	7	7	28	32	5	4.2	12.5	39	46.1%	.380	1.61	6.11	73	0.7	93.8	60.0%	30.1%	47.8%
2021	JUP	A	23	1	0	0	2	2	8^{1}	4	0	3.2	13.0	12	64.7%	.235	0.84	0.00	89	0.2				
2021	MIA	MLB	23	7	8	0	25	25	133	107	6	3.1	10.6	157	39.6%	.307	1.15	2.64	76	2.9	94.8	57.7%	31.0%	54.2%
2022	PNS	AA	24	0	0	0	2	2	8	10	2	0.0	12.4	11	20.8%	.364	1.25	6.75	91	0.1				
2022	JAX	AAA	24	1	1	0	2	2	8	7	1	2.3	15.7	14	29.4%	.375	1.13	5.62	77	0.2				
2022	MIA	MLB	24	4	11	0	23	23	107	116	15	3.8	8.9	106	42.4%	.330	1.50	5.47	122	-0.2	94.7	52.9%	25.8%	53.4%
2023 DC	*MIA*	*MLB*	*25*	*6*	*7*	*0*	*24*	*24*	*114*	*113*	*14*	*3.4*	*9.9*	*126*	*41.0%*	*.321*	*1.37*	*4.17*	*104*	*0.7*	*94.7*	*55.5%*	*28.9%*	*53.4%*

Comparables: Joe Ross (60), Patrick Corbin (58), Travis Wood (57)

It's no secret that Rogers' whole operation is contingent on his changeup. Where the changeup goes, the fastball goes, and Rogers' fastball was horrible in 2022, playing more to its middling shape without the changeup's protection. Rogers made quite a few changes throughout the year—he shifted his position on the rubber toward first base, and his arm slot steadily dropped throughout—but rather than being the sources of his issues, it's more likely that they were either symptoms or attempts at correction. Occam's razor implies that his changeup command just wasn't up to snuff, and we tend to think that's the case. Rogers had a knack for locating his changeup to his arm-side, at the bottom corner of the zone, in 2021. Over the past year, he had trouble spotting it, consistently leaking out to his glove-side. There's little reason to believe Rogers can't get his changeup command dialed in, but we've seen what happens when it isn't.

Sixto Sánchez RHP

Born: 07/29/98 Age: 24 Bats: R Throws: R Height: 6'0" Weight: 234 lb. Origin: International Free Agent, 2015

YEAR	TEAM	LVL	AGE	W	L	SV	G	GS	IP	H	HR	BB/9	K/9	K	GB%	BABIP	WHIP	ERA	DRA-	WARP	MPH	FB%	Whiff%	CSP
2020	MIA	MLB	21	3	2	0	7	7	39	36	3	2.5	7.6	33	58.0%	.303	1.21	3.46	78	0.9	98.2	47.0%	24.9%	50.5%
2023 DC	*MIA*	*MLB*	*24*	*1*	*1*	*0*	*6*	*6*	*25.7*	*26*	*2*	*3.1*	*8.1*	*23*	*50.8%*	*.311*	*1.35*	*3.87*	*99*	*0.2*	*98.2*	*47.0%*	*24.3%*	*50.5%*

Comparables: Deivi García (68), Jacob Turner (66), Henderson Alvarez III (65)

During the abbreviated 2020 season Sánchez made seven MLB starts, in which he looked much like he did in the minor leagues—an ultra-efficient strike thrower who doesn't quite convert those strikes into strikeouts. He more than makes up for the slightly below-average strikeout rate by generating weak contact with his changeup and sinker, which masterfully combine plus sink and run despite being thrown several ticks harder than average. These three traits turn both pitches into heat-seeking missiles, diving and running away from the barrel so hitters are rendered helpless, scraping the top of the ball for weakly hit groundballs. His changeup and sinker are responsible for a 58.0% ground-ball percentage and just 3.8% of plate appearances ending in barrels, both of which are among the best in MLB. There aren't any concerns about his skills as a starting pitcher. The lone concern is that Sánchez hasn't pitched since 2020 and has had two shoulder surgeries since then—although he's expected to be ready by spring training.

Tanner Scott LHP

Born: 07/22/94 Age: 28 Bats: R Throws: L Height: 6'0" Weight: 235 lb. Origin: Round 6, 2014 Draft (#181 overall)

YEAR	TEAM	LVL	AGE	W	L	SV	G	GS	IP	H	HR	BB/9	K/9	K	GB%	BABIP	WHIP	ERA	DRA-	WARP	MPH	FB%	Whiff%	CSP
2020	BAL	MLB	25	0	0	1	25	0	20^2	12	1	4.4	10.0	23	58.0%	.224	1.06	1.31	71	0.6	96.6	61.5%	35.9%	49.4%
2021	BAL	MLB	26	5	4	0	62	0	54	48	6	6.2	11.7	70	52.9%	.318	1.57	5.17	94	0.7	96.8	48.4%	37.2%	51.5%
2022	MIA	MLB	27	4	5	20	67	0	62^2	55	5	6.6	12.9	90	45.6%	.347	1.61	4.31	85	1.1	97.0	37.9%	35.7%	49.0%
2023 DC	*MIA*	*MLB*	*28*	*3*	*2*	*10*	*60*	*0*	*51.7*	*45*	*4*	*5.6*	*12.5*	*72*	*48.9%*	*.335*	*1.50*	*4.20*	*98*	*0.3*	*96.9*	*44.2%*	*34.8%*	*49.5%*

Comparables: Bruce Rondón (66), Wesley Wright (64), Trevor Gott (63)

Last season marked three straight years in which Scott threw his slider more and his fastball less. It seems his slider has reached—or, perhaps, surpassed—its point of diminishing returns, given that it's started to get hit harder and generate whiffs less. The problem remains that Scott can't get his fastball in the zone enough to entice hitters to lift their bats off their shoulders; as his slider usage climbs, hitters are increasingly able to sit on the breaker. With what was virtually a career-high strikeout rate and the worst walk rate of all pitchers to reach 50 innings pitched, Scott has fashioned himself into the high three-quarters delivery version of Jake Diekman.

LINEOUTS

Hitters

HITTER	POS	TEAM	LVL	AGE	PA	R	2B	3B	HR	RBI	BB	K	SB	CS	AVG/OBP/SLG	DRC+	BABIP	BRR	DRP	WARP
Austin Allen	C/DH	MEM	AAA	28	76	7	4	0	2	14	9	19	0	0	.318/.395/.470	99	.413	-0.8	C(16): 0.6	0.2
	C/DH	LV	AAA	28	147	17	11	0	5	26	12	37	0	0	.271/.349/.473	94	.341	-2.2	C(21): 2.1, 1B(1): 0.1	0.4
	C/DH	OAK	MLB	28	16	1	0	0	0	0	1	9	0	0	.071/.188/.071	49	.200	0.3	C(4): -0.2	0.0
Willians Astudillo	3B	JAX	AAA	30	315	36	18	0	16	53	17	16	4	1	.307/.371/.541	139	.281	-0.2	3B(30): -1.9, 2B(6): -1.0, C(5): 0.1	2.0
	3B	MIA	MLB	30	55	5	0	0	1	4	1	3	1	0	.241/.255/.296	110	.240	0.1	3B(10): 0.3, 2B(8): 0.1, 1B(3): 0	0.3
Jacob Berry	3B	JUP	A	21	148	19	7	0	3	24	13	23	1	1	.264/.358/.392	126	.294	-1.2	3B(24): -0.3	0.7
Yiddi Cappe	SS	MRL	ROK	19	132	23	7	0	6	25	9	19	6	4	.305/.364/.517		.316			
	SS	JUP	A	19	167	18	5	1	3	15	6	22	7	1	.278/.299/.380	115	.301	0.6	SS(21): -0.7, 3B(9): -1.3	0.6
Erik González	IF	JAX	AAA	30	402	42	19	1	4	38	28	86	9	2	.284/.336/.373	90	.358	0.6	SS(59): -0.3, 3B(19): 1.7, 1B(14): 1.6	1.1
	IF	MIA	MLB	30	41	4	1	0	0	3	4	12	1	0	.189/.268/.216	78	.280	0.0	SS(8): 0, 3B(7): -0.1, 2B(2): 0	0.0
Joe Mack	C	MRL	ROK	19	31	2	0	0	2	3	4	7	0	0	.296/.387/.519		.333			
	C	JUP	A	19	152	18	4	1	3	12	29	40	0	0	.231/.382/.355	106	.316	-2.2	C(30): 1.5	0.5
Cody Morissette	2B	BEL	A+	22	379	48	17	0	13	51	33	90	4	1	.232/.311/.399	111	.275	0.9	2B(68): 2.4, 3B(13): 0.8	2.0
Nasim Nuñez	SS	BEL	A+	21	378	53	11	3	2	27	71	103	49	11	.247/.390/.323	99	.365	8.1	SS(84): -1.2	1.8
	SS	PNS	AA	21	171	22	6	0	0	14	24	36	21	5	.261/.371/.303	101	.343	-0.2	SS(34): -1.7, 2B(4): -1.2	0.3
Antony Peguero	CF	DSL MIA	ROK	17	217	24	10	1	5	33	13	35	7	6	.286/.355/.423		.327			
Yoffry Solano	IF	DSL MIA	ROK	17	117	17	4	2	0	11	10	19	4	2	.320/.393/.398		.388			
Luke Williams	3B	SAC	AAA	25	41	8	4	0	0	7	3	13	4	2	.378/.415/.486	80	.560	-0.6	2B(3): -0.4, 3B(2): -0.4, SS(2): -0.3	0.1
	3B	MIA	MLB	25	124	20	4	1	1	3	9	40	11	4	.235/.290/.313	70	.351	0.5	LF(25): 1.2, 3B(23): -0.4, 2B(14): 0.1	0.1
	3B	SF	MLB	25	12	1	1	0	0	3	0	4	0	0	.250/.250/.333	92	.375	0.1	3B(8): 0.8, LF(1): 0.1	0.1

After years of trying and failing to stick on a big-league roster in San Diego and Oakland, **Austin Allen** was sent back to his native St. Louis at the trade deadline. After electing free agency in November, he signed a minor-league deal with Miami, where he has a better chance of making the team as a fringey left-handed bench bat than as a legitimate backup catcher. ⚾ DRC+ believes in **Willians Astudillo**, like the friend who stays in your corner when everyone else leaves. It looks at just 28 strikeouts in 588 MLB plate appearances—a full season's worth—along with a perfectly reasonable 16 home runs, and decides he can't *really* deserve that .256 career BABIP. Teams looked at the (lack of) speed, 10.6% career IFFB rate and noted over how many consecutive stints (four) the BABIP had been dismal, deciding Astudillo *did* deserve it. He'll get a chance to prove the doubters wrong—and his buddy DRC+ right—for the NPB's Fukuoka SoftBank Hawks. ⚾ It was expected that **Jacob Berry**, the sixth-overall pick in 2022, would flex his hit tool before the game power showed up. It wasn't so expected that an anemic, 103-mph max exit velo and miserable hard-hit numbers would open questions as to whether the plus hit tool would ever get a chance to play. ⚾ After losing two years of development time, **Yiddi Cappe** made waves in the Florida Complex League, flexing bat-to-ball skills that were much more mature than anticipated. He did see his power and on-base production wane after a promotion, but between the layoff from competition and adjustment to a new level, it was easy to look past a mediocre Low-A line. ⚾ Willie Bloomquist forged a career of more than 1,000 games by playing a lot of positions, mostly poorly. **Erik González** is trying his damndest to do something similar, but his production with the bat (or lack thereof) is looking like it will be his undoing. ⚾ Few things in baseball are as uncertain as a catcher drafted out of high school, but the Marlins doubled down by signing **Joe Mack** to an over-slot deal after drafting him 31st overall in 2021. That he has already hit a baseball 106 mph before turning 20 years old substantiates Miami's confidence; Mack is athletic enough he needn't be an everyday catcher, and he can take a walk. ⚾ On June 16, **Cody Morissette** went 0-for-5, striking out all five times. On June 17, he hit three home runs. Neither game is indicative of his contact-oriented skill set, because baseball is weird. ⚾ There's not really an equivalent in baseball to basketball's 3-and-D player archetype, but **Nasim Nuñez** possesses two valuable skills: baserunning and defense. He boasts elite range at shortstop and swiped 70 bases across two levels last year, which makes him worth watching despite running an on-base percentage higher than his slugging percentage. ⚾ Although no one tool is particularly overwhelming, **Antony Peguero** flexed his feel for hitting in the DSL, striking out just 35 times with a .778 OPS in 50 games. He's one of the Marlins' more advanced hitters in the lower levels despite not yet being 18 at publication; he looks like a corner outfielder, though he's spent most of his time in center field. ⚾ **Yoffry Solano** received the largest bonus of the Marlins' international signing class, and he's justified the choice with strong bat-to-ball skills—albeit without much raw power to show for it as of yet. ⚾ **Luke Williams** runs well and can play multiple positions, but he hits the ball with the authority of Danny Mendick and pops out like Lewin Díaz. At least the rule changes should help the stolen base success rate.

Pitchers

PITCHER	TEAM	LVL	AGE	W	L	SV	G	GS	IP	H	HR	BB/9	K/9	K	GB%	BABIP	WHIP	ERA	DRA-	WARP	MPH	FB%	WHF	CSP
Anthony Bender	MIA	MLB	27	1	3	6	22	0	19^1	17	3	3.7	7.9	17	53.8%	.286	1.29	3.26	104	0.1	97.8	61.3%	28.7%	56.3%
Dax Fulton	BEL	A+	20	5	6	0	20	20	97^1	104	6	3.2	11.1	120	47.7%	.384	1.43	4.07	83	1.8				
	PNS	AA	20	1	1	0	4	3	21	9	2	3.0	12.9	30	66.7%	.175	0.76	2.57	76	0.5				
Bryan Hoeing	PNS	AA	25	2	1	0	4	4	25^2	20	0	1.4	9.1	26	72.5%	.290	0.94	0.35	87	0.4				
	JAX	AAA	25	7	5	0	18	17	94	100	14	3.4	4.7	49	53.2%	.287	1.44	5.07	131	-0.2	92.9	67.0%	10.8%	
	MIA	MLB	25	1	1	0	8	1	12^2	19	5	3.6	4.3	6	52.0%	.318	1.89	12.08	127	-0.1	93.3	72.3%	12.9%	51.4%
Jordan Holloway	JAX	AAA	26	0	1	0	8	2	17^2	12	4	8.2	12.2	24	34.2%	.235	1.58	6.62	99	0.2				
	MIA	MLB	26	0	0	0	1	0	2^2	3	0	3.4	6.7	2	50.0%	.375	1.50	3.37	106	0.0	95.6	22.9%	12.5%	62.4%
Marcus Johnson	JUP	A	21	1	2	0	3	2	12^1	7	2	5.1	17.5	24	40.0%	.278	1.14	5.11	78	0.3	93.0	41.5%	50.5%	
Aneurys Zabala	JAX	AAA	25	0	0	0	17	1	23^2	23	3	10.6	11.4	30	54.2%	.357	2.15	9.51	102	0.3				
	MIA	MLB	25	0	0	0	2	0	2^2	3	0	3.4	6.7	2	25.0%	.375	1.50	0.00	96	0.0	99.2	51.2%	26.3%	57.0%

More than half of the time, **Anthony Bender** throws a 98-mph sinker that runs and dives like hell; a third of the time, he throws a sweeping, dipping slider. Hitters beat the sinker into the ground 69% of the time, and whiffed on 40% of swings at the slider. He doesn't need a bender. Facing a back injury and Tommy John rehab, he'll be unable to show off that stuff until 2024. ⚾ **Dax Fulton** doesn't have the typical new-age stuff (apart from his first name), but he's able to leverage his 6-foot-6 frame with a high release point and three steep pitches. Between the pitch traits and command, he could stick in the rotation as a strike-thrower and legitimate home-run suppressor. ⚾ **Bryan Hoeing** has a curveball that he can make turn left 15 inches at 80 mph, but knowingly chooses to throw a 93-mph sinker 71% of the time. In his big-league debut, he struck out one more hitter than he allowed home runs. ⚾ **Jordan Holloway** can't seem to throw his fastballs, four-seam or two-seam, for strikes. That's a problem! It seems he's trending toward using his slider as his primary offering, which would help—but it wouldn't change the fact that when he *isn't* throwing sliders, he barely throws strikes half of the time. ⚾ Though it was only across 12⅓ innings of Low-A ball, **Marcus Johnson** absolutely dominated, posting a gaudy 47.1% strikeout percentage. His slider is his best pitch, and he's toyed with different breaking-ball shapes, but the X factor might be his sinker—its steep shape pairs well with his steep release. With that arsenal, Johnson has the recipe for whiffs, with a side of groundballs. ⚾ Third-rounder **Karson Milbrandt** can purportedly generate 2800 rpm on his low-90s four-seam fastball, which would make him one of few pitchers who can. His background—he played basketball along with baseball throughout high school, and was called a "difference maker" for a state runner-up squad as a junior—speaks to his athleticism, which should help him repeat his delivery and spot all four of his projectable pitches. ⚾ Between the 2018 and 2021 Drafts, 53 of the 58 pitchers Miami drafted were from the collegiate level. Their first pitcher selected in the 2022 Draft, **Jacob Miller**, was soon to reject a Louisville scholarship offered before he ever pitched in high school. In an organization inundated with high-level pitching talent, perhaps the flamethrower will soon be one among many compelling high-school arms making slow progress through the system—though just one of 10 consecutive pitchers popped after Miller was a high schooler. ⚾ An 11th-round pick out of Stanford, where he was the Pac-12 Pitcher of the Year, **Alex Williams** made two starts in the FCL. The second covered the first three frames of a (seven-inning) no-hitter. He was perfect in the first outing, too, though at some point velocity that barely scrapes 90 mph figures to get him into trouble. ⚾ **Aneurys Zabala** walked 23.5% of hitters in Triple-A, which was (impressively) lower than his strikeout percentage and somehow wasn't even the worst walk rate in Triple-A last year.

NEW YORK METS

Essay by David Roth

Player comments by Allison McCague and BP staff

Before Jacob deGrom's first inning at home in more than a year, the Mets broadcast did not go to commercial break. This was early August, and the Mets were in first place. They were facing a Braves team that had erased a similar Mets lead a year earlier and gone on to win the World Series, and which would go on to pass them down the stretch again. deGrom, who was returning from an absence that was opaque and protracted even by the usual standards that apply to Mets injuries, would look more or less like himself for some brief and dazzling starts, and then look a little bit less like himself for a few after that, and then finally make good on the long-latent threat to leave as a free agent. The Mets team he rejoined would finish with 101 wins and be in the postseason for just three games; in the last of those, their manager would ask umpires to check the unsettlingly red ears of Padres starter Joe Musgrove for a foreign substance that was not there. It was not a dignified end, and the ways in which it was on brand did not reflect any aspects of the brand that Mets fans particularly like.

But at that moment, in the space where local cable advertising would otherwise have been, the Mets season might have been anything. Jacob deGrom could have come back as anyone, up to and including Jacob deGrom; he could also have winced and gritted and disappeared for another 15 months. The team, which had been joyful and fearless all year, could very well have gone on to win the World Series playing that way; they might also have run out of luck in the ways that teams generally do, or in the more florid and tragicomic ways that Mets teams generally do. As deGrom threw his warm-up pitches, a cameraman stationed behind the mound pointed his lens up at the pitcher. That was what people watching at home saw instead of, say, the ad for the New Jersey-based line of water-resistant paving stones in which the grandchildren of the company elfin chief executive spray him with super-soakers—an odd new camera angle on deGrom, himself a more familiar but equally jarring collection of angles in deceptively easy motion; a Lynyrd Skynyrd song playing through the stadium speakers; the plosive sound of the pitches finding the catcher's mitt; first the rustling and then the oddly moving silence of a stadium full of fans who weren't sure whether it was safe to cheer yet. Later in that game, when closer Edwin Díaz came in to

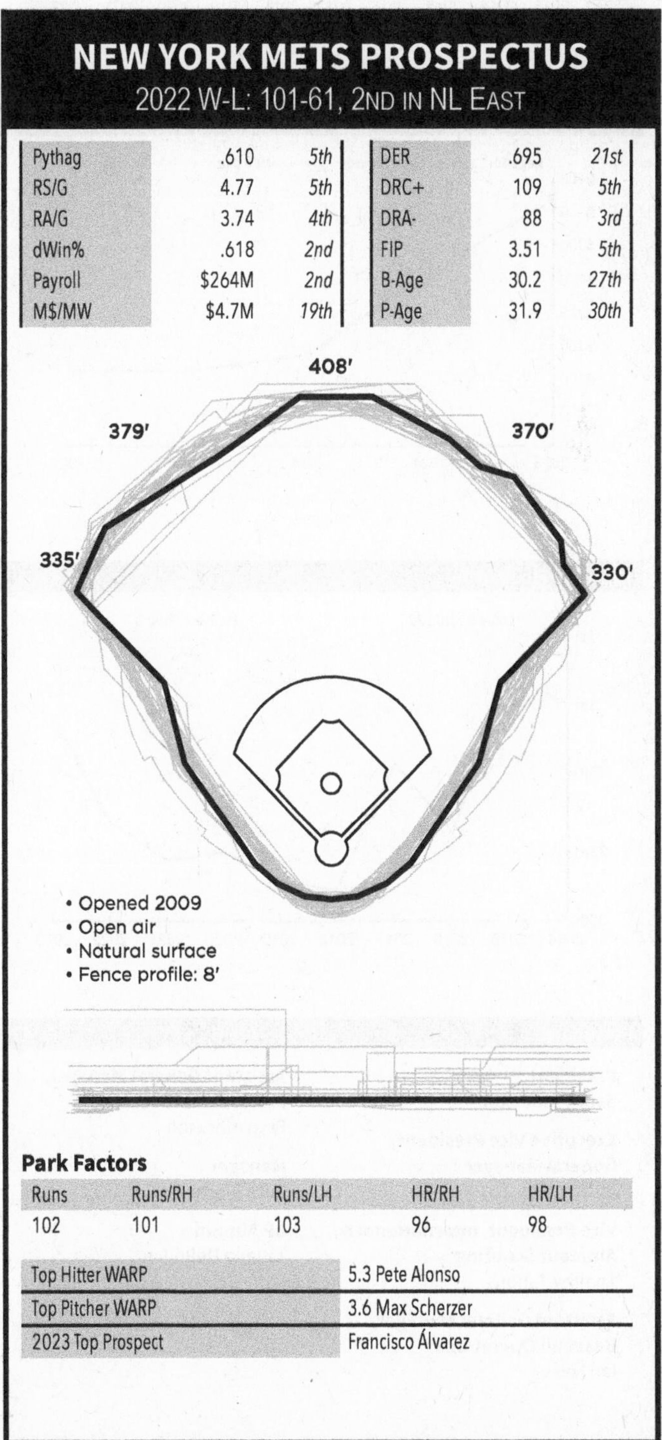

NEW YORK METS PROSPECTUS

2022 W-L: 101-61, 2nd in NL East

Pythag	.610	5th	DER	.695	21st
RS/G	4.77	5th	DRC+	109	5th
RA/G	3.74	4th	DRA-	88	3rd
dWin%	.618	2nd	FIP	3.51	5th
Payroll	$264M	2nd	B-Age	30.2	27th
M$/MW	$4.7M	19th	P-Age	31.9	30th

- Opened 2009
- Open air
- Natural surface
- Fence profile: 8'

Park Factors

Runs	Runs/RH	Runs/LH	HR/RH	HR/LH
102	101	103	96	98

Top Hitter WARP	5.3 Pete Alonso
Top Pitcher WARP	3.6 Max Scherzer
2023 Top Prospect	Francisco Álvarez

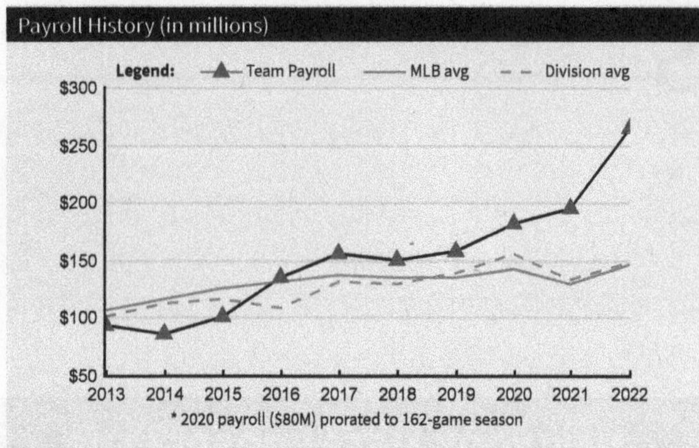

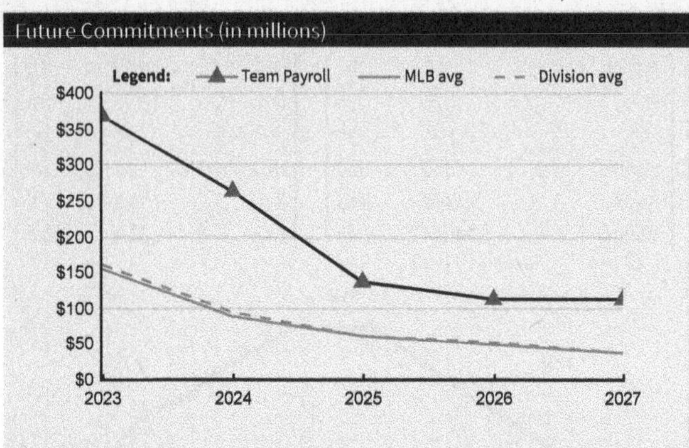

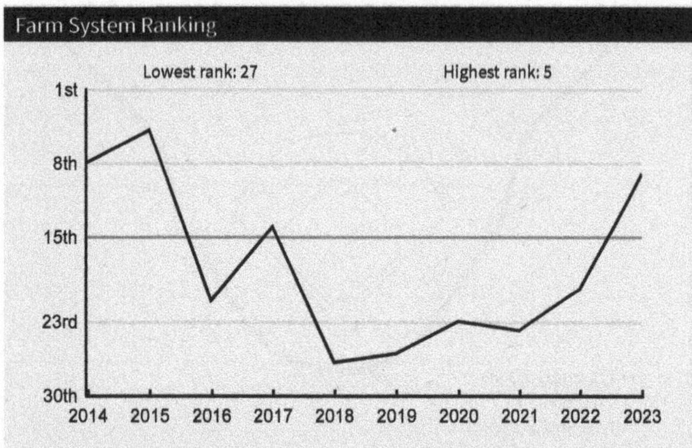

Personnel

President
Sandy Alderson

Executive Vice President, General Manager
Billy Eppler

Vice President, International & Amateur Scouting
Tommy Tanous

Assistant General Manager, Baseball Operations
Ian Levin

Assistant General Manager, Professional Scouting
Bryn Alderson

Manager
Buck Showalter

BP Alumni
Tatiana DeRouen

finish things off, the broadcast again chose the action in the ballpark over the revenue of those paving stone ads. SNY's footage of Díaz's entrance, timed to the stupendously kitschy Klezmer-adjacent trumpet line played by an Australian named Timmy Trumpet on a song called "Narco," was viewed millions of times online and showed up on two ballots in Screen Slate's Best Movies of 2022 poll.

Even for a broadcast as experimental as SNY's, this was new. The Mets' TV team had played around with the format in the past—dropping some animation and theme music every time color commentator Keith Hernandez was moved to tell a story about his friend and mentor Lou Brock, which is roughly fortnightly; throwing a *Kill Bill*-style filter on the glowering face of manager Buck Showalter after a Met got hit by a pitch—but never in a way that actually messed with the money. "It's not something we want to do a lot, because the commercials obviously pay the bills," SNY game director John DeMarsico told *The New York Times*. "We pick our spots and choose wisely, and as long as it doesn't become an everyday thing, we can do things like that and make moments that are special for the folks at home."

The Mets have long been more compelling as a television show than as a baseball team; due to both a generation of willful institutional jankiness and the basic realities of how the human body responds to the stress and strain of playing baseball, their best players have always played on a scalpel's edge. What makes the Mets different in this moment from previous versions of themselves is not just the organization's new willingness to take risks and spend money in pursuit of meaningful moments, but the newfound appreciation of those moments as valuable in their own right.

Here, the current regime benefits greatly by comparison to the petty, peevish, relentlessly anhedonic one it deposed. But treasuring a good time is its own reward. A baseball season is going to go where and how it is going to go, and while some well-spent effort and money can help aim it in one direction or another, there is only so much that can be done to mitigate the chaos inherent in the game. Moment by moment, though, baseball is different—not much less chaotic, really, but much easier to see, and to enjoy. Seasons are shaped the same and fade into each other over time; moments like these help you place yourself within the sweep of it. Baseball is made of them, metaphorically and literally; they add up to seasons, and give them life. If you like baseball, these moments are what you like.

⚾ ⚾ ⚾

The unconscionably rich investor and lifelong Mets fan Steve Cohen, who bought the team in 2021, has said all the things that ambitious owners are supposed to say. On their own, these are not worth very much. Cohen has expressed that he wants the team to compete for the World Series every year, and to do so with the metronomic, luxurious, coolly self-sustaining ease that the Los Angeles Dodgers have demonstrated over the last decade, which are things any fan would want.

It is more meaningful that Cohen has, so far, done the things that an ambitious owner would do if he actually wanted to do all that, which amounts mostly to spending money on big-league talent *and* doing the unglamorous mold-abatement work necessary to turn a proudly backward front office and player development apparatus into suitably state-of-the-art ones. That work is ongoing, both in the way that all sufficiently ambitious work is always ongoing and also because the previous administration's deficits will take years to make up. None of it is easy, although the repeated application of many millions of dollars does help.

"My team is good," Cohen told the *New York Post*, after the team's push to sign Carlos Correa *to play third base* came up short in early December. "But it isn't that much better than last year. If you want a team that's good, this is what it costs. What are you going to do?" Cohen's answer, by that point, was obvious—you spend the necessary money to make the team better whenever and wherever possible. When they failed to land Correa, the Mets' payroll was already well over the fourth and final luxury tax threshold—informally known as The Steve Cohen Tax, given that his combination of (objectively obscene) wealth and (actually rather inspiring) eagerness to spend it improving his baseball team so disturbed his fellow owners that it was instituted more or less in his honor. It is easy to be philosophical about getting curved by Carlos Correa once you have already committed hundreds of millions of dollars in free agent contracts retaining Díaz and Brandon Nimmo while also adding Justin Verlander, Kodai Senga, José Quintana, David Robertson, Adam Ottavino and Omar Narváez along terms ranging from one to eight years in duration. It's easier still when you can afford it. "No one likes to spend money," Cohen said. "But this is the price." Four days before Christmas, after Correa's deal with the Giants fell apart due to team concerns about a long-ago leg injury, the Mets came to an agreement with Correa anyway. That initial deal, a 12-year, $315 million contract, pushed the Mets' total offseason free agent spending north of $800 million, their payroll to an even $385 million, and their luxury tax bill to $111 million. It has not yet been finalized as this book goes to press, and there is some chance that it might not be, but the message is clear enough all the same.

This is, I guess you could say, a start. But even someone as rich as Cohen cannot simply decide to Be The Dodgers and then just make it be so. The Dodgers have built something like the optimal baseball organization—adept and adaptive enough in terms of scouting and player development to continually produce MLB-ready talent up and down the roster, astute enough to turn that talent into blue-chip stars through trades, rich enough to keep every player worth keeping and buy ones as needed. This seems like a reasonable goal for not just any but every baseball team. Most teams, though, will settle for one or maybe two of those pursuits; the third, which is objectively the easiest, generally proves to be the sticking point. No one likes to spend money, as the man said.

But, because that is true—that is, because most baseball owners at this moment are not willing to spend on proven big-league talent, because they don't really care or have to care that much about their team's success—it makes the easy part even easier. When MLB teams talk about sustainability, they are talking, in the euphemistic language of management consultants, about optimizing baseball outcomes while still delivering the profit margin ownership demands. Necessarily, a lot of this is done by taking advantage of the systemic and structural uglinesses that deliver efficiencies in this business, and also every other business. This vision of efficiency is a value-neutral concept that has somehow come to be accepted as something that has merit in its own right; so many of the broader concepts and little instances of micro-arbitrage that once scanned as thrillingly smart new ways to think about baseball have by now been assimilated into something much older and more familiar and less thrilling and notably less laudable, which is Keeping Costs Down.

Once a team's systems are working as they are supposed to work, this can all seem to run on its own—the farm system will provide the cheap young talent, the front office will understand what it has and evaluate it correctly, ownership will provide the resources needed to bring it all together. But while the Mets build the systems that will make that possible—a player development program that actually helps players develop, a front office that understands not just other teams' farm systems but its own—they will have to spend money on big-league talent. It is too soon to know how well this work is going. But, as Scott Boras said after the Mets signed Nimmo, "for four or five years they [are] going to have to be heavy on free agency until the development pool can catch up."

The Mets have to be this way because, under their previous ownership, they were backward in ways that only the strangest and worst MLB organizations are. A connoisseur of executive oafishness might detect, in the finest Wilpon vintages, vinegary notes of Arte Moreno's stubbornness, salty intimations of Jerry Reinsdorf's load-bearing grudgefulness, some funky terroir-specific expressions of Monfort-style whimsicality and Ken Kendrickian peevishness, with the singularly recursive personal pettiness of The House Of Steinbrenner on the nose. It says something about how repellent the Wilpons were that Cohen's gambit, which is turning a singularly sour mom-and-pop organization into one that feels and works much more like every other business currently getting over on everyone on earth, feels so much like an improvement. The Wilpon Mets were already craven and ruthless; they just weren't anything but that. Cohen's program, if it works, might deliver... an organization that is less personal and less compulsive in its cravenness and ruthlessness, but still plenty craven and ruthless in the ways that align with managerial best practices. You know, like the Dodgers.

When he made it, Cohen's initial assessment of the team to the *Post* seemed about right. Last year's team was built to win a World Series and looked like it might, until it didn't; instead of accepting a narrower competitive window or steering into strategic retrenchment, GM Billy Eppler spent Cohen's money building a team that is much more expensive but roughly as likely to win one this year. Instead of resetting the luxury tax, they reset the roster. Adding Correa to the mix, albeit at a position he hasn't played much, represents a tremendous upgrade at one of the few positions where the team was merely average. The rotation is once again dependent on the health of aging Hall of Famers, which is a pretty cool problem to have as such things go; the lineup will be solid and, at its best, infuriating to face. Rising prospects like Francisco Álvarez and Brett Baty, who are nearly ready to contribute at the big-league level, bear the bruises of the previous administration but have time to figure things out. Eppler, who was something like the team's 13th choice for a GM when they brought him in after 2021, has mostly done well evaluating and acquiring big-league talent; the highly regarded player development personnel that the team has brought in and seemingly left alone to do their work will deliver results in time, or not. Cohen, who spent this offseason acting like the team's president of baseball operations, has proven to be decisive, at the very least.

The Mets have a lot of good players and so seem likely to be pretty good in 2023, and for as long as their owner is willing to pay for the necessary talent. This is not high-level analysis, admittedly, but also there is only so much to analyze. Building a good baseball team is not easy, but also only as complicated as it is permitted to become. It will never be perfect and it cannot be permanent, and anyway those are silly things to want. The most a fan can ask, I think, is for their team to act as if every moment might mean something, and to take up the work of creating those moments with some rigor and some joy. I have seen Steve Cohen's political contributions and read about his art collection; I am sure that this is the best and certainly most generous thing he could do with his money. It isn't easy work, either. But so far, so good. ■

—David Roth is a writer and co-owner of Defector.

HITTERS

Pete Alonso 1B Born: 12/07/94 Age: 28 Bats: R Throws: R Height: 6'3" Weight: 245 lb. Origin: Round 2, 2016 Draft (#64 overall)

YEAR	TEAM	LVL	AGE	PA	R	2B	3B	HR	RBI	BB	K	SB	CS	Whiff%	AVG/OBP/SLG	DRC+	BABIP	BRR	DRP	WARP
2020	NYM	MLB	25	239	31	6	0	16	35	24	61	1	0	30.4%	.231/.326/.490	119	.242	-2.5	1B(39): -0.8	0.8
2021	NYM	MLB	26	637	81	27	3	37	94	60	127	3	0	24.9%	.262/.344/.519	128	.274	-1.1	1B(148): -3.1	3.1
2022	NYM	MLB	27	685	95	27	0	40	131	67	128	5	1	24.1%	.271/.352/.518	146	.279	-1.4	1B(134): 0.3	5.1
2023 DC	*NYM*	*MLB*	*28*	*593*	*93*	*24*	*1*	*41*	*113*	*58*	*116*	*3*	*0*	*24.1%*	*.283/.369/.574*	*160*	*.293*	*0.5*	*1B 0*	*5.3*

Comparables: Tony Clark (83), Boog Powell (82), Richie Sexson (81)

Alonso's 2022 season began with a near-death experience. As he was driving to spring training in Port St. Lucie, his truck was struck at high speed by a driver who ran a red light, flipping over three times before coming to rest. Somehow, Alonso kicked out his windshield and emerged from the wreckage with just a scratch on his arm and nothing more. He went on to tell reporters that this spring training and season were special because the harrowing experience was a reminder of the precariousness of it all. The Mets' star first baseman headed into the season determined to make the most of it. And he did, matching Aaron Judge for the RBI lead as his team's leading force on offense and shattering the Mets' single-season RBI record. He may not have nabbed his third consecutive Home Run Derby title, but he still went deep 40 times nonetheless—by far the most potent power threat on a squad that did not hit too many long balls. With his best campaign since his historic rookie season, there is no longer any doubt that Alonso is a franchise player for the Mets—nothing precarious about that.

★ ★ ★ *2023 Top 101 Prospect* **#4** ★ ★ ★

Francisco Álvarez C Born: 11/19/01 Age: 21 Bats: R Throws: R Height: 5'10" Weight: 233 lb. Origin: International Free Agent, 2018

YEAR	TEAM	LVL	AGE	PA	R	2B	3B	HR	RBI	BB	K	SB	CS	Whiff%	AVG/OBP/SLG	DRC+	BABIP	BRR	DRP	WARP
2021	SLU	A	19	67	12	5	0	2	12	15	7	2	2		.417/.567/.646	143	.450	0.1	C(10): -1.5	0.4
2021	BRK	A+	19	333	55	13	1	22	58	40	82	6	3		.247/.351/.538	154	.260	0.8	C(49): -7.6	2.5
2022	BNG	AA	20	296	43	16	0	18	47	36	71	0	0		.277/.368/.553	115	.310	-1.0	C(46): 1.6	1.4
2022	SYR	AAA	20	199	31	6	0	9	31	34	52	0	0	50.0%	.234/.382/.443	109	.283	0.1	C(33): -0.8	0.8
2022	NYM	MLB	20	14	3	1	0	1	1	2	4	0	0	40.0%	.167/.286/.500	92	.143	-0.3	C(2): -0.0	0.0
2023 DC	*NYM*	*MLB*	*21*	*274*	*34*	*11*	*0*	*11*	*35*	*28*	*78*	*0*	*0*	*34.5%*	*.228/.319/.427*	*106*	*.287*	*-1.8*	*C 0*	*0.8*

Comparables: Xander Bogaerts (50), Marc Newfield (44), Carlos Correa (44)

YEAR	TEAM	P. COUNT	FRM RUNS	BLK RUNS	THRW RUNS	TOT RUNS
2021	SLU	1391	-1.3	-0.2	-0.2	-1.7
2021	BRK	6975	-6.7	-1.2	0.9	-6.9
2022	BNG	6924	0.1	0.1	0.8	0.9
2022	SYR	4873	-1.0	-0.2	0.6	-0.6
2022	NYM	190	0.0	0.0		
2023	*NYM*	*6012*	*-2.6*	*-0.3*	*0.3*	*-2.6*

Offensively, the Mets struggled in four ways in 2022: the catching position was a gaping black vortex in the lineup, they failed to find a consistent option at DH, they didn't hit many home runs and they labored against left-handed pitching. Cue Álvarez's entrance music. The hopes of the 2022 season and the legacy of Mike Piazza are a lot to hang on a 20-year-old, but the bright outlook for his future was never going to be impacted by what he did after his call-up to the big leagues in the final week of the regular season. As it turns out, his first major-league hit was a prodigious 439-foot home run that the Mets hope provided a preview of what's to come. Though an ankle injury in the minors this season deepened already existing concerns about Álvarez's defense behind the plate, there is hope that the Mets' catcher of the future never sniffs the minors again, especially after the team sent James McCann to Baltimore.

Jonathan Araúz IF

Born: 08/03/98 Age: 24 Bats: S Throws: R Height: 6'0" Weight: 195 lb. Origin: International Free Agent, 2014

YEAR	TEAM	LVL	AGE	PA	R	2B	3B	HR	RBI	BB	K	SB	CS	Whiff%	AVG/OBP/SLG	DRC+	BABIP	BRR	DRP	WARP
2020	BOS	MLB	21	80	8	2	0	1	9	8	21	0	0	22.0%	.250/.325/.319	85	.340	0.2	2B(16): -0.4, 3B(6): 0, SS(4): 0	0.1
2021	WOR	AAA	22	267	32	8	1	6	30	30	45	2	0		.245/.326/.365	103	.274	-2.3	2B(41): 6.2, SS(13): 2.3, 3B(12): -0.8	1.4
2021	BOS	MLB	22	75	9	3	0	3	8	8	15	0	0	21.1%	.185/.274/.369	101	.191	0.0	SS(13): 0.4, 2B(12): 0, 3B(2): 0	0.3
2022	WOR	AAA	23	99	11	5	0	0	3	7	13	1	0		.185/.242/.239	107	.215	-1.4	2B(16): -2.1, SS(8): -0.4	0.1
2022	NOR	AAA	23	45	4	3	0	0	6	4	9	1	0		.250/.333/.325	107	.323	-1.1	3B(5): -0.3, 2B(2): 0.1, SS(2): -0.5	0.1
2022	BOS	MLB	23	12	1	0	0	0	1	0	3	0	0	18.2%	.000/.000/.000	91		0.1	2B(3): 0.2, SS(3): -0.1	0.0
2022	BAL	MLB	23	29	2	0	0	1	4	1	9	0	0	28.6%	.179/.207/.286	81	.222	0.0	3B(6): 0, 2B(1): 0, SS(1): 0	0.0
2023 non-DC	*NYM*	*MLB*	*24*	*251*	*21*	*9*	*1*	*3*	*21*	*19*	*45*	*1*	*2*	*20.5%*	*.213/.277/.314*	*65*	*.249*	*-0.1*	*2B 0, SS 0*	*-0.5*

Comparables: Richard Urena (53), Andrés Blanco (49), Luis Castillo (49)

You wake up the morning of June 10 and get a call from Chaim Bloom. They need to make room on the 40-man for Rob Refsnyder and have to DFA you two days after calling you back up. Fine. The Orioles get in touch shortly after and you find yourself in Lehigh Valley in a dugout across from a former top pick you were once traded for, in Mark Appel. You collect five hits in that series then get a call from Mike Elias: Ramon Urías is still on the IL with an oblique injury and Baltimore needs somebody to stand at third until he can come back. You're back, baby. In your second game up you're starting and hitting eighth. You step into the box against Dylan Cease and get a 2-1 slider that catches a little too much of the zone. Your eyes light up and you uncork one of the best swings of your life. The ball soars over the wall in right-center 390 feet away; it's just the fifth home run you've hit in the majors. You're Jonathan Araúz, former promising Astros prospect and Red Sox infielder, and you're finally breaking through. Then you go 3-for-20 the rest of your time with the Orioles and hit just .220 with their minor-league affiliates. Elias thanks you for your service but tells you they won't be tendering you a contract in November. You're Jonathan Araúz, former promising prospect, and now former Oriole.

★ ★ ★ *2023 Top 101 Prospect* **#17** ★ ★ ★

Brett Baty 3B/OF

Born: 11/13/99 Age: 23 Bats: L Throws: R Height: 6'3" Weight: 210 lb. Origin: Round 1, 2019 Draft (#12 overall)

YEAR	TEAM	LVL	AGE	PA	R	2B	3B	HR	RBI	BB	K	SB	CS	Whiff%	AVG/OBP/SLG	DRC+	BABIP	BRR	DRP	WARP
2021	SRR	WIN	21	102	16	5	1	1	15	11	31	1	0		.292/.373/.404		.431			
2021	BRK	A+	21	209	27	14	1	7	34	24	53	4	3		.309/.397/.514	118	.402	-0.3	3B(41): 6.7, LF(3): -0.4	1.6
2021	BNG	AA	21	176	16	8	0	5	22	22	45	2	0		.272/.364/.424	91	.350	0.0	3B(24): -0.8, LF(15): 1.4	0.4
2022	BNG	AA	22	394	73	22	0	19	59	46	98	2	3		.312/.406/.544	128	.390	0.0	3B(68): -1.4, LF(9): 0.8	2.2
2022	SYR	AAA	22	26	3	0	0	0	1	3	6	0	1		.364/.462/.364	99	.500	-0.3	3B(4): -0.1, LF(2): 0.2	0.2
2022	NYM	MLB	22	42	4	0	0	2	5	2	8	0	0	23.6%	.184/.244/.342	92	.179	0.0	3B(11): 0	0.1
2023 DC	*NYM*	*MLB*	*23*	*249*	*30*	*11*	*1*	*6*	*27*	*20*	*68*	*2*	*1*	*29.5%*	*.256/.327/.400*	*100*	*.342*	*0.3*	*3B 0, LF 0*	*0.5*

Comparables: Abraham Toro (63), Mat Gamel (60), Juan Francisco (59)

The Mets' no. 2 prospect hit .315/.410/.533 across 89 games at Double-A Binghamton and six games at Triple-A Syracuse before making his big-league debut in August. Initially reluctant to promote Baty, the Mets had their hand forced by injuries to both Eduardo Escobar and Luis Guillorme, leaving them without a reliable everyday option at third base. Baty's sky-high power potential manifested itself right away; he hit a home run in his first major-league at-bat, eliciting the most memorable family reaction since Steven Matz's grandfather's grade-A nuts-going in 2015. However, he managed just six more hits in 42 total plate appearances before his rookie campaign was cut short by a torn UCL in his right thumb just two weeks after his thrilling debut. Latent concerns regarding his defense showed themselves as well. While his throwing arm is a strength, Baty committed two errors at third base and will need to adjust to the pace of big-league play in order to stick at the hot corner. The availability of that gig is, ah, as yet an open question!

Mark Canha LF

Born: 02/15/89 Age: 34 Bats: R Throws: R Height: 6'2" Weight: 209 lb. Origin: Round 7, 2010 Draft (#227 overall)

YEAR	TEAM	LVL	AGE	PA	R	2B	3B	HR	RBI	BB	K	SB	CS	Whiff%	AVG/OBP/SLG	DRC+	BABIP	BRR	DRP	WARP
2020	OAK	MLB	31	243	32	12	2	5	33	37	54	4	0	24.1%	.246/.387/.408	110	.307	-0.8	RF(17): -1, LF(15): 0.4, CF(9): -0.9	0.7
2021	OAK	MLB	32	625	93	22	4	17	61	77	128	12	2	21.5%	.231/.358/.387	114	.274	2.7	LF(106): -4.5, RF(27): -1.8, CF(23): -0.4	3.0
2022	NYM	MLB	33	542	71	24	0	13	61	48	97	3	1	22.1%	.266/.367/.403	119	.309	-3.8	LF(123): -0.7, CF(11): -0.8, RF(6): 0	2.5
2023 DC	*NYM*	*MLB*	*34*	*561*	*74*	*24*	*1*	*16*	*61*	*58*	*111*	*7*	*1*	*21.9%*	*.254/.364/.413*	*122*	*.301*	*3.6*	*LF 0, CF 0*	*3.2*

Comparables: Andrew McCutchen (63), Lu Blue (62), Gene Woodling (62)

In the classic Thanksgiving dinner spread, the self-proclaimed Big League Foodie is the mashed potatoes—unassuming, not the star of the meal, but a consistent and crucial member of the supporting cast that is not polarizing and near-universally appreciated. One of several Mets pre-'22 acquisitions, Canha may not have been the marquee addition that is Max Scherzer or even his former Athletics teammate Starling Marte, but one could argue he was almost as important for the consistency he provided. Canha fit the mold of the Mets' new look offense perfectly, doing in 2022 what he has done his entire career: getting on base and doing so often, to the tune of a .367 on-base percentage. That figure was augmented by a league-leading 28 hit by pitches—Canha the biggest contributor to the 2022 Mets' record-setting number of times plunked in a season. Perhaps most importantly, the Mets' left fielder was able to avoid the hip and back issues that had plagued him in the past, playing in 140 games in 2022, just one shy of his career high from the year before. The cult heroics, soaring bat flips, and fun clubhouse presence? That's just gravy.

Eduardo Escobar 3B

Born: 01/05/89 Age: 34 Bats: S Throws: R Height: 5'10" Weight: 193 lb. Origin: International Free Agent, 2006

YEAR	TEAM	LVL	AGE	PA	R	2B	3B	HR	RBI	BB	K	SB	CS	Whiff%	AVG/OBP/SLG	DRC+	BABIP	BRR	DRP	WARP
2020	AZ	MLB	31	222	22	7	3	4	20	15	41	1	0	21.6%	.212/.270/.335	84	.244	1.0	3B(47): -1.5, 2B(3): -0.1	0.0
2021	MIL	MLB	32	199	27	12	2	6	25	19	39	0	0	22.7%	.268/.342/.458	99	.313	-0.6	3B(34): -1.1, 1B(18): 0	0.4
2021	AZ	MLB	32	400	50	14	3	22	65	29	85	1	0	24.3%	.246/.300/.478	107	.261	0.9	3B(65): -2.2, 2B(42): -0.2	1.6
2022	NYM	MLB	33	542	58	26	4	20	69	40	129	0	2	27.6%	.240/.295/.430	98	.281	2.1	3B(130): -7.7, 2B(2): 0	0.6
2023 DC	*NYM*	*MLB*	*34*	*533*	*62*	*24*	*3*	*20*	*68*	*39*	*120*	*1*	*0*	*26.9%*	*.240/.301/.425*	*96*	*.281*	*2.5*	*3B -3, 2B 0*	*0.8*

Comparables: Toby Harrah (71), Sal Bando (68), Asdrúbal Cabrera (66)

The Mets' inking of Escobar to a two-year, $20 million contract with a 2024 club option kicked off a frenzied 72 hours of free-agent signings that ended with Escobar, Mark Canha, Starling Marte and Max Scherzer all donning orange and blue—the excitement building with each addition before the lockout brought free agent activity to a grinding halt. But it all started with Escobar, who endeared himself to the city of New York with his infectious childlike passion for the game and affection for Brazilian steakhouse chain Fogo de Chão. It was a bookend season for Escobar—a fast start and a strong finish with a prolonged period of struggle in between. He posted a 139 OPS+ in April, but his production plummeted in the summer months, and he soon found himself in the short side of a platoon at third base with lefty utility infielder Luis Guillorme. It made sense, since the switch-hitter's batting average was a full 30 points higher from the right side of the plate with even starker splits with respect to power—a .156 ISO as a left-handed hitter as opposed to a .261 ISO from the right side. But Escobar experienced a renaissance in September, which Mets television play-by-play broadcaster Gary Cohen dubbed The Month of Escobar. Escobar slugged .596 with a .982 OPS in the final 30 games of the regular season. It wasn't quite enough to lead the Mets to an NL East title, but it was probably enough to earn him a nice New York Strip.

Luis Guillorme IF

Born: 09/27/94 Age: 28 Bats: L Throws: R Height: 5'10" Weight: 190 lb. Origin: Round 10, 2013 Draft (#296 overall)

YEAR	TEAM	LVL	AGE	PA	R	2B	3B	HR	RBI	BB	K	SB	CS	Whiff%	AVG/OBP/SLG	DRC+	BABIP	BRR	DRP	WARP
2020	NYM	MLB	25	68	6	6	0	0	9	10	17	2	0	20.7%	.333/.426/.439	90	.463	0.1	2B(17): 0.2, 3B(4): -0.3, SS(3): 0	0.1
2021	SYR	AAA	26	28	4	0	0	0	1	3	2	0	0		.304/.393/.304	112	.318	0.1	2B(3): 0.1, 3B(3): -0.3, SS(3): 0.4	0.2
2021	NYM	MLB	26	156	13	3	0	1	5	23	23	0	2	14.9%	.265/.374/.311	101	.315	-0.1	3B(27): -1.1, 2B(18): 0, SS(11): -0.5	0.4
2022	NYM	MLB	27	335	33	12	1	2	17	34	46	1	0	13.3%	.273/.351/.340	100	.317	-0.5	2B(67): 1.2, 3B(22): 1.3, SS(15): 0	1.2
2023 DC	*NYM*	*MLB*	*28*	*291*	*32*	*11*	*0*	*2*	*25*	*31*	*36*	*2*	*1*	*14.3%*	*.272/.357/.356*	*104*	*.311*	*0.5*	*2B 0, 3B 0*	*1.0*

Comparables: Anderson Hernandez (54), Jonathan Herrera (53), Endy Chavez (53)

Now 28 years old, Guillorme has established himself as the Platonic ideal of a utility infielder. Boasting the silkiest smooth hands and some of the best defensive skills in the league, the Venezuelan native plays all of the infield positions (aside from first base, where the Mets are more than set for a while) and plays them impeccably well. While he will never be the power or base-stealing threat of Francisco Lindor, he has demonstrated the ability to sustain league-average production with the bat with a contact-oriented approach. 2022 represented Guillorme's largest dose of regular at-bats in his career thus far, and he played himself into the long side of a platoon at third base when Eduardo Escobar struggled during much of the summer. When Guillorme went down with a groin injury in August, it quickly became evident just how understatedly valuable he was to the Mets. Twice a spring-training internet darling—once in 2017 for snagging a flying bat out of the air as it hurtled toward the dugout and again in 2021 for working a 22-pitch at-bat against Jordan Hicks that ended in a walk—Guillorme is also simply a pleasure to watch play baseball. Previously somewhat of an up-and-down player, his utility infield role is all but assured moving forward. And as Plato once said, "There is no harm in repeating a good thing."

Travis Jankowski OF

Born: 06/15/91 Age: 32 Bats: L Throws: R Height: 6'2" Weight: 190 lb. Origin: Round 1, 2012 Draft (#44 overall)

YEAR	TEAM	LVL	AGE	PA	R	2B	3B	HR	RBI	BB	K	SB	CS	Whiff%	AVG/OBP/SLG	DRC+	BABIP	BRR	DRP	WARP
2020	CIN	MLB	29	17	3	0	0	0	0	2	7	2	1	33.3%	.067/.176/.067	77	.125	0.1	CF(9): -0.3, RF(3): -0.1	0.0
2021	LHV	AAA	30	72	16	4	0	0	6	15	9	4	3		.304/.451/.375	125	.362	0.5	LF(9): 0.1, CF(5): -0.5, RF(3): -0.2	0.4
2021	PHI	MLB	30	157	24	6	2	1	10	22	29	5	0	18.5%	.252/.364/.351	94	.317	-0.2	CF(45): -1.7, RF(8): 0, LF(6): -0.2	0.3
2022	SYR	AAA	31	165	27	3	1	1	6	31	36	15	1	26.5%	.237/.387/.298	116	.319	2.6	CF(26): 0.1, LF(5): -0.1, RF(3): 0.4	0.9
2022	NYM	MLB	31	63	11	0	0	0	2	8	9	3	0	10.8%	.167/.286/.167	95	.200	-0.1	LF(19): 0.1, RF(12): 0.8, CF(10): 0.5	0.3
2023 non-DC	*NYM*	*MLB*	*32*	*251*	*22*	*7*	*1*	*1*	*19*	*30*	*43*	*10*	*3*	*17.3%*	*.230/.330/.302*	*85*	*.279*	*2.8*	*CF 1, LF 0*	*0.6*

Comparables: Roger Bernadina (54), Otis Nixon (47), Willie Harris (47)

"No one's going to be buying my jersey," Jankowski quipped after scoring three runs in the first game of a doubleheader sweep of the Braves in early May. To his surprise, a couple of weeks later, the Mets were all wearing Jankowski t-shirts during warmups at Citi Field, thanks to the generosity of Eduardo Escobar. To that point entering play on May 14, Jankowski hit .321 in 32 plate appearances with three stolen bases and nine runs scored. Unfortunately, injury befell Jankowski in June and he underwent surgery to repair a fractured metacarpal in his hand and he was unable to reclaim his magic off the bench after that. He was activated from the injured list in mid-July but designated for assignment on August 1 when the Mets acquired Tyler Naquin from the Reds. He was claimed off waivers by the Mariners but unceremoniously DFA'd once more a mere four days later by Seattle. He settled back in the minors with the Mets.

Khalil Lee OF

Born: 06/26/98 Age: 25 Bats: L Throws: L Height: 5'10" Weight: 170 lb. Origin: Round 3, 2016 Draft (#103 overall)

YEAR	TEAM	LVL	AGE	PA	R	2B	3B	HR	RBI	BB	K	SB	CS	Whiff%	AVG/OBP/SLG	DRC+	BABIP	BRR	DRP	WARP
2021	SYR	AAA	23	388	67	20	2	14	37	71	115	8	10		.274/.451/.500	122	.402	-0.3	RF(61): -7.7, CF(26): 6.7, LF(11): -1.0	2.0
2021	NYM	MLB	23	18	2	1	0	0	1	0	13	0	0	55.6%	.056/.056/.111	41	.200		RF(11): -0.6	
2022	SLU	A	24	35	5	3	1	0	2	3	11	1	3	42.9%	.241/.371/.414	93	.389	-1.1	RF(3): -0.4, CF(2): -0.3	-0.1
2022	SYR	AAA	24	418	48	25	0	10	37	47	139	14	3	45.2%	.211/.326/.366	75	.314	1.8	CF(38): -0.8, RF(37): -2.7, LF(23): 0.3	-0.2
2022	NYM	MLB	24	2	1	0	0	1	3	0	0	0	0	0.0%	.500/.500/2.000	94			CF(2): -0.2	
2023 DC	*NYM*	*MLB*	*25*	*30*	*3*	*1*	*0*	*0*	*2*	*2*	*11*	*0*	*1*	*36.3%*	*.214/.312/.352*	*81*	*.348*	*-0.1*	*CF 0*	*0.0*

Comparables: Michael Saunders (53), Lars Anderson (52), Oswaldo Arcia (49)

A combination of on-base ability, speed and raw power fueled Lee's quick ascent in the minor leagues, but he went from being pretty safely in the top ten in the Mets' system entering the 2022 season to being toward the bottom of the top 30 after the draft. He had just two major-league at-bats with the Mets in 2022, and in one of them he hit his first major-league home run, flashing that power potential. But he posted an uninspiring .700 OPS in the minor leagues this year between Triple-A Syracuse and a short stint in Low-A St. Lucie. He is limited offensively by an inability to make contact, elevate the baseball and recognize spin. On defense, his routes render him more likely to stick at a corner outfield position than in center. Squint and hope, and you can see a fourth outfielder.

Francisco Lindor SS

Born: 11/14/93 Age: 29 Bats: S Throws: R Height: 5'11" Weight: 190 lb. Origin: Round 1, 2011 Draft (#8 overall)

YEAR	TEAM	LVL	AGE	PA	R	2B	3B	HR	RBI	BB	K	SB	CS	Whiff%	AVG/OBP/SLG	DRC+	BABIP	BRR	DRP	WARP
2020	CLE	MLB	26	266	30	13	0	8	27	24	41	6	2	20.4%	.258/.335/.415	106	.280	0.0	SS(58): 0.9	1.1
2021	NYM	MLB	27	524	73	16	3	20	63	58	96	10	4	23.3%	.230/.322/.412	105	.248	0.9	SS(124): 0	2.3
2022	NYM	MLB	28	706	98	25	5	26	107	59	133	16	6	23.0%	.270/.339/.449	120	.301	-0.6	SS(159): 0.7	4.0
2023 DC	*NYM*	*MLB*	*29*	*645*	*80*	*27*	*3*	*25*	*90*	*58*	*120*	*14*	*3*	*22.4%*	*.258/.335/.450*	*117*	*.288*	*5.4*	*SS 1*	*4.0*

Comparables: Jim Fregosi (79), Arky Vaughan (79), Joe Sewell (78)

In his second year as a New York Met, Lindor turned his thumbs down upside down (right side up?), putting up the second-best offensive season of his career. It may have been his teammate atop the RBI leaderboard when all was said and done, but Lindor also cracked 100 runs batted in and finished the season with the fifth-best mark in baseball, breaking Carlos Guillen's record for runs driven in by a switch-hitting shortstop in a single season. Lindor and Alonso combined for the most runs batted in of any pair of teammates in the league, and their complementary skill sets—the former still a solidly plus glove man, the latter a masher of the purest sort—are the Mets' pillars.

Lindor decisively silenced the boo birds in 2022, but as many past Mets and stars donning pinstripes across town will tell you, they can rear their ugly heads once more at any time. Lindor's defense all but ensures that he'll remain an effective player as he sets off on his 30s, but an offensive dip could staple an unhappy epilogue to his Big Apple redemption tale. Take away the drama and sign language, though, and what you've got is the closest thing the Mets have to a constant. If the Mets fail to fill out their roster and make up for their power deficit and continue to come up short of the Braves in the NL East, it's likely that Lindor will shoulder an undue amount of the blame. If they bring in a few big names and get the matching big results, it's likely that he'll receive less than his deserved amount of credit.

Starling Marte RF

Born: 10/09/88 Age: 34 Bats: R Throws: R Height: 6'1" Weight: 195 lb. Origin: International Free Agent, 2007

YEAR	TEAM	LVL	AGE	PA	R	2B	3B	HR	RBI	BB	K	SB	CS	Whiff%	AVG/OBP/SLG	DRC+	BABIP	BRR	DRP	WARP
2020	MIA	MLB	31	112	13	6	0	4	13	2	22	5	0	23.5%	.245/.286/.415	108	.275	0.4	CF(28): 0.4	0.6
2020	AZ	MLB	31	138	23	8	1	2	14	10	19	5	2	27.1%	.311/.384/.443	112	.353	0.2	CF(33): -1.2, LF(1): 0	0.5
2021	MIA	MLB	32	275	52	11	1	7	25	32	57	22	3	24.6%	.305/.405/.451	114	.376	2.4	CF(63): 6.5	2.6
2021	OAK	MLB	32	251	37	16	2	5	30	11	42	25	2	24.9%	.312/.355/.462	109	.362	3.7	CF(56): -0.7	1.7
2022	NYM	MLB	33	505	76	24	5	16	63	26	97	18	9	24.3%	.292/.347/.468	119	.340	3.1	RF(116): 0.1	2.9
2023 DC	*NYM*	*MLB*	*34*	*587*	*73*	*27*	*3*	*16*	*69*	*35*	*106*	*27*	*7*	*24.4%*	*.279/.341/.433*	*116*	*.324*	*10.7*	*RF 0, CF 0*	*3.6*

Comparables: Carlos Lee (74), Max Carey (72), Lou Brock (71)

Before the 2022 season, the Mets went and got the best free agent center fielder available, signing Marte to a four-year, $78 million deal in the offseason. For the Mets though, he played right field, which was probably for the best due to a combination of Brandon Nimmo's defensive improvements in center and a career low in sprint speed—the chief contributor to Marte's declining defensive metrics since his arm strength is as, well, strong as ever. Chalk it up to age, various minor lower body injuries he sustained throughout the season or some combination thereof, but Marte was not quite the stolen base threat of years past, stealing fewer than 20 bags for the only time since his rookie season, aside from the shortened 2020 season.

But with the bat, he was everything the Mets could have asked for and then some. He put up a triple slash nearly identical to his career batting line and had the best offensive season of his career by DRC+, making his second All-Star team (and rocking a truly legendary fit on the red carpet). Nestled comfortably between on-base specialist Brandon Nimmo and run-producers Francisco Lindor and Pete Alonso in the batting order, Marte did what the Mets did as a team in 2022: he collected hits in droves despite not hitting the ball very hard. Marte fractured his finger in September, costing him the remainder of his regular season, and while it is difficult to ever reduce the narrative arc of a baseball season to singular events or turning points, it certainly felt like the Mets lost a little of the glue that held it all together when they lost Marte.

Ronny Mauricio SS Born: 04/04/01 Age: 22 Bats: S Throws: R Height: 6'3" Weight: 166 lb. Origin: International Free Agent, 2017

YEAR	TEAM	LVL	AGE	PA	R	2B	3B	HR	RBI	BB	K	SB	CS	Whiff%	AVG/OBP/SLG	DRC+	BABIP	BRR	DRP	WARP
2021	LIC	WIN	20	94	8	5	0	2	8	3	21	1	0		.244/.277/.367		.299			
2021	BRK	A+	20	420	55	14	5	19	63	24	101	9	7		.242/.290/.449	115	.278	0.1	SS(87): 10.9	3.0
2021	BNG	AA	20	33	3	1	0	1	1	2	11	2	0		.323/.364/.452	89	.474	-0.3	SS(8): -0.4	0.0
2022	BNG	AA	21	541	71	26	2	26	89	24	125	20	11		.259/.296/.472	107	.293	0.7	SS(112): -7.5	1.5
2023 non-DC	*NYM*	*MLB*	*22*	*251*	*23*	*9*	*1*	*6*	*26*	*10*	*66*	*4*	*3*	*29.6%*	*.237/.274/.374*	*76*	*.302*	*-3.1*	*SS 0*	*-0.4*

Comparables: Domingo Leyba (77), Alen Hanson (75), J.P. Crawford (67)

Like long distance running, the business of being a prospect is often a cruel and humbling one. Despite more or less putting up the same numbers in Double-A as he did at High-A in 2021 and still showing strong potential at just 21 years old, Mauricio watched as other young talents in the Mets system like Francisco Álvarez, Brett Baty and even Mark Vientos surged past him while he remained on the periphery of the conversation. He's still at shortstop for now, but he may ultimately land at third base or even corner outfield, and his aggressive approach at the plate needs some polishing if he is to harness his plus raw power and punish the right pitches. Sustainable success in the big leagues is a marathon and not a sprint; it might be easier for Mauricio if somebody would at least give him a mile marker.

Jeff McNeil 2B/LF Born: 04/08/92 Age: 31 Bats: L Throws: R Height: 6'1" Weight: 195 lb. Origin: Round 12, 2013 Draft (#356 overall)

YEAR	TEAM	LVL	AGE	PA	R	2B	3B	HR	RBI	BB	K	SB	CS	Whiff%	AVG/OBP/SLG	DRC+	BABIP	BRR	DRP	WARP
2020	NYM	MLB	28	209	19	14	0	4	23	20	24	0	2	17.5%	.311/.383/.454	109	.335	-1.9	LF(28): 1.1, 2B(12): 0.3, 3B(9): -1	0.9
2021	NYM	MLB	29	426	48	19	1	7	35	29	58	3	0	18.2%	.249/.317/.358	94	.276	1.8	2B(79): -0.8, LF(28): 1.3, 3B(2): 0	1.4
2022	NYM	MLB	30	589	73	39	1	9	62	40	61	4	0	16.0%	.326/.382/.454	119	.353	-0.5	2B(106): -0.4, LF(34): 1.6, RF(13): 0.2	3.3
2023 DC	*NYM*	*MLB*	*31*	*581*	*73*	*32*	*2*	*14*	*70*	*41*	*64*	*3*	*1*	*16.4%*	*.303/.369/.452*	*130*	*.328*	*1.3*	*2B 0, RF 0*	*3.9*

Comparables: Robinson Canó (66), Frankie Frisch (66), Dale Mitchell (65)

What a difference a year makes. In 2021, the Flying Squirrel was having heated debates with teammates about which species of his rodent compatriots was spotted in the tunnel at Citi Field and spending the rest of his time slamming his batting helmet down in frustration. In 2022, he won the National League batting title, becoming just the second New York Met to do so. And he did it in an epic sprint to the finish, raising his average 12 points in the final two weeks of the season to overtake Freddie Freeman. No player came to represent the narrative that the 2022 Mets were "lucky" more than McNeil, who has outperformed his xwOBA every season of his career except the aforementioned helmet-slamming 2021. But he didn't accomplish that feat by being lucky; he did it by getting "hitting it where they ain't" down to a science—striking out very rarely, putting lots of balls in play, pulling the ball when teams do not shift against him and hitting it to the opposite field when they do. In this way, McNeil was a microcosm of his team, which achieved great success in 2022 despite not hitting the ball very hard or relying heavily on home runs. And in doing so, he convincingly shook the monkey (or was it a raccoon?) of 2021 off his back, proving it to be an aberration rather than an alarming sign of decline.

Omar Narváez C Born: 02/10/92 Age: 31 Bats: L Throws: R Height: 5'11" Weight: 220 lb. Origin: International Free Agent, 2008

YEAR	TEAM	LVL	AGE	PA	R	2B	3B	HR	RBI	BB	K	SB	CS	Whiff%	AVG/OBP/SLG	DRC+	BABIP	BRR	DRP	WARP
2020	MIL	MLB	28	126	8	4	0	2	10	16	39	0	0	29.6%	.176/.294/.269	78	.254	-0.8	C(39): 5.4	0.6
2021	MIL	MLB	29	445	54	20	0	11	49	41	84	0	0	23.6%	.266/.342/.402	99	.308	-4.2	C(111): 11.7, 2B(1): 0	2.6
2022	MIL	MLB	30	296	21	12	1	4	23	29	57	0	0	23.3%	.206/.292/.305	82	.248	-0.6	C(83): 4.4	0.9
2023 DC	*NYM*	*MLB*	*31*	*260*	*28*	*10*	*0*	*5*	*26*	*24*	*52*	*0*	*0*	*23.1%*	*.247/.329/.371*	*94*	*.300*	*-1.2*	*C 0*	*0.6*

Comparables: Butch Wynegar (79), Geno Petralli (71), Ron Hodges (69)

YEAR	TEAM	P. COUNT	FRM RUNS	BLK RUNS	THRW RUNS	TOT RUNS
2020	MIL	4886	4.9	0.1	0.4	5.4
2021	MIL	14925	13.0	-1.0	1.3	13.3
2022	MIL	11479	5.1	-0.1	0.1	5.1
2023	*NYM*	*9620*	*0.6*	*-0.3*	*0.0*	*0.3*

By his standards, Narváez had the perfect season in 2021. He rebounded offensively at the plate, and the out-of-nowhere improvements to his framing from the previous year held strong, culminating in a career-high WARP. But because Narváez doesn't hit the ball particularly hard, he's granted little room for error. If a few aspects of his approach falter, the whole structure crumbles. That's exactly what happened in 2022, a year in which Narváez saw his DRC+ drop by nearly 20%. He lost a significant amount of exit velocity on balls he hit in the air, as well as a couple of percentage points of in-zone contact rate and line-drive rate. A colossus like Aaron Judge can weather minor regressions like these, but not Narváez. On the bright side, his ability to present balls as strikes hasn't faltered, and such a skill alone is worth millions—until the robot overlords arrive, of course.

Tomás Nido C Born: 04/12/94 Age: 29 Bats: R Throws: R Height: 6'0" Weight: 211 lb. Origin: Round 8, 2012 Draft (#260 overall)

YEAR	TEAM	LVL	AGE	PA	R	2B	3B	HR	RBI	BB	K	SB	CS	Whiff%	AVG/OBP/SLG	DRC+	BABIP	BRR	DRP	WARP
2020	NYM	MLB	26	26	4	1	0	2	6	2	6	0	0	32.7%	.292/.346/.583	104	.313	0.0	C(7): 0.4	0.1
2021	NYM	MLB	27	161	16	5	1	3	13	5	44	1	0	38.0%	.222/.261/.327	75	.292	-1.8	C(52): 8.8	0.9
2022	NYM	MLB	28	313	31	15	0	3	28	14	76	0	0	34.8%	.239/.276/.324	75	.314	-2.1	C(96): 17.2	1.9
2023 DC	*NYM*	*MLB*	*29*	*220*	*21*	*9*	*0*	*4*	*21*	*11*	*58*	*0*	*0*	*34.4%*	*.227/.272/.342*	*66*	*.295*	*-2.1*	*C 10*	*0.7*

Comparables: Sandy Leon (61), Jeff Mathis (59), Matt Walbeck (58)

YEAR	TEAM	P. COUNT	FRM RUNS	BLK RUNS	THRW RUNS	TOT RUNS
2020	NYM	1049	0.8	0.0	0.0	0.9
2021	NYM	5964	8.4	0.1	0.3	8.9
2022	NYM	12294	15.3	0.6	1.1	16.9
2023	*NYM*	*8418*	*9.8*	*0.3*	*0.0*	*10.1*

Beware the Ides of March. Nido batted .417/.440/.583 in 24 at-bats in an abbreviated spring training—just enough to dream of the possibilities of what he could provide with even just a league-average bat. Alas, his bat was once again well below league-average; he didn't hit a home run until September, which prompted the friendly silent treatment from his teammates in the dugout. But Nido's value has always been in his defense; he was the second-best receiver in baseball in 2022 by CDA and was—surprisingly—the only Met named as a finalist for a Gold Glove. Because James McCann was either injured or equally inept with the bat for much of the season, Nido got the lion's share of the playing time behind the dish. But the catching position—even by modern standards—was a black hole for the Mets all season offensively, and while Nido's receiving skills are excellent, it is as apparent as ever that his best role is as a backup. The Mets should have perhaps made better decisions when it comes to the catching position, but as Cassius would say, "The fault, dear Brutus, is not in our stars, but in ourselves."

Brandon Nimmo CF Born: 03/27/93 Age: 30 Bats: L Throws: R Height: 6'3" Weight: 206 lb. Origin: Round 1, 2011 Draft (#13 overall)

YEAR	TEAM	LVL	AGE	PA	R	2B	3B	HR	RBI	BB	K	SB	CS	Whiff%	AVG/OBP/SLG	DRC+	BABIP	BRR	DRP	WARP
2020	NYM	MLB	27	225	33	8	3	8	18	33	43	1	2	21.8%	.280/.404/.484	114	.326	-2.9	CF(44): -2.8, LF(22): 0.3, RF(10): 0.8	0.7
2021	SYR	AAA	28	36	5	1	0	0	0	5	3	0	0		.172/.333/.207	116	.192	-0.1	CF(9): -1.2	0.1
2021	NYM	MLB	28	386	51	17	3	8	28	54	79	5	4	22.7%	.292/.401/.437	111	.366	0.1	CF(84): 3.5, LF(10): 0	2.5
2022	NYM	MLB	29	673	102	30	7	16	64	71	116	3	2	19.5%	.274/.367/.433	115	.317	4.0	CF(151): 1.7	4.3
2023 DC	*NYM*	*MLB*	*30*	*648*	*97*	*28*	*6*	*17*	*65*	*74*	*114*	*5*	*2*	*19.8%*	*.274/.375/.439*	*128*	*.322*	*3.6*	*CF 6*	*5.3*

Comparables: Jim Edmonds (67), Ray Lankford (66), Willie Wilson (64)

Another year, another highlight package full of sprints to first base for the Mets' leadoff man. This season though, a couple of things were different. Most importantly, Nimmo was healthy. He played in 151 games in 2022—a career high and just the second time he's cracked 100 games played in his seven-year tenure in the majors. The other difference was not Nimmo himself, who remained the consistent presence at the top of the Mets' lineup that he's always been; it was the rest of the lineup, which was the best offense Nimmo has ever been a part of in his career.

A combination of these two new factors translated to career highs for Nimmo in hits, runs scored and runs batted in. He also led the league in triples in 2022. Nimmo continued to make strides in center field as well, harnessing his elite sprint speed and the power of positioning to rank in the 91st percentile in outs above average, punctuated by his incredible catch in a crucial August game against the Dodgers to rob Justin Turner of a home run that brought back memories of Endy Chavez in the 2006 NLCS. Over the offseason, the Mets decided to make Nimmo a Met For Life. You'd be surprised how high he ranks on New York's all-time lists already (sixth all-time in OPS+ in franchise history, for instance), and by the time he's through, he's going to own a lot of categories in Queens.

★ ★ ★ *2023 Top 101 Prospect* **#64** ★ ★ ★

Kevin Parada C Born: 08/03/01 Age: 21 Bats: R Throws: R Height: 6'1" Weight: 197 lb. Origin: Round 1, 2022 Draft (#11 overall)

YEAR	TEAM	LVL	AGE	PA	R	2B	3B	HR	RBI	BB	K	SB	CS	Whiff%	AVG/OBP/SLG	DRC+	BABIP	BRR	DRP	WARP
2022	SLU	A	20	41	5	1	0	1	5	10	12	0	1	28.4%	.276/.463/.414	109	.412	-0.3	C(6): -0.2	0.1
2023 non-DC	*NYM*	*MLB*	*21*	*251*	*21*	*9*	*1*	*3*	*21*	*24*	*81*	*1*	*1*	*33.7%*	*.202/.289/.309*	*65*	*.300*	*0.6*	*C 0*	*-0.1*

YEAR	TEAM	P. COUNT	FRM RUNS	BLK RUNS	THRW RUNS	TOT RUNS
2023	*NYM*	*6956*	*-2.9*	*0.5*	*-0.1*	*-2.5*

Parada's mother thought that all it would take was for her son to block one ball behind the plate to realize catcher was not the right position for him. But she was wrong. Fast forward to 2022, and the Georgia Tech product was the Mets' top pick in the draft at no. 11, signing for $5,019,735—a record amount for a player outside of the top ten picks. Despite his unorthodox batting stance, there is little doubt about his ability to hit and hit for power. But his defense behind the plate—particularly his throwing arm—needs some seasoning. You can say it takes a certain amount of masochism to embrace the beatings a backstop takes from an early age. It takes a certain amount of masochism to embrace rooting for the Mets from an early age, too. Between Francisco Álvarez's rapid ascent up the prospect lists and Parada's potential, the Mets have a chance to find themselves with an embarrassment of riches at a position that has been a weakness for many years. They're hoping mother doesn't know best.

★ ★ ★ *2023 Top 101 Prospect* **#101** ★ ★ ★

Alex Ramirez OF Born: 01/13/03 Age: 20 Bats: R Throws: R Height: 6'3" Weight: 170 lb. Origin: International Free Agent, 2019

YEAR	TEAM	LVL	AGE	PA	R	2B	3B	HR	RBI	BB	K	SB	CS	Whiff%	AVG/OBP/SLG	DRC+	BABIP	BRR	DRP	WARP
2021	SLU	A	18	334	41	15	4	5	35	23	104	16	7		.258/.326/.384	84	.376	-3.4	CF(46): 1.7, RF(22): 5.1, LF(5): -0.8	0.8
2022	SLU	A	19	306	40	13	6	6	37	28	68	17	9	30.7%	.284/.359/.443	116	.357	0.9	CF(56): -3.2, LF(3): -0.6, RF(1): 0.1	0.9
2022	BRK	A+	19	246	22	17	1	5	34	16	54	4	7		.278/.329/.427	97	.343	-2.5	CF(34): -2.2, RF(17): -1.4	0.1
2023 non-DC	*NYM*	*MLB*	*20*	*251*	*20*	*11*	*2*	*3*	*22*	*13*	*72*	*7*	*4*	*32.5%*	*.239/.286/.349*	*73*	*.331*	*-3.0*	*LF 0, CF 0*	*-0.5*

Comparables: Jahmai Jones (76), Estevan Florial (66), Cristian Pache (65)

Haunted by the ghost of deadline deals past, the Mets were reluctant to part with their young talent this season. The specter of Pete Crow-Armstrong seemed to loom especially over Ramirez—the current top outfielder in a system that is otherwise rather bereft of outfield talent. After holding his own in the Florida State League as the second-youngest player at the level in 2021, the Dominican native was promoted to High-A and continued to perform well there. Ramírez boasts speed aplenty—bat speed and foot speed alike—which is the gas fueling his upside. But if he fills out and fully leans into being a power-hitting outfielder, he may sacrifice the other side of the equation.

Darin Ruf 1B

Born: 07/28/86 Age: 36 Bats: R Throws: R Height: 6'2" Weight: 232 lb. Origin: Round 20, 2009 Draft (#617 overall)

YEAR	TEAM	LVL	AGE	PA	R	2B	3B	HR	RBI	BB	K	SB	CS	Whiff%	AVG/OBP/SLG	DRC+	BABIP	BRR	DRP	WARP
2020	SF	MLB	33	100	11	6	0	5	18	13	23	1	0	26.3%	.276/.370/.517	118	.322	-1.3	LF(22): -1.3, 1B(4): 0, RF(3): -0.3	0.2
2021	SF	MLB	34	312	41	13	2	16	43	46	87	2	0	25.0%	.271/.385/.519	124	.344	-3.4	1B(44): 0.7, LF(33): -1.8, RF(5): 2.6	1.7
2022	SF	MLB	35	314	46	9	0	11	38	40	85	2	0	27.0%	.216/.328/.373	105	.272	0.9	1B(36): 0.3, LF(28): -0.9, RF(3): -0.1	1.0
2022	NYM	MLB	35	74	6	3	0	0	7	5	20	0	0	29.1%	.152/.216/.197	83	.208	-0.6	1B(9): 0, RF(6): -0.6	-0.1
2023 DC	*NYM*	*MLB*	*36*	*239*	*27*	*10*	*0*	*7*	*26*	*27*	*61*	*1*	*0*	*27.2%*	*.220/.321/.378*	*96*	*.277*	*0.2*	*RF 0, LF 0*	*0.3*

Comparables: Mark Reynolds (54), Steve Pearce (54), Tony Clark (52)

There once was a player named Ruf
Whose tenure was not up to snuff.
  Dealt Davis and Zwack
  Eppler'd like this one back
For the DH did not hit enough.

Mark Vientos 3B

Born: 12/11/99 Age: 23 Bats: R Throws: R Height: 6'4" Weight: 185 lb. Origin: Round 2, 2017 Draft (#59 overall)

YEAR	TEAM	LVL	AGE	PA	R	2B	3B	HR	RBI	BB	K	SB	CS	Whiff%	AVG/OBP/SLG	DRC+	BABIP	BRR	DRP	WARP
2021	BNG	AA	21	306	43	16	0	22	59	26	87	0	1		.281/.346/.580	123	.327	-1.9	3B(41): -4.4, LF(12): -0.2, 1B(11): -0.1	1.1
2021	SYR	AAA	21	43	9	2	0	3	4	7	13	0	1		.278/.395/.583	110	.350	-0.1	3B(9): 1.2, LF(1): -0.1	0.3
2022	SYR	AAA	22	427	66	16	1	24	72	44	122	0	2	33.3%	.280/.358/.519	112	.350	-0.7	3B(59): -2.9, 1B(27): -0.6	1.5
2022	NYM	MLB	22	41	3	1	0	1	3	5	12	0	0	29.7%	.167/.268/.278	94	.217	-0.1	3B(2): -0.3	0.0
2023 DC	*NYM*	*MLB*	*23*	*31*	*3*	*1*	*0*	*1*	*3*	*2*	*8*	*0*	*0*	*32.4%*	*.233/.300/.416*	*95*	*.298*	*-0.4*	*1B 0*	*0.0*

Comparables: Renato Núñez (75), Austin Riley (70), Jeimer Candelario (65)

Young for the level at almost every step of the way in the minor leagues, Vientos demonstrated that he could hit and hit for power, albeit with a lower contact rate in the zone than one would like. A confluence of factors led to his promotion to the big leagues in September at age 22—Luis Guillorme's late-season stint on the injured list, Brett Baty going down with a thumb injury and Darin Ruf failing to uphold his end of the bargain at the DH platoon in the second half. The concerns regarding Vientos' defense are well-established at this point, and the Mets promoted him almost exclusively to take DH at-bats against lefties, against which he has had more success than righties. But at the big-league level, the swing-and-miss issues persisted to the point that he really didn't have much luck against either. The door is ajar on the other side of the platoon this year, opposite Daniel Vogelbach. We'll see if Vientos can make enough contact to push it open.

Daniel Vogelbach DH

Born: 12/17/92 Age: 30 Bats: L Throws: R Height: 6'0" Weight: 270 lb. Origin: Round 2, 2011 Draft (#68 overall)

YEAR	TEAM	LVL	AGE	PA	R	2B	3B	HR	RBI	BB	K	SB	CS	Whiff%	AVG/OBP/SLG	DRC+	BABIP	BRR	DRP	WARP
2020	MIL	MLB	27	67	13	2	0	4	12	8	18	0	0	22.5%	.328/.418/.569	105	.417	-0.3	1B(2): 0.2	0.2
2020	SEA	MLB	27	64	3	1	0	2	4	11	13	0	0	22.1%	.094/.250/.226	93	.079	-0.2		0.1
2020	TOR	MLB	27	5	0	0	0	0	0	1	2	0	0	20.0%	.000/.200/.000	88		0.0		0.0
2021	NAS	AAA	28	65	8	0	0	3	8	16	13	0	0		.313/.477/.500	129	.364	-1.2	1B(16): 0.8	0.3
2021	MIL	MLB	28	258	30	8	0	9	24	43	57	0	0	19.4%	.219/.349/.381	108	.255	-2.9	1B(59): -1.3	0.5
2022	NYM	MLB	29	183	18	9	0	6	25	33	47	0	0	20.8%	.255/.393/.436	108	.333	-0.3		0.7
2022	PIT	MLB	29	278	29	10	1	12	34	40	67	0	0	20.2%	.228/.338/.430	111	.264	0.0	1B(5): -0.2	1.0
2023 DC	*NYM*	*MLB*	*30*	*418*	*56*	*15*	*0*	*16*	*49*	*65*	*87*	*0*	*0*	*20.4%*	*.233/.358/.418*	*117*	*.267*	*-1.7*		*1.4*

Comparables: Justin Smoak (65), J.R. Phillips (55), Chris Davis (54)

In desperate need for an upgrade at the designated hitter position, the Mets acquired Vogelbach at the trading deadline from the Pirates to slot in against right-handed pitchers. Although aesthetically he is an uber-Alonso, his patient style at the plate fit right in with the likes of Mark Canha and Brandon Nimmo. Vogelbach had by far the lowest in-zone swing rate in the majors in 2022, which was the case the year before as well. He put up a solid .255/.393/.436 batting line in 183 plate appearances as a Met, and the goofy style of his home runs (a three-quarter swing, a five-quarter outcome) helped him achieve cult hero status. Picking up Vogelbach's $1.5 million team option for 2023 was a no-brainer, for the reliability of the takes and the radness of the taters.

★ ★ ★ *2023 Top 101 Prospect* **#75** ★ ★ ★

Jett Williams SS

Born: 11/03/03 Age: 19 Bats: R Throws: R Height: 5'8" Weight: 175 lb. Origin: Round 1, 2022 Draft (#14 overall)

YEAR	TEAM	LVL	AGE	PA	R	2B	3B	HR	RBI	BB	K	SB	CS	Whiff%	AVG/OBP/SLG	DRC+	BABIP	BRR	DRP	WARP
2022	MET	ROK	18	41	7	1	1	1	6	4	6	6	0		.250/.366/.438		.259			
2023															*No projection*					

"Man, if you were 6-foot-2, you'd be a top-five draft pick," a scout once told Williams. And they were probably right. As he stands at 5-foot-8, he was drafted 14th overall instead. But his doubters have only made the chip on his shoulder—and his work ethic—bigger. Williams has good plate discipline and bat-to-ball skills and the speed to stick at shortstop, though his arm strength remains an open question. He might well end up at second or in center field, but the position won't much matter as long as he hits how he's supposed to. Short kings and queens, rejoice. The future is bright.

PITCHERS

Matt Allan RHP

Born: 04/17/01 Age: 22 Bats: R Throws: R Height: 6'3" Weight: 225 lb. Origin: Round 3, 2019 Draft (#89 overall)

The best pitcher in the Mets' system when he was drafted in 2019, boasting a mid-90s fastball and one of the best curveballs in his class, Allan has had his development halted in its tracks by the COVID-19 pandemic and injury. He underwent Tommy John surgery in May of 2021, and in January of 2022 he had ulnar transposition surgery as well, rendering his age-21 season his third consecutive one without taking the mound in a professional game. With that long on the sidelines, it's impossible to say whether he will pick up where he left off—with top-of-the-rotation upside—or if the long layoff will rob him of his career.

R.J. Alvarez RHP

Born: 06/08/91 Age: 32 Bats: R Throws: R Height: 6'1" Weight: 230 lb. Origin: Round 3, 2012 Draft (#114 overall)

YEAR	TEAM	LVL	AGE	W	L	SV	G	GS	IP	H	HR	BB/9	K/9	K	GB%	BABIP	WHIP	ERA	DRA-	WARP	MPH	FB%	Whiff%	CSP
2021	NAS	AAA	30	0	3	1	38	0	35^1	34	3	4.6	11.2	44	51.0%	.341	1.47	4.08	89	0.7				
2022	SYR	AAA	31	4	3	4	40	0	45^2	34	3	5.7	8.7	44	47.9%	.263	1.38	3.55	93	0.8				
2022	NYM	MLB	31	0	1	0	1	0	2^1	4	2	11.6	7.7	2	25.0%	.333	3.00	11.57	120	0.0	93.1	51.0%	28.6%	59.2%
2023 DC	*FA*	*MLB*	*32*	*1*	*1*	*0*	*28*	*0*	*25*	*23*	*2*	*5.2*	*8.6*	*23*	*44.8%*	*.301*	*1.53*	*4.88*	*114*	*-0.1*	*93.1*	*51.0%*	*28.4%*	*59.2%*

Comparables: Miguel Socolovich (41), Logan Kensing (40), Josh Judy (40)

Alvarez had last pitched in the majors in 2015, and had since spent time with five different organizations, before the Mets signed him to a minor-league contract in February. He made just one appearance in August, forced into service in long relief just hours after his call-up because of an early exit by Taijuan Walker due to back spasms. He struggled with his command and, in a kind of microcosm of the Mets' eventual division fate, was greeted quite rudely by the Braves' offense in his return to the big leagues.

Jose Butto RHP

Born: 03/19/98 Age: 25 Bats: R Throws: R Height: 6'1" Weight: 202 lb. Origin: International Free Agent, 2017

YEAR	TEAM	LVL	AGE	W	L	SV	G	GS	IP	H	HR	BB/9	K/9	K	GB%	BABIP	WHIP	ERA	DRA-	WARP	MPH	FB%	Whiff%	CSP
2021	BRK	A+	23	1	4	0	12	12	58^1	51	11	2.3	9.3	60	44.1%	.267	1.13	4.32	90	0.8				
2021	BNG	AA	23	3	2	0	8	8	40^1	33	6	2.0	11.2	50	42.7%	.284	1.04	3.12	86	0.7				
2022	BNG	AA	24	6	5	0	20	18	92^1	86	14	3.4	10.5	108	38.9%	.313	1.31	4.00	90	1.7				
2022	SYR	AAA	24	1	1	0	8	7	36^2	26	3	2.2	7.4	30	47.1%	.232	0.95	2.45	84	0.8	94.4	65.0%	0.0%	
2022	NYM	MLB	24	0	0	0	1	1	4	9	2	4.5	11.3	5	25.0%	.500	2.75	15.75	116	0.0	94.8	51.0%	24.5%	53.7%
2023 DC	*NYM*	*MLB*	*25*	*2*	*2*	*0*	*22*	*3*	*31*	*32*	*5*	*3.4*	*7.5*	*25*	*40.8%*	*.302*	*1.43*	*4.89*	*120*	*-0.1*	*94.8*	*51.0%*	*25.5%*	*53.7%*

Comparables: Kyle McPherson (53), Dario Agrazal (51), Tyler Wilson (49)

Butto signed with the Mets as an international free agent in 2017 at the age of 19 and made his major-league debut filling in for the injured Taijuan Walker five years later. Butto's best weapon is his low-80s changeup, which plays excellently off his fastball and which he reliably throws for strikes. Unfortunately, Alec Bohm took one of those changeups deep in Butto's first inning—one of two homers Bohm would hit off him that day. The game turned out to be one of the more memorable ones of the 2022 season, featuring the Mets coming from behind on three different occasions. Looked at charitably, Butto's outing was simply the setup for a Mark Canha bat flip for the ages. The Mets' hope is that Butto's success in 2023 is more direct.

Carlos Carrasco RHP

Born: 03/21/87 Age: 36 Bats: R Throws: R Height: 6'4" Weight: 224 lb. Origin: International Free Agent, 2003

YEAR	TEAM	LVL	AGE	W	L	SV	G	GS	IP	H	HR	BB/9	K/9	K	GB%	BABIP	WHIP	ERA	DRA-	WARP	MPH	FB%	Whiff%	CSP
2020	CLE	MLB	33	3	4	0	12	12	68	55	8	3.6	10.9	82	46.2%	.294	1.21	2.91	76	1.6	93.8	39.3%	32.7%	45.3%
2021	NYM	MLB	34	1	5	0	12	12	53^2	59	12	3.0	8.4	50	43.2%	.299	1.43	6.04	107	0.3	93.3	50.6%	27.4%	52.2%
2022	NYM	MLB	35	15	7	0	29	29	152	161	17	2.4	9.0	152	46.4%	.338	1.33	3.97	99	1.6	93.1	46.8%	27.8%	52.3%
2023 DC	*NYM*	*MLB*	*36*	*7*	*8*	*0*	*24*	*24*	*128.7*	*133*	*16*	*2.8*	*8.5*	*121*	*44.9%*	*.318*	*1.35*	*4.18*	*105*	*0.7*	*93.3*	*46.3%*	*27.4%*	*50.9%*

Comparables: John Lackey (72), Esteban Loaiza (72), Doug Drabek (71)

The exchange between the Mets and Guardians will always be known as "the Francisco Lindor trade," but it was the Carrasco trade, too. After a 2021 riddled with injury, Carrasco improved in his second season in a Mets uniform and demonstrated why he was an underrated part of the deal. Carrasco couldn't match his top-of-the-rotation numbers from his days in Cleveland, but he did give the Mets 152 innings of league-average performance, which was enough in a rotation headlined by Jacob deGrom and Max Scherzer. His most notable bugaboo was his trouble with teams over .500; in 52⅓ innings against such teams, Carrasco posted a 6.71 ERA and a 1.53 WHIP with opponents batting .300 against him in those starts. Amid the Mets' total overhaul of their rotation, the team picked up Carrasco's $14 million option, leaving him in a familiar position: overshadowed and useful. And if you give the Mets a Cookie, they're going to ask for a glass of milk.

Edwin Díaz RHP Born: 03/22/94 Age: 29 Bats: R Throws: R Height: 6'3" Weight: 165 lb. Origin: Round 3, 2012 Draft (#98 overall)

YEAR	TEAM	LVL	AGE	W	L	SV	G	GS	IP	H	HR	BB/9	K/9	K	GB%	BABIP	WHIP	ERA	DRA-	WARP	MPH	FB%	Whiff%	CSP
2020	NYM	MLB	26	2	1	6	26	0	25^{2}	18	2	4.9	17.5	50	45.5%	.381	1.25	1.75	49	1.0	97.9	61.9%	48.2%	43.6%
2021	NYM	MLB	27	5	6	32	63	0	62^{2}	43	3	3.3	12.8	89	32.4%	.308	1.05	3.45	74	1.4	98.9	62.2%	35.1%	51.0%
2022	NYM	MLB	28	3	1	32	61	0	62	34	3	2.6	17.1	118	46.4%	.330	0.84	1.31	42	2.4	99.3	41.9%	50.2%	51.8%
2023 DC	*NYM*	*MLB*	*29*	*3*	*2*	*41*	*58*	*0*	*50.3*	*43*	*5*	*3.4*	*16.7*	*93*	*40.8%*	*.407*	*1.23*	*3.39*	*79*	*0.8*	*98.8*	*54.0%*	*42.7%*	*49.9%*

Comparables: Kenley Jansen (77), Ken Giles (77), David Robertson (75)

Did you know that "Narco"—Díaz's entrance song by Blasterjaxx and Timmy Trumpet that became a viral sensation—actually has lyrics? It's easy to forget amidst the resounding trumpet call that is the real hallmark of the song, but it's true. There is just one verse and it is repeated twice. The last line of that verse: *My goons are strippin' all these cats down to their Underoos*. Díaz likely didn't pick the song for its evocative lyrics, but that line describes exactly what he did to hitters all year long. He pantsed them, day in and day out, inducing cartoonish whiffs that may very well have *literally* had cats down to their Underoos if their pants weren't held up by belts. He struck out over half the batters he faced—a rate over ten percentage points higher than any other reliever in baseball in 2022. Of the Mets' many impending free agents, Díaz was likely the highest on the priority list to retain because he is irreplaceable, both due to his elite level of performance and the show-stopping event his outings have become. The Mets demonstrated this by inking Díaz to a five-year, $102 million dollar contract the day after the World Series concluded—the largest contract ever for a relief pitcher—keeping their star closer in New York long term. Alexa, play "Narco."

Dominic Hamel RHP Born: 03/02/99 Age: 24 Bats: R Throws: R Height: 6'2" Weight: 206 lb. Origin: Round 3, 2021 Draft (#81 overall)

YEAR	TEAM	LVL	AGE	W	L	SV	G	GS	IP	H	HR	BB/9	K/9	K	GB%	BABIP	WHIP	ERA	DRA-	WARP	MPH	FB%	Whiff%	CSP
2022	SLU	A	23	5	2	0	14	13	63^{1}	48	5	4.1	10.1	71	44.1%	.276	1.22	3.84	102	1.0	92.7	55.9%	30.3%	
2022	BRK	A+	23	5	1	0	11	11	55^{2}	35	0	4.0	12.0	74	36.9%	.287	1.08	2.59	84	0.9				
2023 non-DC	*NYM*	*MLB*	*24*	*2*	*2*	*0*	*57*	*0*	*50*	*47*	*6*	*5.3*	*8.4*	*46*	*40.2%*	*.291*	*1.54*	*4.83*	*115*	*-0.2*			*25.1%*	

Comparables: Yefry Ramírez (89), Kyle Cody (85), Chris Vallimont (84)

After getting off to a slow start due to an injury he sustained in spring training, the Mets' 2021 third-round draft pick went on to lead all Mets pitching prospects in batting average against, strikeouts and strikeout rate across Low- and High-A ball. His fastball is of middling velocity but has above-average spin and movement, and is his best offering. He has a full arsenal of secondary pitches as well—a slider, curveball and changeup—but can struggle with his command, which is mostly what is standing between him and an outcome as a mid-rotation starter in the majors.

Elieser Hernandez RHP Born: 05/03/95 Age: 28 Bats: R Throws: R Height: 6'0" Weight: 214 lb. Origin: International Free Agent, 2011

YEAR	TEAM	LVL	AGE	W	L	SV	G	GS	IP	H	HR	BB/9	K/9	K	GB%	BABIP	WHIP	ERA	DRA-	WARP	MPH	FB%	Whiff%	CSP
2020	MIA	MLB	25	1	0	0	6	6	25^{2}	21	5	1.8	11.9	34	33.8%	.267	1.01	3.16	82	0.5	91.4	58.9%	29.2%	56.7%
2021	JAX	AAA	26	0	1	0	5	5	21^{1}	11	3	1.3	13.5	32	35.7%	.205	0.66	2.95	89	0.4				
2021	MIA	MLB	26	1	3	0	11	11	51^{2}	54	13	2.4	9.2	53	38.1%	.293	1.32	4.18	94	0.6	90.9	54.2%	24.1%	60.8%
2022	JAX	AAA	27	4	4	0	12	11	57	51	8	2.7	10.7	68	32.9%	.305	1.19	4.11	85	1.2	91.1	69.9%	22.8%	
2022	MIA	MLB	27	3	6	0	20	10	62^{1}	67	19	3.2	8.7	60	27.6%	.277	1.43	6.35	119	0.0	91.7	50.5%	25.0%	60.5%
2023 DC	*NYM*	*MLB*	*28*	*5*	*3*	*0*	*43*	*4*	*55.3*	*53*	*8*	*2.7*	*8.3*	*51*	*32.6%*	*.290*	*1.25*	*3.96*	*102*	*0.4*	*91.3*	*53.1%*	*25.1%*	*58.6%*

Comparables: Jeff Hoffman (54), Nick Martinez (52), Felix Doubront (51)

Hernandez might throw the most unique pitch in MLB: a breaking ball that moves like a cutter, but with curveball velocity and huge sweep. That he gets plus extension and creates such a low vertical release point should be a boon for his fastball—it has one of the lowest zone-adjusted vertical approach angles in MLB—but its sub-92 mph velocity makes it play down, especially because he doesn't possess a pitch that drops much. His numbers suggest he was probably more unlucky than legitimately bad, but without a tweak to his repertoire, even a 15.1% pop-up rate isn't enough to offset his 2.74 home runs per nine innings.

Tommy Hunter RHP Born: 07/03/86 Age: 37 Bats: R Throws: R Height: 6'3" Weight: 250 lb. Origin: Round 1, 2007 Draft (#54 overall)

YEAR	TEAM	LVL	AGE	W	L	SV	G	GS	IP	H	HR	BB/9	K/9	K	GB%	BABIP	WHIP	ERA	DRA-	WARP	MPH	FB%	Whiff%	CSP
2020	PHI	MLB	33	0	1	1	24	0	24^{2}	22	2	2.2	9.1	25	41.2%	.308	1.14	4.01	86	0.5	91.9	76.8%	25.7%	44.0%
2021	NYM	MLB	34	0	0	0	4	1	8	4	0	3.4	6.7	6	45.5%	.190	0.88	0.00	100	0.1	91.1	86.2%	11.3%	58.9%
2022	SYR	AAA	35	1	0	0	8	0	13^{2}	16	2	0.7	9.2	14	45.7%	.318	1.24	4.61	94	0.2				
2022	NYM	MLB	35	0	1	0	18	0	22^{1}	21	4	2.4	8.9	22	40.9%	.279	1.21	2.42	101	0.2	92.2	85.7%	24.1%	55.0%
2023 DC	*FA*	*MLB*	*36*	*2*	*2*	*0*	*43*	*0*	*37.3*	*38*	*4*	*2.4*	*6.9*	*28*	*43.7%*	*.295*	*1.28*	*3.90*	*102*	*0.1*	*92.0*	*83.0%*	*21.8%*	*51.8%*

Comparables: Lindy McDaniel (67), Anthony Swarzak (63), Don Aase (61)

After achieving cult hero status in 2021 by beginning the season with eight scoreless innings of relief and doing a little jig on first base after hitting a single (RIP Pitchers Who Rake), Hunter missed the rest of the season with a back injury that threatened his career. The multiple disc herniations he suffered caused Hunter such pain that he was not able to lift his infant son. But, 13 months later, Hunter had worked his way back and was pitching on a big-league mound again, making his 2022 Mets debut on June 19. Not only was Hunter able to toe the rubber for his 15th major-league season—an achievement in and of itself—he was effective, contributing 22⅓ solid innings of relief for the Mets during the summer months before his back acted up again in September.

Yoan López RHP Born: 01/02/93 Age: 30 Bats: R Throws: R Height: 6'3" Weight: 208 lb. Origin: International Free Agent, 2015

YEAR	TEAM	LVL	AGE	W	L	SV	G	GS	IP	H	HR	BB/9	K/9	K	GB%	BABIP	WHIP	ERA	DRA-	WARP	MPH	FB%	Whiff%	CSP
2020	AZ	MLB	27	0	1	0	20	0	19^2	21	4	4.1	7.3	16	54.8%	.293	1.53	5.95	106	0.2	95.4	54.7%	25.2%	48.8%
2021	GWN	AAA	28	3	2	2	32	0	32^2	30	3	3.0	9.6	35	52.9%	.329	1.26	3.03	82	0.7				
2021	AZ	MLB	28	0	0	0	13	0	12^1	18	3	4.4	9.5	13	45.2%	.385	1.95	6.57	110	0.1	95.9	51.6%	28.6%	55.7%
2022	SYR	AAA	29	2	2	2	29	0	35	41	4	3.9	9.8	38	56.1%	.359	1.60	5.14	79	0.8				
2022	NYM	MLB	29	1	0	0	8	0	11	14	2	4.1	8.2	10	40.0%	.364	1.73	5.73	112	0.0	96.1	46.2%	28.4%	57.8%
2023 non-DC	*NYM*	*MLB*	*30*	*2*	*2*	*0*	*57*	*0*	*50*	*54*	*6*	*3.8*	*8.2*	*45*	*48.3%*	*.327*	*1.51*	*4.75*	*115*	*-0.2*	*96.0*	*52.4%*	*27.2%*	*52.8%*

Comparables: Ryan Dull (58), Ryan Cook (58), Kevin Quackenbush (56)

López spent the calendar year prior to the start of the 2022 season on a tour of the NL East. He was picked up on waivers and then designated for assignment by the Braves, Phillies and Marlins in short succession before landing with the Mets in late March. The 29-year-old righty racked up frequent flier miles being shuttled back and forth between the minors and the big leagues, and the itinerary was more memorable than the performance. The non-transit moment that stuck most in mind was López falling on the sword and taking a one-game suspension for throwing at Kyle Schwarber—intentionally, as judged by MLB—symbolizing frustrations bubbling over at what turned out to be a record-setting number of Mets hit by pitches in a single season.

Joey Lucchesi LHP Born: 06/06/93 Age: 30 Bats: L Throws: L Height: 6'5" Weight: 225 lb. Origin: Round 4, 2016 Draft (#114 overall)

YEAR	TEAM	LVL	AGE	W	L	SV	G	GS	IP	H	HR	BB/9	K/9	K	GB%	BABIP	WHIP	ERA	DRA-	WARP	MPH	FB%	Whiff%	CSP
2020	SD	MLB	27	0	1	0	3	2	5^2	13	0	3.2	7.9	5	37.5%	.542	2.65	7.94	103	0.1	89.9	65.0%	31.6%	47.7%
2021	NYM	MLB	28	1	4	0	11	8	38^1	34	4	2.6	9.6	41	38.2%	.313	1.17	4.46	96	0.4	91.3	63.3%	23.8%	57.7%
2023 DC	*NYM*	*MLB*	*30*	*3*	*2*	*0*	*22*	*3*	*31.7*	*31*	*4*	*3.0*	*8.3*	*29*	*43.2%*	*.304*	*1.33*	*3.97*	*101*	*0.2*	*90.7*	*64.2%*	*24.6%*	*50.8%*

Comparables: Kevin Gausman (54), Derek Holland (52), Francisco Liriano (51)

Lucchesi's signature "churve" became so legendary in New York, in the half-season he pitched in 2021, that his Mets teammates would raise the "ok" hand sign as a celebration after hits, in an effort to get the scoreboard operators to recognize the churve as an official pitch type. But the Tommy John surgery Lucchesi underwent in June of 2021 cost him the chance to continue the churve recognition campaign in the majors in 2022. Lucchesi began rehabbing in minor-league games in August, pitching in eight games in August in September to the tune of a 2.13 ERA in 12⅔ innings. He should be a viable depth option for the Mets next season.

Adonis Medina RHP Born: 12/18/96 Age: 26 Bats: R Throws: R Height: 6'1" Weight: 187 lb. Origin: International Free Agent, 2014

YEAR	TEAM	LVL	AGE	W	L	SV	G	GS	IP	H	HR	BB/9	K/9	K	GB%	BABIP	WHIP	ERA	DRA-	WARP	MPH	FB%	Whiff%	CSP
2020	PHI	MLB	23	0	1	0	1	1	4	3	0	6.8	9.0	4	81.8%	.273	1.50	4.50	88	0.1	92.3	53.6%	29.7%	42.4%
2021	LHV	AAA	24	4	5	0	17	17	67^2	71	10	3.5	7.3	55	46.8%	.298	1.43	5.05	114	0.4				
2021	PHI	MLB	24	0	0	0	4	1	7^2	9	0	4.7	7.0	6	47.8%	.391	1.70	3.52	120	0.0	92.5	65.0%	26.4%	51.1%
2022	SYR	AAA	25	1	0	1	18	2	31	36	4	4.9	9.6	33	50.5%	.352	1.71	4.65	99	0.4	93.8	54.8%	33.3%	
2022	NYM	MLB	25	1	0	1	14	0	23^2	30	2	2.3	6.5	17	51.2%	.354	1.52	6.08	109	0.1	93.5	47.7%	19.4%	55.2%
2023 non-DC	*NYM*	*MLB*	*26*	*2*	*3*	*0*	*57*	*0*	*50*	*55*	*6*	*3.9*	*6.9*	*38*	*49.5%*	*.316*	*1.54*	*5.40*	*127*	*-0.5*	*93.2*	*51.3%*	*24.1%*	*53.5%*

Comparables: Jake Buchanan (54), Jackson Stephens (53), Robbie Ross Jr. (52)

Medina's first career save was one to remember. In the tenth inning of a June game in Los Angeles, with the tying run on second and other relief options exhausted, Medina found himself on the mound facing Mookie Betts, Freddie Freeman and Trea Turner. He escaped the inning unscathed to lock down the victory. Acquired from the Pirates for cash by the Mets in April, Medina proved an up-and-down middle reliever. He had the ability to pitch multiple innings and occasionally to produce moments like the one in LA, that flashed the potential he showed as a prospect. He carried an ERA under three over multiple stints in the big leagues into August, but a pair of disasters—once in before a second-half send-down and another in his final appearance in September—more than doubled it. Don't let the stats scrub away the specifics, though: the Adonis Medina Game is a crucial entry in the 2022 Mets canon.

Tylor Megill RHP Born: 07/28/95 Age: 27 Bats: R Throws: R Height: 6'7" Weight: 230 lb. Origin: Round 8, 2018 Draft (#230 overall)

YEAR	TEAM	LVL	AGE	W	L	SV	G	GS	IP	H	HR	BB/9	K/9	K	GB%	BABIP	WHIP	ERA	DRA-	WARP	MPH	FB%	Whiff%	CSP
2021	BNG	AA	25	2	1	0	5	5	26	21	1	2.4	14.5	42	58.2%	.370	1.08	3.12	73	0.6				
2021	SYR	AAA	25	0	0	0	3	3	14^1	11	2	3.1	10.7	17	48.6%	.257	1.12	3.77	101	0.2				
2021	NYM	MLB	25	4	6	0	18	18	89^2	88	19	2.7	9.9	99	42.8%	.301	1.28	4.52	81	1.7	94.7	57.6%	26.0%	56.3%
2022	NYM	MLB	26	4	2	0	15	9	47^1	46	7	2.5	9.7	51	40.0%	.310	1.25	5.13	93	0.6	95.9	57.0%	27.6%	56.3%
2023 DC	*NYM*	*MLB*	*27*	*5*	*4*	*0*	*35*	*9*	*70*	*67*	*8*	*3.0*	*10.2*	*79*	*43.2%*	*.327*	*1.30*	*3.71*	*93*	*0.8*	*95.2*	*57.3%*	*27.6%*	*56.3%*

Comparables: Ben Lively (58), Nick Pivetta (57), Tyler Cloyd (56)

After making the transition from the bullpen to the rotation in the minors and putting together a solid rookie campaign in 2021, Megill headed into the 2022 season very much a part of the Mets' starting rotation depth, but still on the outside looking in. That is, until Jacob deGrom went down with a shoulder injury right before the season started and Max Scherzer experienced some hamstring tightness at the end of spring training that delayed his New York debut. Suddenly, Megill was the Opening Day starter, and when he took the mound to fill in for the Mets' ailing aces he looked *very* different from the version of Megill the Mets saw the season before.

Namely, he'd changed his mechanics, added significant velocity to both his fastball and changeup and transformed his slider into a cliff-diving, whiff-inducing machine. The pitcher known to his teammates as "Big Drip" went 4-0 with a 1.93 ERA in April. But as his now-former rotation mate deGrom will tell you, throwing the baseball way harder often comes with a price. In four starts on either side of a monthlong IL stint, Megill was tattooed to the tune of an 11.48 ERA. He suffered a shoulder strain that sidelined him until September, at which point he returned as a reliever and pitched six pedestrian innings out of the bullpen. Megill flashed a new peak. Whether his body lets him stay there is the question.

Bryce Montes de Oca RHP Born: 04/23/96 Age: 27 Bats: R Throws: R Height: 6'7" Weight: 265 lb. Origin: Round 9, 2018 Draft (#260 overall)

YEAR	TEAM	LVL	AGE	W	L	SV	G	GS	IP	H	HR	BB/9	K/9	K	GB%	BABIP	WHIP	ERA	DRA-	WARP	MPH	FB%	Whiff%	CSP
2021	BRK	A+	25	1	3	6	26	0	32^{1}	22	1	7.5	11.7	42	42.1%	.280	1.52	4.73	107	0.1				
2022	BNG	AA	26	1	1	3	14	1	17^{1}	11	0	7.3	12.5	24	65.8%	.289	1.44	3.12	87	0.3				
2022	SYR	AAA	26	2	2	8	30	0	34	24	0	6.4	14.8	56	38.2%	.353	1.41	3.44	65	1.0	98.1	72.5%	40.0%	
2022	NYM	MLB	26	0	0	0	3	0	3^{1}	7	0	5.4	16.2	6	54.5%	.636	2.70	10.80	84	0.1	96.5	77.4%	24.4%	53.3%
2023 DC	*NYM*	*MLB*	*27*	*1*	*1*	*0*	*26*	*0*	*22.3*	*20*	*2*	*6.8*	*11.3*	*28*	*46.1%*	*.323*	*1.65*	*5.09*	*113*	*-0.1*	*96.5*	*77.4%*	*30.6%*	*53.3%*

Comparables: Juan Jaime (48), Jon Edwards (47), Tim Peterson (46)

At age 26, Montes de Oca has already dealt with more injuries than most players do in their entire careers. He was drafted by the Mets in 2018 but did not start pitching in the pros until 2021, undergoing surgeries to his arm, back, shoulder and knee in the interim. But he got his opportunity in 2022 when Trevor May went on the COVID-19 injured list. In the minor leagues, he struck out an eye-popping 72 batters in 47⅓ innings prior to being promoted, but he also walked 35 batters over that span. Montes de Oca made his major-league debut on September 3 and issued a walk and a hit, but was unscored upon. His other two outings were less successful, and his debut campaign was then sadly derailed by yet another injury. The silver lining: The hamstring injury seems unlikely to require an operation.

Stephen Nogosek RHP Born: 01/11/95 Age: 28 Bats: R Throws: R Height: 6'2" Weight: 205 lb. Origin: Round 6, 2016 Draft (#178 overall)

YEAR	TEAM	LVL	AGE	W	L	SV	G	GS	IP	H	HR	BB/9	K/9	K	GB%	BABIP	WHIP	ERA	DRA-	WARP	MPH	FB%	Whiff%	CSP
2021	SYR	AAA	26	1	5	6	27	0	35	35	2	4.1	13.4	52	28.1%	.379	1.46	5.14	81	0.8				
2021	NYM	MLB	26	0	1	0	1	0	3	3	2	0.0	15.0	5	28.6%	.200	1.00	6.00	76	0.1	93.9	62.5%	29.2%	57.0%
2022	SYR	AAA	27	2	0	4	31	0	43	31	2	3.1	11.1	53	38.5%	.284	1.07	2.30	76	1.1				
2022	NYM	MLB	27	1	1	0	12	0	22	20	4	2.9	8.6	21	34.8%	.258	1.23	2.45	104	0.2	95.1	41.6%	22.1%	57.6%
2023 DC	*NYM*	*MLB*	*28*	*1*	*1*	*0*	*26*	*0*	*22.3*	*21*	*2*	*3.6*	*8.3*	*20*	*36.2%*	*.296*	*1.35*	*4.03*	*101*	*0.1*	*95.0*	*45.3%*	*24.4%*	*57.0%*

Comparables: Rowan Wick (51), Evan Scribner (51), Noé Ramirez (50)

Never underestimate the ability of a mustachioed reliever to reinvent himself. The absence of a minor-league season in 2020 gave Nogosek an opportunity to overhaul his repertoire, which had gotten him through the minor leagues but had not yet translated to big-league success. Specifically, he tinkered with his changeup and added a cutter. He struck out a boatload of batters in the minor leagues in 2021, but injury limited his opportunity to showcase his new bag of tricks in the majors. In 2022, he pulled his new cutter out of the hat a whopping 30% of the time and it yielded results—both in Triple-A and in 22 innings in the big leagues. The Mets had to build almost an entire bullpen over the offseason, and Nogosek may have pitched himself into the picture. The magic of the mustache.

Adam Ottavino RHP Born: 11/22/85 Age: 37 Bats: S Throws: R Height: 6'5" Weight: 246 lb. Origin: Round 1, 2006 Draft (#30 overall)

YEAR	TEAM	LVL	AGE	W	L	SV	G	GS	IP	H	HR	BB/9	K/9	K	GB%	BABIP	WHIP	ERA	DRA-	WARP	MPH	FB%	Whiff%	CSP
2020	NYY	MLB	34	2	3	0	24	0	18^{1}	20	2	4.4	12.3	25	52.0%	.375	1.58	5.89	83	0.4	93.5	44.8%	26.5%	53.2%
2021	BOS	MLB	35	7	3	11	69	0	62	55	5	5.1	10.3	71	39.9%	.321	1.45	4.21	101	0.6	95.1	48.6%	27.9%	53.0%
2022	NYM	MLB	36	6	3	3	66	0	65^{2}	48	6	2.2	10.8	79	51.3%	.276	0.97	2.06	73	1.6	94.5	44.8%	29.8%	55.1%
2023 DC	*NYM*	*MLB*	*37*	*2*	*2*	*0*	*58*	*0*	*50.3*	*46*	*5*	*3.9*	*10.5*	*58*	*45.5%*	*.317*	*1.35*	*3.94*	*96*	*0.3*	*94.6*	*45.7%*	*27.8%*	*53.4%*

Comparables: David Weathers (76), Fernando Rodney (75), Octavio Dotel (74)

If Edwin Díaz was the headliner of the Mets bullpen, Ottavino was the overlooked opening act. He was new to these fans and not many of them were wearing his t-shirt, but he took to the stage night after night to warm up the crowd with his patented sweeping slider. Statistically, the veteran righty's 2022 season matched his very best seasons in Colorado. Most notably, he limited his walk percentage to a number in the single digits—something he had not accomplished since 2016. He was not only the most consistent reliever in the Mets bullpen besides Díaz, he was arguably the *only* consistent reliever in the Mets bullpen besides Díaz. By the end of the tour, Mets fans were singing Ottavino's song too. And he performed well enough in his age-36 season that the Mets picked up his record at the merch table. They'll give it a spin and see if it still bangs in 2023.

David Peterson LHP Born: 09/03/95 Age: 27 Bats: L Throws: L Height: 6'6" Weight: 240 lb. Origin: Round 1, 2017 Draft (#20 overall)

YEAR	TEAM	LVL	AGE	W	L	SV	G	GS	IP	H	HR	BB/9	K/9	K	GB%	BABIP	WHIP	ERA	DRA-	WARP	MPH	FB%	Whiff%	CSP
2020	NYM	MLB	24	6	2	0	10	9	49^{2}	36	5	4.3	7.2	40	44.2%	.233	1.21	3.44	113	0.2	92.3	53.2%	26.2%	44.5%
2021	NYM	MLB	25	2	6	0	15	15	66^{2}	64	11	3.9	9.3	69	47.3%	.310	1.40	5.54	100	0.6	92.8	58.6%	25.5%	52.7%
2022	SYR	AAA	26	2	3	0	6	6	26	33	1	3.5	11.8	34	50.7%	.432	1.65	4.85	74	0.7				
2022	NYM	MLB	26	7	5	0	28	19	105^{2}	93	11	4.1	10.7	126	49.1%	.315	1.33	3.83	97	1.2	93.6	49.9%	30.4%	48.9%
2023 DC	*NYM*	*MLB*	*27*	*6*	*5*	*0*	*37*	*11*	*79*	*74*	*8*	*3.9*	*9.9*	*87*	*48.6%*	*.315*	*1.38*	*4.00*	*98*	*0.7*	*93.2*	*52.7%*	*28.6%*	*49.3%*

Comparables: Roenis Elías (64), Dan Straily (64), Jeff Locke (64)

You're at the office holiday party and there's a cookie platter. From across the room, you spot that there's exactly one chocolate chip cookie left. You artfully extricate yourself from the awkward conversation you're having and make a beeline for the cookie…only to find that it's not chocolate chip at all. Despite overall season numbers that seem like an improvement—perhaps even enough of an improvement to make him a viable major-league fifth starter—Peterson remains something different than what the Mets want him to be. Prolonged stints on the injured list by Max Scherzer, Jacob deGrom and Tylor Megill meant that Peterson got his best shot yet at proving himself in the majors. After mixing up his pitch usage in 2021, he returned to his 2020 form, throwing his ineffective sinker a lot less. On the surface, it was a chocolate chip season for the tall lefty, but look closer and you'll find it was a classic oatmeal raisin impostor. Peterson's inability to put batters away consistently gave way to innings that spiraled out of control and pitch counts that snowballed. League-average production from a fifth starter is just fine, but not when he averages less than five innings per start. Down the stretch, the Mets experimented with using him as a reliever, and he may ultimately be relegated to the bullpen permanently if he can't find that putaway pitch. Or perhaps the Mets will simply learn to appreciate oatmeal raisin.

José Quintana LHP

Born: 01/24/89 Age: 34 Bats: R Throws: L Height: 6'1" Weight: 220 lb. Origin: International Free Agent, 2006

YEAR	TEAM	LVL	AGE	W	L	SV	G	GS	IP	H	HR	BB/9	K/9	K	GB%	BABIP	WHIP	ERA	DRA-	WARP	MPH	FB%	Whiff%	CSP
2020	CHC	MLB	31	0	0	0	4	1	10	10	1	2.7	10.8	12	42.3%	.360	1.30	4.50	101	0.1	91.3	60.1%	27.6%	41.5%
2021	SF	MLB	32	0	0	0	5	0	9^{2}	8	3	5.6	11.2	12	48.0%	.227	1.45	4.66	87	0.2	91.8	53.3%	30.0%	53.1%
2021	LAA	MLB	32	0	3	0	24	10	53^{1}	66	9	4.9	12.3	73	44.4%	.401	1.78	6.75	85	0.9	91.7	59.6%	29.2%	51.5%
2022	PIT	MLB	33	3	5	0	20	20	103	100	7	2.7	7.8	89	45.5%	.307	1.27	3.50	112	0.4	91.2	49.5%	25.4%	50.5%
2022	STL	MLB	33	3	2	0	12	12	62^{2}	54	1	2.3	6.9	48	48.6%	.296	1.12	2.01	116	0.1	91.6	57.6%	21.5%	49.9%
2023 DC	*NYM*	*MLB*	*34*	*7*	*8*	*0*	*24*	*24*	*121.3*	*130*	*15*	*3.1*	*8.8*	*118*	*45.6%*	*.331*	*1.42*	*4.38*	*108*	*0.3*	*91.5*	*55.4%*	*24.5%*	*49.8%*

Comparables: Claude Osteen (78), Jim Kaat (76), Andy Pettitte (74)

Quintana and the 2022 Cardinals sounded like a dreamy matchup the second the Pirates agreed to trade him there at last year's deadline, but even the most optimistic predictions would have fallen well short of how things actually went. Not one of the 12 starts Quintana made for St. Louis resulted in more than two earned runs, and his final six yielded just three runs total over 33.1 innings. Sure, there was some clearly unsustainable home run luck involved. But the other reasons Quintana succeeded bore a lot of resemblance to the way the best versions of him always have, and his 32 total starts were a welcome return to the ultra-dependable mid-rotation guy he was for nearly a decade. Throughout his career, Quintana has always been better than the average fan thinks he is. That remains true in his mid-30s, which means Mets fans probably aren't as happy about the news of his acquisition as they should be.

Brooks Raley LHP

Born: 06/29/88 Age: 35 Bats: L Throws: L Height: 6'3" Weight: 200 lb. Origin: Round 6, 2009 Draft (#200 overall)

YEAR	TEAM	LVL	AGE	W	L	SV	G	GS	IP	H	HR	BB/9	K/9	K	GB%	BABIP	WHIP	ERA	DRA-	WARP	MPH	FB%	Whiff%	CSP
2020	CIN	MLB	32	0	0	0	4	0	4	5	0	4.5	13.5	6	45.5%	.455	1.75	9.00	94	0.1	87.5	80.2%	24.3%	46.9%
2020	HOU	MLB	32	0	1	1	17	0	16	8	3	2.3	11.8	21	36.1%	.156	0.75	3.94	77	0.4	87.5	65.1%	33.8%	49.0%
2021	HOU	MLB	33	2	3	2	58	0	49	43	6	2.9	11.9	65	44.6%	.325	1.20	4.78	76	1.1	88.9	54.7%	32.5%	49.8%
2022	TB	MLB	34	1	2	6	60	0	53^{2}	37	3	2.5	10.2	61	38.0%	.256	0.97	2.68	86	0.9	90.9	23.2%	28.0%	49.5%
2023 DC	*NYM*	*MLB*	*35*	*2*	*2*	*0*	*58*	*0*	*50.3*	*45*	*6*	*3.2*	*9.2*	*51*	*40.9%*	*.293*	*1.26*	*3.70*	*94*	*0.4*	*89.8*	*40.1%*	*27.6%*	*49.5%*

Comparables: Andrew Miller (67), Scott Downs (56), Craig Stammen (54)

As is often the case, the Rays asked Raley to throw his best offering more often and it led to success. The lefty features a variety of pitches, but his low-80s slider has long been his best one. Tampa Bay made sure to call for it more often than his low-90s sinker, upper-80s cutter or changeup. That approach led to a more balanced split, with Raley's OPS against right-handers dropping over 220 points from 2021 to 2022. While he might not have been the best pitcher in Tampa Bay's bullpen, Raley certainly looks worthy of the $4.5 million he's guaranteed for 2023. The Mets agreed, nabbing him from the Rays in exchange for a low-level minor leaguer in December.

David Robertson RHP

Born: 04/09/85 Age: 38 Bats: R Throws: R Height: 5'11" Weight: 195 lb. Origin: Round 17, 2006 Draft (#524 overall)

YEAR	TEAM	LVL	AGE	W	L	SV	G	GS	IP	H	HR	BB/9	K/9	K	GB%	BABIP	WHIP	ERA	DRA-	WARP	MPH	FB%	Whiff%	CSP
2021	DUR	AAA	36	0	0	0	6	0	6	4	0	1.5	18.0	12	37.5%	.500	0.83	0.00	76	0.2				
2021	TB	MLB	36	0	0	0	12	1	12	11	2	3.0	12.0	16	40.0%	.321	1.25	4.50	89	0.2	92.2	74.0%	25.8%	60.6%
2022	CHC	MLB	37	3	0	14	36	0	40^{1}	23	4	4.2	11.4	51	47.8%	.216	1.04	2.23	77	0.9	93.5	55.7%	32.7%	55.1%
2022	PHI	MLB	37	1	3	6	22	0	23^{1}	16	2	6.2	11.6	30	43.4%	.275	1.37	2.70	83	0.4	92.5	43.5%	33.5%	51.0%
2023 DC	*NYM*	*MLB*	*38*	*2*	*2*	*0*	*58*	*0*	*50.3*	*42*	*6*	*4.5*	*11.4*	*63*	*43.4%*	*.303*	*1.34*	*3.79*	*93*	*0.4*	*93.1*	*54.2%*	*30.7%*	*54.2%*

Comparables: Michael Jackson (76), Lee Smith (73), Joe Smith (72)

Robertson was one of the best and most consistent relievers in baseball over the first decade of his career. Then Tommy John surgery shut him down for nearly three full seasons, and no one knew quite what to expect upon his return. All the question marks quickly turned to exclamation points, however, as Robertson went right back to doing exactly what he always did. He threw 60 innings for the 10th time in his career, posting an elite strikeout rate and a low home run rate as per usual. He lost velocity and control over the final month of the season—and into the playoffs—but he continued racking up enough strikeouts to push through the late-season fatigue. Signed to a one-year, $10 million contract, expect Robertson to begin 2023 as the final act ahead of the Timmy Trumpet Show.

Max Scherzer RHP Born: 07/27/84 Age: 38 Bats: R Throws: R Height: 6'3" Weight: 208 lb. Origin: Round 1, 2006 Draft (#11 overall)

YEAR	TEAM	LVL	AGE	W	L	SV	G	GS	IP	H	HR	BB/9	K/9	K	GB%	BABIP	WHIP	ERA	DRA-	WARP	MPH	FB%	Whiff%	CSP
2020	WAS	MLB	35	5	4	0	12	12	67^1	70	10	3.1	12.3	92	33.0%	.355	1.38	3.74	79	1.5	94.9	46.0%	32.6%	48.0%
2021	LAD	MLB	36	7	0	0	11	11	68^1	48	5	1.1	11.7	89	34.9%	.269	0.82	1.98	71	1.7	94.6	44.1%	32.3%	54.2%
2021	WAS	MLB	36	8	4	0	19	19	111	71	18	2.3	11.9	147	33.1%	.235	0.89	2.76	71	2.8	94.3	48.3%	35.6%	52.8%
2022	BNG	AA	37	0	0	0	2	2	8	7	1	2.3	15.7	14	50.0%	.353	1.13	4.50	77	0.2				
2022	NYM	MLB	37	11	5	0	23	23	145^1	108	13	1.5	10.7	173	31.1%	.279	0.91	2.29	71	3.6	94.2	45.4%	30.7%	52.9%
2023 DC	*NYM*	*MLB*	*38*	*11*	*8*	*0*	*27*	*27*	*167.7*	*140*	*22*	*2.0*	*10.8*	*201*	*33.4%*	*.292*	*1.06*	*2.78*	*75*	*3.6*	*94.4*	*46.3%*	*31.3%*	*51.9%*

Comparables: Bob Gibson (80), Don Sutton (78), Roger Clemens (77)

If the Francisco Lindor trade and subsequent extension was the first entry in the "Yes, Steve Cohen owns the Mets now" logbook, giving a future Hall of Famer the highest average annual value in major-league history was the second. And in almost every way, Scherzer lived up to the sky-high expectations set for him. By DRA-, he replicated his 2021 season, in which he finished third in the Cy Young balloting. He began the season as the ace of the staff when Jacob deGrom was felled by injury again shortly before Opening Day and was his usual dominant self over the first eight starts. He carried the Mets through the dog days of summer as they battled to stave off the Braves, posting a 2.10 ERA in July and August.

But, there are two elephants in the room—one for the brown eye ("the pitching one") and one for the blue eye ("the sexy one"). The first is an oblique strain that cost him seven weeks on the injured list. In fact, the 145⅓ innings he threw in 2022 were the fewest in his career aside from the pandemic-shortened 2020 season and his debut season in 2008. The second elephant—perhaps related to the first—is the way his season ended. Both in the crucial final series against the Braves that ultimately cost the Mets the NL East and in the Wild Card series against the Padres, Scherzer pitched poorly when the Mets needed him most. That said, Scherzer is guaranteed to return in 2023, and it's hard to imagine the Mets would be unhappy with another overall season like the one he had last year.

Kodai Senga RHP Born: 01/30/93 Age: 30 Bats: L Throws: R Height: 6'1" Weight: 202 lb.

YEAR	TEAM	LVL	AGE	W	L	SV	G	GS	IP	H	HR	BB/9	K/9	K	GB%	BABIP	WHIP	ERA	DRA-	WARP	MPH	FB%	Whiff%	CSP
2023 DC	*NYM*	*MLB*	*30*	*8*	*7*	*0*	*25*	*25*	*132*	*114*	*13*	*3.6*	*10.1*	*148*	*54.5%*	*.301*	*1.26*	*3.22*	*82*	*2.3*			*28.1%*	

Even behind the Mets' reunited pair of number ones, the middle spots in the rotation are crucial ones. Verlander and Scherzer are a combined 77 years old, meaning absences due to injury or preventative rest are less possibilities to hedge against than likelihoods to prepare for. Last year, the gigs went to Taijuan Walker and Chris Bassitt, the former of whom see-sawed between good half-seasons and crummier ones, the latter of whom has already started working through the signs for his first pitch of 2023.

Senga is not without his areas of concern; a high walk rate got him into trouble at times in Japan, and big-league hitters will be eager to test his slider. But what he brings will endear him to those fans tired of Walker's tailing off or Bassitt's indecision. Senga lives on a pair of pitches—a hard, upper-90s fastball and a splitter whose reputation precedes it—that figure to make him a steady presence in a rotation that needs it. Results may vary, but there'll be no mystery to the approach. Any mid-rotation starter worth his salt gives the fans a little extra to rally around, too; the "ghost forkball" should make for some fun costumes and signage.

Drew Smith RHP Born: 09/24/93 Age: 29 Bats: R Throws: R Height: 6'2" Weight: 190 lb. Origin: Round 3, 2015 Draft (#99 overall)

YEAR	TEAM	LVL	AGE	W	L	SV	G	GS	IP	H	HR	BB/9	K/9	K	GB%	BABIP	WHIP	ERA	DRA-	WARP	MPH	FB%	Whiff%	CSP
2020	NYM	MLB	26	0	1	0	8	0	7	6	2	2.6	9.0	7	35.0%	.222	1.14	6.43	103	0.1	95.4	46.8%	39.3%	42.1%
2021	NYM	MLB	27	3	1	0	31	1	41^1	28	7	3.5	8.9	41	34.0%	.212	1.06	2.40	102	0.3	95.1	56.2%	29.1%	55.3%
2022	NYM	MLB	28	3	3	0	44	0	46	38	9	2.9	10.4	53	34.5%	.264	1.15	3.33	86	0.8	96.0	52.6%	31.0%	50.2%
2023 DC	*NYM*	*MLB*	*29*	*2*	*2*	*4*	*58*	*0*	*50.3*	*45*	*7*	*3.4*	*9.6*	*54*	*35.8%*	*.294*	*1.28*	*3.75*	*95*	*0.3*	*95.6*	*53.7%*	*29.1%*	*51.7%*

Comparables: Nick Wittgren (57), Ryan Dull (55), Evan Scribner (55)

Every time Smith looks good enough on the mound that you think the Mets may have successfully developed a relief ace after all, he is felled by injury again. Smith carried a 0.00 ERA until May 13—a scoreless streak of 13⅓ innings, the longest such streak by a reliever to begin a season in Mets history. But Smith scuffled as the dog days of summer set in, posting a 7.56 ERA in seven July appearances. Still, when it all shook out, 2022 was Smith's best season in the big leagues. If he's not a bullpen ace, he is the only core member of the 2022 Mets bullpen that was still under team control when the season ended.

Mike Vasil RHP

Born: 03/19/00 Age: 23 Bats: L Throws: R Height: 6'5" Weight: 225 lb. Origin: Round 8, 2021 Draft (#232 overall)

YEAR	TEAM	LVL	AGE	W	L	SV	G	GS	IP	H	HR	BB/9	K/9	K	GB%	BABIP	WHIP	ERA	DRA-	WARP	MPH	FB%	Whiff%	CSP
2021	MET	ROK	21	0	0	0	3	3	7	3	0	0.0	12.9	10	57.1%	.214	0.43	1.29						
2022	SLU	A	22	3	1	0	9	8	37	26	1	2.7	9.5	39	45.4%	.260	1.00	2.19	93	0.7	94.4	46.5%	31.9%	
2022	BRK	A+	22	1	1	0	8	8	33^1	24	3	4.1	11.9	44	46.8%	.276	1.17	5.13	93	0.3				
2023 non-DC	*NYM*	*MLB*	*23*	*2*	*2*	*0*	*57*	*0*	*50*	*49*	*6*	*4.7*	*7.8*	*43*	*43.5%*	*.294*	*1.51*	*4.67*	*114*	*-0.2*			*25.6%*	

Comparables: Nick Nelson (85), Matt Loosen (84), Spencer Turnbull (84)

Often paired together with his fellow 2021 draftee Dominic Hamel in discussions about starting pitching talent in the Mets' system, Vasil also utilizes a high-spin fastball as a primary weapon that he complements with a curveball, slider and changeup. Like Hamel, Vasil made it to High-A in his first full professional season, though he was not fully healthy. So far, Vasil's success has carried over to the Arizona Fall League, and he has put up a 2.93 ERA in 15⅓ innings for Peoria. The Mets have talked up the dog the pair of righties have in them; now to see about the bark/bite ratio in those puppies.

Justin Verlander RHP

Born: 02/20/83 Age: 40 Bats: R Throws: R Height: 6'5" Weight: 235 lb. Origin: Round 1, 2004 Draft (#2 overall)

YEAR	TEAM	LVL	AGE	W	L	SV	G	GS	IP	H	HR	BB/9	K/9	K	GB%	BABIP	WHIP	ERA	DRA-	WARP	MPH	FB%	Whiff%	CSP
2020	HOU	MLB	37	1	0	0	1	1	6	3	2	1.5	10.5	7	61.5%	.091	0.67	3.00	77	0.1	95.1	54.8%	25.7%	49.5%
2022	HOU	MLB	39	18	4	0	28	28	175	116	12	1.5	9.5	185	37.9%	.240	0.83	1.75	69	4.5	95.1	50.4%	24.3%	55.1%
2023 DC	*NYM*	*MLB*	*40*	*11*	*8*	*0*	*27*	*27*	*167.7*	*143*	*22*	*1.9*	*8.8*	*164*	*37.0%*	*.274*	*1.06*	*2.70*	*75*	*3.5*	*95.0*	*50.4%*	*24.8%*	*53.5%*

Comparables: Roger Clemens (79), Don Sutton (79), Steve Carlton (78)

Rian Johnson's *Glass Onion* skewers the billionaire class for its thoughtless consumption—Edward Norton's character proudly displays a Rothko, hung upside down—but real life is not such a tidy parallel. As much as rival fans want to roast the profligate Steve Cohen for his "AARP rotation," there's nothing to suggest investing in a Verlander, armed with another shiny Cy Young trophy, a brand-new UCL and four years of study with a top-flight organization for pitching development, is a bad buy, especially not on a limited engagement. While the media landscape undoubtedly runs hotter in NYC than H-Town, that shouldn't be a problem for the sangfroid Verlander, who has never shied away from either the spotlight nor from making his opinions known. And unlike Norton's Miles Bron, Cohen has the good sense to only buy art that has a clear top and bottom side.

Lineouts

Hitters

HITTER	POS	TEAM	LVL	AGE	PA	R	2B	3B	HR	RBI	BB	K	SB	CS	AVG/OBP/SLG	DRC+	BABIP	BRR	DRP	WARP
Abraham Almonte	LF	WOR	AAA	33	147	30	4	1	7	24	36	29	5	2	.291/.469/.536	143	.338	1.2	RF(12): -0.9, LF(6): -1.1, CF(5): 0.0	0.9
	LF	NAS	AAA	33	213	36	11	0	11	42	25	48	1	0	.293/.380/.533	127	.339	-1.6	LF(28): -2.0, RF(9): 0.9	1.3
	LF	BOS	MLB	33	37	7	2	0	1	2	1	12	1	0	.257/.297/.400	72	.364	0.6	CF(5): -0.3, LF(3): 0, RF(1): 0	0.0
Terrance Gore	OF	SYR	AAA	31	66	15	0	0	0	4	6	19	9	2	.241/.313/.241	88	.359	2.0	CF(17): -1.0, LF(3): -0.2	0.2
	OF	NYM	MLB	31	8	1	0	0	0	0	0	3	3	0	.143/.143/.143	84	.250	0.8	LF(3): 0, CF(3): 0.2	0.1
Ender Inciarte	OF	SWB	AAA	31	116	12	2	1	4	11	13	17	4	2	.252/.336/.408	116	.268	-0.4	LF(14): -0.1, CF(11): 0.3, RF(6): -0.2	0.3
	OF	NYM	MLB	31	8	1	0	0	0	0	0	0	0	0	.125/.125/.125	94	.125	0.0	LF(6): 0.2, CF(2): -0.0, RF(2): 0.5	0.1
Deven Marrero	IF	SYR	AAA	31	166	23	1	2	3	19	20	34	5	1	.229/.323/.326	105	.280	1.0	SS(23): 0.7, 3B(14): -0.1, 2B(8): 0.4	0.8
	IF	NYM	MLB	31	6	0	0	0	0	0	0	3	1	0	.000/.000/.000	78		0.0	SS(3): 0, 3B(1): 0.1	0.0
Danny Mendick	IF	CLT	AAA	28	39	9	4	0	1	2	3	12	2	2	.303/.378/.515	85	.450	0.8	SS(5): -0.8, 3B(2): -0.4, 2B(1): -0.0	0.0
	IF	CHW	MLB	28	106	22	4	1	3	15	7	23	1	0	.289/.343/.443	102	.352	0.3	SS(22): -0.2, 2B(6): 0.5, 3B(2): -0.2	0.4
Kramer Robertson	IF	SYR	AAA	27	96	16	0	1	1	7	17	14	4	2	.240/.406/.307	125	.283	0.3	SS(12): 1.3, 3B(6): -0.7, 2B(3): 0.4	0.7
	IF	GWN	AAA	27	58	9	3	0	1	6	7	10	4	3	.300/.397/.420	115	.359	1.1	2B(8): -0.2, 3B(5): -1.2	0.4
	IF	MEM	AAA	27	360	56	13	0	9	34	60	79	22	3	.228/.389/.368	127	.284	4.1	SS(46): 1.1, 2B(18): -0.5, 3B(16): 2.5	2.5
	IF	STL	MLB	27	1	0	0	0	0	1	0	0	0	0	.000/.000/.000	95			SS(1): -0.2	0.0

You could've sworn **Abraham Almonte** retired three years ago, but there he was with the Red Sox—his sixth team in the last five seasons—who bought him off the Brewers in late July as emergency roster filler. That's all he offers at this stage of his career. ⚾ As the calendar turned to October, **Terrance Gore** declared that he liked his odds of catching Tom Brady's number of rings. Unfortunately, the 31-year-old pinch-running extraordinaire did not get his fourth ring with the Mets, but he did steal three bases in ten games and picked up his first hit since 2019 to boot. ⚾ The only memorable thing about **Ender Inciarte**'s eight at-bats for the 2022 Mets was the trauma response elicited by the memory of him in a Braves uniform robbing Yoenis Céspedes of a walk-off home run in September 2016. ⚾ Plucked from the Long Island Ducks on a minor-league deal in June, **Deven Marrero** existed in the liminal space between "the Mets have multiple infielders on the injured list" and "the Mets finally called up Brett Baty." ⚾ The darkest timeline of the 2022 White Sox season probably resembled something like **Danny Mendick** becoming a regular part of the starting nine, so invaluable that a season-ending ACL tear in June would leave them scrambling to find an adequate replacement. That is, of course, exactly what happened. ⚾ **Nick Morabito** was the Mets' second-round compensatory pick in the 2022 draft and has baseball in his blood, with a father and uncle who also played. The Virginia native's compact swing and speed on the basepaths generated some buzz, but his first rodeo as a professional did not go well; he collected just two hits in 22 at-bats and struck out 14 times in the Florida Complex League. ⚾ Real college baseball sickos remember **Kramer Robertson** as Alex Bregman's heir as the everyday shortstop at LSU who led the Tigers just two wins shy of a national title in 2017. He now makes a living as a "break glass in case of emergency" shortstop who won't chase Triple-A junk out of the zone.

Pitchers

PITCHER	TEAM	LVL	AGE	W	L	SV	G	GS	IP	H	HR	BB/9	K/9	K	GB%	BABIP	WHIP	ERA	DRA-	WARP	MPH	FB%	WHF	CSP
Jeff Brigham	JAX	AAA	30	3	3	1	30	1	43	35	8	4.4	14.4	69	23.1%	.325	1.30	3.98	81	1.0	94.1	49.6%	20.0%	
	MIA	MLB	30	0	1	1	16	0	24	22	3	3.8	10.5	28	20.6%	.322	1.33	3.38	95	0.3	94.7	42.5%	28.2%	54.8%
Alex Claudio	SYR	AAA	30	3	2	2	34	0	48^1	46	7	2.8	7.8	42	51.0%	.275	1.26	3.91	102	0.6	85.3	44.9%	13.6%	
	NYM	MLB	30	0	0	0	3	0	3^1	1	0	5.4	5.4	2	66.7%	.111	0.90	0.00	112	0.0	85.2	54.0%	25.0%	46.8%
Joel Díaz	SLU	A	18	3	2	0	16	10	55^1	62	7	4.1	8.3	51	42.0%	.340	1.57	5.86	119	0.4	94.2	56.2%	26.5%	
Zach Greene	SWB	AAA	25	9	0	0	48	4	68^1	51	11	4.2	12.6	96	43.1%	.270	1.21	3.42	73	1.9				
Sean Reid-Foley	NYM	MLB	26	0	0	0	7	0	10	7	1	6.3	7.2	8	42.9%	.222	1.40	5.40	114	0.0	96.2	46.6%	31.9%	53.7%
Denyi Reyes	NOR	AAA	25	0	7	1	15	10	54	74	13	1.3	9.0	54	30.8%	.365	1.52	7.17	113	0.4	92.6	35.0%	26.3%	
	BAL	MLB	25	0	0	0	3	1	7^2	8	0	1.2	3.5	3	40.7%	.296	1.17	2.35	120	0.0	92.9	43.6%	19.1%	59.0%
Tayler Saucedo	BUF	AAA	29	1	0	1	20	0	19	14	1	4.7	13.3	28	38.1%	.317	1.26	2.37	74	0.5				
	TOR	MLB	29	0	0	0	4	0	2^2	6	3	3.4	0.0	0	50.0%	.273	2.63	13.50	99	0.0	93.0	47.9%	17.4%	54.2%
Blade Tidwell	SLU	A	21	0	1	0	4	4	8^1	4	0	6.5	9.7	9	40.0%	.200	1.20	2.16	114	0.1	96.1	50.9%	29.2%	
William Woods	GWN	AAA	23	1	1	0	18	0	17^1	13	3	4.7	8.3	16	42.0%	.213	1.27	5.19	97	0.3	95.4	69.0%	20.0%	
	ATL	MLB	23	0	0	0	2	0	2	2	0	4.5	9.0	2	20.0%	.400	1.50	0.00	104	0.0	95.5	67.7%	25.0%	44.3%
Calvin Ziegler	SLU	A	19	0	6	0	16	16	46^2	26	3	6.8	13.5	70	31.9%	.261	1.31	4.44	83	1.1	93.4	65.9%	32.6%	

Jeff Brigham bravely answers the question, "What if you tried to never allow a groundball?" Equipped with a sweeper and a four-seam fastball he pours into the top of the zone, there isn't much opportunity to get on top of the ball—his 22.2% ground-ball rate is half the league average, higher only than that of Sergio Romo. ⚾ The Mets signed **Alex Claudio** to a minor-league deal in the offseason and he very nearly made the Opening Day bullpen just by virtue of being left-handed. As it turned out, Claudio waited until September to see a big-league mound and was unscored upon in three appearances before being designated for assignment. ⚾ The Mets signed **John Curtiss** in April to a big-league deal with a team option for 2023, knowing he would miss the entire 2022 season rehabbing from Tommy John surgery. In doing so, the Mets took a low-risk gamble on one of a seemingly annual parade of arms who broke out as a member of the Rays bullpen. ⚾ After dazzling in the Dominican Summer League in 2021 as a young teen, **Joel Díaz** had a bit of a sophomore slump in his stateside debut. His fastball touches 96, but was hit quite hard in St. Lucie, and it wasn't until he started using his changeup more later in the season that he showed improvement. Since he's just 18, the capacity to improve matters more than the outcomes, for now. ⚾ He isn't overpowering, but **Zach Greene** did an excellent job of fooling International League batters last year, as his K/9 was second best in the league (to Orioles prospect DL Hall, at 14.7). He'll be presumably in the mix to get a look in a middle-relief role in 2023. ⚾ **Sean Reid-Foley** made the Mets' Opening Day bullpen thanks to the expanded 28-man rosters and the promise he showed at the beginning of the 2021 season as a multi-inning option. After ten innings of decidedly mixed results in April, Reid-Foley underwent Tommy John surgery, which ended his season. ⚾ **Denyi Reyes** made his MLB debut for the O's in 2022, showcasing a repertoire wide on variety and light on pure stuff. He carries the somewhat-atypical reliever profile of a command artist who sits 92, with a deep arsenal that doesn't miss many bats. ⚾ A Haverford alumnus, **Stephen Ridings** was a substitute chemistry teacher during the canceled 2020 minor-league season, then was in the Bronx the next summer after a meteoric rise through the Yankees' system. He hit 101 mph on his first—and, to this point, his fastest—pitch in the majors, but a shoulder injury has held him back since his 2021 cameo. ⚾ **Tayler Saucedo** finished the year with more home runs allowed than innings pitched in the majors. He left his fourth appearance with hip discomfort, then was never seen or heard from again (outside of Buffalo, where he spent most of his time rehabbing). ⚾ Some folks, to lightly paraphrase the words of one of America's wisest philosophers Wesley Snipes in the 1998 cinematic classic *Blade*, are always trying to ice skate uphill. In **Blade Tidwell**'s case, the uphill battle is shoulder problems. In the Mets' case, the uphill battle is adding high-upside pitching depth to the minor-league system. They'll try to ice skate uphill together. ⚾ **William Woods** was able to take a fastball that sits in the mid- to high-90s to the major leagues for two relief appearances. While he didn't stick around for long, he did enough to earn lifelong fans from the students and alumni of William Woods University in Missouri. ⚾ Perhaps forever unfairly linked to the Kumar Rocker debacle, **Calvin Ziegler** was the Mets' second-round pick in 2021 and signed underslot to give the Mets the money to pull off the Rocker signing that ultimately never came to pass. The Canadian-born righty flashes fine stuff, but who doesn't these days?

PHILADELPHIA PHILLIES

Essay by Justin Klugh

Player comments by Leo Morgenstern and BP staff

PHILADELPHIA—After an improbable and electrifying October run, the Philadelphia Phillies defeated the Houston Astros in the 2022 World Series, bringing jubilation to their championship-starved city and economic devastation to the food-starved world.

"There's no feeling greater," manager Rob Thomson told reporters as he clutched the trophy in his arms.

Superstar Bryce Harper threw his hands in the air as he shared the moment with his family.

"You dream about this for so long," said the 30-year-old slugger and World Series MVP. "I knew we could do this. It's what we set out to do."

Champagne and tears of joy flowed freely on Broad Street. Elsewhere, world governments enacted doomsday protocols, their dread as intense as the Phanatic's crotch-thrusting during the season's final pitch.

"This is a team of tough, competitive players," said Phillies president of baseball operations Dave Dombrowski. "They played with heart, with skill, and most importantly, without caring that their every action brought the human race closer to its extinction."

Financial recessions have historically hit worldwide economies hard after Phillies championships, such as the ones in 1980 and 2008. Experts forecast that this precedent, in addition to the general sense of "wrongness" felt when a Philadelphia sports team succeeds, will likely have a crippling impact on the global stage. Scholars and analysts remain unable to/uninterested in explaining this phenomenon.

"We could be living in a utopia right now, where the Astros won and everything is good," lamented one downtrodden Houston fan. "Instead, my 36-year-old son and his family are moving into my basement because his company announced massive layoffs the second Seranthony Domínguez struck out Alex Bregman. Thanks a lot, Phillies."

The pending financial collapse is projected to be as swift and severe as the Phillies' turnaround was earlier in the season. After a 22-29 start, Thomson, who took over as manager from Joe Girardi on June 3, led the Phillies to a 65-46 record through the rest of the year.

PHILADELPHIA PHILLIES PROSPECTUS

2022 W-L: 87-75, 3RD IN NL EAST

Pythag	.540	10th	DER	.690	25th
RS/G	4.61	7th	DRC+	104	8th
RA/G	4.23	15th	DRA-	94	10th
dWin%	.557	7th	FIP	3.61	7th
Payroll	$229M	4th	B-Age	28.7	16th
M$/MW	$5.4M	23rd	P-Age	29.6	21st

401'

374'

369'

329'

330'

- Opened 2004
- Open air
- Natural surface
- Fence profile: 6' to 19'

Park Factors

Runs	Runs/RH	Runs/LH	HR/RH	HR/LH
102	103	101	107	104

Top Hitter WARP	4.6 J.T. Realmuto
Top Pitcher WARP	5.1 Aaron Nola
2023 Top Prospect	Andrew Painter

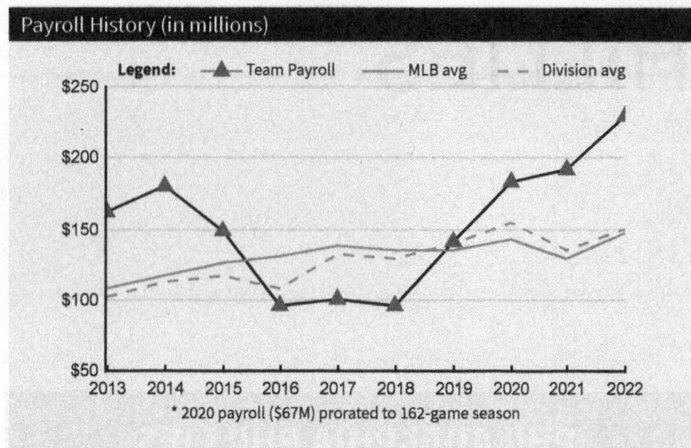

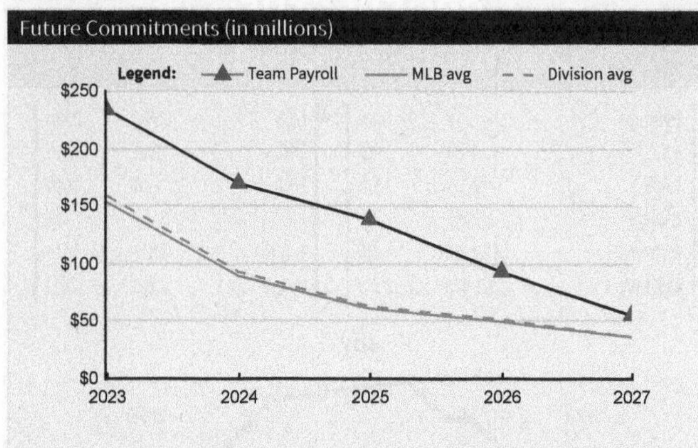

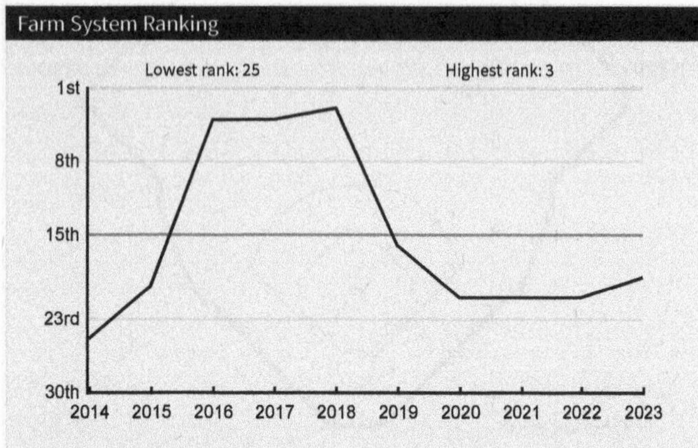

Personnel

President, Baseball Operations
Dave Dombrowski

Vice President, General Manager
Sam Fuld

Assistant General Manager
Ned Rice

Assistant General Manager
Jorge Velandia

Assistant General Manager
Anirudh Kilambi

Manager
Rob Thomson

BP Alumni
Alex Rosen

That marked the third time the Phillies changed managers since 2017: Pete Mackanin was retained after an interim stint due to his familiarity with the roster; Gabe Kapler was brought in as part of a multifaceted analytic push; Girardi was then hired to tap his finger on his chin while surveying the resulting mess of Kapler's tenure. Only midway through 2022, and sort of by accident, did the Phillies find the right man for the job. And it turned out, of course, that he'd been there the entire time.

The promotion of Thomson to manager, scoffed at by many who believed its effect would be limited at best, wound up the catalyst for the Phillies' resurgence. They immediately started hitting, pitching and fielding like a different team, even when key players such as Harper and Jean Segura were lost for weeks and months at a time due to injury. This newfound success was credited to Thomson's player-first approach—similar to that of Charlie Manuel, the last manager to win a World Series in Philadelphia—and led to Thomson being named the 2022 National League Manager of the Year.

"We didn't want to reward the Phillies for their actions, but anyone else receiving this honor would have simply been inexplicable," read the statement from the BBWAA. "We carefully measure a manager's impact in the win column, as well as various other contexts like the challenges they faced and what they were able to accomplish with what they had. It's not just, like, *oh these three teams were really good, so they have the best managers*. That'd be dumb. We wouldn't do that. We're the BBWAA."

Philadelphia's society-threatening win marked the culmination of an ambitious journey embarked upon last offseason. Dombrowski, the billionaire whisperer, convinced owner John Middleton to add both free agents Kyle Schwarber and Nick Castellanos. The moves surprised their fans, gave the team exciting vibes and sent Phillies ownership hurdling over the luxury tax threshold they had shied away from for years. The financial fragility of MLB's reigning bodies had been a topic of great discussion earlier in the year when a labor stoppage enacted by Manfred's office and team owners had delayed the start of the 2022 season.

"That was all because the Phillies seemed like they were getting really good," MLB Commissioner Rob Manfred told reporters. "We had to lie and say it was because baseball can't function without minor leaguers sleeping in their cars. People bought that *very* easily. But no, that whole labor stoppage mess was about seeing the Phillies add Schwarber and Castellanos to their lineup and thinking that they might have a legitimate shot at the title. And we couldn't just stand there and watch that happen. Not with so much at stake. Guess it was all for nothing now."

From June on, the Phillies saw a remarkable pivot from the mediocrity of years past in which a stalled farm system and uninspired play weighed down aggressive spending and trades. With the talent in place, the managerial transition to Thomson seemed to unlock the true potential of stars like Harper, J.T. Realmuto and Schwarber, with additional contributions coming from Rhys Hoskins, Segura and Castellanos. Younger players like Alec Bohm and Bryson Stott found their big-league footing at just the right time, and put together some of the most impressive and crucial at-bats of the Phillies' season, allowing them to complete their two-fold mission to bring a World Series title to Philadelphia and turn America into a third-world country overnight. On the pitching side, Zack Wheeler, Aaron Nola and Ranger Suárez became one of the top trios in baseball. And the relievers put together enough stretches of dominance to help rewrite the narrative of bullpen futility in Philadelphia while simultaneously writing a gospel of doom for the final days of humanity.

From Bohm saying he hated Philadelphia, to Realmuto dodging international vaccine standards, to leaving Clearwater with Odúbel Herrera and Jeurys Familia on the roster, the Phillies had their share of lingering issues. But with the right combination of winning and pandering and not talking about vaccines anymore, the second-half Phillies—with the deadline additions of Brandon Marsh, David Robertson, Edmundo Sosa and Noah Syndergaard—seemed like a completely new team. Their winning ways inoculated them against public outcry.

Upon their victory, nationwide influencers in and outside the government scrambled to respond to the Phillies' catastrophic feel-good story of the summer. President Joe Biden was placed on Air Force One as a security measure to determine how quickly he should bail out banks and airlines. Reviled U.S. politician Ted Cruz was brained by a hurled beer can, despite not being involved with the World Series nor being anywhere near the city of Philadelphia at the time.

And after announcing that he would save the economy and then tweeting "my pronouns are jet/pack," Twitter CEO Elon Musk crashed immediately into a Burger King billboard, leaving his legs comically flailing over a highway. Further pileups and delays were caused by what police called "pointing and laughing, even from drivers who had already crashed their cars and were very much in need of life-saving medical attention."

Assurances from experts that the reality we enjoy is hanging by a delicate thread led to a somber mood in Houston. In front of a crowd of Astros fans watching their life savings melt away, a visibly shaken Manfred handed the trophy over to the Phillies.

"It is my, uh, great honor," Manfred stumbled, interrupted by the scrambling of fighter jets overhead, "to hand you this trophy for your, uh. Your..." Manfred again seemed to stare into space as he considered the haunting future now possible due to the Phillies' win. "... greatness."

Later, Manfred was found by reporters, head in his hands, a lit cigarette between two of his fingers. "I was up there, and, like... Rob [Thomson] was *smiling*," Manfred blurted out with little prompting. "He was smiling. And I was like, what the hell's wrong with this guy? Is he deranged? I leaned away from the mic and said in his ear, *'Do you have any idea what you've done?'* But I don't think he heard me because he just smiled and chuckled and went back to waving at the crowd."'

Manfred and the structure of the MLB postseason had also come under scrutiny this year as the Phillies won series after series while teams that had dominated the regular season, like the Dodgers, Braves, Yankees and Mets, were eliminated. Analysts discovered a massive uptick in whining across these fanbases, which had historically already been amongst baseball's whiniest.

"It's just not fair," one fan said. "Clearly, a system in which the New York Mets cannot succeed is a broken system. This is why I have advocated for baseball to be banned for several decades."

"I couldn't agree more," said a Yankees fan in a half-burned Aaron Judge jersey. "What kind of World Series doesn't have the Yankees in it? As we say in New York anytime we walk on a public street, 'that's garbage!'"

From his billboard, now caked in several days' worth of bird crap, Musk promised to change this, despite having no influence over MLB and its teams.

Manfred said his concern about the Series' outcome had manifested in early November, as the Phillies clinched a World Series berth over the San Diego Padres. It only intensified from there.

"I think it was around Game 3 when they hit all those homers that I leaned over to Joe Torre and said, 'Something is seriously wrong here.'"

"I figured he'd talk me down, you know, tell me I was crazy. But he turns and looks at me—I shit you not—he looks at me like he's just seen behind the curtain of reality and goes, *'Every system enslaves us. Only through our destruction are we set free.'* The hair on my neck stood up. Then he was gone. And then I had to stand up and pretend to cheer for a Brandon Marsh double or something."

The Astros, too, were in a hurry to leave the park and return to their families, suddenly more candid in their answers on any topic, given the encroaching shadow of oblivion.

"I know some brave writers begged Phillies fans not to boo us, but they did," Bregman said, eyes glued to a breaking news report. "That's what ended the World Series for us. We came into this undefeated in the postseason, but that collective *'oooooo'* sound we've heard a thousand times really messed with us, a group of professional athletes who have played in several World Series. Thank you to the writers who tried to reason with Phillies fans, but they're just too brilliant and sinister."

"We cheated every time we played in the World Series, including this one," confessed Astros catcher Martín Maldonado, frantically jamming his belongings in a bag. "Dusty Baker made us take flowers over to the Phillies locker room that we'd bugged with a mic and camera. We said, 'Dusty, how could you of all people do this? Everyone loves you!' He said, 'That's why it's a perfect plan. No one knows that I'm secretly evil. Now stop crying and cheat at baseball with me.' Then he put on the Orbit costume and made a throat-slitting gesture at me."

In the offseason ahead, the Phillies will begin their NL pennant defense. Playing in one of the most competitive divisions in baseball will force them to keep spending on free agents like Trea Turner, who appears to be tightly linked to the Phillies and could replace the offense and speed they'll miss as Harper undergoes Tommy John surgery and sits out the beginning of 2023.

But, as a weeping Manfred told reporters as he boarded his emergency escape jet-copter, "Bryce Harper's elbow health is about to become the least of your problems." Then he and all the MLB owners went to a secret island where rich, useless people go during crises.

Markets crashed around the globe and the New York Stock Exchange exploded exactly at sunrise the following day. But one Philadelphian, whom reporters assumed was part of a line of emigrants fleeing the city, but who was actually just sitting in normal traffic at the Conshohocken Curve, told reporters, "Absolutely, it was worth it. Why? What's happening?" ■

—Justin Klugh is an author of Baseball Prospectus.

HITTERS

Alec Bohm 3B Born: 08/03/96 Age: 26 Bats: R Throws: R Height: 6'5" Weight: 218 lb. Origin: Round 1, 2018 Draft (#3 overall)

YEAR	TEAM	LVL	AGE	PA	R	2B	3B	HR	RBI	BB	K	SB	CS	Whiff%	AVG/OBP/SLG	DRC+	BABIP	BRR	DRP	WARP
2020	PHI	MLB	23	180	24	11	0	4	23	16	36	1	1	25.2%	.338/.400/.481	111	.410	-0.3	3B(38): 0.9, 1B(7): 0	0.7
2021	LHV	AAA	24	68	8	5	0	1	6	7	15	3	1		.271/.353/.407	99	.341	0.2	3B(12): 0.1, 1B(3): -0.5	0.2
2021	PHI	MLB	24	417	46	15	0	7	47	31	111	4	0	26.5%	.247/.305/.342	81	.327	-0.3	3B(103): -0.1, 1B(7): -0.1	0.4
2022	PHI	MLB	25	631	79	24	3	13	72	31	110	2	3	21.1%	.280/.315/.398	103	.319	2.1	3B(135): -4.1, 1B(10): 0	1.6
2023 DC	*PHI*	*MLB*	*26*	*563*	*64*	*22*	*2*	*17*	*65*	*34*	*103*	*7*	*2*	*21.7%*	*.281/.332/.434*	*112*	*.324*	*2.7*	*3B 0, 1B 0*	*2.2*

Comparables: Alex Bregman (56), Pablo Sandoval (55), Ron Santo (54)

The defining moment of Bohm's season came early on, when he made three errors in a single game and attracted mockery from the Philadelphia crowd. The taunting got the best of him, and he was caught on camera muttering five now-infamous words: "I [expletive] hate this place." As the season continued, however, the young third baseman improved at his craft. His range will always be limited, but he cut down on mental errors and made the plays he could get to. Per FRAA, he was still below average, but he was far less of a liability than he had been in 2021. Most importantly, his performance was good enough to stave off calls to move him to first base, where his bat leaves much to be desired—and where there was no room at the inn. Bohm hits for a high average but minimal power, and his walk rate is paltry. He showed encouraging signs of development this season, making more contact, striking out less often and hitting more balls in the air. Even so, his plate discipline is lacking, and he's wasting his power potential by sending too many hard-hit balls into the ground. On the whole, Bohm was a league-average hitter in 2022, and his career trajectory still hinges on his ability to handle third base.

Nick Castellanos RF Born: 03/04/92 Age: 31 Bats: R Throws: R Height: 6'4" Weight: 203 lb. Origin: Round 1, 2010 Draft (#44 overall)

YEAR	TEAM	LVL	AGE	PA	R	2B	3B	HR	RBI	BB	K	SB	CS	Whiff%	AVG/OBP/SLG	DRC+	BABIP	BRR	DRP	WARP
2020	CIN	MLB	28	242	37	11	2	14	34	19	69	0	2	34.2%	.225/.298/.486	103	.257	-1.1	RF(57): -0.9	0.6
2021	CIN	MLB	29	585	95	38	1	34	100	41	121	3	1	30.7%	.309/.362/.576	130	.340	0.5	RF(135): 3.9	4.3
2022	PHI	MLB	30	558	56	27	0	13	62	29	130	7	1	32.1%	.263/.305/.389	93	.326	1.1	RF(121): -3.3, LF(3): -0.2	0.9
2023 DC	*PHI*	*MLB*	*31*	*586*	*68*	*30*	*1*	*21*	*74*	*36*	*140*	*4*	*2*	*31.6%*	*.267/.321/.449*	*110*	*.326*	*0.3*	*RF -2*	*1.7*

Comparables: Ryan Zimmerman (68), Carney Lansford (68), Roberto Clemente (68)

Here's a paradox for you: Castellanos famously thrives in times of tragedy and misfortune. What happens, then, when the biggest tragedy is on the back of his own baseball card? In the first season of a five-year deal, Castellanos put up his worst offensive numbers since 2015. He was still putting the ball in play and getting hits at a decent clip, but his power completely disappeared. His max exit velocity fell, his average exit velocity sank and his hard-hit rate plummeted. He wasn't hitting the ball very hard and, as such, he wasn't mashing nearly as many home runs and extra-base hits. It didn't help that he saw more sliders than ever, which have always been his greatest weakness. It's too soon to say all is lost for the All-Star outfielder in his age-31 season, but his year-over-year decline was sharp and troubling. If only he could go back in time and ask his 2021 self for advice... although that might cause a whole other set of paradoxical problems.

Jake Cave OF

Born: 12/04/92 Age: 30 Bats: L Throws: L Height: 6'0" Weight: 200 lb. Origin: Round 6, 2011 Draft (#209 overall)

YEAR	TEAM	LVL	AGE	PA	R	2B	3B	HR	RBI	BB	K	SB	CS	Whiff%	AVG/OBP/SLG	DRC+	BABIP	BRR	DRP	WARP
2020	MIN	MLB	27	123	17	3	2	4	15	5	44	0	2	39.7%	.221/.285/.389	64	.323	1.0	CF(22): -0.6, RF(12): -0.2, LF(7): 0.9	-0.1
2021	STP	AAA	28	36	6	1	0	1	5	5	10	0	1		.367/.472/.500	98	.526	-0.4	CF(5): 0.3	0.1
2021	MIN	MLB	28	178	14	6	1	3	13	10	62	1	1	32.5%	.189/.249/.293	56	.283	0.7	LF(37): 1.6, CF(29): -0.4, RF(11): -0.9	-0.2
2022	STP	AAA	29	373	63	20	7	14	57	43	93	10	0		.273/.370/.509	107	.343	0.7	CF(45): -3.1, LF(20): 0.2, RF(16): -1.1	0.9
2022	MIN	MLB	29	177	17	7	3	5	20	11	49	2	0	35.2%	.213/.260/.384	77	.268	-1.3	LF(45): 1.1, RF(10): 1, CF(4): -0.3	0.1
2023 DC	*PHI*	*MLB*	*30*	*159*	*17*	*6*	*2*	*4*	*16*	*11*	*47*	*2*	*0*	*32.2%*	*.234/.303/.399*	*89*	*.319*	*2.5*	*RF 1, CF 0*	*0.5*

Comparables: Alex Presley (51), Roger Bernadina (48), Corey Patterson (47)

Afforded another opportunity to avoid the Quad-A tag with near-everyday playing time over the final six weeks, Cave put the label in bold. His Triple-A OPS now stands at .855 over more than 1500 plate appearances, a level Cave hasn't come remotely close to reaching over parts of five big-league seasons. The Twins removed him from the 40-man for the second straight offseason, but this time the Orioles pounced and he didn't make it through waivers. When they tried to get him through waivers, the Phillies grabbed him. Cave has one thing still going for him, from a flexibility standpoint: he has one option left, one more chance to at least change that tag from Quad-A to fourth outfielder.

Kody Clemens 2B

Born: 05/15/96 Age: 27 Bats: L Throws: R Height: 6'1" Weight: 200 lb. Origin: Round 3, 2018 Draft (#79 overall)

YEAR	TEAM	LVL	AGE	PA	R	2B	3B	HR	RBI	BB	K	SB	CS	Whiff%	AVG/OBP/SLG	DRC+	BABIP	BRR	DRP	WARP
2021	TOL	AAA	25	413	66	15	6	18	59	36	94	4	1		.247/.312/.466	105	.278	0.1	2B(72): 5.9, RF(24): 0.2, 1B(7): 0.1	2.1
2022	TOL	AAA	26	264	41	12	6	13	43	20	71	5	2		.274/.327/.535	105	.333	1.5	2B(25): 0.0, 3B(13): 0.8, LF(13): 0.8	1.1
2022	DET	MLB	26	127	13	4	0	5	17	8	33	1	0	27.1%	.145/.197/.308	82	.148	1.7	3B(17): 0.4, 1B(13): 0, 2B(9): -0.6	0.2
2023 DC	*PHI*	*MLB*	*27*	*279*	*24*	*10*	*4*	*7*	*24*	*17*	*75*	*3*	*1*	*29.2%*	*.218/.271/.383*	*76*	*.277*	*3.9*	*2B 0, LF 0*	*0.3*

Comparables: Breyvic Valera (53), Scott Cousins (53), Carlos Asuaje (52)

The Tigers led MLB (non-Ohtani category) in position player pitching appearances with 12, largely thanks to Clemens' seven trips to the mound. That he was more effective at preventing hitters from reaching base than he was at getting there himself isn't quite the burn it sounds like; he retired 20 of the 33 batters he faced, including Ohtani himself (strikeout looking). Still, his line was more reminiscent of his dad at the plate than on the mound—and Roger had the higher OBP, which is absolutely the burn it sounds like. Clemens has some power, is likely to hit more given a larger opportunity and is a solid, versatile defender. The versatility to stand on the mound occasionally, too, isn't likely to earn him any more meaningful playing time, especially now that he's landed in Philadelphia.

Justin Crawford CF

Born: 01/13/04 Age: 19 Bats: L Throws: R Height: 6'3" Weight: 175 lb. Origin: Round 1, 2022 Draft (#17 overall)

YEAR	TEAM	LVL	AGE	PA	R	2B	3B	HR	RBI	BB	K	SB	CS	Whiff%	AVG/OBP/SLG	DRC+	BABIP	BRR	DRP	WARP
2022	PHI	ROK	18	43	6	0	1	0	5	5	6	8	3		.297/.395/.351		.355			
2023 non-DC	*PHI*	*MLB*	*19*	*251*	*17*	*9*	*2*	*2*	*18*	*15*	*96*	*9*	*3*	*38.7%*	*.182/.239/.268*	*36*	*.299*	*1.0*	*CF 0*	*-1.2*

Nearly a decade after selecting J.P. Crawford with the 16th overall pick, the Phillies took a chance on his cousin, Justin, in the first round of the 2022 Draft. Philadelphia hasn't had much success taking high school outfielders in the first round recently (or ever), but clearly the front office thinks things will be different this time around. One reason for their optimism? The young Crawford has a lot in common with his father Carl. (The Crawfords are a talented bunch.) Like his old man, Justin is a speedy outfielder with an impressive glove and solid contact skills. What's more, he's hoping to add power to his game by bulking up ahead of the 2023 MiLB season. With some pop in his bat, he'd have a new tool in his belt that his father never mastered. After inking his deal, Crawford hit well in a handful of games of rookie ball, but he looked overmatched in a small sample at Low-A to end the season.

Darick Hall 1B

Born: 07/25/95 Age: 27 Bats: L Throws: R Height: 6'4" Weight: 232 lb. Origin: Round 14, 2016 Draft (#407 overall)

YEAR	TEAM	LVL	AGE	PA	R	2B	3B	HR	RBI	BB	K	SB	CS	Whiff%	AVG/OBP/SLG	DRC+	BABIP	BRR	DRP	WARP
2020	MOC	WIN	24	91	7	2	0	4	20	11	24	2	1		.227/.352/.413		.271			
2021	LHV	AAA	25	471	46	27	0	14	60	55	100	0	2		.230/.338/.403	108	.270	-3.3	1B(114): 4.6	1.5
2022	LHV	AAA	26	443	59	24	0	28	88	42	100	6	1		.254/.330/.528	129	.268	-2.5	1B(99): -1.6, RF(1): -0.1	2.3
2022	PHI	MLB	26	142	19	8	1	9	16	5	44	0	0	33.8%	.250/.282/.522	90	.301	0.0	1B(7): -0.3	0.1
2023 DC	*PHI*	*MLB*	*27*	*136*	*16*	*6*	*0*	*6*	*18*	*9*	*36*	*0*	*1*	*31.9%*	*.228/.293/.442*	*98*	*.271*	*0.1*	*1B 0*	*0.2*

Comparables: Jesús Aguilar (66), Ji-Man Choi (66), Ben Paulsen (64)

Imagine you're on a game show, and you're presented with several doors. Behind one is a home run, while behind all the others are strikeouts. You must pick a door and hope for the best. That's it. Oh, and you can only open the home run door if the game show host is right-handed. That, you see, is the Darick Hall problem in a nutshell. Hall slugged his way to the big leagues in 2022, hitting 20 bombs in his first 72 Triple-A games. After his call-up, he continued mashing in the majors while filling in for the injured Bryce Harper at DH. When he wasn't hitting home runs, however, Hall struggled to get on base or get ahead of opposing pitchers—and that was with the platoon advantage in nearly every at-bat. What Hall does, he does well, but is it enough to warrant a precious 26-man roster spot? That's the million-dollar question.

Bryce Harper DH

Born: 10/16/92 Age: 30 Bats: L Throws: R Height: 6'3" Weight: 210 lb. Origin: Round 1, 2010 Draft (#1 overall)

YEAR	TEAM	LVL	AGE	PA	R	2B	3B	HR	RBI	BB	K	SB	CS	Whiff%	AVG/OBP/SLG	DRC+	BABIP	BRR	DRP	WARP
2020	PHI	MLB	27	244	41	9	2	13	33	49	43	8	2	28.7%	.268/.420/.542	134	.279	0.2	RF(48): -0.4, CF(3): -0.1	1.7
2021	PHI	MLB	28	599	101	42	1	35	84	100	134	13	3	32.1%	.309/.429/.615	146	.359	-2.0	RF(139): 5.7	5.6
2022	PHI	MLB	29	426	63	28	1	18	65	46	87	11	4	28.6%	.286/.364/.514	127	.324	1.3	RF(8): 0	2.6
2023 DC	*PHI*	*MLB*	*30*	*354*	*51*	*18*	*1*	*18*	*51*	*45*	*72*	*11*	*2*	*28.6%*	*.278/.377/.523*	*148*	*.312*	*3.6*	*RF -1*	*3.0*

Comparables: Johnny Callison (71), Mel Ott (71), Jack Clark (64)

We've already been calling Harper the "$330 million man" since he signed his mega-deal in 2019, but his resemblance to *The Six Million Dollar Man* continues to grow. A year after toughing it out through lingering back issues and a fastball to the face, Harper played through a torn UCL and returned from a broken thumb to lead the Phillies on a miraculous postseason run. The October home runs alone were almost worth the bill, specifically the count-working oppo shot he cracked in Game 5 of the National League Championship Series to get the Phils to the World Series for the first time since 2009, and himself there for the first time in his anointed career. Only flags fly forever, but the image of the swing of Harper's life will linger almost as long. Despite injury after injury, Harper finds a way to come back better and stronger each time. He'll have to continue the pattern in 2023, as he begins the year on the shelf following Tommy John surgery. When he returns mid-season, Bryce Harper will be that man. Count on him to give the club and its fans what they've paid for.

Rhys Hoskins 1B

Born: 03/17/93 Age: 30 Bats: R Throws: R Height: 6'4" Weight: 245 lb. Origin: Round 5, 2014 Draft (#142 overall)

YEAR	TEAM	LVL	AGE	PA	R	2B	3B	HR	RBI	BB	K	SB	CS	Whiff%	AVG/OBP/SLG	DRC+	BABIP	BRR	DRP	WARP
2020	PHI	MLB	27	185	35	9	0	10	26	29	43	1	0	26.6%	.245/.384/.503	122	.276	1.0	1B(40): -1.6	0.8
2021	PHI	MLB	28	443	64	29	0	27	71	47	108	3	2	26.3%	.247/.334/.530	117	.270	-2.3	1B(103): -1.6	1.5
2022	PHI	MLB	29	672	81	33	2	30	79	72	169	2	1	25.8%	.246/.332/.462	115	.292	-3.5	1B(151): -0.1	2.2
2023 DC	*PHI*	*MLB*	*30*	*606*	*84*	*28*	*1*	*30*	*78*	*69*	*148*	*3*	*0*	*25.4%*	*.240/.337/.472*	*121*	*.277*	*0.2*	*1B 0*	*2.5*

Comparables: Mark McGwire (75), Andre Thornton (69), Glenn Davis (67)

The 2017 Taylor Swift album *reputation* seems, at first pass, like a work of vengeance aimed at her various music industry rivals. Upon closer inspection, however, the vast majority of the tracks turn out to be sweet and radiant love songs. The message behind this is clear: one's surface-level reputation is not always an accurate reflection of who that person really is. It's a message that surely rings true for Hoskins, whose reputation has preceded him throughout his big-league career. Not only does he bear the cross of his prodigious rookie season, but he also endures a reputation throughout the Phillies fanbase as both a painfully streaky hitter and a dangerously poor defender. The truth, however, is that Hoskins is actually quite consistent at the plate. He may go through slumps each season, but he's finished all six years of his career with excellent power stats, above-average on-base numbers, and a DRC+ of at least 113. As far as defense goes, he's no Gold Glover out there, but he finished the 2022 season with the best FRAA of his career. Much like *reputation* itself, Hoskins is misunderstood. He's not going to win any major awards, but those that appreciate the kind of player he is know exactly what makes the big fella so special.

Hao Yu Lee IF

Born: 02/03/03 Age: 20 Bats: R Throws: R Height: 5'10" Weight: 190 lb. Origin: International Free Agent, 2021

YEAR	TEAM	LVL	AGE	PA	R	2B	3B	HR	RBI	BB	K	SB	CS	Whiff%	AVG/OBP/SLG	DRC+	BABIP	BRR	DRP	WARP
2021	PHI	ROK	18	25	9	2	2	1	5	3	5	0	0		.364/.440/.773		.438			
2022	CLR	A	19	302	37	11	1	7	50	36	57	10	7	26.0%	.283/.384/.415	133	.338	1.3	SS(23): 0.7, 3B(20): 1.2, 2B(15): 0.8	2.4
2022	JS	A+	19	40	5	3	1	1	2	5	9	3	0		.257/.350/.486	104	.320	-0.2	2B(6): -1.1, SS(3): 0.2	0.0
2023 non-DC	*PHI*	*MLB*	*20*	*251*	*21*	*9*	*1*	*3*	*22*	*18*	*63*	*5*	*3*	*28.7%*	*.223/.287/.329*	*71*	*.292*	*-0.7*	*2B 0, 3B 0*	*-0.3*

Comparables: Juremi Profar (80), Cole Tucker (77), Xavier Edwards (74)

Lee was the breakout hitting prospect of the Phillies' system in 2022. In fact, he proved himself to be one of the best hitters in the low minors. At just 19 years old, he flaunted mature plate discipline skills and flashes of tremendous power. He still must learn how to fully harness his own strength—he only recently bulked up—but the offensive potential is huge. Lee is a versatile infield defender, but his glove doesn't stand out at any position. His big bat will be his carrying tool.

Rafael Marchan C

Born: 02/25/99 Age: 24 Bats: S Throws: R Height: 5'9" Weight: 170 lb. Origin: International Free Agent, 2015

YEAR	TEAM	LVL	AGE	PA	R	2B	3B	HR	RBI	BB	K	SB	CS	Whiff%	AVG/OBP/SLG	DRC+	BABIP	BRR	DRP	WARP
2020	PHI	MLB	21	9	3	0	0	1	3	1	2	0	0	33.3%	.500/.556/.875	107	.600	-0.2	C(3): -0.1	0.0
2021	LHV	AAA	22	265	28	7	0	0	19	23	45	1	0		.203/.283/.232	86	.249	3.4	C(58): -4.6	0.5
2021	PHI	MLB	22	56	7	1	1	1	4	4	10	0	0	15.9%	.231/.286/.346	97	.268	0.0	C(17): -1.8	0.0
2022	LHV	AAA	23	263	26	17	0	4	29	20	24	1	0	10.0%	.233/.316/.358	116	.243	0.1	C(56): 6.0	1.8
2023 DC	*PHI*	*MLB*	*24*	*31*	*2*	*1*	*0*	*0*	*2*	*2*	*4*	*0*	*0*	*17.9%*	*.228/.292/.315*	*72*	*.259*	*0.0*	*C 0*	*0.0*

Comparables: Alexi Casilla (55), Rob Brantly (54), Dioner Navarro (49)

Marchan took several steps in the right direction this past season, cutting down on his strikeouts and finally hitting a few minor-league home runs. Unfortunately, until he can get his natural contact skills to translate into hits on a more consistent basis, he won't be much more than a second-string catcher. Marchan spent the past two seasons as the constant subject of unrealized trade rumors, so perhaps a change of scenery might be what he needs to help him finally figure things out.

YEAR	TEAM	P. COUNT	FRM RUNS	BLK RUNS	THRW RUNS	TOT RUNS
2020	PHI	432	-0.1	0.0	-0.2	-0.3
2021	LHV	8561	-3.6	0.0	-0.2	-3.8
2021	PHI	2072	-1.7	0.0	0.4	-1.3
2022	LHV	8242	5.5	0.6	0.4	6.6
2023	*PHI*	*1202*	*-0.4*	*0.0*	*0.1*	*-0.3*

Brandon Marsh OF Born: 12/18/97 Age: 25 Bats: L Throws: R Height: 6'4" Weight: 215 lb. Origin: Round 2, 2016 Draft (#60 overall)

YEAR	TEAM	LVL	AGE	PA	R	2B	3B	HR	RBI	BB	K	SB	CS	Whiff%	AVG/OBP/SLG	DRC+	BABIP	BRR	DRP	WARP
2021	SL	AAA	23	110	26	5	3	3	8	16	29	2	0		.255/.364/.468	99	.339	2.0	CF(10): 0.8, LF(3): -0.5, RF(1): -0.3	0.5
2021	LAA	MLB	23	260	27	12	3	2	19	20	91	6	1	33.2%	.254/.317/.356	60	.403	1.2	CF(70): -0.4	-0.2
2022	LAA	MLB	24	323	34	9	2	8	37	22	117	8	2	31.3%	.226/.284/.353	59	.341	1.8	LF(77): 5.6, CF(19): -0.4, RF(2): 0.5	0.2
2022	PHI	MLB	24	138	15	9	2	3	15	6	41	2	2	24.8%	.288/.319/.455	75	.398	-1.1	CF(40): 1.7	0.1
2023 DC	*PHI*	*MLB*	*25*	*424*	*46*	*17*	*4*	*10*	*40*	*30*	*137*	*14*	*4*	*28.9%*	*.240/.300/.389*	*84*	*.344*	*8.4*	*CF 2*	*1.5*

Comparables: Michael Brantley (64), Michael Saunders (59), Felix Pie (56)

The Phillies took an *Only Murders in the Building* approach when they traded for Marsh at the 2022 deadline, hoping that by playing the bright young center fielder alongside their two slow-moving old-timers, they could turn the outfield defense into something watchable. However, the jury is still out on whether or not Marsh is truly an elite enough defender to make up for the mediocre outfielders on either side of him. While he has excellent footspeed, you wouldn't necessarily know it from his defensive range in center, and his arm is nothing spectacular. There's certainly nothing wrong with his defense in center, especially if Marsh continues making improvements at the plate. But it's not clear if *any* center fielder could single-handedly solve the problem of the Phillies outfield defense—nor could Mabel solve any mysteries at the Arconia without her septuagenarian companions putting in some work too.

J.T. Realmuto C Born: 03/18/91 Age: 32 Bats: R Throws: R Height: 6'1" Weight: 212 lb. Origin: Round 3, 2010 Draft (#104 overall)

YEAR	TEAM	LVL	AGE	PA	R	2B	3B	HR	RBI	BB	K	SB	CS	Whiff%	AVG/OBP/SLG	DRC+	BABIP	BRR	DRP	WARP
2020	PHI	MLB	29	195	33	6	0	11	32	16	48	4	1	29.8%	.266/.349/.491	109	.307	0.3	C(36): 3.2, 1B(6): 0	1.2
2021	PHI	MLB	30	537	64	25	4	17	73	48	129	13	3	27.0%	.263/.343/.439	100	.325	3.5	C(118): 16.1, 1B(16): -0.1	4.1
2022	PHI	MLB	31	562	75	26	5	22	84	41	119	21	1	25.5%	.276/.342/.478	119	.318	0.5	C(133): 11.5, 1B(3): 0	4.6
2023 DC	*PHI*	*MLB*	*32*	*512*	*60*	*22*	*2*	*19*	*64*	*39*	*113*	*14*	*2*	*25.8%*	*.258/.331/.442*	*113*	*.305*	*8.8*	*C 13*	*5.0*

Comparables: Victor Martinez (84), Don Slaught (83), Ivan Rodríguez (80)

YEAR	TEAM	P. COUNT	FRM RUNS	BLK RUNS	THRW RUNS	TOT RUNS
2020	PHI	5047	3.1	0.0	0.2	3.3
2021	PHI	16465	15.4	0.8	0.3	16.6
2022	PHI	18477	10.2	0.8	0.3	11.3
2023	*PHI*	*16835*	*7.4*	*0.7*	*0.9*	*9.0*

Realmuto was Realmuto again in 2022, finishing with 4+ WARP for the fifth time in the past five full seasons. He got off to a middling start but turned things around in July, producing like one of the best hitters in baseball for the final three months of the year. He finished with the highest DRC+ of his career. Through it all, Realmuto continued to excel in all regards behind the dish. He's an incredible framer and strong blocker, and he boasts the best pop time in baseball. To top it all off, he was the most durable catcher in the sport, too—he caught 17 more games and 127.2 more innings than the next-best backstop. Philadelphia fans have long called Realmuto the best catcher in baseball, but it might be time to think even bigger. #BCIB is settled. Best catcher in franchise history? He's not far off.

Johan Rojas CF Born: 08/14/00 Age: 22 Bats: R Throws: R Height: 6'1" Weight: 165 lb. Origin: International Free Agent, 2018

YEAR	TEAM	LVL	AGE	PA	R	2B	3B	HR	RBI	BB	K	SB	CS	Whiff%	AVG/OBP/SLG	DRC+	BABIP	BRR	DRP	WARP
2021	CLR	A	20	351	51	15	3	7	38	26	69	25	6		.240/.305/.374	100	.283	3.4	CF(66): 11.1, RF(10): -0.7, LF(1): 0.5	2.6
2021	JS	A+	20	74	16	3	1	3	11	7	8	8	3		.344/.419/.563	139	.352	2.5	CF(14): 2.8, LF(2): -0.3, RF(1): -0.0	1.1
2022	JS	A+	21	292	40	12	2	3	22	21	55	33	1		.230/.287/.325	111	.278	2.9	CF(63): 1.8	1.8
2022	REA	AA	21	264	42	8	5	4	16	21	44	29	4		.260/.333/.387	112	.305	5.1	CF(51): 6.5, LF(6): -0.2, RF(1): -0.1	2.4
2023 non-DC	*PHI*	*MLB*	*22*	*251*	*20*	*9*	*2*	*3*	*22*	*13*	*51*	*14*	*4*	*23.7%*	*.230/.280/.335*	*70*	*.283*	*5.1*	*LF 0, CF 0*	*0.3*

Comparables: Greg Golson (57), Mason Williams (51), Che-Hsuan Lin (51)

Rojas could be knocking on the door this season, but several questions persist about his big-league prospects. He has elite speed and plays strong defense in center field, but his bat isn't where it needs to be. He's struggled to unlock his power potential in-game, and although he makes a lot of contact, most of that contact ends up on the ground. Nevertheless, his skills in the field and general athleticism give Rojas a stable floor as a backup center fielder.

Kyle Schwarber LF Born: 03/05/93 Age: 30 Bats: L Throws: R Height: 6'0" Weight: 229 lb. Origin: Round 1, 2014 Draft (#4 overall)

YEAR	TEAM	LVL	AGE	PA	R	2B	3B	HR	RBI	BB	K	SB	CS	Whiff%	AVG/OBP/SLG	DRC+	BABIP	BRR	DRP	WARP
2020	CHC	MLB	27	224	30	6	0	11	24	30	66	1	0	28.2%	.188/.308/.393	96	.219	0.3	LF(48): 0.7	0.6
2021	WAS	MLB	28	303	42	9	0	25	53	31	88	1	1	29.3%	.253/.340/.570	131	.273	-4.3	LF(72): 1.8	2.1
2021	BOS	MLB	28	168	34	10	0	7	18	33	39	0	0	27.4%	.291/.435/.522	117	.364	0.5	LF(15): 1.2, 1B(10): -0.5	1.0
2022	PHI	MLB	29	669	100	21	3	46	94	86	200	10	1	29.3%	.218/.323/.504	125	.240	-1.5	LF(139): -3.8	3.6
2023 DC	*PHI*	*MLB*	*30*	*611*	*96*	*21*	*2*	*42*	*88*	*78*	*166*	*5*	*1*	*28.7%*	*.239/.345/.531*	*136*	*.265*	*3.7*	*LF -7*	*3.8*

Comparables: Adam Dunn (77), Willie Stargell (68), Pete Incaviglia (67)

They say the pen is mightier than the sword, and Schwarber must be inclined to agree. After inking a sizable free agent contract, the lefty had his mightiest season yet, leading the Senior Circuit in home runs, ISO, average exit velocity, barrels, and hard-hit rate. The prototype of a TTO player, Schwarber also finished with the fourth-most walks in the National League and the highest strikeout total in baseball. The strikeouts are a problem, of course, but they're nothing new for Schwarber, and they're far more tenable when they go hand in hand with the earth-shattering power he displayed in 2022. The pen may be mightier than the sword, but Schwarber's trusty Louisville Slugger puts them both to shame.

Edmundo Sosa SS/3B Born: 03/06/96 Age: 27 Bats: R Throws: R Height: 6'0" Weight: 210 lb. Origin: International Free Agent, 2012

YEAR	TEAM	LVL	AGE	PA	R	2B	3B	HR	RBI	BB	K	SB	CS	Whiff%	AVG/OBP/SLG	DRC+	BABIP	BRR	DRP	WARP
2021	STL	MLB	25	326	39	8	4	6	27	17	63	4	4	28.1%	.271/.346/.389	102	.326	0.3	SS(71): 0.9, 2B(25): 0.3, 3B(9): -0.5	1.4
2022	STL	MLB	26	131	17	4	3	0	8	4	38	3	1	34.1%	.189/.244/.270	72	.274	-0.1	SS(34): 0.6, 3B(11): 1	0.1
2022	PHI	MLB	26	59	9	7	1	2	13	1	12	3	0	25.4%	.315/.345/.593	102	.366	0.6	3B(11): 1.6, SS(8): 0.3, LF(2): 0	0.5
2023 DC	*PHI*	*MLB*	*27*	*188*	*19*	*7*	*1*	*3*	*17*	*8*	*42*	*6*	*2*	*29.1%*	*.241/.304/.364*	*87*	*.301*	*2.7*	*2B 0, 3B 0*	*0.5*

Comparables: Hernán Pérez (56), Anderson Hernandez (54), Carlos Sanchez (50)

An anagram is a word, or sometimes a phrase, formed by rearranging the letters from a different word or phrase. All the constituent parts are the same, but changing their location can make a tremendous difference. If, for example, you rearrange the letters in Sosa, you get "O A SS," and that's quite fitting, because *oh, a shortstop* he is. In 2022, a change of location made a tremendous difference for the slick infielder, and his bat lit up after a midsummer move to Philadelphia. No one expects him to keep hitting .300, but he has all the constituent parts to be an excellent utility player. He plays elite defense, runs the bases well, and has potential in his bat. The only thing he can't do is pitch, which makes sense—an anagram for Edmundo is "de-mound."

Bryson Stott MI Born: 10/06/97 Age: 25 Bats: L Throws: R Height: 6'3" Weight: 200 lb. Origin: Round 1, 2019 Draft (#14 overall)

YEAR	TEAM	LVL	AGE	PA	R	2B	3B	HR	RBI	BB	K	SB	CS	Whiff%	AVG/OBP/SLG	DRC+	BABIP	BRR	DRP	WARP
2021	PEJ	WIN	23	119	20	7	1	2	31	24	14	5	3		.318/.445/.489		.333			
2021	JS	A+	23	95	18	4	0	5	10	22	22	3	2		.288/.453/.548	134	.348	1.5	SS(16): -0.0, 2B(6): 0.1	0.8
2021	REA	AA	23	351	49	22	2	10	36	35	78	6	2		.301/.368/.481	109	.368	1.9	SS(71): -3.5, 3B(5): 1.5, 2B(4): 1.0	1.6
2021	LHV	AAA	23	41	4	0	0	1	3	8	8	1	0		.303/.439/.394	111	.375	1.4	SS(10): -2.4	0.1
2022	LHV	AAA	24	40	11	2	1	2	7	3	10	2	0		.333/.375/.611	101	.400	0.3	SS(6): 0.5, 2B(1): 0.4, 3B(1): -0.1	0.2
2022	PHI	MLB	24	466	58	19	2	10	49	36	89	12	4	17.3%	.234/.295/.358	88	.274	1.4	SS(83): -4.2, 2B(47): 1.6, 3B(2): -0.3	0.6
2023 DC	*PHI*	*MLB*	*25*	*481*	*53*	*19*	*3*	*12*	*48*	*39*	*81*	*14*	*3*	*18.5%*	*.254/.319/.397*	*99*	*.288*	*6.3*	*2B 0, SS -1*	*1.9*

Comparables: Jed Lowrie (66), Alberto Gonzalez (66), Darwin Barney (64)

Stott reached the World Series in his very first big-league season, so nobody tell him he plays for the losingest franchise in professional sports history; he might not know yet. The young shortstop improved along with the Phillies throughout the 2022 campaign, starting slow but finding his groove in the summer. At the plate, he showed off stellar pitch recognition skills and a prodigious feel for contact. When he chose to swing, it was nearly impossible to get anything past him. On the flip side, however, he laid off plenty of belt-high heaters over the plate. It would be great if he could do more damage against those fastballs, but if nothing else, at least he knows which pitches he wants to avoid, and he successfully avoids them. On defense, Stott proved to be a better shortstop than was expected. His range was limited, but he did a fine job on the balls he could reach. He still projects as a second baseman in the future—and present, since that's where he'll play most of his games in 2023 thanks to the signing of Tea Turner—but it's good to know he can play a serviceable six if needed.

Garrett Stubbs C Born: 05/26/93 Age: 30 Bats: L Throws: R Height: 5'10" Weight: 170 lb. Origin: Round 8, 2015 Draft (#229 overall)

YEAR	TEAM	LVL	AGE	PA	R	2B	3B	HR	RBI	BB	K	SB	CS	Whiff%	AVG/OBP/SLG	DRC+	BABIP	BRR	DRP	WARP
2020	HOU	MLB	27	10	1	0	0	0	1	0	0	0	1	26.7%	.125/.111/.125	98	.111	-0.5	LF(3): 0	0.0
2021	SUG	AAA	28	146	25	5	0	2	15	30	29	4	0		.265/.418/.363	106	.333	2.1	C(28): -0.1, 2B(6): 0.2	0.9
2021	HOU	MLB	28	38	2	2	0	0	3	2	7	0	0	23.2%	.176/.222/.235	84	.222	0.0	C(14): -0.4, LF(2): -0.1	0.0
2022	PHI	MLB	29	121	19	4	1	5	16	14	30	2	0	21.9%	.264/.350/.462	93	.324	1.5	C(41): -3.9, P(4): 0	0.1
2023 DC	*PHI*	*MLB*	*30*	*121*	*12*	*4*	*0*	*1*	*9*	*12*	*22*	*2*	*0*	*22.0%*	*.216/.307/.319*	*76*	*.260*	*1.2*	*C -2*	*0.0*

Comparables: George Kottaras (54), Michael McKenry (53), Curt Casali (53)

YEAR	TEAM	P. COUNT	FRM RUNS	BLK RUNS	THRW RUNS	TOT RUNS
2020	HOU	400	0.2	0.0	0.0	0.2
2021	SUG	3981	0.3	-0.1	0.0	0.2
2021	HOU	1256	-0.3	0.0	0.0	-0.3
2022	PHI	4789	-4.0	-0.1	-0.3	-4.4
2023	*PHI*	*4810*	*-1.9*	*-0.1*	*0.1*	*-2.0*

Stubbs may have been both the most important and the least essential backup catcher in baseball during the 2022 season. He was blocked from playing time by J.T. Realmuto (coincidentally, the best blocker in baseball), but while he didn't play all that often, Stubbs made the most of the chances he got. By Win Probability Added, he was the sixth-most valuable backstop in the sport. Overall, Stubbs had an excellent season, and while his high batting average and power numbers don't look sustainable, he moves well on the bases and his polished plate discipline is the real deal. Defensively, he grades out as a poor pitch framer but has a strong arm and his pop time is elite.

Trea Turner SS Born: 06/30/93 Age: 30 Bats: R Throws: R Height: 6'2" Weight: 185 lb. Origin: Round 1, 2014 Draft (#13 overall)

YEAR	TEAM	LVL	AGE	PA	R	2B	3B	HR	RBI	BB	K	SB	CS	Whiff%	AVG/OBP/SLG	DRC+	BABIP	BRR	DRP	WARP
2020	WAS	MLB	27	259	46	15	4	12	41	22	36	12	4	19.6%	.335/.394/.588	138	.353	5.3	SS(59): -2.3	2.3
2021	LAD	MLB	28	226	41	17	0	10	28	15	33	11	2	23.2%	.338/.385/.565	125	.361	3.9	2B(49): -0.5, SS(3): 0	1.9
2021	WAS	MLB	28	420	66	17	3	18	49	26	77	21	3	22.8%	.322/.369/.521	123	.363	0.6	SS(95): -0.4	2.7
2022	LAD	MLB	29	708	101	39	4	21	100	45	131	27	3	26.3%	.298/.343/.466	114	.342	-0.8	SS(160): 3.6	3.8
2023 DC	*PHI*	*MLB*	*30*	*622*	*86*	*29*	*3*	*23*	*76*	*43*	*124*	*26*	*3*	*25.3%*	*.299/.354/.489*	*132*	*.349*	*17.2*	*SS 5*	*6.7*

Comparables: Nomar Garciaparra (77), José Reyes (76), Hanley Ramirez (73)

Rickey Henderson. Ozzie Smith. Lou Brock. Paul Molitor. The Hall of Fame has myriad inductees who excelled into their 40s with a slap-and-dash offensive style. Are there even more players who lost their legs somewhere in their 30s? Sure, but there's ample proof that an elite speedster such as Turner isn't predestined to make the Phillies regret paying him through his age-40 season. But this is the *2023 BP Annual*, not the 2033 edition. Philadelphia never adequately filled the shortstop hole left behind by Jimmy Rollins (another fast player who aged well), and Turner is among the game's most well-rounded stars. He's one of just 11 players who eclipsed an average sprint speed of 30.0 ft/s, and none of the others have a track record of productive offense. In year one of his contract, he's a perfect fit for a Phillies lineup that craved a dynamic leadoff hitter at an up-the-middle position. As for his decline phase, put a note on your phone to order that book a decade from now.

PITCHERS

★ ★ ★ *2023 Top 101 Prospect* **#36** ★ ★ ★

Mick Abel RHP Born: 08/18/01 Age: 21 Bats: R Throws: R Height: 6'5" Weight: 190 lb. Origin: Round 1, 2020 Draft (#15 overall)

YEAR	TEAM	LVL	AGE	W	L	SV	G	GS	IP	H	HR	BB/9	K/9	K	GB%	BABIP	WHIP	ERA	DRA-	WARP	MPH	FB%	Whiff%	CSP
2021	CLR	A	19	1	3	0	14	14	44^{2}	27	5	5.4	13.3	66	40.0%	.259	1.21	4.43	78	1.0				
2022	JS	A+	20	7	8	0	18	18	85^{1}	75	6	4.0	10.9	103	39.1%	.315	1.32	4.01	101	0.5				
2022	REA	AA	20	1	3	0	5	5	23	19	5	4.7	10.6	27	27.6%	.264	1.35	3.52	110	0.2				
2023 non-DC	*PHI*	*MLB*	*21*	*2*	*3*	*0*	*57*	*0*	*50*	*51*	*8*	*5.6*	*8.9*	*49*	*37.1%*	*.308*	*1.65*	*5.69*	*131*	*-0.6*			*26.7%*	

Comparables: Julio Rodriguez (77), Matt Manning (75), Grant Holmes (74)

In 2022, Abel continued showing off all the skills that made him a standout prospect to begin with: a mid-90s fastball (with high-90s upside), a strong slider and decent command on all his pitches. Fatigue issues, which plagued him in 2021, were less of a problem, as he looked comfortable pitching further into games. Abel went at least five innings in 14 of his 23 starts, including eight outings of six innings pitched or more. Promoted to Double-A just days after his 21st birthday, he celebrated by upping his whiff rate. He needs to continue generating swings and misses to reach his potential as a top-of-the-rotation arm, but Abel looks ready to make an impact at the big-league level. He should compete for time in the Phillies rotation this season.

José Alvarado LHP Born: 05/21/95 Age: 28 Bats: L Throws: L Height: 6'2" Weight: 245 lb. Origin: International Free Agent, 2012

YEAR	TEAM	LVL	AGE	W	L	SV	G	GS	IP	H	HR	BB/9	K/9	K	GB%	BABIP	WHIP	ERA	DRA-	WARP	MPH	FB%	Whiff%	CSP
2020	TB	MLB	25	0	0	0	9	0	9	9	2	6.0	13.0	13	41.7%	.318	1.67	6.00	98	0.1	97.1	76.8%	28.0%	42.1%
2021	PHI	MLB	26	7	1	5	64	0	55^{2}	42	5	7.6	11.0	68	55.8%	.298	1.60	4.20	102	0.5	99.5	80.6%	33.3%	52.5%
2022	PHI	MLB	27	4	2	2	59	0	51	38	2	4.2	14.3	81	56.5%	.343	1.22	3.18	60	1.6	98.3	98.8%	38.4%	47.2%
2023 DC	*PHI*	*MLB*	*28*	*2*	*2*	*6*	*56*	*0*	*48.7*	*42*	*4*	*5.6*	*13.5*	*73*	*54.0%*	*.348*	*1.48*	*4.11*	*94*	*0.3*	*98.7*	*88.7%*	*34.5%*	*48.6%*

Comparables: Ken Giles (63), Luis Avilán (62), Henry Alberto Rodriguez (61)

Lehigh Valley has been at the epicenter of three momentous revolutions in United States history: the American Revolution, the Industrial Revolution and, most recently, the Alvarado Revolution. In 1777, the Liberty Bell was hidden in Lehigh, keeping it safe from would-be captors during the Revolutionary War. In 1827, the Lehigh Canal opened, and the surrounding area became a central hub of the Industrial Revolution. And in 2022, the Phillies' left-handed reliever was demoted to Triple-A after floundering in the early going. When Alvarado returned, he was a different pitcher. He largely ditched his four-seam and curveball in favor of a cutter, a pitch he began throwing nearly 50% of the time. The result? A 180° revolution. From the day he rejoined the major-league squad until the end of the season, Alvarado struck out 64 batters in 42 appearances, allowing only 36 of the 149 batters he faced to reach base. He transformed from an erratic arm into one of baseball's most reliable left-handed relievers.

Andrew Bellatti RHP Born: 08/05/91 Age: 31 Bats: R Throws: R Height: 6'1" Weight: 190 lb. Origin: Round 12, 2009 Draft (#379 overall)

YEAR	TEAM	LVL	AGE	W	L	SV	G	GS	IP	H	HR	BB/9	K/9	K	GB%	BABIP	WHIP	ERA	DRA-	WARP	MPH	FB%	Whiff%	CSP
2021	JAX	AAA	29	1	2	11	26	0	29^{2}	15	2	3.0	11.5	38	23.4%	.210	0.84	1.52	85	0.6				
2021	MIA	MLB	29	0	0	0	3	0	3^{1}	6	0	5.4	10.8	4	30.8%	.462	2.40	13.50	103	0.0	94.5	54.2%	27.1%	42.7%
2022	PHI	MLB	30	4	4	2	59	1	54^{1}	47	5	4.1	12.9	78	27.0%	.347	1.33	3.31	72	1.3	94.6	40.4%	37.5%	50.0%
2023 DC	*PHI*	*MLB*	*31*	*2*	*2*	*2*	*50*	*0*	*43.3*	*35*	*6*	*3.8*	*11.3*	*54*	*29.9%*	*.285*	*1.23*	*3.59*	*90*	*0.4*	*94.6*	*41.3%*	*33.0%*	*49.5%*

Comparables: Jeurys Familia (40), Jeremy Jeffress (38), Jesus Colome (36)

After making his MLB debut in 2015, Bellatti didn't resurface until 2021—clearly a shrewd political move on his part to skip the entire Trump Presidency. He made another smart decision in 2022, turning his slider into his go-to pitch and, as a result, missing bats like never before. Bellatti proved himself to be a reliable and consistent seventh-inning reliever with a penchant for punchouts, though when he did allow contact, it often led to trouble. Improving his changeup will help him reduce the amount of hard contact he allows going forward.

Connor Brogdon RHP Born: 01/29/95 Age: 28 Bats: R Throws: R Height: 6'6" Weight: 205 lb. Origin: Round 10, 2017 Draft (#293 overall)

YEAR	TEAM	LVL	AGE	W	L	SV	G	GS	IP	H	HR	BB/9	K/9	K	GB%	BABIP	WHIP	ERA	DRA-	WARP	MPH	FB%	Whiff%	CSP
2020	PHI	MLB	25	1	0	0	9	0	11^{1}	5	3	4.0	13.5	17	36.4%	.105	0.88	3.97	83	0.2	95.0	64.7%	32.6%	41.6%
2021	PHI	MLB	26	5	4	1	56	1	57^{2}	47	6	2.8	7.8	50	46.4%	.258	1.13	3.43	96	0.7	95.5	64.4%	29.0%	53.8%
2022	LHV	AAA	27	0	1	2	10	1	9^{1}	8	0	5.8	16.4	17	52.6%	.421	1.50	2.89	74	0.3	93.9	23.1%	20.0%	
2022	PHI	MLB	27	2	2	2	47	0	44	44	6	2.3	10.2	50	31.7%	.319	1.25	3.27	85	0.8	95.4	32.0%	33.2%	53.7%
2023 DC	*PHI*	*MLB*	*28*	*2*	*2*	*0*	*43*	*0*	*38*	*34*	*4*	*3.2*	*9.5*	*40*	*38.7%*	*.294*	*1.25*	*3.53*	*91*	*0.3*	*95.4*	*49.0%*	*31.6%*	*53.0%*

Comparables: Brad Brach (55), David Carpenter (55), Ryan Dull (55)

Brogdon's 2022 season got off to a slow start—quite literally. His four-seam fastball velocity was down almost three miles per hour at the beginning of the year. Never one to blow past hitters with blistering heat, he just needs his four-seam to be fast enough for his best pitch, a changeup, to play. Suffice it to say, it wasn't working that way in April. After an early demotion to search for his missing stuff, Brogdon returned in mid-May looking more like his old self. His velocity didn't get quite as high as it was the year prior, but it was fast enough to complement his changeup, which he used as his primary pitch. He performed like a solid, steadfast middle reliever for the rest of the year. In the postseason, a minor mechanical adjustment helped him add a little extra oomph to his four-seamer, and Brogdon looked downright nasty in each of his World Series outings.

Sam Coonrod RHP Born: 09/22/92 Age: 30 Bats: R Throws: R Height: 6'1" Weight: 225 lb. Origin: Round 5, 2014 Draft (#148 overall)

YEAR	TEAM	LVL	AGE	W	L	SV	G	GS	IP	H	HR	BB/9	K/9	K	GB%	BABIP	WHIP	ERA	DRA-	WARP	MPH	FB%	Whiff%	CSP
2020	SF	MLB	27	0	2	3	18	0	14^{2}	17	2	4.3	9.2	15	45.7%	.341	1.64	9.82	99	0.2	98.0	58.9%	29.1%	48.8%
2021	LHV	AAA	28	0	0	0	5	0	5^{1}	2	1	3.4	6.8	4	46.2%	.083	0.75	1.69	99	0.1				
2021	PHI	MLB	28	2	2	2	42	2	42^{1}	41	5	3.2	10.2	48	56.3%	.316	1.32	4.04	84	0.8	98.1	73.0%	24.9%	54.1%
2022	LHV	AAA	29	1	0	0	9	0	9	12	1	6.0	5.0	5	48.5%	.344	2.00	8.00	130	0.0				
2022	PHI	MLB	29	0	0	0	12	0	12^{2}	12	1	5.0	8.5	12	36.1%	.314	1.50	7.82	112	0.0	96.7	65.7%	20.2%	57.5%
2023 DC	*PHI*	*MLB*	*30*	*2*	*2*	*0*	*43*	*0*	*38*	*39*	*4*	*4.3*	*7.6*	*32*	*48.0%*	*.310*	*1.53*	*4.96*	*118*	*-0.2*	*97.6*	*68.5%*	*23.5%*	*53.4%*

Comparables: Pierce Johnson (64), A.J. Schugel (60), Dan Winkler (60)

Coonrod threw a terrific four-seam fastball in 2021, regularly hitting 100 on the radar gun and regularly making opposing hitters look silly. He tried to throw the four-seam more frequently the following season, but it quickly became clear it was no longer the same pitch, and it wasn't getting the same results. A torn rotator cuff suffered in March seemed to sap his strength, and upon his return from the IL, his fastball looked merely regular. The 2022 season was a lost one for Coonrod, who will look to regain his velocity in 2023.

Hans Crouse RHP Born: 09/15/98 Age: 24 Bats: L Throws: R Height: 6'4" Weight: 180 lb. Origin: Round 2, 2017 Draft (#66 overall)

YEAR	TEAM	LVL	AGE	W	L	SV	G	GS	IP	H	HR	BB/9	K/9	K	GB%	BABIP	WHIP	ERA	DRA-	WARP	MPH	FB%	Whiff%	CSP
2021	FRI	AA	22	3	2	0	13	13	51	27	5	3.4	9.5	54	35.0%	.191	0.90	3.35	94	0.5				
2021	REA	AA	22	2	2	0	6	6	29^{2}	24	3	3.6	11.5	38	28.6%	.313	1.21	2.73	89	0.3				
2021	PHI	MLB	22	0	2	0	2	2	7	4	2	9.0	2.6	2	17.4%	.100	1.57	5.14	156	-0.1	92.8	46.6%	22.2%	48.2%
2022	LHV	AAA	23	0	3	0	5	5	12^{1}	21	2	4.4	9.5	13	27.3%	.452	2.19	13.14	125	0.0				
2023 non-DC	*PHI*	*MLB*	*24*	*2*	*3*	*0*	*57*	*0*	*50*	*51*	*8*	*4.5*	*8.5*	*47*	*32.3%*	*.306*	*1.53*	*5.27*	*125*	*-0.4*	*92.8*	*46.6%*	*28.2%*	*48.2%*

Comparables: Chris Flexen (41), Chase De Jong (40), Robert Gsellman (39)

Crouse made a winning first impression when he arrived in Philadelphia, charming fans with his thick mustache, platinum blonde hair and the kind of goofy smile you wouldn't expect from a guy with so many neck tattoos. Unfortunately, injuries limited him to a handful of Triple-A appearances in 2022, and he didn't look so winsome after that. The luster from his first impression is starting to fade. Between free-agent signings and being surpassed on the minor-league depth chart, Crouse's course might be increasingly charted toward the bullpen.

Seranthony Domínguez RHP Born: 11/25/94 Age: 28 Bats: R Throws: R Height: 6'1" Weight: 225 lb. Origin: International Free Agent, 2011

YEAR	TEAM	LVL	AGE	W	L	SV	G	GS	IP	H	HR	BB/9	K/9	K	GB%	BABIP	WHIP	ERA	DRA-	WARP	MPH	FB%	Whiff%	CSP
2021	REA	AA	26	1	0	0	4	0	5	8	4	5.4	5.4	3	38.1%	.235	2.20	14.40	106	0.0				
2021	LHV	AAA	26	0	1	0	12	0	12^{1}	13	1	5.8	11.7	16	50.0%	.343	1.70	7.30	81	0.3				
2021	PHI	MLB	26	0	0	0	1	0	1	0	0	0.0	9.0	1	50.0%	.000	0.00	0.00			95.0	71.4%	25.0%	63.1%
2022	PHI	MLB	27	6	5	9	54	0	51	36	4	3.9	10.8	61	47.2%	.269	1.14	3.00	79	1.0	98.1	70.1%	32.2%	51.3%
2023 DC	*PHI*	*MLB*	*28*	*2*	*2*	*13*	*50*	*0*	*43.3*	*38*	*5*	*4.5*	*10.5*	*50*	*48.4%*	*.304*	*1.38*	*4.01*	*97*	*0.2*	*98.0*	*69.0%*	*31.1%*	*50.9%*

Comparables: Michael Feliz (63), Ken Giles (62), Henry Alberto Rodriguez (61)

Like a long-lost hero appearing in the distance, Domínguez returned in 2022 to save the Phillies bullpen from the dragon of its own mediocrity. It took him a little while to get going after 852 days on the IL, but eventually, Domínguez looked like the stud reliever he was during his breakout rookie season. By the All-Star Break, he was consistently hitting 98 mph and maxing out over 100 with both his four-seam and his sinker. His slider played off those fastballs perfectly, turning into one of the best whiff pitches in baseball. He allowed his fair share of hard contact, but that comes with the territory when you throw as fast as Domínguez does. He missed enough bats that a few hard-hit balls here and there didn't prove to be a problem. Triceps tendinitis caused a minor setback in August (and he might have come off the IL too soon in September), but he returned to full strength in time for a dominant postseason run. The Phillies envision him protecting leads and slaying late-inning beasts for years to come.

Bailey Falter LHP Born: 04/24/97 Age: 26 Bats: R Throws: L Height: 6'4" Weight: 175 lb. Origin: Round 5, 2015 Draft (#144 overall)

YEAR	TEAM	LVL	AGE	W	L	SV	G	GS	IP	H	HR	BB/9	K/9	K	GB%	BABIP	WHIP	ERA	DRA-	WARP	MPH	FB%	Whiff%	CSP
2021	LHV	AAA	24	2	0	0	8	6	30^{2}	23	3	2.3	12.9	44	44.1%	.308	1.01	1.76	86	0.6				
2021	PHI	MLB	24	2	1	0	22	1	33^{2}	34	5	1.6	9.1	34	37.1%	.315	1.19	5.61	94	0.4	91.9	68.1%	23.3%	55.7%
2022	LHV	AAA	25	4	1	0	9	9	47	25	4	1.1	9.4	49	33.6%	.196	0.66	1.91	82	1.1	92.0	44.8%	24.4%	
2022	PHI	MLB	25	6	4	0	20	16	84	85	16	1.8	7.9	74	34.1%	.292	1.21	3.86	122	-0.1	91.3	64.3%	23.8%	58.1%
2023 DC	*PHI*	*MLB*	*26*	*7*	*7*	*0*	*42*	*17*	*107*	*106*	*16*	*2.1*	*8.3*	*98*	*36.8%*	*.298*	*1.23*	*3.76*	*98*	*0.8*	*91.4*	*65.2%*	*24.9%*	*57.5%*

Comparables: Tyler Alexander (76), Justin Nicolino (76), Gabriel Ynoa (74)

Falter is a hittable pitcher—he throws a lot of pitches in the strike zone, and he doesn't throw them very fast (although his league-best extension helps). His saving grace is that his strike-heavy approach limits free passes, which helps reduce the damage from all those hits. He found a way to further decrease his walk rate in 2022, switching up his pitch mix midseason. His four-seam fastball became his primary pitch, replacing his sinker, and his curveball supplanted his slider as his go-to breaking ball against right-handed batters. Falter remained as hittable as ever, but his walk rate fell to a nearly non-existent level. He showed promise as a back-end starter for the rest of the season.

Craig Kimbrel RHP Born: 05/28/88 Age: 35 Bats: R Throws: R Height: 6'0" Weight: 215 lb. Origin: Round 3, 2008 Draft (#96 overall)

YEAR	TEAM	LVL	AGE	W	L	SV	G	GS	IP	H	HR	BB/9	K/9	K	GB%	BABIP	WHIP	ERA	DRA-	WARP	MPH	FB%	Whiff%	CSP
2020	CHC	MLB	32	0	1	2	18	0	15^{1}	10	2	7.0	16.4	28	33.3%	.320	1.43	5.28	77	0.4	97.1	62.3%	35.4%	42.8%
2021	CHW	MLB	33	2	2	1	24	0	23	18	5	3.9	14.1	36	26.5%	.295	1.22	5.09	87	0.4	96.0	59.3%	40.9%	50.0%
2021	CHC	MLB	33	2	3	23	39	0	36^{2}	13	1	3.2	15.7	64	33.3%	.203	0.71	0.49	68	1.0	97.1	59.3%	44.7%	49.1%
2022	LAD	MLB	34	6	7	22	63	0	60	51	4	4.2	10.8	72	38.7%	.313	1.32	3.75	85	1.0	95.8	68.5%	29.2%	52.8%
2023 DC	*PHI*	*MLB*	*35*	*2*	*2*	*10*	*50*	*0*	*43.3*	*34*	*6*	*4.2*	*11.9*	*57*	*35.5%*	*.286*	*1.25*	*3.60*	*89*	*0.4*	*96.3*	*64.6%*	*32.6%*	*50.3%*

Comparables: Armando Benitez (83), Michael Jackson (82), Joakim Soria (82)

Remember 2012? It was the year of "Call Me Maybe" and the first Avengers movie. The Mayan calendar ended on December 21, but the world kept spinning. Kimbrel became the first-ever qualified reliever to strike out more than 50% of batters faced. Eleven years later, the world is still spinning, Loki is sort of a good guy and Kimbrel's strikeout rate dipped to 27.7%. His fastball velocity was down three ticks from his peak; he entertained a brief, "Hey, I just met you, and this is crazy..." romance with a slider in July before reverting to his trusty curve. He still sticks out his wing like a flightless bird before each pitch, but his stat line is unrecognizable from the days when Curiosity rover first traversed Mars and "Gangnam Style" dominated YouTube.

★ ★ ★ *2023 Top 101 Prospect* **#51** ★ ★ ★

Griff McGarry RHP Born: 06/08/99 Age: 24 Bats: R Throws: R Height: 6'2" Weight: 190 lb. Origin: Round 5, 2021 Draft (#145 overall)

YEAR	TEAM	LVL	AGE	W	L	SV	G	GS	IP	H	HR	BB/9	K/9	K	GB%	BABIP	WHIP	ERA	DRA-	WARP	MPH	FB%	Whiff%	CSP
2021	CLR	A	22	0	0	1	5	1	11	6	0	5.7	18.0	22	52.9%	.353	1.18	3.27	84	0.2				
2021	JS	A+	22	1	0	0	3	3	13^{1}	7	0	4.7	14.2	21	34.6%	.269	1.05	2.70	98	0.1				
2022	JS	A+	23	3	3	0	12	12	46^{2}	33	6	4.6	15.8	82	35.3%	.342	1.22	3.86	84	0.7				
2022	REA	AA	23	1	3	0	8	7	32^{2}	13	1	5.5	10.7	39	44.9%	.176	1.01	2.20	95	0.5				
2022	LHV	AAA	23	0	2	0	7	0	8	7	2	10.1	10.1	9	36.8%	.294	2.00	9.00	101	0.1				
2023 DC	*PHI*	*MLB*	*24*	*1*	*1*	*0*	*4*	*4*	*20.3*	*17*	*3*	*6.8*	*11.5*	*26*	*39.8%*	*.303*	*1.62*	*5.13*	*116*	*0.0*			*30.4%*	

Comparables: Nick Nelson (56), Dellin Betances (53), Josh Staumont (52)

Less than two years ago, McGarry was struggling so badly in college that he lost his spot in the starting rotation. Now, he's on the cusp of making his MLB debut for the defending National League Champions. Command has long been a problem for the right-hander, but his strikeout skills are phenomenal, and he boasts a diverse arsenal of promising pitches. McGarry is still a starting pitcher—he had a bullpen audition in the minors on the chance he could help the major-league squad in their playoff run, but it didn't go well. If he fails in that role, however, his nasty fastball and devastating slider could translate well to a relief role, despite the rough introduction last season.

Francisco Morales RHP Born: 10/27/99 Age: 23 Bats: R Throws: R Height: 6'4" Weight: 185 lb. Origin: International Free Agent, 2016

YEAR	TEAM	LVL	AGE	W	L	SV	G	GS	IP	H	HR	BB/9	K/9	K	GB%	BABIP	WHIP	ERA	DRA-	WARP	MPH	FB%	Whiff%	CSP
2021	REA	AA	21	4	13	0	22	20	83	76	11	6.5	11.9	110	40.8%	.323	1.64	6.94	84	1.4				
2021	LHV	AAA	21	0	1	0	2	2	8^{2}	6	0	7.3	7.3	7	44.0%	.240	1.50	0.00	114	0.1				
2022	REA	AA	22	2	0	1	23	0	30^{1}	9	0	5.0	16.0	54	31.8%	.205	0.86	1.48	72	0.8				
2022	LHV	AAA	22	3	3	2	22	0	20^{2}	24	1	12.2	7.0	16	47.1%	.343	2.52	9.58	147	-0.2				
2022	PHI	MLB	22	0	0	1	3	0	5	2	1	10.8	5.4	3	72.7%	.100	1.60	7.20	122	0.0	95.6	39.2%	26.1%	39.6%
2023 non-DC	*PHI*	*MLB*	*23*	*2*	*3*	*0*	*57*	*0*	*50*	*46*	*6*	*8.0*	*10.3*	*57*	*44.0%*	*.315*	*1.83*	*5.92*	*128*	*-0.5*	*95.6*	*39.2%*	*31.0%*	*39.6%*

Comparables: Arodys Vizcaíno (45), Phillippe Aumont (39), José Leclerc (39)

Morales got off to an incredible start in 2022, striking out nearly half the batters he faced in his first nine appearances. Then things fell apart. For the second straight season, his K/BB plummeted after a promotion to Triple-A, and it was evident his stuff still wasn't ready to play against more mature hitters. Thankfully, Morales has a killer fastball (as long as he can maintain his high velocity) and a nasty slider, and with a little more seasoning (and command), he should soon be ready to take on a role in a big-league bullpen. Which bullpen that will be is unclear, as he was designated for assignment to clear room for Craig Kimbrel.

Nick Nelson RHP
Born: 12/05/95 Age: 27 Bats: R Throws: R Height: 6'1" Weight: 205 lb. Origin: Round 4, 2016 Draft (#128 overall)

YEAR	TEAM	LVL	AGE	W	L	SV	G	GS	IP	H	HR	BB/9	K/9	K	GB%	BABIP	WHIP	ERA	DRA-	WARP	MPH	FB%	Whiff%	CSP
2020	NYY	MLB	24	1	0	0	11	0	20^2	20	4	4.8	7.8	18	55.7%	.281	1.50	4.79	96	0.2	96.5	57.2%	28.1%	44.2%
2021	SWB	AAA	25	3	4	1	29	5	52	50	6	5.0	10.7	62	54.5%	.324	1.52	3.81	84	1.2				
2021	NYY	MLB	25	0	2	0	11	2	14^1	15	0	10.0	13.8	22	35.1%	.405	2.16	8.79	106	0.1	96.6	53.8%	30.7%	52.9%
2022	PHI	MLB	26	3	2	1	47	2	68^2	66	1	4.7	9.0	69	39.1%	.332	1.49	4.85	95	0.9	96.3	51.1%	28.7%	54.7%
2023 DC	*PHI*	*MLB*	*27*	*2*	*2*	*0*	*43*	*0*	*38*	*38*	*4*	*5.1*	*9.3*	*39*	*42.8%*	*.321*	*1.57*	*4.98*	*116*	*-0.2*	*96.4*	*52.2%*	*28.8%*	*53.2%*

Comparables: José Ramirez (66), Josh Staumont (65), Yency Almonte (62)

The crossover in viewership between Major League Baseball and queer, British coming-of-age comedies surely isn't all that high. Still, for the niche group of fans who watch both *Heartstopper* and the Philadelphia Phillies, there are two Nick Nelsons to root for. And while the 27-year-old reliever doesn't have much in common with the teenage rugby captain discovering his own sexuality, the Phillies pitcher did experiment... with his slider in 2022, throwing it with increased velocity and frequency as the season went on. Nelson used the pitch to generate whiffs and weak contact, counterbalancing a rather hittable fastball and a changeup he struggled to locate consistently. For the first time in years, Phillies fans didn't feel their heart stop every time a long reliever entered the game.

Aaron Nola RHP
Born: 06/04/93 Age: 30 Bats: R Throws: R Height: 6'2" Weight: 200 lb. Origin: Round 1, 2014 Draft (#7 overall)

YEAR	TEAM	LVL	AGE	W	L	SV	G	GS	IP	H	HR	BB/9	K/9	K	GB%	BABIP	WHIP	ERA	DRA-	WARP	MPH	FB%	Whiff%	CSP
2020	PHI	MLB	27	5	5	0	12	12	71^1	54	9	2.9	12.1	96	48.8%	.283	1.08	3.28	57	2.3	92.6	46.0%	31.3%	43.5%
2021	PHI	MLB	28	9	9	0	32	32	180^2	165	26	1.9	11.1	223	40.8%	.310	1.13	4.63	74	4.2	92.8	53.2%	28.0%	53.0%
2022	PHI	MLB	29	11	13	0	32	32	205	168	19	1.3	10.3	235	43.1%	.291	0.96	3.25	70	5.1	92.8	52.3%	28.0%	55.4%
2023 DC	*PHI*	*MLB*	*30*	*13*	*8*	*0*	*29*	*29*	*195.3*	*165*	*21*	*1.9*	*9.4*	*204*	*43.4%*	*.284*	*1.06*	*2.55*	*70*	*4.6*	*92.8*	*51.3%*	*27.8%*	*52.5%*

Comparables: Juan Marichal (86), Kevin Appier (85), Justin Verlander (85)

Despite another top-five Cy Young finish and a World Series appearance, Nola remains one of the more underrated aces in baseball. A master of both quantity and quality, he leads the National League in innings pitched over the past six years, and he ranked among the top 10 NL starters in WARP all six seasons. He was in fine form once again in 2022, finishing with the best full-season DRA- of his career. One secret to his success was his four-seam fastball, which he improved upon by adding over 100 RPM in spin—a jump from the 37th to the 56th percentile on Baseball Savant. With a craftier heater to work with, Nola threw first-pitch strikes more than 70% of the time. That helped him limit his walks like never before, and as a result, he finished with the highest strikeout-to-walk ratio in Phillies franchise history. Nola enters his walk year in 2023, hoping for a season that finally does away with his "underrated" label once and for all.

★ ★ ★ *2023 Top 101 Prospect* **#12** ★ ★ ★

Andrew Painter RHP
Born: 04/10/03 Age: 20 Bats: R Throws: R Height: 6'7" Weight: 215 lb. Origin: Round 1, 2021 Draft (#13 overall)

YEAR	TEAM	LVL	AGE	W	L	SV	G	GS	IP	H	HR	BB/9	K/9	K	GB%	BABIP	WHIP	ERA	DRA-	WARP	MPH	FB%	Whiff%	CSP
2021	PHI	ROK	18	0	0	0	4	4	6	4	0	0.0	18.0	12	88.9%	.444	0.67	0.00						
2022	CLR	A	19	1	1	0	9	9	38^2	17	0	3.7	16.1	69	38.1%	.270	0.85	1.40	63	1.3	96.8	66.0%	38.9%	
2022	JS	A+	19	3	0	0	8	8	36^2	25	2	1.7	12.0	49	32.6%	.274	0.87	0.98	83	0.6				
2022	REA	AA	19	2	1	0	5	5	28^1	25	3	0.6	11.8	37	35.3%	.338	0.95	2.54	82	0.6				
2023 DC	*PHI*	*MLB*	*20*	*2*	*2*	*0*	*9*	*9*	*45.7*	*40*	*6*	*3.3*	*9.7*	*49*	*35.6%*	*.291*	*1.27*	*3.76*	*95*	*0.5*			*26.3%*	

Comparables: Francis Martes (71), Julio Teheran (71), Dylan Bundy (68)

Plenty of teenagers spend their summers painting houses or mowing lawns to earn some extra cash. The Phillies are lucky enough to have their own teenage Painter in-house, but they're hoping he spends his summer mowing down batters instead. The top prospect will be 19 years old when the season starts in April, and he's already gearing up to fight for his spot in the big-league rotation. If he makes the Opening Day roster, he'll be the youngest Phillies pitcher to debut in over 40 years. If he starts the year in the minors, he might be the best pitcher down there, and he won't be down for long. He still has room to grow, but he's already throwing a triple-digit heater alongside two plus breaking pitches, so he's well-equipped to do that growing in the majors. The only thing holding Painter back in 2023 will be an innings limit, seeing as he's still pretty new to this whole "professional baseball" thing. That's all the more reason not to waste his precious innings in minor-league games. The kid is ready for the biggest summer job of his life.

Cristopher Sánchez LHP
Born: 12/12/96 Age: 26 Bats: L Throws: L Height: 6'1" Weight: 165 lb. Origin: International Free Agent, 2013

YEAR	TEAM	LVL	AGE	W	L	SV	G	GS	IP	H	HR	BB/9	K/9	K	GB%	BABIP	WHIP	ERA	DRA-	WARP	MPH	FB%	Whiff%	CSP
2021	LHV	AAA	24	5	6	0	19	17	73	58	4	5.9	11.0	89	59.4%	.297	1.45	4.68	97	1.1				
2021	PHI	MLB	24	1	0	0	7	1	12^2	16	1	5.0	9.2	13	59.0%	.417	1.82	4.97	93	0.2	93.9	63.0%	23.8%	54.4%
2022	LHV	AAA	25	2	2	0	15	14	57^1	48	1	3.1	9.1	58	62.8%	.305	1.19	3.14	79	1.4	93.5	44.8%	16.0%	
2022	PHI	MLB	25	2	2	1	15	3	40	38	5	3.8	7.9	35	53.7%	.284	1.38	5.63	108	0.2	93.2	61.0%	19.2%	54.6%
2023 DC	*PHI*	*MLB*	*26*	*4*	*4*	*0*	*26*	*8*	*53.3*	*53*	*4*	*4.2*	*7.3*	*43*	*56.4%*	*.303*	*1.48*	*4.32*	*105*	*0.1*	*93.3*	*61.4%*	*22.3%*	*54.6%*

Comparables: Drew Anderson (60), Austin Gomber (59), Jose Alvarez (56)

Sánchez had a strong year at Triple-A but was inconsistent at the big-league level. He did, however, show promising signs of development, such as adding an extra two ticks on his slider and throwing it more confidently against right-handed hitters. The pitch still lacks horizontal movement, but it played regardless. He might want to consider mixing in his changeup a bit more often overall, as it netted him highest whiffs-per-swing rate. The biggest question facing Sánchez now is whether he'll continue to work as a starter or shift his focus to the bullpen. At 26 years old and entering his 10th year of professional ball, he may be running out of time to develop much further.

Gregory Soto LHP Born: 02/11/95 Age: 28 Bats: L Throws: L Height: 6'1" Weight: 234 lb. Origin: International Free Agent, 2012

YEAR	TEAM	LVL	AGE	W	L	SV	G	GS	IP	H	HR	BB/9	K/9	K	GB%	BABIP	WHIP	ERA	DRA-	WARP	MPH	FB%	Whiff%	CSP
2020	DET	MLB	25	0	1	2	27	0	23	16	2	5.1	11.3	29	53.7%	.269	1.26	4.30	81	0.5	97.4	79.7%	28.8%	48.4%
2021	DET	MLB	26	6	3	18	62	0	63^{2}	46	7	5.7	10.7	76	44.0%	.258	1.35	3.39	99	0.6	98.4	62.4%	31.3%	55.6%
2022	DET	MLB	27	2	11	30	64	0	60^{1}	49	2	5.1	9.0	60	47.5%	.296	1.38	3.28	104	0.4	98.6	77.6%	25.7%	54.0%
2023 DC	*PHI*	*MLB*	*28*	*2*	*2*	*10*	*50*	*0*	*43.3*	*40*	*4*	*5.2*	*9.4*	*45*	*46.6%*	*.305*	*1.51*	*4.42*	*108*	*0.0*	*98.1*	*71.7%*	*26.9%*	*53.8%*

Comparables: Jarlín García (66), Andrew Chafin (66), Robbie Ross Jr. (66)

As Soto's peripherals get worse, his role in the Tigers bullpen grows more prominent. He recorded 30 of the Tigers' 38 saves, converting all but three opportunities. He did so despite a significant plunge in his strikeout rate, driven by an alarming loss of movement on his slider. As if he knew the slider wasn't up to the job, Soto came out fastball-heavy and leaned on both of his heaters more often than the breaker. You'd hope that the walk rate would at least fall in tandem with the breaking ball usage, but the flamethrowing lefty maintained his career-long streak of walking more than five batters per nine. Even so, he still got the job done, partly by ensuring that almost all of the very loud contact against him was on the ground. If the slider doesn't return, it's hard to envision him repeating the trick. Then again, based on his trend lines, he'll walk as many as he strikes out while posting a 2.90 ERA and leading the league in saves. Does that last part seem likely after his acquisition by the Phillies in January? No—but what part of the journey here has seemed likely?

Matt Strahm LHP Born: 11/12/91 Age: 31 Bats: R Throws: L Height: 6'2" Weight: 190 lb. Origin: Round 21, 2012 Draft (#643 overall)

YEAR	TEAM	LVL	AGE	W	L	SV	G	GS	IP	H	HR	BB/9	K/9	K	GB%	BABIP	WHIP	ERA	DRA-	WARP	MPH	FB%	Whiff%	CSP
2020	SD	MLB	28	0	1	0	19	0	20^{2}	14	3	1.7	6.5	15	44.1%	.196	0.87	2.61	99	0.2	93.0	55.8%	22.1%	52.7%
2021	SD	MLB	29	0	1	0	6	1	6^{2}	15	0	1.4	5.4	4	45.2%	.500	2.40	8.10	105	0.0	93.3	56.6%	20.8%	57.5%
2022	BOS	MLB	30	4	4	4	50	0	44^{2}	38	5	3.4	10.5	52	37.0%	.289	1.23	3.83	92	0.6	94.4	53.0%	23.4%	57.8%
2023 DC	*PHI*	*MLB*	*31*	*2*	*2*	*0*	*50*	*0*	*43.3*	*39*	*5*	*2.7*	*8.4*	*40*	*39.2%*	*.285*	*1.22*	*3.65*	*94*	*0.3*	*93.3*	*49.1%*	*24.0%*	*56.3%*

Comparables: Jake Diekman (62), Sam Freeman (58), Xavier Cedeño (57)

Among the dozen Red Sox players who hit the injured list in July, Strahm was quietly one of their biggest losses. The wrist contusion that cost him a month of the season robbed Boston of their top left-handed reliever and one of the few members of their bullpen who could reliably get a strikeout. To make matters worse, Strahm wasn't close to the same pitcher upon his return, going from a 2.61 FIP before his injury to a 5.52 mark afterward. That marked a frustrating end to what had looked like one of Chaim Bloom's savvier signings, with Strahm showing more bat-missing ability than in years prior. He walked more batters, too, but his foundation for future success looks strong thanks to a four-seamer he now throws harder and with less drop. Though they're not so rare a commodity today as in years past, lefties with swing-and-miss stuff still don't grow on trees. That's why Philadelphia gave Strahm a two-year, $15 million deal despite his up-and-down stint with Boston.

Ranger Suárez LHP Born: 08/26/95 Age: 27 Bats: L Throws: L Height: 6'1" Weight: 217 lb. Origin: International Free Agent, 2012

YEAR	TEAM	LVL	AGE	W	L	SV	G	GS	IP	H	HR	BB/9	K/9	K	GB%	BABIP	WHIP	ERA	DRA-	WARP	MPH	FB%	Whiff%	CSP
2020	PHI	MLB	24	0	1	0	3	0	4	10	1	9.0	2.3	1	45.0%	.474	3.50	20.25	160	-0.1	91.4	60.6%	21.4%	38.8%
2021	PHI	MLB	25	8	5	4	39	12	106	73	4	2.8	9.1	107	58.2%	.259	1.00	1.36	85	1.8	93.3	68.2%	27.0%	50.8%
2022	PHI	MLB	26	10	7	0	29	29	155^{1}	149	15	3.4	7.5	129	55.2%	.294	1.33	3.65	117	0.1	92.7	66.9%	21.4%	49.8%
2023 DC	*PHI*	*MLB*	*27*	*9*	*9*	*0*	*27*	*27*	*154*	*156*	*15*	*3.3*	*7.8*	*134*	*55.0%*	*.310*	*1.38*	*3.93*	*99*	*1.1*	*92.9*	*66.5%*	*23.2%*	*49.7%*

Comparables: Felix Doubront (56), Patrick Corbin (55), Jeff Locke (55)

For the third straight season, Suárez got off to a slow start due to factors entirely outside of his control—COVID-19, then COVID-19-related visa problems, then lockout-related visa problems. Thus, he spent the first month of 2022 shaking off the rust. After that, however, he pitched as well as anyone could have reasonably expected. No, he didn't maintain his ridiculously low ERA from 2021, but he lived up to his PECOTA projections with a 3.48 ERA in 132 IP. The southpaw doesn't have overpowering strikeout stuff, but he induces softly hit grounders at an incredible rate. He also does a good job keeping the ball in the yard, since so many of the fly balls he allows are struck to the opposite field. Suárez has established himself as a viable mid-rotation starter, and his maturation gave the Phillies one fewer question mark in the offseason. Now, all they have to worry about is getting him to spring training on time.

Erich Uelmen RHP Born: 05/19/96 Age: 27 Bats: R Throws: R Height: 6'3" Weight: 195 lb. Origin: Round 4, 2017 Draft (#135 overall)

YEAR	TEAM	LVL	AGE	W	L	SV	G	GS	IP	H	HR	BB/9	K/9	K	GB%	BABIP	WHIP	ERA	DRA-	WARP	MPH	FB%	Whiff%	CSP
2021	TNS	AA	25	2	7	2	19	11	69^{2}	64	9	4.0	8.3	64	45.8%	.288	1.36	4.52	106	0.5				
2021	IOW	AAA	25	0	2	0	12	0	20^{2}	22	7	4.4	10.5	24	52.5%	.288	1.55	10.02	80	0.5				
2022	IOW	AAA	26	3	3	6	28	0	42	29	2	4.9	11.1	52	53.0%	.287	1.24	2.79	78	1.0				
2022	CHC	MLB	26	2	1	1	25	0	27	25	3	4.0	7.0	21	47.0%	.275	1.37	4.67	117	0.0	93.7	63.1%	27.7%	47.1%
2023 DC	*PHI*	*MLB*	*27*	*0*	*0*	*0*	*18*	*0*	*16*	*16*	*2*	*4.7*	*8.3*	*14*	*50.4%*	*.306*	*1.53*	*5.13*	*120*	*-0.1*	*93.7*	*63.1%*	*27.2%*	*47.1%*

Comparables: Pierce Johnson (68), Joel Payamps (67), Jared Hughes (65)

Part of a squad of pitchers who have "???" scribbled around their names in various Cubs reports, Uelmen was able to offer signs of success without outright embodying it. He came up throwing a sinker and keeping everything low in the zone, but ultimately in his rookie campaign he tossed a four-seamer and slider nearly as much—with varying degrees of effectiveness. Uelmen will continue to be studied as his role in the bullpen is sorted out, with much of the answer dependent on whether more strikeouts come.

Taijuan Walker RHP

Born: 08/13/92 Age: 30 Bats: R Throws: R Height: 6'4" Weight: 235 lb. Origin: Round 1, 2010 Draft (#43 overall)

YEAR	TEAM	LVL	AGE	W	L	SV	G	GS	IP	H	HR	BB/9	K/9	K	GB%	BABIP	WHIP	ERA	DRA-	WARP	MPH	FB%	Whiff%	CSP
2020	SEA	MLB	27	2	2	0	5	5	27	21	5	2.7	8.3	25	36.8%	.225	1.07	4.00	103	0.3	93.2	46.1%	20.0%	51.3%
2020	TOR	MLB	27	2	1	0	6	6	26[1]	22	3	3.8	8.5	25	39.5%	.260	1.25	1.37	108	0.2	93.3	54.1%	21.0%	46.7%
2021	NYM	MLB	28	7	11	0	30	29	159	133	26	3.1	8.3	146	41.9%	.254	1.18	4.47	96	1.8	94.4	57.1%	23.6%	56.7%
2022	NYM	MLB	29	12	5	0	29	29	157[1]	143	15	2.6	7.6	132	45.9%	.284	1.19	3.49	98	1.7	93.4	45.5%	23.5%	53.4%
2023 DC	*PHI*	*MLB*	*30*	*8*	*8*	*0*	*25*	*25*	*134.7*	*132*	*16*	*3.0*	*7.9*	*118*	*44.4%*	*.298*	*1.31*	*3.82*	*98*	*1.3*	*93.8*	*50.5%*	*23.2%*	*54.3%*

Comparables: Ramon Martinez (74), Pete Harnisch (74), Yovani Gallardo (74)

For the second season in a row, Walker threw more than 150 innings—something he hadn't done for quite some time prior to signing with the Mets. But for the second season in a row, he pitched much better in the first half than in the second half, showing signs of fatigue—like inconsistent velocity—down the stretch. The tacos Walker gave away to fans to benefit charity during the season may have been free, but 150 innings of league-average pitching is not. Walker rode a significant increase in splitter usage—the highest of his career and by far the most since 2019—to a strong year despite the late-season fade. The Mets did not extend Walker a qualifying offer, so the 30-year-old skipped town to the intra-division Phillies.

Zack Wheeler RHP

Born: 05/30/90 Age: 33 Bats: L Throws: R Height: 6'4" Weight: 195 lb. Origin: Round 1, 2009 Draft (#6 overall)

YEAR	TEAM	LVL	AGE	W	L	SV	G	GS	IP	H	HR	BB/9	K/9	K	GB%	BABIP	WHIP	ERA	DRA-	WARP	MPH	FB%	Whiff%	CSP
2020	PHI	MLB	30	4	2	0	11	11	71	67	3	2.0	6.7	53	56.1%	.308	1.17	2.92	81	1.5	97.0	65.7%	22.7%	49.0%
2021	PHI	MLB	31	14	10	0	32	32	213[1]	169	16	1.9	10.4	247	49.1%	.291	1.01	2.78	68	5.6	97.2	60.8%	26.7%	53.7%
2022	PHI	MLB	32	12	7	0	26	26	153	125	13	2.0	9.6	163	45.9%	.287	1.04	2.82	75	3.4	96.0	59.5%	25.2%	52.7%
2023 DC	*PHI*	*MLB*	*33*	*11*	*8*	*0*	*29*	*29*	*177.7*	*157*	*16*	*2.2*	*9.2*	*180*	*47.0%*	*.296*	*1.13*	*2.68*	*73*	*4.0*	*96.7*	*60.5%*	*25.0%*	*52.5%*

Comparables: Bob Welch (77), John Smoltz (76), Bob Gibson (76)

When the New York Mets made the World Series in 2015, an injured Wheeler asked for tickets so he could support his teammates from the stands. His request was denied, and he was told he'd have to pay for his own seats if he wanted to attend. Four years later, when he reached free agency, the Mets apparently showed no interest in bringing him back into the fold. Thus, like the true competitor he is, Wheeler has spent the past three seasons making his former team regret it all. He does just about everything well, racking up strikeouts, limiting walks, pitching deep into games, and inducing soft contact like no one else can. Various injuries limited him to 26 starts this past season, but he was overpowering as usual when he did take the mound. That dominance continued into the postseason, with a particularly remarkable showing in the NLCS. Needless to say, Wheeler didn't have to buy his own World Series tickets in 2022.

Lineouts

Hitters

HITTER	POS	TEAM	LVL	AGE	PA	R	2B	3B	HR	RBI	BB	K	SB	CS	AVG/OBP/SLG	DRC+	BABIP	BRR	DRP	WARP
William Bergolla	SS	DSL PHW	ROK	17	83	18	3	0	0	14	11	3	2	3	.380/.470/.423		.397			
Carlos De La Cruz	LF	JS	A+	22	241	29	10	1	10	24	19	75	5	2	.266/.344/.463	103	.362	0.7	1B(22): -0.6, LF(19): 0.6, RF(8): 0.3	0.8
	LF	REA	AA	22	162	21	12	1	7	23	8	45	1	0	.278/.315/.510	86	.347	-0.1	LF(14): 2.3, RF(12): 1.3, 1B(4): 0.3	0.6
Dalton Guthrie	OF	LHV	AAA	26	374	64	27	1	10	52	24	73	21	6	.302/.363/.476	106	.359	0.0	CF(59): -0.1, RF(25): 2.6, 2B(2): 0.1	2.4
	OF	PHI	MLB	26	28	3	0	0	1	5	6	7	1	0	.333/.500/.476	105	.462	0.0	RF(12): -0.1, 3B(1): 0	0.1
Scott Kingery	MI	LHV	AAA	28	366	51	14	4	7	34	54	108	18	2	.230/.348/.370	85	.330	-0.9	2B(48): 0.8, SS(39): -0.9	0.3
	MI	PHI	MLB	28	0	0	0	0	0	0	0	0	0	0	.000/.000/.000				2B(1): -0.0	
Yairo Munoz	3B	LHV	AAA	27	292	41	15	1	6	37	9	48	13	3	.310/.338/.437	103	.357	0.3	3B(25): 2.3, 2B(17): -1.4, SS(11): 0.2	1.2
	3B	PHI	MLB	27	60	7	2	0	3	7	3	10	1	0	.211/.250/.404	111	.205	0.3	2B(14): -0.2, 3B(8): -0.5, RF(2): 0.3	0.3
Símon Muzziotti	OF	REA	AA	23	165	23	5	4	5	20	19	31	7	3	.259/.339/.455	122	.291	0.7	CF(22): 2.3, LF(10): 0.2, RF(5): 1.2	1.5
	OF	PHI	MLB	23	9	0	0	0	0	0	0	2	0	0	.143/.250/.143	87	.200	-0.4	CF(8): 0	0.0
Josh Ockimey	1B	REA	AA	26	273	33	13	1	9	28	56	76	2	1	.253/.407/.447	111	.348	-0.3	1B(63): -1.2	0.9
	1B	LHV	AAA	26	210	30	8	1	8	27	28	58	1	0	.202/.314/.393	97	.246	-1.9	1B(40): -0.4	0.3
Jhailyn Ortiz	RF	REA	AA	23	505	67	25	2	17	61	43	165	9	2	.237/.319/.415	86	.332	4.5	RF(88): 0.9, CF(11): -0.5, LF(5): -0.2	1.3
Rickardo Perez	C	PHI	ROK	18	93	5	1	0	1	14	7	13	0	1	.349/.387/.398		.389			
Nikau Pouaka-Grego	SS	PHI	ROK	17	125	20	6	1	3	16	16	16	2	2	.301/.424/.466		.333			
Will Toffey	3B	LHV	AAA	27	388	48	23	4	9	37	48	121	9	2	.242/.350/.420	78	.354	-0.4	3B(82): 2.9, LF(10): -0.5, 1B(7): -0.5	0.4
Jordan Viars	DH	PHI	ROK	18	179	28	6	1	2	20	17	40	5	0	.240/.330/.331		.304			
	DH	CLR	A	18	28	2	0	0	0	3	2	9	0	0	.208/.286/.208	91	.313	-0.7	LF(1): -0.4	-0.1
Ethan Wilson	OF	JS	A+	22	458	39	20	2	7	45	28	93	25	7	.238/.290/.344	95	.288	0.9	RF(88): -1.5, CF(5): -0.0, LF(4): -0.5	1.3
	OF	REA	AA	22	78	7	2	0	1	3	5	21	1	2	.214/.286/.286	87	.292	-0.3	LF(14): -0.8, RF(1): -0.1	0.0

William Bergolla Jr. was the gem of the 2022 international signing period for the Phillies. A strong contact hitter with good plate discipline and promise at shortstop, he performed well in his first exposure to pro ball. ⚾ **Carlos De La Cruz** has real power in his bat, but he actually needs to hit the ball for that power to have any effect. If his 2022 season is any indication, he's finally starting to figure that out. ⚾ **Dalton Guthrie** made the Phillies' postseason roster as a defensive replacement/last bat off the bench. That's probably his ceiling as a major leaguer, too. ⚾ The only thing **Scott Kingery** has going for him nowadays is that he's endlessly DFA-able, thanks to the guaranteed millions remaining on his contract. Thus, he could get a major-league call-up even if his Triple-A performance hardly warrants one. It's one of those ultra-rare situations in which having money can help a person achieve something they didn't earn. ⚾ **Yairo Munoz** has worn a lot of red in his career, going from the Cardinals to the Red Sox to the Phillies. Unfortunately, the scarlet on his uniforms hasn't translated to his percentiles on Baseball Savant. He hits like a utility infielder but lacks the high-end defensive skill set such a role requires. ⚾ The scouting report on **Símon Muzziotti** has long been the same: he's a talented center fielder, but his bat needs at least a little pop. In 2022, he put up career-best power numbers, including more home runs than he hit in his first five seasons combined. It's not much, but for Muzziotti, it might be enough. ⚾ **Josh Ockimey** showed promising plate discipline throughout his first year in the Phillies system. If he were a little younger, or if he wasn't limited to first base, his season might have garnered more positive attention. ⚾ **Jhailyn Ortiz** took one step forward and two steps back in 2022. The potential has always been there, but now it's time for him to hit or get off the pot. ⚾ **Rickardo Perez** is still learning to balance his contact skills with his plate discipline, but he has what it takes to be above-average in both areas—with a little power to boot. The next step in his development will be working up to catching a full season after he spent much of 2022 recovering from injury. ⚾ New Zealand-born infielder **Nikau Pouaka-Grego** displayed sound contact skills, excellent plate discipline, and more than a bit of pop in his first pro season, all the more impressive considering he was only 17 years old. ⚾ Growing up in Scotland, **Gabriel Rincones Jr.** didn't have many opportunities to play organized baseball. Nevertheless, he developed into a strong power hitter after moving stateside for high school, and rumor has it he can hit the ball (500 miles). ⚾ Unlike his namesake candy, **Will Toffey** just hasn't been able to stick. The utility man was drafted three times before finally signing in Oakland, and he's been traded three times in the five years since. ⚾ A 2021 third-rounder, **Jordan Viars** was young for his draft class, debuting as a professional at only 17 years old and making quite a splash while doing so. Last year was more of a ripple, statistically, but he retains his youth, bat speed and significant power potential, at least for the moment.

⚾ **Ethan Wilson** struggled at the plate again in his second minor-league season, hitting for even less power than he did the year before. That's not going to cut it for a corner outfielder who was drafted for his hit tool and slugging potential.

Pitchers

PITCHER	TEAM	LVL	AGE	W	L	SV	G	GS	IP	H	HR	BB/9	K/9	K	GB%	BABIP	WHIP	ERA	DRA-	WARP	MPH	FB%	WHF	CSP
Mark Appel	LHV	AAA	30	6	0	5	31	0	40	33	4	3.8	8.1	36	44.6%	.269	1.25	3.15	103	0.5				
	PHI	MLB	30	0	0	0	6	0	10^{1}	9	0	2.6	4.4	5	53.1%	.281	1.16	1.74	113	0.0	95.1	75.2%	21.1%	52.5%
Andrew Baker	JS	A+	22	3	1	0	40	0	43^{2}	41	5	4.9	12.6	61	51.8%	.336	1.49	4.74	92	0.5				
	REA	AA	22	1	0	0	6	0	10^{2}	3	0	4.2	9.3	11	28.6%	.143	0.75	0.84	97	0.2				
Kent Emanuel	CLR	A	30	0	0	0	2	2	6	4	0	1.5	9.0	6	60.0%	.267	0.83	0.00	93	0.1	89.1	45.3%	30.8%	
	LHV	AAA	30	2	2	0	10	10	49^{1}	47	4	1.1	8.0	44	51.7%	.305	1.07	2.37	91	0.9	89.6	43.9%	20.0%	
Damon Jones	PHI	MLB	27	0	0	0	4	0	4^{2}	4	0	9.6	9.6	5	38.5%	.308	1.93	9.64	105	0.0	93.2	62.9%	34.1%	45.1%
James McArthur	REA	AA	25	2	6	0	13	13	57	66	10	4.1	10.3	65	43.6%	.361	1.61	5.05	100	0.8				
Alex McFarlane	CLR	A	21	0	3	0	3	3	8	12	1	3.4	13.5	12	71.4%	.550	1.88	9.00	82	0.2	96.0	39.7%	32.1%	
Erik Miller	REA	AA	24	1	0	0	22	7	36^{1}	25	0	4.2	10.9	44	38.6%	.301	1.16	2.23	79	0.9				
	LHV	AAA	24	0	1	0	10	0	12	14	4	10.5	13.5	18	25.0%	.357	2.33	7.50	103	0.1				
Vinny Nittoli	BUF	AAA	31	0	0	2	10	0	9^{2}	6	0	0.9	14.0	15	35.0%	.300	0.72	2.79	82	0.2				
	SWB	AAA	31	4	1	0	22	4	36^{2}	26	5	3.2	10.8	44	40.9%	.256	1.06	3.44	86	0.8				
	LHV	AAA	31	0	0	0	5	0	5^{2}	8	2	0.0	7.9	5	21.1%	.353	1.41	7.94	96	0.1				
	PHI	MLB	31	0	0	0	2	0	2	0	0	4.5	4.5	1	60.0%	.000	0.50	0.00	108	0.0	92.4	30.0%	25.0%	55.2%
Luis Ortiz	SAC	AAA	26	4	3	2	35	4	67^{1}	68	8	1.7	9.6	72	42.1%	.324	1.20	4.54	80	1.2	94.7	50.4%	24.7%	
	SF	MLB	26	0	0	0	6	0	8^{2}	5	0	3.1	6.2	6	41.7%	.208	0.92	1.04	112	0.0	94.5	49.2%	27.1%	49.4%
Michael Plassmeyer	SAC	AAA	25	0	6	0	11	10	46^{1}	50	15	4.7	9.1	47	37.1%	.299	1.60	7.38	137	-0.8	90.5	43.4%	31.5%	
	LHV	AAA	25	6	3	0	16	16	82	63	12	2.5	9.0	82	36.9%	.249	1.05	2.41	89	1.6	90.1	56.8%	24.0%	
	PHI	MLB	25	0	1	0	2	0	7^{1}	9	1	1.2	8.6	7	47.6%	.400	1.36	3.68	114	0.0	89.1	57.6%	30.6%	54.8%
Tayler Scott	ELP	AAA	30	2	1	3	33	0	40^{2}	41	5	2.4	11.5	52	42.1%	.353	1.28	3.76	76	0.8	93.8	48.8%	35.1%	
	SD	MLB	30	0	1	0	8	0	12	19	1	4.5	9.8	13	47.5%	.462	2.08	6.75	100	0.1	93.6	42.0%	30.1%	50.5%
Noah Skirrow	REA	AA	23	5	8	0	21	21	98^{2}	107	10	2.9	10.5	115	35.2%	.358	1.41	4.65	108	0.9				
	LHV	AAA	23	0	1	0	4	4	21	14	3	3.9	7.7	18	43.6%	.212	1.10	3.00	106	0.2				
Andrew Vasquez	BUF	AAA	28	2	0	1	10	0	11	3	0	1.6	12.3	15	66.7%	.143	0.45	2.45	80	0.3				
	SAC	AAA	28	5	0	1	14	0	16^{1}	13	1	2.8	12.7	23	27.8%	.343	1.10	2.20	90	0.2	88.5	25.5%	29.6%	
	SF	MLB	28	0	0	0	1	0	2	0	0	4.5	18.0	4	50.0%	.000	0.50	0.00	104	0.0	87.6	11.4%	22.2%	55.2%
	TOR	MLB	28	0	0	0	9	0	6^{2}	6	1	4.1	8.1	6	50.0%	.263	1.35	8.10	108	0.0	88.4	33.9%	31.0%	51.1%

Finally reaching the majors at 30 years old, **Mark Appel** was a feel-good story of the 2022 season, as he became the oldest first-overall pick to make his MLB debut. Whatever else he achieves from here on out is icing on the cake. **Andrew Baker** lives in the shadow of another similarly named Phillies right-hander from the 2021 Draft. While he lacks the prospect pedigree of his fellow Andrew, he has proven himself to be nearly as much of a strikeout artist as the Painter himself. **Kent Emanuel** has been dealing with injuries for the past two years and hasn't made an MLB appearance since his brief debut in May 2021. Even if he gets healthy, the odds are stacked against him as a soft-tossing 31-year-old rookie. The ship is starting to sail on **Damon Jones**. He's been treading water at Triple-A for a few years, and he lost most of the 2022 season to shoulder surgery. The southpaw needs to shore up his control, or it won't be long before the clubhouse crew is cleaning out Damon Jones' locker. It doesn't take a genius to figure out **James McArthur** was granting too many walks and hits in 2022. The season represented a step backward for the right-hander, even before an elbow injury ended his year in June. **Alex McFarlane** displayed dominant strikeout stuff in his first taste of pro ball. The 2022 fourth-round pick transitioned to the bullpen in college, but with his intriguing slider/changeup combo and a mid-90s fastball, the Phillies think he has what it takes to make it as a starting pitcher. **Erik Miller** is a strong candidate to transition to a full-time bullpen role, given that he's been in the Phillies organization for four years and has yet to throw even 50 innings in a single season. In 2021, seven years after signing his first professional contract, **Vinny Nittoli** finally made his big-league debut, pitching a single inning for the Mariners. He doubled that total with the Phillies in 2022, so at this rate, he can hope to qualify for the ERA title in time for his 39th birthday. Not the Pirates rookie who debuted this past season throwing 100+, **Luis F. Ortiz**'s most recent stop was as minor-league depth for the Giants in 2022; he wound up making six appearances for the beleaguered San Francisco bullpen, and the Phillies decided they'd seen enough (read: his two remaining options) to claim him on waivers. A soft-throwing left-handed starter without a dependable secondary pitch, **Michael Plassmeyer** needs to throw strikes to succeed. While he had trouble with his control early in 2022, he began to figure things out after a midseason trade to Philadelphia. The first South African-born pitcher in MLB history, **Tayler Scott** has piled up plenty of frequent flyer miles in his career, pitching for seven MLB organizations, with some time in the NPB as well. He was picked up off waivers by the Phillies in September. An undrafted free agent from the class of 2020, **Noah Skirrow** scurried into view with a strong performance in 2022. He upped his strikeout rate while cutting back on the walks, eventually earning an end-of-season call-up to Triple-A. **Andrew Vasquez** is a good reminder that, unless you're Mariano Rivera, one special pitch does not a big leaguer make. The Giants became the latest team to attempt to give his overwhelming curveball a solid supporting cast, and the latest to fail. Philadelphia will take the next turn.

WASHINGTON NATIONALS

Essay by Jarrett Seidler

Player comments by Daniel R. Epstein and BP staff

When Juan Soto took the field for the 2022 Home Run Derby, he knew it was likely the last time he'd don a Nationals jersey on the national stage. Two days earlier, Ken Rosenthal reported Washington's extension negotiations with Soto had broken down. The team's final offer—15 years, $440 million—would have been the largest contract in MLB history by total guarantee, but only the 20th-highest in average annual value, a pittance for the entire prime of one of the game's best hitters. Despite longtime Nationals general manager Mike Rizzo's repeated vows earlier in the spring and summer that he would not trade Soto, the 23-year-old superstar was now very, very publicly on the trade block over two years before his free agency.

Soto told the media that afternoon that he was "really uncomfortable" with the series of events. Then he went out and hit 53 homers in a wildly entertaining Derby, ousting retiring legend Albert Pujols in the semifinals and besting rookie sensation Julio Rodríguez in the finals. A jubilant Soto dropped to one knee upon his victory and launched his bat as high in the air as he could, then held a dance party on the field. It was without a doubt the best moment for the Nationals since their 2019 World Series win, the face of the franchise winning a marquee showcase in great style. How could you not want more of that? How could you decide your team is better off without Soto than with him?

Fifteen days later, Juan Soto was traded to the San Diego Padres.

⚾ ⚾ ⚾

The Soto trade was the end of a long collapse of process for the Nationals, not the beginning. For years, they've just been picking the wrong players.

Rizzo is a scout's scout. It's literally in his blood; his late father Phil was an inaugural member of the Professional Baseball Scouts Hall of Fame. And when the younger Rizzo took over control of the Nationals' baseball operations before the 2009 season, his scouting-above-all mindset was squarely in line with player acquisition orthodoxy, perhaps even a little ahead of the curve. Early on in his tenure, it seemed like they couldn't miss on high draft picks, with a

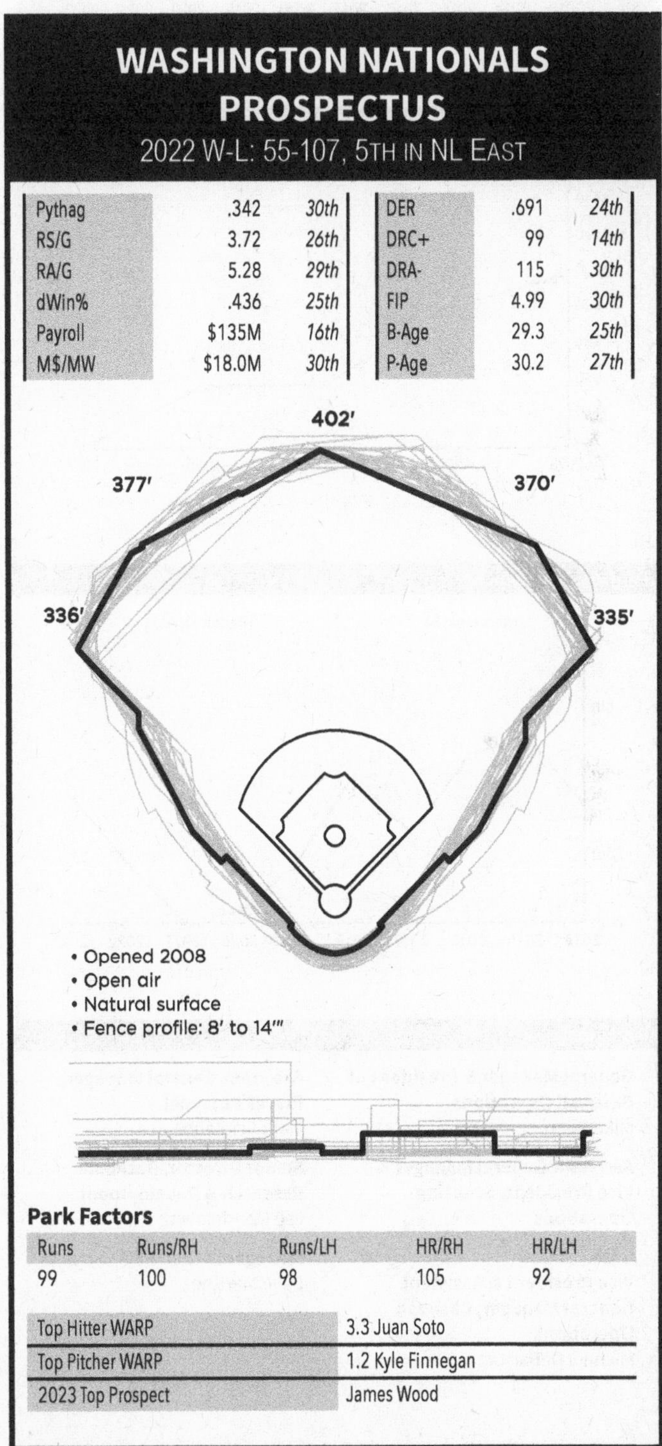

WASHINGTON NATIONALS PROSPECTUS

2022 W-L: 55-107, 5TH IN NL EAST

Pythag	.342	30th	DER	.691	24th
RS/G	3.72	26th	DRC+	99	14th
RA/G	5.28	29th	DRA-	115	30th
dWin%	.436	25th	FIP	4.99	30th
Payroll	$135M	16th	B-Age	29.3	25th
M$/MW	$18.0M	30th	P-Age	30.2	27th

- Opened 2008
- Open air
- Natural surface
- Fence profile: 8' to 14'"

Park Factors

Runs	Runs/RH	Runs/LH	HR/RH	HR/LH
99	100	98	105	92

Top Hitter WARP	3.3 Juan Soto
Top Pitcher WARP	1.2 Kyle Finnegan
2023 Top Prospect	James Wood

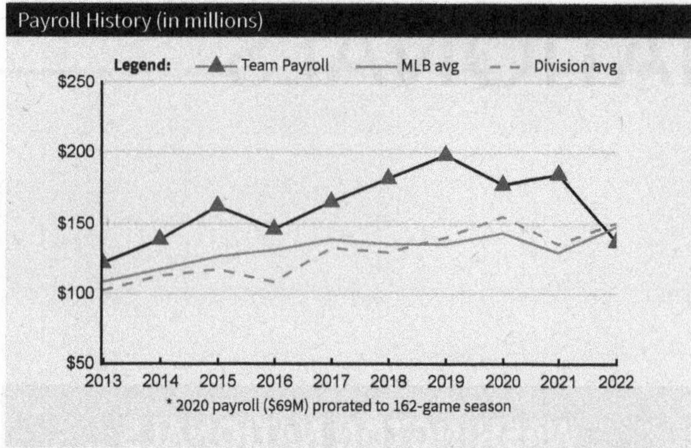

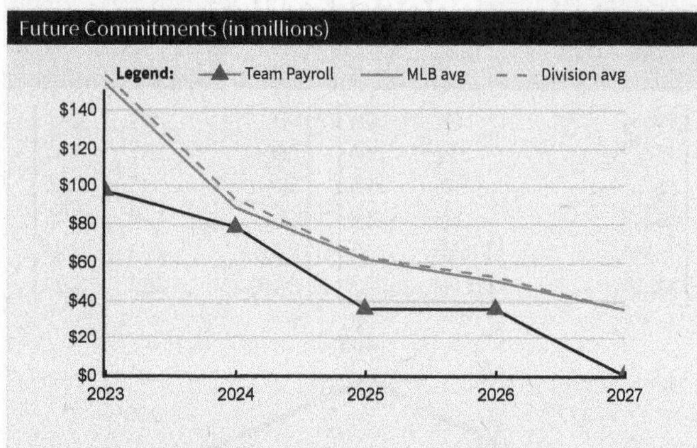

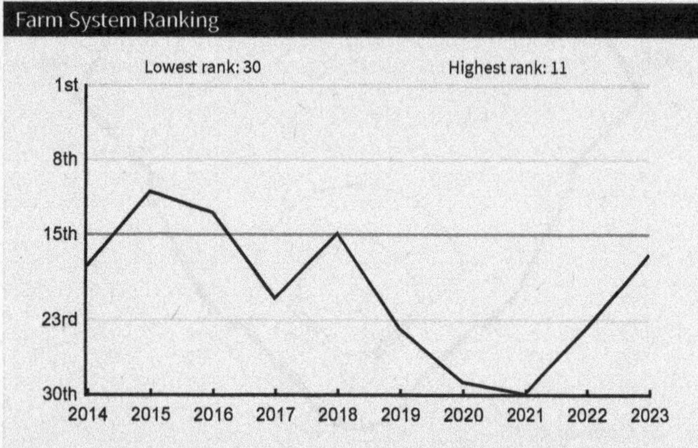

Personnel

General Manager & President of Baseball Operations
Mike Rizzo

Assistant General Manager & Vice President, Scouting Operations
Kris Kline

Vice President & Assistant General Manager, Baseball Operations
Michael DeBartolo

Assistant General Manager, Player Personel
Mark Scialabba

Senior Director, Baseball Research & Development
Lee Mendelowitz

Manager
Dave Martinez

particular knack for getting top talent with signability concerns like Anthony Rendon and Lucas Giolito to fall to them on the board.

But over the last 14 years, the times have changed, while Rizzo has largely stayed the same. Analytics are now embedded in every facet of player acquisition and development across the industry. Washington does use them to a degree, but over time, the Nats have leaned on traditional eyeball scouting more than most—if not all—other organizations. They have very good eyeball scouts, to be sure, but that just is not enough to keep up with the Joneses anymore.

In recent times, the Nationals have systematically overvalued hitters who look good by traditional scouting methods—sweet-looking swings, nice shows of power in batting practice, old-school notions of physical projectability—while ignoring glaring flaws exposed by analytics—poor in-zone contact rates, low exit velocities, high chase rates. Last year, they drafted Elijah Green with the fifth overall pick despite near-historic swing-and-miss concerns; in 2021, they popped Brady House, who struck out almost five times as much as he walked at Low-A. They've been similarly myopic on the pitching side, consistently acquiring pitchers who throw hard but don't get whiffs on their fastballs and have major durability question marks. Before House, they selected four straight pitchers in the first round—Cade Cavalli, Jackson Rutledge, Mason Denaburg and Seth Romero—who threw hard, couldn't get whiffs and got hurt.

As their drafts got worse and worse over the last decade, the Nationals' farm system quickly degraded. They have paired poor drafting with poor player development; there just haven't been success stories of hitters unlocking power from a new swing path or pitchers learning great sweepers to pile up more whiffs. They ranked as a bottom-seven farm system in every season from 2019-22, and that *overstates* what they've gotten out of the minors since Soto graduated. Other than Soto, the last Nationals draft pick or international signee who was a solid regular for the team was Rendon—drafted in 2011.

Nevertheless, Rizzo's keen eye for veteran talent in trades and free agency kept a contending ship afloat for years, and Soto's ascension as a teenage superstar in 2018 looked to extend things indefinitely. Entering 2020, the defending champions were not only looking like one of the best teams in the National League but seemed reasonably well positioned for long-term contention. PECOTA projected Washington as the favorites to win the NL East behind a core of Soto (under team control through 2024), budding superstar shortstop Trea Turner (under team control through 2022) and longtime veteran ace Max Scherzer (signed through 2021). Rendon left as a free agent that offseason, but top prospect Carter Kieboom stood waiting in the wings to seize the third base job. It looked like good times were here to stay in the Navy Yard.

Few things went right in the pandemic-shortened 60-game schedule. Sure, Soto led the league in batting average, OBP and slugging percentage as a 21-year-old, and Turner hit .335; they finished fifth and seventh in MVP voting, respectively. But Scherzer had a down year amidst a host of other injuries and underperformances. They missed a 16-team playoff format by three games.

Rizzo ran it back again in 2021, adding sluggers Kyle Schwarber and Josh Bell to the mix. Entering July, they were right in the middle of the pennant chase, only 2.5 games out of the division lead, and 2020 looked like it might be a blip. Then they skidded out of contention with a pair of five-game losing streaks, and moved to a seller's posture at the deadline.

Trading Scherzer as a rental to bolster a weak farm was a logical move. In a far less logical move, Rizzo sweetened his Scherzer trade with the Dodgers by adding Turner, netting top prospects Keibert Ruiz and Josiah Gray. Combined with a weak farm, moving on from Turner made a Soto trade a virtual inevitability. Without Turner or significant outside spending, Washington simply didn't have enough good players or prospects to compete by 2024—and the Lerner family no longer showed interest in huge free agent deals.

Were the prospects coming back from the Dodgers worth all this trouble? It's early, but signs are pointing toward no. Ruiz is settling in as a decent starting catcher, albeit one who chases outside the zone a ton and doesn't hit the ball very hard yet. Despite plus velocity, Gray's fastball was one of the single worst pitches in the majors last year, and he's going to need improvements in pitch design and usage—things that the Nationals have heretofore proven unable to teach. They're useful players, but neither looks like a future star worth giving up on a contention cycle for.

⚾ ⚾ ⚾

Four years before moving on from Soto, the Nationals were faced with another monumental decision on a face-of-the-franchise outfielder, Bryce Harper. Rizzo almost traded him to the Astros at the 2018 trade deadline for a package of prospects who ultimately didn't amount to much, but ownership stepped in and blocked the trade.

How can you trade Bryce Harper? He presented the same problem, or the same opportunity perceived as a problem, as Soto. Washington tried to extend him instead, ultimately offering a 10-year, $300 million contract that September, but Harper rejected the deal because it had too much deferred money. So the Nationals moved on, choosing to spend much of their Harper budget on Patrick Corbin instead. Flags do fly forever, and one must consider that Corbin was a down-ballot Cy Young candidate and World Series hero in 2019. But he's been one of the worst pitchers in the majors since, while Harper continued to be one of the best hitters in baseball in Philadelphia. It's conceivable that Harper alone would've extended Washington's contention cycle through Soto's prime.

Meanwhile, the Nationals had one of the top prospects in baseball to replace Harper in the outfield. Not Soto, who was already established by then, but Victor Robles, who had recently been the second-best prospect in the entire minors.

The late-2010s were a time of great change in the valuation and development of hitting prospects. Exit velocities and zone-contact percentages have since become a standard part of public player evaluation, but MLB didn't even collect this sort of data in the majors in an organized, encompassing fashion until 2015. It would be a couple more years before Trackman units were fully adopted in the minors and data was freely shared around the industry, and a couple more years after that before public side analysis truly reflected what teams had learned: that it's pretty important to hit the ball hard and make a lot of contact swinging at hittable strikes.

Robles' power was consistently scouted as the weakest of his five tools, with fringe-average to average potential. He was a top prospect regardless because scouts graded him with a plus or plus-plus hit tool and Gold Glove-caliber defense in center field. He came up for good in September 2018, and from then until the end of the 2019 season he slugged .430 with 20 home runs in 683 plate appearances.

Underlying the adequate topline production was an implosion in Robles' hard-hit data. His average exit velocity dropped from 87.7 mph in 2017 to 83.3 mph in 2019, edging out only the historically punchless Billy Hamilton. Robles tried to bulk up before the 2020 season to hit the ball harder, and his batted ball metrics went further in the opposite direction. Entering 2023, Robles has now put up four consecutive seasons of bottom-five average exit velocities and three consecutive seasons of pitiful offensive performance. His vaunted plus-plus hit tool as a prospect has produced a .233 career average.

Replacing Rendon with Kieboom has gone even worse; at least Robles plays a great center. Kieboom has battled a bunch of injuries—he missed all of 2022 after undergoing Tommy John surgery—but when he's been on the field he's been absolutely terrible both at the plate and with the glove. He can't hit a major-league breaking ball to save his life, and his exit velocities have been nearly as poor as Robles'. His hit tool was supposed to carry his offensive game, and instead he's been under the Mendoza Line so far.

So you might think that when choosing the prospects for the Soto trade—a trade in which Rizzo could've selected the best prospects from half the teams in baseball even before throwing in Bell, one of the top rental bats on the market—the Nationals would've learned some lessons about swing decisions, in-zone contact and batted ball data, right?

Well, they really didn't.

The Nats did grab one prospect with unquestionably huge hitting potential in James Wood, San Diego's 2021 second-rounder. The long levers on his 6-foot-7 frame belie above-average contact skills. He blends that contact ability with good swing decisions, and his batted ball data is stellar.

That's the basic framework for a top global hitting prospect—unlike any Washington has developed since Soto—and, indeed, Wood is already the no. 3 prospect in the game. So at least at the top, the Nationals actually did get the right guy back.

The rest of the return...well, it has a lot of familiar-sounding beats that don't bode well for the future. Let's start out with CJ Abrams, a former top-10 global prospect. Like Robles and Kieboom, he projected for a plus-or-better hit tool from a traditional scouting perspective. His exit velocities have been a concern dating back to high school—if you ever see a phrase like "projects for gap power" in a scouting report, that's not a positive—and, sure enough, his hit tool collapsed in the majors as a rookie last year. His already-suspect swing decisions completely fell to pieces too, leading to a chase rate north of 40%, and other than speed and old scouting reports it's hard to find much to like in his offensive profile.

They also got Robert Hassell III, the eighth pick in the 2020 Draft and the no. 26 prospect entering 2022. Hassell has one of those sweet, smooth lefty swings that is guaranteed to make every scout in attendance swoon and project a plus-plus hit tool. But similar to Abrams, he doesn't do anything tangible to actually produce a plus-plus hit tool. He doesn't hit the ball hard, and he makes only an average amount of contact with average swing decisions for his age. His slugging percentage in both High-A and Double-A after the trade started with a two, and his prospect stock is already tanking.

The pitching side of the deal also played to recent form. MacKenzie Gore was the best pitching prospect in the game three years ago before he stopped throwing strikes. He found the plate enough in 2022 to be minimally effective in the majors—although his mid-90s fastball no longer fools anyone—and got included in this trade, right after he bled velocity and ended up on the IL for elbow inflammation. Jarlin Susana is probably the hardest-throwing teenager on the planet, which sounds great except that almost all of the previous hardest-throwing teenagers on the planet didn't turn into productive major leaguers. Will he be the exception? We'll find out some time in the mid-to-late 2020s.

Somehow, Washington made the Soto deal without getting Maryland native Jackson Merrill, San Diego's 2021 first-rounder. Merrill popped up very late in the 2021 draft cycle, going from off the board to the 27th-overall pick in just a couple months, and he's continued on a meteoric rise since then. His swing is not as aesthetically pleasing as Hassell, but he combines great feel for contact with great exit velocities and above-average swing decisions. Basically, he does all of the things Hassell and Abrams don't do. He's a top-15 prospect in the game, and would've been within a stone's throw of Wood to be the top piece in the deal—except he wasn't in it.

⚾ ⚾ ⚾

So how do the Nationals fix their broken development wheel?

The Lerners announced last year that they're exploring selling the team. The easy path is finding some decabillionaire who wants to run a $300 million payroll to turn things around quickly while simultaneously dumping many millions more into developing the superstars of the 2030s. But Jeff Bezos seems more interested in the NFL at the moment.

A more plausible positive trajectory sits an hour-and-a-half north on the Acela train. It wasn't so long ago that the Philadelphia Phillies were right about where Washington is right now. Their major-league club bottomed out pretty hard in the mid-2010s, with a five-year run of 63- to 73-win teams. Worse, they clearly had no idea how to evaluate or develop batters, blowing three consecutive top-10 picks on hitters who couldn't hit, including 2016's first-overall pick, Mickey Moniak. As late as the 2013-14 offseason, their entire analytics department consisted of a part-time extern on loan from the league office.

Eventually, the Phillies realized they had a major problem and made extensive personnel and philosophy changes from top to bottom, culminating with hiring Dave Dombrowski to head their baseball operations two years ago. Dombrowski is just as rooted in old-school team-building as Rizzo, with almost 35 years of experience leading franchises and a longstanding reputation for contention at all costs. But in recent years he's blended his priors with more modern stances, including elevating Sam Fuld, whose expertise lies in analytics and sports science, as his general manager. Their investments in analytics, scouting and player development have led to modest improvements in hitting development outcomes—no superstars yet, though Alec Bohm and Bryson Stott are useful regulars—and they've gotten quite good at unearthing and nurturing young pitchers. To cover that they're still not that great at developing bats, they've aggressively acquired star position players on the open market, including Washington's own departed cornerstones Bryce Harper and Trea Turner.

The Nats can get on that track, if they want to. They've finally started staffing up in analytics, player development and sports science—18 new positions for 2023, per Jesse Dougherty of *The Washington Post*. As in Philadelphia, admitting you're deficient and hiring new faces is the first sign of progress. They landed the second pick in a loaded 2023 Draft, which should provide another near-term boon to the farm. Unlike their last rebuild, they won't get to take slam dunk prospects like Stephen Strasburg and Harper in consecutive years—the new draft lottery and other anti-tanking provisions in the CBA loom large—but they should be able to nab someone to pair with Wood at the top of the farm system.

Having better analytics and smarter people in the lower ranks of the organization is a low bar to clear, which augurs well for the potential quickness of the fix. But those changes won't be enough on their own. The Nationals need more than adjustments at the periphery, an addition to the roster of folks making suggestions. They need a leader who will listen to what they say and, crucially, let it overrule what he and his scouts see. Rizzo must start melding his traditionalist's mindset with today's evaluation and development methods—or whoever ends up owning the team has to replace him with someone who will.

—Jarrett Seidler is an author of Baseball Prospectus.

HITTERS

CJ Abrams SS Born: 10/03/00 Age: 22 Bats: L Throws: R Height: 6'2" Weight: 185 lb. Origin: Round 1, 2019 Draft (#6 overall)

YEAR	TEAM	LVL	AGE	PA	R	2B	3B	HR	RBI	BB	K	SB	CS	Whiff%	AVG/OBP/SLG	DRC+	BABIP	BRR	DRP	WARP
2021	SA	AA	20	183	26	14	0	2	23	15	36	13	2		.296/.363/.420	104	.365	2.7	SS(33): -0.6, 2B(6): -0.5	0.8
2022	ELP	AAA	21	151	35	4	1	7	28	8	25	10	3	25.1%	.314/.364/.507	107	.343	1.3	SS(26): -0.6, 2B(2): 0.2, CF(2): 0.3	0.4
2022	ROC	AAA	21	35	7	2	0	0	2	2	8	4	1		.290/.343/.355	92	.375	0.1	SS(8): -0.5	0.1
2022	SD	MLB	21	139	16	5	0	2	11	4	27	1	2	25.3%	.232/.285/.320	84	.276	0.5	SS(32): -2.2, 2B(13): -0.6, RF(3): -0.1	-0.1
2022	WAS	MLB	21	163	17	7	2	0	10	1	23	6	2	20.3%	.258/.276/.327	81	.301	-2.0	SS(43): -1.3	-0.2
2023 DC	*WAS*	*MLB*	*22*	*534*	*48*	*20*	*3*	*9*	*45*	*22*	*99*	*23*	*6*	*23.4%*	*.258/.304/.366*	*87*	*.307*	*7.1*	*SS 2*	*1.6*

Comparables: Luis Sardinas (66), José Ramírez (65), Ketel Marte (64)

When listening to a podcast on 2x speed, sometimes you miss something important and need to rewind. Obviously, Abrams' rookie season didn't go according to plan, but prior to *THE TRADE*, San Diego had his development on fast-forward. He'd only played 76 games in his entire minor-league career before the Padres named him to their Opening Day roster. In retrospect, this hindered his growth—a 1.7% walk rate with no real power doesn't cut the mustard.

Abrams' upside remains real, but so too do his warts. As such, there seem to be three possible futures we can glean from the infinite.

—In the kindest one, Abrams' hit tool makes a long-anticipated jump to elite levels, and he converts some of his raw pop into game power. His potent bat and outstanding speed and defense make him the preeminent leadoff hitter of his generation.

—In the cruelest timeline, Abrams posts sub-.300 OBPs and fades to black in his late 20s after a few disappointing seasons, receding into history as little more than a footnote in Juan Soto's legend. Of course, no one will remember this the next time a team wants to trade a generational talent for some prospects.

—In the most boring and therefore likely future, Abrams' stellar defense helps make up for a bat that never quite comes around. He's the shortstop version of Victor Robles, basically—a useful player in aggregate, but one who never reaches the heights once promised. But hey, if you're looking to be optimistic, the future hasn't been very boring as of late.

Riley Adams C Born: 06/26/96 Age: 27 Bats: R Throws: R Height: 6'4" Weight: 249 lb. Origin: Round 3, 2017 Draft (#99 overall)

YEAR	TEAM	LVL	AGE	PA	R	2B	3B	HR	RBI	BB	K	SB	CS	Whiff%	AVG/OBP/SLG	DRC+	BABIP	BRR	DRP	WARP
2021	BUF	AAA	25	143	20	6	1	7	17	16	46	0	0		.239/.371/.487	101	.323	-0.6	C(25): -0.8	0.4
2021	WAS	MLB	25	90	11	6	1	2	10	13	28	0	0	25.7%	.268/.422/.465	90	.415	1.5	C(23): -4.8	-0.1
2021	TOR	MLB	25	30	2	2	0	0	0	2	12	0	0	40.4%	.107/.167/.179	70	.188	0.0	C(11): -0.6	
2022	ROC	AAA	26	123	11	8	0	4	17	11	41	0	0		.224/.317/.411	86	.317	0.0	C(21): 1.3, 1B(2): -0.1	0.3
2022	WAS	MLB	26	155	14	4	0	5	10	12	46	0	1	30.2%	.176/.245/.310	85	.220	-0.2	C(44): -10, 1B(1): 0	-0.8
2023 DC	*WAS*	*MLB*	*27*	*218*	*20*	*9*	*0*	*6*	*18*	*19*	*66*	*0*	*1*	*29.3%*	*.207/.296/.360*	*82*	*.279*	*0.2*	*C -13*	*-1.1*

Comparables: Grayson Greiner (69), J.R. Towles (60), Luke Maile (57)

YEAR	TEAM	P. COUNT	FRM RUNS	BLK RUNS	THRW RUNS	TOT RUNS
2021	BUF	3568	-1.1	-0.1	0.1	-1.1
2021	TOR	1110	-0.5	-0.1	0.0	-0.5
2021	WAS	3100	-4.5	-0.1	0.0	-4.5
2022	ROC	3318	0.8	0.0	0.0	0.7
2022	WAS	6092	-9.4	0.1	0.2	-9.1
2023	*WAS*	*8418*	*-12.3*	*-0.1*	*-0.1*	*-12.5*

September 14 was a good day. Adams homered in the third inning and doubled in the eighth. No one stole a base against him and he allowed zero passed balls. The Nationals lost to the Orioles, 6-2, but other than a groundout in the sixth, it was a flawless individual performance for Riley, and he was unquestionably the best player of the game for the losing side. It's important to cherish the good times when they come around. Zooming out to focus on the whole season, he was the worst backstop in the NL by both WARP and FRAA. His lack of competence offensively and defensively casts doubt on whether he can remain the backup catcher even on a rebuilding club, but hey: He'll always have September 14.

Jeimer Candelario 3B Born: 11/24/93 Age: 29 Bats: S Throws: R Height: 6'1" Weight: 216 lb. Origin: International Free Agent, 2010

YEAR	TEAM	LVL	AGE	PA	R	2B	3B	HR	RBI	BB	K	SB	CS	Whiff%	AVG/OBP/SLG	DRC+	BABIP	BRR	DRP	WARP
2020	DET	MLB	26	206	30	11	3	7	29	20	49	1	1	27.8%	.297/.369/.503	109	.372	-0.3	1B(43): -0.4, 3B(10): 0.8	0.7
2021	DET	MLB	27	626	75	42	3	16	67	65	135	0	0	23.5%	.271/.351/.443	106	.333	-1.4	3B(142): 1.7	2.6
2022	DET	MLB	28	467	49	19	2	13	50	28	109	0	1	25.4%	.217/.272/.361	87	.257	-1.1	3B(117): 2	0.5
2023 DC	*WAS*	*MLB*	*29*	*506*	*50*	*24*	*2*	*14*	*50*	*41*	*111*	*0*	*1*	*24.5%*	*.245/.314/.399*	*98*	*.295*	*-3.9*	*3B 0*	*0.5*

Comparables: Mike Mowrey (63), Andy Carey (63), Pablo Sandoval (63)

Perhaps Candelario felt the weight of expectation. That's one explanation for why the third baseman went from back-to-back Tiger of the Year awards, and one of Detroit's more reliable offensive threats, to total bust at the plate. In the prior two seasons, in which no one expected Detroit to do anything, Candelario had been a line-drive hitter with a propensity for rapping doubles. As soon as the Tigers shifted to contention mode, Candy swung more often and did much less upon contact, chasing a season that never materialized. His teammates didn't help to lift that offensive failure from his shoulders; by September, he was on the bench more often than not. Expectations are certainly lower now, since the Tigers didn't even tender him a contract. We'll see if that lightens the load enough to get his bat back on track in DC.

Michael Chavis 1B Born: 08/11/95 Age: 27 Bats: R Throws: R Height: 5'10" Weight: 190 lb. Origin: Round 1, 2014 Draft (#26 overall)

YEAR	TEAM	LVL	AGE	PA	R	2B	3B	HR	RBI	BB	K	SB	CS	Whiff%	AVG/OBP/SLG	DRC+	BABIP	BRR	DRP	WARP
2020	BOS	MLB	24	158	16	5	2	5	19	8	50	3	0	38.3%	.212/.259/.377	76	.280	-1.1	1B(24): -0.6, LF(12): 1.3, 2B(8): 0.8	0.0
2021	WOR	AAA	25	107	19	2	0	6	17	8	30	1	0		.263/.327/.474	106	.311	0.6	1B(18): -1.6, 2B(6): 0.1	0.2
2021	IND	AAA	25	110	19	6	0	8	20	6	26	1	1		.278/.364/.588	118	.302	0.1	2B(10): -1.4, 1B(7): -0.3, 3B(3): 0.2	0.4
2021	PIT	MLB	25	42	4	3	0	1	5	0	10	0	1	23.7%	.357/.357/.500	91	.452	-0.4	2B(7): -0.5, 3B(4): -0.3, 1B(1): 0.1	0.0
2021	BOS	MLB	25	82	12	4	1	2	6	1	32	1	1	44.6%	.190/.207/.342	61	.283	0.8	2B(22): -0.3, 1B(8): 0	-0.1
2022	PIT	MLB	26	426	39	16	3	14	49	19	126	1	1	30.8%	.229/.265/.389	80	.294	-1.0	1B(107): 1.8, 2B(14): 0.3, 3B(9): -0.9	-0.1
2023 non-DC	*WAS*	*MLB*	*27*	*251*	*27*	*9*	*1*	*10*	*32*	*12*	*67*	*1*	*1*	*31.4%*	*.238/.287/.419*	*91*	*.290*	*0.2*	*1B 0, 2B 0*	*0.2*

Comparables: Jeimer Candelario (54), Josh Bell (48), Michael Cuddyer (48)

If you're looking for an object lesson as to why batted-ball metrics aren't the be-all and end-all, Chavis is an excellent case study. His sweet spot percentage, maximum exit velocity, and hard-hit percentage all clock in at, or close to, league-average—if you took the names off their batted-ball profiles, you'd have trouble differentiating Chavis and perennial All-Star Nolan Arenado. The problem is that Chavis swings at everything and has zero plate discipline or zone control. He's also a terrible defender up the middle; while arguably passable at first base, the bat doesn't provide anything near what a major-league team requires from the cold corner. Chavis was unceremoniously designated for assignment and cleared waivers as the season came to a close; he's at a career crossroads entering his age-28 season and joining the Nationals system.

Jeter Downs SS Born: 07/27/98 Age: 24 Bats: R Throws: R Height: 5'11" Weight: 195 lb. Origin: Round 1, 2017 Draft (#32 overall)

YEAR	TEAM	LVL	AGE	PA	R	2B	3B	HR	RBI	BB	K	SB	CS	Whiff%	AVG/OBP/SLG	DRC+	BABIP	BRR	DRP	WARP
2021	SCO	WIN	22	72	9	0	0	5	14	14	18	4	2		.228/.389/.491		.235			
2021	WOR	AAA	22	405	39	9	0	14	39	38	131	18	3		.190/.272/.333	73	.249	2.7	SS(79): -9.3, 2B(21): -1.1	-0.7
2022	WOR	AAA	23	335	56	11	1	16	33	38	99	18	4		.197/.316/.412	104	.235	-0.5	SS(78): 3.6, 3B(3): -0.2, 2B(1): 0.3	1.4
2022	BOS	MLB	23	41	4	1	0	1	4	1	21	0	0	41.2%	.154/.171/.256	53	.278	-0.2	2B(8): 0, 3B(6): 0, SS(3): -0.2	-0.2
2023 DC	*WAS*	*MLB*	*24*	*59*	*5*	*2*	*0*	*1*	*5*	*4*	*19*	*2*	*1*	*35.7%*	*.187/.265/.335*	*63*	*.257*	*1.0*	*SS 0, 2B 0*	*0.0*

Comparables: Daniel Robertson (64), José Peraza (57), Dawel Lugo (55)

"Jeter Downs bad" is both how an out-of-touch person would describe Derek's Marlins tenure *and* a fair assessment of our subject's 2022 season, which was chock full of dispiriting results that led to an offseason DFA. You can start with a second consecutive year spent in Triple-A putting up replacement-level numbers. You can tack on a two-week emergency stay in Boston where he struck out in half his plate appearances. And for good measure, you can sprinkle in some of the increasingly pessimistic takes from scouts and evaluators. The inescapable conclusion is that, barring a full 180 in approach and outcomes, the top prospect involved in the Mookie Betts trade looks like a backup infielder at best. More realistically, he's part of a cautionary tale, reinforcing that one should refrain from trading future Hall of Famers for prospects and tax savings.

Maikel Franco 3B Born: 08/26/92 Age: 30 Bats: R Throws: R Height: 6'1" Weight: 225 lb. Origin: International Free Agent, 2010

YEAR	TEAM	LVL	AGE	PA	R	2B	3B	HR	RBI	BB	K	SB	CS	Whiff%	AVG/OBP/SLG	DRC+	BABIP	BRR	DRP	WARP
2020	KC	MLB	27	243	23	16	0	8	38	16	38	1	0	24.6%	.278/.321/.457	110	.298	0.5	3B(51): 3, 1B(2): 0	1.2
2021	GWN	AAA	28	35	4	0	0	0	0	5	6	0	0		.167/.286/.167	104	.208	-0.2	1B(8): -0.6	0.0
2021	BAL	MLB	28	403	31	22	0	11	47	20	67	0	0	24.1%	.210/.253/.355	87	.225	-1.7	3B(99): -1	0.4
2022	WAS	MLB	29	388	31	15	0	9	39	12	75	1	0	28.0%	.229/.255/.342	89	.262	-1.1	3B(99): -2.7, 1B(4): -0.4	0.0
2023 non-DC	*WAS*	*MLB*	*30*	*251*	*25*	*10*	*0*	*8*	*29*	*13*	*47*	*0*	*0*	*26.8%*	*.236/.280/.397*	*85*	*.261*	*-0.5*	*3B -1, 1B 0*	*-0.1*

Comparables: Joe Dugan (69), Aramis Ramirez (68), Pie Traynor (67)

Man, inebriated, mansplaining OPS+ in a bar: ...SO EVN THO FRANCO HAD A .609 OPS IN 2021 AND A .597 IN 2022, HE WASS A LIL BETTER HITTER IN 2022 BECAUSE OF THE RUN-SCORIG EMVIRONMNT. ITS AJJUSTED, GET IT?!?

Woman, exasperated in that bar: Yes, but according to DRC+, he went from 14% below league-average to 11% below. An improvement of three percentage points is easily within the margin of uncertainty. If anything, it reinforces the expectation that he's a subpar hitter going forward. Like I said 10 minutes ago, he still sucked.

Man: RIGHT... SO... DO U WANNA GO OUT SSOMTIME?

Woman: Tell you what. When Franco gets back up to 2 WARP in a season, I'll get back to you.

Narrator: They never spoke again, and Franco fled to the NPB.

Luis García MI Born: 05/16/00 Age: 23 Bats: L Throws: R Height: 6'2" Weight: 212 lb. Origin: International Free Agent, 2016

YEAR	TEAM	LVL	AGE	PA	R	2B	3B	HR	RBI	BB	K	SB	CS	Whiff%	AVG/OBP/SLG	DRC+	BABIP	BRR	DRP	WARP
2020	WAS	MLB	20	139	18	6	0	2	16	5	29	1	1	29.1%	.276/.302/.366	82	.340	0.0	2B(37): 0.1, SS(3): 0	0.2
2021	ROC	AAA	21	159	26	3	0	13	25	15	26	1	1		.303/.371/.599	147	.288	0.8	SS(28): -0.6, 2B(9): -0.2	1.3
2021	WAS	MLB	21	247	29	18	2	6	22	11	43	0	2	24.5%	.242/.275/.411	86	.273	-1.9	2B(59): 0.2, SS(8): 0.1	0.3
2022	ROC	AAA	22	205	39	7	4	8	32	18	36	3	0		.308/.366/.519	121	.343	-0.9	SS(35): -2.0, 2B(11): 1.0	0.9
2022	WAS	MLB	22	377	29	23	2	7	45	11	84	3	4	27.0%	.275/.295/.408	83	.337	-1.4	SS(59): -7.6, 2B(33): -0.7	-0.6
2023 DC	*WAS*	*MLB*	*23*	*545*	*52*	*22*	*4*	*13*	*53*	*26*	*110*	*5*	*3*	*26.2%*	*.263/.302/.403*	*94*	*.312*	*0.1*	*2B -2, SS -1*	*0.9*

Comparables: Adalberto Mondesi (60), José Reyes (60), Rougned Odor (56)

If you happen to be named Luis García and you reach the major leagues, you must have an inherent aversion to walks. That's a positive for the Luises García on the Astros and Padres, because they're both pitchers with good control. Alas, their commendable walk rates were both more than double that of their namesake's in Washington: His 2.9% walk rate was the lowest for any hitter in MLB (min. 350 PA). He continued to make year-over-year improvements in hard-hit rate, but he doesn't make so much contact that he can overcome averaging roughly three free passes per month. His poor defense compounds the problem, as it's clear that he can't remain up the middle much longer. Thanks to subpar arm strength (another way he's worse than those other Garcías), his future home might be first base. The bar for offense is much higher at the cold corner, so he needs to learn some semblance of plate discipline before he gets there.

Stone Garrett LF Born: 11/22/95 Age: 27 Bats: R Throws: R Height: 6'2" Weight: 195 lb. Origin: Round 8, 2014 Draft (#227 overall)

YEAR	TEAM	LVL	AGE	PA	R	2B	3B	HR	RBI	BB	K	SB	CS	Whiff%	AVG/OBP/SLG	DRC+	BABIP	BRR	DRP	WARP
2021	AMA	AA	25	443	65	19	1	25	81	20	118	17	5		.280/.317/.516	99	.332	0.2	LF(55): -2.8, RF(11): -0.4, 1B(1): 0.0	0.9
2022	RNO	AAA	26	440	73	22	4	28	95	33	105	15	2	30.6%	.275/.332/.568	110	.302	0.0	RF(37): 1.4, LF(36): 0.1, 1B(1): 0.0	2.4
2022	AZ	MLB	26	84	13	8	0	4	10	3	27	3	1	35.0%	.276/.309/.539	92	.370	-0.7	LF(13): -0.4	0.1
2023 DC	*WAS*	*MLB*	*27*	*412*	*40*	*17*	*1*	*14*	*40*	*20*	*119*	*12*	*2*	*33.2%*	*.222/.267/.389*	*76*	*.282*	*4.2*	*LF -1, RF 0*	*0.1*

Comparables: Tommy Pham (63), Scott Van Slyke (55), J.D. Martinez (55)

The sample size is still small, but research now shows that being stabbed by a teammate can cause you to start hitting, as Garrett has finally made good on the promise he showed years ago before a prank went wrong. He's aggressive at the plate, making below-average contact on below-average decisions, but like that friend in pickup basketball who yells "count it!" after winging a shot off the backboard, it's loud when he connects. He'll now ply his trade with the Nationals after the Diamondbacks designated him for assignment in November.

★ ★ ★ *2023 Top 101 Prospect* **#68** ★ ★ ★

Elijah Green OF Born: 12/04/03 Age: 19 Bats: R Throws: R Height: 6'3" Weight: 225 lb. Origin: Round 1, 2022 Draft (#5 overall)

YEAR	TEAM	LVL	AGE	PA	R	2B	3B	HR	RBI	BB	K	SB	CS	Whiff%	AVG/OBP/SLG	DRC+	BABIP	BRR	DRP	WARP
2022	NAT	ROK	18	52	9	4	0	2	9	6	21	1	0		.302/.404/.535		.524			
2023	*No projection*																			

The Nationals' single-season home run record is 46, achieved by Alfonso Soriano in 2006. If anyone currently in the organization has the potential to surpass that mark, it's probably Green. He already possessed grown-man size and strength the day he was drafted fifth overall out of athlete factory/prep school IMG Academy this past July. Remarkably, he also runs the 60-yard dash in under six seconds and his speed could keep him in center despite his bulk. However, in order to crush dingers and steal bags, he'll have to hit the ball. The knock on him leading into the draft was that he swings through too many fastballs, which was reinforced by a 40% strikeout rate in the Florida Complex League. Nevertheless, he has legitimate All-Star tools and several years of development ahead of him in which he can work on catching up to those heaters.

★ ★ ★ *2023 Top 101 Prospect* **#66** ★ ★ ★

Robert Hassell III OF Born: 08/15/01 Age: 21 Bats: L Throws: L Height: 6'2" Weight: 195 lb. Origin: Round 1, 2020 Draft (#8 overall)

YEAR	TEAM	LVL	AGE	PA	R	2B	3B	HR	RBI	BB	K	SB	CS	Whiff%	AVG/OBP/SLG	DRC+	BABIP	BRR	DRP	WARP
2021	LE	A	19	429	77	31	3	7	65	57	74	31	6		.323/.415/.482	125	.385	3.1	CF(84): -3.8, RF(2): -0.1	2.9
2021	FW	A+	19	87	10	2	1	4	11	9	25	3	0		.205/.287/.410	102	.245	-0.3	CF(16): -0.9	0.2
2022	FW	A+	20	346	49	19	1	10	55	38	66	20	3		.299/.379/.467	118	.352	1.7	CF(63): 1.6, LF(2): 0.5	2.0
2022	WIL	A+	20	45	9	1	0	0	3	6	12	3	0		.211/.311/.237	86	.296	0.5	CF(7): 0.6, RF(2): 0.3	0.3
2022	HBG	AA	20	122	9	5	0	1	12	13	35	1	0		.222/.311/.296	82	.319	0.6	CF(27): -1.9	0.2
2023 non-DC	*WAS*	*MLB*	*21*	*251*	*21*	*10*	*1*	*3*	*21*	*20*	*63*	*8*	*2*	*28.3%*	*.231/.297/.333*	*76*	*.306*	*3.6*	*LF 0, CF 0*	*0.4*

Comparables: Engel Beltre (69), Manuel Margot (55), Victor Robles (55)

Washington received an abundance of young players from San Diego this summer, but as one of the top outfield prospects in baseball, Hassell may feel some direct responsibility to eventually replace You Know Who. That's an unfair burden for a young player—that other guy is irreplaceable—but Hassell has the talent to become a middle-of-the-order hitter in his own right. He possesses one of the finest hit tools in the minor leagues as well as above-average speed, but his power is more doubles-in-the-gap than over-the-fence at this point and he might not stick in center long-term. He only reached Double-A at the end of last season and needs to focus on hitting fewer grounders there, but once he's major-league ready, there's a gaping hole in the outfield that the club will keep open for him to fill.

Yadiel Hernandez LF Born: 10/09/87 Age: 35 Bats: L Throws: R Height: 5'10" Weight: 197 lb. Origin: International Free Agent, 2016

YEAR	TEAM	LVL	AGE	PA	R	2B	3B	HR	RBI	BB	K	SB	CS	Whiff%	AVG/OBP/SLG	DRC+	BABIP	BRR	DRP	WARP
2020	HER	WIN	32	212	32	10	1	4	24	34	47	5	2		.339/.448/.475		.444			
2020	WAS	MLB	32	28	3	3	0	1	6	1	12	0	0	32.4%	.192/.214/.423	76	.286	0.0	RF(1): -0.1	0.0
2021	ROC	AAA	33	64	9	2	0	5	12	5	11	0	1		.288/.344/.576	130	.279	-0.2	LF(7): -0.5, RF(4): 0.1, CF(1): -0.0	0.4
2021	WAS	MLB	33	289	33	8	1	9	32	22	59	3	0	28.2%	.273/.329/.413	101	.318	-2.7	LF(48): -3, RF(13): -0.9	0.4
2022	WAS	MLB	34	327	30	16	0	9	41	19	74	2	1	29.5%	.269/.312/.410	92	.326	-1.2	LF(79): -1.4	0.5
2023 non-DC	*WAS*	*MLB*	*35*	*251*	*26*	*9*	*0*	*7*	*29*	*17*	*57*	*1*	*1*	*29.4%*	*.258/.312/.403*	*98*	*.312*	*-0.5*	*LF 0, RF 0*	*0.4*

Comparables: Irv Noren (54), Garret Anderson (53), Jose Cruz (52)

The old adage says, "you can't get off the island by walking," but some exceptions apply. Hernandez *literally* left his native island by walking—he defected from the Cuban National Team in 2015 when they were scrimmaging against U.S. college players in North Carolina. The aphorism isn't true in the figurative sense, either, because drawing walks at the plate is kinda important. He posted elite walk rates in his heyday with Matanzas in Cuba, then pretty good walk rates in the affiliated minors after signing with Washington. Now in his mid-30s, he isn't able to punish pitchers the way he used to when they challenge him in the strike zone, and he was outrighted off the Nats' 40-man roster in November. "You can and should get off the island by walking, which is often correlated with hitting strikes hard," doesn't roll off the tongue, but Hernandez is living proof of its veracity.

Brady House SS Born: 06/04/03 Age: 20 Bats: R Throws: R Height: 6'4" Weight: 215 lb. Origin: Round 1, 2021 Draft (#11 overall)

YEAR	TEAM	LVL	AGE	PA	R	2B	3B	HR	RBI	BB	K	SB	CS	Whiff%	AVG/OBP/SLG	DRC+	BABIP	BRR	DRP	WARP
2021	NAT	ROK	18	66	14	3	0	4	12	7	13	0	0		.322/.394/.576		.357			
2022	FBG	A	19	203	24	8	0	3	31	12	59	1	0		.278/.356/.375	99	.393	2.9	SS(36): -1.1	0.7
2023 non-DC	*WAS*	*MLB*	*20*	*251*	*18*	*9*	*1*	*2*	*19*	*11*	*82*	*0*	*0*	*33.7%*	*.202/.257/.286*	*48*	*.302*	*1.1*	*SS 0*	*-0.8*

Comparables: Adrian Marin (86), Nick Gordon (77), Ruddy Giron (75)

House has a Google problem. If you search for images of his first and last name, the first dozen results are pictures of the 1970s sitcom family's home and the quarterback's multimillion-dollar mansion. When you eventually scroll down far enough to find the Nationals prospect, you'll infer from his size that he could also have a positional problem. He's a shortstop in the same way that Miguel Cabrera and Jim Thome were shortstops when they were teenagers, but fortunately with comparable raw power to boot. Scouts have much more than a hunch that he won't remain up the middle, but if he overcomes his back problems and gets his thunderous batting practice power into games, he might need to hire Tom's realtor someday.

Carter Kieboom 3B Born: 09/03/97 Age: 25 Bats: R Throws: R Height: 6'2" Weight: 200 lb. Origin: Round 1, 2016 Draft (#28 overall)

YEAR	TEAM	LVL	AGE	PA	R	2B	3B	HR	RBI	BB	K	SB	CS	Whiff%	AVG/OBP/SLG	DRC+	BABIP	BRR	DRP	WARP
2020	WAS	MLB	22	122	15	1	0	0	9	17	33	0	1	25.6%	.202/.344/.212	86	.299	0.7	3B(31): -0.8	0.1
2021	ROC	AAA	23	181	26	7	0	5	23	26	31	1	1		.236/.376/.385	123	.268	0.7	3B(40): 3.1	1.4
2021	WAS	MLB	23	249	26	6	0	6	20	25	62	0	0	29.5%	.207/.301/.318	89	.258	-1.1	3B(60): -1.4	0.2
2023 DC	*WAS*	*MLB*	*25*	*288*	*27*	*10*	*0*	*7*	*24*	*31*	*70*	*2*	*1*	*27.7%*	*.228/.327/.363*	*96*	*.287*	*0.1*	*3B -1, SS 0*	*0.3*

Comparables: Luis Urías (54), Brandon Phillips (52), Luis Sardinas (52)

The Gap Year Association, which is a real thing, asserts that gap years must involve "increasing self-awareness, learning about different cultural perspectives, and experimenting with future possible careers." It also states that "taking the time to figure out what success looks like is a necessary step to achieving it." Kieboom's year away from baseball was unplanned—the scourge of Tommy John surgery strikes position players, too—but the Nationals have to hope he made the most of his time off following a massively disappointing start to his big-league career. Perhaps a mental and physical reset for the former 11th-best prospect in baseball will prove beneficial and allow him to visualize his own success. If he doesn't soon improve on his career .087 ISO, 3.2% barrel rate and -2.7 FRAA, "experimenting with possible future careers" will become a more immediate venture.

Joey Meneses 1B Born: 05/06/92 Age: 31 Bats: R Throws: R Height: 6'3" Weight: 215 lb. Origin: International Free Agent, 2011

YEAR	TEAM	LVL	AGE	PA	R	2B	3B	HR	RBI	BB	K	SB	CS	Whiff%	AVG/OBP/SLG	DRC+	BABIP	BRR	DRP	WARP
2020	CUL	WIN	28	239	30	13	0	6	25	16	40	5	3		.251/.305/.393		.280			
2021	CUL	WIN	29	240	23	15	1	7	47	22	26	4	3		.290/.358/.467		.301			
2021	POR	AA	29	207	31	22	1	10	43	12	35	0	1		.303/.348/.590	130	.320	-0.2	RF(22): -2.0, 1B(8): -1.3, LF(8): -1.1	0.9
2021	WOR	AAA	29	162	14	9	2	5	27	13	39	0	0		.260/.315/.452	88	.314	-1.2	RF(21): 0.1, 1B(10): 1.2, LF(3): -0.2	0.2
2022	ROC	AAA	30	414	51	14	1	20	64	32	89	1	0		.286/.341/.489	123	.321	-1.4	1B(64): 3.2, RF(2): -0.5	2.3
2022	WAS	MLB	30	240	33	14	0	13	34	15	52	1	0	23.3%	.324/.367/.563	133	.371	-0.5	1B(40): -0.3, RF(22): -2.2, LF(3): -0.3	1.2
2023 DC	*WAS*	*MLB*	*31*	*592*	*62*	*25*	*1*	*21*	*63*	*38*	*125*	*1*	*0*	*24.1%*	*.256/.307/.424*	*101*	*.296*	*-0.2*	*1B 0, RF 0*	*1.0*

Comparables: Matt McBride (42), Oscar Salazar (40), Chris Colabello (37)

On September 1, Meneses threw a ball to a young girl in the outfield stands named Avery who was enjoying the game with her Little League teammates. Just before it reached her, some jerk jumped in the way and used his height advantage to steal the souvenir from its intended recipient. More on that in a moment.

Meneses never had a chance in the Braves system. He signed with Atlanta in 2011 as a teenager and couldn't get past Double-A before reaching minor-league free agency after the 2017 season. He bounced around in the Phillies and Red Sox organizations as well as Mexico and Japan before latching on with Washington. When he finally got his chance as a 30-year-old rookie, he homered in his big-league debut, then clobbered the best pitching in the world for the rest of the year, a true feel-good story in a Nats season largely bereft of them.

But here's another one: In mid-September, Meneses sent Avery an autographed game ball with a handwritten note signed, "Your friend, Joey." After all, he knows how it feels to be overshadowed.

Victor Robles CF Born: 05/19/97 Age: 26 Bats: R Throws: R Height: 6'0" Weight: 195 lb. Origin: International Free Agent, 2013

YEAR	TEAM	LVL	AGE	PA	R	2B	3B	HR	RBI	BB	K	SB	CS	Whiff%	AVG/OBP/SLG	DRC+	BABIP	BRR	DRP	WARP
2020	WAS	MLB	23	189	20	5	1	3	15	9	53	4	1	27.8%	.220/.293/.315	78	.298	3.5	CF(52): -3.4	0.1
2021	ROC	AAA	24	93	14	8	1	4	8	7	26	6	1		.301/.370/.566	100	.396	0.5	CF(22): 2.5	0.6
2021	WAS	MLB	24	369	37	21	1	2	19	33	85	8	6	25.6%	.203/.310/.295	78	.271	-0.5	CF(104): -0.9	0.4
2022	WAS	MLB	25	407	42	10	2	6	33	17	104	15	4	27.8%	.224/.273/.311	77	.292	0.5	CF(128): -1.7	0.2
2023 DC	*WAS*	*MLB*	*26*	*504*	*52*	*20*	*3*	*13*	*44*	*30*	*126*	*23*	*8*	*26.8%*	*.234/.304/.381*	*90*	*.294*	*4.2*	*CF 0*	*1.3*

Comparables: Rick Manning (50), Milt Cuyler (48), Cesar Cedeno (45)

Robles defends as fiercely as Patrick Swayze in *Road House*, but at the plate, he makes softer contact than Patrick Swayze in *Ghost*. He swung at 52.2% of the pitches he saw in 2022—nearly six points higher than in 2021—but all that did was swell his swinging-strike and chase rates. He finished in the first percentile of just about every Statcast quality-of-contact metric: average exit velocity, hard-hit rate, xwOBA ... you get the idea. His defense is valuable enough to keep him rostered, but there's no Dirty Dancing around the fact that he simply isn't a major league-caliber hitter. At this Point, Break out the "bust" label for the former can't-miss prospect. The Nationals should have Hungry Eyes for a more well-rounded starter in center field.

Keibert Ruiz C Born: 07/20/98 Age: 24 Bats: S Throws: R Height: 6'0" Weight: 225 lb. Origin: International Free Agent, 2015

YEAR	TEAM	LVL	AGE	PA	R	2B	3B	HR	RBI	BB	K	SB	CS	Whiff%	AVG/OBP/SLG	DRC+	BABIP	BRR	DRP	WARP
2020	LAD	MLB	21	8	1	0	0	1	1	0	3	0	0	21.4%	.250/.250/.625	86	.250		C(2): 0.3	0.0
2021	ROC	AAA	22	85	11	6	0	5	14	7	6	0	0		.308/.365/.577	135	.284	-1.3	C(19): 0.5	0.6
2021	OKC	AAA	22	231	39	18	0	16	45	23	27	0	0		.311/.381/.631	140	.293	-1.0	C(44): 2.6	2.2
2021	WAS	MLB	22	89	9	3	0	2	14	6	4	0	0	9.5%	.284/.348/.395	119	.280	-0.6	C(21): 0.2	0.5
2021	LAD	MLB	22	7	1	0	0	1	1	0	5	0	0	54.5%	.143/.143/.571	83			C(2): 0.0	0.0
2022	WAS	MLB	23	433	33	22	0	7	36	30	50	6	1	15.0%	.251/.313/.360	103	.271	0.0	C(106): 3	2.1
2023 DC	*WAS*	*MLB*	*24*	*361*	*36*	*15*	*0*	*11*	*39*	*26*	*40*	*2*	*1*	*14.6%*	*.265/.328/.416*	*110*	*.275*	*0.1*	*C 2*	*2.0*

Comparables: Dioner Navarro (47), Al Lopez (46), Ivan Rodríguez (45)

YEAR	TEAM	P. COUNT	FRM RUNS	BLK RUNS	THRW RUNS	TOT RUNS
2020	LAD	315	-0.1	0.0	0.4	0.3
2021	OKC	6748	3.7	-0.2	0.2	3.7
2021	ROC	2573	1.1	0.1	0.0	1.1
2021	WAS	3216	0.7	0.1	-0.3	0.5
2021	LAD	67	0.0	0.0	0.0	0.0
2022	WAS	15128	1.4	0.2	1.1	2.8
2023	*WAS*	*12025*	*0.9*	*0.3*	*0.0*	*1.2*

What happens when you yell "DON'T PANIC!" in a crowd? Everybody panics. What happens when a stud prospect—not to mention a key part of the return for Max Scherzer and Trea Turner—doesn't immediately become a superstar? It has the same effect—everyone freaks out. But it's okay! Ruiz is fine! His 86.3% contact rate was second-best in MLB among catchers (minimum 100 PA). His DRC+ may seem pedestrian, but it was among the top quartile for his position. Yes, there's a catcher renaissance happening around the league right now, and Ruiz is getting outshined by Adley Rutschman, Will Smith and Sean Murphy, among others. But none of them even made their MLB debuts until their age-24 seasons, whereas Ruiz just completed a full year in the majors in his age-23 campaign. Catchers often develop more slowly and strangely than other players, and Ruiz has proven he's already way ahead of the curve. So... don't panic. DON'T PANIC!

Dominic Smith 1B Born: 06/15/95 Age: 28 Bats: L Throws: L Height: 6'0" Weight: 239 lb. Origin: Round 1, 2013 Draft (#11 overall)

YEAR	TEAM	LVL	AGE	PA	R	2B	3B	HR	RBI	BB	K	SB	CS	Whiff%	AVG/OBP/SLG	DRC+	BABIP	BRR	DRP	WARP
2020	NYM	MLB	25	199	27	21	1	10	42	14	45	0	0	26.0%	.316/.377/.616	111	.368	0.1	1B(25): 0.1, LF(23): -0.2	0.8
2021	NYM	MLB	26	493	43	20	0	11	58	32	112	2	1	27.7%	.244/.304/.363	81	.298	-1.1	LF(114): -3.5, 1B(15): -0.2	0.1
2022	SYR	AAA	27	248	42	11	0	10	38	25	39	4	1	13.5%	.284/.367/.472	119	.306	-0.5	1B(39): 1.0	1.2
2022	NYM	MLB	27	152	11	10	1	0	17	12	37	0	0	26.0%	.194/.276/.284	76	.263	-0.6	1B(37): 0.3	-0.1
2023 DC	*WAS*	*MLB*	*28*	*396*	*39*	*18*	*1*	*12*	*42*	*29*	*81*	*2*	*1*	*24.2%*	*.250/.318/.411*	*103*	*.293*	*0.5*	*1B 0*	*0.8*

Comparables: Domonic Brown (57), Adrián González (55), Casey Kotchman (55)

Heading into the first season of the designated hitter in the National League, the Mets were on everyone's list of which NL teams would benefit the most from the DH. After all, they had Smith, J.D. Davis and Robinson Canó all on the roster and none with an obvious position to play. As it turns out, the Mets had among the worst production in the league from the DH spot in the first half, and none of those players finished the season on the Mets' 26-man roster; all have moved on after the Mets non-tendered Smith this winter. After showing so much promise in the second half of the 2019 season and the pandemic-shortened 2020 season, Smith took a huge step back in 2021 and slid toward the brink of oblivion in 2022.

After being the subject of trade rumors that never materialized just prior to the start of the season, Smith found his roster spot in jeopardy when rosters shrank from 28 to 26 at the start of May. But on April 26, he helped spark a five-run ninth inning for an improbable comeback victory against the Cardinals that bought him another month on the roster, with the Mets opting to cut Canó and eat his cost instead. However, carrying a 59 OPS+ on Memorial Day, Smith was optioned to Triple-A Syracuse. He was called up again in late June, didn't fare any better, sprained his right ankle on July 16 and did not see the big leagues again after the Mets acquired Daniel Vogelbach at the trading deadline. The Nationals will give him a chance to turn things around on a minor-league deal.

Cristhian Vaquero OF Born: 09/13/04 Age: 18 Bats: S Throws: R Height: 6'3" Weight: 180 lb. Origin: International Free Agent, 2022

YEAR	TEAM	LVL	AGE	PA	R	2B	3B	HR	RBI	BB	K	SB	CS	Whiff%	AVG/OBP/SLG	DRC+	BABIP	BRR	DRP	WARP
2022	DSL NAT	ROK	17	216	33	4	4	1	22	33	38	17	7		.256/.379/.341		.317			
2023	*No projection*																			

The Nationals awarded Vaquero a $4.925 million signing bonus, thereby making him the highest-paid international amateur free agent in the 2022 class by nearly a million bucks. Needless to say, he has louder tools than a cadre of chainsaw jugglers, but he's literally still learning the game—he taught himself to switch-hit, like, five minutes ago. Sometimes, the top international amateur turns out like Wander Franco; other times, like Lucius Fox (womp womp). The spectrum of outcomes is as broad as the horizon, but given his tender age and immense talent, there's a chance he could become the centerpiece of the Nationals' rebuild. No, not *this* rebuild—the rebuild after the *next* teardown.

Ildemaro Vargas SS/3B

Born: 07/16/91 Age: 31 Bats: S Throws: R Height: 6'0" Weight: 180 lb. Origin: International Free Agent, 2008

YEAR	TEAM	LVL	AGE	PA	R	2B	3B	HR	RBI	BB	K	SB	CS	Whiff%	AVG/OBP/SLG	DRC+	BABIP	BRR	DRP	WARP
2020	LAR	WIN	28	127	16	4	0	0	15	16	10	5	0		.309/.394/.345		.337			
2020	MIN	MLB	28	24	3	1	1	0	2	1	2	0	0	16.7%	.227/.250/.364	106	.238	-0.4	2B(8): 0.4, 3B(1): 0	0.1
2020	CHC	MLB	28	9	1	0	0	1	1	0	3	0	0	21.4%	.222/.222/.556	102	.200		2B(5): -0.4, 3B(1): 0.5	
2020	AZ	MLB	28	21	2	0	0	0	0	1	5	0	0	21.1%	.150/.190/.150	95	.200	0.1	1B(5): -0.1, 2B(3): 0, 3B(1): 0	0.0
2021	LAR	WIN	29	204	37	10	1	11	40	19	14	3	0		.319/.377/.566		.294			
2021	RNO	AAA	29	268	50	21	0	10	39	16	27	3	1		.313/.351/.518	116	.316	1.3	2B(22): 1.2, SS(22): 0.7, 3B(10): 1.1	1.8
2021	CHC	MLB	29	24	3	2	0	0	2	3	7	1	0	29.7%	.143/.250/.238	93	.214	0.7	2B(4): 0, SS(2): 0	0.1
2021	AZ	MLB	29	46	4	1	1	0	4	3	7	0	0	17.9%	.186/.239/.256	100	.222	-0.4	3B(7): -0.6, 2B(5): -0.1, SS(3): 0	0.1
2021	PIT	MLB	29	13	0	0	0	0	1	0	3	0	0	24.0%	.077/.077/.077	89	.100		3B(3): 0, LF(2): -0.1	
2022	IOW	AAA	30	112	16	3	4	1	7	7	12	1	0		.279/.321/.413	116	.304	0.4	SS(18): 2.1, 2B(5): -0.3, 3B(2): 0.3	0.6
2022	ROC	AAA	30	197	21	11	0	2	18	20	25	2	2		.224/.301/.322	111	.248	1.0	SS(38): -0.1, 2B(7): 0.0, 3B(5): 0.5	1.1
2022	WAS	MLB	30	196	15	13	0	3	19	5	21	3	1	12.4%	.280/.308/.398	109	.301	-0.3	3B(43): -0.3, SS(9): -0.1	0.6
2022	CHC	MLB	30	26	4	0	1	1	4	3	2	0	0	10.0%	.130/.231/.348	107	.100	0.1	SS(6): -1.4, 2B(3): 0	0.0
2023 DC	*WAS*	*MLB*	*31*	*122*	*10*	*5*	*0*	*1*	*10*	*6*	*14*	*0*	*1*	*14.7%*	*.244/.289/.346*	*79*	*.267*	*0.7*	*2B 0, SS 0*	*0.1*

Comparables: Brock Holt (54), Jeff Keppinger (47), Alberto Gonzalez (46)

Ignoring the ethical differences between their chosen professions, Vargas and *Better Call Saul's* Ignacio "Nacho" Varga have a lot in common. There's the name similarity, for one thing. They also both came up in the Desert Southwest (Vargas debuted in Arizona) and make a living playing multiple positions while struggling to rise above their stations. The Nationals are Vargas' Mike Ehrmantraut, then, trying to bring out the best in him and seeing positive characteristics others overlook. His 82.4% out-of-the-zone contact rate was sixth in MLB and his overall contact rate of 89.2% was seventh among hitters with at least 50 PA. *BCS* may have completed its run, but after a modestly successful stint as Washington's utility infielder, Vargas will get at least one more season.

★ ★ ★ *2023 Top 101 Prospect* **#3** ★ ★ ★

James Wood OF

Born: 09/17/02 Age: 20 Bats: L Throws: R Height: 6'7" Weight: 240 lb. Origin: Round 2, 2021 Draft (#62 overall)

YEAR	TEAM	LVL	AGE	PA	R	2B	3B	HR	RBI	BB	K	SB	CS	Whiff%	AVG/OBP/SLG	DRC+	BABIP	BRR	DRP	WARP
2021	PAD	ROK	18	101	18	5	0	3	22	13	32	10	0		.372/.465/.535		.569			
2022	FBG	A	19	93	14	8	0	2	17	10	26	4	0		.293/.366/.463	99	.400	0.8	CF(18): 0.9	0.3
2022	LE	A	19	236	55	19	1	10	45	37	42	15	5		.337/.453/.601	138	.387	1.9	CF(43): 0.2, LF(2): 0.1	0.8
2023 non-DC	*WAS*	*MLB*	*20*	*251*	*22*	*12*	*1*	*4*	*23*	*21*	*62*	*9*	*2*	*27.1%*	*.224/.297/.352*	*80*	*.291*	*2.4*	*LF 0, CF 0*	*0.4*

Comparables: Drew Waters (91), Jarred Kelenic (89), Alek Thomas (89)

Comparing Wood to Aaron Judge is lazy—we get it, they're both 6-foot-7 outfielders—and extremely irresponsible, so we're not going to do it. It doesn't matter that he recorded an eye-popping 112-mph exit velocity as a teenager. Nor does it matter that he possesses freakish speed for someone the size of a defensive end, or that he draws walks with the patience of a monk. That he covers the inner half of the plate better than should be possible for a literal giant? It's neither here nor there. No, juxtaposing him with a 62-homer slugger and MVP is wildly unfair, so we're not going to do it. Besides, given what he did to low-minors pitching with his larger-than-life physique and tools, a superhero comp like Bruce Banner or Clark Kent feels more apropos anyway.

PITCHERS

Cory Abbott RHP

Born: 09/20/95 Age: 27 Bats: R Throws: R Height: 6'1" Weight: 210 lb. Origin: Round 2, 2017 Draft (#67 overall)

YEAR	TEAM	LVL	AGE	W	L	SV	G	GS	IP	H	HR	BB/9	K/9	K	GB%	BABIP	WHIP	ERA	DRA-	WARP	MPH	FB%	Whiff%	CSP
2021	IOW	AAA	25	5	6	0	19	19	96	97	20	5.0	12.2	130	35.1%	.338	1.56	5.91	98	1.4				
2021	CHC	MLB	25	0	0	0	7	1	17^{1}	20	7	5.7	6.2	12	37.3%	.255	1.79	6.75	124	-0.1	92.7	59.1%	20.5%	51.6%
2022	ROC	AAA	26	0	4	0	10	6	28^{1}	30	4	5.4	10.8	34	41.5%	.333	1.66	5.08	87	0.6				
2022	IOW	AAA	26	0	1	0	2	2	6	4	2	3.0	9.0	6	20.0%	.154	1.00	4.50	98	0.1				
2022	WAS	MLB	26	0	5	0	16	9	48	44	12	4.7	8.4	45	28.4%	.248	1.44	5.25	122	-0.1	91.3	50.9%	26.3%	53.8%
2023 DC	*WAS*	*MLB*	*27*	*4*	*4*	*0*	*36*	*6*	*52.7*	*53*	*9*	*4.7*	*8.7*	*50*	*34.7%*	*.299*	*1.54*	*5.24*	*126*	*-0.4*	*91.7*	*52.8%*	*26.5%*	*53.3%*

Comparables: Ben Lively (62), Eddie Butler (60), Mike Wright Jr. (58)

At its core, pitching is an unfair endeavor. You have to throw the ball in the most hittable area—not too close and not too far away, between the knees and letters—but if you make it *too* enticing, your pitch gets creamed. You see, it's not Abbott's fault that he surrendered a home run every four innings on average. The rules are stacked against him. He was just trying to throw strikes (okay, he didn't do that very well either), and those extremely rude batters kept blasting the ball into the air. His astronomical 60% fly-ball rate was the highest in MLB among pitchers with at least 30 innings. One-seventh of the fly balls he induced left the park, which is a reasonable rate, but the sheer quantity of them doomed his season. Again, it's not his fault! Blame the rules that make Abbott aim for the strike zone.

Joan Adon RHP Born: 08/12/98 Age: 24 Bats: R Throws: R Height: 6'2" Weight: 246 lb. Origin: International Free Agent, 2016

YEAR	TEAM	LVL	AGE	W	L	SV	G	GS	IP	H	HR	BB/9	K/9	K	GB%	BABIP	WHIP	ERA	DRA-	WARP	MPH	FB%	Whiff%	CSP
2021	WIL	A+	22	6	4	0	17	17	87	77	7	3.3	9.4	91	46.1%	.299	1.25	4.97	87	1.3				
2021	HBG	AA	22	1	2	0	3	3	14	15	1	3.2	15.4	24	37.1%	.412	1.43	6.43	79	0.3				
2021	WAS	MLB	22	0	0	0	1	1	5^1	6	1	5.1	15.2	9	72.7%	.500	1.69	3.38			95.3	54.3%	33.3%	60.0%
2022	ROC	AAA	23	2	2	0	10	10	42^1	41	5	5.1	9.1	43	50.4%	.316	1.54	4.68	102	0.5				
2022	WAS	MLB	23	1	12	0	14	14	64^2	76	8	5.4	7.7	55	47.1%	.338	1.78	7.10	131	-0.4	95.2	69.4%	16.8%	54.4%
2023 DC	*WAS*	*MLB*	*24*	*3*	*4*	*0*	*14*	*14*	*62.7*	*65*	*7*	*5.0*	*6.9*	*47*	*47.5%*	*.302*	*1.60*	*5.12*	*122*	*-0.2*	*95.2*	*68.5%*	*21.9%*	*54.7%*

Comparables: Andrew Moore (74), Erik Johnson (73), Robert Stephenson (72)

Adon began the season in the starting rotation, but he struggled from the outset. He had difficulty inducing whiffs and consistently locating his breaking pitch, while his fastball was ... you know what? No. Just no. We're not doing this. There's no point in seriously analyzing a dude who coughed up 53 runs in 64⅔ innings, especially when he didn't even give up *that* many home runs! Do you understand how fat and piñata-like his pitches had to be to get singled and doubled into oblivion? In a run-suppressing environment!? *In 2022!?!?* That the Nationals started him 14 times last year tells you everything you need to know about the state of the franchise. Adon is still young and throws hard. Maybe he'll carve out a successful career as a reliever. But in the meantime ... just no.

A.J. Alexy RHP Born: 04/21/98 Age: 25 Bats: R Throws: R Height: 6'4" Weight: 195 lb. Origin: Round 11, 2016 Draft (#341 overall)

YEAR	TEAM	LVL	AGE	W	L	SV	G	GS	IP	H	HR	BB/9	K/9	K	GB%	BABIP	WHIP	ERA	DRA-	WARP	MPH	FB%	Whiff%	CSP
2021	FRI	AA	23	3	1	0	13	7	50^1	30	4	3.8	10.2	57	44.8%	.232	1.01	1.61	93	0.5				
2021	RR	AAA	23	0	0	0	3	3	14^2	9	2	3.7	11.7	19	46.9%	.233	1.02	1.84	91	0.1				
2021	TEX	MLB	23	3	1	0	5	4	23	13	4	6.7	6.7	17	24.2%	.155	1.30	4.70	144	-0.3	93.6	54.5%	22.0%	53.1%
2022	RR	AAA	24	6	6	0	31	16	96	108	25	5.3	9.7	103	35.7%	.329	1.71	5.91	124	-0.8	95.3	49.3%	26.5%	
2022	TEX	MLB	24	1	1	0	4	0	7	10	1	11.6	7.7	6	52.2%	.409	2.71	11.57	126	0.0	94.5	55.9%	18.8%	51.3%
2023 DC	*WAS*	*MLB*	*25*	*0*	*0*	*0*	*15*	*0*	*13*	*13*	*2*	*5.9*	*8.2*	*11*	*37.2%*	*.296*	*1.67*	*5.59*	*130*	*-0.1*	*93.9*	*54.9%*	*23.9%*	*52.5%*

Comparables: Jarred Cosart (62), Nick Tropeano (57), Chi Chi González (55)

If there were ever a season to simply flush down the toilet it would be Alexy's 2022 campaign. He followed up his uneven 2021 MLB debut by getting rag-dolled back at Round Rock, allowing far too many homers and missing fewer bats. Developed mostly as a starter since being drafted in 2016, Alexy moved to the bullpen about halfway through the year. The results were still ugly, but his fastball ticked back up to the 95–97 mph range when deployed in shorter bursts. Alexy isn't *that* far removed from bullying hitters in the upper-minors, and his fastball velocity and four-pitch mix still give him a chance to succeed. But entering his age-25 season and with a modest ceiling, he'll only be allowed to clog up the bases for so long.

Víctor Arano RHP Born: 02/07/95 Age: 28 Bats: R Throws: R Height: 6'2" Weight: 228 lb. Origin: International Free Agent, 2013

YEAR	TEAM	LVL	AGE	W	L	SV	G	GS	IP	H	HR	BB/9	K/9	K	GB%	BABIP	WHIP	ERA	DRA-	WARP	MPH	FB%	Whiff%	CSP
2021	GWN	AAA	26	1	2	2	32	0	36	25	3	3.8	11.3	45	43.9%	.278	1.11	2.50	81	0.9				
2022	WAS	MLB	27	1	1	1	43	0	42	47	5	2.6	9.4	44	52.0%	.347	1.40	4.50	88	0.7	94.2	53.1%	29.6%	53.0%
2023 DC	*WAS*	*MLB*	*28*	*3*	*3*	*0*	*61*	*0*	*52.7*	*50*	*6*	*3.4*	*9.7*	*56*	*46.7%*	*.315*	*1.34*	*3.89*	*98*	*0.3*	*94.1*	*52.7%*	*31.8%*	*52.6%*

Comparables: Dominic Leone (59), Bruce Rondón (52), Jeremy Jeffress (50)

On a 107-loss club, the little victories seem much more significant. On August 18 in San Diego, the Nationals and Padres were tied 1-1 in the bottom of the seventh. The home side loaded the bases with one out, but Arano wriggled free by striking out Trent Grisham and, yes, Juan Soto, who waved through a 96-mph sinker up in the zone. Washington scored two runs in the ninth and won the game, 3-1. The outcomes of that matchup and pivotal plate appearance were both aberrations: The Nationals "improved" to an even 40-80 record with the win, and two other Arano-Soto matchups resulted in a walk and a single. Opposing batters hit .333 off Arano's sinker, and the pitch only induced a 10% whiff rate. But one time, the most patient hitter in MLB swung through it with the game on the line. It was a tiny, massive triumph in a season with precious little to celebrate.

★ ★ ★ *2023 Top 101 Prospect* **#71** ★ ★ ★

Cade Cavalli RHP Born: 08/14/98 Age: 24 Bats: R Throws: R Height: 6'4" Weight: 240 lb. Origin: Round 1, 2020 Draft (#22 overall)

YEAR	TEAM	LVL	AGE	W	L	SV	G	GS	IP	H	HR	BB/9	K/9	K	GB%	BABIP	WHIP	ERA	DRA-	WARP	MPH	FB%	Whiff%	CSP
2021	WIL	A+	22	3	1	0	7	7	40^2	24	1	2.7	15.7	71	49.3%	.329	0.89	1.77	63	1.2				
2021	HBG	AA	22	3	3	0	11	11	58	39	2	5.4	12.4	80	38.3%	.296	1.28	2.79	80	1.1				
2021	ROC	AAA	22	1	5	0	6	6	24^2	33	2	4.7	8.8	24	52.5%	.397	1.86	7.30	109	0.2				
2022	ROC	AAA	23	6	4	0	20	20	97	75	3	3.6	9.6	104	42.6%	.293	1.18	3.71	85	2.0				
2022	WAS	MLB	23	0	1	0	1	1	4^1	6	0	4.2	12.5	6	50.0%	.500	1.85	14.54	94	0.1	95.3	42.4%	28.9%	56.7%
2023 DC	*WAS*	*MLB*	*24*	*5*	*6*	*0*	*21*	*21*	*92.3*	*83*	*8*	*4.4*	*9.8*	*101*	*44.1%*	*.305*	*1.39*	*3.87*	*95*	*1.0*	*95.3*	*42.4%*	*28.6%*	*56.7%*

Comparables: Erik Johnson (48), Daniel Mengden (48), Dylan Cease (47)

Cavalli has been Washington's best pitching prospect since the day he was drafted, so his August 26 debut was one of the few must-watch moments of their season. He lasted just 4⅓ innings, but put all the pros and cons listed in his scouting reports on full display. His lively fastball overwhelmed the Reds lineup at times, and he generated whiffs with both his curveball and changeup. He also plunked three batters and his heat map looked like someone gave a BB gun to a toddler, and shortly after his start he landed on the IL with shoulder inflammation. As such, Cavalli was as advertised: He has ace-caliber stuff with middle-relief command and a violent delivery that some fear could lead to arm injuries. Still, the pure quality of his arsenal should make him a trendy pick for Rookie of the Year if healthy, and he'll have ample opportunities to prove he can remain a starter.

Steve Cishek RHP Born: 06/18/86 Age: 37 Bats: R Throws: R Height: 6'6" Weight: 220 lb. Origin: Round 5, 2007 Draft (#166 overall)

YEAR	TEAM	LVL	AGE	W	L	SV	G	GS	IP	H	HR	BB/9	K/9	K	GB%	BABIP	WHIP	ERA	DRA-	WARP	MPH	FB%	Whiff%	CSP
2020	CHW	MLB	34	0	0	0	22	0	20	21	4	4.1	9.5	21	32.2%	.309	1.50	5.40	131	-0.1	90.5	47.6%	27.2%	46.5%
2021	LAA	MLB	35	0	2	0	74	0	68^1	61	2	5.4	8.4	64	49.7%	.304	1.49	3.42	116	0.1	90.2	61.1%	20.3%	49.1%
2022	WAS	MLB	36	1	4	1	69	0	66^1	54	11	3.7	10.0	74	41.0%	.267	1.22	4.21	92	0.9	89.7	62.4%	26.3%	50.7%
2023 DC	*FA*	*MLB*	*37*	*3*	*3*	*0*	*65*	*0*	*56.3*	*51*	*6*	*4.3*	*8.5*	*53*	*43.9%*	*.288*	*1.40*	*4.39*	*108*	*0.0*	*90.0*	*60.5%*	*23.6%*	*49.1%*

Comparables: Jose Valverde (84), Mike Timlin (83), Grant Balfour (82)

The first thing to know about getting around DC is that you need to stand on the right and walk on the left, especially on metro escalators. Cishek took this way too literally when he signed with the Nationals. He stood tall against right-handed hitters, allowing a meager .194/.290/.300 slash line, but walked plenty of lefties—and just for good measure, he threw them a bunch of gopher balls, too. Overall, he gave up 20% of his career home runs and 22% of his career hit-by-pitches in 2022 despite throwing only 9.6% of his career innings. On a related note, his ground-ball rate was the lowest of his lifetime (excluding the bizarro 2020 season). Perhaps seeing the writing on the wall, Cishek officially called it a career in December after a more-than-respectable 13 years in the big leagues.

Patrick Corbin LHP Born: 07/19/89 Age: 33 Bats: L Throws: L Height: 6'4" Weight: 222 lb. Origin: Round 2, 2009 Draft (#80 overall)

YEAR	TEAM	LVL	AGE	W	L	SV	G	GS	IP	H	HR	BB/9	K/9	K	GB%	BABIP	WHIP	ERA	DRA-	WARP	MPH	FB%	Whiff%	CSP
2020	WAS	MLB	30	2	7	0	11	11	65^2	85	10	2.5	8.2	60	45.2%	.362	1.57	4.66	104	0.6	90.5	52.2%	23.7%	46.2%
2021	WAS	MLB	31	9	16	0	31	31	171^2	192	37	3.1	7.5	143	46.0%	.312	1.47	5.82	117	0.1	92.6	56.4%	25.1%	53.9%
2022	WAS	MLB	32	6	19	0	31	31	152^2	210	27	2.9	7.5	128	44.6%	.365	1.70	6.31	149	-2.4	92.8	62.3%	20.8%	54.8%
2023 DC	*WAS*	*MLB*	*33*	*8*	*10*	*0*	*27*	*27*	*145.7*	*166*	*20*	*2.9*	*7.0*	*113*	*45.2%*	*.318*	*1.46*	*4.76*	*119*	*-0.2*	*92.4*	*58.2%*	*22.6%*	*51.9%*

Comparables: Livan Hernandez (73), Jordan Zimmermann (73), Mark Buehrle (72)

Using metrics that are more predictive and descriptive of performance is a core aspect of the sabermetrics mission, but every now and then the old-fashioned stats tell the story just fine. For example, Corbin had the most losses, hits allowed and earned runs surrendered in MLB in 2022. There's no way to accomplish that unholy trinity without being plainly awful. DRA- concurs—among pitchers who tossed at least 100 innings, he finished dead last. His once-trusty slider lost several inches of movement from its heyday, so he threw more sinkers than ever before, but to no avail. With just under $60 million remaining on his deal through 2024, he is one of the deepest sunk costs in baseball. Want a silver lining? It's quite unlikely that the Nats will have to pay out any of Corbin's contract escalators for earning MVP or Cy Young votes, winning playoff MVPs or making All-Star teams.

Sean Doolittle LHP Born: 09/26/86 Age: 36 Bats: L Throws: L Height: 6'2" Weight: 227 lb. Origin: Round 1, 2007 Draft (#41 overall)

YEAR	TEAM	LVL	AGE	W	L	SV	G	GS	IP	H	HR	BB/9	K/9	K	GB%	BABIP	WHIP	ERA	DRA-	WARP	MPH	FB%	Whiff%	CSP
2020	WAS	MLB	33	0	2	0	11	0	7^2	9	3	4.7	7.0	6	3.8%	.273	1.70	5.87	161	-0.2	90.8	81.9%	18.7%	49.3%
2021	SEA	MLB	34	0	0	0	11	0	11^1	10	1	4.0	9.5	12	21.9%	.290	1.32	4.76	110	0.0	93.6	77.1%	29.3%	57.0%
2021	CIN	MLB	34	3	1	1	45	0	38^1	40	6	4.2	9.6	41	18.6%	.324	1.51	4.46	109	0.2	93.0	89.2%	23.6%	56.9%
2022	WAS	MLB	35	0	0	0	6	0	5^1	1	0	0.0	10.1	6	27.3%	.091	0.19	0.00	94	0.1	94.0	74.5%	35.5%	56.4%
2023 non-DC	*WAS*	*MLB*	*36*	*2*	*2*	*0*	*57*	*0*	*50*	*44*	*8*	*3.4*	*8.7*	*48*	*25.3%*	*.275*	*1.27*	*3.85*	*100*	*0.2*	*93.1*	*86.2%*	*24.5%*	*54.1%*

Comparables: Jake McGee (61), Jake Diekman (60), Tony Sipp (59)

The Nationals' two biggest hits of the 2022 season occurred off the field. One came via their cherry blossom-themed City Connect uniforms; the other a bobblehead of Doolittle wearing one. Few players form as sincere a personal connection with their team's city as he and his wife, Eireann, have—making their offseason home in the District, supporting local indy bookstores, joining the cause for DC statehood and fundraising for SMYAL, an organization empowering Washington's LGBTQ youth. Alas, Doolittle injured his elbow in April and appeared in fewer games last season than the City Connects did (14). He'll return in 2023 as a non-roster invitee to spring training, but if the end of the line is indeed approaching, the Nats need to keep him involved with the organization in some capacity. After all, he's a better hub between team and community than the Navy Yard metro station.

Carl Edwards Jr. RHP Born: 09/03/91 Age: 31 Bats: R Throws: R Height: 6'3" Weight: 170 lb. Origin: Round 48, 2011 Draft (#1464 overall)

YEAR	TEAM	LVL	AGE	W	L	SV	G	GS	IP	H	HR	BB/9	K/9	K	GB%	BABIP	WHIP	ERA	DRA-	WARP	MPH	FB%	Whiff%	CSP
2020	SEA	MLB	28	0	0	1	5	0	4^2	2	0	1.9	11.6	6	60.0%	.200	0.64	1.93	93	0.1	93.5	66.1%	41.7%	47.1%
2021	CLT	AAA	29	0	0	3	10	0	9	4	0	3.0	15.0	15	50.0%	.250	0.78	2.00	80	0.2				
2021	BUF	AAA	29	1	0	0	7	0	7	5	2	0.0	10.3	8	50.0%	.188	0.71	3.86	92	0.1				
2021	ATL	MLB	29	0	0	0	1	0	0^1	3	1	27.0	27.0	1	33.3%	1.000	12.00	81.00	156	0.0	93.2	50.0%	33.3%	43.1%
2021	TOR	MLB	29	0	0	0	6	0	5^1	8	2	3.4	8.4	5	21.1%	.353	1.88	6.75	111	0.0	94.2	68.8%	28.2%	61.5%
2022	ROC	AAA	30	1	0	3	13	0	14^1	3	0	2.5	10.7	17	48.3%	.107	0.49	0.63	78	0.4				
2022	WAS	MLB	30	6	3	2	57	0	62	51	8	3.6	8.1	56	48.3%	.259	1.23	2.76	95	0.8	94.6	67.8%	24.5%	52.1%
2023 DC	*WAS*	*MLB*	*31*	*3*	*3*	*5*	*68*	*0*	*59.3*	*52*	*6*	*3.6*	*9.0*	*59*	*44.4%*	*.287*	*1.29*	*3.40*	*88*	*0.6*	*94.5*	*68.0%*	*28.3%*	*52.0%*

Comparables: Jeremy Jeffress (52), Brad Boxberger (50), Kevin Jepsen (50)

Last year, the Carl's Jr. fast-food chain announced a $500 million rebranding campaign based around the slogan, "Feed Your Happy." Edwards' makeover as a pitcher was less expensive. From 2015-2018, he allowed just 80 hits in 154⅓ innings, though he made up the difference with 84 walks. After three injury-diminished partial seasons, he reemerged in 2022 as a different type of pitcher. He still relies heavily on his fastball, but he induced a 77.2% contact rate—nearly seven points north of his career average. This led to more hits and fewer strikeouts, which he offset by finally tamping down on free passes a bit. Edwards may have rebranded as more of a pitch-to-contact reliever, but what he throws still isn't feeding hitters' happy.

Paolo Espino RHP

Born: 01/10/87 Age: 36 Bats: R Throws: R Height: 5'10" Weight: 211 lb. Origin: Round 10, 2006 Draft (#311 overall)

YEAR	TEAM	LVL	AGE	W	L	SV	G	GS	IP	H	HR	BB/9	K/9	K	GB%	BABIP	WHIP	ERA	DRA-	WARP	MPH	FB%	Whiff%	CSP
2020	TOR	WIN	33	2	3	0	6	6	29	22	2	1.9	6.5	21	34.9%	.238	0.97	3.72						
2020	WAS	MLB	33	0	0	0	2	1	6	8	1	3.0	10.5	7	44.4%	.412	1.67	4.50	78	0.1	90.2	54.5%	28.0%	47.7%
2021	WAS	MLB	34	5	5	1	35	19	109^2	108	19	2.1	7.6	92	35.9%	.283	1.21	4.27	103	0.9	89.1	55.3%	20.2%	58.5%
2022	WAS	MLB	35	0	9	0	42	19	113^1	131	24	1.9	7.3	92	38.8%	.310	1.37	4.84	118	0.1	88.5	48.0%	21.4%	55.7%
2023 DC	*WAS*	*MLB*	*36*	*8*	*8*	*0*	*65*	*12*	*101.7*	*113*	*16*	*2.3*	*6.8*	*77*	*38.1%*	*.306*	*1.37*	*4.58*	*118*	*-0.2*	*88.8*	*51.0%*	*20.9%*	*56.7%*

Comparables: Eric Stults (39), Steven Wright (35), Josh Tomlin (34)

Espino began 2022 on a warpath in his attempt to shatter one of baseball's most vaunted records. As everyone knows, Justin Speier's 35 games finished without recording a save for the 2005 Blue Jays is considered an untouchable milestone. But our protagonist completed 17 of the Nationals' first 59 games this past season, all in losses or rare lopsided victories. He was on pace for a breathtaking 47 games finished sans save until, inexplicably, his quest was derailed when he joined the starting rotation in mid-June and remained a cromulent starter for the remainder of the year. His curveball averaged 73.2 inches of vertical movement, which led MLB by a mile, and his 4.9% walk rate was eighth-best in the NL among pitchers who threw at least 100 innings. Those are nice consolation prizes, but now that Espino has demonstrated his value as a back-end starter, Speier's record remains unassailable.

Erick Fedde RHP

Born: 02/25/93 Age: 30 Bats: R Throws: R Height: 6'4" Weight: 203 lb. Origin: Round 1, 2014 Draft (#18 overall)

YEAR	TEAM	LVL	AGE	W	L	SV	G	GS	IP	H	HR	BB/9	K/9	K	GB%	BABIP	WHIP	ERA	DRA-	WARP	MPH	FB%	Whiff%	CSP
2020	WAS	MLB	27	2	4	0	11	8	50^1	47	10	3.9	5.0	28	55.0%	.234	1.37	4.29	104	0.5	93.7	55.5%	15.3%	46.2%
2021	WAS	MLB	28	7	9	0	29	27	133^1	144	23	3.2	8.6	128	48.4%	.320	1.44	5.47	94	1.7	93.9	43.5%	22.3%	51.7%
2022	WAS	MLB	29	6	13	0	27	27	127	149	21	4.1	6.7	94	42.0%	.321	1.63	5.81	137	-1.2	92.7	39.8%	18.5%	53.5%
2023 DC	*FA*	*MLB*	*30*	*5*	*7*	*0*	*21*	*21*	*99.7*	*110*	*13*	*3.7*	*6.7*	*74*	*45.2%*	*.310*	*1.52*	*4.85*	*120*	*-0.2*	*93.2*	*43.5%*	*19.4%*	*51.8%*

Comparables: Josh Towers (81), Esteban Loaiza (80), Josh Fogg (80)

Pitch classification software is a modern marvel, but it has its drawbacks. Not everything falls neatly into buckets like "cutter" or "slider." The nuance gets lost in the graphs, but sometimes hurlers throw tweener pitches that sort of slurve, churve or clide. This unclassifiable, in-between realm is where Fedde resides. He can vary speeds as well as movement on the horizontal and vertical axes. Call it one pitch, four pitches or 1,000 pitches—how we describe something won't change its nature. Unfortunately, Fedde's nature doesn't fool batters. His 25.2% chase rate was the lowest in MLB among pitchers who tossed at least 100 innings, and his ground-ball and fly-ball rates both took turns in the wrong directions. It's just as well that his pitch arsenal is so difficult to describe because the word "arsenal" implies weaponry and the ability to damage an opponent. Unfortunately, what he throws is mostly just cannon fodder. He'll head overseas after signing with the NC Dinos of the KBO this winter.

Kyle Finnegan RHP

Born: 09/04/91 Age: 31 Bats: R Throws: R Height: 6'2" Weight: 197 lb. Origin: Round 6, 2013 Draft (#191 overall)

YEAR	TEAM	LVL	AGE	W	L	SV	G	GS	IP	H	HR	BB/9	K/9	K	GB%	BABIP	WHIP	ERA	DRA-	WARP	MPH	FB%	Whiff%	CSP
2020	WAS	MLB	28	1	0	0	25	0	24^2	21	2	4.7	9.9	27	50.0%	.297	1.38	2.92	86	0.5	95.2	70.4%	28.3%	51.0%
2021	WAS	MLB	29	5	9	11	68	0	66	64	9	4.6	9.3	68	47.6%	.309	1.48	3.55	96	0.8	95.7	68.4%	25.1%	55.6%
2022	WAS	MLB	30	6	4	11	66	0	66^2	54	9	3.0	9.5	70	47.7%	.269	1.14	3.51	84	1.2	97.1	78.8%	27.6%	56.8%
2023 DC	*WAS*	*MLB*	*31*	*3*	*3*	*21*	*68*	*0*	*59.3*	*56*	*6*	*3.8*	*9.2*	*60*	*47.8%*	*.307*	*1.38*	*3.87*	*98*	*0.3*	*96.3*	*73.7%*	*26.5%*	*55.7%*

Comparables: Buddy Boshers (67), Andrew Kittredge (66), Blake Parker (66)

If Finnegan's 2021 season was like listening to music through laptop speakers, his 2022 was like seeing the band play live—the same songs simply sounded better. Many of his stats were eerily identical to the year prior (some admittedly more consequential than others). His games finished (24), saves (11), home runs allowed (9) and earned runs (26) were exact matches, while his workload, ground-ball rate and K/9 were all in the same ballpark as well. But there were subtle improvements that made a tremendous difference. His sinker was 1.4 mph faster on average, and he used it much more frequently. He cut down on walks and allowed lower-quality contact, which is how he faced 26 fewer batters while recording two more outs. The Nationals should book him another tour as the closer, but this time not only because of a lack of other options. Finnegan's earned his status as a bullpen headliner.

MacKenzie Gore LHP

Born: 02/24/99 Age: 24 Bats: L Throws: L Height: 6'2" Weight: 197 lb. Origin: Round 1, 2017 Draft (#3 overall)

YEAR	TEAM	LVL	AGE	W	L	SV	G	GS	IP	H	HR	BB/9	K/9	K	GB%	BABIP	WHIP	ERA	DRA-	WARP	MPH	FB%	Whiff%	CSP
2021	PAD	ROK	22	1	0	0	3	3	16^1	13	0	2.2	12.1	22	45.9%	.351	1.04	1.65						
2021	SA	AA	22	0	0	0	2	2	9	6	0	8.0	16.0	16	47.1%	.353	1.56	3.00	92	0.1				
2021	ELP	AAA	22	0	2	0	6	6	20	24	3	5.4	8.1	18	46.2%	.339	1.80	5.85	105	0.0				
2022	ROC	AAA	23	0	1	0	4	4	12	16	3	3.0	6.8	9	48.8%	.342	1.67	5.25	113	0.1				
2022	SD	MLB	23	4	4	0	16	13	70	66	7	4.8	9.3	72	37.8%	.312	1.47	4.50	116	0.1	95.0	60.9%	24.2%	55.4%
2023 DC	*WAS*	*MLB*	*24*	*4*	*6*	*0*	*17*	*17*	*80*	*80*	*11*	*4.7*	*8.7*	*77*	*41.0%*	*.306*	*1.53*	*4.94*	*119*	*-0.1*	*95.0*	*60.9%*	*26.0%*	*55.4%*

Comparables: Robbie Erlin (58), Joe Ross (58), Sean Reid-Foley (57)

Gore is the poster boy for nonlinear development. In 2019 and 2020, he was baseball's consensus top pitching prospect. Then he lost consistency with his release point in 2021 and got walloped across four minor-league levels, plus the Arizona Fall League. He found his old self in the spring of 2022 and debuted for the Padres in April. Through June 10, he looked like a Cy Young and Rookie of the Year candidate with a 1.50 ERA and 57 strikeouts in 48 innings. But soon after, his old bugaboos resurfaced. His release points for all his pitches had been nearly identical in April, but by July there were two inches of horizontal separation between his fastball and off-speed stuff, and he lost some velocity along the way. Then he hit the IL with elbow inflammation and got shipped off to Washington. Gore will surely keep his new pitching coaches busy, but can still develop into a different, better type of poster boy—a top-of-the-rotation starter.

Josiah Gray RHP Born: 12/21/97 Age: 25 Bats: R Throws: R Height: 6'1" Weight: 199 lb. Origin: Round 2, 2018 Draft (#72 overall)

YEAR	TEAM	LVL	AGE	W	L	SV	G	GS	IP	H	HR	BB/9	K/9	K	GB%	BABIP	WHIP	ERA	DRA-	WARP	MPH	FB%	Whiff%	CSP
2021	OKC	AAA	23	1	1	0	4	3	15^{2}	8	3	1.1	12.6	22	36.4%	.167	0.64	2.87	85	0.2				
2021	LAD	MLB	23	0	0	0	2	1	8	7	4	5.6	14.6	13	29.4%	.231	1.50	6.75	86	0.1	94.8	50.0%	44.7%	47.7%
2021	WAS	MLB	23	2	2	0	12	12	62^{2}	56	15	4.0	9.0	63	29.6%	.258	1.34	5.31	116	0.1	94.6	51.9%	28.3%	51.9%
2022	WAS	MLB	24	7	10	0	28	28	148^{2}	136	38	4.0	9.3	154	32.9%	.257	1.36	5.02	112	0.6	94.6	43.0%	27.0%	52.5%
2023 DC	*WAS*	*MLB*	*25*	*10*	*9*	*0*	*29*	*29*	*163*	*143*	*23*	*3.7*	*9.6*	*173*	*33.3%*	*.284*	*1.29*	*3.77*	*97*	*1.6*	*94.6*	*45.2%*	*27.8%*	*52.2%*

Comparables: Jarred Cosart (73), Drew Hutchison (72), Joe Ross (71)

There have been 11 Hall of Fame pitchers whose ERAs exceeded 5.00 in their sophomore seasons, including Bob Gibson and Greg Maddux. How many pitchers met that criterion and *didn't* reach the Hall? Let's not get into that. The point is that Gray's disappointing second season isn't a death knell for his career. Both of his breaking pitches are highly effective—he throws the slider predominantly to right-handed hitters and the curve to lefties—but opponents demolished his four-seam fastball to the tune of 24 home runs and a .738 slugging percentage, even though he featured it just 39% of the time. He experimented with a two-seamer late in the year, which could become his go-to fastball in 2023. Whichever heater he throws, it would be in his best interest not to lead the league in both home runs and walks allowed again, but at least he has Phil Niekro for company in that regard. His rotation spot is secure because, well, read the rest of Washington's pitcher comments.

Will Harris RHP Born: 08/28/84 Age: 38 Bats: R Throws: R Height: 6'4" Weight: 234 lb. Origin: Round 9, 2006 Draft (#258 overall)

YEAR	TEAM	LVL	AGE	W	L	SV	G	GS	IP	H	HR	BB/9	K/9	K	GB%	BABIP	WHIP	ERA	DRA-	WARP	MPH	FB%	Whiff%	CSP
2020	WAS	MLB	35	0	1	1	20	0	17^{2}	21	3	4.6	10.7	21	42.6%	.353	1.70	3.06	89	0.3	90.7	77.7%	28.9%	42.6%
2021	WAS	MLB	36	0	1	0	8	0	6	7	1	4.5	13.5	9	33.3%	.353	1.67	9.00	86	0.1	90.2	80.7%	26.5%	55.8%
2023 DC	*FA*	*MLB*	*38*	*1*	*1*	*0*	*28*	*0*	*25*	*26*	*3*	*3.4*	*8.0*	*22*	*45.2%*	*.311*	*1.43*	*4.47*	*112*	*-0.1*	*90.9*	*69.3%*	*25.2%*	*47.0%*

Comparables: Darren O'Day (59), Joe Smith (59), Blake Parker (58)

The thoracic outlet is a thoroughfare for nerves and blood vessels between the collarbone and the first rib. Repeatedly straining the arm—by throwing thousands of pitches over more than 30 years, for example—can cause inflammation that compresses the outlet, potentially leading to circulation issues and nerve damage. Decompression surgery involves removing the rib, scar tissue and possibly certain muscles to relieve the pressure. That's what Harris has been dealing with while he's been absent from MLB action. Many thoracic outlet surgery patients regain normal arm function through physical therapy, but there's nothing normal about repeatedly firing off 90-mph cutters. After a disastrous, aborted rehab attempt, he will have to prove his arm is once again exceptional enough to earn a major-league opportunity at 38 years old.

Hunter Harvey RHP Born: 12/09/94 Age: 28 Bats: R Throws: R Height: 6'2" Weight: 225 lb. Origin: Round 1, 2013 Draft (#22 overall)

YEAR	TEAM	LVL	AGE	W	L	SV	G	GS	IP	H	HR	BB/9	K/9	K	GB%	BABIP	WHIP	ERA	DRA-	WARP	MPH	FB%	Whiff%	CSP
2020	BAL	MLB	25	0	2	0	10	0	8^{2}	8	2	2.1	6.2	6	39.3%	.231	1.15	4.15	115	0.0	97.5	77.2%	23.3%	49.2%
2021	NOR	AAA	26	2	1	0	8	1	10	19	2	1.8	6.3	7	54.8%	.436	2.10	8.10	104	0.1				
2021	BAL	MLB	26	0	0	0	9	0	8^{2}	8	1	3.1	6.2	6	48.1%	.269	1.27	4.15	106	0.1	97.2	64.0%	11.8%	57.8%
2022	WAS	MLB	27	2	1	0	38	0	39^{1}	33	1	2.7	10.3	45	39.0%	.323	1.14	2.52	82	0.7	98.3	77.9%	27.5%	55.4%
2023 DC	*WAS*	*MLB*	*28*	*3*	*3*	*1*	*68*	*0*	*59.3*	*57*	*7*	*3.2*	*8.6*	*56*	*41.8%*	*.301*	*1.33*	*3.98*	*102*	*0.2*	*98.1*	*75.9%*	*24.5%*	*54.9%*

Comparables: Jared Hughes (53), Ryne Stanek (52), Jeremy Jeffress (52)

If a pitcher has an 80-grade fastball, does he need anything else? Harvey's triple-digit four-seamer generated a 27.5% whiff rate and a 33.1% called strikes plus whiffs rate. He consistently located it on the outside corner against right-handed hitters and the upper part of the zone versus lefties. His heater was so dominant that he scarcely used any other offering—his 77% four-seam usage was sixth-highest in MLB and the highest of his career. So what else does he need to succeed? Health, for one thing. Injuries derailed his previous three MLB seasons back in Baltimore and robbed him of two months in 2022, but for the first time in his career, he stayed off the IL long enough to demonstrate how his fastball can dominate with little accompaniment.

Cole Henry RHP Born: 07/15/99 Age: 23 Bats: R Throws: R Height: 6'4" Weight: 215 lb. Origin: Round 2, 2020 Draft (#55 overall)

YEAR	TEAM	LVL	AGE	W	L	SV	G	GS	IP	H	HR	BB/9	K/9	K	GB%	BABIP	WHIP	ERA	DRA-	WARP	MPH	FB%	Whiff%	CSP
2021	WIL	A+	21	3	3	0	9	8	43	23	3	2.3	13.2	63	46.4%	.247	0.79	1.88	74	1.0				
2022	HBG	AA	22	0	0	0	7	7	23^{2}	5	1	3.4	10.6	28	42.6%	.087	0.59	0.76	92	0.4				
2022	ROC	AAA	22	1	0	0	2	2	8	9	1	2.3	6.7	6	38.5%	.320	1.38	4.50	108	0.1				
2023 non-DC	*WAS*	*MLB*	*23*	*2*	*2*	*0*	*57*	*0*	*50*	*46*	*6*	*4.0*	*9.2*	*51*	*43.1%*	*.300*	*1.38*	*4.13*	*102*	*0.1*			*29.1%*	

Comparables: Alex White (56), Sean Reid-Foley (56), Carl Edwards Jr. (56)

Henry absolutely annihilated Double-A hitters in seven starts, striking out 32.9% of opponents and surrendering just five hits in 23⅔ innings. However, according to our super advanced mathematical computations, that's an average of fewer than four innings pitched per start. Two games after his June promotion to Rochester, thoracic outlet syndrome ended Henry's season. "Relief risk" was already stamped in bold print on his profile before the injury; now, it's underlined and italicized. He features three plus pitches—fastball, changeup and slider—but has never accumulated more than 58⅓ innings in a season at any level, and even that modest career high was set in his freshman year at LSU. If he doesn't blow his personal best out of the water soon, he'll have to start throwing those innings one at a time.

Andres Machado RHP

Born: 04/22/93 Age: 30 Bats: R Throws: R Height: 6'0" Weight: 235 lb. Origin: International Free Agent, 2010

YEAR	TEAM	LVL	AGE	W	L	SV	G	GS	IP	H	HR	BB/9	K/9	K	GB%	BABIP	WHIP	ERA	DRA-	WARP	MPH	FB%	Whiff%	CSP
2020	ORI	WIN	27	2	1	0	8	6	25^1	32	1	4.3	5.0	14	61.3%	.365	1.74	3.20						
2021	ROC	AAA	28	0	0	0	11	0	14^2	17	1	2.5	11.7	19	53.5%	.381	1.43	3.68	88	0.3				
2021	WAS	MLB	28	1	2	0	40	0	35^2	30	4	3.8	7.6	30	44.2%	.260	1.26	3.53	109	0.2	94.8	70.8%	22.9%	55.0%
2022	ROC	AAA	29	0	0	0	13	0	17	18	0	2.6	9.5	18	47.9%	.375	1.35	5.82	91	0.3				
2022	WAS	MLB	29	2	0	0	51	0	59^1	55	7	3.9	7.0	46	43.3%	.267	1.37	3.34	112	0.2	95.4	64.6%	24.0%	52.7%
2023 DC	*WAS*	*MLB*	*30*	*3*	*3*	*0*	*68*	*0*	*59.3*	*63*	*7*	*3.9*	*7.0*	*46*	*44.6%*	*.304*	*1.49*	*4.86*	*119*	*-0.4*	*95.2*	*66.6%*	*23.7%*	*53.4%*

Comparables: Gonzalez Germen (53), Rob Scahill (51), Sam Dyson (51)

Machado led Washington pitchers in saves. Not the classic *saves* stat, of which he had none at all, but in rescuing his fellow hurlers from inflated ERAs: He allowed only four of his 25 inherited runners to score in 2022. It isn't clear if this is a repeatable skill or random happenstance—probably the latter—but there's incalculable value in Machado's willingness and ability to clean up teammates' messes when most relievers prefer to start an inning cleanly. Of course, the Nationals still allowed the second-most runs in all of MLB despite his unique aptitude, and his individual performance was otherwise unremarkable. But the staff would have been even more dreadful without Machado saving them from many more disastrous innings, so here's to hoping he gets the props he's due in the clubhouse.

Jake McGee LHP

Born: 08/06/86 Age: 36 Bats: L Throws: L Height: 6'4" Weight: 229 lb. Origin: Round 5, 2004 Draft (#135 overall)

YEAR	TEAM	LVL	AGE	W	L	SV	G	GS	IP	H	HR	BB/9	K/9	K	GB%	BABIP	WHIP	ERA	DRA-	WARP	MPH	FB%	Whiff%	CSP
2020	LAD	MLB	33	3	1	0	24	0	20^1	14	2	1.3	14.6	33	37.2%	.300	0.84	2.66	68	0.6	95.0	97.0%	34.4%	59.0%
2021	SF	MLB	34	3	2	31	62	0	59^2	44	7	1.5	8.7	58	35.5%	.228	0.91	2.72	98	0.6	95.1	90.1%	20.6%	59.0%
2022	MIL	MLB	35	0	0	0	6	0	5^2	7	2	1.6	6.4	4	30.0%	.278	1.41	6.35	110	0.0	94.4	77.4%	14.0%	67.3%
2022	WAS	MLB	35	0	1	0	12	0	10	7	2	4.5	9.0	10	22.2%	.208	1.20	6.30	106	0.1	93.8	80.8%	21.8%	60.7%
2022	SF	MLB	35	1	2	3	24	0	21^1	27	2	2.5	4.6	11	29.1%	.325	1.55	7.17	142	-0.3	94.9	85.2%	19.6%	60.0%
2023 DC	*FA*	*MLB*	*36*	*2*	*2*	*0*	*43*	*0*	*37.3*	*37*	*5*	*2.5*	*8.1*	*33*	*33.9%*	*.296*	*1.28*	*4.04*	*105*	*0.0*	*94.7*	*87.0%*	*22.2%*	*59.1%*

Comparables: Sparky Lyle (70), Mike Stanton (68), John Franco (68)

McGee achieved the trifecta of unwanted player transactions in 2022, getting released, waived and designated for assignment. Despite his advancing age, declining stuff is not to blame here. McGee threw the second-highest percentage of fastballs in the majors, and even though batters slugged .480 against it as opposed to .333 in 2021, its velocity and movement didn't change much. But location is paramount for any one-pitch pitcher, and therein lies the rub. McGee was ahead in the count 45% of the time he threw the culminating pitch in a plate appearance throughout the 2021 season; he trailed in these scenarios just 26% of the time. In 2022, he had the advantage against only 35% of the batters he faced and fell behind in 32% of matchups. Correspondingly, his 15.3% strikeout rate was the worst of his career. He needs to throw strike one more consistently to avoid adding more ugly words to his transactions ledger in 2023.

Tanner Rainey RHP

Born: 12/25/92 Age: 30 Bats: R Throws: R Height: 6'2" Weight: 244 lb. Origin: Round 2, 2015 Draft (#71 overall)

YEAR	TEAM	LVL	AGE	W	L	SV	G	GS	IP	H	HR	BB/9	K/9	K	GB%	BABIP	WHIP	ERA	DRA-	WARP	MPH	FB%	Whiff%	CSP
2020	WAS	MLB	27	1	1	0	20	0	20^1	8	4	3.1	14.2	32	34.3%	.129	0.74	2.66	73	0.5	97.1	60.9%	47.3%	44.4%
2021	ROC	AAA	28	1	0	0	8	1	7^2	3	1	5.9	17.6	15	18.2%	.200	1.04	2.35	77	0.2				
2021	WAS	MLB	28	1	3	3	38	0	31^2	29	6	7.1	11.9	42	24.7%	.307	1.71	7.39	105	0.2	96.4	64.5%	35.6%	53.6%
2022	WAS	MLB	29	1	3	12	29	0	30	26	5	3.9	10.8	36	31.6%	.284	1.30	3.30	91	0.4	97.1	70.3%	33.5%	54.9%
2023 non-DC	*WAS*	*MLB*	*30*	*2*	*2*	*0*	*57*	*0*	*50*	*40*	*7*	*5.0*	*11.5*	*63*	*35.1%*	*.283*	*1.36*	*4.02*	*98*	*0.2*	*97.0*	*67.3%*	*34.7%*	*51.5%*

Comparables: Danny Farquhar (59), JT Chargois (59), Brad Brach (58)

Why do we drive on a parkway and park on a driveway? Is a closer still the closer if he's physically unable to throw a baseball? Can a sunbather get Tanner on a Rainey day? Does a pitcher still have a 97-mph fastball after he tears his UCL? Why is it that when you transport something by car, it's a shipment, but when you transport something by ship, it's called cargo? Would the Nationals have traded Rainey for a mid-level prospect in July if he hadn't succumbed to Tommy John surgery? These are among life's unanswerable questions. Here's one more: Will the high-octane reliever take the mound at all in 2023?

Erasmo Ramírez RHP Born: 05/02/90 Age: 33 Bats: R Throws: R Height: 6'0" Weight: 217 lb. Origin: International Free Agent, 2007

YEAR	TEAM	LVL	AGE	W	L	SV	G	GS	IP	H	HR	BB/9	K/9	K	GB%	BABIP	WHIP	ERA	DRA-	WARP	MPH	FB%	Whiff%	CSP
2020	NYM	MLB	30	0	0	1	6	0	14^1	8	1	2.5	5.7	9	42.5%	.179	0.84	0.63	116	0.0	90.7	44.6%	21.3%	47.9%
2021	TOL	AAA	31	1	0	0	5	0	8	4	0	3.4	11.2	10	47.4%	.211	0.88	3.38	91	0.1				
2021	DET	MLB	31	1	1	0	17	0	26^2	24	4	1.7	6.7	20	37.3%	.253	1.09	5.74	113	0.1	92.5	45.4%	16.8%	62.1%
2022	WAS	MLB	32	4	2	0	60	2	86^1	79	11	1.5	6.4	61	45.1%	.268	1.08	2.92	103	0.7	93.2	43.9%	21.4%	57.2%
2023 DC	*WAS*	*MLB*	*33*	*3*	*3*	*0*	*68*	*0*	*59.3*	*60*	*7*	*2.3*	*6.5*	*42*	*43.5%*	*.290*	*1.28*	*3.86*	*103*	*0.2*	*92.9*	*44.3%*	*21.5%*	*57.5%*

Comparables: Mudcat Grant (62), Anthony Swarzak (60), Jason Grimsley (59)

Whereas some pitchers resemble a Saturday night out at a fancy boutique restaurant, Ramírez is more like a Sunday afternoon Costco trip—everything on his shelves comes in bulk. The grocery list:

- **Innings Pitched**: He led the NL with 80⅔ of them out of the bullpen.
- **Fastballs**: More than 90% of his pitches were either cutters or sinkers.
- **Strikes**: He threw first-pitch strikes 59% of the time and walked just 4% of opposing hitters.
- **Reverse Splits**: His cutter excelled at sawing off lefties, who managed a paltry .588 OPS against him.

He's never going to be Michelin rated, but Ramírez can fill any team's fridge with reliable, multi-inning relief work.

Joe Ross RHP Born: 05/21/93 Age: 30 Bats: R Throws: R Height: 6'4" Weight: 232 lb. Origin: Round 1, 2011 Draft (#25 overall)

YEAR	TEAM	LVL	AGE	W	L	SV	G	GS	IP	H	HR	BB/9	K/9	K	GB%	BABIP	WHIP	ERA	DRA-	WARP	MPH	FB%	Whiff%	CSP
2021	WAS	MLB	28	5	9	0	20	19	108	98	17	2.8	9.1	109	42.7%	.280	1.22	4.17	90	1.6	93.6	63.5%	25.3%	55.3%
2023 DC	*FA*	*MLB*	*30*	*1*	*1*	*0*	*28*	*0*	*25*	*24*	*2*	*3.2*	*8.3*	*23*	*43.3%*	*.300*	*1.33*	*3.99*	*102*	*0.1*	*93.7*	*63.4%*	*25.0%*	*53.4%*

Comparables: Jhoulys Chacín (54), Zach McAllister (52), Vance Worley (52)

Ross spent most of his walk year walking to and from the doctor's office. A procedure to remove bone spurs in his elbow kept him out of action for the first two months of the season. In his one and only rehab appearance on May 24, he tore his UCL and had to undergo his second Tommy John surgery. His only on-field highlight was playing with some adorable puppies from Wolf Trap Animal Rescue on August 26 (you can watch the video on his Twitter page, @JoeRoss21). This was a brilliant career move for Ross: If an MLB executive is going to sign a pitcher whose elbow looks like a crossword puzzle, the guy should at least be willing and able to roll around with some very good doggos in foul territory.

Aníbal Sánchez RHP Born: 02/27/84 Age: 39 Bats: R Throws: R Height: 6'0" Weight: 207 lb. Origin: International Free Agent, 2001

YEAR	TEAM	LVL	AGE	W	L	SV	G	GS	IP	H	HR	BB/9	K/9	K	GB%	BABIP	WHIP	ERA	DRA-	WARP	MPH	FB%	Whiff%	CSP
2020	WAS	MLB	36	4	5	0	11	11	53	70	11	3.1	7.3	43	39.8%	.347	1.66	6.62	121	0.0	89.8	32.6%	23.7%	45.9%
2022	ROC	AAA	38	0	1	0	3	3	12^2	12	0	5.7	9.2	13	35.1%	.324	1.58	4.26	106	0.1				
2022	WAS	MLB	38	4	6	0	14	14	69^1	55	13	4.3	6.2	48	37.2%	.218	1.27	4.28	124	-0.2	89.3	38.9%	19.7%	52.8%
2023 DC	*FA*	*MLB*	*39*	*3*	*4*	*0*	*11*	*11*	*59.7*	*62*	*9*	*4.1*	*6.1*	*40*	*37.8%*	*.285*	*1.49*	*4.90*	*122*	*-0.2*	*89.8*	*36.5%*	*20.2%*	*49.7%*

Comparables: Tim Hudson (73), John Lackey (72), Mike Mussina (69)

Sánchez has been featured in every *Annual* since 2005, which was published nine days before the first spring-training game ever played by a team called the Washington Nationals. His debut comment praised his "excellent fastball" that "absolutely destroyed hitters in the NY-Penn League." Eighteen years later, the hardest heater he threw was just 92 mph. Times have changed: 71 different MLB pitchers threw a changeup 92 mph or faster in 2022, but none of them can replicate *la mariposa*— Sánchez's butterfly change with all the characteristics of a knuckleball that he floated in as daintily as 60 mph. There's nary a pitch ever invented that he doesn't throw—including at least one he concocted himself—but his quantity-over-quality pitch mix led to the worst DRA- of his venerable career. That limits his role to viable innings-eater and mentor on bad teams, but while Sánchez may no longer be good, he's undeniably entertaining.

Stephen Strasburg RHP Born: 07/20/88 Age: 34 Bats: R Throws: R Height: 6'5" Weight: 239 lb. Origin: Round 1, 2009 Draft (#1 overall)

YEAR	TEAM	LVL	AGE	W	L	SV	G	GS	IP	H	HR	BB/9	K/9	K	GB%	BABIP	WHIP	ERA	DRA-	WARP	MPH	FB%	Whiff%	CSP
2020	WAS	MLB	31	0	1	0	2	2	5	8	1	1.8	3.6	2	35.0%	.368	1.80	10.80	108	0.0	92.0	45.8%	26.3%	42.1%
2021	WAS	MLB	32	1	2	0	5	5	21^2	16	4	5.8	8.7	21	37.3%	.218	1.38	4.57	104	0.2	91.5	54.9%	25.0%	52.5%
2022	FBG	A	33	1	1	0	2	2	7^2	3	0	5.9	10.6	9	35.3%	.176	1.04	3.52	102	0.1				
2022	ROC	AAA	33	0	0	0	1	1	6	1	0	1.5	6.0	4	46.7%	.067	0.33	0.00	92	0.1				
2022	WAS	MLB	33	0	1	0	1	1	4^2	8	1	3.9	9.6	5	40.0%	.500	2.14	13.50	109	0.0	90.3	51.8%	20.0%	60.2%
2023 DC	*WAS*	*MLB*	*34*	*4*	*5*	*0*	*16*	*16*	*77.7*	*71*	*9*	*3.9*	*9.1*	*78*	*42.5%*	*.294*	*1.35*	*3.95*	*100*	*0.7*	*93.2*	*49.9%*	*27.1%*	*47.2%*

Comparables: Bob Welch (84), Don Sutton (84), Roger Clemens (82)

When Strasburg was selected with the first overall pick in the 2009 draft, he routinely topped 100 mph. Now 34 years old, he hasn't reached 95 mph even once since winning the 2019 World Series MVP. The "small sample size" disclaimer applies here in the bleakest possible way, as he's only thrown 530 pitches in 31⅓ innings for the Nationals over the past three years. The dreaded thoracic outlet syndrome that ended his 2021 season in July delayed his 2022 debut until June. Then, after just one start, he landed back on the IL with a stress reaction (we've all been there, buddy), which was later determined to be a thoracic outlet syndrome recurrence.

A decade-plus ago while at San Diego State, Strasburg famously added 10 ticks to his heater by laying off the fish tacos, losing weight and getting into better shape. Sadly, there's no simple solution this time around. With four years remaining on his contract, the odds of Strasburg getting and staying healthy, rediscovering his velocity and becoming a reliable pitcher again are long ... about as long as an out-of-shape kid who throws 88 mph developing into the top pick in the draft and generational talent in the first place.

Mason Thompson RHP Born: 02/20/98 Age: 25 Bats: R Throws: R Height: 6'6" Weight: 236 lb. Origin: Round 3, 2016 Draft (#85 overall)

YEAR	TEAM	LVL	AGE	W	L	SV	G	GS	IP	H	HR	BB/9	K/9	K	GB%	BABIP	WHIP	ERA	DRA-	WARP	MPH	FB%	Whiff%	CSP
2021	ELP	AAA	23	3	2	7	23	0	26^2	25	4	2.7	8.1	24	69.2%	.284	1.24	5.74	86	0.3				
2021	SD	MLB	23	0	0	0	4	0	3	4	0	3.0	6.0	2	50.0%	.400	1.67	3.00	95	0.0	98.1	97.7%	28.6%	54.5%
2021	WAS	MLB	23	1	3	0	27	0	21^2	28	4	5.8	8.7	21	50.0%	.364	1.94	4.15	109	0.1	96.0	83.7%	20.1%	52.0%
2022	ROC	AAA	24	0	4	0	11	1	15^1	15	0	2.9	11.2	19	50.0%	.357	1.30	3.52	86	0.3				
2022	WAS	MLB	24	1	1	1	24	0	24^2	19	2	3.3	5.5	15	51.3%	.233	1.14	2.92	106	0.2	95.9	74.5%	23.2%	54.8%
2023 DC	*WAS*	*MLB*	*25*	*3*	*3*	*0*	*68*	*0*	*59.3*	*66*	*7*	*4.4*	*7.1*	*46*	*50.1%*	*.320*	*1.61*	*5.27*	*125*	*-0.5*	*96.1*	*79.4%*	*23.7%*	*53.6%*

Comparables: Alex Burnett (75), J.B. Wendelken (72), Silvino Bracho (69)

Thompson is an exemplar of the Nationals' pitching philosophy (yes, they have one, stop laughing). His slider is inconsistent, sometimes dropping more than a foot, but other times only a few inches and with different degrees of horizontal sweep. Yet opponents hit just .067 against it. The breaking pitch plays up because—like several other pitchers throughout the organization—he throws his fastball more than 70% of the time. In his case, it's a high-90s two-seamer with arm-side run that induced a 54.4% ground-ball rate. Neither of his pitches are swing-and-miss offerings, but it's difficult for batters to prepare for the slider when he throws the two-seamer nearly all the time early in counts. There are whispers he's developing a changeup too, but in the interim, expect him to ride his 75/25 fastball/slider combo as an intriguing member of the Nationals' 2023 relief corps.

Jordan Weems RHP Born: 11/07/92 Age: 30 Bats: L Throws: R Height: 6'4" Weight: 209 lb. Origin: Round 3, 2011 Draft (#111 overall)

YEAR	TEAM	LVL	AGE	W	L	SV	G	GS	IP	H	HR	BB/9	K/9	K	GB%	BABIP	WHIP	ERA	DRA-	WARP	MPH	FB%	Whiff%	CSP
2020	OAK	MLB	27	0	0	0	9	0	14	10	1	4.5	11.6	18	27.3%	.281	1.21	3.21	99	0.2	95.5	62.2%	32.3%	47.5%
2021	RNO	AAA	28	1	1	0	15	0	13^2	15	3	5.3	5.9	9	58.1%	.300	1.68	7.24	103	0.0				
2021	LV	AAA	28	0	2	1	15	0	14^2	17	6	3.7	10.4	17	39.0%	.314	1.57	7.36	89	0.2				
2021	AZ	MLB	28	0	1	0	2	0	1^1	4	1	20.2	20.2	3	60.0%	.750	5.25	47.25	95	0.0	94.8	54.9%	22.7%	49.2%
2021	OAK	MLB	28	0	0	0	5	0	4^1	2	1	6.2	8.3	4	27.3%	.100	1.15	6.23	93	0.1	95.3	62.7%	23.7%	51.5%
2022	ROC	AAA	29	3	2	16	33	0	40	31	4	2.7	11.0	49	33.7%	.297	1.08	2.70	85	0.9				
2022	WAS	MLB	29	0	1	0	32	0	39^2	35	7	2.7	9.3	41	34.5%	.267	1.18	5.22	93	0.5	96.9	63.8%	24.4%	54.2%
2023 DC	*WAS*	*MLB*	*30*	*2*	*2*	*0*	*45*	*0*	*39.3*	*37*	*5*	*3.9*	*8.0*	*35*	*36.7%*	*.280*	*1.37*	*4.22*	*107*	*0.0*	*96.5*	*63.2%*	*27.0%*	*53.1%*

Comparables: Andrew Kittredge (67), Rob Wooten (66), Luke Bard (66)

Watching Weems pitch is like reheating leftover pasta uncovered. If all goes well, you've got a sufficient, unexciting Tuesday lunch. If it doesn't, marinara explodes all over the inside of the microwave, and now you need to get a damp paper towel to clean it because you want to be a considerate coworker, but Linda from Human Resources is getting huffy because she's been tapping her foot behind you for two minutes already while her glare burns a hole in your soul as you try to get the tricky faucet to work right without destroying the paper towel, and you know she's too passive aggressive to say anything to your face, but the next time there's an office birthday, you're DEFINITELY not getting a piece of cake with lettering on it. That said, DRA- thinks he was a bit unlucky last season.

Trevor Williams RHP Born: 04/25/92 Age: 31 Bats: R Throws: R Height: 6'3" Weight: 235 lb. Origin: Round 2, 2013 Draft (#44 overall)

YEAR	TEAM	LVL	AGE	W	L	SV	G	GS	IP	H	HR	BB/9	K/9	K	GB%	BABIP	WHIP	ERA	DRA-	WARP	MPH	FB%	Whiff%	CSP
2020	PIT	MLB	28	2	8	0	11	11	55^1	66	15	3.4	8.0	49	43.3%	.315	1.57	6.18	116	0.1	91.5	51.1%	24.3%	42.6%
2021	IOW	AAA	29	1	0	0	2	2	7	2	0	1.3	6.4	5	60.0%	.111	0.43	0.00	99	0.1				
2021	SYR	AAA	29	1	0	0	2	2	12	9	1	1.5	7.5	10	38.2%	.242	0.92	2.25	101	0.2				
2021	NYM	MLB	29	0	0	0	10	3	32^1	37	1	2.5	8.1	29	42.2%	.367	1.42	3.06	91	0.4	91.2	62.9%	25.3%	49.9%
2021	CHC	MLB	29	4	2	0	13	12	58^2	68	10	3.4	9.4	61	46.6%	.345	1.53	5.06	90	0.9	91.4	56.0%	23.6%	54.2%
2022	NYM	MLB	30	3	5	1	30	9	89^2	87	12	2.3	8.4	84	35.8%	.302	1.23	3.21	103	0.7	90.9	65.7%	23.8%	50.8%
2023 DC	*WAS*	*MLB*	*31*	*9*	*8*	*0*	*69*	*16*	*117.3*	*118*	*16*	*2.7*	*8.0*	*103*	*39.9%*	*.300*	*1.31*	*3.99*	*104*	*0.6*	*91.2*	*61.5%*	*23.3%*	*49.8%*

Comparables: Danny Cox (75), Dick Bosman (75), Ron Reed (74)

Although Javier Báez was the headliner of last year's trade between the Mets and Cubs, it was Williams who had the more lasting impact. He was something of an unsung hero for the 2022 Mets—the last bastion of the team's starting pitching depth and the only man standing between the various injuries endured by the starting rotation and far too many innings pitched by Quad-A types. The tattoo-adorned righty made nine starts in 2022 and pitched to a 4.19 ERA in those contests, but really shined in long relief, posting a 2.47 ERA in 51 innings out of the bullpen. The 2022 Mets may not have gone all the way, but they did corner the market on relievers named Trevor with a good online presence. Now that he's with the Nationals, Williams stands in line to return to his preferred starting role.

Lineouts

Hitters

HITTER	POS	TEAM	LVL	AGE	PA	R	2B	3B	HR	RBI	BB	K	SB	CS	AVG/OBP/SLG	DRC+	BABIP	BRR	DRP	WARP
Jake Alu	3B	HBG	AA	25	325	44	25	1	9	36	32	59	9	1	.281/.360/.470	122	.323	0.6	3B(64): 6.8, LF(4): -0.1, 2B(3): -0.3	2.4
	3B	ROC	AAA	25	242	37	15	1	11	45	19	44	6	2	.323/.372/.553	123	.353	0.8	3B(50): 0.3, 2B(6): -0.6	1.4
Yasel Antuna	LF	WIL	A+	22	415	66	13	1	10	44	72	88	26	6	.235/.372/.370	120	.283	0.8	LF(85): -0.5, RF(4): -0.7	2.0
	LF	HBG	AA	22	108	9	4	0	1	4	17	33	1	2	.143/.278/.220	84	.211	0.6	LF(25): -1.7	0.1
Tres Barrera	C	ROC	AAA	27	206	25	7	1	7	25	20	41	0	2	.254/.338/.424	117	.292	-1.1	C(53): -0.5	0.8
	C	WAS	MLB	27	53	2	1	0	0	4	2	16	0	0	.180/.212/.200	78	.265	-0.5	C(19): 0.2	0.0
Alex Call	OF	COL	AAA	27	305	56	16	1	11	46	49	50	6	0	.280/.418/.494	131	.306	-2.5	CF(22): 0.7, LF(21): 1.6, RF(14): 0.1	2.0
	OF	WAS	MLB	27	115	16	3	1	5	13	11	26	3	3	.245/.330/.441	109	.282	-0.7	LF(27): 0.4, CF(4): 0.3, RF(1): -0.1	0.5
	OF	CLE	MLB	27	16	2	0	0	0	0	4	4	0	0	.167/.375/.167	102	.250	0.5	RF(7): 0.1, CF(2): 0	0.1
Armando Cruz	SS	NAT	ROK	18	226	41	8	2	2	20	11	39	6	5	.275/.320/.362		.329			
Jeremy De La Rosa	CF	FBG	A	20	315	56	19	2	10	57	36	78	26	5	.315/.394/.505	114	.408	-0.1	CF(63): -3.0	0.7
	CF	WIL	A+	20	133	10	4	1	1	10	12	37	13	2	.195/.273/.271	76	.272	0.0	CF(26): 0.5, RF(5): 0.6	0.3
Lucius Fox	MI	ROC	AAA	24	231	28	7	2	4	25	22	61	12	4	.228/.306/.340	87	.305	-0.5	SS(39): 1.5, 2B(14): 0.0	0.4
	MI	WAS	MLB	24	28	2	0	0	0	2	1	9	1	0	.080/.115/.080	77	.125	0.2	SS(6): 0.5, 3B(4): -0.2	0.0
Trey Lipscomb	3B	FBG	A	22	101	15	4	1	1	13	4	19	12	1	.299/.327/.392	97	.364	0.8	3B(22): -1.6	0.2
Josh Palacios	OF	ROC	AAA	26	318	43	12	2	7	44	33	50	19	7	.298/.382/.433	113	.342	1.2	LF(37): 0.1, RF(21): 0.4, CF(4): 0.8	1.7
	OF	WAS	MLB	26	49	8	2	0	0	2	1	15	1	0	.213/.245/.255	67	.313	1.0	RF(12): 0.7, LF(9): 0.1	0.1
Israel Pineda	C	WIL	A+	22	271	31	16	2	8	45	22	70	2	2	.264/.325/.443	106	.335	-1.5	C(55): -6.4	0.2
	C	HBG	AA	22	103	15	3	0	7	21	9	18	1	0	.280/.340/.538	124	.275	0.2	C(22): -2.2	0.4
	C	ROC	AAA	22	26	3	1	0	1	5	5	7	0	0	.095/.269/.286	96	.077	-0.8	C(5): -0.8	-0.1
	C	WAS	MLB	22	14	1	0	0	0	0	1	7	0	0	.077/.143/.077	70	.167	-0.1	C(4): -0.2	0.0
Andrew Stevenson	OF	ROC	AAA	28	604	81	31	9	16	67	46	136	39	7	.279/.344/.457	103	.343	-0.6	CF(63): 1.5, LF(60): -1.7, RF(5): -0.5	1.4
Lane Thomas	OF	WAS	MLB	26	548	62	26	2	17	52	41	132	8	4	.241/.301/.404	98	.291	0.4	LF(73): -1.1, CF(56): -1.7, RF(43): 0.8	1.5
Leonel Valera	SS	GL	A+	22	167	20	3	2	5	21	15	57	11	0	.211/.293/.361	89	.299	1.4	3B(21): -1.7, SS(19): -0.7, 2B(1): -0.2	0.1
	SS	TUL	AA	22	360	61	12	5	13	62	33	119	22	1	.290/.361/.480	85	.419	6.0	SS(78): -7.5, 3B(6): -0.8, 2B(2): 0.1	0.2

Jake Alu plays several positions passably, which would be a high compliment in most other sports. In baseball it means he'll likely never be a regular at any of them, despite hitting well enough in the minors to vie for a major-league bench-warming spot soon. ⚾ **Yasel Antuna** has been in the Nationals' org since the Obama Administration but hasn't yet reached Triple-A. Now that he's dropped several rungs down the defensive ladder from shortstop to left field, time is running out for him to prove he's not the tan suit of prospects. ⚾ **Tres Barrera's** name translates to "Three Barrier." The first two barriers are Keibert Ruiz and Riley Adams. The third is roster limits that keep catcher *numero tres* on the 40-man but off the 26-man most of the time. ⚾ No gratuitous puns here: **Alex Call** finally got the, uh, *ringing phone sound* he had been waiting for since getting drafted in 2016. He proved to be a capable fourth outfielder when the Nationals, er, *summoned* him to perform as such after nabbing him on waivers. Wouldn't you, umm, *consider* that a success? ⚾ **Armando Cruz's** scouting report reads like someone brought their grandma to a nightclub: There's one 70 (defense) surrounded by mostly 20s and 30s (everything bat-related). His power grade needed a fake ID to get past the bouncer. ⚾ Like Billy Mays hawking cleaning products, the Nationals have been overaggressive in their promotion of **Jeremy De La Rosa** since bringing him stateside as a 17-year-old in 2019. He put himself back on the prospect map when repeating Low-A, but proved overmatched in Wilmington at age 20. ⚾ The student who finishes last in their medical school class still becomes a doctor, but you don't want them performing your colonoscopy. **Lucius Fox** became the last player from the 2017 Futures Game to reach the majors and you don't want him performing your colonoscopy either. ⚾ Despite barely playing in his first three seasons at the University of Tennessee, **Trey Lipscomb** exploded with a .355/.428/.717 slash line as a senior in 2022, earning a third-round draft selection. His power disappeared in Fredericksburg, but he's already proven to be a late bloomer. ⚾ **Josh Palacios** was one of only two MLB players with an opposite-field rate greater than 40% (min. 40 PA), which is further evidence that going the other way is not a direct substitute for solid contact. To win a backup outfielder spot—even on the Nationals—he'll need to hit the ball out of the infield more often. ⚾ Backstop **Israel Pineda** drew acclaim from the pitchers he worked with in the minors and has enough power to be worth keeping an eye on. A late-season trip to Washington cemented his humble position as fourth on the Nats' catcher depth chart. ⚾ Admiring **Andrew Stevenson's** Triple-A numbers is like sneaking a pack of gum into your backpack in seventh grade, then whispering to the popular kids on the bus, "Hey guys, wanna see something cool?" It won't make you feel as good as you think it will. ⚾ They're two, they're four, they're six, they're eight / His sprint speed's always pretty great / Dressed in red and white and blue / While hitting for some power, too / The Nats give him the chance to play / And spray singles the other way / Who's the batting order cleanse? / It's **Lane Thomas** (not his friends)! ⚾ An athletic shortstop is dripping with tools and talent, **Leonel Valera** wasn't able to put it all together consistently enough for the Dodgers. He'll take his power-speed (18 HR, 33-for-34 SB) combo to Washington on a minor-league deal.

Pitchers

PITCHER	TEAM	LVL	AGE	W	L	SV	G	GS	IP	H	HR	BB/9	K/9	K	GB%	BABIP	WHIP	ERA	DRA-	WARP	MPH	FB%	WHF	CSP
Gerardo Carrillo	WIL	A+	23	1	0	2	9	0	10	7	1	4.5	9.0	10	44.4%	.231	1.20	3.60	102	0.1				
	HBG	AA	23	1	1	0	10	0	10^1	14	1	7.0	14.8	17	44.8%	.464	2.13	11.32	89	0.2				
Matt Cronin	HBG	AA	24	1	0	0	14	0	16^1	5	0	3.9	12.1	22	26.7%	.167	0.73	0.00	92	0.3				
	ROC	AAA	24	3	1	0	34	0	35^2	30	3	3.8	8.6	34	35.4%	.281	1.26	3.53	100	0.5				
Reed Garrett	ROC	AAA	29	4	4	3	42	0	47^1	40	5	3.4	10.1	53	47.2%	.297	1.23	3.04	77	1.2				
	WAS	MLB	29	0	1	0	7	0	9^1	13	1	7.7	5.8	6	50.0%	.364	2.25	6.75	118	0.0	95.7	69.9%	22.6%	48.8%
Andry Lara	FBG	A	19	3	8	0	23	23	101^1	103	10	3.9	9.3	105	45.6%	.325	1.45	5.51	89	1.7				
Evan Lee	WIL	A+	25	0	1	0	3	3	6	5	0	9.0	9.0	6	31.2%	.313	1.83	4.50	98	0.0				
	HBG	AA	25	0	3	0	7	7	30	25	2	4.5	11.1	37	39.7%	.324	1.33	3.60	94	0.5				
	WAS	MLB	25	0	1	0	4	1	8^2	9	1	7.3	7.3	7	42.9%	.296	1.85	4.15	109	0.0	91.9	52.1%	19.4%	52.5%
Francisco Perez	ROC	AAA	24	1	3	1	45	0	46^2	34	3	6.2	11.8	61	33.6%	.292	1.41	4.82	84	1.0				
	WAS	MLB	24	0	0	0	10	0	8^2	13	2	9.3	7.3	7	43.8%	.367	2.54	7.27	114	0.0	93.3	62.9%	20.7%	52.7%
Seth Romero	HBG	AA	26	0	1	0	5	5	13^2	10	4	7.2	16.5	25	36.0%	.286	1.54	3.95	70	0.4				
Tommy Romero	ROC	AAA	24	3	1	0	6	2	19^1	13	4	4.2	6.5	14	32.1%	.173	1.14	2.33	118	0.1				
	DUR	AAA	24	6	5	1	23	13	66^2	57	12	3.4	7.8	58	36.8%	.251	1.23	3.51	102	0.8	89.3	53.6%	29.7%	
	WAS	MLB	24	0	1	0	1	1	3^2	8	5	9.8	4.9	2	17.6%	.250	3.27	14.73	141	0.0	90.6	57.1%	12.2%	53.4%
	TB	MLB	24	1	0	0	3	1	4^2	3	2	9.6	9.6	5	36.4%	.111	1.71	7.71	114	0.0	90.5	55.0%	28.9%	48.1%
Jackson Rutledge	FBG	A	23	8	6	0	20	20	97^1	106	7	2.7	9.2	99	51.2%	.354	1.39	4.90	89	1.6				
Jarlin Susana	PAD	ROK	18	0	0	0	8	7	29^1	15	1	3.4	13.5	44	56.6%	.269	0.89	2.45						
	FBG	A	18	0	0	0	3	3	10^1	9	1	4.4	11.3	13	38.5%	.320	1.35	2.61	93	0.1				
Jackson Tetreault	ROC	AAA	26	5	3	0	12	12	58	51	10	3.7	8.1	52	43.3%	.255	1.29	4.19	100	0.8				
	WAS	MLB	26	2	2	0	4	4	21	23	4	4.3	3.9	9	40.3%	.260	1.57	5.14	141	-0.2	94.4	57.8%	18.1%	53.1%
Thad Ward	SAL	A	25	0	0	0	2	2	6	2	0	1.5	15.0	10	60.0%	.200	0.50	0.00	84	0.1				
	GVL	A+	25	0	1	0	2	2	7	9	0	5.1	7.7	6	56.0%	.375	1.86	5.14	98	0.1				
	POR	AA	25	0	1	0	7	7	33^1	28	3	3.8	11.1	41	48.8%	.321	1.26	2.43	84	0.7				

Jake Bennett tagged along with Cade Cavalli in high school, college and now in the Nationals' organization. Washington's 2022 second-round pick has a lauded changeup and threw 68% of his pitches for strikes in his final collegiate season, but needs to develop a usable breaking pitch to join his former teammate in the majors. ⚾ Like a race car in need of a pit stop, righty reliever **Gerardo Carrillo** suffered from declining velocity in April and had to be shut down for a while. He ended the year in Harrisburg, right back at his starting point, which is also what a race car does. If only his name were a palindrome. ⚾ **Matt Cronin** is an extremely Nats pitcher in that he throws his fastball nearly 80% of the time because he lacks impactful secondaries. That said, his cheese has great life at the top of the zone, and he should vie for playing time in a wide-open Washington bullpen in 2023. ⚾ You know those ballplayers who rediscover themselves in Japan, then triumphantly return to MLB as regular contributors? **Reed Garrett** isn't yet among them, but he did flaunt a high-90s heater in seven appearances for Washington—all of which came in losses—after two years with the Saitama Seibu Lions. ⚾ **Andry Lara** has a future fifth starter's pitch mix, but his mid-90s fastball and fringy secondaries didn't impress Carolina League batters: His 23.3% strikeout rate was two points below league-average and he allowed a .381 OBP to lefties. ⚾ **Evan Lee** is a developmental victory—a 15th-round draft pick with a decent fastball/curveball combo and a maturing changeup—so *of course* elbow problems shut him down after only four MLB appearances, because the Nats can't have nice things. He rehabbed in Wilmington at the end of the year and should be ready for the start of 2023. ⚾ A classic 95-and-a-slider reliever, lefty **Francisco Perez** would get more mileage out of his arsenal if he could locate either offering in the vicinity of the strike zone. Too bad he failed to do so in either Rochester or Washington. ⚾ **Aldo Ramirez** is an undersized righty in the low minors with no true out pitch, but his stuff plays up due to advanced command—or at least it did in 2021 when he last pitched with a healthy elbow. ⚾ Once again, **Seth Romero** lost most of the year to a bevy of injuries. He rejoined Harrisburg in late August, but he hasn't thrown a competitive pitch in the months of April or May since he was kicked off the University of Houston baseball team in 2017. ⚾ When Icarus flew too close to the sun, the rays melted the wax holding his wings together and he plummeted to the sea. After **Tommy Romero** reached the majors, the Rays waived him and, when Washington claimed him, he plummeted to Rochester, which isn't as bad as drowning in the Mediterranean. ⚾ **Jackson Rutledge** must be a Civil War buff because he spent all season in Fredericksburg rather than moving back to Delaware. He struck out 28% of opposing hitters over his final six starts, so just like the Union in 1865, at least he finished his campaign strong. ⚾ This is the story of **Jarlin Susana** / Who throws the ball harder than anyone can-na / His stateside debut went according to plan-na / One day he hopes he can strike out Mark Canha. ⚾ Beware of misleading first impressions: Righty **Jackson Tetreault** commenced his major-league debut on June 14 by striking out Ronald Acuña Jr. He then promptly walked more batters than he fanned before a shoulder injury ended his season on July 2. ⚾ **Thad Ward** looked good in his return from Tommy John surgery, but that wasn't enough to earn him a 40-man roster spot with Boston in the offseason. The Nats pounced on him in the Rule 5 draft and now hope to turn him into their own version of Garrett Whitlock.

BALTIMORE ORIOLES

Essay by Lauren Theisen

Player comments by Robert Orr and BP staff

The most emotional moment of the Baltimore Orioles' 2022 season only happened because everybody knew the team was giving up. On the afternoon of July 28—the last O's home game before the trade deadline—Trey Mancini came up to bat in the bottom of the eighth and was greeted with a standing ovation from an official crowd of 16,784 at Camden Yards. After going down 0-2 to Tampa pitcher Shawn Armstrong, the Baltimore DH swatted a routine fly ball to right field, where Josh Lowe hustled backward and stuck up his glove to make a catch.

Except the ball didn't find Lowe's glove. In the bright sunlight of a 94-degree Maryland day, Lowe lost track of Mancini's easy out. As punishment, he was bonked in the head like Isaac Newton under an apple tree. Lowe fell to the grass in complete confusion, and the damaging projectile skipped away toward the foul line. While Roman Quinn made the long trek from center to try and retrieve it, Austin Hays scored from second and Mancini took a tour of the bases. Statcast's sprint speed clocked Mancini at 25.6 feet/second last season—499th out of 582 qualified major leaguers—but the Oriole fan favorite was chugging past third when Quinn made his throw home. The ball arrived in René Pinto's glove, just outside the lefty batter's box, with still a few steps remaining for Mancini. But Pinto was slow to get it in front of the plate, and Mancini just barely slid in safe. The official scorer, apparently feeling generous, refused to charge Lowe with an error even as the outfielder showed off a bruise on his left cheek in the postgame, so Mancini was awarded a legit inside-the-park home run.

"A fairy tale has come to life!" Orioles announcer Kevin Brown shouted, punctuating the roar of the fans. Baltimore would go on to win, 3-0, to pull themselves up to 50-49 on the year.

Part of the significance of Trey's magic moment came from the fact that it was Mo Gaba Day at the ballpark. Gaba was a hardcore Orioles and Ravens fan who was honored in several ways by each franchise before he died from cancer at 14 years old in July 2020. Mancini, who himself lost the entirety of his 2020 before coming back from colon cancer, caught the first pitch from Mo's mother Sonsy before this game and made sure to wave to her after he touched the plate. That day would be his last time in the home dugout at Camden Yards.

BALTIMORE ORIOLES PROSPECTUS

2022 W-L: 83-79, 4th in AL East

Pythag	.491	*16th*	DER	.693	*23rd*
RS/G	4.16	*20th*	DRC+	97	*19th*
RA/G	4.25	*17th*	DRA-	105	*20th*
dWin%	.467	*21st*	FIP	4.03	*19th*
Payroll	$44M	*30th*	B-Age	27.4	*9th*
M$/MW	$0.7M	*1st*	P-Age	28.2	*12th*

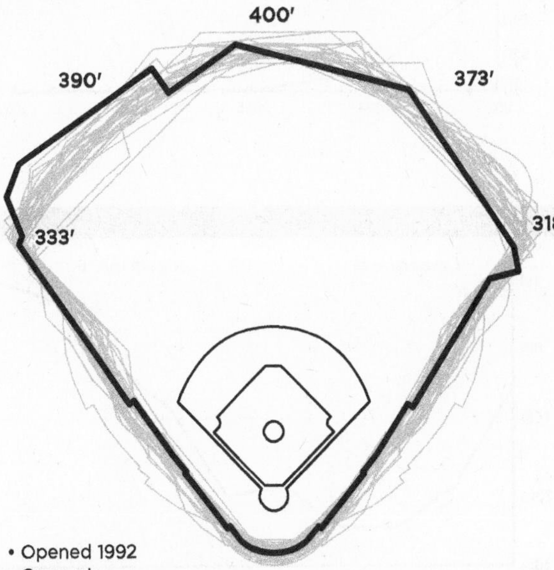

400'

390'

373'

333'

318'

- Opened 1992
- Open air
- Natural surface
- Fence profile: 7'4" to 21'

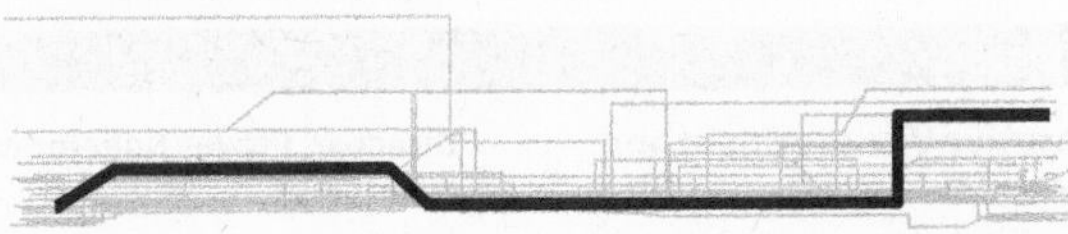

Park Factors

Runs	Runs/RH	Runs/LH	HR/RH	HR/LH
100	98	103	93	108

Top Hitter WARP	4.2 Adley Rutschman
Top Pitcher WARP	1.9 Félix Bautista
2023 Top Prospect	Gunnar Henderson

Payroll History (in millions)

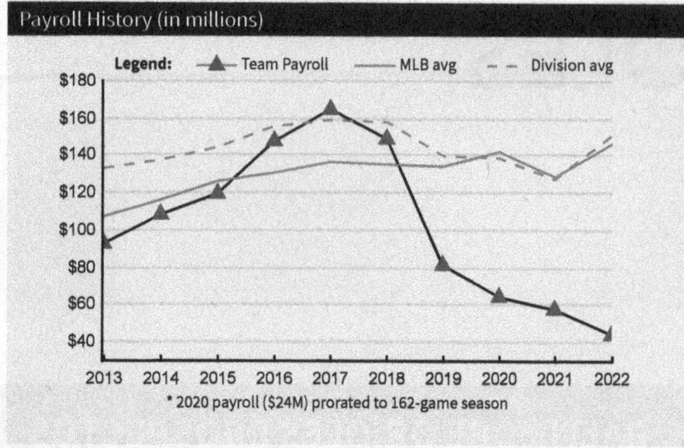

Future Commitments (in millions)

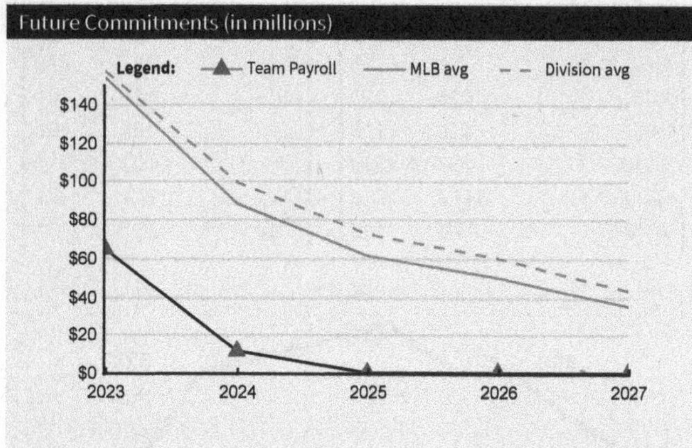

Farm System Ranking

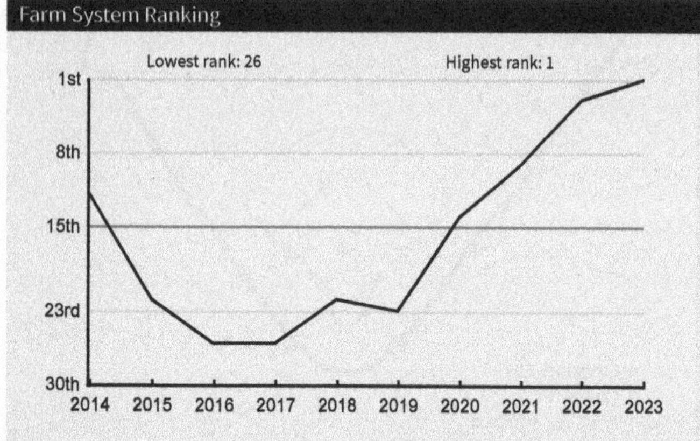

Personnel

Executive Vice President and General Manager
Mike Elias

Vice President & Assistant General Manager, Analytics
Sig Mejdal

Assistant General Manager, Baseball Operations
Eve Rosenbaum

Director, Baseball Systems
Di Zou

Director, Player Development
Matt Blood

Manager
Brandon Hyde

BP Alumni
Kevin Carter
Dan Drullinger

On August 1, to nobody's surprise, the Orioles traded Mancini to the Houston Astros in a deal that netted them a pitching prospect who needed Tommy John and another who had never played above A-ball. Mancini's final moment with the Orioles fans had been special, but the mood around the overachieving ballclub was bleak in the aftermath of his departure.

"We just lost one of the greatest teammates and one of the greatest players," All-Star pitcher Jorge López told the media. Anthony Santander, who's been with the team since 2017, was asked what Mancini had meant to the team and "grabbed a signed Mancini jersey out of his locker and gave it a hug," per the *Baltimore Sun*'s Nathan Ruiz. Mancini himself, talking about saying goodbye to the Orioles' training staff, said, "These are guys who I credit with saving my life two years ago."

The trade quickly became symbolic of not just the misery that has dogged the Orioles since they hit the reset button by trading Manny Machado and basically all of their other top players at the 2018 deadline, but also the seeming refusal to let their customers at least have *some* fun even if it wouldn't directly improve their mathematical chances of winning a title sometime before 2035. In the years after Mike Elias left the Astros to take over as GM from Dan Duquette after that 47-115 campaign, the team's actions gave little reason for optimism. The O's organization showed what felt like a hostile disinterest in their MLB club, washing their hands of pro-caliber players while stocking up on prospects and high draft picks in anticipation of winning further down the road.

Watching in real time, it sucked. The Orioles struggled to even play .350 ball, fielded a mostly anonymous roster of names nobody cared about and all but forfeited multiple seasons as 93-year-old owner Peter Angelos doled out miniscule payrolls even as his team took $600 million from the state of Maryland last year for upgrades to their ballpark, which cost just $110 million to build 30 years ago. The team was a middle finger to its own ticket holders, and especially after an intriguingly decent start to its 2022, the removal of Mancini was agony for any fans craving an accelerated timeline after some better-than-expected results.

It's not fair to say that the Mancini deal actively stopped the Orioles from making the playoffs. He became a liability for the Astros with a -0.5 fWAR, rarely appeared in their own postseason, and likely wouldn't have made up the three games that separated Baltimore from the sixth-place Rays. But the repeatedly unsentimental, almost abrasive transactions that have defined the modern Orioles still give me the creeps even after a 2022 that showed a light at the end of the tunnel. With an 83-79 year marking the first time since 2017 that the O's won more than 54 games in a season, there does seem to be a way out, and the possibility exists that the franchise could actually pull off the often-imitated, rarely-duplicated Astros tank job and recovery. But I'm still stuck looking at their recent past and wondering, What exactly would a successful Orioles team mean to its supporters, after all they've suffered through?

⚾ ⚾ ⚾

In my experience there are roughly two kinds of Orioles fans: the ones who grudgingly accept the argument that tanking is the cost of eventually winning a title, and the ones who want to put bedsheets over their heads and haunt Elias' house until he moves across the country. I side with the latter group, because the idea of fielding a 50-win team year in and year out, while refusing to spend even the relatively small amount of money that could elevate the roster into something that's not completely embarrassing, is unconscionably disgusting to me. I have to confess, even, that I don't particularly *want* the Orioles to find success in this fashion, because I don't want the sacrifice of the last five years to be held up as the model for a championship team.

I don't want to demonize the Elias defenders, though, because they have the same goal as their peers, just a different philosophy on how to reach it. These are the fans still stunned by the Chris Davis contract, which left the Orioles paying $17 million a year for the world's worst hitter, or who favorably compare what the Angels are getting out of Anthony Rendon with what Baltimore got out of Ramón Urías last year for about $35 million less. They understand the logic that MLB's player-payment structure creates a financial incentive toward using inexperienced players at the expense of older free agents, and they've made peace with their team trying to game the system instead of playing nice and generous in a way that could still ultimately fail.

But the other group is clawing their own eyes out because they so badly want to see some guys that win some freaking baseball games. Not just some guys, actually, but *their guys*. Manny Machado, Jonathan Schoop, Renato Núñez, Jonathan Villar, Kevin Gausman, Trey Mancini: So many players created little glimmers of fun for Baltimore fans before they were unceremoniously shipped away and replaced with strangers who couldn't do anything to help the present-day team. Years and years were doomed by this franchise's refusal to try. Now, as players like Adley Rutschman and Gunnar Henderson poke their heads out of the ashes, forming a nucleus that pledges to usher in a new era of success for the Orioles, they have to ask themselves whether or not they can trust the same decision-makers who forced them to sit through all that ugly crap.

⚾ ⚾ ⚾

Jerry Seinfeld has a famous joke about how sports fans are actually cheering for clothes, because the players are always changing, but that doesn't quite cover what it means to really support a team. It's something more akin to a series of arranged marriages, where the fan learns to love (or, sometimes, curse the name of) the guys they get matched up with. Someone like Trey Mancini arrives mostly unknown, a promising but not spectacular prospect who was drafted in the eighth round and worked his way through the minors. He hits three home runs in his first three starts in September 2016. He finishes third in Rookie of the Year voting the following season. He takes a step back in 2018 but plays his butt off for an absolutely dreadful 2019 squad. He misses the next year to undergo chemotherapy. He returns with a very good 2021, again on an awful excuse for a team, and makes the finals of the Home Run Derby and wins Comeback Player of the Year. He keeps it up into 2022 as his boys fight to stay on the right side of .500, and he gets a standing ovation when everyone realizes the white flag is about to be waved. In response, he wills the impossible into existence for one fleeting moment. Orioles fans, though the vast majority haven't said a word to him that wasn't shouted across 20 rows, have lived a little portion of their lives with him. They can feel that lack when he's gone.

Teams *can* lose fans, even if it rarely happens fast. As often as I've heard dramatic renouncements from those attached to perennial heartbreakers like the Toronto Maple Leafs or Detroit Lions, it's usually a gradual process that begins when a franchise decides to no longer provide entertainment, or a reason to care. You start watching the national TV game instead of the local broadcast, because those teams are actually trying to win. You don't go to the ballpark as often, because you can't think of any players who you really want to see live. When you do go, you notice that the names on the backs of the shirts in the crowd are all Hall of Famers, and not anyone actually out there on the field. The bonds fray as the team takes up less and less of your cluttered mind.

So what happens now in Baltimore, particularly among those who have let the Orioles slide down their list of priorities? The expanded playoffs, the hyped-up newcomers, and the encouraging 2022 results all combine to create an Orioles team that, for the first time in a long time, actually shoulders some honest-to-goodness *expectations*, even in a cutthroat division. But for all the relatively unfamiliar faces on this roster, a greater task exists beyond simply winning ballgames.

There's a chance that the team moves backward again this year, and weighing how much to care about a playoff contender will feel like a far-off luxury. But even if Baltimore does start to put it all together, squeezing joy out of a worn-out fanbase isn't as simple as just scoring more runs than you allow. Some fans will be able to get up to speed quickly with newfound success. Others will remember the five years from 2017-21—the casting off of mini-icons, the assertion that bad baseball is the only path to great baseball, the admonishments to understand the wisdom behind 7-2 losses—and manage only a slightly sunnier shade of apathy. That's the problem with the tank-for-a-title routine; until the championship arrives, what might be fun buildup could just as easily be teardown fodder.

Last year's 83 wins might have repaired the bonds a little—and, incidentally, made an argument for the emotional value of at least trying to field a middle-of-the-road team every year—but this is still an unproven group playing in front of a wounded audience. While they can't be literal replacements for the thrown-away opportunities of years gone by, their jobs are to become players deserving of the fans' admiration, worthy of their names on the back of a kid's jersey, and good enough to make this city proud of their team once again. It's not enough for the Orioles to simply end their winning drought. The fans need to feel like it's their guys ending it, and that they can count on those guys to be around tomorrow. ■

—Lauren Theisen is a writer and co-owner of Defector.

HITTERS

Daz Cameron OF

Born: 01/15/97 Age: 26 Bats: R Throws: R Height: 6'2" Weight: 185 lb. Origin: Round 1, 2015 Draft (#37 overall)

YEAR	TEAM	LVL	AGE	PA	R	2B	3B	HR	RBI	BB	K	SB	CS	Whiff%	AVG/OBP/SLG	DRC+	BABIP	BRR	DRP	WARP
2020	DET	MLB	23	59	4	2	1	0	3	2	19	1	0	26.5%	.193/.220/.263	74	.289	-0.5	RF(16): -0.3	-0.1
2021	TOL	AAA	24	181	33	11	2	6	23	15	39	7	3		.296/.365/.500	104	.356	0.8	CF(22): 0.5, RF(10): 1.3, LF(5): -1.1	0.8
2021	DET	MLB	24	115	16	5	0	4	13	10	38	6	0	30.8%	.194/.278/.359	81	.262	1.9	RF(18): -1.2, CF(15): -1.1, LF(1): -0.1	0.1
2022	TOL	AAA	25	430	56	24	2	10	50	37	123	19	4		.240/.312/.392	85	.322	3.2	CF(65): 5.8, RF(33): 0.8	1.3
2022	DET	MLB	25	70	6	3	1	1	8	5	20	2	0	30.7%	.219/.286/.344	81	.302	0.4	RF(14): 0.7, CF(7): -0.8	0.1
2023 non-DC	*BAL*	*MLB*	*26*	*251*	*23*	*10*	*1*	*5*	*25*	*17*	*74*	*6*	*2*	*28.7%*	*.216/.282/.357*	*74*	*.294*	*1.9*	*CF 0, RF 0*	*0.0*

Comparables: Lewis Brinson (51), Danny Bautista (50), Jake Marisnick (50)

We'll spare you the familial comparisons and judge the younger Cameron purely on his own merits. Those have been few and far between to date; another season went by for Daz, spent predominantly at Toledo. That means we still don't have much of a major-league sample on which to base our assessment; perhaps Cameron's extended presence on the Triple-A roster, while the Tigers were busy rolling out a series of sub-par outfield options, speaks for itself. He runs reasonably well, and has the raw pop to hint at more power: His one home run cleared the center field fence in homer-sapping Comerica Park. Much like his playing time, though, it's all very sporadic. His minor-league time has done little to suggest that there's another level to his game, and the glove isn't sufficient to compensate for the bat. This may be his last chance to show some growth before the opportunities vanish altogether.

Robinson Chirinos C

Born: 06/05/84 Age: 39 Bats: R Throws: R Height: 6'1" Weight: 220 lb. Origin: International Free Agent, 2000

YEAR	TEAM	LVL	AGE	PA	R	2B	3B	HR	RBI	BB	K	SB	CS	Whiff%	AVG/OBP/SLG	DRC+	BABIP	BRR	DRP	WARP
2020	TEX	MLB	36	49	3	1	0	0	2	5	12	0	0	33.3%	.119/.224/.143	87	.161	-0.4	C(13): -1.8	-0.1
2020	NYM	MLB	36	33	1	2	0	1	5	1	9	0	0	29.2%	.219/.242/.375	93	.273	0.0	C(12): -0.2	0.1
2021	SWB	AAA	37	45	6	1	0	3	6	9	16	0	0		.278/.422/.556	101	.412	-0.8	C(11): -0.9	0.0
2021	CHC	MLB	37	112	13	5	1	5	15	9	36	0	0	32.9%	.227/.324/.454	83	.304	-1.0	C(27): -0.6	0.1
2022	BAL	MLB	38	220	10	9	0	4	22	19	67	1	0	33.6%	.179/.265/.287	74	.248	-1.7	C(66): -15.2	-1.7
2023 DC	*FA*	*MLB*	*39*	*202*	*20*	*8*	*0*	*6*	*21*	*18*	*61*	*0*	*0*	*33.6%*	*.203/.293/.355*	*79*	*.270*	*-0.7*	*C -8, 2B 0*	*-0.7*

Comparables: Rick Dempsey (70), Jason Varitek (64), Lance Parrish (61)

YEAR	TEAM	P. COUNT	FRM RUNS	BLK RUNS	THRW RUNS	TOT RUNS
2020	NYM	1580	0.0	0.0	0.0	0.0
2020	TEX	1958	-1.8	0.0	0.0	-1.8
2021	SWB	1487	-0.8	0.0	0.0	-0.8
2021	CHC	3394	-0.1	-0.1	0.0	-0.2
2022	BAL	8710	-15.5	-0.1	0.0	-15.5
2023	*FA*	*6956*	*-8.8*	*0.1*	*-0.1*	*-8.8*

The year is 3036. The earth is a scorched wasteland, ravaged by war and environmental upheaval. The soil itself rejected humanity long ago, becoming untenable to supporting the way of life to which we'd grown accustomed. Descendants of the last man have returned to unearth the mysteries of their ancestors. They stumble into a cavernous pit of crumbling stone blocks and long-eroded orange bleachers. The secret they discover is written in their tongue but, to them, the words mean nothing. The message is simple: Robinson Chirinos had 220 plate appearances for the 2022 Orioles.

Franchy Cordero 1B

Born: 09/02/94 Age: 28 Bats: L Throws: R Height: 6'3" Weight: 226 lb. Origin: International Free Agent, 2011

YEAR	TEAM	LVL	AGE	PA	R	2B	3B	HR	RBI	BB	K	SB	CS	Whiff%	AVG/OBP/SLG	DRC+	BABIP	BRR	DRP	WARP
2020	ESC	WIN	25	76	9	2	0	2	10	9	21	0	0		.227/.316/.348		.295			
2020	KC	MLB	25	42	7	3	0	2	7	4	4	1	0	20.2%	.211/.286/.447	106	.188	0.5	RF(8): -0.4, CF(5): -0.6, LF(1): -0.1	0.1
2021	ESC	WIN	26	97	15	5	1	2	10	8	20	1	0		.253/.313/.402		.303			
2021	WOR	AAA	26	335	53	24	2	13	56	42	94	12	1		.300/.398/.533	103	.406	1.0	LF(54): -1.8, 1B(7): -0.6, RF(6): -0.1	1.0
2021	BOS	MLB	26	136	12	6	0	1	9	8	51	1	1	41.9%	.189/.237/.260	48	.307	-0.9	LF(33): 3.1, 1B(11): 0, RF(2): -0.1	-0.2
2022	WOR	AAA	27	136	23	10	0	7	36	15	42	4	2		.325/.397/.590	101	.437	0.0	CF(15): -2.3, RF(9): -0.7, LF(4): 1.3	0.4
2022	BOS	MLB	27	275	36	17	1	8	29	28	92	4	1	37.4%	.219/.300/.397	79	.313	0.4	1B(53): 1.1, RF(26): 1.8, LF(12): 0.3	0.3
2023 DC	*BAL*	*MLB*	*28*	*60*	*6*	*2*	*0*	*2*	*6*	*5*	*20*	*1*	*0*	*37.6%*	*.237/.312/.430*	*99*	*.335*	*0.8*	*1B 0*	*0.2*

Comparables: Jeremy Hermida (53), Todd Dunwoody (52), Melvin Nieves (47)

The beneficiary of Chaim Bloom once again forgetting to sign a right fielder or first baseman, Cordero got another shot at semi-regular playing time in Boston despite his unseemly 2021 season. To his credit, after once more making Triple-A pitchers beg for mercy, he briefly rose to the challenge, posting an .803 OPS in May and showing a more discerning eye at the plate. Such improvements proved fleeting, as Cordero earned a .620 OPS and 37% strikeout rate in June and July that got him sent back to Worcester. A brief return to Boston late in the summer sadly ended with a gnarly ankle injury suffered while "playing" right field. A brutal defender anywhere he goes—the less said about his attempts to man first base, the better—Cordero's only hope of achieving the escape velocity needed to leave Planet Quad-A is to find some semblance of selectivity at the plate. Unless that happens, Franchy's fate is to torture minor-league pitching indefinitely until he decides to give Japan or Korea a go: a move that should probably happen sooner rather than later.

★ ★ ★ *2023 Top 101 Prospect* **#38** ★ ★ ★

Colton Cowser OF

Born: 03/20/00 Age: 23 Bats: L Throws: R Height: 6'3" Weight: 195 lb. Origin: Round 1, 2021 Draft (#5 overall)

YEAR	TEAM	LVL	AGE	PA	R	2B	3B	HR	RBI	BB	K	SB	CS	Whiff%	AVG/OBP/SLG	DRC+	BABIP	BRR	DRP	WARP
2021	ORIO	ROK	21	25	8	3	0	1	8	3	4	3	2		.500/.560/.773		.588			
2021	DEL	A	21	124	22	5	0	1	26	22	19	4	2		.347/.476/.429	124	.418	-1.1	CF(16): -2.8, RF(4): 3.0	0.7
2022	ABD	A+	22	278	42	19	2	4	22	45	79	16	1		.258/.385/.410	112	.374	4.2	CF(41): -3.9, LF(12): -0.1, RF(3): -0.0	1.2
2022	BOW	AA	22	224	49	10	0	10	33	36	57	2	2		.341/.469/.568	127	.446	-1.4	CF(37): -0.2, RF(5): -0.1, LF(3): -0.1	1.3
2022	NOR	AAA	22	124	23	7	0	5	11	13	38	0	0		.219/.339/.429	90	.290	1.8	CF(16): 1.3, RF(9): 0.2, LF(4): 1.1	0.6
2023 DC	*BAL*	*MLB*	*23*	*29*	*2*	*1*	*0*	*0*	*2*	*3*	*8*	*0*	*0*	*29.4%*	*.229/.328/.361*	*92*	*.320*	*0.0*	*CF 0*	*0.1*

Comparables: Josh Reddick (58), Steven Duggar (52), Zach Walters (52)

Like many hitters in the Baltimore system, Cowser appeared at three levels last year. Seen as a corner OF in the 2021 Draft, when he was picked fifth overall, he's tested center field as a pro—and done well enough that he could stick there. His calling card at the plate remains his expert judgement of the zone and willingness to take pitches, making him an on-base heavy contributor. A lefty corner-turned-center fielder with superb discipline is a weird profile, but not entirely unique; a successful development arc for Cowser could end up looking an awful lot like Brandon Nimmo.

Jud Fabian OF

Born: 09/27/00 Age: 22 Bats: R Throws: L Height: 6'1" Weight: 195 lb. Origin: Round 2, 2022 Draft (#67 overall)

YEAR	TEAM	LVL	AGE	PA	R	2B	3B	HR	RBI	BB	K	SB	CS	Whiff%	AVG/OBP/SLG	DRC+	BABIP	BRR	DRP	WARP
2022	DEL	A	21	52	16	7	2	3	9	8	9	0	0		.386/.481/.841	134	.438	0.9	LF(3): 0.2, CF(3): 1.0, RF(2): 0.1	0.6
2022	ABD	A+	21	30	1	1	0	0	4	5	8	0	2		.167/.300/.208	88	.235	-0.3	CF(7): -0.1	0.0
2023 non-DC	*BAL*	*MLB*	*22*	*251*	*23*	*10*	*2*	*6*	*26*	*21*	*79*	*3*	*1*	*34.0%*	*.220/.293/.372*	*81*	*.311*	*2.2*	*LF 0, CF 0*	*0.3*

Comparables: Matt Szczur (66), Edward Olivares (65), Kevin Smith (65)

One of the more divisive prospects in the last few drafts, Fabian was picked by the Red Sox in the second round of the 2021 draft despite concerns about the huge swing-and-miss he displayed in his sophomore season at Florida. They couldn't agree on a signing bonus, and Jud returned to school for his junior season. There, he showed off massive improvements in his plate discipline—he cut his strikeout rate by a quarter, and logged a nearly equal walk rate. Along with the 24 homers, it was clear he'd become a three true outcomes machine. That pattern continued in his first taste of pro ball, after the Orioles selected him with their competitive balance pick: Over 40% of his plate appearances at Delmarva and Aberdeen ended with a walk, strikeout or homer.

Adam Frazier 2B

Born: 12/14/91 Age: 31 Bats: L Throws: R Height: 5'10" Weight: 181 lb. Origin: Round 6, 2013 Draft (#179 overall)

YEAR	TEAM	LVL	AGE	PA	R	2B	3B	HR	RBI	BB	K	SB	CS	Whiff%	AVG/OBP/SLG	DRC+	BABIP	BRR	DRP	WARP
2020	PIT	MLB	28	230	22	7	0	7	23	17	35	1	3	16.5%	.230/.297/.364	98	.246	0.1	2B(41): 1.3, LF(14): 1	0.9
2021	PIT	MLB	29	428	58	28	4	4	32	35	46	5	4	12.2%	.324/.388/.448	109	.359	-1.8	2B(94): -0.9, LF(7): -0.2	1.7
2021	SD	MLB	29	211	25	8	1	1	11	13	23	5	1	13.0%	.267/.327/.335	94	.299	0.0	2B(46): 0.5, LF(5): -0.4	0.6
2022	SEA	MLB	30	602	61	22	4	3	42	46	73	11	6	14.5%	.238/.301/.311	91	.268	-0.7	2B(124): 1.8, RF(21): 0.2, LF(16): 0.4	1.4
2023 DC	*BAL*	*MLB*	*31*	*552*	*59*	*25*	*3*	*10*	*48*	*41*	*65*	*12*	*3*	*14.2%*	*.272/.336/.394*	*105*	*.296*	*4.2*	*2B 2, LF 0*	*2.6*

Comparables: Billy Goodman (71), Johnny Ray (70), Nellie Fox (68)

A player born to be Mic'd Up, Frazier on the field is a never-ending Georgia-accented stream of banter, chatter, patter, attaboy, pep, vim and vigor. He's one of the only players you can plausibly imagine in your adult softball league still taunting the opposing team with "heyyyyy batta batta!" and "we need a pitcher not a belly-itcher!" Affectionately dubbed "Captain Slapdick" by some quarters of Mariners Twitter, the name suggests his loquacious goofiness while also describing his M.O. at the plate. You don't get rich in this game as a thumpless singles hitter with spunk (especially when those singles start to dry up, as they did in 2022), but you can make a career if you've got energy, speed, good contact skills and passing competence at multiple positions. What's more, one of those slappy hits found its way into the right field corner at Rogers Centre in Game Two of the Wild Card series, capping off one of the greatest comebacks in playoff history, carving a forever place for the Captain in Seattle sports lore and giving Frazier a whole lot more stuff to talk about with...well, anyone who'll listen. His new Orioles teammates, perhaps.

Hudson Haskin OF

Born: 12/31/98 Age: 24 Bats: R Throws: R Height: 6'2" Weight: 200 lb. Origin: Round 2, 2020 Draft (#39 overall)

YEAR	TEAM	LVL	AGE	PA	R	2B	3B	HR	RBI	BB	K	SB	CS	Whiff%	AVG/OBP/SLG	DRC+	BABIP	BRR	DRP	WARP
2021	DEL	A	22	254	44	13	1	5	33	22	60	17	5		.276/.377/.415	108	.362	-0.8	CF(39): -1.7, LF(11): -1.5, RF(3): 1.2	0.9
2021	ABD	A+	22	109	15	6	2	0	9	10	18	5	2		.275/.389/.385	114	.342	0.5	CF(23): 2.7, RF(2): -0.4, LF(1): -0.2	0.8
2022	BOW	AA	23	466	58	23	3	15	56	43	101	5	3		.264/.367/.455	124	.313	-2.2	CF(51): -0.9, LF(31): -0.1, RF(22): 1.1	2.4
2023 non-DC	*BAL*	*MLB*	*24*	*251*	*22*	*10*	*1*	*3*	*22*	*17*	*61*	*4*	*2*	*26.8%*	*.225/.301/.337*	*80*	*.291*	*0.5*	*LF 0, CF 0*	*0.1*

Comparables: Greg Allen (66), Donnie Dewees (64), Braden Bishop (63)

The Orioles seem to have one rule when they draft hitters: Did they hit before?

That decision tree goes:
If yes; draft. If no; not interested.

Weirdly enough, it seems to work! Haskin is another example: A distracting ball of energy during his at-bats—he rocks his hips rhythmically while waiting for the pitcher—Haskin hasn't stopped hitting at any point as a pro, managing roughly the same shape of production at each successive level. He won't wow with 500-foot homers or hit .330, but he seems destined to be a steady regular, capably filling out the bottom half of a lineup daily.

Austin Hays OF Born: 07/05/95 Age: 28 Bats: R Throws: R Height: 6'0" Weight: 205 lb. Origin: Round 3, 2016 Draft (#91 overall)

YEAR	TEAM	LVL	AGE	PA	R	2B	3B	HR	RBI	BB	K	SB	CS	Whiff%	AVG/OBP/SLG	DRC+	BABIP	BRR	DRP	WARP
2020	BAL	MLB	24	134	20	2	0	4	9	8	25	2	3	20.2%	.279/.328/.393	104	.316	-0.7	CF(23): -0.2, LF(10): 1.5, RF(3): -0.2	0.5
2021	BAL	MLB	25	529	73	26	4	22	71	28	107	4	3	24.7%	.256/.308/.461	104	.286	3.3	LF(88): 2, RF(54): 5.4, CF(6): -0.4	3.2
2022	BAL	MLB	26	582	66	35	2	16	60	34	114	2	4	23.5%	.250/.306/.413	104	.289	0.2	LF(86): 1.8, RF(58): 0.9, CF(6): -0.1	2.4
2023 DC	*BAL*	*MLB*	*27*	*508*	*57*	*23*	*2*	*18*	*58*	*30*	*92*	*6*	*2*	*23.4%*	*.253/.309/.431*	*108*	*.280*	*1.9*	*LF 1, RF 0*	*2.0*

Comparables: Jerry Morales (57), Vernon Wells (55), Joe Rudi (53)

In his second consecutive season of mostly good health, Hays confirmed the initial impression of a slightly above-average outfielder, who can play center in a pinch and hit .250 with some pop. In fact, he turned in a near-exact replica of his 2021 season in every aspect but one: His 53 extra-base hits were one more than a year prior, but the newly unforgiving left field wall at Camden Yards reduced a half dozen of his home runs into doubles. So while almost everything else about his profile remained static—his walk and strikeout percentages, his whiff rates, his batted ball profile, etc.—his OPS dipped by 50 points. Some home-field advantage, right?

★ ★ ★ *2023 Top 101 Prospect* **#1** ★ ★ ★

Gunnar Henderson SS/3B Born: 06/29/01 Age: 22 Bats: L Throws: R Height: 6'2" Weight: 210 lb. Origin: Round 2, 2019 Draft (#42 overall)

YEAR	TEAM	LVL	AGE	PA	R	2B	3B	HR	RBI	BB	K	SB	CS	Whiff%	AVG/OBP/SLG	DRC+	BABIP	BRR	DRP	WARP
2021	DEL	A	20	157	30	11	1	8	39	14	46	5	1		.312/.369/.574	108	.404	0.8	SS(20): 3.2, 3B(11): 0.2	1.0
2021	ABD	A+	20	289	34	16	3	9	35	40	87	11	1		.230/.343/.432	98	.313	-1.9	SS(40): 4.2, 3B(23): -0.7	0.9
2022	BOW	AA	21	208	41	11	3	8	35	41	38	12	2		.312/.452/.573	138	.350	1.1	3B(27): 0.7, SS(18): 0.1	1.7
2022	NOR	AAA	21	295	60	13	4	11	41	38	78	10	1		.288/.390/.504	110	.374	1.3	SS(32): -1.4, 3B(21): 1.1, 2B(6): 0.0	1.3
2022	BAL	MLB	21	132	12	7	1	4	18	16	34	1	1	26.6%	.259/.348/.440	91	.333	-0.5	3B(24): -0.5, SS(7): -0.2, 2B(3): -0.2	0.1
2023 DC	*BAL*	*MLB*	*22*	*555*	*56*	*24*	*5*	*13*	*49*	*60*	*151*	*11*	*4*	*28.4%*	*.235/.325/.387*	*98*	*.313*	*4.6*	*3B -1, SS 0*	*1.5*

Comparables: Rafael Devers (55), Mookie Betts (53), Eric Hosmer (52)

Perhaps no player better demonstrates how much the Orioles have drilled disciplined swing decisions into their players than Henderson. His 2021 was broadly fine, with flashes of the tools that made him appealing enough to draft straight out of high school in the second round of the 2019 draft, but the 30%+ strikeout rate across three levels was a discouraging sign. Flash forward a season and suddenly Gunnar made some of the best decisions in not only the minors, but all of organized baseball. When he did reach the majors, he chased pitches outside the zone at a Soto-ian clip of just 22.8%. That kind of patience means pitchers had to challenge him more, and from there Gunnar can let the tools do the rest of the work. His cup of coffee in the majors was promising, and he'll likely enter the year as the favorite for AL Rookie of the Year. Of greater concern to Baltimore is ending a seven-year playoff drought. If Gunnar does the former, then the O's stand a good chance of accomplishing the latter.

★ ★ ★ *2023 Top 101 Prospect* **#9** ★ ★ ★

Jackson Holliday SS Born: 12/04/03 Age: 19 Bats: L Throws: R Height: 6'1" Weight: 175 lb. Origin: Round 1, 2022 Draft (#1 overall)

YEAR	TEAM	LVL	AGE	PA	R	2B	3B	HR	RBI	BB	K	SB	CS	Whiff%	AVG/OBP/SLG	DRC+	BABIP	BRR	DRP	WARP
2022	ORI	ROK	18	33	6	1	0	1	3	10	2	3	0		.409/.576/.591		.400			
2022	DEL	A	18	57	8	4	0	0	6	15	10	1	1		.238/.439/.333	124	.313	-0.1	SS(8): -0.4, 2B(4): 0.3	0.3
2023 non-DC	*BAL*	*MLB*	*19*	*251*	*19*	*10*	*1*	*2*	*18*	*25*	*49*	*2*	*1*	*21.8%*	*.189/.278/.280*	*59*	*.233*	*0.4*	*2B 0, SS 0*	*-0.5*

Comparables: Yasel Antuna (83), Michael De León (75), Wenceel Perez (72)

The top pick in the draft, out of Stillwater, OK, and the son of Matt Holliday, Jackson signed for just under the designated slot money, then wowed scouts during his pro debut. He displayed an incredibly refined game for a high schooler—something one might expect from the son of one of the premier hitters of his era. It's no wonder the data-driven Orioles fell in love with Holliday; his combination of elite contact and patience at such a young age hint at great power potential. This is the same bet the Mike Elias Orioles have made over and over again in the draft and—for the most part—you can't argue with the results. There's little reason to think Jackson will be any different.

Heston Kjerstad RF Born: 02/12/99 Age: 24 Bats: L Throws: R Height: 6'3" Weight: 205 lb. Origin: Round 1, 2020 Draft (#2 overall)

YEAR	TEAM	LVL	AGE	PA	R	2B	3B	HR	RBI	BB	K	SB	CS	Whiff%	AVG/OBP/SLG	DRC+	BABIP	BRR	DRP	WARP
2022	DEL	A	23	98	17	9	0	2	17	13	17	0	0		.463/.551/.650	127	.565	-0.4	RF(16): 0.4	0.6
2022	ABD	A+	23	186	28	8	2	3	20	16	47	1	0		.233/.312/.362	77	.302	0.5	RF(31): 1.8	0.3
2023 non-DC	*BAL*	*MLB*	*24*	*251*	*21*	*11*	*1*	*2*	*21*	*17*	*65*	*0*	*0*	*27.6%*	*.227/.294/.327*	*73*	*.305*	*0.7*	*RF 0*	*-0.3*

Comparables: Jonathan Davis (68), Daniel Spingola (60), Kentrail Davis (58)

One of the more cheering developments of the 2022 season was Kjerstad returning to baseball after missing his first two seasons of pro ball with myocarditis. He struggled at points—as one might expect after a multi-year layoff—but by the end of the year he had begun to display the hitting prowess that made him the second overall pick in the 2020 draft, raking all the way through the Arizona Fall League. He was old for the levels at which he appeared—again, two lost seasons—but he will still be just 24 this year, when he has a small but real chance at reaching the majors.

Jorge Mateo SS Born: 06/23/95 Age: 28 Bats: R Throws: R Height: 6'0" Weight: 182 lb. Origin: International Free Agent, 2012

YEAR	TEAM	LVL	AGE	PA	R	2B	3B	HR	RBI	BB	K	SB	CS	Whiff%	AVG/OBP/SLG	DRC+	BABIP	BRR	DRP	WARP
2020	SD	MLB	25	28	4	3	0	0	2	1	11	1	0	35.1%	.154/.185/.269	77	.267	-0.7	2B(5): -0.7, LF(3): -0.4	-0.2
2021	SD	MLB	26	93	10	4	0	2	6	2	27	5	0	31.8%	.207/.250/.322	74	.276	0.8	CF(11): 0.2, 3B(8): 0.7, RF(6): 0.4	0.3
2021	BAL	MLB	26	116	9	7	1	2	8	7	28	5	3	30.6%	.280/.328/.421	91	.359	0.6	2B(18): 1.1, SS(17): 0, 3B(1): -0.2	0.5
2022	BAL	MLB	27	533	63	25	7	13	50	27	147	35	9	31.2%	.221/.267/.379	78	.286	2.0	SS(149): 4.1	0.9
2023 DC	*BAL*	*MLB*	*28*	*337*	*33*	*13*	*3*	*8*	*33*	*17*	*94*	*23*	*9*	*30.5%*	*.228/.276/.378*	*79*	*.297*	*2.1*	*SS 2*	*0.5*

Comparables: Erik González (60), Pat Valaika (59), Freddy Galvis (48)

It's never too late to make good on unfulfilled potential. By the time he was 26, Mateo had already lived the life of a baseball vagabond; cast aside by three orgs, he found his way to Baltimore midway through the 2021 season and got his first consistent run of major-league playing time. A funny thing happened: He played pretty well. Last year, he picked up where he left off with a tidy little season. He qualified for the batting title for the first time and led the AL in stolen bases, edging Cedric Mullins out by one. The batting line took a turn for the worse, and he may not be a daily presence in the next great Orioles lineup, but Mateo is an absolute burner on the basepaths—not a bad thing to be, with the pending rule changes. If only they could make it easier for him to get on base.

★ ★ ★ *2023 Top 101 Prospect* **#69** ★ ★ ★

Coby Mayo 3B Born: 12/10/01 Age: 21 Bats: R Throws: R Height: 6'5" Weight: 215 lb. Origin: Round 4, 2020 Draft (#103 overall)

YEAR	TEAM	LVL	AGE	PA	R	2B	3B	HR	RBI	BB	K	SB	CS	Whiff%	AVG/OBP/SLG	DRC+	BABIP	BRR	DRP	WARP
2021	ORIB	ROK	19	84	17	6	0	3	13	11	13	6	0		.324/.429/.535		.364			
2021	DEL	A	19	125	27	8	1	5	26	16	26	5	0		.311/.416/.547	118	.373	1.3	3B(27): -3.3	0.4
2022	ABD	A+	20	288	50	16	2	14	49	27	62	5	1		.251/.326/.494	142	.275	-1.6	3B(61): 3.2	2.3
2022	BOW	AA	20	145	21	4	0	5	20	12	50	0	0		.250/.331/.398	92	.365	0.5	3B(20): 1.1, 1B(2): -0.4	0.4
2023 non-DC	*BAL*	*MLB*	*21*	*251*	*24*	*10*	*1*	*7*	*27*	*17*	*68*	*2*	*0*	*28.2%*	*.220/.282/.376*	*80*	*.279*	*1.2*	*1B 0, 3B 0*	*0.0*

Comparables: Josh Vitters (65), Blake DeWitt (65), Maikel Franco (59)

It feels like a crime to be named Mayo and play a sport that involves extensive time in the sun, but Baltimore's 2020 fourth-rounder makes it work. A third baseman with a huge frame, Mayo has the massive raw power that fits the traditional profille. He's managed to get much of that power into games without devolving into a real three-true-outcomes profile, too. With solid contact skills and and an idea of the strike zone, Mayo looks like he could be next in line for the Orioles player development boost that Gunnar Henderson received. So if you want to slather him with a little extra upside, we won't judge.

James McCann C Born: 06/13/90 Age: 33 Bats: R Throws: R Height: 6'3" Weight: 220 lb. Origin: Round 2, 2011 Draft (#76 overall)

YEAR	TEAM	LVL	AGE	PA	R	2B	3B	HR	RBI	BB	K	SB	CS	Whiff%	AVG/OBP/SLG	DRC+	BABIP	BRR	DRP	WARP
2020	CHW	MLB	30	111	20	3	0	7	15	8	30	1	1	29.2%	.289/.360/.536	111	.339	-0.4	C(30): 3.5	0.9
2021	NYM	MLB	31	412	29	12	1	10	46	32	115	1	2	27.1%	.232/.294/.349	80	.304	-1.7	C(107): 1.9, 1B(6): -0.3	0.6
2022	NYM	MLB	32	191	19	6	0	3	18	11	46	3	0	28.3%	.195/.257/.282	82	.244	-0.4	C(60): 4, 1B(3): 0	0.7
2023 DC	*BAL*	*MLB*	*33*	*246*	*25*	*8*	*0*	*6*	*24*	*17*	*66*	*2*	*0*	*28.5%*	*.235/.299/.370*	*85*	*.304*	*0.4*	*1B 0, C 0*	*0.3*

Comparables: Yorvit Torrealba (61), Toby Hall (59), Randy Hundley (58)

YEAR	TEAM	P. COUNT	FRM RUNS	BLK RUNS	THRW RUNS	TOT RUNS
2020	CHW	4053	3.3	0.0	0.0	3.3
2021	NYM	13585	0.0	-0.1	0.5	0.4
2022	NYM	7385	4.1	-0.2	0.0	3.9
2023	*BAL*	*6012*	*-0.3*	*-0.1*	*-0.1*	*-0.5*

In Olivia Rodrigo's double-platinum single "traitor," the narrator complains of an ex who didn't *technically* cheat, but nevertheless betrayed her.

And ain't it funny / How you said you were friends?

In 2021, Tómas Nido had 161 PAs, 40% of McCann's total. Last year, he had 122 more.

Loved you at your worst, but that didn't matter.

McCann signed with the Mets a week before the team announced it'd be transitioning into a replacement for team President Sandy Alderson (a job no one seemed to want.) Two years to the day after he signed, New York inked Omar Narváez. A week later and still halfway into his contract, McCann was gone. And he knows the Mets'll never feel sorry.

It took you two weeks, to go off and date her / Guess you didn't cheat, but you're still a traitor.

Ryan Mountcastle 1B Born: 02/18/97 Age: 26 Bats: R Throws: R Height: 6'4" Weight: 230 lb. Origin: Round 1, 2015 Draft (#36 overall)

YEAR	TEAM	LVL	AGE	PA	R	2B	3B	HR	RBI	BB	K	SB	CS	Whiff%	AVG/OBP/SLG	DRC+	BABIP	BRR	DRP	WARP
2020	BAL	MLB	23	140	12	5	0	5	23	11	30	0	1	29.2%	.333/.386/.492	111	.398	-0.8	LF(25): -0.6, 1B(10): -0.2	0.4
2021	BAL	MLB	24	586	77	23	1	33	89	41	161	4	3	31.6%	.255/.309/.487	108	.297	0.3	1B(84): -0.2, LF(21): -1.2	1.9
2022	BAL	MLB	25	609	62	28	1	22	85	43	154	4	1	29.8%	.250/.305/.423	101	.303	0.1	1B(124): -1.8	1.2
2023 DC	*BAL*	*MLB*	*26*	*583*	*67*	*24*	*1*	*25*	*74*	*41*	*143*	*6*	*2*	*29.3%*	*.259/.317/.451*	*112*	*.308*	*1.1*	*1B 0*	*1.9*

Comparables: Brandon Drury (63), Matt Kemp (62), Randal Grichuk (62)

While his name evokes imagery of medieval fortresses in Europe, Mountcastle's season had more in common with Ming dynasty-era China: Overshadowed by a Great Wall. The fireworks he displayed in 2021 were nullified by the bulwark his own organization placed in his home park: Pushed back 10 yards and heightened to 13 feet, the left-field wall robbed Mountcastle of nearly a dozen home runs. The rest of his offensive output remained nearly identical. He even improved in areas that should lead to greater power; by every statistic imaginable he hit the ball harder than when his slugging percentage was 60 points higher. His end-of-season stats may not always reflect it, but Mountcastle can mash. The roomy left field confines also meant that—for the first time as a major leaguer—he took every inning in the field at first base. So maybe the wall wasn't *all* bad.

Cedric Mullins CF

Born: 10/01/94 Age: 28 Bats: L Throws: L Height: 5'8" Weight: 175 lb. Origin: Round 13, 2015 Draft (#403 overall)

YEAR	TEAM	LVL	AGE	PA	R	2B	3B	HR	RBI	BB	K	SB	CS	Whiff%	AVG/OBP/SLG	DRC+	BABIP	BRR	DRP	WARP
2020	BAL	MLB	25	153	16	4	3	3	12	8	37	7	2	22.8%	.271/.315/.407	85	.350	2.1	CF(41): 3.9, LF(4): 1.5, RF(4): 0.2	1.0
2021	BAL	MLB	26	675	91	37	5	30	59	59	125	30	8	21.0%	.291/.360/.518	117	.322	1.1	CF(153): 2.7	4.7
2022	BAL	MLB	27	672	89	32	4	16	64	47	126	34	10	22.5%	.258/.318/.403	98	.299	2.5	CF(150): 3.2	2.9
2023 DC	*BAL*	*MLB*	*28*	*627*	*78*	*28*	*4*	*19*	*57*	*46*	*119*	*29*	*8*	*21.9%*	*.256/.320/.422*	*104*	*.294*	*7.8*	*CF 0*	*3.0*

Comparables: Jackie Bradley Jr. (59), Aaron Hicks (55), Jake Marisnick (54)

After his explosive 2021 breakout, Mullins established some staying power with a solid follow-up. While he wasn't quite the same offensive dynamo this time around—it was always going to be difficult to follow up a 30-30 season—he still turned in an impressive performance, and didn't have to put on the same solo act he did the year prior. As the lineup around him has shuffled and been infused with emergent young talent, Mullins has been the North Star of the Orioles lineup: His 1,315 plate appearances out of the leadoff spot over the past two seasons is the most in the league. There's something to be said for showing up to work every day without fail, and Mullins has done that better than just about anybody else.

★ ★ ★ *2023 Top 101 Prospect* **#82** ★ ★ ★

Connor Norby 2B

Born: 06/08/00 Age: 23 Bats: R Throws: R Height: 5'10" Weight: 187 lb. Origin: Round 2, 2021 Draft (#41 overall)

YEAR	TEAM	LVL	AGE	PA	R	2B	3B	HR	RBI	BB	K	SB	CS	Whiff%	AVG/OBP/SLG	DRC+	BABIP	BRR	DRP	WARP
2021	DEL	A	21	126	17	4	1	3	17	21	28	5	3		.283/.413/.434	113	.352	0.3	2B(26): -0.1	0.6
2022	ABD	A+	22	209	27	7	2	8	20	18	50	6	3		.237/.311/.425	105	.277	0.8	2B(40): -0.0, LF(3): -0.3, SS(1): -0.0	0.7
2022	BOW	AA	22	296	58	14	2	17	46	34	59	10	2		.298/.389/.571	122	.322	-1.3	2B(56): 0.1, LF(7): -0.4	1.3
2022	NOR	AAA	22	42	7	2	0	4	7	3	5	0	1		.359/.405/.718	120	.333	-0.2	2B(6): 1.1, LF(1): 0.2	0.3
2023 non-DC	*BAL*	*MLB*	*23*	*251*	*27*	*9*	*1*	*8*	*29*	*19*	*62*	*4*	*2*	*29.2%*	*.246/.313/.412*	*100*	*.305*	*1.0*	*2B 0, SS 0*	*0.8*

Comparables: Nick Madrigal (64), Scott Kingery (63), Yung-Chi Chen (59)

A data darling for the superb contact ability he showed at East Carolina University ahead of the 2021 draft, Norby took some time to get going before eventually excelling at three levels, performing better after each promotion. He ended his first full professional season by posting an OPS over 1.000 in the final months of the year. His arrow is trending firmly up, having put those heralded bat-to-ball abilities on full display. Firmly established in the high minors, the former second-round pick can be expected to debut sometime in 2023—just two seasons after being drafted—and add to a quickly growing collection of homegrown talent in Baltimore.

Ryan O'Hearn DH

Born: 07/26/93 Age: 29 Bats: L Throws: L Height: 6'3" Weight: 220 lb. Origin: Round 8, 2014 Draft (#243 overall)

YEAR	TEAM	LVL	AGE	PA	R	2B	3B	HR	RBI	BB	K	SB	CS	Whiff%	AVG/OBP/SLG	DRC+	BABIP	BRR	DRP	WARP
2020	KC	MLB	26	132	7	6	0	2	18	18	37	0	0	29.9%	.195/.303/.301	85	.267	-0.9	1B(27): 0.1	0.0
2021	OMA	AAA	27	82	22	4	0	12	25	9	15	3	0		.375/.451/.931	177	.333	1.0	1B(8): 0.8, RF(8): -1.1	1.0
2021	KC	MLB	27	254	23	5	1	9	29	13	71	0	0	29.3%	.225/.268/.369	81	.277	-1.8	RF(25): -1, 1B(20): 0.2, LF(1): 0.1	-0.2
2022	KC	MLB	28	145	14	6	1	1	16	8	35	0	0	24.2%	.239/.290/.321	75	.313	0.1	1B(13): 0, RF(13): -0.8	-0.1
2023 DC	*BAL*	*MLB*	*29*	*31*	*3*	*1*	*0*	*1*	*3*	*2*	*7*	*0*	*0*	*25.5%*	*.244/.307/.441*	*103*	*.279*	*0.1*	*1B 0*	*0.1*

Comparables: Justin Smoak (56), Yonder Alonso (51), Carlos Pena (50)

Bench players these days all sit in the bullpen, and you'll be hard-pressed to find many pinch-anythings strutting out of the dugout, especially as DHs have become universal. Yet O'Hearn, who's long profiled as a lefty power bat, rode the entire major-league season as a late-inning specialist for Mike Matheny to sub in during critical at-bats. His 11 pinch hits led the league, and he appeared in more games as a replacement than a starter. His 1.006 OPS as a pinch-hitter dwarfs his .491 mark when written into the lineup from the start. Usually, this is dismissed as noise around the signal. He has some positional flexibility, so one story to watch could be O'Hearn trying to bring back the whole John Vander Wal thing, which could mark the first time an Irishman ever aspired to be a Dutchman.

Joey Ortiz SS

Born: 07/14/98 Age: 24 Bats: R Throws: R Height: 5'11" Weight: 175 lb. Origin: Round 4, 2019 Draft (#108 overall)

YEAR	TEAM	LVL	AGE	PA	R	2B	3B	HR	RBI	BB	K	SB	CS	Whiff%	AVG/OBP/SLG	DRC+	BABIP	BRR	DRP	WARP
2021	ABD	A+	22	89	14	7	2	0	8	10	18	3	0		.289/.382/.434	104	.373	0.2	SS(14): -0.3, 2B(5): 0.6, 3B(2): 0.3	0.4
2021	BOW	AA	22	67	11	2	0	4	9	6	14	1	0		.233/.313/.467	113	.238	0.8	SS(6): -0.1, 2B(5): 0.3, 3B(2): 0.4	0.4
2022	BOW	AA	23	485	69	28	4	15	71	41	81	2	1		.269/.337/.455	130	.298	-0.1	SS(85): 5.2, 2B(21): 1.5, 3B(2): -0.1	3.7
2022	NOR	AAA	23	115	22	7	2	4	14	9	17	6	1		.346/.400/.567	113	.381	-0.4	SS(17): -1.3, 2B(5): 1.3	0.5
2023 DC	*BAL*	*MLB*	*24*	*130*	*12*	*5*	*0*	*2*	*12*	*8*	*23*	*1*	*0*	*20.0%*	*.248/.304/.375*	*91*	*.290*	*0.8*	*3B 0, SS 0*	*0.3*

Comparables: Brad Miller (66), Erik González (63), Matt Reynolds (63)

A slick-fielding shortstop, Ortiz has a major-league future as an optionable glove on somebody's bench. What decides if he'll be anything more than that is if the gains he made in the hitting department stick after 2022. After an underwhelming end to his campaign in Double-A Bowie the year before, Ortiz took a major step forward in his second go at the level, then hit even better after earning the promotion to Triple-A Norfolk. His smooth glove and the potential for a non-zero bat up the middle makes him one of the more intriguing names to watch in a crowded group of Orioles infield prospects.

Brett Phillips OF Born: 05/30/94 Age: 29 Bats: L Throws: R Height: 6'0" Weight: 195 lb. Origin: Round 6, 2012 Draft (#189 overall)

YEAR	TEAM	LVL	AGE	PA	R	2B	3B	HR	RBI	BB	K	SB	CS	Whiff%	AVG/OBP/SLG	DRC+	BABIP	BRR	DRP	WARP
2020	KC	MLB	26	34	8	0	1	1	2	3	8	3	1	31.6%	.226/.294/.387	89	.273	0.4	CF(11): 0.1, LF(4): -0.1	0.1
2020	TB	MLB	26	25	2	0	1	1	3	5	7	3	0	41.7%	.150/.320/.400	95	.167	0.5	RF(9): 0.9, CF(4): -0.1, LF(3): -0.1	0.2
2021	TB	MLB	27	292	50	9	3	13	44	33	113	14	3	36.3%	.202/.297/.415	74	.295	1.0	CF(52): 1.9, RF(46): 3.9, LF(19): -0.2	0.7
2022	NOR	AAA	28	88	16	1	2	6	17	17	25	1	0		.277/.432/.631	111	.324	-0.1	CF(19): -0.7, LF(2): 0.3, RF(2): -0.2	0.3
2022	BAL	MLB	28	17	1	2	0	0	1	0	9	0	0	35.3%	.118/.118/.235	60	.250	0.1	LF(4): 0.2, RF(2): 0	0.0
2022	TB	MLB	28	208	21	4	0	5	14	16	85	7	0	39.4%	.147/.225/.250	45	.232	1.2	CF(42): 0.5, RF(36): 1.8, P(3): 0.1	-0.3
2023 non-DC	*BAL*	*MLB*	*29*	*251*	*25*	*7*	*2*	*7*	*27*	*25*	*87*	*6*	*1*	*36.0%*	*.199/.288/.366*	*77*	*.286*	*6.3*	*CF 0, RF 0*	*0.6*

Comparables: Ruben Rivera (53), Corey Patterson (51), Nate McLouth (49)

It can be easy to get bogged down in the depressing minutiae of the sport, what with owners being cartoonish villains and teams manipulating service time and circumventing the competitive spirit of the game. The list could go on. So there are times when we need to be reminded of a simple fact: Baseball is a game, and it's meant to be a fun one. And that's where Phillips comes in, galloping in to the mound from center field to lob 50-mph batting practice in a 10-run game—but have a grand old time doing it. Is he only pitching because his team doesn't want to use a real pitcher? Absolutely, but just look at how happy he is! The youthful exuberance! Did that same team DFA Philips mid-season, casting him off to Baltimore? Well yeah, but that's not what we're going for here.

Adley Rutschman C Born: 02/06/98 Age: 25 Bats: S Throws: R Height: 6'2" Weight: 220 lb. Origin: Round 1, 2019 Draft (#1 overall)

YEAR	TEAM	LVL	AGE	PA	R	2B	3B	HR	RBI	BB	K	SB	CS	Whiff%	AVG/OBP/SLG	DRC+	BABIP	BRR	DRP	WARP
2021	BOW	AA	23	358	61	16	0	18	55	55	57	1	2		.271/.392/.508	141	.279	0.3	C(53): 13.8, 1B(20): 0.1	4.4
2021	NOR	AAA	23	185	25	9	2	5	20	24	33	2	2		.312/.405/.490	123	.364	-0.6	C(29): 4.8, 1B(8): -1.3	1.4
2022	NOR	AAA	24	53	5	0	0	3	7	7	6	0	0	9.5%	.233/.377/.442	132	.206	-0.3	C(8): -0.1, 1B(2): -0.1	0.2
2022	BAL	MLB	24	470	70	35	1	13	42	65	86	4	0	17.9%	.254/.362/.445	118	.291	3.8	C(93): 10.7	4.2
2023 DC	*BAL*	*MLB*	*25*	*542*	*61*	*26*	*1*	*17*	*58*	*68*	*88*	*1*	*1*	*17.9%*	*.251/.354/.428*	*121*	*.277*	*-0.1*	*C 17*	*5.0*

Comparables: Tyler Flowers (61), Jordan Luplow (60), Will Smith (59)

YEAR	TEAM	P. COUNT	FRM RUNS	BLK RUNS	THRW RUNS	TOT RUNS
2021	BOW	7738	12.8	0.6	0.8	14.2
2021	NOR	4199	3.2	0.1	0.0	3.3
2022	NOR	1095	0.0	0.1	-0.2	-0.1
2022	BAL	12228	10.7	0.2	-0.3	10.6
2023	*BAL*	*15632*	*15.3*	*0.5*	*-0.2*	*15.6*

We've all had insatiable cravings before—some for pizza, some for a delicious pastry and some for chocolate. When you want it, you just have to have it, although sometimes you have to wait even longer than you expected to enjoy it. But it's always, always, always worth the wait. Orioles fans ran that gamut of emotions with their first taste of Adley: He entered the season with the weight of a franchise on his shoulders, then suffered a triceps injury in the spring that set back his long-awaited debut. When he did finally come up, he sparked a turnaround and blew away every expectation. It would be hard to build a more ideal franchise cornerstone: He rarely chases (23.6% O-Swing rate) and rarely misses (7.3% swinging strike rate). While he doesn't have elite raw pop, he makes the most of it by hitting the ball in the air (38.4% fly-ball rate) and pulling (43.8% of batted balls). Oh, and he's a switch-hitter who was tied for the game's sixth-best catcher by framing runs.

Anthony Santander RF Born: 10/19/94 Age: 28 Bats: S Throws: R Height: 6'2" Weight: 235 lb. Origin: International Free Agent, 2011

YEAR	TEAM	LVL	AGE	PA	R	2B	3B	HR	RBI	BB	K	SB	CS	Whiff%	AVG/OBP/SLG	DRC+	BABIP	BRR	DRP	WARP
2020	BAL	MLB	25	165	24	13	1	11	32	10	25	0	1	25.6%	.261/.315/.575	118	.248	-0.2	RF(35): -0.5, LF(2): -0.2	0.8
2021	BAL	MLB	26	438	54	24	0	18	50	23	101	1	1	25.2%	.241/.286/.433	94	.275	-0.5	RF(81): -7, LF(4): -0.2	0.1
2022	BAL	MLB	27	647	78	24	0	33	89	55	122	0	2	21.5%	.240/.318/.455	123	.248	0.7	RF(84): -6.2, LF(38): -3.8	2.7
2023 DC	*BAL*	*MLB*	*28*	*588*	*69*	*26*	*1*	*29*	*80*	*44*	*109*	*0*	*2*	*21.7%*	*.248/.315/.468*	*114*	*.261*	*-6.4*	*RF -5*	*0.9*

Comparables: Josh Reddick (64), Max Kepler (57), Ruben Sierra (57)

Finally able to put together a full season's worth of at-bats, Santander delivered on the promise he had flashed in parts of previous years—in a big way. Apparently, somebody forgot to tell him the new edition of Camden Yards is a pitcher's safe haven, as Santander socked 15 home runs and put up an OPS of .820 at home on his way to 33 dingers in total, the latter figure among the league's top 15 in an anemic season. His 647 plate appearances surpassed his previous high by more than 200. Is he the focal point of a rebuilt lineup? Not necessarily, but the Orioles have that part figured out already. In Santander, they can safely put one of the better ancillary players in ink, too.

Kyle Stowers OF

Born: 01/02/98 Age: 25 Bats: L Throws: L Height: 6'3" Weight: 200 lb. Origin: Round 2, 2019 Draft (#71 overall)

YEAR	TEAM	LVL	AGE	PA	R	2B	3B	HR	RBI	BB	K	SB	CS	Whiff%	AVG/OBP/SLG	DRC+	BABIP	BRR	DRP	WARP
2021	ABD	A+	23	161	25	6	1	7	32	27	55	3	3		.275/.404/.496	101	.414	-0.2	RF(18): -0.6, LF(10): 0.3, CF(5): -0.1	0.5
2021	BOW	AA	23	276	38	15	0	17	42	34	84	4	1		.283/.377/.561	110	.362	-0.8	RF(48): -2.5, LF(9): 0.1	0.9
2021	NOR	AAA	23	93	10	2	0	3	11	12	32	1	0		.272/.366/.407	82	.413	0.1	RF(19): -0.2, LF(2): -0.2	0.1
2022	NOR	AAA	24	407	54	29	3	19	78	45	104	3	2	27.6%	.264/.357/.527	108	.317	-1.8	CF(44): -1.7, RF(38): -0.2, LF(13): 1.3	1.2
2022	BAL	MLB	24	98	11	4	1	3	11	5	29	0	0	33.0%	.253/.306/.418	75	.339	0.8	LF(13): -0.5, RF(12): 0.8	0.1
2023 DC	*BAL*	*MLB*	*25*	*469*	*52*	*21*	*2*	*18*	*53*	*37*	*140*	*3*	*1*	*32.7%*	*.237/.307/.425*	*98*	*.310*	*1.0*	*RF 0, LF -1*	*0.8*

Comparables: Eric Thames (66), Andre Ethier (62), Scott Schebler (62)

Since being picked in the second round out of Stanford in 2019, Stowers has been known for one thing: hitting the ball very hard. Like many sluggers, though, he's struggled with swing-and-miss issues—he struck out 171 times across three levels in 2021—but working on that part of his game has paid off in a big way. He cut his strikeout rate at Triple-A Norfolk by nearly 10% year-over-year; after a brief cup of coffee in June, Stowers earned a call-up in August and stayed up through the rest of the season. He'll have to adjust to major-league pitching—the strikeouts crept back into his game—but there's a direct path to playing time for him in a Baltimore outfield devoid of power hitters outside of Anthony Santander.

Ramón Urías 3B

Born: 06/03/94 Age: 29 Bats: R Throws: R Height: 6'0" Weight: 190 lb. Origin: International Free Agent, 2010

YEAR	TEAM	LVL	AGE	PA	R	2B	3B	HR	RBI	BB	K	SB	CS	Whiff%	AVG/OBP/SLG	DRC+	BABIP	BRR	DRP	WARP
2020	BAL	MLB	26	27	3	2	0	1	3	2	6	0	0	28.3%	.360/.407/.560	100	.444	-1.0	SS(5): -0.2, 2B(4): 0.2	0.0
2021	NOR	AAA	27	101	14	6	1	4	12	9	25	1	1		.258/.340/.483	105	.317	0.2	2B(11): -0.6, SS(9): -0.6, 3B(4): 1.1	0.4
2021	BAL	MLB	27	296	33	14	0	7	38	28	76	1	2	26.0%	.279/.361/.412	99	.369	0.6	SS(48): 1, 2B(32): 0.2, 3B(10): -0.1	1.2
2022	BAL	MLB	28	445	50	17	1	16	51	30	98	1	0	27.4%	.248/.305/.414	101	.287	-0.8	3B(98): 4.9, 2B(21): 1.8, SS(8): -0.8	1.8
2023 DC	*BAL*	*MLB*	*29*	*290*	*28*	*12*	*0*	*6*	*28*	*22*	*68*	*2*	*1*	*26.9%*	*.245/.314/.376*	*93*	*.307*	*0.0*	*3B 1, 2B 0*	*0.6*

Comparables: Asdrúbal Cabrera (52), Jedd Gyorko (49), Aledmys Díaz (48)

Entering 2022, Urías had played 686 innings in the majors and only 75 had come at third base. That fact made it all the more notable that he won the AL Gold Glove—becoming the first native of Mexico to win one since Fernando Valenzuela—while playing primarily at third base for the first time in his career. Urías continued to swing a roughly league-average bat despite a complete overhaul in his profile: He pulled the ball and hit more fly balls than he had in 2021, obviously trying to hit for more power. Chasing that pop led to him expanding the zone and putting a lot more non-competitive balls in play, which partially explains the nosedive in his formerly stellar on-base skills. Whatever version of Urías the Orioles get this year, it's probably going to be a useful one, since in every big-league stint he's been a competent hitter who excels with the glove all over the infield. Every aspiring contender has a guy like this.

Terrin Vavra UT

Born: 05/12/97 Age: 26 Bats: L Throws: R Height: 6'1" Weight: 200 lb. Origin: Round 3, 2018 Draft (#96 overall)

YEAR	TEAM	LVL	AGE	PA	R	2B	3B	HR	RBI	BB	K	SB	CS	Whiff%	AVG/OBP/SLG	DRC+	BABIP	BRR	DRP	WARP
2021	BOW	AA	24	184	28	10	1	5	20	29	42	6	1		.248/.388/.430	115	.314	-1.0	2B(27): -1.7, CF(9): -1.0, SS(2): 0.3	0.6
2022	NOR	AAA	25	208	34	14	1	2	18	28	36	5	1		.324/.435/.451	116	.400	0.9	2B(22): 0.9, CF(17): -2.3, LF(3): -0.5	0.8
2022	BAL	MLB	25	103	14	2	1	1	12	12	19	0	1	23.2%	.258/.340/.337	95	.310	0.1	2B(15): 0.6, LF(11): -0.1, RF(1): 0	0.3
2023 DC	*BAL*	*MLB*	*26*	*61*	*5*	*2*	*0*	*0*	*5*	*6*	*12*	*0*	*1*	*23.0%*	*.245/.332/.359*	*95*	*.302*	*0.0*	*2B 0, 3B 0*	*0.1*

Comparables: Tommy La Stella (65), Chris Getz (60), JT Riddle (60)

"If you know the enemy and know yourself, you need not fear the result of a hundred battles." Or plate appearances, as it turns out in Vavra's case—although that may not have been what Sun Tzu originally had in mind. The versatile defender came up and knew exactly which archetypal role he was meant to fill: the light-hitting, tough-out utility is a job nearly as old as the sport itself. Vavra made it his own, joining masters of the craft Brendan Donovan and Tony Kemp by lending much-needed length to Baltimore's lineup. There's very little punch, but he's an on-base machine and has DRC+ intrigued. A backup at second base and across the outfield, Vavra is sure to get under the skin of fans of rival clubs with some extraordinarily well-timed bloops.

Max Wagner 3B

Born: 08/19/01 Age: 21 Bats: R Throws: R Height: 6'0" Weight: 215 lb. Origin: Round 2, 2022 Draft (#42 overall)

YEAR	TEAM	LVL	AGE	PA	R	2B	3B	HR	RBI	BB	K	SB	CS	Whiff%	AVG/OBP/SLG	DRC+	BABIP	BRR	DRP	WARP
2022	DEL	A	20	62	9	2	2	1	8	9	13	0	0		.250/.403/.438	107	.314	-0.4	3B(9): 0.5	0.2
2023 non-DC	*BAL*	*MLB*	*21*	*251*	*19*	*9*	*2*	*2*	*20*	*17*	*67*	*1*	*1*	*28.9%*	*.203/.273/.307*	*61*	*.274*	*2.3*	*3B 0*	*-0.5*

Comparables: Travis Denker (76), Jeimer Candelario (75), Jason Taylor (69)

The third pick in the second round of the 2022 Draft, out of Clemson, Wagner is an example of the Orioles' scouting and player development sides working in tandem. A high-risk, high-reward 3B with big power, big strikeout issues and a stance reminiscent of Jorge Soler, the potential is tantalizing—if he can just cut down on the swing-and-miss. That's an area in which the org has excelled, providing confidence in the player dev staff's ability to max (sorry) out his talents. Early returns in his brief cameo in Low- and High-A ball were mixed: a strikeout rate of just 22%, but not much slugging to go along with it. The O's will be looking for a leap forward.

★ ★ ★ *2023 Top 101 Prospect* **#74** ★ ★ ★

Jordan Westburg IF
Born: 02/18/99 Age: 24 Bats: R Throws: R Height: 6'3" Weight: 203 lb. Origin: Round 1, 2020 Draft (#30 overall)

YEAR	TEAM	LVL	AGE	PA	R	2B	3B	HR	RBI	BB	K	SB	CS	Whiff%	AVG/OBP/SLG	DRC+	BABIP	BRR	DRP	WARP
2021	DEL	A	22	91	18	5	1	3	24	12	24	5	1		.366/.484/.592	114	.500	0.8	3B(11): -1.3, SS(8): -0.8	0.3
2021	ABD	A+	22	285	41	16	2	8	41	35	71	9	4		.286/.389/.469	114	.372	0.5	SS(40): 4.4, 3B(20): -2.1	1.6
2021	BOW	AA	22	130	15	6	2	4	14	14	32	3	0		.232/.323/.429	96	.282	0.3	SS(21): 1.7, 3B(5): 0.0	0.5
2022	BOW	AA	23	209	32	14	0	9	32	26	57	3	0		.247/.344/.473	113	.310	1.6	2B(16): -1.8, 3B(16): 1.6, SS(13): -0.3	1.0
2022	NOR	AAA	23	413	64	25	3	18	74	44	90	9	3		.273/.361/.508	113	.318	-1.2	SS(41): -2.9, 2B(24): 0.8, 3B(21): -0.5	1.5
2023 DC	*BAL*	*MLB*	*24*	*97*	*10*	*4*	*0*	*2*	*9*	*8*	*26*	*1*	*0*	*28.8%*	*.236/.309/.383*	*94*	*.309*	*0.5*	*3B 0, SS 0*	*0.2*

Comparables: Todd Frazier (53), Matt Reynolds (53), Jedd Gyorko (53)

Stop us if you've heard it before: The Orioles draft a player. He starts slowly, then makes big strides in game power and patience at the plate after some time in the system. It's a familiar recipe; nearly every Orioles hitting prospect has followed that pattern aside from Adley Rutschman. Westburg—the 30th-overall pick in the 2020 draft—is no different; he began the year repeating Double-A, demonstrating improved decisions and control of the zone to earn a promotion to Norfolk. He dominated the rest of the season in Triple-A and appears on the cusp of joining a growing contingent of talented young hitters in the Baltimore lineup. We don't think Orioles fans will get tired of this repetition any time soon.

Carter Young MI
Born: 01/24/01 Age: 22 Bats: S Throws: R Height: 6'0" Weight: 180 lb. Origin: Round 17, 2022 Draft (#497 overall)

YEAR	TEAM	LVL	AGE	PA	R	2B	3B	HR	RBI	BB	K	SB	CS	Whiff%	AVG/OBP/SLG	DRC+	BABIP	BRR	DRP	WARP
2022	DEL	A	21	71	11	5	1	1	7	5	13	0	0		.246/.296/.400	107	.288	0.2	SS(8): -1.8, 2B(6): -0.1	0.1
2023 non-DC	*BAL*	*MLB*	*22*	*251*	*19*	*10*	*2*	*2*	*20*	*14*	*63*	*0*	*1*	*28.2%*	*.219/.271/.314*	*61*	*.289*	*1.4*	*2B 0, SS 0*	*-0.4*

Comparables: Darwin Barney (89), Dee Strange-Gordon (84), Jonathan Mota (80)

For so prestigious a baseball program, Vanderbilt has had surprisingly few hitters translate college success into a big-league career. Young will be looking to buck that trend after surprising by signing as a 17th-round pick. He's not your typical Day-3 pick, however: He'd garnered some early-round buzz at the beginning of the season before a disappointing campaign, in which he hit .207 with a 29% strikeout rate. Young's calling card is his slick work at shortstop, so the O's need only get his hitting back on track for him to recapture that first-round promise. Early signs were encouraging: He only struck out in 18% of plate appearances at Low-A Delmarva.

PITCHERS

Keegan Akin LHP
Born: 04/01/95 Age: 28 Bats: L Throws: L Height: 5'11" Weight: 235 lb. Origin: Round 2, 2016 Draft (#54 overall)

YEAR	TEAM	LVL	AGE	W	L	SV	G	GS	IP	H	HR	BB/9	K/9	K	GB%	BABIP	WHIP	ERA	DRA-	WARP	MPH	FB%	Whiff%	CSP
2020	BAL	MLB	25	1	2	0	8	6	25^2	27	3	3.5	12.3	35	34.3%	.358	1.44	4.56	94	0.3	92.0	62.0%	28.5%	51.9%
2021	BAL	MLB	26	2	10	0	24	17	95	110	17	3.8	7.8	82	36.6%	.326	1.58	6.63	128	-0.5	92.1	57.2%	21.8%	56.9%
2022	BAL	MLB	27	3	3	2	45	1	81^2	69	10	2.2	8.5	77	48.7%	.269	1.09	3.20	86	1.4	93.8	52.0%	25.8%	58.8%
2023 DC	*BAL*	*MLB*	*28*	*3*	*2*	*0*	*60*	*0*	*51.7*	*52*	*6*	*3.3*	*8.0*	*46*	*42.1%*	*.304*	*1.36*	*3.96*	*102*	*0.3*	*92.8*	*55.3%*	*25.6%*	*57.3%*

Comparables: Steven Brault (65), Nick Pivetta (65), Mike Wright Jr. (62)

Akin transitioned to a long-relief role after two unsuccessful seasons accumulating aches and pains attempting to be a traditional starter. The move seemed to work out for him and Baltimore: He more than halved his ERA year-over-year and solidified himself as a useful part of a competent bullpen. The move to the pen allowed him to pare down his arsenal by ditching an ineffective curve and bumping up the usage of a harder slider that induced more whiffs. It also, predictably, added a tick to the rest of his arsenal—the four-seam jumped from 92–93 to 93–95, and the change from 81–83 to 83–85—which led to more whiffs, and career-best exit velocities and hard-hit rates against. That combination of whiffs plus weak contact is a proven winner.

Bryan Baker RHP
Born: 12/02/94 Age: 28 Bats: R Throws: R Height: 6'6" Weight: 245 lb. Origin: Round 11, 2016 Draft (#320 overall)

YEAR	TEAM	LVL	AGE	W	L	SV	G	GS	IP	H	HR	BB/9	K/9	K	GB%	BABIP	WHIP	ERA	DRA-	WARP	MPH	FB%	Whiff%	CSP
2021	BUF	AAA	26	6	1	11	39	0	41^1	18	1	3.7	10.5	48	41.8%	.175	0.85	1.31	86	0.9				
2021	TOR	MLB	26	0	0	0	1	0	1	1	0	0.0	9.0	1	0.0%	.333	1.00	0.00	93	0.0	94.8	73.7%	40.0%	47.8%
2022	BAL	MLB	27	4	3	1	66	2	69^2	60	3	3.4	9.8	76	41.4%	.311	1.23	3.49	84	1.3	96.6	56.1%	27.4%	55.4%
2023 DC	*BAL*	*MLB*	*28*	*3*	*3*	*0*	*67*	*0*	*58.3*	*52*	*7*	*4.0*	*9.4*	*61*	*40.5%*	*.292*	*1.34*	*3.81*	*96*	*0.4*	*96.5*	*56.3%*	*28.0%*	*55.3%*

Comparables: Wander Suero (79), Rowan Wick (78), Steve Geltz (78)

Baker throws hard: His average fastball velo was over 96 mph. You might expect that from a 6-foot-6, 245-pound hulk of a pitcher. But what minted him as a trusted reliever were the times when he didn't throw as hard: Out of every pitch thrown at least 200 times in the majors last year, his changeup produced the lowest slugging percentage against. No big-league hitter collected an extra-base hit against it. What makes the pitch's success all the more impressive is that Baker didn't even throw it before last year. Which can only lead us to believe that he'll add the league's best curve in 2023, and a knuckleball in 2024.

Mike Baumann RHP

Born: 09/10/95 Age: 27 Bats: R Throws: R Height: 6'4" Weight: 235 lb. Origin: Round 3, 2017 Draft (#98 overall)

YEAR	TEAM	LVL	AGE	W	L	SV	G	GS	IP	H	HR	BB/9	K/9	K	GB%	BABIP	WHIP	ERA	DRA-	WARP	MPH	FB%	Whiff%	CSP
2021	BOW	AA	25	3	2	0	10	10	38^{2}	29	6	4.2	9.1	39	44.2%	.237	1.22	4.89	96	0.4				
2021	NOR	AAA	25	1	1	0	6	6	27	18	0	4.3	8.7	26	37.7%	.261	1.15	2.00	97	0.4				
2021	BAL	MLB	25	1	1	0	4	0	10	13	2	5.4	4.5	5	36.8%	.306	1.90	9.90	133	-0.1	93.7	56.0%	19.8%	58.0%
2022	NOR	AAA	26	2	6	1	20	9	60	54	6	3.8	12.1	81	58.2%	.327	1.32	4.20	66	1.9	95.9	33.3%	23.1%	
2022	BAL	MLB	26	1	3	0	13	4	34^{1}	43	3	2.4	6.0	23	49.6%	.357	1.51	4.72	112	0.1	96.1	48.1%	16.2%	58.1%
2023 DC	*BAL*	*MLB*	*27*	*4*	*3*	*0*	*33*	*3*	*39.3*	*41*	*4*	*4.0*	*6.7*	*29*	*47.8%*	*.303*	*1.49*	*4.43*	*110*	*0.0*	*95.6*	*49.6%*	*21.6%*	*58.1%*

Comparables: Ben Lively (50), Cody Martin (48), Bryan Mitchell (46)

The good: Baumann reeled in the command and (hard) contact problems from 2021, nearly halving his MLB ERA. The bad: Half of a 9.90 ERA is still a large number, and the improved command came at the cost of missing big-league bats—not something at which he was particularly adept in his debut. Still, 2022 represented a step forward for Baumann, the rare contact-manager who throws nearly triple digits. He seems destined for a hybrid role on the Baltimore staff; although he did start four of his final six outings, that may have been borne out of necessity more than an eye to the future. The lurch toward steady competence will do him well as he strives to be the most notable Michael Baumann in baseball.

Félix Bautista RHP

Born: 06/20/95 Age: 28 Bats: R Throws: R Height: 6'5" Weight: 190 lb. Origin: International Free Agent, 2012

YEAR	TEAM	LVL	AGE	W	L	SV	G	GS	IP	H	HR	BB/9	K/9	K	GB%	BABIP	WHIP	ERA	DRA-	WARP	MPH	FB%	Whiff%	CSP
2021	ABD	A+	26	0	2	2	11	0	15	7	1	6.0	16.8	28	30.4%	.273	1.13	1.20	85	0.3				
2021	BOW	AA	26	0	1	4	12	0	13^{1}	2	0	7.4	16.2	24	47.6%	.095	0.98	0.67	85	0.2				
2021	NOR	AAA	26	1	3	5	17	0	18^{1}	11	1	4.4	12.3	25	30.0%	.263	1.09	2.45	85	0.4				
2022	BAL	MLB	27	4	4	15	65	0	65^{2}	38	7	3.2	12.1	88	42.6%	.231	0.93	2.19	64	1.9	99.5	61.3%	33.6%	55.9%
2023 DC	*BAL*	*MLB*	*28*	*3*	*3*	*32*	*67*	*0*	*58.3*	*45*	*7*	*4.6*	*11.8*	*76*	*41.0%*	*.290*	*1.29*	*3.34*	*84*	*0.7*	*99.5*	*61.3%*	*32.8%*	*55.9%*

Comparables: Carlos Ramirez (74), John Axford (70), Danny Barnes (70)

Once your typical-hard throwing minor-league reliever with crazy strikeout totals and even crazier walk numbers, Bautista was always just a tick of command from being a force at the major-league level. In 2022, he got it. And what a revelation he was, mowing down hitters with a high-rise, triple-digits fastball paired with an even filthier splitter—in middle relief at the start of the season, but eventually as the closer once Jorge López was moved at the deadline. By the end of his campaign, the tall righty had transformed ninth innings at Camden Yards into a full-scale event, his entrances accompanied by a light show and Omar's whistle from *The Wire*. Entrenched as the O's main man at the end of the bullpen, Bautista's next step might be solidifying himself as one of the game's most feared relievers.

Kyle Bradish RHP

Born: 09/12/96 Age: 26 Bats: R Throws: R Height: 6'4" Weight: 220 lb. Origin: Round 4, 2018 Draft (#121 overall)

YEAR	TEAM	LVL	AGE	W	L	SV	G	GS	IP	H	HR	BB/9	K/9	K	GB%	BABIP	WHIP	ERA	DRA-	WARP	MPH	FB%	Whiff%	CSP
2021	BOW	AA	24	1	0	0	3	3	13^{2}	7	0	3.3	17.1	26	47.6%	.333	0.88	0.00	84	0.2				
2021	NOR	AAA	24	5	5	0	21	19	86^{2}	85	10	4.1	10.9	105	43.2%	.336	1.43	4.26	93	1.5				
2022	BOW	AA	25	1	0	0	2	2	8	1	0	0.0	10.1	9	43.8%	.063	0.13	0.00	93	0.1				
2022	NOR	AAA	25	2	1	0	4	4	19^{2}	12	1	1.8	10.5	23	50.0%	.234	0.81	1.83	83	0.4				
2022	BAL	MLB	25	4	7	0	23	23	117^{2}	119	17	3.5	8.5	111	45.3%	.314	1.40	4.90	99	1.2	94.9	48.8%	23.6%	56.6%
2023 DC	*BAL*	*MLB*	*26*	*8*	*9*	*0*	*27*	*27*	*137.7*	*138*	*16*	*3.7*	*8.6*	*132*	*45.5%*	*.313*	*1.42*	*4.20*	*105*	*0.8*	*94.9*	*48.8%*	*25.0%*	*56.6%*

Comparables: Anthony DeSclafani (79), David Buchanan (75), Ben Lively (75)

Part of Baltimore's return for sending Dylan Bundy to the Angels, Bradish seems highly qualified to live up to his trade mate's legacy: a baseline of competence, couched by the prevailing sense that there should be more here. There's no question that his stuff is good—a mid-90s fastball along with three usable secondaries (a change, a curve and a hellacious slider). But he scuffled to a 7.38 ERA in his first half-season as a major leaguer, missing too few bats and surrendering too many home runs—even in the pitchers' safe haven that is the renovated Camden Yards. The addition of a sinker seemed to address the long-ball problem and fueled a solid 3.28 ERA after the break, but he still carried a below-average strikeout rate. So what is Bradish? For optimists: a possible mid-rotation arm to dream on. For those less inclined to be hopeful: a worthy heir to Dylan Bundy.

Kyle Gibson RHP

Born: 10/23/87 Age: 35 Bats: R Throws: R Height: 6'6" Weight: 215 lb. Origin: Round 1, 2009 Draft (#22 overall)

YEAR	TEAM	LVL	AGE	W	L	SV	G	GS	IP	H	HR	BB/9	K/9	K	GB%	BABIP	WHIP	ERA	DRA-	WARP	MPH	FB%	Whiff%	CSP
2020	TEX	MLB	32	2	6	0	12	12	67^{1}	73	12	4.0	7.8	58	51.2%	.313	1.53	5.35	103	0.6	92.4	49.4%	23.4%	41.7%
2021	TEX	MLB	33	6	3	0	19	19	113	92	9	3.3	7.5	94	50.9%	.267	1.18	2.87	102	1.0	92.3	59.5%	26.2%	47.7%
2021	PHI	MLB	33	4	6	0	12	11	69	66	8	3.0	8.0	61	53.1%	.294	1.29	5.09	99	0.7	91.8	64.8%	23.3%	47.6%
2022	PHI	MLB	34	10	8	0	31	31	167^{2}	176	24	2.6	7.7	144	45.8%	.309	1.34	5.05	103	1.3	92.0	39.9%	25.1%	52.4%
2023 DC	*BAL*	*MLB*	*35*	*8*	*9*	*0*	*29*	*29*	*142.7*	*148*	*17*	*3.1*	*7.4*	*117*	*47.5%*	*.306*	*1.38*	*4.18*	*106*	*0.7*	*92.2*	*49.5%*	*24.5%*	*48.3%*

Comparables: Jake Westbrook (75), Johnny Cueto (75), Todd Stottlemyre (74)

Gibson had the highest ERA among qualified NL pitchers in 2022, but what really matters in that statement is the word "qualified." The man throws a lot of innings, and as mediocre as those innings can be, his workhorse makeup is still a valuable quality. Since his first full season in 2014, Gibson ranks fifth in innings pitched. He is surrounded on that leaderboard by a collection of far more famous and accomplished names: the likes of Scherzer, Greinke, Cole, Bumgarner, Kershaw and Verlander. The long and short of it is there aren't many back-end starters as durable and consistent as Gibson. He's good for 30 starts a year with a league-average DRA. It's not glamorous, but it gets the job done.

Mychal Givens RHP Born: 05/13/90 Age: 33 Bats: R Throws: R Height: 6'0" Weight: 230 lb. Origin: Round 2, 2009 Draft (#54 overall)

YEAR	TEAM	LVL	AGE	W	L	SV	G	GS	IP	H	HR	BB/9	K/9	K	GB%	BABIP	WHIP	ERA	DRA-	WARP	MPH	FB%	Whiff%	CSP
2020	COL	MLB	30	1	0	1	10	0	9^{1}	9	4	3.9	5.8	6	20.0%	.192	1.39	6.75	179	-0.3	94.9	61.7%	23.9%	48.5%
2020	BAL	MLB	30	0	1	0	12	0	13	7	1	4.2	13.2	19	26.9%	.240	1.00	1.38	101	0.1	94.8	67.7%	30.5%	48.8%
2021	COL	MLB	31	3	2	0	31	0	29^{2}	25	5	4.2	10.3	34	31.1%	.290	1.31	2.73	90	0.4	94.6	46.3%	28.8%	50.2%
2021	CIN	MLB	31	1	1	8	23	0	21^{1}	18	2	5.5	8.4	20	42.4%	.281	1.45	4.22	117	0.0	95.6	47.3%	27.9%	51.2%
2022	NYM	MLB	32	1	1	0	19	1	20^{2}	24	3	2.6	8.7	20	46.7%	.368	1.45	4.79	104	0.2	93.1	56.5%	27.5%	52.7%
2022	CHC	MLB	32	6	2	2	40	0	40^{2}	32	5	4.2	11.3	51	41.4%	.287	1.25	2.66	81	0.8	93.9	49.0%	26.7%	51.6%
2023 DC	*BAL*	*MLB*	*33*	*3*	*2*	*0*	*60*	*0*	*51.7*	*46*	*6*	*3.9*	*9.6*	*55*	*39.2%*	*.290*	*1.32*	*3.79*	*96*	*0.3*	*94.4*	*53.7%*	*27.8%*	*50.9%*

Comparables: Steve Cishek (78), Francisco Rodríguez (74), Luke Gregerson (74)

When the Mets acquired Givens from the Cubs to shore up the non-Edwin Díaz contingent of the bullpen, he reunited with Buck Showalter, who was his manager in Baltimore (where his career began). Givens was having a career year with the Cubs, but got shelled in his first outing as a Met to the tune of five runs in two-thirds of an inning against the lowly Nationals. Givens and his 8.03 August ERA came to represent a trading deadline widely regarded as a failure. But he did quietly turn things around in September, tossing 7⅓ scoreless innings with ten strikeouts before missing the final two weeks of the month on the COVID-19 injured list just as he was hitting his stride. Givens returned to pitch another scoreless frame on the final day of the regular season, ending his season on a note that, while high, was not high enough for his Mets tenure to be considered a success. He returns to Baltimore, the organization that originally drafted him in 2009.

★ ★ ★ *2023 Top 101 Prospect* **#95** ★ ★ ★

DL Hall LHP Born: 09/19/98 Age: 24 Bats: L Throws: L Height: 6'2" Weight: 195 lb. Origin: Round 1, 2017 Draft (#21 overall)

YEAR	TEAM	LVL	AGE	W	L	SV	G	GS	IP	H	HR	BB/9	K/9	K	GB%	BABIP	WHIP	ERA	DRA-	WARP	MPH	FB%	Whiff%	CSP
2021	BOW	AA	22	2	0	0	7	7	31^{2}	16	4	4.5	15.9	56	59.3%	.240	1.01	3.13	80	0.6				
2022	NOR	AAA	23	3	7	0	22	18	76^{2}	62	10	5.8	14.7	125	35.5%	.327	1.45	4.70	60	2.6	97.8	58.0%	32.4%	
2022	BAL	MLB	23	1	1	1	11	1	13^{2}	17	0	4.0	12.5	19	46.2%	.436	1.68	5.93	89	0.2	96.6	52.0%	29.3%	54.2%
2023 DC	*BAL*	*MLB*	*24*	*7*	*3*	*0*	*55*	*3*	*58.3*	*47*	*6*	*5.2*	*11.5*	*74*	*42.8%*	*.294*	*1.39*	*3.74*	*91*	*0.6*	*96.6*	*52.0%*	*32.1%*	*54.2%*

Comparables: Josh Hader (70), Darwinzon Hernandez (59), Renyel Pinto (59)

Perhaps no lefty in the minors possesses the stuff Hall has—he's struck out nearly 33% of the batters he's seen as a professional—but in 2022 he did little to counter the growing chorus of voices who believe him to be a future reliever, some of whom appear to be in the Orioles front office. He made 20 starts prior to his major-league debut, which is good, but only made it through five innings in five of them, which is not so good. He did start when called up to the majors, where he was promptly shelled by the Rays for 3⅔ innings, then returned to the minors—where he came out of the pen for the rest of the season. He ended up making 14 appearances as a reliever across Triple-A and MLB, and the transition seemed to agree with him: He posted a 24:7 strikeout-to-walk ratio across 16⅔ innings. In an era when relievers are more valuable than ever, this shouldn't be looked at as a failure of development as much as a player finding his niche.

Louis Head RHP Born: 04/23/90 Age: 33 Bats: R Throws: R Height: 6'1" Weight: 180 lb. Origin: Round 18, 2012 Draft (#563 overall)

YEAR	TEAM	LVL	AGE	W	L	SV	G	GS	IP	H	HR	BB/9	K/9	K	GB%	BABIP	WHIP	ERA	DRA-	WARP	MPH	FB%	Whiff%	CSP
2021	DUR	AAA	31	0	0	5	26	0	28^{2}	20	2	3.1	11.6	37	47.0%	.281	1.05	2.20	84	0.6				
2021	TB	MLB	31	2	0	0	27	2	35	21	2	2.3	8.2	32	31.1%	.216	0.86	2.31	108	0.2	94.0	52.4%	25.5%	53.5%
2022	NOR	AAA	32	1	1	0	14	0	15^{1}	11	1	10.0	11.2	19	36.4%	.313	1.83	7.04	102	0.2				
2022	MIA	MLB	32	0	0	1	23	0	23^{2}	26	4	4.2	8.7	23	27.4%	.319	1.56	7.23	113	0.1	93.6	38.3%	23.3%	52.9%
2022	BAL	MLB	32	0	0	0	5	0	5	6	0	7.2	5.4	3	38.9%	.333	2.00	1.80	128	0.0	94.0	47.5%	23.9%	47.2%
2023 non-DC	*BAL*	*MLB*	*33*	*2*	*3*	*0*	*57*	*0*	*50*	*49*	*7*	*4.7*	*8.6*	*47*	*35.3%*	*.301*	*1.51*	*5.12*	*122*	*-0.4*	*93.8*	*45.3%*	*24.5%*	*52.6%*

Comparables: Justin Miller (61), Pat Venditte (58), Javy Guerra (55)

Head's lasting legacy may be that he inspired the league to limit to the number of times a team can option a player in a season; the Rays abused the privilege in 2021, sending Head up and down a dozen times. He may be the picturesque example of an anonymous up-down reliever: fastball & slider combo, a few whiffs, capable of eating outs or getting shelled depending on the day. There was a little too much of the latter in 2022, when a 7.23 ERA got him DFA'd out of Miami in July. The Orioles snapped him up and stashed him in the minors until August, then—you guessed it—optioned him again after a few weeks with the club, but just five innings of work. If Head makes it to the majors this year, his team will burn his final option year. Then—after so many bus rides and frequent flyer miles—Louis will finally (hopefully) be able to lay his Head to rest in one place for an entire season.

Dean Kremer RHP

Born: 01/07/96 Age: 27 Bats: R Throws: R Height: 6'2" Weight: 200 lb. Origin: Round 14, 2016 Draft (#431 overall)

YEAR	TEAM	LVL	AGE	W	L	SV	G	GS	IP	H	HR	BB/9	K/9	K	GB%	BABIP	WHIP	ERA	DRA-	WARP	MPH	FB%	Whiff%	CSP
2020	BAL	MLB	24	1	1	0	4	4	18^{2}	15	0	5.8	10.6	22	30.6%	.306	1.45	4.82	101	0.2	92.9	51.2%	26.4%	52.1%
2021	NOR	AAA	25	1	5	0	17	13	62^{1}	61	9	2.9	10.0	69	46.6%	.313	1.30	4.91	87	1.3				
2021	BAL	MLB	25	0	7	0	13	13	53^{2}	63	17	4.2	7.9	47	30.2%	.297	1.64	7.55	140	-0.6	92.6	55.7%	20.4%	57.5%
2022	NOR	AAA	26	0	0	0	2	2	7	1	0	2.6	16.7	13	44.4%	.111	0.43	0.00	75	0.2				
2022	BAL	MLB	26	8	7	0	22	21	125^{1}	123	11	2.4	6.2	87	39.2%	.300	1.25	3.23	110	0.6	91.6	72.3%	22.3%	55.2%
2023 DC	*BAL*	*MLB*	*27*	*8*	*10*	*0*	*27*	*27*	*151.3*	*169*	*23*	*3.2*	*8.2*	*138*	*38.5%*	*.327*	*1.48*	*4.94*	*121*	*-0.4*	*91.9*	*66.7%*	*24.8%*	*55.6%*

Comparables: Chase De Jong (62), Kyle Gibson (60), Vance Worley (60)

Turnarounds don't get much more dramatic than the one Kremer managed between 2021 and 2022. Formerly a strikeout artist who relied on a four-seamer and big, looping curve but didn't get many whiffs with either, Kremer overhauled his repertoire to transition into a contact manager. He added a sinker and boosted his usage of a cutter—both at the expense of his four-seam fastball—and suddenly, nearly 10% more of the batted balls against him were harmless grounders. After allowing 17 homers in 53 disastrous 2021 innings, last year he surrendered just 11 over more than double the workload. The new profile is that of a reliable back-end starter, but it's hard to imagine Kremer can front a rotation if he doesn't improve on the meager, 17% strikeout rate.

Cionel Pérez LHP

Born: 04/21/96 Age: 27 Bats: R Throws: L Height: 5'11" Weight: 162 lb. Origin: International Free Agent, 2016

YEAR	TEAM	LVL	AGE	W	L	SV	G	GS	IP	H	HR	BB/9	K/9	K	GB%	BABIP	WHIP	ERA	DRA-	WARP	MPH	FB%	Whiff%	CSP
2020	HOU	MLB	24	0	0	0	7	0	6^{1}	7	0	8.5	11.4	8	61.1%	.389	2.05	2.84	86	0.1	95.1	62.5%	31.5%	41.8%
2021	LOU	AAA	25	1	2	2	31	0	30^{1}	26	1	3.9	12.2	41	49.3%	.342	1.29	3.26	79	0.7				
2021	CIN	MLB	25	1	2	0	25	0	24	21	5	7.5	9.4	25	51.5%	.262	1.71	6.37	100	0.2	96.2	64.3%	30.3%	53.8%
2022	BAL	MLB	26	7	1	1	66	0	57^{2}	46	2	3.3	8.6	55	51.0%	.284	1.16	1.40	90	0.8	97.2	60.6%	27.5%	55.2%
2023 DC	*BAL*	*MLB*	*27*	*3*	*3*	*1*	*67*	*0*	*58.3*	*57*	*5*	*4.4*	*9.1*	*59*	*50.5%*	*.318*	*1.47*	*4.18*	*103*	*0.2*	*96.8*	*61.7%*	*28.2%*	*53.8%*

Comparables: Chasen Shreve (56), Kyle Ryan (53), Jake McGee (52)

On his third team in as many seasons, Pérez got his first taste of major-league success in Baltimore's bullpen. Though scouts once saw the former Cuban National Series star as a big-league starter, his niche appears to be that of lefty specialist. While that career path's often something of a disappointment, it was a huge step forward for Pérez, who logged more innings in 2022 than across four prior MLB stints. Long held back by wandering command and control, the southpaw found the zone and cut his walk rate in half, allowing the 97-mph heat to play up just as scouts had dreamed. Righties fared scarcely better, with Pérez ultimately preventing runs at a rate that might've been star-making in another era. Instead, O's fans are hoping they've found a long-term contributor in the bullpen—an outcome with which they'd be far from disappointed.

★ ★ ★ *2023 Top 101 Prospect* **#8** ★ ★ ★

Grayson Rodriguez RHP

Born: 11/16/99 Age: 23 Bats: L Throws: R Height: 6'5" Weight: 220 lb. Origin: Round 1, 2018 Draft (#11 overall)

YEAR	TEAM	LVL	AGE	W	L	SV	G	GS	IP	H	HR	BB/9	K/9	K	GB%	BABIP	WHIP	ERA	DRA-	WARP	MPH	FB%	Whiff%	CSP
2021	ABD	A+	21	3	0	0	5	5	23^{1}	11	2	1.9	15.4	40	42.5%	.237	0.69	1.54	69	0.6				
2021	BOW	AA	21	6	1	0	18	18	79^{2}	47	8	2.5	13.7	121	37.8%	.252	0.87	2.60	83	1.4				
2022	NOR	AAA	22	6	1	0	14	14	69^{2}	44	2	2.7	12.5	97	42.1%	.280	0.93	2.20	58	2.5	96.4	50.3%	39.5%	
2023 DC	*BAL*	*MLB*	*23*	*5*	*4*	*0*	*16*	*16*	*76*	*58*	*7*	*3.8*	*11.7*	*99*	*41.9%*	*.291*	*1.19*	*2.86*	*74*	*1.7*			*32.7%*	

Comparables: Tyler Glasnow (65), Chris Archer (56), Archie Bradley (56)

In a system overflowing with future major-league talent, the most obvious shortcoming has been a lack of top-end pitching talent coming through the pipeline. The lone exception to that rule is Rodriguez, unquestionably the most promising of the Orioles' young arms and probably the best pitching prospect in all of baseball entering 2022. He would have shed that prospect label if he had pitched the whole season, but a lat injury ended his year prematurely and guaranteed another winter in the top 10 of prospect lists everywhere. Still, in limited time he picked up right where he'd left off: utterly terrorizing every hitter unfortunate enough to face him, with a fastball that touches triple digits complemented by an uncommonly deep arsenal of plus secondaries. If all goes to plan, G-Rod won't make any more prospect lists after this year, and the Orioles won't have any more questions about producing an ace.

Dillon Tate RHP

Born: 05/01/94 Age: 29 Bats: R Throws: R Height: 6'2" Weight: 195 lb. Origin: Round 1, 2015 Draft (#4 overall)

YEAR	TEAM	LVL	AGE	W	L	SV	G	GS	IP	H	HR	BB/9	K/9	K	GB%	BABIP	WHIP	ERA	DRA-	WARP	MPH	FB%	Whiff%	CSP
2020	BAL	MLB	26	1	1	0	12	0	16^{2}	9	1	2.7	7.6	14	51.2%	.190	0.84	3.24	90	0.3	94.4	57.9%	25.0%	44.6%
2021	BAL	MLB	27	0	6	3	62	0	67^{2}	61	7	3.1	6.5	49	60.1%	.271	1.24	4.39	102	0.5	95.6	60.6%	22.2%	55.9%
2022	BAL	MLB	28	4	4	5	67	0	73^{2}	57	6	2.0	7.3	60	58.9%	.251	0.99	3.05	89	1.1	94.2	51.4%	23.5%	57.7%
2023 DC	*BAL*	*MLB*	*29*	*3*	*3*	*1*	*67*	*0*	*58.3*	*58*	*6*	*2.8*	*7.0*	*45*	*57.8%*	*.295*	*1.31*	*3.90*	*100*	*0.2*	*94.7*	*55.5%*	*23.5%*	*55.8%*

Comparables: Dylan Floro (62), Austin Brice (60), Ryne Stanek (60)

It's probably not the career path he envisioned after being picked fourth overall in 2015, but Tate has fashioned himself into a rock-solid reliever over the last two seasons—and one of the best ground-ball specialists in the game, full stop. He scrapped his four-seam fastball entirely last year in favor of his bowling ball of a 94-mph sinker; nearly 70% of the balls in play against that pitch were weak grounders. He pairs it with the slider against righties and the change against lefties. The beautifully simple game plan made him one of the game's more reliable bullpen arms in 2022. It's not rocket science, but it works.

Nick Vespi LHP Born: 10/10/95 Age: 27 Bats: L Throws: L Height: 6'3" Weight: 215 lb. Origin: Round 18, 2015 Draft (#553 overall)

YEAR	TEAM	LVL	AGE	W	L	SV	G	GS	IP	H	HR	BB/9	K/9	K	GB%	BABIP	WHIP	ERA	DRA-	WARP	MPH	FB%	Whiff%	CSP
2021	BOW	AA	25	1	1	0	14	0	19	9	0	4.3	12.3	26	39.5%	.243	0.95	1.42	82	0.3				
2021	NOR	AAA	25	3	2	1	16	0	19^2	22	6	3.7	11.4	25	44.2%	.348	1.53	6.86	85	0.4				
2022	NOR	AAA	26	2	1	8	26	0	28^2	12	0	1.6	11.3	36	53.3%	.200	0.59	0.00	71	0.8				
2022	BAL	MLB	26	5	0	1	25	0	26^1	29	5	2.7	9.6	28	41.3%	.343	1.41	4.10	88	0.4	88.6	48.7%	31.8%	50.4%
2023 DC	*BAL*	*MLB*	*27*	*1*	*1*	*0*	*30*	*0*	*25.7*	*23*	*2*	*3.4*	*9.0*	*26*	*46.4%*	*.296*	*1.29*	*3.53*	*92*	*0.2*	*88.6*	*48.7%*	*31.6%*	*50.4%*

Comparables: Stephen Tarpley (77), Tyler Kinley (73), Matt Dermody (71)

In 19⅔ innings in Triple-A at the end of the 2021 season, Vespi posted an ERA just a few ticks shy of seven. Not great. Flash forward to 2022, and he flipped the script entirely: zero earned runs allowed in 28⅔ innings at the same level. That utterly dominant performance earned Vespi a call-up to the big leagues for the first time; from there he posted massive reverse splits, but generally seemed like he belonged. His secret? Extreme natural cut on a fastball that causes hitters to guess wrong, despite sitting 88–90. When combined with two distinct breaking balls, Vespi presents hitters with a very uncommon look from the left side. With multiple option years remaining, he's likely carved himself a valuable role as a middle-inning reliever in the Baltimore 'pen.

Austin Voth RHP Born: 06/26/92 Age: 31 Bats: R Throws: R Height: 6'2" Weight: 215 lb. Origin: Round 5, 2013 Draft (#166 overall)

YEAR	TEAM	LVL	AGE	W	L	SV	G	GS	IP	H	HR	BB/9	K/9	K	GB%	BABIP	WHIP	ERA	DRA-	WARP	MPH	FB%	Whiff%	CSP
2020	WAS	MLB	28	2	5	0	11	11	49^2	57	14	3.3	8.0	44	29.6%	.297	1.51	6.34	156	-0.9	92.3	60.8%	22.2%	49.0%
2021	WAS	MLB	29	4	1	0	49	1	57^1	57	10	4.4	9.3	59	38.8%	.320	1.48	5.34	106	0.4	94.2	59.5%	25.2%	52.1%
2022	WAS	MLB	30	0	0	0	19	0	18^2	34	4	2.9	8.7	18	38.6%	.455	2.14	10.12	116	0.0	93.9	43.7%	21.9%	54.8%
2022	BAL	MLB	30	5	4	0	22	17	83	77	10	2.7	7.8	72	32.8%	.283	1.23	3.04	105	0.6	93.6	40.5%	25.4%	54.2%
2023 DC	*BAL*	*MLB*	*31*	*5*	*6*	*0*	*36*	*14*	*83.3*	*86*	*12*	*3.1*	*8.3*	*76*	*35.7%*	*.307*	*1.37*	*4.37*	*111*	*0.1*	*93.5*	*49.5%*	*24.6%*	*52.8%*

Comparables: Sam Gaviglio (48), Iván Nova (46), Lucas Harrell (46)

Last June 1, a report came out in *The Washington Post* that the Nationals had been unsuccessfully attempting to trade Voth to a data-minded club that could make the most of his impressive spin rates (according to Baseball Savant, he has 96th-percentile curve spin and 84th-percentile fastball spin). After being designated for assignment, Voth made the short trip up I-95, where he immediately became one of the first bellwethers signaling that the Orioles now belonged in that group of data-minded outfits. He credited their analytics staff with his in-season turnaround: They scaled back his cutter usage and added a sweeping slider, giving him an impressive five pitches with a whiff-per-swing rate over 20%. This new version of Voth dominated in black and orange, and appears locked into the rotation going forward.

Spenser Watkins RHP Born: 08/27/92 Age: 30 Bats: R Throws: R Height: 6'2" Weight: 185 lb. Origin: Round 30, 2014 Draft (#910 overall)

YEAR	TEAM	LVL	AGE	W	L	SV	G	GS	IP	H	HR	BB/9	K/9	K	GB%	BABIP	WHIP	ERA	DRA-	WARP	MPH	FB%	Whiff%	CSP
2021	NOR	AAA	28	1	2	0	8	6	35^2	28	6	2.8	7.6	30	35.8%	.224	1.09	3.53	112	0.3				
2021	BAL	MLB	28	2	7	0	16	10	54^2	74	14	3.1	5.8	35	33.2%	.326	1.70	8.07	150	-0.9	91.0	46.7%	18.0%	53.7%
2022	NOR	AAA	29	1	0	0	4	4	12^2	8	2	2.1	8.5	12	38.2%	.188	0.87	2.84	91	0.2				
2022	BAL	MLB	29	5	6	0	23	20	105^1	119	11	2.6	5.4	63	41.7%	.308	1.41	4.70	125	-0.3	90.4	68.1%	19.8%	58.1%
2023 DC	*BAL*	*MLB*	*30*	*2*	*2*	*0*	*45*	*0*	*38.7*	*44*	*6*	*2.9*	*5.5*	*23*	*39.7%*	*.304*	*1.47*	*4.99*	*126*	*-0.2*	*90.6*	*61.6%*	*20.6%*	*56.7%*

Comparables: Scott Carroll (55), Sam Gaviglio (52), Zach Neal (49)

In a period of baseball defined by high-powered flamethrowers, Watkins is a relic from a bygone era. He sits 91 mph. He pounds the zone and pitches to contact, and whatever happens after that is in God's hands. There were only 140 pitchers to accumulate 100 or more innings last year, and Watkins' 13.7% strikeout rate was 137th in that group. His swinging strike rate is in the single digits. Gerrit Cole's career strikeout rate is more than double Watkins'. And yet, Watkins did log those innings. Somehow.

Tyler Wells RHP

Born: 08/26/94 Age: 28 Bats: R Throws: R Height: 6'8" Weight: 255 lb. Origin: Round 15, 2016 Draft (#453 overall)

YEAR	TEAM	LVL	AGE	W	L	SV	G	GS	IP	H	HR	BB/9	K/9	K	GB%	BABIP	WHIP	ERA	DRA-	WARP	MPH	FB%	Whiff%	CSP
2021	BAL	MLB	26	2	3	4	44	0	57	40	9	1.9	10.3	65	21.2%	.228	0.91	4.11	93	0.8	95.2	58.7%	28.3%	56.3%
2022	BAL	MLB	27	7	7	0	23	23	103^2	90	16	2.4	6.6	76	36.6%	.247	1.14	4.25	106	0.7	93.8	41.6%	25.1%	55.2%
2023 DC	*BAL*	*MLB*	*28*	*6*	*7*	*0*	*24*	*24*	*109.3*	*107*	*16*	*2.5*	*7.8*	*95*	*33.5%*	*.290*	*1.27*	*3.84*	*101*	*0.6*	*94.2*	*46.6%*	*25.9%*	*55.5%*

Comparables: Steven Brault (70), Austin Voth (63), Dan Straily (62)

Wells ended the 2021 season as one of Brandon Hyde's most trusted late-inning arms. Following years in the metaphorical desert—actually the Twins org, by way of Oklahoma—he seemed to have finally found his way, as a setup man, after Baltimore selected him in the Rule 5 Draft. Then the Orioles unexpectedly stretched him back out into a starter last year, and he was mostly successful in that role, too. The team may have gone to the Wells a bit too much, though: His season was waylaid for over a month by an oblique strain, and shoulder inflammation ended it completely shortly after he returned. It remains unclear whether Wells can carry a starter's full-season workload, and thus the arc his career will take.

Bruce Zimmermann LHP

Born: 02/09/95 Age: 28 Bats: L Throws: L Height: 6'1" Weight: 215 lb. Origin: Round 5, 2017 Draft (#140 overall)

YEAR	TEAM	LVL	AGE	W	L	SV	G	GS	IP	H	HR	BB/9	K/9	K	GB%	BABIP	WHIP	ERA	DRA-	WARP	MPH	FB%	Whiff%	CSP
2020	BAL	MLB	25	0	0	0	2	1	7	6	2	2.6	9.0	7	50.0%	.222	1.14	7.71	110	0.0	91.7	51.4%	19.2%	52.8%
2021	NOR	AAA	26	1	0	0	4	4	15	9	2	3.6	9.0	15	51.4%	.200	1.00	2.40	99	0.2				
2021	BAL	MLB	26	4	5	0	14	13	64^1	75	14	3.1	7.8	56	40.0%	.321	1.51	5.04	123	-0.2	91.6	42.2%	25.6%	53.9%
2022	NOR	AAA	27	5	2	0	14	12	76^1	83	6	2.1	8.7	74	47.9%	.339	1.32	3.77	92	1.3				
2022	BAL	MLB	27	2	5	0	15	13	73^2	97	21	1.5	6.0	49	38.9%	.323	1.48	5.99	155	-1.4	90.9	39.5%	18.8%	57.9%
2023 DC	*BAL*	*MLB*	*28*	*2*	*2*	*0*	*18*	*3*	*25.7*	*29*	*3*	*2.6*	*6.3*	*18*	*41.9%*	*.317*	*1.43*	*4.62*	*118*	*-0.1*	*91.2*	*40.9%*	*23.1%*	*56.1%*

Comparables: Dillon Peters (51), Matthew Boyd (49), Adam Plutko (48)

Zimmermann gave Spenser Watkins a run for his money for the title of least intimidating Orioles starter: Watkins had a K/9 of 5.38 compared to Zimmermann's 5.99. Unfortunately, he wasn't quite as effective; that 5.99 figure also happened to be Zimmermann's ERA. He'll have to figure out how to miss bats or induce weaker contact if he's to remain a part of an improving rotation. For now, his value is directly tied to the multiple option years he has left. As long as he can be stashed in the minors, he provides coveted starter depth.

Lineouts

Hitters

HITTER	POS	TEAM	LVL	AGE	PA	R	2B	3B	HR	RBI	BB	K	SB	CS	AVG/OBP/SLG	DRC+	BABIP	BRR	DRP	WARP
Jesús Aguilar	1B/DH	MIA	MLB	32	456	37	18	0	15	49	27	106	1	0	.236/.286/.388	95	.278	-1.0	1B(57): 1.5, 3B(4): -0.1	0.8
	1B/DH	BAL	MLB	32	51	2	1	0	1	2	1	13	0	0	.224/.240/.306	85	.286	-0.5	1B(6): 0.1	0.0
Leandro Arias	SS	DSL BALB	ROK	17	190	25	7	2	1	15	27	41	10	3	.217/.344/.306		.284			
Dylan Beavers	OF	DEL	A	20	77	13	7	2	0	13	12	11	6	1	.359/.468/.531	122	.434	0.0	RF(9): 0.9, CF(6): -0.4	0.5
Anthony Bemboom	C	NOR	AAA	32	137	18	6	0	3	15	10	28	0	0	.228/.292/.350	100	.266	0.6	C(27): -2.4	0.2
	C	BAL	MLB	32	59	4	2	0	1	1	6	17	0	0	.115/.207/.212	78	.147	0.1	C(21): -0.3	0.0
Collin Burns	SS	ABD	A+	22	344	49	20	0	6	34	27	57	13	3	.269/.337/.392	106	.310	-0.9	SS(74): 7.2, 2B(5): -0.5, LF(1): -0.1	1.9
Lewin Díaz	1B	JAX	AAA	25	368	55	19	1	19	64	32	75	0	0	.252/.323/.492	109	.266	-0.7	1B(82): 0.6	1.4
	1B	MIA	MLB	25	174	12	4	0	5	11	11	54	1	0	.169/.224/.288	67	.214	-0.2	1B(56): 0.8	-0.3
Mark Kolozsvary	C	LOU	AAA	26	142	14	6	0	3	7	13	44	0	0	.168/.293/.294	78	.236	-1.2	C(41): -0.5	-0.1
	C	CIN	MLB	26	21	3	2	0	1	3	1	9	0	0	.200/.238/.450	78	.300	0.1	C(9): -0.6	0.0
Josh Lester	1B	TOL	AAA	27	260	36	16	0	10	39	23	66	2	1	.199/.277/.398	103	.228	-4.6	1B(104): 6.0, RF(13): -2.0, LF(12): 0.5	1.5
	1B	DET	MLB	27	5	0	0	0	0	0	0	3	0	0	.000/.000/.000	65			3B(1): 0	
Richie Martin	SS	NOR	AAA	27	334	51	20	6	2	25	32	66	29	5	.250/.341/.380	95	.316	3.2	SS(32): 1.1, 2B(19): 2.0, LF(13): -0.4	1.4
	SS	BAL	MLB	27	33	4	0	2	0	3	3	10	3	1	.167/.242/.300	81	.250	0.4	2B(10): 0, SS(2): -0.8	0.0
Ryan McKenna	OF	NOR	AAA	25	38	5	0	0	3	6	4	14	0	2	.273/.342/.545	93	.353	0.3	CF(8): 0.1	0.1
	OF	BAL	MLB	25	172	23	10	0	2	11	11	55	2	1	.237/.294/.340	72	.350	-0.1	LF(39): 1.8, RF(31): 0.8, CF(21): 0.3	0.3
Cesar Prieto	IF	ABD	A+	23	105	13	6	0	7	20	5	16	3	1	.340/.381/.619	143	.347	-0.9	SS(10): 1.1, 2B(7): 0.2, 3B(2): -0.3	0.9
	IF	BOW	AA	23	389	44	22	0	4	37	15	58	2	5	.255/.296/.348	91	.294	-1.7	3B(58): 1.6, 2B(24): -2.1, SS(5): -1.1	0.3
John Rhodes	OF	ABD	A+	21	248	43	15	2	5	35	35	50	16	0	.259/.389/.428	125	.318	3.1	RF(23): -1.7, CF(19): 0.1, LF(13): -1.9	1.6
	OF	BOW	AA	21	104	12	3	2	0	9	12	22	0	0	.189/.288/.267	97	.246	-0.1	RF(19): -0.3, LF(4): -0.8, CF(1): -0.2	0.2
Johnny Rizer	OF	NOR	AAA	25	81	13	0	0	5	12	8	27	1	1	.194/.284/.403	94	.225	-1.4	CF(15): -0.2, RF(4): 0.1, LF(2): 0.1	0.0
Braylin Tavera	OF	DSL BALB	ROK	17	185	24	5	0	2	14	36	47	7	4	.243/.411/.319		.347			
Reed Trimble	CF/DH	DEL	A	22	133	19	6	0	2	18	13	28	2	0	.291/.353/.393	109	.356	0.2	CF(16): -0.1, LF(4): 0.2	0.6
Donta' Williams	OF	ABD	A+	23	344	48	14	4	4	42	51	85	23	5	.222/.349/.342	94	.298	1.3	CF(37): 1.2, LF(35): -1.5, RF(7): 0.1	0.8

Exposed to waivers after a disappointing final run in Miami, **Jesús Aguilar** latched on with the Orioles in September as they chased after the final AL Wild Card spot. Alas, his comeback never took off and he would have to settle for one of the less successful revivals by a Jesus figure. ⚾ Lauded for his bat-to-ball ability, switch-hitting shortstop **Leando Arias** has plenty of room to fill out and have his power catch up to his hit tool in the future. If that profile sounds like a lot of club's recent IFA signings, well, yes. ⚾ The Orioles selected **Dylan Beavers** 33rd overall with a comp pick after he made waves at Cal. He resembles many of their recent draftees: slightly unusual setup, great results, even better underlying metrics. And like many other O's prospects, he raked in his first, brief taste of pro ball. If Baltimore's recent track record with this exact kind of hitter is any indication, you can bet on improved swing decisions and power gains in the first full pro assignment. ⚾ Pour one out for nominative determinism. Despite the name, **Anthony Bemboom** doesn't produce much thump with his stick, and instead has played in parts of four seasons because of his experience behind the plate. If you were to google "veteran backup catcher," his picture might well pop up. And that's just fine; it's a role that somebody has to fill. It's just that "Tony Booms" would've been a really, *really* great nickname. ⚾ A sixth round pick out of Tulane in 2021, **Collin Burns** spent all of 2022 in High-A Delmarva, where he played mainly at shortstop and made a lot of contact. The problem? It wasn't always great contact. A slap-hitting, glove-first middle infielder will always have a place in the game, but he'll have to show more thwump to be more than an afterthought on a depth chart someday. ⚾ **Lewin Díaz** remains one of the worst breaking-ball hitters in MLB and, at publication, was well on his way to setting an MLB record for the most times designated for assignment in one offseason. ⚾ **Mark Kolozsvary** is a "glove-first" (read: can't hit) catching "prospect" (read: depth minor-leaguer) who doesn't do the one thing teams want their actual glove-first catching prospects to do, which is frame. He's entering the "optionable third or fourth catcher you try to get through waivers" phase of his career, which led to Baltimore claiming him from Cincinnati over the offseason. ⚾ Long-time Detroit farmhand **Josh Lester** got the tiniest shot of espresso in the big leagues. The slugging first baseman was soon back on the minor-league bus and on his way to lead Triple-A, and all Tigers minor leaguers, in games played and plate appearances. ⚾ Entering last season, **Richie Martin** had two problems: his unreliable health and his reliably punchless bat. He was mostly able to overcome the former, but the extended playing time produced a .380 slugging percentage in Triple-A that confirmed the latter. ⚾ One of the most sacred rituals in any fandom is recalling long-forgotten contributors who provided some spark of hope or moment of glory in the downtrodden years between competitive eras. Rattling off the more notable of these characters earns you acceptance; one-upping your fellow fans by plucking more and more obscure names from memory can be worn like a badge of honor. All of this is to say: It's looking increasingly likely that **Ryan McKenna** is fated to be A Guy Remembered, and maybe sooner than later. ⚾ An over-aged, undersized international signing from Cuba, **Cesar Prieto** raked in High-A before having the bat knocked out of his hands in Double-A. He boasts elite contact skills—he hit .403 in his final year in the Cuban National Series—but he's going to have to prove he can hit for respectable pop in the upper minors to factor into Baltimore's plans. ⚾ The second of three consecutive outfielders picked by Baltimore in the 2021 draft, **John Rhodes** only became eligible after the draft was pushed back a month from June to July, making him one of the younger college players in the 2021 class. He reached Double-A in his first full season as a pro, having dominated High-A with a well-rounded approach and a quick, short swing from the right side. Given his age and approach, there might be more to come. ⚾ **Johnny Rizer** could be a useful org depth piece as a player who can man all three outfield positions, plus run a bit and hit against righties. Should his bat prove more powerful, he might be a ... riser. Sorry. ⚾ **Braylin Tavera** is a well-rounded outfielder who won't turn 18 until February of the year on this book. His $1.7 million signing bonus as an international free agent in 2021 was the largest the franchise has ever given on the market, which is largely a reflection of a longtime disinterest but doesn't detract from a potential five-tool skill set. ⚾ His season didn't get going until July because of a shoulder injury, but the 22-year-old **Reed Trimble**—Baltimore's second-round pick in 2021—hit decently upon his return to action. He'll be looking to hits the ball into the ground less; there's more power in his bat, but he can't get to it as long as over half his contact ends up in the dirt. ⚾ A fourth-round selection in 2021, **Donta' Williams** has a solid approach at the plate—he walked more than he struck out in his final year at Arizona—but has struggled to get to any power in the pros. He runs well and plays a decent center but, until he can make pitchers respect his pop, he may struggle to make an impact as anything other than a bench outfielder who can take a decent at-bat.

Pitchers

PITCHER	TEAM	LVL	AGE	W	L	SV	G	GS	IP	H	HR	BB/9	K/9	K	GB%	BABIP	WHIP	ERA	DRA-	WARP	MPH	FB%	WHF	CSP
Yennier Cano	NOR	AAA	28	0	1	1	11	0	16^{2}	17	3	4.3	10.8	20	51.1%	.318	1.50	4.32	81	0.4				
	STP	AAA	28	1	1	3	20	0	23^{2}	16	2	2.3	9.5	25	64.9%	.259	0.93	1.90	81	0.6				
	MIN	MLB	28	1	0	0	10	0	13^{2}	17	3	7.2	9.2	14	50.0%	.341	2.05	9.22	100	0.1	95.4	40.8%	23.5%	50.7%
	BAL	MLB	28	0	1	0	3	0	4^{1}	9	0	10.4	14.5	7	53.3%	.600	3.23	18.69	75	0.1	95.8	47.3%	21.2%	51.2%
Chris Ellis	BAL	MLB	29	0	0	0	2	2	4^{1}	5	0	12.5	4.2	2	50.0%	.313	2.54	10.38	137	0.0	93.2	45.8%	21.2%	53.9%
Logan Gillaspie	BOW	AA	25	1	0	0	6	0	8	7	0	4.5	12.4	11	40.0%	.350	1.38	3.38	96	0.1				
	NOR	AAA	25	5	3	1	22	0	35^{1}	39	2	2.3	9.7	38	30.5%	.366	1.36	5.09	95	0.6				
	BAL	MLB	25	1	0	0	17	0	17^{1}	20	1	1.6	5.2	10	37.3%	.328	1.33	3.12	115	0.0	95.4	48.1%	18.7%	53.3%
Seth Johnson	BG	A+	23	1	1	0	7	7	27	23	4	3.7	13.7	41	31.0%	.352	1.26	3.00	89	0.4				
Joey Krehbiel	BAL	MLB	29	5	5	1	56	0	57^{2}	53	9	2.8	7.0	45	42.1%	.260	1.23	3.90	112	0.2	94.8	34.5%	22.3%	52.0%
Chayce McDermott	ASH	A+	23	6	1	0	19	10	72	57	9	5.4	14.3	114	46.2%	.318	1.39	5.50	79	1.4				
	BOW	AA	23	1	1	0	6	6	26^{2}	17	7	6.7	12.1	36	35.6%	.192	1.39	6.07	92	0.5				
John Means	BAL	MLB	29	0	0	0	2	2	8	8	0	2.3	7.9	7	36.0%	.320	1.25	3.38	113	0.0	92.1	42.2%	20.5%	53.2%
Cade Povich	CR	A+	22	6	8	0	16	16	78^{2}	71	9	3.0	12.2	107	44.5%	.326	1.23	4.46	83	1.5				
	ABD	A+	22	2	0	0	2	2	12	4	0	1.5	11.3	15	45.8%	.167	0.50	0.00	86	0.2				
	BOW	AA	22	2	2	0	6	5	23^{1}	21	5	4.2	10.0	26	39.4%	.267	1.37	6.94	88	0.4				
Drew Rom	BOW	AA	22	7	2	0	19	18	82^{1}	92	9	3.2	11.0	101	42.9%	.374	1.47	4.37	110	0.7				
	NOR	AAA	22	1	1	0	7	7	37^{2}	38	1	4.3	10.3	43	47.1%	.370	1.49	4.54	94	0.6				
Beau Sulser	IND	AAA	28	1	2	0	3	3	12^{2}	11	1	1.4	9.9	14	41.7%	.286	1.03	2.13	91	0.2				
	NOR	AAA	28	2	2	0	17	3	44	53	4	2.5	9.4	46	41.9%	.374	1.48	4.70	96	0.7	92.5	48.6%	25.0%	
	PIT	MLB	28	0	0	0	4	0	9^{2}	8	1	5.6	9.3	10	41.4%	.250	1.45	3.72	91	0.1	92.0	62.6%	21.2%	55.9%
	BAL	MLB	28	0	0	0	6	0	12^{2}	16	2	2.1	6.4	9	51.2%	.359	1.50	3.55	106	0.1	92.2	57.9%	20.6%	53.2%
Alex Wells	NOR	AAA	25	1	0	0	4	2	11^{1}	11	2	2.4	5.6	7	34.2%	.250	1.24	4.76	109	0.1				
	BAL	MLB	25	0	0	0	2	0	3^{2}	5	2	0.0	14.7	6	40.0%	.375	1.36	4.91	94	0.0	88.7	42.4%	26.3%	62.1%

It was a long and winding road to The Show for **Yennier Cano**. The 28-year-old played in his native Cuba until 2016, signed with the Twins in 2019, played in Puerto Rican Winter League at the end of 2020 and finally made it to the majors in May last year—in his seventh professional season. How did he do? Oh, let's not worry about trivial details. He made it! ⚾ He didn't quite make the Opening Day roster, but for the first time in his career **Chris Ellis** was given a shot, early in a season, to establish himself in a major-league rotation. That fact was made bittersweet when he recorded zero outs, while walking three batters and hitting another, in surrendering five runs against the A's in his second start. He was then promptly shut down with shoulder inflammation. He required arthroscopic surgery and didn't pitch again in 2022. ⚾ An undrafted free agent who bounced between Indy leagues until the Brewers signed him in 2018, **Logan Gillaspie**'s debut made him the 12th major leaguer to hail from California's Oxnard College. He probably won't surpass the careers of Terry Pendleton or Jack Wilson, but can take solace as the baseball team's most successful alum since another former Oriole, Josh Towers. ⚾ The mechanics of it are a little complicated, but the Rays sent **Seth Johnson** to Baltimore when Trey Mancini went to Houston and Jose Siri went to Tampa at the trade deadline. With, potentially, three plus pitches—one a high-90s heater—he immediately becomes one of the most promising pitchers in the O's system. They won't get to see him in action for a while, however: He underwent Tommy John surgery last August. ⚾ Every team needs a **Joey Krehbiel**. Two-thirds of his 56 appearances came before the 8th inning. He came in while his team was trailing or tied far more times than to protect a lead. So while he didn't get many of the important outs, he helped preserve the arms who do. Every team needs a Joey Krehbiel. ⚾ Part of the return for Trey Mancini, this likely reliever posts gaudy strikeout totals, but the equally obscene walk numbers indicate that **Chayce McDermott** doesn't get hitters to [first name] enough. ⚾ You'll be forgiven if you don't remember **John Means** pitching in 2022; he threw just eight innings before he was sidelined with an elbow injury that eventually required Tommy John surgery. It was a particularly disappointing outcome after a promising breakout season. Upon his return, he'll once again look to prove he's not just an average pitcher. ⚾ Sent to Baltimore in exchange for the services of erstwhile closer Jorge López, **Cade Povich**—no relation to Maury—had a rough go of it in Bowie after the trade. He's another to file under the "crafty lefty" tag, relying on command and pitch mix more than overpowering stuff to get outs. Whether he can continue to pile up strikeouts against better hitters remains to be seen; he's one of the few southpaws to watch in this system after DL Hall. ⚾ **Drew Rom** took something of a step back in 2022, with his numbers across the board declining as he moved up the organizational ladder. In an org quickly becoming overstocked with back-end starter-types, a lefty who relies on pitchability may not have as easy a path to the major leagues as it once appeared he would. The O's did indicate they weren't quite ready to give up on him by adding him to their 40-man roster last November. ⚾ The Sulser brothers were like ships passing in the night in Baltimore: The team traded Cole to Miami in April and claimed **Beau Sulser** on waivers in May. Unless Cole takes a trip to Korea, they won't play together in 2023 either: Beau signed a contract to play in the KBO with the KT Wiz in November. ⚾ **Alex Wells** defied the odds and made it to the majors as a southpaw Aussie who topped out at 91.4 mph. That's laudable! Unfortunately for him, major-league hitters feasted on his (lack of) heat; his career MLB ERA (6.60) is more than twice that of his career minor-league ERA (2.89). The dreaded "elbow inflammation" prematurely ended his sophomore season and eventually required Tommy John surgery.

BOSTON RED SOX

Essay by Alex Speier

Player comments by Jon Tayler and BP staff

Where did everyone go?

Little more than four years after the Red Sox authored the most dominant season in franchise history—following a team-record 108 regular-season wins with an 11-3 march through the postseason—nearly all the pillars of that title run had departed. When Xander Bogaerts relocated to San Diego on a staggering 11-year, $280 million deal with the Padres, a dazzling homegrown generation had been almost completely gutted. In his wake—and particularly in the month between his departure and the deal to secure Rafael Devers for $331 million over 11 years—he left not only an incredulous, angry fanbase, but also a team and organization short on the type of star players that have long powered its most successful eras

In 2016, Bogaerts, Mookie Betts and Jackie Bradley Jr. were all elected as All-Star Game starters for the American League. That same year, Andrew Benintendi was the leadoff hitter in the All-Star Futures Game. He was promoted to the big leagues shortly thereafter, with his addition to the aforementioned group representing the opening of a title-contention window. The Sox won their first of three straight AL East championships in 2016, punctuated by the epic 2018 campaign.

Boston built toward 2018 with a sense of World Series-or-bust abandon. Atop (and in no small part because of the financial flexibility afforded by) the remarkable group of young position players, in consecutive offseasons, president of baseball operations Dave Dombrowski signed David Price to a record-setting seven-year, $217 million deal; traded standout prospects Yoán Moncada and Michael Kopech to the White Sox for Chris Sale; and signed J.D. Martinez—a designated hitter!—to a five-year, $110 million contract to serve as a lineup anchor.

The thought process behind such roster construction was clear, just as it has been in every other stop of Dombrowski's career.

"Everyone has different philosophies, but I would say I really believe that you win with star players," Dombrowski said this offseason. "Now, you can't win with star players alone, but you can build around star players. I've really always had that belief."

BOSTON RED SOX PROSPECTUS

2022 W-L: 78-84, 5TH IN AL EAST

Pythag	.468	21st	DER	.688	26th
RS/G	4.54	9th	DRC+	100	12th
RA/G	4.86	25th	DRA-	102	19th
dWin%	.503	17th	FIP	4.17	21st
Payroll	$207M	6th	B-Age	29.3	26th
M$/MW	$6.3M	26th	P-Age	30.4	28th

- Opened 1912
- Open air
- Natural surface
- Fence profile: 3' to 37'

Park Factors

Runs	Runs/RH	Runs/LH	HR/RH	HR/LH
105	107	103	96	83

Top Hitter WARP	4.0 Xander Bogaerts
Top Pitcher WARP	1.5 Garrett Whitlock
2023 Top Prospect	Marcelo Mayer

Payroll History (in millions)

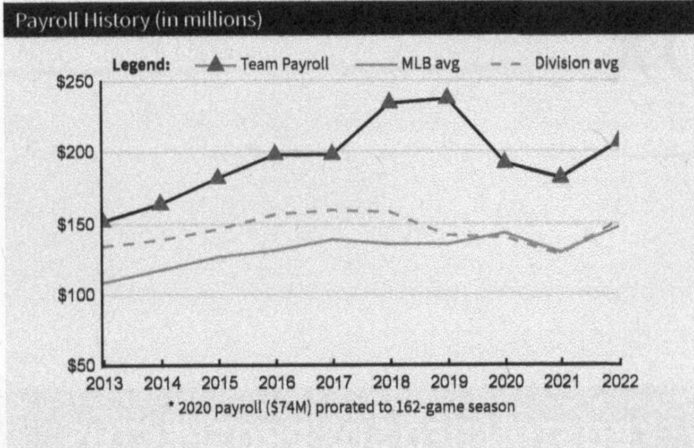

Future Commitments (in millions)

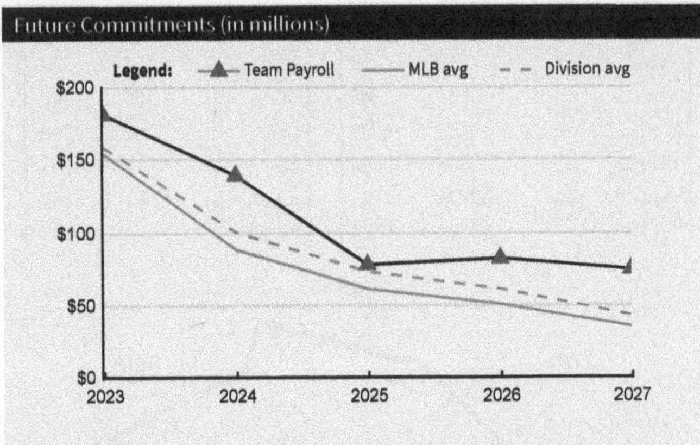

Farm System Ranking

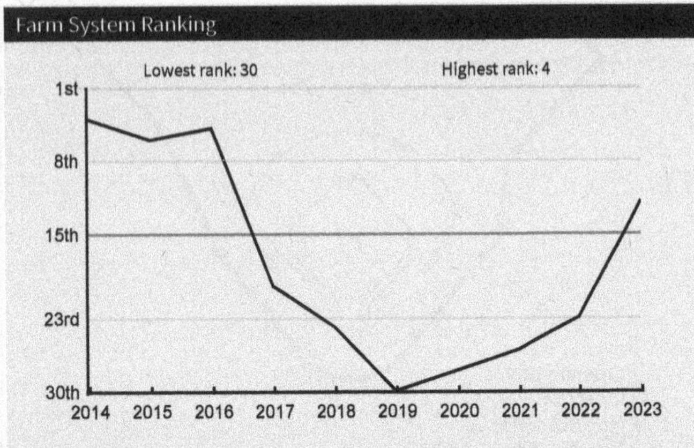

Personnel

Chief Baseball Officer
Chaim Bloom

General Manager
Brian O'Halloran

Executive Vice President, AGM
Raquel Ferreira

Executive Vice President, AGM
Eddie Romero

Senior Vice President, Player Development
Ben Crockett

Senior Vice President, AGM
Michael Groopman

Manager
Alex Cora

BP Alumni
Spencer Bingol
Chaim Bloom
Todd Gold
Mike Groopman
Jason Karegeannes

Dombrowski's Red Sox teams clearly reflected that conviction, with recognizable stars at every turn. Of course, for the Red Sox, such a state of affairs had plenty of precedents.

The Red Sox have long been a team of players with single-name recognition whose numbers are splashed on the backs of jerseys throughout Fenway crowds. Once the team got beyond the post-Ted Williams malaise of the early '60s and entered the era of resurrected hopes that began with the Impossible Dream season of 1967, the club featured one New England household name after another.

Yaz, Fisk, the Gold Dust Twins, Boggs, Clemens, Mo, Nomar, Pedro, Manny, Papi, Schilling, Pedroia, Lester, Betts, among others, created a chain that spanned more than a half-century, with Bogaerts and Devers carrying that baton through the 2022 season.

It wasn't just that the Sox had collected talent: They also possessed players who were performing to the standards of stars. The Sox have had at least two players worth at least 4.0 WARP in 17 of 22 seasons this century. The exceptions were 2022 (when Bogaerts cleared the bar and Devers fell just short at 3.7 WARP), 2020 (the pandemic-shortened season), 2015, 2014 and 2012—all years in which the team finished in last place in the AL East.

During that run, the Sox have experienced the game's greatest pinnacle more often than any other team, with four 21st-century championships in their vault. They also experienced painful nadirs, with five last-place finishes in the last 11 years, also more than any other team in baseball. But even in the years the team cratered, it always featured at least two recognizable pillars who offered the Red Sox both an identity and the promise that, when seasons went off the rails, rapid improvement remained within reach.

In the waning days of 2022, that was no longer the case. The departure of Bogaerts in free agency not only severed the organization's last tie to its 2013 championship team, but also left it without the familiar bright constellation of stars. As of early January, the Sox had just one player—Devers—who projected as a four-win player in 2023. Next closest on the list is the newly signed Masataka Yoshida, who's projected somewhat generously to provide 3.8 WARP.

Was ever a title in this way won?

Technically, yes—though more recently, no. Each of the last five full-season champions had at least three players who posted a WARP of 4.0 or better. That group includes the 2018 Red Sox, who featured four players (Betts, Martinez, Sale and Bogaerts) who performed at such a level.

Going back a bit further, the Giants won the World Series in both 2012 and 2014 when Buster Posey was their lone representative who exceeded 4.0 WARP—though in both cases, Posey not only surpassed that benchmark but *more than doubled it* (8.1 in 2012, 8.2 in 2014). Moreover, in both seasons, the Giants had Madison Bumgarner falling just short of 4.0 WARP in the regular season.

Obviously, the Mike Trout/Shohei Ohtani Angels offer convincing evidence that a couple of megastars aren't sufficient to guarantee success. At the same time, there's been a relatively clear pattern of teams needing stars—plural—to win it all. For the most part, the presence of multiple stars has been a prerequisite to building a championship-caliber team, with the quality of the surrounding players determining whether the team lives up to that potential or ends up being an Anaheim-like disappointment.

Perhaps it is with that loose formula in mind that skepticism about the 2023 Red Sox was widespread by the time the deep end of the free agency pool had been drained in early January. Even with the landmark deal for Devers—a critical rebuttal to growing questions about whether the Sox remained willing to invest at top-of-the-sport levels—questions remained about just how competitive Boston could be. Not only was Bogaerts gone, but the Sox had stood on the sidelines as other big-name free agents came off the board. In a cutthroat American League East, the Sox appeared to lack the depth of high-end talent of their competitors—a surprising development given that they entered the offseason with roughly $100 million in room beneath the $233 million luxury tax threshold.

Chief baseball officer Chaim Bloom said shortly after the 2022 season that the Sox were in a position to consider different moves than they had made during the initial years of his tenure, when he'd signed just one free agent (Trevor Story, on a six-year, $140 million deal) to a deal of more than two years. But beyond the Devers extension, Bloom has continued a pattern of making modest bets with an eye toward raising the team's floor by filling in gaping holes.

The Sox overhauled one area of glaring weakness this winter, attempting to solidify the back end of their bullpen with the additions of Kenley Jansen (two years, $32 million), Chris Martin (two years, $17 million) and lefty Joely Rodríguez (one year, $2 million). The impact of late-inning improvements could be considerable, given that the 2022 Red Sox bullpen blew saves in 13 losses within their division en route to their worst record in franchise history (26-50) in the American League East. Flipping even half of those games would have turned a 78-84 team into a fringe Wild Card contender.

A lineup that struggled with a lack of discipline in 2022 could look considerably different in 2023 with the additions of veteran Justin Turner, rookie Triston Casas (20.0% walk rate in his September call-up) and Yoshida, the NPB star who had roughly twice as many walks as strikeouts last season. Still, that Yoshida's deal proved by far the largest for a player from outside the organization this winter—a five-year, $90 million investment, with an additional $15.375 million posting fee sent to the Orix Buffaloes—speaks to a measured approach, and a far cry from the offseasons of the not-too-distant past in which the Sox were in the mix for the biggest available names.

The pivot isn't entirely shocking. Dombrowski was fired in September 2019 and replaced by Bloom because the team's owners believed Dombrowski's star-collecting model, focused chiefly on concentrating every available resource in the big-league team with minimal regard for depth or the development of the next homegrown core, had left the team in a perilous long-term spot.

Too many long-term deals—seven years for Price, five for Martinez and, of particular note and organizational disagreement, a five-year extension for Sale in the spring of 2019, after he'd been sidelined by shoulder issues for a sizable chunk of 2018—had left the team unable to reshape its roster while ducking under the luxury tax threshold to reset penalties every third year. The team had stars but lacked depth, and also featured a number of high-salaried players whose contributions were minimal. By the end of 2019, the Sox viewed themselves as a team with a huge payroll but little bang for the buck and fearing a future that might look like the post-2011 Phillies and post-2014 Giants and Tigers.

Bloom was hired to overhaul that approach and get the Red Sox past some of their least productive deals with an understanding that painful decisions would be required to do so. He traded Betts and Price to the Dodgers as his first major move in response to the understood need to reset the team's payroll, rebuild its young talent base and start building out the depth of a roster that had become top-heavy. The trade of Benintendi and free-agent departures of Bradley, Bogaerts and Martinez followed.

Bogaerts' departure struck a particular nerve within the fanbase. He'd been the first member of the homegrown wave to truly arrive, emerging as a key contributor to a title in 2013 and a cornerstone by the 2018 championship. He earned recognition as an All-Star four times and played more games at short than anyone in franchise history. The Sox declared repeatedly that re-signing Bogaerts represented their highest priority of the offseason, yet their last offer was more than $100 million less than San Diego's winning bid.

Even beyond the question of what the loss of Bogaerts might mean for the team's competitive fortunes, the Sox recognized the emotional cost of the departure of another beloved, recognizable, homegrown player.

"That's one of the things that's just not pleasant right now, knowing that and still feeling like we should not have gone to that territory [of the Padres' bid] but understanding that emotionally it was going to hit just as hard and maybe even harder given that there are scars from Mookie," said Bloom. "I understand that responsibility [to the fans] and the weight of that. That's really sacred to me. And I try to do right by that every day."

The agreement to retain Devers somewhat dulled the sense of loss, offering evidence that the Red Sox can retain a star who'd been known to the team's fans since his earliest days in the minors. Yet even with that landmark deal, Bloom's deliberate course of team-building has been a difficult one for Red Sox fans to digest. A multi-year Stanford marshmallow experiment was never going to win PR points in a setting where roster-building satisfaction rarely comes from anything but stuffing a damn marshmallow in one's face—and then clamoring for another.

Prior to the agreement with Devers in January, Boston's largest commitment to a player in just over three years following the Dombrowski-to-Bloom transition was the Story deal. During that same time, 14 other teams spanning a range of market sizes—the Angels, Braves (twice), Brewers, Cubs, Dodgers (twice), Mariners, Mets (three times), Nationals, Padres (twice), Phillies, Rangers (three times), Rays, Rockies and Yankees (three times)—all had consummated contracts, whether extensions or free-agent signings, guaranteeing players more than the $140 million of which Story is assured.

Ultimately, of course, payroll size is less important than winning—a fact that the Sox have demonstrated repeatedly over the last 11 years, fielding several last-place clubs while spending more than $200 million on payroll. But can a version of the Red Sox with just a single projected star be successful?

There is a chance, of course, that their players dramatically outperform expectations in 2023. Perhaps Sale or Story can stay intact long enough to reclaim star status. Maybe Yoshida will feature a made-for-Fenway, all-fields, left-handed swing that will make him an offensive force. But for the Sox to have a chance of success in 2023, they will likely need players to perform to levels that they have not in recent years.

The Sox feature a more balanced roster and deeper organization entering 2023 than they did in 2019. Yet improvement in those areas does not represent an endpoint. The commitment to Devers represented an acknowledgement of that notion, and recognition that ultimately, for realistic, sustainable, championship aspirations to seem like anything but an Impossible Dream, the team will have to get back into the business of building around stars. ■

—Alex Speier writes for the Boston Globe.

Hitters

Christian Arroyo 2B

Born: 05/30/95 Age: 28 Bats: R Throws: R Height: 6'1" Weight: 210 lb. Origin: Round 1, 2013 Draft (#25 overall)

YEAR	TEAM	LVL	AGE	PA	R	2B	3B	HR	RBI	BB	K	SB	CS	Whiff%	AVG/OBP/SLG	DRC+	BABIP	BRR	DRP	WARP
2020	CLE	MLB	25	0	0	0	0	0	0	0	0	0	0		.000/.000/.000				3B(1): -0.0	0.0
2020	BOS	MLB	25	54	7	1	0	3	8	4	11	0	0	25.7%	.240/.296/.440	111	.250	0.7	2B(13): 0, SS(2): -0.2	0.3
2021	WOR	AAA	26	38	4	1	0	0	2	2	12	1	0		.091/.184/.121	83	.136	0.3	2B(8): -0.6	0.0
2021	BOS	MLB	26	181	22	12	0	6	25	8	44	1	0	26.7%	.262/.324/.445	98	.325	-0.4	2B(51): 0.8, SS(2): -0.2	0.6
2022	BOS	MLB	27	300	32	16	1	6	36	13	49	5	1	20.6%	.286/.322/.414	104	.326	-2.2	2B(40): -0.6, RF(17): -0.4, SS(14): -0.6	0.6
2023 DC	*BOS*	*MLB*	*28*	*429*	*49*	*20*	*1*	*11*	*46*	*24*	*83*	*6*	*1*	*22.1%*	*.262/.320/.408*	*100*	*.311*	*1.8*	*2B 1, SS -1*	*1.4*

Comparables: Jose Vidro (54), Brandon Phillips (54), Martín Prado (54)

The lasting image of Arroyo's 2022 season is of him standing in Fenway's cavernous right field, arms helplessly outstretched and eyes cast up into an early July evening sky. He was frantically searching for a pop-up off the bat of Joey Gallo that he had lost in the lights, only for the ball to plop some 20 feet behind him for what was charitably scored a triple. It was a play emblematic of both a sloppy Red Sox season and Arroyo's role on what felt like a half-finished roster. Despite spending not a single inning of his professional career off the infield dirt, he was tasked with playing arguably the toughest right field in the majors on a semi-regular basis. To no surprise, he didn't do it well. On a functional team, he's a backup infielder—and a good one, at that—or a short-side platoon partner with some pop and a touch of versatility. But in 2022, he was a square peg jammed repeatedly into a round hole, with predictable results.

★ ★ ★ 2023 Top 101 Prospect **#67** *★ ★ ★*

Miguel Bleis OF

Born: 03/01/04 Age: 19 Bats: R Throws: R Height: 6'3" Weight: 170 lb. Origin: International Free Agent, 2021

YEAR	TEAM	LVL	AGE	PA	R	2B	3B	HR	RBI	BB	K	SB	CS	Whiff%	AVG/OBP/SLG	DRC+	BABIP	BRR	DRP	WARP
2021	DSL RSR	ROK	17	136	17	6	1	4	17	12	25	7	4		.252/.331/.420		.283			
2022	RSX	ROK	18	167	28	14	4	5	27	10	45	18	3		.301/.353/.542		.394			
2023	*No projection*																			

If it weren't for Ceddanne Rafaela's ascension, Bleis would've been the breakout prospect of the year in Boston. The rangy teenager—born seven months before the franchise broke its 86-year championship drought—pasted pitchers in the Florida Complex League, showcasing the potential that earned him a nine-figure signing bonus out of the Dominican Republic in 2021. Bleis fills the entire toolbox, sporting plus bat speed and power that leads to lots of hard contact, big wheels on the basepaths and a fair shot at sticking in center field. A strikeout rate of nearly 27% coupled with a pedestrian walk rate is less encouraging, but there's plenty of time for his approach to improve. Expect to see Bleis jump up Red Sox prospect rankings this year.

★ ★ ★ *2023 Top 101 Prospect* **#35** ★ ★ ★

Triston Casas 1B

Born: 01/15/00 Age: 23 Bats: L Throws: R Height: 6'4" Weight: 252 lb. Origin: Round 1, 2018 Draft (#26 overall)

YEAR	TEAM	LVL	AGE	PA	R	2B	3B	HR	RBI	BB	K	SB	CS	Whiff%	AVG/OBP/SLG	DRC+	BABIP	BRR	DRP	WARP
2021	SCO	WIN	21	97	19	6	0	1	11	17	18	0	1		.372/.495/.487		.475			
2021	POR	AA	21	329	57	12	2	13	52	49	63	6	3		.284/.395/.484	128	.323	-0.8	1B(73): -6.2	1.4
2021	WOR	AAA	21	42	6	3	1	1	7	8	8	1	0		.242/.381/.485	107	.280	-0.4	1B(7): 0.0	0.1
2022	WOR	AAA	22	317	45	20	1	11	38	46	68	0	0		.273/.382/.481	101	.323	0.7	1B(63): -1.1	0.9
2022	BOS	MLB	22	95	11	1	0	5	12	19	23	1	0	26.5%	.197/.358/.408	111	.208	-0.8	1B(27): -1	0.1
2023 DC	*BOS*	*MLB*	*23*	*559*	*66*	*25*	*4*	*15*	*59*	*74*	*135*	*5*	*2*	*28.7%*	*.231/.342/.398*	*106*	*.294*	*2.9*	*1B -1*	*1.4*

Comparables: Dominic Smith (64), Jon Singleton (59), Anthony Rizzo (59)

In an ideal world, Casas would've spent the first half of the season demolishing Triple-A pitching ahead of a midsummer summons to Boston to assume the mantel of franchise first baseman—something the Sox haven't had since Kevin Youkilis retired to become a broadcaster/scally cap model. In the cruel, cold reality in which we instead live, Casas spent most of the year stuck in Worcester and on the injured list, the victim of a right ankle sprain that cost him two months after a hot start. Instead of emerging as the potential missing piece on a contender, the rookie debuted in the majors amid the back stretch of a lost season. Still, Casas quickly showed why he'd been a consensus top prospect, displaying above-average patience and power. Regular contact remains the missing piece of the puzzle, but he's a selective hitter with an excellent eye, and the pending demise of the infield shift should open up holes for his pull-oriented approach. Even if it wasn't a perfect year, Casas' status in the organization hasn't changed: He's the bright and shiny future of a Boston lineup without many long-term anchors.

Bobby Dalbec 1B

Born: 06/29/95 Age: 28 Bats: R Throws: R Height: 6'4" Weight: 227 lb. Origin: Round 4, 2016 Draft (#118 overall)

YEAR	TEAM	LVL	AGE	PA	R	2B	3B	HR	RBI	BB	K	SB	CS	Whiff%	AVG/OBP/SLG	DRC+	BABIP	BRR	DRP	WARP
2020	BOS	MLB	25	92	13	3	0	8	16	10	39	0	0	46.2%	.263/.359/.600	92	.394	-0.6	1B(21): 0.1, 3B(2): 0	0.1
2021	BOS	MLB	26	453	50	21	5	25	78	28	156	2	0	38.2%	.240/.298/.494	90	.316	1.2	1B(123): 2, 3B(14): -0.6	0.7
2022	WOR	AAA	27	53	8	0	0	5	8	3	14	1	0		.250/.302/.563	111	.233	0.2	1B(9): 0.6, 3B(4): -0.8	0.2
2022	BOS	MLB	27	353	40	9	2	12	39	29	118	3	0	35.0%	.215/.283/.369	84	.293	-0.4	1B(89): -1, 3B(24): -0.2, 2B(2): 0	-0.1
2023 DC	*BOS*	*MLB*	*28*	*188*	*25*	*7*	*0*	*10*	*26*	*14*	*60*	*1*	*1*	*35.2%*	*.235/.306/.466*	*107*	*.302*	*1.1*	*1B 0, RF 0*	*0.6*

Comparables: C.J. Cron (54), Ryan Garko (51), Tony Clark (51)

Given the opportunity to cement himself as a starter, or at least a part of the future, in Boston ahead of Triston Casas' arrival, Dalbec took his chance and ran straight into a wall. The second-half surge in 2021 that saved his spot on the roster failed to carry over to a new season. He hit .147/.213/.235 in April with a strikeout rate just shy of 31%, spending most of that first month swinging through fastballs or waving at sliders off the plate. The Sox finally gave up on him in September, demoting Dalbec to make room for Casas and raising the question of what place, if any, he has on this team long-term. His saving graces are his power and continued ability to hit left-handed pitching—a career .855 OPS against southpaws is just about the lone positive stat in his ledger—along with a willingness, if not genuine ability, to fill in at most spots on the infield. But with Casas now ahead of him on the depth chart, it's hard to see where Bobby D. fits with the Red Sox going forward.

Rafael Devers 3B

Born: 10/24/96 Age: 26 Bats: L Throws: R Height: 6'0" Weight: 240 lb. Origin: International Free Agent, 2013

YEAR	TEAM	LVL	AGE	PA	R	2B	3B	HR	RBI	BB	K	SB	CS	Whiff%	AVG/OBP/SLG	DRC+	BABIP	BRR	DRP	WARP
2020	BOS	MLB	23	248	32	16	1	11	43	13	67	0	0	31.8%	.263/.310/.483	84	.325	1.6	3B(57): -1.1	0.2
2021	BOS	MLB	24	664	101	37	1	38	113	62	143	5	5	27.8%	.279/.352/.538	126	.307	2.8	3B(151): -5, 2B(2): 0	4.2
2022	BOS	MLB	25	614	84	42	1	27	88	50	114	3	1	28.2%	.295/.358/.521	132	.329	-1.0	3B(138): -1.2	3.6
2023 DC	*BOS*	*MLB*	*26*	*606*	*92*	*37*	*2*	*31*	*98*	*50*	*129*	*4*	*1*	*27.7%*	*.293/.360/.541*	*148*	*.335*	*0.0*	*3B -3*	*4.5*

Comparables: George Davis (82), George Brett (80), Richie Hebner (78)

There are two ways of looking at the trade that sent Mookie Betts from Boston to Los Angeles. The first is that it represented the craven capitulation of a billionaire owner unwilling to stomach a nine-figure outlay for his team's best player. The second is that it represented the craven capitulation of a billionaire owner unwilling to stomach a nine-figure outlay for his team's best player, but that it had to be done to preserve the payroll space needed to build a balanced roster. Two years after that much-maligned deal, fate again dropped the same problem in John Henry's lap in the form of Devers, who had one season of team control left entering the offseason and a hankering for a Betts-sized contract. This time, Henry blinked: The Sox inked Devers to an 11-year, $331 million extension in January amid the backlash they faced for letting Xander Bogaerts walk to San Diego.

Devers has earned his new deal. Boston's baby-faced third baseman played through pain and cut down on his strikeouts to put up another gaudy offensive season, finishing seventh among all third baseman in WARP and 22nd among all hitters in DRC+. What's more, by FRAA, his defense has gone from "cover the eyes of the children" to acceptable; you'll still get some wild, overly aggressive throws, but he's gone a long way toward cleaning up his work at the hot corner. As one of the best pure hitters in the game set to enter his age-26 season, Devers was going to land a seismic contract one way or another soon. Kudos to the Sox for ponying up for once, even if it means they've only gone one-for-three in locking down their recent homegrown generational talents.

Jarren Duran CF Born: 09/05/96 Age: 26 Bats: L Throws: R Height: 6'2" Weight: 212 lb. Origin: Round 7, 2018 Draft (#220 overall)

YEAR	TEAM	LVL	AGE	PA	R	2B	3B	HR	RBI	BB	K	SB	CS	Whiff%	AVG/OBP/SLG	DRC+	BABIP	BRR	DRP	WARP
2020	CAG	WIN	23	70	14	2	0	0	10	12	14	6	0		.236/.386/.273		.310			
2021	WOR	AAA	24	283	46	11	2	16	36	30	66	16	3		.258/.357/.516	117	.288	1.8	CF(49): -3.3, RF(7): -1.0, LF(2): 0.4	1.3
2021	BOS	MLB	24	112	17	3	2	2	10	4	40	2	1	34.7%	.215/.241/.336	58	.318	0.5	CF(28): -0.2, LF(1): 0	-0.1
2022	WOR	AAA	25	307	49	16	6	10	38	26	73	18	3		.283/.349/.491	101	.352	3.2	CF(58): 0.6, LF(5): 0.3, RF(2): 0.0	1.8
2022	BOS	MLB	25	223	23	14	3	3	17	14	63	7	1	28.3%	.221/.283/.363	69	.302	-0.2	CF(51): 2.1, RF(7): 1.3	0.3
2023 DC	*BOS*	*MLB*	*26*	*275*	*30*	*12*	*4*	*5*	*27*	*17*	*70*	*10*	*2*	*29.2%*	*.244/.305/.392*	*88*	*.322*	*7.2*	*RF 0, LF 0*	*1.0*

Comparables: Laynce Nix (69), Steven Duggar (64), Bradley Zimmer (63)

A quick summary of Duran's depressing 2022 season: After scorching Triple-A for the first three months of the year, he was called up to Boston to be the regular center fielder. Though he started off hot, he missed a crucial series in Toronto in late June because he hadn't gotten the COVID-19 vaccine, then hit .182/.247/.318 over July and August while striking out in about a third of his plate appearances. In late July, he lost a fly ball so thoroughly in the lights at Fenway that, even though it landed a dozen feet behind him, he didn't so much as make a move to retrieve it, resulting in an inside-the-park grand slam. Two weeks later, he got into a verbal fight with some fans in Kansas City after misplaying two fly balls in the same inning. Finally, he was demoted to Triple-A in late August, where he remained until the season's final days. An overly aggressive hitter, terrible defender and poor baserunner despite his blinding speed, Duran is a terrific athlete who desperately needs to get his head straight. At present, he's more fit to patrol Alex Cora's doghouse than Fenway's spacious outfield.

Enrique Hernández CF Born: 08/24/91 Age: 31 Bats: R Throws: R Height: 5'11" Weight: 190 lb. Origin: Round 6, 2009 Draft (#191 overall)

YEAR	TEAM	LVL	AGE	PA	R	2B	3B	HR	RBI	BB	K	SB	CS	Whiff%	AVG/OBP/SLG	DRC+	BABIP	BRR	DRP	WARP
2020	LAD	MLB	28	148	20	8	1	5	20	6	31	0	1	24.5%	.230/.270/.410	93	.260	0.5	2B(30): -0.5, RF(9): -0.5, LF(5): -0.1	0.3
2021	BOS	MLB	29	585	84	35	3	20	60	61	110	1	0	23.6%	.250/.337/.449	109	.278	2.6	CF(93): 7.6, 2B(47): 0.2, SS(8): 0.5	4.1
2022	BOS	MLB	30	402	48	24	0	6	45	34	71	0	2	24.7%	.222/.291/.338	90	.257	1.1	CF(80): -3.8, 2B(11): 0.3, SS(10): 0.6	0.8
2023 DC	*BOS*	*MLB*	*31*	*614*	*82*	*32*	*1*	*22*	*67*	*52*	*121*	*1*	*1*	*24.9%*	*.243/.319/.426*	*104*	*.279*	*0.1*	*CF 2, 2B 0*	*2.3*

Comparables: Mickey Stanley (60), Richard Hidalgo (58), Andruw Jones (58)

A sparkplug in 2021, Hernández sputtered in his second season with the Red Sox, spending most of the year rehabbing a hip injury that never seemed to heal right. Nonetheless, Boston brought him back for '23 on a one-year deal worth $10 million, potentially a sign of how much the front office values his clubhouse presence, versatility and defense in center. Or as an admission that the team can't (or won't) do any better. Or both. Hernández offers plenty of positives despite a total inability to hit right-handed pitching—he posted a .583 OPS against righties last season—and, as the Red Sox learned firsthand with Jarren Duran, a good glove in center can be hard to find. Duran's flop also meant that Boston didn't have anyone ready to take over for Hernández, and the free-agent market looked short on affordable alternative options. It makes plenty of sense to run things back with Kiké and hope for better health, though the tracks need to be laid for his eventual replacement as an everyday option.

Blaze Jordan CI Born: 12/19/02 Age: 20 Bats: R Throws: R Height: 6'2" Weight: 220 lb. Origin: Round 3, 2020 Draft (#89 overall)

YEAR	TEAM	LVL	AGE	PA	R	2B	3B	HR	RBI	BB	K	SB	CS	Whiff%	AVG/OBP/SLG	DRC+	BABIP	BRR	DRP	WARP
2021	RSX	ROK	18	76	12	7	1	4	19	6	13	1	0		.362/.408/.667		.396			
2021	SAL	A	18	38	7	1	0	2	7	2	8	0	0		.250/.289/.444	113	.269	0.3	3B(5): -1.3, 1B(2): 0.2	0.1
2022	SAL	A	19	415	48	29	3	8	57	37	67	4	1		.286/.357/.446	116	.329	1.0	3B(50): -3.8, 1B(34): 5.5	2.4
2022	GVL	A+	19	106	12	1	0	4	11	11	27	1	0		.301/.387/.441	87	.387	-2.2	1B(13): -1.1, 3B(9): -1.5	-0.4
2023 non-DC	*BOS*	*MLB*	*20*	*251*	*21*	*10*	*1*	*3*	*22*	*15*	*64*	*0*	*1*	*32.3%*	*.230/.282/.338*	*71*	*.302*	*1.0*	*1B 0, 3B 0*	*-0.4*

Comparables: Miguel Vargas (77), Anthony Rizzo (62), Nolan Gorman (61)

Blaze Jordan isn't an aptronym; at 6-foot-2 and 220 pounds, he's not the second coming of Juan Pierre or Dee Gordon-Strange. He did set fire to two levels of A-ball, though, as he continued to rise up Boston's prospect rankings. He once again showed the prodigious power that was his calling card as a draft pick of some acclaim, but an even more encouraging development was an increase in walk rate at both Salem and Greenville, where he was nearly four years younger than the average competition. Jordan's bat is going to have to do the heavy lifting for him to meet his ceiling; as a defender, he can hack it at third base but is better suited for first, and as noted already, you're not going to mistake him for Lou Brock on the bases. But so far, so good for the budding slugger at the plate.

Matthew Lugo IF Born: 05/09/01 Age: 22 Bats: R Throws: R Height: 6'1" Weight: 187 lb. Origin: Round 2, 2019 Draft (#69 overall)

YEAR	TEAM	LVL	AGE	PA	R	2B	3B	HR	RBI	BB	K	SB	CS	Whiff%	AVG/OBP/SLG	DRC+	BABIP	BRR	DRP	WARP
2021	SAL	A	20	469	61	21	3	4	50	38	94	15	4		.270/.338/.364	104	.335	0.5	SS(93): 4.0, 2B(6): 0.9	2.2
2022	GVL	A+	21	512	76	25	10	18	78	35	100	20	7		.288/.344/.500	102	.330	-1.3	SS(73): 1.2, 3B(25): -2.4, 2B(7): -0.8	1.3
2023 non-DC	*BOS*	*MLB*	*22*	*251*	*21*	*10*	*2*	*4*	*23*	*13*	*62*	*5*	*1*	*29.7%*	*.240/.288/.363*	*79*	*.311*	*2.6*	*2B 0, 3B 0*	*0.3*

Comparables: Ryan Brett (68), Vidal Bruján (67), Billy Hamilton (67)

After a couple of seasons of looking like a high-round washout, Lugo unexpectedly found his power stroke in High-A, clobbering homers and setting new career highs in both fly-ball and homer-to-fly-ball rate. In doing so, he may have found the ticket to revitalizing his career. The nephew of Carlos Beltrán, Lugo has a compact swing and average or better tools across the board, but his lack of pop and low ceiling defensively seemed to cap his upside as a reserve infielder. But if his newfound ability to drive the ball in the air sticks, he may be able to carve out a role as at least a second-division starter. The path to infield playing time in Boston is crowded, so Lugo needs to keep showing power if he wants to stay on it.

★ ★ ★ *2023 Top 101 Prospect* **#13** ★ ★ ★

Marcelo Mayer SS Born: 12/12/02 Age: 20 Bats: L Throws: R Height: 6'3" Weight: 188 lb. Origin: Round 1, 2021 Draft (#4 overall)

YEAR	TEAM	LVL	AGE	PA	R	2B	3B	HR	RBI	BB	K	SB	CS	Whiff%	AVG/OBP/SLG	DRC+	BABIP	BRR	DRP	WARP
2021	RSX	ROK	18	107	25	4	1	3	17	15	27	7	1		.275/.377/.440		.361			
2022	SAL	A	19	308	46	26	1	9	40	51	78	16	0		.286/.406/.504	121	.375	2.3	SS(58): -0.5	1.8
2022	GVL	A+	19	116	15	4	1	4	13	17	29	1	0		.265/.379/.449	91	.338	0.1	SS(21): 2.3	0.5
2023 non-DC	*BOS*	*MLB*	*20*	*251*	*22*	*11*	*1*	*4*	*23*	*25*	*80*	*5*	*1*	*35.0%*	*.208/.292/.332*	*72*	*.302*	*4.3*	*SS 0*	*0.3*

Comparables: Royce Lewis (68), J.P. Crawford (66), Bo Bichette (65)

Boston's top prospect did nothing to loosen his grip on that spot in 2022, as Mayer adeptly handled both levels of A-ball in his first (mostly) full professional season. He provided both power and patience in steady supply at Salem and Greenville; especially impressive since, at the latter stop, he was nearly four years younger than the average Sally League player. Aside from a wrist sprain that cost him the month of May, his season was a success all the way through. Steady progression doesn't make for the sexiest of updates, but for a Red Sox team facing the departure of its franchise shortstop, having the heir apparent to the position simply keep on chugging is the shiniest of silver linings.

Reese McGuire C Born: 03/02/95 Age: 28 Bats: L Throws: R Height: 6'0" Weight: 218 lb. Origin: Round 1, 2013 Draft (#14 overall)

YEAR	TEAM	LVL	AGE	PA	R	2B	3B	HR	RBI	BB	K	SB	CS	Whiff%	AVG/OBP/SLG	DRC+	BABIP	BRR	DRP	WARP
2020	TOR	MLB	25	45	2	0	0	1	1	0	11	0	0	21.4%	.073/.073/.146	71	.069	-0.3	C(18): -0.6	-0.1
2021	TOR	MLB	26	217	22	15	0	1	10	15	44	0	0	21.6%	.253/.310/.343	81	.318	-0.3	C(73): 7.7	1.2
2022	CHW	MLB	27	166	12	9	0	0	10	6	33	0	0	21.3%	.225/.261/.285	74	.283	-1.8	C(52): 1	0.0
2022	BOS	MLB	27	108	13	5	1	3	12	6	23	1	0	20.9%	.337/.377/.500	94	.411	-0.5	C(32): 0.4	0.3
2023 DC	*BOS*	*MLB*	*28*	*309*	*33*	*14*	*1*	*6*	*32*	*18*	*61*	*1*	*1*	*21.0%*	*.247/.301/.375*	*85*	*.297*	*0.5*	*C 8*	*1.5*

Comparables: Miguel Montero (60), A.J. Pierzynski (57), Brian McCann (55)

YEAR	TEAM	P. COUNT	FRM RUNS	BLK RUNS	THRW RUNS	TOT RUNS
2020	TOR	1815	-0.4	0.0	-0.2	-0.6
2021	TOR	8862	7.9	0.2	0.3	8.5
2022	CHW	6759	1.6	-0.2	-0.3	1.2
2022	BOS	4029	1.5	-0.1	-0.3	1.1
2023	*BOS*	*12025*	*7.0*	*0.0*	*0.2*	*7.2*

The game of musical chairs that took place behind the plate in Boston late in the year after Christian Vázquez's trade clearly rubbed some on the roster the wrong way. McGuire should know, as he's something of an expert on the subject. Added in a deadline deal as part of all that shuffling, the ex-White Sox backstop was a surprising force at the plate with the Red Sox, though he can thank a sky-high BABIP for a lot of his output. His value comes mostly via his glove; he routinely grades out as a plus receiver, and 2022 was no exception. For most nominally contending teams, McGuire would be a backup stapled to the bench four days out of five. Lucky for him, catcher is a gaping maw for the Red Sox; as of December, it seems they'll platoon him with Connor Wong to see what value they can eke out of the position. If that's still the plan come April, don't bet on much offense coming from the catcher's spot in Boston.

★ ★ ★ *2023 Top 101 Prospect* **#73** ★ ★ ★

Ceddanne Rafaela OF/SS Born: 09/18/00 Age: 22 Bats: R Throws: R Height: 5'8" Weight: 152 lb. Origin: International Free Agent, 2017

YEAR	TEAM	LVL	AGE	PA	R	2B	3B	HR	RBI	BB	K	SB	CS	Whiff%	AVG/OBP/SLG	DRC+	BABIP	BRR	DRP	WARP
2021	SAL	A	20	432	73	20	9	10	53	25	79	23	3		.251/.305/.424	110	.288	1.6	CF(52): 7.0, 3B(20): 0.8, SS(16): -0.3	3.1
2022	GVL	A+	21	209	37	17	4	9	36	10	51	14	2		.330/.368/.594	110	.409	0.1	CF(32): -2.4, SS(9): -0.7, 2B(1): -0.2	0.6
2022	POR	AA	21	313	45	15	6	12	50	16	62	14	5		.278/.324/.500	107	.310	-0.5	CF(60): 5.0, SS(12): 1.5	1.8
2023 non-DC	*BOS*	*MLB*	*22*	*251*	*23*	*11*	*4*	*6*	*27*	*10*	*62*	*9*	*3*	*30.1%*	*.245/.285/.407*	*89*	*.308*	*5.0*	*2B 0, 3B 0*	*0.9*

Comparables: Dalton Pompey (76), Teoscar Hernández (74), Brett Phillips (72)

It's hard to find a scouting report on Rafaela that doesn't quickly or prominently mention Mookie Betts, and it's easy to understand why. They're both smaller players — Rafaela is about as big as an average high school junior — whose frames obscure exceptional athleticism. Like Betts, Rafaela boasts lightning-fast hands that power a smooth, quick stroke. He is arguably the best defender in Boston's system, a plus-plus outfielder who can also handle the infield, just like … well, you get the point by now. Those Mookie parallels end mighty quickly once we get to Rafaela's offensive profile, but he had a breakout year at the plate, blitzing High-A pitching to the tune of a .962 OPS. He even held his own in Portland, posting a lower strikeout rate one level up. That type of plate discipline will go a long way toward determining whether the (wildly unfair) Betts comps peter out or pick up steam as he nears his Fenway debut.

Rob Refsnyder OF Born: 03/26/91 Age: 32 Bats: R Throws: R Height: 6'0" Weight: 205 lb. Origin: Round 5, 2012 Draft (#187 overall)

YEAR	TEAM	LVL	AGE	PA	R	2B	3B	HR	RBI	BB	K	SB	CS	Whiff%	AVG/OBP/SLG	DRC+	BABIP	BRR	DRP	WARP
2020	TEX	MLB	29	34	4	1	0	0	1	2	11	0	0	28.6%	.200/.265/.233	84	.300	0.5	1B(4): -0.2, RF(2): 2, LF(1): 0	0.3
2021	STP	AAA	30	80	13	5	0	5	14	12	13	0	0		.318/.425/.621	133	.327	0.9	RF(8): 1.9, LF(3): -0.3	0.8
2021	MIN	MLB	30	157	21	7	0	2	12	17	40	1	0	27.0%	.245/.325/.338	89	.327	-0.5	CF(22): -0.6, LF(20): -0.6, RF(9): -0.7	0.1
2022	WOR	AAA	31	182	31	14	0	6	28	28	42	4	0		.306/.429/.524	123	.386	0.4	RF(20): -0.2, CF(14): -1.4	1.0
2022	BOS	MLB	31	177	25	11	0	6	21	15	46	1	1	24.8%	.307/.384/.497	109	.394	1.8	RF(28): -1.2, CF(17): -0.8, LF(6): 0.5	0.8
2023 DC	*BOS*	*MLB*	*32*	*203*	*25*	*10*	*0*	*5*	*21*	*20*	*47*	*1*	*1*	*24.4%*	*.251/.341/.411*	*107*	*.314*	*0.5*	*CF -1, RF -1*	*0.5*

Comparables: Kevin Frandsen (43), Donovan Solano (43), John Moses (43)

Refsnyder is the latest swing change success story. Formerly a light-hitting utility infielder with a so-so glove, he's transformed himself into a solid outfielder with a decent stick. In particular, he's a demon against lefties, slashing .359/.411/.594 against them last season with a .425 wOBA that ranked 10th in the majors among hitters with 70 or more plate appearances versus southpaws. He's less productive against right-handers, though far more playable than in the past. The key to his newfound success? A flatter swing that resulted in fewer grounders and more hard liners. It feels sustainable, and that gives Refsnyder, who looked to be on his last legs in MLB, a real chance to stick around as an above-average platoon bat and reserve outfielder.

Mikey Romero 2B

Born: 01/12/04 Age: 19 Bats: L Throws: R Height: 6'1" Weight: 175 lb. Origin: Round 1, 2022 Draft (#24 overall)

YEAR	TEAM	LVL	AGE	PA	R	2B	3B	HR	RBI	BB	K	SB	CS	Whiff%	AVG/OBP/SLG	DRC+	BABIP	BRR	DRP	WARP
2022	RSX	ROK	18	43	5	3	0	1	6	7	4	1	0		.250/.372/.417		.258			
2022	SAL	A	18	44	6	4	3	0	11	1	11	1	0		.349/.364/.581	93	.469	0.2	2B(4): 0.2, SS(3): -0.5	0.1
2023 non-DC	*BOS*	*MLB*	*19*	*251*	*19*	*10*	*4*	*3*	*22*	*11*	*67*	*3*	*1*	*28.2%*	*.223/.263/.340*	*62*	*.297*	*3.8*	*2B 0, SS 0*	*-0.1*

Apparently determined to build the whole farm system out of Californian shortstops, Boston tabbed Romero with its first-round pick last summer, marking the third straight year they've taken a high school middle infielder from the Golden State with their top selection. Romero doesn't have the same suite of plus tools that Marcelo Mayer brings to the table and is unlikely to displace his former travel ball teammate at the position long-term, but he's no slouch himself. A contact maven, he excels at squaring up strikes, and while the power in his game is more gap-to-gap than over-the-fence, he profiles as a complete hitter thanks to his excellent bat speed and advanced pitch recognition. Defensively, he should be able to stick at the six as long as needed. It's fun imagining a future Fenway double play combo of Mayer and Romero, even if that theoretical tandem remains years away from the majors.

Trevor Story 2B

Born: 11/15/92 Age: 30 Bats: R Throws: R Height: 6'2" Weight: 213 lb. Origin: Round 1, 2011 Draft (#45 overall)

YEAR	TEAM	LVL	AGE	PA	R	2B	3B	HR	RBI	BB	K	SB	CS	Whiff%	AVG/OBP/SLG	DRC+	BABIP	BRR	DRP	WARP
2020	COL	MLB	27	259	41	13	4	11	28	24	63	15	3	25.7%	.289/.355/.519	110	.354	2.3	SS(57): 2.1	1.5
2021	COL	MLB	28	595	88	34	5	24	75	53	139	20	6	27.5%	.251/.329/.471	105	.293	2.7	SS(138): -2.8	2.5
2022	BOS	MLB	29	396	53	22	0	16	66	32	122	13	0	30.9%	.238/.303/.434	96	.309	2.5	2B(94): 0.2	1.3
2023 DC	*BOS*	*MLB*	*30*	*558*	*72*	*30*	*2*	*24*	*75*	*48*	*158*	*18*	*2*	*29.4%*	*.249/.325/.462*	*113*	*.320*	*10.5*	*SS 0*	*3.6*

Comparables: Vern Stephens (74), Robin Yount (74), Cal Ripken Jr. (74)

Story's 2022 was a stirring tribute to Brian Daubach—he was the hottest hitter on the planet for about six weeks, bookended that run with stretches of empty swings and weak grounders, and mixed in a long stay on the injured list to boot. You can blame some of his struggles on his late start to the year, as he didn't sign until March 23 and missed nearly all of spring training. Of more concern is that he came to the plate with a hyper-aggressive approach that landed him in the bottom quintile of every plate discipline stat in existence, resulting in a worse DRC+ than Kurt Suzuki and Nick Madrigal among many, *many* others. The one plus to his year was how quickly and well he transitioned from shortstop to second base, grading out as an elite defender at the keystone. Of course, with Xander Bogaerts departing for more lucrative pastures, Story seems likely to shift back to the six, where his arm will be in question. If you're reading this blurb and wondering how Javy Báez's writeup got into the Red Sox chapter, you're not alone. Story is a gigantic question mark for 2023 and beyond.

Justin Turner 3B/DH

Born: 11/23/84 Age: 38 Bats: R Throws: R Height: 5'11" Weight: 202 lb. Origin: Round 7, 2006 Draft (#204 overall)

YEAR	TEAM	LVL	AGE	PA	R	2B	3B	HR	RBI	BB	K	SB	CS	Whiff%	AVG/OBP/SLG	DRC+	BABIP	BRR	DRP	WARP
2020	LAD	MLB	35	175	26	9	1	4	23	18	26	1	0	20.5%	.307/.400/.460	119	.347	-1.2	3B(32): -1	0.6
2021	LAD	MLB	36	612	87	22	0	27	87	61	98	3	0	17.7%	.278/.361/.471	121	.292	-2.0	3B(143): -0.5	3.5
2022	LAD	MLB	37	532	61	36	0	13	81	50	89	3	0	20.3%	.278/.350/.438	113	.313	-4.5	3B(66): -1.4	1.5
2023 DC	*BOS*	*MLB*	*38*	*521*	*64*	*27*	*0*	*16*	*66*	*47*	*88*	*1*	*0*	*19.9%*	*.281/.363/.449*	*125*	*.322*	*-1.0*	*3B 0*	*2.4*

Comparables: Aramis Ramirez (78), Adrián Beltré (75), Brooks Robinson (75)

Now that he's teammates with Rafael Devers, Turner's long-prophesied transition off third base has finally transpired. He can now fulfill his destiny as a simple Dude Who Rakes. The raking doesn't happen as freely as it used to, though: His 2022 DRC+ and power output were his worst since the Mets released him in 2013. It's not a question of whether Turner will age gracefully—he already has—but a matter of how much grace he can still muster, especially as he moves into a mostly DH role. Even Nelson Cruz got old eventually. Still, Turner remains a comfortably above-average hitter—just without much power these days. Maybe instead of a Dude Who Rakes, he will be a Dude Who Performs a Somewhat Less Strenuous Yardwork Activity. He can be a Dude Who Leafblows.

Alex Verdugo OF

Born: 05/15/96 Age: 27 Bats: L Throws: L Height: 6'0" Weight: 192 lb. Origin: Round 2, 2014 Draft (#62 overall)

YEAR	TEAM	LVL	AGE	PA	R	2B	3B	HR	RBI	BB	K	SB	CS	Whiff%	AVG/OBP/SLG	DRC+	BABIP	BRR	DRP	WARP
2020	BOS	MLB	24	221	36	16	0	6	15	17	45	4	0	18.8%	.308/.367/.478	97	.371	1.0	RF(31): 2.7, LF(22): 5.6, CF(1): 0	1.5
2021	BOS	MLB	25	604	88	32	2	13	63	51	96	6	2	17.7%	.289/.351/.426	105	.327	-0.7	LF(90): -0.4, CF(42): 1.4, RF(24): 0	2.7
2022	BOS	MLB	26	644	75	39	1	11	74	42	86	1	3	15.5%	.280/.328/.405	105	.309	-1.2	LF(102): 2.9, RF(52): -1.6	2.4
2023 DC	*BOS*	*MLB*	*27*	*596*	*75*	*33*	*2*	*16*	*72*	*43*	*79*	*3*	*1*	*15.8%*	*.292/.351/.448*	*122*	*.322*	*0.2*	*RF -3, LF 0*	*2.6*

Comparables: Derrick May (66), Bill Buckner (64), Carl Crawford (64)

It's probably time to stop expecting more than this from Verdugo. In 2021, he married bad defense and fleeting power with dumb, sweaty baserunning to end up a 2-WARP player. In 2022, he married bad defense and fleeting power with dumber, even glitchier baserunning, plus a lower walk rate, to end up a 2-WARP player. There are few signs that his persistent issues with situational awareness and pitch recognition are being addressed, much less solved. And shifting from center, where he was a mess, to in front of the Green Monster didn't meaningfully improve his defensive metrics. Some peripherals—namely his contact stats and strikeout avoidance—suggest he was better than the final results say. But not by much, and those final results are uninspiring. Working in his favor: he won't turn 27 until May, and he's established a baseline as a useful player. But he now has just two years of team control remaining, and Verdugo's ceiling seems far lower today than it did when Boston acquired him.

Connor Wong C/DH Born: 05/19/96 Age: 27 Bats: R Throws: R Height: 6'1" Weight: 181 lb. Origin: Round 3, 2017 Draft (#100 overall)

YEAR	TEAM	LVL	AGE	PA	R	2B	3B	HR	RBI	BB	K	SB	CS	Whiff%	AVG/OBP/SLG	DRC+	BABIP	BRR	DRP	WARP
2021	WOR	AAA	25	208	22	13	0	8	26	9	58	7	1		.256/.288/.442	87	.323	0.7	C(44): 0.0, 2B(1): -0.4	0.5
2021	BOS	MLB	25	14	3	1	1	0	1	1	7	0	0	46.2%	.308/.357/.538	71	.667	0.6	C(5): -0.1	0.1
2022	WOR	AAA	26	355	47	20	0	15	44	27	80	7	3		.288/.349/.489	109	.341	-1.5	C(54): 4.3, 2B(1): -0.4	1.5
2022	BOS	MLB	26	56	8	3	0	1	7	5	16	0	0	31.1%	.188/.273/.313	85	.250	0.0	C(20): -0.1	0.1
2023 DC	*BOS*	*MLB*	*27*	*245*	*27*	*11*	*1*	*6*	*26*	*14*	*67*	*4*	*1*	*30.6%*	*.242/.298/.390*	*85*	*.321*	*0.9*	*C -1*	*0.5*

Comparables: Grayson Greiner (73), Adam Moore (68), Michael Perez (67)

YEAR	TEAM	P. COUNT	FRM RUNS	BLK RUNS	THRW RUNS	TOT RUNS
2021	WOR	6627	0.3	0.0	0.0	0.3
2021	BOS	499	0.0	0.0	0.0	0.0
2022	WOR	7985	2.9	-0.1	1.0	3.8
2022	BOS	2342	-0.1	0.0	0.1	0.1
2023	*BOS*	*9620*	*-0.8*	*-0.1*	*0.2*	*-0.6*

It's unclear why, after the Red Sox dealt away Christian Vázquez and dumped Kevin Plawecki, they didn't give more rope to Wong. He improved across the board from an already solid 2021 performance in Triple-A, and it's not as if Reese McGuire's upside is high enough (or actually exists at all) to block the man who's ostensibly Boston's catcher of the near future. Then again, Wong's bat grades out as average at best, even for a catcher and even with steps forward in contact rate. And while his defense is good enough to earn him some big-league time, he profiles at present as a weak-side platoon option or high-caliber backup. He seems poised to serve as McGuire's caddy for 2023 unless he can hit his way out of that sad timeshare.

Nick Yorke 2B Born: 04/02/02 Age: 21 Bats: R Throws: R Height: 6'0" Weight: 200 lb. Origin: Round 1, 2020 Draft (#17 overall)

YEAR	TEAM	LVL	AGE	PA	R	2B	3B	HR	RBI	BB	K	SB	CS	Whiff%	AVG/OBP/SLG	DRC+	BABIP	BRR	DRP	WARP
2021	SAL	A	19	346	59	14	4	10	47	41	47	11	8		.323/.413/.500	144	.353	-4.9	2B(66): 7.0	3.0
2021	GVL	A+	19	96	17	6	1	4	15	11	22	2	1		.333/.406/.571	116	.407	0.3	2B(19): -1.0	0.4
2022	GVL	A+	20	373	48	10	1	11	45	33	94	8	4		.231/.303/.365	92	.288	-2.1	2B(68): 5.3	1.0
2023 non-DC	*BOS*	*MLB*	*21*	*251*	*22*	*9*	*1*	*4*	*23*	*16*	*63*	*3*	*2*	*29.4%*	*.230/.288/.344*	*75*	*.297*	*-0.7*	*2B 0*	*-0.2*

Comparables: Heiker Meneses (56), Royce Lewis (54), Manuel Margot (53)

While Boston's farm system saw lots of growth in 2022, Yorke went flying backward after an injury-plagued season with too many strikeouts and pulled groundballs. That'd be concerning for any prospect, but it's especially so for one whose best chance of reaching the majors rests on the strength of his bat. So was Yorke's rough performance just a year-long bad day, or indicative of a larger issue? Probably a little bit of both. Turf toe and wrist soreness bothered him all year and likely explain a good deal of his struggles: Indeed, Yorke looked more like his breakout 2021 self in the Arizona Fall League. At the same time, all those strikeouts are cause for concern if they indicate a permanent change in approach. Given his average-at-best defense and base-running, the calculus for Yorke is simple: regain his magic at the plate, or top out as a back-of-the-roster infielder.

Masataka Yoshida OF Born: 07/15/93 Age: 29 Bats: L Throws: R Height: 5'8" Weight: 176 lb. Origin: International Free Agent, 2022

YEAR	TEAM	LVL	AGE	PA	R	2B	3B	HR	RBI	BB	K	SB	CS	Whiff%	AVG/OBP/SLG	DRC+	BABIP	BRR	DRP	WARP
2023 DC	*BOS*	*MLB*	*29*	*577*	*77*	*30*	*3*	*15*	*70*	*69*	*55*	*0*	*0*	*15.6%*	*.286/.383/.452*	*136*	*.301*	*0.9*	*LF 0*	*3.9*

They say timing is everything, and throughout his career, Yoshida has displayed excellent timing at the plate. During his seven seasons in the NPB, Yoshida hit .326/.419/.538. He never batted under .300 nor posted a sub-.400 OBP after his rookie campaign in 2016. He's walked 13.1% of the time as a pro, and he's averaged 22 homers a year over his past five seasons. Though not an inspiring defender, he can hang in an outfield corner, and he should have time left in his prime as he enters his age-29 season. For the right to see how his skills translate stateside, Boston inked him to a five-year, $90 million contract that also came with a hefty $15 million posting fee.

They say timing is everything, and the Red Sox, per usual, couldn't get theirs right. Outbidding the world for Yoshida—by a good margin, by some accounts—suggested they were back in the business of spending to contend. Instead, Yoshida's signing was quickly followed by Xander Bogaerts' departure, which meant that the average Sox fan didn't care much about their shiny new corner outfielder. That will change if Yoshida hits his top-end projections, which would see him perform along the lines of the guy Andrew Benintendi was supposed to be. But if his power doesn't translate to the majors, or if his hit tool slides from elite to solid, the Sox might once again have replaced a franchise icon with some version of Alex Verdugo.

PITCHERS

Matt Barnes RHP Born: 06/17/90 Age: 33 Bats: R Throws: R Height: 6'4" Weight: 208 lb. Origin: Round 1, 2011 Draft (#19 overall)

YEAR	TEAM	LVL	AGE	W	L	SV	G	GS	IP	H	HR	BB/9	K/9	K	GB%	BABIP	WHIP	ERA	DRA-	WARP	MPH	FB%	Whiff%	CSP
2020	BOS	MLB	30	1	3	9	24	0	23	18	4	5.5	12.1	31	45.5%	.280	1.39	4.30	80	0.5	95.7	54.1%	28.6%	44.9%
2021	BOS	MLB	31	6	5	24	60	0	54^{2}	41	8	3.3	13.8	84	42.2%	.306	1.12	3.79	66	1.5	96.1	49.8%	33.6%	57.3%
2022	BOS	MLB	32	0	4	8	44	0	39^{2}	36	2	4.8	7.7	34	44.1%	.296	1.44	4.31	109	0.2	95.3	45.9%	28.4%	53.2%
2023 DC	*BOS*	*MLB*	*33*	*3*	*3*	*0*	*67*	*0*	*58*	*55*	*7*	*4.4*	*10.0*	*64*	*43.8%*	*.318*	*1.44*	*4.35*	*104*	*0.1*	*95.9*	*48.5%*	*28.9%*	*51.4%*

Comparables: Brad Boxberger (59), Greg Holland (58), Pedro Strop (56)

The monster that swallowed Barnes whole in the second half of 2021 spit him out a mangled wreck, one who posted a 7.94 ERA and 12 walks in 17 innings over the season's first two months before the Red Sox mercifully shut him down with shoulder inflammation. When he returned in August, the results improved to the tune of a 1.59 ERA and 20 strikeouts over his final 22⅔ innings, but without the swing-and-miss stuff and lively fastball that made him an All-Star. Blame the surfeit of injuries that have sapped his arm of its juice, though his velocity did tick up somewhat after his prolonged stay on the injured list. Under contract for one more year, he'll return to Boston's bullpen as its biggest enigma, with error bars that stretch all the way from "dominant closer once more" to "designated for assignment by June 1." Neither outcome should surprise you.

Brayan Bello RHP Born: 05/17/99 Age: 24 Bats: R Throws: R Height: 6'1" Weight: 170 lb. Origin: International Free Agent, 2017

YEAR	TEAM	LVL	AGE	W	L	SV	G	GS	IP	H	HR	BB/9	K/9	K	GB%	BABIP	WHIP	ERA	DRA-	WARP	MPH	FB%	Whiff%	CSP
2021	GVL	A+	22	5	0	0	6	6	31^{2}	25	3	2.0	12.8	45	52.9%	.328	1.01	2.27	69	0.8				
2021	POR	AA	22	2	3	0	15	15	63^{2}	66	5	3.4	12.3	87	44.8%	.381	1.41	4.66	83	1.1				
2022	POR	AA	23	4	2	0	7	7	37^{1}	18	3	2.9	11.6	48	61.0%	.192	0.80	1.69	70	1.1				
2022	WOR	AAA	23	6	2	0	11	10	58^{2}	46	3	3.7	12.4	81	61.5%	.326	1.19	2.76	58	2.1				
2022	BOS	MLB	23	2	8	0	13	11	57^{1}	75	1	4.2	8.6	55	54.9%	.404	1.78	4.71	108	0.3	96.7	53.7%	26.1%	50.6%
2023 DC	*BOS*	*MLB*	*24*	*3*	*4*	*0*	*12*	*12*	*59.3*	*66*	*5*	*4.0*	*9.1*	*60*	*54.3%*	*.352*	*1.55*	*4.90*	*114*	*0.0*	*96.7*	*53.7%*	*29.6%*	*50.6%*

Comparables: Dan Straily (76), Cody Reed (75), Tyler Mahle (75)

Bello's first month in the bigs wasn't pretty. The talented righty, summoned from Triple-A in July to plug one of the many holes in Boston's rotation, seemed to be pitching with his eyes closed at first, walking 11 batters in 16⅓ innings and getting into so many three-ball counts that Blake Snell sued him for copyright infringement. But after a brief bullpen banishment, Bello steadied himself; from his return to the rotation on August 24 through the end of the year, he punched out 40 batters in 40⅓ innings with a 13% swinging-strike rate. His control remained shaky throughout thanks to poor command of his hard-yet-straight four-seamer, and when he did manage to throw it for strikes, batters squared it up well. They had much more trouble with his changeup, which generated a tremendous 44% whiff rate. For all Bello's early struggles, he won't turn 24 until May. Baring major external investments by the Sox, the odds of him exiting spring training with a rotation spot in hand seem high.

Ryan Brasier RHP Born: 08/26/87 Age: 35 Bats: R Throws: R Height: 6'0" Weight: 227 lb. Origin: Round 6, 2007 Draft (#208 overall)

YEAR	TEAM	LVL	AGE	W	L	SV	G	GS	IP	H	HR	BB/9	K/9	K	GB%	BABIP	WHIP	ERA	DRA-	WARP	MPH	FB%	Whiff%	CSP
2020	BOS	MLB	32	1	0	0	25	1	25	24	2	4.0	10.8	30	37.7%	.328	1.40	3.96	92	0.4	96.3	62.0%	34.1%	48.0%
2021	BOS	MLB	33	1	1	0	13	0	12	12	2	3.0	6.8	9	56.8%	.286	1.33	1.50	111	0.0	95.2	68.5%	26.0%	59.4%
2022	BOS	MLB	34	0	3	1	68	0	62^{1}	68	9	1.9	9.2	64	41.1%	.335	1.30	5.78	94	0.8	96.1	55.7%	25.1%	57.9%
2023 DC	*BOS*	*MLB*	*35*	*3*	*3*	*0*	*67*	*0*	*58*	*58*	*7*	*2.7*	*7.4*	*47*	*40.9%*	*.302*	*1.31*	*3.99*	*102*	*0.2*	*96.1*	*58.3%*	*25.7%*	*54.8%*

Comparables: Tommy Hunter (52), Anthony Swarzak (48), Pat Neshek (48)

Among regular Red Sox relievers, Brasier finished second in innings pitched and first in appearances in 2022, which is an indictment of both the front office and manager who stuck with him throughout it all. Though his four-seam fastball ticked up over the course of the year from 93 mph to 96 on average, opposing batters slugged .602 against it, which is a big part of the reason he finished near the bottom of the league in average exit velocity and hard-hit rate. He was useless with runners in scoring position, allowing a .974 OPS in those situations—if the Red Sox were in the process of blowing a late lead, Brasier or Hansel Robles were usually at the center of it. Fittingly, they finished as the bottom two among Boston relievers in Win Probability Added, and by gigantic margins. Brasier's peripherals suggest he deserved better, but you can't blame the vagaries of batted ball luck when every strike you throw gets pummeled. Maybe there's a future in which Brasier holds his velocity gains, uses his plus slider more and carves out a role as a useful middle reliever. But that's his ceiling, and as we just saw, Brasier's floor is awfully low.

Kutter Crawford RHP Born: 04/01/96 Age: 27 Bats: R Throws: R Height: 6'1" Weight: 209 lb. Origin: Round 16, 2017 Draft (#491 overall)

YEAR	TEAM	LVL	AGE	W	L	SV	G	GS	IP	H	HR	BB/9	K/9	K	GB%	BABIP	WHIP	ERA	DRA-	WARP	MPH	FB%	Whiff%	CSP
2021	POR	AA	25	3	2	0	10	10	46^{1}	33	7	1.0	12.4	64	39.8%	.271	0.82	3.30	84	0.8				
2021	WOR	AAA	25	3	4	0	10	9	48^{1}	49	5	2.8	12.5	67	33.1%	.370	1.32	5.21	88	1.0				
2021	BOS	MLB	25	0	1	0	1	1	2	5	1	9.0	9.0	2	11.1%	.500	3.50	22.50	120	0.0	93.4	75.4%	28.1%	49.7%
2022	WOR	AAA	26	1	0	0	6	4	24^{1}	29	5	2.2	8.5	23	38.3%	.316	1.44	5.18	98	0.4				
2022	BOS	MLB	26	3	6	0	21	12	77^{1}	81	12	3.4	9.0	77	31.0%	.322	1.42	5.47	104	0.6	94.8	38.4%	25.6%	56.8%
2023 DC	*BOS*	*MLB*	*27*	*5*	*5*	*0*	*38*	*9*	*71.3*	*71*	*10*	*3.2*	*9.0*	*71*	*34.5%*	*.315*	*1.36*	*4.26*	*106*	*0.3*	*94.7*	*39.6%*	*26.2%*	*56.6%*

Comparables: Chris Stratton (57), Stephen Fife (55), Hector Noesí (54)

One of many bodies shoved into the breach as Boston lost pitchers by the handful, Crawford offered flashes of excellence undermined by long stretches of fifth starter drudgery. Summoned to fill a rotation spot in early June, he ripped off a 2.72 ERA and 42 strikeouts over 43 frames spanning seven starts and a bulk relief appearance, culminating in six strong innings against Houston at the start of August. From there he collapsed, posting a 9.13 ERA over the rest of the month before a shoulder impingement knocked him out for the year. It's tempting to blame the injury for his slide, but things weren't trending well even before his arm started barking. Crawford's four-seamer and cutter are both too hittable, and while his slider and changeup got good results, he barely threw either. There's work to do before he can ascend beyond spot starter/long reliever duties, but Crawford nonetheless represents an improvement over the sort of pitching depth the Sox have called upon in recent seasons.

Jeurys Familia RHP Born: 10/10/89 Age: 33 Bats: R Throws: R Height: 6'3" Weight: 240 lb. Origin: International Free Agent, 2007

YEAR	TEAM	LVL	AGE	W	L	SV	G	GS	IP	H	HR	BB/9	K/9	K	GB%	BABIP	WHIP	ERA	DRA-	WARP	MPH	FB%	Whiff%	CSP
2020	NYM	MLB	30	2	0	0	25	0	26^{2}	20	2	6.4	7.8	23	60.0%	.247	1.46	3.71	91	0.4	96.7	59.8%	27.7%	46.0%
2021	NYM	MLB	31	9	4	1	65	0	59^{1}	57	10	4.1	10.9	72	49.7%	.318	1.42	3.94	80	1.2	96.8	73.5%	27.9%	54.3%
2022	BOS	MLB	32	1	2	0	10	0	10^{1}	10	1	6.1	7.0	8	46.7%	.310	1.65	6.10	108	0.1	94.8	75.6%	24.7%	46.5%
2022	PHI	MLB	32	1	1	0	38	0	34	48	6	4.0	8.7	33	48.6%	.408	1.85	6.09	102	0.3	95.6	73.5%	27.6%	52.8%
2023 non-DC	*BOS*	*MLB*	*33*	*2*	*2*	*0*	*57*	*0*	*50*	*50*	*5*	*4.6*	*8.6*	*47*	*49.1%*	*.323*	*1.53*	*4.65*	*110*	*0.0*	*96.2*	*71.3%*	*27.3%*	*51.1%*

Comparables: David Aardsma (78), Scott Linebrink (78), Joe Smith (77)

Like a DC movie, Boston's Familia experience was predictably bad and took too long to end. Another example of Chaim Bloom filling roster gaps with discarded veterans on their last legs, Familia came to Boston after flunking out of Philadelphia's bullpen in early August. Normally, the Phillies cutting ties with a reliever is a good sign that said pitcher's next stop should be a foreign or independent league. But the Red Sox needed any and all arms, and Familia's was nominally functional. The results were predictable—too many walks and too much hard contact allowed in a baffling number of high-leverage innings ended his Fenway stay after roughly a month, with Familia himself announcing his DFA to the press about 10 minutes after coughing up a game to the Yankees. Given his nonexistent control and declining velocity, don't expect a fun post-credits scene here; no team should bother to expand this universe.

Franklin German RHP Born: 09/22/97 Age: 25 Bats: R Throws: R Height: 6'2" Weight: 195 lb. Origin: Round 4, 2018 Draft (#127 overall)

YEAR	TEAM	LVL	AGE	W	L	SV	G	GS	IP	H	HR	BB/9	K/9	K	GB%	BABIP	WHIP	ERA	DRA-	WARP	MPH	FB%	Whiff%	CSP
2021	POR	AA	23	3	9	2	24	18	84^{1}	99	12	3.2	7.7	72	43.1%	.331	1.53	5.12	108	0.4				
2022	POR	AA	24	3	1	0	11	0	11^{1}	6	0	2.4	14.3	18	38.1%	.286	0.79	3.18	78	0.3				
2022	WOR	AAA	24	2	1	7	32	0	38^{1}	20	2	3.8	10.8	46	44.7%	.217	0.94	2.58	74	1.0				
2022	BOS	MLB	24	0	0	0	5	0	4	7	2	9.0	9.0	4	53.3%	.385	2.75	18.00	109	0.0	97.7	69.0%	13.5%	55.9%
2023 DC	*BOS*	*MLB*	*25*	*1*	*1*	*0*	*29*	*0*	*25.7*	*24*	*3*	*4.3*	*8.3*	*23*	*44.5%*	*.300*	*1.43*	*4.46*	*108*	*0.0*	*97.7*	*69.0%*	*24.9%*	*55.9%*

Comparables: Alberto Cabrera (43), Brady Lail (41), Albert Abreu (41)

Frank German isn't just a description of the historical tribes who came to power in the waning days of the Roman Empire or the country's national character. He's also an ex-Yankees farmhand and Queens native who looks like a potential bullpen piece after racking up lots of strikeouts between Portland and Worcester. German's calling cards are a hard fastball that touches 99 mph and a slider with downward tilt. Holding him back are a lack of a reliable third pitch and some iffy command, and if you're thinking that sounds like every other right-handed reliever you know, well, you're not wrong. In fact, the Germans even have a word for it: *der Jöekellymannderwirft.* German's ceiling is limited, but that shouldn't stop Boston from giving him a spot as a middle reliever and hoping there's some growth potential.

Wikelman Gonzalez RHP Born: 03/25/02 Age: 21 Bats: R Throws: R Height: 6'0" Weight: 167 lb. Origin: International Free Agent, 2018

YEAR	TEAM	LVL	AGE	W	L	SV	G	GS	IP	H	HR	BB/9	K/9	K	GB%	BABIP	WHIP	ERA	DRA-	WARP	MPH	FB%	Whiff%	CSP
2021	RSX	ROK	19	4	2	0	8	7	35	29	1	2.1	11.8	46	40.5%	.337	1.06	3.60						
2021	SAL	A	19	0	0	0	4	4	17^{2}	13	1	4.1	10.2	20	34.8%	.279	1.19	1.53	106	0.1				
2022	SAL	A	20	4	3	0	21	21	81^{1}	63	2	5.3	10.8	98	38.1%	.305	1.36	4.54	99	0.9				
2022	GVL	A+	20	0	0	0	4	4	17	13	0	3.2	12.2	23	42.1%	.342	1.12	2.65	88	0.2				
2023 non-DC	*BOS*	*MLB*	*21*	*2*	*3*	*0*	*57*	*0*	*50*	*49*	*7*	*6.0*	*8.2*	*45*	*37.2%*	*.295*	*1.65*	*5.52*	*127*	*-0.5*			*22.5%*	

Comparables: Jordan Balazovic (79), Emilio Vargas (78), Drew Hutchison (77)

Gonzalez was a big riser on Red Sox prospect lists after his excellent 2021, and he took another step forward last season, albeit a wobblier one. The slight Venezuelan righty was a strikeout machine in Low-A, but too many free passes kept him from working deep into his starts. His command and control waver thanks to an inconsistent release point and funky delivery, though his stuff is plus across the board. He throws a fastball that sits 93–96 mph, a curveball with above-average spin and good break and a devious changeup that disappears into the bottom of the strike zone. Between his age and development, he still has a long way to go before he reaches the majors. But whether he eventually surfaces as a starter, swingman or reliever, Gonzalez offers a lot to be excited about as he continues his climb.

Tanner Houck RHP Born: 06/29/96 Age: 27 Bats: R Throws: R Height: 6'5" Weight: 230 lb. Origin: Round 1, 2017 Draft (#24 overall)

YEAR	TEAM	LVL	AGE	W	L	SV	G	GS	IP	H	HR	BB/9	K/9	K	GB%	BABIP	WHIP	ERA	DRA-	WARP	MPH	FB%	Whiff%	CSP
2020	BOS	MLB	24	3	0	0	3	3	17	6	1	4.8	11.1	21	46.9%	.161	0.88	0.53	88	0.3	92.5	62.3%	27.1%	42.6%
2021	WOR	AAA	25	0	2	0	6	6	21	19	1	3.0	11.1	26	53.7%	.340	1.24	5.14	90	0.4				
2021	BOS	MLB	25	1	5	1	18	13	69	57	4	2.7	11.3	87	48.5%	.319	1.13	3.52	78	1.5	94.3	55.7%	30.9%	49.7%
2022	BOS	MLB	26	5	4	8	32	4	60	49	3	3.3	8.4	56	50.9%	.289	1.18	3.15	93	0.8	95.1	53.2%	29.2%	49.7%
2023 DC	*BOS*	*MLB*	*27*	*3*	*3*	*0*	*67*	*0*	*58*	*58*	*5*	*3.6*	*9.4*	*60*	*49.6%*	*.331*	*1.41*	*4.34*	*104*	*0.3*	*94.6*	*54.9%*	*28.8%*	*49.2%*

Comparables: Alex Colomé (71), John Gant (67), Octavio Dotel (58)

After he provided a late-season jab in the arm for the Red Sox down the stretch in 2021, Boston gave Houck a shot at a regular starting spot to begin '22. Too bad he didn't get his shot in turn. The righty missed a crucial series in Toronto because of his refusal to get the COVID-19 vaccine, which cost him his place in the rotation and left the Red Sox shorthanded for a four-game set, three of which they lost in late-inning meltdowns. Houck stayed in the bullpen from that point forward to try to keep that ailing unit from collapsing, even stepping into the closer role in June and July. The results were uninspiring: He saw a dip in strikeouts and whiffs from the season prior as he labored to throw strikes and command his four-seamer. A back injury then ended his season in August and forced him to undergo surgery. A healthy Houck should play a big part on the Next Good Red Sox Team, whether as a starter or in relief, but he clearly needs to learn to take his medicine.

Kenley Jansen RHP Born: 09/30/87 Age: 35 Bats: S Throws: R Height: 6'5" Weight: 265 lb. Origin: International Free Agent, 2004

YEAR	TEAM	LVL	AGE	W	L	SV	G	GS	IP	H	HR	BB/9	K/9	K	GB%	BABIP	WHIP	ERA	DRA-	WARP	MPH	FB%	Whiff%	CSP
2020	LAD	MLB	32	3	1	11	27	0	24^{1}	19	2	3.3	12.2	33	24.6%	.309	1.15	3.33	91	0.4	91.4	90.4%	30.8%	47.0%
2021	LAD	MLB	33	4	4	38	69	0	69	36	4	4.7	11.2	86	37.3%	.216	1.04	2.22	82	1.3	93.2	84.6%	33.4%	57.7%
2022	ATL	MLB	34	5	2	41	65	0	64	45	8	3.1	12.0	85	29.1%	.259	1.05	3.38	74	1.5	92.6	86.9%	27.7%	57.7%
2023 DC	*BOS*	*MLB*	*35*	*3*	*3*	*34*	*67*	*0*	*58*	*44*	*7*	*3.5*	*10.6*	*68*	*32.9%*	*.275*	*1.16*	*2.94*	*77*	*0.9*	*92.7*	*86.5%*	*28.7%*	*55.6%*

Comparables: Joakim Soria (86), Michael Jackson (85), Francisco Rodríguez (82)

In 1998, Snoop Dogg made the shocking decision to leave the West Coast-centric Death Row Records in favor of No Limit Records. While bringing an iconic California rapper to a Louisiana outfit seemed like a weird combo, Snoop believed No Limit would make "material fittin' to the artist," so he had no worries. That was likely how Jansen felt trading in "California Love" for "Welcome To Atlanta." Part of the new fit for Jansen in Atlanta included bringing the cutter usage rate back over 60% after four straight seasons of decline; against the offering, batters managed their worst batting average since 2016. The ultimate line reflected a version of Jensen we hadn't seen for a couple of seasons—a change in scenery didn't result in a painful change of fortune. It's an approach that The Doggfather would surely appreciate, and one Jansen will now look to emulate over the next two seasons in Boston.

Zack Kelly RHP

Born: 03/03/95 Age: 28 Bats: R Throws: R Height: 6'3" Weight: 205 lb. Origin: Undrafted Free Agent, 2017

YEAR	TEAM	LVL	AGE	W	L	SV	G	GS	IP	H	HR	BB/9	K/9	K	GB%	BABIP	WHIP	ERA	DRA-	WARP	MPH	FB%	Whiff%	CSP
2021	POR	AA	26	3	1	5	21	0	26^{2}	18	1	4.4	13.5	40	59.3%	.321	1.16	1.69	75	0.6				
2021	WOR	AAA	26	1	0	1	15	0	18^{2}	13	1	2.4	14.0	29	45.0%	.308	0.96	2.89	72	0.5				
2022	WOR	AAA	27	6	3	3	44	0	49^{2}	34	2	4.5	13.0	72	45.0%	.302	1.19	2.72	67	1.5				
2022	BOS	MLB	27	1	0	0	13	0	13^{2}	14	2	2.6	7.2	11	45.5%	.286	1.32	3.95	102	0.1	94.9	47.3%	17.6%	58.8%
2023 DC	*BOS*	*MLB*	*28*	*1*	*1*	*0*	*29*	*0*	*25.7*	*24*	*2*	*4.0*	*8.8*	*25*	*47.1%*	*.308*	*1.39*	*4.00*	*98*	*0.1*	*94.9*	*47.3%*	*26.9%*	*58.8%*

Comparables: Tim Peterson (69), Ryan Kelly (68), Rob Wooten (62)

If Kelly sticks in the majors, it'll be because of his changeup. The Division II product and former undrafted free agent put up gaudy strikeout numbers across multiple levels of the minors for Boston in 2021 and '22 on the back of his slow ball, a pitch he taught himself in high school in a homemade pitching lab in his parents' basement. Kelly threw the pitch 40% of the time upon reaching the majors in late August, and though his big whiff numbers didn't make the trip with him from Worcester, the peripherals on his *cambio*—including a .191 expected batting average against—suggest it can be a real weapon. That said, while the pitch has above-average horizontal movement, it lacks dip. Fix that, and his combo of a plus off-speed pitch and a 95-mph fastball make him a viable change-of-pace option in a league full of more generic slider-heavy righties.

Corey Kluber RHP

Born: 04/10/86 Age: 37 Bats: R Throws: R Height: 6'4" Weight: 215 lb. Origin: Round 4, 2007 Draft (#134 overall)

YEAR	TEAM	LVL	AGE	W	L	SV	G	GS	IP	H	HR	BB/9	K/9	K	GB%	BABIP	WHIP	ERA	DRA-	WARP	MPH	FB%	Whiff%	CSP
2020	TEX	MLB	34	0	0	0	1	1	1	0	0	9.0	9.0	1	0.0%	.000	1.00	0.00	90	0.0	91.7	50.0%	12.5%	35.5%
2021	NYY	MLB	35	5	3	0	16	16	80	74	8	3.7	9.2	82	43.0%	.311	1.34	3.83	101	0.7	90.6	29.5%	28.2%	52.2%
2022	TB	MLB	36	10	10	0	31	31	164	178	20	1.2	7.6	139	35.1%	.318	1.21	4.34	105	1.2	89.2	28.3%	23.8%	55.3%
2023 DC	*BOS*	*MLB*	*37*	*7*	*8*	*0*	*24*	*24*	*128.7*	*140*	*18*	*2.4*	*7.6*	*108*	*37.6%*	*.322*	*1.36*	*4.46*	*111*	*0.3*	*89.7*	*29.2%*	*24.9%*	*54.0%*

Comparables: Zack Greinke (73), Max Scherzer (71), Mike Mussina (70)

Serving in the Charlie Morton Memorial Veteran's Spot in the Rays' rotation, Kluber made 30+ starts for the first time since 2018. Mindful of both his age and injury history, Tampa Bay limited Kluber to an average of around five innings per start. He was modestly effective in the role, with fielding-independent stats generally offering a rosier view of his season than traditional numbers. Born in the mid-80s, the right-hander's stuff now lives in a similar range, with all four of his standard offerings coming in below the 90-mph mark. Though his velocity has faded, his accuracy hasn't, as he once again showed the elite command that was a hallmark of his halcyon days in Cleveland. A healthy Kluber looks like he can continue to pitch at the back end of contending rotations until he decides to hang it up, or until his body decides for him. The Red Sox believe that to be the case, signing Kluber to a one-year deal with a club option for 2024.

Chris Martin RHP

Born: 06/02/86 Age: 37 Bats: R Throws: R Height: 6'8" Weight: 225 lb. Origin: Round 21, 2005 Draft (#627 overall)

YEAR	TEAM	LVL	AGE	W	L	SV	G	GS	IP	H	HR	BB/9	K/9	K	GB%	BABIP	WHIP	ERA	DRA-	WARP	MPH	FB%	Whiff%	CSP
2020	ATL	MLB	34	1	1	1	19	0	18	8	1	1.5	10.0	20	38.1%	.171	0.61	1.00	88	0.3	93.7	63.3%	26.7%	48.6%
2021	ATL	MLB	35	2	4	1	46	0	43^{1}	49	4	1.2	6.9	33	48.9%	.338	1.27	3.95	99	0.4	94.5	71.7%	21.1%	59.8%
2022	CHC	MLB	36	1	0	0	34	0	31^{1}	38	5	1.1	11.5	40	51.7%	.393	1.34	4.31	73	0.7	94.5	79.6%	26.6%	55.5%
2022	LAD	MLB	36	3	1	2	26	0	24^{2}	12	1	0.4	12.4	34	42.9%	.200	0.53	1.46	69	0.6	94.6	87.7%	24.9%	58.2%
2023 DC	*BOS*	*MLB*	*37*	*3*	*3*	*2*	*67*	*0*	*58*	*55*	*6*	*1.5*	*8.3*	*53*	*47.2%*	*.303*	*1.12*	*2.95*	*80*	*0.8*	*94.6*	*77.4%*	*23.6%*	*56.5%*

Comparables: Blake Parker (55), Mark Melancon (52), Joe Smith (51)

There's no such thing as a consistent baseball player. They all run hot and cold over the course of a 162-game season, especially relievers, and part of player evaluation is simply knowing when someone's results are due to spring back to their talent level. Martin's first few months with the Cubs weren't as bad as the 42 baserunners he allowed in 31⅓ innings would indicate. However, he wasn't truly as dominant with the Dodgers as the stats suggest, either. On the whole, his 14.8 strikeout-to-walk ratio was exceptional and he quietly pitched at an elite level, but will the Red Sox, who signed him to a two-year, $17.5 million deal this winter, get the Cubs version or the Dodgers version? Most likely some of both.

Bryan Mata RHP

Born: 05/03/99 Age: 24 Bats: R Throws: R Height: 6'3" Weight: 238 lb. Origin: International Free Agent, 2016

YEAR	TEAM	LVL	AGE	W	L	SV	G	GS	IP	H	HR	BB/9	K/9	K	GB%	BABIP	WHIP	ERA	DRA-	WARP	MPH	FB%	Whiff%	CSP
2022	GVL	A+	23	0	1	0	3	3	9	6	1	6.0	15.0	15	50.0%	.294	1.33	4.00	88	0.1				
2022	POR	AA	23	5	2	0	10	9	48^{2}	35	4	4.3	10.7	58	52.2%	.279	1.19	1.85	86	1.0				
2022	WOR	AAA	23	2	0	0	5	5	23^{1}	19	0	5.8	11.6	30	54.5%	.345	1.46	3.47	83	0.5				
2023 DC	*BOS*	*MLB*	*24*	*5*	*4*	*0*	*37*	*8*	*61.3*	*58*	*6*	*5.5*	*9.4*	*63*	*53.3%*	*.316*	*1.57*	*4.71*	*109*	*0.1*			*26.3%*	

Comparables: Sean Reid-Foley (66), Joe Ross (57), Touki Toussaint (56)

Pitchers can find themselves on long, arduous journeys as they recover from Tommy John surgery, and not all of them resurface with their command, control and stuff fully intact. Fortunately, Mata—who blew out his UCL in early 2021—still appears to possess the arsenal that made him a top prospect: a high-velocity fastball, hard slider, workable changeup and developing curve. Upon returning to the mound in 2022, he posted the best strikeout rates of his young career. That said, throwing strikes on the regular remains a challenge for him, as his high-effort delivery once more in part caused his command to come and go at every level of the minors he visited. A future as a major-league reliever—albeit one with high-leverage upside—remains his likeliest outcome.

Kaleb Ort RHP Born: 02/05/92 Age: 31 Bats: R Throws: R Height: 6'4" Weight: 240 lb. Origin: Undrafted Free Agent, 2016

YEAR	TEAM	LVL	AGE	W	L	SV	G	GS	IP	H	HR	BB/9	K/9	K	GB%	BABIP	WHIP	ERA	DRA-	WARP	MPH	FB%	Whiff%	CSP
2021	WOR	AAA	29	1	3	19	42	0	45^1	40	4	4.0	12.3	62	34.5%	.333	1.32	2.98	83	1.0				
2021	BOS	MLB	29	0	0	0	1	0	0^1	1	0	27.0	0.0	0	0.0%	.500	6.00	0.00	132	0.0	95.7	58.3%	20.0%	74.0%
2022	WOR	AAA	30	2	2	16	39	0	40^2	28	1	4.0	11.7	53	37.9%	.293	1.13	2.88	78	1.0				
2022	BOS	MLB	30	1	2	1	25	0	28^1	35	4	4.8	8.6	27	31.1%	.360	1.76	6.35	113	0.1	96.3	59.9%	28.6%	52.5%
2023 DC	*BOS*	*MLB*	*31*	*2*	*2*	*0*	*44*	*0*	*38.7*	*37*	*4*	*4.5*	*9.4*	*40*	*34.8%*	*.321*	*1.48*	*4.56*	*108*	*0.0*	*96.3*	*59.9%*	*28.2%*	*52.8%*

Comparables: Steve Delabar (60), Blake Parker (58), James Hoyt (56)

Somewhere at the edges of our solar system, light-years away from Earth, may lie the Oort Cloud, a theoretical group of icy planetesimals that represent the boundary of the space we know. Why is it theoretical? The Oort Cloud has never been observed. Scientists believe it exists, though, as the source of some of the comets that occasionally come our way. The Ort cloud in Boston, meanwhile, is easily seen by the naked eye, and like the vague, cold, gaseous deep in the void, it also acts as a producer of countless hyper-fast projectiles that fly into the night. What value Ort will provide going forward is about as hard to measure as the space cloud's existence, and about as well understood.

Nick Pivetta RHP Born: 02/14/93 Age: 30 Bats: R Throws: R Height: 6'5" Weight: 214 lb. Origin: Round 4, 2013 Draft (#136 overall)

YEAR	TEAM	LVL	AGE	W	L	SV	G	GS	IP	H	HR	BB/9	K/9	K	GB%	BABIP	WHIP	ERA	DRA-	WARP	MPH	FB%	Whiff%	CSP
2020	BOS	MLB	27	2	0	0	2	2	10	8	1	4.5	11.7	13	29.2%	.304	1.30	1.80	123	0.0	92.6	48.4%	25.0%	45.0%
2020	PHI	MLB	27	0	0	0	3	0	5^2	10	3	1.6	6.4	4	26.1%	.350	1.94	15.88	128	0.0	93.6	51.0%	22.9%	52.7%
2021	BOS	MLB	28	9	8	1	31	30	155	137	24	3.8	10.2	175	38.2%	.290	1.30	4.53	96	1.8	95.0	51.9%	24.6%	56.8%
2022	BOS	MLB	29	10	12	0	33	33	179^2	175	27	3.7	8.8	175	38.5%	.300	1.38	4.56	103	1.5	93.6	51.0%	23.5%	56.6%
2023 DC	*BOS*	*MLB*	*30*	*9*	*9*	*0*	*27*	*27*	*151.3*	*146*	*19*	*3.7*	*9.2*	*155*	*39.0%*	*.313*	*1.38*	*4.10*	*101*	*1.1*	*94.2*	*51.3%*	*24.0%*	*55.9%*

Comparables: Ray Washburn (80), Bill Wegman (74), Kyle Kendrick (72)

The only constants in life are death, taxes and Pivetta ending up with an ERA around 4.50. During a two-month stretch last summer, he was nigh unhittable, posting a 2.18 ERA in 78⅓ innings with just six home runs and 19 walks allowed. In the end, that only made him more frustrating, because per usual, regression loomed—from the beginning of July through the end of the season, he posted a 6.04 ERA, walked nearly four batters per nine and gave up a home run every five innings. For as much promise as he shows and as good as his stuff can look, it's simply too easy for hitters to square Pivetta up, as only his slider produces whiffs on the regular. At this point, he is what he is: a talented yet frustrating rotation piece whose best attribute is his ability to chew up five-inning starts. Hoping for anything more is like waiting for the Earth to spin backward.

Joely Rodríguez LHP Born: 11/14/91 Age: 31 Bats: L Throws: L Height: 6'1" Weight: 200 lb. Origin: International Free Agent, 2009

YEAR	TEAM	LVL	AGE	W	L	SV	G	GS	IP	H	HR	BB/9	K/9	K	GB%	BABIP	WHIP	ERA	DRA-	WARP	MPH	FB%	Whiff%	CSP
2020	TEX	MLB	28	0	0	0	12	0	12^2	8	0	3.6	12.1	17	50.0%	.276	1.03	2.13	75	0.3	94.7	67.2%	26.3%	47.8%
2021	TEX	MLB	29	1	3	1	31	0	27^1	32	3	4.0	9.9	30	63.1%	.363	1.61	5.93	93	0.4	94.1	60.8%	31.1%	49.7%
2021	NYY	MLB	29	1	0	0	21	0	19	21	1	2.8	8.1	17	50.0%	.370	1.42	2.84	96	0.2	94.2	54.3%	31.9%	50.1%
2022	NYM	MLB	30	2	4	0	55	0	50^1	42	3	4.6	10.2	57	53.0%	.307	1.35	4.47	84	0.9	92.9	55.3%	29.6%	50.3%
2023 DC	*BOS*	*MLB*	*31*	*3*	*2*	*0*	*59*	*0*	*51.3*	*50*	*4*	*3.8*	*9.4*	*53*	*56.3%*	*.325*	*1.40*	*3.98*	*97*	*0.3*	*93.5*	*57.5%*	*28.7%*	*49.9%*

Comparables: Fernando Abad (63), Sam Freeman (63), Jake Diekman (61)

Lacking left-handed options out of the bullpen, the Mets traded Miguel Castro to the Yankees in exchange for Rodríguez in a crosstown reliever swap. He was effective against lefties, holding them to a .233 batting average and pitching to a 2.74 ERA against them. But in the era of the three-batter minimum, there's no such thing as a pure lefty specialist, and righties shellacked him. He also pitched far better at Citi Field than he did on the road—over two runs better, in fact. After an awful July, he quietly put together a strong second half: So strong that it convinced the Red Sox to give Rodríguez a one-year deal this winter despite the fact that they extremely do not play at Citi Field.

Chris Sale LHP Born: 03/30/89 Age: 34 Bats: L Throws: L Height: 6'6" Weight: 183 lb. Origin: Round 1, 2010 Draft (#13 overall)

YEAR	TEAM	LVL	AGE	W	L	SV	G	GS	IP	H	HR	BB/9	K/9	K	GB%	BABIP	WHIP	ERA	DRA-	WARP	MPH	FB%	Whiff%	CSP
2021	POR	AA	32	0	0	0	2	2	7^1	6	1	1.2	18.4	15	38.5%	.417	0.95	2.45	74	0.2				
2021	WOR	AAA	32	1	0	0	2	2	9^2	7	0	3.7	14.0	15	28.6%	.333	1.14	0.93	96	0.2				
2021	BOS	MLB	32	5	1	0	9	9	42^2	45	6	2.5	11.0	52	47.0%	.358	1.34	3.16	96	0.5	93.8	49.3%	27.7%	52.0%
2022	BOS	MLB	33	0	1	0	2	2	5^2	5	0	1.6	7.9	5	50.0%	.278	1.06	3.18	125	0.0	94.6	51.0%	12.5%	57.7%
2023 DC	*BOS*	*MLB*	*34*	*7*	*6*	*0*	*22*	*22*	*113.3*	*103*	*12*	*2.9*	*10.8*	*136*	*43.5%*	*.323*	*1.24*	*3.56*	*88*	*1.6*	*93.6*	*48.0%*	*29.8%*	*50.7%*

Comparables: CC Sabathia (76), Pedro Martinez (76), Vida Blue (75)

Sale cost the Red Sox roughly $1.7 million per out recorded in 2022. After spending three months on the injured list recovering from a broken rib suffered while training during the offseason—a winter that itself came after he spent most of 2021 on the shelf recovering from Tommy John surgery—Sale returned to the mound in July. He lasted all of a week before a line drive to the left hand broke his pinky finger and put him back on the IL. It's been a long time, in other words, since we've seen a healthy Sale, and longer still since we've seen the strikeout machine who for years terrorized the AL. Does the latter still exist? His fastball velocity in his two starts was close to its pre-Tommy John levels, and his slider showed more of its trademark sweep. But given his frailty, it's hard to trust that he can stay upright long enough to make a sizable impact beyond the payroll column. There's another $55 million coming his way over the next two years whether he's on the mound or not.

John Schreiber RHP Born: 03/05/94 Age: 29 Bats: R Throws: R Height: 6'2" Weight: 210 lb. Origin: Round 15, 2016 Draft (#445 overall)

YEAR	TEAM	LVL	AGE	W	L	SV	G	GS	IP	H	HR	BB/9	K/9	K	GB%	BABIP	WHIP	ERA	DRA-	WARP	MPH	FB%	Whiff%	CSP
2020	DET	MLB	26	0	1	0	15	0	15^{2}	19	2	2.3	8.0	14	33.3%	.347	1.47	6.32	117	0.0	89.9	52.0%	18.2%	45.0%
2021	WOR	AAA	27	3	3	1	33	8	66^{1}	61	3	3.5	8.8	65	48.7%	.314	1.31	2.71	98	1.0				
2021	BOS	MLB	27	0	0	0	1	0	3	4	0	3.0	15.0	5	42.9%	.571	1.67	3.00	86	0.0	92.2	64.3%	24.0%	48.6%
2022	WOR	AAA	28	2	1	0	7	0	12^{1}	9	2	2.2	10.9	15	50.0%	.250	0.97	1.46	87	0.3				
2022	BOS	MLB	28	4	4	8	64	0	65	45	3	2.6	10.2	74	56.9%	.269	0.98	2.22	75	1.5	94.1	54.8%	32.7%	51.7%
2023 DC	*BOS*	*MLB*	*29*	*3*	*3*	*4*	*67*	*0*	*58*	*53*	*5*	*3.2*	*9.9*	*63*	*50.0%*	*.319*	*1.28*	*3.47*	*87*	*0.6*	*93.5*	*55.2%*	*28.9%*	*50.6%*

Comparables: Evan Scribner (70), Noé Ramirez (70), Giovanny Gallegos (69)

Schreiber's Detroit roots earned him the nickname "8 Mile" from WEEI's Rob Bradford, but if he had sweaty palms or weak knees during the season, it didn't show. The ex-Tigers castoff emerged as Boston's most reliable high-leverage bullpen arm, leading all Red Sox relievers in Win Probability Added and all pitchers on the staff in DRA-. The reasons why are varied: better mechanics; a harder fastball (up nearly 2 mph from 2021); more sliders (his best pitch, with a 43.1% whiff rate and lots of sweep); and an improved two-seamer that earned a Run Value of -7. On top of all that, Schreiber is just plain tough to face, coming at hitters from a nearly sidearm angle and with a four-seamer that appears to rise thanks to one of the flattest vertical approach angles in the majors. One concern for Slim Schreiby: a monster workload that may lead to a heavy arm in 2023—but hopefully not vomit on his sweater. Those white jerseys are hard to clean.

Brandon Walter LHP Born: 09/08/96 Age: 26 Bats: L Throws: L Height: 6'2" Weight: 200 lb. Origin: Round 26, 2019 Draft (#797 overall)

YEAR	TEAM	LVL	AGE	W	L	SV	G	GS	IP	H	HR	BB/9	K/9	K	GB%	BABIP	WHIP	ERA	DRA-	WARP	MPH	FB%	Whiff%	CSP
2021	SAL	A	24	1	1	2	13	2	31	21	0	1.7	13.4	46	67.1%	.288	0.87	1.45	67	0.9				
2021	GVL	A+	24	4	3	0	12	12	58^{1}	46	6	2.2	13.3	86	58.3%	.317	1.03	3.70	73	1.4				
2022	POR	AA	25	2	2	0	9	9	50	36	6	0.5	12.2	68	53.3%	.263	0.78	2.88	71	1.4				
2022	WOR	AAA	25	1	1	0	2	2	7^{2}	9	0	4.7	8.2	7	68.0%	.360	1.70	8.22	107	0.1				
2023 DC	*BOS*	*MLB*	*26*	*1*	*1*	*0*	*4*	*4*	*19.7*	*19*	*2*	*2.5*	*8.5*	*18*	*55.7%*	*.312*	*1.25*	*3.61*	*92*	*0.3*			*27.2%*	

Comparables: Joey Lucchesi (54), Ben Braymer (54), Hiram Burgos (51)

Joe Biden wasn't the only Delaware lefty who had a better 2022 than expected. Once bottom-of-the-system fodder, Walter has emerged as one of Boston's better pitching prospects after back-to-back seasons spent confounding hitters in the high minors. The big velocity jump that accompanied his post-pandemic return—he now sits 93–95 mph and touches 97—and his wipeout slider helped him post the sixth-highest strikeout rate among Double-A starters with 50 or more innings pitched. They also earned him a promotion to Worcester. Sadly, bulging discs in his back ended his season there, but the ceiling here has risen; a future as a shutdown lefty reliever is within reach, and better is possible. Like Uncle Joe, he might be inspiring "Let's go Brandon" chants from the bleachers soon.

Garrett Whitlock RHP Born: 06/11/96 Age: 27 Bats: R Throws: R Height: 6'5" Weight: 225 lb. Origin: Round 18, 2017 Draft (#542 overall)

YEAR	TEAM	LVL	AGE	W	L	SV	G	GS	IP	H	HR	BB/9	K/9	K	GB%	BABIP	WHIP	ERA	DRA-	WARP	MPH	FB%	Whiff%	CSP
2021	BOS	MLB	25	8	4	2	46	0	73^{1}	64	6	2.1	9.9	81	49.7%	.304	1.10	1.96	76	1.6	96.1	62.9%	27.6%	56.0%
2022	BOS	MLB	26	4	2	6	31	9	78^{1}	65	10	1.7	9.4	82	40.8%	.271	1.02	3.45	81	1.5	95.5	62.2%	29.6%	57.7%
2023 DC	*BOS*	*MLB*	*27*	*7*	*6*	*0*	*39*	*17*	*101.3*	*98*	*10*	*2.3*	*9.5*	*106*	*45.3%*	*.324*	*1.23*	*3.46*	*89*	*1.2*	*95.7*	*62.5%*	*28.2%*	*57.0%*

Comparables: Chris Devenski (52), Carlos Villanueva (49), Matt Bowman (49)

Is Whitlock a starter? A reliever? Both? Neither? The Red Sox have yet to make up their minds, shifting him between roles in a manner that seems more based on team need than what's best for the former Rule 5 steal himself—it's probably not a coincidence that Whitlock dealt with a hip injury amidst all the flip-flopping. The arguments in favor of letting him start are obvious: he seemed to solve his issues facing left-handers (they dropped from a .350 wOBA against him in 2021 to just .241 last season), and the value of an above-average starter almost always outstrips the value of an above-average reliever. After an offseason full of bullpen-bolstering moves, it feels as though the Sox want him in the rotation, and reports from beat writers lend further credence to that theory. At worst, Boston knows it has a shutdown reliever here. But if they're gonna give Whitlock another shot at starting, they need to live with that decision for longer than they seemed willing to in 2022.

Josh Winckowski RHP Born: 06/28/98 Age: 25 Bats: R Throws: R Height: 6'4" Weight: 202 lb. Origin: Round 15, 2016 Draft (#462 overall)

YEAR	TEAM	LVL	AGE	W	L	SV	G	GS	IP	H	HR	BB/9	K/9	K	GB%	BABIP	WHIP	ERA	DRA-	WARP	MPH	FB%	Whiff%	CSP
2021	POR	AA	23	8	3	0	21	20	100	100	10	2.7	7.9	88	50.3%	.300	1.30	4.14	100	0.8				
2021	WOR	AAA	23	1	1	0	2	2	12	5	1	2.3	9.8	13	50.0%	.148	0.67	2.25	94	0.2				
2022	WOR	AAA	24	2	4	0	13	12	61^{1}	57	4	2.6	9.1	62	52.9%	.312	1.22	3.82	85	1.3				
2022	BOS	MLB	24	5	7	0	15	14	70^{1}	85	10	3.5	5.6	44	52.3%	.322	1.59	5.89	126	-0.3	93.7	61.7%	17.5%	56.0%
2023 DC	*BOS*	*MLB*	*25*	*1*	*2*	*0*	*6*	*6*	*29*	*33*	*3*	*3.4*	*5.8*	*18*	*51.9%*	*.321*	*1.53*	*4.92*	*119*	*0.0*	*93.7*	*61.7%*	*20.4%*	*56.0%*

Comparables: Paul Blackburn (76), Joe Ross (71), Liam Hendriks (71)

The fruits of the Andrew Benintendi trade have been anything but sweet for Boston. Franchy Cordero is gone; the three lesser prospects acquired are mostly system filler; and Winckowski couldn't carry over his minor-league success to the majors. Only seven pitchers with as many innings had a lower strikeout rate, and they're all in the Dakota Hudson tier of starters entirely dependent on soft contact and low BABIPs. The problem for Winckowski is that he's awful at getting that soft contact. His Baseball Savant page is straight out of Picasso's Blue Period and about as uplifting, as batters hit .344 with a .563 SLG against his sinker. Unless he develops some swing-and-miss secondaries, it's hard to imagine Winckowski becoming anything more than a depth/spot starter.

Lineouts

Hitters

HITTER	POS	TEAM	LVL	AGE	PA	R	2B	3B	HR	RBI	BB	K	SB	CS	AVG/OBP/SLG	DRC+	BABIP	BRR	DRP	WARP
Roman Anthony	CF	RSX	ROK	18	40	5	2	0	0	7	4	4	1	0	.429/.475/.486		.469			
	CF	SAL	A	18	43	2	2	0	0	5	5	4	0	0	.189/.279/.243	110	.206	0.3	CF(8): 0.8	0.2
Alex Binelas	CI	GVL	A+	22	259	41	10	1	14	43	38	69	8	0	.245/.355/.495	108	.285	1.5	1B(29): -0.2, 3B(23): 0.5	1.1
	CI	POR	AA	22	241	30	10	1	11	35	25	78	0	0	.166/.254/.379	87	.192	0.0	3B(40): -1.3, 1B(10): -0.3	0.1
Brainer Bonaci	IF	SAL	A	19	494	86	19	6	6	50	89	89	28	6	.262/.397/.385	119	.319	7.1	2B(57): -0.3, SS(31): 3.5, 3B(10): 0.5	3.6
Yu Chang	IF	CLE	MLB	26	10	0	0	0	0	0	0	7	0	0	.000/.000/.000	64			1B(2): -0.2, 2B(2): 0	
	IF	PIT	MLB	26	49	5	1	0	1	2	4	18	0	1	.167/.286/.262	79	.261	0.2	2B(11): -0.2, 1B(5): 0.2	0.0
	IF	BOS	MLB	26	26	3	2	0	0	1	5	7	0	0	.150/.346/.250	92	.231	0.0	SS(7): -0.3, 2B(4): 0.1	0.0
	IF	TB	MLB	26	105	11	3	0	3	12	7	27	0	0	.260/.305/.385	92	.324	0.8	2B(26): 0.1, SS(9): 0.3, 3B(6): 0.3	0.4
Cutter Coffey	SS	RSX	ROK	18	40	7	1	0	0	0	7	11	1	0	.125/.300/.156		.190			
Narciso Crook	OF	IOW	AAA	26	409	61	21	3	19	67	36	124	13	6	.260/.345/.492	96	.342	2.3	RF(64): -2.0, LF(20): 1.9, 1B(9): 0.9	1.2
	OF	CHC	MLB	26	9	1	1	0	0	2	0	3	0	0	.250/.222/.375	91	.333	-0.4	RF(2): -0.1, CF(1): -0.1	-0.1
Jaylin Davis	OF	WOR	AAA	27	346	43	12	3	7	24	43	107	1	4	.203/.312/.334	79	.288	-1.5	CF(45): 1.1, LF(29): -1.1, RF(13): 0.5	-0.1
	OF	SAC	AAA	27	47	10	3	0	2	7	3	14	3	1	.295/.340/.500	94	.393	0.4	RF(4): -0.8, LF(1): -0.2, CF(1): 0.0	0.0
	OF	BOS	MLB	27	27	4	1	0	0	2	3	11	0	0	.333/.407/.375	77	.615	0.3	CF(4): -0.4, RF(3): 0, LF(1): -0.1	0.0
David Hamilton	MI	POR	AA	24	531	81	16	9	12	42	56	119	70	8	.251/.338/.402	111	.312	6.6	2B(63): 2.6, SS(54): 2.6, CF(2): -0.3	3.3
Ronaldo Hernández	C/DH	WOR	AAA	24	439	50	27	0	17	63	21	92	0	3	.261/.297/.451	98	.295	-0.4	C(67): 1.8	1.3
Gilberto Jimenez	OF	GVL	A+	21	409	49	18	2	5	34	18	100	20	9	.268/.306/.366	71	.351	1.5	RF(47): -0.7, CF(40): -1.9, LF(8): 0.0	0.4
Niko Kavadas	1B	SAL	A	23	254	35	18	1	14	48	54	70	1	1	.286/.453/.609	148	.373	-0.2	1B(42): 3.4	2.6
	1B	GVL	A+	23	161	27	4	0	10	28	32	42	0	0	.308/.472/.592	130	.386	-2.5	1B(30): -0.5	0.7
	1B	POR	AA	23	100	9	3	0	2	10	16	40	0	0	.222/.370/.333	80	.410	-1.1	1B(16): -0.5	-0.1
Tyler McDonough	UT	GVL	A+	23	517	60	23	4	9	48	48	162	21	5	.230/.311/.357	79	.334	2.4	CF(35): 0.7, LF(34): 0.4, 2B(29): -1.8	0.7
Eddinson Paulino	IF	SAL	A	19	539	96	35	10	13	66	64	105	27	5	.266/.359/.469	122	.314	4.2	SS(36): 1.8, 3B(34): 0.1, 2B(30): 1.5	3.7
Kevin Plawecki	C	TEX	MLB	31	11	0	0	0	0	1	0	4	0	0	.273/.273/.273	83	.429	0.0	C(3): -0.0	
	C	BOS	MLB	31	175	15	8	0	1	12	14	28	0	0	.217/.287/.287	95	.256	-0.7	C(58): 1.1	0.6
Corey Rosier	LF	FW	A+	22	373	69	7	8	6	37	54	68	33	4	.263/.381/.396	120	.318	1.9	LF(77): 3.0, CF(7): -0.1	2.2
	LF	GVL	A+	22	93	8	6	0	1	4	11	31	7	1	.163/.272/.275	75	.250	0.5	LF(16): 0.2, RF(5): 0.3, CF(1): -0.2	0.6
Enmanuel Valdez	2B	CC	AA	23	205	40	16	0	11	45	34	47	4	2	.357/.463/.649	132	.438	-2.5	2B(19): -2.3, 3B(14): -1.4, LF(5): -0.0	0.8
	2B	SUG	AAA	23	173	26	10	1	10	32	11	29	1	1	.296/.347/.560	119	.306	-1.9	2B(18): -0.4, LF(9): -0.8, 1B(6): 2.0	0.5
	2B	WOR	AAA	23	195	26	9	1	7	30	19	48	3	0	.237/.309/.422	102	.283	0.0	2B(39): 0.5, 3B(3): -0.1, LF(3): 0.3	0.5

A big lad with a big lefty swing, **Roman Anthony** was Boston's costliest pick in the 2022 draft—despite being taken 79th overall, he signed a $2.5 million over-slot deal, which is late first-round money. That represents a sizable bet both on his North End-ass name and his already-plus power. ⚾ There's not much mystery to **Alex Binelas**' game—he either hits the ball hard or doesn't hit it at all. A whopping 32.4% strikeout rate in Double-A attests to the latter, which limits his ceiling to a three true outcomes bat without the glove to carry him through slumps. ⚾ **Brainer Bonaci's** second go-around in Low-A Salem was a marked improvement on 2021's ugly stint, as the rail-thin youngster showed better patience and contact, albeit with modest power. If he dodges Rule 5 draft displacement he'll return to Boston's system as a glove-first infielder more likely to be a multi-position reserve than a future starter. ⚾ **Yu Chang** was often on the move in 2022, playing for four different MLB teams and two minor-league affiliates with about 2,500 miles between them. He kept landing gigs due to his versatility in the field and kept losing them due to his Gallo-ian whiff rates. ⚾ The Red Sox clearly believe in nominative determinism, which is why they added a **Cutter Coffey** to an organization that already has a Kutter. Unlike the latter, the former doesn't throw a cut fastball, but there's plenty of time for the recent second-round pick to learn one if he can't stick as a position player. ⚾ When the Cubs called up **Narciso Crook** in June, he went 2-for-3 with a double and an RBI—against the Reds, in whose system he'd languished for eight years. Take that, Reds! Back in the minors with the Iowa Cubs, he posted some Crook-ed numbers in July, touching base 36 times from July 23 to July 31. ⚾ Despite spending the season with two organizations perpetually short on outfielders, **Jaylin Davis** couldn't carve out a spot in San Francisco or Boston. He's well-rounded enough to keep earning big-league cameos but flawed enough to suffer long stretches confined to Triple-A. ⚾ Potential utilityman **David Hamilton** has no biological relation to Billy, but you'd be forgiven for thinking otherwise after he led the Eastern League in steals by an absurd margin—26, which was also the gap between nos. 2 and 22. Sadly, he's also Billy's equal with the bat. ⚾ **Ronaldo Hernández** continues to make strides toward his eventual future as a bat-first backup catcher whose definition of the strike zone is purely interpretive. Expect to see him run into the occasional fastball in sporadic MLB action as soon as 2023. ⚾ **Gilberto Jimenez** took a big step back in his first go at High-A. Effectively a slap hitter, he was decidedly below average with the bat even with good speed and an Ichiro-esque BABIP. ⚾ **Niko Kavadas**' Home Run Derby approach—take big cuts at the strikes, spit on everything else—makes him the Greek Jack Cust, or at least Rob Deer's illegitimate demi-god son. It also makes him a longshot to be a regular contributor in the majors. ⚾ **Tyler McDonough**'s name begs to be screamed from the Fenway bleachers in the worst Boston accent you've ever heard, but after a dismal year in Greenville, he's more likely to hear it mangled in a Maine or Rhode Island accent in the near future. ⚾ **Eddinson Paulino**'s first trip to full-season ball was a resounding success, as the young infielder finished third among Low-A players in WARP while maintaining the offensive gains he made in Rookie ball. His next challenge? Finding a long-term defensive home. ⚾ When the Red Sox dumped **Kevin Plawecki** to open up a roster spot for "Frank German," it went over in the clubhouse like a surprise Rob Manfred appearance. It's nice to be loved, but inventing dugout celebrations and post-win anthems will only get you so far when your offense collapses to Jeff Mathis levels. ⚾ **Cory Rosier** is an elite baserunner and defender whose bat lags well behind both of those tools despite him being old for his competition. File him away under "Fifth Outfielders With a Chance to Surprise" if he can learn how to square up strikes and lay off junk. ⚾ Part of the return in the Christian Vázquez trade, **Enmanuel Valdez** has a bat that plays everywhere and a glove that doesn't. Boston will cross its fingers and hope he turns into their very own homegrown Eduardo Escobar.

Pitchers

PITCHER	TEAM	LVL	AGE	W	L	SV	G	GS	IP	H	HR	BB/9	K/9	K	GB%	BABIP	WHIP	ERA	DRA-	WARP	MPH	FB%	WHF	CSP
Eduard Bazardo	WOR	AAA	26	2	4	1	37	4	57^1	65	5	3.0	9.4	60	42.3%	.353	1.47	3.45	94	1.0				
	BOS	MLB	26	1	0	0	12	0	16^1	12	4	2.2	6.1	11	39.6%	.182	0.98	2.76	109	0.1	94.2	45.3%	27.0%	51.5%
Darwinzon Hernandez	WOR	AAA	25	0	3	0	23	7	33	22	3	7.4	13.9	51	33.8%	.297	1.48	5.73	87	0.7				
	BOS	MLB	25	0	1	0	7	0	6^2	14	4	10.8	12.2	9	33.3%	.500	3.30	21.60	119	0.0	94.3	61.0%	33.3%	52.5%
Wyatt Mills	TAC	AAA	27	1	0	0	16	0	19^2	12	1	3.2	7.8	17	53.8%	.216	0.97	1.83	91	0.2	92.0	61.8%	24.4%	
	OMA	AAA	27	2	1	1	13	0	14	7	2	6.4	14.8	23	45.8%	.227	1.21	2.57	78	0.3				
	SEA	MLB	27	0	0	0	8	0	8^2	5	0	3.1	6.2	6	39.1%	.217	0.92	4.15	105	0.1	92.7	76.7%	27.4%	53.4%
	KC	MLB	27	0	1	0	19	0	20^2	21	1	4.4	8.7	20	44.3%	.339	1.50	4.79	102	0.2	91.2	56.1%	28.7%	53.4%
Chris Murphy	POR	AA	24	4	5	0	15	13	76^2	46	6	3.6	10.7	91	35.9%	.229	1.00	2.58	94	1.3				
	WOR	AAA	24	3	6	0	15	15	75^1	77	8	4.9	6.9	58	45.8%	.305	1.57	5.50	127	0.0				
Hirokazu Sawamura	BOS	MLB	34	1	1	0	49	0	50^2	45	4	4.8	7.1	40	49.4%	.273	1.42	3.73	111	0.2	96.2	49.0%	25.2%	52.9%
Connor Seabold	WOR	AAA	26	8	2	0	19	19	86^2	79	7	2.0	9.2	89	38.6%	.303	1.13	3.32	92	1.5				
	BOS	MLB	26	0	4	0	5	5	18^1	35	5	3.9	9.3	19	29.4%	.476	2.35	11.29	122	0.0	92.3	53.5%	25.1%	55.2%
Josh Taylor	WOR	AAA	29	0	2	0	8	4	7^1	10	1	2.5	9.8	8	37.5%	.391	1.64	3.68	98	0.1				

Despite the Red Sox bullpen spending most of the year dousing leads in kerosene, **Eduard Bazardo** couldn't crack the major-league roster until September. Hideous peripherals and a mediocre four-pitch mix are the main reasons why. ⚾ **Darwinzon Hernandez** is your prototypical hard-throwing lefty with wipeout stuff and 20-grade command, and it appears the latter has won out. Seemingly no longer part of Boston's plans, you could even say that nature has selected against him moving on. ⚾ **Wyatt Mills** attacks hitters with a three-pitch mix that is nearly equal parts four-seamer, sinker and slider. In some sense "attacks" might be too literal, as he hit five batters in under 30 innings, and walked a bunch more. He'll try to figure it out in Boston after the Sox dealt Jacob Wallace for him. ⚾ **Chris Murphy** showed just enough in 2022 to earn a 40-man roster spot this winter, but his mediocre four-pitch mix means he's a long shot to contribute to an MLB roster as anything more than a spot starter or bulk reliever. ⚾ Raise your hand if you're surprised that **James Paxton** never made it onto a mound in 2022 because of arm injuries (don't raise your hand if you're Paxton, though, or you might pull something). He'll return to Boston on a cheap one-year option and with a Mass General punch card that's almost full. ⚾ **Hirokazu Sawamura** followed up a decent rookie campaign with a dud. Though he misses plenty of bats, he also misses the plate far too often, leading to a late-August DFA despite the Red Sox's sorry bullpen. ⚾ **Connor Seabold** may not fear the ocean, but he should have a healthier respect for opposing hitters after a season in which he served up meatballs and walks in equal measure. He's a depth arm for now, and one the Red Sox would probably rather leave anchored in Worcester. ⚾ **Josh Taylor** lost his season to a back injury right as he'd made the leap from LOOGY to high-leverage reliever. He joins New York Democrats in the "lefties who didn't show up in 2022" club.

NEW YORK YANKEES

Essay by Steven Goldman
Player comments by Lucas Apostoleris and BP staff

After a season that played out like one of those early 20th-century boardwalk shows in which a horse was ridden off a high-diving platform, Yankees fans—if social media was any evidence— were ready to be done with general manager Brian Cashman and manager Aaron Boone. Owner Hal Steinbrenner was not, choosing not to terminate Boone one year into a three-year-plus-option contract and signing Cashman to a four-year contract extension this winter. Both are bland exemplars of mere competence, lacking in imagination and avoidant of risk. Given a certain amount of money, they will deliver results generally reflective of that investment and no more. This is so well-established by now that it is impossible not to infer that, as long as the team performs at a certain high level, ownership is satisfied to leave the championships to others. The play's the thing, not its denouement, *que sera sera*.

The 2022 Yankees were the ultimate expression of this form of indefinite baseball edging. They did something no other team has ever done, playing a substantial part of the season at a .700 pace, then nearly giving it all back. As of the end of June—coincidentally the Yankees' 77th game, the halfway point of the old 154-game schedule—it seemed like the Yankees had a team for the ages. At 56-21, they were on pace for 118 wins. Just one team in the postwar era had outplayed them over the same span:

.700 STARTS, 1946-2022				
Team	Year	W-L%	W	L
NYY	1998	.740	57	20
NYY	**2022**	**.727**	**56**	**21**
SEA	2001	.727	56	21
CLE	1995	.714	55	22
NYM	1986	.714	55	22
DET	1984	.714	55	22
CIN	1970	.714	55	22
BAL	1969	.714	55	22
BRO	1955	.714	55	22
BRO	1952	.711	54	22
CLE	1954	.701	54	23

NEW YORK YANKEES PROSPECTUS

2022 W-L: 99-63, 1st in AL East

Pythag	.657	*2nd*	DER	.723	*3rd*
RS/G	4.98	*2nd*	DRC+	113	*1st*
RA/G	3.50	*3rd*	DRA-	92	*5th*
dWin%	.613	*3rd*	FIP	3.57	*6th*
Payroll	$246M	*3rd*	B-Age	30.8	*30th*
M$/MW	$4.5M	*17th*	P-Age	29.6	*22nd*

408′ 399′ 385′ 318′ 314′

- Opened 2009
- Open air
- Natural surface
- Fence profile: 8′

Park Factors

Runs	Runs/RH	Runs/LH	HR/RH	HR/LH
99	98	102	100	116

Top Hitter WARP	10.4 Aaron Judge
Top Pitcher WARP	5.0 Gerrit Cole
2023 Top Prospect	Anthony Volpe

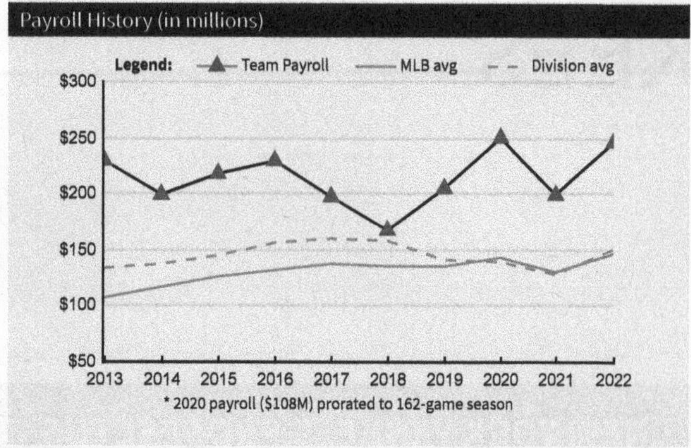

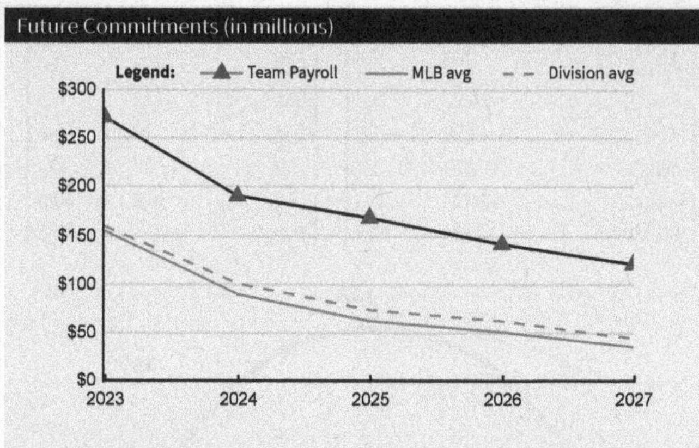

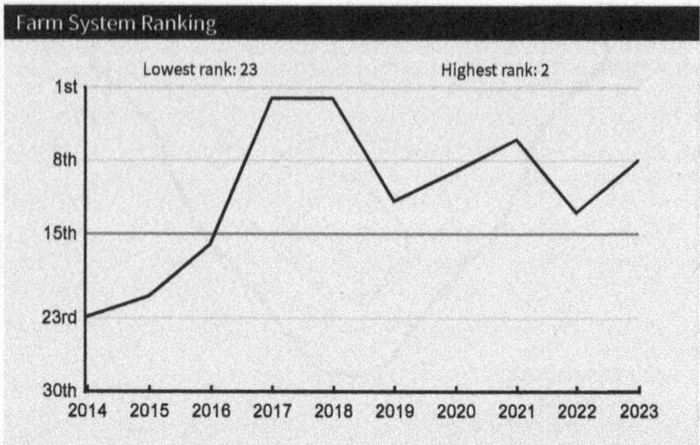

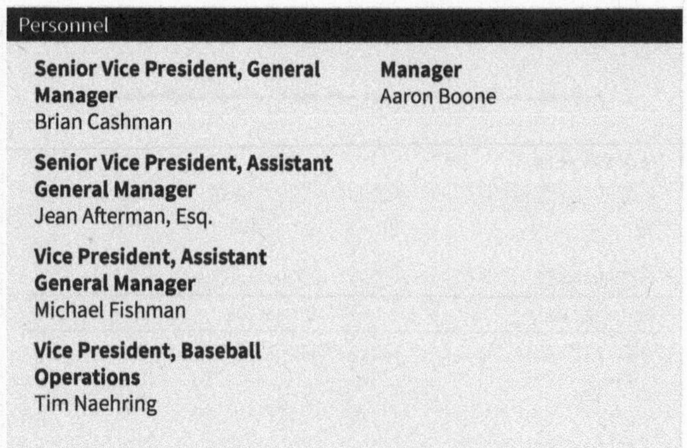
Personnel

Senior Vice President, General Manager
Brian Cashman

Manager
Aaron Boone

Senior Vice President, Assistant General Manager
Jean Afterman, Esq.

Vice President, Assistant General Manager
Michael Fishman

Vice President, Baseball Operations
Tim Naehring

This sort of start is worth only so much: Just four of these 11 teams went on to win the World Series, a testament to the randomness of short series. The 2022 Yankees might have made it through anyway—that coin can flip both ways—but by autumn they were in severe disarray.

The Yankees were legit: Their Pythagorean winning percentage for the first 77 games was .729. Perhaps their early schedule contained a few too many patsies, but given how few teams went to the trouble of fielding a competitive roster in 2022, it can be fairly said that every team in baseball received a similar benefit. In fact, the Yankees acquitted themselves well against their top AL East rivals during this period, going 8-4 against the Blue Jays and 7-3 against the Rays.

There were reasons for doubt: Catcher Jose Trevino was slugging .455, and that seemed unsustainable given his history; Josh Donaldson was struggling to get untracked (he never would); Isiah Kiner-Falefa was hitting exactly like himself, which is to say not enough; Aaron Hicks looked so lost in the field that Boone opted to shift Aaron Judge to center; Joey Gallo's ongoing disintegration had fans delusional, clamoring for the return of Miguel Andújar; Giancarlo Stanton, hitting .285/.339/.523 with 11 home runs through May, commenced a slump from which he would never emerge (he hit .166/.272/.425 the rest of the way, ceasing to make outs only when hobbled by a long bout with Achilles tendinitis). Having begun the season with 12 consecutive scoreless appearances despite a troubling walk rate, closer Aroldis Chapman showed decreased velocity and poor command, was scored upon in five straight appearances, and vanished onto the IL with his own Achilles tendinitis (coded on your doctor's insurance invoice as "a plausible excuse." He subsequently missed time with an infected tattoo, which no one accepted as plausible even if it were true). This, at least, turned into addition by subtraction because it forced Boone to turn to ground-ball machine Clay Holmes in the ninth inning.

It didn't take a Pollyannaish worldview to believe that, if these deficits hadn't dragged the team back to the center by this mature point of the season, they weren't going to. And then the formerly washed-up Matt Carpenter arrived and started bashing away like Babe Ruth. Clearly this was God's chosen team, so blessed as to win despite its flaws.

And then it all stopped.

AFTER .700, 1946-2022				
Team	Year	W-L%	W	L
CLE	1954	.740	57	20
SEA	2001	.706	60	25
CLE	1995	.672	45	22
NYY	1998	.671	57	28
BAL	1969	.635	54	31
NYM	1986	.624	53	32
DET	1984	.576	49	36
BRO	1955	.566	43	33
CIN	1970	.553	47	38
BRO	1952	.545	42	35
NYY	**2022**	**.506**	**43**	**42**

No team has ever had the record the Yankees did to the same point of the season and then posted a losing record the rest of the way. Only a season-closing hot streak, aided by some timely contests against teams that had long since packed it in, saved them from that fate. Even so, unlike any other team to have demonstrated such sustained prowess, the Yankees revealed themselves to have been frauds. They managed to squeak through a five-game American League Division Series against the Guardians by exposing the latter's power-starved offense, but hit only .182/.273/.370 (albeit with nine home runs) themselves. The Astros then punctured any illusions that pitching, home runs and nothing else could get New York through to the World Series by sweeping them in four games. This time the Yankees hit only .162/.232/.269.

It's worth noting that Judge, the eventual American League Most Valuable Player, mostly vanished in October, going 5-for-36 with two home runs, two walks and 15 strikeouts. That is not to tee up Judge for a Steinbrennerian, "Reggie Jackson was Mr. October; Aaron Judge is Mr. May" putdown, but rather to suggest that sans Judge there was very little special about this team. In no way was it *bad*; its poor post-game 77 record was in many ways a function of bad luck and injuries. In aggregate the Yankees continued to outscore opponents handily, and their raw Pythagorean record suggests they should have performed closer to a .617 (a 100-win pace) than .500 mark. Simultaneously, whereas they had had a 17-7 record in one-run games in their first 77 contests, post-game 77 they played more one-run games and lost more of them, with a record of 14-20. When disruption hit, they had all their eggs in one very tall basket, and teams with one star-level performer often struggle to win.

It is tempting to put the onus for the Yankees' freefall on the team's eternally underachieving general manager. That assessment isn't wholly fair; in truth, Cashman may have been flummoxed by short-term inputs that also would have thrown a more intuitive GM. The Yankees were a .500 team in July. The pitching shook a bit, with Gerrit Cole showing signs of the homeritis that would ruin his season, Jameson Taillon and Jordan Montgomery pitching to approximately 5.00 ERAs, Luis Severino and Michael King getting hurt, Domingo Germán looking shaky in his return from a shoulder impingement, and Holmes losing the strike zone. By contrast, the offense looked solid, with Judge, Carpenter, DJ LeMahieu and Anthony Rizzo raking. Even unpredictable players like Hicks and Gleyber Torres were bashing the ball. IKF was hitting a lite-cottage cheese .294, but by his standards those are Derek Jeter numbers.

In short order, three of the top four position players above would get hurt and Hicks would be banished to the dugout with a flaccid bat, but the pitching more or less righted itself. Cashman could not have had foreknowledge that he would soon be down to just one consistently high-achieving hitter. Or that his manager would be reduced to an infantile capacity, helpless as a baby as he was forced to play Marwin Gonzalez at all four corners—and watch as he hit .111 in over 100 plate appearances. Cashman was apparently against throwing Boone a lifeline—surely somewhere in this universe there was someone capable of playing a corner and out-hitting *Marwin Gonzalez*. Hell, even ex-Yankee Mike "Frequent Flier Miles" Ford might have been up to it, and everyone but Boone got to try him in 2022.

Perhaps Boone's petulant postgame press conferences were too delicious an entertainment to preempt with quality players. "It's right in front of us," he said, pounding his hand on the Yankees' dais on August 20. "It's right here. And we can fix it...We can run away with this thing, and we've got the dudes in there to do it." They couldn't fix it, they didn't run away with it and they didn't have the dudes. Boone frequently looked like a toddler who'd had his candy taken away.

Again, that was roughly three weeks in the future as Cashman contemplated his pre-deadline roster. Thus, at the beginning of August, he executed the von Kluck's Turn of trade deadlines, patching what he didn't need to patch and thereby creating vulnerabilities elsewhere. Out went Gallo, Montgomery and a bevy of pitching prospects. In came an injured Harrison Bader, a soon-to-be injured Andrew Benintendi, Frankie Montas, relievers Lou Trivino and Scott Effross and Double-A pitcher Clayton Beeter. Of those acquisitions, the kindest things one can say are that Effross was quite good before tearing his UCL, Bader hit well in the playoffs and that they unwittingly resulted in playing time for rookie Oswaldo Cabrera. It's also worth noting that two of the young pitchers sent to Oakland—Ken Waldichuk and JP Sears—outperformed Montas down the stretch, while in St. Louis, Montgomery outpitched them all.

In his haste to acquire an ostensible top starter, Cashman failed to realize that he needed two outfielders *now*, not one at the deadline and one at a date TBA. Banking on Hicks to stay hot—and that *someone* made the bizarre decision to sign him to a *seven-year* extension in 2019—suggests an inordinate fondness for the former Twins first-rounder that no doubt complicated Cashman's perspective. That said, even an outfield comprising Judge, a high-functioning Hicks (or an ambulatory Bader) and Benintendi would have been overly dependent on Judge delivering the oomph, and that was already the offense's primary problem.

Aside from Judge, the Yankees had several players who were intermittently good, but with the possible exceptions of Rizzo and Carpenter's comet-streak across the sky, there was no one else functioning at a star level. With generally good starting pitching and a strong bullpen despite serious injuries to King, Chad Green and latterly Effross, the Yankees had a good chance to win on any given day. But if things didn't break just right, if Judge didn't hit one or two of his AL record-setting 62 home runs, there wasn't enough offensive consistency to thrive. In short, they needed a Juan Soto (or the nearest facsimile) far more desperately than they needed a Montas or a Luis Castillo.

AARON JUDGE VS. THE YANKEES	
JUDGE THROUGH 77 GAMES	ALL OTHER YANKEES
.282/.360/.619	.203/.315/.407
JUDGE THEREAFTER	**ALL OTHER YANKEES**
.341/.486/.757	.234/.307/.386

It was a very odd team to try to get one's head around, this winning club with what was increasingly a Potemkin village of a record, and as we head into the 2023 season it still is. The decision to retain Judge for $360 million is a double-edged sword. He is 31, prone to injury and unlikely to play at his 2022 level. Re-signing him means that an ownership group that has been squeamish about exceeding the luxury tax threshold has committed $40 million a year to one player through 2031. Signing lefty Carlos Rodón to a six-year, $162 million contract is also a risk given his own injury history and the mismatch between a very effective but fly-ball-prone pitcher and a ballpark in which flies all too easily become souvenirs.

Given these new obligations as well as the $100 million due to Stanton, Cole, Rizzo and LeMahieu, the Yankees are already more than halfway to the $233 million tax-inflection point, and there are still arbitration-driven raises due to Montas, Nestor Cortes, Holmes, Germán, Torres, Jonathan Loáisiga and newly minted Platinum Glover Trevino. This crunch explains why Steinbrenner has become enamored with infield prospects like Anthony Volpe and Oswald Peraza. They're not just young and talented, but they're cheap. Still, if the Yankees are going to staff out a fully rounded roster, they're going to need to take a cue from Steve Cohen or else get creative.

Alas, Steinbrenner isn't much interested in creativity. Boone is a generic manager, unexceptional in both tactics and public-facing personality. Perhaps he excels at the parts of the game the public doesn't see. If so, all credit to him for that, but as the team fell apart in the second half, he gave a good impression of a startled fawn. If there were more aggressive solutions to be tried, he either failed to advocate for them or lost the argument when he did. In short, he's no innovator. The same can be said of Comfortable Shoes Cashman, who has won one World Series in the decades since the team primarily built by Gene Michael aged out. Even if we grant that he was frequently thwarted by the cabal around George Steinbrenner in Tampa through 2005, that still leaves 17 seasons of mixed performances. While the Yankees have reached the postseason 13 times in that span, there has been just the sole pennant, the single championship in 2009. The team's average record in that time is 93-69. Given the resources at Cashman's command, it seems fair to view one of his 93-win seasons differently than we would if it was recorded by a more parsimonious franchise. It is certain that like Boone, Cashman is competent enough to do his job at a respectable level, but he has proven again that he is ruled by a fatal conservatism, as well as a consistent blind spot when it comes to reading the bona fides of available pitchers (call it "going for the Carl Pavano okey-doke").

The team's 2023 chances would seem to be good, with the huge caveat that even with Judge contributing one of the greatest single-season performances in history, this was barely a winning team for over half of last season. If the Yankees receive pitching commensurate with their 2022 level but fail to achieve substantial improvements all around the diamond, they still might not be good enough to win a championship. It is fitting that in a year in which Fred McGriff—who the Yankees had as a prospect but heedlessly threw away for a fungible reliever—will be inducted into the Hall of Fame, the Yankees find themselves in such a confused and confusing place.

It is a team so good, so successful and so expensive that it needs to be rebuilt. Yes, that's a contradiction in terms, but don't feel bad if you don't understand it—neither do the Yankees. ■

—Steven Goldman is a former Editor-in-Chief of Baseball Prospectus.

HITTERS

Harrison Bader CF Born: 06/03/94 Age: 29 Bats: R Throws: R Height: 6'0" Weight: 210 lb. Origin: Round 3, 2015 Draft (#100 overall)

YEAR	TEAM	LVL	AGE	PA	R	2B	3B	HR	RBI	BB	K	SB	CS	Whiff%	AVG/OBP/SLG	DRC+	BABIP	BRR	DRP	WARP
2020	STL	MLB	26	125	21	7	2	4	11	13	40	3	1	28.3%	.226/.336/.443	88	.317	-0.1	CF(49): 0.8	0.3
2021	STL	MLB	27	401	45	21	1	16	50	27	85	9	4	24.8%	.267/.324/.460	102	.306	4.9	CF(103): 7	3.0
2022	STL	MLB	28	264	35	7	3	5	21	13	47	15	2	21.3%	.256/.303/.370	97	.297	3.2	CF(71): 1.1	1.3
2022	NYY	MLB	28	49	3	3	0	0	9	2	15	2	1	28.4%	.217/.245/.283	75	.313	-0.9	CF(14): 0.7	0.0
2023 DC	*NYY*	*MLB*	*29*	*544*	*59*	*21*	*1*	*15*	*56*	*36*	*113*	*25*	*7*	*22.8%*	*.257/.318/.403*	*103*	*.303*	*4.9*	*CF 8*	*3.2*

Comparables: Torii Hunter (59), Carlos Gómez (57), Carl Everett (56)

They say you only get one shot at a first impression, but is that really the case with Bader's relationship with the Yankees and their fans? When the team acquired him from the Cardinals at the trade deadline in a one-for-one swap for Jordan Montgomery, he was in a walking boot, unable to play for another six weeks due to plantar fasciitis—an ominous beginning to a new chapter, especially for a player known for his speed and defense. When Montgomery pitched to an 0.35 ERA over his first four starts and 25⅔ innings with the Cardinals, the trade began to draw the ire of many Yankees fans. But is it really Bader's fault that he was acquired when he was injured? Or that the player for whom he was traded went on to have immediate success with his new team? When Bader socked five postseason homers—just a few weeks after being activated from the injured list—was that the *real* first impression? There certainly wasn't much talk about Jordan Montgomery after that.

Oswaldo Cabrera UT
Born: 03/01/99 Age: 24 Bats: S Throws: R Height: 6'0" Weight: 200 lb. Origin: International Free Agent, 2015

YEAR	TEAM	LVL	AGE	PA	R	2B	3B	HR	RBI	BB	K	SB	CS	Whiff%	AVG/OBP/SLG	DRC+	BABIP	BRR	DRP	WARP
2021	SOM	AA	22	478	61	29	1	24	78	36	118	20	5		.256/.311/.492	111	.295	2.0	2B(43): -0.8, 3B(35): 4.9, SS(24): 3.9	3.1
2021	SWB	AAA	22	36	11	2	1	5	11	5	9	1	0		.500/.583/1.133	134	.625	-0.2	2B(7): 0.0, 3B(1): -0.2, SS(1): -0.2	0.2
2022	SWB	AAA	23	208	29	12	3	8	29	19	55	10	3		.262/.340/.492	97	.331	0.2	2B(21): 4.4, SS(15): 0.5, 3B(6): 0.7	1.1
2022	NYY	MLB	23	171	21	8	1	6	19	15	44	3	2	27.3%	.247/.312/.429	93	.305	-0.6	RF(27): 0.3, LF(9): -0.4, SS(4): 0.9	0.4
2023 DC	*NYY*	*MLB*	*24*	*426*	*43*	*18*	*1*	*15*	*44*	*31*	*109*	*13*	*4*	*27.9%*	*.225/.287/.399*	*85*	*.272*	*3.0*	*LF 0, RF 0*	*0.4*

Comparables: Avisaíl García (59), Starling Marte (58), Jorge Soler (56)

Immediately upon his promotion to the big leagues in mid-August, Cabrera displayed a knack for highlight-reel catches—all around the diamond, too. Just in his first week, he robbed a home run in right field, made a jump-throw play from deep in the shortstop hole and made a running catch at the tarp as a third baseman (sacrificing his body in the process). And then there were the outfield assists. From the time of his outfield debut on August 19 until the end of the season, Cabrera had seven assists, which was the most in the major leagues. It's worth noting that he hadn't played a single professional inning in the outfield until August 10—all of his prior defensive experience had come at either shortstop, second or third. While his success at nabbing baserunners might have something to do with ill-advised aggression against a career infielder playing the outfield, Cabrera displayed a legitimately strong arm: Among outfielders with at least 100 throws last season, his average velocity of 91.3 mph on competitive throws (as flagged by Statcast) put him in the 80th percentile. On top of the defensive prowess, Cabrera rebounded after a rough start to hit .318/.411/.635 over his final 19 regular-season games. With his versatile defensive prowess and solid bat, he figures to give the Yankees plenty of options out of spring training this year.

Willie Calhoun DH/LF
Born: 11/04/94 Age: 28 Bats: L Throws: R Height: 5'8" Weight: 200 lb. Origin: Round 4, 2015 Draft (#132 overall)

YEAR	TEAM	LVL	AGE	PA	R	2B	3B	HR	RBI	BB	K	SB	CS	Whiff%	AVG/OBP/SLG	DRC+	BABIP	BRR	DRP	WARP
2020	TEX	MLB	25	108	3	2	1	1	13	5	17	0	0	14.7%	.190/.231/.260	80	.214	-1.4	LF(8): -0.5	-0.2
2021	TEX	MLB	26	284	26	10	3	6	25	21	34	0	2	16.1%	.250/.310/.381	100	.267	-1.5	LF(41): -2.6	0.5
2022	SAC	AAA	27	170	24	9	0	5	23	19	22	0	0	15.9%	.291/.376/.453	115	.311	-0.4	LF(14): -1.4, RF(5): -0.8, 2B(2): -0.2	0.7
2022	RR	AAA	27	91	18	1	0	5	20	6	13	0	0	15.2%	.217/.264/.410	117	.194	0.6	LF(12): -0.3	0.4
2022	SF	MLB	27	9	0	0	0	0	1	1	2	0	0	21.4%	.125/.222/.125	97	.167	0.2		0.0
2022	TEX	MLB	27	53	7	3	0	1	2	8	6	0	0	12.7%	.136/.283/.273	106	.135	0.7	LF(5): 0.1	0.3
2023 DC	*FA*	*MLB*	*28*	*148*	*16*	*5*	*0*	*4*	*17*	*11*	*20*	*0*	*0*	*16.2%*	*.246/.311/.406*	*100*	*.258*	*-1.1*	*LF -1, 2B 0*	*0.1*

It's always been about the bat with Calhoun. It made him a fourth-round pick by the Dodgers, and a key piece to the trade that sent Yu Darvish from Texas to LA. It earned him his first cup of coffee at age 22, and a 114 DRC+ in 83 games two seasons later. It's also been a pain point of late, as he's struggled to out-hit his defensive inadequacies. When he was optioned to the minors as rosters were trimmed from 28 to 26 on May 1, Calhoun went public with a trade request and aired his complaints with the Rangers attempts to overhaul his swing to avoid consistently grounding into the shift. He wants to get back to his gap-to-gap approach, and those pull-side groundballs might not be so troublesome thanks to the impending shift ban. Calhoun was eventually traded to San Francisco, where his Triple-A numbers improved, but not enough to earn him more than four games in the majors. The Yankees gave him an NRI to big-league camp in late December.

★ ★ ★ *2023 Top 101 Prospect* **#63** ★ ★ ★

Jasson Domínguez OF
Born: 02/07/03 Age: 20 Bats: S Throws: R Height: 5'10" Weight: 190 lb. Origin: International Free Agent, 2019

YEAR	TEAM	LVL	AGE	PA	R	2B	3B	HR	RBI	BB	K	SB	CS	Whiff%	AVG/OBP/SLG	DRC+	BABIP	BRR	DRP	WARP
2021	YNK	ROK	18	27	5	0	0	0	1	6	6	2	0		.200/.407/.200		.286			
2021	TAM	A	18	214	26	9	1	5	18	21	67	7	3		.258/.346/.398	88	.371	0.2	CF(38): -4.4	0.1
2022	TAM	A	19	324	54	17	2	9	36	46	89	19	6	30.0%	.265/.373/.440	104	.360	0.1	CF(65): -2.1	0.7
2022	HV	A+	19	184	33	6	4	6	22	23	34	17	1		.306/.397/.510	113	.353	3.5	CF(35): 1.1	1.7
2023 non-DC	*NYY*	*MLB*	*20*	*251*	*22*	*10*	*2*	*3*	*23*	*20*	*72*	*9*	*3*	*31.3%*	*.226/.294/.344*	*75*	*.313*	*4.0*	*CF 0*	*0.4*

Comparables: Justin Upton (67), Jahmai Jones (67), Heliot Ramos (65)

Obviously, it was never fair to Domínguez to be floating the Mickey Mantle and Mike Trout comparisons when he was a 16-year-old without a professional game under his belt. And when he had a solid yet underwhelming debut last season—despite being one of the youngest players in full-season ball—it only put more fuel to the fire that Domínguez was a disappointment, even though we all knew the expectations were never fair in the first place.

Domínguez's marked improvement in 2022, though, firmly solidifies him as one of the more intriguing prospects in the game. He struggled in April, hitting for a .571 OPS with a bloated 34% strikeout rate and just a three percent walk rate. But by the end of the season, he'd discovered the form many had expected of him: he hit .300/.401/.521—a .923 OPS from August 1 onward, with an impressive 17% strikeout rate against a 14% walk rate. It was against better competition, too: his improvements came on the heels of a midseason promotion to High-A Hudson Valley, and he even got a brief look in Double-A Somerset in the final week of the season, where he was among the league's youngest players. Forget about all the Martian talk and the unnecessary hype, and look at what's there now.

Josh Donaldson 3B Born: 12/08/85 Age: 37 Bats: R Throws: R Height: 6'1" Weight: 210 lb. Origin: Round 1, 2007 Draft (#48 overall)

YEAR	TEAM	LVL	AGE	PA	R	2B	3B	HR	RBI	BB	K	SB	CS	Whiff%	AVG/OBP/SLG	DRC+	BABIP	BRR	DRP	WARP
2020	MIN	MLB	34	102	14	2	0	6	11	18	24	0	0	34.5%	.222/.373/.469	124	.231	0.2	3B(26): 1.6	0.7
2021	MIN	MLB	35	543	73	26	0	26	72	74	114	0	0	27.6%	.247/.352/.475	123	.268	-1.2	3B(92): 1	3.2
2022	NYY	MLB	36	546	59	28	0	15	62	54	148	2	2	33.3%	.222/.308/.374	92	.283	-3.1	3B(104): 0.9	0.6
2023 DC	*NYY*	*MLB*	*37*	*524*	*62*	*22*	*0*	*22*	*64*	*57*	*138*	*1*	*0*	*32.6%*	*.234/.325/.436*	*112*	*.282*	*-1.1*	*3B 0*	*1.7*

Comparables: Ron Cey (73), Scott Rolen (71), Douglas DeCinces (71)

He played good defense, but nothing else about Donaldson's Yankees debut went according to plan; his offensive production dipped below league-average for the first time as a major-league regular, marked by severe regression in his contact and hard-hit numbers. To make matters worse, Donaldson—who doesn't exactly have the reputation as being a particularly well-liked player—earned himself a suspension by the league for an offensive comment made to the White Sox's Tim Anderson during a game in May. Five months of baseball followed, and that remained his most memorable moment of the season.

Estevan Florial CF Born: 11/25/97 Age: 25 Bats: L Throws: R Height: 6'1" Weight: 195 lb. Origin: International Free Agent, 2015

YEAR	TEAM	LVL	AGE	PA	R	2B	3B	HR	RBI	BB	K	SB	CS	Whiff%	AVG/OBP/SLG	DRC+	BABIP	BRR	DRP	WARP
2020	NYY	MLB	22	3	0	0	0	0	0	0	2	0	0	66.7%	.333/.333/.333	93	1.000		CF(1): -0.1	0.0
2021	SOM	AA	23	39	5	2	0	4	6	4	9	0	1		.229/.308/.629	122	.182	-0.7	CF(7): -0.2	0.1
2021	SWB	AAA	23	362	65	17	1	13	41	42	112	13	7		.218/.315/.404	86	.291	1.8	CF(72): -1.4, RF(1): -0.0	0.7
2021	NYY	MLB	23	25	3	2	0	1	2	5	6	1	0	36.7%	.300/.440/.550	97	.385	0.1	CF(11): -0.9	0.0
2022	SWB	AAA	24	461	66	31	2	15	46	54	140	39	10		.283/.368/.481	94	.398	0.9	CF(88): 1.1, RF(10): -0.3, LF(4): 0.6	1.2
2022	NYY	MLB	24	35	4	0	0	0	1	3	13	2	0	46.4%	.097/.200/.097	68	.167	-0.5	CF(14): -0.5, LF(2): 0	-0.1
2023 DC	*NYY*	*MLB*	*25*	*30*	*3*	*1*	*0*	*0*	*2*	*2*	*10*	*1*	*1*	*38.5%*	*.217/.292/.360*	*76*	*.329*	*0.1*	*CF 0*	*0.0*

Comparables: Byron Buxton (60), Brent Clevlen (50), Aaron Hicks (45)

Many Yankees fans were relieved when the team opted not to include Florial in a trade with the Athletics for Sonny Gray. Yes, in 2017. That probably feels like a couple of lifetimes ago, and Florial's career hasn't exactly been on the right trajectory since then. He was set back by a pair of hand injuries suffered in 2018 and 2019, and overall, he quite simply hasn't shown the ability to make the most of his array of tantalizing tools. When he was brought up by the Yankees in mid-August following the continued struggles of Aaron Hicks, it was telling that the team opted to play Florial sparingly before shuttling him back and forth between New York and Scranton. He's entering his age-25 season and has amassed over 800 plate appearances at Triple-A over the past two seasons, so while he's primed for a bigger role at the major-league level in 2023, the production he's shown thus far isn't going to keep him on a roster for very long.

Antonio Gomez C Born: 11/13/01 Age: 21 Bats: R Throws: R Height: 6'2" Weight: 210 lb. Origin: International Free Agent, 2018

YEAR	TEAM	LVL	AGE	PA	R	2B	3B	HR	RBI	BB	K	SB	CS	Whiff%	AVG/OBP/SLG	DRC+	BABIP	BRR	DRP	WARP
2021	YNK	ROK	19	113	18	8	1	2	16	16	31	4	0		.305/.416/.474		.435			
2021	TAM	A	19	71	10	2	0	2	7	10	18	1	0		.197/.310/.328	103	.244	-1.5	C(15): 1.4	0.2
2022	TAM	A	20	370	36	10	2	8	48	35	100	1	3	30.9%	.252/.332/.369	91	.335	-5.4	C(70): 11.0	1.2
2023 non-DC	*NYY*	*MLB*	*21*	*251*	*19*	*8*	*1*	*2*	*19*	*16*	*81*	*0*	*1*	*35.0%*	*.208/.266/.294*	*53*	*.307*	*0.6*	*C 0*	*-0.5*

Comparables: Roberto Peña (68), Francisco Hernandez (68), Deivy Grullón (66)

YEAR	TEAM	P. COUNT	FRM RUNS	BLK RUNS	THRW RUNS	TOT RUNS
2021	TAM	2134	1.1	0.0	0.3	1.4
2022	TAM	9605	11.5	-0.7	0.0	10.7
2023	*NYY*	*6956*	*0.9*	*-0.3*	*0.6*	*1.2*

As far as on-field tools, Gomez is best known for the cannon he possesses for a throwing arm. From an "intangibles" perspective, he's considered to be a leader whose bilinguality has helped form a close relationship with his pitchers. A brutal April at the plate led to a demotion to the Florida Complex League, but after his return to the Tarpons on May 20, Gomez hit for a solid .741 OPS to finish out his season. Gotta have those "tangibles" to throw in.

Ronald Guzmán 1B Born: 10/20/94 Age: 28 Bats: L Throws: L Height: 6'5" Weight: 235 lb. Origin: International Free Agent, 2011

YEAR	TEAM	LVL	AGE	PA	R	2B	3B	HR	RBI	BB	K	SB	CS	Whiff%	AVG/OBP/SLG	DRC+	BABIP	BRR	DRP	WARP
2020	GIG	WIN	25	131	25	3	0	5	13	17	23	2	0		.360/.450/.523		.417			
2020	TEX	MLB	25	86	10	1	1	4	9	7	24	1	0	31.6%	.244/.314/.436	85	.300	0.5	1B(24): 1.3	0.2
2021	TEX	MLB	26	17	1	0	0	1	1	1	6	0	0	40.0%	.063/.118/.250	84			LF(2): -0.1	0.0
2022	SWB	AAA	27	373	51	24	0	16	53	41	100	2	0		.255/.344/.478	94	.314	-0.9	1B(87): -0.2	0.7
2022	NYY	MLB	27	6	0	0	0	0	0	0	5	0	0	69.2%	.000/.000/.000	59				0.0
2023 DC	*FA*	*MLB*	*28*	*148*	*14*	*6*	*0*	*4*	*16*	*13*	*47*	*0*	*0*	*35.0%*	*.214/.294/.366*	*81*	*.297*	*0.2*	*1B 0, LF 0*	*-0.1*

Comparables: Justin Smoak (55), Carlos Pena (52), Logan Morrison (50)

Last summer while he was in Triple-A, Guzmán expressed his desire to become a two-way player; he had been honing his pitching skills in intrasquad practice. Ultimately, he got into one game on the mound with the RailRiders, and even struck someone out. As a position player, Guzmán got a brief shot with the Yankees while Anthony Rizzo was out with a back injury, going 0-6 with five strikeouts and a bases-loaded double play before being outrighted off the roster later that week. Perhaps the Yankees wish they'd asked him to pitch for them instead.

Aaron Hicks OF Born: 10/02/89 Age: 33 Bats: S Throws: R Height: 6'1" Weight: 205 lb. Origin: Round 1, 2008 Draft (#14 overall)

YEAR	TEAM	LVL	AGE	PA	R	2B	3B	HR	RBI	BB	K	SB	CS	Whiff%	AVG/OBP/SLG	DRC+	BABIP	BRR	DRP	WARP
2020	NYY	MLB	30	211	28	10	2	6	21	41	38	4	1	27.9%	.225/.379/.414	118	.256	0.8	CF(50): 4	1.6
2021	NYY	MLB	31	126	13	3	0	4	14	14	30	0	0	29.6%	.194/.294/.333	92	.224	0.7	CF(32): -0.8	0.4
2022	NYY	MLB	32	453	54	9	2	8	40	62	109	10	3	25.9%	.216/.330/.313	94	.279	3.5	CF(81): 0.5, LF(55): 3.2	2.0
2023 DC	*NYY*	*MLB*	*33*	*367*	*40*	*12*	*1*	*12*	*35*	*48*	*79*	*4*	*2*	*26.3%*	*.220/.330/.387*	*101*	*.255*	*1.4*	*LF 2, CF 0*	*1.3*

Comparables: Dwayne Murphy (58), Darren Lewis (58), Lenny Green (53)

The straw is only supposed to break the camel's back once, right? It was a miserable season overall for Hicks, low-lighted by not one, but *two* late-season games against Tampa Bay that sent him to the bench. On August 15, he misplayed a fly ball into a triple and grounded into a bases-loaded double play shortly thereafter. That game seemed to render him unplayable by the Yankees and led to the promotions of Oswaldo Cabrera and Estevan Florial; Hicks started just three games the rest of the month. But after Andrew Benintendi's hamate injury in early September knocked him out for the remainder of the season, Hicks was given yet another chance to redeem himself...which brings us to September 9, when he made yet another key misplay in the outfield and seemed to display a lack of urgency while doing so. This time, Aaron Boone removed Hicks *in the middle of the game*, and he only started four games over the next two weeks. As the Yankees widened their division lead, some playing time opened up for Hicks, and to his credit, he began to turn things around, with a .865 OPS over his final 13 games. But that's too little, and way, way too late.

Kyle Higashioka C Born: 04/20/90 Age: 33 Bats: R Throws: R Height: 6'1" Weight: 202 lb. Origin: Round 7, 2008 Draft (#230 overall)

YEAR	TEAM	LVL	AGE	PA	R	2B	3B	HR	RBI	BB	K	SB	CS	Whiff%	AVG/OBP/SLG	DRC+	BABIP	BRR	DRP	WARP
2020	NYY	MLB	30	48	7	1	0	4	10	0	11	0	0	23.2%	.250/.250/.521	106	.242	-0.1	C(14): 1.9	0.4
2021	NYY	MLB	31	211	20	10	0	10	29	17	59	0	0	31.0%	.181/.246/.389	87	.200	-1.1	C(66): 8.6	1.3
2022	NYY	MLB	32	248	27	7	0	10	31	12	52	0	1	27.2%	.227/.264/.389	97	.246	-0.3	C(82): 9.2	1.8
2023 DC	*NYY*	*MLB*	*33*	*248*	*27*	*9*	*0*	*10*	*28*	*14*	*60*	*0*	*1*	*27.4%*	*.221/.272/.400*	*83*	*.253*	*-0.2*	*C 11*	*1.5*

Comparables: Anthony Recker (56), Dustin Garneau (51), Yan Gomes (48)

YEAR	TEAM	P. COUNT	FRM RUNS	BLK RUNS	THRW RUNS	TOT RUNS
2020	NYY	1794	2.0	0.0	0.0	2.0
2021	NYY	8429	7.7	0.2	0.1	8.1
2022	NYY	10042	9.3	0.0	0.0	9.3
2023	*NYY*	*9620*	*9.6*	*0.1*	*0.2*	*9.9*

Joey Votto, Adam Wainwright, Clayton Kershaw, Miguel Cabrera, Brandon Crawford, Jose Altuve and Salvador Perez. Those household names are the active players who have been with the same organization for longer than Higashioka, who has been playing professionally for the Yankees since 2008. His team has seemed perfectly happy to keep him around all these years, and after working his way up the minor-league ladder for a decade, he's been a perfectly fine backup catcher for the past three seasons, consistently combining excellent defense with just enough pop to assuage an otherwise-lackluster offensive profile.

★ ★ ★ *2023 Top 101 Prospect* **#57** ★ ★ ★

Spencer Jones OF Born: 05/14/01 Age: 22 Bats: L Throws: L Height: 6'7" Weight: 225 lb. Origin: Round 1, 2022 Draft (#25 overall)

YEAR	TEAM	LVL	AGE	PA	R	2B	3B	HR	RBI	BB	K	SB	CS	Whiff%	AVG/OBP/SLG	DRC+	BABIP	BRR	DRP	WARP
2022	TAM	A	21	95	18	5	0	3	8	10	18	10	0	23.6%	.325/.411/.494	113	.387	0.5	CF(18): -0.5	0.4
2023 non-DC	*NYY*	*MLB*	*22*	*251*	*20*	*9*	*1*	*3*	*21*	*16*	*68*	*14*	*1*	*30.1%*	*.226/.286/.324*	*68*	*.307*	*9.4*	*CF 0*	*0.8*

Comparables: Dominic Fletcher (90), Nathan Lukes (89), Andrew Toles (88)

As a 6-foot-7 outfield slugger from California drafted in the first round by the Yankees, the Aaron Judge comps will follow Jones around for a long time. While that's obviously unfair, the former Vanderbilt standout didn't disappoint in his 25-game pro debut last summer. Beyond the impressive slash line, 17 of his 56 balls in his Florida State League cameo were over 100 mph. Breaking home-run records and ascending to Yankee captaincy will have to wait a few years. The reigning AL MVP isn't going anywhere, though.

Aaron Judge OF Born: 04/26/92 Age: 31 Bats: R Throws: R Height: 6'7" Weight: 282 lb. Origin: Round 1, 2013 Draft (#32 overall)

YEAR	TEAM	LVL	AGE	PA	R	2B	3B	HR	RBI	BB	K	SB	CS	Whiff%	AVG/OBP/SLG	DRC+	BABIP	BRR	DRP	WARP
2020	NYY	MLB	28	114	23	3	0	9	22	10	32	0	1	33.5%	.257/.336/.554	112	.283	0.3	RF(25): 1.1	0.6
2021	NYY	MLB	29	633	89	24	0	39	98	75	158	6	1	29.2%	.287/.373/.544	135	.332	-3.6	RF(114): 3.3, CF(23): -1.9	4.4
2022	NYY	MLB	30	696	133	28	0	62	131	111	175	16	3	29.9%	.311/.425/.686	190	.340	3.3	CF(78): -3.6, RF(73): -1.7	9.6
2023 DC	*NYY*	*MLB*	*31*	*621*	*101*	*23*	*0*	*43*	*95*	*90*	*150*	*11*	*3*	*29.4%*	*.281/.391/.581*	*168*	*.312*	*1.3*	*RF 5, CF 0*	*7.2*

Comparables: Sammy Sosa (80), Wally Post (77), Dwight Evans (76)

The historic nature of Judge's offensive prowess has been covered extensively. At this point, we can pretty much gloss over the fact that he set a league record for home runs, almost won the Triple Crown and posted the highest WARP of any offensive player in over a decade (since Albert Pujols in 2009). An aspect of Judge's herculean season that hasn't gotten nearly as much press as his exploits at the plate is the fact that he was essentially playing a new position this year, and a challenging one at that. The ineffectiveness of Aaron Hicks and the injury to Harrison Bader pushed Judge into center field, which accounted for the majority of his defensive innings for the first time in his career—prior to this season, Judge had played only 3.9% of his defensive outfield innings in center. Among players this century with at least 4,000 prior defensive innings in the outfield, that 3.9 rate is the third-lowest for a player who made center their primary outfield position (in 2013, both Andre Ethier and Shin-Soo Choo made the move to CF with less experience in center than Judge did). Not only was it an unusual switch that helped his team fill a hole, Judge was good out there, too: all publicly available metrics pegged him as an above-average defensive center fielder last year, and his arm is nearly as impressive as his bat. Though it's not what people will remember most about his MVP season, Judge's defensive abilities are a big part of what's made him such a superstar.

Isiah Kiner-Falefa SS Born: 03/23/95 Age: 28 Bats: R Throws: R Height: 5'11" Weight: 190 lb. Origin: Round 4, 2013 Draft (#130 overall)

YEAR	TEAM	LVL	AGE	PA	R	2B	3B	HR	RBI	BB	K	SB	CS	Whiff%	AVG/OBP/SLG	DRC+	BABIP	BRR	DRP	WARP
2020	TEX	MLB	25	228	28	4	3	3	10	14	32	8	5	15.8%	.280/.329/.370	103	.316	-0.4	3B(46): 1.7, SS(15): 0.6	0.9
2021	TEX	MLB	26	677	74	25	3	8	53	28	90	20	5	14.6%	.271/.312/.357	95	.304	4.0	SS(156): 2.9	2.7
2022	NYY	MLB	27	531	66	20	0	4	48	35	72	22	4	11.2%	.261/.314/.327	95	.296	1.8	SS(138): 3.7, 3B(6): -0.5	1.9
2023 DC	*NYY*	*MLB*	*28*	*169*	*17*	*6*	*0*	*1*	*13*	*10*	*19*	*6*	*1*	*12.4%*	*.264/.317/.348*	*92*	*.291*	*2.0*	*SS 1, 2B 0*	*0.7*

Comparables: Adeiny Hechavarria (76), Jose Vizcaino (74), Alfredo Griffin (70)

The IKF Experience was divisive from the start, as many Yankees fans were frustrated by the front office's decision to target Kiner-Falefa instead of going for a higher impact player (namely Carlos Correa). He wasn't brought in to do a whole lot with the bat, and he didn't—sure, his high-contact tendencies were useful in situations where the Yankees really needed a base hit, and believe it or not, he had a .424 average in high leverage situations (the fifth-best average in the major leagues last year). But save for those instances, the Yankees essentially punted offense at the shortstop position believing that they would get a premium defender. That didn't really happen either. Despite the fact that Kiner-Falefa is athletic and has good range, he had trouble finishing plays last year due to his weak throwing arm: out of the 37 shortstops that had at least 200 tracked throws in 2022, Kiner-Falefa was 34th in both average (81.1 mph) and max (86 mph) for velocity on competitive throws, as tracked by Statcast. He also became prone to the yips, and his fielding glitches became too much for Aaron Boone to bear. IKF was finally benched during the ALDS. Kiner-Falefa is better suited for a utility role; the defensive versatility he's shown throughout his major-league career thus far is a valuable skill set, but his flaws were exposed front-and-center as the shortstop for a team with World Series aspirations.

DJ LeMahieu IF Born: 07/13/88 Age: 34 Bats: R Throws: R Height: 6'4" Weight: 220 lb. Origin: Round 2, 2009 Draft (#79 overall)

YEAR	TEAM	LVL	AGE	PA	R	2B	3B	HR	RBI	BB	K	SB	CS	Whiff%	AVG/OBP/SLG	DRC+	BABIP	BRR	DRP	WARP
2020	NYY	MLB	31	216	41	10	2	10	27	18	21	3	0	11.2%	.364/.421/.590	146	.370	-0.1	2B(37): 0.1, 1B(11): 0, 3B(11): 0.3	1.9
2021	NYY	MLB	32	679	84	24	1	10	57	73	94	4	2	14.3%	.268/.349/.362	106	.301	-1.4	2B(83): 1.8, 1B(55): 0, 3B(39): -0.8	2.6
2022	NYY	MLB	33	541	74	18	0	12	46	67	71	4	3	15.6%	.261/.357/.377	122	.285	-1.7	3B(47): 0.8, 2B(41): 1.5, 1B(35): 0.7	2.9
2023 DC	*NYY*	*MLB*	*34*	*557*	*72*	*21*	*1*	*12*	*46*	*61*	*75*	*4*	*1*	*15.5%*	*.272/.357/.395*	*117*	*.300*	*0.9*	*3B 1, 1B 0*	*2.5*

Comparables: Bill Mazeroski (74), Omar Infante (73), Red Schoendienst (72)

The 2022 season looked to be a bounceback one for LeMahieu. He was hitting .290/.393/.434 as late as August 8—an improvement of more than 100 points of OPS from his lackluster 2021 campaign, which was marred by a sports hernia. A toe injury caused him to miss much of September and October, and when he did play, his numbers were compromised, to say the least. From August 8 onward, LeMahieu did not have a single extra-base hit in 108 plate appearances. The Yankees are now faced with the harsh reality that LeMahieu, who is entering his age-34 season and has seen his production suffer due to injuries in each of the past two seasons, may need to see a decrease in playing time from what they've expected of him during his tenure in New York. It would be a tough but necessary demotion for a player who has been among the Yankees' most reliable in younger years, and who's signed through 2027.

★ ★ ★ *2023 Top 101 Prospect* **#48** ★ ★ ★

Oswald Peraza SS Born: 06/15/00 Age: 23 Bats: R Throws: R Height: 6'0" Weight: 200 lb. Origin: International Free Agent, 2016

YEAR	TEAM	LVL	AGE	PA	R	2B	3B	HR	RBI	BB	K	SB	CS	Whiff%	AVG/OBP/SLG	DRC+	BABIP	BRR	DRP	WARP
2021	HV	A+	21	127	20	10	0	5	16	12	24	16	1		.306/.386/.532	127	.349	1.0	SS(25): 4.9	1.4
2021	SOM	AA	21	353	51	16	2	12	40	23	82	20	8		.294/.348/.466	102	.362	-2.2	SS(69): -2.7	0.7
2021	SWB	AAA	21	31	5	0	0	1	2	2	5	2	1		.286/.323/.393	98	.304	-0.3	SS(7): 1.5	0.2
2022	SWB	AAA	22	429	57	16	0	19	50	34	100	33	5		.259/.329/.448	100	.302	3.1	SS(89): -1.3, 2B(10): -1.5	1.3
2022	NYY	MLB	22	57	8	3	0	1	2	6	9	2	0	17.7%	.306/.404/.429	108	.359	-1.0	SS(12): 0.7, 2B(4): 0	0.2
2023 DC	*NYY*	*MLB*	*23*	*283*	*28*	*10*	*0*	*6*	*26*	*18*	*63*	*13*	*4*	*27.6%*	*.241/.301/.362*	*87*	*.294*	*3.2*	*SS -2*	*0.5*

Comparables: Willi Castro (68), Reid Brignac (61), Jorge Polanco (60)

If you look at Yankees hitters with at least 50 plate appearances last year, you'll see that Peraza was second in both batting average (to Aaron Judge) and walk-to-strikeout ratio (to DJ LeMahieu). Yes, it's only a few weeks' worth of games, but it was a solid cameo nonetheless for one of the team's top prospects, and it earned him a spot on the ALCS roster. While the crown jewel of the Yankees' farm system is generally considered to be fellow shortstop Anthony Volpe, Peraza is currently the better defensive option of the two and has already debuted. Expect him to stick at short.

Anthony Rizzo 1B Born: 08/08/89 Age: 33 Bats: L Throws: L Height: 6'3" Weight: 240 lb. Origin: Round 6, 2007 Draft (#204 overall)

YEAR	TEAM	LVL	AGE	PA	R	2B	3B	HR	RBI	BB	K	SB	CS	Whiff%	AVG/OBP/SLG	DRC+	BABIP	BRR	DRP	WARP
2020	CHC	MLB	30	243	26	6	0	11	24	28	38	3	1	19.4%	.222/.342/.414	118	.218	-0.6	1B(57): -0.1	1.0
2021	CHC	MLB	31	376	41	16	3	14	40	36	59	4	2	21.0%	.248/.346/.446	112	.261	-1.0	1B(92): -0.8	1.2
2021	NYY	MLB	31	200	32	7	0	8	21	16	28	2	0	20.7%	.249/.340/.428	113	.252	1.7	1B(47): -0.7	0.8
2022	NYY	MLB	32	548	77	21	1	32	75	58	101	6	5	22.8%	.224/.338/.480	130	.216	0.3	1B(120): 0	3.1
2023 DC	*NYY*	*MLB*	*33*	*562*	*70*	*21*	*1*	*26*	*70*	*56*	*95*	*8*	*2*	*22.2%*	*.241/.347/.456*	*123*	*.250*	*3.5*	*1B -1*	*2.7*

Comparables: Kent Hrbek (73), John Olerud (72), Keith Hernandez (72)

With a vacancy at first base after the lockout, the Yankees opted to reunite with Rizzo, whom they'd acquired as a rental at the 2021 trade deadline. Freddie Freeman and Matt Olson had been available options coming off stronger seasons than Rizzo's, but the Yankees never pursued either player too seriously. He's no longer at his peak, but Rizzo still does a good job of controlling the strike zone and—as evidenced by his career-best-tying home run output last year—has been a great fit for the short porch at Yankee Stadium. Though he wasn't the big splash for which Yankees fans were hoping, it turned out they just needed to wait a winter.

Ben Rortvedt C/DH
Born: 09/25/97 Age: 25 Bats: L Throws: R Height: 5'10" Weight: 205 lb. Origin: Round 2, 2016 Draft (#56 overall)

YEAR	TEAM	LVL	AGE	PA	R	2B	3B	HR	RBI	BB	K	SB	CS	Whiff%	AVG/OBP/SLG	DRC+	BABIP	BRR	DRP	WARP
2021	STP	AAA	23	136	18	6	0	5	22	10	35	0	0		.254/.324/.426	91	.313	0.5	C(29): 1.3	0.5
2021	MIN	MLB	23	98	8	1	0	3	7	6	29	0	0	31.6%	.169/.229/.281	76	.211	-0.8	C(39): 2.3	0.3
2022	SWB	AAA	24	177	21	9	0	6	20	18	57	0	0		.221/.307/.396	87	.301	0.1	C(27): 0.4	0.3
2023 DC	*NYY*	*MLB*	*25*	*61*	*6*	*2*	*0*	*1*	*5*	*4*	*18*	*0*	*0*	*33.5%*	*.201/.272/.345*	*67*	*.266*	*-0.6*	*C 1*	*0.0*

Comparables: Chance Sisco (59), Tucker Barnhart (58), Austin Hedges (51)

YEAR	TEAM	P. COUNT	FRM RUNS	BLK RUNS	THRW RUNS	TOT RUNS
2021	STP	4304	2.0	0.0	0.0	2.0
2021	MIN	4482	1.4	0.3	0.0	1.7
2022	SWB	3722	0.8	0.0	0.1	0.9
2023	*NYY*	*2405*	*0.8*	*0.1*	*0.1*	*1.0*

He was supposed to be a big part of the team's future after coming over from Minnesota along with Isiah Kiner-Falefa and Josh Donaldson last spring, but Rortvedt quickly became an afterthought given his inability to stay healthy (and Jose Trevino's emergence). Despite spending a weekend on the big-league roster while Trevino went on paternity leave, Rortvedt saw not a single pitch at the plate or behind it. The wheel of high-hope and low-impact catchers spins. For him, 2022 was a breaking wheel.

Anthony Seigler C/DH
Born: 06/20/99 Age: 24 Bats: S Throws: S Height: 6'0" Weight: 200 lb. Origin: Round 1, 2018 Draft (#23 overall)

YEAR	TEAM	LVL	AGE	PA	R	2B	3B	HR	RBI	BB	K	SB	CS	Whiff%	AVG/OBP/SLG	DRC+	BABIP	BRR	DRP	WARP
2021	HV	A+	22	176	24	12	1	4	24	23	46	1	2		.219/.324/.391	99	.284	-0.6	C(23): 1.2, RF(1): -0.1	0.5
2022	TAM	A	23	101	12	6	0	3	13	25	18	5	0	20.8%	.237/.426/.434	149	.273	-0.9	C(18): 1.0	0.8
2022	HV	A+	23	316	49	15	0	4	32	66	64	11	7		.235/.399/.349	116	.292	1.1	C(47): 2.2	2.1
2023 non-DC	*NYY*	*MLB*	*24*	*251*	*22*	*10*	*0*	*2*	*20*	*32*	*60*	*3*	*2*	*24.5%*	*.193/.305/.291*	*71*	*.254*	*-0.7*	*C 0*	*-0.1*

Comparables: Luis Flores (63), Michael Perez (60), Robbie Perkins (59)

YEAR	TEAM	P. COUNT	FRM RUNS	BLK RUNS	THRW RUNS	TOT RUNS
2021	HV	2915	0.5	-0.1	0.4	0.7
2022	TAM	2665	0.7	0.2	0.1	1.0
2022	HV	6376	-0.4	0.7	2.3	2.6
2023	*NYY*	*6956*	*-0.9*	*0.2*	*0.0*	*-0.6*

Seigler retains some bit of interest as the exceedingly rare switch-hitter/switch-thrower and, after a litany of injuries, was finally able to play regularly in 2022. He's shown an ability to control the strike zone: among batters with at least 300 plate appearances in the South Atlantic League last year, Seigler's BB/K ratio of 1.03 was the best of everyone's. The bat, which remains likelier to define his career, was another story. Seigler hasn't had an easy go of it since being a first-round pick in 2018. If there's a silver lining, two options to choose between are better than one, and baseball has written unlikelier happy stories.

Giancarlo Stanton DH/RF
Born: 11/08/89 Age: 33 Bats: R Throws: R Height: 6'6" Weight: 245 lb. Origin: Round 2, 2007 Draft (#76 overall)

YEAR	TEAM	LVL	AGE	PA	R	2B	3B	HR	RBI	BB	K	SB	CS	Whiff%	AVG/OBP/SLG	DRC+	BABIP	BRR	DRP	WARP
2020	NYY	MLB	30	94	12	7	0	4	11	15	27	1	1	32.7%	.250/.387/.500	100	.333	-0.1		0.2
2021	NYY	MLB	31	579	64	19	0	35	97	63	157	0	0	32.8%	.273/.354/.516	131	.324	-0.9	RF(16): -2, LF(10): -1.8	3.2
2022	NYY	MLB	32	452	53	7	0	31	78	50	137	0	0	36.6%	.211/.297/.462	119	.227	-1.9	RF(34): -1.7, LF(4): -0.4	1.8
2023 DC	*NYY*	*MLB*	*33*	*521*	*70*	*17*	*0*	*33*	*77*	*56*	*155*	*0*	*1*	*35.5%*	*.248/.335/.507*	*131*	*.297*	*-4.1*	*RF -1, LF 0*	*2.4*

Comparables: Jose Canseco (81), Jack Clark (73), Justin Upton (71)

For a while, the big knock on Big G was his ability to stay on the field: from 2019 through 2020, Stanton only appeared in 41 regular-season games, a miniscule 18% of the schedule. The past two seasons may have tempered concerns somewhat, though Stanton did miss about a month and a half with lower leg injuries in 2022 (an ankle injury that cost him two weeks at the end of May, and then Achilles tendonitis that put him on the shelf in August). With Stanton on the other side of 30 now, the Yankees will still presumably manage his workload carefully, locking him in as the team's designated hitter most of the time and trying to keep him off his feet in the outfield when possible. But what's perhaps most concerning about Stanton right now is what he did when he *was* on the field. He still hits the ball harder than just about anyone in the universe, but he just posted the lowest batting average and on-base percentage of his career, as well as the highest strikeout rate since his rookie season with the Marlins in 2010. A driving factor was his inability to time pitches in the strike zone: his in-zone contact rate of 72.9% was not only the lowest of his career and well off his career average of 79.7%, but it was also the fourth-lowest rate in the majors last year among batters with at least 400 plate appearances.

Gleyber Torres 2B
Born: 12/13/96 Age: 26 Bats: R Throws: R Height: 6'1" Weight: 205 lb. Origin: International Free Agent, 2013

YEAR	TEAM	LVL	AGE	PA	R	2B	3B	HR	RBI	BB	K	SB	CS	Whiff%	AVG/OBP/SLG	DRC+	BABIP	BRR	DRP	WARP
2020	NYY	MLB	23	160	17	8	0	3	16	22	28	1	0	28.0%	.243/.356/.368	108	.286	0.2	SS(40): 0.1	0.6
2021	NYY	MLB	24	516	50	22	0	9	51	50	104	14	6	26.3%	.259/.331/.366	96	.314	1.0	SS(108): -2.5, 2B(19): -0.9	1.4
2022	NYY	MLB	25	572	73	28	1	24	76	39	129	10	5	27.1%	.257/.310/.451	112	.295	2.7	2B(124): 3.8, SS(6): -0.2	3.3
2023 DC	*NYY*	*MLB*	*26*	*546*	*63*	*23*	*1*	*21*	*67*	*44*	*112*	*13*	*4*	*26.6%*	*.259/.324/.443*	*113*	*.294*	*1.5*	*2B 2*	*2.7*

Comparables: Carlos Correa (80), Jim Fregosi (78), Bill Mazeroski (71)

One of the biggest disappointments of the 2020-2021 Yankees was the stark downturn in Torres' production, both at the plate and in the field. It wasn't an inexplicable or unexpected development: Torres' impressive power output in 2019 came at a time when the juiced ball was causing *everybody* to hit home runs, and when the deadened ball was put into circulation, players like Torres—not traditionally known for their propensity to hit homers—became particularly susceptible to power outages. On the defensive side, the Yankees made the organizational decision to move him over to shortstop prior to the 2020 season, where he clearly did not appear comfortable; both the eye test and the publicly available metrics agreed that he was a liability. In 2022, Torres moved back to second base full time and saw a positive swing in FRAA, Defensive Runs Saved and Outs Above Average. Even more interesting is Torres' offensive rebound, which is rooted in a tangible improvement in contact quality. Among all MLB hitters who hit at least 300 balls in play in both 2021 and 2022, nobody had a bigger increase in average exit velocity than Torres, who gained 3.3 mph from the previous season. The 2023 season could bring a return of 2019's power, and a long-awaited sequel to the Baby Bombers fun.

Jose Trevino C Born: 11/28/92 Age: 30 Bats: R Throws: R Height: 5'10" Weight: 215 lb. Origin: Round 6, 2014 Draft (#186 overall)

YEAR	TEAM	LVL	AGE	PA	R	2B	3B	HR	RBI	BB	K	SB	CS	Whiff%	AVG/OBP/SLG	DRC+	BABIP	BRR	DRP	WARP
2020	TEX	MLB	27	83	10	8	0	2	9	3	15	0	0	20.2%	.250/.280/.434	99	.279	0.3	C(21): 2.7	0.6
2021	TEX	MLB	28	302	23	14	0	5	30	12	57	1	1	22.6%	.239/.267/.340	84	.279	-1.6	C(88): 14.5	2.0
2022	NYY	MLB	29	353	39	12	1	11	43	15	62	2	1	21.2%	.248/.283/.388	99	.274	0.5	C(112): 20.3	3.5
2023 DC	*NYY*	*MLB*	*30*	*313*	*30*	*12*	*0*	*8*	*31*	*14*	*55*	*2*	*0*	*21.2%*	*.239/.278/.368*	*79*	*.268*	*0.2*	*C 12*	*1.7*

Comparables: Toby Hall (68), Kevin Plawecki (63), Ryan Hanigan (57)

YEAR	TEAM	P. COUNT	FRM RUNS	BLK RUNS	THRW RUNS	TOT RUNS
2020	TEX	2650	2.1	0.0	0.6	2.7
2021	TEX	12070	14.3	0.1	0.3	14.7
2022	NYY	13074	18.5	0.5	1.4	20.4
2023	*NYY*	*12025*	*10.8*	*0.4*	*-0.2*	*11.0*

When the Yankees traded away incumbent catcher Gary Sánchez prior to the start of last season, they didn't have a successor lined up and were looking for someone to step up and take hold of the starting job. Ben Rortvedt, acquired as part of the package for Sánchez, and longtime backup Kyle Higashioka were on the roster throughout spring training, but Rortvedt's oblique injury severely depleted an already questionable platoon. Enter Trevino, who was acquired a week before the start of the regular season. Known as a glove-first catcher, he did more than enough with the bat in the first half of the season, maintaining a .300 average as late as June 14 and earning his first career All-Star nod. The main story was Trevino's defense: his 22.2 Fielding Runs Above Average was the best of any player in the majors last year, contributing to his being one of the league's most valuable catchers. His efforts behind the plate netted him the AL Platinum Glove Award for 2022. By all accounts, Trevino is beloved in the clubhouse, and coming off of last year's breakout it stands to reason that he'll solve the Bronx's backstop problem for a little while.

★ ★ ★ *2023 Top 101 Prospect* **#7** ★ ★ ★

Anthony Volpe SS Born: 04/28/01 Age: 22 Bats: R Throws: R Height: 5'11" Weight: 180 lb. Origin: Round 1, 2019 Draft (#30 overall)

YEAR	TEAM	LVL	AGE	PA	R	2B	3B	HR	RBI	BB	K	SB	CS	Whiff%	AVG/OBP/SLG	DRC+	BABIP	BRR	DRP	WARP
2021	TAM	A	20	257	56	18	5	12	49	51	43	21	5		.302/.455/.623	153	.331	0.4	SS(40): -1.2, 3B(3): -0.3, 2B(1): 0.1	2.3
2021	HV	A+	20	256	57	17	1	15	37	27	58	12	4		.286/.391/.587	132	.319	0.8	SS(45): 0.8, 2B(1): -0.1	1.9
2022	SOM	AA	21	497	71	31	4	18	60	57	88	44	6		.251/.348/.472	123	.272	-2.2	SS(106): -1.7	2.5
2022	SWB	AAA	21	99	15	4	1	3	5	8	30	6	1		.236/.313/.404	87	.321	0.2	SS(21): -1.1	0.1
2023 DC	*NYY*	*MLB*	*22*	*265*	*28*	*12*	*1*	*7*	*26*	*23*	*58*	*13*	*3*	*23.6%*	*.222/.301/.385*	*93*	*.262*	*6.6*	*2B 0, SS 0*	*1.3*

Comparables: Brendan Rodgers (56), J.P. Crawford (54), Jorge Polanco (50)

Whether Volpe breaks in as a shortstop or moves to second base, he has a chance to make an impact with the big-league club in the imminent future. He started the season slow, but hit for a .895 OPS over his last 81 games with Double-A Somerset, earning a promotion to Triple-A Scranton/Wilkes-Barre for September. The Yankees love everything about Volpe and have made it clear over the past year that he's as close to untouchable as anybody from their farm system. Beyond the on-field results he's shown, Volpe's long been praised for his make-up and, despite always being one of the among the younger players at his level, is considered a leader in the clubhouse.

Austin Wells C Born: 07/12/99 Age: 23 Bats: L Throws: R Height: 6'2" Weight: 220 lb. Origin: Round 1, 2020 Draft (#28 overall)

YEAR	TEAM	LVL	AGE	PA	R	2B	3B	HR	RBI	BB	K	SB	CS	Whiff%	AVG/OBP/SLG	DRC+	BABIP	BRR	DRP	WARP
2021	SUR	WIN	21	79	14	5	2	2	18	13	16	1	0		.344/.456/.578		.426			
2021	TAM	A	21	299	61	17	4	9	54	51	62	11	0		.258/.398/.479	122	.306	-1.6	C(47): 0.4	1.5
2021	HV	A+	21	170	21	6	1	7	22	20	55	5	0		.274/.376/.473	97	.393	0.4	C(23): 4.4	0.9
2022	TAM	A	22	34	5	2	0	2	6	8	5	0	0	28.6%	.231/.412/.538	127	.211	-0.4	C(6): 0.7	0.3
2022	HV	A+	22	121	21	7	0	6	16	19	27	9	0		.323/.429/.576	131	.388	-0.5	C(21): 5.7	1.4
2022	SOM	AA	22	247	34	8	1	12	43	29	58	7	0		.261/.360/.479	103	.301	-0.8	C(38): 3.9	1.1
2023 non-DC	*NYY*	*MLB*	*23*	*251*	*25*	*10*	*1*	*6*	*26*	*24*	*67*	*4*	*0*	*29.6%*	*.225/.309/.372*	*89*	*.293*	*2.8*	*C 0*	*0.9*

Comparables: Seth Beer (62), Carlos Santana (59), Luis Exposito (59)

YEAR	TEAM	P. COUNT	FRM RUNS	BLK RUNS	THRW RUNS	TOT RUNS
2021	TAM	6825	-0.9	-0.5	1.5	0.2
2021	HV	3205	3.5	-0.3	0.5	3.8
2022	HV	3208	4.9	0.0	1.0	5.8
2022	SOM	5561	4.1	0.1	0.0	4.3
2023	*NYY*	*6956*	*2.0*	*-0.2*	*-0.2*	*1.6*

On the offensive side, Wells has a smooth, lefty swing that's resulted in solid power numbers, which he combines with good plate discipline. While Wells' defensive game has had its doubters in the industry, there's tangible evidence that he's doing just fine. Wells began a weighted-ball program in 2021 to increase his arm strength, which in turn resulted in a jump in caught stealing percentage from 13% in 2021 to 25% in 2022. Additionally, Wells' 9.4 framing runs in 2022 was 14th-highest among all minor-league catchers last year. If Wells can make the eye hold as he climbs the levels, and if the new workout regimen provides more than a one-year uptick, it's not out of the question that he could feature in a platoon with Jose Trevino.

Pitchers

Albert Abreu RHP
Born: 09/26/95 Age: 27 Bats: R Throws: R Height: 6'2" Weight: 190 lb. Origin: International Free Agent, 2013

YEAR	TEAM	LVL	AGE	W	L	SV	G	GS	IP	H	HR	BB/9	K/9	K	GB%	BABIP	WHIP	ERA	DRA-	WARP	MPH	FB%	Whiff%	CSP
2020	NYY	MLB	24	0	1	0	2	0	1^{1}	4	1	13.5	13.5	2	33.3%	.600	4.50	20.25	156	0.0	96.7	51.2%	33.3%	40.9%
2021	SWB	AAA	25	1	0	2	10	0	16^{2}	10	0	5.9	16.7	31	48.3%	.345	1.26	3.78	69	0.5				
2021	NYY	MLB	25	2	0	1	28	0	36^{2}	27	8	4.7	8.6	35	45.5%	.209	1.25	5.15	116	0.0	98.0	49.1%	26.8%	51.7%
2022	TEX	MLB	26	0	0	0	7	0	8^{2}	4	2	12.5	9.3	9	55.0%	.111	1.85	3.12	105	0.1	97.8	55.1%	30.1%	44.4%
2022	KC	MLB	26	0	0	0	4	0	4^{1}	6	1	8.3	6.2	3	64.3%	.385	2.31	4.15	80	0.1	97.7	57.1%	24.2%	54.8%
2022	NYY	MLB	26	2	2	0	22	0	25^{2}	25	2	2.1	9.1	26	49.3%	.319	1.21	3.16	89	0.4	98.7	63.6%	26.5%	53.8%
2023 DC	*NYY*	*MLB*	*27*	*1*	*1*	*0*	*31*	*0*	*27.3*	*25*	*3*	*5.0*	*8.6*	*26*	*47.8%*	*.294*	*1.50*	*4.53*	*109*	*0.0*	*98.3*	*55.9%*	*27.5%*	*51.4%*

Comparables: Austin Brice (64), Travis Lakins Sr. (64), Michael Blazek (63)

When the Yankees re-acquired Abreu last June, they were convinced that they could fix his approach and get him to finally throw the ball over the plate, a talent that has eluded him throughout his professional career. His control issues were particularly pronounced while he was bouncing around to Texas and Kansas City in the first half of 2022; of course, Abreu had spent the previous five seasons in the Yankees organization, and cited his comfort level with the organization upon his return. To his and the Yankees' credit, Abreu actually did look like a different pitcher when he came back, limiting walks like he's never done before while still striking out over a batter per inning. Home cooking tastes great your first evening back; we'll see if he gets tired of it, or if its medicinal effects carry on.

Clayton Beeter RHP
Born: 10/09/98 Age: 24 Bats: R Throws: R Height: 6'2" Weight: 220 lb. Origin: Round 2, 2020 Draft (#66 overall)

YEAR	TEAM	LVL	AGE	W	L	SV	G	GS	IP	H	HR	BB/9	K/9	K	GB%	BABIP	WHIP	ERA	DRA-	WARP	MPH	FB%	Whiff%	CSP
2021	GL	A+	22	0	4	0	23	22	37^{1}	28	3	3.6	13.3	55	36.7%	.333	1.15	3.13	71	1.0				
2021	TUL	AA	22	0	2	0	5	5	15	10	2	4.2	13.8	23	53.3%	.286	1.13	4.20	71	0.3				
2022	TUL	AA	23	0	3	0	18	16	51^{2}	48	10	6.1	15.3	88	39.8%	.352	1.61	5.75	60	1.5				
2022	SOM	AA	23	0	0	0	7	7	25^{1}	16	1	3.9	14.6	41	46.2%	.306	1.07	2.13	72	0.7				
2023 non-DC	*NYY*	*MLB*	*24*	*2*	*2*	*0*	*57*	*0*	*50*	*42*	*6*	*5.5*	*11.3*	*62*	*41.9%*	*.298*	*1.46*	*4.39*	*104*	*0.1*			*30.0%*	

Comparables: Bryan Abreu (69), Ryan Searle (69), Vince Velasquez (67)

Beeter came over to the Yankees as the return for Joey Gallo last August, and he's acclimated himself nicely to his new organization so far, having assuaged—at least temporarily—the walk and homer concerns that have plagued him throughout his young professional career. He's slowly getting stretched out into a traditional starting pitcher's role; with the Dodgers' organization, he would generally face around 15 batters in his starts, and by the end of the year in the Yankees' system he was up to four or five innings with a longer leash. He seems to love his breaking ball—which is generally in the low- to mid-80s with a vertical curveball shape—and throws it about half the time.

Gerrit Cole RHP
Born: 09/08/90 Age: 32 Bats: R Throws: R Height: 6'4" Weight: 220 lb. Origin: Round 1, 2011 Draft (#1 overall)

YEAR	TEAM	LVL	AGE	W	L	SV	G	GS	IP	H	HR	BB/9	K/9	K	GB%	BABIP	WHIP	ERA	DRA-	WARP	MPH	FB%	Whiff%	CSP
2020	NYY	MLB	29	7	3	0	12	12	73	53	14	2.1	11.6	94	37.1%	.242	0.96	2.84	75	1.8	97.0	52.8%	34.2%	47.3%
2021	NYY	MLB	30	16	8	0	30	30	181^{1}	151	24	2.0	12.1	243	42.5%	.305	1.06	3.23	71	4.5	97.8	48.0%	31.9%	53.6%
2022	NYY	MLB	31	13	8	0	33	33	200^{2}	154	33	2.2	11.5	257	42.0%	.269	1.02	3.50	70	5.0	97.7	57.3%	34.0%	52.6%
2023 DC	*NYY*	*MLB*	*32*	*12*	*7*	*0*	*29*	*29*	*177.7*	*141*	*19*	*2.3*	*11.8*	*233*	*41.5%*	*.296*	*1.04*	*2.28*	*62*	*4.9*	*97.6*	*53.5%*	*32.2%*	*52.0%*

Comparables: John Smoltz (84), Stephen Strasburg (84), Chris Sale (83)

When batters swung at Cole's fastball last year, they missed on 28.9% of their attempts. Among last year's starting pitchers, that puts Cole's heater in the 95th percentile. When they *didn't* miss, though, that was a whole other story. Cole's fastball got torched for a .659 slugging-on-contact rate, which puts him all the way down in the 10th percentile for opposition's contact quality. And that disparity is a good reflection of the Cole narrative: so many games in which he looked like a dominant ace ended up overshadowed by that *one bad pitch*, leading to a career high and league-most 33 home runs allowed on the season.

To try to help his contact-quality issues and get some quick outs early in the count, Cole experimented with a cutter for the first few months of the season, but never seemed to have full confidence in the pitch and shelved it by the end of July. So, this is pretty much who Cole is going to be: the Yankees still regard him as their ace, and make no mistake, he's more than capable of going out and looking the part (let's not forget, he did break Ron Guidry's long-standing team record for strikeouts in a season). But, in case you haven't noticed, Yankees fans are a demanding bunch, and Cole's susceptibility to loud contact could lead to loudening grumbles.

Nestor Cortes LHP

Born: 12/10/94 Age: 28 Bats: R Throws: L Height: 5'11" Weight: 210 lb. Origin: Round 36, 2013 Draft (#1094 overall)

YEAR	TEAM	LVL	AGE	W	L	SV	G	GS	IP	H	HR	BB/9	K/9	K	GB%	BABIP	WHIP	ERA	DRA-	WARP	MPH	FB%	Whiff%	CSP
2020	SEA	MLB	25	0	1	0	5	1	7^{2}	12	6	7.0	9.4	8	35.7%	.286	2.35	15.26	136	-0.1	88.4	40.6%	20.3%	47.6%
2021	SWB	AAA	26	1	1	1	5	1	15	8	1	0.6	10.8	18	37.5%	.226	0.60	1.20	90	0.3				
2021	NYY	MLB	26	2	3	0	22	14	93	75	14	2.4	10.0	103	27.9%	.266	1.08	2.90	99	0.9	89.9	70.3%	23.8%	53.6%
2022	NYY	MLB	27	12	4	0	28	28	158^{1}	108	16	2.2	9.3	163	34.2%	.232	0.92	2.44	87	2.6	91.9	46.7%	24.4%	55.3%
2023 DC	*NYY*	*MLB*	*28*	*9*	*8*	*0*	*27*	*27*	*156.7*	*136*	*22*	*2.6*	*9.3*	*161*	*33.8%*	*.276*	*1.16*	*3.11*	*85*	*2.3*	*91.1*	*53.7%*	*24.4%*	*54.1%*

Comparables: Rafael Montero (41), Caleb Smith (41), Blake Snell (40)

We can talk about the funky arm angles or delivery hitches all day long, but the bottom line is that Cortes has the fourth-best ERA among major-league starting pitchers since 2021, and—spoiler alert—it's not because of the goofy wind-ups. In fact, focusing so heavily on his occasional theatrics on the mound undersells the aspects of his craft that he's worked so hard in recent years to improve. Remember, for much of his professional career, Cortes was considered to be nothing more than an organizational player and was outrighted or DFA'd three times between 2018 and 2020 (including by an Orioles team that went on to lose 115 games). Manager Aaron Boone has specifically cited how Cortes' improved conditioning and physical fitness has helped him improve on the mound; in addition, Cortes has made substantial changes to his pitch shapes over the past few seasons that have enabled him to get a more satisfactory movement profile. That includes a tweak of the grip he uses for his fastball, which now gets some of the most backspin of any four-seamer in the league. And it's not like he's Jamie Moyer out there: he's steadily improved his velocity and now can reach back for 95 mph when he wants to. He might do it in an unorthodox (read: awesome) manner, but Cortes has become one of the league's most successful starting pitchers and deserves a world of credit for making the necessary changes to revitalize his career.

Tyler Danish RHP

Born: 09/12/94 Age: 28 Bats: R Throws: R Height: 6'0" Weight: 200 lb. Origin: Round 2, 2013 Draft (#55 overall)

YEAR	TEAM	LVL	AGE	W	L	SV	G	GS	IP	H	HR	BB/9	K/9	K	GB%	BABIP	WHIP	ERA	DRA-	WARP	MPH	FB%	Whiff%	CSP
2021	RCT	AA	26	1	0	1	3	0	10	4	1	0.0	10.8	12	59.1%	.143	0.40	0.90	95	0.1				
2021	SL	AAA	26	4	3	0	29	3	60^{1}	68	9	2.2	10.0	67	46.3%	.355	1.38	4.33	96	0.4				
2022	WOR	AAA	27	0	0	0	6	0	6^{1}	8	0	4.3	12.8	9	46.7%	.533	1.74	5.68	90	0.1				
2022	BOS	MLB	27	3	1	0	32	0	40^{1}	40	7	2.7	7.1	32	48.8%	.280	1.29	5.13	106	0.3	91.1	44.0%	19.0%	52.4%
2023 DC	*FA*	*MLB*	*28*	*2*	*2*	*0*	*43*	*0*	*37.3*	*40*	*4*	*3.2*	*7.3*	*30*	*47.3%*	*.315*	*1.43*	*4.66*	*114*	*-0.1*	*91.1*	*44.0%*	*24.0%*	*52.4%*

Comparables: Michael Bowden (39), Collin Balester (36), Jordan Lyles (36)

It's a good bet that somewhere in Chaim Bloom's office lies a needlepoint of the proverb, "*One man's trash is another man's treasure.*" But while dumpster diving can occasionally turn up something tasty, Danish was staler than day-old bread. Tossed out by the Angels—a bad sign to begin with—the righty arrived in Boston with a pedestrian arsenal led by a sinker that neither zips nor zags. His three-quarters delivery can occasionally make a batter look foolish, and his curveball gets some awkward swings. He offers little else, though, and any hopes Boston had of unlocking something more never materialized. The world doesn't want for right-handed middle relievers with subpar stuff, but, as the Red Sox just learned, it's tough to build a whole bullpen out of them. Fortunately the Yankees—who signed Danish to a minor-league contract this winter—shouldn't have to.

Scott Effross RHP

Born: 12/28/93 Age: 29 Bats: R Throws: R Height: 6'2" Weight: 202 lb. Origin: Round 15, 2015 Draft (#443 overall)

YEAR	TEAM	LVL	AGE	W	L	SV	G	GS	IP	H	HR	BB/9	K/9	K	GB%	BABIP	WHIP	ERA	DRA-	WARP	MPH	FB%	Whiff%	CSP
2021	TNS	AA	27	3	0	0	8	0	18^{2}	16	2	2.4	9.6	20	50.0%	.292	1.13	2.89	96	0.2				
2021	IOW	AAA	27	4	2	2	23	2	42	28	6	2.1	9.9	46	57.8%	.232	0.90	3.64	85	0.9				
2021	CHC	MLB	27	2	1	0	14	0	14^{2}	13	2	0.6	11.0	18	47.2%	.324	0.95	3.68	82	0.3	90.9	59.5%	30.0%	55.4%
2022	CHC	MLB	28	1	4	1	47	1	44	36	2	2.3	10.2	50	44.8%	.301	1.07	2.66	81	0.9	90.5	45.4%	23.7%	51.7%
2022	NYY	MLB	28	0	0	3	13	0	12^{2}	9	1	2.8	8.5	12	41.2%	.242	1.03	2.13	97	0.1	90.9	44.0%	24.7%	54.7%
2023 non-DC	*NYY*	*MLB*	*29*	*2*	*2*	*0*	*57*	*0*	*50*	*47*	*6*	*2.5*	*8.1*	*44*	*47.2%*	*.291*	*1.23*	*3.54*	*94*	*0.4*	*90.7*	*47.5%*	*24.1%*	*52.9%*

Comparables: Pedro Báez (65), Rob Wooten (63), John Brebbia (62)

The Yankees took a risk when they sent a nearly MLB-ready pitching prospect, Hayden Wesneski, to the Cubs in a one-for-one swap for Effross, a late-bloomer who was still a rookie despite being in his age-28 season. The Cubs weren't going anywhere last year and Effross had been great, so it made sense for the Yankees to bolster their bullpen. Even though Effross impressed when he was on the mound and was immediately entrusted with high-leverage innings, it's hard to imagine the trade looking worse for New York right now. Wesneski was excellent for the South Siders in a 33-inning cameo, and Effross missed much of September with a shoulder strain before succumbing to an even more serious elbow injury that required Tommy John surgery. The guy brought on to provide quick help won't pitch until late in the 2023 season, on the optimistic side.

Deivi García RHP

Born: 05/19/99 Age: 24 Bats: R Throws: R Height: 5'9" Weight: 163 lb. Origin: International Free Agent, 2015

YEAR	TEAM	LVL	AGE	W	L	SV	G	GS	IP	H	HR	BB/9	K/9	K	GB%	BABIP	WHIP	ERA	DRA-	WARP	MPH	FB%	Whiff%	CSP
2020	NYY	MLB	21	3	2	0	6	6	34^{1}	35	6	1.6	8.7	33	34.0%	.293	1.19	4.98	111	0.2	92.0	59.6%	22.8%	50.2%
2021	SWB	AAA	22	3	7	0	24	22	90^{2}	102	21	6.8	9.6	97	29.9%	.333	1.88	6.85	119	0.4				
2021	NYY	MLB	22	0	2	0	2	2	8^{1}	8	1	4.3	7.6	7	23.1%	.280	1.44	6.48	149	-0.1	92.2	41.2%	28.4%	54.3%
2022	SOM	AA	23	2	1	0	6	6	26^{2}	20	6	2.7	12.5	37	45.5%	.233	1.05	5.40	81	0.6				
2022	SWB	AAA	23	2	4	0	14	7	37^{1}	40	7	5.8	9.4	39	27.5%	.324	1.71	7.96	130	-0.1				
2023 DC	*NYY*	*MLB*	*24*	*2*	*2*	*0*	*22*	*3*	*30*	*33*	*5*	*4.9*	*8.5*	*28*	*34.6%*	*.317*	*1.66*	*6.12*	*140*	*-0.4*	*92.1*	*54.0%*	*27.5%*	*51.4%*

Comparables: Tyler Chatwood (47), Jacob Turner (44), Drew Hutchison (41)

The fall from grace has been swift for García. He's gone from starting a playoff game as recently as October 2020 to spending just one day on the major-league roster without getting into a game two years later. García has overhauled his pitch mix and shapes, most calamitously switching up his arm angle in an effort to modify his slider. An exciting young starter can become a dull normal-aged washout in no time.

Domingo Germán RHP

Born: 08/04/92 Age: 30 Bats: R Throws: R Height: 6'2" Weight: 181 lb. Origin: International Free Agent, 2009

YEAR	TEAM	LVL	AGE	W	L	SV	G	GS	IP	H	HR	BB/9	K/9	K	GB%	BABIP	WHIP	ERA	DRA-	WARP	MPH	FB%	Whiff%	CSP
2021	NYY	MLB	28	4	5	0	22	18	98^{1}	89	17	2.5	9.0	98	42.8%	.271	1.18	4.58	95	1.2	93.5	43.7%	30.5%	51.7%
2022	SOM	AA	29	0	0	0	2	2	7^{1}	4	0	0.0	7.4	6	52.6%	.211	0.55	1.23	98	0.1				
2022	SWB	AAA	29	1	0	0	2	2	10	4	0	0.9	4.5	5	55.6%	.148	0.50	0.00	104	0.1				
2022	NYY	MLB	29	2	5	0	15	14	72^{1}	65	11	2.4	7.2	58	40.1%	.262	1.16	3.61	108	0.4	92.7	39.4%	24.4%	56.8%
2023 DC	*NYY*	*MLB*	*30*	*8*	*7*	*0*	*52*	*14*	*105.7*	*104*	*14*	*2.5*	*7.7*	*90*	*42.4%*	*.290*	*1.26*	*3.77*	*100*	*0.9*	*93.2*	*42.3%*	*26.2%*	*53.0%*

Comparables: Anthony DeSclafani (55), Mike Clevinger (55), Bud Norris (54)

He doesn't throw very hard anymore and doesn't strike many guys out anymore, and there's nothing particularly interesting going on in Germán's batted ball profile either (lots of fly balls and a fair amount of hard contact). That being said, when the Yankees were missing Luis Severino due to a lat injury, Germán stepped up and got outs. He's a strike-thrower and was often able to make quick work of batters: his 14.9 pitches per inning was 12th-lowest mark in the league last year, and while that isn't necessarily a repeatable or predictive stat, it provides an excuse to list the names of the far more notable pitchers directly ahead of him on that list: Kershaw, deGrom, McKenzie, McClanahan, Nola, Verlander, Scherzer. With Carlos Rodón joining the club, his rotation status is in jeopardy.

Luis Gil RHP

Born: 06/03/98 Age: 25 Bats: R Throws: R Height: 6'2" Weight: 185 lb. Origin: International Free Agent, 2015

YEAR	TEAM	LVL	AGE	W	L	SV	G	GS	IP	H	HR	BB/9	K/9	K	GB%	BABIP	WHIP	ERA	DRA-	WARP	MPH	FB%	Whiff%	CSP
2021	SOM	AA	23	1	1	0	7	7	30^{2}	24	2	3.8	14.7	50	29.9%	.338	1.21	2.64	80	0.6				
2021	SWB	AAA	23	4	0	1	13	10	48^{2}	35	7	5.9	12.4	67	29.1%	.275	1.38	4.81	84	1.1				
2021	NYY	MLB	23	1	1	0	6	6	29^{1}	20	4	5.8	11.7	38	32.4%	.239	1.33	3.07	100	0.3	96.2	53.4%	31.0%	51.3%
2022	SWB	AAA	24	0	3	0	6	6	21^{2}	21	6	6.2	12.9	31	26.3%	.294	1.66	7.89	104	0.2				
2022	NYY	MLB	24	0	0	0	1	1	4	5	0	4.5	11.3	5	41.7%	.417	1.75	9.00	99	0.0	97.3	59.0%	37.0%	47.8%
2023 non-DC	*NYY*	*MLB*	*25*	*2*	*2*	*0*	*57*	*0*	*50*	*42*	*7*	*5.7*	*11.1*	*61*	*35.1%*	*.292*	*1.48*	*4.48*	*107*	*0.0*	*96.4*	*54.4%*	*30.8%*	*50.7%*

Comparables: Jarred Cosart (63), Chris Archer (61), Jake Faria (59)

"Fastball shape" is a hot term in pitching analysis these days, and Gil's got a good one. The fastballs that are hardest to hit are often those that contain some combination of good velocity, good backspin and a flat angle on their way to home plate. Among fastballs thrown at least 300 times since 2021 and that averaged a 4.5 vertical approach angle or lower—Gil's is at 4.3—the list of pitchers with more velocity and more backspin on their fastballs than Gil possesses is very short: Spencer Strider, Liam Hendriks, Gerrit Cole and, uh, Matt Bush. Basically, Gil's fastball possesses the characteristics often associated with elite heaters, and just that pitch alone makes him look the part of, at the very least, a good late-innings reliever. The elephant in the room: Gil has been on the shelf since last May due to an elbow injury that resulted in Tommy John surgery, so he won't be a factor until at least the second half of 2023. Assuming he's able to come back healthy down the stretch, expect to see his explosive fastball play an important role in the big-league bullpen.

Chad Green RHP

Born: 05/24/91 Age: 32 Bats: L Throws: R Height: 6'3" Weight: 215 lb. Origin: Round 11, 2013 Draft (#336 overall)

YEAR	TEAM	LVL	AGE	W	L	SV	G	GS	IP	H	HR	BB/9	K/9	K	GB%	BABIP	WHIP	ERA	DRA-	WARP	MPH	FB%	Whiff%	CSP
2020	NYY	MLB	29	3	3	1	22	0	25^{2}	13	5	2.8	11.2	32	41.7%	.148	0.82	3.51	82	0.5	95.6	75.1%	31.4%	51.8%
2021	NYY	MLB	30	10	7	6	67	0	83^{2}	57	14	1.8	10.6	99	27.1%	.234	0.88	3.12	86	1.4	95.8	65.5%	32.1%	56.2%
2022	NYY	MLB	31	1	1	1	14	0	15	13	1	3.0	9.6	16	25.0%	.308	1.20	3.00	101	0.1	94.9	63.9%	26.8%	58.3%
2023 DC	*FA*	*MLB*	*32*	*0*	*0*	*0*	*14*	*0*	*12.3*	*10*	*1*	*2.7*	*10.3*	*14*	*31.6%*	*.287*	*1.16*	*3.24*	*86*	*0.1*	*95.8*	*68.6%*	*29.1%*	*54.9%*

Comparables: Liam Hendriks (63), Tommy Hunter (61), Adam Ottavino (59)

From 2017-2021, only five relief pitchers threw more innings than Green, who always took a back seat to the bigger names in the Yankees bullpen but consistently provided steady and reliable results in the later innings. In his final season before his inaugural foray into free agency, Green blew out his elbow on a pickoff throw—yes, a pickoff throw—in a game against the Orioles in May. It's a cruel world out there, and it ain't easy bein' ... a reliever.

Clay Holmes RHP

Born: 03/27/93 Age: 30 Bats: R Throws: R Height: 6'5" Weight: 245 lb. Origin: Round 9, 2011 Draft (#272 overall)

YEAR	TEAM	LVL	AGE	W	L	SV	G	GS	IP	H	HR	BB/9	K/9	K	GB%	BABIP	WHIP	ERA	DRA-	WARP	MPH	FB%	Whiff%	CSP
2020	PIT	MLB	27	0	0	0	1	0	1^{1}	2	0	0.0	6.7	1	60.0%	.400	1.50	0.00	109	0.0	92.6	31.8%	44.4%	36.5%
2021	PIT	MLB	28	3	2	0	44	0	42	35	3	5.4	9.4	44	70.7%	.286	1.43	4.93	98	0.4	96.1	51.2%	27.7%	55.4%
2021	NYY	MLB	28	5	2	0	25	0	28	18	2	1.3	10.9	34	61.5%	.254	0.79	1.61	77	0.6	96.5	73.2%	28.3%	58.0%
2022	NYY	MLB	29	7	4	20	62	0	63^{2}	45	2	2.8	9.2	65	77.0%	.264	1.02	2.54	87	1.0	97.1	80.1%	29.8%	54.1%
2023 DC	*NYY*	*MLB*	*30*	*2*	*2*	*33*	*57*	*0*	*49.3*	*47*	*3*	*3.9*	*9.9*	*54*	*67.5%*	*.321*	*1.39*	*3.91*	*96*	*0.3*	*96.4*	*69.3%*	*28.4%*	*54.0%*

Comparables: Justin Grimm (59), Matt Barnes (58), Alex Colomé (58)

The short story is that Holmes has been an utter revelation since the July 2021 trade that sent him from the Pirates to the Yankees, striking out more batters, walking fewer and throwing his trademark sinker substantially harder in New York than he did during his Pirates career. The improved control is particularly notable, and Holmes claims that it primarily stems from a mechanical tweak that took place prior to the trade—though his new team is obviously the one to reap the benefits. The longer and more complicated story is that 2022 was something of a tale of two seasons for Holmes. Through his first 32 innings last year, his ERA sat at an absurd 0.28; he'd set the franchise record for consecutive scoreless innings, at 31⅓, and walked just three batters while doing so. From that point on, though, he showed glimpses of the control issues that plagued him in Pittsburgh: His walk rate shot up to nearly 12%, and his ERA ballooned to 4.83. A back injury in August and a rotator cuff strain that prematurely ended his regular season were cause for some more concern, though he did end up healthy enough to pitch in the postseason.

Tommy Kahnle RHP

Born: 08/07/89 Age: 33 Bats: R Throws: R Height: 6'1" Weight: 230 lb. Origin: Round 5, 2010 Draft (#175 overall)

YEAR	TEAM	LVL	AGE	W	L	SV	G	GS	IP	H	HR	BB/9	K/9	K	GB%	BABIP	WHIP	ERA	DRA-	WARP	MPH	FB%	Whiff%	CSP
2020	NYY	MLB	30	0	0	0	1	0	1	1	0	9.0	27.0	3	100.0%	.500	2.00	0.00	78	0.0	97.7	35.0%	66.7%	61.0%
2022	OKC	AAA	32	1	0	0	10	0	9^{2}	8	2	2.8	9.3	10	48.1%	.240	1.14	3.72	91	0.1	95.5	39.2%	34.4%	
2022	LAD	MLB	32	0	0	1	13	0	12^{2}	5	2	2.1	9.9	14	65.4%	.125	0.63	2.84	86	0.2	95.5	23.0%	31.9%	58.3%
2023 DC	*NYY*	*MLB*	*33*	*2*	*2*	*0*	*57*	*0*	*49.3*	*45*	*5*	*3.1*	*10.4*	*57*	*48.8%*	*.307*	*1.26*	*3.52*	*90*	*0.5*	*96.2*	*35.3%*	*31.9%*	*51.7%*

Comparables: Brad Boxberger (56), Nick Vincent (55), Mark Melancon (55)

By its nature, a changeup is a variation on the theme of a fastball. What Kahnle throws can't technically be a changeup because it's the headliner rather than the supporting act. In September and October, he featured it nearly 80% of the time. No other pitcher in MLB dared even 60% changeup usage last season. Then again, hardly anyone can throw a 90-mph *cambio* for consistent strikes, inducing swings-and-misses in the strike zone and, on contact, a -14 degree average launch angle. He no longer resembles the fireballer the Yankees once employed, but the Dodgers are more of a come-as-you-are outfit and this edition of Kahnle is just as effective. All he needs is a good nickname for his bread-and-butter offering, because calling it a changeup doesn't do it justice.

Michael King RHP

Born: 05/25/95 Age: 28 Bats: R Throws: R Height: 6'3" Weight: 210 lb. Origin: Round 12, 2016 Draft (#353 overall)

YEAR	TEAM	LVL	AGE	W	L	SV	G	GS	IP	H	HR	BB/9	K/9	K	GB%	BABIP	WHIP	ERA	DRA-	WARP	MPH	FB%	Whiff%	CSP
2020	NYY	MLB	25	1	2	0	9	4	26^{2}	30	5	3.7	8.8	26	40.2%	.325	1.54	7.76	107	0.2	93.2	65.7%	21.3%	48.3%
2021	NYY	MLB	26	2	4	0	22	6	63^{1}	57	6	3.4	8.8	62	45.4%	.291	1.28	3.55	97	0.7	93.6	77.2%	24.9%	55.7%
2022	NYY	MLB	27	6	3	1	34	0	51	35	3	2.8	11.6	66	48.7%	.281	1.00	2.29	70	1.3	96.0	60.0%	36.4%	53.6%
2023 DC	*NYY*	*MLB*	*28*	*3*	*2*	*0*	*57*	*0*	*49.3*	*42*	*5*	*3.1*	*10.1*	*55*	*46.6%*	*.291*	*1.20*	*3.18*	*83*	*0.7*	*94.6*	*68.1%*	*29.7%*	*53.7%*

Comparables: Adam Warren (53), Alex Colomé (51), Andrew Miller (51)

In 2021, King finally found a reliable breaking ball (thanks to then-teammate Corey Kluber), and with a move to the bullpen he simplified his arsenal and picked up a few ticks on his heater. That set the stage for the version of King we saw over the first half of 2022: a bona-fide relief ace touching triple-digits and producing above-average whiff rates on all four of his pitches. An ability to pitch multiple innings out of the pen was a key component of King's game last year, given his recent history as a starter. Unfortunately, his season came to an abrupt halt the weekend after the All-Star break when he fractured his elbow while throwing a slider in a game against the Orioles. Fortunately, he avoided Tommy John surgery and could be back near the start of the season.

Matt Krook LHP

Born: 10/21/94 Age: 28 Bats: L Throws: L Height: 6'4" Weight: 225 lb. Origin: Round 4, 2016 Draft (#125 overall)

YEAR	TEAM	LVL	AGE	W	L	SV	G	GS	IP	H	HR	BB/9	K/9	K	GB%	BABIP	WHIP	ERA	DRA-	WARP	MPH	FB%	Whiff%	CSP
2021	SOM	AA	26	1	1	0	7	7	29^{1}	15	1	3.4	13.5	44	60.3%	.246	0.89	2.15	86	0.5				
2021	SWB	AAA	26	6	5	0	17	14	76^{2}	51	4	5.8	10.3	88	62.8%	.253	1.30	3.17	98	1.1				
2022	SWB	AAA	27	10	7	0	29	22	138^{2}	120	19	4.7	10.1	155	54.6%	.294	1.39	4.09	90	2.6				
2023 DC	*NYY*	*MLB*	*28*	*3*	*2*	*0*	*28*	*3*	*35*	*33*	*3*	*5.3*	*8.9*	*34*	*56.7%*	*.300*	*1.54*	*4.59*	*110*	*0.0*			*31.1%*	

Comparables: Wilmer Font (66), Gregory Infante (57), Fabian Williamson (56)

Krook's been a ground-ball fiend his entire career, and over his past two years at the minors' highest level he's had the highest Triple-A grounder rate, minimum 150 innings, at 58%. For good measure, Krook also set Scranton Wilkes-Barre's franchise record for strikeouts in a season. But despite that sought-after skill set of grounders and strikeouts, there are legitimate questions regarding his velocity and his continued struggle to throw the ball over the plate. The Yankees added him to the 40-man roster after the season, and perhaps a transition to a short relief role will be his ticket to the show.

Jonathan Loáisiga RHP Born: 11/02/94 Age: 28 Bats: R Throws: R Height: 5'11" Weight: 165 lb. Origin: International Free Agent, 2012

YEAR	TEAM	LVL	AGE	W	L	SV	G	GS	IP	H	HR	BB/9	K/9	K	GB%	BABIP	WHIP	ERA	DRA-	WARP	MPH	FB%	Whiff%	CSP
2020	NYY	MLB	25	3	0	0	12	3	23	21	3	2.7	8.6	22	51.5%	.290	1.22	3.52	87	0.4	96.9	67.3%	23.2%	49.9%
2021	NYY	MLB	26	9	4	5	57	0	70^{2}	56	3	2.0	8.8	69	60.5%	.279	1.02	2.17	79	1.4	98.4	58.8%	27.9%	53.0%
2022	NYY	MLB	27	2	3	2	50	0	48	43	3	3.6	6.9	37	59.2%	.278	1.29	4.13	107	0.3	98.2	64.4%	25.5%	49.4%
2023 DC	*NYY*	*MLB*	*28*	*2*	*2*	*9*	*57*	*0*	*49.3*	*53*	*4*	*3.3*	*8.4*	*46*	*55.6%*	*.327*	*1.44*	*4.24*	*105*	*0.1*	*98.0*	*61.7%*	*27.1%*	*50.6%*

Comparables: Justin Grimm (48), J.B. Wendelken (46), Michael Feliz (46)

No American League pitcher with a minimum of 100 innings pitched in the Pandemic Era has allowed a lower average exit velocity than Loáisiga, at 84.1 mph. His contact-management skills were on display even more prominently in the postseason, when he pitched in six games against the notoriously hard-to-whiff Guardians and Astros. He threw 9⅓ innings with just four strikeouts and looked utterly dominant doing so; the 30 balls in play he surrendered in the postseason had an average exit velo of just 75 mph. Loáisiga's season numbers look lackluster, but they were adversely affected by an early-season slump that coincided with a shoulder injury. After the All-Star break, he pitched to 1.82 ERA and a 2.88 FIP. The Yankees view him as one of the linchpins of their bullpen, and his performance down the stretch and in the playoffs marked a return to the form they believe he can sustain.

Ron Marinaccio RHP Born: 07/01/95 Age: 28 Bats: R Throws: R Height: 6'2" Weight: 205 lb. Origin: Round 19, 2017 Draft (#572 overall)

YEAR	TEAM	LVL	AGE	W	L	SV	G	GS	IP	H	HR	BB/9	K/9	K	GB%	BABIP	WHIP	ERA	DRA-	WARP	MPH	FB%	Whiff%	CSP
2021	SOM	AA	25	1	1	3	22	0	39^{2}	17	2	4.3	14.5	64	30.4%	.224	0.91	1.82	73	0.9				
2021	SWB	AAA	25	1	0	2	18	0	26^{2}	18	2	2.7	13.8	41	31.6%	.291	0.97	2.36	72	0.7				
2022	SWB	AAA	26	1	0	0	8	0	9^{2}	10	3	3.7	19.6	21	31.6%	.438	1.45	2.79	63	0.3				
2022	NYY	MLB	26	1	0	0	40	0	44	22	2	4.9	11.5	56	41.5%	.217	1.05	2.05	87	0.7	94.7	44.0%	33.3%	47.1%
2023 DC	*NYY*	*MLB*	*27*	*2*	*2*	*0*	*57*	*0*	*49.3*	*39*	*6*	*4.6*	*11.7*	*64*	*38.0%*	*.288*	*1.30*	*3.74*	*92*	*0.4*	*94.7*	*44.0%*	*34.0%*	*47.1%*

Comparables: Giovanny Gallegos (67), Vic Black (67), Dillon Maples (67)

There hasn't been a whole lot of fanfare around Marinaccio in his professional career, but after his velocity spiked while he trained at home during the canceled MiLB season, a path to the big leagues opened before him. The Yankees suggested that he throw more changeups, which they identified as a plus pitch. He took their advice and ran with it—his changeup was an elite pitch last year, with batters coming up empty on 41% of their swings against it while mustering just a .208 slugging rate when the pitch was put into play. Overall, Marinaccio threw his change for a strike over two-thirds of the time, and the sharp arm-side movement on the pitch made him a tough at-bat against lefties.

Frankie Montas RHP Born: 03/21/93 Age: 30 Bats: R Throws: R Height: 6'2" Weight: 255 lb. Origin: International Free Agent, 2009

YEAR	TEAM	LVL	AGE	W	L	SV	G	GS	IP	H	HR	BB/9	K/9	K	GB%	BABIP	WHIP	ERA	DRA-	WARP	MPH	FB%	Whiff%	CSP
2020	OAK	MLB	27	3	5	0	11	11	53	57	10	3.9	10.2	60	36.6%	.329	1.51	5.60	107	0.3	95.9	62.0%	28.9%	51.3%
2021	OAK	MLB	28	13	9	0	32	32	187	164	20	2.7	10.0	207	42.3%	.298	1.18	3.37	88	2.9	96.5	58.2%	29.7%	52.6%
2022	OAK	MLB	29	4	9	0	19	19	104^{2}	91	12	2.4	9.4	109	44.9%	.290	1.14	3.18	80	2.1	96.1	49.1%	28.0%	52.8%
2022	NYY	MLB	29	1	3	0	8	8	39^{2}	46	6	3.4	7.5	33	43.8%	.325	1.54	6.35	112	0.1	95.9	54.1%	26.8%	53.6%
2023 DC	*NYY*	*MLB*	*30*	*8*	*7*	*0*	*24*	*24*	*128.7*	*118*	*14*	*2.8*	*8.9*	*127*	*43.5%*	*.294*	*1.24*	*3.34*	*88*	*1.9*	*96.2*	*55.2%*	*27.4%*	*52.4%*

Comparables: Justin Masterson (73), Dave Goltz (71), Tyson Ross (70)

On paper, Montas seemed like a perfect fit for the Yankees, who'd been looking for a number-two power arm behind Gerrit Cole, but he was generally terrible for them after they sent a steep prospect package to Oakland for his services at the trade deadline. When he wasn't terrible, he was injured, as a shoulder issue—a recurrence of a similar injury he had in Oakland—kept him on the shelf for much of the last month of the season. The idea of a mighty arm in pinstripes may be a well-worn one, but some command is necessary as well. When Montas got to the Bronx, his BB/9 climbed by a full walk, and all those hard fastballs mostly ended up in locations that had Yankees fans pinching the bridges of their noses.

Wandy Peralta LHP Born: 07/27/91 Age: 31 Bats: L Throws: L Height: 6'0" Weight: 227 lb. Origin: International Free Agent, 2009

YEAR	TEAM	LVL	AGE	W	L	SV	G	GS	IP	H	HR	BB/9	K/9	K	GB%	BABIP	WHIP	ERA	DRA-	WARP	MPH	FB%	Whiff%	CSP
2020	SF	MLB	28	1	1	0	25	0	27^{1}	22	3	3.6	8.2	25	44.7%	.260	1.21	3.29	90	0.4	94.8	35.5%	28.9%	44.9%
2021	SF	MLB	29	2	1	2	10	0	8^{1}	11	1	3.2	8.6	8	53.8%	.400	1.68	5.40	105	0.1	96.3	38.1%	35.8%	54.4%
2021	NYY	MLB	29	3	3	3	46	1	42^{2}	38	5	3.8	7.4	35	57.0%	.268	1.31	2.95	111	0.1	95.1	37.5%	30.0%	48.0%
2022	NYY	MLB	30	3	4	4	56	0	56^{1}	42	2	2.7	7.5	47	53.2%	.260	1.05	2.72	96	0.7	95.6	41.8%	34.0%	48.8%
2023 DC	*NYY*	*MLB*	*31*	*2*	*2*	*4*	*57*	*0*	*49.3*	*51*	*5*	*3.4*	*8.0*	*44*	*52.4%*	*.312*	*1.41*	*4.09*	*103*	*0.1*	*95.4*	*39.2%*	*31.6%*	*47.9%*

Comparables: Sam Freeman (65), Xavier Cedeño (64), Dan Jennings (64)

Since being acquired in May 2021 in a one-for-one swap for outfielder Mike Tauchman, Magic Wandy garnered a reputation with the Yankees for being fearless in pressure situations, and by the end of last season was one of the few relievers that Aaron Boone seemed to trust in tight quarters. In fact, when Boone used him in all five games of their ALDS series against the Guardians, Peralta became the first pitcher ever to appear in every game of a division series. He's leaned hard on his power changeup since coming to the Bronx, and that pitch has helped him mitigate opposite-handed batters (3.28 FIP against righties last year).

Carlos Rodón LHP
Born: 12/10/92 Age: 30 Bats: L Throws: L Height: 6'3" Weight: 245 lb. Origin: Round 1, 2014 Draft (#3 overall)

YEAR	TEAM	LVL	AGE	W	L	SV	G	GS	IP	H	HR	BB/9	K/9	K	GB%	BABIP	WHIP	ERA	DRA-	WARP	MPH	FB%	Whiff%	CSP
2020	CHW	MLB	27	0	2	0	4	2	7^{2}	9	1	3.5	7.0	6	28.0%	.333	1.57	8.22	195	-0.2	93.2	51.1%	23.3%	49.7%
2021	CHW	MLB	28	13	5	0	24	24	132^{2}	91	13	2.4	12.6	185	37.5%	.271	0.96	2.37	69	3.4	95.7	58.6%	33.2%	54.2%
2022	SF	MLB	29	14	8	0	31	31	178	131	12	2.6	12.0	237	34.3%	.295	1.03	2.88	71	4.3	95.6	61.2%	31.3%	56.4%
2023 DC	*NYY*	*MLB*	*30*	*10*	*8*	*0*	*29*	*29*	*160.3*	*129*	*21*	*2.8*	*11.5*	*204*	*36.4%*	*.288*	*1.11*	*2.83*	*76*	*3.3*	*95.5*	*59.8%*	*30.4%*	*55.2%*

Comparables: Chris Sale (79), Tom Glavine (78), CC Sabathia (77)

As an organization, the White Sox have made a variety of head-scratching decisions over the past few years, but nothing puzzled as much as failing to extend a qualifying offer to Rodón after a breakout 2021 that saw him in Cy Young contention. Instead, the Sox gambled that other teams would be scared off by a late-season velocity dip from the oft-injured hurler. As a result, they received neither a compensatory pick nor the services of Rodón, who signed a two-year prove-it deal with San Francisco and spent the rest of the season shoving Chicago's pecuniary down their throats like so many Italian beef sandwiches.

The Giants encouraged Rodón to throw his fastball even higher in the zone, coming in even tighter on righties, allowing him to scrap his ineffective changeup entirely and focus instead on the curve, which he's now throwing harder (+3 mph) and with more drop, although he's still throwing it just five percent of the time. Agent Scott Boras, FBI's Most Wanted for Crimes Against Metaphor, made a tortured comparison to sculptor Auguste Rodin at the GM meetings, but there are no linguistic gymnastics required to understand what Rodón brings as a pitcher: a fastball-slider combo that's among the best in the bigs, and a renewed understanding of what it means to paint the corners.

Clarke Schmidt RHP
Born: 02/20/96 Age: 27 Bats: R Throws: R Height: 6'1" Weight: 200 lb. Origin: Round 1, 2017 Draft (#16 overall)

YEAR	TEAM	LVL	AGE	W	L	SV	G	GS	IP	H	HR	BB/9	K/9	K	GB%	BABIP	WHIP	ERA	DRA-	WARP	MPH	FB%	Whiff%	CSP
2020	NYY	MLB	24	0	1	0	3	1	6^{1}	7	0	7.1	9.9	7	42.1%	.368	1.89	7.11	119	0.0	95.0	54.0%	21.8%	49.7%
2021	SOM	AA	25	0	1	0	2	2	6^{1}	5	2	2.8	7.1	5	47.4%	.176	1.11	4.26	103	0.0				
2021	SWB	AAA	25	0	1	0	6	5	25^{2}	25	4	2.8	11.2	32	52.9%	.318	1.29	2.10	89	0.5				
2021	NYY	MLB	25	0	0	0	2	1	6^{1}	11	1	7.1	8.5	6	57.7%	.417	2.53	5.68	111	0.0	93.0	44.8%	18.6%	50.5%
2022	SWB	AAA	26	2	1	0	8	8	33	26	1	2.5	12.5	46	50.0%	.313	1.06	3.27	73	0.9				
2022	NYY	MLB	26	5	5	2	29	3	57^{2}	46	5	3.6	8.7	56	41.9%	.279	1.20	3.12	96	0.7	94.9	38.8%	26.9%	55.5%
2023 DC	*NYY*	*MLB*	*27*	*7*	*3*	*0*	*54*	*3*	*58*	*54*	*6*	*3.7*	*8.6*	*55*	*46.2%*	*.294*	*1.35*	*3.86*	*98*	*0.4*	*94.7*	*40.3%*	*27.5%*	*54.7%*

Comparables: Adam Warren (49), Tyler Thornburg (49), André Rienzo (48)

Schmidt's most frequently used pitch in 2022 was a hard, sweeping slider in the mid-80s—a pitch that he wasn't even throwing when he broke in with the Yankees a few years ago. It was quite an effective pitch, too, racking up a 41% whiff rate and allowing just a .178 batting average over the course of the regular season. However, Yankees fans are probably going to remember two of Schmidt's sliders in particular: the one that resulted in a walk-off single to Oscar Gonzalez in Game 3 of the ALDS, and the one that Yuli Gurriel hit in the 6th inning of Game 1 of the ALCS that would prove to be the difference in the game. Perhaps as a result, he'll go into spring training battling for the last spot in the bullpen.

Luis Serna RHP
Born: 07/20/04 Age: 18 Bats: R Throws: R Height: 5'11" Weight: 162 lb. Origin: International Free Agent, 2021

YEAR	TEAM	LVL	AGE	W	L	SV	G	GS	IP	H	HR	BB/9	K/9	K	GB%	BABIP	WHIP	ERA	DRA-	WARP	MPH	FB%	Whiff%	CSP
2021	DSL NYY1	ROK	16	1	5	0	12	11	40	25	0	3.8	10.4	46	54.1%	.258	1.05	2.25						
2022	YNK	ROK	17	0	0	0	11	10	41^{1}	33	0	3.7	12.2	56	45.7%	.351	1.21	1.96						
2023	*No projection*																							

If you've followed the Yankees/Red Sox rivalry throughout the 21st century, you probably remember that crazy game in the summer of 2004—you know, the one with the Alex Rodriguez/Jason Varitek brawl, the Bill Mueller walk-off against Mariano Rivera, and a momentum-shift narrative for the ages. Well, Luis Serna was born four days before that. Okay, maybe that means we're all getting old. But also, Serna was the second-youngest player to pitch in the Florida Complex League this year, and, if it helps at all, he's exuded maturity well beyond his years. Serna already features a four-pitch mix, with his calling card being a Bugs Bunny changeup that comes out like a screwball.

Luis Severino RHP
Born: 02/20/94 Age: 29 Bats: R Throws: R Height: 6'2" Weight: 218 lb. Origin: International Free Agent, 2011

YEAR	TEAM	LVL	AGE	W	L	SV	G	GS	IP	H	HR	BB/9	K/9	K	GB%	BABIP	WHIP	ERA	DRA-	WARP	MPH	FB%	Whiff%	CSP
2021	SOM	AA	27	0	0	0	2	2	6^{1}	2	1	1.4	12.8	9	50.0%	.091	0.47	2.84	97	0.1				
2021	NYY	MLB	27	1	0	0	4	0	6	2	0	1.5	12.0	8	41.7%	.167	0.50	0.00	93	0.1	95.2	43.9%	34.1%	47.9%
2022	NYY	MLB	28	7	3	0	19	19	102	72	14	2.6	9.9	112	43.6%	.239	1.00	3.18	78	2.1	96.4	49.2%	27.9%	55.7%
2023 DC	*NYY*	*MLB*	*29*	*8*	*6*	*0*	*24*	*24*	*133.3*	*107*	*13*	*2.9*	*10.4*	*155*	*43.9%*	*.284*	*1.13*	*2.63*	*71*	*2.9*	*96.4*	*49.2%*	*28.9%*	*55.1%*

Comparables: Andy Benes (72), Stephen Strasburg (72), Félix Hernández (71)

When the Yankees placed Severino on the 60-day injured list for a lat strain in July, he wasn't shy about his frustration with the team's decision. He felt that he would be ready to return after a short stint on the shelf, reiterating the point before his first game in September that he had been "anxious to get out there for 45 days." It's easy to empathize with Severino who, heading into the 2022 campaign, had thrown just 27⅔ major-league innings—postseason included—since the start of 2019, but it's also clear to see why the Yankees wanted to be cautious with him given how often injuries have kept him off the field. Lat injury aside, Severino looked a lot like the pitcher he was in 2017-2018, when he was one of the best in the league. His fastball was a tick down on average but still averaged over 96 mph and could reach back for triple digits when he needed to. Severino has also become less predictable since his return, showing some variation in his breaking ball shape and displaying increased confidence in his changeup, especially against same-handed batters: in 2022, 21% of his pitches to righties were changeups, while that mark stood at just under 10% from 2017-2018.

Lou Trivino RHP Born: 10/01/91 Age: 31 Bats: R Throws: R Height: 6'5" Weight: 235 lb. Origin: Round 11, 2013 Draft (#341 overall)

YEAR	TEAM	LVL	AGE	W	L	SV	G	GS	IP	H	HR	BB/9	K/9	K	GB%	BABIP	WHIP	ERA	DRA-	WARP	MPH	FB%	Whiff%	CSP
2020	OAK	MLB	28	0	0	0	20	0	23^{1}	16	3	3.9	10.0	26	40.4%	.241	1.11	3.86	94	0.3	95.6	58.8%	28.5%	45.5%
2021	OAK	MLB	29	7	8	22	71	0	73^{2}	58	5	4.2	8.2	67	47.5%	.269	1.25	3.18	101	0.7	95.9	60.7%	23.8%	53.4%
2022	OAK	MLB	30	1	6	10	39	0	32	46	5	3.9	12.7	45	50.0%	.451	1.88	6.47	75	0.7	95.8	53.0%	27.9%	51.4%
2022	NYY	MLB	30	1	2	1	25	0	21^{2}	18	1	4.2	9.1	22	50.8%	.293	1.29	1.66	99	0.2	95.9	38.9%	27.6%	51.4%
2023 DC	*NYY*	*MLB*	*31*	*2*	*2*	*0*	*57*	*0*	*49.3*	*47*	*5*	*4.0*	*9.1*	*50*	*47.1%*	*.306*	*1.41*	*4.09*	*101*	*0.2*	*96.1*	*54.0%*	*26.3%*	*51.1%*

Comparables: Brad Brach (69), Steve Cishek (69), Pedro Strop (66)

On May 23, when he was still a member of the Oakland Athletics, Trivino debuted a sweeping slider, eschewing the curveball he'd thrown throughout his career for a pitch that operated on a similar plane to his sinking two-seam fastball. From that point on until his trade to the Yankees, Trivino threw his new pitch 24% of the time; with the Yankees (postseason included), he kicked that rate up to 36% while also slashing the usage of his four-seamer in half. Essentially, Trivino simplified his repertoire and began to put a greater emphasis on the pitches with an "east/west" movement profile, something that the Yankees have become known for throughout their organization.

Randy Vasquez RHP Born: 11/03/98 Age: 24 Bats: R Throws: R Height: 6'0" Weight: 165 lb. Origin: International Free Agent, 2018

YEAR	TEAM	LVL	AGE	W	L	SV	G	GS	IP	H	HR	BB/9	K/9	K	GB%	BABIP	WHIP	ERA	DRA-	WARP	MPH	FB%	Whiff%	CSP
2021	TAM	A	22	3	3	0	13	11	50	35	2	4.1	10.4	58	54.7%	.262	1.16	2.34	80	1.1				
2021	HV	A+	22	3	0	0	6	6	36	33	0	2.0	13.3	53	65.9%	.393	1.14	1.75	75	0.8				
2021	SOM	AA	22	2	1	0	4	4	21^{1}	23	2	3.0	8.0	19	52.9%	.309	1.41	4.22	104	0.1				
2022	SOM	AA	23	2	7	0	25	25	115^{1}	106	11	3.2	9.4	120	47.1%	.304	1.27	3.90	95	1.8				
2023 DC	*NYY*	*MLB*	*24*	*0*	*0*	*0*	*3*	*3*	*13*	*13*	*1*	*4.1*	*8.1*	*11*	*50.3%*	*.307*	*1.47*	*4.46*	*110*	*0.0*			*24.3%*	

Comparables: Zach Hedges (79), Austin Voth (78), Jaron Long (77)

Vasquez's high-spin curveball has been well-known in scouting circles for years at this point, and when the results started to come together for him in 2021—including an utterly dominant six-start stretch during his time in Hudson Valley—it wasn't too hard to see him as somebody who would continue to shoot up through the system and make a run at a 2022 roster spot. To that end, it's also not too hard to see last year as a disappointment. He threw a lot more two-seam fastballs, and picked up a cutter in spring training—but counter to what those pitches are typically supposed to do, he got *fewer* groundballs than he had a year prior. While he still spins the heck out of his breaking ball—which looks much more like a sweeping slider now than the hammer curve it used to be—he hasn't yet found a way to maximize the impressive tools he possesses.

Will Warren RHP Born: 06/16/99 Age: 24 Bats: R Throws: R Height: 6'2" Weight: 175 lb. Origin: Round 8, 2021 Draft (#243 overall)

YEAR	TEAM	LVL	AGE	W	L	SV	G	GS	IP	H	HR	BB/9	K/9	K	GB%	BABIP	WHIP	ERA	DRA-	WARP	MPH	FB%	Whiff%	CSP
2022	HV	A+	23	2	3	0	8	8	35	30	2	2.3	10.8	42	57.0%	.333	1.11	3.60	95	0.3				
2022	SOM	AA	23	7	6	0	18	18	94	89	8	3.2	7.9	83	52.5%	.302	1.30	4.02	110	0.8				
2023 non-DC	*NYY*	*MLB*	*24*	*2*	*3*	*0*	*57*	*0*	*50*	*54*	*5*	*4.0*	*6.8*	*37*	*51.7%*	*.311*	*1.53*	*4.88*	*118*	*-0.3*			*22.1%*	

Comparables: Zach Hedges (88), Luis Cessa (83), T.J. Zeuch (83)

Warren throws what Yankees' Director of Pitching Sam Briend calls a "unicorn slider," per a Brendan Kuty *Baseball America* story: a particularly vicious variation of the sweeper that sits in the mid-80s with a video game-like left turn on its way to home plate. It's not all about the slider with him, either; by the end of the season, Warren was utilizing six distinct pitch shapes with elite spin-rates on his breaking balls. His production faded by the end of the season, which isn't too much of a shock considering he spent the majority of his first professional season in Double-A. As a guy who's shown at least one plus pitch combined with the ability to keep the ball on the ground, he's exactly the type of pitcher that the Yankees will envision pitching in the Bronx before too long.

Greg Weissert RHP Born: 02/04/95 Age: 28 Bats: R Throws: R Height: 6'2" Weight: 215 lb. Origin: Round 18, 2016 Draft (#548 overall)

YEAR	TEAM	LVL	AGE	W	L	SV	G	GS	IP	H	HR	BB/9	K/9	K	GB%	BABIP	WHIP	ERA	DRA-	WARP	MPH	FB%	Whiff%	CSP
2021	SOM	AA	26	1	2	4	12	0	12^{2}	9	0	3.6	14.2	20	44.4%	.333	1.11	0.71	85	0.2				
2021	SWB	AAA	26	3	1	2	28	0	36^{2}	20	2	5.4	9.8	40	48.9%	.209	1.15	1.96	94	0.6				
2022	SWB	AAA	27	2	1	18	42	0	48	24	3	3.6	13.1	70	47.4%	.228	0.90	1.69	71	1.4				
2022	NYY	MLB	27	3	0	0	12	0	11^{1}	6	1	4.0	8.7	11	40.0%	.172	0.97	5.56	100	0.1	94.9	53.2%	19.7%	53.7%
2023 DC	*NYY*	*MLB*	*28*	*1*	*1*	*0*	*31*	*0*	*27.3*	*22*	*2*	*4.5*	*9.0*	*27*	*43.9%*	*.265*	*1.30*	*3.57*	*90*	*0.2*	*94.9*	*53.2%*	*27.1%*	*53.7%*

Comparables: Tim Peterson (52), Danny Barnes (52), Arquimedes Caminero (49)

Weissert changed his slider grip a few years ago to mimic Chaz Roe's sweeper, and on average it generated an impressive 18 inches of sweep in 2022—third most among MLB sliders last season. With Weissert set to become a minor-league free agent after the season, the Yankees added him to their 40-man roster in August. Save for a nightmarish debut outing against the Athletics, Weissert performed admirably the rest of the year and seems to be in line for regular work as a middle reliever.

Lineouts

Hitters

HITTER	POS	TEAM	LVL	AGE	PA	R	2B	3B	HR	RBI	BB	K	SB	CS	AVG/OBP/SLG	DRC+	BABIP	BRR	DRP	WARP
Roderick Arias	SS	DSL NYY	ROK	17	140	25	6	2	3	11	28	46	10	2	.194/.379/.370		.305			
Jesus Bastidas	2B	SOM	AA	23	449	56	18	1	18	55	38	115	11	7	.240/.323/.427	98	.289	1.5	2B(92): 2.7, SS(19): -1.9, 3B(2): 0.1	1.4
Wilmer Difo	IF	RNO	AAA	30	306	33	15	0	7	43	20	41	4	2	.269/.311/.398	95	.287	2.1	SS(37): 0.7, 3B(21): -1.0, 2B(4): 0.4	0.9
	IF	AZ	MLB	30	6	0	0	0	0	0	0	1	0	0	.000/.000/.000	96			SS(2): 0, 2B(1): 0	
Elijah Dunham	OF	SOM	AA	24	485	67	26	3	17	63	59	103	37	7	.248/.348/.448	114	.288	0.0	LF(50): 1.2, RF(46): -2.2	2.0
Michael Hermosillo	CF	IOW	AAA	27	26	7	3	1	1	3	4	7	1	1	.400/.500/.800	98	.538	-0.3	LF(1): 0.3, RF(1): 0.2	0.1
	CF	CHC	MLB	27	73	7	2	0	0	4	7	27	1	0	.115/.250/.148	66	.206	-0.1	CF(28): -2.1, LF(1): -0.2	-0.3
Everson Pereira	CF	HV	A+	21	325	55	13	6	9	43	34	87	19	5	.274/.354/.455	96	.363	1.0	CF(58): -5.3, RF(7): 0.4, LF(1): 0.1	0.3
	CF	SOM	AA	21	123	21	4	3	5	13	9	37	2	2	.283/.341/.504	86	.380	-0.8	CF(24): -0.1	0.0
Trey Sweeney	SS	HV	A+	22	458	70	18	4	14	51	59	108	29	2	.241/.350/.415	116	.297	-1.2	SS(87): 5.2	2.7
	SS	SOM	AA	22	50	6	1	0	2	5	7	10	2	1	.233/.340/.395	105	.258	0.0	SS(10): 2.1	0.4

Roderick Arias was a top prospect in the international signing period prior to the 2022 season; despite a delayed start to his season due to an injury, he instantly made an impression by hitting a triple in his first professional at-bat (and proceeded to hit under the Mendoza line). ⚾ **Jesus Bastidas** has exhibited much more power than he did over his first few years in rookie ball, but is still a league-average hitter as a 23-year-old in Double-A. If you squint, you can see a parallel to the improvements made by fellow Venezuelan Oswaldo Cabrera last year, though Bastidas still has a ways to go before he could be viewed as a fit for a big-league roster. ⚾ **Kaleb Cowart** is a familiar name for many due to his long tenure in the Angels organization as a utility player. The update: he now pitches full-time. The jury is still out on whether or not he should keep trying to do so. ⚾ On one hand, **Wilmer Difo** had his best offensive season, rate-stats-wise, since breaking into the league, which is a good line at a party. On the other, it only happened over six plate appearances, which he might want to avoid saying. Maybe he should just talk about the punch. ⚾ **Elijah Dunham** could be considered a victim of the shortened 2020 Rule 4 draft, going undrafted in that year's five rounds. But he quickly pivoted to a free agent deal with the Yankees—spurred on by his former college coach, Casey Dykes, who had recently been hired by New York. Dunham has become a fine low-ceiling prospect, doing many things well without a standout skill. ⚾ Brought on as depth to help cover any outfield spots that opened up, **Michael Hermosillo** could have earned a larger role at any time with consistent good play. He went 2-for-April and 5-for-September in his two biggest chunks of playing time, serving another stint on the 60-day IL in the months between. He was released in October. ⚾ **Everson Pereira** continues to wow and confound in equal measure; in haunting tribute to Aaron Hicks, he looks unstoppable for months at a time, then disappears thanks to injuries and/or poor swing decisions. The Yankees liked him enough to add him to their 40-man roster over the winter but he's not particularly close to making a major-league impact. ⚾ The Yankees' system is loaded with middle-infield prospects alongside **Trey Sweeney**, though the Kentucky native is clearly no slouch himself. He had a fine debut in his first full professional season, and will presumably begin 2023 as Somerset's starting shortstop.

Pitchers

PITCHER	TEAM	LVL	AGE	W	L	SV	G	GS	IP	H	HR	BB/9	K/9	K	GB%	BABIP	WHIP	ERA	DRA-	WARP	MPH	FB%	WHF	CSP
Jhony Brito	SOM	AA	24	5	2	0	8	8	42	36	4	2.4	8.1	38	46.2%	.283	1.12	2.36	100	0.6				
	SWB	AAA	24	6	2	0	18	15	70^{2}	59	5	3.1	6.8	53	52.9%	.266	1.17	3.31	91	1.3				
Jimmy Cordero	SWB	AAA	30	1	1	6	32	0	38^{2}	25	2	3.0	11.6	50	52.2%	.261	0.98	2.09	72	1.1				
Demarcus Evans	RR	AAA	25	2	3	4	32	0	33	22	4	6.0	12.0	44	31.2%	.240	1.33	3.82	94	0.3	90.9	67.2%	31.5%	
Junior Fernández	IND	AAA	25	1	0	0	6	0	8	2	0	6.7	9.0	8	77.8%	.111	1.00	2.25	82	0.2				
	MEM	AAA	25	1	3	5	35	0	36^{1}	47	4	4.2	10.7	43	52.8%	.413	1.76	5.45	84	0.8	98.1	53.0%	15.7%	
	PIT	MLB	25	0	0	0	3	0	3^{1}	1	0	10.8	5.4	2	62.5%	.125	1.50	0.00	94	0.0	98.9	66.7%	13.9%	53.6%
	STL	MLB	25	0	0	0	13	0	15^{1}	17	3	4.7	7.0	12	62.5%	.311	1.63	2.93	106	0.1	98.8	51.3%	30.4%	54.1%
Jack Neely	TAM	A	22	3	1	7	34	0	45^{2}	38	3	4.9	15.6	79	35.8%	.380	1.38	3.94	78	1.2	95.4	50.4%	44.3%	
Matt Sauer	HV	A+	23	5	3	0	18	18	88^{1}	75	8	3.6	10.2	100	35.5%	.305	1.25	3.77	112	0.0				
	SOM	AA	23	0	2	0	4	4	20^{2}	22	5	3.0	14.8	34	36.7%	.386	1.40	7.84	81	0.5				
Tanner Tully	COL	AAA	27	8	6	0	24	20	122	142	12	1.9	7.2	98	47.9%	.335	1.38	4.72	113	0.8				
	CLE	MLB	27	0	0	0	3	0	6	8	1	9.0	3.0	2	36.4%	.333	2.33	6.00	133	0.0	91.4	59.5%	21.1%	55.7%
Art Warren	CIN	MLB	29	2	3	3	39	0	36	37	6	5.5	10.0	40	36.6%	.326	1.64	6.50	104	0.3	93.7	41.7%	29.5%	55.5%

Jhony Brito has never been a flashy pitcher, but he slowly climbed his way through the Yankees' system with good control and an ability to limit homers. He added a couple of ticks to his fastball last year and was sitting at 95 by the summer; the tradeoff, though, was that he ran the highest walk rate of his professional career. ⚾ **Jimmy Cordero** and his biceps have made their way back from Tommy John surgery, and his performance for Scranton Wilkes-Barre yielded his finest results in years. Like pretty much everyone else in the Yankees system, he worked on adding more lateral movement to his breaking ball to better pair with his hard sinker— much to the bewilderment of his International League competition. ⚾ A 25th-round pick way back in 2015, **Demarcus Evans** has consistently run strikeout rates between 30 and 40% while walking almost everyone else he faces. He doesn't throw as hard as you'd expect for someone of his stature, but his fastball has huge carry and life, making him an off-speed pitch away from being an intriguing bullpen option. ⚾ A high-ceiling relief prospect as recently as three years ago, **Junior Fernández** now has a better chance of being a waiver claim a half dozen times or so in the next couple years than he does of getting significant high-leverage work. Pittsburgh plucked him from the Cardinals in September, and he was DFA'd again by the Yankees in December. ⚾ **Jack Neely** had the highest strikeout-per-inning rate of any Florida State League pitcher last year. His control can be shaky, but that plus stuff will lead to a quick rise through at least the lower levels. ⚾ The prospect shine has worn off after a 2019 Tommy John surgery and lackluster minor-league results, but **Matt Sauer** did strike out 17 batters in an August Double-A game—the most of anybody in affiliated baseball last year. ⚾ **Drew Thorpe** hasn't pitched professionally yet, but showed plenty of polish while pitching at Cal Poly. He has a great changeup. ⚾ Did you know **Tanner Tully** struck out Xander Bogaerts in an actual Major League Baseball game last year? Tanner Tully! Xander Bogaerts! Makes you kinda sorta question what you're doing with your life, doesn't it? ⚾ After a flamethrowing debut in 2021, **Art Warren** began shamethrowing (bases on balls) last season. While recovering from a partial UCL tear, it's looking like this season he ain't throwing at all.

TAMPA BAY RAYS

Essay by Bryan Grosnick

Player comments by Tommy Rancel and BP staff

In the late 2000s and early 2010s, after the Great Exorcism of the ~~Devil~~ Rays and their shift from technicolor to sky blue, the team's long-standing run of success was often exemplified by a single player: Ben Zobrist. An indifferent hitter who transformed himself (with help from Jamie Cevallos) into an offensive wrecking ball, Zobrist's calling card was his versatility: He could play anywhere and, as a switch-hitter, always snagged the platoon advantage.

Like Michelle Yeoh last year, Zorilla was everything, everywhere, all at once. An above-average hitter who could play seven positions and sneak into the MVP voting, he created a cottage industry among wannabe stat-heads and fantasy mavens trying to replicate what Tampa had found/created. It seemed that, for years, everyone was asking, "who is the next Ben Zobrist?" Some of the answers were just awful (for example, at one point I really thought it was going to be Arismendy Alcántara), and few players ever truly followed Zobrist's example. This is likely in part because of his singular talents, and in part because teams were unwilling to move their best hitters all across the diamond. But as Russell Carleton pointed out in last year's *Annual*, one of the Rays' guiding principles is "YTFN" ... or "why the f**k not?" That's how Ben Zobrist, elite utility man, was created: because both team and player were courageous and talented enough to try something new.

Now, 15 seasons into the Rays' second act as a franchise, I think we can say we've found the definitive Ben Zobrist comp ... and of course it comes from Tampa Bay. If you're anticipating a long discussion about Brandon Lowe or Isaac Paredes here, fret not. Nor will we discuss Vidal Bruján, or Taylor Walls, or anyone else from the team's seemingly inexhaustible supply of versatile infielders.

No, the next Ben Zobrist isn't a player at all: It's the Tampa Bay Rays front office.

⚾ ⚾ ⚾

Ben Zobrist Rule #1: You have to be consistently good.

When defining what made Zobrist special, you have to start with the thing that was most obvious but never talked about enough: He was just a damn good ballplayer on balance. Though baseball has never been short on utility

TAMPA BAY RAYS PROSPECTUS

2022 W-L: 86-76, 3RD IN AL EAST

Pythag	.537	11th	DER	.712	7th
RS/G	4.11	21st	DRC+	94	25th
RA/G	3.79	6th	DRA-	94	9th
dWin%	.505	16th	FIP	3.71	8th
Payroll	$84M	25th	B-Age	27.6	6th
M$/MW	$1.7M	3rd	P-Age	29.5	18th

404′

370′

370′

315′

322′

- Opened 1990
- Dome
- Synthetic surface
- Fence profile: 5′ to 11′5″

Park Factors

Runs	Runs/RH	Runs/LH	HR/RH	HR/LH
100	100	100	106	100

Top Hitter WARP	3.4 Yandy Díaz
Top Pitcher WARP	4.2 Shane McClanahan
2023 Top Prospect	Curtis Mead

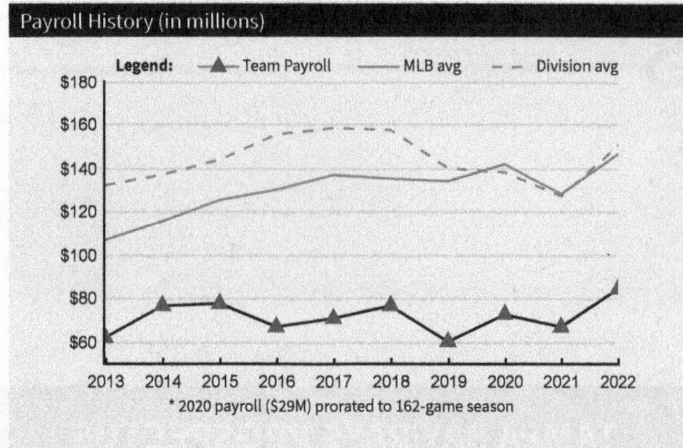

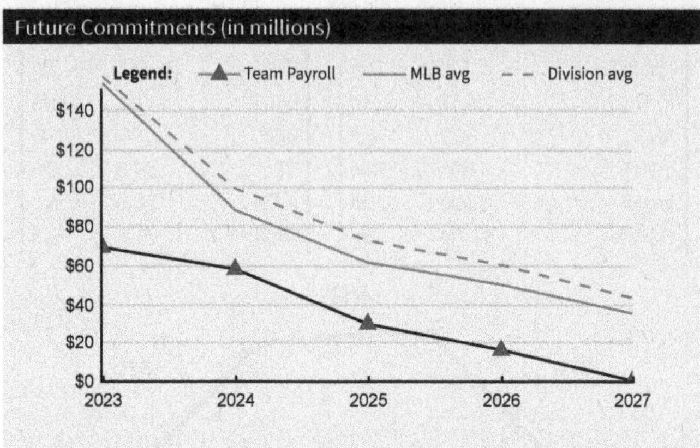

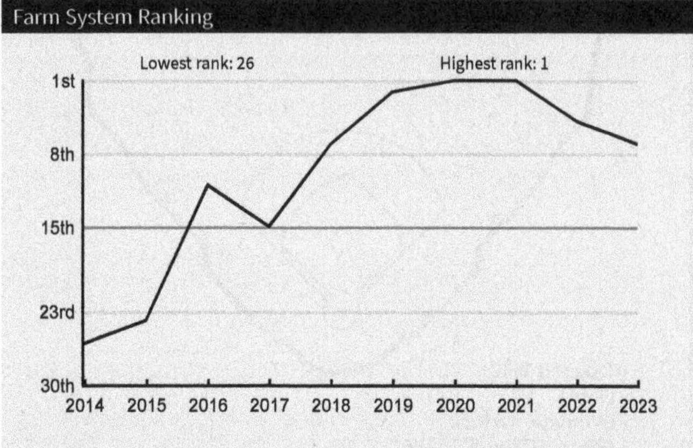

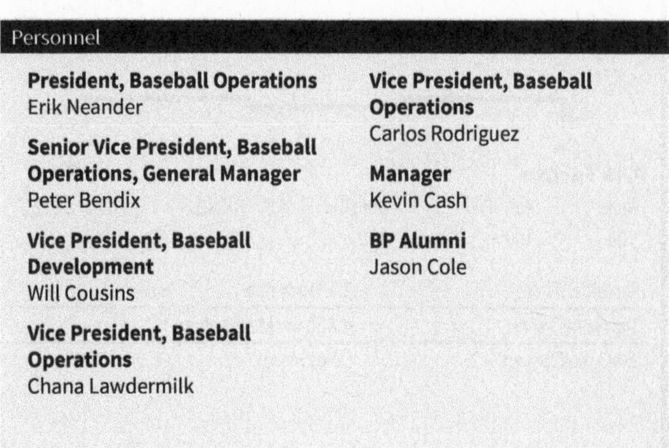
Personnel

President, Baseball Operations
Erik Neander

Senior Vice President, Baseball Operations, General Manager
Peter Bendix

Vice President, Baseball Development
Will Cousins

Vice President, Baseball Operations
Chana Lawdermilk

Vice President, Baseball Operations
Carlos Rodriguez

Manager
Kevin Cash

BP Alumni
Jason Cole

players, most of them carry flaws that hamper their overall value, and/or they've been unable to succeed from season to season. Zobrist was an exception—he would've been an All-Star second baseman or a first-class right fielder in many years even if he never swapped his gloves around, as he posted a DRC+ of 110 or better in every season save one from 2008-2016.

Similarly, the Rays, despite all the hand wringing over their limitations (read: their payroll) as a franchise, have been a consistently good ballclub for a long time. They've made the playoffs in each of the last four seasons. The last year in which they failed to do so—2018—they still won 90 games. Over the past 15 seasons and the whole of their Exorcism Era, they have made eight playoff appearances and earned two World Series berths. They've done all this despite the bitter luck of existing in a division with the Yankees and Red Sox, who've won a combined three World Series and earned 18 playoff appearances in that span. Now they must contend with the upstart Blue Jays, too.

Despite the team's self-imposed payroll constraints, this franchise has held serve with two of the most dominant brands in Major League Baseball over the past decade and a half (if we blithely ignore Commissioner's Trophies). As with Zobrist, the Rays aren't just novel or interesting: they are consistently, reliably good.

The Rays organization also demonstrates how good it is on aggregate in how many members of their front office have moved into leadership roles across the league. Andrew Friedman, a key figure in the Rays' resurgence as their EVP of Baseball Operations and general manager, was lured away by more lucrative pastures in L.A. Matt Silverman, Erik Neander and Peter Bendix have succeeded him, while many of the Rays' other key baseball operations personnel have moved into high-profile roles with other teams. A brief, non-exhaustive list includes Chaim Bloom (Red Sox), James Click (late of the Astros), Andrew Ball (Astros), Matt Arnold (Brewers) and Josh Kalk (Twins).

Some have been more successful than others in their post-Rays careers—more on that later—but it sure seems that, just as many of us spent years trying to find "the next Zobrist," other franchises are intent on finding "the next Rays front office."

*Ben Zobrist Rule #2: You have to be very, very flexible.**

As mentioned before, Zobrist's calling card was his ability to play multiple positions well. Originally a shortstop, he became a pretty remarkable second baseman and an outstanding right fielder, but could acquit himself well enough at any of the seven non-battery positions.

The asterisk next to this rule indicates an important corollary: You can't just carry the potential to be flexible; you have to *actually be adaptable to new situations*. There's no doubt that many high-quality ballplayers could function as elite super-utility players at certain points in their careers (see Trea Turner and Mookie Betts for some recent examples). But while we can assume high-end performance from this genre of player, that's all for naught unless they actually man a spectrum of positions. Even though Zo's main stomping grounds were second base and right field, he consistently put in time all over the diamond, prioritizing flexibility over comfort.

The Rays as an organization have emphasized flexibility out of necessity: They need to be nimble to survive in the face of their payroll restrictions. Over the past several years they have worked around ownership's unfortunate unwillingness to invest in player payroll by:

- Investing in comparatively low-cost areas of the team such as research and development, player development and other front office roles.
- Using the free agent market only to acquire high-variance players on short-term contracts (e.g., Corey Kluber).
- Offering young, unproven players long-term extensions to suppress long-term spending (e.g., Wander Franco).
- Sloughing off their soon-to-be expensive players for ones who are, in general, slightly worse and a lot less expensive (e.g., cutting bait on Austin Meadows, Joey Wendle and José Alvarado).
- Trying to glean value from alternative in-game strategies (e.g., the opener, defensive positioning).

In 2022, for example, the Rays sold high on Wendle and returned Yandy Díaz to his original position, third base, in an attempt to free up the cold corner and DH slots for other hitters. This allowed them to gain unexpected value from roster afterthoughts like Harold Ramírez. For his part, Díaz paid them back by riding high up the league OBP leaderboard: The only regulars who outpaced him were Aaron Judge, Paul Goldschmidt, Yordan Alvarez, Freddie Freeman and Juan Soto.

They moved pitchers between relief and starting roles as necessary to get the most out of their collection of swingmen, leading to breakout seasons from the likes of Drew Rasmussen and Jeffrey Springs. And they experimented with a host of defensive players in a host of roles, most notably at shortstop when Franco sat out a part of the season with injuries.

Knowing the Rays, they'll do it all again in 2023. They'll be ready to move on from Ramirez if he regresses or they feel they can capitalize on his value. They have an army of intriguing arms to switch between the rotation and the bullpen should anyone falter. They are always ready with a Plan B because they have to be. And crucially, more often than not, their Plan Bs are rather good.

⚾ ⚾ ⚾

Ben Zobrist Rule #3: Have several areas of strength, not just one.

Zobrist would not have been so special without having multiple areas in which he excelled. From the jump, he had an outstanding approach at the plate with solid pitch recognition and great patience. He was also a pretty solid shortstop with good footwork and fundamentals and great cognitive gifts for fielding that he could apply anywhere on the diamond. As he emerged as a big leaguer, he added legitimate power—both for raking doubles and putting balls over the fence—making him a real threat for opposing pitchers.

As much as any other franchise, the Rays have a reputation for excellence in a number of different areas of baseball operations. Yes, research and development has been a strength for years, with an analytics department that was well ahead of its time in the mid-aughts. This helped the team benefit from things like OBP and catcher framing before many others.

In more recent years, the team has displayed a particular penchant for player development, especially when it comes to pitchers. They have turned afterthoughts like Ryan Yarborough, Jalen Beeks and Matt Wisler into productive pitchers, and have a cadre of young arms in the minors ready to move into important roles. How do they acquire this talent to begin with? This is a team that shows great ability to self-scout, and to just scout really well overall at the pro level. Far more trades tend to "work out" for the Rays than for their partner teams: we've all seen the famous tweet. The last trades they made that really stung were sending Nathaniel Lowe to the Rangers (for prospects) and Joe Ryan to the Twins (for a Nelson Cruz rental). More often than not, they come out ahead.

In 2022, the front office's range of strengths could be best displayed in the case of Paredes. He was a good but not outstanding Tigers prospect for several years, eventually coming to Tampa Bay in a one-for-one swap for All-Star outfielder Meadows (who himself came to the Rays in one of the most lopsided trades in team history). This deal was, in my view, already a triumph no matter what disaster may befall Paredes or what blessings Meadows heaps upon the Tigers.

First, the Rays accurately self-scouted Meadows, a talented but limited player who had dealt with ups, downs and injuries for years. He didn't fit the Rays' mold as a left field-only defender, and the team could benefit from cutting his (to most teams, negligible) upcoming $4 million arbitration payout. Then, they picked Paredes as a target from the Tigers, noticing his versatility and selectivity, with the hope that maybe he could tap into his raw power eventually. (Hey! That sounds familiar!) After negotiating and closing the deal to bring Paredes in, they used their infield positioning skills and player development chops to help optimize his performance, and voilà: Paredes hit 20 dingers in his first season in Tampa and was the team's second-most productive hitter overall.

It takes a village to raise a child, and it takes a suite of skills to make the Meadows-for-Paredes deal work.

⚾ ⚾ ⚾

Of course, Zobrist didn't finish his career with the Rays, and sadly, that lack of storybook ending is another area of alignment between player and team. The Rays traded away their signature player ahead of the 2015 season, as his arbitration cost was rising and he was nearing a big free agency payday. After stints in Kansas City and Oakland, he had to sign with the Chicago Cubs to chase (and grab) a World Series ring. Over the years, we've seen Rays front office personnel move on in order to do the same. As the organization prides itself on flexibility due to their financial limitations, some top talents—both on the field like Zobrist and in the front office like Friedman, Bloom and Click—will continue to look elsewhere to reach the peak of the baseball world.

And, as alluded to earlier, part of Zobrist's legacy is also one of failed imitators: another connection between the former All-Star and his long-time organization. While more Rays front office expats have succeeded than not, several have failed. Chief among them to date is Bloom, whose run with the Red Sox looks increasingly uninspired despite a surprise 2021 ALCS appearance. Faced with a very Rays-like scenario in which he was (most likely) forced to trade Mookie Betts ahead of free agency, he netted an uninspiring return. Since then, he has not proved gutsy enough to trade other marquee players before letting them walk, as was the case this winter with Xander Bogaerts. He's unearthed a Garrett Whitlock or two, it's true, but the little swings matter less when you get the big ones wrong.

Teams will continue to pilfer Tampa Bay's front office regardless, but some Rays imitators make clear an obvious point of which we nonetheless sometimes lose sight: getting the big stuff right consistently is very hard. Doubtless, there are some things inherent to some front office personnel that just can't be copied, as was very much the case with Zobrist himself.

⚾ ⚾ ⚾

The 2022 Rays were, by most accounts, an unmitigated success, if not to the ultimate level that every team aspires to: No flags fly for coming in third in the division and bowing out in a pair of Wild Card games. They ran something like a $98 million payroll over the course of the season—about 50% lower than league-average—and still managed to contend thanks to the talents of their front office and player base. Their front office has proven over time to be adaptable, capable of doing multiple things well, and able to put a high-performing product on the field.

I'm hesitant to lionize any collection of contributors to a team's on-field performance when they're not the ones in the batter's box or patrolling the lines. But I do think the track record of success in Tampa is worthy of comparison to the outstanding ballplayer who once defined their franchise with his [Liam Neeson voice] particular set of skills. And if you feel that's a bit too complimentary, just keep in mind that Zobrist was never an MVP or a true top-line superstar. Oftentimes, he was not the best or second-best player on his team. We can't calculate the WARP or surplus value for any team's front office, but it's fair to at least note the characteristics that have made the Rays so successful for so long.

Both Zobrist's and this franchise's magic is in their ability and willingness to shift and change and to excel all the while. While it may not last forever, the Rays' success has been born of an ability to grow and adapt while excelling in multiple areas.

As such, it wouldn't surprise me if the next *next* Ben Zobrist pops up in St. Petersburg as well. ■

—Bryan Grosnick is an author of Baseball Prospectus.

HITTERS

Jonathan Aranda IF

Born: 05/23/98 Age: 25 Bats: L Throws: R Height: 6'0" Weight: 210 lb. Origin: International Free Agent, 2015

YEAR	TEAM	LVL	AGE	PA	R	2B	3B	HR	RBI	BB	K	SB	CS	Whiff%	AVG/OBP/SLG	DRC+	BABIP	BRR	DRP	WARP
2020	OBR	WIN	22	159	19	5	2	3	24	11	20	6	0		.333/.390/.458		.369			
2021	OBR	WIN	23	137	12	3	0	2	9	17	24	2	1		.284/.382/.362		.341			
2021	BG	A+	23	89	20	3	0	4	7	9	13	1	0		.351/.449/.554	129	.379	0.6	2B(15): 1.3, 3B(5): 0.3, SS(1): -0.1	0.8
2021	MTG	AA	23	322	53	19	5	10	58	33	63	4	2		.325/.410/.540	129	.383	0.8	1B(48): 1.1, 2B(17): 0.4, 3B(10): -1.6	2.0
2022	DUR	AAA	24	465	71	26	1	18	85	45	100	4	0	25.6%	.318/.394/.521	124	.377	2.6	1B(33): 1.4, 3B(30): 0.6, 2B(25): -0.3	3.0
2022	TB	MLB	24	87	10	4	0	2	6	8	23	0	0	22.4%	.192/.276/.321	86	.245	0.3	2B(13): -0.5, 1B(11): -0.1, 3B(6): 0.1	0.1
2023 DC	*TB*	*MLB*	*25*	*348*	*39*	*15*	*2*	*7*	*33*	*27*	*74*	*1*	*0*	*21.2%*	*.252/.323/.387*	*98*	*.309*	*1.1*	*2B 0, 1B 0*	*0.7*

Comparables: Max Moroff (60), Taylor Green (60), Luis Valbuena (59)

Signed as an international free agent out of Tijuana back in 2015, Aranda has hit ever since turning pro. He was named the 2021 Double-A South MVP and rewarded with a 40-man roster spot in the offseason. That led to Aranda spending most of 2022 in Triple-A Durham, where, as you can see above, he continued to mash despite his lack of size or chrome toolbox. He made his MLB debut in June, but while he started off hot, he followed the example of more veteran Rays hitters by tailing off in September. Not much of a defender, Aranda is nonetheless nominally versatile enough to move around the diamond: He started games at four different positions in the bigs. If he can regain his hitting prowess from the minors, he could be a platoon piece who can play several spots, affording the Rays even more flexibility in both the field and their lineup.

Randy Arozarena OF

Born: 02/28/95 Age: 28 Bats: R Throws: R Height: 5'11" Weight: 185 lb. Origin: International Free Agent, 2016

YEAR	TEAM	LVL	AGE	PA	R	2B	3B	HR	RBI	BB	K	SB	CS	Whiff%	AVG/OBP/SLG	DRC+	BABIP	BRR	DRP	WARP
2020	TB	MLB	25	76	15	2	0	7	11	6	22	4	0	36.8%	.281/.382/.641	120	.306	0.7	LF(14): 1.7, CF(2): 0	0.6
2021	TB	MLB	26	604	94	32	3	20	69	56	170	20	10	32.6%	.274/.356/.459	103	.363	-0.2	LF(81): 4.2, RF(53): 0.5, CF(1): 0.1	2.7
2022	TB	MLB	27	645	72	41	3	20	89	46	156	32	12	28.7%	.263/.327/.445	109	.325	-2.6	LF(104): 2.6, RF(25): 0.9	2.8
2023 DC	*TB*	*MLB*	*28*	*589*	*70*	*30*	*2*	*20*	*70*	*46*	*144*	*30*	*13*	*28.8%*	*.261/.335/.442*	*117*	*.323*	*-2.8*	*LF -1, RF 0*	*2.1*

Comparables: Chris Heisey (62), Khris Davis (60), Jason Bay (58)

Now that the shine of his explosive 2020 debut has worn off, Arozarena has settled in as a pretty good regular. He's proven to be an above-average offensive performer, with a blend of power and speed that puts him in a rare group: He joined Trea Turner and José Ramírez as the only players to post back-to-back 20-homer/20-steal seasons over the last two years, and Arozarena was the only one among that trio to go for 20/30 last season. Although he cut down his strikeout rate by about 4%, he actually chased more pitches out of the zone and took fewer walks. This resulted in a lower average on balls in play and a drop in on-base opportunities. Arozarena doesn't offer much with the glove, but his offense is good enough to keep him in the 2-3-WARP range; a mark that should make him the favorite to win American League Rookie of the Year for a third straight season.

Christian Bethancourt C

Born: 09/02/91 Age: 31 Bats: R Throws: R Height: 6'3" Weight: 205 lb. Origin: International Free Agent, 2008

YEAR	TEAM	LVL	AGE	PA	R	2B	3B	HR	RBI	BB	K	SB	CS	Whiff%	AVG/OBP/SLG	DRC+	BABIP	BRR	DRP	WARP
2020	EST	WIN	28	70	4	3	0	1	5	2	18	1	1		.162/.186/.250		.204			
2021	EST	WIN	29	124	6	4	1	2	15	3	29	0	0		.208/.228/.308		.258			
2021	IND	AAA	29	363	46	18	1	14	60	28	73	4	1		.281/.339/.468	109	.321	1.3	C(28): -2.0, 1B(28): 0.1, RF(12): -1.1	1.3
2022	OAK	MLB	30	182	23	11	0	4	19	10	41	4	1	33.1%	.249/.298/.385	96	.306	-1.3	1B(31): 0.7, C(14): 0.9	0.4
2022	TB	MLB	30	151	16	6	0	7	15	2	39	1	0	36.9%	.255/.265/.436	93	.301	-1.3	C(35): 1.9, 1B(6): 0	0.5
2023 DC	*TB*	*MLB*	*31*	*196*	*19*	*7*	*0*	*6*	*21*	*10*	*52*	*2*	*1*	*33.9%*	*.239/.282/.384*	*81*	*.300*	*0.9*	*C 2*	*0.6*

Comparables: Dioner Navarro (56), Alex Trevino (47), Yadier Molina (46)

YEAR	TEAM	P. COUNT	FRM RUNS	BLK RUNS	THRW RUNS	TOT RUNS
2021	EST	3200			0.0	0.0
2021	IND	4069	-2.3	0.0	0.0	-2.3
2022	OAK	1890	0.2	-0.1	0.4	0.4
2022	TB	4768	1.4	0.1	0.3	1.8
2023	*TB*	*7215*	*1.8*	*0.0*	*0.2*	*1.9*

Talk about persistence. Bethancourt went nearly five years between major-league appearances, a gap that included a stop in South Korea. Once a highly touted prospect, he bounced around the minors (and the world) over the last few years before making it back to the show with the Athletics last April. He would switch bay areas in July, landing in Tampa Bay for the remainder of the season. In a depressed offensive environment, he was just about average at the plate, showing some pop but almost no discipline: Amazingly, he walked just twice in 151 plate appearances with the Rays. Behind the plate, he earned solid marks for framing and threw out 43% of runners. In addition to his work as a backstop, Bethancourt branched out to first base on occasion and made four appearances on the mound to boot. He's not quite Shohei Ohtani yet, but he did well enough to stick around in the majors a bit longer this time, especially if his defensive improvements hold true.

Vidal Bruján UT Born: 02/09/98 Age: 25 Bats: S Throws: R Height: 5'10" Weight: 180 lb. Origin: International Free Agent, 2014

YEAR	TEAM	LVL	AGE	PA	R	2B	3B	HR	RBI	BB	K	SB	CS	Whiff%	AVG/OBP/SLG	DRC+	BABIP	BRR	DRP	WARP
2020	TOR	WIN	22	75	14	2	1	0	5	11	10	10	3		.254/.373/.317		.302			
2021	TOR	WIN	23	69	7	2	1	0	3	6	11	8	3		.206/.275/.270		.250			
2021	DUR	AAA	23	441	77	31	1	12	56	49	68	44	8		.262/.345/.440	116	.290	2.7	2B(29): 0.1, LF(24): 2.8, SS(16): 2.6	2.7
2021	TB	MLB	23	26	3	0	0	0	2	0	8	1	0	20.0%	.077/.077/.077	82	.111	0.2	2B(4): 0.5, RF(2): -0.1	0.1
2022	DUR	AAA	24	290	56	14	3	6	21	27	48	26	13	33.3%	.292/.369/.440	110	.338	0.4	SS(40): 1.2, CF(14): 1.6, 3B(6): -0.8	1.4
2022	TB	MLB	24	162	13	5	0	3	16	12	37	5	5	20.7%	.163/.228/.259	80	.193	-0.2	2B(31): 1.6, RF(19): 0.6, SS(5): 0.4	0.3
2023 DC	*TB*	*MLB*	*25*	*99*	*9*	*4*	*0*	*1*	*8*	*7*	*18*	*6*	*3*	*21.6%*	*.233/.297/.347*	*80*	*.278*	*-2.0*	*SS 0, 2B 0*	*-0.2*

Comparables: Luis Valbuena (69), Arismendy Alcántara (60), Luis Sardinas (57)

Bruján was a regular passenger on the Durham-to-St. Pete shuttle, serving as an on-demand reserve when the Rays needed an extra hand. He had a chance to carve out a larger role over the summer when the team lost their entire middle infield but squandered his opportunity thanks to a total lack of offensive output. Despite his reputation as a contact hitter, he struggled mightily at the plate in the bigs. In his defense, his at-bats were largely scattered, but in Tampa's defense, he's shown very little with the stick to date. He continued to hit in Durham and remains a good, speedy defender who can play six positions. He could earn a regular role if he can fight his way to even average with the bat, but until Bruján starts to look more like a major-league hitter and less like the guy who needed to use the big red bat in whiffle ball just to make contact, his top-of-the-order projection remains in jeopardy.

★ ★ ★ *2023 Top 101 Prospect* **#99** ★ ★ ★

Junior Caminero 3B Born: 07/05/03 Age: 20 Bats: R Throws: R Height: 5'11" Weight: 157 lb. Origin: International Free Agent, 2019

YEAR	TEAM	LVL	AGE	PA	R	2B	3B	HR	RBI	BB	K	SB	CS	Whiff%	AVG/OBP/SLG	DRC+	BABIP	BRR	DRP	WARP
2021	DSL INDR	ROK	17	171	26	8	0	9	33	20	28	2	0		.295/.380/.534		.304			
2022	RAY	ROK	18	154	18	5	1	5	31	15	21	7	1		.326/.403/.492		.349			
2022	CSC	A	18	117	19	2	1	6	20	8	22	5	0		.299/.359/.505	117	.329	1.3	3B(17): -0.4, 2B(2): -0.4	0.7
2023 non-DC	*TB*	*MLB*	*19*	*251*	*21*	*9*	*1*	*4*	*23*	*12*	*63*	*3*	*1*	*28.5%*	*.231/.276/.339*	*68*	*.299*	*2.8*	*1B 0, 2B 0*	*-0.2*

Comparables: Vladimir Guerrero Jr. (91), Josh Vitters (87), Matt Dominguez (87)

You're forgiven if you're not terribly familiar with Caminero, but that sensation won't last long. He's yet another in a long line of Rays low-minors pickups who is destined to become fodder for their vaunted front office efficacy. Plucked from the backfields in exchange for Tobias Myers following a strong performance in the DSL for Cleveland, Caminero torched a combination of the Florida Coast League and Low-A at the age of 18. He parlayed that into a strong performance in the Australian Baseball League, slugging nearly .500 while considerably younger than most of his competition. He's not much of a shortstop and is rough defensively at third right now, but no matter where he settles his bat is likely to play.

Yandy Díaz 3B Born: 08/08/91 Age: 31 Bats: R Throws: R Height: 6'2" Weight: 215 lb. Origin: International Free Agent, 2013

YEAR	TEAM	LVL	AGE	PA	R	2B	3B	HR	RBI	BB	K	SB	CS	Whiff%	AVG/OBP/SLG	DRC+	BABIP	BRR	DRP	WARP
2020	TB	MLB	28	138	16	3	0	2	11	23	17	0	0	15.7%	.307/.428/.386	123	.347	-1.1	3B(25): 0.7, 1B(2): -0.3	0.6
2021	TB	MLB	29	541	62	20	1	13	64	69	85	1	1	19.2%	.256/.353/.387	111	.286	-3.6	1B(81): 1, 3B(58): 1.2	2.1
2022	TB	MLB	30	558	71	33	0	9	57	78	60	3	3	14.4%	.296/.401/.423	132	.323	0.8	3B(102): 2.2, 1B(17): -0.2	3.8
2023 DC	*TB*	*MLB*	*31*	*608*	*80*	*27*	*1*	*16*	*64*	*79*	*79*	*3*	*1*	*15.6%*	*.287/.385/.437*	*136*	*.312*	*-0.4*	*3B 1, 1B 0*	*3.9*

Comparables: Mike Lowell (55), Alberto Callaspo (54), Jeff Cirillo (54)

Though his massive biceps have long belied a lack of in-game power, Díaz remains a very good and important contributor to the Rays lineup. In fact, he was easily the team's best hitter in 2022. For the second time in three seasons, Díaz walked more than he struck out. He reached base in 40% of his plate appearances and topped 40 extra-base hits despite mashing single-digit homers. Altogether, he owns an exceptionally odd profile: He's a muscly ground-ball hitter without great foot speed, yet he hit .323 on balls in play thanks to an ability to routinely aim up the middle and to the opposite field. Out of necessity, he primarily played third base, where he fought his way to pretty close to neutral as a defender. Even if he slides back to the cold corner in 2023, Díaz is a key member of the Rays lineup despite his refusal to take part in the Launch Angle Revolution.

Wander Franco SS Born: 03/01/01 Age: 22 Bats: S Throws: R Height: 5'10" Weight: 189 lb. Origin: International Free Agent, 2017

YEAR	TEAM	LVL	AGE	PA	R	2B	3B	HR	RBI	BB	K	SB	CS	Whiff%	AVG/OBP/SLG	DRC+	BABIP	BRR	DRP	WARP
2021	DUR	AAA	20	180	31	11	6	7	35	14	21	5	4		.313/.372/.583	134	.324	0.6	SS(31): -0.3, 3B(7): 1.1, 2B(3): -0.2	1.4
2021	TB	MLB	20	308	53	18	5	7	39	24	37	2	1	16.4%	.288/.347/.463	113	.311	0.9	SS(63): 1.7, 3B(8): -0.1, 2B(1): 0	1.9
2022	DUR	AAA	21	25	3	2	0	0	2	4	3	0	1	0.0%	.429/.520/.524	117	.500	-0.1	SS(4): 0.0	0.1
2022	TB	MLB	21	344	46	20	3	6	33	26	33	8	0	13.5%	.277/.328/.417	112	.290	1.4	SS(72): -0.8	1.6
2023 DC	*TB*	*MLB*	*22*	*598*	*70*	*29*	*8*	*16*	*74*	*48*	*60*	*9*	*4*	*14.0%*	*.290/.351/.464*	*129*	*.302*	*3.4*	*SS -1*	*4.1*

Comparables: Carlos Correa (72), Rougned Odor (65), Starlin Castro (64)

You know that bumper sticker that says, "not all who wander are lost?" Well, 2022 proved that some Wanders can indeed lose their way, however briefly. After flashing the brilliance everyone figured he would show in 2021, Franco dealt with a variety of injuries that limited him to half a season's worth of games. The good news: None of his maladies should be of long-term concern. He dealt with hamstring and quad issues in the early portion of the year before a right hamate injury required surgery over the summer. But because he's Wander Franco, he returned for the stretch run and found himself in time to hit .322/.381/.471 with 10 extra-base hits over his final 25 contests. Nothing from this campaign should discourage anyone going forward. His tools remain top-notch despite his nagging ailments, and it's notable that he still showed some pop so soon after his hamate issues. Franco remains a five-tool, up-the-middle defender who should compete for end-of-year awards for, let's say, the next 12–15 seasons. Fortunately for the Rays, most of those years will come amid the massive contract extension that Franco signed last winter.

Brandon Lowe 2B Born: 07/06/94 Age: 29 Bats: L Throws: R Height: 5'10" Weight: 185 lb. Origin: Round 3, 2015 Draft (#87 overall)

YEAR	TEAM	LVL	AGE	PA	R	2B	3B	HR	RBI	BB	K	SB	CS	Whiff%	AVG/OBP/SLG	DRC+	BABIP	BRR	DRP	WARP
2020	TB	MLB	25	224	36	9	2	14	37	25	58	3	0	35.8%	.269/.362/.554	110	.309	2.9	2B(44): -0.9, RF(7): 0.5, LF(5): -0.2	1.3
2021	TB	MLB	26	615	97	31	0	39	99	68	167	7	1	32.7%	.247/.340/.523	119	.280	3.4	2B(133): -0.1, LF(10): -0.2, RF(6): -0.2	4.0
2022	TB	MLB	27	266	31	10	2	8	25	27	61	1	0	33.6%	.221/.308/.383	92	.263	-1.6	2B(53): -2, RF(1): 0	0.2
2023 DC	*TB*	*MLB*	*28*	*612*	*84*	*28*	*3*	*28*	*78*	*61*	*159*	*5*	*2*	*32.3%*	*.253/.337/.476*	*122*	*.306*	*3.1*	*2B -1, RF 0*	*3.4*

Comparables: Derek Dietrich (58), Scooter Gennett (57), Danny Espinosa (54)

Lowe was arguably the best player on Tampa Bay's 100-win team in 2021. He belted 70 extra-base hits and paced the Rays in home runs. Entering his age-27 season, he looked poised to become one of the best players in the league that nobody outside of the baseball bubble has ever heard of. Instead, a cranky lower lumbar region limited him to just 65 games. He wasn't great in those contests, but it's clear his back was bothering him even before it forced him to miss time. As long as Lowe fully recovers during the offseason, there's nothing to suggest he can't return to his previous levels of production: even with his balky back, his exit velocity was right around his career norms. On the low (and no, his name still isn't pronounced that way) end, that looks like a .230-ish hitter with 30-homer power. But if Lowe stays healthy and it all clicks, a three- or four-win season from the keystone is within reach.

Josh Lowe RF Born: 02/02/98 Age: 25 Bats: L Throws: R Height: 6'4" Weight: 205 lb. Origin: Round 1, 2016 Draft (#13 overall)

YEAR	TEAM	LVL	AGE	PA	R	2B	3B	HR	RBI	BB	K	SB	CS	Whiff%	AVG/OBP/SLG	DRC+	BABIP	BRR	DRP	WARP
2021	DUR	AAA	23	470	76	28	2	22	78	61	123	26	0		.291/.381/.535	119	.361	4.5	CF(55): -5.9, RF(38): 1.7, LF(11): 2.5	2.9
2021	TB	MLB	23	2	0	0	0	0	0	1	0	1	0	40.0%	1.000/1.000/1.000	96	1.000	0.1	LF(1): 0, RF(1): -0.1	0.0
2022	DUR	AAA	24	351	51	27	2	14	67	44	115	25	2	40.7%	.315/.402/.556	101	.460	-0.9	RF(28): 3.0, CF(24): 0.1, LF(7): -0.4	1.1
2022	TB	MLB	24	198	24	12	2	2	13	15	66	3	0	32.4%	.221/.284/.343	60	.336	0.8	RF(33): 1.5, LF(10): 0.5, CF(9): -0.1	-0.1
2023 DC	*TB*	*MLB*	*25*	*289*	*32*	*14*	*1*	*8*	*30*	*26*	*93*	*11*	*2*	*32.5%*	*.233/.307/.399*	*91*	*.329*	*7.1*	*CF -1, RF 0*	*1.0*

Comparables: Travis Snider (64), Trayvon Robinson (63), Jason Martin (60)

Lowe is not the first highly touted prospect to struggle in his first extended run of big-league action, but that doesn't mean we shouldn't talk about it. Otherwise this comment would be very short. The younger brother of Nathan but of no relation to Brandon, Josh was pretty awful for the 2022 Rays. He struck out in 33% of his at-bats and had a contact rate of 70% when the league average was about six points higher. If you're looking for reasons to be optimistic, Lowe did show some power, racking up 16 extra-base hits in the bigs, plus 43 more in 80 games in Durham. All told, he didn't do enough to prove he's the heir apparent to Kevin Kiermaier in center field, nor did he totally disqualify himself from such a future. After all, if he can hit .240 with some pop and solid defense, he'd be a reasonable facsimile.

★ ★ ★ *2023 Top 101 Prospect* **#81** ★ ★ ★

Kyle Manzardo 1B Born: 07/18/00 Age: 22 Bats: L Throws: R Height: 6'1" Weight: 205 lb. Origin: Round 2, 2021 Draft (#63 overall)

YEAR	TEAM	LVL	AGE	PA	R	2B	3B	HR	RBI	BB	K	SB	CS	Whiff%	AVG/OBP/SLG	DRC+	BABIP	BRR	DRP	WARP
2021	RAY	ROK	20	50	10	5	0	2	8	4	6	0	0		.349/.440/.605		.371			
2022	BG	A+	21	275	53	16	1	17	55	45	46	0	0		.329/.436/.636	155	.343	2.8	1B(52): -0.6	2.7
2022	MTG	AA	21	122	18	10	0	5	26	14	19	1	1		.323/.402/.576	131	.333	0.2	1B(23): 1.3	0.9
2023 non-DC	*TB*	*MLB*	*22*	*251*	*28*	*11*	*1*	*8*	*30*	*25*	*49*	*0*	*0*	*22.9%*	*.253/.335/.424*	*112*	*.293*	*0.3*	*1B 0*	*0.8*

Comparables: Sam Travis (77), Wes Bankston (76), Andrew Benintendi (70)

If you're limited to first base as a prospect, you really need to be able to do one thing well: crush baseballs. Manzardo fit the bill in 2022, with a .327/.426/.617 line split between High- and Double-A. He's not an elite exit velo guy, but he consistently makes hard contact and gets the ball in the air—a good recipe for extra-base hits and homers. He also displays a keen eye at the dish, knowing which pitches he can do the most damage on and which ones he needs to let go. If he can keep doing that all the way up the chain, it won't much matter where he plays (or doesn't) defensively.

Manuel Margot OF Born: 09/28/94 Age: 28 Bats: R Throws: R Height: 5'11" Weight: 180 lb. Origin: International Free Agent, 2011

YEAR	TEAM	LVL	AGE	PA	R	2B	3B	HR	RBI	BB	K	SB	CS	Whiff%	AVG/OBP/SLG	DRC+	BABIP	BRR	DRP	WARP
2020	TB	MLB	25	159	19	9	0	1	11	13	25	12	4	23.7%	.269/.327/.352	100	.317	0.5	CF(21): -0.1, LF(18): -0.1, RF(15): -0.1	0.5
2021	TB	MLB	26	464	55	18	3	10	57	37	70	13	8	20.5%	.254/.313/.382	99	.281	0.9	RF(86): 3.3, LF(24): 1.2, CF(24): 1.3	2.2
2022	TB	MLB	27	363	36	18	2	4	47	24	68	7	3	25.0%	.274/.325/.375	97	.332	1.1	RF(53): 1.3, CF(18): -0.3, LF(8): 0.6	1.2
2023 DC	*TB*	*MLB*	*28*	*441*	*48*	*18*	*2*	*9*	*42*	*34*	*83*	*14*	*6*	*23.4%*	*.256/.317/.385*	*97*	*.300*	*-0.8*	*RF 2, CF 0*	*1.0*

Comparables: Mike Hershberger (74), Cliff Heathcote (66), Jerry White (66)

Margot received a surprising two-year extension with the Rays last April worth almost $20 million guaranteed. That's not a huge commitment for most teams, but Tampa Bay shelling out that kind of cash for a player who's largely been a short-side platoon option suggests they believe Margot can play a larger role going forward. The Rays have younger, faster options in center field, but none have Margot's offensive track record. He turned in another solid—if abbreviated—year, performing just below league-average levels with the bat while playing solid defense across all three outfield spots. He remains a better hitter against lefties but isn't a total zero against same-side pitching. After a knee injury limited him to under 90 games in 2022, Margot will hope to play on a more regular basis in 2023 as his salary increases and he enters his age-28 season. The Rays have to hope he returns to his 2021 levels of production, because, as of December, he is suddenly Tampa Bay's most expensive hitter, set to earn a cool $7 million this season.

★ ★ ★ *2023 Top 101 Prospect* **#16** ★ ★ ★

Curtis Mead 3B/2B Born: 10/26/00 Age: 22 Bats: R Throws: R Height: 6'2" Weight: 171 lb. Origin: International Free Agent, 2018

YEAR	TEAM	LVL	AGE	PA	R	2B	3B	HR	RBI	BB	K	SB	CS	Whiff%	AVG/OBP/SLG	DRC+	BABIP	BRR	DRP	WARP
2020	ADE	WIN	19	76	11	7	0	3	12	3	13	2	0		.347/.382/.569		.393			
2021	SCO	WIN	20	90	16	5	2	3	11	4	13	1	1		.313/.360/.530		.343			
2021	CSC	A	20	211	36	21	1	7	35	15	30	9	2		.356/.408/.586	134	.391	-1.0	3B(25): -0.6, 1B(15): 2.2	1.5
2021	BG	A+	20	233	38	15	1	7	32	19	38	2	2		.282/.348/.466	119	.309	0.4	3B(43): 1.1, 1B(3): 0.1	1.4
2021	DUR	AAA	20	14	3	2	0	1	2	0	3	0	0		.429/.429/.786	97	.500	0.2	3B(4): 0.3	0.1
2022	MTG	AA	21	246	35	21	0	10	36	25	45	6	2		.305/.394/.548	133	.342	-0.3	3B(35): 0.6, 2B(16): -0.1, 1B(3): -0.4	1.6
2022	DUR	AAA	21	85	8	6	0	3	14	11	17	1	0	20.0%	.278/.376/.486	111	.321	0.1	3B(11): -0.8, 2B(4): -0.4	0.2
2023 DC	*TB*	*MLB*	*22*	*97*	*10*	*5*	*0*	*2*	*9*	*6*	*20*	*0*	*1*	*25.6%*	*.242/.305/.381*	*92*	*.293*	*0.0*	*3B 0*	*0.1*

Comparables: Austin Riley (58), Evan Longoria (57), Mookie Betts (54)

Mead continued to hit well as he reached the upper minors. This is important, because hitting is what will get him to the majors and keep him there. Tampa Bay let him keep playing third base, but ultimately his home will be at the cold corner or DH, as he doesn't have the glove or arm to play regularly anywhere else. Now for the good news: Mead has plus raw power and a 60-grade hit tool. His discipline isn't militant, but he walks plenty and he doesn't strike out at an extraordinary rate. Although he has just a handful of games in Durham under his belt, he is close to major-league ready and could get a call up to Tampa Bay in short order when the Rays need a hitter. They'll just also need the roster flexibility to hide his glove.

Francisco Mejía C Born: 10/27/95 Age: 27 Bats: S Throws: R Height: 5'8" Weight: 188 lb. Origin: International Free Agent, 2012

YEAR	TEAM	LVL	AGE	PA	R	2B	3B	HR	RBI	BB	K	SB	CS	Whiff%	AVG/OBP/SLG	DRC+	BABIP	BRR	DRP	WARP
2020	EST	WIN	24	60	4	1	0	1	6	3	14	0	0		.164/.203/.236		.195			
2020	SD	MLB	24	42	5	1	0	1	2	1	9	0	0	24.5%	.077/.143/.179	83	.069	0.5	C(16): -1	0.0
2021	TB	MLB	25	277	31	15	3	6	35	17	49	0	0	20.4%	.260/.322/.416	100	.299	-0.8	C(76): -0.6, 1B(2): 0	1.0
2022	TB	MLB	26	299	32	22	0	6	31	7	65	0	0	23.5%	.242/.264/.381	85	.292	-1.4	C(83): -6.1, 1B(2): 0	-0.3
2023 DC	*TB*	*MLB*	*27*	*283*	*30*	*14*	*1*	*8*	*31*	*13*	*55*	*0*	*0*	*23.0%*	*.251/.296/.412*	*94*	*.289*	*-1.4*	*C -4*	*0.2*

Comparables: Salvador Perez (67), Wilson Ramos (63), Otto Miller (62)

YEAR	TEAM	P. COUNT	FRM RUNS	BLK RUNS	THRW RUNS	TOT RUNS
2020	SD	1616	-1.0	0.0	0.0	-1.0
2021	TB	9353	-2.1	-0.1	0.3	-1.8
2022	TB	10085	-6.7	-0.3	0.4	-6.7
2023	*TB*	*10822*	*-4.2*	*-0.2*	*0.0*	*-4.3*

With Mike Zunino going down early, it appeared Mejía would become the club's primary backstop. Instead, he ended up in a catching timeshare with Christian Bethancourt and René Pinto. Mejía dealt with a shoulder injury of his own during the summer but was largely replacement-level when healthy. A switch-hitter in title, he offers little at the plate as a lefty other than the occasional long ball. Defensively, he is still a poor receiver who does not appear comfortable blocking pitches. The good news for Mejía is catchers as a whole generally stink offensively, and he's only one year removed from providing a serviceable bat. At the same time, a lot of those players are good at catching, which he is decidedly not. Mejía has a tremendous arm and the Rays are not afraid of trying unconventional moves. Perhaps a tour of the diamond wouldn't be the worst idea for the player or club considering he's entering arbitration.

Isaac Paredes IF Born: 02/18/99 Age: 24 Bats: R Throws: R Height: 5'11" Weight: 213 lb. Origin: International Free Agent, 2015

YEAR	TEAM	LVL	AGE	PA	R	2B	3B	HR	RBI	BB	K	SB	CS	Whiff%	AVG/OBP/SLG	DRC+	BABIP	BRR	DRP	WARP
2020	MAZ	WIN	21	177	28	17	0	4	26	27	12	5	0		.379/.480/.579		.389			
2020	DET	MLB	21	108	7	4	0	1	6	8	24	0	0	17.6%	.220/.278/.290	88	.280	-0.3	3B(33): -1.2	0.0
2021	MAZ	WIN	22	181	26	6	0	4	23	37	20	0	0		.282/.436/.408		.305			
2021	TOL	AAA	22	315	39	10	2	11	42	56	47	0	0		.265/.397/.451	128	.281	-2.9	3B(32): 4.4, 2B(22): -1.4, SS(12): 2.4	2.2
2021	DET	MLB	22	85	7	3	1	1	5	10	11	0	0	13.8%	.208/.306/.319	107	.226	-0.7	2B(10): 0.1, 3B(8): 0.1, SS(5): -0.3	0.3
2022	DUR	AAA	23	113	15	7	1	4	18	13	19	0	1		.263/.354/.484	118	.280	0.0	3B(16): 2.1, 2B(6): 1.3, 1B(2): 0.1	0.9
2022	TB	MLB	23	381	48	16	0	20	45	44	67	0	1	16.5%	.205/.304/.435	125	.195	0.8	3B(50): -0.4, 2B(43): 1.1, 1B(29): -0.4	2.3
2023 DC	*TB*	*MLB*	*24*	*430*	*47*	*16*	*1*	*13*	*45*	*48*	*67*	*1*	*1*	*16.3%*	*.228/.326/.389*	*102*	*.244*	*-0.2*	*3B 0, 1B 0*	*0.9*

Comparables: Wilmer Flores (53), Maikel Franco (52), Andy Marte (49)

Paredes was the shiny lotto ticket the Rays received from Detroit in exchange for Austin Meadows' rising salary. Though he arrived as a light-hitting, unathletic second baseman, Tampa found a power-hitting utility infielder once they scratched off a few sections. Paredes' power surge surprised everyone and led to a sterling DRC+ and ISO. That said, he was a one-trick pony at the plate, and while his BABIP was stunningly low there's not much else portending positive regression. The Rays did a good job of moving him around defensively, including getting Paredes to invest in a first baseman's mitt. It was an unconventional way of coaxing 2.5 WARP out of a cast-off, but it worked. He won't be arbitration-eligible for several more seasons, so the Rays have every incentive to see if he can do it again, and then again.

Harold Ramírez DH Born: 09/06/94 Age: 28 Bats: R Throws: R Height: 5'10" Weight: 232 lb. Origin: International Free Agent, 2011

YEAR	TEAM	LVL	AGE	PA	R	2B	3B	HR	RBI	BB	K	SB	CS	Whiff%	AVG/OBP/SLG	DRC+	BABIP	BRR	DRP	WARP
2020	MIA	MLB	25	11	2	0	0	0	1	1	2	0	1	29.2%	.200/.273/.200	96	.250	0.0	RF(2): -0.1, LF(1): 0	0.0
2021	CLE	MLB	26	361	33	21	1	7	41	14	56	3	1	23.8%	.268/.305/.398	96	.301	-1.0	LF(49): -1.2, RF(34): 0.2, CF(20): -0.9	0.8
2022	TB	MLB	27	435	46	24	0	6	58	19	72	3	5	25.4%	.300/.343/.404	106	.350	0.0	1B(32): -1, RF(24): 0, LF(5): 0.6	1.3
2023 DC	*TB*	*MLB*	*28*	*471*	*49*	*22*	*1*	*10*	*51*	*23*	*84*	*6*	*2*	*24.9%*	*.278/.324/.408*	*106*	*.323*	*-0.4*	*1B 0, RF 0*	*1.1*

Comparables: Chris Stynes (56), Alex Ochoa (56), Eddie Rosario (55)

Ramírez was a late addition to the Rays last season, coming over from Chicago in a late-March trade. Despite his belated arrival, he was in the Opening Day lineup as the club's number three hitter and first baseman; a position he had never started at in the majors before 2022. Thanks to roster attrition and his own surprising production, Ramírez emerged as a near-everyday option when healthy. He missed about a month with a fractured thumb but was one of Tampa's more consistent offensive performers otherwise. Although the underlying stats don't support the flashy average he carried, he should be average (if not flashy) at the dish, with room to grow if he can be used in more of a platoon role. Add in his corner outfield experience, and Ramírez is a useful piece who, fortunately for the Rays, is still several years away from free agency.

Jose Siri CF Born: 07/22/95 Age: 27 Bats: R Throws: R Height: 6'2" Weight: 175 lb. Origin: International Free Agent, 2012

YEAR	TEAM	LVL	AGE	PA	R	2B	3B	HR	RBI	BB	K	SB	CS	Whiff%	AVG/OBP/SLG	DRC+	BABIP	BRR	DRP	WARP
2020	GIG	WIN	24	122	21	7	0	3	14	12	34	7	3		.282/.352/.427		.384			
2021	GIG	WIN	25	77	11	2	0	2	3	7	19	6	0		.217/.289/.333		.271			
2021	SUG	AAA	25	397	70	29	4	16	72	26	122	24	3		.318/.369/.552	96	.436	2.6	CF(42): -3.5, RF(30): -0.2, LF(12): 1.0	1.1
2021	HOU	MLB	25	49	10	0	1	4	9	1	17	3	1	36.2%	.304/.347/.609	88	.400	0.5	RF(9): -0.5, CF(5): 0.6, LF(4): -0.2	0.1
2022	SUG	AAA	26	78	17	3	2	9	22	6	20	2	0	36.1%	.296/.346/.775	121	.279	0.7	CF(10): 2.8, RF(4): 0.9	0.8
2022	TB	MLB	26	178	35	9	0	4	14	11	60	8	1	34.9%	.241/.292/.367	73	.353	3.0	CF(54): 3.6	0.8
2022	HOU	MLB	26	147	18	4	2	3	10	9	48	6	1	37.2%	.178/.238/.304	67	.247	1.2	CF(41): 2.7, RF(3): 0.6, LF(2): 0.1	0.4
2023 DC	*TB*	*MLB*	*27*	*480*	*53*	*19*	*4*	*17*	*54*	*28*	*146*	*23*	*5*	*35.4%*	*.232/.283/.411*	*87*	*.304*	*11.7*	*CF 6*	*2.5*

Comparables: Bubba Starling (57), Roman Quinn (54), Jordan Danks (53)

Not many people know this, but in Sabana Grande de Boyá, Dominican Republic, the name "Jose Siri" translates to "Kevin Kiermaier." We know it's weird, but those are the alternative facts. The Rays acquired Siri in a three-team swap at the deadline more due to his promise than actual production. He looks the part of a baseball star and carries himself in such a manner on the field despite not actually being one yet. Like Kiermaier, he is a tremendous defender with an above-average arm and top-end speed. Also like Kiermaier, he makes plenty of outs at the plate. He had slightly better luck on balls in play with the Rays than the Astros and also showed a bit more pop, but still struck out about five times more than he walked. When he did reach base, he showed what a weapon he can be, successfully stealing bases at an 87.5% clip. Kiermaier is the obvious comp, but B.J. Upton would be an even better outcome for both the player and the club.

Taylor Walls IF Born: 07/10/96 Age: 26 Bats: S Throws: R Height: 5'10" Weight: 185 lb. Origin: Round 3, 2017 Draft (#79 overall)

YEAR	TEAM	LVL	AGE	PA	R	2B	3B	HR	RBI	BB	K	SB	CS	Whiff%	AVG/OBP/SLG	DRC+	BABIP	BRR	DRP	WARP
2021	DUR	AAA	24	222	41	9	1	8	29	40	58	10	5		.247/.387/.444	114	.316	1.5	SS(36): 0.8, 2B(10): -0.9, 3B(6): 0.7	1.2
2021	TB	MLB	24	176	15	10	0	1	15	23	49	4	2	26.3%	.211/.314/.296	81	.304	1.2	SS(49): 2.2, 2B(3): 0	0.5
2022	TB	MLB	25	466	53	18	2	8	33	52	120	10	3	25.6%	.172/.268/.285	76	.221	1.4	SS(92): 6.5, 2B(34): 0.2, 3B(25): -0.1	0.9
2023 DC	*TB*	*MLB*	*26*	*184*	*19*	*7*	*1*	*3*	*16*	*20*	*47*	*5*	*2*	*24.9%*	*.211/.304/.345*	*80*	*.274*	*1.4*	*SS 1, 3B 0*	*0.3*

Comparables: Chris Taylor (68), Chin-Lung Hu (63), Kelly Dransfeldt (63)

Walls breached the Rays lineup far more than anticipated in 2022, racking up nearly 500 plate appearances despite not being very good at hitting baseballs. He hit below his listed weight, and his career average now suggests he'll only get hits around one-sixth of the time. Myriad middle infield injuries left Tampa Bay with few options to fill the voids, and to Walls' credit, he was, at the very least, usually available. He has a solid constitution of defensive principles and is a strict proponent of border security along the infield. That's why Kevin Cash elected to use him so much even if his bat proved quite divisive. Because of his defensive ability, Walls will likely stick around the majors for a while, but it would be best for the Rays if he played far less frequently.

PITCHERS

Jason Adam RHP Born: 08/04/91 Age: 31 Bats: R Throws: R Height: 6'3" Weight: 229 lb. Origin: Round 5, 2010 Draft (#149 overall)

YEAR	TEAM	LVL	AGE	W	L	SV	G	GS	IP	H	HR	BB/9	K/9	K	GB%	BABIP	WHIP	ERA	DRA-	WARP	MPH	FB%	Whiff%	CSP
2020	CHC	MLB	28	2	1	0	13	0	13^{2}	9	2	5.3	13.8	21	37.9%	.259	1.24	3.29	86	0.3	94.9	53.8%	41.7%	42.3%
2021	IOW	AAA	29	1	0	1	5	0	6^{1}	4	0	1.4	8.5	6	23.5%	.235	0.79	0.00	100	0.1				
2021	CHC	MLB	29	1	0	0	12	0	10^{2}	10	1	5.1	16.0	19	36.4%	.429	1.50	5.91	71	0.3	94.1	57.3%	34.0%	50.6%
2022	TB	MLB	30	2	3	8	67	0	63^{1}	31	5	2.4	10.7	75	44.2%	.195	0.76	1.56	74	1.5	95.1	32.1%	38.8%	54.2%
2023 DC	*TB*	*MLB*	*31*	*3*	*3*	*12*	*64*	*0*	*55.7*	*43*	*7*	*3.4*	*11.8*	*72*	*38.4%*	*.288*	*1.16*	*3.23*	*82*	*0.7*	*94.9*	*39.5%*	*34.5%*	*51.6%*

Comparables: Chaz Roe (58), Jose Veras (55), Jeremy Jeffress (54)

Adam became the latest in a long line of scrapheap relievers to turn in a career year with the Rays. A former fifth-round pick of the Royals a dozen years ago, he landed with Tampa Bay after bouncing around the majors, showing sporadic promise but never sustaining success. His fastball has always lived in the mid-90s and boasted elite spin rates, and he'd previously complemented it with a few different breaking balls and a changeup. The Rays simplified his approach, scrapping his curveball and evening out the usage of his three remaining pitches. Adam's fastball became a supporting act, while his low-80s slider and second off-speed offering earned more play. The results? Adam became a relief ace, maintaining an above-average strikeout rate while greatly reducing his walks. He induced more groundballs and fewer home runs en route to allowing less than a baserunner per inning. At age 31 he has several years left of team control, which means the Rays will likely get the best out of his career without coughing up much coin. They can't keep getting away with this, can they?

Shawn Armstrong RHP

Born: 09/11/90 Age: 32 Bats: R Throws: R Height: 6'2" Weight: 225 lb. Origin: Round 18, 2011 Draft (#548 overall)

YEAR	TEAM	LVL	AGE	W	L	SV	G	GS	IP	H	HR	BB/9	K/9	K	GB%	BABIP	WHIP	ERA	DRA-	WARP	MPH	FB%	Whiff%	CSP
2020	BAL	MLB	29	2	0	0	14	0	15	9	1	1.8	8.4	14	43.6%	.211	0.80	1.80	91	0.2	90.8	89.0%	26.2%	48.9%
2021	NOR	AAA	30	1	3	0	15	0	17	19	3	3.2	11.1	21	49.0%	.333	1.47	3.18	90	0.3				
2021	DUR	AAA	30	2	1	2	14	0	14	10	1	1.3	12.9	20	45.2%	.310	0.86	2.57	75	0.4				
2021	TB	MLB	30	1	0	0	11	0	16	11	5	2.8	12.4	22	32.4%	.188	1.00	4.50	92	0.2	94.2	85.6%	33.1%	52.8%
2021	BAL	MLB	30	0	0	0	20	0	20	28	5	4.5	9.9	22	31.3%	.371	1.90	8.55	105	0.1	92.2	90.5%	31.1%	51.3%
2022	DUR	AAA	31	0	0	2	7	0	7	5	0	2.6	12.9	10	66.7%	.333	1.00	2.57	79	0.2				
2022	MIA	MLB	31	0	0	0	7	0	6^2	10	1	4.1	6.8	5	38.5%	.360	1.95	10.80	110	0.0	95.1	48.0%	25.0%	50.2%
2022	TB	MLB	31	2	3	2	43	3	55	56	6	2.3	10.0	61	50.0%	.336	1.27	3.60	81	1.1	95.7	66.7%	26.3%	58.7%
2023 DC	*TB*	*MLB*	*32*	*3*	*3*	*0*	*64*	*0*	*55.7*	*53*	*6*	*3.0*	*9.0*	*55*	*43.1%*	*.303*	*1.28*	*3.67*	*94*	*0.4*	*94.3*	*74.2%*	*26.6%*	*54.6%*

Comparables: Heath Hembree (50), Tyler Thornburg (49), Javy Guerra (49)

Stone Cold Shawn Armstrong returned to Tampa Bay last May after a brief, ill-fated stint down south with the Marlins. An arm barn journeyman through and through, he enjoyed some success with the Rays in 2021 and became a steady force for Kevin Cash once back by the bay. The Rays' way for Armstrong is pretty simple: throw things hard. Tampa catchers put the number one sign between their legs (or at least signaled as such via PitchCom) almost 67% of the time Armstrong was on the mound, and the remaining pitches he was asked to throw were mostly variations of his heater. His traditional fastball came in around 95 mph while his cutter flew in just under 93 mph. Both represented increases over his career norms, and Armstrong's harder stuff led to weaker contact from opposing batters: He generated an exit velocity under 87 mph and a ground-ball rate of about 50%. Without a bunch of saves to his name and with two years of arbitration remaining, Armstrong can be kept by the Rays for the next few seasons at reasonable rates. That's probably good for him, too, as it's clear that Armstrong should stay out of Miami.

Shane Baz RHP

Born: 06/17/99 Age: 24 Bats: R Throws: R Height: 6'2" Weight: 190 lb. Origin: Round 1, 2017 Draft (#12 overall)

YEAR	TEAM	LVL	AGE	W	L	SV	G	GS	IP	H	HR	BB/9	K/9	K	GB%	BABIP	WHIP	ERA	DRA-	WARP	MPH	FB%	Whiff%	CSP
2021	MTG	AA	22	2	4	0	7	7	32^2	22	3	0.6	13.5	49	44.8%	.297	0.73	2.48	76	0.7				
2021	DUR	AAA	22	3	0	0	10	10	46	28	6	2.2	12.5	64	39.8%	.242	0.85	1.76	79	1.1				
2021	TB	MLB	22	2	0	0	3	3	13^1	6	3	2.0	12.1	18	39.3%	.120	0.68	2.03	91	0.2	97.2	54.5%	35.3%	53.7%
2022	DUR	AAA	23	0	0	0	4	4	13	8	1	2.8	13.8	20	42.9%	.259	0.92	1.38	80	0.3				
2022	TB	MLB	23	1	2	0	6	6	27	27	5	3.0	10.0	30	44.2%	.306	1.33	5.00	91	0.4	96.1	40.1%	30.6%	56.3%
2023 non-DC	*TB*	*MLB*	*24*	*2*	*2*	*0*	*57*	*0*	*50*	*43*	*6*	*3.1*	*10.9*	*60*	*41.7%*	*.302*	*1.22*	*3.37*	*86*	*0.6*	*96.4*	*43.7%*	*32.4%*	*55.7%*

Comparables: Dylan Cease (81), Tyler Mahle (80), Mitch Keller (80)

Fresh off his impressive rookie season, Baz underwent arthroscopic surgery to remove nomadic fragments in his elbow during the spring, delaying his 2022 debut until the summer. But something seemed off in the six starts he made upon his return, and Baz was soon shut down once more with an elbow sprain. By September we learned that Baz would require Tommy John surgery, which means he'll spend all winter and likely all of next season rehabbing. It's a bummer for both the man himself and the organization, as the brief glimpses we caught of Baz in 2022 saw him feature more sliders with the same premium velocity as in 2021. He'll retain his elite upside even after another surgical procedure, but will not pitch a significant inning for the Rays in 2023 while accruing a year of service time. Sometimes the baseball goods seem needlessly cruel.

Jalen Beeks LHP

Born: 07/10/93 Age: 29 Bats: L Throws: L Height: 5'11" Weight: 215 lb. Origin: Round 12, 2014 Draft (#374 overall)

YEAR	TEAM	LVL	AGE	W	L	SV	G	GS	IP	H	HR	BB/9	K/9	K	GB%	BABIP	WHIP	ERA	DRA-	WARP	MPH	FB%	Whiff%	CSP
2020	TB	MLB	26	1	1	1	12	0	19^1	21	1	1.9	12.1	26	41.2%	.408	1.29	3.26	73	0.5	93.5	42.0%	32.9%	51.1%
2022	TB	MLB	28	2	3	2	42	7	61	49	7	3.2	10.3	70	45.5%	.284	1.16	2.80	86	1.0	95.2	48.1%	31.3%	52.3%
2023 DC	*TB*	*MLB*	*29*	*3*	*3*	*4*	*64*	*0*	*55.7*	*51*	*6*	*3.4*	*9.9*	*61*	*45.2%*	*.307*	*1.31*	*3.78*	*96*	*0.4*	*94.2*	*46.3%*	*29.7%*	*50.4%*

Comparables: Zack Britton (67), Liam Hendriks (67), Alex Colomé (64)

After missing the entire 2021 season recovering from Tommy John surgery, Beeks returned as an effective, flexible piece of the Rays bullpen. He logged 40+ appearances despite right leg injuries that pushed him to the IL twice. He pitched in both long and short relief and served as an opener and a closer when needed. He picked up a few ticks on his fastball post-surgery, going from the low-90s previously to sitting around 95 mph most nights. And his heater was used just as much as his changeup, with that one-two punch making up almost his entire pitch selection. He'll head to arbitration with solid rates, but without much to stand on regarding counting stats. He is, in essence, the platonic ideal of a Tampa Bay Rays pitcher.

★ ★ ★ *2023 Top 101 Prospect* **#23** ★ ★ ★

Taj Bradley RHP

Born: 03/20/01 Age: 22 Bats: R Throws: R Height: 6'2" Weight: 190 lb. Origin: Round 5, 2018 Draft (#150 overall)

YEAR	TEAM	LVL	AGE	W	L	SV	G	GS	IP	H	HR	BB/9	K/9	K	GB%	BABIP	WHIP	ERA	DRA-	WARP	MPH	FB%	Whiff%	CSP
2021	CSC	A	20	9	3	0	15	14	66^2	37	4	2.7	10.9	81	50.3%	.237	0.85	1.76	79	1.5				
2021	BG	A+	20	3	0	0	8	8	36^2	28	4	2.7	10.3	42	47.4%	.267	1.06	1.96	85	0.6				
2022	MTG	AA	21	3	1	0	16	16	74^1	50	4	2.2	10.7	88	39.5%	.266	0.91	1.70	84	1.4				
2022	DUR	AAA	21	4	3	0	12	12	59	55	10	2.3	8.1	53	34.1%	.271	1.19	3.66	93	1.0	94.6	55.5%	23.3%	
2023 DC	*TB*	*MLB*	*22*	*1*	*2*	*0*	*6*	*6*	*30.3*	*30*	*4*	*3.2*	*8.0*	*27*	*41.0%*	*.299*	*1.36*	*4.28*	*108*	*0.1*			*24.8%*	

Comparables: Luis Severino (73), Brady Lail (72), Logan Allen (71)

A fifth-round pick in 2018, Bradley looks poised to become the next pitching prospect the league falls in love with. He has a solid, athletic build that should be able to withstand the workload of the modern-day starter. Bradley works off two plus pitches: a mid-90s fastball and an upper-80s cutter that has late, slider-like break. He also tosses a curveball and a changeup to round out his arsenal, and he shows plus control while aspiring to plus command. After dominating at Double-A Montgomery, Bradley took a slight step back in Durham. But he did so as a 21-year-old, and after finishing the season strong his Triple-A stats look just fine: He held opposing batters to a .189/.226/.347 line with 30 strikeouts and six walks over his final 35 innings. He's likely to make his debut at some point in 2023, at which point we may be able to rebrand The Trop as Taj's Mahal.

Yonny Chirinos RHP

Born: 12/26/93 Age: 29 Bats: R Throws: R Height: 6'2" Weight: 225 lb. Origin: International Free Agent, 2012

YEAR	TEAM	LVL	AGE	W	L	SV	G	GS	IP	H	HR	BB/9	K/9	K	GB%	BABIP	WHIP	ERA	DRA-	WARP	MPH	FB%	Whiff%	CSP
2020	TB	MLB	26	0	0	0	3	3	11^1	14	2	3.2	7.9	10	30.6%	.353	1.59	2.38	118	0.0	93.5	60.5%	30.1%	41.4%
2022	CSC	A	28	0	1	0	3	2	6^1	9	1	2.8	8.5	6	45.5%	.381	1.74	11.37	101	0.1				
2022	DUR	AAA	28	0	0	0	5	5	16	11	2	3.4	7.3	13	54.5%	.220	1.06	2.81	92	0.3	93.7	61.5%	42.1%	
2022	TB	MLB	28	1	0	0	2	1	7	7	0	1.3	7.7	6	77.3%	.318	1.14	0.00	96	0.1	93.6	59.0%	20.4%	58.5%
2023 DC	*TB*	*MLB*	*29*	*5*	*5*	*0*	*40*	*12*	*76.3*	*79*	*9*	*2.8*	*7.5*	*63*	*47.7%*	*.305*	*1.35*	*4.20*	*107*	*0.3*	*93.9*	*57.6%*	*25.7%*	*49.5%*

Comparables: Trevor Williams (52), Nick Tropeano (51), Brad Peacock (51)

Chirinos went more than two full calendar years—from August 16, 2020, to September 7, 2022—between MLB appearances. Initially, his absence was due to the standard year-or-so of rehabilitation that most pitchers must endure post-Tommy John surgery. But as Chirinos neared the end of his initial rehab, he fractured his right elbow while throwing. That makes it all the more impressive that he not only fought his way back to the majors but reintroduced himself to the Rays by tossing three shutout innings in relief. He also became the 25th different pitcher to win a game for the club within one season—a new team record. In limited action, Chirinos showed a similar three-pitch medley (fastball, slider, splitter) with similar velocity and control as before his injuries. Hopefully, he can finally enjoy a healthy offseason that leaves him available to compete for a spot on the Rays' 2023 Opening Day roster.

Garrett Cleavinger LHP

Born: 04/23/94 Age: 29 Bats: R Throws: L Height: 6'1" Weight: 220 lb. Origin: Round 3, 2015 Draft (#102 overall)

YEAR	TEAM	LVL	AGE	W	L	SV	G	GS	IP	H	HR	BB/9	K/9	K	GB%	BABIP	WHIP	ERA	DRA-	WARP	MPH	FB%	Whiff%	CSP
2020	PHI	MLB	26	0	0	0	1	0	0^2	2	1	0.0	13.5	1	66.7%	.500	3.00	13.50	59	0.0	94.3	50.0%	50.0%	62.0%
2021	OKC	AAA	27	1	0	0	11	0	11^2	9	0	3.9	19.3	25	47.1%	.529	1.20	1.54	54	0.3				
2021	LAD	MLB	27	2	4	0	22	1	18	20	4	6.0	10.5	21	48.0%	.356	1.78	3.00	87	0.3	95.9	54.5%	26.1%	53.5%
2022	DUR	AAA	28	0	0	2	9	0	9	2	0	3.0	17.0	17	50.0%	.167	0.56	1.00	69	0.3				
2022	OKC	AAA	28	0	2	1	22	1	29	20	4	5.3	14.6	47	33.3%	.302	1.28	2.79	74	0.6	95.8	37.4%	42.9%	
2022	LAD	MLB	28	0	1	0	4	0	4^1	6	1	6.2	14.5	7	30.8%	.455	2.08	10.38	86	0.1	95.9	51.5%	27.0%	47.8%
2022	TB	MLB	28	1	0	0	13	0	18^2	8	1	1.9	12.1	25	41.0%	.184	0.64	2.41	76	0.4	96.1	54.8%	31.7%	53.8%
2023 DC	*TB*	*MLB*	*29*	*3*	*3*	*0*	*64*	*0*	*55.7*	*44*	*6*	*4.7*	*11.1*	*68*	*43.1%*	*.287*	*1.31*	*3.57*	*88*	*0.6*	*96.0*	*54.1%*	*31.4%*	*52.8%*

Comparables: Chasen Shreve (61), Sam Freeman (59), Jake Diekman (58)

Cleavinger, a former third-round pick of the Orioles, was nabbed by Tampa Bay in a minor trade last August. It was not the first time he was involved in a Rays-related transaction: Cleavinger went to Los Angeles from Baltimore in a three-way deal involving his current club in late 2020. Tampa Bay didn't receive any meaningful returns from that old swap but got immediate results from Cleavinger in 2022. The lefty has always had a big arm and plus breaking ball, but, like many of his ilk, throwing strikes had proved to be a challenge. Though he walked more than a batter every other inning with the Dodgers, you can probably guess what happened once he was traded to the Rays: He dramatically improved his control without seriously hampering his strikeout rate, because of course he did. On the surface, his diet remained the same, as he relied heavily on fastballs and sliders. But a quick check of the recipe list shows he mixed in more sinkers at the expense of his traditional four-seamers. If you're looking for an early 2023 candidate for "Rays pitcher who annoys the rest of the league because they didn't know how good he was until he got to Tampa," Cleavinger is a solid choice.

Zach Eflin RHP Born: 04/08/94 Age: 29 Bats: R Throws: R Height: 6'6" Weight: 220 lb. Origin: Round 1, 2012 Draft (#33 overall)

YEAR	TEAM	LVL	AGE	W	L	SV	G	GS	IP	H	HR	BB/9	K/9	K	GB%	BABIP	WHIP	ERA	DRA-	WARP	MPH	FB%	Whiff%	CSP
2020	PHI	MLB	26	4	2	0	11	10	59	60	8	2.3	10.7	70	46.5%	.347	1.27	3.97	70	1.5	94.1	61.1%	24.0%	48.3%
2021	PHI	MLB	27	4	7	0	18	18	105^{2}	116	15	1.4	8.4	99	43.2%	.328	1.25	4.17	94	1.4	92.8	54.4%	23.0%	54.8%
2022	PHI	MLB	28	3	5	1	20	13	75^{2}	70	8	1.8	7.7	65	45.2%	.282	1.12	4.04	94	1.0	93.1	55.4%	22.2%	52.3%
2023 DC	*TB*	*MLB*	*29*	*7*	*7*	*0*	*24*	*24*	*126.3*	*128*	*15*	*2.0*	*7.9*	*111*	*44.8%*	*.305*	*1.24*	*3.61*	*96*	*1.3*	*93.3*	*55.8%*	*23.0%*	*52.1%*

Comparables: Rick Porcello (78), Oil Can Boyd (77), Rick Wise (77)

Eflin's player comments are beginning to sound a lot like the knights from the Monty Python film—they just keep saying "knee." The right-hander got off to a good start in 2022, doing exactly what he does best: limiting walks and inducing weak contact. He turned his curveball into his go-to breaking pitch (replacing his slider), and the results were excellent. Then, his promising start was interrupted by chronic knee issues, which threatened to cut his season short for a second straight year. However, he fought his way back just in time to become a major bullpen piece for the Phillies' postseason run. He looked healthy and effective in his new role, and his curveball in particular dazzled in October. It was a strong ending to another difficult season: Strong enough that the Rays were willing to make Eflin their highest-paid player this winter, inking him to a three-year, $35 million deal that marks their most expensive foray into free agency as a franchise.

Pete Fairbanks RHP Born: 12/16/93 Age: 29 Bats: R Throws: R Height: 6'6" Weight: 225 lb. Origin: Round 9, 2015 Draft (#258 overall)

YEAR	TEAM	LVL	AGE	W	L	SV	G	GS	IP	H	HR	BB/9	K/9	K	GB%	BABIP	WHIP	ERA	DRA-	WARP	MPH	FB%	Whiff%	CSP
2020	TB	MLB	26	6	3	0	27	2	26^{2}	23	2	4.7	13.2	39	48.4%	.350	1.39	2.70	68	0.8	97.7	57.6%	37.4%	42.5%
2021	TB	MLB	27	3	6	5	47	0	42^{2}	40	2	4.4	11.8	56	42.3%	.349	1.43	3.59	82	0.8	97.5	53.5%	30.6%	55.9%
2022	TB	MLB	28	0	0	8	24	0	24	13	1	1.1	14.2	38	53.3%	.273	0.67	1.13	58	0.8	99.2	61.4%	35.5%	56.2%
2023 DC	*TB*	*MLB*	*29*	*3*	*2*	*17*	*64*	*0*	*55.7*	*46*	*5*	*3.3*	*11.5*	*71*	*47.1%*	*.304*	*1.19*	*2.91*	*75*	*0.9*	*98.0*	*55.7%*	*32.3%*	*52.8%*

Comparables: Ryne Stanek (64), Giovanny Gallegos (63), Steve Cishek (60)

The Rays describe Fairbanks' overall performance as "controlled violence." Up until 2022, the "controlled" part of that description was a misnomer, but the "violence" part has long been evident: Fairbanks throws really hard over and over again and looks like a maniac while doing so. As for control? He walked more than 10% of the batters he faced from 2019-2021 and seemed destined to forever be a wild thrower who got results because his stuff was just that good. But after Fairbanks suffered a torn lat in the spring that sidelined him until mid-summer, he came back a different pitcher. He still featured a violent delivery, but added about two ticks to his fastball—it now *sits* at 99 mph. He also maintained his hard, upper-80s slider. The biggest surprise was that Fairbanks resurfaced with legit control. He also surrendered just one home run, leaving him with tremendous fielding-independent marks. Typically, the Rays avoid using their best reliever to rack up saves, and thanks largely due to missed time, Fairbanks only notched a handful of them last season. Even so, he should see a bump in salary as he goes through the arbitration process for the first time, and if the post-injury version of Fairbanks is the one who's here to stay, the sky's the limit in terms of his future earnings.

Tyler Glasnow RHP Born: 08/23/93 Age: 29 Bats: L Throws: R Height: 6'8" Weight: 225 lb. Origin: Round 5, 2011 Draft (#152 overall)

YEAR	TEAM	LVL	AGE	W	L	SV	G	GS	IP	H	HR	BB/9	K/9	K	GB%	BABIP	WHIP	ERA	DRA-	WARP	MPH	FB%	Whiff%	CSP
2020	TB	MLB	26	5	1	0	11	11	57^{1}	43	11	3.5	14.3	91	40.0%	.281	1.13	4.08	61	1.9	97.2	60.6%	32.8%	45.9%
2021	TB	MLB	27	5	2	0	14	14	88	55	10	2.8	12.6	123	45.3%	.250	0.93	2.66	67	2.4	97.2	51.6%	37.1%	60.4%
2022	DUR	AAA	28	0	0	0	4	4	7	1	0	5.1	18.0	14	12.5%	.125	0.71	1.29	77	0.2				
2022	TB	MLB	28	0	0	0	2	2	6^{2}	4	1	2.7	13.5	10	35.7%	.231	0.90	1.35	84	0.1	97.6	53.5%	32.1%	55.4%
2023 DC	*TB*	*MLB*	*29*	*8*	*6*	*0*	*24*	*24*	*121.3*	*90*	*13*	*3.2*	*12.5*	*168*	*43.4%*	*.291*	*1.11*	*2.48*	*65*	*3.2*	*97.2*	*56.0%*	*33.5%*	*55.0%*

Comparables: Chris Archer (52), Trevor Bauer (49), Tyler Chatwood (48)

Glasnow was arguably pitching better than anyone in the American League in June of 2021 before his elbow started barking at him. Two months later he underwent Tommy John surgery, thereby missing almost the entire 2022 season. He did return in late September to make two abbreviated starts. Once again, he looked like one of the best pitchers in the game for those 6⅔ innings. He featured the same upper-90s fastball and pair of devastating breaking balls as before his injury: a hard, biting slider that sits in the upper 80s to low 90s, plus a low-80s hook with big break. Glasnow should benefit from a normal offseason and, if healthy, is in line to be the Rays' Opening Day starter once more. It may be his last time serving as such in Tampa, as the unique two-year extension he signed will pay him just $5 million and change in 2023 before jumping to $25 million in 2024.

Andrew Kittredge RHP Born: 03/17/90 Age: 33 Bats: R Throws: R Height: 6'1" Weight: 230 lb. Origin: Round 45, 2008 Draft (#1360 overall)

YEAR	TEAM	LVL	AGE	W	L	SV	G	GS	IP	H	HR	BB/9	K/9	K	GB%	BABIP	WHIP	ERA	DRA-	WARP	MPH	FB%	Whiff%	CSP
2020	TB	MLB	30	0	0	1	8	1	8	8	0	2.3	3.4	3	57.7%	.308	1.25	2.25	106	0.1	94.6	47.8%	15.0%	58.8%
2021	TB	MLB	31	9	3	8	57	4	71^{2}	55	7	1.9	9.7	77	53.5%	.268	0.98	1.88	80	1.4	95.5	54.5%	31.2%	53.8%
2022	TB	MLB	32	3	1	5	17	0	20	15	4	0.9	6.3	14	45.8%	.200	0.85	3.15	101	0.2	95.3	59.7%	25.2%	53.0%
2023 DC	*TB*	*MLB*	*33*	*1*	*1*	*0*	*21*	*0*	*18.3*	*19*	*1*	*2.2*	*7.8*	*16*	*49.2%*	*.310*	*1.27*	*3.60*	*95*	*0.1*	*95.3*	*55.8%*	*27.2%*	*52.3%*

Comparables: George Kontos (58), Nick Vincent (58), Pedro Báez (56)

Our big, sleepy boy avoided major surgery in 2021, but alas, he merely delayed the inevitable—his long-balky UCL finally needed Tommy John surgery in June, and he will likely miss most, if not all, of 2023 as a result. Maybe he'll finally get some rest, at least? Prior to his elbow coming apart, Kittredge was on his way to another fine season out of the Rays' bullpen, serving as the de facto closer most nights. He churned through batters with his two-pitch mix: a mid-90s fastball and a hard slider, of course, because he was a reliever in the year 2022. The next time he throws a meaningful major-league pitch, Kittredge will likely be 33, but because he got a late start in the bigs he'll remain under team control for the next several seasons regardless of his health.

Shane McClanahan LHP

Born: 04/28/97 Age: 26 Bats: L Throws: L Height: 6'1" Weight: 200 lb. Origin: Round 1, 2018 Draft (#31 overall)

YEAR	TEAM	LVL	AGE	W	L	SV	G	GS	IP	H	HR	BB/9	K/9	K	GB%	BABIP	WHIP	ERA	DRA-	WARP	MPH	FB%	Whiff%	CSP
2021	TB	MLB	24	10	6	0	25	25	123^{1}	120	14	2.7	10.3	141	45.7%	.330	1.27	3.43	89	1.9	96.8	40.9%	32.1%	56.8%
2022	TB	MLB	25	12	8	0	28	28	166^{1}	116	19	2.1	10.5	194	49.9%	.252	0.93	2.54	70	4.2	97.0	35.7%	34.3%	55.4%
2023 DC	*TB*	*MLB*	*26*	*10*	*7*	*0*	*27*	*27*	*162.3*	*139*	*17*	*2.7*	*11.2*	*201*	*47.9%*	*.308*	*1.16*	*2.82*	*74*	*3.5*	*96.9*	*37.6%*	*32.3%*	*55.9%*

Comparables: Steven Matz (77), Sean Newcomb (75), Jordan Montgomery (75)

McClanahan isn't always first in people's minds, but that's their problem. He was not the first left-handed pitcher selected by the Rays in 2018: That was Matthew Liberatore. Soon after that draft, Tampa Bay traded for an even more highly touted Shane in Baz. Despite a solid rookie season, McClanahan finished third among rookies on his own team in the AL Rookie of the Year vote.

But in 2022, McClanahan stepped out of the shadows. He improved upon his stellar rookie campaign with an even better sophomore season. He upped his strikeouts, lowered his walk rate and allowed fewer hits while inducing groundballs 50% of the time. He was the first pitcher to toe the rubber for the American League All-Star team and finished sixth in the AL Cy Young vote; shoulder and neck injuries caused him to miss time at the end of the season that probably prevented him from finishing even higher.

After showing dazzling stuff in 2021, he diversified his arsenal to become more well-rounded. He dropped a few upper-90 fastballs and hard sliders in favor of a few more curveballs and a lot more split-fingered changeups to great success. That change in pitch selection improved his numbers across the board and allowed the southpaw to dominate across the platoon split, boasting a .192 average against right-handers. No one should overlook McClanahan anymore—he's set to help front the Rays rotation even as numerous talented pitchers around him return to action.

★ ★ ★ *2023 Top 101 Prospect* **#84** ★ ★ ★

Mason Montgomery LHP

Born: 06/17/00 Age: 23 Bats: L Throws: L Height: 6'2" Weight: 195 lb. Origin: Round 6, 2021 Draft (#191 overall)

YEAR	TEAM	LVL	AGE	W	L	SV	G	GS	IP	H	HR	BB/9	K/9	K	GB%	BABIP	WHIP	ERA	DRA-	WARP	MPH	FB%	Whiff%	CSP
2021	RAY	ROK	21	1	0	0	5	4	10^{2}	4	0	0.8	16.9	20	12.5%	.250	0.47	0.84						
2022	BG	A+	22	3	2	0	16	16	69^{2}	49	6	3.5	15.2	118	43.7%	.333	1.09	1.81	73	1.6				
2022	MTG	AA	22	3	1	0	11	11	54^{1}	40	5	2.7	8.8	53	45.6%	.245	1.03	2.48	90	0.8				
2023 non-DC	*TB*	*MLB*	*23*	*2*	*2*	*0*	*57*	*0*	*50*	*48*	*6*	*4.3*	*9.7*	*53*	*43.9%*	*.312*	*1.44*	*4.32*	*106*	*0.1*			*28.0%*	

Comparables: Brian Johnson (87), Steven Brault (86), Zac Lowther (85)

Though he relies on subversion over stuff, Montgomery is a southpaw starter who could be ready for the big leagues just two years after his sixth-round selection in 2021. He blew through the lower minors on the back of a changeup that frankly overpowered High-A hitters, racking up a K% over 40. That dropped substantially upon his arrival in Double-A, but he still flourished thanks to a deceptive delivery that gives batters fits when trying to pick up the ball. In any other org, Montgomery might not be viewed so kindly, but Tampa Bay has made a habit of optimizing guys with weird release points and arm actions. He profiles as a back-end arm for now, but as a Rays prospect he could emerge as a righty with a plus slider at any moment.

Luis Patiño RHP

Born: 10/26/99 Age: 23 Bats: R Throws: R Height: 6'1" Weight: 192 lb. Origin: International Free Agent, 2016

YEAR	TEAM	LVL	AGE	W	L	SV	G	GS	IP	H	HR	BB/9	K/9	K	GB%	BABIP	WHIP	ERA	DRA-	WARP	MPH	FB%	Whiff%	CSP
2020	SD	MLB	20	1	0	0	11	1	17^{1}	18	3	7.3	10.9	21	34.7%	.326	1.85	5.19	117	0.0	96.8	64.8%	26.4%	46.4%
2021	DUR	AAA	21	3	1	0	7	7	29^{1}	23	2	3.4	12.6	41	38.2%	.318	1.16	3.07	88	0.6				
2021	TB	MLB	21	5	3	0	19	15	77^{1}	69	12	3.4	8.6	74	31.7%	.265	1.27	4.31	119	-0.1	96.0	63.7%	25.4%	55.9%
2022	DUR	AAA	22	3	2	0	9	9	34	32	6	3.4	9.0	34	38.1%	.286	1.32	4.50	92	0.6	94.0	47.5%	27.4%	
2022	TB	MLB	22	1	2	0	6	6	20	26	6	5.9	5.0	11	37.0%	.299	1.95	8.10	151	-0.3	94.7	57.3%	21.2%	54.1%
2023 DC	*TB*	*MLB*	*23*	*6*	*6*	*0*	*51*	*9*	*75.7*	*77*	*10*	*4.2*	*7.7*	*65*	*36.4%*	*.298*	*1.49*	*4.73*	*116*	*-0.1*	*95.8*	*62.3%*	*24.8%*	*54.4%*

Comparables: Jacob Turner (59), Bryse Wilson (57), Sean O'Sullivan (56)

Patiño would probably like a mulligan for last season. Poised to serve as a full-fledged member of the Rays rotation, he instead suffered an oblique injury just 13 pitches into his campaign. That kept him sidelined for months, and upon his return he battled blisters, shoulder discomfort and opposing batters to little success—he issued more walks than strikeouts in the majors. His velocity was down across the board, and his fastball spin rate was Carolina Blue on Statcast. Here come the obligatory caveats: Patiño still throws hard, is just a few years removed from ranking as a top prospect and won't turn 24 until October. He hasn't been good yet, but has too much talent to write off. Let's give him a do-over.

Colin Poche LHP

Born: 01/17/94 Age: 29 Bats: L Throws: L Height: 6'3" Weight: 225 lb. Origin: Round 14, 2016 Draft (#419 overall)

YEAR	TEAM	LVL	AGE	W	L	SV	G	GS	IP	H	HR	BB/9	K/9	K	GB%	BABIP	WHIP	ERA	DRA-	WARP	MPH	FB%	Whiff%	CSP
2022	DUR	AAA	28	0	0	1	6	0	6	1	0	3.0	16.5	11	25.0%	.125	0.50	0.00	81	0.1				
2022	TB	MLB	28	4	2	7	65	0	58^{2}	46	11	3.4	9.8	64	31.6%	.238	1.16	3.99	99	0.6	93.5	77.5%	28.0%	55.7%
2023 DC	*TB*	*MLB*	*29*	*3*	*3*	*8*	*64*	*0*	*55.7*	*45*	*7*	*3.4*	*10.4*	*64*	*31.4%*	*.277*	*1.19*	*3.18*	*83*	*0.7*	*93.4*	*79.5%*	*29.7%*	*54.4%*

Comparables: Jake Diekman (74), Danny Coulombe (69), Sam Freeman (69)

When things are going well, you may hear the crowd at The Trop chanting, "Hey, we want some Po-che." When things are going bad, the opposing teams' crowds may be chanting the same thing. Poche returned to the majors after a two-year absence following Tommy John surgery and recovery. Though he only throws his fastball around 93 mph, his unusual delivery and its movement make it the lead offering in his arsenal. He did curb his usage of it a bit, no longer leaning on an extreme 90/10 split between heater and slider—it was more of an 80/20 deal in 2022, so here's to moderation. Alas, his modestly new approach did not really work, as he notched fewer strikeouts and walks while coughing up too many long balls. His seven saves aside, his profile is not conducive to late-inning work. It *is* conducive to tossing another 60 or so innings as a low-leverage option.

Drew Rasmussen RHP Born: 07/27/95 Age: 27 Bats: R Throws: R Height: 6'1" Weight: 211 lb. Origin: Round 6, 2018 Draft (#185 overall)

YEAR	TEAM	LVL	AGE	W	L	SV	G	GS	IP	H	HR	BB/9	K/9	K	GB%	BABIP	WHIP	ERA	DRA-	WARP	MPH	FB%	Whiff%	CSP
2020	MIL	MLB	24	1	0	0	12	0	15^1	17	3	5.3	12.3	21	53.7%	.368	1.70	5.87	84	0.3	98.0	68.2%	32.0%	44.7%
2021	DUR	AAA	25	2	0	1	8	1	11^1	5	0	1.6	18.3	23	60.0%	.333	0.62	0.00	66	0.4				
2021	MIL	MLB	25	0	1	1	15	0	17	13	2	6.4	13.2	25	32.5%	.289	1.47	4.24	82	0.3	97.3	67.7%	30.7%	54.9%
2021	TB	MLB	25	4	0	0	20	10	59	44	3	2.0	7.3	48	50.9%	.248	0.97	2.44	97	0.6	97.4	63.6%	23.5%	56.6%
2022	TB	MLB	26	11	7	0	28	28	146	121	13	1.9	7.7	125	47.0%	.264	1.04	2.84	85	2.6	94.4	72.0%	25.3%	55.6%
2023 DC	*TB*	*MLB*	*27*	*8*	*8*	*0*	*27*	*27*	*143*	*140*	*15*	*2.8*	*8.7*	*138*	*47.3%*	*.309*	*1.29*	*3.57*	*93*	*1.5*	*95.4*	*69.9%*	*26.5%*	*55.2%*

Comparables: Andrew Cashner (62), Brandon Beachy (55), Pete Vuckovich (55)

As with Jeffrey Springs, the Rays plucked Rasmussen from the bullpen and turned him into a better-than-average starting pitcher. Formerly a fastball/slider guy—stop us if you've heard that before—the right-hander added a cutter to give himself a trio of offerings. That cutter comes in a few ticks higher than his slider, but several notches below his mid-90s fastball. Rasmussen had shown decent control previously but also displayed advanced command in 2022. He limited walks and home runs while inducing a ground-ball rate just south of 50%. Better yet, that cutter helped him not only solve the platoon issues that plagued him early in his career but produce reverse splits. Despite his success, the Rays limited his innings somewhat, which they undoubtedly hope will keep his arm healthy, his counting stats low and his salary relatively cheap over the next few seasons.

Jeffrey Springs LHP Born: 09/20/92 Age: 30 Bats: L Throws: L Height: 6'3" Weight: 218 lb. Origin: Round 30, 2015 Draft (#888 overall)

YEAR	TEAM	LVL	AGE	W	L	SV	G	GS	IP	H	HR	BB/9	K/9	K	GB%	BABIP	WHIP	ERA	DRA-	WARP	MPH	FB%	Whiff%	CSP
2020	BOS	MLB	27	0	2	0	16	0	20^1	30	5	3.1	12.4	28	36.5%	.431	1.82	7.08	78	0.5	92.4	46.9%	37.6%	48.0%
2021	TB	MLB	28	5	1	2	43	0	44^2	35	9	2.8	12.7	63	33.3%	.283	1.10	3.43	73	1.1	93.6	41.9%	36.6%	52.3%
2022	TB	MLB	29	9	5	0	33	25	135^1	114	14	2.1	9.6	144	41.0%	.280	1.07	2.46	82	2.5	91.7	40.5%	29.6%	53.3%
2023 DC	*TB*	*MLB*	*30*	*10*	*9*	*0*	*50*	*22*	*142.7*	*137*	*20*	*2.7*	*9.8*	*155*	*38.5%*	*.310*	*1.26*	*3.70*	*96*	*1.1*	*92.1*	*42.2%*	*30.9%*	*52.5%*

Comparables: Fernando Abad (53), Danny Coulombe (51), Jake Diekman (50)

Baseball Twitter loves to talk about the hocus pocus employed by the Rays when it comes to random pitchers joining the franchise and enjoying unparalleled success. Sometimes it seems warranted. Sometimes it's hyperbolic. And sometimes, as in the case of Springs, it makes you ask: *what the absolute hell?!* The Rays picked up Springs in a small trade with the Red Sox in February 2021. He was a serviceable reliever for them in the season that followed, tossing 44 innings in 43 appearances. He never even opened a game. He was fine. And then … the Rays somehow turned him into a really good starting pitcher overnight. The craziest thing is, not much in his profile changed. He still worked off a low-90s fastball, losing some velo as a starter. He threw fewer sliders and more changeups, but nothing earth-shattering. He mixed up his repertoire and threw strikes. He was simply a good reliever who the Rays let try and be good for longer … and it worked! The results are undeniable, though Springs probably needs to do this at least one more time before we buy in long-term. Either way, though: *what the absolute hell?*

Ryan Thompson RHP Born: 06/26/92 Age: 31 Bats: R Throws: R Height: 6'5" Weight: 210 lb. Origin: Round 23, 2014 Draft (#676 overall)

YEAR	TEAM	LVL	AGE	W	L	SV	G	GS	IP	H	HR	BB/9	K/9	K	GB%	BABIP	WHIP	ERA	DRA-	WARP	MPH	FB%	Whiff%	CSP
2020	TB	MLB	28	1	2	1	25	1	26^1	29	4	2.7	7.9	23	59.0%	.316	1.41	4.44	82	0.6	91.5	60.9%	22.2%	54.0%
2021	TB	MLB	29	3	2	0	36	0	34	26	3	2.4	9.8	37	47.7%	.277	1.03	2.38	84	0.6	90.7	60.7%	26.9%	56.5%
2022	TB	MLB	30	3	3	3	47	0	42^2	39	4	2.3	8.2	39	49.6%	.282	1.17	3.80	97	0.5	90.6	58.2%	24.1%	52.5%
2023 DC	*TB*	*MLB*	*31*	*2*	*2*	*0*	*50*	*0*	*43*	*44*	*4*	*3.0*	*8.3*	*39*	*50.6%*	*.312*	*1.35*	*4.02*	*102*	*0.1*	*90.8*	*59.3%*	*24.7%*	*53.9%*

Comparables: Blake Parker (56), Nick Vincent (53), Pedro Báez (52)

You know how when you've played several years into franchise mode in MLB The Show half the rosters are made of auto-generated players? That's sort of how the Rays bullpen operates. Thompson has made at least 25 major-league appearances in each of the last three seasons, accumulating over 100 innings of quality work. But your average fan—hell, even most diehards—wouldn't be able to differentiate him from (fires up random name generator) "Clayworth Stanley," a fictional 95-and-a-slider guy who we'll imagine was drafted in the sixth round two years ago. Thompson doesn't just struggle to stand out because he's a Rays reliever but also because his arsenal is, by today's standards, rather basic. He uses a side-winding motion to induce lots of groundballs with his fastball, and he complements it with—you guessed it—an upper-70s slider. He's even got a nebulous "arm injury" on his résumé now, too. Thompson is the type of guy you'd like to be able to sign to a 10-year, $10 million contract just so you don't have to think about organizational depth for a while. And honestly, if any team were going to actually try that approach, it's Tampa Bay.

Matt Wisler RHP Born: 09/12/92 Age: 30 Bats: R Throws: R Height: 6'3" Weight: 215 lb. Origin: Round 7, 2011 Draft (#233 overall)

YEAR	TEAM	LVL	AGE	W	L	SV	G	GS	IP	H	HR	BB/9	K/9	K	GB%	BABIP	WHIP	ERA	DRA-	WARP	MPH	FB%	Whiff%	CSP
2020	MIN	MLB	27	0	1	1	18	4	25^1	15	2	5.0	12.4	35	23.2%	.241	1.14	1.07	103	0.2	92.1	16.6%	36.1%	49.3%
2021	TB	MLB	28	2	3	1	27	0	29^1	22	2	1.5	11.0	36	22.5%	.290	0.92	2.15	90	0.4	91.6	8.8%	28.1%	59.0%
2021	SF	MLB	28	1	2	0	21	0	19^1	19	4	2.8	12.1	26	30.0%	.326	1.29	6.05	91	0.3	91.9	9.7%	37.5%	61.2%
2022	TB	MLB	29	3	3	1	39	5	44	30	6	2.9	7.2	35	25.2%	.202	1.00	2.25	115	0.1	90.0	8.4%	24.5%	58.1%
2023 non-DC	*TB*	*MLB*	*30*	*2*	*2*	*0*	*57*	*0*	*50*	*47*	*7*	*3.1*	*8.1*	*44*	*29.9%*	*.283*	*1.29*	*3.97*	*103*	*0.1*	*91.2*	*12.4%*	*26.7%*	*56.2%*

Comparables: John Wasdin (74), Tommy Hunter (73), Liam Hendriks (73)

Long removed from his top prospect days, Wisler has been an effective mid-level reliever over the last few seasons. Serving up a steady diet of sliders, he'd posted gaudy strikeout rates in previous years, but not so much in 2022. He lacked control of his yakker at times, leading to more frequent free passes and an ERA that DRA didn't support. He also allowed more fly balls, which predictably led to more homers. All in all, Wisler doesn't offer enough ingredients to be the main course in a bullpen, but he works as a mid-innings appetizer. The pitching-rich Rays had apparently had their fill, and cut Wisler loose in September despite his solid track record. Odds are another team will bite before the winter is over.

LINEOUTS

Hitters

HITTER	POS	TEAM	LVL	AGE	PA	R	2B	3B	HR	RBI	BB	K	SB	CS	AVG/OBP/SLG	DRC+	BABIP	BRR	DRP	WARP
Mason Auer	OF	CSC	A	21	270	46	13	9	4	31	31	48	24	3	.293/.378/.478	127	.348	4.7	RF(40): 1.8, CF(13): 0.5, LF(1): -0.1	2.3
	OF	BG	A+	21	259	38	8	3	11	31	24	62	24	4	.288/.367/.496	109	.346	0.4	CF(39): 2.6, RF(14): 1.3	1.8
Osleivis Basabe	IF	BG	A+	21	236	41	16	2	4	22	16	34	7	5	.315/.370/.463	121	.360	1.3	3B(20): 1.1, SS(16): 1.0, 2B(14): 0.7	1.7
	IF	MTG	AA	21	259	39	23	3	0	25	24	25	14	0	.333/.399/.461	122	.369	2.2	3B(33): 0.5, SS(13): 0.9, 2B(12): -0.1	1.7
Carlos Colmenarez	SS	RAY	ROK	18	153	36	7	3	1	19	17	41	13	2	.254/.379/.381		.365			
Tristan Gray	IF	DUR	AAA	26	500	72	21	0	33	89	30	159	4	2	.225/.282/.487	86	.259	-1.1	SS(66): -0.7, 3B(32): 1.7, 1B(19): -0.6	0.6
Heriberto Hernandez	OF	BG	A+	22	494	70	28	1	24	89	67	155	6	2	.255/.368/.499	119	.346	-1.7	LF(66): 2.4, RF(38): -1.1, 1B(6): -0.6	2.5
Brock Jones	CF	CSC	A	21	62	15	4	1	4	12	12	21	9	3	.286/.419/.653	97	.400	0.4	CF(10): 0.6, LF(3): 1.0	0.3
Greg Jones	SS	MTG	AA	24	358	54	19	3	8	40	27	128	37	5	.238/.318/.392	76	.370	3.1	SS(77): 7.8	1.1
Dominic Keegan	C	CSC	A	21	26	4	0	0	2	6	2	6	0	0	.261/.346/.522	112	.267	-0.2	C(6): -1.4	0.0
Kameron Misner	CF	MTG	AA	24	510	80	25	1	16	62	86	155	32	7	.251/.384/.431	110	.356	-2.2	CF(99): -2.4, RF(11): 0.5, LF(2): -0.1	2.2
René Pinto	C	DUR	AAA	25	306	39	26	2	14	54	22	82	1	0	.266/.320/.521	93	.326	-0.7	C(54): 7.3	1.1
	C	TB	MLB	25	83	5	3	0	2	10	2	35	0	0	.213/.241/.325	55	.349	-0.5	C(25): 2	0.0
Roman Quinn	OF	LHV	AAA	29	25	8	3	0	1	2	8	4	0	1	.294/.520/.647	123	.333	0.0	CF(4): 1.0, RF(1): 0.3	0.1
	OF	OMA	AAA	29	32	5	0	0	2	4	6	10	1	0	.250/.406/.500	102	.308	-0.1	CF(7): -0.1	0.2
	OF	PHI	MLB	29	40	8	1	0	0	3	3	15	4	1	.162/.225/.189	78	.273	0.2	CF(19): -0.5, RF(2): 0.2	0.0
	OF	TB	MLB	29	47	7	2	2	0	4	4	21	0	2	.262/.340/.405	56	.524	-0.6	LF(9): 0, CF(9): -0.4, RF(6): 0.5	-0.2
Luke Raley	1B	DUR	AAA	27	268	39	8	1	14	50	27	73	7	2	.300/.401/.529	104	.383	-2.7	1B(27): -2.0, LF(17): -1.2, RF(6): -0.6	0.5
	1B	TB	MLB	27	72	7	2	0	1	4	7	24	0	0	.197/.306/.279	68	.297	-0.7	RF(8): -1.2, LF(7): -0.2	-0.3
Chandler Simpson	SS	RAY	ROK	21	34	5	3	0	0	3	6	4	8	0	.370/.471/.481		.417			
Carson Williams	SS	CSC	A	19	523	81	22	10	19	70	57	168	28	10	.252/.347/.471	112	.354	-0.5	SS(108): 0.8	2.3

A fifth-round pick in 2021, **Mason Auer** hit .290 with an .859 OPS across two levels. The outfielder spent his fall hitting baseballs in Arizona as a reward, and the high-minors beckon. **Osleivis Basabe** is an up-the-middle player with good contact skills, plus speed and not a ton of power. He's a good half-season away from beat writers and prospect-lovers needing to learn how to spell his first name. **Ryan Cermak**, the 71st player selected in the 2022 draft, has a nice blend of power and athleticism. Though he played some third base at Illinois State, the Rays deployed him exclusively in the outfield in his brief pro debut. The thrifty Rays wrote a $3 million check to sign **Carlos Colmenarez** out of Venezuela based on his potential to become a dynamic player in the middle of the diamond. He made his stateside debut as an 18-year-old in the Complex League. **Tristan Gray** hit a ton of Triple-A home runs but did little else of note at the plate. His game offered more variety in the field, where he appeared at every infield position save for second base in Durham. A catcher-turned-outfielder, **Heriberto Hernandez** continues to show plus power in the minors, but a lot of flaws otherwise. Then again, once upon a time people said the same thing about Nate Lowe ... A first base-only slugger drafted late in the first round, **Xavier Isaac** is going to have to really, really, really hit to make his selection worthwhile. At least he's unlikely to ever be described as a "slapdick prospect!" **Brock Jones** is a lefty outfielder who played safety at Stanford before he focused on hitting baseballs instead of other people. It worked well enough for the Rays to select him in the second round. A 2019 first-rounder, **Greg Jones** has elite athleticism but is swinging and missing his way out of prospectdom as he enters his age-25 season. Former Commodore **Dominic Keegan** is a bat-first catcher with the ability to play first base and left field to boot. A 19th-round pick by the Yankees in 2021, his one-year trip back to Vandy proved wise: The Rays popped him in the fourth round last July. **Kameron Misner** is a tall, left-handed power hitter with the arm, patience and pedigree to profile as a regular in right field. He also struck out nearly a third of the time as a 24-year-old in Double-A. Congrats to catcher **René Pinto** on making it to the majors nearly a decade after he was signed as an IFA out of Venezuela. The nicest thing we can say about his bat is that his pitching staffs reportedly love him. When you Google **Roman Quinn**, it lists him as a "baseball athlete." That's pretty accurate, because he is fast and he does play baseball, but you can't really call him a hitter or a fielder. **Luke Raley** looks like a dude who should hit the baseball really hard, but he hasn't in the majors. Now entering his age-28 season, he'll need to really rally if he wants to lead rallies in Tampa. In **Chandler Simpson**, the Rays have another toolsy, up-the-middle player with questions about how all those skills will coalesce into an actual baseball player. At the very least, the speedy 2022 second-rounder helps assuage the loss of Xavier Edwards within the system. A true shortstop with some ability at the plate, **Carson Williams** is likely at least a year away from earning looks on top-100 prospect lists and, more prestigiously, a full comment instead of a lineout.

Pitchers

PITCHER	TEAM	LVL	AGE	W	L	SV	G	GS	IP	H	HR	BB/9	K/9	K	GB%	BABIP	WHIP	ERA	DRA-	WARP	MPH	FB%	WHF	CSP
Nick Bitsko	RAY	ROK	20	1	2	0	10	8	17	14	0	10.6	7.9	15	54.9%	.275	2.00	7.41						
	CSC	A	20	0	0	0	4	4	9	8	0	7.0	5.0	5	44.8%	.276	1.67	4.00	133	-0.1				
Calvin Faucher	DUR	AAA	26	3	3	1	34	4	43	44	7	4.4	10.9	52	45.4%	.333	1.51	3.56	84	0.9				
	TB	MLB	26	2	3	1	22	0	21^{1}	26	4	4.2	8.9	21	40.6%	.338	1.69	5.48	102	0.2	94.9	59.6%	24.2%	55.0%
Josh Fleming	DUR	AAA	26	9	2	0	15	10	64^{2}	73	4	1.9	6.4	46	62.1%	.356	1.35	3.06	110	0.5	90.9	64.3%	18.5%	
	TB	MLB	26	2	5	0	10	3	35	54	5	3.1	7.5	29	63.8%	.402	1.89	6.43	118	0.0	91.0	70.1%	23.0%	48.7%
Sandy Gaston	CSC	A	20	2	4	3	31	4	54^{2}	33	3	9.2	12.7	77	46.2%	.263	1.63	4.61	83	1.1				
Brendan McKay	CSC	A	26	0	0	0	3	2	8^{2}	7	2	4.2	6.2	6	22.2%	.200	1.27	3.12	118	0.0				
Cole Wilcox	CSC	A	22	0	1	0	4	4	11	8	1	1.6	12.3	15	66.7%	.269	0.91	2.45	66	0.2				

Perhaps best known for hyping up his own stuff virtually, **Nick Bitsko** pitched both professionally and in front of actual people in 2022. He wasn't very good, but still has first-round pedigree and stuff. ⚾ Righty **Calvin Faucher** rode a three-pitch mix all the way to the majors, where he then struggled with control and the long ball. If only he were in an org with a demonstrated track record of getting the most out of dudes with this profile... ⚾ Even if he'd belonged to an organization hard-up for reliever talent, **Josh Fleming** didn't pitch well enough or show good enough stuff to warrant much major-league action in 2022. Factor in that he's a Ray, and it's a miracle he saw any time in the bigs at all. ⚾ **Sandy Gaston** has one of the liveliest arms in the game and a triple-digit fastball that, like most things that fast, proves hard to control. If he learns to do so, he's a potential impact starter. If he doesn't, he won't be. What a guy, that Gaston. ⚾ Former top prospect and draft pick **Brendan McKay** has thrown just 28 professional innings since 2019. He won't throw any in 2023 either after undergoing Tommy John surgery last September, leading the Rays to release him in November amid a big-time roster crunch. ⚾ It was a red-shirt year for righty **Cole Wilcox** in 2022. He recovered from Tommy John surgery to make seven abbreviated starts with an eye toward earning a full-season assignment in 2023.

TORONTO BLUE JAYS

Essay by Blake Murphy

Player comments by Alex Chamberlain and BP staff

In late 2005, Warner Bros. put the world on notice: A new era of superhero movie was upon us.

More than six months before the film would be released, the initial teaser trailer for *Superman Returns* aired. An attempt to capitalize on the guaranteed audience for *Harry Potter and the Goblet of Fire*, the initial and subsequent *Superman Returns* trailers emerged as what may be the first buzzy movie marketing of the early social media era: It was all dramatic music swells and ice-barren landscape and "swoosh" sound effects and Metropolis citizens scanning the signs, and it was *everywhere*.

By the time the movie was released in June of 2006, expectations were through the roof. Still one of the best action movie trailers of all time, *Superman Returns* promised a savvier, grittier and more modern extension of the initial *Superman* franchise. The unknown Brandon Routh would be a breakout star. With a $223-million budget and an estimated $46 million poured into marketing, *Superman Returns* was the can't-miss summer blockbuster of 2006.

And the movie was ... fine? I recently rewatched it to make sure I characterized it properly for this piece. While it doesn't hold up well compared to some of the elite comic book movies that have followed, you can see where it made its imprint and what they were going for. It's not bad, it's just kind of ... there. That happens to be the best description of Routh, too, setting aside his excellent turn in *Scott Pilgrim vs. The World*.

That the movie was largely average makes it a fascinating case study of the start of the internet-buzz-fueled era of cinema. To this day, it holds a 74% score on Rotten Tomatoes and ratings in the six-to-seven range on most user rating sites. It pulled in $391 million at the box office, making it a fiscal success, even if it barely cracked the top 10 for that year.

Despite those modest successes, *Superman Returns* is largely considered a failure. It stands as a cautionary tale about trailer excitement. Warner Bros. opted to scrap a planned sequel, later rebooting the franchise with a lead actor who'd reportedly lost out on the part initially (Henry Cavill). What was an unquestioned win in a vacuum had the outcomes more often associated with an abject failure.

TORONTO BLUE JAYS PROSPECTUS

2022 W-L: 92-70, 2ND IN AL EAST

Pythag	.562	7th	DER	.696	19th
RS/G	4.78	4th	DRC+	112	2nd
RA/G	4.19	13th	DRA-	96	15th
dWin%	.587	6th	FIP	3.83	12th
Payroll	$171M	11th	B-Age	27.5	8th
M$/MW	$3.5M	13th	P-Age	29.8	20th

400′

375′ 375′

328′ 328′

- Opened 1989
- Retractable roof
- Synthetic surface
- Fence profile: 10′

Park Factors

Runs	Runs/RH	Runs/LH	HR/RH	HR/LH
98	97	98	103	96

Top Hitter WARP	4.3 George Springer
Top Pitcher WARP	3.9 Kevin Gausman
2023 Top Prospect	Ricky Tiedemann

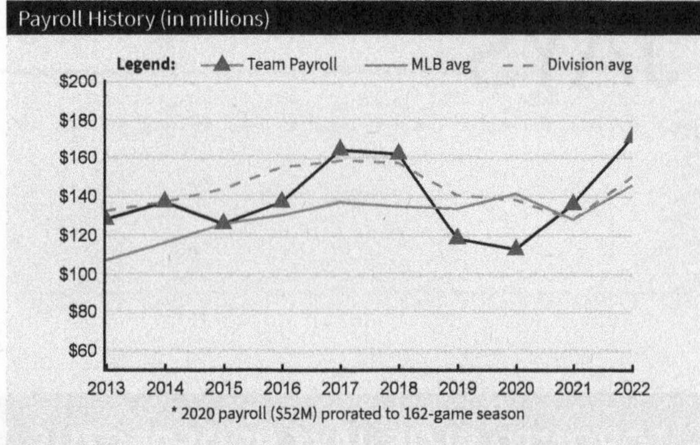

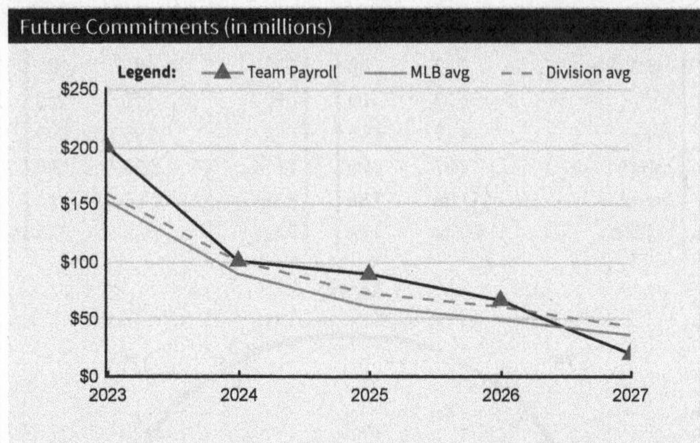

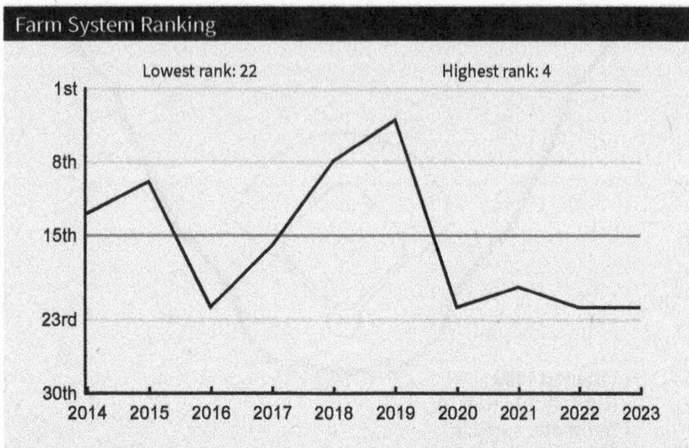

Personnel

President & CEO
Mark A. Shapiro

Executive Vice President, Baseball Operations & General Manager
Ross Atkins

Senior Vice President, Player Personnel
Tony Lacava

Vice President, International Scouting & Baseball Operations
Andrew Tinnish

Assistant General Manager
Joe Sheehan

Assistant General Manager
Michael Murov

Manager
John Schneider

Were Thomas Bayes a film critic, he'd surely have warned about how expectations—our movie-enjoyment priors—can shift our perception. He also probably would have given *Superman Returns* three stars out of five. It was fine.

Also fine: The 2022 Toronto Blue Jays season.

⚾ ⚾ ⚾

It's hard to argue against the season the Blue Jays had this past year. They won 92 games. They made the playoffs (full-season version) for the first time since 2016. Fans returned regularly to Rogers Centre. The young foundation held strong.

If it didn't *feel* like the Jays were a rousing success, that's largely due to the weight of expectations. The 2020 and 2021 seasons were feel-good years, successes still flecked with surprise. The bizarro 2020 season saw the Jays get (kind of) postseason experience and make a number of big moves to signal the future had become the present. With 2021 came an incredible offense, excellent second half of the season and a wild playoff chase that came up just a game short.

"What we did last year was a trailer, now you guys are gonna see the movie," said Vladimir Guerrero Jr. through a translator in March.

And there he summoned them. Expectations.

If the 2022 Blue Jays season taught us anything, it's that the early miles are tougher than the late ones. Technically, Toronto won one more game than the year prior and made the postseason, something that would have been true even in the older, more restrictive playoff format. On results alone, a trip to the Wild Card Series was a step forward, a still-young core getting to taste October baseball as they build for the next few years.

But how they got there, and how they went out, didn't quite involve the fireworks Vladdy predicted. Charlie Montoyo was replaced by John Schneider in the manager's chair in mid-July, at once an admission the team had underperformed to that point and an acknowledgement that a peace-time consigliere was no longer the best choice. On more advanced merit, the team was actually worse, too, losing eight games off of their run-differential-based expected record. Some of the underwhelming specifics—Hyun Jin Ryu needing UCL surgery, Yusei Kikuchi requiring a move to the bullpen, a depth reliever core lacking in the ability to miss bats—are of the sort that every season brings, the ebb and flow of baseball. Others introduce complicated questions about where this team is and where it can go.

What if, for example, the first half of Guerrero's 2021 season was the outlier, not the baseline, and he's closer to 40% above league-average at the plate than a perennial MVP candidate in-waiting? Percentile projections are important! Bo Bichette saved his offensive season with a torrid stretch run while questions cropped back up about his ability to man the shortstop position in a shift-reduced era. George Springer remained excellent but saw his season end with a scary and unfortunate injury, which isn't even the injury he needed addressed via surgery following the season. All of this was hard to square with the homer-pummeling Hydra that Guerrero told us to expect.

Every franchise faces tough ceiling and floor questions. The Jays' front office, though, has planned a window of contention around a young pair of superstars—now expanded to a quartet with Alek Manoah and your Catcher Of The Future of choice. If those superstars are, in actuality, very good players who fall just short of deserving the label? That becomes a problem more serious than false advertising.

That makes the Jays' incremental progression difficult to appreciate. Not only were expectations set higher than a quick two-game exit, the degree of difficulty also increases from here. Guerrero and Bichette are now firmly in their arbitration years, getting more expensive until theoretical long-term deals pay them exponentially more. The top two in the rotation are elite, backed by a carousel of question marks. Generally speaking, there are two primary waves the Jays could focus on: A first wave where their young stars are cheap and they can spend on the Kevin Gausmans of the world to supplement that group, and a second wave where their stars enter their primes and are paid as such, necessitating a much larger budget or a high hit rate on bargain finds at the margins. The former is significantly easier on paper than the latter, especially if you're of the belief that the large-market Jays won't push to the competitive balance tax threshold. Baseball's imbalanced pay system necessitates striking while good young players remain inexpensive, and the Blue Jays used up one more year of that window.

That may not turn out to be an issue. An optimist would look at a playoff berth, additional experience, and confirmation that the floor for the Jays' younger players is considerably high. That core also expanded, as more young players succeeded. Now armed with playoff experience and the pain of blowing an 8-1 lead in an elimination game, the club should be ready to move past any accusations that it wasn't always dialed in as it could be. The Jays remain the envy of no small number of teams: consecutive 90-win seasons, players whose names people know dotting key positions.

Still, relative success isn't what was promised—by Guerrero, or by the gaudiest of the stretches in the 2021 season, or by the not-insubstantial number of analysts and outlets who had the Jays headed for the World Series. So the 2022 season is fine in a vacuum and feels like a missed opportunity at the same time. A mid-July surge after the managerial change—one game featuring a 10th-inning rally bookended by a Vladdy double and a Teoscar Hernández seeing-eye single, another a franchise-record 28-run drubbing of the Red Sox in Boston—was a late tease that a World Series ceiling was still possible. In August, it was the rotation lending confidence, allowing just 23 runs over a 7-1 streak. The pieces were there. Keeping the gears snug was tricky.

Since the 1970s, research on consumer behavior and satisfaction has looked at the expectation-actuality gap. We have a tendency to evaluate outcomes relative to what we expected rather than on their standalone merits. The Orioles were thrilled to have a season where they had a worse outcome than the Blue Jays because they were in an entirely different place on the development and expectation curve. As Tim Robinson taught us: If you think you're going to be eating something ice cold and you bring it up to your lips and it's room temp, it's going to feel like your mouth's on fire.

There was at least some sentiment at the end of the season that the Jays had served room-temp gazpacho, as evidenced by a good-not-great box-office season (12th-highest attendance in franchise history, behind the 2015 and 2016 playoff seasons and a sub-.500 2017). The front office moved swiftly to follow up the Montoyo change by dealing one of the most beloved and longest-tenured Blue Jays in Hernández. Hard decisions were deemed necessary, and more are surely to come.

The expectations only grow from here. The Jays don't have the option of killing a planned sequel, and recasting the leads seems extremely unlikely. (And, to be clear, neither would be all that advisable.) We saw at times how the unfamiliar weight of expectations affected Toronto a year ago, both in how the outcome was perceived and how the team operated day to day. They'll enter the season once again a World Series hopeful.

A team doesn't carry high expectations if they don't have the potential to be great. In that sense, it's difficult for a lofty forecast to be a bad thing. It can be heavy, though, in an industry where adequacy can be quickly cast aside in the pursuit of something better. Routh didn't get to run it back. The Jays do. ■

—Blake Murphy is a Toronto-based writer and host of SportsNets Nation's radio show "Jays Talk Plus."

Hitters

Addison Barger IF

Born: 11/12/99 Age: 23 Bats: L Throws: R Height: 6'0" Weight: 175 lb. Origin: Round 6, 2018 Draft (#176 overall)

YEAR	TEAM	LVL	AGE	PA	R	2B	3B	HR	RBI	BB	K	SB	CS	Whiff%	AVG/OBP/SLG	DRC+	BABIP	BRR	DRP	WARP
2021	DUN	A	21	374	53	21	2	18	80	36	123	7	0		.249/.334/.492	101	.333	-0.6	SS(27): -0.1, 2B(24): -3.0, 3B(13): 0.5	0.7
2022	VAN	A+	22	292	46	21	2	14	53	25	76	7	2		.300/.366/.558	128	.370	0.5	SS(36): -3.4, 3B(19): -1.5	1.4
2022	NH	AA	22	198	26	11	0	9	29	18	50	2	2		.313/.384/.528	104	.390	-1.7	3B(20): 0.1, SS(20): 0.7	0.6
2022	BUF	AAA	22	36	8	1	0	3	9	5	5	0	1		.355/.444/.677	128	.348	0.7	SS(4): 1.0, 3B(3): -0.5	0.3
2023 DC	*TOR*	*MLB*	*23*	*98*	*10*	*4*	*0*	*3*	*10*	*6*	*29*	*0*	*1*	*31.0%*	*.242/.298/.413*	*94*	*.320*	*0.1*	*2B 0, 3B 0*	*0.2*

Comparables: Zach Walters (73), Brad Miller (61), Chris Valaika (60)

Once a strong-armed infielder with questionable pop, Barger broke out in 2022, carrying forward the power spike he enjoyed in 2021 while tightening up his plate discipline. The resulting 26 homers, .308 average and .933 OPS he earned across the three highest minor-league levels landed him a spot on Toronto's 40-man roster in November. Swing-and-miss issues may always color his game; despite his gains at the plate, he still struck out 25% of the time against relatively weak opposition. But his once-latent, now-realized power, paired with his defensive aptitude and versatility, could soon make him a household name. Maybe only in Ontarian households, sure, but in households nonetheless.

Bo Bichette SS

Born: 03/05/98 Age: 25 Bats: R Throws: R Height: 6'0" Weight: 190 lb. Origin: Round 2, 2016 Draft (#66 overall)

YEAR	TEAM	LVL	AGE	PA	R	2B	3B	HR	RBI	BB	K	SB	CS	Whiff%	AVG/OBP/SLG	DRC+	BABIP	BRR	DRP	WARP
2020	TOR	MLB	22	128	18	9	1	5	23	5	27	4	1	21.6%	.301/.328/.512	105	.352	-0.4	SS(26): -0.9	0.3
2021	TOR	MLB	23	690	121	30	1	29	102	40	137	25	1	22.4%	.298/.343/.484	115	.339	3.6	SS(148): 0.4	4.1
2022	TOR	MLB	24	697	91	43	1	24	93	41	155	13	8	23.0%	.290/.333/.469	117	.347	-2.0	SS(157): -6.9	2.7
2023 DC	*TOR*	*MLB*	*25*	*604*	*70*	*29*	*2*	*20*	*77*	*38*	*123*	*21*	*4*	*22.5%*	*.283/.331/.454*	*120*	*.328*	*8.9*	*SS 0*	*4.2*

Comparables: Francisco Lindor (75), Corey Seager (72), Carlos Correa (71)

Bichette has been a paragon of consistency since he debuted four years ago as an elite prospect with MLB-ready polish and power. He's an aggressive, contact-oriented hitter who handles all pitch types well, which bodes well for him as the league rapidly transitions toward elevated triple-digit heat and sweeping sliders. It's unclear what magnitude of aggression would unlock his optimal self—if he was more patient, would that jeopardize the quality of his contact? But, also, why fix what's not broken? Some felt his 2022 campaign left something to be desired, but only those who care about runs and RBI. By most other accounts, he was just as good as, if not better than, in 2021, and he finished the season blisteringly hot, amassing an incredible 54 hits between September and October. That he didn't show visible growth could be a source of disappointment, but it's hard to grow when you are already so, so good. Enjoy Bichette for what he is: a high-floor, high-ceiling franchise cornerstone.

Cavan Biggio IF

Born: 04/11/95 Age: 28 Bats: L Throws: R Height: 6'2" Weight: 200 lb. Origin: Round 5, 2016 Draft (#162 overall)

YEAR	TEAM	LVL	AGE	PA	R	2B	3B	HR	RBI	BB	K	SB	CS	Whiff%	AVG/OBP/SLG	DRC+	BABIP	BRR	DRP	WARP
2020	TOR	MLB	25	265	41	16	0	8	28	41	61	6	0	23.2%	.250/.375/.432	102	.311	1.5	2B(37): -0.2, RF(14): -0.5, 3B(10): -0.1	0.9
2021	BUF	AAA	26	90	15	2	0	3	11	11	26	0	0		.182/.289/.325	85	.224	0.3	3B(9): -0.7, RF(5): -1.1, LF(1): 0.1	0.0
2021	TOR	MLB	26	294	27	10	1	7	27	37	78	3	1	25.8%	.224/.322/.356	87	.290	-0.4	3B(52): 1.1, RF(15): 0.2, 1B(7): 0	0.6
2022	BUF	AAA	27	39	9	3	0	0	3	10	6	2	0		.276/.462/.379	114	.348	0.6	RF(3): 0.2, 1B(2): -0.4, 2B(1): 0.1	0.2
2022	TOR	MLB	27	303	43	18	1	6	24	38	85	2	0	26.0%	.202/.318/.350	82	.275	0.9	2B(49): 1.3, 1B(33): -0.4, RF(7): -0.5	0.3
2023 DC	*TOR*	*MLB*	*28*	*391*	*42*	*16*	*1*	*9*	*36*	*50*	*101*	*4*	*2*	*25.5%*	*.215/.324/.363*	*93*	*.277*	*2.1*	*RF -1, LF 0*	*0.5*

Comparables: Danny Espinosa (62), Jace Peterson (53), Jordany Valdespin (53)

Biggio is an exemplar of the importance of exit velocity in the era of the ever-changing baseball. The stars aligned for his debut season: A relatively bouncy ball enabled his loft-oriented swing to generate a bounty of homers and line drives. But the since-deadened ball has forced hitters who lack natural pop to rely on optimal launch angles for production, and Biggio's swing plane creates too many pop-ups, weak fly balls and strikeouts. The Jays don't appear ready to move on from him just yet, but they weren't shy about enlisting outside help last year, either, as Biggio's overly patient approach and below-average contact skills don't lend themselves to baseball's current offensive environment. Defensive versatility and a glut of free passes should afford Biggio a roster spot, but his contributions as a utility man now lack the coveted "super" prefix.

Matt Chapman 3B

Born: 04/28/93 Age: 30 Bats: R Throws: R Height: 6'0" Weight: 215 lb. Origin: Round 1, 2014 Draft (#25 overall)

YEAR	TEAM	LVL	AGE	PA	R	2B	3B	HR	RBI	BB	K	SB	CS	Whiff%	AVG/OBP/SLG	DRC+	BABIP	BRR	DRP	WARP
2020	OAK	MLB	27	152	22	9	2	10	25	8	54	0	0	36.2%	.232/.276/.535	91	.291	0.3	3B(36): 0.5, SS(1): 0.8	0.4
2021	OAK	MLB	28	622	75	15	3	27	72	80	202	3	2	32.8%	.210/.314/.403	94	.272	3.4	3B(150): 3.1, SS(3): -0.3	2.3
2022	TOR	MLB	29	621	83	27	1	27	76	68	170	2	2	28.7%	.229/.324/.433	109	.277	-0.2	3B(153): 2.3	2.4
2023 DC	*TOR*	*MLB*	*30*	*570*	*72*	*22*	*2*	*29*	*76*	*64*	*155*	*3*	*1*	*28.8%*	*.235/.329/.466*	*119*	*.277*	*1.0*	*3B 3*	*2.9*

Comparables: Bill Melton (79), Eric Chavez (76), Evan Longoria (76)

It seems Chapman's debilitating hip injury is *mostly* in the rearview mirror—his 2022 rebound certainly vindicates Toronto's thrifting at Oakland's offseason garage sale—but so, too, is the MVP-candidate pinnacle of his mid-20s. Indeed, Chapman's debut above the border saw him strike the middle ground between his youthful peak and injury-marred valley. He offloaded some of the whiffs he collected during the pandemic and showcased his usual loud contact. He still suffered from strikeouts and pop-ups—a byproduct of his steep swing—but his bat rose back to above average. He also rehabilitated his defense, though only back to break-even—a welcome upgrade over his initial post-labral tear performance, but a far cry from his tenure as a nightly human highlight reel. Chapman's pending walk year is critical, as walk years tend to be. He successfully clawed back what he lost, but he must ward off Father Time and minimize future losses if he wants to cash in on his first scheduled foray into free agency.

Santiago Espinal 2B

Born: 11/13/94 Age: 28 Bats: R Throws: R Height: 5'10" Weight: 187 lb. Origin: Round 10, 2016 Draft (#298 overall)

YEAR	TEAM	LVL	AGE	PA	R	2B	3B	HR	RBI	BB	K	SB	CS	Whiff%	AVG/OBP/SLG	DRC+	BABIP	BRR	DRP	WARP
2020	TOR	MLB	25	66	10	4	0	0	6	4	16	1	0	25.4%	.267/.308/.333	87	.356	0.1	SS(21): -0.5, P(2): 0, 3B(2): 0	0.1
2021	TOR	MLB	26	246	32	13	1	2	17	22	30	6	1	15.5%	.311/.376/.405	112	.353	0.9	3B(81): 3.2	1.6
2022	TOR	MLB	27	491	51	25	0	7	51	36	68	6	6	15.6%	.267/.322/.370	104	.300	-0.4	2B(120): 0.3, 3B(11): -1.5, SS(11): -0.3	1.5
2023 DC	*TOR*	*MLB*	*28*	*448*	*46*	*18*	*1*	*7*	*41*	*34*	*56*	*11*	*4*	*16.1%*	*.272/.330/.376*	*101*	*.300*	*-0.5*	*2B 1, SS 0*	*1.3*

Comparables: Brock Holt (57), Phil Gosselin (54), César Hernández (54)

You know that significant other you dated a decade ago? The one who never really stood out at the time, but now you can't forget them? The one who—if you're honest with yourself—you've been trying to find again? We've all been there—the Blue Jays included.

Aside from Marcus Semien (who, frankly, was out of Toronto's league), those who have manned the keystone up north haven't held a candle to ex-flame Marco Scutaro. In his place have come a long list of failed trysts with the likes of Cavan Biggio, Aaron Hill, Kelly Johnson, Devon Travis, Munenori Kawasaki, Darwin Barney and Ryan Goins. They all pale in comparison to Scutaro, whose name lingers on the tongue, whose face resurfaces in dreams...

Enter Espinal, who, as a wise man once said, is *a little more of that*, both in performance and stature. As with Scutaro before him, Espinal does scarcely anything with the contact he makes, but he makes so much of it that, by sheer force of will, he creates value. His first All-Star nod could be his last, but he's a versatile, capable infielder with a league-average bat. Looks like Toronto finally found its next match and swiped right.

Vladimir Guerrero Jr. 1B

Born: 03/16/99 Age: 24 Bats: R Throws: R Height: 6'2" Weight: 240 lb. Origin: International Free Agent, 2015

YEAR	TEAM	LVL	AGE	PA	R	2B	3B	HR	RBI	BB	K	SB	CS	Whiff%	AVG/OBP/SLG	DRC+	BABIP	BRR	DRP	WARP
2020	TOR	MLB	21	243	34	13	2	9	33	20	38	1	0	24.7%	.262/.329/.462	116	.282	-0.8	1B(34): -0.2	0.9
2021	TOR	MLB	22	698	123	29	1	48	111	86	110	4	1	27.8%	.311/.401/.601	158	.313	-2.4	1B(133): 0.2	6.4
2022	TOR	MLB	23	706	90	35	0	32	97	58	116	8	3	24.4%	.274/.339/.480	134	.289	-0.9	1B(128): -0.9	4.2
2023 DC	*TOR*	*MLB*	*24*	*601*	*78*	*25*	*1*	*28*	*88*	*57*	*95*	*6*	*2*	*24.4%*	*.287/.361/.502*	*143*	*.302*	*-0.6*	*1B 0*	*4.0*

Comparables: Gary Sheffield (72), Fred Merkle (72), George Davis (71)

If Babe Ruth was the Sultan of Swat, Guerrero Jr. is the Prince of Piss Missiles, the Friar of Frozen Ropes, the Earl of Exit Velocity who lasers 118-mph line drives through outfield walls. His swing is geared toward producing not just enormously loud contact, but also frequent contact: a skill most prodigious sluggers famously lack. It's also a skill that caps his power output; he's physically capable of mashing 50 home runs, as he nearly did in 2021, but his flat swing path suggests he's more likely to routinely post tallies in the mid-30s, as he did last season.

He is inarguably an exceptional hitter, but home run bloodlust is limitless. As such, we have some suggestions as to how Guerrero can eclipse the half-century mark. First, he can feast on more high fastballs. The league is throwing them more and more in general but, as 2022 proved, pitchers are relatively disinclined to adopt that approach against Guerrero specifically. When he sees them, he needs to pounce. Second, he should feast on more first pitches. He saw nine more last season than in 2021, yet swung 65 fewer times, connecting on 11 fewer first-pitch moonshots in the process.

We're picking nits, of course. Guerrero doesn't have to change a thing to remain a top-15 hitter in the league. It may have taken him a couple of seasons to truly arrive, but the fully formed Vladito is every bit as good as advertised.

Miguel Hiraldo 2B

Born: 09/05/00 Age: 22 Bats: R Throws: R Height: 5'11" Weight: 197 lb. Origin: International Free Agent, 2017

YEAR	TEAM	LVL	AGE	PA	R	2B	3B	HR	RBI	BB	K	SB	CS	Whiff%	AVG/OBP/SLG	DRC+	BABIP	BRR	DRP	WARP
2021	DUN	A	20	453	66	26	4	7	52	51	111	29	5		.249/.338/.390	102	.323	0.2	2B(51): -7.5, 3B(37): -1.8	0.6
2022	VAN	A+	21	428	47	19	4	11	55	27	126	28	5		.231/.278/.382	71	.307	0.1	2B(101): -4.0, 3B(4): -1.0	-0.7
2023 non-DC	*TOR*	*MLB*	*22*	*251*	*19*	*10*	*2*	*4*	*22*	*14*	*82*	*9*	*3*	*37.2%*	*.206/.256/.320*	*55*	*.299*	*3.5*	*2B 0, 3B 0*	*-0.3*

Comparables: Gilbert Lara (64), DJ LeMahieu (60), Emilio Guerrero (57)

Hiraldo's standout Rookie League performances as a teenager are starting to feel like they came eons ago. As a 21-year-old at High-A, he fared 29% worse than average, striking out nearly five times more often than he walked. His swing, once holy, now simply appears holey, and rather high-effort, too. His aggression only exacerbates these issues and threatens to jeopardize the hit and raw power tools that once had scouts drooling. Hiraldo allegedly worked with Vancouver's hitting coach last summer to get back on track, and while his results improved in the latter half of the season, his strikeout rate remained staggeringly high. There's plenty of time for him to right the ship, but the Hiraldo of today seems but a specter of the Hiraldo of just a few years ago.

Spencer Horwitz 1B

Born: 11/14/97 Age: 25 Bats: L Throws: R Height: 6'0" Weight: 190 lb. Origin: Round 24, 2019 Draft (#717 overall)

YEAR	TEAM	LVL	AGE	PA	R	2B	3B	HR	RBI	BB	K	SB	CS	Whiff%	AVG/OBP/SLG	DRC+	BABIP	BRR	DRP	WARP
2021	MSS	WIN	23	74	14	4	0	1	12	9	11	4	0		.375/.459/.484		.442			
2021	VAN	A+	23	469	65	28	1	10	62	70	66	4	5		.290/.401/.445	131	.324	1.2	1B(83): 7.3, LF(5): -1.4, 2B(1): 0.1	3.8
2022	NH	AA	24	281	46	19	1	10	39	43	54	3	1		.297/.413/.517	128	.347	0.8	1B(44): 1.5, LF(10): -1.9	1.6
2022	BUF	AAA	24	202	31	14	0	2	12	30	41	4	1		.246/.361/.363	101	.313	-1.2	1B(29): -0.2, LF(10): -0.6, 2B(1): -0.3	0.3
2023 DC	*TOR*	*MLB*	*25*	*98*	*9*	*4*	*0*	*1*	*8*	*10*	*20*	*0*	*1*	*23.5%*	*.229/.315/.350*	*88*	*.282*	*0.2*	*1B 0, LF 0*	*0.0*

Comparables: Jim Gallagher (68), José Marmolejos (65), Travis Shaw (64)

Horwitz pairs a patient approach with a contact-oriented, line-drive swing, cultivating healthy double-digit walk rates and robust slash lines. He has a polished bat that could be ready to contribute to a major-league lineup soon-ish. The last piece of the puzzle is his burgeoning power; it shone through at Double-A but vanished upon his promotion to Buffalo where, for the first time as a professional, he fell a little flat. Horwitz's pop could be the great differentiator between him being good or merely serviceable as a stand-in. He's a first baseman by trade, but the Blue Jays have given him anticipatory reps in left field since they drafted him. In any case, defense won't be his calling card: He'll have to hit his way to continued relevance.

Danny Jansen C

Born: 04/15/95 Age: 28 Bats: R Throws: R Height: 6'2" Weight: 215 lb. Origin: Round 16, 2013 Draft (#475 overall)

YEAR	TEAM	LVL	AGE	PA	R	2B	3B	HR	RBI	BB	K	SB	CS	Whiff%	AVG/OBP/SLG	DRC+	BABIP	BRR	DRP	WARP
2020	TOR	MLB	25	147	18	3	0	6	20	21	31	0	0	24.9%	.183/.313/.358	108	.190	-0.5	C(43): -0.4	0.6
2021	BUF	AAA	26	26	5	0	0	1	4	4	3	0	0		.238/.346/.381	117	.222	-0.1	C(5): -0.0	0.1
2021	TOR	MLB	26	205	32	13	0	11	28	17	44	0	0	25.3%	.223/.299/.473	106	.233	-1.8	C(69): 1.7	1.0
2022	TOR	MLB	27	248	34	10	0	15	44	25	44	1	0	22.0%	.260/.339/.516	133	.255	-0.4	C(63): -0.4	1.8
2023 DC	*TOR*	*MLB*	*28*	*406*	*51*	*16*	*0*	*18*	*51*	*37*	*84*	*0*	*0*	*22.8%*	*.247/.328/.448*	*117*	*.273*	*-2.6*	*C 4*	*2.3*

Comparables: Devin Mesoraco (61), Yasmani Grandal (58), Francisco Cervelli (58)

YEAR	TEAM	P. COUNT	FRM RUNS	BLK RUNS	THRW RUNS	TOT RUNS
2020	TOR	6284	-0.4	0.1	0.0	-0.3
2021	TOR	8117	0.9	0.2	0.0	1.1
2022	TOR	8444	-1.1	0.3	0.4	-0.4
2023	*TOR*	*12025*	*3.1*	*0.1*	*0.3*	*3.5*

A post-hype catching prospect breaking out in the 11th hour of his tenure while younger, potentially superior alternatives breathe down his neck isn't how you'd draw it up, but that may be the scene that's playing out in Toronto. Across two half-seasons accounting for slightly more than 400 plate appearances, Jansen has swatted 23 home runs and compiled a respectable .235/.309/.479 line. Most other teams would love and pay up for a catcher with a league-average bat and a plus glove—something the Jays are likely weighing as Jansen enters arbitration and Alejandro Kirk soars. The Jays' decision to trade away Gabriel Moreno can be seen as a vote of confidence of sorts for Jansen, but Kirk's presence could still leave him on the outside looking in if he fails to quickly validate his long-awaited emergence.

Leo Jimenez SS/DH

Born: 05/17/01 Age: 22 Bats: R Throws: R Height: 5'11" Weight: 215 lb. Origin: International Free Agent, 2017

YEAR	TEAM	LVL	AGE	PA	R	2B	3B	HR	RBI	BB	K	SB	CS	Whiff%	AVG/OBP/SLG	DRC+	BABIP	BRR	DRP	WARP
2021	DUN	A	20	242	35	8	0	1	19	51	35	4	1		.315/.517/.381	145	.388	-0.7	SS(37): -4.4, 2B(12): 0.6	1.6
2022	VAN	A+	21	294	45	14	3	6	40	27	58	7	3		.230/.340/.385	122	.269	-0.3	SS(47): -0.3, 2B(3): -0.3	1.6
2023 non-DC	*TOR*	*MLB*	*22*	*251*	*22*	*9*	*1*	*2*	*20*	*21*	*50*	*1*	*1*	*22.7%*	*.216/.309/.310*	*78*	*.269*	*1.1*	*2B 0, SS 0*	*0.1*

Comparables: Osvaldo Duarte (56), Jonathan Herrera (53), Emilio Guerrero (49)

It somewhat infamously took Jimenez 139 professional games to hit his first home run. It goes without saying, then—although we'll say it anyway—that the six homers he hit in a fraction as many games at High-A last year should be considered quite encouraging. The bulk of Jimenez's future value had previously been tied to his defensive acumen and, within Toronto's system, unrivaled bat-to-ball skills. That he now features nascent power should not be taken lightly. He faced exorbitant odds to replicate his .517 OBP at Low-A Dunedin, and as such, his Vancouver stat line may be disappointing to some. Is he sacrificing too much of his superior contact skills for what ultimately amounts to a handful of taters? Early returns suggest yes, though we're talking about a 300-PA sample size here. Regardless, it's a development that now demands eagle-eyed observation.

Kevin Kiermaier CF

Born: 04/22/90 Age: 33 Bats: L Throws: R Height: 6'1" Weight: 210 lb. Origin: Round 31, 2010 Draft (#941 overall)

YEAR	TEAM	LVL	AGE	PA	R	2B	3B	HR	RBI	BB	K	SB	CS	Whiff%	AVG/OBP/SLG	DRC+	BABIP	BRR	DRP	WARP
2020	TB	MLB	30	159	16	5	3	3	22	20	42	8	1	30.5%	.217/.321/.362	87	.290	0.0	CF(46): 10.3	1.3
2021	TB	MLB	31	390	54	19	7	4	37	33	99	9	5	31.6%	.259/.328/.388	79	.345	3.9	CF(116): 4.4	1.4
2022	TB	MLB	32	221	28	8	0	7	22	14	61	6	1	32.1%	.228/.281/.369	81	.290	-0.7	CF(60): 6	0.9
2023 DC	*TOR*	*MLB*	*33*	*391*	*38*	*15*	*3*	*7*	*34*	*29*	*104*	*9*	*2*	*31.1%*	*.222/.289/.351*	*77*	*.292*	*6.0*	*CF 3*	*0.9*

Comparables: Dave Martinez (63), Mark Kotsay (63), Willie Wilson (60)

Here lies the career of Kevin Kiermaier, Tampa Bay Ray. His gloves were often golden, his bats were mostly driftwood. He dazzled us with defense that made our jaws drop. He also did ... other things ... that made our jaws drop. I'm sure we all remember the time he climbed the center field wall only to have the ball drop 150 feet in front of him, leaving our old friend Daniel Nava (waves to the back of the room) to chase it down from right field. That was our Kev. He really loved surprising us. Who can forget when he inexplicably ran in front of Randy Arozarena to catch a fly ball, then had zero chance of cutting down a tagging runner? Truly the work of a great prankster.

Kevin often called himself "The Outlaw." I never really knew what he meant by that, but looking back, I think it was because he knew how to steal outs both in the field and in the batter's box. Did you know that 69.2% of his Rays plate appearances ended without him reaching base? Sorry, that's not very nice. The Rays paid about $50 million for his services all the while, so perhaps "The Racketeer" is a more appropriate nickname.

We kid, we kid. We hope our dear friend enjoys his time in Toronto, where he'll be adored by half the fanbase for his ability to make leaping catches on routine fly balls while being condemned by the other half for, well, leaping in the air on routine fly balls. In addition to leaving his hips, thumbs, wrists and Achilles in Tampa Bay, the Rays also inherit his son, Jose Siri, who shares a lot of the same qualities, but without millions of guaranteed dollars to his name. Also, he's not as handsome. No one is.

Alejandro Kirk C/DH

Born: 11/06/98 Age: 24 Bats: R Throws: R Height: 5'8" Weight: 245 lb. Origin: International Free Agent, 2016

YEAR	TEAM	LVL	AGE	PA	R	2B	3B	HR	RBI	BB	K	SB	CS	Whiff%	AVG/OBP/SLG	DRC+	BABIP	BRR	DRP	WARP
2020	TOR	MLB	21	25	4	2	0	1	3	1	4	0	0	21.6%	.375/.400/.583	116	.421	-1.3	C(7): -0.8	-0.1
2021	BUF	AAA	22	56	7	3	0	2	13	5	9	0	0		.347/.393/.531	110	.375	0.0	C(10): -1.0	0.2
2021	TOR	MLB	22	189	19	8	0	8	24	19	22	0	0	19.4%	.242/.328/.436	123	.234	-0.6	C(44): 0.9	1.3
2022	TOR	MLB	23	541	59	19	0	14	63	63	58	0	0	15.4%	.285/.372/.415	130	.299	-7.3	C(78): 12.4	4.2
2023 DC	*TOR*	*MLB*	*24*	*500*	*58*	*20*	*1*	*14*	*55*	*55*	*57*	*0*	*1*	*16.0%*	*.279/.365/.429*	*129*	*.293*	*-3.4*	*C 3*	*3.2*

Comparables: Salvador Perez (73), Joe Mauer (65), Jerry May (65)

YEAR	TEAM	P. COUNT	FRM RUNS	BLK RUNS	THRW RUNS	TOT RUNS
2020	TOR	1001	-0.8	0.0	0.0	-0.8
2021	BUF	1421	-0.7	-0.1	0.0	-0.8
2021	TOR	5495	0.6	-0.2	0.5	0.9
2022	TOR	10231	11.0	0.4	0.7	12.1
2023	*TOR*	*10822*	*2.6*	*0.2*	*0.0*	*2.8*

From his superb contact skills and discipline to his modest power but robust slash line, Kirk does a spot-on Buster Posey impression at the plate. That's not hyperbole: The last catcher to record at least 500 plate appearances and hit at least 30% better than average? Posey himself back in 2015. Though Kirk's second-half swoon dampened some enthusiasm for his breakout campaign, his overall accomplishments set him apart from his young, talented game-calling contemporaries.

That said, Kirk enjoys one advantage that was not afforded to Posey for most of his career: He can frequently DH. The Blue Jays deployed him as such 51 times, but don't mistake Toronto's eagerness to keep his bat in the lineup as reluctance to play him in the field. Despite his, erm, unique physique, Kirk was one of baseball's best behind the dish last year, too. He deserves to be a household name, as few catchers do everything better.

Otto Lopez UT

Born: 10/01/98 Age: 24 Bats: R Throws: R Height: 5'10" Weight: 185 lb. Origin: International Free Agent, 2016

YEAR	TEAM	LVL	AGE	PA	R	2B	3B	HR	RBI	BB	K	SB	CS	Whiff%	AVG/OBP/SLG	DRC+	BABIP	BRR	DRP	WARP
2021	NH	AA	22	314	52	24	1	3	39	28	62	7	3		.331/.398/.457	109	.412	0.4	2B(43): -3.4, CF(17): 4.0, LF(3): 2.6	1.8
2021	BUF	AAA	22	194	36	8	3	2	25	13	26	15	1		.289/.347/.405	101	.324	3.3	2B(15): -0.3, LF(15): 3.0, SS(10): -0.5	1.1
2021	TOR	MLB	22	1	0	0	0	0	0	0	1	0	0	66.7%	.000/.000/.000	87				0.0
2022	BUF	AAA	23	391	53	19	6	3	34	41	61	14	5		.297/.378/.415	117	.351	-1.5	2B(36): 0.6, LF(22): 0.6, CF(16): -0.6	1.6
2022	TOR	MLB	23	10	0	0	0	0	3	1	1	0	1	7.1%	.667/.700/.667	95	.750	-0.2	SS(5): 0, 2B(1): 0, CF(1): 0	0.0
2023 DC	*TOR*	*MLB*	*24*	*175*	*19*	*7*	*1*	*1*	*13*	*13*	*30*	*3*	*2*	*20.8%*	*.266/.326/.355*	*97*	*.317*	*-0.3*	*CF 0, SS 0*	*0.3*

Comparables: Hernán Pérez (63), Steve Lombardozzi (63), Dawel Lugo (63)

Lopez employs a somewhat aggressive, highly contact-oriented approach that results in slash lines reminiscent of a bygone era: balanced strikeout and walk rates, healthy batting averages and OBPs and, as suggested by his 5-foot-10, 180-pound frame, a profound lack of thump. He possesses plus speed and carries a versatile glove that should enable him to occupy a utility role, although his arm strength profiles more acceptably from the right side of the infield than the left. All told, Lopez appears to be a low-risk, low-ceiling, MLB-ready role player whom the Blue Jays can plug in anywhere.

Gabriel Martinez OF

Born: 07/24/02 Age: 20 Bats: R Throws: R Height: 6'0" Weight: 170 lb. Origin: International Free Agent, 2018

YEAR	TEAM	LVL	AGE	PA	R	2B	3B	HR	RBI	BB	K	SB	CS	Whiff%	AVG/OBP/SLG	DRC+	BABIP	BRR	DRP	WARP
2021	BLU	ROK	18	125	16	8	0	0	14	21	18	7	2		.330/.448/.410		.393			
2022	DUN	A	19	264	46	14	0	11	46	22	45	3	1	25.0%	.288/.348/.483	129	.314	-3.0	LF(37): -1.9, RF(22): -1.4	0.9
2022	VAN	A+	19	113	11	8	0	3	13	9	17	0	0		.324/.381/.490	120	.361	-2.0	LF(15): 0.5, RF(13): 0.4	0.6
2023 non-DC	*TOR*	*MLB*	*20*	*251*	*23*	*11*	*1*	*5*	*26*	*14*	*57*	*4*	*2*	*27.9%*	*.250/.297/.381*	*87*	*.308*	*-1.5*	*LF 0, CF 0*	*0.0*

Comparables: Randal Grichuk (63), Manuel Margot (63), Carlos Correa (61)

Martinez shows advanced feel at the plate, both irrespective of and because of his age. He brings an aggressive but highly contact-oriented approach that, coupled with his slight frame, is not one that should beget power—long the primary concern with his trajectory. Allow Martinez's 2022 season to assuage those worries. After hitting just two home runs in his first 90-odd games, he mashed 14 across two levels at the tender age of 19, all without compromising his trademark approach. It's a delightful development for the outfielder, indeed. He still has a long path to the bigs ahead, and he needs to sustain this progress, but the questions around his MLB future are starting to transmogrify: not *if*, but *when*.

Orelvis Martinez SS/3B

Born: 11/19/01 Age: 21 Bats: R Throws: R Height: 6'1" Weight: 200 lb. Origin: International Free Agent, 2018

YEAR	TEAM	LVL	AGE	PA	R	2B	3B	HR	RBI	BB	K	SB	CS	Whiff%	AVG/OBP/SLG	DRC+	BABIP	BRR	DRP	WARP
2021	DUN	A	19	326	49	22	2	19	68	33	85	4	1		.279/.369/.572	130	.333	-1.8	SS(46): -5.2, 3B(12): 0.1	1.5
2021	VAN	A+	19	125	17	4	0	9	19	10	28	0	1		.214/.282/.491	125	.197	-0.4	SS(19): -1.1, 3B(6): -0.5	0.6
2022	NH	AA	20	492	57	15	0	30	76	40	140	6	3		.203/.286/.446	96	.217	-3.3	SS(60): -1.3, 3B(43): -0.5	0.8
2023 DC	*TOR*	*MLB*	*21*	*31*	*3*	*1*	*0*	*1*	*3*	*2*	*9*	*0*	*0*	*35.0%*	*.201/.264/.379*	*75*	*.254*	*0.0*	*3B 0*	*0.0*

Comparables: Bo Bichette (66), Javier Báez (59), J.P. Crawford (57)

As a 20-year-old, Martinez hit 30 home runs in just 118 games at Double-A ... and, per DRC+, managed to be *below-average* offensively. When we say Martinez sells out for his power, we mean he sells the heck out, as his approach may be *too* pull- and loft-oriented. His extreme fly-ball slant corroborates his basement-dwelling BABIPs and attests to a worryingly steep swing plane that could prevent him from cleaning up his swing-and-miss issues. Martinez's outcomes (though not his size) echo Chris Carter, who hit some absolute taters but compiled eerily similar fly-ball tendencies, inflated strikeout rates, sunken BABIPs and Mendoza Line batting averages. Despite the warts, Carter *was* an above-average hitter at his five-year peak, providing some hope for Martinez even if he can't evolve. But Carter also promptly, almost instantaneously, flamed out. It's a volatile skill set that could leave Martinez walking a similarly precarious tightrope. At least he has youth and an explosive tool on his side, which is more than can be said for most minor leaguers (and lots of major leaguers, too).

Whit Merrifield UT Born: 01/24/89 Age: 34 Bats: R Throws: R Height: 6'1" Weight: 195 lb. Origin: Round 9, 2010 Draft (#269 overall)

YEAR	TEAM	LVL	AGE	PA	R	2B	3B	HR	RBI	BB	K	SB	CS	Whiff%	AVG/OBP/SLG	DRC+	BABIP	BRR	DRP	WARP
2020	KC	MLB	31	265	38	12	0	9	30	12	33	12	3	16.2%	.282/.325/.440	113	.295	-0.1	RF(34): 0.6, CF(23): -0.8, 2B(15): 0.1	1.3
2021	KC	MLB	32	720	97	42	3	10	74	40	103	40	4	18.2%	.277/.317/.395	95	.309	6.4	2B(149): -2.4, RF(18): 0.7, LF(2): 0	2.5
2022	KC	MLB	33	420	51	23	1	6	42	30	61	15	3	19.0%	.240/.290/.352	96	.266	-0.4	2B(61): 1, RF(33): -0.4, CF(6): -0.2	1.1
2022	TOR	MLB	33	130	19	5	0	5	16	8	24	1	2	21.5%	.281/.323/.446	113	.312	-1.0	2B(22): 0.8, CF(12): -0.2, RF(7): 0.1	0.6
2023 DC	*TOR*	*MLB*	*34*	*553*	*65*	*26*	*1*	*10*	*47*	*35*	*83*	*22*	*2*	*19.1%*	*.263/.312/.384*	*97*	*.294*	*13.1*	*RF 1, LF 0*	*2.5*

Comparables: Red Schoendienst (77), Placido Polanco (77), Brandon Phillips (74)

In Merrifield's last *Annual* comment, we noted that 33 is a precarious year for a ballplayer. Well, about that ... Merrifield struggled mightily against vaccine-related disinformation and fastballs in 2022—against sinkers, specifically, and also unfortunately, because it's a pitch class upon which he had always feasted. His contact skills remained intact, but his diminished ability to square up hard stuff hampered his characteristic line-drive swing, downgrading his once-solid bat to decidedly below-average. His arrival in Toronto from Kansas City did nothing to alleviate his issues; if anything, he looked worse in his new shades of blue, failing to provide his new club with the shot in the arm they'd hoped for. Merrifield's preposterously team-friendly deal expires after this season unless the Blue Jays agree to exercise a relatively exorbitant $18 million mutual option for 2024, which seems unlikely no matter how well Merrifield plays. Ideally, he recaptures his line-drive stroke. But if his struggles persist, he may lose his tag as an everyday regular and cede playing time to Toronto's burgeoning youth movement.

George Springer CF Born: 09/19/89 Age: 33 Bats: R Throws: R Height: 6'3" Weight: 220 lb. Origin: Round 1, 2011 Draft (#11 overall)

YEAR	TEAM	LVL	AGE	PA	R	2B	3B	HR	RBI	BB	K	SB	CS	Whiff%	AVG/OBP/SLG	DRC+	BABIP	BRR	DRP	WARP
2020	HOU	MLB	30	222	37	6	2	14	32	24	38	1	2	25.3%	.265/.359/.540	128	.259	0.3	CF(42): -0.5, RF(9): -0.6	1.4
2021	TOR	MLB	31	342	59	19	1	22	50	37	79	4	1	26.9%	.264/.352/.555	130	.286	-1.0	CF(40): -0.8, RF(4): 0	2.2
2022	TOR	MLB	32	583	89	22	4	25	76	54	100	14	2	28.2%	.267/.342/.472	128	.285	6.2	CF(86): -1.5, RF(26): -0.7	4.3
2023 DC	*TOR*	*MLB*	*33*	*585*	*81*	*21*	*1*	*28*	*75*	*56*	*121*	*11*	*2*	*27.8%*	*.265/.345/.478*	*130*	*.294*	*3.4*	*RF 1, CF 0*	*3.9*

Comparables: Carlos Beltrán (79), Bernie Williams (77), Amos Otis (76)

Ah, the Springer Special: a hugely valuable performance at the plate and at least one guaranteed stint on the Injured List. Throw in some huge hits in key moments, and there you have it. Injuries notwithstanding, his bat has never once graded below average, per DRC+, cementing his status as one of this generation's most talented and consistent hitters. That said, his typical standout production now comes with some red flags. While still a very strong hitter, he posted career-worst marks in indicators such as barrel rate and maximum exit velocity. He was also at his swing-happiest, which cultivated poorer batted ball outcomes and contact rates both in and outside the zone. For some, these fluctuations might be considered aberrations. For a 33-year-old, they skew toward symptoms of decline. With the advent of extracurricular training and highly advanced technologies, seemingly anyone at any time can turn around a career. But, however gracefully he may age into them, Springer is more likely staring down his twilight years. His skills are robust and well-established. It's now a matter of how well he can stave off their erosion.

Yoshi Tsutsugo 1B Born: 11/26/91 Age: 31 Bats: L Throws: R Height: 6'1" Weight: 225 lb. Origin: International Free Agent, 2019

YEAR	TEAM	LVL	AGE	PA	R	2B	3B	HR	RBI	BB	K	SB	CS	Whiff%	AVG/OBP/SLG	DRC+	BABIP	BRR	DRP	WARP
2020	TB	MLB	28	185	27	5	1	8	24	26	50	0	0	23.2%	.197/.314/.395	92	.230	0.6	LF(16): 0.5, 3B(14): -1.1	0.3
2021	OKC	AAA	29	180	28	7	0	10	32	26	32	0	0		.257/.361/.507	121	.252	-0.5	LF(22): -0.1, 1B(19): -2.0	0.8
2021	PIT	MLB	29	144	20	8	1	8	25	15	33	0	1	25.9%	.268/.347/.535	106	.299	-2.7	RF(20): -0.7, 1B(15): 0.1, LF(2): -0.1	0.2
2021	LAD	MLB	29	31	2	0	0	0	2	6	12	0	0	34.6%	.120/.290/.120	69	.231	-0.1	LF(8): -0.3, 1B(1): 0	0.0
2021	TB	MLB	29	87	5	4	0	0	5	8	27	0	0	26.7%	.167/.244/.218	67	.255	-0.8	1B(15): -1	-0.3
2022	BUF	AAA	30	118	15	4	0	5	18	19	38	0	1		.265/.381/.459	100	.375	0.1	LF(11): -0.8, RF(9): 0.7, 1B(1): -0.0	0.5
2022	IND	AAA	30	36	4	2	0	2	12	9	3	0	0		.440/.556/.760	143	.409	-0.4	1B(7): -0.7	0.1
2022	PIT	MLB	30	193	11	4	0	2	19	19	50	0	0	21.5%	.171/.249/.229	69	.221	0.2	1B(35): 0.7	-0.2
2023 non-DC	*TOR*	*MLB*	*31*	*251*	*27*	*9*	*0*	*8*	*29*	*28*	*58*	*0*	*0*	*24.6%*	*.223/.316/.388*	*96*	*.264*	*-0.2*	*LF 0, 1B 0*	*0.3*

Comparables: Mike Jorgensen (52), Travis Ishikawa (51), Ryan Langerhans (51)

Given his prodigious power in Japan—he averaged 30+ home runs in six seasons preceding his stateside arrival—Tsutsugo's debut brought with it a palpable sense of excitement. But his MLB tenure, now spanning three seasons and four orgs, has been nothing short of disastrous. By nearly any measure, Tsutsugo's fabled power has failed to materialize. Paired with a troublesome strikeout rate and one of baseball's worst line-drive rates, it's possible he is irredeemably flawed. His power could eventually emerge—crazier things have happened, it's what makes baseball beautiful—but a ship taking on water won't be saved by a bucket. Maybe a *lot* of buckets, sure, but who has that many buckets? Aaron Judge, maybe? And he's a human aircraft carrier. Just saying, it's probably better for the ship to not start sinking in the first place. You don't want to set sail already relying on buckets.

Daulton Varsho RF Born: 07/02/96 Age: 27 Bats: L Throws: R Height: 5'10" Weight: 207 lb. Origin: Round 2, 2017 Draft (#68 overall)

YEAR	TEAM	LVL	AGE	PA	R	2B	3B	HR	RBI	BB	K	SB	CS	Whiff%	AVG/OBP/SLG	DRC+	BABIP	BRR	DRP	WARP
2020	AZ	MLB	23	115	16	5	2	3	9	12	33	3	1	30.6%	.188/.287/.366	80	.246	0.1	CF(14): 1.9, LF(5): 0.2	0.3
2021	RNO	AAA	24	87	18	6	1	9	25	7	16	2	0		.313/.368/.750	126	.291	0.7	C(11): 0.3, CF(7): -0.3	0.7
2021	AZ	MLB	24	315	41	17	2	11	38	30	67	6	0	24.6%	.246/.318/.437	94	.286	2.6	C(41): -3.9, CF(30): 1.2, LF(12): 1.3	1.3
2022	AZ	MLB	25	592	79	23	3	27	74	46	145	16	6	25.6%	.235/.302/.443	101	.269	5.0	RF(71): 2, CF(54): 1.5, C(31): -2.2	2.7
2023 DC	*TOR*	*MLB*	*26*	*584*	*71*	*24*	*3*	*23*	*68*	*48*	*131*	*15*	*3*	*24.8%*	*.242/.313/.436*	*107*	*.279*	*6.1*	*LF 2, CF 0*	*2.8*

Comparables: Josh Reddick (66), Kendrys Morales (59), Aaron Cunningham (57)

Is Varsho a catcher or a center fielder? As he tries to move toward either position, he becomes humanity's newest example of Zeno's Dichotomy paradox, crossing a distance to the threshold of either position that remains perpetually half a step smaller than the one he previously took. He never gets to a particular destination, but instead remains in the midst of numerous absurd positions, perpetually trying to explain that he's both fast and fast, for a catcher. As long as he retains his penetrating blue eyes (a certainty) and can continue to make incremental improvements as a hitter (a possibility), he will make us forget the absurdities of our reality. His DRC+ has gone up in each of the last two years (94 in 2021 and 101 in 2022) and it will be impossible to overlook how that happened when registering only a fifth of his defensive appearances last year behind the dish compared to half of them the year before. Much of his contact profile looked the same but he was better able to tune into curveballs at the bottom of the zone and remain competitive in two-strike counts, which was previously a problem.

PITCHERS

Brandon Barriera LHP Born: 03/04/04 Age: 19 Bats: L Throws: L Height: 6'2" Weight: 180 lb. Origin: Round 1, 2022 Draft (#23 overall)

The Blue Jays signed Barriera, their 2022 first-rounder, out of high school and away from his Vanderbilt commitment. In doing so, they locked down some of the draft's best capital-S Stuff in his heavy mid-90s fastball, lethal slider and promising changeup—from the left side, no less. The prevailing concern among scouts is his size—at 5-foot-11 and 175 pounds, he won't be mistaken for Alek Manoah—and if he'll hold up under a starter's workload. But he has time to fill out, and even if he didn't, his stuff plays now. The fastball can threaten triple digits, the slider sweeps hard and he sells his changeup with excellent arm speed. A watched egg never hatches, but all eyes will soon be on Barriera as he tries to prove his selection was quite the coup for the Jays.

Anthony Bass RHP Born: 11/01/87 Age: 35 Bats: R Throws: R Height: 6'2" Weight: 205 lb. Origin: Round 5, 2008 Draft (#165 overall)

YEAR	TEAM	LVL	AGE	W	L	SV	G	GS	IP	H	HR	BB/9	K/9	K	GB%	BABIP	WHIP	ERA	DRA	WARP	MPH	FB%	Whiff%	CSP
2020	TOR	MLB	32	2	3	7	26	0	25^{2}	17	2	3.2	7.4	21	61.4%	.224	1.01	3.51	87	0.5	94.8	54.2%	28.0%	44.3%
2021	MIA	MLB	33	3	9	0	70	1	61^{1}	55	11	3.5	8.5	58	44.0%	.272	1.29	3.82	96	0.7	95.4	49.3%	26.9%	55.8%
2022	MIA	MLB	34	2	3	0	45	0	44^{2}	32	1	2.0	9.1	45	38.1%	.265	0.94	1.41	84	0.8	95.5	39.2%	29.4%	58.2%
2022	TOR	MLB	34	2	0	0	28	0	25^{2}	19	5	3.5	9.8	28	45.3%	.237	1.13	1.75	91	0.4	95.4	43.1%	34.7%	54.2%
2023 DC	*TOR*	*MLB*	*35*	*3*	*2*	*2*	*60*	*0*	*52.3*	*48*	*6*	*3.2*	*9.1*	*53*	*44.6%*	*.294*	*1.28*	*3.48*	*92*	*0.4*	*95.4*	*45.9%*	*28.3%*	*54.2%*

Comparables: Clay Carroll (62), Joe Smith (62), Matt Albers (60)

Bass had allowed just one home run in nearly 45 innings with the Marlins before the Jays acquired him at the trade deadline. Naturally, he proceeded to allow five solo shots in just 28 appearances up north. Incredibly—and very fortunately—those five earned runs would be the only ones he'd allow wearing Toronto blue. His increasingly slider-first approach forces hitters to reckon with his best stuff and, at 35, should help him stave off the ruthless aging curve a little while longer. His broader recent track record is characterized by goodness, not last year's greatness, but Bass still proved a-*lure*-ing enough for the Jays to exercise his eminently affordable $3 million club option.

Chris Bassitt RHP Born: 02/22/89 Age: 34 Bats: R Throws: R Height: 6'5" Weight: 217 lb. Origin: Round 16, 2011 Draft (#501 overall)

YEAR	TEAM	LVL	AGE	W	L	SV	G	GS	IP	H	HR	BB/9	K/9	K	GB%	BABIP	WHIP	ERA	DRA	WARP	MPH	FB%	Whiff%	CSP
2020	OAK	MLB	31	5	2	0	11	11	63	56	6	2.4	7.9	55	43.9%	.278	1.16	2.29	90	1.0	92.4	77.5%	23.0%	52.8%
2021	OAK	MLB	32	12	4	0	27	27	157^{1}	127	15	2.2	9.1	159	41.6%	.271	1.06	3.15	86	2.7	92.6	74.0%	23.8%	57.6%
2022	NYM	MLB	33	15	9	0	30	30	181^{2}	159	19	2.4	8.3	167	49.1%	.282	1.14	3.42	92	2.5	93.0	46.4%	23.6%	57.0%
2023 DC	*TOR*	*MLB*	*34*	*9*	*8*	*0*	*27*	*27*	*148.7*	*141*	*17*	*2.6*	*8.6*	*141*	*46.3%*	*.297*	*1.24*	*3.52*	*93*	*1.8*	*92.8*	*60.9%*	*22.9%*	*56.3%*

Comparables: Lance Lynn (76), Todd Stottlemyre (76), Tom Candiotti (74)

If Jacob deGrom and Max Scherzer were the Lennon and McCartney of the Mets' rotation, Bassitt was the George Harrison—a little less heralded, but still essential to making the whole operation click. What Bassitt provided the Mets above all else was consistency; while both deGrom and Scherzer missed chunks of the season due to injury, Bassitt took the ball every fifth day and tossed a career-high 181⅔ innings. That is exactly what the Mets were hoping for when they dealt J.T. Ginn and Adam Oller to Oakland for Bassitt in the immediate aftermath of the lockout, wasting no time supplementing a rotation that lacked depth. And just like how Ravi Shankar teaching Harrison to play the sitar gave The Beatles a new sound, Bassitt's diverse secondary pitch mix injected some variety into the Mets' rotation. While his final two starts may have left a sour taste in many Mets fans' mouths, they do not negate the stretches where he carried the rotation. The Blue Jays clearly think Bassitt's "future still looks good," as Harrison would say, as they signed the 33-year-old to a three-year, $63 million pact in December.

José Berríos RHP Born: 05/27/94 Age: 29 Bats: R Throws: R Height: 6'0" Weight: 205 lb. Origin: Round 1, 2012 Draft (#32 overall)

YEAR	TEAM	LVL	AGE	W	L	SV	G	GS	IP	H	HR	BB/9	K/9	K	GB%	BABIP	WHIP	ERA	DRA-	WARP	MPH	FB%	Whiff%	CSP
2020	MIN	MLB	26	5	4	0	12	12	63	57	8	3.7	9.7	68	40.2%	.295	1.32	4.00	90	1.0	94.4	51.5%	27.4%	47.5%
2021	MIN	MLB	27	7	5	0	20	20	121^2	95	14	2.4	9.3	126	43.2%	.263	1.04	3.48	93	1.6	94.1	56.0%	23.9%	52.8%
2021	TOR	MLB	27	5	4	0	12	12	70^1	64	8	1.7	10.0	78	42.5%	.303	1.09	3.58	88	1.1	93.9	56.8%	22.9%	52.3%
2022	TOR	MLB	28	12	7	0	32	32	172	199	29	2.4	7.8	149	39.7%	.329	1.42	5.23	120	-0.1	94.0	53.7%	21.3%	54.2%
2023 DC	*TOR*	*MLB*	*29*	*8*	*8*	*0*	*25*	*25*	*147.7*	*149*	*20*	*2.5*	*8.4*	*138*	*40.9%*	*.305*	*1.29*	*3.98*	*104*	*1.0*	*93.9*	*54.6%*	*23.1%*	*52.4%*

Comparables: Alex Fernandez (80), Alex Cobb (80), Freddy Garcia (80)

Thanks to the widespread adoption of humidors and an ever-changing ball, hitters are faring worse at present than they have in decades. Can anyone explain, then, how Berríos bombed so spectacularly while MLB was at its pitcher-friendliest? The whole of Berríos has long exceeded the sum of his parts. He thrives—or, uh, thrived—more on contact management than on whiffs, though he was never particularly short on strikeouts, either. Curiously, his pitch usages, velocities and shapes didn't change much last season, which makes his implosion all the more difficult to understand. Once a bastion of consistency, Berríos has to hope his 2022 was an aberration rather than a harbinger of what's to come. To help ensure that's the case, he may try ditching his four-seamer—long his weakest pitch—and replacing it with more of everything else: a plus curve, above-average change and solid sinker. Berríos has too much talent to pitch so poorly: With nine-plus figures still owed to him through 2028, the Jays are literally banking on it.

Adam Cimber RHP Born: 08/15/90 Age: 32 Bats: R Throws: R Height: 6'3" Weight: 195 lb. Origin: Round 9, 2013 Draft (#268 overall)

YEAR	TEAM	LVL	AGE	W	L	SV	G	GS	IP	H	HR	BB/9	K/9	K	GB%	BABIP	WHIP	ERA	DRA-	WARP	MPH	FB%	Whiff%	CSP
2020	CLE	MLB	29	0	1	0	14	0	11^1	13	1	1.6	4.0	5	52.4%	.293	1.32	3.97	107	0.1	86.1	50.8%	22.2%	53.6%
2021	MIA	MLB	30	1	2	0	33	0	34^1	30	0	2.9	5.5	21	49.5%	.291	1.19	2.88	110	0.1	86.9	65.6%	19.1%	55.1%
2021	TOR	MLB	30	2	2	1	39	0	37^1	31	2	1.2	7.2	30	56.5%	.271	0.96	1.69	96	0.4	87.3	70.1%	20.9%	52.0%
2022	TOR	MLB	31	10	6	4	77	0	70^2	66	6	1.7	7.4	58	41.1%	.294	1.12	2.80	100	0.7	86.5	64.7%	20.8%	55.8%
2023 DC	*TOR*	*MLB*	*32*	*2*	*2*	*4*	*54*	*0*	*46.7*	*48*	*5*	*2.4*	*6.9*	*35*	*46.8%*	*.297*	*1.29*	*4.00*	*105*	*0.1*	*86.6*	*65.6%*	*20.6%*	*54.4%*

Comparables: Dan Otero (70), Brandon Kintzler (67), Will Harris (65)

Hitters base their subconscious swing decisions on the untold thousands of pitches they've seen stored in an ever-expanding mental database. Of course, Cimber's pitches look nothing like those pitches. With a topsy-turvy slider and two mid-80s fastballs thrown from knee height, he cultivates conventional bullpen success with an unconventional delivery. Once a fringe-of-the-roster type, the 32-year-old has now tossed over 100 solid innings with Toronto, making this unique side-winder's career arc a true Cimberella story.

Yimi Garcia RHP Born: 08/18/90 Age: 32 Bats: R Throws: R Height: 6'1" Weight: 230 lb. Origin: International Free Agent, 2009

YEAR	TEAM	LVL	AGE	W	L	SV	G	GS	IP	H	HR	BB/9	K/9	K	GB%	BABIP	WHIP	ERA	DRA-	WARP	MPH	FB%	Whiff%	CSP
2020	MIA	MLB	29	3	0	1	14	0	15	9	0	3.0	11.4	19	47.2%	.250	0.93	0.60	77	0.4	94.5	49.4%	29.2%	46.6%
2021	MIA	MLB	30	3	7	15	39	0	36^1	31	5	3.2	8.7	35	39.2%	.271	1.21	3.47	99	0.4	96.0	43.6%	26.6%	56.8%
2021	HOU	MLB	30	1	2	0	23	0	21^1	18	3	2.1	10.5	25	44.6%	.288	1.08	5.48	86	0.4	95.5	48.8%	27.5%	54.6%
2022	TOR	MLB	31	4	5	1	61	0	61	48	6	2.4	8.6	58	40.2%	.258	1.05	3.10	90	0.9	94.6	58.4%	24.1%	54.5%
2023 DC	*TOR*	*MLB*	*32*	*3*	*3*	*0*	*67*	*0*	*58.3*	*51*	*7*	*2.8*	*8.4*	*54*	*39.4%*	*.275*	*1.20*	*3.36*	*91*	*0.5*	*94.9*	*52.1%*	*25.2%*	*53.7%*

Comparables: Kevin Jepsen (54), Brad Boxberger (53), Huston Street (53)

The Blue Jays signed Garcia to a two-year, $11 million deal with a club option last winter, hoping to fortify their bullpen. Fortify it he did, adeptly setting up Jordan Romano all year as one of baseball's more effective relievers. Despite his success, his velo backslid across the board, culminating in all four of his supplemental offerings failing to produce double-digit swinging strike rates—a rare and decidedly ominous feat. As such, Garcia relied heavily on his low arm slot to flatten out, elevate and make effective an otherwise-pedestrian fastball. Should his velo continue to diminish, so too will his room for error.

Kevin Gausman RHP Born: 01/06/91 Age: 32 Bats: L Throws: R Height: 6'2" Weight: 205 lb. Origin: Round 1, 2012 Draft (#4 overall)

YEAR	TEAM	LVL	AGE	W	L	SV	G	GS	IP	H	HR	BB/9	K/9	K	GB%	BABIP	WHIP	ERA	DRA-	WARP	MPH	FB%	Whiff%	CSP
2020	SF	MLB	29	3	3	0	12	10	59^2	50	8	2.4	11.9	79	40.7%	.298	1.11	3.62	68	1.7	95.2	51.1%	33.1%	48.2%
2021	SF	MLB	30	14	6	0	33	33	192	150	20	2.3	10.6	227	41.1%	.275	1.04	2.81	73	4.5	94.8	52.8%	31.4%	57.5%
2022	TOR	MLB	31	12	10	0	31	31	174^2	188	15	1.4	10.6	205	39.5%	.364	1.24	3.35	76	3.9	95.1	48.8%	29.5%	55.3%
2023 DC	*TOR*	*MLB*	*32*	*10*	*8*	*0*	*29*	*29*	*166*	*155*	*20*	*2.0*	*9.6*	*177*	*40.0%*	*.304*	*1.16*	*3.06*	*83*	*2.8*	*94.9*	*51.0%*	*29.2%*	*54.9%*

Comparables: Chris Carpenter (78), Rick Rhoden (75), Esteban Loaiza (74)

In his inaugural season as a Jay, Gausman got "BABIP'd to death"—sophisticated sabermetric parlance that's intended to signal bad luck when hitters make contact. In truth, his biggest blemish is his persistent inability to suppress hard contact. You can hide a wart—just slap a ton of concealer on it and call it a day—but it *will* rear its ugly head. Gausman's didn't stop him from fulfilling his obligations as an ace, but it did lower his ceiling, and perhaps it affected his postseason performance, too. Gausman's splitter remains a heavily featured swing-and-miss pitch and one of MLB's premier weapons. He also mixed in more sliders to give the illusion of a three-pitch arsenal. But he leaves money on the table by using his fastball half the time at the expense of superior alternatives. He'll flash ace-caliber stuff but undercut it of his own accord, content to see his success ebb and flow based on his splitter's effectiveness and the baseball gods' mood every time a hitter connects with his fastball. Even a non-optimized version of Gausman was once more a top-15 pitcher in the game per WARP. It just feels like some minor tweaks could help him become something altogether more.

Drew Hutchison RHP Born: 08/22/90 Age: 32 Bats: L Throws: R Height: 6'3" Weight: 215 lb. Origin: Round 15, 2009 Draft (#460 overall)

YEAR	TEAM	LVL	AGE	W	L	SV	G	GS	IP	H	HR	BB/9	K/9	K	GB%	BABIP	WHIP	ERA	DRA-	WARP	MPH	FB%	Whiff%	CSP
2021	TOL	AAA	30	8	3	0	19	19	88^1	78	8	4.2	9.1	89	41.6%	.299	1.35	3.77	103	1.1				
2021	DET	MLB	30	3	1	0	9	2	21^1	20	1	4.6	4.2	10	48.6%	.279	1.45	2.11	130	-0.1	92.4	52.8%	23.5%	55.8%
2022	TOL	AAA	31	1	1	0	6	3	13^2	11	2	2.0	12.5	19	38.7%	.310	1.02	3.95	82	0.3				
2022	DET	MLB	31	3	9	0	28	18	105^1	114	15	3.6	5.8	68	39.2%	.295	1.48	4.53	136	-0.9	92.8	52.7%	20.1%	55.5%
2023 DC	*FA*	*MLB*	*32*	*2*	*3*	*0*	*9*	*9*	*49.7*	*57*	*7*	*3.9*	*6.2*	*34*	*40.7%*	*.308*	*1.58*	*5.29*	*132*	*-0.4*	*92.7*	*52.7%*	*21.5%*	*55.5%*

Comparables: Jim Slaton (70), Trevor Cahill (64), Rick Wise (62)

Who needed whom more: Hutchison or the Tigers? Since he returned from the indy leagues, Hutchison has signed with the Tigers four times, and been designated for assignment four times. Twice in the course of the first three months of the season, Hutchison was removed from the 40-man, elected free agency and was back with Detroit within a week. The Tigers needed someone who would fill innings all over their pitching staff; Hutchison needed a team that would let him keep pitching in spite of some truly alarming peripherals. The reward for Hutchison's contribution of the second-most innings on the staff was being designated for assignment again at season's end. The hope, of course, is that Detroit will get more out of their younger arms this time around. They better hope so, because their old reliable latched on with the Blue Jays in January.

Yusei Kikuchi LHP Born: 06/17/91 Age: 32 Bats: L Throws: L Height: 6'0" Weight: 205 lb. Origin: International Free Agent, 2019

YEAR	TEAM	LVL	AGE	W	L	SV	G	GS	IP	H	HR	BB/9	K/9	K	GB%	BABIP	WHIP	ERA	DRA-	WARP	MPH	FB%	Whiff%	CSP
2020	SEA	MLB	29	2	4	0	9	9	47	41	3	3.8	9.0	47	52.8%	.306	1.30	5.17	81	1.0	93.6	77.7%	30.0%	50.5%
2021	SEA	MLB	30	7	9	0	29	29	157	145	27	3.6	9.3	163	48.9%	.289	1.32	4.41	95	1.9	93.4	70.7%	27.9%	57.2%
2022	TOR	MLB	31	6	7	1	32	20	100^2	93	23	5.2	11.1	124	44.1%	.293	1.50	5.19	106	0.6	95.0	50.8%	31.1%	54.5%
2023 DC	*TOR*	*MLB*	*32*	*5*	*5*	*0*	*19*	*19*	*87.3*	*75*	*12*	*4.1*	*9.7*	*94*	*46.8%*	*.280*	*1.33*	*3.87*	*99*	*0.8*	*93.9*	*60.7%*	*29.0%*	*54.7%*

Comparables: Brian Anderson (83), Derek Holland (82), Jeff Francis (81)

Much ink has been spilled diagnosing Kikuchi's stateside misfortunes. Well-documented are his NPB workload and MLB's slipperier, less-tacky ball; speculation abounds regarding how Kikuchi has attempted to reconcile the latter. His scattershot changeup, woefully underused, remains his best pitch. Everything else, he grooves, and what Kikuchi grooves, hitters torch. Since his 2019 debut, among pitchers who have thrown at least 7,000 pitches, no one has aided opposing hitters' exit velocities more. The numbers get even uglier if you factor his changeup out of the equation. DRA graciously sees a league-average-ish starter, and other home run-adjusted estimators view Kikuchi through rose-colored glasses as well. But while it's tempting to chalk his struggles up to bad luck, he earns his poor results in part through shoddy pitch selection. Until and unless that changes, his MLB career will feel increasingly unsalvageable.

Adam Kloffenstein RHP Born: 08/25/00 Age: 22 Bats: R Throws: R Height: 6'5" Weight: 243 lb. Origin: Round 3, 2018 Draft (#88 overall)

YEAR	TEAM	LVL	AGE	W	L	SV	G	GS	IP	H	HR	BB/9	K/9	K	GB%	BABIP	WHIP	ERA	DRA-	WARP	MPH	FB%	Whiff%	CSP
2021	VAN	A+	20	7	7	0	23	23	101^1	96	10	5.4	9.5	107	52.9%	.306	1.55	6.22	87	1.5				
2022	VAN	A+	21	0	2	0	6	6	26	28	4	3.5	10.4	30	41.9%	.343	1.46	3.81	95	0.3				
2022	NH	AA	21	2	5	0	19	18	86	98	12	4.7	9.2	88	48.2%	.354	1.66	6.07	99	1.2				
2023 non-DC	*TOR*	*MLB*	*22*	*2*	*3*	*0*	*57*	*0*	*50*	*56*	*7*	*5.7*	*7.8*	*43*	*48.0%*	*.321*	*1.75*	*6.11*	*138*	*-0.8*			*27.3%*	

Comparables: JC Ramírez (82), Gabriel Ynoa (79), Zach Eflin (78)

Before imbuing his creature with life, Dr. Frankenstein had only grand inspirations without intent to produce something hideous or vile. Like the synthesis of the individual limbs of that creature, the assembly of Kloffenstein's arsenal—the sum of its parts—is not exactly easy on the eyes. Kloffenstein piles up whiffs, yet consistent command eludes him, clouding his once-sunny outlook as a rotation piece. His lack of standout stuff belies his 6-foot-5, 240-pound frame, and the big velocity that enticed scouts when he was a prep arm now only surfaces in short bursts. It's unclear what might get him back on track, but at this point a bit of alchemy couldn't hurt.

Adam Macko LHP Born: 12/30/00 Age: 22 Bats: L Throws: L Height: 6'0" Weight: 170 lb. Origin: Round 7, 2019 Draft (#216 overall)

YEAR	TEAM	LVL	AGE	W	L	SV	G	GS	IP	H	HR	BB/9	K/9	K	GB%	BABIP	WHIP	ERA	DRA-	WARP	MPH	FB%	Whiff%	CSP
2021	MOD	A	20	2	2	0	9	9	33^1	29	1	5.7	15.1	56	36.8%	.373	1.50	4.59	104	0.1				
2022	EVE	A+	21	0	2	0	8	8	38^1	33	4	4.7	14.1	60	43.4%	.372	1.38	3.99	83	0.7				
2023 non-DC	*TOR*	*MLB*	*22*	*2*	*3*	*0*	*57*	*0*	*50*	*45*	*7*	*6.0*	*10.3*	*57*	*40.0%*	*.300*	*1.58*	*5.09*	*118*	*-0.3*			*30.2%*	

Comparables: Vince Velasquez (78), Aliangel Lopez (77), Emilio Vargas (75)

At some point, Macko's on-field achievements should outrun his unlikely origin story (Slovakia-to-Ireland-to-Alberta), but the first step for the electric lefty is a prolonged period of health. With various (non-structural) shoulder issues limiting him to only 71⅔ innings over the last two years, Macko has shown glimmers of absolute unhittability with a mid-90s heater paired with a sweeping curve. Command remains the last major performance hurdle, but everything is predicated on his ability to stay healthy. While he was treated as a starter in the Mariners' system, Macko will likely find his home in the bullpen after his November trade to Toronto, but in whatever role, his will surely be the liveliest arm ever to come straight outta Bratislava.

Alek Manoah RHP

Born: 01/09/98 Age: 25 Bats: R Throws: R Height: 6'6" Weight: 285 lb. Origin: Round 1, 2019 Draft (#11 overall)

YEAR	TEAM	LVL	AGE	W	L	SV	G	GS	IP	H	HR	BB/9	K/9	K	GB%	BABIP	WHIP	ERA	DRA-	WARP	MPH	FB%	Whiff%	CSP
2021	BUF	AAA	23	3	0	0	3	3	18	7	1	1.5	13.5	27	40.6%	.194	0.56	0.50	90	0.3				
2021	TOR	MLB	23	9	2	0	20	20	111^{2}	77	12	3.2	10.2	127	39.5%	.246	1.05	3.22	95	1.4	93.3	62.9%	29.9%	52.2%
2022	TOR	MLB	24	16	7	0	31	31	196^{2}	144	16	2.3	8.2	180	37.5%	.245	0.99	2.24	89	3.0	93.7	62.0%	24.9%	53.9%
2023 DC	*TOR*	*MLB*	*25*	*10*	*9*	*0*	*29*	*29*	*174.7*	*156*	*21*	*2.9*	*9.2*	*178*	*38.7%*	*.286*	*1.21*	*3.54*	*93*	*2.1*	*93.6*	*62.3%*	*26.8%*	*53.3%*

Comparables: Zac Gallen (81), Matt Harvey (81), Jack Flaherty (80)

Manoah did more in 2022 of what he did best in his rookie season: keep hitters off-balance. He leverages a low arm slot to create tremendous lateral breaking action. His sinker saws off righties on the inner half and neuters hard contact as effectively as any pitch in baseball. He pounds the top of the zone with his four-seamer to induce whiffs and weak contact galore, and scarcely any slider in the game cuts through the zone more sharply. Evaluators have long expressed concern over the development of his work-in-progress changeup but, as with the rest of his arsenal, it generates feeble swings. Among *cambios*, it induced the most pop-ups on a rate basis and ranked in the top 10% for weak contact. It's not a strikeout pitch, but it is an *out* pitch thanks to Manoah's natural ability to create elite horizontal movement. DRA and ERA don't see eye-to-eye here, as the former is not entirely confident in the legitimacy of Manoah's contact management skills. But the results so far speak volumes, and they declare that Manoah has helped fill one of Toronto's critical top-of-the-rotation roles vacated by José Berríos and Hyun Jin Ryu.

Tim Mayza LHP

Born: 01/15/92 Age: 31 Bats: L Throws: L Height: 6'3" Weight: 213 lb. Origin: Round 12, 2013 Draft (#355 overall)

YEAR	TEAM	LVL	AGE	W	L	SV	G	GS	IP	H	HR	BB/9	K/9	K	GB%	BABIP	WHIP	ERA	DRA-	WARP	MPH	FB%	Whiff%	CSP
2021	TOR	MLB	29	5	2	1	61	0	53	40	5	2.0	9.7	57	57.2%	.265	0.98	3.40	84	0.9	94.1	71.2%	25.4%	52.5%
2022	TOR	MLB	30	8	1	2	63	0	48^{2}	42	7	2.2	8.1	44	56.6%	.273	1.11	3.14	91	0.7	93.7	82.6%	23.2%	50.1%
2023 DC	*TOR*	*MLB*	*31*	*2*	*2*	*0*	*54*	*0*	*46.7*	*47*	*4*	*3.2*	*8.2*	*42*	*53.4%*	*.311*	*1.38*	*4.01*	*103*	*0.1*	*94.0*	*75.5%*	*25.0%*	*49.2%*

Comparables: Jake Diekman (69), Danny Coulombe (66), Sam Freeman (65)

With pitchers shunning their fastballs and embracing their secondaries more than ever before, it's hard to know if Mayza throwing 80% sinkers is cunning or an exercise in denial. His power sinker is losing its power, but its steep entrance through the zone keeps batted balls on the ground. Its complement, a slider, generates its fair share of swings and misses, as sliders tend to do, but its shape lacks elusiveness and has been prone to yielding hard contact. Mayza's approach and results have proven seasonal. In 2023, maybe he'll pitch less to contact like in years past, or maybe he'll settle on throwing *only* sinkers. We won't know until he takes the mound, but given last year's career-best results, he may-za be onto something.

Nate Pearson RHP

Born: 08/20/96 Age: 26 Bats: R Throws: R Height: 6'6" Weight: 255 lb. Origin: Round 1, 2017 Draft (#28 overall)

YEAR	TEAM	LVL	AGE	W	L	SV	G	GS	IP	H	HR	BB/9	K/9	K	GB%	BABIP	WHIP	ERA	DRA-	WARP	MPH	FB%	Whiff%	CSP
2020	TOR	MLB	23	1	0	0	5	4	18	14	5	6.5	8.0	16	38.5%	.191	1.50	6.00	124	0.0	96.3	50.6%	26.3%	44.7%
2021	BUF	AAA	24	1	3	0	12	6	30^{2}	21	4	3.8	12.9	44	36.8%	.266	1.11	4.40	91	0.6				
2021	TOR	MLB	24	1	1	0	12	1	15	14	2	7.2	12.0	20	41.0%	.324	1.73	4.20	102	0.1	97.9	62.8%	33.9%	49.6%
2022	BUF	AAA	25	2	1	0	11	0	12^{2}	7	2	5.0	12.8	18	36.0%	.217	1.11	3.55	84	0.3				
2023 DC	*TOR*	*MLB*	*26*	*5*	*3*	*0*	*43*	*3*	*49.3*	*41*	*6*	*4.7*	*10.1*	*55*	*39.4%*	*.281*	*1.37*	*3.95*	*99*	*0.3*	*97.3*	*57.7%*	*28.5%*	*47.5%*

Comparables: Lucas Sims (66), Chris Flexen (65), Michael Lorenzen (61)

Pearson endured a lengthy bout of mononucleosis and then, during his rehab assignment, a lat strain that sidelined him another 11 weeks. In the end, he threw just over a dozen innings last year, all in the minors and all in relief. That seems to be the role for which the 26-year-old is best suited at this point. The 100-mph heater that tantalized scouts half a decade ago now only emerges in short bursts. In relief, we'll likely see Pearson commit fully to a two-pitch pairing of his four-seamer and slider, thus abandoning the curve and changeup that never came along. (The former wasn't any good, but the latter had a fighting chance once upon a time, mimicking the *cambios* that belong to Lucas Giolito, Kyle Hendricks and teammate Trevor Richards.) Either way, the path ahead is clearer now. It's not the original path; that one was supposed to fast-track him to the front of a big-league rotation, but was littered with potholes and landmines. This new path may be less heralded, but it's a way forward nonetheless. For Pearson's sake—and, selfishly, for our sakes, too—let's hope it's well-paved.

David Phelps RHP

Born: 10/09/86 Age: 36 Bats: R Throws: R Height: 6'2" Weight: 200 lb. Origin: Round 14, 2008 Draft (#440 overall)

YEAR	TEAM	LVL	AGE	W	L	SV	G	GS	IP	H	HR	BB/9	K/9	K	GB%	BABIP	WHIP	ERA	DRA-	WARP	MPH	FB%	Whiff%	CSP
2020	MIL	MLB	33	2	3	0	12	0	13	7	2	1.4	13.8	20	52.0%	.217	0.69	2.77	72	0.3	94.4	41.6%	30.0%	41.7%
2020	PHI	MLB	33	0	1	0	10	0	7^{2}	12	5	3.5	12.9	11	43.5%	.389	1.96	12.91	86	0.1	94.1	52.9%	22.4%	49.2%
2021	TOR	MLB	34	0	0	0	11	1	10^{1}	8	0	3.5	13.1	15	40.9%	.364	1.16	0.87	84	0.2	93.7	40.2%	31.6%	47.2%
2022	TOR	MLB	35	0	2	1	65	1	63^{2}	52	2	4.4	9.0	64	35.8%	.294	1.30	2.83	98	0.7	93.2	41.5%	19.5%	50.7%
2023 non-DC	*TOR*	*MLB*	*36*	*2*	*2*	*0*	*57*	*0*	*50*	*47*	*7*	*4.1*	*8.6*	*48*	*39.2%*	*.287*	*1.40*	*4.40*	*111*	*-0.1*	*93.3*	*42.1%*	*21.6%*	*49.2%*

Comparables: Juan Berenguer (70), Mike Trombley (68), Jason Grimsley (67)

In an era where whiffs reign supreme, Phelps wants nothing to do with them. In fact, he wants nothing to do with swings period, ranking in the bottom one percent of swing rate. With a 3.05 ERA over the last six years, Phelps, sans swinging strikes, steadfastly evades the skills erosion for which he perpetually seems due. As such, he's likely to evade a multi-year deal, too, but so long as teams can go year-to-year with him he's worth the modest gamble.

Zach Pop RHP
Born: 09/20/96 Age: 26 Bats: R Throws: R Height: 6'4" Weight: 220 lb. Origin: Round 7, 2017 Draft (#220 overall)

YEAR	TEAM	LVL	AGE	W	L	SV	G	GS	IP	H	HR	BB/9	K/9	K	GB%	BABIP	WHIP	ERA	DRA-	WARP	MPH	FB%	Whiff%	CSP
2021	MIA	MLB	24	1	0	0	50	0	54^{2}	54	3	4.0	8.4	51	55.8%	.321	1.43	4.12	101	0.5	95.5	67.7%	25.9%	47.8%
2022	JAX	AAA	25	0	1	0	19	0	24^{1}	28	0	3.0	7.4	20	59.5%	.378	1.48	2.22	101	0.3	96.6	84.1%	16.0%	
2022	MIA	MLB	25	2	0	0	18	0	20	23	1	0.9	6.3	14	62.1%	.338	1.25	3.60	101	0.2	96.6	83.5%	19.1%	48.9%
2022	TOR	MLB	25	2	0	0	17	0	19	18	1	0.9	5.2	11	50.0%	.288	1.05	1.89	106	0.1	96.4	70.2%	18.2%	52.0%
2023 DC	*TOR*	*MLB*	*26*	*2*	*2*	*0*	*54*	*0*	*46.7*	*52*	*4*	*3.3*	*6.9*	*35*	*56.3%*	*.323*	*1.49*	*4.63*	*115*	*-0.2*	*96.0*	*71.8%*	*22.8%*	*48.9%*

Comparables: Trevor Gott (65), Evan Phillips (64), Dominic Leone (62)

Pop *should* have nasty stuff—pitches with this type of shape and velocity are usually grounder-inducing sinkers and sharp, whiffy sliders—yet he earns decidedly mediocre results. A culprit could be Pop's inability to replicate his arm slot. He releases his slider, on average, two to three inches lower than his sinker. A couple of inches might as well be a couple of miles to the world's best hitters, who can already differentiate among grips and spin directions out-of-hand without having to distinguish release points. The last thing they need is more help vis-à-vis loose mechanics. If pitch-tipping isn't the perpetrator, small samples could be. But he had a lot of those in the minors, too, and none were particularly compelling. His ceiling was once that of a high-leverage weapon. Now, the Blue Jays would likely be happy to extract adequate middle relief work.

Trevor Richards RHP
Born: 05/15/93 Age: 30 Bats: R Throws: R Height: 6'2" Weight: 205 lb. Origin: Undrafted Free Agent, 2016

YEAR	TEAM	LVL	AGE	W	L	SV	G	GS	IP	H	HR	BB/9	K/9	K	GB%	BABIP	WHIP	ERA	DRA-	WARP	MPH	FB%	Whiff%	CSP
2020	TB	MLB	27	0	0	0	9	4	32	44	6	3.1	7.6	27	33.0%	.362	1.72	5.91	130	-0.2	90.7	50.7%	25.7%	45.7%
2021	DUR	AAA	28	1	0	0	7	0	7^{1}	3	0	1.2	14.7	12	53.8%	.231	0.55	0.00	82	0.2				
2021	MIL	MLB	28	3	0	0	15	0	19^{2}	15	3	4.1	11.4	25	18.8%	.273	1.22	3.20	95	0.2	92.7	58.5%	31.1%	51.1%
2021	TB	MLB	28	0	0	1	6	0	12	9	2	2.3	12.0	16	28.6%	.269	1.00	4.50	92	0.2	92.3	50.3%	31.5%	53.0%
2021	TOR	MLB	28	4	2	0	32	0	32^{2}	16	7	2.8	10.2	37	32.0%	.132	0.80	3.31	103	0.3	93.0	58.1%	35.2%	45.1%
2022	TOR	MLB	29	3	2	0	62	4	64	57	9	4.9	11.5	82	34.4%	.314	1.44	5.34	87	1.0	93.5	44.1%	35.3%	46.1%
2023 DC	*TOR*	*MLB*	*30*	*6*	*4*	*0*	*58*	*4*	*56.3*	*47*	*8*	*3.8*	*10.5*	*65*	*34.4%*	*.281*	*1.27*	*3.59*	*93*	*0.5*	*92.5*	*48.3%*	*32.2%*	*46.9%*

Comparables: Shane Greene (60), Tyler Duffey (57), Joe Kelly (56)

In the paraphrased words of Regina George: "Trevor! Stop trying to make sliders happen!" Richards' slider (the folks at Statcast started labeling it a curve in 2019, but really, it's a slider) has been one of, if not *the* worst of its kind since his 2018 debut. He overhauled his pitch usage to feature his offerings more equitably, meaning more of his top-shelf, knee-buckling changeup that amasses huge whiffs. But it also means more of his abysmally bad breaker, a pitch he can hardly command or reliably throw for strikes. With a two-year strikeout rate north of 30%, a useful relief arm hibernates, but until—*unless*—he whittles down his arsenal to two pitches, it'll be stuck in a long winter's slumber.

Sem Robberse RHP
Born: 10/12/01 Age: 21 Bats: R Throws: R Height: 6'1" Weight: 160 lb. Origin: International Free Agent, 2019

YEAR	TEAM	LVL	AGE	W	L	SV	G	GS	IP	H	HR	BB/9	K/9	K	GB%	BABIP	WHIP	ERA	DRA-	WARP	MPH	FB%	Whiff%	CSP
2021	DUN	A	19	5	4	0	14	12	57^{2}	46	4	3.1	9.5	61	49.4%	.273	1.14	3.90	101	0.6				
2021	VAN	A+	19	0	3	0	7	7	31	39	3	5.2	8.4	29	52.0%	.367	1.84	5.23	114	0.0				
2022	VAN	A+	20	4	4	0	17	17	86^{2}	76	7	2.5	8.1	78	48.6%	.280	1.15	3.12	95	1.0				
2022	NH	AA	20	0	3	0	5	5	24^{2}	19	4	3.6	6.9	19	47.9%	.217	1.18	3.65	104	0.3				
2023 non-DC	*TOR*	*MLB*	*21*	*2*	*3*	*0*	*57*	*0*	*50*	*56*	*6*	*4.3*	*6.2*	*34*	*47.1%*	*.310*	*1.62*	*5.46*	*131*	*-0.6*			*21.7%*	

Comparables: Spencer Adams (73), Jacob Turner (70), Arodys Vizcaíno (68)

When the Blue Jays inked Robberse during the 2018 international signing period, they saw projectability in the Dutchman, an athleticism belied by his slight frame and mid-80s fastball but shown in his command and repeatable delivery. Toronto's intuition proved correct: Robberse's fastball now sits low-90s, and he puts away hitters with a solid-to-plus curve (he features a slider and changeup, too, though both are a bit raw). He's less a flamethrowing strikeout artist and more an efficient, contact-managing *artiste* who may eventually find a home in the back of Toronto's rotation. Most critically, he retains a very, very slight chance of supplanting Bert Blyleven as the foremost Major Leaguer to hail from Zeist, Netherlands.

Jordan Romano RHP
Born: 04/21/93 Age: 30 Bats: R Throws: R Height: 6'5" Weight: 210 lb. Origin: Round 10, 2014 Draft (#294 overall)

YEAR	TEAM	LVL	AGE	W	L	SV	G	GS	IP	H	HR	BB/9	K/9	K	GB%	BABIP	WHIP	ERA	DRA-	WARP	MPH	FB%	Whiff%	CSP
2020	TOR	MLB	27	2	1	2	15	0	14^{2}	8	2	3.1	12.9	21	58.1%	.207	0.89	1.23	70	0.4	96.7	40.3%	43.8%	44.6%
2021	TOR	MLB	28	7	1	23	62	0	63	41	7	3.6	12.1	85	46.5%	.254	1.05	2.14	76	1.4	97.5	63.2%	31.8%	52.8%
2022	TOR	MLB	29	5	4	36	63	0	64	44	4	3.0	10.3	73	44.0%	.258	1.02	2.11	81	1.2	97.0	49.0%	29.8%	55.2%
2023 DC	*TOR*	*MLB*	*30*	*3*	*3*	*36*	*67*	*0*	*58.3*	*49*	*6*	*3.5*	*10.9*	*70*	*44.4%*	*.297*	*1.23*	*3.31*	*85*	*0.7*	*97.1*	*54.7%*	*30.7%*	*53.3%*

Comparables: Brad Brach (69), Pierce Johnson (68), Drew Steckenrider (68)

Flip a coin the next time Romano takes the mound. If heads, you'll get a fastball; if tails, a slider. Romano used his binary approach to pitching to produce a carbon copy of his spectacular 2021 breakout. He coaxes volatile outcomes from his victims—which is what most hitters who face him end up being: *victims*—leaning on his slider for weak grounders, his four-seamer for weak flies and both for whiffs. MLB is flush with filthy, flame-throwing relievers, which is perhaps why it feels as though Romano has yet to garner distinction from much of the baseball-watching diaspora. That should change soon: Among those who have thrown at least 140 innings since the start of 2020, he ranks third in ERA (2.03) and first in both win probability added and FanGraphs' "Clutch" metric. Blue Jays fans: You may proceed to the next comment. Almost everyone else: Yes, Romano is even better than your favorite team's closer.

Hyun Jin Ryu LHP

Born: 03/25/87 Age: 36 Bats: R Throws: L Height: 6'3" Weight: 250 lb. Origin: International Free Agent, 2013

YEAR	TEAM	LVL	AGE	W	L	SV	G	GS	IP	H	HR	BB/9	K/9	K	GB%	BABIP	WHIP	ERA	DRA-	WARP	MPH	FB%	Whiff%	CSP
2020	TOR	MLB	33	5	2	0	12	12	67	60	6	2.3	9.7	72	50.8%	.303	1.15	2.69	71	1.8	89.9	34.7%	26.3%	46.7%
2021	TOR	MLB	34	14	10	0	31	31	169	170	24	2.0	7.6	143	46.2%	.296	1.22	4.37	107	1.0	89.9	36.1%	22.7%	53.4%
2022	TOR	MLB	35	2	0	0	6	6	27	32	5	1.3	5.3	16	45.2%	.307	1.33	5.67	136	-0.2	89.6	42.0%	17.0%	57.3%
2023 DC	*TOR*	*MLB*	*36*	*2*	*2*	*0*	*8*	*8*	*40.3*	*43*	*5*	*2.0*	*6.4*	*28*	*45.7%*	*.298*	*1.29*	*3.82*	*103*	*0.3*	*90.0*	*37.4%*	*21.5%*	*51.7%*

Comparables: Jon Lester (66), Jim Kaat (66), Randy Wolf (65)

Ryu underwent Tommy John surgery in June, mercifully ending his season but calling into question everything thereafter. Depending on his recovery, Ryu could contribute late this year, though probably not meaningfully if his 4.55 ERA as a Jay is any indication. Those theoretical late-season appearances may conclude Ryu's tenure in Toronto and, quite possibly, his career. Allow us, then, to reflect on the good times. Among pitchers who threw at least 800 innings from 2013 through 2020, Ryu ranked 14th in WARP per inning and held a 2.95 ERA—4th-best in MLB, behind only Clayton Kershaw, Jacob deGrom and Max Scherzer. He preceded eight ace-caliber years in MLB with seven ace-caliber years in the KBO, averaging 27 starts, 180 innings and a 2.81 ERA. He was perpetually dwarfed by Kershaw's and Zack Greinke's shadows in Chavez Ravine, and plagued by myriad injuries, including labral and groin tears. Though he succeeded anyway, Ryu never got *quite* the recognition he deserved, our attention too narrowly focused on the lumps and scars and imperfections of each individual tree. Take a step back, see the forest: of everyone to ever do it, Ryu was one of the better ones.

Erik Swanson RHP

Born: 09/04/93 Age: 29 Bats: R Throws: R Height: 6'3" Weight: 222 lb. Origin: Round 8, 2014 Draft (#246 overall)

YEAR	TEAM	LVL	AGE	W	L	SV	G	GS	IP	H	HR	BB/9	K/9	K	GB%	BABIP	WHIP	ERA	DRA-	WARP	MPH	FB%	Whiff%	CSP
2020	SEA	MLB	26	0	2	0	9	0	7^{2}	11	3	2.3	10.6	9	33.3%	.381	1.70	12.91	112	0.0	95.9	74.5%	29.6%	50.8%
2021	SEA	MLB	27	0	3	1	33	2	35^{1}	28	5	2.5	8.9	35	32.7%	.247	1.08	3.31	98	0.4	94.8	59.9%	27.6%	56.4%
2022	SEA	MLB	28	3	2	3	57	1	53^{2}	39	3	1.7	11.7	70	32.8%	.300	0.91	1.68	70	1.3	93.8	54.9%	29.7%	56.6%
2023 DC	*TOR*	*MLB*	*29*	*3*	*2*	*0*	*60*	*0*	*52.3*	*46*	*7*	*2.4*	*9.3*	*54*	*35.2%*	*.279*	*1.15*	*3.19*	*87*	*0.6*	*94.0*	*59.0%*	*27.5%*	*55.4%*

Comparables: Tyler Duffey (52), Dylan Floro (50), Nick Wittgren (50)

After a November trade that had some Jays' fans scratching their heads, Swanson (along with minor-league lefty Adam Macko) arrived from a sparkling season in Seattle (ERA below two, WHIP below one) to a Toronto bullpen in need of late-inning options not named "Jordan Romano." While Teoscar Hernández might have seemed too high a price to pay for the two Ms, don't discount Swanson's ability to be a difference-maker. His Statcast sliders show us deep red just about everywhere but fastball velocity, which is not that surprising given how the Mariners have developed many of their relief arms by encouraging the usage of their stronger secondary pitches. In Swanson's case, an excellent splitter and competent slider play off his mid-90s four-seamer, and this combination led him to be, statistically, the second-most effective reliever by DRA (after Andrés Muñoz) among Los Bomberos in 2022. Inexplicably shelved in the playoffs (but for an inning in the 18-frame marathon elimination game against the Astros), Swanson should be much more than an afterthought as a high-leverage arm in his new digs north of the border.

★ ★ ★ *2023 Top 101 Prospect* **#15** ★ ★ ★

Ricky Tiedemann LHP

Born: 08/18/02 Age: 20 Bats: L Throws: L Height: 6'4" Weight: 220 lb. Origin: Round 3, 2021 Draft (#91 overall)

YEAR	TEAM	LVL	AGE	W	L	SV	G	GS	IP	H	HR	BB/9	K/9	K	GB%	BABIP	WHIP	ERA	DRA-	WARP	MPH	FB%	Whiff%	CSP
2022	DUN	A	19	3	1	0	6	6	30	11	1	3.9	14.7	49	46.8%	.217	0.80	1.80	68	1.0	95.4	58.6%	45.5%	
2022	VAN	A+	19	2	2	0	8	8	37^{2}	23	2	2.9	12.9	54	46.2%	.276	0.93	2.39	87	0.6				
2022	NH	AA	19	0	1	0	4	4	11	5	0	3.3	11.5	14	63.6%	.227	0.82	2.45	90	0.2				
2023 non-DC	*TOR*	*MLB*	*20*	*2*	*2*	*0*	*57*	*0*	*50*	*42*	*6*	*4.9*	*10.8*	*60*	*46.3%*	*.296*	*1.39*	*4.10*	*99*	*0.2*			*30.5%*	

Comparables: John Lamb (49), Deivi García (48), Francis Martes (45)

The Blue Jays' third-rounder in 2021, Tiedemann offers a heavy power sinker that misses bats, a punishing changeup and a developing sweeper. Command remains an issue, but his otherwise top-shelf stuff from the left side has done nothing but devastate opposing hitters. With coal loaded into its boiler, his hype train ripped through three stops, depositing the 20-year-old in Triple-A by August. All told, he compiled a 2.17 ERA, 39% strikeout rate and four times as many Ks as free passes across 18 starts at three levels. His stratospheric, nay, *thermospheric* trajectory is one that could have him knocking down Toronto's door by year's end. He proves that TINSTAAPPBTICTUTBO: There is No Such Thing as a Pitching Prospect, but Tiedemann is Cruelly Tempting Us to Believe Otherwise.

Mitch White RHP

Born: 12/28/94 Age: 28 Bats: R Throws: R Height: 6'3" Weight: 210 lb. Origin: Round 2, 2016 Draft (#65 overall)

YEAR	TEAM	LVL	AGE	W	L	SV	G	GS	IP	H	HR	BB/9	K/9	K	GB%	BABIP	WHIP	ERA	DRA-	WARP	MPH	FB%	Whiff%	CSP
2020	LAD	MLB	25	1	0	0	2	0	3	1	0	3.0	6.0	2	12.5%	.125	0.67	0.00	126	0.0	93.8	50.0%	22.7%	40.5%
2021	RC	A	26	2	0	0	2	2	11^{2}	7	1	0.8	10.8	14	53.8%	.240	0.69	1.54	96	0.1				
2021	OKC	AAA	26	1	0	0	10	7	32	28	1	3.4	11.0	39	38.1%	.325	1.25	1.69	86	0.4				
2021	LAD	MLB	26	1	3	0	21	4	46^{2}	38	6	3.3	9.5	49	47.3%	.258	1.18	3.66	88	0.7	94.6	52.8%	23.0%	57.8%
2022	OKC	AAA	27	2	0	0	2	2	11^{2}	3	0	1.5	7.7	10	55.6%	.111	0.43	0.00	97	0.1	94.6	52.3%	29.2%	
2022	LAD	MLB	27	1	2	0	15	10	56	51	6	3.1	7.6	47	39.6%	.276	1.25	3.70	102	0.5	93.8	52.3%	20.2%	53.0%
2022	TOR	MLB	27	0	5	0	10	8	43	59	3	3.3	6.5	31	45.2%	.368	1.74	7.74	124	-0.1	93.7	51.0%	17.6%	55.4%
2023 DC	*TOR*	*MLB*	*28*	*6*	*5*	*0*	*48*	*8*	*68*	*69*	*8*	*3.1*	*7.0*	*53*	*44.2%*	*.295*	*1.37*	*4.10*	*107*	*0.2*	*94.0*	*52.0%*	*21.6%*	*54.8%*

Comparables: Adrian Houser (52), Rafael Montero (49), Ben Lively (49)

These days, trading with the Dodgers can be terrifying: There's a lurking feeling they see something you don't. Then again, the Jays probably knew what they had in Nick Frasso, who demolished the low minors with an impressive arsenal before getting shipped to Los Angeles for White. Sometimes, you must mortgage your future to improve your present situation—especially if you're a contender. While Frasso represents what *could be*, White represents what *is*—and he's no slouch, either. He exhibits solid command, and his slider is a real weapon, revamped last year by subtracting a tick of velo and adding sweep. (Incidentally, the pitch performed worse than it did in 2021, contributing gently to White's step backward from his promising breakout.) Ultimately, White must confront fastball issues to succeed long-term. He locates it effectively around the zone's edges, but its shape is unspectacular, the kind that big-league hitters see well and square up. Those issues can be remedied or, at the very least, masked, but not when he throws the pitch half the time. White would undoubtedly benefit from seeing his usage better optimized, but the developmentally savvy Dodgers' decision to offload him onto Toronto could signal that a much larger project lies ahead. There it is again, that lurking feeling ...

LINEOUTS

Hitters

HITTER	POS	TEAM	LVL	AGE	PA	R	2B	3B	HR	RBI	BB	K	SB	CS	AVG/OBP/SLG	DRC+	BABIP	BRR	DRP	WARP
Vinny Capra	SS	BUF	AAA	25	222	31	6	1	5	28	29	29	5	2	.283/.378/.403	137	.310	0.5	3B(20): 1.7, SS(20): 0.5, LF(7): 0.1	1.8
	SS	TOR	MLB	25	7	2	0	0	0	0	2	1	0	0	.200/.429/.200	115	.250	0.2	2B(1): 0	0.1
Alex De Jesus	3B	RC	A	20	176	34	9	1	7	22	32	50	2	0	.259/.398/.483	115	.349	-0.7	3B(11): -0.6, SS(11): 1.3	0.9
	3B	GL	A+	20	226	27	11	2	4	26	28	65	0	1	.282/.376/.421	90	.402	-0.3	3B(39): 0.9, SS(3): -0.7	0.3
	3B	VAN	A+	20	104	10	5	0	2	13	12	36	0	0	.211/.298/.333	79	.315	-0.4	SS(17): -2.6, 3B(5): 0.4	0.2
Cade Doughty	2B/3B	DUN	A	21	119	21	5	0	6	24	10	29	3	2	.272/.370/.495	114	.324	1.0	2B(12): -1.9, 3B(11): 2.3	0.7
Josh Kasevich	SS/3B	DUN	A	21	122	18	8	0	0	7	11	9	0	2	.262/.344/.336	130	.283	1.7	SS(16): 2.2, 3B(10): -1.0	1.0
Nathan Lukes	OF	BUF	AAA	27	484	62	25	1	11	61	47	89	20	3	.285/.364/.425	111	.336	-4.2	CF(59): -0.4, RF(24): -0.0, LF(18): 0.4	1.5
Damiano Palmegiani	IF	DUN	A	22	228	30	14	1	11	37	23	47	2	0	.256/.351/.508	132	.279	1.3	3B(41): -2.4, 1B(2): -0.2	1.4
	IF	VAN	A+	22	272	44	11	0	13	46	31	60	3	0	.224/.335/.443	118	.239	0.9	3B(32): 0.2, 1B(21): -0.2	1.4
Tucker Toman	SS	BLU	ROK	18	46	4	3	0	0	5	7	12	0	0	.289/.391/.368		.407			
Bradley Zimmer	CF	PHI	MLB	29	16	4	1	0	0	0	0	4	0	0	.250/.250/.313	80	.333	0.2	CF(9): 1.5	0.2
	CF	TOR	MLB	29	101	14	4	0	2	5	5	41	3	2	.101/.200/.213	49	.152	0.1	CF(88): 1.8, RF(2): 0.1	-0.1

The preeminent bat-to-ball artist in Toronto's system, **Vinny Capra** walked as often as he struck out en route to a healthy 137 DRC+ at Triple-A. His 15-homer pace in Buffalo may overstate his power, but he's nevertheless a high-floor, low-ceiling, MLB-ready bench bat. ⚾ Acquired from the Dodgers alongside Mitch White, **Alex De Jesus** boasts high strikeout rates that mostly wash out his plus raw power. He's patient, flashes in-game pop and is still just 21, but his present and future exude volatility. ⚾ **Cade Doughty** picked up where he left off at LSU, slugging a homer about every 20 PAs thanks to an aggressive, pull-happy approach. The 2022 second-rounder has a coveted combo of power, bat-to-ball ability and a glove that'll play at the four or five, though he'll need to shore up his plate discipline to reach his potential. ⚾ **Josh Kasevich** is a strong defender with a hit tool considered by some to be among the best of the 2022 college class. Though he knocked eight doubles in his 25-game debut, his swing prioritizes contact quantity over quality, leaving him largely devoid of thump. ⚾ You may know him best as one of the dudes traded for Brandon Guyer back in 2016. But after tightening up his plate discipline, adding power to his line-drive stroke and making the Jays' 40-man, **Nathan Lukes'** newest claim to fame, Toronto hopes, will be providing worthwhile outfield depth. ⚾ A Venezuelan-born Canadian you could mistake for being a native Italian, **Damiano Palmegiani** leverages his raw power and steep swing to hit dongs. Though his bat-to-ball skills are impressive for a power hitter, batting average may never be a strength, nor will his defense. ⚾ A 2022 second-rounder, switch-hitting **Tucker Toman** is a natural lefty but is proficient at the plate from the right side as well. His power, bat speed and feel for contact give him a big-league ceiling, though we haven't mentioned his glove yet for a reason. ⚾ **Bradley Zimmer** now boasts the distinction of being reclaimed by a team that DFA'd him earlier the same season. He did nothing to quell longstanding concerns about his futile bat and should generally only be deployed as a defensive replacement.

Pitchers

PITCHER	TEAM	LVL	AGE	W	L	SV	G	GS	IP	H	HR	BB/9	K/9	K	GB%	BABIP	WHIP	ERA	DRA-	WARP	MPH	FB%	WHF	CSP
Irv Carter	BLU	ROK	19	1	3	0	9	6	33^{2}	36	8	2.9	11.2	42	38.9%	.341	1.40	5.88						
	DUN	A	19	0	1	0	4	4	14	14	2	2.6	7.1	11	32.6%	.293	1.29	4.50	120	0.1	92.8	57.0%	24.3%	
Connor Cooke	DUN	A	22	2	5	1	14	8	46^{1}	44	3	2.7	12.2	63	33.6%	.376	1.25	4.86	89	1.0	92.7	47.9%	34.3%	
	VAN	A+	22	0	2	8	11	0	10^{2}	9	2	2.5	10.1	12	26.7%	.250	1.13	6.75	110	0.0				
Brandon Eisert	BUF	AAA	24	4	3	0	45	5	60^{2}	54	8	2.2	11.4	77	42.5%	.319	1.14	3.41	74	1.6				
Bowden Francis	BUF	AAA	26	5	10	0	37	23	98^{1}	108	23	3.9	10.1	110	27.3%	.326	1.54	6.59	123	0.1				
	TOR	MLB	26	0	0	0	1	0	0^{2}	1	0	0.0	13.5	1	100.0%	.500	1.50	0.00	90	0.0	92.1	44.4%	28.6%	70.9%
Matt Gage	BUF	AAA	29	2	2	12	41	0	42^{1}	30	1	3.4	9.8	46	46.2%	.276	1.09	2.34	81	1.0				
	TOR	MLB	29	0	1	0	11	0	13	6	1	4.2	8.3	12	48.4%	.172	0.92	1.38	103	0.1	91.8	89.3%	29.8%	48.9%
Foster Griffin	OMA	AAA	26	4	0	0	20	0	28	19	2	1.9	10.3	32	54.3%	.250	0.89	1.93	77	0.7				
	BUF	AAA	26	2	0	1	18	0	23^{1}	21	1	3.5	9.6	25	54.5%	.308	1.29	2.31	84	0.5				
	KC	MLB	26	0	0	0	5	0	4^{1}	6	0	8.3	4.2	2	35.3%	.400	2.31	12.46	127	0.0	93.6	19.0%	28.6%	56.4%
	TOR	MLB	26	0	0	0	1	0	2	1	0	4.5	9.0	2	60.0%	.200	1.00	0.00	110	0.0	94.1	40.7%	11.1%	55.8%
Thomas Hatch	BUF	AAA	27	8	7	0	28	22	131	127	16	2.6	7.8	113	43.5%	.295	1.26	4.67	93	2.3				
	TOR	MLB	27	0	1	0	1	1	4^{2}	12	3	3.9	7.7	4	52.6%	.563	3.00	19.29	111	0.0	94.2	43.7%	14.6%	57.3%
Adrian Hernandez	BUF	AAA	22	3	0	7	31	0	32^{2}	25	6	4.4	12.1	44	43.4%	.271	1.26	4.96	76	0.8				
Hayden Juenger	NH	AA	21	0	5	0	20	17	56	40	12	3.4	10.8	67	32.1%	.224	1.09	4.02	99	0.8				
	BUF	AAA	21	3	2	2	18	2	32^{2}	23	6	4.4	9.1	33	42.4%	.215	1.19	3.31	91	0.5				
Casey Lawrence	BUF	AAA	34	9	5	0	23	23	126	95	18	1.2	7.6	106	42.3%	.227	0.89	2.79	84	2.7				
	TOR	MLB	34	0	1	0	6	0	18	23	5	2.0	5.5	11	39.7%	.310	1.50	7.50	116	0.0	90.6	37.4%	15.8%	51.2%
Julian Merryweather	BUF	AAA	30	2	0	0	13	0	14^{1}	5	0	3.8	11.3	18	54.8%	.161	0.77	0.00	79	0.4				
	TOR	MLB	30	0	3	0	26	1	26^{2}	31	4	2.4	7.8	23	47.1%	.333	1.43	6.75	99	0.3	97.5	51.6%	22.6%	57.6%
Joey Murray	NH	AA	25	1	1	0	5	4	20^{2}	16	4	5.7	10.0	23	38.9%	.240	1.40	7.84	98	0.3				
Kendry Rojas	DUN	A	19	2	2	0	12	10	39^{2}	36	1	4.3	9.8	43	45.9%	.318	1.39	4.08	101	0.6	90.8	53.0%	30.9%	
Dahian Santos	DUN	A	19	4	5	0	19	14	73^{1}	47	8	4.3	14.7	120	36.4%	.298	1.12	3.44	72	2.2	91.9	48.7%	40.9%	
	VAN	A+	19	0	2	0	4	4	12^{2}	17	3	6.4	15.6	22	37.5%	.483	2.05	10.66	74	0.2				
Trent Thornton	BUF	AAA	28	2	2	3	21	0	28	26	1	3.9	9.6	30	41.8%	.325	1.36	2.89	97	0.4				
	TOR	MLB	28	0	2	0	32	0	46	40	7	3.3	7.2	37	36.6%	.260	1.24	4.11	110	0.2	93.9	46.1%	20.6%	61.2%
Yosver Zulueta	DUN	A	24	0	0	0	3	3	12	9	0	2.3	17.3	23	57.1%	.429	1.00	3.00	68	0.4	97.2	48.9%	45.6%	
	VAN	A+	24	1	3	0	6	6	23^{2}	18	1	4.2	11.8	31	52.6%	.304	1.23	3.80	87	0.4				
	NH	AA	24	1	1	0	9	2	15^{1}	10	1	8.2	14.7	25	38.7%	.300	1.57	4.11	94	0.3				

A renowned prep arm, **Irv Carter**'s first pro reps were unkind to him. Though his size, velo and slider helped him excel as an amateur, he's learning that fastball command and a more fully realized changeup must now fuel his ascent. ⚾ Some unsightly ERAs betray the 31% strikeout rate **Connor Cooke** drummed up in the mid-minors as a starter-turned-closer. The athletic righty impressed out of college and has, ah, *cooked* opposing pro hitters with a four-pitch arsenal led by a running fastball and one of those newfangled sweepy sliders dealt from a low arm slot. ⚾ We can't yet crown **Hagen Danner** as the next Kenley Jansen, but the catcher-turned-fireballer dominated Dunedin hitters with his mid-90s heat in 2021. He spent most of 2022 injured, but enthusiasm for his ascent into Toronto's 'pen lingers. Anyone else suddenly craving ice cream? ⚾ Lefty **Brandon Eisert** has ascended the organizational ladder rapidly, leaving a trail of demolished MiLB hitters in his wake. His low arm slot creates deception and discomfort, masking his low-90s velo and helping his changeup and slider play up. He could serve as a high-leverage weapon out of the bullpen soon. ⚾ His size belies his stuff; at 6-foot-5, 225 pounds, **Bowden Francis** sits low-90s with three decent but underwhelming secondaries. The specs are interesting, but he must address a serious gopher ball issue—over the last two years in the high minors, he's served up nearly two homers per nine. ⚾ He took a circuitous, nearly decade-long journey to the bigs, but **Matt Gage** made it. An overdue transition to relief bought him a new lease on life, and his sweepy cutter could extend that lease long-term, mixed metaphors be damned. ⚾ Acquired by Toronto from the Royals, **Foster Griffin** transitioned to relief and struck out 10 hitters per nine with solid ground-ball tendencies in Buffalo. He leads with his cutter and finishes with a changeup that, at its best, echoes Julio Urías' *cambio*. ⚾ It would be nice if we could use a more flattering pun here—the image of a baby chick emerging from its shell, perhaps. But, after three seasons and 40+ innings of irredeemably bad spot starts, we can't say **Thomas Hatch** has done anything more than lay an egg. ⚾ What he lacks in stature (5-foot-8) and fastball command (12% walk rate the last two years), reliever prospect **Adrian Hernandez** makes up for in, well, a ton of changeups. He's a bit of a one-trick pony, but given his signature pitch's elite spin and devastating run, it's a hell of a trick. ⚾ **Hayden Juenger** hurls from a low slot that gives righties fits, as his fastball sits mid-90s and his slider buckles knees. Command remains elusive—ever moreso as he climbs the ladder—but his potential to garner big strikeout numbers and weak contact could make him a presence in the 'pen. ⚾ **Casey Lawrence** toiled in the minors for a decade before debuting, pitched a year in Japan, spent a year out of baseball completely and then, at 34, returned to the majors with the team that originally signed him. It's a feel-good story, but it'd feel even better had he survived Toronto's winter roster cuts. ⚾ It's awfully bold of **Julian Merryweather** to summon storm clouds wherever he goes despite his sunny surname. Between an endless barrage of injuries and poor performances, Merryweather's MLB career has been plagued by gloom. DRA thinks he could be a league-average arm, but what does it know of unrelenting rain? ⚾ **Joey Murray** is easy to underrate with his low-90s heat and good command from an atypical arm slot. He's also tough to evaluate—he was shut down in May after a ghastly final eight innings of work suggested that something was wrong. Surprise, surprise: Elbow surgery soon followed. ⚾ Only recently did **Kendry Rojas** transition from playing outfield to pitching. Invariably, scouts describe him as "raw." They also anticipate physical maturation that should bring into focus the upside his two pitches offer. ⚾ Like everyone else and their mothers, **Dahian Santos** now throws a sweeper that brings hitters to their knees. His mid-90s fastball belies his small frame and command is not his strong suit, but at just 20 he has an alluring ceiling, Toronto's faith and time on his side. ⚾ The Blue Jays left **Trent Thornton** off their playoff roster, and rightly so—his stuff failed to play up as a starter, and his transition to relief has failed, too. Turns out this rose has a ton of thorns. ⚾ After losing several years to Tommy John surgery and a torn ACL, Rule 5 draft-eligible **Yosver Zulueta** was fast-tracked through Toronto's system so they could see what he's made of. Turns out the answer is big velocity, a wipeout curve and command issues, which means he may be headed for relief work.

Lessons of the Walking Dead

by Rob Mains

The 2022 season was not a banner year for offense. Teams scored only 4.28 runs per game, the lowest output since 2015. They hit the fewest triples per game in MLB history and the second-fewest singles (both excluding 2020, as I'll do throughout this essay). The .243 batting average was fourth-worst, beating only the Deadball 1908 season (.239) and the Deadball II 1967 (.242) and 1968 (.237) seasons. Pitchers had a 3.96 ERA, the lowest since 2015 and only the fifth time since the leagues split into three divisions in 1994 that league-wide ERA fell below 4.00. The reason your fantasy team didn't do as well as you thought it would in WHIP, given the numbers, is that the MLB-wide average of 1.266 was the lowest since 1972, the year that resulted in the American League adopting the designated hitter.

Maybe this will prove to be a nadir. MLB hopes so, obviously. The ban on infield shifts is designed to bolster offense, and the pitch clock should as well. Maybe we'll look back on 2022 as an odd season, an outlier, when offenses were notably bad.

But what if they were even worse than they seemed?

There's a key difference between baseball in 2022 and baseball in the years noted above—1908, 1967, 1968 and 2015. Here's a hint. (Data aren't available for 1908.)

	Runs per Team per 9 Innings	
Season	First Nine Innings	Extra Innings
1967	3.7	3.0
1968	3.5	2.8
2015	4.3	4.0
2022	**4.1**	**10.1**

Here's a similar representation, in chart form, covering the last four full seasons.

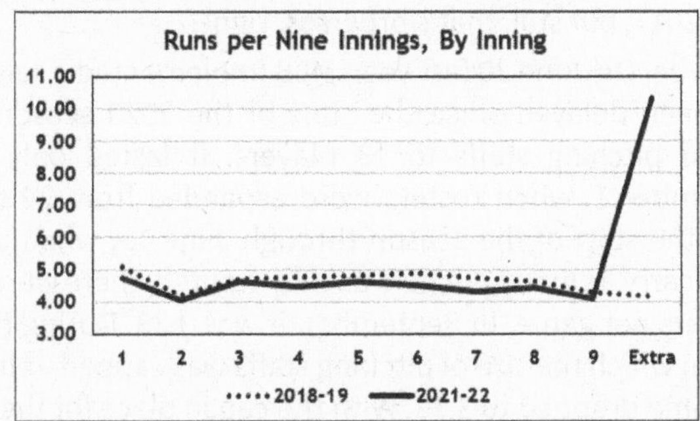

As you can see, prior to the pandemic, there were usually fewer runs scored in extra innings, on a rate basis, than in the first nine innings. That makes sense; teams are often playing for only one run in extra innings. If it's the home team, there's a limit to the number of runs that can be scored to win the game. From 1969-2019, teams scored about 0.9 runs per nine innings in extra innings for every 1.0 they scored in the first nine innings.

And that's how it went throughout baseball history until 2020. In order to shorten games and reduce players' exposure to COVID-19 (supposedly), MLB instituted a new rule that year: After the ninth inning, the player who batted last for a team in the prior inning would start the next inning on second base. The runner on second—there are several terms for it; I prefer, and will use, zombie runner, since they've returned from the dead—drastically changed the scoring profile of extra innings. Instead of 0.9 runs in extra innings for every 1.0 in one through nine, the ratio jumped to more than 2.0: 2.3 in 2021, 2.4 last year. There were 10.5 runs per nine innings in extra innings in 2021, and 10.1 in 2022.

There are many implications of this, of course, but the most profound is to make scoring appear better than it was. MLB teams scored 4.35 runs per nine innings in 2022: 4.28 in the first nine innings, 10.13 thereafter. The figures in 2021 were 4.65 runs per nine innings, with 4.57 in the first nine and 10.53 thereafter. (For 2021, with its seven-inning doubleheaders, I'm counting the first seven innings of twin bills as the first nine, anything after, with zombie runners, as extra innings.) Back in the pre-zombie 2019, the figures were 4.86 runs per nine overall, with 4.88 in frames 1–9 and 4.26 in 10+.

Here's how things looked graphically in the 30-team era.

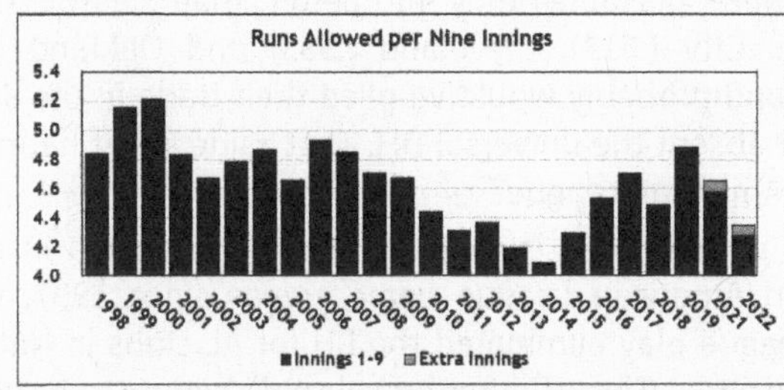

Before the pandemic, extra innings accounted for about 1.9% of innings pitched and 1.7% of runs scored. Since the implementation of the zombie runner, they've accounted for only 1.3% of innings but nearly 3% of runs. The reason you don't see those gray rectangles atop the black bars until 2021 is that the zombie runners have changed the scoring pattern of MLB games. Extra innings now constitute a significant proportion of runs scored. That 4.35 runs scored per nine innings in 2022 was the fifth-lowest of the 30-team era. But in the first nine innings—when the game was played the way it was every season through 2019—4.28 runs per nine innings was third-lowest since 1998, after only 2013 (4.18) and 2014 (4.08). For that matter, 2022's 4.28 figure was the ninth-lowest since the 1977 expansion.

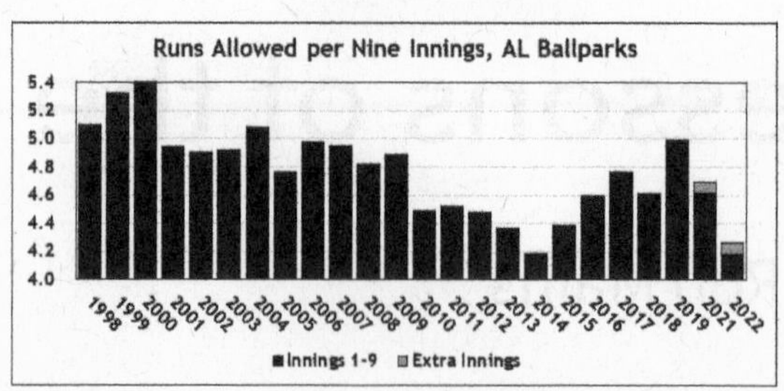

Offense was down a lot in 2022, even more than it appeared, if you exclude the scoring-enhancing contest that's played in games tied after nine innings. But, of course, there was another factor affecting scoring in 2022 (and beyond): The universal designated hitter. In 2021, National League pitchers hit .110/.149/.140. They struck out in 44% of their plate appearances. They were historically awful, and their awfulness was mitigated only slightly by accounting for just 4.9% of plate appearances. That low proportion is due to their batting order position and the frequency of pinch-hitters, not that they were all that great either (.210/.301/.351). All told, the ninth batter in National League lineups hit .166/.229/.256 in 2021.

In 2022, with pitchers no longer batting, National League designated hitters batted .238/.316/.402. That was above average—the league hit .243/.314/.398—and a far cry from the production pitchers and pinch-hitters provided in 2021. So, to isolate the zombie runner impact, we need to look at the American League, where there was not a significant offense-boosting rule change in 2022.

This isn't an apples-to-apples comparison. With the universal DH a permanent change, rather than a short-season one-off as it was in 2020, teams could make long-term plans. There was a brain drain, as it were, of DH types from the American League to the National. The three players with the most plate appearances at DH in the National League last year were Nelson Cruz (signed as a free agent last March 17), Daniel Vogelbach (signed as a free agent March 15) and Luke Voit (traded from the American League on March 18). Granted, Cruz (.648 OPS) and Voit (.652) weren't good. But they were playable—they hit better than Seattle (.615), Kansas City (.613), Cleveland (.585) and Oakland (.559) DHs—and probably would've plied their trade in the Junior Circuit absent the universal DH. That aside, what happened in the American League?

The wrinkle here is that the DH rule has been in effect only in American League *home games* since 1997, when interleague play eliminated the DH for AL clubs in National League parks. These figures include only home games played by American League teams in the 30-team era.

You can see what the issue is here. Overall, American League teams scored 4.22 runs per game in 2022, the second-lowest in the 30-team era, barely ahead of 2014's 4.18. Looking only at games in which the DH was in effect, there were 4.26 runs per nine innings, again barely ahead of the 2014's 4.18 nadir. But if you take out the helium provided by zombie runners, the difference becomes negligible. There were 4.182 runs scored per nine innings in the first nine innings of AL home games in 2014. There were 4.185 in 2022.

And that's not all. In 2014, in AL games with the DH rule in effect, nine position players pitched 8⅓ innings in the first nine innings of games, allowing eight runs. In AL home games in 2022, 57 position players pitched 57⅓ innings in the first nine innings of games and allowed 57 runs. Take away position player pitching, and there were 4.17 runs per nine innings in the first nine of games played in American League parks in 2022, compared to 4.18 in 2014. Stripping out the distortions of the universal DH, zombie runners and position player pitching yields what was the lowest-scoring year in the 30-team era. And it goes back *way* further than that. Excluding the 1981 strike year, *in American League ballparks, scoring in the first nine innings of games in 2022 was the lowest since 1976*, Dusty Baker's age-27 season, nearly half a century ago.

One of the rationales for the zombie runner is that shortening games limits the endless parade of relief pitchers. In 2018, the typical team needed a starting pitcher and 3.36 relievers to complete a ballgame. In 2019, the number of relievers rose to 3.41. In 2021, though, aided by both the zombie runner that shortened extra-inning games and the seven-inning doubleheader rule, relievers per game...wait, they didn't decline, they rose *again*, a little, to 3.44 per team. But last year, they fell to 3.30, the lowest level since...well, since 2017, but still, that's progress, right?

Maybe. On June 20 last year, MLB implemented a rule that had been delayed since the start of the 2020 season that limited pitching staffs to 13 players. It lasted only until September 1, when rosters were expanded from 26 to 28. From the start of the season through June 19, when teams could carry as many pitchers as they wanted, there were 3.38 relievers per game. In September, it was 3.33. During the 73 days in which the size of pitching staffs was capped, relievers per game dropped to 3.19. With the cap in place for the 2023 season, we can expect a figure lower than 2021's. Given that starting pitchers in 2021 were still shaking off rust from a

60-game season, increasing the need for relievers, it seems credible that the zombie runner has decreased reliever usage. A little.

⚾ ⚾ ⚾

The zombie runner is here to stay. Players like it, for the same reason you like working an eight-hour day better than a ten-hour day. Owners like it, because as games go into extra innings, fans leave the ballpark and stop buying concessions—beer sales ended in the seventh!—while hourly employees remain on the clock and you've got to pay to keep the lights on.

Managers and pitching coaches, though, like the zombie runner for strategic reasons. Shorter extra-inning games mean less wear and tear on the bullpen. Pitchers threw 880⅓ extra innings in 2018, and 891 in 2019; that count dropped to 528 in 2022. With a better-rested bullpen, the thinking goes, teams will be better-positioned for the next few games. Playing a 15-inning game on Thursday could put a team at a competitive disadvantage for its upcoming weekend series. The zombie runner could ameliorate this effect.

To check this, I looked at how teams did in the four days (not games, but days) following extra-inning games in 2018 and 2019 compared to how they did in 2021 and 2022. (For 2021, I considered only games that went into the 10th inning or longer; an eight- or nine-inning doubleheader game doesn't count as extra innings in this case). I excluded games against the same opponent during the extra-innings game, since each team has the same handicap and the two teams' won-lost records will be exactly .500. Here's how they did.

Games After Extra Innings	2018-19 W-L	Pct.	2021-22 W-L	Pct.	Difference
1	68-82	.453	83-94	.469	+.012
2	195-222	.468	214-224	.489	+.016
3	325-314	.509	350-348	.501	-.005
4	324-347	.483	362-343	.513	+.036

Overall, teams playing an extra-inning game had a .486 winning percentage against different opponents in the following four days in 2018-19. That rose to .498 in 2021-22. This seems to suggest that teams shrugged off extra-inning games more successfully under zombie runner rules. The differences aren't large—a club would have to play nearly 50 extra-inning games to pick up an extra win two days after the game—but they're consistent.

But this analysis doesn't consider opponent strength. To correct for this, I used the Log5 formula to calculate the expected winning percentage for teams following an extra-innings game, using the two teams' seasonal won-lost records. For example, on July 14, 2019, the Dodgers beat the Red Sox, 7-4, in 12 innings. The next four days, they played the Phillies. Based on their respective records, the Dodgers had an expected winning percentage of .654 per game. Instead, they split the four games. Here's how expected wins compared to actual wins in the last two pre-zombie seasons.

Games After Extra Innings	Expected W-L	Pct.	Actual W-L	Pct.	2018-19 Difference
1	74.4-75.6	.496	68-82	.453	-.043
2	207.7-209.3	.498	195-222	.468	-.030
3	321.8-317.2	.504	325-314	.509	+.005
4	338.5-332.5	.504	324-347	.483	-.022

Based on their opponents, teams playing extra-inning games in 2018 and 2019 could be expected to win 942 of the 1,877 games they played the following four days, a .502 winning percentage. Instead, they won 912, a .486 clip. That's a 16-point decline.

And in zombie world? Here's 2021 and 2022.

Games After Extra Innings	Expected W-L	Pct.	Actual W-L	Pct.	2021-22 Difference
1	88.5-88.5	.500	83-94	.469	-.031
2	220.1-217.9	.502	214-224	.489	-.014
3	349.8-348.2	.501	350-348	.501	+.000
4	352.2-352.8	.500	362-343	.513	+.014

Teams playing extra-inning games with zombie runners still did worse than expected one and two days after the extra-innings game. But the gaps were much diminished compared to the last two pre-zombie years. And they vanish after that.

⚾ ⚾ ⚾

There are, it seems to me, three conclusions here.

First, the zombie runner seems to have delivered on two desired outcomes: fewer relief pitchers per game, and better results for teams following extra-inning games. When your game plan is to use a starter for five innings followed by a procession of one-inning relievers, going beyond the ninth can strain an eight-man bullpen. The zombie runner alleviates that.

Second, the zombie runner, with an assist from position players pitching, papered over a steep decline in offense in 2022. Without those two factors, runs scored in American League home games (removing the effect of the addition of the DH in the National League) were at their lowest level in 46 years.

Finally, aesthetically—ignoring the specific interests of owners, managers and players—fans are split on the zombie runner. Some fans like it. Some (including, I'd wager, most people reading this) don't. But it's here to stay. People attending games lasting more than nine innings will continue to see two separate sports: One, lasting nine innings, in which teams score four to five runs, on average, and another one, after the ninth, in which the rate jumps to over a run per inning.

Thanks for Tom Gieryn for retrieving data for games in AL parks. All other data from Baseball-Reference and Stathead Baseball.

—Rob Mains is an author of Baseball Prospectus.

CHICAGO CUBS

Essay by Noah Frank

Player comments by Justin Klugh and BP staff

One of the more memorable moments of the 2022 Chicago Cubs' season had nothing to do with any of the 74 wins they cobbled together across an unremarkable campaign that did not see them post a winning month until September. It was four minutes and seven seconds of incredible drone video, seamlessly stitched together, opening like Luke Skywalker's Death Star trench run, teetering high above an inbound red line train, swooping and diving down toward the northwest corner of Wrigley Field.

The camera carries us through the Waveland Ave. entrance to Murphy's Bleachers, the beloved pre- and postgame haunt, splitting a crowd of patrons, hurling us out the Sheffield door toward the Harry Caray statue, like one too many Old Styles after a 1:20 p.m. first pitch. From there, though, a theme begins to insist itself upon the untrained eye: the footage stitches the gaudy Gallagher Way offices and plaza that were once parking lots with the timeless marquee; it cuts from Pat Hughes' introduction and Harry-Grossman-invoking-Caray's "let there be light!" proclamation from 8/8/88 straight into the 10-foot cursive, neon-red Budweiser logo atop the monstrous scoreboard in right field; a truly stunning flight *through* the iconic center field scoreboard, dropping along the resplendent, ivy-covered walls, while also scanning every sponsor logo that now interrupts that once-pristine landscape.

It ducks into the front offices to show you the 2016 World Series banner, of course, along with an employee polishing the trophy. It peeks into the clubhouse itself, the spacious, modern ring of blue light and mahogany a far cry from the cramped, outdated quarters formerly tucked under the lower deck down the third base line. It zips down the tunnel over Ian Happ's shoulder, past the batting cage, up the dugout steps and onto the field behind Seiya Suzuki, into a suddenly full ballpark on—as Jon Sciambi has told us from a television monitor somewhere along the journey—the last day of the season. It is an incredible piece of filmmaking. It is nearly as incredible a piece of propaganda.

If I were to ask you, a presumably discerning baseball fan, who the legacy teams of Major League Baseball are, I'd wager that the Cubs would make the cut. Along with the Yankees, Red Sox and Dodgers, few teams have as much of a stake to generational fandom, or are woven within their city's fabric

CHICAGO CUBS PROSPECTUS

2022 W-L: 74-88, 3RD IN NL CENTRAL

Pythag	.451	*22nd*	DER	.702	*15th*
RS/G	4.06	*22nd*	DRC+	95	*21st*
RA/G	4.51	*21st*	DRA-	100	*17th*
dWin%	.486	*19th*	FIP	4.33	*25th*
Payroll	$143M	*14th*	B-Age	28.4	*15th*
M$/MW	$4.8M	*21st*	P-Age	29.7	*15th*

400′
368′
368′
355′
353′

- Opened 1914
- Open air
- Natural surface
- Fence profile: 11′6″ to 15′

Park Factors

Runs	Runs/RH	Runs/LH	HR/RH	HR/LH
105	104	106	110	112

Top Hitter WARP	3.2 Ian Happ
Top Pitcher WARP	2.1 Marcus Stroman
2023 Top Prospect	Pete Crow-Armstrong

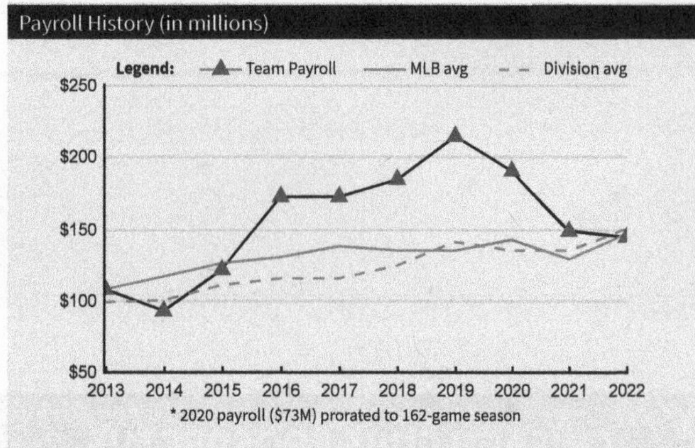

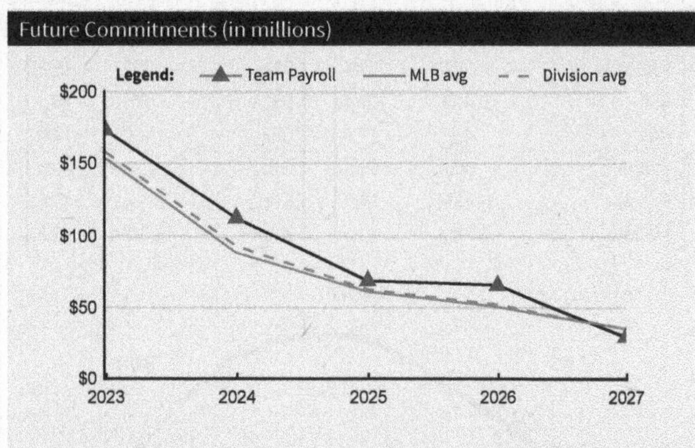

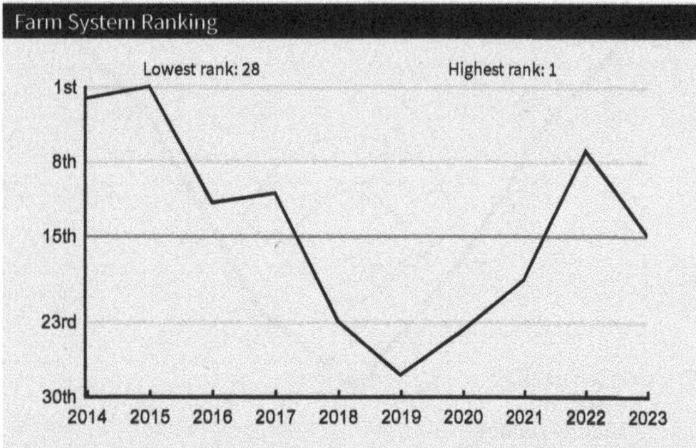

Personnel

President, Baseball Operations
Jed Hoyer

General Manager
Carter Hawkins

Assistant General Manager
Ehsan Bokhari

Assistant General Manager
Jeff Greenberg

Vice President, Player Development
Jared Banner

Vice President, Baseball Operations
Greg Davey

Vice President, Research & Development
Chris Moore

Manager
David Ross

BP Alumni
Bryan Cole
Jeremy Greenhouse

so intractably. Maybe the Giants make your short list as well, perhaps the Cardinals. If you're arguing for any other team, ask yourself this: If someone opened a [team]-themed bar in any American city in which that club didn't play 81 home games annually, would anyone actually patronize it?

The Cubs are so entrenched, it's almost impossible not to think of them being a legacy team forever. And yet, even as they quenched professional sports' most infamous title drought, and even as they "saved" Wrigley Field with some long-overdue renovations, it's starting to feel like they may be losing their grip on that status.

Once the most-ubiquitous team on television, thanks to WGN, the Cubs' move to Marquee Sports Network has eroded no small measure of their presence. Of the 19 teams *Forbes* reported as ranking in the top three primetime broadcasts in their respective markets, the Cubs were not one. And lest you think that day-game-heavy scheduling is to blame, Marquee Sports was down 25% in viewership last year and 56% since it launched. Even if the Cubs develop an over-the-top service for the diehards, a way to watch (most) games without buying into a larger cable or streaming package, the fact is that you can no longer simply turn on your television and watch the Cubs anywhere in America on a summer afternoon without a hefty subscription fee of one kind or another.

The franchise proved, possibly more than any other team in professional sports, that televising games for the masses would not—as popular wisdom once declared—depress attendance, but rather incentivize more people to get out to the ballpark, building a local and national fanbase worthy of envy. The Cubs' current situation is testing the inverse theory—that by making the team increasingly harder to watch, you might erode that foundation.

⚾ ⚾ ⚾

I don't remember the first time I noticed it, but I distinctly remember the feeling of standing in the lower bowl and looking up, away from the emerald grass and vine-obscured brick and seeing the nets, clinging to the underside of the upper deck, nailed in place to collect the crumbling concrete before it dropped on the heads of unsuspecting fans below. This was early in the 2008 season, when I was a media relations intern on the North Side—back when the PR offices were housed in the old, abandoned donut shop just to the west of the marquee, whose roof leaked dramatically when it stormed, raining a waterfall on anyone who dared to cross its threshold.

But while the ballpark itself was falling into disrepair, the state of the franchise had never been more solid. The Cubs cleared 3.3 million fans that season, a cool 40,743 per game, in the hundredth year since their last title. The campaign commenced with an Ernie Banks statue dedication on Opening Day and finished with 98 chants of "Go Cubs Go" before a sweep at the hands of the Dodgers in the Division Series. But it was really something, to see the ballpark very nearly full every single day and night for 81 openings.

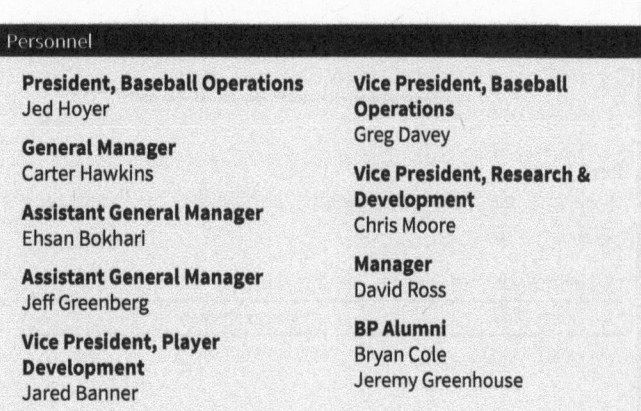

A mark I like to look at for the health of a franchise's support is the single lowest paid attendance number for a home game in any given season. Ticket sales back in 2008 were so robust that the lowest paid attendance could pretty well be explained by the sheer number of comp tickets that had been given away instead of sold (that number, by the way, was 37,812 on April 4 vs. Houston). But when you're not enjoying that kind of day-in, day-out support, the lowest attendance mark of the season more accurately reflects a different kind of number—the actual season ticket base. Your lowest draw is, in essence, a zero-walk-up day, usually an early- or late-season weekday affair, when the kids are in school and the weather more temperamental.

Such inconveniences did not sway a Wrigley crowd back then. But a lot has changed—for better and worse—in the intervening years.

The Cubs drew 32,306 fans per game in 2022, fifth-best in the National League and a mark many clubs would kill for. It was also their lowest seasonal attendance (not counting the COVID-19 years) of the century; to find a lower head count necessitates going all the way back to 1998. Back then, the capacity of the ballpark was just 38,884, a number the club has continuously squeezed upward in the intervening years to 41,649 today. So, while the Cubs have made the playoffs nearly as many times in the last 20 years as they had in the 85 years between 2003 and their last title in 1908, and while the park keeps adding new bells and whistles and expanding its seating capacity, fewer people are showing up to see any of it.

The drone video is framed around the team's final home game of the campaign, but I'd like to draw your attention to the game three days prior. On Thursday, September 29, the Cubs polished off a three-game sweep of the eventual National League Champion Phillies with a 2-0 shutout in front of just 23,425 paid fans.

That number—the 23,425, versus 37,812, 14 years earlier—is the crack in the facade that you only see if you're looking. Perhaps you've noticed it via the ticket-selling emails that never would have hit your inbox just a few years ago, when there was no need to ask. It's certainly a big reason why the club has dropped season ticket prices for 2023 by 5.1%, the largest such drop in a generation.

To be a legacy team, and expect such a team's day-in, day-out fan response, you need to at least try to compete. Great seasons require the unexpected career years of a Mike Fontenot or the temporarily reanimated corpse of a Jim Edmonds. But they don't happen without the quiet, daily consistency of an Aramis Ramirez or Derrek Lee. It wouldn't take a vision quest to see Dansby Swanson potentially filling such a role; one has to squint one's third eye a lot harder to envision Eric Hosmer or Cody Bellinger doing so. Big rotation signing Jameson Taillon has been an exactly league-average pitcher the last two seasons, which means he's been worse over that time than two returning rotation members, Marcus Stroman and Justin Steele. Drew Smyly, returning on a two-year deal, was worse than everyone slated for the rotation plus first man out Adrian Sampson—except for Kyle Hendricks.

More than simple wins and losses, a legacy team needs to provide some greater value for its product—beyond the simple existence of the baseball game itself. Attending a game at Wrigley used to feel like stepping into a living museum, the environment as much a part of the experience as the contest on the field. Now?

That massive, gaudy screen in right field is representative of how, in becoming like everywhere else, Wrigley Field has lost a bit of itself. The scoreboard doesn't add much to the fan experience, especially not at a place like Wrigley. Instead of the views of the neighboring houses and the rooftops across the street, fans are now subjected to even more advertising, both digital and analog, whatever feeds through the LEDs plus that omnipresent, red Budweiser script. It cheapens the experience of what it means to be at Wrigley, all while lining the owners' pockets. And yet, the cost of attendance rises.

While some parks look more like garish megachurches on the sides of the interstate, there are still a few precious, honest-to-goodness cathedrals of the game left. The more generic the environment becomes, the less special the Wrigley experience; the less people have, understandably, been willing to pay. Considering that the average 2022 Cubs game cost fans a staggering $364.83, per *Team Marketing Report*'s Fan Cost Index, second only to a Red Sox game, the aforementioned attendance dip is less surprising.

There have been good outcomes overlooked in all this progress. The Cubs did not abandon their legendary home and flee for the suburbs, like their Atlantan brethren (though the fact that ownership was even willing to even entertain the idea is not the most encouraging sign). The new front offices are airy and spacious. The donut shop, and the trailers that replaced it, are long gone. And plenty of institutional memory remains in the building. Multiple members of my intern class are still working in the front offices, which have expanded greatly in headcount from back then, when they were the smallest in the majors.

It's also not like the Cubs have suddenly changed their stance, and were in any way anathema to the idea of corporate sponsorship in days past. The idea that the Wrigley name itself is separated from the titans of industry is, of course, a falsehood, even if it's one I didn't realize until stumbling upon a replica of the ballpark comprised entirely of various Wrigley gum wrappers at the ESPN Zone in River North as a high schooler. But, to quote singer-songwriter Joe Pug, who launched his music career upon moving to Logan Square in the mid-aughts, "The more I buy, the more I'm bought. And the more I'm bought, the less I cost."

There's a more important flag than the World Series banner that shows up in that drone video. In fact, it shows up no fewer than three times: on the wall at Murphy's, draped over the back of a cyclist whipping down Waveland and in the middle of a Chicago crest painted along an exterior clubhouse wall. It's the W, which we don't even see flown in its official station, atop the flagpole overhanging the center field bleachers.

The official W flag takes the shape of Chicago's variety of breezes, high atop its perch, visible from the red line trains as they approach the south end of the S-turn between the Addison or Sheridan stops. In an age of omnipresent smartphones, the drama and suspense of whether the hometown nine have won or lost may be spoiled, but there is a shared piece of generational fandom in that W—or, just as crucially, in the countervailing L—that flies after each game. That the Cubs willingly "fly the L" tells you a lot about the reverence with which each and every game at Wrigley Field is held, no matter the outcome.

The Cubs did not earn their place as a legacy team by winning championships—this much should be self-evident. That they've become *less* popular just a few years after finally breaking their historic title drought should only reinforce this. Sure, the fanbase wants a competitive product. And it shouldn't be discounted that the Cubs used to be the kind of franchise that would never let a player like Willson Contreras walk, especially not to that boring city 300 miles southwest down I-55.

More than that, the Cubs are only the Cubs because of their preeminent presence on American television screens and because Wrigley Field has, for generations, provided a slice of baseball and America that no other place can quite replicate. Just as it takes generations to build fandom, so it does to build the traditions that make such a place. And just as that fandom can diffuse far more quickly than it was constructed, so can the ties that bind people to a place and make it worth coming to on any given day throughout a baseball season.

The Cubs haven't lost all that magic just yet. But they'd be well-served to consider what makes their home special to begin with and their fandom so widespread, and to preserve that at all costs. Even if it means keeping some things just because people like them, not because they look good on this fiscal year's balance sheet. ■

—Noah Frank is an author of Baseball Prospectus and the Pretty Good newsletter.

HITTERS

Kevin Alcántara OF

Born: 07/12/02 Age: 20 Bats: R Throws: R Height: 6'6" Weight: 188 lb. Origin: International Free Agent, 2018

YEAR	TEAM	LVL	AGE	PA	R	2B	3B	HR	RBI	BB	K	SB	CS	Whiff%	AVG/OBP/SLG	DRC+	BABIP	BRR	DRP	WARP
2021	CUB	ROK	18	107	27	3	5	4	21	13	28	3	0		.337/.415/.609		.443			
2021	YNK	ROK	18	31	5	1	0	1	3	4	8	2	0		.370/.452/.519		.500			
2022	MB	A	19	495	76	19	6	15	85	55	123	14	3		.273/.360/.451	108	.345	2.9	CF(69): 5.7, RF(23): 0.5	2.5
2023 non-DC	*CHC*	*MLB*	*20*	*251*	*21*	*9*	*2*	*4*	*22*	*17*	*80*	*4*	*1*	*36.6%*	*.217/.278/.336*	*67*	*.315*	*2.7*	*CF 0, RF 0*	*-0.1*

Comparables: Johan Mieses (88), Andrew McCutchen (86), Manuel Margot (85)

Alcántara needed nine games of rookie ball for the Cubs to realize he was ready to be somewhere else. He's at least six-and-a-half feet off the ground at all times. His swing is balanced. He hits to all fields. He can read pitch movement. He can run. He can play center field. Maybe he needs to shorten his swing, but that's likely because his wingspan is six-and-a-half feet. He makes you think twice about rounding first. He doesn't strike out much. It won't be that hard for him to get even better. And the day he was born, *Men In Black II* was leading the box office.

Sergio Alcántara IF

Born: 07/10/96 Age: 26 Bats: S Throws: R Height: 5'9" Weight: 151 lb. Origin: International Free Agent, 2012

YEAR	TEAM	LVL	AGE	PA	R	2B	3B	HR	RBI	BB	K	SB	CS	Whiff%	AVG/OBP/SLG	DRC+	BABIP	BRR	DRP	WARP
2020	LIC	WIN	23	82	9	2	1	2	8	8	21	2	0		.257/.346/.400		.333			
2020	DET	MLB	23	23	2	0	1	1	1	2	4	0	0	10.7%	.143/.217/.381	100	.125	0.0	2B(6): 0.1, 3B(6): -0.6	0.0
2021	LIC	WIN	24	86	13	4	1	1	6	16	12	0	1		.290/.419/.420		.333			
2021	IOW	AAA	24	103	19	3	0	3	9	21	23	3	0		.305/.447/.451	125	.393	1.4	SS(23): -2.0, 2B(2): -0.1	0.6
2021	CHC	MLB	24	255	30	6	3	5	17	30	74	3	0	30.1%	.205/.303/.327	80	.280	-0.2	SS(55): -0.5, 2B(22): 1.3, 3B(3): 0	0.3
2022	SD	MLB	25	38	3	0	0	0	3	2	12	0	2	26.7%	.114/.158/.114	75	.167	-0.5	SS(8): -0.1, 2B(7): -0.1, 3B(6): 0.2	-0.1
2022	AZ	MLB	25	186	23	8	1	6	26	10	45	1	0	23.4%	.241/.283/.406	91	.287	1.3	3B(35): -1.2, SS(20): 0, 2B(18): -0.3	0.3
2023 non-DC	*CHC*	*MLB*	*26*	*251*	*21*	*8*	*1*	*3*	*21*	*21*	*60*	*2*	*1*	*24.9%*	*.220/.292/.312*	*68*	*.286*	*0.5*	*SS 1, 3B 0*	*-0.2*

Comparables: Cristhian Adames (58), Robert Andino (55), Kaleb Cowart (53)

Playing defense all around the infield will help you keep a job. Barely cracking an OPS above .600, as Alcántara has, will ensure you're doing that job for three teams in three seasons. What do you have left when the defense takes a step back like it did last year, though? Defensive metrics can be specious at times, but the public-facing ones all agree that the 26-year-old got worse with the leather. A DRC+ in the high-90s had been Alcántara's evergreen ticket to another big-league destination, but if that's gone he might have to get used to riding the minor-league bus.

Moises Ballesteros C/DH

Born: 11/08/03 Age: 19 Bats: L Throws: R Height: 5'10" Weight: 195 lb. Origin: International Free Agent, 2021

YEAR	TEAM	LVL	AGE	PA	R	2B	3B	HR	RBI	BB	K	SB	CS	Whiff%	AVG/OBP/SLG	DRC+	BABIP	BRR	DRP	WARP
2021	DSL CUBR	ROK	17	187	22	10	0	3	25	31	24	6	1		.266/.396/.390		.299			
2022	CUB	ROK	18	110	12	5	0	7	18	13	19	0	0		.268/.355/.536		.268			
2022	MB	A	18	129	17	7	0	3	15	18	28	0	1		.248/.349/.394	104	.300	-1.5	C(18): 0.4	0.3
2023 non-DC	*CHC*	*MLB*	*19*	*251*	*19*	*10*	*1*	*3*	*20*	*18*	*79*	*2*	*1*	*35.1%*	*.204/.267/.303*	*56*	*.295*	*0.6*	*C 0, 1B 0*	*-0.5*

Comparables: Francisco Peña (69), Lana Akau (66), Ramón Flores (65)

YEAR	TEAM	P. COUNT	FRM RUNS	BLK RUNS	THRW RUNS	TOT RUNS
2022	CUB	1596				
2022	MB	2967	-1.3	-0.1	1.1	-0.2
2023	*CHC*	*6956*	*-3.5*	*-0.2*	*-0.3*	*-4.0*

Ballesteros arrived at Low-A Myrtle Beach and immediately homered off the batter's eye. That's the bat he's brought with him everywhere since the Venezuelan youth leagues; it's good enough that his defense can lag behind. With a velvety left-handed cut, he's capable of taking control of the strike zone, though he needs to keep putting the ball in the air to take advantage of the over-the-fence power. His quick arm is held back by a slow body, though plenty of would-be basestealers regretted their decision with Ballesteros behind the plate. This will be a season of growth for the 19-year-old, one that could well see him taking on the upper minors if his rapid progression continues.

Tucker Barnhart C

Born: 01/07/91 Age: 32 Bats: S Throws: R Height: 5'11" Weight: 192 lb. Origin: Round 10, 2009 Draft (#299 overall)

YEAR	TEAM	LVL	AGE	PA	R	2B	3B	HR	RBI	BB	K	SB	CS	Whiff%	AVG/OBP/SLG	DRC+	BABIP	BRR	DRP	WARP
2020	CIN	MLB	29	110	10	3	0	5	13	12	28	0	0	24.6%	.204/.291/.388	94	.231	0.2	C(36): 4.5, 1B(2): 0	0.8
2021	CIN	MLB	30	388	41	21	0	7	48	29	100	0	0	26.2%	.247/.317/.368	78	.324	-2.1	C(102): 7.8, 1B(2): 0	1.1
2022	DET	MLB	31	308	16	10	0	1	16	25	74	0	0	22.6%	.221/.287/.267	74	.296	-0.3	C(92): -4.9	-0.4
2023 DC	*CHC*	*MLB*	*32*	*248*	*23*	*10*	*0*	*4*	*21*	*21*	*53*	*0*	*0*	*23.3%*	*.229/.303/.339*	*77*	*.285*	*-0.8*	*C 1*	*0.2*

Comparables: Bruce Benedict (72), Rick Cerone (70), Francisco Cervelli (65)

YEAR	TEAM	P. COUNT	FRM RUNS	BLK RUNS	THRW RUNS	TOT RUNS
2020	CIN	4801	4.1	0.2	0.0	4.2
2021	CIN	14571	5.3	0.5	0.7	6.5
2022	DET	12823	-5.6	0.5	0.1	-5.0
2023	*CHC*	*9620*	*0.0*	*0.4*	*0.1*	*0.5*

It takes a true team effort to orchestrate an offense as moribund as the 2022 Tigers, especially against right-handed pitching. Detroit's .608 OPS against righties was the lowest team performance since 1972; at 27% below average, it was arguably the worst showing against righties (by sOPS+) of all time. Five of the six teams who performed worse have incomplete data, and the sixth was the 2020 Pirates in a partial season. Nevertheless, Barnhart's .216/.282/.271 line over 238 trips to the plate was a major contributing factor to that futility. The Tigers heavily emphasized getting him into the lineup to gain the platoon advantage, but he found his new home far less conducive to power and threatened only worms with the majority of his batted balls. Still, Detroit didn't trade for Barnhart's bat. It's unfortunate, then, that he also left his glove in Cincinnati. The Cubs will hope for a rebound.

Cody Bellinger CF

Born: 07/13/95 Age: 27 Bats: L Throws: L Height: 6'4" Weight: 203 lb. Origin: Round 4, 2013 Draft (#124 overall)

YEAR	TEAM	LVL	AGE	PA	R	2B	3B	HR	RBI	BB	K	SB	CS	Whiff%	AVG/OBP/SLG	DRC+	BABIP	BRR	DRP	WARP
2020	LAD	MLB	24	243	33	10	0	12	30	30	42	6	1	23.3%	.239/.333/.455	111	.245	0.2	CF(39): 0.8, 1B(19): 0	1.1
2021	LAD	MLB	25	350	39	9	2	10	36	31	94	3	1	29.7%	.165/.240/.302	67	.196	3.6	CF(87): 0, RF(7): 0.2, 1B(4): -0.3	0.3
2022	LAD	MLB	26	550	70	27	3	19	68	38	150	14	3	27.2%	.210/.265/.389	80	.255	2.4	CF(144): 6.7	1.7
2023 DC	*CHC*	*MLB*	*27*	*510*	*58*	*21*	*3*	*24*	*63*	*43*	*114*	*16*	*3*	*27.0%*	*.231/.303/.446*	*99*	*.260*	*7.6*	*CF 7*	*2.9*

Comparables: Mickey Mantle (56), Rick Monday (55), Rowland Office (55)

In 1906, Grantland Rice published "Casey's Revenge," a sequel to Ernest Lawrence Thayer's classic 1888 poem, "Casey at the Bat." The formerly mighty protagonist, having devolved into a shell of himself, was now nicknamed "Strike-Out Casey." The parallel to Bellinger, 117 years later, needs little explanation—nor does the Dodgers' decision to non-tender him. Even in his present, diminished state, Bellinger offers enough value that the Cubs offered him a one-year, $17.5 million contract. He's a highly capable defender in the outfield (and at first base) who wasn't completely terrible against right-handed pitching last year, smashing 17 homers in 390 plate appearances. Most likely, he'll be Chicago's Jason Heyward 2.0, but there's still the latent talent of an MVP deep within him. As Rice wrote, "Fate, though fickle, often gives another chance to men."

David Bote IF

Born: 04/07/93 Age: 30 Bats: R Throws: R Height: 6'1" Weight: 205 lb. Origin: Round 18, 2012 Draft (#554 overall)

YEAR	TEAM	LVL	AGE	PA	R	2B	3B	HR	RBI	BB	K	SB	CS	Whiff%	AVG/OBP/SLG	DRC+	BABIP	BRR	DRP	WARP
2020	CHC	MLB	27	145	15	3	1	7	29	17	40	2	0	27.8%	.200/.303/.408	101	.228	0.3	3B(33): -0.4, 2B(7): 0, 1B(1): 0	0.4
2021	CHC	MLB	28	327	32	10	2	8	35	27	73	0	1	25.0%	.199/.276/.330	84	.235	-1.8	2B(61): 1.4, 3B(24): 0	0.5
2022	IOW	AAA	29	160	14	8	1	3	22	10	39	5	1		.252/.319/.385	90	.320	2.2	2B(16): 1.0, 3B(14): -0.3, SS(3): 0.2	0.6
2022	CHC	MLB	29	127	15	8	0	4	12	6	45	1	0	33.5%	.259/.315/.431	77	.382	0.4	2B(18): 0.7, 3B(16): -0.1, 1B(6): 0	0.1
2023 DC	*CHC*	*MLB*	*30*	*59*	*6*	*2*	*0*	*1*	*5*	*4*	*16*	*0*	*1*	*30.5%*	*.225/.298/.387*	*86*	*.286*	*0.4*	*2B 0, 3B 0*	*0.1*

Comparables: Ryan Flaherty (46), Jayson Nix (46), José Bautista (45)

Bote signed a five-year deal in 2018. Here we are, on the cusp of year four, and he's running out of time to become Ben Zobrist. As Bote has tried to rediscover his ability to hit the ball hard, he's also suffered injuries—just to throw some more obstacles in his path. He started off last season on the 60-day IL, recovering from a shoulder surgery that split his season into a pair of misshapen chunks: between June 24 and August 4, he struck out in 42.4% of plate appearances; September 3 through October 5, he produced the team's second-best OPS (.793), behind only Seiya Suzuki.

★ ★ ★ *2023 Top 101 Prospect* **#80** ★ ★ ★

Owen Caissie OF Born: 07/08/02 Age: 20 Bats: L Throws: R Height: 6'4" Weight: 190 lb. Origin: Round 2, 2020 Draft (#45 overall)

YEAR	TEAM	LVL	AGE	PA	R	2B	3B	HR	RBI	BB	K	SB	CS	Whiff%	AVG/OBP/SLG	DRC+	BABIP	BRR	DRP	WARP
2021	CUB	ROK	18	136	20	7	1	6	20	26	39	1	2		.349/.478/.596		.500			
2021	MB	A	18	90	15	4	0	1	9	16	28	0	0		.233/.367/.329	92	.356	-0.4	LF(14): 0.7	0.2
2022	SB	A+	19	433	57	21	1	11	58	50	124	11	6		.254/.349/.402	94	.350	3.8	RF(77): 1.6, LF(22): -0.2	1.6
2023 non-DC	*CHC*	*MLB*	*20*	*251*	*20*	*10*	*1*	*3*	*21*	*21*	*80*	*2*	*2*	*32.5%*	*.204/.277/.306*	*61*	*.299*	*-0.2*	*LF 0, RF 0*	*-0.8*

Comparables: Dylan Carlson (61), Eric Jenkins (55), Jay Austin (50)

The Cubs' rebuild is at the stage where there's a bunch of teenagers running around still largely identified by the big names they were traded for. In Caissie's case, it's Yu Darvish. That's not to say that Caissie, who turned 20 last July, is going to be (or even has to be) as impactful a player as the Padres' Game 1 starter in the NLCS. That said, Caissie mowed through a pitcher-friendly league in 2021 and earned himself a spot in High-A, where he grounded out for all of April and then was named the Cubs' minor-league player of the month in May. His timing and pitch recognition improved and he got to tell a story everyone wants to hear about a prospect they got for Yu Darvish: He's working, he's adjusting, he's unlocking new dimensions of his game while understanding the mental component of it.

Alexander Canario OF Born: 05/07/00 Age: 23 Bats: R Throws: R Height: 6'1" Weight: 165 lb. Origin: International Free Agent, 2016

YEAR	TEAM	LVL	AGE	PA	R	2B	3B	HR	RBI	BB	K	SB	CS	Whiff%	AVG/OBP/SLG	DRC+	BABIP	BRR	DRP	WARP
2021	SJ	A	21	274	43	14	3	9	29	33	79	15	3		.235/.325/.433	98	.307	1.0	LF(22): 1.9, RF(20): 0.3, CF(14): -1.3	1.0
2021	SB	A+	21	182	19	6	1	9	28	10	46	6	5		.224/.264/.429	106	.248	-1.7	CF(26): 2.1, RF(18): 0.7	0.8
2022	SB	A+	22	100	17	6	0	7	22	10	35	3	0		.281/.360/.584	110	.383	-0.6	RF(12): 0.6, CF(6): -0.8	0.4
2022	TNS	AA	22	350	51	18	2	24	61	36	91	17	3		.248/.329/.552	117	.269	0.0	CF(54): 0.9, RF(22): -0.7, LF(6): 0.3	2.0
2022	IOW	AAA	22	84	16	2	0	6	14	13	21	3	0		.231/.386/.538	115	.231	0.2	RF(7): 1.0, LF(5): -0.5, CF(4): -0.3	0.4
2023 DC	*CHC*	*MLB*	*23*	*96*	*10*	*3*	*0*	*3*	*10*	*7*	*29*	*2*	*1*	*31.4%*	*.207/.276/.396*	*79*	*.264*	*0.9*	*LF 0, CF 0*	*0.1*

It was a strong consolidation year for Canario, who recorded his most games played in a season at 125 while dominating at every stop from High-A to Triple-A, ending the season with 37 home runs. As you might expect, there's plus raw power in the tank, though hit tool concerns mean that he might not end up getting all of it into games at the highest level. A refined approach in 2022 was the key to unlocking his offensive potential, as his pitch recognition and two-strike approach saw major improvements. He's still an aggressive hitter who goes up looking to do damage and is willing to chase out of the zone to try and make it happen. Canario has a high-variance profile ranging anywhere from three-true-outcomes hitter to a middle-of-the-lineup run producer. Which form he ends up taking hinges on how often he can make contact, because the contact is hard when he does connect.

★ ★ ★ *2023 Top 101 Prospect* **#28** ★ ★ ★

Pete Crow-Armstrong OF Born: 03/25/02 Age: 21 Bats: L Throws: L Height: 6'0" Weight: 184 lb. Origin: Round 1, 2020 Draft (#19 overall)

YEAR	TEAM	LVL	AGE	PA	R	2B	3B	HR	RBI	BB	K	SB	CS	Whiff%	AVG/OBP/SLG	DRC+	BABIP	BRR	DRP	WARP
2021	SLU	A	19	32	6	2	0	0	4	7	6	2	3		.417/.563/.500	119	.556	0.1	CF(5): 1.6	0.3
2022	MB	A	20	183	39	5	3	7	27	22	33	13	4		.354/.443/.557	121	.415	0.7	CF(32): 0.9	1.3
2022	SB	A+	20	288	50	15	7	9	34	14	69	19	7		.287/.333/.498	87	.353	0.5	CF(59): 1.7	0.6
2023 non-DC	*CHC*	*MLB*	*21*	*251*	*23*	*9*	*3*	*4*	*25*	*14*	*62*	*11*	*4*	*27.4%*	*.251/.303/.386*	*89*	*.325*	*1.2*	*CF 0*	*0.5*

Comparables: David Dahl (82), Brett Phillips (78), Jordan Schafer (78)

PCA missed 2021 with a torn labrum, but he didn't miss much in 2022. The 20-year-old used 101 games at Low- and High-A to fast-track himself back into the Cubs' top prospect talk. He hits. He scores. He knocks in runs. He steals. He fields. He throws. We don't mean to sound like Jon Hamm narrating Trea Turner's free agency sizzle reel, but PCA does do all of those things well, and as a prospect, it makes him even more thrilling. With a sharp left-handed stroke and a sage, strategic plate approach (for such a young player), he remains Wrigley's center fielder of the future, with space on his mantel for a couple of Gold Gloves. Minor League Baseball agreed with all of this in November, naming him a Midwest League All-Star. Chicago will need a stopgap for the time being, but PCA is on his way.

Brennen Davis OF Born: 11/02/99 Age: 23 Bats: R Throws: R Height: 6'4" Weight: 210 lb. Origin: Round 2, 2018 Draft (#62 overall)

YEAR	TEAM	LVL	AGE	PA	R	2B	3B	HR	RBI	BB	K	SB	CS	Whiff%	AVG/OBP/SLG	DRC+	BABIP	BRR	DRP	WARP
2021	SB	A+	21	32	6	2	0	2	5	3	6	2	0		.321/.406/.607	113	.350	0.0	CF(5): -0.3	0.1
2021	TNS	AA	21	316	50	20	0	13	36	36	97	6	4		.252/.367/.474	105	.344	-1.0	CF(33): 1.0, RF(29): -1.6, LF(8): 1.4	1.1
2021	IOW	AAA	21	68	10	3	0	4	12	11	15	0	0		.268/.397/.536	113	.297	-0.9	RF(9): -2.0, CF(4): -0.2, LF(2): 0.3	0.1
2022	IOW	AAA	22	174	16	6	0	4	13	23	52	0	1		.191/.322/.319	87	.258	-1.4	CF(14): -0.2, LF(13): 0.5, RF(12): -0.8	0.3
2023 non-DC	*CHC*	*MLB*	*23*	*251*	*24*	*10*	*1*	*7*	*26*	*21*	*79*	*2*	*1*	*34.0%*	*.205/.292/.355*	*78*	*.283*	*0.6*	*LF 0, CF 0*	*0.0*

Comparables: Daz Cameron (55), Dalton Pompey (52), Wil Myers (48)

Davis is a top prospect whose 2022 season was defined more by injury than availability: A June surgery was meant to address "lower back tightness" that turned out to be a cluster of troublesome blood vessels pushing up against a nerve. Thereafter, the 23-year-old outfielder went back to work, launching fly balls to all fields with his raw power—until he was dispatched to the Arizona Fall League, where he was pulled off the field after dealing with "general soreness." If there's one guy in this system about whom you don't want to hear vaguely described health problems at this point, it's Davis. But regardless, his ramp-up to 100% remains on track; with the Cubs adding him to the 40-man roster this offseason, expect to see much more of Davis this year, health allowing.

Yan Gomes C

Born: 07/19/87 Age: 35 Bats: R Throws: R Height: 6'2" Weight: 212 lb. Origin: Round 10, 2009 Draft (#310 overall)

YEAR	TEAM	LVL	AGE	PA	R	2B	3B	HR	RBI	BB	K	SB	CS	Whiff%	AVG/OBP/SLG	DRC+	BABIP	BRR	DRP	WARP
2020	WAS	MLB	32	119	14	6	1	4	13	6	22	1	0	22.4%	.284/.319/.468	106	.314	0.2	C(30): -1.9	0.4
2021	OAK	MLB	33	140	19	4	0	5	17	6	31	0	0	22.4%	.221/.264/.366	93	.250	1.3	C(31): -1	0.5
2021	WAS	MLB	33	235	30	11	1	9	35	13	47	0	0	19.2%	.271/.323/.454	107	.309	1.1	C(61): 4.6	1.8
2022	CHC	MLB	34	293	23	12	0	8	31	8	47	2	0	19.4%	.235/.260/.365	93	.252	1.7	C(69): 1.2	1.1
2023 DC	*CHC*	*MLB*	*35*	*356*	*34*	*14*	*0*	*9*	*36*	*18*	*61*	*1*	*0*	*20.3%*	*.248/.298/.380*	*86*	*.281*	*-0.1*	*C 0*	*0.7*

Comparables: Nick Hundley (67), Mike Macfarlane (65), Terry Steinbach (65)

YEAR	TEAM	P. COUNT	FRM RUNS	BLK RUNS	THRW RUNS	TOT RUNS
2020	WAS	4477	-2.7	0.1	0.3	-2.3
2021	WAS	8701	3.4	0.5	-0.3	3.7
2021	OAK	4367	-1.6	0.0	0.1	-1.6
2022	CHC	9685	0.9	0.2	0.2	1.3
2023	*CHC*	*13228*	*-1.9*	*0.2*	*0.0*	*-1.7*

A lot of fans want to believe they can sit through a year of Gomes behind the dish, waiting for one of their catching prospects to mature. But Cubs fans—at least, those minted past 2015—have yet to experience a season without Willson Contreras. Gomes is a 35-year-old makes-everybody-comfortable catcher for whom offensive output is considered a bonus. There are a lot of backstops who fit that latter descriptor, but for seven years Chicago fans haven't had to watch the catcher drive a ball straight into the ground, with runners in scoring position, for the third time in one game. It's a lot to get used to.

Ian Happ LF

Born: 08/12/94 Age: 28 Bats: S Throws: R Height: 6'0" Weight: 205 lb. Origin: Round 1, 2015 Draft (#9 overall)

YEAR	TEAM	LVL	AGE	PA	R	2B	3B	HR	RBI	BB	K	SB	CS	Whiff%	AVG/OBP/SLG	DRC+	BABIP	BRR	DRP	WARP
2020	CHC	MLB	25	231	27	11	1	12	28	30	63	1	3	35.9%	.258/.361/.505	113	.317	-1.6	CF(51): -0.5, LF(28): -0.3, RF(7): 0	0.9
2021	CHC	MLB	26	535	63	20	1	25	66	62	156	9	2	32.4%	.226/.323/.434	102	.281	0.8	LF(65): -1.6, CF(56): -1.5, RF(16): -0.5	2.0
2022	CHC	MLB	27	641	72	42	2	17	72	58	149	9	4	27.2%	.271/.342/.440	107	.336	0.9	LF(146): 4.3, CF(3): 0	3.2
2023 DC	*CHC*	*MLB*	*28*	*583*	*66*	*27*	*2*	*20*	*65*	*58*	*131*	*7*	*2*	*27.4%*	*.249/.333/.428*	*108*	*.299*	*2.7*	*LF 4*	*2.6*

Comparables: Lloyd Moseby (75), Adolfo Phillips (74), Rick Monday (73)

The darling of any team searching for outfield help at the trade deadline, Happ opened his eyes on August 3 and was still wearing a Cubs uniform (probably metaphorically, but possibly literally—they are basically pajamas, after all). It didn't take long for Happ to get more literate reading the ball off the bat in left, so much so that there were advocates trying to put him in the Gold Glove conversation. And why not? It was a year of firsts for the 28-year-old, whose first-half slash line, .274/.364/.443 with 23 doubles, earned him his first All-Star appearance. This breakout came just as the Cubs pushed into the darkest days of a rebuilding phase. Regardless of what was happening around him, Happ kept on making hard contact and hitting doubles in the gap through the season's final days, turning in an outstanding campaign.

Nico Hoerner SS

Born: 05/13/97 Age: 26 Bats: R Throws: R Height: 6'1" Weight: 200 lb. Origin: Round 1, 2018 Draft (#24 overall)

YEAR	TEAM	LVL	AGE	PA	R	2B	3B	HR	RBI	BB	K	SB	CS	Whiff%	AVG/OBP/SLG	DRC+	BABIP	BRR	DRP	WARP
2020	CHC	MLB	23	126	19	4	0	0	13	12	24	3	2	18.3%	.222/.312/.259	94	.279	1.5	2B(37): 0.4, SS(10): 0, 3B(6): -0.6	0.4
2021	IOW	AAA	24	28	3	1	0	0	2	0	6	0	0		.269/.321/.308	89	.350	-0.1	2B(4): 0.1	0.1
2021	CHC	MLB	24	170	13	10	0	0	16	17	25	5	3	18.4%	.302/.382/.369	101	.360	-0.1	2B(30): 1.2, SS(12): -1.2, LF(3): -0.2	0.6
2022	CHC	MLB	25	517	60	22	5	10	55	28	57	20	2	14.2%	.281/.327/.410	111	.300	3.2	SS(133): 0.6	2.7
2023 DC	*CHC*	*MLB*	*26*	*550*	*59*	*23*	*3*	*11*	*57*	*36*	*63*	*20*	*4*	*15.1%*	*.281/.340/.409*	*110*	*.306*	*10.7*	*2B 0, SS 0*	*3.4*

Comparables: Erick Aybar (67), Alex Cintron (64), Chris Owings (62)

After the 2022 Cubs took their team photo in center field, Hoerner went up into the left field bleachers at Wrigley, just walking around and thinking. What about? Maybe how he spent all year proving that he could play shortstop every day, and now might get moved to second if the Cubs acquire a top-tier free agent. Maybe how a stupid tricep injury threw what had been an excellent year in the field and solid year at the plate out of whack. Maybe how once you get that "injury-prone" label slapped on you, it's hard to rip it off. Or maybe he was just thinking about birds, and where they go at night. Who knows.

Eric Hosmer 1B

Born: 10/24/89 Age: 33 Bats: L Throws: L Height: 6'4" Weight: 226 lb. Origin: Round 1, 2008 Draft (#3 overall)

YEAR	TEAM	LVL	AGE	PA	R	2B	3B	HR	RBI	BB	K	SB	CS	Whiff%	AVG/OBP/SLG	DRC+	BABIP	BRR	DRP	WARP
2020	SD	MLB	30	156	23	6	0	9	36	9	28	4	0	20.4%	.287/.333/.517	106	.296	0.0	1B(32): 1.3	0.6
2021	SD	MLB	31	565	53	28	0	12	65	48	99	5	4	22.8%	.269/.337/.395	99	.313	-1.4	1B(131): 1.2	1.1
2022	BOS	MLB	32	50	6	3	0	0	4	4	9	0	0	18.4%	.244/.320/.311	85	.306	-0.9	1B(14): 0	-0.1
2022	SD	MLB	32	369	32	16	0	8	40	33	55	0	0	18.9%	.272/.336/.391	108	.304	-1.5	1B(88): -2.1	0.7
2023 DC	*CHC*	*MLB*	*33*	*433*	*46*	*19*	*1*	*12*	*48*	*35*	*63*	*1*	*1*	*20.1%*	*.272/.337/.421*	*110*	*.300*	*0.1*	*1B 0*	*1.1*

Comparables: Stuffy McInnis (76), Charlie Grimm (75), Ed Kranepool (74)

For about an hour at the trade deadline, Hosmer held the baseball world in his hands, unwilling to accept a move to Washington as part of San Diego's mega-trade for Juan Soto. Chaim Bloom did A.J. Preller a solid and bought Hosmer off the Padres to allow them to finalize the deal, which neatly sums up Hosmer's current standing in the league: trade ballast and roster clutter. An early-season hot streak evaporated by May Day, and he posted a .637 OPS from that point through the end of July. In Boston, he was the band-aid slapped over the stab wound that was first base, and he neither hit well nor lasted long, as a back injury sidelined him for most of the second half. Released by the Red Sox in December, the veteran will cost the Cubs next to nothing—San Diego ate what was left of the mega-deal it gave him in 2018—but he offers little in turn as a ground-and-pound hitter with subpar power. The demise of the infield shift could give him a modest boost, but Hosmer is now strictly a bench bat and veteran presence, and it's hard to argue he should have any role bigger than that.

Nick Madrigal 2B

Born: 03/05/97 Age: 26 Bats: R Throws: R Height: 5'8" Weight: 175 lb. Origin: Round 1, 2018 Draft (#4 overall)

YEAR	TEAM	LVL	AGE	PA	R	2B	3B	HR	RBI	BB	K	SB	CS	Whiff%	AVG/OBP/SLG	DRC+	BABIP	BRR	DRP	WARP
2020	CHW	MLB	23	109	8	3	0	0	11	4	7	2	1	10.8%	.340/.376/.369	117	.365	-1.9	2B(29): -0.2	0.4
2021	CHW	MLB	24	215	30	10	4	2	21	11	17	1	2	8.5%	.305/.349/.425	112	.324	-0.1	2B(53): -0.2	1.1
2022	IOW	AAA	25	43	8	1	0	0	5	3	5	0	0		.308/.372/.333	107	.353	-0.3	2B(10): 0.6	0.2
2022	CHC	MLB	25	228	19	7	0	0	7	14	27	3	1	10.6%	.249/.305/.282	101	.286	0.4	2B(59): 1.5	0.9
2023 DC	*CHC*	*MLB*	*26*	*233*	*25*	*9*	*1*	*1*	*17*	*14*	*17*	*2*	*1*	*10.2%*	*.274/.330/.356*	*97*	*.292*	*1.3*	*2B 0*	*0.6*

Comparables: Steve Lombardozzi (75), César Hernández (64), Ronald Torreyes (60)

Madrigal's role with these Cubs needs some further definition. It could be batting lead-off. Could be off the bench. Could be doing a bad job filling in on the mound after the starter punched a water jug. Madrigal put together a hot August that brought him back to the offensive median, but then a (second) groin strain ended his season weeks early. On the whole, he never really figured it out at the plate—probably the first time that's been true, in Chicago or on the road there. There's more here; as a team that's either fun or rebuilding or both, the Cubs get to let the situation play out.

Zach McKinstry IF

Born: 04/29/95 Age: 28 Bats: L Throws: R Height: 6'0" Weight: 180 lb. Origin: Round 33, 2016 Draft (#1001 overall)

YEAR	TEAM	LVL	AGE	PA	R	2B	3B	HR	RBI	BB	K	SB	CS	Whiff%	AVG/OBP/SLG	DRC+	BABIP	BRR	DRP	WARP
2020	LAD	MLB	25	7	1	1	0	0	0	0	3	0	0	37.5%	.286/.286/.429	78	.500		RF(1): 0.2	
2021	OKC	AAA	26	171	35	8	3	7	21	20	26	4	2		.272/.368/.510	114	.287	1.0	SS(15): -0.7, 2B(12): 3.6, LF(6): 0.7	1.3
2021	LAD	MLB	26	172	19	9	0	7	29	10	50	1	1	26.2%	.215/.263/.405	77	.262	0.0	RF(23): 1, 2B(20): -0.6, LF(14): -0.7	0.0
2022	OKC	AAA	27	223	36	9	4	4	25	27	33	0	3	21.4%	.335/.417/.487	112	.382	-2.2	SS(33): -2.6, 2B(5): -0.3, LF(4): 0.5	0.7
2022	CHC	MLB	27	171	17	6	3	4	12	13	48	7	0	21.1%	.206/.272/.361	75	.272	0.8	3B(21): 0.1, 2B(19): -0.8, SS(9): 0	0.0
2022	LAD	MLB	27	14	4	0	0	1	2	3	4	0	0	24.0%	.091/.286/.364	91		0.1	RF(3): 0.1, 2B(2): 0	0.0
2023 DC	*CHC*	*MLB*	*28*	*129*	*13*	*5*	*1*	*2*	*11*	*10*	*28*	*2*	*0*	*22.5%*	*.234/.305/.378*	*83*	*.288*	*1.7*	*3B 0, RF 0*	*0.2*

Comparables: John Bowker (45), Lucas Duda (43), Kila Ka'aihue (43)

Having lost favor in Los Angeles with a poor offensive showing in 2021, McKinstry worked his way back into the conversation with a few loud months at Triple-A; they were strong enough that the Dodgers traded him to the Cubs for Chris Martin. Once again, the majors failed to bear fruit for the defense-first infielder, but moving to a franchise that's searching for its next identity should ensure regular playing time. That said: September was deemed McKinstry's big chance, with Nick Madrigal's season at an end. The utility struggled to get down the timing for his toe-tap swing and started the month 0-for-15. If you're into half-full glasses, he had nine extra-base hits after snapping the hitless streak.

★ ★ ★ *2023 Top 101 Prospect* **#88** ★ ★ ★

Matt Mervis 1B

Born: 04/16/98 Age: 25 Bats: L Throws: R Height: 6'4" Weight: 225 lb. Origin: Round 39, 2016 Draft (#1174 overall)

YEAR	TEAM	LVL	AGE	PA	R	2B	3B	HR	RBI	BB	K	SB	CS	Whiff%	AVG/OBP/SLG	DRC+	BABIP	BRR	DRP	WARP
2021	MB	A	23	289	38	11	1	9	42	36	66	6	0		.204/.309/.367	106	.236	-0.5	1B(59): 6.6, 3B(1): -0.6, LF(1): -0.6	1.3
2022	SB	A+	24	108	17	9	0	7	29	5	26	0	0		.350/.389/.650	138	.412	1.0	1B(27): 2.3	1.1
2022	TNS	AA	24	230	34	16	1	14	51	20	46	2	0		.300/.370/.596	133	.322	-0.6	1B(36): 3.1	1.8
2022	IOW	AAA	24	240	41	15	1	15	39	25	35	0	0		.297/.383/.593	134	.294	0.5	1B(53): -0.7	1.6
2023 DC	*CHC*	*MLB*	*25*	*402*	*45*	*19*	*2*	*14*	*43*	*27*	*92*	*1*	*0*	*26.0%*	*.243/.306/.427*	*95*	*.290*	*1.2*	*1B 0*	*0.5*

Comparables: Jared Walsh (59), Steve Pearce (56), Andrew Toles (53)

After going undrafted in the five-round, pandemic-shortened 2020 Draft, the Duke University-graduate Mervis sat down and built out a spreadsheet, analyzing which teams offered the best opportunities for development and big-league employment. So far, his choice has been impeccable, as his meteoric rise through the Cubs system has him penciled in for the first-base job in Wrigley in his third professional season. Not content with his regular season, he went on to lead the Arizona Fall League in homers and took the MVP award for its Fall Stars Game. Mervis has a quick swing and long enough arms to cover the outside of the plate, but is also patient enough—and skilled enough at pitch recognition—to spit on pitches that are too good to drive, as evidenced by how some of his singles became walks as he climbed the ladder.

Christopher Morel UT

Born: 06/24/99 Age: 24 Bats: R Throws: R Height: 5'11" Weight: 145 lb. Origin: International Free Agent, 2015

YEAR	TEAM	LVL	AGE	PA	R	2B	3B	HR	RBI	BB	K	SB	CS	Whiff%	AVG/OBP/SLG	DRC+	BABIP	BRR	DRP	WARP
2021	TNS	AA	22	417	59	17	5	17	64	41	124	16	3		.220/.300/.432	98	.276	-0.8	CF(32): -1.9, RF(20): 7.4, 3B(19): -0.5	1.7
2021	IOW	AAA	22	39	6	1	0	1	2	4	10	2	0		.257/.333/.371	88	.333	1.3	3B(4): 0.6, CF(2): -0.4, LF(1): 0.0	0.2
2022	TNS	AA	23	122	22	5	1	7	20	10	30	3	3		.306/.380/.565	110	.366	0.6	CF(18): 0.4, SS(6): 0.4, 3B(4): 0.0	0.7
2022	CHC	MLB	23	425	55	19	4	16	47	38	137	10	7	38.8%	.235/.308/.433	87	.320	1.2	CF(57): -1.1, 2B(33): -0.1, 3B(18): 0.3	0.7
2023 DC	*CHC*	*MLB*	*24*	*432*	*49*	*17*	*5*	*13*	*40*	*34*	*142*	*12*	*7*	*37.1%*	*.221/.292/.393*	*82*	*.312*	*-1.9*	*3B -1, CF -1*	*-0.4*

Comparables: Ian Happ (55), Brett Phillips (53), Dexter Fowler (53)

This past June, one writer called Morel a combination of Javy Báez and Dexter Fowler. By September, he was the first Cubs rookie since Kris Bryant to have 15+ home runs and 10 stolen bases. The center fielder was a high-voltage battery inserted atop of the order, with teammates and coaches lauding his energy, defense, and pop. He needs to strike out less and make more accurate throws to stick, but Cubs fans should be pleased: The first sign the future is arriving is when everybody starts bringing up the past.

Rafael Ortega OF Born: 05/15/91 Age: 32 Bats: L Throws: R Height: 5'11" Weight: 180 lb. Origin: International Free Agent, 2008

YEAR	TEAM	LVL	AGE	PA	R	2B	3B	HR	RBI	BB	K	SB	CS	Whiff%	AVG/OBP/SLG	DRC+	BABIP	BRR	DRP	WARP
2020	ORI	WIN	29	152	23	8	1	4	20	26	15	2	1		.301/.427/.480		.317			
2021	IOW	AAA	30	73	11	3	0	4	11	8	13	1	1		.250/.333/.484	123	.255	-0.2	RF(16): 1.2, C(1): 0.0	0.5
2021	CHC	MLB	30	330	44	14	2	11	33	30	70	12	6	21.5%	.291/.360/.463	103	.349	-0.6	CF(73): -5.9, LF(13): -0.4, RF(13): -0.6	0.7
2022	CHC	MLB	31	371	35	14	1	7	35	44	74	12	7	19.2%	.241/.331/.358	95	.285	-4.0	CF(67): -2.6, RF(19): 0.6, LF(11): -0.1	0.4
2023 DC	*FA*	*MLB*	*32*	*350*	*37*	*14*	*1*	*9*	*39*	*36*	*67*	*9*	*5*	*20.2%*	*.244/.326/.397*	*102*	*.283*	*-1.2*	*CF -3, RF 0*	*0.6*

Comparables: Brock Holt (44), Willie Harris (43), Grégor Blanco (41)

Ortega had an impressive and milestone-filled 2021, featuring a three-homer game and a walk-off bomb to end a 13-game losing streak for Chicago—triggering talk that the Cubs may have stumbled upon someone interesting. While last season saw him develop a charming friendship with a Cubs ball boy named Fabian, on the numbers side everything went in the wrong direction. The Cubs indicated at the start of winter that they'd be interested in acquiring a center fielder, likely ruling out Ortega as a long-term option. Maybe it's for the best—the average ball boy tenure can't be that long, either.

Yohendrick Pinango LF/DH Born: 05/07/02 Age: 21 Bats: L Throws: L Height: 5'11" Weight: 170 lb. Origin: International Free Agent, 2018

YEAR	TEAM	LVL	AGE	PA	R	2B	3B	HR	RBI	BB	K	SB	CS	Whiff%	AVG/OBP/SLG	DRC+	BABIP	BRR	DRP	WARP
2021	MB	A	19	351	50	16	2	4	27	24	57	8	2		.272/.322/.370	104	.317	0.6	LF(41): -5.1, RF(21): 3.0, CF(1): -0.1	1.2
2021	SB	A+	19	105	9	4	1	1	9	7	12	0	0		.289/.343/.381	117	.321	-1.5	LF(22): 1.0, RF(2): 0.2	0.5
2022	SB	A+	20	495	65	24	2	13	63	30	88	14	1		.250/.297/.394	92	.284	2.6	LF(81): -0.6, CF(10): -1.2	1.2
2023 non-DC	*CHC*	*MLB*	*21*	*251*	*20*	*10*	*1*	*3*	*22*	*11*	*49*	*6*	*1*	*22.7%*	*.234/.273/.334*	*67*	*.283*	*2.4*	*LF 0, CF 0*	*-0.2*

Comparables: Leody Taveras (52), Josh Naylor (49), Carlos Tocci (49)

It's easier to hit when you rarely miss the ball! Pinango has a reputation as a guy who makes contact in the same way that other batters breathe: Frequently, naturally and as though he needs to do it to stay alive. His sharp swing makes the lefty a tremendous pure hitter, though most of those hits wind up on the ground. A staggering statistic cited by *Baseball America*: In 2021, at High-A South Bend, Pinango had more multi-hit games than hitless ones. After a winter-ball HBP required surgery (and three screws) on his left pinky ahead of the 2022 campaign, the breakout many were expecting never came.

Reginald Preciado MI Born: 05/16/03 Age: 20 Bats: S Throws: R Height: 6'4" Weight: 185 lb. Origin: International Free Agent, 2019

YEAR	TEAM	LVL	AGE	PA	R	2B	3B	HR	RBI	BB	K	SB	CS	Whiff%	AVG/OBP/SLG	DRC+	BABIP	BRR	DRP	WARP
2021	CUB	ROK	18	154	28	10	3	3	25	11	35	7	1		.333/.383/.511		.423			
2022	CUB	ROK	19	37	5	2	1	0	4	4	14	0	0		.212/.297/.333		.368			
2022	MB	A	19	185	20	6	2	2	24	10	69	3	2		.199/.262/.295	56	.320	-0.5	SS(28): -0.5, 2B(16): 1.7	-0.4
2023 non-DC	*CHC*	*MLB*	*20*	*251*	*16*	*9*	*2*	*2*	*18*	*11*	*103*	*3*	*2*	*41.1%*	*.183/.233/.272*	*32*	*.315*	*1.4*	*2B 0, 3B 0*	*-1.3*

Comparables: Marco Hernández (90), Marten Gasparini (86), Javier Lopez (85)

Preciado is still learning who he is. In a system full of giants, his lanky, still-expanding frame isn't even unique, but he makes contact from the left and right sides—and he can really lay into one on occasion. But he's hungry, and his plate discipline has him biting on more offerings than he should. His Rookie and Low-A numbers aren't exciting, but there's upside here, though it may be easier to see if he moves from shortstop to third and can concentrate on the stick.

Franmil Reyes DH Born: 07/07/95 Age: 28 Bats: R Throws: R Height: 6'5" Weight: 265 lb. Origin: International Free Agent, 2012

YEAR	TEAM	LVL	AGE	PA	R	2B	3B	HR	RBI	BB	K	SB	CS	Whiff%	AVG/OBP/SLG	DRC+	BABIP	BRR	DRP	WARP
2020	CLE	MLB	24	241	27	10	0	9	34	24	69	0	0	38.5%	.275/.344/.450	102	.355	-1.5	LF(1): -0.2	0.5
2021	CLE	MLB	25	466	57	18	2	30	85	43	149	4	1	33.7%	.254/.324/.522	111	.314	-1.6	RF(11): -1	1.5
2022	COL	AAA	26	35	6	2	0	2	7	2	7	0	2		.313/.343/.563	102	.333	-0.7	RF(3): -0.4	0.0
2022	CHC	MLB	26	193	19	8	2	5	19	16	53	0	1	34.3%	.234/.301/.389	87	.305	-0.8	RF(1): 0	0.1
2022	CLE	MLB	26	280	24	9	0	9	28	14	104	2	0	38.8%	.213/.254/.350	69	.309	-1.3	RF(12): -1, LF(2): -0.2	-0.6
2023 non-DC	*CHC*	*MLB*	*27*	*251*	*30*	*9*	*0*	*12*	*35*	*18*	*76*	*0*	*1*	*35.6%*	*.242/.303/.452*	*104*	*.307*	*0.0*	*RF -1, LF 0*	*0.5*

Comparables: Nate Colbert (66), Bob Robertson (66), Wily Mo Pena (65)

Reyes' job as DH is to smash the ball and stay off the field. In 2022, he hit three homers in 12 games as a right fielder, and went 1-for-4 with a double as a left fielder. In 100 contests as a DH, the slugging percentage was .360: He finished with some months over .500, and some closer to .200. After a loud start, Reyes became for the Cubs who he'd been when the Guardians put him on waivers: He hit .195 through May, and .193 in September and October. With only five homers for Chicago, Reyes' music didn't herald a significant offensive threat coming to the plate (though he did slug .536 swinging at the first pitch 56 times). He's still young enough there's hope he's got more smashing to do.

Alfonso Rivas 1B Born: 09/13/96 Age: 26 Bats: L Throws: L Height: 5'11" Weight: 190 lb. Origin: Round 4, 2018 Draft (#113 overall)

YEAR	TEAM	LVL	AGE	PA	R	2B	3B	HR	RBI	BB	K	SB	CS	Whiff%	AVG/OBP/SLG	DRC+	BABIP	BRR	DRP	WARP
2021	IOW	AAA	24	237	22	13	0	4	32	35	49	0	1		.284/.405/.411	115	.361	-2.6	1B(46): 6.6, LF(9): -1.2, RF(1): -0.5	1.2
2021	CHC	MLB	24	49	7	1	0	1	3	4	16	0	0	26.4%	.318/.388/.409	76	.481	0.2	1B(5): 0, LF(5): -0.3, RF(5): -0.3	0.0
2022	IOW	AAA	25	106	15	6	1	1	10	10	28	0	0		.298/.368/.415	91	.409	0.7	LF(10): -0.7, 1B(9): 1.4, RF(1): -0.1	0.2
2022	CHC	MLB	25	287	27	5	2	3	25	29	87	6	1	26.4%	.235/.322/.307	73	.344	1.3	1B(92): -0.6, LF(2): 0.1, RF(1): -0.1	-0.3
2023 non-DC	*CHC*	*MLB*	*26*	*251*	*23*	*9*	*1*	*3*	*20*	*23*	*66*	*2*	*0*	*24.8%*	*.236/.318/.340*	*84*	*.319*	*0.7*	*1B 0, LF 0*	*0.0*

Comparables: Donald Lutz (65), Adron Chambers (61), Chris Shaw (58)

Rivas saw his big-league playing time balloon in 2022, as the guy to come around when the Cubs needed a 27th man for a double-header, or somebody to come fill in when Patrick Wisdom sprained his wrist. He had a particularly exhilarating couple of days in June: He hit a grand slam in a pile-on against the Pirates, and the next night hit an RBI single to key a five-run comeback. Though he's capable of driving a pitcher mad with how long he can stay in the box and fight off pitches, Rivas' absence of power substantially hinders his production. At 26, he's a guy who would benefit from more playing time, to see if he can do more in the box than annoy the pitcher into submission.

Seiya Suzuki RF Born: 08/18/94 Age: 28 Bats: R Throws: R Height: 5'11" Weight: 182 lb. Origin: International Free Agent, 2022

YEAR	TEAM	LVL	AGE	PA	R	2B	3B	HR	RBI	BB	K	SB	CS	Whiff%	AVG/OBP/SLG	DRC+	BABIP	BRR	DRP	WARP
2022	CHC	MLB	27	446	54	22	2	14	46	42	110	9	5	22.9%	.262/.336/.433	105	.326	0.7	RF(106): 5.1	2.2
2023 DC	*CHC*	*MLB*	*28*	*604*	*76*	*28*	*2*	*23*	*67*	*66*	*119*	*10*	*3*	*22.7%*	*.254/.345/.446*	*119*	*.290*	*1.6*	*RF 1*	*2.9*

Comparables: Lyle Mouton (81), Yasiel Puig (81), Joe Gaines (81)

This was an adjustment year for Suzuki, a major signing and presumably big piece of the Cubs' future. And that was the understanding from day one, as he adapted to playing in another country, another city and another league. Things ended up in a strong place: The 28-year-old rookie put together a 116 OPS+ for the year, though DRC+ was less impressed. There were ups and downs: changes made to his stance and his swing; months when he had it and months when he didn't; June lost to a ring finger injury. But Suzuki doesn't swing and miss much, and by the time his season ended for paternity leave, he was doing what he'd been doing in April: Hitting for power to the gaps. The Cubs can afford to be patient with their big international free agent signing, who will begin the 2023 season with greater promise and higher expectations.

Dansby Swanson SS Born: 02/11/94 Age: 29 Bats: R Throws: R Height: 6'1" Weight: 190 lb. Origin: Round 1, 2015 Draft (#1 overall)

YEAR	TEAM	LVL	AGE	PA	R	2B	3B	HR	RBI	BB	K	SB	CS	Whiff%	AVG/OBP/SLG	DRC+	BABIP	BRR	DRP	WARP
2020	ATL	MLB	26	264	49	15	0	10	35	22	71	5	0	31.6%	.274/.345/.464	99	.350	2.2	SS(60): 1.7	1.1
2021	ATL	MLB	27	653	78	33	2	27	88	52	167	9	3	30.5%	.248/.311/.449	98	.297	0.3	SS(159): 2.8	2.5
2022	ATL	MLB	28	696	99	32	1	25	96	49	182	18	7	30.6%	.277/.329/.447	108	.348	6.2	SS(161): 12.4	4.9
2023 DC	*CHC*	*MLB*	*29*	*605*	*70*	*26*	*1*	*23*	*67*	*46*	*156*	*20*	*4*	*30.2%*	*.255/.319/.435*	*104*	*.317*	*7.7*	*SS 8*	*3.7*

Comparables: Dave Concepcion (80), Jay Bell (76), Miguel Tejada (75)

Swanson's career at the plate can be defined by a rolling wOBA chart. In case you don't have one of those handy, just imagine the most volatile roller coaster you can: Swanson's experienced countless peaks and valleys as a batter before generally pulling in with a line right around league-average. Last summer saw the Swansoncoaster reach its apex; he went on a tear unlike anything we'd seen from him, and never dipped to the usual nadir subsequent to one of his hot streaks. Combining his growth with the bat and his typically solid performance with the glove was a surefire recipe for a very timely career year. While Swanson's time in the lineup may be volatile, just remember—nobody gets on a roller coaster unless they want to.

James Triantos 3B Born: 01/29/03 Age: 20 Bats: R Throws: R Height: 6'1" Weight: 195 lb. Origin: Round 2, 2021 Draft (#56 overall)

YEAR	TEAM	LVL	AGE	PA	R	2B	3B	HR	RBI	BB	K	SB	CS	Whiff%	AVG/OBP/SLG	DRC+	BABIP	BRR	DRP	WARP
2021	CUB	ROK	18	109	27	7	1	6	19	7	18	3	3		.327/.376/.594		.351			
2022	MB	A	19	504	74	19	6	7	50	39	81	20	3		.272/.335/.386	112	.315	3.2	3B(104): -6.5	2.0
2023 non-DC	*CHC*	*MLB*	*20*	*251*	*19*	*9*	*2*	*2*	*20*	*13*	*50*	*6*	*1*	*23.2%*	*.233/.279/.326*	*68*	*.289*	*4.2*	*2B 0, 3B 0*	*0.0*

Comparables: Juan Yepez (83), Juremi Profar (80), Edilio Colina (79)

Triantos' approach and compact, right-handed swing often result in hard contact—he's the prototype of a complete batter. Coming up as a pitcher and middle infielder—he hit a homer and pitched a complete game one-hitter, with 12 strikeouts, to secure his final amateur championship—he will likely be neither for Chicago, as he's mostly been a third baseman since going pro. After tearing up rookie ball in 2021, Triantos didn't look lost at High-A, fighting his way back into at-bats, homering in three straight games around the 4th of July and showing the wheels.

Patrick Wisdom 3B Born: 08/27/91 Age: 31 Bats: R Throws: R Height: 6'2" Weight: 220 lb. Origin: Round 1, 2012 Draft (#52 overall)

YEAR	TEAM	LVL	AGE	PA	R	2B	3B	HR	RBI	BB	K	SB	CS	Whiff%	AVG/OBP/SLG	DRC+	BABIP	BRR	DRP	WARP
2020	CHC	MLB	28	2	0	0	0	0	0	0	0	0	0	33.3%	.000/.000/.000	108			1B(2): 0	
2021	IOW	AAA	29	34	7	1	0	3	11	6	12	1	0		.160/.353/.560	107	.091	0.0	3B(3): -0.3, LF(1): 0.0	0.1
2021	CHC	MLB	29	375	54	13	0	28	61	32	153	4	1	41.3%	.231/.305/.518	93	.318	2.4	3B(77): 1.7, LF(15): -0.2, 1B(13): -0.1	1.3
2022	CHC	MLB	30	534	67	28	0	25	66	53	183	8	4	36.3%	.207/.298/.426	93	.274	0.6	3B(105): -2, 1B(18): 1.1, RF(7): -0.3	0.8
2023 DC	*CHC*	*MLB*	*31*	*472*	*56*	*19*	*0*	*25*	*59*	*45*	*163*	*7*	*1*	*36.6%*	*.214/.302/.442*	*97*	*.284*	*2.5*	*3B 0, 1B 0*	*0.9*

Comparables: Todd Frazier (59), Jesús Aguilar (56), Josh Donaldson (53)

Wisdom may not hit righties very well, or have a lot of success at Wrigley Field, and he hit under .200 for the last two months of the season, but last year the 31-year-old utility *did* hit 25 home runs for the second time. He struggles with off-speed stuff, which he's seen more and more as the years have gone by, and he's most effective against hittable fastballs, but you know. Who isn't. Our new DRP metric judges him as a passable defender at multiple positions, so he should stick around as the Cubs hope to enter a new phase.

PITCHERS

Adbert Alzolay RHP Born: 03/01/95 Age: 28 Bats: R Throws: R Height: 6'1" Weight: 208 lb. Origin: International Free Agent, 2012

YEAR	TEAM	LVL	AGE	W	L	SV	G	GS	IP	H	HR	BB/9	K/9	K	GB%	BABIP	WHIP	ERA	DRA-	WARP	MPH	FB%	Whiff%	CSP
2020	CHC	MLB	25	1	1	0	6	4	21^{1}	12	1	5.5	12.2	29	43.2%	.256	1.17	2.95	86	0.3	94.7	52.2%	27.5%	47.1%
2021	CHC	MLB	26	5	13	1	29	21	125^{2}	112	25	2.4	9.2	128	43.8%	.270	1.16	4.58	83	2.3	93.8	52.6%	27.1%	56.4%
2022	IOW	AAA	27	0	1	0	4	4	9^{1}	10	1	5.8	11.6	12	54.2%	.391	1.71	6.75	86	0.2				
2022	CHC	MLB	27	2	1	0	6	0	13^{1}	9	1	1.4	12.8	19	40.0%	.276	0.83	3.38	85	0.2	95.0	47.5%	34.3%	55.9%
2023 DC	*CHC*	*MLB*	*28*	*7*	*3*	*0*	*53*	*3*	*57.3*	*50*	*7*	*3.4*	*10.1*	*64*	*43.2%*	*.299*	*1.26*	*3.52*	*87*	*0.7*	*94.1*	*52.2%*	*28.6%*	*55.0%*

Comparables: Hector Noesí (58), Danny Salazar (58), Dinelson Lamet (58)

Alzolay took a turn as the top pitcher in the Cubs' system before re-injuring a troublesome lat in spring training. When he ran out of gas in the second half, he got bumped into the bullpen, though it didn't dim his star. In limited relief time he thrived, the seamless transition a testament to the depth of the Cubs' arms. Alzolay's prominently used slider became so powerful that it evolved into two different breakers, with one having such severe movement it actually registered as a curve. He came in from the Chicago pen a few times in September and appeared up to the challenge.

Javier Assad RHP Born: 07/30/97 Age: 25 Bats: R Throws: R Height: 6'1" Weight: 200 lb. Origin: International Free Agent, 2015

YEAR	TEAM	LVL	AGE	W	L	SV	G	GS	IP	H	HR	BB/9	K/9	K	GB%	BABIP	WHIP	ERA	DRA-	WARP	MPH	FB%	Whiff%	CSP
2021	TNS	AA	23	4	8	0	21	20	93	111	12	3.1	7.2	74	41.8%	.341	1.54	5.32	119	0.0				
2022	TNS	AA	24	4	1	0	15	14	71^{2}	68	6	3.5	9.3	74	43.3%	.330	1.34	2.51	96	0.9				
2022	IOW	AAA	24	1	2	0	8	7	36^{2}	31	4	1.7	9.1	37	46.1%	.276	1.04	2.95	88	0.7				
2022	CHC	MLB	24	2	2	0	9	8	37^{2}	35	4	4.8	7.2	30	41.4%	.277	1.46	3.11	118	0.0	92.0	79.6%	23.2%	50.9%
2023 DC	*CHC*	*MLB*	*25*	*4*	*3*	*0*	*39*	*3*	*44.7*	*48*	*6*	*3.9*	*7.4*	*36*	*43.0%*	*.316*	*1.52*	*5.06*	*119*	*-0.1*	*92.0*	*79.6%*	*23.3%*	*50.9%*

Comparables: Alec Asher (68), Stephen Fife (68), Chase De Jong (66)

When Assad started the season in Double-A, he was a largely unrecognized Cubs pitching prospect floating in a sea of them. When he walked off the field after his major-league debut in late August, Cubs fans gave him a standing ovation. A lot can change in a couple of months when your sinker starts working. Relying on that pitch, a cutter and a four-seamer, Assad is now a part of the Cubs' legendary organizational pitching depth—which they plan to use both as a wide foundation for their rebuild and as an excuse not to spend a lot in free agency. Once projected to be a guy who could chew through a few innings at the back of a rotation, Assad's 2022 campaign made him part of Chicago's plans.

Brad Boxberger RHP Born: 05/27/88 Age: 35 Bats: R Throws: R Height: 5'10" Weight: 211 lb. Origin: Round 1, 2009 Draft (#43 overall)

YEAR	TEAM	LVL	AGE	W	L	SV	G	GS	IP	H	HR	BB/9	K/9	K	GB%	BABIP	WHIP	ERA	DRA-	WARP	MPH	FB%	Whiff%	CSP
2020	MIA	MLB	32	1	0	0	23	0	18	17	3	4.0	9.0	18	50.0%	.286	1.39	3.00	87	0.3	92.8	55.2%	24.2%	50.6%
2021	MIL	MLB	33	5	4	4	71	0	64^{2}	44	8	3.5	11.6	83	37.1%	.257	1.07	3.34	80	1.3	93.6	56.0%	32.0%	56.2%
2022	MIL	MLB	34	4	3	1	70	0	64	52	6	3.8	9.6	68	33.9%	.284	1.23	2.95	92	0.9	92.9	55.0%	24.5%	56.8%
2023 DC	*CHC*	*MLB*	*35*	*3*	*3*	*0*	*64*	*0*	*56*	*53*	*9*	*4.0*	*9.5*	*59*	*37.6%*	*.299*	*1.40*	*4.53*	*108*	*0.0*	*93.0*	*54.9%*	*26.0%*	*55.6%*

Comparables: Steve Cishek (63), Grant Balfour (63), Greg Holland (63)

Nine out of 10 dentists... er, I mean baseball experts, recommend Boxberger as a durable, reliable setup man suited for any bullpen configuration. The lone dissent comes from pitch-grading models, which tend to dislike all three of his offerings. The weird thing about Boxberger is that he gets away with throwing a ton of pitches in the zone. Common sense dictates that he should be getting punished for his arrogance, but in reality, Boxberger gets rewarded more often than not. As for explanations, two plausible theories stand above the rest. One is that Milwaukee deployed him in optimal situations so as to hide his weaknesses. The other is that Boxberger's stop-then-go delivery and unusually short extension create deception, an aspect for which publicly available models do not account. Whatever the reason may be, Boxberger accumulated a 3.15 ERA in 128⅔ innings for the Brewers. When in doubt, trust the track record—the Cubs did.

Steven Brault LHP Born: 04/29/92 Age: 31 Bats: L Throws: L Height: 6'0" Weight: 195 lb. Origin: Round 11, 2013 Draft (#339 overall)

YEAR	TEAM	LVL	AGE	W	L	SV	G	GS	IP	H	HR	BB/9	K/9	K	GB%	BABIP	WHIP	ERA	DRA-	WARP	MPH	FB%	Whiff%	CSP
2020	PIT	MLB	28	1	3	0	11	10	42^2	29	2	4.6	8.0	38	49.6%	.243	1.20	3.38	107	0.3	92.3	50.7%	23.9%	44.4%
2021	IND	AAA	29	0	1	0	3	3	11	6	2	0.8	7.4	9	53.6%	.154	0.64	1.64	111	0.1				
2021	PIT	MLB	29	0	3	0	7	7	27^2	33	3	3.9	6.2	19	42.1%	.330	1.63	5.86	128	-0.1	90.9	53.8%	20.7%	51.9%
2022	IOW	AAA	30	2	0	0	7	0	6	11	1	7.5	9.0	6	36.4%	.476	2.67	12.00	119	0.0				
2022	CHC	MLB	30	0	0	0	9	0	9	8	0	5.0	8.0	8	44.0%	.320	1.44	3.00	101	0.1	91.0	63.7%	29.7%	53.5%
2023 non-DC	*CHC*	*MLB*	*31*	*2*	*3*	*0*	*57*	*0*	*50*	*51*	*6*	*4.4*	*7.2*	*40*	*44.1%*	*.303*	*1.52*	*5.01*	*118*	*-0.3*	*91.7*	*57.8%*	*23.7%*	*48.1%*

Comparables: Chris Rusin (52), Tommy Milone (49), Héctor Santiago (49)

A free agent who'd wriggled free of the Pirates, Brault used his age-30 season to appear in nine big-league games without allowing an earned run until the last one. But that was after a lat injury prevented him from throwing a pitch, even in the minors, until July 1; what had been a major-league deal was reworked. When he finally got to Wrigley, the sinkerballer reaggravated the left lat—a malady that's becoming a career theme—and was placed on the COVID-19 IL later in the season, resulting in the single-digits innings total. He was pushed through waivers and became a minor-league free agent. He'll need to prove his durability to find a long-term home, though the Cubs brought him on for his final arbitration year.

Anderson Espinoza RHP Born: 03/09/98 Age: 25 Bats: R Throws: R Height: 6'0" Weight: 190 lb. Origin: International Free Agent, 2014

YEAR	TEAM	LVL	AGE	W	L	SV	G	GS	IP	H	HR	BB/9	K/9	K	GB%	BABIP	WHIP	ERA	DRA-	WARP	MPH	FB%	Whiff%	CSP
2021	FW	A+	23	0	1	0	12	12	28^2	29	3	4.1	11.6	37	44.6%	.366	1.47	5.02	76	0.7				
2021	SB	A+	23	1	2	0	5	5	16	10	1	6.2	15.2	27	27.6%	.321	1.31	5.06	74	0.4				
2021	TNS	AA	23	0	0	0	3	3	13^1	11	0	5.4	10.8	16	51.6%	.355	1.43	1.35	93	0.2				
2022	TNS	AA	24	1	4	0	13	12	44^1	40	10	5.1	11.0	54	30.9%	.303	1.47	7.11	121	-0.1				
2022	IOW	AAA	24	1	5	1	8	6	26	32	7	6.6	8.3	24	43.0%	.347	1.96	8.31	109	0.2				
2022	CHC	MLB	24	0	2	0	7	0	18^1	14	4	7.9	9.3	19	43.5%	.238	1.64	5.40	112	0.1	94.1	76.8%	25.4%	48.9%
2023 non-DC	*CHC*	*MLB*	*25*	*2*	*3*	*0*	*57*	*0*	*50*	*51*	*9*	*6.5*	*9.1*	*50*	*40.3%*	*.308*	*1.74*	*6.36*	*138*	*-0.8*	*94.1*	*76.8%*	*24.5%*	*48.9%*

Comparables: Alec Bettinger (48), Pedro Payano (46), Michael King (46)

In March 2021, Espinoza was a young Padres pitching prospect who'd had Tommy John twice and hadn't pitched off a mound since 2016. In March 2022, he was a young Cubs pitching prospect sitting in a dugout, rather than waiting for his next shot in a waiting room. It took Drew Smyly leaving a game with oblique soreness in late May for Espinoza to get in: He pitched four innings, allowing two runs on two hits while striking out six. He would come and go between the minors the rest of the way, as the Cubs veteran starters melted away (the next one Espinoza filled in for was Kyle Hendricks). The Cubs lost all seven of his major-league appearances, and he got tuned up to an 8.31 ERA at Triple-A (though he did make the start in a combined no-hitter), but time is on Espinoza's side. His youth leaves the window open for him to carve out an opportunity in a franchise full of them.

Jeremiah Estrada RHP Born: 11/01/98 Age: 24 Bats: S Throws: R Height: 6'1" Weight: 185 lb. Origin: Round 6, 2017 Draft (#195 overall)

YEAR	TEAM	LVL	AGE	W	L	SV	G	GS	IP	H	HR	BB/9	K/9	K	GB%	BABIP	WHIP	ERA	DRA-	WARP	MPH	FB%	Whiff%	CSP
2021	MB	A	22	1	1	0	11	2	23	18	2	2.3	14.9	38	29.2%	.356	1.04	1.57	64	0.7				
2022	SB	A+	23	2	2	5	15	0	23	14	1	3.9	15.3	39	36.6%	.325	1.04	1.17	64	0.7				
2022	TNS	AA	23	1	0	2	13	0	19^1	11	0	4.2	12.6	27	35.0%	.275	1.03	1.86	83	0.4				
2022	IOW	AAA	23	0	0	2	6	0	6	6	0	1.5	18.0	12	41.7%	.500	1.17	0.00	71	0.2				
2022	CHC	MLB	23	0	0	0	5	0	5^2	6	1	4.8	12.7	8	28.6%	.385	1.59	3.18	91	0.1	96.8	75.2%	31.8%	55.7%
2023 DC	*CHC*	*MLB*	*24*	*1*	*1*	*0*	*21*	*0*	*18.7*	*15*	*2*	*4.2*	*11.4*	*23*	*35.6%*	*.292*	*1.28*	*3.67*	*89*	*0.2*	*96.8*	*75.2%*	*32.6%*	*55.7%*

Comparables: Daniel Webb (42), Michael Tonkin (42), Addison Reed (40)

You hear this story a few times among Cubs pitching prospects: Missed time. Tommy John. Canceled season. Bout with COVID-19. Something to prove. But Estrada's comes with a twist: He adjusted the grip on his slider at High-A South Bend. Suddenly, he was blasting through every level of the Cubs system; he finished his minor-league résumé off with a 1.30 ERA and 78 strikeouts in 48⅓ IP. The 23-year-old was impressive enough that he got to pop out of the Cubs bullpen a few times, and he just kept missing bats in the bigs. If he keeps pitching like that, even a little bit, the Cubs are going to find him a job.

Jackson Ferris LHP Born: 01/15/04 Age: 19 Bats: L Throws: L Height: 6'4" Weight: 195 lb. Origin: Round 2, 2022 Draft (#47 overall)

People think life is so easy for the tall, but we have to deal with low-flying aircraft and reluctantly slam dunking for the crowd. At six-foot-four, Ferris has his own problems. His delivery can look like a machine of a thousand parts working together. Hitters struggle to see what's coming, but Ferris himself struggles to find consistency. That said, his velocity has jumped over the years—from low-90s to high-90s, all while maintaining that low-70s breaking stuff that can make a batter's life flash before their eyes. Ferris has enough promise to be yet another young pitcher who factors into this system; he's tall enough to provide indication of how high the upside goes.

Kyle Hendricks RHP Born: 12/07/89 Age: 33 Bats: R Throws: R Height: 6'3" Weight: 190 lb. Origin: Round 8, 2011 Draft (#264 overall)

YEAR	TEAM	LVL	AGE	W	L	SV	G	GS	IP	H	HR	BB/9	K/9	K	GB%	BABIP	WHIP	ERA	DRA-	WARP	MPH	FB%	Whiff%	CSP
2020	CHC	MLB	30	6	5	0	12	12	81^1	73	10	0.9	7.1	64	47.1%	.272	1.00	2.88	86	1.5	87.6	54.5%	25.0%	51.7%
2021	CHC	MLB	31	14	7	0	32	32	181	200	31	2.2	6.5	131	43.4%	.302	1.35	4.77	115	0.2	87.5	60.5%	20.1%	54.2%
2022	CHC	MLB	32	4	6	0	16	16	84^1	85	15	2.6	7.0	66	36.3%	.285	1.29	4.80	118	0.0	86.9	57.5%	24.0%	51.5%
2023 DC	*CHC*	*MLB*	*33*	*7*	*8*	*0*	*24*	*24*	*126.3*	*132*	*19*	*2.2*	*7.3*	*102*	*40.5%*	*.303*	*1.30*	*4.21*	*106*	*0.7*	*87.2*	*59.1%*	*22.5%*	*53.0%*

Comparables: Charles Nagy (82), Brad Penny (82), Freddy Garcia (81)

Hendricks was out in Arizona as the Cubs finished their season, building up his core strength before tinkering with his delivery to fix a few things. One such thing: since 2014, when he debuted, Hendricks has given up the second-most first inning home runs (41) of any pitcher. Chicago wanted him to play the role of "weathered old-timer" while also rediscovering his spirit and prowess from 2016-17—back when he threw his sinker way more than his other offerings, instead of just slightly more like today. And as anyone who's ever tried to recapture their former glory as they get older will tell you: It's extremely easy and works every time.

Codi Heuer RHP Born: 07/03/96 Age: 27 Bats: R Throws: R Height: 6'5" Weight: 200 lb. Origin: Round 6, 2018 Draft (#168 overall)

YEAR	TEAM	LVL	AGE	W	L	SV	G	GS	IP	H	HR	BB/9	K/9	K	GB%	BABIP	WHIP	ERA	DRA-	WARP	MPH	FB%	Whiff%	CSP
2020	CHW	MLB	23	3	0	1	21	0	23^2	12	1	3.4	9.5	25	50.0%	.193	0.89	1.52	87	0.4	97.8	65.8%	33.9%	46.6%
2021	CHW	MLB	24	4	1	0	40	0	38^2	45	5	2.3	9.1	39	43.1%	.367	1.42	5.12	91	0.5	96.6	53.1%	29.5%	54.9%
2021	CHC	MLB	24	3	3	2	25	0	28^2	20	2	4.1	5.3	17	42.9%	.225	1.15	3.14	121	0.0	95.0	61.2%	25.9%	54.4%
2023 DC	*CHC*	*MLB*	*26*	*2*	*2*	*3*	*43*	*0*	*37.3*	*38*	*4*	*3.5*	*8.4*	*34*	*47.3%*	*.316*	*1.41*	*4.27*	*103*	*0.1*	*96.2*	*58.0%*	*28.3%*	*53.2%*

Comparables: Carlos Estévez (79), Mike Morin (79), Cla Meredith (76)

Heuer put up staggering numbers as a 23-year-old prospect in 2020, a sizzling heater and gutting slider setting him up to dispatch hitters late in games. During a far-less-dominant 2021 campaign he was dealt to the Cubs in the Craig Kimbrel trade, where he managed to find his fastball again for 25 games. Sadly, during last spring training, an MRI revealed Heuer's right UCL had completely ripped off the bone and suddenly his next appearance was pushed back to mid-2023—he might've gone under the knife earlier, but couldn't technically communicate directly with team officials due to the owner-imposed lockout. If things go well, there's a role for Heuer when he gets back, and frankly, he's due for things to get a little better.

Brandon Hughes LHP Born: 12/01/95 Age: 27 Bats: S Throws: L Height: 6'2" Weight: 215 lb. Origin: Round 16, 2017 Draft (#495 overall)

YEAR	TEAM	LVL	AGE	W	L	SV	G	GS	IP	H	HR	BB/9	K/9	K	GB%	BABIP	WHIP	ERA	DRA-	WARP	MPH	FB%	Whiff%	CSP
2021	SB	A+	25	2	1	0	8	0	11^1	7	1	3.2	13.5	17	33.3%	.261	0.97	1.59	86	0.2				
2021	TNS	AA	25	0	0	1	18	0	30^2	24	3	3.8	12.6	43	32.9%	.318	1.21	1.76	78	0.7				
2022	TNS	AA	26	0	0	1	5	0	6^1	1	0	1.4	14.2	10	18.2%	.091	0.32	0.00	92	0.1				
2022	IOW	AAA	26	1	0	0	5	0	10^1	4	0	1.7	10.5	12	31.8%	.182	0.58	0.00	88	0.2				
2022	CHC	MLB	26	2	3	8	57	0	57^2	42	11	3.3	10.6	68	34.0%	.233	1.09	3.12	85	1.0	93.4	53.2%	33.4%	52.7%
2023 DC	*CHC*	*MLB*	*27*	*3*	*3*	*20*	*64*	*0*	*56*	*46*	*8*	*3.5*	*10.7*	*66*	*35.2%*	*.289*	*1.22*	*3.56*	*88*	*0.6*	*93.4*	*53.2%*	*31.2%*	*52.7%*

Comparables: Brad Wieck (58), Ryan O'Rourke (57), Jeff Beliveau (57)

Making his debut in May, Hughes was the first Cubs pitcher since 1974 to strike out the first four MLB batters he faced. He also threw the last pitch of the Chicago season, inducing a flyout to center to seal a 15-2 win. From beginning to end, the 27-year-old lefty (and converted outfielder) established himself as a reliable arm, with a four-seamer to set hitters up and a slider to put them away. Hughes' debut earned him consideration among the crop of promising arms to emerge in Wrigley, and he'll look to solidify a role as a late-inning reliever.

Ryan Jensen RHP Born: 11/23/97 Age: 25 Bats: R Throws: R Height: 6'0" Weight: 190 lb. Origin: Round 1, 2019 Draft (#27 overall)

YEAR	TEAM	LVL	AGE	W	L	SV	G	GS	IP	H	HR	BB/9	K/9	K	GB%	BABIP	WHIP	ERA	DRA-	WARP	MPH	FB%	Whiff%	CSP
2021	SB	A+	23	2	7	0	16	16	62	42	8	3.5	10.9	75	53.3%	.239	1.06	4.50	78	1.4				
2021	TNS	AA	23	1	0	0	4	4	18	14	2	3.5	7.5	15	60.4%	.261	1.17	3.00	99	0.2				
2022	TNS	AA	24	2	4	0	17	17	59^1	44	5	5.9	9.1	60	51.9%	.258	1.40	4.25	98	0.6				
2023 non-DC	*CHC*	*MLB*	*25*	*2*	*3*	*0*	*57*	*0*	*50*	*51*	*6*	*5.8*	*7.8*	*43*	*51.2%*	*.303*	*1.66*	*5.42*	*125*	*-0.5*			*25.9%*	

Comparables: Mike Baumann (73), Aaron Northcraft (73), Michael Kelly (72)

The most important thing Jensen did in 2022 was go on the development list, a "time out" for minor leaguers to fix something away from the heat of competition. There, the wide radius of his delivery was addressed, and when he—or the pod person he was replaced with—returned, his arm action had shortened and remained above his knees. Jensen was able to pitch with more consistency, shrinking his walk total with an output that could suddenly be fine-tuned. After handing out 14 walks in his first 16⅓ innings, he allowed only one in his next 10, attacking the strike zone with a fastball hitting 99 mph and a slider reaching 89. It was a fun three-game stretch; tragically, his command slipped again, and the walks piled up thereafter.

Anthony Kay LHP Born: 03/21/95 Age: 28 Bats: L Throws: L Height: 6'0" Weight: 225 lb. Origin: Round 1, 2016 Draft (#31 overall)

YEAR	TEAM	LVL	AGE	W	L	SV	G	GS	IP	H	HR	BB/9	K/9	K	GB%	BABIP	WHIP	ERA	DRA-	WARP	MPH	FB%	Whiff%	CSP
2020	TOR	MLB	25	2	0	0	13	0	21	22	3	6.0	9.4	22	37.1%	.322	1.71	5.14	114	0.1	93.8	56.5%	26.1%	46.8%
2021	BUF	AAA	26	0	4	0	8	8	26^{1}	31	5	4.4	9.9	29	33.8%	.347	1.67	8.89	109	0.2				
2021	TOR	MLB	26	1	2	0	11	5	33^{2}	38	7	4.8	10.4	39	47.9%	.348	1.66	5.61	100	0.3	94.4	58.4%	25.9%	49.0%
2022	BUF	AAA	27	1	3	0	8	1	14	18	4	7.1	9.6	15	51.2%	.359	2.07	8.36	107	0.1				
2022	TOR	MLB	27	0	0	0	1	0	2	2	0	4.5	13.5	3	20.0%	.400	1.50	4.50	132	0.0	94.5	61.5%	35.3%	40.5%
2023 DC	*CHC*	*MLB*	*28*	*1*	*1*	*0*	*28*	*0*	*24.7*	*25*	*3*	*4.8*	*8.6*	*23*	*44.0%*	*.313*	*1.54*	*4.97*	*115*	*-0.1*	*94.2*	*58.3%*	*25.3%*	*47.5%*

Comparables: Brad Mills (66), Dillon Peters (56), Bryan Mitchell (56)

Sixty-plus minor-league starts with an ERA north of 4.00 would have most minor-leaguers anxiously combing the classifieds, awaiting dreaded news. Most minor-leaguers are not former first-rounders, and former first-rounders are often afforded mighty long leashes. Kay has tinkered with his arsenal over the years, adding a cutter and a slider, then nixing his cutter and changeup as he transitioned to relief. Alas, none of those tweaks has produced particularly encouraging results. In this day and age—and in most of them, really—throwing 60% fastballs alongside secondaries you can't command is a death wish, and Kay's small sample of MLB results attest to that. His full-time transition into the 'pen should make it easier for him to find a role in Toronto, but regardless of how he's deployed, he needs to settle on a suite of offerings that he knows will be effective against big-league hitters.

Mark Leiter Jr. RHP Born: 03/13/91 Age: 32 Bats: R Throws: R Height: 6'0" Weight: 210 lb. Origin: Round 22, 2013 Draft (#661 overall)

YEAR	TEAM	LVL	AGE	W	L	SV	G	GS	IP	H	HR	BB/9	K/9	K	GB%	BABIP	WHIP	ERA	DRA-	WARP	MPH	FB%	Whiff%	CSP
2021	ERI	AA	30	2	4	0	8	4	25^{2}	25	4	2.8	12.3	35	34.8%	.350	1.29	5.26	89	0.4				
2021	TOL	AAA	30	8	4	0	17	15	89	67	10	2.3	11.1	110	46.4%	.275	1.01	3.34	83	2.1				
2022	IOW	AAA	31	0	3	0	6	6	22	21	4	2.5	13.1	32	30.9%	.333	1.23	5.32	79	0.5				
2022	CHC	MLB	31	2	7	3	35	4	67^{2}	52	10	3.3	9.7	73	48.0%	.251	1.14	3.99	85	1.2	91.3	45.9%	29.3%	52.8%
2023 DC	*CHC*	*MLB*	*32*	*3*	*3*	*0*	*64*	*0*	*56*	*52*	*8*	*3.1*	*9.0*	*55*	*44.5%*	*.298*	*1.29*	*4.05*	*99*	*0.3*	*91.3*	*45.9%*	*27.1%*	*52.8%*

Comparables: Carlos Torres (49), Shane Greene (48), Josh A. Smith (48)

Entering the All-Star Break with a 5.35 ERA after surrendering a pair of home runs in his final first-half showing, it appeared Leiter Jr. might flame out of the majors even faster the second time (he pitched in 47 Phillies and Jays games between 2017-18). Instead, across the second half he made as strong a claim for a roster spot as he could, compiling a 2.17 ERA. He enters his age-32 season with six different pitches at his disposal; if not for that finish, he'd be looking at a fight for a middle relief role, potentially in numerous training camps. Especially given the .571 OPS to which he held lefties, though, Leiter earned another long look in Chicago.

Manuel Rodríguez RHP Born: 08/06/96 Age: 26 Bats: R Throws: R Height: 5'11" Weight: 210 lb. Origin: International Free Agent, 2016

YEAR	TEAM	LVL	AGE	W	L	SV	G	GS	IP	H	HR	BB/9	K/9	K	GB%	BABIP	WHIP	ERA	DRA-	WARP	MPH	FB%	Whiff%	CSP
2021	TNS	AA	24	1	1	4	13	0	13^{1}	8	1	6.7	12.8	19	63.0%	.269	1.35	2.03	90	0.2				
2021	IOW	AAA	24	0	0	1	7	0	7^{1}	6	0	2.5	9.8	8	61.1%	.333	1.09	0.00	91	0.1				
2021	CHC	MLB	24	3	3	1	20	0	17^{2}	18	3	6.1	8.2	16	53.7%	.294	1.70	6.11	113	0.0	97.2	71.7%	24.6%	53.9%
2022	IOW	AAA	25	1	0	1	5	0	5	8	2	1.8	18.0	10	36.4%	.667	1.80	9.00	78	0.1				
2022	CHC	MLB	25	2	0	4	14	0	13^{2}	10	1	5.9	5.3	8	52.5%	.231	1.39	3.29	115	0.0	96.0	64.0%	22.4%	45.8%
2023 DC	*CHC*	*MLB*	*26*	*3*	*3*	*3*	*64*	*0*	*56*	*61*	*7*	*5.3*	*9.3*	*57*	*51.4%*	*.342*	*1.69*	*5.72*	*127*	*-0.5*	*96.6*	*68.0%*	*27.9%*	*50.1%*

Comparables: Chad Sobotka (50), Angel Nesbitt (49), Scott Oberg (49)

Rodríguez finished 2021 with a clear task list: Cut down on the walks, maintain the high-90s heaters and continue keeping the ball on the ground. Things had been a bit wobbly in his brief stretch with the big club that year, but he tightened things up a bit in his limited playing time in 2022. Of course, this comes with the caveat that he didn't make his first appearance until late August thanks to a stint on the 60-day IL with an elbow strain, at one point recording a blown save and a win in a single game. He is another example of a pitcher with some promise whom the Cubs had to decide between rostering or risking on waivers.

Michael Rucker RHP Born: 04/27/94 Age: 29 Bats: R Throws: R Height: 6'1" Weight: 195 lb. Origin: Round 11, 2016 Draft (#344 overall)

YEAR	TEAM	LVL	AGE	W	L	SV	G	GS	IP	H	HR	BB/9	K/9	K	GB%	BABIP	WHIP	ERA	DRA-	WARP	MPH	FB%	Whiff%	CSP
2021	IOW	AAA	27	3	0	0	19	0	39^{1}	44	8	2.1	11.2	49	46.7%	.364	1.35	4.81	81	0.9				
2021	CHC	MLB	27	0	0	1	20	0	28^{1}	32	5	3.5	9.5	30	45.8%	.346	1.52	6.99	96	0.3	94.4	61.4%	30.3%	50.6%
2022	IOW	AAA	28	1	0	0	10	0	15^{1}	15	0	4.7	7.6	13	48.9%	.319	1.50	1.17	104	0.2				
2022	CHC	MLB	28	3	1	0	41	0	54^{2}	50	8	3.3	8.2	50	44.7%	.278	1.28	3.95	97	0.6	94.9	44.0%	26.8%	52.3%
2023 DC	*CHC*	*MLB*	*29*	*1*	*1*	*0*	*36*	*0*	*31*	*32*	*4*	*3.4*	*9.1*	*31*	*44.6%*	*.324*	*1.42*	*4.57*	*109*	*0.0*	*94.7*	*49.0%*	*26.2%*	*51.9%*

Comparables: Rob Scahill (64), Tyler Duffey (60), Deolis Guerra (58)

It's a tough time to try and distinguish yourself as a young Cubs pitcher, but Rucker gave it his best shot, allowing three runs in 11 September appearances after being trusted with a more prominent bullpen role. The velocity has historically been higher in a relief role, hitting the mid-90s instead of the low-90s, and it plays up, given that Rucker's command over his changeup and slider is part of what originally got him noticed. There's one word to describe the Cubs staff's second-half performance: solid. After the break, opponents hit under .200 against Rucker at Wrigley Field, and his ERA was cut by nearly half, helping him be just as non-liquid as his teammates.

Adrian Sampson RHP Born: 10/07/91 Age: 31 Bats: R Throws: R Height: 6'2" Weight: 210 lb. Origin: Round 5, 2012 Draft (#166 overall)

YEAR	TEAM	LVL	AGE	W	L	SV	G	GS	IP	H	HR	BB/9	K/9	K	GB%	BABIP	WHIP	ERA	DRA-	WARP	MPH	FB%	Whiff%	CSP
2021	IOW	AAA	29	4	5	0	16	14	81^2	92	19	3.6	6.7	61	37.3%	.304	1.53	4.96	125	0.1				
2021	CHC	MLB	29	1	2	0	10	5	35^1	30	8	2.0	7.1	28	43.7%	.234	1.08	2.80	102	0.3	92.0	58.8%	21.5%	51.9%
2022	IOW	AAA	30	0	3	0	8	6	28^1	29	6	2.2	5.7	18	41.1%	.258	1.27	3.81	117	0.1				
2022	CHC	MLB	30	4	5	0	21	19	104^1	101	10	2.3	6.3	73	41.1%	.288	1.23	3.11	115	0.2	92.4	65.5%	21.1%	50.9%
2023 DC	*CHC*	*MLB*	*31*	*5*	*7*	*0*	*30*	*16*	*85.3*	*99*	*14*	*2.8*	*5.9*	*55*	*40.8%*	*.309*	*1.47*	*5.33*	*128*	*-0.6*	*92.4*	*62.2%*	*20.4%*	*50.9%*

Comparables: Josh Towers (53), Iván Nova (53), Brett Anderson (52)

Sampson made six starts in September, logging a 1.50 ERA across more innings (36) than any other month. That put him among the lowest ERAs in baseball in that span, alongside Yu Darvish and Julio Urías. A few of the five teams he faced were even competitive! (And a few were the Reds.) For a 30-year-old starter who has struggled to find and keep big-league work, that's something, as was crossing the 100-inning threshold for the second time in his career. It's how you get tendered a guaranteed big-league contract for the first time, along with the attendant, low-engagement announcement tweet.

Drew Smyly LHP Born: 06/13/89 Age: 34 Bats: L Throws: L Height: 6'2" Weight: 188 lb. Origin: Round 2, 2010 Draft (#68 overall)

YEAR	TEAM	LVL	AGE	W	L	SV	G	GS	IP	H	HR	BB/9	K/9	K	GB%	BABIP	WHIP	ERA	DRA-	WARP	MPH	FB%	Whiff%	CSP
2020	SF	MLB	31	0	1	0	7	5	26^1	20	2	3.1	14.4	42	41.7%	.310	1.10	3.42	57	0.7	93.8	45.6%	34.7%	50.8%
2021	ATL	MLB	32	11	4	0	29	23	126^2	133	27	2.9	8.3	117	38.4%	.300	1.37	4.48	104	0.9	92.2	46.7%	25.2%	57.9%
2022	CHC	MLB	33	7	8	0	22	22	106^1	101	16	2.2	7.7	91	40.6%	.275	1.19	3.47	110	0.5	92.8	37.6%	25.4%	58.1%
2023 DC	*CHC*	*MLB*	*34*	*7*	*7*	*0*	*44*	*16*	*102.7*	*105*	*16*	*2.8*	*7.7*	*87*	*39.3%*	*.300*	*1.33*	*4.24*	*106*	*0.5*	*92.4*	*42.8%*	*25.8%*	*56.2%*

Comparables: Floyd Bannister (75), Ricky Nolasco (73), Ian Kennedy (72)

Look, you know Smyly. After Tommy John, he was sequestered to a series of minor-league deals, waiting to be signed by weakly smiling GMs looking to fill out pedestrian rotations. Then he helped the Braves win the World Series. Despite a flare-up of oblique soreness in late May and a shoulder issue in September, Smyly kept leaning on his curve and slider to be an effective member of the Cubs' veteran rotational front. He said he wanted to return to Chicago for his age-34 season, and the team proved equally interested; he's back, so you know what to expect.

Justin Steele LHP Born: 07/11/95 Age: 27 Bats: L Throws: L Height: 6'2" Weight: 205 lb. Origin: Round 5, 2014 Draft (#139 overall)

YEAR	TEAM	LVL	AGE	W	L	SV	G	GS	IP	H	HR	BB/9	K/9	K	GB%	BABIP	WHIP	ERA	DRA-	WARP	MPH	FB%	Whiff%	CSP
2021	IOW	AAA	25	2	0	0	9	5	27^1	14	1	4.3	9.5	29	50.7%	.197	0.99	1.32	93	0.5				
2021	CHC	MLB	25	4	4	0	20	9	57	50	12	4.3	9.3	59	49.7%	.264	1.35	4.26	97	0.6	93.3	65.9%	27.6%	54.4%
2022	CHC	MLB	26	4	7	0	24	24	119	111	8	3.8	9.5	126	51.1%	.318	1.35	3.18	93	1.6	92.3	64.3%	24.1%	56.6%
2023 DC	*CHC*	*MLB*	*27*	*7*	*7*	*0*	*24*	*24*	*123.7*	*121*	*13*	*4.2*	*8.7*	*119*	*49.4%*	*.312*	*1.44*	*4.22*	*101*	*0.9*	*92.5*	*64.7%*	*25.2%*	*56.1%*

Comparables: Framber Valdez (60), Drew Pomeranz (58), Héctor Santiago (58)

Steele pitched well enough in 2022 that David Ross gave him a month off at the end of the season (his back issues were also, potentially, a part of this decision). The southpaw was the Cubs' strikeout leader before he went down, having cultivated a 32.7% whiff rate with his signature slider. No Cub ended up topping his 126 punchouts. Steele spent the summer as one of the better arms in baseball, building the confidence of Cubs fans that the light at the end of the tunnel is near. It's probably not, but every time somebody breaks out, they get a little closer.

Marcus Stroman RHP Born: 05/01/91 Age: 32 Bats: R Throws: R Height: 5'7" Weight: 180 lb. Origin: Round 1, 2012 Draft (#22 overall)

YEAR	TEAM	LVL	AGE	W	L	SV	G	GS	IP	H	HR	BB/9	K/9	K	GB%	BABIP	WHIP	ERA	DRA-	WARP	MPH	FB%	Whiff%	CSP
2021	NYM	MLB	30	10	13	0	33	33	179	161	17	2.2	7.9	158	49.5%	.289	1.15	3.02	87	2.9	92.1	43.9%	26.8%	55.0%
2022	CHC	MLB	31	6	7	0	25	25	138^2	123	16	2.3	7.7	119	51.5%	.272	1.15	3.50	90	2.1	92.2	47.8%	22.5%	56.0%
2023 DC	*CHC*	*MLB*	*32*	*9*	*8*	*0*	*27*	*27*	*151.3*	*155*	*15*	*2.5*	*7.0*	*117*	*51.3%*	*.303*	*1.30*	*3.69*	*95*	*1.7*	*92.3*	*44.9%*	*23.4%*	*54.0%*

Comparables: Kevin Brown (78), Roy Oswalt (77), Claude Osteen (77)

Stroman's deal has two more years and a player opt-out clause. That might not line up with the next time the Cubs play in October; after his first year in Chicago, that's a shame. Stroman, despite some shoulder inflammation and a COVID-19 IL stint, was everything the Cubs could have hoped. He had the second-highest strikeout total and strikeout-to-walk ratio on the roster, setting hitters up with a low-90s sinker and finishing them off with his slider. Stro was comfortable enough to profess his love of the Cubs in public, saying he was ready to be recruited by a club just a few pieces away. There are divergent opinions on that matter—but regardless, the Cubs got a good year from a pitcher who wants to play for them.

Jameson Taillon RHP Born: 11/18/91 Age: 31 Bats: R Throws: R Height: 6'5" Weight: 230 lb. Origin: Round 1, 2010 Draft (#2 overall)

YEAR	TEAM	LVL	AGE	W	L	SV	G	GS	IP	H	HR	BB/9	K/9	K	GB%	BABIP	WHIP	ERA	DRA-	WARP	MPH	FB%	Whiff%	CSP
2021	NYY	MLB	29	8	6	0	29	29	144^1	130	24	2.7	8.7	140	33.9%	.273	1.21	4.30	104	1.1	94.0	55.1%	26.5%	55.6%
2022	NYY	MLB	30	14	5	0	32	32	177^1	168	26	1.6	7.7	151	40.4%	.278	1.13	3.91	97	2.0	93.8	57.7%	23.1%	53.4%
2023 DC	*CHC*	*MLB*	*31*	*8*	*8*	*0*	*25*	*25*	*139.7*	*139*	*19*	*2.1*	*7.3*	*113*	*39.5%*	*.292*	*1.23*	*3.72*	*96*	*1.5*	*93.9*	*56.4%*	*23.9%*	*54.1%*

Comparables: Charles Nagy (79), Rick Wise (79), Brad Penny (78)

Taillon has been through significant adversity throughout his career, but has generally been a reliable force in the Yankees' rotation since his acquisition prior to the 2021 season. He's not afraid to make adjustments on the fly; he went from being a sinkerballer in Pittsburgh to a high-heat hurler at the beginning of the Yankees tenure, and since has become much more crafty and unpredictable, adding a cutter in a few weeks into the 2022 season to give him a true six-pitch mix. Thirty-two starts' worth of slightly above-average pitching doesn't grow on trees, and with Taillon entering free agency for the first time this winter, it wasn't a bad time to show off a clean bill of health. He'll join the elder contingent of the Cubs' Spring/Fall rotation.

Keegan Thompson RHP
Born: 03/13/95 Age: 28 Bats: R Throws: R Height: 6'1" Weight: 210 lb. Origin: Round 3, 2017 Draft (#105 overall)

YEAR	TEAM	LVL	AGE	W	L	SV	G	GS	IP	H	HR	BB/9	K/9	K	GB%	BABIP	WHIP	ERA	DRA-	WARP	MPH	FB%	Whiff%	CSP
2021	IOW	AAA	26	0	0	0	4	4	14^{2}	5	0	3.1	9.8	16	34.4%	.156	0.68	0.00	92	0.3				
2021	CHC	MLB	26	3	3	1	32	6	53^{1}	48	9	5.2	9.3	55	42.2%	.273	1.48	3.38	101	0.5	92.7	74.7%	23.8%	56.6%
2022	CHC	MLB	27	10	5	1	29	17	115	103	16	3.4	8.5	108	40.3%	.282	1.27	3.76	103	1.0	93.8	52.3%	24.6%	54.6%
2023 DC	*CHC*	*MLB*	*28*	*9*	*4*	*0*	*67*	*3*	*70.3*	*68*	*10*	*4.0*	*8.9*	*69*	*40.6%*	*.304*	*1.41*	*4.50*	*107*	*0.1*	*93.5*	*58.6%*	*24.4%*	*55.2%*

Comparables: Tyler Pill (65), Nick Pivetta (61), Adrian Houser (60)

Baseball is 80% spreadsheets now. To the folks in the biggest offices with the priciest lunch orders, versatility is value—especially in a rebuild. So Thompson made a lot of friends in the Cubs organization last year by making starts, coming in from the bullpen for high-leverage situations and throwing multiple innings of relief when needed. Part of that cameo in the rotation was due to injury, but the 28-year-old righty continued to provide depth—actual, effective depth, not just a pitcher filling what would otherwise be an empty spreadsheet cell—no matter where he was stationed.

Hayden Wesneski RHP
Born: 12/05/97 Age: 25 Bats: R Throws: R Height: 6'3" Weight: 210 lb. Origin: Round 6, 2019 Draft (#195 overall)

YEAR	TEAM	LVL	AGE	W	L	SV	G	GS	IP	H	HR	BB/9	K/9	K	GB%	BABIP	WHIP	ERA	DRA-	WARP	MPH	FB%	Whiff%	CSP
2021	HV	A+	23	1	1	0	7	7	36^{1}	24	2	2.2	11.6	47	51.9%	.293	0.91	1.49	77	0.8				
2021	SOM	AA	23	8	4	0	15	15	83	76	11	2.4	10.0	92	43.6%	.305	1.18	4.01	94	1.0				
2021	SWB	AAA	23	2	1	0	3	2	11	10	0	4.1	9.8	12	41.4%	.345	1.36	3.27	99	0.2				
2022	SWB	AAA	24	6	7	0	19	19	89^{2}	75	9	2.8	8.3	83	40.9%	.270	1.15	3.51	95	1.5				
2022	IOW	AAA	24	0	2	0	5	4	20^{2}	17	1	3.5	10.0	23	47.2%	.308	1.21	5.66	96	0.3				
2022	CHC	MLB	24	3	2	0	6	4	33	24	3	1.9	9.0	33	46.1%	.244	0.94	2.18	98	0.3	92.4	60.0%	25.7%	56.2%
2023 DC	*CHC*	*MLB*	*25*	*6*	*6*	*0*	*42*	*14*	*90.3*	*89*	*11*	*3.1*	*8.3*	*83*	*44.6%*	*.308*	*1.34*	*4.06*	*100*	*0.6*	*92.4*	*60.0%*	*26.2%*	*56.2%*

Comparables: Joe Ryan (70), A.J. Griffin (69), Kyle Hendricks (67)

The Cubs have struggled to reliably develop pitching, especially starting pitching, so in acquiring Wesneski in a trade for reliever Scott Effross, they imported what they haven't been able to gin up at home. But there's a bit of irony in that deal as well, in that Effross is one of the few pitchers that really did blossom while in Chicago's pipeline. Where Wesneski struggled in four post-trade starts in Iowa, he flourished under the bright lights in Chicago, whiffing a batter per inning in his September call-up. Armed with a fourth-starter's repertoire, Wesneski attacks hitters with a five-pitch mix, including two fastballs, a slider, a cutter and changeup. His success in the majors came from leaning heavily on the slider, his best secondary, throwing it over 30% of the time—good for a plurality of his pitches. Wesneski offers upside beyond the back-of-the-rotation starter he presents as, but he'll need to find another bat-misser among his many offerings to get there.

Rowan Wick RHP
Born: 11/09/92 Age: 30 Bats: L Throws: R Height: 6'3" Weight: 234 lb. Origin: Round 9, 2012 Draft (#300 overall)

YEAR	TEAM	LVL	AGE	W	L	SV	G	GS	IP	H	HR	BB/9	K/9	K	GB%	BABIP	WHIP	ERA	DRA-	WARP	MPH	FB%	Whiff%	CSP
2020	CHC	MLB	27	0	1	4	19	0	17^{1}	18	1	3.1	10.4	20	39.6%	.362	1.38	3.12	97	0.2	95.0	65.8%	25.5%	48.1%
2021	CHC	MLB	28	0	1	5	22	0	23	17	1	5.5	11.3	29	34.5%	.296	1.35	4.30	98	0.2	94.6	68.5%	29.5%	54.4%
2022	CHC	MLB	29	4	7	9	64	0	64	79	9	4.1	9.7	69	43.1%	.378	1.69	4.22	98	0.7	95.1	61.9%	23.6%	56.0%
2023 DC	*CHC*	*MLB*	*30*	*3*	*3*	*6*	*64*	*0*	*56*	*54*	*7*	*4.0*	*9.0*	*55*	*42.8%*	*.311*	*1.42*	*4.28*	*103*	*0.1*	*95.1*	*63.9%*	*25.3%*	*54.5%*

Comparables: Danny Farquhar (64), Evan Scribner (58), Juan Minaya (58)

Right now, there are a lot of job openings on the Cubs pitching staff. One day, you're clapping the dirt out of your cleats while the crowd cheers on some other guy. The next, you're getting his innings because he got moved at the trade deadline. Wick, a 30-year-old Canadian righty closing in on 150 games of big-league experience, had a chance in the second half to finally ink himself into Chicago's depth chart, perhaps as a late-inning relief option. But the inconsistency that's plagued him throughout his career reared its ugly head, and he again finished the year without any certainty about his future (though he did tighten up in September/October, allowing only two runs and four walks in 8⅔ innings).

Jordan Wicks LHP
Born: 09/01/99 Age: 23 Bats: L Throws: L Height: 6'3" Weight: 220 lb. Origin: Round 1, 2021 Draft (#21 overall)

YEAR	TEAM	LVL	AGE	W	L	SV	G	GS	IP	H	HR	BB/9	K/9	K	GB%	BABIP	WHIP	ERA	DRA-	WARP	MPH	FB%	Whiff%	CSP
2021	SB	A+	21	0	0	0	4	4	7	7	0	3.9	6.4	5	37.5%	.304	1.43	5.14	117	0.0				
2022	SB	A+	22	4	3	0	16	16	66^{2}	66	5	2.3	11.6	86	45.1%	.363	1.25	3.65	69	1.8				
2022	TNS	AA	22	0	3	0	8	8	28	24	5	3.5	11.3	35	50.0%	.284	1.25	4.18	83	0.5				
2023 non-DC	*CHC*	*MLB*	*23*	*2*	*2*	*0*	*57*	*0*	*50*	*50*	*6*	*3.9*	*8.4*	*46*	*44.6%*	*.308*	*1.44*	*4.51*	*111*	*-0.1*			*27.5%*	

Comparables: Luis Leroy Cruz (65), Nik Turley (62), Chris Reed (62)

By the end of the season, the best way to find Wicks' name on the internet was in prospective Cubs trade packages for Shohei Ohtani. This at least means he had a good enough year to be considered tradable for one of the two best players on the planet. Wicks was considered a top-10 Cubs prospect at the time of his mid-season promotion to Double-A Tennessee, with his last High-A start being a five-inning, 10-strikeout performance. After allowing 10 hits and four home runs across his first two starts with the Smokies, the 23-year-old settled in for the remainder of the season (barring a disastrous late-August appearance that lasted one inning).

Lineouts

Hitters

HITTER	POS	TEAM	LVL	AGE	PA	R	2B	3B	HR	RBI	BB	K	SB	CS	AVG/OBP/SLG	DRC+	BABIP	BRR	DRP	WARP
Ben DeLuzio	CF	MEM	AAA	27	408	60	16	6	9	49	36	91	30	6	.277/.353/.429	101	.347	2.5	CF(85): -1.6, LF(2): -0.2	1.1
	CF	STL	MLB	27	25	3	1	0	0	0	3	5	0	1	.150/.292/.200	96	.200	-0.2	CF(18): -0.2	0.0
Cristian Hernández	IF	CUB	ROK	18	175	21	4	1	3	21	13	53	6	3	.261/.320/.357		.365			
P.J. Higgins	C/1B	IOW	AAA	29	86	9	8	0	1	17	12	16	1	0	.417/.500/.569	110	.518	0.1	C(13): -0.2, 1B(3): 0.1, 3B(3): -0.4	0.3
	C/1B	CHC	MLB	29	229	23	11	1	6	30	22	58	0	0	.229/.310/.383	91	.290	-2.5	1B(38): 1.7, C(34): -2, 3B(4): -0.6	0.1
Kevin Made	SS	MB	A	19	257	41	14	0	9	30	27	49	0	1	.266/.354/.450	117	.299	1.5	SS(50): -1.6	1.2
	SS	SB	A+	19	151	14	6	1	1	14	19	31	3	0	.162/.267/.246	96	.202	0.8	SS(35): 4.7	1.0
Miles Mastrobuoni	UT	DUR	AAA	26	573	92	32	3	16	64	63	95	23	3	.300/.377/.469	131	.342	0.4	2B(57): -4.0, RF(24): 0.3, LF(19): 1.2	3.5
	UT	TB	MLB	26	17	1	0	0	0	0	1	6	1	0	.188/.235/.188	83	.300	0.6	2B(6): 0, RF(3): 0	0.1
Christopher Paciolla	SS	CUB	ROK	18	25	2	0	0	1	3	2	7	1	0	.143/.280/.286		.154			
Frank Schwindel	1B/DH	IOW	AAA	30	37	5	3	0	1	4	0	8	0	0	.216/.216/.378	92	.250	-1.3	1B(6): 0.3	0.0
	1B/DH	CHC	MLB	30	292	23	11	0	8	36	19	58	0	0	.229/.277/.358	95	.261	-0.6	1B(48): -0.4, P(3): 0	0.4
Andrelton Simmons	MI	IOW	AAA	32	50	3	0	0	1	2	4	13	1	2	.133/.220/.200	92	.161	-0.5	SS(8): 0.0	0.1
	MI	CHC	MLB	32	85	8	1	0	0	7	7	13	4	0	.173/.244/.187	94	.210	0.4	2B(18): 0.8, SS(18): 1	0.4
Nelson Velázquez	OF	TNS	AA	23	94	16	4	1	9	17	14	33	5	2	.288/.394/.700	124	.368	0.2	RF(12): 0.7, CF(8): 0.2	0.7
	OF	IOW	AAA	23	138	21	7	0	6	15	13	50	7	2	.211/.290/.415	67	.294	-0.7	CF(26): 1.4, RF(6): 0.4, LF(3): 0.4	0.0
	OF	CHC	MLB	23	206	20	7	3	6	26	19	65	5	2	.205/.286/.373	80	.281	0.7	CF(32): -0.4, RF(23): 0.9, LF(14): 0.6	0.4

Taking him from unsigned third-round pick out of high school to undrafted out of college to a breakout Triple-A performance in 2019 to a minor-league Rule 5 selection in '21, speedster **Ben DeLuzio**'s route to his big-league debut wasn't quite as fast and effortless as the routes he's run catching fly balls in center. ⓫ A fun thing to do with infielders this young: Wonder if they'll become strong enough to move into a corner, or stay fast enough to play in the middle. A patient and mature hitter for his age, **Cristian Hernández** might need to pack on more muscle to find the power many expect—though that could work against his plus speed. Worth a watch, no matter where on the dirt he ends up. ⓫ After a 2021 season curtailed by a forearm strain, **P.J. Higgins** got to be the back-up he was projected as from May through September—and didn't put up any numbers indicating he'll outgrow that role. ⓫ **Kevin Made** would step in the box and swing at a bee if it got too close. The man's an aggressive swinger, we're saying; if he made contact with that bee, though, it'd go far. He can play any of the infield positions, and his defense has continually improved. But the output dipped severely from Low-A to High-A; it's time for adjustments. Will he leave bees out of it? We can only hope. We're running out of bees. ⓫ Like Starks in Winterfell, there must always be a Ben Zobrist-type in Chicago. Enter **Miles Mastrobuoni**, who the Cubs nabbed from the Rays in November after he posted a strong year in Durham. ⓫ The only position player the Cubs took in their first 14 picks of the 2022 draft, **Christopher Paciolla** still went slightly earlier than projected: Chicago clearly sees something to like. He's a contact-first pull hitter, and maybe a little too much of one: He will need to learn how to hit the ball to all fields, using his tight swing to get the ball in the air more frequently. ⓫ For six weeks, **Frank Schwindel** was among the game's best hitters. Between August 6 and September 17, 2021, the brawny first baseman clubbed 13 home runs. A .369/.416/.711 line in those 38 games powered him to the year's final two NL Rookie of the Month awards. The follow-up was marred by back injuries from spring training onward, and the power never arrived. Now, he'll have another chance to be among the game's best hitters: in a different league, for the Orix Buffaloes. ⓫ A day after the lockout ended, **Andrelton Simmons** signed a one-year, $4 million deal with the Cubs. Due to persistent shoulder woes, he appeared in just 34 major-league games. The legendary defender at shortstop hit .173 in those contests, and was released by the team in early August. ⓫ The Cubs brought **Nelson Velázquez**, their 2021 minor-league leader in RBI, XBH, and TB, up for a May doubleheader; a few weeks later, they recalled him for the rest of the season. The former AFL MVP hit three homers over a three-game, post-break sweep in Philadelphia, bringing his OPS to .843; thereafter, he came plummeting back to earth. He still has fewer than 300 PA of upper-minors experience.

Pitchers

PITCHER	TEAM	LVL	AGE	W	L	SV	G	GS	IP	H	HR	BB/9	K/9	K	GB%	BABIP	WHIP	ERA	DRA-	WARP	MPH	FB%	WHF	CSP
Ben Brown	JS	A+	22	3	5	0	16	15	73	53	7	2.8	12.9	105	43.0%	.291	1.04	3.08	88	1.0				
	TNS	AA	22	3	0	0	7	7	31	33	3	3.8	12.8	44	40.5%	.395	1.48	4.06	91	0.5				
Kervin Castro	SAC	AAA	23	0	4	0	29	0	32^{1}	31	4	6.7	8.9	32	34.8%	.310	1.70	5.57	116	-0.1	93.6	52.4%	28.7%	
	IOW	AAA	23	2	0	1	8	0	13^{2}	7	0	4.6	11.9	18	39.1%	.269	1.02	1.32	77	0.3				
	CHC	MLB	23	0	1	0	8	0	10^{2}	11	3	4.2	5.9	7	41.2%	.258	1.50	7.59	116	0.0	92.8	71.9%	23.6%	53.2%
	SF	MLB	23	0	0	0	2	0	1^{2}	4	0	10.8	21.6	4	40.0%	.800	3.60	27.00	72	0.0	93.8	53.2%	23.5%	43.3%
Luke Farrell	IOW	AAA	31	3	4	0	17	11	59	58	10	4.3	7.5	49	40.7%	.287	1.46	5.03	108	0.5				
	CHC	MLB	31	0	0	0	4	2	11	12	2	2.5	7.4	9	25.0%	.294	1.36	4.09	111	0.0	91.2	51.3%	13.2%	56.3%
	CIN	MLB	31	0	0	0	2	0	4	6	1	9.0	11.3	5	46.2%	.417	2.50	9.00	116	0.0	91.5	42.7%	26.5%	48.8%
Robert Gsellman	IOW	AAA	28	1	4	0	10	9	29	29	3	3.4	6.8	22	47.8%	.302	1.38	6.21	107	0.3				
	CHC	MLB	28	0	2	1	8	0	15^{1}	17	2	1.8	5.3	9	42.3%	.300	1.30	4.70	115	0.0	92.9	56.5%	24.5%	52.3%
DJ Herz	SB	A+	21	2	2	0	17	17	63^{2}	33	3	5.2	14.0	99	41.8%	.252	1.10	2.26	77	1.4				
	TNS	AA	21	1	4	0	9	9	31^{2}	24	5	9.4	11.9	42	35.1%	.275	1.80	8.24	127	-0.1				
Caleb Kilian	IOW	AAA	25	5	4	0	26	26	106^{2}	108	7	5.0	10.5	125	51.5%	.357	1.57	4.22	88	2.0				
	CHC	MLB	25	0	2	0	3	3	11^{1}	11	0	9.5	7.1	9	50.0%	.324	2.03	10.32	116	0.0	94.2	66.8%	16.8%	54.6%
Alec Mills	IOW	AAA	30	0	2	0	4	4	12^{2}	17	2	2.1	7.8	11	44.2%	.366	1.58	4.97	101	0.2				
	CHC	MLB	30	0	1	0	7	2	17^{2}	28	7	1.5	5.6	11	34.3%	.350	1.75	9.68	138	-0.2	88.8	59.9%	15.5%	54.7%
Daniel Palencia	SB	A+	22	1	3	0	21	20	75^{1}	56	7	4.2	11.7	98	46.0%	.290	1.21	3.94	64	2.2				
Ethan Roberts	CHC	MLB	24	0	1	0	9	0	7^{2}	10	3	7.0	10.6	9	36.4%	.368	2.09	8.22	108	0.0	93.9	67.8%	18.4%	56.1%
Eric Stout	IND	AAA	29	1	0	3	11	0	13^{1}	11	0	4.7	10.1	15	44.1%	.324	1.35	0.67	98	0.2				
	IOW	AAA	29	2	2	2	16	1	29^{2}	18	4	6.7	14.6	48	23.7%	.255	1.35	3.94	74	0.8				
	PIT	MLB	29	0	0	1	18	0	18^{2}	22	1	7.2	9.2	19	36.2%	.368	1.98	5.79	126	-0.1	92.1	34.0%	25.6%	48.1%
	CHC	MLB	29	0	0	0	2	0	3^{2}	3	1	2.5	14.7	6	25.0%	.286	1.09	4.91	92	0.1	93.0	40.7%	32.1%	54.3%
Cayne Ueckert	IOW	AAA	26	3	1	0	39	1	50	54	12	9.4	11.3	63	43.3%	.344	2.12	7.74	105	0.5				

Halfway through the season, **Ben Brown** joined the org in the deal that sent David Robertson back to Philadelphia. After his recovery from Tommy John bled right into the 2020 minor-league shutdown, the self-described "instructional-league veteran" made up for lost time by developing a changeup during bullpen work. Also packing a mid-90s heater complemented by a slider and power curve, his ceiling is viewed as a mid-range starter or late-inning reliever. ⚾ A converted catcher with big arm strength, in his 2021 debut **Kervin Castro** allowed no runs in 10 games; last year, he surrendered 14 in 12⅓ innings. Those who put their hopes in his lights-out work during a sample in San Francisco fared about as well as late-stage crypto adopters. His velocity and command dropped off, doing him no favors. ⚾ In four appearances with the Cubs, **Luke Farrell** allowed 12 hits and five earned runs. They designated him for assignment. The Reds grabbed him off waivers in early September, when neither they nor Chicago were playing any kind of impactful baseball. Cincinnati dropped the 31-year-old into two games, in which he allowed six hits, four walks, and four earned runs. They designated him for assignment. ⚾ In May, **Robert Gsellman** was in Chicago, allowing left-handed hitters to tune him up with a 1.027 OPS. In June, the former Met was outrighted. He was released in July. Hopefully he had time for a selfie by that big bean. ⚾ Just one strikeout shy of 100 on the season, **DJ Herz** was promoted out of High-A, where in a recent start he'd punched out 12 of 17 opponents. He got shelled in his first start for the Smokies; it wouldn't be the only time his command (or his defense) would fail him in Double-A. He walked a *ton* of hitters for the rest of the season. The general thought is that there's some raw power in that arm that will yet be harnessed. The Tennessee rotation could be formidable. ⚾ **Cade Horton**, whom the Cubs selected with the seventh overall pick, spent a lot of the year getting right. He spent the first six weeks of his freshman season as an infielder, having missed the prior season recovering from Tommy John. In his first six outings he only once surpassed three innings, but the high-90s heater and wipeout slider returned for Oklahoma's impressive postseason run—in his final collegiate start, he set a single-game NCAA record by striking out 13 Ole Miss hitters. ⚾ After punching holes through Triple-A hitters to kick off the season, necessity required **Caleb Kilian** make three starts for the Cubs in June; he melted down harder and faster with each subsequent outing. Command issues forced him to lean on his sinker a lot more than he'd intended, but the righty—acquired from the Giants in the Kris Bryant trade—remains among Chicago's deep pool of young, talented hurlers. ⚾ Nothing can halt the hype train on a talented left-handed pitcher like consecutive lost seasons. **Brailyn Marquez** underwent surgery on his throwing shoulder in June; the year prior, it was a shoulder strain and a COVID-19 infection. Fortunately, he's just 23 this season, with mid-rotation prospect cache in his pocket and an arm that can unload high-90s heat. ⚾ The Cubs had three more years of control over **Alec Mills**, but decided they didn't want them. He appeared in seven games, logged an ERA close to 10.00 and then underwent back surgery; he didn't appear on the field after July 2. He's now a free agent, and out of minor-league options, if somebody wants to make a starter (or reliever) out of him, they'll have to keep him in the majors. ⚾ Like any teenager, **Nazier Mule** has impressive raw skill waiting to be harnessed. In the case of the Cubs' fourth-round draft pick, that skill includes a fastball that can hit triple digits (but is more effective when he backs off the heat and uses command), a still-inconsistent slider and a changeup as fresh as his professional career. ⚾ There was a point in time when **Daniel Palencia** was considered a throw-in prospect to the Andrew Chafin trade. "Could a throw-in prospect do *this??*" he asked, hurling a 100-mph fastball while developing an unfriendly slider. The answer is yes, a throw-in might be able to, but successfully bringing that stuff to the upper minors would be another matter entirely. ⚾ In the middle of rehabbing a shoulder injury in Iowa, **Ethan Roberts'** elbow went pop; Tommy John came calling. This was particularly frustrating after his smashing 2021, in which he struck out 12 batters per nine innings between Double- and Triple-A. Last year, he showed up with a sharp cutter and slider combo, providing big-league fans just a taste, before the pair of injuries shut things down. He ended the year in Chicago's vast pool of question marks. ⚾ **Eric Stout** resurfaced in the majors after a four-year absence, reinventing himself with a slider-heavy repertoire that led to more strikeouts, but also more walks and indigestion for Pirates fans—which made all too much sense given all the sliders and Stout(s). ⚾ After an electrifying 2021, **Cayne Ueckert** came into training camp with momentum. The buzz tapered off at Triple-A Iowa, where he struggled with command from the get-go, walking 13 in 6⅔ innings during one sad April stretch. He was put on the developmental list in mid-August, and came back two weeks later still looking a bit wobbly. Presumably, the Cubs are hopeful: Everyone likes Raising Ca(y)ne's. ⚾ Through 17 major-league innings, **Brad Wieck** had a 0.00 ERA in 2021. That's not the year on this book, but it is the last time he pitched. If he can make it back from a July Tommy John surgery in time for his age-31 season, there's still hope he can capture the curve that's brought huge strikeout totals—when he's on the field.

CINCINNATI REDS

Essay by Craig Goldstein

Player comments by Jarrett Seidler, Matt Sussman and BP staff

"Like I said the other day, we're aligning our payroll with our resources." —Reds GM Nick Krall, November 2021

It's odd that, even for just a moment, Wade Miley of all people perfectly embodied the current state of baseball. Yet the quote above was issued following the Reds' waiving of Miley, who in 2021 had recorded a 3.37 ERA over 163 innings. He had a reasonable option for a total cost of $10 million for the 2022 season, with a $1 million buyout, which Cincinnati had suddenly become too cheap to pay. Major League Baseball is a "pay for what you'll do rather than what you've done" kinda place these days, and no one was biting on Miley's superficial quality because of underlying fears about his peripheral stats.

So the club waived him. When the Cubs claimed Miley shortly thereafter, Cincinnati rid themselves of the buyout cost. It was a nifty bit of accounting, to be sure: Who wouldn't like to save a cool million in one fell swoop? But at the same time, the symbolism present in an organization valued over $1 billion sidestepping a $1 million hit on a player who had a positive return on investment just the season prior... Well, you could understand why fans might be concerned.

Those concerns came to pass when, following an owner-initiated lockout, a CBA agreement was reached enabling additional free agent spending, among other items. The Reds responded by trading Sonny Gray and his $11.825 million salary to the big-market Twins straight up for their first-round pick, Chase Petty, on March 13. They weren't done, though. The next day, they packaged Jesse Winker, fresh off his All-Star 2021 season, with Eugenio Suárez's bloated contract (we know how that worked out now) and shipped them out to Seattle for a four-player package headlined at the time by pitching prospect Brandon Williamson. PTBNL Connor Phillips now looks like the best piece in that deal.

Between Tucker Barnhart, Gray, Winker and Suárez, the Reds cleared a total of $37,860,714, and that doesn't account for the money taken off the books when Castellanos opted out. Their big winter acquisition was Mike Minor, his 5.05

CINCINNATI REDS PROSPECTUS

2022 W-L: 62-100, 4TH IN NL CENTRAL

Pythag	.394	*25th*	DER	.696	*18th*
RS/G	4.00	*23rd*	DRC+	90	*28th*
RA/G	5.03	*27th*	DRA-	105	*21st*
dWin%	.433	*26th*	FIP	4.60	*29th*
Payroll	$114M	*21st*	B-Age	29.9	*23rd*
M$/MW	$7.0M	*29th*	P-Age	28.2	*11th*

- Opened 2003
- Open air
- Natural surface
- Fence profile: 8' to 12'

Park Factors

Runs	Runs/RH	Runs/LH	HR/RH	HR/LH
108	109	107	123	124

Top Hitter WARP	1.4 TJ Friedl
Top Pitcher WARP	2.2 Hunter Greene
2023 Top Prospect	Elly De La Cruz

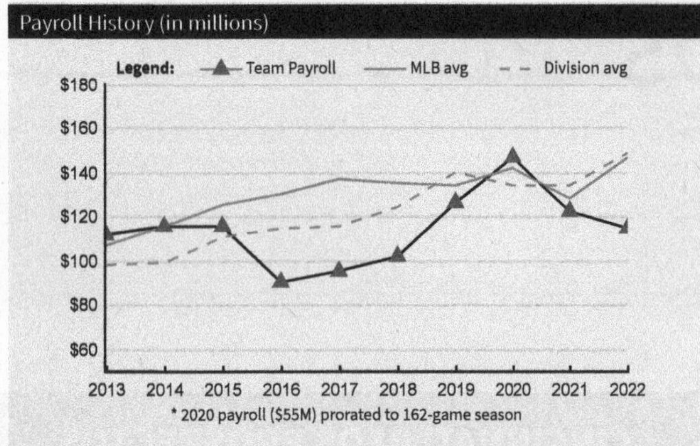

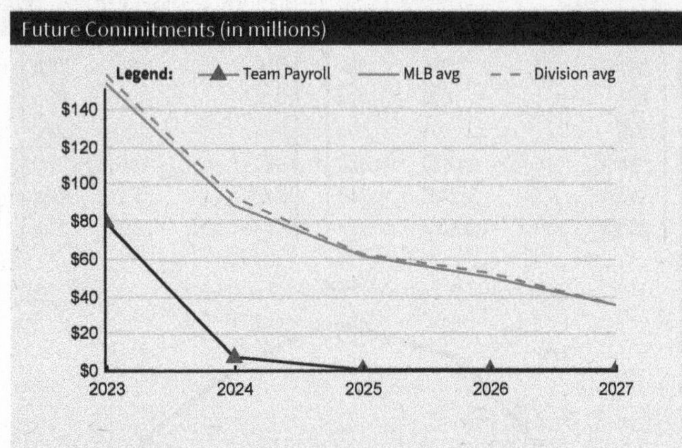

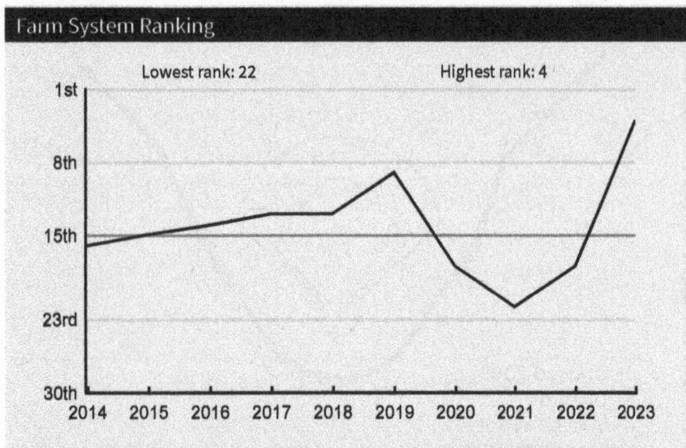

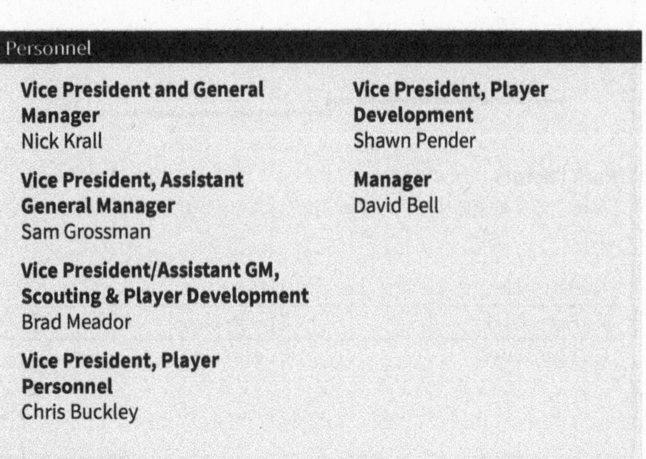
Personnel

Vice President and General Manager
Nick Krall

Vice President, Assistant General Manager
Sam Grossman

Vice President/Assistant GM, Scouting & Player Development
Brad Meador

Vice President, Player Personnel
Chris Buckley

Vice President, Player Development
Shawn Pender

Manager
David Bell

ERA and fly-ball tendencies; after all, who better to pitch in a bandbox? They nabbed Minor in exchange for Amir Garrett, adding $7.275 million to their books.

If there was any confusion about what "aligning our payroll to our resources" meant when Krall said it, by March there wasn't a doubt to be had. Like Baltimore, Detroit and so many other recent rebuilders, the team was going to be blown up—and with it, any near-term hopes for contention. In Cincinnati, though, ownership didn't care to salve the burn.

⚾ ⚾ ⚾

> *"Well, where are you gonna go?" —Phil Castellini, April 12, 2022*

The Reds entered their home opener on April 12 having earned a 2-2 series split against the defending World Series champions in Atlanta. Despite this modest achievement, the fanbase was understandably still focused on the dismantling of the team over the offseason, and the general lack of success the franchise experienced under the Castellinis.

So it came to be that Scott Sloan and Mo Egger asked Phil, son of owner Bob, and President and COO of the Reds, why after 15 years of ownership and little to show for it, a fan's faith should be maintained—in the team, in the direction of the franchise, in the Castellinis?

Phil dropped his mask immediately:

> *That's the other thing, I mean, if you wanna have this debate. Y'know. If you wanna look at what would you do with this team to have it be more profitable, make more money, compete more in the current economic system that this game exists, it would be to pick it up and move it somewhere else. And so be careful what you ask for.*

He considers Reds fans to be a captive audience. That the team's presence is a grace extended to the fans, and that they will either support the team in whatever form the Castellinis opt to provide it, or they will cease to have a team at all.

To hear these people, who already have it so good, essentially tell the fans of a club that gave it the old college try for a total of two seasons—netting two third-place finishes and one expanded playoffs appearance in 2020's shortened season—that they should feel blessed they even have a team is both repugnant and entirely in character. The reply demonstrates the type of contempt that individual teams and the league writ large have demonstrated toward their fans for years now.

It's not enough to be in a great situation, to have that captive audience, to be able to act with impunity. No, it's that the audience must also applaud what the club is doing—even if they're actively taking steps to make the product the audience pays to see worse.

It implies that fans need to give primacy to a club's profit margins and revenue before taking into account their ability and willingness to compete on the field—a willingness that seems to wane more than it waxes. All the while, teams like Cincinnati and ownership groups like the Castellinis' are insulated from the carnage wrought by their apathy toward the quality of the on-field product by national and local television deals that keep the money flowing regardless of the team's record or results.

And the league is only making it easier for owners like Castellini to shield themselves from their fans, frequently opting for deals like those made with Apple and Peacock, taking inventory that was previously available to fans either on their local RSN or via MLB.tv and stuffing it behind yet another paywall. They split their playoff games among a variety of networks, almost all of them on cable, hiding away the league's most dramatic events rather than exposing broader swaths of the country to the game being played at its highest levels. Why? More guaranteed money in the short-term, at the expense of further winnowing what is already the oldest average fanbase among major U.S. sports in the long-term.

⚾ ⚾ ⚾

"If you build it, they will come." —Field of Dreams

The league's only notable departure from this strategy in recent years was the advent of the Field of Dreams game. Played for the first time in 2021, it showcased a powerhouse matchup of the eventual 93-win White Sox against the 92-win Yankees and ended with a dramatic walk-off home run into the Iowa corn stalks off the bat of Tim Anderson.

The event was successful not merely because it featured two good teams and a wildly fun game—though of course that helped—but because the league got its television partner, Fox, to treat it as seriously as it usually treats football. They promoted the game heavily and aired it over broadcast, making it available to a truly national audience. The strategy worked! Fox reeled in more than 5.9 million viewers, making it the most-watched regular-season MLB game in 16 years.

Year two of the event brought a matchup between the "where else are you gonna go" Reds and the post-fire sale Cubs (as though the citizens of Iowa weren't already used to seeing Chicago's non-MLB quality offerings). Rather than ensure that one of the most-watched events of the season was to feature baseball played at its highest level, the league opted for a "local" option, leaning on Chicago's proximity to Iowa, and a historical one in the Reds. It was great to see the old-time uniforms for both the Cubs and Reds—if a bit confusing, as the Cubs unis featured a very Reds-like "C"—but it was also emblematic of the league's indifference toward its current and future fanbases—an indifference that bleeds down to the clubs themselves.

Despite the quality of teams involved, the 2022 Field of Dreams game drew 3.1 million viewers, a significant drop-off from 2021 but still a rousing overall success. Still, it's symbolic of how the league tends to function in regard to having or creating a good product that people want to see, and then taking that existing base of support and squeezing it for all it's worth, rather than rewarding it and enlarging the fanbase. Probably the most exciting part of the 2022 contest, in which the decisive run scored in the top of the first, was that it featured two players named Farmer.

The league, along with its individual clubs, has inverted the *Field of Dreams* message. It's no longer "if you build it, they will come," but rather "we've built it, and there are no other options."

⚾ ⚾ ⚾

"...Just really great to have him here as long as we did, but at the end of the day we had to make ourselves better, um, for the long haul and we felt these four players are gonna help us do that." —Nick Krall, July 30, 2022

On the subject of no other options, the Reds' "need" to align their payroll with their resources and offseason moves left little doubt that the team would continue deconstructing into the 2022 season. When the time came, the front office sent Luis Castillo to Seattle for a package headlined by shortstop prospects Noelvi Marte and Edwin Arroyo. They followed that up by moving Tyler Mahle to Minnesota for Spencer Steer, Christian Encarnacion-Strand and Steve Hajjar. They also landed Padres prospect Victor Acosta for the rental services of Brandon Drury.

Where the offseason trades of Gray, Winker and Suárez were widely panned, the deadline acquisitions were feted, and deservedly so. The Reds injected a ton of upside and talent into a system that had been trending conservative in its recent first-round picks, at least until Elly De La Cruz broke out and they popped Cam Collier with the fifth pick in the 2022 draft.

With that group of players, the Reds now boast one of the better sets of up-the-middle prospects in the minors. De La Cruz is a singular talent, combining the otherworldly dimensions and abilities of Oneil Cruz with an incredible feel for the game. The most concerning thing about him might be that his rise among prospects was so meteoric it calls to mind the many crypto scams that exploded upon impact. The big difference being that the only thing exploding upon impact with De La Cruz's bat is the ball. Marte and Arroyo serve as high-end potential pieces who either have the bat for another position or are good bets to stick at short, respectively.

As moribund as things look at the major-league level more generally, the rotation does provide a few bright spots thanks to the development of Nick Lodolo, Hunter Greene and, to a lesser extent, Graham Ashcraft. Greene closed out the year with four statement starts, where he struck out 37 over 23 innings, walked seven and allowed only 12 hits, good for a 0.78 ERA. It was a strong finish to an up-and-down year, but he really saw things start to click when he upped the usage of his slider. Lodolo fired 103⅓ innings, striking out 131 on the season. He ditched his changeup as the year went along, and also cut down the use of his sinker, throwing his fastball and curve around 35% each by September. It turns out using your best pitches more often is a recipe for success, and his low arm slot makes his fastball up in the zone very difficult for batters to square up. It also opens him up to platoon splits, and the movement on his pitches resulted in a league-leading 19 hit by pitches despite the modest innings totals. Both arms missed time due to injury, so while optimism is warranted, so is caution.

If the Reds are to find success, it will be because of the strong foundation provided by the combination of prospects and early-career pitchers discussed above. And it is to the front office's credit that what looked like it might be a multi-year rebuild on the scale of the Tigers or Orioles might be abbreviated due to the quality of the acquisitions they've made, even as they dismantled the prior attempt at contention at ownership's behest. But it's tough to feel as though Cincinnati is on the verge of success until we understand what success in Cincinnati can look like.

The obvious answer is a division title or two, some playoff wins, possibly a pennant and a World Series win. But there are many shades of success, and absent a willingness to be a full-throated contender, it's hard to conceive of Cincinnati summiting the mountain top when the previous window barely opened before it was slammed shut. Reds fans were rewarded with two years of .513 ball and two third-place finishes as thanks for tolerating four straight seasons where they didn't even crack 70 wins. Next year will mark a decade since they last saw a 90-win team.

So sure, maybe the next decent Reds team isn't that far away, but it's difficult to assume they'll get the rope to find out unless they hit the ground running. If they turn out just okay like the 2020-21 squads, will their window be similarly abbreviated? Will ownership "align their resources" with opportunity? Because even if the prospects pan out, they'll have to spend to keep them—at the extreme end, look at the Mets and Brandon Nimmo or the Yankees and Aaron Judge. Or will the GM be talking about how great it was to have Noelvi Marte for as long as they did, but the Reds need to get better for the long haul?

This process of lengthy rebuilds followed by half-hearted pushes for contention is taking its toll on the fanbase—attendance dropped from the 2.4 million range in the early 2010s down to 1.4 million last year (it was 1.8 million in 2019, before the pandemic). And if this all makes it seem like it would be impossible to build the next generation of Reds fans, well...you're not wrong. Especially when aligning budget with resources means shipping out fan favorites—fan favorites who wanted to stay in Cincinnati—including guys who weren't even costing the Reds a pretty penny. According to former Red Kyle Farmer, the guys the fans grew to love loved them right back, telling Cincinnati.com's Charlie Goldsmith:

> *No one understands that everyone wants to play in Cincinnati... Everyone who comes there wants to stay in Cincinnati. It's not like people who leave are happy to leave. It's that they just can't keep them around. It's kind of sad. Everybody loves Cincinnati. It's a sad thing that we all can't stick around.*

For an ownership group to squander a desirable location just because it's not the most profitable place they could play...to impugn their fans and tell them they're naught but a captive audience who has nowhere else to turn...to intentionally provide a bad product, well—it would be hard to imagine it as a viable business model, if it weren't exactly how the league behaves toward fans nationally.

In Cincinnati, the fans want to root for a winner and the players want to be there to give them one. But the Castellinis' underlying motivations—prioritizing profit margin over competition—are proving that Farmer's analysis that "they just can't keep them around" applies to players and fans alike. ■

—Craig Goldstein is the Editor-in-Chief of Baseball Prospectus.

HITTERS

Aristides Aquino RF Born: 04/22/94 Age: 29 Bats: R Throws: R Height: 6'4" Weight: 220 lb. Origin: International Free Agent, 2011

YEAR	TEAM	LVL	AGE	PA	R	2B	3B	HR	RBI	BB	K	SB	CS	Whiff%	AVG/OBP/SLG	DRC+	BABIP	BRR	DRP	WARP
2020	CIN	MLB	26	56	7	1	0	2	8	6	18	1	0	38.5%	.170/.304/.319	87	.222	0.8	LF(13): -0.5, RF(4): -0.1	0.1
2021	LOU	AAA	27	27	5	2	0	1	5	8	1	0	0		.263/.481/.526	132	.235	0.8	RF(4): 0.5, CF(1): 0.1	0.3
2021	CIN	MLB	27	204	25	6	1	10	23	27	75	2	2	39.5%	.190/.299/.408	77	.253	-1.7	LF(35): -0.2, RF(27): -0.3, CF(14): -0.1	-0.1
2022	LOU	AAA	28	91	18	6	0	8	19	9	33	2	1		.312/.407/.701	90	.432	-0.1	RF(17): -0.8, CF(2): 1.2, LF(1): 0.2	0.2
2022	CIN	MLB	28	276	24	13	0	10	30	17	101	2	3	37.8%	.197/.246/.363	62	.277	0.1	RF(69): -0.6, LF(7): 1, CF(2): 0.3	-0.4
2023 non-DC	*CIN*	*MLB*	*29*	*251*	*30*	*9*	*1*	*13*	*36*	*21*	*80*	*3*	*1*	*37.5%*	*.219/.295/.446*	*99*	*.275*	*0.6*	*RF 2, LF 0*	*0.7*

Comparables: Tyler Moore (49), Mikie Mahtook (48), Hunter Renfroe (47)

Some people just need to see a few Triple-A pitches. Aquino was a case study in how much slumping it would take for a popular player to be designated for assignment. For Aquino, an all-or-nothing slugger with a dangerous throwing arm, it was a 2-for-41 April. After he cleared waivers, he couldn't stay in Triple-A forever without the opposing pitchers filing workplace grievances; his return to the 26-man yielded better results. A month-long injury also gave him a chance to see more minor-league pitches, and Cincinnati used every possible second of his rehab assignment. Despite all the transactional turmoil, Aquino still led the NL in outfield assists. The lesson here: He should start every season "hurt" (like Rodney Dangerfield in *Caddyshack*), and pulverize the Lehigh Valley IronPigs for a few days to get a taste for blood before suiting up in the majors.

★ ★ ★ *2023 Top 101 Prospect* **#61** ★ ★ ★

Edwin Arroyo SS

Born: 08/25/03 Age: 19 Bats: S Throws: S Height: 6'0" Weight: 175 lb. Origin: Round 2, 2021 Draft (#48 overall)

YEAR	TEAM	LVL	AGE	PA	R	2B	3B	HR	RBI	BB	K	SB	CS	Whiff%	AVG/OBP/SLG	DRC+	BABIP	BRR	DRP	WARP
2021	RA12	WIN	17	65	6	3	0	0	2	6	14	1	0		.250/.333/.304		.333			
2021	MRN	ROK	17	86	16	2	0	2	10	10	26	4	1		.211/.337/.324		.295			
2022	DBT	A	18	109	16	6	3	1	16	9	31	4	2	32.1%	.227/.303/.381	80	.318	-0.1	SS(25): 2.8	0.6
2022	MOD	A	18	410	76	19	7	13	67	35	90	21	4		.316/.385/.514	106	.386	3.1	SS(84): 2.6	2.1
2023 non-DC	*CIN*	*MLB*	*19*	*251*	*21*	*9*	*3*	*4*	*23*	*13*	*73*	*7*	*2*	*32.9%*	*.230/.281/.356*	*72*	*.318*	*4.1*	*2B 0, SS 0*	*0.3*

Comparables: Royce Lewis (92), Chris Owings (91), Addison Russell (90)

Coming out of the 2021 draft, Arroyo looked like a premium defensive prospect whose bat was likely to take quite some time to develop—if it ever got there at all. The Mariners aggressively assigned him to full-season ball, and while his glove lived up to billing, it was his offensive game which made unexpected waves. He made more consistent and better contact than expected, and was one of the better hitters in the California League before his midseason inclusion in the Luis Castillo trade. While Noelvi Marte was the headline name in that deal, Arroyo isn't far behind him as a prospect, and could be a star himself if he keeps the chase and swing-and-miss in check. Something to keep an eye on: While Arroyo, a switch-hitter, showed no noticeable platoon splits in overall offensive production, his strikeout rate was nearly 10 percentage points higher hitting from the right side.

Jose Barrero SS

Born: 04/05/98 Age: 25 Bats: R Throws: R Height: 6'2" Weight: 175 lb. Origin: International Free Agent, 2017

YEAR	TEAM	LVL	AGE	PA	R	2B	3B	HR	RBI	BB	K	SB	CS	Whiff%	AVG/OBP/SLG	DRC+	BABIP	BRR	DRP	WARP
2020	CIN	MLB	22	68	4	0	0	0	2	1	26	1	1	40.3%	.194/.206/.194	60	.317	-1.0	SS(21): -1	-0.3
2021	CHA	AA	23	180	31	9	1	6	28	16	40	8	1		.300/.367/.481	121	.362	1.4	SS(37): -0.0	1.1
2021	LOU	AAA	23	200	31	10	0	13	38	20	44	8	3		.306/.392/.594	133	.336	-2.3	SS(43): 4.6, 3B(2): 0.1	1.6
2021	CIN	MLB	23	56	4	4	1	0	3	3	17	1	0	34.6%	.200/.286/.320	72	.303	0.6	SS(9): 0.1, CF(7): -0.5, 2B(2): 0.2	0.1
2022	LOU	AAA	24	237	27	8	1	9	24	11	89	5	2		.209/.262/.377	70	.301	0.3	SS(51): -1.0	-0.2
2022	CIN	MLB	24	174	13	3	0	2	10	9	76	4	1	38.2%	.152/.195/.206	32	.264	0.4	SS(48): -1.3	-1.0
2023 DC	*CIN*	*MLB*	*25*	*92*	*9*	*3*	*0*	*3*	*9*	*4*	*33*	*3*	*1*	*39.0%*	*.210/.269/.377*	*67*	*.306*	*0.4*	*SS -1*	*-0.2*

Comparables: Luis Ordaz (58), Orlando Ramirez (57), Luis Sardinas (56)

He might be the shortstop of the future, but it's been three years so far: That future seems far-flung, one when we're all getting pampered with flying cars and wisecracking robot maids. (Roombas do not joke and therefore cannot be trusted.) Barrero was given a rather extended late-season look at shortstop, and there's only one thing to make of the worst OPS of anyone with at least 100 plate appearances, other than the lumpy doppelgänger who stole and replaced Robinson Canó's body: Barrero is staring a Triple-A assignment right in the mug this year.

Curt Casali C

Born: 11/09/88 Age: 34 Bats: R Throws: R Height: 6'2" Weight: 220 lb. Origin: Round 10, 2011 Draft (#317 overall)

YEAR	TEAM	LVL	AGE	PA	R	2B	3B	HR	RBI	BB	K	SB	CS	Whiff%	AVG/OBP/SLG	DRC+	BABIP	BRR	DRP	WARP
2020	CIN	MLB	31	93	10	3	0	6	8	14	29	2	0	28.2%	.224/.366/.500	108	.268	-0.5	C(29): 1.5	0.5
2021	SF	MLB	32	231	20	11	1	5	26	26	66	0	0	29.7%	.210/.313/.350	82	.287	-1.8	C(64): 0.9	0.4
2022	SEA	MLB	33	50	7	1	0	1	3	9	14	0	0	27.7%	.125/.300/.225	92	.160	0.0	C(15): 0.3	0.2
2022	SF	MLB	33	126	13	3	0	4	14	15	36	0	0	27.8%	.231/.325/.370	91	.300	-0.1	C(39): -3.4, 1B(2): -0.2	-0.1
2023 DC	*CIN*	*MLB*	*34*	*214*	*23*	*8*	*0*	*6*	*21*	*26*	*58*	*0*	*0*	*27.9%*	*.220/.329/.371*	*91*	*.290*	*-1.4*	*C -1*	*0.3*

Comparables: Chris Iannetta (58), Jason LaRue (54), Jim Sundberg (53)

YEAR	TEAM	P. COUNT	FRM RUNS	BLK RUNS	THRW RUNS	TOT RUNS
2020	CIN	3610	1.6	0.0	0.0	1.6
2021	SF	7929	1.5	-0.2	0.0	1.2
2022	SEA	1883	0.3	0.0	0.1	0.4
2022	SF	4825	-2.9	0.0	0.0	-3.0
2023	*CIN*	*7215*	*-0.8*	*0.0*	*-0.1*	*-0.9*

Even with the emerging defensive and offensive solidity of Cal Raleigh, the Mariners found themselves at the trade deadline with a new ace in Luis Castillo, and only Luis Torrens poorly cosplaying as a backup catcher. Enter Casali, in a trade with the Giants, who offered more credibility than the unconvincing Torrens, along with a previously successful working relationship with Castillo in Cincinnati. While Casali caught Castillo several times down the stretch, it was tough to keep Raleigh out of the lineup in a playoff race, so Casali wasn't exactly the Castillo caddy that Jerry Dipoto might have envisioned. Everyone has a part to play, and even if the defensively declining and offensively nugatory Casali served mainly to make their new ace feel at home, you'd have to count the acquisition as the kind of marginally successful move that fills the back pages of countless late-season transaction logs.

★ ★ ★ *2023 Top 101 Prospect* **#49** ★ ★ ★

Cam Collier 3B

Born: 11/20/04 Age: 18 Bats: L Throws: R Height: 6'2" Weight: 210 lb. Origin: Round 1, 2022 Draft (#18 overall)

YEAR	TEAM	LVL	AGE	PA	R	2B	3B	HR	RBI	BB	K	SB	CS	Whiff%	AVG/OBP/SLG	DRC+	BABIP	BRR	DRP	WARP
2022	RED	ROK	17	35	7	1	0	2	4	7	6	0	2		.370/.514/.630		.421			
2023	*No projection*																			

As analytic valuation models became more prevalent in draft rooms over the past decade, certain teams started focusing very heavily on players who are unusually young for their draft class, as potential home-run picks. By age, Collier—the son of itinerant ex-big league utilityman Lou Collier—should be preparing for his senior year of high school at the time of this book's publication. Instead, he pulled a Bryce Harper and got his GED to enroll at Chipola College, long one of the top junior college programs in the country, moving from the 2023 prep draft class to the 2022 college ranks. His outstanding performance, for average and power, against tough competition a minimum of two years older—followed up by a credible pre-draft Cape Cod League cameo—basically broke age-reliant draft models; he was a 17-year-old with the statistical profile of a top-tier 20-year-old prospect. In the mix as high as the first-overall pick, he slipped to the Reds at no. 18 amidst high bonus rumors and signed for a well-above-slot $5 million. He's about as advanced a teenage hitting prospect as you'll ever see, and if this all confirms out against pro pitching he'll soon be one of the best prospects in the game.

★ ★ ★ *2023 Top 101 Prospect* **#5** ★ ★ ★

Elly De La Cruz SS Born: 01/11/02 Age: 21 Bats: S Throws: R Height: 6'5" Weight: 200 lb. Origin: International Free Agent, 2018

YEAR	TEAM	LVL	AGE	PA	R	2B	3B	HR	RBI	BB	K	SB	CS	Whiff%	AVG/OBP/SLG	DRC+	BABIP	BRR	DRP	WARP
2021	RED	ROK	19	55	13	6	2	3	13	4	15	2	0		.400/.455/.780		.531			
2021	DBT	A	19	210	22	12	7	5	29	10	65	8	5		.269/.305/.477	89	.372	-0.7	3B(28): 7.0, SS(20): 2.7	1.2
2022	DAY	A+	20	306	53	14	6	20	52	24	94	28	4		.302/.359/.609	116	.389	1.7	SS(54): -0.2, 3B(14): 0.5	1.7
2022	CHA	AA	20	207	34	17	3	8	34	16	64	19	2		.305/.357/.553	96	.420	2.2	SS(30): 1.3, 3B(10): 0.2	0.9
2023 DC	*CIN*	*MLB*	*21*	*99*	*10*	*4*	*1*	*3*	*11*	*5*	*33*	*5*	*2*	*35.4%*	*.243/.291/.438*	*89*	*.351*	*2.5*	*3B 0, SS 0*	*0.4*

Comparables: Corey Seager (76), Javier Báez (75), Oneil Cruz (73)

No prospect in baseball is more likely to be the best in the game someday than De La Cruz. He has incomparable bat speed; like, close to the guys we're not supposed to comp for bat speed, peak Javier Báez or even Gary Sheffield. He's capable of hitting majestic blasts from both sides of the plate. He's a 70-grade runner. His body control and arm are so good that he might stick at shortstop. Even though he's going to end up bigger than anyone who's ever played the position except Oneil Cruz. His in-zone contact rate is good enough. But—and this is one of those cases where it's very possible nothing before the word "but" ultimately matters—his swing decisions are worse than should be possible for a guy who is hitting .300 with power. Basically, De La Cruz swings at too many pitches; not only offerings out of the strike zone, but ones that he'd need a cricket bat to make contact with. As you can see above, he absolutely demolished Double-A anyway, and that's the level that sinks almost every prospect with swing decisions this bad. If his plate approach improves to even the "normal" kind of below-average, he's going to end up making a bunch of All-Star Games. But—there's that word again—there's literally no comparable player in recent memory who has struck out this much, and walked this little, as a prospect and turned out to be good.

Christian Encarnacion-Strand 3B Born: 12/01/99 Age: 23 Bats: R Throws: R Height: 6'0" Weight: 224 lb. Origin: Round 4, 2021 Draft (#128 overall)

YEAR	TEAM	LVL	AGE	PA	R	2B	3B	HR	RBI	BB	K	SB	CS	Whiff%	AVG/OBP/SLG	DRC+	BABIP	BRR	DRP	WARP
2021	FTM	A	21	92	17	2	2	4	18	5	26	2	0		.391/.424/.598	101	.526	0.2	1B(17): -0.5, 3B(4): 1.1	0.3
2022	CR	A+	22	330	52	23	3	20	68	30	85	7	1		.296/.370/.599	136	.353	1.3	3B(55): -0.6, 1B(2): -0.2	2.3
2022	CHA	AA	22	148	13	6	1	7	29	6	38	0	0		.309/.351/.522	105	.376	-1.0	3B(15): -0.8, 1B(12): -1.0	0.4
2022	WCH	AA	22	60	11	2	1	5	17	4	14	1	1		.333/.400/.685	112	.371	0.2	3B(8): 1.7	0.1
2023 non-DC	*CIN*	*MLB*	*23*	*251*	*26*	*10*	*2*	*8*	*30*	*13*	*74*	*1*	*1*	*32.2%*	*.248/.298/.420*	*95*	*.328*	*1.4*	*1B 0, 3B 0*	*0.5*

Comparables: Nick Senzel (75), Ryan Braun (68), Vinnie Catricala (67)

There's a (possibly apocryphal) story: Positionless slugger Daniel Murphy was once asked to introduce himself to new teammates with his name and defensive position; he responded, "I'm Daniel Murphy and I bat third." Encarnacion-Strand hasn't found a position that's going to work out yet—he played more third base last year than anywhere else, fielding a catastrophic .887 there—but all he's done *everywhere* is hit. He was one of the most productive junior college hitters in the nation in 2019 and 2020 as a Yavapai Roughrider. He was one of the best hitters in the NCAA at Oklahoma State in 2021, and demolished A-ball for a month after the draft. Despite some approach and contact concerns, last season he was one of the leading power hitters in the minors and was one of the biggest prospect names moved at the deadline, in the Tyler Mahle trade. If he keeps hitting the ball hard in the air this much, he'll be introducing himself as a third-slot hitter pretty soon.

Jake Fraley LF Born: 05/25/95 Age: 28 Bats: L Throws: L Height: 6'0" Weight: 195 lb. Origin: Round 2, 2016 Draft (#77 overall)

YEAR	TEAM	LVL	AGE	PA	R	2B	3B	HR	RBI	BB	K	SB	CS	Whiff%	AVG/OBP/SLG	DRC+	BABIP	BRR	DRP	WARP
2020	SEA	MLB	25	29	3	1	1	0	0	2	11	2	1	31.4%	.154/.241/.269	68	.267	0.0	RF(6): -0.1, LF(1): 0.4	0.0
2021	TAC	AAA	26	51	8	1	0	3	7	9	15	3	1		.325/.451/.575	105	.435	0.2	LF(5): 0.3, RF(2): -0.5, CF(1): -0.1	0.2
2021	SEA	MLB	26	265	27	7	0	9	36	46	71	10	2	28.6%	.210/.352/.369	97	.265	1.5	LF(51): -0.3, CF(16): -1.3, RF(6): -0.4	0.8
2022	LOU	AAA	27	48	8	0	0	1	4	7	14	1	0		.268/.375/.341	97	.385	0.1	CF(4): -0.5, RF(4): -0.5	0.0
2022	CIN	MLB	27	247	33	9	0	12	28	26	54	4	1	24.0%	.259/.344/.468	110	.289	0.2	LF(29): 0.7, RF(16): 0.2, CF(7): -0.3	1.1
2023 DC	*CIN*	*MLB*	*28*	*365*	*42*	*14*	*2*	*11*	*39*	*42*	*89*	*8*	*3*	*25.5%*	*.239/.340/.409*	*104*	*.300*	*2.8*	*RF 0, CF 0*	*1.2*

Comparables: Kirk Nieuwenhuis (60), Mark Leonard (58), Lucas Duda (55)

Following Nick Krall's series of reset-button trades, Fraley fit right in with Cincinnati, mostly because he was a warm body and his hair matched the uniform. His presence was an incessant reminder, though, that Eugenio Suárez and Jesse Winker were no longer in the vicinity. At his best, Fraley is basically a slightly younger and redder Winker—someone to sit and wait for bad fastballs, and generally give right-handed pitching a hard time. There's much to be hopeful for, as 11 of Fraley's 12 home runs were in the second half (once an April swoon and pair of injuries were in the rearview). He factors to be the everyday crimson-chinned chum in an outfield corner.

TJ Friedl OF Born: 08/14/95 Age: 27 Bats: L Throws: L Height: 5'10" Weight: 180 lb. Origin: Undrafted Free Agent, 2016

YEAR	TEAM	LVL	AGE	PA	R	2B	3B	HR	RBI	BB	K	SB	CS	Whiff%	AVG/OBP/SLG	DRC+	BABIP	BRR	DRP	WARP
2021	LOU	AAA	25	448	59	15	5	12	36	44	65	13	7		.264/.357/.422	113	.288	2.6	CF(75): -9.0, RF(22): -2.8, LF(20): 1.2	1.5
2021	CIN	MLB	25	36	9	1	0	1	2	4	2	0	0	14.8%	.290/.361/.419	107	.276	0.2	CF(6): -0.7, LF(5): 0.5	0.2
2022	LOU	AAA	26	241	33	9	3	8	38	28	48	10	2		.278/.371/.468	113	.327	-0.2	LF(29): 1.7, CF(27): -2.9, RF(7): 0.0	0.9
2022	CIN	MLB	26	258	33	10	5	8	25	20	40	7	2	20.1%	.240/.314/.436	100	.251	0.8	LF(25): 0, CF(24): -0.6, RF(15): 1	1.0
2023 DC	*CIN*	*MLB*	*27*	*395*	*47*	*14*	*5*	*11*	*40*	*32*	*70*	*9*	*3*	*21.1%*	*.250/.329/.413*	*101*	*.288*	*5.8*	*LF 1, CF 0*	*1.6*

Comparables: Alex Dickerson (52), Kirk Nieuwenhuis (51), Steven Duggar (48)

Freidl held the Reds' distinction for the most triples, tied for the club's most sac flies and nearly took their stolen base crown—all in a half-season's worth of expelled energy. He also had the longest hair of anyone on the team, a real Kevin Sorbo-circa 1990s loaf on his noggin. That's not something that shows up in a box score, at least normally, until a high-and-tight fastball grazed his hair in September and became a hit-by-pitch after video review. We're looking for market inefficiencies, people. No haircuts for any of your batters. Rapunzel that mane out, for the good of your on-base percentage. As one of a few bright spots in a dismal Reds season, the lefty outfielder demonstrated a ton of usefulness thanks to copious amounts of solid contact. That and the hair. The hair has to stay. Nothing short of Fabio on the cover of *IronSword: Wizards and Warriors 2* for the NES.

Austin Hendrick OF Born: 06/15/01 Age: 22 Bats: L Throws: L Height: 6'0" Weight: 195 lb. Origin: Round 1, 2020 Draft (#12 overall)

YEAR	TEAM	LVL	AGE	PA	R	2B	3B	HR	RBI	BB	K	SB	CS	Whiff%	AVG/OBP/SLG	DRC+	BABIP	BRR	DRP	WARP
2021	DBT	A	20	266	30	16	0	7	29	51	100	4	2		.211/.380/.388	93	.363	0.3	RF(56): 3.0, CF(5): -0.3	0.9
2022	DBT	A	21	145	19	4	0	7	21	14	58	2	0	40.0%	.205/.297/.402	80	.302	0.7	RF(29): -1.2, CF(8): 0.0	-0.1
2022	DAY	A+	21	299	39	17	0	14	48	29	107	14	5		.222/.311/.448	74	.308	-0.3	CF(31): -0.7, RF(31): 0.1, LF(2): -0.4	0.1
2023 non-DC	*CIN*	*MLB*	*22*	*251*	*23*	*10*	*0*	*7*	*25*	*20*	*109*	*4*	*2*	*44.7%*	*.191/.266/.338*	*60*	*.329*	*-0.4*	*LF 0, CF 0*	*-0.7*

Comparables: Luis Liberato (62), Jamie Romak (61), Demi Orimoloye (59)

You probably can tell from the low-minors performances, but this is going *very* poorly. Hendrick was an overaged, cold-weather prep prospect with thunderous bat speed but significant swing-and-miss concerns. That section of draftee tends to be very risky, with a small percentage of booms and a lot of busts. Two seasons into his pro career...well, he still flashes very significant power potential on the rare occasions he makes contact. Basically every swing decision or swing-and-miss data point is rough. In short, he fishes out of the zone constantly, and doesn't make a whole lot of contact inside or outside of it. Even A-ball pitchers will eat you alive if you do that. Hendrick is trending strongly into the "bust" group at present.

Jonathan India 2B Born: 12/15/96 Age: 26 Bats: R Throws: R Height: 6'0" Weight: 200 lb. Origin: Round 1, 2018 Draft (#5 overall)

YEAR	TEAM	LVL	AGE	PA	R	2B	3B	HR	RBI	BB	K	SB	CS	Whiff%	AVG/OBP/SLG	DRC+	BABIP	BRR	DRP	WARP
2021	CIN	MLB	24	631	98	34	2	21	69	71	141	12	3	25.1%	.269/.376/.459	108	.326	2.8	2B(148): 1	3.3
2022	CIN	MLB	25	431	48	16	2	10	41	31	94	3	4	23.5%	.249/.327/.378	96	.305	-3.5	2B(86): -3.8	0.3
2023 DC	*CIN*	*MLB*	*26*	*605*	*76*	*26*	*2*	*19*	*63*	*53*	*123*	*10*	*4*	*23.7%*	*.258/.349/.423*	*113*	*.308*	*-1.1*	*2B -3*	*2.2*

Comparables: Ian Kinsler (65), Scooter Gennett (63), Howie Kendrick (62)

Rookie of the Year still carries an unfair connotation—someone who peaked early. That could be from the various Hollandsworths and Hamelins and Cordovi who showed up in the '90s and ruined it for everyone. Recently, though, laureled players had a good streak going: The last NL Rookie of the Year to go their entire career without an All-Star Game selection was Chris Coghlan in 2009. The cohort of active NL ROYs is a short list of the league's inner-circle talents. India deserved his award for a compelling 2021 performance, but the follow-up was lacking: Fronting a power-depleted lineup last year, he got away from his natural swing. Between a host of injuries (including being airlifted out of the Field of Dreams game after fouling one off his knee) and a complete ideological shift in the team's intentions for contention, there are better seasons for India ahead. Based on recent history, you'll eventually see him in a July exhibition game.

Alejo Lopez 2B Born: 05/05/96 Age: 27 Bats: S Throws: R Height: 5'10" Weight: 170 lb. Origin: Round 27, 2015 Draft (#805 overall)

YEAR	TEAM	LVL	AGE	PA	R	2B	3B	HR	RBI	BB	K	SB	CS	Whiff%	AVG/OBP/SLG	DRC+	BABIP	BRR	DRP	WARP
2020	MTY	WIN	24	210	30	9	0	2	22	11	21	6	2		.286/.322/.365		.302			
2021	MOC	WIN	25	143	14	2	1	2	19	22	18	2	0		.235/.357/.319		.260			
2021	CHA	AA	25	119	18	9	0	0	13	12	11	3	1		.362/.437/.448	133	.404	-0.7	2B(21): 0.8	0.8
2021	LOU	AAA	25	290	54	18	0	6	31	33	21	6	2		.303/.386/.446	132	.308	1.5	3B(30): 0.5, 2B(24): 3.2, LF(10): -0.3	2.4
2021	CIN	MLB	25	23	3	0	0	0	0	0	5	0	0	22.9%	.261/.261/.261	96	.333	-0.3	2B(3): 0, 3B(3): -0.3	0.0
2022	LOU	AAA	26	182	14	8	0	3	22	17	21	2	0		.256/.330/.363	109	.273	-0.2	2B(31): -1.0, 3B(7): -0.6, RF(4): -0.2	0.5
2022	CIN	MLB	26	156	15	5	1	1	10	9	21	3	1	16.3%	.262/.314/.331	94	.301	0.9	2B(33): -0.8, 3B(8): 0, LF(4): 0.1	0.4
2023 DC	*CIN*	*MLB*	*27*	*166*	*16*	*7*	*0*	*1*	*14*	*11*	*23*	*3*	*0*	*17.1%*	*.269/.328/.356*	*93*	*.310*	*0.7*	*3B 0, 2B 0*	*0.3*

Comparables: Kelby Tomlinson (66), Ryan Goins (62), Alberto Gonzalez (62)

Are you ready?
Let's do it
I'm in Cincinnati, I wear baseball hats
I'm a little bit useful when I swing my bat
I'm a backup fielder, I ground out a lot
I'm position pitching even when I'm not
I'm a little bit, I'm a little bit
La la la la la la la, a little bit Alejo

Luke Maile C Born: 02/06/91 Age: 32 Bats: R Throws: R Height: 6'3" Weight: 225 lb. Origin: Round 8, 2012 Draft (#272 overall)

YEAR	TEAM	LVL	AGE	PA	R	2B	3B	HR	RBI	BB	K	SB	CS	Whiff%	AVG/OBP/SLG	DRC+	BABIP	BRR	DRP	WARP
2021	NAS	AAA	30	155	17	9	0	1	15	22	50	2	0		.225/.351/.318	77	.359	-0.1	C(41): 8.2, 1B(2): -0.1	0.9
2021	MIL	MLB	30	34	6	4	0	0	3	3	7	0	0	31.6%	.300/.382/.433	89	.391	0.0	C(12): 0.3	0.1
2022	CLE	MLB	31	206	19	10	0	3	17	19	54	0	0	27.6%	.221/.301/.326	81	.291	-1.5	C(76): 1.3	0.3
2023 DC	*CIN*	*MLB*	*32*	*61*	*6*	*2*	*0*	*1*	*5*	*5*	*16*	*0*	*0*	*28.2%*	*.216/.300/.340*	*75*	*.287*	*0.0*	*C 1*	*0.2*

Comparables: Jeff Mathis (63), Martín Maldonado (59), Humberto Quintero (59)

YEAR	TEAM	P. COUNT	FRM RUNS	BLK RUNS	THRW RUNS	TOT RUNS
2021	NAS	5545	8.5	0.0	0.0	8.5
2021	MIL	1125	0.1	0.0	0.0	0.2
2022	CLE	8237	0.6	0.1	0.5	1.2
2023	*CIN*	*2405*	*0.9*	*0.0*	*0.1*	*0.9*

"Our job is to go catch a winner," Maile said while celebrating Cleveland's division title, and truer words have never been spoken. The organization places a premium on the plus receiving skills, leadership and game-calling acumen that Maile provides, particularly with a young pitching staff. He isn't completely useless at the plate, but only with the Guardians can you post a .627 OPS and be considered the offensive juggernaut of the catching corps. A veteran of four organizations but still a year away from free agency, Maile joined the Reds over the winter to see what life is like elsewhere in Ohio. His defensive chops should continue to earn him roster spots while his bats should still be delivered with "Avoid In All Formats" burned into the barrel.

★ ★ ★ *2023 Top 101 Prospect* **#29** ★ ★ ★

Noelvi Marte SS/3B Born: 10/16/01 Age: 21 Bats: R Throws: R Height: 6'1" Weight: 181 lb. Origin: International Free Agent, 2018

YEAR	TEAM	LVL	AGE	PA	R	2B	3B	HR	RBI	BB	K	SB	CS	Whiff%	AVG/OBP/SLG	DRC+	BABIP	BRR	DRP	WARP
2021	MOD	A	19	478	87	24	2	17	69	58	106	23	7		.271/.368/.462	123	.326	4.1	SS(92): -1.1	3.1
2021	EVE	A+	19	33	4	4	0	0	2	2	11	1	0		.290/.333/.419	95	.450	0.4	SS(7): 0.9	0.2
2022	EVE	A+	20	394	62	19	0	15	55	42	84	13	6		.275/.363/.462	115	.321	-1.0	SS(81): -2.8	1.3
2022	DAY	A+	20	126	12	4	0	4	13	17	23	10	3		.292/.397/.443	112	.338	-0.1	SS(23): 0.2	0.4
2023 non-DC	*CIN*	*MLB*	*21*	*251*	*23*	*9*	*0*	*5*	*24*	*20*	*61*	*7*	*3*	*27.5%*	*.227/.296/.346*	*79*	*.288*	*-0.3*	*SS 0*	*0.0*

Comparables: Richard Urena (86), Willi Castro (79), Cole Tucker (78)

Marte had the misfortune to be Seattle's top international free agency signing the year *after* Julio Rodríguez, simply an impossible standard for any normal prospect to live up to. He's quite a good prospect in his own right, though, blending a plus power projection to all fields with a strong sense of what he should swing at. That's led to solid (if not spectacular) performances in the low minors, and enough contact that prior concerns about swing-and-miss are starting to fade. The biggest short-term issue is his future defensive home. He's rapidly losing the agility to play shortstop, and the Reds (who picked him up in the Luis Castillo deadline deal) moved him to third base in the Arizona Fall League. Cincinnati has the best infield depth in the entire minor leagues, and Marte's ultimate landing spot might depend on the other prospects in this chapter as much as himself.

Matt McLain SS Born: 08/06/99 Age: 23 Bats: R Throws: R Height: 5'11" Weight: 180 lb. Origin: Round 1, 2021 Draft (#17 overall)

YEAR	TEAM	LVL	AGE	PA	R	2B	3B	HR	RBI	BB	K	SB	CS	Whiff%	AVG/OBP/SLG	DRC+	BABIP	BRR	DRP	WARP
2021	DAY	A+	21	119	15	6	0	3	19	17	24	10	2		.273/.387/.424	111	.329	0.4	SS(27): 1.3	0.7
2022	CHA	AA	22	452	67	21	5	17	58	70	127	27	3		.232/.363/.453	129	.300	2.5	SS(74): -7.9, 2B(23): -1.3	2.3
2023 non-DC	*CIN*	*MLB*	*23*	*251*	*24*	*9*	*1*	*5*	*24*	*26*	*74*	*10*	*1*	*32.4%*	*.200/.294/.341*	*76*	*.272*	*6.5*	*2B 0, SS 0*	*0.7*

Comparables: Kevin Smith (79), Héctor Gómez (75), Pat Valaika (73)

A year ago, McLain was the clear shortstop of the future in Cincinnati. He'd had a wildly successful pro debut at High-A after a stellar draft year at UCLA, and his main competition within the system (Elly De La Cruz) looked more likely than not to move off the 6 spot. Then McLain—who came into the season touted with a plus hit tool projection—saw his average crater, and strikeout rate skyrocket, at Double-A as he sold out for power. Meanwhile, De La Cruz exploded offensively and now looks he might stay at short, and the Reds traded for Edwin Arroyo, Noelvi Marte, Victor Acosta, and Spencer Steer, creating—by some margin—the best farm depth at the position in the minors. Prospects with good visual hit tool evaluations but iffy contact profiles have tended to fail fairly often, and while McLain has shown a power/speed/patience profile, he needs to get the hit tool fundamentals in better order, or he's going to get overtaken by the new crowd.

Mike Moustakas DH Born: 09/11/88 Age: 34 Bats: L Throws: R Height: 6'0" Weight: 225 lb. Origin: Round 1, 2007 Draft (#2 overall)

YEAR	TEAM	LVL	AGE	PA	R	2B	3B	HR	RBI	BB	K	SB	CS	Whiff%	AVG/OBP/SLG	DRC+	BABIP	BRR	DRP	WARP
2020	CIN	MLB	31	163	13	9	0	8	27	18	36	1	0	24.4%	.230/.331/.468	106	.247	-0.6	2B(32): 1, 1B(10): -0.5, 3B(2): 0	0.6
2021	CIN	MLB	32	206	21	12	0	6	22	18	46	0	0	27.6%	.208/.282/.372	83	.239	-1.1	3B(44): -1.2, 1B(11): -0.3	0.0
2022	CIN	MLB	33	285	30	12	0	7	25	24	75	2	0	29.1%	.214/.295/.345	79	.272	-2.0	3B(25): 0, 1B(24): 1	-0.1
2023 non-DC	*CIN*	*MLB*	*34*	*251*	*28*	*11*	*0*	*10*	*33*	*22*	*57*	*1*	*0*	*28.6%*	*.227/.307/.425*	*101*	*.258*	*-0.3*	*3B 0, 1B 0*	*0.5*

Comparables: Robin Ventura (72), Buddy Bell (63), Adrián Beltré (62)

Dinged up more than an Oldsmobile on a driving range (and equally out of place on the Reds), Moustakas went to the IL six times last year, eventually losing the final month to a calf strain. The burly third baseman was supposed to be a veteran addition to a team looking to compete in the Roaring Twenties. Instead, none of it worked and Moose himself averaged 70 games a year in Cincinnati, with little power while active, before his release with a year remaining on his contract. Just close your eyes and remember him in 2015. It's more fun.

Wil Myers RF Born: 12/10/90 Age: 32 Bats: R Throws: R Height: 6'3" Weight: 207 lb. Origin: Round 3, 2009 Draft (#91 overall)

YEAR	TEAM	LVL	AGE	PA	R	2B	3B	HR	RBI	BB	K	SB	CS	Whiff%	AVG/OBP/SLG	DRC+	BABIP	BRR	DRP	WARP
2020	SD	MLB	29	218	34	14	2	15	40	18	56	2	1	26.4%	.288/.353/.606	121	.331	1.7	RF(52): -3, 1B(2): 0.2	1.1
2021	SD	MLB	30	500	56	24	2	17	63	54	141	8	5	32.0%	.256/.334/.434	97	.333	-1.9	RF(118): -3, LF(13): -0.3	0.8
2022	ELP	AAA	31	38	3	1	0	2	3	3	9	0	0	30.4%	.229/.289/.429	99	.250	-0.5	1B(5): -0.1, RF(1): -0.0	0.0
2022	SD	MLB	31	286	29	15	0	7	41	21	86	2	1	31.3%	.261/.315/.398	83	.357	-0.1	RF(36): -0.3, 1B(25): 0.1, LF(10): -0.8	0.0
2023 DC	CIN	MLB	32	535	60	25	1	21	68	45	158	8	2	30.6%	.248/.319/.438	101	.329	1.4	RF 0, 1B 0	1.2

Comparables: Justin Upton (70), Michael Cuddyer (68), Dwight Evans (66)

It's the end of an era: After he somehow spent his entire Padres career alternating between All-Star level performance and being placed in the team's bargain-bin window, it's over. Wil Myers and his uncontrollable bedhead are finally leaving San Diego.

Though he long struggled with injuries—missing over half of the 2022 season with a thumb contusion and knee inflammation, perhaps compounding his difficulties with off-speed and breaking pitches—Myers should be fondly remembered by Padres fans as one of the longest-tenured players during the rebuild. He finishes sixth all-time on the Padres in home runs—one behind Tony Gwynn—eighth in total bases, and, well, first in strikeouts. The push for the Cincinnati leaderboards begins.

Kevin Newman MI Born: 08/04/93 Age: 29 Bats: R Throws: R Height: 6'0" Weight: 195 lb. Origin: Round 1, 2015 Draft (#19 overall)

YEAR	TEAM	LVL	AGE	PA	R	2B	3B	HR	RBI	BB	K	SB	CS	Whiff%	AVG/OBP/SLG	DRC+	BABIP	BRR	DRP	WARP
2020	PIT	MLB	26	172	12	5	0	1	10	12	21	0	1	14.6%	.224/.281/.276	96	.250	-0.3	SS(23): -0.7, 2B(20): 0.8	0.4
2021	PIT	MLB	27	554	50	22	3	5	39	27	41	6	1	11.9%	.226/.265/.309	80	.236	-0.6	SS(132): 2.1, 2B(15): 0.2	0.8
2022	IND	AAA	28	53	6	3	0	0	6	3	6	0	0		.396/.434/.458	113	.442	0.8	2B(6): -0.1, SS(6): -0.4	0.2
2022	PIT	MLB	28	309	31	18	2	2	24	16	48	8	2	15.3%	.274/.316/.372	98	.322	1.4	2B(42): 0.4, SS(33): -2.3	0.8
2023 DC	CIN	MLB	29	511	53	22	2	8	47	28	62	7	1	15.1%	.265/.313/.375	91	.293	2.6	SS -2, 2B 0	1.0

Comparables: Eduardo Núñez (54), Clint Barmes (54), Yuniesky Betancourt (53)

Though he missed nearly two months with groin and hamstring injuries, when Newman returned to action in early July he posted his first useful season since his 2019 rookie campaign. Still, the output was more acceptable than noteworthy, more decent than spectacular. Even at his best, he remains a below-average hitter, and the carrying tool—defense—doesn't do enough heavy lifting to make him more than a barely passable starter at second base. On a much better team, a regular like Newman could survive as the weakest link in the lineup; on a squad like the Pirates, his deficiencies were a flashing neon sign in a quiet suburban neighborhood at three o'clock in the morning. Newman was traded to the Reds over the winter. Guess which kind of team they're supposed to be this year.

Matt Reynolds IF Born: 12/03/90 Age: 32 Bats: R Throws: R Height: 6'1" Weight: 200 lb. Origin: Round 2, 2012 Draft (#71 overall)

YEAR	TEAM	LVL	AGE	PA	R	2B	3B	HR	RBI	BB	K	SB	CS	Whiff%	AVG/OBP/SLG	DRC+	BABIP	BRR	DRP	WARP
2020	KC	MLB	29	11	1	0	0	0	0	0	7	0	0	30.0%	.000/.000/.000	68		0.3	3B(3): -0.2	0.0
2021	CLT	AAA	30	367	40	20	2	5	35	51	93	5	3		.269/.373/.395	95	.363	-0.5	SS(62): 9.8, 2B(26): 0.6, P(4): -0.1	1.8
2022	NYM	MLB	31	0	0	0	0	0	0	0	0	0	0		.000/.000/.000				RF(1): -0.2	0.0
2022	CIN	MLB	31	272	31	10	1	3	23	26	78	5	0	29.4%	.246/.320/.332	77	.348	0.0	2B(36): -0.7, SS(23): 0.4, 3B(14): -0.2	0.1
2023 DC	CIN	MLB	32	283	27	12	1	4	23	26	80	2	1	28.9%	.225/.305/.335	76	.315	1.0	3B 0, 1B 0	-0.2

Comparables: Omar Quintanilla (45), Craig Paquette (45), Humberto Quintero (43)

Fortune and circumstance—namely, being cut by the Mets and the Reds existing—gave Reynolds more major-league playing time than ever before. Cincinnati needed a stopgap in their infield, and their outfield, and someone to position pitch and to co-sign on this loan—Bob swears we're good for it, we just need to get through the next couple months. Reynolds did just about all that. Prior to 2022, he was Willie Bloomquist minus the playing time; now he really is a Bloomquist reincarnation. That's not a compliment, but it might be good enough for him to get another 250 plate appearances somewhere.

Austin Romine C

Born: 11/22/88 Age: 34 Bats: R Throws: R Height: 6'1" Weight: 216 lb. Origin: Round 2, 2007 Draft (#94 overall)

YEAR	TEAM	LVL	AGE	PA	R	2B	3B	HR	RBI	BB	K	SB	CS	Whiff%	AVG/OBP/SLG	DRC+	BABIP	BRR	DRP	WARP
2020	DET	MLB	31	135	12	5	0	2	17	4	47	0	0	29.9%	.238/.259/.323	65	.354	-1.1	C(37): -1.2, 1B(1): -0.2	-0.3
2021	CHC	MLB	32	62	5	2	0	1	5	2	22	0	0	33.3%	.217/.242/.300	67	.324	0.2	C(21): -1.0	-0.1
2022	SL	AAA	33	39	7	1	0	1	4	5	8	0	0	33.3%	.273/.368/.394	99	.333	0.0	C(9): -0.3	0.1
2022	STL	MLB	33	28	2	1	0	0	0	2	7	0	0	29.5%	.154/.214/.192	85	.211	0.1	C(10): -0.5	0.0
2022	LAA	MLB	33	9	0	0	0	0	0	0	3	0	0	43.8%	.250/.250/.250	90	.400		C(3): -0.2	
2022	CIN	MLB	33	99	8	2	0	3	9	2	36	0	0	34.2%	.147/.173/.263	63	.196	-0.7	C(37): 0.2	-0.1
2023 DC	*FA*	*MLB*	*34*	*148*	*13*	*5*	*0*	*3*	*14*	*7*	*44*	*0*	*0*	*31.8%*	*.220/.262/.342*	*62*	*.296*	*-0.8*	*C 0, 1B 0*	*-0.2*

Comparables: Jeff Mathis (54), Humberto Quintero (50), Chad Moeller (50)

YEAR	TEAM	P. COUNT	FRM RUNS	BLK RUNS	THRW RUNS	TOT RUNS
2020	DET	5408	-1.6	0.0	0.4	-1.1
2021	CHC	2341	-0.8	0.1	0.0	-0.7
2022	SL	1208	-0.4	0.0	0.0	-0.5
2022	STL	1027	-0.5	0.0	0.1	-0.4
2022	CIN	4531	0.4	0.0	0.0	0.4
2022	LAA	404	0.0	0.0	0.0	0.0
2023	*FA*	*6956*	*0.0*	*0.3*	*0.1*	*0.3*

Baseball is full of families. The Alous. The Bells. The Molinas. The Romines are a baseball family by the most technical definition, as they produced three major leaguers in two generations—but good luck naming one. Austin is the last Romine remaining in the league. Older brother Andrew retired a couple years ago, and their father Kevin had seven benchwarming years in Boston. Collectively, the Romine clan owns a .610 OPS, with dad leading the way by a hair. Austin has the most power, nearly double his brother and father's longballs combined in fewer total plate appearances. Since he played for three teams last year, he caught Ohtani, Wainwright and Hunter Greene all in the same season, which is as cool a feat as his brother's nine-position game, or 40% of dad's home runs being walkoffs. Thanksgiving at the Romine household is insufferable.

Nick Senzel CF

Born: 06/29/95 Age: 28 Bats: R Throws: R Height: 6'1" Weight: 205 lb. Origin: Round 1, 2016 Draft (#2 overall)

YEAR	TEAM	LVL	AGE	PA	R	2B	3B	HR	RBI	BB	K	SB	CS	Whiff%	AVG/OBP/SLG	DRC+	BABIP	BRR	DRP	WARP
2020	CIN	MLB	25	78	8	6	0	2	8	6	15	2	1	23.2%	.186/.247/.357	96	.204	-1.5	CF(23): 0.4	0.1
2021	LOU	AAA	26	39	5	3	1	0	2	2	2	0	0		.286/.316/.429	105	.294	-0.4	CF(7): 0.1, SS(2): -0.1	0.1
2021	CIN	MLB	26	124	18	4	0	1	8	12	16	2	5	17.8%	.252/.323/.315	99	.284	-0.7	CF(29): -1.9, 2B(8): 0.1, 3B(3): 0	0.2
2022	CIN	MLB	27	420	45	13	0	5	25	30	76	8	5	21.8%	.231/.296/.306	87	.276	0.2	CF(101): -4.4, 3B(2): -0.1, 2B(1): 0.1	0.4
2023 DC	*CIN*	*MLB*	*28*	*473*	*53*	*20*	*1*	*14*	*49*	*36*	*85*	*9*	*4*	*21.0%*	*.257/.323/.408*	*100*	*.297*	*-1.3*	*CF 0*	*1.1*

Comparables: Cameron Maybin (60), Juan Lagares (57), Leonys Martin (55)

Speed and defense aren't enough to sustain a cult following, unless you're Billy Hamilton or maybe the liquid metal slime from *Dragon Quest*—even then, your best move is running away. Senzel's entire game has been based on being above-average in a number of attributes, as well as being on a fast track to the majors right out of college. The non-batting qualities are all there, but unfortunately batting is a quintessential task of the sport. There were still some positives when Senzel was holding a smooth wooden club: He makes relatively good contact and stays in the zone with moderate zeal. But he's still playing like a fourth outfielder, not a second-overall pick.

Nick Solak LF/DH

Born: 01/11/95 Age: 28 Bats: R Throws: R Height: 5'11" Weight: 185 lb. Origin: Round 2, 2016 Draft (#62 overall)

YEAR	TEAM	LVL	AGE	PA	R	2B	3B	HR	RBI	BB	K	SB	CS	Whiff%	AVG/OBP/SLG	DRC+	BABIP	BRR	DRP	WARP
2020	TEX	MLB	25	233	27	10	0	2	23	18	42	7	1	19.1%	.268/.326/.344	93	.320	3.4	LF(29): -0.9, 2B(17): 1, CF(13): -0.4	0.8
2021	RR	AAA	26	93	15	6	0	1	6	7	16	0	1		.353/.409/.459	101	.426	0.5	2B(15): -0.8	0.3
2021	TEX	MLB	26	511	57	18	2	11	49	34	107	7	5	24.9%	.242/.314/.362	94	.292	-0.8	2B(121): -3.2	1.0
2022	RR	AAA	27	259	38	15	1	10	45	30	51	6	0	21.5%	.278/.371/.489	118	.317	0.4	LF(40): -1.6, CF(2): -0.1, RF(2): -0.3	1.0
2022	TEX	MLB	27	95	14	1	0	3	4	7	19	3	2	24.2%	.207/.309/.329	104	.233	0.6	LF(22): -0.2	0.4
2023 DC	*CIN*	*MLB*	*28*	*229*	*25*	*9*	*0*	*6*	*24*	*18*	*45*	*4*	*1*	*22.4%*	*.252/.331/.400*	*102*	*.298*	*1.1*	*LF 0, CF 0*	*0.6*

Comparables: Logan Forsythe (56), Wilmer Difo (52), Randy Winn (51)

Solak has demonstrated two useful skills over his career: He plays multiple positions and crushes lefties. Or, he did before 2022, at least. Solak hit poorly for six weeks, earned a mid-May demotion and spent the rest of the year shuttling between Round Rock and Arlington before a foot injury ended his season in September. With a wave of young hitters just starting to arrive in Texas, some players are inevitably going to end up on the outside looking in. The Rangers decided Solak should be among them, shipping him to the Reds in exchange for cash just a few days after the World Series.

Spencer Steer IF Born: 12/07/97 Age: 25 Bats: R Throws: R Height: 5'11" Weight: 185 lb. Origin: Round 3, 2019 Draft (#90 overall)

YEAR	TEAM	LVL	AGE	PA	R	2B	3B	HR	RBI	BB	K	SB	CS	Whiff%	AVG/OBP/SLG	DRC+	BABIP	BRR	DRP	WARP
2021	CR	A+	23	208	37	7	1	10	24	35	32	4	4		.274/.409/.506	143	.283	2.5	2B(28): 0.9, SS(7): -0.4, 3B(5): -0.6	1.9
2021	WCH	AA	23	280	45	11	2	14	42	20	73	4	0		.241/.304/.470	99	.274	0.6	3B(36): 2.4, 2B(18): 1.3, SS(8): -1.0	1.1
2022	WCH	AA	24	156	27	13	1	8	30	14	23	1	3		.307/.385/.591	130	.318	-0.5	3B(17): 2.5, SS(9): -1.2, 2B(6): -0.0	1.1
2022	STP	AAA	24	232	39	10	1	12	32	28	43	2	0		.242/.345/.485	119	.248	0.3	3B(26): 0.0, 2B(15): 0.6, SS(4): 0.1	1.0
2022	LOU	AAA	24	104	14	7	0	3	13	9	23	1	0		.293/.375/.467	100	.364	0.5	3B(8): 0.2, SS(7): -1.2, 2B(5): -0.6	0.4
2022	CIN	MLB	24	108	12	5	0	2	8	11	26	0	1	21.2%	.211/.306/.326	87	.269	1.1	3B(14): -0.3, 1B(9): 0.2, 2B(5): -0.3	0.2
2023 DC	*CIN*	*MLB*	*25*	*539*	*56*	*24*	*2*	*15*	*55*	*46*	*108*	*4*	*2*	*22.8%*	*.226/.307/.381*	*87*	*.263*	*0.8*	*3B 0, 2B 0*	*0.3*

Comparables: J.D. Davis (71), James Darnell (70), Taylor Ward (66)

Steer started hitting the ball in the air a ton in 2021; he hit more homers in the minors that season than he'd hit from 2017 to 2019 combined—a period including three years with metal bats at Oregon, a summer on the Cape and his pro debut in the Twins system. That fly-ball frenzy started to tail off when he hit Triple-A, and did so even more upon his September call-up—so that 24-homer season might be something of a mirage. He's never actually hit the ball that hard, so his ultimate output will depend very much on maintaining an optimal vertical spray. Despite the mixed signals on his pop, his stock has shot way up as he's stampeded through the minors, and he was an excellent get for Cincinnati in the Tyler Mahle deal. He's played all around the infield and should be an excellent utility player, even if the power doesn't reappear.

Tyler Stephenson C Born: 08/16/96 Age: 26 Bats: R Throws: R Height: 6'4" Weight: 225 lb. Origin: Round 1, 2015 Draft (#11 overall)

YEAR	TEAM	LVL	AGE	PA	R	2B	3B	HR	RBI	BB	K	SB	CS	Whiff%	AVG/OBP/SLG	DRC+	BABIP	BRR	DRP	WARP
2020	CIN	MLB	23	20	4	0	0	2	6	2	9	0	0	26.7%	.294/.400/.647	92	.500	0.0	C(4): -0.0	0.0
2021	CIN	MLB	24	402	56	21	0	10	45	41	75	0	0	19.0%	.286/.366/.431	106	.333	-1.6	C(78): 2.7, 1B(23): -0.4, LF(1): 0.1	1.9
2022	CIN	MLB	25	183	24	9	0	6	35	12	47	1	0	27.0%	.319/.372/.482	103	.409	-0.3	C(45): -0.6	0.6
2023 DC	*CIN*	*MLB*	*26*	*440*	*45*	*20*	*0*	*10*	*47*	*35*	*98*	*0*	*1*	*23.9%*	*.258/.333/.392*	*99*	*.323*	*-4.0*	*C 0, 1B 0*	*1.0*

Comparables: Jorge Alfaro (70), Wilin Rosario (69), J.T. Realmuto (68)

YEAR	TEAM	P. COUNT	FRM RUNS	BLK RUNS	THRW RUNS	TOT RUNS
2020	CIN	396	0.0	0.0	0.0	0.0
2021	CIN	10089	1.6	-0.1	0.1	1.6
2022	CIN	6198	-0.6	-0.1	0.1	-0.6
2023	*CIN*	*13228*	*-0.2*	*-0.1*	*0.3*	*-0.1*

Those 43 starts behind the flat white pentagon were the most by a Reds catcher last year. It was that kind of season for everybody, but especially for Stephenson, whose bosses cleared roster space in an effort to give him the job. Three separate maladies truncated a season in which he showed some middle-of-the-order might: a concussion, a fractured right thumb and a broken right clavicle. The latter two injuries were sustained on foul tips. This is why catchers hit .180 and we're okay with it.

Joey Votto 1B Born: 09/10/83 Age: 39 Bats: L Throws: R Height: 6'2" Weight: 220 lb. Origin: Round 2, 2002 Draft (#44 overall)

YEAR	TEAM	LVL	AGE	PA	R	2B	3B	HR	RBI	BB	K	SB	CS	Whiff%	AVG/OBP/SLG	DRC+	BABIP	BRR	DRP	WARP
2020	CIN	MLB	36	223	32	8	0	11	22	37	43	0	0	22.5%	.226/.354/.446	119	.235	0.8	1B(50): -2.6	0.8
2021	CIN	MLB	37	533	73	23	1	36	99	77	127	1	0	29.3%	.266/.375/.563	129	.287	-2.1	1B(123): -1.2	2.8
2022	CIN	MLB	38	376	31	18	1	11	41	44	97	0	0	29.7%	.205/.319/.370	88	.257	-2.4	1B(76): -0.6	-0.1
2023 DC	*CIN*	*MLB*	*39*	*561*	*64*	*25*	*1*	*21*	*66*	*69*	*151*	*0*	*0*	*29.4%*	*.231/.337/.417*	*104*	*.294*	*-0.6*	*1B 0*	*1.1*

Comparables: Eddie Murray (75), Todd Helton (75), Jim Bottomley (73)

Votto's lost year, when he was as valuable when not on the field as when available, dipped his career slash line below the .300/.400/.500 barrier for the first time since 2009. That was the year before he became MVP, and was his team's first campaign of the century without Adam Dunn and Ken Griffey Jr.—firmly seating the first baseman atop the list of the most-recognizable Reds. All those years later, he remains the Cincinnati elder statesman. (Not to be confused with the Cincinnati Moeller statesman, Griffey, who began building his legendary reputation at the high school.) Votto might relinquish his title at the end of this year, limping into the final guaranteed season of a 10-year extension thanks to a variety of maladies. The veteran Canadian appears very much at peace at this stage in his career and life, and his ability to rebound likely dictates what happens in future offseasons. In the meantime, Votto's approachability and candor will stretch this summer as long as possible, whether or not it's his last.

PITCHERS

Andrew Abbott LHP Born: 06/01/99 Age: 24 Bats: L Throws: L Height: 6'0" Weight: 180 lb. Origin: Round 2, 2021 Draft (#53 overall)

YEAR	TEAM	LVL	AGE	W	L	SV	G	GS	IP	H	HR	BB/9	K/9	K	GB%	BABIP	WHIP	ERA	DRA-	WARP	MPH	FB%	Whiff%	CSP
2021	DBT	A	22	0	0	0	4	3	11	11	2	3.3	15.5	19	48.0%	.391	1.36	4.91	84	0.2				
2022	DAY	A+	23	3	0	0	5	4	27	16	1	2.3	13.3	40	47.3%	.278	0.85	0.67	76	0.6				
2022	CHA	AA	23	7	7	0	20	20	91	84	7	4.1	11.8	119	43.4%	.360	1.37	4.75	80	1.9				
2023 non-DC	*CIN*	*MLB*	*24*	*2*	*2*	*0*	*57*	*0*	*50*	*48*	*6*	*4.6*	*9.8*	*54*	*44.5%*	*.314*	*1.47*	*4.49*	*108*	*0.0*			*28.8%*	

Comparables: John Gant (73), Steven Matz (71), Sean Nolin (70)

As a result of Cincinnati's investments in pitch design, and a clear turn toward valuing modern stuff metrics, this chapter is going to resemble the Mace Windu fight scene in *Revenge of the Sith*, except with Palpatine yelling "UNLIMITED SPIN!!!!!" instead of "UNLIMITED POWER!!!!" Our first contestant is Abbott, who rode his nasty curve and its wicked spin to a top-15 performance on the minor-league strikeout leaderboard. There are a number of caveats from a traditional scouting perspective here—he's short, his velocity isn't anything special and his command and changeup are works in progress—but the best predictor of whether you can make batters miss is whether you've made batters miss in the past. And his curveball sure looks like a heck of a bat-missing pitch.

Tejay Antone RHP Born: 12/05/93 Age: 29 Bats: R Throws: R Height: 6'4" Weight: 230 lb. Origin: Round 5, 2014 Draft (#155 overall)

YEAR	TEAM	LVL	AGE	W	L	SV	G	GS	IP	H	HR	BB/9	K/9	K	GB%	BABIP	WHIP	ERA	DRA-	WARP	MPH	FB%	Whiff%	CSP
2020	CIN	MLB	26	0	3	0	13	4	35^{1}	20	4	4.1	11.5	45	48.7%	.216	1.02	2.80	77	0.8	95.9	40.5%	34.4%	44.8%
2021	LOU	AAA	27	0	0	1	7	0	6^{2}	4	1	4.1	13.5	10	53.8%	.250	1.05	2.70	82	0.2				
2021	CIN	MLB	27	2	0	3	23	0	33^{2}	17	3	3.5	11.2	42	47.1%	.209	0.89	2.14	80	0.7	97.1	32.3%	33.6%	58.5%
2023 DC	*CIN*	*MLB*	*29*	*3*	*3*	*0*	*69*	*0*	*60*	*53*	*7*	*3.7*	*10.2*	*68*	*48.6%*	*.303*	*1.30*	*3.74*	*90*	*0.6*	*96.6*	*35.8%*	*28.9%*	*52.6%*

Comparables: Charlie Furbush (51), Taylor Hill (49), Josh Collmenter (48)

There are 2,430 games in a major-league season, plus a few dozen postseason games, to go with the other several thousand minor-league bouts. Antone didn't pitch in any of them, as he was recovering from his second Tommy John surgery. Even if he had been tossing 200 innings a season prior, it's easy to forget a pitcher who hasn't been seen in a year given the oversaturation of box scores. The reliever made a ton of batters look foolish with a splendid curveball and was looking like a breakout star halfway through 2021; his presence was certainly missed on a team that permitted over five runs a game. When that first curveball snaps in for strike one, all the memories will come rushing back.

Graham Ashcraft RHP Born: 02/11/98 Age: 25 Bats: L Throws: R Height: 6'2" Weight: 240 lb. Origin: Round 6, 2019 Draft (#174 overall)

YEAR	TEAM	LVL	AGE	W	L	SV	G	GS	IP	H	HR	BB/9	K/9	K	GB%	BABIP	WHIP	ERA	DRA-	WARP	MPH	FB%	Whiff%	CSP
2021	DAY	A+	23	4	1	0	8	8	38^{2}	28	0	3.0	12.8	55	54.5%	.322	1.06	2.33	63	1.2				
2021	CHA	AA	23	7	3	0	14	14	72^{1}	58	4	3.0	9.2	74	59.6%	.287	1.13	3.36	87	1.3				
2022	LOU	AAA	24	3	2	0	8	8	35^{1}	42	0	4.3	8.9	35	66.7%	.359	1.67	2.29	96	0.5				
2022	CIN	MLB	24	5	6	0	19	19	105	119	11	2.6	6.1	71	54.4%	.314	1.42	4.89	120	0.0	97.3	72.2%	18.6%	54.9%
2023 DC	*CIN*	*MLB*	*25*	*8*	*10*	*0*	*27*	*27*	*148.7*	*177*	*14*	*3.5*	*6.2*	*102*	*55.8%*	*.334*	*1.59*	*5.14*	*120*	*-0.3*	*97.3*	*72.2%*	*21.8%*	*54.9%*

Comparables: David Buchanan (73), Ben Lively (71), Dario Agrazal (69)

Ashcraft was one of the biggest beneficiaries of a remaining COVID-19 oddity that affected the 2022 season: the Canadian/American border policy prohibiting unvaccinated players from crossing. Called up as a substitute player to take Tyler Mahle's turn in late May at Rogers Centre, he pitched well enough that the Reds kept him in the rotation for the rest of the year. It was as much due to the injuries and trades around Ashcraft as anything—and he missed part of August and most of September with a biceps issue, after which he got absolutely thrashed for three starts. Ashcraft has premium velocity, regularly hitting 100–101 mph on the radar gun, but both of his fastball types have poor shape and suboptimal movement. That led to a shocking lack of missed bats for a pitcher who throws that hard with a clear plus slider; this sort of issue often works itself out in the bullpen down the road.

Luis Cessa RHP Born: 04/25/92 Age: 31 Bats: R Throws: R Height: 6'0" Weight: 208 lb. Origin: International Free Agent, 2008

YEAR	TEAM	LVL	AGE	W	L	SV	G	GS	IP	H	HR	BB/9	K/9	K	GB%	BABIP	WHIP	ERA	DRA-	WARP	MPH	FB%	Whiff%	CSP
2020	NYY	MLB	28	0	0	1	16	0	21^{2}	20	2	2.9	7.1	17	39.7%	.273	1.25	3.32	119	0.0	93.8	31.1%	27.7%	41.6%
2021	NYY	MLB	29	3	1	0	29	0	38^{1}	31	2	4.0	7.3	31	56.6%	.266	1.25	2.82	107	0.2	93.4	31.0%	27.1%	55.8%
2021	CIN	MLB	29	2	1	0	24	0	26^{1}	24	3	0.7	7.9	23	44.0%	.292	0.99	2.05	95	0.3	94.3	31.6%	26.8%	57.6%
2022	CIN	MLB	30	4	4	0	46	10	80^{2}	76	14	3.1	6.6	59	48.6%	.266	1.29	4.57	111	0.3	93.6	42.3%	22.1%	56.5%
2023 DC	*CIN*	*MLB*	*31*	*8*	*8*	*0*	*63*	*17*	*111.3*	*117*	*13*	*3.3*	*6.9*	*85*	*48.3%*	*.306*	*1.42*	*4.35*	*106*	*0.2*	*93.8*	*38.2%*	*24.5%*	*53.8%*

Comparables: Zach McAllister (61), Alex Colomé (60), Liam Hendriks (57)

For the first time in five years the plurality of Cessa's pitches were fastballs, barely besting his beloved slider. A broadened pitch mix won him some late-season starts. It's a breathtaking example of how much more impact a starter can make: In just over a month of starts, he amassed more innings than in his first 37 appearances—despite not once treading into the seventh inning. It's why pitching coaches scream about getting that third pitch over. It inflates your workload and your paycheck. For the longtime swingman, that third pitch was a changeup. That will decide if he finally hits the triple-digit inning mark for a season, or goes back to tiny bite-sized portions of baseball activities.

Fernando Cruz RHP Born: 03/28/90 Age: 33 Bats: R Throws: R Height: 6'2" Weight: 205 lb. Origin: Round 6, 2007 Draft (#186 overall)

YEAR	TEAM	LVL	AGE	W	L	SV	G	GS	IP	H	HR	BB/9	K/9	K	GB%	BABIP	WHIP	ERA	DRA-	WARP	MPH	FB%	Whiff%	CSP
2022	LOU	AAA	32	4	4	23	51	0	56	39	4	3.1	10.6	66	41.2%	.267	1.04	2.89	79	1.4				
2022	CIN	MLB	32	0	1	0	14	2	14^{2}	9	1	5.5	12.9	21	39.4%	.250	1.23	1.23	84	0.3	94.4	27.6%	37.2%	48.1%
2023 DC	*CIN*	*MLB*	*33*	*2*	*2*	*0*	*54*	*0*	*46.7*	*40*	*6*	*3.9*	*10.3*	*53*	*41.9%*	*.295*	*1.29*	*3.68*	*89*	*0.5*	*94.4*	*27.6%*	*30.7%*	*48.1%*

Comparables: Caleb Thielbar (62), Rafael Dolis (60), Steve Cishek (60)

Cruz was drafted as a position player the same year and round as Anthony Rizzo, who has played over 1,500 major-league games. A year after his switch to the mound, Cruz was released. The son-in-law of former Reds infielder Luis Quinones, his last stat line as an affiliated minor leaguer was back when the Cubs still hadn't won a World Series in some time. Between then and last year, his teams were all based in Puerto Rico, Mexico or New Jersey—the golden triumvirate for diamond dogs with nothing but a decent fastball and a dream. After a modest showing in winter ball, the Reds signed Cruz on a scout recommendation. He became their Triple-A closer thanks to a superior slider and splitter, ultimately becoming the oldest Reds rookie in over 60 years. The split-finger in particular was unhittable: Of the 76 he threw, 42 were swung at, 26 were missed, seven were put into play and only one produced a base hit. The short burst of success coupled with the long road to get here makes Cruz an instant reason to tune in.

Alexis Díaz RHP Born: 09/28/96 Age: 26 Bats: R Throws: R Height: 6'2" Weight: 224 lb. Origin: Round 12, 2015 Draft (#355 overall)

YEAR	TEAM	LVL	AGE	W	L	SV	G	GS	IP	H	HR	BB/9	K/9	K	GB%	BABIP	WHIP	ERA	DRA-	WARP	MPH	FB%	Whiff%	CSP
2021	CHA	AA	24	3	1	2	35	0	42^{1}	30	2	4.3	14.9	70	43.0%	.333	1.18	3.83	68	1.2				
2022	CIN	MLB	25	7	3	10	59	0	63^{2}	28	5	4.7	11.7	83	29.9%	.180	0.96	1.84	76	1.4	95.9	64.9%	36.0%	50.4%
2023 DC	*CIN*	*MLB*	*26*	*3*	*3*	*25*	*77*	*0*	*66.7*	*55*	*10*	*4.9*	*11.8*	*87*	*35.6%*	*.303*	*1.37*	*4.23*	*97*	*0.4*	*95.9*	*64.9%*	*35.4%*	*50.4%*

Comparables: Reyes Moronta (92), Kyle Barraclough (90), Ryan Cook (85)

Imagine this Sisyphean route to the big leagues: a third-day draft selection, a poorly timed Tommy John surgery, six seasons to ascend beyond Class-A ball. After that, any sort of career year might satisfy, but Díaz went further, into genuine name-making territory. Yes, the team was bad, and the bullpen is the widest foxhole from which major leaguers spring, but Díaz started with some low-leverage innings and worked his way into the plurality of the 31 team saves. He even got to choose his own walkout song (Bad Bunny's "Bendiciones"), and was rumored to be a trade target at the deadline. Now, the right-hander's going to be a frontrunner to close out games, thanks to the highest-rpm fastball in the game. It was an incredibly transformative rookie season, a dizzying ascent. The one stinging truth: He had the second-best year in his family, as brother Edwin kinda did better at everything—except for that aforementioned fastball spin. Alexis was especially outdone on his ninth-inning earworm—you can't beat live backing. It's gonna be hard to bring Bad Bunny for a potential save situation, especially if the team is going to lose another 100.

Daniel Duarte RHP Born: 12/04/96 Age: 26 Bats: R Throws: R Height: 6'0" Weight: 170 lb. Origin: International Free Agent, 2013

YEAR	TEAM	LVL	AGE	W	L	SV	G	GS	IP	H	HR	BB/9	K/9	K	GB%	BABIP	WHIP	ERA	DRA-	WARP	MPH	FB%	Whiff%	CSP
2021	DAY	A+	24	0	1	1	4	0	5^{1}	5	0	10.1	6.8	4	26.7%	.333	2.06	3.38	125	0.0				
2021	CHA	AA	24	0	1	6	11	0	12^{1}	14	2	3.6	13.1	18	40.6%	.400	1.54	5.84	84	0.2				
2022	LOU	AAA	25	0	1	0	10	0	7^{2}	8	1	7.0	8.2	7	31.8%	.333	1.83	9.39	101	0.1				
2022	CIN	MLB	25	0	0	0	3	0	2^{2}	3	1	10.1	6.7	2	11.1%	.250	2.25	10.12	117	0.0	96.1	51.9%	11.4%	52.5%
2023 non-DC	*CIN*	*MLB*	*26*	*2*	*3*	*0*	*57*	*0*	*50*	*52*	*9*	*5.7*	*7.7*	*42*	*38.0%*	*.303*	*1.68*	*5.92*	*132*	*-0.6*	*96.1*	*51.9%*	*22.2%*	*52.5%*

Comparables: Angel Nesbitt (31), R.J. Alvarez (29), Zac Reininger (29)

Duarte made the big-league outfit out of spring training last year, and what a ride it was to get there. Originally signed as an international free agent by the Rangers in 2013, he never made full-season ball in five tries, and eventually ended up on loan to the Mexican League. The Royals liked what they saw there enough to select him in the Triple-A phase of the 2017 Rule 5 Draft—the part where everyone who is even remotely a prospect is protected by their original team, and you can select a prospect for low-five figures. From there, he was loaned out again, to the same Mexican club, before spending a couple seasons bouncing around filling holes in Kansas City's A-ball bullpens. The Royals released him after the 2019 season, and he got cut again by the Reds following 2020's abbreviated spring. Duarte went back home to the Mexican League full-time at that point; this is usually where the affiliated baseball story ends, but Cincy kept an eye on him from afar. They needed another arm in the system a year later, and by the end of that season he was hitting the upper-90s with a nasty slider, showcasing himself in the Olympics and meriting a November 2021 addition to the 40-man roster. He made his MLB debut last year but missed most of the summer with an elbow injury; still, no one's forgetting his promising relief arm anymore.

Justin Dunn RHP Born: 09/22/95 Age: 27 Bats: R Throws: R Height: 6'2" Weight: 185 lb. Origin: Round 1, 2016 Draft (#19 overall)

YEAR	TEAM	LVL	AGE	W	L	SV	G	GS	IP	H	HR	BB/9	K/9	K	GB%	BABIP	WHIP	ERA	DRA-	WARP	MPH	FB%	Whiff%	CSP
2020	SEA	MLB	24	4	1	0	10	10	45^{2}	31	10	6.1	7.5	38	32.3%	.179	1.36	4.34	148	-0.7	91.4	54.8%	22.2%	46.2%
2021	SEA	MLB	25	1	3	0	11	11	50^{1}	37	6	5.2	8.8	49	33.8%	.238	1.31	3.75	109	0.2	93.8	51.8%	24.9%	54.9%
2022	LOU	AAA	26	0	3	0	8	8	29	31	4	5.6	8.4	27	36.7%	.314	1.69	6.21	128	0.0				
2022	CIN	MLB	26	1	3	0	7	7	31	32	11	4.9	6.1	21	28.9%	.247	1.58	6.10	150	-0.5	92.3	50.0%	22.3%	55.3%
2023 DC	*CIN*	*MLB*	*27*	*4*	*7*	*0*	*19*	*19*	*89.3*	*91*	*16*	*5.1*	*7.4*	*73*	*34.7%*	*.292*	*1.59*	*5.58*	*126*	*-0.5*	*92.7*	*52.1%*	*23.3%*	*52.7%*

Comparables: Erik Johnson (56), Jeff Locke (55), Daniel Mengden (55)

You could make half of a mighty strong infield with the players Dunn has been traded for in his life. First Robinson Canó as a prospect, then Eugenio Suárez as an injured pitcher—yes, the Reds still acquired him despite knowing about the injury—Dunn was only able to make seven starts in between bouts of shoulder discomfort, while Suárez hit another 30 homers and helped a franchise break a 20-year postseason drought. When Dunn was manning the mound, his fastball was absolutely hammered, allowing at least one home run in each start—making the opposition look like the very infield for which he keeps being dealt.

Buck Farmer RHP Born: 02/20/91 Age: 32 Bats: L Throws: R Height: 6'4" Weight: 232 lb. Origin: Round 5, 2013 Draft (#156 overall)

YEAR	TEAM	LVL	AGE	W	L	SV	G	GS	IP	H	HR	BB/9	K/9	K	GB%	BABIP	WHIP	ERA	DRA-	WARP	MPH	FB%	Whiff%	CSP
2020	DET	MLB	29	1	0	0	23	0	21^1	20	3	2.1	5.9	14	51.4%	.258	1.17	3.80	102	0.2	93.4	52.8%	19.9%	46.4%
2021	RR	AAA	30	2	1	8	15	0	15	11	1	3.6	9.0	15	42.5%	.263	1.13	3.60	87	0.2				
2021	TOL	AAA	30	0	2	0	9	0	11^1	11	0	3.2	5.6	7	36.1%	.306	1.32	3.97	107	0.1				
2021	DET	MLB	30	0	0	0	36	0	35^1	40	9	5.3	9.4	37	37.0%	.313	1.73	6.37	122	-0.1	94.3	47.7%	26.1%	49.7%
2022	LOU	AAA	31	0	3	1	20	0	22^1	18	4	3.6	13.7	34	28.6%	.311	1.21	3.63	78	0.6				
2022	CIN	MLB	31	2	2	2	44	0	47	36	2	4.8	10.3	54	42.0%	.293	1.30	3.83	85	0.8	94.8	44.6%	31.7%	48.0%
2023 DC	*CIN*	*MLB*	*32*	*3*	*3*	*0*	*61*	*0*	*53.3*	*47*	*8*	*4.0*	*9.3*	*55*	*40.1%*	*.288*	*1.34*	*4.07*	*98*	*0.3*	*94.6*	*46.9%*	*29.2%*	*47.7%*

Comparables: Zach McAllister (53), Tyler Thornburg (50), Chris Bootcheck (48)

Being asked to serve as a calming influence, in a bullpen that is constantly being asked to put out fires, and instead just touching the hot burner over and over is a rather sizable favor. The longtime Tigers reliever was briefly thought expendable after a couple of absolute conflagrations spiraled out of control, but after returning for the second half, the veteran put himself in a leading conversation as a late-inning necessity. July onward, the ERA and FIP both ducked below three, and not a single home run was shed—in Cincinnati, of all places. With years of experience and all three pitches preventing forest fires, expect Farmer to irrigate anywhere between the seventh and ninth innings this year.

Hunter Greene RHP Born: 08/06/99 Age: 23 Bats: R Throws: R Height: 6'5" Weight: 230 lb. Origin: Round 1, 2017 Draft (#2 overall)

YEAR	TEAM	LVL	AGE	W	L	SV	G	GS	IP	H	HR	BB/9	K/9	K	GB%	BABIP	WHIP	ERA	DRA-	WARP	MPH	FB%	Whiff%	CSP
2021	CHA	AA	21	5	0	0	7	7	41	27	2	3.1	13.2	60	41.2%	.301	1.00	1.98	92	0.6				
2021	LOU	AAA	21	5	8	0	14	14	65^1	59	11	3.4	10.9	79	45.2%	.306	1.29	4.13	84	1.4				
2022	LOU	AAA	22	0	0	0	3	3	7	6	0	2.6	19.3	15	33.3%	.500	1.14	2.57	70	0.2				
2022	CIN	MLB	22	5	13	0	24	24	125^2	104	24	3.4	11.7	164	30.1%	.281	1.21	4.44	84	2.2	99.2	53.8%	32.0%	52.8%
2023 DC	*CIN*	*MLB*	*23*	*9*	*9*	*0*	*29*	*29*	*154.3*	*131*	*25*	*3.6*	*11.6*	*199*	*35.1%*	*.302*	*1.25*	*3.83*	*91*	*2.0*	*99.2*	*53.8%*	*30.8%*	*52.8%*

Comparables: Luis Severino (68), Taijuan Walker (68), Jack Flaherty (67)

On a quiet, mid-May afternoon against a little-known team called the Pittsburgh Pirates, Greene missed the strike zone for ball four, prompting an eighth-inning pitching change. A rookie starter with three figures of smoke, Greene had just issued his fifth walk, and was up to 118 pitches. He also had not allowed a hit or a run. Greene and reliever Art Warren went on to combine for a no-hitter, but the team still lost, 1-0, making him the first starter since Jered Weaver to take the loss in such a bittersweet fashion. The capacity for more-satisfying gems is ahead: The rookie led his team in all the major categories despite missing over a month with a shoulder strain. Last year was always going to be a summer of setbacks for his club, because that's how the Cincy brass wanted it, but at least Greene finished on a personal positive note—post-injury, he posted a 0.78 ERA across his final four starts. His team lost three of them.

Jeff Hoffman RHP Born: 01/08/93 Age: 30 Bats: R Throws: R Height: 6'5" Weight: 235 lb. Origin: Round 1, 2014 Draft (#9 overall)

YEAR	TEAM	LVL	AGE	W	L	SV	G	GS	IP	H	HR	BB/9	K/9	K	GB%	BABIP	WHIP	ERA	DRA-	WARP	MPH	FB%	Whiff%	CSP
2020	COL	MLB	27	2	1	1	16	0	21^1	32	3	3.8	8.4	20	35.6%	.414	1.92	9.28	120	0.0	94.6	54.6%	22.2%	47.0%
2021	LOU	AAA	28	0	0	0	4	4	15^1	11	2	2.3	11.7	20	32.4%	.265	0.98	1.76	86	0.3				
2021	CIN	MLB	28	3	5	0	31	11	73	70	12	5.5	9.7	79	37.4%	.301	1.58	4.56	107	0.4	94.4	56.0%	29.9%	55.6%
2022	CIN	MLB	29	2	0	0	35	1	44^2	40	5	4.6	9.1	45	28.6%	.289	1.41	3.83	106	0.3	94.5	52.0%	25.6%	53.2%
2023 DC	*FA*	*MLB*	*30*	*2*	*2*	*0*	*43*	*0*	*37.3*	*37*	*6*	*4.3*	*9.1*	*38*	*34.5%*	*.306*	*1.47*	*5.04*	*116*	*-0.2*	*94.4*	*54.8%*	*25.8%*	*53.1%*

Comparables: Billy Buckner (66), Wade LeBlanc (59), Matt Kinney (59)

It was rather hard to find, tucked away behind all of life's little miracles, but Hoffman had a terrific couple of months chucking from the bullpen before his elbow begged for months of rest. He won't need surgery, but the seemingly perpetual prospect who couldn't find a ballpark to match his strengths put up some career numbers—in the half-season when his elbow wasn't a shrieking bundle of nerves yearning for the sweet release of death. There's a usable fastball in there somewhere. It's just hard to hear over the screaming.

Joel Kuhnel RHP Born: 02/19/95 Age: 28 Bats: R Throws: R Height: 6'4" Weight: 280 lb. Origin: Round 11, 2016 Draft (#318 overall)

YEAR	TEAM	LVL	AGE	W	L	SV	G	GS	IP	H	HR	BB/9	K/9	K	GB%	BABIP	WHIP	ERA	DRA-	WARP	MPH	FB%	Whiff%	CSP
2020	CIN	MLB	25	1	0	0	3	0	3	4	2	0.0	9.0	3	30.0%	.250	1.33	6.00	107	0.0	95.7	57.9%	15.8%	48.5%
2022	LOU	AAA	27	0	1	3	10	0	10^1	9	1	0.9	6.1	7	55.9%	.242	0.97	2.61	96	0.2				
2022	CIN	MLB	27	2	3	1	53	0	58	67	8	2.2	8.7	56	53.3%	.347	1.40	6.36	95	0.7	96.2	54.6%	25.3%	54.9%
2023 DC	*CIN*	*MLB*	*28*	*1*	*1*	*0*	*38*	*0*	*33.3*	*35*	*4*	*2.7*	*7.2*	*26*	*50.7%*	*.309*	*1.35*	*4.11*	*101*	*0.1*	*96.2*	*55.0%*	*25.0%*	*54.2%*

Comparables: Noé Ramirez (55), Tayron Guerrero (55), Kevin Quackenbush (54)

For most of the season, Kuhnel ran like a hotel faucet—hotter than hot and colder than cold. The streakiness was a stark improvement over the previous campaign, when he was completely absent. After trying to push through discomfort in the 2020 season, the next year he paid for it: Surgery to repair a torn shoulder capsule precluded all but a few minor-league innings. The slightly smaller version of Jonathan Broxton entered the bullpen a month into the season, immediately oscillating between two extremes. For all the hot/cold turmoil, he limited free passes consistently, which was the commonality in each minor-league success. That's the one thing you want to be lukewarm.

Nick Lodolo LHP Born: 02/05/98 Age: 25 Bats: L Throws: L Height: 6'6" Weight: 205 lb. Origin: Round 1, 2019 Draft (#7 overall)

YEAR	TEAM	LVL	AGE	W	L	SV	G	GS	IP	H	HR	BB/9	K/9	K	GB%	BABIP	WHIP	ERA	DRA-	WARP	MPH	FB%	Whiff%	CSP
2021	CHA	AA	23	2	1	0	10	10	44	31	1	1.8	13.9	68	53.3%	.337	0.91	1.84	77	1.0				
2021	LOU	AAA	23	0	1	0	3	3	6^2	7	2	2.7	13.5	10	56.2%	.357	1.35	5.40	87	0.1				
2022	LOU	AAA	24	0	0	0	3	3	10^2	12	0	1.7	13.5	16	55.6%	.444	1.31	2.53	80	0.3				
2022	CIN	MLB	24	4	7	0	19	19	103^1	90	13	3.4	11.4	131	45.6%	.322	1.25	3.66	87	1.7	94.4	59.1%	30.8%	52.9%
2023 DC	*CIN*	*MLB*	*25*	*9*	*8*	*0*	*29*	*29*	*145.7*	*130*	*18*	*3.2*	*11.3*	*183*	*47.5%*	*.320*	*1.25*	*3.88*	*92*	*1.9*	*94.4*	*59.1%*	*30.3%*	*52.9%*

Comparables: Blake Snell (58), Danny Salazar (58), Sean Newcomb (57)

If you were to redo the 2019 draft, Alek Manoah would certainly be the top pitcher taken, but Lodolo—the first arm chosen—is still likely the second choice. That's especially true after a rookie season in which the legendary K/BB rate in the minors didn't entirely disappear against the continent's most brutal batters. (A league-leading 19 HBP came out of nowhere, from both batters' perspective and Lodolo's.) He peaked in August with consecutive starts featuring 11 strikeouts and no walks; the last rookie to do that was Dwight Gooden. The large glowing question mark remains Lodolo's health. He missed over a month with a bad back, and he's 6-foot-6: That's quite a torso to sustain an especially unnatural arm motion.

Connor Overton RHP Born: 07/24/93 Age: 29 Bats: L Throws: R Height: 6'0" Weight: 190 lb. Origin: Round 15, 2014 Draft (#437 overall)

YEAR	TEAM	LVL	AGE	W	L	SV	G	GS	IP	H	HR	BB/9	K/9	K	GB%	BABIP	WHIP	ERA	DRA-	WARP	MPH	FB%	Whiff%	CSP
2021	BUF	AAA	27	2	1	0	21	7	57^2	52	3	1.6	7.8	50	47.0%	.304	1.08	2.03	105	0.7				
2021	PIT	MLB	27	0	1	0	5	3	8^2	10	2	3.1	11.4	11	32.0%	.348	1.50	8.31	91	0.1	92.0	54.4%	27.0%	51.3%
2021	TOR	MLB	27	0	0	0	4	0	6^2	4	0	2.7	5.4	4	38.9%	.222	0.90	0.00	115	0.0	92.7	49.5%	21.6%	55.6%
2022	LOU	AAA	28	2	3	0	6	4	26^2	22	4	1.7	10.5	31	40.8%	.269	1.01	2.70	89	0.5				
2022	CIN	MLB	28	1	0	0	6	4	33	21	1	3.0	3.8	14	42.4%	.204	0.97	2.73	124	-0.1	91.3	49.0%	16.3%	56.7%
2023 DC	*CIN*	*MLB*	*29*	*8*	*9*	*0*	*52*	*22*	*117.3*	*125*	*16*	*2.9*	*6.4*	*84*	*41.5%*	*.303*	*1.39*	*4.49*	*110*	*0.2*	*91.6*	*50.1%*	*22.4%*	*55.6%*

Comparables: JC Ramírez (49), Andrew Triggs (48), Justin Germano (48)

The Overton window is a political construct, in which ludicrous ideas and thoughts become tolerable and possibly mainstream over time due to a shift in culture and societal tone. For example, the idea of rooting for a sports team in another city, once unthinkable, becomes a logical idea when, suppose, the local team's owner goes into rebuild mode and then dares you to find another allegiance. Twice released as a minor leaguer, Overton's progression into a major leaguer made absolutely zero noise. He was a potentially uplifting story on a dismal team after a 1.82 ERA across four starts, but a back injury wiped out four months. He throws five pitches—all for strikes, though few strikeouts—but he'll be contending for the fifth spot of a major-league rotation, a concept once thought ludicrous when the Marlins released him after his first pro season. Things have shifted.

Chase Petty RHP Born: 04/04/03 Age: 20 Bats: R Throws: R Height: 6'1" Weight: 190 lb. Origin: Round 1, 2021 Draft (#26 overall)

YEAR	TEAM	LVL	AGE	W	L	SV	G	GS	IP	H	HR	BB/9	K/9	K	GB%	BABIP	WHIP	ERA	DRA-	WARP	MPH	FB%	Whiff%	CSP
2022	DBT	A	19	0	4	0	18	13	67^2	57	5	3.2	8.4	63	59.0%	.292	1.20	3.06	101	1.1	93.8	57.6%	27.5%	
2022	DAY	A+	19	1	2	0	7	7	30^2	27	2	2.1	9.7	33	43.5%	.301	1.11	4.40	95	0.4				
2023 non-DC	*CIN*	*MLB*	*20*	*2*	*3*	*0*	*57*	*0*	*50*	*54*	*6*	*4.2*	*6.6*	*36*	*48.8%*	*.308*	*1.56*	*5.31*	*127*	*-0.5*			*23.5%*	

Comparables: Spencer Adams (75), Tyler Danish (71), Jacob Turner (69)

Petty was, at face value, a bit of an odd pick for the Twins in the 2020 Draft: a hard-throwing and wild short prep righty, taken by a team which has otherwise only taken hitters in the first round in the Thad Levine and Derek Falvey era. It probably shouldn't have been a surprise that he was quickly shipped off to Cincinnati—likely the organization most singularly focused on developing raw stuff—straight up for Sonny Gray. Petty dialed his sinking fastball back into the mid-90s in his new organization, and his slider didn't flash plus-plus as often as against overmatched high school kids. But some real development occurred beneath the flashier pieces: His previously barely existent change emerged as a real weapon against lefties, and he threw strikes and pitched well late in the season, as a teenager. If he starts missing more bats with his heater and keeps consolidating his gains, he'll push into Top 101 consideration very quickly.

★ ★ ★ *2023 Top 101 Prospect* **#96** ★ ★ ★

Connor Phillips RHP Born: 05/04/01 Age: 22 Bats: R Throws: R Height: 6'2" Weight: 190 lb. Origin: Round 2, 2020 Draft (#64 overall)

YEAR	TEAM	LVL	AGE	W	L	SV	G	GS	IP	H	HR	BB/9	K/9	K	GB%	BABIP	WHIP	ERA	DRA-	WARP	MPH	FB%	Whiff%	CSP
2021	MOD	A	20	7	3	0	16	16	72	62	1	5.5	13.0	104	41.2%	.361	1.47	4.75	95	0.6				
2022	DAY	A+	21	4	3	0	12	12	64	39	5	4.5	12.7	90	46.5%	.279	1.11	2.95	96	0.8				
2022	CHA	AA	21	1	5	0	12	12	45^2	48	3	6.7	11.8	60	28.7%	.378	1.80	4.93	125	-0.2				
2023 non-DC	*CIN*	*MLB*	*22*	*2*	*3*	*0*	*57*	*0*	*50*	*47*	*7*	*6.5*	*9.5*	*52*	*38.6%*	*.305*	*1.68*	*5.40*	*123*	*-0.4*			*28.7%*	

Comparables: Nick Kingham (76), Jhoan Duran (76), Edwin Díaz (74)

Phillips is yet another acquisition for the Spincinnati pitching project. The player to be named later in the Jesse Winker/Eugenio Suárez trade quickly surpassed perceived headliner Brandon Williamson in prospect cache; throughout the season's first half he pumped high-spin mid- to upper-90s fastballs up in the zone and past beleaguered High-A hitters. He pairs the fastball with two distinct, promising breaking pitches—a slider and a curveball, which both register whiffs when spotted where hitters will swing. That hints at the problem: His sometimes-iffy command and control faltered badly upon promotion to Double-A. Given the nomadic command and a lacking changeup, he might be destined for relief work. In any case, the path to developing top-end starting pitching is to amass prospects with high-end traits and maximize as many as possible, and Phillips is firmly in that mix.

Reiver Sanmartin LHP Born: 04/15/96 Age: 27 Bats: L Throws: L Height: 6'2" Weight: 160 lb. Origin: International Free Agent, 2015

YEAR	TEAM	LVL	AGE	W	L	SV	G	GS	IP	H	HR	BB/9	K/9	K	GB%	BABIP	WHIP	ERA	DRA-	WARP	MPH	FB%	Whiff%	CSP
2021	EST	WIN	25	0	2	0	7	7	31	16	0	3.2	5.5	19	55.2%	.186	0.87	1.45						
2021	CHA	AA	25	2	0	0	4	3	18	8	0	2.5	11.5	23	62.2%	.216	0.72	0.50	90	0.3				
2021	LOU	AAA	25	8	2	0	21	14	82^{1}	80	6	2.5	9.7	89	54.1%	.335	1.25	3.94	93	1.4				
2021	CIN	MLB	25	2	0	0	2	2	11^{2}	12	0	1.5	8.5	11	47.1%	.353	1.20	1.54	80	0.1	89.7	48.1%	31.1%	47.8%
2022	LOU	AAA	26	2	2	0	7	2	18^{1}	24	2	2.0	12.8	26	46.0%	.458	1.53	7.36	81	0.4				
2022	CIN	MLB	26	4	4	0	45	4	57	66	8	4.6	7.4	47	53.9%	.339	1.67	6.32	116	0.1	90.9	41.3%	25.8%	50.4%
2023 DC	*CIN*	*MLB*	*27*	*3*	*3*	*0*	*61*	*0*	*53.3*	*57*	*6*	*3.3*	*8.0*	*47*	*52.4%*	*.324*	*1.44*	*4.38*	*105*	*0.2*	*90.8*	*42.1%*	*26.5%*	*50.1%*

Comparables: Sean Gilmartin (57), Mike Mayers (54), T.J. McFarland (52)

It's unlikely Sanmartin takes the mound in the first inning anytime soon after being rinsed for 25 runs across four starts. He was then sent down for a while, and returned as a rather useful medium-leverage hurler: After his recall, he logged a 3.32 ERA. For left-handed batters, he primarily relies upon a slider—especially in relief; he depends on a so-so changeup to handle the platoon disadvantage. Relying on the softer stuff has helped keep Sanmartin's white sphere out of the atmosphere; he walks too many guys, but that just plays into the southpaw stereotype. There's a pretty good reliever buried under all that ERA.

Lucas Sims RHP Born: 05/10/94 Age: 29 Bats: R Throws: R Height: 6'2" Weight: 225 lb. Origin: Round 1, 2012 Draft (#21 overall)

YEAR	TEAM	LVL	AGE	W	L	SV	G	GS	IP	H	HR	BB/9	K/9	K	GB%	BABIP	WHIP	ERA	DRA-	WARP	MPH	FB%	Whiff%	CSP
2020	CIN	MLB	26	3	0	0	20	0	25^{2}	13	3	3.9	11.9	34	41.8%	.192	0.94	2.45	82	0.5	94.2	48.1%	35.2%	43.0%
2021	CIN	MLB	27	5	3	7	47	0	47	34	6	3.4	14.6	76	26.8%	.308	1.11	4.40	67	1.3	95.3	41.6%	35.5%	54.0%
2022	CIN	MLB	28	1	0	1	6	0	6^{2}	5	0	8.1	6.8	5	52.6%	.263	1.65	9.45	112	0.0	93.8	42.6%	20.8%	46.1%
2023 DC	*CIN*	*MLB*	*29*	*3*	*3*	*3*	*69*	*0*	*60*	*50*	*9*	*4.3*	*11.3*	*75*	*35.2%*	*.294*	*1.32*	*4.06*	*95*	*0.4*	*94.6*	*44.5%*	*30.0%*	*48.8%*

Comparables: Tyler Clippard (53), Michael Lorenzen (51), Collin Balester (50)

If you're not quite familiar with Sims' work, you probably haven't been watching baseball in southern Ohio; if you have been watching, well, you still might have a pass. Sims is somehow the longest-tenured Reds pitcher, joining the team in 2018 and pitching in exactly 100 MLB games since coming over in the Adam Duvall trade. A former first-round draft pick, he's been a rock in their bullpen thanks to a lively fastball, and was one of 53 candidates to close games by the Ohio river in recent seasons. Last year, he wasn't an option due to a back injury, so it's worth tossing the stats into the baler and squeezing them into a nice little cube—he'll try it all again this year.

Brandon Williamson LHP Born: 04/02/98 Age: 25 Bats: R Throws: L Height: 6'6" Weight: 210 lb. Origin: Round 2, 2019 Draft (#59 overall)

YEAR	TEAM	LVL	AGE	W	L	SV	G	GS	IP	H	HR	BB/9	K/9	K	GB%	BABIP	WHIP	ERA	DRA-	WARP	MPH	FB%	Whiff%	CSP
2021	EVE	A+	23	2	1	0	6	6	31	21	4	2.9	17.1	59	44.2%	.354	1.00	3.19	77	0.7				
2021	ARK	AA	23	2	5	0	13	13	67^{1}	62	7	3.1	12.6	94	36.6%	.353	1.26	3.48	77	1.3				
2022	CHA	AA	24	5	2	0	14	14	67^{1}	61	5	5.3	9.9	74	39.1%	.322	1.50	4.14	105	0.5				
2022	LOU	AAA	24	1	5	0	13	13	55^{1}	53	4	6.0	8.0	49	31.9%	.302	1.63	4.07	127	0.0				
2023 DC	*CIN*	*MLB*	*25*	*3*	*4*	*0*	*23*	*8*	*48*	*49*	*7*	*5.3*	*8.3*	*44*	*38.0%*	*.312*	*1.63*	*5.53*	*124*	*-0.3*			*25.2%*	

Comparables: Charlie Leesman (71), Andrew Chafin (69), Adam Scott (69)

Williamson had a rough go of it in a year that might've seen him ascend to The Show. He moved from the Mariners to the Reds ahead of last season, and his new team sent him back to the same Double-A level he dominated in the second half of 2021. Instead of thriving, he stagnated, with the quality of his stuff and his command wavering from start to start; things only got worse after a midseason promotion to Triple-A. Williamson throws four pitches which all flash average to above-average, but lacks a true chase pitch or anything with real deception on it. At his best two years ago, he was able to spot and tunnel everything well enough to run up big rate stats regardless; last year, he couldn't induce swings outside the zone or get enough whiffs inside it, and hitters took first base all too often. There's a mid-rotation starter somewhere in here if you look deep enough, but this was a giant step back.

LINEOUTS

Hitters

HITTER	POS	TEAM	LVL	AGE	PA	R	2B	3B	HR	RBI	BB	K	SB	CS	AVG/OBP/SLG	DRC+	BABIP	BRR	DRP	WARP
Victor Acosta	SS	RED	ROK	18	34	5	4	0	0	1	5	7	0	0	.214/.353/.357		.286			
	SS	PAD	ROK	18	131	17	3	2	2	11	16	30	5	7	.243/.346/.360		.313			
Jay Allen II	CF	DBT	A	19	299	48	13	2	3	21	40	73	31	6	.224/.359/.332	106	.305	1.2	CF(71): 4.8	1.5
	CF	DAY	A+	19	84	13	1	2	0	8	4	19	12	4	.230/.301/.297	90	.304	1.8	CF(16): -0.8	0.2
Albert Almora Jr.	OF	LOU	AAA	28	83	9	4	0	0	7	2	8	0	0	.296/.313/.346	109	.329	0.7	CF(15): 1.6, LF(1): 0.1	0.5
	OF	CIN	MLB	28	235	26	10	1	5	29	17	46	3	2	.223/.282/.349	93	.261	-1.8	RF(28): 1, CF(23): -0.8, LF(17): 0.8	0.5
Ricardo Cabrera	SS	DSL REDS	ROK	17	180	30	6	5	1	19	13	40	5	4	.253/.363/.380		.333			
Tyler Callihan	2B/3B	DBT	A	22	128	18	7	0	3	13	10	19	9	1	.282/.336/.419	121	.313	0.7	2B(28): -0.1, 3B(1): 0.2	0.7
	2B/3B	DAY	A+	22	233	27	12	4	4	20	17	61	6	2	.232/.297/.384	76	.306	0.5	3B(29): -0.5, 2B(23): 1.1	0.1
Allan Cerda	OF	DAY	A+	22	249	38	13	1	13	31	42	91	3	3	.219/.369/.488	104	.320	0.0	CF(38): 0.8, RF(16): -1.3	1.0
	OF	CHA	AA	22	257	36	9	0	11	25	42	77	4	1	.198/.350/.401	107	.250	0.3	RF(39): -0.7, LF(1): 0.1	0.8
Stuart Fairchild	OF	LOU	AAA	26	136	23	6	1	7	16	10	34	5	1	.273/.338/.512	99	.317	1.4	RF(18): 1.3, CF(17): -1.6	0.3
	OF	RNO	AAA	26	43	3	2	0	2	3	4	15	0	1	.162/.279/.378	78	.200	-0.3	LF(3): -0.3, RF(3): -0.1, CF(2): 0.5	0.1
	OF	CIN	MLB	26	99	13	4	1	5	6	8	29	0	2	.279/.374/.523	95	.365	-2.0	LF(20): 0.8, CF(15): 0.2, RF(4): 0.1	0.2
	OF	SF	MLB	26	8	1	0	0	0	0	0	3	0	0	.000/.000/.000	92			CF(5): 0.1	
	OF	SEA	MLB	26	3	0	0	0	0	0	0	2	0	0	.000/.000/.000	88			LF(2): -0.1	0.0
Aramis Garcia	C	CIN	MLB	29	115	6	2	0	1	4	3	34	0	1	.213/.248/.259	67	.301	-0.9	C(41): 6.1, 1B(5): 0	0.5
Colin Moran	CI	LOU	AAA	29	213	21	11	0	7	26	18	54	0	0	.249/.310/.415	91	.306	-3.5	1B(29): 1.8, 3B(11): -1.0	0.1
	CI	CIN	MLB	29	128	11	3	0	5	23	16	30	0	0	.211/.305/.376	96	.234	-1.1	1B(25): -0.2, 3B(14): 0	0.1
Stephen Piscotty	RF/DH	LOU	AAA	31	96	8	3	0	5	14	7	24	0	0	.250/.313/.455	101	.288	-0.2	RF(14): -1.0, LF(1): -0.0	0.4
	RF/DH	OAK	MLB	31	139	12	4	0	5	14	9	48	2	0	.190/.252/.341	82	.253	-1.3	RF(28): -1.7, LF(5): -0.1	-0.2
Chuckie Robinson	C	CHA	AA	27	126	13	5	0	3	13	9	30	4	2	.276/.333/.397	95	.349	-0.8	C(29): -2.5	0.0
	C	LOU	AAA	27	93	11	5	1	2	12	5	19	0	0	.253/.301/.402	95	.303	-1.9	C(27): -0.5	0.0
	C	CIN	MLB	27	60	3	2	0	2	5	0	17	0	0	.136/.136/.271	72	.150	0.1	C(25): -0.8	0.0
Sal Stewart	3B	RED	ROK	18	28	5	4	0	0	5	4	5	0	0	.292/.393/.458		.368			
Logan Tanner	C	DBT	A	21	70	9	3	0	1	7	12	20	1	0	.211/.343/.316	111	.297	-1.1	C(14): 0.2	0.2

Traded for Brandon Drury as part of A.J. Preller's profligate deadline madness, speedy switch-hitting infielder **Victor Acosta** was a top January 2021 international signing who has flashed projectable tools in the international and domestic complexes. His future is a dart throw; but also, Cincinnati got him for literally Brandon Drury. **Jay Allen II** was touted, before and after the 2021 Draft, for his plus power potential—and when challenged by full-season pitching, went out and put up a campaign out of the Myles Straw oeuvre. It's too early to give up entirely, but those great batting practice shows do need to show up against pitchers throwing in anger, sooner or later. He's going down in history as the runner who scored the go-ahead run in Game 7 of the 2016 World Series, but Cincinnati released **Albert Almora Jr.** once it became abundantly clear that situation wasn't going to become possible for them. **Ricardo Cabrera** was one of the top Venezuelan players in the January 2022 international free agency class: a well-rounded, projectable infielder. He should come stateside in 2023 after a solid pro debut in the DSL, and bears close monitoring as a potential spring or summer breakout. Long-touted bat-first infield prospect **Tyler Callihan** was finally healthy enough to play something resembling a full season, and well, if the bat is first, "prospect" might not be used to describe him for much longer. **Allan Cerda** is an old-school three true outcomes outfield prospect who has put up some Adam Dunn-style lines in the minors—so long as you ignore that hitters of this profile who succeed in the majors usually *do* hit for average in the minors. Would you believe Adam Dunn hit .334 as a 21-year-old in the high-minors in 2001? Already on his third organization of the year in July, **Stuart Fairchild** went long in the first pitch he saw with Cincinnati, briefly reminding the Reds why they drafted him, traded him away, and picked him back up off waivers. He saw fairly consistent play in the regular season's last month, showcasing his on-base skills. Backup catcher **Aramis Garcia** turned an Opening Day roster spot for the Reds into being outrighted by the Orioles, and for that reason is no longer invited to do magic tricks for children's birthday parties. Apart from a two-homer game against his ex-team, corner infielder **Colin Moran** had a puzzling post-Pirates season with the Reds—who ultimately released him in September, because the beard can only fashionably match the uniform color for so long before the batting numbers also have also to match the position. The A's released recognizable outfielder **Stephen Piscotty** to make room for Does It Even Matter, That Person Will Be Released In Three Years Anyway To Make Room For The Next Level Of Oakland's Nesting Doll. **Chuckie Robinson** was the extra player called up for the Field of Dreams Game in August and didn't get an at-bat before being sent down, which spawned a bunch of hackneyed Moonlight Graham references. Luckily, he was called back up in August to make his real major-league debut; he went the distance as Cincy's backup catcher. Power-hitting Florida prep third baseman **Sal Stewart** was selected with the first-round compensation pick attached to Nick Castellanos, himself once a power-hitting prep third baseman from Florida taken with a comp first. Since we're deep in echoes of futures past already, there might be drives to deep left field in his (very) distant future. Second-round pick **Logan Tanner** has an absolute cannon for an arm, which is both the most visible and the least important part of a catcher's defensive skill set. His hit tool is currently lagging behind the rest of his skills, which limited his in-game power output in college and has continued to do so early in his pro career.

Pitchers

PITCHER	TEAM	LVL	AGE	W	L	SV	G	GS	IP	H	HR	BB/9	K/9	K	GB%	BABIP	WHIP	ERA	DRA-	WARP	MPH	FB%	WHF	CSP
Chase Anderson	TOL	AAA	34	4	3	0	17	15	70	70	14	3.5	8.0	62	33.6%	.280	1.39	4.63	122	0.1				
	DUR	AAA	34	3	0	1	10	1	10	7	2	1.8	9.0	10	35.7%	.192	0.90	3.60	97	0.1				
	CIN	MLB	34	2	4	0	9	7	24	17	3	5.6	8.6	23	54.8%	.237	1.33	6.37	102	0.2	92.1	39.4%	22.8%	45.6%
Ross Detwiler	LOU	AAA	36	1	0	0	7	0	7	6	0	6.4	9.0	7	36.8%	.333	1.57	3.86	104	0.1				
	CIN	MLB	36	0	2	1	30	0	26^{1}	31	5	3.4	9.6	28	39.5%	.342	1.56	4.44	99	0.3	92.3	50.3%	22.8%	54.0%
Robert Dugger	LOU	AAA	26	2	1	0	14	7	50^{1}	49	5	4.6	7.0	39	34.0%	.303	1.49	4.65	116	0.2				
	DUR	AAA	26	0	2	0	5	5	16	13	2	3.9	7.3	13	45.7%	.250	1.25	3.94	114	0.1				
	CIN	MLB	26	0	1	0	3	1	10^{2}	11	3	5.9	10.1	12	20.7%	.308	1.69	6.75	110	0.1	89.6	40.6%	32.5%	50.1%
	TB	MLB	26	0	0	0	1	0	5^{1}	8	0	0.0	11.8	7	41.2%	.471	1.50	5.06	82	0.1	90.4	49.4%	22.0%	58.9%
Ian Gibaut	COL	AAA	28	2	0	3	17	0	19^{2}	16	0	3.7	8.7	19	51.9%	.308	1.22	3.20	97	0.3				
	CLE	MLB	28	0	0	0	1	0	1^{1}	1	0	0.0	0.0	0	20.0%	.200	0.75	0.00	124	0.0	96.8	67.9%	21.4%	60.1%
	CIN	MLB	28	1	2	1	33	0	34^{2}	38	3	4.7	12.5	48	39.8%	.412	1.62	4.67	79	0.7	95.2	66.2%	25.9%	52.8%
Vladimir Gutierrez	CIN	MLB	26	1	6	0	10	8	36^{2}	46	8	5.9	7.1	29	32.5%	.339	1.91	7.61	155	-0.7	93.1	49.7%	18.1%	53.3%
Steve Hajjar	FTM	A	21	2	2	0	12	12	43^{2}	25	3	4.5	14.6	71	34.2%	.289	1.08	2.47	75	1.2	91.8	62.8%	38.8%	
	DAY	A+	21	0	1	0	2	2	7	4	0	7.7	12.9	10	21.4%	.286	1.43	6.43	108	0.0				
Derek Law	LOU	AAA	31	0	0	0	6	0	8	4	0	3.4	3.4	3	72.7%	.182	0.88	1.13	102	0.1				
	TOL	AAA	31	1	3	15	33	0	39	37	2	2.3	10.2	44	44.9%	.333	1.21	3.23	87	0.8				
	DET	MLB	31	0	1	0	2	0	2	4	1	4.5	9.0	2	33.3%	.375	2.50	4.50	96	0.0	91.7	83.6%	38.5%	53.2%
	CIN	MLB	31	2	2	0	15	0	17^{2}	19	2	3.6	7.6	15	50.0%	.321	1.47	4.08	103	0.1	91.6	70.4%	21.6%	50.8%
Tony Santillan	CIN	MLB	25	0	1	4	21	0	19^{2}	23	1	5.5	9.6	21	28.8%	.386	1.78	5.49	106	0.1	96.4	49.5%	28.2%	56.7%
Jared Solomon	CHA	AA	25	0	0	3	5	0	7	2	0	1.3	7.7	6	56.2%	.125	0.43	0.00	96	0.1				
	LOU	AAA	25	3	2	0	41	0	40^{1}	48	12	6.5	9.8	44	42.0%	.336	1.91	8.93	109	0.4				
	CIN	MLB	25	0	0	0	9	0	8^{1}	8	3	5.4	9.7	9	29.2%	.238	1.56	10.80	102	0.1	95.7	48.4%	30.0%	51.2%
Levi Stoudt	ARK	AA	24	6	6	0	18	18	87	92	13	2.3	8.5	82	40.9%	.315	1.31	5.28	88	1.0				
	LOU	AAA	24	0	2	0	6	6	19	17	0	4.7	7.1	15	30.4%	.304	1.42	3.32	125	0.0				
Justin Wilson	CIN	MLB	34	0	1	0	5	0	3^{2}	3	0	0.0	17.2	7	50.0%	.500	0.82	2.45	82	0.1	95.8	35.2%	44.0%	53.5%

Cincinnati needed an extra starting pitcher to get through the final month, and it was either **Chase Anderson** or forfeit. As they had visitors in from out of town, it would have been rude to cancel. ⚾ Fifteen-year veteran **Ross Detwiler** recorded the first one-out save of his career on August 7. It's the type of awkward accomplishment that would merit a quiet and dignified farewell, but the left-handed strike thrower should still offer some value for a team. ⚾ The suitcase-carrying **Robert Dugger** is quickly becoming the person to call in the tri-state area for a spot start or long relief outing: All four of his appearances lasted at least three innings, and were followed by a trade or a month-long hiatus. ⚾ It's impossible to know how floppy-haired changeup artist **Ian Gibaut** will fit into any bullpen, because by the time you finish this sentence he was just claimed off waivers. ⚾ Please excuse my son for being late this season. He tore his UCL last summer and promises to locate his fastball better. Signed, **Vladimir Gutierrez**'s mother. ⚾ Southpaw **Steve Hajjar** came over in the Tyler Mahle deal. The former Michigan Man has an explosive four-pitch mix—a fastball with great shape, a whiff-heavy changeup and two high-spin breakers for the Spincinnati gods. He needs to stay on the mound and throw more strikes to see a high-end outcome, though. ⚾ **Derek Law** had a 1.13 ERA prior to showing up in Pittsburgh and giving up four runs in one relief appearance. At that point, anti-piracy law was struck down across the land and you were free to re-install Napster. ⚾ Before fastball-slider stalwart **Tony Santillan** missed most of the season to a back strain, he earned the save on Opening Day; for a few months he was one of the cavalcade of late-inning options that gave David Bell some extra wrinkles. ⚾ **Jared Solomon** mixes a mid-90s sinker with a hard slider he's thrown over half the time in the majors. Converted to relief coming off Tommy John, he had no idea where either pitch was going—at any level—and got removed from the 40-man after the season. ⚾ Lehigh product **Levi Stoudt** was an intriguing below-the-fold addition in the Luis Castillo deal. He hasn't pitched much as a pro, but at various times he's flashed big life and velocity with his fastball, plus strong slider shape and an intriguing split-change. He's probably going to end up airing out as a fastball/slider reliever in the end, but he could be a late-innings type. ⚾ Lefty hurler **Justin Wilson** missed all but five games to Tommy John surgery; instinctively, the recovery room nurse on duty traded him for a couple of low-level patients.

MILWAUKEE BREWERS

Essay by Michael Baumann

Player comments by Justin Choi and BP staff

> *"I am the very model of a modern Major-General*
> *I've information vegetable, animal, and mineral*
> *I know the kings of England, and I quote the fights historical*
> *From Marathon to Waterloo, in order categorical"*

You all know the song, from Gilbert and Sullivan's *The Pirates of Penzance*. You might also know that there is an actual list of fights historical to quote from: *The Fifteen Decisive Battles of the World*, written by the English historian Sir Edward Shepherd Creasy in 1851. Therein, Creasy does exactly what the title promises: Lists 15 battles that he believes changed the course of civilization, starting with Marathon and ending with Waterloo.

The list itself is about what you'd expect from a writer of Creasy's time and background (chauvinistic is as good a word as any). But it's a fascinating premise, one that identifies historical watershed moments and invites counterfactuals. If one event, one moment, one individual decision can change the society forever, what are the implications of those decisions?

The Fifteen Decisive Battles of the World is stocked with figures who came to define the great man theory of history. The idea that one person born with exceptional qualities could bend events by talent and force of will was popular among a generation that grew up hearing stories of how Napoleon had nearly conquered the known world. Competing theories of history have since emerged, but the great man theory has never gone away completely, mostly because it flatters people of power and influence who think they have a shot at appearing in *The Thirty Decisive Battles of the World*, whenever that comes out. (It governed Douglas MacArthur's decisions the way the save rule governed the bullpen strategy of turn-of-the-century baseball managers, to give one example.)

But is history determined by the actions of inherently talented individuals, or is it determined by structural and material forces? In other words, do historically influential individuals merely find themselves in the right place at the right time?

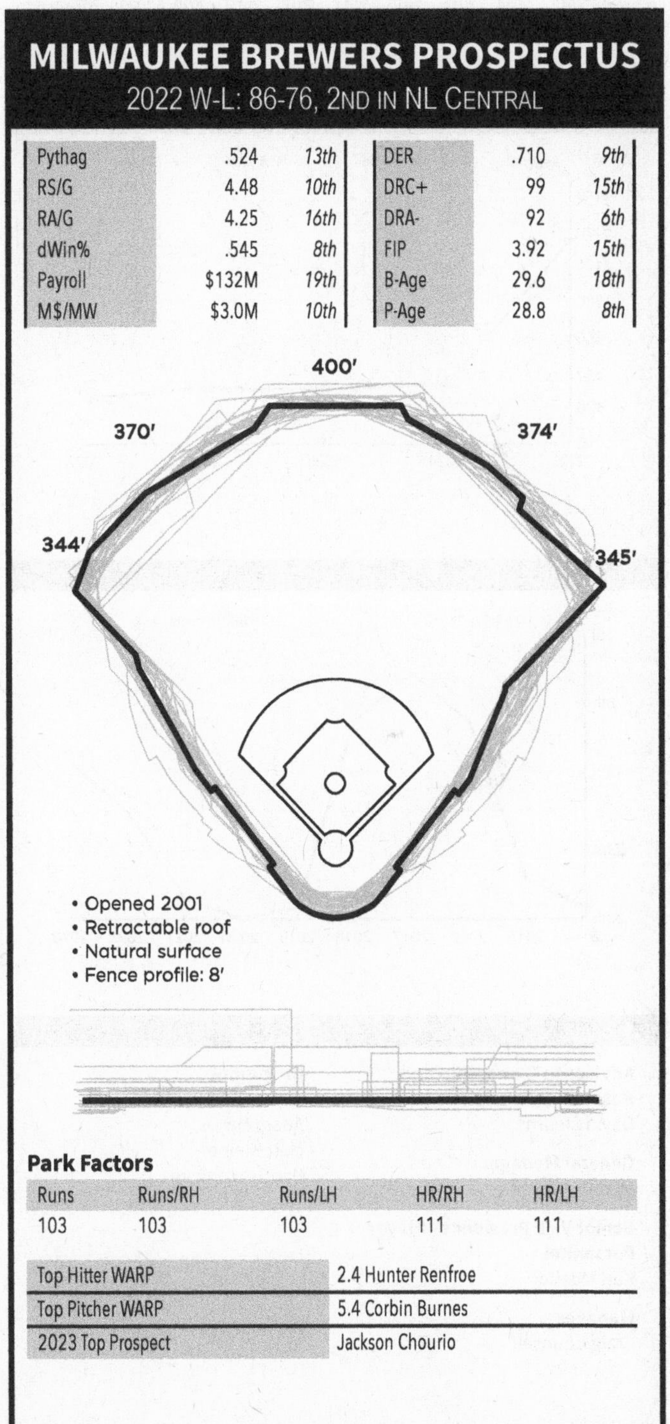

MILWAUKEE BREWERS PROSPECTUS

2022 W-L: 86-76, 2ND IN NL CENTRAL

Pythag	.524	13th	DER	.710	9th
RS/G	4.48	10th	DRC+	99	15th
RA/G	4.25	16th	DRA-	92	6th
dWin%	.545	8th	FIP	3.92	15th
Payroll	$132M	19th	B-Age	29.6	18th
M$/MW	$3.0M	10th	P-Age	28.8	8th

- Opened 2001
- Retractable roof
- Natural surface
- Fence profile: 8'

Park Factors

Runs	Runs/RH	Runs/LH	HR/RH	HR/LH
103	103	103	111	111

Top Hitter WARP	2.4 Hunter Renfroe
Top Pitcher WARP	5.4 Corbin Burnes
2023 Top Prospect	Jackson Chourio

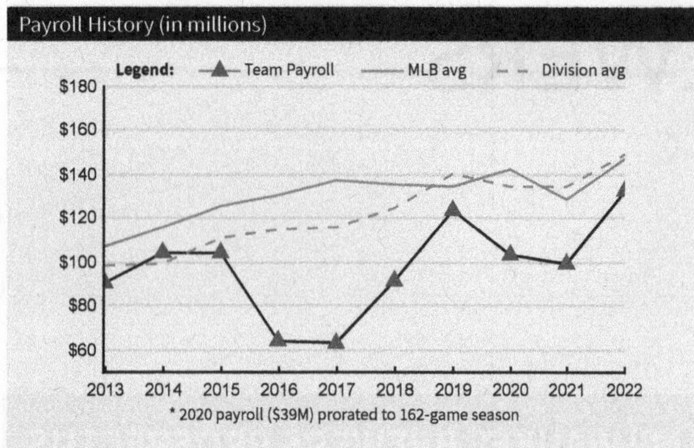

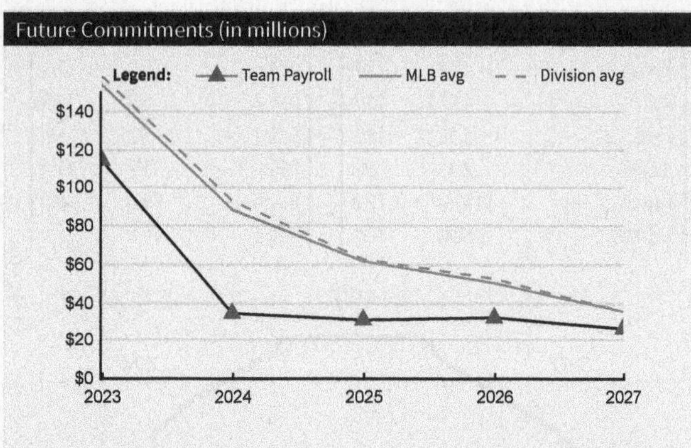

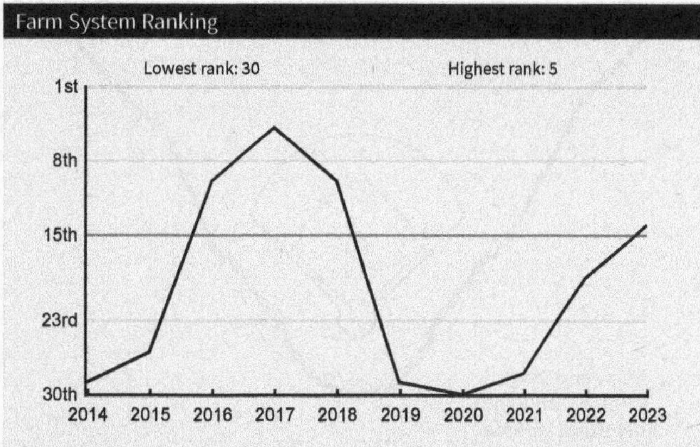

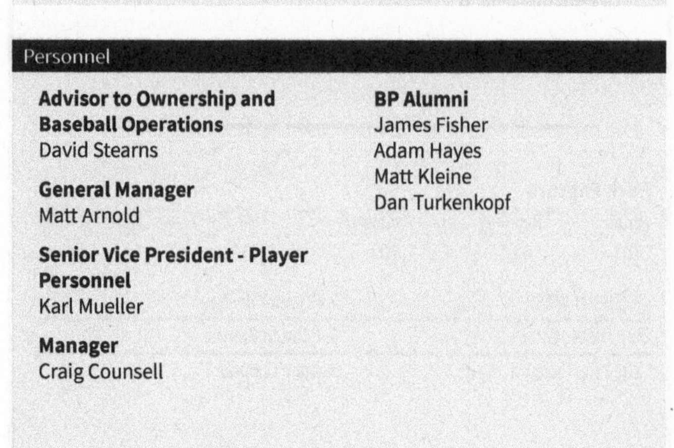
Personnel

Advisor to Ownership and Baseball Operations
David Stearns

General Manager
Matt Arnold

Senior Vice President - Player Personnel
Karl Mueller

Manager
Craig Counsell

BP Alumni
James Fisher
Adam Hayes
Matt Kleine
Dan Turkenkopf

The Milwaukee Brewers are about to find out, as David Stearns has relinquished his title as the Brewers' president of baseball operations.

Adherents of the great man outlook would love Stearns. The very model of a modern general manager, Stearns set about compiling an impressive CV immediately after graduating from Harvard. After a four-year stint in the MLB central office, Stearns worked under two GMs at the bleeding edge of baseball operations: Cleveland's Chris Antonetti and Houston's Jeff Luhnow, who made Stearns his top lieutenant at the age of just 27.

In September 2015, Brewers owner Mark Attanasio made Stearns, then aged just 30, the youngest GM in baseball. At that moment, public opinion of the Astros was at or near its all-time high. Bringing the worst team in baseball back to the playoffs was viewed, correctly, as a tremendous feat of team-building, and Luhnow and his associates were the toast of the baseball world. It was only in the years to come that revelations about workplace culture, the Brandon Taubman incident and the banging scheme would turn the Astros into what they are now. But Stearns, by virtue of leaving when he did, managed to bask in his previous team's glow without being burned by it.

When Attanasio bought the Brewers in the 2004-05 offseason, the club hadn't made the playoffs in 22 years. Incumbent GM Doug Melvin got another decade to turn the team around, which he did, to an extent. Ryan Braun, Prince Fielder and Yovani Gallardo formed a core that kept the team competitive, and Attanasio signed off on the occasional blockbuster trade, acquiring CC Sabathia in 2008 and Zack Greinke in 2011, making the playoffs both years.

But these successes were fleeting, and Stearns was tasked with building a consistent contender. That much he accomplished quickly. Within two seasons of Stearns taking over as GM, the Brewers were a playoff contender; by 2018 they had the best record in the NL and took the Dodgers to Game 7 of the NLCS. In the past six seasons, the Brewers have made the playoffs four times; their only sub-.500 finish came in 2020, when they went 29-31 in the pandemic-shortened season and qualified for the postseason anyway.

The Brewers' road to success was not hewn out of the virgin landscape by sheer force of Stearns' cleverness. It helped that in the late 2010s, most MLB clubs were sitting free agency out completely, leaving top free agents like Yasmani Grandal and Lorenzo Cain available for Milwaukee to scoop up. Most significantly, league-wide commitment to investing in MLB rosters had withered to the point that when the Marlins salary dumped Christian Yelich, Milwaukee—long considered a backwater of the sport—was in a position to pounce. Yelich, of course, turned into the best hitter on the planet the instant he set foot in Wisconsin, like if Popeye's thing was cheese instead of spinach.

But Stearns' tenure has not just been defined by success, it's been defined by *clever* success. The Brewers became one of baseball's premier organizations for pitcher development, turning Corbin Burnes into a Cy Young winner and Josh

Hader, Brandon Woodruff and Freddy Peralta into All-Stars. Under Stearns, Craig Counsell developed a reputation as perhaps the premier tactical manager in the league.

During his tenure as Milwaukee's baseball operations chief, he was an inveterate tinkerer and relentless trader. And not just through the traditional big leaguers-for-prospects swaps most GMs are comfortable making. Stearns loved a challenge trade, and was happy to barter with teams people joke about wanting to avoid—San Diego and Tampa Bay were two of his most frequent partners.

One of Stearns' greatest strengths as a chief of baseball ops has been his willingness to risk being seen to lose a trade, or at least being seen not to win it. It's not a big deal that Trent Grisham leveled up after Stearns traded him—so did Luis Urías, who came the other way. Sure, the Rays got more out of J.P. Feyereisen and Drew Rasmussen than the Brewers could; but that's an acceptable price to pay now that Willy Adames is arguably Milwaukee's best position player.

For a time early this century, the protagonists of baseball were not the players but the executives who shuffled them around the map like, well, Napoleon with an Ivy League MBA. In this post-Theo Epstein, post-Billy Beane world, the pendulum is swinging back in the other direction; but when a team succeeds, as the Brewers have done, a fair chunk of the credit is still reserved for the person who assembled it.

And surely Stearns deserves plenty of praise for his work in Milwaukee. Concurrently with a well-timed financial injection from Attanasio and some exceptional player development work, Stearns turned a small-market also-ran into a perennial contender. The kind of person who views a businessman or a baseball executive as having great man of history potential would consider Stearns the cornerstone of the organization.

We shall see. As of this writing, Stearns plans to see out the final year of his contract as an advisor to general manager Matt Arnold, who had been his right-hand man since their very first days in Milwaukee, back in the fall of 2015.

Stearns says he's stepping back in order to spend time with his family, but it hasn't escaped notice that there are potential spots for him in Houston and in New York, where he grew up. Mets owner Steve Cohen is one of the few people in the world, let alone baseball, who's richer and hedge-fundier than Attanasio, and he has long coveted Stearns to lead the all-conquering team he aims to build. And that de facto capital strike that allowed the Brewers to grab Yelich, Cain, and Grandal for next to nothing? That's over now, as Cohen has brought irresistible financial might to bear on the free agent market. The smallness of Milwaukee's economic base is as evident now as it has been in more than a decade.

The question, then, is where the Brewers are left without their great man of history.

Even if Stearns was especially good at running a baseball operations department—and to be clear, if I owned a team he'd be at or near the top of my list of people I'd want running it—how much of Milwaukee's continued success depends on Stearns, in particular, being the man at the top?

So far this winter, the Brewers have operated as normal. They've stayed out of the deep end of the free agent market, but Arnold has been just as aggressive as Stearns in the trade market. He insinuated himself into the Sean Murphy deal and made off with William Contreras before the A's and Braves realized he'd barely put anything of value into the trade. He traded away two of his best players in 2022—Kolten Wong and Hunter Renfroe—and in turn received an interesting assortment of players but lots of risk.

Contreras and Jesse Winker, who came back in the Wong deal after one troubled season in Seattle, could give the Brewers something they've lacked for years: real offense. Yelich was a one-man rally his first two seasons in Milwaukee—the literal MVP, it bears repeating—but since 2020 his power stroke has disappeared and his offensive production has returned to about the level he was at in Miami. He's still a better-than-average hitter overall, but not providing what the Brewers would hope for from a 31-year-old on a contract worth more than $200 million.

Stearns' Brewers have always been pitching- and defense-focused, but Yelich's decline, the departure of Grandal, the stalled development of Keston Hiura and the retirements of Cain and Ryan Braun have left Milwaukee's offense impotent to the point where the whole team can't compete. This was best illustrated in 2021, when the Brewers won 95 games behind a pitching staff that included four All-Stars, including the Cy Young winner. But come the NLCS, they scored just six runs in a four-game loss.

Changing that takes either a lot of money or a lot of luck. By playing the trade market—and playing it against some pretty savvy operators—Arnold has shown he's no more scared of a bad roll of the dice than Stearns was. If that continues, the Brewers could roll on without a hitch, as other teams have after losing their "genius" head of baseball ops.

In nine years as GM of the Rays, Andrew Friedman made the playoffs four times, with one other 90-win season and won one pennant. In eight ensuing seasons under Matthew Silverman and Erik Neander, the Rays have made the playoffs four times, with one other 90-win season and won one pennant. When the Astros fired Luhnow in the 2019-20 offseason, they'd made the playoffs three straight years, winning two pennants and a World Series. In three seasons under James Click, they made the playoffs three straight years, winning two pennants and a World Series.

When the departure of a talismanic executive coincides with a decline in a franchise's fortunes, there's usually an accompanying reduction in financial commitment from ownership, or some other strife. Epstein is one of the best who ever lived at building a baseball team. But judging by the timing of his departures from the Red Sox and Cubs, he might be even better at knowing when to leave.

As a society, we flatter people at the top of the organizational pyramid. Certainly, leadership is important. Individual leaders can make individual decisions that have massive long-term repercussions. But leaders are not gods. Their influence is limited by the structures in which they operate; in baseball terms, that means market size, resources, facilities, divisional competition, the whims of ownership and even random chance.

A head of baseball ops—a great man of baseball history—can influence a team's fortunes by cunning, competency and charisma. But the weightiest influence that person can exert is not through individual trades or draft picks, but through the construction and maintenance of structures. If there was ever a time when great roster construction was the province of one leader, that time has come and gone. Now Arnold, like Stearns before him, commands hundreds of players, coaches, scouts, analysts and technicians. He might set the agenda and rubber-stamp every signing and hiring, but he won't be in the weeds with intimate knowledge of every aspect of how the next great Brewers team gets constructed. No one who's in charge of an organization that size can be.

It'd be foolish to think that one person, no matter how talented or powerful, could exert more influence on an organization than the scores of people actually doing the legwork. It's their competence and commitment that makes the team run, not the great man's individual capabilities—a lesson that's being learned throughout the business world as this offseason unfolds. However much credit Stearns deserves for building those structures and that culture, the tools that allowed him to build the most successful run in franchise history will be around for Arnold to use throughout his tenure, however long it should last.

On the field as well as off, baseball is a sport that rewards depth, and part of building a durable winning team is accounting for attrition. Players retire, scouts and coaches leave for other jobs, sometimes even the boss decides he's had enough and wants to take a year off. After spending the past seven seasons at Stearns' elbow, Arnold knows how the machine works, and how to keep it ticking over. If the Brewers were actually good these past few years, and not just lucky, you'll barely notice Stearns is no longer in charge.

Running a baseball team is a hard job; it's not like anybody can do it. But it's not so difficult that only a select class of genius is fit to lead. The structure will always outweigh the individual.

—Michael Baumann is a writer of FanGraphs.

HITTERS

Willy Adames SS

Born: 09/02/95 Age: 27 Bats: R Throws: R Height: 6'0" Weight: 210 lb. Origin: International Free Agent, 2015

YEAR	TEAM	LVL	AGE	PA	R	2B	3B	HR	RBI	BB	K	SB	CS	Whiff%	AVG/OBP/SLG	DRC+	BABIP	BRR	DRP	WARP
2020	TB	MLB	24	205	29	15	1	8	23	20	74	2	1	38.7%	.259/.332/.481	85	.388	1.2	SS(53): -1.6	0.2
2021	MIL	MLB	25	413	61	26	0	20	58	47	105	4	2	29.9%	.285/.366/.521	110	.349	0.1	SS(96): -2.8	1.7
2021	TB	MLB	25	142	16	6	1	5	15	10	51	1	2	39.7%	.197/.254/.371	74	.276	-0.3	SS(40): 0.4	0.0
2022	MIL	MLB	26	617	83	31	0	31	98	49	166	8	3	28.1%	.238/.298/.458	105	.278	2.4	SS(136): 9.4	3.6
2023 DC	*MIL*	*MLB*	*27*	*601*	*80*	*28*	*1*	*29*	*79*	*53*	*155*	*7*	*2*	*28.4%*	*.258/.328/.475*	*116*	*.313*	*0.9*	*SS 8*	*3.9*

Comparables: Bill Hall (77), Jorge Polanco (76), Derek Jeter (75)

We're living through the post-launch angle revolution, but that doesn't mean selling out for power is no longer a viable option. Case in point: Since arriving in Milwaukee via a mid-season trade in 2021, Adames has continued to produce more and more fly balls. He's at a point now where two-thirds of his batted balls are airborne, resulting in career highs in barrels and home runs. If there's a downside to this approach, it's that this newfound penchant for elevation is eating into his BABIP. As such, Adames has become yet another player who strikes out uncomfortably often but might be his team's most valuable contributor anyway—like if someone dialed Patrick Wisdom up to 12 and taught him how to pick it at the six. On that note, defensive metrics went all *"humina humina AWOOGA"* over Adames' glove last season, as he became far more adept at handling balls hit directly to him than before. It's unclear what efforts led to such a glow-up, but they should bode well for Adames regardless as enters his second year of arbitration.

Tyler Black 2B

Born: 07/26/00 Age: 22 Bats: L Throws: R Height: 6'2" Weight: 190 lb. Origin: Round 1, 2021 Draft (#33 overall)

YEAR	TEAM	LVL	AGE	PA	R	2B	3B	HR	RBI	BB	K	SB	CS	Whiff%	AVG/OBP/SLG	DRC+	BABIP	BRR	DRP	WARP
2021	CAR	A	20	103	11	4	0	0	6	20	29	3	2		.222/.388/.272	104	.346	-1.3	2B(15): -1.4	0.1
2022	WIS	A+	21	283	45	13	4	4	35	45	44	13	6		.281/.406/.424	120	.330	0.5	2B(30): -2.2, CF(15): -1.4, 3B(6): -0.2	1.1
2023 non-DC	*MIL*	*MLB*	*22*	*251*	*21*	*9*	*2*	*2*	*20*	*26*	*52*	*6*	*3*	*22.4%*	*.222/.314/.316*	*80*	*.282*	*-0.3*	*2B 0, 3B 0*	*0.0*

Comparables: Jose Vallejo (73), Steve Lombardozzi (68), Emilio Bonifácio (68)

Black started 2022 strong in Double-A, walking as often as he struck out, but then the injury bug bit twice: he broke his scapula in July, then his thumb in the AFL. Those maladies cut short a promising season of development. Like many position players in Milwaukee's system, Black features traits favored by statistical models: He's young compared to his peers, has superb plate discipline and bat-to-ball skills, and creates exit velocities that should translate to double-digit home run totals. He'll need to lean on his offensive tools, as he isn't particularly fast, nor is he an adroit defender. He is, at least, a passable second baseman, and his experience around the infield and in center gives him some utility. Not bad for an ostensibly bat-first prospect.

Mike Brosseau 3B Born: 03/15/94 Age: 29 Bats: R Throws: R Height: 5'10" Weight: 205 lb. Origin: Undrafted Free Agent, 2016

YEAR	TEAM	LVL	AGE	PA	R	2B	3B	HR	RBI	BB	K	SB	CS	Whiff%	AVG/OBP/SLG	DRC+	BABIP	BRR	DRP	WARP
2020	TB	MLB	26	98	12	5	1	5	12	8	31	2	0	36.1%	.302/.378/.558	96	.412	-0.5	1B(12): 0.3, 3B(11): -1, 2B(9): -0.2	0.0
2021	DUR	AAA	27	202	25	2	1	8	21	23	50	2	0		.218/.342/.382	108	.259	0.1	3B(28): -3.4, 2B(8): -0.1, 1B(7): 0.2	0.5
2021	TB	MLB	27	169	21	9	0	5	18	15	53	2	0	29.2%	.187/.266/.347	79	.245	0.7	2B(27): -0.1, 3B(23): -1.5, 1B(10): -0.3	0.0
2022	MIL	MLB	28	160	15	5	0	6	23	14	48	2	0	31.1%	.255/.344/.418	93	.345	-0.1	3B(55): -0.6, SS(4): 0.1	0.2
2023 DC	*MIL*	*MLB*	*29*	*197*	*20*	*8*	*0*	*5*	*20*	*17*	*55*	*1*	*1*	*29.9%*	*.220/.306/.368*	*85*	*.289*	*0.7*	*3B 0, 1B 0*	*0.1*

Comparables: Nolan Reimold (55), Neil Walker (54), Aledmys Díaz (53)

Is he way too prone to striking out? Sure. Does he flounder about when facing a right-handed pitcher? Definitely. He's a weak-side platoon option at third base, and not much else. But in Milwaukee, Brosseau re-established himself as a lethal specialist. Not only did he rebound from a woeful offensive performance, but he also embodied the word "clutch." In one September game against the Mets, Brosseau came up to pinch-hit in the seventh inning and launched a cathartic grand slam, the first of his career (and off a right-hander). It'd be naive to count on the clutch-ness continuing, and because Brosseau's output in any given year is highly dependent on BABIP, he's a volatile option. That said, this season will be just his first arbitration-eligible year, and as of now, he fills a useful niche. Brosseau isn't a main ingredient, but he's a spice that can enhance the overall flavor of a roster.

Victor Caratini C Born: 08/17/93 Age: 29 Bats: S Throws: R Height: 6'1" Weight: 215 lb. Origin: Round 2, 2013 Draft (#65 overall)

YEAR	TEAM	LVL	AGE	PA	R	2B	3B	HR	RBI	BB	K	SB	CS	Whiff%	AVG/OBP/SLG	DRC+	BABIP	BRR	DRP	WARP
2020	CHC	MLB	26	132	10	7	0	1	16	12	31	0	1	23.6%	.241/.333/.328	84	.321	-1.3	C(22): 1.1, 1B(3): 0.2	0.2
2021	SD	MLB	27	356	33	9	0	7	39	35	82	2	0	25.5%	.227/.309/.323	87	.281	-1.2	C(101): -3.3, 1B(5): 0	0.5
2022	MIL	MLB	28	314	26	12	0	9	34	31	67	0	0	21.1%	.199/.300/.342	99	.228	-3.6	C(90): 8.2, 1B(2): -0.2	1.6
2023 DC	*MIL*	*MLB*	*29*	*250*	*28*	*10*	*0*	*6*	*26*	*24*	*49*	*0*	*0*	*21.8%*	*.235/.325/.380*	*96*	*.274*	*-1.3*	*C 3*	*1.0*

Comparables: Josh Thole (64), Tucker Barnhart (60), Marc Hill (59)

YEAR	TEAM	P. COUNT	FRM RUNS	BLK RUNS	THRW RUNS	TOT RUNS
2020	CHC	2834	1.1	-0.1	0.0	1.1
2021	SD	13377	-3.4	0.0	0.1	-3.4
2022	MIL	11736	8.5	0.2	-0.3	8.4
2023	*MIL*	*9620*	*2.1*	*0.1*	*0.2*	*2.4*

Don't let the sub-Mendoza batting average fool you. In a world littered with unusable backup catchers, Caratini was to Omar Narváez what Robin is to Batman: a worthy sidekick who follows in his mentor's footsteps but is no slouch himself. One imagines Narváez leading Caratini through various catcher drills down in the Bat Cave, leading to a sudden abundance of framing runs. At the plate, Caratini got on base and slugged enough to where opposing villains couldn't just scoff at him and lob batting practice fastballs. He won't be elevated to main hero status anytime soon—and the world doesn't need another Batman remake anyway—but Caratini the part-time receiver has plenty of value in his own right.

★ ★ ★ *2023 Top 101 Prospect* **#10** ★ ★ ★

Jackson Chourio OF Born: 03/11/04 Age: 19 Bats: R Throws: R Height: 6'1" Weight: 165 lb. Origin: International Free Agent, 2021

YEAR	TEAM	LVL	AGE	PA	R	2B	3B	HR	RBI	BB	K	SB	CS	Whiff%	AVG/OBP/SLG	DRC+	BABIP	BRR	DRP	WARP
2021	DSL BRW2	ROK	17	189	31	7	1	5	25	23	28	8	3		.296/.386/.447		.323			
2022	CAR	A	18	271	51	23	5	12	47	19	76	10	2		.324/.373/.600	117	.423	2.9	CF(57): 7.5	2.3
2022	WIS	A+	18	142	24	6	0	8	24	11	31	4	1		.252/.317/.488	120	.267	0.4	CF(24): 2.3	1.0
2022	BLX	AA	18	26	0	1	0	0	4	2	11	2	1		.087/.154/.130	71	.154	-0.1	CF(5): -0.5	-0.1
2023 non-DC	*MIL*	*MLB*	*19*	*251*	*22*	*11*	*2*	*6*	*26*	*12*	*82*	*5*	*2*	*36.0%*	*.222/.267/.377*	*72*	*.312*	*2.2*	*2B 0, CF 0*	*0.1*

Comparables: Mike Trout (60), Jason Heyward (52), Estevan Florial (52)

You. Yes, you. What were you doing when you were 18 years old? Probably less with your life than Chourio, who's already reached Double-A Biloxi at such a young age. Signed out of Venezuela, he's got the speed to play center, admirable raw power and a controlled swing that lets him access all quadrants of the zone. He's also plenty projectable due to his athleticism, and did we mention he's 18? While Chourio didn't receive much initial hype, he shot up prospect lists after destroying Low-A and holding his own in High-A all when just entering legal adulthood. His aggressive approach will be tested as he faces the more legitimate breaking balls that populate the upper minors, and we've already seen his performance decline some as he's rapidly ascended the ladder. But at age 18, with all his tools and all the time in the world, there's no reason to be anything but optimistic about his future.

William Contreras C/DH Born: 12/24/97 Age: 25 Bats: R Throws: R Height: 6'0" Weight: 180 lb. Origin: International Free Agent, 2015

YEAR	TEAM	LVL	AGE	PA	R	2B	3B	HR	RBI	BB	K	SB	CS	Whiff%	AVG/OBP/SLG	DRC+	BABIP	BRR	DRP	WARP
2020	ATL	MLB	22	10	0	1	0	0	1	0	4	0	0	40.9%	.400/.400/.500	79	.667	-0.3	C(4): -0.1	0.0
2021	LAR	WIN	23	74	9	2	0	2	13	8	14	0	0		.215/.311/.338		.245			
2021	GWN	AAA	23	171	26	8	0	9	29	13	36	0	0		.290/.357/.516	112	.327	0.0	C(34): -1.1	0.7
2021	ATL	MLB	23	185	19	4	1	8	23	19	54	0	0	36.4%	.215/.303/.399	94	.265	0.4	C(49): -5.1	0.2
2022	GWN	AAA	24	51	2	3	0	0	8	3	10	0	0		.292/.333/.354	98	.368	-1.3	C(8): -0.1, LF(1): -0.1, RF(1): -0.0	0.0
2022	ATL	MLB	24	376	51	14	1	20	45	39	104	2	0	34.2%	.278/.354/.506	122	.344	-2.9	C(60): 0.2, LF(1): 0	1.9
2023 DC	*MIL*	*MLB*	*25*	*421*	*46*	*17*	*1*	*14*	*46*	*37*	*115*	*0*	*1*	*33.4%*	*.243/.317/.404*	*97*	*.314*	*-4.7*	*C -3*	*0.3*

Comparables: Javy Lopez (60), Francisco Mejía (58), Jesus Flores (57)

For someone who still has yet to get 162 career games under his belt, Contreras has been setting quite the pace for himself in terms of accolades. He got a World Series ring with the Braves in 2021 and followed that up with a breakout season at the plate. His bat earned him a spot in the All-Star Game as a designated hitter, facilitating an extremely rare occasion: Contreras and his brother, Willson, were both in the lineup, making them only the fifth pair of brothers since 1942 to start in the same All-Star Game. Contreras also followed in his brother's footsteps in posting strong WARP and DRC+ outputs. Many felt as though the Brewers somehow won the "Sean Murphy trade" by nabbing Contreras in exchange for Esteury Ruiz and some pitching depth this winter. Given the success they've had improving the gloves of bat-first catchers in the past, they could help their new backstop earn even more accolades soon.

YEAR	TEAM	P. COUNT	FRM RUNS	BLK RUNS	THRW RUNS	TOT RUNS
2020	ATL	404	0.1	0.0	0.0	0.1
2021	LAR	1492			0.0	0.0
2021	GWN	4102	-0.7	-0.1	0.3	-0.6
2021	ATL	6935	-4.0	-0.5	0.0	-4.5
2022	GWN	1241	-0.3	0.0	0.4	0.0
2022	ATL	8525	-0.8	-0.1	1.2	0.3
2023	*MIL*	*12025*	*-2.0*	*-0.3*	*0.5*	*-1.8*

★ ★ ★ *2023 Top 101 Prospect* **#41** ★ ★ ★

Sal Frelick OF

Born: 04/19/00 Age: 23 Bats: L Throws: R Height: 5'10" Weight: 180 lb. Origin: Round 1, 2021 Draft (#15 overall)

YEAR	TEAM	LVL	AGE	PA	R	2B	3B	HR	RBI	BB	K	SB	CS	Whiff%	AVG/OBP/SLG	DRC+	BABIP	BRR	DRP	WARP
2021	BRWG	ROK	21	17	4	1	1	0	4	2	2	3	0		.467/.529/.667		.538			
2021	CAR	A	21	81	17	6	1	1	12	9	10	6	2		.437/.494/.592	128	.492	0.3	CF(14): 2.3	0.8
2021	WIS	A+	21	71	7	1	1	1	5	10	13	3	0		.167/.296/.267	110	.196	0.1	CF(13): 0.4	0.4
2022	WIS	A+	22	92	12	5	1	2	9	13	14	6	3		.291/.391/.456	128	.333	0.3	CF(17): 0.5	0.9
2022	BLX	AA	22	253	40	12	3	5	25	20	33	9	2		.317/.380/.464	117	.351	-1.0	CF(42): 3.2, LF(6): -0.6, RF(3): -0.3	1.5
2022	NAS	AAA	22	217	38	11	2	4	25	19	16	9	3	11.3%	.365/.435/.508	133	.382	1.6	LF(22): -1.4, CF(17): -1.2, RF(1): -0.2	1.4
2023 DC	*MIL*	*MLB*	*23*	*167*	*18*	*7*	*2*	*2*	*16*	*12*	*22*	*3*	*1*	*17.3%*	*.280/.341/.400*	*107*	*.318*	*1.8*	*LF 0, CF 0*	*0.8*

Comparables: Raimel Tapia (53), Michael Hermosillo (50), Luis Barrera (48)

It's hard to imagine that Frelick, a speedy outfielder with a feel for contact, was once seen as a risky draft pick. But injuries and the pandemic cut his college career short, leaving teams to evaluate him based on potential, not results. Just two seasons into his career, Milwaukee's gamble seems to have paid off handsomely. Though he struggled in his first brief go-around in High-A, Frelick has now slashed and dashed his way through every level of the minors. His hit tool has matured, his plate discipline is admirable and he can flat-out fly—seriously, just look up a video of Frelick running online and prepare to be amazed. Evaluators think he can stay in center, with a soft projected fallback as a plus defender in a corner spot. There are a handful of intriguing upper-level position players in the Brewers organization, and among those who have yet to make their big-league debuts, Frelick should be the first man up. Before long, he may be the first man up in Milwaukee's everyday lineup, too.

Keston Hiura 1B

Born: 08/02/96 Age: 26 Bats: R Throws: R Height: 6'0" Weight: 202 lb. Origin: Round 1, 2017 Draft (#9 overall)

YEAR	TEAM	LVL	AGE	PA	R	2B	3B	HR	RBI	BB	K	SB	CS	Whiff%	AVG/OBP/SLG	DRC+	BABIP	BRR	DRP	WARP
2020	MIL	MLB	23	246	30	4	0	13	32	16	85	3	2	42.7%	.212/.297/.410	92	.273	-0.9	2B(49): -1.7	0.3
2021	NAS	AAA	24	206	22	12	0	8	24	29	69	2	1		.256/.374/.465	100	.375	-0.8	1B(24): -2.6, 2B(23): 4.2	0.6
2021	MIL	MLB	24	197	16	9	1	4	19	14	77	3	0	47.0%	.168/.256/.301	53	.269	-1.4	1B(49): -0.8, 2B(7): -0.3, LF(1): 0	-1.0
2022	NAS	AAA	25	59	8	1	0	6	18	9	15	0	3		.319/.458/.723	119	.346	-0.7	2B(7): -1.2, LF(5): -0.1, 1B(1): 0.4	0.1
2022	MIL	MLB	25	266	34	8	1	14	32	23	111	5	2	40.3%	.226/.316/.449	82	.355	2.0	1B(33): 0.4, 2B(14): -0.2, LF(5): -0.2	0.3
2023 DC	*MIL*	*MLB*	*26*	*235*	*30*	*10*	*0*	*12*	*33*	*20*	*87*	*5*	*3*	*40.1%*	*.246/.336/.488*	*120*	*.362*	*0.1*	*1B 0, 2B 0*	*1.0*

Comparables: Greg Bird (56), Jorge Soler (53), Brandon Drury (52)

Over the years, Hiura has gone from star prospect to breakout candidate to post-hype sleeper to … well, whatever euphemism covers the position-less, part-time role he's now stuck in. A ghastly strikeout rate and an inflated BABIP outweigh the power he showed in his most recent campaign. Worse, he's a complete liability against left-handed pitching; chronic struggles against off-speed pitches and fastballs up-and-in help explain his odd reverse splits. Despite these negatives, Hiura is arguably still worth a major-league roster spot thanks to his pop, and he'd likely get one anyway thanks to his pedigree. But given his lack of minor-league options, he's not a lock to earn one on the team that drafted and developed him. That'd be a bummer for Brewers fans, but sometimes that's the way the cookie crumbles.

Hendry Mendez RF

Born: 11/07/03 Age: 19 Bats: L Throws: L Height: 6'2" Weight: 175 lb. Origin: International Free Agent, 2021

YEAR	TEAM	LVL	AGE	PA	R	2B	3B	HR	RBI	BB	K	SB	CS	Whiff%	AVG/OBP/SLG	DRC+	BABIP	BRR	DRP	WARP
2021	BRWB	ROK	17	74	6	4	2	0	10	10	10	3	1		.333/.425/.460		.396			
2021	DSL BRW1	ROK	17	64	10	5	1	1	9	7	2	0	0		.296/.391/.481		.288			
2022	CAR	A	18	446	47	11	1	5	39	62	70	7	8		.244/.357/.318	115	.286	-4.4	RF(85): -3.3, CF(2): -0.2	1.2
2023 non-DC	*MIL*	*MLB*	*19*	*251*	*19*	*8*	*1*	*1*	*17*	*20*	*45*	*2*	*2*	*20.4%*	*.208/.279/.275*	*60*	*.255*	*-1.8*	*LF 0, CF 0*	*-1.0*

Comparables: Agustin Ruiz (68), Zach Collier (66), Starling Heredia (65)

Only 19 years old as of November, Mendez has been blessed with a natural ability to put balls in play and lay off unattractive pitches. That said, he's burdened by a downward swing that produces an abundance of groundballs *and* pop-ups, which means that, solid OBP aside, his hit tool needs some refinement. Mendez does have raw power, which usually results in satisfyingly loud cracks from his bat. Making sure that sweet noise produces balls that travel beyond the infield will give him a more realistic shot at becoming a solid corner outfielder.

Owen Miller IF

Born: 11/15/96 Age: 26 Bats: R Throws: R Height: 6'0" Weight: 185 lb. Origin: Round 3, 2018 Draft (#84 overall)

YEAR	TEAM	LVL	AGE	PA	R	2B	3B	HR	RBI	BB	K	SB	CS	Whiff%	AVG/OBP/SLG	DRC+	BABIP	BRR	DRP	WARP
2021	COL	AAA	24	206	25	12	1	7	22	21	52	0	0		.297/.374/.489	102	.379	0.4	2B(23): 2.5, 1B(8): -0.4, 3B(8): -1.1	0.7
2021	CLE	MLB	24	202	17	8	0	4	18	9	54	2	0	26.1%	.204/.243/.309	74	.261	-0.9	2B(29): 1.1, 1B(18): 0.3, 3B(7): -1.2	-0.1
2022	CLE	MLB	25	472	53	26	1	6	51	32	93	2	0	18.4%	.243/.301/.351	88	.290	2.0	1B(80): 1.9, 2B(25): 0.4, 3B(4): 0.1	0.9
2023 DC	*MIL*	*MLB*	*26*	*165*	*16*	*8*	*0*	*3*	*17*	*11*	*29*	*0*	*0*	*19.7%*	*.250/.311/.385*	*92*	*.291*	*0.0*	*2B 0, 1B 0*	*0.2*

Comparables: Johnny Giavotella (70), José Pirela (65), Zoilo Almonte (62)

While Steven Kwan was making headlines in April, Miller was quietly slashing .400/.466/.700 and looking like another young breakout star in the Guardians lineup. Then the calendar turned to May and Miller turned into a pumpkin, posting a .222/.278/.305 line the rest of the way. He significantly reduced his whiff rate from his 2021 debut, but pitchers were continually able to tempt Miller with offerings above the zone or just inside, resulting in lots of weak contact and easy outs. He can play an uninspiring second base but was mostly used at the cold corner last year, where his glove was adequate but his lack of power makes him a bad fit. When he's right, Miller has the contact skills and positional flexibility of a useful bench piece. That's likely how the Brewers intend to use him after trading for him in December.

★ ★ ★ *2023 Top 101 Prospect* **#62** ★ ★ ★

Garrett Mitchell OF

Born: 09/04/98 Age: 24 Bats: L Throws: R Height: 6'3" Weight: 215 lb. Origin: Round 1, 2020 Draft (#20 overall)

YEAR	TEAM	LVL	AGE	PA	R	2B	3B	HR	RBI	BB	K	SB	CS	Whiff%	AVG/OBP/SLG	DRC+	BABIP	BRR	DRP	WARP
2021	WIS	A+	22	120	33	5	2	5	20	28	30	12	1		.359/.508/.620	126	.491	0.8	CF(13): -2.5, RF(2): 0.3	0.6
2021	BLX	AA	22	148	16	1	0	3	10	18	41	5	1		.186/.291/.264	84	.247	-0.7	CF(30): 0.9, RF(2): -0.0, LF(1): -0.1	0.2
2022	BLX	AA	23	187	29	9	2	4	25	16	52	7	1		.277/.353/.428	93	.378	1.0	CF(26): -0.7, RF(12): 1.3, LF(3): -0.4	0.6
2022	NAS	AAA	23	85	15	6	0	1	9	10	18	9	0		.342/.435/.466	106	.444	1.7	CF(9): -0.7, RF(5): -0.6, LF(3): -0.1	0.3
2022	MIL	MLB	23	68	9	3	0	2	9	6	28	8	0	31.9%	.311/.373/.459	58	.548	0.9	CF(28): 1.2	0.1
2023 DC	*MIL*	*MLB*	*24*	*434*	*45*	*17*	*3*	*8*	*40*	*39*	*127*	*19*	*4*	*30.5%*	*.232/.310/.357*	*83*	*.325*	*10.4*	*CF 0*	*1.5*

Comparables: Jacoby Ellsbury (64), Adam Eaton (60), Stephen Drew (57)

Called up to the majors in late August, Mitchell needed little time to prove he's the real deal in center with his plus speed and cannon for an arm. As for his prowess at the plate? Despite what his slash line suggests, the jury is still out. A .548 BABIP and a ridiculous strikeout rate make his offensive output hard to take seriously. That said, Mitchell showed off a *below*-average ground-ball rate; notable because his propensity for pounding balls into the dirt in the minors provided sufficient reason for some evaluators to doubt his bat. If that issue has been fixed—and that's a huge if—he could be a franchise cornerstone in the making. But as is so often the case with young hitters, as soon as one flaw is resolved, another rears its ugly head. While most prospects tend to struggle with breaking balls in their early big-league forays, Mitchell demonstrated a considerable weakness against fastballs. That's not an issue he had in the minors, but it bears watching moving forward.

Hedbert Perez OF

Born: 04/04/03 Age: 20 Bats: L Throws: L Height: 5'10" Weight: 160 lb. Origin: International Free Agent, 2019

YEAR	TEAM	LVL	AGE	PA	R	2B	3B	HR	RBI	BB	K	SB	CS	Whiff%	AVG/OBP/SLG	DRC+	BABIP	BRR	DRP	WARP
2021	BRWG	ROK	18	132	19	11	0	6	21	8	34	2	0		.333/.394/.575		.425			
2021	CAR	A	18	68	5	2	0	1	7	1	25	0	0		.169/.206/.246	76	.256	-0.4	CF(16): 2.8, LF(1): -0.1	0.3
2022	CAR	A	19	441	53	23	2	15	57	30	132	9	6		.216/.272/.393	80	.279	-2.6	LF(51): -0.8, CF(26): -0.5, RF(11): 0.5	0.0
2023 non-DC	*MIL*	*MLB*	*20*	*251*	*19*	*10*	*1*	*5*	*22*	*11*	*93*	*3*	*1*	*40.5%*	*.190/.230/.309*	*41*	*.287*	*-0.3*	*LF 0, CF 0*	*-1.3*

Comparables: Jack Suwinski (77), Justin Lopez (68), Everett Williams (66)

Perez's tools are so deafening that they'll probably drown out whatever numbers he puts up in the minors for the time being. Even so, a lackluster triple-slash across 500+ plate appearances in Low-A isn't exactly encouraging, and it's clear Perez isn't yet ready for his next step. His upside—based on a promising hit tool, burgeoning power and a knack for pulling the ball—still outweighs his flaws—namely poor swing decisions and a likely defensive home in an outfield corner. But as Perez gets older, the scales will tip away from hope and toward concern if he fails to evolve as a slugger. That may sound obvious, but it's a good reminder that a hitter's raw ability is usually directly proportional to the how much variance their support systems will tolerate. He turns 20 in April, so while plenty of time remains on the clock, it is indeed ticking.

Jeferson Quero C/DH

Born: 10/08/02 Age: 20 Bats: R Throws: R Height: 5'10" Weight: 165 lb. Origin: International Free Agent, 2019

YEAR	TEAM	LVL	AGE	PA	R	2B	3B	HR	RBI	BB	K	SB	CS	Whiff%	AVG/OBP/SLG	DRC+	BABIP	BRR	DRP	WARP
2021	BRWB	ROK	18	83	15	5	1	2	8	12	10	4	3		.309/.434/.500		.339			
2022	CAR	A	19	320	44	18	1	6	43	28	61	10	2		.278/.345/.412	103	.330	0.5	C(53): 10.1	2.1
2022	WIS	A+	19	85	10	4	1	4	14	2	15	0	0		.313/.329/.530	106	.344	-0.1	C(13): 0.3	0.3
2023 non-DC	*MIL*	*MLB*	*20*	*251*	*21*	*10*	*1*	*3*	*22*	*13*	*59*	*4*	*1*	*27.0%*	*.236/.280/.342*	*70*	*.300*	*1.0*	*C 0*	*0.1*

Comparables: Manuel Margot (66), Jesus Montero (65), Gary Sánchez (63)

YEAR	TEAM	P. COUNT	FRM RUNS	BLK RUNS	THRW RUNS	TOT RUNS
2022	CAR	7853	7.7	1.2	1.4	10.4
2022	WIS	1659	-0.9	0.1	0.0	-0.8
2023	*MIL*	*6956*	*-1.3*	*0.7*	*0.7*	*0.1*

We now have a little more information about Quero following his standout campaign, and it's almost all positive. The Brewers pushed the 20-year-old catcher as far up the ladder as High-A, where his power and burgeoning hit tool were on display. His utter lack of walks is a teeny bit concerning, but overall, Quero impressed both at and behind the plate, showing off a plus arm and impressive overall athleticism. The BP Prospect Team cited Quero as "an athletic fire hydrant with heft, leverage, and loft behind [his] swing." Something else they call him? A breakout candidate to watch headed into 2023.

Jon Singleton 1B

Born: 09/18/91 Age: 31 Bats: L Throws: L Height: 6'2" Weight: 230 lb. Origin: Round 8, 2009 Draft (#257 overall)

YEAR	TEAM	LVL	AGE	PA	R	2B	3B	HR	RBI	BB	K	SB	CS	Whiff%	AVG/OBP/SLG	DRC+	BABIP	BRR	DRP	WARP
2022	NAS	AAA	30	581	84	22	2	24	87	117	161	3	1	27.0%	.219/.375/.434	108	.273	-3.3	1B(111): 3.7	2.2
2023 DC	*MIL*	*MLB*	*31*	*64*	*7*	*2*	*0*	*2*	*6*	*8*	*18*	*0*	*0*	*31.3%*	*.195/.312/.372*	*86*	*.252*	*0.1*	*1B 0*	*0.0*

Comparables: Daric Barton (52), Mark Bellhorn (37), Eric Munson (37)

Yes, that Singleton, the one-time top prospect last seen in affiliated ball back in 2017. Front office advisor Daniel Stearns was an assistant GM for the Astros when they gave him a record-setting five-year contract before he'd notched a single big-league plate appearance, and gave him another chance after seeing him return to the game in an impressive stint in the Mexican independent leagues. Singleton exceeded all expectations, walking in 20.1% of his Triple-A plate appearances, and you could make the argument that baseball is better prepared to accept a low-average, three-true-outcome DH than it was in 2014, particularly in a town where Daniel Vogelbach recently made his home. He re-signed with Milwaukee on another minor-league deal early in the offseason, and while he doesn't fit on the roster as it currently stands, he could be called up early if one of the team's sluggers gets hurt.

Tyrone Taylor OF

Born: 01/22/94 Age: 29 Bats: R Throws: R Height: 6'0" Weight: 194 lb. Origin: Round 2, 2012 Draft (#92 overall)

YEAR	TEAM	LVL	AGE	PA	R	2B	3B	HR	RBI	BB	K	SB	CS	Whiff%	AVG/OBP/SLG	DRC+	BABIP	BRR	DRP	WARP
2020	MIL	MLB	26	41	6	4	0	2	6	2	8	0	0	26.0%	.237/.293/.500	110	.250	-0.1	RF(10): -0.3, CF(9): -0.9, LF(2): -0.2	0.0
2021	NAS	AAA	27	35	10	4	0	3	10	5	4	0	0		.500/.543/.964	136	.478	0.9	CF(7): 0.2, LF(1): 0.1, RF(1): 0.1	0.4
2021	MIL	MLB	27	271	33	9	3	12	43	20	59	6	1	23.6%	.247/.321/.457	102	.277	2.7	LF(37): -1.8, RF(29): -0.9, CF(16): -1.1	0.9
2022	MIL	MLB	28	405	49	21	3	17	51	22	102	3	2	26.5%	.233/.286/.442	93	.272	4.3	CF(84): -2.7, RF(23): -0.9, LF(20): -0.2	1.2
2023 DC	*MIL*	*MLB*	*29*	*526*	*58*	*23*	*3*	*18*	*62*	*32*	*122*	*6*	*1*	*25.5%*	*.235/.296/.412*	*91*	*.279*	*3.6*	*RF -1, CF 0*	*0.9*

Comparables: Juan Rivera (56), Randal Grichuk (55), Yasiel Puig (53)

Once again, Taylor seemed destined to parkour across the outfield as a part-time contributor. But between Lorenzo Cain's departure and Garrett Mitchell's arrival, he assumed the role of chief center fielder and more or less held his own. Taylor put his tools on display across a full-ish season of work, earning acclaim for his speed and quality jumps. He was less impressive at the plate thanks in part to his allergy to walks, but he hit just enough balls hard enough to produce an acceptable—if uninspiring—DRC+. The Brewers have a small army of intriguing outfield prospects flooding through the majors and upper minors, which means Taylor's future in Milwaukee is murky despite his solid showing. But even if he ends up in a different city, he's progressed from questionable prospect to proven commodity.

Rowdy Tellez 1B

Born: 03/16/95 Age: 28 Bats: L Throws: L Height: 6'4" Weight: 255 lb. Origin: Round 30, 2013 Draft (#895 overall)

YEAR	TEAM	LVL	AGE	PA	R	2B	3B	HR	RBI	BB	K	SB	CS	Whiff%	AVG/OBP/SLG	DRC+	BABIP	BRR	DRP	WARP
2020	TOR	MLB	25	127	20	5	0	8	23	11	20	0	1	23.5%	.283/.346/.540	115	.276	-0.1	1B(19): 0.3	0.6
2021	BUF	AAA	26	55	8	4	0	4	11	6	11	0	0		.298/.400/.638	121	.313	0.0	1B(11): 1.2	0.4
2021	MIL	MLB	26	174	22	10	1	7	28	14	32	0	0	21.9%	.272/.333/.481	103	.300	-0.3	1B(46): -0.2	0.4
2021	TOR	MLB	26	151	12	4	1	4	8	9	33	0	0	25.0%	.209/.272/.338	86	.245	0.0	1B(19): -0.5	0.0
2022	MIL	MLB	27	599	67	23	0	35	89	62	121	2	1	23.9%	.219/.306/.461	118	.215	-3.3	1B(139): -1	2.0
2023 DC	*MIL*	*MLB*	*28*	*507*	*64*	*22*	*1*	*26*	*72*	*49*	*100*	*1*	*1*	*23.6%*	*.245/.328/.474*	*117*	*.262*	*-0.2*	*1B -1*	*1.7*

Comparables: Carlos Pena (57), Josh Bell (57), Eric Hosmer (56)

Think about it: In 2022, there were 35 glorious instances in which Tellez leisurely rounded the bases with his jocular mien and imposing frame. Entering the year, there were concerns regarding the first baseman's future as a Brewer; he hit right-handed pitching well, but not well enough to justify a season's worth of plate appearances. Such worries proved unfounded, as Tellez held his ground against lefties and continued to blast righties. The secret? Not much changed in terms of power—his Statcast batted ball numbers are nearly identical to those from 2021—but Tellez slimmed down his chase rate, especially against southpaws. Swinging at fewer balls resulted in more walks, and voilà: Tellez laid the groundwork for a breakout season. Don't mind his paltry average, as the BABIP behind it is freakishly low even after factoring in Tellez's lethargic pace. More aesthetically pleasing dingers await in his future.

Abraham Toro IF

Born: 12/20/96 Age: 26 Bats: S Throws: R Height: 6'0" Weight: 225 lb. Origin: Round 5, 2016 Draft (#157 overall)

YEAR	TEAM	LVL	AGE	PA	R	2B	3B	HR	RBI	BB	K	SB	CS	Whiff%	AVG/OBP/SLG	DRC+	BABIP	BRR	DRP	WARP
2020	HOU	MLB	23	97	13	2	0	3	9	3	23	1	1	23.8%	.149/.237/.276	83	.164	-1.2	3B(14): -0.5, 1B(4): 0.2, 2B(1): 0	-0.1
2021	SUG	AAA	24	68	10	5	1	2	11	11	8	2	1		.352/.485/.593	129	.386	-1.1	3B(8): 1.1, 2B(3): 0.3, 1B(2): 0.1	0.4
2021	HOU	MLB	24	122	17	1	0	6	20	9	21	3	1	18.1%	.211/.287/.385	108	.205	-1.4	3B(30): -1, 1B(2): -0.1	0.3
2021	SEA	MLB	24	253	28	11	0	5	26	22	33	3	2	17.4%	.252/.328/.367	104	.275	-0.9	2B(58): 1, 3B(2): 0	1.1
2022	TAC	AAA	25	69	6	3	1	2	12	10	12	3	0	25.2%	.241/.353/.431	113	.273	0.7	2B(9): -0.6, 3B(5): 1.1	0.4
2022	SEA	MLB	25	352	36	13	1	10	35	22	65	2	0	21.7%	.185/.239/.324	88	.198	-2.3	2B(55): 0.2, 3B(31): 0.6, 1B(1): -0.3	0.3
2023 DC	*MIL*	*MLB*	*26*	*260*	*27*	*11*	*1*	*6*	*27*	*20*	*45*	*3*	*1*	*20.8%*	*.236/.308/.385*	*91*	*.267*	*1.4*	*2B 0, 3B 0*	*0.6*

Comparables: Andy LaRoche (60), Kaleb Cowart (57), Rio Ruiz (57)

The Mariners had to have a lot of stuff go right to survive 352 plate appearances from a poor-fielding utility infielder who notched an OPS well below .600. Prior to 2022, you could at least feign reasons to be optimistic about Toro's development. He showed good bat-to-ball skills coming up through the minors, and he has some speed and power (against right-handers, at least). But we're nearly a thousand major-league plate appearances into his career, and he's still flat-lining at the plate. As a switch-hitter who's still only 26, Toro will likely bounce around the league for a while longer—the Brewers, for their part, found him interesting enough to nab in the Jesse Winker/Kolton Wong swap this winter. But Toro's production needs to take a step forward—probably two steps, if we're being honest—if he wants to stick on a team with designs on playing in October.

Brice Turang SS Born: 11/21/99 Age: 23 Bats: L Throws: R Height: 6'0" Weight: 173 lb. Origin: Round 1, 2018 Draft (#21 overall)

YEAR	TEAM	LVL	AGE	PA	R	2B	3B	HR	RBI	BB	K	SB	CS	Whiff%	AVG/OBP/SLG	DRC+	BABIP	BRR	DRP	WARP
2021	BLX	AA	21	320	40	14	3	5	39	28	48	11	7		.264/.329/.385	107	.300	0.4	SS(71): 2.4	1.5
2021	NAS	AAA	21	176	19	7	0	1	14	32	35	9	2		.245/.381/.315	100	.315	0.1	SS(44): 2.1	0.8
2022	NAS	AAA	22	603	89	24	2	13	78	65	118	34	2	32.1%	.286/.360/.412	109	.342	1.6	SS(104): 0.8, CF(14): -2.2, 3B(8): 0.3	2.6
2023 DC	*MIL*	*MLB*	*23*	*339*	*33*	*12*	*2*	*4*	*29*	*28*	*69*	*11*	*2*	*21.9%*	*.240/.307/.342*	*79*	*.297*	*7.4*	*2B 0, SS 0*	*0.9*

Comparables: Tyler Pastornicky (61), J.P. Crawford (59), Asdrúbal Cabrera (58)

One lament has long emanated from the scouts who evaluate Turang: "If only he had even average power!" Consider their wishes granted. Promoted to Triple-A, Turang launched double-digit home runs for the first time, providing hope he can maintain some semblance of pop as he continues his steady march toward the majors. Other aspects of his game are already advanced—he has an incredible feel for the strike zone, and as a defender, his slick hands allow him to dispose of balls with ease at the six. Oh, and he's a master base-stealer, too. Turang had all the makings of a high-floor, low-variance player, but if he keeps posting slugging percentages that start with a four, he could follow in Andrés Giménez's footsteps as a standout all-around middle infielder.

Luis Urías IF Born: 06/03/97 Age: 26 Bats: R Throws: R Height: 5'9" Weight: 186 lb. Origin: International Free Agent, 2013

YEAR	TEAM	LVL	AGE	PA	R	2B	3B	HR	RBI	BB	K	SB	CS	Whiff%	AVG/OBP/SLG	DRC+	BABIP	BRR	DRP	WARP
2020	MIL	MLB	23	120	11	4	1	0	11	10	32	2	2	22.8%	.239/.308/.294	77	.338	-0.3	3B(30): 0.9, 2B(10): -0.5, SS(8): -0.5	0.0
2021	MIL	MLB	24	570	77	25	1	23	75	63	116	5	1	22.8%	.249/.345/.445	109	.280	-1.0	3B(68): 1.3, SS(68): -1.8, 2B(25): 0.2	2.5
2022	BLX	AA	25	31	4	1	0	0	2	3	7	0	0		.148/.258/.185	102	.200	-0.6	3B(3): 0.1, SS(2): -0.3	0.0
2022	MIL	MLB	25	472	54	17	1	16	47	50	99	1	2	22.2%	.239/.335/.404	111	.274	-0.9	3B(73): 0.4, 2B(46): -0.5, SS(24): -0.8	1.8
2023 DC	*MIL*	*MLB*	*26*	*576*	*71*	*22*	*2*	*20*	*65*	*59*	*114*	*5*	*2*	*22.1%*	*.248/.343/.427*	*113*	*.285*	*0.6*	*3B 0, SS 0*	*2.2*

Comparables: Wilmer Flores (51), Aramis Ramirez (51), José Ramírez (50)

Hot take alert: If Urías called Minute Maid Park his home, he'd be on the same level offensively as Alex Bregman. Hyperbole? Yes, but it's a statement rooted in truth. The two players have a lot in common: They're both third basemen who thrive on exhibiting good plate discipline and maximizing their limited raw power through consistently elevating and pulling the ball, which leads to not-too-dissimilar outputs after adjusting for park factors, sustainability and the like. Granted, the comparison only stands if we isolate the last two years, but the overall point remains: Urías is good, and quite possibly underrated. Despite a month-long absence due to injury, he passed the post-breakout test with flying colors and seems poised to finally cross the 3-WARP threshold.

Felix Valerio 2B Born: 12/26/00 Age: 22 Bats: R Throws: R Height: 5'7" Weight: 165 lb. Origin: International Free Agent, 2018

YEAR	TEAM	LVL	AGE	PA	R	2B	3B	HR	RBI	BB	K	SB	CS	Whiff%	AVG/OBP/SLG	DRC+	BABIP	BRR	DRP	WARP
2021	CAR	A	20	377	71	24	3	6	63	54	49	27	8		.314/.430/.469	135	.354	0.7	2B(40): -4.2, SS(18): -0.5, 3B(17): 2.4	2.5
2021	WIS	A+	20	134	19	13	0	5	16	15	22	4	1		.229/.321/.466	120	.242	-0.6	2B(27): -3.8	0.3
2022	BLX	AA	21	480	60	14	2	12	51	48	80	30	9		.228/.313/.357	106	.249	-1.5	2B(82): 3.3, LF(8): 0.3, 3B(3): 0.1	1.8
2023 non-DC	*MIL*	*MLB*	*22*	*251*	*21*	*10*	*1*	*3*	*22*	*19*	*46*	*10*	*3*	*21.5%*	*.224/.294/.332*	*77*	*.266*	*1.9*	*2B 0, 3B 0*	*0.2*

Comparables: Abiatal Avelino (66), Luis Valbuena (64), Vidal Bruján (63)

Valerio's monster leg kick is evocative of a hulking slugger with huge strikeout tendencies, but he's quite the opposite. Listed somewhat generously as 5-foot-7, the second baseman's swing remains stable despite being max effort, which has led to high contact rates and near-equal walk-to-strikeout ratios. In recent years, Valerio has tried adding power by hitting more fly balls while maintaining his pull-side tendencies. But because he lacks raw strength, that approach might have eaten into his BABIP—fly balls that don't leave the yard are usually easy outs—leading to a statistically poor showing at Double-A Biloxi. Still, Valerio's bat-to-ball skills are such that he should be able to find a middle ground. He has plenty of time to do so, as he's just entering his age-22 season.

★ ★ ★ *2023 Top 101 Prospect* **#65** ★ ★ ★

Joey Wiemer OF Born: 02/11/99 Age: 24 Bats: R Throws: R Height: 6'5" Weight: 215 lb. Origin: Round 4, 2020 Draft (#121 overall)

YEAR	TEAM	LVL	AGE	PA	R	2B	3B	HR	RBI	BB	K	SB	CS	Whiff%	AVG/OBP/SLG	DRC+	BABIP	BRR	DRP	WARP
2021	CAR	A	22	320	53	11	2	13	44	45	69	22	4		.276/.391/.478	126	.326	-0.4	RF(50): 12.5, CF(23): 1.3, LF(5): 0.7	3.4
2021	WIS	A+	22	152	33	7	0	14	33	18	36	8	2		.336/.428/.719	155	.363	-0.1	RF(22): -1.1, CF(4): -1.1	1.2
2022	BLX	AA	23	374	57	19	1	15	47	34	113	25	1		.243/.321/.440	90	.319	4.1	RF(59): 5.8, CF(21): 0.9, LF(2): 0.2	2.5
2022	NAS	AAA	23	174	24	15	1	6	30	21	34	6	2	27.1%	.287/.368/.520	106	.327	-0.2	RF(34): 2.5, CF(2): -0.2	1.0
2023 DC	*MIL*	*MLB*	*24*	*64*	*7*	*2*	*0*	*2*	*7*	*5*	*19*	*2*	*0*	*38.4%*	*.232/.302/.399*	*90*	*.314*	*1.0*	*RF 0*	*0.2*

Comparables: Hunter Renfroe (62), Nick Torres (61), Johan Mieses (58)

Wiemer adopted a new swing in 2021 that helped him convert his raw power into in-game bombs, but it didn't come with a newly discriminating approach. Selling out for launch instead of contact made his strikeout rate balloon; against Double-A pitching, he whiffed over 30% of the time. So did the Brewers ask him to revert back to his old ways? Of course not; they promoted him instead. It didn't make much sense at the time, but boy did it work, as Wiemer dramatically cut his strikeout rate against tougher competition while achieving consistent loft. Unlike many batters with similar profiles, Wiemer is expected to not only stay in right field defensively, but to excel there. His big hacks won't always connect, but with this kind of power he'll only need to every so often to be a viable big-leaguer.

Jesse Winker LF Born: 08/17/93 Age: 29 Bats: L Throws: L Height: 6'3" Weight: 215 lb. Origin: Round 1, 2012 Draft (#49 overall)

YEAR	TEAM	LVL	AGE	PA	R	2B	3B	HR	RBI	BB	K	SB	CS	Whiff%	AVG/OBP/SLG	DRC+	BABIP	BRR	DRP	WARP
2020	CIN	MLB	26	183	27	7	0	12	23	28	46	1	0	29.0%	.255/.388/.544	121	.283	-0.4	LF(15): 0.3, RF(1): 0	0.9
2021	CIN	MLB	27	485	77	32	1	24	71	53	75	1	0	20.2%	.305/.394/.556	136	.324	-0.7	LF(101): -5.1, RF(5): -0.3, CF(1): 0	3.4
2022	SEA	MLB	28	547	51	15	0	14	53	84	103	0	0	19.9%	.219/.344/.344	109	.251	-1.6	LF(118): -7	1.4
2023 DC	*MIL*	*MLB*	*29*	*580*	*81*	*26*	*1*	*21*	*66*	*79*	*98*	*0*	*0*	*19.9%*	*.261/.374/.453*	*130*	*.288*	*-1.8*	*RF 0, LF -1*	*3.0*

Comparables: Carl Yastrzemski (67), Augie Galan (67), Derrick May (66)

Imagine that you've been traded away from a team that seemed utterly indifferent to winning to one whose fans were absolutely ravenous for relevant autumn baseball. You were the principal piece in the trade, the one that garnered the commentary and tweets (even if your fellow traveler was known for his prodigious home runs). You want to impress, you want to be a centerpiece of the offense, but you're not feeling quite right—your neck and shoulder are barking—and it's Just. Not. Happening. It might make you fighting mad—enough so that you take out some aggression when you get plunked in the hip by Angels' righty Andrew Wantz one hot June afternoon, leading to your suspension, along with two of your teammates, and your manager to boot. But your display of bravado didn't make up for your vanished power and disappointingly poor contact. When the news came out a few weeks after the season that you went in for neck and knee surgery, you hoped everyone would understand. With free agency a year away, you've got another chance, now back in the NL Central with the Brewers. Will you fight for it? Your former teammates were reportedly skeptical that you would.

Christian Yelich LF Born: 12/05/91 Age: 31 Bats: L Throws: R Height: 6'3" Weight: 195 lb. Origin: Round 1, 2010 Draft (#23 overall)

YEAR	TEAM	LVL	AGE	PA	R	2B	3B	HR	RBI	BB	K	SB	CS	Whiff%	AVG/OBP/SLG	DRC+	BABIP	BRR	DRP	WARP
2020	MIL	MLB	28	247	39	7	1	12	22	46	76	4	2	33.6%	.205/.356/.430	105	.259	0.4	LF(51): -2.5	0.6
2021	MIL	MLB	29	475	70	19	2	9	51	70	113	9	3	24.9%	.248/.362/.373	93	.321	2.2	LF(107): -0.6	1.5
2022	MIL	MLB	30	671	99	25	4	14	57	88	162	19	3	25.1%	.252/.355/.383	98	.327	2.1	LF(115): 1.5	2.3
2023 DC	*MIL*	*MLB*	*31*	*615*	*78*	*25*	*3*	*19*	*65*	*82*	*134*	*14*	*3*	*25.2%*	*.249/.357/.421*	*116*	*.301*	*7.9*	*LF 9*	*4.4*

Comparables: Tim Raines (72), Carl Yastrzemski (64), Goose Goslin (64)

Farewell to thee, that Yelich of yore, that breakout superstar slugger who was poised to become a perennial MVP candidate. The 2022 season marked the second consecutive full-length campaign in which the Brewers' outfielder reverted to an older, more primitive state: a slap-hitter who drew the occasional walk, but who seldom drove anything out of the ballpark. Yelich didn't add much in the field, either—no defensive metrics liked him, and Baseball Savant corroborated the eye test by ranking his arm strength in the bottom five among regular outfielders. Solid plate discipline and a penchant for line drives grant Yelich a medium-high floor; he's not at risk of falling flat on his face offensively, Cody Bellinger-style. But his most recent season has all but laid to rest any hopes of a drastic rebound. It's taught us, somewhat painfully, to accept that the Yelich of now is likely going to be the Yelich of the foreseeable future.

Freddy Zamora SS Born: 11/01/98 Age: 24 Bats: R Throws: R Height: 6'1" Weight: 190 lb. Origin: Round 2, 2020 Draft (#53 overall)

YEAR	TEAM	LVL	AGE	PA	R	2B	3B	HR	RBI	BB	K	SB	CS	Whiff%	AVG/OBP/SLG	DRC+	BABIP	BRR	DRP	WARP
2021	CAR	A	22	321	58	13	1	5	40	45	57	9	5		.287/.396/.399	118	.344	-0.5	SS(63): 2.8	1.8
2021	WIS	A+	22	92	12	9	0	1	9	12	19	1	0		.342/.435/.494	103	.441	0.3	SS(21): -2.6	0.1
2022	BLX	AA	23	100	10	4	0	1	5	5	22	4	0		.209/.270/.286	97	.261	0.0	SS(23): 0.4, 2B(2): 0.3	0.4
2023 non-DC	*MIL*	*MLB*	*24*	*251*	*21*	*10*	*1*	*2*	*21*	*18*	*53*	*3*	*2*	*22.7%*	*.232/.298/.324*	*75*	*.291*	*-0.2*	*2B 0, SS 0*	*-0.1*

Comparables: Danny Mendick (79), Chase d'Arnaud (70), Luis Gonzalez (69)

The gaps in Zamora's résumé are easily explained: a torn ACL in 2020 prior to being drafted, an erased minor-league season and, most recently, a season-ending shoulder injury that accounts for his poor performance in Double-A. Because of this, it's unfair to label him as a success or failure, or really as anything at all but a work in progress. Even with all the missed time, it is abundantly clear he's a slap hitter whose strength is putting the ball in play. That's no insult, as Zamora should be at least average offensively, and it helps that he's a genuine shortstop with good range and arm strength. Zamora might not be the Brewers' most exciting up-and-comer, but he could still have plenty of value.

PITCHERS

Aaron Ashby LHP Born: 05/24/98 Age: 25 Bats: R Throws: L Height: 6'2" Weight: 181 lb. Origin: Round 4, 2018 Draft (#125 overall)

YEAR	TEAM	LVL	AGE	W	L	SV	G	GS	IP	H	HR	BB/9	K/9	K	GB%	BABIP	WHIP	ERA	DRA-	WARP	MPH	FB%	Whiff%	CSP
2021	NAS	AAA	23	5	4	0	21	12	63^{1}	55	4	4.5	14.2	100	66.9%	.370	1.37	4.41	86	1.4				
2021	MIL	MLB	23	3	2	1	13	4	31^{2}	25	4	3.4	11.1	39	61.7%	.273	1.17	4.55	84	0.6	96.7	36.1%	29.9%	54.9%
2022	MIL	MLB	24	2	10	1	27	19	107^{1}	106	15	3.9	10.6	126	56.1%	.325	1.43	4.44	93	1.4	95.8	37.4%	29.6%	55.8%
2023 DC	*MIL*	*MLB*	*25*	*7*	*7*	*0*	*42*	*16*	*107*	*104*	*10*	*4.4*	*10.0*	*119*	*56.5%*	*.326*	*1.46*	*4.23*	*100*	*0.7*	*96.0*	*37.2%*	*29.8%*	*55.6%*

Comparables: Felix Doubront (58), Brad Hand (57), Nick Tropeano (55)

In 2022, the stage was set for Ashby to find his footing and potentially handle a big-league starter's workload. Unfortunately, sporadic but lengthy trips to the IL meant the rookie was never part of the Brewers rotation for long. When he did manage to take the mound, Ashby offered mixed signals. Despite being the proud owner of four plus pitches used in near-equal measure—Ashby is no fastball extremist, and for good reason—he failed to make noticeable advancements in commanding them. When Ashby is on, he can rack up double-digit strikeouts; in fact, his pitch locations are often outstanding, providing glimpses of a lofty ceiling. But Ashby tends to meander his way into trouble, and in unfavorable counts he's been inept at throwing strikes: Ashby's zone rate when behind in the count was nearly five percentage points below the league-average. It's pretty simple: If he doesn't lick this problem, he's in danger of letting his gaudy stuff go to waste.

Corbin Burnes RHP

Born: 10/22/94 Age: 28 Bats: R Throws: R Height: 6'3" Weight: 225 lb. Origin: Round 4, 2016 Draft (#111 overall)

YEAR	TEAM	LVL	AGE	W	L	SV	G	GS	IP	H	HR	BB/9	K/9	K	GB%	BABIP	WHIP	ERA	DRA-	WARP	MPH	FB%	Whiff%	CSP
2020	MIL	MLB	25	4	1	0	12	9	59^{2}	37	2	3.6	13.3	88	47.2%	.285	1.02	2.11	61	1.9	95.1	67.7%	34.8%	41.0%
2021	MIL	MLB	26	11	5	0	28	28	167	123	7	1.8	12.6	234	49.3%	.309	0.94	2.43	58	5.3	95.5	63.0%	37.0%	52.2%
2022	MIL	MLB	27	12	8	0	33	33	202	144	23	2.3	10.8	243	46.9%	.259	0.97	2.94	67	5.4	95.2	62.7%	35.2%	50.9%
2023 DC	*MIL*	*MLB*	*28*	*11*	*8*	*0*	*29*	*29*	*174.7*	*147*	*17*	*2.5*	*11.4*	*221*	*47.5%*	*.310*	*1.12*	*2.72*	*70*	*4.2*	*95.3*	*63.0%*	*34.8%*	*50.3%*

Comparables: Curt Schilling (75), Bill Stoneman (72), Brandon Morrow (70)

Burnes' award-winning 2021 season was so dominant—he put up the second-lowest FIP of any qualified starter since MLB's integration—that its sequel was bound to feel underwhelming. Fortunately for Burnes, "underwhelming" by his standards includes an ERA that's a hair above three and a league-leading number of swinging strikes. If there's a real nit to pick here, it's that Burnes became more vulnerable to the long ball in his most recent campaign. Maybe that's because hitters have grown accustomed to a cutter-centric repertoire. Or maybe it's because home run rates for pitchers are like trips to the vet as experienced by cats; unpleasant, unpredictable and at times incomprehensible. It was never fair to ask Burnes to suppress hard contact to historically elite levels for a second season in a row. What matters most is that the Brewers ace hasn't seen his stuff deteriorate, remains in control of several pitches and is pitching deeper into games. He's not the baseball community's shiny new toy anymore, but that's only because he's firmly established himself as one of the five-or-so best starting pitchers in the game—and for what it's worth, WARP says he was *the* very best in 2022.

Matt Bush RHP

Born: 02/08/86 Age: 37 Bats: R Throws: R Height: 5'9" Weight: 180 lb. Origin: Round 1, 2004 Draft (#1 overall)

YEAR	TEAM	LVL	AGE	W	L	SV	G	GS	IP	H	HR	BB/9	K/9	K	GB%	BABIP	WHIP	ERA	DRA-	WARP	MPH	FB%	Whiff%	CSP
2021	TEX	MLB	35	0	0	0	4	0	4	4	3	2.3	11.3	5	27.3%	.125	1.25	6.75	96	0.0	95.1	53.6%	31.0%	49.3%
2022	TEX	MLB	36	2	1	1	40	5	36^{2}	27	5	2.5	11.0	45	38.3%	.253	1.01	2.95	78	0.8	97.5	47.6%	30.6%	56.3%
2022	MIL	MLB	36	0	2	2	25	1	23	16	6	3.1	11.3	29	45.5%	.204	1.04	4.30	83	0.4	97.5	51.4%	28.9%	55.4%
2023 DC	*MIL*	*MLB*	*37*	*3*	*2*	*4*	*59*	*0*	*51.3*	*45*	*7*	*3.4*	*9.2*	*52*	*40.1%*	*.283*	*1.25*	*3.70*	*93*	*0.4*	*97.4*	*49.4%*	*27.6%*	*55.6%*

Comparables: Steve Cishek (52), Matt Albers (51), Fernando Rodney (51)

Once considered a lost cause, Bush first surprised the baseball world by returning to the mound, then by turning in a full season's worth of good-to-great relief work. If there's a caveat, it's that Bush, who joined the Brewers at the deadline, experienced a decline in whiff rate down the stretch. That could be attributed to fatigue, or it could be the result of plain variance. But overall, signs point to a pitcher who's regained his health. Look no further than his rejuvenated fastball, an explosive pitch by velocity and movement and one that lets Bush get away with some mistakes down the pipe. For the soon-to-be 37-year-old, what lies ahead is a fight against the inevitable march of time. His stuff will no doubt decline; the questions are when and how fast?

Jake Cousins RHP

Born: 07/14/94 Age: 28 Bats: R Throws: R Height: 6'4" Weight: 185 lb. Origin: Round 20, 2017 Draft (#613 overall)

YEAR	TEAM	LVL	AGE	W	L	SV	G	GS	IP	H	HR	BB/9	K/9	K	GB%	BABIP	WHIP	ERA	DRA-	WARP	MPH	FB%	Whiff%	CSP
2021	BLX	AA	26	0	1	3	8	0	9	6	1	3.0	14.0	14	52.6%	.278	1.00	3.00	91	0.1				
2021	NAS	AAA	26	1	0	1	9	1	9^{2}	6	1	1.9	14.9	16	50.0%	.278	0.83	1.86	79	0.2				
2021	MIL	MLB	26	1	0	0	30	0	30	16	3	5.7	13.2	44	46.6%	.241	1.17	2.70	81	0.6	95.5	37.5%	41.3%	48.3%
2022	NAS	AAA	27	1	0	1	21	0	22^{2}	15	2	4.4	12.3	31	42.3%	.260	1.15	2.78	73	0.6	94.4	40.7%	27.6%	
2022	MIL	MLB	27	2	1	0	12	0	13^{1}	10	1	5.4	14.2	21	50.0%	.333	1.35	2.70	74	0.3	95.8	43.1%	42.4%	49.0%
2023 DC	*MIL*	*MLB*	*28*	*2*	*1*	*0*	*39*	*0*	*34*	*28*	*4*	*4.5*	*13.2*	*50*	*47.3%*	*.327*	*1.33*	*3.89*	*90*	*0.3*	*95.7*	*39.7%*	*38.1%*	*48.6%*

Comparables: John Axford (73), Al Alburquerque (73), Tanner Rainey (72)

There's a secret the Brewers should shove into a safe, then bury six feet under American Family Field. It's how they coerced five more inches of horizontal break out of Cousins' already great slider. Super-sizing his breaking ball helped lift the 28-year-old reliever's strikeout rate and curb his home run rate, but he remained shackled by subpar command. Milwaukee, with its armada of intriguing relievers, treated Cousins as yet a work-in-progress, tossing him back and forth between Triple-A and the majors. It's a luxury the org is uniquely positioned to afford, but no matter what Vikings fans tell you, a full season of Cousins might not be such a scary idea. He may not always know where his pitches are going, but opposing hitters don't either: since 2021, they're averaging just .135 off the slider he throws over half the time.

Robert Gasser LHP

Born: 05/31/99 Age: 24 Bats: L Throws: L Height: 6'1" Weight: 185 lb. Origin: Round 2, 2021 Draft (#71 overall)

YEAR	TEAM	LVL	AGE	W	L	SV	G	GS	IP	H	HR	BB/9	K/9	K	GB%	BABIP	WHIP	ERA	DRA-	WARP	MPH	FB%	Whiff%	CSP
2021	LE	A	22	0	0	0	5	5	14	11	1	1.3	8.4	13	52.8%	.286	0.93	1.29	110	0.0				
2022	FW	A+	23	4	9	0	18	18	90^{1}	86	8	2.8	11.5	115	41.2%	.356	1.26	4.18	96	1.1				
2022	BLX	AA	23	1	1	0	4	4	20^{1}	14	2	3.5	11.5	26	42.6%	.273	1.08	2.21	89	0.3				
2022	NAS	AAA	23	2	2	0	5	5	26^{1}	26	1	5.5	10.6	31	31.0%	.357	1.59	4.44	109	0.2	91.9	74.7%	33.3%	
2023 non-DC	*MIL*	*MLB*	*24*	*2*	*2*	*0*	*57*	*0*	*50*	*48*	*6*	*4.2*	*9.0*	*50*	*40.0%*	*.302*	*1.43*	*4.46*	*109*	*0.0*			*26.1%*	

Comparables: Daniel Mengden (71), Domingo Acevedo (70), Cody Reed (68)

Find someone who loves you as much as the Brewers love pitchers with low arm slots and unorthodox deliveries. Gasser, part of the return in the Josh Hader trade, is a lefty starter who suits Milwaukee's tastes. Though neither the bite nor (ironically) velocity on his fastball impresses, it earns whiffs via an approach angle that's uncomfortable for hitters. As for secondaries, Gasser's slider is his money pitch, benefiting from a wide entry into the zone. His feel for a changeup isn't quite developed yet, but even an average one would greatly increase his big-league viability. As of printing, he's a pitchability-based fifth starter who could grant the Brewers some rotation depth as soon as this season. But this is a Milwaukee pitching project we're talking about here, so who knows what new tricks Gasser will have picked up come spring?

Adrian Houser RHP Born: 02/02/93 Age: 30 Bats: R Throws: R Height: 6'3" Weight: 222 lb. Origin: Round 2, 2011 Draft (#69 overall)

YEAR	TEAM	LVL	AGE	W	L	SV	G	GS	IP	H	HR	BB/9	K/9	K	GB%	BABIP	WHIP	ERA	DRA-	WARP	MPH	FB%	Whiff%	CSP
2020	MIL	MLB	27	1	6	0	12	11	56	63	8	3.4	7.1	44	59.3%	.325	1.50	5.30	93	0.8	93.6	64.0%	22.5%	45.8%
2021	MIL	MLB	28	10	6	0	28	26	142^{1}	118	12	4.0	6.6	105	58.6%	.264	1.28	3.22	102	1.2	93.8	67.6%	18.6%	51.8%
2022	NAS	AAA	29	0	1	0	3	3	8^{1}	6	1	7.6	10.8	10	60.0%	.263	1.56	3.24	95	0.1				
2022	MIL	MLB	29	6	10	0	22	21	102^{2}	103	8	4.1	6.0	69	46.6%	.289	1.46	4.73	123	-0.2	94.0	65.5%	17.1%	51.6%
2023 DC	*MIL*	*MLB*	*30*	*4*	*4*	*0*	*32*	*6*	*56.3*	*60*	*6*	*4.1*	*6.7*	*42*	*51.5%*	*.310*	*1.53*	*4.75*	*114*	*0.0*	*93.9*	*66.4%*	*19.4%*	*50.8%*

Comparables: Rafael Montero (48), Jeff Samardzija (47), Andrew Cashner (45)

Once upon a time, back in May 2021, Houser fanned 10 Marlins in six innings without issuing a single walk, spotting sinker after sinker on the inside corner. He proved that, when everything clicks, he can be an out-making machine. Unfortunately, the knowledge of how he *can* pitch makes watching how he *usually* pitches rather agonizing. The righty is able to keep the ball within the park courtesy of his sinker, but an inability to find the zone or induce chases outside of it has caused his walk rate to balloon. Houser has never been a strikeout artist, and he allows too many hitters to reach base via ball four or hard contact to thrive. Nowadays, he's outclassed by modern pitch-to-contact wizards who can also touch 100 mph with their fastballs. He has his uses, but he could find himself coming out of the bullpen more often than not moving forward.

Eric Lauer LHP Born: 06/03/95 Age: 28 Bats: R Throws: L Height: 6'3" Weight: 228 lb. Origin: Round 1, 2016 Draft (#25 overall)

YEAR	TEAM	LVL	AGE	W	L	SV	G	GS	IP	H	HR	BB/9	K/9	K	GB%	BABIP	WHIP	ERA	DRA-	WARP	MPH	FB%	Whiff%	CSP
2020	MIL	MLB	25	0	2	0	4	2	11	17	2	7.4	9.8	12	21.1%	.417	2.36	13.09	180	-0.4	91.7	52.5%	29.1%	43.4%
2021	MIL	MLB	26	7	5	0	24	20	118^{2}	94	16	3.1	8.9	117	35.3%	.254	1.14	3.19	93	1.6	92.7	44.6%	24.1%	54.8%
2022	MIL	MLB	27	11	7	0	29	29	158^{2}	135	27	3.3	8.9	157	33.9%	.262	1.22	3.69	108	0.9	93.5	43.8%	24.2%	54.7%
2023 DC	*MIL*	*MLB*	*28*	*9*	*8*	*0*	*27*	*27*	*148.7*	*138*	*21*	*3.4*	*9.1*	*150*	*35.2%*	*.297*	*1.31*	*3.86*	*96*	*1.4*	*93.0*	*45.4%*	*24.7%*	*54.1%*

Comparables: José Quintana (79), Donovan Osborne (79), Homer Bailey (79)

Pepperidge Farm remembers when Lauer had a 13.11 K/9 back in April, leading some to crown him as the Brewers' latest pitching development miracle. Given that his pitch mix, stuff and command remained largely the same as before, that narrative always seemed a bit sketchy. Sure enough, as the season progressed, Lauer lapsed into his former role of a solid fourth starter. It serves as a reminder that most baseball players, like most people, don't really change, with teammates like Corbin Burnes the exception rather than the rule. That said, Lauer is still plenty valuable in his own right. While he doesn't have one standout pitch, the lefty features a carousel of four offerings—a four-seamer, cutter, slider and curve—that are all average or a touch above. Being well-rounded is Lauer's true power, and that's not something the Brewers need to try and tweak.

Max Lazar RHP Born: 06/03/99 Age: 24 Bats: R Throws: R Height: 6'1" Weight: 200 lb. Origin: Round 11, 2017 Draft (#324 overall)

YEAR	TEAM	LVL	AGE	W	L	SV	G	GS	IP	H	HR	BB/9	K/9	K	GB%	BABIP	WHIP	ERA	DRA-	WARP	MPH	FB%	Whiff%	CSP
2022	CAR	A	23	0	1	0	3	2	7	6	1	1.3	7.7	6	50.0%	.263	1.00	2.57	102	0.1				
2022	WIS	A+	23	1	0	1	11	6	32	32	5	3.1	5.3	19	53.2%	.260	1.34	4.22	121	0.0				
2023 non-DC	*MIL*	*MLB*	*24*	*2*	*3*	*0*	*57*	*0*	*50*	*59*	*7*	*3.6*	*6.0*	*33*	*45.5%*	*.318*	*1.59*	*5.45*	*131*	*-0.6*			*19.9%*	

Comparables: Zach Thompson (61), Joan Gregorio (59), Parker Markel (54)

It's safe to say the Brewers have a type. Lazar isn't in their system by sheer coincidence; Milwaukee just can't quit pitchers who, despite underwhelming velocity and raw movement, succeed through atypical deliveries and release points. We've seen all types of weird relievers before, but Lazar is especially unique as he throws an effective changeup from an over-the-top arm slot. That's incredibly hard to do. It creates an uncomfortable look for hitters, which nets Lazar tons of swings and misses—or it used to: His strikeout rate plummeted last season in High-A, leading some to wonder if Lazar's unorthodox approach will play against more accomplished, discerning hitters. But there is a precedent for this profile working set by Oliver Drake, meaning there's a chance Lazar develops into a sort of changeup of his own in an arm barn full of generic flamethrowers.

Wade Miley LHP Born: 11/13/86 Age: 36 Bats: L Throws: L Height: 6'2" Weight: 220 lb. Origin: Round 1, 2008 Draft (#43 overall)

YEAR	TEAM	LVL	AGE	W	L	SV	G	GS	IP	H	HR	BB/9	K/9	K	GB%	BABIP	WHIP	ERA	DRA-	WARP	MPH	FB%	Whiff%	CSP
2020	CIN	MLB	33	0	3	0	6	4	14^{1}	15	1	5.7	7.5	12	52.3%	.326	1.67	5.65	110	0.1	90.1	14.0%	30.8%	40.4%
2021	CIN	MLB	34	12	7	0	28	28	163	166	17	2.8	6.9	125	48.0%	.306	1.33	3.37	115	0.2	90.0	17.6%	24.1%	48.6%
2022	SB	A+	35	0	0	0	2	2	6	11	0	1.5	4.5	3	68.0%	.440	2.00	9.00	111	0.0				
2022	IOW	AAA	35	0	0	0	4	4	16	13	1	2.3	6.7	12	52.1%	.261	1.06	2.81	98	0.2				
2022	CHC	MLB	35	2	2	0	9	8	37	31	3	3.4	6.8	28	51.3%	.250	1.22	3.16	129	-0.2	89.0	17.0%	25.3%	49.6%
2023 DC	*MIL*	*MLB*	*36*	*6*	*7*	*0*	*22*	*22*	*113.3*	*127*	*13*	*3.3*	*6.7*	*84*	*49.6%*	*.319*	*1.49*	*4.69*	*114*	*0.1*	*90.0*	*18.3%*	*22.9%*	*47.2%*

Comparables: Mike Flanagan (76), Mark Buehrle (76), Kyle Lohse (76)

Miley's managed to find consistent gigs since 2018 by working out an effective dynamic between his cutter and his changeup. He'll be 36 years old this season, entering his 13th big-league season, and the guy keeps getting work. He made four starts each in the first and second halves of 2022. While solid in both stints, he looked more vulnerable in the latter: opponents' OPS spiked dramatically, from .547 to .704. Miley didn't do himself any favors hurrying back from an injury in the spring, but when unavailable on the mound he found a role in the clubhouse as a reliable source of advice and experience for the myriad young pitchers in the Chicago locker room. The Brewers' staff is far more tenured, but Miley will join it anyway after signing a one-year deal with a mutual 2024 option in January.

Hoby Milner LHP Born: 01/13/91 Age: 32 Bats: L Throws: L Height: 6'3" Weight: 175 lb. Origin: Round 7, 2012 Draft (#248 overall)

YEAR	TEAM	LVL	AGE	W	L	SV	G	GS	IP	H	HR	BB/9	K/9	K	GB%	BABIP	WHIP	ERA	DRA-	WARP	MPH	FB%	Whiff%	CSP
2020	LAA	MLB	29	0	0	0	19	0	13^1	13	5	4.0	8.8	13	38.5%	.235	1.43	8.10	95	0.2	87.9	53.8%	19.8%	49.5%
2021	NAS	AAA	30	1	1	5	30	0	32	19	2	0.6	13.5	48	58.2%	.262	0.66	1.69	71	0.9				
2021	MIL	MLB	30	0	0	0	19	0	21^2	30	8	1.2	12.5	30	26.6%	.400	1.52	5.40	85	0.4	89.2	56.2%	23.5%	55.4%
2022	MIL	MLB	31	3	3	0	67	0	64^2	61	5	2.1	8.9	64	48.9%	.315	1.18	3.76	94	0.8	89.1	47.0%	23.7%	47.3%
2023 DC	*MIL*	*MLB*	*32*	*3*	*2*	*4*	*59*	*0*	*51.3*	*49*	*6*	*2.1*	*8.6*	*48*	*44.5%*	*.298*	*1.19*	*3.51*	*90*	*0.5*	*89.0*	*49.6%*	*23.5%*	*49.1%*

Comparables: Blaine Hardy (63), Sam Freeman (61), Manny Acosta (57)

So you're a LOOGY looking to survive in an era in which baseball has legislated your specific role out of the game. What can you do to go from a one-trick pony to the sort of versatile, reliable reliever who can throw 60+ innings and hold their own against righties? It's simple, really. You need to ditch your sluggish four-seam fastball and replace it with a sinker that's aided by your low arm slot. Then you need to develop a changeup. Oh, and then you need to find an organization that knows when and how to deploy you in your new reality. The survivorship bias is real here, but it couldn't hurt to plaster Milner all over motivational posters for unemployed lefties.

Joel Payamps RHP Born: 04/07/94 Age: 29 Bats: R Throws: R Height: 6'2" Weight: 225 lb. Origin: International Free Agent, 2010

YEAR	TEAM	LVL	AGE	W	L	SV	G	GS	IP	H	HR	BB/9	K/9	K	GB%	BABIP	WHIP	ERA	DRA-	WARP	MPH	FB%	Whiff%	CSP
2020	AZ	MLB	26	0	0	0	2	0	3	2	0	9.0	6.0	2	12.5%	.250	1.67	3.00	162	-0.1	93.9	62.7%	23.5%	45.8%
2021	OMA	AAA	27	1	0	2	8	0	8	10	0	4.5	15.7	14	19.0%	.476	1.75	4.50	88	0.2				
2021	KC	MLB	27	1	1	0	15	1	20^1	23	3	1.3	7.1	16	41.8%	.313	1.28	4.43	103	0.2	95.1	58.4%	17.7%	57.9%
2021	TOR	MLB	27	0	2	0	22	0	30	21	3	3.3	6.6	22	47.1%	.220	1.07	2.70	109	0.1	94.5	61.8%	26.9%	51.8%
2022	OAK	MLB	28	1	3	0	12	0	13	14	2	0.0	5.5	8	55.6%	.279	1.08	3.46	98	0.1	94.3	47.1%	18.2%	58.3%
2022	KC	MLB	28	2	3	0	29	0	42^2	46	5	3.4	7.0	33	52.6%	.313	1.45	3.16	104	0.3	94.8	51.5%	24.0%	55.0%
2023 DC	*MIL*	*MLB*	*29*	*1*	*2*	*0*	*39*	*0*	*34*	*37*	*4*	*2.9*	*7.4*	*28*	*47.0%*	*.318*	*1.41*	*4.49*	*110*	*0.0*	*94.7*	*54.6%*	*24.3%*	*54.9%*

Comparables: Tyler Duffey (52), Dylan Floro (51), Tyler Thornburg (50)

How many teams does a reliever have to suit up for before he officially earns journeyman status? And does it matter how fast he travels from clubhouse to clubhouse, changing uniforms along the way? Maybe we should ask Payamps. After a midseason waiver claim, he joined the Athletics as his fourth team in four years. He was just fine with the Royals before they cut him loose, so the A's brought him on to be something of a seat-filler in their bullpen for the dark days of their latest rebuild. He doesn't walk or strike anyone out, and he gets a pretty high percentage of groundballs for a reliever. Call him a gap-filler or replacement-level if you want, but if he hasn't already earned the journeyman title, he likely will soon; the Brewers nabbed him in the Sean Murphy trade this winter. He has the skills to bounce around the league—and between a few more teams—for at least a few more years.

Freddy Peralta RHP Born: 06/04/96 Age: 27 Bats: R Throws: R Height: 5'11" Weight: 199 lb. Origin: International Free Agent, 2013

YEAR	TEAM	LVL	AGE	W	L	SV	G	GS	IP	H	HR	BB/9	K/9	K	GB%	BABIP	WHIP	ERA	DRA-	WARP	MPH	FB%	Whiff%	CSP
2020	MIL	MLB	24	3	1	0	15	1	29^1	22	2	3.7	14.4	47	33.3%	.333	1.16	3.99	69	0.8	93.3	65.8%	39.8%	40.4%
2021	MIL	MLB	25	10	5	0	28	27	144^1	84	14	3.5	12.2	195	32.1%	.232	0.97	2.81	72	3.5	93.4	53.1%	34.5%	53.2%
2022	MIL	MLB	26	4	4	0	18	17	78	54	6	3.1	9.9	86	39.3%	.247	1.04	3.58	82	1.5	92.8	54.9%	29.7%	52.9%
2023 DC	*MIL*	*MLB*	*27*	*8*	*7*	*0*	*24*	*24*	*138.3*	*115*	*18*	*3.5*	*10.9*	*167*	*36.9%*	*.294*	*1.22*	*3.42*	*85*	*2.1*	*93.2*	*57.3%*	*31.7%*	*51.6%*

Comparables: Chris Archer (66), Lance McCullers Jr. (64), Stephen Strasburg (59)

Injuries are a touchy subject. Visit the comments section of almost any article about an underperforming baseball player (editor's note: do not do this), and chances are, you'll find a debate as to whether various maladies have caused said disappointing outcomes. In Peralta's case, however, there should be little debate—repeated shoulder inflammations and strained lats have caused a dramatic dip in his strikeout rate. Need proof? He lost a ton of sweep on his slider, leaving Peralta with a lethargic breaking ball that just didn't, well, break. He also lost two inches of vertical movement on his otherwise fantastic fastball, and while that didn't result in opposing hitters making harder contact, it did help them stop whiffing on it so much. In retrospect, it's likely Peralta never regained a proper feel for all his pitches amid all the injuries. Even so, he held batters to a .569 OPS, which goes to show that he's still like the biggest kid on the Little League team, capable of crushing the competition even without his A+ stuff. Any version of Peralta in which he's in tune with his mechanics is one that can and will decimate opposing batters.

Ethan Small LHP Born: 02/14/97 Age: 26 Bats: L Throws: L Height: 6'4" Weight: 215 lb. Origin: Round 1, 2019 Draft (#28 overall)

YEAR	TEAM	LVL	AGE	W	L	SV	G	GS	IP	H	HR	BB/9	K/9	K	GB%	BABIP	WHIP	ERA	DRA-	WARP	MPH	FB%	Whiff%	CSP
2021	BLX	AA	24	2	2	0	8	8	41^1	26	1	4.6	14.6	67	39.2%	.342	1.14	1.96	83	0.8				
2021	NAS	AAA	24	2	0	0	9	9	35	27	3	5.4	6.2	24	43.6%	.245	1.37	2.06	117	0.2				
2022	NAS	AAA	25	7	6	0	27	21	103	82	8	5.1	10.0	114	40.7%	.282	1.36	4.46	81	2.4	91.2	61.4%	22.6%	
2022	MIL	MLB	25	0	0	0	2	2	6^1	8	1	11.4	9.9	7	33.3%	.412	2.53	7.11	154	-0.1	91.1	53.0%	33.3%	64.3%
2023 DC	*MIL*	*MLB*	*26*	*2*	*1*	*0*	*16*	*3*	*24.3*	*22*	*3*	*5.7*	*9.7*	*26*	*40.4%*	*.306*	*1.56*	*4.79*	*111*	*0.1*	*91.1*	*53.0%*	*29.6%*	*64.3%*

Comparables: Matthew Boyd (44), Amir Garrett (44), Sam Howard (42)

Some rookies take their cups of coffee like a champ; Small took a sip and singed his tongue. The 26-year-old lefty still has major command issues, made worse by his tendency to induce whiffs in the zone but not out of it (fewer chases equals more walks). His fastball has late life and is deceptive, but it might be too slow to really play at the big-league level. Varying its shape as Nestor Cortes does could be a solution, but for now, strike-throwing is the priority, followed by the continued development of his slider. Based on limited data, it appears to be of the slow, gyro-spin variety, confusing hitters by moving less than expected. The foundation of an effective three-pitch mix still exists in Small's arsenal, but it requires finessing.

Peter Strzelecki RHP

Born: 10/24/94 Age: 28 Bats: R Throws: R Height: 6'2" Weight: 195 lb. Origin: Undrafted Free Agent, 2018

YEAR	TEAM	LVL	AGE	W	L	SV	G	GS	IP	H	HR	BB/9	K/9	K	GB%	BABIP	WHIP	ERA	DRA-	WARP	MPH	FB%	Whiff%	CSP
2021	BLX	AA	26	0	2	1	36	0	47	42	5	3.3	12.4	65	38.9%	.343	1.26	3.45	89	0.8				
2021	NAS	AAA	26	0	0	0	4	0	5	4	1	1.8	10.8	6	38.5%	.300	1.00	3.60	77	0.1				
2022	NAS	AAA	27	4	0	3	27	0	31^2	18	4	2.8	14.2	50	32.8%	.259	0.88	2.84	70	0.9				
2022	MIL	MLB	27	2	1	1	30	0	35	28	2	3.9	10.3	40	31.5%	.295	1.23	2.83	89	0.5	93.5	53.3%	31.0%	51.6%
2023 DC	*MIL*	*MLB*	*28*	*2*	*2*	*0*	*52*	*0*	*45.7*	*39*	*7*	*3.4*	*9.9*	*50*	*34.8%*	*.283*	*1.24*	*3.72*	*93*	*0.4*	*93.5*	*53.3%*	*29.8%*	*51.6%*

Comparables: Carlos Ramirez (79), Jordan Weems (78), Danny Barnes (77)

On the surface, not much is impressive about Strzelecki, who signed as an undrafted free agent in 2018 and made his big-league debut—as well as his *BP Annual* debut—at the age of 27. But the Brewers excel at pitching development, and they've turned Strzelecki into a force to be reckoned with. Since his call-up, he's the proud owner of an excellent DRA and has fanned more than a batter per inning. He features a lower three-quarters arm slot and a crossfire delivery, which helps his otherwise tepid fastball play up and adds horizontal depth to his sweeping slider. The crown jewel of his arsenal, however, might still be in development: he has a devastating changeup, but he's yet to command it with regularity. Even in his current incarnation, Strzelecki is pretty close to his 99th-percentile outcome and deserves a full-time gig in the Brewers bullpen. But if he really figures out that change piece? We might have to start inventing new percentiles.

Devin Williams RHP

Born: 09/21/94 Age: 28 Bats: R Throws: R Height: 6'2" Weight: 200 lb. Origin: Round 2, 2013 Draft (#54 overall)

YEAR	TEAM	LVL	AGE	W	L	SV	G	GS	IP	H	HR	BB/9	K/9	K	GB%	BABIP	WHIP	ERA	DRA-	WARP	MPH	FB%	Whiff%	CSP
2020	MIL	MLB	25	4	1	0	22	0	27	8	1	3.0	17.7	53	61.1%	.200	0.63	0.33	44	1.1	96.7	43.9%	51.8%	41.2%
2021	MIL	MLB	26	8	2	3	58	0	54	36	5	4.7	14.5	87	45.0%	.301	1.19	2.50	65	1.5	95.5	34.7%	42.9%	48.6%
2022	MIL	MLB	27	6	4	15	65	0	60^2	31	2	4.5	14.2	96	50.5%	.266	1.01	1.93	61	1.8	94.1	37.7%	40.8%	48.8%
2023 DC	*MIL*	*MLB*	*28*	*3*	*2*	*32*	*59*	*0*	*51.3*	*46*	*5*	*4.7*	*15.3*	*87*	*47.7%*	*.387*	*1.42*	*4.13*	*93*	*0.4*	*94.9*	*38.1%*	*39.3%*	*47.9%*

Comparables: Nick Vincent (68), Al Alburquerque (68), Reyes Moronta (67)

The untold truth about pitching development is that while adding (or subtracting) movement to a pitch is very much possible, maintaining such tweaks through multiple seasons is much harder. It's the yo-yo effect, but measured through Rapsodo devices instead of weight scales. With that in mind...what the heck, Mr. Williams? Not only did he become one of the league's best relievers by learning a screwball/changeup/whatchamacallit, but he's also kept its movement consistent. You know the deal: It dives and tails further than any other off-speed pitch in existence, allowing him to strike out countless batters *and* run ridiculously low home run rates. When he's healthy, it seems like nothing can stop him—not even a loss in fastball velocity, which Williams compensated for by adding an inch of ride.

Bryse Wilson RHP

Born: 12/20/97 Age: 25 Bats: R Throws: R Height: 6'1" Weight: 250 lb. Origin: Round 4, 2016 Draft (#109 overall)

YEAR	TEAM	LVL	AGE	W	L	SV	G	GS	IP	H	HR	BB/9	K/9	K	GB%	BABIP	WHIP	ERA	DRA-	WARP	MPH	FB%	Whiff%	CSP
2020	ATL	MLB	22	1	0	1	6	2	15^2	18	2	5.2	8.6	15	43.8%	.348	1.72	4.02	106	0.1	93.7	81.8%	21.2%	46.7%
2021	GWN	AAA	23	5	2	0	10	9	55^1	61	8	2.6	6.8	42	40.6%	.321	1.39	4.23	109	0.5				
2021	ATL	MLB	23	2	3	0	8	8	33^2	45	7	3.2	6.1	23	37.6%	.349	1.69	5.88	122	-0.1	93.4	61.5%	23.1%	55.3%
2021	PIT	MLB	23	1	4	0	8	8	40^1	40	8	2.2	5.1	23	33.1%	.252	1.24	4.91	123	-0.1	93.0	65.5%	16.5%	54.0%
2022	IND	AAA	24	5	0	0	6	6	36^1	32	6	1.5	8.4	34	47.2%	.263	1.05	2.97	87	0.7				
2022	PIT	MLB	24	3	9	0	25	20	115^2	132	20	2.5	6.1	79	44.2%	.305	1.42	5.52	127	-0.5	92.7	56.7%	17.6%	56.3%
2023 DC	*MIL*	*MLB*	*25*	*1*	*1*	*0*	*39*	*0*	*34*	*37*	*4*	*2.6*	*5.9*	*22*	*42.3%*	*.297*	*1.37*	*4.46*	*112*	*0.0*	*92.9*	*60.5%*	*20.0%*	*55.0%*

Comparables: Tommy Hunter (69), Jacob Turner (68), Sean O'Sullivan (67)

Throughout the annals of history, there are countless notable figures who might very well have wound up as anonymous unknowns if not for mere happenstance. While he's not *quite* a complete unknown, it's easy to wonder if the Pirates would have bothered acquiring Wilson from Atlanta—if not for one strong start against the Dodgers in the 2020 NLCS. A year and a half into his Pirates tenure, Wilson has been nothing more than a placeholder in the rotation; even the lowly Pirates briefly gave up on that idea, before reverting to Wilson because *someone* needed to eat those innings. A splitter added in the second half helped Wilson to some degree, but not enough to give him many more chances at making his mark. Time will tell if the Brewers see something in him beyond rotation depth.

Brandon Woodruff RHP

Born: 02/10/93 Age: 30 Bats: L Throws: R Height: 6'4" Weight: 243 lb. Origin: Round 11, 2014 Draft (#326 overall)

YEAR	TEAM	LVL	AGE	W	L	SV	G	GS	IP	H	HR	BB/9	K/9	K	GB%	BABIP	WHIP	ERA	DRA-	WARP	MPH	FB%	Whiff%	CSP
2020	MIL	MLB	27	3	5	0	13	13	73^2	55	9	2.2	11.1	91	50.0%	.269	0.99	3.05	62	2.3	96.7	65.1%	29.0%	50.3%
2021	MIL	MLB	28	9	10	0	30	30	179^1	130	18	2.2	10.6	211	41.6%	.264	0.96	2.56	70	4.6	96.6	60.4%	28.4%	55.2%
2022	MIL	MLB	29	13	4	0	27	27	153^1	122	18	2.5	11.2	190	37.4%	.287	1.07	3.05	72	3.7	96.2	59.9%	31.2%	54.5%
2023 DC	*MIL*	*MLB*	*30*	*9*	*7*	*0*	*29*	*29*	*139.7*	*116*	*17*	*2.4*	*11.4*	*177*	*40.8%*	*.300*	*1.10*	*2.78*	*71*	*3.2*	*96.4*	*61.0%*	*30.4%*	*53.9%*

Comparables: Adam Wainwright (90), Stephen Strasburg (85), Justin Verlander (84)

"Well, pack it up boys, it's June, we're terrible, and the season is done," said no veteran baseball fan ever. There's a reason why it ain't over 'til it's over. Throughout April and May, Woodruff looked wrong—he couldn't find the strike zone and was subsequently hit hard. He then missed a month due to an ankle sprain, but when he returned, everything clicked. Shouting "Eureka!" as he ran out of the bullpen naked, Woodruff began dispatching batter after batter from late June onward, restoring his numbers to pleasing, Woodruff-like marks. Early struggles aside, not much changed for the gruff right-hander, but he did reintroduce his old slider, which now drops less and is thrown two ticks harder. It's tough to say which edition is the better pitch, but whichever Woodruff feels most comfortable with is probably the best answer. He's the platonic ideal of an ace, able to rack up whiffs while minimizing hard contact, and 2022 showed that two-and-a-half months of shakiness isn't enough to erase his aura of dominance.

Lineouts

Hitters

HITTER	POS	TEAM	LVL	AGE	PA	R	2B	3B	HR	RBI	BB	K	SB	CS	AVG/OBP/SLG	DRC+	BABIP	BRR	DRP	WARP
Eric Brown Jr.	SS	CAR	A	21	100	16	4	1	3	7	11	17	15	2	.262/.370/.440	121	.292	0.8	SS(17): 1.0, 2B(3): 0.4	0.8
Jonathan Davis	CF	NAS	AAA	30	221	27	11	1	4	22	28	44	14	1	.293/.395/.429	115	.360	3.1	CF(39): 2.4, LF(4): -0.6, RF(2): 0.5	1.4
	CF	MIL	MLB	30	91	9	1	0	0	4	14	26	7	1	.224/.344/.237	80	.340	1.8	CF(34): -1	0.2
Eduardo Garcia	SS	CAR	A	19	372	43	13	3	10	48	19	122	14	2	.262/.309/.403	91	.375	1.1	SS(80): 0.1	0.8
	SS	WIS	A+	19	108	11	3	0	5	17	0	40	1	0	.248/.269/.419	85	.350	-0.1	SS(25): 0.4	0.2
Alex Jackson	C	NAS	AAA	26	119	9	8	1	2	18	12	28	1	0	.225/.319/.382	98	.284	-1.4	C(23): 4.9	0.6
	C	MIL	MLB	26	12	0	0	0	0	0	0	7	0	0	.250/.250/.250	78	.600	0.0	C(4): -0.2	0.0
Robert Moore	MI	CAR	A	20	125	14	8	0	3	14	13	28	6	2	.264/.352/.418	100	.329	0.0	2B(15): 0.8, SS(12): -0.4	0.4
Carlos Rodriguez	OF	WIS	A+	21	166	23	10	1	3	21	18	35	10	3	.268/.355/.415	112	.327	0.3	LF(28): 0.6, CF(7): 0.5, RF(6): 0.2	1.1

When **Eric Brown Jr.** takes a hack his body resembles a helicopter rotor in motion, choppy yet explosive. It's unorthodox, but the first-round pick out of Coastal Carolina has the athleticism to make it work, as well as to display exceptional range at short. ⚾ Like Woody in *Toy Story*, backup center fielder **Jonathan Davis** found himself abandoned upon the arrival of newer, shinier toys. Unlike Woody he's unlikely to bounce back in any sequels. ⚾ A true shortstop prospect, **Eduardo Garcia** reacts quickly to incoming groundballs but not to pitches incoming from the mound. ⚾ The all-power, all-strikeout **Alex Jackson** made just 12 plate appearances due to poor performance, a lack of roster space and injury, making him the Brewers' MFP—Most Forgettable Player. ⚾ The son of longtime Royals architect Dayton, **Robert Moore**'s amateur stock fell because of an uncharacteristically poor 2022 season at Arkansas, but scouts were still enamored with his speed, defensive range and pull-side power. The Brewers stopped his draft day slide near the end of the second round. ⚾ The Brewers may not need more speedy, glove-first fourth outfielders right now, but **Carlos Rodriguez** is on back order in case their stock runs out in a year or two.

Pitchers

PITCHER	TEAM	LVL	AGE	W	L	SV	G	GS	IP	H	HR	BB/9	K/9	K	GB%	BABIP	WHIP	ERA	DRA-	WARP	MPH	FB%	WHF	CSP
Jason Alexander	NAS	AAA	29	8	2	0	13	10	63^{1}	58	5	2.4	6.7	47	57.6%	.285	1.18	2.84	102	0.7				
	MIL	MLB	29	2	3	0	18	11	71^{2}	88	12	3.5	5.8	46	50.6%	.329	1.62	5.40	135	-0.6	92.5	61.1%	17.3%	52.4%
Dylan File	NAS	AAA	26	8	6	0	26	19	114^{1}	107	13	2.7	7.5	95	39.2%	.284	1.23	4.57	121	0.3				
Jandel Gustave	MIL	MLB	29	2	0	0	27	0	28	25	4	3.5	8.7	27	47.5%	.276	1.29	3.86	100	0.3	96.1	63.5%	17.2%	54.5%
Janson Junk	SL	AAA	26	1	7	0	16	15	73^{2}	77	9	2.2	8.4	69	32.3%	.318	1.29	4.64	110	0.0	92.7	44.9%	23.0%	
	LAA	MLB	26	1	1	0	3	2	8^{1}	10	1	3.2	11.9	11	65.2%	.409	1.56	6.48	86	0.1	92.5	43.4%	17.8%	58.2%
Trevor Kelley	NAS	AAA	29	3	3	9	34	0	34^{1}	29	2	2.6	11.0	42	43.2%	.318	1.14	2.36	79	0.8				
	MIL	MLB	29	1	0	0	18	0	23^{2}	25	7	3.4	8.7	23	35.6%	.273	1.44	6.08	106	0.2	90.1	63.9%	23.0%	48.6%
Tyson Miller	RR	AAA	26	4	7	1	29	16	89^{2}	91	14	4.0	11.4	114	45.8%	.344	1.46	4.52	77	1.7	92.1	54.4%	27.9%	
	TEX	MLB	26	1	2	0	4	2	10^{2}	16	1	6.7	6.7	8	44.7%	.405	2.25	10.97	129	-0.1	91.0	59.6%	21.8%	48.7%
Elvis Peguero	SL	AAA	25	4	1	5	38	0	44^{1}	34	2	2.6	10.2	50	57.4%	.283	1.06	2.84	67	1.1	96.8	42.6%	35.0%	
	LAA	MLB	25	0	0	0	13	0	17^{1}	23	4	2.6	6.2	12	50.0%	.339	1.62	6.75	112	0.1	96.7	37.3%	23.9%	52.4%
Luis Perdomo	NAS	AAA	29	2	0	4	24	3	30^{1}	21	2	1.2	9.8	33	56.6%	.257	0.82	2.67	80	0.7				
	MIL	MLB	29	3	0	0	14	0	23^{2}	24	4	1.1	4.6	12	61.3%	.263	1.14	3.80	110	0.1	93.8	56.1%	23.4%	54.3%
Miguel Sánchez	NAS	AAA	28	4	2	1	17	0	19	16	2	2.8	8.5	18	42.0%	.292	1.16	3.79	98	0.3				
	MIL	MLB	28	1	1	0	12	0	13^{1}	12	3	5.4	6.1	9	58.5%	.237	1.50	4.05	114	0.0	94.2	38.9%	24.5%	49.9%
Adam Seminaris	TRI	A+	23	2	2	0	7	5	36^{2}	27	2	2.0	10.6	43	58.4%	.287	0.95	0.98	92	0.5				
	RCT	AA	23	3	4	0	8	7	30^{2}	37	0	4.1	7.9	27	42.9%	.378	1.66	4.70	117	0.0				
	SL	AAA	23	2	5	0	9	9	34^{1}	43	5	4.2	7.1	27	58.9%	.355	1.72	5.24	86	0.4	89.9	60.1%	20.9%	
Russell Smith	WIS	A+	23	2	5	0	15	15	68^{1}	63	8	3.6	8.2	62	36.5%	.276	1.32	4.87	110	0.3				
Collin Wiles	LV	AAA	28	9	11	0	26	26	143^{1}	175	27	1.7	6.7	106	42.6%	.324	1.41	5.40	106	0.3	88.8	75.5%	18.1%	
	OAK	MLB	28	0	0	0	4	0	9^{2}	11	1	1.9	8.4	9	55.2%	.357	1.34	4.66	97	0.1	87.9	74.7%	29.3%	45.0%

Despite an ERA that screams "there is no bigger loser than me," **Jason Alexander** rose to the occasion by eating innings when the Brewers needed them most. To see him pitch is to watch a show about nothing, but he's proven he can provide innings in bulk. ⚾ While **Dylan File** has great command of a four-pitch mix that offsets a lack of velocity, his inability to garner even an average rate of swings-and-misses means that as swingmen go, he's rank-and-File. ⚾ **Jandel Gustave** (noun): A sinkerballer who does not generate groundballs; used as an idiom to describe people or things that do not fulfill their stated purpose, i.e: *My new washing machine is a real Jandel Gustave. I'm going to return it tomorrow.* ⚾ Since **Janson Junk** is never going to escape accusations of nominative determinism despite being a fastball-slider guy, he needs to think outside the box. The classic Chinese "junk" vessel is known for its fully battened sails and versatility as a cargo ship. That's a better reputation for our Junk to aspire to. ⚾ The good news: **Trevor Kelley** recorded career-bests in innings pitched and ERA in 2022. The bad news: Those marks were 23⅔ and 6.08, respectively. ⚾ Fairfield, California is home to both the Jelly Belly candy company's headquarters and right-hander **Tyson Miller**. Alas, much like jelly beans, too much exposure to Miller's ERA can be detrimental to your health. ⚾ **Jacob Misiorowski** is 6-foot-7 with a big frame, routinely touches triple-digits with his fastball and can really spin a slider. Like almost all young pitchers he needs to improve his command and build up his workload, but have we mentioned he's 6-foot-7? ⚾ Acquired by the Angels as part of the return for Andrew Heaney, **Elvis Peguero** had an easily identifiable problem in his small sample of relief innings: He was taken out of the building far too frequently, surrendering a big fly at a rate of more than two per nine innings. Now it's the Brewers' turn to try and fix him. ⚾ After a year spent hurt and/or in minor-league purgatory, **Luis Perdomo** returned to the majors in 2022, chipping in a few multi-inning efforts in various Brewers losses. The four inexplicable triples he hit in 2017 remain the highlight of his career, though we applaud his persistence. ⚾ Some pitchers are artists capable of painting corner after corner with precision. **Miguel Sánchez** is also an artist, but just so happens to take after Jackson Pollock. ⚾ Look, sometimes you have to talk about a guy who doesn't have a compelling backstory or a unique skill set or a pet rosin bag named Edith that he carries with him on road trips. Sometimes, as with **Adam Seminaris**, it's because there's an off-chance he's the next long reliever the Brewers figure out how to fix. It's a thorough book, pal. ⚾ A second-round pick from 2021, **Russell Smith** checks off all the requirements of being a Brewers pitching prospect—superb extension, tricky approach angle, deceptiveness—and expertly commands a changeup, too. ⚾ Blessed with a thunderous arm but no ability to tame it, **Abner Uribe** might be able to get by with his atrocious command as a single-inning reliever who routinely records triple-digit fastballs. They oughta name a podcast after guys like this ... ⚾ After spending 10 years being drafted and developed by the Rangers, **Collin Wiles** finally made his MLB debut for their divisional rivals in Oakland. A pitch-to-contact swingman, he's the type of depth all teams need but none hope to use.

PITTSBURGH PIRATES

Essay by Sarah James

Player comments by Mike Gianella and BP staff

Oscar Levant (1906-1972) was a pianist and TV and radio personality in the '30s, '40s and '50s, known for his acerbic commentary and quick wit. Although Levant had ambitions of becoming a composer himself and found some success in songwriting, he was far better known as an interpreter of the music of his much more famous friend, George Gershwin. "Unsuccessful friend of the famous man" became a part of Levant's public persona, referenced both in his own writings (his 1939 book *A Smattering of Ignorance* contains a chapter called "My Life, Or the Story of George Gershwin") and in writings for him. In the 1946 film *Humoresque*, starring John Garfield as an ambitious young violinist, Levant plays a jaded mentor to Garfield, who warns him about the disappointments of a career in music. "It's not what you are," Levant tells Garfield, "but what you don't become that hurts."

To me, that quote sums up the Pittsburgh Pirates.

I'm too young to remember the Pirates of the early '90s. My Pirates begin just before the Dave Littlefield era. If you're reading this, I don't need to tell you that those teams churned out losing season after losing season. And yet, it felt like each year there was something to hold on to, some kernel of promise for the next season that made this each disappointing yet go down a little easier. If Aramis Ramirez can reach his potential, if Brian Giles stays hot, if we find some pitching and hold on to Jason Kendall—*something*. Every year, it was what we didn't become that hurt, not what we were.

No baseball fan is a stranger to the rebuilding years. You know we're signing up for a slow sport when the game claims to have a massive pace-of-game problem but refuses to end the tradition of stopping to perform a musical number. Baseball moves at its own pace, and as a fan, you tolerate the bad years as part of a plan to one day build your way to something better.

The last few years of watching the Pirates have felt different to me. I no longer see a plan that failed to come together or even a plan that could come together in the future. It's all... well, nothingness.

⚾ ⚾ ⚾

PITTSBURGH PIRATES PROSPECTUS

2022 W-L: 62-100, 5TH IN NL CENTRAL

Pythag	.354	*29th*	DER	.679	*29th*
RS/G	3.65	*27th*	DRC+	90	*27th*
RA/G	5.04	*28th*	DRA-	109	*25th*
dWin%	.409	*28th*	FIP	4.26	*23rd*
Payroll	$56M	*28th*	B-Age	26.8	*1st*
M$/MW	$2.6M	*6th*	P-Age	27.8	*3rd*

399'
389'
375'
325'
320'

- Opened 2001
- Open air
- Natural surface
- Fence profile: 6' to 21'

Park Factors

Runs	Runs/RH	Runs/LH	HR/RH	HR/LH
100	99	101	89	99

Top Hitter WARP	3.5 Bryan Reynolds
Top Pitcher WARP	1.2 Mitch Keller
2023 Top Prospect	Termarr Johnson

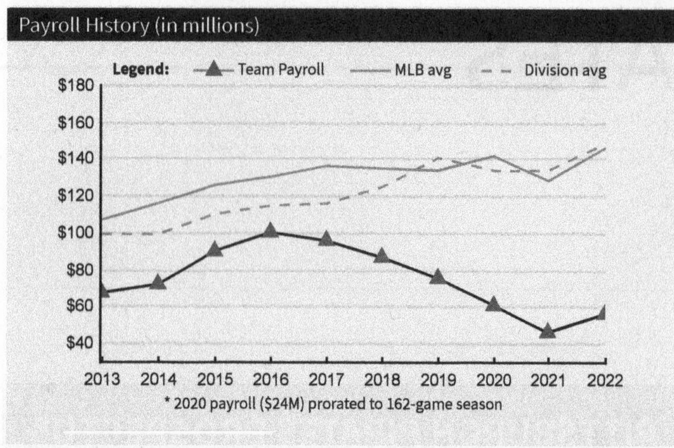

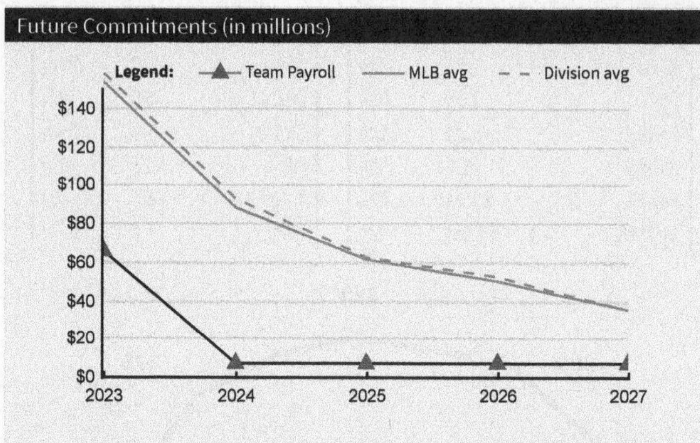

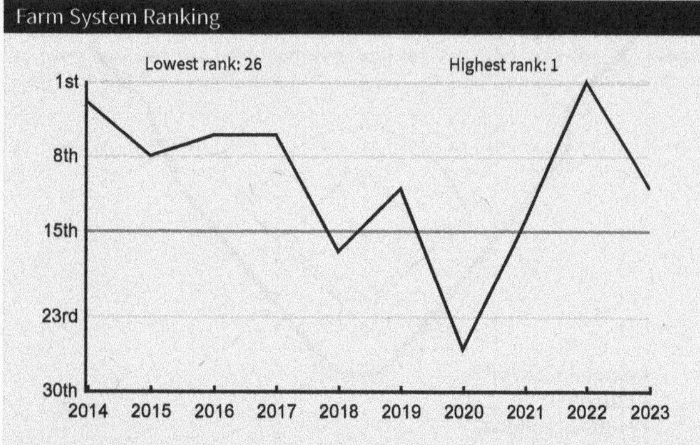

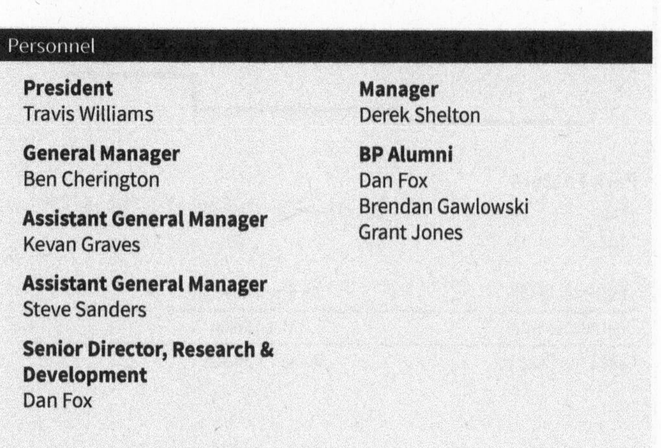
Personnel

President
Travis Williams

General Manager
Ben Cherington

Assistant General Manager
Kevan Graves

Assistant General Manager
Steve Sanders

Senior Director, Research & Development
Dan Fox

Manager
Derek Shelton

BP Alumni
Dan Fox
Brendan Gawlowski
Grant Jones

One of the more exciting parts of the 2022 Pirates season happened off the field. That's not surprising. Not a lot of exciting stuff happened on the field. The Pirates were attempting—as they apparently did 162 times last year—to play the sport of baseball, on a Tuesday night in August against the Boston Red Sox. It was the bottom of the second inning, and the Red Sox were already up 5-0. Red Sox color commentator Dennis Eckersley took the opportunity to opine on the state of the Pirates roster on the Boston broadcast:

> *You talk about a no-name lineup. There's no team like this. I'd love to see some of the service time, if you add it all up, it's not much. You know, we just came from Kansas City, seeing all those young kids... this is different, though. Doesn't it seem different? They have a lot of prospects they are playing over there.*
>
> *...This is a hodgepodge of nothingness. It's ridiculous. It really is. Pathetic.*

The comments quickly flared up among Pirates fans and the team itself. Pirates pitcher Wil Crowe called the remarks "crappy" and "bush league." I agree with the crappy part, or at least I can see how they would make Wil Crowe feel that way. They're not nice remarks. They likely weren't pleasing to Mr. Crowe's ears. It probably would have felt kinder for everyone if Eckersley had taken the "compliment sandwich" approach to feedback. "The Pirates have swell uniforms. The players are a hodgepodge of nothingness. Boy, the stadium is beautiful."

But it's hardly Dennis Eckersley's job to offer constructive criticism to the players of the opposing team, and honestly? It seems he's hardly thinking about the players individually at all. The way he sneers the word "ridiculous" is more of an indictment of the management that put them in this situation. There's a general sense in baseball of what an underdog team that could be competitive in a few years looks like. Solid veterans, exciting prospects, stir in a high-profile free agent signing and bake until John Smoltz is talking all over your dramatic World Series win. This does not in any way describe the 2022 Pittsburgh Pirates, and Eckersley knew it.

It's telling that the Pirates fanbase, on the whole, did not react with the anger that Wil Crowe expressed. There was no mad rush by fans to defend the honor of our baseball boys. Most of the replies to a clip of Eckersley's comments shared by the Twitter account Awful Announcing expressed the online sentiment "Where's the lie?" Some fans even took an ironic pride in the statement. Pittsburgh Clothing Company quickly put out a t-shirt for sale with the phrase, in Pirates black and yellow, of course.

In perhaps the ultimate proof Eckersley had a point, when I went to watch the clip of his comments again, the Pirate at bat was right fielder Bligh Madris, not only someone who I'd forgotten had played for the Pirates but a name I had to rack my brain to ever recall having heard before in my life. (Madris batted .177 over 113 at-bats with the Pirates in 2022 before being DFA'd in September and eventually claimed by Tampa Bay.)

Even Pirates broadcaster Greg Brown seemed to agree, admitting on a radio interview that only hardcore Buccos fans would know many of the names in the Pirates lineup. But Brown took issue with Eckersley's remarks on the "ridiculous" low Pirates payroll. "I would ask, what is more ridiculous, a team with one of the lowest payrolls in baseball being in last place in the NL Central division, or a team with fifth or sixth highest payroll in baseball and is under .500? That's my question."

This question is, with all due respect to Greg Brown, stupid. Of course it's better to spend money and lose a little than not spend money and lose a lot. That's because this is the sport of baseball and not an episode of *Extreme Couponing*. A team that is spending money is at least attempting to build something. The plot of every single movie ever made—this is true—is "Well, we didn't get what we wanted but at least we gave it our all." There are only two instances in which "not trying and losing" is better than "trying and losing." One: You are a teenager, and trying at anything is massive cringe. Two: Your definition of success has nothing to do with winning and losing but instead with how much money you pocketed, such that "losing but saving money" is in fact better than "losing but spending money." But surely a broadcaster who provides objective analysis on the team would never espouse points of view that only make sense if they came from the people who financially benefit from not spending money on the Pirates. So I can't explain Greg Brown's comments.

⚾ ⚾ ⚾

And yet, amongst the hodgepodge that was the 2022 Pirates was one of the three best baseball games I've ever attended in my life.

The first, as anyone writing the Pirates essay for Baseball Prospectus is contractually obligated to mention, was the 2013 Wild Card Game. I won't go into too much detail about the game; you know it already. *Cue-to, Cue-to,* etcetera. Like any good Pittsburgher, I love chanting and waving a towel in the air, so that game delivered big time for me. I was living in Chicago, having just moved there a year earlier. I took the train to Pittsburgh the day before, leaving Chicago at 6:40 at night, getting no sleep on the train, and arriving in town on game day bright and early at 5 am. I took a nap on the floor of my dad's office downtown, the way a five-year-old too sick to go to school might. I was 23 years old.

The second was the same year, 2013, but in Chicago. It was the game the Pirates clinched their playoff berth, the first one since 1992. I went to the game alone, buying the cheapest ticket I could find online and walking over to the stadium from my Lakeview apartment. Living so close to the stadium, I went to games frequently, buying a ticket in the upper levels (or, since this was Wrigley, behind a pole) and then slipping down to the most expensive seat I could sneak into without prompting undue usher attention. That night, I didn't have to sneak. A friend of mine was also at the game, in great seats by the Pirates dugouts with his dad. "There's an open seat right next to us," he texted me. "Come down!" It was September in Chicago. I was in my winter coat, the strange wind patterns of Wrigley blasting cool air on my eyeballs. We were on our feet for the last few outs, although I can't remember if anyone else was. My friend and his dad were Cubs fans, but they were happy for me. We were the underdog, and who doesn't love an underdog?

Those two games remind me what's great about baseball, about sports in general. The community, the connections, the way it makes you feel like a kid again. And despite the hodgepodge of nothingness, we managed to capture it again in 2022, when the Pirates swept the Los Angeles Dodgers.

For some context, I've lived in Los Angeles for seven years and have caught the Pirates when they were in town most seasons. Somehow, every year, I managed to choose the game where the Dodgers would score six runs before I even made it into the stadium. I assumed June 1, 2022, would be the same. The fact that the Pirates had won the last two games against the Dodgers and were up for the sweep only solidified that pessimism in my mind. Surely we didn't have it in us to win three games in a row.

As in the playoff clincher in Chicago, I snuck down to meet up with two friends who were at the game in much better seats than I was willing to pay for. The Pirates scored three runs in the ninth inning to beat the Dodgers 8-4, and we celebrated each one with the same enthusiasm I'd chanted *Cue-to* nine years earlier.

Something intangible came together those three nights, and the Pirates managed to pull together three consecutive wins against a team that would only give away 51 of them all year. But "something intangible coming together" is a plan to win a series, not a season. Granted, the Pirates spent more money this offseason than I expected; also granted, I expected nothing. Is one year of Carlos Santana the ingredient of "high-profile free agent signing" in the underdog champion soup? Will Ji-Man Choi bring a spark of energy and Austin Hedges guiding leadership to the Pirates clubhouse? Maybe. I certainly don't hate any of these moves. But none of it was enough to prevent Bryan Reynolds—maybe the only consistent bright spot in the last two years of Pittsburgh baseball—from requesting a trade. (The Pirates said no.) Clearly, Reynolds isn't seeing a plan, and I tend to agree.

⚾ ⚾ ⚾

I didn't open this essay with a biography of Oscar Levant for my own amusement. (Or at least, not entirely for my own amusement.) Levant, born in Pittsburgh, was a Pirates fan. I live in Los Angeles and the Pirates have been awful for most of my lifetime, so I don't meet a lot of Pirates fans. I had picked up a biography of Levant as research for a historical fiction novel, and when on page 10 I read that his earliest ambition was to play for the Pirates, that he used to spend every day at Forbes Field and memorize box scores, my jaw dropped. Here, somewhere I had never expected—the biography of a classical pianist who died 30 years before I was born—was someone passionate about the same thing I was passionate about.

During his attempt at a composing career, Levant wrote a dirge that was premiered by the Pittsburgh Symphony. According to Sam Kashner's and Nancy Schoenberger's biography of him, Levant told a reporter that a friend had "got off a good crack about 'Dirge' the other day. He wanted to know if I had written it about the Pittsburgh [Pirates] baseball team."

That year was 1939.

The Pirates have been bad for a long time. I'll keep watching, for the community, the connection, the rare moments when the intangible comes together. The rest is just going to hurt. ■

—Sarah James is a historical fiction author.

Hitters

Miguel Andújar LF Born: 03/02/95 Age: 28 Bats: R Throws: R Height: 6'0" Weight: 211 lb. Origin: International Free Agent, 2011

YEAR	TEAM	LVL	AGE	PA	R	2B	3B	HR	RBI	BB	K	SB	CS	Whiff%	AVG/OBP/SLG	DRC+	BABIP	BRR	DRP	WARP
2020	NYY	MLB	25	65	5	2	1	1	5	3	9	0	0	22.1%	.242/.277/.355	103	.269	0.5	LF(7): -0.9, 3B(6): 0.1	0.2
2021	SWB	AAA	26	63	13	1	0	5	13	7	6	0	0		.333/.397/.630	138	.289	-0.2	LF(11): -1.1, 1B(3): -0.1, 3B(1): -0.0	0.3
2021	NYY	MLB	26	162	19	2	0	6	12	7	28	0	1	19.3%	.253/.284/.383	103	.273	-0.6	LF(37): -0.2, 3B(4): -0.1, 1B(2): 0	0.6
2022	SWB	AAA	27	297	42	17	0	13	51	17	35	5	0		.285/.330/.487	121	.287	-1.6	LF(46): 1.1, 3B(19): 1.1	1.4
2022	PIT	MLB	27	40	4	3	1	0	9	2	5	0	1	20.0%	.250/.275/.389	103	.273	-0.4	LF(4): 0.1	0.1
2022	NYY	MLB	27	100	9	2	0	1	8	3	22	4	0	23.8%	.229/.250/.281	88	.284	-0.4	LF(19): 0.1	0.1
2023 DC	*PIT*	*MLB*	*28*	*356*	*37*	*16*	*1*	*11*	*42*	*17*	*58*	*3*	*1*	*21.0%*	*.265/.305/.425*	*103*	*.291*	*1.0*	*LF 1, 1B 0*	*1.0*

Comparables: Danny Santana (50), Adeiny Hechavarria (48), Tony Abreu (48)

Long gone are the days of Andújar as a top third base prospect—his defensive liabilities have pushed him off the hot corner to a primary outfield role these days, and a combination of injuries and unimpressive offense make him look like a shell of the player who hit 47 doubles and was the Rookie of the Year runner-up in 2018. His move to Pittsburgh last September offers him the opportunity of more playing time than he was getting in New York, as he looks to recapture the offensive pop that made him such an intriguing player in the late 2010s.

Ji Hwan Bae UT Born: 07/26/99 Age: 23 Bats: L Throws: R Height: 6'1" Weight: 185 lb. Origin: International Free Agent, 2018

YEAR	TEAM	LVL	AGE	PA	R	2B	3B	HR	RBI	BB	K	SB	CS	Whiff%	AVG/OBP/SLG	DRC+	BABIP	BRR	DRP	WARP
2021	ALT	AA	21	365	63	12	5	7	31	38	83	20	8		.278/.359/.413	103	.352	3.2	2B(65): -8.1, CF(9): 3.4	1.1
2022	IND	AAA	22	473	81	23	6	8	53	48	80	30	8	16.0%	.289/.362/.430	106	.338	5.3	2B(57): -2.4, SS(24): 1.9, CF(20): 0.8	2.1
2022	PIT	MLB	22	37	5	3	0	0	6	2	6	3	0	19.6%	.333/.405/.424	94	.407	1.5	CF(5): 0.1, 2B(4): 0.8, LF(1): 0.1	0.4
2023 DC	*PIT*	*MLB*	*23*	*347*	*36*	*14*	*4*	*4*	*29*	*26*	*67*	*15*	*5*	*20.6%*	*.263/.327/.375*	*95*	*.325*	*6.3*	*2B 0, CF 0*	*1.4*

Comparables: Albert Almora Jr. (65), Erick Aybar (61), Melky Cabrera (60)

Even as a 23-year-old who hadn't logged an inning in the majors before last year, Bae has been the focal point of more controversy than most players experience throughout an entire career. He was signed by the Atlanta Braves as an 18-year-old free agent in 2017, only to have his contract voided two months later by the league. Bae subsequently signed with the Pirates, and was in 2019 suspended for 30 games after being charged and convicted in a Korean court for assaulting his then-girlfriend. The victim told *The Athletic* that she felt the punishment did not go far enough, and expressed desire for his release. The Pirates were unmoved, noting "Ji-Hwan has completed a treatment program." Bae steadily worked his way to the majors and made his Pirates debut in September. He is a solid fielder with gap power and good speed who would slot in as a utility infielder on most teams, but may wind up holding down the keystone for the perpetually talent-starved Pirates.

Rodolfo Castro IF Born: 05/21/99 Age: 24 Bats: S Throws: R Height: 6'0" Weight: 205 lb. Origin: International Free Agent, 2015

YEAR	TEAM	LVL	AGE	PA	R	2B	3B	HR	RBI	BB	K	SB	CS	Whiff%	AVG/OBP/SLG	DRC+	BABIP	BRR	DRP	WARP
2021	ALT	AA	22	312	43	14	1	12	47	19	72	7	4		.242/.295/.425	105	.278	0.9	3B(44): 2.1, 2B(24): 2.6, SS(4): -0.3	1.7
2021	IND	AAA	22	38	7	4	0	3	8	3	11	0	0		.286/.342/.657	107	.333	1.1	3B(4): -0.1, SS(3): -0.3, 2B(1): -0.1	0.2
2021	PIT	MLB	22	93	9	2	0	5	8	6	27	0	0	28.6%	.198/.258/.395	90	.222	-0.2	2B(20): 0.2, 3B(5): 0.8	0.3
2022	IND	AAA	23	314	37	13	2	12	40	32	86	6	3	54.5%	.246/.334/.441	102	.309	0.0	3B(32): 0.9, SS(29): 1.1, 2B(15): 3.7	1.5
2022	PIT	MLB	23	278	25	8	4	11	27	22	74	5	3	32.4%	.233/.299/.427	95	.284	-0.9	2B(32): 1.6, 3B(24): -0.7, SS(19): -0.1	0.6
2023 DC	*PIT*	*MLB*	*24*	*427*	*42*	*17*	*3*	*14*	*44*	*30*	*122*	*8*	*3*	*32.2%*	*.218/.282/.386*	*81*	*.279*	*3.3*	*2B -1, 3B 0*	*0.3*

Comparables: Luis Valbuena (54), Yoán Moncada (53), Mat Gamel (53)

Because he wasn't a highly heralded prospect, Castro found himself fighting for minutes and was removed from the Pirates family plan after a brief stint with the big club in April. A robust showing in the minors provided Pittsburgh with more than enough data, and in early August they added Castro back to their network. A hitter with pitch recognition issues, Castro's in-game ability to knock balls over the fence allowed him to stay in touch with the Pirates' short-term plans. Castro hopes to be part of a new generation of cool, the next vanguard of stars Pittsburgh hopes will connect with the fans; they're done phoning it in and are ready to answer the timeless question "can you hear me now?" Castro might be more of a utility player, and keeping him in a starting role could be a tough cell. (What, did you expect us to ignore the one-game suspension after his cell phone fell out of his pocket on-field?)

Bubba Chandler DH

Born: 09/14/02 Age: 20 Bats: S Throws: R Height: 6'2" Weight: 200 lb. Origin: Round 3, 2021 Draft (#72 overall)

YEAR	TEAM	LVL	AGE	PA	R	2B	3B	HR	RBI	BB	K	SB	CS	Whiff%	AVG/OBP/SLG	DRC+	BABIP	BRR	DRP	WARP
2021	PIRB	ROK	18	37	3	1	0	1	2	5	16	0	0		.167/.324/.300		.308			
2022	PIR	ROK	19	36	8	0	1	3	9	9	6	1	0		.231/.444/.654		.176			
2022	BRD	A	19	88	8	3	1	1	8	11	35	3	0	52.7%	.184/.284/.289	73	.317	-0.1	P(8): -0.1	0.0
2023 non-DC	*PIT*	*MLB*	*20*	*251*	*18*	*9*	*2*	*2*	*19*	*17*	*128*	*3*	*1*	*50.6%*	*.187/.251/.285*	*40*	*.403*	*3.1*	*1B 0, SS 0*	*-1.1*

Comparables: Mike McDade (87), Nellie Rodriguez (82), Chris Carter (81)

For every Pepsi, there are dozens of sodas like Lurvills Delights that didn't make it past the late 19th or early 20th Century. No one sensible would question Chandler's athleticism, and the mere fact that this potential two-way athlete held his own on both sides of the diamond as a teenager in the Florida Complex League is an impressive accomplishment in and of itself. But it's a long road from Bradenton to Pittsburgh (actually, it's several roads; I-95 takes you way too far east) and you can't wish the next Shohei Ohtani into existence simply by cosplaying Jean-Luc Picard and uttering "make it so." The scouting consensus is that Chandler will eventually make his way to the majors as a pitcher, and that his incredible arm is too valuable to risk the experiment for very much longer. Success takes many forms, and Chandler won't be a failure if he "only" pitches, any more than the Lewis Brothers' inability to keep their carbonated soft drink concern afloat meant failure for their successful leather upholstery company, which still exists today.

Ji-Man Choi 1B

Born: 05/19/91 Age: 32 Bats: L Throws: R Height: 6'1" Weight: 260 lb. Origin: International Free Agent, 2009

YEAR	TEAM	LVL	AGE	PA	R	2B	3B	HR	RBI	BB	K	SB	CS	Whiff%	AVG/OBP/SLG	DRC+	BABIP	BRR	DRP	WARP
2020	TB	MLB	29	145	16	13	0	3	16	20	36	0	0	31.8%	.230/.331/.410	89	.291	-0.2	1B(38): -0.6	0.0
2021	DUR	AAA	30	27	4	2	0	0	2	3	7	0	0		.261/.333/.348	93	.353	-1.1	1B(5): 0.3	0.0
2021	TB	MLB	30	305	36	14	0	11	45	45	87	0	0	31.9%	.229/.348/.411	96	.300	-0.2	1B(73): -0.2	0.5
2022	TB	MLB	31	419	36	22	0	11	52	58	123	0	0	32.4%	.233/.341/.388	93	.320	-3.7	1B(98): -2.7	-0.2
2023 DC	*PIT*	*MLB*	*32*	*409*	*45*	*19*	*1*	*13*	*42*	*55*	*116*	*0*	*0*	*31.7%*	*.226/.337/.402*	*104*	*.299*	*-1.4*	*1B 0*	*0.7*

Comparables: Brandon Belt (57), Doug Mientkiewicz (55), Justin Smoak (53)

Choi remains a fan favorite in the Tampa Bay area and around the league. He's an affable character, sort of like what you'd expect Fred Flintstone to look like as a baseball player. For much of his career, he's been a roughly league-average hitter and steady defender at first base. But the problems for the Rays were twofold. First, Choi had been more or less the same guy for several years, steadily getting more expensive but not getting better in turn. And in 2022, Choi took a modest step back at the plate and a bigger one in the field, leading to negative WARP for the second time in three seasons. As a 32-year-old with a history of knee issues, an increasing strikeout rate and declining power, Choi is entering his final year of arbitration at an inopportune time. As such, the Rays chose to yabba dabba do something else at first base moving forward, shipping Choi to the big-money Pirates in early November.

Oneil Cruz SS

Born: 10/04/98 Age: 24 Bats: L Throws: R Height: 6'7" Weight: 220 lb. Origin: International Free Agent, 2015

YEAR	TEAM	LVL	AGE	PA	R	2B	3B	HR	RBI	BB	K	SB	CS	Whiff%	AVG/OBP/SLG	DRC+	BABIP	BRR	DRP	WARP
2021	ALT	AA	22	273	51	15	5	12	40	20	64	18	3		.292/.346/.536	120	.349	2.6	SS(54): -1.7	1.6
2021	IND	AAA	22	29	11	1	0	5	7	8	5	1	0		.524/.655/1.286	147	.545	0.0	SS(5): 1.1	0.3
2021	PIT	MLB	22	9	2	0	0	1	3	0	4	0	0	50.0%	.333/.333/.667	82	.500		SS(2): -0.7	-0.1
2022	IND	AAA	23	247	40	7	3	9	35	30	56	11	6	34.6%	.232/.336/.422	114	.270	1.5	SS(44): 1.5, LF(10): 0.7	1.4
2022	PIT	MLB	23	361	45	13	4	17	54	28	126	11	4	35.5%	.233/.294/.450	81	.317	3.3	SS(79): -1.5	0.5
2023 DC	*PIT*	*MLB*	*24*	*554*	*65*	*21*	*7*	*24*	*65*	*44*	*174*	*22*	*5*	*33.1%*	*.239/.307/.453*	*103*	*.318*	*11.1*	*SS -3*	*2.7*

Comparables: Reid Brignac (63), Adalberto Mondesi (55), Eugenio Suárez (53)

One of the most memorable moments of the 2022 season came on July 6, during an otherwise forgettable 16-0 Yankees shellacking of the hometown heroes at PNC Park. Immediately after an Aaron Judge double in the fifth inning, Cruz ambled toward the second base bag. Real life still photos and exaggerated Internet memes of Judge towering over his opponents have become so mundane that it was surreal to see a player stand next to the 6-foot-7 Judge and match him in size. The term "unicorn" gets bandied about so much when it comes to prospects that it has become tired, overused and meaningless, but Cruz somehow manages to give this cliché new life. He's a magical creature on both sides of the ball: firing laser beams to first like Zeus whipping thunderbolts off Mount Olympus and crushing one-armed home runs over the fence with a mere flick of his enormous arms. Cruz struggled somewhat out of the blocks, but diligently worked to improve his plate discipline and got to the point where his chase rate was better than average in September. He's on the cusp of superstardom, and even if he doesn't get there this year you can see imminent greatness every time this seemingly mythical being graces the diamond.

★ ★ ★ *2023 Top 101 Prospect* **#46** ★ ★ ★

Henry Davis C Born: 09/21/99 Age: 23 Bats: R Throws: R Height: 6'2" Weight: 210 lb. Origin: Round 1, 2021 Draft (#1 overall)

YEAR	TEAM	LVL	AGE	PA	R	2B	3B	HR	RBI	BB	K	SB	CS	Whiff%	AVG/OBP/SLG	DRC+	BABIP	BRR	DRP	WARP
2021	GBO	A+	21	24	6	0	1	2	3	4	8	1	0		.263/.375/.684	100	.300	0.3	C(4): -0.5	0.1
2022	GBO	A+	22	100	18	3	1	5	22	8	18	5	1		.341/.450/.585	134	.383	0.4	C(13): -0.4	0.7
2022	ALT	AA	22	136	19	8	0	4	18	12	30	3	1		.207/.324/.379	104	.244	1.8	C(20): -0.8, RF(2): -0.7	0.5
2023 non-DC	*PIT*	*MLB*	*23*	*251*	*24*	*9*	*2*	*6*	*25*	*17*	*64*	*4*	*1*	*28.3%*	*.223/.304/.366*	*87*	*.285*	*2.3*	*C 0, RF 0*	*0.7*

Comparables: David Rodríguez (73), Koby Clemens (61), Óscar Hernández (60)

YEAR	TEAM	P. COUNT	FRM RUNS	BLK RUNS	THRW RUNS	TOT RUNS
2022	GBO	2123	-0.6	0.2	0.3	-0.1
2022	ALT	3069	-0.4	-0.1	0.2	-0.4
2023	*PIT*	*6956*	*-2.0*	*-0.2*	*-0.1*	*-2.3*

If first-round draft picks are under closer scrutiny than other prospects, then #1 overall picks are constantly under a ptychographic microscope. Davis started the season dominating the competition at High-A Greensboro and quickly earned a promotion to Double-A. Two games later, his left wrist was broken by a pitch, and he was never quite the same. A full offseason of rest and recovery will help, but even then, questions remain about Davis on both sides of the ball. It remains uncertain if he will survive as a catcher; while the bat remains special, there was far more swing and miss than you would expect from an advanced college bat. Davis is more likely to have a successful big-league career than former #1 catching draft picks Steve Chilcott, Danny Goodwin, or Mike Ivie, but that's damning with the faintest of praise—while a solid offensive 1B/DH is nothing to scoff at, it isn't exactly the outcome Pittsburgh fans were dreaming on.

Yordany De Los Santos SS Born: 02/17/05 Age: 18 Bats: R Throws: R Height: 6'1" Weight: 170 lb. Origin: International Free Agent, 2022

YEAR	TEAM	LVL	AGE	PA	R	2B	3B	HR	RBI	BB	K	SB	CS	Whiff%	AVG/OBP/SLG	DRC+	BABIP	BRR	DRP	WARP
2022	DSL PITG	ROK	17	234	35	15	1	1	38	32	45	14	3		.258/.372/.363		.320			
2023										*No projection*										

Lured to the Pirates by a $1.2 million bonus in January 2021, De Los Santos was arguably the crown jewel of the team's most aggressive international signing period ever. He profiles as an extremely athletic infielder with loud tools on both sides of the ball. Scouting reports project him as a future power hitter without enough speed to make an impact on the basepaths, so of course De Los Santos swiped 14 bags in his professional debut. His ceiling hinges upon whether he can stick at short or winds up at the hot corner—but as he's just 17 years old, we won't know the answer to that question until well into the second half of this decade.

Ben Gamel LF Born: 05/17/92 Age: 31 Bats: L Throws: L Height: 5'11" Weight: 180 lb. Origin: Round 10, 2010 Draft (#325 overall)

YEAR	TEAM	LVL	AGE	PA	R	2B	3B	HR	RBI	BB	K	SB	CS	Whiff%	AVG/OBP/SLG	DRC+	BABIP	BRR	DRP	WARP
2020	MIL	MLB	28	127	13	8	1	3	10	13	39	0	2	28.6%	.237/.315/.404	79	.333	-1.8	RF(27): -1, CF(11): -1.6, LF(1): -0.1	-0.4
2021	PIT	MLB	29	383	42	17	3	8	26	48	99	3	6	27.2%	.255/.352/.399	88	.336	-3.0	LF(72): -1.3, RF(18): 1.3, CF(11): -1.5	0.3
2021	CLE	MLB	29	17	1	1	0	0	0	3	6	0	0	27.6%	.071/.235/.143	81	.125	-0.2	CF(9): -0.3	0.0
2022	IND	AAA	30	35	8	1	0	1	3	2	6	0	0		.226/.314/.355	109	.250	0.4	LF(4): -0.4, RF(3): 0.3	0.3
2022	PIT	MLB	30	423	42	20	2	9	46	48	98	5	1	23.8%	.232/.324/.369	92	.291	-1.2	LF(57): -0.7, RF(39): 0.1, 1B(5): 0.2	0.6
2023 DC	*FA*	*MLB*	*31*	*296*	*31*	*13*	*1*	*6*	*31*	*32*	*70*	*3*	*1*	*24.6%*	*.244/.333/.385*	*101*	*.310*	*0.8*	*LF -2, RF 0*	*0.6*

Comparables: Jim Wohlford (57), Henry Rodriguez (55), Ryan Langerhans (54)

Gamel is an adequate backup corner outfielder—thanks to a league-average bat and decent batting eye—but the Pirates allowing him to log over 800 plate appearances across the last two seasons is the major-league equivalent of C. Montgomery Burns installing a "Don't Forget, You're Here Forever" sign in Homer Simpson's workstation. The most amazing part of Gamel's short-lived Pirates journey is the fact that last year propelled him to sixth in plate appearances among Pittsburgh outfielders over the last decade, pushing past Pirates all-time greats John Jaso, Jose Osuna, Corey Dickerson, Travis Snider, and Jose Tabata. Someone must stand out there in left, right, or log time at designated hitter, but it doesn't exactly inspire confidence—or make fans want to rush out and buy a ticket package—when the stopgap solution is Gamel, the rebuilding plan is in Year Seven and the light at the end of the tunnel is an oncoming train.

Nick Gonzales 2B Born: 05/27/99 Age: 24 Bats: R Throws: R Height: 5'10" Weight: 195 lb. Origin: Round 1, 2020 Draft (#7 overall)

YEAR	TEAM	LVL	AGE	PA	R	2B	3B	HR	RBI	BB	K	SB	CS	Whiff%	AVG/OBP/SLG	DRC+	BABIP	BRR	DRP	WARP
2021	PEJ	WIN	22	87	18	4	1	2	13	13	14	4	0		.380/.483/.549		.446			
2021	GBO	A+	22	369	53	23	4	18	54	40	101	7	2		.302/.385/.565	112	.388	-3.4	2B(73): -0.8, SS(1): -0.0	1.2
2022	ALT	AA	23	316	47	20	1	7	33	43	90	5	3		.263/.383/.429	85	.367	-0.5	2B(55): -1.5, SS(14): -1.4	0.0
2023 DC	*PIT*	*MLB*	*24*	*63*	*6*	*3*	*0*	*1*	*5*	*5*	*21*	*0*	*0*	*37.8%*	*.221/.305/.361*	*82*	*.331*	*0.3*	*2B 0*	*0.1*

Comparables: Starlin Rodriguez (67), James Darnell (65), Stephen Bruno (62)

Pittsburgh's first-round pick in 2020, Gonzales hasn't logged nearly as much minor-league time as you'd like to see from a college bat. Thanks to a global pandemic and multiple injuries, he's been limited to 696 professional plate appearances. The most recent culprit was a torn plantar fascia in Gonzales' right foot, sidelining him for 10 weeks. The injury might have been a blessing in disguise, as he struggled in his first high-minors action (.247/.366/.377 slash line pre-injury) and thrived upon his return (.287/.404/.513). To figure out how significant a role Gonzales and his raw talent will play in their long-term plans, though, the Pirates need to see more reps. Given that he turns 24 in May, time is running short to prove major-league pitchers won't exploit his unorthodox swing and batting stance.

Matt Gorski CF Born: 12/22/97 Age: 25 Bats: R Throws: R Height: 6'4" Weight: 198 lb. Origin: Round 2, 2019 Draft (#57 overall)

YEAR	TEAM	LVL	AGE	PA	R	2B	3B	HR	RBI	BB	K	SB	CS	Whiff%	AVG/OBP/SLG	DRC+	BABIP	BRR	DRP	WARP
2021	GBO	A+	23	401	62	18	0	17	56	34	125	18	1		.223/.294/.416	85	.285	2.2	CF(48): 4.8, RF(38): 6.7, 1B(3): -0.3	1.8
2022	GBO	A+	24	146	34	3	2	17	37	17	39	9	1		.294/.377/.754	153	.278	3.4	CF(25): 0.1, 1B(6): 0.5, RF(1): 0.1	2.0
2022	ALT	AA	24	159	27	8	2	6	28	15	47	10	2		.277/.354/.489	100	.375	0.7	CF(16): 1.1, RF(10): -0.3, 1B(6): -0.2	0.7
2023 non-DC	*PIT*	*MLB*	*25*	*251*	*23*	*9*	*1*	*7*	*26*	*17*	*88*	*9*	*1*	*37.8%*	*.209/.271/.358*	*69*	*.302*	*4.8*	*1B 0, LF 0*	*0.2*

Comparables: Brian Barton (57), Skye Bolt (56), Denis Phipps (53)

Gorski is a prospect with tools so loud that you find yourself in your bathrobe and slippers, knocking on his door, politely asking him to keep the noise down. It's 8 a.m. on a Saturday. Some of us are trying to sleep. He obliterated High-A Greensboro, which is something you'd expect from a 24-year-old college draftee; after a late-May promotion to Double-A, a strained quad muscle led to an extended IL stint and limited reps. The center field defense projects as playable in the majors, so if the swing change-driven offensive improvement is legit, then Gorski has moved from the periphery of the Pirates' 40-man roster bubble to the thick of their future plans.

Ke'Bryan Hayes 3B Born: 01/28/97 Age: 26 Bats: R Throws: R Height: 5'10" Weight: 205 lb. Origin: Round 1, 2015 Draft (#32 overall)

YEAR	TEAM	LVL	AGE	PA	R	2B	3B	HR	RBI	BB	K	SB	CS	Whiff%	AVG/OBP/SLG	DRC+	BABIP	BRR	DRP	WARP
2020	PIT	MLB	23	95	17	7	2	5	11	9	20	1	0	18.1%	.376/.442/.682	121	.450	0.7	3B(24): 0.6	0.6
2021	PIT	MLB	24	396	49	20	2	6	38	31	87	9	1	20.5%	.257/.316/.373	86	.321	1.3	3B(95): 1.5	0.9
2022	PIT	MLB	25	560	55	24	3	7	41	48	122	20	5	20.9%	.244/.314/.345	92	.307	2.0	3B(133): 4.9, SS(3): 0	1.6
2023 DC	*PIT*	*MLB*	*26*	*606*	*66*	*28*	*4*	*12*	*55*	*51*	*124*	*21*	*4*	*20.4%*	*.252/.322/.388*	*98*	*.306*	*9.8*	*3B 4*	*2.5*

Comparables: Jeimer Candelario (59), Nolan Arenado (58), Evan Longoria (58)

Are injuries sapping Hayes' power potential, or is he a ground-ball hitter who will never transform into a big-time power bat? Check back next *Annual* to see if we have an answer yet! For the second consecutive season, Hayes muddled through a chronic injury, this time a back issue—which he didn't make any excuses for, but admitted forced him to play through some level of pain all year. After a strong start, he slashed a pedestrian .223/.283/.328 from May 14 onward. Despite the surface numbers, Hayes still hits the ball extremely hard, was arguably the best defensive third baseman in the game and chipped in 20 steals for good measure. The Pirates have no regrets on the $70 million, eight-year extension Hayes signed last April. If there is another gear lurking, he could very well be a living, breathing cheat code at the hot corner. But even if the power never surfaces, Hayes provides enough on-field and off-field value to be a franchise cornerstone.

Austin Hedges C Born: 08/18/92 Age: 30 Bats: R Throws: R Height: 6'1" Weight: 223 lb. Origin: Round 2, 2011 Draft (#82 overall)

YEAR	TEAM	LVL	AGE	PA	R	2B	3B	HR	RBI	BB	K	SB	CS	Whiff%	AVG/OBP/SLG	DRC+	BABIP	BRR	DRP	WARP
2020	SD	MLB	27	71	7	1	0	3	6	6	18	1	1	21.4%	.158/.258/.333	91	.162	-0.3	C(28): -1.4	0.0
2020	CLE	MLB	27	12	0	0	0	0	0	0	5	0	0	40.9%	.083/.083/.083	91	.143		C(6): 0.6	0.1
2021	CLE	MLB	28	312	32	7	0	10	31	15	87	1	0	29.8%	.178/.220/.308	69	.214	1.6	C(87): 8.2	1.1
2022	CLE	MLB	29	338	26	4	0	7	30	25	78	2	0	27.6%	.163/.241/.248	73	.193	-1.7	C(105): 12.5	1.3
2023 DC	*PIT*	*MLB*	*30*	*244*	*24*	*7*	*0*	*7*	*25*	*17*	*60*	*1*	*0*	*27.9%*	*.204/.269/.351*	*69*	*.242*	*0.5*	*C 11*	*1.2*

Comparables: Jeff Mathis (72), Tom Prince (69), Malachi Kittridge (67)

YEAR	TEAM	P. COUNT	FRM RUNS	BLK RUNS	THRW RUNS	TOT RUNS
2020	CLE	585	0.7	0.0	0.0	0.7
2020	SD	2971	-1.4	0.0	0.1	-1.3
2021	CLE	12266	8.0	0.9	0.4	9.3
2022	CLE	12981	10.7	0.3	1.2	12.2
2023	*PIT*	*9620*	*11.4*	*0.3*	*0.1*	*11.8*

"Under heaven all can see beauty as beauty only because there is ugliness." - Lao Tzu, *The Tao Te Ching*

We have many questions. Does the ugliness of a catcher's bat allow us to see the beauty of their defense at all, such that if the catcher suddenly hit well we would not see their defense as beautiful? Or is there a scaled inverse relationship? Can beauty and ugliness in the same object be summed into a single, meaningful value to describe that object's beauty (or ugliness, if that value is negative)? Also, your philosophy seems to say that the best way to make sure the cable bill gets paid is to not pay the cable bill, which will somehow be paid specifically because no action was taken to pay it. Hard to wrap our heads around that, but let's assume that's true. Does that mean a catcher who struggles to hit would improve if he merely stopped trying to improve? (Asking for a friend.)

Connor Joe LF Born: 08/16/92 Age: 30 Bats: R Throws: R Height: 6'0" Weight: 205 lb. Origin: Round 1, 2014 Draft (#39 overall)

YEAR	TEAM	LVL	AGE	PA	R	2B	3B	HR	RBI	BB	K	SB	CS	Whiff%	AVG/OBP/SLG	DRC+	BABIP	BRR	DRP	WARP
2021	ABQ	AAA	28	110	20	7	0	9	25	15	22	1	0		.326/.418/.696	130	.333	-0.3	RF(12): -2.3, 1B(7): 0.6, LF(6): 0.4	0.6
2021	COL	MLB	28	211	23	9	0	8	35	26	41	0	0	23.5%	.285/.379/.469	113	.323	-1.5	LF(32): 0.2, 1B(14): -0.9	0.8
2022	COL	MLB	29	467	56	20	4	7	28	55	97	6	2	21.3%	.238/.338/.359	97	.296	1.1	LF(50): -1.5, 1B(24): -0.9, RF(16): -1.5	0.8
2023 DC	*PIT*	*MLB*	*30*	*321*	*39*	*14*	*1*	*7*	*27*	*36*	*61*	*4*	*1*	*21.7%*	*.241/.339/.387*	*105*	*.284*	*2.1*	*LF 2, RF 0*	*1.2*

Comparables: Brandon Guyer (63), Eric Byrnes (54), Justin Ruggiano (53)

Out to prove he was no average Joe, Connor hit .272/.359/.506 with an 11% walk rate as the Rockies' regular leadoff hitter in April. Coming off his excellent second half in 2021, it looked as if Colorado had found a diamond amidst the coals. But from May 1 onward, the shine wore off: Joe hit just .229/.333/.322 and spent the second half mostly collecting dust on the bench. His sudden emergence and disappearance had some—not us, mind you, but some—asking, "where did you come from, where did you go, where did you come from, Connor Joe?" Alas, it's not entirely clear what caused Joe's numbers to crater. He didn't get hurt or change his approach or alter his mechanics, and it didn't look like opposing pitchers mixed up their gameplans, either. But given his long-standing deficiencies against right-handed pitching (just a .671 OPS last year) and the poor quality of his contact, it shouldn't come as a total surprise that, eventually, the hits just stopped falling in for him. His patience at the plate keeps his floor above subterranean levels, but between his age, iffy offense and poor defense, he's in for a fight to stay on this roster long-term.

★ ★ ★ *2023 Top 101 Prospect* **#31** ★ ★ ★

Termarr Johnson 2B Born: 06/11/04 Age: 19 Bats: L Throws: R Height: 5'7" Weight: 175 lb. Origin: Round 1, 2022 Draft (#4 overall)

YEAR	TEAM	LVL	AGE	PA	R	2B	3B	HR	RBI	BB	K	SB	CS	Whiff%	AVG/OBP/SLG	DRC+	BABIP	BRR	DRP	WARP
2022	PIR	ROK	18	29	0	2	0	0	0	6	8	2	0		.130/.310/.217		.200			
2022	BRD	A	18	53	7	4	0	1	6	10	13	4	1	27.4%	.275/.396/.450	114	.345	0.0	2B(12): -1.6, SS(1): -0.4	0.1
2023 non-DC	*PIT*	*MLB*	*19*	*251*	*19*	*9*	*2*	*2*	*20*	*19*	*77*	*9*	*3*	*32.6%*	*.194/.264/.295*	*53*	*.280*	*2.9*	*2B 0, SS 0*	*-0.4*

Comparables: Rougned Odor (72), Omar Estévez (65), Wendell Rijo (63)

Despite being one of the youngest first-round picks in last year's draft, Johnson had arguably the most advanced hit tool of any high schooler selected. His rapid bat speed, excellent batting eye, and bat-to-ball ability make Johnson's swing a scout's dream. The Pirates nabbed him with the fourth-overall pick, luring him away from a commitment to Arizona State University with a $7.2 million signing bonus. He dominated the Florida State League in a tiny sample, and while there are minor swing-and-miss concerns, it was an extremely successful debut overall. Johnson's short, stocky frame will likely limit him to the keystone defensively, but the bat looks as special as advertised.

Tucupita Marcano UT Born: 09/16/99 Age: 23 Bats: L Throws: R Height: 6'0" Weight: 180 lb. Origin: International Free Agent, 2016

YEAR	TEAM	LVL	AGE	PA	R	2B	3B	HR	RBI	BB	K	SB	CS	Whiff%	AVG/OBP/SLG	DRC+	BABIP	BRR	DRP	WARP
2021	IND	AAA	21	210	29	4	1	1	12	26	33	8	1		.230/.325/.279	97	.275	-1.4	2B(34): 0.9, LF(7): 0.9, 3B(4): -0.8	0.5
2021	ELP	AAA	21	202	31	7	2	6	27	27	26	4	4		.273/.366/.442	112	.287	-0.8	LF(12): -1.0, 2B(11): 1.6, SS(11): -0.6	0.9
2021	SD	MLB	21	50	7	1	0	0	3	6	9	0	1	16.9%	.182/.280/.205	90	.229	0.5	2B(8): 0.3, LF(4): -0.3, RF(4): -0.2	0.2
2022	ALT	AA	22	122	22	7	2	2	13	20	25	4	2		.303/.413/.475	117	.378	-0.4	LF(23): -0.1, 2B(5): -0.7, 3B(3): -0.3	0.4
2022	IND	AAA	22	115	16	5	0	3	9	13	16	1	5		.287/.365/.426	115	.313	0.0	2B(12): -1.9, SS(10): 0.0, 3B(1): -0.2	0.5
2022	PIT	MLB	22	177	18	6	2	2	13	10	44	2	1	20.8%	.206/.256/.306	70	.270	0.2	LF(30): 0, 2B(23): 0.1	-0.1
2023 DC	*PIT*	*MLB*	*23*	*94*	*8*	*3*	*0*	*1*	*7*	*8*	*17*	*1*	*2*	*20.6%*	*.225/.297/.326*	*73*	*.273*	*-0.5*	*LF 0, 2B 0*	*-0.2*

Comparables: Luis Sardinas (56), Hernán Pérez (50), Andrés Blanco (48)

In his first full season in the Pirates organization, Marcano passed a litmus test he couldn't in 2021: succeeding against advanced minor-league pitching. For the second season in a row, though, the bat got knocked out of his hands in the majors. The Pirates coaching staff worked with Marcano to move him away from an extreme ground-ball approach; while they had some success, all it led to was weaker fly-ball outs and fewer weak ground-ball outs. With rule changes coming that will disallow the shift, perhaps Marcano can go back to hitting the ball on the ground, and hope that his above-average speed can be parlayed into a higher OBP. The more likely scenario is that he's more of a utility infielder than a future star.

Cal Mitchell OF Born: 03/08/99 Age: 24 Bats: L Throws: L Height: 6'0" Weight: 205 lb. Origin: Round 2, 2017 Draft (#50 overall)

YEAR	TEAM	LVL	AGE	PA	R	2B	3B	HR	RBI	BB	K	SB	CS	Whiff%	AVG/OBP/SLG	DRC+	BABIP	BRR	DRP	WARP
2021	ALT	AA	22	419	43	19	1	12	61	24	71	6	7		.280/.330/.429	111	.313	-0.4	RF(92): -2.3, LF(5): -0.2	1.6
2021	IND	AAA	22	21	1	1	0	0	1	0	4	0	0		.250/.286/.300	92	.313	0.1	RF(5): -0.7	0.0
2022	IND	AAA	23	261	33	18	2	9	49	17	38	8	1	25.5%	.339/.391/.547	120	.370	-1.2	RF(34): -2.7, LF(17): -0.4, CF(5): -0.3	0.8
2022	PIT	MLB	23	232	21	11	0	5	17	18	52	3	1	26.8%	.226/.286/.349	85	.276	0.2	RF(54): -2.5	0.0
2023 DC	*PIT*	*MLB*	*24*	*392*	*39*	*17*	*2*	*9*	*41*	*23*	*89*	*6*	*3*	*23.9%*	*.256/.309/.396*	*93*	*.316*	*0.0*	*RF -1, CF 0*	*0.4*

Comparables: Trayvon Robinson (56), Aaron Cunningham (56), Jimmy Paredes (53)

Mitchell's rookie year was a mysterious old lady flipping a tarot card revealing a dude who looked exactly like him flying a hot air balloon into power lines. No, it was not good. For a dude whose calling card was supposed to be his hit tool, Mitchell was unable to parlay that into much success in his first taste of major-league action. He particularly struggled against fastballs, as major-league pitchers were able to exploit his weaknesses in the top half of the strike zone. He bounced back in September, and his improved zone command was a hopeful sign, but if the over-the-fence power doesn't translate to the majors, the next card that fortune teller flips is going to be a picture of a despondent young man getting on a bus back to Indianapolis.

Liover Peguero SS Born: 12/31/00 Age: 22 Bats: R Throws: R Height: 6'2" Weight: 200 lb. Origin: International Free Agent, 2017

YEAR	TEAM	LVL	AGE	PA	R	2B	3B	HR	RBI	BB	K	SB	CS	Whiff%	AVG/OBP/SLG	DRC+	BABIP	BRR	DRP	WARP
2021	GBO	A+	20	417	67	19	2	14	45	33	105	28	6		.270/.332/.444	96	.337	-0.6	SS(86): 8.1	1.7
2022	ALT	AA	21	521	65	22	5	10	58	29	111	28	6		.259/.305/.387	97	.316	0.4	SS(94): -3.5, 2B(19): -1.2	1.0
2022	PIT	MLB	21	4	0	0	0	0	0	1	2	0	0	37.5%	.333/.500/.333	91	1.000	0.0	SS(1): 0.1	0.0
2023 non-DC	*PIT*	*MLB*	*22*	*251*	*21*	*9*	*1*	*4*	*23*	*13*	*66*	*9*	*2*	*30.5%*	*.236/.281/.349*	*73*	*.310*	*2.6*	*SS -1, 2B 0*	*0.1*

Comparables: Richard Urena (77), Wilfredo Tovar (64), Jorge Polanco (64)

While Peguero took a slight step backward by the stat line at Double-A last season, he still checks off nearly all the boxes to make him a likely fixture in the Pirates middle infield for years to come. Peguero's athleticism and on-the-field instincts project him as a top-line defender as well as a disruptive force on the basepaths. The thing in question is the bat, which stagnated, particularly after a one-day stint in the bigs in June. The scouting cognoscenti believe most of his issues are tied to pitch recognition, particularly when it comes to off-speed stuff out of the zone—qualifiers that apply to nearly every prospect, even the elite ones. Peguero's struggles mean he's likely ticketed for Double-A again, but the talent and projectability mean he's as capable as anyone in this system of turning it around on a dime.

Bryan Reynolds CF Born: 01/27/95 Age: 28 Bats: S Throws: R Height: 6'3" Weight: 205 lb. Origin: Round 2, 2016 Draft (#59 overall)

YEAR	TEAM	LVL	AGE	PA	R	2B	3B	HR	RBI	BB	K	SB	CS	Whiff%	AVG/OBP/SLG	DRC+	BABIP	BRR	DRP	WARP
2020	PIT	MLB	25	208	24	6	2	7	19	21	57	1	1	27.8%	.189/.275/.357	86	.231	-2.1	LF(37): 3.4, CF(17): 0.5	0.4
2021	PIT	MLB	26	646	93	35	8	24	90	75	119	5	2	23.7%	.302/.390/.522	127	.345	1.4	CF(137): -1.6, LF(17): -0.4	4.8
2022	PIT	MLB	27	614	74	19	4	27	62	56	141	7	3	27.5%	.262/.345/.461	122	.306	1.0	CF(127): -3.4, LF(1): 0.3	3.6
2023 DC	*PIT*	*MLB*	*28*	*604*	*77*	*26*	*5*	*24*	*74*	*58*	*138*	*7*	*2*	*26.8%*	*.276/.359/.482*	*132*	*.333*	*5.0*	*CF -8*	*3.8*

Comparables: Jackie Brandt (85), Max Carey (84), Rickey Henderson (83)

Reynolds followed up his breakthrough campaign with a solid season that didn't nearly measure up. His ability to hit the ball hard and far remained, but opposing pitchers mostly remembered that there weren't many other weapons in the Pirates lineup, which led to fewer good pitches to hit. Reynolds' chase rate shot up, and his batting average predictably plummeted. His center field defense, which looked good in 2021, was well below-average, making him look more suitable as a corner outfielder—and perhaps a left fielder, given the lack of a plus throwing arm. All these deficiencies are picking nits, and won't matter much if Reynolds continues to rake, which he did despite the propensity for the strikeout. Even with the presence of emerging stars Oneil Cruz and Ke'Bryan Hayes, Reynolds remains the centerpiece of the perpetually rebuilding Pirates—at least until he's shipped out as part of the franchise's next Big Effort to Win.

★ ★ ★ *2023 Top 101 Prospect* **#55** ★ ★ ★

Endy Rodriguez C/IF/OF Born: 05/26/00 Age: 23 Bats: S Throws: R Height: 6'0" Weight: 170 lb. Origin: International Free Agent, 2018

YEAR	TEAM	LVL	AGE	PA	R	2B	3B	HR	RBI	BB	K	SB	CS	Whiff%	AVG/OBP/SLG	DRC+	BABIP	BRR	DRP	WARP
2021	BRD	A	21	434	73	25	6	15	73	50	77	2	0		.294/.380/.512	130	.333	-2.3	C(54): -1.5, 1B(18): -1.7, LF(4): -1.2	2.1
2022	GBO	A+	22	370	63	23	3	16	55	42	77	3	3		.302/.392/.544	117	.351	-1.5	C(51): -2.3, 2B(15): 0.9, LF(13): -0.5	1.7
2022	ALT	AA	22	138	27	14	0	8	32	18	21	1	0		.356/.442/.678	135	.378	0.7	C(21): -1.5, 2B(2): -0.8	0.9
2022	IND	AAA	22	23	2	2	1	1	8	0	3	0	0		.455/.435/.773	114	.474	0.0	C(3): 0.1, 2B(1): -0.2	0.1
2023 DC	*PIT*	*MLB*	*23*	*263*	*28*	*14*	*2*	*7*	*28*	*20*	*56*	*0*	*1*	*23.3%*	*.263/.330/.434*	*109*	*.320*	*-2.9*	*C 0*	*0.9*

Comparables: Devin Mesoraco (75), Nathaniel Lowe (72), Ji-Man Choi (63)

YEAR	TEAM	P. COUNT	FRM RUNS	BLK RUNS	THRW RUNS	TOT RUNS
2021	BRD	7964	-2.7	-0.3	1.1	-1.9
2022	GBO	7648	-0.7	-2.5	0.5	-2.7
2022	ALT	2985	-1.2	-0.4	0.4	-1.2
2023	*PIT*	*9620*	*-2.2*	*-1.2*	*0.8*	*-2.6*

A nearly forgotten throw-in from the Joe Musgrove trade two years ago, Rodriguez went from afterthought to integral: He was finally able to tap into his power potential and add to an already impressive offensive tool kit. Rodriguez started the year without a set position, but eventually mostly settled in behind the plate—a sign the organization trusts him, and that maybe he'll even supplant top prospect Henry Davis behind the dish (at least in the short-term). Add to that a confidence that Rodriguez radiates: the idea that he belongs in Pittsburgh *yesterday,* along with a positive, infectious attitude those inside and outside the organization are raving about. It's increasingly likely he makes his big-league debut sometime this year.

Carlos Santana 1B/DH Born: 04/08/86 Age: 37 Bats: S Throws: R Height: 5'11" Weight: 215 lb. Origin: International Free Agent, 2004

YEAR	TEAM	LVL	AGE	PA	R	2B	3B	HR	RBI	BB	K	SB	CS	Whiff%	AVG/OBP/SLG	DRC+	BABIP	BRR	DRP	WARP
2020	CLE	MLB	34	255	34	7	0	8	30	47	43	0	0	20.7%	.199/.349/.350	114	.212	1.0	1B(60): 2.6	1.4
2021	KC	MLB	35	659	66	15	0	19	69	86	102	2	0	22.2%	.214/.319/.342	101	.227	-1.3	1B(136): -1.4	1.2
2022	KC	MLB	36	212	17	10	0	4	21	36	28	0	0	19.3%	.216/.349/.341	117	.236	0.2	1B(42): 0.4	1.0
2022	SEA	MLB	36	294	35	8	0	15	39	35	60	0	0	22.7%	.192/.293/.400	113	.187	1.5	1B(34): 1	1.4
2023 DC	*PIT*	*MLB*	*37*	*509*	*56*	*18*	*1*	*18*	*58*	*68*	*83*	*0*	*0*	*21.6%*	*.226/.335/.401*	*107*	*.240*	*-0.7*	*1B 1*	*1.2*

Comparables: Earl Torgeson (65), Dan Driessen (64), Wally Joyner (62)

In another era, Santana might have been hounded out of the league after posting a Mendoza-adjacent batting average over a three-year span (abbreviated 2020 notwithstanding). We now have the statistical evidence to suggest that (per DRC+, anyway) Santana's bat has been, in fact, slightly better than league-average. For the Mariners, the midseason acquisition of the switch-hitting veteran had as much to do with his leadership as his bat, and it's hard to deny that the team gelled for the stretch run, with Santana offering a few dingers along the way. Like a grizzled gun for hire in a classical Western, he'll mosey along to another clubhouse in need of a mentor and occasional offensive contributor—in this case, the one in PNC Park, as he was signed by the Pirates on a one-year deal last November.

Jack Suwinski OF Born: 07/29/98 Age: 24 Bats: L Throws: L Height: 6'2" Weight: 215 lb. Origin: Round 15, 2016 Draft (#444 overall)

YEAR	TEAM	LVL	AGE	PA	R	2B	3B	HR	RBI	BB	K	SB	CS	Whiff%	AVG/OBP/SLG	DRC+	BABIP	BRR	DRP	WARP
2021	SA	AA	22	267	47	8	4	15	37	45	74	7	6		.269/.398/.551	135	.333	-1.0	RF(60): -2.4, CF(3): 0.2	1.7
2021	ALT	AA	22	182	21	9	0	4	21	25	51	4	2		.252/.359/.391	93	.343	0.7	LF(27): 2.1, RF(10): -0.1	0.7
2022	ALT	AA	23	57	13	8	0	3	13	5	14	1	0		.353/.421/.686	116	.441	0.9	RF(11): -0.9	0.2
2022	IND	AAA	23	130	19	5	0	6	18	11	49	1	0		.214/.285/.410	81	.302	0.9	LF(13): 0.5, CF(9): -0.8, RF(7): -0.6	0.2
2022	PIT	MLB	23	372	45	11	0	19	38	41	114	4	2	30.3%	.202/.298/.411	101	.242	2.5	LF(56): 1.1, RF(38): 1.5, CF(19): 0.6	1.9
2023 DC	*PIT*	*MLB*	*24*	*258*	*26*	*9*	*1*	*8*	*26*	*26*	*81*	*3*	*2*	*30.1%*	*.211/.299/.386*	*85*	*.286*	*1.4*	*LF -1*	*0.2*

Comparables: Travis Snider (54), Michael Conforto (53), Kyle Blanks (51)

It was a debut of fits and starts for the rookie outfielder. Acquired from the Padres at the 2021 trade deadline—as part of a seemingly underwhelming package for Adam Frazier—Suwinski quietly emerged as a prodigious power source. Existing physical strength combined with successful swing and approach changes, giving his batted balls more loft and distance. It was a bumpy ride, laden with inconsistency: While every one of Suwinski's 19 home runs sounded and looked impressive, there was far too much swing and miss for a hitter with little margin for error. On the bright side: Profiled as DH-only heading into the season, Suwinski improved his footwork and outfield routes and went from being a liability to an asset in the field—to the point where the Pirates are considering using him as their starting center fielder.

Travis Swaggerty OF Born: 08/19/97 Age: 25 Bats: L Throws: L Height: 5'10" Weight: 200 lb. Origin: Round 1, 2018 Draft (#10 overall)

YEAR	TEAM	LVL	AGE	PA	R	2B	3B	HR	RBI	BB	K	SB	CS	Whiff%	AVG/OBP/SLG	DRC+	BABIP	BRR	DRP	WARP
2021	IND	AAA	23	48	6	0	0	3	7	6	8	3	0		.220/.333/.439	128	.200	0.2	CF(9): 2.3	0.6
2022	IND	AAA	24	458	55	15	8	9	55	57	117	20	5	47.1%	.254/.348/.399	91	.337	-1.8	CF(56): -0.8, RF(22): -0.0, LF(18): 0.4	0.8
2022	PIT	MLB	24	9	0	0	0	0	0	0	4	0	0	36.8%	.111/.111/.111	66	.200	-0.1	LF(3): -0.3, CF(1): 0	0.0
2023 DC	*PIT*	*MLB*	*25*	*60*	*5*	*2*	*0*	*1*	*5*	*5*	*17*	*1*	*1*	*31.9%*	*.221/.294/.347*	*74*	*.305*	*1.2*	*CF 0, RF 0*	*0.1*

Comparables: Brandon Nimmo (59), Ian Happ (59), Trayvon Robinson (55)

It has been five years since the Pirates nabbed Swaggerty with the #10 overall pick in the 2018 draft; while it's a little too early to deem the outfield prospect a complete bust, it is clear that he's far more likely to be a complementary player than a superstar. A reworked swing at the Pirates' alternate site in 2020 was supposed to unlock more power, but Swaggerty remains more of a singles-and-gaps hitter than an over-the-fence bat. His speed is what's likely to get him to—and keep him in—the majors, particularly in the cavernous outfield corners of PNC Park. It remains possible that enough power will come to make Swaggerty a 20/30 offensive force, but at this point you're looking at a player who will turn 26 this year and hasn't even reached double-digit homers in a professional season.

Lonnie White Jr. OF Born: 12/31/02 Age: 20 Bats: R Throws: R Height: 6'3" Weight: 212 lb. Origin: Round 2, 2021 Draft (#64 overall)

YEAR	TEAM	LVL	AGE	PA	R	2B	3B	HR	RBI	BB	K	SB	CS	Whiff%	AVG/OBP/SLG	DRC+	BABIP	BRR	DRP	WARP
2021	PIRB	ROK	18	33	6	2	0	2	5	2	14	0	0		.258/.303/.516		.400			
2023	*No projection*																			

A two-sport standout out of Malvern High School in suburban Philadelphia, White is an excellent athlete who is still honing his craft on the diamond—and has mostly done that work on the sidelines or in the training room, as injuries wiped out his 2022 almost entirely. The upside is an impact power bat with enough speed to wreak havoc on the basepaths, but 11 games and 40 professional appearances can't tell us anything about White. He has plenty of time to get it going, but the Pirates are hoping that, at the very least, they get a healthy version of their athletic outfielder this year.

PITCHERS

David Bednar RHP Born: 10/10/94 Age: 28 Bats: L Throws: R Height: 6'1" Weight: 250 lb. Origin: Round 35, 2016 Draft (#1044 overall)

YEAR	TEAM	LVL	AGE	W	L	SV	G	GS	IP	H	HR	BB/9	K/9	K	GB%	BABIP	WHIP	ERA	DRA-	WARP	MPH	FB%	Whiff%	CSP
2020	SD	MLB	25	0	0	0	4	0	6^{1}	11	1	2.8	7.1	5	36.0%	.417	2.05	7.11	129	0.0	95.6	59.3%	27.7%	52.0%
2021	PIT	MLB	26	3	1	3	61	0	60^{2}	40	5	2.8	11.4	77	42.1%	.259	0.97	2.23	73	1.4	96.9	55.8%	32.6%	56.1%
2022	PIT	MLB	27	3	4	19	45	0	51^{2}	42	4	2.8	12.0	69	33.1%	.317	1.12	2.61	76	1.1	96.7	53.6%	33.3%	54.9%
2023 DC	*PIT*	*MLB*	*28*	*3*	*3*	*30*	*67*	*0*	*58.3*	*48*	*7*	*3.1*	*11.4*	*74*	*38.1%*	*.302*	*1.18*	*3.11*	*80*	*0.8*	*96.7*	*54.4%*	*32.1%*	*55.2%*

Comparables: Ryan Dull (57), Juan Minaya (54), Nick Vincent (54)

While there's no template for the perfect MLB closer, it sure seems like someone tried—Bednar could've been created in a lab, or imagined in a cocaine-fueled script session for the summer's feel-great generic sports blockbuster: *Local Closer*. Hailing from Mars, Pennsylvania, Bednar went undrafted but kept his dream alive at Lafayette College (motto: "The truth shall set you free"). After finally getting picked up in a draft round that no longer exists, he found his way back home in 2021 as part of a three-way trade for Joe Musgrove. Before long, Bednar and his fireballs found their way into the ninth inning. The only element missing from this storybook ending is a winning franchise, but if the next great Pirates team to grace the western half of the Quaker State is near, Bednar is ready on the hill with nasty stuff and a fiery demeanor.

Tyler Beede RHP Born: 05/23/93 Age: 30 Bats: R Throws: R Height: 6'2" Weight: 216 lb. Origin: Round 1, 2014 Draft (#14 overall)

YEAR	TEAM	LVL	AGE	W	L	SV	G	GS	IP	H	HR	BB/9	K/9	K	GB%	BABIP	WHIP	ERA	DRA-	WARP	MPH	FB%	Whiff%	CSP
2021	SAC	AAA	28	0	6	0	16	16	48^{2}	50	7	8.3	9.2	50	45.5%	.316	1.95	6.66	91	0.5				
2021	SF	MLB	28	0	0	0	1	0	1	2	0	0.0	18.0	2	33.3%	.667	2.00	27.00	99	0.0	96.2	46.4%	40.0%	40.4%
2022	PIT	MLB	29	2	5	0	25	5	51^{2}	57	6	4.0	6.1	35	50.0%	.304	1.55	5.23	127	-0.2	95.9	43.7%	21.6%	52.0%
2022	SF	MLB	29	0	0	0	6	0	9^{2}	14	1	5.6	3.7	4	44.7%	.351	2.07	4.66	113	0.0	95.9	62.9%	12.7%	54.3%
2023 non-DC	*PIT*	*MLB*	*30*	*2*	*3*	*0*	*57*	*0*	*50*	*59*	*6*	*4.8*	*6.8*	*37*	*47.2%*	*.331*	*1.73*	*6.13*	*139*	*-0.8*	*95.4*	*49.8%*	*23.2%*	*50.2%*

Comparables: Chris Stratton (60), Matt Andriese (56), Mike Wright Jr. (56)

Beede believers entered 2022 hopeful the Giants would work their organizational magic and finally help him become a viable rotation piece, but those hopes were unceremoniously dashed in early May when he was designated for assignment. The Pirates scooped him up days later, which as far as reclamation projects are concerned is like shifting from a highly publicized downtown revitalization to a grade schooler's hastily superglued diorama. Beede's fastball remained impressive, but everything else—command, control, and off-speed offerings—was a muddled mess. He managed to spend most of the year in the majors, but while there's still hope he can rediscover the magic that made him a first-round pick way back in 2014, it looks like Beede's future has "capable middle reliever" stamped all over it.

JT Brubaker RHP

Born: 11/17/93 Age: 29 Bats: R Throws: R Height: 6'3" Weight: 185 lb. Origin: Round 6, 2015 Draft (#187 overall)

YEAR	TEAM	LVL	AGE	W	L	SV	G	GS	IP	H	HR	BB/9	K/9	K	GB%	BABIP	WHIP	ERA	DRA-	WARP	MPH	FB%	Whiff%	CSP
2020	PIT	MLB	26	1	3	0	11	9	47^1	48	6	3.2	9.1	48	47.4%	.321	1.37	4.94	86	0.8	93.9	49.8%	27.6%	46.1%
2021	PIT	MLB	27	5	13	0	24	24	124^1	123	28	2.8	9.3	129	42.8%	.289	1.29	5.36	93	1.6	93.3	49.1%	27.4%	55.7%
2022	PIT	MLB	28	3	12	0	28	28	144	157	17	3.4	9.2	147	43.8%	.334	1.47	4.69	105	1.0	93.2	47.8%	27.5%	54.7%
2023 DC	*PIT*	*MLB*	*29*	*9*	*10*	*0*	*29*	*29*	*163*	*162*	*20*	*3.1*	*8.8*	*159*	*44.3%*	*.311*	*1.34*	*4.17*	*104*	*1.0*	*93.3*	*48.5%*	*27.0%*	*54.2%*

Comparables: Anthony DeSclafani (70), Corey Kluber (68), Wade Miley (68)

Brubaker started out last season the way he finished 2021: horribly. After posting a ghastly 6.20 ERA in five April starts, Bru shelved his four-seam fastball in favor of a sinker/slider-heavy approach. This pitch mix change didn't turn Brubaker into an All-Star, but he went from being a borderline major-league starter to an adequate mid-rotation option. This modest improvement, however, got buried by a historically awful won-loss record. Among pitchers with 50+ starts in their first 63 games, only Matt Keough and Andy Ashby had worse won/loss percentages than Brubaker's .243 to start his career. Wins and losses are no way to measure a hurler's effectiveness, and the Pirates' poor offense and inept defense didn't do Brubaker any favors, but the conditions that led to his poor record aren't likely to change in the short-term, either.

Mike Burrows RHP

Born: 11/08/99 Age: 23 Bats: R Throws: R Height: 6'2" Weight: 195 lb. Origin: Round 11, 2018 Draft (#324 overall)

YEAR	TEAM	LVL	AGE	W	L	SV	G	GS	IP	H	HR	BB/9	K/9	K	GB%	BABIP	WHIP	ERA	DRA-	WARP	MPH	FB%	Whiff%	CSP
2021	GBO	A+	21	2	2	0	13	13	49	24	3	3.7	12.1	66	30.8%	.208	0.90	2.20	93	0.6				
2022	ALT	AA	22	4	2	0	12	12	52	38	3	3.3	11.9	69	31.7%	.294	1.10	2.94	93	0.9				
2022	IND	AAA	22	1	4	0	12	10	42^1	45	5	2.6	8.9	42	38.4%	.333	1.35	5.31	99	0.6				
2023 DC	*PIT*	*MLB*	*23*	*1*	*1*	*0*	*22*	*0*	*19.3*	*18*	*2*	*4.0*	*8.3*	*17*	*36.0%*	*.298*	*1.41*	*4.42*	*109*	*0.0*			*25.5%*	

Comparables: Marco Gonzales (72), Luis Gil (71), Yency Almonte (71)

An 11th-round prep pick from Connecticut, Burrows has adroitly climbed both the minor-league ladder and prospect rankings thanks to a combination of a sharp curveball, a mid-90s heater he can dial up to 97, and an improved changeup that adapts a Vulcan split grip to minimize spin. Burrows' rise through the organizational ranks has gone about as well as it possibly can for any high-school draftee, with the exception of health. That's no small matter, though: While Pittsburgh has been rightfully conservative about managing his workloads, Burrows missed time in 2021 due to an oblique injury and was shut down at last season's end with shoulder inflammation. He's still on track to join the Bucs rotation at some point this year, but pitch counts and innings limits will be a thing with this guy, especially right out of the gate.

Roansy Contreras RHP

Born: 11/07/99 Age: 23 Bats: R Throws: R Height: 6'0" Weight: 175 lb. Origin: International Free Agent, 2016

YEAR	TEAM	LVL	AGE	W	L	SV	G	GS	IP	H	HR	BB/9	K/9	K	GB%	BABIP	WHIP	ERA	DRA-	WARP	MPH	FB%	Whiff%	CSP
2021	ALT	AA	21	3	2	0	12	12	54^1	37	5	2.0	12.6	76	48.4%	.267	0.90	2.65	83	1.0				
2021	PIT	MLB	21	0	0	0	1	1	3	3	0	3.0	12.0	4	57.1%	.429	1.33	0.00	84	0.1	96.7	63.0%	27.3%	55.1%
2022	IND	AAA	22	1	1	0	9	9	34^1	29	4	3.4	12.1	46	45.1%	.321	1.22	3.15	75	0.9	97.2	55.4%	25.0%	
2022	PIT	MLB	22	5	5	0	21	18	95	82	13	3.7	8.1	86	36.3%	.257	1.27	3.79	106	0.6	95.8	48.5%	27.6%	53.6%
2023 DC	*PIT*	*MLB*	*23*	*8*	*9*	*0*	*29*	*29*	*139.7*	*129*	*19*	*3.5*	*9.2*	*143*	*39.7%*	*.294*	*1.31*	*3.90*	*99*	*1.2*	*95.8*	*48.8%*	*28.1%*	*53.7%*

Comparables: Lucas Giolito (53), Taijuan Walker (52), Trevor Bauer (51)

The idea that velocity is king has been drummed so consistently into our heads that it's easy to forget not every pitcher needs to, or even should, throw every offering at max effort. Contreras exemplifies the concept that, sometimes, less is more. He started the 2022 campaign guns a-blazing, averaging 97 miles per hour on his fastball. The results were passable, but the Pirates sent him back down to Triple-A in July for additional refinement. When he returned, Contreras was a different pitcher. He could still get to 97 on the gun when necessary, but generally dialed it down two to three ticks, and relied far more on a wipeout slider with wicked horizontal movement. Contreras' ceiling keeps rising, and he has become a vital centerpiece of the (as-yet-theoretical) next Pirates contender.

Wil Crowe RHP

Born: 09/09/94 Age: 28 Bats: R Throws: R Height: 6'2" Weight: 245 lb. Origin: Round 2, 2017 Draft (#65 overall)

YEAR	TEAM	LVL	AGE	W	L	SV	G	GS	IP	H	HR	BB/9	K/9	K	GB%	BABIP	WHIP	ERA	DRA-	WARP	MPH	FB%	Whiff%	CSP
2020	WAS	MLB	25	0	2	0	3	3	8^1	14	5	8.6	8.6	8	27.6%	.375	2.64	11.88	171	-0.2	91.7	57.2%	19.4%	40.5%
2021	PIT	MLB	26	4	8	0	26	25	116^2	126	25	4.4	8.6	111	43.1%	.314	1.57	5.48	106	0.7	93.7	46.7%	25.5%	54.0%
2022	PIT	MLB	27	6	10	4	60	1	76	68	8	4.5	8.1	68	50.2%	.280	1.39	4.38	105	0.5	94.9	37.5%	27.6%	51.2%
2023 DC	*PIT*	*MLB*	*28*	*3*	*3*	*3*	*67*	*0*	*58.3*	*58*	*7*	*4.3*	*8.3*	*54*	*46.4%*	*.310*	*1.48*	*4.56*	*111*	*0.1*	*94.1*	*43.0%*	*26.1%*	*52.4%*

Comparables: Stephen Fife (52), Mike Wright Jr. (51), Ben Lively (51)

"A bird in the hand is worth two in the bush" wasn't a concern for the Pirates when they acquired Crowe as a minor leaguer in December 2020, as part of a modest package for Josh Bell. His stuff isn't just based on a wing and a prayer. Crowe added a changeup that allows him to throw his fastball less, and really goose it when he does. Given that he transitioned from the rotation to a bullpen role last year, no one should expect a Hall of Fame career to magically take flight, but it's also clear that he can rule the roost in the late innings. While Crowe was rarely asked to take the ball in the ninth, he was more than capable. Vulturing four saves might not seem like a big deal, but no one in Pittsburgh could stop raven about Crowe's feat.

Thomas Harrington RHP Born: 07/12/01 Age: 21 Bats: R Throws: R Height: 6'2" Weight: 185 lb. Origin: Round 1, 2022 Draft (#36 overall)

Players generally aren't considered successful until they have not only made it to the majors but thrived there, but this is an extremely narrow definition that implies nearly everyone is a failure. A walk-on at Campbell University who didn't even start pitching until his junior year, Harrington was a late first-round pick by the Pirates a mere year and a half later. That makes him a success by any definition, no matter what happens next. You can hope for more, though: The promising young righty's four-seamer sits in the low-90s but can touch 95 mph, and is complemented by a plus change and a curve and slider that both need refinement. Harrington will make his professional debut this year.

Rich Hill LHP Born: 03/11/80 Age: 43 Bats: L Throws: L Height: 6'5" Weight: 221 lb. Origin: Round 4, 2002 Draft (#112 overall)

YEAR	TEAM	LVL	AGE	W	L	SV	G	GS	IP	H	HR	BB/9	K/9	K	GB%	BABIP	WHIP	ERA	DRA-	WARP	MPH	FB%	Whiff%	CSP
2020	MIN	MLB	40	2	2	0	8	8	38^{2}	28	3	4.0	7.2	31	41.1%	.240	1.16	3.03	115	0.1	87.9	46.8%	16.0%	50.6%
2021	NYM	MLB	41	1	4	0	13	12	63^{1}	62	7	2.7	8.4	59	27.4%	.311	1.28	3.84	103	0.5	87.9	50.4%	22.5%	57.4%
2021	TB	MLB	41	6	4	0	19	19	95^{1}	75	14	3.4	8.6	91	39.8%	.255	1.16	3.87	109	0.4	88.5	49.4%	24.0%	56.3%
2022	BOS	MLB	42	8	7	0	26	26	124^{1}	125	15	2.7	7.9	109	39.6%	.305	1.30	4.27	122	-0.2	88.7	37.8%	22.0%	56.8%
2023 DC	*PIT*	*MLB*	*43*	*6*	*7*	*0*	*22*	*22*	*106.3*	*111*	*16*	*3.1*	*7.6*	*90*	*38.4%*	*.303*	*1.39*	*4.70*	*117*	*-0.1*	*88.5*	*44.3%*	*21.5%*	*56.3%*

Comparables: Steve Carlton (60), Jerry Koosman (58), Randy Johnson (58)

At some point, the steam-powered gears inside Hill's left arm are going to gum up for good, and that will be the end of one of the league's premier journeymen. It looked close to happening in 2022. Injuries kept him off the field for sizable chunks of the year, and he posted his worst DRA- since 2009. Unable to miss bats with regularity and with his fastball trapped in the Phantom Zone, Hill went to his curveball more (though its spin rate remained below its pre-sticky stuff crackdown highs) and mixed in a lot of cutters, hoping that he could trade whiffs for soft contact. But when you're 43 years old and stuck with an 88-mph heater, your margin for error is the width of a hair, making the lefty hard to trust in a regular rotation role. The Pirates look poised to do so anyway, signing Hill to a one-year deal for his 19th(!) season.

Colin Holderman RHP Born: 10/08/95 Age: 27 Bats: R Throws: R Height: 6'7" Weight: 240 lb. Origin: Round 9, 2016 Draft (#280 overall)

YEAR	TEAM	LVL	AGE	W	L	SV	G	GS	IP	H	HR	BB/9	K/9	K	GB%	BABIP	WHIP	ERA	DRA-	WARP	MPH	FB%	Whiff%	CSP
2021	BNG	AA	25	0	2	4	11	2	19^{1}	13	2	2.8	9.3	20	38.0%	.229	0.98	3.26	104	0.1				
2022	SYR	AAA	26	1	0	3	11	0	14^{1}	9	2	1.9	10.7	17	62.9%	.212	0.84	2.51	78	0.4				
2022	PIT	MLB	26	1	0	0	9	0	10^{2}	9	0	5.9	5.1	6	44.1%	.273	1.50	6.75	122	0.0	96.6	49.7%	14.8%	47.1%
2022	NYM	MLB	26	4	0	0	15	0	17^{2}	11	0	3.6	9.2	18	47.6%	.262	1.02	2.04	89	0.3	95.7	50.2%	28.4%	53.4%
2023 DC	*PIT*	*MLB*	*27*	*2*	*3*	*0*	*60*	*0*	*51.7*	*49*	*5*	*4.3*	*7.9*	*45*	*46.8%*	*.291*	*1.42*	*4.34*	*106*	*0.0*	*96.1*	*50.0%*	*25.6%*	*50.5%*

Comparables: Ryan Burr (70), Geoff Hartlieb (68), Hunter Strickland (68)

Pitching is frequently presented as a mysterious enigma no mortal can quite fully comprehend—so when a pitcher "suddenly" gains velocity, it's often digested by the public as something magical that "just happened." The reality is often far more mundane. In Holderman's case, a minor-league coach noticed he was barely using his legs in his delivery. Improvement didn't come overnight, but his velocity eventually jumped from 90 miles per hour to 94–96, also allowing him to sharpen his off-speed stuff. His meteoric rise to the majors earned a key role in a contending Mets bullpen—before the club shipped him off to the Pirates in a July deal for Daniel Vogelbach. The success story was derailed by a shoulder injury in August. If Holderman is healthy this spring, he'll be a key setup piece in the late innings once again.

Jared Jones RHP Born: 08/06/01 Age: 21 Bats: L Throws: R Height: 6'1" Weight: 180 lb. Origin: Round 2, 2020 Draft (#44 overall)

YEAR	TEAM	LVL	AGE	W	L	SV	G	GS	IP	H	HR	BB/9	K/9	K	GB%	BABIP	WHIP	ERA	DRA-	WARP	MPH	FB%	Whiff%	CSP
2021	BRD	A	19	3	6	0	18	15	66	63	6	4.6	14.0	103	45.5%	.385	1.47	4.64	79	1.5				
2022	GBO	A+	20	5	7	0	26	26	122^{2}	115	19	3.7	10.4	142	38.9%	.310	1.35	4.62	94	1.3				
2023 non-DC	*PIT*	*MLB*	*21*	*2*	*3*	*0*	*57*	*0*	*50*	*56*	*9*	*5.2*	*8.7*	*48*	*39.9%*	*.327*	*1.71*	*6.34*	*143*	*-0.9*			*26.4%*	

Comparables: Zach Davies (80), Robert Stephenson (80), Scott Blewett (80)

Blessed with what some believe is the best raw stuff in the Pirates system, Jones remains a work in progress, a tantalizing raw talent who needs plenty of refinement. His heater sits in the mid-90s and can touch 98, but Jones is still mostly too fastball-reliant; things can go south quickly if the offering is missing its spots. The secondary stuff has promise but is inconsistent; the slider has plenty of nasty break and movement, but isn't enough of a go-to just yet. Jones was only 20 years old throughout most of last year, and passed the all-important health and durability test for a young arm getting extended reps for the first time. This year, the hurdle of facing more-polished hitters in the high minors is next on the checklist. Even if the secondaries don't develop, Jones at the very least has a future in a high-leverage relief role.

Mitch Keller RHP Born: 04/04/96 Age: 27 Bats: R Throws: R Height: 6'2" Weight: 220 lb. Origin: Round 2, 2014 Draft (#64 overall)

YEAR	TEAM	LVL	AGE	W	L	SV	G	GS	IP	H	HR	BB/9	K/9	K	GB%	BABIP	WHIP	ERA	DRA-	WARP	MPH	FB%	Whiff%	CSP
2020	PIT	MLB	24	1	1	0	5	5	21^2	9	4	7.5	6.6	16	42.3%	.104	1.25	2.91	129	-0.1	94.2	55.9%	21.2%	43.6%
2021	IND	AAA	25	1	1	0	8	6	28	27	2	4.2	12.5	39	56.0%	.342	1.43	3.21	83	0.6				
2021	PIT	MLB	25	5	11	0	23	23	100^2	131	10	4.4	8.2	92	39.4%	.392	1.79	6.17	116	0.1	94.0	56.8%	20.5%	57.0%
2022	PIT	MLB	26	5	12	0	31	29	159	162	14	3.4	7.8	138	49.1%	.321	1.40	3.91	105	1.2	95.3	55.6%	21.5%	54.9%
2023 DC	*PIT*	*MLB*	*27*	*8*	*10*	*0*	*29*	*29*	*148.7*	*159*	*15*	*3.9*	*8.4*	*138*	*46.8%*	*.329*	*1.50*	*4.72*	*113*	*0.3*	*94.8*	*56.2%*	*22.4%*	*54.8%*

Comparables: Vance Worley (69), Iván Nova (65), Tyler Chatwood (64)

Most of Keller's career has been spent riding the struggle bus, starting wistfully out the window looking for a stop that's still out of view. Last season started out looking like the same old ride before Keller ditched his ineffective four-seamer for a sinking fastball. He went against the modern grain of "throw hard, stupid," lost about two miles per hour off his fastest pitch, and was far more effective. A 3.22 ERA from May 31 until season's end tells part of the story, but it was a launch angle of 7.6 degrees that really drives home the metamorphosis. Among qualified pitchers, that launch angle was sixth-best in the majors, behind only Framber Valdez, Logan Webb, Kyle Wright, Sandy Alcantara, and Max Fried. Keller isn't a surefire guarantee to become the next big thing, but at long last he's reached his destination and can pull the cord—he has an effective pitching approach.

Luis Ortiz RHP Born: 01/27/99 Age: 24 Bats: R Throws: R Height: 6'2" Weight: 240 lb. Origin: International Free Agent, 2018

YEAR	TEAM	LVL	AGE	W	L	SV	G	GS	IP	H	HR	BB/9	K/9	K	GB%	BABIP	WHIP	ERA	DRA-	WARP	MPH	FB%	Whiff%	CSP
2021	BRD	A	22	5	3	0	22	19	87^1	82	5	2.9	11.6	113	51.3%	.344	1.26	3.09	89	1.5				
2022	ALT	AA	23	5	9	0	24	23	114^1	100	19	2.7	9.9	126	46.5%	.288	1.17	4.64	86	2.3				
2022	IND	AAA	23	0	0	0	2	2	10	4	1	3.6	10.8	12	56.0%	.125	0.80	3.60	81	0.2				
2022	PIT	MLB	23	0	2	0	4	4	16	8	1	5.6	9.6	17	42.9%	.171	1.13	4.50	98	0.2	98.6	57.8%	29.8%	52.2%
2023 DC	*PIT*	*MLB*	*24*	*3*	*3*	*0*	*28*	*6*	*46*	*45*	*6*	*3.9*	*8.5*	*43*	*47.2%*	*.304*	*1.43*	*4.50*	*110*	*0.1*	*98.6*	*57.8%*	*27.6%*	*52.2%*

Comparables: Chris Archer (64), Vance Worley (63), Wily Peralta (63)

In the span of 11 months Ortiz went from an interesting High-A live arm, the kind of guy who gets traded for two months of Trevor Rosenthal, to shutting out the Reds over 5⅔ in his MLB debut. An international signing as a 19-year-old in 2019, the Pirates had some time to see if the young right-hander could do the work of establishing himself as a starter—the usual changeup development and search for fastball command. Instead, he dominated the high minors without them, on the back of 98 with extension and a falchion of a slider, charging straight into the big-league club's September rotation. He still could wind up as a reliever—although even that risk suggests he'll be a pretty good one, at least as good as current Trevor Rosenthal.

Johan Oviedo RHP Born: 03/02/98 Age: 25 Bats: R Throws: R Height: 6'5" Weight: 245 lb. Origin: International Free Agent, 2016

YEAR	TEAM	LVL	AGE	W	L	SV	G	GS	IP	H	HR	BB/9	K/9	K	GB%	BABIP	WHIP	ERA	DRA-	WARP	MPH	FB%	Whiff%	CSP
2020	STL	MLB	22	0	3	0	5	5	24^2	24	3	3.6	5.8	16	40.7%	.269	1.38	5.47	138	-0.2	95.0	56.1%	21.5%	47.4%
2021	MEM	AAA	23	1	6	0	12	11	54^1	55	7	4.8	9.8	59	52.0%	.331	1.55	6.13	92	1.0				
2021	STL	MLB	23	0	5	0	14	13	62^1	61	8	5.3	7.4	51	49.0%	.286	1.57	4.91	119	0.0	95.1	53.7%	26.1%	53.5%
2022	IND	AAA	24	0	0	0	5	4	11^1	8	0	2.4	10.3	13	39.3%	.286	0.97	0.79	84	0.2				
2022	MEM	AAA	24	4	2	0	10	10	50	43	14	4.1	9.2	51	45.6%	.238	1.32	5.58	104	0.6	96.2	50.0%	31.4%	
2022	PIT	MLB	24	2	2	0	7	7	30^2	23	1	4.7	8.2	28	56.8%	.253	1.27	3.23	102	0.3	96.7	43.5%	22.4%	54.9%
2022	STL	MLB	24	2	1	0	14	1	25^1	26	4	2.5	9.2	26	43.2%	.314	1.30	3.20	93	0.3	95.7	43.4%	27.5%	57.4%
2023 DC	*PIT*	*MLB*	*25*	*7*	*8*	*0*	*49*	*19*	*107.3*	*110*	*14*	*4.5*	*7.9*	*94*	*48.0%*	*.308*	*1.53*	*4.94*	*118*	*-0.2*	*95.6*	*49.0%*	*25.2%*	*54.1%*

Comparables: Robert Stephenson (61), Jarred Cosart (60), Chris Archer (59)

It might seem premature to give up on a 24-year-old, but in baseball the ticking of the service clock—combined with the loud footfalls of replacements waiting in the high minors—sometimes makes it an imperative to let the dream go. Despite his power stuff and solid delivery, Oviedo's lack of command, and inability to master a third pitch or get lefties out, made the Cardinals surrender to the inevitable and push him to the bullpen. A deadline trade with the Pirates gave Oviedo new life, and after a month in the minors he returned as a starter to mixed results. Pittsburgh is trying to revitalize his changeup, but it's most likely going to be the walks—or lack thereof—that determine whether the Bucs wave the Jolly Roger every fifth day or, like St. Louis before them, raise the white flag.

Quinn Priester RHP Born: 09/15/00 Age: 22 Bats: R Throws: R Height: 6'3" Weight: 210 lb. Origin: Round 1, 2019 Draft (#18 overall)

YEAR	TEAM	LVL	AGE	W	L	SV	G	GS	IP	H	HR	BB/9	K/9	K	GB%	BABIP	WHIP	ERA	DRA-	WARP	MPH	FB%	Whiff%	CSP
2021	GBO	A+	20	7	4	0	20	20	97^2	82	8	3.6	9.0	98	53.7%	.285	1.24	3.04	85	1.7				
2022	ALT	AA	21	4	4	0	15	15	75^1	68	4	2.6	9.0	75	50.2%	.314	1.19	2.87	86	1.5				
2022	IND	AAA	21	1	1	0	2	2	9^1	5	1	6.8	9.6	10	36.4%	.190	1.29	3.86	99	0.1				
2023 DC	*PIT*	*MLB*	*22*	*0*	*0*	*0*	*3*	*3*	*13.3*	*13*	*1*	*4.4*	*7.3*	*10*	*49.5%*	*.303*	*1.50*	*4.57*	*111*	*0.0*			*25.9%*	

Comparables: Peter Lambert (53), Jonathan Pettibone (52), Jacob Turner (51)

Priester's professional career has been disappointing—but only in the way that going to an ice cream parlor, finding out your favorite flavor is out of stock and getting something else instead is disappointing. It isn't exactly what you wanted, but it's still ice cream. Since being drafted in 2019, Priester has lost some velocity off his fastball; it's not the requisite out pitch of an ace. But it has a solid sinking action and is complemented by a sharp breaking curve, along with a *cambio* and slider that markedly improved last season. Analysts are talking about Priester like he's "only" going to be a #2-3 starter and not an ace, but if that's the ultimate outcome then the Pirates and their fans should get some hot fudge, whipped cream, and sprinkles (or jimmies, or whatever they call it in Pittsburgh) and enjoy their ice cream.

Anthony Solometo LHP Born: 12/02/02 Age: 20 Bats: L Throws: L Height: 6'5" Weight: 220 lb. Origin: Round 2, 2021 Draft (#37 overall)

YEAR	TEAM	LVL	AGE	W	L	SV	G	GS	IP	H	HR	BB/9	K/9	K	GB%	BABIP	WHIP	ERA	DRA-	WARP	MPH	FB%	Whiff%	CSP
2022	BRD	A	19	5	1	0	13	8	47^{2}	31	0	3.6	9.6	51	51.8%	.272	1.05	2.64	87	1.1	90.8	61.6%	31.1%	
2023 non-DC	*PIT*	*MLB*	*20*	*2*	*3*	*0*	*57*	*0*	*50*	*53*	*6*	*5.4*	*7.0*	*39*	*46.0%*	*.305*	*1.66*	*5.63*	*131*	*-0.6*			*24.1%*	

Comparables: DL Hall (87), Robbie Ray (86), Stephen Gonsalves (83)

For all the hard and necessary work the Pirates coaching staff put in with their 2021 second-round pick, from the day he was drafted until his professional debut 319 days later, it was an adjustment Solometo made while playing a video game that arguably made the most developmental impact. Solometo noticed, while playing MLB The Show as Zach Wheeler, that he needed to tuck his hands closer to his body during his windup. The mechanical change cleaned up the teenager's somewhat messy, herky-jerky delivery, allowing him to maximize his massive 6-foot-5 frame and bear down on opposing batters. Solometo, like much of the generation of players born this century, embraces data and technology—he managed to do so even without the help of the Pirates' data scientists.

Robert Stephenson RHP Born: 02/24/93 Age: 30 Bats: R Throws: R Height: 6'3" Weight: 205 lb. Origin: Round 1, 2011 Draft (#27 overall)

YEAR	TEAM	LVL	AGE	W	L	SV	G	GS	IP	H	HR	BB/9	K/9	K	GB%	BABIP	WHIP	ERA	DRA-	WARP	MPH	FB%	Whiff%	CSP
2020	CIN	MLB	27	0	0	0	10	0	10	11	8	2.7	11.7	13	23.1%	.167	1.40	9.90	114	0.0	95.1	30.1%	39.5%	45.7%
2021	COL	MLB	28	2	1	1	49	0	46	42	5	3.5	10.2	52	37.6%	.311	1.30	3.13	91	0.6	96.7	49.4%	27.0%	54.9%
2022	PIT	MLB	29	0	1	0	13	0	13^{1}	10	2	0.7	12.1	18	23.3%	.296	0.83	3.38	84	0.2	96.8	28.2%	34.9%	58.4%
2022	COL	MLB	29	2	1	0	45	0	44^{2}	53	8	2.6	7.5	37	27.2%	.324	1.48	6.04	122	-0.1	97.0	53.6%	26.0%	55.3%
2023 DC	*PIT*	*MLB*	*30*	*3*	*3*	*0*	*67*	*0*	*58.3*	*54*	*8*	*3.0*	*8.0*	*51*	*32.4%*	*.281*	*1.26*	*3.74*	*98*	*0.3*	*96.5*	*45.8%*	*28.6%*	*53.5%*

Comparables: Jeanmar Gómez (61), Liam Hendriks (61), Tommy Hunter (57)

TO: Robert Stephenson
FROM: Pittsburgh Pirates, August 27, 2022

Avast, ye matey. Be prepared to undergo a harrowing journey from the mountains of Colorado to the shores of the Allegheny, Monongahela, and Ohio Rivers—it's time to join the brave Pirates of Pittsburgh lore. But batten down the hatches, me hearty, and be ye warned! Ye be entering a forlorn place filled with saddened hearts and many empty seats. But don't worry about the landlubbers or carousers filled with claps of thunder. Ye be joining the mightiest of seadogs on a one-month voyage that will take us to the beginning of October (but no further). For these Pirates aren't searching for booty or sunken treasure, but just looking to play out a baseball season without looking like we're trying to run a rig on the good people of Pittsburgh. Shiver Me Timbers! Every night is like a voyage through a lagoon of sadness, and even though we're standing on dry land it always feels like ye be walking the plank!

Zach Thompson RHP Born: 10/23/93 Age: 29 Bats: R Throws: R Height: 6'7" Weight: 250 lb. Origin: Round 5, 2014 Draft (#138 overall)

YEAR	TEAM	LVL	AGE	W	L	SV	G	GS	IP	H	HR	BB/9	K/9	K	GB%	BABIP	WHIP	ERA	DRA-	WARP	MPH	FB%	Whiff%	CSP
2021	JAX	AAA	27	0	0	1	8	0	15	22	4	1.2	12.6	21	33.3%	.439	1.60	6.60	88	0.3				
2021	MIA	MLB	27	3	7	0	26	14	75	63	6	3.4	7.9	66	42.2%	.273	1.21	3.24	97	0.8	90.0	70.2%	26.8%	52.3%
2022	PIT	MLB	28	3	10	0	29	22	121^{2}	138	19	3.4	6.7	90	45.0%	.309	1.51	5.18	124	-0.3	92.3	37.3%	23.9%	53.1%
2023 non-DC	*PIT*	*MLB*	*29*	*2*	*3*	*0*	*57*	*0*	*50*	*55*	*7*	*3.3*	*7.0*	*39*	*44.3%*	*.315*	*1.48*	*4.86*	*119*	*-0.3*	*91.6*	*47.2%*	*24.9%*	*52.9%*

Comparables: Alec Mills (61), Chasen Bradford (54), Brent Suter (53)

The Marlins' pitching depth allowed them to trade Thompson to the Pirates last winter as part of a package for Jacob Stallings, with the Bucs hoping the late-blooming starter would step right into their rotation without missing a beat. Instead, like a lot of transplants from Florida to the Northeast, he went ice-cold and never completely warmed up. Thompson's four-pitch assortment and excellent cut fastball never really worked in the Iron City, and a changeup that became a weapon in 2021 with severe vertical drop failed him, becoming far more hittable. Thompson was already a pitch-to-contact arm with very little margin for error, so he'll need to go back to the drawing board and conjure up another trick to be more than a long relief arm or spot starter for a team with multiple young, talented arms knocking on the door.

Vince Velasquez RHP Born: 06/07/92 Age: 31 Bats: R Throws: R Height: 6'3" Weight: 212 lb. Origin: Round 2, 2010 Draft (#58 overall)

YEAR	TEAM	LVL	AGE	W	L	SV	G	GS	IP	H	HR	BB/9	K/9	K	GB%	BABIP	WHIP	ERA	DRA-	WARP	MPH	FB%	Whiff%	CSP
2020	PHI	MLB	28	1	1	0	9	7	34	36	5	4.5	12.2	46	43.2%	.373	1.56	5.56	77	0.8	93.9	57.8%	26.8%	48.1%
2021	CLR	A	29	1	0	0	4	2	7	4	1	1.3	15.4	12	30.8%	.250	0.71	2.57	85	0.1				
2021	LHV	AAA	29	0	0	0	2	2	6^{2}	2	1	4.1	16.2	12	22.2%	.125	0.75	2.70	87	0.1				
2021	SD	MLB	29	0	3	0	4	4	12^{2}	15	6	2.8	11.4	16	17.1%	.310	1.50	8.53	94	0.2	93.5	51.3%	34.2%	55.2%
2021	PHI	MLB	29	3	6	0	21	17	81^{2}	76	17	5.0	9.4	85	34.4%	.282	1.48	5.95	110	0.4	93.3	55.7%	25.5%	54.1%
2022	CLT	AAA	30	0	0	0	4	0	5^{2}	5	0	6.4	11.1	7	40.0%	.333	1.59	4.76	93	0.1	93.6	45.0%	25.0%	
2022	CHW	MLB	30	3	3	0	27	9	75^{1}	68	11	3.0	8.2	69	35.9%	.270	1.23	4.78	106	0.5	93.4	52.3%	25.2%	55.7%
2023 DC	*PIT*	*MLB*	*31*	*9*	*9*	*0*	*52*	*22*	*132.3*	*127*	*20*	*3.7*	*9.2*	*135*	*36.0%*	*.300*	*1.37*	*4.41*	*109*	*0.4*	*93.5*	*56.1%*	*26.2%*	*53.0%*

Comparables: Pete Smith (64), Luke Hochevar (63), Don Cardwell (62)

As a kid, the family down the road owned a trampoline. You were so jealous, taking every opportunity to gently hint at an invite. What could be better than owning a trampoline? Just hours of fun bouncing around, sending your friends soaring. It's perfection, objectified. In your ignorance, you failed to notice the dead eyes of the trampoline owner. It was the bane of their existence. Countless ER trips and worries about neighbor kids—yeah, like you, you little brat—coming over and becoming a liability, and what the hell are you supposed to do with it when there's weather anyway? The White Sox saw Velasquez's unfulfilled promise in Philadelphia and, briefly, San Diego, and said "we want that!" There were no broken bones or ER trips, but just as teams have been learning for years, rostering a Velasquez is a lot cooler in theory than in practice.

LINEOUTS

Hitters

HITTER	POS	TEAM	LVL	AGE	PA	R	2B	3B	HR	RBI	BB	K	SB	CS	AVG/OBP/SLG	DRC+	BABIP	BRR	DRP	WARP
Greg Allen	OF	PIT	MLB	29	134	17	4	0	2	8	10	42	8	2	.186/.260/.271	72	.267	1.1	LF(23): 1.4, RF(13): 0.3, CF(11): -0.3	0.3
Zack Collins	1B/C	BUF	AAA	27	155	15	7	1	5	28	32	40	3	0	.195/.361/.398	104	.234	-0.9	1B(14): -0.8, C(12): 0.0	0.4
	1B/C	TOR	MLB	27	79	7	4	0	4	10	6	31	0	0	.194/.266/.417	75	.270	0.5	C(11): -0.6	0.0
	1B/C	PIT	MLB	27	29	2	0	0	0	1	3	10	0	0	.040/.138/.040	73	.063	-0.1	1B(8): 0	0.0
Jason Delay	C	IND	AAA	27	93	10	5	1	0	8	8	15	1	0	.220/.286/.305	96	.265	0.8	C(27): 1.9	0.5
	C	PIT	MLB	27	167	17	6	0	1	11	9	50	0	2	.213/.265/.271	66	.308	-0.5	C(57): 2.8	0.2
José Godoy	C	STP	AAA	27	151	13	5	0	3	14	13	41	0	0	.197/.272/.299	83	.258	-1.1	C(38): 8.4	0.9
	C	IND	AAA	27	42	7	1	0	3	12	1	7	0	0	.333/.357/.590	117	.333	1.1	C(10): 0.4	0.3
	C	PIT	MLB	27	17	1	0	0	0	1	0	7	0	0	.059/.059/.059	68	.100	0.0	C(8): -0.1	0.0
	C	MIN	MLB	27	5	2	0	0	0	0	2	2	0	0	.000/.400/.000	83			C(2): 0.1	0.0
Tyler Heineman	C	PIT	MLB	31	158	14	6	0	0	8	8	13	1	0	.211/.277/.254	97	.233	0.0	C(50): 5.7	1.1
	C	TOR	MLB	31	16	2	2	0	0	1	0	4	0	0	.267/.267/.400	94	.364	-0.1	C(9): -0.1	0.1
Malcom Nunez	1B	SPR	AA	21	350	51	11	0	17	66	48	71	4	2	.255/.360/.463	120	.278	-1.7	1B(68): -1.6, 3B(9): -0.8	0.9
	1B	ALT	AA	21	126	20	5	0	5	21	17	27	1	0	.286/.381/.476	115	.329	-1.5	1B(22): 0.7, 3B(2): 0.7	0.3
Kevin Padlo	IF	IND	AAA	25	96	15	7	0	1	15	9	31	3	0	.279/.344/.395	67	.418	1.1	3B(18): 0.2, 1B(2): 0.1, 2B(1): -0.1	0.2
	IF	TAC	AAA	25	161	18	6	1	4	20	18	41	7	2	.229/.323/.371	88	.292	1.0	3B(19): -2.3, 1B(16): -0.6, 2B(2): 0.4	0.3
	IF	SAC	AAA	25	87	16	3	1	7	16	5	18	3	0	.275/.333/.600	114	.273	0.5	3B(8): -0.6, 1B(7): -0.1, LF(6): -0.3	0.2
	IF	SF	MLB	25	12	0	0	0	0	0	0	4	0	0	.167/.167/.167	89	.250	0.5	3B(3): 0.1, 1B(1): 0	0.1
	IF	PIT	MLB	25	11	0	0	0	0	0	0	1	0	0	.000/.000/.000	105			3B(2): -0.3, 1B(1): -0.2	0.0
	IF	SEA	MLB	25	11	0	1	0	0	3	1	5	0	0	.200/.273/.300	82	.400	0.0	1B(5): 0	0.0
Roberto Pérez	C	PIT	MLB	33	69	8	2	0	2	8	9	25	0	0	.233/.333/.367	81	.364	-0.8	C(20): 1.2	0.1
Canaan Smith-Njigba	OF	IND	AAA	23	218	31	15	3	1	19	33	52	8	3	.277/.387/.408	103	.382	0.6	LF(27): 1.9, RF(13): 0.1, CF(7): -0.4	0.7
	OF	PIT	MLB	23	7	1	1	0	0	0	1	0	0	0	.200/.429/.400	96	.200	0.5	LF(2): 0.3	0.1
Josh VanMeter	IF	IND	AAA	27	38	6	2	0	1	3	7	10	0	1	.161/.316/.323	100	.200	0.2	2B(5): -0.4, 1B(1): 0.5	0.1
	IF	PIT	MLB	27	192	15	5	2	3	14	19	45	4	0	.187/.266/.292	80	.232	0.3	2B(39): -0.3, 1B(21): 0.5	0.1
Ryan Vilade	OF	ABQ	AAA	23	430	64	15	4	5	38	52	69	10	6	.249/.345/.352	93	.291	0.7	RF(64): -2.3, LF(20): 1.2, CF(13): 0.3	1.4

Multiple hamstring injuries kept **Greg Allen** out of action for the first half of the season. He's overexposed as a starting outfielder, but on a Pirates team with few appealing options he got to show off his good glove, steal some bases and be living, breathing proof of the adage that you cannot steal first. ⓫ At 6-foot-5 and 230 pounds, **Tony Blanco Jr.** gets the obligatory "hulking slugger" moniker attached to him whenever he is mentioned. Signed for $900K on international signing day last year, Blanco made his professional debut in the Dominican Summer League in an eight-game trial. ⓫ A former top catching prospect who hasn't worked out on either side of the ball, **Zack Collins** donned the tools of ignorance at two minor-league levels last year, in four cities and two countries. A precipitously high whiff rate and subpar framing skills are a double whammy that have, thus far, been too much for him to overcome. ⓫ **Jason Delay** was drafted on the strength of defense, made it through the minor-league ranks on the strength of his defense, and made his major-league debut last year for his…you guessed it, defense. It should come as no surprise, then, that his offense is about as scintillating as reading an appliance instruction manual. ⓫ Even accounting for the de-emphasis of offensive contributions from behind the plate, **José Godoy** still doesn't contribute nearly enough as a hitter to be anything more than a temporary fill-in and Triple-A insurance policy. ⓫ The Pirates openly praised **Tyler Heineman**'s defense and game-calling abilities behind the plate, but his advanced age and lack of offensive prowess make him more of a temporary stopgap than a long-term solution at catcher. ⓫ **Malcom Nunez's** defensive limitations mean his future is either at DH or as a career minor leaguer. Thankfully for him, the bat is good enough that it might play in the majors—and a midseason trade to the Pirates last year made the glidepath much more accessible. ⓫ **Kevin Padlo** is a good minor-league hitter who hasn't been able to make the final leap to the majors. He has reached the point of his career where he's a popular waiver claim, but is still hoping for an extended opportunity. ⓫ Signed to a one-year, $5 million deal to replace Jacob Stallings last winter, **Roberto Pérez** blew out his hamstring in early May after 69 solid-if-unspectacular plate appearances and missed the remainder of the season. You could say this was the most Pirates thing ever, except there were, as always, oh-so-many things to choose from. ⓫ Bigger isn't always better. **Canaan Smith-Njigba's** thick and powerful upper body should theoretically lead to big-time power outcomes, but instead his hulking size has produced a stiff swing, imbalance and a propensity to hit hard grounders. He was nevertheless promoted to the majors, only to have a wrist injury end his season after three games. ⓫ A cerebral student of the art of hitting, **Josh VanMeter** has been unable to translate his knowledge of the craft into on-field results at the major-league level for any sustainable amount of time. ⓫ The Rockies kept waiting for **Ryan Vilade** to turn into a viable backup outfielder, but he stalled out at Triple-A the last two seasons. He now belongs to Pittsburgh, where there's no such thing as too little production if it comes with a very low price tag.

Pitchers

PITCHER	TEAM	LVL	AGE	W	L	SV	G	GS	IP	H	HR	BB/9	K/9	K	GB%	BABIP	WHIP	ERA	DRA-	WARP	MPH	FB%	WHF	CSP
Cam Alldred	IND	AAA	25	3	3	1	42	2	66^1	66	5	3.4	8.4	62	47.9%	.324	1.37	4.07	94	1.1	88.2	56.5%	50.0%	
	PIT	MLB	25	0	0	0	1	0	1	1	0	0.0	9.0	1	66.7%	.333	1.00	0.00	79	0.0	86.4	50.0%	12.5%	66.0%
Manny Bañuelos	SWB	AAA	31	0	2	0	7	5	30^2	22	0	3.5	8.8	30	46.2%	.275	1.11	2.35	99	0.4				
	PIT	MLB	31	2	1	0	31	0	32^2	25	2	5.0	9.4	34	49.4%	.280	1.32	4.96	92	0.5	93.6	39.3%	28.8%	53.7%
	NYY	MLB	31	0	0	1	4	0	8^1	7	0	3.2	8.6	8	62.5%	.292	1.20	2.16	98	0.1	94.0	50.0%	25.0%	52.9%
Jeremy Beasley	BUF	AAA	26	2	1	1	19	3	38	20	5	2.6	10.2	43	29.5%	.181	0.82	1.89	88	0.7				
	TOR	MLB	26	0	0	0	9	0	15	14	4	3.0	11.4	19	28.9%	.294	1.27	4.80	92	0.2	95.5	61.3%	29.2%	50.6%
Chase De Jong	IND	AAA	28	1	0	0	3	2	13	7	0	3.5	13.2	19	30.8%	.269	0.92	2.08	81	0.3				
	PIT	MLB	28	6	3	1	42	0	71^2	52	10	3.8	7.4	59	32.8%	.225	1.14	2.64	111	0.3	93.0	46.8%	25.2%	55.9%
Yerry De Los Santos	IND	AAA	24	2	0	3	12	0	15^2	8	1	1.1	11.5	20	58.3%	.206	0.64	1.72	77	0.4	95.3	70.8%	21.7%	
	PIT	MLB	24	0	3	3	26	0	25^2	22	3	3.9	9.1	26	52.1%	.275	1.29	4.91	92	0.4	95.4	60.1%	21.3%	47.9%
Jarlín García	SF	MLB	29	1	4	1	58	0	65	60	10	2.5	7.8	56	38.5%	.273	1.20	3.74	98	0.7	93.8	42.9%	25.1%	56.8%
Max Kranick	IND	AAA	24	0	1	0	3	2	6^2	5	2	2.7	5.4	4	39.1%	.143	1.05	2.70	104	0.1				
	PIT	MLB	24	0	0	0	2	0	5	3	0	5.4	7.2	4	25.0%	.250	1.20	0.00	108	0.0	95.3	52.6%	28.1%	41.1%
Dauri Moreta	LOU	AAA	26	3	4	1	28	0	27^1	31	6	4.0	9.2	28	30.4%	.352	1.57	3.95	108	0.2				
	CIN	MLB	26	0	2	1	35	1	38^1	32	10	3.1	9.2	39	32.7%	.234	1.17	5.40	97	0.4	96.3	55.3%	27.7%	54.1%
Dillon Peters	IND	AAA	29	0	0	0	5	0	7^2	5	0	3.5	8.2	7	33.3%	.238	1.04	1.17	103	0.1				
	PIT	MLB	29	5	2	0	22	4	39^1	35	5	3.9	5.9	26	41.8%	.259	1.32	4.58	123	-0.1	92.9	50.3%	20.1%	53.9%
Yohan Ramirez	TAC	AAA	27	0	1	0	4	0	6	8	2	1.5	10.5	7	52.6%	.353	1.50	9.00	84	0.1	95.3	45.5%	31.2%	
	IND	AAA	27	1	0	0	5	0	5^1	1	0	3.4	6.8	4	69.2%	.077	0.56	0.00	94	0.1				
	COL	AAA	27	1	0	0	11	0	10^1	3	0	8.7	11.3	13	61.1%	.167	1.26	4.35	93	0.2				
	PIT	MLB	27	3	1	1	22	0	27	22	1	4.3	7.0	21	54.4%	.276	1.30	3.67	112	0.1	96.0	75.8%	18.2%	54.3%
	SEA	MLB	27	1	0	0	7	0	8^1	7	3	6.5	10.8	10	18.2%	.211	1.56	7.56	102	0.1	94.3	44.9%	41.7%	53.3%
	CLE	MLB	27	0	0	0	1	0	2	3	0	4.5	4.5	1	50.0%	.375	2.00	4.50	102	0.0	95.6	72.5%	0.0%	53.8%
Duane Underwood Jr.	PIT	MLB	27	1	6	1	51	1	57^1	58	1	3.9	8.9	57	50.0%	.333	1.45	4.40	93	0.8	95.8	36.7%	27.4%	54.5%
Cam Vieaux	IND	AAA	28	5	1	2	35	1	50	37	7	2.7	8.5	47	43.0%	.238	1.04	3.06	88	1.0	92.6	57.7%	8.3%	
	PIT	MLB	28	0	0	0	8	0	8^2	15	2	5.2	15.6	15	26.9%	.542	2.31	10.38	77	0.2	93.1	45.2%	24.7%	56.6%
Nathan Webb	NWA	AA	24	0	2	1	20	0	26^1	43	4	6.8	10.3	30	42.9%	.448	2.39	9.57	110	0.0				

"Funky left-hander who people do not take good swings at" isn't a 1930s B-movie palooka, but rather how Pirates manager Derek Shelton described **Cam Alldred**, a soft-tossing southpaw who spent most of last season in Indianapolis dominating Triple-A. Here's hoping his career turns out better than a Wallace Beery wrestling picture. ⚾ **Manny Bañuelos** found his way back to the majors after a two-year international journey that followed him from Taipei to Monterrey. He found a couple of extra ticks on his fastball, but was nevertheless more of a back-end bullpen piece than a vital cog. Still, his next major-league assignment won't require such extensive wanderings. ⚾ A prototypical big college southpaw, **Hunter Barco** underwent Tommy John surgery last May—but that didn't deter the Pirates from drafting him in the second round and adding him to the fold with a $1.525 million signing bonus. He's expected to make his professional debut later this season. ⚾ **Jeremy Beasley** impressively added four miles per hour to his heater and even managed to keep the walks in check, but his pitches had more Elevation than a U2 singles release party in the early 2000s. Unless this improves, like the seminal Irish band Beasley will be Stuck in a Moment (He) Can't Get Out Of (the minors). ⚾ **Chase De Jong** isn't the title character of an international spy thriller, but a fly-ball pitcher who spent years living around the periphery—of both the strike zone and the majors. Prior to last year, his luggage had more tags on it than James Bond's, but he settled in for the Bucs as a low-leverage, middle-relief arm. ⚾ It's too bad Kevin Kramer announced his retirement, because the Pirates could have had a (Kevin) Newman, a Kramer and a **Yerry De Los Santos.** The hard-throwing reliever briefly looked like a top back-end bullpen option, before a shoulder strain sidelined him in August. ⚾ After two years of standout success in San Francisco, **Jarlín García** went back to his changeup heavier ways at the expense of his slider. It wasn't a successful tweak, but after back-to-back years of 65+ innings, the reliable García signed on with the Pirates. ⚾ A present-day starter who might eventually become a future reliever, **Max Kranick** underwent Tommy John surgery last June, making him more of a far-future reliever (cue images of flying cars, teleportation and warp-speed travel). ⚾ **Dauri Moreta** throws a seriously wicked slider—he's induced whiffs on almost half of sliders swung at in his short major-league career—but he doesn't throw it nearly enough, only 23.5% of the time in 2022. He's not in Kansas anymore when throwing a fastball or changeup, though; he either needs to modify his pitch mix, or find another offering he can get past hitters. ⚾ **Dillon Peters** is an artist—not a folk singer from the 1960s, like his name might suggest, but a contemporary control specialist. He doesn't ply his trade with a guitar, but with a baseball and an array of junk that would make fellow junk artist Nik Gentry proud. ⚾ Lots of velocity and an infectiously winning smile and attitude weren't nearly enough to compensate for **Yohan Ramirez's** lack of command. That and the lack of a second workable pitch sent the middle reliever on a journey across three big-league squads in 2022 before he ultimately stuck in Pittsburgh. ⚾ **Duane Underwood Jr.** doesn't have a dominant pitch, but keeps hitters off-balanced with a four-pitch arsenal—including a cutter he added last year. He settled in as a reliable back-end reliever for the Pirates; his greatest value lies in an ability to eat innings. ⚾ **Cam Vieaux** might have just pitched the only 8⅔ innings of his major-league career—but for a guy who spent all of 2020 coaching through the pandemic layoff, that's far from nothing. He was outrighted in September and elected free agency in October. ⚾ A member of the Royals' grounds crew as a high schooler, **Nathan Webb** was DFA'd in November, meaning his days spent raking the infield as a teenager should be the most time he spends in Kauffman Stadium. A strong AFL showing earned him a minors deal and invite to spring training from the Pirates.

ST. LOUIS CARDINALS

Essay by Kelsey McKinney

Player comments by Tony Wolfe and BP staff

There were three Cardinals moments during the 2022 season that will remain branded in the veins on the back of my eyeballs for decades to come. The lost Wild Card games will evaporate from my memory before the first pitch is thrown in April. As will, sadly, the 423-foot homer that Tyler O'Neill rocketed out of the field off of A.J. Minter. The end-of-season push that the Cardinals have made their yearly habit, too, will fade. These are the moments that baseball is made of, but they won't be the ones I remember. Because last year, the St. Louis Cardinals were stealthily one of the silliest teams in baseball.

It is easy to forget that Major League Baseball is a game. There's a seriousness and a reverence that comes with the playoffs and lingers over the winter break. Most people, normal people with normal brains, might forget all of the ridiculous tiny things that happened in the 162 games before the playoffs began. There were so many huge, gigantic swings, so many slippery stolen bases, so many swiftly turned double plays and diving outfield catches and strikes that hung just on the edge of the strike zone for just long enough that the batter didn't even look at the umpire before racking his bat on his shoulder and turning back to the dugout. But those are moments for someone else to remember. Because the ones I want to commemorate in this book—to print out to be remembered—are far, far stupider than that. Baseball is silly. These deserve memorialization, too.

All three important moments feature, front and center, his big smile gleaming under the bright midwest sun, Albert Pujols. In 2023, the Cardinals will need to find a new protagonist, a new place to center the story of their season, because in the last of the legendary first baseman's 22 seasons, everything else fell away.

⚾ ⚾ ⚾

The first moment came so early in the season. It was April 14, 2022. The sun was falling fast, a dark deep shadow crossing from the third-base umpire on the foul line sharp and straight into center-left field. Paul DeJong in the batter's box was drenched in a separate darkness that stretched up the first-base line. Between the two deep shadows, a

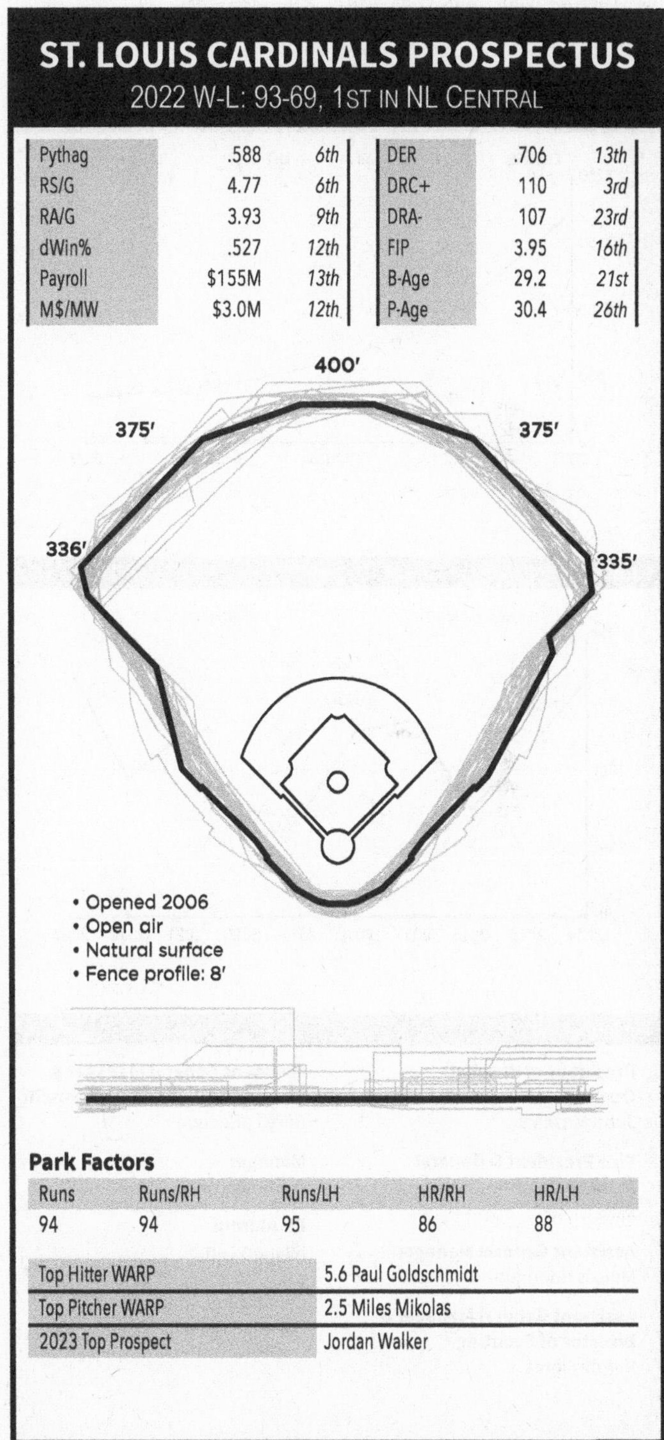

ST. LOUIS CARDINALS PROSPECTUS

2022 W-L: 93-69, 1ST IN NL CENTRAL

Pythag	.588	6th	DER	.706	13th
RS/G	4.77	6th	DRC+	110	3rd
RA/G	3.93	9th	DRA-	107	23rd
dWin%	.527	12th	FIP	3.95	16th
Payroll	$155M	13th	B-Age	29.2	21st
M$/MW	$3.0M	12th	P-Age	30.4	26th

- Opened 2006
- Open air
- Natural surface
- Fence profile: 8'

Park Factors

Runs	Runs/RH	Runs/LH	HR/RH	HR/LH
94	94	95	86	88

Top Hitter WARP	5.6 Paul Goldschmidt
Top Pitcher WARP	2.5 Miles Mikolas
2023 Top Prospect	Jordan Walker

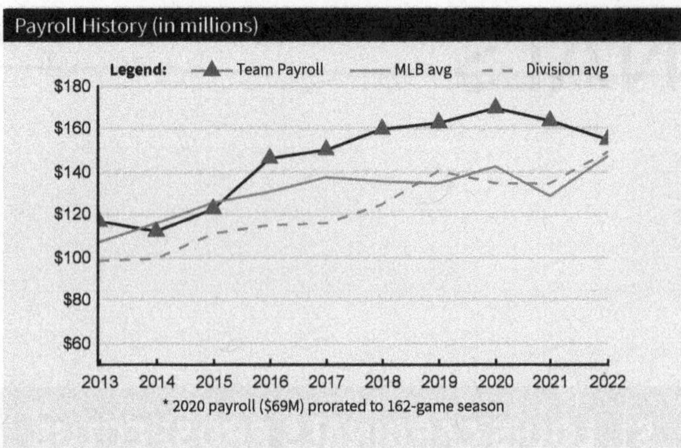

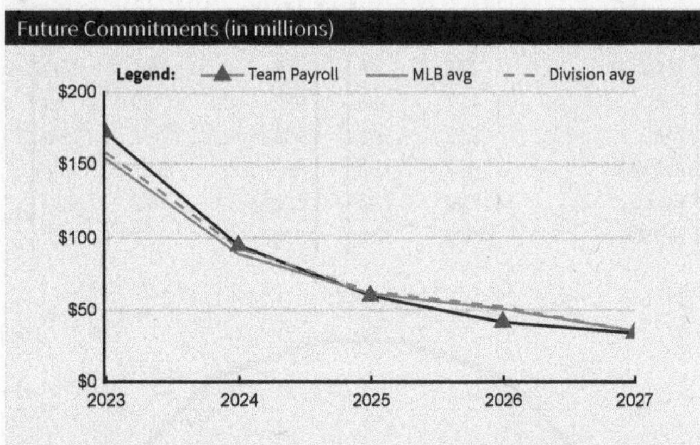

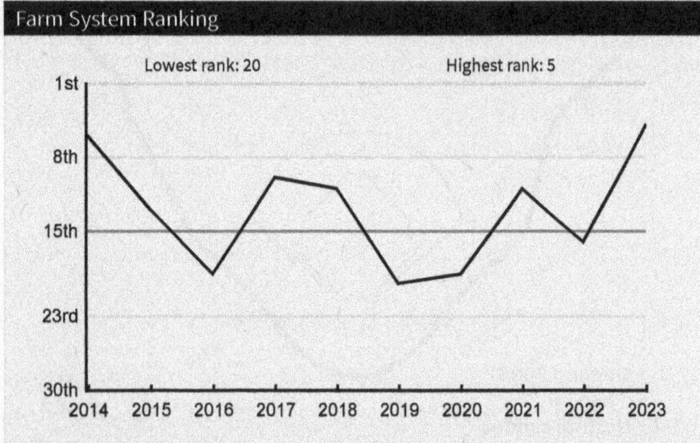

Personnel

President of Baseball Operations
John Mozeliak

Vice President & General Manager
Mike Girsch

Assistant General Manager
Moisés Rodriguez

Assistant General Manager & Director of Scouting
Randy Flores

Assistant General Manager & Director of Player Development
Gary LaRocque

Manager
Oliver Marmol

BP Alumni
Keanan Lamb
Zach Mortimer
Christopher Rodriguez
Mauricio Rubio

hatching pattern appeared across the infield, the sun stark and cold in some places, striped through with darkness projected from the edge of the stadium. The Cardinals were playing the Brewers. The count was 2-1 with one out. Brandon Woodruff was pitching, and on second base stood Albert Pujols.

He was alone out there, a runner in scoring position in an unimportant moment. It was only the top of the second, and the Cardinals were only down one run. There was absolutely no reasonable world in which 42-year-old Albert Pujols should have been given the signal to steal, and yet there he went, lumbering down the baseline, half-heartedly sliding into the tag way ahead of him at third base. The pitch never even made it out of Woodruff's hand. The Brewers pitcher glanced back and second, saw Albert Pujols shuffling down the line, and soft-tossed it right to the third baseman.

Albert Pujols! Stealing! At 42! For no reason! It was doomed to fail and yet here he had gone, risking it! Certainly, the Brewers did not expect it. Perhaps the only element he had on his side was surprise, but that's not nothing. As he trotted into the dugout after being called out, "I don't know what Pujols was thinking there," the announcer said on the broadcast, "It doesn't get much easier than that." And it would be easy to believe him if I hadn't watched this replay 500 times, watched the plodding Pujols put his head down as he ran, and the pitcher overthrow his soft toss to third so badly that the third baseman had to leap into the air, his glove well above the third base bag, and sweep it down. It was only an easy play because Pujols isn't fast. But you can see, if you watch the replay again and again and again, a mild glimmer in his eye. Sometimes, believing something is impossible is the first step to letting the hope of possibility sneak stealthily in.

In a May contest against the Mets, Pujols would successfully steal second. It was his 117th career stolen base. As the announcers explained that the Cardinals wanted to get Pujols into the lineup tonight even though he doesn't hit Scherzer well, the man took off! You can see Scherzer, who is already in motion toward the plate, jerk his head back at the sound of the roaring crowd. Pujols showed no emotion atop second base safely, but in the batter's box, Yadier Molina—another old-timer beating the odds for one last summer—laughed. That day, Pujols' sprint speed was 22.9 feet per second, putting him in the slowest one percent of baseball players and dead last among all players who were not catchers. He knew he was slow. Everyone on that field knew he was slow. It didn't matter. He stood on second base, clocking his 21st of 22 seasons with a successful stolen base.

This was his retirement season, and though Pujols' eyes were always glued on the 700 home-run list, here was something funnier, a little proof that he was enjoying himself, a little "why the hell not?" as a treat.

The second moment I will remember until my death happened that same April week. In a Sunday night game against the Giants, with a huge lead, the Cardinals sent designated hitter Albert Pujols out to the pitcher's mound for the first time in his 22-year career. With his socks high, and his knee covered in dirt, Pujols lobbed the ball to the catcher. The entire stadium stood for him, their smiles so wide you can see them easily on the television, their phones out and pointed toward him, their eyes huge. The Cardinals' bench pressed themselves against the barricade, not one of them seated, laughing to each other. He walked the first batter. Of course he did!

The announcers laughed, questioning whose idea it could be. Pujols' seventh pitch, a strike, set the crowd roaring. Even Giants fans in the stands clapped. Soon after, he recorded his first out. When Evan Longoria hit the ball into left field for a single, he demanded the ball be sent to the dugout as a keepsake. The inning went on for a bit. A double-play ball was outrun by the hitter, and Pujols fist-pumped just a little too early. Even on re-watches, his energy is contagious. He smacks his gum. His grin is bigger than the St. Louis arch, and everyone on the teams and in the stands beams back at him. He gives up a homer to a pitcher, sure. And on the mound, he laughs and laughs. Another homer? Whatever! Leave him out there!

Every time I watch the 10-minute clip of this inning, with its messy pitches and hanging fastballs, my heart grows a size. This is what a retirement season should be. This is what sports should be. There is no reason, up by 13 runs, not to let a guy take a victory lap stand on the mound, let him feel everything that rushes through you when you give up a homer, and pump his fist for the final out. It's the kind of celebration that every great player deserves, but very few get.

It is so rare in any sport, to take a victory lap and feel good at the end of it. It is incredibly difficult to exit well, to retire from a sport you have loved and lived for 22 years at just the right time. "It's my last year and I want to go out with my best. And my best is winning a championship," Pujols said. He didn't get that, obviously. The Cardinals were knocked out of the playoffs early, making them 1-9 in their last 10 postseason games with three straight Wild Card round exits. But maybe these fun, strange moments scattered throughout the season, always full of joy and life, are a better way to say goodbye?

That pitching outing in May, of course, was not the biggest celebration Albert Pujols would get, not even close to the fireworks and praise and glory that came later. To get to the final moment I'll remember, we must first flash back to that big swing, the huge 700th swing.

⚾ ⚾ ⚾

There is a version of history in which we never get to see Albert Pujols step into the box in the top of the fourth against the Dodgers and make that exclusive list. Just before the postseason, reports emerged that Pujols had considered retiring in June, when he had a .425 OPS. It was a simple fix that saved his season and allowed him to hit well again: adjusting the way he held the bat. How many teams could encourage and convince a 42-year-old player to try something new, to stick it out just a little longer? After the All-Star break, Pujols' OPS climbed to 1.105, and the Cardinals' winning percentage rose 100 points to .632. That doesn't happen because one player goes on a hot streak. It happens because a team rallies. Is it any wonder, then, that the Cardinals have been able to turn out homegrown talent like Juan Yepez or Lars Nootbar?

It was the top of the fourth, facing the Dodgers. Tragically, the game was not at home, but the crowd stood for Pujols anyway. They watched him watch the first pitch, a strike from Phil Bickford. Runners on first and second. They watched him watch the second, a ball. The third pitch, dangerously inside, would not survive. His hands are so fast you barely see them before he is slinging the bat onto the ground behind him, leaving the box slowly, his face upturned toward left field where the ball has become a missile, the echo of the crack just fading as it falls into the crowd. Seven hundred home runs: an elite, count-on-one-hand club. Pujols was inducted for his tenacity, for staying to finish it, for still, 22 years into a career, having a swing young batters would kill for.

His beaming face as he rounds the bases will be replayed forever, his gold necklace bouncing wildly as he trots. Everyone will remember how he throws his arms open for his teammates, embraces them tightly as the Dodgers players clap from their various defensive positions. There to greet him were the members of the team who supported him the whole way, players who in any other year, in any other season, might dominate this whole essay themselves. Nolan Arenado and Paul Goldschmidt both had stunning, MVP-quality seasons. Even Molina—who also pitched in the same game as Pujols, retired this year, and was a joy to watch each game—is hard to focus on when you have a man like Pujols rounding those bases. It's almost unfair that this very talented Cardinals team faded so quickly from my memory. But I do remember the clapping. I remember their support. I remember how even Bickford, who gave up the home run, told the press that it was a very special moment, that he could appreciate Pujols' greatness, even at his own expense. History, after all, deserves to be applauded. But that's not how I'll remember that final moment: The moment that lingers is one we didn't get to see.

After that hit, that monumental moment, Pujols went into the tunnel to be alone. Cardinals manager Oliver Marmol saw him crouched there, his head in his hands. "It was just him realizing all that he had accomplished, and it was pretty damn cool," he told MLB.com. Pujols shared so many massive moments with baseball fans, checked almost literally every box one could on the field with them. "It did hit me really hard, because I had felt that weight to deliver for everyone," Pujols told MLB.com. All season, fans got to absorb as much of his legendary play as they could. But in the biggest moment, the one that mattered the most to the history books and perhaps Pujols himself, he relished in the victory alone just as fully.

⚾ ⚾ ⚾

The moments I want to remember from the 2022 St. Louis season are ones that force me to remember how fun and beautiful and affirming this game can be, how well players can be treated and how great they can become. If Pujols' return to St. Louis was initially assumed to be a bit of a nostalgia trip, Pujols rejected that assumption from the beginning. He wanted to do it all, to feel it all, to play every hit, a veritable Vegas residency of a homecoming, a shimmering perfect cap on an incredible career. He got to go out on his terms, with an indelible reminder of his ability. But I want to remember him for that big smile on the field, for the reminder at every turn that baseball can be deeply, truly, fun. ■

—Kelsey McKinney is a writer and co-owner of Defector.

Hitters

Nolan Arenado 3B

Born: 04/16/91 Age: 32 Bats: R Throws: R Height: 6'2" Weight: 215 lb. Origin: Round 2, 2009 Draft (#59 overall)

YEAR	TEAM	LVL	AGE	PA	R	2B	3B	HR	RBI	BB	K	SB	CS	Whiff%	AVG/OBP/SLG	DRC+	BABIP	BRR	DRP	WARP
2020	COL	MLB	29	201	23	9	0	8	26	15	20	0	0	17.9%	.253/.303/.434	115	.241	0.4	3B(48): 4.8	1.4
2021	STL	MLB	30	653	81	34	3	34	105	50	96	2	0	18.5%	.255/.312/.494	120	.249	1.1	3B(155): 6.7	4.6
2022	STL	MLB	31	620	73	42	1	30	103	52	72	5	3	19.1%	.293/.358/.533	142	.290	-0.7	3B(131): 11.1	5.7
2023 DC	*STL*	*MLB*	*32*	*619*	*81*	*32*	*1*	*31*	*95*	*50*	*78*	*3*	*1*	*18.9%*	*.281/.343/.513*	*141*	*.277*	*0.6*	*3B 3*	*4.8*

Comparables: Brooks Robinson (85), Ron Santo (84), Aramis Ramirez (82)

Arenado is an ethereal defender by any standard: the eye test, DRP, our older fielding metrics, everyone else's fielding metrics. The winner of six consecutive NL Platinum Gloves—that's the best defender at any position in the league—his defense has been good enough throughout his career that merely above-average offensive seasons would place him in the MVP conversation. So when he ends up being one of the three or four best hitters in the league, it requires a very strong showing by one of his peers for him to be overshadowed.

As great as his season was, Arenado declined the opportunity to test the free market as a 31-year-old nevertheless at the height of his powers, accepting the remaining five years and $144 million left on his deal with St. Louis. It is the kind of move the Cardinals fans gush over, seeming proof of the ineffable draw of the franchise. Some more cause for future gloating: Between Arenado and Goldschmidt the corners of the Cardinals' infield are pretty well settled for the foreseeable future, and the two veterans should play an important role in molding the next generation of prospects as they mature into big leaguers.

Leonardo Bernal C

Born: 02/13/04 Age: 19 Bats: S Throws: R Height: 6'0" Weight: 200 lb.

YEAR	TEAM	LVL	AGE	PA	R	2B	3B	HR	RBI	BB	K	SB	CS	Whiff%	AVG/OBP/SLG	DRC+	BABIP	BRR	DRP	WARP
2021	DSL CARB	ROK	17	178	23	9	1	5	29	17	28	3	1		.209/.298/.373		.224			
2022	PMB	A	18	171	22	8	1	7	29	12	32	1	1	29.2%	.256/.316/.455	120	.280	-0.5	C(37): 3.5	1.2
2023 non-DC	*STL*	*MLB*	*19*	*251*	*20*	*9*	*1*	*4*	*23*	*12*	*73*	*1*	*1*	*33.8%*	*.224/.269/.337*	*64*	*.306*	*1.0*	*C 0*	*-0.1*

YEAR	TEAM	P. COUNT	FRM RUNS	BLK RUNS	THRW RUNS	TOT RUNS
2022	PMB	4875	4.0	-0.2	-0.2	3.7
2023	*STL*	*6956*	*-3.1*	*-0.3*	*-0.1*	*-3.5*

Bernal's $680,000 bonus made him the biggest-money signing of the Cardinals' 2021 IFA class. They've been concordantly aggressive with the switch-hitting backstop, pushing him to full-season ball last year, where he performed admirably as an 18-year-old. He's a stronger hitter from the left side of the plate, and showed the ability to provide better-than-average exit velocities in the Florida State League. Even from his stronger side, there is more in-zone swing-and-miss than ideal at present. There's a long way to go between the low minors and the majors—but that axiom cuts both ways (fitting for a switch-hitter), as catchers have weird development paths, especially on the offensive side of things. Behind the dish, Bernal is a good receiver with quiet hands whose only significant flaw is fringe arm strength, which he covers for by being quick on the transfer. There's a lot of upside in this profile, but Iván Herrera looms as both a reasonable outcome and a caution against getting too invested this early.

Alec Burleson LF

Born: 11/25/98 Age: 24 Bats: L Throws: L Height: 6'2" Weight: 212 lb. Origin: Round 2, 2020 Draft (#70 overall)

YEAR	TEAM	LVL	AGE	PA	R	2B	3B	HR	RBI	BB	K	SB	CS	Whiff%	AVG/OBP/SLG	DRC+	BABIP	BRR	DRP	WARP
2021	PEO	A+	22	49	8	1	0	4	10	6	15	1	0		.286/.367/.595	121	.333	-0.3	LF(7): 0.1, RF(3): -0.4	0.2
2021	SPR	AA	22	282	34	10	0	14	44	19	59	2	0		.288/.333/.488	113	.321	-0.7	RF(54): -1.9, 1B(1): -0.1, LF(1): 0.0	1.0
2021	MEM	AAA	22	172	19	7	0	4	22	17	27	0	1		.234/.310/.357	106	.260	-0.4	LF(21): -4.2, RF(18): 3.0	0.5
2022	MEM	AAA	23	470	68	25	1	20	87	29	67	4	0	24.8%	.331/.372/.532	121	.350	1.6	LF(71): 0.2, RF(5): -0.8	2.8
2022	STL	MLB	23	53	4	1	0	1	3	5	9	1	0	25.0%	.188/.264/.271	98	.211	0.0	RF(9): -0.2, 1B(6): 0.3, LF(2): 0.1	0.2
2023 DC	*STL*	*MLB*	*24*	*96*	*10*	*3*	*0*	*2*	*10*	*6*	*18*	*0*	*0*	*24.0%*	*.268/.316/.413*	*104*	*.311*	*0.1*	*LF 0*	*0.3*

Stuck as a corner outfielder (and occasional first baseman) defensively, it's going to be all about the bat for Burleson. So far, so good on that front—aside from a rough big-league debut. He's got a bit of a short, uppercut hack early in counts, but will opt for contact over power once he gets to two strikes, which is why his strikeout rate hasn't been overly problematic. Burleson isn't going to be a classic power-first profile from the outfield corners—and won't add much at any position—but he's got just enough in terms of both contact and pop to make it work. He's in a bit of a crowded situation in St. Louis, but he has all the traits of the "annoying Cardinal who burns white-hot for two months" profile, so don't lose track of him.

Dylan Carlson OF

Born: 10/23/98 Age: 24 Bats: S Throws: L Height: 6'2" Weight: 205 lb. Origin: Round 1, 2016 Draft (#33 overall)

YEAR	TEAM	LVL	AGE	PA	R	2B	3B	HR	RBI	BB	K	SB	CS	Whiff%	AVG/OBP/SLG	DRC+	BABIP	BRR	DRP	WARP
2020	STL	MLB	21	119	11	7	1	3	16	8	35	1	1	31.0%	.200/.252/.364	81	.260	-0.6	RF(18): 0.1, CF(17): 0.6, LF(10): 1.6	0.2
2021	STL	MLB	22	619	79	31	4	18	65	57	152	2	1	27.9%	.266/.343/.437	101	.332	1.9	RF(87): 4.5, CF(60): 0.6, LF(9): -0.4	2.9
2022	STL	MLB	23	488	56	30	4	8	42	45	94	5	2	25.7%	.236/.316/.380	96	.281	1.5	CF(73): -0.1, RF(62): 0.5	1.6
2023 DC	*STL*	*MLB*	*24*	*597*	*73*	*29*	*4*	*17*	*61*	*56*	*127*	*5*	*2*	*25.5%*	*.255/.335/.429*	*114*	*.304*	*1.7*	*CF -3, RF 0*	*2.6*

Comparables: Byron Buxton (64), Lastings Milledge (59), Melvin Nieves (58)

Fans and projection systems alike tend to envision player development as a pretty linear process, but that isn't always the case. Take Carlson, for example. At 22, he held a league-average batting line in his first full big-league season while nearing 20 homers. It was only natural for Busch Stadium faithful to expect a big step forward the following year; instead, his home run total was cut in half, while his walk rate regressed and his base-stealing inclinations were a non-factor.

There were gains elsewhere, though. Carlson trimmed his whiff rate, a positive sign that he's not struggling to adjust to major-league pitching. He also took over as the team's center fielder following the injury (and eventual trade) of Harrison Bader and looked quite solid there, despite expectations that he's best suited for a corner. This is still a very young man for someone entering his fourth year of big-league action. That could mean everything or nothing, but you're welcome to dream big.

Willson Contreras C/DH

Born: 05/13/92 Age: 31 Bats: R Throws: R Height: 6'1" Weight: 225 lb. Origin: International Free Agent, 2009

YEAR	TEAM	LVL	AGE	PA	R	2B	3B	HR	RBI	BB	K	SB	CS	Whiff%	AVG/OBP/SLG	DRC+	BABIP	BRR	DRP	WARP
2020	CHC	MLB	28	225	37	10	0	7	26	20	57	1	2	33.7%	.243/.356/.407	109	.307	0.6	C(41): 3.7	1.4
2021	CHC	MLB	29	483	61	20	0	21	57	52	138	5	4	34.6%	.237/.340/.438	101	.298	1.7	C(116): -1.9	2.1
2022	CHC	MLB	30	487	65	23	2	22	55	45	103	4	2	31.2%	.243/.349/.466	126	.270	-1.5	C(72): -2.2	2.7
2023 DC	*STL*	*MLB*	*31*	*601*	*73*	*25*	*1*	*22*	*71*	*57*	*143*	*4*	*2*	*31.1%*	*.240/.341/.426*	*119*	*.287*	*0.8*	*C -4*	*2.9*

Comparables: John Romano (78), Victor Martinez (74), Geovany Soto (72)

YEAR	TEAM	P. COUNT	FRM RUNS	BLK RUNS	THRW RUNS	TOT RUNS
2020	CHC	5378	3.4	0.0	0.0	3.4
2021	CHC	15657	-7.0	0.7	1.4	-4.9
2022	CHC	10500	-2.5	-0.2	0.1	-2.5
2023	*STL*	*14430*	*-6.0*	*0.3*	*0.4*	*-5.4*

"And there goes Willson," Cubs broadcaster Pat Hughes remarked—over a standing ovation—as a pinch-runner replaced Contreras in the club's final home game of the season. After the game, Contreras was the last to leave the field, looking up at the crowd and waving like he was looking through a window into the past one last time. Anybody who thinks catchers aren't supposed to be your biggest offensive threat, and therefore parting with a backstop who mashes is no big deal, hasn't fully comprehended what Contreras did in Chicago. Even at the end of the road, the 30-year-old edged out Ian Happ to lead the team in OBP and SLG. His exit will create holes for Jed Hoyer to fill, not just behind the plate but in the middle of the lineup. But the Cubs are still in the part of their rebuild where people cry and leave town forever, so maybe on that afternoon, no one was thinking about a replacement.

Paul DeJong SS

Born: 08/02/93 Age: 29 Bats: R Throws: R Height: 6'0" Weight: 205 lb. Origin: Round 4, 2015 Draft (#131 overall)

YEAR	TEAM	LVL	AGE	PA	R	2B	3B	HR	RBI	BB	K	SB	CS	Whiff%	AVG/OBP/SLG	DRC+	BABIP	BRR	DRP	WARP
2020	STL	MLB	26	174	17	6	0	3	25	17	50	1	0	32.3%	.250/.322/.349	88	.340	0.0	SS(45): -2.4	0.0
2021	STL	MLB	27	402	44	10	1	19	45	35	103	4	1	27.9%	.197/.284/.390	96	.216	-1.7	SS(107): -1.1	1.0
2022	MEM	AAA	28	230	36	10	0	17	54	20	52	1	1	22.2%	.249/.313/.552	123	.237	1.4	SS(44): 0.0	1.4
2022	STL	MLB	28	237	19	9	0	6	25	21	79	3	2	35.3%	.157/.245/.286	68	.213	-0.7	SS(75): 0.9, 2B(1): 0.2	-0.1
2023 DC	*STL*	*MLB*	*29*	*190*	*21*	*7*	*0*	*7*	*21*	*16*	*55*	*2*	*0*	*31.2%*	*.211/.290/.391*	*88*	*.263*	*0.2*	*SS -1, 2B 0*	*0.2*

Comparables: Chris Speier (64), Garry Templeton (62), Roy Smalley (62)

How much futility at the plate are you willing to tolerate in order to have a defensive wizard at shortstop? It's a question teams in the past have had to ponder regarding players from Omar Vizquel to Jack Wilson, and unfortunately, it seems DeJong has joined that group. Capable of generating value with both the glove and the stick early in his career, the 29-year-old has spent much of the past three seasons struggling to make consistent contact or hit fly balls with authority. And while he can still vacuum up grounders with the best of them, his defensive numbers aren't nearly as consistent as some of the guys mentioned above. To make matters more urgent, his teammate Tommy Edman looked very good at the shortstop position and doesn't come with the same offensive shortcomings. This season is the final guaranteed one of DeJong's contract, and he'll need to make the most of increasingly scarce playing time if he hopes to trigger one of his team options.

Brendan Donovan 2B Born: 01/16/97 Age: 26 Bats: L Throws: R Height: 6'1" Weight: 195 lb. Origin: Round 7, 2018 Draft (#213 overall)

YEAR	TEAM	LVL	AGE	PA	R	2B	3B	HR	RBI	BB	K	SB	CS	Whiff%	AVG/OBP/SLG	DRC+	BABIP	BRR	DRP	WARP
2021	GDD	WIN	24	64	10	5	0	2	8	10	8	2	1		.308/.422/.519		.326			
2021	PEO	A+	24	109	15	6	0	2	13	10	15	7	1		.295/.385/.421	118	.333	0.0	2B(22): -1.5, 3B(1): 0.3, LF(1): -0.0	0.5
2021	SPR	AA	24	219	35	10	1	4	28	25	39	8	5		.319/.411/.449	117	.379	-1.3	3B(18): 0.6, LF(14): -1.5, SS(9): 0.5	1.0
2021	MEM	AAA	24	131	23	5	0	6	25	15	23	4	2		.288/.389/.495	123	.313	0.7	1B(17): -3.0, 3B(12): -1.3, 2B(2): -0.5	0.3
2022	MEM	AAA	25	65	12	3	0	1	6	8	8	0	0	11.4%	.298/.385/.404	120	.333	1.3	3B(7): 0.0, 1B(5): -0.2, 2B(3): 1.3	0.7
2022	STL	MLB	25	468	64	21	1	5	45	60	70	2	3	15.6%	.281/.394/.379	117	.330	1.4	2B(38): 1, 3B(31): 0.9, RF(20): -0.4	2.5
2023 DC	*STL*	*MLB*	*26*	*563*	*65*	*24*	*2*	*7*	*45*	*61*	*79*	*8*	*5*	*16.4%*	*.260/.355/.368*	*109*	*.296*	*-3.8*	*2B 0, RF -1*	*1.5*

Comparables: Anderson Hernandez (50), Oscar Azocar (48), Carlos Sanchez (47)

"Well here he is," BP's prospect scribes wrote in the Cardinals' Top 10 list last spring, "your 24-year-old, seventh-round college bat that is going to outplay this ranking." Indeed, Donovan was designated the 10th-best farmhand in this organization by our team, and when accounting for something known in high academia as "general Cardinals bullshit," that gives him a better outlook than the average team's no. 3 prospect.

Donovan was all over the place as a rookie, in the literal sense. He recorded at least 16 games at six different positions, including DH, and seven more at shortstop. Across a pile of tiny samples, he performed better on the left side of the field than the right side—a surprise given his just-okay arm—but his bat played well everywhere. Thanks to a keen eye and a 92nd percentile whiff rate, he was able to cruise to a well-above-average offensive season despite his lack of power. His rookie year WARP probably isn't far off from his ceiling, but his consistency and versatility will make it difficult for some of the organization's flashier prospects to push him out of the lineup.

Tommy Edman MI Born: 05/09/95 Age: 28 Bats: S Throws: R Height: 5'10" Weight: 180 lb. Origin: Round 6, 2016 Draft (#196 overall)

YEAR	TEAM	LVL	AGE	PA	R	2B	3B	HR	RBI	BB	K	SB	CS	Whiff%	AVG/OBP/SLG	DRC+	BABIP	BRR	DRP	WARP
2020	STL	MLB	25	227	29	7	1	5	26	16	48	2	4	19.1%	.250/.317/.368	95	.301	0.2	3B(31): -0.6, SS(13): 0.1, RF(13): 0.4	0.5
2021	STL	MLB	26	691	91	41	3	11	56	38	95	30	5	15.0%	.262/.308/.387	92	.291	3.8	2B(130): 1.8, RF(41): 0.6, SS(4): 0.2	2.3
2022	STL	MLB	27	630	95	31	4	13	57	46	111	32	3	20.8%	.265/.324/.400	102	.308	4.2	2B(89): 0.6, SS(80): 1.7, 3B(8): -0.2	2.8
2023 DC	*STL*	*MLB*	*28*	*619*	*74*	*29*	*5*	*11*	*54*	*41*	*107*	*28*	*4*	*19.3%*	*.261/.317/.393*	*100*	*.302*	*16.5*	*SS 3, 2B 0*	*3.9*

Comparables: Todd Walker (63), Scooter Gennett (62), Hernán Pérez (61)

Edman has been asked to do a lot since joining the Cardinals midway through the 2019 season as a virtually anonymous prospect. At various points, the team tasked him with holding down second base, third base and right field for extended periods of time, but he received his most difficult assignment in 2022: Fill in as the team's everyday shortstop.

Just how well he handled that assignment depends on which source you consult. Our fielding metrics are the most pessimistic on the job he did, and his modest WARP reflects that. Others, such as Statcast's Outs Above Average, thought he was legitimately the best defender in the sport at the position, leading to borderline MVP-level WAR numbers elsewhere. It is one of the bigger surprises in baseball that Edman has emerged as an everyday starter in each of the last three years, and his ability to handle shortstop as well as he does opens up some crucial flexibility for the Cardinals in other parts of the lineup.

Paul Goldschmidt 1B Born: 09/10/87 Age: 35 Bats: R Throws: R Height: 6'3" Weight: 220 lb. Origin: Round 8, 2009 Draft (#246 overall)

YEAR	TEAM	LVL	AGE	PA	R	2B	3B	HR	RBI	BB	K	SB	CS	Whiff%	AVG/OBP/SLG	DRC+	BABIP	BRR	DRP	WARP
2020	STL	MLB	32	231	31	13	0	6	21	37	43	1	0	23.7%	.304/.417/.466	127	.364	-0.7	1B(52): -0.8	1.1
2021	STL	MLB	33	679	102	36	2	31	99	67	136	12	0	24.9%	.294/.365/.514	127	.331	1.9	1B(153): -1.8	3.8
2022	STL	MLB	34	651	106	41	0	35	115	79	141	7	0	26.8%	.317/.404/.578	154	.368	0.9	1B(128): -1.4	5.6
2023 DC	*STL*	*MLB*	*35*	*639*	*85*	*31*	*1*	*28*	*91*	*72*	*141*	*5*	*1*	*26.5%*	*.285/.370/.500*	*145*	*.334*	*2.0*	*1B 2*	*4.9*

Comparables: Eddie Murray (81), Jeff Bagwell (80), Mark Teixeira (78)

For players outside of the inner-circle Hall of Fame class, the case for entry can often be made or broken by whether or not they're able to add a peak season or two in their mid-30s. It's hard to imagine Joey Votto missing out on the Hall thanks in large part to his 6.5 WARP age-33 season; it's hard to imagine Evan Longoria making it since he hasn't done better than 2.1 WARP since turning 30.

With this in mind, there's probably no player who did more for his eventual Hall chances in 2022 than Goldschmidt. In the year in which he turned 35 years old, he produced his best offensive season in a career not lacking in stellar batting lines. A sluggish first couple of weeks gave way to a torrid 50-game stretch in which he slashed .393/.466/.738, vaulting him well into 1.000+ OPS territory for most of the season en route to earning honor as the NL MVP. He'll still need a graceful back half of his 30s to cement his immortality with voters, but he reset the clock in a way few hitters do at his age, so we're optimistic.

Nolan Gorman 2B Born: 05/10/00 Age: 23 Bats: L Throws: R Height: 6'1" Weight: 210 lb. Origin: Round 1, 2018 Draft (#19 overall)

YEAR	TEAM	LVL	AGE	PA	R	2B	3B	HR	RBI	BB	K	SB	CS	Whiff%	AVG/OBP/SLG	DRC+	BABIP	BRR	DRP	WARP
2021	SPR	AA	21	195	26	6	0	11	27	18	52	4	0		.288/.354/.508	114	.351	0.5	3B(23): -0.6, 2B(16): 2.0	1.1
2021	MEM	AAA	21	328	45	14	1	14	48	20	63	3	0		.274/.320/.465	109	.301	0.2	2B(61): 8.2, 3B(9): 0.4	2.2
2022	MEM	AAA	22	188	35	5	0	16	26	14	69	3	0	34.0%	.275/.330/.585	107	.352	0.0	2B(34): 2.9	0.9
2022	STL	MLB	22	313	44	13	0	14	35	28	103	1	0	34.5%	.226/.300/.420	85	.301	-0.6	2B(68): -1.2	0.2
2023 DC	*STL*	*MLB*	*23*	*303*	*38*	*11*	*1*	*15*	*42*	*22*	*97*	*1*	*1*	*34.2%*	*.241/.303/.468*	*109*	*.308*	*1.0*	*2B -1*	*1.1*

Comparables: Rougned Odor (51), Yoán Moncada (50), Javier Báez (50)

You've read a lot over the last few years about strong hitters whose swings are suboptimal in one way or another, leading to worse results than their raw talent suggests they're capable of. Think of Vladimir Guerrero Jr., the generational prospect still struggling to get his ground-ball rate under 50%, or Christian Yelich, whose brief success in altering the ball's flight path led to back-to-back top-two MVP finishes.

In the context of stories like these, Gorman provokes a sigh of relief. As a rookie, he showed a swing seemingly built in a lab to get absolutely every ounce of his plus-plus power into games. Among players with 300 plate appearances, no one produced a higher sweet spot rate — the percentage of batted balls Statcast measures between launch angles of 8 and 32 degrees—than Gorman, and just one player (Mike Trout) produced a lower ground-ball rate. His biggest problem at the moment is the fact that the Cardinals' infield is going to remain crowded for the foreseeable future, and he isn't close to any of the others as a defender. That doesn't mean he's in danger of being the odd man out long-term, but it could mean that when he slumps—like any young player inevitably does—it will be all the more tempting to get better defenders into the lineup ahead of him.

Iván Herrera C Born: 06/01/00 Age: 23 Bats: R Throws: R Height: 5'11" Weight: 220 lb. Origin: International Free Agent, 2016

YEAR	TEAM	LVL	AGE	PA	R	2B	3B	HR	RBI	BB	K	SB	CS	Whiff%	AVG/OBP/SLG	DRC+	BABIP	BRR	DRP	WARP
2021	SPR	AA	21	437	50	13	0	17	63	60	96	2	3		.231/.346/.408	106	.261	-1.7	C(71): 4.3	2.1
2022	MEM	AAA	22	278	41	10	1	6	34	38	52	5	1	17.5%	.268/.374/.396	119	.318	-1.3	C(57): 5.1	1.8
2022	STL	MLB	22	22	0	0	0	0	1	2	8	0	0	28.2%	.111/.190/.111	78	.182	-0.1	C(11): -0.1	0.0
2023 DC	*STL*	*MLB*	*23*	*61*	*6*	*2*	*0*	*1*	*5*	*5*	*13*	*0*	*0*	*22.0%*	*.221/.305/.332*	*82*	*.272*	*0.1*	*C 0*	*0.1*

Comparables: Austin Romine (55), Wilson Ramos (50), Chance Sisco (50)

YEAR	TEAM	P. COUNT	FRM RUNS	BLK RUNS	THRW RUNS	TOT RUNS
2021	SPR	11097	1.7	-0.4	0.5	1.8
2022	MEM	8682	3.4	0.6	0.8	4.8
2022	STL	994	0.0	0.0	0.0	-0.1
2023	*STL*	*2405*	*0.2*	*0.0*	*0.2*	*0.3*

It was business as usual for Herrera in 2022—he once again made consistent contact, walked a lot, and generally looked like an above-average hitter against pitchers who were several years older. He was sporadically up and down from the minors in the summer while Yadier Molina was on the IL, and while Herrera likely could have benefited from getting an extended period of time to play and learn behind Molina, the Cardinals decided in favor of just getting him everyday reps in Memphis.

Herrera sure looks like Molina physically behind the plate—their listed heights and weights are nearly identical—but their defensive metrics will be very easy to tell apart. It's not a slight to say Herrera doesn't look like one of the best framers to ever live. Still, even after setting aside the shoes he's filling, he's probably going to be an average backstop for the foreseeable future. Nevertheless, he has a good chance to at least be Molina's equal at the plate, which should sustain him enough to be a second-division regular.

Andrew Knizner C Born: 02/03/95 Age: 28 Bats: R Throws: R Height: 6'1" Weight: 225 lb. Origin: Round 7, 2016 Draft (#226 overall)

YEAR	TEAM	LVL	AGE	PA	R	2B	3B	HR	RBI	BB	K	SB	CS	Whiff%	AVG/OBP/SLG	DRC+	BABIP	BRR	DRP	WARP
2020	STL	MLB	25	17	1	1	0	0	4	0	5	0	0	28.9%	.250/.235/.313	89	.333	0.0	C(7): -0.4	0.0
2021	STL	MLB	26	185	18	7	0	1	9	20	39	0	0	24.0%	.174/.281/.236	85	.223	-0.5	C(57): -4.5	-0.1
2022	STL	MLB	27	293	28	10	0	4	25	26	62	0	1	22.8%	.215/.301/.300	89	.268	0.5	C(90): -7, 1B(5): 0	0.0
2023 DC	*STL*	*MLB*	*28*	*216*	*23*	*8*	*0*	*5*	*20*	*19*	*40*	*0*	*0*	*22.7%*	*.232/.313/.358*	*92*	*.269*	*-2.4*	*C -8*	*-0.6*

Comparables: Tony Cruz (65), Carlos Pérez (64), Lou Marson (63)

YEAR	TEAM	P. COUNT	FRM RUNS	BLK RUNS	THRW RUNS	TOT RUNS
2020	STL	679	-0.4	0.0	0.0	-0.4
2021	STL	6775	-5.1	-0.2	-0.2	-5.5
2022	STL	11293	-7.0	0.2	0.0	-6.8
2023	*STL*	*7215*	*-7.9*	*-0.1*	*0.2*	*-7.7*

The last catcher not named Yadier Molina to lead the Cardinals in games caught was Mike Matheny, a man who is now 52 years old and more than a decade into his managerial career. Given that long of a run, you'd hope for a more ceremonious changing of the guard when it finally came to an end than what 2022 gave us. Not only was Molina still on the team when it happened, but his replacement only managed to salvage a replacement-level season by the skin of his teeth.

The last two years have been pretty damning, not only of Knizner's ability to carry over his impressive minor-league batting performance into the majors but also of his ability to improve his very poor framing skills. While the team searches for its starting catcher of the future, it might as well add a backup of the future to its hunt.

Yadier Molina C

Born: 07/13/82 Age: 40 Bats: R Throws: R Height: 5'11" Weight: 225 lb. Origin: Round 4, 2000 Draft (#113 overall)

YEAR	TEAM	LVL	AGE	PA	R	2B	3B	HR	RBI	BB	K	SB	CS	Whiff%	AVG/OBP/SLG	DRC+	BABIP	BRR	DRP	WARP
2020	STL	MLB	37	156	12	2	0	4	16	6	21	0	0	23.9%	.262/.303/.359	108	.281	-1.5	C(42): 0.9, 1B(2): 0	0.6
2021	STL	MLB	38	473	45	19	0	11	66	24	79	3	0	24.0%	.252/.297/.370	93	.283	-2.7	C(118): -0.4, 1B(1): 0	1.3
2022	STL	MLB	39	270	19	8	0	5	24	5	40	2	0	22.0%	.214/.233/.302	85	.234	-1.9	C(77): 1.8	0.5
2023 non-DC	*STL*	*MLB*	*40*	*251*	*24*	*9*	*0*	*6*	*26*	*10*	*42*	*2*	*0*	*22.8%*	*.251/.291/.375*	*84*	*.281*	*-0.3*	*C 0, 1B 0*	*0.4*

Comparables: Ivan Rodríguez (66), Sandy Alomar Jr. (62), Sherm Lollar (58)

YEAR	TEAM	P. COUNT	FRM RUNS	BLK RUNS	THRW RUNS	TOT RUNS
2020	STL	5637	0.5	0.0	0.4	0.9
2021	STL	16610	-0.4	0.0	0.7	0.4
2022	STL	10244	1.6	0.2	0.0	1.8
2023	*STL*	*6956*	*-1.1*	*0.1*	*0.1*	*-1.0*

Of the two Cardinal legends who played their swan song with the club in 2022, there's no argument over which one had the more pleasant tune. As Albert Pujols authored his best season in years and crossed off milestones many had already given up on him reaching, Molina looked in every sense like someone who has spent a downright obscene percentage of his four decades on earth squatting behind a plate, inviting men to hurl projectiles at him, and catching them with more grace than just about anyone who has ever lived.

Still, there were moments. Five home runs. A four-RBI game in San Francisco. Two, as God as our witness, stolen bases. Thanks to Statcast, we know that Molina's average home run trot lasted five seconds longer than when it was first measured in 2015. It's an odd thing to have a number for—a man quantifiably savoring his moments of glory more the likelier they are to be his last. It is also one of the only baseball numbers it is easy to see ourselves in. Who wouldn't, placed on a path with our own mortality visible ahead, walk instead of run?

Lars Nootbaar RF

Born: 09/08/97 Age: 25 Bats: L Throws: R Height: 6'3" Weight: 210 lb. Origin: Round 8, 2018 Draft (#243 overall)

YEAR	TEAM	LVL	AGE	PA	R	2B	3B	HR	RBI	BB	K	SB	CS	Whiff%	AVG/OBP/SLG	DRC+	BABIP	BRR	DRP	WARP
2021	GDD	WIN	23	87	21	6	1	5	13	14	15	0	0		.314/.437/.643		.333			
2021	MEM	AAA	23	136	21	2	1	6	19	17	25	1	3		.308/.404/.496	129	.349	-0.2	RF(27): -1.0, LF(6): 2.4, CF(2): -0.1	1.0
2021	STL	MLB	23	124	15	3	1	5	15	13	28	2	1	26.1%	.239/.317/.422	98	.273	0.9	RF(26): 2.3, LF(9): 0	0.7
2022	MEM	AAA	24	77	13	4	0	4	14	10	19	2	0		.222/.325/.476	111	.233	0.2	RF(10): 0.2, CF(1): 0.0	0.4
2022	STL	MLB	24	347	53	16	3	14	40	51	71	4	1	24.0%	.228/.340/.448	112	.248	-1.0	RF(79): 3.1, CF(12): -0.2, LF(11): 0.2	1.8
2023 DC	*STL*	*MLB*	*25*	*488*	*59*	*17*	*3*	*16*	*53*	*58*	*105*	*10*	*3*	*23.5%*	*.236/.331/.413*	*109*	*.274*	*4.1*	*RF 3, CF 0*	*2.4*

Comparables: Max Kepler (58), Domonic Brown (58), Matt Joyce (54)

The hypothetical, "if it all comes together," gets casually thrown around quite a bit when discussing up-and-coming athletes. But if you're a serious prospect writer, you try to avoid it as much as possible, because it all almost never *does* come together. Sure, this young hitter is big and strong. And yes, he's OK at judging the strike zone. And no, he's not so bad an athlete that it's impossible to imagine him being playable in an outfield corner. But in order to see him as an everyday big leaguer, you'd need to believe he'll never be worse at making contact and judging balls and strikes than he is in the minors, while also maxing out his power capability, and also putting in the work to be a legitimate outfielder. He needs all of *that* to come together, which is a possibility so remote, it isn't even worth ranking him against the rest of the prospects in this organization. Anyway, Lars Nootbaar is probably going to make an All-Star team, and your favorite team's top prospect will not.

Tyler O'Neill LF

Born: 06/22/95 Age: 28 Bats: R Throws: R Height: 5'11" Weight: 200 lb. Origin: Round 3, 2013 Draft (#85 overall)

YEAR	TEAM	LVL	AGE	PA	R	2B	3B	HR	RBI	BB	K	SB	CS	Whiff%	AVG/OBP/SLG	DRC+	BABIP	BRR	DRP	WARP
2020	STL	MLB	25	157	20	5	0	7	19	15	43	3	1	33.9%	.173/.261/.360	95	.189	0.0	LF(48): 0.3	0.4
2021	STL	MLB	26	537	89	26	2	34	80	38	168	15	4	34.8%	.286/.352/.560	120	.366	6.7	LF(131): 9.5	5.1
2022	STL	MLB	27	383	56	11	1	14	58	38	103	14	4	30.8%	.228/.308/.392	96	.277	1.2	LF(83): 1.3, CF(21): 0.5	1.4
2023 DC	*STL*	*MLB*	*28*	*538*	*64*	*20*	*1*	*23*	*70*	*46*	*141*	*22*	*4*	*31.3%*	*.241/.315/.437*	*111*	*.289*	*10.5*	*LF 4, CF 0*	*3.5*

Comparables: Randal Grichuk (56), Carlos González (55), Travis Snider (53)

Hoping to build off a dream 2021 season, O'Neill instead disappointed when he exited the gate slow last year, slashing .195/.256/.297 through his first 32 games before hitting the IL with a shoulder injury. Injuries continued to linger throughout the year, until a hamstring injury piggybacked on his shoulder issues to sap the young slugger's power. His final 19 games of the season were more on par with expectations—a .228/.375/.579 line with eight extra-base hits and 14 walks over his final 72 plate appearances—but they weren't enough to salvage what felt like a lost season. O'Neill remains one of baseball's most exciting athletes with his elite speed and power combination, and it's a welcome sign to see his struggles not stem mainly from whiff issues. With two seasons left until he hits free agency, though, there will be a lot of pressure on him to comfortably re-establish his value in 2023, which will give him the best opportunity to sort out his long-term plans with the organization.

Albert Pujols DH

Born: 01/16/80 Age: 43 Bats: R Throws: R Height: 6'3" Weight: 235 lb. Origin: Round 13, 1999 Draft (#402 overall)

YEAR	TEAM	LVL	AGE	PA	R	2B	3B	HR	RBI	BB	K	SB	CS	Whiff%	AVG/OBP/SLG	DRC+	BABIP	BRR	DRP	WARP
2020	LAA	MLB	40	163	15	8	0	6	25	9	25	0	0	22.2%	.224/.270/.395	102	.230	-0.5	1B(26): -0.5	0.3
2021	LAA	MLB	41	92	9	0	0	5	12	3	13	1	0	23.1%	.198/.250/.372	112	.176	-1.0	1B(20): -0.1	0.2
2021	LAD	MLB	41	204	20	3	0	12	38	11	32	1	0	20.9%	.254/.299/.460	120	.245	0.1	1B(56): 0.7	1.1
2022	STL	MLB	42	351	42	14	0	24	68	28	55	1	2	21.3%	.270/.345/.550	147	.252	-2.9	1B(22): -0.4	2.5
2023 non-DC	*STL*	*MLB*	*43*	*251*	*27*	*8*	*0*	*9*	*31*	*17*	*40*	*1*	*0*	*21.5%*	*.237/.301/.404*	*96*	*.249*	*-0.6*	*1B 0, 3B 0*	*0.2*

Comparables: Tony Perez (64), Eddie Murray (64), Carl Yastrzemski (62)

Everything about Pujols' farewell tour seemed to serve as a direct kick to the groins of Angels fans. It wasn't enough that your same-city rivals picked him up and instantly massaged him into being a more credible hitter than he'd been his last five turns as a Halo. He then went back to the team he played for when he convinced you that you'd signed the Son of God, and proceeded to crush the ball like he never left. It all felt surreal. The 18-game stretch in the summer when he hit eight homers in 53 plate appearances and slashed .438/.491/1.000. The night at Dodger Stadium when Pujols hit his 699th career homer, and then hit his 700th homer *one inning later*. The legend got to retire on a legitimate high note, something that has felt out of the realm of possibility for years. What a tremendous parting gift for Pujols and the organization to share.

★ ★ ★ *2023 Top 101 Prospect* **#2** ★ ★ ★

Jordan Walker OF/3B Born: 05/22/02 Age: 21 Bats: R Throws: R Height: 6'5" Weight: 220 lb. Origin: Round 1, 2020 Draft (#21 overall)

YEAR	TEAM	LVL	AGE	PA	R	2B	3B	HR	RBI	BB	K	SB	CS	Whiff%	AVG/OBP/SLG	DRC+	BABIP	BRR	DRP	WARP
2021	PMB	A	19	122	24	11	1	6	21	18	21	1	0		.374/.475/.687	145	.419	-0.3	3B(22): -3.6	0.6
2021	PEO	A+	19	244	39	14	3	8	27	15	66	13	2		.292/.344/.487	101	.382	-0.5	3B(54): -3.6	0.4
2022	SPR	AA	20	536	100	31	3	19	68	58	116	22	5		.306/.388/.510	98	.365	-1.3	3B(70): -2.6, RF(25): -0.6, CF(4): -1.0	1.4
2023 DC	*STL*	*MLB*	*21*	*298*	*31*	*14*	*2*	*6*	*30*	*22*	*78*	*6*	*2*	*33.0%*	*.251/.315/.398*	*101*	*.328*	*1.3*	*3B 0, RF 0*	*0.7*

Comparables: Rafael Devers (68), Josh Vitters (65), Bo Bichette (64)

As analysts and fans alike racked their brains trying to piece together an appropriate trade package for generational superstar Juan Soto last summer, one name was repeated more than possibly any other. It was that of Walker, a freshly 20-year-old hitter who was already thriving in Double-A for a St. Louis organization that appeared highly motivated to land Soto. In the end, the Nationals chose a different landing spot for their franchise player, which meant Walker stayed put. For a growing contingent of Cardinal fans, that feels like a relief. Historically speaking, the vast majority of players who have shared Walker's size (there aren't many) and raw power (there are fewer still) tend to suffer from contact issues. The ones who can hold their power without lots of whiffs or an overly aggressive approach often glide toward MVP contention. Walker's numbers against older competition and the simple, efficient swing he puts on the ball give him a good chance of falling into the latter group, which means you needn't stress over his inevitable move away from third base.

★ ★ ★ *2023 Top 101 Prospect* **#30** ★ ★ ★

Masyn Winn SS Born: 03/21/02 Age: 21 Bats: R Throws: R Height: 5'11" Weight: 180 lb. Origin: Round 2, 2020 Draft (#54 overall)

YEAR	TEAM	LVL	AGE	PA	R	2B	3B	HR	RBI	BB	K	SB	CS	Whiff%	AVG/OBP/SLG	DRC+	BABIP	BRR	DRP	WARP
2021	PMB	A	19	284	50	15	3	3	34	40	60	16	2		.262/.370/.388	108	.331	3.8	SS(55): 6.5	2.0
2021	PEO	A+	19	154	26	4	2	2	10	6	40	16	3		.209/.240/.304	87	.274	0.7	SS(31): 1.3	0.4
2022	PEO	A+	20	147	22	11	7	1	15	13	29	15	0		.349/.404/.566	132	.431	0.8	SS(28): -0.4	1.1
2022	SPR	AA	20	403	69	25	1	11	48	50	86	28	5		.258/.349/.432	102	.308	5.9	SS(84): 4.5	2.4
2023 non-DC	*STL*	*MLB*	*21*	*251*	*21*	*11*	*3*	*3*	*22*	*19*	*56*	*12*	*3*	*24.3%*	*.228/.293/.353*	*81*	*.289*	*8.0*	*SS 0*	*1.0*

Comparables: Jonathan Araúz (68), Cole Tucker (67), Domingo Leyba (64)

For some of us, a "fallback option" is seeing the 8:00 p.m. screening because we were too late for the 7:00 p.m. one, or getting provolone cheese at the deli counter because they're out of pepper jack. Winn's fallback option is pitching in the major leagues, and he'll only do that if playing shortstop in the bigs doesn't work out for him. Winn could have done either when he entered the draft, but when the Cardinals took him in the second round, they requested he focus on hitting. That's gone pretty well so far, as he made up for his only hiccup—a 36-game dud seeing High-A hitters for the first time—by returning to High-A last year and raking. He has only average home-run pop, but his swing is excellent at finding the gaps and he has easy speed that will add plenty of slugging points the old-fashioned way. The real draw, however, is still his arm. He uncorked a 100-mph throw from shortstop during the Futures Game last summer, showing not only what kind of upside he has in the field, but also what he could offer on the mound should the bat disintegrate. Considering how quickly he's already climbed the minor-league ladder, we wouldn't count on it.

Juan Yepez 1B/DH Born: 02/19/98 Age: 25 Bats: R Throws: R Height: 6'1" Weight: 200 lb. Origin: International Free Agent, 2014

YEAR	TEAM	LVL	AGE	PA	R	2B	3B	HR	RBI	BB	K	SB	CS	Whiff%	AVG/OBP/SLG	DRC+	BABIP	BRR	DRP	WARP
2021	GDD	WIN	23	103	15	8	0	7	26	12	18	1	0		.302/.388/.640		.297			
2021	SPR	AA	23	77	11	4	0	5	14	9	13	0	0		.270/.387/.571	128	.267	-0.7	1B(7): -0.4, LF(5): -0.9, 3B(4): 0.1	0.3
2021	MEM	AAA	23	357	56	25	0	22	63	42	69	1	3		.289/.382/.589	146	.304	-0.2	1B(60): -2.6, 3B(11): -0.6, LF(9): -0.7	2.3
2022	MEM	AAA	24	208	34	9	0	16	53	17	46	0	0	26.5%	.277/.341/.580	126	.283	-0.8	1B(20): -1.3, RF(6): -0.7, 3B(4): 0.5	1.0
2022	STL	MLB	24	274	27	13	0	12	30	16	61	0	0	26.1%	.253/.296/.447	113	.283	0.2	LF(23): -0.9, RF(17): -1.2, 1B(15): 0	0.9
2023 DC	*STL*	*MLB*	*25*	*329*	*38*	*15*	*0*	*13*	*40*	*22*	*74*	*1*	*0*	*26.5%*	*.251/.309/.445*	*110*	*.288*	*-0.4*	*RF 0, LF -1*	*0.8*

Comparables: Stephen Piscotty (52), Jordan Luplow (52), Teoscar Hernández (50)

A year after nearly tripling his previous career-best home run total, Yepez proved his in-game slugging force was here to stay in 2022. His aggressiveness showed itself immediately, as Yepez swung at a rate seven points higher than MLB average and chased nine points more than average. But when he connected, he did so loudly enough that he managed an above-average season in spite of his sub-.300 OBP. The Cardinals tried Yepez in the outfield for 40 games of his rookie year, but he really belongs at first base, and that's if you have to put him on the field at all. Between his defensive limitations and the narrow avenues he uses to get on base, a platoon DH role still seems like the best way to maximize what he adds by being in the game, which makes it disappointing that he didn't really mash against lefties last season the way we hoped he would. As promising as some of the tools are, he's unlikely to beat out some of the other corner bats in this organization for playing time long-term, which makes him an excellent trade candidate if the team wants to package him with someone else to get some veteran help.

PITCHERS

Génesis Cabrera LHP Born: 10/10/96 Age: 26 Bats: L Throws: L Height: 6'2" Weight: 180 lb. Origin: International Free Agent, 2013

YEAR	TEAM	LVL	AGE	W	L	SV	G	GS	IP	H	HR	BB/9	K/9	K	GB%	BABIP	WHIP	ERA	DRA-	WARP	MPH	FB%	Whiff%	CSP
2020	STL	MLB	23	4	1	1	19	0	22^{1}	10	3	6.4	12.9	32	34.1%	.171	1.16	2.42	95	0.3	96.6	56.4%	40.3%	47.3%
2021	STL	MLB	24	4	5	0	71	0	70	52	3	4.6	9.9	77	41.0%	.287	1.26	3.73	93	0.9	97.9	64.5%	26.3%	54.1%
2022	STL	MLB	25	4	2	1	39	0	44^{2}	39	8	4.0	6.4	32	44.9%	.238	1.32	4.63	122	-0.1	96.2	51.6%	23.4%	53.0%
2023 DC	*STL*	*MLB*	*26*	*2*	*2*	*4*	*49*	*0*	*42.7*	*40*	*4*	*4.3*	*8.6*	*40*	*42.0%*	*.295*	*1.41*	*4.08*	*103*	*0.1*	*97.1*	*58.6%*	*26.5%*	*52.7%*

Comparables: Michael Bowden (58), Josh Hader (58), Tim Collins (57)

A string of six appearances over which Cabrera surrendered 11 runs without striking out a single batter triggered the young lefty's demotion in late August, but some of his underlying numbers had been suggesting trouble for most of the year. His fastball lost some of its juice, and when he called upon his secondaries more to pick up the slack on whiffs, they didn't oblige. His frustration was visible at times—like when he spiked the ball on the mound instead of handing it to his manager during a pitching change in July—and eventually, he ran out of ideas and rope. But lefties who throw this hard don't grow on trees, and Cabrera still has an option left. If he can put the ball where it should go—away from barrels and into his manager's hand—he could yet make good.

Jack Flaherty RHP Born: 10/15/95 Age: 27 Bats: R Throws: R Height: 6'4" Weight: 225 lb. Origin: Round 1, 2014 Draft (#34 overall)

YEAR	TEAM	LVL	AGE	W	L	SV	G	GS	IP	H	HR	BB/9	K/9	K	GB%	BABIP	WHIP	ERA	DRA-	WARP	MPH	FB%	Whiff%	CSP
2020	STL	MLB	24	4	3	0	9	9	40^{1}	33	6	3.6	10.9	49	44.1%	.284	1.21	4.91	81	0.9	93.9	55.6%	34.5%	44.6%
2021	STL	MLB	25	9	2	0	17	15	78^{1}	57	12	3.0	9.8	85	39.0%	.236	1.06	3.22	85	1.3	93.7	56.8%	28.0%	55.6%
2022	SPR	AA	26	0	0	0	4	4	16^{2}	13	0	2.2	12.4	23	26.3%	.342	1.02	2.16	73	0.3				
2022	STL	MLB	26	2	1	0	9	8	36	36	4	5.5	8.3	33	41.1%	.314	1.61	4.25	115	0.1	93.1	55.9%	25.8%	52.4%
2023 DC	*STL*	*MLB*	*27*	*7*	*6*	*0*	*22*	*22*	*113.3*	*99*	*13*	*3.5*	*9.8*	*123*	*40.3%*	*.291*	*1.27*	*3.51*	*91*	*1.4*	*93.8*	*56.7%*	*29.0%*	*51.0%*

Comparables: Don Cardwell (73), John Smoltz (73), Ryan Dempster (73)

It's been a rough few years since Flaherty's breakout 2019 campaign. His performance backslid a bit in 2020, before shoulder injuries ate away huge chunks of his 2021-22 seasons. The good news is the last time we saw Flaherty, he was healthy; the bad news is that both his strikeout and walk numbers were veering dramatically in the wrong directions. How much of that was Flaherty still not being all the way back from his injury? We'll likely know the answer to that after his first few weeks of 2023. What we know now is that while his velocity has been trending down for a few years, it has been an incremental dip, and his two best games in terms of fastball velocity last year occurred in his last three starts. His slider also looked quite different than it had before the injuries, showing a few more inches of depth, though oddly enough that led to fewer whiffs. Overall, it isn't much to speculate on, and the Cardinals will just be glad to get a fully healthy Flaherty back before nit-picking his results.

Giovanny Gallegos RHP Born: 08/14/91 Age: 31 Bats: R Throws: R Height: 6'2" Weight: 215 lb. Origin: International Free Agent, 2011

YEAR	TEAM	LVL	AGE	W	L	SV	G	GS	IP	H	HR	BB/9	K/9	K	GB%	BABIP	WHIP	ERA	DRA-	WARP	MPH	FB%	Whiff%	CSP
2020	STL	MLB	28	2	2	4	16	0	15	9	1	2.4	12.6	21	40.6%	.258	0.87	3.60	80	0.3	94.0	48.9%	38.1%	47.5%
2021	STL	MLB	29	6	5	14	73	0	80^{1}	51	6	2.2	10.6	95	32.3%	.247	0.88	3.02	83	1.5	94.6	52.8%	34.8%	54.9%
2022	STL	MLB	30	3	6	14	57	0	59	42	6	2.7	11.1	73	27.1%	.263	1.02	3.05	79	1.2	94.4	48.0%	35.0%	57.0%
2023 DC	*STL*	*MLB*	*31*	*2*	*2*	*4*	*55*	*0*	*48*	*39*	*7*	*2.7*	*11.2*	*60*	*32.0%*	*.285*	*1.12*	*3.02*	*82*	*0.6*	*94.4*	*50.9%*	*33.3%*	*54.6%*

Comparables: Pedro Strop (67), Nick Vincent (67), Ryan Pressly (65)

His role has ebbed and flowed over the years, but the presence really hasn't. For four years, Gallegos has been a durable, dependable high-leverage reliever who can be counted upon as a stopper at any point in a game. Give or take just a couple percentage points, he pretty much gets the same rate of whiffs with both of his two headlining pitches every year. He walks fewer guys than your typical fastball/slider type, and he somehow keeps home runs thoroughly suppressed even as guys hit more and more balls in the air against him. Most fans wouldn't count him among the game's star relievers, but since 2019, just two guys have thrown more innings out of the pen, and only seven have a lower ERA or FIP. The Cardinals just committed to paying him $11 million over the next two seasons; next to the salaries of some of his contemporaries, that looks like an absolute steal.

★ ★ ★ *2023 Top 101 Prospect* **#58** ★ ★ ★

Gordon Graceffo RHP Born: 03/17/00 Age: 23 Bats: R Throws: R Height: 6'4" Weight: 210 lb. Origin: Round 5, 2021 Draft (#151 overall)

YEAR	TEAM	LVL	AGE	W	L	SV	G	GS	IP	H	HR	BB/9	K/9	K	GB%	BABIP	WHIP	ERA	DRA-	WARP	MPH	FB%	Whiff%	CSP
2021	PMB	A	21	1	0	1	11	1	26	28	1	3.1	12.8	37	63.2%	.403	1.42	1.73	87	0.5				
2022	PEO	A+	22	3	2	0	8	8	45^{2}	27	1	0.8	11.0	56	43.7%	.255	0.68	0.99	82	0.9				
2022	SPR	AA	22	7	4	0	18	18	93^{2}	76	16	2.3	8.0	83	45.4%	.237	1.07	3.94	76	1.7				
2023 non-DC	*STL*	*MLB*	*23*	*2*	*2*	*0*	*57*	*0*	*50*	*51*	*6*	*3.0*	*7.6*	*42*	*46.8%*	*.303*	*1.36*	*4.23*	*108*	*0.0*			*26.7%*	

Comparables: Trey Supak (72), Jordan Yamamoto (72), Dean Kremer (70)

Pitchers aren't supposed to be able to show plus command with triple-digit heat, and fifth-round selections aren't supposed to be the best pitching prospects in their organization a year after starting pro ball. In both of these cases, you could call Graceffo a rule-breaker. The right-hander's stuff now dwarfs what he had at Villanova, with the Cardinals pouring a ton of gas into his heater since he was drafted and his breaking balls improving in shape. He raised a few eyebrows throwing to big-league vets in spring training and completely shut down High-A hitters for eight starts before a well-earned Double-A promotion. There, his numbers took a hit, but he did prove he could maintain his stuff deep into games. His large frame and solid command make him a good candidate to eat up innings as a fourth starter.

Ryan Helsley RHP Born: 07/18/94 Age: 28 Bats: R Throws: R Height: 6'2" Weight: 230 lb. Origin: Round 5, 2015 Draft (#161 overall)

YEAR	TEAM	LVL	AGE	W	L	SV	G	GS	IP	H	HR	BB/9	K/9	K	GB%	BABIP	WHIP	ERA	DRA-	WARP	MPH	FB%	Whiff%	CSP
2020	STL	MLB	25	1	1	1	12	0	12	8	3	6.0	7.5	10	33.3%	.167	1.33	5.25	138	-0.1	97.1	43.3%	31.9%	48.1%
2021	STL	MLB	26	6	4	1	51	0	47^{1}	40	4	5.1	8.9	47	41.7%	.283	1.42	4.56	106	0.3	97.7	55.8%	27.3%	56.5%
2022	STL	MLB	27	9	1	19	54	0	64^{2}	28	6	2.8	13.1	94	34.4%	.185	0.74	1.25	64	1.8	99.7	57.0%	37.9%	57.9%
2023 DC	*STL*	*MLB*	*28*	*2*	*2*	*33*	*55*	*0*	*48*	*37*	*6*	*4.0*	*11.2*	*60*	*37.9%*	*.274*	*1.21*	*3.02*	*80*	*0.7*	*98.8*	*55.8%*	*32.5%*	*56.5%*

Comparables: José Ramirez (68), Michael Blazek (68), Brad Boxberger (67)

Once again, a fastball with elite velocity and spin proves to be a hell of a starting point. Prior to 2022, that was all Helsley had — a fastball he threw really hard with tons of carry, but which he also could neither control nor get batters to chase. It rarely got him too far, and he finished 2021 on the bubble of the Cardinals' pen at 27 years old. Then over the offseason, he added a couple ticks and a dash more RPMs to it, began throwing it a little higher in the zone, and bam: He was one of the best relievers in baseball. As had always been the case with Helsley, the fastball was the draw early in the season. But as appearances piled up, his slider took over as the real star of the show. Strikeouts came in bunches and walks plummeted, less due to Helsley suddenly turning into a command maestro than him starting his pitches in spots batters thought they could do damage, only to swing and not come close. It's a trick every pitcher in baseball would love to pull off, but few have the arms for.

★ ★ ★ *2023 Top 101 Prospect* **#43** ★ ★ ★

Tink Hence RHP Born: 08/06/02 Age: 20 Bats: R Throws: R Height: 6'1" Weight: 175 lb. Origin: Round 2, 2020 Draft (#63 overall)

YEAR	TEAM	LVL	AGE	W	L	SV	G	GS	IP	H	HR	BB/9	K/9	K	GB%	BABIP	WHIP	ERA	DRA-	WARP	MPH	FB%	Whiff%	CSP
2021	CAR	ROK	18	0	1	1	8	1	8	11	1	3.4	15.7	14	31.8%	.476	1.75	9.00						
2022	PMB	A	19	0	1	0	16	16	52^{1}	31	1	2.6	13.9	81	54.1%	.309	0.88	1.38	73	1.5	96.3	67.4%	37.2%	
2023 non-DC	*STL*	*MLB*	*20*	*2*	*2*	*0*	*57*	*0*	*50*	*45*	*6*	*4.3*	*9.3*	*51*	*46.7%*	*.293*	*1.39*	*4.02*	*100*	*0.2*			*27.6%*	

Comparables: Noah Syndergaard (92), A.J. Alexy (86), Marcos Diplán (84)

Few players in this organization boast a ceiling as high as that of Hence. The 63rd-overall selection in 2020, he absolutely coasted against A-ball hitters as a teenager last season, overpowering them with mid- to high-90s heat and a series of befuddling secondaries. You might be wondering how a prep arm who was young for his class and that close to dominating Low-A slid to pick 63, or just as likely, you've heard enough about big-armed teenagers to be forming your own guesses. Wildness as an amateur? Violent delivery? Slight frame that poses durability questions? Check, check and check. TINSTAAPP-ish pessimism aside, though, it's hard to brush away the dominance he showed last year, and there's enough room on his body for him to add weight that supports, instead of hinders, his ability to hold his stuff over a starter's workload. As long as he stays healthy, his ascent in prospect rankings should be swift.

Jordan Hicks RHP Born: 09/06/96 Age: 26 Bats: R Throws: R Height: 6'2" Weight: 220 lb. Origin: Round 3, 2015 Draft (#105 overall)

YEAR	TEAM	LVL	AGE	W	L	SV	G	GS	IP	H	HR	BB/9	K/9	K	GB%	BABIP	WHIP	ERA	DRA-	WARP	MPH	FB%	Whiff%	CSP
2021	STL	MLB	24	0	0	0	10	0	10	5	0	9.0	9.0	10	70.8%	.208	1.50	5.40	95	0.1	99.9	68.8%	23.4%	47.8%
2022	STL	MLB	25	3	6	0	35	8	61^{1}	46	5	5.1	9.2	63	58.2%	.268	1.32	4.84	91	0.9	99.5	65.7%	23.9%	55.1%
2023 DC	*STL*	*MLB*	*26*	*1*	*1*	*0*	*31*	*0*	*26.7*	*24*	*2*	*5.7*	*8.6*	*25*	*57.4%*	*.295*	*1.55*	*4.54*	*108*	*0.0*	*99.8*	*65.7%*	*25.2%*	*53.5%*

Comparables: Byung-Hyun Kim (70), Matt Mantei (67), Huston Street (67)

Incomprehensible as it once seemed, the field of pitchers who can throw triple digits is expanding quickly. According to Statcast, there were 3,369 pitches measured at 100 mph or faster in Major League Baseball last year, setting a record that surpassed the previous mark by nearly 73%. In 2018, the first year Hicks pitched in the big leagues, he counted himself among just three pitchers who clocked triple digits at least 100 times. Just four years later, that number expanded to 11. This is bad news for a pitcher like Hicks, for whom the diminishing novelty of velocity coexists with shortcomings in other areas. He can struggle to throw strikes, and when he does put the ball in the zone, batters make contact against him at the same rate they do against Wade Miley. He is coming off his healthiest season since his debut—albeit one that still included a five-week absence thanks to a forearm strain—and his slider is as untouchable as ever. But a triple-digit fastball doesn't automatically buy you a high-leverage spot like it used to, and Hicks' talent level is better suited for a seventh-inning role.

Cooper Hjerpe LHP Born: 03/16/01 Age: 22 Bats: L Throws: L Height: 6'3" Weight: 200 lb. Origin: Round 1, 2022 Draft (#22 overall)

Southpaws who can release the ball from behind a left-handed hitter's back and land it in the zone with velocity and command have a pretty good track record of success in the majors. If they learn a nasty breaking ball, they can become a stud reliever like Andrew Miller, and if they can learn two additional pitches, they might be a frontline starter like Chris Sale. Hjerpe—that's with a silent H, not a silent J—is smaller than those guys, and doesn't throw quite as hard. But he does have three solid pitches, including a low-90s fastball and a changeup that just melts away from right-handed bats, and his delivery has enough deception to really frustrate professional hitters. After he threw more than 100 innings in his final season with Oregon State, St. Louis didn't ask him to appear in a single game the rest of the summer. He'll step on a pro mound for the first time this spring, and if he's added any heat to his fastball the way other Cardinals arms have in the recent past, look out.

Dakota Hudson RHP Born: 09/15/94 Age: 28 Bats: R Throws: R Height: 6'5" Weight: 215 lb. Origin: Round 1, 2016 Draft (#34 overall)

YEAR	TEAM	LVL	AGE	W	L	SV	G	GS	IP	H	HR	BB/9	K/9	K	GB%	BABIP	WHIP	ERA	DRA-	WARP	MPH	FB%	Whiff%	CSP
2020	STL	MLB	25	3	2	0	8	8	39	24	5	3.5	7.2	31	57.7%	.192	1.00	2.77	86	0.7	93.2	58.6%	21.9%	44.5%
2021	SPR	AA	26	1	0	0	3	3	11^{2}	8	0	3.9	5.4	7	56.2%	.250	1.11	0.77	103	0.1				
2021	STL	MLB	26	1	0	0	2	1	8^{2}	7	0	1.0	6.2	6	65.4%	.269	0.92	2.08	106	0.1	92.4	50.4%	16.1%	58.5%
2022	MEM	AAA	27	1	1	0	3	3	21	20	0	3.4	8.1	19	49.2%	.339	1.33	1.71	99	0.3				
2022	STL	MLB	27	8	7	0	27	26	139^{2}	141	9	3.9	5.0	78	53.6%	.303	1.45	4.45	136	-1.2	91.9	54.4%	17.7%	54.2%
2023 DC	*STL*	*MLB*	*28*	*7*	*6*	*0*	*52*	*9*	*90*	*95*	*8*	*4.1*	*5.7*	*56*	*53.8%*	*.298*	*1.52*	*4.55*	*114*	*0.0*	*92.5*	*56.2%*	*19.7%*	*52.0%*

Comparables: Wily Peralta (56), Brandon Morrow (55), Iván Nova (55)

Just about every pitcher on the 2022 Cardinals leaned on the team's spectacular defense for success. It was an integral aspect of how they built the roster, and for the most part, it worked very well. Few of the team's arms, however, tested the limits of that strategy the way Hudson did. Pitching his first full season since undergoing Tommy John surgery, Hudson finished with the second-lowest strikeout rate, fourth-lowest chase rate, and 11th-lowest whiff rate among all pitchers who faced at least 250 batters. At the same time, Hudson ran the lowest GB% of his career, and yielded the highest hard-hit rate as well. Had he not benefited from very good home run luck, the season could have very well turned ugly. He's walked the tightrope for this long without falling, but one would imagine he's likely to be the first pitcher dropped from the rotation as soon as the team has a hot hand in Memphis.

Matthew Liberatore LHP Born: 11/06/99 Age: 23 Bats: L Throws: L Height: 6'4" Weight: 200 lb. Origin: Round 1, 2018 Draft (#16 overall)

YEAR	TEAM	LVL	AGE	W	L	SV	G	GS	IP	H	HR	BB/9	K/9	K	GB%	BABIP	WHIP	ERA	DRA-	WARP	MPH	FB%	Whiff%	CSP
2021	MEM	AAA	21	9	9	0	22	18	124^{2}	123	19	2.4	8.9	123	38.3%	.308	1.25	4.04	104	1.4				
2022	MEM	AAA	22	7	9	0	22	22	115	118	16	3.2	9.1	116	41.8%	.328	1.38	5.17	111	0.8	93.3	46.0%	33.7%	
2022	STL	MLB	22	2	2	0	9	7	34^{2}	42	5	4.7	7.3	28	37.7%	.346	1.73	5.97	144	-0.5	93.6	54.9%	21.8%	53.4%
2023 DC	*STL*	*MLB*	*23*	*4*	*5*	*0*	*16*	*16*	*76*	*76*	*9*	*3.6*	*7.4*	*62*	*41.5%*	*.295*	*1.40*	*4.26*	*109*	*0.2*	*93.6*	*54.9%*	*23.3%*	*53.4%*

Comparables: Sean O'Sullivan (72), Bryse Wilson (71), Jacob Turner (70)

The brief spell in the majors clearly didn't go Liberatore's way, but in truth, he's been struggling to generate positive results since being tested with a Triple-A assignment out of the gate in 2021. To be clear, his numbers that year were perfectly fine for a 21-year-old who'd never pitched above A-ball before. But he did have issues with giving up too much solid contact, and that continued in a repeat of the level in 2022. Liberatore will begin this season as a 23-year-old who still has rookie eligibility, so all of the "pitches beyond his years" statements that have been made about him in the past still qualify. But we do have some more pointed questions this time around. Can he start getting groundballs again? Is his changeup going to be a workable secondary? Will he take charge of a big-league rotation spot before closing in on his 60th Triple-A game? The burden of expectations will start mounting soon.

Steven Matz LHP Born: 05/29/91 Age: 32 Bats: R Throws: L Height: 6'2" Weight: 201 lb. Origin: Round 2, 2009 Draft (#72 overall)

YEAR	TEAM	LVL	AGE	W	L	SV	G	GS	IP	H	HR	BB/9	K/9	K	GB%	BABIP	WHIP	ERA	DRA-	WARP	MPH	FB%	Whiff%	CSP
2020	NYM	MLB	29	0	5	0	9	6	30^{2}	42	14	2.9	10.6	36	33.3%	.346	1.70	9.68	121	0.0	94.8	53.9%	23.4%	46.7%
2021	TOR	MLB	30	14	7	0	29	29	150^{2}	158	18	2.6	8.6	144	45.6%	.321	1.33	3.82	104	1.1	94.5	52.0%	22.2%	56.4%
2022	MEM	AAA	31	0	0	0	6	4	14^{2}	9	1	1.8	11.7	19	45.5%	.250	0.82	1.84	87	0.3				
2022	STL	MLB	31	5	3	0	15	10	48	50	8	1.9	10.1	54	38.3%	.316	1.25	5.25	97	0.5	94.8	48.5%	27.8%	57.8%
2023 DC	*STL*	*MLB*	*32*	*6*	*6*	*0*	*22*	*22*	*111*	*107*	*12*	*2.6*	*9.0*	*110*	*42.8%*	*.307*	*1.26*	*3.54*	*94*	*1.2*	*94.4*	*51.1%*	*24.8%*	*54.8%*

Comparables: Eric Milton (80), Al Jackson (79), Jeff Francis (77)

Six weeks into his first season with the Cardinals, the injury bug that plagued Matz half a decade ago — so, maybe an injury cicada? — resurfaced, and Matz suffered two separate and lengthy IL trips due to shoulder and knee injuries. It was a frustrating setback for him, and it also clouds the vision for any of us who wish to evaluate his season. In a few ways, he looked better than he ever has. The command he boasted of following his excellent finish to 2021 stuck around, and he simultaneously set a personal best for strikeout percentage, to which he can credit a surprising source — his sinker, which induced whiffs on 31.5% of swings. That's a 10-point jump from his previous career best, and eight points higher than that of any starter who threw as many sinkers as Matz did. He can also, however, credit the sinker for the fact that he is as homer-prone as ever, given his habit of throwing it up in the zone. The whole package remains that of a back-end starter, but one that will be difficult for a younger pitcher to usurp.

Michael McGreevy RHP Born: 07/08/00 Age: 22 Bats: L Throws: R Height: 6'4" Weight: 215 lb. Origin: Round 1, 2021 Draft (#18 overall)

YEAR	TEAM	LVL	AGE	W	L	SV	G	GS	IP	H	HR	BB/9	K/9	K	GB%	BABIP	WHIP	ERA	DRA-	WARP	MPH	FB%	Whiff%	CSP
2021	PMB	A	20	0	0	0	5	5	6	10	1	1.5	6.0	4	75.0%	.391	1.83	9.00	111	0.0				
2022	PEO	A+	21	3	1	0	8	8	45^{1}	41	1	0.8	8.1	41	52.3%	.305	0.99	2.58	100	0.4				
2022	SPR	AA	21	6	4	0	20	20	99	109	14	2.4	6.9	76	48.4%	.321	1.36	4.64	102	0.3				
2023 non-DC	*STL*	*MLB*	*22*	*2*	*3*	*0*	*57*	*0*	*50*	*58*	*6*	*2.8*	*5.5*	*30*	*50.4%*	*.311*	*1.48*	*4.78*	*120*	*-0.3*			*18.7%*	

Comparables: Gabriel Ynoa (76), Tyler Phillips (73), Tyler Viza (73)

Since he'd made just five starts in Low-A while showing inconsistent velocity readings, it was surprising to see McGreevy—the Cardinals' 2021 first-round pick—make 20 starts at Double-A in his first full year of pro ball. He didn't get torched there by any means, but he did struggle to strike guys out, as his fastball settled back into the low-90s range instead of the 94–96 he flashed briefly around the time of his draft. Like a few other arms in this system, McGreevy throws tons of strikes—Cardinals Director of Scouting Randy Flores went so far as to say McGreevy had a "phobia" of issuing walks—and that's enough for him to get by with this stuff in the upper minors. But he should be kept at arm's length from the big-league rotation until he can further develop his *cambio* and more successfully nibble at the corners.

Miles Mikolas RHP Born: 08/23/88 Age: 34 Bats: R Throws: R Height: 6'4" Weight: 230 lb. Origin: Round 7, 2009 Draft (#204 overall)

YEAR	TEAM	LVL	AGE	W	L	SV	G	GS	IP	H	HR	BB/9	K/9	K	GB%	BABIP	WHIP	ERA	DRA-	WARP	MPH	FB%	Whiff%	CSP
2021	PEO	A+	32	1	0	0	1	1	7	6	0	0.0	10.3	8	44.4%	.333	0.86	3.86	91	0.1				
2021	SPR	AA	32	1	0	0	2	2	10^1	15	3	2.6	6.1	7	51.5%	.400	1.74	6.97	113	0.0				
2021	MEM	AAA	32	1	1	0	5	5	19^1	17	2	1.4	6.1	13	36.8%	.273	1.03	2.33	111	0.2				
2021	STL	MLB	32	2	3	0	9	9	44^2	43	6	2.2	6.2	31	52.1%	.276	1.21	4.23	100	0.4	93.3	49.8%	17.4%	59.8%
2022	STL	MLB	33	12	13	0	33	32	202^1	170	25	1.7	6.8	153	45.5%	.250	1.03	3.29	95	2.5	93.4	49.7%	18.6%	57.6%
2023 DC	*STL*	*MLB*	*34*	*11*	*9*	*0*	*29*	*29*	*183.7*	*183*	*18*	*2.0*	*6.0*	*121*	*46.4%*	*.284*	*1.22*	*3.33*	*93*	*2.2*	*93.4*	*50.0%*	*18.9%*	*56.6%*

Comparables: Pat Hentgen (74), Kyle Lohse (72), Jeff Suppan (70)

Despite a shoulder injury limiting him to just nine starts from 2020-21, Mikolas returned in '22 as every bit the innings-eating mid-rotation stalwart he was before getting hurt. He finished third in the majors in innings pitched, and showed virtually no loss of velocity — indeed, he threw harder as the season went on. In a rotation without a real star, Mikolas' week-to-week dependability was exactly what the Cardinals needed, and it should make the price tag on the upcoming final year of his contract well worth it.

Jordan Montgomery LHP Born: 12/27/92 Age: 30 Bats: L Throws: L Height: 6'6" Weight: 228 lb. Origin: Round 4, 2014 Draft (#122 overall)

YEAR	TEAM	LVL	AGE	W	L	SV	G	GS	IP	H	HR	BB/9	K/9	K	GB%	BABIP	WHIP	ERA	DRA-	WARP	MPH	FB%	Whiff%	CSP
2020	NYY	MLB	27	2	3	0	10	10	44	48	7	1.8	9.6	47	43.3%	.323	1.30	5.11	87	0.8	92.5	52.3%	28.2%	48.0%
2021	NYY	MLB	28	6	7	0	30	30	157^1	150	19	2.9	9.3	162	42.6%	.308	1.28	3.83	100	1.5	92.1	52.0%	29.2%	55.4%
2022	STL	MLB	29	6	3	0	11	11	63^2	56	6	1.8	8.6	61	48.9%	.287	1.08	3.11	100	0.6	93.3	58.4%	24.3%	55.3%
2022	NYY	MLB	29	3	3	0	21	21	114^2	103	15	1.8	7.6	97	45.3%	.271	1.10	3.69	108	0.6	92.9	47.9%	29.6%	53.9%
2023 DC	*STL*	*MLB*	*30*	*10*	*9*	*0*	*29*	*29*	*160.3*	*158*	*17*	*2.3*	*8.1*	*144*	*45.1%*	*.301*	*1.24*	*3.40*	*92*	*2.0*	*92.7*	*51.9%*	*27.6%*	*54.3%*

Comparables: Andrew Heaney (80), Chris Hammond (79), Aaron Sele (79)

A sinkerballing lefty got traded to a team known for getting the most out of sinkerballers, so obviously after the trade happened, Montgomery suddenly found a lot of success by ... leading with his four-seamer? Don't look at us like that. In his last two months with the Yankees, Montgomery threw his four-seamer about five percent of the time. In 11 starts with St. Louis, he threw it more than 30% of the time, swapping it with his sinker to be his featured fastball. He still got more groundballs with the Cardinals despite this, and out of his first seven starts with the team, he allowed one run or fewer in six of them, making him possibly the most impactful player exchanged at the deadline.

What does this mean? Well, the Cardinals may have unlocked something in the relationship between his four-seamer and changeup that made hitters more likely to roll over on the latter. It also might have just been Montgomery spiking the sinker on his own late in the season, something he also did in 2021 with New York. Maybe it's just small-sample funkiness. Who knows? To be honest, we've never talked about Jordan Montgomery this long without falling asleep before.

Packy Naughton LHP Born: 04/16/96 Age: 27 Bats: R Throws: L Height: 6'2" Weight: 195 lb. Origin: Round 9, 2017 Draft (#257 overall)

YEAR	TEAM	LVL	AGE	W	L	SV	G	GS	IP	H	HR	BB/9	K/9	K	GB%	BABIP	WHIP	ERA	DRA-	WARP	MPH	FB%	Whiff%	CSP
2021	SL	AAA	25	2	2	0	13	9	56^2	69	7	2.1	8.4	53	47.8%	.363	1.45	4.76	94	0.4				
2021	LAA	MLB	25	0	4	0	7	5	22^2	27	3	5.6	4.8	12	50.6%	.308	1.81	6.35	150	-0.4	90.5	56.9%	21.1%	48.0%
2022	MEM	AAA	26	2	1	0	11	0	21^2	21	2	2.1	10.4	25	43.1%	.345	1.20	2.08	90	0.4	92.9	50.0%	38.1%	
2022	STL	MLB	26	0	2	1	26	3	32	39	3	2.0	8.7	31	50.0%	.367	1.44	4.78	95	0.4	92.8	53.7%	27.9%	50.5%
2023 DC	*STL*	*MLB*	*27*	*1*	*1*	*0*	*31*	*0*	*26.7*	*28*	*2*	*2.9*	*7.7*	*22*	*46.6%*	*.319*	*1.40*	*4.22*	*109*	*0.0*	*92.0*	*54.8%*	*25.6%*	*49.6%*

Comparables: Tyler Duffey (59), Garrett Olson (58), Jalen Beeks (55)

For much of the time since Cincinnati made him a ninth-round draft pick in 2017, Naughton has looked like the kind of pitcher who was exactly good enough to eventually make a big-league roster, but never be better than the 23rd or 24th-best guy on the team. His debut with the Angels mostly showcased the low end of what he was capable of—he gave up lots of contact and walked more batters than he struck out—while his follow-up effort after being claimed off waivers by St. Louis represented something closer to his ideal output. He was a death sentence for lefties, thanks to a harder and much more effective four-seamer, and tempted hitters to chase more, leading to a dramatic cut in walks. His appearance in future big-league games will still be a reliable sign things have gotten out of hand for one of the teams present, but those appearances should keep coming as long as there is a need for strike-throwing mop-up types who can occasionally moonlight as a high-leverage lefty specialist.

Andre Pallante RHP Born: 09/18/98 Age: 24 Bats: R Throws: R Height: 6'0" Weight: 203 lb. Origin: Round 4, 2019 Draft (#125 overall)

YEAR	TEAM	LVL	AGE	W	L	SV	G	GS	IP	H	HR	BB/9	K/9	K	GB%	BABIP	WHIP	ERA	DRA-	WARP	MPH	FB%	Whiff%	CSP
2021	SPR	AA	22	4	7	0	21	21	94^{1}	102	8	4.0	7.8	82	60.3%	.331	1.53	3.82	109	0.1				
2022	STL	MLB	23	6	5	0	47	10	108	113	9	3.3	6.1	73	64.4%	.313	1.42	3.17	114	0.3	95.2	63.5%	17.8%	58.1%
2023 DC	*STL*	*MLB*	*24*	*2*	*2*	*0*	*55*	*0*	*48*	*57*	*4*	*4.3*	*5.9*	*31*	*61.6%*	*.325*	*1.66*	*5.21*	*125*	*-0.3*	*95.2*	*63.5%*	*18.8%*	*58.1%*

Comparables: Bryan Augenstein (63), Jose Rodriguez (61), John Gant (59)

Pallante never stopped surprising during his rookie season in St. Louis. The former fourth-round pick had just one full minor-league season under his belt entering 2022, but that didn't stop him from cracking the Opening Day roster, or from logging more than 100 innings without a single demotion or IL stint. Working primarily as a reliever who could plug a hole in the rotation when injuries necessitated it, he ran the second-highest ground-ball rate in the big leagues, trailing only Framber Valdez. Is it good to generate a ton of worm burners with Tommy Edman and Nolan Arenado manning the infield dirt behind you? Check his ERA to find out.

His secret, as discovered by our own Brian Menéndez, was becoming MLB's only pitcher whose four-seamer sinks *more* than his actual sinker does. Perhaps just as interesting—okay, maybe not, the sinking four-seamer is pretty crazy—were his sizable reverse splits, in which lefties produced a wOBA 80 points worse than righties. The Cardinals would do well to give a portion of Pallante's innings to someone who can actually miss a bat or two going forward, but still: More pitchers should be this weird.

Alex Reyes RHP Born: 08/29/94 Age: 28 Bats: R Throws: R Height: 6'4" Weight: 220 lb. Origin: International Free Agent, 2012

YEAR	TEAM	LVL	AGE	W	L	SV	G	GS	IP	H	HR	BB/9	K/9	K	GB%	BABIP	WHIP	ERA	DRA-	WARP	MPH	FB%	Whiff%	CSP
2020	STL	MLB	25	2	1	1	15	1	19^{2}	14	1	6.4	12.4	27	35.6%	.302	1.42	3.20	87	0.3	97.8	60.4%	34.6%	43.2%
2021	STL	MLB	26	10	8	29	69	0	72^{1}	46	9	6.5	11.8	95	36.3%	.233	1.35	3.24	94	0.9	96.9	54.5%	35.2%	52.8%
2023 DC	*FA*	*MLB*	*28*	*1*	*1*	*0*	*28*	*0*	*25*	*20*	*3*	*6.3*	*10.8*	*30*	*37.8%*	*.287*	*1.53*	*4.46*	*107*	*0.0*	*97.0*	*55.6%*	*32.3%*	*51.0%*

Comparables: Arodys Vizcaíno (53), Randall Delgado (49), Archie Bradley (44)

For the fourth time in the last six years following his 2016 debut, Reyes threw fewer than five innings in the majors in 2022. The specific total was zero, as a shoulder injury stopped the follow-up to his first All-Star season — and a year that many hoped would finally establish the Cardinals' closer of the future — before it started. It has been agonizing to see injuries sap what was once game-breaking velocity from his fastball, and diminish someone who once looked like a frontline starter into an inconsistent reliever. After the latest injury, it was hard to see the Cardinals ever giving Reyes a real shot at the rotation again, and they chose not to tender him a contract in November. Perhaps another team will be bold enough to try as he hits the free agent market.

JoJo Romero LHP Born: 09/09/96 Age: 26 Bats: L Throws: L Height: 5'11" Weight: 200 lb. Origin: Round 4, 2016 Draft (#107 overall)

YEAR	TEAM	LVL	AGE	W	L	SV	G	GS	IP	H	HR	BB/9	K/9	K	GB%	BABIP	WHIP	ERA	DRA-	WARP	MPH	FB%	Whiff%	CSP
2020	PHI	MLB	23	0	0	0	12	0	10^{2}	13	1	1.7	8.4	10	48.5%	.387	1.41	7.59	80	0.2	95.1	56.5%	28.6%	48.3%
2021	PHI	MLB	24	0	0	0	11	0	9	12	4	4.0	8.0	8	54.8%	.296	1.78	7.00	86	0.2	94.7	62.8%	20.2%	56.8%
2022	STL	MLB	25	0	0	0	15	0	14^{1}	9	2	5.7	10.0	16	56.2%	.241	1.26	3.77	93	0.2	95.4	46.4%	38.3%	47.2%
2022	PHI	MLB	25	0	0	0	2	0	2	4	1	4.5	4.5	1	62.5%	.429	2.50	13.50	104	0.0	95.2	55.9%	20.0%	50.3%
2023 DC	*STL*	*MLB*	*26*	*1*	*1*	*0*	*24*	*0*	*21.3*	*20*	*2*	*3.9*	*9.5*	*22*	*52.1%*	*.315*	*1.41*	*4.13*	*103*	*0.1*	*95.2*	*53.2%*	*28.5%*	*50.1%*

Comparables: Chasen Shreve (42), Duane Underwood Jr. (42), Robert Carson (41)

Last July, the Cardinals were looking for a way to get something out of infielder Edmundo Sosa when they could no longer afford him a roster spot but didn't have an option to use. That "something" wound up being Romero, a southpaw acquired from the Phillies who had just returned from Tommy John surgery the season prior. The raw numbers after joining St. Louis are nothing special, but it was heartening to see Romero actually gain velocity from his rehab process, as well as more usage from his tantalizing secondary pitches — including a slider that recorded a whiff on 13 of 16 swings against it. He just might be a key piece of this bullpen in 2023.

Chris Stratton RHP Born: 08/22/90 Age: 32 Bats: R Throws: R Height: 6'2" Weight: 205 lb. Origin: Round 1, 2012 Draft (#20 overall)

YEAR	TEAM	LVL	AGE	W	L	SV	G	GS	IP	H	HR	BB/9	K/9	K	GB%	BABIP	WHIP	ERA	DRA-	WARP	MPH	FB%	Whiff%	CSP
2020	PIT	MLB	29	2	1	0	27	0	30	26	3	3.9	11.7	39	48.1%	.303	1.30	3.90	81	0.6	93.5	46.6%	35.3%	43.0%
2021	PIT	MLB	30	7	1	8	68	0	79^{1}	70	9	3.7	9.8	86	41.0%	.293	1.30	3.63	92	1.1	93.2	48.3%	28.1%	55.9%
2022	PIT	MLB	31	5	4	2	40	1	40^{2}	50	4	2.9	8.2	37	39.2%	.368	1.55	5.09	100	0.4	92.8	42.8%	25.7%	53.7%
2022	STL	MLB	31	5	0	0	20	0	22^{2}	22	0	4.8	9.1	23	51.6%	.355	1.50	2.78	95	0.3	93.3	49.6%	27.8%	49.9%
2023 DC	*STL*	*MLB*	*32*	*2*	*2*	*0*	*55*	*0*	*48*	*50*	*5*	*3.7*	*8.9*	*47*	*42.7%*	*.320*	*1.45*	*4.35*	*109*	*0.0*	*93.0*	*47.9%*	*26.8%*	*52.2%*

Comparables: Jim Bouton (65), Doug Brocail (64), Jim Owens (62)

Stratton was a somewhat surprising omission from the Cardinals' Wild Card roster in October, considering the fact that he was a deadline acquisition who yielded just a 1.50 ERA in his final 18 innings of the season. Sent over from Pittsburgh along with José Quintana, Stratton was quickly molded to fit in with the rest of the Cardinals' staff, raising his ground-ball rate by 11 points — quite the magic act considering his most-used pitch is a monster-spin four-seamer up in the zone.

Adam Wainwright RHP

Born: 08/30/81 Age: 41 Bats: R Throws: R Height: 6'7" Weight: 230 lb. Origin: Round 1, 2000 Draft (#29 overall)

YEAR	TEAM	LVL	AGE	W	L	SV	G	GS	IP	H	HR	BB/9	K/9	K	GB%	BABIP	WHIP	ERA	DRA-	WARP	MPH	FB%	Whiff%	CSP
2020	STL	MLB	38	5	3	0	10	10	65^{2}	54	9	2.1	7.4	54	42.9%	.247	1.05	3.15	99	0.8	89.5	36.7%	24.2%	47.2%
2021	STL	MLB	39	17	7	0	32	32	206^{1}	168	21	2.2	7.6	174	47.9%	.257	1.06	3.05	88	3.3	89.2	37.9%	19.9%	56.7%
2022	STL	MLB	40	11	12	0	32	32	191^{2}	192	16	2.5	6.7	143	43.7%	.302	1.28	3.71	111	0.8	88.6	36.5%	16.9%	56.5%
2023 DC	*STL*	*MLB*	*41*	*10*	*11*	*0*	*29*	*29*	*189.3*	*203*	*22*	*2.7*	*6.8*	*142*	*44.5%*	*.305*	*1.37*	*4.22*	*110*	*0.6*	*89.0*	*37.2%*	*18.2%*	*55.2%*

Comparables: Tom Glavine (70), Greg Maddux (70), Tom Seaver (69)

It sure looked foreboding, didn't it? A pillar of frankly astonishing consistency as he approached and then exceeded 40 years old, Wainwright entered the last month of 2022 with a 3.09 ERA and left it having allowed 23 runs in 28 innings across his final six starts of the year. That last month saw him lose a noticeable amount of both velocity and spin, and just like that, the farewell tributes began to write themselves.

Alas, pens down. Wainwright explained in a short Twitter thread that an injury had led him to unwittingly shorten his stride, throwing off his timing and triggering a long list of subtle, but meaningful, mechanical issues. By the time he found the source of the problem, the season was over, but rest assured: He'd fixed it. A few short weeks later, the Cardinals announced an extension. Wainwright's certainly earned the benefit of the doubt this far into his career, and St. Louis is far from the only team who would love to pencil him in as a mid-rotation starter for 2023 — age be damned.

Kodi Whitley RHP

Born: 02/21/95 Age: 28 Bats: R Throws: R Height: 6'3" Weight: 220 lb. Origin: Round 27, 2017 Draft (#814 overall)

YEAR	TEAM	LVL	AGE	W	L	SV	G	GS	IP	H	HR	BB/9	K/9	K	GB%	BABIP	WHIP	ERA	DRA-	WARP	MPH	FB%	Whiff%	CSP
2020	STL	MLB	25	0	0	0	4	0	4^{2}	2	1	1.9	9.6	5	36.4%	.100	0.64	1.93	101	0.1	94.1	53.2%	33.3%	47.6%
2021	MEM	AAA	26	3	0	3	12	0	16	11	1	3.9	11.8	21	24.3%	.278	1.13	1.69	82	0.4				
2021	STL	MLB	26	0	0	0	25	0	25^{1}	15	1	4.3	9.6	27	38.7%	.230	1.07	2.49	92	0.3	93.8	56.9%	31.7%	53.7%
2022	MEM	AAA	27	1	0	3	30	0	32^{2}	33	8	4.4	8.8	32	34.3%	.275	1.50	3.86	114	0.2	93.2	53.6%	14.3%	
2022	STL	MLB	27	2	0	0	14	0	12^{2}	11	2	6.4	8.5	12	41.7%	.265	1.58	5.68	110	0.1	93.6	49.3%	26.2%	55.0%
2023 non-DC	*STL*	*MLB*	*28*	*2*	*2*	*0*	*57*	*0*	*50*	*47*	*6*	*4.4*	*8.6*	*47*	*38.3%*	*.289*	*1.44*	*4.33*	*109*	*0.0*	*93.7*	*53.3%*	*27.4%*	*53.9%*

Comparables: Vic Black (57), Stefan Crichton (54), Steve Geltz (53)

Whitley was an easy guy to point to as a potential breakout for 2022. After all, he was one of the more dependable pitchers down the stretch from the Cardinals' pen the previous year, and at 26, it was his first time seeing extended action against big leaguers. What's concerning about his actual performance last year isn't the 12.2 innings he threw in the majors — it's the 32.2 innings he threw against Triple-A hitters. He continued to get shelled in Memphis, striking out fewer Triple-A hitters than he had big leaguers the previous season, and his FIP ballooned well beyond anything he'd ever posted in the minors. Whitley doesn't throw especially hard, particularly for a right-handed middle reliever, so the location of his fastball as well as his secondaries is exceptionally important for him to have success. His stuff seems intact, so the hope remains that he'll emerge as a solid seventh-inning option for St. Louis going forward.

Jake Woodford RHP

Born: 10/28/96 Age: 26 Bats: R Throws: R Height: 6'4" Weight: 215 lb. Origin: Round 1, 2015 Draft (#39 overall)

YEAR	TEAM	LVL	AGE	W	L	SV	G	GS	IP	H	HR	BB/9	K/9	K	GB%	BABIP	WHIP	ERA	DRA-	WARP	MPH	FB%	Whiff%	CSP
2020	STL	MLB	23	1	0	0	12	1	21	20	7	2.1	6.9	16	45.3%	.228	1.19	5.57	111	0.1	92.3	77.8%	20.4%	48.4%
2021	MEM	AAA	24	2	3	0	7	7	34	41	4	3.2	6.6	25	50.0%	.336	1.56	4.50	111	0.3				
2021	STL	MLB	24	3	4	0	26	8	67^{2}	66	7	3.3	6.7	50	41.9%	.291	1.34	3.99	112	0.2	91.7	63.8%	20.4%	56.4%
2022	MEM	AAA	25	2	3	0	11	10	43	39	2	4.0	8.2	39	48.0%	.306	1.35	3.14	100	0.6	91.9	54.3%	40.0%	
2022	STL	MLB	25	4	0	0	27	1	48^{1}	43	1	2.0	4.5	24	53.3%	.278	1.12	2.23	121	0.0	92.2	59.5%	17.1%	55.7%
2023 DC	*STL*	*MLB*	*26*	*2*	*2*	*0*	*49*	*0*	*42.7*	*47*	*4*	*3.5*	*5.7*	*27*	*48.0%*	*.302*	*1.49*	*4.64*	*117*	*-0.2*	*92.0*	*63.6%*	*19.3%*	*55.3%*

Comparables: Matt Wisler (58), Sun-Woo Kim (55), Gabriel Ynoa (55)

A glimpse into Woodford's nightmares: He's on the mound on a cool night in September, a sparse crowd in the seats, awaiting the sign from his catcher, but something feels off. He looks down and gasps in horror. No, he's not in his underwear, but worse — he's in a Washington Nationals uniform. He fires a fastball toward the plate, and the batter connects on a bouncer to his left. He turns to see not the reliable Tommy Edman running after the ball, but Luis Garcia. The ball skips into right field. This repeats until he wakes up in a sweat to find he fell asleep during *Ozark* again.

To be fair, not all of the credit for Woodford's ground ball-dependent 2.23 ERA belongs to his MLB-best infield defense. He made a big change with his sinker location in 2022, shifting from throwing it low and away from righties to jamming them with it. The result was a nearly 20-point jump in the pitch's ground-ball rate, and all of that weak contact crushed opponents' wOBA by 54 points from the previous season. There isn't much margin for error with Woodford, but as long as the guys can still pick it behind him, he should be a valuable multi-inning guy.

Lineouts

Hitters

HITTER	POS	TEAM	LVL	AGE	PA	R	2B	3B	HR	RBI	BB	K	SB	CS	AVG/OBP/SLG	DRC+	BABIP	BRR	DRP	WARP
Joshua Baez	RF	CAR	ROK	19	43	4	3	0	1	5	5	14	6	1	.237/.326/.395		.348			
	RF	PMB	A	19	79	11	5	1	3	16	11	30	4	3	.286/.418/.540	92	.484	-0.1	RF(12): -1.4, CF(4): 0.4	0.3
Jimmy Crooks III	C	PMB	A	20	96	12	3	2	3	7	12	22	0	0	.266/.396/.468	120	.333	-2.7	C(17): 3.8	0.6
Jonathan Mejia	SS	DSL CAR	ROK	17	208	33	14	3	5	34	33	48	3	2	.267/.418/.479		.348			
Oscar Mercado	OF	COL	AAA	27	190	25	7	3	5	31	18	28	9	4	.281/.363/.449	113	.311	0.7	CF(26): 1.9, LF(14): 1.3, RF(4): 0.3	1.2
	OF	CLE	MLB	27	127	17	6	1	4	16	5	28	2	2	.208/.244/.375	95	.236	1.2	RF(36): -0.5, LF(12): 0.2, CF(4): 0.2	0.4
	OF	PHI	MLB	27	1	0	0	0	0	0	0	1	0	0	.000/.000/.000	85			CF(1): -0.1	0.0
Delvin Pérez	IF	SPR	AA	23	188	26	6	0	2	20	23	48	13	0	.222/.324/.296	84	.301	2.1	SS(34): -0.7, RF(9): -1.6, 3B(6): 0.5	0.3
	IF	MEM	AAA	23	149	19	4	1	3	13	14	38	8	0	.224/.302/.336	89	.290	-0.4	3B(31): -2.5, 2B(9): -0.7, LF(1): -0.1	-0.1

Joshua Baez has cartoonish physical gifts that compare favorably with farmmate Jordan Walker, but will be much more of a long-term project as the organization works to get his whiffs in check. The bust risk is high, but if he booms, you'll be able to hear it from space. ⚾ Fourth round selection **Jimmy Crooks III** doesn't seem likely to steal a starting job behind the plate, but he can have a steady career as a no. 2 backstop thanks to his solid foundation of offensive skills. ⚾ **Jonathan Mejia** was one of the better shortstops available in the 2021-22 international signing class, and is the most interesting one in this system outside of Masyn Winn. Don't get too excited yet about that walk rate against fellow summer-league teenagers, but his feel for hitting is promising and he'll probably stick at the six. ⚾ Nominated last spring for right field duty, continued struggles at the plate and the emergence of another, younger Oscar doomed **Oscar Mercado** to a bit-part role before twice earning his release. He rebounded to put together a solid run in Columbus, but we've seen that film before and know how it ends. ⚾ Skating by on one of the better draft reputations in baseball, the Cardinals' hubris has finally caught up to them, as 2016 first round pick **Delvin Pérez** turned into nothing more than a glove-first fifth infielder. Behind him, all they got out of that draft was Dylan Carlson, Dakota Hudson, Zac Gallen and Tommy Edman. That'll … that'll show 'em.

Pitchers

PITCHER	TEAM	LVL	AGE	W	L	SV	G	GS	IP	H	HR	BB/9	K/9	K	GB%	BABIP	WHIP	ERA	DRA-	WARP	MPH	FB%	WHF	CSP
Aaron Brooks	MEM	AAA	32	5	4	0	15	13	69^{2}	81	9	2.6	7.0	54	49.6%	.335	1.45	5.56	112	0.5	92.8	56.6%	15.8%	
	STL	MLB	32	0	0	0	5	0	9^{1}	11	3	1.9	6.8	7	39.4%	.267	1.39	7.71	114	0.0	93.4	49.4%	19.7%	57.2%
James Naile	MEM	AAA	29	4	3	0	44	3	73^{1}	80	5	2.6	7.9	64	53.7%	.339	1.38	3.31	101	1.0	91.2	79.8%	21.1%	
	STL	MLB	29	0	0	0	7	0	9	8	2	2.0	5.0	5	50.0%	.214	1.11	5.00	106	0.1	91.5	66.7%	19.7%	59.7%
Ljay Newsome	MEM	AAA	25	0	0	0	4	0	5^{2}	5	0	1.6	7.9	5	18.8%	.313	1.06	4.76	98	0.1				
Freddy Pacheco	SPR	AA	24	1	5	8	24	0	28^{1}	20	4	5.1	13.0	41	28.8%	.296	1.27	3.81	74	0.6				
	MEM	AAA	24	2	2	4	26	0	33^{2}	17	2	3.2	11.5	43	38.7%	.208	0.86	2.41	72	0.9				
Inohan Paniagua	PMB	A	22	6	4	0	17	17	99	72	4	2.1	9.7	107	42.9%	.274	0.96	2.18	96	1.8	92.2	61.9%	28.8%	
	PEO	A+	22	2	2	0	8	8	38^{2}	34	8	3.7	8.8	38	33.0%	.260	1.29	4.42	129	-0.2				
Cory Thompson	SPR	AA	27	0	0	0	10	0	11^{2}	14	3	3.1	10.0	13	37.1%	.344	1.54	5.40	90	0.1				
Zack Thompson	MEM	AAA	24	2	3	0	19	10	53^{1}	44	6	3.5	11.3	67	44.9%	.292	1.22	4.73	85	1.1	93.6	52.2%	27.8%	
	STL	MLB	24	1	1	1	22	1	34^{2}	20	3	3.6	7.0	27	54.7%	.185	0.98	2.08	106	0.2	94.9	54.3%	17.6%	57.3%
Drew VerHagen	STL	MLB	31	3	1	0	19	0	21^{2}	27	5	5.8	7.5	18	34.2%	.324	1.89	6.65	131	-0.1	94.9	46.8%	28.4%	50.8%
Jake Walsh	MEM	AAA	26	1	0	6	13	0	15^{1}	11	1	4.1	12.9	22	26.5%	.303	1.17	1.17	89	0.3	95.7	65.1%	16.2%	
	STL	MLB	26	0	1	0	3	0	2^{2}	3	0	6.7	16.9	5	42.9%	.429	1.88	13.50	87	0.0	95.1	61.5%	21.4%	56.1%

From Miles Mikolas to Kwang Hyun Kim to Seung-hwan Oh, the Cardinals have done quite well at bringing in pitchers from the NPB and KBO to plug holes on their own roster. **Aaron Brooks**, one of the best pitchers in South Korea from 2020-21, hoped to be another of the team's success stories in that regard but proved too hittable even against Triple-A hitters. ⚾ St. Louis went hard on college pitching on Day 2 of last year's draft, with Texas southpaw **Pete Hansen** acting as the headliner. He's the cliche crafty lefty through and through, ready to ascend the minors quickly thanks to a reliable four-pitch mix and good strike-throwing ability. ⚾ The Cardinals made **Brycen Mautz** their second-round pick on his 21st birthday last summer. The light beer side of his projection has him as a hard-throwing lefty specialist; his top-shelf liquor outcome sees him bring along his changeup enough to be a no. 4 starter. ⚾ After fighting his way onto the Oakland A's Triple-A roster four separate times from 2016-21 only to spin his tires each time, righty **James Naile** finally got a call-up to St. Louis last year. His sinker hardly spins at all, which is probably why they don't call him James Screw. ⚾ **Ljay Newsome** returned from Tommy John surgery for a handful of minor-league appearances late last year, and appears once again ready to push the limits of how much you can survive on supremely hittable stuff as long as you are almost never missing the strike zone. ⚾ **Freddy Pacheco** is a standard fireballing pen arm who will likely test fans' patience when he first arrives in the majors, but he has better strikeout stuff than many of the club's incumbent relievers and is right on the doorstep after an excellent Triple-A debut. ⚾ With the right-hander already approaching Rule 5 eligibility, the Cardinals asked **Inohan Paniagua** for an enormous innings increase in 2022, which he handled quite well. They're hoping his command is good enough to offset mediocre velocity and make him a back-end rotation option down the line. ⚾ Forget "There Is No Such Thing as a Pitching Prospect." **Wilking Rodriguez** is proof that every pitcher is a prospect forever. Last seen in affiliated ball way back in 2015, he kept showing up in the Venezuelan Winter League, then in 2021 started throwing triple-digits in Mexico. St. Louis nabbed him from the Yankees' back catalogue in one of the last and best picks of this year's Rule 5 draft. ⚾ In 2013, **Cory Thompson** was a prep prospect who could throw in the mid-90s off the mound; the Reds picked him in the fifth round but preferred to use him at shortstop. He still had that velocity when he pitched for the first time in the minors in 2017, and now, a decade after his draft year, he's even added a nice little changeup. He'll be an up-and-down reliever if he gets past some recent UCL trouble. ⚾ Former first-round pick **Zack Thompson** reverted to the bullpen and became a dependable arm for the Cardinals in their playoff hunt last year, but his lack of a reliable bat-missing offering makes him highly volatile going forward. ⚾ **Drew VerHagen** returned from two seasons in Japan to make 19 fairly brutal appearances for St. Louis before finally submitting to hip surgery in August. He's on a two-year deal, so the team will get a chance this spring to pass judgment on just how much the injury may have impacted his lack of control and troubling ground-ball rate. ⚾ Between injuries and the pandemic, **Jake Walsh** has averaged barely 10 innings per year for the last four years. Because of that, he's still pretty unrefined for a pitcher his age, but his surprisingly plucky 12-6 hammer is an intriguing enough secondary to give him some late-bloomer potential.

CHICAGO WHITE SOX

Essay by Tim Marchman

Player comments by Collin Whitchurch and BP staff

A few years ago, when I was working for a sports website, I was responsible for a running feature called Blight Sox, which covered goings-on during the Rick Renteria era in a tone appropriate to their momentousness. "White Sox Outfielder Struggles To Make Contact" was a typical item. So were "Report: White Sox Near Deal With Mike Pelfrey" and "White Sox Manager Lets Emotional Attachment To Mike Pelfrey Get Better Of Him." So was "White Sox Attempt To Lure Fans Using Cheap Cased Meat," which described the team announcing that it would be selling $1 hot dogs at its five remaining home Wednesdays. (This came during a stretch in which they went 1-12, culminating in three straight losses to the Cubs.)

The highlight of my time as editor of this feature came when the team sent me autographed, game-worn Gordon Beckham footwear after I reported that the team had been menacing social-media users by threatening to send it to them if they won a contest. The artifact, previously gazed upon in astonishment by Steve Stone, sits on a shelf behind me, and I was forced to disclose my ownership of it to readers in every story.

With the exception of a few people who wrote me long, bewildered and occasionally anguished emails wondering what my problem with the Sox was, and a smaller number of people who wrote me short, belligerent emails accusing me of having sinister and undisclosed motives, most people seemed to get the point, which was that it was a celebration. The Sox were a terrible team that lost 95 games every year, but there was a purpose to it: The team was committed to young players, seemingly the more or less right ones, and to bringing them along slowly and steadily. The team wasn't idly losing for the sake of it while preaching about a theoretical bright future as part of some deranged accounting exercise, but letting the actual members of the actual team of the future—Tim Anderson, Yoán Moncada, Eloy Jiménez, Lucas Giolito, Dylan Cease, Michael Kopech—learn, grow and improve. If the team occasionally fielded a second baseman whom no one had ever heard of and who seemed not to know which direction you were supposed to run after hitting the ball, they were still a joy to follow. There was nothing much blighted about them at all.

CHICAGO WHITE SOX PROSPECTUS

2022 W-L: 81-81, 2ND IN AL CENTRAL

Pythag	.479	*17th*	DER	.694	*22nd*
RS/G	4.23	*19th*	DRC+	97	*20th*
RA/G	4.43	*20th*	DRA-	96	*14th*
dWin%	.510	*15th*	FIP	3.78	*10th*
Payroll	$193M	*7th*	B-Age	29.8	*20th*
M$/MW	$5.3M	*22nd*	P-Age	30.1	*23rd*

- Opened 1991
- Open air
- Natural surface
- Fence profile: 8′

Park Factors

Runs	Runs/RH	Runs/LH	HR/RH	HR/LH
102	101	103	102	112

Top Hitter WARP	3.7 José Abreu
Top Pitcher WARP	4.5 Dylan Cease
2023 Top Prospect	Colson Montgomery

Payroll History (in millions)

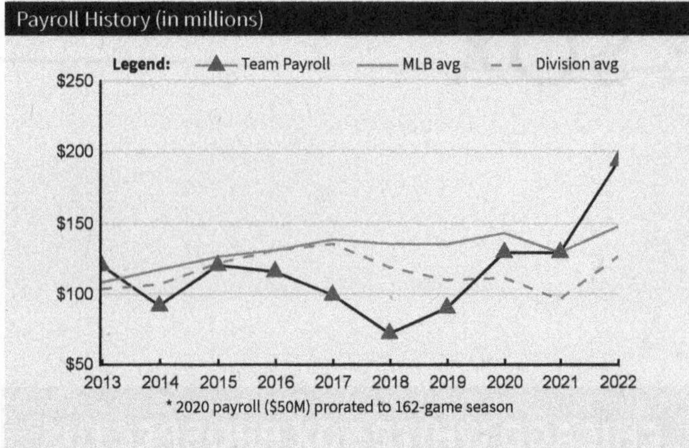

Future Commitments (in millions)

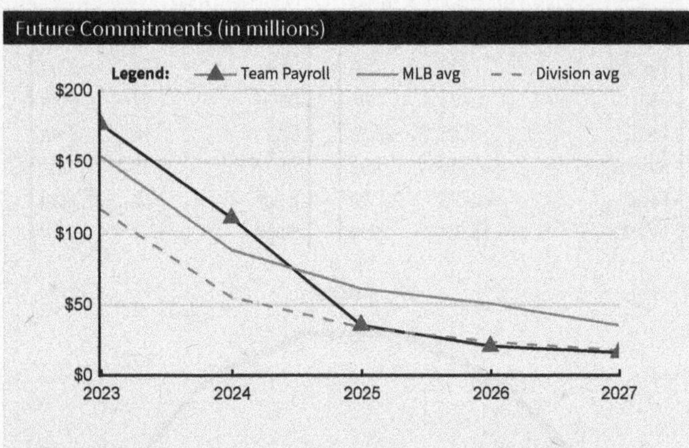

Farm System Ranking

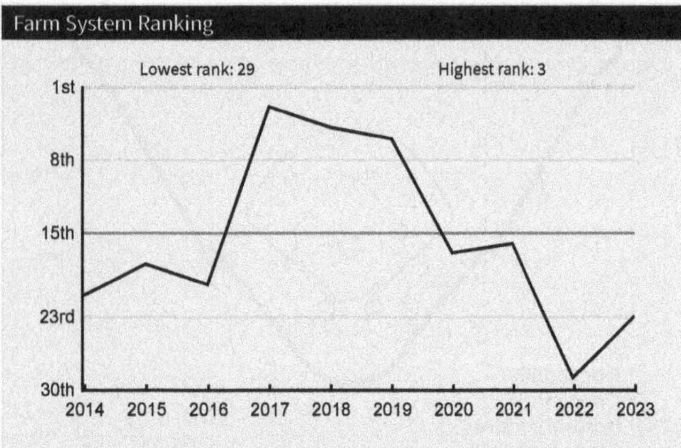

Personnel

Executive Vice President
Ken Williams

Senior Vice President/General Manager
Rick Hahn

Assistant General Manager
Jeremy Haber

Assistant General Manager/ Player Development
Chris Getz

Senior Director of Baseball Operations
Dan Fabian

Manager
Pedro Grifol

BP Alumni
Steffan Segui

This year's team was different, and I don't know how anyone could comprehensively describe the things it did.

A few things do stand out to me, some of them macro and some of them micro. Tony La Russa called for an intentional walk on a 1-2 count. ("That's not even a close call," he said.) He did it again later in the summer, a surprise even from a man who at the apex of his fame in the 1980s made a spectacle of describing the eight possible plays he might call with runners at first and third to the bowtied pundit George Will, at one point throwing himself at the floor.

The team's most common lineup featured four players who would ideally be at first base or not in the field at all, as well as an aging catcher with surgically-repaired knees. That lineup was fielded all of four times, one of the 147 the team rolled out as it dealt with a variety of injuries and cycled through a number of players for various roles, like "outfielder," that it hadn't filled in the offseason despite having well-founded aspirations to winning the World Series.

In May, Byron Buxton hit the longest walk-off home run ever measured by Statcast against the Sox. In July, in a 2-2 game with runners on first and second and none out, AJ Pollock came within an eyelash of a three-run home run but instead hit into a triple play. In a game I selected completely at random because I was sure a randomly selected game would feature something egregiously stupid or dismaying, the Sox gave up 21 runs to the Astros in a game Giolito started, with more innings in which they gave up multiple runs than in which they didn't.

Anderson, Moncada, Jiménez and Luis Robert, the young core of the lineup for whose development Sox fans sacrificed years of overtly watchable baseball, averaged 91 games played apiece. Kopech pitched for months after hearing something pop in his knee, then injured his other knee. Giolito simply pitched poorly. Cease will not be mentioned here as his Cy Young-caliber season contradicts my narrative.

Headline writers described goings-on in an appropriate tone. "Luis Robert on trying to push through his wrist injury: 'It was my mistake,'" was a typical dispatch from *The Athletic*'s excellent Sox writer James Fegan. So was "White Sox searching for meaning while poorly playing out the string." So was "White Sox's dismal fate affirmed after another poor effort against Guardians."

In all, this team seemed, well, blighted. One description of blight I recently read goes:

> *"The filaments are fungus-tubes, and the pear-shaped swelling each carries is a container, like a capsule, which contains the spore of the fungus. The blight fungus consists of these fungus-tubes; they form a vegetable organism of great destructive power; without roots, without flowers, without any differentiation between stem and leaves, which grows and develops within the plant ... As the fungus-tubes, whether originating from large or small spores, work their way through the*

leaf, lengthening and branching, they leave ruin behind, the juices of the leaf are drained and the tissues exhausted."

This description of a sort of anti-life destroying something beautiful and of great value resonated with me.

You can decide for yourself who or what would be the invasive and destructive organism here, and whether it's now gone and has been replaced. (At the end of the season, Rick Hahn said that the ideal new manager would be "someone who understands the way the game has grown and evolved in the last decade or so," suggesting he has some ideas, and the Sox seem to have secured such a person with the hiring of Pedro Grifol.) Complicating the metaphor, though, is that blight leaves behind a black, pulpy mass of rot, whereas if it hardly seems sure that the Sox will be perfectly fine, it seems that they could and perhaps should be.

The case against the Sox is pretty straightforward: They don't have enough good players, and the ones they have aren't good enough. Their best hitters, Jiménez and Andrew Vaughn, don't project as actual star hitters, and have minimal defensive value. Robert appears to have extremely tightly-stretched rubber bands in place of various necessary muscles and tendons, Grandal is paying the price for a lifetime spent squatting and Moncada simply doesn't have the power he'd need to be a true star anymore. Their big offseason signing, Andrew Benintendi—and "big offseason signing" here means that he got the biggest guaranteed free agent contract in team history at five years and $75 million, which would have netted you an All-Star 20 years ago, which is a bit blight-like—is notable mainly for being reliably average and for playing a position at which the Sox might otherwise have fielded a cardboard cutout of Ralph Garr.

The pitching staff is in better shape, but there are some structural similarities to the lineup—its apparent adequacy is more a function of having a lot of guys like Giolito, Cease and Lance Lynn, who seem likely to be not bad or a tick above pretty good—than of having any who seem particularly likely to contend for awards. (I am not mentioning the bullpen here because it contradicts my narrative.) And while it's true that the team's discouraging projections rely on unreliable data collected at the height of a disruptive pandemic and under a manager who may or may not have been awake when charged with running games and instructing players to do things, it's also true that Grifol has never managed a major-league team before. Perhaps there will be an upward swing from [unfocused, ill-prepared, put in the lousiest positions] to [focused, well-prepared, something like optimized], but it's a safer bet that the day-to-day management of the team will, like its better players, be more not bad than actively envy-inducing for fans of other teams.

There is a case, though, for a reasonable optimism. Like five years ago, the team will field guys who aspire to be the sort who might one day be vaguely remembered, and will enter the season without any obvious candidates for several crucial roles. Unlike five years ago, though, they'll enter it with a bit more than half a championship-caliber lineup, perhaps the best and deepest bullpen in baseball and a rotation that's good enough to not get in the way.

The key will perhaps be management. The safe bet is that any improvement in that category will come simply from not being bad—no one will be issuing walks on 1-2 counts, fewer lineups will feature five designated hitters, and the tea leaves suggest that players will not routinely be playing through apparently serious injuries—but you can hope for more, be that savvy strategic and tactical planning and preparation that takes advantage of the improvements in data analysis over the last decade, or players improving because their boss is willing to communicate with them and because they're spending less time figuring out polite ways to tell reporters that they need to watch *Weekend at Bernie's* to get a true read on what the clubhouse looks like behind closed doors.

Those bleak and barren years yielded real talent, and with the exceptions of second base and right field, there isn't a position in the lineup or the rotation where the team doesn't field a player who hasn't been, or doesn't have the talent to be, among the best in the league. All the Sox need is decent health and a bit of luck, and for their important players to not be terrible, and for a couple of them to reach a new level. This is what pretty much every team that considers itself a contender needs—which on the one hand is pretty uninspiring, and on the other isn't bad!

It isn't a particularly insightful thing to say, but it's true: The team should be pretty good, unless it isn't. This is less than anyone who paid to watch Mike Pelfrey start games in 2017 would have hoped for, but more than they might have expected. Whatever rot set in last year, every single one of the players the team chose to build around turned out to be something between useful and a star, and in their better moments, like when they got it together enough to make you think they just might edge their way into the postseason despite everything that went wrong this past year, you could squint and see something worth celebrating. Suffering and boredom aren't always rewarded, but even when they are, they aren't always rewarded immediately. Sometimes you have to wait. ■

—Tim Marchman is a features editor at Motherboard.

Hitters

Tim Anderson SS Born: 06/23/93 Age: 30 Bats: R Throws: R Height: 6'1" Weight: 185 lb. Origin: Round 1, 2013 Draft (#17 overall)

YEAR	TEAM	LVL	AGE	PA	R	2B	3B	HR	RBI	BB	K	SB	CS	Whiff%	AVG/OBP/SLG	DRC+	BABIP	BRR	DRP	WARP
2020	CHW	MLB	27	221	45	11	1	10	21	10	50	5	2	30.9%	.322/.357/.529	112	.383	2.8	SS(49): -1.5	1.1
2021	CHW	MLB	28	551	94	29	2	17	61	22	119	18	7	26.1%	.309/.338/.469	105	.372	6.2	SS(122): 1.8	3.2
2022	CHW	MLB	29	351	50	13	0	6	25	14	55	13	0	23.2%	.301/.339/.395	107	.347	2.6	SS(79): -5.5	1.1
2023 DC	*CHW*	*MLB*	*30*	*595*	*73*	*26*	*1*	*12*	*52*	*27*	*110*	*18*	*4*	*23.5%*	*.291/.329/.409*	*106*	*.345*	*7.0*	*SS -2*	*2.8*

Comparables: Shawon Dunston (82), Bert Campaneris (79), José Reyes (78)

Things that have no practical use unless coupled with something else: a light bulb without electricity; a paint brush without paint; a fish tank without fish; a chess board without pieces; a piece of chalk without a chalkboard; the White Sox offense without Tim Anderson. Between two injuries that cost him most of the season—ending his campaign on August 6—the veteran shortstop continued his usual exploits, again displaying an uncanny ability to hit for a high average while providing passable defense at shortstop. Anderson's speed-based, high-contact game is unique in today's league, and while he'll hit the wrong side of 30 midway through the season, the value of his approach doesn't appear to be going away anytime soon.

Andrew Benintendi LF Born: 07/06/94 Age: 29 Bats: L Throws: L Height: 5'9" Weight: 180 lb. Origin: Round 1, 2015 Draft (#7 overall)

YEAR	TEAM	LVL	AGE	PA	R	2B	3B	HR	RBI	BB	K	SB	CS	Whiff%	AVG/OBP/SLG	DRC+	BABIP	BRR	DRP	WARP
2020	BOS	MLB	25	52	4	1	0	0	1	11	17	1	2	33.3%	.103/.314/.128	77	.182	0.4	LF(13): -0.7	0.0
2021	KC	MLB	26	538	63	27	2	17	73	36	97	8	9	22.7%	.276/.324/.442	101	.309	0.3	LF(129): 3.2	2.4
2022	KC	MLB	27	390	40	14	2	3	39	39	52	4	2	19.8%	.320/.387/.398	114	.366	-1.5	LF(91): -0.6	1.7
2022	NYY	MLB	27	131	14	9	1	2	12	13	25	4	1	23.4%	.254/.331/.404	89	.303	0.1	LF(33): 0.4	0.3
2023 DC	*CHW*	*MLB*	*28*	*560*	*66*	*25*	*2*	*15*	*60*	*51*	*94*	*10*	*3*	*20.9%*	*.282/.354/.436*	*121*	*.322*	*1.2*	*LF 5*	*3.4*

Comparables: Tim Raines (73), Goose Goslin (70), Carl Crawford (69)

When the Yankees acquired Benintendi from the Royals on July 27, the .320 batting average he had at the time was good for third in the American League. The team has made it a point to address lineup diversity—which for this era's Yankees has generally meant an emphasis on adding lefty bats and increasing contact—and Benintendi's skill set made him a sensible target for New York at last year's trade deadline. The sky-high .366 BABIP he was sporting at the time of the trade, unfortunately, crashed down to earth, and when you combine that with a jump in his strikeout rate, you get the much more pedestrian batting line that Benintendi showed in the Bronx. Even worse was the season-ending hamate injury Benintendi suffered on a swing in an early September game against the Rays, rendering him unavailable for the remainder of the season and the team's postseason run. He signed with the White Sox in an immediate contender for most-anonymous five-year deal of all time.

Jake Burger 3B Born: 04/10/96 Age: 27 Bats: R Throws: R Height: 6'2" Weight: 230 lb. Origin: Round 1, 2017 Draft (#11 overall)

YEAR	TEAM	LVL	AGE	PA	R	2B	3B	HR	RBI	BB	K	SB	CS	Whiff%	AVG/OBP/SLG	DRC+	BABIP	BRR	DRP	WARP
2021	CLT	AAA	25	340	46	16	2	18	54	24	91	0	0		.274/.332/.513	102	.330	-2.4	3B(65): 0.0, 2B(5): -0.3	0.9
2021	CHW	MLB	25	42	5	3	1	1	3	4	15	0	0	38.2%	.263/.333/.474	74	.409	-0.2	3B(8): -0.4	-0.1
2022	CLT	AAA	26	168	22	0	2	5	16	18	34	0	1	30.5%	.253/.351/.384	112	.299	-0.5	3B(35): 0.0, 2B(1): -0.2	0.7
2022	CHW	MLB	26	183	20	9	1	8	26	10	56	0	0	35.2%	.250/.302/.458	96	.324	-1.2	3B(37): -1.9	0.0
2023 DC	*CHW*	*MLB*	*27*	*190*	*20*	*7*	*1*	*7*	*21*	*12*	*54*	*0*	*0*	*34.0%*	*.240/.301/.418*	*97*	*.309*	*0.8*	*3B 0, 2B 0*	*0.4*

Comparables: Chris Johnson (74), Gio Urshela (66), Casey McGehee (66)

Enough time has passed since Burger's bout with a myriad of injuries nearly derailed his career that he's now gone from "what a nice story" to "is he really a major leaguer?" The latter question was present before he missed three full years, but initially, amazement over his ascent to the majors kind of overshadowed his shortcomings. To date, Burger remains overmatched at third base—and at the plate against elite pitching. He also lost a considerable amount of weight, which, if it doesn't translate into better results, is also a bummer, because it takes a lot of the fun out of all those beef puns.

Yoelqui Céspedes CF Born: 09/24/97 Age: 25 Bats: R Throws: R Height: 5'9" Weight: 205 lb. Origin: International Free Agent, 2021

YEAR	TEAM	LVL	AGE	PA	R	2B	3B	HR	RBI	BB	K	SB	CS	Whiff%	AVG/OBP/SLG	DRC+	BABIP	BRR	DRP	WARP
2021	GDD	WIN	23	78	8	3	0	0	1	2	22	2	0		.181/.244/.222		.260			
2021	WS	A+	23	199	34	17	0	7	20	13	56	10	2		.278/.355/.494	89	.372	0.5	CF(21): -1.5, RF(3): -0.4	0.2
2021	BIR	AA	23	100	14	3	2	1	7	3	27	8	4		.298/.340/.404	81	.409	-0.2	CF(26): 3.9	0.5
2022	BIR	AA	24	512	65	29	1	17	59	29	154	33	12		.258/.332/.437	78	.349	1.7	CF(101): -0.5, RF(9): 0.5	1.2
2023 DC	*CHW*	*MLB*	*25*	*63*	*5*	*2*	*0*	*1*	*5*	*3*	*21*	*3*	*2*	*40.6%*	*.220/.279/.344*	*68*	*.330*	*0.0*	*RF 0*	*-0.1*

Comparables: Darrell Ceciliani (65), Drew Ferguson (64), Braden Bishop (63)

The thing about untapped potential is that it's yet to be accessed. Like a keg of beer, you need to actually tap the thing for it to be worth a damn. Otherwise it's just a big, heavy hunk of metal taking up space in your parents' garage. To tap a keg, you first need to let it sit for a few hours. Then, lift the handle of the tap to disengage it, line up the bottom of the tap with the mouth of the keg, turn the tap clockwise until you feel resistance (no need to crank on it—just make sure it's snug), push down on the handle and voilà: The keg is tapped. Sounds simple, but it's difficult to master. Untapping potential takes work, too. Even if you've got a carrying skill, say prolific power, learning every step of the process—for example, pitch recognition against advanced competition—is critical. Céspedes' power showed up in a big way in 2022, but there's plenty to draw from the keg before he can be a successful major-leaguer. While his professional debut was delayed by a myriad of issues, at 25, the expiration date looms.

★ ★ ★ *2023 Top 101 Prospect* **#76** ★ ★ ★

Oscar Colas OF Born: 09/17/98 Age: 24 Bats: L Throws: L Height: 6'1" Weight: 209 lb. Origin: International Free Agent, 2022

YEAR	TEAM	LVL	AGE	PA	R	2B	3B	HR	RBI	BB	K	SB	CS	Whiff%	AVG/OBP/SLG	DRC+	BABIP	BRR	DRP	WARP
2022	WS	A+	23	268	37	13	3	7	42	22	54	1	1		.311/.369/.475	108	.375	-1.5	CF(54): -4.0	0.6
2022	BIR	AA	23	225	39	9	1	14	33	14	54	1	2		.306/.364/.563	122	.355	0.7	RF(32): 0.1, CF(12): -1.0	1.6
2022	CLT	AAA	23	33	5	2	0	2	4	2	12	1	1	42.1%	.387/.424/.645	79	.588	0.2	CF(4): 0.3, RF(2): -0.3	0.0
2023 DC	*CHW*	*MLB*	*24*	*491*	*50*	*19*	*3*	*13*	*50*	*28*	*137*	*4*	*1*	*31.5%*	*.247/.299/.395*	*88*	*.325*	*2.2*	*CF 0, RF 0*	*0.5*

Comparables: Adam Haseley (70), Andre Ethier (68), Anthony Webster (66)

Colás started playing professionally, in Cuba, at the age of 17. Over the next four years, both there and in Japan, he elevated himself to one of the sport's top international prospects. More than two years and a multi-million dollar deal passed between his final NPB game and his 2022 MiLB debut, and the wait was worth it. Chicago cautiously assigned him to High-A, but he was in Triple-A Charlotte by the end of the season, leaving a trail of overmatched pitchers in his wake. He's—thus far—gotten away with his aggressiveness at the plate via extraordinary bat-to-ball ability, and his offensive tools portend a good amount of power to go along with a high average. Bigger tests are surely coming for Colás—potentially at the major-league level, this year—but he has all the makings of an elite big-league outfielder.

Leury García UT Born: 03/18/91 Age: 32 Bats: S Throws: R Height: 5'8" Weight: 190 lb. Origin: International Free Agent, 2007

YEAR	TEAM	LVL	AGE	PA	R	2B	3B	HR	RBI	BB	K	SB	CS	Whiff%	AVG/OBP/SLG	DRC+	BABIP	BRR	DRP	WARP
2020	CHW	MLB	29	63	6	1	0	3	8	4	9	0	0	21.3%	.271/.317/.441	108	.277	0.7	SS(10): -0.4, 2B(5): 0.1, RF(3): -0.1	0.3
2021	CHW	MLB	30	474	60	22	4	5	54	41	97	6	2	24.5%	.267/.335/.376	88	.333	3.5	2B(36): 0.9, RF(34): 2.1, LF(26): -0.4	1.6
2022	CHW	MLB	31	315	38	8	0	3	20	7	65	2	0	24.3%	.210/.233/.267	68	.255	2.7	2B(47): 0.1, SS(19): -0.5, RF(15): 1.1	0.1
2023 DC	*CHW*	*MLB*	*32*	*348*	*32*	*13*	*1*	*5*	*29*	*18*	*71*	*4*	*1*	*24.5%*	*.247/.296/.346*	*78*	*.303*	*2.8*	*CF 0, 2B 0*	*0.3*

Comparables: Cookie Rojas (58), Endy Chavez (57), Gary Sutherland (56)

For all of García's faults in 2022, it's important to remember that his appearance in 67 of the White Sox's first 81 games wasn't his fault. He didn't pencil his name into the lineup as the starting second baseman more often than not, or name himself the go-to option behind Tim Anderson at shortstop. As the only player on the roster with the flexibility to field six different positions, García's usage is no surprise; fresh off a new, three-year deal signed before the lockout, Chicago's longest-tenured player did exactly what was asked of him in the field. What *was* García's fault: He was arguably the worst offensive player in baseball with 300 or more plate appearances, posting sub-replacement marks by virtually any metric. It was Tony La Russa's call to play him so frequently, and it was Rick Hahn's choice to put him on the roster to begin with—but nevertheless, García became something of a microcosm of an altogether underwhelming campaign.

Yasmani Grandal C/DH Born: 11/08/88 Age: 34 Bats: S Throws: R Height: 6'2" Weight: 225 lb. Origin: Round 1, 2010 Draft (#12 overall)

YEAR	TEAM	LVL	AGE	PA	R	2B	3B	HR	RBI	BB	K	SB	CS	Whiff%	AVG/OBP/SLG	DRC+	BABIP	BRR	DRP	WARP
2020	CHW	MLB	31	194	27	7	0	8	27	30	58	0	0	30.7%	.230/.351/.422	101	.299	-0.1	C(32): 4.8, 1B(6): -0.1	1.1
2021	CLT	AAA	32	25	3	1	0	1	1	2	8	0	0		.273/.360/.455	95	.385	0.0	C(5): 0.3, 1B(2): 0.0	0.1
2021	CHW	MLB	32	375	60	9	0	23	62	87	82	0	0	24.9%	.240/.420/.520	145	.246	-2.4	C(80): 2.4, 1B(8): 0.3	3.6
2022	CLT	AAA	33	38	6	1	0	2	5	9	2	0	0	23.3%	.379/.526/.621	142	.360	-0.2	1B(6): -0.3, C(5): 0.0	0.2
2022	CHW	MLB	33	376	15	7	0	5	27	45	79	1	0	21.6%	.202/.301/.269	83	.249	-6.1	C(71): 7, 1B(5): 0.2	0.6
2023 DC	*CHW*	*MLB*	*34*	*390*	*45*	*12*	*0*	*13*	*40*	*60*	*74*	*0*	*0*	*22.5%*	*.235/.358/.399*	*114*	*.266*	*-0.4*	*C 10*	*3.1*

Comparables: Brian McCann (74), Del Crandall (68), Chris Iannetta (67)

YEAR	TEAM	P. COUNT	FRM RUNS	BLK RUNS	THRW RUNS	TOT RUNS
2020	CHW	4830	4.8	0.0	0.4	5.1
2021	CHW	10543	2.8	-0.1	0.1	2.8
2022	CHW	9319	6.8	-0.4	0.9	7.3
2023	*CHW*	*13228*	*9.9*	*0.0*	*0.0*	*9.9*

Even if he has never quite returned to the heights he reached in Milwaukee and Los Angeles, the White Sox team-record free agent deal Grandal inked prior to the 2020 season has largely been successful. It was hard to expect his top-of-the-league framing marks to persist forever, and even the rosiest projections of the four years he'd spend on the South Side portended decline in the latter years. While our framing numbers still show Grandal as firmly above-average, everything else cratered in the contract's third year. The myriad of knee and back injuries he's traditionally played through piled up, and while 2021's offensive showcase made a lack of hardiness tenable, last year featured nothing of the sort. In the roughly 100 games that he was healthy enough to take the field, Grandal's power completely evaporated. While he still took a base on balls more often than the average bear, his overall hitting profile slipped to firmly below-average. Grandal has been a unicorn for several years—a backstop who could provide above-average production on both sides of the ball. He'd need to be something even rarer to return to that form as he enters his mid-30s.

Eloy Jiménez DH/LF Born: 11/27/96 Age: 26 Bats: R Throws: R Height: 6'4" Weight: 240 lb. Origin: International Free Agent, 2013

YEAR	TEAM	LVL	AGE	PA	R	2B	3B	HR	RBI	BB	K	SB	CS	Whiff%	AVG/OBP/SLG	DRC+	BABIP	BRR	DRP	WARP
2020	CHW	MLB	23	226	26	14	0	14	41	12	56	0	0	29.2%	.296/.332/.559	121	.340	-0.1	LF(54): -1.7	1.0
2021	CLT	AAA	24	41	3	2	0	1	2	2	14	0	0		.263/.293/.395	78	.375	-0.1	LF(8): 0.6	0.1
2021	CHW	MLB	24	231	23	10	0	10	37	16	57	0	0	33.8%	.249/.303/.437	96	.293	-0.5	LF(37): -2.2	0.4
2022	CLT	AAA	25	63	8	0	0	2	6	6	12	0	0	25.0%	.246/.317/.351	105	.279	-1.5	LF(5): -0.3	0.0
2022	CHW	MLB	25	327	40	12	0	16	54	28	72	0	0	30.5%	.295/.358/.500	124	.337	0.3	LF(30): -0.9	1.8
2023 DC	*CHW*	*MLB*	*26*	*545*	*62*	*22*	*1*	*22*	*71*	*41*	*125*	*0*	*1*	*30.0%*	*.267/.328/.451*	*116*	*.317*	*-3.1*	*LF 0*	*1.7*

Comparables: Matt Kemp (59), Raul Mondesi (58), Jackson Frazier (56)

That so much attention has been paid to Jiménez's adventurously poor defense in left field over the last two years is more or less a byproduct of his bat failing to consistently reach the prodigious heights that were portended. If Jiménez were the middle-of-the-order thumper many predicted when he rose through the ranks of a top prospect, his foibles in left field would be seen as a minor blip more so than a major problem. Nobody cared much, for example, that Manny Ramirez was a whimsical fielder. And there have hardly been any screams of displeasure nowadays when the Astros throw Yordan Alvarez out there. Whether it's playing a below-average left field or becoming a regular DH, Jiménez's value has always lied entirely with his bat. There were more than a few furrowed brows when he was once again injured in April after a slow start, and then hardly set the world on fire immediately upon his return in July.

Then a switch flipped and Jiménez was Jiménez again. He stayed healthy for a majority of the second half, putting up a .948 OPS and slugging 14 home runs after the All-Star break. While he still only played about half of the season because of the aforementioned injury, Jiménez's second half propelled him to the best offensive season, by DRC+, of his career. Now firmly in his mid-20s, expectations have never been higher for Jiménez to reach the lofty heights many envisioned. If his second half is any indication, he's about to reach them. Whether it's while patrolling the outfield or DHing is beside the point.

Yoán Moncada 3B

Born: 05/27/95 Age: 28 Bats: S Throws: R Height: 6'2" Weight: 225 lb. Origin: International Free Agent, 2015

YEAR	TEAM	LVL	AGE	PA	R	2B	3B	HR	RBI	BB	K	SB	CS	Whiff%	AVG/OBP/SLG	DRC+	BABIP	BRR	DRP	WARP
2020	CHW	MLB	25	231	28	8	3	6	24	28	72	0	0	30.7%	.225/.320/.385	84	.315	1.7	3B(52): 0.8	0.4
2021	CHW	MLB	26	616	74	33	1	14	61	84	157	3	2	28.1%	.263/.375/.412	102	.350	-0.8	3B(138): -5	1.6
2022	CLT	AAA	27	25	5	1	0	2	5	2	7	0	1	41.2%	.318/.360/.636	109	.357	-0.3	3B(5): 1.0	0.2
2022	CHW	MLB	27	433	41	18	1	12	51	32	114	2	0	28.0%	.212/.273/.353	82	.265	-0.2	3B(101): 8.8	1.0
2023 DC	*CHW*	*MLB*	*28*	*553*	*63*	*24*	*2*	*19*	*64*	*51*	*140*	*0*	*3*	*27.4%*	*.256/.332/.432*	*110*	*.320*	*-7.3*	*3B 3*	*1.3*

Comparables: Larry Parrish (68), Rick Schu (64), Wayne Garrett (63)

Hamartia, a concept first described by Aristotle, refers to a character's fatal flaw that eventually brings forth their downfall. In most cases, these are character flaws, such as greed, hubris, or ignorance. The causes of Moncada's 2022 failings were external and not internal, but he certainly had a fatal flaw: his legs. The former top prospect limped through the season with a litany of maladies, including a lengthy IL stay because of an oblique strain, a nagging quadriceps injury and another IL trip with a hamstring strain. Injuries are nothing new for Moncada, but when less than 100% in previous seasons, he could provide value by swinging at fewer pitches outside of the strike zone than virtually anyone. But injuries and a prolonged slump at the plate made him press, and in turn Moncada wound up basically halving his walk rate from the year prior while chasing pitches outside of the strike zone at a nearly career-worst rate. The days of Moncada living up to the prospect hype are long gone, but there's still a productive third baseman in there somewhere. He just needs to fend off that fatal flaw.

★ ★ ★ *2023 Top 101 Prospect* **#32** ★ ★ ★

Colson Montgomery SS

Born: 02/27/02 Age: 21 Bats: L Throws: R Height: 6'4" Weight: 205 lb. Origin: Round 1, 2021 Draft (#22 overall)

YEAR	TEAM	LVL	AGE	PA	R	2B	3B	HR	RBI	BB	K	SB	CS	Whiff%	AVG/OBP/SLG	DRC+	BABIP	BRR	DRP	WARP
2021	WSX	ROK	19	111	16	7	0	0	7	13	22	0	1		.287/.396/.362		.375			
2022	KAN	A	20	205	31	12	1	4	26	26	42	0	1		.324/.424/.476	125	.402	1.3	SS(41): 0.1	1.4
2022	WS	A+	20	164	22	4	1	5	14	26	26	1	0		.258/.387/.417	126	.282	-0.7	SS(37): 0.6	1.0
2022	BIR	AA	20	52	5	1	0	2	7	2	15	0	0		.146/.192/.292	99	.156	-0.3	SS(14): -1.5	0.0
2023 non-DC	*CHW*	*MLB*	*21*	*251*	*22*	*9*	*1*	*3*	*22*	*20*	*55*	*0*	*0*	*24.1%*	*.223/.296/.332*	*76*	*.279*	*1.1*	*SS 0*	*0.1*

Comparables: Ian Desmond (58), Kaleb Cowart (52), Ramiro Pena (51)

Perusing Montgomery's minor-league stat line, you might be surprised he got a bit of action at Double-A Birmingham, considering he was drafted out of high school and only in his first full year of pro ball. Unsurprisingly, he struggled, but his placement had more to do with the White Sox "Project Birmingham" initiative that brought basically any prospect worth a damn under one roof for the final month or so of the season. At two other stops, Montgomery more than justified the late-first-round selection, showing strong barrel control that justified the org's decision to move him to full-season ball after just 45 complex games. There are still questions as to whether his power potential will show up in-game, as well as if he has the quickness to stick at shortstop long-term. Despite his cup of coffee in Birmingham, he's still several years from making a difference at the major-league level—but he's done nothing but justify his prospect ranking thus far.

Victor Reyes OF

Born: 10/05/94 Age: 28 Bats: S Throws: R Height: 6'5" Weight: 194 lb. Origin: International Free Agent, 2011

YEAR	TEAM	LVL	AGE	PA	R	2B	3B	HR	RBI	BB	K	SB	CS	Whiff%	AVG/OBP/SLG	DRC+	BABIP	BRR	DRP	WARP
2020	DET	MLB	25	213	30	7	2	4	14	9	45	8	2	26.5%	.277/.315/.391	90	.340	1.7	CF(30): -1.7, LF(22): -0.2, RF(18): 0.1	0.4
2021	TOL	AAA	26	91	13	7	2	1	10	10	17	5	2		.385/.462/.564	110	.475	-0.6	CF(9): 0.1, LF(6): -0.4, RF(4): -1.0	0.2
2021	DET	MLB	26	220	26	10	4	5	22	8	55	5	1	25.6%	.258/.284/.416	89	.327	-0.9	RF(43): 0.4, CF(20): 0.1	0.4
2022	TOL	AAA	27	32	9	1	0	3	5	4	2	1	1		.333/.406/.704	138	.261	-0.4	CF(2): -0.2, RF(2): 0.2	0.2
2022	DET	MLB	27	336	27	19	3	3	34	13	77	2	2	27.5%	.254/.289/.362	81	.322	-1.6	RF(63): -1.5, LF(19): -0.4, CF(8): -0.4	-0.1
2023 non-DC	*CHW*	*MLB*	*28*	*251*	*23*	*11*	*2*	*5*	*26*	*13*	*56*	*5*	*2*	*25.7%*	*.259/.304/.394*	*91*	*.321*	*0.9*	*RF 1, CF -1*	*0.4*

Comparables: Nate Schierholtz (50), Ben Revere (50), Gerardo Parra (50)

In the end, it's difficult to identify a particular mark that Reyes left on the Tigers organization. He was one of the first offseason cuts made after a year in which he received his most major-league opportunities and did the least with them. The season did produce his most momentous play by Championship Win Probability Added: a final-out, walk-off double against ailing then-Padres closer Taylor Rogers in late July. That it ultimately didn't matter at all is fitting. It reinforces the idea that the most lasting mark Reyes left is the tattoo of his shirt, on the calf of an unfortunate Tigers fan who made an ill-timed bet against his own team beating the Astros in 2019.

Luis Robert Jr. CF Born: 08/03/97 Age: 25 Bats: R Throws: R Height: 6'2" Weight: 220 lb. Origin: International Free Agent, 2017

YEAR	TEAM	LVL	AGE	PA	R	2B	3B	HR	RBI	BB	K	SB	CS	Whiff%	AVG/OBP/SLG	DRC+	BABIP	BRR	DRP	WARP
2020	CHW	MLB	22	227	33	8	0	11	31	20	73	9	2	41.7%	.233/.302/.436	92	.300	0.9	CF(56): 6.4	1.2
2021	CLT	AAA	23	36	4	1	0	1	3	5	9	2	0		.276/.417/.414	97	.368	0.5	CF(5): -1.4	0.0
2021	CHW	MLB	23	296	42	22	1	13	43	14	61	6	1	28.4%	.338/.378/.567	122	.394	0.6	CF(67): -0.7	2.1
2022	CHW	MLB	24	401	54	18	0	12	56	17	77	11	3	27.1%	.284/.319/.426	108	.329	1.9	CF(91): -3.9	1.6
2023 DC	*CHW*	*MLB*	*25*	*562*	*68*	*25*	*2*	*19*	*65*	*30*	*116*	*19*	*6*	*27.5%*	*.289/.337/.458*	*121*	*.341*	*4.7*	*CF 0*	*3.6*

Comparables: Matt Kemp (72), Mookie Betts (67), Austin Hays (66)

It's easy to look at Robert's 2022 numbers and be disappointed. While he missed a significant chunk of time for the second straight season, what was more jarring—on the surface—is that he didn't exactly dominate when healthy enough to play. Actually, the term "healthy enough to play" isn't exactly fair, because Robert frequently played when he didn't seem healthy enough to do so; particularly late in the season, he appeared to be trying to prop up a faltering White Sox offense in a futile attempt to save a lost season. Robert had two different IL stints, one with COVID-19 and another with an undisclosed illness, of which the only detail revealed was that he had blurred vision. He also played through a groin injury in April and a hand/wrist issue for the majority of September. The latter malady hindered him to the point that, when he was finally shut down late in the month, he readily admitted trying to play through it was a mistake.

So, what we're left with is a season with a clear "incomplete" grade for a player who many remain hopeful takes the leap into the "best player in baseball" conversation. After showing plenty of flashes of that guy in his rookie year when healthy, he was still there in fits and starts last year. It seems all he needs to get there is a year of good health.

Gavin Sheets RF Born: 04/23/96 Age: 27 Bats: L Throws: L Height: 6'5" Weight: 230 lb. Origin: Round 2, 2017 Draft (#49 overall)

YEAR	TEAM	LVL	AGE	PA	R	2B	3B	HR	RBI	BB	K	SB	CS	Whiff%	AVG/OBP/SLG	DRC+	BABIP	BRR	DRP	WARP
2021	CLT	AAA	25	254	36	15	0	11	46	25	55	1	1		.295/.362/.507	114	.344	0.1	1B(35): 0.5, RF(24): 0.1, LF(2): -0.1	1.1
2021	CHW	MLB	25	179	23	8	0	11	34	16	40	0	0	20.2%	.250/.324/.506	108	.264	-4.3	RF(13): -1.3, 1B(10): 0.1, LF(4): 0	0.1
2022	CLT	AAA	26	39	6	4	0	2	7	2	6	0	0	22.9%	.270/.308/.541	107	.276	0.4	1B(8): 0.9	0.2
2022	CHW	MLB	26	410	34	19	0	15	53	27	86	0	0	22.1%	.241/.295/.411	97	.272	-2.7	RF(85): -3.6, 1B(13): -0.2, LF(3): 0	0.3
2023 DC	*CHW*	*MLB*	*27*	*363*	*38*	*15*	*0*	*11*	*40*	*25*	*67*	*0*	*1*	*21.8%*	*.251/.310/.409*	*98*	*.283*	*-3.2*	*RF -1, 1B 0*	*0.1*

Comparables: Lucas Duda (71), C.J. Cron (66), Kennys Vargas (64)

Sheets is a monster in the batter's box. It's difficult to watch him stand in and not harken back to memories of [insert your choice of left-handed masher from a previous era here]. The problem, however, is that his production as lefty masher looks more like what you'd expect out of [insert light-hitting infielder here] than [insert lefty masher here]. That's not to say that he's powerless, of course. When he hunts out his preferred fastball and makes contact, it's something to behold. Everything that comes between those instances, however, leaves plenty to be desired. Sheets still has a place as a platoon first base/DH type (you straight up do not want him facing a lefty), but his long-term standing in the league is far from secure in an era where [insert lefty masher] types aren't considered as necessary as they once were.

Lenyn Sosa MI Born: 01/25/00 Age: 23 Bats: R Throws: R Height: 6'0" Weight: 180 lb. Origin: International Free Agent, 2016

YEAR	TEAM	LVL	AGE	PA	R	2B	3B	HR	RBI	BB	K	SB	CS	Whiff%	AVG/OBP/SLG	DRC+	BABIP	BRR	DRP	WARP
2021	WS	A+	21	353	45	19	1	10	49	14	77	3	4		.290/.321/.443	98	.349	0.4	SS(64): 5.1, 2B(21): 1.2	1.6
2021	BIR	AA	21	121	10	5	0	1	7	2	28	0	1		.214/.240/.282	77	.273	-0.2	SS(20): 1.9, 2B(9): 0.8, 3B(4): -0.3	0.3
2022	BIR	AA	22	289	47	10	2	14	48	21	40	0	0		.331/.384/.549	136	.340	1.5	SS(35): 2.1, 3B(13): 0.8, 2B(9): 0.3	2.5
2022	CLT	AAA	22	247	30	12	0	9	31	18	43	3	4	20.7%	.296/.352/.469	108	.331	0.3	SS(33): 0.5, 2B(23): -0.6	1.0
2022	CHW	MLB	22	36	3	1	0	1	1	1	12	0	0	27.0%	.114/.139/.229	75	.136	0.8	2B(6): 0.5, SS(5): -0.2	0.1
2023 DC	*CHW*	*MLB*	*23*	*125*	*13*	*5*	*0*	*2*	*12*	*6*	*26*	*0*	*1*	*23.6%*	*.251/.293/.373*	*84*	*.303*	*-0.4*	*SS 0, 2B 0*	*0.0*

Comparables: Hanser Alberto (62), Miguel Andújar (61), José Rondón (59)

Sosa was commonly referred to as a "sleeper" in the White Sox system after something of a breakout 2021, when he displayed a surprising amount of pop, to go along with an impressive hit tool, on his way to Double-A. He continued that ascent last year, mastering the high minors and even getting a (mostly forgettable) cup of coffee at the major-league level. More time at the game's highest level will tell us whether Sosa is a starting middle infielder or merely a competent utility man. Successful organizations need both, of course, so Sosa's future remains bright. Nobody's sleeping on him anymore.

Andrew Vaughn RF Born: 04/03/98 Age: 25 Bats: R Throws: R Height: 6'0" Weight: 215 lb. Origin: Round 1, 2019 Draft (#3 overall)

YEAR	TEAM	LVL	AGE	PA	R	2B	3B	HR	RBI	BB	K	SB	CS	Whiff%	AVG/OBP/SLG	DRC+	BABIP	BRR	DRP	WARP
2021	CHW	MLB	23	469	56	22	0	15	48	41	101	1	1	24.3%	.235/.309/.396	98	.271	-2.4	LF(95): -5.1, RF(18): -2.4, 1B(15): 0.1	0.5
2022	CHW	MLB	24	555	60	28	1	17	76	31	96	0	0	21.0%	.271/.321/.429	109	.301	-5.2	RF(45): -4.2, LF(44): -2.7, 1B(23): 0.6	0.9
2023 DC	*CHW*	*MLB*	*25*	*555*	*61*	*24*	*1*	*16*	*61*	*40*	*97*	*0*	*1*	*21.3%*	*.257/.323/.410*	*107*	*.290*	*-5.2*	*1B -1*	*0.6*

Comparables: Nick Evans (65), Jackson Frazier (64), Nick Swisher (63)

Observing Vaughn's 2022 season in a vacuum, it'd be easy to focus on the negative. He was among the worst defenders in baseball, he was a negative baserunner, and his bat—while sensational at times—was barely enough to prop up those other aspects. However, the former Cal star, as you likely know, is not an outfielder. He was and continues to be a first baseman who has spent the better part of the last two seasons masquerading in the outfield corners. At the plate, the outlook is plenty rosy. In his second full season, he greatly improved his ability to hit right-handed pitching while showcasing the kind of gap-to-gap power that made scouts drool. That Vaughn did all that while playing out of position is impressive enough, and brings with it plenty of optimism that he can become a cornerstone, middle-of-the-order bat for years to come. He just needs to do so while manning first base.

Seby Zavala C/1B

Born: 08/28/93 Age: 29 Bats: R Throws: R Height: 5'11" Weight: 205 lb. Origin: Round 12, 2015 Draft (#352 overall)

YEAR	TEAM	LVL	AGE	PA	R	2B	3B	HR	RBI	BB	K	SB	CS	Whiff%	AVG/OBP/SLG	DRC+	BABIP	BRR	DRP	WARP
2021	CLT	AAA	27	179	19	5	0	8	20	20	75	0	1		.168/.263/.355	70	.240	-0.4	C(35): -2.6, 1B(3): -0.1	-0.2
2021	CHW	MLB	27	104	15	3	0	5	15	6	41	0	0	42.1%	.183/.240/.376	69	.255	0.0	C(33): 0.4	0.1
2022	CLT	AAA	28	169	26	12	0	8	16	26	60	0	0	42.9%	.282/.396/.535	85	.432	-0.5	1B(27): -1.4, C(13): -0.2	0.0
2022	CHW	MLB	28	205	22	14	0	2	21	19	64	0	0	37.6%	.270/.347/.382	74	.404	-1.4	C(58): 5.2, 1B(2): -0.6	0.4
2023 DC	*CHW*	*MLB*	*29*	*183*	*20*	*7*	*0*	*6*	*19*	*16*	*68*	*0*	*0*	*39.6%*	*.216/.297/.386*	*85*	*.324*	*-1.4*	*C 4*	*0.6*

Comparables: Carlos Corporán (57), Curt Casali (54), Chad Wallach (52)

YEAR	TEAM	P. COUNT	FRM RUNS	BLK RUNS	THRW RUNS	TOT RUNS
2021	CLT	5633	-2.0	-0.8	0.2	-2.7
2021	CHW	4374	1.0	-0.3	0.0	0.7
2022	CLT	1752	-0.2	0.1	0.0	-0.2
2022	CHW	7464	5.2	-0.1	0.0	5.1
2023	*CHW*	*7215*	*3.4*	*0.0*	*-0.2*	*3.2*

What makes a good backup catcher? Teams certainly don't anticipate much offense. A good secondary backstop frames well, controls the running game at a decent rate and develops a good rapport with the pitching staff. Anything added by the stick is just a bonus. If a backup catcher did all of those things well...well, they probably wouldn't be a backup. Zavala started the 2022 season firmly third (at best) on the White Sox catching depth chart, behind a perennial All-Star candidate and a guy acquired during spring training. Yasmani Grandal's injury woes afforded Zavala an opportunity, and he performed admirably enough that the White Sox found Reese Maguire expendable come the trade deadline. No, Zavala probably won't put up a .700+ OPS most years—his BABIP shows a boatload of luck. But he threw out runners, framed well and developed a rapport with White Sox pitchers—all the typical duties of his job description. Life is tough for a backup catcher, but there was far from a guarantee Zavala was even that prior to the season. He now pretty firmly is.

PITCHERS

Tanner Banks LHP

Born: 10/24/91 Age: 31 Bats: R Throws: L Height: 6'1" Weight: 210 lb. Origin: Round 18, 2014 Draft (#528 overall)

YEAR	TEAM	LVL	AGE	W	L	SV	G	GS	IP	H	HR	BB/9	K/9	K	GB%	BABIP	WHIP	ERA	DRA-	WARP	MPH	FB%	Whiff%	CSP
2021	CLT	AAA	29	3	3	0	25	5	59^2	69	10	2.0	10.6	70	42.8%	.364	1.37	4.53	93	1.1				
2022	CLT	AAA	30	0	1	0	9	2	17	17	1	2.6	12.7	24	51.2%	.390	1.29	2.65	76	0.4	93.6	39.5%	28.7%	
2022	CHW	MLB	30	2	0	0	35	0	53	42	5	3.1	8.3	49	45.6%	.257	1.13	3.06	91	0.8	93.1	45.2%	19.4%	57.8%
2023 DC	*CHW*	*MLB*	*31*	*1*	*1*	*0*	*32*	*0*	*27.7*	*27*	*3*	*2.7*	*7.0*	*21*	*45.0%*	*.285*	*1.27*	*3.66*	*97*	*0.1*	*93.1*	*45.2%*	*21.4%*	*57.8%*

Comparables: Richard Bleier (46), Vidal Nuño (46), Tommy Layne (45)

On September 18, 2022, Banks pitched the final three innings of what was ultimately an 11-5 White Sox victory over the Tigers. Banks entered with the score 10-4, after two other pitchers had already relieved starter Vince Velasquez—who, crucially, only completed four innings. Standard knowledge of the rules of Major League Baseball would lead you to deduce that the first pitcher who relieved Velasquez—José Ruiz—would get the win, as he came in with the White Sox leading, 7-2. But because of a little-used rule that gives the Official Scorer the ability to award the win "to the pitcher who was the most effective," Banks got the win instead of the blowout, three-inning save fans are likely more familiar with. This was an oddity, which is nothing new for Banks—his rise from organizational arm to major-league contributor at the age of 30 was anything but normal.

Aaron Bummer LHP

Born: 09/21/93 Age: 29 Bats: L Throws: L Height: 6'3" Weight: 215 lb. Origin: Round 19, 2014 Draft (#558 overall)

YEAR	TEAM	LVL	AGE	W	L	SV	G	GS	IP	H	HR	BB/9	K/9	K	GB%	BABIP	WHIP	ERA	DRA-	WARP	MPH	FB%	Whiff%	CSP
2020	CHW	MLB	26	1	0	0	9	0	9^1	5	0	4.8	13.5	14	68.4%	.263	1.07	0.96	75	0.2	96.1	85.1%	35.0%	43.8%
2021	CHW	MLB	27	5	5	2	62	0	56^1	42	3	4.6	12.0	75	76.9%	.298	1.26	3.51	73	1.3	95.4	62.0%	32.3%	53.6%
2022	CHW	MLB	28	2	1	2	32	0	26^2	30	2	3.4	10.1	30	62.7%	.384	1.50	2.36	86	0.5	94.8	63.9%	27.6%	50.1%
2023 DC	*CHW*	*MLB*	*29*	*2*	*2*	*5*	*58*	*0*	*50.3*	*50*	*4*	*4.0*	*10.2*	*57*	*65.6%*	*.337*	*1.44*	*4.04*	*97*	*0.3*	*95.3*	*66.2%*	*28.5%*	*51.4%*

Comparables: Luis Avilán (68), Wesley Wright (63), Rex Brothers (62)

Bummer is undoubtedly tired of the jokes. Any time something goes awry—a bad outing, some bad luck, or something else—he must be accustomed to puns about his last name. How can there not be puns? His surname is an informal noun, commonly uttered when something disappointing happens. When Bummer was on the mound in 2022, there was little room for quips. He remains his effective, bat-missing self...with, still, a few more walks than is preferable out of a late-inning reliever. What's felt like a joke, however, is Bummer's dismal luck with injury. A pair of IL stints significantly limited the lefty for the second time in three seasons, producing far too many utterances of his name as double entendre.

Sean Burke RHP

Born: 12/18/99 Age: 23 Bats: R Throws: R Height: 6'6" Weight: 230 lb. Origin: Round 3, 2021 Draft (#94 overall)

YEAR	TEAM	LVL	AGE	W	L	SV	G	GS	IP	H	HR	BB/9	K/9	K	GB%	BABIP	WHIP	ERA	DRA-	WARP	MPH	FB%	Whiff%	CSP
2021	KAN	A	21	0	1	0	5	5	14	9	0	6.4	12.9	20	43.3%	.321	1.36	3.21	92	0.2				
2022	WS	A+	22	2	1	0	6	5	28	24	3	3.9	10.0	31	30.9%	.318	1.29	2.89	114	0.0				
2022	BIR	AA	22	2	7	0	19	19	73	72	11	4.1	12.2	99	44.8%	.361	1.44	4.81	83	1.4				
2022	CLT	AAA	22	0	2	0	2	2	7	12	1	3.9	9.0	7	34.6%	.440	2.14	11.57	120	0.0	92.9	55.4%	23.3%	
2023 non-DC	*CHW*	*MLB*	*23*	*2*	*3*	*0*	*57*	*0*	*50*	*53*	*8*	*5.2*	*9.2*	*51*	*40.5%*	*.326*	*1.65*	*5.70*	*131*	*-0.6*			*26.0%*	

Comparables: Hunter Wood (55), Carson LaRue (53), Bryan Mitchell (53)

It was, by most accounts, a successful first full pro season for Burke. A third-round college arm drafted in 2021, with an electric fastball and control issues, Burke found his footing fairly well in Double-A Birmingham, missing plenty of bats while fighting occasional bouts with his command. So, basically what you would expect out of a pitching prospect still getting his feet wet. The stuff is worth dreaming on if Burke's command jumps a level or two; a late-season promotion to Triple-A means he could be in the major-league plans sooner than later.

Dylan Cease RHP Born: 12/28/95 Age: 27 Bats: R Throws: R Height: 6'2" Weight: 195 lb. Origin: Round 6, 2014 Draft (#169 overall)

YEAR	TEAM	LVL	AGE	W	L	SV	G	GS	IP	H	HR	BB/9	K/9	K	GB%	BABIP	WHIP	ERA	DRA	WARP	MPH	FB%	Whiff%	CSP
2020	CHW	MLB	24	5	4	0	12	12	58^1	50	12	5.2	6.8	44	39.8%	.239	1.44	4.01	151	-1.0	97.7	47.8%	25.3%	42.4%
2021	CHW	MLB	25	13	7	0	32	32	165^2	139	20	3.7	12.3	226	33.6%	.310	1.25	3.91	77	3.5	96.8	46.8%	34.6%	53.1%
2022	CHW	MLB	26	14	8	0	32	32	184	126	16	3.8	11.1	227	38.7%	.261	1.11	2.20	71	4.5	97.0	40.8%	33.3%	52.5%
2023 DC	*CHW*	*MLB*	*27*	*11*	*9*	*0*	*30*	*30*	*175.3*	*146*	*21*	*3.9*	*11.4*	*222*	*38.4%*	*.301*	*1.27*	*3.38*	*85*	*2.8*	*97.0*	*44.1%*	*32.3%*	*51.3%*

Comparables: Wade Miller (82), Lance McCullers Jr. (82), Catfish Hunter (81)

A perfect relationship isn't perfect because the people involved are 100%, authentically free of faults. No, even happy romances have their fault lines. It's just that everything else is so great that the little things fade away. If your annoying roommate leaves the dirty sponge in the sink, you rage. If your beau does, you don't think twice. If a visitor stays the night and leaves a damp towel on the bathroom floor, you are annoyed. If the love of your life does, you shrug your shoulders and hang it up.

Cease is not a perfect partner. It's difficult to comprehend how a pitcher can be as dominant as he was in 2022 while also leading the majors in walks, but he's a case study: He walked three or more batters in nearly half of his starts this season, but six of those 15 outings also featured eight or nine strikeouts. Of his remaining 17 starts, he punched out at least eight in 12 turns. By all accounts, Cease was one of the most dominant pitchers in baseball. Would the White Sox prefer that dominance came with a few less free passes—which would, in turn, give him more longevity on a start-to-start basis? Sure. But when everything turns out as perfectly as they did in 2022, you look past the little things.

Mike Clevinger RHP Born: 12/21/90 Age: 32 Bats: R Throws: R Height: 6'4" Weight: 215 lb. Origin: Round 4, 2011 Draft (#135 overall)

YEAR	TEAM	LVL	AGE	W	L	SV	G	GS	IP	H	HR	BB/9	K/9	K	GB%	BABIP	WHIP	ERA	DRA-	WARP	MPH	FB%	Whiff%	CSP
2020	SD	MLB	29	2	1	0	4	4	19	14	1	1.4	9.0	19	29.8%	.283	0.89	2.84	100	0.2	95.6	46.1%	28.5%	49.2%
2020	CLE	MLB	29	1	1	0	4	4	22^2	20	5	4.4	8.3	21	36.7%	.273	1.37	3.18	113	0.1	94.5	47.4%	32.1%	46.5%
2022	ELP	AAA	31	0	0	0	2	2	6^2	7	1	2.7	13.5	10	37.5%	.400	1.35	2.70	85	0.1	95.1	47.8%	33.9%	
2022	SD	MLB	31	7	7	0	23	22	114^1	102	20	2.8	7.2	91	35.5%	.250	1.20	4.33	108	0.6	93.5	52.0%	24.4%	55.9%
2023 DC	*CHW*	*MLB*	*32*	*7*	*7*	*0*	*24*	*24*	*123.7*	*117*	*17*	*2.9*	*8.1*	*111*	*36.7%*	*.287*	*1.27*	*3.76*	*98*	*1.1*	*94.1*	*51.3%*	*26.9%*	*53.1%*

Comparables: Russ Ortiz (76), Kevin Appier (75), Joe Horlen (75)

Clevinger didn't have the easiest time after joining the Padres. The long-haired, sunflower-loving, baseball-for-beer-trading pitcher made just four starts with the team in 2020 before being shut down for Tommy John surgery—not pitching again for the team until May 4 last year—strangely enough, against his old team Cleveland. He lasted 4⅔ innings—desperately trying for that last out so he could get the win. The rest of the year, Clevinger battled knee soreness and a trip on the COVID-19 IL.

That may not be what Clevinger dreamed about when he joined up in San Diego, but he was probably happy just to be around. While he was rehabbing in El Paso in April, his flight took a nosedive out of the sky, and the cabin filled with smoke before eventually leveling out at about 5,000 feet before making an emergency landing.

"The guy next to me is trying to keep me calm," Clevinger told *The San Diego Union-Tribune*. "I'm freaking out. ... He's keeping his chill while everyone is crying and freaking out. The flight attendant was crying. Like, she had no bedside manner at all."

So, yeah, a roughly league-average ERA looks pretty good in comparison. He hopes for smoother skies in Chicago.

Jake Diekman LHP Born: 01/21/87 Age: 36 Bats: R Throws: L Height: 6'4" Weight: 195 lb. Origin: Round 30, 2007 Draft (#923 overall)

YEAR	TEAM	LVL	AGE	W	L	SV	G	GS	IP	H	HR	BB/9	K/9	K	GB%	BABIP	WHIP	ERA	DRA-	WARP	MPH	FB%	Whiff%	CSP
2020	OAK	MLB	33	2	0	0	21	0	21^1	8	1	5.1	13.1	31	60.0%	.184	0.94	0.42	62	0.6	95.2	59.3%	40.8%	49.2%
2021	OAK	MLB	34	3	3	7	67	0	60^2	47	10	5.0	12.3	83	34.8%	.282	1.34	3.86	86	1.0	95.6	66.9%	35.1%	52.0%
2022	CHW	MLB	35	0	3	0	26	0	19^1	25	4	5.6	13.0	28	44.6%	.404	1.91	6.52	82	0.4	95.6	69.8%	32.4%	52.9%
2022	BOS	MLB	35	5	1	1	44	0	38^1	27	5	7.0	12.0	51	35.7%	.278	1.49	4.23	102	0.3	95.7	60.5%	33.0%	48.4%
2023 DC	*CHW*	*MLB*	*36*	*2*	*3*	*0*	*58*	*0*	*50.3*	*45*	*7*	*5.7*	*12.1*	*67*	*40.9%*	*.321*	*1.53*	*4.99*	*115*	*-0.2*	*95.6*	*63.2%*	*32.2%*	*50.0%*

Comparables: Jesse Orosco (83), Tippy Martinez (83), Jerry Blevins (83)

Diekman's mid-season move from Boston to the South Side was nothing new to him. The White Sox were the seventh team to employ his services in his 11-year career. Middle relievers switching teams as often as Diekman is typical, especially for those who throw with their left arm. The August 1 trade represented the fourth time he was moved at or near the trade deadline, with the first coming as the "other guy" who moved from Texas to Philadelphia in the Cole Hamels trade back in 2015. Diekman's highly volatile profile—that is to say, a boatload of walks coupled with a boatload of strikeouts—means he shouldn't be too comfortable, no matter where he winds up next. That left arm is made for walkin', after all. Both figuratively and literally.

Matt Foster RHP Born: 01/27/95 Age: 28 Bats: R Throws: R Height: 6'0" Weight: 215 lb. Origin: Round 20, 2016 Draft (#596 overall)

YEAR	TEAM	LVL	AGE	W	L	SV	G	GS	IP	H	HR	BB/9	K/9	K	GB%	BABIP	WHIP	ERA	DRA-	WARP	MPH	FB%	Whiff%	CSP
2020	CHW	MLB	25	6	1	0	23	2	28^2	16	2	2.8	9.7	31	34.8%	.212	0.87	2.20	101	0.3	94.0	57.3%	30.3%	49.1%
2021	CLT	AAA	26	0	2	0	14	0	14^2	14	2	1.2	14.1	23	25.7%	.364	1.09	4.30	76	0.4				
2021	CHW	MLB	26	2	1	1	37	0	39	43	9	3.0	9.2	40	28.6%	.309	1.44	6.00	111	0.1	93.6	67.1%	23.8%	56.8%
2022	CLT	AAA	27	1	0	2	11	0	11	7	0	1.6	11.5	14	28.0%	.280	0.82	0.82	88	0.2	93.9	55.8%	42.1%	
2022	CHW	MLB	27	1	2	1	48	0	45	43	6	3.4	8.4	42	30.6%	.291	1.33	4.40	104	0.3	93.9	52.6%	21.2%	55.4%
2023 DC	*CHW*	*MLB*	*28*	*1*	*1*	*0*	*32*	*0*	*27.7*	*27*	*4*	*3.1*	*8.8*	*27*	*32.9%*	*.298*	*1.31*	*3.96*	*102*	*0.1*	*93.8*	*58.4%*	*24.4%*	*55.0%*

Comparables: Jonathan Holder (70), Justin De Fratus (69), Nick Wittgren (69)

The benefit of hindsight shows us that Foster was probably never going to be as good as his breakout 2020 debut, nor as bad as his hellacious sophomore campaign. Instead, he's settled in as a fairly anonymous middle reliever; the kind of pitcher you don't entirely trust in high-leverage situations, but can safely roster and use in well-chosen spots. Last season was the first where Foster's DRA was even in the same stratosphere as his ERA, proving he's settled in—though his pitch mix remains in flux.

Lucas Giolito RHP

Born: 07/14/94 Age: 28 Bats: R Throws: R Height: 6'6" Weight: 245 lb. Origin: Round 1, 2012 Draft (#16 overall)

YEAR	TEAM	LVL	AGE	W	L	SV	G	GS	IP	H	HR	BB/9	K/9	K	GB%	BABIP	WHIP	ERA	DRA-	WARP	MPH	FB%	Whiff%	CSP
2020	CHW	MLB	25	4	3	0	12	12	72^1	47	8	3.5	12.1	97	43.5%	.255	1.04	3.48	73	1.9	94.2	50.6%	36.6%	46.6%
2021	CHW	MLB	26	11	9	0	31	31	178^2	145	27	2.6	10.1	201	33.3%	.270	1.10	3.53	89	2.7	94.0	43.9%	32.2%	58.9%
2022	CHW	MLB	27	11	9	0	30	30	161^2	171	24	3.4	9.9	177	38.6%	.340	1.44	4.90	106	1.1	92.8	47.7%	28.5%	56.1%
2023 DC	*CHW*	*MLB*	*28*	*10*	*9*	*0*	*29*	*29*	*166*	*150*	*22*	*3.2*	*9.5*	*176*	*38.2%*	*.294*	*1.26*	*3.59*	*93*	*2.0*	*93.5*	*47.4%*	*29.6%*	*55.7%*

Comparables: Joe Coleman (74), John Smoltz (74), Jim Maloney (72)

It's impossible to fully understand how much a bout of COVID-19 might affect any particular professional athlete. So it could be viewed as something of an excuse to assign blame for Giolito's struggles throughout most of the season on his week-long stay on the COVID-19 injured list in May. This much is true, however: He had a 2.70 ERA, with consistent fastball velocity of around 94 mph, through five starts before hitting the list. When he returned, the results were rough, and a lot of that has to do with a nearly two-mph dip in his fastball velocity. Much of Giolito's stark career turnaround years ago was ascribed to an overhaul in his mechanics, which allowed him to create ride on his fastball and tunnel it with his devastating changeup. Whatever the reason, he wasn't doing that in (most of) 2022, and whether or not he can regain that form will go a long way in determining where the Santa Monica native's future lies entering his final season before free agency.

Kendall Graveman RHP

Born: 12/21/90 Age: 32 Bats: R Throws: R Height: 6'2" Weight: 200 lb. Origin: Round 8, 2013 Draft (#235 overall)

YEAR	TEAM	LVL	AGE	W	L	SV	G	GS	IP	H	HR	BB/9	K/9	K	GB%	BABIP	WHIP	ERA	DRA-	WARP	MPH	FB%	Whiff%	CSP
2020	SEA	MLB	29	1	3	0	11	2	18^2	15	2	3.9	7.2	15	48.1%	.250	1.23	5.79	100	0.2	95.0	68.1%	18.6%	47.7%
2021	SEA	MLB	30	4	0	10	30	0	33	15	2	2.2	9.3	34	53.9%	.176	0.70	0.82	86	0.5	96.6	69.1%	24.0%	49.5%
2021	HOU	MLB	30	1	1	0	23	0	23	20	1	4.7	10.6	27	56.1%	.339	1.39	3.13	94	0.3	96.7	74.4%	28.0%	48.4%
2022	CHW	MLB	31	3	4	6	65	0	65	65	5	3.6	9.1	66	54.2%	.324	1.40	3.18	92	0.9	96.8	55.1%	27.1%	51.6%
2023 DC	*CHW*	*MLB*	*32*	*2*	*2*	*18*	*58*	*0*	*50.3*	*51*	*5*	*3.6*	*8.8*	*49*	*52.1%*	*.321*	*1.43*	*4.33*	*106*	*0.1*	*96.6*	*62.0%*	*25.1%*	*50.3%*

Comparables: Jason Grilli (68), LaTroy Hawkins (63), Wily Peralta (62)

In a nutshell, Graveman had a perfectly fine season. While he didn't quite keep pace with the strikeout numbers he posted the season prior nor the run prevention luck he ran into, Graveman was a valuable late-inning bullpen weapon for a team that entered the season with designs on contention. That he was the most notable addition to the White Sox roster in 2022—and wasn't the fire-breathing dragon we saw with Seattle and Houston—made him draw a bit of ire from a fanbase with high expectations. Still, Graveman proved the leap he made in 2021 was no aberration, and he looks the part of a strong late-inning bullpen piece for as long as that right arm continues to fire bullets.

Liam Hendriks RHP

Born: 02/10/89 Age: 34 Bats: R Throws: R Height: 6'0" Weight: 235 lb. Origin: International Free Agent, 2007

YEAR	TEAM	LVL	AGE	W	L	SV	G	GS	IP	H	HR	BB/9	K/9	K	GB%	BABIP	WHIP	ERA	DRA-	WARP	MPH	FB%	Whiff%	CSP
2020	OAK	MLB	31	3	1	14	24	0	25^1	14	1	1.1	13.1	37	28.8%	.260	0.67	1.78	71	0.7	96.2	70.5%	36.2%	49.3%
2021	CHW	MLB	32	8	3	38	69	0	71	45	11	0.9	14.3	113	32.4%	.254	0.73	2.54	59	2.2	97.9	69.0%	38.1%	55.3%
2022	CHW	MLB	33	4	4	37	58	0	57^2	44	7	2.5	13.3	85	34.6%	.303	1.04	2.81	60	1.7	97.8	60.5%	41.4%	51.4%
2023 DC	*CHW*	*MLB*	*34*	*1*	*1*	*11*	*25*	*0*	*22.3*	*17*	*2*	*2.0*	*13.5*	*33*	*34.5%*	*.310*	*1.00*	*2.29*	*61*	*0.5*	*97.6*	*65.9%*	*36.9%*	*52.3%*

Comparables: Tommy Hunter (76), Jason Isringhausen (76), Arthur Rhodes (72)

It's a much tougher burden to be the emotional and vocal leader of a team when nothing is going right. Hendriks took on that mantel upon joining the South Side prior to the 2021 season, and throughout a follow-up campaign that could generously be described as "disappointing," the veteran reliever was often the one offering rallying cry-type quotes that ultimately proved fruitless. He also made headlines when Miguel Cairo took over as acting manager for the ailing Tony La Russa and the team promptly rattled off a hot streak: Many took his quote noting that the White Sox "didn't have that fight earlier" as a shot at the (now-former) skipper.

Hendriks certainly showed plenty of fight throughout a season that began on a rough note, but was soon righted with a month-long IL stay for a forearm strain. He walked twice as many batters as the preceding campaign, but DRA said he was even better than that world-beating showing; while the White Sox limped to the finish line, Hendriks allowed just one earned run over 12 September appearances. Being a hype man on a sinking ship is tough, as is being one of baseball's best closers on a team going nowhere fast. Hendriks stood tall in both roles. In January, he shared a non-Hodgkin's lymphoma diagnosis, putting his pitching on hold for a more pressing fight.

Jared Kelley RHP

Born: 10/03/01 Age: 21 Bats: R Throws: R Height: 6'3" Weight: 230 lb. Origin: Round 2, 2020 Draft (#47 overall)

YEAR	TEAM	LVL	AGE	W	L	SV	G	GS	IP	H	HR	BB/9	K/9	K	GB%	BABIP	WHIP	ERA	DRA-	WARP	MPH	FB%	Whiff%	CSP
2021	KAN	A	19	0	5	0	10	10	21	21	1	9.4	10.7	25	49.2%	.328	2.05	6.86	108	0.1				
2022	KAN	A	20	1	4	0	18	18	64^2	52	6	5.6	8.2	59	52.2%	.264	1.42	3.34	89	1.1				
2022	BIR	AA	20	0	2	0	3	3	12	13	2	5.3	9.0	12	44.8%	.407	1.67	4.50	110	0.1				
2023 non-DC	*CHW*	*MLB*	*21*	*2*	*3*	*0*	*57*	*0*	*50*	*57*	*7*	*7.8*	*7.7*	*42*	*47.0%*	*.324*	*2.00*	*6.98*	*150*	*-1.1*			*24.2%*	

Comparables: Roman Mendez (40), Sean Reid-Foley (38), Matt Manning (38)

Kelley was drafted and signed away from his college commitment because of his plus velocity, advanced changeup and starter's build. Conditioning questions persisted, and have been answered affirmatively, in the form of inconsistent mechanics and form. He only recently became old enough to legally drink, so there's no reason to give up hope yet, but Kelley could (charitably) be described as being a few years away from being a few years away. But what 21-year-old isn't? Michael Harris II? Whatever.

Joe Kelly RHP Born: 06/09/88 Age: 35 Bats: R Throws: R Height: 6'1" Weight: 174 lb. Origin: Round 3, 2009 Draft (#98 overall)

YEAR	TEAM	LVL	AGE	W	L	SV	G	GS	IP	H	HR	BB/9	K/9	K	GB%	BABIP	WHIP	ERA	DRA	WARP	MPH	FB%	Whiff%	CSP
2020	LAD	MLB	32	0	0	0	12	1	10	8	0	6.3	8.1	9	57.7%	.308	1.50	1.80	92	0.1	97.0	36.8%	27.5%	44.4%
2021	LAD	MLB	33	2	0	2	48	0	44	28	3	3.1	10.2	50	58.4%	.227	0.98	2.86	82	0.8	97.8	40.7%	28.2%	56.1%
2022	CHW	MLB	34	1	3	1	43	1	37	36	2	5.6	12.9	53	65.9%	.382	1.59	6.08	76	0.8	97.9	39.5%	34.0%	49.8%
2023 DC	*CHW*	*MLB*	*35*	*3*	*2*	*0*	*58*	*0*	*50.3*	*43*	*4*	*4.4*	*10.7*	*59*	*58.1%*	*.307*	*1.36*	*3.67*	*90*	*0.5*	*97.8*	*41.4%*	*29.1%*	*51.5%*

Comparables: Jason Grilli (76), Jose Mesa (75), Joaquin Benoit (70)

Based on his peripherals, Kelly was every bit as good in his first season on the South Side as he was during his final year in Los Angeles. The problem with expected or deserved statistics is that while they may tell you an individual player's true contribution, it's reality, and not expectation, that matters in the standings and box score. This might be especially true out of the bullpen: Reliever sample sizes are small enough that a few minor swings in luck can change a player's entire season. Even with a career-best strikeout rate, Kelly logged a career-worst ERA. Two stints on the injured list—one to open the campaign and one following a May hamstring strain—certainly didn't help matters. The mechanically driven Kelly struggled with consistency throughout, regressing to the (lack of) control that characterizes his worst years, and that's what people will remember. With another year and at least $10 million left on his contract, the White Sox are stuck hoping for another reversal—in batted ball luck, control, or both.

Michael Kopech RHP Born: 04/30/96 Age: 27 Bats: R Throws: R Height: 6'3" Weight: 210 lb. Origin: Round 1, 2014 Draft (#33 overall)

YEAR	TEAM	LVL	AGE	W	L	SV	G	GS	IP	H	HR	BB/9	K/9	K	GB%	BABIP	WHIP	ERA	DRA	WARP	MPH	FB%	Whiff%	CSP
2021	CHW	MLB	25	4	3	0	44	4	69^1	54	9	3.1	13.4	103	37.6%	.304	1.13	3.50	65	1.8	97.4	64.3%	32.8%	56.5%
2022	CHW	MLB	26	5	9	0	25	25	119^1	85	15	4.3	7.9	105	35.6%	.223	1.19	3.54	105	0.8	95.1	61.8%	24.2%	53.6%
2023 DC	*CHW*	*MLB*	*27*	*7*	*7*	*0*	*24*	*24*	*121.3*	*110*	*16*	*4.0*	*9.2*	*123*	*37.0%*	*.291*	*1.36*	*4.00*	*100*	*0.8*	*95.8*	*62.5%*	*26.8%*	*54.5%*

Comparables: Tyler Glasnow (69), Archie Bradley (64), Lucas Sims (63)

Kopech's whirlwind career took another twist in 2022, as he entered the rotation full-time for the first time since making his MLB debut way back in 2018. The results were...mixed, to say the least. The good was that he surpassed his career high in innings by a long shot. The bad was that he wasn't missing bats in the way many expected before the series of injuries he's suffered the last three years. On the whole, it's another incomplete assessment due to injury—this one a torn meniscus in his knee that bothered him from mid-June until he was finally shut down in September. The White Sox are confident Kopech will return without restriction in time for spring training, and if his career trajectory is to be trusted, expect to be confounded one way or another.

Jimmy Lambert RHP Born: 11/18/94 Age: 28 Bats: R Throws: R Height: 6'2" Weight: 190 lb. Origin: Round 5, 2016 Draft (#146 overall)

YEAR	TEAM	LVL	AGE	W	L	SV	G	GS	IP	H	HR	BB/9	K/9	K	GB%	BABIP	WHIP	ERA	DRA	WARP	MPH	FB%	Whiff%	CSP
2020	CHW	MLB	25	0	0	0	2	0	2	2	0	0.0	9.0	2	33.3%	.333	1.00	0.00	101	0.0	92.9	48.5%	28.6%	50.2%
2021	CLT	AAA	26	3	3	0	19	19	64^1	49	11	4.5	11.5	82	43.1%	.270	1.26	4.76	79	1.6				
2021	CHW	MLB	26	1	1	0	4	3	13	16	3	4.2	6.9	10	21.4%	.333	1.69	6.23	148	-0.2	93.7	52.4%	16.1%	57.6%
2022	CLT	AAA	27	0	3	0	5	5	12^2	21	8	3.6	8.5	12	35.6%	.351	2.05	9.24	121	0.0	92.9	38.9%	26.2%	
2022	CHW	MLB	27	1	2	0	42	2	47	40	4	4.6	8.6	45	35.8%	.279	1.36	3.26	108	0.3	94.4	44.6%	25.8%	55.3%
2023 DC	*CHW*	*MLB*	*28*	*4*	*3*	*0*	*41*	*3*	*46.3*	*48*	*8*	*4.5*	*7.8*	*40*	*37.3%*	*.297*	*1.54*	*5.38*	*130*	*-0.5*	*94.3*	*46.1%*	*24.5%*	*55.6%*

Comparables: Paul Clemens (49), Sean Newcomb (48), Pedro Villarreal (47)

It's mid-August and two supposed World Series contenders are playing in front of a packed house. The game begins with the two Cy Young frontrunners—Justin Verlander and Dylan Cease—on the mound. It's the eighth inning, the game is tied and Jimmy Lambert is on the mound. *Freeze frame* "Yup. That's me. You're probably wondering how I ended up in this situation." The short answer is that Lambert was thrust into high-leverage relief situations out of necessity. The long answer is that another injury early in the season didn't afford him the leash to stretch out into a starter's role. His arsenal played well enough out of the bullpen to gain the trust of Tony La Russa, Ethan Katz & Co., even plagued by the same command issues that made him a tweener to begin with.

Reynaldo López RHP Born: 01/04/94 Age: 29 Bats: R Throws: R Height: 6'1" Weight: 225 lb. Origin: International Free Agent, 2012

YEAR	TEAM	LVL	AGE	W	L	SV	G	GS	IP	H	HR	BB/9	K/9	K	GB%	BABIP	WHIP	ERA	DRA	WARP	MPH	FB%	Whiff%	CSP
2020	CHW	MLB	26	1	3	0	8	8	26^1	28	9	5.1	8.2	24	33.3%	.268	1.63	6.49	133	-0.2	94.5	51.4%	22.2%	48.1%
2021	CLT	AAA	27	1	6	0	10	10	39	53	6	4.8	11.5	50	38.8%	.431	1.90	7.62	110	0.3				
2021	CHW	MLB	27	4	4	0	20	9	57^2	42	10	2.0	8.6	55	39.0%	.222	0.95	3.43	93	0.8	95.9	58.0%	24.7%	55.5%
2022	CHW	MLB	28	6	4	0	61	1	65^1	51	1	1.5	8.7	63	38.8%	.287	0.95	2.76	79	1.3	97.3	54.7%	29.1%	53.3%
2023 DC	*CHW*	*MLB*	*29*	*2*	*2*	*0*	*58*	*0*	*50.3*	*49*	*6*	*2.9*	*8.7*	*48*	*37.5%*	*.305*	*1.30*	*3.85*	*99*	*0.3*	*96.2*	*56.3%*	*26.7%*	*53.1%*

Comparables: Tom Murphy (71), LaTroy Hawkins (70), Wade Davis (69)

"Probably a reliever" is a phrase commonly espoused about young, volatile starting pitching prospects. It was often asserted loudly in the case of López, even as he climbed into the top 30 of our very own prospect rankings. After parts of six seasons in which he intermixed flashes of the potential that made him a top prospect and bouts of inconsistency, we have our answer. López is a reliever, and he spent last year as a pretty good one. The curve and changeup remain virtually nonexistent, but his four-seamer and slider both proved pretty danged good in short bursts. The elite, bat-missing stuff many expected never quite got there, and that will probably prevent him from ever becoming a true back-end staple. But López has carved out a career as a legit bullpen weapon, and that was far from a guarantee in the half-decade he spent floundering as a starter.

Lance Lynn RHP

Born: 05/12/87 Age: 36 Bats: S Throws: R Height: 6'5" Weight: 270 lb. Origin: Round 1, 2008 Draft (#39 overall)

YEAR	TEAM	LVL	AGE	W	L	SV	G	GS	IP	H	HR	BB/9	K/9	K	GB%	BABIP	WHIP	ERA	DRA-	WARP	MPH	FB%	Whiff%	CSP
2020	TEX	MLB	33	6	3	0	13	13	84	64	13	2.7	9.5	89	36.2%	.243	1.06	3.32	92	1.3	93.8	67.5%	25.4%	48.6%
2021	CHW	MLB	34	11	6	0	28	28	157	123	18	2.6	10.1	176	38.8%	.265	1.07	2.69	82	2.9	93.6	62.4%	26.7%	51.9%
2022	CLT	AAA	35	0	1	0	3	3	10	15	2	1.8	7.2	8	45.7%	.394	1.70	9.00	108	0.1	91.4	54.8%	17.2%	
2022	CHW	MLB	35	8	7	0	21	21	121^{2}	120	19	1.4	9.2	124	42.3%	.297	1.14	3.99	86	2.0	92.8	58.2%	28.6%	51.5%
2023 DC	*CHW*	*MLB*	*36*	*10*	*10*	*0*	*29*	*29*	*174.7*	*175*	*23*	*2.2*	*9.1*	*176*	*41.2%*	*.314*	*1.25*	*3.77*	*98*	*1.7*	*93.5*	*62.9%*	*25.9%*	*50.8%*

Comparables: Yu Darvish (79), Zack Greinke (76), Jim Bunning (75)

After Lynn received Cy Young votes in three consecutive years, the White Sox had to feel justified—in both the win-now trade they made to bring him over from Texas, and the extension they handed out to keep him on the South Side through (at least) this season. An offseason knee surgery kept Lynn out until June, and the results were abysmal once he was able to take the mound—producing some consternation about the hefty 35-year-old, particularly when his extension was essentially the White Sox choosing him over Carlos Rodón. (Why not just keep both?) Lynn righted the ship, however, and over 74 innings in the final two months he sported a 2.43 ERA, with 75 strikeouts against just nine walks. He was, essentially, the Cy Young vote-getter we've come to know over the last couple years. Lynn's body type and age has basically everyone waiting for his inevitable decline. It just might not be coming as quickly as his early-season results seemed to indicate.

Davis Martin RHP

Born: 01/04/97 Age: 26 Bats: L Throws: R Height: 6'2" Weight: 200 lb. Origin: Round 14, 2018 Draft (#408 overall)

YEAR	TEAM	LVL	AGE	W	L	SV	G	GS	IP	H	HR	BB/9	K/9	K	GB%	BABIP	WHIP	ERA	DRA-	WARP	MPH	FB%	Whiff%	CSP
2021	WS	A+	24	3	5	0	17	17	67^{2}	80	9	3.5	10.4	78	39.7%	.384	1.57	5.32	112	0.1				
2021	BIR	AA	24	1	2	0	6	6	20^{1}	19	2	3.5	8.9	20	31.6%	.309	1.33	3.54	103	0.2				
2022	BIR	AA	25	2	1	0	5	5	24	23	4	2.6	12.4	33	41.9%	.328	1.25	3.00	90	0.4				
2022	CLT	AAA	25	3	5	0	13	13	53	60	11	3.1	11.2	66	41.1%	.363	1.47	6.11	86	1.1	93.9	50.9%	35.4%	
2022	CHW	MLB	25	3	6	0	14	9	63^{1}	63	8	2.7	6.8	48	37.4%	.293	1.29	4.83	115	0.1	94.1	45.7%	23.6%	57.1%
2023 DC	*CHW*	*MLB*	*26*	*5*	*6*	*0*	*26*	*14*	*85.3*	*97*	*14*	*3.4*	*8.5*	*81*	*39.1%*	*.331*	*1.51*	*5.32*	*128*	*-0.6*	*94.1*	*45.7%*	*26.4%*	*57.1%*

Comparables: Taylor Jordan (76), Anthony DeSclafani (74), Chase De Jong (73)

To say Martin was plucked from obscurity would be an understatement. If a 9 on the prospect Richter Scale is, say, Francisco Álvarez, and a 2 is some common organizational soldier, Martin might not have even registered. And that's in a system that could charitably be described as "shallow." A mechanical tweak allowed him to consistently throw his three off-speed offerings for strikes, and that in turn helped his four-seamer—which could occasionally reach 97—play up. Bouncing in and out of the rotation, and up and down from Triple-A, is a tough life to live, but Martin is at least showing up on the radar now—as an organization soldier, if not more.

José Ruiz RHP

Born: 10/21/94 Age: 28 Bats: R Throws: R Height: 6'1" Weight: 245 lb. Origin: International Free Agent, 2011

YEAR	TEAM	LVL	AGE	W	L	SV	G	GS	IP	H	HR	BB/9	K/9	K	GB%	BABIP	WHIP	ERA	DRA-	WARP	MPH	FB%	Whiff%	CSP
2020	CHW	MLB	25	0	0	0	5	0	4	2	1	0.0	11.3	5	33.3%	.125	0.50	2.25	103	0.0	96.8	58.3%	20.7%	50.6%
2021	CHW	MLB	26	1	3	0	59	0	65	51	8	3.5	8.7	63	41.5%	.247	1.17	3.05	103	0.5	97.2	59.5%	24.0%	57.4%
2022	CHW	MLB	27	1	0	0	63	0	60^{2}	53	9	4.9	10.1	68	42.7%	.284	1.42	4.60	101	0.6	97.1	47.9%	29.3%	51.2%
2023 DC	*CHW*	*MLB*	*28*	*2*	*2*	*0*	*58*	*0*	*50.3*	*47*	*6*	*4.3*	*8.7*	*48*	*41.4%*	*.294*	*1.42*	*4.15*	*103*	*0.1*	*97.0*	*53.5%*	*27.2%*	*53.2%*

Comparables: Trevor Gott (63), Nick Goody (58), Luke Jackson (58)

That Ruiz pitched as much as he did last summer is both a testament to his durability and a statement of how poorly things went for the White Sox. On a team that spent nearly $30 million on one of the best closers in baseball and two proven, veteran, late-inning arms, only Kendall Graveman finished with more pitching appearances than Ruiz. He took the opportunity and transformed from a forgettable, low-leverage middle relief arm into...well, he was still pretty forgettable, but pitched in contests of slightly more consequence. His rise was more a product of necessity than him grabbing the proverbial brass ring, but Ruiz at the very least proved his staying power. Just, ya know, in those forgettable, low-leverage opportunities he's meant for.

Noah Schultz LHP

Born: 08/05/03 Age: 19 Bats: L Throws: L Height: 6'9" Weight: 220 lb. Origin: Round 1, 2022 Draft (#26 overall)

As a 6-foot-9 left-hander with a low-slot delivery, it's easy to look at Schultz and think: "Randy Johnson." OK, it's not *that* easy. It's also not very fair to compare a 19-year-old fresh out of high school to one of the greatest pitchers of his generation (and a pretty danged good photographer, too). Coming from suburban Chicago—not exactly a high school baseball hotbed—and having most of his last two seasons wiped out by COVID-19 and then a bout with mono, Schultz flew somewhat under the radar in his 2022 draft year. Many clubs projected a reliever, and were hesitant of the commitment necessary to buy him out of his Vanderbilt commitment. The White Sox bit, however, giving him an over-slot deal at the end of the first round in hopes that he can develop into a front-end starter with an electric fastball and wipeout slider—even if he's not Big Unit-esque.

Bennett Sousa LHP

Born: 04/06/95 Age: 28 Bats: L Throws: L Height: 6'3" Weight: 220 lb. Origin: Round 10, 2018 Draft (#288 overall)

YEAR	TEAM	LVL	AGE	W	L	SV	G	GS	IP	H	HR	BB/9	K/9	K	GB%	BABIP	WHIP	ERA	DRA-	WARP	MPH	FB%	Whiff%	CSP
2021	BIR	AA	26	0	1	3	20	0	24^{2}	14	4	5.5	13.9	38	46.0%	.217	1.18	3.28	83	0.5				
2021	CLT	AAA	26	4	2	1	21	0	22^{2}	23	3	2.0	13.1	33	35.1%	.370	1.24	3.97	74	0.6				
2022	CLT	AAA	27	2	1	6	28	0	27^{1}	22	4	4.0	11.5	35	52.2%	.286	1.24	3.95	75	0.7	95.3	52.8%	42.5%	
2022	CHW	MLB	27	3	0	1	25	0	20^{1}	25	3	4.4	5.3	12	47.9%	.314	1.72	8.41	116	0.0	94.3	42.7%	26.0%	55.2%
2023 DC	*CHW*	*MLB*	*28*	*0*	*0*	*0*	*19*	*0*	*16.7*	*17*	*2*	*3.9*	*8.9*	*16*	*46.1%*	*.317*	*1.47*	*4.68*	*114*	*-0.1*	*94.3*	*42.7%*	*28.8%*	*55.2%*

Comparables: Tim Peterson (65), Keith Hessler (65), Tyler Kinley (62)

John Philip Sousa, famed composer of American military marches, has living descendants today. Bennett, a mostly anonymous lefty whose major-league debut was marred by too many walks and not enough missed bats, is not one of them. His pitches weren't the most errant by a living Sousa, however. John Philip Sousa IV—yes, that's the famous one's great-grandson—spends his days as a Republican political activist whose claim to fame is spearheading Ben Carson's ill-fated 2016 presidential run. His book, *Ben Carson: Rx for America,* retails for $2.99.

Matthew Thompson RHP

Born: 08/11/00 Age: 22 Bats: R Throws: R Height: 6'3" Weight: 195 lb. Origin: Round 2, 2019 Draft (#45 overall)

YEAR	TEAM	LVL	AGE	W	L	SV	G	GS	IP	H	HR	BB/9	K/9	K	GB%	BABIP	WHIP	ERA	DRA-	WARP	MPH	FB%	Whiff%	CSP
2021	KAN	A	20	2	8	0	19	19	71^{2}	83	7	4.8	9.7	77	42.9%	.384	1.69	5.90	96	0.8				
2022	WS	A+	21	4	5	0	18	18	84^{1}	82	13	3.1	7.8	73	46.7%	.296	1.32	4.70	111	0.1				
2022	BIR	AA	21	0	2	0	7	7	25^{1}	26	3	3.9	11.0	31	29.9%	.359	1.46	5.33	113	0.1				
2023 non-DC	*CHW*	*MLB*	*22*	*2*	*3*	*0*	*57*	*0*	*50*	*53*	*7*	*4.8*	*7.0*	*39*	*40.9%*	*.302*	*1.61*	*5.53*	*131*	*-0.6*			*23.6%*	

Comparables: Jesús Castillo (75), Jacob Nix (75), Andrew Sopko (74)

As an over-slot second-round prep arm, two things are true about Thompson: Expectations have been high regarding his development, and patience is very much needed. If you're the stoic sort, you'll point to the occasional instances during his minor-league journey when the plus stuff has flashed, the curveball has looked the part and he's generally done what's anticipated. Those for whom endurance isn't necessarily a virtue will instead note middling results, shaky command and an inability to miss bats—even before reaching the high minors. As a 2019 draftee, Thompson is one of the many prospects who had a year of development mostly wiped out, and just completed his second year of pro ball. So yes, forbearance remains necessary. But it sure would be nice if his moments when everything seemingly clicked started to appear often, rather than fleetingly.

Norge Vera RHP

Born: 06/01/00 Age: 23 Bats: R Throws: R Height: 6'4" Weight: 185 lb. Origin: International Free Agent, 2021

YEAR	TEAM	LVL	AGE	W	L	SV	G	GS	IP	H	HR	BB/9	K/9	K	GB%	BABIP	WHIP	ERA	DRA-	WARP	MPH	FB%	Whiff%	CSP
2021	DSL WSX	ROK	21	1	0	0	8	7	19	9	0	2.4	16.1	34	73.3%	.300	0.74	0.00						
2022	KAN	A	22	0	2	0	8	8	24	12	1	5.6	13.1	35	51.0%	.229	1.13	1.88	82	0.5				
2022	BIR	AA	22	0	0	0	3	3	8	5	0	13.5	13.5	12	37.5%	.313	2.13	5.62	119	0.0				
2023 non-DC	*CHW*	*MLB*	*23*	*2*	*3*	*0*	*57*	*0*	*50*	*47*	*7*	*8.8*	*10.3*	*57*	*44.9%*	*.306*	*1.92*	*6.16*	*134*	*-0.7*			*26.8%*	

Comparables: John Simms (35), Joe Gardner (34), Brandon Bailey (34)

The latest in a long line of high-profile White Sox international signings out of Cuba, Vera made his highly anticipated debut stateside and promptly proved he was overqualified for Low-A. After burning down Kannapolis for all of 24 innings, he split the rest of the season between High-A and the White Sox prospect camp at Double-A Birmingham, where some rougher edges became apparent. The flamethrower's stuff is undeniable, and his next tasks while ascending up the prospect ladder will be finding consistency with his breaking stuff and—as is the case with nearly every pitching prospect—refining his command. There's a long way to go, but Vera's prospect arrow is pointing up.

LINEOUTS

Hitters

HITTER	POS	TEAM	LVL	AGE	PA	R	2B	3B	HR	RBI	BB	K	SB	CS	AVG/OBP/SLG	DRC+	BABIP	BRR	DRP	WARP
Micker Adolfo	RF	CLT	AAA	25	367	47	18	0	15	37	25	130	8	4	.231/.287/.417	71	.325	-3.4	RF(84): -0.9, LF(4): -0.4, CF(1): -0.0	-0.7
Romy Gonzalez	MI	CLT	AAA	25	135	15	5	0	4	10	13	45	5	2	.198/.281/.339	71	.278	1.0	SS(25): 0.1, 2B(2): 0.1, 3B(1): -0.4	0.0
	MI	CHW	MLB	25	109	15	4	1	2	11	2	39	0	1	.238/.257/.352	57	.354	-1.0	2B(25): 0.2, SS(3): -0.2, RF(2): 0	-0.3
Adam Haseley	OF	CLT	AAA	26	463	59	19	4	15	63	32	78	18	3	.239/.305/.411	98	.259	-0.3	CF(52): -0.4, LF(47): 1.2, RF(2): -0.1	1.3
	OF	CHW	MLB	26	25	4	0	0	0	2	3	7	0	0	.238/.333/.238	80	.357	-0.9	RF(5): -0.1, LF(4): 0.3, CF(3): -0.3	-0.1
Wes Kath	3B	KAN	A	19	449	56	20	1	13	42	60	148	2	0	.238/.343/.397	83	.347	0.3	3B(95): -0.3	0.6
	3B	BIR	AA	19	52	1	1	0	0	3	4	23	0	0	.170/.250/.191	55	.333	-0.6	3B(13): -0.3	-0.2
Mark Payton	OF	CLT	AAA	30	539	85	31	5	25	95	54	76	15	6	.293/.369/.539	124	.301	0.5	CF(69): 0.9, LF(26): -0.3, RF(14): 0.1	3.2
	OF	CHW	MLB	30	25	3	0	0	0	1	4	4	0	0	.143/.280/.143	97	.176	0.4	LF(6): 0.2, RF(3): -0.2, CF(1): -0.1	0.1
Carlos Pérez	C	CLT	AAA	25	465	53	17	1	21	76	34	40	2	2	.254/.316/.450	123	.234	-3.1	C(83): 3.1	2.8
	C	CHW	MLB	25	18	0	2	0	0	2	0	2	0	0	.222/.222/.333	99	.250	0.0	C(6): -0.4	0.0
Bryan Ramos	3B	WS	A+	20	433	64	16	1	19	74	40	71	1	0	.275/.350/.471	125	.291	2.6	3B(86): -0.3	2.6
	3B	BIR	AA	20	86	8	3	0	3	12	5	15	0	1	.225/.279/.375	107	.242	-0.3	3B(10): 0.0, 2B(8): -0.2	0.3
Sebastian Rivero	C	NWA	AA	23	178	22	15	0	5	27	15	38	1	0	.218/.294/.410	95	.250	0.0	C(41): -3.2	0.1
	C	KC	MLB	23	29	2	0	0	0	1	2	10	0	0	.154/.214/.154	78	.250	0.1	C(17): 0.9	0.1
Jose Rodriguez	MI	BIR	AA	21	484	75	21	6	11	68	38	66	40	10	.280/.340/.430	106	.308	3.7	SS(53): -1.0, 2B(43): -0.4	2.0
Yolbert Sánchez	MI	BIR	AA	25	67	7	1	0	0	6	13	7	0	0	.353/.507/.373	130	.409	0.3	2B(8): 0.1, 3B(4): 0.3	0.5
	MI	CLT	AAA	25	479	44	16	1	3	40	27	71	11	9	.280/.324/.341	102	.325	-3.7	2B(70): 2.2, SS(40): 2.3, 3B(3): 0.7	1.6

The good news for **Micker Adolfo** is that he made it through a season healthy for the first time in his career. The bad news is that he still swings at everything, and couldn't carve out a path from Charlotte to Chicago despite an obvious need in the outfield on the South Side. ⚾ Injuries allowed the White Sox to give **Romy Gonzalez** a slightly longer look last season than during his cup of coffee. "Able to play virtually everywhere" is a nice calling card, but unfortunately it doesn't pair very nicely with "doesn't do anything markedly well." ⚾ The Phillies finally gave up on **Adam Haseley** at the end of spring training, moving him to the White Sox for a minor leaguer. After bouncing back and forth between Triple-A and the majors yet again, the former top-10 pick has quickly regressed from "future starting center fielder" to "probably a fourth outfielder" or "is he even that?" ⚾ In his first full pro season, **Wes Kath** displayed all the pitfalls that come with being a prep, bat-first, corner infield prospect who was drafted in the second round with serious concerns about his ability to, ya know, hit the ball. ⚾ The White Sox's injury-plagued campaign forced them to break the "In Case Of Emergency" glass surrounding **Mark Payton**. That he accumulated all of eight games and 25 plate appearances only means he'll be a tough get on the 2022 Chicago White Sox Roster Sporcle quiz. ⚾ The presence of so many veteran backstops on the White Sox 40-man made **Carlos Pérez**'s inclusion surprising. That he saw seven games of major-league action should have been, too—but the injuries had piled up so much by that point, it was hard to be surprised by anything. ⚾ **Bryan Ramos** kept on hitting in his first go-around of full-season ball, showing more than just the raw power that's been present throughout his young career: Also on show was an above-average ability to find the barrel and keen spin recognition. That's particularly good news considering there are plenty of questions as to whether he'll stick at third base as he progresses to higher levels. ⚾ **Sebastian Rivero** failed to stand out amid a deep Royals catching corps, which makes sense since he was squatting the entire time. ⚾ **Jose Rodriguez**'s impressive ascent through the minors has him slowly trending from "notable simply because he's in a bad system" to "notable on his own merit." After showing surprising pop and impressive speed in his first taste at the high minors, he's given the White Sox plenty to dream on. ⚾ If the name **Yolbert Sánchez** gives you the mental image of a slick-fielding, light-hitting infielder, it's likely because you're picturing former White Sox infielder Yolmer, known for his flashy defense and the hole in his bat. You'd also be mostly right, as *this* Sánchez has been identically billed since getting $2.5 million to join the organization out of Cuba. He was also billed as "close to major-league ready" back in 2019, and hasn't yet sniffed the 26-man roster.

Pitchers

PITCHER	TEAM	LVL	AGE	W	L	SV	G	GS	IP	H	HR	BB/9	K/9	K	GB%	BABIP	WHIP	ERA	DRA-	WARP	MPH	FB%	WHF	CSP
Yoan Aybar	BIR	AA	24	0	1	0	10	0	10	11	2	7.2	13.5	15	63.0%	.360	1.90	8.10	80	0.2				
	CLT	AAA	24	1	3	0	33	0	31^{1}	34	8	8.9	10.3	36	34.4%	.317	2.07	8.90	113	0.2	94.9	52.3%	39.3%	
Jason Bilous	BIR	AA	24	5	7	0	19	16	83^{2}	78	10	5.9	11.2	104	40.5%	.322	1.59	5.27	97	1.0				
	CLT	AAA	24	1	4	0	12	5	22	27	4	9.8	11.0	27	35.9%	.383	2.32	10.23	114	0.1	93.9	57.3%	38.0%	
Jonathan Cannon	KAN	A	21	0	0	0	3	3	6^{1}	4	0	2.8	4.3	3	52.9%	.235	0.95	1.42	111	0.0				
Kyle Crick	CLT	AAA	29	1	0	0	6	0	6^{2}	3	1	5.4	12.2	9	78.6%	.154	1.05	2.70	85	0.1	92.8	45.6%	34.6%	
	CHW	MLB	29	2	0	0	14	0	15^{2}	10	0	6.3	10.9	19	32.4%	.294	1.34	4.02	97	0.2	92.5	42.7%	26.5%	50.7%
Andrew Dalquist	WS	A+	21	3	9	0	22	22	90^{2}	106	22	5.3	6.8	69	33.8%	.316	1.75	6.95	130	-0.9				
	BIR	AA	21	0	2	0	4	4	13^{1}	11	1	7.4	7.4	11	51.3%	.263	1.65	3.38	122	0.0				
Nate Fisher	BNG	AA	26	0	1	0	12	2	28^{2}	19	3	3.5	12.6	40	39.4%	.254	1.05	3.77	84	0.6				
	SYR	AAA	26	1	2	0	18	11	56	60	6	3.7	6.4	40	34.3%	.314	1.48	4.34	134	-0.2				
	NYM	MLB	26	0	0	0	1	0	3	1	0	6.0	3.0	1	25.0%	.125	1.00	0.00	108	0.0	92.9	48.0%	18.2%	53.5%
Parker Markel	CLT	AAA	31	1	3	1	24	0	21	28	5	7.7	11.6	27	37.5%	.397	2.19	10.29	111	0.2	95.2	43.3%	26.1%	
	LV	AAA	31	3	0	1	17	0	19	13	2	4.7	13.3	28	35.0%	.289	1.21	1.89	80	0.3	94.6	39.0%	38.0%	
	OAK	MLB	31	0	0	0	3	0	3	1	0	15.0	9.0	3	40.0%	.200	2.00	0.00	108	0.0	95.0	45.9%	27.8%	34.4%
Cristian Mena	KAN	A	19	1	2	0	11	11	53^{2}	45	2	2.5	11.1	66	45.1%	.328	1.12	2.68	86	1.0				
	WS	A+	19	1	3	0	10	10	40^{2}	39	4	4.9	10.4	47	44.5%	.330	1.50	4.65	89	0.5				
	BIR	AA	19	0	1	0	3	3	10	16	1	0.9	11.7	13	35.5%	.500	1.70	6.30	98	0.1				
Nicholas Padilla	SB	A+	25	1	0	1	7	0	10	4	0	4.5	16.2	18	57.1%	.286	0.90	1.80	73	0.2				
	TNS	AA	25	1	1	2	15	0	22^{1}	16	0	5.6	10.1	25	60.3%	.276	1.34	2.82	85	0.4				
	CLT	AAA	25	0	0	0	7	0	6	4	1	6.0	9.0	6	40.0%	.214	1.33	3.00	94	0.1	91.8	56.8%	42.1%	
	IOW	AAA	25	1	0	1	10	0	14^{2}	8	0	4.9	10.4	17	47.1%	.235	1.09	1.23	92	0.3				
	CHC	MLB	25	0	0	0	1	0	1^{2}	2	0	10.8	5.4	1	33.3%	.333	2.40	5.40	99	0.0	93.2	76.9%	16.7%	46.1%
Gregory Santos	SAC	AAA	22	1	2	1	33	0	33	29	4	5.5	9.3	34	52.7%	.287	1.48	4.91	89	0.4	99.1	41.4%	34.4%	
	SF	MLB	22	0	0	0	2	0	3^{2}	3	0	7.4	4.9	2	75.0%	.250	1.64	4.91	110	0.0	98.9	47.8%	20.7%	57.5%
Anderson Severino	CLT	AAA	27	3	4	0	37	0	30	37	6	12.6	10.2	34	43.8%	.373	2.63	11.40	141	-0.2	96.3	64.6%	28.5%	
	CHW	MLB	27	0	0	0	6	0	7^{1}	7	0	4.9	11.0	9	57.9%	.368	1.50	6.14	94	0.1	96.8	64.7%	31.5%	51.2%
Emilio Vargas	BIR	AA	25	4	6	0	18	14	79^{2}	77	10	4.6	9.8	87	45.7%	.318	1.48	5.20	99	0.8				
	CLT	AAA	25	0	3	0	8	5	32^{2}	36	8	3.6	8.0	29	36.0%	.304	1.50	6.61	116	0.2	91.7	50.0%	26.5%	

It's a good thing **Yoan Aybar** throws a lot of gas, because his control issues mean he's going to need a lot of it to travel from organization to organization to organization. (I mean, have you SEEN those gas prices?!) ⚾ When the White Sox added **Jason Bilous** to the 40-man roster after the 2021 season, it was both a sign of the team's belief in his command gains and an indictment of their minor-league pitching depth. Given his high-minors struggles last year, it's clear it was more the latter than the former. ⚾ Third-round over-slot college arm **Jonathan Cannon** is more of a project than your typical college arm, but has the potential of a big-league starting pitcher—if said project is undertaken properly. ⚾ In a surprise, **Kyle Crick** made the White Sox Opening Day roster out of camp, leading some to believe the pitching staff had solved the walk issues that have long plagued the once-promising arm. A monstrous walk rate before a mid-June demotion proved that theory false. ⚾ Tommy John surgery ahead of last season leaves us no closer to learning whether **Garrett Crochet** is a future member of a starting rotation, or merely a flame-throwing reliever with closer potential. ⚾ When **Andrew Dalquist** was given an over-slot deal in the third round of the 2019 Draft, he was seen as a polished high school arm with projectable stuff. While the arsenal has impressed at times, he hasn't shown the kind of polish necessary to reach his mid-rotation potential. ⚾ Of the four Mets in the 0.00 ERA club in 2022, **Nate Fisher** is the most interesting member. In the summer of 2021, he was working at the First National Bank of Omaha in Nebraska. On an August afternoon in Philadelphia the following year, the lefty made his major-league debut at the age of 26 and pitched three scoreless innings of relief in the middle of a division race, paving the way for an improbable come-from-behind Mets victory. ⚾ **Parker Markel** joined his eighth different organization when the White Sox claimed him off waivers from the Athletics in June. He was released two months later, proving the most interesting thing about him remains his tongue-twister of a name. ⚾ At just 19, **Cristian Mena** popped on the radar by posting gaudy strikeout numbers in his first taste of pro ball. As a slighter pitcher without eye-popping velocity, there isn't a ton of projectability—but he's simply stronger command and a good third offering away from becoming a true starting pitching prospect. Easy, right? ⚾ On August 23, **Nicholas Padilla** appeared in the big leagues for the first and only time (so far). He'd surged through the Cubs system and was named their 27th man for a doubleheader. He was out there in the top of the fourth, the crowd tranquilized by an early 5-0 Cardinals lead, facing Paul Goldschmidt with runners in scoring position. Padilla got him to chase low and outside, ending the threat with his first big-league strikeout. Had the score been 3-0 when the inning had started? Yes. Would the Cubs go on to lose 13-3? Yes. But when you're getting your shot, you've got to live in the moment. ⚾ Tommy John surgery has become commonplace enough in baseball that it's almost expected for a young pitcher to get it at some point during their upbringing. So expected is this that the White Sox plucking **Peyton Pallette** in the second round, and signing him to an over-slot bonus, despite him having TJ in January was viewed as a savvy move rather than something constituting a risk. ⚾ The intended story was a redemption year for the triple-digit hurler after his 2021 campaign ended early due to a positive PED test, but in 2022 **Gregory Santos** awoke from uneasy dreams to find himself transformed onto the 60-day IL list with a season-ending groin injury. He'll try to metamorphosize into his ideal form as a setup man or other late-inning reliever next year. ⚾ It took **Anderson Severino** eight years and an organizational change to finally reach the majors, and fewer than eight innings to prove he might not belong there. ⚾ Lat surgery cost **Jonathan Stiever** all of 2022, save for a few Triple-A appearances in late September. Assuming full health in the spring—no simple thing—he'll continue to serve as minor-league depth. ⚾ Still just 26, **Emilio Vargas** has been in pro ball since 2013 and made it to Triple-A for the first time last year. His performance there showed he'll likely remain minor-league pitching depth, either until his career ends or the sun burns out.

CLEVELAND GUARDIANS

Essay by Russell A. Carleton

Player comments by Ken Funck and BP staff

On June 7, 1977, Cleveland used its 15th-round pick in the MLB amateur draft to select Cleveland State University infielder Jerry Dybzinski. Dybzinski eventually made the big-league team in 1980 and played in pieces of six MLB seasons as a utility infielder. Only three of them were with Cleveland. In 1983, "the Dibber" was shipped off to the White Sox for Pat Tabler, a singles-hitting first baseman who was famous for hitting around .500 with the bases loaded. Midway through 1988, Tabler was sent to the Kansas City Royals for pitcher (and future MLB manager) Bud Black. Black was a serviceable starter for Cleveland, but in September 1990, was sent to the Blue Jays in exchange for Alex Sanchez and two other pitchers. Sanchez never put on a Cleveland uniform; in fact, two months later, he was dealt *back* to Toronto, this time for Willie Blair. Blair kicked around the majors for parts of 12 seasons—and wasn't even left-handed—but only one of those years was in Cleveland. In 1991, Blair and catcher Eddie Taubensee were traded to Houston for infielder Dave Rohde and outfielder prospect Kenny Lofton. Lofton turned out to be the better piece of that deal.

As someone who came of age in Cleveland in the 1990s, Lofton will always have a special place in my baseball heart. He's why it broke in March of 1997 when, in a surprise move late in spring training, Cleveland traded Lofton and pitcher Alan Embree to Atlanta for David Justice and Marquis Grissom. It was a weird trade, emotionally. As a Brave, Justice hit a home run that accounted for all the scoring in Game 6 of the 1995 World Series, a game that ended Cleveland's dream run that year. But after putting on a Cleveland jersey, Justice became a key player in their 1997 run to the World Series.

By 2000, Justice was traded to the Yankees for a package of three players, including Ricky Ledee, Zach Day and Jake Westbrook, who became a mainstay in Cleveland's rotation for several years. As you can probably guess by now, Westbrook too was traded, this time in a three-team deal in 2010. In return came Padres prospect and eventual Cy Young Award-winner Corey Kluber. Kluber was the anchor of Cleveland's rotation for the better part of the 2010s, but when health problems arose, he was flipped to the Rangers (for whom he pitched exactly one inning) for Delino DeShields Jr. and current Guardians closer Emmanuel Clase.

CLEVELAND GUARDIANS PROSPECTUS

2022 W-L: 92-70, 1ST IN AL CENTRAL

Pythag	.544	9th	DER	.715	4th
RS/G	4.31	15th	DRC+	100	11th
RA/G	3.91	8th	DRA-	95	12th
dWin%	.536	10th	FIP	3.76	9th
Payroll	$68M	27th	B-Age	26.5	2nd
M$/MW	$1.1M	2nd	P-Age	26.8	1st

405'

370'

375'

325'

325'

- Opened 1994
- Open air
- Natural surface
- Fence profile: 9' to 19'

Park Factors

Runs	Runs/RH	Runs/LH	HR/RH	HR/LH
101	100	101	99	106

Top Hitter WARP	4.8 José Ramírez
Top Pitcher WARP	3.8 Shane Bieber
2023 Top Prospect	Daniel Espino

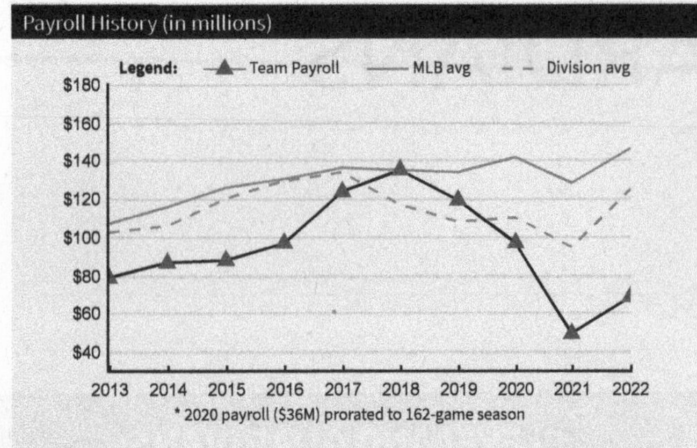

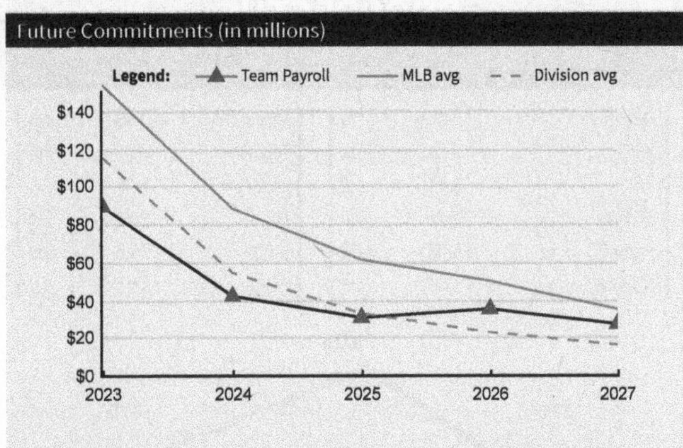

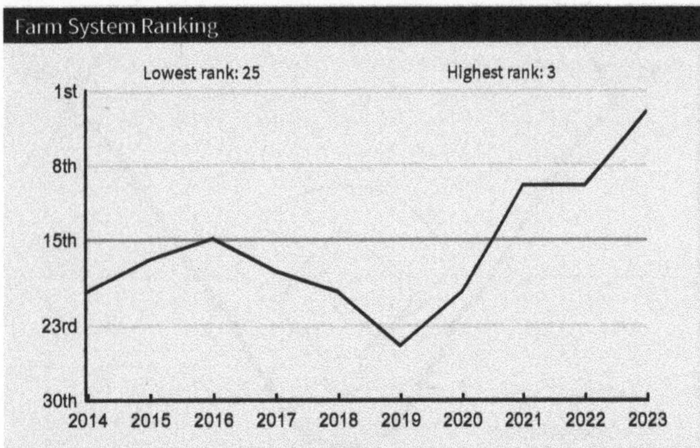

Personnel

President, Baseball Operations
Chris Antonetti

General Manager
Mike Chernoff

Executive Vice President & Assistant General Manager
Matt Forman

Assistant General Manager
Sky Andrecheck

Assistant General Manager
Eric Binder

Assistant General Manager
James Harris

Manager
Terry Francona

BP Alumni
Max Marchi
Chris Mosch
Ethan Purser
Keith Woolner

There's a line of opportunistic swaps that runs through the Cleveland organization from back before I was born to the present day. Necessity being the mother of invention, Cleveland has always had to deal with the burden of being one of the smaller media markets in MLB. Flipping players for what they might fetch before free agency has long been the way in which the team operates.

What's fascinating, though, is that while a churning roster has always been part of the Cleveland experience, the Guardians have one of the longest streaks in MLB of continuity in their front office. After the disastrous 1987 season in which the team went 61-101 after being picked by *Sports Illustrated* to win the World Series, Joe Klein was dismissed from general manager duties, and Cleveland turned to Hank Peters to run the club. That marked the last time that Cleveland would hire a general manager from outside the organization. Peters brought a young John Hart to Cleveland to serve as a lieutenant, then turned the club over to Hart in 1991. When Hart left for Texas, the torch passed to then-Assistant GM Mark Shapiro. Shapiro eventually became club president, with Assistant GM Chris Antonetti moving into the GM chair, and then the President's chair when Shapiro left for the Blue Jays. Current GM Mike Chernoff moved up the ladder as well.

Front office workers have come and gone (and as a responsible journalist, I should point out that I once worked for the club in a consultant role from 2009-12), but there hasn't been a "clear out" since the days of Pat Tabler. There hasn't been much of a need: Even with a shoestring budget, Cleveland has made the playoffs in six of the last 10 seasons.

That odd mix of front office stability and the market demanding that they innovate has empowered the Guardians to take some chances; or, perhaps, it's fairer to say it's *forced* them to. In 2022, the team won 92 games and the AL Central, then advanced to the Division Series, taking the Yankees to five games before bowing out. They did so while hitting 127 home runs during the regular season, second-fewest in MLB. Though they lacked power, the Guardians finished 2022 with the fewest strikeouts of any team and the third-most stolen bases. They earned their superlative strikeout rate by posting the highest contact percentage in the majors. On the basepaths, they benefited from a balanced, deep roster of runners: Amed Rosario (18 steals), Steven Kwan (19), José Ramírez (20), Andrés Giménez (20) and Myles Straw (21) all contributed. Though the team made their mark in the mid-1990s as a group of bashers, the 2022 Cleveland Guardians went back to the 1970s for their approach.

In a game overrun with "three true outcomes" hitters, sometimes the best place to find value is to look for the players that other teams *aren't* thinking about. Three true outcomes hitters can excel, of course, but what if there are other players who can be just as valuable who aren't top-of-mind for other teams? It's a gamble to go against the grain like that, but when you have buy-in from franchise ownership like the Guardians' front office clearly has, you can try some things.

Maybe their shift in approach was accidental. You have to play the cards you're holding, and the Guardians weren't loaded with big boppers. But maybe the whole thing was designed. Cleveland was one of the first teams to hire a Baseball Prospectus writer and analyst to head up their data department (Keith Woolner, who remains there in the role of Principal Data Scientist) back when even having a data department was something significantly above replacement level. Maybe they saw the numbers that follow and decided that, while everyone was zagging, they should zig-a-zig-ahh.

Warning! Gory Mathematical Details Ahead!

Starting in about 2011, and until the last few seasons, there was an upswing in swinging up, demonstrated through these two graphs. They show contact rates on the first pitch of an at-bat compared with contact rates on two-strike pitches, league-wide:

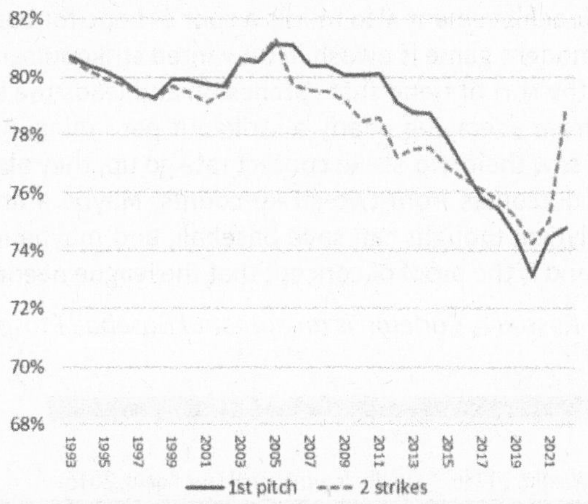

We can see that throughout the 2010s, hitters were consistently swinging and missing more and more on both the first pitch and in two-strike counts. In the first case, that aggressive approach led to more 0-1 counts, and a plate appearance starting with an 0-1 count is about 12 percentage points more likely to end in a strikeout as a 1-0 count. The problem with swinging and missing on a two-strike pitch is obvious. That hitters were being so aggressive in those counts anyway suggests they were making a conscious choice. Why? Because hitters thought they were benefiting from this:

That's slugging percentage on contact (SLGCon) for first pitches and for two-strike pitches. It started spiking in about 2014. There were several factors that played into that: the ball was a little livelier, the infields a little shiftier. With the shift in particular, which increased in usage by an order of magnitude during the 2010s, a lot of hitters talked about their frustrations over hits being "stolen" from them. Some of them took to trying to hit the ball to the one place where the defense couldn't station a fielder: over the wall.

Batters began taking high-risk, low-contact, but also high-power swings. They swung really hard in case they hit it, even on pitches where missing meant an out. Based on SLGCon alone, it worked for a while. When they made contact, the ball went far, and theoretically the corresponding increase in strikeouts was an unfortunate but bearable consequence. If they could turn a few singles into doubles and home runs and the percentages broke right, maybe it was all worth it. There was one minor problem:

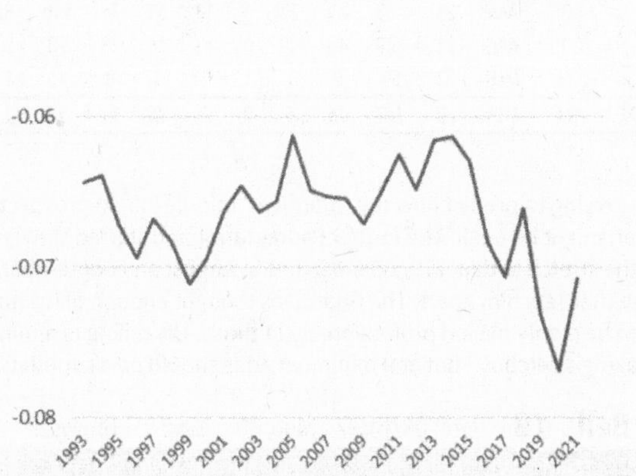

That's a graph showing run expectancy changes for all two-strike counts by year. We know that when a batter makes an out, even if it doesn't end the inning, it becomes less likely that the team will score a run. We also know that when a batter singles, even if it doesn't produce a run, it makes a run more likely. We can monitor those changes. On a two-strike count, we expect that it will trend negative, because there's already a pretty good chance that the batter will strike out. But as the "swing really hard in case you hit it" approach emerged, hitters saw the trend line for run expectancy drop dramatically. It turns out those extra extra-base hits weren't worth all the strikeouts. Teams were better off when they were more invested in making contact than making the scoreboard shoot off fireworks. Those able to identify this shift and adjust their rosters accordingly could potentially have an advantage.

One of the original goals of baseball analytics was to pull the emotionally charged, irrational decision-making out of the game. Bunting felt noble in the moment, but a close look at the numbers showed that it was a bad move. If players were swinging for the fences out of frustration and it was leading to counter-productive behavior, then that's an area for intervention. It's not as simple as saying, "hey, just look at this graph," or "hey, change your behavior." Players' frustrations might be real and warranted, and you have to address it head on. But if you do, you might be able to get players to change their mindsets and maybe ease up just a bit.

It's clear that, for the Guardians, *something* happened between 2021 and 2022. They went from the 20th-best contact percentage in 2021 to the best in 2022. Some of that was due to the introduction of rookie *wunderkind* Kwan (91% contact rate) into the lineup, but there's evidence of some tinkering in other parts of the roster. Rosario, Gimenez and the now-departed Owen Miller all saw five-plus-point jumps in their contact rates. That's the sort of thing that screams, "We did that on purpose."

In a game that has become overrun with "three true outcomes" hitters, Cleveland saw an opportunity to zag where everyone else was zigging. They were able to finish in the middle of the pack in terms of runs scored, even while hitting half the home runs that the Yankees did. With a good pitching staff (the Guardians finished sixth in team ERA and 11th in DRA) and a bit of hustle (first overall in infield hits), they managed 92 wins. The Guardians have proven that you can build a viable major-league offense without asking players to swing for the fences all the time.

The secret might have just been volume. In the last graph above, we saw that since the "swing really hard" approach came into the league, teams began seeing outcomes that were about .01 to .015 runs worse each time up through 2021. That doesn't sound like something worth changing a team's entire approach over until you realize that about half of plate appearances get to two strikes. The average team sees about 6,000 plate appearances in a year, and if we multiply all that out, that could be 30 to 45 runs of value. If a team could reclaim them, that would be very valuable indeed. It seems the Guardians thought so, too.

Their achievement also marks a spot of hope for baseball. If the modern game is awash in unwanted strikeouts, maybe this is the sort of trend that catches on and leads the league away from averaging nearly a strikeout per inning. As MLB hitters saw their two-strike contact rate go up, they also saw better outcomes from two-strike counts. Maybe a little bit of analytical thought can save baseball, and maybe mighty Cleveland is the proof of concept that the league needed.

—Russell A. Carleton is an author of Baseball Prospectus.

HITTERS

Gabriel Arias IF Born: 02/27/00 Age: 23 Bats: R Throws: R Height: 6'1" Weight: 217 lb. Origin: International Free Agent, 2016

YEAR	TEAM	LVL	AGE	PA	R	2B	3B	HR	RBI	BB	K	SB	CS	Whiff%	AVG/OBP/SLG	DRC+	BABIP	BRR	DRP	WARP
2021	COL	AAA	21	483	64	29	3	13	55	39	110	5	1		.284/.348/.454	101	.351	-1.1	SS(82): 0.3, 3B(19): -1.9, 2B(9): -0.3	1.3
2022	COL	AAA	22	323	46	9	0	13	36	25	78	5	1		.240/.310/.406	95	.279	0.6	SS(43): 0.2, 3B(14): -1.2, 1B(10): -0.3	0.7
2022	CLE	MLB	22	57	9	1	1	1	5	8	16	1	0	35.8%	.191/.321/.319	90	.267	0.1	3B(9): -0.4, 2B(3): -0.1, SS(3): -0.1	0.0
2023 DC	*CLE*	*MLB*	*23*	*163*	*16*	*6*	*0*	*3*	*15*	*11*	*45*	*1*	*0*	*34.1%*	*.234/.295/.366*	*83*	*.309*	*0.5*	*3B 0, SS 0*	*0.0*

Comparables: J.P. Crawford (54), Luis Urías (51), Jim Pyburn (49)

If you're trying to predict how the Guardians' middle infield prospect logjam will shake out, the fact that Arias made the postseason roster ahead of Tyler Freeman might be a tell. The former Padres farmhand started slowly in Columbus before needing surgery on his right hand, but he turned things around down the stretch with a .279/.355/.435 line in August and September. Arias is an aggressive batter with a power over hit profile, but it's his glittering defense that sets him apart. The Guardians thought enough of his maturity and glovework to let the 22-year-old start three playoff games at first base, a position he'd only played professionally 11 times. His ceiling is reminiscent of Jeremy Peña—plus shortstop glove and adequate power with occasional out-making stretches—but at a minimum Arias should be a superlative utility man.

Josh Bell 1B Born: 08/14/92 Age: 30 Bats: S Throws: R Height: 6'4" Weight: 261 lb. Origin: Round 2, 2011 Draft (#61 overall)

YEAR	TEAM	LVL	AGE	PA	R	2B	3B	HR	RBI	BB	K	SB	CS	Whiff%	AVG/OBP/SLG	DRC+	BABIP	BRR	DRP	WARP
2020	PIT	MLB	27	223	22	3	0	8	22	22	59	0	0	33.6%	.226/.305/.364	94	.273	-0.6	1B(35): -1.5	0.1
2021	WAS	MLB	28	568	75	24	1	27	88	65	101	0	0	24.1%	.261/.347/.476	127	.276	-3.3	1B(119): -2.2, LF(9): -0.8, RF(1): -0.3	2.6
2022	WAS	MLB	29	437	52	24	3	14	57	49	61	0	1	20.1%	.301/.384/.493	137	.324	-2.6	1B(103): -3.7	2.1
2022	SD	MLB	29	210	26	5	0	3	14	32	41	0	0	24.9%	.192/.316/.271	97	.233	-1.1	1B(21): -0.1	0.3
2023 DC	*CLE*	*MLB*	*30*	*585*	*69*	*24*	*2*	*21*	*71*	*69*	*94*	*0*	*1*	*22.2%*	*.255/.348/.435*	*121*	*.276*	*-2.2*	*1B 0*	*2.2*

Comparables: Joe Judge (81), Tony Clark (78), Anthony Rizzo (78)

Josh Bell is never the Josh Bell you're expecting. After hitting 37 home runs with the Pirates and going to the All-Star Game in 2019, Bell's bat didn't show up for 2020 (or really, the second half of 2019, either). He bounced back in 2021 and was even putting up the best average and on-base marks of his career with Washington in '22 before being traded to San Diego. With the team relying on Bell's bat more than ever after Tatis' suspension, the giant switch-hitter hit more like a pitcher in the days before the universal DH, eventually finding himself in a platoon with another AJ Preller deadline acquisition, Brandon Drury.

This offseason Bell became another player you'd never expect, namely a well-paid Cleveland Guardian. Despite the shock, he's a great fit; the team got a .587 OPS out of the DH spot last year. Still, for someone who is so strong and whose swing can look so good, Bell's lack of power and consistency can drive a fan crazy sometimes. Just don't say that near Bell's father, who may have the title of Most Jacked Dad in the Major Leagues.

Will Benson OF Born: 06/16/98 Age: 25 Bats: L Throws: L Height: 6'5" Weight: 230 lb. Origin: Round 1, 2016 Draft (#14 overall)

YEAR	TEAM	LVL	AGE	PA	R	2B	3B	HR	RBI	BB	K	SB	CS	Whiff%	AVG/OBP/SLG	DRC+	BABIP	BRR	DRP	WARP
2021	AKR	AA	23	332	63	13	5	14	42	60	104	14	3		.221/.374/.469	117	.301	1.0	RF(26): -0.0, CF(23): -2.6, LF(22): -1.6	1.4
2021	COL	AAA	23	107	7	5	1	3	9	14	42	0	2		.161/.271/.333	68	.250	-0.5	LF(10): -0.4, CF(9): 0.0, RF(6): -0.3	-0.1
2022	COL	AAA	24	401	75	20	3	17	45	75	91	16	4		.278/.426/.522	124	.340	-2.5	CF(35): 0.3, LF(27): 0.4, RF(15): 1.1	2.5
2022	CLE	MLB	24	61	8	1	0	0	3	3	19	0	0	30.9%	.182/.250/.200	68	.278	-0.5	CF(10): -0.4, RF(6): -0.2, LF(4): -0.2	-0.2
2023 DC	*CLE*	*MLB*	*25*	*158*	*16*	*5*	*1*	*4*	*15*	*18*	*42*	*4*	*2*	*29.7%*	*.198/.300/.357*	*82*	*.248*	*2.4*	*RF 0, CF 0*	*0.2*

Comparables: Roger Bernadina (57), Brett Phillips (55), Chris Shaw (50)

The story of baseball is one of repetitive disappointment. All but one team either fails to make the playoffs or ends their season glumly watching their opponents celebrate. Most minor leaguers never get a sniff of the bigtime. The majority of plate appearances end with a batter failing to produce, very publicly. Thus when organizations talk about player "makeup," a big part of that is their ability to endure those constant disappointments and keep working. Benson clearly has tremendous makeup, which helped the former first-round prep star survive six years of subpar results and plummeting regard to rework his game and earn his big-league debut. Blessed with size, speed and tremendous raw power, Benson could always work a walk and launch a few bombs, but was a strikeout machine, selling out and swinging through hittable pitches. Last year in Columbus, however, he displayed a more contact-based, all-fields approach, nearly halving his strikeout rate while still drawing walks and hitting the ball hard. Benson has a cannon arm, plays a solid corner outfield and can cover center when necessary. He's always looked the part, and now that he's not whiffing a third of the time he might be able to play the part, at least as a fourth outfielder.

Will Brennan OF Born: 02/02/98 Age: 25 Bats: L Throws: L Height: 6'0" Weight: 200 lb. Origin: Round 8, 2019 Draft (#250 overall)

YEAR	TEAM	LVL	AGE	PA	R	2B	3B	HR	RBI	BB	K	SB	CS	Whiff%	AVG/OBP/SLG	DRC+	BABIP	BRR	DRP	WARP
2021	LC	A+	23	269	42	22	1	4	30	25	43	13	4		.290/.368/.441	116	.339	-0.7	CF(47): 1.2, LF(12): 0.8	1.5
2021	AKR	AA	23	177	28	6	0	2	20	18	29	2	2		.280/.369/.360	107	.328	0.0	CF(20): -2.7, LF(11): -0.9, RF(7): -0.9	0.3
2022	AKR	AA	24	157	16	12	1	4	39	17	16	5	2		.311/.382/.504	130	.319	-0.4	CF(26): -1.0, RF(5): -0.2, LF(3): 0.0	0.8
2022	COL	AAA	24	433	53	28	3	9	68	33	53	15	1		.316/.367/.471	114	.342	-0.2	CF(56): -1.0, LF(17): 0.5, RF(7): 1.0	1.8
2022	CLE	MLB	24	45	6	1	1	1	8	2	4	2	1	17.9%	.357/.400/.500	108	.378	0.6	LF(5): 0, RF(4): -0.5, CF(1): 0	0.2
2023 DC	*CLE*	*MLB*	*25*	*260*	*27*	*12*	*1*	*3*	*24*	*16*	*38*	*5*	*1*	*19.1%*	*.275/.329/.384*	*101*	*.315*	*2.2*	*LF 0, CF 0*	*0.9*

Comparables: Tim Locastro (65), Travis Jankowski (58), Roger Bernadina (57)

Brennan is the sort of unheralded prospect about which observers write "all he does is hit," which isn't true at all; he also plays a steady center field and can be plus in the corners. An eighth-round pick out of Kansas State, Brennan rode his plus hit tool, mature approach and solid fundamentals into the bigs and onto the Guardians' playoff roster last year. His compact, line-drive stroke produces only occasional power, but he grinds out every plate appearance and didn't look overmatched down the stretch in Cleveland. Brennan isn't a future All-Star but has "professional hitter" stenciled all over him, and should carve out a career as a bench bat and the last guy a pitcher wants to see when a strikeout is needed.

Juan Brito 2B Born: 09/24/01 Age: 21 Bats: S Throws: R Height: 5'11" Weight: 162 lb. Origin: International Free Agent, 2018

YEAR	TEAM	LVL	AGE	PA	R	2B	3B	HR	RBI	BB	K	SB	CS	Whiff%	AVG/OBP/SLG	DRC+	BABIP	BRR	DRP	WARP
2021	RCK	ROK	19	109	20	3	0	3	11	15	21	5	4		.295/.406/.432		.354			
2022	FRE	A	20	497	91	29	6	11	72	78	71	17	9		.286/.407/.470	128	.319	-0.9	2B(102): 0.5, SS(4): 0.7	3.3
2023 DC	*CLE*	*MLB*	*21*	*64*	*6*	*2*	*0*	*0*	*5*	*5*	*12*	*0*	*0*	*23.9%*	*.219/.299/.333*	*78*	*.267*	*0.4*	*2B 0, SS 0*	*0.0*

Comparables: Enmanuel Valdez (89), Tony Granadillo (86), Mookie Betts (86)

Brito cruised through his first trip to Low-A, earning more walks than strikeouts and doubling his career home run total in the process. That's good news, because Brito's bat will have to do the heavy lifting given the rest of his profile—without the defensive range to shift to other positions, he's more or less locked into second base. He may rank more highly on prospect lists if he had some more power, but there are tools to like here: an ability to make good contact from both sides of the plate, excellent patience and discipline and a compact swing that lets him turn around fastballs with authority. Keep Brito on your prospect radar as he begins his first season in the Cleveland organization after being dealt from Colorado for Nolan Jones.

Chase DeLauter OF Born: 10/08/01 Age: 21 Bats: L Throws: L Height: 6'4" Weight: 235 lb. Origin: Round 1, 2022 Draft (#16 overall)

The Guardians have outfielders who can make contact and get on base, outfielders with raw power, outfielders that are physical specimens and outfielders who can steal bases and run down fly balls. DeLauter is the only one who has a chance to be all of them at once. Cleveland's top pick in last year's draft combines true five-tool upside with a disciplined approach and the contact skills the organization prizes. Along with easy raw power, DeLauter can steal bases and has the range for center field, though his H-Back frame and plus arm may be a better fit in right. Some scouts have questioned his swing and his Sun Belt Conference pedigree, but the ingredients are here for a potential impact bat.

Tyler Freeman IF Born: 05/21/99 Age: 24 Bats: R Throws: R Height: 6'0" Weight: 190 lb. Origin: Round 2, 2017 Draft (#71 overall)

YEAR	TEAM	LVL	AGE	PA	R	2B	3B	HR	RBI	BB	K	SB	CS	Whiff%	AVG/OBP/SLG	DRC+	BABIP	BRR	DRP	WARP
2021	AKR	AA	22	180	26	14	2	2	19	8	21	4	2		.323/.372/.470	122	.357	-0.8	SS(26): 0.5, 2B(7): -0.2, 3B(7): 0.9	1.1
2022	COL	AAA	23	343	51	7	0	6	44	25	32	6	2		.279/.371/.364	126	.296	0.9	SS(35): -2.6, 2B(33): -0.4, 3B(3): -0.3	1.7
2022	CLE	MLB	23	86	9	3	0	0	3	4	11	1	0	18.7%	.247/.314/.286	102	.284	0.1	3B(11): -0.2, SS(7): 0.5, 2B(4): -0.2	0.3
2023 DC	*CLE*	*MLB*	*24*	*96*	*9*	*3*	*0*	*0*	*7*	*5*	*12*	*1*	*1*	*15.6%*	*.265/.331/.352*	*98*	*.301*	*0.5*	*2B 0, 3B 0*	*0.2*

Comparables: Dawel Lugo (61), Yamaico Navarro (61), Eduardo Núñez (61)

Freeman debuted his well-practiced "Aaron Miles on Steroids, But Not Literally" impression in Cleveland last year as part of their year-long rookie cavalcade, but he wasn't around at the end to hear the applause. Yet another Guardians bat-to-ball savant, Freeman has managed a career .311/.376/.428 minor-league line, with doubles power and infield defense that projects best at the keystone. With the big club, however, Freeman's contact was timid if not downright slappy, resulting in the league's highest percentage of balls hit the other way and only one recorded "barrel" all season; he was sent down in deference to Gabriel Arias at the end of September. By the time the season begins, Freeman will still only be 23, and there's no doubt he *can* hit. It's an open question whether he *will* hit.

Andrés Giménez 2B Born: 09/04/98 Age: 24 Bats: L Throws: R Height: 5'11" Weight: 161 lb. Origin: International Free Agent, 2015

YEAR	TEAM	LVL	AGE	PA	R	2B	3B	HR	RBI	BB	K	SB	CS	Whiff%	AVG/OBP/SLG	DRC+	BABIP	BRR	DRP	WARP
2020	NYM	MLB	21	132	22	3	2	3	12	7	28	8	1	25.7%	.263/.333/.398	91	.318	1.7	SS(23): -1.2, 2B(19): -0.2, 3B(10): 0.1	0.3
2021	COL	AAA	22	233	30	13	1	10	31	12	55	8	4		.287/.342/.502	107	.345	-2.8	SS(32): -0.2, 2B(17): -1.6	0.5
2021	CLE	MLB	22	210	23	10	0	5	16	11	54	11	0	30.5%	.218/.282/.351	77	.273	2.0	SS(42): 0.8, 2B(25): -0.4	0.4
2022	CLE	MLB	23	557	66	26	3	17	69	34	112	20	3	26.7%	.297/.371/.466	115	.353	3.7	2B(125): 3.3, SS(18): 1.9	3.7
2023 DC	*CLE*	*MLB*	*24*	*546*	*64*	*22*	*4*	*16*	*60*	*32*	*120*	*27*	*5*	*26.3%*	*.264/.336/.425*	*111*	*.320*	*15.0*	*2B 1*	*4.0*

Comparables: Francisco Lindor (62), José Ramírez (56), Tony Kubek (54)

Who saw that coming? Giménez bounced back from a disappointing first season in Cleveland to lay claim to the second base job, playing Gold Glove defense and wielding one of the most potent bats in the American League. Giménez is a free swinger who makes plenty of contact despite his propensity to chase, but last year he made a few adjustments to his approach and everything clicked. He walked more (though not a lot), chased less (though still a lot), improved his pitch recognition and worked himself into better counts where he could punish mistakes, resulting in numbers that earned him down-ballot MVP consideration. Some of this may not be sustainable, as his on-base percentage was propped up by 25 plunks and he doesn't hit the ball particularly hard, though the infield hits and hustle doubles his top-end speed generates will help his BABIP and slugging numbers. Giménez just turned 24 so he still has room to improve, but even if his offense slips down a peg, his plus glove in the middle of the diamond makes him a long-term building block.

Oscar Gonzalez RF Born: 01/10/98 Age: 25 Bats: R Throws: R Height: 6'4" Weight: 240 lb. Origin: International Free Agent, 2014

YEAR	TEAM	LVL	AGE	PA	R	2B	3B	HR	RBI	BB	K	SB	CS	Whiff%	AVG/OBP/SLG	DRC+	BABIP	BRR	DRP	WARP
2021	AKR	AA	23	199	31	12	0	13	41	11	36	1	0		.330/.367/.601	142	.353	0.1	RF(21): 2.6, LF(19): 0.2	1.9
2021	COL	AAA	23	305	39	12	1	18	42	11	76	0	1		.269/.305/.503	106	.306	-2.5	RF(46): 0.3, LF(9): 0.7, CF(1): -0.1	1.0
2022	COL	AAA	24	182	21	8	2	9	33	6	26	0	0		.282/.308/.506	120	.286	-0.9	RF(36): 0.3	1.1
2022	CLE	MLB	24	382	39	27	0	11	43	15	75	1	2	26.8%	.296/.327/.461	108	.345	-2.5	RF(84): 2.1	1.4
2023 DC	*CLE*	*MLB*	*25*	*576*	*63*	*26*	*2*	*19*	*75*	*23*	*116*	*1*	*1*	*26.7%*	*.272/.306/.438*	*106*	*.313*	*-0.2*	*RF -3*	*1.2*

Comparables: Anthony Santander (60), Domonic Brown (55), Steven Moya (51)

Who ... plays in the outfield and wears the red C? (Oscar Gonzalez!)

Free-swinging and massive and clutchy is he (Oscar Gonzalez!)

If youthful exuberance be somethin' you wish (Oscar Gonzalez!)

Then watch our young slugger stride to the dish!

Gonzalez began last season in Columbus trying to build on his 2021 high-minors power surge, was called up in May to address Cleveland's perpetual right field void and ended the year as a postseason folk hero. In between he showed the power potential and contact skills of a lineup force alongside the swing percentage and chase rate of a lineup sink. His future likely lies halfway between Eloy Jiménez and Delmon Young, with Gonzalez making improvements to his approach while sending a few more into the bleachers, but never walking enough to get on base at a high rate. Pair that with league-average defense and a strong arm and you've got a good player, not a great one. That's light-years ahead of where the Guardians found themselves last spring.

Steven Kwan LF Born: 09/05/97 Age: 25 Bats: L Throws: L Height: 5'9" Weight: 170 lb. Origin: Round 5, 2018 Draft (#163 overall)

YEAR	TEAM	LVL	AGE	PA	R	2B	3B	HR	RBI	BB	K	SB	CS	Whiff%	AVG/OBP/SLG	DRC+	BABIP	BRR	DRP	WARP
2021	AKR	AA	23	221	42	12	3	7	31	22	23	4	2		.337/.411/.539	135	.354	1.8	CF(24): -1.8, LF(12): 1.7, RF(11): 0.5	1.9
2021	COL	AAA	23	120	23	3	1	5	13	14	8	2	0		.311/.398/.505	137	.300	1.6	CF(21): 2.6, LF(3): -1.2	1.2
2022	CLE	MLB	24	638	89	25	7	6	52	62	60	19	5	9.3%	.298/.373/.400	117	.323	2.7	LF(123): 7.6, RF(20): 0.5, CF(7): 0.1	4.5
2023 DC	*CLE*	*MLB*	*25*	*624*	*81*	*24*	*6*	*11*	*57*	*57*	*50*	*19*	*6*	*9.5%*	*.290/.362/.418*	*122*	*.304*	*9.8*	*LF 11*	*5.4*

Comparables: Adam Eaton (72), Gerardo Parra (71), Yonder Alonso (66)

Kwan spent his rookie year doing everything you'd hope for from an old-school leadoff pest: working long at-bats, drawing walks, looping singles the other way and then hustling or stealing his way into scoring position. He was an instant hero when he went 116 pitches to start his career without a swing-and-miss, but the way he adjusted and thrived after a deep May slump was even more encouraging for his future. The Ambassador was a leader on MLB's youngest team and a Gold Glove defender in left field. The Guardians believe Kwan can develop more pull-side power, but a few more wall-scrapers won't change the shape of his game. It's hard to be a four-win player relying on so many wedge shots down the left field line, but if anyone can, it's this guy.

Bryan Lavastida C Born: 11/27/98 Age: 24 Bats: R Throws: R Height: 6'0" Weight: 200 lb. Origin: Round 15, 2018 Draft (#463 overall)

YEAR	TEAM	LVL	AGE	PA	R	2B	3B	HR	RBI	BB	K	SB	CS	Whiff%	AVG/OBP/SLG	DRC+	BABIP	BRR	DRP	WARP
2021	LC	A+	22	198	32	12	0	5	31	26	30	14	5		.303/.399/.467	124	.336	-0.1	C(38): 11.2	2.2
2021	AKR	AA	22	119	16	7	1	3	17	12	28	2	3		.291/.373/.466	105	.370	0.6	C(15): 0.2	0.5
2022	AKR	AA	23	191	22	4	2	5	14	12	45	5	1		.195/.257/.328	90	.230	-0.9	C(41): -2.2	0.1
2022	COL	AAA	23	168	24	6	2	4	16	16	35	2	1		.224/.315/.374	95	.266	0.2	C(35): -1.3	0.3
2022	CLE	MLB	23	15	0	0	0	0	0	3	4	0	0	33.3%	.083/.267/.083	91	.125	-0.2	C(6): -0.3	0.0
2023 DC	*CLE*	*MLB*	*24*	*61*	*6*	*2*	*0*	*1*	*5*	*4*	*15*	*1*	*0*	*30.3%*	*.217/.285/.329*	*71*	*.280*	*0.7*	*C -1*	*-0.1*

Comparables: Francisco Cervelli (53), Josh Phegley (53), Tucker Barnhart (51)

YEAR	TEAM	P. COUNT	FRM RUNS	BLK RUNS	THRW RUNS	TOT RUNS
2021	LC	5047	10.3	0.6	0.5	11.4
2021	AKR	1984	0.2	0.2	0.0	0.4
2022	AKR	5926	-2.5	-0.3	1.0	-1.8
2022	COL	5237	-2.4	0.0	0.4	-2.1
2022	CLE	613	-0.3	0.0	0.0	-0.4
2023	*CLE*	*2405*	*-1.4*	*0.0*	*0.0*	*-1.5*

The highlight of Lavastida's season was his appearance on the big club's Opening Day roster due to a Luke Maile injury; the lowlight was pretty much everything that followed. The former infielder slumped in Triple-A, missed a month with a hamstring injury and then returned to Akron while Bo Naylor thrived behind the plate in Columbus. Lavastida has worked hard to become an acceptable receiver, and until last year made hard contact with doubles power and a mature approach. Backstops can be slower to develop than a resistance to iocane powder, so there's no reason the 24-year-old can't bounce back and reach his ultimate ceiling as a platoon catcher.

Bo Naylor C Born: 02/21/00 Age: 23 Bats: L Throws: R Height: 6'0" Weight: 205 lb. Origin: Round 1, 2018 Draft (#29 overall)

YEAR	TEAM	LVL	AGE	PA	R	2B	3B	HR	RBI	BB	K	SB	CS	Whiff%	AVG/OBP/SLG	DRC+	BABIP	BRR	DRP	WARP
2021	AKR	AA	21	356	41	13	1	10	44	37	112	10	0		.188/.280/.332	82	.255	-0.5	C(73): 6.7	1.1
2022	AKR	AA	22	220	29	12	2	6	21	45	46	11	3		.271/.427/.471	122	.333	1.3	C(42): -1.1	1.2
2022	COL	AAA	22	290	44	14	2	15	47	37	75	9	1		.257/.366/.514	113	.306	-1.5	C(56): 6.2	1.7
2022	CLE	MLB	22	8	0	0	0	0	0	0	5	0	0	55.6%	.000/.000/.000	70			C(4): -0.0	0.0
2023 DC	*CLE*	*MLB*	*23*	*199*	*19*	*7*	*1*	*5*	*18*	*20*	*55*	*3*	*2*	*27.3%*	*.206/.297/.362*	*81*	*.268*	*1.8*	*C 0*	*0.5*

Comparables: Miguel Montero (67), John Ryan Murphy (57), Jarrod Saltalamacchia (54)

YEAR	TEAM	P. COUNT	FRM RUNS	BLK RUNS	THRW RUNS	TOT RUNS
2021	AKR	10542	5.6	-0.5	1.2	6.3
2022	AKR	5951	-0.8	0.0	0.0	-0.8
2022	COL	8260	5.2	-0.5	0.0	4.7
2022	CLE	227	0.0	0.0	0.0	0.0
2023	*CLE*	*7215*	*0.4*	*-0.4*	*-0.4*	*-0.4*

After a disappointing 2021, Naylor the Younger's second run at the high minors was a resounding success. The athletic catcher showed patience, thump and surprising speed during a 20/20 season that ended with him on the Guardians' playoff roster. Naylor reworked his approach and walked nearly as much as he struck out in Double-A, then launched 15 bombs over half a season in Columbus. No one is going to confuse him with Bob Boone behind the dish, but he has a strong arm and is playable back there. Although he's likely to see his whiff rate spike against major league pitching (who doesn't?), Naylor is ready to prove he can be the rare receiver who can hit near the top of the order.

Josh Naylor 1B Born: 06/22/97 Age: 26 Bats: L Throws: L Height: 5'11" Weight: 250 lb. Origin: Round 1, 2015 Draft (#12 overall)

YEAR	TEAM	LVL	AGE	PA	R	2B	3B	HR	RBI	BB	K	SB	CS	Whiff%	AVG/OBP/SLG	DRC+	BABIP	BRR	DRP	WARP
2020	SD	MLB	23	38	4	0	1	1	4	1	4	1	0	18.6%	.278/.316/.417	100	.290	0.5	RF(4): -0.1, 1B(3): 0, LF(3): 0.1	0.2
2020	CLE	MLB	23	66	9	3	0	0	2	4	8	0	0	13.9%	.230/.277/.279	91	.264	0.8	LF(19): -0.6, 1B(2): 0	0.1
2021	CLE	MLB	24	250	28	13	0	7	21	14	45	1	0	21.3%	.253/.301/.399	95	.287	-1.1	RF(51): -0.3, 1B(15): 0.7	0.4
2022	COL	AAA	25	25	4	2	0	0	5	5	0	0	0		.200/.360/.300	118	.200	-0.8	RF(3): 0.3, 1B(2): -0.1	0.1
2022	CLE	MLB	25	498	47	28	0	20	79	38	80	6	1	19.5%	.256/.319/.452	112	.268	-2.9	1B(88): -0.6, RF(5): -0.4	1.4
2023 DC	*CLE*	*MLB*	*26*	*574*	*63*	*26*	*1*	*18*	*68*	*44*	*89*	*5*	*2*	*19.3%*	*.257/.321/.421*	*107*	*.278*	*0.3*	*1B 0*	*1.4*

Comparables: Jose Tabata (57), Juan Rivera (56), Coco Crisp (55)

Do you like your baseball a little … edgy? Animated? Fiery? Served with a side of kettle-cooked jalapeño shoulder chips? Then whether he's rockin' the baby, asking for all the smoke or just going full-on Taz after a big moment, Naylor the Elder is your guy. After missing the second half of his 2021 season to a gruesome ankle injury, Naylor turned the corner last year and finally melded his enviable combination of power, patience and bat-to-ball skill into big-league production. Battling through lingering ankle soreness and a balky back, Naylor looked comfortable at first base and posted a stellar .283/.334/.522 line against righties, though lefties tied him in knots all season. He's not a 30-homer guy, but with three seasons of club control remaining, Naylor should be able to provide quality power production at discount prices.

Richie Palacios LF Born: 05/16/97 Age: 26 Bats: L Throws: R Height: 5'10" Weight: 180 lb. Origin: Round 3, 2018 Draft (#103 overall)

YEAR	TEAM	LVL	AGE	PA	R	2B	3B	HR	RBI	BB	K	SB	CS	Whiff%	AVG/OBP/SLG	DRC+	BABIP	BRR	DRP	WARP
2021	SCO	WIN	24	93	17	8	1	3	11	13	15	4	1		.269/.387/.513		.300			
2021	AKR	AA	24	283	53	24	3	6	36	33	42	10	3		.299/.389/.496	128	.338	2.3	2B(42): 6.1, CF(10): -0.5, LF(6): -0.0	2.6
2021	COL	AAA	24	145	19	9	1	1	12	25	28	10	0		.292/.434/.416	107	.376	0.8	2B(26): 1.2, CF(6): -0.8	0.7
2022	COL	AAA	25	206	34	10	5	4	36	24	43	12	2		.279/.371/.458	103	.348	1.3	LF(40): -0.4, 2B(3): 0.2, CF(2): 0.5	0.9
2022	CLE	MLB	25	123	7	6	0	0	10	9	20	2	0	16.7%	.232/.293/.286	89	.280	0.7	LF(25): -0.3, 2B(2): 0	0.3
2023 non-DC	*CLE*	*MLB*	*26*	*251*	*23*	*11*	*2*	*3*	*24*	*21*	*44*	*6*	*1*	*21.6%*	*.250/.323/.378*	*97*	*.296*	*4.7*	*LF 0, 2B 0*	*1.0*

Comparables: Rafael Ortega (60), Zoilo Almonte (59), Trevor Crowe (59)

Palacios spent a lot of time last summer traveling between Columbus and Cleveland, doubtless wondering (a) what he needed to do differently to stick with the big club, and (b) why there isn't a Rest Area on I-71 halfway between—there's one outside Mansfield but it's over on U.S. 30, which is just awkward. The answer to the first question is probably "be Steven Kwan," since Palacios has the same high-contact, high-OBP, good speed, low-power offensive profile as the Guardians' breakout left fielder but without the plus defense that would make him an everyday option. The answer to the second question is probably "ask Steven Kwan," since that dude seems like he'd drop everything to get you the answer if he didn't already know it.

José Ramírez 3B Born: 09/17/92 Age: 30 Bats: S Throws: R Height: 5'9" Weight: 190 lb. Origin: International Free Agent, 2009

YEAR	TEAM	LVL	AGE	PA	R	2B	3B	HR	RBI	BB	K	SB	CS	Whiff%	AVG/OBP/SLG	DRC+	BABIP	BRR	DRP	WARP
2020	CLE	MLB	27	254	45	16	1	17	46	31	43	10	3	16.6%	.292/.386/.607	146	.294	0.0	3B(57): 1.3	2.2
2021	CLE	MLB	28	636	111	32	5	36	103	72	87	27	4	15.0%	.266/.355/.538	135	.256	4.1	3B(133): 2	5.5
2022	CLE	MLB	29	685	90	44	5	29	126	69	82	20	7	15.2%	.280/.355/.514	135	.279	0.9	3B(127): 1.3	4.9
2023 DC	*CLE*	*MLB*	*30*	*641*	*89*	*34*	*4*	*33*	*100*	*66*	*81*	*31*	*6*	*15.2%*	*.276/.358/.532*	*146*	*.272*	*15.6*	*3B 1*	*6.7*

Comparables: Brooks Robinson (74), George Kell (73), Ron Santo (70)

Ramírez signed a team-friendly five-year, $124 million extension on Opening Day last year, meaning that baseball's least-hyped superstar will likely remain in Cleveland throughout his prime. How good has he been? Since his 2016 breakout, only five position players (Betts, Arenado, Trout, Judge and Altuve) have posted a higher cumulative WARP, and only Betts is younger than him (by 20 days); in fact, among the top 20 in cumulative wins, only Lindor, Bregman and the Childish Bambino are more than a month younger than Ramírez. As they enter their thirties, all humans begin losing speed, quickness and range, and Ramírez is human (despite much evidence to the contrary). His peerless combination of contact skills, patience and surprising pop should age well, however, so he should continue to be the fountain of joy at the heart of Guardians baseball for the foreseeable future.

Brayan Rocchio MI Born: 01/13/01 Age: 22 Bats: S Throws: R Height: 5'10" Weight: 170 lb. Origin: International Free Agent, 2017

YEAR	TEAM	LVL	AGE	PA	R	2B	3B	HR	RBI	BB	K	SB	CS	Whiff%	AVG/OBP/SLG	DRC+	BABIP	BRR	DRP	WARP
2021	LAG	WIN	20	76	11	6	1	2	6	5	5	2	2		.391/.440/.594		.403			
2021	LC	A+	20	288	45	13	1	9	33	20	65	14	6		.265/.337/.428	108	.319	1.0	SS(36): -1.4, 2B(16): 2.2, 3B(12): 0.3	1.3
2021	AKR	AA	20	203	34	13	4	6	30	13	41	7	4		.293/.360/.505	112	.350	-1.1	SS(43): 1.5, 2B(2): 0.2	1.0
2022	AKR	AA	21	432	62	21	1	13	48	42	81	12	6		.265/.349/.432	114	.302	2.9	SS(51): -2.1, 2B(44): 4.0	2.4
2022	COL	AAA	21	152	21	6	0	5	16	12	21	2	3		.234/.298/.387	112	.241	-0.1	SS(26): -2.9, 2B(8): 0.5	0.4
2023 non-DC	*CLE*	*MLB*	*22*	*251*	*24*	*10*	*1*	*5*	*25*	*16*	*54*	*8*	*4*	*25.3%*	*.244/.304/.371*	*88*	*.298*	*-2.4*	*2B 0, SS 0*	*0.1*

Comparables: Jorge Polanco (73), Adrian Cardenas (70), J.P. Crawford (67)

Of the myriad middle infield prospects in the Cleveland system, Rocchio possesses the broadest set of tools and perhaps the highest upside. A switch-hitting shortstop with soft hands, great range and plus speed, they call Rocchio "The Professor" due to his high baseball IQ. At the plate he has a disciplined approach with strong bat-to-ball skills and developing power, though he'll never be a slugger. Rocchio reached Triple-A as a 21-year-old and struggled down the stretch, but overall he walked more, struck out less and launched a career-high 18 bombs. All the arrows are pointing up, and it's easy to picture Rocchio teaming with fellow Venezuelan Andrés Giménez to form a flashy and productive double play combo for years to come.

Amed Rosario SS Born: 11/20/95 Age: 27 Bats: R Throws: R Height: 6'2" Weight: 190 lb. Origin: International Free Agent, 2012

YEAR	TEAM	LVL	AGE	PA	R	2B	3B	HR	RBI	BB	K	SB	CS	Whiff%	AVG/OBP/SLG	DRC+	BABIP	BRR	DRP	WARP
2020	NYM	MLB	24	147	20	3	1	4	15	4	34	0	1	24.3%	.252/.272/.371	85	.305	0.1	SS(44): -1.5	0.0
2021	CLE	MLB	25	588	77	25	6	11	57	31	120	13	0	24.9%	.282/.321/.409	93	.340	1.0	SS(121): -2.9, CF(18): -0.2	1.4
2022	CLE	MLB	26	670	86	26	9	11	71	25	111	18	4	21.0%	.283/.312/.403	102	.326	2.9	SS(140): 2.3, LF(6): 0.2	2.9
2023 DC	*CLE*	*MLB*	*27*	*612*	*69*	*24*	*6*	*12*	*61*	*28*	*100*	*16*	*4*	*21.4%*	*.282/.320/.411*	*104*	*.323*	*8.5*	*SS 3*	*3.4*

Comparables: Granny Hamner (76), José Reyes (75), Starlin Castro (74)

Rosario may never reach the glorious heights predicted of him during his sepia-tinged days as a Mets prospect, but last year when the Guardians finally just stuck him at shortstop and let him play, he proved to be a key part of their improbable playoff run. His offensive numbers were uncannily similar to his 2021 season, as Rosario rarely walked but consistently put the ball in play and busted out of the box to lead the American League in both infield hits and triples. His defensive metrics varied depending on the system, but most indicated him flashing an above-average glove last year. You know you're doing something right when José Ramírez lobbies for you, joking that he'd pony up $40 million of his own money to help sign you long-term. Rosario may never be an All-Star but has shown he can be an adequate big-league shortstop.

Myles Straw CF

Born: 10/17/94 Age: 28 Bats: R Throws: R Height: 5'10" Weight: 178 lb. Origin: Round 12, 2015 Draft (#349 overall)

YEAR	TEAM	LVL	AGE	PA	R	2B	3B	HR	RBI	BB	K	SB	CS	Whiff%	AVG/OBP/SLG	DRC+	BABIP	BRR	DRP	WARP
2020	HOU	MLB	25	86	8	4	0	0	8	4	22	6	2	19.7%	.207/.244/.256	76	.283	-0.3	CF(27): -1.4, SS(1): 0	-0.1
2021	CLE	MLB	26	268	42	16	0	2	14	29	50	13	1	13.9%	.285/.362/.377	100	.353	2.5	CF(60): 5.2	1.9
2021	HOU	MLB	26	370	44	13	1	2	34	38	71	17	5	13.4%	.262/.339/.326	93	.324	-3.3	CF(96): 8.3	1.8
2022	CLE	MLB	27	596	72	22	3	0	32	54	87	21	1	12.6%	.221/.291/.273	82	.261	2.7	CF(152): 10.8	2.3
2023 DC	*CLE*	*MLB*	*28*	*578*	*64*	*21*	*2*	*5*	*45*	*54*	*89*	*26*	*5*	*13.1%*	*.263/.336/.349*	*96*	*.308*	*11.9*	*CF 4*	*3.1*

Comparables: Billy Hamilton (59), Darren Lewis (56), Delino DeShields (54)

A run prevented is worth the same as a run produced, which is why Straw can make his living as a big-league center fielder despite a complete lack of home run power. In the field he's as rangy, instinctive and reliable as anyone in the game and steals bases at a healthy clip. Yet there's a limit to how much out-making can be papered over, which is why Straw needs to discover what, exactly, he did to offend the baseball gods so deeply. Did he disrespect a streak? Step on a chalked line? Put ketchup on a hot dog? Ghost some deity's oracle? It had to be something, otherwise how can you explain Straw's calamitous drop in OPS when his Statcast, batted ball and plate discipline metrics last year were so similar to those of his non-disastrous 2021 season—in fact, he walked more and struck out less this year, though with a few more grounders and fewer line drives. Moving just a few notches up from "utterly cataclysmic" to "medium awful" would make a huge difference in how much value Straw provides. Who knows, maybe getting a live rooster would help.

Jose Tena MI

Born: 03/20/01 Age: 22 Bats: L Throws: R Height: 5'11" Weight: 190 lb. Origin: International Free Agent, 2017

YEAR	TEAM	LVL	AGE	PA	R	2B	3B	HR	RBI	BB	K	SB	CS	Whiff%	AVG/OBP/SLG	DRC+	BABIP	BRR	DRP	WARP
2021	SCO	WIN	20	75	16	6	1	0	9	10	10	2	1		.387/.467/.516		.444			
2021	LC	A+	20	447	58	25	2	16	58	27	117	10	5		.281/.331/.467	102	.355	1.6	SS(81): -7.3, 3B(13): 0.3, 2B(11): 1.0	1.0
2022	AKR	AA	21	550	74	25	6	13	66	25	138	8	5		.264/.299/.411	86	.332	0.5	SS(71): -0.4, 2B(47): -0.9	0.7
2023 non-DC	*CLE*	*MLB*	*22*	*251*	*21*	*10*	*1*	*4*	*24*	*11*	*67*	*4*	*2*	*29.9%*	*.243/.284/.361*	*75*	*.323*	*0.6*	*2B 0, SS 0*	*0.0*

Comparables: Willi Castro (78), Jorge Polanco (77), J.P. Crawford (60)

Tena sometimes gets lost in the crowd of Guardians middle infield prospects, but his hitting talent is obvious. Saying he has a quick bat is accurate in several ways, as Tena generates impressive bat speed and can put a charge into the pitches he can square up but he's swift to offer at anything and everything he can reach. The more advanced pitchers in Double-A took advantage of his aggressive approach last year and the quality of Tena's contact declined, though he still flashed the surprising raw power that gives him 20-homer potential. More steady than spectacular on the dirt, Tena's upside is Amed Rosario with a bit more power and a bit less speed, but he'll need to improve his approach to reach it.

★ ★ ★ *2023 Top 101 Prospect* **#60** ★ ★ ★

George Valera OF

Born: 11/13/00 Age: 22 Bats: L Throws: L Height: 6'0" Weight: 195 lb. Origin: International Free Agent, 2017

YEAR	TEAM	LVL	AGE	PA	R	2B	3B	HR	RBI	BB	K	SB	CS	Whiff%	AVG/OBP/SLG	DRC+	BABIP	BRR	DRP	WARP
2021	LC	A+	20	263	45	2	4	16	43	55	58	10	5		.256/.430/.548	157	.276	0.4	RF(38): 3.1, CF(12): -0.8, LF(9): -0.5	2.8
2021	AKR	AA	20	100	6	3	0	3	22	11	30	1	0		.267/.340/.407	93	.357	-0.4	RF(10): 3.5, LF(8): 0.6, CF(4): -0.4	0.6
2022	AKR	AA	21	387	64	17	3	15	59	52	100	2	4		.264/.367/.470	109	.332	-2.1	RF(49): -0.2, LF(24): 0.9, CF(12): 2.3	2.1
2022	COL	AAA	21	179	25	8	0	9	23	22	45	0	0		.221/.324/.448	106	.248	-1.0	RF(21): 1.1, LF(13): 0.3	0.6
2023 non-DC	*CLE*	*MLB*	*22*	*251*	*25*	*8*	*2*	*6*	*26*	*25*	*73*	*3*	*1*	*33.3%*	*.219/.305/.366*	*86*	*.294*	*1.1*	*LF 0, CF 0*	*0.2*

Comparables: Jesús Sánchez (57), Carlos González (50), Michael Saunders (48)

There's no longer any doubt about Valera's plate discipline, pitch recognition, on-base skills, raw power, outfield arm or bat flip acumen. What scouts still can't seem to agree on is whether the Bronx-by-way-of-San-Pedro-de-Macoris product will make enough contact to thrive. Some see a hitter with terrific hand-eye coordination who can be fooled by a pitch but still drive it into the alley; others have seen him swing through enough in-zone pitches to fear that his strikeout rate will become untenable when he has to face big-league pitching. Valera has a great eye and works deep counts so walks and whiffs will always be a part of his game, and he showed plenty of thump as a 21-year-old in Triple-A. Our hunch: bet the over.

Mike Zunino C

Born: 03/25/91 Age: 32 Bats: R Throws: R Height: 6'2" Weight: 235 lb. Origin: Round 1, 2012 Draft (#3 overall)

YEAR	TEAM	LVL	AGE	PA	R	2B	3B	HR	RBI	BB	K	SB	CS	Whiff%	AVG/OBP/SLG	DRC+	BABIP	BRR	DRP	WARP
2020	TB	MLB	29	84	8	4	0	4	10	6	37	0	0	40.2%	.147/.238/.360	64	.206	-1.3	C(28): -1.5	-0.4
2021	TB	MLB	30	375	64	11	2	33	62	34	132	0	0	38.8%	.216/.301/.559	122	.231	0.2	C(105): 8.9	3.6
2022	TB	MLB	31	123	7	3	0	5	16	6	46	0	0	40.2%	.148/.195/.304	67	.185	-1.6	C(35): 3.5	0.2
2023 DC	*CLE*	*MLB*	*32*	*374*	*47*	*14*	*0*	*21*	*51*	*28*	*135*	*0*	*0*	*39.1%*	*.207/.279/.443*	*94*	*.267*	*-2.3*	*C 5*	*1.4*

Comparables: Jeff Mathis (67), Chris Snyder (66), Jarrod Saltalamacchia (65)

YEAR	TEAM	P. COUNT	FRM RUNS	BLK RUNS	THRW RUNS	TOT RUNS
2020	TB	3613	-1.4	-0.1	0.0	-1.5
2021	TB	13711	7.7	-0.4	0.6	7.9
2022	TB	4610	3.0	-0.1	0.1	3.0
2023	*CLE*	*14430*	*5.3*	*-0.2*	*0.2*	*5.2*

Zunino's miserable season ended in early June after the veteran backstop underwent surgery for thoracic outlet syndrome. Prior to the diagnosis he tried to play through and manage the ailment in his walk year, but found little success. Coming off his best season at the plate, Zunino regressed badly, looking very much like the player who drew Rays fans' ire in 2020. He continued to strike out at an extraordinary rate while walking less and providing less pop. Still, he's a member of that rare class of ballplayers that can catch competently, and the bar in Cleveland, at least offensively, is literally Austin Hedges. It's too late to ask Zunino to be anything but what he is, but maybe he and the Guardians will get lucky and only see his good days.

PITCHERS

Logan Allen LHP
Born: 09/05/98 Age: 24 Bats: R Throws: L Height: 6'0" Weight: 190 lb. Origin: Round 2, 2020 Draft (#56 overall)

YEAR	TEAM	LVL	AGE	W	L	SV	G	GS	IP	H	HR	BB/9	K/9	K	GB%	BABIP	WHIP	ERA	DRA-	WARP	MPH	FB%	Whiff%	CSP
2021	LC	A+	22	5	0	0	9	9	51^1	37	3	2.3	11.7	67	44.1%	.296	0.97	1.58	80	1.1				
2021	AKR	AA	22	4	0	0	12	10	60	40	9	2.0	11.4	76	28.8%	.238	0.88	2.85	96	0.6				
2022	AKR	AA	23	5	3	0	13	13	73	58	9	2.7	12.8	104	39.0%	.316	1.10	3.33	79	1.8				
2022	COL	AAA	23	4	4	0	14	14	59^2	64	8	4.4	11.0	73	37.3%	.354	1.56	6.49	101	0.8				
2023 non-DC	*CLE*	*MLB*	*24*	*2*	*2*	*0*	*57*	*0*	*50*	*46*	*7*	*3.6*	*9.2*	*51*	*39.0%*	*.291*	*1.32*	*3.97*	*101*	*0.2*			*29.8%*	

Comparables: Marco Gonzales (81), TJ House (79), Kyle Gibson (76)

No, not the lefty reliever the Guardians released last May. Not the outfielder in the Rays system. Not the kid on your youth soccer team whose shoes were always untied (well, theoretically he *could* be that one—our research doesn't go quite that deep). This Logan Allen is the former second-round college lefty longer on pitchability than velocity. Allen has used solid command of his four-pitch mix (low-90s fastball, cutter, slider and potentially plus changeup) to post excellent strikeout numbers in his rapid climb through the minors, though he was roughed up a little after arriving in Triple-A. He's a smallish guy who lacks huge stuff, but he repeats his delivery and always competes. There are enough raw elements here for Cleveland's vaunted pitcher development staff to spin Allen into mid-rotation gold, perhaps as soon as this summer.

★ ★ ★ *2023 Top 101 Prospect* **#52** ★ ★ ★

Tanner Bibee RHP
Born: 03/05/99 Age: 24 Bats: R Throws: R Height: 6'2" Weight: 205 lb. Origin: Round 5, 2021 Draft (#156 overall)

YEAR	TEAM	LVL	AGE	W	L	SV	G	GS	IP	H	HR	BB/9	K/9	K	GB%	BABIP	WHIP	ERA	DRA-	WARP	MPH	FB%	Whiff%	CSP
2022	LC	A+	23	2	1	0	12	12	59	50	8	2.0	13.1	86	37.4%	.344	1.07	2.59	89	1.0				
2022	AKR	AA	23	6	1	0	13	13	73^2	51	4	1.7	9.9	81	34.2%	.260	0.88	1.83	86	1.5				
2023 non-DC	*CLE*	*MLB*	*24*	*2*	*2*	*0*	*57*	*0*	*50*	*48*	*7*	*2.9*	*9.0*	*49*	*36.9%*	*.301*	*1.29*	*3.94*	*101*	*0.2*			*26.1%*	

Comparables: Parker Dunshee (88), Erik Davis (85), Erik Johnson (82)

Few prospects improved their standing as much as Bibee did last summer in his professional debut. Taken in the fifth round out of Cal State Fullerton and billed as a high-floor strike thrower, Bibee blew through the Midwest League like a summer storm before conquering Double-A in his first taste of the upper minors. His command was as advertised, but Bibee's fastball surprisingly sat in the mid-90s and approached triple digits in turbo mode. His secondaries—a sweeping slider, a slow curve and a potentially plus changeup—generated plenty of chases, and Bibee showed he could drop them in the zone when needed for a stolen strike. The Guardians' reputation for pitcher development is well-earned, and Bibee is primed to be their next low-cost, mid-rotation triumph.

Shane Bieber RHP
Born: 05/31/95 Age: 28 Bats: R Throws: R Height: 6'3" Weight: 200 lb. Origin: Round 4, 2016 Draft (#122 overall)

YEAR	TEAM	LVL	AGE	W	L	SV	G	GS	IP	H	HR	BB/9	K/9	K	GB%	BABIP	WHIP	ERA	DRA-	WARP	MPH	FB%	Whiff%	CSP
2020	CLE	MLB	25	8	1	0	12	12	77^1	46	7	2.4	14.2	122	48.4%	.267	0.87	1.63	51	2.9	94.0	51.6%	40.7%	40.1%
2021	CLE	MLB	26	7	4	0	16	16	96^2	84	11	3.1	12.5	134	44.9%	.327	1.21	3.17	75	2.2	92.9	38.8%	36.5%	56.6%
2022	CLE	MLB	27	13	8	0	31	31	200	172	18	1.6	8.9	198	48.1%	.288	1.04	2.88	82	3.8	91.5	34.5%	29.8%	57.3%
2023 DC	*CLE*	*MLB*	*28*	*11*	*9*	*0*	*29*	*29*	*177.7*	*175*	*20*	*2.2*	*9.9*	*196*	*47.3%*	*.323*	*1.23*	*3.42*	*89*	*2.5*	*92.3*	*39.0%*	*31.5%*	*53.6%*

Comparables: Félix Hernández (85), Ben Sheets (83), Aaron Nola (83)

Velo, schmeelo. In his May 7 start against Toronto, Bieber gave up seven runs with three walks and zero strikeouts before leaving in the fourth inning, prompting gale-force tweetstorms about his reduced velocity and "struggles." The air quotes are there because Bieber's FIP after that start was a perfectly fine 3.36, and from that point on the Cleveland ace posted a 2.64 ERA and 2.78 FIP, held opponent batters to a .601 OPS and struck out six for each batter he walked. Bieber may have lost a tick or two off his heater, but his ability to work the edges of the zone and generate chases and whiffs with his devastating secondaries remains intact. Velocity can paper over many sins, but when the rest of your game (including Gold Glove defense) is immaculate, it's not a necessity—*see Maddux, Greg.*

Justin Campbell RHP
Born: 02/14/01 Age: 22 Bats: L Throws: R Height: 6'7" Weight: 219 lb. Origin: Round 1, 2022 Draft (#37 overall)

We're sure you're shocked, SHOCKED, to learn that Cleveland used their supplemental first-rounder on another strike-throwing college arm. Campbell stands out by, well, standing out, as his height and great extension allows him to attack hitters from a steep angle that helps him get as much as he can out of his low-90s fastball. His changeup shows promise, though it could use a little more oomph to better tunnel with the fastball, and he works in a usable slow curve. Campbell has the command profile the Guardians covet and a frame that should support better velocity, marking him as yet another potential mid-rotation piece.

Aaron Civale RHP
Born: 06/12/95 Age: 28 Bats: R Throws: R Height: 6'2" Weight: 215 lb. Origin: Round 3, 2016 Draft (#92 overall)

YEAR	TEAM	LVL	AGE	W	L	SV	G	GS	IP	H	HR	BB/9	K/9	K	GB%	BABIP	WHIP	ERA	DRA-	WARP	MPH	FB%	Whiff%	CSP
2020	CLE	MLB	25	4	6	0	12	12	74	82	11	1.9	8.4	69	45.1%	.333	1.32	4.74	95	1.0	90.3	60.0%	25.0%	47.3%
2021	AKR	AA	26	1	0	0	2	2	7	4	0	3.9	10.3	8	41.2%	.250	1.00	1.29	94	0.1				
2021	CLE	MLB	26	12	5	0	21	21	124^1	108	23	2.2	7.2	99	44.2%	.250	1.12	3.84	111	0.4	90.6	57.9%	21.6%	53.3%
2022	COL	AAA	27	0	0	0	4	4	13^1	14	2	2.7	12.1	18	60.0%	.364	1.35	4.72	81	0.3				
2022	CLE	MLB	27	5	6	0	20	20	97	93	14	2.0	9.1	98	41.4%	.297	1.19	4.92	96	1.1	91.4	30.9%	24.4%	52.3%
2023 DC	*CLE*	*MLB*	*28*	*8*	*7*	*0*	*25*	*25*	*137.3*	*128*	*17*	*2.4*	*8.3*	*126*	*43.6%*	*.289*	*1.20*	*3.37*	*90*	*1.8*	*90.9*	*47.6%*	*24.4%*	*51.4%*

Comparables: Anthony DeSclafani (63), Steven Matz (60), Stephen Fife (60)

Working around three separate stays on the injured list last year, Civale posted the worst ERA of his career despite his best DRA and improved walk, strikeout, chase and swinging strike rates. His six-pitch mix is like a truck stop breakfast scramble, with ingredients of varying quantity and quality that can bring satisfaction or indigestion depending on the day. Last year Civale tossed in more cutters, curveballs and sinkers and fewer sliders, splitters and four-seamers, but produced the same mundane back-of-the-rotation results. There's plenty of value in that, especially when it comes at the Daily Special price point of his pre-arbitration years, but Civale is destined to fill out a rotation, not improve it.

Emmanuel Clase RHP Born: 03/18/98 Age: 25 Bats: R Throws: R Height: 6'2" Weight: 206 lb. Origin: International Free Agent, 2015

YEAR	TEAM	LVL	AGE	W	L	SV	G	GS	IP	H	HR	BB/9	K/9	K	GB%	BABIP	WHIP	ERA	DRA-	WARP	MPH	FB%	Whiff%	CSP
2021	CLE	MLB	23	4	5	24	71	0	69^{2}	51	2	2.1	9.6	74	67.7%	.263	0.96	1.29	76	1.5	100.5	70.2%	33.0%	53.5%
2022	CLE	MLB	24	3	4	42	77	0	72^{2}	43	3	1.2	9.5	77	62.8%	.223	0.73	1.36	71	1.8	99.8	62.0%	30.2%	55.6%
2023 DC	*CLE*	*MLB*	*25*	*3*	*3*	*35*	*69*	*0*	*60*	*55*	*4*	*2.2*	*10.0*	*66*	*62.3%*	*.319*	*1.18*	*2.72*	*73*	*1.1*	*100.1*	*66.4%*	*30.4%*	*54.4%*

Comparables: Huston Street (78), Jonathan Broxton (73), Mark Wohlers (73)

"It's one of those unique pitches where you could tell the hitter what's coming and he's still going to have a hard time hitting it," says Austin Hedges, who should know. Clase's triple-digit cutter is so nasty that hitters call it Ms. Jackson. It kills more worms than your average ice age, is tougher to square up than a sagging Victorian doorway, more difficult to turn on than Broadway at rush hour and harder to elevate than a Thanksgiving discussion with your conspiracy theorist uncle. When you open Clase's Baseball Savant page you can hear Ode to Joy, even if your speakers are on mute. What we're trying to say is Clase is really, really, really good in just about every way you can measure and a few you can't, and should be among the league's best relievers for a long time.

Xzavion Curry RHP Born: 07/27/98 Age: 24 Bats: R Throws: R Height: 6'0" Weight: 195 lb. Origin: Round 7, 2019 Draft (#220 overall)

YEAR	TEAM	LVL	AGE	W	L	SV	G	GS	IP	H	HR	BB/9	K/9	K	GB%	BABIP	WHIP	ERA	DRA-	WARP	MPH	FB%	Whiff%	CSP
2021	LYN	A	22	3	0	0	5	5	25^{1}	12	1	1.4	13.5	38	27.5%	.220	0.63	1.07	72	0.6				
2021	LC	A+	22	5	1	0	13	13	67^{2}	53	10	1.6	10.6	80	30.9%	.261	0.96	2.66	91	1.1				
2022	AKR	AA	23	5	3	0	13	11	69	56	9	2.5	10.4	80	31.7%	.275	1.09	3.65	102	0.9				
2022	COL	AAA	23	4	1	0	12	10	53	50	9	3.9	9.2	54	36.2%	.287	1.38	4.58	103	0.6				
2022	CLE	MLB	23	0	1	0	2	2	9^{1}	13	1	5.8	2.9	3	32.4%	.333	2.04	5.79	142	-0.1	92.5	58.8%	25.4%	51.6%
2023 DC	*CLE*	*MLB*	*24*	*2*	*1*	*0*	*15*	*3*	*24.3*	*24*	*4*	*3.4*	*8.0*	*21*	*34.0%*	*.293*	*1.38*	*4.52*	*114*	*0.0*	*92.5*	*58.8%*	*25.0%*	*51.6%*

Comparables: Erik Johnson (45), Justin Grimm (44), Daniel Mengden (43)

Curry continued to climb the prospect ladder, spending his first full season in the high minors and making his MLB debut alongside his former youth baseball teammate Will Benson. The Georgia Tech product is short on stature and stuff but long on pitchability, slinging his high-spin, low-90s heater from over the top and mixing in a 12-6 curveball and fringy changeup to keep hitters guessing. Although he misses more bats than you would expect and has good control, he contracted a case of the long balls in Columbus that may prove chronic. Curry will likely earn his paychecks in long relief, but if any team can find a way to leverage him into a bigger role, it's the Guardians.

Enyel De Los Santos RHP Born: 12/25/95 Age: 27 Bats: R Throws: R Height: 6'3" Weight: 235 lb. Origin: International Free Agent, 2014

YEAR	TEAM	LVL	AGE	W	L	SV	G	GS	IP	H	HR	BB/9	K/9	K	GB%	BABIP	WHIP	ERA	DRA-	WARP	MPH	FB%	Whiff%	CSP
2021	PIT	MLB	25	1	0	0	7	0	7^{1}	9	1	4.9	7.4	6	24.0%	.348	1.77	4.91	114	0.0	95.1	59.3%	27.8%	52.6%
2021	PHI	MLB	25	1	1	0	26	0	28	34	7	4.5	13.5	42	41.0%	.391	1.71	6.75	76	0.6	95.0	70.7%	33.1%	54.3%
2022	CLE	MLB	26	5	0	1	50	0	53^{1}	40	3	2.9	10.3	61	40.0%	.280	1.07	3.04	78	1.1	95.6	60.4%	30.1%	58.3%
2023 DC	*CLE*	*MLB*	*27*	*2*	*2*	*0*	*57*	*0*	*49*	*43*	*6*	*3.7*	*10.9*	*59*	*40.4%*	*.300*	*1.28*	*3.74*	*94*	*0.3*	*95.3*	*63.3%*	*30.1%*	*56.5%*

Comparables: Lucas Sims (60), Brandon Maurer (58), Robert Stephenson (57)

De Los Santos earned his release from the pitching-starved Pirates after a brief seven-game audition at the end of the 2021 season, only to resurface last year as a key cog in the Guardians' vaunted bullpen. How very Pittsburgh, and how very Cleveland. De Los Santos was at his best down the stretch, hurling mid-90s thunderbolts and whiff-inducing curves and changeups while holding batters to a .171/.244/.195 line after the calendar flipped to September. It's fair to wonder whether his sudden success is sustainable, as he allowed more than his share of lasers that Cleveland's exceptional defense turned into outs and his control was spotty against lefty batters. Still, he has long had the stuff needed to retire big-league hitters and he's started to learn how to use it.

★ ★ ★ *2023 Top 101 Prospect* **#25** ★ ★ ★

Daniel Espino RHP Born: 01/05/01 Age: 22 Bats: R Throws: R Height: 6'2" Weight: 225 lb. Origin: Round 1, 2019 Draft (#24 overall)

YEAR	TEAM	LVL	AGE	W	L	SV	G	GS	IP	H	HR	BB/9	K/9	K	GB%	BABIP	WHIP	ERA	DRA-	WARP	MPH	FB%	Whiff%	CSP
2021	LYN	A	20	1	2	0	10	10	42^{2}	34	2	4.9	13.5	64	48.4%	.352	1.34	3.38	68	1.2				
2021	LC	A+	20	2	6	0	10	10	49	30	7	2.9	16.2	88	31.1%	.280	0.94	4.04	58	1.6				
2022	AKR	AA	21	1	0	0	4	4	18^{1}	9	4	2.0	17.2	35	20.7%	.200	0.71	2.45	71	0.5				
2023 non-DC	*CLE*	*MLB*	*22*	*2*	*2*	*0*	*57*	*0*	*50*	*41*	*8*	*4.5*	*12.3*	*68*	*37.2%*	*.299*	*1.33*	*4.01*	*98*	*0.2*			*35.7%*	

Comparables: Matt Manning (82), Drew Hutchison (80), Mitch Keller (80)

There are no more alarming caveats that can be used to describe pitching prospects than "when healthy." Espino looked like the best hurler in the world (non-deGrom category) last April, absolutely shoving over four Double-A starts that saw him whiff half the batters he faced (!) while unleashing triple-digit heat. Then the young fireballer hit the IL with patellar tendinitis, suffered a sore shoulder while working his way back and never saw the mound again. Espino isn't a one-trick pony, as his slider and curve flashed plus and he displayed tremendous command before his injury. The Guardians hope he'll come out of the offseason intact, and if what he showed last spring is still there the 22-year-old could front the Cleveland rotation for years to come.

Sam Hentges LHP Born: 07/18/96 Age: 26 Bats: L Throws: L Height: 6'6" Weight: 245 lb. Origin: Round 4, 2014 Draft (#128 overall)

YEAR	TEAM	LVL	AGE	W	L	SV	G	GS	IP	H	HR	BB/9	K/9	K	GB%	BABIP	WHIP	ERA	DRA-	WARP	MPH	FB%	Whiff%	CSP
2021	CLE	MLB	24	1	4	0	30	12	68^2	90	10	4.2	8.9	68	45.4%	.386	1.78	6.68	115	0.1	94.6	50.8%	24.1%	54.2%
2022	CLE	MLB	25	3	2	1	57	0	62	41	3	2.8	10.5	72	60.9%	.259	0.97	2.32	79	1.3	96.0	62.9%	30.0%	53.6%
2023 DC	*CLE*	*MLB*	*26*	*3*	*3*	*0*	*63*	*0*	*54.7*	*56*	*5*	*4.0*	*9.1*	*55*	*51.0%*	*.326*	*1.46*	*4.30*	*105*	*0.1*	*95.3*	*56.8%*	*27.4%*	*53.9%*

Comparables: Enny Romero (61), Anthony Misiewicz (61), Lucas Sims (61)

Hentges will be enshrined in Cleveland lore for working the final three scoreless frames of the Guardians' 15-inning, 1-0 victory over the Rays to move out of the Wild Card round, but that was just the cherry on top of his breakthrough campaign. The towering lefty stood tall all year, thriving in his first full season in relief and dominating down the stretch. Hentges posted a 1.39 FIP after the All-Star break, his 0.30 ERA second-half ERA paced the American League and on the year he held lefty batters to a .370 OPS. Liberal application of his mid-90s sinker led to a huge increase in ground-ball outs, while his four-seamer, curve and slider all played up in the 'pen. None of this looks fluky, and Hentges should be a bullpen asset for the foreseeable future.

James Karinchak RHP Born: 09/22/95 Age: 27 Bats: R Throws: R Height: 6'3" Weight: 215 lb. Origin: Round 9, 2017 Draft (#282 overall)

YEAR	TEAM	LVL	AGE	W	L	SV	G	GS	IP	H	HR	BB/9	K/9	K	GB%	BABIP	WHIP	ERA	DRA-	WARP	MPH	FB%	Whiff%	CSP
2020	CLE	MLB	24	1	2	1	27	0	27	14	1	5.3	17.7	53	22.5%	.342	1.11	2.67	62	0.8	95.7	50.2%	45.5%	42.6%
2021	COL	AAA	25	1	1	0	7	0	6	3	1	4.5	13.5	9	33.3%	.182	1.00	3.00	84	0.1				
2021	CLE	MLB	25	7	4	11	60	0	55^1	35	9	5.2	12.7	78	39.8%	.228	1.21	4.07	83	1.0	96.1	67.7%	31.5%	55.7%
2022	COL	AAA	26	1	0	0	12	0	11	10	0	9.0	13.9	17	24.0%	.400	1.91	5.73	96	0.2				
2022	CLE	MLB	26	2	0	3	38	0	39	22	2	4.8	14.3	62	23.7%	.270	1.10	2.08	68	1.0	95.3	59.7%	35.1%	54.1%
2023 DC	*CLE*	*MLB*	*27*	*3*	*3*	*4*	*63*	*0*	*54.7*	*45*	*7*	*5.4*	*13.3*	*80*	*33.2%*	*.322*	*1.43*	*4.16*	*99*	*0.3*	*95.7*	*61.9%*	*33.4%*	*53.2%*

Comparables: Carl Edwards Jr. (58), Nick Goody (55), Corey Knebel (55)

Whether he managed it through improved mechanics or other means, the newly hirsute Karinchak bounced back from his demotion and a sore shoulder that cost him the first half of the year to once again thrive in a setup role. Few pitchers suffered as much reduction in fastball spin and movement as Karinchak did in 2021 after MLB began stricter enforcement of its ban on tacky substances, but last season his heater regained much of its spin and the concomitant extreme rise and run that allows him to bully batsmen with fastballs up in the zone. Karinchak unleashes his heaters and 12-6 power curves from an extreme over-the-top slot that hitters rarely see, and the velocity, unique movement and deceptive delivery combined last year to help him punch out nearly 40% of the batters he faced. A hyperactive, high-effort mound presence casts him perfectly in the beloved "flaky late-inning weapon" role, and as long as he continues to impart his offerings with that much spin, his results will too.

Kirk McCarty LHP Born: 10/12/95 Age: 27 Bats: L Throws: L Height: 5'8" Weight: 185 lb. Origin: Round 7, 2017 Draft (#222 overall)

YEAR	TEAM	LVL	AGE	W	L	SV	G	GS	IP	H	HR	BB/9	K/9	K	GB%	BABIP	WHIP	ERA	DRA-	WARP	MPH	FB%	Whiff%	CSP
2021	COL	AAA	25	9	6	0	24	24	124	117	25	3.2	7.5	104	34.5%	.262	1.30	5.01	113	0.9				
2022	COL	AAA	26	4	1	0	17	8	61^1	57	11	3.4	7.8	53	38.9%	.275	1.30	3.38	113	0.4				
2022	CLE	MLB	26	4	3	0	13	2	37^2	37	11	3.1	6.2	26	37.0%	.241	1.33	4.54	136	-0.3	92.7	38.7%	23.7%	57.3%
2023 DC	*FA*	*MLB*	*27*	*2*	*2*	*0*	*43*	*0*	*37.3*	*41*	*6*	*3.4*	*6.8*	*28*	*37.5%*	*.303*	*1.49*	*5.09*	*127*	*-0.4*	*92.7*	*38.7%*	*23.2%*	*57.3%*

Comparables: Pat Dean (71), Brent Suter (70), David Hale (67)

While his teammates gushed over Sam Hentges and his three-inning Wild Card relief outing, McCarty would be forgiven if he gave a "been there, done that" shrug. On September 17, in the nightcap of a key doubleheader in Minnesota, McCarty was summoned to work the 13th inning and allowed only one ghost runner to score over three innings to earn the win. It was the highlight of a 2022 season that was more eventful than productive for the diminutive lefty, with McCarty making his big-league debut in April and earning a spot on the Wild Card roster in October. In between he repeatedly bounced from the majors to Triple-A, was DFA'd by both the Guardians and Orioles in July, and re-emerged in the Cleveland bullpen down the stretch. That's all a bit more interesting than his stuff, which features a low-90s fastball, a cutter and several fringy secondaries, none of which missed many big-league bats. He'll give it a shot in the KBO though, as he signed on with SSG Landers for 2023.

Triston McKenzie RHP Born: 08/02/97 Age: 25 Bats: R Throws: R Height: 6'5" Weight: 165 lb. Origin: Round 1, 2015 Draft (#42 overall)

YEAR	TEAM	LVL	AGE	W	L	SV	G	GS	IP	H	HR	BB/9	K/9	K	GB%	BABIP	WHIP	ERA	DRA-	WARP	MPH	FB%	Whiff%	CSP
2020	CLE	MLB	22	2	1	0	8	6	33^1	21	6	2.4	11.3	42	40.0%	.217	0.90	3.24	81	0.7	93.1	53.3%	29.2%	45.7%
2021	COL	AAA	23	1	1	0	5	5	21^1	18	5	5.1	9.7	23	26.8%	.255	1.41	2.95	117	0.1				
2021	CLE	MLB	23	5	9	0	25	24	120	84	21	4.4	10.2	136	29.5%	.227	1.18	4.95	104	0.9	92.4	61.4%	27.9%	53.1%
2022	CLE	MLB	24	11	11	0	31	30	191^1	138	25	2.1	8.9	190	33.1%	.238	0.95	2.96	82	3.6	92.7	55.9%	26.7%	58.6%
2023 DC	*CLE*	*MLB*	*25*	*10*	*9*	*0*	*29*	*29*	*169*	*147*	*26*	*3.1*	*9.7*	*181*	*33.2%*	*.280*	*1.22*	*3.51*	*92*	*2.1*	*92.6*	*57.5%*	*27.2%*	*56.1%*

Comparables: Luis Severino (74), Lucas Giolito (73), Ubaldo Jiménez (73)

Can we now all finally stop stressing and obsessing over his willowy build? Dr. Sticks finally overcame the inconsistency that had hitherto defined his major-league career and put together the brilliant season we've long known he's capable of, making 30 starts and ranking among the top 20 MLB starters in WARP, DRA, WHIP, strikeout-to-walk ratio, whiff percentage, chase rate, savvy, resilience, charisma and enthusiasm. McKenzie showed better command of his rising fastball and ditched his changeup in favor of more sliders and curves, trusting both breakers against batters from either side. Fears that he can't bear up to a starter's workload should be assuaged by the .550 OPS he allowed batters during his final six starts. McKenzie has long had the tools and talent to front a rotation, and last year showed he finally put them to their intended use.

Eli Morgan RHP Born: 05/13/96 Age: 27 Bats: R Throws: R Height: 5'10" Weight: 190 lb. Origin: Round 8, 2017 Draft (#252 overall)

YEAR	TEAM	LVL	AGE	W	L	SV	G	GS	IP	H	HR	BB/9	K/9	K	GB%	BABIP	WHIP	ERA	DRA-	WARP	MPH	FB%	Whiff%	CSP
2021	COL	AAA	25	0	1	0	5	5	22^1	20	1	4.4	8.5	21	25.4%	.333	1.39	4.03	120	0.1				
2021	CLE	MLB	25	5	7	0	18	18	89^1	90	20	2.2	8.2	81	30.0%	.282	1.25	5.34	120	-0.1	90.6	49.8%	22.9%	55.1%
2022	CLE	MLB	26	5	3	0	50	1	66^2	46	10	1.8	9.7	72	30.8%	.226	0.88	3.38	86	1.1	92.4	55.3%	26.7%	56.6%
2023 DC	*CLE*	*MLB*	*27*	*2*	*2*	*0*	*57*	*0*	*49*	*45*	*7*	*2.6*	*8.0*	*44*	*31.9%*	*.273*	*1.20*	*3.65*	*98*	*0.3*	*91.5*	*52.5%*	*25.6%*	*55.8%*

Comparables: Tyler Duffey (70), André Rienzo (69), Trent Thornton (64)

The Guardians clearly noticed the huge dropoff in Morgan's 2021 performance against hitters during his second time through the order (.939 OPS) compared to the first (.690 OPS), and understandably decided a move to the bullpen would limit his exposure. Their plan worked, especially in the first half of the season when Morgan's rising fastball found a little more giddy-up and his ultra-slow changeup was mystifying. Morgan has a deceptive, high-slot delivery that makes it hard for hitters to lock in on his pitches, and the extra fastball velocity gives them even less time to differentiate between his heater, slider and *cambio*. He gives up a lot of fly balls so home runs will always be an imminent threat, but Morgan's pitch mix makes him effective against both righties and lefties and can make him a weapon in middle relief.

Cody Morris RHP Born: 11/04/96 Age: 26 Bats: R Throws: R Height: 6'4" Weight: 205 lb. Origin: Round 7, 2018 Draft (#223 overall)

YEAR	TEAM	LVL	AGE	W	L	SV	G	GS	IP	H	HR	BB/9	K/9	K	GB%	BABIP	WHIP	ERA	DRA-	WARP	MPH	FB%	Whiff%	CSP
2021	AKR	AA	24	0	0	0	5	5	20	14	1	3.2	13.1	29	38.1%	.317	1.05	1.35	91	0.3				
2021	COL	AAA	24	2	2	0	9	8	36^2	25	1	2.9	12.8	52	43.8%	.304	1.01	1.72	76	1.0				
2022	GUA	ROK	25	0	0	0	3	3	6	4	0	0.0	13.5	9	46.2%	.308	0.67	0.00						
2022	COL	AAA	25	0	0	1	6	3	15^1	5	2	3.5	17.6	30	45.5%	.150	0.72	2.35	59	0.5				
2022	CLE	MLB	25	1	2	0	7	5	23^2	21	3	4.6	8.7	23	36.9%	.290	1.39	2.28	109	0.1	93.5	75.7%	28.7%	53.7%
2023 DC	*CLE*	*MLB*	*26*	*7*	*5*	*0*	*53*	*9*	*82*	*72*	*10*	*4.0*	*11.0*	*100*	*40.7%*	*.307*	*1.33*	*3.80*	*95*	*0.8*	*93.5*	*75.7%*	*30.1%*	*53.7%*

Comparables: Framber Valdez (71), Jefry Rodriguez (69), Domingo Germán (68)

Morris is blessed with an ideal starter's frame and high-octane stuff, but injuries and inconsistency have kept him from reaching the promised land. His shoulder began barking during spring training and kept him off the mound until July, but when he finally arrived in Columbus he dominated, whiffing more than half the batters he faced. Morris made five uneven starts for the Guardians down the stretch but showed plenty of upside, particularly in his plus changeup that produced copious empty swings. His mid-90s fastball has plenty of spin, ride and arm-side run and Morris has a usable cutter and curve, but his command comes and goes. Morris needs to stay healthy and do a better job avoiding the heart of the plate to reach his mid-rotation upside.

Konnor Pilkington LHP Born: 09/12/97 Age: 25 Bats: L Throws: L Height: 6'3" Weight: 240 lb. Origin: Round 3, 2018 Draft (#81 overall)

YEAR	TEAM	LVL	AGE	W	L	SV	G	GS	IP	H	HR	BB/9	K/9	K	GB%	BABIP	WHIP	ERA	DRA-	WARP	MPH	FB%	Whiff%	CSP
2021	AKR	AA	23	3	2	0	8	7	38^2	25	2	4.2	11.4	49	39.1%	.271	1.11	2.33	87	0.6				
2021	BIR	AA	23	4	4	0	14	14	62	36	9	3.0	10.3	71	43.5%	.209	0.92	3.48	89	1.1				
2022	COL	AAA	24	3	5	0	13	12	56^2	59	8	4.1	9.2	58	37.0%	.325	1.50	5.88	106	0.5				
2022	CLE	MLB	24	1	2	0	15	11	58	53	6	5.0	7.8	50	39.7%	.280	1.47	3.88	131	-0.4	92.3	63.5%	28.0%	52.2%
2023 DC	*CLE*	*MLB*	*25*	*4*	*4*	*0*	*31*	*6*	*51*	*51*	*7*	*4.7*	*8.4*	*47*	*39.5%*	*.305*	*1.53*	*4.95*	*119*	*-0.1*	*92.3*	*63.5%*	*27.7%*	*52.2%*

Comparables: Anthony Banda (76), Jeff Locke (72), Tyler Matzek (69)

A command-over-stuff lefty from Mississippi State, Pilkington spent last year bouncing between Columbus and Cleveland without distinguishing himself in either place—when Baseball Savant lists the 2022 version of Patrick Corbin as one of your Statcast *doppelgängers*, well, ouch. Pilkington deploys his changeup, slider and curve in an attempt to keep hitters from timing up his low-90s fastball with some success, as his four-seamer generated an impressive 25.1% whiff rate last year. On the other hand, for a strike-thrower he spent a lot of time working outside the zone without generating many chases and issued too many free passes. Pilkington needs to trust his stuff and cut down on the walks to survive in a big-league rotation, though more likely he'll serve best as quality rotation depth in Triple-A.

Zach Plesac RHP Born: 01/21/95 Age: 28 Bats: R Throws: R Height: 6'3" Weight: 220 lb. Origin: Round 12, 2016 Draft (#362 overall)

YEAR	TEAM	LVL	AGE	W	L	SV	G	GS	IP	H	HR	BB/9	K/9	K	GB%	BABIP	WHIP	ERA	DRA-	WARP	MPH	FB%	Whiff%	CSP
2020	CLE	MLB	25	4	2	0	8	8	55^1	38	8	1.0	9.3	57	38.0%	.224	0.80	2.28	88	1.0	93.0	37.6%	29.8%	50.9%
2021	CLE	MLB	26	10	6	0	25	25	142^2	137	23	2.1	6.3	100	44.5%	.264	1.20	4.67	120	-0.2	93.1	41.9%	23.2%	55.2%
2022	CLE	MLB	27	3	12	0	25	24	131^2	136	19	2.6	6.8	100	40.0%	.288	1.32	4.31	118	0.1	92.3	42.9%	22.1%	56.0%
2023 DC	*CLE*	*MLB*	*28*	*8*	*8*	*0*	*25*	*25*	*139.7*	*143*	*19*	*2.4*	*6.9*	*107*	*41.3%*	*.294*	*1.29*	*3.97*	*104*	*0.9*	*92.8*	*42.9%*	*23.5%*	*54.8%*

Comparables: Anthony DeSclafani (60), Jerad Eickhoff (59), Jakob Junis (58)

In the seventh inning of his August 27 start, Plesac gave up his third solo home run of the game and punched the ground in frustration, breaking his pinky and consequently missing all of September. Cleveland immediately plated three runs to award Plesac the 4-3 comeback win and went 22-9 during Plesac's absence. Given (a) this was the second time Plesac had lost time due to an anger-related hand injury in two years; (b) he also had been caught in 2020 unapologetically flouting COVID-19 protocols; and (c) this was Plesac's third and final win of the year, and one of only nine team wins in Plesac's 24 starts, it's natural to wonder whether the Guardians would have been better off without him. Plesac's mediocre ERA is belied by his sky-high DRA and subpar peripherals, as he's never been able to build on his promising 2020 campaign to become anything more than fungible rotation filler. If he doesn't stop giving his employers extra reasons to doubt him he'll soon run out of chances to do so.

Cal Quantrill RHP Born: 02/10/95 Age: 28 Bats: L Throws: R Height: 6'3" Weight: 195 lb. Origin: Round 1, 2016 Draft (#8 overall)

YEAR	TEAM	LVL	AGE	W	L	SV	G	GS	IP	H	HR	BB/9	K/9	K	GB%	BABIP	WHIP	ERA	DRA-	WARP	MPH	FB%	Whiff%	CSP
2020	SD	MLB	25	2	0	1	10	1	17^{1}	17	2	3.1	9.3	18	43.8%	.333	1.33	2.60	92	0.3	94.8	52.1%	24.3%	44.3%
2020	CLE	MLB	25	0	0	0	8	2	14^{2}	14	2	1.2	8.0	13	45.5%	.286	1.09	1.84	99	0.1	95.2	56.7%	26.1%	50.1%
2021	CLE	MLB	26	8	3	0	40	22	149^{2}	129	16	2.8	7.3	121	42.8%	.270	1.18	2.89	108	0.8	94.0	77.1%	22.2%	53.0%
2022	CLE	MLB	27	15	5	0	32	32	186^{1}	178	21	2.3	6.2	128	41.2%	.280	1.21	3.38	111	0.8	93.9	47.9%	18.5%	52.3%
2023 DC	*CLE*	*MLB*	*28*	*9*	*10*	*0*	*29*	*29*	*163*	*172*	*18*	*2.7*	*6.6*	*120*	*42.0%*	*.303*	*1.35*	*4.08*	*105*	*0.7*	*94.0*	*58.5%*	*20.9%*	*51.6%*

Comparables: Trevor Williams (79), Kyle Gibson (72), Jakob Junis (71)

There's a longstanding myth that bumblebees shouldn't be able to fly as their wings, at least mathematically, are too small to carry their weight. Of course bumblebees can and do fly, and scientists with high-speed cameras were eventually able to determine that bees' wings generate tiny hurricanes as they rotate to generate the requisite lift. Those scientists should now point those cameras at Quantrill, who mathematically should not be able to consistently succeed in the middle of a 21st century rotation. The Pride of Port Hope has low strikeout and whiff rates, subpar velocity, and none of his offerings have great movement or the extreme high or low spin that leads to success. He throws a sinker without much sink and a cutter without much cut, neither of which produce copious groundballs. His DRA annually screams "replacement level," at least when it isn't yawning. So how does he do it? Our theory is that Quantrill's offerings generate tiny hurricanes on the way to the plate, moving each pitch slightly up or down or away—just enough to force weak contact which Cleveland's stellar defense converts into outs. His extremely high contact rate on pitches out of the zone, above-average chase rate and low exit velocities support this theory, but the most compelling evidence can be seen on the scoreboard and in the win column. Here's hoping Quantrill can keep on flying, for it would be a sad world indeed without bumblebees.

Nick Sandlin RHP Born: 01/10/97 Age: 26 Bats: R Throws: R Height: 5'11" Weight: 175 lb. Origin: Round 2, 2018 Draft (#67 overall)

YEAR	TEAM	LVL	AGE	W	L	SV	G	GS	IP	H	HR	BB/9	K/9	K	GB%	BABIP	WHIP	ERA	DRA-	WARP	MPH	FB%	Whiff%	CSP
2021	CLE	MLB	24	1	1	0	34	0	33^{2}	21	2	4.5	12.8	48	41.7%	.271	1.13	2.94	77	0.7	94.8	51.3%	33.1%	52.0%
2022	COL	AAA	25	0	0	0	5	0	4^{1}	3	1	8.3	6.2	3	33.3%	.200	1.62	8.31	102	0.1				
2022	CLE	MLB	25	5	2	0	46	0	44	27	2	4.9	8.4	41	55.4%	.227	1.16	2.25	102	0.4	93.8	47.7%	27.6%	50.4%
2023 DC	*CLE*	*MLB*	*26*	*2*	*2*	*0*	*57*	*0*	*49*	*45*	*5*	*5.5*	*10.2*	*56*	*48.8%*	*.308*	*1.53*	*4.73*	*111*	*-0.1*	*94.2*	*49.1%*	*29.3%*	*51.0%*

Comparables: Arodys Vizcaíno (58), José Leclerc (57), David McKay (54)

Sandlin has yet to duplicate his impressive minor-league strikeout numbers on the big stage, but his side-arm delivery and wiffle-ball slider are still hell on wheels against same-side batters. Uncomfortable righties slashed a punchless .149/.265/.238 when facing him, while lefties weren't much better at barreling him up—though they were able to wait him out and drew plenty of walks. His frisbee, sinker and splitter produce a ton of groundballs, and Sandlin works in enough four-seamers at the top of the zone to change eye levels and keep batters guessing. If spotted correctly, Sandlin can thrive as a situational reliever, and even a small improvement in his iffy command would put him in line for more high-leverage innings.

Bryan Shaw RHP Born: 11/08/87 Age: 35 Bats: S Throws: R Height: 6'1" Weight: 226 lb. Origin: Round 2, 2008 Draft (#73 overall)

YEAR	TEAM	LVL	AGE	W	L	SV	G	GS	IP	H	HR	BB/9	K/9	K	GB%	BABIP	WHIP	ERA	DRA-	WARP	MPH	FB%	Whiff%	CSP
2020	SEA	MLB	32	1	0	0	6	0	6	13	1	9.0	6.0	4	55.6%	.462	3.17	18.00	114	0.0	92.5	52.3%	20.0%	41.4%
2021	CLE	MLB	33	6	7	2	81	0	77^{1}	69	10	4.4	8.3	71	46.0%	.277	1.38	3.49	110	0.3	92.7	79.3%	25.7%	51.2%
2022	CLE	MLB	34	6	2	1	60	2	58^{1}	58	9	4.0	8.0	52	49.2%	.288	1.44	5.40	109	0.3	93.4	82.2%	21.8%	53.5%
2023 DC	*FA*	*MLB*	*35*	*2*	*2*	*0*	*50*	*0*	*43.7*	*45*	*5*	*4.3*	*7.2*	*35*	*47.8%*	*.303*	*1.51*	*4.72*	*116*	*-0.2*	*93.0*	*79.2%*	*23.1%*	*51.1%*

Comparables: Joe Smith (74), Francisco Rodríguez (74), Dan Miceli (73)

Baseball Prospectus alum and front-office fixture Kevin Goldstein once explained why, despite the large pool of similar talent available, the same few veterans keep getting signed as catching depth: They're good dudes. It's easy for fans to forget that a ballpark is a workplace and, all other things being equal, there are some folks you'd rather work with and some you'd rather not. Cleveland didn't re-sign the rubber-armed Shaw last year to get big outs; six other relievers worked in higher-leverage situations. They signed him to be Uncle Bryan to their cadre of young arms, to share his experience, to keep everyone loose, to play cribbage with Tito and oh, by the way, occasionally soak up a few unimportant innings. Shaw was designated for assignment before season's end, but traveled with the team during the playoffs anyway after accepting his minor-league assignment. Good dude.

Trevor Stephan RHP Born: 11/25/95 Age: 27 Bats: R Throws: R Height: 6'5" Weight: 225 lb. Origin: Round 3, 2017 Draft (#92 overall)

YEAR	TEAM	LVL	AGE	W	L	SV	G	GS	IP	H	HR	BB/9	K/9	K	GB%	BABIP	WHIP	ERA	DRA-	WARP	MPH	FB%	Whiff%	CSP
2021	CLE	MLB	25	3	1	1	43	0	63^{1}	58	15	4.4	10.7	75	32.9%	.272	1.41	4.41	100	0.6	96.4	59.7%	30.2%	53.5%
2022	CLE	MLB	26	6	5	3	66	0	63^{2}	57	3	2.5	11.6	82	47.2%	.344	1.18	2.69	72	1.5	96.8	47.5%	35.5%	52.9%
2023 DC	*CLE*	*MLB*	*27*	*3*	*3*	*2*	*63*	*0*	*54.7*	*49*	*5*	*3.5*	*10.4*	*63*	*41.5%*	*.308*	*1.28*	*3.60*	*91*	*0.5*	*96.6*	*53.2%*	*31.6%*	*53.2%*

Comparables: Matt Barnes (76), Michael Feliz (74), Josh Staumont (73)

There was magic in Cleveland's bullpen air last season, and perhaps the most charmed was Stephan, who went from live-armed Rule 5 pick to bullpen leviathan over the course of a year. It wasn't pixie dust that brought about this metamorphosis but better application of the split-fingered fastball. Before this season, Stephan had lived and died by his high-90s fastball and sweeping slider, especially against right-handed batters. But the best hitters in the world can turn around anyone's heater if they know it's coming, and righties did so against him in 2021 with a .525 slugging percentage. Last year, however, Stephan deployed his splitter against them and the difference was gasp-inducing. Righties couldn't sit on the heater, couldn't touch the splitter or slider, and posted a .207/.263/.293 line with only one home run. Now that he's cracked the code, Stephan should feature prominently in batter's nightmares for years to come.

Touki Toussaint RHP Born: 06/20/96 Age: 27 Bats: R Throws: R Height: 6'3" Weight: 215 lb. Origin: Round 1, 2014 Draft (#16 overall)

YEAR	TEAM	LVL	AGE	W	L	SV	G	GS	IP	H	HR	BB/9	K/9	K	GB%	BABIP	WHIP	ERA	DRA-	WARP	MPH	FB%	Whiff%	CSP
2020	ATL	MLB	24	0	2	0	7	5	24^1	27	7	5.9	11.1	30	37.7%	.328	1.77	8.88	100	0.3	94.2	41.1%	31.9%	42.2%
2021	GWN	AAA	25	2	1	0	7	4	20^2	12	1	5.2	12.2	28	61.0%	.275	1.16	3.48	83	0.5				
2021	ATL	MLB	25	3	3	0	11	10	50	43	11	4.0	8.6	48	46.4%	.252	1.30	4.50	100	0.5	92.8	51.6%	25.6%	55.8%
2022	GWN	AAA	26	2	2	0	13	8	41^2	42	7	5.4	11.4	53	49.1%	.340	1.61	6.26	84	0.9				
2022	SL	AAA	26	0	1	0	9	3	13^2	13	3	7.2	5.9	9	48.8%	.263	1.76	3.95	123	-0.1	91.8	66.8%	15.2%	
2022	LAA	MLB	26	1	1	0	8	2	25^1	15	2	6.8	9.2	26	50.8%	.228	1.34	4.62	98	0.3	92.1	46.9%	29.7%	47.7%
2023 DC	*FA*	*MLB*	*27*	*2*	*2*	*0*	*43*	*0*	*37.3*	*36*	*5*	*5.8*	*9.3*	*38*	*47.6%*	*.305*	*1.62*	*5.46*	*125*	*-0.3*	*92.9*	*48.2%*	*27.7%*	*49.3%*

Comparables: Chris Archer (52), Robert Stephenson (50), Jake Faria (50)

Just 18-or-so months ago, Triston McKenzie was out there on the mound, looking for all the world like he was throwing with his eyes closed. Given his ascension, teams figured to take an extra-long look at Toussaint, who was non-tendered by the Angels after they signed the pitcher's polar opposite in Tyler Anderson. You can understand the impulse: The former first-rounder has shown flashes of greatness in the past, and a lot of smart baseball people need to prove how smart they are. But fixing him won't be easy. Toussaint led the league (min. 20 IP) by starting off the count 1-0 54.6% of the time—the gap between him and second place was equal to the one between second and 18th. The man simply cannot throw strikes, no matter the pitch, no matter the batter, no matter the count…and yet the Guardians, perhaps remembering their good work with McKenzie, gave Toussaint a minor-league deal in January. If they can't get him right, it's likely no one can.

★ ★ ★ *2023 Top 101 Prospect* **#26** ★ ★ ★

Gavin Williams RHP Born: 07/26/99 Age: 23 Bats: L Throws: R Height: 6'6" Weight: 255 lb. Origin: Round 1, 2021 Draft (#23 overall)

YEAR	TEAM	LVL	AGE	W	L	SV	G	GS	IP	H	HR	BB/9	K/9	K	GB%	BABIP	WHIP	ERA	DRA-	WARP	MPH	FB%	Whiff%	CSP
2022	LC	A+	22	2	1	0	9	9	45	25	0	2.8	13.4	67	40.5%	.298	0.87	1.40	73	1.1				
2022	AKR	AA	22	3	3	0	16	16	70	44	9	3.3	10.5	82	35.5%	.219	1.00	2.31	79	1.7				
2023 non-DC	*CLE*	*MLB*	*23*	*2*	*2*	*0*	*57*	*0*	*50*	*45*	*7*	*4.2*	*9.8*	*54*	*38.5%*	*.293*	*1.37*	*4.19*	*103*	*0.1*			*28.2%*	

Comparables: Spencer Howard (92), Corbin Burnes (90), Dellin Betances (87)

Last year Williams did exactly what you would hope a first-round college arm would do in his first pro season: dominate High-A, struggle a bit when he can't just overpower Double-A hitters with velocity and end the season as a pitcher, not a thrower. His high-90s fastball has plenty of life and Williams abets it with two solid breakers and an improving changeup, giving him a starter's arsenal to go along with his ideal frame. He repeats his delivery well and his control, always important to the walk-loathing Cleveland staff, was better than advertised. Nothing is guaranteed for pitching prospects, but it's easy to picture Williams moving quickly and reaching his second starter ceiling.

Lineouts

Hitters

HITTER	POS	TEAM	LVL	AGE	PA	R	2B	3B	HR	RBI	BB	K	SB	CS	AVG/OBP/SLG	DRC+	BABIP	BRR	DRP	WARP
Bobby Bradley	1B	COL	AAA	26	198	24	10	0	7	30	19	74	0	1	.174/.268/.359	67	.237	-0.3	1B(36): 2.1	-0.1
	1B	CLE	MLB	26	17	1	0	0	0	0	0	9	0	0	.118/.118/.118	52	.250	-0.1	1B(7): -0.1	-0.1
Jaison Chourio	CF	DSL CLER	ROK	17	175	32	7	3	1	28	40	22	14	4	.280/.446/.402		.324			
Jake Fox	UT	LYN	A	19	470	74	25	4	5	44	74	90	21	3	.247/.381/.374	136	.307	3.9	2B(61): 1.1, CF(31): 0.5, 3B(6): -1.3	3.9
Angel Genao	SS	GUA	ROK	18	171	22	6	1	2	18	16	40	6	3	.322/.394/.416		.422			
	SS	LYN	A	18	33	3	1	0	0	3	4	5	0	1	.179/.303/.214	110	.217	-0.1	SS(6): -0.2, 3B(2): 0.6	0.2
Petey Halpin	CF	LC	A+	20	434	68	21	4	6	36	45	92	16	7	.262/.346/.385	103	.330	3.1	CF(94): 0.6, RF(9): 0.8	2.5
Angel Martinez	MI	LC	A+	20	331	46	17	3	10	27	40	58	10	6	.288/.384/.477	121	.330	-2.3	SS(50): -3.2, 2B(23): 0.1, 3B(4): -0.1	1.3
	MI	AKR	AA	20	103	10	6	1	3	17	12	18	2	1	.244/.356/.451	116	.266	0.2	2B(19): -2.5, SS(4): 1.9	0.4
Jhonkensy Noel	RF	LC	A+	20	252	35	9	0	19	42	18	80	1	0	.219/.286/.509	114	.237	-1.7	3B(24): -3.3, RF(17): -1.6, 1B(6): 1.3	0.6
	RF	AKR	AA	20	278	43	16	2	13	42	30	63	2	0	.242/.338/.488	119	.271	-1.5	RF(33): 0.4, LF(16): -0.2, 1B(9): 0.3	1.5
Milan Tolentino	IF	LYN	A	20	205	33	12	0	1	26	32	44	8	1	.333/.434/.423	113	.433	1.7	SS(22): -0.4, 3B(13): -2.0, 2B(9): -0.7	0.8
	IF	LC	A+	20	291	39	18	0	3	28	44	92	21	2	.221/.344/.332	83	.340	2.6	SS(45): 1.6, 3B(12): -1.3, 2B(11): -0.4	0.6

After almost a decade on hold awaiting an agent who could help fix **Bobby Bradley**'s recurrent BSOD (Billion Strikeouts of Death) error, the Guardians finally hung up last summer. ⚾ Though he doesn't have quite as much helium as his older brother Jackson, switch-hitting center fielder **Jaison Chourio** wowed with speed, patience, plus defense, power potential and tremendous bat-to-ball skills as a teenager in the Dominican Summer League. He's one to watch. ⚾ Had you not noticed the chapter heading, you'd still probably assume **Jake Fox** is a Guardians middle infield prospect given his high-floor, solid approach, hit-over-power profile. He's no shortstop, but is fine at the keystone and could become a useful bench bat. ⚾ Had you not noticed the chapter heading, you'd still probably assume **Angel Genao** is a Guardians middle infield prospect given his high-floor, solid approach, hit-over-power profile. He's a solid shortstop, would be plus at the keystone and could become a useful bench bat. ⚾ Fleet center fielder **Petey Halpin** has a balanced, line-drive swing that generates hard contact and began generating a little more home run thump as the season wore on. He has enough bat and glove to succeed as a spare outfielder even if the power remains on permanent back order. ⚾ Switch-hitting shortstop and noted Brayan Rocchio impersonator **Angel Martinez** made it to Double-A as a 20-year-old on the strength of his silky smooth defense, discerning approach, developing pop and high baseball IQ. There may be a cavalry charge of Guardians middle infield prospects ahead of him right now, but he's coming up fast on the outside. ⚾ After tryouts at all four corners it's clear that the only place **Jhonkensy Noel** profiles as a potential big leaguer is in the batter's box. So far his legitimate light-tower power has managed to overshadow his hacktastic approach, but until he unwraps better contact skills he's doomed to follow the Franmil Reyes career path. ⚾ Exceptional leather work is **Milan Tolentino**'s carrying tool, but the young shortstop flashed solid on-base skills and surprising speed as he worked his way up to the Midwest League. If he maintains his batting eye and patient approach in Double-A he'll increase his prospect standing with a quickness.

Pitchers

PITCHER	TEAM	LVL	AGE	W	L	SV	G	GS	IP	H	HR	BB/9	K/9	K	GB%	BABIP	WHIP	ERA	DRA-	WARP	MPH	FB%	WHF	CSP
Peyton Battenfield	COL	AAA	24	8	6	0	28	28	153^{2}	138	17	3.3	6.4	109	39.2%	.267	1.27	3.63	103	1.9				
Tanner Burns	AKR	AA	23	3	7	0	21	21	88^{2}	75	14	4.6	9.3	92	34.7%	.269	1.35	3.55	108	0.8				
Joey Cantillo	AKR	AA	22	4	3	0	14	13	60^{2}	38	2	4.2	12.9	87	41.7%	.288	1.09	1.93	77	1.5				
Hunter Gaddis	AKR	AA	24	4	3	0	15	14	76^{1}	63	12	3.1	12.0	102	24.3%	.302	1.17	4.24	102	0.9				
	COL	AAA	24	4	3	0	9	9	45	27	5	3.0	11.2	56	28.2%	.224	0.93	3.60	91	0.8				
	CLE	MLB	24	0	2	0	2	2	7^{1}	15	7	3.7	6.1	5	18.8%	.320	2.45	18.41	137	-0.1	93.5	53.2%	20.0%	55.2%
Anthony Gose	CLE	MLB	31	3	0	0	22	0	21	15	4	6.0	12.0	28	26.5%	.244	1.38	4.71	96	0.2	97.6	64.8%	33.5%	51.2%
Tim Herrin	AKR	AA	25	0	1	1	12	0	22^{1}	17	1	2.4	14.9	37	52.3%	.372	1.03	2.01	66	0.7				
	COL	AAA	25	1	3	1	34	2	47	46	6	3.3	12.3	64	49.6%	.345	1.34	4.98	72	1.3				
Doug Nikhazy	LC	A+	22	4	4	0	21	21	93	59	8	6.6	11.4	118	40.5%	.252	1.37	3.19	94	1.2				
	AKR	AA	22	0	2	0	3	3	9^{1}	14	1	10.6	9.6	10	53.3%	.448	2.68	11.57	116	0.1				

A four-pitch mix and above-average command make **Peyton Battenfield** a solid back-end starting option. He chewed through more than 150 Triple-A innings, and should be ready to serve when called upon in the majors in 2023. ⚾ The Cleveland system has more low ceilings and high floors than a Munchkin City skyscraper, so former top pick **Tanner Burns** fits right in. His workmanlike three-pitch mix is solid enough to earn innings at the end of the rotation, but spotty command will likely keep him from being much more. ⚾ **Joey Cantillo** has never gotten much prospect love but has done nothing but thrive on the mound, returning from two lost seasons to overpower Double-A hitters with his baffling changeup and improving fastball. Health and better control headline his to-do list, but he always misses bats and has plenty of sleeper appeal. ⚾ Hulking right-hander **Hunter Gaddis** lived out his fondest dreams by making two major-league starts and his worst nightmares by allowing seven home runs, including a team-record-tying 5 against the White Sox. On the bright side, he can now brag about sharing a record with Luis Tiant. ⚾ **Anthony Gose** proved his spirit was willing by spending a half-season in the Cleveland 'pen years after washing out as an outfielder in the Tigers system; he also proved that flesh is weak by suffering an arm injury that eventually required Tommy John surgery. Here's hoping he finds a happier cliché to embody when he returns in 2024. ⚾ Stuff, headlined by high-90s heat, was never a question for **Ethan Hankins**. But health always was, even before he missed two full seasons to Tommy John surgery. It feels like he's lost diggity-seven years or so of development time, but if anyone can get him back on track quickly it's the Guardians. ⚾ Never a heralded prospect, former 29th-rounder **Tim Herrin** threw it in another gear in his climb through the high minors, striking out batters with high-90s heat, including seven consecutive Omaha hitters in one bullpen game start. He's looking to make the case as the second lefty in Cleveland's pen behind Sam Hentges. ⚾ Armed with a potentially plus changeup, a low-90s fastball and two immature breaking balls, beefy lefty **Parker Messick** was a dominant force at Florida State and earned second round money; we'll see this year how well his stuff plays against professional hitters. ⚾ His stuff, reputation and demeanor may have been "polished college lefty" but in his pro debut **Doug Nikhazy**'s elevated walk and whiff rates shouted "fireballing relief prospect." His low-90s fastball and potentially plus breakers missed more bats than expected but, unlike every other kid entering the workforce, he'll need to rediscover the control he displayed during his university days to succeed. ⚾ Cleveland drafted 17-year-old Flornadian prep star **Jacob Zibin** and gave him the largest bonus ever awarded a 10th-round pick, betting on his youth, mid-90s fastball and excellent changeup. We're telling you this because when the Guardians hone in on pitching prospects they're usually worth paying attention to. Also because it gives us a chance to coin the portmanteau "Flornadian."

DETROIT TIGERS

Essay by Maitreyi Anantharaman

Player comments by Darius Austin and BP staff

On one of those last glorious days Michigan gives you in October before she remembers herself and turns to ice, I was on the second floor of the team store at Comerica Park, feeling clear-eyed as ever. The Tigers were hosting their not-quite-annual "garage sale," a chance to comb through years' worth of surplus inventory and see if you couldn't dig up some treasure for yourself. (You couldn't.) Halloween was a few weeks away, and the timing felt appropriate. The whole place recalled some terrible haunted house. Every ghost, every skeleton, every bad decision the Tigers had made in the last 10 years hung there on the clearance racks, ready to spook the unsuspecting. Beware those Jordan Zimmermann jerseys lurking in the corner.

My brother, nine years old the last time the Tigers played postseason games and suddenly a rather tall kid finishing up his college applications, reached into a tote of game-used "mystery baseballs." He fished out one brown paper lump and turned it over in his palm, like he was inspecting a piece of produce. Encouraged by the result, he added it to our pile of utility infielder shirseys. We paid and stepped back into the sun, proud of the amazing deals we'd found on junk. When my brother read aloud the ball's provenance later—thrown to an ailing Victor Martínez by an even more ailing Homer Bailey in 2018—he did so the way Charlie Brown tells the other trick-or-treaters he got a rock. It was brave of the Tigers to do this, I thought, to remind us just how much bad baseball we'd watched and forgotten.

Here is how 2022 was supposed to go in Detroit: The Tigers would call up two of baseball's best prospects, and they would join a 77-win roster already beefed up in the offseason by fine-if-not-great free agents. This was the "flipping the switch" stage of the rebuild. After he hit an Opening Day walk-off double, new Tiger Javy Báez addressed the crowd while a teammate poured cups of water down his head. "Fans," Báez said, leaning into the microphone, an almost solemn look on his face. "It's not going to be easy this year. But it's going to be fun."

He went 1-for-2. It would end up the most difficult and least fun Tigers season in memory, defined by historically and uniformly low offensive output. Everyone—free agents, hyped rookies, reliable veterans—underperformed. You couldn't at all tell the difference between the rebuilding team

DETROIT TIGERS PROSPECTUS

2022 W-L: 66-96, 4th in AL Central

Pythag	.390	*27th*	DER	.704	*14th*
RS/G	3.44	*30th*	DRC+	84	*30th*
RA/G	4.40	*19th*	DRA-	109	*26th*
dWin%	.377	*30th*	FIP	4.16	*20th*
Payroll	$135M	*17th*	B-Age	28.5	*14th*
M$/MW	$6.6M	*27th*	P-Age	27.8	*4th*

420′
370′
365′
345′
330′

- Opened 2000
- Open air
- Natural surface
- Fence profile: 6′10″ to 14′

Park Factors

Runs	Runs/RH	Runs/LH	HR/RH	HR/LH
94	94	94	85	81

Top Hitter WARP	2.2 Javier Báez
Top Pitcher WARP	1.7 Alex Lange
2023 Top Prospect	Jace Jung

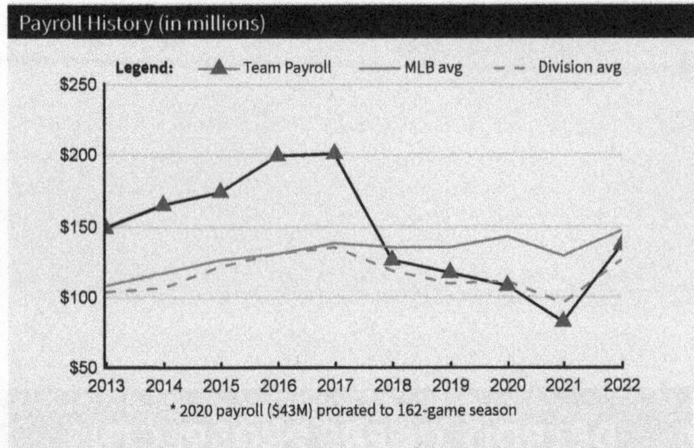

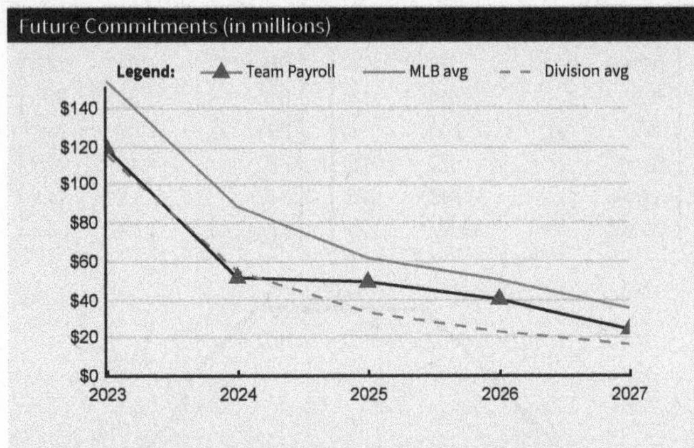

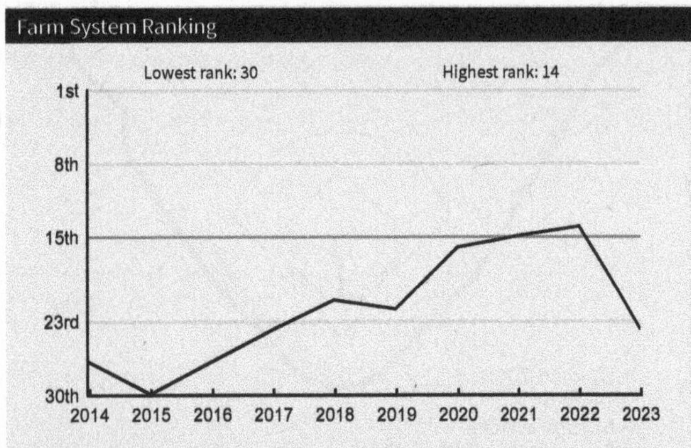

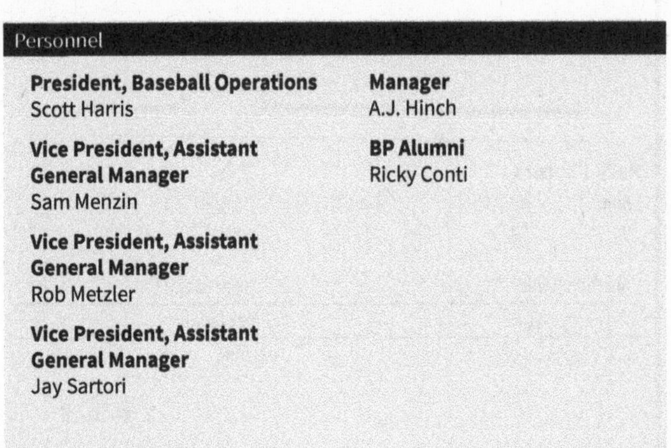
Personnel

President, Baseball Operations
Scott Harris

Vice President, Assistant General Manager
Sam Menzin

Vice President, Assistant General Manager
Rob Metzler

Vice President, Assistant General Manager
Jay Sartori

Manager
A.J. Hinch

BP Alumni
Ricky Conti

and the one rebuilt. Both teams began their seasons 9-23, but where the 2021 team played respectable, above-.500 baseball afterward, the 2022 team made no such recovery. A six-game win streak in July prompted third-base coach Ramón Santiago to shave his head, in celebration of a turning point. The Tigers won five of their next 20 games.

What the Tigers lacked in power—their 110 home runs were the fewest hit by any team in baseball—they made up for in striking out a lot and never walking. Among their regular statistical neighbors were the Oakland Athletics and Pittsburgh Pirates, teams designed to perform this way. The Tigers settled into something like MLB's saddest quadrant, which was to be bad without even meaning to. Fans in Detroit had spent the lockout craving resolution, ready to watch competitive baseball again. After one dismal game against the Rangers, I joked to a friend that a second bout of labor strife would be nice.

In team sports, there is the concept of the "burn-the-tape game," the loss so complete and irredeemable that to reflect on it would be a waste of time. The idea might sit wrong with a sportswriter, inclined to mine meaning from everything. But sportswriting's for chumps, and burning the tape is a much healthier way to live. By May it was clear that 2022 would not be the Tigers' year. The early returns were in, and the Everyone Has Their Career-Worst Season At The Same Time strategy, if inventive, had led nowhere. Before the tape could be burned, though, there were 100+ games left to play.

How to stay entertained in the meantime? You could look forward, carve away the lineup filler and limit your focus to the prospects, who seemed to be holding up OK, even if they weren't hitting like superstars. They called each other best friends and gave *aw, shucks* interviews. The 22-year-old first baseman Spencer Torkelson began most of his answers with "gosh." Riley Greene, a 21-year-old center fielder, sometimes got so flustered in front of cameras that he said adorably, egregiously untrue things like, "I've been telling a lot of people this offense is really, really good" and "This lineup can put up runs in any scenario at any time."

You could also look backward, and you were encouraged to. The front office endeavored to wring as much fan goodwill as it could from a 39-year-old Miguel Cabrera. Next to the Comerica Park scoreboard, above the brick wall in left field, an enormous tote board tracked MIGGY MILESTONES. These were sweet until he reached both milestones—he poked a 3,000th hit into right field in April—and the numbers turned odd and unromantic. 3,057 hits. 504 home runs. We'd unwrapped all the gifts, but no one could bear to take down the Christmas tree.

You could forget the offense altogether, though the situation on the other side of the ball wasn't so rosy either. The list of starting pitchers used reached 17 names at the end of the season. Eduardo Rodriguez disappeared for two months sorting through a marital issue. By the time Tarik Skubal left an August game with "arm fatigue," it felt only right that the budding ace should join the rest of the rotation on the injured list. Really, he had been cheating fate. The relievers, meanwhile, figured into the season like the crushing twist of an O. Henry story. They formed the elite, eclectic bullpen denied to the best Tigers lineups of the 2010s, and they were wasted now on a team who seldom gave them a lead to hold. Contemporary bullpens draw their share of suspicion for draining baseball of its drama and variety. But the Tigers' bullpen was the team's lone source of style. "They all have their own schtick," said catcher Tucker Barnhart, after showing them off one evening in Toronto. Jason Foley threw fantastic turbo sinkers for automatic groundballs. Joe Jiménez and his lively fastball rebounded from two tragic seasons. Alex Lange wore a sleeveless turtleneck beneath his jersey, even in 90-degree weather, and warmed up to Aerosmith. His two-seamers, like they'd been designed with Pitching Ninja in mind, broke in the shape of question marks at the plate.

The distractions compelled me less than the problem itself did. No baseball player on this baseball team could hit a baseball. What made this problem so difficult was that nothing could be done about it. By me, I mean. One of life's mandates is to alleviate suffering in any way you can—holding doors open, rustling up spare change. In baseball, you must sit helplessly there as Robbie Grossman takes an unwise cut and shambles back to the dugout.

Of course, you can yell. Some people yelled. They booed Báez's hopeful flailing. They tweeted that Torkelson should not overthink things, and should be more thoughtful in the batter's box, and should fix his long swing, and should make his swing less compact. But yelling only effected catharsis, and what I wanted more than that was diagnosis, to understand the problem better, even if I couldn't solve it. By August, I was hitting-obsessed. I watched slowed-down swings on YouTube and learned to spot hitches from blurry stills. I committed launch angles and exit velos and heat maps to memory. I read books with pleasing little diagrams, all laying out the joints of the human body like furniture parts; they just had to be screwed together the right way.

The back cover of Ted Williams' guide to hitting promised "THE SECRETS OF HIP AND WRIST ACTION." But the most interesting chapter, to me, concerned the role of guesswork in the batter's box. Williams proposed that while the gap between the known and the unknown couldn't ever be closed, it could at least be made smaller. "You work from a frame of reference, you learn what you might expect in certain instances, and you guess from there," he wrote. The best hitters honed those frames of reference so that they stepped to the plate needing little luck to go their way. Good things happened to them more often than not.

For months, I told myself the Tigers' season was tape to be burned. No lessons could be learned from it. Run the whole thing back, and there's no way it goes this poorly again. It was a comforting belief, and an easy one to hold. An entire language exists to divorce inputs from outputs; there are always BABIP gods and slumps and injury bugs to be blamed. But it isn't a wholly convincing language. Maybe there is value in the sportswriter's impulse, to cut through superstition, to tell a story of cause and effect. The Tigers made decisions. Most of the decisions were bad. The decisions produced a range of potential outcomes, and within the range was this one: the team of hopeless free swingers. They were unlucky, sure, in all the normal ways teams are unlucky. Injuries piled up. The plucky stars of the 2021 season faded. But other teams faced those problems and withstood them. That the Tigers couldn't was no coincidence.

The Athletic's Ken Rosenthal told this story in a June column about Detroit's "perfect storm of calamities." Fundamental failures in international scouting, player development, free agent signings and trades had set the team up perfectly to be felled by any stroke of bad luck. In his story, Rosenthal reported that rival executives doubted general manager Al Avila was "creative and savvy enough to build a consistent winner." When Avila was fired midseason, after seven years in charge, the only real surprise was the timing. The bill for all the Jordan Zimmermann jerseys had finally come due.

The new president of baseball operations, introduced one afternoon in mid-September, spoke in pithy but unmannered sentences, all with subjects and verbs and beginnings and endings. Thirty-six with a younger face, Scott Harris had kept reassuring company. The names he dropped were impeccable MLB mononyms: Theo. Jed. Farhan. Where Avila had gestured broadly and never quite convincingly at "using more technology," Harris called himself an "information-first" executive, which sounded wise and interesting, whatever it meant. There were no revelations in his first press conference, just the essential facts of baseball: He believed pitchers should throw strikes. He believed hitters should swing at good pitches. Even so, we oohed and aahed. One night, as he explained OPS+ to the Tigers broadcast booth during an in-game interview, I remembered a friend's lukewarm appraisal of her sister's new boyfriend, some perfectly average guy all the exes made seem like a dreamboat.

The state of Major League Baseball is such that Harris' job, at the helm of a 66-win team, could be called an attractive one. In a thrifty AL Central, half the work is just to try. Tie outputs back to inputs, and suddenly assembling a good baseball team starts to look simple. The shrewdest executive will insist this takes great time and patience, but a Tigers fan knows it doesn't need to. Whenever the timeline of a rebuild seems daunting and necessarily epochal, it helps to think of the 2006 team: American League champions three seasons after losing 119 games. When I was younger, that team seemed propelled by a force that could never be replicated. But what was the force, really? Management's consistent effort. Ownership's checkbook. Great free agents. Draft picks panning out. A truer story went that the Tigers made decisions. Most of the decisions were good. The decisions produced a range of potential outcomes, and within the range was this one: the team for whom everything went right. In the thrill of the moment, we called the whole thing magic. ■

—Maitreyi Anantharaman is a writer and co-owner of Defector

HITTERS

Akil Baddoo OF
Born: 08/16/98 Age: 24 Bats: L Throws: L Height: 6'1" Weight: 214 lb. Origin: Round 2, 2016 Draft (#74 overall)

YEAR	TEAM	LVL	AGE	PA	R	2B	3B	HR	RBI	BB	K	SB	CS	Whiff%	AVG/OBP/SLG	DRC+	BABIP	BRR	DRP	WARP
2021	DET	MLB	22	461	60	20	7	13	55	45	122	18	4	30.5%	.259/.330/.436	90	.335	2.5	CF(66): 2.7, LF(56): 3.4, RF(5): 0	2.1
2022	TOL	AAA	23	131	14	9	2	3	15	19	26	7	4		.300/.405/.500	109	.366	-1.2	LF(18): -0.5, CF(10): 1.0, RF(1): -0.1	0.6
2022	DET	MLB	23	225	30	3	2	2	9	24	64	9	6	28.5%	.204/.289/.269	73	.289	1.6	LF(50): 3.4, CF(16): 0.7	0.6
2023 DC	*DET*	*MLB*	*24*	*456*	*46*	*16*	*7*	*10*	*36*	*46*	*112*	*29*	*11*	*27.8%*	*.232/.314/.385*	*93*	*.297*	*7.1*	*LF 2, CF 0*	*1.6*

Comparables: Carlos González (53), Bobby Abreu (52), Josh Naylor (51)

It's worth remembering that 2022 was only Baddoo's second season above High-A, that he played most of it as a 23-year-old and that he looked very much like a major leaguer when he handled Triple-A with ease. The fact that Baddoo was facing Triple-A pitching at all speaks to the precipitous decline he suffered, after a debut that suggested he was destined to join the select club of great Rule-5 picks. His power almost entirely evaporated, a demotion coming mid-way through a streak of 48 MLB games and 137 plate appearances between extra-base hits. He's still fun, and quick and capable of taking a walk. That might be all he is.

Javier Báez SS
Born: 12/01/92 Age: 30 Bats: R Throws: R Height: 6'0" Weight: 190 lb. Origin: Round 1, 2011 Draft (#9 overall)

YEAR	TEAM	LVL	AGE	PA	R	2B	3B	HR	RBI	BB	K	SB	CS	Whiff%	AVG/OBP/SLG	DRC+	BABIP	BRR	DRP	WARP
2020	CHC	MLB	27	235	27	9	1	8	24	7	75	3	0	38.0%	.203/.238/.360	77	.262	0.5	SS(56): 6.6	0.7
2021	NYM	MLB	28	186	32	9	0	9	22	13	53	5	2	39.6%	.299/.371/.515	103	.390	1.0	2B(35): -0.6, SS(12): 1.2	0.9
2021	CHC	MLB	28	361	48	9	2	22	65	15	131	13	3	41.1%	.248/.292/.484	92	.330	-1.3	SS(88): 0.2	0.8
2022	DET	MLB	29	590	64	27	4	17	67	26	147	9	2	35.8%	.238/.278/.393	91	.292	5.0	SS(133): 3.2	2.1
2023 DC	*DET*	*MLB*	*30*	*582*	*55*	*24*	*3*	*18*	*59*	*28*	*160*	*12*	*2*	*35.9%*	*.244/.288/.406*	*95*	*.309*	*7.8*	*SS 5*	*2.7*

Comparables: Robin Yount (68), Joe Cronin (68), Matt Williams (66)

Calling Báez a league-average player probably makes people mad at WAR, in its various iterations, rather than providing consolation to Tigers fans. That doesn't make it less true. He remains a solid defensive shortstop and a plus baserunner. His .671 OPS wasn't nearly as disastrous as it sounds given that the league average was a mere .706, the worst since 2014. He still has the bat speed to destroy a baseball and looked much more like peak Báez in the final month, when he slashed .293/.322/.509 with six homers. Even a frustrated Tigers fan who acknowledges last season was average, though, might also justifiably say that six-year, $140 million deals shouldn't be handed out to average players—not least those with severe approach problems. For some reason, it took opposing batteries this long to decide that they'd be better off throwing more secondaries if Báez was just going to swing violently at them outside the zone. For the first time ever, under half of the pitches he saw were fastballs, and considerably so at 44.8%. WAR is good for telling us what players are worth even when we're mad at them. It's not so good at making them less maddening.

Miguel Cabrera DH
Born: 04/18/83 Age: 40 Bats: R Throws: R Height: 6'4" Weight: 267 lb. Origin: International Free Agent, 1999

YEAR	TEAM	LVL	AGE	PA	R	2B	3B	HR	RBI	BB	K	SB	CS	Whiff%	AVG/OBP/SLG	DRC+	BABIP	BRR	DRP	WARP
2020	DET	MLB	37	231	28	4	0	10	35	24	51	1	0	31.6%	.250/.329/.417	113	.283	-1.1		0.8
2021	DET	MLB	38	526	48	16	0	15	75	40	118	0	0	25.8%	.256/.316/.386	99	.305	-5.6	1B(44): 0	0.5
2022	DET	MLB	39	433	25	10	0	5	43	28	101	1	0	27.1%	.254/.305/.317	85	.324	-2.3		0.0
2023 DC	*DET*	*MLB*	*40*	*474*	*39*	*15*	*0*	*9*	*41*	*33*	*108*	*1*	*0*	*26.9%*	*.250/.307/.352*	*86*	*.310*	*-0.8*		*-0.2*

Comparables: Eddie Murray (69), Albert Pujols (67), Steve Garvey (64)

He did it: 3000. Unlike Albert Pujols, who needed an improbable second-half surge to take him past 700 homers, his fellow future Hall-of-Famer was almost inevitably going to reach his milestone. Cabrera was hitting over .300 on April 23 when the moment came, a rare event in the latter years of his career, but his campaign ended up being the antithesis of Pujols' rediscovery of his peak form. The hit itself wasn't even a showcase of Cabrera's once-singular talent: a mild, opposite-field grounder off perhaps the most hittable pitcher in the majors in 2022, Antonio Senzatela (13 hits per nine), during a game in which the Tigers recorded 20 total hits.

It was still gratifying to have a moment to remember all that Cabrera has done, in a season that mostly highlighted what he has lost. Only two players with 400+ plate appearances had a lower ISO—the speedy and defensively talented Nicky Lopez and Myles Straw. His body continues to let him down, as more biceps trouble and a balky knee contributed to that power outage. Cabrera is set to return in 2023 for what will be his last year, in a part-time role that's desperately necessary if the Tigers aim to contend. The veteran first baseman, now 25th all-time on the hits leaderboard, only needs two more to pass Ichiro and another 54 to join the top 20. Regardless of any further milestones, Cabrera is in the club. It's likely he's the last member for a decade. He could be the last member altogether. So here's to Cabrera, and 3,000, and a career that's no less remarkable for how it's ending.

Kerry Carpenter OF Born: 09/02/97 Age: 25 Bats: L Throws: R Height: 6'2" Weight: 220 lb. Origin: Round 19, 2019 Draft (#562 overall)

YEAR	TEAM	LVL	AGE	PA	R	2B	3B	HR	RBI	BB	K	SB	CS	Whiff%	AVG/OBP/SLG	DRC+	BABIP	BRR	DRP	WARP
2021	ERI	AA	23	461	57	24	1	15	74	29	94	5	6		.262/.319/.433	104	.299	-0.4	LF(69): 0.6, RF(27): -6.1, CF(2): -0.1	1.0
2022	ERI	AA	24	262	43	16	0	22	48	16	72	1	3		.304/.359/.646	136	.347	0.2	RF(29): -0.6, LF(26): -0.2	1.6
2022	TOL	AAA	24	138	17	11	1	8	27	17	17	2	7		.331/.420/.644	133	.330	-0.6	LF(28): 0.7, RF(3): -0.3	0.8
2022	DET	MLB	24	113	16	4	1	6	10	6	32	0	0	27.8%	.252/.310/.485	92	.303	0.3	LF(12): 0.3, RF(8): -0.1	0.3
2023 DC	*DET*	*MLB*	*25*	*458*	*42*	*20*	*3*	*14*	*46*	*26*	*109*	*6*	*4*	*25.6%*	*.238/.291/.406*	*94*	*.284*	*-2.4*	*LF 0, RF 0*	*0.3*

Comparables: Lucas Duda (62), David Cooper (61), Mike Carp (61)

While the major-league club was searching desperately for any positive offensive contribution, Carpenter was busy fashioning a monstrous line in the minors. After three months of dismantling Double-A pitching and another six weeks of doing the same at Toledo, the outfielder got the call and hammered his way to a team-leading .795 OPS. His six big-league blasts also ensured that he led the entire organization in home runs, with 36. Carpenter's squat, torque-heavy swing will lead to a bundle of strikeouts, but when he nails a pitch, he's capable of clearing the fence to all fields. How often he can do that will determine whether he's able to craft a productive major-league career.

Harold Castro IF Born: 11/30/93 Age: 29 Bats: L Throws: R Height: 5'10" Weight: 195 lb. Origin: International Free Agent, 2011

YEAR	TEAM	LVL	AGE	PA	R	2B	3B	HR	RBI	BB	K	SB	CS	Whiff%	AVG/OBP/SLG	DRC+	BABIP	BRR	DRP	WARP
2020	DET	MLB	26	54	6	4	0	0	3	5	11	0	0	24.3%	.347/.407/.429	92	.447	0.3	LF(6): -0.4, 3B(4): 0, RF(4): -0.1	0.1
2021	DET	MLB	27	339	35	13	1	3	37	14	72	1	1	26.0%	.283/.310/.359	84	.351	-1.7	SS(43): 0.2, 2B(33): -0.6, 1B(15): 0.6	0.3
2022	DET	MLB	28	443	37	21	2	7	47	17	79	0	1	19.9%	.271/.300/.381	90	.318	0.3	1B(50): -0.4, 3B(25): 0.4, SS(19): -1.3	0.5
2023 DC	*FA*	*MLB*	*29*	*350*	*31*	*13*	*1*	*5*	*33*	*16*	*62*	*0*	*1*	*20.9%*	*.271/.308/.368*	*87*	*.321*	*-3.8*	*SS -1, 2B 0*	*-0.3*

Comparables: Wilmer Difo (47), Larry Bowa (45), Alex Sanchez (45)

Castro's career-high plate appearance total had nothing to do with his production, which remains relentlessly subpar. He still plays everywhere, more because of previous experience around the diamond rather than any positive defensive contribution. He took a few more turns as Pitchin' Harold, where he was about as effective as he was as a hitter. It's true that he started relatively well offensively, and his batting average-driven line held up for a while. By the end of the season, however, he was there just because the Tigers looked at their list of options and decided he might conceivably be a better choice than Spencer Torkelson, or Jonathan Schoop, or Jeimer Candelario. They weren't wrong; he out-hit them all. There's some value to knowing what you're getting. Unlike his teammates, Castro did exactly what he was expected to.

Brendon Davis 3B Born: 07/28/97 Age: 25 Bats: R Throws: R Height: 6'4" Weight: 185 lb. Origin: Round 5, 2015 Draft (#162 overall)

YEAR	TEAM	LVL	AGE	PA	R	2B	3B	HR	RBI	BB	K	SB	CS	Whiff%	AVG/OBP/SLG	DRC+	BABIP	BRR	DRP	WARP
2021	TRI	A+	23	282	41	17	3	14	40	19	75	9	3		.280/.337/.535	117	.337	1.6	3B(41): -1.2, SS(10): -0.1, 2B(8): 0.3	1.4
2021	RCT	AA	23	131	25	4	1	8	18	18	34	4	0		.268/.366/.536	111	.310	-0.4	2B(9): 0.0, 3B(9): -1.1, SS(7): 0.4	0.6
2021	SL	AAA	23	133	25	8	2	8	25	10	28	3	1		.333/.409/.641	121	.383	0.3	SS(20): -0.3, LF(8): -1.3, 3B(3): 0.5	0.7
2022	SL	AAA	24	159	24	10	1	6	25	18	31	2	2	27.2%	.243/.333/.463	98	.265	-0.4	3B(10): 2.1, SS(9): -0.8, RF(8): 0.9	0.4
2022	TOL	AAA	24	430	54	19	2	14	47	55	104	6	4		.232/.342/.409	91	.284	-1.5	3B(44): -1.3, RF(39): -2.6, SS(10): -0.3	1.1
2022	DET	MLB	24	11	2	0	0	0	0	1	3	1	0	36.4%	.200/.273/.200	91	.286	-0.1	RF(2): 0.1, 3B(1): -0.3	0.0
2023 non-DC	*DET*	*MLB*	*25*	*251*	*24*	*10*	*1*	*6*	*26*	*21*	*76*	*1*	*1*	*32.6%*	*.218/.294/.366*	*80*	*.297*	*0.0*	*RF 0, 3B 0*	*-0.1*

Comparables: José Osuna (40), Mark Zagunis (39), George Springer (39)

Davis did get to make his major-league debut—although not with the Angels, as one might have expected when he sped through their system in 2021. When Los Angeles dropped him from their 40-man in May after a middling start, it was the Tigers who pounced on waivers and who finally gave him his cup of coffee in a very late-season call-up. The offensive performance in the minors remained more lukewarm than scalding, then went ice-cold when he hit the bigs. Davis did continue to showcase his defensive versatility, predominantly featuring at third base and right field but playing every position but pitcher and catcher. It took Davis four organizations and seven positions to get to the majors; he'll have to hit a bit more to avoid adding to the former tallies in the near future.

Dillon Dingler C Born: 09/17/98 Age: 24 Bats: R Throws: R Height: 6'3" Weight: 210 lb. Origin: Round 2, 2020 Draft (#38 overall)

YEAR	TEAM	LVL	AGE	PA	R	2B	3B	HR	RBI	BB	K	SB	CS	Whiff%	AVG/OBP/SLG	DRC+	BABIP	BRR	DRP	WARP
2021	WM	A+	22	141	25	6	1	8	24	13	36	0	0		.287/.376/.549	127	.342	2.1	C(24): 4.8	1.5
2021	ERI	AA	22	208	24	3	3	4	20	9	62	1	0		.202/.264/.314	82	.272	-0.3	C(40): 5.5	0.8
2022	ERI	AA	23	448	56	22	3	14	58	45	143	1	0		.238/.333/.419	97	.335	0.7	C(82): 9.6	2.1
2023 non-DC	*DET*	*MLB*	*24*	*251*	*21*	*9*	*1*	*4*	*23*	*16*	*84*	*0*	*0*	*33.8%*	*.200/.269/.323*	*61*	*.292*	*1.4*	*C 0*	*-0.1*

Comparables: Óscar Hernández (76), David Rodríguez (74), Phil Avlas (67)

YEAR	TEAM	P. COUNT	FRM RUNS	BLK RUNS	THRW RUNS	TOT RUNS
2021	WM	3574	3.5	-0.3	1.4	4.5
2021	ERI	5952	4.4	0.5	0.8	5.7
2022	ERI	11712	6.3	-0.1	1.7	7.9
2023	*DET*	*6956*	*1.8*	*-0.2*	*0.9*	*2.5*

The Tigers would like to drop a few Ls from their record. Dion Dinger sounds like a slugger who could help them do that. Dillon Dingler...well, he still might, but questions about the hit tool remain. He did rebound from a tough debut at Double-A to show more of the power that means he isn't a glove-only catcher. He also maintained the quality defensive work, rating as one of the level's finest players behind the plate. The concern is that 32% strikeout rates don't tend to improve as you face tougher competition, which could well prevent him from logging those dingers. Teams have become ever more accepting of almost any offensive performance at catcher if it comes with plus glovework. As the robo-zone looms, however, it would benefit Dingler to fully unleash the slugger within.

Mario Feliciano C

Born: 11/20/98 Age: 24 Bats: R Throws: R Height: 6'1" Weight: 200 lb. Origin: Round 2, 2016 Draft (#75 overall)

YEAR	TEAM	LVL	AGE	PA	R	2B	3B	HR	RBI	BB	K	SB	CS	Whiff%	AVG/OBP/SLG	DRC+	BABIP	BRR	DRP	WARP
2021	BRWG	ROK	22	29	7	3	1	0	4	1	6	0	0		.360/.448/.560		.474			
2021	NAS	AAA	22	114	12	2	0	3	19	4	26	1	0		.210/.246/.314	87	.241	0.7	C(30): 1.8	0.5
2021	MIL	MLB	22	1	1	0	0	0	0	1	0	0	0	33.3%	.000/1.000/.000	110		0.1		0.0
2022	NAS	AAA	23	311	31	14	0	6	38	18	52	2	2	11.5%	.274/.326/.386	102	.314	-1.3	C(65): -3.7	0.5
2022	MIL	MLB	23	5	0	0	0	0	0	1	1	0	0	22.2%	.250/.400/.250	94	.333	-0.1	C(2): 0	0.0
2023 DC	*DET*	*MLB*	*24*	*29*	*2*	*1*	*0*	*0*	*2*	*1*	*5*	*0*	*0*	*27.0%*	*.246/.293/.360*	*85*	*.292*	*0.1*	*C 0*	*0.1*

Comparables: Pedro Severino (53), Gary Sánchez (51), Eduardo Núñez (50)

YEAR	TEAM	P. COUNT	FRM RUNS	BLK RUNS	THRW RUNS	TOT RUNS
2021	NAS	4160	2.5	-0.1	0.0	2.4
2022	NAS	9427	-3.3	-0.7	0.7	-3.3
2022	MIL	192	0.0	0.0	0.0	0.0
2023	*DET*	*1202*	*0.2*	*0.0*	*-0.1*	*0.1*

Once a promising prospect with a decent hit tool and above-average power, Feliciano no longer seems like a lock to stick behind the plate full-time. That'd matter a little less if his bat looked "*good* good" and not just "good for a catcher," but, like his work behind the dish, it hasn't progressed quite as hoped. Injuries may be partially to blame, as may be a year lost to the pandemic. He's no longer the "catcher of the future" in Milwaukee, nor even their third backstop after being exposed to waivers and picked up by Detroit—a new org to wait for something special.

Riley Greene CF

Born: 09/28/00 Age: 22 Bats: L Throws: L Height: 6'3" Weight: 200 lb. Origin: Round 1, 2019 Draft (#5 overall)

YEAR	TEAM	LVL	AGE	PA	R	2B	3B	HR	RBI	BB	K	SB	CS	Whiff%	AVG/OBP/SLG	DRC+	BABIP	BRR	DRP	WARP
2021	ERI	AA	20	373	59	16	5	16	54	41	102	12	1		.298/.381/.525	112	.386	1.8	CF(73): 5.6, RF(6): -0.5, LF(5): -1.0	2.4
2021	TOL	AAA	20	185	36	9	3	8	30	22	51	4	0		.308/.400/.553	105	.406	1.5	RF(15): -0.0, LF(13): -1.7, CF(13): -0.8	0.6
2022	TOL	AAA	21	68	10	4	0	1	6	6	14	3	0		.274/.338/.387	101	.340	1.2	CF(14): -0.9, RF(1): 0.1	0.2
2022	DET	MLB	21	418	46	18	4	5	42	36	120	1	4	25.5%	.253/.321/.362	78	.354	-3.1	CF(93): 1.1	0.2
2023 DC	*DET*	*MLB*	*22*	*609*	*64*	*22*	*9*	*13*	*45*	*51*	*151*	*11*	*3*	*25.6%*	*.248/.319/.393*	*97*	*.320*	*11.7*	*CF 7*	*3.6*

Comparables: Melky Cabrera (53), Lastings Milledge (50), Leody Taveras (49)

Riding a wave of preseason positivity, the Tigers were all set to open the campaign with the dynamic Greene on the roster when he fouled a ball off his foot late in the spring. He continued the at-bat against Gerrit Cole, rapped a long double to the center field wall and scored before he consulted medical personnel, later discovering his foot was broken. He was finally able to make his debut two and a half months later with the Tigers sitting at a miserable 25-40. After two weeks he was at the top of the lineup; 93 games later he was voted Tiger of the Year. That's not to say there weren't struggles. Greene's OPS sank as low as .607 in mid-August, and a near-30% strikeout rate speaks to some approach issues that will need to be resolved; if anything, he was a little too passive. Nevertheless, he demonstrated his array of tools and, perhaps more importantly, offered hope that things might be better next season—which might make him Tiger of the Year in itself.

Eric Haase C

Born: 12/18/92 Age: 30 Bats: R Throws: R Height: 5'10" Weight: 210 lb. Origin: Round 7, 2011 Draft (#218 overall)

YEAR	TEAM	LVL	AGE	PA	R	2B	3B	HR	RBI	BB	K	SB	CS	Whiff%	AVG/OBP/SLG	DRC+	BABIP	BRR	DRP	WARP
2020	DET	MLB	27	19	1	0	0	0	2	1	6	0	0	39.5%	.176/.211/.176	87	.250	0.0	C(7): -0.0	0.0
2021	TOL	AAA	28	28	3	3	0	1	5	5	10	1	0		.348/.464/.609	87	.583	0.2	C(4): 0.0, LF(3): -0.3	0.0
2021	DET	MLB	28	381	48	12	1	22	61	26	119	2	0	34.7%	.231/.286/.459	103	.278	1.1	C(66): -7.3, LF(22): -1	0.9
2022	DET	MLB	29	351	41	17	1	14	44	24	97	0	0	32.8%	.254/.305/.443	106	.316	0.0	C(84): -7.6, LF(11): -0.1	0.7
2023 DC	*DET*	*MLB*	*30*	*355*	*34*	*12*	*1*	*13*	*37*	*25*	*100*	*1*	*0*	*32.9%*	*.229/.288/.405*	*94*	*.285*	*1.2*	*LF 0, C -5*	*0.3*

Comparables: Michael McKenry (58), Welington Castillo (58), Kelly Shoppach (57)

YEAR	TEAM	P. COUNT	FRM RUNS	BLK RUNS	THRW RUNS	TOT RUNS
2020	DET	778	0.0	0.0	0.1	0.1
2021	DET	9170	-6.1	0.1	0.1	-5.9
2022	DET	10053	-6.9	-0.7	0.0	-7.6
2023	*DET*	*8418*	*-5.9*	*-0.1*	*0.1*	*-6.0*

Above, you see the line of the most valuable hitter on the 2022 Detroit Tigers. As late as June 10, Haase's OPS was below .500 and his season looked to be going the way of his team's: nowhere. From then on, he slashed .283/.330/.508. If that were his full-season line, it might seem entirely reasonable that Haase was Detroit's best offensive performer. Instead, all it took was another good-for-a-catcher season that essentially replicated his 2021. He remains a flawed, streaky power threat with the bat and a catcher best utilized somewhere other than behind the plate. What he shouldn't be is a team's best hitter.

★ ★ ★ *2023 Top 101 Prospect* **#86** ★ ★ ★

Jace Jung 2B

Born: 10/04/00 Age: 22 Bats: L Throws: R Height: 6'0" Weight: 205 lb. Origin: Round 1, 2022 Draft (#12 overall)

YEAR	TEAM	LVL	AGE	PA	R	2B	3B	HR	RBI	BB	K	SB	CS	Whiff%	AVG/OBP/SLG	DRC+	BABIP	BRR	DRP	WARP
2022	WM	A+	21	134	16	6	1	1	13	25	28	1	0		.231/.373/.333	104	.300	-1.6	2B(27): 3.4	0.6
2023 non-DC	*DET*	*MLB*	*22*	*251*	*22*	*9*	*1*	*3*	*21*	*26*	*70*	*0*	*1*	*31.0%*	*.206/.297/.315*	*71*	*.285*	*1.5*	*2B 0*	*0.0*

Comparables: Luis Alejandro Basabe (87), Max Moroff (86), Josh Johnson (86)

Just a couple months before his brother Josh made his major-league debut, Jung emulated him by being drafted in the first round out of Texas Tech, three years later. Jung the younger (Junger?) has a more unconventional setup, holding his bat perpendicular to the ground, and is likely to be confined to the right side of the infield. Although he didn't get to it often in his pro debut, he has plenty of power, plus an advanced approach that was far more evident. The defensive limitations put plenty of pressure on the bat, but if he lives up to his college pedigree he'll be emulating his brother again before long, and it might not take him three years to do it.

★ ★ ★ *2023 Top 101 Prospect* **#98** ★ ★ ★

Colt Keith 3B Born: 08/14/01 Age: 21 Bats: L Throws: R Height: 6'3" Weight: 211 lb. Origin: Round 5, 2020 Draft (#132 overall)

YEAR	TEAM	LVL	AGE	PA	R	2B	3B	HR	RBI	BB	K	SB	CS	Whiff%	AVG/OBP/SLG	DRC+	BABIP	BRR	DRP	WARP
2021	LAK	A	19	181	32	6	3	1	21	30	39	4	1		.320/.436/.422	117	.422	1.4	3B(27): 3.3, 2B(14): -1.3	1.2
2021	WM	A+	19	76	7	1	1	1	6	8	27	0	0		.162/.250/.250	80	.250	0.9	3B(15): 1.1, 2B(2): -0.4	0.2
2022	WM	A+	20	216	38	14	3	9	31	22	42	4	0		.301/.370/.544	138	.343	1.6	3B(27): -2.0, 2B(13): 0.2	1.5
2023 non-DC	*DET*	*MLB*	*21*	*251*	*22*	*9*	*2*	*4*	*23*	*20*	*67*	*1*	*1*	*29.7%*	*.238/.304/.360*	*84*	*.320*	*2.5*	*2B 0, 3B 0*	*0.3*

Comparables: Trey Michalczewski (68), Marcos Vechionacci (63), Eric Hosmer (62)

Keith hit his stride right out of the gate at West Michigan, galloping to a .290 average at the end of April. He quickly turned on the power, too: By the time a shoulder injury felled him in early June, he had 26 extra-base knocks in 48 games, clearing the fence nine times. He proved that the earlier success was no fluke in the AFL, where he displayed an outstanding approach by walking almost as often as he struck out. While the race to the majors is far from run, Keith's clearly leading the pack of Detroit hitting prospects.

Justyn-Henry Malloy LF Born: 02/19/00 Age: 23 Bats: R Throws: R Height: 6'3" Weight: 212 lb. Origin: Round 6, 2021 Draft (#187 overall)

YEAR	TEAM	LVL	AGE	PA	R	2B	3B	HR	RBI	BB	K	SB	CS	Whiff%	AVG/OBP/SLG	DRC+	BABIP	BRR	DRP	WARP
2021	AUG	A	21	147	23	5	0	5	21	24	30	4	2		.270/.388/.434	123	.318	-0.4	3B(31): -1.4, LF(1): -0.0	0.6
2022	ROM	A+	22	320	51	16	0	10	44	47	73	3	0		.304/.409/.479	126	.376	1.0	3B(51): -1.9, LF(3): -0.6	1.6
2022	MIS	AA	22	238	35	11	0	6	31	43	60	0	0		.268/.403/.421	113	.354	0.9	LF(51): -1.9	0.8
2022	GWN	AAA	22	33	5	1	0	1	6	7	5	2	0		.280/.424/.440	116	.300	-1.4	LF(7): 0.7	0.1
2023 non-DC	*DET*	*MLB*	*23*	*251*	*25*	*10*	*0*	*5*	*24*	*27*	*64*	*1*	*1*	*27.1%*	*.229/.320/.354*	*89*	*.298*	*0.0*	*3B 0, LF 0*	*0.2*

Comparables: Tito Polo (51), Ramon Hernandez (50), Lorenzo Cain (50)

If anybody knows about taking a chance and running with it, it's Malloy. After only getting 39 at-bats in two seasons at Vanderbilt, he transferred to Georgia Tech and wound up playing himself into the sixth round of the 2021 Draft. After beginning his first full pro season in High-A, Malloy hit and hit (and walked) at each level, winding up at Triple-A. The bat will need to propel him to the majors, as he's still something of a question mark as a third baseman—especially as it comes to his throwing arm. Even if he moves forward as a left fielder—which only became more likely when he was swapped to Detroit (along with 80-grade name/LHP Jake Higginbotham) for reliever Joe Jiménez—Malloy has taken every chance he's gotten so far; there's no reason to think he won't continue to make things happen for himself.

Nick Maton SS Born: 02/18/97 Age: 26 Bats: L Throws: R Height: 6'2" Weight: 178 lb. Origin: Round 7, 2017 Draft (#203 overall)

YEAR	TEAM	LVL	AGE	PA	R	2B	3B	HR	RBI	BB	K	SB	CS	Whiff%	AVG/OBP/SLG	DRC+	BABIP	BRR	DRP	WARP
2021	LHV	AAA	24	252	29	11	2	5	27	38	60	3	2		.199/.332/.345	97	.252	-1.4	SS(38): -3.6, 2B(15): 0.3, 3B(13): 0.2	0.3
2021	PHI	MLB	24	131	16	7	1	2	14	10	39	2	0	31.3%	.256/.323/.385	70	.364	1.8	2B(21): -0.5, SS(20): 0.1	0.1
2022	LHV	AAA	25	250	33	20	1	5	35	34	55	3	1	40.0%	.261/.368/.436	100	.327	1.6	SS(46): -4.0, 2B(9): -0.6, 3B(1): -0.1	0.5
2022	PHI	MLB	25	85	13	2	1	5	17	10	29	0	0	35.4%	.250/.341/.514	88	.325	0.9	2B(10): -0.1, LF(10): 0.1, RF(10): -0.3	0.2
2023 DC	*DET*	*MLB*	*26*	*216*	*23*	*9*	*1*	*4*	*19*	*20*	*60*	*2*	*1*	*30.7%*	*.217/.299/.359*	*79*	*.293*	*1.3*	*3B 0, 2B 0*	*0.0*

Comparables: Brandon Lowe (60), Tzu-Wei Lin (55), Chris Nelson (54)

When Maton hits the ball, he can *really* hit the ball—he sees four-seamers expertly and crushes them with abandon. The problem, unfortunately, is what happens the rest of the time. He chases breaking balls and off-speed pitches on both sides of the plate, and he strikes out a ton. Thus, he's a much better hitter when he gets ahead in the count, but he tends to fall behind far more often. His defensive versatility is an asset, but he isn't elite at any position. Maton provides flexibility off the bench, but his shortcomings on both sides of the ball prevent him from offering a whole lot more than that.

Austin Meadows OF Born: 05/03/95 Age: 28 Bats: L Throws: L Height: 6'3" Weight: 225 lb. Origin: Round 1, 2013 Draft (#9 overall)

YEAR	TEAM	LVL	AGE	PA	R	2B	3B	HR	RBI	BB	K	SB	CS	Whiff%	AVG/OBP/SLG	DRC+	BABIP	BRR	DRP	WARP
2020	TB	MLB	25	152	19	8	1	4	13	17	50	2	1	31.4%	.205/.296/.371	73	.288	0.1	LF(23): -0.7, RF(4): 0.1	-0.1
2021	TB	MLB	26	591	79	29	3	27	106	59	122	4	3	24.4%	.234/.315/.458	104	.249	-1.9	LF(78): 1, RF(1): -0.6	2.0
2022	TOL	AAA	27	39	4	0	0	1	4	4	7	0	0		.147/.231/.235	103	.148	0.4	RF(7): -0.6	0.1
2022	DET	MLB	27	147	9	6	2	0	11	16	17	0	1	13.4%	.250/.347/.328	105	.288	-1.7	RF(18): -0.7, LF(15): -0.2	0.2
2023 DC	*DET*	*MLB*	*28*	*515*	*56*	*21*	*4*	*19*	*56*	*50*	*82*	*6*	*1*	*19.0%*	*.254/.333/.449*	*121*	*.270*	*5.0*	*RF 3*	*3.3*

Comparables: Nick Markakis (60), Jay Bruce (59), Domonic Brown (58)

A litany of health complications kept Meadows off the field after his trade from the Rays, from vertigo to COVID-19 and Achilles tendinitis. Toward the end of the season, however, Meadows revealed that he needed to take more time away to deal with his mental health. It was the kind of disclosure that would have been unthinkable in most environments in the not-too-distant past, let alone professional sports. We can only applaud Meadows for his courage and honesty, and hope that he will make others feel capable of asking for help if they need it.

Parker Meadows CF Born: 11/02/99 Age: 23 Bats: L Throws: R Height: 6'5" Weight: 205 lb. Origin: Round 2, 2018 Draft (#44 overall)

YEAR	TEAM	LVL	AGE	PA	R	2B	3B	HR	RBI	BB	K	SB	CS	Whiff%	AVG/OBP/SLG	DRC+	BABIP	BRR	DRP	WARP
2021	WM	A+	21	408	50	15	2	8	44	37	99	9	8		.208/.290/.330	94	.261	1.7	CF(73): -2.0, RF(13): -0.8, LF(4): 0.1	1.0
2022	WM	A+	22	67	16	4	1	4	7	4	18	0	0		.230/.288/.525	126	.256	1.0	CF(12): -0.7, RF(1): -0.1	0.4
2022	ERI	AA	22	489	64	21	6	16	51	52	90	17	2		.275/.354/.466	117	.309	0.2	CF(109): 2.2, RF(3): 0.9	2.7
2023 non-DC	*DET*	*MLB*	*23*	*251*	*22*	*9*	*1*	*5*	*24*	*18*	*61*	*4*	*2*	*26.7%*	*.221/.283/.348*	*74*	*.277*	*1.0*	*CF 0, RF 0*	*0.0*

Comparables: Juan Lagares (57), John Matulia (54), Luis Barrera (51)

Parker Meadows has the sound of a retirement community (and there is, in fact, one in Hampshire, England); not the ideal vibe for a young athlete who had started to look like he might never get his high-end tools into games. A better start to the retread at High-A earned him a promotion to Erie, and Meadows finally took his career in a different direction. His five-category performance was far more like what evaluators had hoped for based on his athletic abilities. The glove is good enough in center that he can afford to hit a little less and still be a valuable player. One thing's for sure: Retirement's the last thing on anyone's mind after this season.

Jake Rogers C Born: 04/18/95 Age: 28 Bats: R Throws: R Height: 6'1" Weight: 201 lb. Origin: Round 3, 2016 Draft (#97 overall)

YEAR	TEAM	LVL	AGE	PA	R	2B	3B	HR	RBI	BB	K	SB	CS	Whiff%	AVG/OBP/SLG	DRC+	BABIP	BRR	DRP	WARP
2021	DET	MLB	26	127	17	5	3	6	17	11	46	1	0	37.9%	.239/.306/.496	82	.344	-0.2	C(37): -3, P(1): -0.4	-0.1
2023 DC	*DET*	*MLB*	*28*	*357*	*35*	*13*	*2*	*12*	*34*	*33*	*115*	*0*	*2*	*34.7%*	*.205/.288/.382*	*87*	*.272*	*-5.1*	*C -7*	*-0.6*

Comparables: Cameron Rupp (62), Sandy Leon (59), Tomás Nido (56)

YEAR	TEAM	P. COUNT	FRM RUNS	BLK RUNS	THRW RUNS	TOT RUNS
2021	DET	5067	-2.4	-0.2	0.1	-2.5
2023	*DET*	*14430*	*-6.5*	*-0.5*	*-0.2*	*-7.2*

Although Rogers didn't succeed in his bid to return from September 2021 Tommy John surgery before the season was over, there wasn't much need to rush back and stop someone else taking his role. Tigers catchers combined for 0.4 WARP on the season, almost exclusively thanks to Eric Haase's bat. Rogers hasn't been a plus defensive catcher in the majors, either, but his minor-league numbers are far more promising: when the bar is "better behind the plate than Eric Haase," there's not a ton of pressure on Rogers' glove.

Jonathan Schoop 2B Born: 10/16/91 Age: 31 Bats: R Throws: R Height: 6'1" Weight: 247 lb. Origin: International Free Agent, 2008

YEAR	TEAM	LVL	AGE	PA	R	2B	3B	HR	RBI	BB	K	SB	CS	Whiff%	AVG/OBP/SLG	DRC+	BABIP	BRR	DRP	WARP
2020	DET	MLB	28	177	26	4	2	8	23	8	39	0	0	27.8%	.278/.324/.475	107	.316	0.2	2B(44): -0.9	0.7
2021	DET	MLB	29	674	85	30	1	22	84	37	133	2	0	24.6%	.278/.320/.435	106	.317	0.5	1B(114): 2.2, 2B(38): -0.3, 3B(1): 0	2.4
2022	DET	MLB	30	510	48	23	1	11	38	19	107	5	0	28.2%	.202/.239/.322	77	.234	-1.0	2B(129): 4.5, 1B(2): 0	0.5
2023 DC	*DET*	*MLB*	*31*	*536*	*50*	*21*	*1*	*15*	*49*	*26*	*110*	*1*	*1*	*27.2%*	*.240/.285/.384*	*88*	*.276*	*0.1*	*2B 2*	*1.0*

Comparables: Bill Mazeroski (70), Roberto Alomar (69), Dave Cash (69)

No advanced forecasting system is required to predict some volatility in Schoop's heavily average-dependent offensive production. A time machine would have been required, though, to foresee the extent of his collapse at the plate. In some ways Schoop traveled back in time—to his first full season in 2014, when he looked every bit the inexperienced 22-year-old. Since then he has always been able to outpace that line, both in terms of average and power. While our eye might drift to that BABIP mark, a career-worst ISO was even more responsible. Although Schoop didn't seem to know what was coming at the plate, he certainly did in the field, where he put together a superlative defensive season that led the league in Outs Above Average. If we built a Schoop-scope to tell us what the future holds, we'd see a low walk rate, plenty of aggression at the plate and elite glovework—an increasingly clear part of the picture. The rest remains murky.

Spencer Torkelson 1B Born: 08/26/99 Age: 23 Bats: R Throws: R Height: 6'1" Weight: 220 lb. Origin: Round 1, 2020 Draft (#1 overall)

YEAR	TEAM	LVL	AGE	PA	R	2B	3B	HR	RBI	BB	K	SB	CS	Whiff%	AVG/OBP/SLG	DRC+	BABIP	BRR	DRP	WARP
2021	WM	A+	21	141	21	11	1	5	28	24	28	3	2		.312/.440/.569	128	.363	0.4	3B(16): -0.1, 1B(15): 0.0	0.9
2021	ERI	AA	21	212	33	10	0	14	36	30	50	1	1		.263/.373/.560	139	.278	-0.5	3B(27): -1.5, 1B(23): 0.0	1.4
2021	TOL	AAA	21	177	35	8	1	11	27	23	36	1	0		.238/.350/.531	120	.233	-0.1	1B(37): -1.0	0.7
2022	TOL	AAA	22	155	18	6	0	5	18	23	41	1	1		.229/.348/.389	98	.294	-0.6	1B(31): -0.0	0.3
2022	DET	MLB	22	404	38	16	1	8	28	37	99	0	1	25.6%	.203/.285/.319	85	.255	-0.4	1B(109): -1.8	-0.1
2023 DC	*DET*	*MLB*	*23*	*508*	*48*	*19*	*1*	*16*	*47*	*50*	*121*	*2*	*1*	*26.2%*	*.221/.306/.382*	*95*	*.263*	*0.8*	*1B 0*	*0.5*

Comparables: Jon Singleton (54), Chris Marrero (53), Luis Rengifo (53)

What a spectacular year it was for rookies. Julio Rodríguez, Spencer Strider, Adley Rutschman...the list goes on. Torkelson was a leading candidate to be on that list, an Opening Day starter with arguably the most polished bat in the minors—or so we thought. Instead of battling with his peers for a Rookie of the Year award, he was engaged in a season-long struggle with the Mendoza Line, which he barely won. The number one overall pick in 2020 did display plus power on occasion, plus a discerning eye at the plate; the strikeout rate wasn't prohibitively high, either. It just seemed that the contact he did make wasn't consistent enough, that his timing wasn't quite right in too many of his at-bats. That's a good sign in the sense that most of the components are there, a bad one given he couldn't figure out how to improve over 400+ plate appearances. Not being on the Rookie of the Year shortlist is now the least of Tork's concerns. He'd settle for not appearing on another list: first-round busts.

Matt Vierling OF Born: 09/16/96 Age: 26 Bats: R Throws: R Height: 6'3" Weight: 205 lb. Origin: Round 5, 2018 Draft (#137 overall)

YEAR	TEAM	LVL	AGE	PA	R	2B	3B	HR	RBI	BB	K	SB	CS	Whiff%	AVG/OBP/SLG	DRC+	BABIP	BRR	DRP	WARP
2021	REA	AA	24	102	16	6	1	6	16	12	18	5	1		.345/.422/.644	136	.369	-0.1	CF(15): -1.0, RF(10): 4.5	1.1
2021	LHV	AAA	24	236	25	6	1	5	31	24	46	5	1		.248/.331/.359	99	.291	-0.8	LF(20): 2.5, RF(17): -1.6, 3B(11): 1.8	1.0
2021	PHI	MLB	24	77	11	3	1	2	6	4	20	2	0	24.2%	.324/.364/.479	92	.420	-0.4	1B(9): 0.2, CF(8): -0.3, LF(7): 0.3	0.2
2022	LHV	AAA	25	95	15	6	2	2	9	10	15	8	2		.271/.347/.459	117	.309	0.7	CF(16): -0.5, LF(3): -0.2, 1B(1): -0.0	0.4
2022	PHI	MLB	25	357	41	12	2	6	32	23	70	7	4	19.6%	.246/.297/.351	93	.290	-0.6	CF(61): -0.1, RF(37): 0.6, LF(30): 0.5	1.0
2023 DC	*DET*	*MLB*	*26*	*227*	*25*	*9*	*1*	*5*	*22*	*15*	*41*	*8*	*3*	*19.7%*	*.254/.314/.393*	*96*	*.293*	*2.3*	*LF 0, CF 0*	*0.7*

Comparables: Abraham Almonte (54), Tony Cruz (52), Albert Almora Jr. (50)

Vierling made a grand entrance with some grand exit velocity in 2021, going from unranked prospect to 2022 Opening Day center fielder faster than a ball coming off his own bat. He has since proven himself to be a capable hitter against southpaws and a quick enough fielder to survive in center, but his ineptitude against right-handed pitching will prevent him from being any more than the short side of a platoon. He'll take those limited talents to Detroit after the Tigers picked him up in a swap headlined by Gregory Soto in January.

PITCHERS

Tyler Alexander LHP Born: 07/14/94 Age: 28 Bats: R Throws: L Height: 6'2" Weight: 203 lb. Origin: Round 2, 2015 Draft (#65 overall)

YEAR	TEAM	LVL	AGE	W	L	SV	G	GS	IP	H	HR	BB/9	K/9	K	GB%	BABIP	WHIP	ERA	DRA-	WARP	MPH	FB%	Whiff%	CSP
2020	DET	MLB	25	2	3	0	14	2	36^1	39	8	2.2	8.4	34	45.7%	.320	1.32	3.96	105	0.3	90.2	62.1%	21.9%	46.2%
2021	DET	MLB	26	2	4	0	41	15	106^1	106	16	2.4	7.4	87	38.0%	.285	1.26	3.81	119	-0.1	88.8	71.5%	20.0%	53.5%
2022	TOL	AAA	27	1	1	0	5	1	9	12	1	1.0	8.0	8	45.2%	.367	1.44	8.00	98	0.1				
2022	DET	MLB	27	4	11	0	27	17	101	108	18	2.2	5.4	61	35.9%	.281	1.32	4.81	143	-1.3	90.2	43.1%	17.1%	55.7%
2023 DC	*DET*	*MLB*	*28*	*2*	*3*	*0*	*63*	*0*	*54.7*	*64*	*8*	*2.4*	*5.8*	*35*	*38.1%*	*.309*	*1.45*	*4.97*	*130*	*-0.5*	*89.7*	*56.7%*	*19.0%*	*53.8%*

Comparables: Brett Oberholtzer (63), Adam Morgan (61), Aaron Laffey (60)

For a player who has one of the least-impressive strikeout rates in the majors, Alexander has found himself flirting with history at least twice more than you'd expect. His nine-consecutive-strikeout relief appearance in 2020 was joined by last September's no-hit bid, broken up in the seventh by Ryan Mountcastle. Alexander was already in a position that he ought to occupy less as that game's starter; he's far better-suited to mopping up in relief. Letting him face righties too often is a recipe for disaster, and his kitchen-sink approach and 90-mph heat aren't nearly so deceptive when opponents get multiple chances to figure out the trick. To Alexander's credit, he filled innings that the Tigers desperately needed to be filled, and gave fans something to cheer at the end of a season with very little. Next season, he'll have a 12% strikeout rate and make a run at the single-game strikeout record.

Matthew Boyd LHP Born: 02/02/91 Age: 32 Bats: L Throws: L Height: 6'3" Weight: 223 lb. Origin: Round 6, 2013 Draft (#175 overall)

YEAR	TEAM	LVL	AGE	W	L	SV	G	GS	IP	H	HR	BB/9	K/9	K	GB%	BABIP	WHIP	ERA	DRA-	WARP	MPH	FB%	Whiff%	CSP
2020	DET	MLB	29	3	7	0	12	12	60^1	67	15	3.3	9.0	60	37.5%	.310	1.48	6.71	133	-0.4	91.8	52.7%	27.9%	45.5%
2021	TOL	AAA	30	0	0	0	3	3	9^1	5	0	0.0	10.6	11	45.0%	.250	0.54	0.00	94	0.2				
2021	DET	MLB	30	3	8	0	15	15	78^2	77	9	2.6	7.7	67	38.3%	.296	1.27	3.89	113	0.2	92.1	47.5%	22.6%	55.6%
2022	TAC	AAA	31	1	1	0	6	0	8	4	1	0.0	15.7	14	42.9%	.231	0.50	2.25	79	0.1	92.6	41.6%	47.4%	
2022	SEA	MLB	31	2	0	0	10	0	13^1	5	0	5.4	8.8	13	41.9%	.167	0.98	1.35	102	0.1	92.1	47.4%	30.0%	47.7%
2023 DC	*DET*	*MLB*	*32*	*7*	*7*	*0*	*33*	*19*	*107.3*	*96*	*14*	*2.9*	*9.8*	*116*	*38.4%*	*.289*	*1.21*	*3.47*	*94*	*1.1*	*92.1*	*50.7%*	*28.1%*	*50.6%*

Comparables: Bruce Hurst (80), Wade Miley (79), Rick Honeycutt (78)

Signed by the Giants on a one-year deal before the 2022 season, Boyd only wore the orange and black while rehabbing from flexor tendon surgery. Flipped to his hometown Mariners at the trade deadline, the lefty eventually found a September role out of the bullpen, where his slider appeared to be fully intact, even if his command was lagging behind. With this late-season reminder of his signature pitch, Boyd piqued the interest of his erstwhile team, the Tigers, who signed him on a one-year deal. After all, you can't spell Matthew Boyd without "B," "T," and "D"...Back To Detroit.

Beau Brieske RHP Born: 04/05/98 Age: 25 Bats: R Throws: R Height: 6'3" Weight: 200 lb. Origin: Round 27, 2019 Draft (#802 overall)

YEAR	TEAM	LVL	AGE	W	L	SV	G	GS	IP	H	HR	BB/9	K/9	K	GB%	BABIP	WHIP	ERA	DRA-	WARP	MPH	FB%	Whiff%	CSP
2021	WM	A+	23	6	3	0	13	13	62^2	49	5	2.2	10.9	76	35.4%	.289	1.02	3.45	77	1.4				
2021	ERI	AA	23	3	1	0	8	8	44	36	2	1.6	8.2	40	41.3%	.286	1.00	2.66	108	0.2				
2022	TOL	AAA	24	0	2	0	4	4	17^1	17	3	2.6	9.9	19	39.1%	.326	1.27	4.15	99	0.2				
2022	DET	MLB	24	3	6	0	15	15	81^2	73	14	2.8	6.0	54	37.1%	.242	1.20	4.19	116	0.1	94.3	53.3%	17.7%	56.3%
2023 DC	*DET*	*MLB*	*25*	*3*	*3*	*0*	*20*	*6*	*45.7*	*50*	*6*	*3.1*	*6.2*	*31*	*38.1%*	*.298*	*1.44*	*4.71*	*123*	*-0.2*	*94.3*	*53.3%*	*21.9%*	*56.3%*

Comparables: Jharel Cotton (73), David Buchanan (70), Williams Pérez (68)

Try saying it a few times. Beau Brieske. Bo Brisk-ee. Bobriskee. It's one of those names that rolls right off the tongue, no matter how briskly you say it. His return from the injured list after some mid-season biceps tendinitis was anything but brisk. The Tigers exercised an abundance of caution, letting his recovery extend throughout most of the second half before shutting him down rather than risk any further injury just for a start or two. It was otherwise a respectable rookie season for the 27th-rounder, who has largely defied draft-slot expectations throughout his time in the minors despite the pandemic arriving just a few months after he joined the organization. His half-season in the rotation didn't blow anyone away, but his five-pitch arsenal, promising velocity and spin rates should ensure that Tigers fans will be rolling that name off their tongues in the future.

Alex Faedo **RHP** Born: 11/12/95 Age: 27 Bats: R Throws: R Height: 6'5" Weight: 225 lb. Origin: Round 1, 2017 Draft (#18 overall)

YEAR	TEAM	LVL	AGE	W	L	SV	G	GS	IP	H	HR	BB/9	K/9	K	GB%	BABIP	WHIP	ERA	DRA-	WARP	MPH	FB%	Whiff%	CSP
2022	LAK	A	26	1	1	0	3	1	10^2	6	0	2.5	10.1	12	38.5%	.231	0.84	2.53	93	0.2	93.4	56.1%	41.6%	
2022	DET	MLB	26	1	5	0	12	12	53^2	63	7	4.2	7.4	44	31.0%	.335	1.64	5.53	129	-0.3	92.9	51.8%	24.4%	56.0%
2023 DC	*DET*	*MLB*	*27*	*4*	*3*	*0*	*32*	*4*	*46*	*46*	*7*	*3.5*	*8.0*	*41*	*32.5%*	*.291*	*1.40*	*4.58*	*119*	*-0.1*	*92.9*	*51.8%*	*27.0%*	*56.0%*

Comparables: Hector Noesí (71), Nick Martinez (68), Glenn Sparkman (67)

Faedo's rookie season began with seven straight starts of at least five innings and two earned runs or less. That was followed by 21 earned runs in just 16⅔ innings across his final five outings. The hip surgery that ended his season offers at least one explanation for the abrupt reversal of fortunes. A less optimistic possibility: The mediocre fastball performance, and a changeup that did little to distract hitters from the heater, caught up with him. If you're a Tigers fan still leaning into optimism, we salute you.

★ ★ ★ *2023 Top 101 Prospect* **#87** ★ ★ ★

Wilmer Flores **RHP** Born: 02/20/01 Age: 22 Bats: R Throws: R Height: 6'4" Weight: 225 lb. Origin: International Free Agent, 2020

YEAR	TEAM	LVL	AGE	W	L	SV	G	GS	IP	H	HR	BB/9	K/9	K	GB%	BABIP	WHIP	ERA	DRA-	WARP	MPH	FB%	Whiff%	CSP
2021	TIGW	ROK	20	2	1	0	3	2	13	15	0	1.4	12.5	18	58.8%	.441	1.31	4.85						
2021	LAK	A	20	4	3	0	11	11	53	47	1	3.7	12.2	72	52.4%	.368	1.30	3.40	99	0.6				
2022	WM	A+	21	1	0	0	6	5	19^2	14	2	0.9	16.0	35	57.9%	.333	0.81	1.83	67	0.5				
2022	ERI	AA	21	6	4	0	19	19	83^2	67	8	2.3	10.2	95	45.7%	.280	1.05	3.01	89	1.6				
2023 non-DC	*DET*	*MLB*	*22*	*2*	*2*	*0*	*57*	*0*	*50*	*49*	*6*	*3.3*	*8.8*	*48*	*47.8%*	*.309*	*1.36*	*4.17*	*104*	*0.1*			*25.3%*	

Comparables: Drew Hutchison (82), Matt Manning (80), Edwin Escobar (79)

No, not that one. This is a different one. It is his brother, though. They also have another brother called Wilmer. This Flores (Wilmer De Jesus, as opposed to Wilmer Alejandro, ten years his senior) won't get confused with his veteran sibling if they're ever on the same field. He's taller, for one, and an exciting pitching prospect. While a third pitch remains a work in progress, his high-nineties fastball and hard curve made short work of Double-A hitters, earning him Tigers Minor League Player of the Year honors. It looks ever more likely that he'll share a big-league diamond with his brother at some point, an impressive outcome for one of many undrafted free agents from the abbreviated 2022 draft.

Jason Foley **RHP** Born: 11/01/95 Age: 27 Bats: R Throws: R Height: 6'4" Weight: 215 lb. Origin: Undrafted Free Agent, 2016

YEAR	TEAM	LVL	AGE	W	L	SV	G	GS	IP	H	HR	BB/9	K/9	K	GB%	BABIP	WHIP	ERA	DRA-	WARP	MPH	FB%	Whiff%	CSP
2021	TOL	AAA	25	1	1	2	32	0	34^2	34	5	4.9	9.3	36	55.3%	.330	1.53	4.41	95	0.6				
2021	DET	MLB	25	0	0	0	11	0	10^1	8	1	4.4	5.2	6	58.1%	.233	1.26	2.61	119	0.0	96.3	72.2%	17.9%	51.4%
2022	TOL	AAA	26	1	0	0	4	0	5	5	1	1.8	10.8	6	57.1%	.308	1.20	3.60	96	0.1				
2022	DET	MLB	26	1	0	0	60	0	60^1	72	2	1.6	6.4	43	56.5%	.355	1.38	3.88	102	0.5	96.5	69.6%	16.7%	59.4%
2023 DC	*DET*	*MLB*	*27*	*3*	*3*	*0*	*70*	*0*	*61*	*74*	*6*	*3.3*	*6.3*	*42*	*54.8%*	*.331*	*1.58*	*5.19*	*128*	*-0.6*	*96.4*	*70.0%*	*19.4%*	*58.3%*

Comparables: Kevin McCarthy (50), Zac Reininger (48), Logan Ondrusek (47)

It's tough to convince DRA when you don't strike anyone out. Foley was the only one of the 53 pitchers who threw at least 40 frames with a strikeout rate below 17% to register even close to a league-average mark. He did so by filling up the zone with his hard, plunging sinker, an approach that slashed his walk rate and ensured most of the batted balls against him went straight into the ground. Batters rarely swing and miss against Foley—frequently hitting him extremely hard—but try as they might, they can't elevate that sinker as it squirms away from the barrel of the bat. Only three of the 301 players to face him in the majors managed to hit a home run. In the absence of walks or extra-base hits, Foley just has to keep on generating those grounders and hope more of them find an infielder than the space between.

Bryan Garcia **RHP** Born: 04/19/95 Age: 28 Bats: R Throws: R Height: 6'1" Weight: 205 lb. Origin: Round 6, 2016 Draft (#175 overall)

YEAR	TEAM	LVL	AGE	W	L	SV	G	GS	IP	H	HR	BB/9	K/9	K	GB%	BABIP	WHIP	ERA	DRA-	WARP	MPH	FB%	Whiff%	CSP
2020	DET	MLB	25	2	1	4	26	0	21^2	18	0	4.2	5.0	12	42.9%	.257	1.29	1.66	127	-0.1	94.6	64.2%	20.1%	47.1%
2021	TOL	AAA	26	0	1	1	19	0	23^1	25	3	3.1	7.3	19	40.0%	.306	1.41	5.40	96	0.4				
2021	DET	MLB	26	3	2	2	39	0	39^1	48	10	5.7	7.3	32	35.3%	.314	1.86	7.55	146	-0.6	94.2	55.8%	22.8%	53.4%
2022	TOL	AAA	27	5	3	1	39	11	85^1	77	11	3.6	7.3	69	37.6%	.276	1.30	3.80	106	0.9				
2022	DET	MLB	27	2	0	0	4	4	20^1	14	3	4.4	7.5	17	42.6%	.216	1.18	3.54	112	0.1	93.0	49.4%	24.8%	57.5%
2023 DC	*FA*	*MLB*	*28*	*2*	*2*	*0*	*7*	*7*	*39.7*	*41*	*5*	*4.3*	*6.9*	*30*	*39.5%*	*.296*	*1.53*	*4.86*	*122*	*-0.1*	*93.9*	*55.1%*	*24.0%*	*53.4%*

Comparables: Justin De Fratus (58), Jimmy Yacabonis (57), Jonathan Holder (55)

This would be a great place to compile a list of Tigers pitchers who finished the season on the 60-day IL, except then there would be no room to talk about Garcia. His season perhaps says enough about the state of Detroit's rotation as it is. Six years after he was drafted, the Tigers handed Garcia his first-ever professional start, for Toledo. Less than three weeks later, he was starting in the majors against the Blue Jays. All things considered, it went reasonably well. Sure, he lost a tick off his already underwhelming fastball, was lucky to escape a six-walk game in his second start unscathed, and the peripherals were unkind. Nevertheless, he didn't get blown up, earned a couple of wins and, most importantly for this team, stayed healthy so they could call on him a couple more times for some much-needed turns. The Tigers used 17 starting pitchers in total, one fewer than the opener-happy Rays. One mark of a more-settled 2023 would be a shorter list.

Rony García RHP Born: 12/19/97 Age: 25 Bats: R Throws: R Height: 6'3" Weight: 200 lb. Origin: International Free Agent, 2015

YEAR	TEAM	LVL	AGE	W	L	SV	G	GS	IP	H	HR	BB/9	K/9	K	GB%	BABIP	WHIP	ERA	DRA-	WARP	MPH	FB%	Whiff%	CSP
2020	DET	MLB	22	1	0	0	15	2	21	25	7	3.9	6.0	14	34.2%	.273	1.62	8.14	151	-0.3	93.1	84.7%	20.0%	45.9%
2021	TOL	AAA	23	0	1	0	4	4	19^{2}	13	4	4.6	11.0	24	40.4%	.209	1.17	3.20	104	0.2				
2021	DET	MLB	23	0	0	0	2	0	3^{2}	1	1	4.9	4.9	2	25.0%	.000	0.82	2.45	103	0.0	92.1	60.7%	10.0%	56.1%
2022	DET	MLB	24	3	3	0	16	8	51	40	9	2.3	8.5	48	31.2%	.235	1.04	4.41	104	0.4	92.9	58.1%	21.7%	53.0%
2023 DC	*DET*	*MLB*	*25*	*2*	*2*	*0*	*49*	*0*	*42.7*	*42*	*6*	*3.6*	*7.7*	*36*	*34.6%*	*.287*	*1.40*	*4.63*	*120*	*-0.2*	*92.9*	*62.9%*	*22.7%*	*51.9%*

Comparables: Robert Stephenson (62), Gabriel Ynoa (62), Zack Littell (57)

A contender for weirdest wild pitch of the season came in mid-April: García unwittingly summed up how things were about to go for the Tigers when a cracked fingernail caused him to spike a delivery straight into the mound during a bullpen appearance. The ball bounced off toward first base, and García's season soon took an unexpected turn: He went from low-leverage innings to the rotation in a month as Detroit's staff fell victim to numerous injuries. The former Rule 5 pick battled through a series of starts, his heavy strike-throwing approach and underwhelming stuff proving an unsurprisingly poor combination given wider exposure. A shoulder injury felled him in late June, and he was able to make only one appearance in the final three months—a far more predictable development in the context of Detroit's season.

★ ★ ★ *2023 Top 101 Prospect* **#91** ★ ★ ★

Jackson Jobe RHP Born: 07/30/02 Age: 20 Bats: R Throws: R Height: 6'2" Weight: 190 lb. Origin: Round 1, 2021 Draft (#3 overall)

YEAR	TEAM	LVL	AGE	W	L	SV	G	GS	IP	H	HR	BB/9	K/9	K	GB%	BABIP	WHIP	ERA	DRA-	WARP	MPH	FB%	Whiff%	CSP
2022	LAK	A	19	2	5	0	18	18	61^{2}	59	12	3.6	10.4	71	40.2%	.299	1.36	4.52	103	0.9	94.7	58.9%	28.7%	
2022	WM	A+	19	2	0	0	3	3	15^{2}	10	2	2.9	5.7	10	40.4%	.178	0.96	1.15	115	0.0				
2023 non-DC	*DET*	*MLB*	*20*	*2*	*3*	*0*	*57*	*0*	*50*	*58*	*10*	*4.8*	*6.9*	*38*	*39.1%*	*.311*	*1.70*	*6.40*	*147*	*-1.0*			*22.9%*	

Comparables: Simeon Woods Richardson (75), Franklin Pérez (72), Francis Martes (69)

While they've largely made it to the bigs, Tigers first-round picks haven't contributed much to the major-league team in recent years, especially pitchers. Corey Knebel's success never came in a Detroit uniform, meaning that Nick Castellanos, a supplemental pick in 2010, was the only first-rounder to make a lasting impact for the Tigers since Rick Porcello (2007). The jury remains out on several others, including those who have reached the majors but are yet to fulfill that promise—Casey Mize and Spencer Torkelson. For much of the year, Jobe's first pro season didn't necessarily suggest he'd buck the trend, as he sported a 5.14 ERA and .811 OPS against at the end of July. The raw stuff was still there, however, with the slider often looking like a major league-quality out pitch; the work to boost his fastball spin rate paid off, too. The Tigers saw enough in his development to promote him to West Michigan for the final three starts of the year. The Justin Verlander bar is too high for anyone, but there are plenty of reasons to believe that Jobe can at least clear the Porcello threshold—a loftier aim than the Jacob Turner or Beau Burrows benchmarks.

Alex Lange RHP Born: 10/02/95 Age: 27 Bats: R Throws: R Height: 6'3" Weight: 202 lb. Origin: Round 1, 2017 Draft (#30 overall)

YEAR	TEAM	LVL	AGE	W	L	SV	G	GS	IP	H	HR	BB/9	K/9	K	GB%	BABIP	WHIP	ERA	DRA-	WARP	MPH	FB%	Whiff%	CSP
2021	TOL	AAA	25	2	1	1	19	0	21^{2}	22	0	7.1	11.2	27	33.9%	.393	1.80	4.57	95	0.4				
2021	DET	MLB	25	1	3	1	36	0	35^{2}	37	5	4.0	9.8	39	44.2%	.323	1.49	4.04	97	0.4	96.6	45.7%	32.1%	51.7%
2022	DET	MLB	26	7	4	0	71	0	63^{1}	48	5	4.4	11.7	82	54.2%	.295	1.25	3.69	68	1.7	96.3	31.7%	44.3%	49.0%
2023 DC	*DET*	*MLB*	*27*	*3*	*3*	*24*	*70*	*0*	*61*	*54*	*5*	*4.8*	*11.0*	*74*	*48.6%*	*.316*	*1.43*	*4.05*	*100*	*0.3*	*96.4*	*36.1%*	*36.2%*	*49.9%*

Comparables: Ryne Stanek (75), Josh Staumont (74), Ryan Cook (74)

Aside from a walk percentage with one more digit than you'd like, Lange's second campaign was exactly what the Tigers would've wanted to see. Trading his four-seam for an often violently swerving sinker and leaning heavily on his breaking ball, the 2017 first-rounder became a ground-ball machine with a healthy helping of whiffs. Both that breaker and his changeup made hitters miss on more than half of their swings, helping him to finish as a top-20 pitcher in DRA (among those with at least 50 frames). Curtailing the free passes could firmly establish Lange among the league's upper echelon of bullpen arms.

Zach Logue LHP Born: 04/23/96 Age: 27 Bats: L Throws: L Height: 6'0" Weight: 165 lb. Origin: Round 9, 2017 Draft (#279 overall)

YEAR	TEAM	LVL	AGE	W	L	SV	G	GS	IP	H	HR	BB/9	K/9	K	GB%	BABIP	WHIP	ERA	DRA-	WARP	MPH	FB%	Whiff%	CSP
2021	NH	AA	25	3	1	0	7	7	35^{2}	33	6	1.8	12.9	51	36.1%	.351	1.12	4.54	83	0.6				
2021	BUF	AAA	25	9	3	0	18	17	89^{1}	79	9	2.0	9.4	93	37.7%	.295	1.11	3.32	92	1.7				
2022	LV	AAA	26	3	6	0	17	17	78^{2}	119	25	4.3	6.8	59	32.1%	.370	2.00	8.12	151	-2.0	90.0	73.2%	19.5%	
2022	OAK	MLB	26	3	8	0	14	10	57	68	13	3.2	6.6	42	30.1%	.309	1.54	6.79	156	-1.1	89.8	70.6%	21.7%	53.8%
2023 DC	*DET*	*MLB*	*27*	*0*	*0*	*0*	*14*	*0*	*12*	*13*	*2*	*3.4*	*6.8*	*9*	*33.7%*	*.303*	*1.52*	*5.49*	*139*	*-0.2*	*89.8*	*70.6%*	*21.5%*	*53.8%*

Comparables: Dillon Peters (65), Pat Dean (62), Chris Rusin (61)

It takes real skill to succeed as an MLB starting pitcher with a 90-mph fastball. Veterans like Clayton Kershaw and Zack Greinke use their years of experience to mitigate their lack of cheese, out-thinking opposing hitters. Pitchers like Tyler Anderson and Corey Kluber limit mistakes, refusing to walk hitters and limiting their homers. Unicorns like Rich Hill and Kyle Hendricks spam their signature pitches, using these offerings to confound their opponents. Unfortunately, Logue hasn't yet found his niche. His 2022 debut was uninspiring, as he saw his minor-league strikeout rate dip considerably in the bigs, and buffeted four very solid starts with about half a dozen more that could charitably be described as "messy." Any pitcher who can get any big-leaguers out deserves respect, but Logue faces an uphill climb to become anything more than the least memorable part of the Matt Chapman trade.

Michael Lorenzen RHP Born: 01/04/92 Age: 31 Bats: R Throws: R Height: 6'3" Weight: 217 lb. Origin: Round 1, 2013 Draft (#38 overall)

YEAR	TEAM	LVL	AGE	W	L	SV	G	GS	IP	H	HR	BB/9	K/9	K	GB%	BABIP	WHIP	ERA	DRA-	WARP	MPH	FB%	Whiff%	CSP
2020	CIN	MLB	28	3	1	0	18	2	33^2	30	3	4.5	9.4	35	50.0%	.300	1.40	4.28	87	0.6	96.8	40.5%	35.5%	40.6%
2021	CIN	MLB	29	1	2	4	27	0	29	26	2	4.3	6.5	21	42.7%	.279	1.38	5.59	126	-0.1	96.6	36.2%	26.5%	52.3%
2022	IE	A	30	0	0	0	1	1	6	4	1	3.0	7.5	5	66.7%	.214	1.00	3.00	107	0.0				
2022	SL	AAA	30	0	2	0	2	2	6^2	10	2	2.7	10.8	8	22.7%	.400	1.80	10.80	110	0.0	94.4	35.9%	25.8%	
2022	LAA	MLB	30	8	6	0	18	18	97^2	81	11	4.1	7.8	85	50.7%	.262	1.28	4.24	100	0.9	94.5	44.0%	25.3%	52.2%
2023 DC	*DET*	*MLB*	*31*	*5*	*6*	*0*	*19*	*19*	*99*	*95*	*9*	*3.9*	*7.8*	*86*	*48.0%*	*.295*	*1.40*	*3.91*	*102*	*0.6*	*95.3*	*41.5%*	*25.8%*	*49.9%*

Comparables: Tyler Clippard (69), Kyle Farnsworth (66), C.J. Nitkowski (64)

Lorenzen wasn't shy about wanting a chance to start. The Angels, who in recent years have struggled to find enough men to do it, said they'd give him the chance. That made things a little awkward for GM Perry Minasian, who spent the spring telling fans that he was still looking for upgrades in the rotation, even though the newly signed Lorenzen was the most obvious choice to get bumped back to the bullpen if L.A. landed a bigger name. In the end, it all worked out...sort of. The Anaheim native did just fine in the fifth starter role until a shoulder injury took out a chunk of his summer. Meanwhile, the team got its best production out of the rotation in years, only to have offensive depth tank their season for a change. Even when healthy, Lorenzen struggled with his cutter in 2022 and largely shelved it to mix in more of his other four pitches. But given that he finished strong in his five post-injury starts and didn't show any discernible fatigue working into the middle innings, it looks like Lorenzen has earned himself another shot at starting, this time for the Tigers on another one-year deal.

Matt Manning RHP Born: 01/28/98 Age: 25 Bats: R Throws: R Height: 6'6" Weight: 195 lb. Origin: Round 1, 2016 Draft (#9 overall)

YEAR	TEAM	LVL	AGE	W	L	SV	G	GS	IP	H	HR	BB/9	K/9	K	GB%	BABIP	WHIP	ERA	DRA-	WARP	MPH	FB%	Whiff%	CSP
2021	TOL	AAA	23	1	3	0	7	7	32^1	40	11	2.8	10.0	36	34.7%	.337	1.55	8.07	110	0.3				
2021	DET	MLB	23	4	7	0	18	18	85^1	96	10	3.5	6.0	57	44.7%	.306	1.51	5.80	127	-0.4	93.7	60.8%	16.8%	57.7%
2022	TOL	AAA	24	1	1	0	6	6	20^1	19	0	4.4	10.2	23	47.2%	.358	1.43	2.66	93	0.3				
2022	DET	MLB	24	2	3	0	12	12	63	55	6	2.7	6.9	48	41.0%	.259	1.17	3.43	102	0.5	93.3	59.1%	22.4%	56.5%
2023 DC	*DET*	*MLB*	*25*	*7*	*9*	*0*	*25*	*25*	*134.7*	*143*	*15*	*3.5*	*6.9*	*103*	*43.2%*	*.303*	*1.45*	*4.39*	*114*	*0.2*	*93.5*	*60.0%*	*21.9%*	*57.1%*

Comparables: Jarred Cosart (70), Zach Eflin (69), Drew Hutchison (69)

Things that make you go mmmm: Manning's four-seam holding opponents to a sub-.200 average and .054 ISO. Things that make you go hmmm: the rest of the tall right-hander's pitches performing worse than his number one, in some cases considerably so. Double-M missed a large chunk of the year with a shoulder strain and, when he returned, had clearly dropped his arm slot compared to his debut season. It's not that he wasn't still getting swing and misses, with both slider and changeup drawing whiffs on more of a third of swings. Consistency was the issue, as both pitches plus his once-trusty curve wandered all over the zone. That shows up in his performances: six or seven frames of scoreless ball when the command was on, abbreviated more-walk-than-strikeout starts when it wasn't. Since a forearm strain also cut his season slightly short, it's fair to say Manning didn't have the ideal year for development. He's always gonna make someone sweat; whether it's opponents or Tigers fans depends on the command.

Casey Mize RHP Born: 05/01/97 Age: 26 Bats: R Throws: R Height: 6'3" Weight: 212 lb. Origin: Round 1, 2018 Draft (#1 overall)

YEAR	TEAM	LVL	AGE	W	L	SV	G	GS	IP	H	HR	BB/9	K/9	K	GB%	BABIP	WHIP	ERA	DRA-	WARP	MPH	FB%	Whiff%	CSP
2020	DET	MLB	23	0	3	0	7	7	28^1	29	7	4.1	8.3	26	38.2%	.268	1.48	6.99	118	0.0	93.1	72.0%	23.7%	44.7%
2021	DET	MLB	24	7	9	0	30	30	150^1	130	24	2.5	7.1	118	48.0%	.254	1.14	3.71	107	0.9	93.8	52.0%	22.7%	55.3%
2022	DET	MLB	25	0	1	0	2	2	10	13	1	1.8	3.6	4	35.9%	.316	1.50	5.40	121	0.0	94.0	50.9%	12.0%	57.1%
2023 DC	*DET*	*MLB*	*26*	*0*	*1*	*0*	*3*	*3*	*15*	*16*	*1*	*3.0*	*6.1*	*10*	*44.2%*	*.297*	*1.41*	*4.56*	*118*	*0.0*	*93.7*	*54.4%*	*21.3%*	*54.1%*

Comparables: Daniel Mengden (65), Kyle Drabek (64), Erik Johnson (63)

The competition for Most Disappointing Tiger in 2022 is fierce. Mize didn't pitch enough to rival some of his teammates' dismal on-field performances. Few players are more emblematic of Detroit's rebuild, however. Selected after a season in which the Tigers lost 98 games and while they were in the process of losing 98 more, Mize was some distant light at the end of a long tunnel, a polished college pitcher who was already accomplished enough that you could see him playing a key role in a competitive Tigers team by, say, his age-25 season. Two starts into said season, elbow discomfort sent Mize to the IL, from which he never returned. Although his UCL was never torn, further tests in June—after some failed rehab—revealed that Tommy John surgery would nevertheless be necessary, if Mize was to return to full strength. It's still not clear that Mize will be a significant member of the next good Tigers team, nor will he return until 2024, at the absolute earliest. That 2014 playoff appearance is starting to feel awfully long ago.

Daniel Norris LHP Born: 04/25/93 Age: 30 Bats: L Throws: L Height: 6'2" Weight: 207 lb. Origin: Round 2, 2011 Draft (#74 overall)

YEAR	TEAM	LVL	AGE	W	L	SV	G	GS	IP	H	HR	BB/9	K/9	K	GB%	BABIP	WHIP	ERA	DRA-	WARP	MPH	FB%	Whiff%	CSP
2020	DET	MLB	27	3	1	0	14	1	27^{2}	25	2	2.3	9.1	28	56.2%	.295	1.16	3.25	83	0.5	92.8	47.6%	27.6%	48.2%
2021	MIL	MLB	28	1	0	0	18	0	20^{1}	17	5	6.6	8.0	18	41.4%	.231	1.57	6.64	121	0.0	92.8	52.4%	25.7%	51.8%
2021	DET	MLB	28	1	3	1	38	0	36^{2}	38	4	3.7	9.8	40	49.0%	.354	1.45	5.89	92	0.5	93.0	44.6%	28.4%	55.6%
2022	TOL	AAA	29	0	0	0	3	3	8^{2}	5	0	2.1	5.2	5	30.8%	.192	0.81	2.08	119	0.0				
2022	DET	MLB	29	2	0	0	14	2	28^{2}	22	4	2.5	7.2	23	48.8%	.237	1.05	3.45	104	0.2	90.8	45.8%	28.9%	55.3%
2022	CHC	MLB	29	0	4	0	27	1	30	23	7	6.3	12.9	43	42.6%	.262	1.47	6.90	75	0.7	92.0	39.2%	33.7%	51.5%
2023 DC	*FA*	*MLB*	*30*	*2*	*2*	*0*	*50*	*0*	*43.7*	*38*	*5*	*3.7*	*10.1*	*49*	*44.1%*	*.297*	*1.30*	*3.61*	*95*	*0.3*	*91.9*	*46.3%*	*28.3%*	*52.2%*

Comparables: Randy Lerch (65), Ross Detwiler (60), Chuck Stobbs (59)

For someone whose whole vibe screams journeyman, Norris might have become unusually comfortable in Detroit. His first foray away from the Tigers, with the Brewers in July 2021, came six years to the day after the deadline day trade that brought him there. He couldn't keep the walks under control, there or with NL Central rivals Chicago—where he signed his first free agent deal, only to be designated for assignment before July was out. Just under a year after he left the organization, Detroit brought him back. By mid-August, he was back on their major-league roster. While he didn't stick in their makeshift rotation very long, he did look far more settled from a control perspective. Norris has never walked fewer than five batters per nine at any of his other major-league stops. With Detroit, he's below three.

Michael Pineda RHP Born: 01/18/89 Age: 34 Bats: R Throws: R Height: 6'7" Weight: 280 lb. Origin: International Free Agent, 2005

YEAR	TEAM	LVL	AGE	W	L	SV	G	GS	IP	H	HR	BB/9	K/9	K	GB%	BABIP	WHIP	ERA	DRA-	WARP	MPH	FB%	Whiff%	CSP
2020	MIN	MLB	31	2	0	0	5	5	26^{2}	25	0	2.4	8.4	25	37.2%	.321	1.20	3.38	95	0.4	92.3	50.1%	29.3%	47.1%
2021	MIN	MLB	32	9	8	0	22	21	109^{1}	114	17	1.7	7.2	88	39.5%	.297	1.23	3.62	110	0.5	90.8	54.1%	22.1%	56.8%
2022	TOL	AAA	33	1	2	0	7	6	25	30	2	1.8	7.6	21	36.2%	.359	1.40	4.68	107	0.2				
2022	DET	MLB	33	2	7	0	11	11	46^{2}	58	13	1.5	5.0	26	39.2%	.294	1.41	5.79	136	-0.4	90.2	59.2%	17.6%	59.1%
2023 non-DC	*DET*	*MLB*	*34*	*2*	*2*	*0*	*57*	*0*	*50*	*56*	*6*	*2.1*	*5.9*	*32*	*38.9%*	*.302*	*1.35*	*4.24*	*115*	*-0.2*	*91.1*	*55.4%*	*22.1%*	*55.1%*

Comparables: Aaron Sele (81), Joel Pineiro (79), Kevin Millwood (78)

On April 17, 2011, Pineda hurled a fastball 100.4 mph. Eleven years later, he sat 90 and had two starts where he wasn't even able to break the 91-mph barrier. To his credit, not many pitchers stick around long enough to lose double digits from their fastball. Unfortunately, Pineda isn't likely to stick around much longer to lose any more. For a while he made it work with the Tigers, between a broken finger and a triceps issue, keeping his team in the game in most starts until late July, when he had a sub-4.00 ERA. His final three outings—two prior to the triceps injury, one after—encompassed nine innings, five home runs and 15 earned runs in total. Detroit, ravaged as they were by other injuries, decided they'd rather take a look at their few remaining healthy arms than hand any more starts to Pineda. It's tough to envision a team emulating the Tigers and utilizing Pineda at the back of their rotation for some veteran presence, not least because his presence isn't all that reliable.

Eduardo Rodriguez LHP Born: 04/07/93 Age: 30 Bats: L Throws: L Height: 6'2" Weight: 231 lb. Origin: International Free Agent, 2010

YEAR	TEAM	LVL	AGE	W	L	SV	G	GS	IP	H	HR	BB/9	K/9	K	GB%	BABIP	WHIP	ERA	DRA-	WARP	MPH	FB%	Whiff%	CSP
2021	BOS	MLB	28	13	8	0	32	31	157^{2}	172	19	2.7	10.6	185	44.0%	.364	1.39	4.74	91	2.2	92.7	51.5%	26.4%	52.2%
2022	TOL	AAA	29	1	0	0	3	3	15	8	0	1.2	15.6	26	61.5%	.308	0.67	0.60	66	0.5				
2022	DET	MLB	29	5	5	0	17	17	91	87	12	3.4	7.1	72	42.8%	.279	1.33	4.05	117	0.1	92.0	55.1%	18.0%	52.2%
2023 DC	*DET*	*MLB*	*30*	*9*	*9*	*0*	*29*	*29*	*160.3*	*159*	*16*	*3.1*	*8.2*	*146*	*44.7%*	*.305*	*1.34*	*3.71*	*99*	*1.4*	*92.5*	*53.2%*	*22.7%*	*50.3%*

Comparables: Jon Lester (80), Johnny Podres (79), CC Sabathia (78)

One reason that optimism swirled around the Tigers prior to Opening Day was the signing of Rodriguez to a five-year, $77 million deal. It felt like a strong move to supplement a young core of Tigers pitching that carried much promise but lacked experience. Rodriguez had over 850 innings and 153 major-league starts to his name when he entered the season, including 30+ start campaigns in both 2019 and 2021. He added far less than the Tigers hoped to that total: A trip to the IL with a ribcage sprain turned into an extended, largely unexplained move to the restricted list, for what was vaguely described as family matters. After weeks of radio silence and uncertainty over whether he would return at all, Rodriguez got back in touch with the team and returned in late August after a rehab assignment. His uneven return can easily be attributed to his heavily interrupted season. Let's hope Rodriguez is in a better place personally, and what the Tigers were looking for may follow.

Elvin Rodriguez RHP Born: 03/31/98 Age: 25 Bats: R Throws: R Height: 6'3" Weight: 160 lb. Origin: International Free Agent, 2014

YEAR	TEAM	LVL	AGE	W	L	SV	G	GS	IP	H	HR	BB/9	K/9	K	GB%	BABIP	WHIP	ERA	DRA-	WARP	MPH	FB%	Whiff%	CSP
2021	ERI	AA	23	4	6	0	18	18	75^{2}	69	18	3.4	9.5	80	28.6%	.262	1.30	5.83	111	0.2				
2022	TOL	AAA	24	6	4	0	23	21	99^{1}	115	17	3.3	8.2	91	40.3%	.334	1.52	4.98	123	0.2				
2022	DET	MLB	24	0	4	0	7	5	29^{2}	42	12	4.6	7.6	25	35.3%	.333	1.92	10.62	129	-0.2	93.3	53.9%	16.9%	55.2%
2023 non-DC	*DET*	*MLB*	*25*	*2*	*3*	*0*	*57*	*0*	*50*	*55*	*8*	*3.9*	*6.6*	*36*	*36.3%*	*.297*	*1.54*	*5.43*	*137*	*-0.7*	*93.3*	*53.9%*	*21.4%*	*55.2%*

Comparables: Joe Ross (66), Chase De Jong (65), Paul Blackburn (65)

Rodriguez has a well-documented excuse for the 10 earned runs he allowed to the Yankees in early June: He was tipping his pitches. Anthony Rizzo confessed as much to Tucker Barnhart later in the same game, and a day later the event was thoroughly broken down by Jomboy on Twitter. Even as it became apparent that something was up, the pitching-starved Tigers let Rodriguez wear it for as long as they could. Maybe tipping was also the problem when he gave up eight runs the week after, or six on the final day of the season, or on any of the five occasions when he surrendered five or more runs in the minors. The pedestrian fastball, without workable secondaries to keep hitters off balance, might also have something to do with it. It would help if they didn't know what was coming, though.

Tarik Skubal LHP Born: 11/20/96 Age: 26 Bats: R Throws: L Height: 6'3" Weight: 240 lb. Origin: Round 9, 2018 Draft (#255 overall)

YEAR	TEAM	LVL	AGE	W	L	SV	G	GS	IP	H	HR	BB/9	K/9	K	GB%	BABIP	WHIP	ERA	DRA-	WARP	MPH	FB%	Whiff%	CSP
2020	DET	MLB	23	1	4	0	8	7	32	28	9	3.1	10.4	37	27.4%	.253	1.22	5.62	142	-0.3	94.5	60.1%	29.5%	46.4%
2021	DET	MLB	24	8	12	0	31	29	149^{1}	141	35	2.8	9.9	164	38.4%	.278	1.26	4.34	103	1.2	94.5	56.0%	26.9%	58.4%
2022	DET	MLB	25	7	8	0	21	21	117^{2}	104	9	2.4	8.9	117	46.2%	.301	1.16	3.52	92	1.6	94.6	48.0%	26.5%	56.7%
2023 DC	*DET*	*MLB*	*26*	*5*	*4*	*0*	*14*	*14*	*80*	*73*	*8*	*2.9*	*9.0*	*80*	*42.4%*	*.293*	*1.24*	*3.34*	*91*	*1.0*	*94.6*	*52.6%*	*27.0%*	*56.8%*

Comparables: Drew Smyly (69), José Quintana (68), Mike Minor (67)

Even as Detroit's season was bursting into flames around him, Skubal was evading the disasters that befell most of his teammates and single-handedly making a bid to rescue the Tigers rotation from total disappointment. Two months into the season, he had a 2.33 ERA and 70 strikeouts in 65⅔ frames, armed with a changeup that had enhanced bat-missing action and an increased focus on his hard slider. No good action movie comes without some genuine obstacles for the hero to overcome, and the young right-hander's started in June: His control began to waver and his old nemesis, the homer, emerged to wreak havoc. He appeared to be moving into the redemptive, victorious final act when arm fatigue took a dark turn into flexor tendon surgery, reminding us that this was just the 2022 Tigers—not an action movie at all. Although his final start came on August 1, Skubal still led the rotation in games started, innings pitched and WARP. Since he's unlikely to be ready for Opening Day, repeating as leader will either mean a total blockbuster of a season, or that the rest of the team has produced a sequel even worse than the original.

Spencer Turnbull RHP Born: 09/18/92 Age: 30 Bats: R Throws: R Height: 6'3" Weight: 210 lb. Origin: Round 2, 2014 Draft (#63 overall)

YEAR	TEAM	LVL	AGE	W	L	SV	G	GS	IP	H	HR	BB/9	K/9	K	GB%	BABIP	WHIP	ERA	DRA-	WARP	MPH	FB%	Whiff%	CSP
2020	DET	MLB	27	4	4	0	11	11	56^{2}	47	2	4.6	8.1	51	48.8%	.288	1.34	3.97	91	0.9	94.4	66.0%	28.3%	45.5%
2021	DET	MLB	28	4	2	0	9	9	50	37	2	2.2	7.9	44	57.1%	.255	0.98	2.88	92	0.7	94.5	60.5%	23.4%	54.4%
2023 DC	*DET*	*MLB*	*30*	*6*	*7*	*0*	*22*	*22*	*115.7*	*117*	*11*	*3.5*	*7.8*	*99*	*50.9%*	*.307*	*1.41*	*4.21*	*108*	*0.5*	*94.2*	*63.7%*	*24.8%*	*48.7%*

Comparables: Jimmy Nelson (67), Chris Bassitt (66), Anthony DeSclafani (63)

In late July, almost exactly a year after he underwent Tommy John surgery, the Tigers announced that Turnbull wouldn't make it back in 2022. A standard 14-month timeframe would have returned the righty in late September, and the incentive to do so at that point would merely have been to see him healthy on a mound. There is a theoretical situation in which, at some point in the not-too-distant future, the Tigers actually have to make some difficult decisions about who fits in the rotation—a puzzle they'd have to factor Turnbull into. It's a problem they'd desperately love to have after dealing with the reverse all season.

Will Vest RHP Born: 06/06/95 Age: 28 Bats: R Throws: R Height: 6'0" Weight: 180 lb. Origin: Round 12, 2017 Draft (#365 overall)

YEAR	TEAM	LVL	AGE	W	L	SV	G	GS	IP	H	HR	BB/9	K/9	K	GB%	BABIP	WHIP	ERA	DRA-	WARP	MPH	FB%	Whiff%	CSP
2021	TOL	AAA	26	1	3	2	23	0	25^{2}	27	3	2.8	8.8	25	52.6%	.333	1.36	4.91	85	0.5				
2021	SEA	MLB	26	1	0	0	32	0	35	38	2	4.6	6.9	27	39.8%	.343	1.60	6.17	122	-0.1	93.7	56.9%	22.8%	54.2%
2022	DET	MLB	27	3	3	1	59	2	63	62	6	3.1	9.0	63	49.2%	.320	1.33	4.00	87	1.0	95.3	56.3%	23.8%	56.3%
2023 DC	*DET*	*MLB*	*28*	*3*	*3*	*3*	*70*	*0*	*61*	*62*	*6*	*3.7*	*8.3*	*56*	*47.9%*	*.313*	*1.44*	*4.30*	*109*	*0.0*	*94.8*	*56.5%*	*24.3%*	*55.7%*

Comparables: Dean Kiekhefer (68), Tim Peterson (68), Jimmy Cordero (65)

Are you ready to read about a nice, positive season? Vest, simply put, got better. He threw harder and improved his slider location. He struck more batters out and walked fewer. He recorded his first save and welcomed his first child to the world. He was a steady, reliable presence in the middle of the Tigers bullpen. It was essentially the kind of typical improvement you'd like to see from a player as they gain experience in the majors. That's it. Nothing alarming or depressing. No, really.

Joey Wentz LHP Born: 10/06/97 Age: 25 Bats: L Throws: L Height: 6'5" Weight: 220 lb. Origin: Round 1, 2016 Draft (#40 overall)

YEAR	TEAM	LVL	AGE	W	L	SV	G	GS	IP	H	HR	BB/9	K/9	K	GB%	BABIP	WHIP	ERA	DRA-	WARP	MPH	FB%	Whiff%	CSP
2021	LAK	A	23	0	3	0	5	5	18^{2}	23	5	3.9	11.6	24	34.6%	.383	1.66	6.75	110	0.1				
2021	ERI	AA	23	0	4	0	13	13	53^{1}	41	7	5.6	9.8	58	33.3%	.256	1.39	3.71	109	0.2				
2022	TOL	AAA	24	2	2	0	12	11	48^{1}	37	6	3.7	9.9	53	39.3%	.267	1.18	3.17	86	1.0				
2022	DET	MLB	24	2	2	0	7	7	32^{2}	23	2	3.6	7.4	27	40.4%	.228	1.10	3.03	111	0.1	92.0	77.0%	21.4%	53.9%
2023 DC	*DET*	*MLB*	*25*	*4*	*5*	*0*	*26*	*12*	*67.7*	*66*	*9*	*4.6*	*8.2*	*61*	*38.5%*	*.289*	*1.48*	*4.57*	*116*	*0.0*	*92.0*	*77.0%*	*24.3%*	*53.9%*

Comparables: Danny Duffy (63), Adalberto Mejía (61), Chris Archer (61)

When it comes to Promotions That Preceded Unfortunate Events, only former British Prime Minister Liz Truss can rival Wentz on the 2022 shortlist. The Tigers prospect was lit up by the notoriously lifeless bats of the Oakland Athletics in his debut, allowing six runs while recording a paltry eight outs. Wentz didn't let his disastrous debut bother him. After being sent back to the minors and dealing with a shoulder injury that kept him out until late July, he allowed only four runs over his next seven outings. He then returned to the majors and surrendered just five more earned runs over his final five starts. To underline the point, he took the opportunity of extra innings in the AFL to allow only six baserunners to reach over 12 scoreless frames. Too many walks and the lack of a standout secondary threaten to limit his ceiling, although a new cutter provides an intriguing alternative—one that offers more promise than Truss' economic plans.

Lineouts

Hitters

HITTER	POS	TEAM	LVL	AGE	PA	R	2B	3B	HR	RBI	BB	K	SB	CS	AVG/OBP/SLG	DRC+	BABIP	BRR	DRP	WARP
Roberto Campos	OF	LAK	A	19	448	52	26	5	5	50	40	97	7	3	.258/.326/.385	93	.326	1.6	CF(67): -6.0, RF(28): -1.6, LF(8): -0.4	0.3
Samuel Gil	SS	DSL TIG2	ROK	17	193	32	10	2	2	26	25	33	7	0	.255/.363/.376		.308			
Peyton Graham	SS	LAK	A	21	113	19	5	1	1	13	10	29	7	1	.270/.345/.370	92	.366	2.9	SS(14): 2.7, 2B(5): 0.7, 3B(2): 0.6	0.9
Andy Ibáñez	IF	RR	AAA	29	315	38	18	1	6	31	28	48	5	2	.255/.330/.390	95	.288	-3.5	1B(31): 0.4, 3B(27): -2.0, 2B(3): -0.0	0.2
	IF	TEX	MLB	29	128	13	4	0	1	9	9	21	3	0	.218/.273/.277	96	.258	-0.3	3B(25): -1.2, 1B(6): 0.2, 2B(2): 0.2	0.1
Ryan Kreidler	IF	TOL	AAA	24	250	29	12	2	8	22	36	72	15	1	.213/.352/.411	90	.280	0.8	SS(26): 3.6, 2B(12): 0.6, 3B(11): -0.4	0.9
	IF	DET	MLB	24	84	8	1	0	1	6	6	22	0	1	.178/.244/.233	79	.231	0.6	3B(13): 0.3, SS(13): -0.7, 2B(2): 0	0.0
Andre Lipcius	3B/2B	ERI	AA	24	372	52	20	1	9	39	61	56	12	1	.264/.392/.426	128	.295	-1.2	3B(61): -0.7, 2B(14): 0.6, 1B(1): 0.2	2.1
	3B/2B	TOL	AAA	24	188	18	13	1	3	24	25	33	1	3	.302/.388/.453	108	.354	0.5	3B(25): -1.4, 2B(20): -0.2	0.6
Tyler Nevin	CI	NOR	AAA	25	191	30	8	1	7	36	21	36	4	0	.291/.382/.479	115	.333	0.2	3B(25): 0.1, 1B(15): -0.1, RF(4): -0.3	0.8
	CI	BAL	MLB	25	184	17	4	0	2	16	20	46	0	0	.197/.299/.261	85	.259	-0.8	3B(44): -2, 1B(8): -0.2, LF(2): 0	-0.2
Javier Osorio	SS	DSL TIG1	ROK	17	178	17	5	0	1	12	16	68	15	3	.175/.281/.227		.302			
Izaac Pacheco	3B	LAK	A	19	371	54	21	2	8	39	38	80	12	4	.267/.342/.415	103	.328	-0.3	3B(63): 5.6, SS(18): 1.5	1.9
	3B	WM	A+	19	73	9	2	0	3	13	9	17	0	1	.183/.274/.367	103	.182	-0.3	3B(15): -0.8, SS(2): -0.4	0.1
Jermaine Palacios	IF	STP	AAA	25	428	70	28	0	14	60	34	102	12	9	.283/.341/.462	92	.350	0.2	SS(56): -2.2, 3B(33): 1.6, LF(6): 0.1	0.9
	IF	MIN	MLB	25	77	8	0	0	2	6	4	27	0	0	.143/.184/.229	72	.186	-0.4	SS(14): -0.8, 2B(12): -0.6	-0.2
Michael Papierski	C	SUG	AAA	26	108	12	3	0	1	15	14	9	0	0	.211/.324/.278	117	.220	-1.2	C(11): -1.1, 1B(9): -0.5	0.3
	C	SAC	AAA	26	57	5	2	0	2	13	3	18	0	0	.208/.246/.358	88	.265	-0.1	C(11): 0.9, 1B(2): -0.3	0.1
	C	LOU	AAA	26	57	6	2	0	3	13	9	12	0	0	.298/.421/.532	119	.344	-1.0	C(16): -0.1	0.1
	C	CIN	MLB	26	93	6	1	0	1	4	9	22	0	0	.159/.242/.207	83	.203	-0.7	C(34): 0	0.1
	C	SF	MLB	26	10	1	0	0	0	0	1	4	0	0	.000/.100/.000	83			C(4): 0.1, 1B(1): -0.0	0.0
Wenceel Perez	2B/DH	WM	A+	22	236	35	13	5	9	38	27	38	13	1	.286/.364/.529	138	.309	0.1	2B(30): 0.2, 3B(7): 0.2	1.8
	2B/DH	ERI	AA	22	171	28	10	5	5	28	15	23	5	4	.307/.374/.540	128	.328	-0.2	2B(30): -1.1	0.9
Donny Sands	C/DH	LHV	AAA	26	242	41	9	0	5	34	38	44	1	0	.308/.413/.428	126	.368	-0.2	C(35): 0.5, 1B(1): -0.2	1.4
	C/DH	PHI	MLB	26	4	0	0	0	0	0	1	1	0	0	.000/.250/.000	88		0.0		0.0
Cristian Santana	IF	LAK	A	18	340	52	13	0	9	30	54	88	10	5	.215/.379/.366	109	.281	0.7	SS(34): -2.5, 2B(29): 0.7, 3B(11): 0.1	1.2
Zack Short	SS	TOL	AAA	27	559	79	31	1	11	60	88	149	11	5	.229/.355/.373	96	.308	0.4	SS(87): 5.6, 2B(15): 0.1, LF(4): 0.9	2.0
	SS	DET	MLB	27	13	2	0	0	0	2	2	5	1	0	.000/.154/.000	84		0.3	SS(4): 0.4, 2B(2): 0.4	0.1

The long-awaited full-season debut of **Roberto Campos** didn't produce the gaudiest numbers. He did flash his power promise on a wider stage, with an opposite-field blast in a spring training win, and—as one of the youngest players in the Florida State League—performed more than well enough to maintain the prospect intrigue going forward. ⚾ The second seven-figure shortstop of the Tigers' January 2022 class, and one of three Venezuelans, **Samuel Gil** displayed a mature approach in the DSL that was commensurate with his reputation as an advanced, intelligent ballplayer/teenager. ⚾ Detroit's efforts to move out of their rebuild phase as rapidly as possible extended to the draft, where they exclusively selected college hitters. Overslot selection **Peyton Graham** was one of the higher-rated college bats, but underwhelming contact rates in A-ball may cause the Tigers to think twice about moving him quickly. ⚾ Nominally a bat-first second baseman, **Andy Ibáñez** couldn't hit and appeared most often at third base in 2022, where his glove was mediocre. His ugly season earned him a ride on the waiver wire, where the Tigers picked him up in early November. ⚾ A surprising offensive outburst in 2021 from **Ryan Kreidler** now looks more like a case of the boy who cried breakout: His bat slipped back to mediocre at Toledo, and proved almost non-existent under the scrutiny of the majors. ⚾ By walking almost as often as he struck out, making a ton of contact and taking reps at all four infield positions, **Andre Lipcius** proved he has the kind of approach and versatility that will earn him big-league opportunities in the very near future. ⚾ Phil Nevin played first and third and had a career slugging percentage of .472, with 208 home runs. His son **Tyler Nevin** plays first and third too, but his career slugging percentage (.292) and home run total (three) aren't quite there yet. He's rapidly becoming a corner bat who doesn't hit like a corner bat, and he's out of minor-league options. Thus it came as no surprise when he was removed from the Orioles' 40-man roster over the offseason to make room for James McCann —given McCann's recent performance, not an encouraging sign for his chances of catching up to dad. ⚾ Detroit's top international signing of the period ending January 2022, **Javier Osorio** has a frame that promises more power and a strong arm, with the glove to stick at shortstop—or at least to provide more confidence on the latter front than the average 17-year-old. ⚾ **Izaac Pacheco** graduated to High-A as a 19-year-old, part of an impressive first full pro campaign. The initial transition was a challenge, but his growing power—and the gains he's already made with his approach—suggest Tigers fans can continue to hope he's their third baseman of the future. ⚾ No major leaguer has ever gone a single month of at least 35 plate appearances without recording a hit. Fringy utilityman **Jermaine Palacios** started September hitless in his first 36 before ruining his chance at history with three hits in the final game of the month. ⚾ Have catching equipment, will travel. Last season, **Michael Papierski** got traded to the Giants to fill in for Joey Bart and within six weeks was claimed off waivers by the Reds to fill in for Tyler Stephenson; he was claimed again by Detroit in October. This is the exact type of transaction chain our sabermetric forefathers conceived of when coming up with the concept of "replacement level." ⚾ Patience paid off for both **Wenceel Perez** backers and the Dominican infielder, who turned some of his long-observed offensive promise into genuine production with significant improvements to his approach. ⚾ **Donny Sands** deserves a shot at a major-league job, but the sands of playing time weren't kind to him in 2022. He had a career year at Triple-A but was blocked at the major-league level. He has a better shot in Detroit, where J.T. Realmuto doesn't play. ⚾ Not content with making dueling Wilmer Floreses a possibility, the Tigers are now working on confronting us with more than one **Cristian Santana**. Detroit's version is seven years the junior of the Reds farmhand, however, and given that he handled an aggressive full-season assignment with relative maturity, might have a better shot at an extended major-league career. ⚾ Another year, another comment befitting **Zack Short**'s name. Beyond his walk rate, at Triple-A he gave the Tigers few reasons to give him a longer look in the majors, and the odds are against him extending the length of this comment in the future.

Pitchers

PITCHER	TEAM	LVL	AGE	W	L	SV	G	GS	IP	H	HR	BB/9	K/9	K	GB%	BABIP	WHIP	ERA	DRA-	WARP	MPH	FB%	WHF	CSP
Luis Castillo	TOL	AAA	27	4	1	0	40	0	41^{1}	39	2	2.4	8.5	39	50.9%	.327	1.21	1.74	88	0.8				
	DET	MLB	27	0	0	0	3	0	3^{2}	2	0	0.0	9.8	4	70.0%	.200	0.55	0.00	92	0.1	93.8	53.3%	22.6%	48.0%
José Cisnero	TOL	AAA	33	1	0	0	6	0	5^{2}	3	0	1.6	9.5	6	50.0%	.214	0.71	3.18	91	0.1				
	DET	MLB	33	1	0	0	28	0	25	15	0	6.8	8.3	23	37.1%	.242	1.36	1.08	105	0.2	95.6	67.9%	28.9%	53.3%
Angel De Jesus	TOL	AAA	25	5	1	1	44	0	47^{2}	34	4	3.8	8.3	44	38.6%	.234	1.13	4.15	104	0.6				
	DET	MLB	25	0	0	0	8	0	12^{2}	9	2	2.8	5.0	7	36.6%	.179	1.03	2.13	109	0.1	94.6	54.9%	19.8%	59.4%
Garrett Hill	ERI	AA	26	2	0	0	7	7	32	19	3	2.8	14.6	52	33.9%	.271	0.91	2.25	81	0.7				
	TOL	AAA	26	2	2	0	8	8	37^{2}	31	4	3.6	11.0	46	31.2%	.293	1.22	4.06	99	0.5				
	DET	MLB	26	3	3	0	17	8	60^{1}	53	8	4.3	6.0	40	34.7%	.247	1.36	4.03	134	-0.5	92.0	59.3%	19.7%	55.4%
Ty Madden	WM	A+	22	6	4	0	19	19	87	69	10	2.7	8.7	84	32.1%	.254	1.09	3.10	123	-0.2				
	ERI	AA	22	2	2	0	7	7	35^{2}	28	6	3.0	12.4	49	46.9%	.293	1.12	2.78	72	1.0				
Tyler Mattison	TIG	ROK	22	0	1	1	3	1	7	4	0	2.6	10.3	8	43.8%	.250	0.86	1.29						
	LAK	A	22	7	0	1	24	0	32^{2}	25	2	4.7	12.7	46	39.2%	.319	1.29	5.23	83	0.8	94.5	75.8%	33.1%	
Reese Olson	ERI	AA	22	8	6	0	26	25	119^{2}	109	15	2.9	12.6	168	42.1%	.337	1.23	4.14	70	3.4				
Wily Peralta	TOL	AAA	33	0	0	1	5	0	5^{1}	7	0	5.1	13.5	8	40.0%	.467	1.88	3.38	91	0.1				
	DET	MLB	33	2	0	0	28	1	38^{1}	34	2	5.6	7.5	32	45.9%	.294	1.51	2.58	113	0.1	95.6	49.4%	21.4%	55.4%
Dylan Smith	WM	A+	22	8	6	0	20	19	83^{1}	78	6	2.3	9.3	86	43.5%	.312	1.19	4.00	102	0.7				
Brendan White	ERI	AA	23	6	5	9	48	0	67^{1}	44	3	2.3	9.8	73	55.6%	.246	0.91	2.67	86	1.4				

One benefit of a book is that you can't look at this **Luis Castillo** comment and suddenly find you're reading about the Mariners ace. This Castillo has a ways to go to match the other's name recognition, but the minor-league signing was one of Toledo's best relievers and earned a much-deserved cup of coffee. ⚾ **José Cisnero** recorded the lowest ERA in major-league history among pitchers who threw at least 25 innings and walked more than six batters per nine. It's possible that this approach isn't sustainable. ⚾ Watching **Angel De Jesus** pitch did not qualify as a religious experience, unless you worship at Our Righty of Inconsistent Command. His strikeout advantage has steadily waned as he's faced more competent hitters, and the punchouts almost disappeared altogether at the highest level. ⚾ **Kyle Funkhouser** never got an opportunity to find his rhythm after a shoulder injury kept him off the Opening Day roster and ultimately required surgery in late July. ⚾ **Sean Guenther** was a control artist during his time in the minors, throwing 69% of his pitches for strikes. His sweeper was potent enough to overwhelm hitters through Triple-A, but his middling fastball shape and velocity portend continued struggles given more major-league time—unless it ceases to be his primary pitch. ⚾ If only he could / Get a few more whiffs / He might be a back-end starter / He's throwing ninety-two / His name is **Garrett Hill** / He's running up that walk rate. ⚾ **Tanner Kohlhepp** was busy giving opponents fits with his whippy side-arm delivery in spring training—until a forearm injury delayed his start to the season. That turned out to be a torn UCL, meaning he'll have to wait until mid-2023 to test out that delivery in his first pro games. ⚾ Once considered a 95-and-a-slider guy, **Ty Madden** has rapidly transitioned to a five-pitch arsenal and addressed a lot of the concerns over whether he could stick in the rotation. Testing that repertoire over a larger sample at the upper levels is next—but judging by his first seven Double-A outings, it's going to play. ⚾ Bryant University alum **Tyler Mattison** shifted to relief, and used his high fastball and developing changeup to punch out a third of batters he faced in A-ball. He kept it up throughout the AFL, all the way to the Fall Stars Game. ⚾ Al Avila is not going to be remembered particularly fondly by a Tigers fanbase that was more than ready for the rebuild to end, rather than shift into a new and stranger phase. Getting **Reese Olson** in exchange for a couple of months of Daniel Norris might be one redeeming transaction—the righty started dominating with his curveball and slider, striking out nearly one in three batters he saw. ⚾ He may still have little idea of where the ball is going, but **Wily Peralta** remained effective at keeping runs off the board with his atypically balanced pitch distribution. In the end, it was not his performance that counted against him so much as his age, as the Tigers moved into "evaluating for the future" mode. ⚾ A back injury interrupted **Dylan Smith**'s debut pro season for a month; it may also have given him the reset he needed after a miserable June. There's work to do on the back end of his arsenal, but his 2.74 ERA and 69:13 strikeout-to-walk ratio outside of June speaks to the upside. ⚾ In a bullpen that currently rosters three Rule 5 picks (two taken, one returned), it's not hard to imagine **Brendan White** finding his way into regular work. He's a certified personal trainer with a deep interest in biomechanics, and happened to stumble into a high-spin slider that looks capable of drawing chases at the major-league level.

KANSAS CITY ROYALS

Essay by Daniel R. Epstein

Player comments by Nathan Graham, Matt Sussman and BP staff

When does one era end and a new one begin? Sometimes there are neon signs heralding the shift, such as a handful of massive free-agent signings or metamorphic trades. Other times, the signpost is hidden in the foliage. We speed right past it none the wiser, only acknowledging the pivot point in retrospect years later.

The end of the "Holy Crap, We Won the World Series!" Era in Kansas City was impossible to miss. The Lorenzo Cain/Eric Hosmer/Mike Moustakas core and exceptional bullpen pieces had all departed by mid-2018, turning the franchise over to Whit Merrifield, Salvador Perez and a mostly replacement-level supporting cast.

It's that post-championship stretch—the Merrifield Era, as we'll call it—that's only recently concluded, and in a manner far more subtle. Those years were defined by quaint small ball and roster decisions revealing an out-of-touch front office that had been lapped several times by their forward-thinking rivals.

Merrifield's trade to Toronto on August 2 wasn't an obvious era-shifting moment, but in moving on from their front man, the Royals turned the page on the type of baseball he exemplified. He was the archetype for a speedy, scrappy, no-days-off, outdated style of play. Beyond that, his trade signaled that clinging to an unproductive fan favorite to shill tragicomic nostalgia was no longer more important than winning.

The Royals appear on the precipice of something new—or at least something foreign to Kansas City baseball: A revamped, modern coaching staff that can lead a new wave of young talent with a contemporary approach to the game. It's a sea change in philosophy signifying a renaissance for an organization that too often seemed left in the analytical dark ages. Perhaps the best way to understand the Royals right now is through several distinct changes that, as a whole, signal an organization on the brink of something entirely different—and hopefully better.

⚾ ⚾ ⚾

KANSAS CITY ROYALS PROSPECTUS

2022 W-L: 65-97, 5th in AL Central

Pythag	.391	*26th*	DER	.678	*30th*
RS/G	3.95	*24th*	DRC+	95	*23rd*
RA/G	5.00	*26th*	DRA-	110	*27th*
dWin%	.436	*24th*	FIP	4.42	*27th*
Payroll	$95M	*23rd*	B-Age	27.6	*5th*
M$/MW	$4.5M	*18th*	P-Age	27.8	*5th*

410′
387′ 387′
330′ 330′

- Opened 1973
- Open air
- Natural surface
- Fence profile: 9′ to 11′

Park Factors

Runs	Runs/RH	Runs/LH	HR/RH	HR/LH
97	98	97	77	79

Top Hitter WARP	2.0 Bobby Witt Jr.
Top Pitcher WARP	2.9 Brady Singer
2023 Top Prospect	Gavin Cross

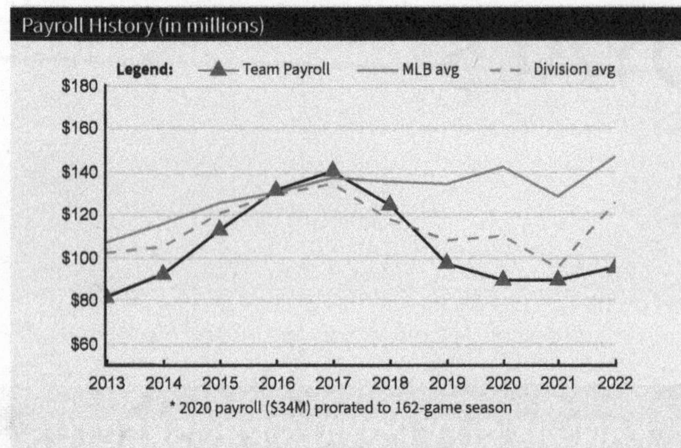

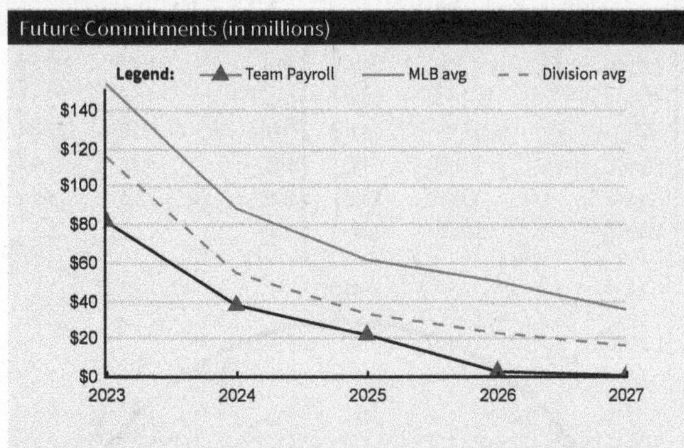

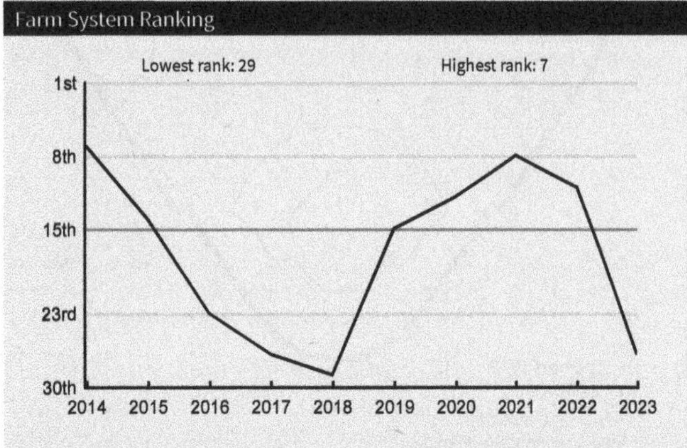

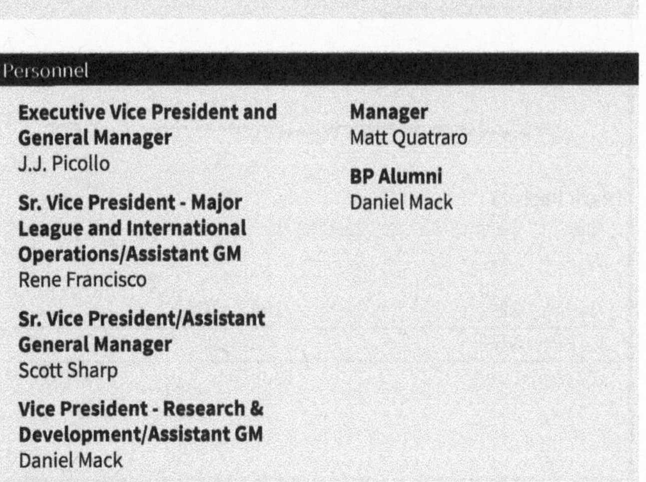
Personnel

Executive Vice President and General Manager
J.J. Picollo

Sr. Vice President - Major League and International Operations/Assistant GM
Rene Francisco

Sr. Vice President/Assistant General Manager
Scott Sharp

Vice President - Research & Development/Assistant GM
Daniel Mack

Manager
Matt Quatraro

BP Alumni
Daniel Mack

"Most teams have the same amount of data. It's a matter of opening up the lines of communication between field staff, front office, R&D, strength and conditioning, everybody."

When Matt Quatraro made that statement in his first press conference as the newly hired manager on November 3, it felt as though the Royals jumped forward two decades.

Every manager in franchise history, all the way through Mike Matheny, seemed to be chasing the hit-and-run ghosts of Cookie Rojas and Willie Wilson. Using data to inform coaching and in-game managerial decisions has never been a given in Kansas City, but Quatraro previously served as bench coach for the Tampa Bay Rays, the model of a cutting-edge, low-payroll organization. On his first day on the job, he announced that not only are they going to make the most of the data they have (of course they are, doesn't everybody?), but also implied he's at the forefront of one of the next frontiers in analytics: fostering communication throughout the organization, and approaching coaching as an exercise in teaching and managing relationships.

Quatraro isn't the only decision-maker from a savvy franchise that the Royals imported this winter. They replaced embattled pitching coach Cal Eldred with Brian Sweeney from the Cleveland Guardians and Zach Bove from the Minnesota Twins. Both have a reputation for meticulous research, using as much data and video as they can acquire to make analytically informed coaching recommendations. Sweeney in particular can point to a record of working with pitching-forward playoff teams since 2018. Just as important as their analytical acumen, both also have reputations as outstanding communicators. The more the players can understand and buy into what the data says, the more they can maximize their ability.

Not everyone is new, though. General manager J.J. Picollo took over for longtime shot-caller Dayton Moore in September. He was long Moore's understudy and has been a Royals employee since 2006. But organizational balance has some value as well—too many internal promotions and it can be hard to keep up with the league; too many external hires and the franchise loses its soul. Quatraro made it clear that communication is tantamount to success; as such, keeping some of the pre-established relationships between the front office, the players and the community makes sense.

And so the franchise has (mostly) cleaned house this offseason, assembling a new coaching staff with excellent credentials as analysts and communicators. It remains to be seen how they'll make their mark, and Picollo still needs to prove he's more than just Moore's flunky.

But at least Quatraro nailed the introductory presser. That's a good start.

⚾ ⚾ ⚾

Over the past few years, we've all learned the importance of taking a sick day when we're under the weather. It's not just about oneself; it's about the germs we bring to work and spread to those around us. When professional athletes take the field at less than 100%, their performance isn't contagious like a virus, but it still affects their coworkers.

Ballplayers benefit from a game off here and there to help their bodies recover from the rigors of playing nearly every day from April through September. Most organizations believe that an elite player can be more productive playing 155 games than 162.

But for a long time, the Royals weren't one of them. From 2016-2021, there were 22 players in MLB who participated in all 162 games in a season. Six of them were Royals, and that doesn't even include Perez's 2021 season in which he set a record for someone who primarily plays catcher by appearing in 161 games.

Seasons with 162 Games Played	WARP	Following Seasons' Total Games Played	Following Season's WARP
2016 Alcides Escobar	1.2	162	1.6
2017 Alcides Escobar	1.6	140	-0.4
2017 Eric Hosmer	3.0	157	0.1
2019 Whit Merrifield	3.0	60*	1.4*
2019 Jorge Soler	4.4	43*	0.0*
2021 Whit Merrifield	4.1	139	1.5

**Pandemic-shortened 60-game season*

The streak of 553 consecutive games from Merrifield was the longest in MLB since Miguel Tejada's 1,152-game streak terminated in 2007. If he hadn't hurt his toe, which finally caused him to miss a start, Merrifield would have lost the streak anyway just a few days later: He was one of 10 unvaccinated Royals[1] forbidden from entering Canada for the Blue Jays series from July 14-16. Ironically, the Royals later traded him to the Jays in August, which apparently compelled Merrifield to get his shots. Perhaps he believed it simply wasn't worthwhile to get the COVID-19 vaccine for a sub-.500 Royals team? Using that as the criterion for an important health decision feels like bunting with a runner on second and one out, but it's tough to view his about-face any other way.

Merrifield's motives aside, the top active games-played streak on the Royals now belongs to MJ Melendez, who has played in a modest 31 straight. Bobby Witt Jr., meanwhile, led the team with "only" 150 games played last season. It seems that the Royals no longer perceive playing every single day to be as important or beneficial long-term as playing at the highest possible level most of the time—but not all the time. In other words, the organization has finally discovered what the rest of MLB already knew.

⚾ ⚾ ⚾

The sea changes to the coaching staff and front office are just now underway, but there's an on-field transformation already in progress. The Royals' average age was 27.2 years last season, which was the second-youngest roster in MLB and the youngest in Kansas City since 2012. Appropriately, the youngest player on the team is already the face of the franchise.

On May 2, the Royals lost to the Cardinals 1-0 and Bobby Witt Jr. was pressing. He beat out an infield single in his first plate appearance of the day, though a soft grounder to shortstop was hardly worth celebrating. With a runner on second and two outs in the fourth, he hit a weak infield popup on a middle-middle curveball to end the inning. Then he struck out swinging in the seventh. His slash line read .221/.250/.312 and he still had no home runs.

Witt was the foremost prospect not just in the Royals system, but in all of affiliated baseball, having earned Baseball Prospectus' top overall ranking prior to the 2022 season. There were no weaknesses in his scouting report whatsoever—he made lots of contact, hit the ball hard, kept a low ground-ball rate, stole bases and played solid defense at shortstop. The team believed in him enough to start him at third base as a 21-year-old on Opening Day.

Witt was the centerpiece of a rebuilding farm system that had previously cratered to rank 29th in baseball in 2018, per BP's experts. In 2023, the system is on the decline again, but graduations are now the primary culprit. Last year, six of their top-10 preseason prospects exhausted their rookie eligibility: Witt (no. 1), Melendez (2), Nick Pratto (3), Kyle Isbel (7), Vinnie Pasquantino (8) and Jackson Kowar (9). Not all of them excelled—Kowar and Pratto failed to stick in the majors—but others met or surpassed expectations, including Drew Waters, who ranked eighth on Atlanta's preseason top-10 list.

Kansas City had not let young players drive the direction of the franchise in many years, not necessarily because they refused to hand them the keys, but because there weren't any capable drivers. They didn't have a single player on BP's 2017 Top 101 Prospects list. In 2018, their only ranked prospect was no. 75 Seuly Matias. Prior to Witt, their last prospect in the top-10 overall was no. 7 Mike Moustakas way back in 2011.

The day after their 1-0 loss to the Cardinals, St. Louis starter Dakota Hudson threw Witt an 88-mph changeup diving down and out of the strike zone, but the young superstar-in-waiting clobbered it 417 feet into the Kauffman Stadium stands. He didn't win Rookie of the Year, as many predicted he might, but he did post a better-than-average barrel rate (8.7%), hard-hit rate (38.7%) and contact rate (77.4%), while his 30.4 ft/s sprint speed tied for second-best in MLB. It was a commendable 2.0-WARP rookie campaign that portends better days to come, and the youth movement he spearheads remains as promising as any in Kansas City in at least ten years.

⚾ ⚾ ⚾

Playing youth for youth's sake isn't enough to take the Royals northward in the AL Central standings. The young players they employ must prove themselves capable of playing a different, better brand of baseball.

To that end, if Nicky Lopez and Adalberto Mondesi are Formula One race cars, Vinnie Pasquantino is the food truck in the parking lot. His speed grade on the 20–80 scouting scale is on par with his belt size. Playing him at first base is like texting your ex at 2 a.m.—just because you can do it doesn't mean it's a good idea. Yet after just 72 games in the majors, he's unquestionably a cornerstone of the franchise.

Pasquantino is the least Royals-esque player the team has had in recent memory. He became the first Kansas City hitter with more walks than strikeouts in a season since Alberto Callaspo and Coco Crisp in 2009 (min. 100 PA).[2] The franchise has historically never been known for producing sluggers—no Royal authored a 40-homer season until Jorge Soler in 2019—but in his rookie year, Pasquantino's 46.9% hard-hit rate ranked in the 84th percentile. What's more, 22.2% of his swings resulted in a >95-mph batted ball, which was fourth-best in MLB.

Even during the slash-and-dash 1970s, it wasn't usually Frank White or Freddie Patek sparking the offense. If Witt hopes to play the part of George Brett in the reenactment of the Royals' halcyon days, Pasquantino is John Mayberry—the mashing 1B/DH who led the AL in walks twice and OBP once. That role had been vacant for the duration of the Merrifield Era, as indicated by the Royals' MLB rankings in home runs and walks since 2016:

Year	HR (MLB Rank)	BB (MLB Rank)
2016	122 (27th)	382 (30th)
2017	193 (20th)	390 (30th)
2018	155 (26th)	427 (28th)
2019	162 (28th)	456 (26th)
2020	68 (20th)	172 (25th)
2021	163 (27th)	421 (30th)
2022	138 (26th)	460 (20th)

Getting on base and clearing the fences are two of the skills most strongly correlated with scoring runs. However, the things Pasquantino does well weren't valued as highly by Kansas City as they were by other clubs. The few major-league free agents they've signed in recent years include Billy Hamilton, Michael A. Taylor and two ill-advised reunions with a past-his-prime Alex Gordon. They also traded Mike Moustakas for Brett Phillips and Jorge López. For some reason, Paulo Orlando was around for a while.

One player alone can't reverse the tide of feeble offense. The club needs several more productive hitters to build a successful modern lineup. But there hasn't been anyone like Pasquantino in their dugout in a very long time.

⚾ ⚾ ⚾

The Merrifield Era of quirky, bizarre, somewhat entertaining and ultimately inadequate baseball in which the organization fell behind the times is over. Merrifield himself could get away with his slappy, low walks/low power style, but most others don't make enough decent contact or add sufficient value with their gloves and on the basepaths to be productive playing that way. It seems that the Royals have finally learned that lesson.

The 2023 Royals will likely not be a particularly good baseball team. They have many problems to fix, and they've only started to show signs of addressing some of them. To name one of their nastiest messes, the pitching staff was the only one in MLB last season with a K-BB% lower than 10%. For context, 11 of the 12 teams with the highest K-BB% reached the playoffs. That can't be completely rectified in just one year.

Still, there are indications that they're approaching the game from a different angle. Playing better baseball—not merely fast baseball with fan-favorite players who never miss a game, but actual winning baseball—seems to be the priority, which hasn't always been the case since 2016.

The next era of Royals baseball may or may not be better than the previous one, but with a focus on smarter decisions, better communication and a handful of young players worth building around, it has already yielded a modicum of something powerful, dangerous, and largely absent during Merrifield's tenure: Hope.

—Daniel R. Epstein is an author of Baseball Prospectus.

---

1. Andrew Benintendi, Dylan Coleman, Hunter Dozier, Cam Gallagher, Kyle Isbel, Brad Keller, MJ Melendez, Brady Singer, Michael A. Taylor and Whit Merrifield

2. Carlos Santana also had more walks than strikeouts for the Royals in 2022, but over the full season, including his time with the Mariners, he had more strikeouts than walks.

Hitters

★ ★ ★ *2023 Top 101 Prospect* **#70** ★ ★ ★

Gavin Cross OF
Born: 02/13/01 Age: 22 Bats: L Throws: L Height: 6'3" Weight: 210 lb. Origin: Round 1, 2022 Draft (#9 overall)

YEAR	TEAM	LVL	AGE	PA	R	2B	3B	HR	RBI	BB	K	SB	CS	Whiff%	AVG/OBP/SLG	DRC+	BABIP	BRR	DRP	WARP
2022	COL	A	21	123	20	5	2	7	22	22	31	4	2		.293/.423/.596	113	.355	-2.0	CF(22): -0.5	0.2
2023 non-DC	*KC*	*MLB*	*22*	*251*	*24*	*9*	*2*	*6*	*25*	*23*	*82*	*4*	*2*	*35.4%*	*.209/.291/.359*	*78*	*.300*	*1.1*	*CF 0*	*0.1*

Comparables: LeVon Washington (85), Derek Fisher (82), Brian Goodwin (81)

Three years spent as one of the top hitters in the ACC put Cross on every team's radar going into last summer's draft. A high-floor prospect with solid tools across the board, he lasted all the way until the ninth overall selection due to a perceived lack of upside. But the Royals saw some untapped power remaining in his left-handed swing, and he put it on display post-draft, albeit against Low-A pitching. His future defensive home is likely a corner outfield spot, but his bat is more than capable of propping up a modest slide down the defensive spectrum.

Hunter Dozier 1B
Born: 08/22/91 Age: 31 Bats: R Throws: R Height: 6'4" Weight: 220 lb. Origin: Round 1, 2013 Draft (#8 overall)

YEAR	TEAM	LVL	AGE	PA	R	2B	3B	HR	RBI	BB	K	SB	CS	Whiff%	AVG/OBP/SLG	DRC+	BABIP	BRR	DRP	WARP
2020	KC	MLB	28	186	29	4	2	6	12	27	48	4	0	30.9%	.228/.344/.392	105	.288	0.5	1B(28): 0.2, RF(18): -1.6, LF(2): -0.4	0.5
2021	KC	MLB	29	543	55	27	6	16	54	43	154	5	4	32.3%	.216/.285/.394	82	.276	0.8	RF(60): -0.6, 3B(57): -1.1, 1B(19): -0.1	0.3
2022	KC	MLB	30	500	51	26	4	12	41	34	125	4	3	29.1%	.236/.292/.387	88	.298	-5.4	1B(42): 0.3, RF(35): -1.3, 3B(27): -0.5	-0.2
2023 DC	*KC*	*MLB*	*31*	*395*	*39*	*17*	*3*	*11*	*41*	*29*	*104*	*5*	*1*	*29.3%*	*.239/.303/.405*	*96*	*.305*	*4.4*	*3B -1, 1B 0*	*0.9*

Comparables: Todd Benzinger (66), Eduardo Perez (63), Mark Whiten (63)

It's funny how individual baseball games are long, yet the career of a ballplayer can flash before your eyes. One minute you're eyeing a prospect, and the next you're watching a 30-year-old riding out a player-friendly deal, chasing the sequel to his One Good Year for the better part of an entire franchise rebuild. Dozier was just two plate appearances shy of qualifying for rate-stat leaderboards. Had he been penciled into the lineup for another agonizing 8-2 loss or two, he would've ranked among the lower fifth of batters league-wide for average, OBP and slugging. He retains nominal positional flexibility and can notch the occasional extra-base hit, but would be unlikely to garner much playing time on any roster with at least two quality corner outfielders. Fortunately, he plays for the Royals.

Tyler Gentry RF
Born: 02/01/99 Age: 24 Bats: R Throws: R Height: 6'2" Weight: 210 lb. Origin: Round 3, 2020 Draft (#76 overall)

YEAR	TEAM	LVL	AGE	PA	R	2B	3B	HR	RBI	BB	K	SB	CS	Whiff%	AVG/OBP/SLG	DRC+	BABIP	BRR	DRP	WARP
2021	QC	A+	22	186	29	10	0	6	28	29	55	4	0		.259/.395/.449	101	.360	-1.3	RF(37): 1.3, LF(5): 0.2, CF(1): -0.2	0.6
2022	QC	A+	23	152	22	6	1	5	23	20	39	2	2		.336/.434/.516	126	.447	-0.9	RF(27): 0.4	0.8
2022	NWA	AA	23	331	57	16	0	16	63	40	66	8	4		.321/.417/.555	129	.362	-0.9	RF(34): 1.8, LF(20): 0.6	3.2
2023 non-DC	*KC*	*MLB*	*24*	*251*	*26*	*10*	*0*	*6*	*27*	*23*	*66*	*2*	*1*	*27.4%*	*.243/.329/.383*	*98*	*.319*	*-0.1*	*LF 0, RF 0*	*0.5*

Comparables: Alfredo Marte (73), Francisco Peguero (70), Evan Bigley (70)

A knee injury prematurely ended Gentry's 2021 season, but he returned fully healthy last year and became Kansas City's breakout minor-league hitter. Physical and strong, he hunts fastballs in hitter's counts, making loud contact to all fields. Better yet, he's more than just a slugger, possessing plus contact ability and a solid command of the strike zone. Defensively, Gentry is a classic corner outfielder with enough arm strength to handle right field. The Royals aren't shy about promoting players when they're ready, and last season saw a wave of new faces join the big-league lineup. That prospect attrition, coupled with Gentry's own progress, makes him arguably the best bat remaining in the Royals farm system.

Brewer Hicklen OF
Born: 02/09/96 Age: 27 Bats: R Throws: R Height: 6'2" Weight: 208 lb. Origin: Round 7, 2017 Draft (#210 overall)

YEAR	TEAM	LVL	AGE	PA	R	2B	3B	HR	RBI	BB	K	SB	CS	Whiff%	AVG/OBP/SLG	DRC+	BABIP	BRR	DRP	WARP
2021	NWA	AA	25	424	70	15	3	16	57	52	132	40	4		.243/.346/.434	91	.333	5.2	LF(63): -2.2, RF(37): 3.8, CF(3): 0.1	1.5
2022	OMA	AAA	26	559	85	30	4	28	85	58	202	35	2		.248/.348/.502	88	.360	3.6	RF(84): 0.5, LF(34): 2.2, CF(16): -1.4	1.9
2022	KC	MLB	26	4	1	0	0	0	0	0	4	0	0	71.4%	.000/.000/.000	74		-0.6	RF(2): 0, CF(1): 0.1	-0.1
2023 non-DC	*KC*	*MLB*	*27*	*251*	*27*	*9*	*1*	*8*	*30*	*20*	*92*	*12*	*4*	*38.4%*	*.223/.303/.403*	*91*	*.333*	*4.2*	*RF 0, CF 0*	*0.7*

Comparables: Melky Mesa (63), Jason Dubois (61), Justin Maxwell (59)

Hicklen's two trips to the big leagues didn't amount to much—four times walking up to the plate, four times walking back after strike three. And yes, one of those trips was to Toronto to help backfill a number of unvaccinated colleagues. But the Alabama native did a bunch of damage to Omaha scoreboards behind the scenes. His 60+ Triple-A extra-base hits prove he's got some USDA certified Grade-AAAA beef, while his 200+ strikeouts suggest he's cut from the Mark Reynolds cloth. His 35 steals basically make him Reynolds being chased by Wile E. Coyote.

Kyle Isbel OF
Born: 03/03/97 Age: 26 Bats: L Throws: R Height: 5'11" Weight: 190 lb. Origin: Round 3, 2018 Draft (#94 overall)

YEAR	TEAM	LVL	AGE	PA	R	2B	3B	HR	RBI	BB	K	SB	CS	Whiff%	AVG/OBP/SLG	DRC+	BABIP	BRR	DRP	WARP
2021	OMA	AAA	24	451	62	18	3	15	55	45	91	22	5		.269/.357/.444	108	.314	-1.1	CF(55): -5.5, RF(26): 5.0, LF(19): -1.9	1.6
2021	KC	MLB	24	83	16	5	2	1	7	7	23	2	0	24.2%	.276/.337/.434	83	.385	1.1	RF(14): 0.6, CF(9): -0.1, LF(4): 0	0.3
2022	KC	MLB	25	278	32	10	4	5	28	16	75	9	6	22.1%	.211/.264/.340	73	.275	1.5	RF(49): 2.3, CF(30): -0.4, LF(29): 1.4	0.5
2023 DC	*KC*	*MLB*	*26*	*344*	*32*	*14*	*3*	*8*	*31*	*23*	*75*	*17*	*7*	*21.7%*	*.235/.297/.384*	*89*	*.285*	*2.8*	*LF 2, RF 1*	*1.0*

Comparables: Pablo Reyes (67), Travis Snider (64), Jackie Bradley Jr. (61)

Per MLB Savant, Enrique Hernández was the best in baseball at getting outfield jumps in 2021, earning four feet over the league average and finishing a foot better than anyone else. Isbel, once thought to be a solid hitting prospect without a position, upended his profile by playing a darn good right field in 2022 and besting Hernández at this particular metric, which tracks how much positive ground a fielder covers the first three seconds after contact. As such, the questions surrounding Isbel have now flipped: He can patrol any outfield position and likely will for the Royals, but will hitting like *that* let his glove stay in the lineup? After all, there's only one person who is permitted by law to make a career out of terrific jumps and that is Super Mario, in theaters April 7.

Carter Jensen DH/C

Born: 07/03/03 Age: 20 Bats: L Throws: R Height: 6'1" Weight: 210 lb. Origin: Round 3, 2021 Draft (#78 overall)

YEAR	TEAM	LVL	AGE	PA	R	2B	3B	HR	RBI	BB	K	SB	CS	Whiff%	AVG/OBP/SLG	DRC+	BABIP	BRR	DRP	WARP
2021	ROYG	ROK	17	65	8	1	1	1	7	10	19	4	0		.273/.385/.382		.400			
2022	COL	A	18	485	66	24	2	11	50	83	103	8	6		.226/.363/.382	117	.275	-2.8	C(46): 1.3	2.2
2023 non-DC	*KC*	*MLB*	*19*	*251*	*21*	*10*	*1*	*3*	*21*	*25*	*65*	*2*	*2*	*28.5%*	*.193/.280/.303*	*62*	*.256*	*-1.0*	*C 0*	*-0.4*

Comparables: Chris Parmelee (64), Isael Soto (60), Jack Suwinski (59)

YEAR	TEAM	P. COUNT	FRM RUNS	BLK RUNS	THRW RUNS	TOT RUNS
2022	COL	6704	1.7	-1.6	0.9	1.1
2023	*KC*	*6956*	*-1.5*	*-1.4*	*0.4*	*-2.5*

Don't scout Jensen's final slash line. An ice-cold start as a teenager in High-A obscures that he was one of the hottest hitters in the Carolina League during the second half of the season. He possesses an exceptional eye and controls the zone well, and his simple, quick swing produces hard contact. The hope is that his in-game power continues to grow as he matures. Overall, Jensen has an impressive offensive profile—so impressive, in fact, that the Royals may choose to slide him out from behind the plate and into a corner spot if his glove continues to lag behind his bat.

Nick Loftin CF

Born: 09/25/98 Age: 24 Bats: R Throws: R Height: 6'1" Weight: 180 lb. Origin: Round 1, 2020 Draft (#32 overall)

YEAR	TEAM	LVL	AGE	PA	R	2B	3B	HR	RBI	BB	K	SB	CS	Whiff%	AVG/OBP/SLG	DRC+	BABIP	BRR	DRP	WARP
2021	QC	A+	22	410	67	22	5	10	57	42	60	11	2		.289/.373/.463	122	.323	1.6	SS(47): -3.9, 2B(21): 1.0, 3B(11): -0.2	2.1
2022	NWA	AA	23	425	78	17	1	12	47	45	57	24	4		.270/.354/.421	108	.288	0.8	CF(53): -1.4, 2B(19): -1.6, SS(6): 0.5	1.4
2022	OMA	AAA	23	168	26	7	0	5	19	10	41	5	2		.216/.280/.359	89	.259	0.3	3B(24): -1.9, CF(9): -1.4, LF(4): 0.5	0.0
2023 non-DC	*KC*	*MLB*	*24*	*251*	*22*	*9*	*1*	*4*	*24*	*18*	*46*	*6*	*1*	*21.6%*	*.229/.294/.348*	*80*	*.268*	*2.8*	*2B 0, 3B 0*	*0.3*

The 32nd-overall pick in the 2020 draft looked to be on the express train to Kansas City in 2022, earning a bump from Double-A Northwest Arkansas to Triple-A Omaha in August. A smooth and versatile defender, Loftin predominantly played center field, though he also showed up at second, third, short and left. His late-season promotion was well-earned, but the wheels fell off offensively in the PCL—generally not how things go in the offense-friendly league. He did pick things up at the end of the season, slashing .260/.362/.400 from September 9 through September 28. Loftin is a contact-heavy hitter who likes to put his speed to use once he gets on base, and one imagines the new pickoff rule will only help him in that endeavor. He profiles as a second-division, bottom-third hitter, or possibly a supersub type on a playoff-bound team.

Nicky Lopez IF

Born: 03/13/95 Age: 28 Bats: L Throws: R Height: 5'11" Weight: 180 lb. Origin: Round 5, 2016 Draft (#163 overall)

YEAR	TEAM	LVL	AGE	PA	R	2B	3B	HR	RBI	BB	K	SB	CS	Whiff%	AVG/OBP/SLG	DRC+	BABIP	BRR	DRP	WARP
2020	KC	MLB	25	192	15	8	0	1	13	18	41	0	5	21.1%	.201/.286/.266	77	.260	-0.2	2B(53): 0.4, SS(4): 0	0.1
2021	KC	MLB	26	565	78	21	6	2	43	49	74	22	1	15.6%	.300/.365/.378	102	.347	5.4	SS(148): 8.4, 2B(4): 0.2	3.6
2022	KC	MLB	27	480	51	12	4	0	20	29	63	13	3	17.5%	.227/.281/.273	79	.265	2.5	2B(68): -2.5, SS(52): 4.2, 3B(30): 0.3	0.7
2023 DC	*KC*	*MLB*	*28*	*376*	*35*	*13*	*3*	*3*	*28*	*26*	*49*	*8*	*3*	*16.9%*	*.258/.318/.348*	*88*	*.294*	*3.7*	*2B 0, SS 1*	*1.0*

Comparables: Ehire Adrianza (64), Omar Quintanilla (63), Chris Getz (62)

Just as sure as a baseball player named "Nicky" is bound to hit for average and play middle infield, so will a paragraph on a below-average major leaguer's strengths include intangibles and work ethic. Indeed, Lopez is a nine-hole slap-hitter whose power comes in the form of static electricity. Last year he hit one ball farther than 360 feet, but his low strikeout rate and off-the-field contributions, which led to a Roberto Clemente Award nomination, kept him in good graces. After a 3-1 win in Toronto, one for which many of his unvaccinated teammates were unable to travel, Lopez called the victory an "unselfish win." He officially had zero home runs, but after review, that one oughta count.

MJ Melendez C

Born: 11/29/98 Age: 24 Bats: L Throws: R Height: 6'1" Weight: 190 lb. Origin: Round 2, 2017 Draft (#52 overall)

YEAR	TEAM	LVL	AGE	PA	R	2B	3B	HR	RBI	BB	K	SB	CS	Whiff%	AVG/OBP/SLG	DRC+	BABIP	BRR	DRP	WARP
2021	NWA	AA	22	347	58	18	0	28	65	43	76	2	4		.285/.372/.628	143	.286	-0.7	C(52): -3.5	2.6
2021	OMA	AAA	22	184	37	4	3	13	38	32	39	1	2		.293/.413/.620	128	.310	-1.4	C(29): -2.3, 3B(9): 0.5	0.9
2022	OMA	AAA	23	91	7	4	0	2	6	13	22	3	0		.167/.286/.295	97	.204	0.7	C(15): 0.6, RF(2): 0.5	0.4
2022	KC	MLB	23	534	57	21	3	18	62	66	131	2	3	27.8%	.217/.313/.393	98	.258	-3.3	C(78): -18.8, LF(23): 0.4, RF(16): 0.5	-0.6
2023 DC	*KC*	*MLB*	*24*	*522*	*62*	*21*	*4*	*19*	*52*	*62*	*120*	*5*	*3*	*28.5%*	*.225/.320/.423*	*109*	*.261*	*3.2*	*LF 0, RF 0*	*0.5*

Comparables: John Ryan Murphy (61), Jarrod Saltalamacchia (61), Blake Swihart (56)

YEAR	TEAM	P. COUNT	FRM RUNS	BLK RUNS	THRW RUNS	TOT RUNS
2021	NWA	7563	-3.1	-0.5	-0.3	-3.8
2021	OMA	4340	-2.6	-0.3	0.2	-2.7
2022	OMA	2202	0.3	-0.2	0.3	0.4
2022	KC	9969	-17.5	-1.1	0.0	-18.6
2023	*KC*	*9620*	*-18.1*	*-0.8*	*0.0*	*-19.0*

There's a very narrow but specific reason to be hopeful about Kansas City's lineup: Melendez and Bobby Witt Jr. are the first Royals rookie pair to each hit 15 home runs in their debut seasons since Bo Jackson and Kevin Seitzer 35 years ago. Homers solve and absolve everything in today's environment, and they're the main aspect of the rookie catcher/outfielder's game that will levitate his status. His positional flexibility can also keep him afloat, although a readout of his catching data makes one think, hey, here's a fine outfielder. Or failing that, a DH. Or failing that, a coach. There are just so many potential jobs in baseball for Melendez, but a lot of them can wait so long as he keeps bashing the long ball.

Adalberto Mondesi SS Born: 07/27/95 Age: 27 Bats: S Throws: R Height: 6'1" Weight: 200 lb. Origin: International Free Agent, 2011

YEAR	TEAM	LVL	AGE	PA	R	2B	3B	HR	RBI	BB	K	SB	CS	Whiff%	AVG/OBP/SLG	DRC+	BABIP	BRR	DRP	WARP
2020	KC	MLB	24	233	33	11	3	6	22	11	70	24	8	40.4%	.256/.294/.416	75	.350	0.4	SS(59): 1	0.1
2021	KC	MLB	25	136	19	8	1	6	17	6	43	15	1	35.8%	.230/.271/.452	78	.299	0.6	3B(20): 1.8, SS(11): -0.2	0.3
2022	KC	MLB	26	54	3	0	0	0	3	4	20	5	0	43.9%	.140/.204/.140	62	.233	0.8	SS(15): 0.2	0.0
2023 DC	*KC*	*MLB*	*27*	*322*	*28*	*13*	*4*	*8*	*30*	*17*	*98*	*28*	*7*	*37.7%*	*.224/.272/.374*	*74*	*.305*	*12.4*	*SS 1, 3B 0*	*1.2*

Comparables: Javier Báez (46), Wilmer Flores (45), Troy Tulowitzki (44)

Mondesi tore his ACL during an attempted steal last April, making 2022 his shortest season to date. Since becoming the first player to make his debut in the World Series—as a teen, no less—he's stayed healthy for just the one full season: ironically, the pandemic-shortened one. All told, he's averaging about 50 major-league games per calendar year. There just isn't much to say about a wonderful player who can't keep all his physical appendages in harmony. Well, not much to say with an optimistic bent, at least, which is the tendency we all have each offseason. Whether all the collective hospital visits are a result of bad luck or simply a Calvinistic inevitability, he's missing the years in which his speed was going to be at its peak. A completely healthy Mondesi might have upwards of 300 steals by now, possibly leading active players. Instead, he's 21st between Charlie Blackmon and Michael Brantley, who are nearly a decade older. So let's all suck it up and say it again together before Lucy yanks the football away once more: Here's hoping he's healthy this year.

Edward Olivares OF Born: 03/06/96 Age: 27 Bats: R Throws: R Height: 6'2" Weight: 190 lb. Origin: International Free Agent, 2014

YEAR	TEAM	LVL	AGE	PA	R	2B	3B	HR	RBI	BB	K	SB	CS	Whiff%	AVG/OBP/SLG	DRC+	BABIP	BRR	DRP	WARP
2021	OMA	AAA	25	292	54	12	3	15	36	29	46	12	4		.313/.397/.559	133	.333	-0.4	CF(39): -3.2, LF(13): 0.4, RF(10): -1.6	1.6
2021	KC	MLB	25	111	14	2	0	5	12	5	19	2	2	24.3%	.238/.291/.406	106	.244	-0.7	RF(22): 0.8, LF(11): 0.3, CF(4): -0.1	0.5
2022	OMA	AAA	26	86	13	7	0	1	11	8	14	2	1		.269/.337/.397	97	.317	-1.8	RF(15): -0.7, LF(6): 0.5	0.1
2022	KC	MLB	26	174	24	8	0	4	15	10	36	2	3	24.7%	.286/.333/.410	101	.344	0.0	RF(27): -0.1, LF(12): 0.3, CF(1): 0	0.6
2023 DC	*KC*	*MLB*	*27*	*418*	*39*	*17*	*2*	*8*	*38*	*27*	*84*	*14*	*6*	*24.0%*	*.254/.313/.384*	*96*	*.306*	*-1.1*	*RF -1, LF 0*	*0.4*

Comparables: Charlie Blackmon (65), Stephen Piscotty (59), Austin Slater (55)

Every fanbase languishing through the "not really trying years" wants the hot-hitting minor-league outfielder to come up for a little while to see what they can do. Olivares, with a career Triple-A slugging percentage of .521, was that outfielder in 2022. He played every day down the stretch when there was high demand for anyone in Kansas City who could put the ball in play. He also has the requisite speed and controllable cost that ticks the boxes for starched suits and polyester-draped diehards alike, so there's a good chance he'll be a primary outfielder this year. The only question is, who's going to replace Olivares as the Triple-A outfielder fans will clamor for once he slumps?

Vinnie Pasquantino DH/1B Born: 10/10/97 Age: 25 Bats: L Throws: L Height: 6'4" Weight: 245 lb. Origin: Round 11, 2019 Draft (#319 overall)

YEAR	TEAM	LVL	AGE	PA	R	2B	3B	HR	RBI	BB	K	SB	CS	Whiff%	AVG/OBP/SLG	DRC+	BABIP	BRR	DRP	WARP
2021	QC	A+	23	276	44	20	3	13	42	33	38	4	0		.291/.384/.565	144	.298	-1.5	1B(52): 5.0	2.5
2021	NWA	AA	23	237	35	17	0	11	42	31	26	2	0		.310/.405/.560	140	.307	0.1	1B(54): -2.8	1.5
2022	OMA	AAA	24	313	52	17	2	18	70	40	39	3	1		.277/.371/.561	135	.258	-0.9	1B(34): 0.9	2.1
2022	KC	MLB	24	298	25	10	0	10	26	35	34	1	0	14.9%	.295/.383/.450	133	.306	-0.4	1B(37): -0.7	1.7
2023 DC	*KC*	*MLB*	*25*	*590*	*64*	*27*	*3*	*17*	*63*	*60*	*74*	*4*	*1*	*16.8%*	*.260/.342/.427*	*120*	*.274*	*2.6*	*1B 0*	*2.6*

Comparables: Mitch Moreland (71), C.J. Cron (70), David Cooper (69)

In his third major-league game, Pasquantino's first hit went long and far. It screamed over the outfielders' collective heads, clanged around the top of the wall and bounced back into play. The young lad hustled in for a double and felt good about it. It was a distinctively folksy moment in the game, as Pasquantino evokes all the shades of Billy Butler: a fresh-faced, defensively-limited basher. The difference? Pasquantino may have even more power than Country Breakfast. For example, a few seconds after the rookie trotted into the keystone base, the umpire present for the aforementioned line drive ruled that it had cleared the hallowed yellow line for a home run. You see, when Pasquantino gets a hold of one, it's usually not just going to be a double. Royals fans are going to have fun watching him flick fly balls well over the fence as they shout all sorts of Italian nonsense while he circles the bases. They'll yell "*colazione nazione*," perhaps.

Salvador Perez C/DH Born: 05/10/90 Age: 33 Bats: R Throws: R Height: 6'3" Weight: 255 lb. Origin: International Free Agent, 2006

YEAR	TEAM	LVL	AGE	PA	R	2B	3B	HR	RBI	BB	K	SB	CS	Whiff%	AVG/OBP/SLG	DRC+	BABIP	BRR	DRP	WARP
2020	KC	MLB	30	156	22	12	0	11	32	3	36	1	0	26.9%	.333/.353/.633	122	.375	-0.6	C(34): 1.5, 1B(3): 0	1.1
2021	KC	MLB	31	665	88	24	0	48	121	28	170	1	0	33.6%	.273/.316/.544	130	.298	-0.5	C(124): -14.6	3.5
2022	KC	MLB	32	473	48	23	1	23	76	18	109	0	0	31.6%	.254/.292/.465	114	.285	-2.1	C(77): -13.5	0.7
2023 DC	*KC*	*MLB*	*33*	*596*	*70*	*25*	*1*	*28*	*76*	*25*	*153*	*0*	*0*	*31.6%*	*.259/.301/.464*	*115*	*.306*	*-2.9*	*C -10*	*1.5*

Comparables: Ted Simmons (77), Ivan Rodríguez (76), Joe Torre (73)

YEAR	TEAM	P. COUNT	FRM RUNS	BLK RUNS	THRW RUNS	TOT RUNS
2020	KC	4651	1.4	0.1	0.0	1.5
2021	KC	17285	-14.3	-1.2	0.7	-14.8
2022	KC	10818	-14.2	0.0	0.1	-14.2
2023	*KC*	*13228*	*-10.9*	*-0.1*	*0.1*	*-10.9*

Yadier Molina and Kurt Suzuki retired this winter, which cleared some nobility in the catching ranks. Perez is now the active leader in games caught and has years left ahead of him to pad his lead. It is officially time to start cobbling together a Hall of Fame case for the man. He's not there yet, but his trajectory is promising. He's already among history's best offensive catchers, ranking 15th in homers, and he's one of seven catchers with at least five Gold Gloves. The only backstops joining him on both those lists are Iván Rodríguez and Johnny Bench. Perez also has a World Series MVP to his name thrown in for a dash of flavor. He's suffered some injuries to random limbs and appendages as of late, but the torn UCL in his thumb he suffered in June, which normally takes a couple months to rehab, only forced him out for five weeks. His first game back, he conked a three-run parabola. Watch the current monarch of backstops while you can, and enjoy the rest of the ride.

Nick Pratto 1B Born: 10/06/98 Age: 24 Bats: L Throws: L Height: 6'1" Weight: 215 lb. Origin: Round 1, 2017 Draft (#14 overall)

YEAR	TEAM	LVL	AGE	PA	R	2B	3B	HR	RBI	BB	K	SB	CS	Whiff%	AVG/OBP/SLG	DRC+	BABIP	BRR	DRP	WARP
2021	NWA	AA	22	275	44	13	4	15	43	46	80	7	5		.271/.404/.570	121	.349	-1.8	1B(61): -0.8	1.2
2021	OMA	AAA	22	270	54	15	3	21	55	37	77	5	0		.259/.367/.634	119	.282	1.0	1B(52): -1.0, RF(3): -0.1	1.2
2022	OMA	AAA	23	374	57	10	3	17	47	59	114	8	2		.228/.369/.449	106	.299	-0.2	1B(58): -2.7, LF(13): 1.2, RF(8): -0.6	1.1
2022	KC	MLB	23	182	18	9	1	7	20	19	66	0	0	34.5%	.184/.271/.386	72	.250	-1.2	1B(43): 0.4, LF(7): -0.1, RF(1): 0.1	-0.3
2023 DC	*KC*	*MLB*	*24*	*224*	*23*	*9*	*2*	*7*	*22*	*24*	*74*	*2*	*1*	*33.7%*	*.213/.308/.399*	*96*	*.298*	*1.4*	*1B 0*	*0.3*

Comparables: Brandon Allen (66), Justin Smoak (62), Josh Bell (57)

First basemen can have all the patient approaches and quality at-bats they want, but at the end of the day the demand of someone playing that position is best symbolized by a face-painted fan mashing their fists in their basket of nachos and screaming, "More dingers!" And while you can question the method of their criticism, they're not wrong. If Pratto is going to survive in the majors, it will be by his mammoth moonshot measurements. Despite a humbling overall debut, it took him just four days after getting called up to sock his first homer, and his first walk-off job came a few weeks after that. He's likely to see plenty of time at first base for the Royals this year, so pound your fists in joy (or disapproval) accordingly.

Michael A. Taylor CF Born: 03/26/91 Age: 32 Bats: R Throws: R Height: 6'4" Weight: 215 lb. Origin: Round 6, 2009 Draft (#172 overall)

YEAR	TEAM	LVL	AGE	PA	R	2B	3B	HR	RBI	BB	K	SB	CS	Whiff%	AVG/OBP/SLG	DRC+	BABIP	BRR	DRP	WARP
2020	WAS	MLB	29	99	11	6	0	5	16	6	27	0	0	28.7%	.196/.253/.424	94	.217	-0.8	LF(14): -0.1, CF(11): -0.7, RF(11): 0.1	0.1
2021	KC	MLB	30	528	58	16	1	12	54	33	144	14	7	31.3%	.244/.297/.356	83	.319	2.5	CF(139): 15.6	2.9
2022	KC	MLB	31	456	49	10	3	9	43	35	109	4	2	29.1%	.254/.313/.357	92	.321	1.2	CF(123): 6.2, P(1): 0	2.0
2023 DC	*KC*	*MLB*	*32*	*472*	*46*	*17*	*2*	*12*	*44*	*33*	*121*	*7*	*2*	*29.4%*	*.250/.308/.386*	*93*	*.319*	*2.7*	*CF 12*	*2.5*

Comparables: Jim Busby (71), Omar Moreno (62), Billy Hatcher (58)

Taylor is an excellent fielder who turns singles into outs and extra bases into singles, but he largely does the same thing when he's the one holding the bat. Twenty years ago he'd have been a leadoff hitter, but not even the 2022 Royals were gullible enough to fall for the ol' "fast person bats first" ruse. The veteran vacuum cleaner did post career bests in strikeout and walk rates, but both were still below the league average. His well-established skills and weaknesses will keep him in the lineup's lower third indefinitely.

Drew Waters OF Born: 12/30/98 Age: 24 Bats: S Throws: R Height: 6'2" Weight: 185 lb. Origin: Round 2, 2017 Draft (#41 overall)

YEAR	TEAM	LVL	AGE	PA	R	2B	3B	HR	RBI	BB	K	SB	CS	Whiff%	AVG/OBP/SLG	DRC+	BABIP	BRR	DRP	WARP
2021	GWN	AAA	22	459	70	22	1	11	37	47	142	28	9		.240/.329/.381	85	.341	2.1	LF(44): 4.3, CF(38): 6.2, RF(25): 2.8	2.2
2022	GWN	AAA	23	210	26	7	3	5	16	16	57	5	1		.246/.305/.393	83	.321	1.4	CF(44): 3.8, RF(1): -0.2	0.7
2022	OMA	AAA	23	143	29	5	2	7	17	20	41	13	0		.295/.399/.541	99	.392	1.1	CF(21): 0.4, LF(2): 0.5, RF(2): -0.2	0.5
2022	KC	MLB	23	109	14	6	1	5	18	12	40	0	0	32.5%	.240/.324/.479	82	.353	-0.8	RF(17): -1.3, CF(12): -2, LF(4): -0.1	-0.3
2023 DC	*KC*	*MLB*	*24*	*274*	*26*	*12*	*3*	*5*	*23*	*23*	*83*	*10*	*2*	*31.4%*	*.231/.304/.373*	*86*	*.326*	*5.9*	*RF 1, CF -3*	*0.6*

Comparables: Nick Williams (52), Jesse Winker (50), Tyler O'Neill (49)

The Royals rolled the dice when they sent their competitive balance-round draft pick to the Braves for Waters, a former top prospect who'd stalled out offensively in Triple-A. Their gamble paid off almost instantly, as Waters used his intriguing power-speed combination to great effect in Omaha, earning a late-season promotion to Kansas City. Though he posted a gnarly strikeout rate in the bigs, he made a good enough overall impression that it seems like the Braves should've just tried promoting him as a means of fixing him. He'll be in the outfield mix for the Royals this season. (Oh, and because you're wondering, Atlanta popped prep arm JR Ritchie with the Royals' 35th overall selection. Check back in a decade or so to see how that one worked out.)

Peyton Wilson 2B/CF Born: 11/01/99 Age: 23 Bats: S Throws: R Height: 5'9" Weight: 180 lb. Origin: Round 2, 2021 Draft (#66 overall)

YEAR	TEAM	LVL	AGE	PA	R	2B	3B	HR	RBI	BB	K	SB	CS	Whiff%	AVG/OBP/SLG	DRC+	BABIP	BRR	DRP	WARP
2021	ROYG	ROK	21	41	7	3	1	1	7	5	10	2	2		.219/.366/.469		.273			
2021	COL	A	21	46	6	3	1	0	1	4	10	5	0		.231/.326/.359	106	.300	0.4	2B(11): 0.3	0.2
2022	QC	A+	22	390	60	16	3	14	44	41	97	23	2		.268/.359/.456	107	.335	2.5	2B(51): -3.3, CF(35): -2.3	1.8
2023 non-DC	*KC*	*MLB*	*23*	*251*	*21*	*9*	*1*	*4*	*23*	*17*	*71*	*9*	*2*	*30.5%*	*.215/.281/.333*	*69*	*.291*	*5.7*	*2B 0, CF 0*	*0.4*

Comparables: Jemile Weeks (87), Devin Mann (85), Eric Sogard (84)

The Royals have definitely had a type when it comes to draftees in the past few years. They've gravitated toward advanced college hitters who, despite lacking loud tools, are solid across the board and close to major-league ready. Wilson fits the mold perfectly with his bat, above-average speed and sneaky pop. His athleticism allows him to play multiple positions, regularly seeing time in both the infield and outfield. He's a low-ceiling, high-floor prospect who, like Kansas City's last batch of rookies, should move quickly through the organization.

Bobby Witt Jr. SS/3B Born: 06/14/00 Age: 23 Bats: R Throws: R Height: 6'1" Weight: 200 lb. Origin: Round 1, 2019 Draft (#2 overall)

YEAR	TEAM	LVL	AGE	PA	R	2B	3B	HR	RBI	BB	K	SB	CS	Whiff%	AVG/OBP/SLG	DRC+	BABIP	BRR	DRP	WARP
2021	NWA	AA	21	279	44	11	4	16	51	25	67	14	8		.295/.369/.570	120	.339	1.1	SS(50): -1.7, 3B(8): -1.1	1.4
2021	OMA	AAA	21	285	55	24	0	17	46	26	64	15	3		.285/.352/.581	114	.314	-0.1	SS(52): -4.8, 3B(10): -1.4	0.8
2022	KC	MLB	22	632	82	31	6	20	80	30	135	30	7	25.1%	.254/.294/.428	99	.295	6.6	SS(98): -15, 3B(55): 0.3	0.9
2023 DC	*KC*	*MLB*	*23*	*608*	*76*	*29*	*5*	*24*	*67*	*35*	*128*	*31*	*10*	*25.4%*	*.265/.315/.466*	*118*	*.304*	*6.3*	*SS -8, 3B 0*	*2.8*

Comparables: Corey Seager (75), Adalberto Mondesi (73), Gleyber Torres (73)

Witt Jr. entered the year facing sky-high expectations as BP's top prospect and the presumptive AL Rookie of the Year. Though he fell short of earning those honors, he nonetheless acquitted himself well in his first MLB season. He joined Tommie Agee, Mitchell Page, Devon White and Mike Trout as the fifth rookie ever to have at least 20 homers and 30 steals. Witt has the distinction of nailing those numbers exactly, and as such gets to be mentioned in the same breath as Trout—even though *he* had 30 and 49 as a rookie—because that's how echelons work. Witt used his power and speed to fight his way to league-average production at the plate despite a paltry walk rate. The physical base the Royals rookie swiped for his 30th steal was sent to Cooperstown, no doubt for safekeeping, so no one would ever steal it again. So that's two aspects of the game—offense and base-running—in which Witt looked up to snuff in his debut. As for fielding? Well, let's just say he's in jeopardy of joining Page as the only player among those aforementioned standout rookies to not win multiple Gold Gloves. The eye test says his work at third was less bad than his work at short, but there's still plenty of time for him to improve on the dirt as he enters his sophomore season at the ripe old age of 22.

PITCHERS

Scott Barlow RHP Born: 12/18/92 Age: 30 Bats: R Throws: R Height: 6'3" Weight: 210 lb. Origin: Round 6, 2011 Draft (#194 overall)

YEAR	TEAM	LVL	AGE	W	L	SV	G	GS	IP	H	HR	BB/9	K/9	K	GB%	BABIP	WHIP	ERA	DRA-	WARP	MPH	FB%	Whiff%	CSP
2020	KC	MLB	27	2	1	2	32	0	30	27	4	2.7	11.7	39	45.3%	.324	1.20	4.20	79	0.6	95.1	37.3%	37.6%	43.0%
2021	KC	MLB	28	5	3	16	71	0	74^1	61	4	3.4	11.0	91	38.9%	.315	1.20	2.42	84	1.3	95.5	33.4%	35.4%	51.5%
2022	KC	MLB	29	7	4	24	69	0	74^1	52	9	2.7	9.3	77	46.8%	.240	1.00	2.18	78	1.6	93.6	24.3%	32.4%	50.8%
2023 DC	*KC*	*MLB*	*30*	*3*	*3*	*25*	*65*	*0*	*56.3*	*51*	*5*	*3.3*	*10.6*	*66*	*43.5%*	*.318*	*1.29*	*3.49*	*91*	*0.5*	*94.5*	*30.9%*	*32.3%*	*49.6%*

Comparables: Bobby Parnell (60), Chris Devenski (59), Andrew Chafin (59)

It's March, and your team is so perfect there is no need to make any baseball trades. However, it's going to be April and May soon, and suddenly your team's bullpen will be in dire need of a couple of magicians. Barlow has the hair and goatee for it. He's also got the breaking stuff to pull off some daring escapes, as he's shown over the last few years in Kansas City. His arsenal is above average across the board except for his largely ornamental fastball, but he's found success working off his slider and finishing batters with his curve. He keeps batted stuff on the ground, and he limits free passes. In short, he's exactly the type of Houdini you want in the eighth or ninth inning when you're in a pennant race. But remember, your team doesn't need him … yet.

Jake Brentz LHP Born: 09/14/94 Age: 28 Bats: L Throws: L Height: 6'1" Weight: 205 lb. Origin: Round 11, 2013 Draft (#325 overall)

YEAR	TEAM	LVL	AGE	W	L	SV	G	GS	IP	H	HR	BB/9	K/9	K	GB%	BABIP	WHIP	ERA	DRA-	WARP	MPH	FB%	Whiff%	CSP
2021	KC	MLB	26	5	2	2	72	0	64	45	7	5.2	10.7	76	48.1%	.255	1.28	3.66	95	0.8	97.0	59.5%	30.2%	51.4%
2022	KC	MLB	27	0	3	0	8	0	5^1	11	1	16.9	15.2	9	33.3%	.625	3.94	23.63	100	0.1	96.2	61.6%	32.0%	46.7%
2023 DC	*FA*	*MLB*	*28*	*1*	*1*	*0*	*28*	*0*	*25*	*21*	*2*	*5.9*	*10.3*	*28*	*45.8%*	*.301*	*1.53*	*4.51*	*109*	*0.0*	*96.9*	*59.8%*	*28.7%*	*50.6%*

Comparables: Hunter Cervenka (73), Darin Downs (66), Rowan Wick (63)

A year after serving as the reliable southpaw in Kansas City's bullpen, Brentz fell apart. His April began miserably and ended worse: 11 of the final 16 batters he faced went on to score. Perhaps he was feeling the early effects of the elbow injury that'd require Tommy John surgery come July, or maybe those 16 batters picked up on something else. Either way, you can't blame 'em for keeping their big ol' traps shut as they circled the bases. Brentz has legit swing-and-miss, triple-digit stuff when healthy—a rarity among lefties in particular—so despite his control issues and the DFA he earned in November, he'll likely keep getting chances somewhere. At the very least we'll see his name pop up in beat writers' spring-training columns for years to come until he either locks down a steady job or tires of cleanly sailing his pitches to the backstop.

Kris Bubic LHP Born: 08/19/97 Age: 25 Bats: L Throws: L Height: 6'3" Weight: 225 lb. Origin: Round 1, 2018 Draft (#40 overall)

YEAR	TEAM	LVL	AGE	W	L	SV	G	GS	IP	H	HR	BB/9	K/9	K	GB%	BABIP	WHIP	ERA	DRA-	WARP	MPH	FB%	Whiff%	CSP
2020	KC	MLB	22	1	6	0	10	10	50	52	8	4.0	8.8	49	45.0%	.312	1.48	4.32	109	0.3	91.6	54.2%	24.9%	48.0%
2021	KC	MLB	23	6	7	0	29	20	130	121	22	4.1	7.9	114	47.1%	.280	1.38	4.43	123	-0.4	90.9	52.0%	23.5%	54.3%
2022	OMA	AAA	24	0	2	0	3	3	13^2	14	2	2.6	11.2	17	32.4%	.343	1.32	6.59	95	0.2				
2022	KC	MLB	24	3	13	0	28	27	129	156	18	4.4	7.7	110	41.0%	.353	1.70	5.58	132	-0.9	91.9	50.5%	21.3%	55.9%
2023 DC	*KC*	*MLB*	*25*	*5*	*6*	*0*	*19*	*19*	*97*	*103*	*10*	*4.1*	*8.1*	*87*	*42.9%*	*.321*	*1.52*	*4.70*	*117*	*0.0*	*91.5*	*51.5%*	*23.0%*	*54.4%*

Comparables: Brett Oberholtzer (76), Zack Britton (75), Chris Volstad (75)

The easiest way to avoid posting the worst ERA in a given season is to simply take up falconry instead of baseball. Another strategy is to exist at the same time as 40% of the 2022 Nationals rotation. Yet another method? Pitch so few innings that some of the league's other erstwhile starters beat you in a race to the bottom. Such was Bubic's way, as he allowed so many walks, homers and runs that he averaged fewer than seven outs in his first six starts of the year. After a short trip to find himself in Omaha (where ERA indicates he came closer to finding South Dakota), he returned to Kansas City and at least helped the Royals get through the season. He's got a very fine curveball, but the opposition simply knows to wait for his fastball. It's the best way to avoid looking silly against his breaker, with the easiest way still being taking up falconry.

Taylor Clarke RHP Born: 05/13/93 Age: 30 Bats: R Throws: R Height: 6'4" Weight: 217 lb. Origin: Round 3, 2015 Draft (#76 overall)

YEAR	TEAM	LVL	AGE	W	L	SV	G	GS	IP	H	HR	BB/9	K/9	K	GB%	BABIP	WHIP	ERA	DRA-	WARP	MPH	FB%	Whiff%	CSP
2020	AZ	MLB	27	3	0	0	12	5	43^1	35	8	4.4	8.3	40	44.3%	.237	1.29	4.36	108	0.3	94.4	45.5%	22.3%	45.7%
2021	RNO	AAA	28	1	0	0	7	0	7	6	0	2.6	10.3	8	58.8%	.353	1.14	0.00	84	0.1				
2021	AZ	MLB	28	1	3	0	43	0	43^1	52	4	2.9	8.1	39	37.6%	.350	1.52	4.98	103	0.3	95.7	53.4%	22.7%	53.9%
2022	KC	MLB	29	3	1	3	47	0	49	50	6	1.5	8.8	48	36.3%	.314	1.18	4.04	87	0.8	95.8	42.4%	25.2%	54.7%
2023 DC	*KC*	*MLB*	*30*	*2*	*2*	*0*	*58*	*0*	*50*	*50*	*6*	*2.7*	*7.9*	*43*	*39.0%*	*.301*	*1.31*	*3.90*	*105*	*0.1*	*95.2*	*47.7%*	*24.2%*	*51.4%*

Comparables: Chris Stratton (65), Mike Wright Jr. (60), Vidal Nuño (57)

Pining to stand out in a sea of relievers featuring heat and a slider, Clarke became a late-inning liaison for Mike Matheny by avoiding ball four. In the 46 instances in which Clarke missed the zone three times in one PA, batters reached base less than a quarter of the time. This is, simply put, an astonishing accomplishment. The league average OBP for a three-ball count last year was .548. The only other times in history a pitcher had 40 three-ball counts and an OBP split under .300 were Dennis Eckersley's 1991 All-Star season and mighty Josh Tomlin's 2019 campaign. Of the three, Clarke performed the best in those situations by far. This is not necessarily a projectable skill, but it's one worth celebrating, especially when relievers don't have much to hang their hats on beyond saves and beard length.

Dylan Coleman RHP Born: 09/16/96 Age: 26 Bats: R Throws: R Height: 6'5" Weight: 230 lb. Origin: Round 4, 2018 Draft (#111 overall)

YEAR	TEAM	LVL	AGE	W	L	SV	G	GS	IP	H	HR	BB/9	K/9	K	GB%	BABIP	WHIP	ERA	DRA-	WARP	MPH	FB%	Whiff%	CSP
2021	NWA	AA	24	1	1	4	18	0	24^2	19	2	1.8	13.5	37	50.9%	.333	0.97	2.92	69	0.6				
2021	OMA	AAA	24	4	0	3	27	0	33	19	2	4.6	15.3	56	36.2%	.304	1.09	3.55	66	1.0				
2021	KC	MLB	24	0	0	0	5	0	6^1	5	0	1.4	9.9	7	23.5%	.294	0.95	1.42	98	0.0	98.3	60.6%	26.8%	56.1%
2022	KC	MLB	25	5	2	0	68	0	68	47	5	4.9	9.4	71	41.7%	.247	1.24	2.78	85	1.2	97.6	57.5%	31.3%	51.3%
2023 DC	*KC*	*MLB*	*26*	*3*	*3*	*2*	*65*	*0*	*56.3*	*48*	*5*	*4.6*	*10.3*	*64*	*42.4%*	*.299*	*1.37*	*3.73*	*94*	*0.4*	*97.7*	*57.7%*	*30.7%*	*51.6%*

Comparables: Chad Sobotka (78), Reyes Moronta (76), Brian Ellington (75)

Two-pitch ponies need to do *something* to separate themselves from the herd of hard-throwing relievers before they can even be noted as two-pitch ponies. Nobody likes the term, which is why nobody uses it. Coleman, a throw-in from the late-2020 Trevor Rosenthal trade with the Padres, has a fastball that reaches triple digits to go with the requisite snappy slider. He used them to strike down a third of all minor leaguers he faced. In the majors, Coleman's walk rate has been high, but then again so is the number of whiffs he's produced. Last season, he began to pull away from the pack by becoming one of Mike Matheny's least apocalyptic late-inning choices. One less ideal way to stand out? Coleman missed his team's road trip to Toronto due to his lack of vaccination. Though on the 2022 Royals roster, perhaps that helped him blend in.

Jose Cuas RHP Born: 06/28/94 Age: 29 Bats: R Throws: R Height: 6'3" Weight: 195 lb. Origin: Round 11, 2015 Draft (#331 overall)

YEAR	TEAM	LVL	AGE	W	L	SV	G	GS	IP	H	HR	BB/9	K/9	K	GB%	BABIP	WHIP	ERA	DRA-	WARP	MPH	FB%	Whiff%	CSP
2021	NWA	AA	27	3	1	3	22	0	32^1	31	1	1.9	8.9	32	53.3%	.333	1.18	1.95	81	0.6				
2021	OMA	AAA	27	1	0	0	3	0	5	2	0	1.8	7.2	4	50.0%	.167	0.60	0.00	83	0.1				
2022	OMA	AAA	28	0	3	3	22	0	22^1	17	1	2.8	8.5	21	62.5%	.262	1.07	1.61	91	0.4				
2022	KC	MLB	28	4	2	1	47	0	37^2	39	2	5.7	8.1	34	49.1%	.327	1.67	3.58	107	0.2	93.1	62.3%	26.1%	52.4%
2023 DC	*KC*	*MLB*	*29*	*2*	*2*	*0*	*58*	*0*	*50*	*51*	*4*	*4.0*	*7.5*	*41*	*50.1%*	*.308*	*1.46*	*4.46*	*111*	*-0.1*	*93.1*	*62.3%*	*24.8%*	*52.4%*

Way back in 2015, the Brewers drafted this University of Maryland shortstop and the world didn't think much of it. Two years later he was converted to a pitcher, and a year later released. He got another chance with the Diamondbacks but, despite posting terrific numbers, was cut loose at the start of the pandemic. He began working as a FedEx delivery driver in his native New York City to support his family, but through the help of his brother Alex, a sports trainer, Cuas gave his dream one more shot in 2021. The Royals signed him out of the Atlantic League, and minor leaguers rarely touched his mid-90s sinker that comes from a true sidearm angle. On May 31, he entered his first MLB game and notched a strikeout to start his career. With all due respect to FedEx, Cuas' new deliveries are much more interesting.

Amir Garrett LHP Born: 05/03/92 Age: 31 Bats: R Throws: L Height: 6'5" Weight: 239 lb. Origin: Round 22, 2011 Draft (#685 overall)

YEAR	TEAM	LVL	AGE	W	L	SV	G	GS	IP	H	HR	BB/9	K/9	K	GB%	BABIP	WHIP	ERA	DRA-	WARP	MPH	FB%	Whiff%	CSP
2020	CIN	MLB	28	1	0	1	21	0	18^1	10	4	3.4	12.8	26	44.4%	.188	0.93	2.45	77	0.4	94.9	44.5%	43.7%	40.6%
2021	CIN	MLB	29	0	4	7	63	0	47^2	46	9	5.5	11.5	61	50.4%	.322	1.57	6.04	83	0.8	95.0	49.0%	33.7%	55.0%
2022	KC	MLB	30	3	1	0	60	0	45^1	28	0	6.4	9.7	49	38.2%	.255	1.32	4.96	100	0.4	94.1	43.8%	26.4%	51.5%
2023 DC	*KC*	*MLB*	*31*	*2*	*2*	*0*	*58*	*0*	*50*	*43*	*5*	*5.5*	*11.0*	*61*	*44.1%*	*.305*	*1.47*	*4.20*	*103*	*0.1*	*94.6*	*45.4%*	*30.2%*	*50.5%*

Comparables: Zack Britton (68), Andrew Chafin (64), J.C. Romero (62)

When Garrett upgraded home ballparks from the bandbox in Cincinnati to Kansas City's more forgiving confines, the hope was that his homer rate would fall in turn. Well, fall it did ... all the way down to zero. Incredibly, Garrett and Minnesota's Jovani Moran became the first pitchers since Andrew Chafin in 2018 to throw at least 40 innings without surrendering a single longball. It's a wild accomplishment, especially for someone as wild as Garrett. Now for the bad news: The last time a pitcher had as high an ERA without coughing up a homer? Dennis Powell in 1990. "Well *he* didn't have to face Aaron Judge," you might say, but neither did Garrett last season.

Jonathan Heasley RHP

Born: 01/27/97 Age: 26 Bats: R Throws: R Height: 6'3" Weight: 225 lb. Origin: Round 13, 2018 Draft (#392 overall)

YEAR	TEAM	LVL	AGE	W	L	SV	G	GS	IP	H	HR	BB/9	K/9	K	GB%	BABIP	WHIP	ERA	DRA-	WARP	MPH	FB%	Whiff%	CSP
2021	NWA	AA	24	7	3	0	22	21	105^{1}	95	18	2.9	10.3	120	39.0%	.303	1.22	3.33	89	1.4				
2021	KC	MLB	24	1	1	0	3	3	14^{2}	15	3	1.8	3.7	6	45.8%	.267	1.23	4.91	129	-0.1	93.8	49.6%	12.5%	52.5%
2022	OMA	AAA	25	1	2	0	9	9	39^{1}	35	7	2.3	10.3	45	42.9%	.289	1.14	4.35	83	0.9				
2022	KC	MLB	25	4	10	0	21	21	104	108	19	4.1	6.1	70	36.8%	.276	1.49	5.28	134	-0.8	93.4	48.7%	19.7%	55.5%
2023 DC	*KC*	*MLB*	*26*	*3*	*5*	*0*	*14*	*14*	*71.3*	*77*	*10*	*3.5*	*6.8*	*54*	*39.7%*	*.304*	*1.48*	*4.99*	*127*	*-0.4*	*93.5*	*48.8%*	*20.8%*	*55.2%*

Comparables: Daniel Wright (75), Josh Tomlin (75), Barry Enright (75)

Heasley is a baseball character straight out of a Disney film with his scruffy mullet complementing a stand-alone mustache. His aesthetic has just one flaw, though: sometimes he throws up. No, not up in the zone, but rather via his digestive system. He was taken out of a game last August after 4⅔ scoreless innings and two dry heaves. "Nothing I can do to stop it," Heasley told MLB.com afterwards. He attributed his condition to adrenaline and competitiveness, the mix of which "goes straight to my stomach, and sometimes, it comes out." He said this also happened before every one of his high school football games, as well as before some of his earlier outings. His esophagus can only hope he can stay in the rotation; otherwise the bullpen may need some extra buckets.

Carlos Hernández RHP

Born: 03/11/97 Age: 26 Bats: R Throws: R Height: 6'4" Weight: 245 lb. Origin: International Free Agent, 2016

YEAR	TEAM	LVL	AGE	W	L	SV	G	GS	IP	H	HR	BB/9	K/9	K	GB%	BABIP	WHIP	ERA	DRA-	WARP	MPH	FB%	Whiff%	CSP
2020	KC	MLB	23	0	1	0	5	3	14^{2}	19	4	3.7	8.0	13	42.6%	.349	1.70	4.91	103	0.1	96.3	51.4%	25.4%	48.3%
2021	OMA	AAA	24	2	1	0	6	6	26^{1}	28	6	2.1	8.9	26	43.6%	.306	1.29	4.44	112	0.2				
2021	KC	MLB	24	6	2	0	24	11	85^{2}	69	7	4.3	7.8	74	40.2%	.267	1.28	3.68	115	0.1	97.3	55.9%	25.8%	51.9%
2022	OMA	AAA	25	2	4	0	12	11	50	39	7	3.4	7.9	44	36.6%	.232	1.16	3.78	97	0.7				
2022	KC	MLB	25	0	5	0	27	7	56	72	7	5.0	5.6	35	36.7%	.339	1.84	7.39	146	-0.8	97.2	50.0%	23.7%	54.3%
2023 DC	*KC*	*MLB*	*26*	*3*	*3*	*0*	*65*	*0*	*56.3*	*60*	*7*	*4.0*	*7.3*	*46*	*38.7%*	*.308*	*1.51*	*4.82*	*121*	*-0.3*	*97.2*	*52.9%*	*24.6%*	*52.8%*

Comparables: Anthony Swarzak (63), Bronson Arroyo (63), Sean O'Sullivan (63)

He'll always be best known as the pitcher who jumped from rookie ball in 2019 to the majors in 2020, but Hernández was most notable last season for the large step he took backward. Batters figured out how to handle his fastball, and it didn't help that he left a lot of them in the middle of the zone. He was jettisoned from the rotation in mid-May as a result, though he'd eventually return to Kansas City as a reliever, faring slightly better in some low-leverage work. Though he's aged out of prospect-dom, Hernández is still very much a work in progress. In some ways, that's refreshing to think about. In others, it's a very Kansas City Royals sentiment.

Brad Keller RHP

Born: 07/27/95 Age: 27 Bats: R Throws: R Height: 6'5" Weight: 255 lb. Origin: Round 8, 2013 Draft (#240 overall)

YEAR	TEAM	LVL	AGE	W	L	SV	G	GS	IP	H	HR	BB/9	K/9	K	GB%	BABIP	WHIP	ERA	DRA-	WARP	MPH	FB%	Whiff%	CSP
2020	KC	MLB	24	5	3	0	9	9	54^{2}	39	2	2.8	5.8	35	51.6%	.233	1.02	2.47	94	0.8	92.9	59.2%	19.5%	49.1%
2021	KC	MLB	25	8	12	0	26	26	133^{2}	158	18	4.3	8.1	120	48.3%	.347	1.66	5.39	126	-0.5	93.9	60.9%	22.4%	55.5%
2022	KC	MLB	26	6	14	1	35	22	139^{2}	153	17	3.7	6.6	102	52.2%	.311	1.50	5.09	109	0.7	94.1	59.4%	21.7%	56.8%
2023 DC	*KC*	*MLB*	*27*	*6*	*6*	*0*	*51*	*8*	*81.3*	*92*	*7*	*3.8*	*6.7*	*60*	*51.0%*	*.325*	*1.56*	*4.76*	*118*	*-0.1*	*93.9*	*60.9%*	*22.1%*	*54.3%*

Comparables: Jimmy Jones (80), Nathan Eovaldi (80), Storm Davis (79)

There's never a great time to relegate a familiar starter to the bullpen. But it seemed a bit harsh that the Royals did so with Keller after his eight-run, three-inning start against the Dodgers in August—by no means an outing rife with reasons for optimism, but neither one that especially mattered to a fourth-place team. Nonetheless, Keller had been taking the mound every fifth day for quite some time, all the while trying to slalom through the red flags that were his low strikeout numbers. During his month in bullpen purgatory, the sinkerballer saw his slider become more effective, averaging nearly a K per frame. So he *can* miss bats, it turns out. The question simply becomes whether he can do so across 50 innings of above-average pitching, or if he's destined to once more toss 150 or so that pitching coaches watch through their palms.

Ben Kudrna RHP

Born: 01/30/03 Age: 20 Bats: R Throws: R Height: 6'3" Weight: 175 lb. Origin: Round 2, 2021 Draft (#43 overall)

YEAR	TEAM	LVL	AGE	W	L	SV	G	GS	IP	H	HR	BB/9	K/9	K	GB%	BABIP	WHIP	ERA	DRA-	WARP	MPH	FB%	Whiff%	CSP
2022	COL	A	19	2	5	0	17	17	72^{1}	66	4	4.0	7.6	61	39.4%	.292	1.35	3.48	112	0.3				
2023 non-DC	*KC*	*MLB*	*20*	*2*	*3*	*0*	*57*	*0*	*50*	*57*	*8*	*5.5*	*6.1*	*33*	*38.2%*	*.307*	*1.76*	*6.30*	*145*	*-0.9*			*20.5%*	

Comparables: Eric Pardinho (92), Mike Soroka (84), Eduardo Rodriguez (84)

The Royals went heavy on prep arms in the 2021 draft, and in their first full professional seasons, it was Kudrna who established himself as the cream of the crop. A big, projectable righty, he performed well as a teenager in the Carolina League. His strikeout numbers weren't great, but they should improve as he physically matures and his fastball gains velocity. He pairs the heater with a power slider and an improving changeup. It's an advanced repertoire for a young player, and one that gives him arguably the highest upside in the organization.

Asa Lacy LHP Born: 06/02/99 Age: 24 Bats: L Throws: L Height: 6'4" Weight: 215 lb. Origin: Round 1, 2020 Draft (#4 overall)

YEAR	TEAM	LVL	AGE	W	L	SV	G	GS	IP	H	HR	BB/9	K/9	K	GB%	BABIP	WHIP	ERA	DRA-	WARP	MPH	FB%	Whiff%	CSP
2021	QC	A+	22	2	5	0	14	14	52	41	5	7.1	13.7	79	33.0%	.346	1.58	5.19	81	1.1				
2022	ROY	ROK	23	1	0	0	4	2	8	4	1	15.7	11.2	10	44.4%	.176	2.25	9.00						
2022	NWA	AA	23	1	2	0	11	3	20	9	2	12.6	11.3	25	50.0%	.167	1.85	11.25	127	-0.2				
2023 non-DC	*KC*	*MLB*	*24*	*2*	*3*	*0*	*57*	*0*	*50*	*50*	*8*	*10.1*	*10.8*	*59*	*40.4%*	*.325*	*2.12*	*7.83*	*156*	*-1.2*			*31.9%*	

Comparables: Matt Krook (76), Edgar Olmos (75), Blake Taylor (73)

A dominant SEC pitcher with a classic starter's build and top-shelf stuff, Lacy was supposed to move up the ladder quickly and become an anchor of the major-league staff. Instead, injuries have limited him to just 80 professional innings since he was drafted fourth overall in 2020. During his time on the mound he's been wildly inconsistent, showing flashes of an elite repertoire but too often struggling to find the strike zone. The hope is that shoulder and back issues contributed to his lack of control, and that a healthy start to 2023 could get him back on track. He'll turn 24 mid-season, though, and instead of entering his prime, Lacy is already facing a make-or-break point in his career.

Jordan Lyles RHP Born: 10/19/90 Age: 32 Bats: R Throws: R Height: 6'5" Weight: 230 lb. Origin: Round 1, 2008 Draft (#38 overall)

YEAR	TEAM	LVL	AGE	W	L	SV	G	GS	IP	H	HR	BB/9	K/9	K	GB%	BABIP	WHIP	ERA	DRA-	WARP	MPH	FB%	Whiff%	CSP
2020	TEX	MLB	29	1	6	0	12	9	57^2	67	12	3.6	5.6	36	40.5%	.286	1.56	7.02	143	-0.7	92.4	48.1%	16.9%	48.6%
2021	TEX	MLB	30	10	13	0	32	30	180	194	38	2.8	7.3	146	36.8%	.300	1.39	5.15	134	-1.5	93.0	48.5%	23.7%	55.0%
2022	BAL	MLB	31	12	11	0	32	32	179	196	26	2.6	7.2	144	39.8%	.313	1.39	4.42	120	-0.1	91.7	49.3%	21.8%	54.5%
2023 DC	*KC*	*MLB*	*32*	*7*	*8*	*0*	*24*	*24*	*133.3*	*140*	*17*	*2.9*	*6.8*	*100*	*39.3%*	*.301*	*1.37*	*4.25*	*112*	*0.2*	*92.3*	*49.2%*	*21.8%*	*53.4%*

Comparables: Homer Bailey (66), Edgar Gonzalez (65), Rick Wise (64)

Only 18 starters have pitched 350 or more innings over the last two seasons. That list includes luminaries such as Sandy Alcantara, Zack Wheeler and Gerrit Cole. It also includes Lyles, who you may not have expected. Has he thrown the same type of 350 innings as those aforementioned, Cy Young-caliber pitchers? No, not even close. But there's an intrinsic value to soaking up that many innings; the Orioles bullpen had the ninth-best ERA in the league, and at least some of that can be attributed to this Steady Eddie giving them a break on his turns through the rotation. He went five innings or more in 25 of his 32 starts. And so, Lyles—whose early career was marred by a litany of injuries—joins Kansas City as an unlikely but reliable free agent workhorse, ready to chew up outs in the back half of the Royals rotation.

Daniel Lynch LHP Born: 11/17/96 Age: 26 Bats: L Throws: L Height: 6'6" Weight: 200 lb. Origin: Round 1, 2018 Draft (#34 overall)

YEAR	TEAM	LVL	AGE	W	L	SV	G	GS	IP	H	HR	BB/9	K/9	K	GB%	BABIP	WHIP	ERA	DRA-	WARP	MPH	FB%	Whiff%	CSP
2021	OMA	AAA	24	4	3	0	12	11	57	74	10	2.8	9.8	62	44.8%	.390	1.61	5.84	98	0.8				
2021	KC	MLB	24	4	6	0	15	15	68	80	9	4.1	7.3	55	38.9%	.336	1.63	5.69	152	-1.2	93.7	52.5%	25.8%	51.7%
2022	OMA	AAA	25	0	0	0	2	2	7	7	0	3.9	10.3	8	42.1%	.368	1.43	3.86	94	0.1				
2022	KC	MLB	25	4	13	0	27	27	131^2	155	21	3.6	8.3	122	42.0%	.337	1.57	5.13	124	-0.4	94.2	46.2%	25.4%	53.8%
2023 DC	*KC*	*MLB*	*26*	*7*	*9*	*0*	*27*	*27*	*132*	*146*	*16*	*3.6*	*8.3*	*122*	*42.3%*	*.331*	*1.50*	*4.79*	*119*	*-0.2*	*94.0*	*48.0%*	*26.2%*	*53.2%*

Comparables: Dallas Keuchel (79), Brett Oberholtzer (77), Eric Skoglund (77)

For many years it seemed as though Dayton Moore's draft strategy involved listing as many college pitchers as he could from memory and selecting exclusively from that group. To his credit, a lot of his picks have made the major-league rotation. But to his demise, few have stood out, which is likely a big reason why Moore is no longer making decisions for the Royals. Lynch is a poster child for the group, a requisite tall lefty with electric stuff who gives up far too many walks and homers nonetheless. In some ways, he was dealt a tough hand; he faced right-handed hitters 87% of the time last season, while the league-average for southpaws was down around 74%. Of course, that does not excuse the .287/.348/.455 line righties posted against him. Lynch's size, track record and left-handedness will afford him a few more chances to make future Royals GMs look smart, but only if righties stop making Lynch look quite so dumb.

Anthony Misiewicz LHP Born: 11/01/94 Age: 28 Bats: R Throws: L Height: 6'1" Weight: 196 lb. Origin: Round 18, 2015 Draft (#545 overall)

YEAR	TEAM	LVL	AGE	W	L	SV	G	GS	IP	H	HR	BB/9	K/9	K	GB%	BABIP	WHIP	ERA	DRA-	WARP	MPH	FB%	Whiff%	CSP
2020	SEA	MLB	25	0	2	0	21	0	20	20	2	2.7	11.3	25	31.4%	.367	1.30	4.05	87	0.4	91.0	76.8%	31.6%	44.7%
2021	SEA	MLB	26	5	5	0	66	0	54^2	61	7	2.5	8.7	53	43.1%	.340	1.39	4.61	95	0.6	92.5	68.8%	26.3%	55.1%
2022	TAC	AAA	27	0	0	0	13	0	12^1	10	2	4.4	9.5	13	54.3%	.242	1.30	3.65	87	0.2	93.8	37.1%	18.8%	
2022	OMA	AAA	27	2	1	0	8	0	6^2	3	2	1.4	9.5	7	37.5%	.071	0.60	4.05	96	0.1				
2022	SEA	MLB	27	0	1	0	17	0	13^2	14	1	4.0	5.3	8	32.6%	.310	1.46	4.61	108	0.1	93.0	26.9%	20.9%	55.6%
2022	KC	MLB	27	1	1	0	15	0	15^1	13	3	2.3	11.2	19	43.9%	.270	1.11	4.11	88	0.2	94.3	30.5%	27.5%	56.2%
2023 DC	*KC*	*MLB*	*28*	*2*	*2*	*0*	*58*	*0*	*50*	*52*	*6*	*3.0*	*8.3*	*46*	*41.8%*	*.314*	*1.38*	*4.21*	*110*	*-0.1*	*92.7*	*55.4%*	*24.7%*	*54.1%*

Comparables: Brooks Pounders (63), Wandy Peralta (63), Sean Gilmartin (62)

Last year there were four pitchers who had a relief outing of at least two innings where every out recorded was by strikeout. Misiewicz was one such pitcher to accomplish the feat a month after relocating to the Royals in the ol' cash considerations corollary. After the Mariners' trade for Ryan Borucki bogarted Misiewicz's opportunities—and probably his favorite chair, too—the native Michigander rediscovered some success with his cut fastball in Kansas City, using it to get swings and misses (which is not really what a cutter is supposed to do, but nobody questions the results). Long has baseball missed the perfect combination of un-hittability and un-pronounceability in a lefty reliever: ever since the retirement of Marc Rzepczynski, really. But Mi-, Misiew-, uh, Anthony could fill that role.

Frank Mozzicato LHP Born: 06/19/03 Age: 20 Bats: L Throws: L Height: 6'3" Weight: 175 lb. Origin: Round 1, 2021 Draft (#7 overall)

YEAR	TEAM	LVL	AGE	W	L	SV	G	GS	IP	H	HR	BB/9	K/9	K	GB%	BABIP	WHIP	ERA	DRA-	WARP	MPH	FB%	Whiff%	CSP
2022	COL	A	19	2	6	0	19	19	69	55	6	6.7	11.6	89	53.4%	.314	1.54	4.30	73	1.7				
2023 non-DC	*KC*	*MLB*	*20*	*2*	*3*	*0*	*57*	*0*	*50*	*55*	*7*	*8.1*	*8.4*	*46*	*48.0%*	*.322*	*2.00*	*6.99*	*149*	*-1.0*			*25.1%*	

Comparables: Robbie Ray (89), DL Hall (87), Grant Holmes (87)

Mozzicato's overall numbers from his first professional season look pedestrian, which could be seen as disappointing for the seventh overall selection in the previous year's draft. However, there was some improvement each month during his time in the Carolina League, as he became more in tune with how to use his advanced stuff and get hitters out. His curve is a legitimate out pitch and his changeup showed flashes as the year progressed. It's worth remembering he's a young, former cold weather prep pick who is still finding his way. Mozzicato is going to be a slow burn as a prospect, but he seems to at least be trending in the right direction.

Cody Poteet RHP Born: 07/30/94 Age: 28 Bats: R Throws: R Height: 6'1" Weight: 190 lb. Origin: Round 4, 2015 Draft (#116 overall)

YEAR	TEAM	LVL	AGE	W	L	SV	G	GS	IP	H	HR	BB/9	K/9	K	GB%	BABIP	WHIP	ERA	DRA-	WARP	MPH	FB%	Whiff%	CSP
2021	JAX	AAA	26	1	0	0	2	2	8	6	1	3.4	13.5	12	29.4%	.313	1.13	3.38	102	0.1				
2021	MIA	MLB	26	2	3	0	7	7	30^2	25	7	4.7	9.4	32	33.3%	.234	1.34	4.99	106	0.2	93.8	48.7%	24.1%	57.8%
2022	MIA	MLB	27	0	1	0	12	2	28	23	4	3.5	6.8	21	52.4%	.244	1.21	3.86	107	0.2	94.7	37.5%	29.9%	55.6%
2023 non-DC	*KC*	*MLB*	*28*	*2*	*2*	*0*	*57*	*0*	*50*	*47*	*6*	*3.6*	*8.2*	*45*	*44.2%*	*.290*	*1.35*	*3.94*	*101*	*0.2*	*94.3*	*42.9%*	*27.4%*	*56.6%*

Comparables: Taylor Clarke (63), Stephen Fife (61), Tyler Pill (58)

A four-seam fastball-heavy approach wasn't working for Poteet, so he folded in a sinker and made the changeup his primary offering. That created a much more groundball-oriented profile, but he still walked too many hitters to accommodate such a low strikeout percentage. Given that his most unique trait is his ability to spin his breakers nearly 3,000 RPM, it's a wonder he hasn't attempted to weaponize his curveball or slider more. In years past, a move to Kansas City on a minor-league deal might mean an abrupt end to those wonderings. Instead, with new, analytically minded pitching coach Brian Sweeney aboard, Poteet is one to watch in a developing rotation.

Brady Singer RHP Born: 08/04/96 Age: 26 Bats: R Throws: R Height: 6'5" Weight: 215 lb. Origin: Round 1, 2018 Draft (#18 overall)

YEAR	TEAM	LVL	AGE	W	L	SV	G	GS	IP	H	HR	BB/9	K/9	K	GB%	BABIP	WHIP	ERA	DRA-	WARP	MPH	FB%	Whiff%	CSP
2020	KC	MLB	23	4	5	0	12	12	64^1	52	8	3.2	8.5	61	53.7%	.260	1.17	4.06	79	1.3	93.5	57.9%	24.3%	48.3%
2021	OMA	AAA	24	0	2	0	2	2	4^2	8	1	1.9	3.9	2	52.6%	.412	1.93	13.50	109	0.0				
2021	KC	MLB	24	5	10	0	27	27	128^1	146	14	3.7	9.2	131	50.6%	.350	1.55	4.91	103	1.0	93.8	58.0%	25.3%	54.5%
2022	OMA	AAA	25	1	0	0	3	3	13^2	8	3	2.6	7.2	11	57.9%	.143	0.88	3.29	100	0.2				
2022	KC	MLB	25	10	5	0	27	24	153^1	140	18	2.1	8.8	150	47.8%	.303	1.14	3.23	82	2.9	93.8	54.3%	23.0%	57.2%
2023 DC	*KC*	*MLB*	*26*	*9*	*9*	*0*	*29*	*29*	*154.3*	*159*	*14*	*2.8*	*8.2*	*140*	*49.7%*	*.318*	*1.34*	*3.93*	*102*	*1.2*	*93.8*	*56.1%*	*23.3%*	*55.2%*

Comparables: Alex Cobb (73), Danny Salazar (71), Vance Worley (71)

In 2017, Jason Vargas won 18 games for the Royals: an astounding stat for many reasons, but perhaps most of all because it continues to make Vargas relevant today. You see, that marked the last time a Kansas City pitcher notched at least 10 wins in a season until Singer went on a bit of a September tear, allowing one run across 20 innings to triumph in three straight games. He did so after not making the rotation out of spring training, taking a demotion for a couple weeks, then finally starting a game in the majors in mid-May. The former first-rounder finally seemed to "put it all together," as the coaches say, with a reformed sinker and an improved off-speed pitch. He even might be "Jason Vargas good" now, which is something coaches almost never say.

Collin Snider RHP Born: 10/10/95 Age: 27 Bats: R Throws: R Height: 6'4" Weight: 195 lb. Origin: Round 12, 2017 Draft (#360 overall)

YEAR	TEAM	LVL	AGE	W	L	SV	G	GS	IP	H	HR	BB/9	K/9	K	GB%	BABIP	WHIP	ERA	DRA-	WARP	MPH	FB%	Whiff%	CSP
2021	NWA	AA	25	2	1	3	27	0	36^1	32	1	3.5	10.2	41	47.9%	.333	1.27	2.97	91	0.4				
2021	OMA	AAA	25	3	2	0	21	0	30	39	7	3.6	6.9	23	52.9%	.337	1.70	6.30	114	0.2				
2022	OMA	AAA	26	2	1	0	20	0	21^2	18	1	6.6	5.4	13	60.3%	.254	1.57	5.40	116	0.1				
2022	KC	MLB	26	4	2	0	42	0	34^1	40	3	3.9	5.8	22	50.0%	.343	1.60	6.55	122	0.0	96.2	48.7%	20.9%	50.0%
2023 DC	*KC*	*MLB*	*27*	*1*	*2*	*0*	*43*	*0*	*37.7*	*45*	*4*	*4.5*	*6.4*	*26*	*51.4%*	*.331*	*1.70*	*5.82*	*137*	*-0.6*	*96.2*	*48.7%*	*20.7%*	*50.0%*

Comparables: Preston Claiborne (72), Ryan Kelly (71), A.J. Achter (71)

Snider made it to the majors by ditching his four-seamer for a wily sinker. He made the team, so in some ways you can't argue with the results. After his first six scoreless outings, however, he left plenty of room for disagreement. Snider's above-average vertical break on the pitch kept most of the contact he surrendered rolling around in ballparks rather than in stands, but hitters smacked him around nonetheless for lots of ground-ball hits. One of many recent hard-throwing Vanderbilt pitchers, he tosses the type of pitch mix that works in theory to eliminate middle-inning catastrophes, but, lo and behold, that wasn't the case in 2022. Looks like we can argue over his switch to the sinker after all.

Josh Staumont RHP Born: 12/21/93 Age: 29 Bats: R Throws: R Height: 6'3" Weight: 200 lb. Origin: Round 2, 2015 Draft (#64 overall)

YEAR	TEAM	LVL	AGE	W	L	SV	G	GS	IP	H	HR	BB/9	K/9	K	GB%	BABIP	WHIP	ERA	DRA-	WARP	MPH	FB%	Whiff%	CSP
2020	KC	MLB	26	2	1	0	26	0	25^{2}	20	2	5.6	13.0	37	28.6%	.333	1.40	2.45	98	0.3	98.2	72.5%	36.7%	45.8%
2021	KC	MLB	27	4	3	5	64	0	65^{2}	43	6	3.7	9.9	72	38.7%	.236	1.07	2.88	91	0.9	96.7	65.3%	26.7%	55.7%
2022	KC	MLB	28	3	3	3	42	0	37^{2}	37	3	6.9	10.3	43	28.2%	.343	1.75	6.45	99	0.4	96.4	65.3%	27.5%	53.5%
2023 DC	*KC*	*MLB*	*29*	*2*	*2*	*1*	*58*	*0*	*50*	*42*	*5*	*5.2*	*9.5*	*53*	*35.1%*	*.281*	*1.42*	*4.01*	*101*	*0.2*	*96.7*	*66.4%*	*27.9%*	*53.3%*

Comparables: Justin Grimm (69), Ryan Cook (67), Ryne Stanek (66)

Many moons ago, Ichiro famously, uh, colorfully described to Bob Costas how warm Kansas City gets in August. His metaphor would seem PG compared to how Staumont would likely recount said time of year after a rough campaign. In his eight appearances in the eighth month of 2022, Staumont posted a 16.71 ERA before getting sidelined by biceps tendinitis. Unfortunately, he'd only just returned from a month-long hiatus nursing a bad neck. Prior to those maladies, he'd used his mid- to upper-90s fastball to serve as a dependable bullpen option, even notching a couple of saves. But injuries tend to gradually get worse as the season wears on, a reality we usually see baked into a reliever's final season statistics. For Staumont in particular, it was baked in worse than two rats in a sock.

Ryan Yarbrough LHP Born: 12/31/91 Age: 31 Bats: R Throws: L Height: 6'5" Weight: 205 lb. Origin: Round 4, 2014 Draft (#111 overall)

YEAR	TEAM	LVL	AGE	W	L	SV	G	GS	IP	H	HR	BB/9	K/9	K	GB%	BABIP	WHIP	ERA	DRA-	WARP	MPH	FB%	Whiff%	CSP
2020	TB	MLB	28	1	4	0	11	9	55^{2}	54	5	1.9	7.1	44	40.9%	.299	1.19	3.56	99	0.6	84.6	59.4%	27.7%	48.6%
2021	TB	MLB	29	9	7	0	30	21	155	163	25	1.6	6.8	117	35.0%	.293	1.23	5.11	125	-0.6	83.0	54.0%	21.2%	52.3%
2022	DUR	AAA	30	2	2	0	7	7	27^{2}	32	3	3.9	8.5	26	37.9%	.345	1.59	4.55	120	0.1				
2022	TB	MLB	30	3	8	0	20	9	80	88	12	2.5	6.9	61	37.2%	.306	1.38	4.50	131	-0.5	83.8	49.1%	22.2%	53.6%
2023 DC	*KC*	*MLB*	*31*	*8*	*8*	*0*	*57*	*14*	*106*	*112*	*12*	*2.2*	*6.4*	*75*	*37.5%*	*.300*	*1.31*	*4.17*	*111*	*0.1*	*83.8*	*53.8%*	*22.2%*	*52.1%*

Comparables: Doug Rau (83), Dennis Rasmussen (82), Scott McGregor (82)

Nobody would ever peg Yarbrough as a rebel, but while the league zigs, the southpaw continues to zag. In an era dominated by velocity, over 50% of Yarbrough's pitches came in under 80 mph. The throwback thrower tossed Watergate sliders around 72 mph and Saturday Night Fever curveballs a few ticks higher. His cutter got physical around 82, while his Top Gun was a seldom-used fastball that topped out around 86. His retro style worked for a few years, but not in 2022. His strikeout rate is still well below average while his home run rate is above. He has been able to limit walks in his career, but even that wasn't the case last year. Previously an underrated, underpaid starter without the actual starts to his name, he now appears to be a replacement-level (or worse) pitcher regardless of his role. The Royals offered him a one-year, $3 million deal to see if he can unearth his former magic.

Angel Zerpa LHP Born: 09/27/99 Age: 23 Bats: L Throws: L Height: 6'0" Weight: 220 lb. Origin: International Free Agent, 2016

YEAR	TEAM	LVL	AGE	W	L	SV	G	GS	IP	H	HR	BB/9	K/9	K	GB%	BABIP	WHIP	ERA	DRA-	WARP	MPH	FB%	Whiff%	CSP
2021	QC	A+	21	4	0	0	8	8	41^{2}	32	2	1.7	11.4	53	44.2%	.297	0.96	2.59	83	0.8				
2021	NWA	AA	21	0	3	0	13	13	45^{1}	51	7	3.8	10.7	54	47.6%	.370	1.54	5.96	88	0.6				
2021	KC	MLB	21	0	1	0	1	1	5	3	0	1.8	7.2	4	40.0%	.214	0.80	0.00	117	0.0	94.4	67.6%		
2022	NWA	AA	22	2	5	0	13	13	64	70	7	3.0	9.7	69	46.5%	.354	1.42	4.36	81	1.0				
2022	OMA	AAA	22	0	0	0	6	6	7^{2}	2	0	4.7	0.0	0	58.3%	.083	0.78	1.17	111	0.0				
2022	KC	MLB	22	2	1	0	3	2	11	9	2	2.5	2.5	3	50.0%	.194	1.09	1.64	139	-0.1	94.1	59.2%	10.3%	58.7%
2023 DC	*KC*	*MLB*	*23*	*2*	*2*	*0*	*17*	*3*	*26.3*	*31*	*2*	*3.8*	*6.2*	*18*	*47.2%*	*.327*	*1.60*	*5.34*	*131*	*-0.2*	*94.2*	*61.3%*	*19.2%*	*44.4%*

Comparables: Yohander Méndez (34), Daniel Norris (29), Adalberto Mejía (27)

Zerpa has thrown only 25 innings above Double-A, but they've all been pretty great. His two starts last season produced a five-inning, one-run gem against the Blue Jays and a four-inning, one-run outing against the Angels. Royals coaches are reportedly over the moon with his mound presence and mentality, and his stuff is nothing to sneeze at, either: The southpaw has a sinker, slider and changeup, and he commands them all well. A knee injury in his L.A. outing prevented Zerpa from building on his promising start, but don't sleep on him as an impactful member of the Royals pitching staff in 2023, which will be his age-23 season.

LINEOUTS

Hitters

HITTER	POS	TEAM	LVL	AGE	PA	R	2B	3B	HR	RBI	BB	K	SB	CS	AVG/OBP/SLG	DRC+	BABIP	BRR	DRP	WARP
Nate Eaton	RF	NWA	AA	25	159	23	4	1	4	19	11	29	12	1	.271/.331/.400	102	.309	1.4	3B(23): 1.8, RF(8): 1.0, LF(3): -0.2	1.3
	RF	OMA	AAA	25	229	33	10	3	9	32	21	48	11	4	.295/.376/.510	106	.345	0.1	RF(34): 0.4, CF(10): -1.3, LF(5): 0.1	0.9
	RF	KC	MLB	25	122	16	4	3	1	12	10	30	11	1	.264/.331/.387	87	.346	1.9	RF(20): 1.7, 3B(15): -1, LF(6): -0.1	0.5
Maikel Garcia	SS	NWA	AA	22	369	63	24	1	4	33	41	60	27	3	.291/.369/.409	111	.345	1.7	SS(78): 0.3	1.9
	SS	OMA	AAA	22	186	41	10	0	7	28	17	42	12	5	.274/.341/.463	106	.322	-0.3	SS(39): -1.2	0.5
	SS	KC	MLB	22	23	1	1	0	0	2	1	5	0	0	.318/.348/.364	89	.412	-0.3	SS(8): -0.1	0.0
Michael Massey	2B	NWA	AA	24	248	36	15	0	9	48	21	54	9	2	.305/.359/.495	101	.356	0.9	2B(46): 0.9	0.8
	2B	OMA	AAA	24	143	21	13	0	7	29	13	35	4	0	.325/.392/.595	101	.395	0.1	2B(28): 2.0, 3B(2): 1.1	0.7
	2B	KC	MLB	24	194	16	9	1	4	17	9	46	3	0	.243/.307/.376	83	.304	0.1	2B(48): -2.3, 3B(1): -0.1	0.0
Erick Peña	CF	COL	A	19	326	25	10	1	9	36	41	121	6	5	.149/.258/.288	69	.216	0.1	CF(79): 2.1, RF(2): -0.1	-0.4
Samad Taylor	2B/LF	BUF	AAA	23	280	41	10	2	9	45	28	62	23	5	.258/.337/.426	112	.305	1.9	2B(39): 0.2, LF(25): 1.8, SS(1): -0.0	1.4
Luca Tresh	C/DH	QC	A+	22	347	48	15	1	14	54	41	85	3	3	.273/.360/.470	127	.332	-0.5	C(49): -4.0	1.7
	C/DH	NWA	AA	22	106	16	4	0	5	14	13	25	1	0	.253/.358/.462	112	.295	0.2	C(23): -1.1	0.4
Cayden Wallace	3B	COL	A	20	122	15	7	3	2	16	12	22	8	1	.294/.369/.468	112	.353	-1.8	3B(25): -0.2	0.4

How is utility player **Nate Eaton** like a clothing store's assistant manager on Adderall? Both have lots of speed but shouldn't let their Gap power get to their heads. ⚾ With the Royals in desperate need of infielders, young **Maikel Garcia** debuted out of Double-A, displaying decent bat-to-ball skills across nine big-league games, all on the road. Nobody tell him about the fountain in Kauffman; it's always fun to watch a player's reaction the first time they see it. ⚾ **Michael Massey** spelled Whit Merrifield in Toronto because of *that* whole ordeal, then usurped his playing time when his predecessor was dealt there. If he can bring his minor-league power with him in 2023, he'll embody the OPS of the Massey's. ⚾ No one is making Carlos Beltrán comps anymore about **Erick Peña**—at least not anyone who saw him play last season. He was a trainwreck in the Carolina League, suffering a complete collapse of his hit tool against Low-A pitching. ⚾ Rumors of a Whit Merrifield trade swirled forever in Kansas City, so when they finally pulled the trigger, their return of **Samad Taylor** and Max Castillo seemed underwhelming. But while a top prospect he may never be, Taylor could contribute in the majors soon thanks to his speed and defensive versatility. ⚾ Looks like we can chalk **Luca Tresh**'s poor post-draft numbers up to fatigue, as his 2022 output was more in line with expectations. The young backstop is still raw behind the dish, but at it he's shown he can get his plus raw power into games without zapping his contact ability. ⚾ One of the top power hitters in the SEC, **Caden Wallace**'s physicality and bat speed produce impressive exit velocities. There are still questions as to if he'll make enough contact against advanced pitching, but if he puts those to rest, the recent second-rounder will profile as an everyday player.

Pitchers

PITCHER	TEAM	LVL	AGE	W	L	SV	G	GS	IP	H	HR	BB/9	K/9	K	GB%	BABIP	WHIP	ERA	DRA-	WARP	MPH	FB%	WHF	CSP
Jonathan Bowlan	ROY	ROK	25	0	1	0	7	7	19^{1}	29	1	1.9	12.1	26	36.2%	.491	1.71	5.12						
	NWA	AA	25	1	3	0	9	9	39	51	7	3.9	6.9	30	42.4%	.352	1.74	6.92	135	-0.6				
Max Castillo	NH	AA	23	3	1	0	6	6	29	21	3	4.3	10.9	35	49.3%	.261	1.21	3.10	86	0.6				
	OMA	AAA	23	1	1	0	7	6	21^{1}	35	3	3.8	9.3	22	32.5%	.416	2.06	8.44	117	0.1				
	BUF	AAA	23	2	0	0	5	3	27^{1}	10	2	3.3	9.5	29	45.0%	.138	0.73	0.66	87	0.6				
	KC	MLB	23	0	2	0	5	4	18^{2}	23	4	4.8	8.2	17	40.0%	.345	1.77	9.16	116	0.0	92.5	46.0%	23.1%	52.1%
	TOR	MLB	23	0	0	0	9	2	20^{2}	15	4	2.2	8.7	20	51.8%	.212	0.97	3.05	96	0.2	93.5	50.9%	25.3%	48.9%
Ben Hernandez	COL	A	20	1	7	0	23	23	77	83	7	4.7	8.3	71	49.6%	.342	1.60	5.38	110	0.4				
Andrew Hoffmann	ROM	A+	22	7	2	0	15	15	80	63	9	2.4	10.1	90	46.6%	.277	1.05	2.36	91	1.0				
	NWA	AA	22	2	4	0	9	9	39^{1}	50	5	4.6	6.9	30	31.8%	.354	1.78	6.64	147	-0.9				
Jackson Kowar	OMA	AAA	25	4	10	0	20	20	83^{1}	95	14	4.6	9.5	88	42.7%	.348	1.66	6.16	108	0.8				
	KC	MLB	25	0	0	0	7	0	15^{2}	27	4	6.3	9.8	17	50.0%	.460	2.43	9.77	100	0.1	95.7	46.6%	26.1%	54.1%
Daniel Mengden	OMA	AAA	29	7	7	0	25	20	109	106	24	4.6	7.7	93	44.9%	.276	1.49	5.20	118	0.5				
	KC	MLB	29	0	1	1	5	1	7	10	1	1.3	10.3	8	34.8%	.409	1.57	5.14	92	0.1	92.6	29.4%	21.7%	65.0%
T.J. Sikkema	HV	A+	23	1	1	0	11	10	36^{1}	21	3	2.2	13.4	54	47.9%	.257	0.83	2.48	82	0.6				
	NWA	AA	23	0	5	0	8	8	32^{2}	42	6	4.1	8.0	29	56.5%	.360	1.74	7.44	118	-0.2				
Jacob Wallace	POR	AA	23	8	2	1	47	0	56^{2}	35	7	7.8	12.1	76	39.3%	.243	1.48	3.81	86	1.1				
Beck Way	QC	A+	22	3	3	0	7	7	35^{2}	24	1	4.3	11.9	47	41.0%	.288	1.15	3.79	90	0.5				
	HV	A+	22	5	5	0	15	15	72^{1}	55	9	3.2	10.0	80	46.1%	.271	1.12	3.73	95	0.7				

A strong 2019 campaign put **Jonathan Bowlan** on the prospect radar, but Tommy John surgery and other obstacles have slowed his path toward becoming a future back-end starter. We know that command can be the last piece to return to pitchers post-TJ, and that proved true for Bowlan in his Texas League stint. ⚾ The Royals asked for righty **Max Castillo** in return for Whit Merrifield because they liked his changeup so much, but then again all baseball trades are basically changeups when you think about it. ⚾ Hard contact and a lack of command plagued **Ben Hernandez** all season long in the Carolina League. A former second-round selection, he has the pedigree and tools to be a quality big-league starter but has yet to put it all together on the mound. ⚾ Dominant in the early season for Atlanta's High-A squad, **Andrew Hoffmann** was moved to Kansas City via trade. He quickly fit in with his new organization by walking more batters and giving up hard contact in bunches. ⚾ Six major leaguers have career ERAs above 10 with at least 40 innings pitched, but **Jackson Kowar** can scratch his name off that rolodex if his next 3⅔ innings are of the shutout variety. After that, it's up to him if he wants to return to the naughty list. ⚾ **Daniel Mengden** serves as a proof that a cool mustache can take you far in this game, but not as far as his fastballs tend to travel once they make contact with enemy bats. ⚾ Part of the return from the Yankees in the Andrew Benintendi deal, prospect **T.J. Sikkema**'s funky delivery and sweeping breaking pitches make him especially tough on left-handed hitters. The Royals used him in a starting role after the trade, but a move to the 'pen could be imminent for the 24-year-old. ⚾ **Jacob Wallace** raises the haunting question, "What if Matt Barnes, but with a bad breaking ball?" The answer is a pitcher with tons of strikeouts and walks who's condemned to up-and-down reliever hell unless his command jumps at least a grade (if not two). The Royals nabbed him for the low cost of Wyatt Mills this winter. ⚾ Throw hard, mix in a slider: This is the **Beck Way**, who came to Kansas City by way of New York after the Yankees beckoned for Andrew Benintendi.

MINNESOTA TWINS

Essay by Whitney McIntosh

Player comments by Darius Austin and BP staff

In June of 1890, *The New York Times* blared a headline with a St. Paul, Minn., dateline: "CENSUS-BRED BITTERNESS." Distrust in the Twin Cities had come to a head, as seven census takers from Minneapolis had been detained by a U.S. Marshal for allegedly padding the population count. The eastern twin passed St. Paul in population for the first time in the 1880 census, and the latter took it personally, further stoking a rumbling competitiveness that had mushroomed between the two cities since their incorporation near the middle of the century.

Allegations flew. That the St. Paul U.S. District Attorney opted not to prosecute because he was actually a resident of Minneapolis. That the supposed scheme was on the orders of the Republican National Party in the hopes of bolstering support for President Benjamin Harrison, who had been elected despite losing the popular vote. That a Minneapolis government inspector was secretly working in the interest of St. Paul. Some St. Paul business leaders and citizens vowed to "descend upon Washington" to secure a special prosecutor's impartiality. *The Times* calls St. Paul "jealous" and Minneapolis refers to the entire thing as "a great game of bluff" ... but still detains St. Paul census takers in kind, for the same allegations levied in the opposite direction.

Eventually, federal officials did a recount without either city's participation and Minneapolis would come out ahead by many thousands. It's the type of situation where the end result seems so obvious looking at it from an outside perspective, but the Twin Cities insisted on going about everything the messiest way possible.

Similar nonsense would happen nearly a century later when, in 1965, Minneapolis and St. Paul changed over to Daylight Savings Time two weeks apart despite state law mandating clocks change on May 23. By this point the rivalry felt like a truly internal affair, given that urban sprawl had essentially conjoined the two cities. Minneapolis' mayor declared, "Obedience to state law is an elementary lesson in civics that we all should have learned in sixth grade," and St. Paul essentially responded with "there are plenty of laws broken that you don't enforce all the time," which isn't the airtight argument they may have intended. Commuters between each city had to reset their watches on their way to work and then on the way home again, and some offices

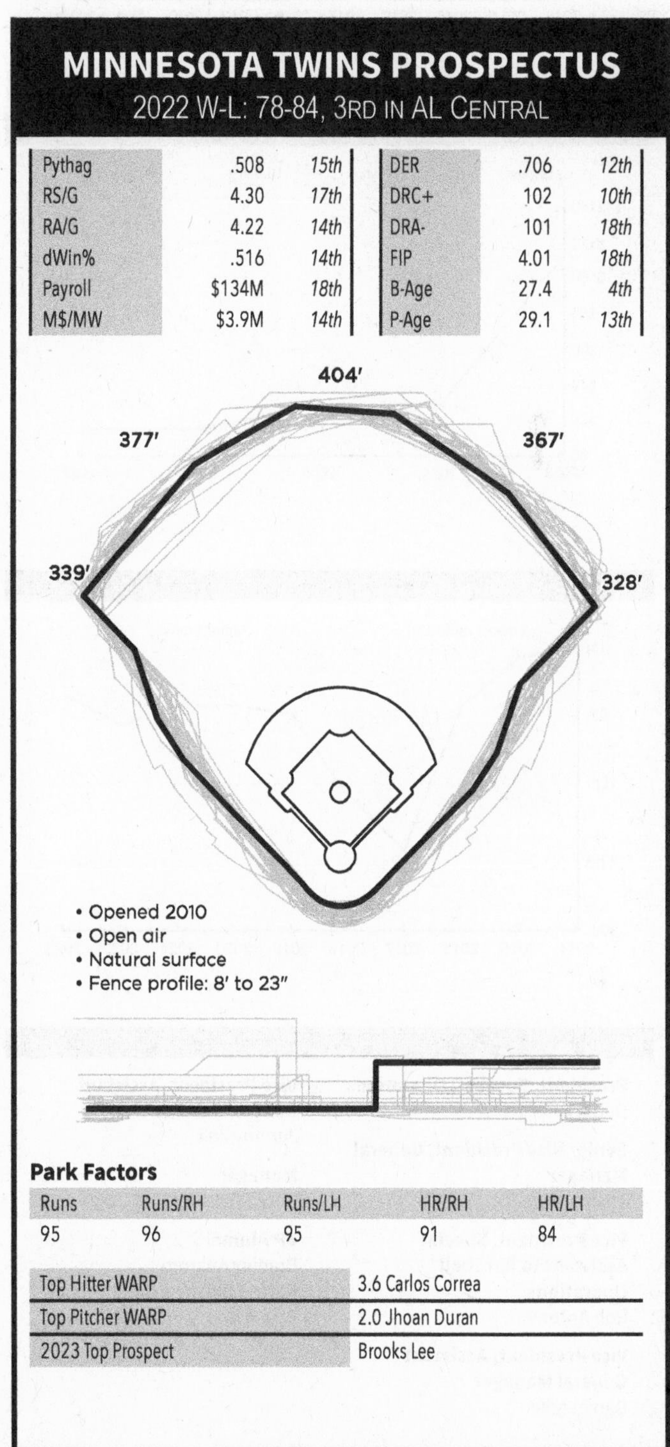

MINNESOTA TWINS PROSPECTUS

2022 W-L: 78-84, 3RD IN AL CENTRAL

Pythag	.508	*15th*	DER	.706	*12th*
RS/G	4.30	*17th*	DRC+	102	*10th*
RA/G	4.22	*14th*	DRA-	101	*18th*
dWin%	.516	*14th*	FIP	4.01	*18th*
Payroll	$134M	*18th*	B-Age	27.4	*4th*
M$/MW	$3.9M	*14th*	P-Age	29.1	*13th*

- Opened 2010
- Open air
- Natural surface
- Fence profile: 8' to 23"

Park Factors

Runs	Runs/RH	Runs/LH	HR/RH	HR/LH
95	96	95	91	84

Top Hitter WARP	3.6 Carlos Correa
Top Pitcher WARP	2.0 Jhoan Duran
2023 Top Prospect	Brooks Lee

Payroll History (in millions)

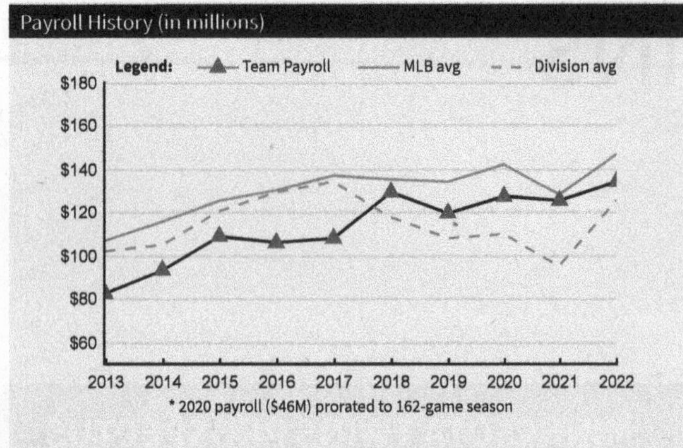

Future Commitments (in millions)

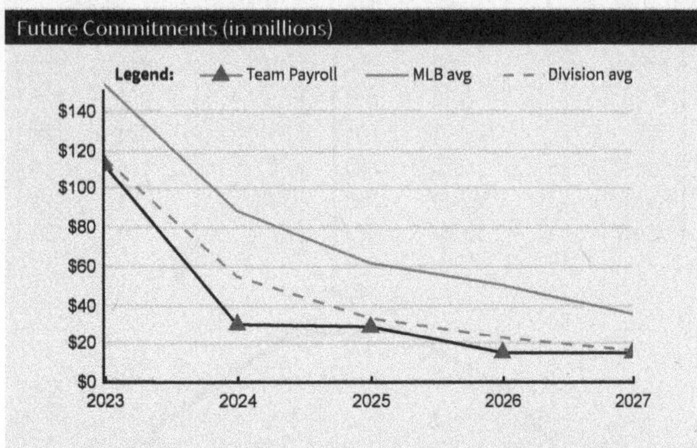

Farm System Ranking

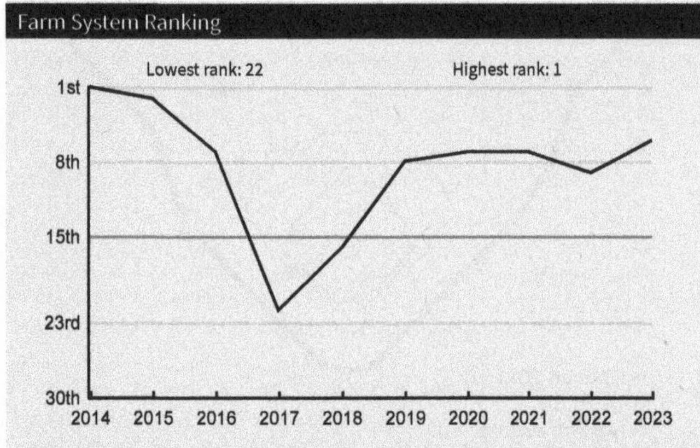

Personnel

President, Baseball Operations
Derek Falvey

Senior Vice President, General Manager
Thad Levine

Vice President, Special Assistant to Baseball Operations
Rob Antony

Vice President, Assistant General Manager
Daniel Adler

Vice President, Assistant General Manager
Jeremy Zoll

Manager
Rocco Baldelli

BP Alumni
Bradley Ankrom
Kevin Goldstein
Ezra Wise

reportedly changed their clocks begrudgingly but then adjusted workers' hours in kind as a corresponding move. A real Escher painting of a situation, to the benefit of basically no one.

It's part of a decades-long pattern of the Twin Cities butting heads in a manner that foregrounded blind pride and immense stubbornness, always seeming to make it harder on themselves than strictly necessary. Their history reminds you less of siblings than of *Sesame Street*'s Two-Headed Monster, with one head trying to practice piano while the other head tries to hear what it sounds like when you mash all the piano keys at once. It's a metropolitan area at war with itself, with a baseball team now following suit, with the type of anecdotes that make you go "Can't we just settle on something and move on with our lives?"

⚾ ⚾ ⚾

The modern Twins reject logical roster construction strategies. Rather than just go with the straightforward options, buy or sell, they manage to identify the most difficult path to success and bushwhack their way through it with muddled-yet-predictable results. It's not as if there is no optimism to be found, and there are clear upsides to the current squad—nearly every player offers a 90th-percentile projection worth dreaming on—but in the "great game of bluff" that is the AL Central right now the Twins are perhaps one of the teams with the most unintelligible reasoning as to why they do what they do.

The most obvious instances of upside are also two of the most electric talents Target Field has ever seen. But that pair of crowd-pleasing players are also facing serious injury woes ... again. And the space between the best- and worst-case scenarios is wider than the Mississippi, with the ceiling for each player masking deeper and more widespread worries about where exactly this team could be headed.

Byron Buxton and Royce Lewis, the Twins' no. 1 picks (in Lewis' case, first overall) in the 2012 and 2017 MLB drafts, respectively, are quickly becoming a matching set for all of the most depressing reasons. And with the Twins' offseason consisting of a handful of supporting moves but nothing close to a big splash, a lot hangs on these two becoming consistent and healthy at the same time. Buxton has only broken the 100-game threshold once in his major league career, and although his 2022 injuries were not so frequent or varied as in previous years, he played only 92 games due to hip problems that eventually put him on the injured list, before undergoing season-ending surgery to remedy an ailing right knee.

Buxton was one of only two people in the 2022 starting lineup not named Carlos Correa to put up at least three WARP (the third, AL batting champion Luis Arraez), and his .526 slugging percentage was nearly 80 points higher than Correa's. That doesn't even get into his defense, which provided a few thousand endlessly rewatchable moments, give or take. "If he's healthy, it's as good as any free agency signing" is one of the most meaningless front office clichés each offseason or trade deadline, but boy if it hasn't applied perfectly to Buxton for multiple years running. And may for years more, considering the seven-year, $100 million contract extension inked over the 2021-22 offseason even in light of his full injury ledger.

Lewis, meanwhile, may have even more of a fraught future after tearing the same ACL two years in a row. The concept of bad luck almost doesn't begin to cover another top draft pick who can make plays like the one on which he was injured—high-baseball IQ, running-backward-on-the-track plays—suffering repeated severe injuries. He's optimistic his recovery will be faster than the first time, which seems equal parts medical insight and insistent emotional optimism, the need to believe that it couldn't possibly be as bad as what he already pushed through during his lost 2021. Based on what Lewis has shown when he's gotten big-league chances, that optimism is both understandable and pitiable.

Even players like Trevor Larnach and Alex Kirilloff, both just in their mid-20s, could be tremendous pieces, if those pieces can hold together. Kirilloff too had surgery on the same body part two years in a row, in his case the right wrist, and really how many guys on one team can have matching surgeries in consecutive seasons before this starts to get downright creepy? Even so, when he's been on the field he's put up respectable numbers in various roles. Larnach's stat line is similarly comforting as a solid outfield bat, but contains one fluke injury (hand contusion in 2021) and one a bit more hope-dampening (core muscle strain in 2022). They're not necessarily built to be the headliners here, which is completely fine, but there's only so much space for enjoyably competent middleground guys before the whole endeavor starts crumbling under that weight.

It's especially true given the condition of the team's pitching staff, which stands as both a marvelous recovery from the desolation that was the Happ-Shoemaker-Dobnak summer of 2021, and a testament to the limitations of how quickly a team can rearm themselves. A rotation led by Sonny Gray, Tyler Mahle and Joe Ryan will keep the team in a lot of games, yet dominate very few of them. Because of the vanilla-light-yogurt quality of the rotation, all of those upside players, at this point in their careers or injury patterns, are far more important and intriguing as part of a more expansive picture than they are as individual pieces. Yet in Minnesota, they have nothing to coalesce around in order to transform into something mightier.

Putting aside as best you can what actually ended up unfolding during the rest of Correa's offseason—which is admittedly a very, very hard request—the Twins barely broke a sweat with the effort they put in trying to retain him. A reported $285 million over 10 years isn't a complete dereliction of duty, especially when you put those numbers up against the Twins' history of free-agent spending. Yet it's a little like offering to help a buddy move after you've already heard they hired a moving company. You know what the landscape looks like, and are aware you're probably off the hook.

With their All-Star shortstop, the rest of the roster still wouldn't have been perfect, but they would've been able to use Correa as a load-bearing beam as they figured out how specifically to continue building around him this offseason. He appeared to like being on the Twins and the Twins liked him, but the lure of teams with a more concrete direction, and a more Keynesian mentality toward spending, still won out in the end. Unable to commit, the team found itself in offseason no-man's land.

⚾ ⚾ ⚾

Minnesota's 89-loss 2021 season should have been a wake-up call, underlining the importance of having at least one star to build around. They determined, correctly, that said star was not Josh Donaldson. They'd already lost Kenta Maeda to Tommy John surgery, but chose to double down on the soft-tossing veteran approach with Chris Archer (don't they know that type of move only ever works for the Dodgers and Rays?). Ultimately, there were too many holes to plug. It's not reasonable to expect Max Kepler's home run count and OPS to rebound suddenly in his age-30 season. And even if he was dealt a month ago by the time you're reading this, what does that return even look like as far as true additive pieces for the Twins?

This club, as constructed right now, is committed to playing chess when actually these types of decisions are most often checkers. Pick a path, put the pieces into place, and know what you have to do if Plan A falls apart. But without Correa, the Twins don't even have an identifiable Plan A. It's all muddled, with the prevailing strategy seeming to be waiting and seeing how many times the middling AL Central falls into their laps in the next decade as other teams cycle in and out of performance windows.

It's going to take some big moves to avoid stumbling into the same ravine year in and year out. The 2023 roster is one that includes both the highest strikeout rate (Joey Gallo, 39.8%) and lowest (Arraez, 7.1%) in the same lineup, and the type of player that is more likely to be on the trade block this season is the latter. Which might actually be the best lane forward for this team, because at the very least it would be a lane and it would be moving forward. Instead, the roster is stocked with high-variance veterans who look to average out to set up a .500 team, unless they all have career years at the same time. The all-or-nothing Gallo, who was signed to complete the outfield, is a perfect example of this. Faced with no other options, the team's plan is to put it all on red.

You don't get extra wins added to your record for being too cute by half. If you did, the Twins would more frequently be seeded in a slot that didn't require losing to the Yankees in October every couple of years. At some point, you have to commit to some of the obvious things. Spending money, for example, or realizing luck isn't going to suddenly tilt your way after beating up on you for years, and coming to terms with the kind of team you're actually working with rather than waiting for a different type of roster construction to fall into your lap.

⚾ ⚾ ⚾

Here's the lousiest part about all that Twin Cities drama: St. Paul and Minneapolis weren't even originally the Twin Cities. According to the Minnesota Historical Society, the original twins were actually Minneapolis and St. Anthony, which the former absorbed in 1872. St. Paul was a few miles away, across the river. They weren't even a problem for each other until they came looking for one. The Twins, too, just can't stop making life needlessly difficult for themselves.

You have to at least hope that, for those alive in 1890 to witness that census mishmash firsthand, the entertainment factor of watching it unfold mostly counterbalanced all of the trouble it involved. Without some level of amusement, watching well-meaning people tangle themselves up in that type of complicated problem solving can't have been easy to stomach. Maybe this Twins team won't require anything quite as drastic as that level of counterbalancing, thanks to all that aforementioned upside. But if the dominoes tilt toward things completely falling apart, at least all signs point to some gratifying, entertaining moments—or at least unforgettable zaniness—to make it far easier if they fall a bit short on the field.

Or they could just convince the rest of the league the Trade Deadline is actually two weeks later than it is, and capitalize on the market while everyone else's clocks are wrong. ■

—Whitney McIntosh is a baseball editor who lives in New York.

HITTERS

Luis Arraez 1B Born: 04/09/97 Age: 26 Bats: L Throws: R Height: 5'10" Weight: 175 lb. Origin: International Free Agent, 2013

YEAR	TEAM	LVL	AGE	PA	R	2B	3B	HR	RBI	BB	K	SB	CS	Whiff%	AVG/OBP/SLG	DRC+	BABIP	BRR	DRP	WARP
2020	MIN	MLB	23	121	16	9	0	0	13	8	11	0	0	10.1%	.321/.364/.402	101	.353	-0.6	2B(31): -0.5	0.3
2021	MIN	MLB	24	479	58	17	6	2	42	43	48	2	2	10.7%	.294/.357/.376	102	.323	1.2	3B(55): 0.2, 2B(48): 2.7, LF(27): 2.6	2.5
2022	MIN	MLB	25	603	88	31	1	8	49	50	43	4	4	7.1%	.316/.375/.420	123	.331	-2.0	1B(65): 2.8, 2B(41): 0.4, 3B(7): -0.2	3.2
2023 DC	*MIN*	*MLB*	*26*	*614*	*74*	*26*	*3*	*8*	*52*	*53*	*39*	*7*	*2*	*8.2%*	*.312/.375/.416*	*128*	*.325*	*1.7*	*1B 0, 3B 0*	*3.4*

Comparables: A.J. Pierzynski (54), Joe Panik (53), Yoán Moncada (52)

Arraez technically won the batting title at his first opportunity—he didn't qualify in any of his first three seasons. But from the moment the contact wizard came up, he'd been on the shortlist of players most likely to win the crown. In his first complete campaign he increased an already superlative contact rate to nearly 93%, including a ludicrous 90.1% on pitches outside the zone. He recorded the lowest qualified strikeout rate by any batter in a full season since 2015, and beat out the 2022 runner-up, Steven Kwan, by more than two percentage points. He's not without flaws at the plate—not merely his lack of power but also his platoon split, where even his average lags by almost 70 points. (This drew Minnesota the ire of some Aaron Judge Triple Crown hopefuls when Arraez sat against certain southpaws.) The utility remains an anachronistic delight, reminiscent of an era when people really cared about the batting title. Rob Manfred is working on the cloning technology at this very moment.

Byron Buxton CF/DH Born: 12/18/93 Age: 29 Bats: R Throws: R Height: 6'2" Weight: 190 lb. Origin: Round 1, 2012 Draft (#2 overall)

YEAR	TEAM	LVL	AGE	PA	R	2B	3B	HR	RBI	BB	K	SB	CS	Whiff%	AVG/OBP/SLG	DRC+	BABIP	BRR	DRP	WARP
2020	MIN	MLB	26	135	19	3	0	13	27	2	36	2	1	28.9%	.254/.267/.577	121	.241	0.6	CF(39): 3.3	1.2
2021	STP	AAA	27	26	6	2	1	3	9	2	3	0	0		.409/.423/1.000	134	.333	0.1	CF(6): -0.2	0.2
2021	MIN	MLB	27	254	50	23	0	19	32	13	62	9	1	29.2%	.306/.358/.647	135	.344	1.8	CF(60): 7.5	3.2
2022	MIN	MLB	28	382	61	13	3	28	51	34	116	6	0	34.0%	.224/.306/.526	121	.244	1.9	CF(57): 3.5	2.8
2023 DC	*MIN*	*MLB*	*29*	*543*	*70*	*25*	*3*	*29*	*70*	*40*	*157*	*7*	*2*	*32.7%*	*.240/.306/.489*	*120*	*.286*	*4.0*	*CF 5*	*3.8*

Comparables: Adam Jones (70), Andre Dawson (68), Carlos Gómez (65)

There are certain hallmarks of a Buxton season that we could do without. Those would be the injuries and the corresponding plate appearance total, well below qualifying status. Yet they remained indelibly stamped on yet another campaign. Instead, it was the batting average and speed that looked less Buxtonesque than usual: He attempted steals at a career-low rate, and took the extra base less often than all but his debut season. A nagging hip injury that ultimately ended his season was undoubtedly a factor. It made less difference to his production than it would for most players, since the .300+ ISO and superlative defense remained intact to keep Buxton on pace for yet another MVP-caliber year. It's thrilling to imagine what a season when we could drop the "on-pace" qualifier might look like. As the Twins outfielder enters the final year of his twenties, we're still having to use our imagination.

Johan Camargo SS

Born: 12/13/93 Age: 29 Bats: S Throws: R Height: 6'0" Weight: 195 lb. Origin: International Free Agent, 2010

YEAR	TEAM	LVL	AGE	PA	R	2B	3B	HR	RBI	BB	K	SB	CS	Whiff%	AVG/OBP/SLG	DRC+	BABIP	BRR	DRP	WARP
2020	AGU	WIN	26	61	4	1	0	0	7	7	7	0	0		.212/.311/.231		.239			
2020	ATL	MLB	26	127	16	8	0	4	9	6	35	0	0	33.9%	.200/.244/.367	80	.247	0.6	2B(21): 0.2, 3B(10): -1.5	0.0
2021	GWN	AAA	27	436	70	24	4	19	67	47	72	0	1		.326/.401/.557	136	.361	-0.7	1B(59): -4.0, 3B(47): -1.1, RF(1): 0.0	2.3
2021	ATL	MLB	27	18	1	0	0	0	0	2	6	0	0	34.5%	.000/.111/.000	87			2B(1): 0	
2022	LHV	AAA	28	167	19	6	0	2	23	21	25	0	0		.213/.311/.298	110	.237	0.1	3B(10): -0.5, 1B(6): -1.2, SS(4): -0.8	0.4
2022	PHI	MLB	28	166	8	3	0	3	15	13	37	0	0	24.9%	.237/.297/.316	91	.295	0.9	SS(26): 0.1, 3B(13): -1.1, 2B(9): 0.3	0.3
2023 non-DC	*MIN*	*MLB*	*29*	*251*	*25*	*10*	*0*	*6*	*26*	*20*	*47*	*0*	*0*	*24.2%*	*.249/.314/.386*	*95*	*.290*	*0.1*	*3B 0, 1B 0*	*0.4*

Comparables: Joe Panik (50), Cory Spangenberg (49), Johnny Giavotella (47)

Ever since a head-turning sophomore season in 2018, Camargo has struggled to keep up with big-league pitching. In 2022, he struggled against minor-league pitching as well. His defensive versatility is nice—he played all four infield positions this past year—but his glove just isn't a strong enough carrying tool if he can't reach base.

Willi Castro UT

Born: 04/24/97 Age: 26 Bats: S Throws: R Height: 6'1" Weight: 206 lb. Origin: International Free Agent, 2013

YEAR	TEAM	LVL	AGE	PA	R	2B	3B	HR	RBI	BB	K	SB	CS	Whiff%	AVG/OBP/SLG	DRC+	BABIP	BRR	DRP	WARP
2020	DET	MLB	23	140	21	4	2	6	24	7	38	0	1	30.8%	.349/.381/.550	99	.448	-1.7	SS(27): -1.2, 3B(8): -0.9, 2B(1): 0	0.0
2021	DET	MLB	24	450	56	15	6	9	38	23	109	9	4	29.4%	.220/.273/.351	76	.275	1.4	2B(91): -3.7, SS(20): 0.5, LF(10): 0.4	0.0
2022	TOL	AAA	25	36	2	2	0	0	1	2	10	3	1		.265/.306/.324	97	.375	0.3	2B(2): 0.1, SS(2): -0.7, CF(2): 0.2	0.1
2022	DET	MLB	25	392	47	18	2	8	31	15	82	9	4	28.6%	.241/.284/.367	88	.288	1.1	RF(40): 2.8, LF(27): -0.4, 2B(16): -0.7	0.9
2023 DC	*FA*	*MLB*	*26*	*350*	*35*	*14*	*2*	*9*	*38*	*17*	*82*	*10*	*3*	*28.1%*	*.255/.305/.398*	*93*	*.315*	*4.8*	*2B -1, SS -1*	*1.0*

Comparables: Reid Brignac (63), Ted Martinez (55), Albert Almora Jr. (54)

From utility infielder to utility everything, Castro expanded his résumé considerably. He was the only player in the majors to appear in double-digit games at each of the middle infield spots and all three outfield positions, and he tossed in six games at the hot corner, too. While he didn't spend long enough anywhere to register particularly meaningful fielding data, indications are that he fielded respectably everywhere, if not spectacularly, with enough arm strength to play right. That's promising for his major-league longevity, since he remains subpar at the plate, capable of occasionally crushing a pitch—but far more often, reaching for one that he should have no business chasing. If the tools had shown through a little more offensively, he might have convinced the Twins to give him more than a minor-league deal.

Gilberto Celestino CF

Born: 02/13/99 Age: 24 Bats: R Throws: L Height: 6'0" Weight: 170 lb. Origin: International Free Agent, 2015

YEAR	TEAM	LVL	AGE	PA	R	2B	3B	HR	RBI	BB	K	SB	CS	Whiff%	AVG/OBP/SLG	DRC+	BABIP	BRR	DRP	WARP
2021	WCH	AA	22	96	10	5	0	2	7	11	24	0	1		.250/.344/.381	95	.328	0.1	CF(12): -0.5, RF(6): 0.3, LF(1): -0.2	0.2
2021	STP	AAA	22	211	27	13	0	5	24	24	43	4	0		.290/.384/.443	101	.356	-1.2	CF(23): -5.1, RF(17): 1.0, LF(3): 0.1	0.2
2021	MIN	MLB	22	62	7	3	0	2	3	3	14	0	0	23.1%	.136/.177/.288	94	.140	-0.3	CF(22): -1.3, RF(2): 1.1	0.2
2022	MIN	MLB	23	347	30	12	1	2	24	32	77	4	1	23.4%	.238/.313/.302	87	.310	-3.8	CF(90): -3.7, LF(28): 0.1, RF(8): -0.3	-0.1
2023 DC	*MIN*	*MLB*	*24*	*184*	*17*	*7*	*0*	*2*	*14*	*16*	*38*	*2*	*1*	*23.5%*	*.233/.305/.334*	*84*	*.286*	*0.4*	*CF 0, LF 0*	*0.1*

Comparables: Darren Lewis (55), Jake Marisnick (54), Rich Becker (50)

The possibility of Celestino reaching his ceiling looks ever more distant. After spending almost the entire year on the major-league roster, it's clear that his bat needs truly stellar defensive work to justify a starting role—but the glove was merely good rather than transcendental. The failure to launch at the plate is a major hurdle. No batter who stepped into the box as often as Celestino came close to his near-60% ground-ball rate, a tendency he's not quick enough to take full advantage of. A healthier Twins team will surely leave him grounded on the bench, as a glove-first fourth outfielder. While no one's expecting him to be a star at this point, Celestino will need to aim a little higher to be sure he's in the dugout at all.

Kyle Farmer SS/3B

Born: 08/17/90 Age: 32 Bats: R Throws: R Height: 6'0" Weight: 205 lb. Origin: Round 8, 2013 Draft (#244 overall)

YEAR	TEAM	LVL	AGE	PA	R	2B	3B	HR	RBI	BB	K	SB	CS	Whiff%	AVG/OBP/SLG	DRC+	BABIP	BRR	DRP	WARP
2020	CIN	MLB	29	70	4	3	0	0	4	5	13	1	0	25.0%	.266/.329/.313	96	.333	-0.4	SS(15): 0.1, 2B(13): 0.5, 3B(2): 0.1	0.2
2021	CIN	MLB	30	529	60	22	2	16	63	22	97	2	3	20.0%	.263/.316/.416	98	.296	1.0	SS(121): 0.4, 3B(10): 0.1, 2B(9): -0.2	1.9
2022	CIN	MLB	31	583	58	25	1	14	78	33	99	4	3	19.1%	.255/.315/.386	101	.286	-3.7	SS(98): -1.6, 3B(36): 0	1.2
2023 DC	*MIN*	*MLB*	*32*	*466*	*44*	*20*	*1*	*9*	*44*	*25*	*78*	*3*	*1*	*19.6%*	*.251/.308/.373*	*93*	*.284*	*0.6*	*SS 0, 3B 0*	*0.9*

Comparables: Ivy Olson (49), Miguel Rojas (49), Jeff Keppinger (49)

Farmer is a proven 30-30 talent, provided the 30s stand for homers and HBPs and you add both numbers up over the last two seasons. (Hey, it still creates a list of just seven major leaguers.) If that's not an acceptable use of the 30-30 club, then Farmer is a member of the 30-30-30 club: homers and HBPs (over two seasons) and his age. It's just a number, and he broke into regular major-league play after his twenties. All of those numbers belie for what he's been most known: reliable defense, which he can provide from a number of positions, though he was locked at shortstop for the past couple years—before Brandon Drury got his trade deadline lottery ticket. There aren't a lot of defensive stats where 30 is an interesting or impressive total, but maybe Farmer can find a way.

Joey Gallo OF Born: 11/19/93 Age: 29 Bats: L Throws: R Height: 6'5" Weight: 250 lb. Origin: Round 1, 2012 Draft (#39 overall)

YEAR	TEAM	LVL	AGE	PA	R	2B	3B	HR	RBI	BB	K	SB	CS	Whiff%	AVG/OBP/SLG	DRC+	BABIP	BRR	DRP	WARP
2020	TEX	MLB	26	226	23	8	0	10	26	29	79	2	0	37.5%	.181/.301/.378	77	.240	2.3	RF(53): 1.9	0.5
2021	TEX	MLB	27	388	57	6	1	25	55	74	125	6	0	39.3%	.223/.379/.490	122	.275	-0.3	RF(83): 7.2	2.9
2021	NYY	MLB	27	228	33	7	0	13	22	37	88	0	0	38.8%	.160/.303/.404	81	.193	1.0	LF(51): -0.1, RF(9): -0.4	0.3
2022	LAD	MLB	28	137	16	4	1	7	23	16	57	1	0	40.5%	.162/.277/.393	72	.222	-0.8	LF(32): -0.9, RF(10): 0, 1B(1): 0	-0.2
2022	NYY	MLB	28	273	32	4	1	12	24	40	106	2	0	40.9%	.159/.282/.339	73	.217	1.4	LF(45): 0, RF(38): 1.4, CF(1): 0.2	0.3
2023 DC	*MIN*	*MLB*	*29*	*465*	*57*	*15*	*1*	*24*	*58*	*67*	*164*	*3*	*0*	*39.6%*	*.201/.323/.434*	*112*	*.264*	*1.9*	*LF -2, RF 1*	*1.8*

Comparables: Adam Dunn (56), Barry Bonds (53), Jay Bruce (51)

On Opening Day last season, the Yankees started two corner outfielders in the final year of their contracts. Aaron Judge enjoyed the greatest walk year in the history of the sport. Gallo...did the opposite. He lost all semblance of pitch recognition and his out-of-the-zone swing rate climbed from 22.7% in 2021, to 33.0%. He swung and missed 356 times—producing a strikeout rate of just under 40% and a walk rate that plummeted from 18.0% to 13.7%. Even after his merciful trade to the Dodgers, chants of *"Jo-ey GAL-lo!"* taunted underperforming Yankees down the stretch. Judge's 2022 will be revered alongside Ruth and Maris for eternity, but Gallo will also be remembered in the Bronx for years to come—except as a nasty epithet.

Kyle Garlick OF Born: 01/26/92 Age: 31 Bats: R Throws: R Height: 6'1" Weight: 210 lb. Origin: Round 28, 2015 Draft (#852 overall)

YEAR	TEAM	LVL	AGE	PA	R	2B	3B	HR	RBI	BB	K	SB	CS	Whiff%	AVG/OBP/SLG	DRC+	BABIP	BRR	DRP	WARP
2020	PHI	MLB	28	23	0	1	0	0	3	0	7	0	0	32.3%	.136/.174/.182	81	.200	-0.1	LF(5): -0.5, RF(5): -0.2	-0.1
2021	MIN	MLB	29	107	17	8	0	5	10	6	32	1	0	28.9%	.232/.280/.465	90	.286	-0.2	RF(18): 2.1, LF(12): -0.6, CF(5): -0.4	0.3
2022	STP	AAA	30	46	5	1	1	3	7	6	16	0	0		.250/.348/.550	95	.333	-1.0	LF(6): -0.7, RF(1): -0.2	-0.1
2022	MIN	MLB	30	162	23	3	0	9	18	8	48	0	0	34.8%	.233/.284/.433	106	.277	0.6	LF(27): -1.2, RF(23): -1.4	0.4
2023 DC	*MIN*	*MLB*	*31*	*100*	*10*	*4*	*0*	*3*	*10*	*6*	*31*	*0*	*0*	*33.7%*	*.221/.280/.398*	*87*	*.289*	*0.2*	*LF 0*	*0.0*

Comparables: Adam Duvall (59), Jason Bay (57), Josh Willingham (56)

You might as well start calling lefties vampires when Garlick's around, since he continued to repel their efforts with an .805 OPS. He was bitten by something else instead: the injury bug. Calf, hamstring and ribcage issues sent him to the injured list three times by the start of August, then a wrist sprain felled him for good in mid-September. That made it seven total IL trips for Garlick as a Twin, after three in a similarly unfortunate 2021 campaign. Short-side platoon bat is a precarious role to begin with. The injuries may well drive a stake into the heart of Garlick's major-league career.

Nick Gordon UT Born: 10/24/95 Age: 27 Bats: L Throws: R Height: 6'0" Weight: 160 lb. Origin: Round 1, 2014 Draft (#5 overall)

YEAR	TEAM	LVL	AGE	PA	R	2B	3B	HR	RBI	BB	K	SB	CS	Whiff%	AVG/OBP/SLG	DRC+	BABIP	BRR	DRP	WARP
2021	STP	AAA	25	77	11	0	1	3	9	6	12	7	2		.282/.338/.437	112	.304	-1.2	SS(11): -1.3, CF(2): -0.2, 2B(1): 0.0	0.1
2021	MIN	MLB	25	216	19	9	1	4	23	12	55	10	1	28.4%	.240/.292/.355	77	.310	0.3	CF(34): -3.7, 2B(17): 0.1, SS(14): 0.1	-0.1
2022	MIN	MLB	26	443	45	28	4	9	50	19	105	6	4	27.9%	.272/.316/.427	89	.340	-1.3	LF(62): 0.5, CF(38): -2.6, 2B(36): -1.6	0.2
2023 DC	*MIN*	*MLB*	*27*	*255*	*24*	*11*	*2*	*5*	*24*	*13*	*62*	*7*	*2*	*27.8%*	*.250/.299/.387*	*91*	*.315*	*2.4*	*2B -1, LF 0*	*0.6*

Comparables: Steven Duggar (60), Ángel Pagán (51), Marwin Gonzalez (50)

No team lost more (projected) WARP to injuries than the Twins in 2022. If it hadn't been for Gordon, things could have been even worse. He covered for Byron Buxton in center, for Alex Kirilloff in left and for Jorge Polanco at second. He showed far more pop than you'd expect given his frame, and hit for average despite a hyper-aggressive approach. Whether he ought to be starting every day, as the injuries demanded he did for much of the season, is a different matter. Whatever his role, the Twins know they can count on him to fill it.

Ryan Jeffers C Born: 06/03/97 Age: 26 Bats: R Throws: R Height: 6'4" Weight: 235 lb. Origin: Round 2, 2018 Draft (#59 overall)

YEAR	TEAM	LVL	AGE	PA	R	2B	3B	HR	RBI	BB	K	SB	CS	Whiff%	AVG/OBP/SLG	DRC+	BABIP	BRR	DRP	WARP
2020	MIN	MLB	23	62	5	0	0	3	7	5	19	0	0	33.3%	.273/.355/.436	103	.364	-0.9	C(25): 0.9	0.2
2021	STP	AAA	24	103	13	4	0	5	16	16	26	0	0		.217/.340/.446	116	.236	0.2	C(13): 1.2, 1B(1): -0.1	0.7
2021	MIN	MLB	24	293	28	10	1	14	35	22	108	0	1	34.4%	.199/.270/.401	83	.269	-2.3	C(84): 5.8	1.0
2022	STP	AAA	25	39	5	1	0	3	7	4	4	1	0		.229/.308/.514	120	.179	0.0	C(4): 0.1	0.2
2022	MIN	MLB	25	236	25	10	1	7	27	23	62	0	0	22.7%	.208/.285/.363	89	.259	0.4	C(59): 5	1.1
2023 DC	*MIN*	*MLB*	*26*	*215*	*23*	*8*	*0*	*8*	*23*	*18*	*53*	*0*	*0*	*25.3%*	*.225/.300/.402*	*96*	*.266*	*-1.8*	*C 4*	*1.0*

Comparables: Yasmani Grandal (65), Joe Oliver (62), Matt Wieters (60)

YEAR	TEAM	P. COUNT	FRM RUNS	BLK RUNS	THRW RUNS	TOT RUNS
2020	MIN	2804	0.6	0.0	0.3	0.9
2021	STP	2087	1.3	0.0	0.0	1.3
2021	MIN	11035	5.3	0.3	0.2	5.8
2022	MIN	8105	4.7	-0.1	0.3	4.9
2023	*MIN*	*8418*	*4.4*	*0.0*	*-0.1*	*4.4*

Time and time again we have seen catchers with the defensive chops to stick in the majors take multiple seasons to drag their bat up to respectability. Jeffers definitely has the glove to keep a place in the starting lineup. He's not an elite framer but he is clearly above-average, and he holds his own with blocking and throwing. It's not as though he's a zero at the plate, either, taking free passes at an above-average clip and flashing high-end power. As the prospect of the automated strike zone looms, however, his framing contributions may be rendered moot, putting a clock on the bat's development. Jeffers isn't too far away from being a 20+ homer backstop with (at least) an average OBP, but last year a broken thumb cost him precious months of development time. He has at least one more year to show he belongs in the lineup without the framing.

Max Kepler RF Born: 02/10/93 Age: 30 Bats: L Throws: L Height: 6'4" Weight: 225 lb. Origin: International Free Agent, 2009

YEAR	TEAM	LVL	AGE	PA	R	2B	3B	HR	RBI	BB	K	SB	CS	Whiff%	AVG/OBP/SLG	DRC+	BABIP	BRR	DRP	WARP
2020	MIN	MLB	27	196	27	9	0	9	23	22	36	3	0	21.2%	.228/.321/.439	108	.236	-0.7	RF(44): 1, CF(2): 0	0.8
2021	MIN	MLB	28	490	61	21	4	19	54	54	96	10	0	23.0%	.211/.306/.413	99	.225	3.3	RF(97): 1.3, CF(22): -1.2	1.8
2022	MIN	MLB	29	446	54	18	1	9	43	49	66	3	2	19.9%	.227/.318/.348	102	.249	1.2	RF(110): 6.3, CF(3): -0.2	2.2
2023 DC	*MIN*	*MLB*	*30*	*441*	*45*	*18*	*1*	*12*	*44*	*47*	*73*	*5*	*1*	*20.5%*	*.224/.316/.378*	*100*	*.245*	*2.4*	*RF 2*	*1.3*

Comparables: Terry Puhl (66), Harry Hooper (65), Nick Markakis (63)

Kepler's commitment to low BABIPs remains unparalleled. Now running a league-leading streak of five straight campaigns in which under a quarter of his balls in play turned into hits, the German somehow managed to do so with a quite considerable shift in his batted ball mix. He posted his highest ground-ball rate since he was a rookie while popping up at a career-low rate. The results stubbornly remained the same, in terms of both BABIP and his overall offensive production—which was essentially average yet again, thanks to his similarly consistent walk rate and the league taking a collective dive in power along with him. We can call him unlucky, and project that the new positioning rules will be a boon for the oft-shifted Kepler. If we look up in October 2023 and he has a .240 BABIP, we'll just have to admire the commitment to the bit.

Alex Kirilloff LF Born: 11/09/97 Age: 25 Bats: L Throws: L Height: 6'2" Weight: 195 lb. Origin: Round 1, 2016 Draft (#15 overall)

YEAR	TEAM	LVL	AGE	PA	R	2B	3B	HR	RBI	BB	K	SB	CS	Whiff%	AVG/OBP/SLG	DRC+	BABIP	BRR	DRP	WARP
2021	MIN	MLB	23	231	23	11	1	8	34	14	52	1	1	26.9%	.251/.299/.423	90	.295	0.1	1B(29): -1, RF(27): 1.4, LF(13): -0.5	0.3
2022	STP	AAA	24	157	33	7	0	10	32	22	26	1	0		.359/.465/.641	139	.389	0.0	1B(14): -1.6, LF(14): 0.7, RF(1): 0.3	1.0
2022	MIN	MLB	24	156	14	7	0	3	21	5	36	0	0	20.1%	.250/.290/.361	80	.308	-1.8	LF(21): 0.2, 1B(18): -0.3, RF(8): -0.2	-0.2
2023 DC	*MIN*	*MLB*	*25*	*397*	*40*	*17*	*1*	*10*	*43*	*26*	*79*	*1*	*0*	*23.4%*	*.262/.320/.411*	*107*	*.306*	*0.8*	*LF -2, 1B 0*	*0.9*

Comparables: Eddie Rosario (58), Jeimer Candelario (56), Brad Fullmer (55)

If it is, in fact, all in the wrist, it's little surprise that Kirilloff didn't have it at all in his sophomore season. Looking to improve on a rookie year that started well, before wrist trouble first spoiled his production and then led to surgery, the former top prospect instead found that his wrist was still bothering him from day one. It turns out that it was not in the wrist in this case, "it" being space. A lack of it between the bones in that joint led to pain that rendered his once-lauded swing almost useless. The solution sounds as unpleasant as the pain: Kirilloff had a second surgery, this time to have his ulna broken and shortened, followed by the insertion of a metal plate, all in an effort to reintroduce some of that space. If that made you wince just reading it, think about how it must have felt every time Kirilloff swung, if this was deemed to be the solution. There's a long way between here and the plus offensive contributor he was supposed to be. Being able to swing pain-free would be a great start.

Trevor Larnach OF Born: 02/26/97 Age: 26 Bats: L Throws: R Height: 6'4" Weight: 223 lb. Origin: Round 1, 2018 Draft (#20 overall)

YEAR	TEAM	LVL	AGE	PA	R	2B	3B	HR	RBI	BB	K	SB	CS	Whiff%	AVG/OBP/SLG	DRC+	BABIP	BRR	DRP	WARP
2021	STP	AAA	24	62	13	1	0	3	7	6	21	0	0		.176/.323/.373	90	.222	0.8	RF(6): 0.4, LF(2): 0.4	0.3
2021	MIN	MLB	24	301	29	12	0	7	28	31	104	1	0	39.0%	.223/.322/.350	72	.338	-0.8	LF(60): -3.9, RF(20): 1.8	-0.3
2022	STP	AAA	25	41	1	0	0	0	2	4	11	0	0		.222/.293/.222	88	.308	-0.4	LF(4): -0.5, RF(3): 0.4	0.0
2022	MIN	MLB	25	180	22	13	0	5	18	18	57	0	0	39.7%	.231/.306/.406	79	.320	-0.3	LF(33): 0.3, RF(11): 0.7	0.2
2023 DC	*MIN*	*MLB*	*26*	*296*	*30*	*12*	*0*	*8*	*29*	*28*	*99*	*0*	*0*	*38.1%*	*.230/.313/.386*	*95*	*.331*	*-2.4*	*LF 0, RF 0*	*0.2*

Comparables: Christin Stewart (64), Derek Fisher (55), Kirk Nieuwenhuis (53)

It has often felt like Larnach is tied to fellow bat-first, lefty-swinging corner type Alex Kirilloff—in more than just profile. They're separated by only eight months in age, spent most of their time in the minors jostling for position on prospect lists and now have compiled a relatively comparable amount of major-league playing time. That proximity has regrettably extended to both their offensive performances and their health since they made the majors. Larnach arguably has the advantage in that his wrist isn't too painful for him to swing effectively, but he too missed a sizable chunk of the season, not playing at all over the final three months after core muscle surgery. He undoubtedly has massive power, but has yet to prove he can consistently mash something other than a fastball, most notably off-speed stuff. If Larnach and Kirilloff must insist on matching each other so closely, some progression at the plate and seasons of full health would do Minnesota's offense wonders.

★ ★ ★ *2023 Top 101 Prospect* **#37** ★ ★ ★

Brooks Lee SS Born: 02/14/01 Age: 22 Bats: S Throws: R Height: 6'2" Weight: 205 lb. Origin: Round 1, 2022 Draft (#8 overall)

YEAR	TEAM	LVL	AGE	PA	R	2B	3B	HR	RBI	BB	K	SB	CS	Whiff%	AVG/OBP/SLG	DRC+	BABIP	BRR	DRP	WARP
2022	CR	A+	21	114	14	4	0	4	12	16	18	0	2		.289/.395/.454	114	.320	-1.9	SS(20): -1.0	0.3
2023 non-DC	*MIN*	*MLB*	*22*	*251*	*21*	*9*	*1*	*3*	*21*	*20*	*57*	*1*	*0*	*26.4%*	*.229/.299/.327*	*76*	*.291*	*1.1*	*SS 0*	*0.1*

Comparables: C.J. Hinojosa (87), Luis Rengifo (86), Didi Gregorius (84)

In the conversation for the first overall pick and ranked in the top five of the draft class by many evaluators, nobody—including the Twins front office—expected Lee to be available when the eighth pick rolled around. Lee quickly set about making it look like a steal. After a year in which he'd crushed NCAA pitching and put up similar numbers with a wood bat in the Cape Cod League, the Cal Poly star's approach and bat-to-ball skills looked far too accomplished for High-A, too. A mere 25 games after making his debut at the level, the Twins bumped him up to Double-A. Although he isn't expected to stick at shortstop long-term, the bat is starting to look like it will play anywhere.

Sandy Leon C

Born: 03/13/89 Age: 34 Bats: S Throws: R Height: 5'10" Weight: 235 lb. Origin: International Free Agent, 2007

YEAR	TEAM	LVL	AGE	PA	R	2B	3B	HR	RBI	BB	K	SB	CS	Whiff%	AVG/OBP/SLG	DRC+	BABIP	BRR	DRP	WARP
2020	CLE	MLB	31	81	4	1	0	2	4	14	21	0	0	30.6%	.136/.296/.242	93	.163	-1.1	C(24): 1.6	0.3
2021	MIA	MLB	32	220	15	5	0	4	14	12	65	0	0	27.1%	.183/.237/.267	63	.244	-1.6	C(60): 0.2, P(6): 0, 3B(1): 0	-0.2
2022	LOU	AAA	33	84	5	3	0	1	7	10	12	0	0		.222/.321/.306	116	.250	-1.4	C(26): 4.0	0.6
2022	CLE	MLB	33	21	0	0	0	0	0	6	4	0	0	25.0%	.133/.381/.133	101	.182	0.0	C(8): 0.6	0.1
2022	MIN	MLB	33	65	6	3	0	0	4	7	23	0	0	25.4%	.179/.270/.232	69	.303	-1.2	C(25): 1.1	0.0
2023 DC	*FA*	*MLB*	*34*	*148*	*13*	*5*	*0*	*3*	*13*	*14*	*36*	*0*	*0*	*23.6%*	*.192/.278/.303*	*62*	*.239*	*-0.9*	*C 1, 3B 0*	*-0.1*

Comparables: Jeff Mathis (61), Tom Prince (55), Chad Moeller (54)

YEAR	TEAM	P. COUNT	FRM RUNS	BLK RUNS	THRW RUNS	TOT RUNS
2020	CLE	3027	0.9	0.0	0.3	1.2
2021	MIA	6933	0.0	0.1	0.1	0.1
2022	LOU	3381	2.1	0.3	1.2	3.5
2022	MIN	2874	1.2	0.0	0.1	1.3
2022	CLE	885	0.5	0.0	0.0	0.5
2023	*FA*	*6956*	*1.2*	*0.0*	*-0.2*	*1.0*

Little speaks to Leon's defensive ability more than his now five-season streak of an OPS starting with a five. Slightly waning powers behind the plate turned him into something of a nomad in 2023, as he took a trip around the Central division before becoming the latest in a long line of Twins injuries when a torn meniscus ended his season. In a season almost devoid of highlights, he did reprise his pitching role once in wildly successful fashion, setting down all six Tigers he faced to become the first position player since Jason Lane in 2014 to face at least six batters without allowing a baserunner. You, the reader, can decide whether that highlight says more about Leon or the 2022 Tigers.

★ ★ ★ *2023 Top 101 Prospect* **#40** ★ ★ ★

Royce Lewis SS

Born: 06/05/99 Age: 24 Bats: R Throws: R Height: 6'2" Weight: 200 lb. Origin: Round 1, 2017 Draft (#1 overall)

YEAR	TEAM	LVL	AGE	PA	R	2B	3B	HR	RBI	BB	K	SB	CS	Whiff%	AVG/OBP/SLG	DRC+	BABIP	BRR	DRP	WARP
2022	STP	AAA	23	153	30	12	1	5	14	18	32	12	2		.313/.405/.534	116	.379	-0.3	SS(26): -0.5, 3B(2): 0.1, LF(2): 0.2	0.7
2022	MIN	MLB	23	41	5	4	0	2	5	1	5	0	0	16.7%	.300/.317/.550	114	.303	0.5	SS(11): -0.7, CF(1): 0	0.2
2023 DC	*MIN*	*MLB*	*24*	*276*	*28*	*12*	*1*	*7*	*27*	*19*	*56*	*10*	*3*	*25.0%*	*.245/.303/.394*	*97*	*.287*	*2.5*	*SS -1*	*0.9*

Comparables: Richard Urena (57), Wilmer Flores (56), Ketel Marte (56)

After two completely lost seasons, things were finally looking up for Lewis. He ripped through Triple-A in his first month at the level and quickly earned a call-up to the Show. He was sent back down, but was soon back in the bigs when the Twins outfield situation presented what looked like an extended opportunity to prove himself. Three innings into his first big-league appearance in center field, Lewis tracked back to make a spectacular catch at the wall and crashed into it. The grimace on his face as he lay on the ground said it all: A few days later, it was announced that Lewis would need a second surgery to repair the ACL that he'd torn just 15 months earlier. Most people would feel like giving up then and there, but Lewis remained resolutely positive—even in the immediate aftermath, he announced his desire to get back to full strength to help the team as soon as possible and noted the benefits that having gone through the rehab process already would bring. We know he has the attitude. His debut flashed the talent. Now he just needs the health.

Austin Martin SS

Born: 03/23/99 Age: 24 Bats: R Throws: R Height: 6'0" Weight: 185 lb. Origin: Round 1, 2020 Draft (#5 overall)

YEAR	TEAM	LVL	AGE	PA	R	2B	3B	HR	RBI	BB	K	SB	CS	Whiff%	AVG/OBP/SLG	DRC+	BABIP	BRR	DRP	WARP
2021	NH	AA	22	250	43	10	2	2	16	37	53	9	3		.281/.424/.383	116	.368	0.8	SS(27): 1.1, CF(26): 4.5	1.9
2021	WCH	AA	22	168	24	8	0	3	19	23	30	5	1		.254/.399/.381	112	.304	1.6	CF(20): 1.0, SS(16): -2.3	0.8
2022	WCH	AA	23	406	59	13	3	2	32	47	54	34	5		.241/.367/.315	102	.280	2.3	SS(70): -4.0, 2B(7): 0.3, CF(7): 1.7	1.4
2023 non-DC	*MIN*	*MLB*	*24*	*251*	*22*	*8*	*1*	*2*	*19*	*23*	*46*	*9*	*1*	*20.6%*	*.226/.323/.311*	*83*	*.278*	*4.9*	*2B 0, SS 0*	*0.7*

Comparables: Trevor Crowe (82), Nate Samson (75), Nick Ahmed (71)

Martin continued to display an outstanding approach at the plate, walking almost as often as he struck out. Unfortunately, when he made contact with the ball, it was a different story. Notching a mere 18 extra-base hits in 90 games in his second go-around at Double-A raised significant questions about whether he'll have enough power to be a major-league regular. In Martin's defense, he did miss over a month with a wrist injury and there were flashes of more power in September, when he tripled his homer total for the season—plus in the Arizona Fall League. He'll need to show he can maintain it over more than a month to have any chance of making a difference in the majors.

Jose Miranda IF

Born: 06/29/98 Age: 25 Bats: R Throws: R Height: 6'2" Weight: 210 lb. Origin: Round 2, 2016 Draft (#73 overall)

YEAR	TEAM	LVL	AGE	PA	R	2B	3B	HR	RBI	BB	K	SB	CS	Whiff%	AVG/OBP/SLG	DRC+	BABIP	BRR	DRP	WARP
2020	CAG	WIN	22	61	10	6	0	1	8	6	10	0	0		.302/.377/.472		.349			
2021	WCH	AA	23	218	36	8	0	13	38	17	25	4	2		.345/.408/.588	148	.342	0.9	3B(15): 1.3, 1B(14): 1.0, 2B(14): 0.2	2.2
2021	STP	AAA	23	373	61	24	0	17	56	25	49	0	2		.343/.397/.563	133	.362	-2.7	3B(39): -0.9, 2B(20): 0.8, 1B(14): -0.3	2.2
2022	STP	AAA	24	95	10	10	0	2	12	5	14	0	0		.256/.295/.442	103	.274	0.3	3B(14): 1.9, 1B(5): 0.4	0.6
2022	MIN	MLB	24	483	45	25	0	15	66	28	91	1	1	24.2%	.268/.325/.426	111	.307	0.1	1B(77): 1.8, 3B(34): -0.5	1.8
2023 DC	*MIN*	*MLB*	*25*	*578*	*61*	*28*	*1*	*17*	*64*	*34*	*102*	*2*	*2*	*23.0%*	*.261/.315/.420*	*108*	*.291*	*-1.6*	*3B -1, 1B -1*	*1.3*

Comparables: Kendrys Morales (60), Brandon Snyder (56), Juan Rivera (54)

When Miranda was batting under .100 almost three weeks after his call-up, his chances of sticking around on the roster seemed low. The Twins, short of multiple corner infield options already and confident that the Puerto Rican's minor-league breakout in 2021 wasn't a mirage, stuck with him. The rest of the way, he slashed .292/.349/.458, justifying Minnesota's faith and scouting reports alike. Those reports were more or less borne out in the manner of the production, too: Miranda was aggressive at the plate, expanding the zone frequently but making contact more often than not when he did, keeping the strikeout rate below 20%. His fence-clearing power was all to the pull side, in line with raw pop that's middling rather than high-end, but should play given the bat-to-ball skills; the pop has room to grow if he elevates more often. Whether he can play a respectable third base regularly is more of a question, and there's more pressure on that power to develop if he can't. Wherever the power settles, the Twins have a plus young hitter on their hands. It was worth having a little patience.

Jorge Polanco 2B Born: 07/05/93 Age: 30 Bats: S Throws: R Height: 5'11" Weight: 208 lb. Origin: International Free Agent, 2009

YEAR	TEAM	LVL	AGE	PA	R	2B	3B	HR	RBI	BB	K	SB	CS	Whiff%	AVG/OBP/SLG	DRC+	BABIP	BRR	DRP	WARP
2020	MIN	MLB	26	226	22	8	0	4	19	13	35	4	2	16.8%	.258/.304/.354	97	.292	-0.5	SS(53): -1	0.4
2021	MIN	MLB	27	644	97	35	2	33	98	45	118	11	6	19.8%	.269/.323/.503	120	.282	1.2	2B(120): 1.7, SS(39): -0.9	4.1
2022	MIN	MLB	28	445	54	16	0	16	56	64	95	3	3	25.7%	.235/.346/.405	115	.269	1.1	2B(97): 1.4, SS(6): 0.8	2.5
2023 DC	*MIN*	*MLB*	*29*	*567*	*66*	*24*	*2*	*19*	*60*	*63*	*127*	*9*	*2*	*23.6%*	*.246/.334/.423*	*114*	*.290*	*3.4*	*2B 0, SS 0*	*3.0*

Comparables: Starlin Castro (78), Tony Fernandez (77), Rabbit Maranville (75)

Polanco's something of an ironman, even if the stats don't show it. He has only topped 150 only games twice, thanks to a combination of some bizarre handling as a prospect, a PED suspension and a nagging ankle injury. Abbreviated seasons don't help, either. It's therefore surprising to learn that until a back injury in June, the long-time Twin had never been on the injured list in the major leagues. That doesn't mean that injuries haven't bothered him: The aforementioned ankle has been surgically repaired on multiple occasions, and while he returned quickly from the back issue, it was his knee that proved problematic. He attempted to play through inflammation after first injuring it in mid-August, but this was one joint issue he couldn't tough out. He didn't play after August 27 and was forced to watch an ailing Twins team collapse out of the playoff race. In between the health woes, he was essentially just as valuable a hitter as the year prior, albeit more patient, with a pitches-per-plate-appearance mark that would have ranked in the top five had he qualified. He just needs a chance to exercise that patience at the plate more often, rather than recovering on the bench.

★ ★ ★ *2023 Top 101 Prospect* **#42** ★ ★ ★

Emmanuel Rodriguez OF Born: 02/28/03 Age: 20 Bats: L Throws: L Height: 5'10" Weight: 210 lb. Origin: International Free Agent, 2019

YEAR	TEAM	LVL	AGE	PA	R	2B	3B	HR	RBI	BB	K	SB	CS	Whiff%	AVG/OBP/SLG	DRC+	BABIP	BRR	DRP	WARP
2021	TWI	ROK	18	153	31	5	2	10	23	23	56	9	4		.214/.346/.524		.279			
2022	FTM	A	19	199	35	5	3	9	25	57	52	11	5	32.6%	.272/.492/.551	153	.364	1.6	CF(37): -0.2, RF(4): -0.4	1.7
2023 non-DC	*MIN*	*MLB*	*20*	*251*	*27*	*8*	*3*	*6*	*27*	*37*	*84*	*8*	*4*	*35.9%*	*.221/.345/.384*	*103*	*.333*	*1.0*	*LF 0, CF 0*	*0.9*

Comparables: Khalil Lee (74), Akil Baddoo (74), Drew Waters (70)

Nobody with even 100 plate appearances in A-ball came remotely close to Rodriguez and his staggering 28.6% walk rate, part of an almost Bondsian stat line in his first full-season assignment. He's bursting with power and energy at the plate, on the basepaths and in the field. In other words, wherever he is, he's getting after it—and yet it's not uncontrolled aggression, as those plate discipline numbers testify. A knee injury was the one blemish on the season, preventing the teenager from adding to his video-game numbers...for now. There are always many more hurdles to clear when talking about prospects this far out, including health, but there's no doubt about one thing: The tools are there for star-level production.

Christian Vázquez C Born: 08/21/90 Age: 32 Bats: R Throws: R Height: 5'9" Weight: 205 lb. Origin: Round 9, 2008 Draft (#292 overall)

YEAR	TEAM	LVL	AGE	PA	R	2B	3B	HR	RBI	BB	K	SB	CS	Whiff%	AVG/OBP/SLG	DRC+	BABIP	BRR	DRP	WARP
2020	BOS	MLB	29	189	22	9	0	7	23	16	43	4	3	22.9%	.283/.344/.457	104	.341	-1.4	C(42): 4.3	1.0
2021	BOS	MLB	30	498	51	23	1	6	49	33	84	8	4	17.6%	.258/.308/.352	89	.301	0.9	C(132): 4, 2B(2): 0	1.9
2022	HOU	MLB	31	108	8	3	0	1	10	4	18	0	2	17.5%	.250/.278/.308	95	.294	-2.0	C(30): 0.6	0.2
2022	BOS	MLB	31	318	33	20	0	8	42	18	51	1	2	17.1%	.282/.327/.432	109	.315	-2.2	C(78): 8.9, 1B(9): 0.8	2.3
2023 DC	*MIN*	*MLB*	*32*	*352*	*34*	*15*	*0*	*8*	*35*	*21*	*56*	*5*	*2*	*17.6%*	*.264/.312/.395*	*99*	*.294*	*0.4*	*C 5*	*1.9*

Comparables: Yadier Molina (71), Mike Heath (67), Dioner Navarro (66)

YEAR	TEAM	P. COUNT	FRM RUNS	BLK RUNS	THRW RUNS	TOT RUNS
2020	BOS	6333	4.9	-0.1	-0.2	4.6
2021	BOS	18097	3.9	0.5	0.7	5.1
2022	HOU	3647	0.6	-0.1	0.0	0.6
2022	BOS	10710	8.3	0.2	0.4	8.9
2023	*MIN*	*13228*	*5.2*	*-0.2*	*-0.2*	*4.8*

The focus of one of the less confounding transactions of Chaim Bloom's 2022 as an imminently expiring contract on a team in free-fall, Vázquez also looked to be the ideal solution for one of the few deficiencies Houston had: offensive production at catcher. The Red Sox did get worse, playing sub-.500 ball the rest of the way; the Astros did get better, owning the best record in baseball after Vázquez's arrival and then going on to win the World Series. Whether the longtime Boston catcher had anything to do with that is dubious. His average was superior to Martín Maldonado's, but unlike his Puerto Rican compatriot he offered almost no power. The upshot was that Vázquez's line as an Astro was somehow slightly worse than Maldonado's season-long mark, albeit with a far superior DRC+; consequently, he took a back seat to Maldonado in both the regular season and the playoffs. Vázquez has settled in as a very middle-of-the-road catcher, a good but not elite defender with a bat that—tenure in Houston aside—usually won't tank offensive production the way backstop bats normally do. His 3-year, $30 million deal with Minnesota therefore felt extremely appropriate.

Matt Wallner RF Born: 12/12/97 Age: 25 Bats: L Throws: R Height: 6'5" Weight: 220 lb. Origin: Round 1, 2019 Draft (#39 overall)

YEAR	TEAM	LVL	AGE	PA	R	2B	3B	HR	RBI	BB	K	SB	CS	Whiff%	AVG/OBP/SLG	DRC+	BABIP	BRR	DRP	WARP
2021	SCO	WIN	23	79	11	2	0	6	15	9	27	0	0		.303/.405/.606		.412			
2021	CR	A+	23	294	39	14	2	15	47	28	98	0	1		.264/.350/.508	103	.363	-1.2	RF(55): -7.1, LF(2): -0.2	0.2
2022	WCH	AA	24	342	61	15	1	21	64	62	107	8	5		.299/.436/.597	111	.407	1.3	RF(66): 0.3, LF(1): -0.6	2.7
2022	STP	AAA	24	229	29	17	3	6	31	35	63	1	0		.247/.376/.463	85	.339	-2.2	RF(36): -0.2, LF(4): 0.3	0.2
2022	MIN	MLB	24	65	4	3	0	2	10	6	25	1	0	38.1%	.228/.323/.386	67	.367	0.3	RF(16): -0.3	-0.1
2023 DC	*MIN*	*MLB*	*25*	*124*	*12*	*5*	*0*	*3*	*11*	*13*	*43*	*1*	*1*	*38.2%*	*.215/.312/.367*	*90*	*.323*	*-0.1*	*RF 0*	*0.1*

Comparables: Billy McKinney (59), Brandon Allen (57), Matt Lawton (55)

Power was never likely to be the obstacle for Wallner. Still, it's reassuring that he cleared that hurdle. The corner outfielder built on his promising 2021, blasting his way through the two highest levels of the minors and breaking into the big leagues. While only two baseballs cleared the fence in his cup of coffee, one was all it took for the Statcast seal of approval: A near-114 mph skyscraper that immediately placed Wallner among the league's upper echelon in exit velocity. If he is going to run into a wall, it'll be because of those times he didn't make contact, which comprised almost 40% of his trips to the plate. If he can tone down the strikeouts a little, he has the power to smash his way through that final barrier and secure regular major-league work.

PITCHERS

Jhoan Duran RHP Born: 01/08/98 Age: 25 Bats: R Throws: R Height: 6'5" Weight: 230 lb. Origin: International Free Agent, 2014

YEAR	TEAM	LVL	AGE	W	L	SV	G	GS	IP	H	HR	BB/9	K/9	K	GB%	BABIP	WHIP	ERA	DRA-	WARP	MPH	FB%	Whiff%	CSP
2021	STP	AAA	23	0	3	0	5	4	16	16	1	7.3	12.4	22	62.5%	.385	1.81	5.06	85	0.3				
2022	MIN	MLB	24	2	4	8	57	0	67^2	50	6	2.1	11.8	89	59.2%	.295	0.98	1.86	61	2.0	100.5	65.5%	34.7%	55.4%
2023 DC	*MIN*	*MLB*	*25*	*3*	*3*	*6*	*71*	*0*	*61.7*	*56*	*6*	*3.7*	*11.2*	*76*	*57.0%*	*.320*	*1.32*	*3.58*	*91*	*0.5*	*100.5*	*65.5%*	*33.1%*	*55.4%*

Comparables: Brandon Maurer (78), Jeurys Familia (75), Archie Bradley (74)

In a year when the sweeper dominated the conversation about pitch design, Duran announced his arrival in the major leagues with a different weapon: a 97-mph, split-fingered sinker, known as his "splinker." Befitting the unique name, and entirely unlike the sweeper, Duran alone is capable of producing the offering—a violently swerving, ostensibly off-speed pitch that's about as off-speed as the Yankees are small-market, except the rookie *does* throw his fastball even harder. The four-seam topped out at 103 mph, another late-breaking monstrosity that he used to both catch hitters looking (on the corner) and draw flailing swinging strikes (in on their hands). That sounds like more than enough, but Duran—almost exclusively a starter until 2022—made hitters' lives even more miserable with a hard curve that drew whiffs on nearly half of swings. It's no surprise that he was one of the most dominant relievers in baseball. If he can effectively incorporate a slider that made occasional cameo appearances, hitters might as well turn around and start walking back to the dugout before they even get in the box.

Sonny Gray RHP Born: 11/07/89 Age: 33 Bats: R Throws: R Height: 5'10" Weight: 195 lb. Origin: Round 1, 2011 Draft (#18 overall)

YEAR	TEAM	LVL	AGE	W	L	SV	G	GS	IP	H	HR	BB/9	K/9	K	GB%	BABIP	WHIP	ERA	DRA-	WARP	MPH	FB%	Whiff%	CSP
2020	CIN	MLB	30	5	3	0	11	11	56	42	4	4.2	11.6	72	51.9%	.290	1.21	3.70	67	1.5	93.3	55.1%	29.6%	44.7%
2021	CIN	MLB	31	7	9	0	26	26	135^1	115	19	3.3	10.3	155	48.2%	.282	1.22	4.19	81	2.6	92.4	58.4%	26.2%	55.6%
2022	MIN	MLB	32	8	5	0	24	24	119^2	99	11	2.7	8.8	117	44.1%	.278	1.13	3.08	88	1.9	92.2	54.2%	22.2%	55.1%
2023 DC	*MIN*	*MLB*	*33*	*8*	*8*	*0*	*25*	*25*	*134.7*	*123*	*14*	*3.3*	*8.0*	*120*	*45.9%*	*.284*	*1.29*	*3.53*	*94*	*1.5*	*92.6*	*55.2%*	*24.0%*	*52.6%*

Comparables: Bob Welch (80), Jim Palmer (79), Roger Clemens (78)

Gray has become one of the game's most reliable pitchers, which doesn't necessarily mean what you think it means. Yes, he's reliably above-average at run prevention, giving the Twins exactly what they wanted when they swapped him for 2021 first-rounder Chase Petty. He experienced the drop in home run rate that would be projected when moving from dinger-friendly Cincinnati to homer-suppressing Minnesota. Unfortunately, the reliability extends to traits you'd rather not have. Gray has started 30 games just once since 2015; he was also, reliably, back on the injured list a couple more times. He also embodies modern pitching usage in that when on the mound, he rarely exceeded 90 pitches or got deep into the third time through the lineup. Of course, he's reliably aging too, losing a tiny bit more velocity every season. He's still more than good enough to justify the Twins picking up his $12.5 million contract option for a year in which he's very likely to keep runs off the board, miss a handful of starts and throw ever-so-slightly less hard.

Ronny Henriquez RHP Born: 06/20/00 Age: 23 Bats: R Throws: R Height: 5'10" Weight: 155 lb. Origin: International Free Agent, 2017

YEAR	TEAM	LVL	AGE	W	L	SV	G	GS	IP	H	HR	BB/9	K/9	K	GB%	BABIP	WHIP	ERA	DRA-	WARP	MPH	FB%	Whiff%	CSP
2021	HIC	A+	21	1	3	0	5	5	24	13	2	3.0	10.1	27	42.4%	.193	0.88	3.75	94	0.3				
2021	FRI	AA	21	4	4	0	16	11	69^2	65	15	2.2	10.1	78	43.6%	.279	1.18	5.04	76	1.3				
2022	STP	AAA	22	3	4	1	24	14	95^1	99	19	3.1	10.0	106	44.0%	.323	1.38	5.66	87	1.9				
2022	MIN	MLB	22	0	1	0	3	0	11^2	8	1	2.3	6.9	9	52.8%	.200	0.94	2.31	104	0.1	93.4	24.3%	23.5%	51.8%
2023 DC	*MIN*	*MLB*	*23*	*5*	*3*	*0*	*45*	*3*	*50.7*	*53*	*7*	*3.4*	*8.2*	*46*	*44.4%*	*.307*	*1.43*	*4.70*	*120*	*-0.2*	*93.4*	*24.3%*	*27.2%*	*51.8%*

Comparables: Zach Lee (49), Jaime Barría (49), Robert Gsellman (49)

All three of his debut-season appearances may have come in relief, but Henriquez's usage in those outings point toward a looming tryout in the big-league rotation. Acquired along with the immediately traded Isiah Kiner-Falefa in the deal that sent Mitch Garver to Texas, Henriquez got a September call-up and faced 20 and 18 batters, respectively, in his first two showings. He then closed out a third by holding the Tigers to a single hit over three scoreless frames. He also continued a regular theme of his career: being younger than almost everyone he faced. Of the 27 batters he saw, only Riley Greene and Livan Soto were younger than the 22-year-old. Henriquez primarily worked with his slider and changeup in the bigs, relegating his four-seam to a third pitch. That might have been for the best given how major-league hitters treated his heat when they got the chance. He'll need to show that was just a small-sample blip if he's going to make the most of any rotation opportunity. For now, the Twins look like they have the better chance of winning the Mitch Garver trade.

Griffin Jax RHP Born: 11/22/94 Age: 28 Bats: R Throws: R Height: 6'2" Weight: 195 lb. Origin: Round 3, 2016 Draft (#93 overall)

YEAR	TEAM	LVL	AGE	W	L	SV	G	GS	IP	H	HR	BB/9	K/9	K	GB%	BABIP	WHIP	ERA	DRA-	WARP	MPH	FB%	Whiff%	CSP
2021	STP	AAA	26	4	1	0	8	8	40^{2}	37	2	3.5	8.0	36	39.8%	.302	1.30	3.76	114	0.3				
2021	MIN	MLB	26	4	5	0	18	14	82	82	23	3.2	7.1	65	31.8%	.248	1.35	6.37	142	-1.1	92.8	45.9%	21.3%	55.8%
2022	MIN	MLB	27	7	4	1	65	0	72^{1}	56	7	2.5	9.7	78	45.5%	.271	1.05	3.36	81	1.4	95.5	33.6%	29.6%	55.7%
2023 DC	*MIN*	*MLB*	*28*	*3*	*3*	*2*	*71*	*0*	*61.7*	*53*	*6*	*2.9*	*8.0*	*54*	*41.5%*	*.273*	*1.19*	*3.11*	*86*	*0.8*	*94.2*	*39.4%*	*25.9%*	*55.7%*

Comparables: Tyler Pill (70), Shane Greene (69), Jeremy Hefner (69)

After watching Jax's arsenal fail to penetrate opponents' defenses in the rotation, the Twins moved the righty to the bullpen. The transition allowed him to minimize his fastball usage and instead make the slider his primary weapon. The transformation was stark. Jax increased his strikeout rate by almost 50%, dispatching foes with that sweeping slider on 59 occasions. As they repeatedly flailed helplessly at breakers that ended up well outside the zone, Jax quickly moved up the bullpen hierarchy and became one of Rocco Baldelli's more trusted high-leverage options. Despite gaining almost three ticks, the heater remained a blunt tool, while the changeup flashed some promise as an alternative method of attack. Jax may not be master of all his weapons, but the slider alone is good enough to keep calling on him when a lead needs to be defended.

Jorge López RHP Born: 02/10/93 Age: 30 Bats: R Throws: R Height: 6'3" Weight: 200 lb. Origin: Round 2, 2011 Draft (#70 overall)

YEAR	TEAM	LVL	AGE	W	L	SV	G	GS	IP	H	HR	BB/9	K/9	K	GB%	BABIP	WHIP	ERA	DRA-	WARP	MPH	FB%	Whiff%	CSP
2020	KC	MLB	27	0	0	0	1	0	0^{2}	3	0	0.0	0.0	0	40.0%	.600	4.50	27.00	172	0.0	94.1	55.0%	0.0%	58.2%
2020	BAL	MLB	27	2	2	0	9	6	38^{1}	43	7	2.8	6.6	28	50.0%	.305	1.43	6.34	99	0.4	93.8	60.2%	22.0%	50.1%
2021	BAL	MLB	28	3	14	0	33	25	121^{2}	142	21	4.1	8.3	112	50.4%	.341	1.63	6.07	111	0.4	95.4	57.9%	20.6%	55.9%
2022	MIN	MLB	29	0	1	4	23	0	22^{2}	23	1	5.6	7.1	18	55.2%	.333	1.63	4.37	113	0.1	97.4	54.7%	21.7%	56.8%
2022	BAL	MLB	29	4	6	19	44	0	48^{1}	30	3	3.2	10.1	54	59.5%	.231	0.97	1.68	77	1.0	98.1	55.1%	25.5%	59.5%
2023 DC	*MIN*	*MLB*	*30*	*3*	*3*	*30*	*71*	*0*	*61.7*	*60*	*6*	*3.8*	*8.4*	*57*	*52.2%*	*.304*	*1.40*	*4.16*	*106*	*0.2*	*95.9*	*56.6%*	*22.8%*	*55.1%*

Comparables: Hector Noesí (56), Nick Tropeano (48), Brad Peacock (48)

One of the first signs that the Orioles were turning the corner from basement-dweller to genuine contender: Converted bullpen weapon López throwing nasty, triple-digit sinkers out of the gate. One of the many signs that the Baltimore front office was still looking firmly to the future: Trading López and his miniscule ERA to Minnesota at the deadline, with his former club firmly in the mix for a playoff spot. Naturally, Mike Elias' timing was impeccable—López's control wavered and his production slid, while Baltimore got four arms back in return. He still has two more years of arbitration left to make good in Minnesota's bullpen. For all the sense the swap made in an objective, dispassionate way, it was the worst of both worlds—simultaneously a disheartening moment in an otherwise-resurgent Baltimore season, without ever providing the Twins a much-needed uplift.

Kenta Maeda RHP Born: 04/11/88 Age: 35 Bats: R Throws: R Height: 6'1" Weight: 185 lb. Origin: International Free Agent, 2016

YEAR	TEAM	LVL	AGE	W	L	SV	G	GS	IP	H	HR	BB/9	K/9	K	GB%	BABIP	WHIP	ERA	DRA-	WARP	MPH	FB%	Whiff%	CSP
2020	MIN	MLB	32	6	1	0	11	11	66^{2}	40	9	1.4	10.8	80	47.5%	.208	0.75	2.70	61	2.1	91.5	25.9%	34.8%	44.4%
2021	MIN	MLB	33	6	5	0	21	21	106^{1}	106	16	2.7	9.6	113	39.0%	.318	1.30	4.66	101	1.0	90.5	31.2%	29.5%	52.5%
2023 DC	*MIN*	*MLB*	*35*	*6*	*6*	*0*	*21*	*21*	*107.3*	*97*	*13*	*2.7*	*9.0*	*107*	*40.6%*	*.288*	*1.21*	*3.32*	*91*	*1.4*	*91.2*	*31.6%*	*28.9%*	*49.3%*

Comparables: Zack Greinke (83), Don Sutton (81), Kevin Gross (80)

There was some hope that Maeda would make a late-season cameo for the Twins. If the season had gone better for his team, perhaps it's more likely he would have. In late August, Derek Falvey indicated Minnesota wouldn't be aggressive with Maeda's Tommy John recovery, while leaving open the possibility that he could appear if the team made a deep playoff run. At that point, Minnesota had already coughed up the division lead to Cleveland, which had been as large as 5.5 games in late May and remained at 4.5 as late as July 5. Maeda's chances of a postseason contribution rapidly evaporated; the Twins were the worst team in the AL Central the rest of the way, winning a mere 11 games in September as the Guardians led baseball with 24 victories. Reports indicate that Maeda's rehab is progressing as expected and he should play a significant role in 2023, the last year of his deal. Hopefully that expectation isn't as ill-fated as the suggestion of that playoff run.

Tyler Mahle RHP Born: 09/29/94 Age: 28 Bats: R Throws: R Height: 6'3" Weight: 210 lb. Origin: Round 7, 2013 Draft (#225 overall)

YEAR	TEAM	LVL	AGE	W	L	SV	G	GS	IP	H	HR	BB/9	K/9	K	GB%	BABIP	WHIP	ERA	DRA-	WARP	MPH	FB%	Whiff%	CSP
2020	CIN	MLB	25	2	2	0	10	9	47^{2}	34	6	4.0	11.3	60	30.2%	.255	1.15	3.59	97	0.6	94.2	55.9%	33.8%	43.6%
2021	CIN	MLB	26	13	6	0	33	33	180	158	24	3.2	10.5	210	41.7%	.303	1.23	3.75	83	3.3	94.2	53.0%	28.5%	53.3%
2022	MIN	MLB	27	1	1	0	4	4	16^{1}	13	4	2.2	6.6	12	29.8%	.209	1.04	4.41	119	0.0	92.1	56.9%	21.5%	53.6%
2022	CIN	MLB	27	5	7	0	19	19	104^{1}	91	12	3.4	9.8	114	36.5%	.290	1.25	4.40	87	1.7	93.7	51.2%	27.8%	51.9%
2023 DC	*MIN*	*MLB*	*28*	*7*	*7*	*0*	*24*	*24*	*123.7*	*108*	*14*	*3.2*	*9.4*	*130*	*38.5%*	*.286*	*1.24*	*3.32*	*90*	*1.7*	*93.9*	*53.2%*	*27.5%*	*51.6%*

Comparables: Homer Bailey (85), Matt Garza (80), Dan Haren (80)

There's no place like home, which in Mahle's case has never been a good thing. He ranks behind only Josiah Gray among active starters for highest home run rate at home. Mahle was freed from Cincy when the Twins made a bid to bolster their rotation at the deadline, but things didn't begin well when he allowed three bombs in his first Minnesota start against the Blue Jays. Shoulder inflammation made matters worse, limiting him to four turns in a Twins uniform. In theory, Mahle should benefit greatly from Target Field, which saw almost 50 fewer homers than Great American Ball Park in 2022 and rates as slightly below-average for round-trippers—while GABP boosts homers more than anywhere else. In practice, he'll have to get on the mound more often to see if the fly balls actually stay in the park.

Trevor Megill RHP Born: 12/05/93 Age: 29 Bats: L Throws: R Height: 6'8" Weight: 250 lb. Origin: Round 7, 2015 Draft (#207 overall)

YEAR	TEAM	LVL	AGE	W	L	SV	G	GS	IP	H	HR	BB/9	K/9	K	GB%	BABIP	WHIP	ERA	DRA-	WARP	MPH	FB%	Whiff%	CSP
2021	IOW	AAA	27	0	0	1	12	0	14	12	2	5.1	12.9	20	44.1%	.313	1.43	5.14	88	0.3				
2021	CHC	MLB	27	1	2	0	28	0	23^2	36	7	3.0	11.4	30	38.2%	.426	1.86	8.37	89	0.4	96.5	66.5%	25.5%	55.1%
2022	STP	AAA	28	0	2	2	10	0	12	11	2	3.0	12.0	16	44.4%	.391	1.25	3.00	79	0.3				
2022	MIN	MLB	28	4	3	0	39	0	45	50	4	3.4	9.8	49	44.2%	.368	1.49	4.80	89	0.7	98.2	55.4%	25.3%	58.0%
2023 DC	*MIN*	*MLB*	*29*	*3*	*3*	*0*	*71*	*0*	*61.7*	*59*	*7*	*3.4*	*9.3*	*63*	*42.2%*	*.310*	*1.35*	*3.87*	*100*	*0.2*	*97.6*	*58.8%*	*26.3%*	*57.1%*

Comparables: Noé Ramirez (66), Stefan Crichton (65), Andrew Kittredge (64)

He didn't draw the same attention as his younger brother Tylor did with his early-season success in New York, nor is it easy to stand out on a team where one of your bullpen colleagues throws 103. Still, Megill's velocity bump made him one of the lesser-known of the 33 pitchers to hurl a pitch at least 101 mph; his average four-seam velocity of 98 mph tied for 19th. Of course, triple-digit fastballs without much wiggle won't beat a lot of major leaguers, and his secondaries, while blessed with massive movement, are—unsurprisingly—inconsistently located. Refining those would ensure a great deal more attention.

Jovani Moran LHP Born: 04/24/97 Age: 26 Bats: L Throws: L Height: 6'1" Weight: 167 lb. Origin: Round 7, 2015 Draft (#200 overall)

YEAR	TEAM	LVL	AGE	W	L	SV	G	GS	IP	H	HR	BB/9	K/9	K	GB%	BABIP	WHIP	ERA	DRA-	WARP	MPH	FB%	Whiff%	CSP
2021	WCH	AA	24	2	1	2	20	0	37^2	14	3	3.3	15.3	64	42.6%	.190	0.74	1.91	52	1.3				
2021	STP	AAA	24	2	1	1	15	0	29^2	14	3	5.5	13.7	45	46.4%	.212	1.08	3.03	74	0.9				
2021	MIN	MLB	24	0	0	0	5	0	8	9	0	7.9	11.2	10	42.9%	.429	2.00	7.87	109	0.0	92.7	52.5%	37.5%	47.9%
2022	STP	AAA	25	1	2	0	20	0	24	25	2	5.2	16.1	43	50.9%	.451	1.63	6.00	59	0.8				
2022	MIN	MLB	25	0	1	1	31	0	40^2	25	0	4.0	12.0	54	50.0%	.272	1.06	2.21	74	0.9	93.4	51.0%	39.0%	52.6%
2023 DC	*MIN*	*MLB*	*26*	*3*	*3*	*0*	*71*	*0*	*61.7*	*48*	*6*	*5.1*	*12.5*	*85*	*46.0%*	*.302*	*1.35*	*3.45*	*86*	*0.7*	*93.3*	*51.3%*	*37.4%*	*51.9%*

Comparables: Paul Fry (71), Eury De La Rosa (68), J.B. Wendelken (67)

For all the success he had, Moran made the trip between Minneapolis and St. Paul surprisingly often. His first call-up saw him strike out five of the nine batters he faced over two appearances before being sent back down. There were four distinct major-league stints in total, and each time he left opponents flailing helplessly as the bottom dropped out of his changeup. The *cambio*, used so often it's almost his primary pitch, has an effective 10-mph separation from his fastball; Moran now repeats the release well, basically giving hitters a 50-50 guess as to what's coming. When they get the change, they failed over 90% of the time, batting .093 against the pitch. Control remains an issue—Moran hasn't had a walk rate in the single digits since rookie ball—but since the next batter is likely to go down swinging on the change, it's tough to worry about it.

Bailey Ober RHP Born: 07/12/95 Age: 27 Bats: R Throws: R Height: 6'9" Weight: 260 lb. Origin: Round 12, 2017 Draft (#346 overall)

YEAR	TEAM	LVL	AGE	W	L	SV	G	GS	IP	H	HR	BB/9	K/9	K	GB%	BABIP	WHIP	ERA	DRA-	WARP	MPH	FB%	Whiff%	CSP
2021	STP	AAA	25	1	0	0	4	4	16	13	0	2.8	11.8	21	48.7%	.333	1.13	2.81	97	0.3				
2021	MIN	MLB	25	3	3	0	20	20	92^1	92	20	1.9	9.4	96	33.5%	.296	1.20	4.19	101	0.8	92.5	58.0%	24.7%	52.7%
2022	FTM	A	26	0	0	0	2	2	7	4	1	1.3	7.7	6	44.4%	.176	0.71	1.29	106	0.1	91.7	42.6%	27.1%	
2022	STP	AAA	26	0	1	0	2	2	9^2	5	2	1.9	12.1	13	52.4%	.158	0.72	4.66	79	0.2				
2022	MIN	MLB	26	2	3	0	11	11	56	48	4	1.8	8.2	51	28.8%	.278	1.05	3.21	102	0.5	91.7	49.1%	27.6%	53.3%
2023 DC	*MIN*	*MLB*	*27*	*7*	*7*	*0*	*24*	*24*	*123.7*	*120*	*17*	*2.1*	*8.8*	*120*	*34.5%*	*.298*	*1.22*	*3.57*	*98*	*1.2*	*92.2*	*54.1%*	*26.5%*	*53.0%*

Comparables: Jimmy Nelson (66), Anthony DeSclafani (66), Scott Baker (64)

It felt like that, for a playoff contender, the Twins were oberconfident about what they'd get out of their pitching staff in 2022—especially in their rotation. Those questions were pervasive, from past talent level to experience. None of the unit had come close to 30 starts the year before; most, including Ober, had never done it at all. It turned out that the tall righty wasn't oberrated at all based on his 2021 performance; he more or less replicated that showing, continuing to demonstrate good control, a decent whiff rate and oberall the profile of a league-average starter—the kind of guy who's just there, anchoring the staff without being particularly noticeable. The problem, as with much of the roster, was that Minnesota only got that performance ober a third of a season, due to a groin strain. The 2022 Twins would not have been dramatically better if they'd had him all year, but it's easy to underestimate the value of an Ober holding everything together.

Chris Paddack RHP Born: 01/08/96 Age: 27 Bats: R Throws: R Height: 6'5" Weight: 217 lb. Origin: Round 8, 2015 Draft (#236 overall)

YEAR	TEAM	LVL	AGE	W	L	SV	G	GS	IP	H	HR	BB/9	K/9	K	GB%	BABIP	WHIP	ERA	DRA-	WARP	MPH	FB%	Whiff%	CSP
2020	SD	MLB	24	4	5	0	12	12	59	60	14	1.8	8.8	58	46.8%	.289	1.22	4.73	86	1.1	94.1	61.5%	26.0%	48.8%
2021	SD	MLB	25	7	7	0	23	22	108^1	115	15	1.8	8.2	99	42.4%	.317	1.26	5.07	91	1.5	94.9	61.5%	24.7%	57.4%
2022	MIN	MLB	26	1	2	0	5	5	22^1	25	0	0.8	8.1	20	44.3%	.357	1.21	4.03	98	0.2	93.3	52.3%	25.7%	62.4%
2023 DC	*MIN*	*MLB*	*27*	*1*	*1*	*0*	*4*	*4*	*23*	*23*	*2*	*2.2*	*8.3*	*21*	*43.1%*	*.306*	*1.24*	*3.44*	*94*	*0.3*	*94.4*	*60.2%*	*25.6%*	*55.2%*

Comparables: Vance Worley (74), Scott Baker (73), Danny Salazar (71)

A second Tommy John surgery does not automatically signal the end of a career. Paddack can take heart from the careers of Nathan Eovaldi and Jameson Taillon, both of whom had their second procedure in their mid-20s and returned to compile highly productive seasons in the rotation. Unlike those starters, the former Padre has yet to pass 150 innings in a season prior to his repeat surgery and now will almost certainly not do so before his 28th birthday. The Twins traded away Taylor Rogers in the hope that Paddack could rediscover his standout rookie form. The move brought some changes, including a move away from that once-trusty four-seamer to a more balanced arsenal, but a UCL (that may not have fully recovered from a September 2021 sprain) gave out five starts in. Paddack seems better-placed than most to navigate the loss of command that often affects hurlers, post-TJ. That rookie form, on the other hand, is likely to remain elusive.

Emilio Pagán RHP Born: 05/07/91 Age: 32 Bats: L Throws: R Height: 6'2" Weight: 208 lb. Origin: Round 10, 2013 Draft (#297 overall)

YEAR	TEAM	LVL	AGE	W	L	SV	G	GS	IP	H	HR	BB/9	K/9	K	GB%	BABIP	WHIP	ERA	DRA-	WARP	MPH	FB%	Whiff%	CSP
2020	SD	MLB	29	0	1	2	22	0	22	14	4	3.7	9.4	23	30.9%	.196	1.05	4.50	112	0.1	93.7	97.8%	26.7%	46.5%
2021	SD	MLB	30	4	3	0	67	0	63^{1}	56	16	2.6	9.8	69	23.0%	.253	1.17	4.83	109	0.3	94.2	98.9%	29.8%	55.3%
2022	MIN	MLB	31	4	6	9	59	0	63	60	12	3.7	12.0	84	39.9%	.320	1.37	4.43	77	1.3	95.8	51.9%	30.6%	52.4%
2023 DC	*MIN*	*MLB*	*32*	*3*	*3*	*2*	*71*	*0*	*61.7*	*50*	*8*	*3.1*	*9.8*	*67*	*33.6%*	*.266*	*1.15*	*3.04*	*85*	*0.7*	*95.0*	*76.7%*	*29.4%*	*52.7%*

Comparables: Brad Brach (73), Josh Fields (68), Pedro Báez (66)

Pagán's efforts to recapture his 2019 form with the same pitch mix were unsuccessful, so he tried adding not one but two more offerings. The first, a splitter, helped him to bump his ground-ball rate to a career high and generated a healthy amount of whiffs. The second, a slider, appeared briefly mid-season and mostly when ahead to right-handed batters. A curveball re-joined the repertoire late in the season and flashed plus depth, along with an even better ground-ball rate. The Twins reliever still gets crushed when he leaves one out over the middle of the zone, and he's issuing too many free passes to feel comfortable with that home run rate. Nonetheless, his final month of the season, after the curve returned, was the closest he's looked to elite in years. Maintaining that throughout the upcoming season would set Pagán up nicely for free agency.

★ ★ ★ *2023 Top 101 Prospect* **#53** ★ ★ ★

Marco Raya RHP Born: 08/07/02 Age: 20 Bats: R Throws: R Height: 6'1" Weight: 170 lb. Origin: Round 4, 2020 Draft (#128 overall)

YEAR	TEAM	LVL	AGE	W	L	SV	G	GS	IP	H	HR	BB/9	K/9	K	GB%	BABIP	WHIP	ERA	DRA-	WARP	MPH	FB%	Whiff%	CSP
2022	FTM	A	19	3	2	0	19	17	65	47	8	3.2	10.5	76	43.5%	.255	1.08	3.05	96	1.2	94.9	44.0%	31.3%	
2023 non-DC	*MIN*	*MLB*	*20*	*2*	*3*	*0*	*57*	*0*	*50*	*52*	*9*	*4.5*	*7.0*	*39*	*40.7%*	*.291*	*1.55*	*5.39*	*130*	*-0.6*			*24.1%*	

Comparables: Germán Márquez (86), Michael Kopech (84), Ian Anderson (84)

Armed with a pair of obscenely filthy breaking balls, Raya demonstrated that he has the stuff to be one of the very best pitching prospects in baseball. The distinct lack of professional innings tells you why he isn't even more highly-regarded: His stature, injury history, and total lack of experience pitching deep into games are potential bullpen markers. In other words, all he has to do to surge to the top of the 101 is show he can hold up as a starter—and pitching prospects never fail that test, right?

Joe Ryan RHP Born: 06/05/96 Age: 27 Bats: R Throws: R Height: 6'2" Weight: 205 lb. Origin: Round 7, 2018 Draft (#210 overall)

YEAR	TEAM	LVL	AGE	W	L	SV	G	GS	IP	H	HR	BB/9	K/9	K	GB%	BABIP	WHIP	ERA	DRA-	WARP	MPH	FB%	Whiff%	CSP
2021	DUR	AAA	25	4	3	0	12	11	57	35	8	1.6	11.8	75	32.3%	.227	0.79	3.63	87	1.2				
2021	STP	AAA	25	0	0	0	2	2	9	5	1	2.0	17.0	17	66.7%	.286	0.78	2.00	87	0.2				
2021	MIN	MLB	25	2	1	0	5	5	26^{2}	16	4	1.7	10.1	30	26.2%	.197	0.79	4.05	104	0.2	91.2	66.0%	23.4%	56.2%
2022	MIN	MLB	26	13	8	0	27	27	147	115	20	2.9	9.2	151	27.8%	.253	1.10	3.55	99	1.5	92.2	60.0%	25.8%	54.9%
2023 DC	*MIN*	*MLB*	*27*	*9*	*8*	*0*	*27*	*27*	*148.7*	*122*	*20*	*2.7*	*9.7*	*160*	*29.9%*	*.270*	*1.13*	*3.03*	*85*	*2.4*	*92.1*	*60.7%*	*26.5%*	*55.1%*

Comparables: Dinelson Lamet (73), Kyle Hendricks (67), Danny Salazar (65)

Hit the fastball. I dare you. Go on, hit it. I'll throw it all the time. Right there, at the top of the zone. Nothing? I'll give you another. Can't hit it, can you? C'mon, it's only 92. Alright, I'll toss you a slider or changeup now and then. I shouldn't, but I'm feeling generous. After that you're getting another fastball, though. Top of the zone. I'll give you a hint: My arm slot's kinda low, and it's comin' in pretty flat. Harder than it looks, isn't it? Better luck next time.

Aaron Sanchez RHP Born: 07/01/92 Age: 31 Bats: R Throws: R Height: 6'4" Weight: 212 lb. Origin: Round 1, 2010 Draft (#34 overall)

YEAR	TEAM	LVL	AGE	W	L	SV	G	GS	IP	H	HR	BB/9	K/9	K	GB%	BABIP	WHIP	ERA	DRA-	WARP	MPH	FB%	Whiff%	CSP
2021	SAC	AAA	28	1	1	0	6	6	17^{1}	24	4	5.2	5.7	11	42.9%	.339	1.96	7.79	130	-0.2				
2021	SF	MLB	28	1	1	0	9	7	35^{1}	32	2	3.8	6.6	26	53.2%	.275	1.33	3.06	106	0.2	90.4	49.4%	20.6%	54.1%
2022	ROC	AAA	29	1	0	0	3	3	15	17	2	3.0	6.0	10	43.5%	.341	1.47	3.60	109	0.1				
2022	STP	AAA	29	3	2	0	10	10	47^{1}	43	7	2.9	6.3	33	44.1%	.263	1.23	3.80	115	0.3				
2022	MIN	MLB	29	0	1	0	8	3	28^{2}	31	2	2.2	7.8	25	56.8%	.337	1.33	4.71	96	0.3	92.5	54.9%	18.2%	54.1%
2022	WAS	MLB	29	3	3	0	7	7	31^{1}	47	6	2.3	4.6	16	49.1%	.376	1.76	8.33	132	-0.2	92.0	67.9%	18.1%	58.2%
2023 DC	*FA*	*MLB*	*30*	*3*	*4*	*0*	*13*	*13*	*59.7*	*69*	*7*	*3.3*	*5.9*	*39*	*49.3%*	*.312*	*1.52*	*5.06*	*126*	*-0.3*	*92.3*	*57.8%*	*19.2%*	*53.0%*

Comparables: Stan Bahnsen (70), Jason Marquis (69), Milt Pappas (68)

Sanchez recovered a couple more ticks of his lost velocity, posted a new career-best walk rate (5.5%) and essentially managed to stay healthy all season. Those are the positives. Unfortunately, the majority of the batted balls recorded against the one-time AL ERA leader were returned harder than he could throw them. No one who pitched as often allowed hard-hit batted balls as frequently; 48% of them were hit at least 95 mph. Since Sanchez has never been in the business of missing that many bats, it was a sub-optimal combination. He was also a little unlucky, since he's still good at generating grounders, but when almost 80% of your pitches end up in play and they don't move like they used to, you're at the mercy of fortune. Still, Sanchez was offered an extended look by two pitching-needy teams, and there are always more of those.

Cole Sands RHP

Born: 07/17/97 Age: 25 Bats: R Throws: R Height: 6'3" Weight: 215 lb. Origin: Round 5, 2018 Draft (#154 overall)

YEAR	TEAM	LVL	AGE	W	L	SV	G	GS	IP	H	HR	BB/9	K/9	K	GB%	BABIP	WHIP	ERA	DRA-	WARP	MPH	FB%	Whiff%	CSP
2021	WCH	AA	23	4	2	0	19	18	80^1	59	6	3.9	10.8	96	40.1%	.277	1.17	2.46	78	1.5				
2022	STP	AAA	24	3	6	0	19	13	61^2	78	9	3.5	10.5	72	39.5%	.397	1.65	5.55	105	0.6				
2022	MIN	MLB	24	0	3	1	11	3	30^2	35	4	3.8	8.2	28	44.4%	.326	1.57	5.87	113	0.1	91.9	50.1%	22.7%	52.4%
2023 DC	*MIN*	*MLB*	*25*	*2*	*1*	*0*	*17*	*3*	*25*	*24*	*2*	*3.7*	*8.4*	*23*	*41.5%*	*.304*	*1.40*	*4.12*	*105*	*0.1*	*91.9*	*50.1%*	*24.4%*	*52.4%*

Comparables: Frankie Montas (66), Jordan Yamamoto (66), Keyvius Sampson (66)

You know what they say about Sands: it gets everywhere. The Twins prospect began his season with five frames of one-hit ball at Triple-A, and ended it with a four-inning save in Minnesota's final game. In between, it was a season that matched his uneven usage, lacking consistency and stability. Sands made seven trips between Triple-A and the big leagues, plus one to the injured list with each team. He was employed as a starter and in relief, both long and short. His pitch count undulated by 40 or 50 between outings on more than one occasion. His control was coarse, but the grains of more promise were there, notably with his high-spin curveball. As debut seasons go, it was fine. Sands will hope that the major-league roster spot doesn't keep slipping through his fingers quite so often in his second year.

Devin Smeltzer LHP

Born: 09/07/95 Age: 27 Bats: R Throws: L Height: 6'3" Weight: 195 lb. Origin: Round 5, 2016 Draft (#161 overall)

YEAR	TEAM	LVL	AGE	W	L	SV	G	GS	IP	H	HR	BB/9	K/9	K	GB%	BABIP	WHIP	ERA	DRA-	WARP	MPH	FB%	Whiff%	CSP
2020	MIN	MLB	24	2	0	0	7	1	16	19	2	2.8	8.4	15	35.3%	.354	1.50	6.75	113	0.1	87.8	33.2%	25.0%	49.3%
2021	MIN	MLB	25	0	0	0	1	0	4^2	1	0	1.9	5.8	3	45.5%	.091	0.43	0.00	94	0.1	85.9	40.4%	25.9%	64.5%
2022	STP	AAA	26	3	4	0	15	9	50	64	10	2.9	8.5	47	38.8%	.353	1.60	7.56	121	0.1				
2022	MIN	MLB	26	5	2	0	15	12	70^1	67	13	2.4	5.1	40	37.4%	.254	1.22	3.71	137	-0.7	89.0	50.0%	18.6%	54.2%
2023 non-DC	*MIN*	*MLB*	*27*	*2*	*3*	*0*	*57*	*0*	*50*	*57*	*7*	*2.8*	*6.1*	*33*	*38.5%*	*.304*	*1.45*	*5.00*	*129*	*-0.5*	*88.8*	*47.7%*	*20.5%*	*53.7%*

Comparables: Paul Blackburn (63), Daniel Norris (60), Chase De Jong (59)

The kitchen sink was thrown at Smeltzer's opponents in an effort to support his sub-14% strikeout rate. It mostly worked, at least on the surface and in the majors; at Triple-A, the batted-ball fortune went down the drain. His distracting delivery, and willingness to throw his curve and change almost as often as his "heater" to righties, seemed to keep them off-balanced enough to cap that all-crucial BABIP; he also mixed in a promising cutter at times. He still doesn't seem to know what to do with lefties, however: He remained reliant on his mediocre four-seam, and the reverse split persisted in a .308/.368/.539 line. His employers were unimpressed with the junkballing lefty's performance regardless of run prevention, outrighting him in October.

Caleb Thielbar LHP

Born: 01/31/87 Age: 36 Bats: R Throws: L Height: 6'0" Weight: 205 lb. Origin: Round 18, 2009 Draft (#556 overall)

YEAR	TEAM	LVL	AGE	W	L	SV	G	GS	IP	H	HR	BB/9	K/9	K	GB%	BABIP	WHIP	ERA	DRA-	WARP	MPH	FB%	Whiff%	CSP
2020	MIN	MLB	33	2	1	0	17	0	20	14	0	4.1	9.9	22	27.5%	.275	1.15	2.25	104	0.2	90.1	54.4%	29.4%	51.4%
2021	MIN	MLB	34	7	0	0	59	0	64	55	8	2.8	10.8	77	30.7%	.303	1.17	3.23	92	0.9	91.5	49.0%	26.5%	59.0%
2022	MIN	MLB	35	4	3	1	67	0	59^1	51	5	2.7	12.1	80	29.9%	.324	1.16	3.49	71	1.5	93.0	49.4%	30.3%	57.6%
2023 DC	*MIN*	*MLB*	*36*	*3*	*3*	*0*	*71*	*0*	*61.7*	*52*	*7*	*2.9*	*9.8*	*67*	*32.2%*	*.279*	*1.16*	*3.02*	*84*	*0.8*	*92.1*	*49.7%*	*27.3%*	*57.6%*

Comparables: Jake Diekman (53), Randy Choate (49), Pat Neshek (48)

Thielbar's mid-30s renaissance keeps getting more remarkable. First, it was impressive that he even made it back at all, after four years away from the bigs and a short-lived retirement. Then he went from a solid small-sample season to a full, good year in the Twins bullpen. Not content with that, Thielbar added a tick and a half to his fastball velocity, throwing harder than ever in his age-35 season and finishing with an identical DRA- to Guardians closer Emmanuel Clase. Thielbar's ERA told a different story for most of the year; a pair of blow-ups against the Dodgers and Red Sox in mid-April saw him give up seven earned while recording a single out. At that point, he had zero strikeouts and a 23.63 ERA. For the remainder, he whiffed 80 across 56⅔ frames with a 2.54 ERA. Only 11 players throwing 50 or more innings have ever posted a strikeout rate as high as Thielbar's at 35 or older. Following the Nelson Cruz trajectory as a lefty reliever will be tough to maintain for the rest of his 30s. However long this lasts, he deserves credit for a year as one of the best relievers in baseball.

Louie Varland RHP

Born: 12/09/97 Age: 25 Bats: L Throws: R Height: 6'1" Weight: 205 lb. Origin: Round 15, 2019 Draft (#449 overall)

YEAR	TEAM	LVL	AGE	W	L	SV	G	GS	IP	H	HR	BB/9	K/9	K	GB%	BABIP	WHIP	ERA	DRA-	WARP	MPH	FB%	Whiff%	CSP
2021	FTM	A	23	4	2	0	10	8	47^1	41	2	3.0	14.5	76	45.7%	.379	1.20	2.09	82	1.0				
2021	CR	A+	23	6	2	0	10	10	55^2	41	4	2.3	10.7	66	37.4%	.276	0.99	2.10	87	1.0				
2022	WCH	AA	24	7	4	0	20	19	105	102	14	3.3	10.2	119	40.3%	.320	1.34	3.34	82	1.6				
2022	STP	AAA	24	1	1	0	4	4	21^1	15	1	1.3	11.4	27	36.5%	.275	0.84	1.69	81	0.5				
2022	MIN	MLB	24	1	2	0	5	5	26	26	4	2.1	7.3	21	38.5%	.297	1.23	3.81	111	0.1	93.9	47.9%	19.9%	58.1%
2023 DC	*MIN*	*MLB*	*25*	*3*	*4*	*0*	*12*	*12*	*63.3*	*64*	*8*	*3.4*	*7.3*	*51*	*40.1%*	*.296*	*1.39*	*4.21*	*110*	*0.2*	*93.9*	*47.9%*	*24.0%*	*58.1%*

Comparables: Tyler Duffey (84), Jimmy Nelson (82), Ben Lively (79)

In the first inning of his first three major-league starts, Varland faced: Aaron Judge; José Ramírez; and then Mike Trout and Shohei Ohtani back-to-back. He retired Judge (strikeout), Trout (deep flyout) and Ohtani (hard groundout), while Ramírez homered. That feels on the precarious side of fine, which is kind of how Varland's debut was overall. It certainly didn't reach the heights of his first four starts at Triple-A, in which he struck out nearly a third of opponents and allowed just four runs to earn a rapid promotion. Striking out that many hitters in the majors, with his mid-90s fastball and fairly middle-of-the-road stuff, was never likely. Instead, Varland filled up the zone, ranking third in zone percentage among starters with at least 20 innings pitched. Indiscriminately throwing strikes might not keep working against big leaguers if he can't refine his command; it certainly won't against Judge and company in the long-term. Varland did enough to show that a long-term outlook is possible, though, which is all we can ask at this stage of his career.

Josh Winder RHP Born: 10/11/96 Age: 26 Bats: R Throws: R Height: 6'5" Weight: 210 lb. Origin: Round 7, 2018 Draft (#214 overall)

YEAR	TEAM	LVL	AGE	W	L	SV	G	GS	IP	H	HR	BB/9	K/9	K	GB%	BABIP	WHIP	ERA	DRA-	WARP	MPH	FB%	Whiff%	CSP
2021	WCH	AA	24	3	0	0	10	10	54^{2}	41	5	1.6	10.7	65	40.6%	.281	0.93	1.98	88	0.7				
2021	STP	AAA	24	1	0	0	4	4	17^{1}	14	4	1.6	7.8	15	32.7%	.222	0.98	4.67	111	0.1				
2022	STP	AAA	25	0	0	0	5	5	16	11	3	3.4	6.2	11	37.5%	.178	1.06	3.38	110	0.1				
2022	MIN	MLB	25	4	6	0	15	11	67	69	11	2.4	6.3	47	34.1%	.282	1.30	4.70	125	-0.2	94.2	40.5%	22.2%	53.7%
2023 DC	*MIN*	*MLB*	*26*	*4*	*4*	*0*	*34*	*6*	*56.3*	*57*	*8*	*2.9*	*7.2*	*45*	*35.9%*	*.287*	*1.33*	*4.19*	*112*	*0.1*	*94.2*	*40.5%*	*24.1%*	*53.7%*

Comparables: Hiram Burgos (80), Tyler Duffey (77), Taylor Jordan (75)

Here's a pitcher scary story in two words: shoulder injury. Add a third to make it terrifying: recurring shoulder injury. It could be much worse for Winder: He hasn't required surgery as a result of his impingement problems, and he was throwing just as hard in September as he was in April. On the flip side, it doesn't feel particularly reassuring to know that the team has no idea why this keeps happening. That feels like a sign that it's going to keep happening, although there's no real way of knowing. If you're in the market for more horror, here's another two-word scary story: bad fastball. No pitcher who threw at least 300 four-seamers had a worse xwOBA on the pitch than Winder at .495; opponents slugged a largely deserved .713 against it. Ideally, the root cause of the impingement can be fixed and it makes the fastball better. If not, it might be time to hide behind the couch.

Simeon Woods Richardson RHP Born: 09/27/00 Age: 22 Bats: R Throws: R Height: 6'3" Weight: 210 lb. Origin: Round 2, 2018 Draft (#48 overall)

YEAR	TEAM	LVL	AGE	W	L	SV	G	GS	IP	H	HR	BB/9	K/9	K	GB%	BABIP	WHIP	ERA	DRA-	WARP	MPH	FB%	Whiff%	CSP
2021	NH	AA	20	2	4	0	11	11	45^{1}	42	5	5.2	13.3	67	32.4%	.359	1.50	5.76	86	0.7				
2021	WCH	AA	20	1	1	0	4	3	8	6	0	9.0	11.2	10	38.1%	.316	1.75	6.75	101	0.1				
2022	WCH	AA	21	3	3	0	16	15	70^{2}	56	4	3.3	9.8	77	42.5%	.294	1.16	3.06	77	1.3				
2022	STP	AAA	21	2	0	0	7	7	36^{2}	21	2	2.5	9.3	38	46.2%	.213	0.85	2.21	79	0.9				
2022	MIN	MLB	21	0	1	0	1	1	5	3	1	3.6	5.4	3	20.0%	.143	1.00	3.60	120	0.0	91.1	54.9%	19.2%	51.8%
2023 DC	*MIN*	*MLB*	*22*	*1*	*1*	*0*	*4*	*4*	*21.7*	*20*	*2*	*4.3*	*8.6*	*20*	*41.0%*	*.302*	*1.43*	*4.06*	*104*	*0.1*	*91.1*	*54.9%*	*26.6%*	*51.8%*

Comparables: Carlos Martinez (48), Jacob Turner (47), Deivi García (45)

After a good minor-league campaign restored some of the sheen to Woods Richardson's profile, he made his major-league debut during the season's final weekend. If a little of that prospect glow was back, it wasn't exactly polished by the debut: He sat a touch below 91, and allowed hard contact that he was largely fortunate to see fly into a teammate's glove. Still, the arsenal is now deep enough to help Woods Richardson hold down a back-end rotation slot. His extreme over-the-top arm slot may cause some serious issues with fastball shape if he can't keep the heater up in the zone, though, and he doesn't project to have the kind of stuff that will let him get away with an elevated walk rate. He looks set to provide much-needed innings of some sort for Minnesota in the near future. Whether he'll be merely filling those frames or brightening the Twins' outlook is down to that command.

Lineouts

Hitters

HITTER	POS	TEAM	LVL	AGE	PA	R	2B	3B	HR	RBI	BB	K	SB	CS	AVG/OBP/SLG	DRC+	BABIP	BRR	DRP	WARP
Tim Beckham	DH	STP	AAA	32	143	18	6	0	5	31	14	31	2	1	.413/.483/.579	109	.522	0.1	2B(10): -1.5, 3B(9): -0.6, 1B(5): 0.3	0.4
	DH	MIN	MLB	32	25	1	0	0	0	1	0	9	0	0	.080/.080/.080	78	.125	0.2	LF(4): 0, 1B(2): 0.1	0.0
Keoni Cavaco	3B	FTM	A	21	396	34	18	5	11	59	22	138	7	4	.231/.275/.397	74	.332	-4.0	3B(80): -1.4	-0.4
Mark Contreras	OF	STP	AAA	27	423	64	21	1	15	59	37	125	23	2	.237/.317/.418	78	.311	0.3	CF(46): -3.7, RF(31): -0.6, LF(14): 1.7	0.5
	OF	MIN	MLB	27	61	9	1	0	3	6	1	21	1	0	.121/.148/.293	69	.114	0.6	CF(13): -0.5, RF(9): -0.3, LF(3): 0	0.0
Billy Hamilton	CF	TAC	AAA	31	95	11	2	0	0	5	9	25	4	0	.186/.263/.209	78	.262	-0.2	CF(15): -1.6, LF(6): -0.2	0.2
	CF	MIA	MLB	31	15	9	0	0	0	0	1	8	7	0	.077/.143/.077	70	.200	0.4	LF(6): 0.1, CF(5): -0.2	0.0
	CF	MIN	MLB	31	8	4	0	0	0	0	1	4	3	1	.000/.125/.000	80		0.1	LF(6): -0.1, 2B(1): 0	0.0
Caleb Hamilton	C	STP	AAA	27	251	34	10	0	11	43	43	67	1	0	.233/.367/.442	113	.287	0.6	C(31): 1.1, 3B(11): -0.9, 1B(4): 0.1	1.2
	C	MIN	MLB	27	23	5	0	0	1	1	4	14	0	0	.056/.227/.222	56		0.2	C(11): 0.6, 1B(6): -0.2	0.0
Alex Isola	DH	WCH	AA	23	247	33	9	0	10	40	32	45	0	1	.286/.377/.471	122	.314	-4.2	C(18): 0.9, 1B(17): -0.1	1.0
Edouard Julien	2B	WCH	AA	23	508	77	19	3	17	67	98	125	19	7	.300/.441/.490	128	.393	-2.0	2B(94): -8.2	2.2
Yasser Mercedes	OF	DSL TWI	ROK	17	176	34	13	3	4	20	18	35	30	5	.355/.420/.555		.432			
Noah Miller	SS	FTM	A	19	469	62	12	4	2	24	76	110	23	7	.211/.348/.279	110	.287	-1.6	SS(98): 5.5	2.2
Tanner Schobel	2B/3B	FTM	A	21	120	11	3	0	1	10	18	23	6	1	.242/.367/.303	118	.303	-1.4	2B(19): 1.8, 3B(6): -1.2, SS(3): 0.1	0.5

Tim Beckham returned to the majors for the first time since 2019, logging a pair of singles in nearly four weeks on the roster; you'd still prefer his big-league output over the past few seasons to that of Stephen Strasburg, who succeeded him as first overall pick. **Keoni Cavaco** started to show some of the power that would make an elevated strikeout rate more palatable. Unfortunately, the punchouts came even more frequently in his second go-around at Low-A, making it look ever more likely that he won't live up to first-round expectations. Ninth-round pick **Mark Contreras** finally got the call, to cover for a glut of outfield injuries. He showcased his good glove, powerful arm and a whole lot of swing and miss. If the Twins outfield is as healthy as it was in 2022, he'll get more opportunities to cut down on those whiffs—although his minor-league track record doesn't bode well. It would be easy to call **Billy Hamilton** the new Terrance Gore, except that the original Terrance Gore is a year younger. Regardless, the now-journeyman speedster has a shot at becoming the active career stolen base leader, if he can run this pinch-runner and outfield replacement tightrope for long enough. Six years after he was drafted, third baseman-turned catcher **Caleb Hamilton** three-true-outcomed his way to his first above-average line in full-season ball, plus a promotion to the majors. The balance between the outcomes went askew when he got there, and he was ejected from the 40-man at season's end. He hasn't quite put the ISO in **Alex Isola** yet, but the former 29th-round catcher has progressed just enough with the bat to compensate for his lack of progression with the glove, opening up the possibility of carving out a role as a corner infielder. There's plenty of doubt as to whether **Edouard Julien** can handle second, or whether he can make regular contact against advanced pitching, or whether he'll ever hit lefties (.210/.373/.276 last year). Given all that, the fact that we're still including him here says something about the other kinds of things he *can* do. "The best or nothing," the Mercedes-Benz slogan, doubles as a good summary of excessively binary prospect discourse. While **Yasser Mercedes**' career has a far wider range of potential outcomes than that, he shaded heavily to the former after the Twins spent $1.7 million on him, with a DSL campaign that demonstrated blistering speed, great defense and developing power. He. Gets. On. Base. **Noah Miller** didn't do a ton else at the plate to inspire confidence in his first full season, true. Since he was younger than most of his competition and has the potential to stick at short, though, that approach may yet prove to be enough for a big-league role. While second-rounder **Tanner Schobel** may not be a high-ceiling type, he led Virginia Tech with 19 home runs in his final college season. He had a harder time clearing the fence in his first taste of pro ball, but he maintained the outstanding approach that gives him a solid offensive floor.

Pitchers

PITCHER	TEAM	LVL	AGE	W	L	SV	G	GS	IP	H	HR	BB/9	K/9	K	GB%	BABIP	WHIP	ERA	DRA-	WARP	MPH	FB%	WHF	CSP
Jorge Alcala	MIN	MLB	26	0	0	0	2	0	2^{1}	2	0	7.7	7.7	2	50.0%	.333	1.71	0.00	104	0.0	94.9	37.5%	35.3%	58.7%
Jordan Balazovic	STP	AAA	23	0	7	0	22	21	70^{2}	102	20	4.5	9.7	76	40.4%	.392	1.94	7.39	126	0.0				
Matt Canterino	WCH	AA	24	0	1	0	11	10	34^{1}	17	1	5.8	13.1	50	26.4%	.229	1.14	1.83	73	0.7				
Jharel Cotton	STP	AAA	30	4	1	1	22	0	25	17	4	3.6	14.0	39	26.4%	.265	1.08	2.88	73	0.7				
	MIN	MLB	30	2	2	0	25	0	35	23	7	4.1	8.0	31	29.5%	.182	1.11	2.83	116	0.1	93.1	46.7%	25.5%	56.8%
	SF	MLB	30	2	0	0	5	0	8	11	0	4.5	9.0	8	32.0%	.440	1.88	6.75	108	0.0	91.8	35.8%	25.3%	51.7%
Danny Coulombe	MIN	MLB	32	0	0	0	10	0	12^{1}	7	0	6.6	6.6	9	37.1%	.200	1.30	1.46	113	0.0	91.7	36.9%	30.4%	50.4%
Randy Dobnak	STP	AAA	27	1	2	0	8	3	20	18	3	7.2	8.6	19	45.6%	.278	1.70	5.40	106	0.2				
David Festa	FTM	A	22	2	1	0	5	5	24	12	1	2.3	12.4	33	50.0%	.234	0.75	1.50	75	0.7	95.8	54.0%	36.8%	
	CR	A+	22	7	3	0	16	13	79^{2}	67	5	3.2	8.5	75	49.3%	.294	1.19	2.71	92	1.1				
Oliver Ortega	SL	AAA	25	2	1	2	23	0	25^{2}	34	3	2.8	9.5	27	46.3%	.392	1.64	5.96	93	0.3	96.1	52.6%	25.8%	
	LAA	MLB	25	1	3	1	27	0	34	32	5	4.8	8.7	33	50.0%	.300	1.47	3.71	94	0.4	96.0	60.7%	23.8%	54.9%
Jhon Romero	MIN	MLB	27	0	0	0	4	0	5	9	0	1.8	10.8	6	70.6%	.529	2.00	3.60	90	0.1	94.6	54.4%	28.3%	53.0%
Joe Smith	MIN	MLB	38	1	1	0	34	0	27^{1}	33	7	3.0	5.6	17	56.8%	.295	1.54	4.61	118	0.0	84.5	72.7%	17.6%	52.5%
Cody Stashak	MIN	MLB	28	3	0	0	11	0	16^{1}	16	1	0.0	8.3	15	26.0%	.306	0.98	3.86	101	0.2	90.7	48.9%	28.0%	58.7%
Tyler Thornburg	STP	AAA	33	1	0	0	13	0	14^{1}	17	1	3.8	9.4	15	56.8%	.372	1.60	5.65	94	0.2				
	ATL	MLB	33	0	0	0	9	0	9^{1}	12	0	4.8	9.6	10	25.0%	.375	1.82	3.86	105	0.1	93.8	54.9%	24.7%	49.9%
	MIN	MLB	33	0	1	0	5	0	9^{2}	4	1	5.6	3.7	4	41.4%	.107	1.03	2.79	121	0.0	93.4	62.4%	14.3%	51.5%

Sometimes it's just obvious you don't have it. **Jorge Alcala** topped out at 98 mph in his final outing of 2021, so it was glaring when he couldn't hit 95 in his first of 2022. He ended up throwing only 59 total pitches all season. His elbow was the cause, albeit not in the way you might immediately think: He underwent arthroscopic debridement surgery in August and is expected to be ready for the spring. Looking to thrust himself into Minnesota's major-league plans, **Jordan Balazovic** instead lost the first month to a knee sprain, spent much of the season on a limited pitch count—on a quest to rediscover his form—and gave up a truly astounding number of homers. The score's against him. A better September offered a glimmer of hope. By the time **Matt Canterino** returns from his August 2022 Tommy John surgery, he will—at best—be approaching his 26th birthday, with 85 professional innings pitched. While the brief but dominant stint at Double-A showed his starting potential, volume alone is starting to dictate a bullpen role—if he can even stay healthy enough for that. The Twins were able to get **Jharel Cotton** through waivers three times and stash him in St Paul for whenever they needed another arm. A fourth DFA proved to be one too many, as the Giants stepped in, but Cotton seems to be at the point of his career when he'll always be available again sooner rather than later. Ever-committed to the art of deception, lefty **Danny Coulombe** added a little side-to-side shimmy to start his delivery. Whether his body objected to the motion or the timing was coincidental, his troublesome hip cost him most of the season and ultimately required labrum surgery in late July. The middle finger strain that ended **Randy Dobnak**'s 2021 was so persistent that he landed on the 60-day IL to start the year. He was thus restricted to giving injuries just the one finger for most of the year—but he did have both functioning in September, when he was outrighted to Triple-A. Thirteenth-rounder **David Festa** has added a few ticks since college, now sitting mid-nineties with his heater, and is showing enough development with his slider and changeup to suggest he might be one of the biggest bargains of the 2021 draft. You'd think we'd have accumulated all the baseball statistics we could ever possibly need, yet there's no convenient way to look up how many curveballs **Oliver Ortega** spiked in front of the plate last season, and whether that number led the league (the rough estimates: 19, and probably?). **Connor Prielipp**'s upside was highlighted by his first four starts for Alabama, in which he struck out 35 over 21 scoreless innings. That was in 2020. The pandemic and then Tommy John surgery combined to ensure he only threw seven more innings in college, but pre-draft workouts were enough to convince the Twins to give him $1.8 million in the second round. Claimed on waivers from the Nationals in March, **Jhon Romero** suffered a season-ending biceps injury before the end of his first month in Minnesota. At least he had company on the IL: Two other right-handed pitchers were already there, and three more joined him by May 10. When is it time to hang it up? It might be when you're 38, you throw 86 and over a quarter of the fly balls you allow leave the park. **Joe Smith** does still get groundballs, though. **Cody Stashak** cleaned up his walk rate to start the season, facing 65 batters without handing out a single free pass. Unfortunately, the next thing that needed to be cleaned up was the labrum in his shoulder, which is why he didn't get to face any more opponents. Veteran righty **Tyler Thornburg** has now recovered from both thoracic outlet syndrome and Tommy John surgery to pitch in the majors again, and he did so in 2022 with his velocity intact. His already fringy control, sadly, was less preserved, and we're long past the era where a superficially good ERA will make teams overlook a near 1:1 strikeout-to-walk ratio.

Rule Changes, Risk Tolerance and the Sean Murphy Trade

by Jeff Quinton

Every little bit counts
Though it may not count for much
Could be long forgotten
By the time you add 'em up
Could be too little too late, sorry
—James McMurtry, "Every Little Bit Counts"

⚾ ⚾ ⚾

On September 9, 2022, MLB Commissioner Rob Manfred held a press conference to discuss the significant rule changes coming in 2023. Per Manfred, these changes—a pitch clock, limits on defensive shifts and bigger bases—were being implemented with the fans in mind. At his press conference, he specifically said:

> *Our guiding star in thinking about changes to the game has always been our fans. 'What do our fans want to see on the field?' We've conducted thorough and ongoing research with our fans, and certain things are really clear. Number one, fans want games with better pace. Two, fans want more action, more balls in play. And three, fans want to see more of the athleticism of our great players.*

These rule changes should help the game better serve these things that fans, per MLB's research, want. This season, we'll get to see what their effects are on the broader fan experience.

But for many fans—those of us helplessly drawn to the game no matter what rule, enforcement or baseball composition changes Manfred enacts—it will be more interesting to see how *teams* respond to these pending rule changes. How will player evaluation and acquisition change? How will teams adjust their in-game strategies? What will they be trying to accomplish by doing so?

To some extent, we'll have to wait to see. But based on what we know about human behavior as it relates to risk-based decision-making—and based on how teams have already reacted this off-season—we can make some educated guesses as to how teams will respond en masse. From there, we can decipher what those responses say about the states of their organizations and, maybe more importantly, the state of baseball in general.

⚾ ⚾ ⚾

Luckily for us, in December the Atlanta Braves, Milwaukee Brewers and Oakland Athletics made a trade that provides insight into how teams are factoring rule changes into their strategies, roster-building and decision-making processes.

A quick breakdown of the transaction in question, just so we have all the cards on the table:

- From the A's, the Braves acquired catcher Sean Murphy—a 28-year-old above-average hitter and great defensive catcher, especially in terms of his impact on mitigating the run game. After acquiring Murphy, Atlanta inked him to a six-year, $73 million extension that tacks on three years to the three he had remaining under team control.
- To acquire Murphy, the Braves sent William Contreras, a 24-year-old All-Star, bat-first catcher with five years left on his rookie contract, and RHP Justin Yeager to the Brewers. Atlanta also shipped a trio of pitching prospects—LHP Kyle Muller, RHP Freddy Tarnok and RHP Royber Salinas—to the A's.
- Additionally, the A's acquired Esteury Ruiz from the Brewers. A true burner heading into his age-24 season, Ruiz tore up the high-minors last year and could be an impact talent if he can become an average hitter in the majors, which is a far from certain outcome given. Along with Muller—who BP ranks as a top-101 prospect—Ruiz is considered the prize of the deal for Oakland.
- (To be as thorough as possible, we'll note that catcher Manny Piña went from Milwaukee to Oakland in the deal, while reliever Joel Payamps went the other way. But for our purposes today that's of little consequence.)

The consensus analysis of the trade indicates that the Brewers were the big winners for landing Contreras—a young, high-floor hitter with upside should they prove able to improve his defense as they have with other bat-first catchers—for relatively little. The consensus also says that the A's should have gotten more for Murphy, and that, while the Braves likely acquired the best player in the deal, Contreras was a steep price to pay for him.

If we take that analysis at face value, it makes the decisions made by these teams worthy of further exploration within the context of how MLB's rule changes may have influenced their decisions. Specifically, they raise the following questions: Why did the A's choose to move their most valuable trade chip for such a seemingly risky return? How did the Brewers get involved? And why did the Braves feel the need to play musical chairs at catcher to only get slightly better in the short-term?

As we endeavor to answer these questions, we turn to psychologists Amos Tversky and Daniel Kahneman, who developed "Prospect Theory" in 1974. It describes how people make decisions that involve risk and uncertainty. Specifically, Prospect Theory proposed a challenge (or correction, even) to the prevailing economic theory at the time, "Expected Utility Theory," which posits that everyone tackles risk-based choices the same way.

Prospect Theory, in contrast, posits that reference points matter. For a tangible example, it suggests that someone worried about eviction might make a different choice than someone who has incredible financial security. Per Kahneman, in *Thinking, Fast and Slow*:

> *In bad choices, where a sure loss is compared to a larger loss that is merely probable, diminishing sensitivity causes risk-seeking behavior.*

Here we see an explanation for the A's part in this trade, and really in how they operate in general. Because ownership is unwilling to spend to retain top talent like Murphy (or Matt Olson, or Frankie Montas, or Chris Bassitt or ... well, you get it) or surround those players with viable supporting casts, Oakland's front office is constantly operating in an environment in which loss is inevitable. All too often, the A's must decide whether to a) trade their best players near the heights of their value, thus becoming less competitive in the short term, or b) risk retaining said players past their peak value and missing the playoffs anyway.

This explains why, per Prospect Theory, they are more likely to be drawn to boom-or-bust prospects like Ruiz. Just like how underdogs in college bowl games run lots of trick plays or how financially challenged people are more likely to buy lottery tickets, the A's are more willing to gamble because they aren't likely to win otherwise. When we remember that Ruiz's chief attributes are speed and athleticism, we can also interpret his inclusion in the deal as an attempt by Oakland to be aggressive in response to rule changes that should make defense and baserunning matter more. They're simply willing to entertain levels of risk that more stable and resource-rich organizations are not.

⚾ ⚾ ⚾

So, how do the Brewers factor into all this? Well, Prospect Theory cuts multiple ways. Look at another part of the same passage from *Thinking, Fast and Slow*:

> *In mixed gambles, where both a gain and a loss are possible, loss aversion causes extremely risk-averse choices.*

This means that other organizations looking to improve—those in a better position than the A's, such as the Brewers—are likely to be far more risk-*averse* when trading, because any trade for them is inherently a "mixed gamble." Put more plainly, the players most teams make available in trades will inherently be more volatile, while the players the A's need to provide in return must make their trade partners feel safer in their decision-making.

In some ways, this is nothing new: rebuilding teams take fliers on "riskier" prospects all the time. But the pending rule changes provide opportunities for franchises like Oakland to double-down on their risk tolerance, to apply it to broader swaths of roster reconstruction. The A's are likely to be willing to take on more risk in incorporating the impact of rule changes into their player valuations and strategies. Conversely, other teams like the Brewers are likely to be more risk-averse in doing so.

A player like Ruiz, whose value as a baserunner could see a significant increase with the rule changes, then becomes exactly the kind of player that the A's would value more than other teams. He also becomes the exact kind of player that the Brewers are happy to trade for a more traditionally productive player like Contreras. Perhaps the Brewers were less motivated by the rule changes themselves than they were an opportunity to use the shifting landscape to mitigate risk, acquiring known commodities for relative unknowns that may possess more upside. But this too, in a way, *is* a response to the rule changes: While the A's are leaning into them, the Brewers are doubling down on an approach that's already made them successful.

⚾ ⚾ ⚾

The A's being more risk-seeking in their decision-making as it relates to the rule change makes sense, as does the Brewers looking to benefit from said risk-seeking behavior without accepting much risk of their own. What we've not yet addressed is what the Braves were likely thinking.

At first glance, it looks like they willingly chose to partake in a "mixed gamble." That does not make much sense for a team that's one season removed from a World Series title, and which has a young, contracted core of players that is the envy of the league. One would think that, if any front office would have cause to be risk-averse, it would be Atlanta's.

That said, as Prospect Theory highlights, risk tolerance depends on reference point. While many front offices could be putting their jobs on the line by getting a Contreras-Murphy swap wrong, the calculus is different for those secure in their roles. We can see, then, how the Braves envision going from Contreras to Murphy as less of a mixed gamble and, instead, maybe the best way to optimize their chances in their current window. This is especially true given the potential impact rule changes could have on the value of Murphy's influence on the running game vs. Contreras' bat. More plainly, it is not a stretch to see how Braves GM and president of baseball ops Alex Anthopoulos and co. could be thinking that they are playing with house money. Given the choices between two *good* options, they feel empowered to be aggressive in betting on the one that could have outsized value in baseball's new environment.

Another factor that may have influenced Atlanta's decision-making? Anthopoulos' experience and tenure. It gives him an advantage in that he can operate purely from a standpoint of trying to maximize future expected value, and not from the very human standpoint of protecting his own job security.

In *Thinking, Fast and Slow*, Kahneman notes the impact experience has on decision-making:

> *The experimental economist John List, who has studied trading at baseball card conventions, found that novice traders were reluctant to part with the cards they owned, but that this reluctance eventually disappeared with trading experience.*

We don't need to look far back in time to find another example of an experienced front office leader with job security proving more willing than his peers to let rule changes impact roster construction. Last offseason, the Dave Dombrowski-helmed Phillies jumped the market in aggressively reacting to the NL adoption of the DH by signing Kyle Schwarber and Nick Castellanos only days apart despite already having a roster long on bat-first players. Though the Phillies did not have Atlanta's recent track record of success to lean on, Dombrowski—thanks to his experience and standing in the game—is among the least risk-averse shot-callers in the game today. He likely *did* act purely with intent to maximize win totals, and we saw his approach rewarded, as Castellanos and especially Schwarber played major roles in Philadelphia's run to the World Series. The Braves can only hope that their aggressive approach to swapping out Contreras for Murphy provides similar dividends.

⚾ ⚾ ⚾

So, which approach to reacting to the rule changes is best? Will it be aggressiveness or restraint that's more richly rewarded? As with most questions, the answer is that it depends, but if the past is any indication, teams stand to benefit by being aggressive in their response. As such, the risk-taking A's, opportunistic Brewers and aggressive Braves may all, in their own ways, be ahead of the curve compared to teams that stood pat this winter.

That said, there is one more factor from a game theory-ish standpoint that we have not yet discussed, which is that we are likely only at the beginning of an era that will be rife with rule changes. With more changes coming—robot umps, further pitcher usage restrictions and other attempts to speed up the game—teams may feel less certain than ever about which player archetypes will be most valuable in the near-term future.

The way value in a controlled construct like baseball works, though, is that as it decreases somewhere it therefore increases somewhere else. In this case, as long-term value decreases due to uncertainty, short-term value—in other words, major-league players who are valuable under the current construct—increases. Combine this with the new, larger playoff format, and we *should* see more teams spending and trading to win right now. Conversely, we *should* see fewer teams adopting the multi-year, complete teardowns that have long been in vogue, because teams should be less certain about what they are building toward.

We have run into the word *should* a lot here, and if you have made it this far in this essay, you probably are invested enough in baseball to know that the ways in which teams *should* and *do* operate are often quite different. This is because we—fans and observers of the game—work under the impression that teams should be trying to maximize their chances of winning (and, if it matters, that such winning will bring in money for the owners). But recent history suggests that, for many franchises, being able to accurately forecast profits is often more important than maximizing wins and even revenues.

Sadly, if the past is any indicator, instead of seeing teams react to these dynamics by being aggressive, we will likely hear these dynamics used as a crutch for even more risk-averse decision-making and, with it, reduced spending. Yes, spending will be record-breaking (as has been revenue). But it will likely fall short of the heights it could reach if all teams were interested in maximizing their chances of winning.

Then again, if you want to believe that's too pessimistic a view of how teams will continue to respond to rule changes, you need not look further than the previously deputized Kahneman, who said:

> *We're generally overconfident in our opinions and our impressions and judgements.*

Here's hoping that applies to the prior few paragraphs.

⚾ ⚾ ⚾

The highs are slightly higher,
The lows are just as low
A mild improvement on the average even so
—James McMurtry, "Every Little Bit Counts"

—Jeff Quinton is a former author of Baseball Prospectus.

ARIZONA DIAMONDBACKS

Essay by Zach Crizer

Player comments by Tim Jackson and BP staff

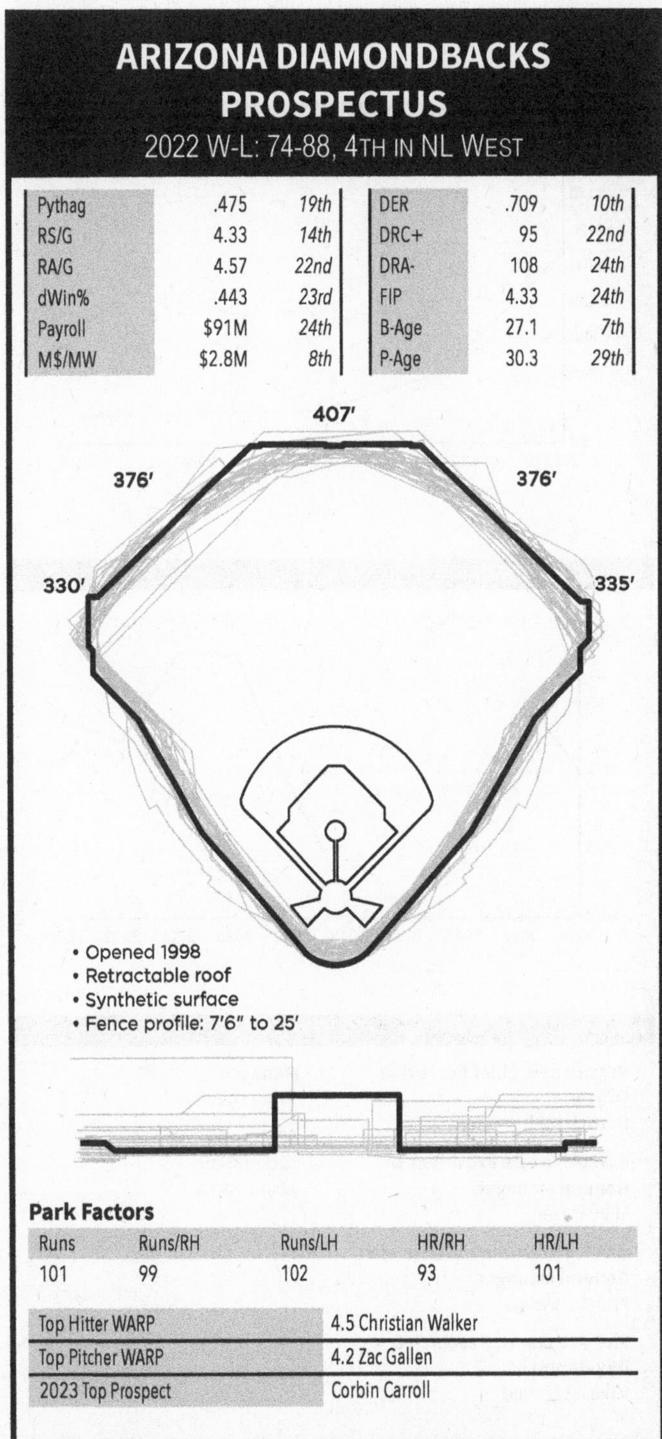

ARIZONA DIAMONDBACKS PROSPECTUS

2022 W-L: 74-88, 4TH IN NL WEST

Pythag	.475	19th	DER	.709	10th
RS/G	4.33	14th	DRC+	95	22nd
RA/G	4.57	22nd	DRA-	108	24th
dWin%	.443	23rd	FIP	4.33	24th
Payroll	$91M	24th	B-Age	27.1	7th
M$/MW	$2.8M	8th	P-Age	30.3	29th

- Opened 1998
- Retractable roof
- Synthetic surface
- Fence profile: 7'6" to 25'

Park Factors

Runs	Runs/RH	Runs/LH	HR/RH	HR/LH
101	99	102	93	101

Top Hitter WARP	4.5 Christian Walker
Top Pitcher WARP	4.2 Zac Gallen
2023 Top Prospect	Corbin Carroll

About 272 miles west of Phoenix, the desert rises into a tormented pile of sun-baked rocks. Swallowed by a landscape that feels more like the moon than earth, air feels like a pleasant surprise. Anything more, anything actively encouraging, would seem too much to ask. But you're here because more is promised.

Carving through the arid terrain on a dusty path, only miniature crimson cacti cling to the hillsides—until you look up after a deep descent and notice a rush of green peeking above the jagged land ahead. Further down, in a narrow pocket, luscious palm trees burst out of a thriving oasis.

Now a feature in Joshua Tree National Park dubbed Fortynine Palms Oasis, this is one of several points of refuge that once helped Native Americans—and still helps many animal species—survive high in the harsh Mojave Desert. It is a blip of awe-inspiring natural prosperity achieved in the shadow of California's more fertile coast. And it really is in the shadow: The Mojave exists because mountain ranges block the rain that might allow more life to thrive here, save the region's scant precipitation for the more favorably situated areas to the west.

This is a place where existential challenge and reality bleed into one. It's a place the Arizona Diamondbacks know well. They also live in the daunting shadow of resource-rich California powers—the Los Angeles Dodgers, San Francisco Giants and San Diego Padres. And their path to success in the National League West can appear similarly remote.

Now five seasons removed from their last postseason appearance, the D'Backs are scanning that space that may or may not exist between the immense natural barriers and the horizon—seeking that unlikely, almost-inexplicable haven where they can thrive despite the conditions.

The stars assembling in Los Angeles, San Francisco and San Diego are clearly visible in Arizona. Buoyed by recent 100-win seasons and playoff runs, the division's top powers are behaving as if they intend to stay there, year in and year out. Two division rivals are likely to enter the season among MLB's top 10 payrolls, as the Padres continue their fireworks show and the Dodgers remain the Dodgers. The Giants

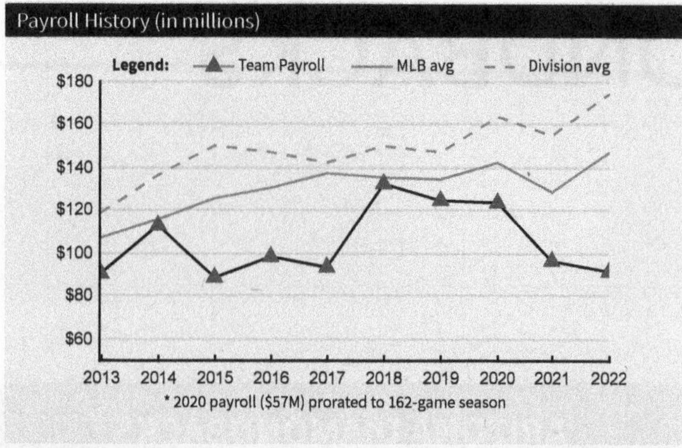

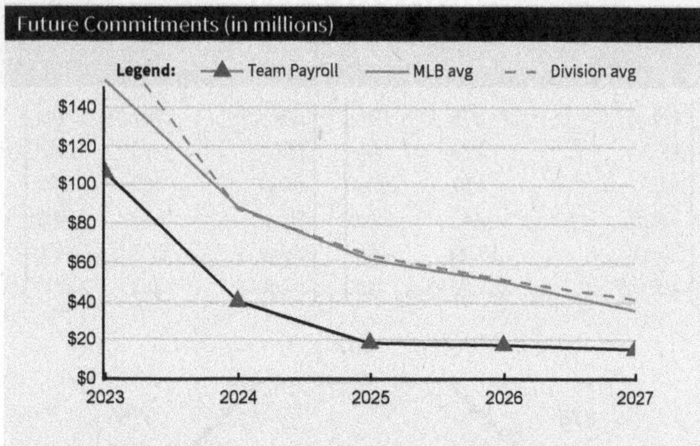

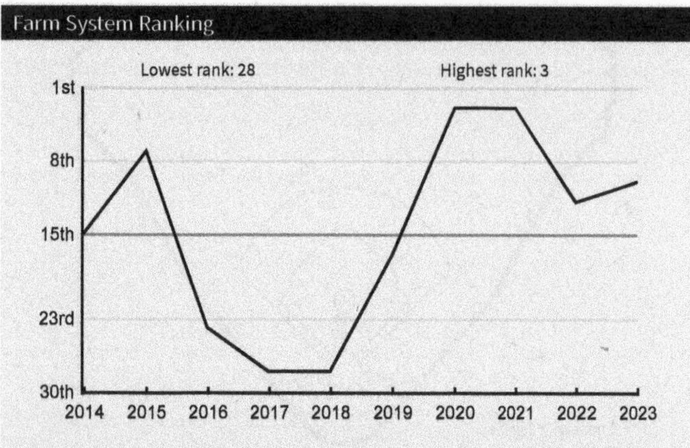

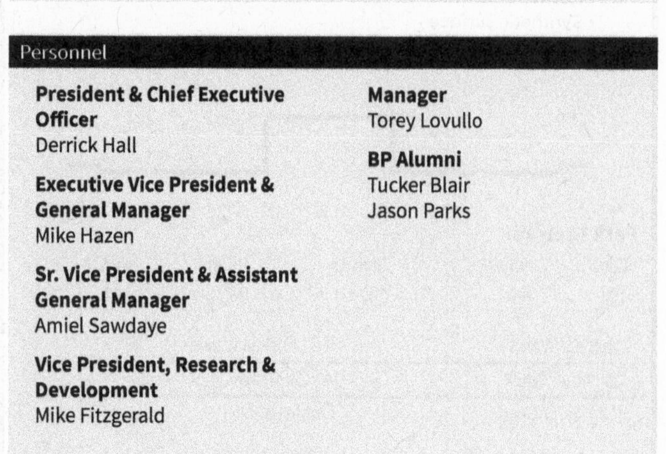
Personnel

President & Chief Executive Officer
Derrick Hall

Executive Vice President & General Manager
Mike Hazen

Sr. Vice President & Assistant General Manager
Amiel Sawdaye

Vice President, Research & Development
Mike Fitzgerald

Manager
Torey Lovullo

BP Alumni
Tucker Blair
Jason Parks

clearly have the intent to flex financial muscle as they head into a new era and the patience to follow the plan, no matter the pains of building a consistent contender.

The D'Backs work on a less perennial timeline. Their payroll, under team owner Ken Kendrick, hasn't ranked in the top half of the league on Opening Day since 2014. Last year, slashed down to pre-2016 levels, it ranked 24th. Fans appear unhappy with the latest drift toward irrelevance, with seasonal attendance falling short of the club's 2,000,000-fan projection by nearly a fifth. Potential issues with the cables that open the roof were discovered too close to last season's onset to address; throughout the summer games were played in literal as well as metaphoric shadow as the roof remained closed, the most obvious of a slew of issues piling up at Chase Field.

We have seen teams faced with similarly challenging divisions take extreme measures: The Baltimore Orioles used the controlled burn of a multiyear tank; the Washington Nationals traded off a World Series core in less than three years; the Tampa Bay Rays live in a spin cycle of their own creation. Despite bottoming out with a 52-win bruise of a campaign in 2021, the Diamondbacks have made relatively few sudden movements. (The franchise's rare momentous pivots have not proven rewarding: Zack Greinke's $206 million deal only covered one playoff berth, whereas discarded face of the franchise Paul Goldschmidt won NL MVP for the Cardinals in 2022 on a cheaper contract.)

Adapting to life in the desert can look a lot like doing nothing. The enormous Saguaro cactus native to Arizona grows at a glacial pace. Even though they can stretch to 60 feet in height, they might stand only an inch and a half high at age 10. The real development is happening below the surface. And that has been the story of the recent D'Backs under general manager Mike Hazen.

They've been collecting and storing talent. Conserving and growing potential. They agreed to a contract extension with Ketel Marte prior to 2022 that pays the positionally flexible All-Star a reasonable $15.2 million per year through at least 2027. They signed starting pitcher Merrill Kelly to an extension that could keep him in Arizona through 2025, just as his velocity ticked up and he embarked on the most successful season of his late-blooming big-league career. They held onto emerging contributors, like powerful first baseman Christian Walker and out-of-the-blue relief ace Joe Mantiply, who certainly would have had trade suitors.

Heading into last winter, Hazen signaled the team's focus by insisting that a sudden surplus of major-league outfielders wouldn't be exchanged for future value. "We're kind of moving past the prospect stage," he told *The Arizona Republic*, saying the intent would be to bring back immediate contributors.

Like stones marking off a navigable, if tenuous, way forward, there's a promise embedded in there: Something is going to rise from the nothingness.

⚾ ⚾ ⚾

Oases in the wasteland that separates Arizona from their glitzy rivals are fueled by groundswells. Really deep, really old groundswells. Movement along fault lines in Southern California is responsible for pushing water to the surface and sustaining palm trees, bighorn sheep and a bevy of other life forms that wouldn't seem to stand a chance. The first outward evidence of a groundswell in Arizona bubbled up in 2022.

Several existing major leaguers took significant steps forward: Zac Gallen reasserted himself as an ace with a headline-grabbing scoreless streak, 2.54 ERA and career-best 75 DRA-. Walker put up a line worthy of the cold corner, crushing 36 homers while slashing his strikeout rate and chase rate. Daulton Varsho completed a dumbfounding dance around the top of the defensive spectrum by shifting his primary position from catcher to the outfield…and immediately rating as the most valuable outfield defender in baseball by Statcast's Outs Above Average metric. The superlative metrics stem largely from excellent reads and excellent range, especially tracking down would-be extra-base hits whacked toward the wall. Josh Rojas, the most anonymous prospect the D'Backs landed when they traded Greinke halfway through his contract, evolved into a useful utility player who stole 23 bases.

Then the prospects started sprouting. Some of them were very much fledgling, far from final products. Outfielder Alek Thomas and shortstop Geraldo Perdomo took their lumps, especially at the plate, as they adjusted to the majors. Others announced their presence more forcefully. The brightest glimmer of hope emanates from Corbin Carroll. The 22-year-old outfielder rebounded from a 2021 shoulder injury to torch Double-A and Triple-A, en route to a promising 32-game MLB debut. The 5-foot-10 lefty hits, walks and runs—and maybe strikes out a tad more than you'd expect, looking at his compact physique. He will enter 2023 as the rookie to beat in the NL, and a threat to go 20/20.

Three or more rookie arms figure to be in play for the major-league rotation, most notably Brandon Pfaadt and Drey Jameson—a fireballer who already impressed in a cup of coffee. More top picks, largely on the position player front, are marinating lower in the system.

While Varsho and fellow OF/C Cooper Hummel ended up on the move, the players for whom they were traded, Gabriel Moreno, Lourdes Gurriel Jr. and Kyle Lewis, are at least as geared toward present-day relevance. Gurriel (entering his walk year) and Lewis are the established names and bats, but it's Moreno on whom hope is pinned: The Blue Jays' top-ranked prospect coming into 2022, the catcher checked every box at Triple-A before impressing with the bat (113 DRC+) in a short big-league sample. Hazen said he expected that after a year in the big leagues, "I make a phone call on this player and I don't get a response."

The roots are in place. Growth is expected now; Hazen and manager Torey Lovullo have a wizened guide on hand who's helped to develop a young team before. Brent Strom, the 74-year-old master pitching coach whose fingerprints are all over the Astros' recent success, joined Arizona in a bit of a surprise move after the 2021 season. In his Houston days, Strom famously advised pitchers to prey on hitters' homer-focused uppercut swings: High fastballs, with the spin to impart the appearance of "rise."

It was a simple insight that took a lot of complex knowledge to relay and execute. In full effect, it altered the trajectories of several careers—most notably Justin Verlander's and Gerrit Cole's—and ultimately the entire environment to which it was originally reacting.

⚾ ⚾ ⚾

The line between surviving and thriving can get hazy in the heat of intense competition. And at the extremes—of earth's environment, of baseball's bewildering season—the distinction often depends purely on timing. Ask the Padres, after a validating NLCS run followed a tense slog of a season. Or the Dodgers, after the bottom instantly fell out of a 111-win season. Ask the humble cactus, which wildly varies its water intake and storage based on the time of year.

There's also more cosmic timing at play. The D'Backs are assembling their promising collection of potential stars as the Dodgers and Padres spend hundreds and hundreds of millions to stockpile confirmed stars, yes, but they're also doing it as MLB switches to a balanced schedule. In 2022, Arizona went 5-14 against the Dodgers, and 5-14 against the Padres. (They managed a healthy 10-9 mark against the Giants in San Francisco's return to the realm of normal gravitational laws.)

In 2023, and moving forward, every MLB team will play all 29 other teams. To make room, they will see each divisional foe 13 times instead of 19. In their place, Arizona will have more games against the AL West, and the weak AL Central, but also matchups with the similarly difficult AL East titans (whom they didn't face at all in 2022). The Texas Rangers will be their "natural rivals" for a four-game interleague slate, which may have been a luckier draw ahead of their momentous offseason. It could be worse: The Colorado Rockies wound up tied to the Houston Astros.

It's borderline impossible to project the strength of individual season schedules in advance, but in a longer view, the balanced schedule—combined with the expanded postseason format that took effect last season—gives Arizona precious breathing room. Finishing sixth in the NL is more than attainable. Placing a distant third in the division and nevertheless reaching the World Series, as the Philadelphia Phillies did, doesn't feel any less glorious. Even winding up fourth in the division and making the postseason is now technically possible, if unlikely.

That's not to say the D'Backs should limit their ambitions or curb their dreams. Ideally, success breeds the resources to ensure more success—just as the humans once sustained by a precious oasis worked toward its preservation. But as many current MLB ownership groups prefer, the Diamondbacks are going to rest the bulk of their hopes on hope, on the promise just over that next bluff.

Products of time. Products of careful cultivation. And yes, products of chance.

⚾ ⚾ ⚾

After you reach the Fortynine Palms Oasis, after you get a full sense of its triumph over the elements, you retrace your steps. Successful baseball teams do this, too. Winning sets a more urgent clock, poses more direct questions. The youngest, brightest stars—will they accept long-term extensions? The veteran additions—are their contracts up? The original core reaching five, six years of service time and free agency—are they decamping for greener pastures?

It's painful but gratifying. When, in bygone eras, hopes were fulfilled in the oasis—by MVP awards or Cy Youngs or champagne celebrations—the faces and numbers and batting stances seared themselves into place. Even in their seasons of absence, they remain affirmations of possibility—once-questionable seeds that undeniably bore fruit. It can be done. In that place. In new forms.

On the trek back, the natural instinct is to peer over your shoulder. Your eye can't help but catch on the palm fronds. Up and up you climb, and the flash of green still hovers above the threat of the rocks. Winded, you stop and fully turn around, immediately alighting on the oasis from a vista where you'd swear there was nothing but desert visible before. ■

—Zach Crizer is an editor of Yahoo.com.

HITTERS

Nick Ahmed SS

Born: 03/15/90 Age: 33 Bats: R Throws: R Height: 6'2" Weight: 201 lb. Origin: Round 2, 2011 Draft (#85 overall)

YEAR	TEAM	LVL	AGE	PA	R	2B	3B	HR	RBI	BB	K	SB	CS	Whiff%	AVG/OBP/SLG	DRC+	BABIP	BRR	DRP	WARP
2020	AZ	MLB	30	217	29	10	1	5	29	18	46	4	0	27.6%	.266/.327/.402	96	.324	0.5	SS(57): -0.3	0.5
2021	AZ	MLB	31	473	46	30	3	5	38	34	104	7	2	26.8%	.221/.280/.339	75	.279	0.6	SS(127): 4.6	0.7
2022	AZ	MLB	32	54	7	2	0	3	7	2	15	0	1	24.8%	.231/.259/.442	95	.265	-0.3	SS(16): -0.6	0.0
2023 DC	*AZ*	*MLB*	*33*	*382*	*38*	*19*	*2*	*7*	*35*	*27*	*80*	*5*	*1*	*25.8%*	*.226/.287/.358*	*79*	*.273*	*2.2*	*SS 3*	*0.6*

Comparables: Jason Bartlett (70), Larry Bowa (69), Leo Durocher (67)

After the bizarro 2020 season and a down 2021 campaign, Ahmed was surely hoping for a bounce-back campaign. That didn't happen, though, because he needed shoulder surgery after playing in just 17 games. In his brief time before getting hurt, he knocked three homers, but was also hitting groundballs at a career-high rate. One of those things would have had to relent over the course of the season, and, given his track record and the realities of small sample sizes, the grounder rate was more concerning than the homers were encouraging. Like a vinyl LP, he'll give it another spin at 33, hoping to come back in vogue in what will be a contract year.

Seth Beer 1B/DH

Born: 09/18/96 Age: 26 Bats: L Throws: R Height: 6'3" Weight: 213 lb. Origin: Round 1, 2018 Draft (#28 overall)

YEAR	TEAM	LVL	AGE	PA	R	2B	3B	HR	RBI	BB	K	SB	CS	Whiff%	AVG/OBP/SLG	DRC+	BABIP	BRR	DRP	WARP
2021	RNO	AAA	24	435	73	33	0	16	59	39	76	0	0		.287/.398/.511	117	.321	-3.0	1B(91): 0.4	1.7
2021	AZ	MLB	24	10	4	1	0	1	3	1	3	0	0	28.6%	.444/.500/.889	80	.600	0.0		0.0
2022	RNO	AAA	25	402	56	20	1	14	62	44	68	0	1	27.5%	.242/.361/.435	107	.259	-1.4	1B(66): -2.6	1.1
2022	AZ	MLB	25	126	4	3	0	1	9	11	31	0	0	28.7%	.189/.278/.243	72	.250	-1.6	1B(5): -0.1	-0.3
2023 DC	*AZ*	*MLB*	*26*	*97*	*9*	*4*	*0*	*2*	*9*	*7*	*23*	*0*	*0*	*27.8%*	*.224/.318/.365*	*91*	*.281*	*-0.4*	*1B 0*	*0.0*

Comparables: Chris Shaw (63), Ryan O'Hearn (62), Greg Bird (58)

It was a flat year for Beer. He wasn't firkin around but it sure seemed that way. His sub-.200 batting average was the yeast of his issues. He had the worst power performance of his career, too, barley ever racking up extra bases when in the majors. He was better in the minors, but not good enough to hop over any of the myriad options on the depth chart. Concerns about whether he'll be able to deliver on the game's biggest stage are more than pint-sized at this point. He'll need to mash, and soon, if he wants to regain any of his stout prospect status.

★ ★ ★ *2023 Top 101 Prospect* **#6** ★ ★ ★

Corbin Carroll OF

Born: 08/21/00 Age: 22 Bats: L Throws: L Height: 5'10" Weight: 165 lb. Origin: Round 1, 2019 Draft (#16 overall)

YEAR	TEAM	LVL	AGE	PA	R	2B	3B	HR	RBI	BB	K	SB	CS	Whiff%	AVG/OBP/SLG	DRC+	BABIP	BRR	DRP	WARP
2021	HIL	A+	20	29	9	1	2	2	5	6	7	3	1		.435/.552/.913	113	.571	-0.4	CF(7): 0.7	0.2
2022	AMA	AA	21	277	62	11	8	16	39	41	68	20	3		.313/.430/.643	125	.379	2.4	CF(35): 1.1, RF(9): -0.9, LF(2): -0.1	2.1
2022	RNO	AAA	21	157	25	11	0	7	22	24	36	11	2	25.1%	.287/.408/.535	114	.345	1.8	CF(19): 2.1, RF(9): 0.1, LF(5): 0.3	1.4
2022	AZ	MLB	21	115	13	9	2	4	14	8	31	2	1	29.1%	.260/.330/.500	92	.333	-0.2	LF(25): 1.2, CF(5): 0.3, RF(2): 0.4	0.4
2023 DC	*AZ*	*MLB*	*22*	*468*	*53*	*21*	*9*	*14*	*50*	*45*	*123*	*14*	*5*	*27.4%*	*.242/.330/.439*	*106*	*.316*	*6.2*	*CF 0, RF 0*	*2.3*

Comparables: Andrew Benintendi (61), Christian Yelich (61), Mookie Betts (57)

As one of the game's top prospects, Carroll delivered examples of his immense tools in his big-league debut. He has the speed to be an antagonist on the basepaths, logging infield hits no player has any business legging out and going first to third like it's nothing. He could turn into an outright menace with the new pickoff rules, which he has already taken advantage of in his time in the minors. He'll use that speed to track down balls in the gaps, too, with perhaps only Jesus Christ saving more. At the plate, though, he had trouble adjusting to velocity, registering a wOBA of just .283 on pitches coming in at 94+ mph—some 40 points under the league average, and 60 off his mark on slower offerings. Pitchers might be tempted to challenge him with fastballs until he makes them regret it. His hardest hit ball of the year (107.5 mph) came in his third-to-last game of the season off a 96-mph Brandon Woodruff heater. Whether that was a one-off or the sign of an early adjustment could determine whether Carroll is commended for his high floor or pushing his high ceiling.

Diego Castillo SS

Born: 10/28/97 Age: 25 Bats: R Throws: R Height: 5'11" Weight: 185 lb. Origin: International Free Agent, 2014

YEAR	TEAM	LVL	AGE	PA	R	2B	3B	HR	RBI	BB	K	SB	CS	Whiff%	AVG/OBP/SLG	DRC+	BABIP	BRR	DRP	WARP
2021	ALT	AA	23	121	11	3	0	5	16	10	9	1	2		.282/.342/.445	137	.271	-1.7	SS(12): -0.9, 2B(9): -2.6, 3B(7): 1.0	0.5
2021	SOM	AA	23	249	44	18	0	11	32	21	34	8	3		.277/.345/.504	135	.283	1.1	2B(23): 0.9, 3B(14): -1.1, SS(14): 1.5	2.1
2021	IND	AAA	23	70	18	3	0	3	7	13	13	0	0		.278/.414/.500	117	.300	0.2	SS(9): -0.9, 2B(6): -1.1, 3B(2): -0.1	0.2
2022	IND	AAA	24	151	21	6	0	3	12	14	33	2	1		.246/.331/.358	101	.306	0.6	SS(15): -0.7, 3B(7): -0.1, 2B(5): 0.1	0.5
2022	PIT	MLB	24	283	28	13	0	11	29	14	75	1	1	26.8%	.206/.251/.382	92	.239	0.7	SS(32): 1.1, 2B(28): -0.6, RF(22): -0.9	0.7
2023 DC	*AZ*	*MLB*	*25*	*63*	*5*	*2*	*0*	*1*	*5*	*4*	*13*	*0*	*0*	*25.2%*	*.212/.270/.332*	*66*	*.256*	*0.1*	*SS 0, 2B 0*	*-0.1*

Comparables: Pat Valaika (56), Anderson Hernandez (55), Ian Desmond (54)

The phrase "scouting versus sabermetrics" conjures images of a violent battle; heck, there's a weapon nestled right in the terminology. However, the two don't represent a duality but rather a yin and yang: a multilayered set of forces not in opposition but interconnected. The scouting wisdom on Castillo throughout his minor-league career was that he was "skills over tools" and wouldn't do enough to break into the bigs, but he defied the odds with a strong spring training and broke camp with the Pirates in April. Then the shortcomings that the scouts warned about reared their ugly heads: Castillo started swinging for the fences and mostly missing. There's a future here, but as more of an around-the-diamond utility player than a star. At least the D'Backs, who traded for him in December, have a track record of maximizing those players.

Deyvison De Los Santos 3B

Born: 06/21/03 Age: 20 Bats: R Throws: R Height: 6'1" Weight: 185 lb. Origin: International Free Agent, 2019

YEAR	TEAM	LVL	AGE	PA	R	2B	3B	HR	RBI	BB	K	SB	CS	Whiff%	AVG/OBP/SLG	DRC+	BABIP	BRR	DRP	WARP
2021	DIA	ROK	18	95	19	4	2	5	17	13	24	1	1		.329/.421/.610		.415			
2021	VIS	A	18	160	26	12	0	3	20	13	43	2	0		.276/.340/.421	95	.374	1.0	3B(35): 5.8, 1B(1): -0.0	1.0
2022	VIS	A	19	349	43	18	2	12	67	22	84	4	1		.329/.370/.513	98	.404	-1.4	3B(59): -3.2, 1B(14): -1.4	0.5
2022	HIL	A+	19	166	24	9	0	9	33	7	54	1	0		.278/.307/.506	103	.365	-2.8	3B(29): -1.6, 1B(7): 0.6	0.1
2022	AMA	AA	19	45	5	2	0	1	6	5	9	0	0		.231/.333/.359	100	.276	0.0	3B(6): -0.9, 1B(4): 0.3	0.1
2023 non-DC	*AZ*	*MLB*	*20*	*251*	*21*	*10*	*1*	*4*	*23*	*11*	*79*	*0*	*1*	*35.9%*	*.231/.271/.342*	*66*	*.327*	*0.5*	*1B 0, 3B 0*	*-0.5*

Comparables: Vladimir Guerrero Jr. (76), Hudson Potts (74), Ronald Acuña Jr. (62)

De Los Santos boasts the kind of heft that clearly set him apart from players at the lower levels. His stout frame might mean that he makes his way across the diamond to first base sooner rather than later, but it also means that when he makes contact it produces a different sound than that of his peers. As is the case with many players who have such talent, he wants to show it off as often as he can. Exercising a bit of patience and swinging from the calves instead of the heels might mean his homers go five feet shorter; it also might mean he hits a lot more of them.

Lourdes Gurriel Jr. LF

Born: 10/10/93 Age: 29 Bats: R Throws: R Height: 6'4" Weight: 215 lb. Origin: International Free Agent, 2016

YEAR	TEAM	LVL	AGE	PA	R	2B	3B	HR	RBI	BB	K	SB	CS	Whiff%	AVG/OBP/SLG	DRC+	BABIP	BRR	DRP	WARP
2020	TOR	MLB	26	224	28	14	0	11	33	14	48	3	1	26.3%	.308/.348/.534	120	.351	-0.4	LF(53): 0.4	1.2
2021	TOR	MLB	27	541	62	28	2	21	84	32	102	1	3	24.3%	.276/.319/.466	107	.305	-2.6	LF(119): 6, 1B(11): 0	2.8
2022	TOR	MLB	28	493	52	32	1	5	52	31	83	3	4	21.2%	.291/.343/.400	104	.346	-0.4	LF(105): -4, 1B(8): 0	1.4
2023 DC	*AZ*	*MLB*	*29*	*558*	*63*	*29*	*1*	*16*	*65*	*36*	*96*	*5*	*1*	*21.9%*	*.278/.332/.440*	*115*	*.315*	*0.5*	*LF -5*	*1.8*

Comparables: Starling Marte (65), Eddie Rosario (63), Cleon Jones (63)

It's minutes before midnight on New Year's Eve. Gurriel Jr. opens Instagram, pulls up his self-facing camera, flashes a beautiful smile and punches in a caption: New Year, New Me. (He adds a kissy face emoji for good measure, deletes it and changes it to a flexing bicep, but that's neither here nor there.) He's probably right. Every year, Gurriel seems to present a new version of himself. He tweaks his approach, generally making more contact at the expense of his power, which bottomed out last year in near-alarming fashion. Yet his DRC+ hardly budged: He both changes and remains the same. The good news is Gurriel's power outage may not be entirely due to his approach. It turns out he was dealing with a bum wrist that bothered him for months and that he had to remedy with surgery in October. It's possible, then, that his evolving plate discipline will only serve to raise his floor, and that his power will return to pre-injury levels. If that's the case, Gurriel's next New Year's post may capture his head scraping up against an awfully high ceiling. The Diamondbacks proved willing to bet on such an outcome, nabbing Gurriel and Gabriel Moreno in exchange for Dalton Varsho in December.

★ ★ ★ *2023 Top 101 Prospect* **#33** ★ ★ ★

Druw Jones OF

Born: 11/28/03 Age: 19 Bats: R Throws: R Height: 6'4" Weight: 180 lb. Origin: Round 1, 2022 Draft (#2 overall)

Some organizations tend to have a type and, weirdly, Arizona's might be guys who hurt their shoulders shortly after signing. Jones hurt his shoulder while taking BP with the team and required surgery. He joins Jordan Lawlar and Corbin Carroll before him. The injury isn't a long-term concern and he still promises gold glove-caliber defense with dynamic abilities at the plate, headlined by massive power. If that report sounds familiar, it's because it's a carbon copy of his dad's (Andruw Jones). No, there is nothing that makes you feel old quite like learning about a professional athlete's child going pro.

Carson Kelly C Born: 07/14/94 Age: 28 Bats: R Throws: R Height: 6'2" Weight: 212 lb. Origin: Round 2, 2012 Draft (#86 overall)

YEAR	TEAM	LVL	AGE	PA	R	2B	3B	HR	RBI	BB	K	SB	CS	Whiff%	AVG/OBP/SLG	DRC+	BABIP	BRR	DRP	WARP
2020	AZ	MLB	25	129	11	5	0	5	19	6	29	0	0	26.8%	.221/.264/.385	93	.250	-0.7	C(38): 5	0.8
2021	AZ	MLB	26	359	41	11	1	13	46	44	74	0	0	25.1%	.240/.343/.411	113	.270	-2.4	C(91): 1.8	2.1
2022	AZ	MLB	27	354	40	18	0	7	35	29	71	2	0	21.0%	.211/.282/.334	91	.247	-1.7	C(100): 1.4	0.9
2023 DC	*AZ*	*MLB*	*28*	*403*	*45*	*17*	*0*	*13*	*44*	*39*	*74*	*0*	*0*	*22.1%*	*.238/.321/.401*	*102*	*.265*	*-2.6*	*C 0*	*1.3*

Comparables: Austin Hedges (54), Tim Blackwell (52), Ben Davis (52)

YEAR	TEAM	P. COUNT	FRM RUNS	BLK RUNS	THRW RUNS	TOT RUNS
2020	AZ	4964	4.8	0.0	0.3	5.0
2021	AZ	11892	1.5	0.3	0.0	1.8
2022	AZ	12479	0.6	0.2	0.8	1.6
2023	*AZ*	*14430*	*0.2*	*0.2*	*-0.6*	*-0.2*

Kelly's game has played on the edge over the course of his career, often alternating between seasons of good-for-a-catcher and regular-good. This year was more the former than the latter. Despite his typically discerning eye that allowed him to avoid chasing and make more contact than average, creating an ideal batted ball mix, he started to watch more pitches sail over the plate in 2022. Pitchers weren't afraid of him. So it goes when your average exit velo on balls in the air leaves you in the lower half of the league. Kelly has two years left to prove that he belongs in the team's plans as they crack open their next contention window, but given their acquisition of Gabriel Moreno, it might be less than that. Kelly hits enough to clear the bar at catcher, but, like a middling breakfast cereal, also leaves you wanting more.

Buddy Kennedy 3B Born: 10/05/98 Age: 24 Bats: R Throws: R Height: 6'1" Weight: 190 lb. Origin: Round 5, 2017 Draft (#142 overall)

YEAR	TEAM	LVL	AGE	PA	R	2B	3B	HR	RBI	BB	K	SB	CS	Whiff%	AVG/OBP/SLG	DRC+	BABIP	BRR	DRP	WARP
2021	SRR	WIN	22	64	10	3	0	2	7	7	16	0	0		.236/.328/.400		.289			
2021	HIL	A+	22	127	15	5	0	5	20	11	25	9	2		.315/.386/.495	118	.361	0.2	3B(16): 3.3, 1B(5): 1.1, 2B(4): -0.3	1.1
2021	AMA	AA	22	279	46	6	2	17	40	39	73	7	2		.278/.384/.536	115	.331	-0.4	3B(55): 2.0, 2B(7): -0.5	1.4
2022	RNO	AAA	23	394	55	14	3	7	40	54	76	8	4	18.8%	.261/.363/.385	101	.311	-2.6	3B(45): 0.4, 2B(23): -2.5, LF(9): -0.1	0.8
2022	AZ	MLB	23	94	10	2	2	1	12	8	23	0	0	21.5%	.217/.287/.325	85	.279	0.1	2B(22): 0.6, 3B(2): -0.2	0.2
2023 non-DC	*AZ*	*MLB*	*24*	*251*	*24*	*8*	*1*	*5*	*24*	*24*	*52*	*2*	*1*	*21.8%*	*.229/.309/.353*	*86*	*.276*	*1.3*	*3B 0, 2B 0*	*0.3*

Comparables: Dawel Lugo (69), Matt Antonelli (66), Andy LaRoche (58)

The grandson of former Phillie and Brewer Don Money, he's proof for all time that Kennedys come from Money. The former fifth-rounder broke through to the big leagues last year but his pop—by which we mean power, not father—was nowhere to be found. In 62 batted ball events, he registered only one barrel, which is a worse rate than one of the most light-hitting players in the game (and teammate), Geraldo Perdomo. Kennedy didn't have it with him in Triple-A, either. It was last seen in Double-A, happily hopping over fences, and would like to come home. If found, please call (602) 514-8400.

★ ★ ★ *2023 Top 101 Prospect* **#24** ★ ★ ★

Jordan Lawlar SS Born: 07/17/02 Age: 20 Bats: R Throws: R Height: 6'2" Weight: 190 lb. Origin: Round 1, 2021 Draft (#6 overall)

YEAR	TEAM	LVL	AGE	PA	R	2B	3B	HR	RBI	BB	K	SB	CS	Whiff%	AVG/OBP/SLG	DRC+	BABIP	BRR	DRP	WARP
2022	VIS	A	19	208	44	9	4	9	32	27	48	24	4		.351/.447/.603	120	.437	1.0	SS(37): -1.1	1.1
2022	HIL	A+	19	130	31	8	2	3	17	16	33	13	1		.288/.385/.477	109	.382	3.6	SS(27): -1.8	0.8
2022	AMA	AA	19	97	18	0	0	4	11	10	28	2	1		.212/.299/.353	85	.259	0.2	SS(17): -0.2	0.1
2023 non-DC	*AZ*	*MLB*	*20*	*251*	*23*	*9*	*2*	*4*	*24*	*19*	*76*	*11*	*3*	*34.2%*	*.226/.296/.357*	*79*	*.318*	*6.7*	*SS 0*	*0.8*

Comparables: Heiker Meneses (58), Xander Bogaerts (55), Matt Dominguez (55)

Lawlar showed no residual effects from shoulder surgery that ended his 2021 season, as he zoomed through three levels of the minors last year. That doesn't count a short stint in the complex league in June. Overall, he slashed .301/.401/.509 as a 19-year-old who had made it to Double-A fast enough to rack up nearly 100 plate appearances before the campaign wrapped. His range is good enough to keep him at short, but his inconsistent arm strength might make him best suited for the keystone. His eye is good enough to maintain a high walk rate, which means he'll offer a high floor if he stays on his current trajectory. His bat and speed mean the sky is still the limit.

Kyle Lewis DH Born: 07/13/95 Age: 27 Bats: R Throws: R Height: 6'4" Weight: 222 lb. Origin: Round 1, 2016 Draft (#11 overall)

YEAR	TEAM	LVL	AGE	PA	R	2B	3B	HR	RBI	BB	K	SB	CS	Whiff%	AVG/OBP/SLG	DRC+	BABIP	BRR	DRP	WARP
2020	SEA	MLB	24	242	37	3	0	11	28	34	71	5	1	36.3%	.262/.364/.437	105	.341	2.2	CF(57): -4.5	0.7
2021	SEA	MLB	25	147	15	4	0	5	11	16	37	2	0	34.2%	.246/.333/.392	101	.307	-0.4	CF(34): -3.4	0.2
2022	TAC	AAA	26	174	29	4	0	12	34	26	45	0	0	34.1%	.245/.362/.517	111	.267	-1.2	LF(8): -1.0	0.5
2022	SEA	MLB	26	62	6	0	0	3	5	5	19	0	0	39.2%	.143/.226/.304	95	.147	-0.3	RF(3): -0.6, LF(1): -0.3	0.0
2023 DC	*AZ*	*MLB*	*27*	*339*	*39*	*12*	*0*	*13*	*40*	*35*	*105*	*3*	*1*	*35.2%*	*.234/.319/.417*	*102*	*.312*	*1.2*	*CF 0, RF 0*	*1.0*

Comparables: Wily Mo Pena (54), Matt Murton (52), Aaron Cunningham (51)

Lewis would probably lobby for a permanent switch to a 60-game season, as that proved the exact window of health that allowed him to showcase his power and defense on the way to an AL Rookie of the Year award in 2020. Before and after those magical two months, it's been short stretches of health alternated with longer periods of rehab and recovery. Yet for all of the time Lewis has missed with his troubled right knee, it was a concussion from a José Urquidy HBP that wiped away most of his 2022. And so, here we are, the 27-year-old looking again for a nice, healthy run of games. Centuries of medical advice would at least approve of traveling to a warmer, drier southern climate in which to recuperate.

Evan Longoria 3B Born: 10/07/85 Age: 37 Bats: R Throws: R Height: 6'1" Weight: 213 lb. Origin: Round 1, 2006 Draft (#3 overall)

YEAR	TEAM	LVL	AGE	PA	R	2B	3B	HR	RBI	BB	K	SB	CS	Whiff%	AVG/OBP/SLG	DRC+	BABIP	BRR	DRP	WARP
2020	SF	MLB	34	209	26	10	1	7	28	11	39	0	1	21.0%	.254/.297/.425	103	.280	-1.3	3B(52): 0.9	0.5
2021	SF	MLB	35	291	45	17	0	13	46	35	68	1	1	25.2%	.261/.351/.482	118	.305	-0.6	3B(78): 2.3	1.8
2022	SAC	AAA	36	25	3	2	0	0	0	1	8	0	0	32.6%	.333/.360/.417	78	.500	-1.5	3B(4): -0.6	-0.2
2022	SF	MLB	36	298	31	13	0	14	42	27	83	0	0	29.2%	.244/.315/.451	106	.297	-1.2	3B(68): -0.7	0.8
2023 DC	*AZ*	*MLB*	*37*	*375*	*42*	*17*	*1*	*14*	*45*	*33*	*96*	*0*	*0*	*28.5%*	*.235/.310/.418*	*100*	*.287*	*-2.3*	*3B 0*	*0.5*

Comparables: Scott Rolen (82), Matt Williams (77), Brooks Robinson (75)

The 2017 *Annual* comment on Longoria, already the 10th written about him, referenced Joseph Campbell's "monomyth," or the hero's journey, positioning Longo at the precipice of his "ultimate battle"—the end of the story. Returning to the theme in 2020's comment, the cycle restarted in San Francisco and with a second chance at a ring. But after the Giants declined to pick up his option, it seems like it's time to look at a different role for Longoria: not as the hero, but the mentor figure who aids the hero on their quest, only to take a step back at the crisis moment, forcing the real protagonist to go it alone. It's a cruel metaphor that makes a 37-year-old baseballer his sport's Gandalf, but baseball is not renowned for its kindness, and Gandalf probably enjoyed a very nice retirement "outside of time and space"—which for Longoria would be Arizona.

Ketel Marte 2B Born: 10/12/93 Age: 29 Bats: S Throws: R Height: 6'1" Weight: 210 lb. Origin: International Free Agent, 2010

YEAR	TEAM	LVL	AGE	PA	R	2B	3B	HR	RBI	BB	K	SB	CS	Whiff%	AVG/OBP/SLG	DRC+	BABIP	BRR	DRP	WARP
2020	AZ	MLB	26	195	19	14	1	2	17	7	21	1	0	14.1%	.287/.323/.409	101	.311	-0.6	2B(41): 0.8, CF(3): -0.1, SS(2): 0	0.7
2021	AZ	MLB	27	374	52	29	1	14	50	31	60	2	0	17.3%	.318/.377/.532	124	.352	-0.1	CF(71): -10.8, 2B(20): 0.1	1.5
2022	AZ	MLB	28	558	68	42	2	12	52	55	101	5	1	20.6%	.240/.321/.407	104	.276	2.7	2B(94): 0.9	2.2
2023 DC	*AZ*	*MLB*	*29*	*574*	*74*	*35*	*4*	*18*	*64*	*51*	*95*	*4*	*1*	*19.8%*	*.267/.341/.460*	*120*	*.299*	*3.1*	*2B 1*	*3.4*

Comparables: Lou Whitaker (67), Billy Herman (66), Starlin Castro (65)

If you've ever taken the hour-long commute between Alexandria, Indiana, home to the world's largest ball of paint, and Mount Sterling, Ohio, infamous residence of a billboard that reads "HELL IS REAL," well, sorry about that. But also, having journeyed from a starting point of something that is both uniquely fascinating, yet still fairly anonymous, all the way to, well...hell, you'd be well-suited to describe Marte's last few seasons.

Ok, maybe that's dramatic. He hasn't been a below-average bat since he was a 22-year-old in 2016, and he's played defense at up-the-middle spots his whole career. But he still lost time to injury this season and dealt with other nicks, and spontaneously flashed his elite skill more often than he wielded it. He tallied one fewer barrel this year (24) than he did last year despite 115 additional batted ball events, and more pull-heavy approach than ever. Selling out for power best works when you can actually get to your power, and Marte needs his: When he slugs over .500, he's a borderline elite bat. When he doesn't, he's much more pedestrian. Throw in losing a half-step defensively between a combination of injury and age, and he looked watered down last year. Suddenly Marte's outlook is dotted with "ifs"—never a welcome sign for a player's profile—but we know there's a uniquely fascinating player in there somewhere. Without a rebound in the power department, though, well...the heat in Arizona is real enough.

Jake McCarthy OF Born: 07/30/97 Age: 25 Bats: L Throws: L Height: 6'2" Weight: 215 lb. Origin: Round 1, 2018 Draft (#39 overall)

YEAR	TEAM	LVL	AGE	PA	R	2B	3B	HR	RBI	BB	K	SB	CS	Whiff%	AVG/OBP/SLG	DRC+	BABIP	BRR	DRP	WARP
2021	AMA	AA	23	156	25	8	4	6	23	17	46	17	1		.241/.333/.489	100	.318	2.1	LF(13): -2.4, CF(11): -2.7, RF(6): -1.3	0.0
2021	RNO	AAA	23	212	38	6	7	9	31	20	49	12	3		.262/.330/.508	104	.306	1.2	CF(25): -1.4, RF(14): -3.5, 1B(6): -0.4	0.4
2021	AZ	MLB	23	70	11	3	0	2	4	8	23	3	2	41.3%	.220/.333/.373	76	.324	1.2	CF(14): -0.7, RF(6): 3.4	0.5
2022	RNO	AAA	24	165	33	11	3	5	27	19	22	11	4	22.4%	.369/.457/.596	118	.412	-1.2	CF(17): -1.0, RF(13): -1.1, 1B(3): -0.1	0.4
2022	AZ	MLB	24	354	53	16	3	8	43	23	76	23	3	28.1%	.283/.342/.427	95	.349	3.8	RF(47): 0.4, LF(32): 1.2, CF(12): 0.8	1.5
2023 DC	*AZ*	*MLB*	*25*	*455*	*48*	*20*	*7*	*8*	*45*	*34*	*105*	*30*	*7*	*28.1%*	*.256/.325/.404*	*98*	*.328*	*16.0*	*RF -5, LF 0*	*2.1*

Comparables: Corey Hart (59), Josh Reddick (57), Kevin Kiermaier (55)

McCarthy demonstrated skills growth in 2022 that would have been unfair to expect before the season, and did it mostly by swinging at anything that came over the plate and spitting on offerings off of it—good strategy. His controlled aggression and resulting performance have given the Diamondbacks a good problem once he was recalled in mid-July, forcing them to find plate appearances for him despite having roughly several thousand outfield options, including numerous top prospects (they opted to address this issue by trading a catcher/outfielder for a catcher and an outfielder). His exit velocities are below-average despite a swing change that helped him tap into more power and he hits a ton of grounders (nearly two for every fly ball). It's unclear whether he's a speed-power guy or just a speed guy who had a nice half season. How the organization handles his sudden interjection could mold the team, whether he's a part of it or traded to help fill holes elsewhere on the roster.

Ivan Melendez CI Born: 01/24/00 Age: 23 Bats: R Throws: R Height: 6'3" Weight: 225 lb. Origin: Round 2, 2022 Draft (#43 overall)

YEAR	TEAM	LVL	AGE	PA	R	2B	3B	HR	RBI	BB	K	SB	CS	Whiff%	AVG/OBP/SLG	DRC+	BABIP	BRR	DRP	WARP
2022	VIS	A	22	106	11	3	1	3	8	10	20	0	0		.207/.349/.368	107	.234	-0.9	1B(14): -0.2, 3B(10): -0.4	0.3
2023 non-DC	*AZ*	*MLB*	*23*	*251*	*20*	*9*	*2*	*3*	*20*	*15*	*69*	*0*	*0*	*31.4%*	*.198/.270/.300*	*58*	*.269*	*1.6*	*1B 0, 3B 0*	*-0.8*

Comparables: Eric Campbell (84), Skyler Ewing (80), Brock Stassi (79)

Melendez closed out his college career in style, earning the Golden Spikes Award after breaking Kris Bryant's record for most home runs in the BBCOR era (32). The University of Texas grad boasts a nickname (The Hispanic Titanic) equal to that of his achievement. There's some irony to the nickname since the nominal third baseman showed the range of an iceberg in his 10-game showing after signing. While a cold corner is what ultimately felled the actual Titanic, it will be the best spot to hide Melendez's glove, other than DH. But this second-round selection wasn't made for his defense, but rather the thunder he brings with his bat. He offers a consistent stroke and incredible strength, allowing him to capitalize on mistake offerings. His uppercut swing does heavy damage to anything he catches out in front of the plate, but also offers exploitable holes that could sink his professional career.

Gabriel Moreno C Born: 02/14/00 Age: 23 Bats: R Throws: R Height: 5'11" Weight: 195 lb. Origin: International Free Agent, 2016

YEAR	TEAM	LVL	AGE	PA	R	2B	3B	HR	RBI	BB	K	SB	CS	Whiff%	AVG/OBP/SLG	DRC+	BABIP	BRR	DRP	WARP
2020	LAR	WIN	20	70	12	5	0	1	11	11	6	1	0		.373/.471/.508		.404			
2021	MSS	WIN	21	100	16	11	0	1	18	13	13	0	0		.329/.410/.494		.370			
2021	LAR	WIN	21	73	11	0	1	1	8	11	11	2	0		.279/.397/.361		.327			
2021	NH	AA	21	145	29	9	1	8	45	14	22	1	2		.373/.441/.651	147	.398	0.6	C(27): -2.9, 3B(1): -0.1	1.1
2022	BUF	AAA	22	267	35	16	0	3	39	24	45	7	1		.315/.386/.420	115	.377	-2.8	C(51): -2.3	0.8
2022	TOR	MLB	22	73	10	1	0	1	7	4	8	0	0	19.7%	.319/.356/.377	113	.350	0.7	C(19): 1.3, 3B(1): 0	0.6
2023 DC	*AZ*	*MLB*	*23*	*60*	*6*	*2*	*0*	*1*	*6*	*3*	*9*	*0*	*1*	*19.4%*	*.272/.329/.397*	*105*	*.313*	*0.0*	*C 2*	*0.4*

Comparables: Salvador Perez (62), John Ryan Murphy (57), Francisco Mejía (56)

YEAR	TEAM	P. COUNT	FRM RUNS	BLK RUNS	THRW RUNS	TOT RUNS
2021	MSS	1282			0.4	0.4
2021	NH	4215	-2.5	0.1	0.0	-2.4
2022	BUF	7046	-3.2	0.1	0.4	-2.7
2022	TOR	2527	1.1	0.0	0.0	1.1
2023	*AZ*	*2405*	*1.4*	*0.0*	*0.0*	*1.4*

After hitting a home run every four games in 2021, Moreno socked a donger just once every 20ish contests in 2022, dampening excitement about the previous year's power surge. Despite the dearth of home runs, his prospect stock kept rising, as his line-drive swing, coupled with fantastic bat-to-ball skills, helped him put an absolute boatload of balls into play. It underscored that any power Moreno offers is merely an added bonus, because his hit tool is top-shelf, and not only when you grade on the catching prospect curve. With both Alejandro Kirk and Danny Jansen ahead of him in Toronto, the Jays dealt Moreno to the DBacks—along with Loudres Gurriel Jr.—for Dalton Varsho, who was once upon a time a promising young catcher himself. Moreno's path to everyday playing time is much clearer in the desert than it was up north, and a breakout campaign could be on the horizon.

Geraldo Perdomo SS Born: 10/22/99 Age: 23 Bats: S Throws: R Height: 6'2" Weight: 203 lb. Origin: International Free Agent, 2016

YEAR	TEAM	LVL	AGE	PA	R	2B	3B	HR	RBI	BB	K	SB	CS	Whiff%	AVG/OBP/SLG	DRC+	BABIP	BRR	DRP	WARP
2021	AMA	AA	21	344	51	8	5	6	32	47	81	8	5		.231/.351/.357	104	.299	0.3	SS(82): 1.6	1.4
2021	AZ	MLB	21	37	5	3	1	0	1	6	6	0	0	28.0%	.258/.378/.419	103	.320	-0.2	SS(10): -0.3	0.1
2022	AZ	MLB	22	500	58	10	2	5	40	50	103	9	2	18.9%	.195/.285/.262	74	.243	2.5	SS(140): 5.3, 3B(6): 0.1, 2B(2): 0	0.9
2023 DC	*AZ*	*MLB*	*23*	*181*	*18*	*5*	*1*	*2*	*14*	*18*	*33*	*4*	*2*	*19.3%*	*.226/.318/.329*	*82*	*.272*	*1.0*	*SS 2*	*0.5*

Comparables: Abraham O. Nunez (62), Luis Ordaz (62), Gary Disarcina (61)

When considering Perdomo's overall contributions, it is important to remember that his last name translates to "I forgive," because you certainly can't forget that no other shortstop with as many plate appearances had a worse DRC+ than him. He also had the lowest maximum exit velocity. He knows how to take a walk, but given his paltry slugging percentage, pitchers have no reason not to throw him strikes. He's only 23, but it's hard to project growth in his bat and keep a straight face, but his defense still ultimately plays above average and provides a space for him on the roster, at least until someone more exciting like Blaze Alexander or Jordan Lawlar comes along.

Emmanuel Rivera 3B Born: 06/29/96 Age: 27 Bats: R Throws: R Height: 6'2" Weight: 225 lb. Origin: Round 19, 2015 Draft (#579 overall)

YEAR	TEAM	LVL	AGE	PA	R	2B	3B	HR	RBI	BB	K	SB	CS	Whiff%	AVG/OBP/SLG	DRC+	BABIP	BRR	DRP	WARP
2020	MAY	WIN	24	73	12	6	0	3	9	6	13	3	0		.292/.342/.523		.314			
2021	OMA	AAA	25	282	48	17	2	19	57	22	58	3	0		.286/.348/.592	126	.300	-1.7	3B(45): 3.1, 1B(9): 0.9	1.9
2021	KC	MLB	25	98	13	4	0	1	5	8	21	2	0	25.3%	.256/.316/.333	91	.324	0.6	3B(28): 0, 1B(1): 0	0.3
2022	OMA	AAA	26	85	12	5	1	3	5	10	16	1	0		.307/.388/.520	107	.357	-0.1	3B(19): -2.5	0.1
2022	KC	MLB	26	211	24	8	3	6	22	11	46	0	0	23.4%	.237/.284/.399	94	.281	0.0	3B(57): 4.3, 1B(1): 0	0.8
2022	AZ	MLB	26	148	22	8	0	6	18	12	37	1	2	29.4%	.227/.304/.424	105	.267	1.7	3B(29): 0.9, 1B(4): -0.2	0.7
2023 DC	*AZ*	*MLB*	*27*	*320*	*33*	*14*	*2*	*8*	*33*	*21*	*69*	*3*	*0*	*26.0%*	*.240/.300/.391*	*90*	*.288*	*1.5*	*3B 0*	*0.4*

Comparables: Luis Jimenez (59), Chris Johnson (58), Chris Nelson (56)

After a hamate injury followed a power breakout in Triple-A in 2021, we were left to wonder if Rivera's ability to bop was real or not. He hit six home runs in 63 games with the Royals this year, seemingly giving us an answer (no). Then he got traded to the Diamondbacks and hit six home runs in 38 games, seemingly giving us another answer (yes). Given the lack of clarity, we could query a Magic 8 Ball, but it would only tell us to "ask again later." Having a lot of questions about what you are as a player at 26 generally isn't a positive trait, but it beats *knowing* if you're not much of one. But between who he was traded for (Luke Weaver), and how the Diamondbacks are positioning him (either a bench bat behind Evan Longoria or short-side platoon bat with Josh Rojas), they're giving some pretty strong hints.

Josh Rojas 3B Born: 06/30/94 Age: 29 Bats: L Throws: R Height: 6'1" Weight: 207 lb. Origin: Round 26, 2017 Draft (#781 overall)

YEAR	TEAM	LVL	AGE	PA	R	2B	3B	HR	RBI	BB	K	SB	CS	Whiff%	AVG/OBP/SLG	DRC+	BABIP	BRR	DRP	WARP
2020	AZ	MLB	26	70	9	0	0	0	2	7	16	1	1	25.6%	.180/.257/.180	76	.234	0.9	2B(8): 0, SS(2): 0.1, LF(1): 0	0.1
2021	AZ	MLB	27	550	69	32	3	11	44	58	137	9	4	23.6%	.264/.341/.411	88	.345	1.2	2B(55): -1.6, SS(42): -1.1, RF(37): 0.3	1.0
2022	AZ	MLB	28	510	66	25	1	9	56	55	98	23	3	22.3%	.269/.349/.391	98	.323	2.3	3B(89): -4.4, 2B(26): -0.6	0.9
2023 DC	*AZ*	*MLB*	*29*	*395*	*49*	*19*	*2*	*9*	*35*	*43*	*84*	*17*	*4*	*22.5%*	*.255/.341/.404*	*106*	*.314*	*8.0*	*2B -1, 3B 0*	*2.0*

Comparables: Fernando Vina (54), Tony Kemp (48), Jonathan Villar (47)

Rojas is a versatile defender in the sense he can peddle his below-average glove in a number of spots. Okay, "glove" is the wrong substitute for "defense" there, as there's nothing *particularly* wrong with the leather. It's his weak arm that causes problems, accounting for 10 of his 16 errors, and no doubt applying pressure on him to rush some other plays that resulted in fielding errors. We know, we know, errors aren't an enlightened statistic, but here they underscore the point. Rojas doesn't do enough to make up for the glove when at the dish, checking in around average offensively thanks to a passive approach that borders on comatose. Maybe the package plays up in a utility role, where some of his various liabilities can be hidden, but if he approaches 500 plate appearances in 2023, something will have gone wrong.

Pavin Smith RF

Born: 02/06/96 Age: 27 Bats: L Throws: L Height: 6'2" Weight: 208 lb. Origin: Round 1, 2017 Draft (#7 overall)

YEAR	TEAM	LVL	AGE	PA	R	2B	3B	HR	RBI	BB	K	SB	CS	Whiff%	AVG/OBP/SLG	DRC+	BABIP	BRR	DRP	WARP
2020	AZ	MLB	24	44	7	0	1	1	4	5	8	1	0	23.8%	.270/.341/.405	95	.300	-0.8	1B(5): -0.1, LF(3): 0.1, RF(2): -0.2	0.0
2021	AZ	MLB	25	545	68	27	4	11	49	42	106	1	0	17.2%	.267/.328/.404	91	.319	-3.4	1B(54): -0.4, RF(53): -2.8, CF(39): -3.5	-0.1
2022	AZ	MLB	26	277	24	9	0	9	33	28	67	1	0	21.8%	.220/.300/.367	90	.262	0.2	RF(43): -0.5, 1B(10): -0.3	0.4
2023 DC	*AZ*	*MLB*	*27*	*173*	*19*	*7*	*1*	*4*	*17*	*15*	*31*	*0*	*0*	*19.6%*	*.246/.319/.401*	*98*	*.283*	*0.8*	*1B 0*	*0.3*

Comparables: John Mabry (65), Tyler Collins (59), Lucas Duda (59)

In 866 career plate appearances across three big league campaigns, Smith has only sniffed being an average hitter. As a player with a corner-only profile, that's a tough sell. He takes walks at a rate higher than most hitters, has shown an ability to make good contact on pitches high in the zone, and occasionally drive ones down low, but he's never been able to do both at the same time with enough authority to truly stake claim to a roster spot. Smith still has options, so is likely to stick on the roster for a bit longer despite Arizona's logjam in the outfield and at first base. That's good because having to tell a guy named Pavin Smith to hit the road would be a bit too on the nose.

Alek Thomas CF

Born: 04/28/00 Age: 23 Bats: L Throws: L Height: 5'11" Weight: 175 lb. Origin: Round 2, 2018 Draft (#63 overall)

YEAR	TEAM	LVL	AGE	PA	R	2B	3B	HR	RBI	BB	K	SB	CS	Whiff%	AVG/OBP/SLG	DRC+	BABIP	BRR	DRP	WARP
2021	AMA	AA	21	329	54	18	8	10	41	37	65	8	5		.283/.374/.507	119	.335	-0.6	CF(45): -1.2, RF(18): 0.5, LF(10): -0.3	1.6
2021	RNO	AAA	21	166	32	11	4	8	18	15	34	5	4		.369/.434/.658	119	.439	0.4	CF(31): 4.1, LF(1): -0.0, RF(1): -0.1	1.4
2022	RNO	AAA	22	131	25	11	1	4	19	14	18	5	2	21.0%	.322/.397/.539	110	.351	-1.8	CF(26): 1.0, RF(2): 0.2, LF(1): -0.0	0.4
2022	AZ	MLB	22	411	45	17	1	8	39	22	74	4	3	24.9%	.231/.275/.344	81	.263	3.1	CF(112): 5.5	1.5
2023 DC	*AZ*	*MLB*	*23*	*231*	*25*	*10*	*3*	*4*	*22*	*15*	*43*	*4*	*1*	*24.8%*	*.264/.322/.410*	*101*	*.316*	*1.6*	*CF 0, RF 0*	*0.8*

Comparables: Byron Buxton (60), Felix Pie (58), Melky Cabrera (57)

His overall stat line might not reflect it, but Thomas showed the skills that made him a top prospect throughout his debut. There have only been 15 others who have debuted at his age and position in the last 20 years to hit as many homers as he did. He's also shown that when he gets into it, he *really* gets into it, registering a max exit velocity better than 65% of the league. Overall, the league was more willing to chase last year (29.3%) compared to 2021 (27.6%), which makes his willingness to do it (33.4%) a little more palatable. The issue could still be pitch selection, though. While more and more batters are attuned to attacking only the pitches that enter their nitro zone, Thomas was repeatedly coaxed into reaching for pitches away. Still, this is a solid baseline for a dude who plays a smooth center field.

Christian Walker 1B

Born: 03/28/91 Age: 32 Bats: R Throws: R Height: 6'0" Weight: 208 lb. Origin: Round 4, 2012 Draft (#132 overall)

YEAR	TEAM	LVL	AGE	PA	R	2B	3B	HR	RBI	BB	K	SB	CS	Whiff%	AVG/OBP/SLG	DRC+	BABIP	BRR	DRP	WARP
2020	AZ	MLB	29	243	35	18	1	7	34	19	50	1	1	27.1%	.271/.333/.459	101	.317	0.7	1B(43): 0	0.6
2021	AZ	MLB	30	445	55	23	1	10	46	38	106	0	0	27.4%	.244/.315/.382	92	.307	2.9	1B(107): -4.2	0.4
2022	AZ	MLB	31	667	84	25	2	36	94	69	131	2	2	24.6%	.242/.327/.477	131	.248	-0.1	1B(150): 2.9	4.1
2023 DC	*AZ*	*MLB*	*32*	*622*	*73*	*27*	*2*	*25*	*81*	*61*	*125*	*0*	*1*	*25.0%*	*.248/.331/.444*	*115*	*.279*	*-2.4*	*1B 1*	*1.9*

Comparables: David Segui (74), Babe Dahlgren (71), Justin Smoak (69)

A quick look at Walker's line this past season suggests he decided to be an upgraded version of who he was three years ago. He drove the ball better than all but a handful of players in 2022 and hit more homers than an even smaller handful. If he continues at this pace, we'll be dealing with some incredibly small hands. Speaking of small hands, he became as picky at the plate as your average toddler, leading to the best strikeout rate and second-highest walk rate of his career. You might think there is room for him to be more dynamic with the bat if you look at his BABIP (.248), but lower figures are bound to happen when you insist on hitting everything in the air (44.2% fly-ball rate). He remains a first baseman in his 30s with break-even defense who will have a thin margin for error, even if his track record buys him more time if he struggles again.

PITCHERS

Madison Bumgarner LHP

Born: 08/01/89 Age: 33 Bats: R Throws: L Height: 6'4" Weight: 257 lb. Origin: Round 1, 2007 Draft (#10 overall)

YEAR	TEAM	LVL	AGE	W	L	SV	G	GS	IP	H	HR	BB/9	K/9	K	GB%	BABIP	WHIP	ERA	DRA-	WARP	MPH	FB%	Whiff%	CSP
2020	AZ	MLB	30	1	4	0	9	9	41^{2}	47	13	2.8	6.5	30	33.3%	.266	1.44	6.48	190	-1.4	88.4	39.9%	17.4%	47.7%
2021	AZ	MLB	31	7	10	0	26	26	146^{1}	134	24	2.4	7.6	124	33.0%	.267	1.18	4.67	113	0.4	90.4	36.5%	21.6%	56.7%
2022	AZ	MLB	32	7	15	0	30	30	158^{2}	179	25	2.8	6.4	112	36.6%	.307	1.44	4.88	145	-2.2	91.0	33.4%	18.2%	53.5%
2023 DC	*AZ*	*MLB*	*33*	*8*	*10*	*0*	*27*	*27*	*151.3*	*161*	*24*	*2.7*	*6.4*	*108*	*35.9%*	*.295*	*1.36*	*4.66*	*118*	*-0.1*	*90.7*	*36.2%*	*19.4%*	*53.4%*

Comparables: CC Sabathia (71), Vida Blue (68), Frank Tanana (65)

Armed with catchy hooks and lyrics laced with longing, pop punk surged to the forefront of the music world in the early 2000s. As time passed, the choruses and nostalgia slowly lost their grip and the genre's popularity faded. Bumgarner's career has followed a similar arc: undeniable electricity to questionable contributions. Sure, he made 30 turns through the rotation and threw nearly 160 innings in 2022, but that's about as close as we can get to saying he was helpful. His strikeout rate continued to sink and hitters could sit on his once-fearsome breaking ball. He relied more on a changeup than he ever has, a Matt Skiba trying to prop up his shell of a blink-182. That's where the metaphor runs dry; in this case the Tom DeLonge of fastball velocity isn't coming back.

Miguel Castro RHP

Born: 12/24/94 Age: 28 Bats: R Throws: R Height: 6'7" Weight: 201 lb. Origin: International Free Agent, 2012

YEAR	TEAM	LVL	AGE	W	L	SV	G	GS	IP	H	HR	BB/9	K/9	K	GB%	BABIP	WHIP	ERA	DRA-	WARP	MPH	FB%	Whiff%	CSP
2020	NYM	MLB	25	1	2	0	10	0	9	11	1	8.0	14.0	14	43.5%	.455	2.11	4.00	86	0.2	98.8	55.2%	37.1%	44.5%
2020	BAL	MLB	25	1	0	1	16	0	15^2	17	3	2.9	13.8	24	57.5%	.378	1.40	4.02	65	0.5	98.0	47.4%	26.7%	48.8%
2021	NYM	MLB	26	3	4	0	69	2	70^1	48	7	5.5	9.9	77	51.4%	.241	1.29	3.45	94	0.9	98.2	43.5%	32.5%	50.3%
2022	NYY	MLB	27	5	0	0	34	0	29	27	2	4.7	9.6	31	47.5%	.321	1.45	4.03	97	0.3	98.0	36.8%	32.3%	49.7%
2023 DC	*AZ*	*MLB*	*28*	*2*	*2*	*0*	*49*	*0*	*42.7*	*36*	*4*	*4.8*	*9.8*	*47*	*49.8%*	*.293*	*1.38*	*3.79*	*93*	*0.3*	*98.1*	*43.4%*	*31.0%*	*48.9%*

Comparables: Michael Jackson (56), Arodys Vizcaíno (55), Eric O'Flaherty (53)

There has never been a question about Castro's tantalizing stuff—he's had the upper-90s-with-movement thing down since he was coming up through Toronto's system in the mid-2010s. What still plagues him is lack of command, and only recently has he exhibited an ability to rack up strikeouts with any kind of regularity. He's been roughly a league-average pitcher for years now, and a shoulder strain—his first significant injury since his minor league days—wiped out much of his season after the All-Star break and raised questions about his health as he headed to free agency for the first time. It didn't stop Arizona from inking him on a one-year deal with a club option, though.

Zach Davies RHP

Born: 02/07/93 Age: 30 Bats: R Throws: R Height: 6'0" Weight: 180 lb. Origin: Round 26, 2011 Draft (#785 overall)

YEAR	TEAM	LVL	AGE	W	L	SV	G	GS	IP	H	HR	BB/9	K/9	K	GB%	BABIP	WHIP	ERA	DRA-	WARP	MPH	FB%	Whiff%	CSP
2020	SD	MLB	27	7	4	0	12	12	69^1	55	9	2.5	8.2	63	40.7%	.250	1.07	2.73	91	1.1	88.6	39.1%	25.6%	43.7%
2021	CHC	MLB	28	6	12	0	32	32	148	162	25	4.6	6.9	114	41.4%	.311	1.60	5.78	121	-0.3	88.1	52.3%	22.5%	49.4%
2022	AZ	MLB	29	2	5	0	27	27	134^1	122	21	3.5	6.8	102	42.0%	.258	1.30	4.09	115	0.2	89.5	54.1%	21.5%	51.5%
2023 DC	*AZ*	*MLB*	*30*	*7*	*8*	*0*	*24*	*24*	*121.3*	*120*	*15*	*3.6*	*6.6*	*89*	*41.9%*	*.287*	*1.39*	*4.17*	*106*	*0.7*	*88.8*	*51.8%*	*22.1%*	*49.1%*

Comparables: Danny Cox (81), Sidney Ponson (81), Mike Pelfrey (79)

On his fourth team in four years, Davies occasioned all the enthusiasm of a wall being painted taupe and drying over the course of a few especially hot days in mid-August. His changeup was less effective than it typically has been, and batters were therefore less willing to offer at it—it generated fewer chases and strikeouts than it has since 2018. Perhaps it's a blip on the radar, or perhaps the righty's most faithful offering is slowly ghosting him. The Diamondbacks brought him back on a one-year deal, but he needs to find another wrinkle if he wants to keep what little relevance he has intact.

Zac Gallen RHP

Born: 08/03/95 Age: 27 Bats: R Throws: R Height: 6'2" Weight: 189 lb. Origin: Round 3, 2016 Draft (#106 overall)

YEAR	TEAM	LVL	AGE	W	L	SV	G	GS	IP	H	HR	BB/9	K/9	K	GB%	BABIP	WHIP	ERA	DRA-	WARP	MPH	FB%	Whiff%	CSP
2020	AZ	MLB	24	3	2	0	12	12	72	55	9	3.1	10.3	82	46.4%	.269	1.11	2.75	76	1.7	93.1	39.2%	30.4%	42.4%
2021	AZ	MLB	25	4	10	0	23	23	121^1	108	19	3.6	10.3	139	43.6%	.289	1.29	4.30	83	2.1	93.4	61.3%	23.6%	51.8%
2022	AZ	MLB	26	12	4	0	31	31	184	121	15	2.3	9.4	192	45.6%	.237	0.91	2.54	75	4.2	94.0	48.1%	23.1%	51.6%
2023 DC	*AZ*	*MLB*	*27*	*10*	*8*	*0*	*27*	*27*	*156.7*	*132*	*16*	*2.9*	*9.6*	*166*	*44.9%*	*.287*	*1.17*	*2.99*	*79*	*3.0*	*93.7*	*51.2%*	*24.5%*	*50.3%*

Comparables: Noah Syndergaard (78), José Berríos (77), Chris Archer (74)

The story of seemingly every breakout pitching year, these days, centers on pitch mix. It's true that Gallen reworked his percentages a bit, favoring cutters and curveballs and minimizing sliders. But Gallen's 2022 wasn't the product of some clever tinkering; he was (to adopt the phrasing of the 1980s dungaree-and-motor-oil dad he looks like) a whole new souped-up machine.

After a down 2021, he got more chases on every single pitch type. His velocity ticked up, but what he talks most proudly about is his bespoke batter-by-batter sequencing, and the best version of Gallen we've yet seen was hugging curves, changing gears and flooring it on straightaways to great effect. Listen to that baby purr.

Kevin Ginkel RHP

Born: 03/24/94 Age: 29 Bats: L Throws: R Height: 6'4" Weight: 235 lb. Origin: Round 22, 2016 Draft (#659 overall)

YEAR	TEAM	LVL	AGE	W	L	SV	G	GS	IP	H	HR	BB/9	K/9	K	GB%	BABIP	WHIP	ERA	DRA-	WARP	MPH	FB%	Whiff%	CSP
2020	AZ	MLB	26	0	2	1	19	0	16	21	3	7.3	10.1	18	29.2%	.400	2.13	6.75	129	-0.1	95.5	59.7%	32.9%	42.5%
2021	AZ	MLB	27	0	1	0	32	0	28^1	30	7	4.4	9.8	31	41.5%	.311	1.55	6.35	100	0.3	94.9	59.3%	25.3%	53.4%
2022	RNO	AAA	28	2	1	9	30	0	30^2	23	1	3.5	13.2	45	43.1%	.344	1.14	1.17	73	0.7	96.1	66.2%	34.4%	
2022	AZ	MLB	28	1	1	1	30	0	29^1	27	1	3.4	9.2	30	50.0%	.321	1.30	3.38	91	0.4	96.3	62.0%	27.1%	55.4%
2023 DC	*AZ*	*MLB*	*29*	*3*	*3*	*15*	*63*	*0*	*55*	*51*	*5*	*4.0*	*9.6*	*58*	*42.4%*	*.308*	*1.37*	*3.84*	*95*	*0.4*	*95.5*	*60.0%*	*28.1%*	*51.8%*

Comparables: Nick Vincent (69), Kevin Quackenbush (67), Ryan Cook (67)

For the first time, Ginkel's average four-seamer sat above 96 mph, as if he'd been slowly soaking up the desert heat and had finally been able to channel it into his arm. Not so coincidentally, he also had the longest stretch of success in his career. The zapped-up number one let him pepper the zone more often but with less consequence, as shown by a hard-hit rate (32.9%) that continued to drop well below the league average (38.2%) despite batters making just as much contact in that context. His slider generated more swings and misses than average, too, and when batters did connect, they drove it into the ground at a maddening rate.

Tommy Henry LHP
Born: 07/29/97 Age: 25 Bats: L Throws: L Height: 6'3" Weight: 205 lb. Origin: Round 2, 2019 Draft (#74 overall)

YEAR	TEAM	LVL	AGE	W	L	SV	G	GS	IP	H	HR	BB/9	K/9	K	GB%	BABIP	WHIP	ERA	DRA-	WARP	MPH	FB%	Whiff%	CSP
2021	AMA	AA	23	4	6	0	23	23	115^{2}	116	24	4.1	10.5	135	38.7%	.335	1.46	5.21	84	1.8				
2022	RNO	AAA	24	4	4	0	21	21	113	103	11	3.6	8.2	103	44.1%	.295	1.31	3.74	90	1.3	92.1	57.5%	26.4%	
2022	AZ	MLB	24	3	4	0	9	9	47	47	10	4.0	6.9	36	38.6%	.276	1.45	5.36	137	-0.4	91.5	55.8%	23.4%	56.8%
2023 DC	*AZ*	*MLB*	*25*	*1*	*2*	*0*	*6*	*6*	*28.3*	*30*	*4*	*4.3*	*7.8*	*24*	*41.0%*	*.312*	*1.56*	*5.28*	*126*	*-0.1*	*91.5*	*55.8%*	*24.5%*	*56.8%*

Comparables: Andrew Suárez (80), Ben Lively (80), Brett Oberholtzer (79)

"Tommy Henry" is a cover name for an operative at France's Deuxième Bureau that continued secret intelligence operations through World War II despite being formally dissolved in 1940. It's so nondescript because it had to be unassuming to pass off as an American traveling in Europe for business, and Johnny Mainstreet was deemed to be too on the nose. Coincidentally, "undistinguished" also describes Henry's walk rate, which has been below-average as a professional. Paired with shrug-worthy stuff, it could ticket him for the bullpen, where he'd become even more unassuming. That could be helpful, considering how things are heating up in Marrakesh.

Drey Jameson RHP
Born: 08/17/97 Age: 25 Bats: R Throws: R Height: 6'0" Weight: 165 lb. Origin: Round 1, 2019 Draft (#34 overall)

YEAR	TEAM	LVL	AGE	W	L	SV	G	GS	IP	H	HR	BB/9	K/9	K	GB%	BABIP	WHIP	ERA	DRA-	WARP	MPH	FB%	Whiff%	CSP
2021	HIL	A+	23	2	4	0	13	12	64^{1}	60	9	2.5	10.8	77	52.6%	.319	1.21	3.92	95	0.7				
2021	AMA	AA	23	3	2	0	8	8	46^{1}	38	6	3.5	13.2	68	38.5%	.327	1.21	4.08	79	0.9				
2022	AMA	AA	24	2	1	0	4	4	18^{2}	13	0	1.9	11.1	23	55.8%	.302	0.91	2.41	63	0.5				
2022	RNO	AAA	24	5	12	0	22	21	114	139	21	3.3	8.6	109	48.2%	.351	1.59	6.95	101	0.6	95.9	63.7%	24.6%	
2022	AZ	MLB	24	3	0	0	4	4	24^{1}	20	2	2.6	8.9	24	56.1%	.281	1.11	1.48	90	0.4	95.1	62.3%	26.3%	59.4%
2023 DC	*AZ*	*MLB*	*25*	*4*	*5*	*0*	*17*	*17*	*80*	*87*	*10*	*3.5*	*8.4*	*74*	*49.8%*	*.327*	*1.48*	*4.88*	*117*	*0.0*	*95.1*	*62.3%*	*24.9%*	*59.4%*

Comparables: Zach Plesac (73), Taylor Jungmann (70), A.J. Griffin (70)

After spending most of the year in Triple-A and getting knocked around in the hitter-friendly confines of the Pacific Coast League, Jameson was called up and made four useful starts, going at least 5⅓ innings in each of them. The high-octane hurler touched triple digits multiple times, and will sit 95–97 with his fastballs (plural). He'll throw the four-seamer up in the zone for whiffs, and use the sinker to induce weak contact. His slider is his best secondary, often causing batters to feel like a crypto wallet as they come up empty following a big hack. He'll mix in a more vertical curveball and a weak changeup, but will mostly lean on the fastballs and slider—which he showed tighter command of in his debut than in Triple-A. A shorter pitcher, the preference for a shallower arsenal and effort in his delivery might add up to a bullpen future, but the Diamondbacks will give him every opportunity to show what he can do in the rotation.

Bryce Jarvis RHP
Born: 12/26/97 Age: 25 Bats: L Throws: R Height: 6'2" Weight: 195 lb. Origin: Round 1, 2020 Draft (#18 overall)

YEAR	TEAM	LVL	AGE	W	L	SV	G	GS	IP	H	HR	BB/9	K/9	K	GB%	BABIP	WHIP	ERA	DRA-	WARP	MPH	FB%	Whiff%	CSP
2021	HIL	A+	23	1	2	0	7	7	37^{1}	30	4	3.1	10.1	42	31.6%	.283	1.15	3.62	95	0.4				
2021	AMA	AA	23	1	2	0	8	8	35	32	8	4.4	10.3	40	43.6%	.286	1.40	5.66	106	0.1				
2022	AMA	AA	24	3	6	0	25	25	106^{2}	141	27	5.1	9.3	110	39.3%	.381	1.88	8.27	119	-0.7				
2023 non-DC	*AZ*	*MLB*	*25*	*2*	*3*	*0*	*57*	*0*	*50*	*56*	*10*	*5.3*	*7.7*	*42*	*39.6%*	*.312*	*1.72*	*6.34*	*145*	*-1.0*			*25.4%*	

Comparables: Kyle McGowin (79), Jon Harris (78), Thomas Eshelman (78)

With a walk rate pushing 12%, Jarvis still hasn't regained the command he had before his velocity spiked in college. The former first-rounder has given up a larger rate of free passes at each level. He has a busy motion and uses a lot of north-south movement to get to his mid-90s velo. Overall, his inefficiency has made it hard to know what to expect in a given outing other than a bunch of hits and homers allowed, if 2022 is to be taken seriously. Given the depth throughout the organization his skills, once re-established, could be best leveraged in a relief role.

Merrill Kelly RHP
Born: 10/14/88 Age: 34 Bats: R Throws: R Height: 6'2" Weight: 202 lb. Origin: Round 8, 2010 Draft (#251 overall)

YEAR	TEAM	LVL	AGE	W	L	SV	G	GS	IP	H	HR	BB/9	K/9	K	GB%	BABIP	WHIP	ERA	DRA-	WARP	MPH	FB%	Whiff%	CSP
2020	AZ	MLB	31	3	2	0	5	5	31^{1}	26	5	1.4	8.3	29	45.6%	.247	0.99	2.59	87	0.6	91.5	65.5%	23.5%	51.3%
2021	AZ	MLB	32	7	11	0	27	27	158	163	21	2.3	7.4	130	43.3%	.305	1.29	4.44	97	1.7	91.6	65.2%	20.4%	55.6%
2022	AZ	MLB	33	13	8	0	33	33	200^{1}	167	21	2.7	8.0	177	42.9%	.269	1.14	3.37	92	2.8	92.1	65.8%	23.6%	54.1%
2023 DC	*AZ*	*MLB*	*34*	*9*	*9*	*0*	*29*	*29*	*163*	*160*	*20*	*2.7*	*7.8*	*141*	*42.7%*	*.298*	*1.29*	*3.76*	*97*	*1.6*	*91.8*	*65.5%*	*22.5%*	*53.9%*

Comparables: Jeff Samardzija (80), Bob Purkey (80), Kevin Tapani (79)

A casual glance at Kelly's 2022 season makes it appear like the rest of his major league seasons, in that it resembles room-temperature soda: sweet and with casual bubbles, but short of refreshing. He deserves more, though, mostly because of how it can be broken up so comically. Against anyone except the Dodgers (28 starts), he was easily the best he's ever been, posting a sub-2.50 ERA. Against the Dodgers (five starts), he posted an 8.25 ERA. Those games against LA can't be wished away, but that doesn't change how his fastball was back above 92 mph and got more swings and misses than ever, or how he upped his changeup usage to career highs in addition to getting an elite rate of grounders with it (nearly 63%). The overall results are thoroughly unassuming, but the parts under the hood are distinctly different; now a combination of some of his best traits from earlier iterations.

Joe Mantiply LHP Born: 03/01/91 Age: 32 Bats: R Throws: L Height: 6'4" Weight: 219 lb. Origin: Round 27, 2013 Draft (#816 overall)

YEAR	TEAM	LVL	AGE	W	L	SV	G	GS	IP	H	HR	BB/9	K/9	K	GB%	BABIP	WHIP	ERA	DRA-	WARP	MPH	FB%	Whiff%	CSP
2020	AZ	MLB	29	0	0	0	4	0	2^1	3	0	15.4	7.7	2	44.4%	.333	3.00	15.43	100	0.0	91.1	47.4%	26.1%	48.0%
2021	AZ	MLB	30	0	3	0	57	0	39^2	45	1	3.9	8.6	38	44.6%	.370	1.56	3.40	89	0.6	91.1	51.4%	28.1%	55.8%
2022	AZ	MLB	31	2	5	2	69	0	60	59	6	0.9	9.2	61	54.3%	.319	1.08	2.85	82	1.1	90.3	43.8%	29.3%	54.3%
2023 DC	*AZ*	*MLB*	*32*	*3*	*3*	*8*	*63*	*0*	*55*	*59*	*5*	*2.4*	*8.6*	*52*	*50.2%*	*.330*	*1.34*	*4.02*	*101*	*0.2*	*90.6*	*46.5%*	*28.0%*	*54.6%*

Comparables: Zac Rosscup (39), Sam Freeman (38), Jake Diekman (36)

With his sinker-slider combo, Mantiply likes to party like it's 1994. He also throws a changeup that is a legitimate third offering. In another ode to '94, he's keen on bouncy balls, using all three offerings to coax grounders from whoever is in the batter's box. If all else fails, he's demonstrated an ability to use his off-speed pitches to get swinging strikes at an above-average rate. On top of all this, only 10 relievers averaged lower velocity on their fastball last year. Whenever someone gripes about the modern pitcher, they should be handed a grainy-picture VHS—their favorite way to consume media—with all of Mantiply's outings. A fruitful find in minor-league free agency back in 2020, the Diamondbacks are hoping Mantiply's All-Star 2022 is the genesis of a storybook second half of his career.

Corbin Martin RHP Born: 12/28/95 Age: 27 Bats: R Throws: R Height: 6'2" Weight: 225 lb. Origin: Round 2, 2017 Draft (#56 overall)

YEAR	TEAM	LVL	AGE	W	L	SV	G	GS	IP	H	HR	BB/9	K/9	K	GB%	BABIP	WHIP	ERA	DRA-	WARP	MPH	FB%	Whiff%	CSP
2021	RNO	AAA	25	2	0	0	6	6	27^1	31	7	6.3	9.9	30	40.5%	.316	1.83	5.93	109	0.0				
2021	AZ	MLB	25	0	3	0	5	3	16	23	5	7.9	7.3	13	29.3%	.353	2.31	10.69	129	-0.1	94.1	63.7%	19.4%	55.5%
2022	RNO	AAA	26	6	7	0	17	17	77	86	15	3.5	9.2	79	39.1%	.330	1.51	6.08	107	0.1	93.4	55.8%	27.8%	
2022	AZ	MLB	26	0	1	0	7	2	22^1	25	3	4.8	8.5	21	27.9%	.344	1.66	4.84	119	0.0	94.0	54.8%	26.6%	50.7%
2023 DC	*AZ*	*MLB*	*27*	*5*	*4*	*0*	*53*	*4*	*57.3*	*60*	*9*	*4.6*	*7.9*	*50*	*37.1%*	*.308*	*1.57*	*5.28*	*125*	*-0.4*	*94.2*	*58.7%*	*24.6%*	*51.6%*

Comparables: Jeff Hoffman (73), Eddie Butler (70), Chi Chi González (69)

Martin's trajectory continues downward, toward a narrative in which we talk about him in terms of before his Tommy John surgery. His velocity failed to bounce back to pre-TJ levels, and instead of sitting 95+, he's now squarely at 94. Maybe that doesn't sound like a lot to you, but it means a lot in terms of run prevention. His spin rates continue to slip and his breaking balls have less drop than average. The sample size is modest but these are all things that can be meaningful quickly.

Scott McGough RHP Born: 10/31/89 Age: 33 Bats: R Throws: R Height: 5'11" Weight: 190 lb. Origin: Round 5, 2011 Draft (#164 overall)

YEAR	TEAM	LVL	AGE	W	L	SV	G	GS	IP	H	HR	BB/9	K/9	K	GB%	BABIP	WHIP	ERA	DRA-	WARP	MPH	FB%	Whiff%	CSP
2023 DC	*AZ*	*MLB*	*33*	*3*	*3*	*0*	*63*	*0*	*55*	*49*	*7*	*3.0*	*9.4*	*57*	*45.8%*	*.294*	*1.24*	*3.50*	*90*	*0.5*			*26.8%*	

Comparables: Josh Judy (42), R.J. Alvarez (41), Mark Hamburger (41)

As with so many of us, it took McGough nearly until his 30s to figure things out. After getting battered around Triple-A for years, he found his niche relieving and then closing with the Yakult Swallows of the NPB, striking out 10 batters per nine in a league that averages a hair over seven. In the past two seasons, though, he's not only missed bats, he'd stopped giving up square contact at all, allowing just a baserunner per inning. The Diamondbacks have had some luck with retrieving pitchers from overseas, and they'll be thrilled if they tap even a fraction of the magic that they've gotten out of Merrill Kelly.

Mark Melancon RHP Born: 03/28/85 Age: 38 Bats: R Throws: R Height: 6'1" Weight: 215 lb. Origin: Round 9, 2006 Draft (#284 overall)

YEAR	TEAM	LVL	AGE	W	L	SV	G	GS	IP	H	HR	BB/9	K/9	K	GB%	BABIP	WHIP	ERA	DRA-	WARP	MPH	FB%	Whiff%	CSP
2020	ATL	MLB	35	2	1	11	23	0	22^2	22	1	2.8	5.6	14	58.3%	.300	1.28	2.78	100	0.2	92.0	57.9%	19.6%	45.7%
2021	SD	MLB	36	4	3	39	64	0	64^2	54	4	3.5	8.2	59	56.7%	.284	1.22	2.23	92	0.9	92.1	65.3%	21.0%	54.5%
2022	AZ	MLB	37	3	10	18	62	0	56	63	5	3.4	5.6	35	43.2%	.315	1.50	4.66	124	-0.1	90.8	65.8%	20.9%	53.7%
2023 DC	*AZ*	*MLB*	*38*	*3*	*3*	*10*	*63*	*0*	*55*	*65*	*6*	*3.5*	*6.6*	*40*	*49.1%*	*.332*	*1.57*	*5.10*	*122*	*-0.4*	*91.5*	*65.1%*	*21.0%*	*52.4%*

Comparables: Chad Qualls (81), Mike Timlin (80), Joakim Soria (80)

Melancon carried on in 2022 as he did in 2021, which isn't terribly endearing. He is one of two qualified relievers in the entire league to have registered a second consecutive season of a strikeout-minus-walk rate in the single digits. The league average hovers above 14%. Melancon has long survived on the margins, making sub-par strikeout rates work on the back of high ground-ball rates and weak contact. His first year in the desert saw those margins evaporate, as his strikeout percentage dropped a full eight percentage points, below even the paltry 14.7% he put up in Atlanta in 2020. Unlike in Atlanta, he couldn't keep the ball on the ground, registering a career-low figure. That wasn't all—career-worsts in average exit velocity allowed and launch angle meant the additional balls in play were going for extra bases. Melancon still excels at keeping the ball in the park and his multi-year deal will likely keep him in uniform, but things aren't trending up as he enters his age-38 season.

Ryne Nelson RHP Born: 02/01/98 Age: 25 Bats: R Throws: R Height: 6'3" Weight: 184 lb. Origin: Round 2, 2019 Draft (#56 overall)

YEAR	TEAM	LVL	AGE	W	L	SV	G	GS	IP	H	HR	BB/9	K/9	K	GB%	BABIP	WHIP	ERA	DRA-	WARP	MPH	FB%	Whiff%	CSP
2021	HIL	A+	23	4	1	0	8	8	39^{1}	21	3	3.2	13.5	59	29.5%	.240	0.89	2.52	85	0.6				
2021	AMA	AA	23	3	3	0	14	14	77	66	13	3.0	12.2	104	38.0%	.312	1.19	3.51	89	0.9				
2022	RNO	AAA	24	10	5	0	26	26	136	142	25	3.1	8.5	128	36.0%	.301	1.39	5.43	108	0.1	93.5	62.4%	23.6%	
2022	AZ	MLB	24	1	1	0	3	3	18^{1}	9	2	2.9	7.9	16	25.5%	.156	0.82	1.47	104	0.1	94.5	69.6%	23.6%	60.9%
2023 DC	*AZ*	*MLB*	*25*	*3*	*4*	*0*	*14*	*14*	*65.3*	*65*	*10*	*3.6*	*8.6*	*62*	*35.2%*	*.301*	*1.40*	*4.57*	*113*	*0.1*	*94.5*	*69.6%*	*24.3%*	*60.9%*

Comparables: Joe Ryan (74), Zach Plesac (68), A.J. Griffin (67)

Nelson spent the 2022 season piling up innings at Triple-A and throwing lots of fastballs, which runs counterintuitive to today's starting pitchers but might still work for him. He registered three encouraging big-league starts in which he threw just over 18 innings with mid-90s velocity before inflammation in his right scapula shut him down for the year. That fastball might not look special in terms of velocity, often sitting around 94 mph, but it has almost pure backspin and can be deadly up in the zone. He sprinkled in an even amount of sliders and curves, but it wasn't enough to see if he'll have the stuff to stick in the rotation. If he does, his methodical but reliable delivery helps him retain the command to find success there.

★ ★ ★ *2023 Top 101 Prospect* **#83** ★ ★ ★

Brandon Pfaadt RHP Born: 10/15/98 Age: 24 Bats: R Throws: R Height: 6'4" Weight: 220 lb. Origin: Round 5, 2020 Draft (#149 overall)

YEAR	TEAM	LVL	AGE	W	L	SV	G	GS	IP	H	HR	BB/9	K/9	K	GB%	BABIP	WHIP	ERA	DRA-	WARP	MPH	FB%	Whiff%	CSP
2021	VIS	A	22	2	2	0	7	7	40^{1}	29	5	1.6	12.7	57	40.0%	.267	0.89	3.12	94	0.4				
2021	HIL	A+	22	5	4	0	9	9	58	39	5	2.2	10.4	67	39.9%	.246	0.91	2.48	100	0.5				
2021	AMA	AA	22	1	1	0	6	6	33^{1}	37	12	1.9	9.7	36	30.6%	.291	1.32	4.59	99	0.2				
2022	AMA	AA	23	6	6	0	19	19	105^{1}	113	19	1.6	12.3	144	34.9%	.372	1.25	4.53	68	2.5				
2022	RNO	AAA	23	5	1	0	10	10	61^{2}	47	9	2.0	10.8	74	29.8%	.270	0.99	2.63	102	0.3	93.7	54.2%	33.5%	
2023 DC	*AZ*	*MLB*	*24*	*0*	*0*	*0*	*3*	*3*	*13.3*	*13*	*2*	*2.4*	*9.4*	*14*	*35.7%*	*.297*	*1.23*	*4.05*	*104*	*0.1*			*28.8%*	

Comparables: Matt Bowman (73), Erik Johnson (72), Nick Nelson (71)

Pfaadt pitched at both levels of the upper minors in 2022 and arguably looked better than he did when he was nasty at the lower levels in 2021, striking out more batters while walking fewer. He garnered at least 10 strikeouts five times, all in the second half of the season. A high set with his arms from the windup allows for a whippy arm motion to the plate that hides the ball well and creates good plane on his offerings. He leans on his running low- to mid-90s fastball, a sweeping slider and an average change, and can control the entire arsenal. He hasn't quite captured can-do dad energy with cut-off dungarees, but if anyone sees him in some jorts this spring he might be trying to be the next Zac Gallen.

Caleb Smith LHP Born: 07/28/91 Age: 31 Bats: R Throws: L Height: 6'0" Weight: 207 lb. Origin: Round 14, 2013 Draft (#434 overall)

YEAR	TEAM	LVL	AGE	W	L	SV	G	GS	IP	H	HR	BB/9	K/9	K	GB%	BABIP	WHIP	ERA	DRA-	WARP	MPH	FB%	Whiff%	CSP
2020	MIA	MLB	28	0	0	0	1	1	3	1	1	18.0	9.0	3	0.0%	.000	2.33	3.00	156	-0.1	92.7	54.3%	46.4%	36.3%
2020	AZ	MLB	28	0	0	0	4	3	11	5	2	4.9	9.8	12	33.3%	.120	1.00	2.45	133	-0.1	91.8	50.3%	31.8%	46.7%
2021	AZ	MLB	29	4	9	0	45	13	113^{2}	93	20	5.0	9.8	124	27.5%	.256	1.37	4.83	102	1.0	91.5	48.1%	27.4%	54.4%
2022	RNO	AAA	30	1	0	0	4	0	9^{2}	8	1	0.9	7.4	8	32.0%	.292	0.93	0.93	99	0.1	90.4	36.2%	38.3%	
2022	AZ	MLB	30	1	3	0	44	1	70	57	14	5.0	8.4	65	29.9%	.236	1.37	4.11	122	-0.1	91.8	45.7%	28.8%	55.2%
2023 non-DC	*AZ*	*MLB*	*31*	*2*	*2*	*0*	*57*	*0*	*50*	*44*	*7*	*4.4*	*9.3*	*51*	*29.5%*	*.279*	*1.37*	*4.20*	*104*	*0.1*	*91.6*	*48.4%*	*28.7%*	*52.8%*

Comparables: Adam Warren (42), T.J. McFarland (42), Chris Rusin (41)

We're deep enough into Smith's career that we can say concerns about his ability to control the zone have manifested and are no longer hypothetical. The only major league season in which he had a single-digit walk rate happened three years ago and it was still worse than average. His fastball became far less intimidating in 2022, garnering fewer chases, fewer swinging strikes overall and leading to more free passes. It also overshadowed how batters had a hard time teeing up his slider and changeup. When your primary pitch is a stinker and you give up a lot of contact in the air, you're cooking up a bad time.

Blake Walston LHP Born: 06/28/01 Age: 22 Bats: L Throws: L Height: 6'5" Weight: 175 lb. Origin: Round 1, 2019 Draft (#26 overall)

YEAR	TEAM	LVL	AGE	W	L	SV	G	GS	IP	H	HR	BB/9	K/9	K	GB%	BABIP	WHIP	ERA	DRA-	WARP	MPH	FB%	Whiff%	CSP
2021	VIS	A	20	2	2	0	8	8	43^{1}	34	4	3.5	12.5	60	43.7%	.303	1.18	3.32	86	0.6				
2021	HIL	A+	20	2	3	0	11	11	52^{1}	52	12	2.8	9.8	57	36.8%	.288	1.30	4.13	120	-0.2				
2022	HIL	A+	21	1	0	0	4	4	17^{2}	13	0	3.6	13.8	27	48.7%	.333	1.13	2.55	81	0.3				
2022	AMA	AA	21	7	3	0	21	21	106^{1}	115	16	3.3	9.3	110	34.0%	.345	1.45	5.16	83	1.6				
2023 DC	*AZ*	*MLB*	*22*	*0*	*1*	*0*	*3*	*3*	*13*	*14*	*2*	*4.0*	*8.3*	*12*	*38.3%*	*.313*	*1.52*	*5.31*	*127*	*-0.1*			*24.0%*	

Comparables: Tyler Viza (80), Gabriel Ynoa (75), Domingo Robles (75)

Nearly the size of an Ent, Walston is still learning to control his limbs and the wind they weaponize when wielded at batters. He's getting there, though, as his fastball still puts in work despite having middling velocity. When the season finally came to an end he struck out more batters than average—about a quarter of them—and walked fewer than average. He allowed too many baserunners and still needs to grow (figuratively speaking), but has delivered enough on his projectability to be a solid overall prospect. He has a fallback option as a reliever with a sweeping slider that will be rough on lefties, but his changeup is good enough to inspire belief he can stick in the rotation.

Lineouts

Hitters

HITTER	POS	TEAM	LVL	AGE	PA	R	2B	3B	HR	RBI	BB	K	SB	CS	AVG/OBP/SLG	DRC+	BABIP	BRR	DRP	WARP
Blaze Alexander	SS	AMA	AA	23	363	48	17	3	17	54	33	92	10	6	.306/.388/.539	95	.383	-0.9	SS(70): 0.7, 2B(11): 0.4, 3B(8): -0.1	0.9
	SS	RNO	AAA	23	34	8	1	0	2	4	4	8	0	0	.259/.412/.519	101	.294	1.1	SS(6): 0.7, 2B(1): 1.5, 3B(1): -0.2	0.4
Ryan Bliss	SS	HIL	A+	22	484	68	19	3	10	37	43	118	31	12	.214/.298/.343	87	.268	0.7	SS(84): 4.0, 2B(24): 0.4	1.3
Gavin Conticello	3B	DIAR	ROK	19	146	17	7	2	2	19	15	47	3	1	.246/.329/.381		.363			
	3B	VIS	A	19	125	16	3	2	1	12	14	38	1	1	.210/.328/.305	84	.313	-1.5	3B(25): -0.0, 1B(7): -0.7	-0.1
Adrian Del Castillo	C	HIL	A+	22	324	30	17	2	7	30	31	70	5	0	.199/.287/.346	97	.237	-2.4	C(54): 11.6	1.8
Dominic Fletcher	OF	AMA	AA	24	142	28	6	2	7	34	13	25	4	2	.346/.408/.591	106	.385	0.5	RF(18): 1.4, CF(6): -1.1, LF(2): 0.2	0.7
	OF	RNO	AAA	24	449	70	29	8	5	38	42	88	5	6	.301/.368/.452	99	.369	-5.4	CF(74): 8.2, RF(21): 1.3, LF(4): 0.9	1.9
Jose Herrera	C	RNO	AAA	25	104	16	3	0	2	14	12	10	0	0	.341/.423/.440	124	.367	-0.5	C(22): -0.5	0.6
	C	AZ	MLB	25	124	9	2	0	0	5	9	34	0	0	.189/.250/.207	72	.273	-0.6	C(46): -0.3	-0.1
Caleb Roberts	C	HIL	A+	22	465	57	24	3	9	55	60	127	17	5	.234/.353/.380	106	.320	1.2	LF(30): 0.4, C(28): -6.4, 1B(22): 0.8	1.9
	C	AMA	AA	22	33	4	2	1	0	5	2	6	0	1	.323/.364/.452	98	.400	-2.2	C(5): -0.2, RF(3): 0.2, 1B(2): -0.3	-0.2
Ali Sánchez	C	MEM	AAA	25	123	15	5	0	4	12	13	29	1	0	.255/.333/.409	104	.312	-0.1	C(27): 3.5	0.6
	C	TOL	AAA	25	168	23	9	0	2	21	22	48	1	0	.268/.369/.373	87	.383	1.3	C(38): 3.9, 1B(4): -0.1	0.8
A.J. Vukovich	3B	HIL	A+	20	448	55	26	2	15	69	18	105	35	4	.274/.308/.450	113	.330	1.1	3B(76): -4.5, LF(10): -0.6, RF(10): 0.8	1.8
	3B	AMA	AA	20	45	6	0	0	2	9	1	13	1	0	.295/.311/.432	92	.379	-0.2	LF(7): -0.3, 3B(4): -1.1	0.0
Andy Yerzy	1B/C	AMA	AA	23	346	45	15	1	12	38	50	85	1	0	.220/.338/.402	88	.265	-1.6	1B(48): -3.5, C(31): 2.3, P(1): -0.0	0.2

Contrary to what one may think, **Blaze Alexander** is not the protagonist in a new young adult trilogy doing battle with a dystopian government via somehow charming acts of arson. He is instead a minor leaguer who popped big time at the upper levels. Similarly, though, he could become a heartthrob in short order. ⓫ The good news is **Ryan Bliss** made it to High-A last year. The less good news is he wasn't especially good with the bat, so he stayed there all season, waiting for his pull-side power to travel with him. ⓫ **Gavin Conticello** is a three-true-outcomes hitter who is yet to flash the most important outcome—homers—in the minors. He's some bacon short of a BLT. ⓫ A purported bat-first catcher, **Adrian Del Castillo** hasn't yet hit much in High-A ball. "Nothing-first catcher" doesn't have the same ring to it. ⓫ **Dominic Fletcher** appeared to be in line for major-league work, given both his résumé and the roster in front of him. Then the Diamondbacks went out and got both Lourdes Gurriel Jr. and Kyle Lewis, having remembered that his fancy numbers aren't all that fancy in the blast furnace that is the PCL. ⓫ **Jose Herrera**'s debut didn't look all that special. However, he did display his excellent eye at the plate, chasing pitches at a favorable rate (24.9%) comparable to established MLB veterans. He doesn't have power to make pitchers pay, but will get on base and can play sturdy defense. That's spicy for a backup catcher. ⓫ As a backstop with a knack for getting on base, **Caleb Roberts** has posted fine-for-a-catcher lines and teased a bit more when promoted to the high minors. ⓫ Just as Yadier Molina's time behind the plate for the Cardinals was coming to an end, his longtime backup **Ali Sánchez** was designated for assignment and claimed by the Tigers. While he didn't get to add to his major-league playing time, it may be of some consolation that he's unlikely to be stuck behind a catcher of such longevity again. ⓫ An impressive athlete with surprising speed for how strong he his, **A.J. Vukovich** is a hard contact merchant who strikes out often and is allergic to walks. As far as we know, the makers of Claritin haven't addressed that last part. ⓫ **Andy Yerzy** adjusted to Double-A in his second go-round, perhaps reigniting his chance to be a guy who hits well enough for a catcher.

Pitchers

PITCHER	TEAM	LVL	AGE	W	L	SV	G	GS	IP	H	HR	BB/9	K/9	K	GB%	BABIP	WHIP	ERA	DRA-	WARP	MPH	FB%	WHF	CSP
Luke Albright	HIL	A+	22	6	10	0	26	26	123	125	17	4.1	9.5	130	31.4%	.321	1.47	5.49	114	0.1				
J.B. Bukauskas	RNO	AAA	25	0	1	1	21	0	20^{1}	21	1	1.8	8.4	19	45.5%	.370	1.23	2.66	95	0.2	94.2	53.2%	28.3%	
Humberto Castellanos	AZ	MLB	24	3	2	0	11	9	44^{1}	50	7	2.4	6.5	32	33.6%	.312	1.40	5.68	125	-0.2	90.1	43.0%	17.8%	56.3%
Slade Cecconi	AMA	AA	23	7	6	0	26	25	129^{2}	139	22	2.2	8.8	127	38.5%	.313	1.32	4.37	81	2.1				
Sam Clay	ROC	AAA	29	1	2	0	21	0	20^{1}	22	2	3.1	8.9	20	63.5%	.328	1.43	3.10	96	0.3				
	SYR	AAA	29	4	1	0	19	0	22^{2}	22	1	4.0	9.9	25	66.1%	.368	1.41	3.97	89	0.4				
	NYM	MLB	29	0	0	0	1	0	1	1	0	9.0	18.0	2	100.0%	.333	2.00	0.00	87	0.0	93.3	64.0%	28.6%	59.0%
	WAS	MLB	29	0	0	0	6	0	4^{1}	3	1	6.2	6.2	3	76.9%	.182	1.38	10.38	96	0.1	91.6	77.3%	20.0%	56.0%
Hugh Fisher	HIL	A+	23	3	5	0	39	0	39^{1}	39	4	7.3	11.9	52	62.1%	.354	1.81	8.01	121	-0.1				
Luis Frías	RNO	AAA	24	3	2	0	27	3	47^{1}	44	6	4.9	14.1	74	38.7%	.362	1.48	3.99	75	1.0	96.4	54.1%	35.0%	
	AZ	MLB	24	1	1	0	15	0	17	23	1	9.0	7.4	14	41.4%	.386	2.35	10.59	128	-0.1	96.9	62.4%	23.6%	56.4%
Tyler Gilbert	RNO	AAA	28	4	4	0	11	10	44	55	11	4.9	5.3	26	29.7%	.306	1.80	7.57	157	-1.2	89.7	37.5%	19.6%	
	AZ	MLB	28	0	3	0	8	7	34^{1}	33	8	2.6	5.2	20	32.5%	.238	1.25	5.24	151	-0.6	89.6	40.4%	19.9%	57.1%
Conor Grammes	HIL	A+	24	1	1	0	12	0	18	14	2	6.5	16.5	33	44.1%	.375	1.50	8.50	78	0.4				
Ryan Hendrix	LOU	AAA	27	1	1	0	42	0	38^{2}	33	3	7.2	12.3	53	54.3%	.337	1.66	5.12	84	0.8				
	CIN	MLB	27	0	0	0	9	0	8^{1}	9	0	6.5	9.7	9	52.4%	.429	1.80	5.40	101	0.1	94.6	46.9%	39.3%	49.6%
Tyler Holton	RNO	AAA	26	5	0	1	24	2	44^{2}	39	5	3.4	8.7	43	39.8%	.291	1.25	4.43	92	0.5	89.2	63.8%	29.7%	
	AZ	MLB	26	0	0	0	10	0	9	8	1	2.0	6.0	6	30.0%	.241	1.11	3.00	112	0.0	90.0	52.8%	29.6%	53.7%
Keynan Middleton	RNO	AAA	28	2	0	1	17	0	17	8	1	3.7	12.7	24	45.7%	.206	0.88	2.12	77	0.3	95.9	54.8%	37.9%	
	AZ	MLB	28	1	2	0	18	0	17	16	5	1.6	7.9	15	26.0%	.250	1.12	5.29	109	0.1	94.9	50.4%	36.6%	60.2%
Kyle Nelson	AZ	MLB	25	2	1	0	43	1	37	26	1	3.4	7.3	30	39.4%	.243	1.08	2.19	98	0.4	91.8	36.3%	26.0%	50.6%
Chad Patrick	HIL	A+	23	3	0	0	6	6	28^{2}	26	1	3.1	9.4	30	32.9%	.313	1.26	3.77	108	0.1				
Scott Randall	HIL	A+	23	6	7	0	21	21	108^{1}	101	14	2.1	8.6	104	37.3%	.294	1.16	3.82	108	0.5				
Jake Rice	HIL	A+	24	3	0	1	11	0	14	8	0	3.9	13.5	21	40.7%	.296	1.00	2.57	86	0.2				
	AMA	AA	24	1	0	0	24	0	25	35	9	6.5	7.9	22	30.9%	.361	2.12	9.36	143	-0.5				
Jacob Steinmetz	DIAR	ROK	18	0	7	0	11	7	24	28	1	7.5	10.1	27	50.0%	.415	2.00	7.87						
Cole Sulser	MIA	MLB	32	1	4	2	39	0	34	39	6	4.2	10.1	38	40.0%	.375	1.62	5.29	97	0.4	92.0	49.6%	30.7%	56.0%
Edwin Uceta	RNO	AAA	24	6	1	0	28	5	50	35	9	5.4	12.6	70	37.6%	.260	1.30	4.86	78	0.9	93.0	54.1%	37.6%	
	AZ	MLB	24	0	0	0	10	0	17	14	2	3.7	6.9	13	44.2%	.240	1.24	5.82	108	0.1	93.4	55.5%	24.8%	49.6%
Carlos Vargas	AKR	AA	22	3	3	1	19	0	24^{1}	25	1	4.4	7.8	21	60.3%	.333	1.52	4.81	97	0.4				
	COL	AAA	22	1	0	0	8	0	10	8	1	4.5	14.4	16	65.0%	.368	1.30	0.90	75	0.2				
Taylor Widener	RNO	AAA	27	2	2	0	27	0	36^{2}	40	5	2.9	11.5	47	28.0%	.368	1.42	5.40	104	0.1	93.6	67.3%	25.9%	
	AZ	MLB	27	0	1	0	14	0	17^{1}	22	2	2.6	7.3	14	31.7%	.345	1.56	3.63	117	0.0	94.0	68.4%	20.1%	57.7%

His ERA will say otherwise, but **Luke Albright** made incremental improvements once he made it to High-A. He still has some way to go before he's lights out. ⚾ Sent to the minors in July after making it back from a shoulder injury, **J.B. Bukauskas** didn't throw a major-league pitch in 2022. The reliever was good when healthy, though, as evidenced by his career-best walk rate, and should get another chance to break into the big leagues. ⚾ As a control artist who walks hitters less than his peers and doesn't strike anyone out, **Humberto Castellanos** is hoping to revive the Carlos Silva lifestyle, at least when he's back from Tommy John Surgery. ⚾ **Slade Cecconi** is the classic equation: High-90s fastball + groovy slider + ?? = useful big-league arm. For now we're solving for the unknown, the known variables having been taken care of. ⚾ **Sam Clay** molded a 0.00 ERA with the Mets out of a single appearance in August. He'll probably have to take on any number of roles to prove himself worthy of more big-league time, but he's probably fairly malleable. ⚾ When last seen, **Stefan Crichton**'s velocity was fading from a Polaroid picture. Now out of options and sitting below 91 with his heater, he'll have a hard time generating the 1.21 gigawatts to come back and stay in the big-league picture. ⚾ Unfortunately, **Hugh Fisher** walks a ton of guys. Fortunately, he generates a ton of groundballs. He'll need more of the latter than the former to bait the organization into promoting him further. ⚾ **Luis Frías** has a fastball that looks nasty by the old wisdom—that is to say, it pushes the upper 90s—but it just doesn't miss many bats. His power breaker isn't good enough to offset that or the control issues that have plagued him as a professional. ⚾ If you search "**Tyler Gilbert**" on Twitter, you'll find a bunch of influencer-like videos of a woman that are captioned in a foreign language. Averaging 89 on a heater isn't a great recipe for the baseball Tyler Gilbert to become the more famous one. ⚾ **Conor Grammes** was a three-year, two-way guy for Xavier University who had big reliever stuff but command that would make Ricky Vaughn blush. He could move quickly now that he's recovered from Tommy John surgery. ⚾ It's tempting to make a Jimi reference, but organizational reliever **Ryan Hendrix** is more analogous to character actress Leslie, who plays the medical examiner in the *Law and Order* universe in that he makes a brief appearance at the beginning, to provide exposition. ⚾ Low-octane **Tyler Holton** comes armed with a changeup that falls with style and a loopy, effective curveball. His fastball is best compared to a limp handshake. Perhaps just wave to him. ⚾ **Keynan Middleton** has logged just over 85 major-league innings in the last five seasons. His walk rate was a career-best, but his fastball velocity sunk below 95 mph again and his ERA broke 5.00 for the second time in three years. ⚾ In his first extended performance at the big-league level, **Kyle Nelson** recorded sparkling surface-level stats. Head down to the basement, though, and you'll find a combination of strikeout, home run, and ground-ball rates that make for a very shaky foundation. ⚾ **Chad Patrick** had his least Chad season as a professional yet, but did it at the highest level he's seen yet and still flashed dreamy stuff. ⚾ With a tidy changeup, solid control and two first names, **Scott Randall** is able to keep walks down and stay in the game. ⚾ **Jake Rice** struggled to use his flat fastball and breaker combo in Double-A as effectively as he did in the low minors. It's not couscous for concern yet, though, but will be if the problems get bulgur. ⚾ **Landon Sims** maintained his nasty stuff when transitioning to the rotation in college, if not his velocity, racking up 27 Ks in 15⅔ innings before needing Tommy John. He'll need to attack rehab like he did batters but the first-round pick showcased a dynamic fastball/slider combo and a high-effort delivery when healthy. ⚾ **Jacob Steinmetz** walked more than a retiree who's taken up residence near the boardwalk and enjoys beating the crowds in the morning. He also flashed stuff that could compete with deep fried oreos for a delightful snack. Getting consistent control of his levers would prove a wild ride. ⚾ If **Cole Sulser** can make a pattern out of being traded, put on waivers following that season and then posting the best season of his career after getting picked up, this is going to look like a great acquisition for the D'Backs in 2024. ⚾ **Edwin Uceta** has gone from possible starter to probable reliever but currently leans too heavily on a fastball that's far too hittable (57% fly balls), and not enough on his changeup and slider, which each generate grounders at elite levels. ⚾ **Carlos Vargas** is a prototypical live-armed relief prospect, with triple-digit heat, a sharp-breaking slider and questionable control, plus Tommy John on his résumé. ⚾ In a year when the D'Backs went through more relievers than Joseph Smith had wives, they elected not to give **Taylor Widener** much of a shot in the bullpen. Perhaps that, and the 22 hits accumulated against by just 82 big-league opponents, says more about him than his serviceable ERA.

COLORADO ROCKIES

Essay by Sam Miller

Player comments by Jon Tayler and BP staff

> *But the great fact was the land itself, which seemed to overwhelm the little beginnings of human society that struggled in its sombre wastes. It was from facing this vast hardness that the boy's mouth had become so bitter; because he felt that men were too weak to make any mark here.*
> *—Willa Cather, O Pioneers!*

To talk about the Rockies, let's talk about the Astros.

In June 1969, at the close of the Astros' first calendar decade as a baseball franchise, a sportswriter wrote a column with this headline: "Expansion Astros Gain Maturity." Houston finished the year 81-81, their first season without a losing record.

In June 1979, at the close of the Astros' *second* decade, the Associated Press wrote a column with this headline: "Expansion Astros Charge In Front Of Longtime N.L. Powers." Those Astros would falter in September but finish in second place—their highest finish ever—with 89 wins, a new franchise best.

In the 1980s, they made the playoffs for the first time. In the 1990s, they won 52% of their games, which is still their winningest decade as a franchise. In the 2000s, they made the World Series for the first time. In the 2010s, they won it for the first time. In 2022, of course, they won it again, behind one of the half-dozen best pitching staffs in American League history.

These are the questions: When, precisely, did Houston stop being an expansion team? And when will the Rockies?

⚾ ⚾ ⚾

In 1987, Colorado Senator Tim Wirth organized a congressional task force to encourage MLB to add new teams. The implied threat was that if the league wouldn't expand, it would face a Senatorial challenge to its anti-trust exemption. "For years, it has been argued that expansion will not take place until major-league baseball is forced into it," a wire report explained. Wirth and his state ended up with their team, as did Florida Senator Connie Mack III, who had been another active lobbyist for expansion.

COLORADO ROCKIES PROSPECTUS

2022 W-L: 68-94, 5TH IN NL WEST

Pythag	.394	24th	DER	.679	28th
RS/G	4.31	16th	DRC+	97	17th
RA/G	5.39	30th	DRA-	114	29th
dWin%	.432	27th	FIP	4.39	26th
Payroll	$131M	20th	B-Age	29.7	22nd
M$/MW	$5.7M	24th	P-Age	29.2	14th

415′ 390′ 375′ 347′ 350′

- Opened 1995
- Open air
- Natural surface
- Fence profile: 8′ to 16′6″

Park Factors

Runs	Runs/RH	Runs/LH	HR/RH	HR/LH
105	105	105	104	107

Top Hitter WARP	3.0 Brendan Rodgers
Top Pitcher WARP	1.4 Daniel Bard
2023 Top Prospect	Ezequiel Tovar

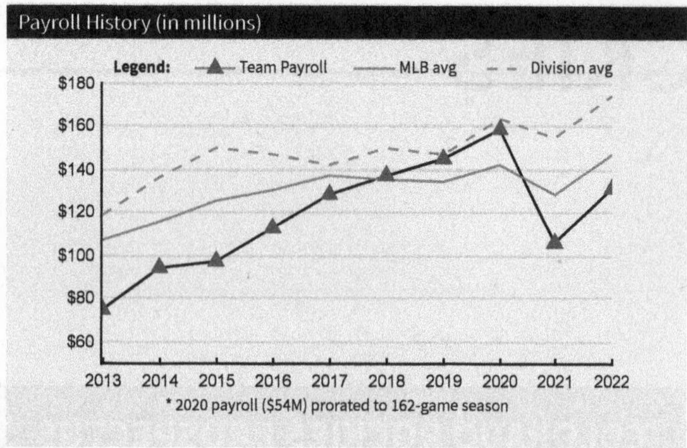

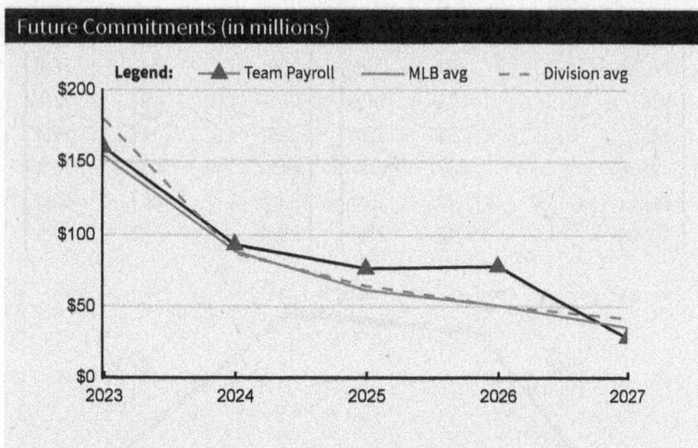

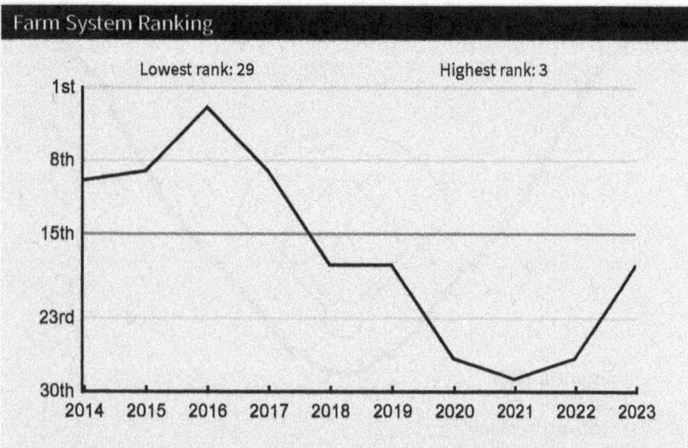

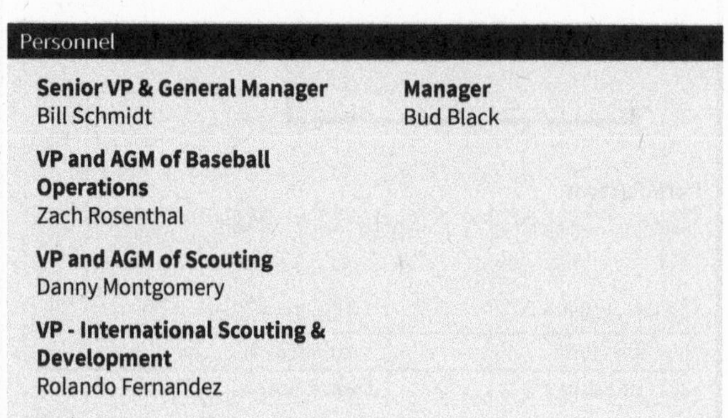
Personnel

Senior VP & General Manager
Bill Schmidt

Manager
Bud Black

VP and AGM of Baseball Operations
Zach Rosenthal

VP and AGM of Scouting
Danny Montgomery

VP - International Scouting & Development
Rolando Fernandez

In the 30 years since, neither the Rockies or the Marlins have won a division title (though the Marlins have won two World Series as Wild Card entries). Neither team has won more than 92 games in a season. Both teams are, in their history, hundreds of games under .500: 374 games below square for Miami, 294 for Colorado.

An underrated aspect of modern baseball is how long the stink of expansion takes to wear off. To get back to the Astros: On September 12 last year, behind a grand slam by Alex Bregman, the Astros beat the Angels 12-4. That moved Houston's all-time record to 4,815-4,814. They were, finally, over .500.

Which is mildly interesting, but what's more interesting is that they're the only expansion team over .500. Fourteen teams, all extant for at least 26 seasons and as long as 62 seasons, and every single one of them had been a historical loser until September 12, 2022.

I first heard that fun fact in 2011, when Chris Jaffe wrote about it for *The Hardball Times*. Expansion teams lose a lot early on, go into win-debt and take a long time to win enough games to get back to even, fine. But in the 12 seasons since Jaffe's article, the 14 non-original teams are collectively 522 games under .500. These expansion teams are all ancient by now. Four of them pre-date Ringo Starr joining the Beatles and James Bond on the big screen and Roger Angell writing about ball. How could they *still* be disadvantaged?

Now, spread among 14 teams over a dozen seasons, 522 games is not a huge deficit. On average, expansion teams since the Jaffe article have won about 79.5 games per season, while original teams have won about 82.3—much less than the effect of home-field advantage, for example.

But those extra few wins seem to make a big difference on the margins. Since 1998, expansion teams have represented 47% of the league's teams. During that time, non-expansion teams have averaged twice as many playoff appearances as expansion teams, winning 71% of division titles and 18 of the 25 World Series.

⚾ ⚾ ⚾

But being an expansion team is not one experience, it's two.

We can see this when we look at the 14 expansion teams' performance by age (i.e. in their first year, second year, third year). When big-league teams are one year old, they've collectively won about 38% of their games. At 62 years old, they've collectively won 44% of games—but that's just the 2022 Angels and the 2022 Rangers (who were born in 1961 as the second Washington Senators), so it's not all that definitive.

In five-year blocks, we can see the progression a bit more convincingly:

Years	W-L%
1-5	.423
6-10	.468
11-20	.495
21-30	.494
31-40	.478
41-62	.498

Or:

Years	W-L%
1-7	.435
8-62	.492

The bulk of the win debt comes early, and that phase lasts for close to a decade, as non-incumbent teams struggle under a number of structural disadvantages. They lack farm depth built up over several years, they often inherit uninviting multi-use stadiums, they lose a lot of games—and are thus less appealing to free agents—and they have yet to cultivate durable, generational fanbases. That's the first phase of being a franchise team.

After seven to 10 years, the gap between old teams and "new" teams shrinks down to a very small difference—but, crucially, still a difference. This tells us something else: There are persistent disadvantages these franchises face long, long, long, long, long after the first waves of personnel have turned over. The disadvantage typically comes down to one of two geographical quandaries: 1) There's some reason big-league baseball hadn't been played (or hadn't stuck) in that city before, or 2) There was already a baseball team playing there.

So, for example, Seattle has to travel farther than everybody else—a small disadvantage that persists. Toronto has the inconvenience of being in a different country than everybody else. Washington has the not-actually-local locals problem. Milwaukee and Kansas City have small metro areas that had previously been abandoned by other teams. And almost every expansion team has, for a while, the mile-wide, inch-deep problem with their fans: Nobody who controls a credit card grew up with the team. There's no mythology to market around. It takes 20 years before even a marginal old-timers game can be staged.

Many of these disadvantages shrink over time. Houston's first park (built atop an oily swamp) had a legendary mosquito problem, but eventually they replaced the swamp stadium and the mosquitos became just a part of the lore. The Diamondbacks were born in a small market, but Metro Phoenix's population has nearly doubled since 1997, and the Diamondbacks have moved from small market to medium-big without having to pack. Over their first 45 seasons, the Rangers had cumulative winning records in April and May and June but losing records through the brutally hot September and August and (especially) July months, a seemingly unsolvable climate problem. Then they finally built a dome.

So the trajectory of an expansion team is this: First, you're an "expansion team" in the sense that the league charges you a ton of money up front to field a team that has very few good players and no depth and you have to fight hard for every fan and the stadium is primarily used for rodeos or whatever. Then, the years pass, you build your farm system, you replace your swamp park, you figure out what you're doing—and then you're an "expansion team" in the sense that you have to play in a city that was the 15th- or 20th- or 25th-best option for placing a baseball team. This disadvantage shrinks until it's only a trickle, you hope.

The Mets and Angels—playing in the market shadow of the most popular and valuable franchises in the sport—are still expansion teams, but only faintly. The Astros and Rangers (née Senators) probably aren't.

⚾ ⚾ ⚾

The Rockies are obviously way past the phase of expansion in which David Nied was their Opening Day starter, they had two fewer minor-league affiliates than anybody else and every one of those affiliates had a losing record. But they're still stuck in a place where winning baseball seems close to untenable. Thanks to the altitude in Denver, the club starts every year with disadvantages, which can be summed up like this:

- It's hard to develop young pitching in such a hostile environment;
- It's hard to attract established pitchers to such a hostile environment;
- The cumulative effect of this hostile environment means Colorado needs more pitchers than the average team, because their pitchers throw more high-stress pitches and in a more physically depleting environment;
- The hangover effect of altitude wrecks Colorado hitters on the road, so that the offense becomes basically hopeless when it leaves its home park. The Rockies have been an above-average road offense... once. In 1997.

A further complication: Altitude has not, to understate things, been neutralized. While the first few years of the humidor (in the mid-aughts) were somewhat successful at bringing the Rockies' home/road splits back to earth, that hasn't been the case lately. In 2022, their tOPS+ at home—which measures one split against the non-split numbers—was 125, the 11th-highest in the franchise's 30 seasons.

If playing in an extreme ballpark is the Rockies' main disadvantage, this year's rule changes seem designed to make things worse. Limiting pickoff attempts and expanding the size of the bases will make baserunners more dangerous; Rockies pitchers regularly face the most batters with runners on base. (They're fourth in the NL in pickoff attempts since 2017.) Imposing pitch clocks will force pitchers to work more quickly; pitchers at altitude are already prone to fatigue because of the thin air. (Rockies pitchers have the third-slowest pace among NL pitchers since 2010.) Banning the shift will make balls put in play more productive; the Rockies' pitchers have the NL's lowest strikeout rate in three of the past four seasons, and thus typically allow the most balls in play.

⚾ ⚾ ⚾

On the other hand, the Rockies shifted less than any team in baseball last year, which isn't necessarily a bad thing—there are cases to be made for and against any strategy. But when an approach is apparently so effective that *the league bans it*, it's probably not the place to be counterintuitive.

This is not a franchise that looks poised to discover any secret formulas. Their analytics department was depleted to one person after the pandemic season, according to *The Athletic*'s Nick Groke, and the Research & Development director they recruited in late 2021 lasted only five months in the job. (It took five more months to replace him with an in-house promotion.) I'm willing to believe Bud Black is great at a thousand managerial things. But he's 15 years into his career, he's never finished first and he's won one postseason game. Change won't start internally.

It's always been tempting to think that the Rockies' way out of this phase of expansion would be finding the One Neat Trick, and at this point we've seen the franchise try about 30 neat tricks that failed. Black is the personification of the latest gambit, which we might call Strength In Stability. The Rockies' nine projected starting position players and top five starting pitchers this year will be playing, on average, their fifth season with the club. (In the NL West, only the Dodgers can compare.) And extensions, not acquisitions, have been the front office's priority. Since the end of the 2021 season, the Rockies have agreed to long extensions with Antonio Senzatela, which will keep him in purple through his 10th big-league season; Kyle Freeland, through his 10th; and Ryan McMahon, through his 11th. They also extended Elias Díaz, a 31-year-old catcher with 3.9 career WARP, for three years; in July they extended their 37-year-old closer, Daniel Bard, for two years. There's a logic here: If the terrain is brutal and you find a crop that won't immediately wilt, you'll keep trying that crop. But not wilting isn't the same as flourishing, and the Rockies have merely locked in the league's most stable 70-some-win team.

In 2017, when the Rockies were still trying the High-Spin Relievers neat trick and the Stockpile Pitching Prospects neat trick and Black was their brand-new manager, *Sports Illustrated*'s Albert Chen went to Colorado to talk to the people who'd tried to win there. He came away with a fatalistic conclusion: "This much is clear: If there's a solution to the greatest puzzle in baseball, the Rockies now understand, it's simply being better—better at drafting players, better at developing them; better at finding cheap, undervalued pitchers; better at staying strong and healthy."

But that's not a strategy, it's a tautology. Everybody is trying to do that. The Rockies might do it, and if they do, you probably won't even notice. Being better probably gets them to 83 wins in a good year. To 92 in the best one.

—Sam Miller is a former Editor-in-Chief of Baseball Prospectus.

HITTERS

★ ★ ★ *2023 Top 101 Prospect* **#44** ★ ★ ★

Adael Amador SS Born: 04/11/03 Age: 20 Bats: S Throws: R Height: 6'0" Weight: 160 lb. Origin: International Free Agent, 2019

YEAR	TEAM	LVL	AGE	PA	R	2B	3B	HR	RBI	BB	K	SB	CS	Whiff%	AVG/OBP/SLG	DRC+	BABIP	BRR	DRP	WARP
2021	RCK	ROK	18	200	41	10	1	4	24	27	29	10	7		.299/.394/.445		.331			
2022	FRE	A	19	555	100	24	0	15	57	87	67	26	12		.292/.415/.445	122	.312	4.3	SS(108): -4.8, 2B(7): -1.4	3.1
2023 non-DC	*COL*	*MLB*	*20*	*251*	*22*	*9*	*0*	*3*	*21*	*23*	*41*	*7*	*4*	*20.5%*	*.224/.304/.318*	*78*	*.261*	*-2.0*	*2B 0, SS 0*	*-0.2*

Comparables: Daniel Robertson (87), Brad Harman (85), Jake Hager (84)

Ezequiel Tovar is the presumptive shortstop of the future in Colorado, but should he stumble, Rockies fans can hope for Amador to take his place. The 19-year-old followed up a solid rookie season in Arizona with an equally strong year with Low-A Fresno, showing an advanced feel for hitting from both sides of the plate and a terrific eye to go with it. Power will never be his strength, though he's added muscle since being signed, and his baserunning is a work in progress. The tools are all there, though, for an above-average middle infielder or, at the low end, a valuable utility player whose contact-heavy approach would work well in Colorado's thin air.

Jordan Beck OF Born: 04/19/01 Age: 22 Bats: R Throws: R Height: 6'3" Weight: 225 lb. Origin: Round 1, 2022 Draft (#38 overall)

YEAR	TEAM	LVL	AGE	PA	R	2B	3B	HR	RBI	BB	K	SB	CS	Whiff%	AVG/OBP/SLG	DRC+	BABIP	BRR	DRP	WARP
2022	RCK	ROK	21	57	9	5	0	1	10	8	11	0	0		.306/.404/.469		.378			
2022	FRE	A	21	52	11	2	0	2	9	13	9	0	0		.282/.462/.487	119	.321	0.6	RF(6): 0.4, LF(3): 1.1	0.4
2023 non-DC	*COL*	*MLB*	*22*	*251*	*21*	*9*	*1*	*3*	*21*	*26*	*77*	*0*	*0*	*33.7%*	*.200/.290/.306*	*67*	*.289*	*1.4*	*LF 0, RF 0*	*-0.4*

Comparables: Mark Zagunis (86), Matt Joyce (81), Pedro Gonzalez (81)

If you could design a prototypical right fielder you'd probably end up with a player who looks like Beck. The former Volunteer brings above-average power, good speed and a plus arm to the table. While he needs to work on making contact, he didn't struggle in short stints in either the Rookie League or Low-A. His first real challenge will come next year in High-A, which will mark Beck's first exposure to older and better competition. If he can handle that assignment the road to Coors Field could be a short one. Then again this is a Beck we're talking about, so perhaps he'll head to Red Rocks instead.

Warming Bernabel 3B

Born: 06/06/02 Age: 21 Bats: R Throws: R Height: 6'0" Weight: 180 lb. Origin: International Free Agent, 2018

YEAR	TEAM	LVL	AGE	PA	R	2B	3B	HR	RBI	BB	K	SB	CS	Whiff%	AVG/OBP/SLG	DRC+	BABIP	BRR	DRP	WARP
2021	RCK	ROK	19	86	18	5	0	6	31	5	12	5	1		.432/.453/.743		.426			
2021	FRE	A	19	94	9	6	0	1	7	7	14	4	1		.205/.287/.313	111	.232	-0.9	3B(17): 0.6	0.4
2022	FRE	A	20	300	52	19	0	10	54	29	39	21	6		.317/.390/.504	127	.336	-1.1	3B(64): 1.8	2.1
2022	SPO	A+	20	109	18	7	0	4	17	2	17	2	2		.305/.315/.486	114	.329	0.1	3B(25): -0.7	0.4
2023 non-DC	*COL*	*MLB*	*21*	*251*	*21*	*11*	*0*	*4*	*23*	*13*	*49*	*7*	*4*	*25.1%*	*.238/.285/.350*	*75*	*.284*	*-3.0*	*3B 0*	*-0.6*

Comparables: Juan Silverio (69), Aderlin Rodríguez (67), Dustin Geiger (63)

Bernabel's prospect stock cooled slightly after a blazing run on the backfields in Arizona turned into a frosty stay in Fresno. But the lanky third baseman heated back up in 2022, torching Low-A pitching before holding his own against tougher, older competition in High-A Spokane. An aggressive hitter, Bernabel balances his propensity to hack with a gorgeous, textbook swing that produces good contact on the regular, and his power has begun to bloom. How well his approach holds up as he climbs the ladder will largely determine whether he continues to rise on prospect lists or freezes in place.

Charlie Blackmon DH/RF

Born: 07/01/86 Age: 37 Bats: L Throws: L Height: 6'3" Weight: 221 lb. Origin: Round 2, 2008 Draft (#72 overall)

YEAR	TEAM	LVL	AGE	PA	R	2B	3B	HR	RBI	BB	K	SB	CS	Whiff%	AVG/OBP/SLG	DRC+	BABIP	BRR	DRP	WARP
2020	COL	MLB	33	247	31	12	1	6	42	19	44	2	1	23.5%	.303/.356/.448	99	.347	0.4	RF(50): 2.9	1.0
2021	COL	MLB	34	582	76	25	4	13	78	54	91	3	0	20.4%	.270/.351/.411	103	.305	-0.6	RF(137): 7.3	2.6
2022	COL	MLB	35	577	60	22	6	16	78	32	109	4	1	21.5%	.264/.314/.419	97	.304	0.7	RF(51): -1.1	1.2
2023 DC	*COL*	*MLB*	*36*	*533*	*64*	*23*	*5*	*16*	*58*	*35*	*97*	*4*	*1*	*21.4%*	*.271/.333/.442*	*111*	*.313*	*5.9*	*RF 0*	*2.2*

Comparables: Paul Waner (73), Ken Griffey (71), Jerry Lynch (71)

Blackmon's gradual decline continued apace, with the hirsute veteran recording his third straight season of roughly league-average production. A drop in walk rate and uptick in strikeouts undermined his 2022 efforts, and even his drug of choice—the stat-boosting hitters' haven that is Coors Field—could only do so much. He was once again a no-show on the road, hitting .241/.288/.376 away from Colorado. What offensive value he does provide is limited to the occasional line drive or mistake pitch he drives into the right field seats; most of what he puts in play is softly struck and on the ground. Set to turn 37 in July, at a point where pitchers throw fastballs by him with impunity and no longer a regular outfielder, Blackmon is likely looking at his last year as a major leaguer. Here's hoping he can turn back the clock long enough to give the fans of the only team he's ever known a happy farewell.

Sean Bouchard LF

Born: 05/16/96 Age: 27 Bats: R Throws: R Height: 6'3" Weight: 215 lb. Origin: Round 9, 2017 Draft (#266 overall)

YEAR	TEAM	LVL	AGE	PA	R	2B	3B	HR	RBI	BB	K	SB	CS	Whiff%	AVG/OBP/SLG	DRC+	BABIP	BRR	DRP	WARP
2021	HFD	AA	25	381	58	30	3	14	46	33	101	8	4		.266/.336/.494	104	.336	0.1	LF(37): 0.3, 1B(25): 2.0, 3B(9): -1.3	1.4
2022	ABQ	AAA	26	312	61	15	6	20	56	44	70	12	2	28.7%	.300/.404/.635	120	.333	0.7	LF(25): -0.2, 1B(21): 0.4, RF(18): 0.7	1.9
2022	COL	MLB	26	97	9	6	0	3	11	21	25	0	0	27.8%	.297/.454/.500	117	.404	-0.8	LF(26): -1.5	0.3
2023 DC	*COL*	*MLB*	*27*	*188*	*21*	*9*	*1*	*5*	*19*	*21*	*51*	*4*	*1*	*29.1%*	*.230/.330/.414*	*103*	*.303*	*2.0*	*LF 0, RF 0*	*0.7*

Comparables: Scott Van Slyke (68), Tommy Pham (64), J.D. Martinez (64)

If you were unfamiliar with Bouchard before he popped up on the Rockies' roster in June, that's understandable. The UCLA product hasn't been a presence on prospect lists, and his name had never earned a mention in these pages. But an impressive final month of the season helped him emerge from anonymity. He carried over a spike in walk rate at Triple-A to the majors, where he routinely spat on outside pitches—his 19.8% chase rate was 10 points better than the league average. What's more, he showed improving power as he climbed the minor-league ladder. The sky-high BABIP that partially fueled his success is unlikely to hold, but his patience and developing pop should help Bouchard in the roster battles to come.

Kris Bryant LF

Born: 01/04/92 Age: 31 Bats: R Throws: R Height: 6'5" Weight: 230 lb. Origin: Round 1, 2013 Draft (#2 overall)

YEAR	TEAM	LVL	AGE	PA	R	2B	3B	HR	RBI	BB	K	SB	CS	Whiff%	AVG/OBP/SLG	DRC+	BABIP	BRR	DRP	WARP
2020	CHC	MLB	28	147	20	5	1	4	11	12	40	0	0	29.5%	.206/.293/.351	94	.264	0.3	3B(27): 0.6, LF(4): 1, 1B(1): 0	0.5
2021	CHC	MLB	29	374	58	19	2	18	51	39	89	4	2	27.4%	.267/.358/.503	113	.314	0.4	3B(29): -0.1, LF(29): -0.3, RF(28): -1.4	1.7
2021	SF	MLB	29	212	28	13	0	7	22	23	46	6	0	29.0%	.262/.344/.444	106	.311	2.3	3B(26): 0.1, LF(19): 0.7, RF(11): 0.5	1.2
2022	COL	MLB	30	181	28	12	0	5	14	17	27	0	0	21.5%	.306/.376/.475	122	.338	1.4	LF(30): -0.9	1.1
2023 DC	*COL*	*MLB*	*31*	*577*	*77*	*29*	*1*	*20*	*60*	*56*	*114*	*3*	*1*	*24.9%*	*.268/.355/.452*	*123*	*.314*	*1.0*	*LF -1*	*2.9*

Comparables: David Wright (82), Chipper Jones (80), Evan Longoria (80)

Bryant isn't someone you'd call relatable, what with his World Series ring, Bobby Sherman good looks and the hundreds of millions of dollars in his bank account. But 2022 showed him to be just like regular folks in that his back gave out on him the second he turned 30. Lower back soreness cost Bryant most of May and June, and a bout of plantar fasciitis knocked him out for the season at the end of July. Amid those maladies he produced as you'd expect, his offensive numbers a near carbon copy of 2021. Unfortunately, so were his defensive metrics, with all the advanced stats grading the small sample of his work in left field—his full-time home now—anywhere from below average to flat-out awful. The Rockies didn't try Bryant anywhere else, eschewing the versatility that made him valuable in Chicago. Defense aside, Colorado presumably would be happy with their marquee addition simply staying healthy enough to stand in the box four times a game for six straight months. Hopefully he spends the offseason getting right and coming to terms with what all 30-somethings must: rest, recovery and stretching are *very* important.

C.J. Cron 1B Born: 01/05/90 Age: 33 Bats: R Throws: R Height: 6'4" Weight: 235 lb. Origin: Round 1, 2011 Draft (#17 overall)

YEAR	TEAM	LVL	AGE	PA	R	2B	3B	HR	RBI	BB	K	SB	CS	Whiff%	AVG/OBP/SLG	DRC+	BABIP	BRR	DRP	WARP
2020	DET	MLB	30	52	9	3	0	4	8	9	16	0	0	31.3%	.190/.346/.548	105	.182	-0.1	1B(13): 0	0.1
2021	COL	MLB	31	547	70	31	1	28	92	60	117	1	0	27.5%	.281/.375/.530	127	.316	-1.6	1B(130): 0.3	2.9
2022	COL	MLB	32	632	79	28	3	29	102	43	164	0	0	24.3%	.257/.315/.468	109	.307	-0.4	1B(121): 0.2	2.0
2023 DC	*COL*	*MLB*	*33*	*582*	*70*	*27*	*1*	*27*	*78*	*46*	*125*	*0*	*0*	*24.6%*	*.252/.327/.463*	*115*	*.286*	*-0.2*	*1B 0*	*1.9*

Comparables: Greg Colbrunn (83), Paul Konerko (82), Gil Hodges (79)

Through the first three-plus months of the season Cron continued to look like one of the smartest signings in Rockies history. Building on the excellent 2021 that earned him a two-year extension, he hit .298/.350/.552 with 21 homers in the first half and made the All-Star team for the first time. But the Cron who went to Los Angeles never came back: Instead, the pod person who replaced him hit a miserable .197/.263/.341 with just eight homers after the break. Maybe getting plunked on the left wrist the week before the Midsummer Classic had something to do with his downturn, or maybe the corned beef and cabbage at Musso & Frank just didn't sit right. Whatever the reason, it has to be concerning for the Rockies that one of the core pieces of their lineup—one who turned 33 in January and who seems to have at least one foot over the cliff's edge—is coming off such a dismal stretch. As Cron eyes free agency next winter, it's got to be concerning for him personally, too.

Yonathan Daza CF Born: 02/28/94 Age: 29 Bats: R Throws: R Height: 6'2" Weight: 207 lb. Origin: International Free Agent, 2010

YEAR	TEAM	LVL	AGE	PA	R	2B	3B	HR	RBI	BB	K	SB	CS	Whiff%	AVG/OBP/SLG	DRC+	BABIP	BRR	DRP	WARP
2021	ABQ	AAA	27	26	4	0	0	0	2	0	4	1	0		.308/.308/.308	96	.364	-0.5	CF(4): -0.1, LF(1): -0.1, RF(1): -0.3	0.0
2021	COL	MLB	27	331	26	12	2	2	30	21	60	2	1	19.9%	.282/.332/.355	90	.346	0.2	CF(57): -2.1, RF(22): 1.3, LF(12): 0.2	0.9
2022	COL	MLB	28	408	56	21	2	2	34	26	58	0	3	18.8%	.301/.349/.384	106	.347	1.1	CF(92): -6.5, LF(27): 0.7	1.3
2023 DC	*COL*	*MLB*	*29*	*442*	*47*	*20*	*2*	*4*	*35*	*28*	*65*	*4*	*1*	*19.0%*	*.282/.336/.376*	*99*	*.331*	*2.3*	*CF -7, LF 0*	*0.7*

Comparables: Adam Engel (59), Craig Gentry (53), Endy Chavez (52)

Given ample playing time despite his subpar work at the plate and woeful numbers in the field, Daza was at least able to improve on the former, going from below league-average offensively to just over it. He can thank an inflated BABIP for that: There's no power to speak of here, and Daza's walk rate and overall selectivity barely budged from 2021. On top of that, advanced metrics continued to cast shade on his defense—among fancy defensive stats only FRAA had him finishing in the black, and not by much. As such, it's hard to understand how he finished the season as the Rockies' leader in games played in center, though the fact that Randal Grichuk is second on that list may explain it somewhat. Daza is better suited to be a fourth or fifth outfielder than a starter, and a team that's trying to contend may be better off replacing him altogether.

Elias Díaz C Born: 11/17/90 Age: 32 Bats: R Throws: R Height: 6'1" Weight: 223 lb. Origin: International Free Agent, 2008

YEAR	TEAM	LVL	AGE	PA	R	2B	3B	HR	RBI	BB	K	SB	CS	Whiff%	AVG/OBP/SLG	DRC+	BABIP	BRR	DRP	WARP
2020	COL	MLB	29	73	4	2	0	2	9	5	15	0	0	27.9%	.235/.288/.353	97	.275	-0.1	C(24): 0.5	0.3
2021	COL	MLB	30	371	52	18	1	18	44	30	60	0	0	24.1%	.246/.310/.464	115	.249	-1.8	C(98): 6.1	2.7
2022	COL	MLB	31	381	29	18	2	9	51	25	82	0	1	22.7%	.228/.281/.368	90	.270	-2.4	C(104): -8.9	-0.3
2023 DC	*COL*	*MLB*	*32*	*412*	*43*	*18*	*1*	*12*	*44*	*29*	*75*	*0*	*0*	*23.0%*	*.242/.302/.397*	*91*	*.273*	*-1.6*	*C -8*	*0.0*

Comparables: Travis d'Arnaud (62), Sandy Leon (58), Ramon Hernandez (57)

YEAR	TEAM	P. COUNT	FRM RUNS	BLK RUNS	THRW RUNS	TOT RUNS
2020	COL	2173	0.5	0.0	0.0	0.5
2021	COL	12793	1.0	-0.1	1.7	2.6
2022	COL	14059	-10.3	-0.3	1.1	-9.5
2023	*COL*	*15632*	*-7.5*	*-0.5*	*0.1*	*-7.8*

Raise your hand if you thought Díaz's transformation from noodle bat to roughly league-average at the age of 30 was going to stick. Spoiler alert: It didn't. The former scrap-heap success story saw his numbers fall back down to earth thanks to a big jump in strikeouts and a big dip in power. He was borderline unplayable everywhere, but especially away from Coors, posting a .517 OPS—yes, .517—and all of two home runs on the road. And as a defender he was a disaster, ranking 106th out of 109 qualified catchers in CDA. Add it all up and you get a player who finished with less WARP at his position than Anthony Bemboom and Sandy Leon. It's nice that Díaz snuck in a good year in 2021, but a franchise catcher he most certainly is not.

Yanquiel Fernandez RF Born: 01/01/03 Age: 20 Bats: L Throws: L Height: 6'2" Weight: 198 lb. Origin: International Free Agent, 2019

YEAR	TEAM	LVL	AGE	PA	R	2B	3B	HR	RBI	BB	K	SB	CS	Whiff%	AVG/OBP/SLG	DRC+	BABIP	BRR	DRP	WARP
2021	DSL ROC	ROK	18	202	29	17	0	6	34	22	26	0	0		.333/.406/.531		.361			
2022	FRE	A	19	523	76	33	5	21	109	39	114	5	1		.284/.340/.507	108	.330	-3.3	RF(90): 0.9	2.1
2023 non-DC	*COL*	*MLB*	*20*	*251*	*21*	*11*	*1*	*5*	*24*	*12*	*71*	*0*	*1*	*32.7%*	*.223/.267/.356*	*69*	*.297*	*1.3*	*1B 0, RF 0*	*-0.4*

Comparables: Carlos González (90), Caleb Gindl (85), Justin Williams (83)

Fernandez has drawn Yordan Alvarez comparisons in his short time with the Rockies, and it's easy to see why. Big and muscular, the Cuban product boasts lots of power in his bat, frequently barreling up balls in a loud Dominican Summer League stint in 2021. He didn't ace his first real test in '22 when he made the jump to Low-A, nor did he stare blankly before filling in bubbles at random. His power was still evident, and while his strikeout rate ballooned it did so to reasonable levels for a 19-year-old tackling full-season ball for the first time. Fernandez will need to watch his plate discipline if he wants to keep those Alvarez comps coming, but it seems within his power to do so.

Randal Grichuk OF Born: 08/13/91 Age: 31 Bats: R Throws: R Height: 6'2" Weight: 216 lb. Origin: Round 1, 2009 Draft (#24 overall)

YEAR	TEAM	LVL	AGE	PA	R	2B	3B	HR	RBI	BB	K	SB	CS	Whiff%	AVG/OBP/SLG	DRC+	BABIP	BRR	DRP	WARP
2020	TOR	MLB	28	231	38	9	0	12	35	13	49	1	1	23.1%	.273/.312/.481	112	.299	-0.1	CF(48): -4.9	0.6
2021	TOR	MLB	29	545	59	25	1	22	81	27	114	0	3	23.2%	.241/.281/.423	94	.266	-1.6	CF(96): -6.9, RF(71): 0.8	0.8
2022	COL	MLB	30	538	60	21	3	19	73	24	127	4	0	24.7%	.259/.299/.425	97	.309	-0.4	RF(106): -4.2, CF(52): -3.6	0.7
2023 DC	*COL*	*MLB*	*31*	*497*	*52*	*21*	*2*	*18*	*58*	*25*	*106*	*3*	*1*	*24.0%*	*.242/.290/.413*	*89*	*.280*	*2.1*	*RF 1, CF 0*	*0.8*

Comparables: Red Murray (71), Gary Matthews (69), Vernon Wells (68)

On paper, it was a match made in heaven: Grichuk, one of the game's premier grip-and-rip sluggers, getting regular playing time in a stadium that nitro boosts fly balls and offers immense power alleys for right-handed hitters. And boy did he take advantage of his new home, slashing a meaty .307/.338/.513 in Coors. All's well that ends well, right? Not so much, given that pesky "you have to play half the season on the road" thing, where Grichuk hit a putrid .205/.257/.326. Or the fact that right-handed pitchers, who only make up, oh, 75% of the league, held him to a .620 OPS and struck him out a quarter of the time. Or that those big ol' power alleys have to be patrolled when you're not at the plate, and that's very much not Grichuk's bag. Add it all up and that's how a player seemingly designed in a lab to succeed at Coors ends up posting fewer WARP than Jake Marisnick despite finishing with more plate appearances than Mike Trout.

Nolan Jones RF Born: 05/07/98 Age: 25 Bats: L Throws: R Height: 6'4" Weight: 195 lb. Origin: Round 2, 2016 Draft (#55 overall)

YEAR	TEAM	LVL	AGE	PA	R	2B	3B	HR	RBI	BB	K	SB	CS	Whiff%	AVG/OBP/SLG	DRC+	BABIP	BRR	DRP	WARP
2021	COL	AAA	23	407	60	25	1	13	48	59	122	10	2		.238/.356/.431	99	.327	3.8	3B(67): 2.4, RF(25): 1.0, 1B(1): -0.1	1.8
2022	COL	AAA	24	248	44	11	1	9	43	31	64	4	1		.276/.368/.463	111	.352	-0.4	RF(42): -2.9, LF(2): -0.4	1.2
2022	CLE	MLB	24	94	10	5	0	2	13	8	31	0	0	30.1%	.244/.309/.372	68	.358	-0.9	RF(22): 0.3	-0.2
2023 DC	*COL*	*MLB*	*25*	*318*	*34*	*13*	*1*	*10*	*32*	*31*	*92*	*5*	*1*	*28.6%*	*.238/.321/.407*	*98*	*.318*	*1.7*	*RF 1, 3B 0*	*0.8*

Comparables: Willy García (53), Ben Gamel (51), Domonic Brown (50)

Jones is a former top prospect who finds himself firmly in post-hype territory. His long-anticipated move to the corner outfield is complete, with his strong arm fitting well in right, and he continues to work deep counts, draw lots of walks and strike out a ton. Unfortunately, he's yet to launch 20 home runs in a season despite plus raw power that scouts have long expected to show up between the lines. Jones made his big-league debut with the Guardians last season and started off strong, but a deep August slump (five singles in 30 at-bats with no walks and 14 whiffs) led to exile in Columbus, and he was left off a playoff roster that included rookie outfielders Will Benson and Will Brennan. Even if his power never develops, Jones has enough on-base skill to become the next Robbie Grossman, but he'd best get started soon. The Rockies will give him some chances to do so after acquiring him in a challenge trade for Juan Brito in November.

Dyan Jorge SS Born: 03/18/03 Age: 20 Bats: R Throws: R Height: 6'3" Weight: 170 lb. Origin: International Free Agent, 2022

YEAR	TEAM	LVL	AGE	PA	R	2B	3B	HR	RBI	BB	K	SB	CS	Whiff%	AVG/OBP/SLG	DRC+	BABIP	BRR	DRP	WARP
2022	DSL COL	ROK	19	218	35	11	1	4	20	23	31	13	10		.319/.404/.450		.365			
2023	*No projection*																			

The recipient of the biggest international signing bonus in franchise history ($2.8 million), Jorge has yet to come stateside, but his strong production in the Dominican Summer League should see him start the coming season in Arizona. His loud tools were all on display at the plate and on the bases in the DSL, though he's not yet a savvy base-stealer. While his future defensive home is up in the air, Colorado stuck him at shortstop and will presumably let him prove he can't stick there. His 16 errors in 51 games at the six suggest that a move down the defensive spectrum may come sooner rather than later, but at his age, lots of errors are more of a "needs improvement" than an outright "fail" on the report card. We'll get a better sense of just what the Rockies have in Jorge once he's climbed a few more rungs of the ladder.

Grant Lavigne 1B Born: 08/27/99 Age: 23 Bats: L Throws: R Height: 6'4" Weight: 220 lb. Origin: Round 1, 2018 Draft (#42 overall)

YEAR	TEAM	LVL	AGE	PA	R	2B	3B	HR	RBI	BB	K	SB	CS	Whiff%	AVG/OBP/SLG	DRC+	BABIP	BRR	DRP	WARP
2021	FRE	A	21	308	49	13	4	7	40	39	73	7	2		.281/.388/.442	113	.365	2.0	1B(64): -6.6	0.8
2021	SPO	A+	21	139	17	5	1	2	18	22	39	2	1		.225/.362/.342	94	.319	0.5	1B(30): -1.7	0.1
2022	SPO	A+	22	282	41	16	3	5	38	36	68	2	3		.315/.406/.469	108	.418	-0.5	1B(61): 0.7	1.0
2022	HFD	AA	22	242	29	7	2	5	24	32	66	0	0		.245/.347/.370	81	.333	-1.1	1B(41): -1.3	-0.1
2023 non-DC	*COL*	*MLB*	*23*	*251*	*21*	*8*	*1*	*2*	*20*	*23*	*75*	*2*	*2*	*32.2%*	*.220/.299/.315*	*71*	*.319*	*0.4*	*1B 0*	*-0.5*

Comparables: Nathaniel Lowe (54), Gavin LaValley (50), Chris Parmelee (49)

Lavigne is less climbing the organizational ladder than hanging off each rung and insisting to everyone below him that he's moving, so don't rush him. He finally made the jump to Double-A after repeating High-A and mostly solving it, and it's reassuring that the good plate discipline he showed in Spokane went with him to Hartford. That said, Lavigne's stay in Connecticut was otherwise uninspiring, as he's yet to truly get his power into games. The big lefty has been consistent in his ability to figure things out in his second go at each level, but Colorado has to be a bit frustrated that his progress has been so incremental.

Ryan McMahon 3B

Born: 12/14/94 Age: 28 Bats: L Throws: R Height: 6'2" Weight: 219 lb. Origin: Round 2, 2013 Draft (#42 overall)

YEAR	TEAM	LVL	AGE	PA	R	2B	3B	HR	RBI	BB	K	SB	CS	Whiff%	AVG/OBP/SLG	DRC+	BABIP	BRR	DRP	WARP
2020	COL	MLB	25	193	23	6	1	9	26	18	66	0	1	31.6%	.215/.295/.419	78	.286	-0.6	2B(33): -1.7, 3B(14): 0, 1B(12): -0.1	-0.2
2021	COL	MLB	26	596	80	32	1	23	86	59	147	6	2	29.2%	.254/.331/.449	99	.306	0.6	3B(113): 0.3, 2B(52): -1.1	1.9
2022	COL	MLB	27	597	67	23	3	20	67	60	158	7	3	28.2%	.246/.327/.414	96	.311	-0.2	3B(145): -4.5, 2B(10): -0.4, 1B(1): 0	0.7
2023 DC	*COL*	*MLB*	*28*	*537*	*65*	*23*	*3*	*22*	*65*	*55*	*133*	*8*	*2*	*28.1%*	*.252/.337/.455*	*114*	*.307*	*4.1*	*3B 0, 2B 0*	*2.5*

Comparables: Howard Johnson (59), Roy Howell (58), Dan Meyer (57)

McMahon is the baseball equivalent of a take a penny leave a penny tray: For every contribution he makes, another seems to disappear. His galoot-level power is impressive, and he'll send poorly located fastballs and middle-middle changeups deep into the night. If the league outlawed sliders, he'd be all set, but they won't, so he isn't. He doesn't get his power into games consistently enough, and the Coors Effect remains in full effect for him on the road. As for his defensive aptitude? That's up to interpretation. Outs Above Average and DRS love him, FRAA hates him and UZR can't make up its mind. If nothing else, we know for sure that he made three times as many errors at third just one year after finishing as a Gold Glove finalist, so we'll say he's regressed. McMahon only works as a viable starter on a nominal contender if he can be solidly above average in one way or another, and his boom-or-bust approach at the plate means that's unlikely to be with the bat. If his glove doesn't show up either, he's a drain overall. Good thing the Rockies didn't recently give him a $70 million extension through the next five years!

Elehuris Montero IF

Born: 08/17/98 Age: 24 Bats: R Throws: R Height: 6'3" Weight: 235 lb. Origin: International Free Agent, 2014

YEAR	TEAM	LVL	AGE	PA	R	2B	3B	HR	RBI	BB	K	SB	CS	Whiff%	AVG/OBP/SLG	DRC+	BABIP	BRR	DRP	WARP
2021	EST	WIN	22	158	12	4	1	2	15	16	35	1	0		.221/.297/.307		.276			
2021	HFD	AA	22	379	46	11	1	22	69	43	90	0	0		.279/.361/.523	124	.309	0.2	3B(42): -0.4, 1B(40): -3.0	1.9
2021	ABQ	AAA	22	121	23	9	1	6	17	10	20	0	0		.278/.355/.546	114	.293	-1.2	3B(19): 0.2, 1B(9): -0.9	0.4
2022	ABQ	AAA	23	297	44	10	2	15	54	27	63	4	2	29.9%	.310/.392/.541	114	.354	1.6	3B(37): -5.0, 1B(20): -0.6	1.0
2022	COL	MLB	23	185	21	15	1	6	20	8	60	0	0	35.5%	.233/.270/.432	78	.318	0.8	3B(23): 0.7, 1B(16): 0	0.1
2023 DC	*COL*	*MLB*	*24*	*157*	*17*	*6*	*0*	*5*	*17*	*10*	*44*	*0*	*0*	*32.8%*	*.237/.299/.414*	*92*	*.305*	*0.4*	*3B 0, 1B 0*	*0.1*

Comparables: Kris Bryant (58), Will Middlebrooks (58), Miguel Andújar (57)

Ryan McMahon's extension ostensibly closes the door on Montero becoming the Rockies' primary third baseman any time soon. McMahon's deal might not look so smart at the moment, but the decision to block Montero looks just fine. After an MLB debut in which he posted a worse strikeout-to-walk ratio than Javier Báez, Montero's odds of earning every day playing time in Colorado look slim. If he wasn't facing a fastball, he had no chance at the plate, posting a 47.9% whiff rate on breaking balls and a 56.9% mark against off-speed pitches. To be fair, his MLB stats came in a relatively small sample, and he's walloped Triple-A pitching across 400+ PA. But Montero's plate discipline stats in Albuquerque were closer to acceptable than exceptional. Perhaps another year spent seeing MLB-caliber curves and changeups will help Montero perform better against them. He'd better hope that's the case, as his best chance at seeing at-bats in Denver will likely come while playing first base, where the bar for offensive performance is even higher than at the hot corner.

Benny Montgomery CF

Born: 09/09/02 Age: 20 Bats: R Throws: R Height: 6'4" Weight: 200 lb. Origin: Round 1, 2021 Draft (#8 overall)

YEAR	TEAM	LVL	AGE	PA	R	2B	3B	HR	RBI	BB	K	SB	CS	Whiff%	AVG/OBP/SLG	DRC+	BABIP	BRR	DRP	WARP
2021	RCK	ROK	18	52	7	0	1	0	6	5	9	5	1		.340/.404/.383		.421			
2022	FRE	A	19	264	48	20	3	6	42	21	71	9	1		.313/.394/.502	93	.429	0.5	CF(44): -0.8	0.5
2023 non-DC	*COL*	*MLB*	*20*	*251*	*19*	*11*	*2*	*2*	*20*	*13*	*86*	*4*	*1*	*37.5%*	*.213/.269/.315*	*59*	*.326*	*2.9*	*CF 0*	*-0.2*

Comparables: Albert Almora Jr. (83), Drew Waters (83), Andrew McCutchen (80)

Despite a swing best described as "having a lot going on," all Montgomery has done in his short pro career is hit. His Low-A debut was hampered by injuries but he still put up a strong triple-slash against older competition. He's fast enough to create plenty of infield singles and turn balls in the gap into instant doubles. Holding him back—aside from all the dip and wiggle in his stance—are mediocre plate discipline and struggles squaring up balls on the inner half of the strike zone. He faces far fewer questions about his defense, as he's top-tier in center thanks to his 70-grade wheels. Benny has the jets, but can he transcend his weird swing to end up wonderful? Here's to hoping he can, because the league could always use more Hunter Pence cosplayers.

Brendan Rodgers 2B

Born: 08/09/96 Age: 26 Bats: R Throws: R Height: 6'0" Weight: 204 lb. Origin: Round 1, 2015 Draft (#3 overall)

YEAR	TEAM	LVL	AGE	PA	R	2B	3B	HR	RBI	BB	K	SB	CS	Whiff%	AVG/OBP/SLG	DRC+	BABIP	BRR	DRP	WARP
2020	COL	MLB	23	21	1	1	0	0	2	0	6	0	0	30.6%	.095/.095/.143	83	.133	0.0	2B(5): 0	0.0
2021	COL	MLB	24	415	49	21	3	15	51	19	84	0	0	23.0%	.284/.328/.470	102	.328	0.3	2B(81): 1.7, SS(26): -0.4	1.8
2022	COL	MLB	25	581	72	30	3	13	63	46	101	0	0	22.8%	.266/.325/.408	108	.304	0.4	2B(134): 5.3	2.9
2023 DC	*COL*	*MLB*	*26*	*545*	*59*	*26*	*3*	*13*	*55*	*37*	*101*	*0*	*0*	*22.4%*	*.264/.326/.407*	*102*	*.312*	*-1.2*	*2B 2*	*1.8*

Comparables: Carlos Sanchez (63), Robinson Canó (56), Brandon Phillips (55)

Trevor Story's departure didn't result in Rodgers manning shortstop, but he settled in just fine at second base, particularly with the glove. The keystone is a better spot for him anyway given his lackluster arm strength, though his range toward first isn't ideal. Either way, the Rockies will live with it, especially since he only just reached arbitration eligibility. Cheap production will always be endearing to a franchise like Colorado, though it's worth wondering if Rodgers' development will keep pace with his price tag as he goes forward. For a second straight year, there was no progress in his numbers against righties (a .647 OPS), and he's an indifferent baserunner. This likely isn't the future the Rockies envisioned when they tabbed Rodgers in the draft eight years ago, and those 70th-percentile outcomes just aren't as interesting to cover as the extremes in either direction. Still, so long as his offense is good enough and his defense is above-average, Rodgers will have a job in Colorado.

Drew Romo C/DH Born: 08/29/01 Age: 21 Bats: S Throws: R Height: 6'1" Weight: 205 lb. Origin: Round 1, 2020 Draft (#35 overall)

YEAR	TEAM	LVL	AGE	PA	R	2B	3B	HR	RBI	BB	K	SB	CS	Whiff%	AVG/OBP/SLG	DRC+	BABIP	BRR	DRP	WARP
2021	FRE	A	19	339	48	17	2	6	47	19	50	23	6		.314/.345/.439	121	.348	1.2	C(69): 12.8	3.2
2022	SPO	A+	20	420	52	19	5	5	58	35	81	18	3		.254/.321/.372	100	.306	0.0	C(57): 8.3	2.0
2023 non-DC	*COL*	*MLB*	*21*	*251*	*19*	*10*	*1*	*2*	*20*	*14*	*53*	*8*	*3*	*25.1%*	*.231/.278/.323*	*67*	*.289*	*3.3*	*C 0*	*0.2*

Comparables: Neil Walker (71), Austin Romine (69), Austin Hedges (66)

YEAR	TEAM	P. COUNT	FRM RUNS	BLK RUNS	THRW RUNS	TOT RUNS
2021	FRE	9773	11.8	1.8	0.5	14.1
2022	SPO	7764	9.4	0.2	-0.3	9.3
2023	*COL*	*6956*	*3.5*	*0.6*	*-0.1*	*3.9*

Romo's road to the majors was always likely to be a long one, and his year at High-A isn't going to speed things up. His bat didn't survive the season, with a bad second-half slump (.173/.262/.241 from July 1 onward) tanking his numbers overall. Even in his best months, there wasn't much thump in his swing despite the plus or better grades on his raw power. Romo is a strong defender, though, giving him a realistic shot at reaching the big leagues eventually even if his offense doesn't make the leap beyond "a more patient Austin Nola." Given that he only just turned old enough to enjoy a Coors Light legally, there's still time for his hitting to take a step forward.

Brian Serven C Born: 05/05/95 Age: 28 Bats: R Throws: R Height: 6'0" Weight: 207 lb. Origin: Round 5, 2016 Draft (#140 overall)

YEAR	TEAM	LVL	AGE	PA	R	2B	3B	HR	RBI	BB	K	SB	CS	Whiff%	AVG/OBP/SLG	DRC+	BABIP	BRR	DRP	WARP
2021	ABQ	AAA	26	276	36	12	2	16	38	16	61	1	0		.250/.308/.504	104	.266	-1.3	C(66): 3.2	1.4
2022	ABQ	AAA	27	96	18	3	0	5	11	16	15	0	0	27.2%	.273/.406/.506	119	.276	-0.8	C(22): 2.1	0.6
2022	COL	MLB	27	205	19	4	1	6	16	13	44	0	0	27.2%	.203/.261/.332	92	.232	-0.9	C(59): 10.1	1.6
2023 DC	*COL*	*MLB*	*28*	*210*	*21*	*8*	*1*	*5*	*19*	*14*	*44*	*0*	*0*	*27.9%*	*.213/.282/.347*	*72*	*.255*	*-1.6*	*C 11*	*1.1*

Comparables: Carlos Corporán (68), Chad Wallach (68), Adam Moore (68)

YEAR	TEAM	P. COUNT	FRM RUNS	BLK RUNS	THRW RUNS	TOT RUNS
2021	ABQ	9789	0.3	-0.1	0.8	1.1
2022	ABQ	3286	1.9	0.0	0.0	1.9
2022	COL	7949	9.7	0.1	-0.1	9.7
2023	*COL*	*8418*	*11.3*	*0.0*	*0.0*	*11.3*

Brian was Serven career backup catcher vibes in his rookie season, marrying some fantastic defense with three or four empty plate appearances every four or five days. The advanced stats love his glove, particularly his framing ability; by Framing Runs, he ranked 10th in the majors, albeit in a far smaller sample than his starting counterparts. On offense, he's miles behind instead of high—too many whiffs with too aggressive an approach left him toward the bottom of the leaderboard at his position in DRC+, and that's with the average catcher hitting like a 1990s backup middle infielder. The good news is that his defense will carry his bat. The bad news is that framing is where he grades out best, and an automatic strike zone would slash that value significantly. If the Cyberdyne offices where MLB is creating its robo umps get blown up this offseason, that's probably Serven trying his best to escape his pending obsolescence.

Sterlin Thompson 3B Born: 06/26/01 Age: 22 Bats: L Throws: R Height: 6'4" Weight: 200 lb. Origin: Round 1, 2022 Draft (#31 overall)

YEAR	TEAM	LVL	AGE	PA	R	2B	3B	HR	RBI	BB	K	SB	CS	Whiff%	AVG/OBP/SLG	DRC+	BABIP	BRR	DRP	WARP
2022	RCK	ROK	21	61	9	3	0	1	6	2	16	1	0		.273/.328/.382		.359			
2022	FRE	A	21	50	9	4	0	1	4	3	12	2	0		.348/.380/.500	95	.441	0.2	3B(11): -1.5	0.0
2023 non-DC	*COL*	*MLB*	*22*	*251*	*19*	*10*	*1*	*2*	*20*	*15*	*70*	*4*	*1*	*30.7%*	*.215/.269/.308*	*58*	*.297*	*2.4*	*3B 0*	*-0.6*

It's hard and a little unfair to try to project out the entirety of a professional career for someone who was drafted last summer, but for Thompson, it's pretty clear that his path will go one of two ways. Either he'll figure out how to handle non-fastballs and improve his defense enough to carve out a role as a versatile major-leaguer, or he'll be spending the bulk of his best years tattooing mediocre heaters all over Japan and Korea. The overall package offers lots to like—a good swing from the left side, plenty of raw power, consistent demolition of fastballs—but also lots that remain a work in progress. In particular, he's stretched at second base and looks average in the outfield—the missing g in his name apparently stands for "glove." He'll need to rely on his bat and better pitch recognition to pull ahead of the seemingly 40 or 50 similarly built lefty-hitting outfielders crowding Colorado's system.

Michael Toglia 1B Born: 08/16/98 Age: 24 Bats: S Throws: L Height: 6'5" Weight: 226 lb. Origin: Round 1, 2019 Draft (#23 overall)

YEAR	TEAM	LVL	AGE	PA	R	2B	3B	HR	RBI	BB	K	SB	CS	Whiff%	AVG/OBP/SLG	DRC+	BABIP	BRR	DRP	WARP
2021	SRR	WIN	22	105	10	2	1	3	12	12	26	1	0		.264/.343/.407		.328			
2021	SPO	A+	22	330	50	10	2	17	66	42	91	7	3		.234/.333/.465	108	.275	2.0	1B(67): 11.8	2.5
2021	HFD	AA	22	169	16	10	1	5	18	23	51	3	0		.217/.331/.406	93	.295	-2.3	1B(41): 4.3	0.5
2022	HFD	AA	23	420	63	13	1	23	66	51	127	7	1		.234/.329/.466	113	.286	1.9	1B(86): 0.8, RF(6): -0.5	2.0
2022	ABQ	AAA	23	75	11	7	0	7	17	9	22	0	1	26.8%	.333/.413/.758	114	.405	-2.3	1B(13): 0.2, RF(3): -0.2	0.1
2022	COL	MLB	23	120	10	8	2	2	12	9	44	1	1	33.8%	.216/.275/.378	65	.338	-0.4	RF(17): -0.8, 1B(15): 1.6	-0.2
2023 DC	*COL*	*MLB*	*24*	*163*	*16*	*6*	*1*	*5*	*17*	*14*	*50*	*1*	*1*	*33.1%*	*.207/.283/.380*	*76*	*.277*	*1.2*	*RF -1, 1B 0*	*-0.2*

Comparables: Moisés Sierra (60), Brandon Allen (60), Max Kepler (51)

The idea of Toglia's gorilla-level power showing out in the spacious confines of Coors Field is drool-worthy. Pitchers, though, have to be salivating at the thought of getting to face a hitter who apparently doesn't know what a curveball or slider is. The big first baseman's hit tool hasn't progressed as he's worked his way through the minors, and his first taste of Double-A and its better caliber of off-speed and breaking pitches brought him to his knees. Nor did a month spent in the majors at the end of the year go any better: His strikeout rate would've been the worst in the league by two points if he'd had enough plate appearances to qualify. That's a big obstacle in the way of Toglia establishing himself as a long-term first baseman, which is an especially bitter pill to swallow given that he's a terrific defender. Right now, he just doesn't provide enough offense to justify a roster spot, even with his gargantuan raw power, plus glove and propensity for drawing walks.

★ ★ ★ *2023 Top 101 Prospect* **#21** ★ ★ ★

Ezequiel Tovar SS Born: 08/01/01 Age: 21 Bats: R Throws: R Height: 6'0" Weight: 162 lb. Origin: International Free Agent, 2017

YEAR	TEAM	LVL	AGE	PA	R	2B	3B	HR	RBI	BB	K	SB	CS	Whiff%	AVG/OBP/SLG	DRC+	BABIP	BRR	DRP	WARP
2021	SRR	WIN	19	96	10	2	0	3	10	5	20	2	0		.161/.219/.287		.167			
2021	FRE	A	19	326	60	21	3	11	54	14	38	21	4		.309/.346/.510	132	.320	2.5	SS(64): 8.1	3.3
2021	SPO	A+	19	143	19	9	0	4	18	3	19	3	2		.239/.266/.396	115	.252	-1.0	SS(32): -1.8	0.4
2022	HFD	AA	20	295	39	15	3	13	47	25	64	17	3		.318/.386/.545	113	.378	1.4	SS(64): 0.9	1.6
2022	COL	MLB	20	35	2	1	0	1	2	2	9	0	0	32.4%	.212/.257/.333	96	.261	-0.1	SS(9): -0.4	0.0
2023 DC	*COL*	*MLB*	*21*	*429*	*43*	*19*	*3*	*10*	*42*	*21*	*96*	*10*	*4*	*28.4%*	*.246/.294/.390*	*86*	*.302*	*2.0*	*SS -1, 2B 0*	*0.5*

Comparables: Carlos Correa (58), Xander Bogaerts (56), Starlin Castro (53)

In the Book of Ezekiel, the aforementioned prophet receives a vision of a valley of dry bones that gradually reconstitute themselves into living humans—the exiled Israelites resurrected and ready to return to the promised land. In Tovar, the Rockies likely see a vision of a franchise shortstop reborn, or at least one less skeletal and more muscular than their present alternatives. Despite a rough go at High-A and in the Arizona Fall League in 2021, Colorado aggressively promoted Tovar to Double-A to start last season. He rewarded that decision by bashing Eastern League pitching at just 20 years old. He did so well that he got both Triple-A and MLB cups of coffee—the latter of which proved to be too hot for him to gulp down, but again, we're talking about a kid who started the year two levels below the majors and who won't turn 22 until August. There are no questions about Tovar's defense, which is already starter-caliber and could reach Gold Glove levels in the future. What has to be especially reassuring for the Rockies is how he rediscovered his line-drive stroke and power at Hartford while also showing better plate discipline. He may not be the second coming of Troy Tulowitzki, but Tovar is no false prophet—he's the real deal at shortstop, and should be for a long time.

Alan Trejo SS Born: 05/30/96 Age: 27 Bats: R Throws: R Height: 6'2" Weight: 205 lb. Origin: Round 16, 2017 Draft (#476 overall)

YEAR	TEAM	LVL	AGE	PA	R	2B	3B	HR	RBI	BB	K	SB	CS	Whiff%	AVG/OBP/SLG	DRC+	BABIP	BRR	DRP	WARP
2021	ABQ	AAA	25	363	56	34	6	17	72	23	78	2	4		.278/.324/.569	100	.314	-2.7	SS(75): 7.5, 2B(10): 0.0, 3B(2): 0.1	1.6
2021	COL	MLB	25	50	7	2	0	1	3	3	15	0	0	27.1%	.217/.260/.326	81	.290	1.1	2B(10): 0.2, SS(9): 0	0.2
2022	ABQ	AAA	26	293	46	20	1	16	52	10	64	2	2	25.6%	.296/.331/.551	98	.330	0.5	SS(53): 0.9, 2B(10): 1.6, 3B(3): -0.3	1.0
2022	COL	MLB	26	125	15	6	0	4	17	5	31	1	2	25.3%	.271/.312/.424	94	.337	0.4	SS(20): -2, 2B(13): -0.6, 3B(2): 0.1	0.1
2023 DC	*COL*	*MLB*	*27*	*277*	*27*	*14*	*1*	*6*	*27*	*12*	*62*	*3*	*1*	*25.7%*	*.232/.276/.376*	*74*	*.284*	*0.6*	*SS -1, 2B 0*	*-0.1*

Comparables: Chris Nelson (67), José Pirela (62), Jedd Gyorko (60)

For the second straight year, Trejo found himself mired in New Mexico, spending most of his season toiling in Triple-A and stuck behind Brendan Rodgers and José Iglesias at the major-league level. And for the second straight year, he easily handled the PCL, taking advantage of its many launching pads to post a whopping .255 ISO that somehow ranked only 19th in the league among hitters with 250 or more plate appearances. (Fun fact: That ISO would've tied him with Austin Riley for sixth in the majors among qualified hitters. The PCL is less a baseball league than a place where pitchers go to die.) Trejo's surprising power makes him an intriguing utility infielder candidate for Colorado, and he helped his own case by hitting a stellar .291/.341/.468 in September with the big-league club. The main thing holding him back, save the players in front of him, is his plate discipline; even in that nice September run, he walked just four times in 85 plate appearances. Still, it would behoove the Rockies to give Trejo room to grow, as a third long stint in Albuquerque isn't going to teach him anything more or us anything more about him.

★ ★ ★ *2023 Top 101 Prospect* **#34** ★ ★ ★

Zac Veen OF Born: 12/12/01 Age: 21 Bats: L Throws: R Height: 6'4" Weight: 190 lb. Origin: Round 1, 2020 Draft (#9 overall)

YEAR	TEAM	LVL	AGE	PA	R	2B	3B	HR	RBI	BB	K	SB	CS	Whiff%	AVG/OBP/SLG	DRC+	BABIP	BRR	DRP	WARP
2021	FRE	A	19	479	83	27	4	15	75	64	126	36	17		.301/.399/.501	117	.396	-1.7	RF(69): -0.2, LF(26): 2.2	2.6
2022	SPO	A+	20	400	72	19	3	11	60	50	90	50	4		.269/.368/.439	100	.332	6.7	RF(77): 3.3, LF(2): -0.1	2.6
2022	HFD	AA	20	141	12	4	0	1	7	14	42	5	5		.177/.262/.234	71	.253	-0.7	RF(33): -1.1	-0.2
2023 non-DC	*COL*	*MLB*	*21*	*251*	*21*	*9*	*1*	*4*	*22*	*21*	*71*	*14*	*5*	*33.1%*	*.216/.288/.327*	*70*	*.297*	*0.8*	*LF 0, RF 0*	*-0.3*

Comparables: Jorge Bonifacio (68), Justin Williams (61), Carlos González (57)

Veen's run through the minor leagues continued apace last year, with Colorado's top outfield prospect successfully hitting his way through High-A and earning a brief promotion to end the year. He cleared an .800 OPS each month in Spokane, and while Hartford ate him up, that's to be expected for a 20-year-old whose professional experience amounted to fewer than 900 PA prior. Even in Connecticut, all his tools were on display; an excellent left-handed stroke, plus-plus speed and burgeoning power. The latter is probably the biggest question mark in his profile at this point—his all-fields approach makes him a dangerous hitter, but it would be nice to see him pull the ball in the air more often. Right now, his pop is more raw than realized, and that could cap his ceiling at "good starter" instead of "perennial All-Star," especially since defensively he's a corner outfielder through and through. Again though, he's young, and the beauty of youth lies in how many years you still have left in front of you. He'll return to Double-A looking to take the next step forward as a hitter.

Pitchers

Daniel Bard RHP Born: 06/25/85 Age: 38 Bats: R Throws: R Height: 6'4" Weight: 215 lb. Origin: Round 1, 2006 Draft (#28 overall)

YEAR	TEAM	LVL	AGE	W	L	SV	G	GS	IP	H	HR	BB/9	K/9	K	GB%	BABIP	WHIP	ERA	DRA-	WARP	MPH	FB%	Whiff%	CSP
2020	COL	MLB	35	4	2	6	23	0	24^2	22	2	3.6	9.9	27	48.5%	.313	1.30	3.65	83	0.5	97.2	56.4%	28.7%	52.2%
2021	COL	MLB	36	7	8	20	67	0	65^2	69	8	4.9	11.0	80	42.0%	.355	1.60	5.21	87	1.0	97.6	48.5%	29.7%	52.3%
2022	COL	MLB	37	6	4	34	57	0	60^1	35	3	3.7	10.3	69	51.4%	.221	0.99	1.79	75	1.4	98.1	55.3%	27.6%	56.1%
2023 DC	*COL*	*MLB*	*38*	*3*	*3*	*28*	*62*	*0*	*53.7*	*50*	*6*	*4.1*	*9.3*	*55*	*47.2%*	*.305*	*1.39*	*4.18*	*100*	*0.2*	*97.8*	*52.4%*	*27.0%*	*54.0%*

Comparables: Mark Melancon (60), Pat Neshek (60), Steve Cishek (60)

It's very easy (and usually fun, too) to snark on the Rockies for doing things that they and they alone find necessary or smart. Case in point: Giving Bard, a reliever who was fully out of baseball five years ago, a two-year contract extension in the midst of his age-37 season. Given the state of the roster, it's hard to argue that doubling down on Bard's unlikely resurgence is the best way to spend what limited resources the team has. On the other hand: good for the Rockies, and good for Bard. His comeback with Colorado is a terrific story, his fastball is humming again at 97 mph and touching 100, and while his peripherals suggest he's not a dominant closer, he's good enough that a $19 million guarantee doesn't feel like a huge risk. There's something to be said, too, for retaining good players instead of coldly flipping them for lottery tickets. It may not be "smart baseball" according to some, but it's far from the dumbest thing to happen at Coors Field, and it may well be the nicest.

Jake Bird RHP Born: 12/04/95 Age: 27 Bats: R Throws: R Height: 6'3" Weight: 200 lb. Origin: Round 5, 2018 Draft (#156 overall)

YEAR	TEAM	LVL	AGE	W	L	SV	G	GS	IP	H	HR	BB/9	K/9	K	GB%	BABIP	WHIP	ERA	DRA-	WARP	MPH	FB%	Whiff%	CSP
2021	HFD	AA	25	1	0	0	10	1	20^1	20	1	3.1	10.2	23	71.9%	.339	1.33	2.21	90	0.3				
2021	ABQ	AAA	25	5	1	0	29	1	38^1	34	3	4.5	8.5	36	64.8%	.304	1.38	3.99	84	0.5				
2022	ABQ	AAA	26	2	2	2	22	0	26	16	3	3.1	11.8	34	63.3%	.228	0.96	2.77	69	0.6	94.7	48.2%	34.3%	
2022	COL	MLB	26	2	4	0	38	0	47^2	45	7	4.3	7.9	42	54.2%	.284	1.43	4.91	104	0.4	95.1	57.7%	20.8%	55.6%
2023 DC	*COL*	*MLB*	*27*	*3*	*3*	*0*	*62*	*0*	*53.7*	*56*	*5*	*4.4*	*7.5*	*44*	*57.3%*	*.314*	*1.54*	*4.97*	*116*	*-0.2*	*95.1*	*57.7%*	*23.5%*	*55.6%*

Comparables: Miguel Sánchez (76), Brian Ellington (74), Mike McClendon (74)

Despite getting the call to the majors midway through the season, Bird saw enough action to rank third in innings pitched and fifth in appearances among Colorado's beleaguered relief corps. Durability aside, they weren't very impactful innings—something his results and peripherals agree on—as it's hard to thrive in Coors Field when you lack a true plus pitch. Bird's high-spin curveball gets whiffs coming from his three-quarters slot, and his 95-mph sinker is tough to square up, but he needs to generate more whiffs and improve his control if he's to build on his rookie campaign. He may want to begin by reworking a cutter that all too frequently drifts over the heart of the plate.

Alex Colomé RHP Born: 12/31/88 Age: 34 Bats: R Throws: R Height: 6'1" Weight: 225 lb. Origin: International Free Agent, 2007

YEAR	TEAM	LVL	AGE	W	L	SV	G	GS	IP	H	HR	BB/9	K/9	K	GB%	BABIP	WHIP	ERA	DRA-	WARP	MPH	FB%	Whiff%	CSP
2020	CHW	MLB	31	2	0	12	21	0	22^1	13	0	3.2	6.4	16	51.6%	.203	0.94	0.81	103	0.2	94.6	28.4%	30.9%	41.2%
2021	MIN	MLB	32	4	4	17	67	0	65	68	8	3.2	8.0	58	52.7%	.306	1.40	4.15	114	0.1	93.9	29.4%	27.1%	56.2%
2022	COL	MLB	33	2	7	4	53	0	47	57	5	4.2	6.1	32	55.3%	.335	1.68	5.74	122	-0.1	94.5	15.6%	20.0%	51.5%
2023 DC	*FA*	*MLB*	*34*	*2*	*2*	*0*	*43*	*0*	*37.3*	*41*	*4*	*3.8*	*6.3*	*26*	*51.5%*	*.312*	*1.52*	*4.88*	*117*	*-0.2*	*94.3*	*23.9%*	*23.7%*	*51.8%*

Comparables: Kevin Gregg (77), Mark Melancon (74), Mike MacDougal (73)

Colomé and Coors Field were a match made in hell. A pitcher who categorically refuses to strike hitters out and models his game on inducing contact is the last person who should agree to take money from the Rockies. Then again, after his mediocre 2021 in Minnesota, there likely weren't many teams beating down his door. The veteran's performance in Colorado won't bring many suitors calling this winter, either. His strikeout rate dipped to an alarmingly low 14.9% and his 8.6% swinging-strike rate was in the bottom 20 among relievers with 40 or more innings pitched. It's hard, if not impossible, to be a viable reliever when you're not getting whiffs, and even more so when your walk rate spikes as Colomé's did. The next stop on this train is likely a non-roster invitation to spring training, hopefully with a team far, far away from Coors.

Jackson Cox RHP Born: 09/25/03 Age: 19 Bats: R Throws: R Height: 6'1" Weight: 185 lb. Origin: Round 2, 2022 Draft (#50 overall)

Like a hit from Dead or Alive, Cox's curveball will spin you right 'round, baby, right 'round. His Uncle Charlie routinely cracks 3,000 RPM on its way to the plate with slider-like movement, making it a potential plus-plus pitch and the best offering in his arsenal. His fastball is less exciting, usually floating in at 92 mph but flashing higher, and his changeup shows promise but isn't as developed. On the plus side, Cox threw strikes regularly in his high school career, demonstrating an ability to focus in the face of what one can only assume was a tidal wave of sophomoric, name-based taunts. His curveball/control combo give him a reliever's floor, but he has the potential to aspire to more if his fastball and changeup can catch up.

Ryan Feltner RHP Born: 09/02/96 Age: 26 Bats: R Throws: R Height: 6'4" Weight: 190 lb. Origin: Round 4, 2018 Draft (#126 overall)

YEAR	TEAM	LVL	AGE	W	L	SV	G	GS	IP	H	HR	BB/9	K/9	K	GB%	BABIP	WHIP	ERA	DRA-	WARP	MPH	FB%	Whiff%	CSP
2021	SPO	A+	24	3	1	0	7	7	37^1	26	1	4.3	10.8	45	42.4%	.275	1.18	2.17	90	0.5				
2021	HFD	AA	24	5	2	0	13	13	72^2	68	7	2.7	9.9	80	37.9%	.324	1.24	2.85	100	0.6				
2021	COL	MLB	24	0	1	0	2	2	6^1	9	3	7.1	8.5	6	9.5%	.333	2.21	11.37	115	0.0	92.7	54.2%	32.1%	53.9%
2022	ABQ	AAA	25	5	1	0	11	11	51^2	49	5	3.1	10.5	60	41.1%	.326	1.30	3.83	90	0.6	94.8	52.7%	27.2%	
2022	COL	MLB	25	4	9	0	20	19	97^1	102	16	3.2	7.8	84	41.4%	.300	1.41	5.83	114	0.2	94.2	55.5%	20.8%	54.6%
2023 DC	*COL*	*MLB*	*26*	*6*	*8*	*0*	*24*	*24*	*114*	*121*	*16*	*3.7*	*7.6*	*96*	*40.7%*	*.313*	*1.48*	*4.89*	*117*	*0.0*	*94.1*	*55.4%*	*22.9%*	*54.5%*

Comparables: Taylor Jordan (78), Hiram Burgos (75), Tyler Duffey (74)

There's nothing wrong with being average. That can get lost in a society that demands you never stop grinding, hustling or scrapping, and in an industry ruled by the Ricky Bobby mentality of being last if you're not first. The creamy middle is a perfectly comfortable place to be more often than not, and with the right attitude, accepting one's place there can be downright freeing. But "average" is, obviously, entirely relative, and Coors Field is a place that takes average pitchers and turns them into doormats. Pity poor Feltner, then, who would probably crank out a bunch of fine, nondescript innings somewhere like Cleveland or Pittsburgh but instead had to watch his mediocre stuff take a weekly beating in Colorado. An okay back-end starter anywhere else, he's merely a depth option in the thin mountain air.

Kyle Freeland LHP Born: 05/14/93 Age: 30 Bats: L Throws: L Height: 6'4" Weight: 204 lb. Origin: Round 1, 2014 Draft (#8 overall)

YEAR	TEAM	LVL	AGE	W	L	SV	G	GS	IP	H	HR	BB/9	K/9	K	GB%	BABIP	WHIP	ERA	DRA-	WARP	MPH	FB%	Whiff%	CSP
2020	COL	MLB	27	2	3	0	13	13	70^2	77	9	2.9	5.9	46	50.0%	.305	1.42	4.33	111	0.4	92.0	33.4%	20.6%	45.6%
2021	ABQ	AAA	28	1	1	0	2	2	10	4	0	1.8	3.6	4	76.7%	.133	0.60	1.80	102	0.0				
2021	COL	MLB	28	7	8	0	23	23	120^2	133	20	2.8	7.8	105	44.0%	.328	1.42	4.33	103	1.0	91.5	41.4%	21.5%	52.5%
2022	COL	MLB	29	9	11	0	31	31	174^2	193	19	2.7	6.8	131	42.2%	.319	1.41	4.53	126	-0.7	90.2	45.3%	20.8%	53.0%
2023 DC	*COL*	*MLB*	*30*	*8*	*9*	*0*	*27*	*27*	*148.7*	*157*	*18*	*2.9*	*6.6*	*109*	*44.1%*	*.305*	*1.38*	*4.36*	*108*	*0.6*	*90.9*	*43.5%*	*21.1%*	*51.4%*

Comparables: John Danks (84), Martín Pérez (83), Claude Osteen (81)

Jon Gray's departure from Colorado was a boon for Freeland: The same offseason that the former left for Texas, the latter scored a five-year, $65 million extension that will likely keep him in black and purple for the balance of his career. It's a big reward for a lefty who has made a living out of league-average results, both suffering and benefiting from Coors. He's a bad fit for the park given his allergy to strikeouts (which his 6.00 ERA at home last year attests to), but his overall results look that much better in its context. Still, it's odd that the team chose to give more money to Freeland than Gray—a categorically better starter—and over more years to boot (Fun fact: Freeland's contract is the biggest for a Rockies pitcher since Darryl Kile's). That may just be what it takes to keep players in Denver, even when they're hometown kids who'd probably struggle to get three years guaranteed anywhere else. As such, pitching in Colorado will remain Freeland's gain and his bane for the foreseeable future.

Lucas Gilbreath LHP Born: 03/05/96 Age: 27 Bats: L Throws: L Height: 6'1" Weight: 185 lb. Origin: Round 7, 2017 Draft (#206 overall)

YEAR	TEAM	LVL	AGE	W	L	SV	G	GS	IP	H	HR	BB/9	K/9	K	GB%	BABIP	WHIP	ERA	DRA-	WARP	MPH	FB%	Whiff%	CSP
2021	COL	MLB	25	3	2	1	47	1	42^2	33	5	4.9	9.3	44	45.3%	.250	1.31	3.38	95	0.5	93.6	63.1%	29.9%	53.5%
2022	COL	MLB	26	2	0	0	47	0	43	37	2	5.4	10.3	49	45.4%	.333	1.47	4.19	93	0.6	93.9	73.3%	29.5%	49.5%
2023 DC	*COL*	*MLB*	*27*	*3*	*3*	*0*	*62*	*0*	*53.7*	*53*	*7*	*5.2*	*9.7*	*58*	*46.1%*	*.319*	*1.56*	*5.05*	*115*	*-0.2*	*93.8*	*69.1%*	*28.6%*	*51.1%*

Comparables: Sam Freeman (69), Jake Diekman (69), Jonny Venters (68)

Gilbreath's 2022 was a near carbon-copy of his 2021, from the number of appearances he made down to the stats that peg him as "middle relief and nothing more." If you didn't look for Gilbreath in the box score you'd likely never find him; he showed up mostly in the seventh inning to flick low-90s fastballs and a slurvy slider from the left side. That slider remains his best pitch, as hitters had a somewhat easier time squaring up his fastball than in the previous year. Without a third pitch to turn to—he has a splitter that exists in name only—he's going to have a hard time climbing out of his place in the bullpen hierarchy. That's not inherently a bad thing; if the definition of insanity is doing the same thing repeatedly and expecting different results, then the definition of stability is looking up to see Gilbreath on the mound cranking out the same acceptable inning *ad infinitum*.

Austin Gomber LHP Born: 11/23/93 Age: 29 Bats: L Throws: L Height: 6'5" Weight: 220 lb. Origin: Round 4, 2014 Draft (#135 overall)

YEAR	TEAM	LVL	AGE	W	L	SV	G	GS	IP	H	HR	BB/9	K/9	K	GB%	BABIP	WHIP	ERA	DRA-	WARP	MPH	FB%	Whiff%	CSP
2020	STL	MLB	26	1	1	0	14	4	29	19	1	4.7	8.4	27	48.0%	.243	1.17	1.86	95	0.3	92.8	52.5%	26.6%	48.3%
2021	COL	MLB	27	9	9	0	23	23	115^1	102	20	3.2	8.8	113	43.2%	.265	1.24	4.53	99	1.1	91.9	40.7%	26.0%	56.6%
2022	COL	MLB	28	5	7	0	33	17	124^2	137	20	2.5	6.9	95	42.0%	.310	1.37	5.56	121	-0.1	91.3	40.7%	22.2%	54.6%
2023 DC	*COL*	*MLB*	*29*	*9*	*7*	*0*	*66*	*11*	*104.7*	*107*	*12*	*3.0*	*7.0*	*81*	*42.6%*	*.304*	*1.36*	*4.12*	*103*	*0.6*	*91.6*	*41.5%*	*23.4%*	*54.9%*

Comparables: Wade Miley (56), Chris Rusin (56), Tommy Milone (55)

Gomber has a last name that sounds like a Midwestern epithet—"Aw jeez Midge, I just saw that gomber neighbor of ours spit out yer tuna apple casserole!"—and 2022 stats that are about as appealing as a bowl of lutefisk. Coming off back surgery that derailed his 2021, the lefty threw up an ERA just shy of 6.00 before getting booted from the rotation in late July. He wasn't all that much better as a reliever, sporting a 4.54 ERA and just 28 strikeouts in 35 innings out of the 'pen. The plus curveball that boosted his prospect status in St. Louis—a pitch that lost a ton of bite and solicited fewer whiffs last season—has apparently abandoned him. Worse yet was his fastball, against which opposing batters hit an absurd .376 with a .618 slugging percentage—its plus-21 run value was fifth worst in the league. With his four-seamer puttering in around 91 mph and his Uncle Charlie still AWOL, Gomber is a bad bet to rebound without some serious changes to his arsenal.

Gabriel Hughes RHP Born: 08/22/01 Age: 21 Bats: R Throws: R Height: 6'4" Weight: 220 lb. Origin: Round 1, 2022 Draft (#10 overall)

YEAR	TEAM	LVL	AGE	W	L	SV	G	GS	IP	H	HR	BB/9	K/9	K	GB%	BABIP	WHIP	ERA	DRA-	WARP	MPH	FB%	Whiff%	CSP
2023 non-DC	*COL*	*MLB*	*21*	*2*	*3*	*0*	*57*	*0*	*50*	*57*	*7*	*5.8*	*6.1*	*33*	*44.8%*	*.308*	*1.79*	*6.30*	*143*	*-0.9*			*22.0%*	

The Rockies have a mixed track record when spending high draft picks on pitchers. Tyler Anderson, Jon Gray and Kyle Freeland were all notable successes (relatively, anyway), but in the eight years since Freeland went eighth overall, Colorado has mostly steered away from or whiffed badly on blue-chip pitchers. Enter Hughes, the first starter the Rockies have nabbed in the first round since Ryan Rolison back in 2018. On the surface, he's everything you'd want in a top-of-the-rotation prospect. Built like an NFL quarterback? Check. Boasts a hard fastball that already sits in the mid-90s? Check. Has workable secondaries with plus characteristics? Check: His sweeping slider hits 90 on the gun, and his changeup looked very good in college. Throws strikes and attacks hitters? Check. All the pieces are there for Hughes to do what Rolison and Riley Pint and the rest haven't been able to: make it to Denver in one piece.

Tyler Kinley RHP Born: 01/31/91 Age: 32 Bats: R Throws: R Height: 6'4" Weight: 220 lb. Origin: Round 16, 2013 Draft (#472 overall)

YEAR	TEAM	LVL	AGE	W	L	SV	G	GS	IP	H	HR	BB/9	K/9	K	GB%	BABIP	WHIP	ERA	DRA-	WARP	MPH	FB%	Whiff%	CSP
2020	COL	MLB	29	0	2	0	24	0	23^{2}	13	2	4.6	9.9	26	45.5%	.212	1.06	5.32	90	0.4	95.9	33.6%	36.2%	44.0%
2021	COL	MLB	30	3	2	0	70	0	70^{1}	59	12	3.3	8.7	68	38.7%	.253	1.21	4.73	99	0.7	96.1	43.4%	29.2%	56.3%
2022	COL	MLB	31	1	1	0	25	0	24	21	0	2.3	10.1	27	39.4%	.318	1.13	0.75	85	0.4	95.8	46.5%	32.3%	58.2%
2023 DC	*COL*	*MLB*	*32*	*2*	*2*	*0*	*48*	*0*	*41.7*	*40*	*5*	*3.8*	*9.2*	*43*	*40.9%*	*.310*	*1.39*	*4.27*	*103*	*0.1*	*95.8*	*42.9%*	*29.8%*	*53.7%*

Comparables: Brad Brach (67), Dan Otero (65), Josh Fields (65)

Pity Kinley, who finally seemed to have figured things out. Armed with one of the best sliders on the planet and a 96-mph fastball, he'd nonetheless long struggled to find consistency or success thanks to a total lack of control. But through the first three months of the 2022 season, suddenly he'd righted the ship, firing strikes with precision and wiping out batters with that slider, which earned a gaudy 47% whiff rate. Alas, the baseball gods are all too often cruel. On June 8, Kinley came out, threw an inning against the Giants with two strikeouts and a walk, and then didn't take the mound again for the rest of the year. The culprit: a flexor tear in his right elbow that required surgery to repair in July. It's a nasty reminder that pitchers break, but the Rockies were willing to bet on a full recovery, inking Kinley to a three-year, $6.25 million deal with incentives just before Thanksgiving.

Dinelson Lamet RHP Born: 07/18/92 Age: 30 Bats: R Throws: R Height: 6'3" Weight: 228 lb. Origin: International Free Agent, 2014

YEAR	TEAM	LVL	AGE	W	L	SV	G	GS	IP	H	HR	BB/9	K/9	K	GB%	BABIP	WHIP	ERA	DRA-	WARP	MPH	FB%	Whiff%	CSP
2020	SD	MLB	27	3	1	0	12	12	69	39	5	2.6	12.1	93	38.0%	.234	0.86	2.09	65	2.1	97.0	46.5%	32.6%	47.0%
2021	SD	MLB	28	2	4	0	22	9	47	48	6	4.2	10.9	57	39.1%	.347	1.49	4.40	86	0.8	95.4	48.2%	32.3%	55.0%
2022	SA	AA	29	0	0	0	6	0	7	10	2	1.3	11.6	9	36.4%	.400	1.57	3.86	89	0.1				
2022	ELP	AAA	29	0	1	0	11	0	11^{2}	8	0	3.9	13.9	18	50.0%	.308	1.11	0.77	67	0.3	96.4	48.0%	32.4%	
2022	SD	MLB	29	0	1	0	13	0	12^{1}	16	2	6.6	11.7	16	33.3%	.412	2.03	9.49	91	0.2	95.6	42.2%	38.3%	58.8%
2022	COL	MLB	29	1	1	0	19	0	20	14	2	4.5	13.1	29	33.3%	.279	1.20	4.05	79	0.4	95.5	48.4%	40.7%	57.2%
2023 DC	*COL*	*MLB*	*30*	*3*	*2*	*0*	*62*	*0*	*53.7*	*45*	*7*	*3.8*	*11.8*	*71*	*37.7%*	*.306*	*1.26*	*3.63*	*88*	*0.7*	*96.0*	*48.1%*	*33.3%*	*52.6%*

Comparables: Danny Salazar (49), Kendall Graveman (48), Joe Kelly (48)

Lamet's up-and-down career took its latest and strangest turn midseason when he was surprisingly included in San Diego's trade for Josh Hader, then waived by Milwaukee barely a day later. Much to the horror of everyone hoping for the live-armed Lamet to end up somewhere safe and secure, it was the Rockies who snagged him shortly thereafter. Injuries have taken their toll on Lamet, pushing him into the relief role that many long feared was in his future. Regardless of his job or landing spot, Lamet's biggest issue at present is that his fastball doesn't really work, both because he has a bad habit of throwing it straight down the middle and because it has below-average vertical and horizontal movement. His slider still brings tears to batters' eyes—he registered a 52.3% whiff rate with it on the year—but until his four-seamer improves, Lamet will remain but a dream for spring. With just one year of team control left, he's running out of time to turn his potential into production.

Germán Márquez RHP Born: 02/22/95 Age: 28 Bats: R Throws: R Height: 6'1" Weight: 230 lb. Origin: International Free Agent, 2011

YEAR	TEAM	LVL	AGE	W	L	SV	G	GS	IP	H	HR	BB/9	K/9	K	GB%	BABIP	WHIP	ERA	DRA-	WARP	MPH	FB%	Whiff%	CSP
2020	COL	MLB	25	4	6	0	13	13	81^{2}	78	6	2.8	8.0	73	50.4%	.300	1.26	3.75	77	1.7	95.7	52.4%	26.3%	50.2%
2021	COL	MLB	26	12	11	0	32	32	180	165	21	3.2	8.8	176	51.3%	.297	1.27	4.40	85	3.1	94.9	53.0%	27.5%	57.8%
2022	COL	MLB	27	9	13	0	31	31	181^{2}	185	30	3.1	7.4	150	48.2%	.292	1.37	5.00	108	1.0	95.4	54.1%	23.1%	58.2%
2023 DC	*COL*	*MLB*	*28*	*10*	*9*	*0*	*29*	*29*	*172*	*170*	*17*	*3.0*	*8.1*	*154*	*49.1%*	*.310*	*1.33*	*3.76*	*94*	*1.9*	*95.3*	*53.4%*	*25.0%*	*56.6%*

Comparables: Julio Teheran (76), Sidney Ponson (74), Jonathon Niese (73)

Looking at Márquez's 2022 stats is enough to make your head hurt. Once you dive into the driving factors behind what was the worst season of his career, you'll get a full-on migraine. Somehow, Márquez tripled the number of sinkers he threw but ended up with a worse ground-ball rate. His decision to toss more worm-killers at the expense of his four-seamer looks to have backfired horrifically, as the pitch earned a .328 BAA and .567 SLG. By Run Value, it graded out as (somehow only) the 10th-worst sinker in the league. So Márquez's main issue was pitch selection then, right? Not so fast. Turns out he didn't really have a choice but to rely on his sinker, as his four-seamer was (somehow) even worse! In short, neither of his heaters had anything near above-average movement. It's enough to make you wonder if he'd be better off junking them both and becoming a pure breaking ball/off-speed guy. That sounds like a terrible idea for a pitcher in Coors, but could it really end up any worse than his sinker-heavy approach to 2022? Facing what might mercifully be his last year in Colorado, Márquez suddenly has a lot to figure out if he wants to return to being a valuable innings-eater in any home park.

Carson Palmquist LHP Born: 10/17/00 Age: 22 Bats: L Throws: L Height: 6'3" Weight: 185 lb. Origin: Round 3, 2022 Draft (#88 overall)

The ceiling on a lefty who doesn't have premium velocity or excellent command is about as high as those in the Shire, but maybe Palmquist, the Rockies' most recent third-rounder, can transcend those limitations in the right role. He was both a starter and a closer in college at Miami, and his stuff plays better out of the bullpen. His velocity is closer to the mid-90s as a reliever, and his low-slot delivery has a stronger chance of keeping batters wrong-footed in limited looks. Ultimately, his secondaries—a tight slider and a changeup with good fade—may make all the difference, as they can help keep batters off his fastball. If not, well, the world needs left-handed ditch diggers, too.

Antonio Senzatela RHP Born: 01/21/95 Age: 28 Bats: R Throws: R Height: 6'1" Weight: 236 lb. Origin: International Free Agent, 2011

YEAR	TEAM	LVL	AGE	W	L	SV	G	GS	IP	H	HR	BB/9	K/9	K	GB%	BABIP	WHIP	ERA	DRA-	WARP	MPH	FB%	Whiff%	CSP
2020	COL	MLB	25	5	3	0	12	12	73^{1}	71	9	2.2	5.0	41	50.8%	.268	1.21	3.44	99	0.9	94.4	56.0%	18.5%	48.4%
2021	COL	MLB	26	4	10	0	28	28	156^{2}	178	12	1.8	6.0	105	50.4%	.326	1.34	4.42	106	1.0	94.8	56.1%	19.8%	56.3%
2022	ABQ	AAA	27	1	0	0	2	2	9	12	2	2.0	0.0	0	48.6%	.303	1.56	5.00	124	-0.1	94.8	55.7%	7.0%	
2022	COL	MLB	27	3	7	0	19	19	92^{1}	133	9	2.2	5.3	54	48.9%	.386	1.69	5.07	137	-0.9	94.3	59.2%	16.3%	54.3%
2023 DC	*COL*	*MLB*	*28*	*7*	*10*	*0*	*27*	*27*	*143*	*177*	*15*	*2.4*	*5.3*	*84*	*49.6%*	*.331*	*1.51*	*5.03*	*122*	*-0.4*	*94.5*	*58.1%*	*17.8%*	*53.6%*

Comparables: Jeff Suppan (82), Ricky Bones (80), Mike Leake (79)

Here's an incomplete list of things easier to do than survive in Coors Field with a strikeout rate that starts with a one: Climb Mount Everest on stilts; perform open-heart surgery blindfolded; get through a Thanksgiving dinner without hearing the word "woke" used entirely wrong and said with pure contempt. Painful as they may be, all of those endeavors sound far more fun than enduring the season Senzatela had. He finished the year with a bottom-10 WARP (right next to Chad Kuhl, fittingly) and tied with the remains of Dallas Keuchel in DRA-. He struggled through a spate of leg, back and arm injuries that culminated with a torn ACL in August that will keep him off a major-league mound until at least May. This is probably the right place to note that 2022 marked the first season of a five-year deal that will pay Senzatela $50.5 million. His lack of swing-and-miss offerings and overall average profile already made that contract look questionable. Now it looks downright disastrous.

Brent Suter LHP Born: 08/29/89 Age: 33 Bats: L Throws: L Height: 6'4" Weight: 213 lb. Origin: Round 31, 2012 Draft (#965 overall)

YEAR	TEAM	LVL	AGE	W	L	SV	G	GS	IP	H	HR	BB/9	K/9	K	GB%	BABIP	WHIP	ERA	DRA-	WARP	MPH	FB%	Whiff%	CSP
2020	MIL	MLB	30	2	0	0	16	4	31^{2}	30	4	1.4	10.8	38	52.9%	.321	1.11	3.13	73	0.8	85.7	79.1%	31.1%	47.3%
2021	MIL	MLB	31	12	5	1	61	1	73^{1}	72	9	2.9	8.5	69	52.1%	.303	1.31	3.07	96	0.8	87.5	77.1%	21.2%	53.1%
2022	MIL	MLB	32	5	3	0	54	0	66^{2}	58	9	3.0	7.2	53	43.8%	.266	1.20	3.78	110	0.3	86.6	70.6%	27.0%	56.7%
2023 DC	*COL*	*MLB*	*33*	*3*	*3*	*3*	*62*	*0*	*53.7*	*55*	*6*	*2.8*	*8.1*	*48*	*45.8%*	*.313*	*1.34*	*4.05*	*101*	*0.2*	*86.9*	*74.4%*	*24.9%*	*54.1%*

Comparables: Chris Rusin (51), Donne Wall (51), Brian Duensing (50)

The term "unicorn" gets thrown around, arguably too often, when describing relievers with funky deliveries and eclectic repertoires. But Suter truly stands out in a sea of un-horned reliever workhorses, and that's for one particular reason: his unwavering faith (i.e. over 60% usage) in his 87-mph fastball. His belief is grounded in the pitch's atypical movement which, combined with Suter's excellent command, allows him to induce pop-ups and weak fly balls despite his lack of premium velocity. But last season, his dogmatic faith in his fastball faltered, as opposing hitters produced a .397 wOBA against it, up markedly from the .302 average it earned a season prior. It might be time to wonder if Suter's magic has worn off, but true unicorns always have more of it in store. He just needs to allow two or three fewer homers next season for what makes him special to shine through—a task that became far more daunting when the Rockies claimed him off waivers in November.

José Ureña RHP Born: 09/12/91 Age: 31 Bats: R Throws: R Height: 6'2" Weight: 208 lb. Origin: International Free Agent, 2008

YEAR	TEAM	LVL	AGE	W	L	SV	G	GS	IP	H	HR	BB/9	K/9	K	GB%	BABIP	WHIP	ERA	DRA-	WARP	MPH	FB%	Whiff%	CSP
2020	MIA	MLB	28	0	3	0	5	5	23^{1}	22	4	5.0	5.8	15	45.9%	.257	1.50	5.40	122	0.0	95.6	60.9%	27.1%	47.1%
2021	DET	MLB	29	4	8	0	26	18	100^{2}	119	14	3.8	6.0	67	52.8%	.319	1.60	5.81	130	-0.6	94.1	63.9%	20.5%	52.0%
2022	ABQ	AAA	30	0	1	0	5	5	21	33	1	5.1	6.0	14	54.1%	.438	2.14	7.29	99	0.1	96.5	45.5%	27.7%	
2022	MIL	MLB	30	0	0	0	4	0	7^{2}	7	1	5.9	3.5	3	42.9%	.222	1.57	3.52	119	0.0	95.9	59.5%	21.6%	54.6%
2022	COL	MLB	30	3	8	0	17	17	89^{1}	102	10	3.8	6.0	60	50.8%	.321	1.57	5.14	129	-0.5	95.7	59.6%	19.5%	48.1%
2023 DC	*COL*	*MLB*	*31*	*6*	*8*	*0*	*22*	*22*	*117.7*	*136*	*14*	*4.0*	*6.2*	*81*	*50.3%*	*.322*	*1.60*	*5.25*	*123*	*-0.5*	*95.2*	*61.6%*	*21.2%*	*49.3%*

Comparables: Jose Lima (72), Brandon McCarthy (71), Mike Pelfrey (70)

Ureña is, at this point in his career, definitively a bad pitcher. He doesn't strike out enough hitters, he walks too many, gives up too much hard contact and all four of his pitches are average at best. But the Rockies apparently saw something in the man whom three other organizations have given up on, including the pitching-savvy Brewers. Maybe it's his 96-mph sinker, the cheat code that the franchise keeps trying to input in order to counter Coors' deleterious high-altitude impact on fly balls. It's not a bad idea in theory, but Ureña is the wrong person to try and execute it given his awful control and command. More likely, it's the fact that all those non-competitive innings he threw last year cost a grand total of $700,000. If Coors is going to turn every pitcher who steps onto its mound into a human piñata, you might as well get one cheap—a role that Ureña will fill once again this year for a modest salary of $3 million.

LINEOUTS

Hitters

HITTER	POS	TEAM	LVL	AGE	PA	R	2B	3B	HR	RBI	BB	K	SB	CS	AVG/OBP/SLG	DRC+	BABIP	BRR	DRP	WARP
Wynton Bernard	CF	ABQ	AAA	31	475	95	31	8	21	92	39	67	30	5	.333/.387/.590	116	.353	1.3	CF(90): -4.4, LF(10): -1.0, RF(5): 0.5	1.8
	CF	COL	MLB	31	42	9	1	0	0	3	0	8	3	1	.286/.286/.310	92	.353	0.1	CF(10): 1.1, LF(1): 0.1, RF(1): 0.1	0.3
Brenton Doyle	OF	HFD	AA	24	507	74	21	3	23	68	23	158	23	3	.246/.287/.450	88	.314	2.8	CF(88): 12.0, RF(28): 1.3	2.2
	OF	ABQ	AAA	24	41	8	1	2	3	9	5	13	0	0	.389/.463/.778	94	.550	0.1	CF(5): 1.3, RF(3): -1.0, LF(1): -0.3	0.2
Jameson Hannah	OF	HFD	AA	24	114	16	5	1	1	4	12	25	7	0	.273/.351/.374	100	.356	2.0	CF(15): 0.1, LF(12): -0.7, RF(1): -0.3	0.4
Dom Nuñez	C	ABQ	AAA	27	285	36	13	3	5	29	34	70	1	1	.223/.319/.360	91	.287	0.2	C(52): -6.5	-0.1
	C	COL	MLB	27	41	3	1	0	0	2	6	10	0	0	.121/.244/.152	83	.160	0.6	C(14): -0.2	0.1
Aaron Schunk	3B	HFD	AA	24	497	62	32	1	14	77	36	115	6	2	.258/.316/.427	94	.312	1.9	3B(112): 0.8, 2B(10): -0.7	1.2

After 10 years, nearly 900 minor-league games and countless bus rides, **Wynton Bernard** finally realized his major-league dreams at 31 when the Rockies called him up mid-August. Kudos to him for persevering long past the point when most would've hung up their spikes. ⓫ Filled with more helium than a Macy's Thanksgiving Day Parade float thanks to a solid 2021 in High-A, **Brenton Doyle** struggled mightily in his first exposure to more advanced pitching. His big, uppercut swing leads to too many strikeouts, even if it also helps him mash some majestic taters. ⓫ **Jameson Hannah** continues to project as this generation's Ben Revere: a speedy, smooth fielder who'll be lucky if his MLB home run total cracks single digits. ⓫ **Dom Nuñez** needs to change his first name to Sub. His whiff-heavy approach negates his power and cost him a shot at regular backup duties in Colorado, making him a minor-league depth piece at best. ⓫ **Aaron Schunk**'s last name is the sound his prospect stock made as it tumbled like a stone last offseason. An okay year in Double-A revitalized it somewhat, but as with cryptocurrency, it's smart to be weary of Schunk costs.

Pitchers

PITCHER	TEAM	LVL	AGE	W	L	SV	G	GS	IP	H	HR	BB/9	K/9	K	GB%	BABIP	WHIP	ERA	DRA-	WARP	MPH	FB%	WHF	CSP
Ty Blach	ABQ	AAA	31	1	5	0	15	1	36	44	3	2.0	5.0	20	46.9%	.331	1.44	4.50	113	-0.1	91.0	51.3%	17.5%	
	COL	MLB	31	1	0	1	24	1	44^{1}	51	4	2.2	5.9	29	41.7%	.322	1.40	5.89	116	0.1	91.2	55.0%	20.0%	58.4%
Jhoulys Chacín	COL	MLB	34	4	2	0	35	0	47^{1}	55	7	4.0	7.0	37	38.4%	.316	1.61	7.61	121	-0.1	93.2	44.5%	20.9%	53.9%
Noah Davis	HFD	AA	25	8	8	0	26	26	133^{1}	133	26	4.1	10.3	152	34.2%	.319	1.45	5.54	122	0.3				
	COL	MLB	25	0	0	0	1	0	1	3	1	9.0	18.0	2	50.0%	.667	4.00	18.00	108	0.0	94.8	37.5%	25.0%	59.9%
Jaden Hill	RCK	ROK	22	0	0	0	7	7	10^{1}	11	0	3.5	9.6	11	44.8%	.379	1.45	3.48						
	FRE	A	22	0	0	0	3	3	7^{1}	7	0	2.5	17.2	14	38.5%	.538	1.23	2.45	78	0.1				
Pierce Johnson	ELP	AAA	31	0	0	1	5	0	5	2	0	0.0	10.8	6	54.5%	.182	0.40	1.80	90	0.1	94.0	46.4%	40.0%	
	SD	MLB	31	1	2	0	15	0	14^{1}	14	1	5.0	13.2	21	57.1%	.382	1.53	5.02	73	0.3	94.9	38.6%	28.0%	59.4%
Victor Juarez	FRE	A	19	6	5	0	21	21	103	102	15	2.9	8.7	100	42.9%	.313	1.31	4.98	108	-0.4				
Peter Lambert	ABQ	AAA	25	0	2	0	4	4	8^{2}	11	0	6.2	11.4	11	37.5%	.458	1.96	6.23	89	0.1	93.9	41.3%	31.9%	
Justin Lawrence	ABQ	AAA	27	1	0	1	28	0	29^{1}	17	2	4.0	15.0	49	40.7%	.288	1.02	3.07	72	0.7	96.3	54.7%	36.2%	
	COL	MLB	27	3	1	1	38	0	42^{2}	44	3	4.6	10.1	48	50.0%	.350	1.55	5.70	92	0.6	95.3	55.3%	24.7%	53.4%
Chris McMahon	RCK	ROK	23	0	0	0	4	2	10^{2}	17	1	2.5	7.6	9	37.8%	.444	1.88	2.53						
	SPO	A+	23	1	0	0	4	4	18	30	4	1.0	8.0	16	37.1%	.448	1.78	7.00	116	0.0				
Riley Pint	HFD	AA	24	2	1	0	38	0	42^{2}	31	4	6.1	11.6	55	54.8%	.303	1.41	4.64	90	0.8				
Joe Rock	SPO	A+	21	7	8	0	20	20	107^{2}	87	10	3.8	9.1	109	44.7%	.270	1.23	4.43	103	0.8				
	HFD	AA	21	0	0	0	2	2	8	9	2	5.6	12.4	11	45.5%	.350	1.75	10.12	84	0.2				
Jordy Vargas	RCK	ROK	18	2	1	0	7	5	26^{2}	13	0	1.4	13.5	40	49.1%	.245	0.64	2.36						
	FRE	A	18	2	0	0	6	6	24^{2}	20	5	4.7	8.8	24	44.6%	.250	1.34	3.65	106	-0.1				
Sam Weatherly	RCK	ROK	23	0	1	0	4	2	7^{2}	8	1	1.2	21.1	18	35.7%	.538	1.17	3.52						
T.J. Zeuch	LOU	AAA	26	0	1	0	5	5	22^{1}	18	2	4.0	10.5	26	60.7%	.296	1.25	3.63	91	0.4				
	MEM	AAA	26	0	4	0	5	5	19^{1}	39	6	5.1	9.3	20	36.8%	.532	2.59	11.64	117	0.1	93.0	46.0%	27.0%	
	CIN	MLB	26	0	3	0	3	3	10^{2}	24	5	5.9	4.2	5	49.0%	.432	2.91	15.19	158	-0.2	91.9	44.0%	15.9%	52.1%

After two years lost in the wilderness, **Ty Blach** reemerged in the majors as a swingman/long reliever in the single worst stadium imaginable for a soft-tossing pitcher with zero swing-and-miss stuff. It went about as well as you'd expect, though he was at least able to nudge his career strikeout rate over five. ⚾ On September 15, the Rockies put an end to a failed reunion tour, releasing **Jhoulys Chacín** after a brutal summer of nominal relief work. Once the bright and shiny future of the franchise over a decade ago, he's now back-of-the-bullpen fodder for any team ready to settle for below league-average production at minimal cost. ⚾ A funhouse mirror version of Dustin May, **Noah Davis** showed why no one claimed him in last year's Rule 5 draft by getting smashed in Double-A. His lone MLB appearance revealed his true colors as a three-true-outcomes pitcher: he faced seven batters, walked two, struck out two and gave up a homer. ⚾ Back from Tommy John surgery, **Jaden Hill** impressed in a handful of outings late in the season, showing the power fastball that makes him a potential late-inning relief weapon if he can stay healthy and continue developing his secondaries. ⚾ While a pierced johnson is its own special kind of injury, this **Pierce Johnson** missed most of the season with right forearm tendonitis. After returning in September he pitched 4⅓ scoreless innings in the postseason, setting up a one-year deal with the Rockies sure to inflict even more pain. ⚾ Colorado gave **Victor Juarez** an aggressive assignment, sending him to Low-A at 18. The results were mixed, but he held his own against much older competition—he was the youngest player on Fresno's roster—while seeing his fastball velocity spike to 92–95 mph. ⚾ **Peter Lambert** has barely pitched since the start of 2019 thanks to Tommy John surgery and its after-effects. If he can return to the mound in '23, it'll be as rotation depth in the upper minors as he rebuilds his stamina. ⚾ **Justin Lawrence** seems to have figured out how to throw strikes regularly, taking his walk rate from Rick Ankiel-esque to something more Joe Kelly-adjacent. Somehow, that hasn't resulted in more whiffs yet. ⚾ A lat strain cost **Chris McMahon** most of a crucial season; set to turn 24 in February, he has yet to get out of High-A. He must be dying to move to Hartford, a feeling that no one in human history has ever before experienced. ⚾ **Scott Oberg**'s on-field career is likely over thanks to blood clots in his arm that have kept him off the field since 2019. Fortunately, the down time let him get involved in Colorado's scouting department, where he'll look to start his next journey. ⚾ Congrats to **Helcris Olivarez** on finally posting a walk rate under four per nine on the season. Too bad that was because a left shoulder strain limited him to a single game on the year. ⚾ **Riley Pint** seemed tapped before the season started, but his retirement proved brief. His return to the game was more along the lines of Michael Jordan on the Wizards than anything inspirational, as his control remained well below average. ⚾ MLB is saturated with fastball-slider righties, but what **Joe Rock** dares to ask is, "what if that package, but from the left side?" If he truly wants to find out he'll need to improve his fastball command and velocity. ⚾ Shoulder surgery kept **Ryan Rolison** off the mound entirely in 2022 after a 2021 season mostly lost to appendicitis and a fractured hand. As such, he's yet to fulfill his destiny as an up-and-down spot starter who never makes it through the fifth inning. ⚾ Being a highly touted Rockies pitching prospect is like being the biggest lobster in the tank at a seafood restaurant, futilely trying to snap the rubber bands around your claws so that you don't get thrown into the pot of boiling water. **Jordy Vargas** is still a few years away from cooking at Coors Field, but he retains intriguing upside even if his first stateside stint was a mixed bag. ⚾ A strained left shoulder kept **Sam Weatherly** on the shelf for nearly the entire season. Too bad it wasn't an illness that sidelined him instead, or we could've described him as being under the Weath [a giant cane begins to appear from off stage]. ⚾ **T.J. Zeuch**'s last name is pronounced 'Zoik,' as in the cartoonish sound made by the vaudeville hook the manager used to yank him off the mound after each disastrous start.

LOS ANGELES DODGERS

Essay by Megan Gailey

Player comments by Daniel R. Epstein, Dustin Nosler and BP staff

I grew up in Indianapolis, a sports-obsessed city without an MLB team. As a diehard sports fan, from a hometown that loves basketball and football almost as much as Ranch dressing and church, it always felt like we were missing something. Don't let me fool you, Indy had and continues to have baseball in the Indianapolis Indians. Victory Field is gorgeous, the games are fun and there are fireworks, which was almost all that was needed to convince 8-year-old me that I was seeing the big leagues. It feels like the athletes need you just as much as you need them. As someone with codependency issues, this is more or less my dream scenario.

Post-college, I made the requisite Midwestern pilgrimage to Chicago. I wound up close enough to Wrigley Field that my roommates and I got that yearly spring mailing from the city. I'm paraphrasing but I think it went something like: "Happy baseball season! Sorry about all the guys that are about to pee in your yard." I saw my fair share of good (and very bad) Cubs teams, drank Old Style and frequented the Clark Street Taco Bell (RIP). Still, the Irish Catholic in me was somehow pulled to the Ozzie Guillen White Sox—I love a team with a chip on its shoulder.

From Chicago, I went off to NYC. The Mets had cheaper tickets, but people look hotter in the Yankees cap. I say all of this to admit: none of these casual fandoms ever felt exactly right. Yes, I metaphorically dated four teams—I got around, okay!—but was never willing to commit. I was the classic 30-something man who refused to meet his longtime girlfriend's parents...but for, er, baseball.

The truth is I didn't even know I was holding back until I came to Los Angeles. Fate's first indication that the Dodgers were going to be for me was when I got to do stand-up on *Conan*, my very first time on TV. I wanted to look great. I searched high and low for the right outfit and wound up buying a dress in my favorite color, "Colts blue." A cameraman held it up to get the lighting right and said, "Great dress, Dodgers blue." I did my set, had the time of my life, ate the obligatory In & Out and flew back to New York City to be at my nannying job the next day.

LOS ANGELES DODGERS PROSPECTUS

2022 W-L: 111-51, 1ST IN NL WEST

Pythag	.716	1st	DER	.732	1st
RS/G	5.23	1st	DRC+	106	7th
RA/G	3.17	1st	DRA-	89	4th
dWin%	.602	5th	FIP	3.46	4th
Payroll	$281M	1st	B-Age	30.2	28th
M$/MW	$4.2M	16th	P-Age	29.3	17th

395′

375′ 375′

330′ 330′

- Opened 1962
- Open air
- Natural surface
- Fence profile: 4′ to 8′

Park Factors

Runs	Runs/RH	Runs/LH	HR/RH	HR/LH
104	106	100	120	104

Top Hitter WARP	6.4 Mookie Betts
Top Pitcher WARP	2.6 Julio Urías
2023 Top Prospect	Diego Cartaya

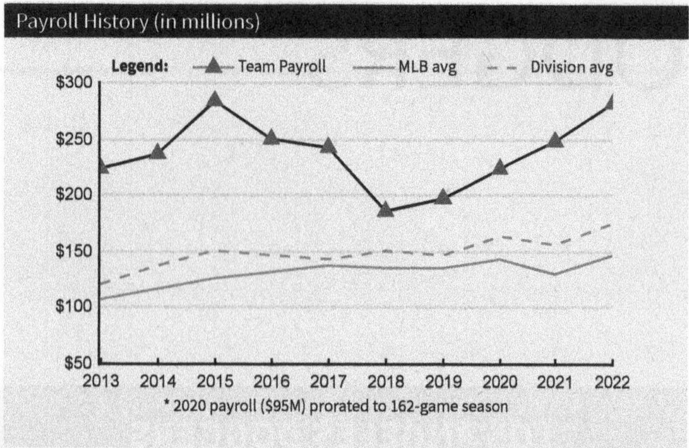

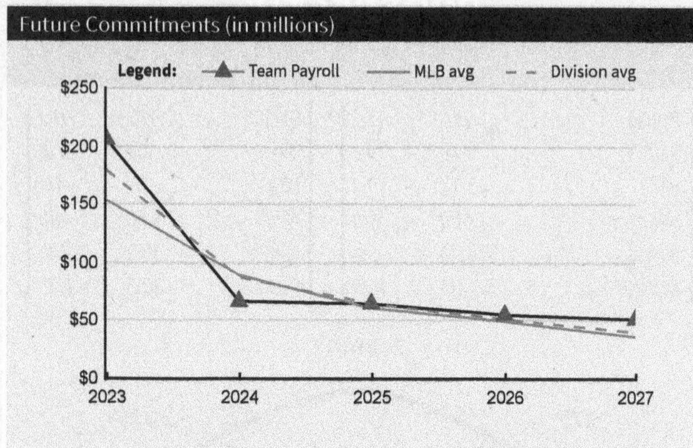

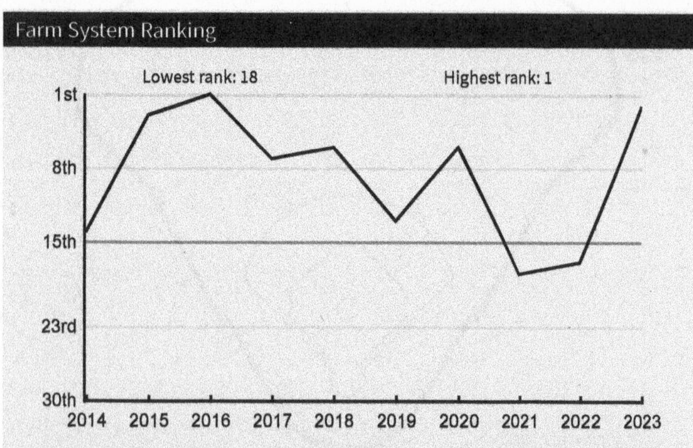

Personnel

President, Baseball Operations
Andrew Friedman

Executive Vice President & General Manager
Brandon Gomes

Senior Vice President, Baseball Operations
Josh Byrnes

Vice President & Assistant General Manager
Jeffrey Kingston

Vice President & Assistant General Manager
Alex Slater

Manager
Dave Roberts

I moved to LA in 2016, and that summer I had the hottest first date of my baseball life. My manager (very LA) took me as a guest of her company to sit behind home plate (very very LA) at Dodger damn Stadium. I'm talking about the seats Mary Hart sits in. I "love" sports but I love free food and drinks. Being only a nascent celebrity myself, I gawked at my higher-listed colleagues—movie stars, musicians, agents, the full Hollywood bingo card. But the real charm for me, and the proof that I was not yet totally ruined by my rocket ship of fame, was that there were families everywhere. (Or, at least, more than you see at Soho House.) An 18-month-old was sitting next to me. A toddler! We both sat there, guests of guests made comfortable by the sport. Both chomping on nachos. Both drooling. You get the idea.

The game itself was almost incidental, but it did not disappoint. My first in-person Dodgers home run was hit by my shining compatriot in red-headedness: Justin Turner.

What I felt that day was the real thing...for, er, baseball. Whenever any friends or family visit, now, I take them to see the Dodgers. I brought my parents, one of whom was having severe mobility issues, to a game. We climbed up the Vin Scully Avenue hill, climbed up more stairs to our section and just as I could feel my dad getting too tired to go much further, we arrived at our very high seats. We settled in, took a deep breath and then the team honored a World War II veteran by having him throw out the first pitch. My parents and I sat there sobbing. I tear up thinking about it now. The sun was setting, the palm trees were sparkling and the tribute to this nonagenarian lifelong Dodgers fan was gorgeous.

The Dodgers' popularity doesn't just come from the stadium, uniforms or nachos, of course. The team is consistently great. They go out and get the players they want; they contend with the perennial regularity of A24 at the Oscars. They're persistent players in free agency and at the trade deadline. And because of the organization's willingness to bring in fresh faces, the Dodgers' lineup ends up mirroring LA's population: at once new to town and emblematic of it.

The 2022 Dodgers were powered by three superstar transplants: Mookie Betts, Freddie Freeman and Trea Turner. These players called Boston, Atlanta and Washington home before winding up in Southern California. I'm sure I don't need to point out to you, the astute Baseball Prospectus reader, that I am just like these extremely talented men. Stay with me now! Mookie, Freddie, Trea and I all started our (illustrious) careers elsewhere. We all found success in smaller markets but had more to prove. And when the opportunity for a bigger stage came knocking, we took that leap! I am Mookie. Mookie is me!

Living in an all-new city can be a little isolating. You have to make new friends, find your chosen family, create new memories. It helps to have common interests. My friends and I like to sit around and talk about the worst shows we've ever done. Mookie, Freddie and Trea (the last of the list since having pulled the unusual follow-up of decamping to Philly) liked to mash baseballs.

LA gets a lot of flack for being flashy, expensive and out of touch. (So, incidentally, do the Dodgers, who by the time you read this will probably have replaced Turner with your team's star shortstop.) Some of these critiques have their merits. But what they ignore is that Los Angeles is a city of almost four million people, and only like one percent of those people are Kardashians and *Entourage* actors. The rest of LA is made up of "regular people" (as I like to call them from the backs of my increasingly decadent limousines): families, nurses, Hollywood's laborers, folks who could never afford a BBL or tell you what it stands for. (It stands for Brazilian Butt Lift.) And even in this bizarro city, the Dodgers serve the function that the Red Sox do in Boston, and the Reds do in Cincinnati. Everybody, workaday production assistant and crypto-fraud-committing A-lister alike, cares about them. Everyone shares in the civic pride—the specifically Angelan joy of pummeling other cities with their own expats—and everybody fosters the same worry and sharpens the same unacknowledged inferiority complex when another year of dominance comes and goes with just a short-season championship to show for it.

As of right now, Los Angeles is home to two NBA franchises, two NFL teams, an NHL team, three soccer teams and all of UCLA's and USC's sports. Not to mention movies, TV shows, award ceremonies, the LA Philharmonic, the beach, Adele singing on a mountaintop, etc. The Rams played in a home game for their Super Bowl win and I had to tell people it was even happening. There's a lot going on, and we're all too self-obsessed to register most of it. But you don't choose to pay attention to the Dodgers, any more than you choose to pay attention to the beating of your own heart. They're just there.

I now live 10 minutes from Dodgers Stadium. We recently invited everyone on our street over to hang out in our driveway. Very Midwest meets LA; you can't say I don't remember where I came from! As we made small talk, I heard my husband ask one of the men that had been in our neighborhood for three generations, "Are you Lakers fans?" (It must be noted that my husband loves LeBron and is more loyal to him than I would ever ask him to be to me). Our neighbor's response was, "I'm a Dodgers fan."

The first sporting event my husband and I brought our son to was a Dodgers game. He was three months old and as I changed a dirty diaper in the stadium parking lot, I wondered why I had brought an infant to this place. But we had this event on the calendar before I even gave birth because it was Filipino Heritage Night. My husband is Filipino and my son is biracial, and once we got inside the stadium we saw other Filipino babies and families everywhere. We also saw my extended, and very white, and heavily freckled family there; I'd chosen this sacred location for them to meet our baby. Granted, my child is too young for nachos, yet, and I'm not sure he can detail the differences in Mookie's and Freddie's batting styles. And, absolutely, he will be free to make his own decisions in due time.

Still, it is every parent's dream that their child finds love in their life. And when mine gets serious with a baseball team, I hope he chooses right. ■

—Megan Gailey is a comedian, podcaster and writer in Los Angeles.

Hitters

Jacob Amaya SS Born: 09/03/98 Age: 24 Bats: R Throws: R Height: 6'0" Weight: 180 lb. Origin: Round 11, 2017 Draft (#340 overall)

YEAR	TEAM	LVL	AGE	PA	R	2B	3B	HR	RBI	BB	K	SB	CS	Whiff%	AVG/OBP/SLG	DRC+	BABIP	BRR	DRP	WARP
2021	GDD	WIN	22	67	14	3	0	3	6	13	13	1	1		.333/.463/.556		.395			
2021	TUL	AA	22	476	60	15	1	12	47	52	103	5	0		.216/.303/.343	94	.254	-0.9	SS(112): -3.8	0.7
2022	TUL	AA	23	216	39	10	3	9	26	32	29	3	1		.264/.370/.500	120	.267	1.4	SS(49): -2.2	1.2
2022	OKC	AAA	23	351	46	10	1	8	45	49	83	3	1	26.0%	.259/.368/.381	102	.329	-0.3	SS(80): 0.9, 2B(4): -0.4	1.1
2023 DC	*LAD*	*MLB*	*24*	*169*	*17*	*6*	*1*	*3*	*14*	*17*	*39*	*0*	*1*	*23.7%*	*.210/.296/.324*	*73*	*.266*	*0.7*	*2B 0, SS 0*	*0.0*

Comparables: Orlando Calixte (60), Abiatal Avelino (58), Ehire Adrianza (53)

Heading into the offseason, the consensus was that the Dodgers were going to secure a long-term option at shortstop. They could have re-signed Trea Turner, or dipped into the free-agent market for another of the premium shortstops available. Fast-forward to now—well, that didn't happen. What does this have to do with Amaya? The 24-year-old could be in line to get playing time in Los Angeles, seeing as Gavin Lux is atop the Dodgers' shortstop depth chart. That's not going to end well for anyone except Amaya. His numbers look more pedestrian than one would think after a hot start (.957 OPS through May), but an ice-cold June and July (.601 OPS)—that also included a promotion to Triple-A—dampened his overall production. He finished the season on a stronger note (.854 OPS over the final two months) and his glove never slumped. If (when) Lux falters at shortstop, Amaya might be the beneficiary.

Austin Barnes C Born: 12/28/89 Age: 33 Bats: R Throws: R Height: 5'10" Weight: 187 lb. Origin: Round 9, 2011 Draft (#283 overall)

YEAR	TEAM	LVL	AGE	PA	R	2B	3B	HR	RBI	BB	K	SB	CS	Whiff%	AVG/OBP/SLG	DRC+	BABIP	BRR	DRP	WARP
2020	LAD	MLB	30	104	14	3	0	1	9	13	24	3	0	25.0%	.244/.353/.314	95	.323	0.6	C(28): 3.3	0.7
2021	LAD	MLB	31	225	28	8	0	6	23	20	56	1	0	26.9%	.215/.299/.345	85	.268	0.7	C(52): 4.5, 2B(7): 0	1.0
2022	LAD	MLB	32	212	31	6	0	8	26	27	37	2	1	17.7%	.212/.324/.380	111	.222	0.4	C(55): 8.8	2.0
2023 DC	*LAD*	*MLB*	*33*	*220*	*26*	*8*	*0*	*6*	*23*	*24*	*45*	*3*	*0*	*20.7%*	*.234/.332/.387*	*100*	*.276*	*1.3*	*C 7*	*1.7*

Comparables: Chad Moeller (55), Martín Maldonado (54), Lenny Webster (53)

YEAR	TEAM	P. COUNT	FRM RUNS	BLK RUNS	THRW RUNS	TOT RUNS
2020	LAD	3848	3.4	0.0	0.0	3.4
2021	LAD	6843	5.3	0.0	0.5	5.8
2022	LAD	7463	8.2	0.2	0.4	8.8
2023	*LAD*	*8418*	*7.2*	*0.2*	*-0.2*	*7.3*

The movie about Barnes' career would be a sci-fi thriller, in which a man fights desperately to stave off obsoletion from robots taking over the world. Okay, maybe not *the world*—just the strike zone. Most of Barnes' value derives from elite pitch framing, which will disappear as soon as MLB adopts automated balls and strikes. After the film establishes world-building and plot, the second act is about him proving he can actually hit. He always drew tons of walks (12.1% career rate), but his contact rate jumped from 76% in 2021 to 84.2% last season. That contact wasn't particularly high quality, but Barnes deserved better than an absurdly low .222 BABIP. The movie's climax takes place in 2023, when he must show whether the improvements are sustainable. If so, he may remain the best backup catcher in MLB—even if the robots take control. (It seems likely that some form of robo umps will be implemented in 2024, probably with a challenge system.)

Mookie Betts RF

Born: 10/07/92 Age: 30 Bats: R Throws: R Height: 5'9" Weight: 180 lb. Origin: Round 5, 2011 Draft (#172 overall)

YEAR	TEAM	LVL	AGE	PA	R	2B	3B	HR	RBI	BB	K	SB	CS	Whiff%	AVG/OBP/SLG	DRC+	BABIP	BRR	DRP	WARP
2020	LAD	MLB	27	246	47	9	1	16	39	24	38	10	2	13.8%	.292/.366/.562	133	.289	3.7	RF(52): 3.6, 2B(1): 0.1, CF(1): 0	2.5
2021	LAD	MLB	28	550	93	29	3	23	58	68	86	10	5	16.8%	.264/.367/.487	124	.276	-1.3	RF(98): 0.2, CF(30): -1.8, 2B(7): -0.3	3.1
2022	LAD	MLB	29	639	117	40	3	35	82	55	104	12	2	16.5%	.269/.340/.533	133	.272	4.5	RF(136): 6.1, 2B(7): 0.3	5.6
2023 DC	*LAD*	*MLB*	*30*	*647*	*102*	*34*	*2*	*30*	*80*	*63*	*94*	*14*	*3*	*16.5%*	*.269/.351/.497*	*132*	*.279*	*6.8*	*RF 16*	*6.3*

Comparables: Al Kaline (81), Ruben Sierra (76), Dave Winfield (76)

Betts' dalliance with second base is now an annual fling. For the second straight year, he played seven games at the keystone, starting five—to the delight of fantasy players everywhere. At his regular position, he won his fifth Fielding Bible award and sixth Gold Glove. On top of that, he set a career high in home runs, recorded double-digit steals for the eighth consecutive season and achieved his fourth top-five MVP finish. It's not enough for him to dominate every facet of the game as a hitter, baserunner and outfielder—he also has to remind everyone that, yes, he could be a great middle infielder if need be. He's one of baseball's few flawless players, and possesses more talent than the rules of the game allow him to display at any given time.

★ ★ ★ *2023 Top 101 Prospect* **#59** ★ ★ ★

Michael Busch 2B

Born: 11/09/97 Age: 25 Bats: L Throws: R Height: 6'1" Weight: 210 lb. Origin: Round 1, 2019 Draft (#31 overall)

YEAR	TEAM	LVL	AGE	PA	R	2B	3B	HR	RBI	BB	K	SB	CS	Whiff%	AVG/OBP/SLG	DRC+	BABIP	BRR	DRP	WARP
2021	TUL	AA	23	495	84	27	1	20	67	70	129	2	3		.267/.386/.484	112	.337	0.4	2B(88): 7.2, 1B(11): -0.1	3.0
2022	TUL	AA	24	137	31	6	0	11	29	24	36	1	0		.306/.445/.667	127	.355	0.1	2B(26): -0.7, LF(2): 0.4	0.8
2022	OKC	AAA	24	504	87	32	0	21	79	50	131	3	2	26.6%	.266/.343/.480	98	.327	-2.4	2B(93): -3.6, LF(11): -0.2	0.7
2023 DC	*LAD*	*MLB*	*25*	*204*	*23*	*9*	*0*	*6*	*22*	*18*	*57*	*1*	*0*	*28.3%*	*.222/.303/.382*	*88*	*.291*	*0.1*	*2B 0, LF 0*	*0.2*

Comparables: Mike Baxter (59), Kennys Vargas (57), Bruce Caldwell (57)

The second of two first-rounders selected by LA in 2019, Busch has separated himself from Kody Hoese—a full-fledged bust at this point. If he played almost anywhere but in the Dodgers' organization, Busch probably would have made his MLB debut by now. He had nothing left to prove in the minors after July, but he lacked the *Veteran Presence* many teams have come to love. That, and there was literally no playing time for him in Los Angeles. He's a bat-first "second baseman" who might end up as a first baseman or left fielder. He's heading into his age-25 season and has all the makings of the next Max Muncy—the rectangular one, not the teenager (coincidentally) drafted by the Athletics. And like the quadrilateral Dodger slugger, Busch is going to make it on the strength of his bat (even if Muncy's defense is underrated by most).

★ ★ ★ *2023 Top 101 Prospect* **#19** ★ ★ ★

Diego Cartaya C

Born: 09/07/01 Age: 21 Bats: R Throws: R Height: 6'3" Weight: 219 lb. Origin: International Free Agent, 2018

YEAR	TEAM	LVL	AGE	PA	R	2B	3B	HR	RBI	BB	K	SB	CS	Whiff%	AVG/OBP/SLG	DRC+	BABIP	BRR	DRP	WARP
2021	RC	A	19	137	31	6	0	10	31	18	37	0	0		.298/.409/.614	119	.353	0.5	C(31): -4.0	0.4
2022	RC	A	20	163	31	9	1	9	31	23	44	0	0		.260/.405/.550	118	.321	0.1	C(23): -1.5	0.7
2022	GL	A+	20	282	43	13	0	13	41	40	75	1	0		.251/.379/.476	109	.310	0.6	C(41): -2.6	1.1
2023 non-DC	*LAD*	*MLB*	*21*	*251*	*24*	*10*	*0*	*6*	*26*	*22*	*80*	*0*	*0*	*34.4%*	*.203/.291/.348*	*76*	*.283*	*0.2*	*C 0*	*0.2*

Comparables: Francisco Mejía (58), A.J. Jimenez (55), Jorge Alfaro (54)

YEAR	TEAM	P. COUNT	FRM RUNS	BLK RUNS	THRW RUNS	TOT RUNS
2021	RC	4422	-3.7	-1.0	1.0	-3.8
2022	RC	3762	-1.4	-0.9	0.9	-1.3
2022	GL	6178	-2.6	-1.2	1.9	-1.9
2023	*LAD*	*6956*	*-3.5*	*-1.2*	*0.0*	*-4.7*

Cartaya is often compared to a certain Kansas City Royal backstop who also hails from Venezuela, but the younger backstop has a much more rounded offensive approach. Cartaya's contact rates could use a bit of work, but he has the plate discipline thing down—through A-ball, at least. There were early rumblings that he might have to move from behind the dish, but the 20-year-old quashed any talk of that by displaying surprising agility for a kid his size and a cannon of an arm. He's probably still 18-24 months away from the majors, but when he arrives, he's likely to stick. He's such a high-quality prospect that he might incentivize the Dodgers to move Will Smith from behind the plate.

Freddie Freeman 1B Born: 09/12/89 Age: 33 Bats: L Throws: R Height: 6'5" Weight: 220 lb. Origin: Round 2, 2007 Draft (#78 overall)

YEAR	TEAM	LVL	AGE	PA	R	2B	3B	HR	RBI	BB	K	SB	CS	Whiff%	AVG/OBP/SLG	DRC+	BABIP	BRR	DRP	WARP
2020	ATL	MLB	30	262	51	23	1	13	53	45	37	2	0	20.1%	.341/.462/.640	148	.366	-1.1	1B(58): 2	2.2
2021	ATL	MLB	31	695	120	25	2	31	83	85	107	8	3	21.0%	.300/.393/.503	134	.321	2.3	1B(159): 0.4	4.7
2022	LAD	MLB	32	708	117	47	2	21	100	84	102	13	3	19.5%	.325/.407/.511	136	.359	0.0	1B(159): 1.7	4.7
2023 DC	*LAD*	*MLB*	*33*	*663*	*100*	*34*	*2*	*24*	*89*	*79*	*93*	*8*	*1*	*19.7%*	*.302/.392/.499*	*150*	*.327*	*2.7*	*1B 2*	*5.6*

Comparables: Keith Hernandez (79), Eddie Murray (78), Boog Powell (77)

In his first season in Chavez Ravine, Freeman was like Big Worm from *Friday*—as emotional as he was formidable. His tearful return to Atlanta resurfaced old emotions and he ultimately fired his representation within a week. His final plate appearance of 2022 left everyone choked up for a different reason, as he swung through an 0-2 slider from Josh Hader to end the Dodgers' playoff run. Despite the tears along the way, it was one of his best campaigns. He led the NL in on-base percentage, doubles, plate appearances, hits (199) and runs scored (117). If the team advances deeper into the postseason in 2023, he'll be the guy driving the ice cream truck.

Jason Heyward OF Born: 08/09/89 Age: 33 Bats: L Throws: L Height: 6'5" Weight: 240 lb. Origin: Round 1, 2007 Draft (#14 overall)

YEAR	TEAM	LVL	AGE	PA	R	2B	3B	HR	RBI	BB	K	SB	CS	Whiff%	AVG/OBP/SLG	DRC+	BABIP	BRR	DRP	WARP
2020	CHC	MLB	30	181	20	6	2	6	22	30	37	2	0	23.6%	.265/.392/.456	113	.311	2.0	RF(50): 0.9	1.1
2021	CHC	MLB	31	353	35	15	2	8	30	27	68	5	1	23.8%	.214/.280/.347	82	.247	2.4	RF(97): 1.8	0.6
2022	CHC	MLB	32	151	15	5	1	1	10	11	32	1	0	27.9%	.204/.278/.277	77	.260	0.9	CF(26): -1.1, RF(21): -0.5	0.0
2023 non-DC	*LAD*	*MLB*	*33*	*251*	*25*	*9*	*1*	*6*	*26*	*22*	*54*	*2*	*1*	*26.0%*	*.233/.309/.371*	*90*	*.280*	*0.6*	*RF 0, CF 0*	*0.4*

Comparables: Ruben Sierra (63), Johnny Callison (60), Rusty Staub (58)

The Cubs announced that Heyward would not return for 2023 back in early August. As the team has slowly, gently—but not super reluctantly—ushered its former core out the door, Heyward's departure did not seem to be as mourned as many of the others. This is due to the polarizing nature of a starter who fields better than he hits and then misses huge chunks of time due to injury. But no one can question his legacy as the rain delay inspirational speech-giver who spurred the Cubs to win the 2016 World Series. Signed by the Dodgers to a minor-league deal, Heyward leaves Chicago as a champion, a curse-breaker and a Gold Glover.

Eddys Leonard SS Born: 11/10/00 Age: 22 Bats: R Throws: R Height: 5'11" Weight: 195 lb. Origin: International Free Agent, 2017

YEAR	TEAM	LVL	AGE	PA	R	2B	3B	HR	RBI	BB	K	SB	CS	Whiff%	AVG/OBP/SLG	DRC+	BABIP	BRR	DRP	WARP
2021	RC	A	20	308	59	19	2	14	57	34	74	6	2		.295/.399/.544	122	.362	-0.1	SS(32): -1.0, 2B(16): 1.2, 3B(9): 1.1	1.9
2021	GL	A+	20	184	30	10	2	8	24	17	42	3	1		.299/.375/.530	117	.360	-0.4	3B(15): -2.1, 2B(11): -1.1, CF(11): -1.1	0.4
2022	GL	A+	21	566	80	32	4	15	61	45	119	4	4		.264/.348/.435	109	.317	1.3	SS(104): -7.0, 2B(8): 0.9, 3B(7): -0.5	2.0
2023 non-DC	*LAD*	*MLB*	*22*	*251*	*23*	*11*	*1*	*5*	*24*	*15*	*64*	*3*	*1*	*30.4%*	*.232/.297/.364*	*83*	*.303*	*0.0*	*2B 0, 3B 0*	*0.2*

Comparables: Aderlin Rodríguez (67), Dawel Lugo (63), Aaron Cunningham (62)

Somewhat surprisingly added to the Dodgers' 40-man roster in 2021 after a breakout season, Leonard didn't enjoy the same success across a full run of the Midwest League. Still, the future utility man was solid enough that he'll likely progress to the Texas League this season, so he's unlikely to eddy in High-A. With the way the Dodgers tend to covet versatile position players, Leonard could find himself in Los Angeles by 2024 as a potential replacement for Chris Taylor—probably his best comp. For Leonard's sake, here's hoping he can keep the strikeouts in check, because he probably won't walk enough to keep pitchers honest.

Gavin Lux 2B Born: 11/23/97 Age: 25 Bats: L Throws: R Height: 6'2" Weight: 190 lb. Origin: Round 1, 2016 Draft (#20 overall)

YEAR	TEAM	LVL	AGE	PA	R	2B	3B	HR	RBI	BB	K	SB	CS	Whiff%	AVG/OBP/SLG	DRC+	BABIP	BRR	DRP	WARP
2020	LAD	MLB	22	69	8	2	0	3	8	6	19	1	0	26.1%	.175/.246/.349	86	.195	0.4	2B(18): -0.1	0.1
2021	OKC	AAA	23	74	18	4	0	1	10	6	15	0	0		.279/.338/.382	92	.346	1.0	2B(8): 0.1, 3B(4): -0.1, LF(1): 3.1	0.5
2021	LAD	MLB	23	381	49	12	4	7	46	41	83	4	1	23.1%	.242/.328/.364	90	.300	1.9	SS(59): -1.1, 2B(27): 0.6, LF(11): -0.1	1.1
2022	LAD	MLB	24	471	66	20	7	6	42	47	95	7	2	23.3%	.276/.346/.399	94	.341	-1.1	2B(102): -2.9, LF(28): 0.7, SS(9): -0.6	0.7
2023 DC	*LAD*	*MLB*	*25*	*552*	*69*	*21*	*7*	*14*	*62*	*55*	*115*	*11*	*2*	*23.0%*	*.269/.346/.428*	*114*	*.326*	*8.8*	*SS 4, 2B 0*	*3.9*

Comparables: Asdrúbal Cabrera (54), Luis Sardinas (53), Lou Whitaker (52)

It's time to part ways with our expectations of Lux from when he was a consensus top-five prospect. The problem isn't the player himself; it's that our collective belief in him was unreasonable. (That should make him feel better, right?) He popped 26 homers in Double-A and Triple-A in 2019, which was part of the basis for our excitement. It turns out that 2019 was an aberrative season across the board and he's one of many players who couldn't sustain his power spike. Now he has just 18 home runs in 1,003 major-league plate appearances and a ground-ball rate approaching 50%. On the bright side, his DRC+ has gained an average of five points each year. If he sustains that rate of progress, he should finally be above average by 2024. See? The key to successful post-prospect relationships is setting a low bar. Optimists are never pleasantly surprised.

J.D. Martinez DH Born: 08/21/87 Age: 35 Bats: R Throws: R Height: 6'3" Weight: 230 lb. Origin: Round 20, 2009 Draft (#611 overall)

YEAR	TEAM	LVL	AGE	PA	R	2B	3B	HR	RBI	BB	K	SB	CS	Whiff%	AVG/OBP/SLG	DRC+	BABIP	BRR	DRP	WARP
2020	BOS	MLB	32	237	22	16	0	7	27	22	59	1	0	28.1%	.213/.291/.389	90	.259	-2.0	RF(4): -0.7, LF(3): -0.6	0.0
2021	BOS	MLB	33	634	92	42	3	28	99	55	150	0	0	29.3%	.286/.349/.518	117	.340	-2.6	LF(30): 1.3, RF(8): 0.3	2.9
2022	BOS	MLB	34	596	76	43	1	16	62	52	145	0	0	30.1%	.274/.341/.448	106	.345	-4.8		1.3
2023 DC	*LAD*	*MLB*	*35*	*538*	*77*	*30*	*1*	*30*	*86*	*46*	*130*	*0*	*0*	*29.9%*	*.278/.348/.528*	*134*	*.327*	*-1.2*	*LF 0*	*3.1*

Comparables: Bob Watson (71), Joe Adcock (69), Willie Horton (69)

The days of Martinez profiling as the league's premier designated hitter—and one of the league's best pure hitters in general—have finally come to an end. A creaky, wheezing season full of medium-deep flyouts saw him hit all of five homers through May, and the rest of his campaign was punctuated by several more weeks-long dinger-less stretches. His 2022 season was the second out of the last three in which he produced negative run value on pitches out over the heart of the plate, as his ability to punish strikes continued to devolve. Kick that leg out, and the whole table tends to go with it. Equally worrisome were the drops in homers and extra-base hits to right and right-center, as Martinez's whole-field approach was long a hallmark of his success. All told, he looked little like the once-fearsome hitter who more than justified his five-year, $110 million Red Sox contract through his 2018, 2019 and 2021 performances. Now 35 years old and offering zero value with his glove or legs, Martinez may not have much left to offer, save for patience at the plate and sage advice to younger hitters. By reuniting the All-Star with the man who helped reinvent his swing in the first place (hitting coach Robert Van Scoyoc), the Dodgers will pay to find out if he can win back some ground from Father Time, however briefly.

Max Muncy IF

Born: 08/25/90 Age: 32 Bats: L Throws: R Height: 6'0" Weight: 215 lb. Origin: Round 5, 2012 Draft (#169 overall)

YEAR	TEAM	LVL	AGE	PA	R	2B	3B	HR	RBI	BB	K	SB	CS	Whiff%	AVG/OBP/SLG	DRC+	BABIP	BRR	DRP	WARP
2020	LAD	MLB	29	248	36	4	0	12	27	39	60	1	0	26.8%	.192/.331/.389	104	.203	0.9	1B(35): -1.1, 3B(16): 1.5, 2B(12): 0.1	0.9
2021	LAD	MLB	30	592	95	26	2	36	94	83	120	2	1	23.3%	.249/.368/.527	130	.257	0.8	1B(122): 0.7, 2B(39): -0.5, 3B(7): -0.1	3.8
2022	LAD	MLB	31	565	69	22	1	21	69	90	141	2	0	26.2%	.196/.329/.384	101	.227	-0.6	3B(84): 0.7, 2B(31): -0.1, 1B(3): -0.2	1.5
2023 DC	*LAD*	*MLB*	*32*	*565*	*82*	*21*	*1*	*30*	*81*	*84*	*131*	*0*	*1*	*25.9%*	*.237/.362/.484*	*134*	*.263*	*0.3*	*3B -1, 2B 0*	*3.6*

Comparables: Chris Davis (62), Mike Hegan (59), Dave Bergman (59)

Oh no! You've cracked your phone screen. You have three choices: repair it, replace it or live with it.

Oh no! Max Muncy suffered his worst year as a Dodger. The organization had the same three choices. Would a swing change fix things? He still hit the ball as hard as ever, and maintained his normal strikeout and walk rates. His 49.5% fly-ball rate and 49.2% pull rate were significantly higher than his career averages, which might imply more power—except that his HR/FB ratio was nearly halved, to 13%. In other words, Muncy sacrificed some hits all over the field for fly balls, but they largely wound up as lazy flies to right. Even when you can see the damage, it's not so easy to fix the crack.

That said, the infielder was rejuvenated in the second half, with more extra-base hits after August 1 than in his campaign's first four months; his home run off Yu Darvish briefly gave the Dodgers a lead in Game 2 of the NLDS. Los Angeles decided to live with him for now when they exercised his 2023 option, but it'll take more to forget the cracks.

James Outman OF

Born: 05/14/97 Age: 26 Bats: L Throws: R Height: 6'3" Weight: 215 lb. Origin: Round 7, 2018 Draft (#224 overall)

YEAR	TEAM	LVL	AGE	PA	R	2B	3B	HR	RBI	BB	K	SB	CS	Whiff%	AVG/OBP/SLG	DRC+	BABIP	BRR	DRP	WARP
2021	GDD	WIN	24	83	17	7	1	3	11	15	23	2	1		.284/.422/.552		.390			
2021	GL	A+	24	304	50	12	8	9	30	45	88	21	2		.250/.385/.472	120	.349	1.4	CF(51): -6.5, RF(13): 1.6	1.4
2021	TUL	AA	24	187	40	9	1	9	24	18	51	2	2		.289/.369/.518	98	.368	0.7	CF(36): 1.6, RF(3): -0.1	0.8
2022	TUL	AA	25	307	59	17	1	16	45	38	89	7	3		.295/.394/.552	107	.386	0.6	CF(33): -0.1, LF(20): 0.2, RF(12): 1.4	1.4
2022	OKC	AAA	25	252	42	14	6	15	61	32	63	6	1	28.9%	.292/.390/.627	112	.343	-2.4	RF(44): 2.9, CF(6): 1.1, LF(3): 0.5	1.2
2022	LAD	MLB	25	16	6	2	0	1	3	2	7	0	0	38.7%	.462/.563/.846	67	1.000	0.4	LF(3): 0.2	0.0
2023 DC	*LAD*	*MLB*	*26*	*440*	*54*	*18*	*6*	*14*	*51*	*42*	*132*	*6*	*2*	*31.6%*	*.225/.312/.419*	*96*	*.302*	*4.0*	*LF 1, CF 0*	*1.4*

Comparables: Brandon Boggs (63), Josh Rojas (61), Tyler Moore (56)

The way Dodgers fans revere any prospect who comes up and produces immediately, you'd think Outman was the next coming of Duke Snider: He went 3-for-4 with a home run in his MLB debut, continuing to endear himself to LA faithful for another three games before returning to Oklahoma City.
The former Sacramento State Hornet launched 31 home runs between Double-A and Triple-A after mashing 18 in his pro debut in 2021. Strikeouts are a concern, as he struck out 27.2% of the time in the minors and in seven of his 16 plate appearances in the majors; his pitch recognition and plate discipline will determine his future at the dish. While he's not going to maintain a 282 OPS+, he's a quality prospect, known more for his glove than his bat—a legitimate center fielder with an above-average throwing arm. Much like the Dodgers' shortstop situation, the state of center field is fluid; Outman could see substantial playing time and a chance to build on his fan-favorite résumé.

★ ★ ★ *2023 Top 101 Prospect* **#90** ★ ★ ★

Andy Pages OF

Born: 12/08/00 Age: 22 Bats: R Throws: R Height: 6'1" Weight: 212 lb. Origin: International Free Agent, 2018

YEAR	TEAM	LVL	AGE	PA	R	2B	3B	HR	RBI	BB	K	SB	CS	Whiff%	AVG/OBP/SLG	DRC+	BABIP	BRR	DRP	WARP
2021	GL	A+	20	538	96	25	1	31	88	77	132	6	3		.265/.394/.539	139	.305	1.4	RF(83): 4.4, CF(27): -5.2	4.3
2022	TUL	AA	21	296	33	15	2	12	41	34	67	3	1		.239/.351/.458	97	.277	1.6	RF(49): -0.3, CF(10): -0.6, LF(4): -0.3	1.4
2023 DC	*LAD*	*MLB*	*22*	*101*	*11*	*4*	*0*	*3*	*10*	*8*	*26*	*1*	*0*	*27.3%*	*.209/.295/.378*	*81*	*.261*	*0.1*	*CF 0, RF 0*	*0.0*

Comparables: Wladimir Balentien (71), Randal Grichuk (69), Franmil Reyes (66)

Blessed with the best power tool in the Dodgers' farm system, Pages was added to the 40-man roster over the winter and—with the way the LA outfield situation currently looks over the next few years—is in a prime position to get meaningful plate appearances, perhaps as early as this summer. He also had a brief, impressive stint in the 2022 Arizona Fall League that saw him hit .296/.398/.506 with five home runs in 98 plate appearances. He profiles as a right fielder, but with Betts in the fold, Pages could see most of his time in left field, should he remain a Dodger in the short- and long-term.

★ ★ ★ *2023 Top 101 Prospect* **#56** ★ ★ ★

Dalton Rushing C
Born: 02/21/01 Age: 22 Bats: L Throws: R Height: 6'1" Weight: 220 lb. Origin: Round 2, 2022 Draft (#40 overall)

YEAR	TEAM	LVL	AGE	PA	R	2B	3B	HR	RBI	BB	K	SB	CS	Whiff%	AVG/OBP/SLG	DRC+	BABIP	BRR	DRP	WARP
2022	RC	A	21	128	27	11	0	8	30	21	21	1	0		.424/.539/.778	134	.472	0.5	C(17): 1.4, 1B(5): -0.5	1.1
2023 non-DC	*LAD*	*MLB*	*22*	*251*	*25*	*11*	*1*	*5*	*26*	*22*	*61*	*0*	*0*	*27.5%*	*.236/.319/.378*	*94*	*.298*	*0.6*	*C 0, 1B 0*	*0.7*

Comparables: Kyle Schwarber (83), Tim Federowicz (77), J.R. Towles (75)

YEAR	TEAM	P. COUNT	FRM RUNS	BLK RUNS	THRW RUNS	TOT RUNS
2022	RC	2546	1.1	-0.5	0.7	1.3
2023	*LAD*	*6956*	*-0.7*	*-1.0*	*-0.1*	*-1.8*

"The Dodgers did it again," is a common refrain when it comes to their draft picks. They haven't been perfect in the Friedman era, but Rushing might be another one they got right. The catcher—because the Dodgers don't have enough quality catching prospects—hit the ground running in A-ball. The rate stats he posted in 30 games were even better than in his junior season at Louisville; while he's not going to hit .400 as a professional, the bat-first catcher is someone to watch. There are questions about his long-term viability behind the plate, but if he can stick, he'll be among the game's best catching prospects. If he has to move to, say, first base, he'll have plenty of bat for the position.

Will Smith C
Born: 03/28/95 Age: 28 Bats: R Throws: R Height: 5'10" Weight: 195 lb. Origin: Round 1, 2016 Draft (#32 overall)

YEAR	TEAM	LVL	AGE	PA	R	2B	3B	HR	RBI	BB	K	SB	CS	Whiff%	AVG/OBP/SLG	DRC+	BABIP	BRR	DRP	WARP
2020	LAD	MLB	25	137	23	9	0	8	25	20	22	0	0	15.5%	.289/.401/.579	133	.294	-1.0	C(34): -3.1	0.6
2021	LAD	MLB	26	501	71	19	2	25	76	58	101	3	0	21.2%	.258/.365/.495	125	.274	-1.1	C(117): 6.3, 3B(1): 0	4.2
2022	LAD	MLB	27	578	68	26	3	24	87	56	96	1	0	19.5%	.260/.343/.465	122	.276	-1.9	C(109): 7.1	4.1
2023 DC	*LAD*	*MLB*	*28*	*490*	*66*	*20*	*1*	*25*	*73*	*50*	*85*	*0*	*0*	*19.4%*	*.262/.355/.492*	*130*	*.277*	*-1.0*	*C 2*	*3.7*

Comparables: Willson Contreras (65), Carlos Santana (63), Buster Posey (62)

YEAR	TEAM	P. COUNT	FRM RUNS	BLK RUNS	THRW RUNS	TOT RUNS
2020	LAD	4351	-3.0	0.1	0.1	-2.8
2021	LAD	16176	8.8	-0.3	0.4	8.9
2022	LAD	15036	5.9	0.0	1.4	7.4
2023	*LAD*	*15632*	*3.8*	*0.1*	*0.0*	*3.9*

Smith isn't the best catcher in MLB at any given skill. He lacks the bat control and patience of Alejandro Kirk, the power of Salvador Perez, the wheels of J.T. Realmuto and the defensive acumen of Jose Trevino. However, he ranges from "pretty good" to "top two or three" in each category. He made slight approach changes last year, increasing his contact rate—particularly on off-speed pitches out of the zone—and reducing both his strikeout and walk rates. More importantly, the tweaks earned him more fastballs, which he absolutely clobbers—he has a career .571 slugging percentage against them. Smith is greater than the sum of his parts, but each part is nevertheless impressive in its own right.

Chris Taylor LF
Born: 08/29/90 Age: 32 Bats: R Throws: R Height: 6'1" Weight: 196 lb. Origin: Round 5, 2012 Draft (#161 overall)

YEAR	TEAM	LVL	AGE	PA	R	2B	3B	HR	RBI	BB	K	SB	CS	Whiff%	AVG/OBP/SLG	DRC+	BABIP	BRR	DRP	WARP
2020	LAD	MLB	29	214	30	10	2	8	32	26	55	3	2	32.7%	.270/.366/.476	106	.344	-0.4	SS(20): 0, LF(19): 1.8, 2B(13): 0	0.9
2021	LAD	MLB	30	582	92	25	4	20	73	63	167	13	1	32.7%	.254/.344/.438	97	.337	0.6	CF(61): -3, 2B(46): -1.1, LF(30): -0.7	1.5
2022	LAD	MLB	31	454	45	25	3	10	43	44	160	10	1	39.9%	.221/.304/.373	70	.336	-0.6	LF(80): 0.7, 2B(22): 0.1, CF(10): -0.3	-0.2
2023 DC	*LAD*	*MLB*	*32*	*573*	*72*	*27*	*3*	*22*	*68*	*56*	*198*	*10*	*2*	*37.8%*	*.238/.325/.439*	*104*	*.346*	*6.5*	*2B 0, LF 0*	*2.5*

Comparables: Billy Rogell (61), Mariano Duncan (58), Ian Desmond (57)

OFFICIAL STATEMENT FROM BASEBALL PROSPECTUS: We understand that words have immense power and we must wield them carefully. To that end, we apologize for Taylor's comment in the 2022 *Annual*, which said, *"Never compare a player to Ben Zobrist, as that player will ultimately be a worse version of Ben Zobrist. At the risk of receiving the electronic equivalent of a fastball to the ribs, Taylor is as close as the baseball world has seen since Zobrist retired."* Immediately thereafter, Taylor became the second player ever with 160 strikeouts and no more than 10 home runs in a season (Austin Jackson did it twice). We are deeply sorry for the jinx that transformed him from Zobrist into Leury García. We apologize to Mr. Taylor, the Dodgers and their fans.

Trayce Thompson OF
Born: 03/15/91 Age: 32 Bats: R Throws: R Height: 6'3" Weight: 225 lb. Origin: Round 2, 2009 Draft (#61 overall)

YEAR	TEAM	LVL	AGE	PA	R	2B	3B	HR	RBI	BB	K	SB	CS	Whiff%	AVG/OBP/SLG	DRC+	BABIP	BRR	DRP	WARP
2021	IOW	AAA	30	358	48	14	1	21	63	45	116	3	1		.233/.344/.492	101	.296	-1.0	CF(42): -2.5, RF(23): 0.8, LF(13): -0.1	1.0
2021	CHC	MLB	30	35	6	1	0	4	9	7	11	2	0	28.3%	.250/.400/.714	111	.231	-0.1	RF(8): -0.9, CF(3): -0.2	0.0
2022	ELP	AAA	31	65	16	4	0	9	17	7	18	1	0	38.9%	.316/.385/.860	125	.290	-0.5	CF(7): -0.4, RF(7): 1.2, LF(2): -0.0	0.3
2022	TOL	AAA	31	105	17	7	1	8	19	7	30	1	1		.299/.352/.639	104	.356	0.1	LF(15): 0.6, RF(6): -0.5	0.5
2022	SD	MLB	31	16	1	0	0	0	2	2	7	0	1	37.1%	.071/.188/.071	79	.143	-0.4	RF(6): 0.2, LF(1): 0	0.0
2022	LAD	MLB	31	239	35	14	1	13	39	30	86	4	0	37.8%	.268/.364/.537	98	.389	1.9	LF(35): -0.2, RF(23): -0.3, CF(18): -0.4	0.8
2023 DC	*LAD*	*MLB*	*32*	*495*	*63*	*19*	*2*	*25*	*66*	*50*	*177*	*7*	*1*	*36.9%*	*.217/.305/.444*	*97*	*.297*	*3.4*	*CF 3, LF 0*	*1.8*

Comparables: Franklin Gutierrez (47), Dexter Fowler (46), Jayson Werth (44)

You're forgiven for doing a double-take at Thompson's DRC+ listed above. The 38-point difference between his 135 OPS+ and 97 DRC+ was five points larger than any other hitter's in MLB (minimum 250 PA). There's certainly nothing wrong with his 92.2-mph average exit velocity, which was tied for 15th in the league. That indicates he should do well on balls hit into play, but scorching the ball on contact only matters so much for someone with a 36.5% strikeout rate. From a three-true-outcomes perspective, his revival looks a lot like peak Joey Gallo—another player who DRC+ never loved as much as you might think—and, well, look what happened to Gallo when his BABIP and walk rate crash landed. His 2023 campaign will be yet another miniature referendum on whether he can thrive while striking out more than a third of the time.

★ ★ ★ *2023 Top 101 Prospect* **#39** ★ ★ ★

Miguel Vargas 3B/OF Born: 11/17/99 Age: 23 Bats: R Throws: R Height: 6'3" Weight: 205 lb. Origin: International Free Agent, 2017

YEAR	TEAM	LVL	AGE	PA	R	2B	3B	HR	RBI	BB	K	SB	CS	Whiff%	AVG/OBP/SLG	DRC+	BABIP	BRR	DRP	WARP
2021	GL	A+	21	172	31	11	1	7	16	9	32	4	0		.314/.366/.532	121	.353	-1.1	3B(31): -1.9, 2B(2): -0.6, 1B(1): -0.0	0.6
2021	TUL	AA	21	370	67	16	1	16	60	36	57	7	1		.321/.386/.523	125	.344	1.0	3B(53): -0.4, 2B(15): -1.0, 1B(9): 0.1	2.2
2022	OKC	AAA	22	520	100	32	4	17	82	71	76	16	5	20.8%	.304/.404/.511	120	.331	1.4	3B(74): -1.0, LF(23): -1.0, 2B(7): -0.5	2.7
2022	LAD	MLB	22	50	4	1	0	1	8	2	13	1	0	24.3%	.170/.200/.255	82	.206	0.3	1B(8): 0, LF(7): -1.1	-0.1
2023 DC	*LAD*	*MLB*	*23*	*367*	*40*	*17*	*1*	*9*	*39*	*30*	*67*	*8*	*1*	*22.2%*	*.256/.326/.405*	*101*	*.297*	*3.4*	*LF 0, 1B 0*	*1.1*

Comparables: Josh Vitters (60), Brandon Drury (58), Randal Grichuk (58)

If you're looking for one of the game's most underrated prospects, you've found him in Vargas. He has done nothing but hit since being an inconspicuous, $300,000 international amateur signing in September 2017. He was a 3/4/5 guy in Triple-A, which earned him the proverbial cup of coffee with the big-league club. His numbers there belied an average exit velocity 1.3-mph harder than MLB average, a hard-hit rate 4.2 percentage points better than league-average and a 92.7-mph average exit velo on plate appearances ending in fastballs—even though he was 2-for-23 in such at-bats. Atypically, he needs to elevate *less*, as he ran a 25.9-degree launch angle and 51.4% fly-ball rate. With Ginger Jesus signing in Boston, the Dodgers are going all-in on Vargas at the hot corner—if that seems risky, it's not the first time he's been underappreciated.

Jorbit Vivas 2B Born: 03/09/01 Age: 22 Bats: L Throws: R Height: 5'10" Weight: 171 lb. Origin: International Free Agent, 2017

YEAR	TEAM	LVL	AGE	PA	R	2B	3B	HR	RBI	BB	K	SB	CS	Whiff%	AVG/OBP/SLG	DRC+	BABIP	BRR	DRP	WARP
2021	RC	A	20	375	73	20	4	13	73	27	42	5	3		.311/.389/.515	140	.322	-0.7	2B(38): -1.0, 3B(34): 2.6, SS(2): -0.1	3.0
2021	GL	A+	20	102	12	6	0	1	14	13	13	3	1		.318/.422/.424	121	.361	-0.7	3B(14): 0.0, 2B(9): -1.3	0.4
2022	GL	A+	21	570	73	19	7	10	66	63	58	2	1		.269/.374/.401	112	.285	-3.0	2B(91): 0.4, 3B(33): -1.9	2.1
2023 non-DC	*LAD*	*MLB*	*22*	*251*	*23*	*9*	*2*	*3*	*23*	*18*	*34*	*4*	*2*	*19.3%*	*.241/.315/.351*	*89*	*.272*	*0.8*	*2B 0, 3B 0*	*0.4*

Comparables: Travis Denker (73), Steve Lombardozzi (69), Jesmuel Valentín (67)

Similar to Eddys Leonard in that he was added to the 40-man roster before playing above A-ball, Vivas' production dipped from 2021 to '22. He doesn't have as much value upside as Leonard, as he's more limited defensively—he's basically a second baseman posing as a utility player. He did walk more than he struck out, but his bat lacks the thump to keep pitchers at the next level honest. Until he proves otherwise, his ceiling is limited, but we've seen the Dodgers' player developmental machine do much wilder things over the years than enliven this profile.

PITCHERS

Yency Almonte RHP Born: 06/04/94 Age: 29 Bats: R Throws: R Height: 6'5" Weight: 223 lb. Origin: Round 17, 2012 Draft (#537 overall)

YEAR	TEAM	LVL	AGE	W	L	SV	G	GS	IP	H	HR	BB/9	K/9	K	GB%	BABIP	WHIP	ERA	DRA-	WARP	MPH	FB%	Whiff%	CSP
2020	COL	MLB	26	3	0	1	24	0	27^2	25	2	2.0	7.5	23	55.6%	.291	1.12	2.93	86	0.5	94.8	42.8%	28.1%	44.7%
2021	COL	MLB	27	1	3	0	48	0	47^2	47	9	5.5	8.9	47	42.3%	.297	1.59	7.55	114	0.1	94.3	48.8%	26.8%	50.1%
2022	OKC	AAA	28	0	1	3	14	0	18	14	3	0.5	14.0	28	66.7%	.306	0.83	4.00	61	0.5	95.2	47.2%	44.7%	
2022	LAD	MLB	28	0	0	1	33	0	35^1	18	2	2.5	8.4	33	50.0%	.186	0.79	1.02	89	0.5	95.9	45.9%	34.0%	50.8%
2023 DC	*LAD*	*MLB*	*29*	*3*	*3*	*2*	*64*	*0*	*56*	*52*	*6*	*3.6*	*9.3*	*57*	*48.2%*	*.301*	*1.33*	*3.93*	*97*	*0.3*	*95.0*	*47.9%*	*31.3%*	*49.0%*

Comparables: Evan Marshall (62), Austin Brice (61), Dominic Leone (60)

Almonte is hardly the first pitcher to flourish after descending from the Rocky Mountains, but his breakout is about more than simply leaving Colorado. He became a sinker/sweeper thrower with the Dodgers after four years as an unexceptional four-seamer/slider/changeup arm with the Rockies and was practically unhittable. He threw 158 sinkers in 2022 and allowed only two extra-base hits on the offering. In transforming from a slider into a sweeper, his breaking pitch increased its horizontal movement from 7.5 inches to 11.5. After July 4, he gave up only three hits over 14⅔ innings for the remainder of the regular season—though there was a seven-week layover on the IL. His flashy new repertoire fueled his success more than the new digs, but he certainly seems happier pitching closer to sea level.

Phil Bickford RHP Born: 07/10/95 Age: 27 Bats: R Throws: R Height: 6'4" Weight: 200 lb. Origin: Round 1, 2015 Draft (#18 overall)

YEAR	TEAM	LVL	AGE	W	L	SV	G	GS	IP	H	HR	BB/9	K/9	K	GB%	BABIP	WHIP	ERA	DRA-	WARP	MPH	FB%	Whiff%	CSP
2020	MIL	MLB	24	0	0	0	1	0	1	4	0	0.0	18.0	2	0.0%	.800	4.00	36.00	127	0.0	89.6	84.8%	25.0%	56.8%
2021	OKC	AAA	25	1	0	0	5	0	5	5	0	0.0	21.6	12	44.4%	.556	1.00	5.40	74	0.1				
2021	MIL	MLB	25	0	0	0	1	0	1	2	1	9.0	0.0	0	20.0%	.250	3.00	18.00	97	0.0	92.8	84.2%	23.5%	49.4%
2021	LAD	MLB	25	4	2	1	56	0	50^1	34	6	3.2	10.5	59	47.1%	.243	1.03	2.50	80	1.0	94.1	63.3%	30.2%	58.5%
2022	OKC	AAA	26	0	0	0	6	0	5	4	2	5.4	10.8	6	53.8%	.182	1.40	9.00	90	0.1	92.8	74.2%	21.3%	
2022	LAD	MLB	26	2	1	0	60	0	61	53	12	2.1	9.9	67	37.2%	.270	1.10	4.72	86	1.0	94.2	68.1%	25.2%	55.8%
2023 DC	*LAD*	*MLB*	*27*	*2*	*2*	*0*	*57*	*0*	*49.7*	*47*	*7*	*3.1*	*9.8*	*54*	*39.5%*	*.304*	*1.29*	*4.02*	*100*	*0.2*	*94.1*	*66.9%*	*26.1%*	*56.6%*

Comparables: Bruce Rondón (64), Ken Giles (64), Nick Goody (63)

Through no fault of his own, Bickford briefly became the enemy in his own ballpark. On September 23, the Dodger Stadium faithful stood at attention, phones at the ready, silently praying for their own reliever to make a mistake. When he delivered, they erupted into tumultuous cheers as Albert Pujols rounded the bases for the 700th time. A few days later, Bickford landed on the IL with shoulder fatigue and missed the postseason. Aside from giving up three homers in his final two outings, when he may have been injured, he compiled a better season than his 4.72 ERA indicates. His mid-90s fastball has good spin and movement characteristics and he usually locates his slider well, but the one he hung for The Machine is how he'll be remembered forever.

Walker Buehler RHP Born: 07/28/94 Age: 28 Bats: R Throws: R Height: 6'2" Weight: 185 lb. Origin: Round 1, 2015 Draft (#24 overall)

YEAR	TEAM	LVL	AGE	W	L	SV	G	GS	IP	H	HR	BB/9	K/9	K	GB%	BABIP	WHIP	ERA	DRA-	WARP	MPH	FB%	Whiff%	CSP
2020	LAD	MLB	25	1	0	0	8	8	36^2	24	7	2.7	10.3	42	36.6%	.198	0.95	3.44	84	0.7	96.8	62.3%	28.4%	48.4%
2021	LAD	MLB	26	16	4	0	33	33	207^2	149	19	2.3	9.2	212	43.9%	.250	0.97	2.47	77	4.4	95.5	52.0%	26.5%	56.0%
2022	LAD	MLB	27	6	3	0	12	12	65	67	8	2.4	8.0	58	47.7%	.312	1.29	4.02	97	0.7	95.4	38.9%	24.8%	52.8%
2023 non-DC	*LAD*	*MLB*	*28*	*3*	*2*	*0*	*57*	*0*	*50*	*45*	*5*	*2.5*	*8.6*	*47*	*45.4%*	*.292*	*1.19*	*3.19*	*84*	*0.6*	*95.8*	*50.9%*	*25.8%*	*53.9%*

Comparables: Jim Palmer (91), Roger Clemens (90), Félix Hernández (89)

Buehler isn't injured. He's leading a Martian colonization mission to establish sustainable extraterrestrial living. He's part of a deep-sea research initiative tracking a rare species of squid that secretes cancer-destroying enzymes. He's volunteering in refugee camps feeding malnourished children from war-torn lands. He's developing a new type of pitch that moves like an upside-down curveball. He's performing emergency medical care for endangered koalas in Australia's eucalyptus forests. He's inventing a car engine that runs on landfill garbage, emits only clean, potable water and smells like springtime rain. Tell yourself whatever you want, except that he's recovering from his second Tommy John surgery. There's no need to confront the terrifying truth until 2024.

Caleb Ferguson LHP Born: 07/02/96 Age: 27 Bats: R Throws: L Height: 6'3" Weight: 226 lb. Origin: Round 38, 2014 Draft (#1149 overall)

YEAR	TEAM	LVL	AGE	W	L	SV	G	GS	IP	H	HR	BB/9	K/9	K	GB%	BABIP	WHIP	ERA	DRA-	WARP	MPH	FB%	Whiff%	CSP
2020	LAD	MLB	23	2	1	0	21	1	18^2	16	4	1.4	13.0	27	51.1%	.293	1.02	2.89	65	0.6	95.4	79.6%	29.1%	51.9%
2022	OKC	AAA	25	0	1	0	10	2	7^1	10	1	4.9	16.0	13	42.1%	.500	1.91	7.36	76	0.1	94.5	70.3%	34.2%	
2022	LAD	MLB	25	1	0	0	37	1	34^2	23	1	4.4	9.6	37	41.9%	.259	1.15	1.82	100	0.3	94.8	66.9%	26.8%	55.9%
2023 DC	*LAD*	*MLB*	*26*	*3*	*3*	*0*	*64*	*0*	*56*	*48*	*6*	*4.4*	*11.2*	*69*	*43.2%*	*.309*	*1.35*	*3.81*	*91*	*0.5*	*94.9*	*71.4%*	*28.1%*	*53.9%*

Comparables: Tim Collins (56), Arodys Vizcaíno (51), Eric O'Flaherty (51)

Ferguson's season was like a black-and-white animated Tim Burton film. His elbow came back from the dead (Tommy John surgery), and everything seemed wonderful on the surface (1.82 ERA). But deep within, something indefinable was…off. His curveball, which hadn't been seen since 2019, reappeared from the great beyond along with his elbow and completely smothered his cutter, which he didn't throw even once in 2022. The walk and strikeout rates both jumped in the wrong direction. An extremely fortunate 3.4% home run-to-fly-ball rate papered over some of the problems, and his fastball still has a good shape that prevents too much loud contact. Unless he can tame his wildness and re-locate a consistent secondary offering, though, the dead shall rise and reclaim the Earth! Or… he'll just be a boring, average reliever instead of a pretty good one. Same thing.

J.P. Feyereisen RHP Born: 02/07/93 Age: 30 Bats: R Throws: R Height: 6'2" Weight: 215 lb. Origin: Round 16, 2014 Draft (#488 overall)

YEAR	TEAM	LVL	AGE	W	L	SV	G	GS	IP	H	HR	BB/9	K/9	K	GB%	BABIP	WHIP	ERA	DRA-	WARP	MPH	FB%	Whiff%	CSP
2020	MIL	MLB	27	0	0	0	6	0	9^1	4	3	4.8	6.8	7	33.3%	.048	0.96	5.79	116	0.0	93.6	54.0%	34.7%	39.1%
2021	MIL	MLB	28	0	2	0	21	0	19^1	10	2	5.1	9.3	20	47.8%	.186	1.09	3.26	110	0.1	93.7	41.1%	42.6%	45.5%
2021	TB	MLB	28	4	2	3	34	0	36^2	26	3	5.4	8.1	33	31.4%	.235	1.31	2.45	117	0.0	93.1	56.7%	31.6%	45.3%
2022	TB	MLB	29	4	0	1	22	2	24^1	7	0	1.8	9.2	25	33.9%	.125	0.49	0.00	90	0.4	92.7	44.5%	33.5%	53.0%
2023 DC	*LAD*	*MLB*	*30*	*1*	*1*	*0*	*28*	*0*	*24.7*	*22*	*3*	*4.1*	*10.3*	*28*	*36.9%*	*.298*	*1.36*	*4.00*	*98*	*0.1*	*93.1*	*49.6%*	*32.3%*	*47.2%*

Comparables: Danny Farquhar (56), Gregory Infante (53), Evan Scribner (53)

Feyereisen was on pace for an all-time reliever season with the Rays—just look at that scoreless innings streak—before a shoulder injury shut him down in June, then again for good in early September as he tried to work his way back to the mound. He threw fewer low-90s fastballs in favor of more upper-80s changeups, continuing to mix in sliders as well. As a result, he saw increased effectiveness against batters on both sides of the dish, and flashed the potential to become a legit relief ace even with some run-related regression likely looming. All in all, Feyereisen only dominated in a small sample, but at his best he's a highly effective bullpen arm with several years of team control remaining. He just needs to ensure his right shoulder stays intact, but the Dodgers thought he was worth the gamble, acquiring him in December for "Jeff Belge."

★ ★ ★ *2023 Top 101 Prospect* **#79** ★ ★ ★

Nick Frasso RHP

Born: 10/18/98 Age: 24 Bats: R Throws: R Height: 6'5" Weight: 200 lb. Origin: Round 4, 2020 Draft (#106 overall)

YEAR	TEAM	LVL	AGE	W	L	SV	G	GS	IP	H	HR	BB/9	K/9	K	GB%	BABIP	WHIP	ERA	DRA-	WARP	MPH	FB%	Whiff%	CSP
2021	DUN	A	22	0	0	0	3	2	5	3	0	3.6	14.4	8	45.5%	.273	1.00	0.00	96	0.1				
2022	DUN	A	23	0	0	0	7	7	25^2	13	0	2.8	14.7	42	40.4%	.277	0.82	0.70	75	0.7	95.8	62.4%	46.1%	
2022	VAN	A+	23	0	0	0	3	3	11	3	1	1.6	12.3	15	40.9%	.095	0.45	0.82	91	0.2				
2022	TUL	AA	23	0	0	0	4	4	11^2	12	1	5.4	7.7	10	35.1%	.306	1.63	5.40	116	-0.1				
2023 non-DC	*LAD*	*MLB*	*24*	*2*	*2*	*0*	*57*	*0*	*50*	*48*	*6*	*4.2*	*10.1*	*55*	*40.9%*	*.314*	*1.43*	*4.42*	*108*	*0.0*			*29.9%*	

Comparables: Cale Coshow (64), Ryne Stanek (63), Brett Conine (62)

A seemingly innocuous acquisition at the 2022 trade deadline, Frasso has catapulted himself to knocking on the door of top prospectdom. His Trackman numbers are off the charts, and the fact that the Dodgers were able to get him from another org is incredible, much less for depth starter Mitch White. He can hit triple-digits with his heater, while sitting in the mid- to upper-90s, while peppering the upper third of the zone from a vertical slot. His slider might not pop visually but works well off the plus-plus fastball as it dips under bats at the last second. The changeup is a clear third offering but will flash plus potential. He's already 23 and carries a fair bit of relief risk thanks to funky mechanics. If he can hold up as a starter—a fair question given prior elbow surgery—he could make for a high-strikeout option in the middle of a rotation. Seriously, why do teams even trade with Friedman anymore?

Tony Gonsolin RHP

Born: 05/14/94 Age: 29 Bats: R Throws: R Height: 6'3" Weight: 205 lb. Origin: Round 9, 2016 Draft (#281 overall)

YEAR	TEAM	LVL	AGE	W	L	SV	G	GS	IP	H	HR	BB/9	K/9	K	GB%	BABIP	WHIP	ERA	DRA-	WARP	MPH	FB%	Whiff%	CSP
2020	LAD	MLB	26	2	2	0	9	8	46^2	32	2	1.4	8.9	46	33.6%	.252	0.84	2.31	85	0.8	95.1	47.5%	29.8%	47.3%
2021	OKC	AAA	27	0	0	0	3	3	10^1	6	2	2.6	7.8	9	35.7%	.154	0.87	3.48	106	0.0				
2021	LAD	MLB	27	4	1	0	15	13	55^2	41	8	5.5	10.5	65	36.4%	.254	1.35	3.23	98	0.6	93.9	43.6%	29.7%	54.3%
2022	LAD	MLB	28	16	1	0	24	24	130^1	79	11	2.4	8.2	119	42.9%	.207	0.87	2.14	83	2.4	93.3	39.1%	27.1%	57.2%
2023 DC	*LAD*	*MLB*	*29*	*9*	*8*	*0*	*27*	*27*	*145.7*	*127*	*17*	*3.2*	*8.3*	*135*	*40.9%*	*.275*	*1.23*	*3.33*	*87*	*2.2*	*93.6*	*41.5%*	*27.4%*	*54.8%*

Comparables: Mike Clevinger (62), Tyson Ross (60), Chris Young (59)

You know that recurring third-grade nightmare you have? The one where you write *3 x 5 = 14* on the board and the teacher quips, "Close only counts in horseshoes and hand grenades!" Well, guess what! Mrs. Thomas is WRONG! It counts in pitching, too. In 2021, Gonsolin induced a 27.2% strikeout rate, getting batters to chase diving splitters and sliders down and out of the strike zone. Of course, the byproduct was an untenable 14.2% walk rate. He was close, yet so far away. So what made things work this time around? Mrs. Thomas would say that Gonsolin showed his work: His 2022 zone map reflects that he threw his splitter and slider for strikes with far more consistency; though his strikeout rate dropped, he improved his DRA- by 15 points. In sacrificing some whiffs, he halved his walk rate and generated more weak contact. Turns out, he was close. There's just no point arguing with grown-ups, especially math teachers in nightmares.

Brusdar Graterol RHP

Born: 08/26/98 Age: 24 Bats: R Throws: R Height: 6'1" Weight: 265 lb. Origin: International Free Agent, 2014

YEAR	TEAM	LVL	AGE	W	L	SV	G	GS	IP	H	HR	BB/9	K/9	K	GB%	BABIP	WHIP	ERA	DRA-	WARP	MPH	FB%	Whiff%	CSP
2020	LAD	MLB	21	1	2	0	23	2	23^1	18	1	1.2	5.0	13	63.8%	.250	0.90	3.09	94	0.3	99.3	70.8%	15.2%	54.3%
2021	OKC	AAA	22	2	2	1	17	0	16^2	12	1	2.7	10.8	20	73.8%	.268	1.02	6.48	83	0.3				
2021	LAD	MLB	22	3	0	0	34	1	33^1	34	2	3.5	7.3	27	57.7%	.314	1.41	4.59	104	0.2	100.0	68.5%	19.0%	61.0%
2022	LAD	MLB	23	2	4	4	46	1	49^2	39	3	1.8	7.8	43	63.8%	.261	0.99	3.26	87	0.8	99.8	53.1%	21.1%	57.9%
2023 DC	*LAD*	*MLB*	*24*	*7*	*4*	*0*	*67*	*3*	*59*	*62*	*5*	*3.2*	*7.2*	*47*	*60.6%*	*.313*	*1.40*	*4.18*	*103*	*0.2*	*99.8*	*60.4%*	*21.8%*	*58.3%*

Comparables: Caleb Ferguson (59), Roberto Osuna (56), Joel Zumaya (55)

What if Sidd Finch—*Sports Illustrated*'s 1985 April Fools prank pitcher who could throw 168 mph—couldn't strike anybody out? Graterol is as close as it comes to such an absurdity. His heater travels faster than a rumor, but his 21.8% strikeout rate—his best since his 9⅔-inning debut in 2019—was below league-average. However, he only (unintentionally) walked nine of 197 batters faced, and his supercharged sinker prompted a 63.1% ground-ball rate, sixth in MLB (min. 40 innings). Just as he demonstrates that high velocity doesn't always convert into whiffs, Graterol is also proof that succeeding without strikeouts is no hoax.

Michael Grove RHP

Born: 12/18/96 Age: 26 Bats: R Throws: R Height: 6'3" Weight: 200 lb. Origin: Round 2, 2018 Draft (#68 overall)

YEAR	TEAM	LVL	AGE	W	L	SV	G	GS	IP	H	HR	BB/9	K/9	K	GB%	BABIP	WHIP	ERA	DRA-	WARP	MPH	FB%	Whiff%	CSP
2021	TUL	AA	24	1	4	0	21	19	71	85	19	5.3	11.2	88	34.8%	.351	1.79	7.86	93	0.7				
2022	TUL	AA	25	0	1	0	5	5	16^1	11	1	2.8	12.1	22	45.0%	.256	0.98	2.76	69	0.4				
2022	OKC	AAA	25	1	4	0	14	12	59^2	56	10	3.2	10.3	68	40.0%	.297	1.29	4.07	87	0.8	94.4	53.9%	26.3%	
2022	LAD	MLB	25	1	0	0	7	6	29^1	32	6	3.1	7.4	24	40.4%	.280	1.43	4.60	105	0.2	94.2	51.1%	22.4%	58.4%
2023 DC	*LAD*	*MLB*	*26*	*4*	*4*	*0*	*29*	*8*	*55.7*	*61*	*10*	*4.0*	*8.2*	*50*	*39.2%*	*.316*	*1.54*	*5.39*	*127*	*-0.3*	*94.2*	*51.1%*	*24.5%*	*58.4%*

Comparables: Daniel Wright (73), Chase De Jong (73), Jimmy Nelson (72)

Despite an ERA that topped 8.00 for most of 2021, the Dodgers still chose to add Grove to the 40-man roster. That proved to be a shrewd move, as he made his MLB debut in 2022 and was, well, a big bowl of fine. Considering he has a career minor-league ERA of 5.84, the fact Grove threw any kind of meaningful innings for LA is remarkable. The numbers don't tell the entire story—his stuff is a lot better than the stats would have you believe. With the ever-changing role of the pitcher, Grove looks like a solid bet to be a contributor via the multi-inning reliever role, or even as a spot starter. If he played for, say, the Pirates, he'd probably be their no. 4 starter, in line for 160 innings of pain. Instead, the Dodgers will look to maximize his potential by minimizing his exposure.

Daniel Hudson RHP
Born: 03/09/87 Age: 36 Bats: R Throws: R Height: 6'3" Weight: 215 lb. Origin: Round 5, 2008 Draft (#150 overall)

YEAR	TEAM	LVL	AGE	W	L	SV	G	GS	IP	H	HR	BB/9	K/9	K	GB%	BABIP	WHIP	ERA	DRA-	WARP	MPH	FB%	Whiff%	CSP
2020	WAS	MLB	33	3	2	10	21	0	20^{2}	15	6	4.8	12.2	28	18.0%	.209	1.26	6.10	112	0.1	96.6	75.9%	31.2%	51.7%
2021	SD	MLB	34	1	2	0	23	0	19	17	4	4.3	12.8	27	27.7%	.302	1.37	5.21	91	0.3	96.9	61.9%	34.1%	55.1%
2021	WAS	MLB	34	4	1	0	31	0	32^{2}	23	4	1.9	13.2	48	29.2%	.279	0.92	2.20	77	0.7	97.1	72.7%	34.5%	54.6%
2022	LAD	MLB	35	2	3	5	25	0	24^{1}	17	1	1.8	11.1	30	51.7%	.276	0.90	2.22	75	0.5	97.1	54.7%	34.1%	54.3%
2023 DC	*LAD*	*MLB*	*36*	*2*	*2*	*26*	*57*	*0*	*49.7*	*42*	*7*	*3.2*	*10.8*	*59*	*37.4%*	*.294*	*1.21*	*3.57*	*89*	*0.5*	*96.8*	*66.2%*	*30.2%*	*53.1%*

Comparables: Wade Davis (69), Jason Isringhausen (68), Tommy Hunter (63)

To avoid Vietnam, Gregg Allman of The Allman Brothers drew a bullseye on his shoe, then shot himself in the foot. Hudson has no bullet wounds, but he's just as quintessential a Dodger. They're his seventh big-league team in 13 seasons—insert *Ramblin' Man* joke here— and somehow, they got him to throw more strikes and create more favorable contact than ever before. Sound similar to, like, every other Dodgers reliever? A 53.4% ground-ball rate was nearly twice as high as Hudson recorded in 2021. Like so many other Dodgers, however—the baseball kind and the draft kind—injuries took him out of action. Hudson tore his ACL fielding a grounder on June 24, but the team remained confident enough to extend him. He should recur as an important member of their bullpen, possibly as soon as Opening Day.

Andre Jackson RHP
Born: 05/01/96 Age: 27 Bats: R Throws: R Height: 6'3" Weight: 210 lb. Origin: Round 12, 2017 Draft (#370 overall)

YEAR	TEAM	LVL	AGE	W	L	SV	G	GS	IP	H	HR	BB/9	K/9	K	GB%	BABIP	WHIP	ERA	DRA-	WARP	MPH	FB%	Whiff%	CSP
2021	TUL	AA	25	3	2	0	15	13	63^{1}	46	12	2.8	10.7	75	31.8%	.239	1.04	3.27	82	1.1				
2021	OKC	AAA	25	2	3	0	6	5	26^{1}	26	6	3.1	7.9	23	35.4%	.263	1.33	5.13	99	0.1				
2021	LAD	MLB	25	0	1	1	3	0	11^{2}	10	1	4.6	7.7	10	26.5%	.290	1.37	2.31	100	0.1	92.1	58.8%	29.9%	57.3%
2022	OKC	AAA	26	2	7	1	21	19	75^{2}	68	10	7.3	9.0	76	47.0%	.280	1.70	5.00	86	1.0	93.7	47.9%	27.8%	
2022	LAD	MLB	26	0	0	1	4	0	9^{2}	9	0	3.7	8.4	9	48.3%	.321	1.34	1.86	93	0.1	95.0	36.5%	26.2%	61.7%
2023 DC	*LAD*	*MLB*	*27*	*2*	*2*	*0*	*24*	*3*	*25*	*24*	*3*	*5.2*	*8.3*	*23*	*42.3%*	*.293*	*1.54*	*4.83*	*114*	*0.0*	*93.6*	*47.4%*	*26.7%*	*59.5%*

Comparables: Jefry Rodriguez (41), Adam Plutko (39), Mike Clevinger (39)

Trevor Hoffman might be the best example of a fastball-changeup pitcher being successful in the majors. Jackson's first two seasons as a major-leaguer saw him throw his fastball 41.7% of the time, and his changeup at a 45.9% clip. Granted, it's only 21⅓ innings of work, but it's a glimpse of what the future could hold. If he's to remain a starting pitcher, Jackson will probably have to develop a usable breaking pitch: Of his 355 MLB pitches, only 44 (35 sliders, nine curveballs) of them had any kind of tilt. With or without a breaker, Jackson may not be the next Hoffman, but he might not need one to carve out a solid career as a multi-inning reliever.

Clayton Kershaw LHP
Born: 03/19/88 Age: 35 Bats: L Throws: L Height: 6'4" Weight: 225 lb. Origin: Round 1, 2006 Draft (#7 overall)

YEAR	TEAM	LVL	AGE	W	L	SV	G	GS	IP	H	HR	BB/9	K/9	K	GB%	BABIP	WHIP	ERA	DRA-	WARP	MPH	FB%	Whiff%	CSP
2020	LAD	MLB	32	6	2	0	10	10	58^{1}	41	8	1.2	9.6	62	52.7%	.232	0.84	2.16	71	1.6	91.6	40.8%	27.7%	51.5%
2021	LAD	MLB	33	10	8	0	22	22	121^{2}	103	15	1.6	10.7	144	48.0%	.292	1.02	3.55	73	2.9	90.7	36.9%	34.8%	57.6%
2022	LAD	MLB	34	12	3	0	22	22	126^{1}	96	10	1.6	9.8	137	47.1%	.269	0.94	2.28	81	2.5	90.8	40.4%	29.3%	55.2%
2023 DC	*LAD*	*MLB*	*35*	*8*	*6*	*0*	*24*	*24*	*133.3*	*117*	*17*	*1.8*	*9.7*	*143*	*46.7%*	*.291*	*1.09*	*2.77*	*74*	*2.9*	*90.8*	*39.9%*	*29.3%*	*54.2%*

Comparables: Roger Clemens (79), Don Sutton (79), Steve Carlton (77)

The baseball world might not be familiar with him just yet, but Kershaw is one of the better up-and-coming southpaws in the Dodgers organization. They've already given him a few sips of coffee in the majors, during which he has racked up 2,807 strikeouts in only 2,581 innings. He's a former first-round pick with an ideal frame to handle a starter's workload who has succeeded at every level thus far. He features a three-pitch mix of a four-seamer, slider and curve from an over-the-top release point, utilizing all three offerings against both lefties and righties. Though his fastball velocity is underwhelming, he compensates with heavy slider usage as well as command that flashes double plus. He won't appear on any prospect lists due to barely squeaking past rookie eligibility, but this young star has a bright future in Dodger blue.

Dustin May RHP
Born: 09/06/97 Age: 25 Bats: R Throws: R Height: 6'6" Weight: 180 lb. Origin: Round 3, 2016 Draft (#101 overall)

YEAR	TEAM	LVL	AGE	W	L	SV	G	GS	IP	H	HR	BB/9	K/9	K	GB%	BABIP	WHIP	ERA	DRA-	WARP	MPH	FB%	Whiff%	CSP
2020	LAD	MLB	22	3	1	0	12	10	56	45	9	2.6	7.1	44	53.4%	.235	1.09	2.57	82	1.1	97.4	81.5%	19.2%	53.3%
2021	LAD	MLB	23	1	1	0	5	5	23	16	4	2.3	13.7	35	54.9%	.255	0.96	2.74	69	0.6	98.0	77.3%	32.3%	57.5%
2022	OKC	AAA	24	1	0	0	5	5	19	14	2	2.8	15.6	33	45.0%	.316	1.05	1.89	63	0.5	97.4	55.3%	34.0%	
2022	LAD	MLB	24	2	3	0	6	6	30	21	3	4.2	8.7	29	50.6%	.237	1.17	4.50	99	0.3	97.7	51.9%	29.7%	52.3%
2023 DC	*LAD*	*MLB*	*25*	*8*	*6*	*0*	*24*	*24*	*123.7*	*107*	*12*	*3.2*	*10.8*	*149*	*50.1%*	*.308*	*1.22*	*3.24*	*81*	*2.2*	*97.4*	*70.7%*	*28.0%*	*53.7%*

Comparables: Jack Flaherty (59), Carlos Martinez (59), Shelby Miller (59)

Tommy John surgery cost May most of 2021 and 2022, but he came back throwing nearly as hard as he did pre-surgery and actually saw a slight increase in his four-seam fastball (+50 RPM) and curveball (+91 RPM) spin rates. Durability could be something to monitor from here on out, as his MLB career high in innings is 56—professionally, he maxed out at 141⅓ frames between the minors and majors in 2019. It's his second year back from TJ, which tends to be when pitchers really regain steam. Before you know it, he'll be eliminating hitters again the way he eliminates unsuspecting animals—for sport (check his Instagram).

★ ★ ★ *2023 Top 101 Prospect* **#27** ★ ★ ★

Bobby Miller RHP

Born: 04/05/99 Age: 24 Bats: L Throws: R Height: 6'5" Weight: 220 lb. Origin: Round 1, 2020 Draft (#29 overall)

YEAR	TEAM	LVL	AGE	W	L	SV	G	GS	IP	H	HR	BB/9	K/9	K	GB%	BABIP	WHIP	ERA	DRA-	WARP	MPH	FB%	Whiff%	CSP
2021	GL	A+	22	2	2	0	14	11	47	30	1	2.1	10.7	56	45.6%	.257	0.87	1.91	84	1.0				
2021	TUL	AA	22	0	0	0	3	3	9^{1}	10	1	1.9	13.5	14	52.0%	.375	1.29	4.82	70	0.1				
2022	TUL	AA	23	6	6	0	20	19	91	78	8	3.1	11.6	117	49.4%	.311	1.20	4.45	61	2.5				
2022	OKC	AAA	23	1	1	0	4	4	21^{1}	17	4	2.5	11.8	28	56.0%	.283	1.08	3.38	75	0.4	98.8	52.6%	25.8%	
2023 DC	*LAD*	*MLB*	*24*	*2*	*1*	*0*	*17*	*3*	*26*	*23*	*2*	*3.4*	*8.7*	*25*	*48.9%*	*.291*	*1.28*	*3.54*	*89*	*0.3*			*24.8%*	

Comparables: Andrew Heaney (79), Adam Warren (79), Daniel Gossett (78)

The Dodgers' 2020 first-rounder (29th overall, if you can believe it) has opened some eyes since being popped. He started the 2022 Futures Game at Dodger Stadium and struck out Jasson Domínguez, Anthony Volpe and Matt Wallner. Sure, he gave up a run and walked Gunnar Henderson to lead off the game, which goes to show the good and not-so-good when it comes to Miller as a prospect. He logged a career high in innings and, going into his age-24 season, should see Chavez Ravine at some point in 2023. He's armed with a legitimate high-90s fastball that might actually be behind his other offerings. His other three pitches—changeup, curveball, slider—all grade out as plus or better. Combine that with a starter's frame, and you have a pitcher who could headline a rotation.

Shelby Miller RHP

Born: 10/10/90 Age: 32 Bats: R Throws: R Height: 6'3" Weight: 225 lb. Origin: Round 1, 2009 Draft (#19 overall)

YEAR	TEAM	LVL	AGE	W	L	SV	G	GS	IP	H	HR	BB/9	K/9	K	GB%	BABIP	WHIP	ERA	DRA-	WARP	MPH	FB%	Whiff%	CSP
2021	IND	AAA	30	2	1	0	10	1	14	10	1	1.9	14.1	22	41.9%	.300	0.93	3.86	78	0.4				
2021	IOW	AAA	30	0	0	0	3	3	10^{1}	4	1	5.2	13.1	15	47.6%	.150	0.97	1.74	99	0.1				
2021	PIT	MLB	30	0	1	0	10	0	10^{2}	9	3	5.1	5.9	7	36.7%	.222	1.41	5.06	126	0.0	93.8	58.0%	29.6%	59.5%
2021	CHC	MLB	30	0	0	0	3	0	2	7	0	22.5	4.5	1	41.7%	.583	6.00	31.50	115	0.0	93.8	75.3%	10.8%	53.6%
2022	SWB	AAA	31	2	2	4	16	0	21	13	1	2.6	10.7	25	30.8%	.240	0.90	1.71	95	0.3				
2022	SAC	AAA	31	0	2	8	27	1	32^{1}	25	3	4.2	12.2	44	32.9%	.306	1.24	3.62	90	0.4	94.1	49.9%	31.1%	
2022	SF	MLB	31	0	1	0	4	0	7	6	0	3.9	18.0	14	23.1%	.462	1.29	6.43	75	0.2	94.2	44.9%	22.0%	59.3%
2023 DC	*LAD*	*MLB*	*32*	*1*	*1*	*0*	*36*	*0*	*31*	*28*	*4*	*4.4*	*8.5*	*29*	*37.9%*	*.286*	*1.41*	*4.24*	*104*	*0.1*	*94.1*	*61.4%*	*24.7%*	*55.4%*

Comparables: Wily Peralta (63), Ismael Valdez (60), Joel Pineiro (59)

Here's all you need to know about baseball: The most chaotic, absurd, beautiful, stupid thing that can possibly happen almost always will. Miller is back. That's ridiculous enough as it is, but forget what you remember about him. His career strikeout rate is just 19.2%, but in a cameo with the Giants last year, he struck out 14 of the 30 batters he faced. When he was a starter, he featured five different pitches—and a slider wasn't one of them. Now, it's his primary weapon. Baseball being baseball, there's only one way this can go: Miller will earn the closer job by May, strike out Dansby Swanson in a high-leverage situation and win the pennant against the Braves with Dave Stewart seated in the first row.

★ ★ ★ *2023 Top 101 Prospect* **#54** ★ ★ ★

Nick Nastrini RHP

Born: 02/18/00 Age: 23 Bats: R Throws: R Height: 6'3" Weight: 215 lb. Origin: Round 4, 2021 Draft (#131 overall)

YEAR	TEAM	LVL	AGE	W	L	SV	G	GS	IP	H	HR	BB/9	K/9	K	GB%	BABIP	WHIP	ERA	DRA-	WARP	MPH	FB%	Whiff%	CSP
2021	RC	A	21	0	0	0	6	6	13	6	2	4.8	20.8	30	56.2%	.286	1.00	2.08	74	0.3				
2022	GL	A+	22	5	3	0	21	21	86^{1}	61	12	4.1	13.2	127	37.8%	.271	1.16	3.86	81	1.7				
2022	TUL	AA	22	1	1	0	6	6	30^{1}	14	5	4.7	12.5	42	35.6%	.167	0.99	4.15	74	0.6				
2023 non-DC	*LAD*	*MLB*	*23*	*2*	*2*	*0*	*57*	*0*	*50*	*43*	*8*	*5.4*	*10.7*	*59*	*38.6%*	*.287*	*1.47*	*4.75*	*113*	*-0.1*			*31.8%*	

Comparables: Ryan Helsley (75), André Rienzo (75), Dylan Cease (74)

There's something about the Dodgers and fourth-round draft picks. From Joe Thurston to Dee Strange-Gordon to Cody Bellinger to Nastrini—and everyone in between—the Dodgers have had success popping players in the fourth. Nastrini has a chance to be one of the best. After an injury-riddled career at UCLA that saw him log just 66⅔ innings, he almost doubled that in 2022 and saw his stuff take a step forward. He's not in the Miller or Stone prospect strata yet, but he has a chance to get there, if his command and control take a step forward and—more importantly—he stays healthy. He struck out more than 35% of the batters he faced and allowed a .178 batting average against. Those are elite-level numbers from a once-unheralded draft pick. He could boom in 2023.

Ryan Pepiot RHP

Born: 08/21/97 Age: 25 Bats: R Throws: R Height: 6'3" Weight: 215 lb. Origin: Round 3, 2019 Draft (#102 overall)

YEAR	TEAM	LVL	AGE	W	L	SV	G	GS	IP	H	HR	BB/9	K/9	K	GB%	BABIP	WHIP	ERA	DRA-	WARP	MPH	FB%	Whiff%	CSP
2021	TUL	AA	23	3	4	0	15	13	59^{2}	30	7	3.9	12.2	81	32.5%	.198	0.94	2.87	70	1.4				
2021	OKC	AAA	23	2	5	0	11	9	41^{2}	54	12	4.5	9.9	46	40.6%	.350	1.80	7.13	99	0.2				
2022	OKC	AAA	24	9	1	0	19	17	91^{1}	62	10	3.5	11.2	114	39.4%	.263	1.07	2.56	80	1.6	94.0	75.4%	31.8%	
2022	LAD	MLB	24	3	0	0	9	7	36^{1}	26	6	6.7	10.4	42	26.1%	.244	1.46	3.47	110	0.2	93.6	74.4%	28.4%	47.4%
2023 DC	*LAD*	*MLB*	*25*	*6*	*5*	*0*	*39*	*11*	*78*	*65*	*12*	*4.8*	*10.0*	*87*	*35.6%*	*.274*	*1.37*	*4.24*	*102*	*0.5*	*93.6*	*74.4%*	*28.6%*	*47.4%*

Comparables: Adbert Alzolay (79), John Gant (72), Alex Colomé (70)

Pepiot is a dead ringer for Q from *Impractical Jokers*, but his control problems are no laughing matter. Walking 27 opponents in his 36⅓-inning debut earns a thumbs down. His changeup truly is a 70-grade offering, though, averaging 9.2 inches of arm-side run. It pairs well with his mid-90s four-seamer, as he throws both pitches from a nearly identical release point. Neither lefties nor righties could do anything with his change, so it's surprising that he only featured it 25% of the time. His third option was a little slider/cutter thingy that rarely fooled batters. Finding a more effective third pitch would keep him in the rotation mix, but he needs to locate better and avoid free passes if he wants to win a joker vs. joker challenge for a major-league roster spot.

Evan Phillips RHP
Born: 09/11/94 Age: 28 Bats: R Throws: R Height: 6'2" Weight: 215 lb. Origin: Round 17, 2015 Draft (#510 overall)

YEAR	TEAM	LVL	AGE	W	L	SV	G	GS	IP	H	HR	BB/9	K/9	K	GB%	BABIP	WHIP	ERA	DRA-	WARP	MPH	FB%	Whiff%	CSP
2020	BAL	MLB	25	1	1	0	14	0	14^1	14	1	6.3	12.6	20	44.4%	.371	1.67	5.02	85	0.3	94.8	67.4%	27.3%	52.9%
2021	NOR	AAA	26	1	1	0	18	0	25	21	5	5.0	12.6	35	36.8%	.308	1.40	5.04	86	0.5				
2021	LAD	MLB	26	1	1	0	7	0	10^1	8	0	4.4	7.8	9	54.8%	.258	1.26	3.48	101	0.1	95.5	40.8%	22.9%	58.4%
2021	TB	MLB	26	0	0	1	1	0	3	3	1	0.0	6.0	2	40.0%	.222	1.00	3.00	112	0.0	96.1	65.1%	21.7%	61.1%
2022	LAD	MLB	27	7	3	2	64	0	63	33	2	2.1	11.0	77	45.7%	.228	0.76	1.14	71	1.5	94.8	55.9%	30.7%	54.8%
2023 DC	*LAD*	*MLB*	*28*	*3*	*3*	*12*	*64*	*0*	*56*	*48*	*6*	*3.6*	*10.9*	*68*	*44.2%*	*.305*	*1.27*	*3.61*	*88*	*0.6*	*94.9*	*56.7%*	*28.3%*	*54.4%*

Comparables: J.B. Wendelken (70), Trevor Gott (67), Bruce Rondón (65)

With the Dodgers moving on from the Craig Kimbrel experience—and what an experience it was—Phillips could be in line for more save opportunities. But for Dave Roberts, Phillips has become a valuable fireman—a reliever who can come in at any time and get out of a jam. That's wild to think considering the Dodgers plucked him off waivers from Tampa Bay in mid-August 2021. The Rays tried to sneak him through waivers, having just signed him as a free agent when the Orioles cut him, but it's the Dodgers who have turned him into one of baseball's most effective relievers. Per Statcast, he was in MLB's 93rd percentile by exit velocity against and hard-hit percentage, as well as the 98th percentile by expected batting average and expected slugging percentage. What changed? He added a sweeper slider upon landing in LA in 2021, which he throws ~40% of the time. He also added a cut fastball in 2022 that reduced the amount he threw his four-seamer. Less exposure on the four-seamer (.368 batting average against in 2021) plus a couple elite secondaries led to Phillips' ascension.

David Price LHP
Born: 08/26/85 Age: 37 Bats: L Throws: L Height: 6'5" Weight: 215 lb. Origin: Round 1, 2007 Draft (#1 overall)

YEAR	TEAM	LVL	AGE	W	L	SV	G	GS	IP	H	HR	BB/9	K/9	K	GB%	BABIP	WHIP	ERA	DRA-	WARP	MPH	FB%	Whiff%	CSP
2021	LAD	MLB	35	5	2	1	39	11	73^2	79	8	3.2	7.1	58	48.9%	.314	1.43	4.03	105	0.5	93.0	52.8%	21.1%	61.2%
2022	LAD	MLB	36	2	0	2	40	0	40^1	38	6	2.0	8.3	37	55.4%	.281	1.17	2.45	94	0.5	92.4	67.1%	18.6%	60.1%
2023 non-DC	*FA*	*MLB*	*37*	*2*	*2*	*0*	*57*	*0*	*50*	*55*	*6*	*2.9*	*7.3*	*40*	*48.3%*	*.317*	*1.43*	*4.66*	*114*	*-0.2*	*92.6*	*57.0%*	*20.5%*	*57.9%*

Comparables: CC Sabathia (73), Jon Lester (71), Al Downing (69)

When a prominent player retires, it's like encasing his statistics and accomplishments in lucite. They're preserved for eternity, no longer prone to erosion, fortification or the whims of fate. The surrounding narrative or analysis of the metrics may change over time, but the numbers never will again. Now that Price's career is almost certainly engraved onto forever, we can reflect on his 14-year career including 400 appearances, 322 starts and 2,143⅔ innings. He became the first no. 1 draft pick to win a Cy Young and, along with Gerrit Cole and Stephen Strasburg, broke the jinx over pitchers selected first overall. That's just the first draft of his legacy. It may be tweaked and prodded by our children and grandchildren, but no matter which lens future generations use to interpret his numbers, it was a damn fine career.

★ ★ ★ *2023 Top 101 Prospect* **#50** ★ ★ ★

Gavin Stone RHP
Born: 10/15/98 Age: 24 Bats: R Throws: R Height: 6'1" Weight: 175 lb. Origin: Round 5, 2020 Draft (#159 overall)

YEAR	TEAM	LVL	AGE	W	L	SV	G	GS	IP	H	HR	BB/9	K/9	K	GB%	BABIP	WHIP	ERA	DRA-	WARP	MPH	FB%	Whiff%	CSP
2021	RC	A	22	1	2	0	18	17	70	69	5	2.6	13.0	101	46.9%	.381	1.27	3.73	90	0.8				
2021	GL	A+	22	1	0	0	5	5	21	18	2	2.1	15.9	37	56.1%	.410	1.10	3.86	60	0.7				
2022	GL	A+	23	1	1	0	6	6	25	19	1	2.2	10.1	28	53.8%	.281	1.00	1.44	79	0.5				
2022	TUL	AA	23	6	4	0	14	13	73^1	59	1	3.7	13.1	107	44.0%	.356	1.21	1.60	57	2.2				
2022	OKC	AAA	23	2	1	0	6	6	23^1	14	1	3.1	12.7	33	46.0%	.265	0.94	1.16	71	0.5	95.4	48.0%	38.6%	
2023 DC	*LAD*	*MLB*	*24*	*3*	*2*	*0*	*25*	*4*	*40.3*	*36*	*4*	*3.7*	*10.1*	*45*	*46.4%*	*.306*	*1.30*	*3.44*	*86*	*0.6*			*30.5%*	

Comparables: Erik Johnson (80), Rogelio Armenteros (79), Daniel Gossett (78)

The 2020 draft is shaping up to be one of the best in the Friedman/Billy Gasparino era. The Dodgers only had six selections (thanks, COVID-19), and their final pick could eventually rival their first for best pick of the draft. Stone came off a solid 2021 season with an elite 2022 that saw him post a sub-1.50 ERA across three combined levels, striking out almost 34% of batters faced. He has one of the best changeups in the minors, and backs it up with a fastball that holds its velocity late into outings and a quality slider to keep hitters honest. For a guy listed at 175 pounds, there will always be concerns about remaining a starting pitcher—especially since he threw just 102⅔ collegiate innings. However, the Dodgers have been successful at developing guys without prototypical starter's frames; so far, Stone looks like he's on that path.

Noah Syndergaard RHP Born: 08/29/92 Age: 30 Bats: L Throws: R Height: 6'6" Weight: 242 lb. Origin: Round 1, 2010 Draft (#38 overall)

YEAR	TEAM	LVL	AGE	W	L	SV	G	GS	IP	H	HR	BB/9	K/9	K	GB%	BABIP	WHIP	ERA	DRA-	WARP	MPH	FB%	Whiff%	CSP
2021	NYM	MLB	28	0	1	0	2	2	2	3	1	0.0	9.0	2	16.7%	.400	1.50	9.00	145	0.0	94.8	57.7%	21.4%	59.6%
2022	PHI	MLB	29	5	2	0	10	9	54^{2}	63	5	1.5	5.1	31	39.0%	.320	1.32	4.12	129	-0.3	93.4	47.6%	15.9%	55.5%
2022	LAA	MLB	29	5	8	0	15	15	80	75	9	2.5	7.2	64	44.4%	.277	1.21	3.83	105	0.6	94.3	47.1%	23.0%	56.9%
2023 DC	*LAD*	*MLB*	*30*	*5*	*5*	*0*	*19*	*19*	*91.3*	*94*	*9*	*2.3*	*6.8*	*69*	*43.7%*	*.304*	*1.30*	*3.75*	*97*	*0.9*	*95.0*	*50.6%*	*22.7%*	*54.4%*

Comparables: Bill Gullickson (82), Matt Harvey (81), Roy Oswalt (80)

When *Thor: Love and Thunder* was released many were left disappointed, with critics noting the new film wasn't quite as fresh or fast-paced as the previous entry in the Thor canon. Indeed, *Thor: Ragnarok* set a high bar years earlier, and the next installment just wasn't the same. It still made for an entertaining two hours, sure, but it seemed like the Norse god had lost some of his electricity after a few years away from the screen. Syndergaard returned in 2022 after nearly two full years off the mound, and while he still looked like a capable back-end starter, he was no longer the flamethrowing ace who earned his deific nickname. His fastball sat several miles per hour slower than it did in his heyday, and he succeeded by deftly mixing and locating his pitches rather than blowing past hitters with burning heat. A midseason trade to the Phillies saw Syndergaard drop his four-seam fastball almost entirely, instead relying heavily on his sinker and a newer, faster slider. The results were mixed, much like the reviews for *Thor: Love and Thunder.* But hey, there's nothing like a move to Hollywood to overhaul the script for the next sequel.

Julio Urías LHP Born: 08/12/96 Age: 26 Bats: L Throws: L Height: 6'0" Weight: 225 lb. Origin: International Free Agent, 2012

YEAR	TEAM	LVL	AGE	W	L	SV	G	GS	IP	H	HR	BB/9	K/9	K	GB%	BABIP	WHIP	ERA	DRA-	WARP	MPH	FB%	Whiff%	CSP
2020	LAD	MLB	23	3	0	0	11	10	55	45	5	2.9	7.4	45	32.3%	.256	1.15	3.27	118	0.1	94.2	56.3%	26.0%	52.7%
2021	LAD	MLB	24	20	3	0	32	32	185^{2}	151	19	1.8	9.5	195	40.0%	.276	1.02	2.96	78	3.7	94.3	48.4%	24.4%	57.7%
2022	LAD	MLB	25	17	7	0	31	31	175	127	23	2.1	8.5	166	38.8%	.229	0.96	2.16	90	2.6	93.2	49.2%	23.9%	57.1%
2023 DC	*LAD*	*MLB*	*26*	*11*	*8*	*0*	*29*	*29*	*169*	*147*	*20*	*2.4*	*8.2*	*154*	*39.2%*	*.276*	*1.14*	*2.95*	*79*	*3.3*	*93.8*	*50.2%*	*24.9%*	*56.3%*

Comparables: Don Gullett (66), Don Drysdale (65), Félix Hernández (63)

Urías finally laid to rest a few of the nagging narratives pestering him throughout his career:

1. "He's so young!" Now 26 years old, he's officially in his prime.
2. "He's not durable enough!" He has missed only one start in the last three years.
3. "He's not a true ace!" About that…

His fastball won't blow anyone away, at 93 mph, but it has an elite, 2,488-rpm spin rate and its 11:45 perceived spin direction is almost perfectly vertical—an ideal recipe for lazy fly balls. His 45.2% fly-ball rate was the second-highest in MLB among qualified pitchers, yet he wasn't burned by tons of home runs. Mix in a healthy dose of excellent, high-spin curveballs and some quality changeups to keep righties honest, and you've got a legitimate, narrative-busting ace.

Alex Vesia LHP Born: 04/11/96 Age: 27 Bats: L Throws: L Height: 6'1" Weight: 209 lb. Origin: Round 17, 2018 Draft (#507 overall)

YEAR	TEAM	LVL	AGE	W	L	SV	G	GS	IP	H	HR	BB/9	K/9	K	GB%	BABIP	WHIP	ERA	DRA-	WARP	MPH	FB%	Whiff%	CSP
2020	MIA	MLB	24	0	1	0	5	0	4^{1}	7	3	14.5	10.4	5	20.0%	.333	3.23	18.69	168	-0.1	91.8	72.9%	28.3%	47.1%
2021	OKC	AAA	25	0	0	2	9	0	9	3	0	3.0	19.0	19	44.4%	.333	0.67	1.00	67	0.2				
2021	LAD	MLB	25	3	1	1	41	0	40	17	6	5.0	12.2	54	25.3%	.143	0.98	2.25	83	0.7	93.9	72.4%	38.5%	52.8%
2022	LAD	MLB	26	5	0	1	63	0	54^{1}	37	2	4.0	13.1	79	34.4%	.297	1.12	2.15	73	1.3	94.2	63.1%	33.8%	54.5%
2023 DC	*LAD*	*MLB*	*27*	*3*	*3*	*0*	*64*	*0*	*56*	*44*	*7*	*4.5*	*12.3*	*76*	*33.8%*	*.297*	*1.28*	*3.60*	*86*	*0.6*	*94.0*	*66.5%*	*34.0%*	*53.6%*

Comparables: Diego Castillo (72), Tommy Kahnle (71), Aaron Bummer (71)

Vesia vs. Jake Cronenworth was exactly the matchup the Dodgers wanted. Their seven previous meetings, going back to 2020, resulted in four strikeouts, a single to left field, a lazy fly out and a weak grounder to first. Vesia threw 21 total pitches, 11 of which were called or swinging strikes. His fastball-slider combo spelled near-certain doom for left-handed hitters all season: He held 79 same-side batters to a .130/.218/.130 slash, with 32 strikeouts. Everything seemed tilted in the pitcher's favor as the adversaries squared off, in the seventh inning of NLDS Game 4, yet as everyone who watches enough baseball already knows, that's when it's most likely to break the other way. Once again the Dodgers' premier lefty reliever in 2023, expect Vesia to avenge the two-run single that prematurely ended their postseason run—perhaps seven times.

Lineouts

Hitters

HITTER	POS	TEAM	LVL	AGE	PA	R	2B	3B	HR	RBI	BB	K	SB	CS	AVG/OBP/SLG	DRC+	BABIP	BRR	DRP	WARP
Hanser Alberto	IF	LAD	MLB	29	159	13	9	2	2	15	3	25	0	1	.244/.258/.365	93	.279	-0.7	2B(37): 0.1, 3B(20): 0.7, P(10): 0	0.3
Rayne Doncon	SS	DOD	ROK	18	215	28	16	1	9	38	15	38	6	2	.256/.307/.482		.275			
	SS	RC	A	18	43	6	0	0	3	8	3	5	0	0	.250/.302/.475	110	.219	-1.2	SS(10): -0.1	0.1
Yonny Hernandez	IF	RNO	AAA	24	295	49	6	6	1	31	35	47	30	5	.244/.353/.328	105	.297	4.2	2B(44): -0.5, SS(12): 0.6, 3B(11): 1.3	1.6
	IF	AZ	MLB	24	28	2	0	0	0	0	2	4	2	0	.083/.154/.083	93	.100	0.7	3B(10): 1.1, 2B(2): 0	0.3
Brandon Lewis	CI	TUL	AA	23	436	60	19	0	24	71	28	147	0	1	.209/.271/.438	83	.257	-0.4	1B(64): -0.4, 3B(34): -1.4, 2B(1): -0.1	0.0
Jason Martin	OF	OKC	AAA	26	544	100	25	5	32	107	68	135	8	5	.285/.374/.564	119	.332	-0.4	RF(72): 0.0, LF(26): 1.0, CF(21): -0.2	2.8
Patrick Mazeika	C	SAC	AAA	28	55	9	2	0	2	6	3	5	0	0	.235/.291/.392	112	.227	-2.0	C(8): 0.3, 1B(4): -0.5	0.1
	C	SYR	AAA	28	133	10	2	0	2	12	15	18	0	0	.261/.383/.333	117	.297	-2.2	C(13): 1.0, 1B(9): -1.0	0.3
	C	NYM	MLB	28	72	4	4	0	1	6	2	9	0	0	.191/.214/.294	90	.207	0.0	C(22): 1, 1B(2): 0	0.3
Samuel Munoz	DH	DSL LADM	ROK	17	210	39	12	5	1	42	26	34	4	5	.347/.429/.491		.407			
Kevin Pillar	OF	OKC	AAA	33	176	42	7	3	10	40	20	22	2	1	.315/.398/.604	136	.306	0.5	CF(22): 0.8, RF(8): -0.4, LF(4): 0.5	1.3
	OF	LAD	MLB	33	13	1	1	0	0	0	1	4	0	0	.083/.154/.167	85	.125	-0.4	LF(4): 0, CF(1): 0.1	0.0
Jose Ramos	OF	RC	A	21	138	20	3	3	6	23	18	36	2	0	.277/.391/.518	109	.342	0.7	RF(19): 0.4, CF(11): 0.2	0.8
	OF	GL	A+	21	407	63	19	3	19	74	39	133	2	0	.240/.322/.467	102	.322	0.1	CF(43): -0.0, RF(41): 1.1	1.6
Logan Wagner	3B/2B	DOD	ROK	18	58	8	1	0	0	6	7	12	2	1	.220/.328/.240		.289			
Ryan Ward	LF	TUL	AA	24	506	62	18	2	28	78	39	116	5	1	.255/.319/.486	102	.281	-1.8	LF(84): 2.0, RF(4): 0.3, 1B(3): -0.3	1.4

Pitching can lead to injuries, which is why the position player who takes the hill is usually the most expendable on the roster. **Hanser Alberto** pitched 10 times in 2022. He had as many walks on the mound as he did at the plate (three). ⚾ Remember Alfonso Soriano? Well, **Rayne Doncon** might be him, time-traveling from the past under a different name. That's a bit presumptuous to say about a 19-year-old, but they both hail from San Pedro de Macoris, started as infielders and have similar actions at the plate. Doncon might be the biggest boom-or-bust prospect in the system. ⚾ **Yonny Hernandez** dealt with injuries last year and never had a chance to get going in the big leagues. Already flipped between Arizona, Oakland and Los Angeles over the offseason, he'll get a shot to be *some* organization's notorious "sum greater than his parts" player, with a chance to make a sneaky impact. ⚾ If Mark Trumbo was still playing, he'd probably identify with **Brandon Lewis**. The large adult son launched 24 home runs in Double-A (after 30 in A-ball in 2021), but did so with a 6.4% walk rate and 33.7% strikeout rate. In fact, if Lewis ascended to Trumbo's level, he'd be a quality major leaguer. However, that is the 100th percentile outcome for the corner infielder. ⚾ After a banner season in Triple-A without touching the majors, the only practical move for **Jason Martin** was to go to the Korea Baseball Organization. The NC Dinos landed him and, considering his impressive performance in 2022, Martin should thrive in the KBO. ⚾ "Bat-first third catcher" is a tough role to carve out, and **Patrick Mazeika** ran out of time to do so with the Mets this year. After a catch-and-release stint with the Giants, he's found a new team that needs backstop insurance, as most teams do. ⚾ The recipient of the largest international bonus the Dodgers doled out in 2022, it isn't quite clear where **Samuel Muñoz** is going to play in the field—outfield, third, or first—but the hope is that he'll mash wherever, as he did as a 17-year-old in the DSL. He could be stateside by 2023. ⚾ At age 33, **Kevin Pillar** dominated Triple-A for two months, which is like a dad joining his kid's dodgeball game and taking it way too seriously. He hurt his shoulder on a slide, in his fourth game after getting called up—which is what usually happens when dad gets too intense about dodgeball. ⚾ The Spider-Man pointing meme may never be more appropriate than when it comes to Pages and **Jose Ramos**. Both are profile right fielders, both have massive power (career MiLB OPS within .054 points of one other) and their birthdays are separated by 24 days. The main difference: Ramos hasn't played above A-ball, while Pages is on the brink of Triple-A (or the majors). ⚾ The largest over-slot signing (by percentage) for the Dodgers in the 2022 draft, **Logan Wagner** impressed LA scouts enough for them to commit $600,000 to him. The high-school shortstop is a surefire bet to end up at second or third base in the pros. He'll go as far as his bat takes him. ⚾ The Dodgers lost Ryan Noda in the Rule 5 Draft. To cope with that, they have **Ryan Ward**. The 2019 eighth-rounder has back-to-back seasons of 27 and 28 home runs and an .800+ OPS. He's limited defensively, but he has LF/DH written all over him.

Pitchers

PITCHER	TEAM	LVL	AGE	W	L	SV	G	GS	IP	H	HR	BB/9	K/9	K	GB%	BABIP	WHIP	ERA	DRA-	WARP	MPH	FB%	WHF	CSP
Justin Bruihl	OKC	AAA	25	3	1	0	25	1	30^1	32	2	5.9	7.1	24	38.8%	.313	1.71	3.56	107	0.0	87.2	73.5%	24.7%	
	LAD	MLB	25	1	1	1	24	0	23^2	22	4	2.3	4.9	13	35.9%	.254	1.18	3.80	115	0.1	86.9	80.1%	24.4%	63.3%
Maddux Bruns	RC	A	20	0	3	0	21	21	44^1	36	1	9.1	13.6	67	38.5%	.368	1.83	5.68	120	-0.5				
Victor González	OKC	AAA	26	1	0	0	12	0	11^2	10	1	3.9	7.7	10	65.7%	.265	1.29	3.09	86	0.2	94.7	68.4%	23.3%	
Ben Harris	RC	A	22	1	1	3	22	0	27^2	23	1	7.2	19.2	59	50.0%	.512	1.63	5.53	59	0.8				
	GL	A+	22	3	0	4	22	3	28	9	1	4.8	15.4	48	32.6%	.195	0.86	1.93	67	0.8				
Heath Hembree	OKC	AAA	33	1	0	1	10	0	9^1	7	2	1.9	13.5	14	39.1%	.263	0.96	4.82	75	0.2	95.3	60.1%	31.5%	
	PIT	MLB	33	2	0	0	20	0	16^1	17	5	7.7	6.6	12	25.0%	.255	1.90	7.16	141	-0.2	94.2	50.3%	20.2%	55.5%
	LAD	MLB	33	1	1	0	6	0	5^2	9	1	4.8	7.9	5	28.6%	.400	2.12	7.94	108	0.0	94.8	58.9%	13.0%	59.5%
Peter Heubeck	RC	A	19	0	1	0	15	13	31^2	22	7	7.1	11.9	42	36.1%	.231	1.48	7.39	104	0.0				
Landon Knack	TUL	AA	24	2	10	0	17	17	64^2	64	8	3.8	11.1	80	34.7%	.341	1.41	5.01	74	1.3				
Ronan Kopp	RC	A	19	5	2	1	24	9	57^2	36	3	5.8	15.9	102	49.1%	.308	1.27	2.81	71	1.1				
Emmet Sheehan	GL	A+	22	7	2	0	18	12	63^2	41	2	4.0	14.3	101	41.1%	.310	1.08	2.83	71	1.6				
Blake Treinen	OKC	AAA	34	0	0	0	7	0	6	8	0	1.5	13.5	9	52.6%	.421	1.50	4.50	79	0.1	95.7	45.4%	29.1%	
	LAD	MLB	34	1	1	0	5	0	5	1	1	1.8	10.8	6	60.0%	.000	0.40	1.80	94	0.1	96.6	43.5%	26.5%	61.7%

Pretend **Justin Bruihl** releases a pitch as you start reading this lineout. As you wait for it to arrive, you look up his numbers. He fanned just 13 of 100 batters faced last season and only three of his 341 pitches reached 90 mph. Thud! At last, the ball reaches the catcher's mitt. ⚾ There might not be a pitcher with better stuff (31% strikeout rate) in the Dodgers' org than **Maddux Bruns**. However, there also might not be a pitcher with more shaky command/control (20.8 BB%). Yes, he's named after Greg Maddux. No, he doesn't—nor will he ever likely—have anything close to Greg's mastery when it comes to commanding the baseball. Still, it's easy to dream on Bruns' stuff. ⚾ It was the best laid plan of mice and men, as Vin Scully used to say. The Dodgers acquired **Danny Duffy** at the 2021 trade deadline to help bolster the staff. He didn't throw a pitch. They re-signed him to an incentive-laden deal for 2022 and threw just 6⅔ innings across three minor-league levels for LA. His career might be on its last legs. ⚾ **Victor González** spent the first half of 2022 injured and the second half rehabbing in the minors. In the postseason, he was, "in the conversation for the next round," according to Dave Roberts. That next round never came, so he'll try to rejoin "the conversation" in spring training. ⚾ Quick, who led Minor League Baseball in strikeout percentage (minimum 50 IP)? If you guessed **Ben Harris**, you'd be correct. The unsung eighth-round draft pick in 2021 struck out 45% of the batters he faced in his first full season in the minors. Don't look up his walk rate, though. ⚾ After 16⅓ innings of 7.16 ERA-ball for the Pirates, **Heath Hembree** got a shot with the Dodgers. He lasted 5⅔ innings with LA and posted a 7.94 ERA. In his last 99 innings (since 2020), he has pitched for six teams and has an ERA just south of seven. Not great! ⚾ **Peter Heubeck**, the 2021 second-rounder, doesn't have the stuff of Maddux Bruns nor the polish of Gavin Stone, landing somewhere in between on both counts. The Dodgers development history bodes well for him, but he'll need to show more durability and an uptick in stuff if he's going to take the next step. ⚾ Once on the fast path to the majors, **Landon Knack**'s progress hit a speed bump in 2022, as he dealt with injuries that limited him to fewer than 65 innings—still a career-best. His stuff took a step back (velocity in the low-90s rather than mid-90s) and his future might ultimately be in the bullpen. ⚾ He's funky. He has the stuff. He's **Ronan Kopp**! The 6-foot-7 lefty quietly put together one of the better seasons in the system (38.4% strikeout rate) after having been a 12th-round, junior college draftee in 2021. The Double-A proving ground awaits sometime this year, which will give a better feel for Kopp's future—but he's a lefty who's breathing, so he has a chance. He also has premium stuff, which helps. ⚾ The Dodgers paid **Jimmy Nelson** $700,000 not to pitch in 2022, just so they could have the option to retain his services for 2023. They declined it. Make your own conclusions about what that means for his career. ⚾ No relation to Joe, **Emmet Sheehan** is similar to his draft classmate Nick Nastrini in terms of being injured in college and improving as a professional. The sample size is small (83⅔ innings in 2021-22), but the early returns are encouraging (29.1% strikeout-minus-walk rate). ⚾ What's the difference between a pack of Big League Chew and **Blake Treinen's** right shoulder? Big League Chew is still good after it's been torn open. Also, it will be present at baseball games in 2023.

SAN DIEGO PADRES

Essay by Shaker Samman

Player comments by Michael Clair and BP staff

The thing about San Diego is it's never been particularly noteworthy. It's warm and sits on miles of beautiful Pacific Ocean coastline; so does Los Angeles. It's beautiful, and has a seemingly endless parade of stellar burrito haunts; so does the Bay Area. It's, at times, soulless and corporate; so is every other facet of modern life. It's not a particularly exciting, or inviting, or memorable city. It does not exist to solve a problem or answer a question beyond "how high could an orca jump to catch a piece of fish?" (Pretty high, by the way.)

It's through this lens that I view the San Diego Padres; the white bread of Major League Baseball. In 54 tries, the Padres have reached the playoffs seven times—their fans had to wait 10 years for their first winning season, and six more for their first World Series appearance, losing in five games to the Detroit Tigers. Fourteen years later, they finally made it back to the Fall Classic, this time being swept by the Yankees.

That disappointment begat a half-decade of sub-mediocrity that, save for two NLDS appearances in the mid-2000s (remember when Mike Piazza was on the Padres? Me neither), gave way to another 12 years without a postseason appearance.

There were some glimmers of hope here and there. Adrián González was a bright spot until he was shipped to Boston. Miguel Tejada nearly helped San Diego to the playoffs in one of his twilight seasons. By 2018, though, most of the excitement around the Padres centered around what could happen in the future. The farm system, led by a kid named Fernando Tatis Jr., was the best in the sport, and beyond him, there seemed to be more than enough talent to turn the team around.

But that kind of thinking can be a double-edged sword; success is always right around the corner, until someone else swoops in and takes it away. The annals of baseball history are littered with teams that refused to take advantage of the luxury of young talent, never built around it and watched their championship ambitions wither away. Not every big-name prospect from the top-ranked 2018 and 2019 Padres farm systems has made their marks for San Diego, or even

SAN DIEGO PADRES PROSPECTUS

2022 W-L: 89-73, 2ND IN NL WEST

Pythag	.530	*12th*	DER	.711	*8th*
RS/G	4.35	*13th*	DRC+	100	*13th*
RA/G	4.07	*10th*	DRA-	93	*7th*
dWin%	.544	*9th*	FIP	3.83	*11th*
Payroll	$211M	*5th*	B-Age	28.8	*12th*
M$/MW	$4.7M	*20th*	P-Age	30.8	*25th*

396'
367'
382'
336'
322'

- Opened 2004
- Open air
- Natural surface
- Fence profile: 5' to 12'

Park Factors

Runs	Runs/RH	Runs/LH	HR/RH	HR/LH
98	97	98	100	99

Top Hitter WARP	4.5 Manny Machado
Top Pitcher WARP	4.3 Yu Darvish
2023 Top Prospect	Jackson Merrill

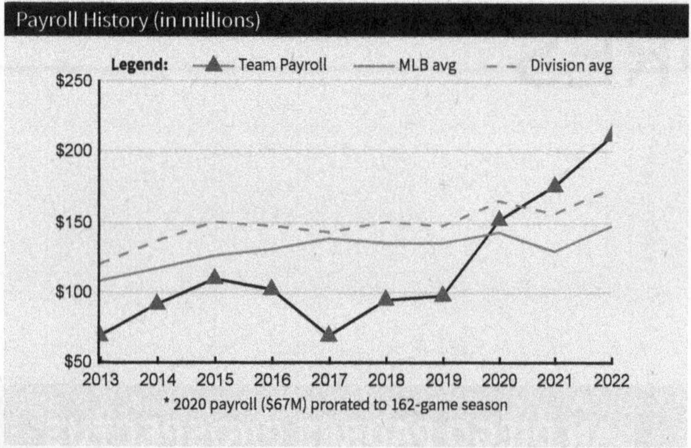

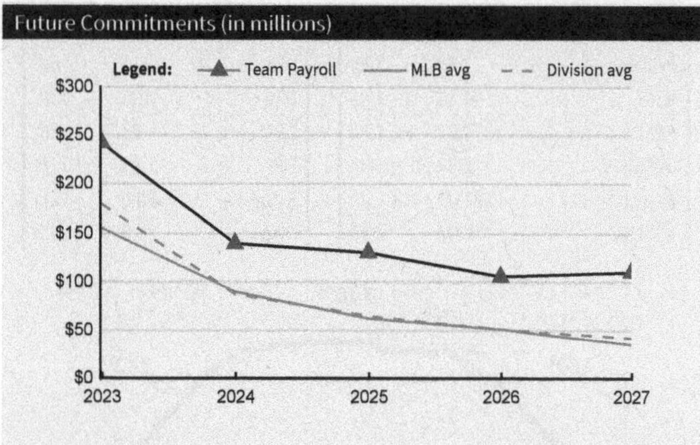

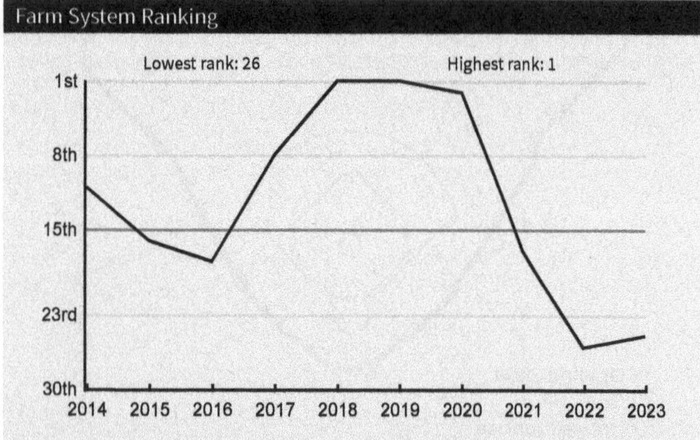

Personnel

President of Baseball Operations & General Manager
A.J. Preller

Vice President, Assistant General Manager
Fred Uhlman, Jr.

Vice President, Assistant General Manager
Josh Stein

Vice President, Baseball Operations
Nick Ennis

Senior Advisor/Director of Player Personnel
Logan White

Manager
Bob Melvin

in the pros. A few fizzled out. One became a superstar. But it's the ones in between that outline how San Diego turned a basement dweller into a bona fide World Series contender.

Between Tatis and the $300 million man, Manny Machado, the Padres understood they had the spine of what could become something exciting. But filling in the rest of a championship-caliber roster isn't straightforward. San Diego flipped top prospects like Francisco Mejía, Josh Naylor and Cal Quantrill for lights-out arms like Blake Snell, Mike Clevinger and Yu Darvish. Taylor Trammell turned into starting catcher Austin Nola, Hunter Renfroe into Jake Cronenworth.

A.J. Preller started to do what you do when you understand something special might be just around the corner, adding complementary players to smooth out the edges. Then in the span of about 48 hours in early August, the Padres turned into genuine contenders. Trades for Josh Hader and Brandon Drury bolstered the rotation and the infield. Josh Bell arrived to add some muscle to the middle of the order. But none of that compared to what happened when they pushed their chips into the center of the table.

Juan Soto. Him. The kind of guy whose name you scribbled into your English notebooks, surrounded by hearts and flowers and a half-dozen block-Ses—you know the ones. Soto is everything you want from a baseball player. It's not just his numbers, which place him among the best to ever swing a bat, even at just 24 years old. It's what bringing him to San Diego represents. Soto is the centerpiece of Preller's project—the player the Padres were building around long before he boarded a plane from Washington. Barring injury, Soto will likely spend the next few seasons of his career launching balls into orbit and collecting accolades. In a few years, he'll have a chance to become the first $500 million man in American sports, with the Padres surely a suitor. And he's already in San Diego—doesn't the incumbent always have the advantage?

It's stunning, not just because it's happening here, but that it's happening at all. The Padres are unique in the modern landscape—they're a historically insignificant team playing in the 27th-biggest market in the country in a sport where checks are cashed, win or lose. And yet, they're trying.

Trying is, mathematically speaking, 100% harder than not trying. Coasting is so easy, and grifting is second nature. It's unimaginably easy to not try to do anything ever for any reason at all. Especially when not trying means collecting gargantuan sums of money with little to no effort required.

The last decade of American life has lowered expectations we hold for those in power, and it can feel comparatively trivial to point out how disappointing it is to see owners phoning it in. Professional baseball is entertainment; that's what sport is. It matters in an enigmatic way. It doesn't solve crises or save folks from hunger, but it unites communities and builds a common bond.

Unfortunately, it's business, too. The spreadsheets and formulas, too convoluted for my smooth caveman brain to understand, say Player A is worth X and Player B is worth Y. They took over baseball because they were meant, at least in theory, to help build a team efficiently. They do that pretty well. But they also opened the door for bad actors to exploit an already broken system.

Baseball teams refuse to open their books, so there's no way of knowing just how large a profit they're turning (at least outside of Atlanta), but it's hard to imagine any team having a net income that wouldn't make Scrooge McDuck blush. Between MLB's traditional TV deals with Turner and ESPN, its new streaming offerings with Apple and NBC, and the contracts teams sign individually with their regional sports networks like Bally, teams are pulling in more than $100 million in revenue before selling a single ticket. All 30 teams received a $30 million payment in 2022 from the sale of the final 15% of BAMTech not already owned by Disney, the third such windfall in six years.

Despite a slight dip thanks to that whole COVID thing, MLB's total revenue has skyrocketed in the last decade. In 2012, Major League Baseball generated $6.81 billion to be dispersed to teams and players. In 2019, that figure climbed to $10.37 billion, before settling at $9.56 billion in 2021. But spending, on the whole, hasn't kept up with growth. In 2021, 12 teams fielded rosters with lower total payrolls than the league average in 2012 (about $107 million), and three—Pittsburgh ($54.3 million), Cleveland ($50.7M) and Baltimore ($42.4M)—somehow spent less on players than the Astros did nine years prior.

And while teams like the Orioles, A's and Marlins—all of whom play in larger media markets than the Padres—have allowed richer clubs to strip them for parts, San Diego has done the opposite, buying up star players, assembling a collection of talent that should compete for the World Series year-in and year-out.

Not all of their decisions have worked out. They say the specter of no. 30 still haunts Beer Alley in the concourse behind home plate, and Tatis' road back from the wrist injury that cost him the first half of the 2022 season was waylaid by an 80-game suspension after testing positive for performance-enhancing drugs. He'll miss the first 20 games of the 2023 season as penance, too. Not so long ago, he was the West Coast answer to Soto; now he's a massive question mark and a sobering reminder of the speed of change in this league. It would've been easy to take his absence, for the entirety of year two of 14 and part of year three, as a sign to step back and assess next steps. But unlike other teams, content to keep the treadmill of mediocrity humming along, the Padres aspire for something more, and their fans are better off for it.

In the years before their spending spree, the Padres typically ranked in the middle of the pack in attendance, even despite their meager payroll. For most owners, that would've been good enough. A sizable town with impeccable weather and a beloved stadium on the water is a printing press, no matter the quality on the field. Making things even easier: Since the Chargers left, they're the only game in town as far as men's big four sports go. But the Padres wanted more, and their fans did, too. Seeing San Diego reach the 2020 NLDS meant something to a city that hadn't experienced postseason baseball in 14 years. In 2021, the Padres welcomed the third-most visitors of any ballclub in the country. In 2022, they brought in nearly three million fans—good for fifth. The Padres gave good baseball to San Diego, and San Diego gave thanks in return.

That trend will likely continue this spring, after the Padres again swiped a sought-after star, this time gifting former Red Sox shortstop Xander Bogaerts $280 million over 11 years to bring his talents to San Diego. When Soto and Bell were announced as Padres in August, franchise owner Peter Seider said, "the art of the possible is here." As puzzling a sentiment as that remains, maybe this is what he meant: For the first time in a long time, maybe even the first time, period, San Diego is undeniable.

The Padres are just a few months removed from finally—improbably—slaying the Dodgers, upending what many believed was one of the best teams of all time. The ride ended in the NLCS, but the front office promptly went to work putting together a roster that's well-positioned to make it back—or go all the way. As Los Angeles sat on their hands all offseason, San Diego got better. They made the big-ticket signing, sure; they also made smart complementary deals, like bringing in Matt Carpenter fresh off a comeback season in New York, snagging Seth Lugo out from under the Mets' noses or even keeping Robert Suarez from chasing glory elsewhere. In a vacuum, those sorts of moves are all commendable; viewed alongside the others the Padres have made in the past few seasons, they're the kind that could deliver championships.

No team—not the Dodgers, or Yankees, or Braves or Mets—boasts a lineup that's clearly more threatening, at least on paper, after Preller went out and added a third star shortstop to go with the first two. Soto, Machado, Tatis and Bogaerts could all be the best players on nearly any other team in the sport. In Cronenworth, the Padres have a fourth All-Star infielder, plus supplementary players like Nola and Ha-Seong Kim (so many infielders). There's no doubt things could get murky in the rotation when Lugo and Nick Martinez, who barely combined for qualified status, are filling out the rotation. But when the postseason comes, you really only need three starters, plus a handful of guys who can be counted on when the going gets tough. That lineup, plus the trio of Darvish, Snell and Joe Musgrove in the rotation and backed up by Hader in the bullpen, have positioned San Diego for a season that could surpass even their grandest expectations.

The NL West is wide open—the Padres saw to that when they crowbarred themselves past the Dodgers in the NLDS. I don't know if this is the year the Padres finally win the

World Series. Even beyond questions about Tatis' return, or the infield Tetris game tasked to manager Bob Melvin, there are still so many unknowns.

Baseball is random. Teams play 162 games over six-plus months—nearly double what any other American professional league puts on—and determine without a sliver of a doubt the best teams each regular season. And then, after working so hard to build these conclusions, baseball lights them ablaze, and throws teams into the deep end. Years of development and teambuilding and spending can end in a mid-week game that shares a timeslot with *Bachelor in Paradise*. It's silly to predict that any team will win it all before the year starts—just ask Dave Roberts.

So I'm not sure if the Padres will climb the mountaintop. But I do know they'll have a shot. A team that spent the overwhelming majority of its history in the doldrums, only occasionally sticking its head out from the depths of the National League to remind us of their existence, could finally—maybe—do what their entire existence has built toward. And even if this isn't the year, and San Diego fans have to wait at least a little longer, that they're this close is worth so much more than what it cost to build this team.

There are the big numbers, like the total payroll, or the count of fans in attendance or the sheer number of bases that will soon be collected by the most daunting lineup around. But in the end, they don't mean much, whether the Padres win the World Series or not. The point of a grand experiment isn't the conclusion; it's the process. What matters is how they got here—to the head table, with the big dogs—and that they got here at all. It's the effort that counts. And it's thrilling to watch them try. ■

—Shaker Samman is a writer and editor in Los Angeles.

HITTERS

José Azocar OF Born: 05/11/96 Age: 27 Bats: R Throws: R Height: 5'11" Weight: 181 lb. Origin: International Free Agent, 2012

YEAR	TEAM	LVL	AGE	PA	R	2B	3B	HR	RBI	BB	K	SB	CS	Whiff%	AVG/OBP/SLG	DRC+	BABIP	BRR	DRP	WARP
2021	SA	AA	25	343	46	8	6	9	43	35	71	15	11		.276/.360/.432	121	.333	0.3	CF(74): -5.6, RF(1): -0.2	1.5
2021	ELP	AAA	25	201	26	14	8	0	27	6	45	17	3		.289/.308/.447	83	.369	0.9	CF(39): -2.4, RF(5): 1.1, LF(3): -0.3	0.2
2022	ELP	AAA	26	105	11	6	0	5	16	7	24	3	1	25.3%	.306/.352/.520	99	.362	0.2	CF(21): 0.7, LF(1): -0.1, RF(1): 0.7	0.4
2022	SD	MLB	26	216	24	9	3	0	10	12	44	5	6	24.6%	.257/.298/.332	87	.327	0.4	RF(49): 1.3, CF(35): 0.2, LF(21): 0.4	0.6
2023 DC	*SD*	*MLB*	*27*	*251*	*26*	*9*	*2*	*4*	*25*	*13*	*54*	*11*	*4*	*24.4%*	*.257/.301/.375*	*87*	*.317*	*2.4*	*LF 1, CF 0*	*0.6*

Comparables: Noel Cuevas (53), Mitch Haniger (49), Juan Lagares (49)

Nicknamed "Azúcar" for how sweet he looks while running down balls in the field with his lightning-quick speed, Azocar finally made his big-league debut 10 years after originally signing with the Tigers thanks to some early-season injuries in the Padres outfield. He soon earned manager Bob Melvin's trust and briefly took over center field from a struggling Trent Grisham. Strikeouts and plate discipline have long been Azocar's main problems, and he spent the previous winter working extensively with a pitching machine, calling out if the spheres hurled at him were strikes or balls. He may never make enough solid contact to start, but with his legs and his glove a future as a fourth outfielder and defensive replacement is well within his reach.

Xander Bogaerts SS Born: 10/01/92 Age: 30 Bats: R Throws: R Height: 6'2" Weight: 218 lb. Origin: International Free Agent, 2009

YEAR	TEAM	LVL	AGE	PA	R	2B	3B	HR	RBI	BB	K	SB	CS	Whiff%	AVG/OBP/SLG	DRC+	BABIP	BRR	DRP	WARP
2020	BOS	MLB	27	225	36	8	0	11	28	21	41	8	0	23.0%	.300/.364/.502	123	.329	1.6	SS(53): -3	1.2
2021	BOS	MLB	28	603	90	34	1	23	79	62	113	5	1	22.0%	.295/.370/.493	126	.333	0.0	SS(138): -1	4.0
2022	BOS	MLB	29	631	84	38	0	15	73	57	118	8	2	24.8%	.307/.377/.456	123	.362	1.4	SS(146): -5	3.4
2023 DC	*SD*	*MLB*	*30*	*599*	*75*	*30*	*1*	*21*	*81*	*56*	*118*	*12*	*1*	*24.1%*	*.282/.356/.463*	*130*	*.325*	*5.0*	*SS -3*	*4.2*

Comparables: Lou Boudreau (80), José Reyes (77), Robin Yount (75)

When the Padres inked Bogaerts to a stunning 11-year, $280 million contract in December, it was tempting to let John Henry and co. off the hook. After all, it's easy to argue against giving any 30-year-old that much guaranteed money over that period of time. But the issue isn't that the Red Sox failed to match San Diego's exorbitant offer once Bogaerts reached free agency: it's that they ever let the heart and soul of their franchise reach free agency at all.

Clearly frustrated by Boston's low-ball extension offer from the winter of '21, Bogaerts cited how tough the 2022 season was for him at several points. That didn't stop him from posting his fifth straight campaign with a DRC+ of 120 or better, or from tying Corey Seager for the most WARP among regular shortstops. The Padres proved willing to reward Bogaerts for that consistency, while the Sox brass were once more left holding an "at least we tried" poster in front of their increasingly incredulous fanbase.

So why did Boston balk on re-signing its star player *this* time around? Likely because he'd just turned 30, and because his defense slipped from excellent in 2021 to average last season (though defensive metrics have never known what to make of his glove), rekindling rumors of a potential move down the defensive spectrum. Of course, he more than makes up for those modest warts by owning one of the game's most reliably excellent bats and being one of its most durable players—he set the all-time Red Sox record for games started at shortstop last season.

Boston's loss is San Diego's gain, as Bogey figures to help anchor a wildly exciting lineup. In some ways it's a loss for all of us, though, as we may never again hear someone say "Xander Bogaerts" in a molasses-thick Masshole accent.

Luis Campusano C Born: 09/29/98 Age: 24 Bats: R Throws: R Height: 5'11" Weight: 232 lb. Origin: Round 2, 2017 Draft (#39 overall)

YEAR	TEAM	LVL	AGE	PA	R	2B	3B	HR	RBI	BB	K	SB	CS	Whiff%	AVG/OBP/SLG	DRC+	BABIP	BRR	DRP	WARP
2020	SD	MLB	21	4	2	0	0	1	1	0	2	0	0	37.5%	.333/.500/1.333	103		0.0		0.0
2021	ELP	AAA	22	326	47	21	3	15	45	27	66	1	0		.295/.365/.541	111	.335	-0.8	C(62): 1.8, 1B(3): -0.1	1.7
2021	SD	MLB	22	38	0	0	0	0	1	4	11	0	0	37.9%	.088/.184/.088	76	.130	-1.3	C(9): -0.4	-0.1
2022	ELP	AAA	23	358	62	15	1	14	60	33	62	0	0	24.9%	.298/.363/.483	104	.328	-0.5	C(61): -8.9	0.3
2022	SD	MLB	23	50	4	1	0	1	5	1	11	0	0	31.7%	.250/.260/.333	94	.297	-0.5	C(10): -0.4	0.0
2023 DC	*SD*	*MLB*	*24*	*224*	*25*	*8*	*0*	*6*	*24*	*15*	*48*	*0*	*0*	*28.5%*	*.247/.306/.390*	*93*	*.294*	*0.1*	*C -2*	*0.4*

Comparables: Francisco Mejía (80), Hank Conger (61), Austin Hedges (59)

YEAR	TEAM	P. COUNT	FRM RUNS	BLK RUNS	THRW RUNS	TOT RUNS
2021	ELP	8976	2.6	-0.2	0.6	3.0
2021	SD	1331	-0.3	0.0	0.0	-0.3
2022	ELP	9726	-7.7	-0.2	-0.5	-8.4
2022	SD	1357	-0.3	0.0	0.1	-0.2
2023	*SD*	*7215*	*-1.5*	*0.1*	*0.0*	*-1.3*

For three straight years, Campusano had been a top-100 MLB prospect. For three straight years, he received little tastes of the big leagues. And for three straight years, he's looked *not quite ready* for big-league time. But hey, he's a 24-year-old catcher with an advanced approach at the plate and the kind of power that could see him pop 30+ home runs given enough playing time. Though the Padres didn't play him much in the regular *or* postseason, they still thought enough of him to keep him on their playoff roster. The only thing harder to predict than a pitching prospect is a catching one, but Campusano seems as sure a bet as there is. Let's not go all the way in on the Matt Wieters memes just yet.

Matt Carpenter DH Born: 11/26/85 Age: 37 Bats: L Throws: R Height: 6'4" Weight: 210 lb. Origin: Round 13, 2009 Draft (#399 overall)

YEAR	TEAM	LVL	AGE	PA	R	2B	3B	HR	RBI	BB	K	SB	CS	Whiff%	AVG/OBP/SLG	DRC+	BABIP	BRR	DRP	WARP
2020	STL	MLB	34	169	22	6	0	4	24	23	48	0	0	33.4%	.186/.325/.314	89	.250	0.1	3B(30): -2, 1B(6): -0.1	0.0
2021	STL	MLB	35	249	18	11	1	3	21	35	77	2	0	29.7%	.169/.305/.275	72	.250	-1.7	2B(34): -1.4, 1B(14): 1, 3B(6): -0.1	-0.2
2022	RR	AAA	36	95	15	5	2	6	19	14	20	1	1	23.1%	.275/.379/.613	118	.291	0.0	1B(19): -1.6, 3B(1): -0.5	0.3
2022	NYY	MLB	36	154	28	9	0	15	37	19	35	0	0	23.6%	.305/.412/.727	144	.304	-0.3	RF(12): -0.4, 1B(5): 0, LF(3): -0.2	1.1
2023 DC	*SD*	*MLB*	*37*	*341*	*39*	*15*	*1*	*11*	*37*	*40*	*85*	*2*	*0*	*26.0%*	*.215/.321/.396*	*99*	*.261*	*1.0*	*LF 0, 1B 0*	*0.7*

Comparables: Robin Ventura (59), Wade Boggs (59), Will Clark (58)

Carpenter had an ISO of .422 last year—.422! He only played in 47 games, but still. Setting the seasonal minimum at a modest 150 plate appearances, there've only been five seasons post-integration with a higher ISO than his last year, and they all belonged to either Barry Bonds or Mark McGwire. Carpenter had been in an extended decline phase at the tail end of his time in St. Louis, but he placed a call to Joey Votto to seek out advice and came away dedicated to the craft of lofting the ball. Combine career-on-the-line desperation, wisdom from a Canadian hitting seer and the short porch at Yankee Stadium, and stir.

Jake Cronenworth 2B Born: 01/21/94 Age: 29 Bats: L Throws: R Height: 6'0" Weight: 187 lb. Origin: Round 7, 2015 Draft (#208 overall)

YEAR	TEAM	LVL	AGE	PA	R	2B	3B	HR	RBI	BB	K	SB	CS	Whiff%	AVG/OBP/SLG	DRC+	BABIP	BRR	DRP	WARP
2020	SD	MLB	26	192	26	15	3	4	20	18	30	3	1	16.7%	.285/.354/.477	102	.324	-0.8	2B(38): 0.4, SS(11): -0.1, 1B(10): 0.1	0.6
2021	SD	MLB	27	643	94	33	7	21	71	55	90	4	3	13.8%	.266/.340/.460	113	.283	-1.3	2B(94): -1.7, SS(41): 0.4, 1B(24): -0.2	2.9
2022	SD	MLB	28	684	88	31	4	17	88	70	131	3	0	18.0%	.240/.333/.394	103	.277	2.6	2B(147): -2.5, 1B(20): -0.2, SS(9): -0.1	2.3
2023 DC	*SD*	*MLB*	*29*	*612*	*76*	*28*	*5*	*18*	*71*	*58*	*107*	*3*	*1*	*16.9%*	*.253/.338/.426*	*114*	*.286*	*3.9*	*1B 0, 2B 0*	*2.4*

Comparables: Adam Frazier (62), Brian Roberts (56), Johnny Evers (53)

The night is chilly. The tree limbs, knobby and gnarled, reach out for you. A breeze kicks up, scattering brown-and-gold leaves behind you. An owl hoots…you, my friend, have just found yourself trapped in THE CRONE ZONE. For the second straight year, Cronenworth's overall production went down while his strikeouts ticked up. But once again, The Withered Old Crone of San Diego continued to play solid defense at second base and hit for some pop. Through spells and incantations, he found himself responsible for some of the team's biggest hits—chief among them the home run that guaranteed the Padres a trip to the playoffs and the eventual series-winner against the Dodgers in the NLDS. Cronenworth battled a finger injury last year, which could explain his struggles at the plate and the lowest average exit velocity of his career. An eye of newt or just some good old ol' R&R should have him fresh and ready for 2023.

Adam Engel OF Born: 12/09/91 Age: 31 Bats: R Throws: R Height: 6'2" Weight: 215 lb. Origin: Round 19, 2013 Draft (#573 overall)

YEAR	TEAM	LVL	AGE	PA	R	2B	3B	HR	RBI	BB	K	SB	CS	Whiff%	AVG/OBP/SLG	DRC+	BABIP	BRR	DRP	WARP
2020	CHW	MLB	28	93	11	5	1	3	12	3	19	1	0	26.5%	.295/.333/.477	99	.348	0.3	RF(25): 0.9, LF(9): 1.3, CF(3): 0.9	0.6
2021	CLT	AAA	29	60	7	2	0	2	5	3	16	5	0		.222/.283/.370	94	.270	-0.1	CF(8): -0.7, RF(5): 1.6	0.2
2021	CHW	MLB	29	140	21	9	0	7	18	11	31	7	1	27.1%	.252/.336/.496	106	.279	-0.3	CF(26): 0.6, RF(10): 1.5, LF(4): 0.8	0.9
2022	CHW	MLB	30	260	32	13	1	2	17	11	76	12	4	34.4%	.224/.269/.310	66	.317	-1.2	CF(57): 1.8, RF(55): 1.4, LF(3): 0.1	0.0
2023 DC	*SD*	*MLB*	*31*	*198*	*20*	*8*	*1*	*5*	*20*	*10*	*58*	*11*	*3*	*32.0%*	*.227/.283/.369*	*79*	*.304*	*5.4*	*CF 1, RF 0*	*0.7*

Comparables: Craig Gentry (52), Brandon Barnes (50), Drew Stubbs (49)

Engel is a perfectly serviceable fourth outfielder. He's proven that much for a majority of his career, plugging holes when injuries occur, coming in as a defensive replacement, pinch running and generally being available and reliable where needed. During that same period of time, however, Engel was regularly exposed as underqualified whenever he was handed any semblance of regular playing time. The White Sox were trotting out first base/DH types in the outfield in 2022, and injuries limited erstwhile starting center fielder Luis Robert to fewer than 100 games. So Engel was overexposed, struggling to hit his weight while playing defense that was hardly up to the standards of his reputation. There's little glory in a fourth outfielder's job, and even less when you're playing more than a fourth outfielder should. He might end up overexposed again in San Diego, at least until Fernando Tatis Jr. returns to the lineup.

Trent Grisham CF

Born: 11/01/96 Age: 26 Bats: L Throws: L Height: 5'11" Weight: 224 lb. Origin: Round 1, 2015 Draft (#15 overall)

YEAR	TEAM	LVL	AGE	PA	R	2B	3B	HR	RBI	BB	K	SB	CS	Whiff%	AVG/OBP/SLG	DRC+	BABIP	BRR	DRP	WARP
2020	SD	MLB	23	252	42	8	3	10	26	31	64	10	1	24.4%	.251/.352/.456	96	.310	-1.8	CF(59): 6.1	1.1
2021	SD	MLB	24	527	61	28	3	15	62	54	119	13	5	21.9%	.242/.327/.413	96	.292	1.7	CF(127): 1.5	2.3
2022	SD	MLB	25	524	58	16	2	17	53	57	150	7	1	26.6%	.184/.284/.341	82	.231	0.7	CF(148): 1.7	1.1
2023 DC	*SD*	*MLB*	*26*	*487*	*60*	*18*	*3*	*16*	*50*	*52*	*120*	*12*	*3*	*24.8%*	*.217/.311/.394*	*95*	*.263*	*7.1*	*CF 10*	*3.0*

Comparables: Joc Pederson (56), Dexter Fowler (49), Jake Marisnick (48)

With runners on first and second, the Padres down a run and Austin Nola on deck with one out in what would be the Padres final game of the year, Bob Melvin called for the bunt. Grisham, who was at the plate after going hitless in the NLCS, weakly grounded back to pitcher Ranger Suárez for an out. In some ways, the decision was understandable—Grisham is so streaky he should be a spokesperson for Windex—but it was a tough way to help end a season. Given his power and superlative glove in the outfield, Grisham stands a decent chance to be the starting center fielder for San Diego when Opening Day rolls around next year. But given Grisham's ups and downs, don't be surprised if Fernando Tatis Jr. eventually takes his job.

Ha-Seong Kim SS

Born: 10/17/95 Age: 27 Bats: R Throws: R Height: 5'9" Weight: 168 lb. Origin: International Free Agent, 2020

YEAR	TEAM	LVL	AGE	PA	R	2B	3B	HR	RBI	BB	K	SB	CS	Whiff%	AVG/OBP/SLG	DRC+	BABIP	BRR	DRP	WARP
2021	SD	MLB	25	298	27	12	2	8	34	22	71	6	1	21.8%	.202/.270/.352	82	.241	2.7	SS(35): -0.4, 3B(23): -0.5, 2B(21): 0.6	0.6
2022	SD	MLB	26	582	58	29	3	11	59	51	100	12	2	19.2%	.251/.325/.383	103	.290	1.9	SS(131): 4.7, 3B(24): -0.5	2.7
2023 DC	*SD*	*MLB*	*27*	*564*	*63*	*23*	*2*	*16*	*59*	*50*	*90*	*13*	*3*	*19.4%*	*.235/.311/.385*	*96*	*.257*	*4.6*	*2B 0, SS 1*	*1.9*

Comparables: Elvis Andrus (80), Jose Offerman (78), Freddie Patek (78)

If there was one beneficiary of Fernando Tatis Jr. missing all of 2022, it was Kim. After being handed the everyday shortstop job he showed off the superlative glove that makes him worth starting no matter what he gives you with the bat. Of course, Kim also hits like he fields, with a jittery step and plenty of energy—it's fitting that he gifted his former KBO teammates a coffee truck for their own postseason battle. He attacks first pitches the way he races across the infield for foul balls, making him a fan-favorite in San Diego and the recipient of more than a few "Ha-Seong Kim! Ha-Seong Kim!" chants down the stretch. On a team with Manny Machado, Xander Bogaerts and (presumably) a healthy Tatis, Kim figures to see less playing time next season. But when he does take the field, he should shine as the glue guy with the golden glove.

Manny Machado 3B

Born: 07/06/92 Age: 31 Bats: R Throws: R Height: 6'3" Weight: 218 lb. Origin: Round 1, 2010 Draft (#3 overall)

YEAR	TEAM	LVL	AGE	PA	R	2B	3B	HR	RBI	BB	K	SB	CS	Whiff%	AVG/OBP/SLG	DRC+	BABIP	BRR	DRP	WARP
2020	SD	MLB	27	254	44	12	1	16	47	26	37	6	3	21.7%	.304/.370/.580	139	.297	-0.8	3B(56): 0	1.7
2021	SD	MLB	28	640	92	31	2	28	106	63	102	12	3	23.1%	.278/.347/.489	123	.290	2.3	3B(144): 4.8	4.8
2022	SD	MLB	29	644	100	37	1	32	102	63	133	9	1	24.9%	.298/.366/.531	139	.337	2.3	3B(134): -0.4	4.8
2023 DC	*SD*	*MLB*	*30*	*646*	*93*	*29*	*1*	*36*	*105*	*63*	*118*	*9*	*2*	*24.3%*	*.282/.355/.528*	*144*	*.298*	*3.5*	*3B 1*	*5.3*

Comparables: George Davis (71), Brooks Robinson (69), Adrián Beltré (68)

Machado's public persona has gone through more critical reexaminations than Nicolas Cage. There was Machado, the hotshot superstar stud. Then there was Machado, the truculent, immature player. Then there was Machado, the complementary piece. And now Machado, the team leader who has the makings of what could be a Hall of Fame career as he enters his 30s.

When Bob Melvin exploded on the Padres during their late-season swoon, it was Machado who called a players-only meeting the next day to emphasize the details. While we can debate how smart it is to do so, Machado has played through injuries each of the last two seasons with the Padres—something his teammates view with great respect. And when the Padres defeated the Dodgers in the NLDS, it was Machado who celebrated the loudest, champagne running down his bare chest.

Fernando Tatis Jr. may be the face of the team, Xander Bogaerts its flashiest newcomer and Juan Soto its best overall player, but Machado is the heart of this Padres club. That's something not a lot of people would have expected given his early career, but hey, who among us hasn't grown up a bit in their late-20s?

Joshua Mears OF

Born: 02/21/01 Age: 22 Bats: R Throws: R Height: 6'3" Weight: 230 lb. Origin: Round 2, 2019 Draft (#48 overall)

YEAR	TEAM	LVL	AGE	PA	R	2B	3B	HR	RBI	BB	K	SB	CS	Whiff%	AVG/OBP/SLG	DRC+	BABIP	BRR	DRP	WARP
2021	LE	A	20	291	45	10	4	17	48	36	114	10	5		.244/.368/.529	105	.375	-1.2	RF(35): 0.8, CF(16): -1.5, LF(7): 1.1	1.1
2022	PAD	ROK	21	66	10	6	1	3	10	8	26	2	0		.268/.364/.571		.429			
2022	FW	A+	21	207	29	11	0	14	34	16	90	1	1		.223/.304/.511	93	.333	0.6	RF(25): -1.4, CF(19): 2.3	0.6
2022	SA	AA	21	94	9	2	0	5	15	10	45	1	0		.169/.266/.373	60	.273	-0.1	CF(24): 0.1	-0.2
2023 non-DC	*SD*	*MLB*	*22*	*251*	*27*	*9*	*1*	*10*	*32*	*17*	*116*	*4*	*1*	*45.3%*	*.206/.276/.403*	*79*	*.358*	*1.4*	*CF 0, RF 0*	*0.1*

Comparables: Johan Mieses (61), Greg Golson (56), Sean Henry (56)

We all know the feeling. When we pimp and preen in the mirror and flash our most rakish grins, we feel pretty good about what stares back at us. Then we see our faces in pictures and shudder, thinking "is this what everyone else truly sees?" Mears can sympathize. When he looks in the mirror, he likely sees the impressive size that's helped him hit 46 homer runs in just over 200 pro games and launch a 117-mph laser beam last spring training. But the rest of us can't help but notice a strikeout rate that would make Adam Dunn weep: Mears whiffed at a nearly 50% clip in Double-A. No matter how much pop he provides, he needs to rein in the strikeouts if he wants more Instagram-able moments.

★ ★ ★ *2023 Top 101 Prospect* **#14** ★ ★ ★

Jackson Merrill SS

Born: 04/19/03 Age: 20 Bats: L Throws: R Height: 6'3" Weight: 195 lb. Origin: Round 1, 2021 Draft (#27 overall)

YEAR	TEAM	LVL	AGE	PA	R	2B	3B	HR	RBI	BB	K	SB	CS	Whiff%	AVG/OBP/SLG	DRC+	BABIP	BRR	DRP	WARP
2021	PAD	ROK	18	120	19	7	2	0	10	10	27	5	1		.280/.339/.383		.370			
2022	PAD	ROK	19	31	5	3	1	1	6	1	2	3	0		.433/.452/.700		.444			
2022	LE	A	19	219	33	10	3	5	34	19	42	8	5		.325/.387/.482	111	.393	1.4	SS(42): -1.3	0.9
2023 non-DC	*SD*	*MLB*	*20*	*251*	*19*	*9*	*2*	*2*	*20*	*14*	*52*	*6*	*3*	*22.4%*	*.232/.280/.322*	*68*	*.290*	*-0.4*	*SS 0*	*-0.3*

Comparables: Hanser Alberto (87), Royce Lewis (85), Alen Hanson (80)

The Padres don't have a director of player development: They have a warlock of scouting. Merrill wasn't widely considered a first-rounder until a week before the 2021 draft, when he blasted a ball clear out of Camden Yards. The Padres scooped him up with the 27th pick soon thereafter. He was rumored to be included in the Juan Soto trade—Merrill said he knew it was down to him or James Wood to be sent to Washington—but San Diego held onto the shortstop prospect, invoking a protection charm. Though he missed time with a wrist injury in 2022—one that usually saps power—he still hammered the ball when he returned, then put on a show in the Arizona Fall League. Not expected to be MLB-ready until 2025 or so, Merrill may eventually outgrow shortstop, but given the strange workings in San Diego, he may just grow to be 8-feet tall, weigh a whopping 410 pounds and still produce Gold Glove defense.

Austin Nola C

Born: 12/28/89 Age: 33 Bats: R Throws: R Height: 6'0" Weight: 197 lb. Origin: Round 5, 2012 Draft (#167 overall)

YEAR	TEAM	LVL	AGE	PA	R	2B	3B	HR	RBI	BB	K	SB	CS	Whiff%	AVG/OBP/SLG	DRC+	BABIP	BRR	DRP	WARP
2020	SD	MLB	30	74	9	4	0	2	9	9	17	0	0	22.4%	.222/.324/.381	106	.267	0.7	C(17): 2	0.6
2020	SEA	MLB	30	110	15	5	1	5	19	9	17	0	0	18.5%	.306/.373/.531	122	.325	-0.3	C(27): 0.9, 1B(2): 0, 3B(1): -0.3	0.7
2021	ELP	AAA	31	39	3	1	0	1	4	5	7	0	0		.303/.410/.424	102	.360	-0.4	1B(4): 0.1, C(3): 0.3	0.1
2021	SD	MLB	31	194	15	12	0	2	29	14	19	0	1	12.2%	.272/.340/.376	106	.292	0.9	C(48): -1.9, 2B(4): 0	0.9
2022	SD	MLB	32	397	40	15	0	4	40	34	60	2	1	14.5%	.251/.321/.329	99	.284	-0.7	C(101): -5.5	0.7
2023 DC	*SD*	*MLB*	*33*	*432*	*48*	*18*	*0*	*10*	*44*	*36*	*57*	*1*	*1*	*15.3%*	*.260/.333/.390*	*106*	*.283*	*-0.1*	*C -7*	*1.1*

Comparables: Jonathan Lucroy (54), Dioner Navarro (54), A.J. Ellis (51)

YEAR	TEAM	P. COUNT	FRM RUNS	BLK RUNS	THRW RUNS	TOT RUNS
2020	SEA	3547	0.6	0.1	0.3	0.9
2020	SD	2167	2.0	0.0	0.0	2.0
2021	SD	6719	-1.8	-0.2	0.1	-1.9
2022	SD	13572	-7.5	0.0	1.4	-6.1
2023	*SD*	*14430*	*-5.1*	*0.2*	*-0.2*	*-5.1*

The 32-year-old former shortstop may not be flashy. He may not have much power. But he played solid defense, called a good game and gave manager Bob Melvin someone he could pencil in every single day behind the dish even as the Fernando Tatis Jr. drama overshadowed the team, Juan Soto briefly forgot how to hit and Josh Hader worked his way back from mechanical madness. Nola faced off against his brother Aaron in the NLCS, marking the first time brother batted against brother in postseason history. Austin laced an 0-2 sinker into the outfield for an RBI single in the Padres' Game 2 victory and forced his dad—wearing a Padres cap and Phillies jersey—to have a complete existential breakdown. "That was the best game and the worst game, all in one," A.J. Nola said. "Words can't even describe how difficult that was."

Yendry Rojas SS

Born: 01/27/05 Age: 18 Bats: L Throws: R Height: 6'0" Weight: 185 lb. Origin: International Free Agent, 2022

YEAR	TEAM	LVL	AGE	PA	R	2B	3B	HR	RBI	BB	K	SB	CS	Whiff%	AVG/OBP/SLG	DRC+	BABIP	BRR	DRP	WARP
2022	DSL PAD	ROK	17	187	29	4	4	0	18	26	23	14	6		.279/.373/.357		.316			
2023	*No projection*																			

Signed for $1.3 million in January 2022 after earning comps to studs like Yoán Moncada, Rojas looked the part in his debut as a 17-year-old in the Dominican Summer League. He owns a dynamic left-handed swing and an impressive frame for his age, very much looking the part of a bat-first infielder already. He played shortstop last season, but some expect he'll start sliding down the defensive spectrum as he gets older. Then again, couldn't you say the same about any of us? We just keep sliding lower and lower down the spectrum of whatever career we've chosen until the day we turn to dust. Eat at Arby's.

Eguy Rosario IF

Born: 08/25/99 Age: 23 Bats: R Throws: R Height: 5'9" Weight: 150 lb. Origin: International Free Agent, 2015

YEAR	TEAM	LVL	AGE	PA	R	2B	3B	HR	RBI	BB	K	SB	CS	Whiff%	AVG/OBP/SLG	DRC+	BABIP	BRR	DRP	WARP
2020	MAR	WIN	20	112	18	6	2	0	14	7	13	8	0		.327/.393/.429		.368			
2021	PEJ	WIN	21	73	9	3	0	1	12	8	13	2	2		.250/.342/.344		.300			
2021	SA	AA	21	481	65	31	3	12	61	49	109	30	14		.281/.360/.455	110	.349	-4.6	SS(69): -3.3, 2B(38): 4.2, 3B(7): 0.6	1.7
2022	ELP	AAA	22	564	98	34	4	22	81	59	109	21	8	27.4%	.288/.368/.508	111	.325	0.8	2B(54): -1.6, SS(37): 0.0, 3B(35): 1.6	2.5
2022	SD	MLB	22	6	0	0	0	0	0	1	2	0	0	44.4%	.200/.333/.200	86	.333	0.0	SS(2): -0.5	0.0
2023 DC	*SD*	*MLB*	*23*	*135*	*14*	*6*	*0*	*3*	*13*	*10*	*31*	*4*	*3*	*28.5%*	*.235/.302/.375*	*88*	*.291*	*-0.4*	*SS 0, 2B 0*	*0.1*

Comparables: Josh Vitters (55), Asdrúbal Cabrera (54), Cheslor Cuthbert (52)

It's a fitting name because, just by looking at him, you'd think Rosario was just e *guy*. Standing 5-foot-9 and weighing in at 150 pounds, he could be your barista, the film major down the street who keeps asking you, "Have you even watched, I mean *really* watched '8 ½,'" or the best player on the local high school's badminton team. Instead, he's a multi-position, basestealing threat with a smooth swing that lets him put up power numbers you wouldn't expect given his frame. This past year was his best yet, as he reached that symmetrically beautiful 20/20 mark in Triple-A and earned a short trip to the majors. Given how many positions he can play, don't be surprised if the Padres find a way to get Rosario into the lineup next year.

Juan Soto RF Born: 10/25/98 Age: 24 Bats: L Throws: L Height: 6'2" Weight: 224 lb. Origin: International Free Agent, 2015

YEAR	TEAM	LVL	AGE	PA	R	2B	3B	HR	RBI	BB	K	SB	CS	Whiff%	AVG/OBP/SLG	DRC+	BABIP	BRR	DRP	WARP
2020	WAS	MLB	21	196	39	14	0	13	37	41	28	6	2	21.5%	.351/.490/.695	163	.363	-0.3	LF(36): -0.9, RF(6): -0.5	1.9
2021	WAS	MLB	22	654	111	20	2	29	95	145	93	9	7	20.0%	.313/.465/.534	164	.332	-1.3	RF(144): 4.4	7.4
2022	SD	MLB	23	228	31	8	1	6	16	44	34	0	0	17.5%	.236/.388/.390	122	.261	-1.7	RF(52): -0.1	1.1
2022	WAS	MLB	23	436	62	17	1	21	46	91	62	6	2	20.2%	.246/.408/.485	156	.243	-1.7	RF(99): 1.2	4.2
2023 DC	*SD*	*MLB*	*24*	*629*	*106*	*24*	*3*	*33*	*92*	*129*	*91*	*11*	*3*	*19.1%*	*.290/.440/.557*	*181*	*.296*	*5.7*	*RF 1, LF 0*	*8.3*

Comparables: Bryce Harper (77), Mel Ott (71), Johnny Callison (66)

The air crackles around Soto every time he steps into the box, gets into his squat and stares down the pitcher with a look that screams, "I will eat you alive, bones and all, if given the opportunity." He spits at pitches that barely miss the strike zone, reaching 500 walks faster than any other player in history, as if he alone could power robotic umpires if we could simply harness his vision. When he swings, he creates so much torque that he seems to split atoms all on his own.

That's why A.J. Preller opened up his farm system and kept layering players atop one another until the Nationals finally said, "That's enough." When you get a chance to acquire a player like Soto, you roll the dice and gamble everything. He isn't a once-in-a-generation player: he's a once-in-a-sporting history-type player. Soto made more contact out of the zone than ever before, saw his laser beam batted balls find gloves like never before, suffered a career-low BABIP and hit just .202 in his first 35 games with his new team…and was still nearly 50% better than league-average. When you get a chance to acquire a player like Soto, you take it.

Fernando Tatis Jr. SS Born: 01/02/99 Age: 24 Bats: R Throws: R Height: 6'3" Weight: 217 lb. Origin: International Free Agent, 2015

YEAR	TEAM	LVL	AGE	PA	R	2B	3B	HR	RBI	BB	K	SB	CS	Whiff%	AVG/OBP/SLG	DRC+	BABIP	BRR	DRP	WARP
2020	SD	MLB	21	257	50	11	2	17	45	27	61	11	3	28.2%	.277/.366/.571	124	.306	1.3	SS(57): -0.7	1.6
2021	SD	MLB	22	546	99	31	0	42	97	62	153	25	4	34.8%	.282/.364/.611	144	.324	2.8	SS(102): -0.7, RF(20): 2.1, CF(7): 0.8	5.5
2023 DC	*SD*	*MLB*	*24*	*558*	*94*	*24*	*3*	*34*	*84*	*66*	*146*	*25*	*9*	*31.8%*	*.277/.370/.556*	*154*	*.327*	*3.4*	*RF -1, CF 0*	*5.2*

The only thing more tired than Game of Thrones references are debates about PEDs in baseball. Thanks to Tatis' mortifying last 12 months, we have cause to engage in both. While rehabbing from his latest shoulder separation and a wrist injury suffered in an off-season motorcycle accident, Tatis was suspended 80 games last August for testing positive for the banned substance clostebol. And so the "next face of baseball" completed a fall from grace so stunning, swift and unsatisfying it's a wonder D.B. Weiss and David Benioff weren't involved.

Assuming Tatis emerges from this offseason a healthy, hale and humbled 24-year-old—far from a sure bet—he should return to major-league game action in late April. He'll join a very different Padres team than the one he left, both in composition—hello, Juan Soto and Xander Bogaerts—and attitude. After Tatis' suspension, quotes from A.J. Preller, Bob Melvin and Joe Musgrove, among others, suggested their young superstar had all but lost the clubhouse through his off-field antics and occasional on-field meltdowns. He returns not as a conquering hero, but as just one of a half-dozen megastars uniting to take down the *real* enemy up the coast. Preller and co. loaded up on those stars to win, of course, but perhaps also to send a not-so-subtle message to their $340 million man: We want you, but we don't *need* you, and we won't wait for you forever.

If we know anything about Tatis, it's that he can change narratives in the blink of an eye. He can restore his good standing by doing what earned him the mantel of baseball's savior in the first place: mashing at the plate, electrifying on the bases and wowing in the field, even if he'll now do so on the grass instead of the dirt. Tatis isn't the best player in baseball—maybe not even on his own team anymore—but he's still its most exciting. His return to health, happiness and glory would benefit not just San Diego but the entire sport.

Samuel Zavala OF Born: 07/15/04 Age: 18 Bats: L Throws: L Height: 6'1" Weight: 175 lb. Origin: International Free Agent, 2021

YEAR	TEAM	LVL	AGE	PA	R	2B	3B	HR	RBI	BB	K	SB	CS	Whiff%	AVG/OBP/SLG	DRC+	BABIP	BRR	DRP	WARP
2021	DSL PAD	ROK	16	235	44	16	6	3	40	32	36	11	7		.297/.400/.487		.344			
2022	PAD	ROK	17	35	6	3	1	1	6	4	11	0	0		.345/.412/.621		.500			
2022	LE	A	17	141	24	6	2	7	26	19	37	5	3		.254/.355/.508	110	.308	-1.8	CF(20): -0.2, RF(12): -0.6	0.2
2023 non-DC	*SD*	*MLB*	*18*	*251*	*20*	*9*	*2*	*4*	*22*	*18*	*82*	*6*	*3*	*35.5%*	*.198/.263/.324*	*59*	*.287*	*-0.1*	*CF 0, RF 0*	*-0.6*

Comparables: Fernando Martinez (70), Angel Villalona (49), Jose Tabata (46)

Signed for $1.2 million as a 16-year-old out of Venezuela in January 2021, Zavala made his stateside debut this season and immediately looked like the kind of player to whom you would hand $1.2 million. Like a lot of young hitters he has to work on his plate discipline, but it's easier to imagine a bright future for a guy who can swing the bat like Zavala than some dude who can take a walk, but whose swing resembles Goofy's in "How to Play Baseball." Hopefully he'll grow into more power, but bashing seven homers in just 141 PA while still a teenager is plenty impressive, even in the Cal League.

Pitchers

Ryan Bergert RHP

Born: 03/08/00 Age: 23 Bats: R Throws: R Height: 6'1" Weight: 210 lb. Origin: Round 6, 2021 Draft (#190 overall)

YEAR	TEAM	LVL	AGE	W	L	SV	G	GS	IP	H	HR	BB/9	K/9	K	GB%	BABIP	WHIP	ERA	DRA-	WARP	MPH	FB%	Whiff%	CSP
2021	PAD	ROK	21	1	0	1	7	3	11	3	0	0.0	11.5	14	52.2%	.130	0.27	0.00						
2022	FW	A+	22	4	10	0	24	24	103^1	124	18	3.7	11.2	129	37.7%	.377	1.61	5.84	93	1.4				
2023 non-DC	*SD*	*MLB*	*23*	*2*	*3*	*0*	*57*	*0*	*50*	*56*	*9*	*4.8*	*7.9*	*44*	*38.4%*	*.316*	*1.66*	*5.99*	*140*	*-0.8*			*24.9%*	

Comparables: Justin Slaten (91), Jeremy Beasley (91), Taylor Williams (90)

Signed for $500,000 out of West Virginia in 2021 despite not pitching that spring because of an arm injury, Bergert is easy to dream on. Mid-90s fastball? Check. Good slider? Check. Injuries clouding the last few years, allowing one to only imagine the big, bright future? Check, check and check. Bergert pitched his first full season this past year, and while it wasn't always great, it didn't do anything to tarnish those lovely prospect visions. He didn't only start, he did it across an entire campaign. Everything else was gravy, baby.

Nabil Crismatt RHP

Born: 12/25/94 Age: 28 Bats: R Throws: R Height: 6'1" Weight: 220 lb. Origin: International Free Agent, 2011

YEAR	TEAM	LVL	AGE	W	L	SV	G	GS	IP	H	HR	BB/9	K/9	K	GB%	BABIP	WHIP	ERA	DRA-	WARP	MPH	FB%	Whiff%	CSP
2020	STL	MLB	25	0	0	0	6	0	8^1	6	2	1.1	8.6	8	50.0%	.200	0.84	3.24	101	0.1	89.8	41.2%	27.4%	46.9%
2021	SD	MLB	26	3	1	0	45	0	81^1	87	10	2.7	7.9	71	50.8%	.326	1.36	3.76	93	1.0	90.2	25.1%	26.1%	52.5%
2022	SD	MLB	27	5	2	0	50	1	67^1	57	5	2.9	8.7	65	49.7%	.280	1.17	2.94	89	1.0	90.6	29.4%	26.7%	53.6%
2023 DC	*SD*	*MLB*	*28*	*2*	*2*	*0*	*50*	*0*	*43.7*	*45*	*5*	*2.9*	*8.2*	*40*	*48.7%*	*.308*	*1.34*	*4.15*	*106*	*0.1*	*90.4*	*27.7%*	*27.2%*	*52.9%*

Comparables: Tyler Duffey (48), Mike Mayers (45), Pedro Villarreal (44)

If ever there was a player to make the "velo isn't everything" crowd go wild, it's Crismatt. Despite leading all Padres relievers—save for Nick Martinez, who made 10 starts—in innings pitched, while *also* posting a sub-3.00 ERA and solid strikeout numbers, it was Crismatt who was sent down at the end of September when Craig Stammen came off the injured list. That's just the way of the modern world when you're a reliever with a fastball that scrapes 90 mph the way you scrape your spoon on the edge of the empty peanut butter jar. Delicious? Yes. But you'll always be looking for something else to eat.

Yu Darvish RHP

Born: 08/16/86 Age: 36 Bats: R Throws: R Height: 6'5" Weight: 220 lb. Origin: International Free Agent, 2012

YEAR	TEAM	LVL	AGE	W	L	SV	G	GS	IP	H	HR	BB/9	K/9	K	GB%	BABIP	WHIP	ERA	DRA-	WARP	MPH	FB%	Whiff%	CSP
2020	CHC	MLB	33	8	3	0	12	12	76	59	5	1.7	11.0	93	42.8%	.297	0.96	2.01	64	2.3	95.5	30.1%	32.2%	52.9%
2021	SD	MLB	34	8	11	0	30	30	166^1	138	28	2.4	10.8	199	36.5%	.274	1.09	4.22	77	3.6	94.4	33.0%	27.4%	57.8%
2022	SD	MLB	35	16	8	0	30	30	194^2	148	22	1.7	9.1	197	37.7%	.251	0.95	3.10	76	4.3	94.8	39.1%	25.2%	59.2%
2023 DC	*SD*	*MLB*	*36*	*12*	*9*	*0*	*29*	*29*	*198*	*173*	*27*	*2.2*	*8.8*	*193*	*38.5%*	*.275*	*1.12*	*3.08*	*85*	*3.2*	*94.6*	*36.3%*	*25.6%*	*56.9%*

Comparables: Justin Verlander (85), Jim Bunning (85), Tom Seaver (84)

Leave it to the man who's thrown roughly 8,000 pitches (give or take) to have what was arguably his best year at the age of 35. On a Padres team that could have sputtered and died during a rough second-half stretch, Darvish went supernova. He posted a 1.85 September ERA while picking up the win in five of his six starts. That led Darvish to winning what was somehow the first Player of the Week Award of his career. Entering his age-36 season, Darvish doesn't seem to be losing anything at all. That's good news, because we could all benefit from some more time watching someone that funny on Twitter, who looked that good in underwear ads (look them up!) and who approaches the art of pitching with such gusto.

Luis García RHP

Born: 01/30/87 Age: 36 Bats: R Throws: R Height: 6'2" Weight: 240 lb. Origin: International Free Agent, 2017

YEAR	TEAM	LVL	AGE	W	L	SV	G	GS	IP	H	HR	BB/9	K/9	K	GB%	BABIP	WHIP	ERA	DRA-	WARP	MPH	FB%	Whiff%	CSP
2020	TEX	MLB	33	0	2	0	11	2	8^1	10	1	9.7	11.9	11	48.0%	.375	2.28	7.56	96	0.1	96.8	56.5%	30.6%	44.4%
2021	SWB	AAA	34	1	2	11	18	0	17^1	16	2	1.6	9.9	19	59.6%	.311	1.10	3.63	84	0.4				
2021	STL	MLB	34	1	1	2	34	0	33^1	25	2	2.2	9.2	34	46.7%	.256	0.99	3.24	92	0.5	98.5	59.5%	32.1%	60.1%
2022	SD	MLB	35	4	6	3	64	0	61	57	3	2.5	10.0	68	53.3%	.327	1.21	3.39	77	1.3	98.7	55.1%	30.0%	54.9%
2023 DC	*SD*	*MLB*	*36*	*2*	*2*	*0*	*50*	*0*	*43.7*	*43*	*4*	*3.1*	*8.9*	*43*	*50.4%*	*.311*	*1.33*	*3.81*	*97*	*0.2*	*98.3*	*54.9%*	*28.8%*	*53.6%*

Comparables: Will Harris (61), Joe Smith (57), Shawn Kelley (57)

Ten years ago, García was out of baseball. Having failed to escape A-ball with the Nationals—and with his fastball topping out at a very pedestrian 87 mph—García called it a day. He became a barber in New Jersey, then a mover because his haircutting skills weren't all that sharp. But then, as reported by Kevin Acee in the *San Diego Union-Tribune*, García's minor-league teammate, Luis Ferraro, told García he'd had a dream…one that featured García back on the mound. Come 2022, García isn't just in the majors, but he's got one of the most electric arms in the sport. At an age when some guys are contemplating retirement, he looks fresher than ever. He's got a 99-mph fastball and a wipeout slider that batters whiffed on 57% of the time, making him one of the most reliable relievers in the San Diego 'pen. The point of all of this: Listen to prophetic dreams.

Josh Hader LHP Born: 04/07/94 Age: 29 Bats: L Throws: L Height: 6'3" Weight: 180 lb. Origin: Round 19, 2012 Draft (#582 overall)

YEAR	TEAM	LVL	AGE	W	L	SV	G	GS	IP	H	HR	BB/9	K/9	K	GB%	BABIP	WHIP	ERA	DRA-	WARP	MPH	FB%	Whiff%	CSP
2020	MIL	MLB	26	1	2	13	21	0	19	8	3	4.7	14.7	31	26.5%	.161	0.95	3.79	83	0.4	94.9	67.7%	38.7%	43.8%
2021	MIL	MLB	27	4	2	34	60	0	58^{2}	25	3	3.7	15.6	102	31.2%	.237	0.84	1.23	64	1.6	96.5	65.5%	45.2%	48.8%
2022	MIL	MLB	28	1	4	29	37	0	34	26	7	3.2	15.6	59	30.4%	.306	1.12	4.24	67	0.9	97.3	65.9%	38.4%	48.0%
2022	SD	MLB	28	1	1	7	19	0	16	17	1	5.1	12.4	22	31.8%	.372	1.63	7.31	96	0.2	97.7	76.0%	33.8%	52.5%
2023 DC	*SD*	*MLB*	*29*	*3*	*2*	*36*	*57*	*0*	*49.3*	*36*	*6*	*3.6*	*14.3*	*78*	*31.0%*	*.310*	*1.15*	*3.03*	*76*	*0.8*	*96.7*	*70.0%*	*38.1%*	*48.3%*

Comparables: Aroldis Chapman (70), Jeurys Familia (67), Craig Kimbrel (65)

For five years, Hader was a cheat code; a nearly unhittable blur of limbs, hair and sweeping sliders called forth from the Brewers bullpen. But as relievers and our old high school significant others so often teach us, good things can only be temporary. So it went with Hader. He continued to pile up strikeouts, but he also allowed plenty of game-tying and -winning runs to score. After the Padres rolled the dice on his bounceback and acquired him in exchange for Dinelson Lamet, Taylor Rogers, Esteury Ruiz and Robert "Fart" Gasser, his performance dipped even further and he was pulled from closing duties. After a few days off, Hader looked like his usual self by the end of the season, but the margin between being the game's best closer and a guy in Triple-A saying "I'm just trying to figure out a few things, mechanically" is razor-thin.

Jagger Haynes LHP Born: 09/20/02 Age: 20 Bats: L Throws: L Height: 6'3" Weight: 170 lb. Origin: Round 5, 2020 Draft (#139 overall)

He missed his senior year of high school baseball because of COVID-19. Then, he needed Tommy John surgery. A fifth-round draft pick from back in 2020, he hasn't pitched an inning of professional baseball for the organization. But not all is lost: Haynes was the youngest pitcher picked that year and the Padres called him "the steal of the draft." He's still young enough and has enough promise that such a sentiment could eventually ring true. And with a name like Jagger, he could be going strong well into his mid-60s.

Tim Hill LHP Born: 02/10/90 Age: 33 Bats: R Throws: L Height: 6'4" Weight: 200 lb. Origin: Round 32, 2014 Draft (#963 overall)

YEAR	TEAM	LVL	AGE	W	L	SV	G	GS	IP	H	HR	BB/9	K/9	K	GB%	BABIP	WHIP	ERA	DRA-	WARP	MPH	FB%	Whiff%	CSP
2020	SD	MLB	30	3	0	0	23	0	18	17	3	3.0	10.0	20	52.9%	.292	1.28	4.50	72	0.4	90.6	89.9%	22.8%	46.7%
2021	SD	MLB	31	6	6	1	78	0	59^{2}	51	9	3.5	8.4	56	58.8%	.264	1.24	3.62	88	0.9	91.8	84.5%	23.0%	54.1%
2022	SD	MLB	32	3	0	0	55	0	48	45	1	2.6	4.7	25	59.0%	.284	1.23	3.56	116	0.1	90.1	90.9%	15.6%	53.3%
2023 DC	*SD*	*MLB*	*33*	*2*	*2*	*0*	*50*	*0*	*43.7*	*50*	*4*	*3.3*	*6.8*	*33*	*56.7%*	*.326*	*1.52*	*4.84*	*118*	*-0.2*	*90.8*	*86.9%*	*19.8%*	*52.7%*

Comparables: Tommy Layne (70), Will Harris (66), Grant Dayton (66)

All glory to the sinker, that democratic bringer of burned worms, that most deceptive pitch that dominates not by sheer force, but by using the hubris of batters' very own swings against them. The 2022 season saw the great return of the sinker, and Hill was one of its most effective wielders. The side-winding lefty upped his sinker usage to career highs, saw his strikeout rate crater to nearly half his career mark and his ERA still dip to a career-best. That's what happens when you induce some well-placed grounders from nearly 60% of batters.

Alek Jacob RHP Born: 06/16/98 Age: 25 Bats: L Throws: R Height: 6'3" Weight: 190 lb. Origin: Round 16, 2021 Draft (#490 overall)

YEAR	TEAM	LVL	AGE	W	L	SV	G	GS	IP	H	HR	BB/9	K/9	K	GB%	BABIP	WHIP	ERA	DRA-	WARP	MPH	FB%	Whiff%	CSP
2021	LE	A	23	2	0	2	12	0	18^{2}	12	0	1.0	12.5	26	50.0%	.316	0.75	0.00	91	0.2				
2022	FW	A+	24	3	0	0	4	0	9	4	0	0.0	16.0	16	53.3%	.267	0.44	0.00	75	0.2				
2022	SA	AA	24	1	0	2	23	1	34^{1}	27	1	2.6	11.3	43	40.5%	.313	1.08	1.83	79	0.6				
2022	ELP	AAA	24	1	1	2	16	0	13^{2}	18	4	3.3	11.9	18	33.3%	.368	1.68	6.59	99	0.1	86.3	49.0%	22.1%	
2023 non-DC	*SD*	*MLB*	*25*	*2*	*2*	*0*	*57*	*0*	*50*	*44*	*5*	*3.1*	*9.0*	*49*	*41.6%*	*.288*	*1.23*	*3.44*	*90*	*0.5*			*27.2%*	

Comparables: Tyler Kinley (71), Edgar Santana (70), César Vargas (70)

Jacob has all the tools to become your favorite baseball internet personality's most annoying obsession. He was a 16th-round selection (oh yeah!) from Gonzaga (home of Jason Bay?! Ooh baby!) who throws in the upper-80s (that's the stuff) from a funky arm angle. (HELL YES!) Though he hit a wall in Triple-A last year, Jacob's ability to throw strikes and pile up strikeouts has him just a phone call away from San Diego. When he gets there, a sea of people will be ready to let you know they knew about him first.

Kevin Kopps RHP Born: 03/02/97 Age: 26 Bats: R Throws: R Height: 6'0" Weight: 200 lb. Origin: Round 3, 2021 Draft (#99 overall)

YEAR	TEAM	LVL	AGE	W	L	SV	G	GS	IP	H	HR	BB/9	K/9	K	GB%	BABIP	WHIP	ERA	DRA-	WARP	MPH	FB%	Whiff%	CSP
2021	FW	A+	24	1	0	3	8	0	8	2	0	4.5	11.2	10	60.0%	.133	0.75	0.00	97	0.1				
2022	SA	AA	25	1	2	4	42	3	54^{1}	44	4	5.6	9.9	60	53.5%	.290	1.44	4.14	87	0.7				
2023 non-DC	*SD*	*MLB*	*26*	*2*	*3*	*0*	*57*	*0*	*50*	*50*	*5*	*6.4*	*9.1*	*50*	*50.8%*	*.317*	*1.71*	*5.51*	*124*	*-0.4*			*28.2%*	

Comparables: Gerardo Reyes (66), Tom Hackimer (66), Arquimedes Caminero (66)

There aren't many 25-year-olds with only two years of pro experience and a low-90s fastball who are worth writing about, but those players don't have Kopps' cutter. It's a true wonder-pitch that helped him earn a Golden Spikes Award, Dick Howser Trophy and honors as the SEC Pitcher of the Year. It's even been compared to the slidey-cutty mythical "gyroball" that Daisuke Matsuzaka threw. If Mariano Rivera could make an entire Hall of Fame career out of a cutter, then Kopps can probably get at least a nice little stretch in the majors out of his.

Dylan Lesko RHP Born: 09/07/03 Age: 19 Bats: R Throws: R Height: 6'2" Weight: 195 lb. Origin: Round 1, 2022 Draft (#15 overall)

Remember when teams could just unload gobs of cash on young players in the draft and reap the rewards? MLB has tried to put the kibosh on that, but the Padres are still finding ways to snatch up the best players with money. In the running to go first overall thanks to a mid-90s fastball, a killer change and a developing curveball with good spin, Lesko fell to 15th due to Tommy John surgery, and the Padres paid him $3.9 million to rehab with them and resume pitching in 2023. If you want to stay in the running with the Dodgers and their never-ending Scrooge McDuck-style money pit, these are the chances you have to take.

Seth Lugo RHP Born: 11/17/89 Age: 33 Bats: R Throws: R Height: 6'4" Weight: 225 lb. Origin: Round 34, 2011 Draft (#1032 overall)

YEAR	TEAM	LVL	AGE	W	L	SV	G	GS	IP	H	HR	BB/9	K/9	K	GB%	BABIP	WHIP	ERA	DRA-	WARP	MPH	FB%	Whiff%	CSP
2020	NYM	MLB	30	3	4	3	16	7	36^{2}	40	8	2.5	11.5	47	50.5%	.344	1.36	5.15	71	0.9	93.4	55.4%	30.1%	48.1%
2021	NYM	MLB	31	4	3	1	46	0	46^{1}	41	6	3.7	10.7	55	41.7%	.307	1.29	3.50	87	0.8	94.0	54.1%	31.0%	56.3%
2022	NYM	MLB	32	3	2	3	62	0	65	58	9	2.5	9.6	69	45.1%	.283	1.17	3.60	86	1.1	94.5	51.2%	23.7%	56.5%
2023 DC	*SD*	*MLB*	*33*	*8*	*8*	*0*	*46*	*21*	*125*	*119*	*15*	*3.0*	*9.2*	*127*	*44.5%*	*.304*	*1.28*	*3.65*	*95*	*1.0*	*94.2*	*53.3%*	*25.1%*	*54.7%*

Comparables: Joe Kelly (73), Jose Mesa (72), Craig Stammen (72)

Lugo's final season before free agency was a carbon copy of his 2021 campaign. Although not the shutdown fireman he once was when he first broke out as a reliever, Lugo still put together a perfectly acceptable age-32 season. A 34th-round pick in 2011, Lugo has had much more success out of the bullpen than as a starter over the course of his seven-year career. But he never stopped wishing he could return to the rotation—an opportunity the Padres will reportedly give him after signing Lugo to a $15 million deal this winter. His bread and butter remains a high-spin curveball, which was as effective as ever in 2022, holding hitters to just a .184 batting average.

Nick Martinez RHP Born: 08/05/90 Age: 32 Bats: L Throws: R Height: 6'1" Weight: 200 lb. Origin: Round 18, 2011 Draft (#564 overall)

YEAR	TEAM	LVL	AGE	W	L	SV	G	GS	IP	H	HR	BB/9	K/9	K	GB%	BABIP	WHIP	ERA	DRA-	WARP	MPH	FB%	Whiff%	CSP
2022	SD	MLB	31	4	4	8	47	10	106^{1}	96	15	3.5	8.0	95	47.4%	.276	1.29	3.47	102	0.9	93.4	40.8%	25.6%	54.0%
2023 DC	*SD*	*MLB*	*32*	*8*	*8*	*0*	*36*	*24*	*137.3*	*132*	*15*	*3.6*	*7.8*	*118*	*49.8%*	*.292*	*1.36*	*3.86*	*99*	*1.0*	*93.4*	*40.8%*	*24.5%*	*54.0%*

Comparables: Jeff Suppan (67), Reggie Cleveland (67), Brian Anderson (66)

After struggling for four years with the Rangers, Martinez headed to Japan where he…continued to struggle. But after he spent an offseason going deep into Driveline and Rapsodo's online courses—one imagines a lot of days of visiting the library to use their computer room—he became a full pitching analytics dude, and everything changed. His 90-mph fastball ticked up to 94, and his slider and changeup picked up spin. That led to a 1.60 ERA with the SoftBank Hawks and a subsequent $6 million contract with the Padres for 2022. While he held his own in the rotation, he eventually found his calling as one of the few dependable relievers in a bullpen of madness. San Diego rewarded him with a new three-year deal this winter.

Adam Mazur RHP Born: 04/20/01 Age: 22 Bats: R Throws: R Height: 6'2" Weight: 180 lb. Origin: Round 2, 2022 Draft (#53 overall)

If you've ever thought it's unfair that we ask 18-year-olds to know what they want to do with the rest of their lives when they're just leaving high school, well, Mazur probably agrees. He spent two years at South Dakota State without a pitching coach, putting up the kind of ERA that would look better as a GPA. After getting an invite to the Cape Cod League and transferring to the University of Iowa, Mazur rediscovered himself. He ditched the two-seamer and relied on his mid-90s fastball, hard slider and even his changeup to post a 1.55 ERA for the Wareham Gateman and then the seventh-best batting average against in college. The Padres subsequently nabbed him with the 53rd overall pick in the 2022 draft.

Adrian Morejon LHP Born: 02/27/99 Age: 24 Bats: L Throws: L Height: 5'11" Weight: 224 lb. Origin: International Free Agent, 2016

YEAR	TEAM	LVL	AGE	W	L	SV	G	GS	IP	H	HR	BB/9	K/9	K	GB%	BABIP	WHIP	ERA	DRA-	WARP	MPH	FB%	Whiff%	CSP
2020	SD	MLB	21	2	2	0	9	4	19^{1}	20	7	1.9	11.6	25	46.0%	.302	1.24	4.66	73	0.4	96.8	56.2%	28.5%	46.5%
2021	SD	MLB	22	0	0	0	2	2	4^{2}	5	2	3.9	5.8	3	53.3%	.231	1.50	3.86	110	0.0	96.7	62.5%	30.8%	59.7%
2022	SA	AA	23	0	0	0	5	0	7	1	0	2.6	10.3	8	58.3%	.083	0.43	0.00	93	0.1				
2022	SD	MLB	23	5	1	0	26	0	34	31	4	2.4	7.4	28	33.0%	.273	1.18	4.24	108	0.2	96.8	69.1%	24.1%	57.9%
2023 DC	*SD*	*MLB*	*24*	*6*	*5*	*0*	*50*	*6*	*65.7*	*66*	*9*	*3.2*	*8.6*	*62*	*39.9%*	*.305*	*1.36*	*4.28*	*109*	*0.1*	*96.8*	*65.3%*	*26.0%*	*55.4%*

Comparables: Wilbur Wood (48), Caleb Ferguson (48), Miguel Castro (43)

For all those expecting a long joke about Garfield Minus Garfield—the extremely dark post-modern take on Garfield that features *only* Jon speaking to himself and asking the heavens, "who ate my lasagna?"—well, we're sorry to tell you that our protagonist's last name is not pronounced "More Jon" (who can say no?), but "Moe-re-hoan." He posted a career high in innings pitched last season despite being more or less the same pitcher he's always been: a replacement-level one. He's only entering his age-25 campaign, but Morejon needs to do more if we're to see more of him.

Joe Musgrove RHP Born: 12/04/92 Age: 30 Bats: R Throws: R Height: 6'5" Weight: 230 lb. Origin: Round 1, 2011 Draft (#46 overall)

YEAR	TEAM	LVL	AGE	W	L	SV	G	GS	IP	H	HR	BB/9	K/9	K	GB%	BABIP	WHIP	ERA	DRA-	WARP	MPH	FB%	Whiff%	CSP
2020	PIT	MLB	27	1	5	0	8	8	39^2	33	5	3.6	12.5	55	47.3%	.318	1.24	3.86	70	1.1	92.7	39.1%	33.0%	45.8%
2021	SD	MLB	28	11	9	0	32	31	181^1	142	22	2.7	10.1	203	44.2%	.268	1.08	3.18	79	3.8	93.4	25.8%	29.7%	54.8%
2022	SD	MLB	29	10	7	0	30	30	181	154	22	2.1	9.1	184	44.9%	.277	1.08	2.93	84	3.2	92.8	30.2%	25.6%	54.0%
2023 DC	*SD*	*MLB*	*30*	*12*	*9*	*0*	*29*	*29*	*186.3*	*164*	*20*	*2.5*	*9.0*	*186*	*44.9%*	*.286*	*1.15*	*3.10*	*83*	*3.2*	*93.0*	*31.2%*	*26.7%*	*53.4%*

Comparables: Johnny Cueto (76), Brad Penny (76), Jim Slaton (75)

Vincent Van Gogh. Spock. And now, Joe Musgrove. Yes, the Padres' hometown pitcher, the one who threw the first no-hitter in team history and who gritted his way through San Diego's upset over the Dodgers, will in part be remembered for his ears, and how slick they appeared in his Wild Card start against the Mets. Just as Italo Calvino wrote, "It is not the voice that commands the story: It is the ear," and so it will go with Musgrove's 2022 season. After a hot start, he swooned along with his teammates before picking it up late to help the Padres in their deepest playoff run since 1998. Along the way, he earned a five-year, $100 million deal with the team in August, ensuring that he'll be wearing Jake Peavy's old number in San Diego for a long time to come. The next time someone checks for something behind Musgrove's ear, they're likely to find more than just a quarter.

Drew Pomeranz LHP Born: 11/22/88 Age: 34 Bats: R Throws: L Height: 6'5" Weight: 246 lb. Origin: Round 1, 2010 Draft (#5 overall)

YEAR	TEAM	LVL	AGE	W	L	SV	G	GS	IP	H	HR	BB/9	K/9	K	GB%	BABIP	WHIP	ERA	DRA-	WARP	MPH	FB%	Whiff%	CSP
2020	SD	MLB	31	1	0	4	20	0	18^2	9	1	4.8	14.0	29	47.1%	.242	1.02	1.45	73	0.5	94.6	79.6%	34.7%	47.9%
2021	SD	MLB	32	1	0	0	27	0	25^2	19	2	3.5	10.5	30	45.2%	.283	1.13	1.75	88	0.4	94.1	75.3%	27.4%	55.6%
2023 DC	*SD*	*MLB*	*34*	*2*	*2*	*4*	*44*	*0*	*38.3*	*35*	*5*	*4.4*	*9.7*	*41*	*41.1%*	*.299*	*1.41*	*4.17*	*103*	*0.1*	*93.3*	*71.6%*	*25.0%*	*50.7%*

Comparables: Don Larsen (63), Juan Pizarro (62), Oliver Pérez (58)

We could tell you that Pomeranz is one of baseball's most effective relievers when healthy. We could tell you he has a curveball that batters are truly unable to hit. We could tell you that A.J. Preller is hopeful that Pomeranz will be healthy come spring training, and that he could be the biggest addition to a San Diego bullpen that lost several arms to free agency this winter. What we *need* to tell you, though, is this: His great-grandfather was a man named Garland Buckeye who played in the majors and the NFL...and was sentenced to six months in prison for his part in a slot machine ring. That doesn't tell you much about Pomeranz, but really, you needed to know.

Blake Snell LHP Born: 12/04/92 Age: 30 Bats: L Throws: L Height: 6'4" Weight: 225 lb. Origin: Round 1, 2011 Draft (#52 overall)

YEAR	TEAM	LVL	AGE	W	L	SV	G	GS	IP	H	HR	BB/9	K/9	K	GB%	BABIP	WHIP	ERA	DRA-	WARP	MPH	FB%	Whiff%	CSP
2020	TB	MLB	27	4	2	0	11	11	50	42	10	3.2	11.3	63	48.4%	.288	1.20	3.24	73	1.3	95.3	50.6%	34.0%	41.3%
2021	SD	MLB	28	7	6	0	27	27	128^2	101	16	4.8	11.9	170	39.0%	.296	1.32	4.20	86	2.2	95.3	52.4%	31.8%	54.8%
2022	SD	MLB	29	8	10	0	24	24	128	103	11	3.6	12.0	171	36.7%	.308	1.20	3.38	70	3.2	95.8	55.5%	32.9%	53.5%
2023 DC	*SD*	*MLB*	*30*	*9*	*8*	*0*	*29*	*29*	*148.7*	*121*	*18*	*3.7*	*11.3*	*187*	*38.9%*	*.294*	*1.23*	*3.12*	*81*	*2.7*	*95.6*	*53.3%*	*32.7%*	*51.8%*

Comparables: Steve Carlton (80), Chris Sale (80), Gio González (79)

On September 21, Snell faced off against the Cardinals while the Padres were trying to lock up the NL Wild Card, and the left-hander went off. He hit 99 mph on the radar gun for the first time in his career and had a no-hitter going until Albert Pujols sent a bleeder through the hole in the shift. ("Which won't be a thing next year!" Snell is surely telling himself while rewatching the footage on repeat this winter.) Snell then finished off the inning by getting his 13th strikeout—a career high. But the most shocking thing wasn't the no-hitter—he's got the stuff—or the 13th K, but that he pitched seven innings for the second consecutive start and second time all year. Forget whether Kevin Cash should have lifted him in the 2020 World Series: Snell has only pitched more than 6⅓ innings in a start 22 times since 2018, his Cy Young season. That's once more than Cole Hamels, who hasn't pitched since 2020, and is tied with Dylan Bundy, who has a 5.02 ERA in that time span. Obviously, some of Snell's shorter starts were a function of pitching for the Rays, who make sure their pitching coach gets 10,000 steps in every game. But the other reason is that, despite his amazing stuff, Snell nibbles more than a rabbit on a diet.

Robby Snelling LHP Born: 12/19/03 Age: 19 Bats: R Throws: L Height: 6'3" Weight: 210 lb. Origin: Round 1, 2022 Draft (#39 overall)

Get ready for a whole lot of Darin Erstad-esque "This guy is a football player out on the mound" comments. A star quarterback and linebacker at McQueen High School in Reno, Nevada, Snelling was set to be a two-sport star at Arizona before the school made a head coaching change. So, after the left-hander with a 97-mph fastball absolutely obliterated the opposition—he posted a 0.56 ERA with a state-record 146 strikeouts and just six walks in 62⅓ innings—he joined up with the Padres for a cool $3 million. Of course, when he set the K record, Snelling went full football player. As he told Nevada Sportsnet: "My catcher came out, and I didn't even know what I was at. 'The umpire asked if you wanted to keep the ball,' and I was like, 'Why?' And he's like, 'Well you just broke the record.' I was like 'Oh, OK that's really cool. I'll toss it back in.'"

Robert Suarez RHP Born: 03/01/91 Age: 32 Bats: R Throws: R Height: 6'2" Weight: 210 lb. Origin: International Free Agent, 2021

YEAR	TEAM	LVL	AGE	W	L	SV	G	GS	IP	H	HR	BB/9	K/9	K	GB%	BABIP	WHIP	ERA	DRA-	WARP	MPH	FB%	Whiff%	CSP
2022	SD	MLB	31	5	1	1	45	0	47^2	29	4	4.0	11.5	61	42.9%	.250	1.05	2.27	77	1.0	97.5	73.5%	25.0%	52.6%
2023 DC	*SD*	*MLB*	*32*	*2*	*2*	*4*	*50*	*0*	*43.7*	*35*	*4*	*3.5*	*8.7*	*42*	*53.1%*	*.265*	*1.20*	*2.96*	*79*	*0.6*	*97.5*	*73.5%*	*24.9%*	*52.6%*

Comparables: Pedro Strop (75), Steve Cishek (75), Cory Gearrin (74)

It's a sad day when your "Road to the Show" wish fulfillment requires you to cut your age in half (or more) when playing MLB: The Show. That's why it's great when players like Suarez come through. Making his MLB debut at the geriatric age of 31, Suarez has a career route as non-traditional as that of your high school friend who tried to go pro in hacky sack after he dropped out of UVM. Suarez started playing professionally in Mexico and headed to Japan, where he played in the NPB's minor-league system before he got his chance with the Hanshin Tigers at the age of 29 in 2020. A successful two-year stint as a Tiger led to Suarez signing with the Padres, where he emerged as an eminently useful pitcher. San Diego rewarded him with a $46 million deal that could keep him in the brown and gold through 2027. Maybe that friend of yours ended up making his hacky sack career work, too.

Ryan Weathers LHP Born: 12/17/99 Age: 23 Bats: R Throws: L Height: 6'1" Weight: 230 lb. Origin: Round 1, 2018 Draft (#7 overall)

YEAR	TEAM	LVL	AGE	W	L	SV	G	GS	IP	H	HR	BB/9	K/9	K	GB%	BABIP	WHIP	ERA	DRA-	WARP	MPH	FB%	Whiff%	CSP
2021	ELP	AAA	21	1	0	0	2	2	10	13	2	1.8	9.9	11	46.7%	.393	1.50	3.60	106	0.0				
2021	SD	MLB	21	4	7	1	30	18	94^2	101	20	2.9	6.8	72	43.6%	.299	1.38	5.32	115	0.1	94.0	62.2%	18.8%	54.5%
2022	ELP	AAA	22	7	7	0	31	22	123	163	31	4.2	6.4	88	35.7%	.346	1.79	6.73	140	-2.3	94.1	51.7%	22.3%	
2022	SD	MLB	22	0	0	0	1	1	3^2	6	0	9.8	7.4	3	50.0%	.429	2.73	9.82	157	-0.1	94.2	50.6%	25.6%	51.7%
2023 DC	*SD*	*MLB*	*23*	*2*	*2*	*0*	*16*	*4*	*30.7*	*37*	*5*	*3.9*	*6.6*	*22*	*41.1%*	*.318*	*1.63*	*5.89*	*140*	*-0.4*	*94.0*	*61.4%*	*20.9%*	*54.3%*

Comparables: Bryse Wilson (47), Ryan Feierabend (46), Lucas Giolito (46)

Marcel Proust once wrote, "A change in the weather is sufficient to recreate the world and ourselves." Change may be necessary for the Padres' young left-hander. After making his big-league debut in the 2020 postseason and starting 2021 looking like a future star, Weathers has seen things turn decidedly less sunny. The Padres have tinkered with his fastball, swapped out his curve for a slide piece and shuffled him from rotation to bullpen to everything in between. It hasn't worked—he had the highest opponents' batting average and HR/9 in all the affiliated minor leagues while seeing his walk rate spike as well. He's still young, has a mid-90s fastball and hails from a family loaded with athletes—his dad, David, was a former MLB reliever, while his sister Karly is the only freshman on the Alabama women's basketball team this year—so his story isn't finished. But for now, a George Carlin quote comes to mind: "Weather forecast for tonight: Dark."

Steven Wilson RHP Born: 08/24/94 Age: 28 Bats: R Throws: R Height: 6'3" Weight: 221 lb. Origin: Round 8, 2018 Draft (#231 overall)

YEAR	TEAM	LVL	AGE	W	L	SV	G	GS	IP	H	HR	BB/9	K/9	K	GB%	BABIP	WHIP	ERA	DRA-	WARP	MPH	FB%	Whiff%	CSP
2021	ELP	AAA	26	4	0	0	28	0	39^1	22	7	3.2	14.4	63	26.9%	.211	0.92	3.43	72	0.8				
2022	SD	MLB	27	4	2	1	50	1	53	36	7	3.4	9.0	53	22.5%	.223	1.06	3.06	104	0.4	95.2	52.2%	28.5%	53.6%
2023 DC	*SD*	*MLB*	*28*	*2*	*2*	*0*	*50*	*0*	*43.7*	*36*	*7*	*3.7*	*9.5*	*46*	*29.1%*	*.267*	*1.26*	*3.76*	*97*	*0.2*	*95.2*	*52.2%*	*29.9%*	*53.6%*

Comparables: Rowan Wick (76), Steve Geltz (76), Jimmie Sherfy (76)

A six-year college student, Wilson ended up finishing his college career with two degrees—one in economics, the other in business analytics—to go with one Tommy John surgery and a blown-out shoulder. That's more likely to be the background of a guy wearing a Patagonia vest either on Wall Street or in the front office—not a 27-year-old who made an impact as a rookie. Relying primarily on a fastball and slider mix, Wilson is a truly modern pitcher. His fastball sits at the top of the zone and he throws his slider in the bottom. He collects tons of fly balls and held opponents to a .188 batting average against. Wilson has plenty of fallback options should his MLB career stall out, but it doesn't look likely to do so very soon.

Lineouts

Hitters

HITTER	POS	TEAM	LVL	AGE	PA	R	2B	3B	HR	RBI	BB	K	SB	CS	AVG/OBP/SLG	DRC+	BABIP	BRR	DRP	WARP
Matthew Batten	IF	ELP	AAA	27	378	63	17	1	12	46	47	73	18	2	.289/.382/.458	116	.339	1.7	SS(36): 2.5, 3B(34): -0.7, 2B(10): -1.3	2.1
	IF	SD	MLB	27	22	0	1	0	0	1	2	6	0	0	.105/.227/.158	92	.154	-0.3	3B(7): -0.3, 2B(5): 0	0.0
Matt Beaty	RF	ELP	AAA	29	145	19	2	1	2	13	14	27	0	0	.270/.366/.349	105	.330	-0.7	RF(15): -2.7, LF(9): 0.1	0.2
	RF	SD	MLB	29	47	6	1	1	0	1	2	8	0	0	.093/.170/.163	86	.114	0.9	RF(10): -0.3, LF(2): -0.2	0.1
Korry Howell	UT	SA	AA	23	184	37	8	4	6	20	25	52	12	1	.253/.390/.486	104	.344	4.1	CF(17): 0.5, LF(15): -0.5, 2B(10): 2.7	1.0
Tirso Ornelas	LF	SA	AA	22	492	62	28	2	7	51	43	85	7	2	.288/.355/.408	102	.342	1.5	LF(104): -0.6, 1B(1): 0.1, RF(1): -0.5	1.3
Brett Sullivan	C	ELP	AAA	28	475	73	28	6	9	81	38	58	3	0	.285/.339/.444	98	.302	2.0	C(64): 2.1, 3B(15): -0.7, LF(13): -1.6	1.5
Preston Tucker	LF/DH	GWN	AAA	31	311	37	16	0	9	47	30	49	1	0	.267/.347/.426	113	.290	-0.5	LF(40): -3.2, RF(9): -0.9	1.0

Even if **Matthew Batten** never reaches the majors again, he's already beat the odds as a New England-born, 32nd-round draft pick who's played every position except catcher in his professional career. After a few solid seasons as a utility guy with some pop, **Matt Beaty** managed just 20 games and an absolutely ghastly batting line due in large part to shoulder impingements. He just needs to keep telling himself, "The only thing keeping Beaty from Beauty is U." **Korry Howell** grew up a White Sox superfan and can name every player from 2005-07. (Finally! A baseball player who also wants to remember some guys!) With emerging power, 70-grade speed and a solid glove, he can man any position up the middle. Drafted in the fourth round and signed away from a Georgia Tech commitment, **Lamar King Jr.** is a big-bodied, power-hitting catcher who shares a frame with his father, a former Seattle Seahawks defensive end. A Vancouver, B.C. native, King could eventually challenge Matt Stairs for the title of MLB's beefiest boy from Canada. Signed for $1 million, **Daniel Montesino** is a power-hitting outfielder, though really his bat will determine where, or if, teams squeeze him onto the roster. He had Tommy John surgery and missed all of 2022. The streaky **Tirso Ornelas** at least ended the season on a high-note: The outfielder went 12-for-43 with two doubles, a homer and six RBI in the last 10 games. In total, 2022 was his best year yet after two rough campaigns and a lost year due to COVID-19, but for a guy with his tools and penchant for striking out, you'd like to see a lot more than just seven home runs. Part of the return from the Brewers in the Victor Caratini trade, **Brett Sullivan** has a steady glove and enough of a bat to be someone's backup catcher next season. For the first time since early 2019, **Preston Tucker** played baseball games stateside, looking to repeat the mashing he did for the Kia Tigers in the KBO. Tucker once again proved himself a fully capable hitter at the Triple-A level—maybe that's worth trading Gwangju for Gwinnett?

Pitchers

PITCHER	TEAM	LVL	AGE	W	L	SV	G	GS	IP	H	HR	BB/9	K/9	K	GB%	BABIP	WHIP	ERA	DRA-	WARP	MPH	FB%	WHF	CSP
Austin Adams	SD	MLB	31	1	0	0	2	0	2^1	0	0	11.6	7.7	2	100.0%	.000	1.29	0.00	103	0.0	92.8	21.3%	29.4%	51.6%
Michel Baez	LE	A	26	0	0	0	4	2	7^2	3	0	1.2	10.6	9	50.0%	.188	0.52	1.17	92	0.1				
	SA	AA	26	4	1	1	13	0	18^2	10	3	1.9	11.6	24	48.8%	.184	0.75	2.41	65	0.5				
	ELP	AAA	26	1	2	0	24	0	21^1	27	3	7.6	10.1	24	38.1%	.400	2.11	8.44	103	0.1	94.5	50.2%	29.9%	
	SD	MLB	26	0	0	0	2	0	2	1	0	0.0	9.0	2	40.0%	.200	0.50	0.00	95	0.0	94.7	56.0%	16.7%	49.1%
José Castillo	LE	A	26	0	0	0	5	0	5^1	4	0	1.7	11.8	7	78.6%	.286	0.94	0.00	94	0.0				
	ELP	AAA	26	3	2	3	43	0	43^1	43	3	4.2	12.0	58	42.3%	.396	1.45	2.91	78	0.8	94.4	43.7%	36.0%	
	SD	MLB	26	0	0	0	1	0	1	1	0	9.0	9.0	1	66.7%	.333	2.00	9.00	88	0.0	94.6	50.0%	30.0%	54.2%
Efrain Contreras	FW	A+	22	0	5	0	17	17	53^1	64	7	4.2	10.8	64	42.8%	.396	1.67	5.74	108	0.3				
Jay Groome	POR	AA	23	3	4	0	16	14	76^2	58	11	4.5	9.5	81	45.0%	.250	1.25	3.52	99	1.0				
	WOR	AAA	23	1	1	0	3	3	16	17	2	3.9	8.4	15	35.4%	.326	1.50	3.94	99	0.2				
	ELP	AAA	23	3	2	0	10	10	51^1	52	4	3.3	7.7	44	38.2%	.324	1.38	3.16	106	0.1	92.3	54.2%	20.5%	
Garrett Hawkins	LE	A	22	5	5	0	17	17	77^2	73	9	2.3	12.5	108	31.6%	.348	1.20	3.94	81	1.0				
	FW	A+	22	0	3	0	4	4	15^1	22	6	5.9	7.0	12	26.8%	.320	2.09	8.80	162	-0.3				
Brent Honeywell Jr.	LV	AAA	27	0	3	0	11	0	17^1	28	7	3.6	10.9	21	35.7%	.447	2.02	7.79	88	0.2	93.7	43.3%	28.8%	
Jairo Iriarte	LE	A	20	4	7	0	21	18	91^1	83	13	4.1	10.7	109	39.2%	.304	1.37	5.12	96	0.4				
Ray Kerr	ELP	AAA	27	5	0	3	46	0	44^1	45	4	7.3	13.6	67	40.6%	.423	1.83	5.08	67	1.1	95.7	68.3%	35.9%	
	SD	MLB	27	0	0	0	7	0	5	3	1	7.2	5.4	3	21.4%	.154	1.40	9.00	117	0.0	94.8	71.6%	25.6%	52.2%
Reiss Knehr	ELP	AAA	25	4	4	1	32	15	87^2	89	18	5.6	9.4	92	40.7%	.302	1.64	6.88	100	0.5	93.4	51.7%	25.0%	
	SD	MLB	25	0	0	0	5	1	13^2	11	1	2.6	6.6	10	29.3%	.250	1.10	3.95	117	0.0	92.9	50.8%	14.2%	54.3%
Victor Lizarraga	LE	A	18	8	3	0	20	19	94^1	87	5	3.2	9.1	95	48.1%	.313	1.28	3.43	97	0.3				
Moises Lugo	SA	AA	23	6	0	2	28	1	62^1	41	4	4.9	12.3	85	30.7%	.278	1.20	2.74	64	1.6				
	ELP	AAA	23	2	0	0	11	0	10^1	11	2	4.4	10.5	12	36.7%	.321	1.55	6.10	92	0.1	94.0	47.6%	33.3%	
Sean Poppen	RNO	AAA	28	0	3	1	21	0	25^1	26	1	2.5	6.8	19	40.5%	.321	1.30	4.62	115	-0.1	93.9	56.6%	22.2%	
	AZ	MLB	28	2	2	0	29	0	28^2	27	5	3.8	6.9	22	35.3%	.278	1.36	4.40	111	0.1	94.6	62.2%	16.0%	58.6%
Noel Vela	FW	A+	23	6	7	0	20	20	87	74	6	4.9	10.4	101	44.2%	.312	1.39	3.83	88	1.4				
	SA	AA	23	1	3	0	9	4	22^2	25	1	7.9	9.5	24	50.0%	.381	1.99	6.35	119	-0.1				
Jackson Wolf	FW	A+	23	7	8	0	23	22	119	91	16	3.3	10.1	134	35.6%	.262	1.13	4.01	117	0.1				
	SA	AA	23	0	2	0	2	2	10^2	12	1	5.1	6.7	8	37.1%	.324	1.69	8.44	136	-0.2				

The good news? **Austin Adams** hit zero batters in 2022 after hitting a whopping 24 of them in just 52⅔ IP in 2021. The bad news? He pitched only 2⅔ innings after suffering a forearm strain. He had surgery in August and will likely miss a chunk of next year as well, meaning batters can safely enter the box for at least a few more months. ⚾ After missing all of 2021 post-Tommy John surgery, **Michel Baez** pitched at four different levels in 2022. He enjoyed some highs—taking part in a minor-league no hitter and reaching the majors—and the lowest of lows, coughing up eight runs in a third of an inning in a rough El Paso outing. ⚾ Oh, the frailty of the human body. After looking like one of the best young left-handed relievers in 2018, **José Castillo** pitched just two-thirds of an inning in 2019, missed the 2020 season with a lat strain and a torn ligament in his hand and missed 2021 with Tommy John surgery. That he made the majors at all in 2022 is a testament to perseverance and true devotion to this very silly game. ⚾ **Efrain Contreras** finally got back on the mound after hurting himself in his final start of 2019, requiring Tommy John surgery. A strike-throwing, short-and-stout teapot, he looked solid in the Arizona Fall League and could eventually find himself at the back of a big-league rotation. ⚾ It took just a few extra years and unloading Eric Hosmer's contract, but San Diego finally became betrothed to **Jay Groome**, who they reportedly had a pre-draft deal with in 2017 before the Red Sox plucked him first. His fastball doesn't flash the upper '90s like it once did, but he's added a slider and changeup in recent years and he finally topped 100 innings in a professional campaign. ⚾ A bespectacled hurler out of British Columbia? Yes, please. After playing in the MLB Draft League due to COVID-19 restrictions in Canada, **Garrett Hawkins** landed with the Padresin the ninth round. He's got a fastball that can touch the mid-90s and some off-speed pitches you can dream on. ⚾ Finishing the season healthy is about as big a win as we can hope for with **Brent Honeywell** these days. Yet another elbow injury slowed his development and wrecked his control, but there remains hope that the screwball artist could find himself in a relief role in 2023. ⚾ Armed with a mid-90s fastball, a biting two-seamer and a high-80s changeup that can regularly flummox batters, **Jairo Iriarte** has plenty of tools in his arsenal. He needs to greatly improve his control and command, but at just 21 years old, time is on his side. ⚾ Acquired from the Mariners as part of the Adam Frazier deal, **Ray Kerr** made his big-league debut at the age of 27. Though he has a five-pitch mix, he may want to cut down on his selection: He walked a whopping 40 batters in 49⅓ innings between Triple-A and MLB. ⚾ If you're reading this on a bus, take a quick look to your left or right: There's a decent chance **Reiss Knehr** might be with you. The Padres called up and sent down Knehr six different times in 2022. He responded with solid, unspectacular outings that might keep him on a similar trajectory for years. ⚾ Though he'll need to add some strength if he wants to stick as a starter, **Victor Lizarraga** has the kind of upside that would make any farm director salivate. The Padres gave him two consecutive aggressive promotions, including to the California League, where he was the youngest arm around. ⚾ Plucked in the 11th round of the Amateur Draft and given an above-slot bonus of $400,000 to skip going to Wake Forest, **Isaiah Lowe** features a mid-90s fastball, a sweeping slider and a boosted bank account. ⚾ **Moises Lugo**'s ascent through the Padres system picked up some steam when the team moved him into a full-time relief role in 2022. He was already a reliever in all but name, as he owns a potent fastball/slider combo but only a murky sense as to the direction of home plate. ⚾ Lightly bearded so as to keep from looking like Sheldon Cooper, **Sean Poppen** couldn't get chases on either his sinker or his slider, with each becoming loosey-goosey instead of maintaining their tighter side-to-side wiggle. Instead of poppin', they were ploppin' out of the zone, creating a stark drop in strikeouts and effectiveness. ⚾ A former 28th-round pick—a round that doesn't even exist anymore—**Noel Vela** took a few years to really get going. After Vela added a few ticks of velo, the left-hander now sits in the mid-90s and has a chance to stick in a rotation, though he needs to cut down on his walks. ⚾ Plucked out of Duke in the third round for a cool $800,000 signing bonus, **Henry Williams** isn't one of those college arms who is on the cusp of the majors. For one, he had Tommy John surgery and threw a total of 37⅔ innings in college. For another, he hails from Darien, CT, a cold-weather town that limited his time on the mound. ⚾ No, he's not the title character in CBS' new werewolf procedural, "Lycan, Oklahoma." Instead, **Jackson Wolf** is a lean, Chris Sale-esque 6-foot-7 pitcher, but his fastball sits in the upper-80s. The only thing rarer than that combination may be an actual werewolf detective.

SAN FRANCISCO GIANTS

Essay by Patrick Dubuque

Player comments by Kate Preusser and BP staff

A year ago, it was a challenge to talk about the San Francisco Giants, a team that spat in the face of projection systems and pundits alike, reanimating the corpses of 35-year-old men with the necromancy of "platooning" and "individualized coaching." It remains a challenge with the latest edition, if for the opposite reason. The 2022 Giants, cresting the wave of 2021's expectations, collapsed with all the weight and predictability of a Dostoevsky novel. If their crime last year was upending our collective wisdom about what makes successful baseball teams, this year was their punishment.

The illusions all vanished. All those mid-thirties veterans who had discovered the fountain of youth lost it again, as Brandon Belt, Brandan Crawford and Darin Ruf withered before our eyes. The clever substitutions transformed into an open audition, as the team gave plate appearances to a league-high 37 different position players, picking through the league's dumpster to try and squeeze talent out of busted prospects like Lewis Brinson, Willie Calhoun, Luke Williams and Yermín Mercedes. The waiver wire magic that had brought the team LaMonte Wade Jr. and Donovan Solano was dispelled when it came time to replace Buster Posey.

Other elements of the team suffered as well. The organization maintained its aptitude for rehabilitating starting pitching, getting rewarded for its faith in acquisitions like Carlos Rodón and Alex Cobb, but an anonymous bullpen that largely succeeded by eschewing both strikeouts and walks in favor of weak contact maintained exactly one of those traits. It almost didn't matter, because they could no longer benefit from balls in play; where the team betrayed its age most was on the field, where a collection of creaky backs and stiff joints combined to provide the league's worst defense.

Despite all this, the Giants did maintain line of sight with a Wild Card spot through the All-Star break, at which point they immediately lost seven straight, then did so again to close out August. From a traditional analytics standpoint, the near future for the Giants went dark in an instant. As Farhan Zaidi and Gabe Kapler took over an aging roster and arid farm system, the decision to maintain the Belt-Crawford-Posey core and paper over the edges with Anthony DeSclafani types

SAN FRANCISCO GIANTS PROSPECTUS

2022 W-L: 81-81, 3RD IN NL WEST

Pythag	.513	14th	DER	.681	27th
RS/G	4.42	11th	DRC+	98	16th
RA/G	4.30	18th	DRA-	94	8th
dWin%	.530	11th	FIP	3.41	2nd
Payroll	$155M	12th	B-Age	30.6	29th
M$/MW	$4.2M	15th	P-Age	29.6	19th

391′ 364′ 415′ 339′ 309′

- Opened 2000
- Open air
- Natural surface
- Fence profile: 8′ to 25′

Park Factors

Runs	Runs/RH	Runs/LH	HR/RH	HR/LH
98	99	98	92	78

Top Hitter WARP	2.6 Wilmer Flores
Top Pitcher WARP	4.3 Carlos Rodón
2023 Top Prospect	Marco Luciano

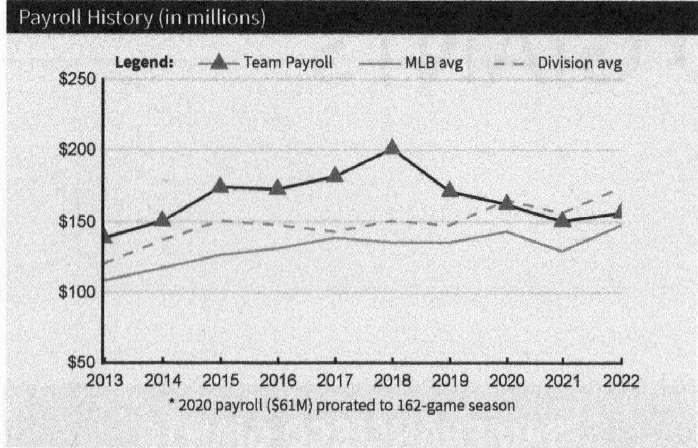

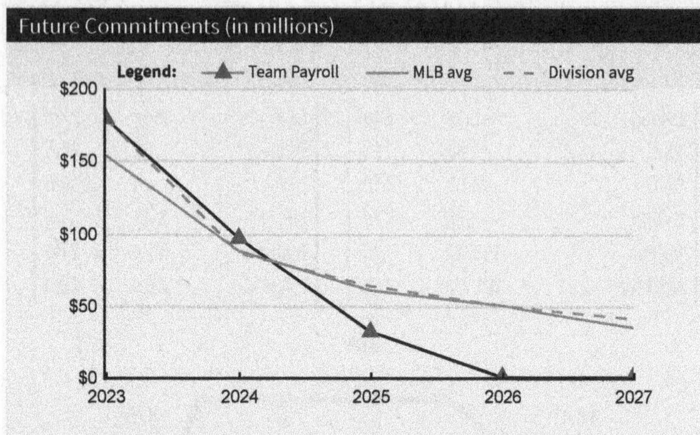

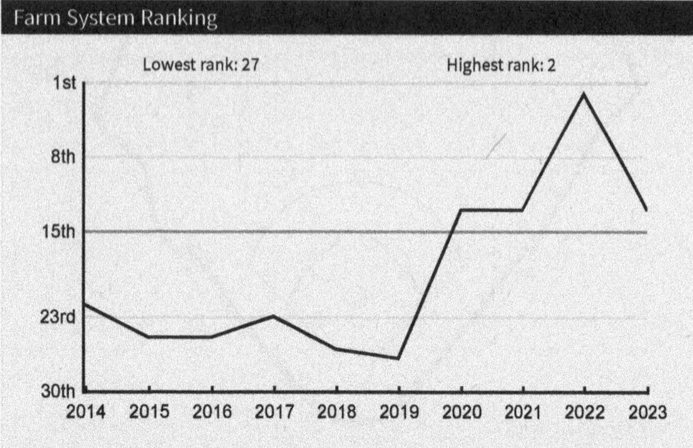

Personnel

President of Baseball Operations
Farhan Zaidi

General Manager
Pete Putila

Vice President & Assistant General Manager
Jeremy Shelley

Vice President of Baseball Resources & Development
Yeshayah Goldfarb

Vice President, Baseball Analytics
Paul Bien

Manager
Gabe Kapler

felt at first like window dressing, an admirable level of professionalism amidst the dirty, methodical work of modernizing the franchise's infrastructure. Then 2021 blinded everyone, and for a moment it was impossible to tell what had happened, and what it meant.

Turns out it didn't mean anything, and that's what made it special.

There's a great scene in the Anne Washburn work *Mr. Burns, a Post-Electric Play*, where two people fight about a cartoon. It would probably help to describe the situation: In the near future, America suffers from a full-scale nuclear apocalypse, and a few ragged survivors in the woods fend off despair by collectively remembering *The Simpsons* episode "Cape Feare," in which Sideshow Bob tries to murder Bart. Fast-forward 10 years, and in a world without electricity, these men and women have devoted their lives to reproducing the show as a series of stage plays, complete with commercials and practical effects, a desperate attempt to cling to a better past. As we watch them rehearse, struggle with production and argue about presentation, two of the actors get into an argument over the realism of an oil smudge on a character's face.

> *QUINCY: This is a cartoon. That's what we're doing. A cartoon. You keep trying to turn it into a Drama.*
>
> *MARIA: I'm not trying to turn it into a Drama Quincy. I'm trying to create a...richer sense of reality and that's part of what makes it funny; things are funniest when they're true. (To everyone.) Right?*
>
> *She gets no playback.*
>
> *QUINCY: I just think, if we're giving everything motivation, then where's the power, where's the joy. No motivation, no consequence, that's the point of a cartoon. Where else do we get to experience that, nowhere.*
>
> *MARIA: I'm just saying I think we have a chance to like, to like, engage at the same time with, like...larger...are we just entertaining them? We have an opportunity to provide...meaning.*
>
> *QUINCY: Things aren't funny when they're true they're awful. Meaning is everywhere. We get meaning for free, whether we like it or not. Meaningless Entertainment, on the other hand, is actually really hard.*

Mr. Burns premiered in 2014, and if it didn't presage the collapse of society, it certainly did nail the crisis of comedy in a world suddenly in visible decline. *The Simpsons* shambles on, but the ethos of a world resetting every 22 minutes, still natural in 1989, is next to extinct in 2022; even the cartoons, including creator Matt Groening's, now have arcs.

There's a correlation at play between the slow death of the episodic nature of television, serials and comic strips, and the growing realization that our world, too, is beyond the point of resetting. It's impossible now to shake the feeling that these characters and settings aren't non-renewable resources. The audience feels this invisible clock in the background, ticking. Only one form of entertainment truly resets the pins each year, attempts at pure untethered escapism: sports.

Or at least it used to. A while back baseball got hooked on narrative continuity as well as tanking drove teams to exchange "wait 'til next year" for "wait 'til next cycle." It was no longer possible to simply dispose of an at-bat, a game, a season; suddenly it was all data, and thus all meaningful. It left many wondering where the joy had gone. And then came this team that was funny because it was so impossible, because it rejected every rule. It was funny the way that *The Simpsons* were funny, in 1989, and in how everything has caught up to them. It was the theater of the absurd.

⚾ ⚾ ⚾

The 2022 San Francisco Giants provided a service. Not the one that people in the Bay Area would have liked, of course, though that's often the way. The strain of the 2021 club was its incorporation; baseball, like life, is a series of patterns and rules. The fun for so many fans, and the work of the teams they root for, is to ride one step ahead of the knowledge, like surfing a wave of information, knowing a little bit more a little bit earlier than everyone else. That Giants club did not cooperate with this metaphor; they didn't make enough sense to adapt to. It was too much disbelief to suspend.

In his 1982 novel, *Life, the Universe and Everything*, Douglas Adams invented a cloaking device called the SEP Field, short for "Somebody Else's Problem." The title hints at an *Ikiru*-style bureaucratic buck-passing, but the actual idea behind it is somewhat less satirical and more psychological. As his character Ford Prefect puts it, "An SEP is something we can't see, or don't see, or our brain doesn't let us see, because we think that it's somebody else's problem...The brain just edits it out, it's like a blind spot." The phenomenon is mirrored in the famous 1999 "Invisible Gorilla" study by Daniel Simons and Christopher Chabris, in which subjects tasked with focusing their attention on counting the number of passes in a basketball game failed to notice a man walk across the screen in a gorilla suit. It was later shown that even when they were forewarned about the gorilla, they still missed it; the task had shrunk the subjects' world to a wireframe, and the gorilla didn't fit in it.

The only hole in Adams' thesis of the SEP is not that the brain would ignore a phenomenon or a fact that could not acclimate to its present worldview; we've all seen far too much evidence to the contrary to deny that. Instead, it's the idea that it would do so effortlessly. Anyone with young children knows how difficult it is, even subconsciously, to ignore something that does not want to be ignored. The people roaming about in Adams' novel would ignore the shiny white spaceship, but they'd be vaguely irritated. It would generate strain.

The 2021 Giants were, for those who like to or are compelled to analyze baseball, a source of great strain. They tormented the teams staring enviously up at them in the standings, not least of which being the dynastic Los Angeles Dodgers themselves. And they required, if not a re-evaluation of the expertise of critics, no small effort in pretending that they'd seen it all along. Only a few blessed souls, mostly in the Bay Area, could enjoy the team as the house money that it certainly was, the gold vein discovered in the hills. Everyone wanted to be the ones to solve the riddle, to deconstruct and ruin the joke.

And now, thanks to the miserable 2022 San Francisco Giants, they are free.

⚾ ⚾ ⚾

A year from now, it'll be an unenviable task to talk about the San Francisco Giants, a team that will have won its share of games but almost certainly not enough to conquer a contentious National League West. For a moment the path forward seemed so clear: A smiling Carlos Correa holding up his orange no. 1 jersey in front of the flashing lights and microphones, evolving how we would tell their story.

These 2023 San Francisco Giants wouldn't really be the 2023 Giants anymore. They'd just be the Giants. Correa would be under contract with the team for 13 years, an eternity in baseball time; not one teammate, except perhaps under the perfect circumstances, Logan Webb, would remain by the end. Correa might not have remained himself. It's too far in the future to see. But the Giants would still be the Giants. The names on the backs of the jerseys will be different, and they'll sport a dozen alternate jerseys in varying shades of cream, but they'll be the same ballclub, just as they were 13 years ago, and 13 years before that.

The mission of the modern incarnation of this franchise is to exist out of time, reject cycles. As with their rivals down the coast, team president Farhan Zaidi has begun to build an infrastructure and an engine to create perpetual motion. The coaching and training aspects of the program quickly made themselves evident, while the development and scouting side continues to accelerate as the team's farm system slowly builds up to speed. The Giants could have, and were indeed expected, to tear down during this part of the process, as so many other "smart" teams have, since major-league success is incidental at best for this part of the plan.

And then, once again, everything changed. It all became like a dream sequence, a lazy piece of sitcom writing. The morning of Correa's press conference, his family in town, ready to do some house-shopping, a terse communication was released by the team. Twelve hours later, it was announced that the All-Star shortstop was now a third baseman for the New York Mets. The Giants' front office had spotted something in the medical reports and voided the deal. And at that moment, next year's San Francisco Giants suddenly looked a lot like last year's San Francisco Giants. The story wrapped up, but the show didn't end.

We've spent the better part of a decade fretting about the plague upon the sport that is tanking, how the spirit of *Moneyball* has allowed teams to twist the message and manipulate their way into years of non-competitive baseball. Now, with Correa's eventual contract and other megadeals that have defined the 2022-23 offseason, we're seeing a potential way out of the mess. If the old way of baseball was wrapping everything up in 22 minutes, and the modern age reflects the multi-season arc, what we're approaching now is a postmodern baseball that resembles an extended universe: singular movies set within a greater canon. Each creation is separate, and yet beholden to the overarching formula. Bad movies (and everything else) can still happen, but it's not reflective of the greater work.

The Giants appeared to be on a path toward perpetual contention, committed to justifying the existence of their star shortstop and his salary, like signing up for a year-long gym membership on New Year's Day. Until they stared 13 years in the future with Correa's reassembled leg and blinked. Instead, they've chosen to bring in equally damaged, if more temporary, players in Mitch Haniger and Michael Conforto. They've committed to the bit of resuscitating pitching careers, this time with Sean Manaea and Taylor Rogers. While the construction of the dynasty goes on in the background, the current roster still feels surprisingly divorced from it, as though they were two separate projects altogether.

In a league where teams are either good or bad, but always with driven, wearying purpose, San Francisco has chosen to be neither, seeking only to provide that rare, golden opportunity for meaningless entertainment. If the 2023 Giants are good, and they have the upside to squeak their way into qualifying for it, it'll feel, as it always has, like house money. It's the best kind of money there is.

The other truth, perhaps not a kind one, about modern media concerns the growing power of hype. People spend more time reflecting on stories, through their fandom and through external sources of consumption, than they do actually watching the stories. In this way, baseball is actually the frontrunner of the phenomenon; after all, it's why you're reading this book. It's not that this level of analysis is evil in any way, but Adams' SEP field still exists, and there's still that eternal strain of enjoying the spontaneity of a thing and the desire to understand and thus destroy it. In baseball, the latter has set the former to rout, compelling us to understand every trend and explain every joke.

We'd ruin the 2021 Giants, too, if we could, but luckily they're now beyond our reach. ■

—Patrick Dubuque is an editor of Baseball Prospectus.

HITTERS

Aeverson Arteaga SS

Born: 03/16/03 Age: 20 Bats: R Throws: R Height: 6'1" Weight: 170 lb. Origin: International Free Agent, 2019

YEAR	TEAM	LVL	AGE	PA	R	2B	3B	HR	RBI	BB	K	SB	CS	Whiff%	AVG/OBP/SLG	DRC+	BABIP	BRR	DRP	WARP
2021	GNTO	ROK	18	226	42	12	1	9	43	23	69	8	0		.294/.367/.503		.398			
2022	SJ	A	19	565	87	35	2	14	84	49	155	11	6		.270/.345/.431	91	.362	-1.3	SS(118): 4.2	1.4
2023 non-DC	*SF*	*MLB*	*20*	*251*	*19*	*11*	*1*	*3*	*21*	*14*	*83*	*2*	*1*	*35.2%*	*.210/.262/.315*	*55*	*.308*	*0.4*	*3B 0, SS 0*	*-0.7*

Comparables: Andrew Velazquez (89), Cole Tucker (78), Juremi Profar (72)

If you've never understood the baseball cliche of "slick infielder," watch Arteaga, who flows like water across the diamond, subsuming baseballs into his current before channeling them with his powerful arm to his fellow defenders. Eat your heart out, Marvel Studios. As for the bat, Arteaga held up well in his first full season of stateside ball, but had a tendency to hunt mistakes like Thanos searching out the Infinity Stones. Who doesn't love a nice shiny hanging slider? As he moves up and faces better pitching, though, a refinement in approach will be necessary: No need to woo Lady Dinger when Lady Double will do.

Joey Bart C

Born: 12/15/96 Age: 26 Bats: R Throws: R Height: 6'2" Weight: 238 lb. Origin: Round 1, 2018 Draft (#2 overall)

YEAR	TEAM	LVL	AGE	PA	R	2B	3B	HR	RBI	BB	K	SB	CS	Whiff%	AVG/OBP/SLG	DRC+	BABIP	BRR	DRP	WARP
2020	SF	MLB	23	111	15	5	2	0	7	3	41	0	0	34.5%	.233/.288/.320	62	.387	-0.1	C(32): 2.6	0.1
2021	SAC	AAA	24	279	37	15	0	10	46	21	82	0	0		.294/.358/.472	92	.398	-1.5	C(63): 8.8	1.4
2021	SF	MLB	24	6	1	0	0	0	1	0	2	0	0	33.3%	.333/.333/.333	96	.500	0.1	C(1): -0.1	0.0
2022	SAC	AAA	25	31	5	0	0	1	4	2	6	0	0	22.6%	.286/.355/.393	104	.333	-0.3	C(7): -0.3	0.1
2022	SF	MLB	25	291	34	6	0	11	25	26	112	2	1	38.2%	.215/.296/.364	71	.326	1.0	C(93): -2.6	-0.1
2023 DC	*SF*	*MLB*	*26*	*369*	*38*	*13*	*1*	*12*	*37*	*26*	*132*	*1*	*1*	*35.4%*	*.224/.294/.380*	*83*	*.331*	*1.1*	*C 1*	*0.8*

Comparables: Jarrod Saltalamacchia (60), Victor Caratini (59), Mike Fitzgerald (58)

YEAR	TEAM	P. COUNT	FRM RUNS	BLK RUNS	THRW RUNS	TOT RUNS
2020	SF	4088	2.0	0.0	0.5	2.6
2021	SAC	9190	2.5	0.0	2.5	5.1
2021	SF	140	0.0	0.0	0.0	0.0
2022	SAC	1047	-0.5	0.0	0.4	-0.1
2022	SF	11566	-2.8	-0.2	0.3	-2.6
2023	*SF*	*14430*	*1.3*	*0.0*	*-0.3*	*1.0*

That rookie backstop in Baltimore is really messing with people's conceptions of what a young top catching prospect's trajectory looks like. Often, it looks a lot more like Bart's, or Luis Campusano's, or Cal Raleigh's, or Sam Huff's: fits and starts, before ascending to a full-time role. And that's assuming consistent health for the most physically punishing role in baseball.

After being recalled from Triple-A in July, El Barto enacted a late-season swing change, lowering his hands while standing more upright, that helped him be shorter to the ball and finally unlock that big righty power; he slugged .517 in August. But he'll have to prove those changes are here to stay, which means first he'll have to earn the starting job. There's also the issue of his defense: Bart is often a one-knee-down catcher, which is great for catching pitchers like the sinker-heavy Logan Webb, but that setup can cost players agility behind the plate, as reflected in his FRAA. He's also not a great pitch framer, although the utility of that skill may be going the way of rotary phones, and his strong arm is one that will play even in the robo-ump era. Viva El Barto.

Vaun Brown OF

Born: 06/23/98 Age: 25 Bats: R Throws: R Height: 6'1" Weight: 215 lb. Origin: Round 10, 2021 Draft (#296 overall)

YEAR	TEAM	LVL	AGE	PA	R	2B	3B	HR	RBI	BB	K	SB	CS	Whiff%	AVG/OBP/SLG	DRC+	BABIP	BRR	DRP	WARP
2021	GNTO	ROK	23	98	24	7	4	2	14	7	29	8	1		.354/.480/.620		.542			
2022	SJ	A	24	262	50	14	5	14	41	25	67	23	3		.346/.427/.636	116	.439	0.6	LF(35): 1.1, CF(11): 1.4, RF(3): -0.3	1.4
2022	EUG	A+	24	194	50	10	2	9	34	22	52	21	3		.350/.454/.611	115	.460	4.5	RF(25): 0.1, LF(8): -0.3, CF(3): -0.2	1.6
2023 non-DC	*SF*	*MLB*	*25*	*251*	*25*	*10*	*2*	*6*	*28*	*17*	*80*	*12*	*4*	*35.0%*	*.242/.312/.404*	*95*	*.345*	*3.8*	*LF 0, CF 0*	*0.8*

Comparables: Mitch Haniger (58), Jarrod Dyson (55), Terry Evans (54)

It's odd that the Giants, usually super-aggressive with their prospects, kept the 24-year-old at San Jose for so long to beat up on hapless Cal League pitching—but then, everyone is still learning about what the tooled-up, jacked-up outfielder can do on the field. A late bloomer who hit no home runs in high school and had to fight for playing time at D-II Florida Southeastern, Brown thundered all the way up to Double-A despite what scouts see as a grooved swing that might leave him vulnerable to pitches at the top of the zone. That could be a disastrous trait with the premium velocity of Double-A pitching, but at least now the caveat "old for the level" can be shed in evaluating his performance, even if the tradeoff is slightly less swoony numbers.

Michael Conforto RF

Born: 03/01/93 Age: 30 Bats: L Throws: R Height: 6'1" Weight: 215 lb. Origin: Round 1, 2014 Draft (#10 overall)

YEAR	TEAM	LVL	AGE	PA	R	2B	3B	HR	RBI	BB	K	SB	CS	Whiff%	AVG/OBP/SLG	DRC+	BABIP	BRR	DRP	WARP
2020	NYM	MLB	27	233	40	12	0	9	31	24	57	3	3	26.0%	.322/.412/.515	105	.412	0.2	RF(52): 5.8	1.5
2021	NYM	MLB	28	479	52	20	0	14	55	59	104	1	0	23.5%	.232/.344/.384	102	.276	0.0	RF(117): -3.2	1.2
2023 DC	*SF*	*MLB*	*30*	*376*	*42*	*16*	*1*	*12*	*42*	*42*	*75*	*0*	*4*	*23.5%*	*.249/.349/.421*	*119*	*.290*	*-11.8*	*RF 0, LF 0*	*0.3*

In last year's *Annual* we wrote that Conforto was taking a calculated risk by declining the Mets' qualifying offer. Sometimes, gambles don't work out: Conforto sat out the entire 2022 season after undergoing shoulder surgery last April. He's resurfaced as a San Francisco-bound consolation prize, signing a two-year, $36 million deal with the Giants shortly after their pact with Carlos Correa fell through. Now reportedly fully healthy, Conforto will look to resume his up-and-down career. The outfielder was excellent in 2017, 2019 and 2020 but pedestrian in 2018 and 2021, battling various injuries all the while. Of particular concern in his final season with the Mets were declining power and line-drive rates, though his plate discipline remained strong. Even at his worst, he gets on base at a high clip, plays solid outfield defense and spits out about 2 WARP, and he retains the upside to be about twice that valuable. Should he reach at least 350 PA, he'll earn an opt-out clause after the 2023 season, which means his Giants career is almost sure to be either brief or disappointing.

Brandon Crawford SS

Born: 01/21/87 Age: 36 Bats: L Throws: R Height: 6'1" Weight: 223 lb. Origin: Round 4, 2008 Draft (#117 overall)

YEAR	TEAM	LVL	AGE	PA	R	2B	3B	HR	RBI	BB	K	SB	CS	Whiff%	AVG/OBP/SLG	DRC+	BABIP	BRR	DRP	WARP
2020	SF	MLB	33	193	26	12	0	8	28	15	47	1	2	31.6%	.256/.326/.465	94	.303	0.1	SS(53): 0.2	0.4
2021	SF	MLB	34	549	79	30	3	24	90	56	105	11	3	29.3%	.298/.373/.522	122	.334	-2.1	SS(135): 3	3.6
2022	SF	MLB	35	458	50	15	2	9	52	39	98	1	1	31.9%	.231/.308/.344	87	.280	-1.2	SS(116): -4	0.2
2023 DC	*SF*	*MLB*	*36*	*530*	*51*	*23*	*2*	*12*	*52*	*47*	*120*	*5*	*1*	*31.1%*	*.242/.320/.376*	*95*	*.301*	*2.3*	*SS 3*	*1.7*

Comparables: Don Kessinger (67), Dave Bancroft (66), Carlos Guillen (63)

The hot-cold empathy gap is a cognitive bias wherein a person in a "hot" state, driven by visceral feeling, makes decisions their "coolheaded" counterpart would never agree to—like Jekyll and Hyde, but if the serum was hunger or lust or one's franchise shortstop posting a career-high DRC+ in his age-34 season. This delirium caused the normally sangfroid Farhan Zaidi to re-up Crawford's chokehold on the shortstop position in San Francisco for another two years, a hot-state decision rewarded by an ice-cold performance at the plate, with Crawford posting career-lows in every offensive category. More troublingly, his normally sure-handed defense took a hit as well, grading poorly in several metrics. Extending Crawford bought the Giants some time to figure out if Marco Luciano is the shortstop or third baseman of the future, but a year of that has already elapsed; meanwhile, the empathy gap from fans grows larger.

J.D. Davis DH

Born: 04/27/93 Age: 30 Bats: R Throws: R Height: 6'3" Weight: 218 lb. Origin: Round 3, 2014 Draft (#75 overall)

YEAR	TEAM	LVL	AGE	PA	R	2B	3B	HR	RBI	BB	K	SB	CS	Whiff%	AVG/OBP/SLG	DRC+	BABIP	BRR	DRP	WARP
2020	NYM	MLB	27	229	26	9	0	6	19	31	56	0	0	29.3%	.247/.371/.389	107	.318	-1.4	3B(34): -0.2, LF(8): -0.2	0.6
2021	SYR	AAA	28	49	8	4	0	4	7	10	14	0	0		.316/.469/.737	112	.400	0.3	3B(10): -0.2, 1B(3): 0.1	0.2
2021	NYM	MLB	28	211	18	12	0	5	23	24	68	1	0	41.0%	.285/.384/.436	85	.426	-2.1	3B(50): -1.6	0.0
2022	NYM	MLB	29	207	26	8	1	4	21	20	66	1	1	37.2%	.238/.324/.359	83	.345	-0.5	3B(12): -0.3, 1B(4): -0.1	0.0
2022	SF	MLB	29	158	20	8	0	8	14	19	56	0	0	37.8%	.263/.361/.496	95	.384	-0.9	3B(18): -0.2, 1B(14): -0.1	0.1
2023 DC	*SF*	*MLB*	*30*	*434*	*49*	*19*	*1*	*16*	*50*	*47*	*135*	*1*	*0*	*36.8%*	*.245/.341/.431*	*115*	*.338*	*-0.1*	*3B -1, 1B 0*	*1.4*

Comparables: Chris Taylor (59), Chris Johnson (57), Craig Monroe (56)

The king of wanderlust, Davis enjoyed his best stretch of play after being flipped to the Giants in the Darin Ruf deal since...2019, when he was first dealt to the Mets from the Astros. However comfortable the Elk Grove native might have been on his home turf, with friends and family in regular attendance, he also credited his improvements in The Bay to a path to regular playing time. That path widened when the Giants neglected to pick up Evan Longoria's option, indicating Davis should have the opportunity to share hot corner duties with David Villar or Casey Schmitt. In order to secure the lion's share there with the plate discipline-conscious Giants, he'll need to mitigate a strikeout rate that has steadily crept upward over the past two seasons while continuing to show he can hit lefties and righties equally well, and move from "liability" defense at third to "passable." Take a cue from Belle and Sebastian, J.D., and let your wandering days be over.

Isan Díaz IF

Born: 05/27/96 Age: 27 Bats: L Throws: R Height: 5'11" Weight: 201 lb. Origin: Round 2, 2014 Draft (#70 overall)

YEAR	TEAM	LVL	AGE	PA	R	2B	3B	HR	RBI	BB	K	SB	CS	Whiff%	AVG/OBP/SLG	DRC+	BABIP	BRR	DRP	WARP
2020	MIA	MLB	24	22	3	0	0	0	1	0	7	0	0	32.4%	.182/.182/.182	74	.267	0.0	2B(7): 0.2	0.0
2021	JAX	AAA	25	116	16	8	1	5	15	11	30	0	2		.243/.328/.485	108	.294	-2.0	3B(20): 2.2, 2B(8): -1.3	0.4
2021	MIA	MLB	25	278	25	9	0	4	17	34	73	1	1	31.8%	.193/.293/.282	71	.256	-1.2	3B(37): 0.7, 2B(35): 0	-0.1
2022	SAC	AAA	26	332	60	12	2	23	61	43	82	7	2	32.6%	.275/.377/.574	120	.306	1.0	2B(57): -1.7, SS(14): -0.1, 3B(10): -1.7	0.7
2023 DC	*SF*	*MLB*	*27*	*63*	*6*	*2*	*0*	*2*	*6*	*6*	*18*	*0*	*0*	*32.1%*	*.218/.306/.391*	*93*	*.289*	*0.3*	*2B 0, SS 0*	*0.2*

Comparables: Luis Valbuena (57), Josh Bell (55), Cristhian Adames (48)

The last piece of the Christian Yelich trade officially left the Marlins organization when the Fish swapped him to the Giants for cash or a PTBNL early in the 2022 season; the Giants liked what they saw so much (like 23 homers for Sacramento) they added him to their 40-man roster even after the injury-prone Díaz suffered a season-ending oblique injury. Headed into his age-27 season, Díaz will get another chance to rediscover his prospect promise, this time without the pressure of having been traded for a franchise player.

Thairo Estrada MI

Born: 02/22/96 Age: 27 Bats: R Throws: R Height: 5'10" Weight: 185 lb. Origin: International Free Agent, 2012

YEAR	TEAM	LVL	AGE	PA	R	2B	3B	HR	RBI	BB	K	SB	CS	Whiff%	AVG/OBP/SLG	DRC+	BABIP	BRR	DRP	WARP
2020	NYY	MLB	24	52	8	0	0	1	3	1	19	1	0	29.4%	.167/.231/.229	76	.250	0.3	2B(20): -0.6, 3B(6): 0	0.0
2021	SAC	AAA	25	233	37	14	1	9	40	20	35	6	4		.333/.399/.538	123	.367	-1.0	SS(30): -6.0, 2B(16): 2.0, 3B(2): 0.1	1.0
2021	SF	MLB	25	132	19	4	0	7	22	9	23	1	0	19.0%	.273/.333/.479	114	.286	1.2	SS(19): -0.3, 2B(16): -0.3, 3B(4): 0	0.8
2022	SF	MLB	26	541	71	23	2	14	62	33	89	21	6	20.0%	.260/.322/.402	112	.290	1.2	2B(102): -1.2, SS(37): 0.7, LF(18): -0.1	2.6
2023 DC	*SF*	*MLB*	*27*	*455*	*44*	*18*	*2*	*9*	*42*	*28*	*75*	*15*	*4*	*20.2%*	*.254/.316/.377*	*97*	*.291*	*2.8*	*2B 0, SS 0*	*1.5*

Comparables: Howie Kendrick (64), Felix Millan (59), Bill Mazeroski (58)

Mauricio Dubón probably owes Estrada a cut of his World Series winnings, as Estrada's play rendered Dubón superfluous on San Francisco's roster. Mid-season, the Giants flipped Dubón to the eventual WS champs in exchange for catcher Michael Papierski, who they then DFA'd a month later. What baseball fan's heart doesn't quicken over a good old roster-crunch trade?

But while Dubón might have the ring, Estrada has the heart of Giants fans, who appreciate his knack for clutch hits (an OPS of 1.136 in "late and close" games). Estrada was even a Silver Slugger finalist in the inaugural year of including utility players in the award. Giants fans might like shiny things, but they'll marry Thairo with paper rings, especially if he keeps turning up in clutch moments. In chasing a real ring, however, Giants brass may need to look for a utility infielder who can handle the "fielder" part of the job description.

Wilmer Flores IF

Born: 08/06/91 Age: 31 Bats: R Throws: R Height: 6'2" Weight: 213 lb. Origin: International Free Agent, 2007

YEAR	TEAM	LVL	AGE	PA	R	2B	3B	HR	RBI	BB	K	SB	CS	Whiff%	AVG/OBP/SLG	DRC+	BABIP	BRR	DRP	WARP
2020	SF	MLB	28	213	30	11	1	12	32	13	36	1	0	17.8%	.268/.315/.515	118	.272	-1.2	1B(14): 1.6, 2B(14): 0.1, 3B(3): -0.2	1.1
2021	SF	MLB	29	436	57	16	1	18	53	41	56	1	0	16.6%	.262/.335/.447	122	.264	-2.2	3B(58): -0.5, 1B(34): -0.6, 2B(30): 0.3	2.3
2022	SF	MLB	30	602	72	28	1	19	71	59	103	0	0	18.8%	.229/.316/.394	111	.246	-1.0	2B(61): 2, 1B(45): -0.5, 3B(34): 1.2	2.6
2023 DC	*SF*	*MLB*	*31*	*545*	*58*	*23*	*1*	*18*	*59*	*49*	*85*	*0*	*0*	*18.2%*	*.243/.321/.406*	*104*	*.261*	*-1.7*	*3B 0, 2B 0*	*1.2*

Comparables: Pie Traynor (65), Willie Jones (65), Brooks Robinson (64)

Every family has that one pot, the one that's been in the family for so long you're not exactly sure which relative it belonged to, only that it predates your existence on this planet and will live on long after you have shuffled off this mortal coil. If that pot was a baseball player, it would be Flores: around forever with the attendant dings of years of service; reliable if unspectacular, both at the plate and in the field. Flores maintained the offensive improvements he made in 2021—erasing handedness splits, walking more—and also hit a career-high 19 homers, second-most on the team. The family pot isn't the nicest. It's scuffed in places and made out of materials that are almost certainly carcinogenic, by a company that no longer exists if it ever did at all—but, like Flores, you can't imagine being without it.

Luis González OF Born: 09/10/95 Age: 27 Bats: L Throws: L Height: 6'1" Weight: 185 lb. Origin: Round 3, 2017 Draft (#87 overall)

YEAR	TEAM	LVL	AGE	PA	R	2B	3B	HR	RBI	BB	K	SB	CS	Whiff%	AVG/OBP/SLG	DRC+	BABIP	BRR	DRP	WARP
2020	CHW	MLB	24	2	1	0	0	0	0	0	1	0	0	100.0%	.000/.500/.000	76		0.1	LF(1): 0, CF(1): -0.2	0.0
2021	CLT	AAA	25	163	24	4	0	7	20	22	41	9	2		.241/.352/.423	110	.289	0.7	CF(26): -3.6, RF(5): -1.1, LF(4): -0.6	0.3
2021	CHW	MLB	25	11	2	2	0	0	0	3	2	0	0	25.0%	.250/.455/.500	93	.333	-0.2	RF(3): 1.3, LF(2): 0.1	0.1
2022	SAC	AAA	26	92	15	1	0	6	13	15	22	4	2	23.3%	.289/.402/.539	118	.327	0.2	CF(7): 0.5, RF(5): -0.2, LF(3): 0.0	0.5
2022	SF	MLB	26	350	31	17	2	4	36	30	75	10	2	23.3%	.254/.323/.360	85	.316	1.8	RF(69): 1.4, LF(52): 2, CF(6): -0.3	1.0
2023 DC	*SF*	*MLB*	*27*	*248*	*26*	*10*	*1*	*5*	*24*	*22*	*53*	*8*	*2*	*23.5%*	*.240/.317/.379*	*94*	*.292*	*4.6*	*RF -1, CF 0*	*0.8*

Comparables: Jeremy Reed (52), Randy Winn (51), Tyler Naquin (50)

It's no surprise González led the 2022 Giants in pitching appearances by position players, as he's blessed with an arm that looks like it makes a sound ("pew pew!") when he fires the ball in from the outfield. He's also one of just a few Giants semi-regulars to provide actual defensive value in 2022. As a righty-mashing platoon bat, he currently projects as a fine fourth outfielder who gets love on social media for his defense, occasional clutch homers, and rare instances of doing yeoman's work on the mound; relying on him for more diminishes the return on the gifts he does bring.

Mitch Haniger RF Born: 12/23/90 Age: 32 Bats: R Throws: R Height: 6'2" Weight: 214 lb. Origin: Round 1, 2012 Draft (#38 overall)

YEAR	TEAM	LVL	AGE	PA	R	2B	3B	HR	RBI	BB	K	SB	CS	Whiff%	AVG/OBP/SLG	DRC+	BABIP	BRR	DRP	WARP
2021	SEA	MLB	30	691	110	23	2	39	100	54	169	1	0	29.8%	.253/.318/.485	117	.281	-1.9	RF(123): -2.8	2.9
2022	TAC	AAA	31	33	5	0	0	2	6	10	3	0	0	17.6%	.238/.515/.524	125	.188	0.5	RF(4): 0.1	0.3
2022	SEA	MLB	31	247	31	8	0	11	34	20	65	0	0	29.6%	.246/.308/.429	100	.293	0.5	RF(47): -2.8	0.5
2023 DC	*SF*	*MLB*	*32*	*428*	*51*	*16*	*1*	*17*	*50*	*38*	*108*	*0*	*0*	*28.5%*	*.248/.325/.436*	*112*	*.301*	*0.4*	*RF 0*	*1.4*

Comparables: Jermaine Dye (73), Brian Jordan (71), Ken Singleton (69)

Time's arrow doesn't freeze in mid-air for injury rehabilitation, and it moved ineluctably forward through Haniger's lost age-28 and age-29 seasons (though the pandemic would have truncated the latter, regardless). If you're reading this, you likely know of Haniger's absolutely excruciating medical woes, the severity of which can be summarized in "ruptured testicle eventually leads to major back and core surgeries (yes, plural)." Haniger's early career showcased his do-it-all abilities as an athletic power and average (with a bit of speed) right fielder, encapsulated in a 2018 when he was worth nearly four wins. 2021 saw a shift to a power-forward profile, followed by a 2022 dominated by a high-ankle sprain that cost him two-thirds of the season. The speed and average have diminished, leaving his plus power, although if anyone can claw back some altitude on the aging curve, it might be the relentlessly hard-working outfielder. Bottom line: Haniger and the Giants—his new, hometown team—will welcome an extended period of robust health to call back the skills and vibe that made him such a fan and clubhouse favorite in Seattle.

★ ★ ★ *2023 Top 101 Prospect* **#18** ★ ★ ★

Marco Luciano SS Born: 09/10/01 Age: 21 Bats: R Throws: R Height: 6'2" Weight: 178 lb. Origin: International Free Agent, 2018

YEAR	TEAM	LVL	AGE	PA	R	2B	3B	HR	RBI	BB	K	SB	CS	Whiff%	AVG/OBP/SLG	DRC+	BABIP	BRR	DRP	WARP
2021	SCO	WIN	19	87	7	0	0	3	13	11	28	0	1		.253/.356/.373		.364			
2021	SJ	A	19	308	52	14	3	18	57	38	68	5	5		.278/.373/.556	129	.309	-0.9	SS(60): -0.1	1.9
2021	EUG	A+	19	145	16	3	2	1	14	10	54	1	0		.217/.283/.295	69	.351	-0.1	SS(29): -1.2	-0.3
2022	GNTB	ROK	20	27	6	2	0	1	6	4	7	0	0		.318/.444/.545		.429			
2022	EUG	A+	20	230	27	10	0	10	30	22	51	0	0		.263/.339/.459	112	.303	-0.1	SS(51): 2.1	1.3
2023 non-DC	*SF*	*MLB*	*21*	*251*	*23*	*9*	*1*	*6*	*26*	*18*	*70*	*3*	*1*	*30.5%*	*.222/.284/.361*	*77*	*.291*	*0.2*	*SS 0*	*0.0*

Comparables: Cole Tucker (72), Richard Urena (69), Jonathan Araúz (68)

After a Hobbes-ian introduction to High-A in 2021 (nasty, brutish, short), the Giants sent Luciano to repeat the level in 2022, only to see him miss three months of the season with a lower back strain, possibly caused by toting around all the expectations that have so far been placed on the organization's top prospect. Upon his return, Luciano mostly picked up where he'd left off in the Great Northwest, showcasing improved plate discipline that allows him to get to his immense power, and recording his first Double-A hit in the Eastern League playoffs. Eager to get him more at-bats, the Giants signed off on letting Luciano play for the Estrellas Orientales in LIDOM this year, allowing him to face more seasoned competition in the DR, but he's been slowed by injury there, too. Fans of nominative determinism will note that the root luc- means "light." Prospect evaluators remain confident that even with the spotty year, Luciano will be shining at Oracle Park before long.

Luis Matos CF Born: 01/28/02 Age: 21 Bats: R Throws: R Height: 5'11" Weight: 160 lb. Origin: International Free Agent, 2018

YEAR	TEAM	LVL	AGE	PA	R	2B	3B	HR	RBI	BB	K	SB	CS	Whiff%	AVG/OBP/SLG	DRC+	BABIP	BRR	DRP	WARP
2021	SJ	A	19	491	84	35	1	15	86	28	61	21	5		.313/.358/.494	129	.332	1.2	CF(86): -4.7, RF(14): -2.9, LF(4): 0.0	3.0
2022	EUG	A+	20	407	55	14	1	11	43	27	65	11	3		.211/.275/.344	98	.226	0.5	CF(74): 3.1, RF(9): -0.1	1.3
2023 non-DC	*SF*	*MLB*	*21*	*251*	*21*	*10*	*1*	*4*	*23*	*11*	*48*	*6*	*2*	*26.0%*	*.225/.269/.342*	*69*	*.265*	*2.0*	*CF 0, RF 0*	*-0.1*

Comparables: Angel Morales (69), John Drennen (69), Teodoro Martinez (68)

Matos has a beautifully balanced swing modeled after his idol, Ronald Acuña Jr., that seems to attract baseballs like a magnet. The Giants want him to be more selective, though, and attack pitches he can damage. That didn't happen this season; like so many other prospects used to playing in warmer climes, Matos struggled in the offense-dampening Northwest League. Back in the familiar environs of the desert, he stuck the landing on his season with a star turn in the AFL, winning Defensive Player of the Year and showing what kind of contact he can make when the sun shines.

Grant McCray CF Born: 12/07/00 Age: 22 Bats: L Throws: R Height: 6'2" Weight: 190 lb. Origin: Round 3, 2019 Draft (#87 overall)

YEAR	TEAM	LVL	AGE	PA	R	2B	3B	HR	RBI	BB	K	SB	CS	Whiff%	AVG/OBP/SLG	DRC+	BABIP	BRR	DRP	WARP
2021	GNTO	ROK	20	65	16	3	1	1	6	9	20	3	1		.309/.400/.455		.457			
2021	SJ	A	20	88	8	2	2	2	12	6	30	4	1		.250/.299/.400	76	.367	-0.7	CF(18): 1.8, LF(6): 0.2	0.2
2022	SJ	A	21	507	92	21	9	21	69	58	148	35	10		.291/.383/.525	100	.391	0.4	CF(91): -0.6, RF(2): 0.2	1.4
2022	EUG	A+	21	62	12	2	0	2	10	9	22	8	0		.269/.387/.423	95	.429	1.2	CF(13): -1.0	0.1
2023 non-DC	*SF*	*MLB*	*22*	*251*	*22*	*9*	*3*	*5*	*24*	*18*	*93*	*11*	*4*	*38.9%*	*.214/.278/.347*	*68*	*.337*	*2.5*	*CF 0, RF 0*	*0.0*

Comparables: Luis Liberato (69), Steven Moya (67), Starling Marte (67)

McCray's middle name is Snow, and it might be easier to karaoke the 1993 hit "Informer" than to understand his Byzantine swing mechanics. When he makes contact, the ball goes far, but striking out a third of the time against bad Cal League pitching is not rock steady. Above-average defense in center with plus speed on the bases (he was the first ever San Jose Giant to post a 20/20 season) give him a safe floor as a fourth outfielder even if the bat doesn't go licky boom boom now.

Yermín Mercedes DH/1B Born: 02/14/93 Age: 30 Bats: R Throws: R Height: 5'11" Weight: 245 lb. Origin: International Free Agent, 2011

YEAR	TEAM	LVL	AGE	PA	R	2B	3B	HR	RBI	BB	K	SB	CS	Whiff%	AVG/OBP/SLG	DRC+	BABIP	BRR	DRP	WARP
2020	LIC	WIN	27	95	9	2	0	2	16	7	9	0	1		.276/.326/.368		.286			
2020	CHW	MLB	27	1	0	0	0	0	0	0	0	0	0	0.0%	.000/.000/.000	94				0.0
2021	LIC	WIN	28	68	3	2	0	1	7	3	6	0	0		.190/.221/.270		.190			
2021	CLT	AAA	28	239	32	7	1	11	29	11	39	3	0		.275/.318/.464	106	.287	-1.0	1B(19): -3.5, C(18): -1.1, 3B(1): -0.0	0.3
2021	CHW	MLB	28	262	26	9	1	7	37	20	46	0	1	22.0%	.271/.328/.404	105	.309	-0.9	C(2): 0	0.7
2022	SAC	AAA	29	158	17	5	0	8	19	13	34	2	0	30.2%	.268/.329/.472	105	.294	-1.6	1B(21): -0.1, C(2): -0.0, LF(2): -0.2	0.4
2022	CLT	AAA	29	109	14	5	0	4	13	20	24	5	1	36.8%	.230/.376/.425	108	.267	0.2	1B(9): 1.3	0.3
2022	SF	MLB	29	83	9	5	0	1	8	9	17	0	0	22.9%	.233/.325/.342	106	.291	-0.6	LF(8): -0.2, 1B(4): 0	0.2
2023 DC	*FA*	*MLB*	*30*	*148*	*16*	*5*	*0*	*5*	*17*	*12*	*31*	*1*	*1*	*26.7%*	*.245/.314/.408*	*101*	*.282*	*0.4*	*1B 0, LF 0*	*0.6*

Comparables: Darin Ruf (55), Josh Satin (49), Luke Voit (49)

It's hard not to feel bad for Mercedes, whose big-league path in 2021 was derailed partly by a septuagenarian blinkered into obsolescence by the Unwritten Rules, and partly by his own inability to cope with the sudden, intense pressure of becoming an overnight MLB sensation. It was the baseball player version of the bends. But things didn't get much better with the Giants, who declined to bring back the defensively-limited slugger after a brief tenure. Mercedes will audition for a future big-league job this off-season playing with the Tigres del Licey, which will hopefully provide adequate decompression before he surfaces in MLB's waters again.

Joc Pederson LF Born: 04/21/92 Age: 31 Bats: L Throws: L Height: 6'1" Weight: 220 lb. Origin: Round 11, 2010 Draft (#352 overall)

YEAR	TEAM	LVL	AGE	PA	R	2B	3B	HR	RBI	BB	K	SB	CS	Whiff%	AVG/OBP/SLG	DRC+	BABIP	BRR	DRP	WARP
2020	LAD	MLB	28	138	21	4	0	7	16	11	34	1	0	31.0%	.190/.285/.397	99	.200	-1.0	LF(23): -0.9, RF(8): 1.5	0.3
2021	ATL	MLB	29	194	20	8	1	7	22	17	43	0	0	25.7%	.249/.325/.428	97	.290	-1.9	RF(36): 0.1, CF(24): -0.8	0.4
2021	CHC	MLB	29	287	35	11	2	11	39	22	74	2	3	26.7%	.230/.300/.418	85	.274	0.5	LF(66): -2.2, RF(3): -0.4, CF(2): 0	0.3
2022	SF	MLB	30	433	57	19	3	23	70	42	100	3	2	24.6%	.274/.353/.521	124	.310	-1.7	LF(102): -3.1, RF(18): 0.1	2.2
2023 DC	*SF*	*MLB*	*31*	*592*	*77*	*24*	*3*	*30*	*82*	*54*	*125*	*3*	*0*	*24.6%*	*.248/.329/.481*	*127*	*.269*	*3.2*	*LF -4*	*3.1*

Comparables: Luis Gonzalez (63), Lou Brock (63), Bob Skinner (62)

An LMFAO song that gained sentience, Pederson brings the party wherever he goes, coast to coast, black tie optional but pearls required. Party Joc secured a big payday when he smartly took his hometown Giants up on their qualifying offer to be around for a good time, if not a long time. The new shift restrictions should help the pull-happy lefty, whose bat nonetheless makes the bass drop in Oracle Park: his barrel rate in 2022 ranked up among the league's best sluggers as he led the team in shots! shots! shots! (Everybody...else was hitting singles). Unfortunately there's no new rule coming where plodding corner outfielders are allowed to ride hoverboards and hold cartoonishly oversized butterfly nets, so he'll need to be in a DH-dominant role or paired with a truly elite center fielder in order to maintain the value he brings at the plate. If $20M seems like a hefty price to pay for this kind of player, congratulations on not having had to watch the Giants try to create offense this past season.

Heliot Ramos OF Born: 09/07/99 Age: 23 Bats: R Throws: R Height: 6'1" Weight: 188 lb. Origin: Round 1, 2017 Draft (#19 overall)

YEAR	TEAM	LVL	AGE	PA	R	2B	3B	HR	RBI	BB	K	SB	CS	Whiff%	AVG/OBP/SLG	DRC+	BABIP	BRR	DRP	WARP
2021	RIC	AA	21	266	36	14	1	10	26	27	73	7	2		.237/.323/.432	104	.301	0.0	CF(58): -3.2	0.7
2021	SAC	AAA	21	229	30	11	2	4	30	15	65	8	2		.272/.323/.399	78	.375	2.9	CF(32): -2.4, RF(17): 1.2	0.3
2022	SAC	AAA	22	475	61	17	1	11	45	41	112	6	6	30.5%	.227/.305/.349	76	.283	0.2	CF(49): -4.5, RF(33): -2.6, LF(21): 1.6	-0.5
2022	SF	MLB	22	22	4	0	0	0	0	2	6	0	0	41.5%	.100/.182/.100	95	.143	0.2	RF(6): -0.2, LF(3): -0.3	0.0
2023 DC	*SF*	*MLB*	*23*	*61*	*5*	*2*	*0*	*1*	*5*	*4*	*18*	*1*	*0*	*32.8%*	*.221/.284/.340*	*72*	*.307*	*0.2*	*RF 0, LF 0*	*-0.1*

Comparables: Wil Myers (44), Carlos Tocci (42), Domingo Santana (40)

"There's always someone younger and hungrier coming down the stairs after you." Cristal Connors (Gina Gershon) is referring to Vegas showgirls in the eponymous 1995 film, but it's true for prospect rankings, as well. Every year there's another class of players wanting to impress, and the brightest star in San Francisco's low-ceiling system has been eclipsed. Ramos lit up the hitter-friendly California League as a 19-year-old, but has never recaptured that starshine, which hasn't stopped the Giants from aggressively promoting him up through the system despite middling results against older competition. On the way, his body has made him more a corner outfielder than the center fielder he was projected to be, which puts more pressure on the bat. While he has plus power, the plate discipline improvements he made at Triple-A this year have to stick in order for him to get to it, and slugging just .350 in the hitter-friendly PCL isn't exactly encouraging. At the upper minors with a bevy of young and hungry players coming down the stairs behind him, Ramos is running thin on time to show that his name belongs in lights.

★ ★ ★ *2023 Top 101 Prospect* **#94** ★ ★ ★

Casey Schmitt 3B Born: 03/01/99 Age: 24 Bats: R Throws: R Height: 6'2" Weight: 215 lb. Origin: Round 2, 2020 Draft (#49 overall)

YEAR	TEAM	LVL	AGE	PA	R	2B	3B	HR	RBI	BB	K	SB	CS	Whiff%	AVG/OBP/SLG	DRC+	BABIP	BRR	DRP	WARP
2021	SJ	A	22	280	36	14	1	8	29	22	44	2	2		.247/.318/.406	110	.269	0.4	3B(50): 6.0	1.7
2022	EUG	A+	23	383	58	14	1	17	59	42	86	1	2		.273/.363/.474	127	.319	1.1	3B(50): -2.2, SS(40): -1.4	2.1
2022	RIC	AA	23	127	13	10	1	3	16	6	29	2	0		.342/.378/.517	92	.432	1.3	3B(29): -1.1	0.2
2023 DC	*SF*	*MLB*	*24*	*29*	*2*	*1*	*0*	*0*	*2*	*1*	*7*	*0*	*0*	*28.2%*	*.234/.291/.355*	*78*	*.300*	*0.1*	*3B 0*	*0.0*

Comparables: Chris Johnson (69), Danny Valencia (64), Michael Griffin (61)

Schmitt's Creek was more of a trickle in his 2021 pro debut. But, to put the numbers in context, he was coming off the COVID layoff year, and also played through a broken nose suffered in June when he was hit by a pitch, before another HBP ended his season early. Schmitt got his redemption arc this season, though, sailing through the minors with the ease of an Alexis Rose hair toss. He's now in line to provide consistent, above-average defense at third; in the box, he has a contact-oriented approach and sees the best success when he's driving the ball all over the field rather than chasing homers off inexperienced pitcher mistakes, as he was in the low minors. The Giants somewhat hastily promoted him to Triple-A to get him on the right coast, and while he'll need to keep showing that consistency before he takes the ride down I-80 for good, this is still a glow-up worthy of the Rose family.

Austin Slater CF Born: 12/13/92 Age: 30 Bats: R Throws: R Height: 6'1" Weight: 204 lb. Origin: Round 8, 2014 Draft (#238 overall)

YEAR	TEAM	LVL	AGE	PA	R	2B	3B	HR	RBI	BB	K	SB	CS	Whiff%	AVG/OBP/SLG	DRC+	BABIP	BRR	DRP	WARP
2020	SF	MLB	27	104	18	2	1	5	7	16	22	8	1	25.3%	.282/.408/.506	119	.328	0.9	RF(9): 0.7, LF(3): -0.1	0.7
2021	SF	MLB	28	306	39	12	1	12	32	28	84	15	2	30.2%	.241/.320/.423	101	.303	1.5	CF(77): -2.1, LF(37): -0.9, RF(24): -0.5	1.1
2022	SF	MLB	29	325	49	15	2	7	34	40	89	12	1	31.4%	.264/.366/.408	104	.361	2.4	CF(106): -1.1, LF(16): 0.1, RF(14): -0.3	1.4
2023 DC	*SF*	*MLB*	*30*	*250*	*29*	*10*	*1*	*5*	*20*	*28*	*69*	*9*	*2*	*30.8%*	*.239/.339/.379*	*103*	*.326*	*4.8*	*CF 0, LF 0*	*1.3*

Comparables: George Springer (53), Chris Taylor (52), Robbie Grossman (52)

If you're named like the popular jock antagonist in an 80s teen romcom you should swing the part, and Slater does, with big, aggressive right-handed hacks that would never clue in a new observer that he was once afflicted with the dreaded Stanford Swing. Unfortunately, even with a swing with more loft, he's still prone to hitting the ball on the ground, despite an above-average barrel rate. Perplexing, but change does take time. If the Giants upgrade their outfield and reduce Slater to a part-time role, they can take comfort in the fact that his OPS as a pinch-hitter (min. 100 PAs) is best in baseball history—yes, better than Literally Ted Williams. We'll take that bet down the ski slopes.

David Villar IF Born: 01/27/97 Age: 26 Bats: R Throws: R Height: 6'1" Weight: 215 lb. Origin: Round 11, 2018 Draft (#316 overall)

YEAR	TEAM	LVL	AGE	PA	R	2B	3B	HR	RBI	BB	K	SB	CS	Whiff%	AVG/OBP/SLG	DRC+	BABIP	BRR	DRP	WARP
2021	RIC	AA	24	446	70	29	0	20	58	46	112	5	1		.275/.374/.506	123	.340	1.5	3B(92): 1.1, 1B(13): 0.3	2.8
2022	SAC	AAA	25	366	67	19	1	27	82	55	93	1	1	31.1%	.275/.404/.617	130	.306	0.5	3B(51): 1.1, 1B(16): 1.6, 2B(15): -0.9	2.7
2022	SF	MLB	25	181	21	6	1	9	24	18	58	0	1	37.2%	.231/.331/.455	102	.300	-0.7	3B(27): 0.3, 1B(11): 1.5, 2B(6): 0.1	0.6
2023 DC	*SF*	*MLB*	*26*	*381*	*41*	*16*	*1*	*12*	*40*	*37*	*117*	*1*	*0*	*34.1%*	*.222/.317/.396*	*98*	*.301*	*0.4*	*3B 0, 2B 0*	*0.7*

Comparables: Travis Metcalf (67), Danny Valencia (65), J.D. Davis (62)

Villar has a track record of mashing in the minors, and although that didn't initially carry over during his big-league debut in place of the injured Evan Longoria, he returned from Triple-A in September and finished the season strong, hitting eight of his nine homers that month. Villar has gap-to-gap power that translated into a top-10 homer performance in the hitter-friendly PCL but is likely more doubles power in Oracle Park. The profile is perked up by his defensive flexibility, as he was one of five Giants position players to post a positive DRS mark in 2022, and one of three who played more than 200 innings. He could find regular playing time at third base if he could just lay off a ding-dang slider. Perhaps he could pretend it's a throw from his less-accurate Giants infield teammates.

LaMonte Wade Jr. RF Born: 01/01/94 Age: 29 Bats: L Throws: L Height: 6'1" Weight: 205 lb. Origin: Round 9, 2015 Draft (#260 overall)

YEAR	TEAM	LVL	AGE	PA	R	2B	3B	HR	RBI	BB	K	SB	CS	Whiff%	AVG/OBP/SLG	DRC+	BABIP	BRR	DRP	WARP
2020	MIN	MLB	26	44	3	3	0	0	1	4	9	1	1	15.4%	.231/.318/.308	94	.300	-0.1	1B(4): -0.1, CF(4): -0.2, LF(3): 0	0.0
2021	SAC	AAA	27	59	12	2	0	3	8	14	13	0	1		.244/.424/.489	118	.276	0.1	LF(5): 1.5, RF(5): -0.8, CF(3): -0.3	0.4
2021	SF	MLB	27	381	52	17	3	18	56	33	89	6	1	20.1%	.253/.326/.482	107	.289	0.0	RF(52): -2.4, LF(42): -2.7, 1B(31): -0.2	0.9
2022	SAC	AAA	28	58	11	4	0	2	11	10	6	0	0	20.5%	.250/.397/.477	112	.237	0.5	LF(6): -0.2, 1B(4): -0.2, RF(2): 0.1	0.2
2022	SF	MLB	28	251	29	7	1	8	26	26	51	1	0	18.2%	.207/.305/.359	99	.233	1.2	RF(33): -3.1, 1B(22): 1.3, LF(19): -0.2	0.6
2023 DC	*SF*	*MLB*	*29*	*430*	*51*	*16*	*2*	*12*	*40*	*45*	*78*	*4*	*1*	*18.9%*	*.232/.325/.387*	*101*	*.262*	*3.0*	*1B 0, LF 0*	*1.0*

Comparables: Abraham Almonte (59), Mike Baxter (48), Roger Bernadina (47)

Wade Jr. missed the opening half of the season with a knee injury, and when he returned, it was as a diminished version of the player who earned the moniker "Late Night LaMonte" in 2021 for his knack for late-inning clutch hits. He's still well above league-average at finding barrels, and his batted ball profile suggests that with regular playing time and an off-season to calm down his inflamed knee, he's a solid rebound candidate—maybe more than solid, once the shift is eliminated. "Clutch Hits at the 11th Hour" Guy is fun, but not really a sustainable gig; "Controls the Zone Well Enough to Earn Walks or Pitches to Hit" Guy has less snap as a nickname but much more staying power.

Donovan Walton IF Born: 05/25/94 Age: 29 Bats: L Throws: R Height: 5'10" Weight: 190 lb. Origin: Round 5, 2016 Draft (#147 overall)

YEAR	TEAM	LVL	AGE	PA	R	2B	3B	HR	RBI	BB	K	SB	CS	Whiff%	AVG/OBP/SLG	DRC+	BABIP	BRR	DRP	WARP
2020	SEA	MLB	26	14	0	1	0	0	3	1	5	0	1	42.9%	.154/.214/.231	77	.250	0.0	SS(4): 0.2, 2B(1): 0	0.0
2021	TAC	AAA	27	334	50	20	1	13	60	35	36	1	3		.304/.395/.519	123	.305	0.6	SS(46): 4.2, 2B(20): -2.1, LF(3): -0.5	2.3
2021	SEA	MLB	27	69	6	2	1	2	7	4	15	1	0	26.6%	.206/.254/.365	87	.239	-0.9	2B(14): -0.5, LF(5): -0.6, 3B(2): 0.1	-0.1
2022	TAC	AAA	28	57	10	4	2	1	5	6	6	2	1	13.7%	.294/.368/.510	108	.318	0.3	SS(7): 0.4, 2B(2): 0.4, 3B(1): -0.3	0.1
2022	SAC	AAA	28	88	10	6	0	1	7	12	13	3	0	20.9%	.225/.345/.352	101	.263	0.3	2B(7): -1.4, SS(7): 0.1, LF(4): -0.5	0.2
2022	SEA	MLB	28	0	1	0	0	0	0	0	0	0	0		.000/.000/.000				3B(1): -0.0	0.0
2022	SF	MLB	28	78	8	8	0	1	8	1	16	0	0	17.0%	.158/.179/.303	77	.186	0.0	2B(14): 0.4, SS(12): -1.3	-0.1
2023 non-DC	*SF*	*MLB*	*29*	*251*	*23*	*11*	*1*	*4*	*23*	*18*	*39*	*2*	*1*	*21.1%*	*.233/.302/.353*	*85*	*.265*	*-1.2*	*SS 0, 2B 0*	*0.1*

Comparables: Ryan Goins (60), JT Riddle (56), Eric Sogard (56)

With no disrespect intended to either party, Walton is what people thought Steven Kwan was going to be: a disciplined hitter with a preternatural ability to make contact, plus defense and a lunchpail work ethic rounding out the package. He remains a solid utility infield option but unfortunately hasn't yet found the success at the plate that Kwan enjoyed right out of the gates of his MLB career. However, he might have the best strike zone awareness in the organization, and the Giants love that for him (and for them). He was also one of precious few surehanded infield defenders for the 2022 Giants, which is why his pitchers love him.

Mike Yastrzemski OF Born: 08/23/90 Age: 32 Bats: L Throws: L Height: 5'10" Weight: 178 lb. Origin: Round 14, 2013 Draft (#429 overall)

YEAR	TEAM	LVL	AGE	PA	R	2B	3B	HR	RBI	BB	K	SB	CS	Whiff%	AVG/OBP/SLG	DRC+	BABIP	BRR	DRP	WARP
2020	SF	MLB	29	225	39	14	4	10	35	30	55	2	1	24.9%	.297/.400/.568	111	.370	-0.1	RF(31): 1.6, CF(24): -0.2, LF(8): -0.2	1.1
2021	SF	MLB	30	532	75	28	3	25	71	51	131	4	0	24.4%	.224/.311/.457	100	.254	2.3	RF(115): -2, CF(34): 0.1	1.8
2022	SF	MLB	31	558	73	31	2	17	57	61	141	5	1	22.9%	.214/.305/.392	93	.261	2.4	RF(104): 0.7, CF(93): -0.1	1.7
2023 DC	*SF*	*MLB*	*32*	*484*	*56*	*24*	*4*	*16*	*52*	*50*	*108*	*4*	*1*	*22.9%*	*.230/.319/.421*	*105*	*.272*	*3.6*	*CF 5, RF 2*	*2.7*

Comparables: Ryan Ludwick (51), Chris Coghlan (47), Will Venable (47)

The band Yaz (Yazoo in the US), composed of Alison Moyet and Depeche Mode's Vince Clarke, had exactly one (1) megahit: the angsty, romantic, synth-rich ballad "Only You." Only Yaz provided the Giants with consistent, above-average defense this season, proving his ability to play center is a feature, not a bug. The 2022 Giants needed much more than the love he gave at the plate, but there's a chance that being another year removed from a hand injury that sapped power and playing time in 2021 helps him recapture his early-career excitement. That's a torch song we can get behind.

PITCHERS

John Brebbia RHP Born: 05/30/90 Age: 33 Bats: L Throws: R Height: 6'1" Weight: 200 lb. Origin: Round 30, 2011 Draft (#929 overall)

YEAR	TEAM	LVL	AGE	W	L	SV	G	GS	IP	H	HR	BB/9	K/9	K	GB%	BABIP	WHIP	ERA	DRA-	WARP	MPH	FB%	Whiff%	CSP
2021	SAC	AAA	31	3	0	0	17	2	15^1	9	2	2.9	15.8	27	35.7%	.269	0.91	2.93	69	0.4				
2021	SF	MLB	31	0	1	0	18	0	18^1	25	4	2.0	10.8	22	27.1%	.389	1.58	5.89	92	0.2	93.3	49.1%	23.0%	58.4%
2022	SF	MLB	32	6	2	0	76	11	68	71	5	2.4	7.1	54	35.8%	.317	1.31	3.18	107	0.4	94.4	46.0%	23.4%	56.4%
2023 DC	*SF*	*MLB*	*33*	*2*	*2*	*0*	*59*	*0*	*51.3*	*51*	*6*	*2.8*	*8.0*	*45*	*33.4%*	*.300*	*1.31*	*3.97*	*104*	*0.1*	*94.1*	*48.4%*	*24.7%*	*55.6%*

Comparables: Dan Otero (74), Justin Miller (70), Javy Guerra (69)

The Final Boss of the Quirky Bullpen Guy, Brebbia was known to celebrate Valentine's Day by handing out roses around the Cardinals' complex during spring training, and shows up on getaway days with only the top and bottom parts of his dress shirt buttoned, allowing the middle to flap in the breeze. He reads 500-page ethnologies, with footnotes and everything. He thinks the Giants-Dodgers rivalry is funny, actually. He begins the season clean-shaven and then allows his beard to grow until it requires management from the DNR.

That last bit might be connected to some superstition, since he's seen his career almost-end twice. Brebbia was cut loose by the Cards after having TJ surgery and struggled with the Giants last year in his recovery season, but the Giants' patience was rewarded this year as Brebbia rebounded to become a pitching staff stalwart, a versatile spot starter-slash-reliable bullpen arm. He's a perfect fit for San Francisco on and off the field, proving that sometimes a quirk of fate is the best quirk of all.

Alex Cobb RHP Born: 10/07/87 Age: 35 Bats: R Throws: R Height: 6'3" Weight: 205 lb. Origin: Round 4, 2006 Draft (#109 overall)

YEAR	TEAM	LVL	AGE	W	L	SV	G	GS	IP	H	HR	BB/9	K/9	K	GB%	BABIP	WHIP	ERA	DRA-	WARP	MPH	FB%	Whiff%	CSP
2020	BAL	MLB	32	2	5	0	10	10	52^1	52	8	3.1	6.5	38	54.2%	.275	1.34	4.30	95	0.7	92.6	48.1%	23.6%	48.9%
2021	LAA	MLB	33	8	3	0	18	18	93^1	85	5	3.2	9.5	98	53.3%	.316	1.26	3.76	89	1.4	92.7	46.7%	26.6%	50.6%
2022	SF	MLB	34	7	8	0	28	28	149^2	152	9	2.6	9.1	151	60.3%	.338	1.30	3.73	83	2.8	94.8	42.7%	24.8%	53.2%
2023 DC	*SF*	*MLB*	*35*	*9*	*9*	*0*	*25*	*25*	*152.7*	*161*	*15*	*2.9*	*8.1*	*137*	*56.4%*	*.322*	*1.38*	*4.02*	*102*	*1.1*	*93.9*	*44.5%*	*24.0%*	*51.9%*

Comparables: Freddy Garcia (77), Tim Hudson (76), Justin Verlander (75)

There's a proverb in Spanish, *más sabe el diablo por viejo que por diablo*: the devil knows more because he's old rather than because he's a supernatural being. Maybe Cobb is a little of both, as at age 35 he had his best year in a career that's spanned over a decade. His splitter has always been a maleficent entity, but this year Cobb also punched up his fastball by two ticks, at one point hitting 97 mph, a new career high. Add in his posting career-best numbers despite forfeiting pretty much the whole month of June, and it certainly seems to suggest the presence of the dark arts.

Reggie Crawford LHP Born: 12/04/00 Age: 22 Bats: L Throws: L Height: 6'4" Weight: 235 lb. Origin: Round 1, 2022 Draft (#30 overall)

Spare a thought for those bereft of talent because Crawford has been given all of it. As a pitching prospect, the southpaw possesses a high-90s fastball plus a hard slider, and he spent his rehab from TJ studying up on a changeup that he's begun implementing. As a hitter, he has plus raw power from the left side. And as a person, he has the magnetic personality of a superstar in the making, thanks in part to his unique background. Crawford was more known as a swimming standout at his Pennsylvania high school and only played baseball for his school rather than on the expensive, elite travel teams; he credits the 5 AM wakeups for swim practice with instilling the discipline that has him known now as "Reggie Regimen." Two-way players usually get pushed into one lane or the other by the time they make it to pro ball, but because Crawford was coming off TJ surgery, the Giants had him hit in the AZL this year, where he showed he can hit and play a competent first base, because why not just do all the things well. Free idea for Giants social: Find archived website of Chuck Norris Facts, search + replace "Norris" with "Crawford," profit. You're welcome.

Anthony DeSclafani RHP Born: 04/18/90 Age: 33 Bats: R Throws: R Height: 6'2" Weight: 195 lb. Origin: Round 6, 2011 Draft (#199 overall)

YEAR	TEAM	LVL	AGE	W	L	SV	G	GS	IP	H	HR	BB/9	K/9	K	GB%	BABIP	WHIP	ERA	DRA-	WARP	MPH	FB%	Whiff%	CSP
2020	CIN	MLB	30	1	2	0	9	7	33^2	41	7	4.3	6.7	25	39.5%	.318	1.69	7.22	136	-0.3	95.1	51.3%	23.2%	42.2%
2021	SF	MLB	31	13	7	0	31	31	167^2	141	19	2.3	8.2	152	43.3%	.268	1.09	3.17	86	2.8	94.2	45.7%	24.1%	56.5%
2022	SF	MLB	32	0	2	0	5	5	19	34	4	1.9	8.1	17	43.1%	.448	2.00	6.63	103	0.2	92.8	42.6%	22.9%	57.0%
2023 DC	*SF*	*MLB*	*33*	*6*	*7*	*0*	*22*	*22*	*115.7*	*122*	*14*	*2.7*	*7.5*	*96*	*43.1%*	*.310*	*1.36*	*4.18*	*108*	*0.5*	*94.3*	*47.9%*	*23.1%*	*53.4%*

Comparables: Joe Blanton (78), Frank Lary (77), Rick Wise (77)

Some guys just can't catch a break. Vacuumed away from the Blue Jays in a controversial trade by a pompous popinjay of an owner who ran the Marlins with the same degree of feel as Elon running Twitter, he was traded to an even more impecunious owner in Cincinnati before finally breaking west like a baseball-throwing Fievel. By the Golden Gate, Disco enjoyed both a more capacious home park and a tweak to his arsenal that swapped out two lesser pitches (fastball and changeup) for a sinker-slider-curve mix. Everything seemed on track for him to settle comfortably at the rear of San Francisco's rotation, notching a couple wins and cheerfully eating innings, until an ankle injury on his plant foot effectively canceled his season. He'll try to captain his own destiny in the final year of his contract.

Camilo Doval RHP Born: 07/04/97 Age: 26 Bats: R Throws: R Height: 6'2" Weight: 185 lb. Origin: International Free Agent, 2015

YEAR	TEAM	LVL	AGE	W	L	SV	G	GS	IP	H	HR	BB/9	K/9	K	GB%	BABIP	WHIP	ERA	DRA-	WARP	MPH	FB%	Whiff%	CSP
2021	SAC	AAA	23	3	0	1	28	0	30^2	28	3	7.0	12.9	44	50.7%	.362	1.70	4.99	86	0.4				
2021	SF	MLB	23	5	1	3	29	0	27	19	4	3.0	12.3	37	50.0%	.259	1.04	3.00	73	0.6	98.8	41.6%	33.5%	53.0%
2022	SF	MLB	24	6	6	27	68	0	67^2	54	4	4.0	10.6	80	57.2%	.298	1.24	2.53	81	1.3	99.0	56.4%	30.7%	51.5%
2023 DC	*SF*	*MLB*	*25*	*3*	*2*	*31*	*59*	*0*	*51.3*	*46*	*4*	*4.8*	*10.3*	*58*	*52.7%*	*.313*	*1.43*	*3.93*	*96*	*0.3*	*98.9*	*52.9%*	*31.4%*	*51.8%*

Comparables: Ken Giles (86), Kelvin Herrera (81), Bruce Rondón (81)

When the Ghostbusters shoot from their proton packs the rule is "don't cross the streams," which—spoiler alert!—they do anyway, because that's how they bust the ghosts, or whatever. Doval's pitches work kind of the same way, in that they are waves of obliterative energy, sometimes directionally unpredictable, that often cross streams thanks to his highly consistent release point. This leaves batters guessing as to whether they're chasing his slider, fastball, or two-seamer. Because the stuff moves so much, there's always a risk of a higher walk rate or a slider winding up in the wrong place, but despite a moderate sophomore slump, the 25-year-old is poised to be one of the best closers in the game, provided you ain't afraid of no ghosts (the pitch clock).

★ ★ ★ *2023 Top 101 Prospect* **#20** ★ ★ ★

Kyle Harrison LHP Born: 08/12/01 Age: 21 Bats: R Throws: L Height: 6'2" Weight: 200 lb. Origin: Round 3, 2020 Draft (#85 overall)

YEAR	TEAM	LVL	AGE	W	L	SV	G	GS	IP	H	HR	BB/9	K/9	K	GB%	BABIP	WHIP	ERA	DRA-	WARP	MPH	FB%	Whiff%	CSP
2021	SJ	A	19	4	3	0	23	23	98^2	86	3	4.7	14.3	157	49.1%	.393	1.40	3.19	82	1.7				
2022	EUG	A+	20	0	1	0	7	7	29	19	2	3.1	18.3	59	43.8%	.378	1.00	1.55	63	0.8				
2022	RIC	AA	20	4	2	0	18	18	84	60	11	4.2	13.6	127	34.1%	.301	1.18	3.11	84	1.8				
2023 DC	*SF*	*MLB*	*21*	*0*	*0*	*0*	*3*	*3*	*14.3*	*12*	*1*	*5.1*	*11.4*	*18*	*40.7%*	*.304*	*1.42*	*4.25*	*102*	*0.1*			*32.7%*	

Comparables: Henry Owens (84), Stephen Gonsalves (81), Jesse Biddle (81)

It might not be quite Beatles-level stardom, but Isn't It A Pity that San Francisco hasn't had a pitching prospect this hotly anticipated since the last great lefty Giant, Madison Bumgarner. It's understandable Giants fans have their Minds Set On this young lefty, who features an exceptional mid-90s fastball and a wipeout slider. When Harrison joins the rotation, the Giants will need to Handle Him With Care, as he hit a career high in innings pitched last season, but his ability to rack up strikeouts on a more contact-oriented pitching staff will soon have Giants fans saying Here Comes the Sun.

Sean Hjelle RHP Born: 05/07/97 Age: 26 Bats: R Throws: R Height: 6'11" Weight: 228 lb. Origin: Round 2, 2018 Draft (#45 overall)

YEAR	TEAM	LVL	AGE	W	L	SV	G	GS	IP	H	HR	BB/9	K/9	K	GB%	BABIP	WHIP	ERA	DRA-	WARP	MPH	FB%	Whiff%	CSP
2021	RIC	AA	24	3	2	0	14	14	65^{2}	60	8	2.6	9.5	69	55.2%	.299	1.20	3.15	93	0.8				
2021	SAC	AAA	24	2	6	0	10	10	53^{1}	67	6	4.9	5.9	35	54.6%	.345	1.80	5.74	111	-0.1				
2022	SAC	AAA	25	6	8	0	22	22	97	112	11	3.5	7.4	80	56.1%	.334	1.55	4.92	103	0.4	92.9	58.9%	20.8%	
2022	SF	MLB	25	1	2	0	8	0	25	33	3	2.9	10.1	28	59.0%	.400	1.64	5.76	89	0.4	93.8	55.1%	20.5%	59.1%
2023 DC	*SF*	*MLB*	*26*	*4*	*3*	*0*	*36*	*3*	*41.3*	*46*	*4*	*3.6*	*6.9*	*31*	*56.5%*	*.321*	*1.52*	*4.85*	*118*	*-0.2*	*93.8*	*55.1%*	*21.3%*	*59.1%*

Comparables: Brandon Workman (72), Logan Darnell (67), Thomas Eshelman (66)

For all the brouhaha about his height, a three-quarter arm slot actually means the 6-foot-11 Hjelle has a release point around MLB average: 6.3 feet, virtually identical to that of Zack Greinke (who stands an MLB-average 6-foot-2). Every tall kid can relate to just wanting to be normal once in a while. Maybe dropping the release point helped Hjelle find consistency with both that and his mechanics, which are remarkably clean for such a tall pitcher—corralling all those limbs is not a task for the faint of heart. The tradeoff here is there's no wacky wizard pitch generated by all these extra feet; it's just a nice arsenal geared toward weak contact. For a second-rounder and the tallest MLB pitcher ever (tie), that might feel like a bit of a disappointment, but so what? Better working than weird.

Jakob Junis RHP Born: 09/16/92 Age: 30 Bats: R Throws: R Height: 6'3" Weight: 220 lb. Origin: Round 29, 2011 Draft (#876 overall)

YEAR	TEAM	LVL	AGE	W	L	SV	G	GS	IP	H	HR	BB/9	K/9	K	GB%	BABIP	WHIP	ERA	DRA-	WARP	MPH	FB%	Whiff%	CSP
2020	KC	MLB	27	0	2	0	8	6	25^{1}	35	7	2.1	6.8	19	46.0%	.350	1.62	6.39	114	0.1	91.2	49.2%	20.5%	51.6%
2021	OMA	AAA	28	0	2	0	6	6	17^{2}	22	4	4.1	9.2	18	48.2%	.346	1.70	5.60	109	0.2				
2021	KC	MLB	28	2	4	0	16	6	39^{1}	43	7	2.7	9.4	41	43.5%	.333	1.40	5.26	94	0.5	90.0	37.0%	25.6%	55.0%
2022	SAC	AAA	29	0	1	0	3	3	11^{1}	19	5	3.2	7.1	9	39.0%	.389	2.03	8.74	109	0.0	90.2	58.0%	26.6%	
2022	SF	MLB	29	5	7	0	23	17	112	120	13	2.0	7.9	98	42.7%	.318	1.29	4.42	99	1.2	91.9	32.7%	21.7%	56.5%
2023 DC	*SF*	*MLB*	*30*	*7*	*3*	*0*	*55*	*3*	*59.7*	*64*	*8*	*2.6*	*7.6*	*50*	*43.0%*	*.315*	*1.37*	*4.37*	*112*	*0.1*	*91.5*	*38.5%*	*22.5%*	*54.0%*

Comparables: Sidney Ponson (86), Jeff Francis (85), Josh Fogg (85)

His 2022 was that classic of Russian literature, *One Day in the Life of Jakob Junis*: Wake up, follow the boss' instructions to dump his cutter and four-seam and increase his changeup, sinker and slider usage, all while fixing command issues; see strikeout rate dip. Minimize hard contact; see defense boot ball. Provide 100 innings-plus of workmanlike pitching; get shuttled to bullpen as swingman while rotation spot is given to top prospect. It's an unglamorous life, that which is lived by back-end starters, but as the wise General Kutuzov reflects in *War and Peace*, his two greatest warriors are patience and time, and Junis still has a fair—although not infinite—amount of both.

Sam Long LHP Born: 07/08/95 Age: 27 Bats: L Throws: L Height: 6'1" Weight: 185 lb. Origin: Round 18, 2016 Draft (#540 overall)

YEAR	TEAM	LVL	AGE	W	L	SV	G	GS	IP	H	HR	BB/9	K/9	K	GB%	BABIP	WHIP	ERA	DRA-	WARP	MPH	FB%	Whiff%	CSP
2021	RIC	AA	25	0	1	0	4	4	15	12	0	2.4	13.2	22	41.2%	.353	1.07	3.00	89	0.2				
2021	SAC	AAA	25	1	0	0	11	3	26^{1}	16	2	3.1	10.6	31	45.2%	.233	0.95	2.05	84	0.4				
2021	SF	MLB	25	2	1	0	12	5	40^{2}	37	5	3.3	8.4	38	39.2%	.278	1.28	5.53	99	0.4	92.7	43.2%	21.4%	57.9%
2022	SAC	AAA	26	1	0	0	8	3	16^{2}	11	2	8.6	8.6	16	30.4%	.205	1.62	4.32	109	0.0	93.6	52.9%	23.1%	
2022	SF	MLB	26	1	3	1	28	6	42^{1}	39	8	3.0	7.0	33	38.3%	.250	1.25	3.61	112	0.1	94.7	44.0%	25.4%	58.2%
2023 DC	*SF*	*MLB*	*27*	*6*	*3*	*0*	*49*	*3*	*55*	*53*	*6*	*4.0*	*7.5*	*46*	*39.4%*	*.291*	*1.42*	*4.26*	*108*	*0.1*	*93.8*	*43.7%*	*24.3%*	*58.1%*

Comparables: Jefry Rodriguez (57), Alex Young (55), Tyler Duffey (51)

In 2021, Long ranked 37th in baseball in tempo; respectable, but well behind several of his teammates. The Giants, who encourage their pitchers to work quickly, challenged Long to shave some time off his delivery, and he did, jumping all the way to seventh in tempo in 2022 while also adding a couple ticks to his average fastball. Unfortunately, that quicker pace didn't deliver better results; Long's strikeout rate fell off some while hitters barreled him up more. As anyone new to an exercise regimen will tell you, it's annoying to feel like you're doing all the right things and not getting the benefits, but as Long is just 80 innings into his big-league career, he's got a...while to figure it out. First, though, he'll have to work around the oblique injury that cut his season short in late August.

Sean Manaea LHP Born: 02/01/92 Age: 31 Bats: R Throws: L Height: 6'5" Weight: 245 lb. Origin: Round 1, 2013 Draft (#34 overall)

YEAR	TEAM	LVL	AGE	W	L	SV	G	GS	IP	H	HR	BB/9	K/9	K	GB%	BABIP	WHIP	ERA	DRA-	WARP	MPH	FB%	Whiff%	CSP
2020	OAK	MLB	28	4	3	0	11	11	54	57	7	1.3	7.5	45	50.0%	.311	1.20	4.50	86	1.0	90.4	54.3%	22.1%	50.5%
2021	OAK	MLB	29	11	10	0	32	32	179^{1}	179	25	2.1	9.7	194	41.8%	.318	1.23	3.91	91	2.5	92.3	60.1%	27.0%	57.9%
2022	SD	MLB	30	8	9	0	30	28	158	155	29	2.8	8.9	156	37.4%	.292	1.30	4.96	114	0.4	91.2	60.9%	25.6%	56.7%
2023 DC	*SF*	*MLB*	*31*	*7*	*7*	*0*	*22*	*22*	*117.7*	*116*	*17*	*2.5*	*8.4*	*109*	*40.1%*	*.298*	*1.26*	*3.82*	*101*	*0.9*	*91.6*	*60.1%*	*25.4%*	*56.5%*

Comparables: Joe Blanton (80), Claude Osteen (80), Jimmy Key (78)

Most of us struggle with imposter syndrome, with the belief that we don't actually know what we're doing and one day we'll be found out. Usually, that's all just in our heads and we simply have to continue living with anxiety for all the days in our lives. For Manaea, it seemingly happened. After posting a 4.11 ERA in the first half of the season, he became a self-driving Tesla car about to run into a person. Everything stopped working. Manaea posted a 6.44 ERA in the second half while giving up 15 HRs in just 57⅓ innings pitched. "At this point, it's whatever I can do to help the team," Manaea said after being pulled from the rotation. "If that's not pitching, then sure." Hardly the words you want to hear from one of your four best starting pitchers.

Yunior Marte RHP

Born: 02/02/95 Age: 28 Bats: R Throws: R Height: 6'2" Weight: 180 lb. Origin: International Free Agent, 2012

YEAR	TEAM	LVL	AGE	W	L	SV	G	GS	IP	H	HR	BB/9	K/9	K	GB%	BABIP	WHIP	ERA	DRA-	WARP	MPH	FB%	Whiff%	CSP
2021	SAC	AAA	26	0	3	4	43	1	56^{2}	60	4	3.7	9.8	62	51.5%	.348	1.46	3.49	87	0.7				
2022	SAC	AAA	27	1	1	3	25	0	25^{2}	9	4	3.2	12.3	35	40.0%	.109	0.70	3.16	78	0.5	97.4	51.8%	36.6%	
2022	SF	MLB	27	1	1	0	39	0	48	47	5	4.1	8.3	44	50.0%	.307	1.44	5.44	102	0.4	97.3	61.9%	26.3%	52.1%
2023 DC	*PHI*	*MLB*	*28*	*2*	*2*	*0*	*43*	*0*	*38*	*36*	*3*	*4.0*	*8.7*	*36*	*47.8%*	*.307*	*1.41*	*4.12*	*103*	*0.1*	*97.3*	*61.9%*	*27.3%*	*52.1%*

Comparables: Noé Ramirez (70), Tayler Scott (70), Yacksel Ríos (69)

Hidden under Marte's meh numbers are some exciting peripherals; looking through them is like picking up a rice cake to find it's stuffed with luscious salted caramel. In this case, the ooey-gooey filling is an ability to limit hard contact and keep batters from squaring up his upper-90s running fastball and tightly spinning slider. As an older prospect, Marte is easy to overlook, having spent years as a Royals farmhand before signing with the Giants as a minor-league free agent, but the Giants knew what they were doing when they opted to protect him on the 40-man prior to the 2021 Rule 5 draft. With the delicious raw stuff he possesses plus the quality of Giants' pitching development, it seems a safe bet he won't be overlooked much longer.

Randy Rodriguez RHP

Born: 09/05/99 Age: 23 Bats: R Throws: R Height: 6'0" Weight: 166 lb. Origin: International Free Agent, 2017

YEAR	TEAM	LVL	AGE	W	L	SV	G	GS	IP	H	HR	BB/9	K/9	K	GB%	BABIP	WHIP	ERA	DRA-	WARP	MPH	FB%	Whiff%	CSP
2021	SJ	A	21	6	3	2	32	0	62	44	0	3.3	14.7	101	36.2%	.346	1.08	1.74	88	0.8				
2022	EUG	A+	22	2	3	0	16	13	50^{2}	35	5	4.3	12.6	71	22.3%	.280	1.16	3.38	96	0.6				
2022	RIC	AA	22	0	1	0	6	0	10	7	2	7.2	17.1	19	36.8%	.294	1.50	6.30	77	0.3				
2022	SAC	AAA	22	0	1	0	5	0	6	3	0	16.5	10.5	7	57.1%	.214	2.33	10.50	101	0.0	94.2	49.7%	34.0%	
2023 DC	*SF*	*MLB*	*23*	*0*	*0*	*0*	*19*	*0*	*17*	*14*	*2*	*6.0*	*10.5*	*19*	*32.6%*	*.289*	*1.51*	*4.74*	*112*	*0.0*			*29.2%*	

Comparables: Cody Martin (38), Seranthony Domínguez (37), Nestor Molina (37)

After Rodriguez had an absolutely dominant 2021 out of San Jose's bullpen, the Giants made the curious decision to try to stretch him out as a starter in Eugene this season, where the 22-year-old adapted to a new pitching role and a brand-new climate as well. Still, a 98-mph fastball with late life and a near-flat VAA will keep one warm even out in the PNW wilds; he pairs that with a hard slider with two-plane break that's helped him rack up gaudy strikeout totals even as the Giants throw challenge after challenge at him. He also throws a passable changeup, but that may get shelved if the Giants go all-in on a relief role for him, as seems likely.

Taylor Rogers LHP

Born: 12/17/90 Age: 32 Bats: L Throws: L Height: 6'3" Weight: 190 lb. Origin: Round 11, 2012 Draft (#340 overall)

YEAR	TEAM	LVL	AGE	W	L	SV	G	GS	IP	H	HR	BB/9	K/9	K	GB%	BABIP	WHIP	ERA	DRA-	WARP	MPH	FB%	Whiff%	CSP
2020	MIN	MLB	29	2	4	9	21	0	20	26	2	1.8	10.8	24	43.5%	.400	1.50	4.05	88	0.4	94.8	54.5%	23.6%	55.3%
2021	MIN	MLB	30	2	4	9	40	0	40^{1}	38	4	1.8	13.2	59	48.5%	.366	1.14	3.35	64	1.1	95.9	45.8%	29.6%	56.3%
2022	MIL	MLB	31	3	3	3	24	0	23	20	6	3.9	14.1	36	37.3%	.318	1.30	5.48	81	0.5	93.9	39.0%	32.3%	58.0%
2022	SD	MLB	31	1	5	28	42	0	41^{1}	37	1	2.0	10.5	48	44.0%	.333	1.11	4.35	86	0.7	94.6	45.2%	30.6%	55.1%
2023 DC	*SF*	*MLB*	*32*	*3*	*2*	*0*	*59*	*0*	*51.3*	*43*	*5*	*2.3*	*11.4*	*64*	*44.0%*	*.309*	*1.10*	*2.86*	*76*	*0.8*	*94.8*	*45.6%*	*28.3%*	*55.7%*

Comparables: Justin Wilson (69), Jose Alvarez (67), Ryan Pressly (67)

As Rogers can attest, it's rough business being a reliever. In smaller groupings of innings, the usual volatility present in pitching is magnified, meaning results often don't reflect actual skill. Compared to last season—or his entire career, for that matter—Rogers experienced only marginal setbacks in fielding-independent areas. But his ERA ballooned in 2022, and a midseason trade to Milwaukee did him no favors. That said, Rogers can't only blame variance and bad luck, as he isn't quite the same pitcher he used to be. His slight drop in fastball velocity isn't alarming in and of itself. But what might be is his modified breaking ball, which now moves a ton horizontally but cost him three ticks of velo. Such a drastic drop seems intentional, and may have been ill-advised: his slider returned more hard contact than usual, and its more distinct shape may have helped hitters better identify his sinker, which is an inferior pitch. Despite his down year, Rogers landed a three-year pact from the Giants to join his twin brother, Tyler, in their bullpen. Perhaps part of his sales pitch included junking his new junk-ball.

Tyler Rogers RHP

Born: 12/17/90 Age: 32 Bats: R Throws: R Height: 6'3" Weight: 181 lb. Origin: Round 10, 2013 Draft (#312 overall)

YEAR	TEAM	LVL	AGE	W	L	SV	G	GS	IP	H	HR	BB/9	K/9	K	GB%	BABIP	WHIP	ERA	DRA-	WARP	MPH	FB%	Whiff%	CSP
2020	SF	MLB	29	3	3	3	29	0	28	31	2	1.9	8.7	27	53.5%	.349	1.32	4.50	82	0.6	82.4	63.8%	24.2%	52.1%
2021	SF	MLB	30	7	1	13	80	0	81	74	5	1.4	6.1	55	57.3%	.279	1.07	2.22	99	0.8	82.9	57.4%	16.6%	54.0%
2022	SF	MLB	31	3	4	0	68	0	75^{2}	73	3	2.7	5.8	49	55.6%	.294	1.27	3.57	113	0.2	83.2	53.9%	19.3%	55.2%
2023 DC	*SF*	*MLB*	*32*	*2*	*3*	*3*	*59*	*0*	*51.3*	*56*	*4*	*2.7*	*6.0*	*34*	*55.9%*	*.311*	*1.39*	*4.27*	*109*	*0.0*	*83.0*	*56.5%*	*19.3%*	*54.5%*

Comparables: Blake Parker (71), Nick Vincent (71), Brad Brach (68)

Rogers the (minimally) Younger attracts attention primarily for two things: 1) his knuckle-scraping submarine delivery resulting in a slider that resembles a riseball in softball; and 2) his twin brother, who you literally just read about in the comment above. The real curiosity here, though, is his continued success despite his striking absolutely no one out, walking a few more batters than he probably should and getting next to nothing in the whiffs department. None of that matters, though, when one is able to elicit essentially double the MLB average for weak contact. Batters might not be swinging and missing, but the quality of contact they're making is less "big leagues," more "middle school dance." A weak rollover on a slider isn't going to go "sword and K strut" viral, but the outs count the same.

Ross Stripling RHP

Born: 11/23/89 Age: 33 Bats: R Throws: R Height: 6'1" Weight: 215 lb. Origin: Round 5, 2012 Draft (#176 overall)

YEAR	TEAM	LVL	AGE	W	L	SV	G	GS	IP	H	HR	BB/9	K/9	K	GB%	BABIP	WHIP	ERA	DRA-	WARP	MPH	FB%	Whiff%	CSP
2020	LAD	MLB	30	3	1	0	7	7	33^{2}	38	12	2.9	7.2	27	33.3%	.268	1.46	5.61	117	0.1	91.7	45.2%	16.0%	52.9%
2020	TOR	MLB	30	0	2	1	5	2	15^{2}	18	1	4.0	7.5	13	56.0%	.347	1.60	6.32	110	0.1	91.7	41.4%	25.2%	51.1%
2021	TOR	MLB	31	5	7	0	24	19	101^{1}	99	23	2.7	8.3	94	35.4%	.270	1.27	4.80	110	0.4	91.9	51.3%	24.2%	57.3%
2022	TOR	MLB	32	10	4	1	32	24	134^{1}	117	12	1.3	7.4	111	44.2%	.269	1.02	3.01	89	2.1	91.8	41.0%	23.5%	55.8%
2023 DC	*SF*	*MLB*	*33*	*10*	*9*	*0*	*60*	*21*	*141.7*	*143*	*16*	*2.1*	*7.5*	*117*	*42.2%*	*.302*	*1.25*	*3.57*	*96*	*1.4*	*91.7*	*44.3%*	*23.0%*	*55.3%*

Comparables: Ed Whitson (69), Dennis Martinez (68), Jordan Zimmermann (67)

Stripling's arrival in Toronto can best be described as turbulent, to say nothing of the conditions of the commercial flight that deposited him there. After 117 ghastly innings, it seemed wisest to chalk up Stripling's acquisition as a failure—a low-cost, low-risk failure, but a failure nonetheless. In no other sport can the succession of a player's lows and highs cause such extraordinary whiplash. Stripling concluded his 2022 campaign having established not only career highs in games started and innings pitched, but also a career-best ERA. After his bad four-seamer eclipsed 50% usage in 2021, he scaled it back to roughly one-third of the time and relied more heavily on his changeup, which he managed to flatten out while also dialing back its velocity. It fueled his best swinging strike rate in half a decade and helped him produce almost as many WARP as in his previous three seasons combined. That said, he's not in the clear yet. Recent success aside, he's 33 with one out pitch and a suboptimal fastball. Interestingly, he introduced a heavy sinker that appears ultra-steep thanks to his 12 o'clock release point. He only used it seven percent of the time, but it could pad his longevity. The Giants clearly believe it will, as they gave Stripling a two-year, $25 million deal in December.

Thomas Szapucki LHP

Born: 06/12/96 Age: 27 Bats: R Throws: L Height: 6'2" Weight: 210 lb. Origin: Round 5, 2015 Draft (#149 overall)

YEAR	TEAM	LVL	AGE	W	L	SV	G	GS	IP	H	HR	BB/9	K/9	K	GB%	BABIP	WHIP	ERA	DRA-	WARP	MPH	FB%	Whiff%	CSP
2021	SYR	AAA	25	0	4	0	10	9	41^{2}	42	5	6.0	8.9	41	36.1%	.322	1.68	4.10	114	0.3				
2021	NYM	MLB	25	0	0	0	1	0	3^{2}	7	2	7.4	9.8	4	38.5%	.455	2.73	14.73	120	0.0	91.0	68.3%	29.0%	50.4%
2022	SYR	AAA	26	2	6	0	18	16	64	54	5	4.1	12.2	87	44.6%	.343	1.30	3.38	73	1.8				
2022	SAC	AAA	26	0	0	0	7	0	8^{1}	7	0	3.2	16.2	15	37.5%	.438	1.20	1.08	79	0.1	95.9	64.2%	43.1%	
2022	NYM	MLB	26	0	1	0	1	1	1^{1}	7	4	20.2	13.5	2	12.5%	.750	7.50	60.75	239	-0.1	95.0	57.1%	23.5%	47.7%
2022	SF	MLB	26	0	0	0	10	0	13^{2}	12	2	2.6	10.5	16	32.4%	.313	1.17	1.98	92	0.2	95.4	61.6%	23.9%	56.4%
2023 DC	*SF*	*MLB*	*27*	*4*	*3*	*0*	*36*	*3*	*41.3*	*36*	*4*	*4.5*	*9.2*	*42*	*39.3%*	*.290*	*1.39*	*4.06*	*101*	*0.2*	*94.6*	*62.1%*	*27.7%*	*54.3%*

Comparables: T.J. McFarland (48), Sean Gilmartin (47), Nik Turley (46)

A year ago, after Tommy John surgery, Szapucki was hanging out in the low 90s with his fastball while clinging to a starting role in the Mets system. In his debut for the Giants, after coming over in the Darin Ruf trade, he was at 97–98, with an obscene 13 inches of vertical drop. And for his next trick, Szapucki throws a slurve that tunnels neatly with that heavily dropping fastball, eliciting some truly hideous swings. Mets fans are always convinced ownership has traded away the next great thing for magic beans. Watching Szapucki climb up that beanstalk and become a Giant, one could easily conclude they might have a point.

Logan Webb RHP

Born: 11/18/96 Age: 26 Bats: R Throws: R Height: 6'1" Weight: 220 lb. Origin: Round 4, 2014 Draft (#118 overall)

YEAR	TEAM	LVL	AGE	W	L	SV	G	GS	IP	H	HR	BB/9	K/9	K	GB%	BABIP	WHIP	ERA	DRA-	WARP	MPH	FB%	Whiff%	CSP
2020	SF	MLB	23	3	4	0	13	11	54^{1}	61	4	4.0	7.6	46	52.1%	.350	1.56	5.47	97	0.7	92.5	53.9%	22.9%	47.2%
2021	SF	MLB	24	11	3	0	27	26	148^{1}	128	9	2.2	9.6	158	60.9%	.312	1.11	3.03	71	3.5	93.0	49.1%	28.8%	53.3%
2022	SF	MLB	25	15	9	0	32	32	192^{1}	174	11	2.3	7.6	163	56.6%	.294	1.16	2.90	91	2.7	92.0	36.2%	24.1%	52.9%
2023 DC	*SF*	*MLB*	*26*	*10*	*9*	*0*	*27*	*27*	*165*	*172*	*13*	*2.7*	*8.1*	*149*	*56.6%*	*.324*	*1.35*	*3.83*	*98*	*1.6*	*92.4*	*42.5%*	*25.2%*	*52.3%*

Comparables: Tyler Mahle (61), Aaron Nola (59), Tyler Chatwood (58)

It says a lot about where the Giants are currently that Webb is the ace of their rotation. That's not to take away from his accomplishments, but in a division featuring Walker Buehler and the perpetual-motion machine of Dodgers player development, the Big Three of the Padres' rotation, and the slate of young pitching coming down the pipeline in Arizona, it's like San Francisco is turning up at a black tie event in a Canadian tuxedo. To be fair, Britney and Justin made that look good back in the early 2000s, and a sinker-slider, pitch-to-contact lefty is appropriate to that era. Call him a throwback and appreciate his ability to limit barrels and keep the ball on the ground, grinding deep into games, while hoping the Giants get a little more razzle-dazzle at the top of the rotation to keep up with the (Bobby) Millers.

Alex Wood LHP

Born: 01/12/91 Age: 32 Bats: R Throws: L Height: 6'4" Weight: 215 lb. Origin: Round 2, 2012 Draft (#85 overall)

YEAR	TEAM	LVL	AGE	W	L	SV	G	GS	IP	H	HR	BB/9	K/9	K	GB%	BABIP	WHIP	ERA	DRA-	WARP	MPH	FB%	Whiff%	CSP
2020	LAD	MLB	29	0	1	0	9	2	12^{2}	17	2	4.3	10.7	15	39.0%	.385	1.82	6.39	105	0.1	91.4	48.2%	28.7%	45.3%
2021	SF	MLB	30	10	4	0	26	26	138^{2}	125	14	2.5	9.9	152	50.0%	.305	1.18	3.83	85	2.4	91.9	46.4%	27.6%	54.2%
2022	SF	MLB	31	8	12	0	26	26	130^{2}	132	17	2.1	9.0	131	48.7%	.317	1.24	5.10	100	1.2	92.4	45.5%	25.0%	53.2%
2023 DC	*SF*	*MLB*	*32*	*7*	*7*	*0*	*22*	*22*	*122.3*	*123*	*13*	*2.5*	*8.6*	*116*	*48.1%*	*.315*	*1.28*	*3.81*	*98*	*1.1*	*92.1*	*46.1%*	*25.3%*	*53.1%*

Comparables: Mike Hampton (76), Danny Jackson (73), Brett Anderson (73)

In the early 20th century, wealthy folks afflicted with long-term illnesses were prescribed a "fresh-air cure," in which they repaired to literally greener pastures. In traveling up I-5 from smoggy LA to the Bay's breezes, Wood seems to have found a cure for what's ailed him, posting back-to-back mostly-healthy years for the first time since 2017-18. "Mostly" is admittedly doing some heavy lifting there, as his season ended a month early due to a left shoulder impingement, but there's an expected injury risk baked into Wood's delivery, which may generously be called "unorthodox" and ungenerously called "elderly draft horse at the Christmas tree farm starting out on its 15th sleigh ride of the day." Wood had periods of inconsistency—the slider that was so good last year was more capricious this year, as sliders are wont to be—but the groundballer was mostly hurt by the Giants' abysmal infield defense, as he posted better defensive metrics than many infield regulars. The fresh air cure can only do so much.

Miguel Yajure RHP

Born: 05/01/98 Age: 25 Bats: R Throws: R Height: 6'1" Weight: 215 lb. Origin: International Free Agent, 2015

YEAR	TEAM	LVL	AGE	W	L	SV	G	GS	IP	H	HR	BB/9	K/9	K	GB%	BABIP	WHIP	ERA	DRA-	WARP	MPH	FB%	Whiff%	CSP
2020	NYY	MLB	22	0	0	0	3	0	7	3	1	6.4	10.3	8	40.0%	.143	1.14	1.29	96	0.1	91.9	50.0%	22.0%	43.7%
2021	IND	AAA	23	2	3	0	9	9	43^{2}	33	6	2.7	8.2	40	45.4%	.239	1.05	3.09	99	0.6				
2021	PIT	MLB	23	0	2	0	4	3	15	17	6	4.2	6.6	11	34.7%	.256	1.60	8.40	122	0.0	90.2	49.4%	21.4%	58.1%
2022	IND	AAA	24	4	4	0	16	14	54^{2}	59	7	3.8	8.7	53	38.9%	.325	1.50	6.09	107	0.5	91.7	48.3%	33.3%	
2022	PIT	MLB	24	1	1	1	12	1	24^{1}	31	3	5.9	5.9	16	43.5%	.341	1.93	8.88	135	-0.2	93.3	36.7%	22.3%	51.0%
2023 DC	*SF*	*MLB*	*25*	*0*	*0*	*0*	*13*	*0*	*11.3*	*11*	*1*	*4.1*	*7.2*	*9*	*42.6%*	*.304*	*1.50*	*4.78*	*118*	*0.0*	*92.4*	*41.1%*	*23.8%*	*52.2%*

Comparables: Rafael Montero (66), Matt Wisler (66), Jacob Turner (66)

"The velocity is back!" It's not what you want to hear if you're a police officer after you've stopped someone for speeding, or a scientist tracking a meteor hurtling toward Earth, but those four words are magical if you're a pitcher. Yajure's fastball velocity jumped from 91 miles per hour in 2021 to 93 last season. He didn't spend much time in the majors, but given his age and gradual recovery from a 2021 elbow scare his latest sample was seen as a key developmental step. Yajure has five pitches he can throw for strikes and has an excellent chance of playing some sort of role for the Giants this year.

Alex Young LHP

Born: 09/09/93 Age: 29 Bats: L Throws: L Height: 6'3" Weight: 220 lb. Origin: Round 2, 2015 Draft (#43 overall)

YEAR	TEAM	LVL	AGE	W	L	SV	G	GS	IP	H	HR	BB/9	K/9	K	GB%	BABIP	WHIP	ERA	DRA-	WARP	MPH	FB%	Whiff%	CSP
2020	AZ	MLB	26	2	4	0	15	7	46^{1}	51	11	2.7	7.6	39	36.7%	.288	1.40	5.44	135	-0.4	89.8	54.6%	24.5%	46.7%
2021	COL	AAA	27	0	0	0	8	0	9	8	1	4.0	7.0	7	46.2%	.292	1.33	5.00	96	0.1				
2021	CLE	MLB	27	0	0	0	10	0	10^{1}	15	1	6.1	4.4	5	46.2%	.368	2.13	7.84	132	-0.1	90.0	70.7%	15.7%	54.7%
2021	AZ	MLB	27	2	6	0	30	2	41^{2}	50	11	4.3	8.2	38	44.8%	.322	1.68	6.26	106	0.3	89.2	59.9%	29.7%	53.4%
2022	COL	AAA	28	3	0	1	30	0	32	30	5	2.0	13.2	47	51.9%	.347	1.16	3.66	65	1.0				
2022	CLE	MLB	28	0	0	0	1	0	0^{1}	1	0	0.0	27.0	1	100.0%	1.000	3.00	0.00	5	0.0	90.4	16.7%	75.0%	60.9%
2022	SF	MLB	28	1	1	0	24	1	26^{1}	28	0	3.8	6.8	20	53.7%	.341	1.48	2.39	99	0.3	90.9	27.6%	30.7%	48.6%
2023 DC	*FA*	*MLB*	*29*	*2*	*2*	*0*	*43*	*0*	*37.3*	*38*	*4*	*3.4*	*9.1*	*37*	*47.1%*	*.325*	*1.41*	*4.33*	*108*	*0.0*	*89.7*	*51.4%*	*30.4%*	*49.4%*

Comparables: Tyler Duffey (58), Vidal Nuño (55), Matt Maloney (54)

The problem with being a collector of things is sometimes it becomes difficult to locate the off switch, and suddenly you find yourself in possession of a thousand ceramic frogs, or enough cookie jars that you have to rent a storage space to store them, or a stable full of soft-tossing lefties. The Giants went out and acquired Young from the Guardians anyway, dramatically altering his pitch mix to feature the curveball and changeup while fading his fastball. The curve looks to be a burgeoning weapon against righties, especially as he's shown more willingness to throw it inside at a hitter's knees. It's too early to tell whether that tweak will unlock more strikeout potential for Young, but only the collector knows the true value of their collection.

LINEOUTS

Hitters

HITTER	POS	TEAM	LVL	AGE	PA	R	2B	3B	HR	RBI	BB	K	SB	CS	AVG/OBP/SLG	DRC+	BABIP	BRR	DRP	WARP
Austin Dean	OF	SAC	AAA	28	438	68	17	5	17	55	38	94	10	2	.268/.345/.467	112	.313	-1.5	RF(59): 0.3, LF(27): 0.2, CF(8): -0.6	1.9
	OF	SF	MLB	28	9	1	0	0	0	0	1	0	0	0	.375/.444/.375	104	.375	-0.1	LF(3): 0	0.0
Bryce Johnson	CF	SAC	AAA	26	352	41	11	4	5	36	33	90	31	5	.290/.369/.401	94	.391	2.4	CF(67): 0.7, LF(15): 0.3, RF(9): -0.7	0.7
	CF	SF	MLB	26	19	1	0	0	0	2	1	7	0	0	.111/.158/.111	85	.182	-0.1	CF(7): -0.1, RF(4): 0, LF(1): 0	0.0
Andrew Knapp	C	SAC	AAA	30	142	20	7	0	8	26	13	35	1	1	.276/.352/.520	107	.321	0.0	C(25): 2.0, 1B(6): -0.8	0.5
	C	TAC	AAA	30	88	8	7	0	4	11	4	22	0	0	.198/.250/.432	97	.214	-1.4	C(19): 0.4, 1B(2): 0.7, LF(1): -0.2	0.3
	C	SEA	MLB	30	4	0	0	0	0	0	0	3	0	0	.000/.000/.000	75		-0.1	C(2): -0.1	0.0
	C	PIT	MLB	30	35	2	1	0	0	2	3	9	0	0	.129/.229/.161	86	.182	-0.1	C(11): -1.1	0.0
	C	SF	MLB	30	7	2	0	0	0	2	2	0	0	0	.250/.429/.250	108	.200	0.3	C(3): -0.1	0.0
Ford Proctor	C	DUR	AAA	25	317	27	7	0	6	28	44	95	3	2	.213/.329/.306	83	.304	-2.5	C(52): 3.0, 3B(10): -0.0, 2B(4): -0.1	0.6
	C	SAC	AAA	25	142	19	3	0	6	14	24	38	0	0	.267/.390/.448	105	.342	0.4	3B(16): 0.7, 2B(8): 0.9, C(4): 0.2	0.3
	C	SF	MLB	25	22	3	0	0	1	6	2	3	0	0	.111/.182/.278	97	.063	0.1	2B(6): -0.3	0.0
Jason Vosler	IF	SAC	AAA	28	398	52	13	1	18	47	34	100	4	0	.242/.311/.433	100	.285	1.3	3B(34): -1.3, 1B(28): 1.2, LF(19): -0.2	1.2
	IF	SF	MLB	28	111	14	6	1	4	12	10	29	1	1	.265/.342/.469	89	.333	-0.5	3B(29): -0.4, LF(3): -0.1, 1B(2): 0.2	0.0
Brett Wisely	IF	MTG	AA	23	500	84	23	6	15	56	62	104	31	11	.274/.371/.460	111	.329	-3.0	2B(54): 4.1, SS(18): -0.8, 1B(17): -0.3	2.0
Austin Wynns	C	LHV	AAA	31	134	21	5	0	3	20	28	18	1	0	.365/.504/.500	146	.422	0.5	C(28): -1.0	1.1
	C	SF	MLB	31	177	14	7	0	3	21	10	38	0	0	.259/.313/.358	93	.320	-1.0	C(57): 3.7	0.8

After an injury-riddled 2021, the Giants were hoping for a rebound season from **Austin Dean**, who'd showed some signs of being a late bloomer in the power department; he did hit 17 homers for Sacramento, but apparently there wasn't enough bloom on the rose for San Francisco to add him to the 40-man, and he'll search for a new team this off-season. ⚾ If **Bryce Johnson** can hit even a little bit, there's a spot for him in San Francisco's slow-footed outfield, which could use the Triple-A stolen base leader. If he remains a BABIP-fueled Quad-A player, though, there are worse outcomes than being summoned on occasion by the big-league club as an injury replacement/extra outfielder/playoff turbo button. ⚾ **Andrew Knapp** played for three organizations in five different cities in 2022, so we'll forgive him his less-than-stellar slash line and just be impressed at his packing skills. Offensive woes aside, MLB-experienced catching depth is always in demand, so the Knappsack should be loaded up and ready to find a new club this spring. ⚾ **Ford Proctor's** name might sound like an extra from The Crucible, although his full name (Jay Clifford Proctor IV) is more Gatsby. On the field, his AP Lit pick is A Thousand Acres, representing all the positions he's able to play—yes, including catcher. ⚾ **Jason Vosler** attended Don Bosco Prep in New Jersey, named after the Catholic saint who revolutionized the teaching of poor children during the Industrial Revolution with the mind-blowing pedagogy of "be nice to them." In the spirit of the Don, we will focus on the power numbers that led to a .200 point jump in his OPS this year, and nothing else. ⚾ The Giants acted quickly to grab **Brett Wisely** from the Rays, hours after Joc Pederson accepted the qualifying offer, which made him the team's primary DH, which made Tommy La Stella expendable. Wisely's a bat-first infielder who can fake shortstop, unlike his predecessor. ⚾ **Austin Wynns**' Twitter bio still lists him as a member of the Baltimore Orioles hashtag BIRDLAND, even though the account is in active use, which is some of the most powerful baseball Wife Guy energy we've ever seen. Dance with the one that brought you, etc. It's also a savvy play as the Giants continue collecting a backlog of backstops in SF.

Pitchers

PITCHER	TEAM	LVL	AGE	W	L	SV	G	GS	IP	H	HR	BB/9	K/9	K	GB%	BABIP	WHIP	ERA	DRA-	WARP	MPH	FB%	WHF	CSP
Scott Alexander	SF	MLB	32	0	0	2	17	4	17^1	12	1	0.5	5.2	10	75.0%	.216	0.75	1.04	106	0.1	92.2	71.5%	25.5%	54.9%
Jose Alvarez	SF	MLB	33	2	1	1	21	0	15^1	17	3	5.3	8.8	15	44.9%	.311	1.70	5.28	100	0.2	90.9	54.9%	23.3%	49.6%
Mason Black	SJ	A	22	1	1	0	8	8	34^1	25	1	2.1	11.5	44	60.2%	.293	0.96	1.57	81	0.5				
	EUG	A+	22	5	3	0	16	16	77^2	70	11	3.2	10.7	92	43.5%	.312	1.26	3.94	97	0.7				
Dominic Leone	SF	MLB	30	4	5	3	55	0	49^1	55	6	4.4	9.5	52	39.0%	.353	1.60	4.01	94	0.6	94.5	64.5%	35.8%	51.2%
Mauricio Llovera	SAC	AAA	26	2	0	1	15	0	20	13	0	1.8	12.6	28	51.1%	.289	0.85	0.00	73	0.4	96.2	48.4%	32.1%	
	SF	MLB	26	0	0	0	17	1	16^1	14	2	4.4	11.0	20	45.5%	.286	1.35	4.41	85	0.3	95.2	44.4%	30.3%	51.9%
Cole Waites	EUG	A+	24	1	1	1	13	0	12^2	10	1	2.8	19.2	27	42.9%	.450	1.11	3.55	70	0.3				
	RIC	AA	24	2	2	4	18	0	21	12	0	6.4	16.3	38	34.2%	.324	1.29	1.71	75	0.6				
	SAC	AAA	24	1	0	1	7	0	8	3	0	3.4	12.4	11	50.0%	.214	0.75	0.00	84	0.1	95.7	67.7%	31.5%	
	SF	MLB	24	0	0	0	7	0	5^2	6	1	6.4	6.4	4	41.2%	.313	1.76	3.18	107	0.0	96.0	70.2%	17.3%	55.4%

The Giants continued their "hot pitchers in your area" strategy by picking up Santa Rosa-born **Scott Alexander**, who'd dealt with shoulder inflammation with the Dodgers in '21. He's an extreme ground-ball pitcher, which seems like a mismatch for the Giants' virulently poor infield defense in 2022, but maybe Zaidi and Co. have an answer for the "???" before the "step three: profit" stage. ⚾ When healthy, **Jose Alvarez** was a key part of the Giants' improbable 2021 run, but the injury monster reared up again in 2022, and the particularly scary "elbow inflammation" one at that, curtailing his season and limiting his effectiveness when he was on the mound. Coming into his age-34 season it's possible "La Llave" ("The Key") has run out of locks to try. ⚾ **Mason Black** has a starting pitcher's build but not yet a starting pitcher's arsenal. The mid-90s high-spin fastball/sinker duo is an excellent one-two punch, and he throws a sweeping slider that can get whiffs when he can land it, but he needs one other reliable offering—either the change or a splitter—in order to become a rotation mainstay. ⚾ The Giants seem intent on cornering the market on relievers named Sam who grew up in Northern California. **Sam Delaplane** has been dealt some arm injuries, but when healthy has had one of the best strikeout pitches in the minors, a double-plus slider that makes batters both hoot and holler with rage as they flail after it. ⚾ A career-low ERA and friendly BABIP last year masked a troubling drop in strikeouts that seemed to hit, Cinderella-like, right at the stroke of **Dominic Leone**'s 30th birthday. The Giants released him this September after a bout with elbow inflammation to look for another dance partner at the ball. ⚾ The Giants love to target relievers from organizations they feel don't make the most of their prospects, and **Mauricio Llovera**, formerly of the Phillies, is a poster child for this. Since signing on with San Francisco in 2021, he's struck out a higher percentage of batters than ever, partly thanks to a fastball that touches 98 paired with a sweeping slider. ⚾ **Cole Waites** was a dizzying spectator experience in his short MLB stint, both for the corkscrew torsion of his follow-through, and the centrifugal force of the runners circling the bases around him. He's a fastball-slider guy who relies on high velocity over movement, so getting that four-seamer near the plate will be a necessity, or else someone is going to wind up sick. ⚾ The Giants popped lefty **Carson Whisenhunt** with their 2022 second-round pick despite his modest upside and the suspension for banned substance use he'd earned earlier in his collegiate career. He has a plus curveball but has yet to throw 100 innings between college and the pros.

HOUSTON ASTROS

Essay by Ted Walker
Player comments by BP staff

At dawn every school day, I serve as barkeep behind our kitchen island, slinging milk and waffles while Astrid, age 10, and Everett, age 8, pepper me with questions. Good questions. Life questions. *How does a battleship float?* Physics, most likely. *Where is the end of space?* There isn't one, next question. *Are the Astros still cheating?* Time to put on my parenting hat and work my way through carefully. I don't know if they are cheating anymore, but I don't think so. *But they did cheat, right?* That's right, and they got caught and punished. Sort of. Well, the organization was punished. *What other baseball players have cheated?* The Black Sox were paid by bad guys to lose on purpose. King Kelly used to skip second base when nobody was looking. In the '90s, a lot of people took medicine called steroids to make them stronger when they weren't allowed to. *Jose Altuve never took steroids, though, right?* That's right. *And the Astros are really good now, without cheating?* Well, you can see that. My chin is typically in my hands by this point, my expression veiled by a gauze of melancholy woven together with golden thread. The golden thread of relentless victory. This complex textile is their birthright.

Sailing back to calmer waters, they change the subject to catching. *This is how you frame, right dad?* I throw Astrid an invisible pitch. She cups her hand around it so it catches the edge of her waffle. *Why did you like being a catcher?* Best position in baseball. I was involved in every play, could see everything. Catchers are the field generals. *Were you a good catcher?* I was okay. *But you played in college so you have to be…pretty good?* I have answered these questions many times; they enjoy their predictability and their cadence. My career as a Division III backup catcher toiling in the chilly foothills of the Green Mountains of Vermont holds for them, I think, the wonderment of what other lives your parents have led.

Who is the best catcher right now? Come on, too easy: Machete. Martín Maldonado. You can't get a ball past him. What color is his hair today, you don't even know! *But he's a terrible hitter, right, dad?* They start to defend him before I can, then we join in a chorus. He's so good that he could hit for a zero average and still start in the playoffs. *Great defensive catchers are so rare it doesn't matter if they can hit.* Darn tootin', I say, drawing a sip of joe from my mug inscribed

HOUSTON ASTROS PROSPECTUS

2022 W-L: 106-56, 1st in AL West

Pythag	.654	*3rd*	DER	.724	*2nd*
RS/G	4.55	*8th*	DRC+	109	*4th*
RA/G	3.20	*2nd*	DRA-	86	*1st*
dWin%	.622	*1st*	FIP	3.28	*1st*
Payroll	$175M	*10th*	B-Age	29.7	*24th*
M$/MW	$2.7M	*7th*	P-Age	29.6	*16th*

409′
362′
373′
315′
326′

- Opened 2000
- Retractable roof
- Natural surface
- Fence profile: 7′ to 25′

Park Factors

Runs	Runs/RH	Runs/LH	HR/RH	HR/LH
101	102	99	117	98

Top Hitter WARP	6.0 Yordan Alvarez
Top Pitcher WARP	4.5 Justin Verlander
2023 Top Prospect	Hunter Brown

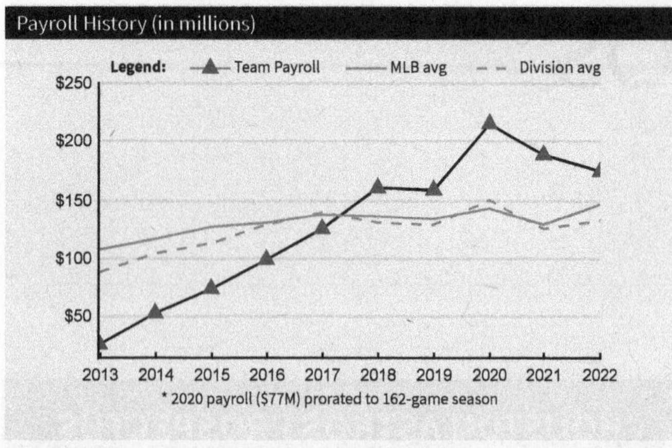

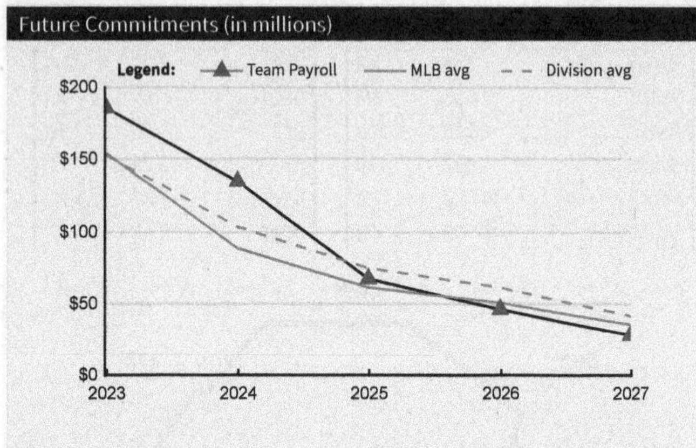

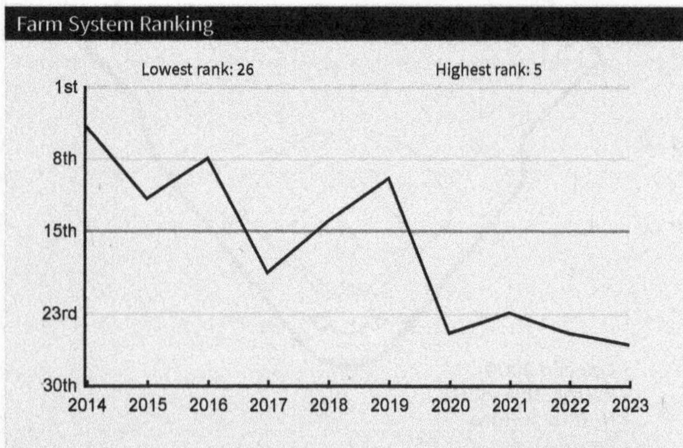

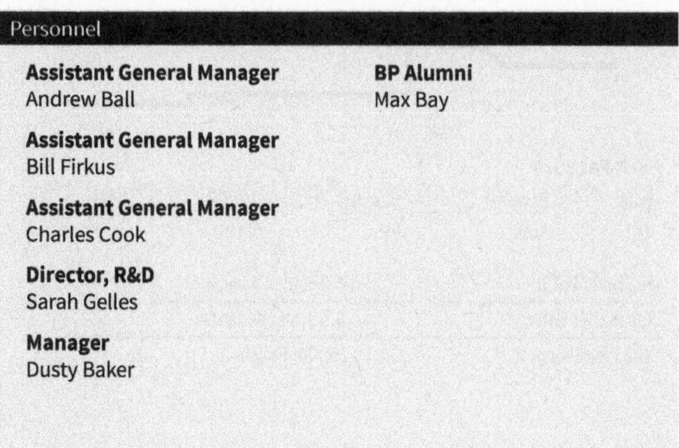
Personnel

Assistant General Manager
Andrew Ball

Assistant General Manager
Bill Firkus

Assistant General Manager
Charles Cook

Director, R&D
Sarah Gelles

Manager
Dusty Baker

BP Alumni
Max Bay

DAD JOKES SERVED DAILY. He once wore a Father's Day tie over his chest protector, in a game! And imagine it, he played out the end of the season and the playoffs with a broken hand and a sports hernia. *What is a sportsermia?* He won't let this team be disrespected without a fight. He said it straight to the camera: they asked for Houston, they got Houston. *Is that why they were yelling that at the parade?* Something like that.

This fall, Astrid dedicated herself to catching. I took the news as calmly as she delivered it. We attend the extra pitching clinics, where she is the only catcher. Pitchers want all the attention, she tells me. I nod, playing it cool. A coach spends some time with her. Glove-hand thumb down, back straight. Astrid nods with every bit of knowledge. I quietly offer a supplemental tip and she narrows her eyes like a viper. We save our catching for breakfast.

Maldonado catches a pitch like river water moving around a rock. Astrid's form is compact and by the book, more akin to the fundamentally flawless Astros defensive legend Brad Ausmus. Her back is straight and her knees are off the ground, perfectly parallel, in the old style. Her throwing arm is placed behind her back, like that of an embassy guard upon arrival of a foreign dignitary. When a ball is in the dirt, she flicks her glove over with seemingly little effort. You're a natural, I tell her, but I don't look up from the fried eggs. The pan is hot, but I play it cool.

Tuesday morning, the day after the World Series victory parade. This isn't normal, you know, I tell them as I slide them bananas and peanut butter. From their parade float, Framber Valdez and Héctor Neris doused us in suds. *What is this?!* Everett yelled. Beer, I said. *Héctor Neris sprayed us with beer!* Maldy hung out on the dad float with Verlander. For 50 years we didn't win a thing, I tell them. They wring every bit of joy from the victories—after the last out, we hugged in a jumping, rotating circle—but as Astros fans they've glimpsed the other side of the coin. In the heat of the 2021 World Series, their sweet, beloved 12-year-old cousin, a Braves fan, flamed us with a "trashstros" text. Everett and Astrid must have seen the cloud pass over my face. After that, their questions took on a searching tone, as did my answers. *Are they the trashstros?* No, they aren't. *He said they are trash.* He is saying what he's hearing.

On a team of such broad-based excellence, Maldonado is an unlikely deity. Kyle Tucker is tall and lanky in the DiMaggio mold. Alex Bregman, the indefatigable gym rat and quote-unquote baseball guy, is a middleweight who uses every muscle in a perfectly efficient swing. Yordan Alvarez scratches his back on mountain peaks and guzzles lakes dry. Justin Verlander will have his face on a plaque in due time. Maldonado batted below the Mendoza line, and advanced stats don't pretty up the picture. But, according to his teammates and coaches, he is an indispensable communicator and a preparation obsessive. As a bilingual catcher, he imparts his deep knowledge to every pitcher directly. Ryan Pressly described an apparently typical scene in which a single blue glow emanates from one seat of an otherwise dark and sleeping airplane cabin. It's Maldonado, building his own scouting report for the next game, to supplement the report already provided by the team. In 2021, Red Sox manager Alex Cora reflected on the source of the trouncing they endured at the hands of the Astros in the ALCS: "Brent Strom and Martín Maldonado. Two of the smartest people in baseball."

Midseason, *Houston Chronicle* writer Danielle Lerner prodded him about his poor hitting. "I get frustrated, yes," he told her. "Overall, I know there is a reason why they got me here. I'm doing what I was supposed to do, taking care of my pitchers. That's my number one priority." I once heard an interview with his mother in the stands, who admitted she gave him a hard time about his batting average. In October, cries of "trick or treat" were matched in volume only by those "bench Maldy." I was susceptible to the impulse. No matter how great the lineup overall, the automatic out elicits a deep desire to amputate the diseased limb. Midseason pickup Christian Vázquez was a perfectly rational alternative, and indeed he started a good number of games in the second half. But Maldy caught the lion's share of starts from Justin Verlander and Framber Valdez during their stellar years. Dusty Baker defends his lineup choices like few others. "He's my field general," he said in July under questioning. "He studies like crazy."

In a World Series-winning year, the endgame can grab all of the oxygen. But the soul of the 2022 season for our family was cemented on July 3, against the Angels and starting pitcher Shohei Ohtani. The family was there, in person, to see Shohei, but we left with another name in our throats. In the top of the fifth, Los Angeles Angel Taylor Ward flipped a single to Tucker in right field. Tucker blithely tossed it in to Altuve. As we, like most of the crowd, turned our attention to the next hitter, the first-base umpire suddenly threw his arms out, calling Ward safe. Safe from what, we had no idea. But we saw Maldonado striding back to home plate from first, telling Baker in the dugout to review the play. We learned by watching the big screen that while Ward had rounded first, with first baseman Yuli Gurriel near the outfield grass, Maldy had moved in to cover the bag. Altuve clocked the maneuver and whipped the ball to his catcher. Ward saw it happening, but with his back to first he blindly and futilely attempted to find the base with his heel as Maldonado put the tag on. Upon review, the New York review crew called him out. We screamed the name of Machete into the pale green rafters of Minute Maid Park.

Most pundits, by season's end, talked about how probable an Astros World Series was. In late October 2022, Timothy Jackson wrote in BP's digital pages that "[the Astros] are a machine with parts you can see and products you can imagine in action without knowing much — beyond how you'll get a win at the end, but full well knowing you will get a win." Maldonado's efforts, though, his insights and adjustments, are invisible to the naked eye and resistant to analysis. What trace does an inkling leave in the cloud? What algorithm can predict one man's shift of a couple of inches at a pivotal moment in a World Series game to raise the probability of his success from meager to merely plain awful?

On November 5, in the last game of the 2022 Classic, Maldonado stepped a bit closer to home plate against Zack Wheeler, who had dominated that night with his tailing heater and held a 1-0 lead. When one of those fastballs tailed into the batter's box, Maldy was waiting. He took the pitch off the elbow and took his base. While Maldy would be forced out at second on an Altuve fielder's choice, shortstop Jeremy Peña ran Wheeler from the game a batter later with a single. Soon after, Alvarez sealed up the season with his last home run of the playoffs. As loud as Minute Maid Park was when Yordan's bomb cleared the batter's eye in dead center field, it was just as still and quiet on the early-morning airplane plane full of sleeping Astros when (in my imagination) Martín Maldonado found, on his fifth or sixth pass through Zach Wheeler's scouting report, a tendency to let the ball run in just a little against right-handed batters, giving him just enough knowledge to step into the path of a near-miracle.

Catchers take part in every play. This is the standard pitch to youngsters: for the small price of an armful of bruises you'll never taste boredom on the ballfield again! I lean on the idea on Astrid's tough days. With their omnipresence on screen, major league catchers shape the game as fans know it, too. As we see it. Baseball is the cadence of the catcher's pitch-calling, their subtle moves to get in position, their receiving, their particular style of throwing the ball back to the pitcher. How much of a season quite literally centers around the catcher! Machete framed our year in baseball.

As a catcher, I'm not a Machete, Astrid says, accurately. The fall softball season is over. A time of reflection has settled in. I miss watching her catch already, her consistency and confidence, which improved so much in that short season. I must wait until spring to again marvel at the way she pounds her glove twice before putting her hand cleanly behind her back. Watching her catch, the world falls away, as the world would recede when I caught a game. *As a catcher, I'm more of an Astrid,* she says.

José Abreu has since joined the Astros as a free agent. Over oatmeal laced with honey and peanut butter, the kids and I touch base. On his facial hair (awesome pirate beard), his country of origin (Cuba, like Yordan and Yuli), his demeanor (not feisty). Everett is a first baseman, constantly scanning the horizon for new heroes. We will get to know Abreu in our way, the way we came to know Maldonado. There are many conversations to come. I think I know how they will go, but I know better than to think I'm right; the pleasure is in learning just how it is that I will be wrong. *I'm, like, an Anthony Rizzo, says Everett. I wonder if I'm a José Abreu.* We'll see, I tell him. We shall see.

—Ted Walker is the co-founder of the former baseball blog Pitchers & Poets.

Hitters

José Abreu 1B

Born: 01/29/87 Age: 36 Bats: R Throws: R Height: 6'3" Weight: 235 lb. Origin: International Free Agent, 2013

YEAR	TEAM	LVL	AGE	PA	R	2B	3B	HR	RBI	BB	K	SB	CS	Whiff%	AVG/OBP/SLG	DRC+	BABIP	BRR	DRP	WARP
2020	CHW	MLB	33	262	43	15	0	19	60	18	59	0	0	30.1%	.317/.370/.617	141	.350	-1.9	1B(54): 0.6	1.8
2021	CHW	MLB	34	659	86	30	2	30	117	61	143	1	0	27.4%	.261/.351/.481	120	.293	1.3	1B(135): 1	3.3
2022	CHW	MLB	35	679	85	40	0	15	75	62	110	0	0	23.1%	.304/.378/.446	125	.350	1.5	1B(128): 0.1	3.7
2023 DC	*HOU*	*MLB*	*36*	*602*	*76*	*29*	*1*	*23*	*80*	*51*	*110*	*0*	*0*	*24.1%*	*.280/.355/.468*	*129*	*.314*	*-1.4*	*1B 1*	*3.0*

Comparables: Eddie Murray (86), Steve Garvey (84), George Burns (83)

A funny thing happened to Abreu on his way to the standard mid-30s downturn: He turned into prime Mark Grace. The longtime '90s Cub, you'll remember, was never a prototypical first baseman. Instead of being stretched at the seams with muscles and hitting 450-foot blasts, he plied his trade for 16 years using a keen eye and scarcely matched bat-to-ball ability. This comp is a stretch, of course, because Abreu's 62 walks would've represented Grace's 11th-best full-season mark, and his 110 strikeouts were nearly double that of the Little Hurt's largest tally. But it's a different game these days, and what Abreu lost in power—his 15 home runs in 157 games were the fewest in his MLB career, even factoring in 2020—he made up for with the best contact rate and OBP of his career. Those walk and strikeout marks also represented high-water marks (over a full season). Even before he signed a $50 million extension in November 2019, many were presaging Abreu's downfall, but it still hasn't arrived. The Astros are betting it won't for at least another three years.

Jose Altuve 2B

Born: 05/06/90 Age: 33 Bats: R Throws: R Height: 5'6" Weight: 166 lb. Origin: International Free Agent, 2007

YEAR	TEAM	LVL	AGE	PA	R	2B	3B	HR	RBI	BB	K	SB	CS	Whiff%	AVG/OBP/SLG	DRC+	BABIP	BRR	DRP	WARP
2020	HOU	MLB	30	210	32	9	0	5	18	17	39	2	3	20.4%	.219/.286/.344	92	.250	1.6	2B(48): -0.6	0.6
2021	HOU	MLB	31	678	117	32	1	31	83	66	91	5	3	16.1%	.278/.350/.489	126	.280	2.3	2B(144): 2.1	5.1
2022	HOU	MLB	32	604	103	39	0	28	57	66	87	18	1	16.4%	.300/.387/.533	145	.315	0.1	2B(135): -2.3	4.9
2023 DC	*HOU*	*MLB*	*33*	*648*	*101*	*29*	*1*	*28*	*75*	*65*	*82*	*13*	*2*	*16.6%*	*.284/.363/.491*	*138*	*.289*	*4.4*	*2B 1*	*5.5*

Comparables: Roberto Alomar (79), Billy Herman (75), Frankie Frisch (74)

"I am large, I contain multitudes." - Whitman

"I am small, I contain multitudes." - Hit Man

A consistent hitter in the macro sense, Altuve can be prone to streaks of utter helplessness, as evidenced by his 0-for-23 start to the playoffs that somehow looked even worse than that stat line suggests. Then he hit .314 to close out the title run, because he's Jose Altuve. A slugger by any definition of the word, his power carries far beyond the Crawford Boxes. No longer one of the fastest players in baseball (though still no slowpoke), he went three full seasons without double-digit steals, only to eclipse that mark this year yet somehow be *less* valuable on the bases.

What makes 'Tuve excellent is the same thing that makes him disappear, on occasion: an aggressiveness in the batter's box that turns first pitches into OK Corral showdowns. When he's on, nobody in the game has a quicker draw, and Altuve leaps on "get-ahead" four-seamers to set off an Astros rally or put a run on the board all on his own. When he's off, he plunks a slider into the dirt, shakes his head and spends the next hour getting antsy for another chance. Such variance is, aesthetically and analytically, out of keeping with the tenets of contemporary baseball and in particular of the Houston Astros. (He is in every way—size, selection, swing—Yordan Alvarez's opposite.) Two titles in, though, nobody can say it doesn't work.

Yordan Alvarez DH/LF

Born: 06/27/97 Age: 26 Bats: L Throws: R Height: 6'5" Weight: 225 lb. Origin: International Free Agent, 2016

YEAR	TEAM	LVL	AGE	PA	R	2B	3B	HR	RBI	BB	K	SB	CS	Whiff%	AVG/OBP/SLG	DRC+	BABIP	BRR	DRP	WARP
2020	HOU	MLB	23	9	2	0	0	1	4	0	1	0	0	14.3%	.250/.333/.625	95	.167	0.5		0.1
2021	HOU	MLB	24	598	92	35	1	33	104	50	145	1	0	22.7%	.277/.346/.531	118	.320	1.6	LF(41): -0.3	3.1
2022	HOU	MLB	25	561	95	29	2	37	97	78	106	1	1	23.4%	.306/.406/.613	156	.320	-0.2	LF(56): -0.2	5.3
2023 DC	*HOU*	*MLB*	*26*	*604*	*93*	*29*	*2*	*37*	*103*	*75*	*129*	*0*	*1*	*23.0%*	*.293/.388/.572*	*164*	*.323*	*-3.5*	*LF 0*	*5.6*

Comparables: Anthony Rizzo (62), Justin Morneau (62), Billy Butler (61)

We can quantify just about everything that happens on the baseball field. Whether it's exit velocity, chase rate, walks, DRC+, hell, even arm strength, Alvarez ranks at or near the top of the leaderboard. Still, there are mysteries we can't quantify. If we could, though, it's safe to say Alvarez would be off the charts for "that feeling in your bones when this guy comes to the plate."

A tree trunk of a man, with the plate discipline and confidence of a 15-year veteran, Alvarez completed just his second full season in 2022. He's only 87 days older than wunderkind teammate Jeremy Peña. Yet, his 6-foot-5 frame engulfs the batter's box in a way that commands respect. His sheer gravity seems to warp home plate into a fun house mirror, taking every pitch and distorting it into a beach ball thrown right down the middle. If there's a way to beat him, no one has found it yet. He inflicts pain on lefties and righties with equal disdain. He slugged .572 against fastballs and .570 against breaking balls, which is terrifying enough before you see his .821 mark against off-speed offerings. He bookended the Astros' playoff run with two of the most majestic home runs in living memory. His second-decker off Robbie Ray supplied the highest WPA of any play in playoff history, and his vaporization of a 99-mph fastball off Jose Alvarado the highest WTF of any play in the Astros' books.

Both pitchers were brought in specifically to face Alvarez. It didn't work. It never works. Alvarez is inevitable. You can feel it in your bones.

Colin Barber OF Born: 12/04/00 Age: 22 Bats: L Throws: L Height: 6'0" Weight: 200 lb. Origin: Round 4, 2019 Draft (#136 overall)

YEAR	TEAM	LVL	AGE	PA	R	2B	3B	HR	RBI	BB	K	SB	CS	Whiff%	AVG/OBP/SLG	DRC+	BABIP	BRR	DRP	WARP
2021	ASH	A+	20	53	10	1	0	3	7	9	22	1	1		.214/.365/.452	76	.353	0.7	RF(7): 0.5, LF(5): -0.5, CF(3): -0.8	0.0
2022	ASH	A+	21	260	35	10	1	7	33	30	57	7	4		.298/.408/.450	113	.374	-0.8	CF(20): -0.3, RF(19): -0.7, LF(15): -1.6	0.8
2023 non-DC	*HOU*	*MLB*	*22*	*251*	*22*	*9*	*1*	*3*	*22*	*20*	*67*	*3*	*1*	*28.3%*	*.220/.300/.327*	*75*	*.296*	*-0.2*	*LF 0, CF 0*	*-0.2*

Comparables: Danry Vasquez (75), Trayvon Robinson (74), Brandon Nimmo (73)

Barber got a lot of behind-the-curtain buzz over the past few years, gaining a reputation for loud contact in mostly unseen-to-the-public places like a hastily organized Illinois 2020 pandemic summer league, the alternate site and the instructional leagues. His 2021 season was extremely truncated due to a shoulder injury, so 2022 represented his first extended game action in affiliated ball. While he played pretty well overall, showing off solid contact abilities and a strong plate approach, the big pop didn't actually show up in games. Without hitting the ball hard his profile starts to look a wee bit tweenerish—a little light on the glove for center, a little light on the bat for the corners—so let's hope he starts putting a bit more of a charge into it.

Michael Brantley DH/LF Born: 05/15/87 Age: 36 Bats: L Throws: L Height: 6'2" Weight: 209 lb. Origin: Round 7, 2005 Draft (#205 overall)

YEAR	TEAM	LVL	AGE	PA	R	2B	3B	HR	RBI	BB	K	SB	CS	Whiff%	AVG/OBP/SLG	DRC+	BABIP	BRR	DRP	WARP
2020	HOU	MLB	33	187	24	15	0	5	22	17	28	2	0	16.4%	.300/.364/.476	104	.336	-2.2	LF(19): 3	0.7
2021	HOU	MLB	34	508	68	29	3	8	47	33	53	1	0	11.0%	.311/.362/.437	110	.337	-0.4	LF(84): -2.6, RF(8): -0.5	2.0
2022	HOU	MLB	35	277	28	14	1	5	26	31	30	1	1	12.7%	.288/.370/.416	115	.311	-1.9	LF(29): -1.3	0.9
2023 DC	*HOU*	*MLB*	*36*	*516*	*67*	*25*	*1*	*12*	*55*	*45*	*56*	*2*	*0*	*12.7%*	*.294/.361/.440*	*127*	*.312*	*0.8*	*LF 3*	*3.2*

Comparables: Lou Brock (74), Heinie Manush (71), Garret Anderson (69)

For the first time since 2017, Brantley played in fewer than 75% of possible games in a season, thanks to a shoulder injury that ended his campaign in June. For the second season in a row, his OPS sat below .800. These details sound like they portray a player at the edge of the cliff with rocks crumbling beneath their foot, and yet, Brantley still has one the unique skill sets in the league. Despite not having the power he used to—he had more homers in his Astros debut in 2019 (19) than the last three years combined (18)—there is no one who makes as much contact as him while also driving the ball as hard. He'll play more DH than outfield at this point but an unmatched carrying tool makes that palatable, as long as his surgically repaired shoulder can hold up. That's a big "if" for a guy who will play most of the season at 36.

Alex Bregman 3B Born: 03/30/94 Age: 29 Bats: R Throws: R Height: 6'0" Weight: 192 lb. Origin: Round 1, 2015 Draft (#2 overall)

YEAR	TEAM	LVL	AGE	PA	R	2B	3B	HR	RBI	BB	K	SB	CS	Whiff%	AVG/OBP/SLG	DRC+	BABIP	BRR	DRP	WARP
2020	HOU	MLB	26	180	19	12	1	6	22	24	26	0	0	14.7%	.242/.350/.451	116	.254	0.0	3B(42): -1.2	0.7
2021	SUG	AAA	27	44	6	3	0	1	5	7	2	0	0		.250/.386/.417	118	.242	-1.1	3B(10): 1.7	0.3
2021	HOU	MLB	27	400	54	17	0	12	55	44	53	1	0	13.5%	.270/.355/.422	119	.286	-0.8	3B(90): -2.5	2.0
2022	HOU	MLB	28	656	93	38	0	23	93	87	77	1	2	14.9%	.259/.366/.454	133	.260	0.6	3B(154): 5.4	4.9
2023 DC	*HOU*	*MLB*	*29*	*600*	*79*	*28*	*1*	*25*	*81*	*78*	*73*	*2*	*0*	*14.6%*	*.267/.374/.475*	*138*	*.270*	*-0.3*	*3B 2*	*4.2*

Comparables: Ron Santo (80), Richie Hebner (79), Scott Rolen (78)

Bregman posted his healthiest campaign since 2019 last year, which, coincidentally, yielded his most productive one since then, too. He's never played as many games in a single season and hit so few homers (23), which might suggest he's fighting off a power outage despite a rebound in that department. The narrative can be shaded differently if you acknowledge the late-season increase in slugging that got him over the 20-homer mark. He also maintained it through the playoffs, where he hit four more long balls and his eight total extra-base knocks accounted for more than half of his hits. Over the course of the year, he saw a lot more sliders, but it's unclear why the opposition thought that would be a valid strategy: He generated a .386 wOBA against them, tied for the best mark of his career and his best number since 2018.

Bregman's defense also rebounded from bad to neutral this year. He isn't exactly playing at peak anymore, but still being able to produce four-win seasons means he's one of the best third basemen in the league, a necessity for a team with offensive depth that is still impressive but slowly dissipating. Though there have been a few more ebbs and flows to Bregman's trajectory than Astros fans might have preferred from such a touted young player, they can't quibble with the general arc. The plucky tagalong on one title team becomes the old head on another.

Jason Castro C Born: 06/18/87 Age: 36 Bats: L Throws: R Height: 6'3" Weight: 215 lb. Origin: Round 1, 2008 Draft (#10 overall)

YEAR	TEAM	LVL	AGE	PA	R	2B	3B	HR	RBI	BB	K	SB	CS	Whiff%	AVG/OBP/SLG	DRC+	BABIP	BRR	DRP	WARP
2020	SD	MLB	33	30	3	5	0	0	3	2	10	0	0	30.4%	.179/.233/.357	70	.278	-0.7	C(9): 0.1	-0.1
2020	LAA	MLB	33	62	5	4	0	2	6	10	23	0	0	36.5%	.192/.323/.385	73	.296	-0.1	C(17): 2	0.2
2021	HOU	MLB	34	179	22	7	0	8	21	25	54	0	0	35.1%	.235/.356/.443	93	.310	-1.6	C(52): -0.7	0.4
2022	HOU	MLB	35	88	6	2	0	1	3	8	40	1	0	42.4%	.115/.205/.179	44	.211	-0.2	C(30): -0.5	-0.3
2023 DC	*FA*	*MLB*	*36*	*148*	*15*	*5*	*0*	*4*	*16*	*16*	*53*	*0*	*0*	*38.1%*	*.208/.309/.369*	*86*	*.311*	*0.0*	*C 0*	*0.3*

Comparables: Brian Schneider (64), Dave Valle (61), Darrell Porter (60)

YEAR	TEAM	P. COUNT	FRM RUNS	BLK RUNS	THRW RUNS	TOT RUNS
2020	LAA	2172	2.0	0.0	0.0	2.0
2020	SD	1135	0.0	-0.1	0.0	0.0
2021	HOU	5964	-1.2	-0.2	0.5	-0.8
2022	HOU	3202	-0.9	-0.1	0.4	-0.6
2023	*FA*	*6956*	*0.5*	*-0.1*	*0.0*	*0.3*

Castro the Astro had the best seat in the house for some truly terrible baseball at the start of his career. A first-round pick by Houston in 2008, he just missed out on a 2017 ring, leaving for Minnesota in free agency that off-season. He returned to the 'Stros in 2021 and punched in for some off-the-bench duty during their playoff run, even clocking a homer against Boston. But age finally caught up with the catcher last year, and knee surgery rendered him unfit for any postseason participation in what would become the franchise's second Castro-adjacent title. Still, Castro got his ring before he retired, giving a grace note of human wisdom to the otherwise optimized club. Hang around long enough, and what you missed out on might be given back, in some small way.

J.C. Correa C Born: 09/15/98 Age: 24 Bats: R Throws: R Height: 6'0" Weight: 200 lb. Origin: Round 38, 2019 Draft (#1156 overall)

YEAR	TEAM	LVL	AGE	PA	R	2B	3B	HR	RBI	BB	K	SB	CS	Whiff%	AVG/OBP/SLG	DRC+	BABIP	BRR	DRP	WARP
2021	FAY	A	22	255	44	19	2	5	32	28	30	7	7		.306/.392/.477	128	.335	-2.0	SS(30): 0.4, 1B(11): 0.3, 3B(9): 2.5	1.6
2021	ASH	A+	22	193	33	13	0	4	25	7	29	3	2		.314/.337/.449	110	.353	-0.4	2B(14): -0.7, 3B(13): -1.5, 1B(8): -0.5	0.5
2022	ASH	A+	23	453	59	29	1	8	64	37	36	1	2		.309/.364/.446	121	.317	-3.0	C(65): -15.2, 2B(20): -0.4, 3B(15): -0.6	0.6
2023 non-DC	*HOU*	*MLB*	*24*	*251*	*21*	*12*	*1*	*2*	*22*	*15*	*31*	*2*	*1*	*16.1%*	*.264/.313/.361*	*91*	*.296*	*-1.8*	*C 0, 1B 0*	*0.3*

Comparables: Gerson Montilla (73), Jose Trevino (68), Tyler Bortnick (68)

YEAR	TEAM	P. COUNT	FRM RUNS	BLK RUNS	THRW RUNS	TOT RUNS
2022	ASH	10351	-13.2	-3.5	2.2	-14.5
2023	*HOU*	*6956*	*-6.2*	*-1.9*	*-0.4*	*-8.4*

The younger brother of departed Astros superstar Carlos Correa, J.C. has an uphill battle to top Carlos at most things on the field, but when he graduated from Lamar University he became the first person in his family to earn a bachelor's degree. Take that, big bro. Correa the Younger was taken twice by the Astros as a very late courtesy pick before finally signing as a 2020 undrafted free agent for the princely sum of $20,000. Carlos isn't here anymore, but his little brother turned out to be no nepotism signing; he's displayed some of the best bat-to-ball ability in the low-minors and is now a real prospect in his own right. And an interesting one on defense, too, logging at least 15 games at catcher, second and third base.

Mauricio Dubón UT Born: 07/19/94 Age: 28 Bats: R Throws: R Height: 6'0" Weight: 173 lb. Origin: Round 26, 2013 Draft (#773 overall)

YEAR	TEAM	LVL	AGE	PA	R	2B	3B	HR	RBI	BB	K	SB	CS	Whiff%	AVG/OBP/SLG	DRC+	BABIP	BRR	DRP	WARP
2020	SF	MLB	25	177	21	4	1	4	19	15	36	2	3	24.3%	.274/.337/.389	101	.328	-0.9	CF(44): -1.2, 2B(8): -0.1, SS(8): 0.1	0.4
2021	SAC	AAA	26	283	41	13	2	8	31	29	38	9	3		.332/.410/.498	117	.365	2.0	SS(51): -3.2, 2B(3): 1.2, LF(3): -0.7	1.5
2021	SF	MLB	26	187	20	9	0	5	22	9	41	2	1	23.0%	.240/.278/.377	90	.282	-2.4	CF(27): -1.1, SS(21): -0.3, 2B(20): 0.2	0.1
2022	SF	MLB	27	49	10	1	0	2	8	1	4	0	0	14.8%	.239/.245/.391	110	.214	-0.4	CF(14): -0.4, SS(4): -0.5, 3B(3): -0.3	0.1
2022	HOU	MLB	27	216	21	8	0	3	16	12	26	2	3	15.5%	.208/.254/.294	93	.222	0.3	CF(45): 0.6, SS(17): 0.5, 2B(16): -0.5	0.8
2023 DC	*HOU*	*MLB*	*28*	*258*	*28*	*9*	*0*	*6*	*27*	*15*	*34*	*6*	*3*	*17.0%*	*.262/.312/.391*	*96*	*.282*	*-0.9*	*CF 0, LF 0*	*0.5*

Comparables: Donovan Solano (48), Brian L. Hunter (47), Cameron Maybin (46)

Dubón's time in San Francisco ended without him ever elevating his bat to a level that would earn him everyday starts. That didn't change in Houston, but his ability to fill in extremely competently at both shortstop and center field ensured that he played a semi-regular role for the World Series champions right up through the Fall Classic itself. While there are probably teams for which Dubón would find his name written in the starting lineup far more often, a role which shades toward his defensive versatility continues to look like the most appropriate use of his skills.

Drew Gilbert CF Born: 09/27/00 Age: 22 Bats: L Throws: L Height: 5'9" Weight: 185 lb. Origin: Round 1, 2022 Draft (#28 overall)

YEAR	TEAM	LVL	AGE	PA	R	2B	3B	HR	RBI	BB	K	SB	CS	Whiff%	AVG/OBP/SLG	DRC+	BABIP	BRR	DRP	WARP
2022	FAY	A	21	22	4	0	0	1	2	1	0	3	1		.238/.273/.381	122	.200	-0.1	CF(5): -0.1	0.1
2023 non-DC	*HOU*	*MLB*	*22*	*251*	*21*	*9*	*1*	*3*	*22*	*15*	*54*	*15*	*6*	*25.6%*	*.236/.290/.333*	*74*	*.294*	*1.6*	*CF 0*	*0.1*

Is there more first-round pressure on a pick if the drafting team hasn't had a first-round choice in three years? Gilbert has the college numbers to support the selection, posting a 1.128 OPS in his final season for a Tennessee team that dominated the SEC. His offensive prowess is backed by dynamic center field defense, including an arm that can fire 90+ mph fastballs off the mound, a relic of Gilbert's time as a premium high school pitcher. Most importantly, he has enough swag for three first-rounders, earning himself the moniker of Bat Flip King in college. He also has enough hustle for three—perhaps even *too much*, as his first pro season ended early when he dislocated his right elbow running into the center field wall.

Korey Lee C/DH Born: 07/25/98 Age: 24 Bats: R Throws: R Height: 6'2" Weight: 210 lb. Origin: Round 1, 2019 Draft (#32 overall)

YEAR	TEAM	LVL	AGE	PA	R	2B	3B	HR	RBI	BB	K	SB	CS	Whiff%	AVG/OBP/SLG	DRC+	BABIP	BRR	DRP	WARP
2021	GDD	WIN	22	71	8	2	0	1	6	9	19	1	0		.258/.352/.339		.357			
2021	ASH	A+	22	121	24	5	0	3	14	12	24	1	0		.330/.397/.459	112	.402	-0.6	C(20): -0.5, 3B(2): 0.3	0.5
2021	CC	AA	22	203	25	9	1	8	27	17	35	3	1		.254/.320/.443	116	.275	1.3	C(38): -1.6, 3B(4): -0.1, 1B(3): 0.2	1.1
2021	SUG	AAA	22	38	2	4	0	0	4	2	9	0	0		.229/.263/.343	83	.296	0.1	C(4): -0.5, 1B(2): -0.6	-0.1
2022	SUG	AAA	23	446	74	20	2	25	76	36	127	12	1	32.9%	.238/.307/.483	93	.281	2.1	C(66): 4.2, LF(2): 0.1, 1B(1): -0.0	1.5
2022	HOU	MLB	23	26	1	2	0	0	4	1	9	0	0	30.0%	.160/.192/.240	79	.250	-0.2	C(12): -1.2	-0.1
2023 DC	*HOU*	*MLB*	*24*	*217*	*22*	*8*	*0*	*6*	*22*	*13*	*61*	*3*	*0*	*30.7%*	*.211/.266/.364*	*70*	*.267*	*0.8*	*C -12*	*-1.2*

Comparables: Danny Jansen (71), Devin Mesoraco (64), John Ryan Murphy (63)

YEAR	TEAM	P. COUNT	FRM RUNS	BLK RUNS	THRW RUNS	TOT RUNS
2021	ASH	2963	-0.5	-0.1	-0.2	-0.8
2021	CC	5226	-1.3	-0.9	0.1	-2.0
2022	SUG	10554	4.9	-1.0	0.0	3.9
2022	HOU	1041	-1.3	0.0	0.0	-1.3
2023	*HOU*	*8418*	*-11.5*	*-0.4*	*-0.3*	*-12.3*

The lone thermal exhaust port in the Astros' Death Star over the past half-decade has been the catching position, staffed by a carousel of defense-first backstops heavy on the leadership and light on the in-box skills. Lee, already praised for his defense behind the plate, will have this season to learn the first part of that equation from Martín Maldonado while attempting to make up ground on the offensive side after a disappointing season at Triple-A Sugar Land. There, despite walloping 25 homers in the PCL's hitter-friendly parks, he spent the rest of the time hitting the ball either A) on the ground or B) not at all. The Astros are so loaded they have been able to absorb subpar production behind the dish, partially as a tradeoff for excellent support of the pitching staff, but Lee will have to show he is the droid catcher of the future Jim Crane's been looking for, or risk being sent into the garbage chute.

Pedro Leon CF Born: 05/28/98 Age: 25 Bats: R Throws: R Height: 5'10" Weight: 170 lb. Origin: International Free Agent, 2021

YEAR	TEAM	LVL	AGE	PA	R	2B	3B	HR	RBI	BB	K	SB	CS	Whiff%	AVG/OBP/SLG	DRC+	BABIP	BRR	DRP	WARP
2021	GDD	WIN	23	84	9	3	0	1	9	13	20	4	1		.257/.381/.343		.347			
2021	CC	AA	23	217	29	7	1	9	33	25	67	13	8		.249/.359/.443	101	.339	0.3	SS(41): -3.9, CF(9): 0.1	0.3
2021	SUG	AAA	23	75	11	2	0	0	2	14	23	4	2		.131/.293/.164	77	.211	0.2	SS(7): -0.5, 3B(6): -1.2, CF(4): 0.4	-0.1
2022	SUG	AAA	24	504	71	27	3	17	63	71	145	38	18	31.3%	.228/.365/.431	97	.306	-5.0	CF(53): 0.8, RF(33): -0.7, 2B(20): 1.4	1.0
2023 DC	*HOU*	*MLB*	*25*	*168*	*17*	*6*	*0*	*4*	*14*	*17*	*52*	*10*	*6*	*31.8%*	*.197/.299/.338*	*78*	*.274*	*-3.1*	*CF 0, RF 0*	*-0.4*

Comparables: Pat Valaika (64), Erik González (55), Deven Marrero (54)

Owner of one of the loudest power/speed potential packages in the minors, Leon is a diminutive dynamo. He comes at the ball with a ferocious, short uppercut, generating top-end exit velocity; he had a bunch of batted balls over 110 mph and maxed out over 113 in 2022. While his plate approach is solid enough for a healthy walk rate, his hit tool lags behind due to mediocre bat-to-ball. He's only hit .225 so far in two seasons in the American minors, and while the underlying fundamentals support a better average eventually, the maxim that hitters hit applies in inverse to Leon. Houston has tried him at both middle infield spots with mixed success due to reliability issues, and his long-term home is probably in center, where his plus-plus speed and strong arm play best. Leon has an intriguing mix of higher-end abilities, and he might have some late development relative to his age because of limited professional experience.

Joey Loperfido UT Born: 05/11/99 Age: 24 Bats: L Throws: R Height: 6'4" Weight: 195 lb. Origin: Round 7, 2021 Draft (#208 overall)

YEAR	TEAM	LVL	AGE	PA	R	2B	3B	HR	RBI	BB	K	SB	CS	Whiff%	AVG/OBP/SLG	DRC+	BABIP	BRR	DRP	WARP
2021	FAY	A	22	87	10	4	0	2	6	8	31	1	0		.116/.276/.261	85	.158	1.2	LF(7): 0.7, RF(5): -1.0, CF(4): -0.2	0.2
2022	FAY	A	23	348	51	17	3	9	45	40	76	30	9		.304/.399/.473	125	.379	-2.2	1B(27): 1.6, 2B(26): 1.3, CF(15): 0.4	2.3
2022	ASH	A+	23	113	19	8	1	3	24	13	25	2	2		.354/.434/.552	105	.443	-0.1	1B(5): -0.3, RF(5): -0.1, LF(4): 0.5	0.3
2023 non-DC	*HOU*	*MLB*	*24*	*251*	*22*	*10*	*1*	*4*	*23*	*18*	*68*	*9*	*3*	*29.5%*	*.226/.296/.343*	*77*	*.305*	*0.7*	*1B 0, 2B 0*	*-0.1*

Comparables: Logan Parker (72), Dylan Moore (69), Mickey Gasper (69)

His surname could be related to the Latin *perfidus*, meaning "incredulous," which is also the sensation one might feel looking at the unheralded seventh-rounder's stat line after his first full pro season. The Astros were cautious with Loperfido in 2022 after a slow start and an injury-shortened draft-year season, taking time to work with the Duke product on quieting and shortening up his swing, which helped solve some strikeout issues that had plagued him since college. The tougher task of the high minors still lies ahead, as he's already creeping into his mid-20s, but with a proven ability to improve on and off the field and praise heaped upon him for his work ethic by Houston's coaching staff, the results Loperfido's seeing look significantly more credible.

Bligh Madris RF Born: 02/29/96 Age: 27 Bats: L Throws: R Height: 6'0" Weight: 208 lb. Origin: Round 9, 2017 Draft (#268 overall)

YEAR	TEAM	LVL	AGE	PA	R	2B	3B	HR	RBI	BB	K	SB	CS	Whiff%	AVG/OBP/SLG	DRC+	BABIP	BRR	DRP	WARP
2020	BRI	WIN	24	98	12	5	0	3	10	12	15	1	0		.259/.347/.424		.279			
2021	IND	AAA	25	385	43	25	1	9	55	40	70	2	4		.272/.352/.434	108	.314	-4.4	RF(49): -4.7, LF(33): -1.9	0.6
2022	IND	AAA	26	288	34	19	4	7	34	29	63	4	2	20.0%	.294/.366/.482	102	.364	-3.0	RF(30): 0.9, 1B(12): -2.2, LF(10): 1.8	0.9
2022	DUR	AAA	26	46	11	3	0	4	15	4	11	0	0	13.3%	.317/.370/.683	110	.333	0.1	LF(6): -0.3, CF(4): -0.1, RF(1): -0.0	0.1
2022	PIT	MLB	26	123	10	7	0	1	7	10	31	2	1	26.8%	.177/.244/.265	70	.235	-0.2	RF(19): -0.3, 1B(9): -1, LF(5): 0.1	-0.3
2023 DC	*HOU*	*MLB*	*27*	*32*	*3*	*1*	*0*	*0*	*3*	*2*	*7*	*0*	*0*	*27.5%*	*.227/.290/.356*	*79*	*.284*	*0.0*	*LF 0*	*0.0*

Comparables: Scott Cousins (64), Chris Herrmann (59), Bryan Petersen (56)

Madris' 123 MLB plate appearances to date might make him look like nothing more than a pedestrian afterthought among the 20,000+ players to reach the majors, but to a tiny archipelago in the Pacific, Madris is so much more: the first Palauan to don a major league uniform, the product of a baseball-crazy culture that has been part of Palau's social fabric for nearly 100 years. Madris' auspicious, three-hit debut in June was followed by far more bad days than good, but not all achievements on the diamond should be measured solely by statistical success. The joy and pride of a nation matters, and, by that metric, for at least a few days this summer Madris was among the league's most important players.

Martín Maldonado C Born: 08/16/86 Age: 36 Bats: R Throws: R Height: 6'0" Weight: 230 lb. Origin: Round 27, 2004 Draft (#803 overall)

YEAR	TEAM	LVL	AGE	PA	R	2B	3B	HR	RBI	BB	K	SB	CS	Whiff%	AVG/OBP/SLG	DRC+	BABIP	BRR	DRP	WARP
2020	HOU	MLB	33	165	19	4	0	6	24	27	51	1	0	29.2%	.215/.350/.378	92	.295	-1.7	C(47): -3.2	-0.1
2021	HOU	MLB	34	426	40	10	1	12	36	47	127	0	0	28.8%	.172/.272/.300	75	.221	-3.0	C(123): -0.5	0.1
2022	HOU	MLB	35	379	40	12	0	15	45	22	116	0	0	32.2%	.186/.248/.352	73	.228	-2.5	C(113): 6.7	0.6
2023 DC	*HOU*	*MLB*	*36*	*372*	*39*	*12*	*0*	*12*	*37*	*30*	*112*	*0*	*0*	*31.4%*	*.197/.275/.345*	*68*	*.257*	*-1.9*	*C 4*	*0.1*

Comparables: Jeff Mathis (70), Duffy Dyer (68), Steve Yeager (65)

YEAR	TEAM	P. COUNT	FRM RUNS	BLK RUNS	THRW RUNS	TOT RUNS
2020	HOU	6449	-2.8	0.0	0.0	-2.8
2021	HOU	16739	2.1	-0.4	0.1	1.8
2022	HOU	15040	6.6	-0.1	0.3	6.8
2023	*HOU*	*14430*	*1.7*	*0.0*	*-0.1*	*1.6*

Find someone who believes in you like the Astros believe in Maldonado. The latest exhibit in Houston's commitment to the backstop's skills that don't involve the bat: The aftermath of a deadline trade for Red Sox catcher Christian Vázquez, owner of at least as prominent a share of playing time behind the dish and a batting average that Maldonado could only dream of. Would Houston move to a more equitable timeshare, or finally tire of their sub-Mendoza line production behind the plate and relegate him to second catcher duty? Of course not. Oh, Vázquez got a look-in more often than Jason Castro or Korey Lee had, but Maldonado outpaced him in starts 36-24 over those final 60 games, and when the business end of the season rolled around, it was Maldonado calling the shots behind the plate, starting 11 of the 13 games in Houston's triumphant postseason run. Perhaps before his career is over, his production at the plate will finally drop to a point that the Astros will no longer rely on him behind it, but at this stage it's very hard to imagine that there's any level of performance that would precipitate such an unthinkable event.

Chas McCormick OF Born: 04/19/95 Age: 28 Bats: R Throws: L Height: 6'0" Weight: 208 lb. Origin: Round 21, 2017 Draft (#631 overall)

YEAR	TEAM	LVL	AGE	PA	R	2B	3B	HR	RBI	BB	K	SB	CS	Whiff%	AVG/OBP/SLG	DRC+	BABIP	BRR	DRP	WARP
2021	HOU	MLB	26	320	47	12	0	14	50	25	104	4	2	35.5%	.257/.319/.447	88	.341	-2.7	LF(51): -0.4, CF(33): -0.6, RF(22): 2.7	0.6
2022	HOU	MLB	27	407	47	12	2	14	44	46	106	4	3	32.5%	.245/.332/.407	101	.308	-2.4	LF(64): -0.4, CF(60): 0.5, RF(17): 0.9	1.3
2023 DC	*HOU*	*MLB*	*28*	*296*	*33*	*9*	*1*	*9*	*29*	*30*	*81*	*4*	*2*	*32.1%*	*.232/.318/.384*	*94*	*.301*	*0.7*	*CF 1, RF 0*	*0.8*

Comparables: Chris Heisey (63), Khris Davis (59), Scott Van Slyke (58)

The league-average center fielder last year slashed .237/.303/.389, making McCormick's line look sharp even before you acknowledge the steps forward he made in on-base percentage and strikeout rate compared to his 2021 season. He took those steps by going to an aggressive approach at the plate, and by tuning into changeups (.382 wOBA) and four-seamers (.446). He does have a weak spot, though, and that's sliders, against which he generated a woeful .134 wOBA. We're not the only ones with those numbers, of course, so expect McCormick to have to improve just to stay level, as teams throw sweeper-happy righties at him. Even with his solid defense, he'll remain a fine-not-excellent option in center.

Jake Meyers CF Born: 06/18/96 Age: 27 Bats: R Throws: L Height: 6'0" Weight: 200 lb. Origin: Round 13, 2017 Draft (#391 overall)

YEAR	TEAM	LVL	AGE	PA	R	2B	3B	HR	RBI	BB	K	SB	CS	Whiff%	AVG/OBP/SLG	DRC+	BABIP	BRR	DRP	WARP
2021	SUG	AAA	25	304	52	17	2	16	51	25	59	10	3		.343/.408/.598	126	.389	-1.0	CF(25): 2.9, RF(20): 8.1, LF(16): 2.5	3.2
2021	HOU	MLB	25	163	22	8	0	6	28	10	50	3	0	29.2%	.260/.323/.438	86	.352	1.3	CF(39): -0.8, LF(4): -0.2, RF(3): 0.1	0.4
2022	SUG	AAA	26	170	26	6	1	7	18	25	30	2	0	25.0%	.306/.406/.507	122	.343	0.8	CF(30): 3.2	1.2
2022	HOU	MLB	26	160	13	6	2	1	15	7	54	2	1	31.2%	.227/.269/.313	62	.344	-0.9	CF(51): 0.7	-0.2
2023 DC	*HOU*	*MLB*	*27*	*227*	*22*	*9*	*1*	*5*	*21*	*15*	*58*	*2*	*1*	*28.8%*	*.231/.294/.363*	*81*	*.296*	*1.6*	*CF 4*	*0.8*

Comparables: Billy Burns (64), Roman Quinn (57), Justin Maxwell (56)

The shoulder injury that Meyers sustained in the 2021 playoffs had a lingering impact all season long, first pushing him to the 60-day injured list and keeping him out until June and limiting him to an OPS that was worse than nearly 90% of players who had at least as many plate appearances as he did. In total, he only got to the plate in the major leagues 160 times and took 52 games to reach that mark. When compared to his time in the minors, where he had more plate appearances in fewer games and was much better overall, it's clear he wasn't much of an option for the Astros even when he was in the big leagues. He was kept off the roster in the ALCS and World Series, and will need to make a lot of noise to seize playing time from Chas McCormick.

Jeremy Peña SS Born: 09/22/97 Age: 25 Bats: R Throws: R Height: 6'0" Weight: 202 lb. Origin: Round 3, 2018 Draft (#102 overall)

YEAR	TEAM	LVL	AGE	PA	R	2B	3B	HR	RBI	BB	K	SB	CS	Whiff%	AVG/OBP/SLG	DRC+	BABIP	BRR	DRP	WARP
2020	EST	WIN	22	129	18	2	2	3	9	7	23	7	0		.306/.349/.430		.358			
2021	EST	WIN	23	134	18	6	1	2	15	11	32	7	2		.291/.364/.410		.381			
2021	AST	ROK	23	27	3	1	1	0	2	2	6	1	0		.348/.444/.478		.471			
2021	SUG	AAA	23	133	22	4	2	10	19	6	35	5	1		.287/.346/.598	106	.325	1.1	SS(25): 2.2, 3B(2): 0.0	0.8
2022	HOU	MLB	24	558	72	20	2	22	63	22	135	11	2	29.9%	.253/.289/.426	95	.298	1.1	SS(134): -6.5	0.8
2023 DC	*HOU*	*MLB*	*25*	*588*	*65*	*20*	*3*	*19*	*63*	*28*	*146*	*15*	*4*	*29.5%*	*.252/.298/.408*	*93*	*.309*	*5.4*	*SS 0*	*1.8*

Comparables: Trea Turner (71), Tim Anderson (67), Juan Uribe (65)

Surrounded by questions about how much his brief Triple-A power breakout was real, Peña more than answered the bell in 2022. His 22 home runs were the fifth-most by a rookie shortstop all time, tying him with the very dude he was replacing in Carlos Correa. Peña might have hit more, too, if it weren't for Houston's loaded roster and flimsy division limiting him to only 136 games where he often hit at the bottom of the lineup. His biggest issue was laying off breakers down and away, leading to the highest strikeout rate of any regular on the squad. Whether he can improve on that will be worth watching, considering Houston's recent history with being one of the most disciplined clubs at the plate in the league by walk and strikeout rates. Beyond the dingers, he also graded out mostly favorable as a defender, particularly by Statcast's Outs Above Average, where he ranked 12th of 37 qualified shortstops. He's already got a firm grip on the six and with a tweak or two could be a star—a profile he previewed for us throughout Houston's World Series run.

Kyle Tucker RF Born: 01/17/97 Age: 26 Bats: L Throws: R Height: 6'4" Weight: 199 lb. Origin: Round 1, 2015 Draft (#5 overall)

YEAR	TEAM	LVL	AGE	PA	R	2B	3B	HR	RBI	BB	K	SB	CS	Whiff%	AVG/OBP/SLG	DRC+	BABIP	BRR	DRP	WARP
2020	HOU	MLB	23	228	33	12	6	9	42	18	46	8	1	22.5%	.268/.325/.512	98	.303	0.1	LF(41): 1.4, RF(7): 0.2	0.8
2021	HOU	MLB	24	567	83	37	3	30	92	53	90	14	2	20.4%	.294/.359/.557	130	.304	1.8	RF(133): 0.7, CF(4): 0	4.0
2022	HOU	MLB	25	609	71	28	1	30	107	59	95	25	4	20.0%	.257/.330/.478	123	.261	0.5	RF(147): -0.3	3.5
2023 DC	*HOU*	*MLB*	*26*	*576*	*79*	*26*	*3*	*28*	*85*	*54*	*88*	*31*	*5*	*19.9%*	*.272/.345/.504*	*136*	*.279*	*16.0*	*RF 9*	*6.4*

Comparables: Anthony Rizzo (57), Johnny Callison (55), Jay Bruce (54)

It's weird to think there could be an underrated World Series champ, and yet Tucker fits the bill. Somehow, 2022 was only his second full pro season, thanks to the pandemic-shortened year and the Astros slow-playing their last top-five draft pick—as if to savor it—for the two seasons prior. The opposite of Fox News aficionados, fans of rival AL West teams already feel like they've seen enough of Tucker, whose patience at the plate feels more appropriate to a 10-year vet. It is very difficult to bait him into bad swings, but if a pitcher puts the ball in the heart of the plate, only two other hitters—Harper and Judge—create more run value on those pitches. The one slider that isn't maxed out on Tucker's profile is speed, but with smart base-running and savvy defensive positioning in Houston's fun-sized park, even that potential weakness has been neutralized. Limiting the shift (he was shifted against over 90% of the time last season) should help boost him from "reserve All-Star" to "starting All-Star" in 2023, and build him a fanbase outside of the AL West.

Will Wagner IF Born: 07/29/98 Age: 24 Bats: L Throws: R Height: 6'0" Weight: 210 lb. Origin: Round 18, 2021 Draft (#538 overall)

YEAR	TEAM	LVL	AGE	PA	R	2B	3B	HR	RBI	BB	K	SB	CS	Whiff%	AVG/OBP/SLG	DRC+	BABIP	BRR	DRP	WARP
2021	FAY	A	22	134	22	8	1	2	14	16	33	5	0		.299/.388/.436	104	.402	2.4	2B(14): 1.1, 3B(8): -1.4, SS(7): 1.0	0.7
2022	ASH	A+	23	199	22	7	1	4	25	32	41	3	1		.276/.392/.405	110	.339	-2.5	3B(16): -0.8, 2B(12): -0.8, 1B(11): 1.1	0.5
2022	CC	AA	23	298	40	12	2	6	28	35	57	5	1		.251/.361/.386	103	.302	-2.4	2B(41): 2.5, 3B(21): -0.6, 1B(9): -1.1	0.8
2023 non-DC	*HOU*	*MLB*	*24*	*251*	*22*	*9*	*1*	*3*	*21*	*23*	*55*	*2*	*0*	*22.4%*	*.225/.306/.327*	*80*	*.284*	*1.8*	*1B 0, 2B 0*	*0.1*

Comparables: Ryan Flaherty (66), Matt Cusick (62), Drew Dosch (61)

Growing up, most of us were lucky to get a few swings in before our dad's arm gave out after a dozen 67-mph "heaters" in the batting cage. Wagner was 12 years old when his dad, Billy, retired an All-Star with plenty of gas left in the tank. That would certainly help explain the advanced hit tool he's shown so far. He's played all over the infield, though the lack of power means the bat probably only plays as a utility player. He has good command of the strike zone and puts the ball in play consistently with his opposite-field approach.

PITCHERS

Bryan Abreu RHP Born: 04/22/97 Age: 26 Bats: R Throws: R Height: 6'1" Weight: 225 lb. Origin: International Free Agent, 2013

YEAR	TEAM	LVL	AGE	W	L	SV	G	GS	IP	H	HR	BB/9	K/9	K	GB%	BABIP	WHIP	ERA	DRA-	WARP	MPH	FB%	Whiff%	CSP
2020	HOU	MLB	23	0	0	0	4	0	3^1	1	0	18.9	8.1	3	37.5%	.125	2.40	2.70	123	0.0	92.9	35.5%	23.5%	36.7%
2021	TOR	WIN	24	1	4	0	7	7	26	23	0	3.8	9.7	28	55.2%	.315	1.31	2.42						
2021	SUG	AAA	24	0	0	0	15	0	15^1	11	0	7.6	14.1	24	51.6%	.355	1.57	1.76	64	0.4				
2021	HOU	MLB	24	3	3	1	31	0	36	35	4	4.5	9.0	36	48.1%	.310	1.47	5.75	106	0.2	95.7	45.3%	31.1%	50.9%
2022	HOU	MLB	25	4	0	2	55	0	60^1	45	2	3.9	13.1	88	47.7%	.336	1.18	1.94	64	1.7	97.3	45.6%	39.1%	50.0%
2023 DC	*HOU*	*MLB*	*26*	*3*	*3*	*0*	*63*	*0*	*55*	*45*	*6*	*4.9*	*12.5*	*76*	*46.9%*	*.315*	*1.38*	*3.81*	*91*	*0.5*	*96.6*	*44.9%*	*35.3%*	*49.8%*

Comparables: Carlos Contreras (57), Dan Altavilla (56), Carl Edwards Jr. (55)

With a fastball that touches triple digits and a slider that seemingly teleports to the catcher's mitt, Abreu makes hitters look like they'd rather be anywhere than in the batter's box. Perhaps no pitch demonstrates that more than the last one he threw. With the Phillies four outs away from elimination in Game 6 of the World Series, in stepped Kyle Schwarber—brazenly nonchalant after his team was no-hit just three days prior, and an hour removed from a missile to right field that could have been the fodder of legend were it not for the nuclear blast to center field from Yordan Alvarez that followed. Two perfunctory hacks on 3,000+ rpm buzzsaw sliders allowed reality to finally set in. There was no escape. The National League home run champ literally bent the knee and offered a feeble bunt attempt on a 98-mph heater that sealed the same fate for him as almost every hitter who sees Abreu: a slow walk back to the bench wondering what in God's name just happened.

Brandon Bielak RHP Born: 04/02/96 Age: 27 Bats: L Throws: R Height: 6'2" Weight: 208 lb. Origin: Round 11, 2017 Draft (#331 overall)

YEAR	TEAM	LVL	AGE	W	L	SV	G	GS	IP	H	HR	BB/9	K/9	K	GB%	BABIP	WHIP	ERA	DRA-	WARP	MPH	FB%	Whiff%	CSP
2020	HOU	MLB	24	3	3	0	12	6	32	39	9	4.8	7.3	26	35.9%	.323	1.75	6.75	147	-0.5	92.9	63.8%	27.5%	44.4%
2021	SUG	AAA	25	2	0	0	6	3	17^1	16	0	2.1	11.4	22	54.3%	.348	1.15	2.08	83	0.3				
2021	HOU	MLB	25	3	4	1	28	2	50	48	5	3.8	8.3	46	45.3%	.305	1.38	4.50	109	0.2	93.9	61.1%	25.4%	56.0%
2022	SUG	AAA	26	3	6	0	23	14	88^2	82	5	4.4	8.7	86	44.1%	.308	1.41	3.15	86	1.2	93.5	52.9%	26.9%	
2022	HOU	MLB	26	0	0	0	5	0	12^1	11	2	2.9	8.8	12	51.4%	.273	1.22	3.65	98	0.1	93.5	59.3%	19.8%	60.5%
2023 DC	*HOU*	*MLB*	*27*	*5*	*3*	*0*	*41*	*3*	*46*	*46*	*4*	*4.1*	*7.8*	*40*	*44.7%*	*.303*	*1.46*	*4.36*	*108*	*0.1*	*93.6*	*61.4%*	*24.7%*	*53.9%*

Comparables: Adam Warren (61), Justin Grimm (60), Lance Cormier (56)

Bielak spent most of the season in the minors, a testament to Houston's pitching depth more than a commentary on his abilities. He still allowed a lot of baserunners in Triple-A, however, so maybe it's more 50-50. In his 12⅓ big-league innings, he completely ditched his cutter, leaving him with four offerings. He's the typical Astros pitcher who works the top of the zone with his fastball and the bottom of it with his breakers, his changeup playing anywhere gloveside. He remains a depth piece for the club.

★ ★ ★ *2023 Top 101 Prospect* **#45** ★ ★ ★

Hunter Brown RHP Born: 08/29/98 Age: 24 Bats: R Throws: R Height: 6'2" Weight: 212 lb. Origin: Round 5, 2019 Draft (#166 overall)

YEAR	TEAM	LVL	AGE	W	L	SV	G	GS	IP	H	HR	BB/9	K/9	K	GB%	BABIP	WHIP	ERA	DRA-	WARP	MPH	FB%	Whiff%	CSP
2021	CC	AA	22	1	4	1	13	11	49^1	45	6	5.3	13.9	76	45.5%	.379	1.50	4.20	96	0.4				
2021	SUG	AAA	22	5	1	0	11	8	51	47	6	3.7	9.7	55	52.5%	.311	1.33	3.88	84	0.7				
2022	SUG	AAA	23	9	4	1	23	14	106	70	5	3.8	11.4	134	54.3%	.271	1.08	2.55	67	2.7	96.3	52.8%	29.0%	
2022	HOU	MLB	23	2	0	0	7	2	20^1	15	0	3.1	9.7	22	64.7%	.294	1.08	0.89	90	0.3	96.8	53.1%	22.9%	58.3%
2023 DC	*HOU*	*MLB*	*24*	*8*	*6*	*0*	*50*	*12*	*100.3*	*93*	*10*	*4.3*	*9.3*	*103*	*53.8%*	*.302*	*1.41*	*3.92*	*97*	*0.8*	*96.8*	*53.1%*	*25.2%*	*58.3%*

Comparables: Anthony Reyes (71), Robinson Tejeda (67), Chris Archer (67)

If imitation is the most sincere form of flattery, Brown must make Justin Verlander feel like a king. A carbon-copy delivery has allowed the fifth-round pick to blossom into a budding star, carving up Triple-A hitters only because the Astros rotation was too deep to make room for him. Owner of the fastest slider this side of Adam Levine into your DMs, Brown has electric stuff and the command to put all four pitches anywhere he wants. The Astros should have the luxury of limiting his innings, as he's only been a starter for three seasons, maxing out at 126 innings. Still, expect him to be a mainstay in the rotation for the foreseeable future.

Austin Davis LHP

Born: 02/03/93 Age: 30 Bats: L Throws: L Height: 6'4" Weight: 235 lb. Origin: Round 12, 2014 Draft (#352 overall)

YEAR	TEAM	LVL	AGE	W	L	SV	G	GS	IP	H	HR	BB/9	K/9	K	GB%	BABIP	WHIP	ERA	DRA-	WARP	MPH	FB%	Whiff%	CSP
2020	PIT	MLB	27	0	0	0	5	0	3^{2}	1	0	2.5	7.4	3	75.0%	.125	0.55	2.45	93	0.1	93.1	58.5%	36.8%	46.8%
2020	PHI	MLB	27	0	0	0	4	0	3	10	1	3.0	6.0	2	58.8%	.563	3.67	21.00	88	0.1	94.1	50.0%	30.2%	48.9%
2021	IND	AAA	28	0	1	0	11	0	14	6	0	3.2	11.6	18	34.6%	.231	0.79	2.57	93	0.2				
2021	PIT	MLB	28	0	1	0	10	0	9^{2}	6	2	4.7	10.2	11	40.0%	.174	1.14	5.59	87	0.2	93.8	62.3%	27.9%	51.6%
2021	BOS	MLB	28	1	1	0	19	0	16^{2}	18	2	3.8	9.2	17	49.0%	.327	1.50	4.86	103	0.1	93.6	46.4%	25.9%	50.8%
2022	MIN	MLB	29	0	0	0	2	0	1^{2}	1	0	21.6	16.2	3	33.3%	.333	3.00	16.20	168	0.0	94.6	50.0%	45.0%	43.6%
2022	BOS	MLB	29	2	1	0	50	3	54^{1}	56	5	4.8	10.1	61	32.1%	.336	1.56	5.47	103	0.4	94.1	45.4%	25.5%	52.6%
2023 non-DC	*HOU*	*MLB*	*30*	*2*	*2*	*0*	*57*	*0*	*50*	*45*	*6*	*4.5*	*9.5*	*52*	*38.4%*	*.295*	*1.42*	*4.20*	*106*	*0.0*	*94.0*	*48.0%*	*27.6%*	*51.8%*

Comparables: Danny Coulombe (65), Sam Freeman (62), Dan Jennings (61)

On June 12, Davis had a 1.46 ERA for Boston after reeling off 13 straight scoreless outings. Three months later, he was electing free agency after having been designated for assignment a second time in the space of two weeks. Less changed between those two points than you might think. Davis issued a few more walks, yet he was hardly a paragon of control in those first two-plus months, averaging a walk every other inning. When hitters made contact in the second half, however, things went much, much worse. Reliever volatility remains inescapable.

Luis Garcia RHP

Born: 12/13/96 Age: 26 Bats: R Throws: R Height: 6'1" Weight: 244 lb. Origin: International Free Agent, 2017

YEAR	TEAM	LVL	AGE	W	L	SV	G	GS	IP	H	HR	BB/9	K/9	K	GB%	BABIP	WHIP	ERA	DRA-	WARP	MPH	FB%	Whiff%	CSP
2020	HOU	MLB	23	0	1	0	5	1	12^{1}	7	1	3.6	6.6	9	41.2%	.182	0.97	2.92	117	0.0	93.9	62.1%	26.1%	44.9%
2021	HOU	MLB	24	11	8	0	30	28	155^{1}	132	19	2.9	9.7	167	38.3%	.288	1.17	3.30	90	2.3	92.4	67.2%	30.6%	55.6%
2022	HOU	MLB	25	15	8	0	28	28	157^{1}	131	23	2.7	9.0	157	37.0%	.261	1.13	3.72	89	2.4	94.1	42.3%	29.2%	56.9%
2023 DC	*HOU*	*MLB*	*26*	*8*	*7*	*0*	*24*	*24*	*131*	*116*	*18*	*3.2*	*8.6*	*125*	*38.2%*	*.276*	*1.24*	*3.43*	*91*	*1.6*	*93.4*	*53.3%*	*29.5%*	*56.1%*

Comparables: Daniel Mengden (53), Jake Odorizzi (52), Matt Garza (51)

A very important thought appears to have occurred to either Garcia, Martín Maldonado, or someone else who influences how often the young righty throws his pitches: No-one can hit his cutter. It drew whiffs on an incredible 42.9% of swings. Opponents recorded an average of .149 against it, second to only Jose Alvarado among those with at least 200 thrown, and comfortably first among starting pitchers. This began to be fully weaponized in early May, when Garcia's usage of the pitch surged over 30% and lived there for the rest of the month, and much of the rest of the season. His four-seam remains less effective and the other secondaries less consistent, which might be why the Astros cut back on his usage when the postseason rolled around, limiting him to two extra-inning emergencies. One of those was the 18-inning epic which saw Garcia earn the win by allowing just two runners to reach base over five frames by relying most heavily on—you guessed it—the cutter. The obvious next step is confounded by one key issue: Garcia doesn't throw the pitch for strikes often, making it hard to employ regularly as his primary offering.

Cristian Javier RHP

Born: 03/26/97 Age: 26 Bats: R Throws: R Height: 6'1" Weight: 213 lb. Origin: International Free Agent, 2015

YEAR	TEAM	LVL	AGE	W	L	SV	G	GS	IP	H	HR	BB/9	K/9	K	GB%	BABIP	WHIP	ERA	DRA-	WARP	MPH	FB%	Whiff%	CSP
2020	HOU	MLB	23	5	2	0	12	10	54^{1}	36	11	3.0	8.9	54	29.3%	.194	0.99	3.48	115	0.2	92.3	63.1%	22.5%	47.7%
2021	HOU	MLB	24	4	1	2	36	9	101^{1}	67	16	4.7	11.5	130	27.4%	.235	1.18	3.55	96	1.2	93.6	59.4%	31.8%	51.6%
2022	HOU	MLB	25	11	9	0	30	25	148^{2}	89	17	3.1	11.7	194	25.2%	.229	0.95	2.54	73	3.5	94.0	59.9%	30.4%	53.9%
2023 DC	*HOU*	*MLB*	*26*	*9*	*7*	*0*	*25*	*25*	*142.3*	*104*	*21*	*3.9*	*11.0*	*173*	*27.7%*	*.254*	*1.17*	*3.10*	*81*	*2.5*	*93.7*	*60.1%*	*30.1%*	*52.5%*

Comparables: Blake Snell (65), Zack Wheeler (63), Matt Moore (63)

Prior to 2022, Javier served as a Tao-like presence on Houston's pitching staff, remaining fluid and moving wherever he needed to go, from the rotation to relief. His nasty fastball-slider combo and high walk rate tabbed him for the bullpen more than not, but that changed this year. He's never thrown so many innings and had a walk rate so low. Though he still gave up free passes more than nearly 80% of pitchers who threw at least 100 innings, he also struck out more than all but two of them.

It's hard to overstate the quality of his stuff. His motion to the plate creates a flat plane for his mid-90s heater, which is so good at eating batters up that it lets him throw it almost 60% of the time. It also sets the stage for his frisbee-like slider to create some truly ugly whiffs. Javier also managed to use his curveball just enough to be considered more than a show-me pitch, providing an offering that left-handed hitters have to account for. He upped the chase and swinging strike rates on that pitch, too. In all, his progress fueled two no-hitters, including one in the World Series, and another high-water mark for Houston's pitching development.

Seth Martinez RHP Born: 08/29/94 Age: 28 Bats: R Throws: R Height: 6'2" Weight: 200 lb. Origin: Round 17, 2016 Draft (#502 overall)

YEAR	TEAM	LVL	AGE	W	L	SV	G	GS	IP	H	HR	BB/9	K/9	K	GB%	BABIP	WHIP	ERA	DRA-	WARP	MPH	FB%	Whiff%	CSP
2021	SUG	AAA	26	5	3	0	36	0	57^{2}	35	5	3.1	12.2	78	41.1%	.242	0.95	2.81	74	1.2				
2021	HOU	MLB	26	0	0	0	3	0	3	5	0	9.0	9.0	3	30.0%	.500	2.67	15.00	123	0.0	89.8	71.4%	24.0%	56.8%
2022	SUG	AAA	27	2	1	0	14	0	15	10	2	3.6	9.0	15	51.3%	.216	1.07	3.60	96	0.1	91.5	53.3%	31.0%	
2022	HOU	MLB	27	1	1	0	29	0	38^{2}	26	3	3.3	8.8	38	40.2%	.235	1.03	2.09	95	0.5	91.5	53.4%	25.6%	53.1%
2023 DC	*HOU*	*MLB*	*28*	*2*	*2*	*0*	*50*	*0*	*44*	*39*	*5*	*3.7*	*8.5*	*41*	*42.3%*	*.280*	*1.31*	*3.73*	*96*	*0.3*	*91.4*	*54.7%*	*25.9%*	*53.3%*

Comparables: Hunter Strickland (79), Brandon Cunniff (78), Danny Barnes (77)

Rule 5 draft selectees who stick with their big-league clubs enjoy built-in coverage due to the unorthodox nature of their baseball journeys, but Martinez takes it a step further, as the Astros plucked him out of Oakland's system as part of the 2020 minor-league phase of the Rule 5 draft. What that means is not only did the A's fail to protect him on the 40-man despite excellent numbers between both the High- and Double-A, levels, they also left him off the protected list for their Triple-A club that year—a year, followed by another year, that was not particularly flush with Oakland pitching prospects knocking down MLB's door. A command-control righty, Martinez's fastball is below-average in velocity but plays up thanks to deception and his ability to create boatloads of weak contact, and Houston's vaunted pitching development has helped him maximize his strikeout potential. That translates into free pitching depth for an AL West rival that doesn't need it; good for the Astros and for Martinez, who projects to see more big-league time in 2023. And a pretty tough look for Oakland's player identification and development departments, or at least the resources allocated therein.

Phil Maton RHP Born: 03/25/93 Age: 30 Bats: R Throws: R Height: 6'2" Weight: 206 lb. Origin: Round 20, 2015 Draft (#597 overall)

YEAR	TEAM	LVL	AGE	W	L	SV	G	GS	IP	H	HR	BB/9	K/9	K	GB%	BABIP	WHIP	ERA	DRA-	WARP	MPH	FB%	Whiff%	CSP
2020	CLE	MLB	27	3	3	0	23	0	21^{2}	23	1	2.5	13.3	32	44.4%	.415	1.34	4.57	68	0.6	92.7	79.7%	37.3%	48.0%
2021	CLE	MLB	28	2	0	0	38	1	41^{1}	36	4	4.4	13.3	61	40.4%	.356	1.35	4.57	69	1.1	91.8	61.8%	38.0%	52.7%
2021	HOU	MLB	28	4	0	0	27	0	25^{1}	28	2	4.3	8.5	24	38.8%	.333	1.58	4.97	112	0.1	91.2	47.4%	29.7%	52.0%
2022	HOU	MLB	29	0	2	0	67	0	65^{2}	58	10	3.3	10.0	73	36.9%	.291	1.25	3.84	93	0.9	91.0	49.8%	30.3%	52.0%
2023 DC	*HOU*	*MLB*	*30*	*3*	*3*	*0*	*70*	*0*	*60.3*	*54*	*7*	*3.6*	*10.3*	*69*	*39.8%*	*.302*	*1.30*	*3.91*	*97*	*0.3*	*91.3*	*56.5%*	*30.8%*	*51.7%*

Comparables: Jeremy Jeffress (64), Noé Ramirez (63), Nick Wittgren (61)

Hamartia, a term coined by Aristotle in the Poetics, refers to the error of judgment that brings about a tragic hero's downfall: Othello's jealousy that leads to him strangling Desdemona, or Victor Frankenstein's hubris that causes him to create the monster. Sometimes the hamartia is a complex intersection, hard to simplify into one word—like Gatsby's combination of superficial consumerism, naivete and obsession with the past—but it all ends in tragedy. Whatever hamartia swirled about Maton, causing him to punch a locker in frustration after a poor outing in the regular-season finale is unknown, but the result—a broken pinky finger that sidelined him for the entirety of the Astros' playoff run—is familiar to anyone who took high school English. Maton will try to get his hamartia under control before hitting free agency in 2024; trusting the improvements he's made in Houston, which has optimized the low-velo Spin King for weak contact, while recognizing that the life of a reliever means being constantly at the whim of the baseball gods, is a good place to start.

Lance McCullers Jr. RHP Born: 10/02/93 Age: 29 Bats: L Throws: R Height: 6'1" Weight: 202 lb. Origin: Round 1, 2012 Draft (#41 overall)

YEAR	TEAM	LVL	AGE	W	L	SV	G	GS	IP	H	HR	BB/9	K/9	K	GB%	BABIP	WHIP	ERA	DRA-	WARP	MPH	FB%	Whiff%	CSP
2020	HOU	MLB	26	3	3	0	11	11	55	44	5	3.3	9.2	56	58.9%	.279	1.16	3.93	71	1.5	93.9	44.1%	29.7%	44.6%
2021	HOU	MLB	27	13	5	0	28	28	162^{1}	122	13	4.2	10.3	185	56.4%	.273	1.22	3.16	83	3.0	94.0	35.6%	30.3%	53.5%
2022	SUG	AAA	28	0	0	0	3	3	11^{1}	13	2	5.6	11.1	14	50.0%	.367	1.76	7.15	92	0.1	92.5	40.7%	22.1%	
2022	HOU	MLB	28	4	2	0	8	8	47^{2}	37	4	4.2	9.4	50	50.4%	.277	1.24	2.27	91	0.7	92.7	30.4%	27.1%	52.7%
2023 DC	*HOU*	*MLB*	*29*	*8*	*7*	*0*	*24*	*24*	*136*	*120*	*14*	*4.1*	*9.0*	*136*	*53.1%*	*.289*	*1.34*	*3.74*	*94*	*1.5*	*93.7*	*35.6%*	*27.6%*	*52.1%*

Comparables: Ramon Martinez (85), Stephen Strasburg (83), Andy Benes (82)

During the lockout, McCullers indicated that the exclusion from team staff and facilities had set him back in his recovery from a flexor strain. It would be another five months from the end of the lockout before he made his season debut, after he had initially been expected to be ready for spring training before the shutdown. If you were making a list of players who could do without extra complications when it came to health, McCullers would be toward the top. Both his start and innings totals from 2021 were comfortably a career high, and that forearm had prevented him from appearing beyond the Division Series. Even the 2022 playoffs produced another slice of McCullers injury drama, in the most bizarre way, when his surgically repaired elbow was accidentally struck by a champagne bottle during their ALDS celebration, forcing his subsequent start to be pushed back a day. The remainder of his deal with the Astros should feature more settled offseasons. That's good news because when healthy, he remains a dynamic mid-rotation option with the upside for more.

Rafael Montero RHP

Born: 10/17/90 Age: 32 Bats: R Throws: R Height: 6'0" Weight: 190 lb. Origin: International Free Agent, 2011

YEAR	TEAM	LVL	AGE	W	L	SV	G	GS	IP	H	HR	BB/9	K/9	K	GB%	BABIP	WHIP	ERA	DRA-	WARP	MPH	FB%	Whiff%	CSP
2020	TEX	MLB	29	0	1	8	17	0	17^{2}	12	2	3.1	9.7	19	26.7%	.238	1.02	4.08	109	0.1	95.6	72.0%	25.0%	49.0%
2021	SEA	MLB	30	5	3	7	40	0	43^{1}	56	4	3.1	7.7	37	55.1%	.366	1.64	7.27	102	0.4	95.6	61.4%	22.4%	50.3%
2021	HOU	MLB	30	0	1	0	4	0	6	3	0	3.0	7.5	5	50.0%	.214	0.83	0.00	104	0.0	95.8	66.3%	29.3%	52.1%
2022	HOU	MLB	31	5	2	14	71	0	68^{1}	47	3	3.0	9.6	73	51.7%	.262	1.02	2.37	79	1.4	96.4	68.4%	28.3%	48.0%
2023 DC	*HOU*	*MLB*	*32*	*3*	*3*	*2*	*63*	*0*	*55*	*51*	*5*	*3.1*	*9.2*	*56*	*48.9%*	*.303*	*1.27*	*3.44*	*89*	*0.5*	*96.0*	*65.3%*	*26.0%*	*48.7%*

Comparables: Zach McAllister (50), Liam Hendriks (49), Tommy Hunter (48)

The song everyone thinks is called "Call Me By Your Name" is actually called "Montero"—the given first name of the rapper Lil Nas X—and is about celebrating one's true self. It'd be a good walkout song for the Astros pitcher, who bounced through three different organizations before finding his true self in Houston, where the advice seemed to be: Damn the walks, throw your four-seam fastball more, and harder, if possible. As instructed, he threw his four-seamer about 12 percentage points more often in 2022, with a velocity bump pushing the offering over 96 mph on average. He also walked even more batters than he did with Seattle, a club that emphasizes controlling the zone, but made up for it by spiking his strikeout rate from the 17th to the 75th percentile, punching out 27% of batters faced. Montero went from struggling with the Mariners to helping eliminate them from the playoffs en route to a World Series ring, proving that you're always your best self when you're yourself, first and foremost.

Héctor Neris RHP

Born: 06/14/89 Age: 34 Bats: R Throws: R Height: 6'2" Weight: 227 lb. Origin: International Free Agent, 2010

YEAR	TEAM	LVL	AGE	W	L	SV	G	GS	IP	H	HR	BB/9	K/9	K	GB%	BABIP	WHIP	ERA	DRA-	WARP	MPH	FB%	Whiff%	CSP
2020	PHI	MLB	31	2	2	5	24	0	21^{2}	24	0	5.4	11.2	27	39.7%	.381	1.71	4.57	89	0.3	94.2	51.9%	39.1%	41.0%
2021	PHI	MLB	32	4	7	12	74	0	74^{1}	55	12	3.9	11.9	98	48.9%	.264	1.17	3.63	77	1.6	94.6	55.9%	34.3%	52.1%
2022	HOU	MLB	33	6	4	3	70	0	65^{1}	49	3	2.3	10.9	79	34.2%	.293	1.01	3.72	76	1.4	94.5	62.5%	30.5%	57.1%
2023 DC	*HOU*	*MLB*	*34*	*3*	*3*	*6*	*70*	*0*	*60.3*	*51*	*8*	*3.3*	*10.0*	*67*	*39.8%*	*.280*	*1.22*	*3.52*	*91*	*0.5*	*94.5*	*55.9%*	*31.6%*	*51.9%*

Comparables: Brad Brach (65), Darren O'Day (64), Steve Cishek (64)

Baseball is a game of trade-offs, and Neris never had a problem generating strikeouts. That dominance has been oft-threatened by walks and homers, increasingly so in the former case in recent years, a problem driven almost exclusively by opposite-handed hitters. Houston had a simple, if somewhat counter-intuitive solution: Neris became an exclusively four-seam/splitter pitcher against lefties, still tossing the split regularly but relying on the heater more often than before when he needed a strike. Against righties, he threw both *less* often and made his sinker the primary pitch, frequently running it inside and catching hitters looking. The altered approach allowed Neris to slash both his walk and homer rates, while becoming a little more hittable, as might be expected when cutting back on one of the game's filthiest pitches. The end result? More or less the same as what it had been in 2021. Neris is already one of the better relievers in baseball, so perhaps it's greedy to expect more, but there's always that hope that a slightly different combination of trade-offs will be truly optimal.

Ryan Pressly RHP

Born: 12/15/88 Age: 34 Bats: R Throws: R Height: 6'2" Weight: 206 lb. Origin: Round 11, 2007 Draft (#354 overall)

YEAR	TEAM	LVL	AGE	W	L	SV	G	GS	IP	H	HR	BB/9	K/9	K	GB%	BABIP	WHIP	ERA	DRA-	WARP	MPH	FB%	Whiff%	CSP
2020	HOU	MLB	31	1	3	12	23	0	21	21	2	3.0	12.4	29	48.1%	.365	1.33	3.43	73	0.5	94.6	37.1%	36.5%	45.2%
2021	HOU	MLB	32	5	3	26	64	0	64	49	4	1.8	11.4	81	55.1%	.298	0.97	2.25	70	1.6	95.5	39.6%	32.0%	58.5%
2022	HOU	MLB	33	3	3	33	50	0	48^{1}	30	4	2.4	12.1	65	44.2%	.265	0.89	2.98	69	1.2	94.6	32.5%	39.1%	51.2%
2023 DC	*HOU*	*MLB*	*34*	*3*	*2*	*36*	*63*	*0*	*55*	*45*	*5*	*2.5*	*11.1*	*68*	*48.7%*	*.296*	*1.10*	*2.53*	*68*	*1.1*	*95.1*	*36.2%*	*33.8%*	*53.1%*

Comparables: Darren O'Day (83), Jonathan Papelbon (82), Mike Timlin (81)

If you were 34 and coming off the best season of your career by K-BB%—a leading in-season indicator of pitcher performance—perhaps you would look at other relievers and casually sing "You don't im-Pressly me much." Maybe if you had the most saves of your career despite the fewest appearances in a full season you'd wax poetic to your manager, saying "look how far we've come, baby." And if batters made less contact than they ever had against you, you'd probably walk out to the mound confidently professing that you're goin' out tonight, feelin' alright, gonna let it all hang out. You'd probably even have no inhibitions, make no conditions, and get a little outta line. And it would all be perfectly acceptable, because you'd be one of the top relievers in the league, countering a gradual velocity loss with more and more breakers.

Ryne Stanek RHP

Born: 07/26/91 Age: 31 Bats: R Throws: R Height: 6'4" Weight: 226 lb. Origin: Round 1, 2013 Draft (#29 overall)

YEAR	TEAM	LVL	AGE	W	L	SV	G	GS	IP	H	HR	BB/9	K/9	K	GB%	BABIP	WHIP	ERA	DRA-	WARP	MPH	FB%	Whiff%	CSP
2020	MIA	MLB	28	0	0	0	9	0	10	11	3	7.2	9.9	11	34.5%	.308	1.90	7.20	123	0.0	95.9	43.9%	33.7%	42.9%
2021	HOU	MLB	29	3	5	2	72	0	68^{1}	46	8	4.9	10.9	83	33.3%	.242	1.21	3.42	95	0.8	97.8	59.7%	32.7%	51.7%
2022	HOU	MLB	30	2	1	1	59	0	54^{2}	36	2	5.1	10.2	62	38.9%	.264	1.23	1.15	92	0.8	98.5	58.4%	35.1%	50.5%
2023 DC	*HOU*	*MLB*	*31*	*3*	*3*	*0*	*63*	*0*	*55*	*45*	*8*	*5.0*	*11.0*	*67*	*36.3%*	*.283*	*1.38*	*3.91*	*96*	*0.3*	*98.0*	*57.9%*	*32.7%*	*49.3%*

Comparables: Pedro Strop (71), Matt Barnes (70), Brad Boxberger (70)

WARP might suggest that Stanek wasn't as sharp in 2022 as he was in 2021, but that's like saying your Ginsu knife only cuts through full shoes and steel cans, not construction-grade beams. He allowed an earned run in just six of his 59 appearances. Results-based gains in stats like home run rate and pop-up rate were supported by processed-based tweaks in pitch location, where his fastball rode higher and his splitter tumbled lower with more regularity. Little things like that, which can boost a pitcher from below-average at getting chases to average, scale big.

Blake Taylor LHP

Born: 08/17/95 Age: 27 Bats: L Throws: L Height: 6'3" Weight: 220 lb. Origin: Round 2, 2013 Draft (#51 overall)

YEAR	TEAM	LVL	AGE	W	L	SV	G	GS	IP	H	HR	BB/9	K/9	K	GB%	BABIP	WHIP	ERA	DRA-	WARP	MPH	FB%	Whiff%	CSP
2020	HOU	MLB	24	2	1	1	22	0	20^{2}	13	2	5.2	7.4	17	50.0%	.196	1.21	2.18	93	0.3	93.8	76.5%	19.9%	50.5%
2021	HOU	MLB	25	4	4	0	51	0	42^{2}	38	6	4.6	8.6	41	40.0%	.271	1.41	3.16	117	0.0	93.1	72.5%	24.6%	49.8%
2022	SUG	AAA	26	2	0	0	11	1	10^{2}	6	1	5.9	5.9	7	53.6%	.185	1.22	5.06	109	0.0	92.2	66.5%	23.0%	
2022	HOU	MLB	26	1	1	0	19	0	16	15	1	5.6	5.1	9	45.5%	.259	1.56	3.94	124	0.0	92.8	73.6%	20.1%	47.3%
2023 DC	*HOU*	*MLB*	*27*	*1*	*1*	*0*	*25*	*0*	*22*	*22*	*2*	*4.7*	*7.0*	*17*	*46.1%*	*.294*	*1.55*	*4.85*	*118*	*-0.1*	*93.1*	*73.5%*	*22.3%*	*49.2%*

Comparables: A.J. Minter (60), Paul Fry (59), Kyle Ryan (59)

Taylor is an outlier with the Astros, who don't stress over free passes as long as pitchers also strike out boatloads of batters, preferably with primo velocity. Taylor doesn't do that, instead inducing weak contact with his high-spin fastball, which he throws almost 75% of the time, the 11th-highest usage of a four-seamer in MLB. It's a narrow band for success, but it's worked for the lefty so far. An elbow injury shelved him for most of 2022, making it hard to discern if it was the inflamed elbow, early-season rust or hitters figuring out his One Weird Trick to Making Outs that caused the downtick in performance.

Miguel Ullola RHP

Born: 06/19/02 Age: 21 Bats: R Throws: R Height: 6'1" Weight: 184 lb. Origin: International Free Agent, 2021

YEAR	TEAM	LVL	AGE	W	L	SV	G	GS	IP	H	HR	BB/9	K/9	K	GB%	BABIP	WHIP	ERA	DRA-	WARP	MPH	FB%	Whiff%	CSP
2021	DSL AST	ROK	19	1	1	0	8	5	21^{1}	10	1	7.2	14.3	34	44.7%	.243	1.27	4.22						
2022	FAY	A	20	2	2	2	22	11	72	39	3	6.9	15.0	120	40.5%	.281	1.31	3.25	74	1.8				
2023 non-DC	*HOU*	*MLB*	*21*	*2*	*3*	*0*	*57*	*0*	*50*	*45*	*8*	*8.2*	*10.6*	*59*	*39.6%*	*.299*	*1.82*	*6.09*	*133*	*-0.6*			*31.9%*	

Comparables: Joe Boyle (93), Bryan Abreu (92), Chris Anderson (91)

The Astros have done incredibly well in scouting and developing international free agent pitchers who are older than the typical signing age of 16 or 17. That cohort includes most of their current starting rotation—Framber Valdez, Cristian Javier, José Urquidy and Luis Garcia were all signed for five-figure bonuses, and all but Javier were over 18 when signed (he was a week short of his 18th birthday). The next contributor to come out of this group very well might be Ullola, signed two years ago at age 18 for $75,000. He has one of the best swing-and-miss profiles on his fastball in the entire minors; his mid-90s velocity is augmented with demented bat-missing movement, and his slider is a pretty nifty weapon too. His command is god-awful and he walked over a batter an inning in his starts. He struck out 76 in 42⅓ relief innings with a 1.70 ERA and a respectable walk rate, and if he can continue to generally get it close to his target out of the bullpen he's going to be a monster reliever no more than a few years from now.

José Urquidy RHP

Born: 05/01/95 Age: 28 Bats: R Throws: R Height: 6'0" Weight: 217 lb. Origin: International Free Agent, 2015

YEAR	TEAM	LVL	AGE	W	L	SV	G	GS	IP	H	HR	BB/9	K/9	K	GB%	BABIP	WHIP	ERA	DRA-	WARP	MPH	FB%	Whiff%	CSP
2020	HOU	MLB	25	1	1	0	5	5	29^{2}	22	4	2.4	5.2	17	35.6%	.209	1.01	2.73	133	-0.2	93.4	54.5%	20.9%	52.8%
2021	HOU	MLB	26	8	3	0	20	20	107	87	17	1.6	7.6	90	31.7%	.239	0.99	3.62	104	0.7	92.7	55.0%	25.1%	59.3%
2022	HOU	MLB	27	13	8	0	29	28	164^{1}	154	29	2.1	7.3	134	36.3%	.264	1.17	3.94	109	0.8	93.5	57.6%	22.3%	56.3%
2023 DC	*HOU*	*MLB*	*28*	*9*	*8*	*0*	*27*	*27*	*151.3*	*143*	*22*	*2.1*	*6.8*	*114*	*36.1%*	*.271*	*1.18*	*3.45*	*94*	*1.7*	*93.3*	*56.3%*	*23.6%*	*56.8%*

Comparables: Clay Buchholz (59), Jerad Eickhoff (58), Stephen Fife (57)

Urquidy remains somewhat of an enigma. A career high in innings pitched answered some questions about durability after a barking shoulder dogged him in 2021, and a consistent year-to-year line indicated that yes, even with a Savant page covered in more blue than an Yves Klein painting, he could continue to be an acronym-buster. A heroic turn in the World Series to save the bullpen after Lance McCullers' Oprah-style homer giveaway left a positive final impression. For those who watched his season, though, it was impossible to guess which Urquidy would be on the mound that day: The weak contact-inducer with excellent command, or the meatball-tosser serving up his own home run giveaway (fourth-most in the AL) and hitting more batters (7) than in his previous three seasons combined (3). The Astros didn't trust Urquidy with a starting role in the playoffs, and didn't play him at all against the Mariners, owners of a season-long OPS of .938 against him. With Justin Verlander departing and the farm thinned out, Urquidy's spot at the back half of Houston's rotation seems set for now—once the armchair GMs stop hypothetically trading him away for Bryan Reynolds, at least.

Framber Valdez LHP

Born: 11/19/93 Age: 29 Bats: R Throws: L Height: 5'11" Weight: 239 lb. Origin: International Free Agent, 2015

YEAR	TEAM	LVL	AGE	W	L	SV	G	GS	IP	H	HR	BB/9	K/9	K	GB%	BABIP	WHIP	ERA	DRA-	WARP	MPH	FB%	Whiff%	CSP
2020	HOU	MLB	26	5	3	0	11	10	70^{2}	63	5	2.0	9.7	76	59.7%	.314	1.12	3.57	65	2.1	93.1	58.6%	24.4%	52.4%
2021	HOU	MLB	27	11	6	0	22	22	134^{2}	110	12	3.9	8.4	125	70.1%	.268	1.25	3.14	94	1.7	92.6	57.2%	26.3%	56.4%
2022	HOU	MLB	28	17	6	0	31	31	201^{1}	166	11	3.0	8.7	194	66.5%	.286	1.16	2.82	87	3.3	94.1	53.0%	25.7%	59.4%
2023 DC	*HOU*	*MLB*	*29*	*11*	*10*	*0*	*30*	*30*	*187.7*	*185*	*15*	*3.4*	*8.6*	*179*	*65.8%*	*.313*	*1.37*	*3.76*	*95*	*2.1*	*93.5*	*55.2%*	*25.3%*	*57.2%*

Comparables: CC Sabathia (76), Bob Gibson (74), Chris Sale (73)

Whether it's coming from the pitching coach or the team psychologist Valdez credits with his newfound ability to handle adversity on the mound, the advice is the same: stay grounded. The absurd 66% ground-ball rate he earned was a full 10 points better than the next closest qualified pitcher in 2022. His mid-90s sinker drops off quicker than a teenager riding to the mall with their parents and his curveball is one of the best in the game today, generating whiffs on nearly half of swings. Critics could say he doesn't always know where his pitches are going, but they move so much it hardly matters. Martín Maldonado would routinely set up right down the middle as if to remind Valdez he just has to get in the general area of the plate to succeed. He proved that and more, posting a major league-record 25 consecutive quality starts. Then, after imploding in the 2021 World Series, Valdez was at his best when the lights were brightest last year, striking out 27 and allowing just two earned runs in his final three starts of the Astros World Series run.

Forrest Whitley RHP

Born: 09/15/97 Age: 25 Bats: R Throws: R Height: 6'7" Weight: 238 lb. Origin: Round 1, 2016 Draft (#17 overall)

YEAR	TEAM	LVL	AGE	W	L	SV	G	GS	IP	H	HR	BB/9	K/9	K	GB%	BABIP	WHIP	ERA	DRA-	WARP	MPH	FB%	Whiff%	CSP
2022	SUG	AAA	24	0	2	0	10	8	33	32	2	6.8	9.8	36	47.4%	.326	1.73	7.09	94	0.3	95.1	50.2%	25.1%	
2023 DC	*HOU*	*MLB*	*25*	*1*	*2*	*0*	*6*	*6*	*29.7*	*28*	*3*	*5.8*	*9.5*	*31*	*43.3%*	*.308*	*1.61*	*5.09*	*118*	*0.0*			*26.2%*	

Comparables: Manny Bañuelos (46), Tyler Skaggs (43), Alex Reyes (35)

Once the top pitching prospect in the sport, Whitley is coming off not just a lost season but a lost half-decade. Since the end of the 2017 season, he's thrown just a total of 126 competitive innings scattered throughout the minors (plus another 51 if you want to count a pair of Arizona Fall League stints). In 2018, he got hit with a drug suspension and then had oblique and lat issues. In 2019, he battled shoulder fatigue and mechanical problems. In 2020, his forearm barked ramping up during summer camp and he never really got going. In 2021, the same thing happened in spring training, and he ended up having Tommy John surgery that March. His 2022 encore was brutal, and he missed more time with bicep and shoulder issues—but he was consistently throwing in the mid-90s, and the return year from TJS is also rough. If he can stay on the mound and throw strikes...well, it was five Taylor Swift albums ago, but you can dream on him recapturing that top pitching prospect form.

Lineouts

Hitters

HITTER	POS	TEAM	LVL	AGE	PA	R	2B	3B	HR	RBI	BB	K	SB	CS	AVG/OBP/SLG	DRC+	BABIP	BRR	DRP	WARP
Rylan Bannon	3B/DH	NOR	AAA	26	326	45	14	1	11	58	45	87	6	1	.229/.347/.407	98	.292	0.0	3B(53): -2.1, 2B(6): -0.3	1.1
	3B/DH	GWN	AAA	26	85	12	4	0	2	19	14	13	4	0	.328/.447/.478	120	.370	1.9	3B(16): 1.7, 2B(3): -0.1	0.3
	3B/DH	ATL	MLB	26	0	0	0	0	0	0	0	0	0	0	.000/.000/.000				2B(1): -0.1	0.0
	3B/DH	BAL	MLB	26	15	0	0	0	0	0	0	5	0	0	.143/.200/.143	87	.222	0.1	3B(3): 0	0.0
Luke Berryhill	C	CC	AA	24	432	67	18	0	12	60	63	122	5	2	.256/.380/.409	94	.348	-1.6	C(41): 4.9, 1B(32): 1.7, LF(4): 0.0	1.4
Logan Cerny	OF	FAY	A	22	372	59	16	4	15	54	47	110	35	7	.253/.360/.472	132	.337	-0.3	CF(34): -0.6, RF(19): 1.0, LF(17): -0.8	2.4
Ryan Clifford	LF	ASO	ROK	18	50	8	3	0	1	5	12	16	2	0	.222/.440/.389		.368			
	LF	FAY	A	18	51	5	2	0	1	5	10	15	0	0	.268/.412/.390	101	.400	-0.2	LF(7): -0.6, 1B(2): 0.3, RF(2): 0.2	0.2
Zach Dezenzo	IF	FAY	A	22	117	13	3	0	4	15	12	37	4	0	.255/.342/.402	95	.355	0.8	3B(15): 2.4, 1B(5): -0.4, 2B(3): -0.7	0.5
Yainer Diaz	C	CC	AA	23	267	37	13	3	9	48	21	40	1	0	.316/.367/.504	115	.345	0.6	1B(26): 2.4, C(23): -0.8, RF(4): -0.2	1.5
	C	SUG	AAA	23	219	38	9	1	16	48	13	39	1	0	.294/.342/.587	119	.291	0.4	C(27): -7.1, 1B(10): 1.0, LF(1): -0.1	0.6
	C	HOU	MLB	23	9	0	1	0	0	1	1	2	0	0	.125/.222/.250	90	.167		C(2): 0.1	0.0
Justin Dirden	OF	CC	AA	24	407	64	32	5	20	73	41	94	7	2	.324/.411/.616	121	.391	1.0	CF(38): -2.1, LF(26): -0.4, RF(20): -1.5	1.7
	OF	SUG	AAA	24	142	18	8	0	4	28	10	40	5	1	.242/.305/.398	81	.318	-0.4	RF(15): 0.9, CF(10): 0.4, LF(5): 0.4	0.2
Cristian Gonzalez	SS	ASH	A+	20	445	54	18	1	10	48	29	127	1	2	.227/.283/.350	72	.302	-0.9	SS(76): -1.9, 3B(11): 0.6	-0.3
David Hensley	IF	SUG	AAA	26	464	80	30	4	10	57	80	103	20	7	.298/.420/.478	116	.383	-1.2	SS(33): -3.8, 3B(24): -0.4, 2B(23): -0.3	1.9
	IF	HOU	MLB	26	34	7	2	1	1	5	5	6	0	0	.345/.441/.586	109	.409	0.2	2B(5): -0.1, 3B(3): 0.1, SS(2): 0	0.1
Corey Julks	3B	SUG	AAA	26	590	100	21	4	31	89	56	128	22	5	.270/.351/.503	133	.301	-0.3	3B(49): -1.1, RF(38): -1.1, LF(25): -1.7	3.6
J.J. Matijevic	1B	SUG	AAA	26	282	46	16	2	16	54	33	68	10	2	.285/.372/.561	114	.331	1.2	1B(41): -0.5, LF(19): 1.2	1.4
	1B	HOU	MLB	26	71	7	2	0	2	5	2	25	1	0	.209/.254/.328	68	.300	0.0	1B(10): 0	-0.1
Jacob Melton	CF	FAY	A	21	86	11	6	0	4	13	11	20	4	2	.324/.424/.577	114	.396	-1.0	CF(15): -0.3, RF(1): -0.0	0.3
Joe Perez	3B	ASO	ROK	22	26	2	1	0	0	2	0	7	0	0	.308/.308/.346		.421			
	3B	CC	AA	22	284	30	16	0	6	28	26	70	3	0	.265/.335/.397	91	.343	-1.3	3B(40): -0.5, RF(9): -1.2, LF(8): -0.9	0.1
	3B	SUG	AAA	22	35	6	1	0	1	6	6	6	0	0	.483/.571/.621	108	.591	-0.1	3B(5): 0.5, LF(1): 0.3, RF(1): 0.1	0.2
	3B	HOU	MLB	22	1	0	0	0	0	0	0	1	0	0	.000/.000/.000	80			3B(1): -0.5	
Tyler Whitaker	RF	FAY	A	19	150	4	3	1	0	11	9	59	3	2	.146/.213/.182	85	.253	-0.6	RF(48): -0.4, 3B(27): -3.5, SS(22): 0.1	0.0

Rylan Bannon made it to the bigs, and got a handful of games under his belt. He currently finds himself in a state of purgatory: Teams still want to have his bat in their organization, but they don't want to see him starting for their team. ⚾ Quietly acquired from the Reds before the 2021 season, **Luke Berryhill** has done all you can ask a catching prospect to do—get on base and keep the other team off of it. Splitting time between first and catcher speaks more to health than defensive ability, as his framing and arm were both above-average in limited playing time after fracturing his finger in July. ⚾ **Logan Cerny** fits the Astros' recent center fielder-mold, in that he can play there while hitting with enough pop to banish platoon-mates. Weighing that with his near-30% strikeout rate in A-ball means he isn't quite clear of them yet, or even close to a major-league piece. ⚾ An 11th-round pick with a second-round bonus, **Ryan Clifford** signed with the Astros for $1.2 million. Turns out his commitment to Vanderbilt was all bark and no bite. The smooth-swinging lefty has plenty of pop with room to grow in his big frame. ⚾ **Zach Dezenzo** traded one college town for another after being drafted out of The Ohio State University in the 12th round, but brought his strikeout issues from Columbus to Low-A Fayetteville. Luckily, he's landed with an organization that teaches master classes in prospect development. ⚾ As a bat-first catcher, **Yainier Diaz** flopped in an espresso-sized call-up but still produced well in the minors this year. His bat will have to be his carrying tool. Unfortunately, science doesn't yet have the capability to fuse him with Martín Maldonado to form one fully-functioning catcher. ⚾ Former undrafted free agent **Justin Dirden** lacks conventional standout tools, but he's driven the ball in the air consistently at most levels of the minors over the past two seasons. If he keeps mashing righties like this, he's going to force his way into Houston's major-league picture pretty soon. ⚾ Imposing shortstop **Cristian Gonzalez** continued to be years younger than his competition, as Houston had him spend the entire year at High-A as a 20-year-old. He also continued to look out of his depth, but flashed just enough power to dream on a viable bat at a more age-appropriate stage of his career. ⚾ With an eye at the plate that has racked up double-digit walk rates more than not, **David Hensley** has a skill the Astros prioritize. He strikes out more than most of their dudes, though, and he's tabbed more for DH and bench duties since his primary position is occupied by one of the best second basemen in the league. ⚾ **Corey Julks** has been hitting the ball harder and harder over the past two seasons, and was only one dinger short of the Pacific Coast League home run crown last year. Although he went unselected in Rule 5, he's still a sneaky candidate to play his way into a part-time role this season. ⚾ A jovial fellow popular with teammates and fans alike, **J.J. Matijevic's** profile—a power-over-hit, possible corner outfielder but more 1B/DH type—is less of an easy sell at the big-league level, especially with the strikeouts dimming the power output. ⚾ Second-round pick **Jacob Melton** hits the ball really, really hard—a foundational skill shared by many Houston hitting prospects—but also has some concerning swing-and-miss tendencies. He has a higher chance at stardom than most college hitters taken outside of the first round, but also a higher chance to top out whiffing too much at Double-A. ⚾ It's a good thing **Joe Perez** isn't pitching any more. An oblique injury was the latest in the litany of ailments that has limited him to barely 1,000 plate appearances as a pro. The former two-way high school star needs plenty more reps and a continuation of his impressive Triple-A debut to distinguish himself from Houston's other depth options. ⚾ Because they lost their first two picks in the 2020 and 2021 drafts as part of the banging scheme penalties, the Astros took some massive swings for upside on the picks they had left. Their first pick in 2021, projectable power merchant **Tyler Whitaker**, has taken some massive swings himself as a pro, few of which have made contact with a baseball.

Pitchers

PITCHER	TEAM	LVL	AGE	W	L	SV	G	GS	IP	H	HR	BB/9	K/9	K	GB%	BABIP	WHIP	ERA	DRA-	WARP	MPH	FB%	WHF	CSP
Spencer Arrighetti	ASH	A+	22	6	5	2	22	13	85^{2}	88	6	4.8	13.0	124	42.1%	.390	1.56	5.04	91	1.0				
	CC	AA	22	1	1	0	5	4	21	13	3	3.9	12.0	28	38.6%	.244	1.05	3.43	67	0.4				
Edinson Batista	FAY	A	20	8	3	0	21	8	93^{1}	59	3	4.1	10.9	113	50.5%	.258	1.09	2.60	88	1.6				
	ASH	A+	20	1	0	0	3	2	14^{1}	9	2	5.7	8.8	14	52.8%	.206	1.26	3.14	92	0.2				
Ronel Blanco	SUG	AAA	28	4	7	5	44	0	44^{2}	35	8	3.8	11.7	58	43.5%	.273	1.21	3.63	70	1.0	96.0	47.7%	40.8%	
	HOU	MLB	28	0	0	0	7	0	6^{1}	8	1	5.7	9.9	7	25.0%	.368	1.89	7.11	107	0.0	95.6	45.8%	34.3%	54.2%
Shawn Dubin	SUG	AAA	26	3	5	0	23	12	58^{1}	52	3	4.9	12.3	80	46.7%	.368	1.44	4.78	74	1.2	96.8	50.1%	29.5%	
J.P. France	SUG	AAA	27	3	4	3	34	15	110^{2}	99	15	4.1	11.1	136	33.7%	.304	1.36	3.90	81	1.9	91.7	63.4%	30.3%	
Colton Gordon	ASB	ROK	23	0	1	0	4	4	7	3	0	1.3	14.1	11	42.9%	.214	0.57	0.00						
	ASO	ROK	23	0	0	0	2	1	6	6	1	1.5	16.5	11	30.0%	.455	1.17	4.50						
	FAY	A	23	0	0	0	5	3	20^{1}	13	1	1.3	12.0	27	53.3%	.273	0.79	2.21	74	0.5				
	ASH	A+	23	2	0	1	4	3	20^{1}	13	2	1.3	12.8	29	34.1%	.262	0.79	2.66	68	0.4				
Jayden Murray	MTG	AA	25	8	2	0	16	15	76^{1}	65	9	2.7	7.7	65	51.1%	.257	1.15	2.83	98	0.9				
	CC	AA	25	0	2	0	6	6	27^{1}	24	3	3.6	8.6	26	48.1%	.288	1.28	4.28	95	0.2				
Parker Mushinski	SUG	AAA	26	2	2	0	38	0	40^{2}	28	3	4.2	9.1	41	57.8%	.240	1.16	2.66	75	0.8	90.4	62.5%	28.9%	
	HOU	MLB	26	0	0	0	7	0	7^{1}	5	0	3.7	9.8	8	50.0%	.278	1.09	3.68	91	0.1	88.3	48.6%	38.2%	52.9%
Enoli Paredes	SUG	AAA	26	5	4	12	50	0	54^{2}	34	4	5.1	13.3	81	41.4%	.273	1.19	2.63	64	1.5	95.3	61.2%	33.0%	
	HOU	MLB	26	0	0	0	3	0	3	3	0	9.0	6.0	2	44.4%	.333	2.00	3.00	106	0.0	95.1	86.0%	18.5%	58.7%
Misael Tamarez	CC	AA	22	3	6	1	24	19	103^{1}	76	18	4.8	10.6	122	41.0%	.249	1.27	4.62	71	2.3				
	SUG	AAA	22	1	1	0	4	4	18	6	2	7.5	10.0	20	40.5%	.114	1.17	2.50	98	0.1	94.3	43.6%	31.9%	

His palms are sweaty, **Spencer Arrighetti** / A local product from the sixth round but he might be ready / His curve is, just a reserve pitch, but the scouts have said he, could pop off / he goes up into the 90s, with a strange arm slot / his slider's "wow," everybody knows him now / he takes the mound, winds up, strikes you out /   Upon promotion to High-A, **Edinson Batista** wasn't as sharp as he was in lower levels, posting a lower strikeout rate and higher walk rate. His projectable profile lacks big-time stuff but is one that the organization has found ways to make serviceable at the big-league level.   A position player until he was 18, **Ronel Blanco** was 22 by the time he was signed by the Astros for a mere $5,000. Six years later, he earned his way onto the Opening Day roster with a strong spring, becoming the latest in a long line of pitching development successes.   **Trey Dombroski** used his plus-plus command to dominate many of the nation's top college hitters in the Cape Cod League in 2021 and continued to roll for the Monmouth Hawks in the 2022 season. He lasted until the fourth round because he sits on either side of 90 with his fastball; professional pitch design could be a boon for him.   **Shawn Dubin** is a Georgetown product—no, not that one, the one where Billy Ray Cyrus went on a baseball scholarship—who missed out on an MLB debut in 2022 due to a forearm strain. He'll take the Old Town Road to Houston as soon as a spot becomes available, where he'll deploy his upper-90s fastball and two-plane slider to achy-breaky some bats.   Houston added **J.P. France** to the 40-man after the season. It's unusual to see a 27-year-old with no MLB experience or real prospect buzz protected from Rule 5, yet France has been one of the more effective pitchers in Triple-A over the last two seasons, with a five-pitch mix that moves in all kinds of directions; he can serve in any role as a depth arm.   Many players struggle with control upon their return from Tommy John surgery. Underslot 2021 draftee **Colton Gordon** seems to be managing alright. He averaged under a walk per start while dominating with his deceptive heater in his pro debut.   The Astros emphasized proximity—each of their first 10 picks were college players—and strike-throwers in their draft selections. That philosophy was embodied by third-rounder **Michael Knorr**, a tall righty with a deep arsenal and a stellar K:BB ratio in his dominant season at Coastal Carolina.   Acquired by Houston from the Rays in the three-way Trey Mancini deal, **Jayden Murray** is a Very Astros Pitching Prospect—a former 23rd-round pick out of a Division III school who just gets outs as a 95-and-a-slider type. He projects as a back-of-the-rotation starter or middle relief type.   We're not saying the Astros have a type, but **Parker Mushinski** makes up for a low-90s fastball with a spin rate that's reminiscent of several other arms in their bullpen. Although those other arms also made it difficult for Mushinski to get much of a chance, he has the capability, and the curveball, to turn major league hitters' legs to mush.   As another high-strikeout, high-walk reliever in the team's system, **Enoli Paredes** will have to either power up or corral his stuff to get back to the major leagues and be a meaningful piece.   *taps ear* I'm being told we have another recent low budget IFA signing to discuss. Well, here's **Misael Tamarez**, he throws an overpowering mid-90s fastball that induces bad swings and needs a better breaking or off-speed offering, with his breaking ball showing the most potential so far. Does this profile sound familiar by the end of this chapter?   **Andrew Taylor** has a fastball that sits in the low 90s but has elite traits, which provide a strong foundation to build on for the organization's industry-leading pitching development.

LOS ANGELES ANGELS

Essay by Grant Brisbee

Player comments by Patrick Dubuque and BP staff

How?

There are a lot of questions concerning the operations and general efficacy of Angels Baseball LP, but they all branch out from this mother question. This is a team with two of the most exciting players the sport has ever seen. Both of them, together on the same team at the same time, baseballing better than almost anyone has ever baseballed in history. Yet the team is kinda awful. How?

This will be the Angels' second Baseball Prospectus *Annual* essay in a row to invoke the name "'Tungsten Arm' O'Doyle," and it's absolutely necessary. It's malpractice to not invoke it, like the sign of peace at a Catholic Mass. Every season, the Angels have the same task as every other team—to acquire and deploy the 26 best players they can find—and they've somehow wormed their way into position to have one of the greatest head starts on that task *in baseball history*. Every season, they lose more games than the Akron Groomsmen lost in any year during the 1920s.

Imagine a league-wide draft of every active major and minor leaguer before every season. There's one every offseason, so don't worry about owner-friendly contracts and team control. Just look for the players who can help their teams win in the following season. You're taking Shohei Ohtani and Mike Trout with the first two picks, right? Even if you'd pick differently, you're not making fun of another team for those picks.

The Angels were 73-89 last season. They were 77-85 the season before. You can explain some of this away with injuries and pandemics and general malaise, but take a trip back to 2015, when Jered Weaver and C.J. Wilson were heading up the rotation. Do you remember how innocent you were in 2015? That's the last time the Angels won more games than they lost, even though they've enjoyed one of the greatest one-two cornerstones in the history of roster-building since then.

How?

Howwwwwwwwwwwwww?

Well, it starts with the other 24 spots on the roster. During this hypothetical draft, the Angels set up their auto-draft on a flip phone and took an extended whiz. Bill James famously said that the best organizations look at what players can do,

LOS ANGELES ANGELS PROSPECTUS

2022 W-L: 73-89, 3RD IN AL WEST

Pythag	.468	*20th*	DER	.714	*5th*
RS/G	3.85	*25th*	DRC+	95	*24th*
RA/G	4.12	*11th*	DRA-	95	*13th*
dWin%	.496	*18th*	FIP	3.95	*17th*
Payroll	$189M	*8th*	B-Age	28.5	*17th*
M$/MW	$6.9M	*28th*	P-Age	27.7	*6th*

400′ 387′ 370′ 330′ 330′

- Opened 1966
- Open air
- Natural surface
- Fence profile: 4′6″ to 8′

Park Factors

Runs	Runs/RH	Runs/LH	HR/RH	HR/LH
100	98	103	102	108

Top Hitter WARP	4.7 Mike Trout
Top Pitcher WARP	5.1 Shohei Ohtani
2023 Top Prospect	Zach Neto

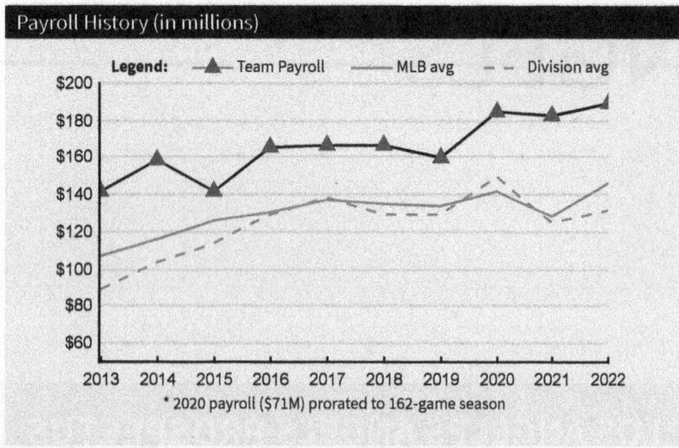

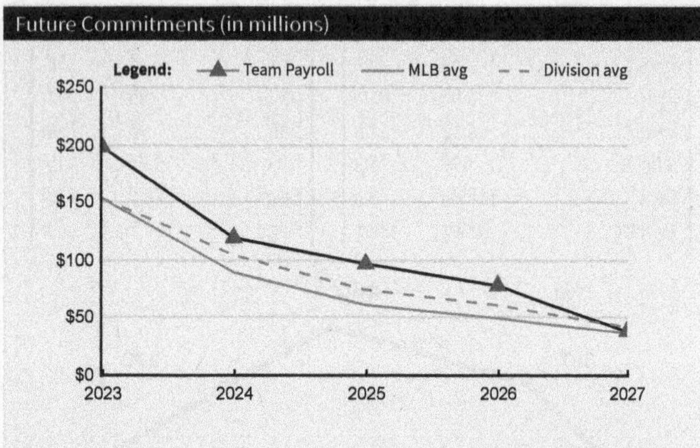

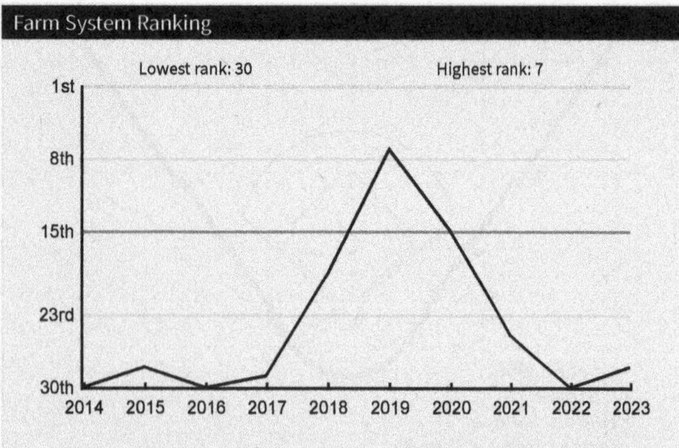

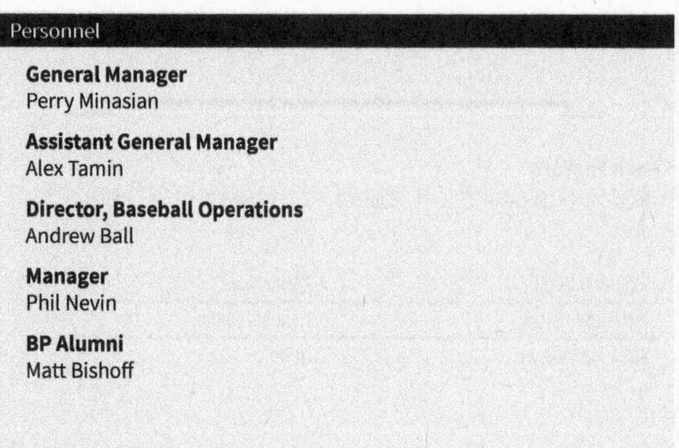
Personnel

General Manager
Perry Minasian

Assistant General Manager
Alex Tamin

Director, Baseball Operations
Andrew Ball

Manager
Phil Nevin

BP Alumni
Matt Bishoff

not what they can't do. But when you're evaluating the Angels, don't look at the players who are helping them. Look at the players who *aren't* helping. They've flipped the sabermetric truism on its head. With the Angels, you have to ignore the generational superstars and focus on the unhelpful players.

There are a lot of them. My multi-part documentary on PBS will be titled, *A Preponderance of Unhelpful Players*. Viewer discretion is advised.

Last season, five Angels batters had a DRC+ below 75 across at least 285 trips to the plate. Since Los Angeles joined the league in 1961, only seven teams had more players with such a low DRC+ receive at least 200 plate appearances. The 2022 Angels had five such members, and they averaged more than 350 PA. Is that cherry picking? Of course it is. But the point isn't to prove that the Angels were the worst team ever. It's to answer that initial question: How? That's how. Teams usually don't have that many players doing so little, so often. The 2022 Angels had players like Andrew Velazquez, whose .540 OPS actually *improved* his career OPS.

The Onion published an article in 2004 with the headline, "Yee-Haw! My Vote Cancels Out Y'all's!," in which the (fictional) author wrote:

> *Now, you probably waste a whole lotta good-fishin' Saturdays readin' yourself the papers, watchin' all the talk on the TV, and sittin' around thinkin' real hard about which way you gonna vote. Well, it's a real shame, then, ain't it, that all that time you spend in real careful considerin' don't count for nothin', once my vote runs y'all's right off the road.*

It's like that, but with OPS, ERA and WARP. Ohtani and Trout are trying, friends, they're really trying. But, yee-haw, someone else's feckless 0-for-5 or blown save cancels them out. And because there are only two superstars and a lot more un-superstars on the roster, it gets messy quick.

Before assigning blame, take a moment to recognize that there were defensible decisions that just didn't work out for the 2022 Angels. It was possible to be skeptical about the long-term productivity of Anthony Rendon when the Angels signed him, but nobody saw him immediately losing every last scrap of his power and missing huge chunks of consecutive seasons.

The Angels thought Max Stassi had turned a corner offensively, giving them a backstop who could excel on both sides of the ball. They even extended him ahead of the season. He then turned in one of the worst offensive seasons from a catcher—any catcher—since the turn of the millennium. Can't plan for that. Oh, the defense fell off a cliff, too. In 2021, he was second in the league by Catcher Defensive Adjustment. Catchers don't have to hit well, but only if they catch well. Stassi did neither.

Jared Walsh, a literal All-Star in 2021, stopped hitting. He had the 11th-worst OPS of any first baseman with at least 450 PA since the Angels joined the league in 1961. If it makes

Angels fans feel better, Casey Kotchman takes *two* of the spots above Walsh, and neither of those seasons were with the Angels.

(No: Casey Kotchman factlets do not make Angels fans feel better.)

Rendon, Stassi and Walsh were three entirely unhelpful players who were (reasonably!) expected to be much, much more, and they canceled out the two super-duper-duper stars. The early-season surge from the Angels was so believable because we didn't know that that trio would tank. It's not as if this roster was built with an open tryout after Ohtani and Trout. There was money spent and reasonable decisions were made. Noah Syndergaard was an absolutely inspired decision for a team in the Angels' position. There's an alternate universe where that signing is the best of the previous offseason.

But the starting pitching wasn't the problem this time. The Angels' pitching staff enjoyed its best adjusted ERA since 2008, when they won 100 games. They've been around for 62 seasons now, and last season's ERA+ was the 12th-best in franchise history. Every team with a better rotation by that metric was .500 or better, and the 2022 Angels most certainly weren't, but at least it's not the same old problem.

This isn't like the 2019 team that had 600 plate appearances from a 27-year-old Trout and 425 PA from a 24-year-old Ohtani, but was still messing around with Trevor Cahill, Matt Harvey and a gaggle of starting pitchers who were 23 or younger, with 10 or more starts and an unfortunate ERA. This club could pitch a little bit, at least. Ohtani was the 28-start marvel, of course, but Patrick Sandoval was outstanding, Reid Detmers was solid and José Suarez is trending in the right direction. Michael Lorenzen even helped out a bit, although he had exactly zero pinch-hitting appearances. (If there's one team that should believe in the concept of a two-way player...)

The bullpen wasn't as good as the rotation, though, and didn't miss bats. The Angels ranked 25th of 30 teams in K/9 from relievers, and finished 19th in reliever DRA- compared to 11th for the rotation. They weren't terrible as a unit, but as with the lineup, far too much time went to unhelpful players: 116 combined innings were given to Mike Mayers (5.68 ERA), Tucker Davidson (6.87 ERA), and Chase Silseth (6.59 ERA). Not helping matters: They shipped Raisel Iglesias to Atlanta at the trade deadline, eight months after they signed him to a four-year deal, in a functional salary dump (there, he posted a 0.34 ERA). That's another good way for a team to waste the performances of two of the greatest baseball players to ever live.

The cruelest part of this is that there are other teams that excel at the very thing the Angels are so bad at. The Rays aren't so good at the "getting Mike Trout or Shohei Ohtani" part of roster construction, but they can build a rotation, bullpen and bench that's 56 deep and filled with surprisingly effective create-a-players. Even if you ignore the Giants' 107-win season, they still finished .500 last season with a philosophy of limiting the players who have no business being on the roster. It's possible for a team to be strong around the margins without overextending itself, and those gains would be worth exponentially more with such a head start.

The Angels didn't need to throw nine-figure contracts at the premium free agents this offseason. Even if they had signed a premium player to a Rendon-sized contract—with a guarantee of him providing the Rendon-sized production they were expecting from the actual Rendon—it still wouldn't have addressed what this organization is lacking: not superstars, but players to stand guard outside the vault that contains the 10-to-15 WARP they're expecting every season from just two players.

Tyler Anderson should help. His contract looks like a relative bargain now that the offseason dust has settled on an extravagant free agent market. He's not the specific answer, but he's a part of the larger answer. More helpful players. Fewer unhelpful players. Maybe it really is that simple. Even compared to the inherently sketchy genre of baseball players known as relievers, Carlos Estévez seems like a bit of a gamble, but he's still advancing the correct philosophy.

The new ideology, more than anything else, will answer the questions that are bothering the Angels. Forget about Joe Maddon, Phil Nevin, Mike Scioscia or the ghost of Bill Rigney. This isn't a manager problem. It's not a one-weird-trick solution. (Though if owner Arte Moreno does sell the team ahead of Opening Day, as purported, it'll be much easier to believe a refreshed outlook has taken root.) They'll need help with the players filling out the roster beyond the obvious superstars. They'll need to reinvent players like Anthony Rendon, Max Stassi, Jared Walsh and Jo Adell. They'll need to hug players like Taylor Ward and tell them how much they appreciate them for being helpful and normal.

To that end, the Angels brought on Hunter Renfroe and Gio Urshela in trades, plus Brandon Drury in free agency. They're under-the-radar, but none has had a campaign that could be described as "historically terrible." Suddenly, Velasquez remains on the 40-man, but is (at best) third on the depth chart for shortstops, where he belongs. If Adell's breakout is ever going to come, it'll be via a bench role or injury replacement. Should any of last season's implosions repeat, there's enough depth to cast them off.

They'll still need to figure out why Walsh can be a Ward one year but not the next, and they'll need to prevent Ward from being a Walsh. It would help if they had a robust farm system, so let's just check where they ranked in last season's Baseball Prospectus organizational rankings:

> *30. Los Angeles Angels*
>
> *Strengths: Theoretically, a couple of close-to-the-majors mid-rotation starters*

Weaknesses: The group of bats here wouldn't be that inspiring, even if they had a track record of developing bats in the last decade, which they don't.

Oh no. Things look slightly better this season, but the Angels' system is again expected to be squarely in the bottom five. Logan O'Hoppe and Zach Neto are the only impact players anywhere near the majors.

It's certainly possible that the Angels figure this stuff out before the start of the season. You don't have to travel too far to find teams that thrived while adding supplementary and complementary players by the dozen. If the Angels can do that and keep everyone healthy, they won't just threaten .500. They'll threaten the Astros.

So that's my diagnosis of how the Angels inspired the legend of "'Tungsten Arm' O'Doyle," and my prescription for how to cure it. Turns out they needed more good players.

Which, when you put it like that...

This will be the third season of the Perry Minasian reign. The processes and the people should be mostly in place. His well-oiled machinery should be puffing steam and tooting away, in theory. This was the offseason to fix a dozen roster problems rather than slapping another star on top of the roster. Because, again, the Angels have rough approximations of Babe Ruth and Willie Mays on the roster, that's plenty of star power.

The Angels still have one of the greatest head starts for 7.69% of a roster that any team has ever had. This is the season when it could finally pay off. It's also the season where the dream and the impossibly enviable core could be broken up forever. No matter what this year looks like, if Ohtani leaves, that's the story of their next offseason. And he made it clear that the options are winning or moving, saying he had "a rather negative impression" of his penultimate year under contract. Judging by the tens of millions Ohtani risked to come to MLB earlier, a big enough figure in free agency might not overcome another losing season. No pressure, Perry and Phil.

If the season is just as messy next year, the answer will be simple: What difference would it have made anyway? If the Angels can't win with Trout and Ohtani, how can they win with an older, far more expensive Ohtani? What's the point of any of this, man?

The season is here, though, so the questions get kicked down the road to next offseason (or when the Angels' postseason hopes disappear in another 14-game losing streak). The goal is to not have a preponderance of bad players. Get more of the good ones. It seems simple, but if it were, we wouldn't be back here asking the same question every winter. This time next year, either things will be different, or we'll be asking one question.

How?

—Grant Brisbee writes about the Giants and MLB for The Athletic.

Hitters

Jo Adell LF Born: 04/08/99 Age: 24 Bats: R Throws: R Height: 6'3" Weight: 215 lb. Origin: Round 1, 2017 Draft (#10 overall)

YEAR	TEAM	LVL	AGE	PA	R	2B	3B	HR	RBI	BB	K	SB	CS	Whiff%	AVG/OBP/SLG	DRC+	BABIP	BRR	DRP	WARP
2020	LAA	MLB	21	132	9	4	0	3	7	7	55	0	1	42.1%	.161/.212/.266	51	.258	0.2	RF(34): -2.1, CF(4): -0.1	-0.6
2021	SL	AAA	22	339	57	17	4	23	69	22	99	8	2		.289/.342/.592	107	.351	1.7	CF(28): 0.1, LF(24): -1.2, RF(18): 1.8	1.7
2021	LAA	MLB	22	140	17	5	2	4	26	8	32	2	1	29.6%	.246/.295/.408	93	.298	0.5	LF(25): -1.1, RF(19): 3.4	0.6
2022	SL	AAA	23	180	35	15	0	13	33	20	56	3	2	30.7%	.239/.333/.587	100	.273	1.9	LF(23): -0.8, RF(15): -1.1	0.6
2022	LAA	MLB	23	285	22	12	2	8	27	11	107	4	2	36.4%	.224/.264/.373	61	.338	0.8	LF(69): 0.3, RF(15): -0.6	-0.4
2023 DC	*LAA*	*MLB*	*24*	*94*	*10*	*4*	*0*	*4*	*11*	*5*	*30*	*1*	*1*	*33.7%*	*.227/.281/.433*	*93*	*.293*	*0.0*	*LF 0, RF 0*	*0.1*

Comparables: Byron Buxton (52), Cameron Maybin (49), Kyle Tucker (47)

OK, first comment of the chapter. They're fun to write! And to start, we have... oh. Oh no.

Let's just lay it out there: Adell can't hit the ball. Sometimes his swing gets called "complicated," other times "long" or "noisy." Angels hitting coach Jeremy Reed, who had a bit of an Adell-esque career himself, tried to mix things up by getting him to hit more like Luis Rengifo, which does not, at first blush, inspire a ton of confidence. But it's understandable. Adell isn't one of those guys who makes poor swing decisions; he's not swinging at ball one and two to put himself in a hole. The former top prospect is swinging at *strike* one and two, which is a much more difficult problem to solve—his contact rate on pitches in the zone last year was among the ten worst in baseball, reaching Gallo-ian depths of bat-to-ball ability. Even as LA's crowded outfield opened up before him due to injuries, he found himself on the short side of a platoon with Mickey Moniak. Adell can still run and he still has power, so he'll get at least one more shot to prove he can be, well, if not a star, then maybe, like, Brian Goodwin?

Man, what a depressing sentence. Are they all going to be like this? They are, aren't they.

Brandon Drury IF

Born: 08/21/92 Age: 30 Bats: R Throws: R Height: 6'2" Weight: 230 lb. Origin: Round 13, 2010 Draft (#404 overall)

YEAR	TEAM	LVL	AGE	PA	R	2B	3B	HR	RBI	BB	K	SB	CS	Whiff%	AVG/OBP/SLG	DRC+	BABIP	BRR	DRP	WARP
2020	TOR	MLB	27	49	3	1	0	0	1	2	9	0	0	18.4%	.152/.184/.174	87	.184	-0.4	3B(16): 0.5, 2B(4): 0, SS(2): 0	0.1
2021	SYR	AAA	28	236	28	14	0	9	32	19	49	0	0		.257/.318/.449	107	.291	-1.9	3B(23): -1.4, 1B(17): 0.5, 2B(10): -1.0	0.5
2021	NYM	MLB	28	88	7	5	0	4	14	3	22	0	0	24.0%	.274/.307/.476	96	.328	-0.4	3B(7): -0.3, LF(6): -0.2, RF(6): -0.8	0.1
2022	SD	MLB	29	183	25	9	0	8	28	9	42	0	1	22.9%	.238/.290/.435	98	.267	-1.2	1B(21): 0.6, 2B(7): 0.3, 3B(5): -0.4	0.3
2022	CIN	MLB	29	385	62	22	2	20	59	29	84	2	2	20.7%	.274/.335/.520	120	.306	-2.4	3B(62): -2.3, 2B(20): 0.4, 1B(9): 0	1.4
2023 DC	*LAA*	*MLB*	*30*	*504*	*58*	*23*	*1*	*19*	*57*	*32*	*99*	*0*	*1*	*21.8%*	*.246/.301/.428*	*103*	*.272*	*-3.9*	*2B 0, 3B 0*	*0.9*

Comparables: Aramis Ramirez (72), Gary Gaetti (65), Brooks Robinson (65)

Drury has been traded three times in his career and DFA'd twice. He has signed two minor-league deals, including one with the Reds before the 2022 season. After a career spent moving around from position to position and team to team like the human version of the bouncing DVD logo, no one saw his '22 breakout coming. But in undoing his attempts to become the latest launch-angle revolution dude, Drury saw all the benefits he was looking for, including an uptick in barrels and a career-high in home runs. He was even a part of one of AJ Preller's patented trade-for-everyone July moves. After hitting a grand slam in his first at-bat with the Padres, Drury looked more like the spare part he was previously, but he got to play in the postseason and earn himself a nice payday with the Angels, who inked him to a two-year, $17 million deal.

David Fletcher MI

Born: 05/31/94 Age: 29 Bats: R Throws: R Height: 5'9" Weight: 185 lb. Origin: Round 6, 2015 Draft (#195 overall)

YEAR	TEAM	LVL	AGE	PA	R	2B	3B	HR	RBI	BB	K	SB	CS	Whiff%	AVG/OBP/SLG	DRC+	BABIP	BRR	DRP	WARP
2020	LAA	MLB	26	230	31	13	0	3	18	20	25	2	1	8.6%	.319/.376/.425	115	.348	0.3	SS(27): 0, 2B(15): -0.4, 3B(8): -0.3	1.1
2021	LAA	MLB	27	665	74	27	3	2	47	31	60	15	3	9.5%	.262/.297/.324	85	.287	1.9	2B(142): -2.2, SS(20): -0.3	1.1
2022	SL	AAA	28	51	3	1	0	0	1	2	7	1	0	15.5%	.204/.235/.224	98	.238	0.5	SS(7): -0.9, 2B(3): 0.2	0.1
2022	LAA	MLB	28	228	20	9	1	2	17	7	16	1	0	12.2%	.255/.288/.333	100	.268	-1.0	2B(44): 0.7, SS(36): 1.5	0.8
2023 DC	*LAA*	*MLB*	*29*	*528*	*59*	*21*	*2*	*6*	*43*	*28*	*51*	*8*	*2*	*11.3%*	*.278/.320/.371*	*97*	*.298*	*3.4*	*SS 1, 2B 0*	*1.8*

Comparables: Lenny Harris (76), Wally Backman (76), Duane Kuiper (73)

Modern society has long wrestled with the value of that ubiquitous keystone of small talk, the question "what do you do?" For some, it's a natural way of learning about people and finding common interests. For others, it yields both instant social stratification and a worrisome conflation of work and identity. We are not, it's worth reminding us, what we do. For Fletcher, that axiom is vital. What he did is right there above this paragraph, but that's not who he is or what happened to him: namely a nagging hip strain that consumed months of the season, followed by a hand contusion that, thanks to the triage tent that was the team's infield, he was forced to play through. By September 14 his hand hurt so badly that he couldn't physically swing the bat; instead Fletcher bunted in all three of his plate appearances, even when he had two strikes. DRC+ remains faithful, remembering the bat-to-ball skills that made him a .300 hitter in the past. Meanwhile, at parties, when people ask him what he does, Fletcher can fire back an old Sartre quote: "Freedom is what we do with what's been done to us."

Mike Ford 1B/DH

Born: 07/04/92 Age: 31 Bats: L Throws: R Height: 6'0" Weight: 225 lb. Origin: Undrafted Free Agent, 2013

YEAR	TEAM	LVL	AGE	PA	R	2B	3B	HR	RBI	BB	K	SB	CS	Whiff%	AVG/OBP/SLG	DRC+	BABIP	BRR	DRP	WARP
2020	NYY	MLB	27	84	5	4	0	2	11	7	16	0	0	26.1%	.135/.226/.270	90	.140	0.0	1B(13): -0.1	0.1
2021	SWB	AAA	28	29	3	0	0	0	1	3	8	0	0		.083/.207/.083	92	.118	-0.2	1B(6): -0.1	0.0
2021	ROC	AAA	28	116	10	5	0	3	12	11	32	0	0		.202/.284/.337	91	.261	0.3	1B(21): -0.8	0.1
2021	DUR	AAA	28	162	22	5	1	11	31	21	41	1	0		.243/.346/.529	120	.261	-0.2	1B(19): -0.5, 3B(6): 0.3	0.7
2021	NYY	MLB	28	72	6	0	0	3	5	11	23	0	0	30.0%	.133/.278/.283	89	.147	-0.9	1B(21): 0.6	0.0
2022	TAC	AAA	29	47	10	1	0	2	5	5	4	0	0	16.9%	.317/.404/.488	119	.314	0.5	1B(5): -0.2, P(2): 0.1	0.1
2022	GWN	AAA	29	53	2	6	0	0	3	11	7	0	0		.238/.396/.381	119	.286	-2.0	1B(8): -0.5	0.1
2022	LAA	MLB	29	99	8	4	0	3	5	8	26	0	0	20.4%	.231/.293/.374	83	.290	-1.1	1B(27): -0.1	-0.1
2022	SEA	MLB	29	38	1	1	0	0	3	8	12	0	0	28.9%	.172/.368/.207	87	.294	-0.6	1B(1): -0.0	
2022	SF	MLB	29	4	0	0	0	0	2	0	0	0	0	20.0%	.250/.250/.250	102	.250		1B(1): -0.1	0.0
2022	ATL	MLB	29	8	0	0	0	0	0	1	2	0	0	16.7%	.000/.125/.000	88			P(1): -0.0	0.0
2023 DC	*FA*	*MLB*	*30*	*148*	*16*	*5*	*0*	*5*	*18*	*16*	*30*	*0*	*0*	*22.2%*	*.218/.312/.395*	*97*	*.243*	*-0.1*	*1B 0, 3B 0*	*0.1*

Comparables: Justin Smoak (50), J.R. Phillips (50), Mike Baxter (48)

The most vital statistics of all for Ford: Five dress shirts, two pairs of pants and some shorts and T-shirts. The journeyman's journeyman played for eight different teams in 2022—four major and four minor—as he continued his personal quest to live in the same place for more than two consecutive weeks. It's a common lamentation, and not untrue, that we'll never know what guys like this would do with regular playing time. But in Ford's case, the answer is pretty clear: The real journey he needs to make is back in time to a previous era. He's a fastball hitter who'll sit the bat on his shoulder until he gets a fastball count, and he'll make an out if he doesn't. His career splits are illuminating, as he's assembled a .987 OPS when ahead in the count and a .324 mark when behind in it. Now that seemingly half the pitchers in the league use a breaking ball as their primary weapon—and with little room for the lefty-killing pinch-hitter—Ford is likely doomed to measure out the rest of his career in stops made at the Hudson News.

Denzer Guzman SS

Born: 02/08/04 Age: 19 Bats: R Throws: R Height: 6'1" Weight: 180 lb. Origin: International Free Agent, 2021

YEAR	TEAM	LVL	AGE	PA	R	2B	3B	HR	RBI	BB	K	SB	CS	Whiff%	AVG/OBP/SLG	DRC+	BABIP	BRR	DRP	WARP
2021	DSL ANG	ROK	17	164	21	10	1	3	27	20	24	11	7		.213/.311/.362		.233			
2022	ANG	ROK	18	211	38	11	3	3	33	15	44	3	1		.286/.341/.422		.354			
2022	IE	A	18	23	2	0	0	0	2	6	10	1	0		.176/.391/.176	82	.429	0.3	SS(5): -0.6	0.0
2023 non-DC	*LAA*	*MLB*	*19*	*251*	*19*	*9*	*2*	*2*	*19*	*20*	*105*	*7*	*2*	*41.8%*	*.193/.266/.285*	*48*	*.344*	*2.6*	*SS 0*	*-0.6*

Guzman is just the latest in a long line of men to play an important role in baseball's ecosystem: the 18-year-old complex prospect. In an age where the sport grows increasingly quantified and granular, where we're only years away from players' high school essays on *The Crucible* getting added into their statistical profiles, the international prospect remains a legend cloaked in mystery, an old-fashioned yarn of a hero. Sure, everything else about baseball's international system is horrific garbage, its corruption mirrored only by its profitability, but it's nice that teams have a vague sense of optimism that some impending prodigy is out there just waiting to take shape. Guzman is that for the Angels: His feel for hitting translated well to the complex league where, as an 18-year-old, he also showed a promising touch of doubles power. It's enough to dream on, and if it isn't, it will be again soon.

Jeremiah Jackson IF Born: 03/26/00 Age: 23 Bats: R Throws: R Height: 6'0" Weight: 165 lb. Origin: Round 2, 2018 Draft (#57 overall)

YEAR	TEAM	LVL	AGE	PA	R	2B	3B	HR	RBI	BB	K	SB	CS	Whiff%	AVG/OBP/SLG	DRC+	BABIP	BRR	DRP	WARP
2021	GDD	WIN	21	61	10	1	0	3	10	2	23	0	1		.161/.213/.339		.194			
2021	IE	A	21	196	29	14	3	8	46	24	65	11	3		.263/.352/.527	101	.367	-1.3	SS(31): -1.2, 2B(9): -0.4	0.4
2022	RCT	AA	22	351	44	16	0	14	44	38	77	7	4		.215/.308/.404	97	.239	1.7	2B(33): -0.8, SS(31): -2.0, 3B(10): 0.7	0.8
2023 non-DC	*LAA*	*MLB*	*23*	*251*	*22*	*10*	*1*	*5*	*24*	*19*	*77*	*5*	*2*	*36.4%*	*.202/.271/.334*	*66*	*.279*	*1.3*	*2B 0, 3B 0*	*-0.2*

Comparables: Eliezer Álvarez (68), Kristopher Negrón (57), Vinny Capra (57)

For four years we were all writing and reading the same thing about Jackson: he'll have incredible power for a shortstop, assuming he fields well enough to be a shortstop. Also, each time he makes contact with a pitch, it feels like it could be his last. For those four years in which he haunted the back half of Angels top-10 lists, we reached the same conclusion: Double-A would be the proving ground, the point at which his swing-and-miss would either improve or destroy him. That's over and done with, and now we have to figure out what the hell happened. Jackson struck out at a career-low clip as a Trash Panda without sacrificing much in the way of walks, yet the results looked awful anyway thanks to that ridiculously low BABIP. To make matters even more confusing, he started off the year on fire before going through a 6-for-70 stretch, then spent some time late in the season trying out left field. In the end, no one's questions got answered and no one was particularly satisfied. But hey, what's one more year of waiting?

Jake Lamb 1B Born: 10/09/90 Age: 32 Bats: L Throws: R Height: 6'3" Weight: 215 lb. Origin: Round 6, 2012 Draft (#213 overall)

YEAR	TEAM	LVL	AGE	PA	R	2B	3B	HR	RBI	BB	K	SB	CS	Whiff%	AVG/OBP/SLG	DRC+	BABIP	BRR	DRP	WARP
2020	OAK	MLB	29	49	5	4	0	3	9	2	8	0	0	21.6%	.267/.327/.556	100	.265	0.8	3B(11): 0.4	0.2
2020	AZ	MLB	29	50	2	1	0	0	1	6	17	0	1	31.0%	.116/.240/.140	70	.192	-0.2	1B(12): -1, 3B(3): 0	-0.2
2021	CLT	AAA	30	69	6	5	0	3	8	8	15	0	0		.246/.333/.475	109	.279	0.7	RF(10): -0.6, 3B(5): -0.5	0.3
2021	CHW	MLB	30	131	20	2	0	6	13	17	38	0	0	27.1%	.212/.321/.389	91	.261	-0.1	LF(16): -0.5, RF(9): -0.6, 3B(6): -0.2	0.1
2021	TOR	MLB	30	39	5	2	0	1	6	5	13	0	0	26.4%	.129/.256/.290	75	.158	-0.3	3B(10): 0, 1B(1): 0	0.0
2022	OKC	AAA	31	276	44	12	0	15	50	39	74	1	1	30.4%	.290/.395/.537	119	.359	0.6	1B(34): -0.7, 3B(3): 0.1, LF(3): -0.3	1.4
2022	LAD	MLB	31	77	10	5	1	2	4	8	24	0	1	30.8%	.239/.338/.433	77	.341	-0.4	LF(9): -0.3	-0.1
2022	SEA	MLB	31	34	3	1	0	1	2	3	14	0	0	32.0%	.167/.265/.300	70	.267	-1.0	RF(6): -0.1, LF(5): -0.2, 3B(4): -0.1	-0.2
2023 non-DC	*LAA*	*MLB*	*32*	*251*	*27*	*10*	*0*	*9*	*29*	*27*	*74*	*1*	*0*	*30.0%*	*.211/.307/.388*	*92*	*.273*	*-0.3*	*3B 0, RF 0*	*0.2*

Comparables: Howard Johnson (60), Darrell Evans (57), Eddie Yost (56)

You could fire up a montage of Lamb's career to Supertramp's "Take the Long Way Home." After coming into his own as a lefty power bat with the Diamondbacks in 2016 and 2017, injuries, severe platoon splits and defensive limitations have led to an itinerant career at the ends of various benches in Oakland, Toronto, Chicago (Southside) and Los Angeles (the real one), eventually to be traded to his hometown Mariners last August. Alas, the homecoming was brief, as an underperforming Lamb was designated for assignment within two months. Another team willing to take a chance on a resurgence of Lamb's bat may yet keep the montage from its final verse: "When you look through the years and see what you could have been / Oh, what you might have been / If you would have more time."

Mickey Moniak OF Born: 05/13/98 Age: 25 Bats: L Throws: R Height: 6'2" Weight: 195 lb. Origin: Round 1, 2016 Draft (#1 overall)

YEAR	TEAM	LVL	AGE	PA	R	2B	3B	HR	RBI	BB	K	SB	CS	Whiff%	AVG/OBP/SLG	DRC+	BABIP	BRR	DRP	WARP
2020	PHI	MLB	22	18	3	0	0	0	0	4	6	0	0	50.0%	.214/.389/.214	86	.375	0.1	LF(5): -0.3, RF(1): 0	0.0
2021	LHV	AAA	23	409	42	15	8	15	65	31	101	5	2		.238/.299/.447	97	.280	-1.7	CF(59): -6.0, LF(25): 0.1, RF(10): -0.0	0.6
2021	PHI	MLB	23	37	3	0	0	1	3	3	16	0	0	41.7%	.091/.167/.182	65	.125	0.5	CF(8): -0.4, RF(3): -0.1	0.0
2022	REA	AA	24	25	5	1	1	1	6	1	6	0	0		.391/.400/.652	105	.471	0.4	CF(5): -1.1	0.0
2022	LHV	AAA	24	91	14	5	0	5	8	8	22	5	3		.277/.341/.518	106	.321	0.3	CF(19): -0.0	0.4
2022	LAA	MLB	24	62	9	2	1	3	6	1	25	1	0	40.4%	.200/.226/.417	70	.281	-0.3	LF(13): -0.2, CF(6): -0.4	-0.1
2022	PHI	MLB	24	50	4	1	0	0	2	3	19	0	0	34.3%	.130/.184/.152	59	.222	0.5	CF(15): -0.2	0.0
2023 DC	*LAA*	*MLB*	*25*	*254*	*24*	*9*	*3*	*6*	*24*	*15*	*80*	*4*	*2*	*33.6%*	*.212/.266/.372*	*68*	*.291*	*3.6*	*CF 0, LF 0*	*0.1*

Comparables: Arismendy Alcántara (60), Brett Phillips (59), Todd Dunwoody (56)

There was a time when a notable Mickey landing with the Angels would have represented incredible brand synergy in a way that reflected positively on the ballclub and player alike. That synergy still exists, but these days it casts a much darker pall. Moniak ending up in Anaheim initially looked to prove a fundamental truth: Multiply two negatives and you get a positive. In this case, the Angels' negative aura and Moniak's negative OPS+ multiplied to create an 11-game run in which the former first overall pick recorded three home runs—tripling his career total—and an .881 OPS (with a .661 SLG). The problem? He notched 12 strikeouts to zero walks in that time, and in the following eight games produced a .285 OPS. He was then felled by a hit-by-pitch to the hand, and, to add insult to injury, he didn't even get to take first base; he'd offered at the pitch, because of course he did. He left the game in an 0-2 count with the bases loaded and no one out. His replacement struck out. So did the next two batters. The Angels didn't score in the inning. So much for the place where dreams come true.

★ ★ ★ *2023 Top 101 Prospect* **#47** ★ ★ ★

Zach Neto SS Born: 01/31/01 Age: 22 Bats: R Throws: R Height: 6'0" Weight: 185 lb. Origin: Round 1, 2022 Draft (#13 overall)

YEAR	TEAM	LVL	AGE	PA	R	2B	3B	HR	RBI	BB	K	SB	CS	Whiff%	AVG/OBP/SLG	DRC+	BABIP	BRR	DRP	WARP
2022	TRI	A+	21	31	2	0	1	1	4	4	4	1	0		.200/.355/.400	113	.200	-0.3	SS(6): -0.1	0.1
2022	RCT	AA	21	136	22	9	0	4	23	8	29	4	2		.320/.382/.492	99	.389	-0.6	SS(28): -0.3	0.3
2023 non-DC	*LAA*	*MLB*	*22*	*251*	*21*	*10*	*2*	*3*	*22*	*15*	*60*	*4*	*2*	*27.3%*	*.231/.294/.341*	*77*	*.298*	*1.3*	*SS 0*	*0.1*

Comparables: Jose Martinez (87), Luis Rengifo (80), Mauricio Dubón (77)

The Angels' first-round pick in the 2022 draft, Neto's swing might be the closest thing baseball has to a crane kick. Just as the pitcher steps into his delivery, Neto lifts his front leg high in the air and holds it there for just a moment. Then he brings it back down, but not quite all the way, dangling his foot just above the ground. This last little step is his timing device—he turns his foot as he plants, generating the torque for his swing. With two strikes, he dispenses with the kick but keeps the rotation, nearly facing the cleats of his left foot toward the pitcher, generating a lovely, violent whiplash of a swing. So far, it's working. His hand-eye coordination is his leading skill, while his other tools hover around "acceptable," with enough pull-side power to get the job done and enough hustle to look fast. He's also a lock to stay at short, which is a nice skill to pair with his roundhouse worthy of a green belt.

★ ★ ★ *2023 Top 101 Prospect* **#77** ★ ★ ★

Logan O'Hoppe C Born: 02/09/00 Age: 23 Bats: R Throws: R Height: 6'2" Weight: 185 lb. Origin: Round 23, 2018 Draft (#677 overall)

YEAR	TEAM	LVL	AGE	PA	R	2B	3B	HR	RBI	BB	K	SB	CS	Whiff%	AVG/OBP/SLG	DRC+	BABIP	BRR	DRP	WARP
2021	PEJ	WIN	21	100	19	8	0	3	17	21	15	3	1		.299/.440/.519		.328			
2021	JS	A+	21	358	43	17	2	13	48	30	63	6	3		.270/.335/.459	124	.294	0.2	C(60): 3.2	2.4
2021	REA	AA	21	57	6	1	0	3	7	1	9	0	0		.296/.333/.481	109	.310	-0.3	C(11): -0.5	0.2
2021	LHV	AAA	21	23	2	1	0	1	3	2	4	0	0		.190/.261/.381	102	.188	0.0	C(5): -0.3	0.1
2022	RCT	AA	22	131	24	3	0	11	33	29	22	1	2		.306/.473/.673	167	.288	0.1	C(27): 1.9	1.0
2022	REA	AA	22	316	48	11	1	15	45	41	52	6	2		.275/.392/.496	142	.289	-0.1	C(58): -0.5	2.3
2022	LAA	MLB	22	16	1	0	0	0	2	2	3	0	0	36.7%	.286/.375/.286	101	.364	-0.4	C(5): 0.4	0.1
2023 DC	*LAA*	*MLB*	*23*	*253*	*28*	*8*	*1*	*7*	*25*	*24*	*51*	*3*	*1*	*24.1%*	*.236/.321/.388*	*101*	*.271*	*1.1*	*C -4*	*0.7*

Comparables: Wilin Rosario (62), John Ryan Murphy (55), Austin Romine (54)

YEAR	TEAM	P. COUNT	FRM RUNS	BLK RUNS	THRW RUNS	TOT RUNS
2021	PEJ	1520			0.0	0.0
2021	JS	8805	4.1	-0.1	0.0	4.0
2021	REA	1517	-0.6	-0.1	0.2	-0.4
2021	LHV	819	-0.2	0.0	0.0	-0.2
2022	REA	8259	-1.1	0.4	0.0	-0.6
2022	RCT	3867	2.0	-0.1	0.0	1.9
2022	LAA	638	-0.2	0.0	0.0	-0.2
2023	*LAA*	*9620*	*-3.3*	*0.2*	*0.2*	*-2.9*

Let's not beat around the bush: It was a weird trade. Despite having Max Stassi on board for two more seasons, the Angels couldn't pass up a chance to sell not-low on struggling center fielder Brandon Marsh, picking up the highly regarded (but statistically average) O'Hoppe from the Phillies. Then, immediately, both players kicked it into another gear. O'Hoppe is a button-masher of a hitter, standing directly over the plate and uppercutting everything he can reach into the sun. Sometimes, the baseball doesn't pass through the plane he's chosen to swing on, which leads to infield flies and other weak contact. But when he does connect, as he did often in Rocket City, he's got the raw power to do damage. He's an average receiver with an average arm, so it wouldn't be surprising to see him split time with the more defensively advanced Stassi, at least in the early going. He'll find his way into some homer-related highlight reels regardless.

Shohei Ohtani RHP/DH Born: 07/05/94 Age: 29 Bats: L Throws: R Height: 6'4" Weight: 210 lb. Origin: International Free Agent, 2017

YEAR	TEAM	LVL	AGE	PA	R	2B	3B	HR	RBI	BB	K	SB	CS	Whiff%	AVG/OBP/SLG	DRC+	BABIP	BRR	DRP	WARP
2020	LAA	MLB	25	175	23	6	0	7	24	22	50	7	1	32.2%	.190/.291/.366	84	.229	1.1	P(2): -0.0	0.2
2021	LAA	MLB	26	639	103	26	8	46	100	96	189	26	10	35.2%	.257/.372/.592	132	.303	-0.5	P(23): -0.1, LF(1): 0	5.2
2022	LAA	MLB	27	666	90	30	6	34	95	72	161	11	9	28.1%	.273/.356/.519	122	.320	0.6	P(28): 0	3.4
2023 DC	*LAA*	*MLB*	*28*	*616*	*92*	*25*	*6*	*35*	*86*	*69*	*150*	*21*	*7*	*28.6%*	*.276/.363/.540*	*145*	*.322*	*7.9*		*5.3*

Comparables: Reggie Jefferson (81), Boog Powell (79), Richie Sexson (78)

YEAR	TEAM	LVL	AGE	W	L	SV	G	GS	IP	H	HR	BB/9	K/9	K	GB%	BABIP	WHIP	ERA	DRA-	WARP	MPH	FB%	Whiff%	CSP
2020	LAA	MLB	25	0	1	0	2	2	1^{2}	3	0	43.2	16.2	3	40.0%	.600	6.60	37.80	136	0.0	94.3	48.8%	24.0%	39.8%
2021	LAA	MLB	26	9	2	0	23	23	130^{1}	98	15	3.0	10.8	156	44.9%	.271	1.09	3.18	76	2.9	95.0	56.2%	28.9%	56.4%
2022	LAA	MLB	27	15	9	0	28	28	166	124	14	2.4	11.9	219	41.9%	.289	1.01	2.33	59	5.1	97.5	31.3%	33.1%	55.8%
2023 DC	*LAA*	*MLB*	*28*	*10*	*7*	*0*	*27*	*27*	*162.3*	*130*	*18*	*3.0*	*10.9*	*196*	*43.2%*	*.285*	*1.14*	*2.75*	*73*	*3.6*	*96.6*	*40.5%*	*31.3%*	*55.8%*

There's no shortage of topics into which we could delve in this space: That Ohtani, just a year away from free agency, told the Japanese press he was disappointed with the state of the Angels. Or that only a generational season by Aaron Judge—one so powerful it made people care about Roger Maris—stood in the way of his second consecutive MVP. Or the boring but important demand for more appreciation that, in watching Ohtani, we are still somehow in the middle of something we will talk about for the rest of our lives, a redefinition of what greatness looks like.

But perhaps the best subject is how Ohtani keeps finding new ways to delight, such as in his August 15 start against the Mariners when he decided, out of nowhere, to throw a sinker that touched 100 mph. The Angels lost 6-2 that day, because of course they did; Aaron Loup gave up four unearned runs in the ninth. But even as fans and critics argued whether WAR accurately reflected all of Ohtani's value, it was clear that it could never summarize his talent. Incredibly, it feels as though there are pitches and possibilities left for Ohtani to unlock. Some will never be; the ninth-inning Ohtani who can really let it rip, the graceful Ohtani patrolling center field. We'll never get to see all of them concurrently, but we've seen enough to imagine what they'd be like. That, more than anything, proves his greatness.

Adrian Placencia MI Born: 06/02/03 Age: 20 Bats: S Throws: R Height: 5'11" Weight: 155 lb. Origin: International Free Agent, 2019

YEAR	TEAM	LVL	AGE	PA	R	2B	3B	HR	RBI	BB	K	SB	CS	Whiff%	AVG/OBP/SLG	DRC+	BABIP	BRR	DRP	WARP
2021	ANG	ROK	18	175	29	3	3	5	19	28	49	4	2		.175/.326/.343		.225			
2022	IE	A	19	469	83	23	2	13	64	76	142	21	8		.254/.387/.427	85	.367	-0.4	2B(67): 5.0, SS(32): 0.5	0.9
2023 non-DC	*LAA*	*MLB*	*20*	*251*	*21*	*10*	*1*	*3*	*21*	*23*	*96*	*6*	*3*	*42.5%*	*.199/.283/.307*	*61*	*.329*	*0.0*	*2B 0, SS 0*	*-0.5*

Comparables: Luis Alejandro Basabe (80), Dilson Herrera (80), Esteury Ruiz (79)

Sometimes all you can ask of a prospect, especially in a system like LA's, is that they give you something to dream on. Placencia, a 2019 international signee, recovered from a brutal first tour of the States, and he possesses an encouraging combination of skills. He can hit the ball hard, he can run, he can take a walk. But as of yet, the middle infielder can't really do any of them consistently, or even at the same time, and that walk rate is more about passivity and stretching counts than high-grade pitch selection. He's also a teenager, and a welterweight at that, so from a fan standpoint all you can really do is stash him away in the box of cables in your mind. That said, you can't just get rid of a perfectly good cable. It might be useful later.

★ ★ ★ *2023 Top 101 Prospect* **#89** ★ ★ ★

Edgar Quero C Born: 04/06/03 Age: 20 Bats: S Throws: R Height: 5'11" Weight: 170 lb. Origin: International Free Agent, 2021

YEAR	TEAM	LVL	AGE	PA	R	2B	3B	HR	RBI	BB	K	SB	CS	Whiff%	AVG/OBP/SLG	DRC+	BABIP	BRR	DRP	WARP
2021	ANG	ROK	18	116	21	8	1	4	24	23	28	1	1		.253/.440/.506		.327			
2021	IE	A	18	42	2	2	0	1	6	5	16	1	0		.206/.310/.353	84	.316	-0.8	C(9): -0.6	-0.1
2022	IE	A	19	515	86	35	2	17	75	73	91	12	5		.312/.435/.530	139	.360	-2.5	C(80): -11.0	2.9
2023 non-DC	*LAA*	*MLB*	*20*	*251*	*22*	*12*	*1*	*4*	*23*	*21*	*60*	*2*	*2*	*27.2%*	*.222/.302/.341*	*80*	*.286*	*-0.1*	*C 0*	*0.3*

Comparables: Gary Sánchez (81), Travis d'Arnaud (72), Chase Vallot (70)

YEAR	TEAM	P. COUNT	FRM RUNS	BLK RUNS	THRW RUNS	TOT RUNS
2021	IE	1468	-0.5	0.0	0.0	-0.5
2022	IE	11910	-11.4	0.9	-0.5	-11.0
2023	*LAA*	*6956*	*-5.2*	*0.1*	*0.2*	*-4.9*

The Angels farm system feels like when you fire up Netflix and watch a period piece, and the movie starts with a 20-second establishing shot of some windswept grassland—a heath, maybe? Every single British novel written between 1750-1900 really cared about heaths, or moors, or gorses, or some other word for unattractive field—and you realize, OK, we're going to be here for a while. Quero is a good prospect, a switch-hitting catcher with quality bat control, a fair amount of pull power and the athleticism and makeup to become a capable defender (if that's still required in the future). He's also, like so much of the farm, years away from the majors, and it's going to be a real test of patience waiting for him to arrive. It's a long, metaphorical path, and one needs to be careful treading it; apparently, people used to just fall into swamps in the middle of England and die.

Anthony Rendon 3B Born: 06/06/90 Age: 33 Bats: R Throws: R Height: 6'1" Weight: 200 lb. Origin: Round 1, 2011 Draft (#6 overall)

YEAR	TEAM	LVL	AGE	PA	R	2B	3B	HR	RBI	BB	K	SB	CS	Whiff%	AVG/OBP/SLG	DRC+	BABIP	BRR	DRP	WARP
2020	LAA	MLB	30	232	29	11	1	9	31	38	31	0	0	14.7%	.286/.418/.497	138	.302	1.0	3B(52): -0.5	1.7
2021	LAA	MLB	31	249	24	13	0	6	34	29	41	0	0	17.3%	.240/.329/.382	103	.267	-0.8	3B(57): -0.3	0.8
2022	LAA	MLB	32	193	15	10	0	5	24	23	35	2	0	19.6%	.229/.326/.380	109	.258	0.4	3B(47): 1.6	0.9
2023 DC	*LAA*	*MLB*	*33*	*519*	*61*	*25*	*1*	*17*	*59*	*62*	*88*	*1*	*0*	*18.4%*	*.255/.353/.433*	*122*	*.282*	*-0.4*	*3B 2*	*2.6*

Comparables: Heinie Groh (78), Buddy Bell (75), Carney Lansford (74)

Years from now, people are only going to remember one thing about Rendon's 2022: That he returned from a season-ending wrist injury a week before the actual season's end so that he could serve out a five-game suspension. And that he was bad, so ok, people are going to remember *two* things about Rendon's 2022. He wasn't bad before he got hurt, but injuries and COVID have obscured his natural aging process. The former All-Star's footspeed has slowed considerably over the last three years, but that was never a sizable part of his game. More worrisome are his fading contact skills and his three-year drop in BABIP, which correlates primarily with the fact that his fly balls are no longer clearing the walls the way they used to. Rendon hits it in the air about five percentage points more than the league, yet only managed a .624 OPS on flies, which is an ominous combination. The ball may change tomorrow—it may have changed yesterday—but if it doesn't, the third baseman may have to admit that time passed during his injury stints, and adjust his approach for more modest aims.

Hunter Renfroe RF Born: 01/28/92 Age: 31 Bats: R Throws: R Height: 6'1" Weight: 230 lb. Origin: Round 1, 2013 Draft (#13 overall)

YEAR	TEAM	LVL	AGE	PA	R	2B	3B	HR	RBI	BB	K	SB	CS	Whiff%	AVG/OBP/SLG	DRC+	BABIP	BRR	DRP	WARP
2020	TB	MLB	28	139	18	5	0	8	22	14	37	2	0	32.1%	.156/.252/.393	104	.141	-0.3	RF(39): 0.9, 1B(2): 0	0.5
2021	BOS	MLB	29	572	89	33	0	31	96	44	130	1	2	25.9%	.259/.315/.501	116	.284	-1.7	RF(138): 6.8, CF(8): -0.5	3.3
2022	MIL	MLB	30	522	62	23	1	29	72	39	121	1	1	27.0%	.255/.315/.492	116	.281	-1.0	RF(118): -5.7	1.8
2023 DC	*LAA*	*MLB*	*31*	*494*	*63*	*20*	*0*	*27*	*69*	*39*	*110*	*1*	*0*	*26.5%*	*.247/.311/.483*	*118*	*.266*	*-0.4*	*RF -3, LF 0*	*1.8*

Comparables: Jay Buhner (74), Glenallen Hill (73), Dwight Evans (72)

It took two legitimate prospects for the Brewers to rid themselves of Jackie Bradley Jr.'s contract, but getting Renfroe in return for what we now know was a rental season certainly eased the pain. A Mike Trout doppelganger—neck and all—Renfroe carried the adjustments he made in his successful 2021 stint in Boston over to a strong season in Milwaukee. That adjustment? Basically, he's started swinging more often. It may cost him a few walks per year, but it's increased his rate of contact, which in turn grants him more access to his famed raw power. He was Mr. Consistent as a Brewer; by almost all measures, there wasn't a single month in which he was below-average offensively. Despite the depressed offensive environment and some time missed due to leg injuries, he posted the same strong DRC+ as with the Red Sox, helping to make up for what FRAA sees as some defensive deficiencies. With two consecutive strong seasons under his belt and a year of team control remaining, Renfroe would seem to have plenty of value ... yet it didn't cost the Angels all that much—just a trio of bottom-of-the-roster pitchers—to become his third team in as many seasons. It seems odd, but at least Renfroe can now befuddle innocent camera crews by playing next to his more famous and gifted aesthetic twin out West.

Luis Rengifo IF Born: 02/26/97 Age: 26 Bats: S Throws: R Height: 5'10" Weight: 195 lb. Origin: International Free Agent, 2013

YEAR	TEAM	LVL	AGE	PA	R	2B	3B	HR	RBI	BB	K	SB	CS	Whiff%	AVG/OBP/SLG	DRC+	BABIP	BRR	DRP	WARP
2020	LAA	MLB	23	106	12	1	0	1	3	14	26	3	1	24.5%	.156/.269/.200	87	.206	1.3	2B(32): 0.3, 3B(1): 0.4, SS(1): -0.2	0.4
2021	SL	AAA	24	228	46	16	4	8	32	17	32	13	5		.329/.386/.560	120	.357	-0.8	SS(37): -1.4, 2B(15): -0.8	1.0
2021	LAA	MLB	24	190	22	1	0	6	18	9	38	1	0	27.2%	.201/.246/.310	86	.220	2.2	SS(26): -0.8, RF(14): 0.3, 3B(12): -0.3	0.4
2022	SL	AAA	25	112	19	5	2	4	15	12	24	2	2	27.8%	.313/.384/.525	107	.375	2.1	SS(16): 1.2, 2B(5): 0.2, 3B(3): -0.5	0.7
2022	LAA	MLB	25	511	45	22	4	17	52	17	79	6	2	21.5%	.264/.294/.429	103	.285	4.2	2B(99): -1.3, 3B(39): 0.6, SS(19): 0.2	2.1
2023 DC	*LAA*	*MLB*	*26*	*263*	*28*	*10*	*2*	*6*	*25*	*14*	*49*	*5*	*2*	*22.6%*	*.254/.303/.392*	*93*	*.295*	*1.3*	*SS 0, 2B 0*	*0.6*

Comparables: Brandon Phillips (63), Eduardo Escobar (60), Erick Aybar (58)

One of the knock-on effects of a continually underperforming ballclub—beyond the losing and the excuses for losing, and the promises about how the losing will stop—is a sort of natural fatigue. When the inevitable injuries hit and the larder is bare, the first call usually goes to the 30-year-old Triple-A lifers, the Jack Mayfields and Brian Morans of the baseball world. But then *those* guys get hurt, too, and there's little choice or disincentive but to call up the 21-year-old kid out of Double-A, with arms like pool noodles and a helmet two sizes too big. Then next year, the same thing happens, and again after that.

So when Rengifo got the call in early May to stand in for a wounded David Fletcher, you could understand the lack of excitement. After all, it was already his fourth major-league tour of duty, and he had more than 700 mediocre plate appearances under his belt. You can also understand why that reaction was a bit unfair; the utility infielder was only 25, right around the age when fans should be getting to know him instead of getting sick of him. Rengifo does have some warts; his fielding can be choppy, and he's too aggressive at the plate, failing to take advantage when the count gets in his favor. But he's also capable of hitting with authority and spreading the ball to all fields, and he should produce enough to last until some other kid has to look bad filling in for him someday.

Max Stassi C Born: 03/15/91 Age: 32 Bats: R Throws: R Height: 5'10" Weight: 200 lb. Origin: Round 4, 2009 Draft (#123 overall)

YEAR	TEAM	LVL	AGE	PA	R	2B	3B	HR	RBI	BB	K	SB	CS	Whiff%	AVG/OBP/SLG	DRC+	BABIP	BRR	DRP	WARP
2020	LAA	MLB	29	105	12	2	0	7	20	11	21	0	0	26.5%	.278/.352/.533	127	.277	-1.3	C(31): 1.9	0.8
2021	LAA	MLB	30	319	45	11	1	13	35	28	101	0	0	31.2%	.241/.326/.426	90	.325	-2.3	C(86): 14.4	2.2
2022	LAA	MLB	31	375	32	12	1	9	30	38	112	0	0	33.9%	.180/.267/.303	74	.239	-2.0	C(97): 0.4	0.0
2023 DC	*LAA*	*MLB*	*32*	*321*	*33*	*11*	*0*	*10*	*31*	*29*	*97*	*0*	*0*	*32.9%*	*.211/.295/.365*	*83*	*.279*	*-1.6*	*C 11*	*1.5*

Comparables: Sandy Leon (56), Martín Maldonado (55), Jeff Mathis (55)

YEAR	TEAM	P. COUNT	FRM RUNS	BLK RUNS	THRW RUNS	TOT RUNS
2020	LAA	4049	1.2	0.1	0.5	1.8
2021	LAA	11913	15.4	0.5	0.4	16.3
2022	LAA	13467	1.2	-0.4	0.2	1.0
2023	*LAA*	*12025*	*11.0*	*0.0*	*0.0*	*11.0*

In March, the Angels rewarded Stassi for two productive semi-seasons by buying out his first two years of free agency. By July, they'd traded one of their young outfielders for a top catching prospect. Stassi enjoyed his first truly healthy season in 2022, minus a couple of weeks with COVID-19, yet his offensive production was the worst of his career and his framing numbers collapsed. The backstop has undergone swing overhauls before, and he likely will again with the team parting ways with hitting coach Jeremy Reed. Whatever that next swing looks like, it had better start covering the high ones: Stassi hit just .129 on pitches in or above the top third of the zone, killing his chances of barreling anything up. It's not a good sign when your catcher notches more than a third of his singles on infield hits because he can only make contact with pitches at his knees.

Kurt Suzuki C Born: 10/04/83 Age: 39 Bats: R Throws: R Height: 5'11" Weight: 210 lb. Origin: Round 2, 2004 Draft (#67 overall)

YEAR	TEAM	LVL	AGE	PA	R	2B	3B	HR	RBI	BB	K	SB	CS	Whiff%	AVG/OBP/SLG	DRC+	BABIP	BRR	DRP	WARP
2020	WAS	MLB	36	129	15	8	0	2	17	11	19	1	0	16.9%	.270/.349/.396	105	.301	-2.2	C(30): -3.6	0.0
2021	LAA	MLB	37	247	17	8	0	6	16	12	44	0	0	21.8%	.224/.294/.342	93	.250	0.0	C(69): -6.5	0.2
2022	LAA	MLB	38	159	10	4	0	4	15	15	29	0	0	21.1%	.180/.266/.295	97	.194	-0.7	C(44): -7.8	-0.4
2023 DC	*FA*	*MLB*	*39*	*202*	*20*	*7*	*0*	*5*	*21*	*14*	*33*	*0*	*0*	*21.3%*	*.229/.303/.368*	*88*	*.251*	*-1.7*	*C -8, 1B 0*	*-0.6*

Comparables: Yadier Molina (61), Sherm Lollar (60), Sandy Alomar Jr. (58)

YEAR	TEAM	P. COUNT	FRM RUNS	BLK RUNS	THRW RUNS	TOT RUNS
2020	WAS	4520	-4.1	0.0	0.5	-3.6
2021	LAA	9696	-5.4	-0.7	0.3	-5.7
2022	LAA	5878	-8.5	0.1	0.6	-7.8
2023	*FA*	*6956*	*-7.8*	*-0.1*	*0.1*	*-7.8*

Suzuki called it a 16-year career late in the 2022 season, and now that we can take it all in, we can say it was a pretty weird one. An indifferent defender from the start, the Hawaiian gave away 12 wins with the glove over his career, nearly half of what he supplied with the bat. Even that would have stunned a time traveler from a decade ago given that Suzuki couldn't really hit in his twenties. But not only did he outlive the rise of framing metrics, he made it to the era when catchers stopped hitting, such that his league-average offensive production felt at times like gaining an extra DH. And now that he's gone, it'll be time for the robot umps to eliminate framing altogether. Timing truly is everything, but we can't really say Suzuki was too early or too late. He simply did certain things well enough at certain times for long enough to earn a World Series ring and finish 12th all-time in catcher putouts. His was a weird career, yes, but in unique ways a successful one.

Matt Thaiss C Born: 05/06/95 Age: 28 Bats: L Throws: R Height: 6'0" Weight: 215 lb. Origin: Round 1, 2016 Draft (#16 overall)

YEAR	TEAM	LVL	AGE	PA	R	2B	3B	HR	RBI	BB	K	SB	CS	Whiff%	AVG/OBP/SLG	DRC+	BABIP	BRR	DRP	WARP
2020	LAA	MLB	25	25	3	0	0	1	1	4	8	0	0	32.1%	.143/.280/.286	84	.167	-0.2	1B(2): 0.2, 2B(1): 0	0.0
2021	SL	AAA	26	449	71	23	4	17	69	60	92	2	1		.280/.383/.496	110	.325	-2.2	C(54): 2.9, 1B(17): -0.9, 3B(3): -0.4	2.0
2021	LAA	MLB	26	8	1	0	0	0	0	1	1	0	0	15.4%	.143/.250/.143	90	.167	-0.1	1B(2): -0.1	0.0
2022	SL	AAA	27	332	46	16	3	10	48	43	61	7	0	26.6%	.268/.364/.451	103	.306	-1.0	C(45): -3.2, 1B(6): -0.6, 3B(1): -0.1	0.6
2022	LAA	MLB	27	81	9	1	0	2	8	11	24	1	0	34.2%	.217/.321/.319	82	.295	0.1	C(14): -0.9, 1B(11): -0.1, 3B(3): -0.1	0.0
2023 DC	*LAA*	*MLB*	*28*	*190*	*18*	*7*	*1*	*3*	*15*	*19*	*51*	*1*	*1*	*31.2%*	*.209/.297/.330*	*75*	*.278*	*1.2*	*1B 0, C -1*	*-0.2*

Comparables: Justin Smoak (56), Cody Asche (55), Brandon Allen (52)

Long before *Moneyball*, one of the early epiphanies of baseball research was that certain players were being wasted in the minors. The first Erubiel Durazo was actually Ken Phelps, a sluggish platoon slugger who could—and did—produce given the right situation. There was some hope at the time that smarter baseball management would lead to the end of the fabled Quad-A slugger. Close to four decades later, it hasn't, and Thaiss is just another example of a player thrown in front of the cannon fire in spots in which he can't succeed. The Angels immediately converted Thaiss, a bat-first college catcher, to the corners, only to watch his bat wither in the harsh, bright lights. Five years of development later, the team decided that if he was going to hit like a backup catcher, he may as well field like one, too. So that's exactly what he did. Reports are that he worked very hard, just as he always has. It just wasn't enough. There's no way to know what Thaiss could have been, given a different path, but with Max Stassi under contract and Logan O'Hoppe waiting in the wings, it's easy to guess what he will be soon.

Mike Trout CF Born: 08/07/91 Age: 31 Bats: R Throws: R Height: 6'2" Weight: 235 lb. Origin: Round 1, 2009 Draft (#25 overall)

YEAR	TEAM	LVL	AGE	PA	R	2B	3B	HR	RBI	BB	K	SB	CS	Whiff%	AVG/OBP/SLG	DRC+	BABIP	BRR	DRP	WARP
2020	LAA	MLB	28	241	41	9	2	17	46	35	56	1	1	19.5%	.281/.390/.603	131	.300	1.2	CF(52): -2.4	1.6
2021	LAA	MLB	29	146	23	8	1	8	18	27	41	2	0	27.5%	.333/.466/.624	124	.456	1.0	CF(36): -1.6	1.0
2022	LAA	MLB	30	499	85	28	2	40	80	54	139	1	0	30.4%	.283/.369/.630	154	.323	-1.4	CF(111): 4.2	5.4
2023 DC	*LAA*	*MLB*	*31*	*572*	*92*	*24*	*2*	*41*	*92*	*70*	*166*	*0*	*2*	*28.6%*	*.278/.376/.590*	*163*	*.333*	*-5.8*	*CF 5*	*6.0*

Comparables: Mickey Mantle (80), Ken Griffey Jr. (73), Cesar Cedeno (71)

Trout is in his thirties. He's also been on the planet for 30+ years, but that's not what the first sentence means. The future inner-circle Hall of Famer embodies what it is to be 31, to feel the dip in one's stomach after the roller coaster lurches past its apex. After the awe of his arrival, what distinguished Trout was how methodically he took his perfection and improved upon it. One year he emerged in the spring having suddenly improved his route-running. Another year he just decided to stop chasing low pitches. Like so many of the all-time greats, he treated each of his mistakes as a puzzle, and most of the time, he solved them.

And now Trout's in his thirties. He's not worse than he used to be, he's just available in lesser quantities. When he went down with a back injury in the summer, a story came out that the issue was degenerative, and that even if he did return, he would never be quite the same. Trout vociferously denied the charge and resurfaced after a month to hit .308/.370/.688, squashing all short-term doubts—but like the best works of fiction, it took hold because it felt so true. Two seasons of nicks and scrapes and hideous *mortality* led everyone to assume the worst, because it fit narratively. This is what happens in your thirties: you fall, like you always fell, but you never quite get all the way back up.

Trout could. That's a tautology: Mike Trout can do anything, because that's what it means to be Mike Trout. Granted, he has more puzzles to solve heading into 2023 than ever before, as the time off has made him more aggressive at the plate, chasing and whiffing more. He's also, still, the greatest baseball player of his generation, mortality and all.

Gio Urshela 3B Born: 10/11/91 Age: 31 Bats: R Throws: R Height: 6'0" Weight: 215 lb. Origin: International Free Agent, 2008

YEAR	TEAM	LVL	AGE	PA	R	2B	3B	HR	RBI	BB	K	SB	CS	Whiff%	AVG/OBP/SLG	DRC+	BABIP	BRR	DRP	WARP
2020	NYY	MLB	28	174	24	11	0	6	30	18	25	1	0	20.3%	.298/.368/.490	123	.315	-0.6	3B(43): 2.3	1.1
2021	NYY	MLB	29	442	42	18	2	14	49	20	109	1	0	25.1%	.267/.301/.419	93	.329	-3.1	3B(96): -1.8, SS(28): -0.4	0.6
2022	MIN	MLB	30	551	61	27	3	13	64	41	96	1	0	21.4%	.285/.338/.429	113	.326	-2.3	3B(136): 0.1, SS(2): -0.4	1.9
2023 DC	*LAA*	*MLB*	*31*	*322*	*35*	*14*	*0*	*9*	*35*	*21*	*57*	*0*	*0*	*21.9%*	*.271/.324/.422*	*109*	*.306*	*-0.1*	*SS 1, 3B 0*	*1.4*

Comparables: George Kell (69), Carney Lansford (68), Buddy Bell (67)

The trade that brought Urshela and Gary Sánchez to Minnesota, and sent Josh Donaldson and Isiah Kiner-Falefa to New York, can hardly be described as an unqualified success. There's also no doubt about which part was the win for Minnesota, though. They swapped $50 million of guaranteed money on Donaldson's deal—and what turned out to be the worst offensive season since he reached stardom—for a far more productive Urshela still in his arbitration years. There's still something jarring about the shape of Urshela's production compared to his reputation as a prospect, which continues to be good-bat-over-mediocre-glove if you consult most defensive metrics. As long as Urshela keeps getting it done with the bat, he'll continue to hold down a regular role in an infield—this season he'll do so for the Angels after yet another trade.

Andrew Velazquez SS Born: 07/14/94 Age: 28 Bats: S Throws: R Height: 5'9" Weight: 170 lb. Origin: Round 7, 2012 Draft (#243 overall)

YEAR	TEAM	LVL	AGE	PA	R	2B	3B	HR	RBI	BB	K	SB	CS	Whiff%	AVG/OBP/SLG	DRC+	BABIP	BRR	DRP	WARP
2020	BAL	MLB	25	77	11	1	1	0	3	10	23	4	2	30.6%	.159/.274/.206	79	.250	0.7	SS(30): 0.5, LF(7): -0.2, CF(3): 0.2	0.2
2021	SWB	AAA	26	306	40	20	3	7	46	37	87	29	3		.273/.362/.451	89	.378	0.8	SS(42): -5.9, 2B(24): 1.6, 3B(10): -1.4	0.1
2021	NYY	MLB	26	68	11	4	1	1	6	1	23	4	1	34.4%	.224/.235/.358	71	.326	1.1	SS(28): -0.6	0.0
2022	LAA	MLB	27	349	37	8	0	9	28	15	119	17	1	35.0%	.196/.236/.304	60	.274	3.3	SS(124): 2.5	0.0
2023 DC	*LAA*	*MLB*	*28*	*29*	*2*	*1*	*0*	*0*	*2*	*1*	*9*	*1*	*0*	*33.9%*	*.209/.265/.331*	*60*	*.293*	*1.1*	*SS 0*	*0.1*

Comparables: Reid Brignac (55), Felix Martinez (55), Mike Benjamin (53)

The nice thing about a 2022 Velazquez plate appearance is that there was never much suspense. Everything was decided by that first pitch: When the toothpick-wielding infielder swung at it, he hit .248/.265/.397, including six of his nine home runs. If he took it ... well, it was all over. He hit just .155/.214/.232, even after watching ball one fly by. It was never part of the plan for this minor-league free agent to start 100 games at shortstop for a major-league ballclub. Even with his strong glovework, he's not making anyone in Anaheim forget Andrelton Simmons. But when the left side of your infield falls apart like a Jenga tower, well, this is what happens.

Arol Vera SS Born: 09/12/02 Age: 20 Bats: S Throws: R Height: 6'2" Weight: 170 lb. Origin: International Free Agent, 2019

YEAR	TEAM	LVL	AGE	PA	R	2B	3B	HR	RBI	BB	K	SB	CS	Whiff%	AVG/OBP/SLG	DRC+	BABIP	BRR	DRP	WARP
2021	ANG	ROK	18	164	24	16	3	0	17	12	39	2	2		.317/.384/.469		.426			
2021	IE	A	18	90	10	0	0	0	5	6	20	9	2		.280/.344/.280	100	.371	0.2	SS(12): 1.0, 2B(7): 0.3	0.4
2022	IE	A	19	551	71	16	4	4	59	53	149	19	7		.207/.291/.281	73	.287	1.7	SS(93): -0.2, 2B(23): -2.1, 3B(1): -0.1	-0.4
2023 non-DC	*LAA*	*MLB*	*20*	*251*	*16*	*8*	*1*	*1*	*16*	*15*	*79*	*7*	*2*	*33.5%*	*.192/.246/.255*	*36*	*.283*	*1.0*	*2B 0, 3B 0*	*-1.2*

Comparables: Juan Diaz (83), Jose Vinicio (81), Sergio Alcántara (78)

Writing about prospects isn't easy. You don't want to be too critical of a young man whose entire corporeal existence has coincided with the broadcast life of the cartoon *Kim Possible.* But Vera's 2022 season underscored an Angels farm system defined by the philosophy that potential is just another way of saying "not having had time to fail." The Venezuelan infielder remains a glove-first prospect, a description that would have been true even if it weren't by default, as his power potential was always going to manifest farther down the road if at all. But Vera's BABIP crashed like MLB's official crypto partner and took everything in his batting line with it. There's nothing you can really do, as a writer, except note that maybe it'll come together next year, or the year after, until either it does or you just don't write about him anymore at all.

Jared Walsh 1B Born: 07/30/93 Age: 29 Bats: L Throws: L Height: 6'0" Weight: 210 lb. Origin: Round 39, 2015 Draft (#1185 overall)

YEAR	TEAM	LVL	AGE	PA	R	2B	3B	HR	RBI	BB	K	SB	CS	Whiff%	AVG/OBP/SLG	DRC+	BABIP	BRR	DRP	WARP
2020	LAA	MLB	26	108	19	4	2	9	26	5	15	0	0	22.8%	.293/.324/.646	121	.256	0.3	1B(29): -0.7, RF(2): -0.2	0.5
2021	LAA	MLB	27	585	70	34	1	29	98	48	152	2	1	26.0%	.277/.340/.509	109	.335	0.5	1B(128): -0.2, RF(18): -1.4	1.9
2022	LAA	MLB	28	454	41	18	2	15	44	27	138	2	1	27.7%	.215/.269/.374	74	.281	-1.8	1B(118): 0.2, LF(2): 0	-0.7
2023 DC	*LAA*	*MLB*	*29*	*480*	*52*	*22*	*1*	*18*	*57*	*33*	*126*	*1*	*1*	*26.8%*	*.238/.300/.421*	*96*	*.293*	*0.4*	*1B 0*	*0.5*

Comparables: Tyler White (55), Doug Mientkiewicz (53), Gerald Perry (51)

It's unfortunate, for our purposes, that the letter R comes after L in the dictionary, because it would be better to discuss Walsh after Taylor Ward in this chapter rather than before him. After all, the slugging first baseman was the team's breakout story of 2021 before tumbling, as Angels so often do, back to Earth. But they're not the same player; Walsh isn't even the same player as himself, in a way. A boom-or-bust swinger even at his apex, the sophomore saw a jump in pitches in the zone in 2022. That cut into his walk rate, and Walsh couldn't create a corresponding rise in contact to shave his strikeouts in turn. But the real story here is that Walsh was clearly broken by the summer, managing just a .133 average and .213 slugging percentage from July forward. He underwent thoracic outlet syndrome surgery in September, and should be on a timetable to start the 2023 season, hitting behind and fielding in front of L.A.'s more recent breakout story.

Taylor Ward RF Born: 12/14/93 Age: 29 Bats: R Throws: R Height: 6'1" Weight: 200 lb. Origin: Round 1, 2015 Draft (#26 overall)

YEAR	TEAM	LVL	AGE	PA	R	2B	3B	HR	RBI	BB	K	SB	CS	Whiff%	AVG/OBP/SLG	DRC+	BABIP	BRR	DRP	WARP
2020	LAA	MLB	26	102	16	6	2	0	5	8	28	2	0	23.6%	.277/.333/.383	85	.394	1.3	RF(19): -0.2, LF(17): -0.1, 1B(2): 0	0.2
2021	SL	AAA	27	59	15	9	0	4	10	9	12	2	0		.429/.525/.857	113	.515	0.6	LF(7): -0.7, RF(5): -0.8, CF(1): 0.8	0.3
2021	LAA	MLB	27	237	33	15	0	8	33	20	55	1	1	25.1%	.250/.332/.438	98	.301	0.7	RF(51): -0.9, LF(18): -0.1, CF(12): -0.3	0.6
2022	LAA	MLB	28	564	73	22	2	23	65	60	120	5	3	22.1%	.281/.360/.473	126	.325	3.0	RF(125): -1.7, CF(7): 0.2	3.6
2023 DC	*LAA*	*MLB*	*29*	*586*	*74*	*25*	*1*	*21*	*66*	*59*	*125*	*5*	*2*	*22.7%*	*.268/.349/.448*	*123*	*.314*	*1.2*	*LF -2, RF -1*	*2.8*

Comparables: Nelson Cruz (58), Hank Bauer (53), Craig Monroe (52)

So much of life is overcorrecting: midterm elections, fad diets, generational parenting styles, replacing players' coaches with hardliners and vice versa. The wayward journey of one Matt Thaiss was to some degree a reaction to the story of Ward, another first-round catcher who spent three years failing to catch. Ward moved to third only to be blocked by Anthony Rendon's sentient corpse before finally finding, at age 27, his role in the outfield. Was his development stunted? Given that his improvement in 2022 was "do everything about hitting better," it's hard to say. Ward chased fewer pitches, made better contact and hit the ball harder and higher in the air. Only a collision with a wall put a dent in his breakout season, sending him into a midsummer slump before he pulled himself out of the skid by year's end. Angels fans are understandably worried that Ward's production will careen back to Earth, but while his counting numbers vacillated between angelic and Los Angeles Angelic, the plate discipline beneath them held firm. Ward is here to stay, as much as anyone on this team is.

Pitchers

Tyler Anderson LHP
Born: 12/30/89 Age: 33 Bats: L Throws: L Height: 6'2" Weight: 220 lb. Origin: Round 1, 2011 Draft (#20 overall)

YEAR	TEAM	LVL	AGE	W	L	SV	G	GS	IP	H	HR	BB/9	K/9	K	GB%	BABIP	WHIP	ERA	DRA-	WARP	MPH	FB%	Whiff%	CSP
2020	SF	MLB	30	4	3	0	13	11	59^{2}	58	5	3.8	6.2	41	28.9%	.288	1.39	4.37	156	-1.1	90.2	47.0%	24.6%	47.2%
2021	PIT	MLB	31	5	8	0	18	18	103^{1}	99	16	2.2	7.5	86	36.5%	.280	1.20	4.35	109	0.5	90.2	45.8%	24.5%	57.9%
2021	SEA	MLB	31	2	3	0	13	13	63^{2}	71	11	1.8	6.8	48	32.1%	.303	1.32	4.81	127	-0.3	90.6	50.3%	21.6%	55.9%
2022	LAD	MLB	32	15	5	0	30	28	178^{2}	145	14	1.7	7.0	138	39.9%	.257	1.00	2.57	98	1.9	90.6	45.0%	24.4%	55.9%
2023 DC	*LAA*	*MLB*	*33*	*9*	*9*	*0*	*27*	*27*	*154*	*154*	*20*	*2.3*	*6.7*	*114*	*37.9%*	*.284*	*1.25*	*3.72*	*101*	*1.2*	*90.5*	*46.2%*	*23.9%*	*55.4%*

Comparables: Wade Miley (78), Claude Osteen (78), Mark Buehrle (78)

A year ago, Anderson signed a one-year, $8 million deal with the Dodgers. This offseason, he received a three-year, $36 million contract from the Angels. In between, he compiled the most successful season of his career and made his first All-Star team. He still throws in the low 90s and struck out only 19.5% of opposing hitters, but his average exit velocity and hard-hit rate both placed in the 98th percentile and his 4.8% walk rate was a career best. Reworking his changeup was the biggest catalyst for his soft-contact revolution. By adding six inches of break to the offering, he reduced right-handed hitters' OPS against him from .774 in 2021 to .615 last year. Apparently, that extra drop was worth a 17-point DRA- improvement and a $28 million free-agency glow-up.

Sam Bachman RHP
Born: 09/30/99 Age: 23 Bats: R Throws: R Height: 6'1" Weight: 235 lb. Origin: Round 1, 2021 Draft (#9 overall)

YEAR	TEAM	LVL	AGE	W	L	SV	G	GS	IP	H	HR	BB/9	K/9	K	GB%	BABIP	WHIP	ERA	DRA-	WARP	MPH	FB%	Whiff%	CSP
2021	TRI	A+	21	0	2	0	5	5	14^{1}	13	1	2.5	9.4	15	65.8%	.324	1.19	3.77	109	0.0				
2022	RCT	AA	22	1	1	0	12	12	43^{2}	41	4	5.2	6.2	30	54.1%	.282	1.51	3.92	115	0.1				
2023 non-DC	*LAA*	*MLB*	*23*	*2*	*3*	*0*	*57*	*0*	*50*	*59*	*6*	*5.7*	*7.1*	*39*	*53.0%*	*.333*	*1.82*	*6.30*	*141*	*-0.8*			*24.3%*	

Comparables: Josh Sborz (67), Conner Greene (67), Justin Donatella (65)

As a rule, it doesn't do much to assuage injury concerns when you lose the better part of two months to bicep inflammation. And it doesn't silence the whispers of reliever risk when you can't get ramped up enough to manage a starter's workload—Bachman saw the fifth inning just once all season, and it was in his final start. Combine his maladies with a loss of velocity and what was already a fastball-slider profile, and things start to look a little grim. Bachman is just 23 years of age, but he's already discovering one of the terrors of getting old: it becomes hard to tell if you're spending your life recovering from some nagging injury, or just spending your life. A clean start in 2023 will either offer hope or answers.

Jaime Barría RHP
Born: 07/18/96 Age: 26 Bats: R Throws: R Height: 6'1" Weight: 210 lb. Origin: International Free Agent, 2013

YEAR	TEAM	LVL	AGE	W	L	SV	G	GS	IP	H	HR	BB/9	K/9	K	GB%	BABIP	WHIP	ERA	DRA-	WARP	MPH	FB%	Whiff%	CSP
2020	LAA	MLB	23	1	0	0	7	5	32^{1}	27	3	2.5	7.5	27	33.7%	.261	1.11	3.62	113	0.1	92.2	43.1%	23.1%	49.9%
2021	SL	AAA	24	3	2	0	10	10	49	54	10	1.5	6.2	34	36.5%	.280	1.27	4.41	133	-0.8				
2021	LAA	MLB	24	2	4	0	13	11	56^{2}	70	8	3.0	5.6	35	43.8%	.333	1.57	4.61	132	-0.4	93.1	55.1%	19.1%	53.8%
2022	LAA	MLB	25	3	3	0	35	1	79^{1}	63	11	2.2	6.1	54	40.0%	.230	1.03	2.61	107	0.5	92.0	39.3%	23.1%	57.8%
2023 DC	*LAA*	*MLB*	*26*	*3*	*3*	*0*	*68*	*0*	*59*	*61*	*8*	*2.6*	*6.7*	*43*	*40.5%*	*.292*	*1.33*	*4.24*	*111*	*0.0*	*92.3*	*43.7%*	*22.4%*	*54.3%*

Comparables: Chris Volstad (67), Sean O'Sullivan (66), Jacob Turner (65)

Barría had the best season of his young career in 2022, which is a charitable way of saying that it was physically impossible to remember any of it. Bounced into a longman role after the team's myriad starting pitching acquisitions flopped, he thrived in the glow of lowered expectations, giving up the usual amount of contact on his nonthreatening four-pitch mix. How'd he outperform his peripherals, you ask? As a slop-baller happy to live in the zone and avoid a 1-0 count, he should be particularly prone to first-pitch swings. Instead, hitters managed only to swat just .143 with a .225 slugging percentage against him to open their at-bats. That trend is unlikely to continue, so if Barría is going to succeed going forward, he's going to have to risk pitching up with his middling fastball to get strikeouts, or down with his breaking pitches to hunt for grounders. Everything's in no man's land right now, floating above the knees, and men don't tend to survive in no man's land for very long.

Ky Bush LHP
Born: 11/12/99 Age: 23 Bats: L Throws: L Height: 6'6" Weight: 240 lb. Origin: Round 2, 2021 Draft (#45 overall)

YEAR	TEAM	LVL	AGE	W	L	SV	G	GS	IP	H	HR	BB/9	K/9	K	GB%	BABIP	WHIP	ERA	DRA-	WARP	MPH	FB%	Whiff%	CSP
2021	TRI	A+	21	0	2	0	5	5	12	14	0	3.8	15.0	20	46.4%	.500	1.58	4.50	103	0.1				
2022	RCT	AA	22	7	4	0	21	21	103	93	14	2.5	8.8	101	44.7%	.282	1.18	3.67	93	1.4				
2023 non-DC	*LAA*	*MLB*	*23*	*2*	*3*	*0*	*57*	*0*	*50*	*54*	*7*	*3.7*	*8.1*	*44*	*44.9%*	*.321*	*1.51*	*4.99*	*121*	*-0.3*			*26.4%*	

Comparables: Osvaldo Hernandez (66), Alex Wells (65), Nick Kingham (65)

People talk about "reliever risk" all the time, but there are relievers, and then there are *relievers*. A sizable southpaw, Bush could profile as the latter. He's still starting for now, having put together a solid performance in the Southern League, tamping down on the walks that formed one of his pre-draft red flags. Others remain: his curveball and change still need work to reach average, and there's a real possibility that he reaches the majors as a fastball-slider guy. That said, the fastball is nice and heavy and capable of missing bats, so if he does wind up a reliever, it'll likely be of the late-inning variety. One aspect of his development that appears certain, however: With each passing year, Bush looks increasingly like actor Tim Curry. You want to get into a hitter's head by making him guess whether you'll throw the off-speed, but making him remember all the one-liners from *Clue* is better than nothing.

Griffin Canning RHP Born: 05/11/96 Age: 27 Bats: R Throws: R Height: 6'2" Weight: 180 lb. Origin: Round 2, 2017 Draft (#47 overall)

YEAR	TEAM	LVL	AGE	W	L	SV	G	GS	IP	H	HR	BB/9	K/9	K	GB%	BABIP	WHIP	ERA	DRA-	WARP	MPH	FB%	Whiff%	CSP
2020	LAA	MLB	24	2	3	0	11	11	56¹	54	8	3.7	8.9	56	36.1%	.307	1.37	3.99	109	0.3	92.2	60.4%	27.3%	44.2%
2021	LAA	MLB	25	5	4	0	14	13	62²	65	14	4.0	8.9	62	36.0%	.298	1.48	5.60	118	0.0	93.7	40.7%	30.3%	55.4%
2023 DC	*LAA*	*MLB*	*27*	*2*	*2*	*0*	*16*	*3*	*26*	*25*	*3*	*4.1*	*9.0*	*26*	*38.6%*	*.304*	*1.45*	*4.67*	*114*	*0.0*	*93.1*	*53.5%*	*29.0%*	*49.8%*

Comparables: Vance Worley (67), Daniel Hudson (66), Nick Tropeano (66)

Backbones are fragile, mysterious, terrifying things. The worst part about back pain: It never truly disappears, it just goes into hiding, waiting for that moment you awkwardly reach for a glass of water on the end table. Canning, whose rough 2021 season was cut short by a stress fracture in his lower back, ran into setbacks in both March and June, scuttling his 2022 as well. In consultation with team doctors, he opted to avoid surgery. According to the Johns Hopkins Medicine website, the basic risk factors for such stress fractures are "being human and walking upright," both of which will be required of the 26-year-old, so it's hard to feel optimistic, especially given his struggles before the injury. If all goes well, he'll report to Salt Lake in April and pace himself in recovery, while both he and his team will try to avoid making any sudden moves.

Tucker Davidson LHP Born: 03/25/96 Age: 27 Bats: L Throws: L Height: 6'2" Weight: 215 lb. Origin: Round 19, 2016 Draft (#559 overall)

YEAR	TEAM	LVL	AGE	W	L	SV	G	GS	IP	H	HR	BB/9	K/9	K	GB%	BABIP	WHIP	ERA	DRA-	WARP	MPH	FB%	Whiff%	CSP
2020	ATL	MLB	24	0	1	0	1	1	1²	3	1	21.6	10.8	2	28.6%	.333	4.20	10.80	126	0.0	91.8	75.5%	16.7%	42.5%
2021	GWN	AAA	25	2	2	0	4	4	23	11	2	2.0	11.0	28	54.9%	.184	0.70	1.17	85	0.4				
2021	ATL	MLB	25	0	0	0	4	4	20	15	3	3.6	8.1	18	42.1%	.226	1.15	3.60	100	0.2	93.3	49.8%	27.5%	56.0%
2022	GWN	AAA	26	3	7	0	15	15	80¹	82	14	2.7	10.8	96	45.7%	.327	1.32	4.59	81	1.9				
2022	ATL	MLB	26	1	2	0	4	3	15¹	15	0	7.6	5.9	10	46.0%	.300	1.83	6.46	137	-0.1	93.9	46.4%	25.6%	54.4%
2022	LAA	MLB	26	1	5	0	8	8	36²	39	7	5.4	5.6	23	42.6%	.278	1.66	6.87	140	-0.4	92.7	41.5%	21.2%	57.3%
2023 DC	*LAA*	*MLB*	*27*	*6*	*6*	*0*	*50*	*9*	*79*	*80*	*10*	*4.2*	*8.1*	*71*	*45.0%*	*.304*	*1.48*	*4.59*	*113*	*0.1*	*93.1*	*45.1%*	*25.4%*	*56.0%*

Comparables: Andrew Heaney (72), Jeff Locke (70), Daniel Mengden (67)

Every year, the Atlanta Braves reach into the inky well of abyssal terror behind their stadium and pull out three rookie starting pitchers. The following season, one of them becomes an All-Star, one gets hurt and the other becomes Davidson. The southpaw got tucked into the Raisel Iglesias trade at the 2022 deadline, hidden in Jesse Chavez's luggage, and apparently wasn't able to get his command through security. The Angels asked Davidson to throw his slider more, which made sense; it's easily his best pitch, and really the only one that can reliably miss bats. But it's hard to make batters chase when you're always behind in the count, and both his hard pitches are too straight and too slow to be relied on. At least he, Sean Newcomb and Bryse Wilson can get together, have coffee and share thoughts.

Reid Detmers LHP Born: 07/08/99 Age: 23 Bats: L Throws: L Height: 6'2" Weight: 210 lb. Origin: Round 1, 2020 Draft (#10 overall)

YEAR	TEAM	LVL	AGE	W	L	SV	G	GS	IP	H	HR	BB/9	K/9	K	GB%	BABIP	WHIP	ERA	DRA-	WARP	MPH	FB%	Whiff%	CSP
2021	RCT	AA	21	2	4	0	12	12	54	45	10	3.0	16.2	97	33.9%	.361	1.17	3.50	69	1.4				
2021	SL	AAA	21	1	0	0	2	2	8	7	0	1.1	12.4	11	31.6%	.368	1.00	1.13	97	0.0				
2021	LAA	MLB	21	1	3	0	5	5	20²	26	5	4.8	8.3	19	33.3%	.328	1.79	7.40	143	-0.3	93.1	45.1%	27.1%	56.8%
2022	SL	AAA	22	0	0	0	1	1	6	3	1	1.5	21.0	14	14.3%	.333	0.67	1.50	82	0.1	94.3	45.6%	37.2%	
2022	LAA	MLB	22	7	6	0	25	25	129	110	13	3.2	8.5	122	36.1%	.278	1.21	3.77	103	1.0	93.3	45.0%	25.5%	55.0%
2023 DC	*LAA*	*MLB*	*23*	*7*	*9*	*0*	*27*	*27*	*132*	*126*	*20*	*3.5*	*9.0*	*132*	*36.4%*	*.294*	*1.35*	*4.26*	*108*	*0.6*	*93.3*	*45.0%*	*27.2%*	*55.2%*

Comparables: José Suarez (72), Tyler Skaggs (64), Jonathon Niese (62)

(DAVID ATTENBOROUGH VOICE) At the end of the pupal phase, the Angels top pitching prospect undergoes a metamorphosis, shedding its adolescent pitch movement and taking on a less threatening appearance. Rather than predate, the creature becomes shy, foraging for strikes on the remote edges of the strike zone, seeking sustenance. As it reaches maturity, the pitching prospect will begin its migratory pattern, relocating each winter to a new burrow, unable to return to its previous lodgings. This phase can last anywhere from three to eight years before the aging creature, no longer able to feed or protect itself, devotes its final years to passing along its knowledge to the next generation. (ATTENBOROUGH'S VOICE GROWS MELANCHOLY) But these are dangerous times for the species. Rising velocities and changing shift patterns have left the Angels pitching prospect with scarce hunting grounds. Without intervention, the entire species may face extinction in these harsh, bitter, modern climes.

Carlos Estévez RHP Born: 12/28/92 Age: 30 Bats: R Throws: R Height: 6'6" Weight: 277 lb. Origin: International Free Agent, 2011

YEAR	TEAM	LVL	AGE	W	L	SV	G	GS	IP	H	HR	BB/9	K/9	K	GB%	BABIP	WHIP	ERA	DRA-	WARP	MPH	FB%	Whiff%	CSP
2020	COL	MLB	27	1	3	1	26	0	24	33	6	3.4	10.1	27	29.9%	.380	1.75	7.50	124	0.0	97.0	61.5%	25.1%	50.2%
2021	COL	MLB	28	3	5	11	64	0	61²	71	8	3.1	8.8	60	44.9%	.354	1.49	4.38	98	0.6	97.3	65.8%	24.6%	56.4%
2022	COL	MLB	29	4	4	2	62	0	57	44	7	3.6	8.5	54	35.7%	.247	1.18	3.47	98	0.6	97.7	70.5%	21.7%	52.9%
2023 DC	*LAA*	*MLB*	*30*	*3*	*3*	*2*	*61*	*0*	*53*	*49*	*6*	*3.3*	*7.4*	*44*	*38.7%*	*.278*	*1.30*	*3.73*	*98*	*0.3*	*97.5*	*68.0%*	*23.9%*	*53.8%*

Comparables: Jeremy Jeffress (68), Drew Storen (66), Manny Corpas (66)

Estévez's ERA dropped almost a full run from his uneven 2021, but his peripherals didn't follow, as he allowed too many walks and too much hard contact without the whiffs to even it all out. His slider remains unhittable, but that's mostly a product of it routinely avoiding the strike zone; its 21.4% whiff rate is both pedestrian and represents a five-point dip from the year prior. Nor does his 97-mph fastball produce the kind of numbers you'd expect. Righty relievers who feature fastball/slider combos and spotty command are a dime a dozen these days. Somehow, that didn't stop the Angels from giving Estévez $13.5 million on a two-year deal.

Jimmy Herget RHP Born: 09/09/93 Age: 29 Bats: R Throws: R Height: 6'3" Weight: 170 lb. Origin: Round 6, 2015 Draft (#175 overall)

YEAR	TEAM	LVL	AGE	W	L	SV	G	GS	IP	H	HR	BB/9	K/9	K	GB%	BABIP	WHIP	ERA	DRA-	WARP	MPH	FB%	Whiff%	CSP
2020	TEX	MLB	26	1	0	0	20	1	19^2	13	2	6.4	7.8	17	35.2%	.216	1.37	3.20	125	0.0	93.3	54.3%	25.7%	49.8%
2021	RR	AAA	27	2	2	3	27	0	37^2	28	5	2.9	11.5	48	33.0%	.250	1.06	2.63	98	0.2				
2021	TEX	MLB	27	0	1	0	4	0	4	5	1	0.0	4.5	2	40.0%	.286	1.25	9.00	109	0.0	91.2	46.3%	25.9%	61.5%
2021	LAA	MLB	27	2	2	0	14	0	14^2	15	0	2.5	11.0	18	44.4%	.417	1.30	4.30	93	0.2	91.1	49.4%	33.0%	53.8%
2022	LAA	MLB	28	2	1	9	49	1	69	48	4	2.0	8.2	63	41.1%	.246	0.91	2.48	83	1.3	90.8	31.3%	25.3%	55.5%
2023 DC	*LAA*	*MLB*	*29*	*3*	*3*	*16*	*68*	*0*	*59*	*56*	*8*	*3.4*	*8.8*	*58*	*38.5%*	*.297*	*1.33*	*4.06*	*103*	*0.1*	*91.2*	*37.2%*	*26.8%*	*54.5%*

Comparables: Mark Melancon (57), Brad Boxberger (56), Kevin Jepsen (55)

In addition to being a quality reliever, Herget is the owner of one of the most underrated deliveries in the major leagues. Staring in for the sign, he sets up through a small, wearied shrug of the shoulders, steps forward lazily with his front foot, then whips the ball nearly from the side before his leg motion sweeps him away to face first base, as if commiserating with some unseen bystander. The effect is marvelously dismissive, especially against right-handers, who often walked back to the dugout looking for their own invisible companions to yell at. Despite the side-arming, Herget isn't too vulnerable against lefties, mostly because his slider barely slides, breaking just faintly at the end of its path like a pedestrian that politely steps out of the way on the sidewalk. He was given the opportunity to lead L.A.'s closer committee after Raisel Iglesias' departure, and he made the most of the opportunity, giving up runs in just three of his 24 games after the deadline.

Ben Joyce RHP Born: 09/17/00 Age: 22 Bats: R Throws: R Height: 6'5" Weight: 225 lb. Origin: Round 3, 2022 Draft (#89 overall)

YEAR	TEAM	LVL	AGE	W	L	SV	G	GS	IP	H	HR	BB/9	K/9	K	GB%	BABIP	WHIP	ERA	DRA-	WARP	MPH	FB%	Whiff%	CSP
2022	RCT	AA	21	1	0	1	13	0	13	11	0	2.8	13.8	20	46.7%	.367	1.15	2.08	80	0.3				
2023 non-DC	*LAA*	*MLB*	*22*	*2*	*2*	*0*	*57*	*0*	*50*	*45*	*6*	*4.6*	*8.8*	*49*	*43.8%*	*.289*	*1.43*	*4.43*	*108*	*0.0*			*27.7%*	

Comparables: Johnny Barbato (88), Sam Tuivailala (87), Jhan Mariñez (86)

A lack of innings—and a career destined to be spent in the bullpen—pushed Joyce into the third round of the 2022 draft. But the argument could easily be made that the latter mitigates concerns about the former. This is not a man who needs to spend years honing his secondaries or searching for a changeup that could allow him to start. He *is* a man who should maximize each of the bullets left in his right arm. You see, we're burying the lede here a bit. Joyce touched 105 mph on his fastball in college, and saw no error in translation when he unleashed it on the Southern League. His slider, which comes in 15 mph slower, has the potential to be average, and he'll have plenty of time to hone it while hitters try to keep up with his heat. Health will always be a concern, but barring injury, Joyce might be able to reach the majors by next fall, lack of experience be damned.

Aaron Loup LHP Born: 12/19/87 Age: 35 Bats: L Throws: L Height: 5'11" Weight: 210 lb. Origin: Round 9, 2009 Draft (#280 overall)

YEAR	TEAM	LVL	AGE	W	L	SV	G	GS	IP	H	HR	BB/9	K/9	K	GB%	BABIP	WHIP	ERA	DRA-	WARP	MPH	FB%	Whiff%	CSP
2020	TB	MLB	32	3	2	0	24	0	25	17	3	1.4	7.9	22	39.4%	.230	0.84	2.52	89	0.4	92.3	49.9%	19.8%	54.9%
2021	NYM	MLB	33	6	0	0	65	2	56^2	37	1	2.5	9.1	57	51.8%	.259	0.94	0.95	84	1.0	92.5	51.9%	27.1%	54.3%
2022	LAA	MLB	34	0	5	1	65	0	58^2	54	4	3.4	8.0	52	48.9%	.287	1.30	3.84	101	0.5	91.3	48.7%	24.4%	52.1%
2023 DC	*LAA*	*MLB*	*35*	*3*	*3*	*0*	*61*	*0*	*53*	*55*	*6*	*3.3*	*8.7*	*51*	*48.3%*	*.316*	*1.40*	*4.57*	*113*	*-0.1*	*91.8*	*49.9%*	*24.2%*	*53.1%*

Comparables: Jake Diekman (70), Randy Choate (66), Steve Cishek (66)

We have nothing against the French horn, which is a noble instrument. But the Angels employing Loup, one of the game's preeminent lefty specialists, was like including one in a three-piece band. The southpaw couldn't follow up on his career year with the Mets, in part because of a bad strand rate and in part because of small sample variation. But mostly, he simply stopped missing bats with his primary weapon, his sinker. The good news is that the pitch wasn't quantifiably different than in years past—down a tick in velocity, perhaps, but still boasting excellent movement—so it's fair to expect some positive regression for Loup in the second leg of his two-year sentence in LA.

Mike Mayers RHP Born: 12/06/91 Age: 31 Bats: R Throws: R Height: 6'2" Weight: 220 lb. Origin: Round 3, 2013 Draft (#93 overall)

YEAR	TEAM	LVL	AGE	W	L	SV	G	GS	IP	H	HR	BB/9	K/9	K	GB%	BABIP	WHIP	ERA	DRA-	WARP	MPH	FB%	Whiff%	CSP
2020	LAA	MLB	28	2	0	2	29	0	30	18	2	2.7	12.9	43	32.4%	.242	0.90	2.10	75	0.7	92.9	57.8%	35.7%	45.4%
2021	LAA	MLB	29	5	5	2	72	2	75	71	11	3.1	10.8	90	35.7%	.326	1.29	3.84	85	1.3	93.4	68.4%	29.2%	51.3%
2022	SL	AAA	30	0	3	0	8	8	33	30	7	4.6	9.3	34	31.6%	.261	1.42	6.27	121	-0.2	93.3	39.5%	27.1%	
2022	LAA	MLB	30	1	1	0	24	3	50^2	52	15	3.2	8.0	45	38.6%	.259	1.38	5.68	106	0.3	93.8	46.7%	26.1%	53.0%
2023 DC	*FA*	*MLB*	*31*	*2*	*2*	*0*	*50*	*0*	*43.7*	*43*	*7*	*3.6*	*9.1*	*44*	*36.1%*	*.304*	*1.40*	*4.55*	*113*	*-0.1*	*93.6*	*57.6%*	*26.9%*	*51.0%*

Comparables: Alex Wilson (52), Noé Ramirez (52), Jim Johnson (51)

Mayers used to be an important part of the Baseball Prospectus *Annual* process. When it came time to assign that 2,100th player, the editors would ask, "Well, is this guy more important than Mike Mayers?" He was one of those middle relievers who you only knew about if he was on your team, useless for fantasy and with no real upside, but always, ceaselessly *around*. But the Mendoza Line isn't really .200 anymore, and Mayers isn't that last guy in the book—first because he was actually pretty good for a bit, working in a cutter and getting whiffs, and now because he's bad enough to be interesting. Nothing worked for Mayers in 2022, which is remarkable because the man tried everything, throwing six different pitches. He's getting batters to chase, but he's no longer getting them to miss. Without the advantage of being ahead in the count all the time, he's going to get compared to some other 95-and-a-slider guy next year. Unless he rebounds, he may finally miss the cut.

José Quijada LHP Born: 11/09/95 Age: 27 Bats: L Throws: L Height: 5'11" Weight: 215 lb. Origin: International Free Agent, 2013

YEAR	TEAM	LVL	AGE	W	L	SV	G	GS	IP	H	HR	BB/9	K/9	K	GB%	BABIP	WHIP	ERA	DRA-	WARP	MPH	FB%	Whiff%	CSP
2020	LAA	MLB	24	0	1	0	6	0	3^2	6	1	4.9	14.7	6	36.4%	.500	2.18	7.36	70	0.1	93.5	68.5%	33.3%	48.4%
2021	SL	AAA	25	3	1	1	22	0	29^1	17	2	3.4	11.4	37	46.3%	.231	0.95	1.53	79	0.5				
2021	LAA	MLB	25	0	2	0	26	0	25^2	20	2	5.3	13.3	38	39.3%	.333	1.36	4.56	73	0.6	93.8	73.3%	31.7%	48.6%
2022	LAA	MLB	26	0	5	3	42	0	40^2	25	5	4.6	11.5	52	33.0%	.225	1.13	3.98	83	0.8	94.7	84.9%	32.4%	49.9%
2023 DC	*LAA*	*MLB*	*27*	*3*	*2*	*2*	*61*	*0*	*53*	*42*	*7*	*4.8*	*11.4*	*67*	*37.6%*	*.280*	*1.33*	*3.75*	*93*	*0.4*	*94.3*	*79.3%*	*31.5%*	*48.5%*

Comparables: Corey Knebel (67), A.J. Minter (65), Ken Giles (65)

One of the trends of modern analytical thinking is that pitchers should throw their best pitches more often, so Quijada went ahead and upped his four-seam usage from 73% to 87%. That might sound dangerous, but there's little risk in being predictable if no one knows where the one pitch you throw all the time is going to go. Besides, the southpaw doesn't seem particularly incentivized to care; he actually got more swinging strikes than called ones, a rare feat among pitchers lacking elite whiff rates. The extra tick he found on his pitches last year certainly helped, but deception remains his number one weapon. His delivery is short and violent, often concluding with the baseball equivalent of jazz hands, as he hops and windmills to maintain balance in his follow-through. At least the entertainment value of watching him work helps mitigate how random middle relievers have helped thrust the sport into three-true-outcomes hell; only 53% of batters managed to put the ball in play against Quijada, hitting .179 against that ever-present fastball.

Patrick Sandoval LHP Born: 10/18/96 Age: 26 Bats: L Throws: L Height: 6'3" Weight: 190 lb. Origin: Round 11, 2015 Draft (#319 overall)

YEAR	TEAM	LVL	AGE	W	L	SV	G	GS	IP	H	HR	BB/9	K/9	K	GB%	BABIP	WHIP	ERA	DRA-	WARP	MPH	FB%	Whiff%	CSP
2020	LAA	MLB	23	1	5	0	9	6	36^2	37	10	2.9	8.1	33	55.3%	.260	1.34	5.65	88	0.6	93.0	44.6%	27.6%	47.7%
2021	LAA	MLB	24	3	6	1	17	14	87	69	11	3.7	9.7	94	50.7%	.266	1.21	3.62	92	1.2	93.5	43.1%	34.0%	52.1%
2022	LAA	MLB	25	6	9	0	27	27	148^2	139	8	3.6	9.1	151	46.6%	.320	1.34	2.91	93	2.0	93.4	37.0%	29.7%	54.1%
2023 DC	*LAA*	*MLB*	*26*	*9*	*9*	*0*	*27*	*27*	*154*	*147*	*15*	*3.8*	*9.6*	*163*	*48.0%*	*.312*	*1.38*	*3.83*	*97*	*1.5*	*93.4*	*39.6%*	*30.5%*	*52.7%*

Comparables: Jake Odorizzi (65), Robbie Ray (64), Chris Archer (62)

Did Sandoval have a breakout year? The traditional stats clearly think so, but DRA is more suspicious. In order to understand its cynicism, you have to look under the hood: BABIP regression is a 2012 talking point, but it's relevant here. Sandoval suddenly gave up half the homers he used to despite a career-low ground-ball rate and a tick upwards in contact rate, and our advanced metrics are always going to bet against that. An additional wrinkle is the sudden weakness of his four-seam fastball, which he tried to mitigate by throwing less often as the year went on. It's not necessarily a *bad* pitch, but the way he throws it makes it very heavy, and instead of aiming it down and racking up the grounders, he threw it at the top of the zone in search of strikeouts. Despite the weirdness, Sandoval is a good starting pitcher. He'll just need to iron out a few things to meet the standard 2022 set for him.

Chase Silseth RHP Born: 05/18/00 Age: 23 Bats: R Throws: R Height: 6'0" Weight: 217 lb. Origin: Round 11, 2021 Draft (#321 overall)

YEAR	TEAM	LVL	AGE	W	L	SV	G	GS	IP	H	HR	BB/9	K/9	K	GB%	BABIP	WHIP	ERA	DRA-	WARP	MPH	FB%	Whiff%	CSP
2022	RCT	AA	22	7	0	0	15	15	83	52	11	2.9	11.9	110	48.9%	.247	0.95	2.28	74	2.0				
2022	LAA	MLB	22	1	3	0	7	7	28^2	33	7	3.8	7.5	24	44.6%	.310	1.57	6.59	110	0.1	95.7	46.3%	26.1%	55.0%
2023 DC	*LAA*	*MLB*	*23*	*1*	*2*	*0*	*6*	*6*	*29*	*29*	*4*	*3.9*	*9.0*	*29*	*45.9%*	*.307*	*1.44*	*4.52*	*111*	*0.1*	*95.7*	*46.3%*	*28.2%*	*55.0%*

Comparables: Casey Kelly (74), Spencer Howard (72), Lucas Sims (71)

An 11th-rounder in 2021, Silseth made his major-league debut in May of 2022. That kind of race through the minors is usually reserved for an early-round reliever, but impressively, Silseth did it as a starter, jumping straight to Double-A to open his first full minor-league season. He excelled there thanks to a reliance on a previously seldom-thrown splitter, using his new off-speed offering to pick up, ahem, chases by the bushel. His split-finger works so well because he can also run his fastball into the upper 90s, though it lacks the ideal shape to elicit whiffs. He'll also offer an inconsistent slider, and will show a curve and a two-seamer, but none stand out, and therein lies the problem. Big-league hitters caught on to Silseth's two-pitch approach, and as such he saw his Double-A strikeout rate nearly halved in the majors. He has mid-rotation upside if he finds a more consistent breaker or better fastball shape. But even if he's "just" a back-end starter, the Angels have to be happy with their double-digit-round selection.

José Suarez LHP Born: 01/03/98 Age: 25 Bats: L Throws: L Height: 5'10" Weight: 225 lb. Origin: International Free Agent, 2014

YEAR	TEAM	LVL	AGE	W	L	SV	G	GS	IP	H	HR	BB/9	K/9	K	GB%	BABIP	WHIP	ERA	DRA-	WARP	MPH	FB%	Whiff%	CSP
2020	LAA	MLB	22	0	2	0	2	2	2^1	10	1	19.3	7.7	2	46.7%	.643	6.43	38.57	252	-0.2	93.1	45.5%	32.4%	38.3%
2021	SL	AAA	23	0	0	0	2	2	6	8	0	1.5	6.0	4	50.0%	.364	1.50	1.50	110	0.0				
2021	LAA	MLB	23	8	8	0	23	14	98^1	85	11	3.3	7.8	85	47.6%	.269	1.23	3.75	106	0.6	92.8	47.6%	25.8%	53.3%
2022	SL	AAA	24	1	1	0	4	3	16^2	18	3	4.3	9.2	17	22.0%	.319	1.56	8.64	123	-0.1	91.9	53.3%	30.5%	
2022	LAA	MLB	24	8	8	0	22	20	109	103	14	2.7	8.5	103	40.7%	.290	1.25	3.96	102	0.9	92.6	42.6%	24.5%	55.6%
2023 DC	*LAA*	*MLB*	*25*	*7*	*8*	*0*	*25*	*25*	*124.3*	*124*	*16*	*3.5*	*8.1*	*111*	*41.3%*	*.298*	*1.38*	*4.31*	*109*	*0.4*	*92.6*	*44.9%*	*25.9%*	*53.7%*

Comparables: Tyler Skaggs (69), Chris Tillman (59), Jonathon Niese (59)

Everyone wants to send Brusdar Graterol back in time to break Babe Ruth's brain and leave him a haunted shell. No one ever talks about using their time machine to send Suarez back to the 1980s so that he can be properly appreciated. In those contact-happy days of yore, the five-pitch lefty would have been a minor celebrity, keeping everything down, mixing speeds, raking in those Orel Hershiser-level local TV endorsements. In these dark times, Suarez will have to be content with keeping everything down, mixing speeds and holding down a job on a second-division team. Now approaching his mid-20s, Suarez has the potential to serve as a long-term, mid-rotation stalwart. That may not get the kids excited these days, but Angels fans should be thrilled given their team's sordid history of developing pitching.

Ryan Tepera RHP Born: 11/03/87 Age: 35 Bats: R Throws: R Height: 6'1" Weight: 195 lb. Origin: Round 19, 2009 Draft (#580 overall)

YEAR	TEAM	LVL	AGE	W	L	SV	G	GS	IP	H	HR	BB/9	K/9	K	GB%	BABIP	WHIP	ERA	DRA-	WARP	MPH	FB%	Whiff%	CSP
2020	CHC	MLB	32	0	1	0	21	0	20^{2}	17	2	5.2	13.5	31	40.0%	.349	1.40	3.92	82	0.4	94.1	46.1%	44.0%	35.8%
2021	CHW	MLB	33	0	0	1	22	0	18	13	1	3.5	12.0	24	37.2%	.286	1.11	2.50	87	0.3	93.0	45.6%	35.9%	46.7%
2021	CHC	MLB	33	0	2	1	43	0	43^{1}	22	3	2.5	10.4	50	46.0%	.196	0.78	2.91	81	0.8	93.7	43.3%	35.0%	51.8%
2022	LAA	MLB	34	5	4	6	59	0	57^{1}	42	7	3.1	7.4	47	40.5%	.226	1.08	3.61	94	0.7	92.8	48.3%	30.7%	48.9%
2023 DC	*LAA*	*MLB*	*35*	*3*	*3*	*20*	*61*	*0*	*53*	*49*	*6*	*3.6*	*9.1*	*53*	*41.7%*	*.293*	*1.33*	*3.91*	*99*	*0.2*	*93.2*	*46.9%*	*30.9%*	*47.8%*

Comparables: Luis García (66), Will Harris (63), Santiago Casilla (63)

The final numbers make it look like Tepera put together a fairly average year, given his usual standards. But the process by which he earned those numbers felt like anything but average. The middle reliever scattered four months of ERAs starting with ones and twos around a pair in the sevens, and neither he, nor anyone with a rooting interest in watching him, ever felt comfortable. Frustrated with the idea that hitters were starting to key on his fastball, the 35-year-old broke out a new, slower slider with more movement, and found success using it as an improved version of his changeup. It's good to see youngish people improving themselves, but in all likelihood, this was more just small-sample variation than some fundamental flaw he was able to fix. Perry Minasian has stated that his bullpen will undergo renovations this offseason, but, as Tepera is in the second year of a two-year contract, his job seems safe.

Andrew Wantz RHP Born: 10/13/95 Age: 27 Bats: R Throws: R Height: 6'4" Weight: 235 lb. Origin: Round 7, 2018 Draft (#211 overall)

YEAR	TEAM	LVL	AGE	W	L	SV	G	GS	IP	H	HR	BB/9	K/9	K	GB%	BABIP	WHIP	ERA	DRA-	WARP	MPH	FB%	Whiff%	CSP
2021	SL	AAA	25	1	0	0	12	5	30^{1}	22	2	1.8	8.9	30	47.5%	.256	0.92	1.78	94	0.2				
2021	LAA	MLB	25	1	0	0	21	0	27^{1}	23	5	3.6	12.5	38	29.9%	.290	1.24	4.94	82	0.5	92.5	75.4%	30.3%	53.9%
2022	SL	AAA	26	1	1	0	10	0	15^{2}	11	3	1.7	9.8	17	40.0%	.222	0.89	2.87	89	0.2	93.5	47.5%	35.7%	
2022	LAA	MLB	26	2	1	0	42	1	50^{1}	37	8	3.8	9.3	52	29.5%	.240	1.15	3.22	102	0.4	93.8	49.5%	32.1%	52.5%
2023 DC	*LAA*	*MLB*	*27*	*3*	*3*	*0*	*61*	*0*	*53*	*47*	*8*	*3.5*	*10.1*	*59*	*34.4%*	*.288*	*1.28*	*3.87*	*99*	*0.3*	*93.4*	*57.3%*	*30.1%*	*52.9%*

Comparables: Hansel Robles (70), Dan Altavilla (69), Louis Coleman (69)

He couldn't quite one-up John Lannan, who was famously ejected in his MLB debut, but Wantz made some measure of history by getting tossed just 12 pitches into his first (and so far only) career start after plunking Jesse Winker, instigating a benches-clearing brawl. The attention that drew was a bit ironic, because the former seventh-rounder enjoyed a forgettable, productive season in a relief otherwise. He keeps his fastball up and buries his slider down and away, often out of the zone where hitters can only wave at it. He's the prototypical modern reliever, earning whiffs with all four of his pitches but giving up loud contact on those rare occasions when a hitter guesses right. Some men are just born into the right era; 10 years ago, Wantz might have lost his roster spot in favor of a bench bat, but two years ago the Angels may have doomed him by forcing him into a starting role. Middle relief is where Wantz belongs, and that's where he looks to stay.

Lineouts

Hitters

HITTER	POS	TEAM	LVL	AGE	PA	R	2B	3B	HR	RBI	BB	K	SB	CS	AVG/OBP/SLG	DRC+	BABIP	BRR	DRP	WARP
Jordyn Adams	OF	TRI	A+	22	249	31	11	3	0	22	21	54	18	3	.228/.308/.306	98	.299	0.5	CF(49): -2.4	0.7
	OF	RCT	AA	22	236	33	7	2	4	20	21	70	15	0	.249/.326/.359	79	.350	2.3	CF(27): -3.6, RF(19): 1.8, LF(16): -0.7	0.1
Werner Blakely	3B/DH	IE	A	20	235	36	13	2	5	40	45	70	24	2	.295/.447/.470	106	.450	1.2	3B(34): -2.8	0.8
Steven Duggar	OF	RR	AAA	28	50	5	2	0	1	5	11	13	3	0	.184/.360/.316	95	.240	-1.7	RF(7): -1.6, CF(4): 0.3, LF(1): -0.2	0.0
	OF	SL	AAA	28	37	3	1	0	2	2	3	14	1	0	.147/.216/.353	85	.167	0.0	CF(9): -0.5	0.0
	OF	SAC	AAA	28	53	8	1	0	1	5	3	18	2	0	.204/.264/.286	75	.300	0.8	CF(9): 0.2	0.0
	OF	SF	MLB	28	39	2	3	0	0	4	2	16	4	0	.194/.231/.278	64	.333	0.5	CF(12): 0.1	0.0
	OF	TEX	MLB	28	19	2	0	0	0	0	2	12	1	1	.176/.263/.176	41	.600	-0.1	LF(5): 0, CF(4): 0	-0.1
	OF	LAA	MLB	28	22	3	0	1	0	0	3	13	0	0	.053/.182/.158	60	.167	-0.3	LF(8): 0.2, CF(2): 0.1	0.0
Juan Lagares	OF	SL	AAA	33	29	3	2	1	0	6	3	4	0	1	.308/.379/.462	104	.364	0.5	LF(3): -0.0, RF(3): 0.1	0.1
	OF	LAA	MLB	33	62	4	2	1	0	0	2	15	0	0	.183/.210/.250	86	.244	0.0	RF(9): -0.3, CF(8): -0.2, LF(5): -0.4	0.0
Kyren Paris	MI	TRI	A+	20	392	58	18	5	8	32	49	117	28	4	.229/.345/.387	104	.330	3.7	SS(60): -6.4, 2B(26): -0.1	1.2
	MI	RCT	AA	20	51	11	2	0	3	8	10	14	5	0	.359/.510/.641	109	.500	-0.2	2B(13): -0.5	0.1
Alexander Ramirez	RF	IE	A	19	520	67	24	5	8	59	31	160	21	8	.229/.290/.352	79	.326	5.4	RF(96): 5.2, LF(14): 1.1, CF(8): -0.3	0.9
Magneuris Sierra	CF	SL	AAA	26	311	49	10	4	7	45	24	51	22	5	.297/.358/.437	107	.339	3.9	CF(65): -0.1, RF(5): -0.3, LF(2): -0.2	1.9
	CF	LAA	MLB	26	96	7	1	3	0	5	4	25	6	1	.165/.200/.242	64	.227	0.7	CF(28): 1.1, LF(17): 0.5, RF(2): 0.1	0.2
Livan Soto	MI	RCT	AA	22	543	69	17	1	6	57	71	102	18	8	.281/.379/.362	98	.345	-0.6	SS(68): 6.1, 2B(42): 2.9, 3B(7): -0.0	2.3
	MI	LAA	MLB	22	59	9	5	1	1	9	2	13	1	1	.400/.414/.582	83	.500	0.2	SS(18): -1.3, 3B(1): 0	0.0
Michael Stefanic	2B	SL	AAA	26	346	50	14	3	4	37	48	22	4	2	.314/.422/.425	130	.326	-1.4	2B(68): -0.7, 3B(6): 1.1	2.2
	2B	LAA	MLB	26	69	5	2	0	0	0	5	12	0	0	.197/.279/.230	96	.245	0.1	2B(22): 0.1	0.2

Jordyn Adams cut his strikeout rate more than 15 percentage points and received a midsummer promotion to Double-A. Good thing this is a lineout and there isn't room to describe anything else about his season or his prospect status. ⚾ Third baseman prospect **Werner Blakely** unlocked "doubles power" in his skill tree, but he'll still need to put points into "two-strike contact" and "throwing to first baseman" as he levels up to High-A next season. ⚾ **Steven Duggar** played on six professional teams in 2022 and hit above .200 for one of them. He didn't hit above .205 for any of them. It's hard to find MLB work as a platoon fourth outfielder, especially when the team most likely to roster one is the one that traded him away. ⚾ The Angels brought back **Juan Lagares** as outfield insurance in 2022, and he answered by helping his team win a pennant and slugging .464 ... in the Korea Baseball Organization. ⚾ Some hitters earn walks because pitchers are afraid of them. Others, because they're afraid of pitchers. The Angels won't always have **Kyren Paris**, what with the reserve clause being dead and all, but since he falls squarely in the latter camp it might not matter much anyway. ⚾ Outfield prospect **Alexander Ramirez** spent his season in Low-A striking out five times for every walk. He can hit the ball a very long way, but until he can stop staring at each new breaking ball with the object permanence of an infant under a bedsheet, it's not going to matter much. ⚾ Six-year veteran **Magneuris Sierra** only needs one moonshot to catch up to Max Scherzer on the all-time home run leaderboard. And yes, Max Scherzer has one career home run. ⚾ You gotta love a small sample in which a .400/.414/.582 slash line nets an 83 DRC+, but **Livan Soto** showed up to the bigs hacking, and the metrics are impartial arbiters of justice. Ironically, his eye is ordinarily his best trait as a hitter; it's usually his lack of pop that does him in. He'll need to thwack balls past the infield in larger samples to carve out a lasting utility role in the majors. ⚾ **Michael Stefanic** has a good eye and a good beard, and he hit two balls past the outfielders out of 52 balls in play. He'll stick around the majors for a couple of years, mostly fouling off pitches and working eight-pitch at-bats that end with weak grounders to second. Get excited.

Pitchers

PITCHER	TEAM	LVL	AGE	W	L	SV	G	GS	IP	H	HR	BB/9	K/9	K	GB%	BABIP	WHIP	ERA	DRA-	WARP	MPH	FB%	WHF	CSP
Kyle Barraclough	SL	AAA	32	4	3	2	41	0	45	31	3	5.6	12.2	61	49.5%	.286	1.31	3.00	68	1.1	92.2	41.2%	34.1%	
	LAA	MLB	32	0	1	0	8	0	9	7	0	4.0	9.0	9	25.0%	.292	1.22	3.00	98	0.1	93.2	46.0%	37.7%	53.9%
Caden Dana	ANG	ROK	18	0	0	0	3	3	6^{2}	6	0	0.0	8.1	6	42.1%	.316	0.90	1.35						
Davis Daniel	SL	AAA	25	6	7	0	21	21	102^{1}	92	14	2.8	7.3	83	37.7%	.265	1.21	4.49	115	-0.3	91.0	55.2%	22.5%	
Jhonathan Diaz	SL	AAA	25	3	1	0	10	10	47	44	4	3.8	8.8	46	47.8%	.310	1.36	4.98	91	0.5	90.7	55.6%	26.5%	
	LAA	MLB	25	1	1	0	4	3	15^{1}	13	1	5.9	6.5	11	51.1%	.273	1.50	2.93	128	-0.1	90.6	50.0%	22.0%	46.9%
Landon Marceaux	TRI	A+	22	4	5	0	16	16	85	64	5	1.5	7.3	69	57.1%	.246	0.92	2.65	94	1.0				
Jose Marte	SL	AAA	26	0	2	3	34	0	34^{2}	27	4	6.0	11.9	46	47.6%	.295	1.44	5.45	75	0.7	96.4	51.8%	32.6%	
	LAA	MLB	26	0	0	0	11	0	11	8	2	14.7	12.3	15	16.0%	.261	2.36	7.36	111	0.0	96.5	50.6%	27.1%	45.7%
Robinson Pina	TRI	A+	23	6	6	1	18	13	81^{2}	71	7	2.6	12.9	117	32.5%	.348	1.16	3.31	74	1.9				
Kenny Rosenberg	ANG	ROK	26	0	2	0	3	2	6	8	1	1.5	9.0	6	63.2%	.389	1.50	7.50						
	SL	AAA	26	2	5	0	14	13	62^{2}	50	9	3.9	8.9	62	40.1%	.255	1.23	3.16	90	0.7	90.7	45.1%	30.2%	
	LAA	MLB	26	0	0	0	3	1	10^{2}	9	1	5.1	6.7	8	27.3%	.250	1.41	4.22	136	-0.1	90.6	45.1%	22.0%	51.2%
César Valdez	SL	AAA	37	10	5	0	23	23	146^{1}	138	14	1.4	7.6	123	51.5%	.293	1.09	3.94	84	2.3	84.9	26.9%	27.7%	
	LAA	MLB	37	0	0	0	1	0	1	2	0	0.0	0.0	0	80.0%	.400	2.00	9.00	112	0.0	86.3	12.5%	9.1%	62.5%
Connor Van Scoyoc	IE	A	22	11	5	0	23	22	120	103	10	2.9	10.5	140	52.4%	.302	1.18	4.28	81	1.6				
Austin Warren	SL	AAA	26	2	0	1	29	0	34	23	2	4.5	7.9	30	54.3%	.228	1.18	2.12	86	0.5	93.4	53.7%	27.4%	
	LAA	MLB	26	2	0	0	14	0	16	19	3	2.8	5.1	9	35.7%	.308	1.50	5.62	118	0.0	93.8	54.1%	17.3%	57.1%
Zack Weiss	SL	AAA	30	2	3	3	43	0	50	44	6	3.8	11.7	65	35.9%	.304	1.30	4.50	84	0.8	94.4	40.0%	32.1%	
	LAA	MLB	30	0	1	0	12	0	13^{1}	7	2	4.7	12.1	18	33.3%	.185	1.05	3.38	84	0.2	94.4	37.8%	41.1%	51.4%

A closer of the future for a future that never happened, **Kyle Barraclough** never did cut down the walks that stood in the way of his dreams. His arm's not what it used to be, but he can still be an effective reliever if he stays wild in fastball counts and avoids the homer, as he did to some modest success in 2022.

Caden Dana is a pitcher with an ETA around the last year of the Anthony Rendon contract, so it would be irresponsible to assign him any description that might stoke the slightest bit of hype. The Kentucky commit signed a record deal for a post-tenth-round pick, breaking the previous record held by ... the Angels, last year, with a pitcher who isn't even getting a lineout in this book.

In almost any other year as an Angels Triple-A starter, **Davis Daniel** would have traded in his punch card—make 12 starts, get one MLB promotion free—and enjoyed his month eating decent meals. Instead, he had to spend the whole year cobbling together a mid-four ERA in Utah for nothing.

Jhonathan Diaz is a former minor-league free agent and one of the Angels' 2021 developmental successes, mixing four pitches from the left side. As Triple-A starter depth goes, he's of the "break glass in case of emergency" variety.

Jake Madden is no Ben Joyce—his fastball "only" reaches 98 mph—but he's got a better chance to start someday. That won't happen soon, however, as the Angels opted to lock him in an underground bunker and make him draw strike zones hundreds of times a day rather than let him pitch post-draft.

Back in the old days, **Landon Marceaux** wouldn't have stood a chance as a starter, as passable changeups were required for graduation and fastballs were obligatory in obvious counts. Alas, his low-90s velo would've played better back then—in today's game, he has to use his breaking pitches as his primaries as he clings to the edges of the zone.

Fun fact: **Jose Marte** led the league in something! Less fun fact (for him): That thing was three-true-outcome rate among pitchers with more than three innings pitched (60.3%).

Robinson Pina has always had electric stuff and sporadic command, so after he struggled in Double-A in 2021, the Angels escorted him back to the Northwest League rather than force the issue. The future reliever resumed his destruction of High-A batters via an improving splitter, then skipped straight to Salt Lake to end the season.

Seven seasons into his career, **Chris Rodriguez** has amassed fewer innings (127⅔) than Reid Detmers did last season alone. The dynamic right-hander has long seemed a better fit for the bullpen—now he needs to prove he's still dynamic at all a year after shoulder surgery.

Kenny Rosenberg holds the distinction of being the only pitcher taken in the 2022 Rule 5 draft to reach the majors last year. He almost certainly holds other distinctions, but these were not made available by the time this book went to press.

César Valdez pitched one whole big-league inning at the age of 37, which gives us a chance to print a final goodbye to the changeup king. Other pitchers might throw harder, or strike out more batters, or win more glory. No one else did it by treating baseball like a game of rock-paper-scissors and, for 17 professional seasons, only throwing paper, over and over.

Connor Van Scoyoc is your run-of-the-mill projectable righty with a low-90s fastball and two potentially workable secondaries, which makes for a more than acceptable outcome for an 11th-round pick. He has a first-round delivery, though: mechanically simple, upright, and with a satisfyingly late snap that makes his pitches look better than they actually are.

"Now dear," your mother says from the front seat, "we have a perfectly good **Austin Warren** at home." Alas, the Austin Warren at home is also Austin Warren.

After four long years, **Zack Weiss** finally got a chance to shave infinity off his career ERA. He seemed to have lost his command after that fateful four-batter, four-run day back in 2018, but given the stuff he flashed in his short return, he's a potentially useful bullpen piece.

OAKLAND ATHLETICS

Essay by Dan Moore

Player comments by Bryan Grosnick and BP staff

Typically, what baseball fans want most out of their preseason analysis is insight into whether and by what means their favorite team might find success on the field in the coming year. In Oakland heading into 2023, what fans will care most about regards business that'll transpire almost entirely *off* the field—that is, in the A's corporate headquarters and in dimly lit boardrooms cloistered deep within Oakland's City Hall. How the A's actually play feels inconsequential in comparison.

There are two reasons for this focus. Both evince something elemental about the state of baseball in Oakland today.

The first has to do with hope. For 25 years now, rooting for the A's has felt a lot like being caught in a toxic relationship—beguiling when it's good, belittling the rest of the time. This is, on the one hand, a product of owner John Fisher and team president Dave Kaval's peculiar approach to fan-service, which revolves around taunting fans online, gaslighting them in the news and repelling them in person; ahead of the 2022 A's home opener, Fisher purged the Oakland Coliseum of most of its concessions and many of its contractors, which had the maximally insulting effect of guaranteeing that at a game attended by fewer than 18,000 people, what fans *had* shown up would nevertheless have to wait 30 minutes anytime they wanted a hot dog or a beer. Though in truth A's fans have become inured to this kind of neglect. We could live with it, if we had to. We don't need nice things—we in fact quite like the Coliseum, along with the feral cats who've colonized it—and we don't need to be coddled. What's far more draining, I think, is how Fisher approaches the actual *baseball* part of the fan-franchise relationship. It's an operating strategy by now so infamous it boasts its own sobriquet: "Moneyball."

Now, if you live somewhere other than Oakland, you might understand "Moneyball" in anodyne scientific terms—as shorthand, perhaps, for a once-prescient approach to scouting and analytics popularized by Brad Pitt. A's fans, however, know that "Moneyball" was never about analytics or scouting so much as it was about compensating for our owners' conspicuous frugality. The strategy is simple, on paper—it's a recipe for prying open windows of contention without ever having to pay good players market-rate

OAKLAND ATHLETICS PROSPECTUS

2022 W-L: 60-102, 5th in AL West

Pythag	.364	*28th*	DER	.698	*17th*
RS/G	3.51	*29th*	DRC+	91	*26th*
RA/G	4.75	*24th*	DRA-	112	*28th*
dWin%	.387	*29th*	FIP	4.42	*28th*
Payroll	$48M	*29th*	B-Age	28.9	*11th*
M$/MW	$2.4M	*5th*	P-Age	28.4	*9th*

400'

362' 362'

330' 330'

- Opened 1966
- Open air
- Natural surface
- Fence profile: 8' to 15'

Park Factors

Runs	Runs/RH	Runs/LH	HR/RH	HR/LH
97	95	99	92	102

Top Hitter WARP	4.0 Sean Murphy
Top Pitcher WARP	2.1 Frankie Montas
2023 Top Prospect	Tyler Soderstrom

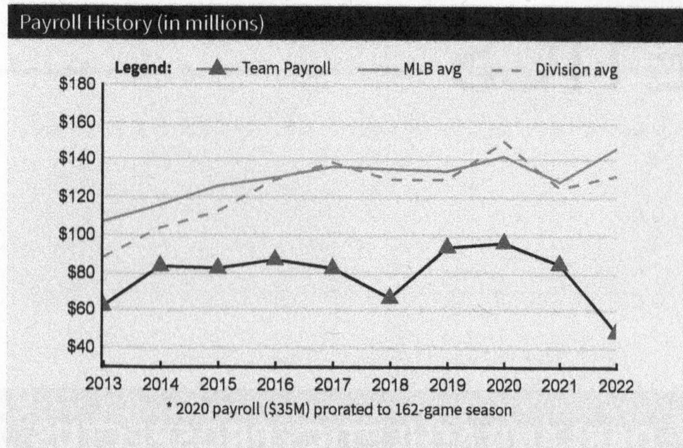

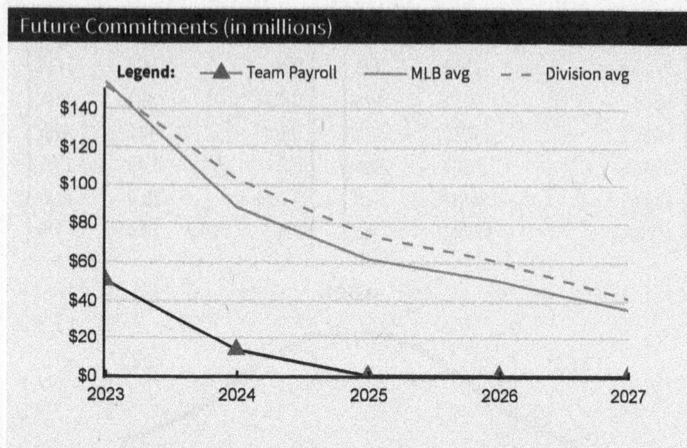

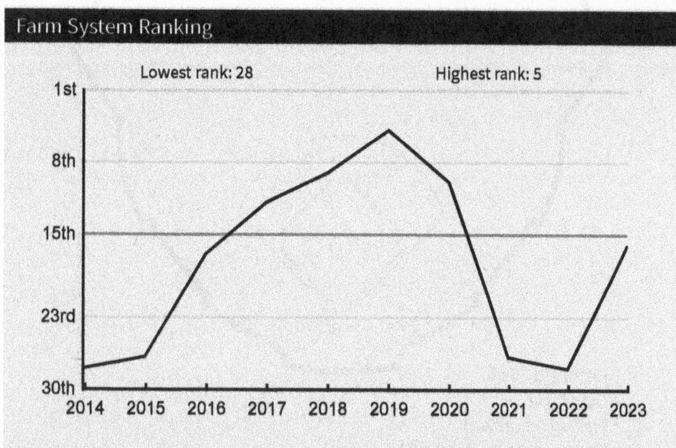

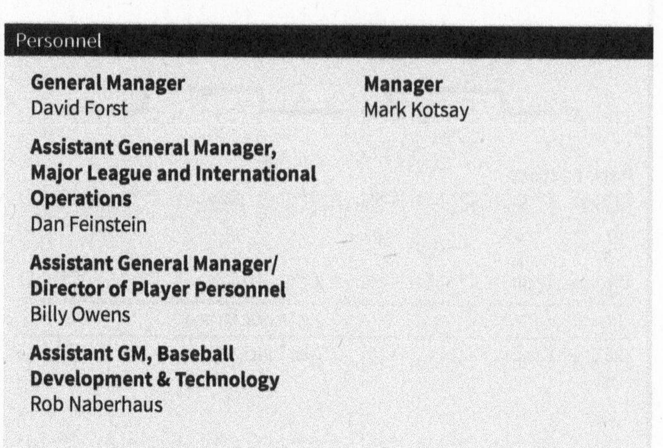
Personnel

General Manager
David Forst

Assistant General Manager, Major League and International Operations
Dan Feinstein

Assistant General Manager/ Director of Player Personnel
Billy Owens

Assistant GM, Baseball Development & Technology
Rob Naberhaus

Manager
Mark Kotsay

contracts—and in the years since former A's GM Billy Beane pioneered it, in the early 2000's, it has been co-opted by all manner of economically conservative team owners in cities all around the league. But nowhere has "Moneyball" been embraced so militantly. In Oakland, we do not rebuild only with chagrin, nor stretch to re-sign marquee players in special, okay-we're-really-going-for-it scenarios. We rebuild relentlessly—with industry—and we *never* re-sign good players, no matter the dynastic potential of doing so. It's fundamental, by this point, to our organizational ethos. It feels like a curse.

Don't get me wrong. Rebuilding with purpose is better than never rebuilding at all—see: Rockies, Colorado—and rebuilding the "Moneyball" way has been proven to work, to an extent. The A's haven't won a World Series since 1989, but over Beane's tenure with the team (he took over as GM in 1998, and is now a "senior advisor" to Fisher), the A's have won seven AL West division titles and four Wild Card spots. The 2002 team that author Michael Lewis dramatized in his 2003 book still stands as one of the most exciting teams in baseball history.

But "Moneyball" is also punishingly taxing. With each rebuild, the A's not only consign themselves to several years of non-competitive play—last season was the second-worst season in the history of the A's tenure in Oakland—they sever fans brutally from whole, fresh crops of young and exciting players with whom they'd only recently started forming bonds. This most recent rendition, initiated in the fall of 2021, has seen the A's trade away or let go of Matt Chapman, Matt Olson, Starling Marte, Chris Bassitt, Sean Murphy, Sean Manaea, Frankie Montas and Lou Trivino: every member of the 2021 starting lineup, basically.

This works on fans like cancer treatment. You see it in the stands. (Last season, by a Bash-Brother sized margin, the A's ranked dead last in attendance.) You see it on social media. (Last spring, after the A's traded Matt Olson, one fan memorably tweeted, "The good news about being an Oakland A's fan is someday I'll die.") And you can just sort of *feel* it, in the air. When I run into Giants fans at the grocery store these days, most spare me the limp, sympathetic nod more typically offered the visibly ill. In the eyes of Major League Baseball, "Moneyball" has reduced A's fans—who rank among the most vociferous and charismatic in baseball—to the diminutive status of the game's soot-dusted Tiny Tims.

So fans hate "Moneyball," is the point. Yet that hatred is precisely why many in Oakland have invested so much hope into the A's off-field business this year: it presents as a chance at liberation—at the end of "Moneyball."

This is not conjecture; rather, it comes straight from Fisher and Kaval.

The business in question pertains to negotiations that are ongoing between Fisher and the Oakland City Council over whether, and with what amount of public financing, the A's should be allowed to construct a new stadium on Oakland's waterfront, a mile south of downtown. The proposed stadium is massive, is in fact not just a stadium but a $12 billion stadium "district"—the sort *every* team owner wants to build these days, all the better for capturing auxiliary revenues—complete with condos, hotels, parks and apartment buildings. It also remains far from certain whether they will ever be allowed to build it. One complication is funding. Though Fisher and Kaval have touted the stadium project as totally "privately funded," the project is in fact not viable without many seismic infrastructural improvements to the area around the stadium, which the A's are asking the city to fund, to the tune of many hundreds of millions of dollars. Which is a problem for several reasons, chief among them that political appetite in Oakland for subsidizing pro sports is, shall we say, less than voracious; the city is still paying off the $223 million in municipal bonds it issued Al Davis in 1995. And yet, the parties continue to haggle—a vote over a final developer agreement is expected sometime this year. Central to the pitch: that a new stadium will be the thing that finally allows Fisher a less crushingly frugal way of doing business.

"This is why we need a new stadium," Kaval recently told the *San Francisco Chronicle*. "In order for us to retain our talent, to have a much higher payroll, we need higher revenues. That comes with a new fan-friendly facility."

Now, fans should parse such comments with several souvenir cups' worth of high-quality salt. It is dubious that a new stadium will magically turn Fisher into some kind of beneficent spender—a beautiful new stadium had no such effect on Robert Nutting, owner of the Pittsburgh Pirates—and Fisher himself hardly inspires faith. The man, it merits noting, is heir to the Gap Inc. fortune, and has a personal net worth north of $2 billion; he's never been wanting for money to spend. But it's understandable why fans might be willing to buy into the dream he's selling. Fisher is perhaps the least subtle of the unsubtle coterie of MLB owners who don't even try to compete, and he's conditioned fans to believe that perpetually shortchanged is how this team simply has to operate. That's never been true, as fans know damn well, but for a long-suffering fanbase adept at finding creative things to root for, the prospect of things *actually* changing is nevertheless tantalizing.

Unfortunately, hope for the end of "Moneyball" is not the only reason A's fans care so much about this blasted stadium business.

A far more transfixing—not to mention representative—reason is fear. Flashback to May 2021, when MLB commissioner Rob Manfred issued a statement bemoaning "the rate of progress of the A's ballpark effort" in Oakland. Fisher and Kaval had been working for several years by that point to advance their real estate ambitions. But in part because the A's flatly refuse to build their new stadium at the Coliseum site, in East Oakland, progress had been slow. Manfred's statement parroted Fisher and Kaval's party line that the Coliseum site was "not a viable option for the future vision of baseball," but, more importantly, it also instructed Fisher and Kaval to begin to "explore other markets while they continue to pursue a waterfront ballpark in Oakland." The "other markets" were in fact one, Las Vegas, and promptly thereafter, Fisher and Kaval announced that they'd placed offers on stadium sites all around Sin City. Reporting in Oakland—though still imbued with hints of hope—has been tinged by anxiety ever since. Fisher and Kaval's commentary, meanwhile, has grown reliably darker and more foreboding. As Kaval also put it to the *San Francisco Chronicle*, "I just cannot stress enough...our future completely is dependent on what happens with the stadium. It's kind of everything."

Once again, one counsels salt. It's not unusual for team owners keen on extorting their host city to make these kinds of threats. And though the stadium project still faces a sizable financial shortfall—and though Fisher has insisted it's on Oakland to find a way to plug the gap—given how much time and money the A's have invested into the effort so far, it's hard to believe that Fisher would allow the deal to fail on account of a few hundred million dollars he'd likely recoup. (Plus, politicians in Nevada have insisted there's no more appetite in Las Vegas for subsidizing Fisher than there is in Oakland—which makes the Vegas threat look slightly more like a bluff than Fisher and Kaval might prefer.)

And yet, none of this will be much consolation for fans. For all of Fisher's neglect, the prospect of losing the A's hangs heavy over fans. And whether it's fear or hope that's captured their attention, the end result is the same. As long as the A's future in Oakland remains uncertain, held hostage by our owners, the experience of rooting for them will remain unpleasant and deadening, like a kind of purgatory. What A's baseball has become known for—empty seats, feral cats, "Moneyball" working for Fisher like a crutch and on fans like a cudgel—it will remain.

This is the truly unfortunate part. Baseball is a business, yes. But it is also undeniably more than that, and it remains most fulfilling and transportive when one can believe—for a strike, a series, a summer, a season—that it's more of that ineffable "other" thing. It's categorically *less* fulfilling when maintaining such faith is impossible. So it has been in Oakland for a while. Occasionally, of course, fans catch the upswing of a rebuild, and reasons for excitement emerge. This season, it's technically possible that the prospects the A's have acquired over the last few years—Ken Waldichuk and JP Sears, picked up in the Montas trade; reliever A.J. Puk, the sixth overall pick from 2016; Shea Langeliers, former ninth overall pick scooped up in the Olson trade; most recently, Esteury Ruiz, a speedster acquired in the widely panned Murphy deal—bloom earlier than expected, and lead a march toward the postseason. Crazier things have happened. The A's were not really expected to be competitive in 2002, either.

More than likely, however, the A's will turn out to be very bad—worse, even, than last year—and unless Fisher announces he's had some Dickensian change of heart, all summer fans will find their attention drawn away from the diamond and up toward sternly closed doors. Again. The story of baseball in Oakland will continue to revolve—necessarily—around term sheets and tax dollars, instead of box scores and batting averages.

This is, objectively, I think, a suboptimal way to experience what Roger Angell once called "the sunshine game." Personally, that A's fans are once again being subjected to such a sunless version of the sport we love fills me with something like shame. I wish I could write this team off almost as much as I wish I was writing a different kind of preseason analysis, at least until Fisher sells to someone who gives a damn. But I can't. I hold onto the hope of a better tomorrow—of a return to something like the late 1980s, a dynasty that shines like an Atlantis in my mind—and I remain in thrall to the fear that that tomorrow will never come.

Most A's fans I know are in the same boat. The question before us, then, is what to do with our energy and interest? Hold onto the hope, or give in to the fear? The only rational answer, I think, is to try for the former. It's a matter, ultimately, of self-preservation. The 2023 campaign might simultaneously be the least competitive yet most consequential season in the history of Oakland A's baseball. It could be strange and stressful. Hope—for this chapter of A's history to end; for the A's to remain in Oakland; for the team to start burnishing a different kind of reputation, one more in line with the colorful audacity of our abundant past, as opposed to the pitiable poverty of our protracted present—will sustain us. Picture it, and go nuts. It's Opening Day, 2033. Fisher, in a final fit of pique, has sold the A's to Joe Lacob. Ruiz, whom Lacob has recently re-signed to another multi-year extension, is still batting leadoff. The stands are full. And everyone in them is happy, in part because we've forgotten what it was like to root for the A's back when we had to spend each offseason sour and fearful. By this point in time, we may have even forgotten that we ever had to play "Moneyball," instead of baseball, at all.

It's a nice thought, isn't it? Right. Now hold onto it in your mind. Or keep it somewhere you can find it. In the months ahead, it might be all we have. ■

—Dan Moore is a writer and editor based in the Bay Area.

HITTERS

Nick Allen MI Born: 10/08/98 Age: 24 Bats: R Throws: R Height: 5'8" Weight: 166 lb. Origin: Round 3, 2017 Draft (#81 overall)

YEAR	TEAM	LVL	AGE	PA	R	2B	3B	HR	RBI	BB	K	SB	CS	Whiff%	AVG/OBP/SLG	DRC+	BABIP	BRR	DRP	WARP
2021	MID	AA	22	229	31	9	2	6	31	18	46	8	6		.319/.374/.471	111	.381	-0.8	SS(26): -1.6, 2B(22): 3.0	1.1
2021	LV	AAA	22	151	17	8	0	0	10	11	30	4	1		.243/.302/.301	84	.308	0.8	SS(22): -2.0, 2B(14): 0.6	0.1
2022	LV	AAA	23	206	31	10	0	2	16	27	34	10	2	24.2%	.266/.371/.358	100	.321	1.8	SS(39): 2.6, 2B(7): -0.5	0.9
2022	OAK	MLB	23	326	31	13	0	4	19	19	64	3	2	23.2%	.207/.256/.291	82	.250	-2.3	SS(60): 6.5, 2B(43): 0	0.8
2023 DC	*OAK*	*MLB*	*24*	*521*	*43*	*19*	*2*	*4*	*35*	*36*	*103*	*13*	*4*	*23.5%*	*.231/.290/.315*	*72*	*.283*	*1.0*	*SS 5*	*0.4*

Comparables: Daniel Castro (76), Dixon Machado (75), Marwin Gonzalez (66)

Allen's big-league debut was more fraught than most, as the dynamic defender was tasked with replacing a resurgent Elvis Andrus, who'd been released in a naked attempt to help reduce costs. The good news: Allen was billed as a stellar glove at the six, and in the field the former Olympian did not disappoint. But he didn't merely fail to adequately replace Andrus at the plate—he may have had A's fans pining for the days of Franklin Barreto's or Adam Rosales' bats. Add up the good (glove) and the bad (bat) and Allen wasn't quite ready to emerge as a competent regular on a team bereft of them, but his glovework should afford him ample chance to do so.

Euribiel Angeles IF Born: 05/11/02 Age: 21 Bats: R Throws: R Height: 5'11" Weight: 175 lb. Origin: International Free Agent, 2018

YEAR	TEAM	LVL	AGE	PA	R	2B	3B	HR	RBI	BB	K	SB	CS	Whiff%	AVG/OBP/SLG	DRC+	BABIP	BRR	DRP	WARP
2021	LE	A	19	405	65	22	6	3	56	32	61	18	6		.343/.397/.461	117	.399	1.3	SS(41): 0.2, 2B(28): -1.2, 3B(14): -0.9	2.0
2021	FW	A+	19	86	12	4	0	1	8	8	16	1	1		.264/.369/.361	104	.327	1.6	3B(9): 0.4, SS(8): 0.8, 2B(1): 0.1	0.6
2022	LAN	A+	20	388	29	19	1	2	32	17	58	8	6		.278/.316/.353	108	.325	-1.9	SS(49): -0.5, 2B(34): 1.4, 3B(5): -0.3	1.4
2023 non-DC	*OAK*	*MLB*	*21*	*251*	*20*	*10*	*1*	*1*	*20*	*11*	*40*	*6*	*4*	*20.1%*	*.261/.301/.342*	*80*	*.308*	*-1.2*	*2B 0, 3B 0*	*-0.1*

Comparables: Hanser Alberto (70), Richard Urena (65), Josh Vitters (62)

After winning a minor-league batting title at the age of 19, any misstep was going to make Angeles' follow-up campaign look disappointing. Perhaps that's why it feels as though his unremarkable first season in Oakland's system was so underwhelming. Despite boasting outstanding hand-eye coordination and bat-to-ball skills, Angeles took his hyper-aggressive approach at the plate a bit too far. He struggled to get on base much until the end of the year, then appeared in just 23 games between August and September. It remains to be seen if Angeles—the key piece headed back to the A's in the Sean Manaea trade—will emerge as an everyday option at second base or as more of a contact-first utilityman. Either way, he'll need to lay off advanced breaking pitches if he wants to earn another batting title in the future.

Skye Bolt CF Born: 01/15/94 Age: 29 Bats: S Throws: R Height: 6'2" Weight: 180 lb. Origin: Round 4, 2015 Draft (#128 overall)

YEAR	TEAM	LVL	AGE	PA	R	2B	3B	HR	RBI	BB	K	SB	CS	Whiff%	AVG/OBP/SLG	DRC+	BABIP	BRR	DRP	WARP
2021	LV	AAA	27	199	41	12	2	9	29	32	43	5	0		.387/.492/.650	131	.482	2.3	CF(41): 1.9, LF(4): 0.0, RF(4): -0.4	1.9
2021	SF	MLB	27	1	0	0	0	0	0	0	1	0	0	33.3%	.000/.000/.000	91			LF(1): -0.2	0.0
2021	OAK	MLB	27	59	5	1	0	1	4	1	14	2	0	23.2%	.089/.105/.161	80	.098	0.3	CF(16): -1.3, LF(5): -0.2, RF(4): -0.1	0.0
2022	LV	AAA	28	104	15	7	0	4	23	7	23	1	1	21.7%	.326/.385/.526	98	.397	-0.1	CF(14): 0.2, RF(4): -0.4, LF(3): -0.2	0.2
2022	OAK	MLB	28	116	10	2	0	4	13	7	30	5	0	28.8%	.198/.259/.330	90	.233	2.0	CF(36): -0.9, RF(5): -0.3, LF(2): 0	0.4
2023 non-DC	*OAK*	*MLB*	*29*	*251*	*24*	*9*	*1*	*6*	*27*	*18*	*62*	*4*	*1*	*26.2%*	*.234/.297/.379*	*86*	*.293*	*2.6*	*CF 1, RF 0*	*0.7*

Comparables: Logan Schafer (56), Keon Broxton (56), Joe Mather (53)

If Bolt were a superhero, as his name implies, he'd be one cut from Spider-Man's cloth. He's agile and well-liked, but most of all he's inherited some Peter Parker-ass luck, always catching bad breaks despite good intentions. Just look at his 2022: Even though he logged the most MLB plate appearances of his career, he struggled at the plate, suffered three injuries (including two leg issues that threaten to rob him of his best asset, his speed) and even vomited mid-game after eating a bad sausage. Despite all this, he battled on and earned his hero moment: an August walk-off homer against the Marlins that would fit as a splash page in any comic book climax.

Henry Bolte OF Born: 08/04/03 Age: 19 Bats: R Throws: R Height: 6'3" Weight: 195 lb. Origin: Round 2, 2022 Draft (#56 overall)

YEAR	TEAM	LVL	AGE	PA	R	2B	3B	HR	RBI	BB	K	SB	CS	Whiff%	AVG/OBP/SLG	DRC+	BABIP	BRR	DRP	WARP
2022	ATH	ROK	18	39	5	0	0	0	2	5	19	0	1		.212/.333/.212		.500			
2023										*No projection*										

Few ballplayers have a shorter distance between their old stomping grounds (Palo Alto High School) and their MLB club's stadium (RingCentral Coliseum), but that doesn't mean that Bolte is close to the majors. The 19-year-old was the A's second-round pick based on his high-end athleticism, projectable physicality and enough raw power to break a dormitory window during the Area Code Games. But as many toolsy prep hitters learn the hard way, the road to the majors is paved by making consistent contact against high-end pitching. Bolte's young enough yet to shorten his swing path and prove he can square up more advanced offerings, but he's still a long way off for someone oh-so-close.

Jonah Bride 2B Born: 12/27/95 Age: 27 Bats: R Throws: R Height: 5'10" Weight: 200 lb. Origin: Round 23, 2018 Draft (#683 overall)

YEAR	TEAM	LVL	AGE	PA	R	2B	3B	HR	RBI	BB	K	SB	CS	Whiff%	AVG/OBP/SLG	DRC+	BABIP	BRR	DRP	WARP
2021	MSS	WIN	25	71	15	2	0	3	8	16	12	0	0		.250/.451/.462		.270			
2021	MID	AA	25	334	45	11	2	9	49	57	57	2	0		.265/.407/.424	132	.302	0.0	1B(45): -2.2, 3B(16): 0.5, 2B(9): 0.8	2.1
2022	MID	AA	26	87	18	9	0	4	22	11	11	0	0		.315/.402/.603	125	.317	0.4	C(10): -0.5, 3B(2): 0.1, 2B(1): -0.3	0.5
2022	LV	AAA	26	78	14	6	0	2	10	13	12	0	0	14.9%	.393/.526/.590	124	.468	-0.3	3B(7): 1.7, 2B(5): -0.8, 1B(3): 0.2	0.5
2022	OAK	MLB	26	187	17	4	0	1	6	19	32	1	0	17.1%	.204/.301/.247	97	.246	-2.3	2B(32): -1.1, 3B(21): 0.5, 1B(5): 0	0.2
2023 DC	*OAK*	*MLB*	*27*	*233*	*22*	*8*	*0*	*4*	*19*	*24*	*37*	*0*	*1*	*16.6%*	*.245/.336/.368*	*104*	*.277*	*0.6*	*2B 0, 3B 0*	*0.7*

Comparables: Paul Faries (51), Rob Refsnyder (50), Kyle Farmer (47)

The late-career pickup of a catcher's mitt certainly makes Bride more interesting, but has it really made the young utility player *better*? Before donning the tools of ignorance occasionally, he was rapidly aging out of prospectdom, as his above-average approach and contact skills weren't sharp enough tools to peg him as an MLB regular. Developing as a receiver is probably his best way to consistently make a roster, as it seems more likely that he can stand out behind the plate than at it. In short, it's smart for the A's to groom this Bride as a part-time backstop before they make a long-term commitment to him.

Seth Brown 1B Born: 07/13/92 Age: 30 Bats: L Throws: L Height: 6'1" Weight: 223 lb. Origin: Round 19, 2015 Draft (#578 overall)

YEAR	TEAM	LVL	AGE	PA	R	2B	3B	HR	RBI	BB	K	SB	CS	Whiff%	AVG/OBP/SLG	DRC+	BABIP	BRR	DRP	WARP
2020	OAK	MLB	27	5	0	0	0	0	0	0	2	0	0	55.6%	.000/.000/.000	84			1B(3): 0	
2021	OAK	MLB	28	307	43	13	1	20	48	23	89	4	1	32.4%	.214/.274/.480	99	.230	-1.4	RF(75): -1.7, LF(19): -0.5, 1B(6): 0.1	0.8
2022	OAK	MLB	29	382	36	19	2	17	49	29	92	8	1	29.7%	.231/.293/.443	105	.264	1.4	1B(84): 0, LF(38): -0.6, RF(32): -1.1	1.5
2023 DC	*OAK*	*MLB*	*30*	*538*	*55*	*22*	*3*	*25*	*62*	*45*	*146*	*10*	*3*	*29.8%*	*.235/.302/.450*	*104*	*.281*	*6.3*	*1B 0, CF 0*	*1.8*

Comparables: Luke Voit (58), Justin Bour (57), Logan Morrison (54)

Perhaps no one benefited more from Oakland's most recent teardown than Brown, which is ironic considering how tough the task of filling Matt Olson's shoes appeared to be. Instead of working half a corner outfield platoon, the big lefty emerged as a consistent presence in the center of Oakland's ever-shifting lineup. Splitting time between first base and the outfield, he made room for new players to get reps while swinging a reliable bat. He even shed his platoon label, facing southpaws with regularity by season's end. Better yet, Brown boosted his OPS by almost 200 points in the second half, morphing into a player more like Olson than we ever thought possible ... in that he could either be a steady, middle-of-the-order presence on the next good A's team, or valuable enough to be dealt for another wave of prospects.

Lawrence Butler RF Born: 07/10/00 Age: 22 Bats: L Throws: R Height: 6'3" Weight: 210 lb. Origin: Round 6, 2018 Draft (#173 overall)

YEAR	TEAM	LVL	AGE	PA	R	2B	3B	HR	RBI	BB	K	SB	CS	Whiff%	AVG/OBP/SLG	DRC+	BABIP	BRR	DRP	WARP
2021	STK	A	20	396	62	20	4	17	67	55	131	26	4		.263/.364/.499	104	.370	0.6	1B(47): -2.3, LF(25): 0.1, CF(11): 0.2	1.2
2021	LAN	A+	20	54	14	4	0	2	8	4	15	3	1		.340/.389/.540	95	.455	-0.5	1B(6): 2.0, RF(6): -0.6, CF(1): 0.2	0.2
2022	LAN	A+	21	333	52	19	3	11	41	40	105	13	5		.270/.357/.468	104	.384	-0.9	RF(40): -0.7, CF(13): 0.2, 1B(11): -0.8	1.7
2023 non-DC	*OAK*	*MLB*	*22*	*251*	*23*	*10*	*1*	*5*	*25*	*20*	*89*	*6*	*2*	*35.7%*	*.216/.284/.357*	*73*	*.326*	*2.0*	*1B 0, LF 0*	*-0.1*

Comparables: Ronald Guzmán (57), Casey Craig (56), Carlos Peguero (56)

Sometimes the fit is just too good: Butler is certainly *Athletic*. It's no surprise that the chiseled first baseman/outfielder hit the Arizona Fall League ahead of Oakland adding him to the 40-man roster: He needs the extra reps to prove he's more than a low-minors lottery ticket. Like most minor-league hitters, he struggles with off-speed pitches, but unlike many of his peers, he has a body that gives him perhaps the best pure power of any player in Oakland's system. He's also a plus runner with a solid approach, so there's hope that, even if he never makes consistent contact, he could emerge as a fine platoon first baseman with a fairly unique skill set.

Denzel Clarke CF Born: 05/01/00 Age: 23 Bats: R Throws: R Height: 6'5" Weight: 220 lb. Origin: Round 4, 2021 Draft (#127 overall)

YEAR	TEAM	LVL	AGE	PA	R	2B	3B	HR	RBI	BB	K	SB	CS	Whiff%	AVG/OBP/SLG	DRC+	BABIP	BRR	DRP	WARP
2022	STK	A	22	193	37	14	2	7	26	28	56	14	2		.295/.420/.545	119	.411	-1.5	CF(31): -0.2, RF(9): 0.5	0.8
2022	LAN	A+	22	218	30	9	2	8	21	28	79	16	1		.209/.317/.406	105	.307	1.0	CF(47): 5.0, RF(1): 0.3	1.2
2023 non-DC	*OAK*	*MLB*	*23*	*251*	*22*	*10*	*2*	*4*	*23*	*22*	*97*	*11*	*2*	*39.2%*	*.202/.285/.334*	*69*	*.329*	*6.7*	*LF 0, CF 0*	*0.4*

Comparables: Yusuf Carter (75), Brandon Downes (75), Jake Meyers (71)

We're still working on embedding video into the pages of this book, but if that tech existed, this would be the spot where we'd use it. Clarke's highlight-reel catch in last year's All-Star Futures Game is worth seeking out, and demonstrates the Canadian's world-class explosiveness and athleticism. He's already a gifted defender—even if his massive frame means he may eventually play most often in a corner—but he needs to work on his hitting skills after getting a later start in the sport. On a similar note, he still needs to figure out premium velocity and unlock some in-game power, too. Hopefully, his bat progresses to the point where his glove gets some play because if he eventually works his way up to the majors, we'll be raving about Clarke's GIF-able tools for years to come.

Ernie Clement 3B Born: 03/22/96 Age: 27 Bats: R Throws: R Height: 6'0" Weight: 170 lb. Origin: Round 4, 2017 Draft (#132 overall)

YEAR	TEAM	LVL	AGE	PA	R	2B	3B	HR	RBI	BB	K	SB	CS	Whiff%	AVG/OBP/SLG	DRC+	BABIP	BRR	DRP	WARP
2021	COL	AAA	25	138	11	12	1	1	10	9	22	2	1		.250/.294/.387	95	.288	0.2	3B(12): -1.4, SS(8): 1.3, 2B(7): 0.3	0.5
2021	CLE	MLB	25	133	16	4	0	3	9	7	19	0	1	16.5%	.231/.285/.339	98	.253	0.0	2B(22): -1, 3B(16): -1.1, LF(2): 0	0.2
2022	COL	AAA	26	87	13	2	1	4	17	6	8	0	0		.238/.291/.438	124	.221	0.3	2B(9): -0.6, 3B(8): -0.0, SS(6): 1.1	0.6
2022	CLE	MLB	26	161	18	3	0	0	6	11	24	0	1	16.3%	.200/.264/.221	91	.238	-2.4	3B(26): -1.2, 2B(15): 0.3, LF(11): -0.3	-0.1
2022	OAK	MLB	26	18	1	1	0	0	0	0	2	0	0	13.6%	.056/.056/.111	102	.063	-0.1	3B(4): -0.1, SS(1): -0.2	0.0
2023 non-DC	*OAK*	*MLB*	*27*	*251*	*19*	*9*	*1*	*3*	*18*	*14*	*33*	*4*	*3*	*16.5%*	*.236/.287/.330*	*74*	*.262*	*-0.5*	*3B 0, 2B 0*	*-0.2*

Comparables: Danny Worth (55), Emmanuel Burriss (54), Deven Marrero (54)

In his brief career Clement has come to epitomize the difference between "high contact" and "good contact." The fleet utility man is tough to strike out but rarely hits the ball hard or where they ain't, leading to a surprisingly low career batting average on balls in play and minimal over-the-fence power. Add in his aversion to walks and Clement does little to help his team at the dish. On the plus side he's a reliable glove anywhere on the diamond, though he's a bit stretched at shortstop or center field. The Guardians cut bait on Clement during their September pennant push, but the less aspirational A's grabbed him with the hope they can teach him the difference between a pitch he can hit and a pitch he should hit.

Aledmys Díaz UT Born: 08/01/90 Age: 32 Bats: R Throws: R Height: 6'1" Weight: 195 lb. Origin: International Free Agent, 2014

YEAR	TEAM	LVL	AGE	PA	R	2B	3B	HR	RBI	BB	K	SB	CS	Whiff%	AVG/OBP/SLG	DRC+	BABIP	BRR	DRP	WARP
2020	HOU	MLB	29	59	8	5	0	3	6	1	12	0	0	26.5%	.241/.254/.483	104	.256	0.7	2B(10): 0.3, 3B(3): 0, 1B(2): -0.1	0.3
2021	HOU	MLB	30	319	28	19	0	8	45	16	62	0	1	22.5%	.259/.317/.405	98	.304	-4.7	3B(30): -0.1, LF(15): -0.4, 2B(13): 0	0.4
2022	HOU	MLB	31	327	35	13	0	12	38	18	53	1	1	22.7%	.243/.287/.403	106	.256	-1.5	LF(28): 0.1, 2B(22): -0.2, SS(18): -1.5	0.9
2023 DC	*OAK*	*MLB*	*32*	*442*	*41*	*18*	*0*	*13*	*42*	*27*	*71*	*1*	*0*	*22.7%*	*.248/.302/.395*	*98*	*.269*	*-0.5*	*3B 1, 2B 0*	*0.9*

Comparables: Jim Fregosi (74), Hanley Ramirez (73), Harvey Kuenn (73)

One of Díaz's final acts as an Astro may also turn out to be his most memorable. The utilityman had the chance to be the extra-innings hero when he pinch-hit with Houston, down to their final out in Game 1 of the 2022 World Series. With two on and the Astros trailing by a run, Díaz not-so-subtly dropped his elbow into the path of a David Robertson inside curveball. He then suffered the ignominy of being called back to the box by umpire James Hoye after he'd trotted off toward first, informed in no uncertain terms that he had leaned into the pitch. Díaz subsequently grounded out to end the game and would never get on base as an Astro again. Now that he has a World Series ring, Díaz presumably decided it was time for something different—perhaps an opportunity to be more than just a utility player. He has yet to record 500 plate appearances in a season, but he'll soon get his best chance yet to do so after signing a two-year, $14.5 million deal with the A's. High-stakes moments are likely to be harder to come by.

Jordan Diaz DH Born: 08/13/00 Age: 22 Bats: R Throws: R Height: 5'10" Weight: 175 lb. Origin: International Free Agent, 2016

YEAR	TEAM	LVL	AGE	PA	R	2B	3B	HR	RBI	BB	K	SB	CS	Whiff%	AVG/OBP/SLG	DRC+	BABIP	BRR	DRP	WARP
2021	LAN	A+	20	365	46	24	1	13	56	25	58	2	3		.288/.337/.483	124	.311	0.2	3B(52): -4.5, 1B(23): 1.9, LF(4): -0.7	1.8
2022	MID	AA	21	407	48	26	0	15	58	22	61	0	0		.319/.361/.507	111	.348	0.8	1B(41): -2.5, 3B(7): -1.4, LF(2): -0.3	1.3
2022	LV	AAA	21	120	19	8	1	4	25	6	15	0	0	18.6%	.348/.383/.545	109	.372	-0.8	1B(3): -0.1, 2B(3): -0.8, 3B(3): -0.2	0.3
2022	OAK	MLB	21	51	3	3	0	0	1	2	7	0	0	20.4%	.265/.294/.327	103	.310	-0.2	2B(12): -1.2, 1B(1): 0	0.0
2023 DC	*OAK*	*MLB*	*22*	*198*	*17*	*8*	*0*	*4*	*18*	*9*	*33*	*0*	*0*	*22.0%*	*.268/.305/.396*	*99*	*.303*	*-0.9*	*2B -1, 1B 0*	*0.2*

Comparables: Luis Sardinas (62), Jose Altuve (57), Mark Lewis (57)

If at this time last year you projected Diaz would get regular reps in Oakland *at the keystone* of all places, then you probably drive either a DeLorean or a TARDIS. Sure, his reputation for having outstanding contact skills was well known, but it looked like he'd slide down the defensive spectrum to first base, not cop a few starts from Tony Kemp up the middle. Instead, Diaz mastered the Texas League and the PCL in his first stints at both stops and survived his trial-by-fire at second base all the while. As such, he looks like a non-traditional utility player: a right-handed bat who can stand at any base in the infield and wear down an opposing pitcher before lining the ball into play. All he needs now is to add a little oomph to that compact swing and he'll have mastered space, time and a potential long-term roster spot.

Zack Gelof 2B/3B Born: 10/19/99 Age: 23 Bats: R Throws: R Height: 6'3" Weight: 205 lb. Origin: Round 2, 2021 Draft (#60 overall)

YEAR	TEAM	LVL	AGE	PA	R	2B	3B	HR	RBI	BB	K	SB	CS	Whiff%	AVG/OBP/SLG	DRC+	BABIP	BRR	DRP	WARP
2021	STK	A	21	145	26	8	1	7	22	19	36	11	2		.298/.393/.548	120	.366	1.5	3B(30): -6.8	0.3
2021	LV	AAA	21	13	3	1	0	0	6	1	2	0	0		.583/.615/.667	90	.700	0.8	3B(3): 0.2	0.1
2022	MID	AA	22	402	54	16	2	13	61	47	110	9	2		.271/.356/.438	102	.358	-0.3	2B(53): -2.3, 3B(26): -1.9, CF(1): 0.5	0.8
2022	LV	AAA	22	38	7	1	0	5	5	3	11	1	0	30.4%	.257/.316/.714	103	.211	0.5	2B(9): -1.1	0.1
2023 DC	*OAK*	*MLB*	*23*	*29*	*2*	*1*	*0*	*0*	*2*	*2*	*8*	*0*	*0*	*31.3%*	*.227/.293/.369*	*85*	*.302*	*0.1*	*3B 0*	*0.0*

Comparables: Jimmy Paredes (63), Jesmuel Valentín (62), Aarom Baldiris (57)

Gelof has been a fast mover since his 2021 signing, spending most of the past year in Double-A before a late-season promotion to Las Vegas. He then put up a strong showing in the AFL, where he was a near-miss for the Fall Stars Game. He didn't post the eye-popping numbers you'd hope for from a bat-first third base prospect—in part because he missed about six weeks with a labrum tear in his non-throwing shoulder—but then again, maybe he's not going to be a third baseman after all. Gelof got plenty of reps at the keystone in 2022 and played there almost exclusively in Arizona. There's solid upside here, and he'll likely get his first crack at the big leagues sometime in 2023.

Tony Kemp 2B/LF Born: 10/31/91 Age: 31 Bats: L Throws: R Height: 5'6" Weight: 160 lb. Origin: Round 5, 2013 Draft (#137 overall)

YEAR	TEAM	LVL	AGE	PA	R	2B	3B	HR	RBI	BB	K	SB	CS	Whiff%	AVG/OBP/SLG	DRC+	BABIP	BRR	DRP	WARP
2020	OAK	MLB	28	114	15	5	0	0	4	15	14	3	1	13.6%	.247/.363/.301	101	.284	1.1	2B(43): 0.1, LF(3): -0.2	0.5
2021	OAK	MLB	29	397	54	16	3	8	37	52	51	8	2	15.6%	.279/.382/.418	110	.304	2.6	2B(89): -0.4, LF(49): -0.3, SS(1): 0	2.2
2022	OAK	MLB	30	558	61	24	2	7	46	45	69	11	1	13.2%	.235/.307/.334	94	.259	2.9	2B(89): 0.2, LF(65): -3.2	1.3
2023 DC	*OAK*	*MLB*	*31*	*512*	*50*	*19*	*3*	*8*	*36*	*47*	*56*	*10*	*2*	*14.0%*	*.251/.330/.361*	*98*	*.270*	*6.5*	*LF 1, 2B 1*	*2.0*

Comparables: Mark Lemke (51), Dee Strange-Gordon (49), Ehire Adrianza (49)

Too much of the commentary about Kemp and players like him focuses on what he lacks: vertical inches, towering home runs or dollars on a big-time free agent contract. Instead, let's focus on what he has in abundance: speed, versatility and toughness. Setting the table for one of the American League's most dismal offenses would take a toll on anyone, and Kemp's first-half performance was a step down from his breakout 2021 campaign. But Kemp was in many ways the rhythm section of the Athletics, a consistent presence with a grinder mentality who picked up the tempo in the second half. He may not have stolen many bases, but he was a top-20 base-runner overall by our BRR metric, and he seamlessly shifted from infield to outfield as the situation demanded. As second-division regulars go, Kemp is first class.

Shea Langeliers C Born: 11/18/97 Age: 25 Bats: R Throws: R Height: 6'0" Weight: 205 lb. Origin: Round 1, 2019 Draft (#9 overall)

YEAR	TEAM	LVL	AGE	PA	R	2B	3B	HR	RBI	BB	K	SB	CS	Whiff%	AVG/OBP/SLG	DRC+	BABIP	BRR	DRP	WARP
2021	MIS	AA	23	370	56	13	0	22	52	36	97	1	0		.258/.338/.498	136	.299	0.3	C(79): -12.9	1.6
2021	GWN	AAA	23	14	3	2	0	0	1	3	6	0	0		.182/.357/.364	79	.400	-0.3	C(3): 0.3	0.0
2022	LV	AAA	24	402	62	19	2	19	56	43	88	5	1	29.6%	.283/.366/.510	97	.327	-2.2	C(79): -7.3	0.2
2022	OAK	MLB	24	153	14	10	1	6	22	9	53	0	0	42.9%	.218/.261/.430	79	.294	-0.5	C(17): -0.4	0.0
2023 DC	*OAK*	*MLB*	*25*	*496*	*44*	*19*	*1*	*15*	*47*	*35*	*163*	*3*	*1*	*36.6%*	*.221/.282/.375*	*81*	*.303*	*0.6*	*C -3*	*0.1*

Comparables: Kennys Vargas (69), Chris Carter (65), Yan Gomes (65)

YEAR	TEAM	P. COUNT	FRM RUNS	BLK RUNS	THRW RUNS	TOT RUNS
2021	MIS	11234	-13.8	0.4	0.5	-13.0
2022	LV	11624	-7.0	0.1	0.4	-6.5
2022	OAK	2299	-0.5	-0.1	0.2	-0.4
2023	*OAK*	*12025*	*-2.2*	*-0.3*	*-0.2*	*-2.7*

At the end of Steven King's *The Langoliers*, the protagonists have landed in an airport and are waiting for time to catch up to them. Sound familiar, Shea? After a year in Atlanta's system where he emerged as one of the best catching prospects in baseball, he was traded to Oakland on the cusp of his emergence so he could … sit behind one of the game's finest backstops in Sean Murphy and fill in as a designated hitter. Oh, and fellow highly touted backstops Tyler Soderstrom and Daniel Susac are now breathing down his neck. A position switch is out of the question: Langeliers has to stay behind the plate, as his pop time was one of the best in baseball, and there are too many holes in his swing for his bat to carry him in a corner. The A's apparently agreed, shipping Murphy to the Braves for an … interesting … return in December. It's Langeliers' job to keep or to lose now, at least until he gets expensive.

Ramón Laureano OF

Born: 07/15/94 Age: 28 Bats: R Throws: R Height: 5'11" Weight: 203 lb. Origin: Round 16, 2014 Draft (#466 overall)

YEAR	TEAM	LVL	AGE	PA	R	2B	3B	HR	RBI	BB	K	SB	CS	Whiff%	AVG/OBP/SLG	DRC+	BABIP	BRR	DRP	WARP
2020	OAK	MLB	25	222	27	8	1	6	25	24	58	2	1	25.0%	.213/.338/.366	98	.270	0.6	CF(53): 0.7	0.8
2021	OAK	MLB	26	378	43	21	2	14	39	27	98	12	5	27.1%	.246/.317/.443	100	.304	-0.4	CF(75): 1.9, RF(8): 1.4	1.8
2022	LV	AAA	27	44	10	2	0	0	2	5	11	2	0	27.9%	.135/.273/.189	90	.192	2.1	RF(5): 1.2, CF(3): -0.5	0.4
2022	OAK	MLB	27	383	49	18	0	13	34	25	104	11	6	30.4%	.211/.287/.376	94	.262	-0.6	RF(71): 1, CF(34): -2.5	0.7
2023 DC	*OAK*	*MLB*	*28*	*561*	*56*	*23*	*2*	*18*	*52*	*40*	*149*	*22*	*7*	*28.7%*	*.230/.305/.398*	*97*	*.286*	*3.5*	*RF -4, CF -1*	*0.8*

Comparables: Matt Kemp (64), Austin Jackson (63), Richard Hidalgo (58)

With apologies to Stomper, the real elephant in the room at the start of the A's season was Laureano's PED suspension. It cost him April, but upon his return, he appeared in much the same shape as in previous years. His arm and speed on the bases were still there, and compared to the rest of Oakland's roster, he was a dynamic power hitter. But by the second half, it became clear that he was not the same defensive player as earlier in his career. A hamstring injury derailed his last couple of weeks of the season, and that might've been for the best—his numbers in August and September were dreadful, including zero walks in 86 plate appearances. If either his lower body injury or questionable approach lingers he may profile better as a third or fourth outfielder on a good team than as an ascending star on a bad one.

Jed Lowrie DH

Born: 04/17/84 Age: 39 Bats: S Throws: R Height: 6'0" Weight: 180 lb. Origin: Round 1, 2005 Draft (#45 overall)

YEAR	TEAM	LVL	AGE	PA	R	2B	3B	HR	RBI	BB	K	SB	CS	Whiff%	AVG/OBP/SLG	DRC+	BABIP	BRR	DRP	WARP
2021	OAK	MLB	37	512	55	28	0	14	69	49	108	0	0	24.3%	.245/.318/.398	98	.289	-3.5	2B(71): 1.2, 3B(1): 0	1.2
2022	OAK	MLB	38	184	14	5	0	3	16	15	39	1	0	25.6%	.180/.245/.263	86	.213	0.1	1B(3): -0.3, 2B(2): 0.1	0.1
2023 non-DC	*OAK*	*MLB*	*39*	*251*	*24*	*11*	*0*	*6*	*26*	*20*	*56*	*0*	*0*	*25.1%*	*.234/.300/.372*	*85*	*.282*	*-0.5*	*2B 1, 1B 0*	*0.3*

Comparables: Cal Ripken Jr. (60), Rich Aurilia (60), Alan Trammell (58)

Lowrie's shapeshifter of a career likely ends not where it began in Boston, but on the east side of the San Francisco Bay, where it peaked half a decade ago. His MLB journey took him all over the country (Texas and both coasts) and the infield (almost 500 starts at both second base and shortstop, and over 100 more at the corners). He balanced All-Star-level seasons with injury-shortened ones, plus the occasional misfires like his Mets contract and historically dire postseason performance. Despite all the changes, the fits, the starts and the injured list stints, he remained something of a prototypical A's player for the post-*Moneyball* era: hardly ever in high demand, possessed of patience, versatility and a little pop, and long willing to grind it out in one of the league's most barren markets.

Vimael Machín 3B

Born: 09/25/93 Age: 29 Bats: L Throws: R Height: 5'11" Weight: 185 lb. Origin: Round 10, 2015 Draft (#293 overall)

YEAR	TEAM	LVL	AGE	PA	R	2B	3B	HR	RBI	BB	K	SB	CS	Whiff%	AVG/OBP/SLG	DRC+	BABIP	BRR	DRP	WARP
2020	CAG	WIN	26	69	8	2	0	0	7	6	8	1	0		.345/.435/.379		.392			
2020	OAK	MLB	26	71	11	2	0	0	0	8	10	0	0	20.8%	.206/.296/.238	93	.245	1.6	3B(10): 0.6, SS(6): -0.5, 2B(3): 0.1	0.3
2021	CAG	WIN	27	123	17	8	0	2	18	12	9	1	0		.287/.374/.417		.299			
2021	LV	AAA	27	393	65	17	6	11	58	49	72	2	1		.295/.389/.479	109	.344	0.6	3B(58): -4.0, 2B(26): 0.7, SS(4): 0.7	1.5
2021	OAK	MLB	27	37	1	0	0	0	1	3	10	0	0	28.8%	.125/.200/.125	79	.182	-0.2	SS(8): -0.2, 2B(3): 0.1, 3B(3): 0.1	0.0
2022	LV	AAA	28	292	41	16	3	4	49	33	30	0	0	12.5%	.324/.401/.457	117	.353	-0.1	3B(36): -0.8, SS(16): -0.1, 2B(11): 0.8	1.4
2022	OAK	MLB	28	253	26	12	0	1	13	25	47	1	1	17.9%	.220/.300/.287	90	.270	-1.0	3B(68): 0.6, SS(1): 0	0.3
2023 non-DC	*OAK*	*MLB*	*29*	*251*	*23*	*9*	*1*	*3*	*23*	*23*	*38*	*1*	*0*	*17.6%*	*.248/.323/.356*	*92*	*.283*	*0.6*	*3B 0, 2B 0*	*0.3*

Comparables: Ed Giovanola (51), Matt Tolbert (50), Logan Schafer (49)

In Robert Jordan's seminal fantasy series *The Wheel of Time*, **Machin** Shin is the black wind of madness. Omnipresent, lurking and **filling the gaps** in the dark corners of the Ways, it forces the protagonists out of their alternate dimension and **back up** to the real world. This being is mostly formless and intangible, never truly **in the field** of vision, and has no distinct plot **utility** other than to evoke a sense of danger. Though **never making solid contact** with the heroes from Emond's Field, this presence **lurks in the background**, a constant reminder that we are **nearly powerless** against fear ... and in Vimael's case, also against anything off-speed.

Max Muncy SS

Born: 08/25/02 Age: 20 Bats: R Throws: R Height: 6'1" Weight: 180 lb. Origin: Round 1, 2021 Draft (#25 overall)

YEAR	TEAM	LVL	AGE	PA	R	2B	3B	HR	RBI	BB	K	SB	CS	Whiff%	AVG/OBP/SLG	DRC+	BABIP	BRR	DRP	WARP
2021	ATH	ROK	18	34	3	0	0	0	4	3	12	1	0		.129/.206/.129		.211			
2022	STK	A	19	365	50	16	1	16	51	51	109	6	5		.230/.352/.447	108	.298	2.5	SS(77): -1.1, 2B(2): 0.1	1.6
2022	LAN	A+	19	190	19	12	2	3	19	18	60	13	1		.226/.305/.375	84	.327	1.7	SS(35): 1.4	0.5
2023 non-DC	*OAK*	*MLB*	*20*	*251*	*20*	*10*	*1*	*4*	*22*	*19*	*88*	*5*	*2*	*35.4%*	*.191/.263/.312*	*55*	*.287*	*1.3*	*2B 0, SS 0*	*-0.5*

Comparables: Hanser Alberto (55), Ian Desmond (54), Lucius Fox (54)

What are the odds that two MLB players would share not only the same name, but also kick off their careers with the same franchise? Somewhere between "getting struck by lightning" and "hitting the Powerball number" exist the Maxes Muncy, the younger of whom is starting to translate his power into on-field production as he enters his age-20 season. He's far more athletic than his cross-state counterpart in L.A.—yes, both in team *and* in physicality—but there are still questions as to if he can make consistent contact. Barring massive progress, they're likely to linger until, one way or another, there's only one Max Muncy left in affiliated baseball.

Sheldon Neuse IF
Born: 12/10/94 Age: 28 Bats: R Throws: R Height: 6'0" Weight: 232 lb. Origin: Round 2, 2016 Draft (#58 overall)

YEAR	TEAM	LVL	AGE	PA	R	2B	3B	HR	RBI	BB	K	SB	CS	Whiff%	AVG/OBP/SLG	DRC+	BABIP	BRR	DRP	WARP
2021	OKC	AAA	26	349	57	13	3	13	56	29	84	6	0		.293/.352/.478	103	.357	2.6	2B(30): -0.3, 3B(20): 1.1, SS(17): -0.8	1.7
2021	LAD	MLB	26	66	6	1	0	3	4	1	26	1	1	40.0%	.169/.182/.323	73	.222	0.1	2B(13): -0.3, 3B(8): -0.3, LF(4): -0.3	-0.1
2022	LV	AAA	27	113	14	6	1	5	20	3	22	2	0	21.4%	.398/.407/.611	101	.458	0.5	3B(13): 1.4, 2B(4): -0.1, SS(3): -0.1	0.5
2022	OAK	MLB	27	293	25	4	2	4	26	20	80	6	1	27.1%	.214/.273/.288	76	.289	0.6	3B(44): -2, 2B(23): -0.5, 1B(13): 0	-0.2
2023 non-DC	*OAK*	*MLB*	*28*	*251*	*22*	*8*	*1*	*4*	*23*	*14*	*64*	*1*	*1*	*26.9%*	*.247/.296/.350*	*78*	*.324*	*1.1*	*3B 0, 2B 0*	*0.0*

Comparables: Deven Marrero (57), Emmanuel Burriss (56), Danny Worth (55)

This past season Neuse was given more chances than ever to prove that his minor-league power numbers could translate to The Show. Unfortunately, he only managed 10 extra-base hits in a half-season's worth of plate appearances, making his second stint in Oakland as uninspiring as his first. While it's easy to look upon his big-league performance with dismay, a glass-is-half-full take looks like this: He's a pretty great Triple-A hitter! Neuse may yet get more chances to prove he can reach base often enough to slot in as an MLB utility man. Until then, he'll be the type of player who can crush it in the second-best league in the country and fill in when a second-division team needs an injury replacement.

Cristian Pache CF
Born: 11/19/98 Age: 24 Bats: R Throws: R Height: 6'2" Weight: 215 lb. Origin: International Free Agent, 2015

YEAR	TEAM	LVL	AGE	PA	R	2B	3B	HR	RBI	BB	K	SB	CS	Whiff%	AVG/OBP/SLG	DRC+	BABIP	BRR	DRP	WARP
2020	ATL	MLB	21	4	0	0	0	0	0	0	2	0	0	33.3%	.250/.250/.250	96	.500		LF(2): 0.2	0.0
2021	GWN	AAA	22	353	50	15	0	11	44	30	97	9	7		.265/.330/.414	89	.347	0.6	CF(79): -3.9, RF(4): 0.1	0.5
2021	ATL	MLB	22	68	6	3	0	1	4	2	25	0	0	36.9%	.111/.152/.206	65	.162	1.2	CF(22): -1.7	-0.1
2022	LV	AAA	23	171	15	8	1	4	20	11	39	1	1	27.5%	.248/.298/.389	80	.302	0.3	CF(39): -3.1, LF(1): 0.1, RF(1): 0.1	-0.3
2022	OAK	MLB	23	260	18	5	2	3	18	15	70	2	2	31.0%	.166/.218/.241	68	.220	2.4	CF(90): -0.8	0.1
2023 DC	*OAK*	*MLB*	*24*	*244*	*18*	*8*	*1*	*3*	*18*	*14*	*65*	*4*	*3*	*30.4%*	*.218/.267/.324*	*65*	*.287*	*-1.4*	*CF 0, LF 0*	*-0.5*

Comparables: Magneuris Sierra (46), Melky Cabrera (45), Byron Buxton (43)

It was easy to call Pache a change-of-scenery candidate ahead of his trade to Oakland in the Matt Olson deal. Despite scuffling in the upper minors, he had (and has) the physical tools and prospect pedigree to emerge as an elite defensive center fielder and everyday contributor. But there's no way to sugarcoat it: Pache was an absolute disaster at the plate in 2022. He was almost completely unable to clear the infield, beating everything into the ground or popping it straight up into the sky. He was better in a limited sample in Las Vegas, but only in the sense that he couldn't possibly have been worse than he was in the bigs. Now entering his age-24 season, Pache is seemingly in need of a complete swing overhaul if he wants to stay in the majors as anything more than a defensive replacement.

Jace Peterson 3B
Born: 05/09/90 Age: 33 Bats: L Throws: R Height: 6'0" Weight: 215 lb. Origin: Round 1, 2011 Draft (#58 overall)

YEAR	TEAM	LVL	AGE	PA	R	2B	3B	HR	RBI	BB	K	SB	CS	Whiff%	AVG/OBP/SLG	DRC+	BABIP	BRR	DRP	WARP
2020	MIL	MLB	30	61	6	1	0	2	5	15	20	1	0	34.6%	.200/.393/.356	97	.292	-0.4	RF(13): -0.5, 1B(4): 0, 3B(4): 0	0.0
2021	NAS	AAA	31	64	12	4	0	5	19	9	19	1	0		.236/.344/.582	122	.258	-0.2	2B(7): -0.6, 1B(3): 0.0, 3B(3): 0.0	0.3
2021	MIL	MLB	31	302	36	11	1	6	31	38	68	10	1	27.3%	.247/.348/.367	90	.310	3.1	2B(35): -0.6, 1B(26): 0, RF(17): 0.2	0.9
2022	MIL	MLB	32	328	44	14	2	8	34	33	85	12	1	27.1%	.236/.316/.382	87	.303	1.8	3B(86): -1, RF(12): 1, 1B(5): 0	0.6
2023 DC	*OAK*	*MLB*	*33*	*392*	*34*	*15*	*1*	*9*	*33*	*40*	*93*	*11*	*2*	*27.0%*	*.221/.308/.359*	*87*	*.273*	*7.0*	*3B 0, 2B 0*	*0.9*

Comparables: Nick Punto (65), Mark McLemore (57), Mike Gallego (53)

Capable of playing a plethora of positions? Check. Good baserunning instincts? Check. A surprisingly solid bat, considering he's often subject to the pinch-hit penalty? Check. Peterson's well-rounded skill set basically looks the same from season to season, but he went the extra mile in his most recent one, hitting for a bit more power and swiping more bases without meaningfully succumbing to the league-wide drop-off in offense. Every good team needs a competent, reliable utility guy, but they're often underappreciated and altogether rarer than you might think. The Brewers were lucky they got to rely on Peterson: There aren't many players you can slot into second base *or* left field without inadvertently creating fodder for sports fail compilations on YouTube. The A's will now benefit from his versatility after inking him to a two-year deal this winter.

Manny Piña C
Born: 06/05/87 Age: 36 Bats: R Throws: R Height: 6'0" Weight: 222 lb. Origin: International Free Agent, 2004

YEAR	TEAM	LVL	AGE	PA	R	2B	3B	HR	RBI	BB	K	SB	CS	Whiff%	AVG/OBP/SLG	DRC+	BABIP	BRR	DRP	WARP
2020	MIL	MLB	33	45	4	1	0	2	5	3	11	0	0	27.6%	.231/.333/.410	100	.269	-0.2	C(13): 1.7	0.3
2021	MIL	MLB	34	208	27	6	0	13	33	22	38	0	0	23.8%	.189/.293/.439	111	.162	0.4	C(65): 5.9	1.8
2022	ATL	MLB	35	17	1	0	0	0	2	1	1	0	0	13.8%	.143/.235/.143	107	.143	0.3	C(5): 0.1	0.1
2023 DC	*OAK*	*MLB*	*36*	*283*	*23*	*9*	*0*	*6*	*23*	*24*	*59*	*0*	*0*	*23.5%*	*.217/.299/.338*	*82*	*.257*	*-2.6*	*C 8*	*0.9*

Comparables: Chris Iannetta (50), Miguel Olivo (48), Ramon Hernandez (48)

YEAR	TEAM	P. COUNT	FRM RUNS	BLK RUNS	THRW RUNS	TOT RUNS
2020	MIL	1750	1.7	0.0	0.0	1.7
2021	MIL	7534	4.4	0.6	0.4	5.3
2022	ATL	787	0.0	0.0	0.0	0.0
2023	*OAK*	*9620*	*6.8*	*0.2*	*-0.3*	*6.7*

On April 24, Piña made a nifty play on a broken-bat dribbler. Though the ball was nearer to the mound, the backstop fielded it with his bare hand, whirled and fired, nabbing Jorge Soler with a looping, off-balance throw. This ended up being the highlight of Piña's season, as the veteran produced virtually no offense in the handful of games in which he appeared. As it turns out, Piña got off to a slow start with his bat for good reason: The wrist discomfort he'd been suffering was discovered to be ligament and cartilage damage, requiring season-ending surgery. Once Piña returns, the grind of being a veteran backup catcher awaits, the same as it ever was—only now he'll be grinding in Oakland.

Esteury Ruiz OF Born: 02/15/99 Age: 24 Bats: R Throws: R Height: 6'0" Weight: 169 lb. Origin: International Free Agent, 2015

YEAR	TEAM	LVL	AGE	PA	R	2B	3B	HR	RBI	BB	K	SB	CS	Whiff%	AVG/OBP/SLG	DRC+	BABIP	BRR	DRP	WARP
2021	SA	AA	22	353	52	16	2	10	42	28	73	36	7		.249/.328/.411	106	.294	1.7	LF(32): 6.0, CF(26): 0.6, RF(20): 0.7	2.2
2022	SA	AA	23	232	54	17	2	9	37	32	40	37	5		.344/.474/.611	141	.398	1.1	CF(42): -1.8	2.0
2022	ELP	AAA	23	142	30	6	0	4	9	20	25	23	4	26.7%	.315/.457/.477	111	.378	0.3	CF(14): -0.6, RF(13): 2.3, LF(2): 0.1	0.5
2022	NAS	AAA	23	167	30	10	0	3	19	14	29	25	5	25.0%	.329/.402/.459	106	.395	1.9	LF(15): -0.1, CF(14): -0.0, RF(3): 0.5	0.6
2022	SD	MLB	23	27	1	1	1	0	2	0	5	1	2	23.1%	.222/.222/.333	94	.273	-0.5	RF(6): 0.1, LF(5): -0.7, CF(5): -0.2	-0.1
2022	MIL	MLB	23	9	2	0	0	0	0	1	2	0	0	22.2%	.000/.111/.000	91		0.0	LF(2): 0	0.0
2023 DC	*OAK*	*MLB*	*24*	*335*	*31*	*13*	*1*	*7*	*29*	*26*	*71*	*36*	*7*	*24.9%*	*.247/.324/.376*	*99*	*.299*	*14.8*	*CF 0, LF 0*	*2.4*

Comparables: Junior Lake (58), Trayvon Robinson (52), Starling Marte (52)

Ruiz went on a tear to begin 2022, prompting some to anoint him a top prospect. But underlying data revealed poor exit velocities, and we can infer that a good chunk of Ruiz's extra-base hits were the product of his speed rather than his power. Once a future Padre, Ruiz came to Milwaukee in the now-infamous Josh Hader trade before getting shipped to Oakland this winter as part of the Sean Murphy deal. His big-league debut with the Brewers highlighted several weaknesses, such as a lack of plate discipline and poor pitch recognition. That doesn't signify that Ruiz's recent minor-league heroics are meaningless—he now projects to have a slightly better hit tool than before—but, as Flavor Flav says, don't believe the hype. He looks more like a backup outfielder and legitimate stolen base threat than a future regular, but perhaps the A's see something in his profile that most don't.

Kevin Smith SS/3B Born: 07/04/96 Age: 27 Bats: R Throws: R Height: 6'0" Weight: 190 lb. Origin: Round 4, 2017 Draft (#129 overall)

YEAR	TEAM	LVL	AGE	PA	R	2B	3B	HR	RBI	BB	K	SB	CS	Whiff%	AVG/OBP/SLG	DRC+	BABIP	BRR	DRP	WARP
2021	BUF	AAA	24	410	65	27	4	21	69	46	97	18	3		.285/.370/.561	130	.333	0.6	SS(66): 6.3, 3B(17): 2.1, LF(4): 0.2	3.5
2021	TOR	MLB	24	36	2	0	0	1	1	3	11	0	0	33.8%	.094/.194/.188	87	.100	0.5	3B(14): 0.2, LF(1): -0.1	0.1
2022	LV	AAA	25	370	44	16	2	13	49	29	112	6	1	31.9%	.268/.331/.446	77	.360	-0.4	SS(78): -0.6, 3B(7): -0.8	-0.2
2022	OAK	MLB	25	151	9	9	1	2	13	7	42	4	0	30.6%	.180/.216/.302	74	.237	-0.7	3B(39): 1.2, SS(10): -0.9	-0.1
2023 DC	*OAK*	*MLB*	*26*	*93*	*8*	*3*	*0*	*3*	*9*	*5*	*26*	*1*	*1*	*31.5%*	*.224/.277/.397*	*86*	*.283*	*1.0*	*3B 0, SS 0*	*0.2*

Comparables: Chris Taylor (69), Josh Bell (67), Yadiel Rivera (66)

In what could be considered an inversion of the career arc of the critically acclaimed director with whom he shares a name, Smith started his season with a *Jay and Silent Bob Reboot*-level whimper. Anointed the Opening Day third baseman after the Matt Chapman trade, Smith pressed at the plate and swiftly found himself at a *Yoga Hosers*-esque nadir. Though his slump persisted, once back in Las Vegas he produced a solid run of hits, much as his namesake did in the 90s. If he can stay his aggression and take his dinger-happy approach with him back to Oakland, his future—unlike his "View Askewniverse" counterpart's—can still be bright.

★ ★ ★ *2023 Top 101 Prospect* **#78** ★ ★ ★

Tyler Soderstrom 1B/C Born: 11/24/01 Age: 21 Bats: L Throws: R Height: 6'2" Weight: 200 lb. Origin: Round 1, 2020 Draft (#26 overall)

YEAR	TEAM	LVL	AGE	PA	R	2B	3B	HR	RBI	BB	K	SB	CS	Whiff%	AVG/OBP/SLG	DRC+	BABIP	BRR	DRP	WARP
2021	STK	A	19	254	39	20	1	12	49	27	61	2	1		.306/.390/.568	125	.373	-1.2	C(38): -3.6, 1B(9): -1.0	1.0
2022	LAN	A+	20	371	47	19	3	20	71	29	99	0	0		.260/.323/.513	123	.306	0.1	1B(39): -0.2, C(31): 1.6	2.1
2022	MID	AA	20	147	17	1	2	8	28	10	33	0	1		.278/.327/.496	118	.305	-0.3	1B(17): -0.1, C(16): -0.1	0.7
2022	LV	AAA	20	38	2	1	0	1	6	1	13	0	0	33.3%	.297/.316/.405	82	.435	0.3	C(5): -0.3, 1B(3): 0.4	0.1
2023 DC	*OAK*	*MLB*	*21*	*133*	*12*	*5*	*0*	*4*	*12*	*7*	*37*	*0*	*1*	*29.4%*	*.229/.279/.390*	*82*	*.292*	*0.3*	*C 0, 1B 0*	*0.1*

Comparables: Josh Naylor (63), Chris Marrero (63), Nick Williams (58)

YEAR	TEAM	P. COUNT	FRM RUNS	BLK RUNS	THRW RUNS	TOT RUNS
2021	STK	5254	-2.2	-1.5	0.3	-3.5
2022	LAN	3857	2.0	-0.2	0.0	1.8
2022	MID	2091	-0.8	-0.1	0.8	-0.1
2022	LV	766	-0.1	0.0	0.0	-0.1
2023	*OAK*	*2405*	*-0.5*	*-0.2*	*0.0*	*-0.7*

It was an interesting year for the A's top prospect. He ranked 23rd on BP's preseason top-101 list, then tumbled to 47th in our midseason top-50 update. Despite that, he ended the season with 29 homers across three minor-league levels and looking very much like a guy who'll be ready for a major-league call-up early in 2023. So what gives? Despite adding size and strength to his frame, Soderstrom never truly dominated at any level offensively. He struggled through a thumb injury at the start of the season, and, though he's still getting reps as a catcher, it looks as if he'll be moving to a less strenuous position sooner rather than later—especially with the defensively gifted Shea Langeliers now in the organization. If Soderstrom is to excel as a hit-tool-focused first baseman, he'll need to put the ball in the air more. Should he prove able to do so, he could produce roughly along the lines of former Athletic Yonder Alonso's All-Star season back in 2017. If he doesn't? Well, no one look at Alonso's 2016 campaign in the green and gold, because that could be Soderstrom's floor.

Daniel Susac DH/C

Born: 05/14/01 Age: 22 Bats: R Throws: R Height: 6'4" Weight: 218 lb. Origin: Round 1, 2022 Draft (#19 overall)

YEAR	TEAM	LVL	AGE	PA	R	2B	3B	HR	RBI	BB	K	SB	CS	Whiff%	AVG/OBP/SLG	DRC+	BABIP	BRR	DRP	WARP
2022	STK	A	21	107	14	7	0	1	13	7	25	0	0		.286/.346/.388	92	.375	-1.2	C(11): -0.1	0.1
2023 non-DC	*OAK*	*MLB*	*22*	*251*	*18*	*10*	*1*	*1*	*19*	*14*	*62*	*0*	*0*	*26.8%*	*.217/.269/.298*	*57*	*.289*	*0.7*	*C 0*	*-0.3*

Comparables: Henry Wrigley (79), Luken Baker (77), Manuel Rodriguez (77)

YEAR	TEAM	P. COUNT	FRM RUNS	BLK RUNS	THRW RUNS	TOT RUNS
2022	STK	1601	0.4	-0.3	0.1	0.2
2023	*OAK*	*6956*	*-1.3*	*-0.9*	*0.0*	*-2.2*

Chosen 19th overall in the 2022 MLB Draft, Susac get his plaudits for potential, makeup and MLB bloodlines: all things that could make for an outstanding major leaguer. Of course, he'll also need to defend, and hit, and actually *perform* on the field as well. Fortunately, he had a solid pro debut in Stockton, showing some of the best hit and power tools of any of the team's recent draftees. The expectation is that he can grow into a solid, bat-first backstop. Given the hit rate on most of Oakland's recent first-rounders, they'll just be hoping his career surpasses his brother Andrew's pedestrian MLB run.

Stephen Vogt DH

Born: 11/01/84 Age: 38 Bats: L Throws: R Height: 6'0" Weight: 216 lb. Origin: Round 12, 2007 Draft (#365 overall)

YEAR	TEAM	LVL	AGE	PA	R	2B	3B	HR	RBI	BB	K	SB	CS	Whiff%	AVG/OBP/SLG	DRC+	BABIP	BRR	DRP	WARP
2020	AZ	MLB	35	81	6	5	0	1	7	8	18	0	0	19.6%	.167/.247/.278	81	.204	-0.4	C(23): 1.8, 1B(1): 0	0.2
2021	ATL	MLB	36	87	7	0	0	2	8	8	20	0	0	24.9%	.167/.241/.244	81	.193	0.4	C(23): 0.4	0.2
2021	AZ	MLB	36	151	17	6	1	5	17	18	36	0	0	27.2%	.212/.307/.386	94	.253	-1.2	C(40): 2.1, 1B(2): 0	0.6
2022	OAK	MLB	37	191	18	4	1	7	23	17	46	1	0	27.0%	.161/.241/.321	89	.168	1.3	C(19): -1.6, 1B(17): 0	0.3
2023 non-DC	*FA*	*MLB*	*38*	*251*	*23*	*9*	*0*	*6*	*26*	*21*	*62*	*0*	*0*	*27.0%*	*.200/.272/.342*	*68*	*.244*	*0.2*	*C -4, 1B 0*	*-0.6*

Comparables: John Roseboro (66), A.J. Pierzynski (65), Tim McCarver (63)

YEAR	TEAM	P. COUNT	FRM RUNS	BLK RUNS	THRW RUNS	TOT RUNS
2020	AZ	2961	1.7	0.0	0.1	1.7
2021	AZ	5282	0.9	0.0	0.2	1.1
2021	ATL	3089	0.5	-0.1	0.0	0.4
2022	OAK	2234	-1.5	-0.1	0.0	-1.6
2023	*FA*	*6956*	*-3.8*	*-0.1*	*0.0*	*-4.0*

For a poetic celebration of Vogt's outstanding connection with the fans in Oakland, check out Patrick Dubuque's edition of Box Score Banter at the BP website, entitled "Vogt to Adjourn." For a prosaic accounting of Vogt's life and times both on and off the field, we direct you toward his robust Wikipedia page, authored mostly by Colin McEvoy and swamped with 340 independent citations. If you want to keep things real, re-read his stat line above, which was dismal even for a backup catcher on an awful team. And if you want to see magic, watch two videos: first, the one with Vogt's children announcing him for his first at-bat in his final ballgame, and then another of him launching a ball over the fence hours later in his last professional plate appearance. To see the future, listen to the ways his teammates gush over him, or how Craig Counsell sells him as a future manager. To see one man who exemplifies the best of baseball in so many ways, just look to Stephen Vogt.

PITCHERS

Domingo Acevedo RHP

Born: 03/06/94 Age: 29 Bats: R Throws: R Height: 6'7" Weight: 240 lb. Origin: International Free Agent, 2012

YEAR	TEAM	LVL	AGE	W	L	SV	G	GS	IP	H	HR	BB/9	K/9	K	GB%	BABIP	WHIP	ERA	DRA-	WARP	MPH	FB%	Whiff%	CSP
2021	LV	AAA	27	2	0	9	30	0	32^2	22	3	1.7	14.6	53	25.8%	.302	0.86	2.48	70	0.7				
2021	OAK	MLB	27	0	0	0	10	0	11	9	3	3.3	7.4	9	41.9%	.214	1.18	3.27	105	0.1	92.8	50.6%	28.4%	56.6%
2022	OAK	MLB	28	0	1	0	18	0	18^2	18	4	1.9	8.2	17	39.9%	.280	1.18	3.86	97	0.8	93.3	43.3%	31.4%	57.2%
2023 DC	*OAK*	*MLB*	*29*	*3*	*3*	*2*	*64*	*0*	*55.7*	*52*	*8*	*2.7*	*9.0*	*55*	*38.5%*	*.290*	*1.24*	*3.66*	*98*	*0.3*	*93.2*	*44.1%*	*30.8%*	*57.1%*

Comparables: Rafael Montero (54), Tyler Duffey (53), Pierce Johnson (53)

Acevedo's imposing presence and visage don't quite match his stuff anymore: Instead of the fireballing tyro who drew intrigue in the Yankees' farm system, he's now an even-keeled vet who deals two off-speed pitches, soothing crowds and quieting bats as he guides late leads home. Long past his days as an intriguing prospect, the big man has resurfaced in Oakland as a righty-killer who pitches to contact, but with a changeup that gives him a weapon against lefties, too. He could eventually be half of a lefty-righty closing tandem, but until then, he's a reliable late-inning option who gets by with a much different skill set than the premium velocity upon which his hat used to hang.

Paul Blackburn RHP

Born: 12/04/93 Age: 29 Bats: R Throws: R Height: 6'1" Weight: 196 lb. Origin: Round 1, 2012 Draft (#56 overall)

YEAR	TEAM	LVL	AGE	W	L	SV	G	GS	IP	H	HR	BB/9	K/9	K	GB%	BABIP	WHIP	ERA	DRA-	WARP	MPH	FB%	Whiff%	CSP
2020	OAK	MLB	26	0	1	0	1	1	2^1	5	0	7.7	7.7	2	50.0%	.500	3.00	27.00	128	0.0	89.8	68.8%	10.5%	43.6%
2021	LV	AAA	27	4	7	0	17	16	88^2	114	8	2.7	8.1	80	54.6%	.376	1.59	4.97	91	0.9				
2021	OAK	MLB	27	1	4	0	9	9	38^1	52	8	2.3	6.1	26	51.1%	.341	1.62	5.87	122	-0.1	90.3	74.0%	15.7%	50.3%
2022	OAK	MLB	28	7	6	0	21	21	111^1	110	15	2.4	7.2	89	46.6%	.291	1.26	4.28	108	0.6	91.9	45.8%	23.7%	53.6%
2023 DC	*OAK*	*MLB*	*29*	*5*	*6*	*0*	*19*	*19*	*101*	*109*	*12*	*2.6*	*6.5*	*73*	*48.7%*	*.303*	*1.38*	*4.22*	*110*	*0.3*	*91.4*	*52.8%*	*21.4%*	*52.5%*

Comparables: Iván Nova (69), Chi Chi González (68), Jeff Karstens (68)

Perhaps last season's most unlikely All-Star, Blackburn was on fire in the first half. After many years of false starts due to injuries, he became the A's unquestioned ace through newfound confidence in his curveball, missing bats at a higher rate than ever before while still limiting walks and inducing grounders with his sinker. Sure, the wheels fell off in July around that Midsummer Classic nod, but it's tough to know exactly why: Pessimists will argue that opposing hitters figured out his seven-pitch mix, while the hopeful will point to the torn finger tendon that eventually sidelined Blackburn for the last several weeks of the season. Either way, just a few extra swings and misses shifts his profile from the rear to the middle of the rotation. On a team like the A's, that could mean more mid-season accolades await him in the near future.

Jeff Criswell RHP Born: 03/10/99 Age: 24 Bats: R Throws: R Height: 6'4" Weight: 225 lb. Origin: Round 2, 2020 Draft (#58 overall)

YEAR	TEAM	LVL	AGE	W	L	SV	G	GS	IP	H	HR	BB/9	K/9	K	GB%	BABIP	WHIP	ERA	DRA-	WARP	MPH	FB%	Whiff%	CSP
2021	LAN	A+	22	0	0	0	5	5	12	9	1	3.0	9.0	12	54.5%	.250	1.08	4.50	95	0.2				
2022	LAN	A+	23	2	3	0	10	10	50	37	7	3.2	10.4	58	48.8%	.254	1.10	3.78	91	0.7				
2022	MID	AA	23	2	6	0	12	9	57^{2}	61	6	3.7	8.9	57	33.3%	.335	1.47	4.21	88	0.7				
2022	LV	AAA	23	0	1	0	2	2	10^{2}	10	0	2.5	3.4	4	28.6%	.286	1.22	4.22	184	-0.2	91.8	44.2%	20.9%	
2023 non-DC	*COL*	*MLB*	*24*	*2*	*3*	*0*	*57*	*0*	*50*	*54*	*7*	*4.4*	*7.3*	*40*	*40.5%*	*.310*	*1.58*	*5.30*	*127*	*-0.5*			*23.9%*	

Comparables: Matt Bowman (59), Andrew Moore (58), Trent Thornton (57)

Ever since his time at the University of Michigan, Criswell struggled to stay healthy ... until 2022, that is. Finally hale and hearty, the A's shot him up the minor-league ladder as he produced performances more solid than outstanding. You might think that to be purely positive, but his rapid rise came with some downside: He ended the season pitching at the dreaded Las Vegas Ballpark, home to inflated ERAs and outrageous offensive numbers—not the best fit for his homer-prone ways. While it was encouraging to watch Criswell put his talents on display for a full season, there's still a lot of effort in his delivery, and he never posted standout numbers at any level. That said, he offers big-time velocity and two off-speeds with potential, which means he's likely to make the big leagues in some capacity sooner rather than later ... provided he stays healthy.

Ryan Cusick RHP Born: 11/12/99 Age: 23 Bats: R Throws: R Height: 6'6" Weight: 235 lb. Origin: Round 1, 2021 Draft (#24 overall)

YEAR	TEAM	LVL	AGE	W	L	SV	G	GS	IP	H	HR	BB/9	K/9	K	GB%	BABIP	WHIP	ERA	DRA-	WARP	MPH	FB%	Whiff%	CSP
2021	AUG	A	21	0	1	0	6	6	16^{1}	15	1	2.2	18.7	34	57.1%	.519	1.16	2.76	57	0.5				
2022	MID	AA	22	1	6	0	12	9	41	53	4	6.6	9.4	43	31.7%	.402	2.02	7.02	122	-0.4				
2023 non-DC	*OAK*	*MLB*	*23*	*2*	*3*	*0*	*57*	*0*	*50*	*53*	*8*	*6.0*	*8.4*	*46*	*38.7%*	*.316*	*1.74*	*5.99*	*136*	*-0.7*			*25.8%*	

Comparables: Albert Abreu (78), Pedro Avila (77), Isaac Anderson (76)

Cusick has a chance to be the third MLBer to come out of Avon Old Farms High School in Connecticut—following Juan Nieves and George Springer—but his first year in the A's organization wasn't exactly evocative of his alma mater's *Gilmore Girls* vibe. Though his pop culture references weren't oblique, his core injury was, and the only "will-they-or-won't-they" relationship that Cusick demonstrates in baseball is one with the strike zone. Time for another year in the life.

Gunnar Hoglund RHP Born: 12/17/99 Age: 23 Bats: L Throws: R Height: 6'4" Weight: 220 lb. Origin: Round 1, 2021 Draft (#19 overall)

YEAR	TEAM	LVL	AGE	W	L	SV	G	GS	IP	H	HR	BB/9	K/9	K	GB%	BABIP	WHIP	ERA	DRA-	WARP	MPH	FB%	Whiff%	CSP
2023 non-DC	*OAK*	*MLB*	*23*	*2*	*3*	*0*	*57*	*0*	*50*	*57*	*7*	*5.4*	*6.7*	*37*	*43.4%*	*.319*	*1.76*	*6.14*	*140*	*-0.8*			*22.7%*	

Comparables: Yaya Chentouf (26), Harol González (26), Gabe Friese (26)

The fulcrum on which the Matt Chapman trade balances, Hoglund finally made his pro debut late last season, allowing the A's front office and fans alike to exhale. Soon after, they inhaled sharply: Hoglund lasted all of three innings in Stockton before he returned to the ether *a la* Brigadoon, but with less singing. Though concerns over bicep tightness temporarily ended his comeback before it really began, the polished righty should move quickly when (if?) he proves healthy. With three solid pitches and good command, he could be every bit as valuable as the third baseman he was traded for ... eventually.

Cole Irvin LHP Born: 01/31/94 Age: 29 Bats: L Throws: L Height: 6'4" Weight: 217 lb. Origin: Round 5, 2016 Draft (#137 overall)

YEAR	TEAM	LVL	AGE	W	L	SV	G	GS	IP	H	HR	BB/9	K/9	K	GB%	BABIP	WHIP	ERA	DRA-	WARP	MPH	FB%	Whiff%	CSP
2020	PHI	MLB	26	0	1	0	3	0	3^{2}	11	1	2.5	9.8	4	35.3%	.625	3.27	17.18	107	0.0	92.8	52.4%	14.0%	50.1%
2021	OAK	MLB	27	10	15	0	32	32	178^{1}	195	23	2.1	6.3	125	37.5%	.305	1.33	4.24	130	-1.1	90.8	59.9%	19.4%	56.2%
2022	OAK	MLB	28	9	13	0	30	30	181	174	25	1.8	6.4	128	37.0%	.274	1.16	3.98	117	0.2	90.6	61.0%	20.5%	56.7%
2023 DC	*OAK*	*MLB*	*29*	*9*	*10*	*0*	*29*	*29*	*169*	*177*	*23*	*2.0*	*6.5*	*122*	*37.8%*	*.292*	*1.28*	*3.88*	*106*	*0.7*	*90.7*	*60.1%*	*20.9%*	*56.1%*

Comparables: Wade Miley (71), Marco Gonzales (69), Tommy Milone (66)

Oakland's ironman of a southpaw has a dubious statistical record to go along with his white-knuckle grip on a rotation spot. For the second year in a row, he was one of the least effective starting pitchers in baseball per both stats and the eye test despite logging the 25th most innings in the majors over that stretch. He doesn't miss bats *or* starts, which makes him a drain from a WARP perspective but a valuable asset for a team so dedicated to, uh, experimenting with its 40-man roster. Until the day comes once more when the A's rotation is chock full of talented starters, Irvin will be the back-of-the-rotation rock that keeps the pitching staff as stable as it can be.

Zach Jackson RHP Born: 12/25/94 Age: 28 Bats: R Throws: R Height: 6'4" Weight: 230 lb. Origin: Round 3, 2016 Draft (#102 overall)

YEAR	TEAM	LVL	AGE	W	L	SV	G	GS	IP	H	HR	BB/9	K/9	K	GB%	BABIP	WHIP	ERA	DRA-	WARP	MPH	FB%	Whiff%	CSP
2021	MID	AA	26	1	1	5	14	0	16^{1}	7	0	3.9	18.7	34	54.5%	.333	0.86	0.55	57	0.5				
2021	LV	AAA	26	1	1	1	11	0	11^{2}	11	1	4.6	10.0	13	41.4%	.333	1.46	5.40	94	0.1				
2022	OAK	MLB	27	2	3	3	54	0	48	28	1	6.2	12.6	67	27.0%	.278	1.27	3.00	80	1.0	94.6	54.3%	33.6%	54.0%
2023 DC	*OAK*	*MLB*	*28*	*3*	*3*	*7*	*64*	*0*	*55.7*	*44*	*7*	*5.6*	*11.9*	*73*	*36.1%*	*.289*	*1.42*	*4.04*	*99*	*0.3*	*94.6*	*54.3%*	*32.9%*	*54.0%*

Comparables: Danny Farquhar (64), Jose De La Torre (63), Tommy Kahnle (63)

Do we overuse the term "effectively wild" these days? Probably, but that's because more pitchers than ever have eschewed control in favor of physics-defying movement and drool-inducing velocity. But even among pitchers in the Ricky Vaughn mode, Jackson walks a *lot* of dudes. Only three other relievers with as many innings allowed more free passes, but his sizzling fastball and hellacious curve made him Oakland's season leader in ERA and strikeout rate. A shoulder issue ended his campaign early, but he'll be a bullpen stalwart so long as he keeps opposing hitters flailing.

Dany Jiménez RHP Born: 12/23/93 Age: 29 Bats: R Throws: R Height: 6'1" Weight: 182 lb. Origin: International Free Agent, 2015

YEAR	TEAM	LVL	AGE	W	L	SV	G	GS	IP	H	HR	BB/9	K/9	K	GB%	BABIP	WHIP	ERA	DRA-	WARP	MPH	FB%	Whiff%	CSP
2020	SF	MLB	26	0	0	0	2	0	1^1	1	0	20.2	6.7	1	50.0%	.250	3.00	6.75	105	0.0	93.1	51.4%	27.3%	45.1%
2021	BUF	AAA	27	3	3	3	39	1	44^2	29	5	5.0	14.7	73	39.3%	.289	1.21	2.22	71	1.3				
2022	OAK	MLB	28	3	4	11	34	0	34^1	23	2	4.7	8.9	34	43.0%	.231	1.19	3.41	95	0.4	94.2	38.4%	35.1%	55.8%
2023 DC	*OAK*	*MLB*	*29*	*3*	*3*	*2*	*64*	*0*	*55.7*	*48*	*7*	*4.8*	*11.1*	*68*	*42.2%*	*.298*	*1.40*	*3.95*	*98*	*0.3*	*94.2*	*38.8%*	*34.7%*	*55.5%*

Comparables: Dillon Maples (57), Tyler Kinley (57), Austin Adams (57)

The poster boy for running it back, Jiménez was twice taken in the Rule 5 draft by a Bay Area team only to be returned to his original squad in Toronto. After all that, he eventually signed with Oakland of his own accord, because if at first you don't succeed, just keep throwing. *La Muerte* won the job as the A's closer by spamming his "curveball"—PitchInfo calls it a slider—in much the same way your friend from third grade spammed the *hadouken* in Street Fighter II. All those reps worked, and now Jiménez is an established late-inning reliever despite his fleeting dominance and health. That breaking pitch is a beast, though—he racked up whiffs with it about 20% of the time—so as long as that keeps its shape, he could repeat his 2022 success next season. And hey, if there's one thing he's really good at, it's repeating!

James Kaprielian RHP Born: 03/02/94 Age: 29 Bats: R Throws: R Height: 6'3" Weight: 225 lb. Origin: Round 1, 2015 Draft (#16 overall)

YEAR	TEAM	LVL	AGE	W	L	SV	G	GS	IP	H	HR	BB/9	K/9	K	GB%	BABIP	WHIP	ERA	DRA-	WARP	MPH	FB%	Whiff%	CSP
2020	OAK	MLB	26	0	0	0	2	0	3^2	4	2	4.9	9.8	4	36.4%	.222	1.64	7.36	125	0.0	95.1	69.0%	37.5%	37.4%
2021	OAK	MLB	27	8	5	0	24	21	119^1	105	19	3.1	9.3	123	33.6%	.276	1.22	4.07	108	0.6	93.1	58.8%	27.3%	52.3%
2022	LV	AAA	28	0	1	0	2	2	8^2	12	1	5.2	7.3	7	20.7%	.393	1.96	9.35	131	-0.1	92.9	57.4%	27.8%	
2022	OAK	MLB	28	5	9	0	26	26	134	121	16	4.0	6.6	98	37.3%	.264	1.34	4.23	125	-0.4	94.1	54.5%	21.1%	52.6%
2023 DC	*OAK*	*MLB*	*29*	*6*	*8*	*0*	*22*	*22*	*117.7*	*117*	*17*	*3.6*	*7.7*	*100*	*35.7%*	*.289*	*1.39*	*4.38*	*113*	*0.1*	*93.7*	*56.4%*	*24.2%*	*52.3%*

Comparables: Chad Bettis (55), Andrew Cashner (52), Matt Shoemaker (52)

The story goes like this: A man puts on a shirt. He has done this nearly 9,000 times before (trust us, we did the math), but this time, something goes horribly wrong. While stretching out his arm, he slides his hand across a poster on the wall, delivering an epic paper cut to his pitching hand and temporarily risking his livelihood. Perhaps when he read last year's *Annual,* Kaprielian saw that we wrote he'd "suffered every conceivable arm injury" and took it as a challenge? Nevertheless, he went from being a replaceable, workaday starter pre-injury to finishing his season on a high note, flashing some of the mid-rotation potential he once carried before the myriad injuries slowed him down. We can only hope that he doesn't find some new and inventive way to get banged up next season—let's keep him away from John Smoltz's iron—but if he does, may Kaprielian rebound just as well as he did after Shirtgate.

Adrián Martínez RHP Born: 12/10/96 Age: 26 Bats: R Throws: R Height: 6'2" Weight: 215 lb. Origin: International Free Agent, 2015

YEAR	TEAM	LVL	AGE	W	L	SV	G	GS	IP	H	HR	BB/9	K/9	K	GB%	BABIP	WHIP	ERA	DRA-	WARP	MPH	FB%	Whiff%	CSP
2021	SA	AA	24	7	3	0	17	13	80^2	64	4	2.7	9.3	83	43.7%	.284	1.09	2.34	74	1.7				
2021	ELP	AAA	24	1	2	0	9	9	44^1	50	6	3.5	7.9	39	54.7%	.338	1.51	5.28	86	0.6				
2022	LV	AAA	25	5	7	0	18	18	89^2	94	24	3.3	10.0	100	45.4%	.308	1.42	5.72	81	1.5	93.6	53.5%	29.0%	
2022	OAK	MLB	25	4	6	0	12	12	57^2	69	13	3.0	8.3	53	41.3%	.327	1.53	6.24	108	0.3	93.9	50.3%	24.1%	55.8%
2023 DC	*OAK*	*MLB*	*26*	*2*	*2*	*0*	*18*	*4*	*35*	*36*	*5*	*3.4*	*7.8*	*30*	*44.3%*	*.300*	*1.42*	*4.62*	*117*	*0.0*	*93.9*	*50.3%*	*24.6%*	*55.8%*

Comparables: Tyler Duffey (71), James Marvel (69), Taylor Jordan (69)

A rookie strikeout artist, Martínez had an inauspicious debut upon replacing Sean Manaea in Oakland's rotation. After bouncing between Triple-A and the majors for much of the season, he finally stuck as a starter with the A's come late August. Though his numbers don't inspire, he flashed enough in his final seven outings to suggest he can develop into a decent back-end option. The owner of a plus changeup, Martínez needs to develop his breakers to help limit the mistakes that led him to cough up more than a homer per start—especially since half his outings came in the cavernous RingCentral Coliseum. Until and unless that happens, he may fit better as a swingman who rarely faces a lineup more than twice through the order.

Trevor May RHP Born: 09/23/89 Age: 33 Bats: R Throws: R Height: 6'5" Weight: 240 lb. Origin: Round 4, 2008 Draft (#136 overall)

YEAR	TEAM	LVL	AGE	W	L	SV	G	GS	IP	H	HR	BB/9	K/9	K	GB%	BABIP	WHIP	ERA	DRA-	WARP	MPH	FB%	Whiff%	CSP
2020	MIN	MLB	30	1	0	2	24	0	23^1	20	5	2.7	14.7	38	25.5%	.326	1.16	3.86	86	0.4	96.6	51.7%	43.0%	45.3%
2021	NYM	MLB	31	7	3	4	68	0	62^2	55	10	3.4	11.9	83	35.8%	.302	1.26	3.59	80	1.2	96.7	60.3%	32.7%	54.3%
2022	NYM	MLB	32	2	0	1	26	0	25	27	4	3.2	10.8	30	29.2%	.338	1.44	5.04	96	0.3	96.3	52.5%	30.6%	57.0%
2023 DC	*OAK*	*MLB*	*33*	*3*	*3*	*11*	*64*	*0*	*55.7*	*51*	*7*	*3.3*	*10.5*	*65*	*33.6%*	*.303*	*1.28*	*3.69*	*96*	*0.3*	*96.4*	*57.7%*	*30.8%*	*52.8%*

Comparables: Matt Albers (61), Scott Linebrink (59), Tommy Hunter (58)

It was a tumultuous season for May, who lost two things in 2022: his cat Donny—beloved by his owners and the internet alike—and his chance to be part of Edwin Díaz's supporting cast as one of the Mets' primary setup men. Attempting to pitch through a triceps issue in April, May posted an unsightly 8.64 ERA in 8⅓ innings before hitting the injured list with what turned out to be a stress reaction in his right humerus that sidelined him for three months. The Mets' most online player became less so, posting only his famous "Let's Go Mets" tweets after wins, accompanied by a series of emojis representing the key contributors to the victory. He returned in August, and his 8⅓ innings in that month were a bit better, resulting in a 4.32 ERA. He was also placed on the COVID-19 injured list down the stretch, so he only pitched, you guessed it, 8⅓ innings in September and October, and across that span he halved his ERA again to a mark of 2.16. His 2022 season was a true statistical oddity: Three chunks of exactly 8⅓ innings, his ERA across each chunk halved each time. May himself recently pointed out on Twitter the cruel irony of May being the worst month of his career historically (this year it was the month in which he suffered his injury), quipping, "Like, why you gotta do me like that?" Perhaps it will prove kinder to him in Oakland, where he'll look to pitch at least until this season's trade deadline.

Luis Medina RHP Born: 05/03/99 Age: 24 Bats: R Throws: R Height: 6'1" Weight: 175 lb. Origin: International Free Agent, 2015

YEAR	TEAM	LVL	AGE	W	L	SV	G	GS	IP	H	HR	BB/9	K/9	K	GB%	BABIP	WHIP	ERA	DRA-	WARP	MPH	FB%	Whiff%	CSP
2021	HV	A+	22	2	1	0	7	7	32^2	18	4	5.2	13.8	50	50.0%	.241	1.13	2.76	79	0.7				
2021	SOM	AA	22	4	3	0	15	14	73^2	65	7	5.0	10.1	83	50.5%	.314	1.44	3.67	84	1.2				
2022	MID	AA	23	1	4	0	7	7	20^2	35	3	9.6	11.3	26	46.2%	.516	2.76	11.76	114	-0.1				
2022	SOM	AA	23	4	3	0	17	17	72	46	4	5.0	10.1	81	51.4%	.240	1.19	3.38	80	1.7				
2023 DC	*OAK*	*MLB*	*24*	*0*	*0*	*0*	*14*	*0*	*12.3*	*12*	*1*	*6.9*	*8.8*	*12*	*49.0%*	*.312*	*1.79*	*5.75*	*130*	*-0.1*			*27.7%*	

Comparables: Alex Colomé (68), Jordan Yamamoto (66), Trey Supak (64)

He's got elite velocity and big movement on his secondaries, yet Medina remains in no man's land as a prospect even after changing coasts. His raw stuff and three-pitch mix signal frontline starter, but they're paired with plenty of red flags: He doesn't go deep into games, his fastball is a bit too true and he's never had more than a passing interest in the strike zone. So will his future lie in the rotation or in relief? As pitching staffs move beyond traditional roles, Medina may find himself as something of a hybrid; he could throw several innings out of the 'pen or be a short-burst starter. With his eye-popping talent and relatively clean medical history, we can be all but certain that Medina will be afforded many more years to figure it out. As to whether he'll emerge as an ace, a closer or something in between? That remains anyone's guess.

Sam Moll LHP Born: 01/03/92 Age: 31 Bats: L Throws: L Height: 5'9" Weight: 190 lb. Origin: Round 3, 2013 Draft (#77 overall)

YEAR	TEAM	LVL	AGE	W	L	SV	G	GS	IP	H	HR	BB/9	K/9	K	GB%	BABIP	WHIP	ERA	DRA-	WARP	MPH	FB%	Whiff%	CSP
2021	RNO	AAA	29	0	0	0	21	0	21^2	19	3	6.2	12.5	30	44.4%	.314	1.57	5.82	77	0.4				
2021	LV	AAA	29	1	1	2	12	0	13^2	12	2	3.3	11.2	17	57.6%	.323	1.24	2.63	80	0.2				
2021	OAK	MLB	29	0	0	0	8	0	10^1	8	1	4.4	7.0	8	44.8%	.250	1.26	3.48	113	0.0	93.7	55.1%	16.7%	55.2%
2022	OAK	MLB	30	2	1	0	53	0	43^1	33	5	4.6	9.6	46	50.0%	.252	1.27	2.91	93	0.6	93.6	44.6%	24.7%	53.8%
2023 DC	*OAK*	*MLB*	*31*	*3*	*3*	*0*	*64*	*0*	*55.7*	*52*	*6*	*4.7*	*8.8*	*54*	*48.4%*	*.293*	*1.46*	*4.32*	*107*	*0.0*	*93.6*	*46.2%*	*24.6%*	*54.0%*

Comparables: Buddy Boshers (47), Sam Freeman (46), Scott Alexander (45)

Congrats to Moll, who has graduated from glib gangster puns and Triple-A to a late-career surge as a serious southpaw reliever. As a sinker-slider guy, he's obviously far more effective against fellow lefties, but he held his own against right-handers; a necessity in MLB now that the three-batter minimum rule is in place. His slider has improved greatly over the last two years and has turned into a real swing-and-miss pitch, making him an ideal second lefty in any team's bullpen—even if said bullpen has few leads to protect.

★ ★ ★ *2023 Top 101 Prospect* ***#92*** ★ ★ ★

Kyle Muller LHP Born: 10/07/97 Age: 25 Bats: R Throws: L Height: 6'7" Weight: 250 lb. Origin: Round 2, 2016 Draft (#44 overall)

YEAR	TEAM	LVL	AGE	W	L	SV	G	GS	IP	H	HR	BB/9	K/9	K	GB%	BABIP	WHIP	ERA	DRA-	WARP	MPH	FB%	Whiff%	CSP
2021	GWN	AAA	23	5	4	0	17	17	79^2	66	9	4.7	10.5	93	41.6%	.286	1.36	3.39	78	2.0				
2021	ATL	MLB	23	2	4	0	9	8	36^2	26	2	4.9	9.1	37	37.5%	.261	1.25	4.17	106	0.2	93.4	42.4%	31.4%	54.2%
2022	GWN	AAA	24	6	8	0	23	23	134^2	119	14	2.7	10.6	159	46.6%	.325	1.18	3.41	79	3.3	94.8	47.5%	32.4%	
2022	ATL	MLB	24	1	1	0	3	3	12^1	13	2	5.8	8.8	12	41.0%	.306	1.70	8.03	129	-0.1	94.4	46.8%	26.9%	57.2%
2023 DC	*OAK*	*MLB*	*25*	*4*	*5*	*0*	*16*	*16*	*77.7*	*72*	*8*	*4.2*	*9.3*	*80*	*43.1%*	*.301*	*1.40*	*3.97*	*101*	*0.6*	*93.7*	*43.8%*	*28.3%*	*55.1%*

Comparables: Danny Duffy (68), Mitch Keller (67), Travis Wood (66)

For the second season in a row, Muller absolutely tore up Triple-A. He cut down on walks while continuing to strike out batters at a high rate. In total, he's tossed over 200 innings in Gwinnett now, giving every indication that he's mastered the level. Muller even earned a few big-league starts, and while the turns he took were unspectacular at best, his breaking pitches produced some encouraging results and gave fans something to mull over. This should be the year where we see if what Muller has figured out in Triple-A can translate to the majors, especially since the path to starts in Oakland—where Muller was traded as a key part of the Sean Murphy deal—is clearer than in Atlanta.

Adam Oller RHP Born: 10/17/94 Age: 28 Bats: R Throws: R Height: 6'4" Weight: 225 lb. Origin: Round 20, 2016 Draft (#615 overall)

YEAR	TEAM	LVL	AGE	W	L	SV	G	GS	IP	H	HR	BB/9	K/9	K	GB%	BABIP	WHIP	ERA	DRA-	WARP	MPH	FB%	Whiff%	CSP
2021	BNG	AA	26	5	3	0	15	15	76	66	8	3.4	11.3	95	47.2%	.310	1.25	4.03	84	1.3				
2021	SYR	AAA	26	4	1	0	8	8	44	27	1	3.7	8.8	43	34.2%	.241	1.02	2.45	95	0.7				
2022	LV	AAA	27	3	0	0	7	7	31^2	29	0	4.8	9.1	32	38.2%	.330	1.45	3.69	102	0.1	93.4	71.2%	26.0%	
2022	OAK	MLB	27	2	8	0	19	14	74^1	82	17	4.7	5.6	46	32.8%	.280	1.63	6.30	166	-1.8	92.6	67.9%	21.2%	51.7%
2023 DC	*OAK*	*MLB*	*28*	*5*	*3*	*0*	*46*	*3*	*51.7*	*54*	*7*	*4.4*	*7.0*	*40*	*37.1%*	*.296*	*1.55*	*5.13*	*126*	*-0.3*	*92.6*	*67.9%*	*22.6%*	*51.7%*

Comparables: Glenn Sparkman (67), Sam Gaviglio (62), Anthony Lerew (61)

It was supposed to be a charming success story when Oller, freshly arrived from the Mets, made the Athletics' Opening Day rotation, ostensibly as a replacement for the player he was dealt for, Chris Bassitt. Unfortunately, the 27-year-old got absolutely housed in his first MLB start, and things didn't improve much from there. He lost his spot in the rotation after just four outings, bouncing between starting and relieving for Oakland and Las Vegas for the remainder of the season. While in the bigs he was startlingly ineffective, and his body language suggested he would rather suffer a public colonoscopy than attack opposing hitters. The quality of his stuff, his number of minor-league options remaining and the team he now plays for mean he'll likely get every opportunity to pitch in similar roles over the next few seasons. And hey, for both Oller and the A's, at least there's nowhere to go but up.

A.J. Puk LHP
Born: 04/25/95 Age: 28 Bats: L Throws: L Height: 6'7" Weight: 248 lb. Origin: Round 1, 2016 Draft (#6 overall)

YEAR	TEAM	LVL	AGE	W	L	SV	G	GS	IP	H	HR	BB/9	K/9	K	GB%	BABIP	WHIP	ERA	DRA-	WARP	MPH	FB%	Whiff%	CSP
2021	LV	AAA	26	2	5	1	29	4	48^{2}	61	12	3.5	10.7	58	39.5%	.363	1.64	6.10	91	0.5				
2021	OAK	MLB	26	0	3	0	12	0	13^{1}	18	1	4.0	10.8	16	52.4%	.415	1.80	6.07	96	0.2	96.0	65.0%	24.5%	57.2%
2022	OAK	MLB	27	4	3	4	62	0	66^{1}	53	7	3.1	10.3	76	42.7%	.286	1.15	3.12	83	1.2	96.7	61.8%	29.1%	54.1%
2023 DC	*OAK*	*MLB*	*28*	*7*	*3*	*4*	*60*	*3*	*64*	*60*	*8*	*3.5*	*10.2*	*73*	*43.5%*	*.310*	*1.34*	*4.11*	*104*	*0.2*	*96.6*	*62.3%*	*28.3%*	*54.4%*

Comparables: Andrew Chafin (48), Michael Feliz (46), Sam Howard (46)

For a huge dude with a Dorito-colored beard, world-class velocity and a history as a top-10 draft selection, Puk had kind of a quiet season out of the bullpen. Finally able to stay upright and with a functioning left arm for a full season, the University of Florida product nonetheless proved that his ultimate role will be that of a late-inning fireman. No longer a potential ace, he's leaning more and more on a slider that has added depth and is a reliable companion to his 97-mph heater. Is he in the upper echelon of swing-and-miss relievers? Not yet, but staying healthy will go a long way toward enabling him to move from solid late-inning hurler to true relief ace.

Drew Rucinski RHP
Born: 12/30/88 Age: 34 Bats: R Throws: R Height: 6'2" Weight: 190 lb. Origin: Undrafted Free Agent, 2011

YEAR	TEAM	LVL	AGE	W	L	SV	G	GS	IP	H	HR	BB/9	K/9	K	GB%	BABIP	WHIP	ERA	DRA-	WARP	MPH	FB%	Whiff%	CSP
2023 DC	*OAK*	*MLB*	*34*	*5*	*6*	*0*	*19*	*19*	*97*	*95*	*12*	*2.8*	*7.3*	*78*	*41.6%*	*.287*	*1.29*	*3.76*	*101*	*0.8*			*23.9%*	

Comparables: Gonzalez Germen (44), Rob Scahill (43), Shane Greene (42)

Rucinski is the latest in a growing line of MLB pitchers who turned to the KBO in order to rehabilitate their careers. The A's are making a short-term bet that he can return to the majors and have success *a la* Chris Flexen or Merrill Kelly. As one of the better starters in South Korea over the past four years, Rucinski built his stamina and actually added some velocity, giving him the potential to step in and immediately add value to a depleted A's staff. Sure, there's a chance he could go the Josh Lindblom route, but given that he was brought in on a one-year, $3 million contract, he's exactly the kind of upside play that fits a team in Oakland's ugly situation.

JP Sears LHP
Born: 02/19/96 Age: 27 Bats: R Throws: L Height: 5'11" Weight: 180 lb. Origin: Round 11, 2017 Draft (#333 overall)

YEAR	TEAM	LVL	AGE	W	L	SV	G	GS	IP	H	HR	BB/9	K/9	K	GB%	BABIP	WHIP	ERA	DRA-	WARP	MPH	FB%	Whiff%	CSP
2021	SOM	AA	25	3	2	1	15	8	50^{2}	45	6	3.2	12.6	71	47.5%	.351	1.24	4.09	89	0.7				
2021	SWB	AAA	25	7	0	0	10	10	53^{1}	41	5	1.9	11.0	65	39.8%	.298	0.98	2.87	88	1.1				
2022	SWB	AAA	26	1	1	0	11	9	43	24	3	1.5	11.5	55	41.0%	.216	0.72	1.67	71	1.2				
2022	OAK	MLB	26	3	3	0	10	9	48	53	7	3.4	6.8	36	39.3%	.322	1.48	4.69	137	-0.5	93.0	55.2%	19.4%	54.3%
2022	NYY	MLB	26	3	0	0	7	2	22	14	1	2.0	6.1	15	43.5%	.213	0.86	2.05	121	0.0	93.6	60.1%	21.6%	54.0%
2023 DC	*OAK*	*MLB*	*27*	*5*	*6*	*0*	*21*	*21*	*96.7*	*96*	*12*	*2.9*	*7.6*	*82*	*41.7%*	*.295*	*1.32*	*3.89*	*103*	*0.6*	*93.2*	*56.6%*	*23.4%*	*54.2%*

Comparables: Matthew Boyd (64), Ryan Yarbrough (63), Dillon Peters (62)

Another interesting hurler plucked from the Yankees' catalog via the Frankie Montas trade, Sears moved quickly to plug a gaping hole in the A's major-league rotation. His strongest pitches are his fastball and a slider he aims at the back feet of right-handed hitters, but make no mistake: he's a command-and-control artist, not a purveyor of premium stuff. Because of that, he wasn't able to recreate the gaudy strikeout numbers he posted in the minors once facing the best hitters in the world. That said, *this* Sears has a meaningful future, at least. He may just spend it closer to the middle or back end of a rotation than toward the front of one.

Freddy Tarnok RHP
Born: 11/24/98 Age: 24 Bats: R Throws: R Height: 6'3" Weight: 185 lb. Origin: Round 3, 2017 Draft (#80 overall)

YEAR	TEAM	LVL	AGE	W	L	SV	G	GS	IP	H	HR	BB/9	K/9	K	GB%	BABIP	WHIP	ERA	DRA-	WARP	MPH	FB%	Whiff%	CSP
2021	ROM	A+	22	3	2	0	7	5	28^{1}	21	6	4.1	15.2	48	34.5%	.306	1.20	4.76	74	0.7				
2021	MIS	AA	22	3	2	0	9	9	45	35	2	3.0	12.2	61	33.3%	.324	1.11	2.60	81	0.9				
2022	MIS	AA	23	2	2	0	15	15	62^{2}	54	8	3.9	10.8	75	32.7%	.293	1.29	4.31	106	0.4				
2022	GWN	AAA	23	2	1	0	10	8	44	38	7	3.5	10.0	49	42.4%	.279	1.25	3.68	83	1.0	95.2	37.4%	13.7%	
2022	ATL	MLB	23	0	0	0	1	0	0^{2}	1	0	0.0	13.5	1	50.0%	.500	1.50	0.00	98	0.0	96.4	50.0%	66.7%	54.0%
2023 DC	*OAK*	*MLB*	*24*	*1*	*1*	*0*	*35*	*0*	*30.7*	*30*	*4*	*4.2*	*8.9*	*30*	*37.8%*	*.297*	*1.44*	*4.52*	*113*	*-0.1*	*96.4*	*50.0%*	*26.6%*	*54.0%*

Comparables: Touki Toussaint (45), Michael Fulmer (44), Rafael Montero (44)

Tarnok's steady rise through the minors finally paid off in 2022, as he made his major-league debut with the Braves in one solitary relief appearance. He earned his cup of coffee through a seamless jump from Double-A to Triple-A, keeping his walk rate in line while striking out more than a quarter of the batters he faced. Tarnok's fastball reached as high as 98 mph, and he paired it with a nasty (if somewhat easy to identify) curveball and developing slider. An underrated part of the Sean Murphy trade, he should get a chance to start in Oakland soon.

★ ★ ★ *2023 Top 101 Prospect* **#97** ★ ★ ★

Ken Waldichuk LHP Born: 01/08/98 Age: 25 Bats: L Throws: L Height: 6'4" Weight: 220 lb. Origin: Round 5, 2019 Draft (#165 overall)

YEAR	TEAM	LVL	AGE	W	L	SV	G	GS	IP	H	HR	BB/9	K/9	K	GB%	BABIP	WHIP	ERA	DRA-	WARP	MPH	FB%	Whiff%	CSP
2021	HV	A+	23	2	0	0	7	7	30^2	12	0	3.8	16.1	55	31.1%	.267	0.82	0.00	82	0.6				
2021	SOM	AA	23	4	3	0	16	14	79^1	64	13	4.3	12.3	108	36.7%	.293	1.29	4.20	87	1.2				
2022	SOM	AA	24	4	0	0	6	6	28^2	16	2	3.1	14.4	46	52.7%	.264	0.91	1.26	78	0.7				
2022	SWB	AAA	24	2	3	0	11	11	47^2	38	5	4.3	13.2	70	40.7%	.333	1.28	3.59	75	1.3				
2022	LV	AAA	24	0	1	0	4	4	18^2	20	3	1.4	10.1	21	38.9%	.333	1.23	3.38	95	0.2	94.5	58.7%	31.8%	
2022	OAK	MLB	24	2	2	0	7	7	34^2	32	5	2.6	8.6	33	36.4%	.287	1.21	4.93	121	0.0	94.3	56.5%	25.3%	53.7%
2023 DC	*OAK*	*MLB*	*25*	*5*	*6*	*0*	*19*	*19*	*91.3*	*80*	*12*	*4.0*	*9.5*	*96*	*39.7%*	*.283*	*1.33*	*3.88*	*100*	*0.8*	*94.3*	*56.5%*	*29.1%*	*53.7%*

Comparables: Matthew Boyd (74), Ben Lively (71), Wade Miley (70)

A strikeout machine with two deceptively powerful pitches, Waldichuk emerged as one of the game's top left-handed pitching prospects before heading to Oakland in the Frankie Montas trade. The A's wasted no time putting him on the bump in the big leagues where, for the first time in his career, the 24-year-old failed to strike out more than a batter per inning. While he didn't thrive in his first taste of MLB action, he didn't implode, either, though DRA suggests he's lucky his ERA started with a 4. It's uncertain whether his swing-and-miss skills will translate completely to the majors, but for now it looks like his floor is that of a solid rotation piece. He's got the upside to toss the occasional masterpiece, too.

Lineouts

Hitters

HITTER	POS	TEAM	LVL	AGE	PA	R	2B	3B	HR	RBI	BB	K	SB	CS	AVG/OBP/SLG	DRC+	BABIP	BRR	DRP	WARP
Brayan Buelvas	OF	LAN	A+	20	260	28	14	1	7	26	17	57	7	4	.195/.265/.352	103	.225	-0.3	CF(33): 0.0, RF(23): 0.8, LF(9): -0.7	0.8
Conner Capel	OF	MEM	AAA	25	377	52	18	3	10	38	50	62	19	8	.258/.361/.425	118	.292	-2.2	RF(52): 0.2, LF(19): 0.8, CF(11): -0.5	2.0
	OF	LV	AAA	25	32	4	2	0	0	4	3	8	2	1	.321/.406/.393	87	.450	0.2	LF(5): -0.5, RF(2): -0.2, CF(1): -0.3	0.2
	OF	OAK	MLB	25	40	6	0	1	2	9	4	8	1	1	.371/.425/.600	112	.423	-0.5	RF(13): 2.1	0.3
	OF	STL	MLB	25	19	1	0	0	1	2	1	2	0	0	.176/.211/.353	104	.133	0.0	RF(5): 0.2	0.1
Dermis Garcia	1B	LV	AAA	24	278	51	15	1	13	44	32	83	4	1	.264/.349/.498	85	.338	0.7	1B(47): 1.3, LF(1): -0.0	0.4
	1B	OAK	MLB	24	125	13	6	0	5	20	8	55	0	0	.207/.264/.388	66	.339	-0.2	1B(35): -0.2, LF(1): 0	-0.3
Brett Harris	3B	LAN	A+	24	123	22	7	0	7	18	19	21	0	0	.304/.415/.578	157	.320	-0.1	3B(23): -0.9, 2B(4): -0.9	1.0
	3B	MID	AA	24	360	51	15	2	10	45	31	62	11	5	.286/.361/.441	112	.327	-0.2	3B(66): 0.2, 2B(17): -0.6	1.5
David MacKinnon	1B	SL	AAA	27	273	47	19	4	14	45	42	51	2	2	.324/.429/.631	134	.360	-0.5	1B(57): 0.6	1.7
	1B	LV	AAA	27	73	6	5	0	1	9	7	12	0	0	.297/.370/.422	102	.346	-0.1	3B(10): 0.4, 1B(4): -0.2	0.5
	1B	LAA	MLB	27	43	0	0	0	0	6	5	12	0	0	.189/.279/.189	85	.269	-0.1	1B(7): -0.2, 3B(5): -0.3	0.0
	1B	OAK	MLB	27	14	2	0	0	0	0	1	5	0	0	.000/.071/.000	93		0.1	1B(5): 0.1	0.0
Billy McKinney	RF	LV	AAA	27	293	48	13	5	12	49	36	83	2	0	.295/.396/.530	96	.397	2.3	RF(19): 1.0, 1B(16): -1.4, CF(14): 0.0	0.9
	RF	OAK	MLB	27	57	3	1	0	1	4	4	16	0	0	.096/.158/.173	75	.111	-0.4	RF(10): 0.1, 1B(7): 0.8, LF(4): 0	0.0
Pablo Reyes	IF	NAS	AAA	28	432	63	27	2	11	59	39	67	15	7	.273/.348/.439	112	.305	-1.9	2B(50): 1.7, 3B(17): 1.0, SS(14): 0.4	2.0
	IF	MIL	MLB	28	16	1	0	0	0	0	1	2	0	0	.267/.313/.267	104	.308	0.1	SS(3): -0.1, 3B(2): 0.5	0.1
Brent Rooker	LF	OMA	AAA	27	92	16	8	0	9	32	9	25	0	1	.338/.424/.775	121	.391	-1.1	LF(12): 0.7, RF(2): -0.2	0.3
	LF	ELP	AAA	27	273	55	19	0	19	55	37	78	5	1	.272/.385/.605	113	.323	2.3	LF(30): 0.2, RF(21): 1.3	1.0
	LF	KC	MLB	27	29	1	1	0	0	2	3	7	0	0	.160/.276/.200	94	.222	-0.1	LF(6): 0.2	0.1
	LF	SD	MLB	27	7	0	0	0	0	0	0	4	0	0	.000/.000/.000	96			LF(2): -0.3	
Cal Stevenson	OF	DUR	AAA	25	203	29	7	1	2	17	31	42	9	2	.265/.376/.353	111	.339	2.0	CF(45): 4.5, LF(9): 0.1	1.4
	OF	LV	AAA	25	104	23	2	2	4	19	14	12	7	1	.322/.413/.529	125	.329	1.2	RF(11): 1.0, LF(9): -0.2, CF(5): -0.5	0.7
	OF	OAK	MLB	25	71	5	3	0	0	1	8	23	1	1	.167/.261/.217	69	.263	-0.1	CF(22): -1, RF(2): 0, LF(1): 0	-0.1
Cody Thomas	LF	LV	AAA	27	39	3	3	0	1	8	2	13	0	0	.200/.256/.371	83	.273	-0.1	LF(5): -0.2	0.0
	LF	OAK	MLB	27	32	1	0	0	0	0	2	12	0	0	.267/.313/.267	66	.444	0.4	LF(10): -0.1	0.0

Toolsy outfielder **Brayan Buelvas** spent most of 2022 as one of the youngest players in the Midwest League but was clearly challenged by the aggressive assignment. He'll have plenty more chances to bring his athleticism, foot speed and raw power to bear in his age-21 season. ⚾ An .875 OPS looks pretty dang sweet on the back of a baseball card, even when it's only 59 plate appearances. **Conner Capel** should get plenty of run to prove how real his small sample success was this coming season. ⚾ University of Michigan product **Clark Elliott** isn't just a thinking man's ballplayer, but a man who thinks about thinking: His college course of study was cognitive science. The 2022 draft pick will work to bring the brain-body connection to bear as a contact-first corner outfielder. ⚾ **Dermis Garcia** finally has some skin in the game, having made his MLB debut more than six years after signing as a big-time IFA. He has impressive power but led all hitters with more than 100 PA in strikeout rate, making him an iffy bet for a long stay in the bigs. ⚾ Infield prospect **Brett Harris** showed out in his first full season in the A's organization, but he was expected to as an age-24 player in Lansing and Midland. At least he's positioned himself to perhaps make the majors by 25. ⚾ First baseman **David MacKinnon** is a Quad-A southpaw-smasher who couldn't hold down the short side of a Seth Brown platoon. He's more likely to be a star in Korea, Japan or Las Vegas than a regular in Oakland. ⚾ Everything comes full circle eventually, and that includes **Billy McKinney** returning to the A's. Unfortunately, there was also a full circle at the front of his batting average (.096). ⚾ It's said that if a **Pablo Reyes** emerges from Triple-A and sees its shadow, his team's injury woes will continue for six more weeks. Otherwise, their player depth will remain intact. ⚾ Baseball transactions are like games of chess, and when the Royals traded for Quad-A masher **Brent Rooker**, an outfielder who can move in any orthogonal direction, he was castled to Omaha in order to protect the king before being DFA'd and picked up by Oakland. ⚾ **Cal Stevenson** is your stereotypical fifth outfielder: he can hit a little, run a little and play all three outfield positions. ⚾ **Cody Thomas** suffered an Achilles injury that kept him out for much of last season, which is ironic for someone with the athleticism of a Greek demigod. Try not to confuse him with Colby. ⚾ **Colby Thomas** could be a dynamic two-way outfielder. The Mercer University product racked up Division I dingers before pre-draft labrum surgery, and A's scouting director Eric Kubota raved about his maximum exit velocities. Try not to confuse him with Cody.

Pitchers

PITCHER	TEAM	LVL	AGE	W	L	SV	G	GS	IP	H	HR	BB/9	K/9	K	GB%	BABIP	WHIP	ERA	DRA-	WARP	MPH	FB%	WHF	CSP
Tyler Cyr	LHV	AAA	29	2	3	6	35	0	36	26	0	4.5	9.3	37	51.6%	.280	1.22	2.50	86	0.7	93.7	58.3%	50.0%	
	LV	AAA	29	0	0	0	4	0	5	7	1	9.0	14.4	8	46.2%	.500	2.40	5.40	80	0.1	94.6	74.1%	32.6%	
	OAK	MLB	29	1	0	0	11	0	13	9	1	3.5	11.1	16	53.3%	.276	1.08	2.08	88	0.2	93.9	65.6%	27.2%	58.4%
	PHI	MLB	29	0	0	0	1	0	0^1	2	1	0.0	0.0	0	0.0%	.500	6.00	27.00	47	0.0	94.0	88.9%	0.0%	65.1%
Joey Estes	LAN	A+	20	3	7	0	20	20	91	86	17	3.0	9.1	92	32.4%	.291	1.27	4.55	126	-0.3				
J.T. Ginn	ATH	ROK	23	0	0	0	2	2	7	4	0	0.0	6.4	5	84.2%	.211	0.57	0.00						
	MID	AA	23	1	4	0	10	10	35^1	38	3	3.6	10.4	41	58.3%	.350	1.47	6.11	71	0.8				
Hogan Harris	LAN	A+	25	0	1	0	7	7	13	5	0	4.8	12.5	18	42.3%	.192	0.92	1.38	92	0.2				
	MID	AA	25	1	0	0	8	7	32^1	15	0	5.3	13.4	48	43.5%	.242	1.05	1.67	70	0.7				
	LV	AAA	25	1	3	0	8	8	28^1	31	6	5.4	12.4	39	33.3%	.362	1.69	6.35	93	0.3	92.9	71.1%	32.4%	
Daulton Jefferies	OAK	MLB	26	1	7	0	8	8	39^1	46	4	1.8	6.4	28	46.3%	.323	1.37	5.72	114	0.1	92.7	45.1%	22.7%	54.4%
Jared Koenig	LV	AAA	28	6	6	0	20	18	107	112	13	2.5	8.7	104	43.4%	.329	1.33	4.71	88	1.4	88.9	78.2%	24.4%	
	OAK	MLB	28	1	3	0	10	5	39^1	40	4	3.4	5.0	22	48.9%	.277	1.40	5.72	139	-0.4	88.7	64.9%	15.1%	55.6%
Mason Miller	LAN	A+	23	0	1	0	3	3	7	3	1	2.6	16.7	13	45.5%	.200	0.71	3.86	78	0.2				
Austin Pruitt	LV	AAA	32	1	0	1	12	0	22	20	0	0.8	8.2	20	37.9%	.308	1.00	3.27	89	0.3	91.4	42.2%	29.2%	
	OAK	MLB	32	0	1	1	39	1	55^1	48	11	1.5	6.2	38	46.0%	.224	1.03	4.23	108	0.3	91.6	34.4%	24.9%	52.4%
Norge Ruiz	LV	AAA	28	5	1	2	31	0	41	36	5	3.5	8.6	39	58.5%	.274	1.27	3.73	85	0.6	92.9	44.7%	24.7%	
	OAK	MLB	28	0	1	0	14	0	19	30	4	3.3	8.5	18	38.8%	.413	1.95	7.11	107	0.1	93.2	44.8%	21.3%	60.1%
Sam Selman	LV	AAA	31	2	0	6	28	0	35	20	2	4.6	9.3	36	39.5%	.214	1.09	2.83	97	0.3	89.9	56.8%	28.3%	
	OAK	MLB	31	0	0	0	16	0	18^1	16	4	2.5	8.8	18	33.3%	.255	1.15	4.91	99	0.2	89.5	52.9%	23.0%	51.2%
Chad Smith	ABQ	AAA	27	1	2	12	32	0	35	27	6	2.8	10.3	40	60.0%	.266	1.09	3.09	72	0.8	96.1	44.6%	34.4%	
	COL	MLB	27	0	1	0	15	0	18	16	2	7.5	11.5	23	55.6%	.326	1.72	7.50	87	0.3	95.7	66.5%	32.3%	48.9%
Kirby Snead	LV	AAA	27	2	0	1	11	0	13^2	13	1	2.0	13.2	20	51.5%	.375	1.17	4.61	76	0.3	93.8	52.5%	30.9%	
	OAK	MLB	27	1	1	1	46	0	44^2	56	5	4.4	7.1	35	43.0%	.352	1.75	5.84	124	-0.1	93.5	55.6%	20.1%	53.6%
Kyle Virbitsky	STK	A	23	5	4	0	16	15	86^2	101	9	2.1	10.3	99	46.3%	.371	1.40	4.78	86	0.9				
	LAN	A+	23	2	3	0	7	7	39^2	35	9	2.3	9.3	41	39.4%	.263	1.13	4.31	96	0.5				
Jake Walkinshaw	LAN	A+	25	3	1	0	9	8	40	37	5	2.5	9.7	43	54.1%	.302	1.20	3.83	87	0.7				
	LV	AAA	25	1	0	1	6	0	18^1	21	3	2.0	5.4	11	39.1%	.295	1.36	3.44	116	-0.1	92.8	54.1%	14.5%	
Chen Zhong-Ao Zhuang	STK	A	21	0	4	0	8	8	42	46	9	1.9	9.2	43	41.7%	.301	1.31	4.71	101	0.0				

Mid-season waiver claim **Tyler Cyr** went to college in Daytona Beach and, like the stock cars circling the international speedway, this reliever's best offering moves to the right and sneaks up on you. Off the strength of his changeup—learned from fellow Bay Area hurler Tim Lincecum—he may have finally earned a regular bullpen role. ⚾ All **Joey Estes** did last year is lead his Lansing teammates in every major rate stat, emerging as one of the more intriguing up-and-coming arms in the organization. Only just entering his age-21 season, the righty prep product is doing his part to improve the A's return for Matt Olson. ⚾ Once considered the crown jewel of last winter's Chris Bassitt deal, **J.T. Ginn** simply hasn't thrown enough innings for us to know if he's worthy of that billing. A forearm issue limited him to just 12 minor-league starts, though an impressive run in the AFL offers hope he's regained his mid-rotation upside. ⚾ This winter, burly right-hander **Deolis Guerra** will celebrate the 15th anniversary of his inclusion in the Johan Santana trade by recovering from UCL reconstruction and trying to prove his *cambio* still belongs in a big-league bullpen. ⚾ Let me tell ya something, brother: **Hogan Harris** earned a 40-man spot by eating his vitamins, saying his prayers and recovering from Tommy John surgery to post a breakout Triple-A campaign. Whatcha gonna do when he runs wild—no really, he misses both lots of bats and sometimes the strike zone entirely—on you? ⚾ Jefferies has battled injuries his entire pro career, but even for him 2022 felt catastrophic. He had part of his rib removed during a thoracic outlet decompression procedure in June, and in September he endured his second Tommy John surgery. Is there anything left of the pitcher he was at Berkeley or who flashed mid-rotation potential in the minors? Here's hoping for 2024. ⚾ The owner of an outstanding story deserving of more words than you'll find in this lineout, **Jared Koenig** made his minor-league debut in 2021 at age 27 and his MLB debut last year at 28. The former Indy Ball standout throws everything but the kitchen sink and profiles as an up-and-down lefty swingman. ⚾ Righty **Mason Miller** turned heads last season, hitting 101 mph with his fastball and impressing in both the minors and AFL. He's probably a reliever long-term, but he could be an interesting one in the majors pretty soon. ⚾ Kudos to **Austin Pruitt**, who topped 77 innings between Las Vegas and Oakland last year as he stayed fully healthy for the first time since 2019. That said, he's homer-prone, out of options and nearing arbitration at 32, so expect him to sign a minor-league contract (or two) before the season starts. ⚾ **Norge Ruiz** possesses the stereotypical tricksy repertoire of Cubano hurlers of the past and present, but his results are less like peak Montreal Expo Liván Hernández than they are like late-career Atlanta Brave Liván Hernández. ⚾ Returning to the Bay Area after a brief stop down the Pacific Coast Highway, **Sam Selman** hinted at putting it all together in short relief bursts. Unfortunately, addressing his longstanding control issues came at the cost of a goosed-up home run rate and decreased effectiveness against lefties. ⚾ **Chad Smith** faced 85 batters with the Rockies and walked or struck out nearly half of them. The remainder spent their time smashing his 96-mph sinker all over the park. His slider is a legit weapon, but he's got little beyond it. ⚾ After a fine April, southpaw reliever **Kirby Snead** allowed runs in 37% of his appearances over the rest of the season. Not many pitchers can maintain a role in a bullpen with that kind of performance, but not many belong to teams that lose 100 games either. ⚾ Big **Kyle Virbitsky** is an outlier both in terms of height and outcomes: The tall righty out of Happy Valley grabs strikeouts by the handful without top-end velocity, and he pounds the zone to minimize free passes. He could move quickly up the minor-league ladder in 2023. ⚾ **Jake Walkinshaw** pitches like a guy who works in baseball R&D during the offseason—he tunnels his pitches well, adds velocity when he needs it and is still adjusting his slider to make it more effective. Will he emerge from the morass of Triple-A swingmen as he refines his craft? More research (and development) is needed. ⚾ It was an impressive, if abbreviated, stateside debut for **Chen Zhong-Ao Zhuang**, a starter signed out of Taiwan in November 2021. He battled injury issues in Stockton but pounded the strike zone with an intriguing four-pitch mix when healthy.

SEATTLE MARINERS

Essay by Robert O'Connell

Player comments by Jon Hegglund and BP staff

I'll take a start over a finish any day, no matter how hopeless the former and how triumphant the latter. Give me the training montage over the big showdown, the leadoff single over the three-run blast. So it is with even the sweetest baseball seasons. A championship has its melancholy aspect, the swirl of confetti signaling it's time to set the book down. April and May might still be endless.

The story of the 2022 Seattle Mariners was built around an ending. One night in September, late in a Northwestern ninth inning, Cal Raleigh got into a 3-2 changeup and held his bat in the air like a flare. The ball bent around the foul pole. The home run meant a 2-1 Mariners win, which meant the team would reach the postseason for the first time since 2001. Raleigh skipped into his trot; his teammates jumped the dugout fence; his triumphant twirl of lumber nearly clocked one or two of them. Twenty-one years of irrelevance and false hope and something either just shy or far short of adequacy was erased, and you could practically hear the orchestra swelling into the major chord. Great! Hooray! But also, blech.

The story of the '22 Mariners also centered on a beginning, of course, but that beginning was so heralded that it felt somehow ending-ish, as if the arrival of the hero made the actual carrying out of his scripted tasks a formality. Julio Rodríguez closed a loop that opened with the farewells of Ken Griffey Jr. and Ichiro. He arrived and seems already permanent, an etching of airborne snags and mad dashes and big airy homers from that big airy loop of his swing. His age, his frame and the still-sometimes-frantic aspect to his movement suggest progress to come, of course, but they suggest it so strongly that it seems foregone. Julio is here, and what does he do? He hits missiles, runs like a lightning bolt, jumps high and throws hard, and he gets better at doing each of those things every day.

The happiest stretch of 2022's happiest season, then, seemed to me to come at the turn of August, when the Mariners traded for Luis Castillo. It's as worn and wonderful as a beginning gets: a stranger comes to town, with 97 miles-per-hour on his hip. Sending off prospects for the best available pitcher in the game signaled buy-in from management, and Castillo may well have provided the last margins that got Seattle to the playoffs. Still, the narrative

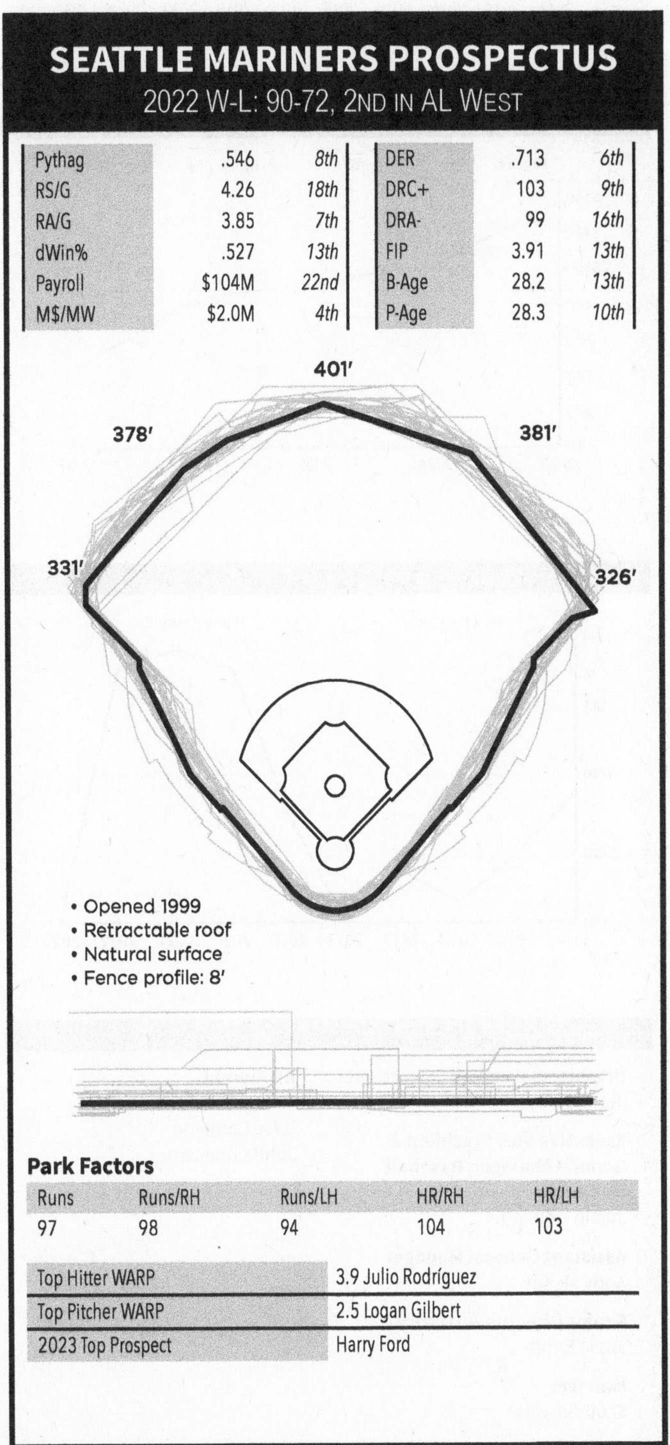

SEATTLE MARINERS PROSPECTUS

2022 W-L: 90-72, 2ND IN AL WEST

Pythag	.546	*8th*	DER	.713	*6th*
RS/G	4.26	*18th*	DRC+	103	*9th*
RA/G	3.85	*7th*	DRA-	99	*16th*
dWin%	.527	*13th*	FIP	3.91	*13th*
Payroll	$104M	*22nd*	B-Age	28.2	*13th*
M$/MW	$2.0M	*4th*	P-Age	28.3	*10th*

- Opened 1999
- Retractable roof
- Natural surface
- Fence profile: 8'

Park Factors

Runs	Runs/RH	Runs/LH	HR/RH	HR/LH
97	98	94	104	103

Top Hitter WARP	3.9 Julio Rodríguez
Top Pitcher WARP	2.5 Logan Gilbert
2023 Top Prospect	Harry Ford

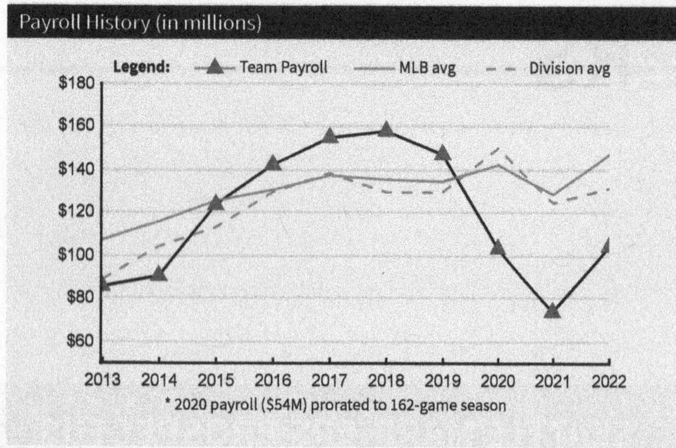

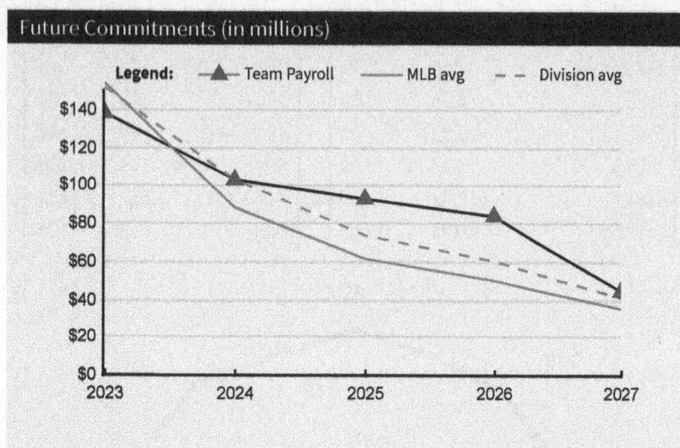

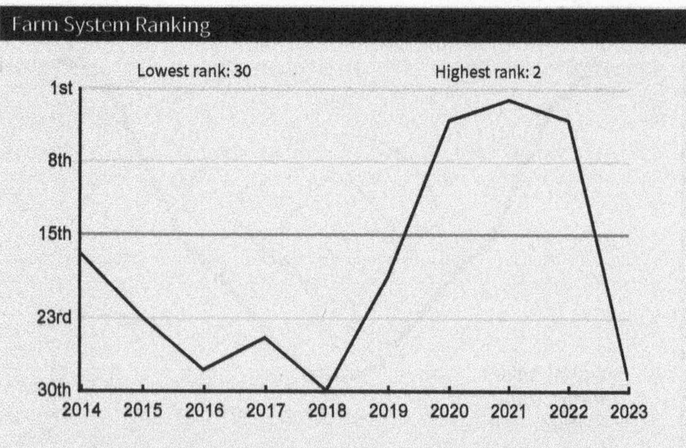

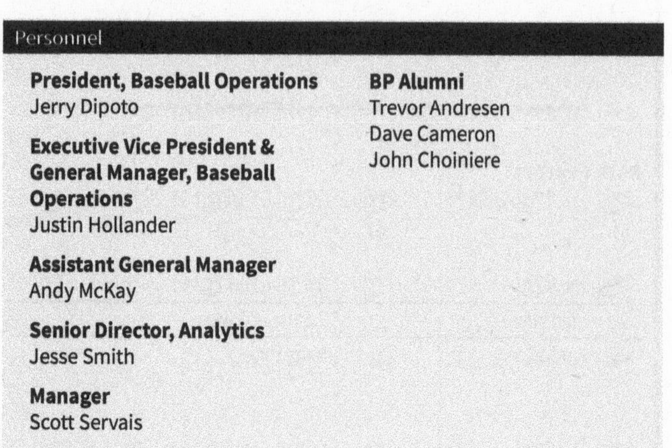
Personnel

President, Baseball Operations
Jerry Dipoto

Executive Vice President & General Manager, Baseball Operations
Justin Hollander

Assistant General Manager
Andy McKay

Senior Director, Analytics
Jesse Smith

Manager
Scott Servais

BP Alumni
Trevor Andresen
Dave Cameron
John Choiniere

purpose trumped the symbolic or practical ones. Castillo put on the teal and told the lie that good openings do. Something new is happening, and it'll last forever.

⚾ ⚾ ⚾

"We've got a chance to do something really big here this year," Seattle manager Scott Servais said after the deadline deal that brought Castillo to Seattle. "You have to step out and take a chance once in a while if you ultimately want to get the reward, take a little risk. Dominant starting pitcher, and I'm anxious to meet him."

One can forgive the paltry time scale: the managerial one-day-at-a-time-dictate, the looming possibility of a playoff berth and the questionable status of Castillo long-term (he'd not yet agreed to an extension with the Mariners) meant that October was about as far-off a horizon as Servais could see. But the rest of his words were shot through with the pure, avid possibility of it all, with first steps and nervy determination and the potential of immense reward, in the near or distant future.

The first day Castillo climbed the bump for the Mariners, he struck out eight Yankees over 6⅔ innings in a breezy win. The numbers didn't mean as much as how he got them. Over the first four months of the season, the Mariners' rotation had been charming and mostly effective; Logan Gilbert's fastball ran straight at hitters, and Marco Gonzales' changeup ducked out of their sight. But Castillo was something else. Tall, languid and long-levered, he threw with an economy of motion that suggested success as a birthright, not as a reward for fallow decades of toil. He notched his first strikeout on a high heater buzzing the top of the zone, minimal effort and maximum thrust. The next was on a slider, low and in. After another fastball K—this one aimed at the outside edge and then *whooshing* off of it—out came the changeup. This was the strange light mottling the leaves of the untraveled path, the different smell to the air. Josh Donaldson swung like he'd never seen a pitch like it. The Mariners hadn't either, at least coming from someone wearing their colors. (Late-career Félix's had the style, not the speed.)

His next time out, again against the Yankees, Castillo worked eight shutout innings, each of them crucial in a 1-0 extra-inning win. "That was the coolest game I've ever been a part of," Seattle reliever Matt Brash said.

Of course it was. That's the kind of baseball game players like Castillo make possible, the kind of avenue a character like Castillo opens up. For the rest of the summer and into the fall, he wasn't untouchable; the Mariners won six of his 11 regular-season starts as he put up a 3.11 ERA. His mode of excellence, though, was its own reward. What does it feel like, to play for or follow a team that for years has held fast to crumbs of luck and tried to maximize dwindling percentages, and then one day to see a hand like that let go of pitches like those? I'd imagine it feels like you've got important places to go.

⚾ ⚾ ⚾

If the front half of the Mariners' season was characterized by conscious optimism—willing the bat and hairstyles of Eugenio Suárez to keep mashing homers and summoning good vibes, the eye of Raleigh to stay just to the right side of passable, the tendons and ligaments of Rodríguez to remain unhampered—the post-Castillo chapter carried a sense of things falling into place. Gilbert and Robbie Ray, the latter of whom was miscast as an imported ace savior, were alright as a number one and two, but they shined as a two and three. Players forced into something like stardom, namely Suárez and Raleigh, could take a step back and focus on what they did best: cranking big extra-base hits, conceiving of and executing Art Deco bleach jobs, embracing nicknames that the denizens of Seattle had to explain to their parents.

In September, Castillo signed an extension with Seattle, joining Rodríguez, who'd inked his own in August. If everything goes according to plan for the Mariners, players like J.P. Crawford and Suárez and Raleigh will be replaced—upgraded—in time, but contenders are always shot through with their sort: guys who might dully gather their numbers on sub-.500 clubs and who, buoyed by winners, are revealed to have lovable and groovy it-factors. (Kolten Wong is a candidate here; Teoscar Hernández is, happily, overqualified.) There's a multiplying effect, in mood if not in data. Dudes like Castillo make guys like them matter more, give their slash singles and aberrant walks and moments of web-gem inspiration a big contextual glow-up.

The Mariners might have made the playoffs sans Castillo, but they couldn't have held to the same version of hope this offseason without him. Before those starts against the Yankees, this was a club that had clawed its way upward and could as easily slide back. Now it's one with an ace to set next to its center field superstar for—what a luxury of a phrase—*the foreseeable future*. The team can tell its fans that this is just getting going, and the fans can believe it.

Castillo pitched twice for the Mariners in the postseason. The first start was chock full of statistical and spiritual Ace Shit. Castillo went 7⅓ shutout innings, survived the Blue Jays' lineup three times, fanned Vladdy Guerrero Jr. on his way out. The pressure of the only playoff game he'd ever worked in front of a non-COVID-tamped audience didn't faze but emboldened Castillo. I don't know if the clutch gene exists, but I know who I'd pick for the medical trial.

Castillo's second and final start came against the Astros in the ALDS, and although he lost it—he fired a fastball just off the plate against Yordan Alvarez; Alvarez reached out and thwacked it a mile to the opposite field; some far-off planets made entirely of metal scraped against each other, creating a galaxy-wide show of sparks and recreating the exact sounds of *Led Zeppelin III*—he did nothing to diminish his earned standing. For seven more innings, in the sweatiest of environs, he gave the most decorated postseason lineup of its generation a fair and honest fight. Sequencing his pitches with the step-ahead caginess of a seasoned vet, he powered them with the hot-burning fuel of someone who hasn't gotten to do something like this all that often. His fastball put Jose Altuve on his heels. His changeup was a lockpick, releasing him from jams.

Strange as it might have been to say at the time—especially with almost the whole baseball universe cheering plucky Seattle on against the wicked Astros—the outcome didn't particularly matter. Seattle lost the series, three games to none, but Castillo didn't join the club to do anything as mundane as "win the 2022 championship." He doesn't promise a trophy, but represents an invitation to something more sprawling and layered than a season. The last month of the Mariners' 2022 was baseball at its most pulse-quickening: opportunity approaching and narrowing, massive stakes getting massiver, generational curses coming to rest on individual shoulders. This is where the team lives now. There's plenty more to come. ■

—Robert O'Connell covers basketball for the Wall Street Journal.

⚾ ⚾ ⚾

HITTERS

Jonatan Clase CF Born: 05/23/02 Age: 21 Bats: S Throws: R Height: 5'8" Weight: 150 lb. Origin: International Free Agent, 2018

YEAR	TEAM	LVL	AGE	PA	R	2B	3B	HR	RBI	BB	K	SB	CS	Whiff%	AVG/OBP/SLG	DRC+	BABIP	BRR	DRP	WARP
2021	MRN	ROK	19	57	12	1	0	2	10	6	15	16	0		.245/.333/.388		.303			
2022	MOD	A	20	499	91	22	11	13	49	65	133	55	10		.267/.373/.463	101	.358	3.6	CF(95): -0.5, LF(5): 0.1	1.8
2023 non-DC	*SEA*	*MLB*	*21*	*251*	*21*	*9*	*3*	*4*	*23*	*20*	*82*	*16*	*4*	*34.6%*	*.207/.278/.338*	*67*	*.303*	*7.3*	*LF 0, CF 0*	*0.5*

Comparables: Sean Henry (86), Daz Cameron (85), Teoscar Hernández (84)

Clase came into rookie ball from the Dominican Republic in 2019, and paired his 80-grade speed with a walk rate approaching 20%. The real sickos would say "now let's add some power," and Clase did just that in a 2022 full season at... well, Low-A. The center fielder, with some newfound bulk, buttressed his 55 steals with 13 bombs in his age-20 season. We hear there's already a pretty good power/speed/defense guy playing center field in Seattle for the next couple decades or so, but if Clase continues his improbable arc through the minors, an excess of tooled-up hitters at a premium defensive position will be, to put it mildly, a good problem for the Mariners to have.

J.P. Crawford SS Born: 01/11/95 Age: 28 Bats: L Throws: R Height: 6'2" Weight: 202 lb. Origin: Round 1, 2013 Draft (#16 overall)

YEAR	TEAM	LVL	AGE	PA	R	2B	3B	HR	RBI	BB	K	SB	CS	Whiff%	AVG/OBP/SLG	DRC+	BABIP	BRR	DRP	WARP
2020	SEA	MLB	25	232	33	7	2	2	24	23	39	6	3	18.3%	.255/.336/.338	93	.303	2.8	SS(53): 2.4	1.0
2021	SEA	MLB	26	687	89	37	0	9	54	58	114	3	6	15.6%	.273/.338/.376	92	.320	-2.0	SS(160): 2.4	1.8
2022	SEA	MLB	27	603	57	24	3	6	42	68	80	3	2	14.4%	.243/.339/.336	102	.275	0.0	SS(144): 0.2	2.1
2023 DC	*SEA*	*MLB*	*28*	*629*	*71*	*25*	*2*	*11*	*54*	*65*	*87*	*6*	*2*	*14.7%*	*.258/.340/.380*	*108*	*.283*	*1.9*	*SS 5*	*3.2*

Comparables: Everth Cabrera (76), Ed Brinkman (74), Spike Owen (70)

One of several Mariners whose statistical output doesn't quite measure up to his vibes factor, Crawford entered the 2022 season fresh off of signing a five-year extension that indicated his role as a key foundation piece of the NextGen Mariners. As if to will that optimistic outlook into reality, manager Scott Servais ended up slotting Crawford into a top-five batting order position in 97 of his 144 games. While the 28-year-old has consistently been able to take a walk, his hard-hit rate is befitting of a ninth-place hitter whose contributions lie with defense and speed. And about those… In 2022, Crawford's defense, by nearly all metrics, declined significantly (with an Outs Above Average that placed him last among full-time major-league shortstops), and his sprint speed is well below average. The club appears to remain committed to Crawford as the preferred shortstop option heading into 2023, and he is a core element in the team's fizzing chemistry, but it's hard not to see Crawford as a conspicuous weakness at a position that, for championship caliber teams, is nearly always a strength.

★ ★ ★ *2023 Top 101 Prospect* **#85** ★ ★ ★

Harry Ford C Born: 02/21/03 Age: 20 Bats: R Throws: R Height: 5'10" Weight: 200 lb. Origin: Round 1, 2021 Draft (#12 overall)

YEAR	TEAM	LVL	AGE	PA	R	2B	3B	HR	RBI	BB	K	SB	CS	Whiff%	AVG/OBP/SLG	DRC+	BABIP	BRR	DRP	WARP
2021	MRN	ROK	18	65	12	7	0	3	10	9	14	3	0		.291/.400/.582		.342			
2022	MOD	A	19	499	89	23	4	11	65	88	115	23	5		.274/.425/.438	116	.358	-0.6	C(54): 7.5	3.1
2023 non-DC	*SEA*	*MLB*	*20*	*251*	*22*	*9*	*1*	*3*	*21*	*25*	*72*	*5*	*2*	*31.3%*	*.208/.301/.317*	*74*	*.293*	*2.6*	*C 0*	*0.4*

Comparables: Angel Salome (83), Bo Naylor (82), Iván Herrera (80)

YEAR	TEAM	P. COUNT	FRM RUNS	BLK RUNS	THRW RUNS	TOT RUNS
2022	MOD	8140	5.7	0.8	-0.2	6.3
2023	*SEA*	*6956*	*-0.2*	*0.4*	*0.1*	*0.4*

What are they even doing in the Catcher Factory these days? As if they weren't happy enough creating a defensively impeccable on-base machine (The Rutschman 3000) or the guy who could double as a base-stealing outfielder when needed (The Varsh-o-matic), now they're trying to give us a backstop who has a superlative batting eye, blazing speed, a decent bit of pop and the defensive ability to stick at the position. Perhaps the Ford C 20/20 won't deliver on all of its advertised promises, but the development path will surely be fun to watch.

Ty France 1B Born: 07/13/94 Age: 28 Bats: R Throws: R Height: 5'11" Weight: 215 lb. Origin: Round 34, 2015 Draft (#1017 overall)

YEAR	TEAM	LVL	AGE	PA	R	2B	3B	HR	RBI	BB	K	SB	CS	Whiff%	AVG/OBP/SLG	DRC+	BABIP	BRR	DRP	WARP
2020	SD	MLB	25	61	9	4	0	2	10	5	15	0	0	26.8%	.309/.377/.491	98	.395	0.7	1B(5): -0.1, 3B(2): -0.2	0.2
2020	SEA	MLB	25	94	10	5	1	2	13	6	22	0	0	24.2%	.302/.362/.453	100	.387	-0.2	2B(10): -0.6, 3B(4): -0.5	0.1
2021	SEA	MLB	26	650	85	32	1	18	73	46	106	0	0	19.1%	.291/.368/.445	119	.327	0.5	1B(106): 2, 2B(21): 0.2, 3B(5): 0.1	3.4
2022	SEA	MLB	27	613	65	27	1	20	84	35	94	0	0	19.3%	.276/.340/.437	123	.299	-1.7	1B(127): 0.4, 3B(6): -0.2, 2B(1): 0	2.8
2023 DC	*SEA*	*MLB*	*28*	*604*	*66*	*25*	*1*	*15*	*63*	*39*	*95*	*0*	*0*	*19.2%*	*.276/.346/.416*	*117*	*.308*	*-1.2*	*1B 1, 3B 0*	*2.1*

Comparables: C.J. Cron (60), Garrett Atkins (58), Josh Bell (58)

After the singular excellence of Julio, it's an understatement to say that the Mariners' lineup contained quite a few high-variance bats—which makes France's steadiness a welcome, and indeed necessary, component of this mercurial offense. France gets his bat to the ball with the skill to frequently find a place where defenders are not, and while his exit velocities amble along in the slow lane, he can yank one to the pull side on a semi-regular basis. Add in the strong defense at the cold corner, and France is essentially what the M's thought Evan White would be. A wrist injury likely contributed to a deflated second half, but a healthy France should spend quite a bit of time at or around first base—whether he's arrived via bat or glove.

Sam Haggerty UT Born: 05/26/94 Age: 29 Bats: S Throws: R Height: 5'11" Weight: 175 lb. Origin: Round 24, 2015 Draft (#724 overall)

YEAR	TEAM	LVL	AGE	PA	R	2B	3B	HR	RBI	BB	K	SB	CS	Whiff%	AVG/OBP/SLG	DRC+	BABIP	BRR	DRP	WARP
2020	SEA	MLB	26	54	7	4	0	1	6	4	16	4	0	36.2%	.260/.315/.400	87	.364	1.0	LF(10): -0.7, 3B(1): 0, RF(1): 0.1	0.1
2021	SEA	MLB	27	94	15	3	0	2	5	6	28	5	1	31.5%	.186/.247/.291	79	.250	0.3	LF(20): 1.2, RF(6): -0.4, 2B(4): 0.2	0.2
2022	TAC	AAA	28	179	28	11	2	6	25	18	34	15	1	26.8%	.283/.369/.500	109	.325	1.5	2B(29): 1.0, SS(7): -1.0, CF(2): 0.7	0.9
2022	SEA	MLB	28	201	29	9	1	5	23	18	53	13	1	28.8%	.256/.335/.403	95	.333	1.8	RF(37): 0.6, LF(33): 1.8, CF(6): 0.3	1.0
2023 DC	*SEA*	*MLB*	*29*	*249*	*24*	*9*	*2*	*4*	*21*	*20*	*63*	*15*	*2*	*28.5%*	*.223/.294/.347*	*81*	*.286*	*9.2*	*2B 0, RF 0*	*1.1*

Comparables: Justin Ruggiano (54), Rob Ducey (53), Marlon Byrd (51)

The 2022 Mariners were oddly filled with lovable fan favorites whose appeal couldn't always be captured by a stat line. "Ham Swaggerty" was one such personality, endearing himself to fans with an all-out defensive style, electric speed and even the occasional dinger here and there. Even though his ascendance was largely due to a shortage of healthy outfielders, Haggerty gave the offense a late-season spark until he injured his groin stealing his 13th base of the year in the season's final week. In the cold, statistical light of day, Haggerty is probably best cast as a fourth outfielder, with his defense and switch hitting particularly useful traits, and his mediocre contact skills less so. In Jerry Dipoto's optimal 2023 roster construction, Haggerty will be most beloved as a bit player rather than an everyday fixture.

Teoscar Hernández RF Born: 10/15/92 Age: 30 Bats: R Throws: R Height: 6'2" Weight: 215 lb. Origin: International Free Agent, 2011

YEAR	TEAM	LVL	AGE	PA	R	2B	3B	HR	RBI	BB	K	SB	CS	Whiff%	AVG/OBP/SLG	DRC+	BABIP	BRR	DRP	WARP
2020	TOR	MLB	27	207	33	7	0	16	34	14	63	6	1	34.9%	.289/.340/.579	117	.348	-0.5	RF(40): 4.9, CF(9): 0.8	1.6
2021	TOR	MLB	28	595	92	29	0	32	116	36	148	12	4	31.9%	.296/.346/.524	118	.352	0.6	RF(110): 5, LF(58): -1.6	3.6
2022	TOR	MLB	29	535	71	35	1	25	77	34	152	6	3	35.1%	.267/.316/.491	112	.335	2.4	RF(117): 2.4, LF(8): -0.8	2.8
2023 DC	*SEA*	*MLB*	*30*	*588*	*65*	*26*	*2*	*25*	*76*	*40*	*165*	*11*	*4*	*34.2%*	*.254/.309/.453*	*109*	*.316*	*1.2*	*RF -1*	*1.8*

Comparables: Gary Matthews (71), Mike Marshall (71), Sammy Sosa (70)

The oblique strain Hernández suffered in April looked like it would derail his season. Upon returning in early May, he hit groundballs at a 60% clip and slashed a woeful .151/.195/.233. But on May 31, things started to turn around. He hit two doubles—doubling his total from his first 24 games—and went on to slash .285/.331/.536 with 23 home runs the rest of the way. He was the Blue Jays' best hitter during that span, as the defining characteristics of his 2020-2021 breakout—40-homer power and a line drive-inflated BABIP—shone once more upon his return to health. Those early-season stats still count, of course, so we know we're tastefully cherry-picking here. But even if Hernández is "only" as good as his final stat line suggests—dreadful month of May included—he remains an exceptionally good baseball player. If he's truly as gifted as his output *without* May, well, he's a down-ballot MVP candidate. Despite having just one year of team control remaining, Hernández's bat remains tempting enough for the Mariners to part with Erik Swanson and change for it in November. He'll now look to help anchor Seattle's lineup.

Jarred Kelenic OF Born: 07/16/99 Age: 23 Bats: L Throws: L Height: 6'1" Weight: 206 lb. Origin: Round 1, 2018 Draft (#6 overall)

YEAR	TEAM	LVL	AGE	PA	R	2B	3B	HR	RBI	BB	K	SB	CS	Whiff%	AVG/OBP/SLG	DRC+	BABIP	BRR	DRP	WARP
2021	TAC	AAA	21	143	29	9	1	9	28	15	22	6	1		.320/.392/.624	125	.323	-1.5	LF(11): -1.5, CF(11): 0.2, RF(6): 0.4	0.7
2021	SEA	MLB	21	377	41	13	1	14	43	36	106	6	4	26.9%	.181/.265/.350	77	.216	-0.1	CF(77): -4, LF(14): -1.5, RF(3): -0.1	-0.1
2022	TAC	AAA	22	394	58	32	3	18	65	35	82	9	4	26.1%	.295/.365/.557	108	.339	1.5	RF(28): 0.3, CF(25): 2.2, LF(22): -1.0	2.1
2022	SEA	MLB	22	181	20	5	1	7	17	16	61	5	2	33.4%	.141/.221/.313	70	.167	-0.4	CF(24): -0.2, RF(24): -0.3, LF(3): 0.2	-0.1
2023 DC	*SEA*	*MLB*	*23*	*421*	*45*	*18*	*2*	*16*	*45*	*34*	*119*	*8*	*3*	*29.8%*	*.218/.286/.411*	*92*	*.267*	*1.6*	*LF 0, CF -1*	*0.6*

Comparables: Chad Hermansen (54), Byron Buxton (52), Roger Cedeno (49)

Prospects begin with varying degrees and layers of uncertainty and, over time, these broad questions narrow to a fine point regarding what will, or won't, make them major-league players. In Kelenic's case, the remaining uncertainty is now focused down to one hard question: *Can he hit anything that isn't a fastball*? A quick glance at his pitch type splits suggests that, as of yet, the answer is an emphatic "no." If you go deeper in the splits, noting some swing adjustments and improved results last September, you might ever-so-slightly upgrade your answer to an uncertain "maybe?" It's hard to calculate the developmental issues that attended the chaos of the pandemic year, and then throw in the overwhelming expectations from a success-starved Seattle fanbase, so these crumbs of hope may have to suffice to feed hopeful M's supporters through the long winter months. Does Kelenic merit this kind of patience? He has the pedigree, raw talent and total commitment to his team to deserve all the patience in the world. But, in 2022, the Mariners made the transition from "win someday" to "win now," and Kelenic's ability to hit breaking and off-speed pitches will soon—like, really really soon—determine whether he plays his hoped-for role as a key player on the new, good Mariners.

Cade Marlowe CF Born: 06/24/97 Age: 26 Bats: L Throws: R Height: 6'1" Weight: 210 lb. Origin: Round 20, 2019 Draft (#606 overall)

YEAR	TEAM	LVL	AGE	PA	R	2B	3B	HR	RBI	BB	K	SB	CS	Whiff%	AVG/OBP/SLG	DRC+	BABIP	BRR	DRP	WARP
2021	PEJ	WIN	24	92	18	5	0	0	7	17	23	7	0		.233/.385/.301		.340			
2021	MOD	A	24	160	35	6	5	6	29	24	40	11	2		.301/.406/.556	127	.382	0.9	LF(20): -2.7, CF(7): -1.3, RF(1): -0.2	0.8
2021	EVE	A+	24	325	52	18	5	20	77	36	91	12	7		.259/.345/.566	113	.307	-3.5	RF(39): 0.4, CF(16): -0.4, LF(10): -0.9	1.2
2022	ARK	AA	25	518	75	18	4	20	86	55	133	36	10		.291/.380/.483	101	.369	2.0	CF(113): 2.9, LF(1): -0.1	2.0
2022	TAC	AAA	25	60	8	3	1	3	16	7	23	6	0	38.3%	.250/.350/.519	79	.385	0.7	CF(5): 0.6, LF(4): 0.6, RF(4): 0.5	0.2
2023 DC	*SEA*	*MLB*	*26*	*30*	*3*	*1*	*0*	*0*	*3*	*2*	*9*	*1*	*0*	*33.8%*	*.220/.289/.387*	*87*	*.290*	*0.7*	*LF 0*	*0.1*

In 1593, eminent dramatist and 29-year-old Christopher Marlowe was stabbed to death in a London bar fight, cutting short a career of astonishingly modern, violent works and launching centuries of speculation into the reason for his death, most notably a persistent(ly deranged) theory he'd faked his demise to ghostwrite the works of one William Shakespeare—with whom his oeuvre shares passing similarities. This Marlowe is a few years short of 29, but as long as he remains in Seattle he, too, will languish in the shadow of someone with a similar output in the nascent days of his career.

Lazaro Montes OF Born: 10/22/04 Age: 18 Bats: L Throws: R Height: 6'3" Weight: 210 lb. Origin: International Free Agent, 2022

YEAR	TEAM	LVL	AGE	PA	R	2B	3B	HR	RBI	BB	K	SB	CS	Whiff%	AVG/OBP/SLG	DRC+	BABIP	BRR	DRP	WARP
2022	DSL SEA	ROK	17	223	34	13	5	10	41	35	74	3	1		.284/.422/.585		.421			
2023															*No projection*					

An 18-year-old in a large human frame, Montes has drawn comparisons to another left-handed slugger, his fellow Cuban Yordan Alvarez. Lest we get ahead of ourselves, the 2022 signee is years away from competing on the same stage as the Astro superstar, but he does have the seeds of an impact power and on-base slugger. While his short DSL season was plenty encouraging, Montes will have to cut down on the swing-and-miss as he moves through the minors.

Dylan Moore UT

Born: 08/02/92 Age: 30 Bats: R Throws: R Height: 6'0" Weight: 205 lb. Origin: Round 7, 2015 Draft (#198 overall)

YEAR	TEAM	LVL	AGE	PA	R	2B	3B	HR	RBI	BB	K	SB	CS	Whiff%	AVG/OBP/SLG	DRC+	BABIP	BRR	DRP	WARP
2020	SEA	MLB	27	159	26	9	0	8	17	14	43	12	5	27.2%	.255/.358/.496	113	.314	1.6	LF(13): 0, RF(13): 2.9, 2B(10): -0.7	1.1
2021	SEA	MLB	28	377	42	11	2	12	43	40	111	21	5	25.9%	.181/.276/.334	85	.229	-0.3	2B(66): -1.1, LF(48): 0.6, 3B(10): 0	0.5
2022	SEA	MLB	29	255	41	11	2	6	24	34	75	21	8	27.8%	.224/.368/.385	96	.320	2.3	RF(39): -0.5, SS(26): -0.3, LF(18): 0.4	0.9
2023 DC	*SEA*	*MLB*	*30*	*379*	*41*	*14*	*1*	*12*	*36*	*42*	*106*	*34*	*7*	*27.0%*	*.209/.322/.385*	*98*	*.267*	*13.4*	*3B 0, SS 0*	*2.3*

Comparables: Jayson Nix (58), Ernie Young (50), Keon Broxton (50)

It would make sense to say "we're still waiting to find out who the real Dylan Moore is" if he were, say, a 25-year-old post-prospect fresh off of an uneven-but-promising major-league debut. But as the chiseled utility man passes into his thirties and his fifth season with the Mariners, his profile is still a bit of a head-scratcher. He's positionally versatile, but the fielding metrics have bounced around wildly. When you watch him you see the power to the pull side, but he still owns a career slugging percentage under .400. He's improved his walk rates, but his quality of contact and strikeout rates remain underwhelming. One thing we can say about Moore: He's faster than you'd think to look at his frame—but when you realize he's built like a tailback, the speed makes a bit more sense. On a competitive roster, Moore is a second-base/corner-outfield supersub, or possibly a starter in a short-side platoon. But even if his skills are difficult to pin down, they generally add up to something worthwhile.

Tom Murphy C

Born: 04/03/91 Age: 32 Bats: R Throws: R Height: 6'1" Weight: 206 lb. Origin: Round 3, 2012 Draft (#105 overall)

YEAR	TEAM	LVL	AGE	PA	R	2B	3B	HR	RBI	BB	K	SB	CS	Whiff%	AVG/OBP/SLG	DRC+	BABIP	BRR	DRP	WARP
2021	SEA	MLB	30	325	35	8	0	11	34	40	99	0	0	33.2%	.202/.304/.350	90	.265	0.2	C(88): 2.6	1.2
2022	SEA	MLB	31	42	9	2	0	1	1	8	13	0	0	33.3%	.303/.439/.455	84	.474	0.2	C(12): 0.4	0.1
2023 DC	*SEA*	*MLB*	*32*	*252*	*27*	*9*	*0*	*9*	*25*	*29*	*77*	*0*	*0*	*32.6%*	*.215/.313/.388*	*95*	*.284*	*-1.9*	*C 1*	*0.5*

Comparables: Kelly Shoppach (59), David Ross (57), Charles Johnson (56)

YEAR	TEAM	P. COUNT	FRM RUNS	BLK RUNS	THRW RUNS	TOT RUNS
2021	SEA	12065	1.1	0.1	0.9	2.1
2022	SEA	1582	0.5	0.0	0.0	0.5
2023	*SEA*	*7215*	*0.3*	*0.0*	*0.5*	*0.8*

Murphy got off to a hot, small-sample start in April before being sidelined with a dislocated left shoulder in early May. Eventually, this ailment led to labrum surgery and a lost season. While Murphy was sidelined, Cal Raleigh emerged as a backstop who could offer both offense and defense and became the de facto starter for the team. Murphy's path forward depends, first and foremost, on his injury recovery and whether he will be able to retain his previous skills both behind and at the plate—with the caveat that neither offensive nor defensive metrics were above average. It's certainly concerning that Murphy's least objectionable hitting skill was his power, as a balky shoulder could easily drain that away in a hurry. Presuming game-readiness, it might be a fortuitous outcome that the 31-year-old is eased back in as Raleigh's understudy as he works his way toward full health in his final arbitration year.

AJ Pollock OF

Born: 12/05/87 Age: 35 Bats: R Throws: R Height: 6'1" Weight: 210 lb. Origin: Round 1, 2009 Draft (#17 overall)

YEAR	TEAM	LVL	AGE	PA	R	2B	3B	HR	RBI	BB	K	SB	CS	Whiff%	AVG/OBP/SLG	DRC+	BABIP	BRR	DRP	WARP
2020	LAD	MLB	32	210	30	9	0	16	34	12	45	2	2	24.5%	.276/.314/.566	119	.277	0.0	LF(27): -2.2, CF(16): -0.9	0.8
2021	LAD	MLB	33	422	53	27	1	21	69	30	80	9	1	24.3%	.297/.355/.536	119	.326	-0.5	LF(103): 0.2, CF(8): -0.5	2.5
2022	CHW	MLB	34	527	61	26	1	14	56	32	98	3	1	24.8%	.245/.292/.389	97	.278	-2.7	LF(107): -0.4, CF(37): -2.8, RF(14): -0.2	0.9
2023 DC	*SEA*	*MLB*	*35*	*438*	*49*	*21*	*1*	*16*	*56*	*28*	*87*	*5*	*0*	*24.6%*	*.260/.314/.441*	*108*	*.295*	*2.2*	*LF 0, RF 0*	*1.7*

Comparables: Torii Hunter (76), Bernie Williams (75), Garry Maddox (74)

Pollock was an imperfect solution to the White Sox's right field problem, even when they acquired him from Los Angeles for Craig Kimbrel a week before the season opener. The sometime center fielder had been, in some ways, a perfect fit in Los Angeles; the team's depth and a forward-thinking staff helped optimize his time on the field. In Chicago, he regularly did what he's always done: hit left-handed pitching. He also did something he hadn't since 2015: get through an entire season healthy. What Pollock didn't do is solve Chicago's outfield problem. His declining defensive skills hardly made a difference when the team was regularly trotting out first baseman at either corner, and like many teammates, he handled right-handed pitching like a replacement-level player. Pollock is a fine platoon outfielder at this stage in his career. With Seattle, he's finally found a team that can afford to use him that way.

Cal Raleigh C

Born: 11/26/96 Age: 26 Bats: S Throws: R Height: 6'3" Weight: 235 lb. Origin: Round 3, 2018 Draft (#90 overall)

YEAR	TEAM	LVL	AGE	PA	R	2B	3B	HR	RBI	BB	K	SB	CS	Whiff%	AVG/OBP/SLG	DRC+	BABIP	BRR	DRP	WARP
2021	TAC	AAA	24	199	34	21	1	9	36	14	25	3	2		.324/.377/.608	124	.327	0.4	C(34): 7.2, 1B(2): -0.0	2.0
2021	SEA	MLB	24	148	6	12	0	2	13	7	52	0	0	33.1%	.180/.223/.309	53	.267	0.0	C(43): 4	0.1
2022	TAC	AAA	25	30	4	2	0	1	4	2	7	0	0	25.6%	.286/.333/.464	98	.350	0.0	C(5): -0.2	0.1
2022	SEA	MLB	25	415	46	20	1	27	63	38	122	1	0	32.2%	.211/.284/.489	115	.226	-0.2	C(115): 11	3.4
2023 DC	*SEA*	*MLB*	*26*	*438*	*50*	*21*	*1*	*21*	*54*	*33*	*121*	*2*	*1*	*31.2%*	*.221/.286/.445*	*99*	*.257*	*-0.1*	*C 12*	*2.7*

Comparables: J.P. Arencibia (75), Sean Murphy (73), Yan Gomes (70)

YEAR	TEAM	P. COUNT	FRM RUNS	BLK RUNS	THRW RUNS	TOT RUNS
2021	TAC	5098	7.4	0.0	0.0	7.4
2021	SEA	5497	3.9	-0.1	0.0	3.8
2022	SEA	14649	11.4	0.1	-0.2	11.4
2023	*SEA*	*14430*	*12.0*	*-0.1*	*0.3*	*12.2*

There were a handful of games in 2021 when the Mariners effectively started three catchers: Raleigh behind the dish, Luis Torrens at first base and Tom Murphy at DH. At the risk of understatement, this is Not What You Want. What a difference a year makes. Murphy got knocked out early in the year, and Torrens showed little as either hitter or backstop. This opened a pathway to a starting job so wide that even Raleigh's legendary and prodigious backside could comfortably fit through with plenty of clearance. And while Raleigh was by no means perfect, he hit plenty of well-timed dingers and backed his way into Seattle hearts as the one and only Big Dumper. Perhaps the most impressive development in Raleigh's season was his defense: He became a pitch-framing wizard and an effective extinguisher of would-be basestealers. All of this added up to a three-plus win season (eighth-best among catchers) and one less roster problem that Jerry Dipoto needs to solve heading into 2023.

Julio Rodríguez CF Born: 12/29/00 Age: 22 Bats: R Throws: R Height: 6'3" Weight: 228 lb. Origin: International Free Agent, 2017

YEAR	TEAM	LVL	AGE	PA	R	2B	3B	HR	RBI	BB	K	SB	CS	Whiff%	AVG/OBP/SLG	DRC+	BABIP	BRR	DRP	WARP
2020	ESC	WIN	19	64	4	1	1	0	7	6	16	3	0		.196/.297/.250		.275			
2021	EVE	A+	20	134	29	8	2	6	21	14	29	5	1		.325/.410/.581	114	.390	0.6	RF(19): 1.8, LF(1): -0.1, CF(1): -0.2	0.8
2021	ARK	AA	20	206	35	11	0	7	26	29	37	16	4		.362/.461/.546	125	.431	0.9	RF(20): 4.0, CF(12): -0.6, LF(9): -0.9	1.6
2022	SEA	MLB	21	560	84	25	3	28	75	40	145	25	7	30.4%	.284/.345/.509	124	.345	0.5	CF(130): -2.3	3.5
2023 DC	*SEA*	*MLB*	*22*	*595*	*75*	*25*	*3*	*26*	*73*	*45*	*145*	*30*	*9*	*29.7%*	*.283/.347/.490*	*134*	*.341*	*7.7*	*CF -4*	*4.7*

Comparables: Victor Robles (68), Mike Trout (59), Mookie Betts (58)

On August 26, 2022, Rodríguez signed a massive extension with the Mariners that could conceivably turn out to be an 18-year deal worth nearly half a billion dollars. With this extension, the measure of time has changed in Seattle. Before, the M's were a team whose fans experienced time as a series of arrhythmic jumps: sudden spikes of fleeting hope followed by longer waves of despair. With the extension of Julio, they are now a franchise plotting their success over a decades-long sweep of years. Who can say how long Jerry Dipoto's or Scott Servais' tenure will be, but now the Mariners are now on Julio time, a player-centric mission mapped out even longer than the epochs defined by Junior, Edgar and Ichiro.

None of this would have seemed especially likely back in April, when Rodríguez started his major-league career with a tepid .544 OPS, zero home runs and a K percentage within shouting distance of 40 (albeit with 10 (!) out-of-zone third-strike calls). But Rodríguez's increased speed was abundantly in evidence, as he stole nine bags in that month and, defensively, demonstrated that, yes, he *is* a center fielder. Fast-forward, montage-style, through a season that only improved from May Day onward, highlighted by a star-making (if runner-up) turn in the Home Run Derby and what seemed like nightly heroics in the Mariners' run to their first playoff bid in 21 years. Rodríguez is somehow a fully-fashioned power, speed and defensive maestro at the tender age of 21. We can quibble about the swing-and-miss, but even that minor fault measurably improved in the season's second half. In a fitting exclamation point to his wondrous debut, Rodríguez was a near-unanimous Rookie of the Year award winner.

When Rodríguez signed his extension, it crystallized a vision, opening up a portal into the late 2030s. It's strange to think about the future that far ahead; it seems ever more foreclosed, obscured, like a sudden fog bank when you sail out into the Sound on a clammy June morning. Now the Mariners have a cornerstone for the franchise that presumes a future longer that some low-lying Puget Sound real estate might stay above water. The world is warming, the seas are rising; what an odd time to feel hope in Seattle. But hope they feel, and it goes by the name of Julio.

Eugenio Suárez 3B Born: 07/18/91 Age: 31 Bats: R Throws: R Height: 5'11" Weight: 213 lb. Origin: International Free Agent, 2008

YEAR	TEAM	LVL	AGE	PA	R	2B	3B	HR	RBI	BB	K	SB	CS	Whiff%	AVG/OBP/SLG	DRC+	BABIP	BRR	DRP	WARP
2020	CIN	MLB	28	231	29	8	0	15	38	30	67	2	0	31.7%	.202/.312/.470	111	.214	0.1	3B(57): 1.8	1.1
2021	CIN	MLB	29	574	71	23	0	31	79	56	171	0	1	29.5%	.198/.286/.428	94	.224	-6.4	3B(104): -1.1, SS(34): 0.1	0.8
2022	SEA	MLB	30	629	76	24	2	31	87	73	196	0	0	33.1%	.236/.332/.459	113	.302	-1.2	3B(130): -1.6	2.3
2023 DC	*SEA*	*MLB*	*31*	*578*	*70*	*20*	*1*	*32*	*77*	*63*	*177*	*0*	*1*	*32.1%*	*.230/.325/.470*	*117*	*.281*	*-0.4*	*3B 1*	*2.4*

Comparables: Howard Johnson (69), Bob Bailey (69), Evan Longoria (69)

Suárez is here to provide two things: dingers and vibes, and when the dingers are flowing the vibes are, as the irrepressibly upbeat third-baseman will tell you, only good. Suárez came to the Mariners as the ostensible contract dump in the "Jesse Winker trade," and while Winker struggled mightily in the early season, it was largely Suárez's home runs and sunny press conferences that kept (some) Seattle fans from prematurely declaring the trade a catastrophe. As the season rounded into form, and Suárez kept up his slugging ways, the acquisition of the erstwhile Red looks to be a considerable win for the Mariners, as they appear to have found a reasonable facsimile of 2019 Suárez, when adjusted for the vastly different offensive environments of Cincinnati and Seattle. And beyond this: Seattle gains the more intangible, and seemingly endless, supply of vibes that keep an exciting young team cohesive, loose and happy.

Taylor Trammell OF Born: 09/13/97 Age: 25 Bats: L Throws: L Height: 6'2" Weight: 220 lb. Origin: Round 1, 2016 Draft (#35 overall)

YEAR	TEAM	LVL	AGE	PA	R	2B	3B	HR	RBI	BB	K	SB	CS	Whiff%	AVG/OBP/SLG	DRC+	BABIP	BRR	DRP	WARP
2021	TAC	AAA	23	323	43	15	1	12	49	40	74	8	2		.263/.362/.456	95	.313	1.1	CF(32): -2.9, RF(30): -0.0, LF(5): -0.1	0.7
2021	SEA	MLB	23	178	23	7	0	8	18	17	75	2	3	43.4%	.160/.256/.359	62	.233	-0.6	CF(37): 0.3, LF(14): -0.4	-0.2
2022	TAC	AAA	24	98	18	6	0	5	12	11	17	8	1	27.6%	.333/.408/.575	114	.369	1.2	LF(7): 1.0, RF(7): -0.9, CF(4): -0.2	0.5
2022	SEA	MLB	24	117	15	9	0	4	10	13	33	2	1	33.7%	.196/.284/.402	87	.242	-0.2	RF(34): 0.6, CF(7): 0.1, LF(3): 0.1	0.2
2023 DC	*SEA*	*MLB*	*25*	*347*	*33*	*13*	*1*	*9*	*31*	*33*	*97*	*12*	*3*	*34.2%*	*.211/.292/.352*	*80*	*.273*	*5.7*	*RF 0, LF 0*	*0.4*

Comparables: Michael Saunders (55), Josh Reddick (51), Jackie Bradley Jr. (50)

You might, squinting just so at Trammell's offensive stat line, see your way to cutting him some slack if you assumed that he was a defense-first center fielder. Open your eyes fully, however, and you see a 75 DRC+ in a major-league sample approaching 300 plate appearances and defense suited for center only in emergency situations. While Trammell has a decent eye and a modicum of power, the contact skills are simply not at a sustainable level for a big-league job. Look for Trammell to be part of the standing reserve at Tacoma, if he's not given a new start with a new team.

Evan White 1B Born: 04/26/96 Age: 27 Bats: R Throws: L Height: 6'3" Weight: 219 lb. Origin: Round 1, 2017 Draft (#17 overall)

YEAR	TEAM	LVL	AGE	PA	R	2B	3B	HR	RBI	BB	K	SB	CS	Whiff%	AVG/OBP/SLG	DRC+	BABIP	BRR	DRP	WARP
2020	SEA	MLB	24	202	19	7	0	8	26	18	84	1	2	38.1%	.176/.252/.346	66	.264	-0.4	1B(54): -0.3	-0.5
2021	SEA	MLB	25	104	8	3	0	2	9	6	31	0	0	29.9%	.144/.202/.237	73	.188	0.0	1B(30): -0.4	-0.2
2022	TAC	AAA	26	107	14	5	0	7	16	13	23	0	0	27.4%	.204/.308/.484	110	.190	-0.5	1B(21): -0.5	0.3
2023 DC	*SEA*	*MLB*	*27*	*99*	*10*	*3*	*0*	*3*	*11*	*7*	*28*	*0*	*0*	*30.6%*	*.220/.288/.397*	*88*	*.275*	*-1.7*	*1B 0*	*-0.2*

Comparables: Alfredo Marte (64), Joey Terdoslavich (60), Jim Tatum (60)

The modest contract extension that buys out a player's pre-arbitration years before his major-league debut—that has to be a bit of a conundrum for a player. Is it a concession to self-doubt after years of success at every level? Or is it a wise move to ensure that one gets fast-tracked to the big-league roster and eventually leaves baseball with enough money to live happily ever after? Like Jon Singleton and Scott Kingery before him, Evan White did not initially pan out in his extension-motivated promotion to the bigs, struggling to find an offensive identity as first a contact guy and then a power guy. After two partial years in Seattle and only a 70 DRC+ to show for it, White spent most of 2022 recovering from sports hernia surgery. If you're looking for glimmers of hope, there was an intriguing power surge when he finally made it to Triple-A Tacoma in September. But barring an improbable age-27 leap forward, White seems to have made a smart decision in getting the bag before he gets bounced from the bigs.

Kolten Wong 2B

Born: 10/10/90 Age: 32 Bats: L Throws: R Height: 5'7" Weight: 185 lb. Origin: Round 1, 2011 Draft (#22 overall)

YEAR	TEAM	LVL	AGE	PA	R	2B	3B	HR	RBI	BB	K	SB	CS	Whiff%	AVG/OBP/SLG	DRC+	BABIP	BRR	DRP	WARP
2020	STL	MLB	29	208	26	4	2	1	16	20	30	5	2	16.2%	.265/.350/.326	95	.311	2.1	2B(53): 0.2	0.8
2021	MIL	MLB	30	492	70	32	2	14	50	31	83	12	5	18.9%	.272/.335/.447	98	.305	2.0	2B(113): 1.3	2.0
2022	MIL	MLB	31	497	65	24	4	15	47	46	88	17	6	20.4%	.251/.339/.430	107	.280	-0.8	2B(131): -4.4	1.4
2023 DC	*SEA*	*MLB*	*32*	*569*	*65*	*25*	*2*	*14*	*52*	*48*	*92*	*16*	*4*	*19.7%*	*.250/.329/.396*	*108*	*.276*	*4.5*	*2B 0*	*2.7*

Comparables: Brian Roberts (67), Julian Javier (65), Roberto Alomar (65)

Let's start with the good news: Wong repeated his strong 2021 campaign with the bat, doing a little bit of everything at the plate. He hit for an okay average, showed some power and stole a base here and there, and while he doesn't stand out in any one offensive category, he's average or better across the board. Now for the bad news: For some inexplicable reason, Wong committed numerous mistakes in the infield that belied his reputation as an elite defender. All the major defensive metrics agreed that Wong took a step back on defense, as did the simplest metric of all, errors. Tough to watch as it was, Wong's 2022 performance in the field seems like an anomaly: A player's defense does worsen with age, but it almost never falls off a cliff like this. The Mariners were willing to bet on such, as they nabbed Wong from the Brewers for Jesse Winker and Abraham Toro right before the winter meetings.

Cole Young SS

Born: 07/29/03 Age: 19 Bats: L Throws: R Height: 6'0" Weight: 180 lb. Origin: Round 1, 2022 Draft (#21 overall)

YEAR	TEAM	LVL	AGE	PA	R	2B	3B	HR	RBI	BB	K	SB	CS	Whiff%	AVG/OBP/SLG	DRC+	BABIP	BRR	DRP	WARP
2022	MRN	ROK	18	26	6	1	1	0	5	4	4	3	0		.333/.423/.476		.389			
2022	MOD	A	18	45	11	0	0	2	9	4	4	1	2		.385/.422/.538	118	.371	-0.3	SS(8): -0.3, 2B(2): 0.3	0.2
2023 non-DC	*SEA*	*MLB*	*19*	*251*	*20*	*9*	*1*	*2*	*21*	*15*	*44*	*4*	*4*	*21.0%*	*.241/.292/.329*	*74*	*.287*	*-2.5*	*2B 0, SS 0*	*-0.4*

A high-school shortstop with the athletic ability to stay at the position, Young was the M's first pick in the 2022 amateur draft. Offensively, he leads with the hit tool, and in a small sample at Low-A last season, his batting average offered compelling evidence of his bat-to-ball skill. Even if the power only ends up touching league-average, Young offers a high-enough floor, both offensively and defensively, to suggest he'll move quickly up the organizational ladder. It helps that a higher-profile shortstop prospect closer to the majors was moved at last summer's trade deadline.

PITCHERS

Ryan Borucki LHP

Born: 03/31/94 Age: 29 Bats: L Throws: L Height: 6'4" Weight: 210 lb. Origin: Round 15, 2012 Draft (#475 overall)

YEAR	TEAM	LVL	AGE	W	L	SV	G	GS	IP	H	HR	BB/9	K/9	K	GB%	BABIP	WHIP	ERA	DRA-	WARP	MPH	FB%	Whiff%	CSP
2020	TOR	MLB	26	1	1	0	21	0	16^{2}	12	1	6.5	11.3	21	35.0%	.282	1.44	2.70	96	0.2	94.9	47.8%	32.6%	41.0%
2021	BUF	AAA	27	0	0	0	9	0	9^{1}	5	0	7.7	11.6	12	52.6%	.263	1.39	2.89	89	0.2				
2021	TOR	MLB	27	3	1	0	24	0	23^{2}	18	5	4.2	8.0	21	61.5%	.220	1.23	4.94	102	0.2	95.5	58.3%	29.3%	53.9%
2022	SEA	MLB	28	2	0	0	21	0	19	17	4	2.8	6.2	13	53.4%	.241	1.21	4.26	99	0.2	95.0	53.5%	23.8%	54.2%
2022	TOR	MLB	28	0	0	0	11	0	6^{1}	7	2	7.1	11.4	8	36.8%	.313	1.89	9.95	82	0.1	95.1	43.2%	33.3%	49.6%
2023 non-DC	*CHC*	*MLB*	*29*	*2*	*2*	*0*	*57*	*0*	*50*	*49*	*5*	*4.8*	*9.0*	*49*	*48.8%*	*.306*	*1.52*	*4.60*	*112*	*-0.1*	*95.0*	*52.4%*	*27.4%*	*50.6%*

Comparables: Amir Garrett (56), Zack Britton (56), Brett Cecil (53)

Borucki must feel like the universe has doubly conspired against him: first, with a body that regularly breaks down, and second, with a rule—the three-batter minimum—that has effectively legislated erstwhile LOOGYs out of the game. Even with these two strikes against him, Borucki remains a useful guy to have hanging out at the back of your bullpen if you need a ground-ball or strikeout-inducing slider against a lefty to get out of a jam. What's left of the southpaw's utility, however, is predicated on his good health, and with 2022 ending with an IL stint for an ominous-sounding flexor strain, Borucki has to be shaking his (healthy right) arm at the cruel, indifferent gods of the game.

Matt Brash RHP

Born: 05/12/98 Age: 25 Bats: R Throws: R Height: 6'1" Weight: 173 lb. Origin: Round 4, 2019 Draft (#113 overall)

YEAR	TEAM	LVL	AGE	W	L	SV	G	GS	IP	H	HR	BB/9	K/9	K	GB%	BABIP	WHIP	ERA	DRA-	WARP	MPH	FB%	Whiff%	CSP
2021	EVE	A+	23	3	2	1	10	9	42^{1}	31	3	5.3	13.2	62	51.1%	.315	1.32	2.55	92	0.5				
2021	ARK	AA	23	3	2	0	10	10	55	32	3	3.8	13.1	80	45.4%	.252	1.00	2.13	78	1.0				
2022	TAC	AAA	24	0	1	3	22	0	26	19	4	4.8	14.2	41	50.0%	.319	1.27	3.46	65	0.7	98.2	48.4%	33.2%	
2022	SEA	MLB	24	4	4	0	39	5	50^{2}	46	3	5.9	11.0	62	51.2%	.355	1.56	4.44	89	0.8	97.1	35.9%	31.6%	52.6%
2023 DC	*SEA*	*MLB*	*25*	*2*	*2*	*0*	*55*	*0*	*47.7*	*40*	*5*	*5.5*	*11.0*	*58*	*49.4%*	*.296*	*1.46*	*3.95*	*96*	*0.3*	*97.1*	*35.9%*	*31.3%*	*52.6%*

Comparables: Tommy Kahnle (74), Carlos Contreras (73), Taylor Hearn (72)

Brash encountered the starter/reliever fork in the road in 2022, and he seemingly took a decisive 'penward turn. One can be forgiven for holding onto Spencer-Strider-ish dreams of a starting Brash, but where the Atlanta hurler succeeds with the heat, Brash needs to establish his extreme breaking stuff to excel, which did not prove easy in his early-season rotation role (and his 7.65 ERA as a starter testifies to the command difficulties). Even if you note that Brash gained a measure of command while in Triple-A, you have to look at the Mariners' crowded rotation as the most definitive sign that Brash's future in Seattle lies with the firefighting work of Los Bomberos, especially when his is one of the most powerful hoses in the squad.

Diego Castillo RHP Born: 01/18/94 Age: 29 Bats: R Throws: R Height: 6'3" Weight: 268 lb. Origin: International Free Agent, 2014

YEAR	TEAM	LVL	AGE	W	L	SV	G	GS	IP	H	HR	BB/9	K/9	K	GB%	BABIP	WHIP	ERA	DRA-	WARP	MPH	FB%	Whiff%	CSP
2020	TB	MLB	26	3	0	4	22	0	21^{2}	12	3	4.6	9.6	23	59.3%	.176	1.06	1.66	81	0.5	96.3	35.3%	38.2%	46.6%
2021	SEA	MLB	27	3	1	2	24	0	22	14	4	2.9	10.6	26	54.9%	.213	0.95	2.86	88	0.4	94.5	39.9%	29.7%	52.6%
2021	TB	MLB	27	2	4	14	37	0	36^{1}	26	5	2.5	12.1	49	44.7%	.269	0.99	2.72	67	1.0	95.1	29.6%	34.6%	54.1%
2022	SEA	MLB	28	7	3	7	59	0	54^{1}	40	5	3.6	8.8	53	46.2%	.250	1.14	3.64	93	0.7	95.5	36.7%	26.5%	54.7%
2023 DC	*SEA*	*MLB*	*29*	*2*	*2*	*4*	*55*	*0*	*47.7*	*43*	*5*	*3.7*	*9.4*	*49*	*48.5%*	*.295*	*1.32*	*3.69*	*95*	*0.3*	*95.7*	*37.2%*	*29.5%*	*52.7%*

Comparables: Brad Boxberger (77), Tommy Kahnle (72), Brian Wilson (72)

Castillo might be one of the most "he is who he is" players in the game: Over the past three seasons, he's thrown his slider and sinker in a reliable 2:1 ratio, the former mostly getting a nasty downward hook while the latter blows in at the mid-90s, with the late arm-side movement a bear for hitters sitting on the slidepiece. These descriptions have been qualified with "mostly," however. As consistent as the approach is, the occasional cement-mixer slider sneaks by, just asking for a pounding, and the command on the fastball is just shaky enough to induce minor tension headaches, if not full-blown migraines. But even with the walks and ERA edging a little higher in 2022, Castillo is perfectly suited to a late-inning situational role rather than being a capital-C Closer, and the Mariners, like the Rays before them, have followed this blueprint. Seattle's marketing department is much better, so rather than being a mere replacement part in an anonymously competent Tampa bullpen, Castillo now features as a key fireman in the vaunted brigade of Los Bomberos, which sounds like a hell of a lot more fun.

Luis Castillo RHP Born: 12/12/92 Age: 30 Bats: R Throws: R Height: 6'2" Weight: 200 lb. Origin: International Free Agent, 2012

YEAR	TEAM	LVL	AGE	W	L	SV	G	GS	IP	H	HR	BB/9	K/9	K	GB%	BABIP	WHIP	ERA	DRA-	WARP	MPH	FB%	Whiff%	CSP
2020	CIN	MLB	27	4	6	0	12	12	70	62	5	3.1	11.4	89	58.4%	.329	1.23	3.21	61	2.3	97.6	52.3%	32.8%	48.7%
2021	CIN	MLB	28	8	16	0	33	33	187^{2}	181	19	3.6	9.2	192	55.6%	.323	1.36	3.98	89	2.9	97.4	52.2%	28.9%	49.8%
2022	LOU	AAA	29	0	0	0	2	2	8	5	0	5.6	13.5	12	58.8%	.294	1.25	0.00	85	0.2				
2022	SEA	MLB	29	4	2	0	11	11	65^{1}	55	6	2.3	10.6	77	45.8%	.302	1.10	3.17	72	1.6	97.3	61.1%	29.3%	54.2%
2022	CIN	MLB	29	4	4	0	14	14	85	63	7	3.0	9.5	90	46.9%	.257	1.07	2.86	81	1.6	97.0	53.4%	26.6%	53.7%
2023 DC	*SEA*	*MLB*	*30*	*11*	*8*	*0*	*29*	*29*	*172*	*148*	*15*	*3.4*	*9.4*	*179*	*50.7%*	*.288*	*1.24*	*3.08*	*82*	*3.0*	*97.2*	*53.8%*	*29.0%*	*50.3%*

Comparables: Kevin Appier (87), Jake Peavy (86), Bartolo Colon (85)

For years, if you thought "Luis Castillo" your next thought was probably "changeup," but Castillo's evolution has seen him rely more and more on a lethal fastball combination—both two- and four-seamer nosing triple digit velocities with dizzying arm-side run on the former and turbo rising action on the latter. Yes, the changeup can still be elite, and Castillo has found ways to mix in the slider more when the change isn't at its best. With his velocity and pitch-selection leveling up, getting out of Cincinnati for the more pitcher-friendly environment of T-Mobile Park is the cherry on top of this ace sundae. Both Castillo and the Mariners seemed to realize this could be the beginning of a beautiful friendship when the deadline trade acquisition signed a five-year extension to stay in the PNW and become the number-one starter in an increasingly fearsome rotation.

Matt Festa RHP Born: 03/11/93 Age: 30 Bats: R Throws: R Height: 6'1" Weight: 195 lb. Origin: Round 7, 2016 Draft (#207 overall)

YEAR	TEAM	LVL	AGE	W	L	SV	G	GS	IP	H	HR	BB/9	K/9	K	GB%	BABIP	WHIP	ERA	DRA-	WARP	MPH	FB%	Whiff%	CSP
2021	TAC	AAA	28	4	1	1	19	0	21^{1}	17	4	1.3	13.1	31	38.8%	.289	0.94	2.95	78	0.4				
2022	TAC	AAA	29	1	0	0	6	0	6^{2}	2	0	2.7	14.9	11	63.6%	.182	0.60	0.00	74	0.1	92.7	51.1%	37.2%	
2022	SEA	MLB	29	2	0	2	53	0	54	43	10	3.0	10.7	64	39.3%	.268	1.13	4.17	82	1.0	92.7	43.4%	30.5%	52.1%
2023 DC	*SEA*	*MLB*	*30*	*2*	*2*	*0*	*55*	*0*	*47.7*	*41*	*6*	*3.3*	*10.3*	*54*	*40.3%*	*.287*	*1.24*	*3.58*	*94*	*0.4*	*92.7*	*44.4%*	*29.1%*	*51.8%*

Comparables: JT Chargois (60), Evan Scribner (59), Brandon Gomes (58)

The word "festa" comes from Latin, originally denoting a religious celebration, but generally used in Italian these days to mean "party" or "feast." Festa, the pitcher, finally got to celebrate some good times after several years in the minors, punctuated by two cups of coffee—really, shots of espresso—in 2018 and 2019. The 2022 version of Festa showed up to the party with baseball's trendiest pitch: the sweeper, which gave the righty a legit strikeout weapon against both sides. The four-seamer he pairs it with may be more of a wingman, but sometimes, it only takes two to make a thing go right. Party on, Matt.

Chris Flexen RHP Born: 07/01/94 Age: 29 Bats: R Throws: R Height: 6'3" Weight: 219 lb. Origin: Round 14, 2012 Draft (#440 overall)

YEAR	TEAM	LVL	AGE	W	L	SV	G	GS	IP	H	HR	BB/9	K/9	K	GB%	BABIP	WHIP	ERA	DRA-	WARP	MPH	FB%	Whiff%	CSP
2021	SEA	MLB	26	14	6	0	31	31	179^{2}	185	19	2.0	6.3	125	42.3%	.300	1.25	3.61	112	0.5	92.8	40.0%	19.3%	57.0%
2022	SEA	MLB	27	8	9	2	33	22	137^{2}	132	17	3.3	6.2	95	33.9%	.273	1.33	3.73	124	-0.4	91.9	39.6%	21.8%	52.4%
2023 DC	*SEA*	*MLB*	*28*	*8*	*6*	*0*	*58*	*9*	*93.7*	*99*	*13*	*3.0*	*6.7*	*70*	*37.6%*	*.294*	*1.40*	*4.38*	*114*	*0.1*	*92.4*	*40.1%*	*22.1%*	*54.5%*

Comparables: José Ureña (58), Jeff Locke (58), Rafael Montero (56)

Two homonyms for Flexen's last name come immediately to mind: one describes a confident display of strength, and one speaks to an ability to adapt to different demands and situations. With an arsenal that relies less on power than guile and generous ballpark dimensions, the former option here is probably not a fit. But, with the quick advance of Logan Gilbert and George Kirby to locked-in rotation roles, the right-hander was converted into jack-of-all-innings reliever over the season's final two months. Flexen proved to be quite capable in the latter sense of the word, with a sub-two ERA as a reliever. Plenty of starters have had trouble with a mid-season push to the 'pen, but Chris? He's Flexen.

Walter Ford RHP
Born: 12/28/04 Age: 18 Bats: R Throws: R Height: 6'3" Weight: 198 lb. Origin: Round 2, 2022 Draft (#74 overall)

With a name that sounds like a studio actor from the golden age of cinema, shaggy locks and a boyish face that would make him at home as an extra in the baseball scenes of *Everybody Wants Some!* and an entirely unsubtle nickname and Twitter handle (@Vanilla_Missile), Ford was not shy about introducing himself to the Mariners' fanbase as a pitcher that would strike fear into AL West lineups in the coming years (as evidenced by a widely liked-and-RTed True Detective tweet with a bawling Matthew McConaughey). But what about Ford, the pitcher? He'll enter his minor-league career in 2023 as an 18-year-old, and he'll have plenty of time to fill out his lanky frame, add some burn to a mid-90s heater, and develop his slider and change. He might be siloed for a while, but set your countdown for a few years when the Missile is ready for launch.

Logan Gilbert RHP
Born: 05/05/97 Age: 26 Bats: R Throws: R Height: 6'6" Weight: 215 lb. Origin: Round 1, 2018 Draft (#14 overall)

YEAR	TEAM	LVL	AGE	W	L	SV	G	GS	IP	H	HR	BB/9	K/9	K	GB%	BABIP	WHIP	ERA	DRA-	WARP	MPH	FB%	Whiff%	CSP
2021	SEA	MLB	24	6	5	0	24	24	119^1	112	17	2.1	9.7	128	32.6%	.295	1.17	4.68	96	1.4	95.4	61.5%	27.2%	57.3%
2022	SEA	MLB	25	13	6	0	32	32	185^2	170	19	2.4	8.4	174	36.3%	.294	1.18	3.20	93	2.5	96.2	55.3%	24.3%	57.6%
2023 DC	*SEA*	*MLB*	*26*	*10*	*9*	*0*	*29*	*29*	*169*	*157*	*22*	*2.6*	*8.2*	*154*	*36.4%*	*.282*	*1.22*	*3.47*	*94*	*1.9*	*96.0*	*57.5%*	*25.4%*	*57.5%*

Comparables: Steven Matz (66), Aaron Civale (65), Daniel Mengden (64)

Gilbert is exceptionally good at throwing his fastball for strikes, which sounds like a compliment but sort of is and sort of isn't. Because he relies so heavily on the heater (55% of his 2022 pitches), hitters have been able to sit on it fairly comfortably, even as it comes in at the mid to upper 90s. But the fastball does provide a foundation for further experiments with his pitch mix, as well as a floor for his performance. Gilbert, like many Mariners, is now mixing in a two-seam version of the fastball and trying to decide which of his breaking pitches—slider or curve—is the better secondary. Given the Mariners' success with developing arsenals at the major-league level, there's no reason to be anything but optimistic for Gilbert, even if the young righty is still a work-in-progress.

Marco Gonzales LHP
Born: 02/16/92 Age: 31 Bats: L Throws: L Height: 6'1" Weight: 205 lb. Origin: Round 1, 2013 Draft (#19 overall)

YEAR	TEAM	LVL	AGE	W	L	SV	G	GS	IP	H	HR	BB/9	K/9	K	GB%	BABIP	WHIP	ERA	DRA-	WARP	MPH	FB%	Whiff%	CSP
2020	SEA	MLB	28	7	2	0	11	11	69^2	59	8	0.9	8.3	64	37.6%	.263	0.95	3.10	94	0.9	88.4	45.2%	19.7%	52.9%
2021	SEA	MLB	29	10	6	0	25	25	143^1	125	29	2.6	6.8	108	33.0%	.240	1.17	3.96	131	-1.0	88.5	50.4%	20.5%	52.0%
2022	SEA	MLB	30	10	15	0	32	32	183	194	30	2.5	5.1	103	42.2%	.278	1.33	4.13	146	-2.6	88.6	36.6%	18.3%	50.5%
2023 DC	*SEA*	*MLB*	*31*	*8*	*9*	*0*	*25*	*25*	*145*	*153*	*21*	*2.5*	*6.2*	*99*	*40.0%*	*.288*	*1.34*	*4.22*	*112*	*0.3*	*88.6*	*41.9%*	*19.4%*	*51.3%*

Comparables: Jason Vargas (76), Jarrod Washburn (70), Paul Maholm (69)

Gonzales' facade of surface-stat respectability cannot conceal the fact that he is, by no small margin, the worst pitcher in the majors at striking batters out. Surviving with plus command around the edge of the zone and thereby generating weak contact, Gonzales has, over the last few years, managed to capably eat innings like so many fried clams from Ivar's. But his is a profile with warning signs flashing like strobes: a fastball velocity tucked well into the 80s, Statcast sliders full of icy blue and DRAs north of six for two years running. With the signing of Robbie Ray, the trade for (and subsequent extension of) Luis Castillo, and the precocious MLB-ready performances of Logan Gilbert and George Kirby, Gonzales can now assume his most fitting role: a back-end starter holding a place for the arrival of more minor-league arms (or another free-agent or trade acquisition)—unless the collapse of his performance to the level of his peripherals gets there first.

Trevor Gott RHP
Born: 08/26/92 Age: 30 Bats: R Throws: R Height: 5'10" Weight: 182 lb. Origin: Round 6, 2013 Draft (#178 overall)

YEAR	TEAM	LVL	AGE	W	L	SV	G	GS	IP	H	HR	BB/9	K/9	K	GB%	BABIP	WHIP	ERA	DRA-	WARP	MPH	FB%	Whiff%	CSP
2020	SF	MLB	27	1	2	4	15	0	11^2	13	7	6.2	6.2	8	20.0%	.182	1.80	10.03	219	-0.6	95.4	64.1%	24.7%	42.9%
2021	SAC	AAA	28	1	3	3	43	1	41^2	37	4	3.5	11.4	53	41.6%	.340	1.27	4.10	79	0.7				
2022	MIL	MLB	29	3	4	0	45	0	45^2	35	8	2.4	8.7	44	44.1%	.227	1.03	4.14	93	0.6	95.3	54.8%	25.7%	49.6%
2023 DC	*SEA*	*MLB*	*30*	*2*	*2*	*0*	*55*	*0*	*47.7*	*44*	*5*	*3.2*	*9.2*	*48*	*43.0%*	*.296*	*1.29*	*3.71*	*97*	*0.3*	*95.2*	*60.3%*	*26.6%*	*48.4%*

Comparables: Jeremy Jeffress (61), Dan Miceli (60), Jesus Colome (60)

Call it a slider, call it a cutter, call it what you want. Nomenclature aside, it's clear that increased reliance on a faster, snappier breaking ball has given new life to Gott's career. Designated for assignment by the Giants in 2020, Gott laid low in the minors throughout 2021. Last offseason, the Brewers offered him a contract and (presumably) suggested that he adjust his repertoire. It worked. There may be further changes ahead: Gott's final regular-season outing, in which he allowed two home runs on two four-seam fastballs, could inspire him to ditch the pitch altogether and go the Collin McHugh route. That just might work, too.

Emerson Hancock RHP
Born: 05/31/99 Age: 24 Bats: R Throws: R Height: 6'4" Weight: 213 lb. Origin: Round 1, 2020 Draft (#6 overall)

YEAR	TEAM	LVL	AGE	W	L	SV	G	GS	IP	H	HR	BB/9	K/9	K	GB%	BABIP	WHIP	ERA	DRA-	WARP	MPH	FB%	Whiff%	CSP
2021	EVE	A+	22	2	0	0	9	9	31	19	1	3.8	8.7	30	57.0%	.231	1.03	2.32	100	0.2				
2021	ARK	AA	22	1	1	0	3	3	13^2	10	0	2.6	8.6	13	36.8%	.263	1.02	3.29	95	0.1				
2022	ARK	AA	23	7	4	0	21	21	98^1	80	16	3.5	8.4	92	34.5%	.245	1.20	3.75	91	0.9				
2023 DC	*SEA*	*MLB*	*24*	*1*	*2*	*0*	*6*	*6*	*29*	*29*	*4*	*4.5*	*7.0*	*22*	*40.7%*	*.284*	*1.51*	*4.89*	*122*	*-0.1*			*22.6%*	

Comparables: Drew Anderson (84), Brandon Bielak (81), Lay Batista (81)

With a name that sounds more like a financial services company than a starting pitcher, Hancock seemed like a money pick in the first round of the 2020 draft. Health challenges have followed the former Georgia hurler in his pro years, most recently a lat strain that delayed his 2022 start at Double-A Arkansas. Once up and running, Hancock was solid, if not dominant, giving up a few too many homers and walks to really make the top-line stats shine. With a diverse portfolio of pitches, Hancock still seems a safe, high-floor bet, and a strong, healthy 2023 start at Triple-A should see his line go up, perhaps all the way to Seattle.

George Kirby RHP Born: 02/04/98 Age: 25 Bats: R Throws: R Height: 6'4" Weight: 215 lb. Origin: Round 1, 2019 Draft (#20 overall)

YEAR	TEAM	LVL	AGE	W	L	SV	G	GS	IP	H	HR	BB/9	K/9	K	GB%	BABIP	WHIP	ERA	DRA-	WARP	MPH	FB%	Whiff%	CSP
2021	EVE	A+	23	4	2	0	9	9	41^{2}	33	1	1.7	11.2	52	58.3%	.317	0.98	2.38	83	0.7				
2021	ARK	AA	23	1	1	0	6	6	26	25	0	2.4	9.7	28	48.6%	.338	1.23	2.77	83	0.4				
2022	ARK	AA	24	2	0	0	5	5	24^{2}	17	3	1.8	11.7	32	43.6%	.269	0.89	1.82	65	0.6				
2022	SEA	MLB	24	8	5	0	25	25	130	135	13	1.5	9.2	133	45.3%	.332	1.21	3.39	87	2.1	95.3	57.6%	21.2%	56.6%
2023 DC	*SEA*	*MLB*	*25*	*8*	*8*	*0*	*25*	*25*	*142.3*	*141*	*15*	*2.2*	*8.2*	*129*	*46.2%*	*.301*	*1.24*	*3.47*	*94*	*1.7*	*95.3*	*57.6%*	*23.6%*	*56.6%*

Comparables: A.J. Griffin (69), Luis Castillo (67), Tyler Duffey (66)

The Mariners would not have been able to experience the heartbreak of the 18-inning playoff elimination against the Astros if not for Kirby's absolute dominance for the first seven of those frames. Though his performance that afternoon will largely be lost to history, it was a fitting culmination of his splendid rookie season in Seattle. Like his rotation-mate Logan Gilbert, Kirby has leaned on the four-seam fastball, and also like Gilbert, he began to mix in a two-seamer as the season progressed (throwing more sinkers than four-seamers in that final October game). Kirby arrived in the majors with preternatural command, mid-90s velocity and a deep arsenal of secondary pitches. Even as he refines his pitch mix going forward, Kirby has the toolset of a pitcher who is already worthy of the front end of many rotations, with the potential to become something truly superlative.

Bryce Miller RHP Born: 08/23/98 Age: 24 Bats: R Throws: R Height: 6'2" Weight: 180 lb. Origin: Round 4, 2021 Draft (#113 overall)

YEAR	TEAM	LVL	AGE	W	L	SV	G	GS	IP	H	HR	BB/9	K/9	K	GB%	BABIP	WHIP	ERA	DRA-	WARP	MPH	FB%	Whiff%	CSP
2021	MOD	A	22	0	0	0	5	3	9^{1}	15	0	1.9	14.5	15	53.6%	.556	1.82	4.82	81	0.1				
2022	EVE	A+	23	3	3	0	16	15	77^{2}	54	7	2.9	11.5	99	45.7%	.264	1.02	3.24	80	1.5				
2022	ARK	AA	23	4	1	0	10	10	50^{2}	34	3	3.4	10.8	61	43.0%	.263	1.05	3.20	64	1.1				
2023 non-DC	*SEA*	*MLB*	*24*	*2*	*2*	*0*	*57*	*0*	*50*	*47*	*6*	*4.1*	*8.5*	*47*	*44.4%*	*.298*	*1.41*	*4.23*	*105*	*0.1*			*25.2%*	

Comparables: Erik Johnson (76), Bailey Ober (75), Logan Gilbert (74)

Lost among the pop-up breakout of Taylor Dollard and the prospect hype of Emerson Hancock, perhaps the most exciting story in the rotation at Double-A Arkansas was the accelerating progress of righty power arm Miller. Sharing both a mustachioed mien and fire fastball with Atlanta rookie Spencer Strider, Miller leads with a near-100 mph heater and finishes with a nasty, hard slidepiece. The continued development of his curve and changeup likely determines whether he follows the starting or relief path, but for now the Mariners should be happy that their stacked major-league staff has a passel of advanced arms ready to add even more depth.

Andrés Muñoz RHP Born: 01/16/99 Age: 24 Bats: R Throws: R Height: 6'2" Weight: 222 lb. Origin: International Free Agent, 2015

YEAR	TEAM	LVL	AGE	W	L	SV	G	GS	IP	H	HR	BB/9	K/9	K	GB%	BABIP	WHIP	ERA	DRA-	WARP	MPH	FB%	Whiff%	CSP
2021	SEA	MLB	22	0	0	0	1	0	0^{2}	0	0	27.0	13.5	1	100.0%	.000	3.00	0.00			99.7	70.6%	25.0%	46.8%
2022	SEA	MLB	23	2	5	4	64	0	65	43	5	2.1	13.3	96	52.6%	.297	0.89	2.49	54	2.2	100.4	35.4%	42.0%	49.9%
2023 DC	*SEA*	*MLB*	*24*	*2*	*2*	*10*	*55*	*0*	*47.7*	*37*	*4*	*3.6*	*13.6*	*72*	*48.5%*	*.318*	*1.18*	*2.94*	*75*	*0.8*	*100.4*	*38.7%*	*38.2%*	*49.6%*

Comparables: Tim Collins (62), Francisco Rodríguez (60), Huston Street (58)

After a late-2021 taste that allowed the Mariners to exhale in relief that Muñoz's post-TJ velocity was intact, the righty started 2022 with heat but also a fair amount of rust. After a mid-season switch to a harder slider, Muñoz became almost literally unhittable. Most relievers would be happy with a fastball that tops out at 103 mph, but for Muñoz, it's his secondary pitch, as he now features a harder, low-90s slider with excellent command, making him one of many Seattle pitchers to level up their effectiveness by paring down, or slightly adjusting, their arsenals. Of course, with the new-school Mariners, this does not mean that Muñoz is locked in as a closer—he only tallied four saves—but that doesn't mean he's not in the inner circle of late-inning stoppers across the league.

Penn Murfee RHP Born: 05/02/94 Age: 29 Bats: R Throws: R Height: 6'2" Weight: 195 lb. Origin: Round 33, 2018 Draft (#988 overall)

YEAR	TEAM	LVL	AGE	W	L	SV	G	GS	IP	H	HR	BB/9	K/9	K	GB%	BABIP	WHIP	ERA	DRA-	WARP	MPH	FB%	Whiff%	CSP
2021	ARK	AA	27	5	2	0	10	10	52^{1}	50	9	3.4	10.7	62	40.1%	.308	1.34	4.13	101	0.3				
2021	TAC	AAA	27	2	1	0	16	4	26^{1}	22	2	5.1	12.0	35	41.3%	.328	1.41	4.44	91	0.2				
2022	TAC	AAA	28	2	0	2	5	0	8	1	0	2.3	11.2	10	42.9%	.077	0.38	0.00	90	0.1	89.5	44.8%	29.5%	
2022	SEA	MLB	28	4	0	0	64	1	69^{1}	48	7	2.3	9.9	76	33.0%	.243	0.95	2.99	82	1.3	89.1	49.0%	25.0%	52.5%
2023 DC	*SEA*	*MLB*	*29*	*2*	*2*	*0*	*55*	*0*	*47.7*	*43*	*6*	*3.3*	*8.9*	*46*	*37.9%*	*.282*	*1.28*	*3.82*	*100*	*0.2*	*89.1*	*49.0%*	*25.3%*	*52.5%*

Comparables: Tyler Kinley (55), Seth Lugo (55), Robert Coello (54)

Murphy's Law famously postulates that "anything that can go wrong, will go wrong." Murfee's Law, by contrast, states that "if you are a low-arm-slot, slider-heavy reliever, any physical proximity to Paul Sewald will turn you into his doppelgänger." Where the former law seems to apply almost universally, the latter is specific to one player, who, in his rookie season, became a key stepping stone in delivering leads to the late-inning triumvirate of Castillo, Sewald and Muñoz. Murfee's game is all about deception, not fire, but you wouldn't know that to look at his strikeout numbers (high) and exit velocities (low). In bullpens, as in life, Murphy's Law can strike at any time, but after a solid 2022, the smart money is on Murfee's Law for now.

Robbie Ray LHP Born: 10/01/91 Age: 31 Bats: L Throws: L Height: 6'2" Weight: 225 lb. Origin: Round 12, 2010 Draft (#356 overall)

YEAR	TEAM	LVL	AGE	W	L	SV	G	GS	IP	H	HR	BB/9	K/9	K	GB%	BABIP	WHIP	ERA	DRA-	WARP	MPH	FB%	Whiff%	CSP
2020	AZ	MLB	28	1	4	0	7	7	31	31	9	9.0	12.5	43	20.3%	.314	2.00	7.84	164	-0.7	93.8	52.5%	33.3%	39.5%
2020	TOR	MLB	28	1	1	0	5	4	20^{2}	22	4	6.1	10.9	25	31.0%	.333	1.74	4.79	162	-0.5	93.8	54.1%	32.6%	44.9%
2021	TOR	MLB	29	13	7	0	32	32	193^{1}	150	33	2.4	11.5	248	37.1%	.269	1.04	2.84	82	3.6	94.8	59.8%	32.4%	54.1%
2022	SEA	MLB	30	12	12	0	32	32	189	163	32	3.0	10.1	212	38.5%	.284	1.19	3.71	96	2.2	93.6	60.1%	30.1%	52.6%
2023 DC	*SEA*	*MLB*	*31*	*10*	*9*	*0*	*29*	*29*	*169*	*146*	*26*	*3.3*	*10.4*	*194*	*37.8%*	*.283*	*1.23*	*3.49*	*92*	*2.1*	*93.9*	*58.6%*	*30.2%*	*51.3%*

Comparables: Jon Lester (78), Mark Langston (76), Gio González (76)

As the calendar layers more pages over the bitter end to Ray's season—a questionable, and ultimately ill-fated, decision to bring him in as a reliever to face one of the best hitters in baseball in a high-leverage playoff situation—we can look with a detached eye on the arc of the southpaw's reinvention. Sure, there was a step back from what was unquestionably a career year in Toronto, but 2022 Ray seems to have decisively shed his wild-and-wooly former skin and left it to desiccate in the Arizona desert. With a simplified arsenal consisting exclusively of two fastballs and a slider, Ray commands each of his offerings well, with the downside being that with increased strikes come more home runs, a problem that has not been fixed even with the move to spacious T-Mobile Park. It has to be noted, as well, that Ray seemed gassed in September, leading to a few stat-line marring performances. The good far outweighs the bad, however, and while the Cy Young may have been a one-time deal, we can now consider applying an adjective to Ray that no one ever thought would describe the lefty: reliable.

Casey Sadler RHP Born: 07/13/90 Age: 32 Bats: R Throws: R Height: 6'3" Weight: 223 lb. Origin: Round 25, 2010 Draft (#747 overall)

YEAR	TEAM	LVL	AGE	W	L	SV	G	GS	IP	H	HR	BB/9	K/9	K	GB%	BABIP	WHIP	ERA	DRA-	WARP	MPH	FB%	Whiff%	CSP
2020	SEA	MLB	29	1	2	0	7	0	10	7	1	3.6	10.8	12	38.5%	.240	1.10	4.50	93	0.1	92.7	33.5%	28.8%	48.4%
2020	CHC	MLB	29	0	0	0	10	0	9^{1}	8	2	7.7	8.7	9	44.4%	.250	1.71	5.79	122	0.0	93.2	37.4%	31.2%	39.5%
2021	SEA	MLB	30	0	1	0	42	0	40^{1}	19	1	2.2	8.3	37	63.9%	.188	0.72	0.67	84	0.7	93.2	27.5%	23.7%	52.2%
2023 non-DC	*SEA*	*MLB*	*32*	*2*	*2*	*0*	*57*	*0*	*50*	*49*	*5*	*3.1*	*8.0*	*44*	*51.7%*	*.302*	*1.32*	*3.76*	*97*	*0.3*	*93.2*	*31.7%*	*25.2%*	*48.7%*

Comparables: Liam Hendriks (42), Tommy Hunter (38), Tyler Thornburg (37)

After a stellar 2021, Sadler's follow-up season was over before it began, as he succumbed to a shoulder injury and subsequent surgery in spring training. Rather than wait around to see if post-surgery Sadler could recapture that former magic, the Mariners placed him on waivers in the offseason to ease a 40-man roster crunch. They haven't forgotten what the righty did in 2021, however, as he re-upped with Seattle on a minor-league deal.

Paul Sewald RHP Born: 05/26/90 Age: 33 Bats: R Throws: R Height: 6'3" Weight: 219 lb. Origin: Round 10, 2012 Draft (#320 overall)

YEAR	TEAM	LVL	AGE	W	L	SV	G	GS	IP	H	HR	BB/9	K/9	K	GB%	BABIP	WHIP	ERA	DRA-	WARP	MPH	FB%	Whiff%	CSP
2020	NYM	MLB	30	0	0	0	5	0	6	12	1	6.0	3.0	2	35.7%	.407	2.67	13.50	147	-0.1	92.0	59.7%	16.4%	46.4%
2021	SEA	MLB	31	10	3	11	62	0	64^{2}	42	10	3.3	14.5	104	25.9%	.256	1.02	3.06	62	1.9	92.4	58.3%	36.5%	54.2%
2022	SEA	MLB	32	5	4	20	65	0	64	32	10	2.4	10.1	72	30.9%	.159	0.77	2.67	81	1.2	92.7	51.4%	34.2%	53.9%
2023 DC	*SEA*	*MLB*	*33*	*2*	*2*	*26*	*55*	*0*	*47.7*	*36*	*6*	*2.9*	*11.0*	*58*	*30.4%*	*.268*	*1.10*	*2.80*	*76*	*0.8*	*92.5*	*55.5%*	*31.9%*	*53.8%*

Comparables: Kirby Yates (79), Brad Brach (74), Pedro Báez (71)

After a breakout in his age-31 season, Sewald largely maintained his successes of the previous year. A simple but effective pitch mix—nearly 50/50 between the four-seamer and sweeping slider—nets the righty plenty of strikeouts, but he does suffer the consequences of the occasional meatball left up in the zone. One can quibble with a DRA that puts him in the merely "good" rather than "lethal" reliever bucket (we can thank his ridiculous .158 BABIP for that), but for now Sewald retains his spot as the member of Los Bomberos who usually douses the last of the opponent's flames.

Justus Sheffield LHP Born: 05/13/96 Age: 27 Bats: L Throws: L Height: 5'10" Weight: 224 lb. Origin: Round 1, 2014 Draft (#31 overall)

YEAR	TEAM	LVL	AGE	W	L	SV	G	GS	IP	H	HR	BB/9	K/9	K	GB%	BABIP	WHIP	ERA	DRA-	WARP	MPH	FB%	Whiff%	CSP
2020	SEA	MLB	24	4	3	0	10	10	55^{1}	52	2	3.3	7.8	48	49.7%	.314	1.30	3.58	94	0.8	92.0	48.0%	19.8%	48.0%
2021	TAC	AAA	25	0	1	0	5	2	8^{1}	8	1	7.6	15.1	14	38.9%	.412	1.80	8.64	85	0.1				
2021	SEA	MLB	25	7	8	0	21	15	80^{1}	105	14	4.8	7.1	63	45.6%	.351	1.84	6.83	142	-1.0	92.4	47.4%	19.9%	55.1%
2022	TAC	AAA	26	6	8	0	24	24	103	138	19	4.1	7.5	86	47.5%	.365	1.80	6.99	122	-0.8	91.0	47.2%	19.6%	
2022	SEA	MLB	26	1	0	0	6	1	11^{2}	9	1	4.6	5.4	7	56.8%	.222	1.29	3.86	114	0.0	91.9	46.9%	14.9%	57.1%
2023 DC	*SEA*	*MLB*	*27*	*3*	*3*	*0*	*27*	*3*	*34.7*	*41*	*5*	*4.4*	*6.2*	*23*	*48.4%*	*.319*	*1.70*	*5.89*	*139*	*-0.5*	*92.3*	*47.5%*	*20.0%*	*52.9%*

Comparables: Brett Oberholtzer (67), Zack Britton (60), Joe Ross (59)

After a handful of early-season appearances out of the 'pen, Sheffield languished in Tacoma until he was called up as the 29th man to start against the Tigers on the season's penultimate day. That performance showed the essence of the late-era Justus Sheffield Experience: five innings of underwhelming stuff, iffy command and too many hard-hit balls. The fact that the lefty was called up only to make numbers in a meaningless game is a harsh reminder of how far the former prospect has fallen. The stuff seems to have stalled out below the standard to be a useful starter, and maybe the last hope is to see what, if anything, can be tweaked to make him effective in relief.

Gabe Speier LHP Born: 04/12/95 Age: 28 Bats: L Throws: L Height: 5'11" Weight: 200 lb. Origin: Round 19, 2013 Draft (#563 overall)

YEAR	TEAM	LVL	AGE	W	L	SV	G	GS	IP	H	HR	BB/9	K/9	K	GB%	BABIP	WHIP	ERA	DRA-	WARP	MPH	FB%	Whiff%	CSP
2020	KC	MLB	25	0	1	0	8	0	5^2	9	1	6.4	9.5	6	45.0%	.421	2.29	7.94	100	0.1	92.2	54.1%	30.4%	42.4%
2021	OMA	AAA	26	3	0	5	45	0	45^1	45	5	1.8	11.3	57	53.7%	.345	1.19	2.98	81	1.1				
2021	KC	MLB	26	0	0	0	7	0	7^2	10	0	0.0	5.9	5	44.4%	.370	1.30	1.17	103	0.1	94.1	61.9%	22.0%	63.0%
2022	OMA	AAA	27	1	3	0	30	0	26^2	51	11	4.0	11.5	34	42.7%	.482	2.36	14.51	104	0.3				
2022	KC	MLB	27	0	1	0	17	1	19^1	16	2	2.3	6.5	14	44.8%	.250	1.09	2.33	102	0.2	93.9	55.7%	20.3%	55.0%
2023 DC	*SEA*	*MLB*	*28*	*2*	*2*	*0*	*49*	*0*	*42.3*	*47*	*6*	*3.3*	*8.1*	*38*	*44.8%*	*.324*	*1.50*	*4.95*	*122*	*-0.3*	*93.8*	*57.0%*	*24.6%*	*53.9%*

Comparables: Scott Alexander (46), Jhan Mariñez (45), Sam Freeman (45)

That's not a misprint: Speier's ERA in Triple-A was over six times higher than his major-league mark. The sinker-slider lefty, who's been involved in numerous trades involving everyone from Rick Porcello to Dansby Swanson, made the Royals' Opening Day roster. He looked to be a bright spot, dashing through 11⅓ innings with nary a run allowed to begin 2022. Alas, he ended the year grinding it out in Omaha, where worse control and an absurd BABIP conspired to give him some unsightly top-line results. In that sense, his Triple-A ERA can be taken as a misprint, but one Speier himself has to edit if he wants to resurface in Kansas City.

Drew Steckenrider RHP Born: 01/10/91 Age: 32 Bats: R Throws: R Height: 6'4" Weight: 235 lb. Origin: Round 8, 2012 Draft (#257 overall)

YEAR	TEAM	LVL	AGE	W	L	SV	G	GS	IP	H	HR	BB/9	K/9	K	GB%	BABIP	WHIP	ERA	DRA-	WARP	MPH	FB%	Whiff%	CSP
2021	SEA	MLB	30	5	2	14	62	0	67^2	52	5	2.3	7.7	58	38.3%	.258	1.02	2.00	103	0.5	94.2	66.0%	20.6%	57.9%
2022	TAC	AAA	31	4	0	3	23	0	25^1	29	6	6.0	7.5	21	50.6%	.291	1.82	4.62	104	0.1	94.6	55.7%	21.2%	
2022	SEA	MLB	31	0	2	2	16	0	14^1	21	2	3.1	6.3	10	32.1%	.373	1.81	5.65	126	-0.1	94.6	65.0%	20.8%	54.7%
2023 non-DC	*SEA*	*MLB*	*32*	*2*	*2*	*0*	*57*	*0*	*50*	*50*	*7*	*3.8*	*7.2*	*40*	*39.7%*	*.289*	*1.43*	*4.46*	*114*	*-0.2*	*94.3*	*65.5%*	*21.5%*	*56.6%*

Comparables: Louis Coleman (67), Brad Brach (65), Kirby Yates (65)

Former part-time closer Steckenrider was already walking a fine line with his diminished skills, and that line faded even more in 2022. After coming back from elbow issues in 2021, he became the rare fastball-changeup reliever, and subsequently demonstrated why this combination is, in fact, rare. Without anything bendy, Steckenrider relied on middling velocity and iffy command that, in 2021, outran his DRA by nearly three runs, though in retrospect you can see plenty of luck in a low BABIP and high strand rate. But his strikeouts were at nearly half the pace of his Marlins heyday, so it seemed only a matter of time before the peripherals would catch up to his performance. And, in 2022, they did. With a deep bullpen, the Mariners could afford to send him to Tacoma, which is where he ended last year, and where he'll likely begin the next one.

LINEOUTS

Hitters

HITTER	POS	TEAM	LVL	AGE	PA	R	2B	3B	HR	RBI	BB	K	SB	CS	AVG/OBP/SLG	DRC+	BABIP	BRR	DRP	WARP
Michael Arroyo	SS	DSL SEA	ROK	17	199	46	10	2	4	22	27	33	4	4	.314/.457/.484		.370			
Zach DeLoach	OF	ARK	AA	23	499	79	15	3	14	73	71	119	4	1	.258/.369/.409	95	.324	-0.3	RF(71): 1.4, LF(25): 0.4	1.9
Drew Ellis	IF	RNO	AAA	26	179	27	12	1	4	28	33	38	2	0	.217/.369/.399	109	.265	-0.1	3B(23): -1.2, 2B(3): -0.0	0.6
	IF	TAC	AAA	26	289	34	15	1	15	39	41	79	4	3	.231/.346/.488	106	.272	-4.6	3B(31): 0.8, 2B(20): -0.6, 1B(14): 2.2	0.9
	IF	AZ	MLB	26	14	2	1	0	0	1	1	6	0	0	.154/.214/.231	81	.286	0.2	3B(6): 0.1	0.0
	IF	SEA	MLB	26	3	0	0	0	0	0	0	1	0	0	.333/.333/.333	92	.500	-0.1	3B(1): 0.1	0.0
Gabriel Gonzalez	LF	MRN	ROK	18	140	20	9	0	5	17	8	21	5	3	.357/.421/.548		.400			
	LF	MOD	A	18	150	31	5	1	2	17	13	21	4	1	.286/.400/.389	113	.330	0.4	LF(29): -0.5, RF(2): -0.1	0.7
Cooper Hummel	LF	RNO	AAA	27	156	31	8	1	6	19	24	40	3	4	.310/.423/.527	98	.405	0.0	LF(14): 1.0, RF(5): 0.9, C(3): -0.1	0.8
	LF	AZ	MLB	27	201	20	8	3	3	17	23	64	4	1	.176/.274/.307	71	.255	1.1	LF(21): -0.8, C(18): -3.5	-0.4
Carlos Jimenez	CF	DSL SEA	ROK	19	126	26	5	3	6	17	28	34	13	5	.255/.429/.564		.321			
Tyler Locklear	3B	MOD	A	21	133	19	5	0	7	29	7	29	0	0	.282/.353/.504	116	.313	-1.0	3B(22): -0.9, 1B(5): -0.3	0.5
Spencer Packard	LF	EVE	A+	24	307	43	15	1	12	37	41	47	5	1	.282/.397/.490	150	.303	-1.1	LF(42): -2.2, RF(9): -0.9, CF(5): 1.1	2.3
Alberto Rodriguez	RF	EVE	A+	21	382	42	23	3	6	35	32	100	5	3	.263/.330/.399	94	.353	-4.9	RF(92): -0.4, CF(8): -0.3, LF(4): 1.1	0.7
Axel Sanchez	MI	MRN	ROK	19	99	15	5	2	2	9	11	20	9	2	.267/.354/.442		.323			
	MI	MOD	A	19	152	27	13	2	8	37	15	42	4	1	.305/.401/.618	104	.395	-0.2	SS(28): 1.6, 2B(4): -0.8, 3B(1): 0.1	0.6
	MI	EVE	A+	19	34	0	1	0	0	1	0	9	0	0	.235/.235/.265	76	.320	-0.6	2B(7): -0.0, 3B(1): -0.0	-0.1

A 17-year-old from Colombia, **Michael Arroyo** has been described as a "shortstop for now," which implies a move to second or third base eventually. Regardless of position, the bet here is on the hit tool, which he displayed in abundance during his DSL stint in 2022. As with all teenagers of slightish build, the power is in the future, if at all. You want a 24-year-old corner outfield college bat to blow through Double-A, but **Zach DeLoach** sort of ambled along, with the kind of middling power and good on-base skills that can get you to Tacoma, if not further up I-5. Picked up off of waivers from the D-Backs, former Louisvillian **Drew Ellis** once profiled as a decent three-true-outcomes corner infield bat, but the three outcomes now maybe add up to one and a half (with the "one" being the unfortunate one), and with limited defensive skills, the corner potential is rapidly skewing toward the colder side of the diamond. Rather than dissipate into the ether of abstractions that usually surround teenage prospects, we might simply note that **Gabriel Gonzalez**, before his 19th birthday, has already notched an OBP of .400 in 150 plate appearances at Low-A. That seems a solid foundation on which the athletic corner outfielder might develop more precise adjectives to describe his game. A kind-of catcher and not-really batter who spent as much time in the outfield and DH as behind the plate, **Cooper Hummel's** season was also Arizona's in a nutshell: weird and a bit much, like a Martin Short character you grimaced at as he entered the frame. Athletic teenage outfielders are an outsized demographic among recent high-school draftees and international signees, but **Carlos Jimenez** stands out for both impressive power and an elite walk rate in his two DSL campaigns. As he moves stateside, he's worth watching as closely as he watches pitches thrown his way. A masher out of Virginia Commonwealth, 2022 second-round pick **Tyler Locklear** may not have a good long-term fit at a defensive position, but when the frequent blasts come with a strong OBP, you sort of mentally pencil in "1B/DH" next to his name and get back to enjoying the dingers. Though just getting to High-A in his age-24 season, high-contact outfielder **Spencer Packard** upped his walk rate to become an on-base machine. Sure, an old-for-level guy with middling power may not get your blood pumping, but with a touch more strength to the bat he could become relevant sooner than later, if ever. A short and wide-bodied corner outfielder who showed some 2021 promise in Low-A, **Alberto Rodriguez** seemed stuck in neutral in his age-21 season at High-A Everett, with the hit tool remaining solid but little power to complement it. The development needs to happen sooner than later if he hopes to double the Rodriguez outfield population in Seattle someday. Noelvi Marte left an offensive void among Mariners' shortstop prospects when he was traded to the Reds, but **Axel Sanchez** responded to this deficit with a late-season offensive surge at Low-A. A glove-first prospect signed out of the Dominican Republic in 2019, Sanchez showed some power and patience at Modesto. The patience seems baked-in, but whether the power remains sustainable as he goes up the levels is the big question.

Pitchers

PITCHER	TEAM	LVL	AGE	W	L	SV	G	GS	IP	H	HR	BB/9	K/9	K	GB%	BABIP	WHIP	ERA	DRA-	WARP	MPH	FB%	WHF	CSP
Brennan Bernardino	TAC	AAA	30	2	0	2	23	0	32^{2}	18	1	2.8	9.6	35	55.8%	.224	0.86	2.20	82	0.5	92.0	55.2%	27.4%	
	SEA	MLB	30	0	1	0	2	0	2^{1}	3	0	7.7	0.0	0	45.5%	.273	2.14	3.86	114	0.0	92.4	63.4%	0.0%	61.4%
Prelander Berroa	EVE	A+	22	2	2	0	13	13	52^{1}	29	2	5.5	13.9	81	49.0%	.276	1.17	2.41	78	1.1				
	EUG	A+	22	0	0	0	4	4	13^{1}	5	0	4.0	10.8	16	32.0%	.200	0.83	0.67	88	0.2				
	ARK	AA	22	2	1	0	9	9	35	20	3	6.4	13.6	53	46.4%	.262	1.29	4.37	69	0.8				
Taylor Dollard	ARK	AA	23	16	2	0	27	27	144	106	9	1.9	8.2	131	40.0%	.251	0.95	2.25	73	2.9				
Travis Kuhn	ARK	AA	24	3	3	3	50	0	59^{1}	43	3	5.3	10.8	71	38.8%	.286	1.31	4.10	95	0.4				
Michael Morales	MOD	A	19	5	7	0	26	26	120^{1}	143	14	3.7	9.3	125	42.1%	.359	1.60	5.91	117	-1.1				
Juan Then	ARK	AA	22	0	1	0	10	0	10	11	2	2.7	12.6	14	25.9%	.360	1.40	5.40	88	0.1				
Justin Topa	NAS	AAA	31	2	0	0	17	0	18^{2}	23	0	3.9	8.2	17	59.3%	.390	1.66	4.34	100	0.2				
	MIL	MLB	31	0	0	0	7	0	7^{1}	9	0	4.9	4.9	4	74.1%	.333	1.77	4.91	111	0.0	95.6	68.8%	13.7%	47.3%

Homer could have written another *Odyssey* about 30-year-old rookie reliever **Brennan Bernardino**, whose career has traversed the North American continent—the lefty went from Reds farmhand, to indy ball in Canada, to the Mexican League, before his debut in July, when he gave up a walk-off hit in Houston to Yordan Alvarez. Even Homer would have shied away from such heavy-handed foreshadowing, however. Acquired from the Giants in the midseason, **Prelander Berroa** is a power arm who misses his catchers' targets almost as much as he misses swinging bats. His path to the majors is almost certainly via the bullpen, but without a dramatic improvement in command, it could all just amount to a missed opportunity. What is a Dollard worth these days? Based on baseball-card stats alone (a 16-2 record, with a 2.25 ERA), **Taylor Dollard**'s 2022 season at Double-A is worth your attention. Digging deeper, his excellent command of a solid four-pitch mix might even be worth your excitement. A little more fastball sauce could make him worth a look in the majors in 2023. So many high-school pitchers present a fundamental problem of ontology as they move through the minors—What is he? Is he a starter? Is he a reliever? A 2022 draftee with a big body, power arm, and precociously deep arsenal, **Ashton Izzi** hopes to quickly answer the existential question posed by his last name. Bootstrap fables can justifiably get eye-rolls, but **Travis Kuhn** has been a self-motivated success story. Left to train for and by himself over the pandemic, the righty transformed himself from low-minors relief fodder to a legit bullpen prospect, adding a few ticks to his fastball and some serious spin to his slider. You could say he has a Kuhn-do attitude. Only turning 20 near the end of last season, **Michael Morales** was a mainstay in the rotation at Low-A Modesto. He has a varied arsenal and precocious approach—his nickname is "The Sponge"—but he needs to refine his command so he can more often be the wiper, and not the wipee. Sometimes you can see it coming from miles away: the starter with a high-effort delivery, a near-triple-digit heater and command issues reaches his ultimate destination. For **Juan Then**, that is the 'pen. Kink-shaming is usually a no-no, but considering that the Brewers' fetish for sinker-slider relievers led them to try out **Justin Topa** for the third year in a row, someone oughta bonk them on the head and send 'em to Horny Jail. Give them credit, though, they tried to break the habit by shipping him to the Mariners in January.

TEXAS RANGERS

Essay by Kennedi Landry

Player comments by Eli Walsh and BP staff

Deep in the heart of Arlington, Texas, Ray Davis shares a city and a parking lot with one of American sports' most prominent, hands-on owners and general managers in Jerry Jones of the Dallas Cowboys. The two billionaires also share a Metroplex with yet another outspoken owner in the Mavericks' Mark Cuban, who spends his offseasons starring on ABC's entrepreneurial hit show, *Shark Tank*.

Through all the chatter, interviews and press conferences, Davis has remained elusive over the last decade since becoming majority owner of the Rangers in 2010. Even in the last year, as the Rangers have risen up MLB's payroll ladder, Davis rarely makes an appearance, rarely grants interviews, rarely sits at a podium.

When asked a question at Bruce Bochy's introductory press conference, he appeared shocked that a media member would want to hear his voice on an impactful hire. At the press conferences introducing Corey Seager and Marcus Semien last winter, he sat silently in the front row of the audience as agent Scott Boras and general manager Chris Young fielded questions, allowing other faces to take the credit for the seemingly miraculous signings, even as he provided the millions of dollars behind the scenes.

But on a day in mid-August, Davis—the notorious "Undercover Billionaire," as he was dubbed in a *D Magazine* article in 2012—channeled his DFW counterparts to deliver a simple message: He's tired of losing. It was the first time in my two years covering the team that he sat at a podium and fielded questions from the media contingent, and likely the first time in his entire tenure as owner that he was quite so forward on any topic, much less the on-field product.

In the midst of the Rangers' sixth straight losing season, Davis became impatient with the slow-moving rebuild process. While the club looked to be coming out on the other side sooner rather than later, Davis said he isn't a good loser. He wanted to treat this organization and fanbase with a sense of urgency with regards to winning, now and in the future.

On that day—August 17—Davis relieved president of baseball operations Jon Daniels of his duties, just two days after Daniels did the same to manager Chris Woodward. Young, the Rangers' general manager since late 2020, was left

TEXAS RANGERS PROSPECTUS

2022 W-L: 68-94, 4TH IN AL WEST

Pythag	.477	18th	DER	.698	16th
RS/G	4.36	12th	DRC+	97	18th
RA/G	4.59	23rd	DRA-	106	22nd
dWin%	.460	22nd	FIP	4.18	22nd
Payroll	$142M	15th	B-Age	28.5	10th
M$/MW	$6.3M	25th	P-Age	28.7	7th

407′ 372′ 374′ 329′ 326′

- Opened 2020
- Retractable roof
- Synthetic surface
- Fence profile: 7′ to 10′ (estimate)

Park Factors

Runs	Runs/RH	Runs/LH	HR/RH	HR/LH
100	100	99	109	104

Top Hitter WARP	4.2 Corey Seager
Top Pitcher WARP	2.3 Jon Gray
2023 Top Prospect	Evan Carter

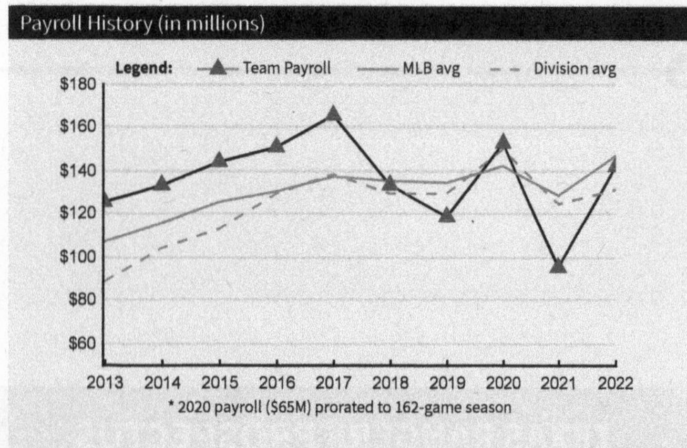

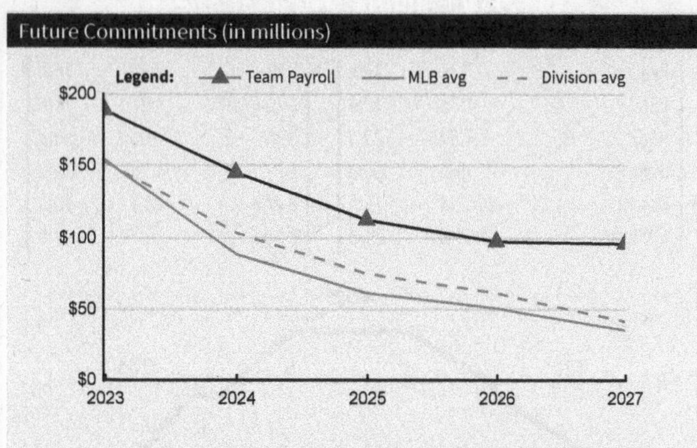

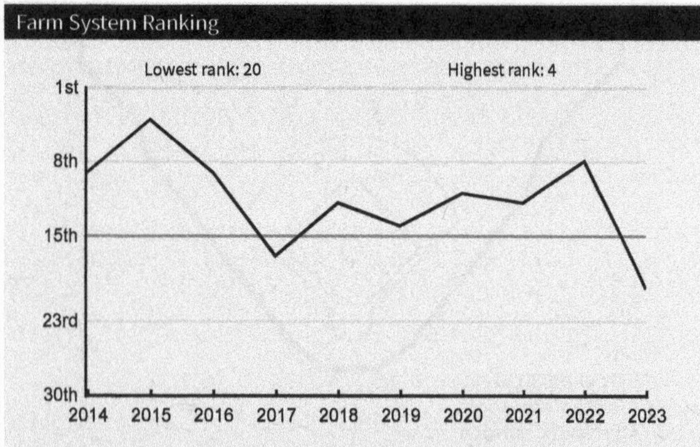

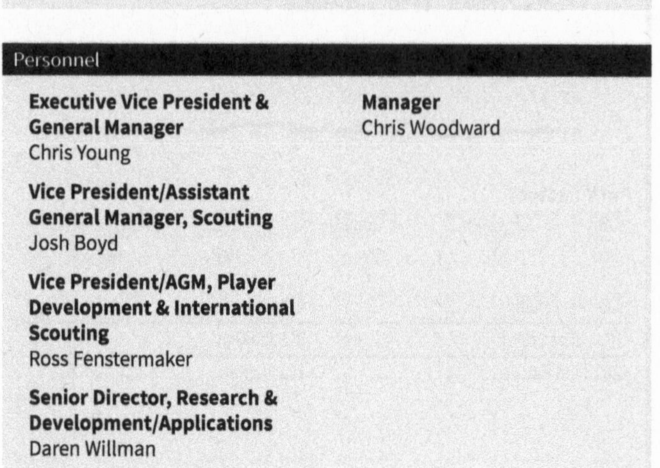
Personnel

Executive Vice President & General Manager
Chris Young

Vice President/Assistant General Manager, Scouting
Josh Boyd

Vice President/AGM, Player Development & International Scouting
Ross Fenstermaker

Senior Director, Research & Development/Applications
Daren Willman

Manager
Chris Woodward

stunned by the move and waited two days to even address the media about his new role as the head of the baseball operations department. Davis, sitting alone at the podium in the Globe Life Field media room for the first time, took it upon himself to usher in a new era of Texas Rangers baseball.

It was a shocking move, letting go of Daniels. But maybe it shouldn't have been, considering the results. Since winning back-to-back American League pennants in 2010-11, the Rangers have appeared in the postseason only three times, never advancing past the Division Series. The 2020 season featured the club's lowest winning percentage (.367) since 1985, and 2021 handed the Rangers their first 100-loss season since 1973, their second year in Texas.

Last season was supposed to be a step forward, but ended with just eight more wins than the previous summer and a fourth-place finish in the AL West, due in large part to an astonishingly unlucky 15-35 record in one-run games.

Davis simply ran out of goodwill. "Chris is the right guy to lead us forward," he said that day in August. And sure, it's Young's team now. It has to be, after his own shock at his predecessor's dismissal. But maybe it's a blessing that the Rangers are no longer in Daniels' shadow. There are no more what-ifs, of two barely missed World Series championships or the failed core of prospects that followed as the organization tried to extend its golden era.

It *is* a new era of Texas Rangers baseball. Young will have to be the right guy to move it forward.

⚾ ⚾ ⚾

"We're not where we need to be in terms of a championship-caliber club," Young said at his end-of-season press conference, another first without Daniels by his side.

"Championship culture" has become sort of a buzzword within the Rangers organization for the last year or two. Young was clearly right that they lacked it, but what makes a championship-caliber club, really? The Rangers had periods of success in the late 1990s and the early 2010s, but championship culture never became synonymous with Texas' baseball club. Is it simply winning a championship? Competing year in and year out? Or something altogether intangible?

Young referenced Seager and Semien. The two middle-infield pillars represent the intangibles of an everyday big leaguer: the preparation, the care they bring into the clubhouse daily, the "winning mentality." A championship culture requires championship-caliber players who stick around long enough to build championship-caliber clubs. Bringing a few stars to Texas was just the start. Almost every move the Rangers have made in the past year-plus—from the free-agent stunners in December 2021 to the hiring of Bochy and inking of Jacob deGrom this offseason—has been with the intent to build that culture, to return to playoff contention and challenge the Astros in the American League West, "in 2023 and beyond."

It was also all done with the recognition that Texas isn't quite there yet. The Rangers flip-flopped the traditional construction of a championship baseball team by adding their big-name free agent signings before the top-ranked prospects reached the big leagues. They worked proactively instead of adding later, when needed. And something like that has its pros and cons.

Typically, a 68-94 record doesn't indicate a team on the precipice of a playoff run, but it was a disparate campaign: The four batters making up the offensive core—Seager, Semien, Nathaniel Lowe, and Adolis García—each logged at least 25 home runs. They were basically the sole drivers of a Rangers offense that disappeared by the bottom of the lineup, give or take one Jonah Heim. Seager and Semien didn't have their best years, but were steady forces in the batter's box and on either side of second base. García kept coming up in big moments with a bat flip and a strut around the bases, though DRC+ (100) was noncommittal. Lowe was the breakout star of the year, with a shiny new Silver Slugger Award to his name and a .302 batting average to go along with it. Top prospect Josh Jung got a cup of coffee in September and will be a popular preseason pick for Rookie of the Year.

The pitching has a longer climb. Texas finished 22nd in MLB with a 4.22 ERA, only a slight improvement from 23rd (4.79 ERA) in 2021. The bullpen struggled mightily and a number of blown leads contributed to the futility in one-run games. By DRA-, the relief corps ranked 22nd, and the starting pitchers fared no better. Jon Gray, brought on with the other pre-lockout signings to stabilize the rotation, failed to blossom away from the thin Colorado air. Their best starter in his stead, Martín Pérez, accepted a qualifying offer last November, perhaps a surer indicator of looming regression than his series of one-year deals preceding it.

So, Young and Davis both entered the offseason with one clear goal above all: To improve the starting rotation. More than anything, they needed a bona fide ace. They answered that call with another big splash in free agency, signing deGrom before baseball's annual winter meetings. It was Young's first big signing as the sole leader of Texas' baseball operations; deGrom, like Seager and Semien before him, raved about the "vision" Young had for building a perennial contender. The two star middle infielders were just the start. deGrom is the newest addition to a group that could lay the groundwork for years of title runs.

"It was the vision of building something special and winning for a long time," deGrom said of his decision to sign with Texas. "I want to play this game for a long time and want to win. Hearing that from [Young] and Bochy and ultimately getting to meet Ray [Davis] at the end, everybody having that same vision, everything lined up. This is where I wanted to be."

Young has, in a short time, proven himself the type of general manager who can sell a vision and a process, even as he leads a franchise with little historical success. He's honest and transparent with free agents, who know it's not a simple road to the top—especially not in a division with the reigning World Series champion Houston Astros. But Young is intent on building *something* in Texas.

There's no doubt that a healthy deGrom, whom Young called one of the greatest pitchers of this generation, is foundational. As a two-time National League Cy Young Award winner, a four-time All-Star, the 2014 NL Rookie of the Year, the ERA title winner in 2018 (1.70) and the owner of a career ERA+ of 155 (66 DRA-), he immediately improves any rotation he joins—as long as he can take the mound, a major caveat after two seasons that fail to combine for qualified status.

Not content to depend on one pitcher's arm, the Rangers also brought on Andrew Heaney and Nathan Eovaldi in free agency, additionally picking up Jake Odorizzi in a trade with Atlanta and summarily pushing him off the five-starter depth chart. It won't be a truly formidable group without deGrom, but even average pitching would represent a major step forward.

All the puzzle pieces are there and the stars may be slowly aligning as the seeds of a championship team take root at Globe Life Field. It stands to reason Young isn't quite done yet.

⚾ ⚾ ⚾

Rewind to November 1, 2010. Bochy's Giants defeated Ron Washington's Rangers at Rangers Ballpark in Arlington, Texas, bringing the city of San Francisco its first World Series and the club its first since relocating to the West Coast from New York.

Daniels was the architect of that Rangers team: The first of back-to-back World Series heartbreaks, it seems like a lifetime ago. As the front office tried to extend the window of contention, it became clear that a full-scale rebuild would follow before the end of the decade. And it has. It seemed Daniels might hold on until the next good Texas team, before a season that had higher expectations than the previous two still ended in more than 90 losses. The rebuild is finally nearing its end, but Daniels won't be a through-line.

Meanwhile, Bochy won two more World Series in San Francisco before retiring following the 2019 season. Now he's back, at the helm of a team that was in desperate need of a strong figurehead. The hire was evidence of a new era and new leadership; the first big splash of Young's tenure. Bochy was lured out of retirement with the promise of, you guessed it, a championship culture in Texas. Despite winning three World Series titles and having a near-perfect chance at Cooperstown, a competitive fire still burns within Bochy. He said he'd only return to a dugout for the "right fit." The Rangers, for whatever reason, were that fit.

"Anybody who's got three rings obviously has a clue what they're doing as far as winning at the major-league level goes," said the first baseman Lowe. "It's nice to have somebody in the manager's spot that knows what it takes to win a World Series. He's going to bring everything that he can bring going forward and we're just going to get better. There's no other option for us besides getting better."

Bochy doesn't come out of retirement without the chance to build something like in San Francisco. Young doesn't commit fully to the legendary skipper without believing Texas can field a squad capable of doing that. The offensive nucleus is well above-average and locked up for years to come. The rotation—deGrom, Gray, Pérez, Heaney, Eovaldi—is as complete and stable as a group of 30-something pitchers can be.

It's far from perfect, but things are coming into focus.

How full-circle would it be for Bochy to help deliver a World Series to the Rangers, the club he prevented from capturing one in the first place? For all the tearing down and building back up and tearing down again the Rangers have done this century, Young and Bochy have given the organization a true direction. It's not the first time there's been hope for baseball in Texas, but it feels like the light at the end of the tunnel after 50 years in Arlington without a World Series.

"You will get the parade you deserve," Daniels told Rangers fans in a statement after his dismissal. It may not happen in 2023. It probably won't, if we're all being honest with ourselves. But this is—hopefully—just the start.

—Kennedi Landry covers the Texas Rangers for MLB.com.

Hitters

Luisangel Acuña MI Born: 03/12/02 Age: 21 Bats: R Throws: R Height: 5'10" Weight: 181 lb. Origin: International Free Agent, 2018

YEAR	TEAM	LVL	AGE	PA	R	2B	3B	HR	RBI	BB	K	SB	CS	Whiff%	AVG/OBP/SLG	DRC+	BABIP	BRR	DRP	WARP
2021	DE	A	19	473	77	15	3	12	74	49	110	44	11		.266/.345/.404	106	.329	1.9	SS(42): 1.5, 2B(36): 1.0	2.1
2022	HIC	A+	20	240	45	10	0	8	29	34	60	28	6		.317/.417/.483	108	.416	2.0	SS(37): -1.9, 2B(9): -0.4	1.0
2022	FRI	AA	20	169	21	6	2	3	18	17	36	12	3		.224/.302/.349	89	.274	1.1	SS(24): 0.5, 2B(13): 1.1	0.5
2023 non-DC	*TEX*	*MLB*	*21*	*251*	*22*	*9*	*1*	*4*	*23*	*20*	*70*	*14*	*4*	*32.5%*	*.231/.296/.340*	*78*	*.315*	*3.7*	*2B 0, SS 0*	*0.4*

Comparables: Cole Tucker (72), Lucius Fox (67), Richard Urena (66)

By now, you probably know Acuña either as the kid brother of Ronald or from his frequent comments on MLB's Instagram posts. Though he lacks the superstar ceiling of his older brother, the 20-year-old Acuña has made himself into a fine prospect in his own right after clobbering the Sally League. He slowed up a bit after a promotion to Double-A, but his walk and strikeout rates remained encouraging as he faced better, older competition. A lithe, gifted athlete, Acuña profiles as an up-the-middle defender, and so far he's only played at second and short as a pro. Those spots are spoken for long-term in Texas, of course, so something may have to give if Acuña soon masters upper-minors pitching. Fortunately, employing too many good middle infielders is a "problem" any organization would love to have.

★ ★ ★ *2023 Top 101 Prospect* **#22** ★ ★ ★

Evan Carter OF Born: 08/29/02 Age: 20 Bats: L Throws: R Height: 6'4" Weight: 190 lb. Origin: Round 2, 2020 Draft (#50 overall)

YEAR	TEAM	LVL	AGE	PA	R	2B	3B	HR	RBI	BB	K	SB	CS	Whiff%	AVG/OBP/SLG	DRC+	BABIP	BRR	DRP	WARP
2021	DE	A	18	146	22	8	1	2	12	34	28	12	4		.236/.438/.387	121	.299	-2.0	CF(30): -4.0	0.4
2022	HIC	A+	19	447	78	18	10	11	66	59	75	26	12		.287/.388/.476	137	.329	-2.1	CF(72): -0.2, LF(8): 1.1, RF(3): 0.0	3.1
2022	FRI	AA	19	28	8	3	0	1	7	5	6	2	1		.429/.536/.714	104	.533	0.2	RF(3): 0.4, CF(2): 0.2	0.2
2023 non-DC	*TEX*	*MLB*	*20*	*251*	*23*	*10*	*3*	*3*	*23*	*25*	*53*	*10*	*4*	*25.3%*	*.233/.320/.365*	*93*	*.291*	*0.5*	*LF 0, CF 0*	*0.5*

Comparables: Jason Heyward (63), Ronald Acuña Jr. (56), Heliot Ramos (56)

Carter showed preternatural plate discipline as a teenager for the Wood Ducks in 2021 before a stress fracture in his back wiped out the majority of his pro debut. That led to some concerns about whether the sweet-swinging lefty's offensive ceiling would remain as high as it seemed. No one's asking those questions anymore after Carter torched the Sally League and, most importantly, stayed healthy all season. The Tennessee native is arguably the most dynamic talent in the organization now as a bona fide five-tool outfield prospect—his rapid ascension through the minors means you can name-drop him right alongside Josh Jung and Jack Leiter when talking about impact future Rangers. A 2023 big-league debut isn't out of the question, and in time we may be asking if this is the best Carter to come out of the south since *Tha Carter III*.

Charlie Culberson 3B Born: 04/10/89 Age: 34 Bats: R Throws: R Height: 6'1" Weight: 200 lb. Origin: Round 1, 2007 Draft (#51 overall)

YEAR	TEAM	LVL	AGE	PA	R	2B	3B	HR	RBI	BB	K	SB	CS	Whiff%	AVG/OBP/SLG	DRC+	BABIP	BRR	DRP	WARP
2020	ATL	MLB	31	7	2	1	0	0	1	0	4	0	0	44.4%	.143/.143/.286	86	.333	-0.8	1B(4): 0, 2B(1): 0	-0.1
2021	TEX	MLB	32	271	23	15	2	5	22	17	64	7	1	31.2%	.243/.296/.381	83	.307	0.4	3B(68): -1.6, LF(6): 0.5, 1B(4): 0	0.3
2022	TEX	MLB	33	124	19	6	0	2	12	5	31	2	3	30.9%	.252/.283/.357	84	.329	0.0	3B(25): -1.9, LF(12): -0.4, 2B(11): -0.1	-0.1
2023 DC	*FA*	*MLB*	*34*	*148*	*12*	*6*	*0*	*2*	*13*	*8*	*38*	*5*	*1*	*30.5%*	*.228/.279/.338*	*70*	*.299*	*2.3*	*3B 0, LF 0*	*0.0*

Comparables: Michael Young (46), Rich Aurilia (45), Carlos Guillen (44)

Wario Dansby Swanson logged another roughly replacement-level season in 2022, playing all over the diamond and posting a respectable but ultimately empty slash line. Such is the life of the journeyman bench bat. Most of Culberson's time in the first half was spent at the hot corner, but he saw his at-bats diminish as the year wore on as the Rangers turned to younger and more promising players like Josh Jung and Ezequiel Duran. For the sake of the memes, we can only hope that Culberson, still a free agent, latches on in Chicago with Swanson.

Ezequiel Duran IF Born: 05/22/99 Age: 24 Bats: R Throws: R Height: 5'11" Weight: 185 lb. Origin: International Free Agent, 2017

YEAR	TEAM	LVL	AGE	PA	R	2B	3B	HR	RBI	BB	K	SB	CS	Whiff%	AVG/OBP/SLG	DRC+	BABIP	BRR	DRP	WARP
2021	HIC	A+	22	174	25	7	0	7	31	12	59	7	2		.229/.287/.408	81	.309	-0.9	SS(25): 2.3, 2B(4): 0.3, 3B(3): -0.2	0.3
2021	HV	A+	22	297	42	15	6	12	48	28	71	12	7		.290/.374/.533	124	.354	-2.2	2B(42): 7.4, SS(16): -1.9	2.0
2022	FRI	AA	23	200	34	24	1	7	31	14	36	7	2		.317/.365/.574	113	.359	0.2	SS(24): -1.7, 2B(15): -0.9, 3B(4): -0.1	0.7
2022	RR	AAA	23	155	18	9	0	9	26	7	43	7	5	25.7%	.283/.316/.531	95	.337	-0.7	CF(10): -0.1, SS(9): -0.3, 3B(6): 0.1	0.2
2022	TEX	MLB	23	220	25	10	1	5	25	12	54	4	1	29.3%	.236/.277/.365	84	.295	1.0	3B(51): -3.5, 2B(9): -0.5	-0.2
2023 DC	*TEX*	*MLB*	*24*	*184*	*16*	*8*	*1*	*4*	*16*	*10*	*48*	*6*	*2*	*28.7%*	*.237/.285/.377*	*81*	*.303*	*0.5*	*3B 0, 2B 0*	*0.0*

Comparables: Yamaico Navarro (55), Eduardo Núñez (55), Jordan Luplow (55)

It may not show in his lackluster major-league slash line, but Duran can mash. The infielder has flashed above-average power potential, bordering on plus, since before the pandemic, and did so again in both Double- and Triple-A last season. He's also carried swing-and-miss issues, as evidenced by his nearly 5:1 K/BB ratio in the majors. Still, there are plenty of reasons to be bullish on the lightning in Duran's bat. The real question is where he's going to play defensively, as both middle infield spots in Texas look to be occupied for the better part of the next decade and fellow prospect Josh Jung is likely to get a long look at the hot corner. In an apparent nod to this logjam, Duran got some in-game reps in the outfield in Round Rock. That could point to where the Rangers plan to trot him out next season to keep his promising bat in the lineup.

Justin Foscue 2B Born: 03/02/99 Age: 24 Bats: R Throws: R Height: 6'0" Weight: 205 lb. Origin: Round 1, 2020 Draft (#14 overall)

YEAR	TEAM	LVL	AGE	PA	R	2B	3B	HR	RBI	BB	K	SB	CS	Whiff%	AVG/OBP/SLG	DRC+	BABIP	BRR	DRP	WARP
2021	SUR	WIN	22	89	15	4	0	5	14	15	23	3	1		.257/.416/.529		.310			
2021	HIC	A+	22	150	34	11	1	14	35	16	39	1	1		.296/.407/.736	127	.315	0.7	2B(29): -0.2	1.0
2021	FRI	AA	22	104	14	7	0	2	13	8	29	0	1		.247/.317/.387	84	.333	-1.6	2B(24): -0.7	-0.1
2022	FRI	AA	23	460	60	31	1	15	81	45	66	3	4		.288/.367/.483	118	.308	0.3	2B(76): 1.7, 3B(12): 0.3	2.5
2023 non-DC	*TEX*	*MLB*	*24*	*251*	*26*	*12*	*1*	*7*	*28*	*17*	*46*	*0*	*1*	*20.3%*	*.244/.310/.406*	*99*	*.277*	*-0.6*	*2B 0, 3B 0*	*0.6*

Comparables: Nick Solak (77), Tony Kemp (74), Christopher Bostick (72)

Some players are destined to receive the "he can hit" superlative ad nauseum from coaches and commentators alike. You will most likely hear Foscue garner a "he can hit" more than once if and when he reaches the majors. He's shown excellent feel for the strike zone since his early days at Mississippi State and hits pretty much anywhere he plays. That brings us to Foscue's main issue: Where will he play? He's not much of a (Dr. Evil quote fingers) "fielder," and is blocked in the org at his best (read: least-worst) positions of second and third base. Nathaniel Lowe has taken a hold of the cold corner gig, which means Foscue's best odds of seeing playing time may need to come at DH, as an oft-played super-sub or with a different org altogether. Defensive quandary aside, it's likely that the Huntsville, Alabama, product will soon find his way into a lineup. After all, he can hit.

Adolis García OF Born: 03/02/93 Age: 30 Bats: R Throws: R Height: 6'1" Weight: 205 lb. Origin: International Free Agent, 2017

YEAR	TEAM	LVL	AGE	PA	R	2B	3B	HR	RBI	BB	K	SB	CS	Whiff%	AVG/OBP/SLG	DRC+	BABIP	BRR	DRP	WARP
2020	TEX	MLB	27	7	0	0	0	0	0	1	4	0	0	46.2%	.000/.143/.000	79			LF(3): -0.3	
2021	TEX	MLB	28	622	77	26	2	31	90	32	194	16	5	34.2%	.243/.286/.454	92	.306	1.3	CF(79): 3, RF(51): 11.1, LF(9): 0.1	3.2
2022	TEX	MLB	29	657	88	34	5	27	101	40	183	25	6	33.5%	.250/.300/.456	100	.309	1.2	RF(93): 6.3, CF(57): 0.4	2.9
2023 DC	*TEX*	*MLB*	*30*	*581*	*61*	*24*	*3*	*25*	*70*	*33*	*170*	*20*	*7*	*33.2%*	*.239/.291/.443*	*98*	*.299*	*4.0*	*RF 1, CF 0*	*1.6*

Comparables: Nelson Cruz (69), Chris Denorfia (67), Lorenzo Cain (64)

In October 2006, Arizona Cardinals head coach Dennis Green infamously lost his temper after his team blew a 20-0 halftime lead to the Chicago Bears, ranting "they are who we thought they were" after his foe's comeback win. Well, it appears García is who we thought he was, both for better and for worse. While his first half in 2021 was as explosive as his second half was anemic, the end result was a slugging defensive whiz with a ton of punchouts and an allergy to walks. His defensive value dipped in 2022 as he shifted from center to right, but he was largely the same player as in his rookie year, just without such pronounced peaks and valleys. That makes García eminently useful, as reflected by his six combined WARP over the past two seasons. As the Rangers edge toward competing they'll likely want to drop him some in the batting order, but it seems like García will stick around longer than one would've expected when he was slugging .370 in 2021's second half.

Mitch Garver DH Born: 01/15/91 Age: 32 Bats: R Throws: R Height: 6'1" Weight: 220 lb. Origin: Round 9, 2013 Draft (#260 overall)

YEAR	TEAM	LVL	AGE	PA	R	2B	3B	HR	RBI	BB	K	SB	CS	Whiff%	AVG/OBP/SLG	DRC+	BABIP	BRR	DRP	WARP
2020	MIN	MLB	29	81	8	1	0	2	5	7	37	0	0	39.6%	.167/.247/.264	56	.294	0.0	C(22): -0.6, 1B(1): 0	-0.2
2021	MIN	MLB	30	243	29	15	0	13	34	31	71	1	1	30.0%	.256/.358/.517	111	.320	0.7	C(59): 0.9, 1B(4): 0.4	1.5
2022	TEX	MLB	31	215	23	7	0	10	24	23	53	1	1	25.3%	.207/.298/.404	108	.228	1.1	C(14): 0.6	1.0
2023 DC	*TEX*	*MLB*	*32*	*400*	*45*	*15*	*1*	*17*	*45*	*44*	*103*	*2*	*1*	*26.7%*	*.234/.328/.438*	*111*	*.280*	*0.4*	*C -2*	*1.4*

Comparables: Welington Castillo (60), Chris Hoiles (59), Mike Napoli (57)

YEAR	TEAM	P. COUNT	FRM RUNS	BLK RUNS	THRW RUNS	TOT RUNS
2020	MIN	2772	-0.6	0.0	0.0	-0.6
2021	MIN	7509	1.6	-0.1	0.1	1.6
2022	TEX	2081	0.5	0.0	0.1	0.6
2023	*TEX*	*7215*	*-2.0*	*-0.1*	*-0.1*	*-2.2*

It's tempting to look at Garver's season and call it, as the kids would say, "mid." A nearly league-average DRC+ from a bat-first player will do that. But a brief look under the hood shows Garver was compromised by batted ball chicanery, a bout with COVID-19 and a flexor tendon injury that ultimately ended his season in July. When healthy, Garver suffered what would have been the fifth lowest BABIP in the league if he'd seen enough plate appearances to qualify. That's a nice way of saying he can probably still hit. There's no nice way to say he's not going to supplant Jonah Heim defensively behind the plate, and now that he's coming off his fifth-straight injury-marred campaign he may be best served spending less time donning the tools of ignorance altogether.

Dustin Harris LF/DH Born: 07/08/99 Age: 23 Bats: L Throws: R Height: 6'2" Weight: 185 lb. Origin: Round 11, 2019 Draft (#344 overall)

YEAR	TEAM	LVL	AGE	PA	R	2B	3B	HR	RBI	BB	K	SB	CS	Whiff%	AVG/OBP/SLG	DRC+	BABIP	BRR	DRP	WARP
2021	DE	A	21	306	54	11	3	10	53	34	48	20	1		.301/.389/.483	130	.329	0.1	1B(50): 1.9, 3B(13): -0.9	1.9
2021	HIC	A+	21	160	32	10	0	10	32	13	25	5	1		.372/.425/.648	144	.396	-0.6	1B(24): -1.8, 3B(11): -0.2	1.0
2022	FRI	AA	22	382	58	16	2	17	66	42	74	19	5		.257/.346/.471	112	.279	-1.1	LF(58): -0.9, 1B(6): 0.8	1.3
2023 DC	*TEX*	*MLB*	*23*	*128*	*12*	*4*	*0*	*3*	*12*	*9*	*26*	*4*	*2*	*23.9%*	*.238/.301/.386*	*91*	*.277*	*0.2*	*LF 0*	*0.2*

Comparables: Dwight Smith Jr. (60), David Cooper (59), Thomas Neal (59)

Harris had only ever mashed in the low-level minors as a teenager when the Athletics traded him to Texas for Mike Minor. Well, Harris is now at the ripe old age of 23, and he's only ever mashed through the middle and upper minors, too. Defensively, he's bounced from third base to first to left field and hasn't been particularly playable in any of those places. He also continues to access more of his raw power in games and even went two-for-three with a stolen base in the Futures Game. Given the defensive concerns, he'll have to hit his way into whatever role he eventually lands in the bigs. So far, all signs suggest he'll be able to do so.

Jonah Heim C Born: 06/27/95 Age: 28 Bats: S Throws: R Height: 6'4" Weight: 220 lb. Origin: Round 4, 2013 Draft (#129 overall)

YEAR	TEAM	LVL	AGE	PA	R	2B	3B	HR	RBI	BB	K	SB	CS	Whiff%	AVG/OBP/SLG	DRC+	BABIP	BRR	DRP	WARP
2020	OAK	MLB	25	41	5	0	0	0	5	3	3	0	0	10.9%	.211/.268/.211	103	.229	-0.2	C(12): 0.1	0.2
2021	TEX	MLB	26	285	22	13	0	10	32	15	58	3	1	21.6%	.196/.239/.358	86	.210	-0.9	C(78): 11.1	1.7
2022	TEX	MLB	27	450	51	20	1	16	48	41	87	2	0	21.6%	.227/.298/.399	106	.249	-0.9	C(111): 12	3.1
2023 DC	*TEX*	*MLB*	*28*	*354*	*34*	*14*	*0*	*10*	*35*	*28*	*65*	*2*	*0*	*21.2%*	*.233/.298/.386*	*90*	*.260*	*0.0*	*C 9*	*1.8*

Comparables: Bobby Wilson (59), Tony Sanchez (58), Steve Clevenger (56)

YEAR	TEAM	P. COUNT	FRM RUNS	BLK RUNS	THRW RUNS	TOT RUNS
2020	OAK	1456	0.1	0.0	0.0	0.1
2021	TEX	10395	10.9	-0.3	0.3	11.0
2022	TEX	14678	12.2	-0.2	0.3	12.3
2023	*TEX*	*13228*	*9.6*	*-0.2*	*0.0*	*9.4*

Between 2014 and 2016, YouTube creators Taylor Ramos and Tony Zhou produced a series of 18 video essays focused on film editing and cinematography, including features on the work of directors Edgar Wright and the Coen brothers. That series, *Every Frame a Painting*, has since garnered north of 100 million views. Heim's work behind the plate hasn't been seen or celebrated as often, but his framing certainly is artistic. Best of all for the Rangers, his hitting ability is no longer a work of abstract expressionism: He does just enough at the dish now to ensure he'll get enough playing time to display his brilliance behind it.

Sam Huff C Born: 01/14/98 Age: 25 Bats: R Throws: R Height: 6'5" Weight: 240 lb. Origin: Round 7, 2016 Draft (#219 overall)

YEAR	TEAM	LVL	AGE	PA	R	2B	3B	HR	RBI	BB	K	SB	CS	Whiff%	AVG/OBP/SLG	DRC+	BABIP	BRR	DRP	WARP
2020	TEX	MLB	22	33	5	3	0	3	4	2	11	0	0	40.7%	.355/.394/.742	96	.471	-0.7	C(10): -1.2	-0.1
2021	RAN	ROK	23	33	6	2	0	3	6	3	11	0	0		.276/.364/.655		.333			
2021	FRI	AA	23	191	24	5	0	10	23	16	77	0	0		.237/.309/.439	70	.360	-0.1	1B(34): -0.8	-0.3
2021	RR	AAA	23	25	4	1	0	3	7	2	9	0	0		.273/.320/.727	90	.273	0.0	1B(4): -0.5	0.0
2022	RR	AAA	24	274	46	4	0	21	50	25	85	0	0	34.4%	.260/.336/.533	110	.307	-1.7	C(44): 2.7	1.2
2022	TEX	MLB	24	132	9	4	0	4	10	11	42	1	0	39.0%	.240/.303/.372	81	.333	0.7	C(29): 0.7, 1B(6): -0.4	0.2
2023 DC	*TEX*	*MLB*	*25*	*124*	*13*	*3*	*0*	*6*	*14*	*9*	*44*	*0*	*0*	*37.3%*	*.235/.298/.440*	*98*	*.325*	*-0.5*	*C -1*	*0.2*

Comparables: Nick Evans (50), Brian McRae (48), Michael Barrett (47)

YEAR	TEAM	P. COUNT	FRM RUNS	BLK RUNS	THRW RUNS	TOT RUNS
2020	TEX	1459	-1.2	0.0	0.0	-1.2
2022	RR	6770	3.3	-0.5	-0.2	2.5
2022	TEX	3846	0.5	-0.2	0.2	0.6
2023	*TEX*	*3608*	*-1.0*	*-0.1*	*0.0*	*-1.1*

It feels like Huff has been around for about a decade, floating around the league as an emergency catcher behind glass that is rarely broken. Turns out that's not the case, and Huff is still in his mid-20s. Bully for him! Just please don't look at his K/BB ratios if you value your health—usually when you see a Huff whiff *this* badly, it means Aubrey is running for a school board seat. Sam isn't the first mountain of a man employed by the Rangers who swings hard enough and misses often enough to be considered a small wind turbine. But unlike Joey Gallo, Huff isn't particularly athletic, which leads to another problem with his profile—he's not a very good catcher. Bleacher Creatures beware: When Huff runs into one, you'll know it. But most of the time, you'll only feel his presence when you detect a stiff breeze.

★ ★ ★ *2023 Top 101 Prospect* **#100** ★ ★ ★

Josh Jung 3B Born: 02/12/98 Age: 25 Bats: R Throws: R Height: 6'2" Weight: 214 lb. Origin: Round 1, 2019 Draft (#8 overall)

YEAR	TEAM	LVL	AGE	PA	R	2B	3B	HR	RBI	BB	K	SB	CS	Whiff%	AVG/OBP/SLG	DRC+	BABIP	BRR	DRP	WARP
2021	FRI	AA	23	186	25	8	1	10	40	13	42	2	2		.308/.366/.544	114	.356	-1.9	3B(32): 0.2	0.7
2021	RR	AAA	23	156	29	14	0	9	21	18	34	0	0		.348/.436/.652	125	.413	-0.4	3B(24): 1.3	1.1
2022	RAN	ROK	24	29	4	0	0	3	5	3	5	0	0		.240/.345/.600		.176			
2022	RR	AAA	24	106	15	7	0	6	24	4	30	1	0	29.1%	.273/.321/.525	97	.333	-0.2	3B(18): -0.2	0.2
2022	TEX	MLB	24	102	9	4	1	5	14	4	39	2	0	30.1%	.204/.235/.418	77	.278	0.2	3B(25): 1.3	0.1
2023 DC	*TEX*	*MLB*	*25*	*514*	*47*	*22*	*2*	*16*	*49*	*29*	*142*	*4*	*1*	*29.3%*	*.228/.281/.387*	*82*	*.289*	*1.6*	*3B 0*	*0.1*

Comparables: Matt Chapman (65), Brandon Laird (65), Chris Johnson (64)

We could fill this entire book with the names of former prospects whose bright futures were prematurely extinguished by injuries both fluky and persistent. With that in mind, let's count ourselves lucky that Jung appeared in the majors at all in 2022. Since the Rangers drafted the San Antonio product eighth overall out of Texas Tech in 2019, Jung has lost game reps due to the pandemic, a knee injury and a torn labrum in his left shoulder. There's never been much doubt that Jung can rake—he did so in college and at every stop in the minors—but his timeline to do so in the majors has been delayed multiple times. Given his hitting and medical track records, we can look past his strikeout rate and 42nd percentile maximum exit velocity and instead celebrate how Jung mashed extra-base hits and held his own defensively in his big-league debut. He has an everyday role at the hot corner pretty much guaranteed to start 2023 and, health permitting, he's likely to stay there a while.

Nathaniel Lowe 1B

Born: 07/07/95 Age: 28 Bats: L Throws: R Height: 6'4" Weight: 220 lb. Origin: Round 13, 2016 Draft (#390 overall)

YEAR	TEAM	LVL	AGE	PA	R	2B	3B	HR	RBI	BB	K	SB	CS	Whiff%	AVG/OBP/SLG	DRC+	BABIP	BRR	DRP	WARP
2020	TB	MLB	24	76	10	2	0	4	11	9	28	1	0	29.4%	.224/.316/.433	85	.314	0.0	1B(15): -0.2, 3B(2): 0	0.0
2021	TEX	MLB	25	642	75	24	3	18	72	80	162	8	0	23.6%	.264/.357/.415	101	.339	-1.3	1B(148): 1.3, 3B(1): 0.5	1.5
2022	TEX	MLB	26	645	74	26	3	27	76	48	147	2	2	24.9%	.302/.358/.492	120	.363	-3.5	1B(153): -0.4	2.5
2023 DC	*TEX*	*MLB*	*27*	*609*	*65*	*24*	*1*	*19*	*65*	*55*	*148*	*3*	*1*	*24.4%*	*.272/.342/.430*	*115*	*.339*	*1.1*	*1B 0*	*2.1*

Comparables: Brandon Belt (67), Josh Bell (66), Joey Votto (63)

Pending the development of the outfielders Tampa Bay received in the 2020 deal that brought him to Texas, Lowe might end up as the rare player the Rays regret trading away. He was a fine hitter in 2021 but got even better in 2022 after upping his swing rate from just under 45% to 52% while cutting back on his whiffs. He also cut his ground-ball rate by nearly seven percentage points and bumped his fly-ball rate by more than three percentage points, resulting in a career high in homers. As a result, he was the most consistent hitter in the Rangers lineup. Lowe was not an unheralded prospect, but the ceiling for bat-first first basemen—he's still not anything better than average defensively—is only so high. That said, it seems like Lowe has reached his. He won't post such a high BABIP every season, but he's cemented himself as a durable, middle-of-the-order slugger.

Brad Miller 3B

Born: 10/18/89 Age: 33 Bats: L Throws: R Height: 6'2" Weight: 195 lb. Origin: Round 2, 2011 Draft (#62 overall)

YEAR	TEAM	LVL	AGE	PA	R	2B	3B	HR	RBI	BB	K	SB	CS	Whiff%	AVG/OBP/SLG	DRC+	BABIP	BRR	DRP	WARP
2020	STL	MLB	30	171	21	8	1	7	25	25	46	1	0	35.7%	.232/.357/.451	104	.289	0.3	3B(15): -0.6, SS(2): 0, 2B(1): -0.4	0.4
2021	PHI	MLB	31	377	53	9	3	20	49	45	112	3	0	31.0%	.227/.321/.453	100	.276	-0.6	1B(58): 0, RF(14): -0.5, 2B(13): -0.8	0.9
2022	TEX	MLB	32	241	20	3	0	7	32	18	70	4	2	36.4%	.212/.270/.320	78	.274	1.1	LF(28): -1.5, 3B(27): -0.7, RF(3): 0	-0.1
2023 DC	*TEX*	*MLB*	*33*	*257*	*27*	*8*	*1*	*10*	*27*	*24*	*79*	*3*	*1*	*34.7%*	*.224/.303/.406*	*94*	*.292*	*1.9*		*0.4*

Comparables: Dick McAuliffe (55), José Reyes (54), Asdrúbal Cabrera (52)

In the first leg of his two-year deal Miller had arguably his worst season in the majors, suffering a complete loss of power even against right-handers and posting a career-worst slugging percentage and walk rate. He also dealt with an assortment of hip and neck injuries that may have led in part to a career-low maximum exit velocity. There are a dozen other ways to illustrate that it was never Miller Time in Arlington last season, but you get the idea. It's possible that 2022 wasn't a blinking red light indicating that he's washed. There's also a chance that Miller is done living the high life.

Corey Seager SS

Born: 04/27/94 Age: 29 Bats: L Throws: R Height: 6'4" Weight: 215 lb. Origin: Round 1, 2012 Draft (#18 overall)

YEAR	TEAM	LVL	AGE	PA	R	2B	3B	HR	RBI	BB	K	SB	CS	Whiff%	AVG/OBP/SLG	DRC+	BABIP	BRR	DRP	WARP
2020	LAD	MLB	26	232	38	12	1	15	41	17	37	1	0	25.8%	.307/.358/.585	124	.309	-1.3	SS(43): -0.1	1.2
2021	LAD	MLB	27	409	54	22	3	16	57	48	66	1	1	28.0%	.306/.394/.521	122	.336	-1.1	SS(92): -0.5	2.5
2022	TEX	MLB	28	663	91	24	1	33	83	58	103	3	0	26.6%	.245/.317/.455	122	.242	1.6	SS(144): 0.1	4.0
2023 DC	*TEX*	*MLB*	*29*	*597*	*72*	*26*	*1*	*25*	*68*	*54*	*105*	*0*	*0*	*26.2%*	*.267/.341/.464*	*124*	*.290*	*-0.1*	*SS 1*	*3.7*

Comparables: Arky Vaughan (79), Cal Ripken Jr. (76), Joe Sewell (76)

Thanks to a career high in homers and his first All-Star selection since 2017, you could argue Seager's Rangers debut was largely successful. You could also point to his career-worst on-base and slugging percentages (in a full season, at least) and lament that Seager is still owed roughly $290 million over the next nine years. The good news is that much of his batted-ball profile and swing tendencies were right in line with his career averages, and Seager still finished top-20 in the league in DRC+, flanked by fellow stars like Kyle Tucker and Will Smith. A significant part of the Rangers' ostensible return to contention rests upon Seager's shoulders, and the smart money is on his non-homer counting stats returning to their Dodgersian levels. Of course, there remains a small but non-zero chance that 2022 marked the ominous beginning of a very surprising, depressing and expensive decline for Texas' biggest acquisition in a decade. That's the magic of playing in free agency, baby. You never *really* know what you're gonna get.

Marcus Semien 2B

Born: 09/17/90 Age: 32 Bats: R Throws: R Height: 6'0" Weight: 195 lb. Origin: Round 6, 2011 Draft (#201 overall)

YEAR	TEAM	LVL	AGE	PA	R	2B	3B	HR	RBI	BB	K	SB	CS	Whiff%	AVG/OBP/SLG	DRC+	BABIP	BRR	DRP	WARP
2020	OAK	MLB	29	236	28	9	1	7	23	25	50	4	0	23.3%	.223/.305/.374	99	.260	1.4	SS(53): 1.1	0.9
2021	TOR	MLB	30	724	115	39	2	45	102	66	146	15	1	21.5%	.265/.334/.538	126	.276	4.1	2B(147): 0.5, SS(21): -1	5.4
2022	TEX	MLB	31	724	101	31	5	26	83	53	120	25	8	20.6%	.248/.304/.429	112	.263	4.3	2B(148): 4.2, SS(17): -1.2	4.1
2023 DC	*TEX*	*MLB*	*32*	*650*	*81*	*28*	*3*	*27*	*68*	*51*	*112*	*20*	*4*	*20.8%*	*.256/.318/.453*	*113*	*.274*	*8.6*	*2B 3, SS 0*	*4.2*

Comparables: Eric McNair (69), Asdrúbal Cabrera (69), Clete Boyer (66)

Semien parlayed his pyrotechnic 2021 into a seven-year, nine-figure deal before the lockout and almost immediately fell on his face, failing to hit his first homer until May 28 and hitting under .200 until June 7. After that he was excellent, but few seemed to notice given the Rangers' overall mediocrity. Semien slashed .272/.326/.493 over the last four months of the year and remained as durable and defensively capable as ever. Much like Corey Seager, Semien will probably be just fine after his rough acclimation period, which is not a prediction some would have felt comfortable making as recently as Memorial Day. The Rangers have about 150 million reasons remaining to pray his early-season stumbles were indeed as fluky as they seem.

Josh H. Smith 3B Born: 08/07/97 Age: 25 Bats: L Throws: R Height: 5'10" Weight: 172 lb. Origin: Round 2, 2019 Draft (#67 overall)

YEAR	TEAM	LVL	AGE	PA	R	2B	3B	HR	RBI	BB	K	SB	CS	Whiff%	AVG/OBP/SLG	DRC+	BABIP	BRR	DRP	WARP
2021	TAM	A	23	50	15	0	0	6	15	7	6	5	0		.333/.480/.795	138	.259	1.1	SS(7): -0.4, 2B(1): -0.0	0.4
2021	HIC	A+	23	49	10	3	0	1	7	2	9	2	0		.295/.367/.432	105	.353	-0.1	SS(9): 1.0	0.3
2021	HV	A+	23	125	29	12	3	3	9	16	27	12	3		.320/.435/.583	109	.411	-0.3	SS(23): 3.6	0.8
2021	FRI	AA	23	127	12	5	0	3	10	18	20	7	2		.294/.425/.431	124	.338	-0.1	SS(30): -1.8	0.6
2022	RR	AAA	24	261	45	13	4	6	45	33	54	9	4	20.7%	.290/.395/.466	112	.358	0.1	3B(20): -0.8, SS(17): 1.5, CF(16): -1.2	1.0
2022	TEX	MLB	24	253	23	5	0	2	16	28	50	4	3	23.8%	.197/.307/.249	83	.244	-1.1	3B(36): 1.2, LF(24): -0.1, SS(6): -0.2	0.2
2023 DC	*TEX*	*MLB*	*25*	*391*	*44*	*15*	*2*	*9*	*33*	*38*	*80*	*13*	*3*	*22.4%*	*.242/.335/.386*	*105*	*.288*	*4.2*	*LF 0, SS 0*	*1.6*

Comparables: Josh Bell (62), JaCoby Jones (59), J.D. Davis (58)

Who among us can ever forget Zooey Deschanel's transcendent line in the 2009 film *500 Days of Summer,* "I love The Smiths?" Rangers fans were reciting it non-stop in July, when our protagonist hustled for an inside-the-park home run for his first major-league dinger. He didn't do all that much else in his rookie campaign, but Smith showed good speed and discipline and an ability to play all over the place, appearing at second base, third base, shortstop and left field. While Smith's not all that explosive, he will probably grow to annoy the fanbases of opposing teams as any good utility player should. Zooey's got a point: What's not to love?

Leody Taveras CF Born: 09/08/98 Age: 24 Bats: S Throws: R Height: 6'2" Weight: 195 lb. Origin: International Free Agent, 2015

YEAR	TEAM	LVL	AGE	PA	R	2B	3B	HR	RBI	BB	K	SB	CS	Whiff%	AVG/OBP/SLG	DRC+	BABIP	BRR	DRP	WARP
2020	TEX	MLB	21	134	20	6	1	4	6	14	43	8	0	30.4%	.227/.308/.395	80	.319	2.3	CF(33): 1	0.4
2021	AGU	WIN	22	175	27	5	1	2	19	24	23	11	1		.274/.379/.363		.309			
2021	RR	AAA	22	381	57	19	2	17	55	49	95	13	5		.245/.343/.475	98	.287	1.2	CF(70): 4.9, LF(9): 3.0, RF(2): 0.1	2.1
2021	TEX	MLB	22	185	14	6	2	3	9	9	60	10	1	26.9%	.161/.207/.270	62	.225	2.5	CF(48): 3.4	0.5
2022	RR	AAA	23	221	34	12	3	7	29	14	48	7	4	21.5%	.294/.335/.485	99	.349	-0.2	CF(24): 2.4, LF(14): -0.5, RF(10): -1.1	0.5
2022	TEX	MLB	23	341	39	14	2	5	34	21	88	11	5	29.0%	.261/.309/.366	81	.344	1.1	CF(93): 4.8	1.1
2023 DC	*TEX*	*MLB*	*24*	*516*	*49*	*19*	*4*	*11*	*43*	*35*	*129*	*21*	*4*	*26.4%*	*.233/.287/.362*	*78*	*.295*	*11.6*	*CF 3*	*1.7*

Comparables: Anthony Gose (62), Byron Buxton (60), Carlos Gómez (53)

Taveras looked rejuvenated at Round Rock over the first two months of the season, and while the former top prospect didn't carry his modest power rebound with him to Arlington, he didn't look bereft of offensive potential as he did in 2021. Taveras' lifetime slugging percentage across six minor-league seasons spanning more than 600 games is .384. He's never going to be much of a power threat, but that doesn't have to be a deal-breaker when you have 96th percentile sprint speed and 98th percentile arm strength. Taveras still looks like a future Gold Glove candidate in center, which means he's eminently playable if he can just fight his way to something like an 85 or 90 DRC+. Regardless of how he gets there, he'd be wise to add some production to his offensive game soon, as Texas' next wave of high-ceiling prospects in the mirror may be closer than they appear.

Bubba Thompson OF Born: 06/09/98 Age: 25 Bats: R Throws: R Height: 6'2" Weight: 197 lb. Origin: Round 1, 2017 Draft (#26 overall)

YEAR	TEAM	LVL	AGE	PA	R	2B	3B	HR	RBI	BB	K	SB	CS	Whiff%	AVG/OBP/SLG	DRC+	BABIP	BRR	DRP	WARP
2021	FRI	AA	23	470	73	23	9	16	52	29	121	25	8		.275/.325/.483	97	.347	1.5	CF(68): -3.1, LF(16): 1.8, RF(10): 0.4	1.3
2022	RR	AAA	24	375	77	12	4	13	48	22	95	49	3	33.0%	.303/.355/.474	85	.385	8.5	CF(51): 0.3, LF(20): 0.6, RF(9): -0.5	0.9
2022	TEX	MLB	24	181	18	5	0	1	9	7	56	18	3	33.2%	.265/.302/.312	67	.389	0.6	LF(35): 2.3, RF(10): 1, CF(9): 0.3	0.3
2023 DC	*TEX*	*MLB*	*25*	*359*	*35*	*12*	*3*	*7*	*32*	*18*	*104*	*35*	*7*	*32.6%*	*.244/.289/.374*	*81*	*.330*	*19.1*	*RF -1, LF 1*	*2.1*

Comparables: Zoilo Almonte (67), Alfredo Marte (65), Austin Slater (63)

Just 26 players in major-league history have had Leslie as their given first name. Many of them went by shorter versions like Les, or by nicknames such as Bullet Joe or Buster. Now we can add Bubba to the list, and as of last summer, he was the only active major leaguer with either name. A blistering 80 games in Round Rock earned the speedy outfielder his first call-up. He wasn't very good at the plate, with a 37th percentile max exit velocity undermining a solid batting average. Despite owning the second-best sprint speed in the majors, he wasn't particularly good in the field, either. But given his wheels, Thompson may be able to stick around for a bit, even if he ultimately ends up a pinch-running threat and reserve outfielder. At the very least, he can probably count on being the only Bubba in the league for a while: Pittsburgh's Bubba Chandler still hasn't reached Double-A.

Aaron Zavala RF Born: 06/24/00 Age: 23 Bats: L Throws: R Height: 6'0" Weight: 193 lb. Origin: Round 2, 2021 Draft (#38 overall)

YEAR	TEAM	LVL	AGE	PA	R	2B	3B	HR	RBI	BB	K	SB	CS	Whiff%	AVG/OBP/SLG	DRC+	BABIP	BRR	DRP	WARP
2021	RAN	ROK	21	26	5	1	0	0	2	3	7	2	0		.273/.385/.318		.400			
2021	DE	A	21	67	13	4	0	1	7	10	13	7	0		.302/.433/.434	122	.375	-0.2	RF(10): -1.3, LF(1): 0.4	0.3
2022	HIC	A+	22	375	61	10	3	11	41	68	79	10	5		.278/.424/.441	133	.344	1.2	RF(67): -0.5, CF(6): -0.2	2.8
2022	FRI	AA	22	139	28	8	0	5	21	21	29	4	1		.277/.410/.482	116	.329	0.7	RF(24): -0.5	0.9
2023 non-DC	*TEX*	*MLB*	*23*	*251*	*25*	*9*	*1*	*4*	*24*	*28*	*61*	*4*	*2*	*27.0%*	*.227/.328/.352*	*92*	*.294*	*1.1*	*LF 0, CF 0*	*0.4*

Comparables: Trevor Larnach (72), Kelly Dugan (72), Zoilo Almonte (71)

A second-round pick out of Oregon in 2021, Zavala has done nothing but hit since his pro debut. The 22-year-old doesn't possess a ton of over-the-fence power, as his swing is more geared toward producing line drives. But he looks like a plug-and-play leadoff hitter who will take a lot of walks and make a lot of solid contact, and there's plenty of value in that. Zavala will likely have to succeed as such, as defensively he profiles as a corner outfielder who may lack the arm strength to play right. But even if his upside is relatively modest, teams tend to find a spot for dudes with this type of control over both their own bats and the strike zone.

Pitchers

Joe Barlow RHP Born: 09/28/95 Age: 27 Bats: R Throws: R Height: 6'2" Weight: 210 lb. Origin: Round 11, 2016 Draft (#339 overall)

YEAR	TEAM	LVL	AGE	W	L	SV	G	GS	IP	H	HR	BB/9	K/9	K	GB%	BABIP	WHIP	ERA	DRA-	WARP	MPH	FB%	Whiff%	CSP
2021	RR	AAA	25	0	1	7	17	0	21	8	1	3.4	12.4	29	34.1%	.175	0.76	2.57	84	0.3				
2021	TEX	MLB	25	0	2	11	31	0	29	12	2	3.7	8.4	27	38.9%	.143	0.83	1.55	112	0.1	94.6	46.6%	25.9%	54.4%
2022	FRI	AA	26	1	0	0	3	0	5^1	1	0	3.4	8.4	5	50.0%	.083	0.56	0.00	86	0.1				
2022	TEX	MLB	26	3	1	13	35	0	35	27	5	3.3	7.2	28	36.6%	.229	1.14	3.86	106	0.2	94.8	31.0%	27.1%	55.0%
2023 DC	*TEX*	*MLB*	*27*	*2*	*2*	*0*	*58*	*0*	*50.3*	*45*	*6*	*4.5*	*9.2*	*51*	*38.1%*	*.286*	*1.40*	*4.09*	*102*	*0.2*	*94.7*	*37.0%*	*28.0%*	*54.8%*

Comparables: Nick Goody (63), Diego Castillo (62), Keynan Middleton (61)

Barlow set the bar high (yes, we know, we're sorry) for himself as an out-of-nowhere impact rookie in 2021. He entered the 2022 season as the Rangers' closer, but lost the job after consecutive blown saves in mid-July. A pair of IL stints for blister issues allowed some of his bullpen mates to pass him on the depth chart, as did Barlow's propensity for allowing more homers while missing fewer bats than a season ago. Is the 27-year-old righty just a poster boy for reliever volatility, or can he re-earn high-leverage work once afforded a full offseason to get right? It's probably best to hope for the middle ground and pencil in Barlow as no better than a set-up option until he proves otherwise. In other words, it's time to set the bar a little, well …

Brock Burke LHP Born: 08/04/96 Age: 26 Bats: L Throws: L Height: 6'4" Weight: 210 lb. Origin: Round 3, 2014 Draft (#96 overall)

YEAR	TEAM	LVL	AGE	W	L	SV	G	GS	IP	H	HR	BB/9	K/9	K	GB%	BABIP	WHIP	ERA	DRA-	WARP	MPH	FB%	Whiff%	CSP
2021	RR	AAA	24	1	5	0	21	20	77^2	76	13	3.6	11.2	97	42.2%	.330	1.38	5.68	86	1.1				
2022	TEX	MLB	25	7	5	0	52	0	82^1	63	9	2.6	9.8	90	37.7%	.271	1.06	1.97	85	1.4	94.8	78.6%	25.0%	53.5%
2023 DC	*TEX*	*MLB*	*26*	*2*	*2*	*5*	*58*	*0*	*50.3*	*46*	*6*	*3.3*	*8.7*	*48*	*40.7%*	*.287*	*1.29*	*3.72*	*97*	*0.3*	*94.6*	*77.2%*	*24.4%*	*53.2%*

Comparables: Lucas Sims (65), Cody Reed (57), Kyle Ryan (55)

Heading into 2022, Burke had only two stints as a professional in which he posted a sub-3.00 ERA while throwing a meaningful number of innings. The first came in 2017, when Burke was 20 years old and besting Low-A hitters as a member of the Rays system. The next came in 2018, when Burke impressed in Double-A. It looked like he may never pull off that feat again after a few lost seasons and some shoulder injuries, but he ticked the box once more last year, and crucially, this time he did it in the majors. Burke resurfaced as a shutdown reliever and joined Matt Moore as one of the two best southpaws in the Rangers bullpen. Should we expect him to do it again? Maybe not, since his average exit velocity, hard-hit percentage and chase rate were all below average, according to Statcast. That said, Burke is still just 26, and though an assortment of higher-ceiling pitching prospects is en route to Texas, he might've found a role he can settle into.

Jacob deGrom RHP Born: 06/19/88 Age: 35 Bats: L Throws: R Height: 6'4" Weight: 180 lb. Origin: Round 9, 2010 Draft (#272 overall)

YEAR	TEAM	LVL	AGE	W	L	SV	G	GS	IP	H	HR	BB/9	K/9	K	GB%	BABIP	WHIP	ERA	DRA-	WARP	MPH	FB%	Whiff%	CSP
2020	NYM	MLB	32	4	2	0	12	12	68	47	7	2.4	13.8	104	42.5%	.288	0.96	2.38	55	2.4	98.8	44.9%	41.0%	44.2%
2021	NYM	MLB	33	7	2	0	15	15	92	40	6	1.1	14.3	146	44.6%	.213	0.55	1.08	52	3.2	99.5	57.6%	41.7%	47.1%
2022	SYR	AAA	34	0	1	0	2	2	8	4	2	4.5	11.2	10	23.5%	.133	1.00	4.50	93	0.1				
2022	NYM	MLB	34	5	4	0	11	11	64^1	40	9	1.1	14.3	102	38.8%	.261	0.75	3.08	59	2.0	99.0	47.5%	41.9%	49.7%
2023 DC	*TEX*	*MLB*	*35*	*8*	*4*	*0*	*19*	*19*	*114.7*	*78*	*12*	*1.8*	*13.6*	*172*	*41.5%*	*.286*	*0.89*	*1.52*	*43*	*4.4*	*98.7*	*50.3%*	*38.0%*	*47.1%*

Comparables: Bob Gibson (87), Tom Seaver (85), Max Scherzer (85)

Last year in this space, deGrom was compared to Prometheus, who subverted the gods by stealing their fire. In several versions of the myth, Prometheus was eventually freed from his eternal torment by the hero Hercules. Much like the Greek hero, after spending years living among the gods, deGrom is contending with the fact that he is indeed part mortal after all. When he made his return from a stress reaction in his scapula on August 2, tasked with carrying the Mets to the gates of Olympus alongside Max Scherzer, he certainly appeared deGromian, striking out batters at the same prodigious rate as he did in his injury-shortened 2021. But he was vulnerable to the long ball in a way he hasn't been since before his run with the divine. Though we are not used to seeing deGrom's ERA begin with the number three, his DRA was lower than it was in either of his Cy Young seasons. That was enough for him to begin the next chapter of his career in Texas with a five-year, $185 million deal in hand in an effort to finally go the distance.

Dane Dunning RHP Born: 12/20/94 Age: 28 Bats: R Throws: R Height: 6'4" Weight: 225 lb. Origin: Round 1, 2016 Draft (#29 overall)

YEAR	TEAM	LVL	AGE	W	L	SV	G	GS	IP	H	HR	BB/9	K/9	K	GB%	BABIP	WHIP	ERA	DRA-	WARP	MPH	FB%	Whiff%	CSP
2020	CHW	MLB	25	2	0	0	7	7	34	25	4	3.4	9.3	35	44.6%	.239	1.12	3.97	93	0.5	92.0	60.6%	27.6%	44.0%
2021	TEX	MLB	26	5	10	0	27	25	117^2	126	13	3.3	8.7	114	53.6%	.339	1.44	4.51	102	1.0	90.4	60.8%	23.4%	55.2%
2022	TEX	MLB	27	4	8	0	29	29	153^1	158	20	3.6	8.0	137	51.5%	.314	1.43	4.46	112	0.5	89.2	52.0%	24.7%	50.1%
2023 DC	*TEX*	*MLB*	*28*	*6*	*6*	*0*	*38*	*12*	*88.3*	*92*	*10*	*3.6*	*8.7*	*85*	*51.3%*	*.319*	*1.45*	*4.56*	*112*	*0.2*	*89.8*	*55.6%*	*24.5%*	*51.4%*

Comparables: Zack Wheeler (75), Stephen Fife (74), Jordan Montgomery (73)

Dunning has settled in as the archetypal back-end starter as he continues to incrementally build up his workload more than three years removed from Tommy John surgery. That's not necessarily a pejorative, though he's yet to offer better than league-average production over a full season per WARP, DRA- or pretty much any other advanced metric. Boring pitchers with decent command and average stuff still have value in the bigs so long as they can gobble up innings—ask Jordan Lyles, who just reached 10 years of service time despite a career DRA- of 106. Dunning will never be particularly exciting or aesthetically pleasing to watch, but as far as back-of-the-rotation fillers go, you could do a lot worse.

Nathan Eovaldi RHP Born: 02/13/90 Age: 33 Bats: R Throws: R Height: 6'2" Weight: 217 lb. Origin: Round 11, 2008 Draft (#337 overall)

YEAR	TEAM	LVL	AGE	W	L	SV	G	GS	IP	H	HR	BB/9	K/9	K	GB%	BABIP	WHIP	ERA	DRA-	WARP	MPH	FB%	Whiff%	CSP
2020	BOS	MLB	30	4	2	0	9	9	48^1	51	8	1.3	9.7	52	49.3%	.339	1.20	3.72	74	1.2	97.6	37.7%	28.1%	49.9%
2021	BOS	MLB	31	11	9	0	32	32	182^1	182	15	1.7	9.6	195	42.1%	.327	1.19	3.75	85	3.2	97.0	42.3%	26.0%	58.0%
2022	WOR	AAA	32	0	0	0	2	2	6	8	2	3.0	12.0	8	31.6%	.400	1.67	7.50	93	0.1				
2022	BOS	MLB	32	6	3	0	20	20	109^1	115	21	1.6	8.5	103	47.3%	.300	1.23	3.87	92	1.5	96.1	38.5%	25.4%	54.9%
2023 DC	*TEX*	*MLB*	*33*	*8*	*8*	*0*	*25*	*25*	*142.3*	*141*	*17*	*2.1*	*8.3*	*131*	*45.2%*	*.302*	*1.22*	*3.45*	*92*	*1.7*	*96.8*	*40.6%*	*25.1%*	*55.5%*

Comparables: Milt Pappas (71), Rick Wise (70), Homer Bailey (70)

The four-year, $68 million deal the Red Sox gave Eovaldi after his 2018 postseason heroics bought them roughly 400 innings of good-but-not-great pitching, undercut by his perpetual twin bugaboos: injuries and home runs. Both sank his 2022, as he lost several weeks to back and shoulder inflammation and finished with the second-worst home run rate among starters with 100 or more innings pitched. Those injuries also sapped his fastball of its premium velocity; from June onward, his four-seamer was mostly stuck in the low- to mid-90s as opposed to its usual 96+ mph home. That's not the most reassuring combo for the righty, but the end result was still a starter who, by DRA-, ranked alongside Pablo López, Logan Webb and Chris Bassitt—in other words, a mid-rotation arm with no. 1 upside when it's all clicking. That's something any contender could use, and the Rangers now fancy themselves as such after signing Eovaldi to a two-year deal with an option to slot in the middle of their rebuilt rotation.

Jon Gray RHP Born: 11/05/91 Age: 31 Bats: R Throws: R Height: 6'4" Weight: 225 lb. Origin: Round 1, 2013 Draft (#3 overall)

YEAR	TEAM	LVL	AGE	W	L	SV	G	GS	IP	H	HR	BB/9	K/9	K	GB%	BABIP	WHIP	ERA	DRA-	WARP	MPH	FB%	Whiff%	CSP
2020	COL	MLB	28	2	4	0	8	8	39	45	6	2.5	5.1	22	36.7%	.293	1.44	6.69	134	-0.3	94.1	49.4%	22.1%	47.4%
2021	COL	MLB	29	8	12	0	29	29	149	140	21	3.5	9.5	157	47.7%	.299	1.33	4.59	85	2.6	95.1	47.6%	26.9%	57.2%
2022	TEX	MLB	30	7	7	0	24	24	127^1	105	17	2.8	9.5	134	43.9%	.271	1.13	3.96	83	2.3	96.0	50.6%	26.1%	55.1%
2023 DC	*TEX*	*MLB*	*31*	*8*	*8*	*0*	*25*	*25*	*142.3*	*132*	*16*	*3.1*	*8.5*	*134*	*45.0%*	*.289*	*1.27*	*3.53*	*93*	*1.7*	*95.5*	*49.6%*	*25.6%*	*54.7%*

Comparables: Kevin Brown (77), Mike Moore (77), Ricky Nolasco (76)

Not many starting pitchers find sustained success in Colorado. Not all of them find it once they escape its low-gravity science experiment of a ballpark, either. Outside of the modest post-Coors peaks enjoyed by Ubaldo Jiménez and Jhoulys Chacín, there are relatively few examples that inspire confidence. As such, it was fair to wonder if Gray would remain the frustrating but talented pitcher we saw in Denver once he fled for the more terrestrial pitching environment in Arlington. Well, it turns out he's fine. Just fine, though. His counting stats? Fine. Rate stats? Not great, but not bad either. Advanced metrics? You guessed it, they're fine. Gray will never be a workhorse—his latest injury was an oblique issue that kept him out for more than a month—but as far as mid-rotation arms go, you can trust him more often than not. He's ... well, he's fine.

Andrew Heaney LHP Born: 06/05/91 Age: 32 Bats: L Throws: L Height: 6'2" Weight: 200 lb. Origin: Round 1, 2012 Draft (#9 overall)

YEAR	TEAM	LVL	AGE	W	L	SV	G	GS	IP	H	HR	BB/9	K/9	K	GB%	BABIP	WHIP	ERA	DRA-	WARP	MPH	FB%	Whiff%	CSP
2020	LAA	MLB	29	4	3	0	12	12	66^2	63	9	2.6	9.5	70	38.3%	.302	1.23	4.46	92	1.0	91.7	58.0%	28.0%	50.1%
2021	NYY	MLB	30	2	2	0	12	5	35^2	38	13	2.5	9.3	37	32.7%	.266	1.35	7.32	129	-0.2	92.0	58.8%	23.6%	51.3%
2021	LAA	MLB	30	6	7	0	18	18	94	92	16	3.0	10.8	113	34.0%	.319	1.31	5.27	95	1.1	92.1	59.7%	29.7%	49.7%
2022	OKC	AAA	31	0	1	0	2	2	7^1	4	0	0.0	12.3	10	60.0%	.267	0.55	1.23	77	0.1	92.1	65.3%	30.4%	
2022	LAD	MLB	31	4	4	0	16	14	72^2	60	14	2.4	13.6	110	34.9%	.293	1.09	3.10	70	1.8	93.0	62.5%	36.1%	50.8%
2023 DC	*TEX*	*MLB*	*32*	*7*	*6*	*0*	*22*	*22*	*120*	*97*	*17*	*2.5*	*11.0*	*147*	*36.5%*	*.280*	*1.09*	*2.93*	*78*	*2.3*	*92.4*	*60.1%*	*30.7%*	*50.1%*

Comparables: Derek Holland (76), Gavin Floyd (74), Jeff Francis (74)

Midlife crises have an unfair reputation. They're great! You get to do all kinds of fun stuff like drive fast cars and take cool vacations. Heaney's career year exhibited many of the symptoms of the standard existential despair. He ditched his old curveball for the newer, sexier sweeper that all the young folks rave about these days. When he returned from the IL (again) in August, his fastball was a full tick harder than he'd ever thrown it before. The new look suited him well. His 35.5% strikeout rate was 10 points higher than his career average. However, his old self still shone through—in between two IL stints, he surrendered 14 home runs in 72⅔ innings and his 47.7% hard-hit rate was sixth-worst in MLB. Now that he's jet-setting to Texas, the Rangers will find out if he's truly a whole new man, or he merely went through a phase.

Taylor Hearn LHP Born: 08/30/94 Age: 28 Bats: L Throws: L Height: 6'6" Weight: 230 lb. Origin: Round 5, 2015 Draft (#164 overall)

YEAR	TEAM	LVL	AGE	W	L	SV	G	GS	IP	H	HR	BB/9	K/9	K	GB%	BABIP	WHIP	ERA	DRA-	WARP	MPH	FB%	Whiff%	CSP
2020	TEX	MLB	25	0	0	0	14	0	17^1	13	2	5.7	11.9	23	26.8%	.282	1.38	3.63	103	0.2	95.2	60.5%	24.5%	50.2%
2021	TEX	MLB	26	6	6	0	42	11	104^1	96	17	3.6	7.9	92	38.9%	.277	1.32	4.66	120	-0.1	94.8	67.9%	23.1%	56.5%
2022	RR	AAA	27	1	0	0	3	2	12	8	3	4.5	15.0	20	8.7%	.250	1.17	6.00	106	0.0	95.0	74.1%	46.6%	
2022	TEX	MLB	27	6	8	1	31	13	100	107	11	3.9	8.7	97	37.6%	.327	1.50	5.13	120	-0.1	94.7	65.2%	22.3%	54.2%
2023 DC	*TEX*	*MLB*	*28*	*2*	*2*	*0*	*52*	*0*	*44.7*	*42*	*6*	*4.0*	*8.9*	*44*	*36.9%*	*.294*	*1.40*	*4.25*	*106*	*0.1*	*94.8*	*66.0%*	*24.8%*	*54.9%*

Comparables: Garrett Mock (62), Lenny DiNardo (61), Sean Gilmartin (56)

Hearn never reached his potential as a starter but looked much feistier as a reliever in 2022. Out of the 'pen, he had a better K/BB ratio, a lower WHIP by more than half a baserunner and a lower BABIP. He showcased good velocity as well, touching as high as 98 mph. Nevertheless, DRA- and WARP looked at his unsightly ERA and thought, "ya know what, that seems about right." As such, 2022 was likely Hearn's last shot at establishing a place in the Rangers' rapidly improving rotation; a notion that seems even more true in the wake of their off-season acquisitions of Jacob deGrom, Andrew Heaney, Nathan Eovaldi and Jake Odorizzi. Hearn may have missed his chance to start long-term, but teams will always find a place for lefty relievers with credible fastballs and sliders.

Jonathan Hernández RHP Born: 07/06/96 Age: 27 Bats: R Throws: R Height: 6'3" Weight: 190 lb. Origin: International Free Agent, 2013

YEAR	TEAM	LVL	AGE	W	L	SV	G	GS	IP	H	HR	BB/9	K/9	K	GB%	BABIP	WHIP	ERA	DRA-	WARP	MPH	FB%	Whiff%	CSP
2020	TEX	MLB	23	5	1	0	27	0	31	24	2	2.3	9.0	31	45.1%	.278	1.03	2.90	84	0.6	97.9	47.5%	33.8%	44.3%
2022	RR	AAA	25	0	2	0	15	0	13^1	13	1	8.8	10.8	16	55.6%	.343	1.95	4.05	87	0.2	97.8	41.8%	39.4%	
2022	TEX	MLB	25	2	3	4	29	0	30^1	26	2	5.0	8.0	27	60.5%	.289	1.42	2.97	106	0.2	98.0	43.2%	30.8%	52.3%
2023 DC	*TEX*	*MLB*	*26*	*2*	*3*	*9*	*58*	*0*	*50.3*	*49*	*6*	*5.2*	*9.2*	*51*	*53.0%*	*.308*	*1.55*	*4.72*	*113*	*-0.1*	*97.9*	*45.0%*	*31.5%*	*48.5%*

Comparables: Jeremy Jeffress (61), Johnny Barbato (58), Trevor Gott (57)

After missing all of 2021 recovering from Tommy John surgery, Hernández returned in July and was once again a quality late-inning reliever for most of the second half. He was even better than it may appear when you consider that one blow-up outing on September 1, in which he allowed four runs in a third of an inning, inflated his ERA at the time by more than two full runs. What matters most is that the velocity and movement profiles of his pitches looked virtually unchanged from before the injury. If the Rangers start playing more meaningful games soon, don't be surprised if a healthy Hernández is the one closing them out.

Spencer Howard RHP Born: 07/28/96 Age: 26 Bats: R Throws: R Height: 6'3" Weight: 210 lb. Origin: Round 2, 2017 Draft (#45 overall)

YEAR	TEAM	LVL	AGE	W	L	SV	G	GS	IP	H	HR	BB/9	K/9	K	GB%	BABIP	WHIP	ERA	DRA-	WARP	MPH	FB%	Whiff%	CSP
2020	PHI	MLB	23	1	2	0	6	6	24^1	30	6	3.7	8.5	23	38.0%	.329	1.64	5.92	110	0.1	94.4	56.5%	25.7%	52.2%
2021	LHV	AAA	24	1	0	0	6	6	21^2	13	1	3.7	11.6	28	37.5%	.255	1.02	1.25	96	0.4				
2021	TEX	MLB	24	0	3	0	8	8	21^1	28	5	4.2	8.9	21	38.0%	.348	1.78	9.70	124	-0.1	93.2	75.4%	23.3%	55.3%
2021	PHI	MLB	24	0	2	0	11	7	28^1	25	2	5.4	9.8	31	34.2%	.311	1.48	5.72	99	0.3	94.6	70.5%	26.9%	57.6%
2022	RR	AAA	25	3	6	0	14	12	59	53	6	3.8	11.1	73	34.0%	.320	1.32	4.73	96	0.5	94.8	55.7%	28.3%	
2022	TEX	MLB	25	2	4	0	10	8	37^2	50	12	3.6	7.6	32	39.7%	.319	1.73	7.41	133	-0.3	94.4	50.3%	17.8%	58.0%
2023 DC	*TEX*	*MLB*	*26*	*4*	*3*	*0*	*35*	*3*	*43*	*43*	*5*	*3.8*	*7.8*	*37*	*38.2%*	*.300*	*1.44*	*4.46*	*112*	*0.1*	*94.2*	*60.9%*	*23.2%*	*56.6%*

Comparables: Casey Kelly (73), Liam Hendriks (72), Robert Stephenson (72)

Howard received a score of just 28% on Metacritic as well as seven Razzie Award nominations. He even won four of them! Though some may consider him among the worst characters ever put to film, Howard should be lauded for destroying the Dark Overlord of the Universe and saving Eart- oh …oh, our apologies. It seems we've mixed up our notes and are writing about *Howard the Duck (1986)*. Let's see now, *this* lame-duck Howard once again pitched poorly, allowing far too many hits and home runs. And when he wasn't doing that, he was hurt. We, uh, we think we'd rather watch the old Marvel movie for now.

Dallas Keuchel LHP Born: 01/01/88 Age: 35 Bats: L Throws: L Height: 6'2" Weight: 205 lb. Origin: Round 7, 2009 Draft (#221 overall)

YEAR	TEAM	LVL	AGE	W	L	SV	G	GS	IP	H	HR	BB/9	K/9	K	GB%	BABIP	WHIP	ERA	DRA-	WARP	MPH	FB%	Whiff%	CSP
2020	CHW	MLB	32	6	2	0	11	11	63^1	52	2	2.4	6.0	42	52.0%	.258	1.09	1.99	100	0.7	86.4	65.3%	23.8%	44.0%
2021	CHW	MLB	33	9	9	0	32	30	162	189	25	3.3	5.3	95	54.7%	.308	1.53	5.28	147	-2.5	87.1	64.3%	21.0%	48.8%
2022	DIAB	ROK	34	0	1	0	1	1	7	5	0	1.3	16.7	13	69.2%	.385	0.86	2.57						
2022	RR	AAA	34	1	0	0	4	4	23^1	13	1	4.2	8.5	22	62.1%	.211	1.03	2.31	83	0.4	87.3	57.7%	26.4%	
2022	TEX	MLB	34	0	2	0	2	2	10	18	1	3.6	6.3	7	51.3%	.447	2.20	12.60	115	0.0	86.9	72.4%	27.4%	46.6%
2022	CHW	MLB	34	2	5	0	8	8	32	49	6	5.6	5.6	20	51.6%	.364	2.16	7.87	163	-0.7	87.1	63.9%	20.7%	48.1%
2022	AZ	MLB	34	0	2	0	4	4	18^2	27	4	3.4	8.7	18	48.4%	.383	1.82	9.64	104	0.1	87.2	65.3%	21.9%	46.3%
2023 non-DC	*TEX*	*MLB*	*35*	*2*	*3*	*0*	*57*	*0*	*50*	*55*	*5*	*3.7*	*6.1*	*33*	*53.1%*	*.307*	*1.53*	*4.75*	*118*	*-0.3*	*87.1*	*65.9%*	*21.8%*	*47.0%*

Comparables: Shawn Estes (74), CC Sabathia (73), Frank Viola (73)

Let's play a game: Which 2010s Cy Young winner looks more surprising in retrospect, R.A. Dickey or Keuchel? Dickey has, of course, been out of the league for quite some time, but Keuchel now looks poised to join him, as he's been pitching like someone missing a UCL since April 2021. Over his past two seasons, three teams and 222 innings pitched, Keuchel has allowed 283 hits and 157 earned runs. When we asked DRA to spit out a number for that timeframe, it politely declined out of respect for the southpaw's career. It's wild to think that, only two seasons ago, Keuchel finished fifth in Cy Young voting in the pandemic-shortened 2020 season. It's even more wild to think any team could look at his past 24 months and elect to put him back on the mound. Sometimes, you've got to know when to fold 'em. But even when you haven't folded in time, you can always, *always*, walk away.

José Leclerc RHP Born: 12/19/93 Age: 29 Bats: R Throws: R Height: 6'0" Weight: 195 lb. Origin: International Free Agent, 2010

YEAR	TEAM	LVL	AGE	W	L	SV	G	GS	IP	H	HR	BB/9	K/9	K	GB%	BABIP	WHIP	ERA	DRA-	WARP	MPH	FB%	Whiff%	CSP
2020	TEX	MLB	26	0	0	1	2	0	2	2	0	9.0	13.5	3	0.0%	.400	2.00	4.50	98	0.0	94.7	57.4%	43.8%	33.1%
2022	RR	AAA	28	0	1	0	7	0	6^2	5	0	6.8	10.8	8	37.5%	.313	1.50	5.40	97	0.0	95.5	47.0%	36.8%	
2022	TEX	MLB	28	0	3	7	39	0	47^2	33	5	4.0	10.2	54	29.2%	.243	1.13	2.83	93	0.6	96.5	36.6%	37.7%	48.8%
2023 DC	*TEX*	*MLB*	*29*	*3*	*2*	*22*	*58*	*0*	*50.3*	*39*	*6*	*4.4*	*10.8*	*60*	*33.3%*	*.275*	*1.28*	*3.56*	*90*	*0.5*	*96.5*	*40.9%*	*35.7%*	*46.9%*

Comparables: Ken Giles (55), Corey Knebel (54), Joakim Soria (52)

There are only two active professional athletes with the surname Leclerc. One of them, Charles, is a Monaco-born driver for Ferrari's Formula 1 racing team. In the modern F1, Ferrari is more or less an analog for the Wilpon-era Mets; expensive and bumbling and rife with underperforming stars. Such is the case with Charles Leclerc, Ferrari's 25-year-old superstar whose potential to win the circuit's driver championship in 2022 was undone largely by poor in-race strategy. The *other* Leclerc resides in the Rangers bullpen—perhaps a less prestigious assignment than that of a globe-trotting racecar driver, but José arguably had a much more enjoyable season. After missing most of 2020 with shoulder issues and all of 2021 recovering from Tommy John surgery, Leclerc returned with a healthy arm and racked up more saves than any non-Barlow in Texas' bullpen. He has the formula to serve as one of the Rangers' best bullpen arms in 2023.

Jack Leiter RHP Born: 04/21/00 Age: 23 Bats: R Throws: R Height: 6'1" Weight: 205 lb. Origin: Round 1, 2021 Draft (#2 overall)

YEAR	TEAM	LVL	AGE	W	L	SV	G	GS	IP	H	HR	BB/9	K/9	K	GB%	BABIP	WHIP	ERA	DRA-	WARP	MPH	FB%	Whiff%	CSP
2022	FRI	AA	22	3	10	0	23	22	92^{2}	88	11	5.4	10.6	109	36.0%	.322	1.55	5.54	88	1.1				
2023 non-DC	*TEX*	*MLB*	*23*	*2*	*3*	*0*	*57*	*0*	*50*	*50*	*8*	*6.1*	*8.3*	*46*	*38.4%*	*.295*	*1.68*	*5.71*	*131*	*-0.6*			*25.5%*	

Comparables: Chi Chi González (85), Anthony Ranaudo (84), Dan Cortes (83)

Even when you consider his aggressive Double-A assignment, Leiter's pro debut was rough. Command was never Leiter's carrying tool at Vanderbilt, but he threw enough good strikes with three advanced pitches to regularly mow down SEC lineups. But the hitters Leiter faced in the Texas League provided a tougher challenge than those at Tennessee or Mississippi State, and they punished his mistakes accordingly. Despite his ugly overall Frisco stat line, there were still some positives: Leiter struck out plenty of hitters, and his high-spin fastball, diving curveball and sweeping slider continued to flash as plus-or-better pitches. His adjustment period may take longer than some hoped, but Leiter has the stuff to help anchor the Rangers rotation by the end of 2023.

Jake Odorizzi RHP Born: 03/27/90 Age: 33 Bats: R Throws: R Height: 6'2" Weight: 190 lb. Origin: Round 1, 2008 Draft (#32 overall)

YEAR	TEAM	LVL	AGE	W	L	SV	G	GS	IP	H	HR	BB/9	K/9	K	GB%	BABIP	WHIP	ERA	DRA-	WARP	MPH	FB%	Whiff%	CSP
2020	MIN	MLB	30	0	1	0	4	4	13^{2}	16	4	2.0	7.9	12	34.9%	.308	1.39	6.59	117	0.0	93.2	41.8%	19.9%	45.1%
2021	SUG	AAA	31	0	1	0	2	2	7^{2}	10	1	1.2	12.9	11	66.7%	.450	1.43	4.70	86	0.1				
2021	HOU	MLB	31	6	7	0	24	23	104^{2}	97	16	2.9	7.8	91	35.5%	.276	1.25	4.21	116	0.1	92.3	55.4%	22.0%	52.1%
2022	ATL	MLB	32	2	3	0	10	10	46^{1}	54	9	3.5	7.8	40	32.9%	.321	1.55	5.24	126	-0.2	92.1	47.5%	24.4%	51.6%
2022	HOU	MLB	32	4	3	0	12	12	60	52	5	2.6	6.9	46	31.1%	.270	1.15	3.75	111	0.2	92.5	54.6%	20.3%	56.2%
2023 DC	*TEX*	*MLB*	*33*	*6*	*6*	*0*	*38*	*12*	*85.7*	*85*	*13*	*3.0*	*7.4*	*70*	*34.3%*	*.288*	*1.33*	*4.08*	*106*	*0.4*	*92.4*	*53.5%*	*22.8%*	*51.8%*

Comparables: Doyle Alexander (79), Ricky Nolasco (76), Mike Moore (74)

When Odorizzi was traded to the Braves near the trade deadline, it was cause for celebration in Atlanta—not because of his arrival, but because it closed the book on the tenure of onetime closer Will Smith, for whom he was swapped. Unfortunately, it didn't take long for the new group of fans to realize what Astros faithful had already learned: The 2019 version of Odorizzi who earned 2+ WARP has long been gone. In his place exists a back-of-the-rotation veteran who does little but eat innings. The Rangers still found his profile more palatable than Kolby Allard's, whom they shipped back to Atlanta for Odorizzi in November.

Glenn Otto RHP Born: 03/11/96 Age: 27 Bats: R Throws: R Height: 6'3" Weight: 240 lb. Origin: Round 5, 2017 Draft (#152 overall)

YEAR	TEAM	LVL	AGE	W	L	SV	G	GS	IP	H	HR	BB/9	K/9	K	GB%	BABIP	WHIP	ERA	DRA-	WARP	MPH	FB%	Whiff%	CSP
2021	SOM	AA	25	6	3	0	11	10	65^{1}	46	6	1.9	14.2	103	38.1%	.315	0.92	3.17	86	1.0				
2021	SWB	AAA	25	1	0	0	2	2	10^{1}	14	0	2.6	10.5	12	33.3%	.424	1.65	4.35	104	0.1				
2021	RR	AAA	25	2	1	0	4	4	20	13	0	3.2	8.6	19	49.0%	.255	1.00	2.70	100	0.1				
2021	TEX	MLB	25	0	3	0	6	6	23^{1}	32	2	3.1	10.8	28	43.8%	.429	1.71	9.26	99	0.2	92.8	48.9%	22.1%	59.8%
2022	RR	AAA	26	0	1	0	3	3	9^{2}	8	1	2.8	11.2	12	48.0%	.292	1.14	2.79	90	0.1	93.2	55.8%	22.5%	
2022	TEX	MLB	26	7	10	0	27	27	135^{2}	119	21	4.1	7.1	107	42.6%	.257	1.33	4.64	118	0.1	92.2	50.2%	23.2%	53.9%
2023 DC	*TEX*	*MLB*	*27*	*0*	*1*	*0*	*3*	*3*	*16*	*16*	*2*	*4.0*	*8.3*	*14*	*42.9%*	*.309*	*1.47*	*4.60*	*113*	*0.0*	*92.3*	*50.0%*	*24.3%*	*54.7%*

Comparables: Jimmy Nelson (68), Tyler Cloyd (65), Matthew Boyd (64)

Otto raised his profile in the Yankees' system in 2021 after tightening up his command and adding a new slider, then was promptly shipped off to Texas as one of the players exchanged for Joey Gallo. Gallo mostly stunk in pinstripes, it's true, but Otto hasn't been much better since arriving in Arlington. He gave back a lot of the command gains he made and allowed a whole bunch of homers. He also stopped striking hitters out—an issue that had never plagued Otto at any stop in the minors. As a starter, Otto threw his fastball or slider more than three-fourths of the time over the last two seasons, meaning he was already at risk of moving to the bullpen. It'd be no surprise if his lackluster Rangers debut hastened that transition.

Martín Pérez LHP Born: 04/04/91 Age: 32 Bats: L Throws: L Height: 6'0" Weight: 200 lb. Origin: International Free Agent, 2007

YEAR	TEAM	LVL	AGE	W	L	SV	G	GS	IP	H	HR	BB/9	K/9	K	GB%	BABIP	WHIP	ERA	DRA-	WARP	MPH	FB%	Whiff%	CSP
2020	BOS	MLB	29	3	5	0	12	12	62	55	8	4.1	6.7	46	38.4%	.267	1.34	4.50	141	-0.7	90.6	65.1%	22.3%	46.3%
2021	BOS	MLB	30	7	8	0	36	22	114	136	19	2.8	7.7	97	43.2%	.337	1.51	4.74	132	-0.8	91.7	67.4%	19.4%	53.2%
2022	TEX	MLB	31	12	8	0	32	32	196^{1}	178	11	3.2	7.7	169	50.2%	.298	1.26	2.89	109	1.0	92.8	43.3%	21.1%	48.3%
2023 DC	*TEX*	*MLB*	*32*	*9*	*10*	*0*	*29*	*29*	*163*	*167*	*17*	*3.3*	*7.4*	*133*	*47.8%*	*.303*	*1.39*	*4.01*	*103*	*1.1*	*92.3*	*55.1%*	*20.6%*	*49.0%*

Comparables: Claude Osteen (69), Jim Kaat (68), Mark Buehrle (68)

There were many points throughout 2022—when he shut out the Astros in mid-May, when he carried a sub-2.00 ERA through late June, and especially when he threw a scoreless inning in the All-Star Game—when most baseball fans and observers had the same thought: *What the hell has gotten into Martín Pérez?!* In his age-31 season, Pérez posted far and away the best numbers of his career, making up for some of the negative WARP he'd generated over the last decade. What's most surprising is he did so without a sudden velocity spike or wildly different batted-ball profile—he just had more success pitching on the corners, got better results with his changeup and stopped allowing home runs. Who knows if any of this is sustainable or if Pérez can be a capital-d Dude going forward, but at the very least he's pitched himself back from the brink of major-league relevance, accepting Texas' qualifying offer for 2023.

Brock Porter RHP Born: 06/03/03 Age: 20 Bats: R Throws: R Height: 6'4" Weight: 208 lb. Origin: Round 4, 2022 Draft (#109 overall)

A Michigan prep star, Porter was viewed as one of the best overall pitching talents in the 2022 draft. He posted an absurd 115 strikeouts in 58 innings and tossed three (3!) no-hitters in the spring, but there was no guarantee he'd go pro and skip out on his commitment to Clemson. Then the Rangers offered him nearly $4 million after popping him in the fourth round, and the Tigers' loss became Texas' gain as Porter immediately became one of the more intriguing arms in their system. Tall and strong with a whippy arm and projectable frame, Porter can run his fastball into the high 90s with a changeup, slider and curveball that all have the potential to be average or better. We all know about the risks involved with projecting prep arms, but Porter has the ceiling to emerge as one of the org's top overall prospects in short order.

Cole Ragans LHP Born: 12/12/97 Age: 25 Bats: L Throws: L Height: 6'4" Weight: 190 lb. Origin: Round 1, 2016 Draft (#30 overall)

YEAR	TEAM	LVL	AGE	W	L	SV	G	GS	IP	H	HR	BB/9	K/9	K	GB%	BABIP	WHIP	ERA	DRA-	WARP	MPH	FB%	Whiff%	CSP
2021	HIC	A+	23	1	2	0	10	10	44^1	34	4	2.8	11.0	54	40.4%	.300	1.08	3.25	84	0.8				
2021	FRI	AA	23	3	1	0	9	7	36^1	39	8	5.0	8.2	33	31.5%	.301	1.62	5.70	123	-0.2				
2022	FRI	AA	24	5	3	0	10	10	51^1	41	6	3.3	11.4	65	42.3%	.299	1.17	2.81	67	1.2				
2022	RR	AAA	24	3	2	0	8	8	43^1	34	4	2.5	10.0	48	47.4%	.273	1.06	3.32	81	0.7	92.1	62.6%	27.2%	
2022	TEX	MLB	24	0	3	0	9	9	40	43	6	3.6	6.1	27	36.6%	.296	1.48	4.95	144	-0.5	91.6	60.9%	22.5%	51.0%
2023 DC	*TEX*	*MLB*	*25*	*3*	*2*	*0*	*29*	*3*	*37.7*	*40*	*5*	*4.0*	*7.3*	*30*	*40.0%*	*.303*	*1.51*	*4.96*	*122*	*-0.1*	*91.6*	*60.9%*	*25.9%*	*51.0%*

Comparables: Matthew Boyd (82), Cody Anderson (74), Jimmy Nelson (73)

Ragans didn't pitch in affiliated ball for nearly four years due to the pandemic and back-to-back Tommy John surgeries, the second of which became necessary after he re-tore his ligament just before returning to game action in 2019. The former first-rounder stayed relatively healthy and put it all together for the first time in 2022, walking fewer hitters, missing more bats and throwing more innings than in any other season in his career. Once oft-comped to Cole Hamels, Ragans profiles more in the Marco Gonzales vein these days. But don't let that modest downgrade in projection dull the shine on Ragans' incredible story: few prep arms with two elbow scars make it this far.

Kumar Rocker RHP Born: 11/22/99 Age: 23 Bats: R Throws: R Height: 6'5" Weight: 245 lb. Origin: Round 1, 2022 Draft (#3 overall)

Filmmaker J.J. Abrams is well known for the "mystery box" concept used in his movies and TV shows, introducing plot threads and story elements that are kept deliberately murky so as to both hold the viewer's attention and allow their imagination to fill in the missing details. In that vein, Rocker's career arc to date has more or less been another *Cloverfield* sequel, with a surprising number of unknowns surrounding arguably the most famous pitching prospect of the last decade. The Mets drafted Rocker 10th overall in the 2021 draft but failed to come to terms with the former College World Series MVP, citing injury concerns. Rocker subsequently underwent minor shoulder surgery and pitched in indy ball, looking good enough in the process that the Rangers somewhat surprisingly popped him third overall last season. Turns out his arm *wasn't* dead the whole time, and that being drafted by the Mets is really just a stand-in analogy for purgatory. Some things remain in Rocker's own mystery box—his arm health and long-term upside among them—but there's no denying he's built like a tight end and features at least two plus pitches. Some argue Rocker could already be pitching in a big-league rotation, and at the very least the Rangers hope he joins fellow former Vanderbilt standout Jack Leiter in theirs by season's end.

Ricky Vanasco RHP Born: 10/13/98 Age: 24 Bats: R Throws: R Height: 6'3" Weight: 180 lb. Origin: Round 15, 2017 Draft (#464 overall)

YEAR	TEAM	LVL	AGE	W	L	SV	G	GS	IP	H	HR	BB/9	K/9	K	GB%	BABIP	WHIP	ERA	DRA-	WARP	MPH	FB%	Whiff%	CSP
2022	HIC	A+	23	3	5	0	21	21	84^1	78	12	5.0	11.8	111	42.4%	.333	1.48	4.48	100	0.6				
2022	FRI	AA	23	0	0	0	2	2	8	11	2	5.6	7.9	7	37.0%	.360	2.00	6.75	129	-0.1				
2023 non-DC	*TEX*	*MLB*	*24*	*2*	*3*	*0*	*57*	*0*	*50*	*52*	*8*	*6.2*	*9.1*	*50*	*41.2%*	*.316*	*1.74*	*5.83*	*132*	*-0.6*			*24.1%*	

Comparables: Tayler Scott (45), Oscar De La Cruz (44), Corey Oswalt (43)

After losing 2020 to the pandemic and 2021 to Tommy John surgery and rehab, Vanasco, a former 15th-round pick, finally escaped the low minors last season. Upon resurfacing, he looked like a potential reliever long-term, as evidenced by his 12.6% walk rate, good-not-great strikeout numbers and reliance on a fastball/curveball combination. His fastball velocity and general arm strength also come with question marks, as he touched 98 mph as recently as the 2021 Arizona Instructional League but more often sat in the low-90s during 2022. His prospect shine has worn off over the last few years, but Vanasco still has time to impact a major-league roster in some way.

Owen White RHP Born: 08/09/99 Age: 23 Bats: R Throws: R Height: 6'3" Weight: 199 lb. Origin: Round 2, 2018 Draft (#55 overall)

YEAR	TEAM	LVL	AGE	W	L	SV	G	GS	IP	H	HR	BB/9	K/9	K	GB%	BABIP	WHIP	ERA	DRA-	WARP	MPH	FB%	Whiff%	CSP
2021	SUR	WIN	21	5	0	0	6	6	28^1	20	1	4.1	9.2	29	39.4%	.271	1.16	1.91					37.0%	
2021	DE	A	21	3	1	0	8	8	33^1	25	2	3.2	14.6	54	41.2%	.348	1.11	3.24	68	0.7				
2022	HIC	A+	22	6	2	0	11	10	58^2	51	7	2.9	12.4	81	43.7%	.326	1.19	3.99	87	0.9				
2022	FRI	AA	22	3	0	0	4	4	21^2	19	1	1.7	9.6	23	50.9%	.327	1.06	2.49	80	0.4				
2023 non-DC	*TEX*	*MLB*	*23*	*2*	*2*	*0*	*57*	*0*	*50*	*49*	*6*	*3.9*	*9.7*	*53*	*43.5%*	*.316*	*1.42*	*4.33*	*106*	*0.0*			*27.6%*	

Comparables: Dan Straily (77), Aaron Blair (77), Chris Flexen (76)

White—a 2018 high school draftee—saw his first three professional seasons wiped out or truncated by, in order: Tommy John surgery, the pandemic and a broken hand. When he's been healthy, though, he's dominated, as he did in High-A and the Arizona Fall League in 2021. White's 2022 season marked something of a breakout as he bullied hitters in the Sally League and at Double-A Frisco before landing on the injured list in mid-July with what the Rangers called "forearm fatigue." It wasn't a particularly surprising nor reassuring revelation as White built up his workload after two lost seasons. He wouldn't reappear until the Texas League playoffs in late September, when he struck out six in two perfect innings in the last game of the season. With a mid-90s fastball and three average-or-better secondaries, White has become arguably the best Rangers pitching prospect not named Leiter. When his body cooperates, that is.

Cole Winn RHP Born: 11/25/99 Age: 23 Bats: R Throws: R Height: 6'2" Weight: 190 lb. Origin: Round 1, 2018 Draft (#15 overall)

YEAR	TEAM	LVL	AGE	W	L	SV	G	GS	IP	H	HR	BB/9	K/9	K	GB%	BABIP	WHIP	ERA	DRA-	WARP	MPH	FB%	Whiff%	CSP
2021	FRI	AA	21	3	3	0	19	19	78	38	6	3.0	11.2	97	36.7%	.198	0.82	2.31	84	1.2				
2021	RR	AAA	21	1	0	0	2	2	8	5	1	5.6	11.2	10	30.0%	.211	1.25	3.38	101	0.0				
2022	RR	AAA	22	9	8	0	28	28	121^{2}	125	13	6.4	9.1	123	39.8%	.326	1.74	6.51	105	0.3	93.8	41.9%	27.2%	
2023 DC	*TEX*	*MLB*	*23*	*0*	*1*	*0*	*3*	*3*	*14.3*	*14*	*1*	*5.6*	*8.2*	*13*	*40.8%*	*.293*	*1.60*	*5.04*	*120*	*0.0*			*25.2%*	

Comparables: Luis Severino (59), Michael Kopech (58), Matt Wisler (56)

Winn looked to be on the cusp of his major-league debut after a sterling 2021 season in Double-A followed by a brief cameo in Round Rock that cemented his status as one of the organization's better arms. Alas, he followed that campaign by getting absolutely pantsed in the Pacific Coast League through much of 2022. Winn's performance was perplexing, as he seemingly lost the ability to command the ball. Odder still is that his homer rate stayed relatively steady despite the PCL's many high-altitude locales. Winn is still just 23 and has the stuff to settle in as a mid-rotation starter in the majors thanks to his four average-or-better pitches. But that can't happen until he finds the strike zone again.

Lineouts

Hitters

HITTER	POS	TEAM	LVL	AGE	PA	R	2B	3B	HR	RBI	BB	K	SB	CS	AVG/OBP/SLG	DRC+	BABIP	BRR	DRP	WARP
Maximo Acosta	SS	DE	A	19	456	62	26	1	4	35	40	87	44	17	.262/.341/.361	100	.325	4.0	SS(76): 0.2, 2B(29): 1.6	1.9
Danyer Cueva	2B	RAN	ROK	18	189	39	10	1	5	31	10	40	3	2	.330/.376/.483		.405			
Gleider Figuereo	DH/3B	RAN	ROK	18	146	29	5	5	9	31	15	33	7	1	.280/.363/.616		.302			
	DH/3B	DE	A	18	26	0	0	0	0	1	2	8	0	0	.208/.269/.208	88	.313	0.0	3B(2): 0.1	0.1
Anthony Gutierrez	OF	DSL TEXR	ROK	17	103	22	8	0	3	16	8	18	5	3	.352/.408/.538		.403			
	OF	RAN	ROK	17	87	13	5	2	1	8	3	16	6	3	.259/.299/.407		.308			
Mark Mathias	2B	NAS	AAA	27	202	20	8	1	8	30	27	48	8	3	.318/.421/.518	120	.400	-0.1	2B(32): 1.3, 3B(17): -0.7	1.0
	2B	RR	AAA	27	35	7	2	0	1	4	4	9	5	0	.345/.429/.517	92	.450	0.7	2B(6): -0.9, LF(2): -0.3	0.2
	2B	MIL	MLB	27	17	2	0	0	1	4	0	4	1	0	.125/.118/.313	95	.083	0.1	2B(6): -0.1	0.0
	2B	TEX	MLB	27	74	11	3	0	5	16	9	26	2	0	.277/.365/.554	99	.382	0.9	1B(3): 0, 3B(2): 0, LF(2): 0.3	0.3
Yeison Morrobel	OF	RAN	ROK	18	173	31	13	1	3	21	17	34	5	5	.329/.405/.487		.405			
	OF	DE	A	18	29	3	1	0	0	3	3	6	2	1	.231/.310/.269	102	.300	-0.3	RF(5): 0.2, LF(2): -0.1	0.1
Jonathan Ornelas	SS/3B	FRI	AA	22	580	84	20	2	14	64	45	121	14	6	.299/.360/.425	108	.365	-1.4	SS(86): 7.6, 3B(29): 2.7, 2B(4): 0.7	3.3
Yohel Pozo	C	RR	AAA	25	267	37	21	0	6	38	11	32	0	1	.320/.352/.474	100	.347	-0.9	C(30): -0.2, 1B(11): 0.1	0.7

A 2019 signee out of Venezuela, **Maximo Acosta** has yet to grow into much game power but showcases solid tools, an up-the-middle defensive profile and an 80-grade name. He stole 2.3 bases per year spent on earth as a 19-year-old in full-season ball. ⚾ **Danyer Cueva** was part of the Rangers' 2021 international class and profiles as an eventual up-the-middle bat with a good feel for hitting from the left side. It's good he's got time to add pop to his 6-foot-1, 160-pound frame, because right now he offers less consistent power than ERCOT. ⚾ Dominican teenager **Gleider Figuereo** dominated at the Rangers' complex over the summer with a sweet left-handed swing. Though he's already moved to third base, he looks likely to grow into enough power for his bat to play just fine there. ⚾ Teenage outfielder **Anthony Gutierrez** already has huge pop, but at 6-foot-3 and 180 pounds, he's got room to add good weight and, theoretically, even more power. The Rangers sure do have a type, don't they? ⚾ **Mark Mathias**' star burned bright for about a month after he was acquired from the Brewers. But that supernova resulted in a black hole that sucked in his bat and spit out a 1-for-19 mark to finish the season. ⚾ Teenager **Yeison Morrobel** played stateside for the first time since the Rangers signed him for $1.8 million in 2021. He showed an advanced feel for the strike zone in Low-A, along with a frame that should allow him to grow into more power as he gets older. ⚾ **Jonathan Ornelas** had a bit of a breakout at Double-A Frisco, spraying line drives all over the place and playing all over it as well. Alas, the future utilityman also posted middling strikeout and walk rates, as he has at every level of full-season ball. ⚾ Texas took Georgia prep infielder **Chandler Pollard** in the fifth round of the 2022 draft. His in-game power is still MIA, but he did steal 59 bases in 61 attempts, the sixth-most among all high schoolers in the country. ⚾ Though he didn't get a second shot with the Rangers after his 2021 debut, **Yohel Pozo** had a nice season at Triple-A Round Rock where he showed off some doubles power. If his defense ever improves, he could have a nice career as a backup backstop.

Pitchers

PITCHER	TEAM	LVL	AGE	W	L	SV	G	GS	IP	H	HR	BB/9	K/9	K	GB%	BABIP	WHIP	ERA	DRA-	WARP	MPH	FB%	WHF	CSP
Kohei Arihara	RR	AAA	29	3	6	0	19	15	74	80	10	2.3	7.8	64	52.4%	.317	1.34	4.86	90	0.8	91.0	36.4%	23.7%	
	TEX	MLB	29	1	3	0	5	4	20	36	4	5.0	6.3	14	48.8%	.427	2.35	9.45	130	-0.1	91.0	27.9%	22.0%	48.3%
Mitch Bratt	DE	A	18	5	5	0	19	18	80^2	66	4	3.1	11.0	99	41.2%	.310	1.17	2.45	95	1.1				
Kyle Cody	RAN	ROK	27	1	0	0	8	0	10^2	9	0	2.5	15.2	18	50.0%	.450	1.13	0.84						
	RR	AAA	27	0	0	1	12	2	19^2	20	1	2.3	9.6	21	47.2%	.365	1.27	3.66	85	0.3	93.6	42.1%	31.8%	
Greg Holland	TEX	MLB	36	0	1	0	5	0	4^2	6	3	1.9	9.6	5	50.0%	.273	1.50	7.71	96	0.1	93.7	30.0%	29.0%	55.2%
Antoine Kelly	WIS	A+	22	2	4	0	19	19	91	60	6	5.1	11.8	119	45.1%	.271	1.23	3.86	83	1.7				
	FRI	AA	22	0	0	0	7	5	18^2	12	0	9.2	11.6	24	43.6%	.308	1.66	7.23	133	-0.3				
Zak Kent	FRI	AA	24	2	3	0	19	19	82^2	83	11	3.3	9.5	87	47.6%	.329	1.37	4.68	80	1.4				
	RR	AAA	24	1	1	0	5	5	27	17	2	4.3	7.7	23	47.2%	.214	1.11	1.67	98	0.2	92.2	45.3%	22.9%	
John King	RR	AAA	27	2	1	0	14	0	17^1	20	5	3.6	9.3	18	57.4%	.306	1.56	7.27	83	0.3	93.2	51.4%	20.9%	
	TEX	MLB	27	1	4	0	39	0	51^1	61	5	2.5	5.3	30	63.3%	.327	1.46	4.03	122	-0.1	92.6	52.3%	19.8%	53.4%
Brett Martin	TEX	MLB	27	1	7	3	55	1	50	50	4	3.2	7.2	40	48.7%	.309	1.36	4.14	101	0.4	93.5	45.3%	24.6%	53.5%
Spencer Patton	RR	AAA	34	4	2	1	24	0	29^1	33	8	5.2	12.3	40	38.5%	.368	1.70	6.44	91	0.3	92.7	57.0%	29.6%	
	TEX	MLB	34	0	0	0	7	0	7	4	1	3.9	6.4	5	52.6%	.167	1.00	3.86	112	0.0	92.4	48.6%	25.0%	47.9%
Tekoah Roby	HIC	A+	20	3	11	0	22	21	104^2	95	19	3.0	10.8	126	38.5%	.298	1.24	4.64	96	1.0				
Yerry Rodriguez	RR	AAA	24	4	1	4	49	5	59	60	9	4.9	11.1	73	46.0%	.336	1.56	4.27	84	0.9	97.2	55.4%	28.7%	
	TEX	MLB	24	0	0	0	1	0	1	1	0	0.0	9.0	1	66.7%	.333	1.00	0.00	95	0.0	98.1	55.6%	9.1%	57.7%
Josh Sborz	RR	AAA	28	3	0	1	19	1	22^1	11	2	4.4	12.1	30	36.2%	.205	0.99	1.61	82	0.4	96.9	50.9%	38.9%	
	TEX	MLB	28	1	0	0	19	1	22^1	25	4	4.4	12.9	32	29.8%	.396	1.61	6.45	76	0.5	97.0	51.8%	35.3%	51.6%
Nick Snyder	RR	AAA	26	2	2	2	41	1	38	36	5	4.3	12.1	51	40.4%	.348	1.42	4.97	79	0.7	95.7	90.0%	36.3%	
	TEX	MLB	26	0	0	0	2	0	1	1	0	27.0	0.0	0	50.0%	.250	4.00	18.00	109	0.0	96.4	84.8%	9.1%	54.5%
Jesus Tinoco	RR	AAA	27	1	2	13	35	0	44	33	3	3.5	10.4	51	59.5%	.278	1.14	3.27	69	1.1	96.0	45.7%	33.9%	
	TEX	MLB	27	0	0	0	17	2	20^2	12	2	4.4	7.8	18	34.5%	.189	1.06	2.18	105	0.2	95.9	48.0%	24.8%	52.9%

Kohei Arihara might exit stateside baseball as quickly as he arrived after making a five-game cameo in Arlington that was somehow worse than his 2021 debut. He'll enter 2023 as a 30-year-old who walks too many, doesn't strike anyone out and can't keep the ball off the barrel. ⚾ Canadian southpaw **Mitch Bratt** has an intriguing three-pitch mix, quality command of it and one of the more unfortunate spoonerisms in baseball. At just 19, he's a ways away from helping out the big-league team, but he's an arm to keep an eye on. ⚾ The 6-foot-7 **Kyle Cody**—whose middle name is David, giving him the coveted three-first-names moniker—returned from shoulder surgery to throw his highest innings total (30⅓, including Complex League action) since 2017. While he may not be a starter anymore, he has a chance to get back to a major-league bullpen in 2023. ⚾ The Rangers likely wish they'd gone Dutch on the $2.1 million they gave **Greg Holland** for five mostly mediocre appearances. Though he was DFAd in mid-April, he'd just reached 10 years of service time, so even if this is it for the pride of Western Carolina University, at least he's gained access to the league's maximum pension. ⚾ Acquired from the Brewers as part of the return for Matt Bush, **Antoine Kelly** likely caught Texas' eye with his high-90s fastball and darting slider. A thoracic outlet surgery survivor, his medical history, walk rates and only passable changeup mean he profiles best as a reliever. He could be a pretty nasty one, though. ⚾ **Zak Kent** profiles as a future candidate for the back end of a rotation with his solid fastball/slider/changeup mix and sturdy frame. He's on the cusp of his major-league debut after making five starts at Round Rock to end 2022. ⚾ Surprisingly, the British monarchy only includes one King John, who reigned in England during the sealing of the Magna Carta. Relatedly, there's only been one **John King** in major-league history, but unlike the monarch he can hit 94 from the left side. ⚾ **Brett Martin** is, by pretty much any measure, the *most accomplished* player ever drafted out of Walters State Community College. But unless he has a late-career breakout, he might not ever be the *most well-known* baseballer from his alma mater; the Rays drafted former teammate Brent Honeywell Jr. two rounds before him back in 2014. ⚾ If you don't read past 2021, **Spencer Patton** has a nice story, as he returned to affiliated ball a cromulent reliever after four years pitching in Japan. Alas, even the good stories must end: Patton struggled in both Triple-A and Texas in 2022, earning a mid-August release. ⚾ The exquisitely named **Tekoah Roby** rebounded from a 2021 campaign cut short by an elbow sprain to make all of his scheduled starts at High-A Hickory. His second half was much better than his first, and he finished the season on a high, punching out 12 in just five innings against the Rome Braves. ⚾ **Yerry Rodriguez** throws the ball very (yerry?) hard, but doesn't generate quite as many whiffs as you'd like due to the pitch's sinking action. He throws plenty of strikes, though, and should be contributing in the Rangers' bullpen in short order. ⚾ Despite his unsightly ERA, **Josh Sborz** was in the midst of his best season in the majors per both DRA- and strikeout rate before elbow troubles cut his season short. Don't ask him about it—it's a bit of a Sborz spot. ⚾ The Rangers announced a Snyder cut of their own when they sent hard-throwing righty **Nick Snyder** to Round Rock for the rest of 2022 after he allowed two runs and three walks in two early-season appearances. ⚾ Though he no longer had Coors as an excuse, **Jesus Tinoco** was the same as ever in Texas, walking far too many hitters for someone with a paltry strikeout rate. That said, a low BABIP helped him earn some outs and land a deal with NPB's Saitama Seibu Lions over the offseason.

FREE AGENTS

HITTERS

Jorge Alfaro C Born: 06/11/93 Age: 30 Bats: R Throws: R Height: 6'3" Weight: 230 lb. Origin: International Free Agent, 2010

YEAR	TEAM	LVL	AGE	PA	R	2B	3B	HR	RBI	BB	K	SB	CS	Whiff%	AVG/OBP/SLG	DRC+	BABIP	BRR	DRP	WARP
2020	MIA	MLB	27	100	12	2	0	3	16	4	36	2	0	41.7%	.226/.280/.344	74	.333	0.1	C(29): -4.8, RF(1): 0.1	-0.4
2021	MIA	MLB	28	311	22	15	1	4	30	11	99	8	1	33.1%	.244/.283/.342	61	.354	-0.5	C(61): 5.2, LF(21): 0.9, 1B(3): -0.1	0.3
2022	SD	MLB	29	274	25	14	0	7	40	11	98	1	0	37.9%	.246/.285/.383	62	.364	0.7	C(65): -0.2	-0.2
2023 DC	*FA*	*MLB*	*30*	*296*	*31*	*12*	*0*	*10*	*35*	*14*	*97*	*4*	*1*	*36.6%*	*.246/.296/.407*	*91*	*.342*	*1.8*	*LF 0, C 0*	*1.0*

Comparables: Wilson Ramos (60), Welington Castillo (59), Tyler Flowers (56)

YEAR	TEAM	P. COUNT	FRM RUNS	BLK RUNS	THRW RUNS	TOT RUNS
2020	MIA	3746	-4.9	0.0	0.1	-4.8
2021	MIA	7948	4.9	-0.9	0.3	4.4
2022	SD	8855	-1.7	-0.4	0.5	-1.7
2023	*FA*	*6956*	*0.9*	*-0.4*	*-0.1*	*0.5*

Have you ever held a plate of fresh-out-of-the-oven chocolate chip cookies in front of a three-year-old and tried to get them to wait for it, telling them they'll enjoy it *that much more* if they can just hold off a few minutes so the roof of their mouth doesn't immediately melt off? That's how it is telling Alfaro to show some patience at the plate. As if he was playing every game on a speed run, Alfaro swung at the fifth-highest percentage of first pitches in the league, struck out at the eighth-highest rate and walked at the 24th-lowest rate (min. 200 plate appearances) in the majors. Not that he didn't have his moments: Alfaro finished the year with four walk-off hits, including a game-winning home run on Mother's Day and (somehow) a walk-off walk. Alas, after his power dried up—he hit one home run in 30 games from July onward—the Padres non-tendered the former top prospect in November.

Brian Anderson 3B Born: 05/19/93 Age: 30 Bats: R Throws: R Height: 6'3" Weight: 208 lb. Origin: Round 3, 2014 Draft (#76 overall)

YEAR	TEAM	LVL	AGE	PA	R	2B	3B	HR	RBI	BB	K	SB	CS	Whiff%	AVG/OBP/SLG	DRC+	BABIP	BRR	DRP	WARP
2020	MIA	MLB	27	229	27	7	1	11	38	22	66	0	0	34.5%	.255/.345/.465	108	.323	-0.2	3B(56): 0.2, 1B(1): -0.1	0.8
2021	MIA	MLB	28	264	24	9	0	7	28	26	65	5	0	28.2%	.249/.337/.378	93	.317	0.4	3B(65): 2.1, SS(1): 0	0.9
2022	JAX	AAA	29	28	4	2	0	2	2	2	10	0	0		.231/.286/.538	89	.286	-0.1	3B(2): -0.2, RF(2): -0.2, LF(1): -0.3	0.0
2022	MIA	MLB	29	383	43	16	1	8	28	37	101	1	0	30.3%	.222/.311/.346	90	.291	-0.2	3B(48): -1.2, RF(36): -0.2, LF(8): 0.1	0.4
2023 DC	*FA*	*MLB*	*30*	*451*	*47*	*19*	*1*	*12*	*48*	*43*	*112*	*3*	*0*	*29.8%*	*.231/.320/.379*	*96*	*.292*	*1.2*	*3B 0, RF -1*	*0.8*

Comparables: Mark Teahen (67), Jim Davenport (65), Billy Nash (65)

During his three-year ascent from 2018 to 2020, Anderson combined reliable defense at third base and in right field with above-average results with the bat. His max exit velos suggested that, if he were to elevate the ball more consistently, he might elevate himself to an All-Star caliber player; for this reason, he was a popular breakout candidate. Pitchers have adjusted by throwing Anderson fewer fastballs, and locating them in areas where he's struggled to do much damage. His own adjustment has been for the worse: A much more aggressive approach against non-fastballs has coincided with higher chase and whiff rates. It could be that he's gotten in his own head, or perhaps he lost his swing. Whatever the case, Anderson lost the ability to hit anything that's not a fastball. As a result, the Marlins declined to tender his contract.

Elvis Andrus SS Born: 08/26/88 Age: 34 Bats: R Throws: R Height: 6'0" Weight: 210 lb. Origin: International Free Agent, 2005

YEAR	TEAM	LVL	AGE	PA	R	2B	3B	HR	RBI	BB	K	SB	CS	Whiff%	AVG/OBP/SLG	DRC+	BABIP	BRR	DRP	WARP
2020	TEX	MLB	31	111	11	5	0	3	7	8	15	3	1	19.5%	.194/.252/.330	98	.200	0.2	SS(29): -1.3	0.2
2021	OAK	MLB	32	541	60	25	2	3	37	31	81	12	2	19.6%	.243/.294/.320	85	.283	3.0	SS(143): -3.4	0.9
2022	CHW	MLB	33	191	25	8	0	9	28	9	30	11	0	21.0%	.271/.309/.464	116	.282	2.4	SS(42): 2.5	1.5
2022	OAK	MLB	33	386	41	24	0	8	30	30	62	7	4	21.5%	.237/.301/.373	104	.268	2.1	SS(101): 0.3	1.7
2023 DC	*FA*	*MLB*	*34*	*498*	*49*	*23*	*1*	*12*	*53*	*32*	*79*	*16*	*3*	*21.1%*	*.252/.306/.389*	*95*	*.281*	*7.6*	*SS 2*	*2.1*

Comparables: Edgar Renteria (66), Don Kessinger (65), Alan Trammell (64)

Andrus' best offensive season in a half-decade wasn't satisfying enough for the offensively starved Athletics, whose desire to lose as many games as possible led them to release the veteran outright in mid-August after no market materialized for him at the trade deadline. The $15 million vesting option he was on pace to collect to match surely had nothing to do with his DFA. Down one All-Star shortstop, the White Sox scooped a former one up, and he was a godsend down the stretch, tapping into power he hadn't shown since 2017 while playing passable defense in Tim Anderson's stead. The version of Andrus the Rangers signed to an eight-year deal isn't coming back as he enters his mid-30s, but with a boatload of cash already pocketed, he can continue plying his trade for as long as he sees fit as either a utility infielder or second-division starter.

Brandon Belt 1B Born: 04/20/88 Age: 35 Bats: L Throws: L Height: 6'3" Weight: 231 lb. Origin: Round 5, 2009 Draft (#147 overall)

YEAR	TEAM	LVL	AGE	PA	R	2B	3B	HR	RBI	BB	K	SB	CS	Whiff%	AVG/OBP/SLG	DRC+	BABIP	BRR	DRP	WARP
2020	SF	MLB	32	179	25	13	1	9	30	30	36	0	0	23.6%	.309/.425/.591	128	.356	0.2	1B(47): 0.6	1.1
2021	SF	MLB	33	381	65	14	2	29	59	48	103	3	2	28.0%	.274/.378/.597	145	.309	-1.3	1B(93): -1	2.8
2022	SF	MLB	34	298	25	9	1	8	23	37	81	1	0	32.4%	.213/.326/.350	89	.277	0.9	1B(63): -2.3	0.1
2023 DC	*TOR*	*MLB*	*35*	*350*	*41*	*14*	*1*	*13*	*43*	*43*	*98*	*1*	*0*	*30.6%*	*.228/.335/.413*	*107*	*.293*	*0.7*	*1B 0*	*0.9*

Comparables: Boog Powell (70), Tony Clark (67), John Olerud (67)

Belt has been a Giant so long that as a prospect he threatened to put Aubrey Huff, the ex-player turned amateur shitposter turned failed school board candidate, out of a job. The road hasn't always been smooth for Bad Luck Belt, who's had to battle both his own body and armchair GMs over his tenure in the Bay, but he's one of the core players who will forever be associated with the great Giants teams of the 2010s, so much so that the team recognized him this season with a charmingly cringe Opening Day ceremony where he rode out onto the field on a motorized boat, the electrical tape "C" for Captain still taped on his uniform. Unfortunately, that might have been the high point of his 2022 season, which wasn't a regression so much as a full-on grounding at the hands of Father Time. It's possible someone takes a flier on the soon-to-be 35-year-old as a DH, banking on at least a partial rebound; it's more likely Belt quietly, gracefully calls it a career. Whichever route he chooses, it's a safe bet that Belt, unlike the man whose job he eventually took, won't spend his retirement systematically lighting the dearly held goodwill of a fanbase on fire. The "C" doesn't stand for "crackpot," after all.

Kole Calhoun OF Born: 10/14/87 Age: 35 Bats: L Throws: L Height: 5'10" Weight: 205 lb. Origin: Round 8, 2010 Draft (#264 overall)

YEAR	TEAM	LVL	AGE	PA	R	2B	3B	HR	RBI	BB	K	SB	CS	Whiff%	AVG/OBP/SLG	DRC+	BABIP	BRR	DRP	WARP
2020	AZ	MLB	32	228	35	9	0	16	40	28	50	1	1	32.7%	.226/.338/.526	118	.211	0.5	RF(48): -0.5	1.2
2021	AZ	MLB	33	182	17	8	0	5	17	15	41	1	0	31.9%	.235/.297/.373	87	.281	-0.1	RF(39): -2.3	0.0
2022	TEX	MLB	34	424	36	14	1	12	49	27	136	3	2	36.2%	.196/.257/.330	68	.263	-1.5	RF(75): -3.5, LF(29): -1.6	-1.1
2023 DC	*FA*	*MLB*	*35*	*296*	*30*	*11*	*0*	*10*	*34*	*23*	*87*	*2*	*0*	*35.0%*	*.210/.282/.376*	*79*	*.267*	*0.3*	*RF -1, LF 0*	*-0.2*

Comparables: Nick Markakis (67), Tommy Griffith (66), Bill Nicholson (65)

Calhoun posted exactly one month—May—with an OPS over .600, had one of the worst defensive seasons of his career, his worst overall season by WARP and *still* suited up for 125 games for the Rangers. Paging Chris Young: You might want to get to work looking for some outfield depth. It's no surprise that Texas declined his $5.5 million club option for 2023, which means the veteran outfielder can only hope to latch on as the fifth outfielder on a contender or in a mentorship role with a rebuilding squad. It's also possible that no one bites, and that the Red Baron's career is crash landing to an end. If that's the case, don't let his dud of a year in Arlington overshadow a solid, if uneven, 10-year career spent almost wholly in the AL West.

Carlos Correa SS Born: 09/22/94 Age: 28 Bats: R Throws: R Height: 6'4" Weight: 220 lb. Origin: Round 1, 2012 Draft (#1 overall)

YEAR	TEAM	LVL	AGE	PA	R	2B	3B	HR	RBI	BB	K	SB	CS	Whiff%	AVG/OBP/SLG	DRC+	BABIP	BRR	DRP	WARP
2020	HOU	MLB	25	221	22	9	0	5	25	16	49	0	0	24.3%	.264/.326/.383	93	.324	0.1	SS(57): 2	0.7
2021	HOU	MLB	26	640	104	34	1	26	92	75	116	0	0	20.9%	.279/.366/.485	126	.308	0.3	SS(148): 2.2	4.7
2022	MIN	MLB	27	590	70	24	1	22	64	61	121	0	1	22.1%	.291/.366/.467	125	.339	-1.9	SS(132): 1	3.6
2023 DC	*FA*	*MLB*	*28*	*519*	*70*	*22*	*1*	*22*	*76*	*54*	*98*	*0*	*0*	*21.5%*	*.280/.361/.479*	*134*	*.314*	*-2.8*	*SS 3*	*3.8*

Comparables: Jim Fregosi (84), Travis Jackson (80), Cal Ripken Jr. (78)

In the absence of a contract offer that fit his requirements last offseason, Correa pivoted to a three-year deal that still awarded him the second-highest AAV ever for a position player—while also ensuring he would be able to take another shot at free agency after each season. His year in Minnesota was good enough that he exercised the first opt-out, having reaffirmed his elite offensive skills after the slowest of starts. Correa didn't only show his flexibility in contract talks: The notorious stathead reportedly offered trade advice to his new front office ahead of the deadline, then turned in a performance as a TV analyst that suggested he won't have much trouble finding another job when he stops playing.

Perhaps someday, Correa will be willing to provide his own analysis of how his wild offseason played out. As of printing, the All-Star was still negotiating with the Mets after medical concerns submarined the 13-year, $350 million pact he reportedly had with the Giants. It feels as though his Mets deal is likely to get done in some fashion after all the noise Steve Cohen made about Correa being the missing piece his roster needs. Should that not prove true, Correa may be playing on a year-to-year contract on a more permanent basis.

Nelson Cruz DH Born: 07/01/80 Age: 43 Bats: R Throws: R Height: 6'2" Weight: 230 lb. Origin: International Free Agent, 1998

YEAR	TEAM	LVL	AGE	PA	R	2B	3B	HR	RBI	BB	K	SB	CS	Whiff%	AVG/OBP/SLG	DRC+	BABIP	BRR	DRP	WARP
2020	MIN	MLB	39	214	33	6	0	16	33	25	58	0	0	34.2%	.303/.397/.595	142	.360	-0.6		1.5
2021	TB	MLB	40	238	35	8	0	13	36	16	63	0	0	32.4%	.226/.283/.442	100	.252	0.7	1B(1): 0	0.6
2021	MIN	MLB	40	346	44	13	1	19	50	35	63	3	0	29.3%	.294/.370/.537	138	.308	-2.6		2.1
2022	WAS	MLB	41	507	50	16	0	10	64	49	119	4	0	32.0%	.234/.313/.337	94	.295	-2.9		0.6
2023 DC	*FA*	*MLB*	*42*	*296*	*34*	*10*	*0*	*11*	*37*	*27*	*70*	*0*	*0*	*31.8%*	*.246/.325/.416*	*105*	*.294*	*-0.5*	*1B 1*	*0.6*

Comparables: Frank Robinson (64), Hank Aaron (64), Tony Perez (62)

It can be hard to recognize when you've hung around too long. One day, you're Steve "The Hair" Harrington—the coolest, most popular guy at Hawkins High. The next, you're wearing a dopey Scoops Ahoy sailor's uniform and your friends are all suspiciously young for you. Cruz was a legend in his day and remains a sage mentor to younger players, but his 2022 ISO of .103—less than half of his career .241 mark—suggests it's time for him to stop trying to relive his glory days. That's one of the Stranger Things about both life and baseball—there's a sharp, sudden drop from being voted prom king to striking out with every girl at Starcourt Mall and Family Video. Or just plain striking out.

Corey Dickerson LF/DH Born: 05/22/89 Age: 34 Bats: L Throws: R Height: 6'1" Weight: 200 lb. Origin: Round 8, 2010 Draft (#260 overall)

YEAR	TEAM	LVL	AGE	PA	R	2B	3B	HR	RBI	BB	K	SB	CS	Whiff%	AVG/OBP/SLG	DRC+	BABIP	BRR	DRP	WARP
2020	MIA	MLB	31	210	25	5	1	7	17	15	35	1	1	25.7%	.258/.311/.402	101	.283	0.8	LF(46): -0.8, RF(1): 0	0.6
2021	MIA	MLB	32	225	27	12	3	2	14	16	45	2	4	24.6%	.263/.324/.380	85	.327	1.5	LF(52): 1.2	0.7
2021	TOR	MLB	32	140	16	6	2	4	15	9	23	4	1	23.9%	.282/.329/.450	99	.317	0.1	LF(25): -0.7, CF(10): -0.1, RF(5): 0.2	0.4
2022	STL	MLB	33	297	28	17	1	6	36	12	48	0	0	22.8%	.267/.300/.399	93	.301	-1.1	LF(60): 0.6, RF(10): 0.4	0.7
2023 DC	*FA*	*MLB*	*34*	*249*	*25*	*12*	*1*	*6*	*28*	*14*	*42*	*1*	*1*	*23.3%*	*.269/.315/.420*	*103*	*.305*	*0.9*	*LF 0, RF 0*	*0.8*

Comparables: Leon Wagner (80), Lou Brock (79), Al Martin (79)

Dickerson's propensity for turning up in places that make fans think, "huh, wonder how he's going to get any playing time there," and somehow playing 60% of that team's games continued unabated in St. Louis last year. At 33, he's at the stage where the career numbers that have been his calling cards—his .281 batting average, his .836 OPS against right-handers—will be more and more at odds with reasonable projections for the seasons ahead of him. But he'll make the fifth outfielder spot on your roster much less likely to be a black hole than your standard Quad-A filler will, and that's worth the $2-3 million or so upcharge it takes to sign him these days.

Matt Duffy IF Born: 01/15/91 Age: 32 Bats: R Throws: R Height: 6'2" Weight: 190 lb. Origin: Round 18, 2012 Draft (#568 overall)

YEAR	TEAM	LVL	AGE	PA	R	2B	3B	HR	RBI	BB	K	SB	CS	Whiff%	AVG/OBP/SLG	DRC+	BABIP	BRR	DRP	WARP
2021	CHC	MLB	30	322	45	12	0	5	30	25	63	8	1	15.3%	.287/.357/.381	101	.351	3.3	3B(56): -0.6, 2B(21): -2.3, SS(5): -0.1	1.2
2022	SL	AAA	31	38	4	0	0	1	2	2	8	0	0	15.7%	.171/.237/.257	96	.192	0.3	3B(4): -0.2, 1B(2): 0.4, 2B(1): -0.1	0.1
2022	LAA	MLB	31	247	14	8	0	2	16	17	50	0	0	21.8%	.250/.308/.311	90	.313	1.4	3B(42): -1.5, 1B(21): -0.1, 2B(17): 0.1	0.3
2023 DC	*FA*	*MLB*	*32*	*249*	*23*	*9*	*0*	*3*	*22*	*18*	*46*	*2*	*1*	*19.5%*	*.259/.325/.350*	*91*	*.312*	*0.8*	*3B 0, 2B 0*	*0.3*

Comparables: Luis Castillo (61), Bob Aspromonte (59), Buddy Bell (59)

It's hard to justify your job as a backup if you're always needing backup yourself. Duffy lost another two months last season to back spasms, just 10 days after starter Anthony Rendon's campaign all but ended due to a wrist injury. There's no real way to know how much the pain was affecting Duffy's play given that he slugged .246 in June, but didn't fare much better during his nominally healthy months. He provides so many of the things you want from a veteran utilityman: he grinds, he works counts, he plays multiple positions. He just doesn't do any of them enough, and now he's reached the age where most people hurt their backs all the time for no reason. We might be at the point where, instead of requiring a Plan C to roster him, Duffy is the Plan C himself.

Adam Duvall OF Born: 09/04/88 Age: 34 Bats: R Throws: R Height: 6'1" Weight: 215 lb. Origin: Round 11, 2010 Draft (#348 overall)

YEAR	TEAM	LVL	AGE	PA	R	2B	3B	HR	RBI	BB	K	SB	CS	Whiff%	AVG/OBP/SLG	DRC+	BABIP	BRR	DRP	WARP
2020	ATL	MLB	31	209	34	8	0	16	33	15	54	0	0	27.1%	.237/.301/.532	117	.240	0.3	LF(45): -2, RF(17): -1.1	0.8
2021	MIA	MLB	32	339	41	10	1	22	68	21	105	5	0	28.8%	.229/.277/.478	98	.263	-1.2	RF(66): 6, LF(16): -1.1, CF(8): -0.1	1.3
2021	ATL	MLB	32	216	26	7	1	16	45	14	69	0	0	29.9%	.226/.287/.513	104	.254	-0.1	LF(35): 2.5, CF(22): -1, RF(11): -0.5	1.0
2022	ATL	MLB	33	315	39	16	1	12	36	21	101	0	2	29.2%	.213/.276/.401	84	.278	-0.3	CF(44): -1.5, LF(35): 0.3, RF(11): -0.1	0.3
2023 DC	*FA*	*MLB*	*34*	*249*	*29*	*9*	*0*	*13*	*35*	*16*	*73*	*1*	*0*	*29.0%*	*.217/.281/.438*	*94*	*.257*	*0.6*	*LF 0, RF 1*	*0.6*

Comparables: Gary Redus (63), Greg Vaughn (60), Dave Kingman (60)

Duvall has worn an Atlanta jersey during every season since 2018; last year was the first one in which things didn't go particularly well. The understanding when you bring in Duvall is that while he'll whiff on a ton of pitches, it'll all work out in the end when he eventually sends left-handed pitching to the moon. That agreement didn't hold true last season, as Duvall struck out plenty while failing to bring his production and power to his usual standard. His rough season culminated in Duvall jamming his wrist against the wall while chasing a fly ball. He tore a tendon sheath in his left wrist and went under the knife to end his season. All arrangements have to come to an end eventually. Still, if Duvall is healthy he usually provides power and steady defense to boot.

Robbie Grossman OF Born: 09/16/89 Age: 33 Bats: S Throws: L Height: 6'0" Weight: 209 lb. Origin: Round 6, 2008 Draft (#174 overall)

YEAR	TEAM	LVL	AGE	PA	R	2B	3B	HR	RBI	BB	K	SB	CS	Whiff%	AVG/OBP/SLG	DRC+	BABIP	BRR	DRP	WARP
2020	OAK	MLB	30	192	23	12	2	8	23	21	38	8	1	18.4%	.241/.344/.482	109	.267	0.9	LF(46): 0.5, CF(2): -0.1, RF(1): 0	0.9
2021	DET	MLB	31	671	88	23	3	23	67	98	155	20	5	21.6%	.239/.357/.415	111	.286	1.4	LF(82): -1.9, RF(73): -1.7	2.9
2022	ATL	MLB	32	157	16	6	0	5	22	18	39	3	1	24.0%	.217/.306/.370	100	.263	1.2	RF(25): -0.3, LF(23): -0.2	0.6
2022	DET	MLB	32	320	24	13	1	2	23	38	90	3	1	23.9%	.205/.313/.282	76	.293	-1.6	LF(46): 0, RF(34): 0.3	-0.1
2023 DC	*FA*	*MLB*	*33*	*350*	*37*	*14*	*1*	*9*	*37*	*42*	*86*	*7*	*1*	*23.1%*	*.220/.323/.365*	*93*	*.277*	*3.1*	*LF 2, RF 1*	*1.1*

Comparables: Dave Collins (57), Greg Gross (56), Luis Gonzalez (53)

If there's a silver lining that Grossman can take from this past season, it's that he figured out how to consistently hit against lefties. The bad news is that right-handed pitchers also exist and they absolutely befuddled him all season, which likely explains the precipitous drop in DRC+. It doesn't help that his strikeout rate continued to rise as he put up one of the lowest contact percentages of his career. On top of that, he hasn't been consistently hitting the ball hard when he does make contact. Hopefully 2022 was just a gross outlier.

Yuli Gurriel 1B Born: 06/09/84 Age: 39 Bats: R Throws: R Height: 6'0" Weight: 215 lb. Origin: International Free Agent, 2016

YEAR	TEAM	LVL	AGE	PA	R	2B	3B	HR	RBI	BB	K	SB	CS	Whiff%	AVG/OBP/SLG	DRC+	BABIP	BRR	DRP	WARP
2020	HOU	MLB	36	230	27	12	1	6	22	12	27	0	1	15.6%	.232/.274/.384	98	.235	-1.0	1B(55): -0.5	0.3
2021	HOU	MLB	37	605	83	31	0	15	81	59	68	1	1	13.9%	.319/.383/.462	126	.336	-1.0	1B(142): 0.6	3.2
2022	HOU	MLB	38	584	53	40	0	8	53	30	73	8	0	14.3%	.242/.288/.360	95	.266	-0.9	1B(142): 1.6	0.9
2023 DC	*FA*	*MLB*	*39*	*451*	*47*	*24*	*0*	*12*	*52*	*29*	*48*	*2*	*1*	*14.7%*	*.272/.326/.423*	*110*	*.285*	*0.1*	*1B 1, 3B 0*	*1.3*

Comparables: Rod Carew (78), Mark Grace (77), Steve Garvey (74)

Say one thing for Gurriel: he remains elite at avoiding strikeouts. That his 12.5% strikeout rate represented a career worst is testament to the stellar job he has done at putting bat to ball since arriving in the States. Sadly, that's where the good ends in 2022, not least because Gurriel was one of the least-threatening players in the league when said contact was made. With diminishing power, an increased vulnerability to fastballs and a major swoon over the season's final third, the 38-year-old looked every bit his age, a number that has been hitherto easy to forget given the timing of his arrival in the majors and the quality of his performance throughout. A strong postseason helped to earn himself another ring and generate some hope heading into free agency. Wherever Gurriel ends up, whether he can reverse this decline or not, he'll carry on putting the bat on the ball.

César Hernández 2B Born: 05/23/90 Age: 33 Bats: S Throws: R Height: 5'10" Weight: 183 lb. Origin: International Free Agent, 2006

YEAR	TEAM	LVL	AGE	PA	R	2B	3B	HR	RBI	BB	K	SB	CS	Whiff%	AVG/OBP/SLG	DRC+	BABIP	BRR	DRP	WARP
2020	CLE	MLB	30	261	35	20	0	3	20	24	57	0	0	20.1%	.283/.355/.408	92	.364	0.2	2B(58): 0.4	0.7
2021	CHW	MLB	31	217	24	4	0	3	15	21	45	1	1	19.8%	.232/.309/.299	88	.286	-1.1	2B(53): -0.8	0.3
2021	CLE	MLB	31	420	60	17	2	18	47	38	90	0	0	23.6%	.231/.307/.431	104	.256	-1.1	2B(89): 0.2	1.6
2022	WAS	MLB	32	617	64	28	4	1	34	45	114	10	4	20.9%	.248/.311/.318	84	.309	0.0	2B(126): -1.8, LF(10): 0.7, 3B(9): -0.5	0.6
2023 DC	*FA*	*MLB*	*33*	*451*	*45*	*18*	*1*	*9*	*46*	*35*	*86*	*5*	*2*	*20.8%*	*.254/.319/.378*	*95*	*.301*	*1.2*	*2B 0, LF 0*	*1.1*

Comparables: Luis Castillo (66), Brian Roberts (66), Jim Gantner (65)

Across MLB, batters hit 729 fewer home runs in 2022 than in 2021. That's an overall 12.3% decline, but the deader baseball affected some more than others. Enter Hernández, whose homer total dropped from 21 down to just one. Even during his salad days with Philadelphia and Cleveland, power was never his defining trait, and most of his 21 '21 dingers were wall-scrapers that wouldn't have cleared the fence in every big-league park. As it turns out, a little more drag on the baseball turned those first-row souvenirs into outs. He only hit 22 batted balls at least 350 feet in '22, compared to 47 the year prior. It's not all the baseball's fault though: His innate power has declined as rapidly as his defensive range as he's pushed into his 30s. As such, it's unlikely a team will rely on Hernández to be an everyday player moving forward no matter how aerodynamic the baseball may or may not be.

José Iglesias SS Born: 01/05/90 Age: 33 Bats: R Throws: R Height: 5'11" Weight: 195 lb. Origin: International Free Agent, 2009

YEAR	TEAM	LVL	AGE	PA	R	2B	3B	HR	RBI	BB	K	SB	CS	Whiff%	AVG/OBP/SLG	DRC+	BABIP	BRR	DRP	WARP
2020	BAL	MLB	30	150	16	17	0	3	24	3	17	0	0	14.5%	.373/.400/.556	119	.407	-0.6	SS(24): -0.2	0.7
2021	BOS	MLB	31	64	8	4	1	1	7	3	9	0	0	14.7%	.356/.406/.508	111	.408	-1.3	2B(18): 0.5, SS(5): -0.1	0.2
2021	LAA	MLB	31	447	57	23	1	8	41	18	66	5	2	19.5%	.259/.295/.375	90	.291	0.0	SS(114): -3.5	0.7
2022	COL	MLB	32	467	48	30	0	3	47	17	56	2	3	13.2%	.292/.328/.380	104	.326	-1.1	SS(116): 4.8	2.1
2023 DC	*FA*	*MLB*	*33*	*451*	*41*	*24*	*1*	*6*	*43*	*19*	*51*	*3*	*1*	*14.7%*	*.275/.315/.382*	*96*	*.302*	*0.6*	*SS 0, 2B 0*	*1.1*

Comparables: Luis Aparicio (71), Rafael Furcal (68), Edgar Renteria (68)

The first hit of Iglesias' 2022 season wasn't one for the record books—it was the 924th of his 11-year career for the sixth team he's been a part of. But once he reached first base, he started to cry—he'd notched his first MLB hit that his father, Candelario, hadn't seen, as he'd passed away shortly before the season began. Iglesias did his late father proud all year long, tacking on 127 more knocks en route to his best season by WARP since his 2019 campaign in Cincinnati. This time around, the metrics say he was more valuable with the bat than the glove. That's not a good sign for Iglesias going forward: His defense has kept him in the majors this long, but by FRAA, he's now been a negative at shortstop for three years running. Plus, it's not as if his offense is suddenly at peak A-Rod levels—roughly league-average with no power is the best you can expect, and that's what the Rockies got for their modest investment. As such, Iglesias is more apt to serve as a stopgap infielder for rebuilding clubs than a key piece on a contender.

Tommy La Stella DH Born: 01/31/89 Age: 34 Bats: L Throws: R Height: 5'11" Weight: 180 lb. Origin: Round 8, 2011 Draft (#266 overall)

YEAR	TEAM	LVL	AGE	PA	R	2B	3B	HR	RBI	BB	K	SB	CS	Whiff%	AVG/OBP/SLG	DRC+	BABIP	BRR	DRP	WARP
2020	OAK	MLB	31	111	16	6	2	1	11	12	5	0	0	10.9%	.289/.369/.423	113	.293	0.1	2B(18): -1.3, 3B(6): -0.1	0.4
2020	LAA	MLB	31	117	15	8	0	4	14	15	7	1	0	11.5%	.273/.371/.475	119	.258	-1.7	2B(15): -0.4, 1B(10): 0.2	0.4
2021	SAC	AAA	32	38	8	2	0	0	2	7	5	0	0		.200/.351/.267	104	.240	0.6	2B(6): 0.2, 3B(2): -0.1, 1B(1): -0.1	0.2
2021	SF	MLB	32	242	26	11	1	7	27	18	26	0	0	12.3%	.250/.308/.405	108	.255	0.6	2B(54): -0.7, 3B(5): 0	1.1
2022	SAC	AAA	33	48	8	2	0	2	7	9	7	0	0	14.5%	.316/.458/.526	122	.345	-1.0	2B(8): -1.0, 3B(2): 0.0	0.1
2022	SF	MLB	33	195	17	14	0	2	14	11	30	0	0	16.8%	.239/.282/.350	86	.272	-0.8	3B(6): -0.2, 1B(3): 0.1, 2B(3): 0.2	0.1
2023 non-DC	*FA*	*MLB*	*34*	*251*	*26*	*11*	*0*	*5*	*22*	*20*	*28*	*0*	*0*	*14.9%*	*.251/.317/.377*	*96*	*.267*	*-0.4*	*2B 0, 3B 0*	*0.4*

Comparables: Brian Roberts (57), Orlando Hudson (53), Jim Gantner (50)

It was a disappointing season for La Stella, who began and ended the season on the IL, the first stretch after a prolonged recovery from off-season surgery on his Achilles tendons—note the *s*—and the second time with neck spasms. When asked about where La Stella had gone after his clubhouse locker was emptied out before the Giants' final homestand, Gabe Kapler reasserted that "he's still very much a part of this team," which is one of those "people asking a lot of questions already answered by my shirt..." moments. Within months, said shirt met the same fate as the ones printed for losing Super Bowl teams.

Trey Mancini DH Born: 03/18/92 Age: 31 Bats: R Throws: R Height: 6'3" Weight: 230 lb. Origin: Round 8, 2013 Draft (#249 overall)

YEAR	TEAM	LVL	AGE	PA	R	2B	3B	HR	RBI	BB	K	SB	CS	Whiff%	AVG/OBP/SLG	DRC+	BABIP	BRR	DRP	WARP
2021	BAL	MLB	29	616	77	33	1	21	71	51	143	0	0	29.5%	.255/.326/.432	103	.308	-1.5	1B(77): 0.6	1.4
2022	HOU	MLB	30	186	17	7	0	8	22	18	49	0	0	27.1%	.176/.258/.364	94	.191	-0.6	LF(17): -0.1, 1B(10): 0.1, RF(1): -0.1	0.3
2022	BAL	MLB	30	401	39	16	1	10	41	35	86	0	0	27.6%	.268/.347/.404	108	.326	-0.5	1B(29): -1, RF(10): -1.2, LF(3): 0.2	1.1
2023 DC	*FA*	*MLB*	*31*	*498*	*60*	*21*	*1*	*20*	*66*	*44*	*110*	*0*	*0*	*27.3%*	*.253/.330/.446*	*115*	*.293*	*-1.5*	*1B 1, LF 0*	*1.6*

Comparables: Ken Henderson (69), Bob Watson (69), Eric Karros (68)

That Mancini is in possession of a World Series ring is one of the few great justices visited upon the sport by the nameless, faceless baseball gods in their limitless capriciousness. Ignore the fact that, upon being traded to Houston, Mancini's bat turned into one of those fake-out cakes instead of solid lumber; the flip side of the Crawford Boxes is they can make a righty hitter's eyes bug out like a Tex Avery cartoon. Slightly more difficult to ignore is the season-long trend of a dip in hard-hit rate and max exit velocity and generally less thumping of the ball from a player whose sole goal is to thump baseballs, but ignore it you must, because this is all you need to know: Trey Mancini, who went toe-to-toe with a particularly insidious form of cancer and emerged on the other side; who donates his time and energy to helping others in the same unfortunate predicament; who is one of baseball's truly Good Guys; *that* Trey Mancini is in possession of a World Series ring, and—in this one case, if no others—the cosmic scales are balanced.

Andrew McCutchen DH Born: 10/10/86 Age: 36 Bats: R Throws: R Height: 5'11" Weight: 195 lb. Origin: Round 1, 2005 Draft (#11 overall)

YEAR	TEAM	LVL	AGE	PA	R	2B	3B	HR	RBI	BB	K	SB	CS	Whiff%	AVG/OBP/SLG	DRC+	BABIP	BRR	DRP	WARP
2020	PHI	MLB	33	241	32	9	0	10	34	22	48	4	0	22.0%	.253/.324/.433	109	.281	-1.2	LF(39): -1.8	0.6
2021	PHI	MLB	34	574	78	24	1	27	80	81	132	6	1	25.7%	.222/.334/.444	108	.242	0.9	LF(135): -3	2.5
2022	MIL	MLB	35	580	66	25	0	17	69	57	124	8	6	24.2%	.237/.316/.384	97	.278	-2.5	LF(31): -0.1, RF(19): 0.1, CF(3): 0.2	1.1
2023 DC	*FA*	*MLB*	*36*	*397*	*45*	*16*	*0*	*14*	*48*	*43*	*85*	*5*	*2*	*24.5%*	*.239/.327/.410*	*105*	*.278*	*1.2*	*LF 2, RF 0*	*1.6*

Comparables: Amos Otis (75), Chet Lemon (75), Cesar Cedeno (74)

Two decades ago, the Billy Beane-led A's signed late-career David Justice to a one-year deal based on their assumption that a hitter's plate discipline is largely impervious to age. It worked out for Oakland, but alas, the same strategy didn't pay off for the 2022 Brewers. A modern-day Justice, McCutchen didn't get on base or hit for power as often as his new employers likely hoped. His swing rate jumped by four percentage points, and he routinely went after bad pitches he used to take. Fewer walks, limited pop and way too many DH appearances culminated in just a fraction of a win above replacement for the former MVP. Soon to turn 36, McCutchen may still shine if used in certain spots, but his days as a full-time contributor seem like they should be over.

Tyler Naquin OF Born: 04/24/91 Age: 32 Bats: L Throws: R Height: 6'2" Weight: 195 lb. Origin: Round 1, 2012 Draft (#15 overall)

YEAR	TEAM	LVL	AGE	PA	R	2B	3B	HR	RBI	BB	K	SB	CS	Whiff%	AVG/OBP/SLG	DRC+	BABIP	BRR	DRP	WARP
2020	CLE	MLB	29	141	15	8	1	4	20	5	40	0	1	30.9%	.218/.248/.383	73	.275	-1.1	RF(39): -0.7	-0.2
2021	CIN	MLB	30	454	52	24	2	19	70	35	106	5	3	23.8%	.270/.333/.477	101	.318	-2.6	CF(92): -3.5, LF(22): -0.8, RF(21): -0.3	1.1
2022	CIN	MLB	31	204	29	12	2	7	33	13	53	3	2	27.4%	.246/.305/.444	89	.307	0.6	RF(42): -0.9	0.3
2022	NYM	MLB	31	130	18	7	2	4	13	6	40	1	0	35.2%	.203/.246/.390	72	.266	0.8	RF(26): -0.8, LF(15): -0.6, CF(2): 0	-0.1
2023 DC	*FA*	*MLB*	*32*	*296*	*33*	*14*	*1*	*12*	*39*	*19*	*80*	*4*	*1*	*28.7%*	*.249/.305/.447*	*104*	*.309*	*2.0*	*RF -1, CF -1*	*0.9*

Comparables: Denard Span (54), David Murphy (52), Andre Ethier (51)

It's getting late. But, it's not time for bed yet. It's too late to invest the mental energy into starting the latest Netflix dramedy everyone is talking about, but it's too early for the most depraved reality TV. That's how you end up watching multiple hours of Love It or List It on HGTV. That's also something of an analogy for how you end up with 130 plate appearances of Naquin after a deadline deal. After a hot start with the Mets in August, Naquin's production dropped off rather precipitously in September, and his overall Mets batting average ended up hovering just above the Mendoza line—more than 40 points lower than that of his first half with the Reds. But the Mets needed a fourth outfielder, and nothing else was on.

Rougned Odor 2B Born: 02/03/94 Age: 29 Bats: L Throws: R Height: 5'11" Weight: 200 lb. Origin: International Free Agent, 2011

YEAR	TEAM	LVL	AGE	PA	R	2B	3B	HR	RBI	BB	K	SB	CS	Whiff%	AVG/OBP/SLG	DRC+	BABIP	BRR	DRP	WARP
2020	TEX	MLB	26	148	15	4	0	10	30	7	47	0	1	26.0%	.167/.209/.413	78	.157	-0.2	2B(37): -0.1	0.1
2021	NYY	MLB	27	361	42	12	0	15	39	27	100	0	1	28.7%	.202/.286/.379	82	.242	0.7	2B(74): 0, 3B(33): 1.8	0.7
2022	BAL	MLB	28	472	49	19	3	13	53	32	109	6	1	27.4%	.207/.275/.357	83	.244	0.7	2B(129): -3, 3B(2): -0.1	0.3
2023 DC	*FA*	*MLB*	*29*	*350*	*41*	*13*	*1*	*16*	*47*	*26*	*91*	*4*	*2*	*27.4%*	*.225/.298/.430*	*99*	*.263*	*1.3*	*2B -2, 3B 0*	*0.9*

Comparables: Joe Morgan (68), Roberto Alomar (59), Rennie Stennett (58)

"Rougie" played the role of veteran vibes guy for the Orioles in 2022, though some fans were left questioning if that job truly necessitated him playing as much as he did. For a team that was just a few favorable bounces shy of qualifying for the postseason, giving nearly 500 plate appearances to a player with an 83 DRC+ was puzzling to say the least. How valuable could those infielder-initiated mound visits really be? Nonetheless, manager Brandon Hyde persisted with penciling Odor's name into the lineup whenever possible, and in return he authored the modern Rougned Odor season: lots of personality, a little bit of pop and a lot less time on base.

David Peralta LF

Born: 08/14/87 Age: 35 Bats: L Throws: L Height: 6'1" Weight: 210 lb. Origin: International Free Agent, 2005

YEAR	TEAM	LVL	AGE	PA	R	2B	3B	HR	RBI	BB	K	SB	CS	Whiff%	AVG/OBP/SLG	DRC+	BABIP	BRR	DRP	WARP
2020	AZ	MLB	32	218	19	10	1	5	34	13	45	1	0	21.1%	.300/.339/.433	90	.361	0.4	LF(45): 1.2	0.5
2021	AZ	MLB	33	538	57	30	8	8	63	46	92	2	1	21.2%	.259/.325/.402	91	.303	-0.4	LF(137): -0.1	1.4
2022	TB	MLB	34	180	10	11	1	0	18	14	40	0	1	23.1%	.255/.317/.335	80	.331	0.8	LF(38): -0.6	0.1
2022	AZ	MLB	34	310	29	19	2	12	41	27	74	1	2	28.1%	.248/.316/.460	98	.292	-3.1	LF(75): -1.4	0.5
2023 DC	*FA*	*MLB*	*35*	*350*	*40*	*17*	*2*	*12*	*45*	*28*	*75*	*1*	*1*	*25.3%*	*.263/.329/.452*	*115*	*.309*	*1.1*	*LF 2, 1B 0*	*1.8*

Comparables: Charlie Jamieson (76), Ken Griffey (75), Jerry Lynch (74)

When the Rays acquired Peralta from Arizona last summer, they thought they were adding some much-needed thump to their lineup—after all, Peralta slugged quite well in his half-season with the snakes. But while he maintained his average and on-base ability in Tampa, he provided almost no pop: his ISO fell from .212 in the desert to .081 in the swamp. Peralta is now a 35-year-old platoon bat who saw his power vanish and who, despite placing as a finalist for a Gold Glove in left field, saw his defense begin to regress last season. He may soon be grateful for the existence of the universal DH.

Tommy Pham LF

Born: 03/08/88 Age: 35 Bats: R Throws: R Height: 6'1" Weight: 223 lb. Origin: Round 16, 2006 Draft (#496 overall)

YEAR	TEAM	LVL	AGE	PA	R	2B	3B	HR	RBI	BB	K	SB	CS	Whiff%	AVG/OBP/SLG	DRC+	BABIP	BRR	DRP	WARP
2020	SD	MLB	32	125	13	2	0	3	12	15	27	6	0	27.0%	.211/.312/.312	96	.253	0.3	LF(18): -0.3	0.3
2021	SD	MLB	33	561	74	24	2	15	49	78	128	14	6	23.4%	.229/.340/.383	101	.280	0.3	LF(113): -5.3, CF(11): -0.9, RF(1): 0	1.6
2022	BOS	MLB	34	235	32	12	0	6	24	14	67	1	1	23.3%	.234/.298/.374	83	.310	0.8	LF(51): -2.5	0.1
2022	CIN	MLB	34	387	57	11	1	11	39	42	100	7	2	27.6%	.238/.320/.374	97	.300	1.8	LF(83): -3.9	0.9
2023 DC	*FA*	*MLB*	*35*	*451*	*50*	*17*	*1*	*14*	*53*	*45*	*110*	*7*	*2*	*25.5%*	*.240/.324/.402*	*102*	*.295*	*2.3*	*LF -3, CF 0*	*1.1*

Comparables: Roy White (64), Dexter Fowler (64), Merv Rettenmund (63)

At this point in his career, Pham is more random scandal generator than productive baseball player. Last season, he made more headlines for slapping Joc Pederson over a fantasy football season gone wrong than for anything he did at the plate, where he scalded the ball for a week or so each month before vanishing for the next fortnight. All that hard contact couldn't make up for strikeout and walk rates each moving in the wrong direction, or defense that grades out as average at best when in left field. Still unable to hit anything with break or fade, Pham now finds himself in the itinerant veteran portion of his career and looks best suited for a fourth outfielder gig. His future teammates may want to hold their fantasy draft before he signs, just to be safe.

Chad Pinder LF

Born: 03/29/92 Age: 31 Bats: R Throws: R Height: 6'2" Weight: 210 lb. Origin: Round 2, 2013 Draft (#71 overall)

YEAR	TEAM	LVL	AGE	PA	R	2B	3B	HR	RBI	BB	K	SB	CS	Whiff%	AVG/OBP/SLG	DRC+	BABIP	BRR	DRP	WARP
2020	OAK	MLB	28	61	8	3	0	2	8	5	13	0	0	21.7%	.232/.295/.393	100	.268	0.1	2B(13): -0.1, 3B(7): 0.2	0.2
2021	LV	AAA	29	31	6	2	0	2	10	2	8	0	0		.286/.323/.571	99	.316	-0.5	SS(3): 0.1, RF(3): -0.4	0.0
2021	OAK	MLB	29	233	30	16	1	6	27	16	62	1	0	28.1%	.243/.300/.411	88	.313	1.3	RF(39): -2.4, LF(17): -1.6, SS(8): 0.2	0.3
2022	OAK	MLB	30	379	38	18	0	12	42	14	118	2	0	34.4%	.235/.263/.385	82	.313	-0.9	LF(64): -2.9, RF(30): -0.3, 3B(9): -0.1	-0.1
2023 DC	*FA*	*MLB*	*31*	*296*	*29*	*13*	*0*	*9*	*34*	*16*	*90*	*0*	*0*	*32.8%*	*.232/.281/.390*	*82*	*.309*	*-0.1*	*LF 1, RF 0*	*0.0*

Comparables: Scott Hairston (60), Ben Francisco (59), Chris Heisey (58)

One of the game's signature utility players may have aged out of his versatility and into a platoon outfielder role at just the wrong time. The first-time free agent remains a solid offensive player against southpaws—he makes enough contact and has enough pop to compensate for his hyper-aggressive approach—but he hardly roamed the dirt at all last season in Oakland, and a great deal of his value had traditionally derived from his ability to cover any position save the battery. His defense has never been better than average at best, but as he enters his 30s, Pinder may fit best as a different kind of super-sub now: a lefty-smashing pinch-hit specialist on a contender.

Nick Plummer OF

Born: 07/31/96 Age: 26 Bats: L Throws: L Height: 5'10" Weight: 200 lb. Origin: Round 1, 2015 Draft (#23 overall)

YEAR	TEAM	LVL	AGE	PA	R	2B	3B	HR	RBI	BB	K	SB	CS	Whiff%	AVG/OBP/SLG	DRC+	BABIP	BRR	DRP	WARP
2021	SPR	AA	24	376	52	17	4	13	46	53	108	9	8		.283/.404/.489	110	.393	-0.1	LF(33): -5.0, CF(33): -2.5, RF(17): -0.4	0.8
2021	MEM	AAA	24	102	19	3	2	2	8	20	18	4	1		.267/.455/.440	126	.327	1.1	LF(20): -0.8, CF(4): -0.4, RF(1): -0.2	0.6
2022	SYR	AAA	25	270	29	12	0	7	41	25	80	8	4		.238/.330/.379	83	.327	-2.7	LF(23): -2.6, RF(22): -1.4, CF(16): -1.4	-0.7
2022	NYM	MLB	25	31	4	1	0	2	6	1	12	0	0	36.2%	.138/.194/.379	71	.133	-0.1	RF(5): -0.4, LF(4): 0.1	0.0
2023 non-DC	*FA*	*MLB*	*26*	*251*	*22*	*9*	*1*	*4*	*23*	*21*	*85*	*3*	*1*	*35.0%*	*.198/.284/.320*	*66*	*.297*	*-0.4*	*LF 0, RF 0*	*-0.5*

Comparables: Chris McGuiness (52), Donald Lutz (51), Jeremy Hazelbaker (49)

Surprising performances from ancillary players are one of the trappings of a 100-win season, and Plummer was one such player who got his moment in the sun for the Mets. Striding to the plate to the Super Mario theme song, Plummer notched his first career hit with a game-tying home run in the bottom of the ninth inning off Corey Knebel on May 29, setting up for a Mets walk-off victory in the tenth. He followed up those heroics with a three-hit, four-RBI performance on Memorial Day. He only played in 14 games in 2022, but the outfielder who the Mets signed as a minor-league free agent in November had an outsized impact. Maybe Chris Pratt will play him in the movie about the 2022 Mets.

Jurickson Profar LF Born: 02/20/93 Age: 30 Bats: S Throws: R Height: 6'0" Weight: 184 lb. Origin: International Free Agent, 2009

YEAR	TEAM	LVL	AGE	PA	R	2B	3B	HR	RBI	BB	K	SB	CS	Whiff%	AVG/OBP/SLG	DRC+	BABIP	BRR	DRP	WARP
2020	SD	MLB	27	202	28	6	0	7	25	15	28	7	1	20.2%	.278/.343/.428	112	.293	2.2	LF(36): 1.3, 2B(17): 0.1, RF(2): 0.1	1.3
2021	SD	MLB	28	412	47	17	2	4	33	49	65	10	5	18.0%	.227/.329/.320	97	.266	4.1	LF(36): -0.6, RF(29): -2.4, 1B(20): -0.4	1.3
2022	SD	MLB	29	658	82	36	2	15	58	73	103	5	1	18.9%	.243/.331/.391	109	.272	0.1	LF(146): -5.5	2.3
2023 DC	*FA*	*MLB*	*30*	*498*	*52*	*23*	*1*	*12*	*53*	*56*	*73*	*6*	*1*	*18.6%*	*.238/.333/.384*	*104*	*.261*	*0.9*	*LF -9, RF 0*	*0.5*

Comparables: Eddie Miksis (52), Eddie Yost (51), Danny Heep (50)

Ask your doctor about Profar, the do-it-all antihistamine and sensual aid for all former top prospects. Side effects include:

- Hitting for moderate power
- Drawing a fair share of walks
- An ability to play multiple positions (though its brand-new formulation is specifically made for left field!)

Simply apply anywhere you would like in the batting order and allow 3-6 weeks for maximum effect to take hold. Call your doctor if you end up holding onto the ball for four hours to allow a runner to take third base.

Gary Sánchez C Born: 12/02/92 Age: 30 Bats: R Throws: R Height: 6'2" Weight: 230 lb. Origin: International Free Agent, 2009

YEAR	TEAM	LVL	AGE	PA	R	2B	3B	HR	RBI	BB	K	SB	CS	Whiff%	AVG/OBP/SLG	DRC+	BABIP	BRR	DRP	WARP
2020	TOR	WIN	27	62	5	4	0	2	10	6	19	0	0		.245/.355/.434		.344			
2020	NYY	MLB	27	178	19	4	0	10	24	18	64	0	0	34.0%	.147/.253/.365	88	.159	-0.8	C(41): -0.8	0.2
2021	NYY	MLB	28	440	54	13	1	23	54	52	121	0	0	29.4%	.204/.307/.423	108	.230	-1.0	C(110): -1.2	2.0
2022	MIN	MLB	29	471	42	24	0	16	61	40	136	2	0	30.8%	.205/.282/.377	87	.257	-0.5	C(91): 4.7, 1B(1): 0	1.3
2023 DC	*FA*	*MLB*	*30*	*350*	*42*	*13*	*0*	*16*	*47*	*33*	*94*	*0*	*0*	*30.3%*	*.212/.300/.423*	*98*	*.246*	*-2.5*	*C 0, 1B 0*	*0.9*

Comparables: Steve Yeager (75), Frankie Hayes (70), Yasmani Grandal (68)

YEAR	TEAM	P. COUNT	FRM RUNS	BLK RUNS	THRW RUNS	TOT RUNS
2020	NYY	5546	-0.3	-0.1	-0.2	-0.7
2021	NYY	14761	-1.7	-1.6	0.2	-3.1
2022	MIN	11847	4.8	0.0	0.0	4.8
2023	*FA*	*6956*	*-0.4*	*-0.3*	*0.1*	*-0.6*

If the alternative hypothesis was that a change of scenery would help Sánchez rediscover his best form, the null hypothesis cannot be rejected on the available evidence. The former Yankee was handed the most plate appearances since his monster 2017 season, and responded with the opposite of that campaign. His ISO sank below .200 for the first time in his career, and the miserable batting average that plagued his later Bronx years persisted. Through all his other struggles, Sánchez used to be a lock for a plus offensive contribution. Last year, he was not only a clearly worse-than-average hitter, he was indistinguishable from the average backstop at the plate. Minnesota did help in one regard: Both his framing and blocking improved significantly from the performances that drew so much ire in the Bronx. Sánchez retains the raw pop to be one of the league's most explosive offensive catchers, which might encourage teams to keep running their own experiments for a few years further. As he moves into his age-30 season, though, it seems ever-more-likely his formula for success won't be rediscovered.

Miguel Sanó 1B Born: 05/11/93 Age: 30 Bats: R Throws: R Height: 6'4" Weight: 272 lb. Origin: International Free Agent, 2009

YEAR	TEAM	LVL	AGE	PA	R	2B	3B	HR	RBI	BB	K	SB	CS	Whiff%	AVG/OBP/SLG	DRC+	BABIP	BRR	DRP	WARP
2020	MIN	MLB	27	205	31	12	0	13	25	18	90	0	0	42.6%	.204/.278/.478	81	.301	1.9	1B(52): -0.1	0.2
2021	MIN	MLB	28	532	68	24	0	30	75	59	183	2	1	38.2%	.223/.312/.466	105	.291	-0.5	1B(118): -0.9, 3B(9): 0.4	1.4
2022	STP	AAA	29	26	5	2	0	3	7	3	10	0	0		.348/.423/.826	81	.500	-0.4	1B(6): -0.7	-0.1
2022	MIN	MLB	29	71	1	0	0	1	3	9	25	1	0	37.2%	.083/.211/.133	80	.114	-1.3	1B(19): 0.6	-0.1
2023 DC	*FA*	*MLB*	*30*	*148*	*19*	*5*	*0*	*8*	*23*	*16*	*50*	*0*	*1*	*37.0%*	*.229/.319/.479*	*115*	*.297*	*0.1*	*1B 0, 3B 0*	*0.5*

Comparables: Mark Reynolds (73), Troy Glaus (66), Bob Robertson (65)

This is the way Sanó in Minnesota ends; not with a bang but with a whimper. Sanó, so known for the former, produced only the latter, the last year of his twenties devoid of promise. A torn meniscus robbed him of the chance to contribute for most of the season, to be fair. Maybe one of his patented hot streaks would have followed the empty start, if he'd been given enough time. Instead all we're left with is hollow: a batting average that never started with anything but a zero, the usual alarming strikeout rate without the explosive power. A brief return in late July added more nothing to the line before the knee returned him to the IL. The Twins had little choice but to decline his contract option, ending a 13-year relationship.

Donovan Solano DH Born: 12/17/87 Age: 35 Bats: R Throws: R Height: 5'8" Weight: 210 lb. Origin: International Free Agent, 2005

YEAR	TEAM	LVL	AGE	PA	R	2B	3B	HR	RBI	BB	K	SB	CS	Whiff%	AVG/OBP/SLG	DRC+	BABIP	BRR	DRP	WARP
2020	SF	MLB	32	203	22	15	1	3	29	10	39	0	0	22.0%	.326/.365/.463	101	.396	-1.7	2B(45): -2.1, 3B(5): -0.4, SS(2): 0	0.3
2021	SF	MLB	33	344	35	17	0	7	31	25	58	2	0	20.3%	.280/.344/.404	105	.321	-0.6	2B(91): 0.4, SS(2): 0	1.5
2022	LOU	AAA	34	34	2	4	0	1	3	2	4	0	0		.345/.412/.586	108	.360	-0.2	3B(6): -0.4, SS(1): -0.2	0.1
2022	CIN	MLB	34	304	22	16	0	4	24	19	61	0	0	21.1%	.284/.339/.385	96	.349	-0.7	1B(26): -0.4, 3B(16): -0.1, 2B(7): -0.1	0.4
2023 DC	*FA*	*MLB*	*35*	*249*	*24*	*12*	*0*	*4*	*24*	*15*	*47*	*0*	*0*	*21.8%*	*.269/.325/.380*	*98*	*.324*	*-0.4*	*2B 0, 3B 0*	*0.6*

Comparables: Julian Javier (70), Brandon Phillips (68), Frank White (64)

You know that elderly dude at the gym who shoots about 200 free throws a day? That's Solano in the lineup, except it's plain old singles. That's right, reliable base hits. Seeing-eye loafers. After about two months of plate appearances, the 35-year-old sported a .333 batting average. His late-stage baseball career, in which he grew from organizational depth to a guy crouching by himself whackin' liners, is a remarkable feat. The average fell off some, but expect those singles to keep bringing Solano work. They might not be the same as home runs, but just like all those free throws, singles are still fun to watch for anyone who shows up just to sit down and keep score.

Raimel Tapia OF

Born: 02/04/94 Age: 29 Bats: L Throws: L Height: 6'3" Weight: 175 lb. Origin: International Free Agent, 2010

YEAR	TEAM	LVL	AGE	PA	R	2B	3B	HR	RBI	BB	K	SB	CS	Whiff%	AVG/OBP/SLG	DRC+	BABIP	BRR	DRP	WARP
2020	COL	MLB	26	206	26	8	2	1	17	14	38	8	2	18.9%	.321/.369/.402	91	.392	2.4	LF(36): 1.7, RF(3): -0.2	0.7
2021	COL	MLB	27	533	69	26	2	6	50	40	70	20	6	14.8%	.273/.327/.372	92	.306	3.6	LF(118): 6.3, RF(4): 0.5, CF(3): -0.1	2.5
2022	TOR	MLB	28	433	47	20	3	7	52	16	81	8	2	21.4%	.265/.292/.380	87	.315	1.4	LF(64): 1.5, CF(38): 0.3, RF(32): -0.5	1.0
2023 DC	*FA*	*MLB*	*29*	*350*	*31*	*16*	*2*	*4*	*32*	*20*	*58*	*13*	*3*	*19.9%*	*.267/.312/.371*	*91*	*.314*	*6.6*	*LF 1, CF 0*	*1.2*

Comparables: Eddie Rosario (57), Coco Crisp (56), Nate Schierholtz (54)

Tapia joined the Blue Jays as, at best, their fourth outfielder, and more realistically their fifth. He finished the season starting semi-regularly to spell the starters who were either hurt or underperforming. Unfortunately, Tapia did much of the latter himself. To no one's surprise, leaving Denver's thin air did nothing to improve his outcomes. He derives much of his utility from his legs—a skill that soured in 2022 as his speed visibly eroded, causing his baserunning and defense to wilt. His plate discipline took a nosedive, too, as he encountered a significant increase in off-speed stuff. Tapia is on the right side of 30, but the waning value of his contributions caused the Blue Jays to non-tender him in November. He'll likely be relegated to fourth or fifth outfielder duties once more should he sign with a contender.

Luis Torrens C

Born: 05/02/96 Age: 27 Bats: R Throws: R Height: 6'0" Weight: 217 lb. Origin: International Free Agent, 2013

YEAR	TEAM	LVL	AGE	PA	R	2B	3B	HR	RBI	BB	K	SB	CS	Whiff%	AVG/OBP/SLG	DRC+	BABIP	BRR	DRP	WARP
2020	SD	MLB	24	13	0	1	0	0	0	1	2	0	0	27.8%	.273/.333/.364	99	.333	-0.4	C(7): -0.4	0.0
2020	SEA	MLB	24	65	5	4	0	1	6	6	13	0	0	19.8%	.254/.323/.373	104	.311	-0.1	C(17): -2.2	0.0
2021	TAC	AAA	25	85	12	4	0	6	19	10	22	0	0		.219/.318/.521	104	.217	0.0	C(9): 0.1, 1B(8): 0.2	0.3
2021	SEA	MLB	25	378	39	16	2	15	47	28	99	0	0	27.4%	.243/.299/.431	97	.294	-0.6	C(35): -5.3, 1B(5): 0, 3B(2): 0	0.4
2022	TAC	AAA	26	68	7	5	0	3	15	5	18	0	0	27.7%	.279/.324/.508	94	.333	-0.9	C(10): 0.4, 2B(4): -0.5, 1B(2): 0.0	0.1
2022	SEA	MLB	26	166	13	2	0	3	15	12	50	0	0	26.7%	.225/.283/.298	79	.310	0.8	C(42): -4.6, 2B(2): 0	-0.2
2023 DC	*FA*	*MLB*	*27*	*202*	*19*	*8*	*0*	*5*	*21*	*15*	*49*	*0*	*0*	*26.5%*	*.224/.288/.362*	*79*	*.277*	*-1.0*	*C -8, 1B 0*	*-0.8*

Comparables: Jack Boyle (51), Fred Kendall (47), Tom Egan (45)

YEAR	TEAM	P. COUNT	FRM RUNS	BLK RUNS	THRW RUNS	TOT RUNS
2020	SEA	2281	-2.1	-0.1	0.0	-2.2
2020	SD	597	-0.4	0.0	0.1	-0.4
2021	TAC	1166	0.3	0.0	0.0	0.3
2021	SEA	4805	-5.6	-0.2	0.5	-5.3
2022	TAC	1554	0.0	0.0	0.4	0.4
2022	SEA	4943	-4.7	-0.1	0.1	-4.7
2023	*FA*	*6956*	*-7.7*	*-0.1*	*0.0*	*-7.8*

For a while, Torrens was bobbing along as a nominal catcher with enough thump with the bat to justify his role on a major-league roster. The 2022 year saw both facets of Torrens' game sink well below the replacement-level surface. With Tom Murphy sidelined for the year in May due to labrum surgery, Torrens was forced into occasional appearances behind the dish because, well, Cal Raleigh can't catch *every* game. But the defense didn't even touch backup standards, as the M's acquired Curt Casali at the deadline to spell Raleigh. And the bat suffered a considerable drop-off, with the previous year's power vanishing in the mists over Elliott Bay. If you call yourself a catcher, you should probably be able to catch. And, if you identify as a designated hitter, well… you know. At the moment, Torrens can't plausibly wear either label, which goes a long way toward explaining why he was non-tendered by the Mariners in November.

Luke Voit DH

Born: 02/13/91 Age: 32 Bats: R Throws: R Height: 6'3" Weight: 255 lb. Origin: Round 22, 2013 Draft (#665 overall)

YEAR	TEAM	LVL	AGE	PA	R	2B	3B	HR	RBI	BB	K	SB	CS	Whiff%	AVG/OBP/SLG	DRC+	BABIP	BRR	DRP	WARP
2020	NYY	MLB	29	234	41	5	0	22	52	17	54	0	0	27.6%	.277/.338/.610	144	.268	-0.4	1B(48): -0.5	1.7
2021	SWB	AAA	30	36	8	3	0	4	9	3	8	0	0		.344/.417/.813	125	.350	-0.2	1B(6): -0.2	0.2
2021	NYY	MLB	30	241	26	7	1	11	35	21	74	0	0	40.5%	.239/.328/.437	95	.313	-1.3	1B(42): -1.1	0.2
2022	WAS	MLB	31	224	17	4	0	9	21	16	69	0	0	32.3%	.228/.295/.381	92	.294	-1.3	1B(26): 0	0.1
2022	SD	MLB	31	344	38	18	0	13	48	39	110	1	1	40.7%	.225/.317/.416	94	.302	-1.4	1B(11): 0	0.4
2023 DC	*FA*	*MLB*	*32*	*451*	*57*	*17*	*1*	*22*	*64*	*42*	*144*	*0*	*0*	*37.8%*	*.239/.323/.456*	*112*	*.313*	*-0.3*	*1B 0*	*1.2*

Comparables: Justin Bour (65), Cecil Fielder (61), Brian Daubach (59)

In 2020, Voit belted 22 home runs to lead MLB. In 2022, he hit 22 home runs and tied for 55th. Granted, the schedule was 102 games longer, but he still paced the bigs in two categories: Trades Thrown Into at the Last Minute Because Eric Hosmer Has a Limited No-Trade Clause (1) and Uniform Buttons Unfastened (3). Voit may have the physique and fashion sense of Gaston, but facing left-handed pitching, he hit like LeFou. He's always carried curious reverse platoon tendencies, but his .271 SLG against lefties last season was ghastly. Overall, his 18.7% swinging-strike rate was up more than five points from two years prior. As such, he's unlikely to be the Belle of the ball in free agency. *Noooo oooone whiffed like Luke Voit, declined swift like Luke Voit, yet the Nationals batted him fifth like Luke Voit.*

PITCHERS

Chris Archer RHP

Born: 09/26/88 Age: 34 Bats: R Throws: R Height: 6'2" Weight: 195 lb. Origin: Round 5, 2006 Draft (#161 overall)

YEAR	TEAM	LVL	AGE	W	L	SV	G	GS	IP	H	HR	BB/9	K/9	K	GB%	BABIP	WHIP	ERA	DRA-	WARP	MPH	FB%	Whiff%	CSP
2021	DUR	AAA	32	0	1	0	5	5	14	9	3	1.9	10.3	16	40.0%	.188	0.86	3.86	98	0.2				
2021	TB	MLB	32	1	1	0	6	5	19^1	18	3	3.7	9.8	21	31.5%	.294	1.34	4.66	115	0.0	92.3	45.0%	29.3%	55.8%
2022	MIN	MLB	33	2	8	0	25	25	102^2	87	12	4.2	7.4	84	43.5%	.260	1.31	4.56	113	0.3	93.3	35.7%	24.2%	54.4%
2023 DC	*FA*	*MLB*	*34*	*4*	*6*	*0*	*18*	*18*	*79.7*	*81*	*11*	*4.2*	*8.0*	*71*	*41.5%*	*.299*	*1.49*	*4.76*	*120*	*-0.2*	*93.4*	*39.6%*	*25.2%*	*52.8%*

Comparables: Bob Welch (78), Ken Hill (76), Bobby Witt (75)

Twenty batters: that was the limit. Not 18, which would make the most sense had the Twins decided that Archer was best suited to twice-through-the order usage. Not a certain pitch count; although Archer was largely held under 80, he had games of 88 and 90 pitches. No, 20 was the exact number of batters faced at which Minnesota yanked Archer on seven occasions, regardless of how his start was going. It wasn't tied to the incentive-laden contract the former Ray signed, which rewarded him for appearances. Whatever the reason, it didn't help a great deal. Archer mainly relies on two pitches: These days, the fastball lacks both movement and velocity, and the slider has lost its bat-missing vertical break. It probably *did* help that Archer didn't have to face the third or fourth hitters in a lineup for a third time, but we might have reached the point in his career when he should be facing a lot fewer than 20 batters per game.

Archie Bradley RHP

Born: 08/10/92 Age: 30 Bats: R Throws: R Height: 6'4" Weight: 215 lb. Origin: Round 1, 2011 Draft (#7 overall)

YEAR	TEAM	LVL	AGE	W	L	SV	G	GS	IP	H	HR	BB/9	K/9	K	GB%	BABIP	WHIP	ERA	DRA-	WARP	MPH	FB%	Whiff%	CSP
2020	CIN	MLB	27	1	0	0	6	0	7^2	4	1	0.0	7.0	6	50.0%	.143	0.52	1.17	110	0.0	94.3	65.3%	21.3%	50.4%
2020	AZ	MLB	27	1	0	6	10	0	10^2	13	0	2.5	10.1	12	31.0%	.448	1.50	4.22	97	0.1	94.1	66.5%	24.6%	48.3%
2021	PHI	MLB	28	7	3	2	53	0	51	51	5	3.9	7.1	40	56.0%	.299	1.43	3.71	107	0.3	94.2	70.5%	17.6%	52.8%
2022	SL	AAA	29	1	0	0	4	0	5^2	6	1	0.0	4.8	3	65.0%	.263	1.06	3.18	96	0.0	91.9	64.1%	17.8%	
2022	LAA	MLB	29	0	1	2	21	0	18^2	17	1	3.4	7.2	15	58.9%	.291	1.29	4.82	97	0.2	93.6	57.0%	20.3%	57.0%
2023 DC	*FA*	*MLB*	*30*	*2*	*2*	*0*	*43*	*0*	*37.3*	*40*	*3*	*3.6*	*7.1*	*29*	*52.9%*	*.313*	*1.49*	*4.54*	*112*	*-0.1*	*94.4*	*67.0%*	*20.7%*	*52.0%*

Comparables: Jeff Robinson (76), Tyler Clippard (73), Larry Sherry (71)

How rough was Bradley's season with the Angels? Andrew Wantz drilled Jesse Winker in the glute with a fastball, and it broke Bradley's arm. OK, sure, there was an intermediary step, as both benches cleared and Bradley, who had the misfortune of positioning himself in the dugout rather than in the pen that day, tumbled over the railing and planted his palm to break his fall, fracturing his elbow. The slip effectively wiped out the majority of his season, which also managed to include abdominal and forearm strains. When he did get out there, the former closer was mildly effective, but also demonstrated how he'll be a former closer from now on. His days of striking out batters with an upper-90s fastball are long gone, as he's wisely ditched his flagging four-seam for a sinker and the groundballs it offers.

Zack Britton LHP

Born: 12/22/87 Age: 35 Bats: L Throws: L Height: 6'1" Weight: 200 lb. Origin: Round 3, 2006 Draft (#85 overall)

YEAR	TEAM	LVL	AGE	W	L	SV	G	GS	IP	H	HR	BB/9	K/9	K	GB%	BABIP	WHIP	ERA	DRA-	WARP	MPH	FB%	Whiff%	CSP
2020	NYY	MLB	32	1	2	8	20	0	19	12	0	3.3	7.6	16	71.7%	.226	1.00	1.89	90	0.3	95.0	80.3%	25.8%	38.4%
2021	NYY	MLB	33	0	1	1	22	0	18^1	17	2	6.9	7.9	16	68.0%	.313	1.69	5.89	117	0.0	92.6	84.1%	25.2%	48.0%
2022	NYY	MLB	34	0	0	0	3	0	0^2	1	0	81.0	13.5	1	50.0%	.500	10.50	13.50	90	0.0	92.9	80.6%	25.0%	28.7%
2023 DC	*FA*	*MLB*	*35*	*1*	*1*	*0*	*28*	*0*	*25*	*26*	*2*	*6.0*	*8.1*	*22*	*67.5%*	*.320*	*1.73*	*5.31*	*122*	*-0.2*	*93.9*	*83.8%*	*24.6%*	*42.2%*

Comparables: Jason Isringhausen (67), J.C. Romero (66), Arthur Rhodes (65)

Britton desperately wanted to get back on the mound before the conclusion of the 2022 season, and to his credit, he did. He fast-tracked his recovery from September 2021 UCL construction surgery and got into a few games with the Yankees a year later. Unfortunately for him and the Yankees, Britton exhibited similarly diminished velocity as he did leading up to his injury, threw over half his pitches for balls, and ultimately left in the middle of an at-bat in just his third game of the season with what the team described as "arm fatigue." Any team that signs him will be getting a reclamation project, not a dominant lefty reliever.

Dylan Bundy RHP

Born: 11/15/92 Age: 30 Bats: S Throws: R Height: 6'1" Weight: 225 lb. Origin: Round 1, 2011 Draft (#4 overall)

YEAR	TEAM	LVL	AGE	W	L	SV	G	GS	IP	H	HR	BB/9	K/9	K	GB%	BABIP	WHIP	ERA	DRA-	WARP	MPH	FB%	Whiff%	CSP
2020	LAA	MLB	27	6	3	0	11	11	65^2	51	5	2.3	9.9	72	41.0%	.274	1.04	3.29	81	1.4	90.4	41.9%	29.5%	49.3%
2021	LAA	MLB	28	2	9	0	23	19	90^2	89	20	3.4	8.3	84	40.3%	.275	1.36	6.06	112	0.3	90.9	51.5%	23.1%	57.2%
2022	MIN	MLB	29	8	8	0	29	29	140	151	24	1.8	6.0	94	33.8%	.285	1.28	4.89	124	-0.3	89.1	46.7%	21.3%	58.2%
2023 DC	*FA*	*MLB*	*30*	*6*	*8*	*0*	*25*	*25*	*120*	*129*	*17*	*2.5*	*6.8*	*90*	*36.4%*	*.299*	*1.36*	*4.39*	*117*	*0.0*	*90.0*	*47.9%*	*23.2%*	*55.2%*

Comparables: Ken Brett (60), Edwin Jackson (58), Homer Bailey (58)

It's not really all downhill from 30. Just ask Justin Verlander or Nelson Cruz. For every aging curve-defying success story, though, there are many more players who feel the constraints of age in a far more typical manner. Then there are the Bundies of the world, who get started a little early on the downhill slope. Far from reversing the velocity decline that accompanied the rapid unraveling of his 2021 season, Bundy came out throwing exactly as hard as he had been in September of that year—and lost another half-tick as the season progressed. The result was easily the worst season of his career by DRA- and a below-replacement-level campaign. To Bundy's credit, the heater isn't playing any worse than when he threw 95 and he displayed an ability to get ahead in the count more often, mitigating his strikeout rate with fewer free passes. The problem is that it was never his best pitch, and everything else has performed worse as the velocity has dropped. At 30, he has the benefit of experience on his side. If the downhill slope continues, he won't have the benefit of anything else, including a big-league roster spot.

Andrew Chafin LHP

Born: 06/17/90 Age: 33 Bats: R Throws: L Height: 6'2" Weight: 235 lb. Origin: Round 1, 2011 Draft (#43 overall)

YEAR	TEAM	LVL	AGE	W	L	SV	G	GS	IP	H	HR	BB/9	K/9	K	GB%	BABIP	WHIP	ERA	DRA-	WARP	MPH	FB%	Whiff%	CSP
2020	CHC	MLB	30	0	1	1	4	0	3	2	1	3.0	9.0	3	62.5%	.143	1.00	3.00	110	0.0	93.7	81.4%	21.1%	42.1%
2020	AZ	MLB	30	1	1	0	11	0	6^{2}	9	1	5.4	13.5	10	31.6%	.444	1.95	8.10	81	0.1	93.7	70.9%	27.8%	45.9%
2021	OAK	MLB	31	2	2	5	28	0	29^{1}	24	3	2.1	8.3	27	36.6%	.266	1.06	1.53	104	0.2	91.3	75.0%	24.2%	53.2%
2021	CHC	MLB	31	0	2	0	43	0	39^{1}	21	1	2.7	8.5	37	49.5%	.204	0.84	2.06	89	0.6	92.7	71.2%	27.3%	57.1%
2022	DET	MLB	32	2	3	3	64	0	57^{1}	48	5	3.0	10.5	67	50.0%	.293	1.17	2.83	78	1.2	91.8	67.7%	31.7%	51.5%
2023 DC	*FA*	*MLB*	*33*	*2*	*2*	*0*	*50*	*0*	*43.7*	*40*	*4*	*3.1*	*9.5*	*46*	*46.9%*	*.302*	*1.27*	*3.36*	*90*	*0.4*	*92.2*	*69.1%*	*29.3%*	*52.0%*

Comparables: Justin Wilson (65), Jake Diekman (64), Alan Embree (60)

If 2021 proved that Chafin could sufficiently hold his own against righties and shed the LOOGY tag in a post-LOOGY world, last season demonstrated that he could go one step further. The veteran lefty held right-handers to a .586 OPS and posted a better strikeout minus walk percentage than he did against same-handed hitters. The key, it seemed, was fully shifting the orientation of his relatively pedestrian fastballs: He rarely threw the four-seam to righties, and turned to his sinker three-quarters of the time on the first pitch or if the batter was ahead. Against lefties, the four-seamer remained his primary offering. It helps that he is able to adjust each pitch's relative movement profiles, to spot both low and away as required, severely restricting the extra-base hits he allows. When Chafin had hitters from either side where he wanted them, he turned to that trusty slider to finish the job. The result was a second straight year as one of the most effective relievers in baseball, with no qualifiers required.

Aroldis Chapman LHP

Born: 02/28/88 Age: 35 Bats: L Throws: L Height: 6'4" Weight: 218 lb. Origin: International Free Agent, 2010

YEAR	TEAM	LVL	AGE	W	L	SV	G	GS	IP	H	HR	BB/9	K/9	K	GB%	BABIP	WHIP	ERA	DRA-	WARP	MPH	FB%	Whiff%	CSP
2020	NYY	MLB	32	1	1	3	13	0	11^{2}	6	2	3.1	17.0	22	27.8%	.250	0.86	3.09	77	0.3	98.1	76.9%	41.6%	50.4%
2021	NYY	MLB	33	6	4	30	61	0	56^{1}	36	9	6.1	15.5	97	41.9%	.287	1.31	3.36	66	1.5	98.5	62.3%	39.8%	54.7%
2022	NYY	MLB	34	4	4	9	43	0	36^{1}	24	4	6.9	10.7	43	35.6%	.241	1.43	4.46	110	0.2	97.8	60.5%	33.8%	53.7%
2023 DC	*FA*	*MLB*	*35*	*2*	*2*	*0*	*43*	*0*	*37.3*	*29*	*5*	*5.7*	*12.9*	*53*	*39.6%*	*.300*	*1.42*	*4.03*	*96*	*0.2*	*98.2*	*63.3%*	*34.0%*	*53.2%*

Comparables: Randy Myers (80), Armando Benitez (78), Jesse Orosco (78)

Chapman pitched poorly when he was on the field and alienated himself from the team when he was off it, most notably by failing to show up for a mandatory team workout prior to the postseason. His pitching-related struggles were best exemplified by an absolutely remarkable inability to throw the ball over the plate whenever a runner got on base. Of the 100 batters he faced last year with the bases empty, just eight of them reached via walk. But with runners on base, that tidy 8% walk rate shot up to an untenable 33%, by far the worst mark in the majors in that situation. Factor in that he had a career-low strikeout rate and a career-high ERA (both by a lot) AND that he'll be 35 this year, and there's really not a whole lot that's good to say about the pitcher who was once the game's primo velo-peddler.

Johnny Cueto RHP

Born: 02/15/86 Age: 37 Bats: R Throws: R Height: 5'11" Weight: 229 lb. Origin: International Free Agent, 2004

YEAR	TEAM	LVL	AGE	W	L	SV	G	GS	IP	H	HR	BB/9	K/9	K	GB%	BABIP	WHIP	ERA	DRA-	WARP	MPH	FB%	Whiff%	CSP
2020	SF	MLB	34	2	3	0	12	12	63^{1}	61	9	3.7	8.0	56	42.2%	.284	1.37	5.40	109	0.4	91.4	43.5%	20.0%	44.0%
2021	SF	MLB	35	7	7	0	22	21	114^{2}	127	15	2.4	7.7	98	37.2%	.336	1.37	4.08	100	1.1	92.0	51.4%	22.9%	54.1%
2022	CLT	AAA	36	0	1	0	4	4	15^{2}	15	3	2.3	9.8	17	57.1%	.308	1.21	5.17	85	0.3	90.8	39.4%	28.1%	
2022	CHW	MLB	36	8	10	0	25	24	158^{1}	161	15	1.9	5.8	102	42.0%	.296	1.23	3.35	116	0.2	91.5	43.0%	17.6%	51.5%
2023 DC	*FA*	*MLB*	*37*	*8*	*8*	*0*	*23*	*23*	*139.7*	*155*	*18*	*2.5*	*6.1*	*95*	*41.4%*	*.307*	*1.39*	*4.40*	*113*	*0.2*	*91.7*	*45.9%*	*19.4%*	*51.3%*

Comparables: Kevin Millwood (80), Tim Hudson (76), Jim Palmer (75)

ESPN's Jeff Passan wrote a feature story about Cueto in May, calling the veteran "the most interesting man in baseball" while detailing the tricked-out ambulance he bought and equipped with 22 speakers, among other eccentricities. That's likely nothing new to longtime followers of his Instagram, who are familiar with Cueto's affinity for horses, dancing and fine cuisine. What was surprising, likely, was that he regained on-field relevance. A minor-league signing by the White Sox in spring training after his big San Francisco contract fizzled, Cueto was thrust into the rotation thanks to injuries. He wound up with his highest innings total since 2017, and lowest ERA over a full season since 2016. The decline we saw with the Giants was still apparent, highlighted by a strikeout rate straight out of the 1980s, but Cueto proved valuable as a back-end workhorse. Injury risk and advanced age mean the phrase "rotation depth" is going to be most associated with Cueto, rather than any flowery epithets from his heyday, but he remains an absorbing personality—both on the mound and on social media.

Tyler Duffey RHP

Born: 12/27/90 Age: 32 Bats: R Throws: R Height: 6'3" Weight: 220 lb. Origin: Round 5, 2012 Draft (#160 overall)

YEAR	TEAM	LVL	AGE	W	L	SV	G	GS	IP	H	HR	BB/9	K/9	K	GB%	BABIP	WHIP	ERA	DRA-	WARP	MPH	FB%	Whiff%	CSP
2020	MIN	MLB	29	1	1	0	22	0	24	13	2	2.3	11.6	31	55.6%	.212	0.79	1.88	70	0.7	92.8	43.8%	36.4%	42.7%
2021	MIN	MLB	30	3	3	3	64	0	62^{1}	48	4	4.0	8.8	61	45.4%	.278	1.22	3.18	101	0.6	92.6	48.7%	23.6%	52.1%
2022	SWB	AAA	31	1	1	1	7	0	6	11	1	1.5	12.0	8	9.5%	.500	2.00	10.50	99	0.1				
2022	RR	AAA	31	1	0	0	4	0	5	5	0	7.2	9.0	5	40.0%	.333	1.80	0.00	99	0.0	91.6	51.0%	30.2%	
2022	MIN	MLB	31	2	4	2	40	0	44	45	8	3.1	8.0	39	45.4%	.303	1.36	4.91	101	0.4	92.4	51.1%	25.1%	50.8%
2023 DC	*FA*	*MLB*	*32*	*2*	*2*	*0*	*43*	*0*	*37.3*	*37*	*4*	*3.4*	*9.2*	*38*	*43.1%*	*.314*	*1.38*	*4.13*	*106*	*0.0*	*92.7*	*49.8%*	*26.3%*	*50.2%*

Comparables: Steve Karsay (80), Mike MacDougal (78), Kameron Loe (76)

It's hard work being a middle reliever. On July 24, Duffey had worked his way down to a respectable 3.86 ERA, having shrugged off a rough patch with 13 consecutive scoreless appearances, five of them for more than three outs. A week later he was unemployed. He signed with Texas and languished in Round Rock, then gambled on a spot opening up with the Yankees, moving to Scranton. The call never came. If Duffey saw decay in his pitches, it actually happened in 2021, when his trusty curveball stopped luring bats out of the zone, but it didn't really get tagged until last year. Based on the peripherals, it's not hard to believe that he's good enough to catch on somewhere for seventh-inning work, but based on those same peripherals, it's not hard to care if it isn't your team of choice.

Michael Fulmer RHP Born: 03/15/93 Age: 30 Bats: R Throws: R Height: 6'3" Weight: 224 lb. Origin: Round 1, 2011 Draft (#44 overall)

YEAR	TEAM	LVL	AGE	W	L	SV	G	GS	IP	H	HR	BB/9	K/9	K	GB%	BABIP	WHIP	ERA	DRA-	WARP	MPH	FB%	Whiff%	CSP
2020	DET	MLB	27	0	2	0	10	10	27^{2}	45	8	3.9	6.5	20	35.9%	.394	2.06	8.78	153	-0.5	93.1	62.3%	19.3%	43.2%
2021	DET	MLB	28	5	6	14	52	4	69^{2}	69	7	2.6	9.4	73	45.7%	.323	1.28	2.97	86	1.1	95.8	45.8%	29.8%	49.8%
2022	MIN	MLB	29	2	2	1	26	0	24^{1}	30	3	3.0	8.1	22	37.3%	.375	1.56	3.70	111	0.1	94.6	30.8%	28.0%	45.7%
2022	DET	MLB	29	3	4	2	41	0	39^{1}	29	1	4.6	8.9	39	32.7%	.264	1.25	3.20	99	0.4	94.5	26.8%	29.6%	53.3%
2023 DC	*FA*	*MLB*	*30*	*2*	*2*	*0*	*57*	*0*	*50*	*47*	*5*	*3.5*	*8.6*	*47*	*40.3%*	*.295*	*1.33*	*3.85*	*101*	*0.2*	*94.8*	*39.5%*	*27.4%*	*49.3%*

Comparables: Scott Bankhead (72), Tom Murphy (69), Wade Davis (66)

In his first full season pitching exclusively out of the bullpen, Fulmer embraced the freedom that the role offers him and leaned even more heavily on his slider. His fastball losing a tick may have had something to do with it. Just like his post-TJ 2020 season, the four-seam was easy fodder for hitters when Fulmer couldn't sit 95. No matter; he hurled slider after slider, turning to it almost two-thirds of the time. It worked well enough that the Twins traded for him mid-season, and he remained effective enough through the year's end. There aren't many new places for Fulmer to go from here, unless he can try out throwing 80% sliders if the rest of the arsenal gets any worse.

Zack Greinke RHP Born: 10/21/83 Age: 39 Bats: R Throws: R Height: 6'2" Weight: 200 lb. Origin: Round 1, 2002 Draft (#6 overall)

YEAR	TEAM	LVL	AGE	W	L	SV	G	GS	IP	H	HR	BB/9	K/9	K	GB%	BABIP	WHIP	ERA	DRA-	WARP	MPH	FB%	Whiff%	CSP
2020	HOU	MLB	36	3	3	0	12	12	67	67	6	1.2	9.0	67	41.8%	.321	1.13	4.03	83	1.4	88.2	42.4%	27.8%	45.2%
2021	HOU	MLB	37	11	6	0	30	29	171	164	30	1.9	6.3	120	44.9%	.264	1.17	4.16	115	0.3	89.0	45.9%	21.7%	53.0%
2022	OMA	AAA	38	2	0	0	2	2	12	7	1	0.8	6.0	8	45.5%	.188	0.67	2.25	98	0.2				
2022	KC	MLB	38	4	9	0	26	26	137	157	14	1.8	4.8	73	41.1%	.306	1.34	3.68	130	-0.8	89.2	41.4%	17.4%	53.5%
2023 DC	*FA*	*MLB*	*39*	*6*	*8*	*0*	*23*	*23*	*119.7*	*136*	*13*	*1.9*	*5.4*	*72*	*42.1%*	*.310*	*1.35*	*4.10*	*111*	*0.3*	*89.2*	*43.8%*	*20.1%*	*51.6%*

Comparables: Greg Maddux (73), Bert Blyleven (72), Don Sutton (71)

At some point soon will come that unforgiving yet cathartic moment when all 30 teams say "You, Zack Greinke, yes you ... we don't want you pitching for us." Last year, that number was still only at 29, as the Royals decided to make their rotation retro by offering their former ace a mid-March contract. The last time Greinke had pitched in Royals blue, his rotation-mates included Brian Bannister, Luke Hochevar and Bruce Chen. His contributions to the organization were vast, from his Cy Young season in 2009 to the many pieces of Kansas City's eventual World Series teams acquired via Greinke's trade to Milwaukee. His return in the flesh to The K brought back many pleasant memories, even if his production, solid ERA aside, was subpar. Greinke has been a treat to watch his entire career. Pretty soon, all 30 teams will be sad to see him go.

Brad Hand LHP Born: 03/20/90 Age: 33 Bats: L Throws: L Height: 6'3" Weight: 224 lb. Origin: Round 2, 2008 Draft (#52 overall)

YEAR	TEAM	LVL	AGE	W	L	SV	G	GS	IP	H	HR	BB/9	K/9	K	GB%	BABIP	WHIP	ERA	DRA-	WARP	MPH	FB%	Whiff%	CSP
2020	CLE	MLB	30	2	1	16	23	0	22	13	0	1.6	11.9	29	26.5%	.265	0.77	2.05	101	0.2	91.6	48.1%	24.8%	51.9%
2021	NYM	MLB	31	1	0	0	16	0	13^{1}	12	1	3.4	9.4	14	48.6%	.324	1.28	2.70	90	0.2	92.7	62.0%	22.8%	53.3%
2021	WAS	MLB	31	5	5	21	41	0	42^{2}	31	5	3.8	8.9	42	40.2%	.239	1.15	3.59	103	0.3	93.2	56.1%	19.8%	56.6%
2021	TOR	MLB	31	0	2	0	11	0	8^{2}	13	3	3.1	5.2	5	30.3%	.333	1.85	7.27	119	0.0	93.1	56.7%	22.2%	57.1%
2022	PHI	MLB	32	3	2	5	55	0	45	37	2	4.6	7.6	38	40.5%	.273	1.33	2.80	115	0.1	92.7	47.9%	18.6%	55.9%
2023 DC	*FA*	*MLB*	*33*	*2*	*2*	*0*	*43*	*0*	*37.3*	*34*	*4*	*3.7*	*7.6*	*31*	*39.0%*	*.280*	*1.34*	*4.19*	*105*	*0.1*	*92.7*	*51.5%*	*21.8%*	*54.9%*

Comparables: Dave Righetti (65), Arthur Rhodes (64), Dennys Reyes (61)

There was a time when Hand's slider was one of the best breaking pitches in baseball, but time is fleeting, and madness takes its toll. Over the past five seasons, his slider has gotten less and less effective, to the point where it's no longer a productive out pitch. Opposing hitters have learned to lay off his breaking balls outside the zone, and his strikeout-to-walk ratio has come crashing down as a result. The one thing Hand did really well in 2022 was limit home runs, but considering the number of hard-hit fly balls he allowed, don't expect him to keep that up. His season was rocky, and with the way things are trending, a horror show could be soon to come. Oh Brad!

Ian Kennedy RHP Born: 12/19/84 Age: 38 Bats: R Throws: R Height: 6'0" Weight: 210 lb. Origin: Round 1, 2006 Draft (#21 overall)

YEAR	TEAM	LVL	AGE	W	L	SV	G	GS	IP	H	HR	BB/9	K/9	K	GB%	BABIP	WHIP	ERA	DRA-	WARP	MPH	FB%	Whiff%	CSP
2020	KC	MLB	35	0	2	0	15	1	14	20	7	3.2	9.6	15	37.5%	.325	1.79	9.00	120	0.0	93.9	49.8%	21.5%	51.2%
2021	TEX	MLB	36	0	0	16	32	0	32^{1}	27	5	1.9	9.7	35	28.6%	.278	1.05	2.51	100	0.3	94.5	82.6%	29.0%	61.0%
2021	PHI	MLB	36	3	1	10	23	0	24	18	7	3.8	10.1	27	19.0%	.200	1.17	4.12	119	0.0	94.0	82.4%	26.3%	52.0%
2022	AZ	MLB	37	4	7	10	57	0	50^{1}	57	11	3.9	7.9	44	24.4%	.301	1.57	5.36	127	-0.2	93.3	81.3%	19.4%	56.0%
2023 DC	*FA*	*MLB*	*38*	*2*	*2*	*0*	*43*	*0*	*37.3*	*37*	*6*	*3.3*	*7.4*	*30*	*29.1%*	*.287*	*1.37*	*4.49*	*114*	*-0.1*	*93.8*	*77.7%*	*21.9%*	*55.2%*

Comparables: Cal Eldred (73), Floyd Bannister (65), Edinson Volquez (65)

For the better part of his 16-year career, Kennedy has basically been the big-league equivalent of a snake plant: He just needs water every now and then, is really hard to kill and should occasionally get re-potted. That may not be the best metaphor anymore, though. Struggles that bubbled to the surface after a 2021 trade to Philadelphia persisted, his fastball velocity took a step back and he allowed baserunners at an alarming rate. It culminated in his worst DRA- since the Yankees last tried using him as a starter 15 years ago. At this point, he feels more like a battery in the TV remote that has finally given out.

Corey Knebel RHP Born: 11/26/91 Age: 31 Bats: R Throws: R Height: 6'3" Weight: 224 lb. Origin: Round 1, 2013 Draft (#39 overall)

YEAR	TEAM	LVL	AGE	W	L	SV	G	GS	IP	H	HR	BB/9	K/9	K	GB%	BABIP	WHIP	ERA	DRA-	WARP	MPH	FB%	Whiff%	CSP
2020	MIL	MLB	28	0	0	0	15	0	13^1	15	4	5.4	10.1	15	33.3%	.314	1.73	6.07	116	0.0	94.6	62.7%	21.8%	45.9%
2021	LAD	MLB	29	4	0	3	27	4	25^2	16	2	3.2	10.5	30	45.9%	.233	0.97	2.45	89	0.4	96.4	58.1%	31.1%	56.1%
2022	PHI	MLB	30	3	5	12	46	0	44^2	33	4	5.6	8.3	41	38.2%	.244	1.37	3.43	106	0.3	95.9	69.9%	27.2%	52.4%
2023 DC	*FA*	*MLB*	*31*	*2*	*2*	*0*	*43*	*0*	*37.3*	*33*	*5*	*4.5*	*10.5*	*43*	*40.3%*	*.302*	*1.40*	*4.20*	*102*	*0.1*	*95.9*	*66.3%*	*28.1%*	*52.6%*

Comparables: David Robertson (68), David Riske (65), Trevor Rosenthal (64)

The Phillies spent $10 million on Corey in 2022, but the hotline didn't bling. His fastball velocity was down to start the season and batters were seeing his curveball better than they had in years. He threw a ton of pitches outside the zone, and opposing hitters kept their bats on their shoulders. Knebel started to look better in July, picking up heat with his heater and missing more bats with his curve, but a lat strain in August ended his season for good. Health has long been an issue for Knebel. Now it seems he can add "fastball velocity" and "throwing strikes" to his growing list of concerns.

Chad Kuhl RHP Born: 09/10/92 Age: 30 Bats: R Throws: R Height: 6'3" Weight: 205 lb. Origin: Round 9, 2013 Draft (#269 overall)

YEAR	TEAM	LVL	AGE	W	L	SV	G	GS	IP	H	HR	BB/9	K/9	K	GB%	BABIP	WHIP	ERA	DRA-	WARP	MPH	FB%	Whiff%	CSP
2020	PIT	MLB	27	2	3	0	11	9	46^1	35	8	5.4	8.5	44	41.8%	.239	1.36	4.27	107	0.3	94.1	43.9%	27.0%	44.2%
2021	IND	AAA	28	0	0	0	2	2	6^1	2	0	4.3	12.8	9	50.0%	.167	0.79	1.42	102	0.1				
2021	PIT	MLB	28	5	7	0	28	14	80^1	73	13	4.7	8.4	75	43.9%	.288	1.43	4.82	106	0.5	94.4	38.4%	27.0%	53.5%
2022	COL	MLB	29	6	11	0	27	27	137	155	25	3.8	7.2	110	36.7%	.313	1.55	5.72	131	-0.9	93.0	45.0%	23.7%	55.0%
2023 DC	*FA*	*MLB*	*30*	*6*	*8*	*0*	*23*	*23*	*119.7*	*127*	*17*	*4.2*	*7.8*	*103*	*39.1%*	*.315*	*1.53*	*5.13*	*120*	*-0.2*	*93.5*	*43.0%*	*24.7%*	*53.5%*

Comparables: Jason Jennings (80), Oil Can Boyd (78), Sidney Ponson (78)

As far as pitchers go, Kuhl is an extraordinarily bad fit for a place like Colorado. His fastball tops out at 93 mph, and his best weapon, a curveball, had to fight the flattening effect of the thin air a mile above sea level. Unsurprisingly, the result was your standard journeyman Rockies season: an ERA flirting with 6.00, a bunch of starts that were over before the fifth inning and a bottom-15 WARP among qualified starters. An added wrinkle was Kuhl's decision to shelve his mediocre fastball and replace it with an even worse sinker, one that was blasted to hell and back via a .367 batting average against, .599 slugging percentage against and .446 wOBA. Aside from a slider that graded out positively, there's not much here of interest. Kuhl's market this winter will likely be ... well, you know.

Mike Minor LHP Born: 12/26/87 Age: 35 Bats: R Throws: L Height: 6'4" Weight: 210 lb. Origin: Round 1, 2009 Draft (#7 overall)

YEAR	TEAM	LVL	AGE	W	L	SV	G	GS	IP	H	HR	BB/9	K/9	K	GB%	BABIP	WHIP	ERA	DRA-	WARP	MPH	FB%	Whiff%	CSP
2020	TEX	MLB	32	0	5	0	7	7	35^1	35	7	3.3	8.9	35	38.3%	.280	1.36	5.60	120	0.0	90.9	43.8%	24.6%	51.1%
2020	OAK	MLB	32	1	1	0	5	4	21^1	15	4	3.0	11.4	27	28.6%	.244	1.03	5.48	95	0.3	90.9	62.7%	32.1%	49.5%
2021	KC	MLB	33	8	12	0	28	28	158^2	156	26	2.3	8.5	149	38.4%	.291	1.24	5.05	110	0.7	91.1	42.8%	24.4%	52.8%
2022	LOU	AAA	34	1	2	0	4	4	16	15	3	0.6	11.2	20	36.4%	.293	1.00	3.38	90	0.3				
2022	CIN	MLB	34	4	12	0	19	19	98	120	24	3.7	7.0	76	33.7%	.312	1.63	6.06	162	-2.2	90.4	41.5%	20.1%	53.0%
2023 DC	*FA*	*MLB*	*35*	*4*	*5*	*0*	*15*	*15*	*79.7*	*84*	*14*	*2.9*	*6.5*	*58*	*35.7%*	*.293*	*1.38*	*4.73*	*115*	*0.1*	*91.1*	*43.5%*	*21.6%*	*52.0%*

Comparables: Mike Moore (70), CC Sabathia (67), Frank Viola (67)

Minor joined the Reds last year in a spring-training swap for Amir Garrett and was intended as an innings eater. Unfortunately, at his advanced (for sports) age of 34, the veteran lefty digested the innings as if they were cheese, and it was 10 p.m., and he had just gotten home from a long day at the office—meeting after meeting, all these meetings could have been emails—*I should have gone grocery shopping during the weekend when I had the chance, all I had in the fridge was some Babybels*. This wasn't a good idea. *This happens every time I go for the cheese late at night. My digestive tract is not what it used to be. I have a lot of things to think about*—not just eating habits, but life choices. He's now a free agent.

Matt Moore LHP Born: 06/18/89 Age: 34 Bats: L Throws: L Height: 6'3" Weight: 210 lb. Origin: Round 8, 2007 Draft (#245 overall)

YEAR	TEAM	LVL	AGE	W	L	SV	G	GS	IP	H	HR	BB/9	K/9	K	GB%	BABIP	WHIP	ERA	DRA-	WARP	MPH	FB%	Whiff%	CSP
2021	LHV	AAA	32	0	2	0	5	5	19^1	20	5	5.1	10.2	22	20.8%	.313	1.60	4.66	124	0.0				
2021	PHI	MLB	32	2	4	0	24	13	73	78	15	4.7	7.8	63	37.7%	.303	1.59	6.29	120	-0.1	92.6	56.7%	22.0%	51.9%
2022	RR	AAA	33	1	0	0	2	0	5	2	0	1.8	12.6	7	33.3%	.250	0.60	0.00	90	0.1	93.9	55.2%	39.4%	
2022	TEX	MLB	33	5	2	5	63	0	74	49	3	4.6	10.1	83	44.0%	.257	1.18	1.95	87	1.2	94.0	45.0%	31.3%	53.6%
2023 DC	*FA*	*MLB*	*34*	*3*	*3*	*0*	*65*	*0*	*56.3*	*52*	*8*	*4.3*	*9.6*	*60*	*40.8%*	*.294*	*1.40*	*4.27*	*106*	*0.1*	*93.4*	*50.1%*	*27.2%*	*52.9%*

Comparables: Derek Holland (61), Randy Wolf (61), Danny Jackson (60)

Moore is not the first post-prospect with big stuff and bigger walk rates to flourish after a move to the bullpen, but can anyone say they saw *this* level of success coming? After all, this is the same Moore who received a pink slip from a team as starved for pitching as the 2021 Phillies. Nevertheless, Moore persisted. He dropped his fastball usage from around 55% to under 45% and more than doubled his use of his breaker, spinning it 38% of the time. Moore's curve yielded an average launch angle of -3 degrees, which contributed to what was easily the best home run rate of his career. The 33-year-old may never start again, but he clearly has, *ahem*, Moore left in the tank as a reliever.

Craig Stammen RHP Born: 03/09/84 Age: 39 Bats: R Throws: R Height: 6'2" Weight: 228 lb. Origin: Round 12, 2005 Draft (#354 overall)

YEAR	TEAM	LVL	AGE	W	L	SV	G	GS	IP	H	HR	BB/9	K/9	K	GB%	BABIP	WHIP	ERA	DRA-	WARP	MPH	FB%	Whiff%	CSP
2020	SD	MLB	36	4	2	0	24	0	24	27	2	1.5	7.5	20	57.0%	.333	1.29	5.62	82	0.5	91.8	86.7%	24.1%	49.3%
2021	SD	MLB	37	6	3	1	67	4	88^1	79	13	1.3	8.5	83	55.1%	.273	1.04	3.06	81	1.7	91.7	70.0%	24.1%	55.2%
2022	SD	MLB	38	1	2	0	33	1	40^2	45	9	2.2	7.7	35	50.4%	.300	1.35	4.43	102	0.4	91.4	55.1%	26.3%	54.4%
2023 DC	*FA*	*MLB*	*39*	*2*	*2*	*0*	*50*	*0*	*43.7*	*46*	*4*	*2.1*	*8.0*	*38*	*51.8%*	*.316*	*1.28*	*3.71*	*97*	*0.2*	*91.8*	*69.2%*	*24.8%*	*53.2%*

Comparables: LaTroy Hawkins (76), Dennis Lamp (73), Jose Mesa (72)

Since joining the Padres prior to the 2017 season, Stammen has thrown 383.1 innings, more than any other reliever. With a mid-90s sinker and an aversion to walks, Stammen was always the pitcher the Padres could count on regardless of the situation. He could finish off games, come in during the middle innings and—as he did on the final day of the season—save the staff for another game.

After he missed two months with a shoulder injury and struggled when on the mound, the Padres told the reliever that he would be left off the Wild Card roster. So, on the last day of the regular season, they asked Stammen to go as long as he could. The low-velo hurler tossed 69 pitches—his most since 2010—and ate as many frames as he could for his club.

Now a free agent, the 39-year-old Stammen may be done in San Diego, but he should be remembered fondly by Padres fans for a long time.

Hunter Strickland RHP Born: 09/24/88 Age: 34 Bats: R Throws: R Height: 6'3" Weight: 225 lb. Origin: Round 18, 2007 Draft (#564 overall)

YEAR	TEAM	LVL	AGE	W	L	SV	G	GS	IP	H	HR	BB/9	K/9	K	GB%	BABIP	WHIP	ERA	DRA-	WARP	MPH	FB%	Whiff%	CSP
2020	NYM	MLB	31	0	1	0	4	0	3^1	5	0	2.7	10.8	4	72.7%	.455	1.80	8.10	80	0.1	95.9	57.4%	25.0%	47.9%
2021	MIL	MLB	32	3	2	0	35	0	36^1	21	4	3.0	9.4	38	31.1%	.198	0.91	1.73	99	0.3	94.9	55.6%	30.4%	53.7%
2021	TB	MLB	32	0	0	0	13	0	16	14	1	3.4	9.0	16	40.9%	.302	1.25	1.69	101	0.1	94.7	56.2%	26.0%	52.7%
2021	LAA	MLB	32	0	0	0	9	0	6^1	11	3	5.7	5.7	4	34.6%	.364	2.37	9.95	133	0.0	95.1	65.9%	17.5%	55.4%
2022	CIN	MLB	33	3	3	7	66	0	62^1	61	8	4.8	8.7	60	34.2%	.301	1.51	4.91	117	0.0	95.1	57.9%	27.8%	52.4%
2023 DC	*FA*	*MLB*	*34*	*2*	*2*	*0*	*57*	*0*	*50*	*48*	*8*	*4.0*	*8.5*	*47*	*35.9%*	*.294*	*1.42*	*4.74*	*112*	*-0.1*	*95.1*	*57.9%*	*26.8%*	*52.6%*

Comparables: Javy Guerra (55), Santiago Casilla (54), Nick Vincent (53)

Strickland was given his second chance to close games, and the first since 2018 with the Giants. After going 7-for-11 in save opportunities, and without a Slurpee machine in sight, he was relegated back to hard-throwing middle reliever, and his numbers became much more palatable. From here on out it's going to be one-year deals for the nine-year vet—sometimes a playoff team, sometimes a real stinker—for as long as he wants to be paid to watch the first six innings of a game from behind the outfield fence.

Michael Wacha RHP Born: 07/01/91 Age: 32 Bats: R Throws: R Height: 6'6" Weight: 215 lb. Origin: Round 1, 2012 Draft (#19 overall)

YEAR	TEAM	LVL	AGE	W	L	SV	G	GS	IP	H	HR	BB/9	K/9	K	GB%	BABIP	WHIP	ERA	DRA-	WARP	MPH	FB%	Whiff%	CSP
2020	NYM	MLB	28	1	4	0	8	7	34	46	9	1.9	9.8	37	36.4%	.366	1.56	6.62	104	0.3	93.8	42.5%	24.6%	49.4%
2021	TB	MLB	29	3	5	0	29	23	124^2	132	23	2.2	8.7	121	41.9%	.313	1.31	5.05	99	1.2	94.1	39.7%	23.1%	56.6%
2022	BOS	MLB	30	11	2	0	23	23	127^1	111	18	2.2	7.4	104	41.2%	.260	1.12	3.32	102	1.1	93.2	45.4%	20.7%	55.3%
2023 DC	*FA*	*MLB*	*31*	*7*	*7*	*0*	*22*	*22*	*119.7*	*119*	*14*	*2.5*	*7.1*	*94*	*42.1%*	*.298*	*1.28*	*3.70*	*96*	*1.2*	*93.5*	*43.9%*	*21.7%*	*54.3%*

Comparables: Milt Pappas (76), Bill Gullickson (74), Ismael Valdez (73)

Wacha is a sabermetric case study in how your eyes can lie to you. His sub-3.50 ERA was built on avoiding walks and hard contact; flinging precise changeups and cutters, he perfectly embodied the "crafty veteran" trope. So how did he end up, per the advanced numbers, posting a season right in line with (if not worse than) the three boring-as-oatmeal years before his apparent Boston renaissance? He barely struck anyone out, and on top of that, he benefited from a BABIP that was tied for 18th lowest among starters with 120 or more innings. His quality-of-contact stats aren't much prettier. That's why all the major pitching-independent metrics—DRA, FIP, xERA, etc.—paint Wacha as closer to a 5.00 ERA pitcher than the mid-rotation stalwart his surface stats suggest. Nonetheless, he'll likely earn a decent multi-year deal this winter—one that his new team may end up regretting if (or, more likely, when) the luck that propelled his 2022 dries up.

Luke Weaver RHP Born: 08/21/93 Age: 29 Bats: R Throws: R Height: 6'2" Weight: 183 lb. Origin: Round 1, 2014 Draft (#27 overall)

YEAR	TEAM	LVL	AGE	W	L	SV	G	GS	IP	H	HR	BB/9	K/9	K	GB%	BABIP	WHIP	ERA	DRA-	WARP	MPH	FB%	Whiff%	CSP
2020	AZ	MLB	26	1	9	0	12	12	52	63	10	3.1	9.5	55	32.7%	.349	1.56	6.58	120	0.0	94.0	54.0%	24.9%	48.5%
2021	RNO	AAA	27	0	0	0	2	2	7	6	0	5.1	15.4	12	33.3%	.400	1.43	3.86	84	0.1				
2021	AZ	MLB	27	3	6	0	13	13	65^2	58	11	2.7	8.5	62	37.5%	.266	1.19	4.25	96	0.7	93.7	61.9%	23.8%	55.1%
2022	RNO	AAA	28	0	0	0	2	1	6	6	1	3.0	7.5	5	27.8%	.294	1.33	3.00	113	0.0	94.1	60.2%	28.0%	
2022	KC	MLB	28	0	0	0	14	0	19^1	28	0	3.7	8.8	19	40.9%	.424	1.86	5.59	105	0.1	95.4	57.1%	21.3%	54.7%
2022	AZ	MLB	28	1	1	0	12	1	16^1	24	1	2.8	10.5	19	40.7%	.434	1.78	7.71	88	0.3	94.5	63.6%	24.7%	53.4%
2023 DC	*FA*	*MLB*	*29*	*2*	*2*	*0*	*43*	*0*	*37.3*	*37*	*5*	*3.0*	*8.0*	*33*	*38.8%*	*.294*	*1.33*	*4.02*	*106*	*0.0*	*94.2*	*58.6%*	*23.9%*	*52.5%*

Comparables: Wily Peralta (64), Mike Minor (59), Jon Gray (59)

A bigger Royals reclamation project than Prince Harry, Weaver failed to win a rotation spot out of spring training for the Diamondbacks. He nonetheless went on to pitch to varying degrees of success depending on which stat you like: his ERA was unsightly, his FIP was tiny and his DRA split the middle. His tumultuous era in the desert came to an end in August, when he was shipped to Kansas City. He tossed only a handful of innings as a Royal, was claimed off waivers by Seattle this winter, and was then non-tendered shortly thereafter. Now unencumbered by the need to live up to his inclusion in the Paul Goldschmidt trade—and with some very decent peripheral numbers—Weaver might finally be able to perform in a high-leverage hurling role sans pressure. We can only hope he finds some stability, because with all his drastic fluctuations it's a wonder he finds pants that fit.

Lineouts

Hitters

HITTER	POS	TEAM	LVL	AGE	PA	R	2B	3B	HR	RBI	BB	K	SB	CS	AVG/OBP/SLG	DRC+	BABIP	BRR	DRP	WARP
Luis Barrera	OF	LV	AAA	26	348	55	16	7	8	45	29	68	9	3	.263/.329/.436	99	.310	0.7	CF(35): 1.8, RF(26): 0.5, LF(23): 0.4	1.5
	OF	OAK	MLB	26	85	3	5	0	1	7	6	17	3	0	.234/.294/.338	89	.283	-1.5	LF(16): 1.1, RF(16): 0.1, CF(1): 0.1	0.1
Jackie Bradley Jr.	OF	BOS	MLB	32	290	21	19	1	3	29	17	58	2	3	.210/.257/.321	77	.257	0.2	RF(71): 1.3, CF(29): -0.2	0.2
	OF	TOR	MLB	32	80	9	4	0	1	9	7	19	0	0	.178/.250/.274	79	.226	-0.2	CF(26): -0.7, RF(20): 0.1	0.0
Lewis Brinson	OF	SUG	AAA	28	364	61	21	2	22	63	26	102	5	3	.299/.356/.574	114	.370	0.9	RF(30): 0.7, CF(27): -0.9, LF(16): 0.1	1.6
	OF	SF	MLB	28	39	5	2	0	3	4	2	14	1	0	.167/.211/.472	96	.158	-0.7	CF(15): -0.7	0.0
Marwin Gonzalez	UT	NYY	MLB	33	207	20	7	0	6	18	14	54	3	0	.185/.255/.321	83	.222	-1.2	SS(20): -0.2, RF(20): -0.1, LF(16): -0.7	-0.3
Josh Harrison	2B	CHW	MLB	34	425	50	19	2	7	27	21	71	2	1	.256/.317/.370	96	.297	-3.7	2B(90): -2.1, 3B(23): 1.3	0.6
Tim Locastro	OF	SWB	AAA	29	191	27	13	2	3	18	12	38	7	1	.240/.332/.395	101	.294	-0.4	CF(16): -2.1, LF(15): 1.0, RF(12): 0.6	0.3
	OF	NYY	MLB	29	46	13	1	0	2	4	2	7	8	2	.186/.239/.349	105	.176	0.3	LF(11): 0.1, CF(9): 0, RF(7): 0	0.2
Michael Perez	C	IND	AAA	29	27	3	1	0	0	2	10	5	0	0	.294/.556/.353	120	.417	-0.9	C(7): 0.7	0.1
	C	SYR	AAA	29	65	3	2	0	2	10	3	18	0	0	.183/.231/.317	85	.220	-0.2	C(15): -1.2	0.1
	C	PIT	MLB	29	116	8	0	0	6	11	8	26	1	0	.150/.209/.318	87	.133	0.3	C(38): 2.7	0.6
	C	NYM	MLB	29	16	2	0	0	0	3	2	6	0	0	.143/.250/.143	76	.250	0.0	C(6): -0.2	0.0
Edwin Ríos	3B/DH	OKC	AAA	28	218	32	17	0	9	39	20	66	0	1	.259/.339/.492	83	.339	-1.0	3B(33): -0.1	0.1
	3B/DH	LAD	MLB	28	92	12	1	0	7	17	5	36	0	1	.244/.293/.500	72	.326	-0.1	1B(4): 0, 3B(4): 0.3	-0.1

Longtime A's farmhand **Luis Barrera** had his moment in his 32-game run last year; his first (and so far only) big-league home run was a walk-off blast on May 14. The left-handed outfielder is known for his speed, which he'll use to try and catch on as a fifth outfielder somewhere. ⚾ After earning a DFA in his second stint with Boston, **Jackie Bradley Jr.** joined Toronto as a defensive reinforcement. He can still go get it in the outfield, but his bat has degraded such that the light at the end of the tunnel, once just a pinprick, has come screaming into view. ⚾ The McKinsey Group's sixth lever to success for organizations is "the right organizational structure and governance," which is what **Lewis Brinson** will be looking for as he signs on with potentially his potentially sixth organization. Hopefully whoever it is can govern him out of chasing so many pitches. His career is the reason prospect evaluators have trust issues. ⚾ He can't really hit anymore, but **Marwin Gonzalez** filled in all around the diamond—he played everywhere but catcher and center field, including a mop-up inning on the mound. The ringing-est endorsement of how valuable that stopgap glovework can be? He stayed on the Yankees roster throughout the regular season and first round of the playoffs. ⚾ **Josh Harrison**'s distinctive skill has long been getting out of pickles on the base paths; last season, he got himself out of the pickle of not hitting for the first few months, recovering to post an acceptable final line. A return to the White Sox at his $5.5 million option price tag didn't make sense for the club. As such, he'll have to find another short-term dill elsewhere. ⚾ **Tim Locastro** has become known for two things since first becoming a major leaguer: he's really fast, and he gets hit by a lot of pitches. There's not a whole lot to work with otherwise. It isn't fair to consider him as one-dimensional as, say, Terrance Gore, but Locastro has shown himself to be most valuable as a late-inning pinch-runner. ⚾ So woeful was the Mets' catching situation by midseason that they acquired **Michael Perez** from the Pirates for cash considerations ahead of the trading deadline. Pérez appeared in six games for the Mets in August when Tomás Nido spent a short stint on the COVID-19 injured list and collected just two hits over that span, but both of them drove in runs. ⚾ Big Daddy **Edwin Rios** was a surprising non-tender. He dealt with a significant hamstring injury (#TrueDodger) that landed him in Triple-A after he missed nearly 40% of the season because of it. At least he'll always have the memory of being the Dodgers' third baseman in the final two innings of their 2020 World Series-clinching game.

Pitchers

PITCHER	TEAM	LVL	AGE	W	L	SV	G	GS	IP	H	HR	BB/9	K/9	K	GB%	BABIP	WHIP	ERA	DRA-	WARP	MPH	FB%	WHF	CSP
Josh James	SUG	AAA	29	1	0	4	28	0	25^{2}	32	4	6.0	10.2	29	42.5%	.368	1.91	7.01	102	0.1	94.0	65.6%	26.0%	
Zack Littell	SAC	AAA	26	0	1	0	13	1	13^{1}	14	3	2.7	8.8	13	46.2%	.306	1.35	6.75	94	0.1	94.4	47.5%	31.8%	
	SF	MLB	26	3	3	1	39	0	44^{1}	48	8	2.6	7.9	39	43.1%	.310	1.38	5.08	103	0.4	94.5	50.7%	27.3%	54.6%
Sean Newcomb	IOW	AAA	29	1	1	1	12	1	24	12	1	6.7	11.6	31	46.0%	.224	1.25	3.38	84	0.5				
	ATL	MLB	29	0	0	0	3	0	5	7	1	7.2	7.2	4	27.8%	.353	2.20	7.20	116	0.0	94.6	89.7%	12.8%	57.2%
	CHC	MLB	29	2	1	0	17	1	22^{2}	26	7	6.0	9.5	24	34.8%	.306	1.81	9.13	114	0.1	93.6	84.8%	22.6%	55.5%
Garrett Richards	TEX	MLB	34	1	1	1	32	2	42^{2}	44	3	2.7	7.6	36	51.9%	.315	1.34	5.27	102	0.4	94.5	25.3%	26.1%	53.7%
Sergio Romo	SEA	MLB	39	0	0	0	17	0	14^{1}	18	6	2.5	6.9	11	18.4%	.279	1.53	8.16	135	-0.1	85.8	39.3%	20.6%	50.0%
	TOR	MLB	39	0	1	0	6	0	3^{2}	1	1	4.9	7.4	3	11.1%	.000	0.82	4.91	114	0.0	84.3	23.3%	29.2%	49.1%
Will Smith	ATL	MLB	32	0	1	5	41	0	37	35	7	5.1	10.0	41	34.6%	.280	1.51	4.38	103	0.3	92.3	41.8%	28.8%	51.4%
	HOU	MLB	32	0	2	0	24	0	22	23	2	1.6	9.8	24	33.9%	.350	1.23	3.27	85	0.4	91.9	41.5%	35.3%	52.1%

The Amazing Slider-Man ran into one enemy that couldn't be easily dispatched at the plate: Tommy John surgery robbed **Luke Jackson** of this entire season, but he'll surely be back to slinging sliders for one team or another once he's healthy. ⚾ Hip. Hamstring. Back. Lat. Arm. In some respects it's impressive that **Josh James** has pitched much at all since his 2019 breakout, given the parts of his body that have let him down. The performance has understandably suffered, to the point that Houston non-tendered him. ⚾ **Zack Littell** is probably most famous for chirping at manager Gabe Kapler for removing him for a left-on-left platoon in a late-season game against Atlanta. The two retreated to the clubhouse to discuss matters further, which led Kapler later to declaim "we're gonna appreciate and respect the highest level of teammate behavior, always" which is Kapler-speak for "get this person out of my face, immediately." His wish was granted when Littell elected free agency at the end of the season. ⚾ After five seasons, **Sean Newcomb**'s career as a not-quite-there-yet reliever in Atlanta came to an end when he was swapped to the Cubs for Jesse Chavez. About four of the 17 appearances the lefty made for Chicago, between waiver wire sojourns, could be considered complete disasters; the stuff that came in between those wasn't particularly enticing. ⚾ Baseball Reference shows one of **Garrett Richards**' nicknames to be Garrrrrett. That's five Rs, if you're counting, which is 11 fewer than he allowed across his final nine appearances with the Rangers before they DFA'd him in August. ⚾ Nine glorious seasons in San Francisco preceded six inglorious campaigns with seven other teams. Glory aside, **Sergio Romo** compiled a 3.21 ERA across 821 games—good for 49th all-time—all while beating the odds as a frisbee-slider-throwing soft-tosser. And hey, he'll always have that backward K. ⚾ Wake up, sheeple, **Trevor Rosenthal** isn't real: His 2020 resurgence was a pandemic-induced fever dream conjured by your feeble mind. He was not with the Brewers. He does not exist. And yes, he'll probably notch a handful of saves somewhere next season anyway. ⚾ Because the universe requires balance, there had to be a **Will Smith** that was prone to *getting* slapped while on the big stage. The former closer obliged, and will hope to get (Chris) rocked less at his next stop.

Fates and Futures

by Marc Normandin

John Helyar's vital baseball text, *Lords of the Realm*, was named that for a reason. For decades, Major League Baseball's owners styled themselves and acted as the unquestioned, unimpeachable lords of the realm of professional baseball. They'd go to war with upstart leagues, crushing these tiny rebellions and often absorbing them into their kingdom before they could grow into something larger and more dangerous—like, say, an alternative for the serfs they had control over. One that would have ended up being expensive for them, once they had to compete with.

These feudalistic analogies worked well for Helyar and analysis of the MLB of the past, as, until the big league players unionized for real, they didn't have a Magna Carta moment. The owners would occasionally grant the players a pittance to quell the rising tensions—like when a higher minimum salary and the concept of Murphy Money was introduced after labor lawyer Robert Murphy nearly got the Pirates to strike in protest of the reserve clause in 1946—but the idea that both the players and the owners were on any kind of equal footing, or that the players had actual rights and a say in their wellbeing, was preposterous to the owners across the league.

Hell, things were still like that for years and years and *years* after the Players Association formed and collective bargaining had become the norm. The lords were not keen on giving up what they felt was rightfully theirs. If you keep up with the news around the league—and you're reading this annual look at the state of things, so it's safe to say you do—they still aren't. But at least the presence of the MLBPA keeps the owners and the league from being able to act on those impulses in the way they would have 60 years prior.

At least, at the major-league level, anyway. Minor League Baseball's players were still subject to the whims of the MLB owners who paid their salaries and decided their fates. It was there that the feudalistic dreams of the lords lived on, where something approaching the reserve clause's control over players' fates and compensation could continue to persist. The players weren't organized, so there was nothing stopping the lords from directing their barons—the lesser owners of minor-league franchises—to make sure that life remained difficult for the serfs, and to be their eyes and ears if any potential rebellious behavior was on the rise. The parallels run out, and not in a good way; at least serfs had a place to live while they worked. Minor-league players had to pay for their own living space, for their own equipment and for their own meals for decades.

This is also in the past, however. Or, is on the way to being past. Minor-league players are now organized as well, in their own bargaining sub-unit under the larger MLBPA umbrella. There are myriad reasons why this couldn't happen until now. When the PA first seriously organized under executive director Marvin Miller in the '60s, the infrastructure simply wasn't there on the financial or technological sides to form a union of that size and scope, and future attempts at including minor-league players were met with (legally permissible) stonewalling from MLB's owners. (MLB and the PA had already agreed to the scope of the bargaining unit, so any attempts to expand that, such as during the 1994 strike, needed MLB's approval, which they of course were not going to give.) In 2022, however, with the players finally prepared to be unionized—the most vital and overlooked step that had been missing until now—and the PA ready to represent them in a *separate* unit, the last vestiges of MLB's feudalistic past are now on the verge of disappearing forever.

No longer will MLB be allowed to decide that they're going to shrink Minor League Baseball by disaffiliating dozens of teams, as they did before the 2021 season. No longer will wages be something that MLB can lobby Congress to suppress, as they did when they snuck the Save America's Pastime Act into a federal spending omnibus no one had the time to read before they voted on it. The league agreed to pay for players' housing prior to the 2022 season as a concession they hoped would stop any further thoughts of formally organizing, and while the results of that process weren't entirely satisfactory to the players, the key thing is that the concept existed before collective bargaining and will now continue to exist because of that precedent. This time around, due to unionizing, the players have a seat at the table to iron out all of those wrinkly details that should have been taken care of in the first place.

Exactly what the players end up agreeing to in their first-ever collective bargaining agreement with MLB is unknown at this time. Details on the opening negotiations have not yet emerged, and owners have thus far resisted their instincts of leaking to the more willing, mouthpiece-y portions of the press. What we do know, though, is that MLB can't force anything upon these minor leaguers any longer. A living, year-round wage that includes pay for spring training is on the table, to go along with improved housing plans, more robust health insurance, offseason training programs that players don't have to work a second job to fund, team-provided meals that even the Oakland A's won't be able to cheap out on and maybe even a little less team control over these players.

It's hard to overstate how much control over minor-league players' lives MLB's owners have. The existing Uniform Player Contract outright states that, "This Minor League Uniform Player Contract obligates Player to perform professional services on a calendar year basis, regardless of the fact that salary payments are to be made only during the actual championship playing season in which Player performs ... Player's physical condition is important to the safety and welfare of Player and to the success of Club. Thus, to enable Player to become properly fit for Player's duties under this Minor League Uniform Player Contract, Club may require Player's playing condition and weight during the off-season."

Or shorter, "You might not be getting paid in the winter, but don't forget that we own you."

The current UPC actually gives MLB the rights to *the likenesses of minor-league players*: once they had signed that Uniform Player Contract, they no longer owned their own faces and couldn't profit off of them, but MLB could. Which they did, once Sony's *MLB: The Show* video game franchise introduced real, playable minor-league players.

You can rip all of that up, though, just like the UPC that their big-league cousins operated under in the years before their first CBA: they're going to start over from scratch, and the players don't have to sign anything that forces them to continue to exist in such a state. If MLB is going to profit off of their likenesses in a video game, the players will be able to, as well. Minor-league players might even be able to get control of their own likenesses just like MLB's players have, creating revenue streams for the players (and the PA that represents them) that did not previously exist.

There have been significant moments in MLB's labor history since the signing of the first-ever CBA in North American professional sports in 1968, but what we saw occur within 2022 is as meaningful as any of them. At the big-league level, the players finally regrouped and rebuffed the ever-encroaching owners, who had been slowly rolling back gains made by the players in prior decades and setting themselves up to crush the union's power with an unnecessary lockout. MLB's owners have been quiet since the end of a lockout in which the players showed they could push back and pick up some wins once again, clearly regrouping for whatever the next plan of attack is going to be, like they did in the years after their defeat in the 1994-1995 strike that their actions forced into being. That would have been momentous on its own, but coupled with the unionization of the minor leaguers? There remains plenty to criticize in how 2022 went for the sport and the league, but on the labor side, things have maybe never been more promising, as now the thousands and thousands of minor-league players finally have the voice and seat they've desperately needed for a century.

Minor-league players are in control of their own fates and futures in a way they never have been before, and it's because the lords no longer wield the authority over them that they once did. It happened over five decades ago in the majors, and changed everything in a power struggle that hasn't yet been settled. The same is going to occur for minor-league players now, and while that struggle will also not be settled immediately, the fact it can be contested at all is the victory. ■

—Marc Normandin is an editor of Baseball Prospectus.

Top 101 Prospects

by Jeffrey Paternostro, Jarrett Seidler, Nathan Graham and Ben Spanier

1.) Gunnar Henderson, SS/3B, Baltimore Orioles

Sam Miller once wrote that "we're each of us a single machine, and all the little parts of that machine thrive off each other in some way that brings them all up or down together." So what happens when those little parts work together to pull an already very good prospect skyward? Henderson provides the answer, as he jumped from "interesting power/speed shortstop with hit tool questions" to "the best prospect in baseball." Over the course of 2022, Henderson's power projection ticked up from plus to plus-plus. His bat-to-ball abilities improved from below-average to solid-average or even a touch higher. He not only started chasing less but began taking pitcher's strikes early in the count and fouling them off in two-strike counts. All of those micro improvements led to one macro outcome: He's an exponentially better hitting prospect now because he makes more contact and does a lot more damage when he does. After spending the bulk of 2021 at High-A, where he hit .230 with a 30% strikeout rate, Henderson torched both levels of the upper minors all spring and summer—much of that before he could legally drink—to the score of a .297/.416/.531 slash line. Called up to the show that never ends on the last day of August to bolster Baltimore's unexpected playoff chase, he ended the season hitting .259/.348/.440 at age 21 in the majors while falling just short of losing rookie eligibility. We don't expect him to leave the dirt at Camden Yards for a very, very long time.

2.) Jordan Walker, OF/3B, St. Louis Cardinals

Walker began the season as a 19-year-old in Double-A and posted a near-.300/.400/.500 batting line. If he doesn't have the most raw power in the minors he's within a shout of the top of the list. While he still hits the ball on the ground a bit too much to get his 80-grade pop into games consistently, he started lifting the ball more over the course of the 2022 season. Walker knocked more than half his home runs after July 1, and he tightened up his ability to make contact in the zone as well. Walker is listed at 6-foot-5 and 220 pounds and both those measurements look light nowadays, so he's going to deal with some swing-and-miss given how long it will take his arms to get the bat through the zone. He's officially grown off third base as well, spending most of the latter half of the season in the outfield. The Cards are trying him a bit in center field—and he's still an above-average runner—but right field might be his ultimate home, where he should slug enough to be a star. Walker enters the 2023 season as a 20-year-old on the cusp of the majors and one of the top prospects in baseball.

3.) James Wood, OF, Washington Nationals

One of the single most important skills for a hitting prospect is the ability to make contact within the strike zone. Scouts express this as "bat-to-ball," analysts as "Z-Contact" or its inverse, "In-Zone Whiff." Unlike for the majors, you can't go on our website or FanGraphs or Baseball Savant or anywhere else to find it comprehensively for minor leaguers (at least not yet), but it's incredibly important. It was considered Wood's major flaw out of the draft, except then he went to Low-A and displayed superior in-zone contact ability—both from an eye-scouting perspective and an analytical one—to most of the hitters surrounding him near the top of this list. Given that he already had among the highest power potentials in the entire minor leagues and makes solid swing decisions...well, he missed some time last year with knee and wrist injuries, but other than that there's not much to nitpick here. If the Juan Soto trade ends up working out for Washington, Wood will probably be the reason why.

4.) Francisco Álvarez, C, New York Mets

Álvarez is a short, wide backstop who was a fringy defender behind the plate before his offseason ankle surgery. He must really be able to hit, huh? Well, he's hit 51 dingers the last two seasons in the minors in just a shade over 200 games. Álvarez is plenty twitchy at the plate where he flashes plus-plus bat speed and raw power. He can get a bit pull-happy and has an expansive view of what he can hit hard, but he's been one of the youngest players at every minor-league stop and he's the first notable catching prospect to debut at 20 years old since Dioner Navarro. He's about as high-variance as you will find in a top-five prospect. If Álvarez can't catch, he's not athletic enough to play elsewhere in the field, and while he could hit enough to be a good designated hitter, we don't really rank future DHs this high. If he can stick behind the plate—and there has been some year-over-year improvement in his receiving—well, how many catchers out there are banging 30+ home runs?

5.) Elly De La Cruz, SS, Cincinnati Reds

De La Cruz has the best chance of any prospect to be a franchise-defining, face-of-baseball kind of superstar. He's an electric athlete, with a mix of fast-twitch movements, body control, size and speed, which is unparalleled across the minors. He has true top-of-the-line bat speed with surprisingly strong barrel control from both sides of the plate. If just *one thing* clicks a little bit more for him, he's going to be a superstar. But at present, he simply chases outside the zone way, way, **way** too much. Like, "as much as anyone in the majors but Javier Báez" too much—and that's against minor-league pitching. De La Cruz hasn't actually needed to improve his approach to perform yet—he hit .304 and slugged .586 last year, as neither High-A nor Double-A pitchers could actually exploit his love for swinging at breaking balls low and fastballs high, which speaks to the special nature of his bat. When and if that day comes, he'll either make the adjustment and become one of the best players in the game, or "what if Elly De La Cruz made average swing decisions?" will become a question we ask ourselves for decades to come.

6.) Corbin Carroll, OF, Arizona Diamondbacks

Carroll has recovered nicely from a shoulder injury that cost him almost all of the 2021 season. He posted a 1.000 OPS in the upper minors—despite a mere 29 full-season plate appearances previously—and added an .830 OPS in the majors at the end of 2022. Amarillo, Reno and Chase Field are three very nice places to hit mind you, and Carroll posted a pretty significant platoon split. If we nitpick further, his contact rates and exit velocities were just "fine," and he isn't the most natural center fielder despite good foot speed. Carroll also doesn't have a real weakness in his game; he's a potential 20/20 outfielder who should get on base and impact the game with his speed. He's the favorite for 2023 National League Rookie of the Year, and as likely to be a perennial above-average regular as anyone in the top 10 other than Henderson. All our nitpicks just mean he's the sixth-best prospect in baseball rather than the second.

7.) Anthony Volpe, SS, New York Yankees

"Anthony Volpe will have to be ___ to validate himself in view of [insert angsty Yankee fan's grievance with the organization here]" will never be an easy bar to clear, especially for a prospect who, despite his universally agreed upon global top-10 status, is a sum-over-parts type of talent. All of those parts are above-average or better, of course, which is what gives this Jersey guy a chance to be the Yanks' best first-round outcome since Aaron Judge. Volpe maintains his hit tool well even with a very modern swing designed to lift the ball as much as possible, and his glove, arm and instincts make him a good shortstop who may profile more cleanly as a very good third baseman. He also generates additional value with his opportunistic baserunning and feel for the game. He'll be up sometime in 2023. So, an infielder who makes multiple All-Star games probably clears the bar. (Alright, who are we kidding? He needs to win a World Series.)

8.) Grayson Rodriguez, RHP, Baltimore Orioles

Rodriguez remains the best pitching prospect in baseball due to a combination of some major service time shenanigans and a minor lat injury. Oh, and the stuff. The stuff is really good. He came out dominating Triple-A as he has every other stop on the Orioles organizational ladder. He flashes five potential above-average pitches including a mid-90s—touching higher—fastball and a potential plus-plus change and slider. The curve and cutter are pretty good as well. Rodriguez didn't always have the breaking balls working for him consistently—especially post-injury—but his arsenal is so deep he can pick and choose what looks good on the menu from start to start. And when the full five-course Michelin-starred meal is on offer, he looks like a budding ace. His command is maybe a bit too far to the fringe side of average to project as a no. 1 starter quite yet, so look for Baltimore to have Rodriguez work on that in Norfolk for, oh, let's say the first three or four weeks of 2023.

9.) Jackson Holliday, SS, Baltimore Orioles

In a year's time, Holliday went from a projected second-round pick who might head to Oklahoma State to play for his uncle to the 1.1 pick and a spot atop a trio of brilliant emerging prospects named Jackson. As the pre-draft process unfolded, Holliday emerged late as the best prospect in the class, pairing incredibly advanced swing decisions with a tremendous feel for contact; his chase and zone-contact rates are just stupendous for his age, and we know in 2023 that's what drives a lot of hit tool development. Holliday has decent power projection too, and on top of it all he's likely to stick at shortstop from a talent perspective, although the Orioles have three other middle infielders on this list, so where everyone plays in 2025 is a ball still up in the air. Matt Holliday made seven All-Star teams and tallied over 40 WARP, so it's going to be quite an uphill climb for his son to become the best player at Christmas dinner. But it's possible.

10.) Jackson Chourio, OF, Milwaukee Brewers

Chourio might end up an interesting test case in the sometimes tense relationship between traditional eye-scouting and modern batted ball data. On one hand it is beautiful to watch him play—the Maracaibo, Venezuela native is a superior athlete who runs and throws well enough to stick in center long-term, and at the dish he showcases an explosive swing with advanced balance and torque designed to get as much power as he can out of his frame. On the other hand, that frame isn't huge, and there is room for improvement in both swing decisions and quality of contact. What can't be debated is Chourio's precociousness—the man was born in 2004 and dominated full-season ball as an 18-year-old (.324/.373/.600 at Low-A, .252/.317/.488 at High-A), drawing comparisons to Trout, Harper and Stanton. It remains possible that he blitzes Double-A and Triple-A in short order and ends the conversation before it can begin.

11.) Eury Pérez, RHP, Miami Marlins

The towering righty—now listed at 6-foot-8, and that might be short—kept climbing up the ranks by reaching Double-A a week before his 19th birthday and striking out 110 batters over 77 innings. Ho-hum, totally normal stuff. Pérez has a full four-pitch mix now and they're all pretty developed. His fastball easily sits in the mid-90s and regularly gets into the upper-90s; it doesn't have true bat-missing shape so it has induced more weak contact over swinging strikes, but it's still a decent fastball. He already had a breaking ball that flashed plus dating back to 2021, and he's more recently added a hard slider that is also going to be an above-average to plus offering. His changeup has also flashed huge in bursts, although he hasn't leaned on it a ton yet, and it's worth noting that Miami has shown elite skill at maximizing that particular pitch, sometimes at the MLB level. Pérez fills up the zone and gets both chases and whiffs. Overall, he has everything you could want in an elite pitching prospect short of an obvious 80-grade pitch. He only pitched four innings after the first week of August while battling a reported minor shoulder issue.

12.) Andrew Painter, RHP, Philadelphia Phillies

As good as Pérez is, he may not even have the best pure stuff for a teenage pitching giant who has already reached Double-A. Painter, who reached that level for a five-start end-of-season run (with a strikeout-to-walk ratio of 37:2), throws a tick or two harder than Pérez, regularly hitting triple-digits. And his heater *does* have carry and movement that misses bats up and out of the zone. Painter primarily throws two breaking balls off his fastball, a diving curve and a sweeping slider, both of which only have above-average visual properties but miss bats at plus to plus-plus levels. His changeup is lagging currently but should improve with additional use. Painter has yet to be challenged as a pro and, coming off one of the best modern minor-league pitching campaigns by a teenager, it's plausible he opens 2023 in the majors while still just 19.

13.) Marcelo Mayer, SS, Boston Red Sox

Mayer might have been the top hitting talent in the 2021 amateur class at the time of the draft, and 18 months or so later, he still only ranks behind James Wood. Drafting is an inexact science, but Mayer's talent isn't mere hypothesis at this point. He hit for average and power across both A-ball levels and showed off enough faculty in the field that we are a bit more confident he sticks at shortstop than we were on draft day. Mayer may not end up with a true plus tool in his locker—although both hit and power have more than a puncher's chance—so his level-by-level progression will be important to watch. He will get to Double-A at some point in 2023, perhaps even starting there—pack layers for Portland in April, Marcelo—and his Eastern League performance will either stamp him as a top-10 prospect in baseball or reveal the cracks in the offensive tools.

14.) Jackson Merrill, SS, San Diego Padres

This has been one heck of a two-year rocketship ride. Merrill was largely unknown to amateur scouts entering the 2021 prep season, an obscure kid from suburban Maryland who hadn't done much on the showcase scene before the pandemic hit. A couple months before the draft, his name started being whispered about in hushed tones by the few who had seen him as one of the secret best prospects in the draft due to late physical and hit tool development. Then general managers started showing up in Severna Park, and it became clear he was going to go in the top few rounds of the 2021 Draft as a potential star two-way shortstop. Despite the lack of foundation, the risk-tolerant Padres ultimately popped him with the 27th pick. After looking the part in the complex after the draft, Merrill was a top priority follow coming into 2022, where he promptly displayed a preternatural feel for hard contact despite having little experience hitting off anyone better than Annapolis-area high school pitchers and missing a bunch of time with a wrist injury. He does hit the ball way too much on the ground at present, but it's his only analytic flaw—and perhaps the only thing stopping him from being the best prospect in baseball in a year's time.

15.) Ricky Tiedemann, LHP, Toronto Blue Jays

It will take a few years to suss out the player development effects from the lost 2020 pandemic season. One thing it did do was send some prep players—who may have broken out and become major draft prospects—to college. Tiedemann was one such arm, heading off to junior college and becoming a 2021 third-rounder, the Golden West Rustlers' highest draft pick since Keith Kaub in 1986. Tiedemann's velocity popped into the mid-90s by the time fall instructs rolled around and he spent 2022 blitzing three levels of the minors, whiffing almost 40% of the batters he faced. His slider was the big riser in 2022, while he held his velocity gains, giving him two potential plus-plus pitches with a pretty good change to boot. There's a bit more uncertainty with Tiedemann compared to the arms ahead of him. He tossed just 78 innings last year following a short JuCo season in 2021 and a lost season in 2020. But he's merely a year away from erasing those concerns, and if he does this will likely be the last time we get to rank him. So let's just get our marker down under the wire here: Tiedemann has a good shot to be a top-of-the-rotation lefty, anchoring the Blue Jays rotation with Alek Manoah for years.

16.) Curtis Mead, 3B/2B, Tampa Bay Rays

Curtis Mead is an extremely good hitting prospect, justifying an aggressive ranking despite a murky and not altogether encouraging defensive outlook. The guy just hits, slashing .305/.394/.548 at Double-A in 2022 and following it up with .278/.377/.486 in a brief Triple-A campaign. He hits the ball early, hits it often and hits it very hard. He has a longish swing but a quick bat, and a plus power outcome is well within reason. What position will he be playing? TBD. He is still primarily a third baseman, but his actions and arm there aren't great. In the past, it may have been tempting to stick him at second despite his limited athleticism, but the new shift rules will make that difficult. First base is his likely landing spot, and that'll do just fine if he keeps hitting. Oh, and he's from Australia. We meant to make a joke about that.

17.) Brett Baty, 3B/OF, New York Mets

At a glance, Baty's 2022—.315/.410/.533 in the high-minors with the Mets briefly entrusting him with a regular job in a desperate pennant race before he hurt his thumb—seems valedictory. Under the hood, there's some real concern. Despite occasional glimpses of progress, Baty has continued to hit the ball on the ground way more than you want an emerging power threat to do. In practice, that means although he already hits the ball harder than most major-leaguers and flashes 80-grade power when he does lift and drive it, it's hard to actually project him for 30+ homers in the majors without changes. Things aren't much clearer for him in the field; despite decent fluidity and a big arm, he's never displayed a consistently reliable glove at third, and his frame is on the larger side for the hot corner anyway. Recent developments in Flushing threaten to push him to the outfield—where he's made occasional forays already but needs more experience—if he remains a Met at all.

18.) Marco Luciano, SS, San Francisco Giants

The zeal of the convert has its limits. Luciano dropped stateside and onto prospect writers' radars just as minor-league exit velocity was becoming more widely available, and subsequently a factor in things like...well, this list. His second appearance on our Top 101—this is year four—noted his 119-mph home run in fall instructs. But after four years, Luciano is still in High-A, has yet to dominate a minor-league level and dealt with a back strain that cost him two months of the 2022 season. Perhaps that is a bit unfair. He had a great stretch in Eugene before the back injury, showing both mechanical and approach improvements at the plate. He's still playing shortstop everyday and faced only a handful of pitchers younger than him in the Northwest League. He's stagnated a bit in recent years, but with tools like these—as John Darnielle once wrote—something here will eventually have to explode, have to explode.

19.) Diego Cartaya, C, Los Angeles Dodgers

Cartaya stands out on the diamond, both for his physical size and his ability to impact the baseball at the plate. He's always been viewed as a hit-first prospect since coming stateside in 2019, but he's made strides with the glove, becoming a passable receiver behind the plate. Despite his lack of foot speed, he has enough lateral quickness to block well and a strong enough throwing arm to keep opponents from running wild on the bases. The Dodgers also love the soft skills he displays, raving about his leadership and ability to handle a pitching staff. The defensive gains are a bonus, but the carrying tools remain with his bat. He has double-plus power and he does pretty well getting to it in-game, recognizing spin well and having a feel for the barrel. There's still plenty of polishing remaining before Cartaya is big league-ready, but if it all comes together he'll become a power-hitting backstop, a rare commodity in today's game.

20.) Kyle Harrison, LHP, San Francisco Giants

Harrison has an analytically friendly modern starting arsenal. He comes from a very low arm slot for a starting pitcher and primarily works off two pitches that play well from that angle. His fastball velocity and spin is just fine—yes, low-to mid-90s is "just fine" now—but it plays well and induces plenty of swings-and-misses up in the zone due to his slot and the deception of perceived rise. The fastball tunnels well with his out-pitch, a dastardly sweeping slider that he uses to beat batters around the edge of the zone. He also mixes in a changeup with above-average potential. Harrison could use some improvements in command, but his fastball/slider combination gives him top-of-the-rotation potential.

21.) Ezequiel Tovar, SS, Colorado Rockies

Tovar is as complete a shortstop prospect as you will find in the minors. He's the best shortstop glove thus far on our list, a polished present plus defender who does everything well in the field. He will hit for average, hit for power—Coors won't hurt on either account—and he's a heady baserunner, if only a solid runner. He was the second-youngest player in the majors when he debuted in September. So why isn't Tovar up with the top shortstop prospects above? Well, we think he will hit for average, but that average will be in the .270 range—in a vacuum; again, Coors—and he was overmatched by better spin at times in Double-A. He needs to fill out and get stronger—especially in his upper half—to tap into the present sneaky pop. We think these things will all happen, and he will be one of the youngest players in the National League again in 2023, where he might just put some pressure on Corbin Carroll for that Rookie of the Year crown. But they haven't happened yet.

22.) Evan Carter, OF, Texas Rangers

Amidst the never-ending story that is the Rangers attempting to develop a hitting prospect to preconceived expectations, Carter represents the possibility for an apotheosis of sorts. Unlike top Texas prospects from 101s past, Carter is not a player outfitted with speed, defensive skills and elite athleticism who needs simply to develop the most difficult of tools, the ability to hit, in order to become a star. It isn't that Carter doesn't possess those traits—he does, in spades. What differentiates him from the others is that there are indications in his offensive performance that he shares characteristics with the types of prospects who become successful big-league hitters. Carter is extremely selective at the plate and makes excellent swing decisions, producing rock-solid numbers (.287/.388/.476 at High-A Hickory) that earned him a late-season taste of Double-A as a 19-year-old. The frame is still a bit willowy and he doesn't currently hit the ball extremely hard, so pop may be the last tool to appear.

23.) Taj Bradley, RHP, Tampa Bay Rays

Like his org-mate Curtis Mead, Bradley has acquitted himself well in Triple-A and should expect to debut sometime in 2023. Once an overslot fifth-round prep, the now-21-year-old has pretty clearly been the top non-Shane Baz Rays pitching prospect since mid-2021, when he was striking out all comers in the lower minors with an analytically appealing mid-90s fastball, a killer cut/slider thing and a very good curve. At one point it was fun to discuss Bradley's future role —the Rays, creative or nickel-and-dime depending on your vantage, would certainly find an interesting way to deploy him, even if not as a strict starter or reliever. A year of dominance in the upper minors—he would boast a 1.70 ERA and 30.9% strikeout rate over 74⅓ Double-A innings before drifting a bit nearer to earth following the midseason promotion to Durham—made it clear that Bradley projects as a starting pitcher. The question now: Will his health hold up better than it has for other recent Rays power arms?

24.) Jordan Lawlar, SS, Arizona Diamondbacks

You could argue, as we did, that Lawlar was the best prep shortstop prospect in the 2021 draft class. While perhaps lacking the same upside with the bat as Mayer, he was the more advanced hitter and that bore out in their first pro seasons. Lawlar made it all the way to Double-A in his age-19 season, hitting .300 with power. He has less projection in his bat, though, and his propensity to swing-and-miss in the zone is a concern, underpinning a strikeout rate that's a tad higher than you'd like for a plus, but not elite offensive profile. Lawlar has also looked a bit more like a second baseman than a shortstop in the pros, with throwing being a particular issue—he's the second of three Diamondbacks first-round picks who've suffered horrible shoulder injuries that you will encounter on this list. So no, we don't think he's the best prep prospect in his class anymore, but he's still a very, very good one.

25.) Daniel Espino, RHP, Cleveland Guardians

If we had run a Top 101 Prospects list in late-April 2022, Espino would've easily been in the top half-dozen, and perhaps even at no. 1 overall. For a few weeks there, he looked like the best pitching prospect in recent memory. Espino was nuking Double-A hitters with three offerings projecting in the plus-plus to 80-grade band: a fastball hitting triple-digits with killer characteristics, one of the best sliders in the entire minors and a distinct downer breaking ball. He struck out 35 in 18⅓ innings over his first four starts, and was headed toward having a big impact on the pennant race. Then he was shut down with a reported knee injury. He never got back into games, and by the summer the Guardians acknowledged he was battling shoulder soreness. Given that his huge jump in stuff was almost immediately followed by a barking shoulder, we certainly have significant concerns about sustainability and durability. But man, it's the best stuff on the list.

26.) Gavin Williams, RHP, Cleveland Guardians

Speaking of Guardians pitchers with latent medical concerns, we wrote last year that if Williams sustained the health and performance he showed during the 2021 college season, he'd very quickly be one of the top pitching prospects in the minors. Well, he more or less did, and here he is. This isn't the world's most complicated profile, and it's extremely Guardians in the way that they maximize every college pitching prospect possible. Williams throws strong characteristic mid- to upper-90s fastballs, plus some sliders, up in the zone, and everything else down. At present he leans most on his slider out of his secondary offerings, although his curveball is more consistent and he's also developing a useful changeup. He's had two clean, dominant seasons in a row, and the years where he was struggling with ineffectiveness and injury in the East Carolina bullpen are now long in the rearview mirror.

27.) Bobby Miller, RHP, Los Angeles Dodgers

You'll notice a theme as you read through the reports on Dodgers' pitchers on this list—they have power stuff with less than ideal command—and nobody fits that profile better than Miller. His four-seam fastball flirts with triple digits, has decent ride and holds its velocity deep into games. He'll even mix in an occasional sinking two-seamer to keep hitters honest. The breaking stuff, a 12-5 curve and power slider, both have the makings of knee-buckling offerings that can miss bats. Throw in the change, which has excellent velocity separation, and you have the repertoire of a front-line starter. He got hit a little harder than expected during his time in the hitter-friendly Texas League but looked more the part of top prospect after his late-season promotion to the PCL. While his command isn't great and he could use a bit more polish in the upper minors, Miller is another weapon the Dodgers can utilize down the stretch in 2023.

28.) Pete Crow-Armstrong, OF, Chicago Cubs

Part of the prospect haul the Cubs garnered in their 2021 selloff, PCA used his first healthy minor-league season to plant his flag as the top prospect in the organization. An intense competitor with a high motor, he's an excellent defender whose plus range and instincts will allow him to patrol center field in Wrigley for the foreseeable future. The defense and speed give him a reasonably high floor but it's the bat that will have him in future All-Star conversations. He's an intelligent hitter, always tinkering and making adjustments to maximize his simple, efficient swing. Exceptional bat control and speed make for plenty of loud contact off the bat. While he's never going to be a slugger, he added some physical strength while rehabbing a shoulder injury, and that led to an increase in the over-the-fence power last season. Crow-Armstrong should serve as a table-setter atop the lineup for the next competitive Cubs team.

29.) Noelvi Marte, SS/3B, Cincinnati Reds

Marte was a casualty of the Mariners going all in at the deadline in an attempt to end their long playoff drought. It worked out for them, but for Marte, joining the Reds meant being part of an organization deep in shortstop talent. Cincinnati sent him to the AFL to get some reps at third but he struggled there, committing six errors in just 20 games. It really doesn't matter where he winds up defensively—the bat is the calling card in the profile. He possesses double-plus raw power and he knows how to get to it in-game without sacrificing contact ability. His approach at the plate is advanced, especially for a young player, as he commands the zone well and punishes mistakes. The jump to Double-A can be daunting, and he's sure to be tested by the advanced arms of the Southern League this year, but his huge offensive upside gives Cincinnati something to dream on no matter where he lands defensively.

30.) Masyn Winn, SS, St. Louis Cardinals

Drafted as a two-way player, there's not a lot of talk about Winn returning to the mound now that his bat has taken a large step forward. He looked overmatched in his initial professional season, getting overpowered by High-A pitching. He spent the following offseason getting stronger and more physical, and the results showed it in 2022. Pitchers could no longer overwhelm him with velocity as he began to impact the ball with more frequency. His throwing arm from short is unrivaled and he's not too shabby with the glove either. Those tools, plus his quick hands and excellent range, will make him an everyday player at the six.

31.) Termarr Johnson, 2B, Pittsburgh Pirates

Maybe we can give the Pirates credit here—they didn't galaxy brain this one. The 2022 fourth overall pick is this high on the list for a reason: we have a reasonably high degree of confidence that he will attain a plus hit tool. Despite being vertically challenged as professional athletes go, Johnson is a strong kid with a quick bat who barrels the ball hard and with consistency despite interesting swing mechanics. He is also pretty advanced already for a prep bat—he did well (.275/.396/.450) in a late season assignment to the Florida State League and could open 2023 at High-A if the organization is so inclined. He is a second baseman through and through, which limits his upside a bit, but his hitting ability and potential above-average power output from the left side are star-quality at the keystone.

32.) Colson Montgomery, SS, Chicago White Sox

If it is possible to be an immediately successful first-round pick who already looks like a developmental win, yet at the same time be a bit underwhelming, Montgomery is pulling it off. He packs a plus hit tool projection, but nothing else really pops despite a surprisingly advanced profile for a prep hitter that should allow him to matriculate quickly. His plate approach is very good, and excellent barrel feel and an ability to pick up spin enabled him to dominate Low-A and hold his own in High-A as a 20-year-old, slashing .324/.424/.477 and .258/.387/.417, respectively, over a combined 369 plate appearances at those levels. His power hasn't really manifested yet (though there should be more in that large frame), and the defense certainly could be better. Athleticism is present but foot speed is not, so there will be limited ancillary value to round out the profile. In the end Montgomery will have to hit and hit for power, and we think he will.

33.) Druw Jones, OF, Arizona Diamondbacks

The no. 2 pick in the 2022 Draft, Jones is a phenomenal defender in center field already, following in the footsteps of his 10-time Gold Glove-winning father. He's a plus-plus runner and thrower who takes brilliant routes: he's really the total package out there. At the plate, he brings a classic, smooth swing and a lot of bat speed. His power projection is above-average, albeit geared for opposite-field power over pull power at the moment. We don't have any professional data at all on Jones, because he suffered a severe shoulder injury while taking swings after signing and before even getting into a complex game. (Along with the severe shoulder injuries Carroll and Lawlar suffered in 2021, that means all three top Arizona outfield prospects have missed many months recently with similar, unusual injuries. No, we don't know what's in the water there.) We'll see how his bat plays against pro pitching this summer.

34.) Zac Veen, OF, Colorado Rockies

Veen's sweet lefty swing and projectable frame will tick every box for your more traditional scouting eye. He's a plus runner who swiped 55 bags last year while only getting caught nine times. Sure, the stat line doesn't pop, and he struggled after a promotion to Double-A, but he was only 20 and his skill set is sure to blossom soon enough, right? Maybe! He'll show you plus raw pop at 5 PM, but he doesn't actually hit the ball in games harder than his org-mate Ezequiel Tovar (despite looking like he should) and he hits the ball on the ground far too often to make consistent use of his power, anyway. The speed that makes him such an effective base-stealer isn't quite enough to let him play center field. Veen's swing remains one to dream on, and he isn't that far off from boasting an impact power/speed combo and starting everyday in Coors, but we're still mostly dreaming at present.

35.) Triston Casas, 1B, Boston Red Sox

The December DFA of Eric Hosmer (we hardly knew ye) seems to all but guarantee that Casas will be manning first during the vast majority of this season's Red Sox games. We don't expect an easy learning curve. Boston's lineup is short on thump after losing a lot of their old homegrown talent, and cheap production from new homegrown talent will be vital. Casas actually hasn't hit as many minor-league homers as you think, massive 6-foot-4 frame notwithstanding, but the raw pop is in there and he exhibits traits consistent with a plus hit grade. Casas struggled in his September cameo last season, but a few more oppo shots over the Monster against Gerrit Cole should get him in good with the Fenway faithful.

36.) Mick Abel, RHP, Philadelphia Phillies

Abel had the slight misfortune of being drafted a year ahead of Andrew Painter, a player with roughly the same profile who has better stuff and is moving much faster. But there's absolutely nothing wrong with Abel, who is exactly where you want a prep first-round pitcher to be entering his age-21 season. He throws in the mid- to upper-90s with good but not elite fastball characteristics, getting a solid number of whiffs. His best pitch is his slider, which visually presents as plus-plus but doesn't induce an overwhelming amount of chase outside the zone because it doesn't tunnel ideally with the rest of his arsenal. His curveball and changeup are both consistently average. He throws strikes but sometimes nibbles too much. He's a fairly high probability mid-rotation starter. He's just not Andrew Painter.

37.) Brooks Lee, SS, Minnesota Twins

Lee might be the polar opposite of Zac Veen. He looks like he learned to swing a Louisville Slugger by watching a Rankin/Bass animation of Hunter Pence. But all Lee's ever done is hit baseballs and hit them hard, including posting a ludicrous .400 batting average in the tough environs of the Cape Cod League. He hit almost as well across his sophomore and junior seasons at Cal-Poly and kept on hitting after the Twins made him the ninth pick in last summer's draft. Lee is a bit barrel-chested for shortstop—although he's twitchier and more athletic than you'd think given the frame—but should fit just fine at third base, where he may hit .300 now and again. He should settle in as a perennial plus hit/plus power bat at the hot corner, and will have a plus-plus "funny Twitter clips of weird swings that end up as doubles in the gap" game if nothing else. Assuming that Twitter is still up and running by the time he reaches the majors, that is.

38.) Colton Cowser, OF, Baltimore Orioles

Cowser's about as good of a prospect as you'd expect the no. 5 pick two years ago to be, but the *shape* of his projected performance has changed fairly substantially since he was drafted. His plate discipline has been great for as long as he's been a relevant prospect, but the strong contact ability we projected at Sam Houston State and even in the lowest rungs of Baltimore's system wilted in 2022 as he went up the organizational ladder. Cowser piled up 174 strikeouts between High-A, Double-A and Triple-A, and if you don't swing a whole lot and run up that many strikeouts, it means you're swinging through an awful lot of hittable pitches in the zone (and probably taking a few too many, too). To his credit, he's lifting and driving the ball on contact more than expected, so his game power projection is trending up even as he's connecting less. On the opposite side of the ball, he now projects to stay in center and maybe even excel there: a surprise given that he seemed likely to move to a corner just a year ago. In all, he's gone from a contact-first corner masher to a three-true-outcomes center field archetype before he's even hit the majors. Prospects, man.

39.) Miguel Vargas, 3B/OF, Los Angeles Dodgers

Rough debuts haven't derailed Vargas in the past. While the sweet swinger has posted a .300-or-better average at five out of six stops over the last three minor-league seasons, he came out the gates professionally with a .115/.148/.154 line back in the Cuban National Series over eight games. At age 14. Compared to that, his .170/.200/.255 big-league debut isn't so sour. Vargas' intervening work has honed his swing to a fine point: it is short to the ball and stays in the zone a long time, covering all quadrants. He has solid-average power that plays up because of how frequently he makes contact. He's no hacker, though, walking at an above-average clip throughout the upper minors. A third baseman by trade, the Dodgers have moved Vargas all over defensively, including having him take balls at first, second and left. That forced versatility is more representative of how much they want his bat in the lineup than some sort of endorsement of his ability to handle all of these positions with aplomb. He's a capable defender at third, but his skills would likely shine most at first base.

40.) Royce Lewis, SS, Minnesota Twins

Lewis made his big-league debut last May, a spot start made necessary by Carlos Correa's brief trip to the IL. Now that Correa is a free agent, the (other) former first-overall pick may be back to reclaim the future that was once his. It's been a long time coming for the (still just) 23-year-old, who has had to battle through horrible issues with his swing mechanics and even worse injuries in order to even get to this point. He's filled out some and may eventually have to move off short, though he is fine there for now. More importantly, his elite bat speed has not been diminished, and his swing is correctly modulated to create power. Lewis even posted a Correa-like OPS+ of 145 over the tantalizing 40 at-bats he managed before going down with his second serious knee injury. Now, he just needs to do the one thing in the game that is more difficult than hitting—stay healthy—and the world is his.

41.) Sal Frelick, OF, Milwaukee Brewers

We all have aesthetic preferences when it comes to baseball players. You might like Rich Hill's big, arcing lefty curveball, the direct, no-nonsense violence of a Giancarlo Stanton laser beam to the opposite field, or Jazz Chisholm Jr., full stop. I'm sure there is an audience out there for Sal Frelick, too—the universe contains multitudes—but a hit-first, left field prospect with a good approach is not high on our list of favorite archetypes. We are fond of the occasional scouting platitude though, and Frelick embodies one of our favorite tautologies: "Hitters hit." Frelick hit .331 across three levels and looked like a potential future batting champ, short to the ball with good wrists able to drive the outside pitch the other way, and punish pitchers that challenged him inside. He picks his pitches well too, and while his home run totals might only go as high as a Spinal Tap amp, Frelick will be the perfect complement to a Brewers lineup that has been awfully reliant on the long ball the last few seasons.

42.) Emmanuel Rodriguez, OF, Minnesota Twins

A recurring question from our readership, paraphrased: Who on this list is most likely to take a jump into the top 10 next year? This is of course merely a disguised dynasty league question, but it provides a useful frame for this blurb. Our answer: Emmanuel Rodriguez. We don't know if he would have gotten there with a full, healthy season for Fort Myers—he missed the second half of the season with a torn meniscus—but early signs were pointing way up. Rodriguez was crushing the Florida State League as a 19-year-old, showing a remarkably disciplined approach and punishing anything in the zone. All five tools flashed in short bursts in 2022. The knee injury might force him to a corner—and that was a possibility regardless, despite good foot speed—but Rodriguez's potential impact with the bat is equal to those in the top 10 right now. And if you want to expand on our opening question even further, he's one of a small handful of prospects outside the top 20 who have a chance to be the best prospect in baseball someday.

43.) Tink Hence, RHP, St. Louis Cardinals

The Cardinals picked three times in the first 63 picks in the 2020 Draft and Hence is the *lowest*-ranked of the three; their next pick, outfielder Alec Burleson, came reasonably close to making this list himself. Suffice to say, that has a chance to be a legendary class even though it was only a five-round draft. St. Louis has been extremely cautious with Hence, keeping him in extended spring training for most of 2021 and then limiting him to a series of one-inning complex appearances that summer. His 2022 debut was delayed until mid-May, he pitched with a lot of extra rest and never even went five innings, so he only threw 56⅓ of them in the regular season. But when he was on the mound he was simply sensational, toying with Low-A hitters while showing plus-or-better projections on his fastball, breaking ball and changeup. He continued to shine in the Arizona Fall League, where he got classmate Jordan Walker to fly out in the Fall Stars Game. We have little idea if he can handle anything resembling a true starting workload, but the sky's the limit if he can.

44.) Adael Amador, SS, Colorado Rockies

The Rockies don't lack for interesting middle infield prospects. Amador is a couple levels behind Ezequiel Tovar, but has far more advanced bat-to-ball skills despite spending his entire 2022 season in A-ball. He's a switch-hitter with 70-grade bat speed who sprays hard line drives to the outfield seemingly at will. He walked more than he struck out last year, and while he doesn't really look to lift the ball now, at least average power is possible given how much hard contact he makes. The profile is bat-first (and maybe second and third). Amador is an above-average runner but a bit too aggressive on the bases at present, and his infield actions will likely force him to second base in the medium term. Still, the hit tool is a true carrying tool, and the 19-year-old has at least a plus one.

45.) Hunter Brown, RHP, Houston Astros

You may remember Brown from his scoreless 12th and 13th innings in the ALDS Game 3 marathon. The Astros called him up for a pair of early-September spot starts in place of Justin Verlander, and he pitched well enough in them to earn a lower-leverage spot in the playoff bullpen. He's able to carry mid- to high-90s with high spin as a starter or a reliever, although his movement profile is average so the pitch isn't a complete monster. His out-pitch is a plus-plus downer of a curveball that shows hard, late break. He also mixes in one of the hardest sliders you'll see, in the low- to mid-90s and overlapping some in the same velocity band as his fastball; some pitch classifications classify it as a cutter despite the slidery break. He rarely uses his changeup but has shown some ability to get whiffs with it, too. Brown is a higher-effort pitcher with mediocre command, and that could push him into a full-time bullpen role, although the Astros have been more malleable than most with pitching roles and are likely to give him every chance to start.

46.) Henry Davis, C, Pittsburgh Pirates

Davis is either too high or too low on this list, depending on who you ask. He is a catcher with obvious plus power (that's good) who might not be all that good at the finer points of catching (that's bad). The bat speed is elite and he hits the ball hard (that's good) but he tends to swing through too many pitches in the zone and struggled at Double-A—his .207/.324/.379 Altoona slash line contrasts dramatically with his .342/.450/.585 Greensboro output—amid an injury-riddled 2022 (that's bad). The massive upside inherent in his profile is still present, but so is the significant risk. His age-23 season will be an important one.

47.) Zach Neto, SS, Los Angeles Angels

The 2022 college hitter class was pretty deep at the top, but there wasn't really a clear, standout top option. Neto ended up the sixth college bat taken, going 13th overall. Perhaps he slid a bit due to the level of competition in the Big South conference, but Neto dominated there, hitting over .400 his sophomore and junior seasons for Campbell. Modern draft models tend not to see as big a gap between the Big South and the SEC as pundits might proffer, and Neto promptly hit .300 in his pro debut, most of which was spent in Double-A. Neto is likely to stick at shortstop all the way to the majors, and while it remains to be seen how much power he will generate with wood bats, everything else looks on target to make him a plus major league regular as soon as 2023.

48.) Oswald Peraza, SS, New York Yankees

After making a brief cameo in the playoffs that probably should have been less brief, Peraza seems the odds-on favorite to break camp as New York's (or in the event of a major trade, someone else's) starter at the six. The best infield defender in the org, he plays a stress-free shortstop and seems ready to contribute with the bat. A gap power guy who has been tapping into some over-the-fence pop, Peraza boasts very good in-zone contact rates and can be an above-average offensive producer despite pedestrian pitch selection abilities. Throw in some speed and baserunning ability and you've got a solid contributor at a premium position, something that every team needs.

49.) Cam Collier, 3B, Cincinnati Reds

Collier went down a road paved by Bryce Harper, getting his GED two years early and heading to a JuCo powerhouse in what should've been his high school junior season, ultimately reclassifying for the draft a year before he'd have been eligible by graduating high school. Playing for Chipola College at age 17, Collier hit .333 with power, thereby breaking a bunch of draft model inputs that weigh age and college performance heavily. He then broke the models a little more with a cameo as the youngest player in recent Cape Cod League memory. Eligible for the 2022 Draft still four months shy of his 18th birthday, he slid down to the 18th pick and signed for a well above-slot $5 million bonus. Collier is a skills ahead of tools player right now, driven by bat-to-ball ability. While he's still very young and further physical growth is quite possible, he's not really hitting the ball that hard and his power projection is questionable at present. He's a suitable match for third base with the glove. He's likely to be one of the youngest players in full-season ball this year.

50.) Gavin Stone, RHP, Los Angeles Dodgers

A former small college bullpen arm, Stone followed up his breakout 2021 by becoming the most dominant pitcher in minor-league baseball last year. A large part of his success is due to his devastating changeup, which is quite possibly the best secondary pitch in the minors. It's a true bat-misser that tunnels well off of his mid-90s fastball. The slider also plays up from the change, breaking sharply glove-side and generating plenty of weak contact. He's proven himself to be a durable starter over the last two years, logging over 200 innings without missing any time due to injury. Stone might not have the upside of Bobby Miller, but he's very close and it's likely he gets a chance to make his debut in Los Angeles sometime in 2023.

51.) Griff McGarry, RHP, Philadelphia Phillies

A recurring theme of modern pitching prospect analysis is that everyone has great stuff now; at least every prospect a devoted fan is likely to know about. McGarry throws distinct four-seam and two-seam fastballs in the mid- to high-90s; the four-seamer gets whiffs up in the zone and the two-seamer has demon sinker properties and almost acts as a changeup at fastball velocity. His slider has taken a big step forward to become a potential out-pitch, overtaking a curveball that flashes plus itself, as his primary secondary offering. Yes, his changeup isn't much to look at, and yes, his command is still pretty spotty even if tremendously improved (he spent most of his college career walking around a batter an inning), but McGarry has the type of pitch mix where you kind of just have to ignore the bad parts and hope for the best. The Phillies tried him out of the bullpen late in the 2022 season in Triple-A in the hopes he could impact the pennant race. It didn't go great, so he might have less of an impact-reliever fallback than you'd think, given the profile.

52.) Tanner Bibee, RHP, Cleveland Guardians

Tell me if you've heard this story before: The Guardians drafted a command-first day-two college pitcher (in this case a 2021 fifth-rounder out of Cal State-Fullerton) with low-90s velocity, below-average stuff and no apparent projectability. By the end of his first full pro season, his velocity had jumped four or five ticks and he was striking out the world with a plus sweeping slider while still displaying pinpoint command and a usable change. Bibee struck out 167 batters last year in 132⅔ innings between High-A and Double-A after striking out 67 batters in 89⅔ innings in the Big West Conference the year before. There was just no way to see that coming, except that Cleveland keeps getting the same velocity and slider bumps out of the command-first college pitcher cohort year after year, a credit to their amateur acquisition and pitching development program alike.

53.) Marco Raya, RHP, Minnesota Twins

Modern pitching prospect evaluation is balancing ever more hellacious stuff—in this instance mid-90s heat with two potential plus-or-better breakers—against more conservative usage patterns. Raya had a barking shoulder in 2021 and only pitched into the sixth inning once in 2022. So there's an open question as to whether his stuff can hold up over longer stretches, especially since Raya is on the shorter and slighter side. On the other hand, we don't expect our major-league starters to throw much more than 150 innings in a season nowadays, and there are all sorts of roles you can carve out between starter and one-inning reliever. On the other, *other* hand, if Raya shows he can hold up as that 150-inning arm in 2023, he'll be one of the best pitching prospects around.

54.) Nick Nastrini, RHP, Los Angeles Dodgers

Once on the brink of quitting baseball due to the yips after thoracic outlet surgery, Nastrini has worked his way back, harnessing his electric stuff to become one of the top arms in a deep Dodgers system. His fastball easily sits in the mid-90s with some ride up in the zone and he pairs it well with a plus changeup. His breaking pitches both flash as future swing-and-miss offerings, with the sweeping slider currently ahead of the curve developmentally. It's a quality repertoire, nearly as good as both Gavin Stone's and Bobby Miller's, but Nastrini's command and control started off so poor that he massively improved in hitting his spots and still only got to fringe-average. Given the history of walks and injury, he still carries major bullpen risk.

55.) Endy Rodriguez, C/IF/OF, Pittsburgh Pirates

Not that the Steve Cohen Mets care, but they probably lost their end of the Joey Lucchesi trade. Rodriguez made himself an elite hitting prospect during the second half of the 2022 season—the April version of him would not have placed here—and he plays catcher (and second, first and left field). Note that we didn't say he is a catcher—his receiving isn't great and his bat seems to be jolting him through the system more quickly than he can improve his skills behind the dish. We think he will ultimately be playing a lot of corner outfield, where his athleticism allows him to profile well. But listen, the man hits. The game power can get to plus, and a midseason stance adjustment has him tapping into an above-average hit tool. And he's a switch-hitter. How the Pirates manage the contradictions in his profile and where they see his ultimate defensive home are the questions we're keeping an eye on as Rodriguez begins 2023, likely at Triple-A.

56.) Dalton Rushing, C, Los Angeles Dodgers

It's very rare for a player selected outside of the first round to make the next winter's Top 101. When it does happen, it's usually at the bottom of the list, and it's usually a player who got pushed out because of bonus demands or similar weirdness. Rushing was last summer's 40th pick—the Dodgers' "first-rounder," but penalized 10 spots for luxury tax infractions, in fact—as a one-year college wonder who spent the early part of his career at Louisville stuck behind Henry Davis. After signing, Rushing blitzed the California League like he was playing The Show on rookie mode, hitting .404/.522/.740 in 30 games and walking as much as he struck out. We suspect his line would've been taken more seriously if he had hit a little *less*, because what he did was so absurd that it was easy to discount. The top-line average and power was underpinned by truly impressive batted ball data; nearly everything he hit was in the air and really freakin' hard. The Dodgers already have an embarrassment of catching riches between fellow former Louisville Cardinal Will Smith and Diego Cartaya, but that's why they're the Dodgers.

57.) Spencer Jones, OF, New York Yankees

Speaking of on-brand 2022 picks who probably should've gone earlier, the Yankees nabbed this super-sized exit velocity kingpin with endless Aaron Judge comps with the no. 25 pick. Once one of the top prep prospects for the 2019 Draft—as a left-handed pitcher—Jones honored his commitment to Vanderbilt and ended up giving up pitching when chronic elbow issues turned into Tommy John surgery. He finally got to focus on hitting and playing the outfield full-time in 2022 and exploded, hitting the ball as consistently hard as any player in the nation. He continued vaporizing baseballs in the Low-A Florida State League, spawning regular social media video threads of triple-digit exit velos, and he made a lot more contact than you'd expect for a behemoth swinging out of his shoes. If Jones continues to keep the swing-and-miss manageable...well, those Judge comps will get more pointed, even if they're impossible to live up to.

58.) Gordon Graceffo, RHP, St. Louis Cardinals

Graceffo started trending up almost immediately after he was drafted as a 2021 fifth-rounder out of Villanova—a jump in velocity to the mid-90s helped him post a 1.73 ERA in his pro debut and earn a mention in our Cardinals list that fall. The true breakout came last season as he tore his way through the Midwest League before finishing up the year with an impressive Double-A campaign. He has all the makings of a future major-league starter: a strong frame, an advanced changeup and the ability to pound the strike zone. Graceffo's track record of success is rather short and he needs to find a consistent breaking pitch—his slider is more promising than his curveball at the moment—but he's really close to earning starter's innings in St. Louis.

59.) Michael Busch, 2B, Los Angeles Dodgers

Busch was mostly a first baseman who moonlighted in the outfield in college, but the Dodgers pushed him up the defensive spectrum to second after drafting him in 2019. Despite being a major college first-rounder who has had success at every level, he's moved fairly slowly through the system, including beginning 2022 by repeating Double-A after spending a full and productive 2021 there. Busch doesn't do any one thing at an incredible level at the plate, but he hits the ball hard enough and makes good enough decisions to carry average bat-to-ball ability. The defense at the keystone isn't superb, but he should survive the elimination of the shift. He's ready for major-league time and likely to just be a good, solid bat who can stand at second or any corner.

60.) George Valera, OF, Cleveland Guardians

On the subject of baseball aesthetics, Valera's swing has long been a particular favorite of our staff. It's more outsider art than Rembrandt, the work of a true iconoclast, but the commercial viability is starting to come into question. The art world might love a shark in formaldehyde—just ask Steve Cohen—but in the prospect world we need some rigorous form under the bouts of postmodern improvisation. That is all to say, Valera didn't really make enough contact in the upper minors last year. The power looks effortless even when he doesn't completely square a pitch, but there are in fact more moving parts than a Collectif Scale installation. The in-zone swing-and-miss is a problem and drove his batting average down into the .250 range. Valera has a great approach and will do enough damage on contact that he can be a good major leaguer—even as a corner outfielder—if he doesn't give back anymore hit tool, but that last step up is the steepest. Still, we are excited to see Valera's magnum opus, *The Physical Impossibility of Whiff in the Mind of Someone Swinging*, when it comes to a major-league ballpark near you.

61.) Edwin Arroyo, SS, Cincinnati Reds

Arroyo broke out in the first half of 2022 as one of the youngest players in the Cal League. Drafted as a glove-first prep talent in 2021 by the Mariners, his bat has quickly caught up. Arroyo showed feel for contact from both sides of the plate and burgeoning pull-side pop. His slick glove was on display night in and night out, as well. Shipped off to Cincinnati—by way of Daytona—as part of the Luis Castillo return, Arroyo struggled a bit in his new digs. But that all adds up to a month of a bit more swing-and-miss, which you wouldn't even notice if it weren't a separate row on his player card. And that's before we get into how much of a pain it can be to focus on baseball when you've just moved across the country to a new organization. His overall line—.297/.368/.486 in Low-A, while playing most of the season at 18—and the top-notch live reports point to a true breakout, and Arroyo may have another gear if he can more consistently tap into his power.

62.) Garrett Mitchell, OF, Milwaukee Brewers

Speaking of tapping into power, Mitchell has now made it all the way to the majors without ever hitting more than eight home runs in a season—including his time with ping bats at UCLA—despite looking the part of a middle-of-the-order thumper. He's played more like a table-setter, using his elite foot speed on the bases and in the outfield. He's had durability issues throughout his pro career—an oblique injury cost him time in 2022—and his MLB debut featured a frightening amount of swing-and-miss. If he can iron that issue out with more reps, his hit tool, speed and defense should give him a fairly high floor as a regular center fielder. That's just an okay outcome for the 62nd best prospect in baseball, but we'll keep baking in that 10% chance he starts hitting home runs and becomes a real star.

63.) Jasson Domínguez, OF, New York Yankees

The discourse around "The Martian" has been going on for what feels like an interminable length of time, and likely will continue interminably, as Domínguez probably isn't too close to making his debut despite finishing 2022 at Double-A. No, he isn't Mickey Mantle, nor is he Mike Trout, and he might not even be Bryan Reynolds. He is, however, a very good prospect. He isn't as fast as you think, he's probably a corner outfielder and he doesn't hit the ball prodigiously hard, at least consistently. But when he does get into one the high-end exit velos are very nice, and his production at High-A and Double-A (.306/.397/.510 and .266/.374/.440, respectively) was impressive when factoring in his age—yes, he is still a teenager. Above-average big-league production is the likely outcome, even if it falls short of superstardom.

64.) Kevin Parada, C, New York Mets

The Mets got one of the best college players in the draft when Parada slid to the 11th pick. A draft-eligible sophomore, he slugged .700 for the Georgia Tech Ramblin' Wreck, following up on an almost-as-good freshman campaign. Parada has a bit of an unusual setup, starting with the bat pointed almost directly toward the ground, but he has good enough wrists to make it work and is strong enough to wring plus power out of the resulting swing. He's a two-way catcher, although the defensive skills aren't as loud as those at the plate, and we could list all the usual caveats about non-elite catching prospects and their potential offensive regression. But for now, let's just enjoy the potential plus outcome that Parada carries in his locker.

65.) Joey Wiemer, OF, Milwaukee Brewers

Major League Baseball tilts more and more toward the three true outcomes every year. A lot of that is due to spiking K-rates as pitching just gets better and better. But if you can hit enough home runs and generate enough wind energy to power a few Wisconsin counties, you'll find yourself in the lineup every day. That's the gambit Wiemer plays every time he steps up to the plate. He swings hard in case he hits it. He swings up, which means there are holes to exploit. But he also knows when not to swing, which means he can pile up walks—that *other* true outcome. It's a precarious balancing act. He's a pretty good runner and right fielder, but those are "nice to haves." The 30 home runs are the "have to have." Wiemer has that kind of power, and he was very good in Triple-A after scuffling a bit in the Southern League to start 2022.

66.) Robert Hassell III, OF, Washington Nationals

A former top-10 selection and one of the top prospect bats for San Diego, Hassell was a key piece in the deadline deal that sent Juan Soto to the Padres. In him the Nationals have an athletic, projectable player with a knack for finding the barrel and enough range and arm to hold down center field. His inability to generate much loft and weak exit velocities were concerning even before he suffered a broken hamate bone late in the season, but now the lack of hard contact is even more magnified. The contact ability, speed and defense give Hassell a relatively high floor, but unless he begins to impact the ball more consistently, the profile is going to lack high-impact upside.

67.) Miguel Bleis, OF, Boston Red Sox

Signed for $1.5 million out of the Dominican Republic a mere two years ago, Bleis is another name outside the top 20 who has a chance to be an elite prospect down the road. The complex-level stats were good, but keeping stats on the backfields seems a bit silly. The tools are even better: all five are checked off, including potential plus center field defense. His swing decisions are ponderous at times, his approach too aggressive overall, but Bleis has that scout-friendly swing that marries power and contact and plays well analytically, too. He just has to get a bit better at picking which pitches to play with, which is only one of the toughest things in baseball to do.

68.) Elijah Green, OF, Washington Nationals

Green is the player with the highest variance on this list. You can find scouts who think he's a near-generational talent, the kind of athlete who comes into baseball once or twice a decade. If he hits their view of his reasonable upside, he'll be a future MVP because of his explosive bat speed, immense power potential, lightning speed and great swing. But you can find just as many others who think he's going to struggle to make it out of A-ball because of contact problems, the magnitude of which are unusual for such a high pick; he's pretty hopeless against velocity up in the zone at present, specifically. His in-zone contact woes are just brutal, and an anchor attached to any sort of hit tool projection. Green's whiff rates were alarming even against prep pitching, and he was basically a windmill at the complex after the draft. One of two things is going to happen here, probably pretty quickly: He's going to improve his bat-to-ball skills *a lot*, or he's going to start hitting for really low averages with a really high number of strikeouts.

69.) Coby Mayo, 3B, Baltimore Orioles

Have the Orioles cracked the code on hitting development? They keep getting huge gains out of all of their top hitting prospects, some rather unexpected. Mayo is a big, hulking corner prospect—currently a third baseman, maybe an outfielder or first baseman down the road—and he checks the boxes for traditional power projectability. He hasn't really had his huge breakout a la Gunnar Henderson yet, but he's pretty well-rounded at the plate for his experience and age—he reached Double-A at 20 after only playing 95 games between Low-A and High-A—with decent contact and discipline skills. Mayo's profile hasn't fully coalesced to a star projection quite yet, though the same could be said for Henderson just a year ago.

70.) Gavin Cross, OF, Kansas City Royals

Another top college bat—this one with bona fide major conference production—Cross is an advanced slugger who should move quickly through the minors and reach Kansas City as a good corner outfielder capable of hitting .280 and swatting 25+ bombs. The power may play a bit above that; he's strong and knows how to use the length and leverage in his swing to inflict maximum damage. The hit tool might come in a bit below that average, given his expansive view on what breaking balls he should be swinging at. Cross is perhaps a bit of a dull subject as a polished college offensive player of the Michael Conforto variety. That's still a player every team would love to have, even if every team doesn't have one.

71.) Cade Cavalli, RHP, Washington Nationals

On the flip side of all of the pitchers with ideal modern stuff who get more whiffs than it looks like they should is Cavalli, who is a 2010s scout's dream but who has induced consistently underwhelming swing-and-miss rates in the upper minors. Cavalli throws his fastball in the mid- to upper-90s and scrapes triple-digits, but with very generic movement. In the 2020s, fastballs in the 95–97-mph range with a little sink just don't generate elite whiff rates, even in Triple-A. Both his curveball and slider have flashed plus but don't get enough chases, with the curve lately further ahead, and his changeup flashes average. Cavalli is headed down the path of a frustrating but effective mid-rotation starter outcome where you always think he should be better based on the radar gun and visual movement. All of this comes with the caveat that he came down with shoulder soreness after his late-August debut and was never able to ramp back up before season's end—and that injuries were a recurring problem for him in college.

72.) Max Meyer, RHP, Miami Marlins

Meyer shares some of Cavalli's knocks in that the optics of his mid- to upper-90s fastball are better than their pedestrian underlying shape, which causes them to miss fewer bats than you'd otherwise think. Where Meyer excels is with his plus-plus slider, which has nuked hitters dating back to college and was continuing to obliterate them for a short time in the bigs. His changeup was also developing on schedule, but he blew out his elbow in the first inning of his second major-league start last July. Dating back to his college days, there have been concerns that Meyer's ultimate home would be in the bullpen, as he's a smaller pitcher with a high-octane fastball/slider combo. An elbow reconstruction is unlikely to quell those concerns. Given that he's going to miss most or all of the 2023 season on rehab, we'll likely be confronted with ranking him again next year.

73.) Ceddanne Rafaela, OF/SS, Boston Red Sox

The loyal rooters of New England might not want to hear it right now, but Rafaela may just be Boston's next homegrown fan favorite (and it will be many years before he hits free agency). The Curaçaon isn't a huge guy—listed at 5-foot-8 and probably closer to 150 than 200 pounds—but he is an excellent athlete with a smooth explosiveness to his game. His wiry strength and quick, loose stroke at the dish have him spraying liners gap-to-gap and should get him to average or slightly above game power at the highest level. He also has a hit tool that should reach average or better and is a quick and savvy baserunner. Rafaela plays a very cool center field and handles shortstop, too, with the potential to cover other spots around the diamond. The 21-year-old was a massive hit at High-A Greenville (.330/.368/.594) and adjusted well to Double-A breaking stuff following a June promotion (.278/.324/.500). Turbocharged Enrique Hernández might be in play.

74.) Jordan Westburg, IF, Baltimore Orioles

Westburg's offensive improvements in 2022 didn't get blared through a bullhorn like Gunnar Henderson's, but they were notable just the same. Previously showing a collection of mostly average tools as a high-floor college bat, Westburg traded off a bit of batting average for some real game power improvements—a more than fair bargain. He's started ratcheting up earlier in his swing, and while that's added to his whiff rates, he's gained bat speed, lift and pull-side pop. Westburg is also a versatile infielder who can move around second, third and short, giving you adequate to above-average defense wherever Henderson isn't playing that day. While he won't ever be first—or now perhaps even second—among Orioles infield prospects, he's no third banana.

75.) Jett Williams, SS, New York Mets

This has been said so much over the last year that it's a bit trite, but once more with feeling: If Williams—listed at 5-foot-8 and perhaps not even that tall—was 6-foot-2, he'd have been one of the top few picks in the 2022 Draft. (That anecdote should reinforce how specially the similarly statured Termarr Johnson's hit tool is viewed.) Instead, he's a short king who fell all the way to the Mets at no. 14. He had one of the best contact profiles in the draft class, a clear benefit to shorter levers that has been a noticeable industry trend recently, and has a surprising bit of pop for his size. We're listing Williams as a shortstop because the Mets announced him as a shortstop and that's where he played in the complex, but he's much more likely to be a second baseman or even a center fielder over the long haul—his arm doesn't project for the left half of the infield. Regardless of where he plays defensively, Williams projects as well as a natural hitter as you can without significant pro data to confirm.

76.) Oscar Colás, OF, Chicago White Sox

Colás may seem low here considering his strong second-half campaign at Double-A Birmingham and proximity to the majors. It is true that the now-24-year-old boasts wicked bat speed and massive power, and he seems a little less old for his levels when considering that he essentially took the prior two years off from professional baseball (2019 saw him take his at-bats in Cuba and Japan). Still, his swing decisions are not especially strong, and while he should provide solid defense, it will be in a corner, as he doesn't have enough speed or baserunning ability to add value around the edges. We see him as someone who can impact the middle of the lineup with his left-handed power production, but relying on him as a starter from day one may be a risky proposition.

77.) Logan O'Hoppe, C, Los Angeles Angels

Last July, the Phillies traded O'Hoppe—a near-ready catching prospect totally and utterly blocked by J.T. Realmuto—for Brandon Marsh, the no. 44 prospect from 2021. It was a rare one-for-one trade of young players with considerable upside—Marsh might yet be a star because of his defense and how much damage he can do on contact. Meanwhile, O'Hoppe swatted 26 long balls between his two Double-A clubs, and he doesn't chase or miss within the zone all that much. He doesn't really have huge raw power potential, but he's getting to every bit of what he has under the lights. The Angels gave him a one-week trial run at catcher at the end of 2022, and he should take over the full-time gig from Max Stassi imminently.

78.) Tyler Soderstrom, 1B/C, Oakland Athletics

Even with the current selloff happening in Oakland, Soderstrom remains the top prospect for the Athletics. A hit tool-driven catcher when drafted 26th overall in 2020, it's likely he makes the move to first to get his near big league-ready bat in the lineup rather than develop behind the plate. His offensive skills are strong enough to handle the move down the defensive spectrum, with a combination of an advanced feel at the plate and the ability to hit for over-the-fence power. Take a look at the current depth chart for Oakland and you'll realize that not only is Soderstrom the best prospect in the organization, he might just be the best hitter at the major-league level as well.

79.) Nick Frasso, RHP, Los Angeles Dodgers

I want you to know that I'm happy for you
I wish nothing but the best for you both
An older version of me
Does he throw a hundred like me?
Would he go down on an in-zone slider?
Does he pitch adequately?
And would he throw it zippy?
I'm sure he'd make a really excellent starter

Cause the stuff that you gave that we made
Wasn't able to make it enough for you to get pitch design, no
And every time you start Mitch White
Does he know how you told me
You'd make my sweeper slide?
Until my elbow died, 'til it died, but it's back alive

And I'm here to remind you
Of the mess you left when you traded me
It's not fair to deny me
Of the whiffs I bear that you gave to me
You, you, you oughta know

80.) Owen Caissie, OF, Chicago Cubs

Maybe they wanted to see how he would handle advanced pitching, or maybe they thought spending spring in the upper Midwest would remind him of his Ontario home. Either way, the Cubs gave Caissie an aggressive High-A assignment to begin his age-19 season. He struggled early but looked more comfortable and more the part of slugging corner outfielder as the season progressed. He'll need to work on getting the ball in the air more consistently to take full advantage of his plus bat speed and physical strength. He's a fairly well-rounded hitter at the plate, showing a good amount of barrel control and a command of the strike zone. Defensively, the glove is improving and he has more than enough arm to handle right field. Caissie can get overlooked in the Cubs' vastly improved system, but he has the tools to become a middle of the order run producer for the next competitive team on the North Side.

81.) Kyle Manzardo, 1B, Tampa Bay Rays

You can find a lot of things Manzardo isn't—defensively gifted for one, as he's limited to first base. Of impressive stature, for another, as he's just 6-foot-1, 205 pounds. He only boasts average power, and his swing setup and mechanics can look frantic to the naked eye. But he's an absolute masher at the plate, and he does the one thing that matters most: *he hits*. He cranked out a .327/.426/.617 line between High-A and Double-A last year, and his ability to mash is grounded in tangible things he excels at. While Manzardo may never hit 115-mph moonshots, his swing constantly produces hard contact in the air. He doesn't chase terrible pitches, and he makes more than his share of contact. He just hits, even if absolutely none of it looks or seems right.

82.) Connor Norby, 2B, Baltimore Orioles

Speaking of college bats in strong drafting and development organizations getting to all of their power in games, Norby also has merely average raw power. Nevertheless, he socked 29 home runs last year across three levels, far exceeding any reasonable expectations. The rest of the profile has a ton of "average to above-average" attached—he projects in that band on his contact, swing decisions, overall hit tool projection and second base defense—and frankly his power will probably recede back into that area as well. It's worth noting that Baltimore is completely overloaded with middle infielders in their system and Norby is likely the weakest defender of the crop; he doesn't have the arm to play short and might end up in the outfield.

83.) Brandon Pfaadt, RHP, Arizona Diamondbacks

Pfaadt throws a pretty standard array of above-average pitches, but lacks a clear plus attribute other than command. His fastball ranges from the low-90s up to 95 on the regular, with enough spin and carry that it gets past more hitters at the top of the strike zone than you would expect. He pairs that with a solid sweeping slider, a change that flashes above-average but with less consistency, and a curveball. He has very good command and control, and while there's nothing in the arsenal that looks better than a 55-grade pitch, he should get enough chases and whiffs on the edges of the zone to become a mid-rotation starter.

84.) Mason Montgomery, LHP, Tampa Bay Rays

The modern version of a crafty lefty profile, Montgomery has an odd, extremely short arm path that creates significant visual deception. That lends both his low-90s fastball and changeup some baffling extra oomph, and the Texas Tech product struck out 171 batters in 124 innings mostly off those two offerings. Despite the strange-looking mechanics, he repeats his delivery very well and hits his spots. His arm action is less well suited for a breaking ball, and improvements in his slider would enhance things even further. The Rays are well known for maximizing swing-and-miss from oddball release points and arm actions—they love creating different looks on the arm clock—so Montgomery is a great match for his organization.

85.) Harry Ford, C, Seattle Mariners

Ford has a weird but neat grouping of outlier skills. He's one of the speediest catchers in affiliated baseball. His swing decisions are about as good as you're going to see out of a teenage hitter, which allow him to maximize average-to-above contact and power abilities. He hasn't caught a ton yet—the Mariners never made him catch two games in a row last year—but he graded out as an excellent framer in the 54 games in which he donned the tools of ignorance. He's a candidate to play elsewhere on the field if the position ends up holding his bat back, and his athleticism would provide more defensive options than a standard backstop's would. After posting a pretty representative .274/.425/.439 line at Low-A, he basically carried his parents' home country of Great Britain through World Baseball Classic qualifying last fall. Expect to see him as one of the featured players for a very fun British squad in the main tournament in March.

86.) Jace Jung, 2B, Detroit Tigers

The last and only other time Detroit picked 12th in the amateur draft they did pretty well, selecting future World Series hero Kirk Gibson. Jung has a long way to go to match Gibby's career, but he was one of the top college bats available last July. He features a profile that is entirely dependent on his ability to impact the ball at the plate. The setup is unconventional but the swing is quick and direct, making hard contact to all fields. He also displays an advanced approach, commanding the zone well, which helps him get to most of his plus-raw pop. Everything in the field is fringe-average at best, with his range, quickness and arm strength limiting him to somewhere on the right side of the infield and putting a ton of pressure on the bat.

87.) Wilmer Flores, RHP, Detroit Tigers

A 2020 undrafted free agent, Flores followed up his breakout in 2021 with an even more impressive sophomore campaign, striking out over 30% of opposing hitters and showing a much improved cutter/slider. The new breaker combines with his mid-90s fastball and above-average curve to give him a more complete repertoire. His stuff is quality, but not quite on par with the eye-popping, high-upside offerings that you might see featured by pitchers toward the top of the list. However, you won't find anyone in Detroit crying if Flores the Younger becomes a middle-of-the-rotation workhorse.

88.) Matt Mervis, 1B, Chicago Cubs

Another 2020 undrafted free agent with limited defensive skills and a slugging percentage that started with a three in his first professional season, Mervis was not on anyone's prospect radar to begin the season. However, getting away from pitcher-friendly Myrtle Beach and implementing a more disciplined approach helped unlock his immense raw pop and rocket him up the organizational ladder. There's more than just a slugger in the profile: He has enough bat speed to catch up to velocity and he's shown enough contact ability to keep his strikeout rate in an acceptable range. After missing out on José Abreu in free agency, the Cubs are willing to trot out Eric Hosmer at first base at the season's onset, but sooner than later Mervis should get a chance to provide consistent thunder to a lineup that desperately needs it.

89.) Edgar Quero, C, Los Angeles Angels

Not to be confused with Jeferson Quero, a pretty good Brewers catching prospect himself, Edgar torched the pitching in the Cal League as a 19-year-old, posting a .965 OPS. The switch-hitting backstop shows plus power and contact ability from both sides of the plate. Behind it, the arm and athleticism are strong assets, but his receiving is going to need work. That kind of fine glovework is a teachable skill, but Quero is a long way from being a major-league factor. This is a long-term value list though, and if he is even an average defender in time, his bat could make him one of the top five or so catchers in baseball.

90.) Andy Pages, OF, Los Angeles Dodgers

After punishing Midwest League pitching in 2021 and establishing himself as the top power-hitting prospect in the organization, Pages was tested this past season by the advanced pitching in Double-A. The slugging dipped, but he still managed an elite fly-ball rate and continued to post a very manageable 25% strikeout rate. Despite concerns about his hit tool, he still has two double-plus-graded tools in his pop and his cannon of an arm in the outfield, both which rank among the best in all of minor-league baseball. Pages might not be a perennial All-Star, but he's got what it takes to become an everyday corner outfielder.

91.) Jackson Jobe, RHP, Detroit Tigers

Jobe was the first prep pitcher taken in the 2021 draft, but back issues limited him to just 77 innings last season, and when on the bump his command came and went. He has the kind of stuff that, well, gets you drafted third overall. Jobe fires mid-90s heat that can beat batters up in the zone, backed by a potential plus-plus spin-monster slider that rips off late, two-plane break, leaving A-ball hitters flailing at air. The changeup is also developing apace, but everything was a little too hittable in 2022. Jobe has as much upside as the low-minors arms already effusively praised in these pages like Tink Hence and Marco Raya, but is a bit further behind at present with higher relief risk.

92.) Kyle Muller, LHP, Oakland Athletics

This year's "prospect fatigue" entry, Muller feels like he should have established himself as a frustrating mid-rotation starter or dominant late-inning reliever by this point. He's struck out a batter per inning in the majors, and it's not hard to see why. His fastball is mid-90s from the left side with good extension, and he features two bat-missing breaking balls. Muller is a very modern pitching prospect, but he was never able to outpitch his command and control issues and establish himself in Atlanta. A trade to Oakland for Sean Murphy puts him in a much better situation to get the ball every fifth day, so this will likely be the last time we rank him. And despite his major-league struggles, he was very good in Triple-A last year. Muller is one of many prospect arms that's a grade or so of command away from having top-of-the-rotation impact. He likely won't get to it, but again, he should be a good, if frustrating mid-rotation starter in Oakland.

93.) Jose Salas, IF, Miami Marlins

As we've remarked before in these pages, there are worse strategies than just filling the tail end of these lists with good shortstop prospects. Salas played a bit all over the infield in 2022, but spent the majority of his games at the six, and should be just fine there. And one of the advantages inherent in being a shortstop prospect is that you have a ways to slide down the defensive spectrum before it puts real pressure on your bat. Salas is a contact merchant at present, but hits the ball decently hard for a 19-year-old in A-ball. If he grows off shortstop he'll likely grow into enough power to balance it out, and he'll likely be an above-average defender wherever he lands. The one concern with Salas is that he may lack a carrying tool, but when infield prospects in this range of the list find one, they often end up much higher in a year's time.

94.) Casey Schmitt, 3B, San Francisco Giants

To prospect rankers, a great glove at third will get you as much attention as cinephiles give to the Best Art Direction Oscar, but Schmitt's defense might be the *Barry Lyndon* of this category. It ranks among the best in the minors. He tossed in 21 homers across three levels in 2022, and while the pop is mostly pull-side—and he struck out more as he went up the ladder—good third base defenders in this range can sometimes go Matt Chapman and then we don't get another chance to rank them.

95.) DL Hall, LHP, Baltimore Orioles

DL Hall strides toward the Orioles mound
In his left arm great stuff can be found

Fastball and slider, plus is the word

Total package says starter the third

But then his pitches move far and wide
Walks are a problem we can't elide

DL Hall, inevitably then
Takes his free passes to the Camden bullpen

96.) Connor Phillips, RHP, Cincinnati Reds

What do David Ortiz, Moises Alou, Jesse Orosco and Phillips have in common? All were included as the PTBNL in trades that shipped them away from their original teams. Phillips topped out in Double-A last year, so there's a long way to go before he's on the same level as his trade add-on counterparts, but the tools are apparent. It starts with his high-octane fastball. With plenty of life and high-90s velocity, he uses it up in the zone to generate plenty of awkward, late swings. The secondaries are inconsistent, but both his 12-to-6 curve and sweeping slider show signs of being plus future offerings. The effort in his delivery will likely keep him from ever having pinpoint command, but his athleticism should allow him to control his repertoire. There's a good deal of reliever risk in his profile but there's also a chance he puts it all together and becomes a front-line starter.

97.) Ken Waldichuk, LHP, Oakland Athletics

A crafty lefty who actually has good stuff, Waldichuk is one of the more distinctive arms to arise from the Yankees' pitching development lab. Sent over to Oakland as the centerpiece of last deadline's Frankie Montas deal, the former fifth-rounder runs his heater well into the mid-90s and throws one of those fashionable sweeping sliders along with a legit changeup that also gets more than its share of whiffs. Both secondaries offer a substantial speed differential from the fastball, and the deception created by his tall frame hurling those pitches from a low three-quarters slot doesn't make him any easier to square up. Waldichuk made his debut late in 2022, and there should be nothing but wide-open spaces in Oakland's rotation next season.

98.) Colt Keith, 3B, Detroit Tigers

Had it not been for a midseason shoulder injury, Keith might have climbed even higher on this list. He was in the midst of a breakout season at High-A, hitting for average and a newfound amount of power. Surgery was reportedly not required, and he showed no ill-effects upon his return to action in the Arizona Fall League, leading his Salt River squad in most offensive categories. He's still raw in the field and a bit stiff in his actions at third but should develop into an adequate defender as he garners more experience. He looked the part of a burgeoning power-hitting infielder in 2022 and we look forward to seeing if he continues to grow into the role next season.

99.) Junior Caminero, 3B, Tampa Bay Rays

Just stop dealing low, low-minors players to the Rays. Tampa flipped Tobias Myers to Cleveland rather than add him to the 40-man in the 2021-22 offseason and got back Caminero, who had spent 2021 in the Dominican Summer League. He got stateside complex time this past summer and was so good there that he was bumped to full-season ball as an 18-year-old. He kept hitting thereafter, and while he's going to have to move off shortstop—and is already playing a fair bit of third base—his lightning-quick bat and strong approach should get him over the hot corner's higher offensive bar in due time. We're not saying he's going to end up like Curtis Mead, but we're not *not* saying it either.

100.) Josh Jung, 3B, Texas Rangers

Our no. 1 prospect emphatically stamped that ranking in permanent ink with his major-league performance. Our no. 100 prospect homered in his first Rangers at-bat and then struck out in almost 40% of the subsequent ones. Jung has been snakebitten with injuries during his pro career, but had always hit when on the field...right up until they added a third deck to the stadiums. Now, if you are still eligible for one of these lists, your MLB time won't be a significant sample, but there were some warning signs in his gaudy Triple-A numbers, too. His contact rates and exit velocities are fairly pedestrian, and he chases a bit more than you'd prefer. Jung has improved a lot as a defender, but he's going to be a bat-first third baseman, and his bat isn't quite there yet.

101.) Alex Ramirez, OF, New York Mets

A seven-figure IFA signing in 2019, Ramirez has done just about everything you'd ask of that kind of prospect so far. He held his own in the Florida State League (or Low-A Southeast or whatever it was called for that one regrettable year) as an 18-year-old in 2021. He was better than that in 2022 and took the step up to High-A Brooklyn in stride. He hits the ball very hard, though not in the air as much as you'd like, and has a bit of a noisy swing with a bit too many whiffs in it at the moment. He's a good runner but a bit of a ponderous center fielder. He won't be able to legally drink when we lock the 2024 Top 101, in which he might rank 75 spots higher or not really be in consideration for. This list is—as our predecessors have always emphasized—a snapshot in time.

MLB Managers

Craig Counsell wRM+: 105

TEAM	YEAR	W	L	Pythag +/-	Avg PC	100+ P	120+ P	QS	REL	REL w Zero R	IBB	PH	PH Avg	PH HR	SB2	CS2	SB3	CS3	SAC Att	SAC %	POS SAC	Squeeze
MIL	2018	96	67	4	85.5	16	0	51	559	407	34	286	.243	10	97	26	28	8	41	71	6	0
MIL	2019	89	73	8	84.3	16	0	34	588	395	28	314	.190	8	79	18	22	6	33	61	5	1
MIL	2020	29	31	1	81.2	3	0	15	189	124	1	65	.271	1	14	10	1	1	1	0	0	0
MIL	2021	95	67	0	83.8	23	0	70	533	378	19	292	.163	7	74	20	8	1	36	69	5	2
MIL	2022	86	76	1	88.6	33	0	63	548	386	12	124	.284	5	90	22	5	7	15	73	11	0

Aaron Boone wRM+: 103

TEAM	YEAR	W	L	Pythag +/-	Avg PC	100+ P	120+ P	QS	REL	REL w Zero R	IBB	PH	PH Avg	PH HR	SB2	CS2	SB3	CS3	SAC Att	SAC %	POS SAC	Squeeze
NYY	2018	100	62	0	88.2	33	0	67	508	368	9	70	.203	1	54	19	9	1	19	53	10	0
NYY	2019	103	59	3	79.4	20	0	53	545	371	12	57	.231	4	46	20	9	1	20	50	6	2
NYY	2020	33	27	-2	81.4	11	0	18	175	114	5	36	.233	1	23	6	4	1	5	20	1	0
NYY	2021	92	70	6	84.8	24	1	51	512	350	10	94	.218	3	54	15	9	5	12	83	9	0
NYY	2022	99	63	-9	87.3	31	0	68	507	374	10	93	.187	2	83	28	20	7	24	58	14	2

Alex Cora wRM+: 103

TEAM	YEAR	W	L	Pythag +/-	Avg PC	100+ P	120+ P	QS	REL	REL w Zero R	IBB	PH	PH Avg	PH HR	SB2	CS2	SB3	CS3	SAC Att	SAC %	POS SAC	Squeeze
BOS	2018	108	54	3	88.8	42	0	67	535	383	8	96	.202	2	109	25	16	5	9	78	7	0
BOS	2019	84	78	-4	86.6	48	0	55	632	431	22	123	.330	5	59	26	9	5	26	77	18	0
BOS	2021	92	70	3	84.9	18	0	39	563	393	31	93	.221	1	32	16	8	5	15	67	10	0
BOS	2022	78	84	3	82.0	14	0	46	576	386	17	91	.244	3	45	18	7	2	18	67	12	1

Scott Servais wRM+: 103

TEAM	YEAR	W	L	Pythag +/-	Avg PC	100+ P	120+ P	QS	REL	REL w Zero R	IBB	PH	PH Avg	PH HR	SB2	CS2	SB3	CS3	SAC Att	SAC %	POS SAC	Squeeze
SEA	2018	89	73	12	86.4	31	0	66	537	387	21	102	.230	2	69	34	10	2	46	63	27	1
SEA	2019	68	94	0	76.0	20	0	51	538	328	25	81	.243	2	104	42	10	4	18	78	11	0
SEA	2020	27	33	2	84.2	7	0	25	189	120	7	26	.211	0	48	15	2	1	5	60	3	0
SEA	2021	90	72	15	84.7	22	0	55	584	414	23	101	.264	3	58	24	6	0	23	39	9	0
SEA	2022	90	72	1	90.0	34	0	79	536	404	24	127	.257	6	75	24	8	3	15	60	9	0

Kevin Cash wRM+: 102

TEAM	YEAR	W	L	Pythag +/-	Avg PC	100+ P	120+ P	QS	REL	REL w Zero R	IBB	PH	PH Avg	PH HR	SB2	CS2	SB3	CS3	SAC Att	SAC %	POS SAC	Squeeze
TB	2018	90	72	1	63.0	22	0	39	553	363	34	109	.198	1	117	45	11	5	52	54	28	5
TB	2019	96	66	2	69.8	22	0	53	603	413	27	130	.204	3	82	31	10	4	15	53	8	1
TB	2020	40	20	3	71.2	5	0	7	219	155	4	66	.259	0	42	8	6	1	1	0	0	0
TB	2021	100	62	-3	72.7	15	0	33	531	364	27	120	.250	3	81	40	8	3	9	67	6	0
TB	2022	86	76	-2	72.3	1	0	52	573	404	15	114	.260	2	82	29	13	9	12	58	7	0

Tony La Russa wRM+: 101

TEAM	YEAR	W	L	Pythag +/-	Avg PC	100+ P	120+ P	QS	REL	REL w Zero R	IBB	PH	PH Avg	PH HR	SB2	CS2	SB3	CS3	SAC Att	SAC %	POS SAC	Squeeze
CHW	2021	93	69	-6	89.0	42	0	57	512	358	16	83	.162	3	43	19	13	2	35	69	24	2
CHW	2022	76	75	2	88.9	31	0	62	513	357	14	65	.237	1	39	9	14	0	24	67	16	1

Mark Kotsay wRM+: 101

TEAM	YEAR	W	L	Pythag +/-	Avg PC	100+ P	120+ P	QS	REL	REL w Zero R	IBB	PH	PH Avg	PH HR	SB2	CS2	SB3	CS3	SAC Att	SAC %	POS SAC	Squeeze
OAK	2022	60	102	3	84.0	15	0	47	530	365	37	163	.193	3	71	20	7	3	31	71	22	1

Don Mattingly wRM+: 101

TEAM	YEAR	W	L	Pythag +/-	Avg PC	100+ P	120+ P	QS	REL	REL w Zero R	IBB	PH	PH Avg	PH HR	SB2	CS2	SB3	CS3	SAC Att	SAC %	POS SAC	Squeeze
MIA	2018	63	98	7	88.0	29	0	57	546	367	73	281	.177	6	40	29	5	3	47	68	12	1
MIA	2019	57	105	-2	91.3	33	0	60	539	369	52	290	.214	9	49	26	6	1	53	58	8	2
MIA	2020	31	29	5	76.7	1	0	16	215	148	14	36	.233	0	41	10	7	5	9	67	6	1
MIA	2021	67	95	-4	79.0	11	0	49	596	417	43	270	.185	3	93	26	13	5	50	60	11	1
MIA	2022	68	93	-1	87.8	30	0	64	526	370	19	89	.221	1	105	23	16	4	10	50	5	1

Chris Woodward wRM+: 100

TEAM	YEAR	W	L	Pythag +/-	Avg PC	100+ P	120+ P	QS	REL	REL w Zero R	IBB	PH	PH Avg	PH HR	SB2	CS2	SB3	CS3	SAC Att	SAC %	POS SAC	Squeeze
TEX	2019	78	84	4	87.0	60	1	55	500	306	11	82	.214	4	109	33	20	5	25	68	16	0
TEX	2020	22	38	2	83.5	18	0	17	204	128	3	30	.208	0	41	13	8	1	7	14	2	0
TEX	2021	60	102	0	81.2	14	1	50	507	331	11	89	.218	1	94	25	9	2	30	53	15	1
TEX	2022	51	63	-6	80.8	13	0	37	384	259	12	105	.250	4	76	22	13	4	18	39	7	2

Charlie Montoyo wRM+: 100

TEAM	YEAR	W	L	Pythag +/-	Avg PC	100+ P	120+ P	QS	REL	REL w Zero R	IBB	PH	PH Avg	PH HR	SB2	CS2	SB3	CS3	SAC Att	SAC %	POS SAC	Squeeze
TOR	2019	67	95	-3	76.0	19	0	40	591	377	25	79	.154	2	40	16	10	4	19	74	14	1
TOR	2020	32	28	3	76.1	1	0	11	226	141	7	37	.133	0	23	6	10	0	11	73	8	0
TOR	2021	91	71	-9	85.5	28	0	68	537	375	10	100	.167	0	72	15	10	6	18	56	7	1
TOR	2022	45	42	1	81.2	10	0	37	315	218	7	55	.234	0	30	13	2	2	8	75	7	0

Buck Showalter wRM+: 100

TEAM	YEAR	W	L	Pythag +/-	Avg PC	100+ P	120+ P	QS	REL	REL w Zero R	IBB	PH	PH Avg	PH HR	SB2	CS2	SB3	CS3	SAC Att	SAC %	POS SAC	Squeeze
BAL	2018	47	115	-6	87.8	35	1	64	490	304	29	98	.212	2	73	17	8	5	28	46	12	1
NYM	2022	101	61	1	86.8	29	0	72	483	342	13	98	.145	1	53	20	7	3	30	67	20	2

Bob Melvin wRM+: 100

TEAM	YEAR	W	L	Pythag +/-	Avg PC	100+ P	120+ P	QS	REL	REL w Zero R	IBB	PH	PH Avg	PH HR	SB2	CS2	SB3	CS3	SAC Att	SAC %	POS SAC	Squeeze
OAK	2018	97	65	1	80.6	14	0	62	578	427	19	135	.256	3	31	20	3	1	10	60	6	0
OAK	2019	97	65	-1	88.7	30	1	78	547	393	19	116	.235	5	45	20	6	1	11	64	6	0
OAK	2020	36	24	1	81.4	4	0	19	181	137	6	32	.103	1	25	2	1	1	3	67	2	0
OAK	2021	86	76	-1	88.5	28	0	76	504	348	11	158	.241	5	70	15	19	7	21	81	13	1
SD	2022	89	73	3	91.5	40	0	84	488	338	6	108	.188	1	45	20	4	3	34	50	17	1

Rocco Baldelli wRM+: 100

TEAM	YEAR	W	L	Pythag +/-	Avg PC	100+ P	120+ P	QS	REL	REL w Zero R	IBB	PH	PH Avg	PH HR	SB2	CS2	SB3	CS3	SAC Att	SAC %	POS SAC	Squeeze
MIN	2019	101	61	3	89.6	34	0	67	524	379	10	83	.258	2	27	20	1	0	18	56	7	0
MIN	2020	36	24	-1	77.0	4	0	16	202	141	0	29	.250	0	14	7	0	0	5	40	2	1
MIN	2021	73	89	3	81.5	17	0	32	529	355	13	112	.196	0	48	15	7	0	13	54	6	1
MIN	2022	78	84	-4	78.5	9	0	35	549	377	19	121	.192	0	34	14	4	2	15	67	10	2

Phil Nevin wRM+: 100

TEAM	YEAR	W	L	Pythag +/-	Avg PC	100+ P	120+ P	QS	REL	REL w Zero R	IBB	PH	PH Avg	PH HR	SB2	CS2	SB3	CS3	SAC Att	SAC %	POS SAC	Squeeze
LAA	2022	46	59	1	87.4	14	0	32	312	206	15	81	.118	1	39	9	7	3	26	54	14	1

Oliver Marmol wRM+: 100

TEAM	YEAR	W	L	Pythag +/-	Avg PC	100+ P	120+ P	QS	REL	REL w Zero R	IBB	PH	PH Avg	PH HR	SB2	CS2	SB3	CS3	SAC Att	SAC %	POS SAC	Squeeze
STL	2022	93	69	-3	87.6	31	1	62	466	326	11	126	.167	5	85	22	10	2	9	56	5	0

David Bell wRM+: 100

TEAM	YEAR	W	L	Pythag +/-	Avg PC	100+ P	120+ P	QS	REL	REL w Zero R	IBB	PH	PH Avg	PH HR	SB2	CS2	SB3	CS3	SAC Att	SAC %	POS SAC	Squeeze
CIN	2019	75	87	-5	91.6	47	0	65	535	375	31	316	.179	9	73	33	7	4	45	67	2	2
CIN	2020	31	29	1	89.1	18	0	26	168	114	6	68	.228	3	27	8	2	2	1	0	0	0
CIN	2021	83	79	-1	90.0	44	0	68	579	391	30	300	.188	6	28	20	8	4	50	68	5	0
CIN	2022	62	100	-1	86.9	40	1	51	574	390	21	117	.172	1	53	30	5	4	20	60	12	0

Brandon Hyde wRM+: 100

TEAM	YEAR	W	L	Pythag +/-	Avg PC	100+ P	120+ P	QS	REL	REL w Zero R	IBB	PH	PH Avg	PH HR	SB2	CS2	SB3	CS3	SAC Att	SAC %	POS SAC	Squeeze
BAL	2019	54	108	-4	85.1	17	0	41	534	310	11	126	.195	2	72	25	11	5	43	51	19	2
BAL	2020	25	35	-3	75.6	0	0	10	207	138	2	43	.184	2	17	11	2	1	18	83	15	0
BAL	2021	52	110	0	79.4	7	0	31	569	348	12	85	.233	1	47	23	6	0	23	61	13	2
BAL	2022	83	79	4	80.1	12	0	41	541	381	8	94	.200	1	81	26	14	7	26	46	12	0

Bud Black wRM+: 100

TEAM	YEAR	W	L	Pythag +/-	Avg PC	100+ P	120+ P	QS	REL	REL w Zero R	IBB	PH	PH Avg	PH HR	SB2	CS2	SB3	CS3	SAC Att	SAC %	POS SAC	Squeeze
COL	2018	91	72	6	92.2	42	0	84	518	361	24	273	.242	8	91	34	4	0	67	63	11	1
COL	2019	71	91	1	87.6	23	0	46	590	386	33	301	.188	13	63	31	8	0	73	70	10	3
COL	2020	26	34	3	86.1	8	0	28	189	108	5	51	.186	1	37	8	5	0	12	58	7	0
COL	2021	74	87	-1	82.8	13	0	68	543	353	19	278	.233	10	70	21	6	2	71	68	10	4
COL	2022	68	94	5	87.6	21	0	64	497	316	12	37	.267	1	41	19	4	0	17	59	10	0

Dusty Baker Jr. wRM+: 100

TEAM	YEAR	W	L	Pythag +/-	Avg PC	100+ P	120+ P	QS	REL	REL w Zero R	IBB	PH	PH Avg	PH HR	SB2	CS2	SB3	CS3	SAC Att	SAC %	POS SAC	Squeeze
HOU	2020	29	31	-1	83.4	8	0	25	193	122	7	28	.208	0	20	10	2	1	8	75	6	0
HOU	2021	95	67	-7	88.1	28	0	66	512	349	12	94	.235	3	49	11	4	5	16	56	9	1
HOU	2022	106	56	-2	91.9	35	0	94	480	373	6	81	.250	1	72	17	9	2	18	50	9	1

Terry Francona wRM+: 100

TEAM	YEAR	W	L	Pythag +/-	Avg PC	100+ P	120+ P	QS	REL	REL w Zero R	IBB	PH	PH Avg	PH HR	SB2	CS2	SB3	CS3	SAC Att	SAC %	POS SAC	Squeeze
CLE	2018	91	71	-9	96.9	79	2	98	509	361	29	97	.241	2	118	34	15	4	45	56	23	0
CLE	2019	93	69	-1	93.6	76	3	81	522	372	19	100	.213	2	92	28	10	5	62	64	38	0
CLE	2020	35	25	0	92.2	20	0	37	181	130	8	37	.188	0	24	7	2	2	16	38	7	1
CLE	2021	50	49	4	83.0	18	1	30	330	238	6	68	.169	2	43	10	6	1	20	65	13	0
CLE	2022	92	70	3	87.7	11	0	75	507	377	14	96	.227	0	110	25	10	3	29	76	22	1

A.J. Hinch wRM+: 100

TEAM	YEAR	W	L	Pythag +/-	Avg PC	100+ P	120+ P	QS	REL	REL w Zero R	IBB	PH	PH Avg	PH HR	SB2	CS2	SB3	CS3	SAC Att	SAC %	POS SAC	Squeeze
HOU	2018	103	59	-9	95.7	67	1	97	510	396	4	91	.167	1	63	22	8	3	20	70	14	6
HOU	2019	107	55	-2	91.6	55	0	89	492	354	0	81	.175	3	58	24	8	2	19	53	9	1
DET	2021	77	85	3	78.8	6	0	47	577	384	10	72	.266	3	78	21	10	4	22	77	15	3
DET	2022	66	96	5	81.3	9	0	46	581	423	9	85	.169	0	43	23	4	1	15	60	9	0

Mike Matheny wRM+: 99

TEAM	YEAR	W	L	Pythag +/-	Avg PC	100+ P	120+ P	QS	REL	REL w Zero R	IBB	PH	PH Avg	PH HR	SB2	CS2	SB3	CS3	SAC Att	SAC %	POS SAC	Squeeze
STL	2018	47	46	-1	92.9	15	0	42	322	213	24	136	.179	2	32	19	1	2	38	76	8	2
KC	2020	26	34	-1	78.2	9	0	11	232	167	7	50	.200	3	38	17	11	4	19	42	8	0
KC	2021	74	88	4	84.8	22	0	51	556	371	16	80	.219	1	92	28	32	6	55	56	28	2
KC	2022	65	96	3	86.7	13	0	51	558	381	15	91	.304	1	97	30	8	4	34	59	20	1

Rob Thomson wRM+: 99

TEAM	YEAR	W	L	Pythag +/-	Avg PC	100+ P	120+ P	QS	REL	REL w Zero R	IBB	PH	PH Avg	PH HR	SB2	CS2	SB3	CS3	SAC Att	SAC %	POS SAC	Squeeze
PHI	2022	65	46	3	86.2	20	0	55	340	241	7	60	.264	3	62	23	10	0	10	30	3	0

Derek Shelton wRM+: 99

TEAM	YEAR	W	L	Pythag +/-	Avg PC	100+ P	120+ P	QS	REL	REL w Zero R	IBB	PH	PH Avg	PH HR	SB2	CS2	SB3	CS3	SAC Att	SAC %	POS SAC	Squeeze
PIT	2020	19	41	-2	82.1	6	0	9	210	136	3	26	.160	0	14	9	2	3	9	78	7	0
PIT	2021	61	101	5	79.7	3	0	25	583	400	26	290	.232	9	56	26	4	3	54	57	9	1
PIT	2022	62	100	6	79.4	6	0	38	504	313	23	129	.161	3	75	28	15	3	32	56	18	1

Dave Martinez wRM+: 99

TEAM	YEAR	W	L	Pythag +/-	Avg PC	100+ P	120+ P	QS	REL	REL w Zero R	IBB	PH	PH Avg	PH HR	SB2	CS2	SB3	CS3	SAC Att	SAC %	POS SAC	Squeeze
WAS	2018	82	80	-9	94.0	66	1	74	563	409	37	293	.176	4	99	31	20	3	67	61	13	0
WAS	2019	93	69	-3	94.4	62	0	87	530	364	41	253	.261	5	97	26	18	3	84	57	20	2
WAS	2020	26	34	-3	87.8	18	0	16	202	139	22	31	.321	0	29	11	5	1	12	42	5	0
WAS	2021	65	97	-6	84.3	24	0	50	569	370	46	282	.242	6	52	24	5	3	64	59	10	1
WAS	2022	55	107	1	85.0	17	0	30	588	417	12	67	.306	2	69	27	5	6	42	48	20	1

David Ross wRM+: 98

TEAM	YEAR	W	L	Pythag +/-	Avg PC	100+ P	120+ P	QS	REL	REL w Zero R	IBB	PH	PH Avg	PH HR	SB2	CS2	SB3	CS3	SAC Att	SAC %	POS SAC	Squeeze
CHC	2020	34	26	1	84.6	10	0	30	188	128	7	51	.114	1	21	10	2	0	2	50	1	0
CHC	2021	71	91	4	80.1	14	0	43	599	424	25	308	.257	6	75	31	9	2	55	73	9	2
CHC	2022	74	88	2	81.0	9	0	48	528	345	19	132	.150	4	93	34	19	5	34	56	19	0

Gabe Kapler wRM+: 98

TEAM	YEAR	W	L	Pythag +/-	Avg PC	100+ P	120+ P	QS	REL	REL w Zero R	IBB	PH	PH Avg	PH HR	SB2	CS2	SB3	CS3	SAC Att	SAC %	POS SAC	Squeeze
PHI	2018	80	82	5	87.8	38	0	71	596	432	35	295	.207	5	64	20	3	6	48	67	6	0
PHI	2019	81	81	2	89.0	38	0	58	564	401	38	310	.201	9	65	15	12	1	55	62	11	1
SF	2020	29	31	-1	81.9	10	0	11	236	173	2	73	.267	4	19	7	0	1	4	100	4	0
SF	2021	107	55	2	80.8	12	0	63	599	452	20	407	.199	18	62	12	6	5	52	69	7	1
SF	2022	81	81	-2	79.2	21	0	55	576	394	16	256	.241	5	61	14	3	1	15	40	6	0

Brian Snitker wRM+: 97

TEAM	YEAR	W	L	Pythag +/-	Avg PC	100+ P	120+ P	QS	REL	REL w Zero R	IBB	PH	PH Avg	PH HR	SB2	CS2	SB3	CS3	SAC Att	SAC %	POS SAC	Squeeze
ATL	2018	90	72	-3	90.7	39	1	70	553	397	43	247	.202	7	75	28	13	7	65	75	13	3
ATL	2019	97	65	5	88.0	25	0	76	576	411	33	262	.247	9	82	25	8	3	34	74	3	2
ATL	2020	35	25	-1	73.2	2	0	13	228	159	13	29	.200	1	21	4	2	0	3	33	1	0
ATL	2021	88	73	-7	85.3	13	0	67	581	415	34	272	.184	10	56	16	2	3	41	78	8	1
ATL	2022	101	61	-1	90.4	34	0	69	518	380	21	47	.225	0	75	30	12	0	3	33	1	0

Torey Lovullo wRM+: 97

TEAM	YEAR	W	L	Pythag +/-	Avg PC	100+ P	120+ P	QS	REL	REL w Zero R	IBB	PH	PH Avg	PH HR	SB2	CS2	SB3	CS3	SAC Att	SAC %	POS SAC	Squeeze
AZ	2018	82	80	-5	92.7	36	0	78	574	434	43	257	.202	5	62	22	18	4	61	62	10	0
AZ	2019	85	77	-3	88.8	32	0	67	557	390	38	256	.221	12	84	12	3	2	51	61	5	2
AZ	2020	25	35	-2	84.5	2	0	13	200	131	20	27	.000	0	22	6	1	1	4	25	1	0
AZ	2021	52	110	-7	83.6	15	0	41	566	350	45	338	.205	10	38	16	5	0	42	76	6	0
AZ	2022	74	88	-3	88.0	24	0	55	546	371	18	147	.189	4	89	25	14	3	52	60	32	3

Dave Roberts wRM+: 96

TEAM	YEAR	W	L	Pythag +/-	Avg PC	100+ P	120+ P	QS	REL	REL w Zero R	IBB	PH	PH Avg	PH HR	SB2	CS2	SB3	CS3	SAC Att	SAC %	POS SAC	Squeeze
LAD	2018	92	71	-11	86.3	22	0	79	593	441	39	354	.238	9	57	20	18	1	57	68	9	3
LAD	2019	106	56	-4	85.8	24	0	80	545	390	24	307	.234	13	52	10	4	0	64	86	3	3
LAD	2020	43	17	-1	72.8	0	0	18	249	191	4	41	.194	1	25	6	4	1	6	50	3	1
LAD	2021	106	56	-5	80.6	29	1	74	600	446	43	276	.201	9	49	14	15	4	37	86	3	5
LAD	2022	111	51	-8	82.9	6	1	68	563	429	13	83	.219	3	90	17	9	2	8	38	3	0

2023 PECOTA Projected Standings

AL East	Sim W	Sim L	Sim W%	RS	RA	Div %	WC %	Playoff %	WS %
New York Yankees	100.1	61.9	.618	733	558	80.7	17.9	98.6	17.8
Toronto Blue Jays	89.5	72.5	.552	731	644	11.2	57.7	68.9	3.9
Tampa Bay Rays	87.9	74.1	.543	699	628	6.7	54.6	61.3	2.5
Boston Red Sox	81.8	80.2	.505	769	745	1.3	24.2	25.5	0.9
Baltimore Orioles	73.3	88.7	.452	662	716	0.1	3.0	3.1	0.0
AL Central	**Sim W**	**Sim L**	**Sim W%**	**RS**	**RA**	**Div %**	**WC %**	**Playoff %**	**WS %**
Cleveland Guardians	88.3	73.7	.545	714	661	51.5	16.3	67.8	3.4
Minnesota Twins	86.6	75.4	.535	657	620	39.8	19.4	59.2	2.9
Chicago White Sox	79.4	82.6	.490	673	696	8.7	8.1	16.8	0.5
Detroit Tigers	63.1	98.9	.390	566	726	0.0	0.0	0.0	0.0
Kansas City Royals	62.1	99.9	.383	620	804	0.0	0.0	0.0	0.0
AL West	**Sim W**	**Sim L**	**Sim W%**	**RS**	**RA**	**Div %**	**WC %**	**Playoff %**	**WS %**
Houston Astros	96.9	65.1	.598	781	635	80.8	15.4	96.2	12.6
Los Angeles Angels	86.5	75.5	.534	745	691	11.9	41.9	53.8	3.1
Seattle Mariners	84.1	77.9	.519	679	646	5.8	30.4	36.2	1.1
Texas Rangers	79.1	82.9	.488	637	651	1.5	11.1	12.6	0.1
Oakland Athletics	60.5	101.5	.373	544	717	0.0	0.0	0.0	0.0

NL East	Sim W	Sim L	Sim W%	RS	RA	Div %	WC %	Playoff %	WS %
New York Mets	97.7	64.3	.603	803	646	61.2	36.2	97.4	11.4
Atlanta Braves	91.5	70.5	.565	730	632	19.7	62.6	82.3	4.5
Philadelphia Phillies	91.8	70.2	.567	752	654	19.1	62.9	82.0	4.2
Miami Marlins	74.5	87.5	.460	622	674	0.0	4.1	4.1	0.0
Washington Nationals	59.5	102.5	.367	588	782	0.0	0.0	0.0	0.0
NL Central	**Sim W**	**Sim L**	**Sim W%**	**RS**	**RA**	**Div %**	**WC %**	**Playoff %**	**WS %**
St. Louis Cardinals	88.8	73.2	.548	750	690	58.1	12.8	70.9	4.2
Milwaukee Brewers	86.4	75.6	.533	720	681	39.8	17.4	57.2	2.4
Chicago Cubs	73.3	88.7	.452	669	749	1.1	1.6	2.7	0.0
Pittsburgh Pirates	71.5	90.5	.441	644	737	0.9	0.7	1.6	0.0
Cincinnati Reds	65.8	96.2	.406	665	820	0.1	0.3	0.4	0.0
NL West	**Sim W**	**Sim L**	**Sim W%**	**RS**	**RA**	**Div %**	**WC %**	**Playoff %**	**WS %**
Los Angeles Dodgers	102.1	59.9	.630	824	628	73.0	26.9	99.9	16.7
San Diego Padres	96.6	65.4	.596	803	660	27.0	69.0	96.0	7.8
San Francisco Giants	75.9	86.1	.469	672	715	0.0	5.0	5.0	0.0
Arizona Diamondbacks	70.8	91.2	.437	674	765	0.0	0.5	0.5	0.0
Colorado Rockies	64.4	97.6	.398	673	828	0.0	0.0	0.0	0.0

2023 PECOTA Leaderboards

Catcher DRC+

Rank	Name	Team	DRC+
1	Will Smith	LAD	130
2	Alejandro Kirk	TOR	129
3	Adley Rutschman	BAL	121
4	W. Contreras	STL	119
5	Sean Murphy	ATL	117
5	Danny Jansen	TOR	117
7	Salvador Perez	KC	115
8	Yasmani Grandal	CHW	114
9	J.T. Realmuto	PHI	113
10	Keibert Ruiz	WAS	110
11	MJ Melendez	KC	109
12	Austin Nola	SD	106
13	Gabriel Moreno	AZ	105
14	Carson Kelly	AZ	102
15	Logan O'Hoppe	LAA	101

First Base DRC+

Rank	Name	Team	DRC+
1	Pete Alonso	NYM	160
2	Freddie Freeman	LAD	150
3	Paul Goldschmidt	STL	145
4	V. Guerrero	TOR	143
5	José Abreu	HOU	129
6	Luis Arraez	MIN	128
7	Matt Olson	ATL	127
8	Anthony Rizzo	NYY	123
9	Rhys Hoskins	PHI	121
9	Josh Bell	CLE	121
11	V. Pasquantino	KC	120
11	Keston Hiura	MIL	120
13	Rowdy Tellez	MIL	117
13	Ty France	SEA	117
15	Christian Walker	AZ	115

Second Base DRC+

Rank	Name	Team	DRC+
1	Jose Altuve	HOU	138
2	Jeff McNeil	NYM	130
3	Brandon Lowe	TB	122
4	Ketel Marte	AZ	120
5	Jorge Polanco	MIN	114
5	Gavin Lux	LAD	114
5	Jake Cronenworth	SD	114
8	Gleyber Torres	NYY	113
8	Trevor Story	BOS	113
8	Marcus Semien	TEX	113
8	Jonathan India	CIN	113
12	Andrés Giménez	CLE	111
13	Nolan Gorman	STL	109
13	Brendan Donovan	STL	109
15	Kolten Wong	SEA	108

Shortstop DRC+

Rank	Name	Team	DRC+
1	Carlos Correa	FA	134
2	Trea Turner	PHI	132
3	Xander Bogaerts	SD	130
4	Wander Franco	TB	129
5	Corey Seager	TEX	124
6	Bo Bichette	TOR	120
7	Bobby Witt Jr.	KC	118
8	Francisco Lindor	NYM	117
9	Willy Adames	MIL	116
10	Nico Hoerner	CHC	110
11	J.P. Crawford	SEA	108
12	Tim Anderson	CHW	106
13	Dansby Swanson	CHC	104
13	Amed Rosario	CLE	104
15	Oneil Cruz	PIT	103

Third Base DRC+

Rank	Name	Team	DRC+
1	Rafael Devers	BOS	148
2	José Ramírez	CLE	146
3	Manny Machado	SD	144
4	Austin Riley	ATL	141
4	Nolan Arenado	STL	141
6	Alex Bregman	HOU	138
7	Yandy Díaz	TB	136
8	Max Muncy	LAD	134
9	Justin Turner	BOS	125
10	Anthony Rendon	LAA	122
11	Matt Chapman	TOR	119
12	Eugenio Suárez	SEA	117
12	DJ LeMahieu	NYY	117
14	Ryan McMahon	COL	114
15	Luis Urías	MIL	113

Designated Hitter DRC+

Rank	Name	Team	DRC+
1	Yordan Alvarez	HOU	164
2	Bryce Harper	PHI	148
3	Shohei Ohtani	LAA	145
4	J.D. Martinez	LAD	134
5	G. Stanton	NYY	131
6	Michael Brantley	HOU	127
7	Marcell Ozuna	ATL	118
8	Daniel Vogelbach	NYM	117
9	Eloy Jiménez	CHW	116
10	Trey Mancini	FA	115
10	J.D. Davis	SF	115
12	Luke Voit	FA	112
13	Mitch Garver	TEX	111
13	Charlie Blackmon	COL	111
15	Harold Ramírez	TB	106

Left Field DRC+

Rank	Name	Team	DRC+
1	Kyle Schwarber	PHI	136
2	Jesse Winker	MIL	130
3	Joc Pederson	SF	127
4	Kris Bryant	COL	123
5	Alex Verdugo	BOS	122
5	Steven Kwan	CLE	122
5	Mark Canha	NYM	122
8	A. Benintendi	CHW	121
9	Randy Arozarena	TB	117
10	Christian Yelich	MIL	116
11	David Peralta	FA	115
11	L. Gurriel	AZ	115
13	Jorge Soler	MIA	113
14	Joey Gallo	MIN	112
15	Tyler O'Neill	STL	111

Center Field DRC+

Rank	Name	Team	DRC+
1	Aaron Judge	NYY	168
2	Mike Trout	LAA	163
3	Julio Rodríguez	SEA	134
4	Bryan Reynolds	PIT	132
5	George Springer	TOR	130
6	Luis Robert Jr.	CHW	121
7	Byron Buxton	MIN	120
8	Dylan Carlson	STL	114
9	Cedric Mullins	BAL	104
9	E. Hernandez	BOS	104
11	Austin Slater	SF	103
11	Harrison Bader	NYY	103
13	Rafael Ortega	CHC	102
14	Alek Thomas	AZ	101
14	Aaron Hicks	NYY	101

Right Field DRC+

Rank	Name	Team	DRC+
1	Juan Soto	SD	181
2	Ronald Acuña Jr.	ATL	148
3	Kyle Tucker	HOU	136
4	Mookie Betts	LAD	132
5	Brandon Nimmo	NYM	128
6	Taylor Ward	LAA	123
7	Austin Meadows	DET	121
8	Seiya Suzuki	CHC	119
9	Hunter Renfroe	LAA	118
10	Starling Marte	NYM	116
11	A. Santander	BAL	114
12	Mitch Haniger	SF	112
13	Nick Castellanos	PHI	110
14	Lars Nootbaar	STL	109
14	T. Hernandez	SEA	109

Catcher DRP

Rank	Name	Team	DRP
1	Adley Rutschman	BAL	17.1
2	J.T. Realmuto	PHI	12.7
3	Jose Trevino	NYY	12.0
4	Cal Raleigh	SEA	11.5
5	Brian Serven	COL	11.2
5	Austin Hedges	PIT	11.2
7	Max Stassi	LAA	10.9
8	Kyle Higashioka	NYY	10.8
9	Tomás Nido	NYM	9.8
10	Yasmani Grandal	CHW	9.6
11	Jonah Heim	TEX	8.8
12	Manny Piña	OAK	7.6
12	Reese McGuire	BOS	7.6
14	Austin Barnes	LAD	6.8
15	C. Vazquez	MIN	5.1

First Base DRP

Rank	Name	Team	DRP
1	Paul Goldschmidt	STL	2.1
2	Freddie Freeman	LAD	1.9
3	Yuli Gurriel	FA	1.2
4	Christian Walker	AZ	1.0
4	José Abreu	HOU	1.0
6	Matt Olson	ATL	0.6
6	Ty France	SEA	0.6
8	Donovan Solano	FA	0.5
8	Carlos Santana	PIT	0.5
8	Ryan Mountcastle	BAL	0.5
8	Luis Arraez	MIN	0.5
12	Jared Walsh	LAA	0.4
13	Joey Votto	CIN	0.3
13	Darin Ruf	NYM	0.3
13	Joey Meneses	WAS	0.3

Second Base DRP

Rank	Name	Team	DRP
1	Gavin Lux	LAD	3.9
2	Tommy Edman	STL	3.2
3	Marcus Semien	TEX	2.7
4	Adam Frazier	BAL	2.2
5	Jonathan Schoop	DET	2.1
5	Brendan Rodgers	COL	2.1
7	Tony Kemp	OAK	1.7
8	Gleyber Torres	NYY	1.6
9	David Fletcher	LAA	1.5
10	Jose Altuve	HOU	1.2
11	Ozzie Albies	ATL	1.1
12	Josh Harrison	FA	1.0
13	Nicky Lopez	KC	0.9
13	Jon Berti	MIA	0.9
15	Ketel Marte	AZ	0.7

Shortstop DRP

Rank	Name	Team	DRP
1	Dansby Swanson	CHC	7.8
2	Willy Adames	MIL	7.6
3	Nick Allen	OAK	5.3
4	Javier Báez	DET	5.1
5	J.P. Crawford	SEA	4.8
6	Trea Turner	PHI	4.7
7	Carlos Correa	FA	3.3
8	Amed Rosario	CLE	3.0
8	Nick Ahmed	AZ	3.0
10	Brandon Crawford	SF	2.7
11	Geraldo Perdomo	AZ	2.2
12	Miguel Rojas	MIA	2.1
13	CJ Abrams	WAS	2.0
14	Jorge Mateo	BAL	1.6
14	Elvis Andrus	FA	1.6

Third Base DRP

Rank	Name	Team	DRP
1	Ke'Bryan Hayes	PIT	4.2
2	Yoán Moncada	CHW	3.1
3	Nolan Arenado	STL	3.0
4	Matt Chapman	TOR	2.7
5	Austin Riley	ATL	2.6
6	Anthony Rendon	LAA	1.6
6	Alex Bregman	HOU	1.6
8	Joey Wendle	MIA	1.5
8	Gio Urshela	LAA	1.5
10	DJ LeMahieu	NYY	1.2
11	Ramón Urías	BAL	1.1
12	Yandy Díaz	TB	1.0
13	Eugenio Suárez	SEA	0.8
14	Manny Machado	SD	0.6
15	José Ramírez	CLE	0.5

Left Field DRP

Rank	Name	Team	DRP
1	Steven Kwan	CLE	11.3
2	Christian Yelich	MIL	9.2
3	A. Benintendi	CHW	5.5
4	Tyler O'Neill	STL	3.8
4	Ian Happ	CHC	3.8
6	Trayce Thompson	LAD	2.9
6	Robbie Grossman	FA	2.9
8	Eddie Rosario	ATL	2.1
8	David Peralta	FA	2.1
10	Akil Baddoo	DET	2.0
11	Brandon Marsh	PHI	1.7
12	Billy Hamilton	MIN	1.2
13	Raimel Tapia	FA	1.1
13	Chas McCormick	HOU	1.1
13	Connor Joe	PIT	1.1

Center Field DRP

Rank	Name	Team	DRP
1	M. Taylor	KC	11.6
2	Trent Grisham	SD	10.5
3	Harrison Bader	NYY	8.3
4	Riley Greene	DET	7.1
5	Cody Bellinger	CHC	7.0
6	Jose Siri	TB	5.7
7	Mike Trout	LAA	5.0
8	Byron Buxton	MIN	4.6
9	Aaron Judge	NYY	4.5
10	Jake Meyers	HOU	4.3
11	Myles Straw	CLE	3.6
12	Leody Taveras	TEX	3.4
13	Kevin Kiermaier	TOR	2.6
14	Magneuris Sierra	LAA	2.0
15	Aaron Hicks	NYY	1.9

Right Field DRP

Rank	Name	Team	DRP
1	Mookie Betts	LAD	15.8
2	Kyle Tucker	HOU	8.8
3	Ronald Acuña Jr.	ATL	6.7
4	Brandon Nimmo	NYM	6.4
5	Mike Yastrzemski	SF	6.3
6	Kyle Isbel	KC	3.4
7	Lars Nootbaar	STL	3.3
8	Austin Meadows	DET	3.2
9	Manuel Margot	TB	2.6
10	J. Bradley	FA	2.4
11	Max Kepler	MIN	1.9
12	Daulton Varsho	TOR	1.6
13	Adolis García	TEX	1.1
13	José Azocar	SD	1.1
15	Seiya Suzuki	CHC	1.0

Catcher WARP

Rank	Name	Team	WARP
1	Adley Rutschman	BAL	5.0
1	J.T. Realmuto	PHI	5.0
3	Will Smith	LAD	3.7
4	Alejandro Kirk	TOR	3.2
5	Yasmani Grandal	CHW	3.1
6	Sean Murphy	ATL	3.0
7	W. Contreras	STL	2.9
8	Cal Raleigh	SEA	2.7
9	Danny Jansen	TOR	2.3
10	Keibert Ruiz	WAS	2.0
11	C. Vazquez	MIN	1.9
12	Jonah Heim	TEX	1.8
13	Jose Trevino	NYY	1.7
13	Austin Barnes	LAD	1.7
15	Max Stassi	LAA	1.5

First Base WARP

Rank	Name	Team	WARP
1	Freddie Freeman	LAD	5.6
2	Pete Alonso	NYM	5.3
3	Paul Goldschmidt	STL	4.9
4	V. Guerrero	TOR	4.0
5	Luis Arraez	MIN	3.4
6	Matt Olson	ATL	3.0
6	José Abreu	HOU	3.0
8	Anthony Rizzo	NYY	2.7
9	V. Pasquantino	KC	2.6
10	Rhys Hoskins	PHI	2.5
11	Josh Bell	CLE	2.2
12	Nathaniel Lowe	TEX	2.1
12	Ty France	SEA	2.1
14	Christian Walker	AZ	1.9
14	Ryan Mountcastle	BAL	1.9

Second Base WARP

Rank	Name	Team	WARP
1	Jose Altuve	HOU	5.5
2	Marcus Semien	TEX	4.2
3	Andrés Giménez	CLE	4.0
4	Jeff McNeil	NYM	3.9
4	Gavin Lux	LAD	3.9
4	Tommy Edman	STL	3.9
7	Trevor Story	BOS	3.6
8	Ketel Marte	AZ	3.4
8	Brandon Lowe	TB	3.4
10	Jorge Polanco	MIN	3.0
11	Kolten Wong	SEA	2.7
11	Gleyber Torres	NYY	2.7
13	Adam Frazier	BAL	2.6
13	J. Chisholm	MIA	2.6
13	Jon Berti	MIA	2.6

Shortstop WARP

Rank	Name	Team	WARP
1	Trea Turner	PHI	6.7
2	Xander Bogaerts	SD	4.2
2	Bo Bichette	TOR	4.2
4	Wander Franco	TB	4.1
5	Francisco Lindor	NYM	4.0
6	Willy Adames	MIL	3.9
7	Carlos Correa	FA	3.8
8	Dansby Swanson	CHC	3.7
8	Corey Seager	TEX	3.7
10	Amed Rosario	CLE	3.4
10	Nico Hoerner	CHC	3.4
12	J.P. Crawford	SEA	3.2
13	Bobby Witt Jr.	KC	2.8
13	Tim Anderson	CHW	2.8
15	Oneil Cruz	PIT	2.7

Third Base WARP

Rank	Name	Team	WARP
1	José Ramírez	CLE	6.7
2	Manny Machado	SD	5.3
3	Nolan Arenado	STL	4.8
4	Austin Riley	ATL	4.7
5	Rafael Devers	BOS	4.5
6	Alex Bregman	HOU	4.2
7	Yandy Díaz	TB	3.9
8	Max Muncy	LAD	3.6
9	Matt Chapman	TOR	2.9
10	Anthony Rendon	LAA	2.6
11	Ryan McMahon	COL	2.5
11	DJ LeMahieu	NYY	2.5
11	Ke'Bryan Hayes	PIT	2.5
14	Justin Turner	BOS	2.4
14	Eugenio Suárez	SEA	2.4

Designated Hitter WARP

Rank	Name	Team	WARP
1	Yordan Alvarez	HOU	5.6
2	Shohei Ohtani	LAA	5.3
3	Michael Brantley	HOU	3.2
4	J.D. Martinez	LAD	3.1
5	Bryce Harper	PHI	3.0
6	G. Stanton	NYY	2.4
7	Charlie Blackmon	COL	2.2
8	Eloy Jiménez	CHW	1.7
9	Andrew McCutchen	FA	1.6
9	Trey Mancini	FA	1.6
11	Daniel Vogelbach	NYM	1.4
11	Mitch Garver	TEX	1.4
11	J.D. Davis	SF	1.4
14	Luke Voit	FA	1.2
15	Harold Ramírez	TB	1.1

Left Field WARP

Rank	Name	Team	WARP
1	Steven Kwan	CLE	5.4
2	Christian Yelich	MIL	4.4
3	Kyle Schwarber	PHI	3.8
4	Tyler O'Neill	STL	3.5
5	A. Benintendi	CHW	3.4
6	Mark Canha	NYM	3.2
7	Joc Pederson	SF	3.1
8	Jesse Winker	MIL	3.0
9	Kris Bryant	COL	2.9
10	Alex Verdugo	BOS	2.6
10	Ian Happ	CHC	2.6
12	Chris Taylor	LAD	2.5
13	Esteury Ruiz	OAK	2.4
14	Corbin Carroll	AZ	2.3
15	Bubba Thompson	TEX	2.1

Center Field WARP

Rank	Name	Team	WARP
1	Aaron Judge	NYY	7.2
2	Mike Trout	LAA	6.0
3	Julio Rodríguez	SEA	4.7
4	George Springer	TOR	3.9
5	Bryan Reynolds	PIT	3.8
5	Byron Buxton	MIN	3.8
7	Luis Robert Jr.	CHW	3.6
7	Riley Greene	DET	3.6
9	Harrison Bader	NYY	3.2
10	Myles Straw	CLE	3.1
11	Cedric Mullins	BAL	3.0
11	Trent Grisham	SD	3.0
13	Cody Bellinger	CHC	2.9
14	Dylan Carlson	STL	2.6
15	M. Taylor	KC	2.5

Right Field WARP

Rank	Name	Team	WARP
1	Juan Soto	SD	8.3
2	Kyle Tucker	HOU	6.4
3	Mookie Betts	LAD	6.3
4	Ronald Acuña Jr.	ATL	6.1
5	Brandon Nimmo	NYM	5.3
6	Starling Marte	NYM	3.6
7	Austin Meadows	DET	3.3
8	Seiya Suzuki	CHC	2.9
9	Taylor Ward	LAA	2.8
9	Daulton Varsho	TOR	2.8
11	Mike Yastrzemski	SF	2.7
12	Lars Nootbaar	STL	2.4
13	Dylan Moore	SEA	2.3
14	Jake McCarthy	AZ	2.1
15	Hunter Renfroe	LAA	1.8

Batting Average

Rank	Name	Team	BA
1	Luis Arraez	MIN	.312
2	Jeff McNeil	NYM	.303
3	Freddie Freeman	LAD	.302
4	Trea Turner	PHI	.299
5	Michael Brantley	HOU	.294
6	Rafael Devers	BOS	.293
6	Yordan Alvarez	HOU	.293
8	Alex Verdugo	BOS	.292
9	Tim Anderson	CHW	.291
10	Juan Soto	SD	.290
10	Steven Kwan	CLE	.290
10	Wander Franco	TB	.290
13	Luis Robert Jr.	CHW	.289
14	V. Guerrero	TOR	.287
14	Yandy Díaz	TB	.287
16	Masataka Yoshida	BOS	.286
17	Paul Goldschmidt	STL	.285
18	Jose Altuve	HOU	.284
19	Julio Rodríguez	SEA	.283
19	Bo Bichette	TOR	.283
19	Pete Alonso	NYM	.283
22	Amed Rosario	CLE	.282
22	Manny Machado	SD	.282
22	Yonathan Daza	COL	.282
22	Xander Bogaerts	SD	.282

On-Base Percentage

Rank	Name	Team	OBP
1	Juan Soto	SD	.440
2	Freddie Freeman	LAD	.392
3	Aaron Judge	NYY	.391
4	Yordan Alvarez	HOU	.388
5	Yandy Díaz	TB	.385
6	Masataka Yoshida	BOS	.383
7	Bryce Harper	PHI	.377
7	Ronald Acuña Jr.	ATL	.377
9	Mike Trout	LAA	.376
10	Brandon Nimmo	NYM	.375
10	Luis Arraez	MIN	.375
12	Jesse Winker	MIL	.374
12	Alex Bregman	HOU	.374
14	F. Tatis	SD	.370
14	Paul Goldschmidt	STL	.370
16	Jeff McNeil	NYM	.369
16	Pete Alonso	NYM	.369
18	Alejandro Kirk	TOR	.365
19	Mark Canha	NYM	.364
20	Justin Turner	BOS	.363
20	Shohei Ohtani	LAA	.363
20	Jose Altuve	HOU	.363
23	Max Muncy	LAD	.362
23	Steven Kwan	CLE	.362
25	V. Guerrero	TOR	.361

Slugging Percentage

Rank	Name	Team	SLG
1	Mike Trout	LAA	.590
2	Aaron Judge	NYY	.581
3	Pete Alonso	NYM	.574
4	Yordan Alvarez	HOU	.572
5	Juan Soto	SD	.557
6	F. Tatis	SD	.556
7	Rafael Devers	BOS	.541
8	Shohei Ohtani	LAA	.540
9	José Ramírez	CLE	.532
10	Kyle Schwarber	PHI	.531
11	J.D. Martinez	LAD	.528
11	Manny Machado	SD	.528
13	Bryce Harper	PHI	.523
14	Austin Riley	ATL	.518
15	Nolan Arenado	STL	.513
16	G. Stanton	NYY	.507
16	Ronald Acuña Jr.	ATL	.507
18	Kyle Tucker	HOU	.504
19	V. Guerrero	TOR	.502
20	Paul Goldschmidt	STL	.500
21	Freddie Freeman	LAD	.499
22	Mookie Betts	LAD	.497
23	Will Smith	LAD	.492
24	Jose Altuve	HOU	.491
25	Julio Rodríguez	SEA	.490

Isolated Slugging Percentage

Rank	Name	Team	ISO
1	Mike Trout	LAA	.313
2	Aaron Judge	NYY	.300
3	Kyle Schwarber	PHI	.292
4	Pete Alonso	NYM	.290
5	Yordan Alvarez	HOU	.280
6	F. Tatis	SD	.279
7	Juan Soto	SD	.267
8	Shohei Ohtani	LAA	.265
9	G. Stanton	NYY	.259
10	José Ramírez	CLE	.256
11	Miguel Sanó	FA	.250
11	J.D. Martinez	LAD	.250
13	Rafael Devers	BOS	.248
13	Byron Buxton	MIN	.248
15	Max Muncy	LAD	.247
16	Manny Machado	SD	.246
17	Bryce Harper	PHI	.245
18	Austin Riley	ATL	.242
18	Keston Hiura	MIL	.242
20	Eugenio Suárez	SEA	.240
21	Mike Zunino	CLE	.236
21	Hunter Renfroe	LAA	.236
21	Matt Olson	ATL	.236
24	Joc Pederson	SF	.233
24	Joey Gallo	MIN	.233

OPS

Rank	Name	Team	OPS
1	Juan Soto	SD	.997
2	Aaron Judge	NYY	.972
3	Mike Trout	LAA	.967
4	Yordan Alvarez	HOU	.960
5	Pete Alonso	NYM	.942
6	F. Tatis	SD	.926
7	Shohei Ohtani	LAA	.903
8	Bryce Harper	PHI	.901
9	Rafael Devers	BOS	.900
10	Freddie Freeman	LAD	.891
11	José Ramírez	CLE	.890
12	Ronald Acuña Jr.	ATL	.884
13	Manny Machado	SD	.883
14	J.D. Martinez	LAD	.877
15	Kyle Schwarber	PHI	.876
16	Paul Goldschmidt	STL	.869
17	Austin Riley	ATL	.866
18	V. Guerrero	TOR	.863
19	Nolan Arenado	STL	.857
20	Jose Altuve	HOU	.855
21	Kyle Tucker	HOU	.849
21	Alex Bregman	HOU	.849
21	Mookie Betts	LAD	.849
24	Will Smith	LAD	.847
25	Max Muncy	LAD	.846

BABIP

Rank	Name	Team	BABIP
1	Keston Hiura	MIL	.362
2	Elly De La Cruz	CIN	.351
3	Trea Turner	PHI	.349
4	Khalil Lee	NYM	.348
5	Chris Taylor	LAD	.346
6	Tim Anderson	CHW	.345
7	Brandon Marsh	PHI	.344
7	Brenton Doyle	COL	.344
9	Brett Baty	NYM	.342
9	Jorge Alfaro	FA	.342
11	Julio Rodríguez	SEA	.341
11	Luis Robert Jr.	CHW	.341
13	Nathaniel Lowe	TEX	.339
14	J.D. Davis	SF	.338
15	Rafael Devers	BOS	.335
15	Franchy Cordero	BAL	.335
17	Paul Goldschmidt	STL	.334
18	Marcus Wilson	SEA	.333
18	Mike Trout	LAA	.333
18	Bryan Reynolds	PIT	.333
21	Cody Thomas	OAK	.332
21	J. Encarnacion	MIA	.332
23	Blake Sabol	PIT	.331
23	Trevor Larnach	MIN	.331
23	Nick Gonzales	PIT	.331

Runs Scored

Rank	Name	Team	R
1	Juan Soto	SD	106
2	Mookie Betts	LAD	102
2	Ronald Acuña Jr.	ATL	102
4	Aaron Judge	NYY	101
4	Jose Altuve	HOU	101
6	Freddie Freeman	LAD	100
7	Brandon Nimmo	NYM	97
8	Kyle Schwarber	PHI	96
9	F. Tatis	SD	94
10	Manny Machado	SD	93
10	Yordan Alvarez	HOU	93
10	Pete Alonso	NYM	93
13	Mike Trout	LAA	92
13	Shohei Ohtani	LAA	92
13	Rafael Devers	BOS	92
16	José Ramírez	CLE	89
17	Trea Turner	PHI	86
18	Paul Goldschmidt	STL	85
19	Austin Riley	ATL	84
19	Brandon Lowe	TB	84
19	Rhys Hoskins	PHI	84
22	Matt Olson	ATL	83
23	Max Muncy	LAD	82
23	E. Hernandez	BOS	82
25	Jesse Winker	MIL	81

Runs Batted In

Rank	Name	Team	RBI
1	Pete Alonso	NYM	113
2	Manny Machado	SD	105
3	Yordan Alvarez	HOU	103
4	José Ramírez	CLE	100
5	Rafael Devers	BOS	98
6	Aaron Judge	NYY	95
6	Nolan Arenado	STL	95
8	Austin Riley	ATL	93
9	Mike Trout	LAA	92
9	Juan Soto	SD	92
11	Paul Goldschmidt	STL	91
12	Francisco Lindor	NYM	90
13	Freddie Freeman	LAD	89
14	Kyle Schwarber	PHI	88
14	V. Guerrero	TOR	88
16	Matt Olson	ATL	86
16	Shohei Ohtani	LAA	86
16	J.D. Martinez	LAD	86
19	Kyle Tucker	HOU	85
20	F. Tatis	SD	84
21	Joc Pederson	SF	82
22	Christian Walker	AZ	81
22	Max Muncy	LAD	81
22	Alex Bregman	HOU	81
22	Xander Bogaerts	SD	81

Home Runs

Rank	Name	Team	HR
1	Aaron Judge	NYY	43
2	Kyle Schwarber	PHI	42
3	Mike Trout	LAA	41
3	Pete Alonso	NYM	41
5	Yordan Alvarez	HOU	37
6	Manny Machado	SD	36
7	Shohei Ohtani	LAA	35
8	F. Tatis	SD	34
8	Austin Riley	ATL	34
10	G. Stanton	NYY	33
10	Juan Soto	SD	33
10	José Ramírez	CLE	33
10	Matt Olson	ATL	33
14	Eugenio Suárez	SEA	32
15	Rafael Devers	BOS	31
15	Nolan Arenado	STL	31
15	Ronald Acuña Jr.	ATL	31
18	Joc Pederson	SF	30
18	Max Muncy	LAD	30
18	J.D. Martinez	LAD	30
18	Rhys Hoskins	PHI	30
18	Mookie Betts	LAD	30
23	A. Santander	BAL	29
23	Matt Chapman	TOR	29
23	Byron Buxton	MIN	29

Stolen Bases

Rank	Name	Team	SB
1	Ronald Acuña Jr.	ATL	40
2	Esteury Ruiz	OAK	36
3	Bubba Thompson	TEX	35
3	J. Chisholm	MIA	35
5	Dylan Moore	SEA	34
6	Jon Berti	MIA	32
7	Bobby Witt Jr.	KC	31
7	Kyle Tucker	HOU	31
7	José Ramírez	CLE	31
10	Julio Rodríguez	SEA	30
10	Jake McCarthy	AZ	30
10	Randy Arozarena	TB	30
13	Cedric Mullins	BAL	29
13	Akil Baddoo	DET	29
15	A. Mondesi	KC	28
15	Tommy Edman	STL	28
17	Starling Marte	NYM	27
17	Andrés Giménez	CLE	27
19	Trea Turner	PHI	26
19	Myles Straw	CLE	26
21	F. Tatis	SD	25
21	Harrison Bader	NYY	25
23	Jose Siri	TB	23
23	Victor Robles	WAS	23
23	Jorge Mateo	BAL	23

Walk Rate

Rank	Name	Team	BB%
1	Juan Soto	SD	20.6
2	Daniel Vogelbach	NYM	15.7
3	Yasmani Grandal	CHW	15.4
4	Max Muncy	LAD	15.0
5	Aaron Judge	NYY	14.6
6	Joey Gallo	MIN	14.5
7	Edouard Julien	MIN	13.9
8	Jon Singleton	MIL	13.8
8	Jesse Winker	MIL	13.8
10	Ji-Man Choi	PIT	13.5
10	Carlos Santana	PIT	13.5
12	Christian Yelich	MIL	13.4
13	Aaron Hicks	NYY	13.3
14	Triston Casas	BOS	13.2
15	Alex Bregman	HOU	13.1
15	Yandy Díaz	TB	13.1
17	Cavan Biggio	TOR	13.0
18	Bryce Harper	PHI	12.9
19	Kyle Schwarber	PHI	12.8
20	Adley Rutschman	BAL	12.7
21	Zack Collins	PIT	12.6
22	Brandon Belt	FA	12.5
22	Yordan Alvarez	HOU	12.5
24	Joey Votto	CIN	12.3
24	Mike Trout	LAA	12.3

Strikeout Rate

Rank	Name	Team	K%
1	W. Astudillo	MIA	6.1
2	Luis Arraez	MIN	6.5
3	Nick Madrigal	CHC	7.6
4	Steven Kwan	CLE	8.1
5	Masataka Yoshida	BOS	9.7
6	David Fletcher	LAA	9.8
7	Wander Franco	TB	10.1
8	Yuli Gurriel	FA	10.8
9	Michael Brantley	HOU	11.0
10	Jeff McNeil	NYM	11.1
10	Tony Kemp	OAK	11.1
12	Keibert Ruiz	WAS	11.2
13	Michael Stefanic	LAA	11.5
13	José Iglesias	FA	11.5
15	Alejandro Kirk	TOR	11.6
15	Nico Hoerner	CHC	11.6
17	I. Kiner-Falefa	NYY	11.7
18	Ildemaro Vargas	WAS	11.8
18	Adam Frazier	BAL	11.8
20	Carlos Pérez	CHW	12.0
21	Alex Bregman	HOU	12.2
22	Kevin Newman	CIN	12.3
22	Miguel Rojas	MIA	12.3
24	Luis Guillorme	NYM	12.6
25	Nolan Arenado	STL	12.7

Catcher Defense Added

Rank	Name	Team	Total Runs
1	Adley Rutschman	BAL	15.6
2	Cal Raleigh	SEA	12.2
3	Austin Hedges	PIT	11.8
4	Brian Serven	COL	11.3
5	Max Stassi	LAA	11.0
5	Jose Trevino	NYY	11.0
7	Tomás Nido	NYM	10.1
8	Kyle Higashioka	NYY	9.9
8	Yasmani Grandal	CHW	9.9
10	Jonah Heim	TEX	9.4
11	J.T. Realmuto	PHI	9.0
12	Austin Barnes	LAD	7.3
13	Reese McGuire	BOS	7.2
14	Manny Piña	OAK	6.7
15	Mike Zunino	CLE	5.2
16	C. Vazquez	MIN	4.8
17	Ryan Jeffers	MIN	4.4
18	Will Smith	LAD	3.9
19	Danny Jansen	TOR	3.5
20	Seby Zavala	CHW	3.2
21	René Pinto	TB	3.1
22	Travis d'Arnaud	ATL	3.0
22	Sean Murphy	ATL	3.0
24	Alejandro Kirk	TOR	2.8
25	Victor Caratini	MIL	2.4

Framing Runs

Rank	Name	Team	Framing Runs
1	Adley Rutschman	BAL	15.3
2	Cal Raleigh	SEA	12.0
3	Austin Hedges	PIT	11.4
4	Brian Serven	COL	11.3
5	Max Stassi	LAA	11.0
6	Jose Trevino	NYY	10.8
7	Yasmani Grandal	CHW	9.9
8	Tomás Nido	NYM	9.8
9	Jonah Heim	TEX	9.6
9	Kyle Higashioka	NYY	9.6
11	J.T. Realmuto	PHI	7.4
12	Austin Barnes	LAD	7.2
13	Reese McGuire	BOS	7.0
14	Manny Piña	OAK	6.8
15	Mike Zunino	CLE	5.3
16	C. Vazquez	MIN	5.2
17	Ryan Jeffers	MIN	4.4
18	Will Smith	LAD	3.8
19	Seby Zavala	CHW	3.4
20	René Pinto	TB	3.3
21	Danny Jansen	TOR	3.1
22	Travis d'Arnaud	ATL	2.9
23	Alejandro Kirk	TOR	2.6
24	Sean Murphy	ATL	2.5
25	Victor Caratini	MIL	2.1

Called Strikes Above Average

Rank	Name	Team	CSAA
1	Brian Serven	COL	.018
2	Austin Hedges	PIT	.016
2	Tomás Nido	NYM	.016
4	Kyle Higashioka	NYY	.013
4	Adley Rutschman	BAL	.013
6	Max Stassi	LAA	.012
6	Jose Trevino	NYY	.012
8	Austin Barnes	LAD	.011
8	Cal Raleigh	SEA	.011
10	Yasmani Grandal	CHW	.010
10	Jonah Heim	TEX	.010
12	Manny Piña	OAK	.009
13	Gabriel Moreno	AZ	.008
13	Reese McGuire	BOS	.008
15	René Pinto	TB	.007
15	Ryan Jeffers	MIN	.007
17	Seby Zavala	CHW	.006
17	J.T. Realmuto	PHI	.006
19	Travis d'Arnaud	ATL	.005
19	C. Vazquez	MIN	.005
19	Anthony Bemboom	BAL	.005
19	Payton Henry	MIL	.005
19	Mike Zunino	CLE	.005
19	Luke Maile	CIN	.005
19	Jason Delay	PIT	.005

Throwing Runs

Rank	Name	Team	Throwing Runs
1	J.T. Realmuto	PHI	0.9
2	W. Contreras	MIL	0.5
2	Tom Murphy	SEA	0.5
4	W. Contreras	STL	0.4
5	Danny Jansen	TOR	0.3
5	Tyler Stephenson	CIN	0.3
5	Cal Raleigh	SEA	0.3
8	Logan O'Hoppe	LAA	0.2
8	Connor Wong	BOS	0.2
8	Andrew Knizner	STL	0.2
8	Kyle Higashioka	NYY	0.2
8	Jose Herrera	AZ	0.2
8	Sean Murphy	ATL	0.2
8	C. Bethancourt	TB	0.2
8	Victor Caratini	MIL	0.2
8	Reese McGuire	BOS	0.2
8	Iván Herrera	STL	0.2
8	Mike Zunino	CLE	0.2
19	Elias Díaz	COL	0.1
19	Eric Haase	DET	0.1
19	Nick Fortes	MIA	0.1
19	Luke Maile	CIN	0.1
19	Chadwick Tromp	ATL	0.1
19	Salvador Perez	KC	0.1
19	Garrett Stubbs	PHI	0.1

Blocking Runs

Rank	Name	Team	Blocking Runs
1	J.T. Realmuto	PHI	0.7
2	Adley Rutschman	BAL	0.5
2	Jacob Stallings	MIA	0.5
4	Tucker Barnhart	CHC	0.4
4	Jose Trevino	NYY	0.4
6	Austin Hedges	PIT	0.3
6	Keibert Ruiz	WAS	0.3
6	Sean Murphy	ATL	0.3
6	Tomás Nido	NYM	0.3
6	W. Contreras	STL	0.3
11	Austin Barnes	LAD	0.2
11	Manny Piña	OAK	0.2
11	Austin Nola	SD	0.2
11	Alejandro Kirk	TOR	0.2
11	Carson Kelly	AZ	0.2
11	Yan Gomes	CHC	0.2
11	Logan O'Hoppe	LAA	0.2
18	Luis Campusano	SD	0.1
18	Victor Caratini	MIL	0.1
18	Carlos Pérez	CHW	0.1
18	Will Smith	LAD	0.1
18	Travis d'Arnaud	ATL	0.1
18	Danny Jansen	TOR	0.1
18	Kyle Higashioka	NYY	0.1
25	Ryan Jeffers	MIN	0.0

Swipe Rate Above Average

Rank	Name	Team	SRAA
1	Tom Murphy	SEA	-.022
1	Iván Herrera	STL	-.022
3	Chadwick Tromp	ATL	-.018
3	J.T. Realmuto	PHI	-.018
5	W. Contreras	MIL	-.014
6	Freddy Fermin	KC	-.013
7	Jose Herrera	AZ	-.012
8	Andrew Knizner	STL	-.010
8	Mark Kolozsvary	BAL	-.010
10	Danny Jansen	TOR	-.009
10	Luke Maile	CIN	-.009
10	Logan O'Hoppe	LAA	-.009
10	Connor Wong	BOS	-.009
14	C. Bethancourt	TB	-.008
14	Tyler Stephenson	CIN	-.008
16	Kyle Higashioka	NYY	-.007
16	W. Contreras	STL	-.007
16	Anthony Bemboom	BAL	-.007
16	Cal Raleigh	SEA	-.007
20	Victor Caratini	MIL	-.006
21	Eric Haase	DET	-.005
21	Reese McGuire	BOS	-.005
21	Payton Henry	MIL	-.005
21	Nick Fortes	MIA	-.005
25	Garrett Stubbs	PHI	-.004

AL Hitter WARP

Rank	Name	Team	WARP
1	Aaron Judge	NYY	7.2
2	José Ramírez	CLE	6.7
3	Kyle Tucker	HOU	6.4
4	Mike Trout	LAA	6.0
5	Yordan Alvarez	HOU	5.6
6	Jose Altuve	HOU	5.5
7	Steven Kwan	CLE	5.4
8	Shohei Ohtani	LAA	5.3
9	Adley Rutschman	BAL	5.0
10	Julio Rodríguez	SEA	4.7
11	Rafael Devers	BOS	4.5
12	Marcus Semien	TEX	4.2
12	Alex Bregman	HOU	4.2
12	Bo Bichette	TOR	4.2
15	Wander Franco	TB	4.1
16	V. Guerrero	TOR	4.0
16	Andrés Giménez	CLE	4.0
18	Masataka Yoshida	BOS	3.9
18	George Springer	TOR	3.9
18	Yandy Díaz	TB	3.9
21	Byron Buxton	MIN	3.8
22	Corey Seager	TEX	3.7
23	Trevor Story	BOS	3.6
23	Luis Robert Jr.	CHW	3.6
23	Riley Greene	DET	3.6

NL Hitter WARP

Rank	Name	Team	WARP
1	Juan Soto	SD	8.3
2	Trea Turner	PHI	6.7
3	Mookie Betts	LAD	6.3
4	Ronald Acuña Jr.	ATL	6.1
5	Freddie Freeman	LAD	5.6
6	Brandon Nimmo	NYM	5.3
6	Manny Machado	SD	5.3
6	Pete Alonso	NYM	5.3
9	F. Tatis	SD	5.2
10	J.T. Realmuto	PHI	5.0
11	Paul Goldschmidt	STL	4.9
12	Nolan Arenado	STL	4.8
13	Austin Riley	ATL	4.7
14	Christian Yelich	MIL	4.4
15	Xander Bogaerts	SD	4.2
16	Francisco Lindor	NYM	4.0
17	Jeff McNeil	NYM	3.9
17	Gavin Lux	LAD	3.9
17	Tommy Edman	STL	3.9
17	Willy Adames	MIL	3.9
21	Kyle Schwarber	PHI	3.8
21	Bryan Reynolds	PIT	3.8
23	Dansby Swanson	CHC	3.7
23	Will Smith	LAD	3.7
25	Max Muncy	LAD	3.6

WARP

Rank	Name	Team	WARP
1	Juan Soto	SD	8.3
2	Aaron Judge	NYY	7.2
3	Trea Turner	PHI	6.7
3	José Ramírez	CLE	6.7
5	Kyle Tucker	HOU	6.4
6	Mookie Betts	LAD	6.3
7	Ronald Acuña Jr.	ATL	6.1
8	Mike Trout	LAA	6.0
9	Freddie Freeman	LAD	5.6
9	Yordan Alvarez	HOU	5.6
11	Jose Altuve	HOU	5.5
12	Steven Kwan	CLE	5.4
13	Shohei Ohtani	LAA	5.3
13	Brandon Nimmo	NYM	5.3
13	Manny Machado	SD	5.3
13	Pete Alonso	NYM	5.3
17	F. Tatis	SD	5.2
18	Adley Rutschman	BAL	5.0
18	J.T. Realmuto	PHI	5.0
20	Paul Goldschmidt	STL	4.9
21	Nolan Arenado	STL	4.8
22	Julio Rodríguez	SEA	4.7
22	Austin Riley	ATL	4.7
24	Rafael Devers	BOS	4.5
25	Christian Yelich	MIL	4.4
26	Marcus Semien	TEX	4.2
26	Alex Bregman	HOU	4.2
26	Xander Bogaerts	SD	4.2
26	Bo Bichette	TOR	4.2
30	Wander Franco	TB	4.1
31	Francisco Lindor	NYM	4.0
31	V. Guerrero	TOR	4.0
31	Andrés Giménez	CLE	4.0
34	Masataka Yoshida	BOS	3.9
34	George Springer	TOR	3.9
34	Jeff McNeil	NYM	3.9
34	Gavin Lux	LAD	3.9
34	Tommy Edman	STL	3.9
34	Yandy Díaz	TB	3.9
34	Willy Adames	MIL	3.9
41	Kyle Schwarber	PHI	3.8
41	Bryan Reynolds	PIT	3.8
41	Carlos Correa	FA	3.8
41	Byron Buxton	MIN	3.8
45	Dansby Swanson	CHC	3.7
45	Will Smith	LAD	3.7
45	Corey Seager	TEX	3.7
48	Trevor Story	BOS	3.6
48	Luis Robert Jr.	CHW	3.6
48	Max Muncy	LAD	3.6

DRC+

Rank	Name	Team	DRC+
1	Juan Soto	SD	181
2	Aaron Judge	NYY	168
3	Yordan Alvarez	HOU	164
4	Mike Trout	LAA	163
5	Pete Alonso	NYM	160
6	F. Tatis	SD	154
7	Freddie Freeman	LAD	150
8	Bryce Harper	PHI	148
8	Rafael Devers	BOS	148
8	Ronald Acuña Jr.	ATL	148
11	José Ramírez	CLE	146
12	Shohei Ohtani	LAA	145
12	Paul Goldschmidt	STL	145
14	Manny Machado	SD	144
15	V. Guerrero	TOR	143
16	Austin Riley	ATL	141
16	Nolan Arenado	STL	141
18	Alex Bregman	HOU	138
18	Jose Altuve	HOU	138
20	Masataka Yoshida	BOS	136
20	Kyle Tucker	HOU	136
20	Kyle Schwarber	PHI	136
20	Yandy Díaz	TB	136
24	Julio Rodríguez	SEA	134
24	Max Muncy	LAD	134
24	J.D. Martinez	LAD	134
24	Carlos Correa	FA	134
28	Trea Turner	PHI	132
28	Bryan Reynolds	PIT	132
28	Mookie Betts	LAD	132
31	G. Stanton	NYY	131
32	Jesse Winker	MIL	130
32	George Springer	TOR	130
32	Will Smith	LAD	130
32	Jeff McNeil	NYM	130
32	Xander Bogaerts	SD	130
37	Alejandro Kirk	TOR	129
37	Wander Franco	TB	129
37	José Abreu	HOU	129
40	Brandon Nimmo	NYM	128
40	Luis Arraez	MIN	128
42	Joc Pederson	SF	127
42	Matt Olson	ATL	127
42	Michael Brantley	HOU	127
45	Justin Turner	BOS	125
46	Corey Seager	TEX	124
47	Taylor Ward	LAA	123
47	Anthony Rizzo	NYY	123
47	Kris Bryant	COL	123
50	Alex Verdugo	BOS	122

Earned Run Average - Starters

Rank	Name	Team	ERA
1	Jacob deGrom	TEX	1.52
2	Gerrit Cole	NYY	2.28
3	Tyler Glasnow	TB	2.48
4	Aaron Nola	PHI	2.55
5	Luis Severino	NYY	2.63
6	Zack Wheeler	PHI	2.68
7	Justin Verlander	NYM	2.70
8	Corbin Burnes	MIL	2.72
9	Shohei Ohtani	LAA	2.75
10	Clayton Kershaw	LAD	2.77
11	Max Scherzer	NYM	2.78
11	Brandon Woodruff	MIL	2.78
13	Shane McClanahan	TB	2.82
14	Carlos Rodón	NYY	2.83
15	Sandy Alcantara	MIA	2.84
16	G. Rodriguez	BAL	2.86
17	Andrew Heaney	TEX	2.93
18	Julio Urías	LAD	2.95
19	Zac Gallen	AZ	2.99
20	Joe Ryan	MIN	3.03
21	Kevin Gausman	TOR	3.06
22	Luis Castillo	SEA	3.08
22	Yu Darvish	SD	3.08
24	Cristian Javier	HOU	3.10
24	Joe Musgrove	SD	3.10

Strikeout Percentage - Starters

Rank	Name	Team	K%
1	Jacob deGrom	TEX	39.0%
2	Tyler Glasnow	TB	34.0%
3	Spencer Strider	ATL	33.9%
4	Gerrit Cole	NYY	32.8%
5	Brandon Woodruff	MIL	31.3%
6	G. Rodriguez	BAL	31.2%
7	Carlos Rodón	NYY	31.1%
8	Corbin Burnes	MIL	30.9%
9	Hunter Greene	CIN	30.7%
10	Blake Snell	SD	30.1%
11	Shane McClanahan	TB	30.0%
11	Dylan Cease	CHW	30.0%
11	Andrew Heaney	TEX	30.0%
14	Max Scherzer	NYM	29.9%
15	Cristian Javier	HOU	29.4%
15	Nick Lodolo	CIN	29.4%
15	Shohei Ohtani	LAA	29.4%
18	Freddy Peralta	MIL	28.8%
19	Chris Sale	BOS	28.6%
20	Dustin May	LAD	28.5%
21	Cody Morris	CLE	28.4%
22	Luis Severino	NYY	28.3%
23	Robbie Ray	SEA	27.3%
24	Tylor Megill	NYM	26.8%
24	Clayton Kershaw	LAD	26.8%

Walk Percentage - Starters

Rank	Name	Team	BB%
1	Zack Greinke	FA	5.0%
2	Clayton Kershaw	LAD	5.1%
3	Hyun Jin Ryu	TOR	5.2%
3	Justin Verlander	NYM	5.2%
3	Jacob deGrom	TEX	5.2%
6	Aaron Nola	PHI	5.3%
6	Cole Irvin	OAK	5.3%
8	Zach Eflin	TB	5.4%
8	Kevin Gausman	TOR	5.4%
8	Miles Mikolas	STL	5.4%
11	Max Scherzer	NYM	5.5%
12	Nathan Eovaldi	TEX	5.6%
12	Ross Stripling	SF	5.6%
14	Bailey Falter	PHI	5.7%
14	Jameson Taillon	CHC	5.7%
14	Bailey Ober	MIN	5.7%
14	José Urquidy	HOU	5.7%
18	Max Fried	ATL	5.8%
18	Ryan Yarbrough	KC	5.8%
18	John Means	BAL	5.8%
21	Lance Lynn	CHW	5.9%
21	George Kirby	SEA	5.9%
21	Shane Bieber	CLE	5.9%
21	Zack Wheeler	PHI	5.9%
21	Kyle Hendricks	CHC	5.9%

Earned Run Average - Relievers

Rank	Name	Team	ERA
1	Liam Hendriks	CHW	2.29
2	Raisel Iglesias	ATL	2.53
2	Ryan Pressly	HOU	2.53
4	Emmanuel Clase	CLE	2.72
5	Paul Sewald	SEA	2.80
6	A.J. Minter	ATL	2.82
7	Taylor Rogers	SF	2.86
8	Pete Fairbanks	TB	2.91
9	Kenley Jansen	BOS	2.94
9	Andrés Muñoz	SEA	2.94
11	Chris Martin	BOS	2.95
12	Robert Suarez	SD	2.96
13	G. Gallegos	STL	3.02
13	Ryan Helsley	STL	3.02
13	Caleb Thielbar	MIN	3.02
16	Josh Hader	SD	3.03
17	Emilio Pagán	MIN	3.04
18	Dylan Lee	ATL	3.06
19	David Bednar	PIT	3.11
19	Griffin Jax	MIN	3.11
21	Michael King	NYY	3.18
21	Colin Poche	TB	3.18
23	Erik Swanson	TOR	3.19
24	Nic Enright	CLE	3.21
25	Jason Adam	TB	3.23

Strikeout Percentage - Relievers

Rank	Name	Team	K%
1	Edwin Díaz	NYM	43.6%
2	Devin Williams	MIL	38.4%
3	Josh Hader	SD	38.2%
4	Liam Hendriks	CHW	37.7%
5	Andrés Muñoz	SEA	35.8%
6	José Alvarado	PHI	33.6%
6	Jake Cousins	MIL	33.6%
8	James Karinchak	CLE	33.5%
9	Aroldis Chapman	FA	32.3%
10	Alex Vesia	LAD	32.2%
11	Jovani Moran	MIN	31.9%
12	Bryan Abreu	HOU	31.6%
13	Jason Adam	TB	31.3%
14	Craig Kimbrel	PHI	31.2%
14	Dinelson Lamet	COL	31.2%
16	Jimmy Nelson	LAD	31.1%
17	Félix Bautista	BAL	30.9%
17	Austin Adams	SD	30.9%
19	Pete Fairbanks	TB	30.8%
20	Taylor Rogers	SF	30.7%
20	Tanner Scott	MIA	30.7%
20	David Bednar	PIT	30.7%
23	Ryan Pressly	HOU	30.4%
23	G. Gallegos	STL	30.4%
25	Alexis Díaz	CIN	30.2%

Walk Percentage - Relievers

Rank	Name	Team	BB%
1	Chris Martin	BOS	4.0%
2	Richard Bleier	MIA	5.3%
3	Craig Stammen	FA	5.4%
3	Easton McGee	TB	5.4%
5	Denyi Reyes	NYM	5.6%
6	Hoby Milner	MIL	5.7%
6	Liam Hendriks	CHW	5.7%
6	Chris Paddack	MIN	5.7%
9	Andrew Kittredge	TB	5.8%
10	Tyler Alexander	DET	5.9%
11	Emmanuel Clase	CLE	6.0%
11	Erasmo Ramírez	WAS	6.0%
13	Adam Cimber	TOR	6.1%
13	Dylan Lee	ATL	6.1%
13	Cody Stashak	MIN	6.1%
16	Taylor Rogers	SF	6.2%
16	Joe Mantiply	AZ	6.2%
18	Raisel Iglesias	ATL	6.3%
18	Tommy Hunter	NYM	6.3%
20	Brandon Pfaadt	AZ	6.5%
20	Aaron Brooks	STL	6.5%
20	Erik Swanson	TOR	6.5%
20	Bruce Zimmermann	BAL	6.5%
20	Luis Perdomo	MIL	6.5%
20	Brandon Walter	BOS	6.5%

Wins

Rank	Name	Team	W
1	Aaron Nola	PHI	13
1	Sandy Alcantara	MIA	13
3	Joe Musgrove	SD	12
3	Yu Darvish	SD	12
3	Gerrit Cole	NYY	12
6	Zack Wheeler	PHI	11
6	Justin Verlander	NYM	11
6	Framber Valdez	HOU	11
6	Julio Urías	LAD	11
6	Max Scherzer	NYM	11
6	Miles Mikolas	STL	11
6	Pablo López	MIA	11
6	Max Fried	ATL	11
6	Dylan Cease	CHW	11
6	Luis Castillo	SEA	11
6	Corbin Burnes	MIL	11
6	Shane Bieber	CLE	11
18	Kyle Wright	ATL	10
18	Logan Webb	SF	10
18	Adam Wainwright	STL	10
18	Ross Stripling	SF	10
18	Jeffrey Springs	TB	10
18	Carlos Rodón	NYY	10
18	Robbie Ray	SEA	10
18	Shohei Ohtani	LAA	10

Strikeouts

Rank	Name	Team	K
1	Gerrit Cole	NYY	233
2	Dylan Cease	CHW	222
3	Corbin Burnes	MIL	221
4	Carlos Rodón	NYY	204
4	Aaron Nola	PHI	204
6	Spencer Strider	ATL	203
7	Max Scherzer	NYM	201
7	Shane McClanahan	TB	201
9	Hunter Greene	CIN	199
10	Sandy Alcantara	MIA	198
11	Shohei Ohtani	LAA	196
11	Shane Bieber	CLE	196
13	Robbie Ray	SEA	194
14	Yu Darvish	SD	193
15	Blake Snell	SD	187
16	Joe Musgrove	SD	186
17	Nick Lodolo	CIN	183
18	Triston McKenzie	CLE	181
19	Zack Wheeler	PHI	180
20	Framber Valdez	HOU	179
20	Luis Castillo	SEA	179
22	Alek Manoah	TOR	178
23	Brandon Woodruff	MIL	177
23	Kevin Gausman	TOR	177
25	Lance Lynn	CHW	176

WHIP - Starters

Rank	Name	Team	WHIP
1	Jacob deGrom	TEX	0.89
2	Gerrit Cole	NYY	1.04
3	Aaron Nola	PHI	1.06
3	Max Scherzer	NYM	1.06
3	Justin Verlander	NYM	1.06
6	Andrew Heaney	TEX	1.09
6	Clayton Kershaw	LAD	1.09
8	Brandon Woodruff	MIL	1.10
9	Tyler Glasnow	TB	1.11
9	Carlos Rodón	NYY	1.11
11	Corbin Burnes	MIL	1.12
11	Yu Darvish	SD	1.12
13	Joe Ryan	MIN	1.13
13	Luis Severino	NYY	1.13
13	Zack Wheeler	PHI	1.13
16	Shohei Ohtani	LAA	1.14
16	Julio Urías	LAD	1.14
18	Sandy Alcantara	MIA	1.15
18	Joe Musgrove	SD	1.15
20	Nestor Cortes	NYY	1.16
20	Kevin Gausman	TOR	1.16
20	Shane McClanahan	TB	1.16
23	Zac Gallen	AZ	1.17
23	Cristian Javier	HOU	1.17
25	José Urquidy	HOU	1.18

Saves

Rank	Name	Team	SV
1	Edwin Díaz	NYM	41
2	Jordan Romano	TOR	36
2	Ryan Pressly	HOU	36
2	Josh Hader	SD	36
5	Emmanuel Clase	CLE	35
6	Kenley Jansen	BOS	34
7	Raisel Iglesias	ATL	33
7	Clay Holmes	NYY	33
7	Ryan Helsley	STL	33
10	Devin Williams	MIL	32
10	Félix Bautista	BAL	32
12	Camilo Doval	SF	31
13	Jorge López	MIN	30
13	David Bednar	PIT	30
15	Daniel Bard	COL	28
16	Paul Sewald	SEA	26
16	Daniel Hudson	LAD	26
18	Dylan Floro	MIA	25
18	Alexis Díaz	CIN	25
18	Scott Barlow	KC	25
21	Alex Lange	DET	24
22	José Leclerc	TEX	22
23	Kyle Finnegan	WAS	21
24	Ryan Tepera	LAA	20
24	Brandon Hughes	CHC	20

Holds

Rank	Name	Team	HLD
1	Griffin Jax	MIN	22
1	Jhoan Duran	MIN	22
3	Will Vest	DET	21
3	Lucas Sims	CIN	21
3	Héctor Neris	HOU	21
3	Carl Edwards Jr.	WAS	21
3	José Cisnero	DET	21
8	Dillon Tate	BAL	20
8	John Schreiber	BOS	20
8	Evan Phillips	LAD	20
8	Cionel Pérez	BAL	20
8	Chris Martin	BOS	20
8	Wil Crowe	PIT	20
8	Dylan Coleman	KC	20
15	Rowan Wick	CHC	19
15	Brent Suter	COL	19
15	Trevor Stephan	CLE	19
15	Ryne Stanek	HOU	19
15	Manuel Rodríguez	CHC	19
15	José Quijada	LAA	19
15	Rafael Montero	HOU	19
15	Joe Mantiply	AZ	19
15	James Karinchak	CLE	19
15	Brusdar Graterol	LAD	19
15	Carlos Estévez	LAA	19

WHIP - Relievers

Rank	Name	Team	WHIP
1	Liam Hendriks	CHW	1.00
2	Raisel Iglesias	ATL	1.07
3	Ryan Pressly	HOU	1.10
3	Taylor Rogers	SF	1.10
3	Paul Sewald	SEA	1.10
6	G. Gallegos	STL	1.12
6	Chris Martin	BOS	1.12
8	Dylan Lee	ATL	1.13
9	Josh Hader	SD	1.15
9	Emilio Pagán	MIN	1.15
9	Erik Swanson	TOR	1.15
12	Jason Adam	TB	1.16
12	Nic Enright	CLE	1.16
12	Chad Green	NYY	1.16
12	Kenley Jansen	BOS	1.16
12	A.J. Minter	ATL	1.16
12	Caleb Thielbar	MIN	1.16
18	David Bednar	PIT	1.18
18	Emmanuel Clase	CLE	1.18
18	Andrés Muñoz	SEA	1.18
18	Cody Stashak	MIN	1.18
22	Pete Fairbanks	TB	1.19
22	Griffin Jax	MIN	1.19
22	Hoby Milner	MIL	1.19
22	Colin Poche	TB	1.19

Fastball Velocity - Starters

Rank	Name	Team	FB Velo
1	Hunter Greene	CIN	99
1	Jacob deGrom	TEX	99
1	Luis Ortiz	PIT	99
4	Spencer Strider	ATL	98
4	Sixto Sánchez	MIA	98
4	Sandy Alcantara	MIA	98
4	Gerrit Cole	NYY	98
8	Dustin May	LAD	97
8	Graham Ashcraft	CIN	97
8	Tyler Glasnow	TB	97
8	Luis Castillo	SEA	97
8	Dylan Cease	CHW	97
8	Shane McClanahan	TB	97
8	Nathan Eovaldi	TEX	97
8	Hunter Brown	HOU	97
8	Adrian Morejon	SD	97
8	Brayan Bello	BOS	97
8	Zack Wheeler	PHI	97
8	Shohei Ohtani	LAA	97
20	Brandon Woodruff	MIL	96
20	Luis Severino	NYY	96
20	Frankie Montas	NYY	96
20	Edward Cabrera	MIA	96
20	Logan Gilbert	SEA	96
20	Aaron Ashby	MIL	96

Groundball Rate - Starters

Rank	Name	Team	GB%
1	Framber Valdez	HOU	65.8%
2	Josh Fleming	TB	59.1%
3	Logan Webb	SF	56.6%
4	Aaron Ashby	MIL	56.5%
5	C. Sanchez	PHI	56.4%
5	Alex Cobb	SF	56.4%
7	Graham Ashcraft	CIN	55.8%
8	Bryan Hoeing	MIA	55.2%
9	Ranger Suárez	PHI	55.0%
10	Kodai Senga	NYM	54.5%
11	Brayan Bello	BOS	54.3%
12	Dakota Hudson	STL	53.8%
12	Hunter Brown	HOU	53.8%
14	Bryan Mata	BOS	53.3%
15	L. McCullers	HOU	53.1%
16	Mike Soroka	ATL	52.9%
17	Kyle Wright	ATL	52.6%
18	Bryce Elder	ATL	52.3%
19	Sandy Alcantara	MIA	52.1%
20	Josh Winckowski	BOS	51.9%
21	Adrian Houser	MIL	51.5%
22	Marcus Stroman	CHC	51.3%
22	Dane Dunning	TEX	51.3%
24	Brad Keller	KC	51.0%
25	Spencer Turnbull	DET	50.9%

Whiff Rate - Starters

Rank	Name	Team	Whiff%
1	Jacob deGrom	TEX	38.0%
2	Corbin Burnes	MIL	34.8%
3	Spencer Strider	ATL	34.5%
4	Tyler Glasnow	TB	33.5%
5	Blake Snell	SD	32.7%
5	G. Rodriguez	BAL	32.7%
7	Shane McClanahan	TB	32.3%
7	Dylan Cease	CHW	32.3%
9	Gerrit Cole	NYY	32.2%
10	Freddy Peralta	MIL	31.7%
11	Shane Bieber	CLE	31.5%
12	Edward Cabrera	MIA	31.4%
13	Max Scherzer	NYM	31.3%
13	Shohei Ohtani	LAA	31.3%
15	Jesús Luzardo	MIA	31.0%
16	Jeffrey Springs	TB	30.9%
17	Hunter Greene	CIN	30.8%
18	Andrew Heaney	TEX	30.7%
19	Patrick Sandoval	LAA	30.5%
20	Brandon Woodruff	MIL	30.4%
20	Carlos Rodón	NYY	30.4%
22	Nick Lodolo	CIN	30.3%
23	Robbie Ray	SEA	30.2%
24	Cody Morris	CLE	30.1%
24	Cristian Javier	HOU	30.1%

Fastball Velocity - Relievers

Rank	Name	Team	FB Velo
1	Jhoan Duran	MIN	100
1	Andrés Muñoz	SEA	100
1	Emmanuel Clase	CLE	100
1	Brusdar Graterol	LAD	100
1	Jordan Hicks	STL	100
1	Félix Bautista	BAL	100
7	Aneurys Zabala	MIA	99
7	Camilo Doval	SF	99
7	Edwin Díaz	NYM	99
7	Ryan Helsley	STL	99
7	José Alvarado	PHI	99
7	Gregory Santos	CHW	99
13	Luis García	SD	98
13	Albert Abreu	NYY	98
13	Aroldis Chapman	FA	98
13	Trevor Rosenthal	FA	98
13	Hunter Harvey	WAS	98
13	Gregory Soto	PHI	98
13	Yerry Rodriguez	TEX	98
13	Miguel Castro	AZ	98
13	Junior Fernández	NYY	98
13	J. Loaisiga	NYY	98
13	Pete Fairbanks	TB	98
13	S. Dominguez	PHI	98
13	Nick Snyder	TEX	98

Groundball Rate - Relievers

Rank	Name	Team	GB%
1	Clay Holmes	NYY	67.5%
1	Zack Britton	FA	67.5%
3	Aaron Bummer	CHW	65.6%
4	Scott Alexander	SF	64.2%
5	Emmanuel Clase	CLE	62.3%
6	Andre Pallante	STL	61.6%
7	Brusdar Graterol	LAD	60.6%
8	Adam Kolarek	OAK	60.0%
9	John King	TEX	59.1%
10	Joe Kelly	CHW	58.1%
11	Dillon Tate	BAL	57.8%
12	Jordan Hicks	STL	57.4%
13	Jake Bird	COL	57.3%
14	Jhoan Duran	MIN	57.0%
14	Richard Bleier	MIA	57.0%
16	Matt Krook	NYY	56.7%
16	Tim Hill	SD	56.7%
18	Chad Smith	OAK	56.6%
18	Cam Robinson	MIL	56.6%
20	Sean Hjelle	SF	56.5%
21	Joely Rodríguez	BOS	56.3%
21	Zach Pop	TOR	56.3%
23	Tyler Rogers	SF	55.9%
24	Brandon Walter	BOS	55.7%
24	Justin Topa	SEA	55.7%

Whiff Rate - Relievers

Rank	Name	Team	Whiff%
1	Edwin Díaz	NYM	42.7%
2	Devin Williams	MIL	39.3%
3	Andrés Muñoz	SEA	38.2%
4	Josh Hader	SD	38.1%
4	Jake Cousins	MIL	38.1%
6	Jovani Moran	MIN	37.4%
7	Liam Hendriks	CHW	36.9%
8	Alex Lange	DET	36.2%
9	José Leclerc	TEX	35.7%
10	Alexis Díaz	CIN	35.4%
11	Bryan Abreu	HOU	35.3%
12	Tanner Scott	MIA	34.8%
13	Dany Jiménez	OAK	34.7%
14	José Alvarado	PHI	34.5%
14	Jason Adam	TB	34.5%
16	Raisel Iglesias	ATL	34.2%
17	Alex Vesia	LAD	34.0%
17	Ron Marinaccio	NYY	34.0%
17	Aroldis Chapman	FA	34.0%
20	Ryan Pressly	HOU	33.8%
21	Ronel Blanco	HOU	33.5%
22	Seth Romero	WAS	33.4%
22	James Karinchak	CLE	33.4%
24	Dinelson Lamet	COL	33.3%
24	G. Gallegos	STL	33.3%

Batting Average Against

Rank	Name	Team	AVG
1	Jacob deGrom	TEX	.190
2	Cristian Javier	HOU	.200
3	Tyler Glasnow	TB	.203
3	Josh Hader	SD	.203
5	Ryan Helsley	STL	.208
5	G. Rodriguez	BAL	.208
7	Liam Hendriks	CHW	.209
7	Kenley Jansen	BOS	.209
7	Paul Sewald	SEA	.209
10	Félix Bautista	BAL	.210
10	Jovani Moran	MIN	.210
12	Andrés Muñoz	SEA	.211
12	Enoli Paredes	HOU	.211
14	Jason Adam	TB	.212
14	Aroldis Chapman	FA	.212
14	José Leclerc	TEX	.212
14	José Quijada	LAA	.212
14	Spencer Strider	ATL	.212
14	Alex Vesia	LAD	.212
20	Gerrit Cole	NYY	.213
20	Craig Kimbrel	PHI	.213
20	Ron Marinaccio	NYY	.213
23	G. Cleavinger	TB	.214
24	Jake Walsh	STL	.215
24	Greg Weissert	NYY	.215

Slugging Percent Against

Rank	Name	Team	SLG
1	Jacob deGrom	TEX	.327
2	Jovani Moran	MIN	.341
3	Emmanuel Clase	CLE	.343
3	Andrés Muñoz	SEA	.343
5	G. Rodriguez	BAL	.345
6	Tyler Glasnow	TB	.346
7	Luis Severino	NYY	.348
8	Joe Kelly	CHW	.352
9	Luis Castillo	SEA	.353
9	Gerrit Cole	NYY	.353
9	Robert Suarez	SD	.353
12	Clay Holmes	NYY	.354
12	Greg Weissert	NYY	.354
14	José Alvarado	PHI	.355
14	Pete Fairbanks	TB	.355
14	Ryan Pressly	HOU	.355
14	Andrew Vasquez	PHI	.355
18	Shawn Dubin	HOU	.356
19	Corbin Burnes	MIL	.357
19	G. Cleavinger	TB	.357
19	Enoli Paredes	HOU	.357
22	Shohei Ohtani	LAA	.358
22	Tanner Scott	MIA	.358
24	Bryan Abreu	HOU	.359
24	Félix Bautista	BAL	.359

AL WARP

Rank	Name	Team	WARP
1	Gerrit Cole	NYY	4.9
2	Jacob deGrom	TEX	4.4
3	Shohei Ohtani	LAA	3.6
4	Shane McClanahan	TB	3.5
5	Carlos Rodón	NYY	3.3
6	Tyler Glasnow	TB	3.2
7	Luis Castillo	SEA	3.0
8	Luis Severino	NYY	2.9
9	Kevin Gausman	TOR	2.8
9	Dylan Cease	CHW	2.8
11	Cristian Javier	HOU	2.5
11	Shane Bieber	CLE	2.5
13	Joe Ryan	MIN	2.4
14	Andrew Heaney	TEX	2.3
14	Nestor Cortes	NYY	2.3
16	Framber Valdez	HOU	2.1
16	Robbie Ray	SEA	2.1
16	Triston McKenzie	CLE	2.1
16	Alek Manoah	TOR	2.1
20	Lucas Giolito	CHW	2.0
21	Frankie Montas	NYY	1.9
21	Logan Gilbert	SEA	1.9
23	Aaron Civale	CLE	1.8
23	Chris Bassitt	TOR	1.8
25	José Urquidy	HOU	1.7

NL WARP

Rank	Name	Team	WARP
1	Aaron Nola	PHI	4.6
2	Corbin Burnes	MIL	4.2
2	Sandy Alcantara	MIA	4.2
4	Zack Wheeler	PHI	4.0
5	Max Scherzer	NYM	3.6
6	Justin Verlander	NYM	3.5
7	Julio Urías	LAD	3.3
8	Brandon Woodruff	MIL	3.2
8	Joe Musgrove	SD	3.2
8	Yu Darvish	SD	3.2
11	Zac Gallen	AZ	3.0
12	Clayton Kershaw	LAD	2.9
13	Max Fried	ATL	2.8
14	Blake Snell	SD	2.7
15	Pablo López	MIA	2.6
16	Spencer Strider	ATL	2.5
17	Kodai Senga	NYM	2.3
18	Miles Mikolas	STL	2.2
18	Dustin May	LAD	2.2
18	Tony Gonsolin	LAD	2.2
21	Freddy Peralta	MIL	2.1
21	Charlie Morton	ATL	2.1
23	Kyle Wright	ATL	2.0
23	J. Montgomery	STL	2.0
23	Hunter Greene	CIN	2.0

WARP

Rank	Name	Team	WARP
1	Gerrit Cole	NYY	4.9
2	Aaron Nola	PHI	4.6
3	Jacob deGrom	TEX	4.4
4	Corbin Burnes	MIL	4.2
4	Sandy Alcantara	MIA	4.2
6	Zack Wheeler	PHI	4.0
7	Max Scherzer	NYM	3.6
7	Shohei Ohtani	LAA	3.6
9	Justin Verlander	NYM	3.5
9	Shane McClanahan	TB	3.5
11	Julio Urías	LAD	3.3
11	Carlos Rodón	NYY	3.3
13	Brandon Woodruff	MIL	3.2
13	Joe Musgrove	SD	3.2
13	Tyler Glasnow	TB	3.2
13	Yu Darvish	SD	3.2
17	Zac Gallen	AZ	3.0
17	Luis Castillo	SEA	3.0
19	Luis Severino	NYY	2.9
19	Clayton Kershaw	LAD	2.9
21	Kevin Gausman	TOR	2.8
21	Max Fried	ATL	2.8
21	Dylan Cease	CHW	2.8
24	Blake Snell	SD	2.7
25	Pablo López	MIA	2.6
26	Spencer Strider	ATL	2.5
26	Cristian Javier	HOU	2.5
26	Shane Bieber	CLE	2.5
29	Joe Ryan	MIN	2.4
30	Kodai Senga	NYM	2.3
30	Andrew Heaney	TEX	2.3
30	Nestor Cortes	NYY	2.3
33	Miles Mikolas	STL	2.2
33	Dustin May	LAD	2.2
33	Tony Gonsolin	LAD	2.2
36	Framber Valdez	HOU	2.1
36	Robbie Ray	SEA	2.1
36	Freddy Peralta	MIL	2.1
36	Charlie Morton	ATL	2.1
36	Triston McKenzie	CLE	2.1
36	Alek Manoah	TOR	2.1
42	Kyle Wright	ATL	2.0
42	J. Montgomery	STL	2.0
42	Hunter Greene	CIN	2.0
42	Lucas Giolito	CHW	2.0
46	Frankie Montas	NYY	1.9
46	Germán Márquez	COL	1.9
46	Jesús Luzardo	MIA	1.9
46	Nick Lodolo	CIN	1.9
46	Logan Gilbert	SEA	1.9

DRA- Starters

Rank	Name	Team	DRA-
1	Jacob deGrom	TEX	43
2	Gerrit Cole	NYY	62
3	Tyler Glasnow	TB	65
4	Corbin Burnes	MIL	70
4	Aaron Nola	PHI	70
6	Luis Severino	NYY	71
6	Brandon Woodruff	MIL	71
8	Shohei Ohtani	LAA	73
8	Zack Wheeler	PHI	73
10	Clayton Kershaw	LAD	74
10	Shane McClanahan	TB	74
10	G. Rodriguez	BAL	74
13	Max Scherzer	NYM	75
13	Justin Verlander	NYM	75
15	Carlos Rodón	NYY	76
16	Sandy Alcantara	MIA	78
16	Andrew Heaney	TEX	78
18	Zac Gallen	AZ	79
18	Spencer Strider	ATL	79
18	Julio Urías	LAD	79
21	Cristian Javier	HOU	81
21	Dustin May	LAD	81
21	Blake Snell	SD	81
24	Luis Castillo	SEA	82
24	Kodai Senga	NYM	82
26	Kevin Gausman	TOR	83
26	Jesús Luzardo	MIA	83
26	Joe Musgrove	SD	83
29	Dylan Cease	CHW	85
29	Nestor Cortes	NYY	85
29	Yu Darvish	SD	85
29	Freddy Peralta	MIL	85
29	Joe Ryan	MIN	85
34	Max Fried	ATL	86
35	Tony Gonsolin	LAD	87
35	Pablo López	MIA	87
37	Frankie Montas	NYY	88
37	Chris Sale	BOS	88
39	Shane Bieber	CLE	89
39	Charlie Morton	ATL	89
39	Garrett Whitlock	BOS	89
42	Aaron Civale	CLE	90
42	Tyler Mahle	MIN	90
44	Jack Flaherty	STL	91
44	Luis Garcia	HOU	91
44	Hunter Greene	CIN	91
44	Kenta Maeda	MIN	91
44	Tarik Skubal	DET	91
49	Nathan Eovaldi	TEX	92
49	Nick Lodolo	CIN	92

DRA- Relievers

Rank	Name	Team	DRA-
1	Liam Hendriks	CHW	61
2	Ryan Pressly	HOU	68
3	Raisel Iglesias	ATL	70
4	Emmanuel Clase	CLE	73
5	Pete Fairbanks	TB	75
5	Andrés Muñoz	SEA	75
7	Josh Hader	SD	76
7	A.J. Minter	ATL	76
7	Taylor Rogers	SF	76
7	Paul Sewald	SEA	76
11	Kenley Jansen	BOS	77
12	Edwin Díaz	NYM	79
12	Robert Suarez	SD	79
14	David Bednar	PIT	80
14	Ryan Helsley	STL	80
14	Chris Martin	BOS	80
17	Jason Adam	TB	82
17	G. Gallegos	STL	82
17	Pierce Johnson	COL	82
20	Michael King	NYY	83
20	Colin Poche	TB	83
22	Félix Bautista	BAL	84
22	Stephen Ridings	NYM	84
22	Caleb Thielbar	MIN	84
25	Dylan Lee	ATL	85
25	Emilio Pagán	MIN	85
25	Jordan Romano	TOR	85
28	Nic Enright	CLE	86
28	Chad Green	NYY	86
28	Griffin Jax	MIN	86
28	Jovani Moran	MIN	86
28	Gavin Stone	LAD	86
28	Alex Vesia	LAD	86
34	Adbert Alzolay	CHC	87
34	John Schreiber	BOS	87
34	Erik Swanson	TOR	87
37	José Castillo	SD	88
37	G. Cleavinger	TB	88
37	Carl Edwards Jr.	WAS	88
37	Brandon Hughes	CHC	88
37	Dinelson Lamet	COL	88
37	Evan Phillips	LAD	88
43	Fernando Cruz	CIN	89
43	Shawn Dubin	HOU	89
43	Jeremiah Estrada	CHC	89
43	Daniel Hudson	LAD	89
43	Craig Kimbrel	PHI	89
43	Bobby Miller	LAD	89
43	Rafael Montero	HOU	89
43	Michael Tonkin	ATL	89

Team Codes

CODE	TEAM	LG	AFF	NAME
ABD	Aberdeen	SAL	Orioles	IronBirds
ABQ	Albuquerque	PCL	Rockies	Isotopes
ADE	Adelaide	ABL	-	Giants
AGS	Aguascalientes	MEX	-	Rieleros
AGU	Aguilas	LIDOM	-	Aguilas
AKR	Akron	EAS	Guardians	RubberDucks
ALT	Altoona	EAS	Pirates	Curve
AMA	Amarillo	TEX	D-backs	Sod Poodles
ANG	ACL Angels	ACL	Angels	ACL Angels
ANG	AZL Angels	AZL	Angels	AZL Angels
ARA	Aragua	LVBP	Tigres	Tigres
ARK	Arkansas	TEX	Mariners	Travelers
ASB	FCL Astros Blue		Astros	FCL Astros Blue
ASGO	AZL Athletics Gold	AZL	Athletics	AZL Athletics Gold
ASGR	AZL Athletics Green	AZL	Athletics	AZL Athletics Green
ASH	Asheville	SAL	Astros	Tourists
ASO	FCL Astros Orange		Astros	FCL Astros Orange
AST	FCL Astros	FCL	Astros	FCL Astros
AST	GCL Astros	GCL	Astros	GCL Astros
ATH	ACL Athletics	ACL	Athletics	ACL Athletics
ATL	Atlanta	NL	-	Braves
AUG	Augusta	CAR	Braves	GreenJackets
AZ	Arizona	NL	-	D-backs
BAL	Baltimore	AL	-	Orioles
BEL	Beloit	MID	Marlins	Sky Carp
BEL	Beloit	A+ C	Marlins	Snappers
BG	Bowling Green	SAL	Rays	Hot Rods
BIR	Birmingham	SOU	White Sox	Barons
BLU	FCL Blue Jays		Blue Jays	FCL Blue Jays
BLU	GCL Blue Jays	GCL	Blue Jays	GCL Blue Jays
BLX	Biloxi	SOU	Brewers	Shuckers
BNG	Binghamton	EAS	Mets	Rumble Ponies
BOS	Boston	AL	-	Red Sox
BOW	Bowie	EAS	Orioles	Baysox
BRA	FCL Braves		Braves	FCL Braves
BRA	GCL Braves	GCL	Braves	GCL Braves
BRB	AZL Brewers Blue	AZL	Brewers	AZL Brewers Blue
BRD	Bradenton	FSL	Pirates	Marauders
BRG	AZL Brewers Gold	AZL	Brewers	AZL Brewers Gold
BRI	Brisbane	ABL	Bandits	Bandits
BRK	Brooklyn	SAL	Mets	Cyclones
BRWB	ACL Brewers Blue	ACL	Brewers	ACL Brewers Blue
BRWG	ACL Brewers Gold	ACL	Brewers	ACL Brewers Gold
BUF	Buffalo	INT	Blue Jays	Bisons
BUR	Burlington	MID	Angels	Bees
CAG	Caguas	PWL	Caguas	Caguas
CAM	Campeche	MEX	-	Piratas
CAN	Canberra	ABL	Cavalry	Cavalry
CAR	Carolina	CAR	Brewers	Mudcats
CAR	FCL Cardinals		Cardinals	FCL Cardinals
CAR	GCL Cardinals	GCL	Cardinals	GCL Cardinals

CODE	TEAM	LG	AFF	NAME
CAR	Carolina	PWL	Carolina	Carolina
CAR	Caracas	LVBP	Leones	Leones
CC	Corpus Christi	TEX	Astros	Hooks
CHA	Charlotte	INT	White Sox	Knights
CHA	Charlotte	FSL	Rays	Stone Crabs
CHA	Chattanooga	SOU	Reds	Lookouts
CHC	Chi Cubs	NL	-	Cubs
CIN	Cincinnati	NL	-	Reds
CLE	Cleveland	AL	-	Guardians
CLE	Cleveland	AL	-	Guardians
CLI	Clinton	MID	Marlins	LumberKings
CLR	Clearwater	FSL	Phillies	Threshers
CLT	Charlotte	INT	White Sox	Knights
COL	Colombia	CS	-	Colombia
COL	Colorado	NL	-	Rockies
COL	Columbia	CAR	Royals	Fireflies
COL	Columbus	INT	Guardians	Clippers
CR	Cedar Rapids	MID	Twins	Kernels
CSC	Charleston	CAR	Rays	RiverDogs
CUB	ACL Cubs	ACL	Cubs	ACL Cubs
CUBB	AZL Cubs Blue	AZL	Cubs	AZL Cubs Blue
CUBR	AZL Cubs Red	AZL	Cubs	AZL Cubs Red
CUL	Culiacan	LMP	-	Culiacan
CHW	Chi White Sox	AL	-	White Sox
DAY	Dayton	MID	Reds	Dragons
DBT	Daytona	FSL	Reds	Tortugas
DE	Down East	CAR	Rangers	Wood Ducks
DEL	Delmarva	CAR	Orioles	Shorebirds
DET	Detroit	AL	-	Tigers
DIA	ACL D-backs	ACL	D-backs	ACL D-backs
DIA	AZL D-backs	AZL	D-backs	AZL D-backs
DIA2	ACL D-backs 2	ACL	D-backs	ACL D-backs 2
DIAB	ACL D-backs Black	ACL	D-backs	ACL D-backs Black
DIAR	ACL D-backs Red	ACL	D-backs	ACL D-backs Red
DOD	ACL Dodgers	ACL	Dodgers	ACL Dodgers
DOD1	AZL Dodgers 1	AZL	Dodgers	AZL Dodgers 1
DOD2	AZL Dodgers 2	AZL	Dodgers	AZL Dodgers 2
DR	Dom. Rep.	CS	-	Dom. Rep.
DSL ANG	DSL Angels	DSL	Angels	DSL Angels
DSL AST	DSL Astros	DSL	Astros	DSL Astros
DSL ATH	DSL Athletics	DSL	Athletics	DSL Athletics
DSL BALB	DSL BAL Black	DSL	Orioles	DSL BAL Black
DSL BALO	DSL BAL Orange	DSL	Orioles	DSL BAL Orange
DSL BAU	DSL Dodgers Bautista	DSL	Dodgers	DSL Dodgers Bautista
DSL BLJ	DSL Blue Jays	DSL	Blue Jays	DSL Blue Jays
DSL BOSB	DSL BOS Blue	DSL	Red Sox	DSL BOS Blue
DSL BOSR	DSL BOS Red	DSL	Red Sox	DSL BOS Red
DSL BRA	DSL Braves	DSL	Braves	DSL Braves
DSL BRW	DSL Brewers	DSL	Brewers	DSL Brewers
DSL BRW1	DSL Brewers1	DSL	Brewers	DSL Brewers1

CODE	TEAM	LG	AFF	NAME
DSL BRW1	DSL Brewers 1	DSL	Brewers	DSL Brewers 1
DSL BRW2	DSL Brewers2	DSL	Brewers	DSL Brewers2
DSL BRW2	DSL Brewers 2	DSL	Brewers	DSL Brewers 2
DSL CAR	DSL Cardinals	DSL	Cardinals	DSL Cardinals
DSL CARB	DSL Cardinals Blue	DSL	Cardinals	DSL Cardinals Blue
DSL CARR	DSL Cardinals Red	DSL	Cardinals	DSL Cardinals Red
DSL CLEB	DSL CLE Blue	DSL	Guardians	DSL CLE Blue
DSL CLER	DSL CLE Red	DSL	Guardians	DSL CLE Red
DSL COL	DSL Colorado	DSL	Rockies	DSL Colorado
DSL COOP	DSL MIL/TOR	DSL	DSL MIL/ TOR	DSL MIL/TOR
DSL CUBB	DSL Cubs Blue	DSL	Cubs	DSL Cubs Blue
DSL CUBR	DSL Cubs Red	DSL	Cubs	DSL Cubs Red
DSL DB1	DSL D-backs1	DSL	D-backs	DSL D-backs1
DSL DB2	DSL D-backs2	DSL	D-backs	DSL D-backs2
DSL DBB	DSL D-backs Black	DSL	D-backs	DSL D-backs Black
DSL DBR	DSL D-backs Red	DSL	D-backs	DSL D-backs Red
DSL GIA	DSL Giants1	DSL	Giants	DSL Giants1
DSL GIB	DSL Giants Black	DSL	Giants	DSL Giants Black
DSL GIO	DSL Giants Orange	DSL	Giants	DSL Giants Orange
DSL GIT	DSL Giants2	DSL	Giants	DSL Giants2
DSL HOUB	DSL HOU Blue	DSL	Astros	DSL HOU Blue
DSL HOUO	DSL HOU Orange	DSL	Astros	DSL HOU Orange
DSL IND1	DSL Guardians1	DSL	Guardians	DSL Guardians1
DSL IND2	DSL Guardians2	DSL	Guardians	DSL Guardians2
DSL INDB	DSL Guardians Blue	DSL	Guardians	DSL Guardians Blue
DSL INDR	DSL Guardians Red	DSL	Guardians	DSL Guardians Red
DSL KCG	DSL KC Glass	DSL	Royals	DSL KC Glass
DSL KCS	DSL KC Stewart	DSL	Royals	DSL KC Stewart
DSL LADB	DSL LAD Bautista	DSL	Dodgers	DSL LAD Bautista
DSL LADM	DSL LAD Mega	DSL	Dodgers	DSL LAD Mega
DSL MET1	DSL Mets1	DSL	Mets	DSL Mets1
DSL MET1	DSL Mets 1	DSL	Mets	DSL Mets 1
DSL MET2	DSL Mets2	DSL	Mets	DSL Mets2
DSL MET2	DSL Mets 2	DSL	Mets	DSL Mets 2
DSL MIA	DSL Marlins	DSL	Marlins	DSL Marlins
DSL MIA	DSL Miami	DSL	Marlins	DSL Miami
DSL MRL	DSL Marlins	DSL	Marlins	DSL Marlins
DSL NAT	DSL Nationals	DSL	Nationals	DSL Nationals
DSL NYY	DSL NYY Yankees	DSL	Yankees	DSL NYY Yankees
DSL NYY	DSL Yankees	DSL	Yankees	DSL Yankees
DSL NYY1	DSL Yankees1	DSL	Yankees	DSL Yankees1
DSL NYY2	DSL Yankees2	DSL	Yankees	DSL Yankees2
DSL NYYB	DSL NYY Bombers	DSL	Yankees	DSL NYY Bombers
DSL OR1	DSL Orioles1	DSL	Orioles	DSL Orioles1
DSL OR2	DSL Orioles2	DSL	Orioles	DSL Orioles2
DSL PAD	DSL Padres	DSL	Padres	DSL Padres
DSL PHR	DSL Phillies Red	DSL	Phillies	DSL Phillies Red
DSL PHW	DSL Phillies White	DSL	Phillies	DSL Phillies White
DSL PIR1	DSL Pirates1	DSL	Pirates	DSL Pirates1
DSL PIR2	DSL Pirates2	DSL	Pirates	DSL Pirates2
DSL PIRB	DSL Pirates Black	DSL	Pirates	DSL Pirates Black
DSL PIRG	DSL Pirates Gold	DSL	Pirates	DSL Pirates Gold
DSL PITB	DSL PIT Black	DSL	Pirates	DSL PIT Black
DSL PITG	DSL PIT Gold	DSL	Pirates	DSL PIT Gold
DSL RAN2	DSL Rangers2	DSL	Rangers	DSL Rangers2
DSL RAY	DSL Rays	DSL	Rays	DSL Rays
DSL RAY1	DSL Rays1	DSL	Rays	DSL Rays1
DSL RAY2	DSL Rays2	DSL	Rays	DSL Rays2
DSL REDS	DSL Reds	DSL	Reds	DSL Reds
DSL RGR1	DSL Rangers1	DSL	Rangers	DSL Rangers1
DSL RGR2	DSL Rangers2	DSL	Rangers	DSL Rangers2
DSL ROC	DSL Rockies	DSL	Rockies	DSL Rockies

CODE	TEAM	LG	AFF	NAME
DSL ROY1	DSL Royals1	DSL	Royals	DSL Royals1
DSL ROY2	DSL Royals2	DSL	Royals	DSL Royals2
DSL ROYB	DSL Royals Blue	DSL	Royals	DSL Royals Blue
DSL ROYW	DSL Royals White	DSL	Royals	DSL Royals White
DSL RSB	DSL Red Sox Blue	DSL	Red Sox	DSL Red Sox Blue
DSL RSR	DSL Red Sox Red	DSL	Red Sox	DSL Red Sox Red
DSL SEA	DSL Mariners	DSL	Mariners	DSL Mariners
DSL SHO	DSL Dodgers Shoemaker	DSL	Dodgers	Dodgers Shoemaker
DSL TB	DSL Tampa Bay	DSL	Rays	DSL Tampa Bay
DSL TB1	DSL Rays1	DSL	Rays	DSL Rays1
DSL TB2	DSL Rays2	DSL	Rays	DSL Rays2
DSL TEXB	DSL TEX Blue	DSL	Rangers	DSL TEX Blue
DSL TEXR	DSL TEX Red	DSL	Rangers	DSL TEX Red
DSL TIG	DSL Tigers	DSL	Tigers	DSL Tigers
DSL TIG1	DSL Tigers1	DSL	Tigers	DSL Tigers1
DSL TIG1	DSL Tigers 1	DSL	Tigers	DSL Tigers 1
DSL TIG2	DSL Tigers2	DSL	Tigers	DSL Tigers2
DSL TIG2	DSL Tigers 2	DSL	Tigers	DSL Tigers 2
DSL TWI	DSL Twins	DSL	Twins	DSL Twins
DSL WSX	DSL White Sox	DSL	White Sox	DSL White Sox
DUN	Dunedin	FSL	Blue Jays	Blue Jays
DUR	Durham	INT	Rays	Bulls
DUR	Durango	MEX	-	Generales
ELP	El Paso	PCL	Padres	Chihuahuas
ERI	Erie	EAS	Tigers	SeaWolves
ESC	Escogido	LIDOM	-	Leones
EST	Estrellas	LIDOM	-	Estrellas
EUG	Eugene	NWL	Giants	Emeralds
EVE	Everett	NWL	Mariners	AquaSox
FAY	Fayetteville	CAR	Astros	Woodpeckers
FBG	Fredericksburg	CAR	Nationals	Nationals
FLO	Florida	FSL	Braves	Fire Frogs
FRE	Frederick	CAR	Orioles	Keys
FRE	Fresno	CAL	Rockies	Grizzlies
FRI	Frisco	TEX	Rangers	RoughRiders
FTM	Fort Myers	FSL	Twins	Mighty Mussels
FW	Fort Wayne	MID	Padres	TinCaps
GBO	Greensboro	SAL	Pirates	Grasshoppers
GDD	Glendale	AFL	-	Desert Dogs
GIB	AZL Giants Black	AZL	Giants	AZL Giants Black
GIG	Gigantes	LIDOM	-	Gigantes
GIO	AZL Giants Orange	AZL	Giants	AZL Giants Orange
GL	Great Lakes	MID	Dodgers	Loons
GNTB	ACL Giants Black	ACL	Giants	ACL Giants Black
GNTO	ACL Giants Orange	ACL	Giants	ACL Giants Orange
GSV	Guasave	LMP	-	Guasave
GUA	ACL Guardians	ACL	Guardians	ACL Guardians
GVL	Greenville	SAL	Red Sox	Drive
GWN	Gwinnett	INT	Braves	Stripers
HAG	Hagerstown	SAL	Nationals	Suns
HBG	Harrisburg	EAS	Nationals	Senators
HER	Hermosillo	LMP	-	Hermosillo
HFD	Hartford	EAS	Rockies	Yard Goats
HIC	Hickory	SAL	Rangers	Crawdads
HIL	Hillsboro	NWL	D-backs	Hops
HOU	Houston	AL	-	Astros
HV	Hudson Valley	SAL	Yankees	Renegades
IE	Inland Empire	CAL	Angels	66ers
IND	ACL Guardians	ACL	Guardians	ACL Guardians
IND	Indianapolis	INT	Pirates	Indianapolis
INDB	AZL Guardians Blue	AZL	Guardians	AZL Guardians Blue
INDR	AZL Guardians Red	AZL	Guardians	AZL Guardians Red
IOW	Iowa	INT	Cubs	Cubs

CODE	TEAM	LG	AFF	NAME
JAL	Jalisco	LMP	-	Jalisco
JAX	Jacksonville	INT	Marlins	Jumbo Shrimp
JS	Jersey Shore	SAL	Phillies	BlueClaws
JUP	Jupiter	FSL	Marlins	Hammerheads
JXN	Jackson	SOU	D-backs	Generals
KAN	Kannapolis	CAR	White Sox	Cannon Ballers
KC	Kane County	MID	D-backs	Cougars
KC	Kansas City	AL	-	Royals
LAA	LA Angels	AL	-	Angels
LAD	LA Dodgers	NL	-	Dodgers
LAG	Laguna	MEX	-	Algodoneros
LAG	La Guaira	LVBP	Tiburones	Tiburones
LAK	Lakeland	FSL	Tigers	Flying Tigers
LAN	Lancaster	CAL	Rockies	JetHawks
LAN	Lansing	MID	Athletics	Lugnuts
LAR	Lara	LVBP	Cardenales	Cardenales
LAR	Dos Laredos	MEX	-	Tecolotes
LC	Lake County	MID	Guardians	Captains
LE	Lake Elsinore	CAL	Padres	Storm
LEO	Leon	MEX	-	Bravos
LEX	Lexington	SAL	Royals	Legends
LHV	Lehigh Valley	INT	Phillies	IronPigs
LIC	Licey	LIDOM	-	Tigres
LOU	Louisville	INT	Reds	Bats
LV	Las Vegas	PCL	Athletics	Aviators
LWD	Lakewood	SAL	Phillies	BlueClaws
LYN	Lynchburg	CAR	Guardians	Hillcats
MAG	Magallanes	LVBP	Navegantes	Navegantes
MAN	Manati	PWL	Manati	Manati
MAR	AZL Mariners	AZL	Mariners	AZL Mariners
MAR	Margarita	LVBP	Bravos	Bravos
MAY	Mayaguez	PWL	Mayaguez	Mayaguez
MAZ	Mazatlan	LMP	-	Mazatlan
MB	Myrtle Beach	CAR	Cubs	Pelicans
MEL	Melbourne	ABL	Aces	Aces
MEM	Memphis	INT	Cardinals	Redbirds
MET	FCL Mets		Mets	FCL Mets
MEX	Mexico	MEX	-	Diablos Rojos
MEX	Mexico	CS	-	Mexico
MIA	Miami	NL	-	Marlins
MID	Midland	TEX	Athletics	RockHounds
MIL	Milwaukee	NL	-	Brewers
MIN	Minnesota	AL	-	Twins
MIS	Mississippi	SOU	Braves	Braves
MOC	Los Mochis	LMP	-	Los Mochis
MOD	Modesto	CAL	Mariners	Nuts
MRL	FCL Marlins		Marlins	FCL Marlins
MRL	GCL Marlins	GCL	Marlins	GCL Marlins
MRN	ACL Mariners	ACL	Mariners	ACL Mariners
MSS	Mesa	AFL	-	Solar Sox
MTG	Montgomery	SOU	Rays	Biscuits
MTS	GCL Mets	GCL	Mets	GCL Mets
MTY	Monterrey	LMP	-	Sultanes
MVA	Monclova	MEX	-	Acereros
MXC	Mexicali	LMP	-	Mexicali
NAS	Nashville	INT	Brewers	Sounds
NAT	FCL Nationals		Nationals	FCL Nationals
NAT	GCL Nationals	GCL	Nationals	GCL Nationals
NAV	Navojoa	LMP	-	Navojoa
NH	New Hampshire	EAS	Blue Jays	Fisher Cats
NOR	Norfolk	INT	Orioles	Tides
NWA	NW Arkansas	TEX	Royals	Naturals
NYM	NY Mets	NL	-	Mets
NYY	NY Yankees	AL	-	Yankees
OAK	Oakland	AL	-	Athletics
OAX	Oaxaca	MEX	-	Guerreros
OBR	Obregon	LMP	-	Obregon
OKC	Okla. City	PCL	Dodgers	Dodgers
OMA	Omaha	INT	Royals	Storm Chasers
ORI	Caribes	LVBP	Caribes	Caribes
ORI	FCL Orioles		Orioles	FCL Orioles
ORI	GCL Orioles	GCL	Orioles	GCL Orioles
ORIB	FCL Orioles Black	FCL	Orioles	FCL Orioles Black
ORIO	FCL Orioles Orange	FCL	Orioles	FCL Orioles Orange
PAD	ACL Padres	ACL	Padres	ACL Padres
PAN	Panama	CS	-	Panama
PAW	Pawtucket	INT	Red Sox	Red Sox
PEJ	Peoria	AFL	-	Javelinas
PEO	Peoria	MID	Cardinals	Chiefs
PER	Perth	ABL	Heat	Heat
PHE	GCL Phillies East	GCL	Phillies	GCL Phillies East
PHI	FCL Phillies		Phillies	FCL Phillies
PHI	Philadelphia	NL	-	Phillies
PHW	GCL Phillies West	GCL	Phillies	GCL Phillies West
PIR	FCL Pirates		Pirates	FCL Pirates
PIR	GCL Pirates	GCL	Pirates	GCL Pirates
PIRB	FCL Pirates Black	FCL	Pirates	FCL Pirates Black
PIRG	FCL Pirates Gold	FCL	Pirates	FCL Pirates Gold
PIT	Pittsburgh	NL	-	Pirates
PMB	Palm Beach	FSL	Cardinals	Cardinals
PNS	Pensacola	SOU	Marlins	Blue Wahoos
POR	Portland	EAS	Red Sox	Sea Dogs
PUE	Puebla	MEX	-	Pericos
PUR	Puerto Rico	CS	-	Puerto Rico
QC	Quad Cities	MID	Royals	River Bandits
RA12	RA12	PWL	-	RA12
RAN	ACL Rangers	ACL	Rangers	ACL Rangers
RAN	AZL Rangers	AZL	Rangers	AZL Rangers
RAY	FCL Rays		Rays	FCL Rays
RAY	GCL Rays	GCL	Rays	GCL Rays
RC	Rancho Cuca.	CAL	Dodgers	Quakes
RCK	ACL Rockies	ACL	Rockies	ACL Rockies
RCT	Rocket City	SOU	Angels	Trash Pandas
REA	Reading	EAS	Phillies	Fightin Phils
RED	ACL Reds	ACL	Reds	ACL Reds
RED	AZL Reds	AZL	Reds	AZL Reds
RIC	Richmond	EAS	Giants	Flying Squirrels
RNO	Reno	PCL	D-backs	Aces
ROC	Rochester	INT	Nationals	Red Wings
ROM	Rome	SAL	Braves	Braves
ROY	ACL Royals	ACL	Royals	ACL Royals
ROY	AZL Royals	AZL	Royals	AZL Royals
ROYB	ACL Royals Blue	ACL	Royals	ACL Royals Blue
ROYG	ACL Royals Gold	ACL	Royals	ACL Royals Gold
RR	Round Rock	PCL	Rangers	Express
RSX	FCL Red Sox		Red Sox	FCL Red Sox
RSX	GCL Red Sox	GCL	Red Sox	GCL Red Sox
SA	San Antonio	TEX	Padres	Missions
SAC	Sacramento	PCL	Giants	River Cats
SAL	Salem	CAR	Red Sox	Red Sox
SAL	Saltillo	MEX	-	Saraperos
SAN	Santurce	PWL	Santurce	Santurce
SB	South Bend	MID	Cubs	Cubs
SCO	Scottsdale	AFL	-	Scorpions
SD	San Diego	NL	-	Padres
SD1	AZL Padres 1	AZL	Padres	AZL Padres 1
SD2	AZL Padres 2	AZL	Padres	AZL Padres 2
SEA	Seattle	AL	-	Mariners

CODE	TEAM	LG	AFF	NAME
SF	San Francisco	NL	-	Giants
SJ	San Jose	CAL	Giants	Giants
SL	Salt Lake	PCL	Angels	Bees
SLU	St. Lucie	FSL	Mets	Mets
SOM	Somerset	EAS	Yankees	Patriots
SPO	Spokane	NWL	Rockies	Spokane
SPR	Springfield	TEX	Cardinals	Cardinals
SRR	Salt River	AFL	-	Rafters
STK	Stockton	CAL	Athletics	Ports
STL	St. Louis	NL	-	Cardinals
STL	St. Lucie	FSL	Mets	Mets
STP	St. Paul	INT	Twins	Saints
SUG	Sugar Land	AAA W	Astros	Skeeters
SUG	Sugar Land	PCL	Astros	Space Cowboys
SUR	Surprise	AFL	-	Saguaros
SWB	Scranton/WB	INT	Yankees	RailRiders
SYD	Sydney	ABL	Blue Sox	Blue Sox
SYR	Syracuse	INT	Mets	Mets
TAB	Tabasco	MEX	-	Olmecas
TAC	Tacoma	PCL	Mariners	Rainiers
TAM	Tampa	FSL	Yankees	Tarpons
TB	Tampa Bay	AL	-	Rays
TDN	Tren del Norte		-	Tren del Norte
TEX	Texas	AL	-	Rangers
TIG	FCL Tigers		Tigers	FCL Tigers
TIG	GCL Tigers East	GCL	Tigers	GCL Tigers East
TIG	Quintana Roo	MEX	-	Tigres
TIGE	FCL Tigers East	FCL	Tigers	FCL Tigers East
TIGW	FCL Tigers West	FCL	Tigers	FCL Tigers West
TIJ	Tijuana	MEX	-	Toros
TIW	GCL Tigers West	GCL	Tigers	GCL Tigers West
TNS	Tennessee	SOU	Cubs	Smokies
TOL	Toledo	INT	Tigers	Mud Hens
TOR	Toronto	AL	-	Blue Jays
TOR	Toros	LIDOM	-	Toros
TRI	Tri-City	NWL	Angels	Dust Devils
TRN	Trenton	EAS	Yankees	Thunder
TUL	Tulsa	TEX	Dodgers	Drillers
TWI	FCL Twins		Twins	FCL Twins
TWI	GCL Twins	GCL	Twins	GCL Twins
VAN	Vancouver	NWL	Blue Jays	Canadians
VEN	Venezuela	CS	-	Venezuela
VIS	Visalia	CAL	D-backs	Rawhide
WCH	Wichita	TEX	Twins	Wind Surge
WIL	Wilmington	SAL	Nationals	Blue Rocks
WIS	Wisconsin	MID	Brewers	Timber Rattlers
WM	West Michigan	MID	Tigers	Whitecaps
WOR	Worcester	INT	Red Sox	Red Sox
WS	Winston-Salem	SAL	White Sox	Dash
WAS	Washington	NL	-	Nationals
WSX	ACL White Sox	ACL	White Sox	ACL White Sox
WSX	AZL White Sox	AZL	White Sox	AZL White Sox
WV	West Virginia	SAL	Mariners	Power
YAE	GCL Yankees East	GCL	Yankees	GCL Yankees East
YAW	GCL Yankees West	GCL	Yankees	GCL Yankees West
YNK	FCL Yankees		Yankees	FCL Yankees
YUC	Yucatan	MEX	-	Leones
ZUL	Zulia	LVBP	Aguilas	Aguilas

Contributors

Biographies

Mikey Ajeto is a Filipino community organizer struggling for a free and sovereign Philippines. He's watched the Mariners on purpose for over two decades and is a contributor for Baseball Prospectus.

Maitreyi Anantharaman is a staff writer at Defector. She lives in Ann Arbor, Michigan.

Lucas Apostoleris is a musician living in Miami, FL. When he isn't performing or writing music, there's a good chance that he's thinking about baseball. He has worked as a writer and researcher at Baseball Prospectus since 2019, and he's previously been published at outlets such as ESPN and FanGraphs.

Robert Au is the Director of Operations at Baseball Prospectus. His San Francisco Bay Area household includes three other humans and a heat-seeking cat.

Darius Austin is a fantasy writer and depth chart administrator at Baseball Prospectus. He has been thinking about stolen bases more than you.

Michael Baumann is a writer at FanGraphs. Previously, he was a staff writer at The Ringer and D1Baseball. His work has appeared at Grantland, Baseball Prospectus, Vice, The Atlantic, and ESPN.com.

Demetrius Bell is an Atlanta-based writer whose work can be found on plenty of websites on the internet (including baseballprospectus.com) and also in multiple editions of this esteemed annual publication. Currently, you can find him writing about baseball for SBNation.com and for the Atlanta Braves blog on the SB Nation network known as Battery Power. You can also follow him on Twitter (assuming the website still exists by the time you are reading this) under the handle of @fergoe.

Grant Brisbee writes for The Athletic and is negotiating his midlife crisis through his record collection. Have boxes of records you don't know what to do with? Are your parents cleaning their garage? Well, you know where to find ol' Grant on Twitter. Rock, soul, jazz, rap, folk, Scandinavian black metal, weirdo Moog records, all genres, really, get in touch and I will take those suckers off your hands, they help me forget how lonely and bleak and fragile this existence really is. No Eagles.

Shawn Brody is a former writer for Beyond the Box Score and BP Mets. He now works for the BP Stats team on PECOTA and other assorted projects, happy he gets to do research without the need to write about it. He lives with his wife in Austin, Texas.

Russell A. Carleton lives in Atlanta with his wife (who is awesome) and five kids. He is the author of the forthcoming book *The New Ballgame: The Not-So-Hidden Forces Shaping Baseball* from Triumph Books, available in June 2023.

Ben Carsley is a senior author at Baseball Prospectus. When he's not writing about baseball, Ben can be found cooking, drinking wine, making nihilistic puns and losing NFL parlays. By day, he manages a team of SEO analysts and content writers who are fairly convinced he's Ron Swanson.

Alex Chamberlain writes for FanGraphs sometimes. He likes pitching and other topics about which he is probably not well-suited to write. He supposes he is known for his Pitch Leaderboard, which he hopes has helped advance understanding and analysis of pitching. Mostly he is the always-tired father of a precocious two-year-old.

Justin Choi is a contributing writer at FanGraphs. When he's not thinking about baseball, he tries his best to be an acceptable college student. He finds that one is easier than the other.

Michael Clair writes for MLB.com and believes that no run expectancy chart could possibly capture the beauty and art of a finely placed sacrificial bunt. Follow him @michaelsclair or just around the Zumiez at the local mall.

Zach Crizer is a baseball writer at Yahoo Sports, and a former columnist for Baseball Prospectus. He lives in New York City.

Patrick Dubuque has served at Baseball Prospectus as writer, editor, and guy whose ideas seem like too much work since 2015. He lives in the Pacific Northwest with his wife Kjersten and his two children, who serve as the opposition party.

Daniel R. Epstein is an elementary special education teacher and union president in Central Jersey. He writes for Baseball Prospectus and Off the Bench Baseball. He also serves as Co-Director of the Internet Baseball Writers Association of America.

Noah Frank is a writer whose work used to appear at Baseball Prospectus. It still does, but it used to, too. He writes a newsletter called Pretty Good, which aspires to its name in quality.

Ken Funck has contributed to the Baseball Prospectus *Annual* each year since 2009, during which time saplings became trees, children blossomed into adults and baseball analytics grew from nerdy outsider subculture to core organizational competency. Ken lives outside Madison, Wisconsin in a tidy home decorated in the Midwest Nice style alongside his wife Stephanie, an ideal travel companion and the worst choice to participate in any focus group.

Megan Gailey is a comedian and writer living in Los Angeles, CA.

Mike Gianella is a senior fantasy baseball writer at Baseball Prospectus. He lives in suburban Philadelphia with his wife, two awesome children, and three cats. He's still a Mets fan, for some stupid reason.

Steven Goldman, former BP editor-in-chief and current consulting editor, edited, co-edited and contributed to multiple volumes of this book and was also responsible for BP's books *Mind Game*, *It Ain't Over 'Til It's Over*, and *Extra Innings: More Baseball Between the Numbers*. He's also the author of the Casey Stengel biography *Forging Genius* and *Baseball's Brief Lives: Player Stories Inspired by the Infinite Inning*, presented by BP. His work has appeared in numerous other places ranging from Deadspin to The Daily Beast. He's the host of the long-running Infinite Inning podcast, which sits at the crossroads of baseball, history, politics, and culture. All of the above originates from New Jersey, where he resides with his wife, son, occasionally his daughter, two cats, and an unmanageable number of books, the mass of which has only grown since the last edition.

Craig Goldstein is the editor-in-chief of Baseball Prospectus. His work has appeared in Sports Illustrated, Vice Sports, Fox Sports MLB/JABO and SB Nation MLB. He lives in Maryland, where he spends just the right amount of time not being remotely normal, and bless him for it.

Nathan Graham is a member of the Baseball Prospectus prospect team, specifically covering the Midwest League. In his free time, he enjoys spending time with his 80-grade cat, Nugget, and his fringe-average family.

Bryan Grosnick is an author of Baseball Prospectus and has consulted for an MLB franchise. This is his ninth consecutive appearance in the *Annual*, for which he is extremely thankful. He lives in New England with his dazzling and brilliant wife, two outstanding sons, and—as of this book's publication—a player to be named later.

Jon Hegglund lives in an alternate universe where Aaron Judge and Carlos Correa lead the 2025 San Francisco Giants to a Wild Card spot and subsequent heartbreaking Division Series exit against the Cardinals. He is a ghost that haunts the hallways of the fantasy offices at BP.

Tim Jackson is a writer and educator. He spent his summer Sundays at Veterans Stadium with his aunt and four brothers, where the Phillies taught him that winning isn't everything.

Sarah James is a historical fiction author currently living in Los Angeles. Her debut novel *The Woman with Two Shadows* came out in 2022, and her second book *Last Night at the Hollywood Canteen* is forthcoming from Sourcebooks. Everything she knows about baseball, she learned from the 1949 Gene Kelly/Frank Sinatra film *Take Me Out to the Ball Game*.

Jonathan Judge is a lawyer who also designs statistics and models for Baseball Prospectus. He believes in hierarchical (modeling) structures, full paragraph justification, and two spaces between sentences. *[We did not leave this in for him. -ed.]*

Justin Klugh is a writer and contributor to Baseball Prospectus. His work has also appeared in the Philadelphia Inquirer, Baltimore Magazine, FanGraphs, and SB Nation MLB. He currently hosts the podcast, "The Dirty Inning," a theatrical retelling of the dumbest innings in Phillies history.

Kennedi Landry covers the Texas Rangers for MLB.com. She was born and raised in New Orleans before attending LSU for college and continuing her lifelong fandom of all Tigers sports. When not at the ballpark, she enjoys good books, good wine, good music and laying by her apartment complex pool.

Rob Mains is a writer at Baseball Prospectus, where his career in finance is distressingly handy in discussing the game today. He lives in a redoubt in upstate New York, surrounded by Finger Lakes wine, waging a lonely battle to preserve the Chicago Manual of Style usage of the word only. He has never played Wordle.

Tim Marchman is a features editor at Motherboard. He lives in Philadelphia, surrounded by hiking equipment and old periodicals.

Allison McCague is a geneticist and science policy professional living in Washington DC, but holding steadfastly to her hometown roots by keeping at least a dozen New Jersey bagels in Ziploc bags in her freezer at any given time. She is also a writer and podcaster at Amazin' Avenue, the Mets' SB Nation community; her baseball writing has also appeared in Baseball Prospectus and FanGraphs. Her favorite things include craft breweries, Earl Grey tea, running, books and Gary Cohen saying "Oh wow!"

Whitney McIntosh is a baseball editor whose work has appeared in The Guardian, Racquet Magazine, and for a few years SB Nation MLB. She lives in New York City, where she is trying to figure out how many public places you can wear a neon Padres City Connect jersey while still following the dress code, and is recovering from a stressful autumn contemplating Rafael Devers' free agency.

Kelsey McKinney is a writer and co-owner at Defector Media where she also hosts the podcast Normal Gossip. Her first book, *God Spare The Girls* was published in 2021, and she is always, always keeping boxscore in pen like an idiot.

Andrew Mearns is the managing editor of Pinstripe Alley, the Yankees' SB Nation blog, where he first started writing in 2012. He also previously wrote for Cut4 at MLB.com, where he hopes his tribute to the glory of batdogs will never get lost in the digital ether (long live Rookie). He will never stop loving Robinson Canó, Andrew McCutchen, or Masahiro Tanaka.

Sam Miller is a former Editor-in-Chief of Baseball Prospectus.

Dan Moore is a writer and editor based in the Bay Area. He's a contributor to The Ringer, the San Francisco Chronicle, and Oaklandside Magazine. His essay, "What Do Cities Lose When They Lose Pro Sports" was a Pocket "Best of 2022" selection.

Leo Morgenstern is a contributing writer at FanGraphs and an editor at Just Baseball Media. His Phillies coverage has appeared on all corners of the internet. He also writes for the Canadian satire website The Beaverton, where his pitches about the Blue Jays all sharing one really big hat keep getting rejected for some reason.

Blake Murphy is a Toronto-based writer and sports radio host, most relevantly the host of the national Toronto Blue Jays analysis show "Jays Talk Plus" (JT+). As the show title suggests, Blake endeavors for all of his work to approximate league average. If Eric Hinske is reading this, let's talk tattoos and Pantera.

Santul Nerkar is an editor and reporter at FiveThirtyEight. He lives in New York City.

Marc Normandin writes on baseball's labor issues and more at marcnormandin.com, which you can read for free but support through his Patreon. He writes regularly for Baseball Prospectus, and his other baseball work has appeared at SB Nation, Defector, Deadspin, Sports Illustrated, ESPN, Sports on Earth, The Guardian, The Nation, FAIR, TalkPoverty, and other places, too, but please don't make him remember how long he's been doing this. You can also read his takes on video games at Retro XP and Paste Magazine.

Dustin Nosler is one of the co-founders of Dodgers Digest. His work has also appeared at The Hardball Times and SB Nation. He resides in Stockton, CA with his wife and their horde of cats and dogs.

Robert O'Connell writes about basketball for the Wall Street Journal. Previously, he covered sports for Defector, Sports Illustrated, The New York Times, The Atlantic and other outlets.

Robert Orr is a baseball nerd in Philadelphia by way of Virginia Tech. In his free time, he (mostly) enjoys the local nine and procrastinating before stressing out to meet deadlines.

Jeffrey Paternostro is the Lead Prospect Writer and Multimedia Production Manager for Baseball Prospectus. He has written and podcasted for Baseball Prospectus since 2015. He now drives up and down I-15 among these ridiculous mountains with a weird flavored soda in the cupholder and '70s Japanese jazz fusion on the speakers.

Harry Pavlidis is the Director of R&D at Baseball Prospectus.

Amy Pircher is a software designer for NASA JPL by day and Baseball Prospectus by night. Her cats think she should do neither.

Kate Preusser is a contributor at Baseball Prospectus and editor-in-chief at SB Nation's Lookout Landing, where she writes about the Mariners and spends too much time considering the hip-size-to-power ratio of Dylan Moore.

Jeff Quinton is a procurement professional who lives and works in his home state of New Jersey. His hobbies include cooking, grocery shopping, spending time with his wife and son, going to the shore, and being from central Jersey.

Tommy Rancel a.k.a. Pen Griffey Jr has previously written for ESPN, The Athletic, FanGraphs and the Baseball Prospectus Annual. He lives in the Tampa Bay area with his wife Jamie and their five children.

David Roth is a co-founder and co-owner at Defector.com, and the co-host of the podcasts The Distraction, which is mostly about sports, and It's Christmastown, which is entirely about Hallmark movies. His writing has appeared in New York, The New Yorker, The New Republic, and The Baffler.

Shaker Samman is a writer based in Los Angeles. His work has previously appeared in Sports Illustrated, The Ringer, The Guardian, and Slate, and was selected as part of The Year's Best Sports Writing 2022. His time at Baseball Prospectus was mostly spent googling the first 13 games of Chris Shelton's 2006 season, just to make sure they actually happened. Don't follow him on Twitter.

Ginny Searle is a writer and editor for Baseball Prospectus whose work has appeared in various outlets. She lives in Los Angeles, where her sleeping and eating habits concern friends and acquaintances alike.

Jarrett Seidler is the Senior Prospect Writer for Baseball Prospectus. He also co-hosts For All You Kids Out There, a weekly BP podcast which is occasionally about the Mets. As a lifelong New Jersey resident, he puts salt, pepper and ketchup on most breakfast sandwiches.

Ben Spanier is a graduate student in North Carolina who enjoys reading, listening to indie rock music and attending minor league baseball games during the few weeks of the year in which it is neither too hot nor too cold.

Alex Speier has covered the Red Sox for more than two decades, currently doing so for the Boston Globe. In his free time, he gets peppered with questions from a nine-year-old about the Hall of Fame worthiness of everyone from Shohei Ohtani to Juan Yepez.

Matt Sussman is an IT professional from Ohio who is the head drawmaster of the Bowling Green Curling Club and often tells Baseball Prospectus whenever former baseball players turn 50 years old.

Jon Tayler is an editor at FanGraphs and 11-time runner-up for People's Sexiest Man of the Year award. His work has appeared primarily there and in Sports Illustrated, and also the March 27, 1995 issue of The New Yorker, which he ghost-wrote in its entirety. He lives in New York City and will thank you not to make eye contact if you see or pass him in the street.

Lauren Theisen is a co-owner and a blog girl at Defector, where she writes about hockey prospects, pro wrestling pay-per-views, and everything in between.

Ted Walker works in development at Rice University in Houston, Texas. In the 2010s he co-wrote the baseball blog Pitchers & Poets with Eric Nusbaum. Today, he co-hosts the notebook and stationery podcast Take Note.

Eli Walsh is a reporter and contributes to Baseball Prospectus' prospect team with coverage of the California League's North Division. He lives in the San Francisco Bay Area and serves as BP's resident emo music scholar.

Collin Whitchurch is a senior editor at the Action Network, having fully embraced the fact that legal sports betting is consuming the world and all our lives (whether you like it or not). He lives in Austin, TX and spends most of his free time hate-watching movies you probably love and obsessing over video games he's too embarrassed to admit the names of here.

Tony Wolfe is a writer and communications specialist who has covered Major League Baseball for Red Reporter and FanGraphs, as well as high school and college sports for various newspapers in Ohio and West Virginia. He lives in Columbus, OH with his wife and a nice young man (dog) named Carl.

Acknowledgments

This book is dedicated to our friend Rob McQuown.

Thanks for the research, and for everything else.

Michael Ajeto: My dad, Cesar, who would get home from work and fall asleep watching Mariners baseball with me; Paul Sewald, for helping me feel like a kid watching baseball again; Craig Goldstein, Ginny Searle, Patrick Dubuque, and every other editor who have entertained my midnight Slack DMs and made my words prettier than they would have been otherwise.

Maitreyi Anantharaman: Tigers beat writers cover the team with rigor and curiosity, and their work informed this essay. Dan Dickerson, the voice of Tigers baseball, made the dreariest season a pleasure.

Lucas Apostoleris: Thanks to everyone in the BP Stats slack for being a great support system. In addition, I greatly appreciate the help of the editorial staff (Craig, Patrick, Robert, Ginny, and Ben) for fixing up all my words. Also, a particular thank you to Harry Pavlidis, whom I've worked with in some capacity or another for over a decade and is directly responsible for my involvement with BP. I owe him quite a lot.

Robert Au: Thank you to the human and feline members of my family for bringing me joy and love. To those of you who have departed, I miss you. Thanks again to everyone on the BP stats team for your camaraderie and hard work, to Kathy Woolner and Rob Mains for their patience and diligence, and to Craig Goldstein for inviting me to this crazy world in the first place.

Darius Austin: All those who have contributed to the depth charts in 2022: Rob Mains, Robert Au, Randy Holt, Derek Albin, Brian Duricy, Craig Goldstein, Tim McCullough & Kaz Yamazaki. The BP Fantasy team, including Tim Jackson & Mark Barry, for their inspiration, advice and hard work. The Bat Flips and Nerds team, an endlessly reliable source of daft takes and Wade Miley content: John McGee, Tom Pringle, Ben Carter, Russell Eassom, Rob Noverraz, Rachel Steinberg & Gavin Tramps.

Michael Baumann: To Kate White, without whose limitless off-the-field support I could accomplish nothing. To Craig Goldstein, who invited me back to the *Annual*. To Ryan O'Hanlon, Megan Schuster, and Ben Glicksman, the editors who made me the writer I am today. And to my current editor, Meg Rowley, who probably wishes they'd made me into a different writer.

Demetrius Bell: Patricia Bell, Garry Bell, Sheretha Bell, Deronne Floyd, Gaurav Vedak, Kris Willis, the entire team at Battery Power and everybody who's given my work a read, a click, or even just a passing glance.

Grant Brisbee: Craig Wright at SOU, who set me on this path. Rob Neyer, who taught me where "only" goes in a sentence. Jeff Sullivan, who taught me to look for the weird little nuggets. Marc Normandin, who taught me how the real world affects the sports world. Sam Miller, who asked for my first BP essay. Uh, this was a horrible idea, and I'm going to forget someone or run out of space, uh, Whitney McIntosh, Blez, Jon Bois, Lindsey Adler, Andy Baggarly, Melissa Lockard, dammit, Bryan Murphy, Brian Floyd, I'm so sorry that I omitted so many people, ugh.

Shawn Brody: Thank you to my wife, Grace, for your patience in tolerating my perpetually inconsistent schedule and incoherent rants. Thank you to my mom, dad, brother, friends, and family for all the support. Thank you to R.J. Anderson, Harry Pavlidis, Cory Frontin, and the rest of the BP Stats team for all the help and assistance in solving any problem.

Ben Carsley: The ever-patient Allyson Carsley, Bob, Bernadette and Elizabeth Carsley, Bret Sayre, Craig Goldstein, Sam Miller, Patrick Dubuque, Xander Bogaerts, Mary Donovan, Daniel Ohman and the C-4 Content Team.

Alex Chamberlain: Thank you, Remi, for everything that you are. May you forever be inquisitive and empathic and ridiculously silly and, most importantly, rid of Diseased

Baseball Brain. Thank you, Jill, for supporting my writing, even though it's never actually "just 20 more minutes." Thank you, Patrick Dubuque, for inviting me back this year to ruin another chapter. Thank you, Meg Rowley, for tolerating my frantic Slack messages and editing my painfully overwritten articles and overuse of adverbs and hyphens. Thank you, friends and readers—this paragraph wouldn't exist without you.

Justin Choi: I would first like to thank Ben Carsley, who guided me through my first time contributing to the *Annual* with patience and understanding. I'd also like to thank Meg Rowley, whose feedback and advice have pushed me to become a better and more mature writer. Lastly, much love goes out to Mom and Dad, who may not always understand what their son is doing on his laptop, but are unconditionally supportive nonetheless.

Michael Clair: Thanks much to the creative geniuses at BP, my colleagues at the MLB mothership for their guidance, support, and intelligence, and my amazing wife for unflagging support when it's time to talk about Willians Astudillo.

Zach Crizer: Craig Goldstein, R.J. Anderson, Hannah Keyser, Matthew Stein, Jason Catania, Jeff Gold, Steph Bauman, Scott and Amy.

Patrick Dubuque: To Kjersten, Sylvie and Felix, this year and all years.

Daniel R. Epstein: Thanks to Heather, Andrew, Sofia, Ronni and Ray, Theresa and Joe, the members of a very good band called The Subway Ghosts (Davy Andrews, Michael Clair, and Mike Petriello), Jonathan Becker and the IBWAA, Max Frankel and Sean Morash from Off the Bench Baseball, the NASA and RRBL Strat-O-Matic leagues, Luis Guillorme, I suppose J Shin, and especially Sydney Bergman for all her help with the Nationals comments and for not judging me too harshly for stalking Luke Voit's grandmother.

Noah Frank: I'd like to thank the city of Chicago for all it gave me as a young man trying to find my way in the world and in baseball. Thanks to Josh and Chris from Ivy & Coney, to the 2008 Cubs intern class, to the Loyola Chicago Law School Class of 2010, to Peter Chase for the opportunity, and to Jimmy Bank for the advice. Last but not least, thanks to the drunk woman with the southern drawl leaving the luxury suites who embraced me as I was carrying postgame notes up the ramp to the press box one sweltering, summer afternoon and whispered in my ear, "Goodbye. I love you."

Ken Funck: R.J. Anderson, Steph Bee, Ben Carsley, Patrick Dubuque, Aaron Gleeman, Steven Goldman, Craig Goldstein, Christina Kahrl, King Kaufman, Ben Lindbergh, Sam Miller, Robert O'Connell, John Perrotto, Bret Sayre, Ginny Searle, Cecilia Tan, Jason Wojciechowski and anyone else who has worked their editorial magic on my behalf.

Mike Gianella: My wife Colleen and children Lucy and Elliot. Bret Sayre, Tim Jackson and everyone on the awesome fantasy team at Baseball Prospectus. Alex Patton, Steve Gardner, Peter Kreutzer, Jeff Erickson, Eric Karabell, Tristan Cockcroft and so many others in the fantasy industry whose advice and contributions were instrumental along the way.

Steven Goldman: As always, immeasurable gratitude to Stefanie, Sarah, Clemens, Reuven, Eliane, Ilana, Andy, Rick, Cliff, Raven, and Charity for believing.

Craig Goldstein: Katherine and Charlie Pappas, Laurie Gross, Harvey Goldstein, Alexis Goldstein, Tony Pappas, Patrick Dubuque, Ben Carsley, Robert O'Connell, Ginny Searle, R.J. Anderson, Bret Sayre, Sam Miller, Jason Wojciechowski, Marc Normandin, Steven Goldman, Tim Jackson, Rob McQuown, Jacob Raim, Harry Pavlidis, Jeffrey Paternostro, Tom Gieryn, Robert Orr, Mikey Ajeto, Brian Menéndez, Jonathan Judge, Rob Mains, Jason Parks, Ben Lindbergh, the BP Prospect Team, Jarrett Seidler, Zach Mortimer, Tucker Blair, Ethan Purser, Mike Ferrin, Tommy Rancel, Michael Baumann, Meg Rowley, James Fegan, Emma Baccellieri, Shakeia Taylor, Mauricio Rubio, Zach Crizer, Robert Au.

Nathan Graham: Thanks to my wife, Emily, for running the show while I spend time at various Rust Belt minor league stadiums. Thanks, Mom and Dad, for the constant encouragement, even if you're not sure what I do. Thanks to Jeffrey, Jarrett, and the rest of the prospect team for putting together top-notch minor league coverage. Finally, thanks to all the scouts, team personnel, and front office staff for letting me pick your brains and helping me along the way.

Bryan Grosnick: Sarah Grosnick, Luke Grosnick, Miles Grosnick, Phil and Debbie Grosnick, Craig Goldstein, Bret Sayre, Ben Carsley, Nathaniel Stoltz, Ginny Searle, Patrick Dubuque, Jarrett Seidler, Jeffrey Paternostro, R.J. Anderson, Jason Wojciechowski, Sam Miller, the BP Stats team, and the data providers at Baseball Prospectus, FanGraphs, Baseball-Reference, Baseball Savant and Brooks Baseball.

Jon Hegglund: Thank you to the editors at Baseball Prospectus who have annually exercised questionable judgement and taste in their invitations for me to write for this august publication. Special thanks to Mikey Ajeto, who generously told me what to think about certain Mariners pitchers (all errors of fact, evaluation, and prose style are my own). As always, my family: Emily and Oscar (the humans), Ruthie and Louise (the cats), and Vinny (the dog).

Tim Jackson: Thank you to my wife and dog for their infinite patience and generous understanding of "a few more minutes."

Sarah James: Thanks to BP for this opportunity, to Tony Wirt for his feedback, and to Pirates Twitter. The community around our team almost makes up for...the team.

Justin Klugh: My thanks goes as always to my beautiful wife Aviva, for her endless support despite profound indifference to baseball. Also my parents, grandparents, and sisters for a lifelong love of the game, as well as Liz Roscher, Trevor Strunk, John Stolnis, Chris Jones, and Mike Robertson for the extra eyes and ears they're always willing to give my work.

Kennedi Landry: Thanks to my best friend, Madison, who I don't think has ever read a single baseball story I've written, but will always click on it for the engagement. Thanks to my parents, who actually do read everything, and to my boyfriend Joey for listening to my endless Texas Rangers rants despite being a Mets fan. Thanks to Nana and Paige in the "Taylor Swift for Rangers GM" group chat for keeping me sane with jokes, memes and group facetimes. Most of all, thanks to my grandmother, who passed away while I was writing the draft for this and was my biggest supporter. She would have loved to have a print copy of the book to show anybody and everybody that came to the house.

Rob Mains: My mother, Rhoda Mains, for instilling a love of the game, and my wife, Amy Durland, for encouraging me to pursue it and often not regretting having done so. Martín Alonso, José Hernández, Marco Gámez, Pepe Latorre, and Fernando Battaglini for making BP en español, our daily Spanish-language content, a reality. Craig Goldstein, Ginny Searle, and Marc Normandin for putting up with my overuse of charts and tables. AM and PM for who they are.

Tim Marchman: Julia Marchman, Firebolt, Oliver, and River.

Allison McCague: Thank you, Dad, for cursing/blessing me with my deep, passionate love of baseball and my Mets fandom. Thank you, Mom and Ryan, for putting up with it and always cheering me on in everything that I do. Thank you to all the folks at Baseball Prospectus, particularly Jeff Paternostro and Jarrett Seidler for their friendship, wisdom, and late-night chats on various messaging platforms. Thank you to the beautiful "chatters" and all my baseball Twitter friends; you are truly the best. Thank you to my inimitable A Pod of Their Own co-hosts Linda Surovich, Maggie Wiggin, and Kellyanne Healey and to our "podcast dad" Brian Salvatore for always being in our corner and editing my on-air rants down to a reasonable volume. I am immensely grateful for the support and generosity of all our APOTO friends for continuing to listen to our words and supporting the Dollars for Dingers fundraiser every fall; it means so much to me. There are not enough words in this book or any book to articulate my gratitude for the Amazin' Avenue community, through which I have found boundless baseball knowledge, support, friendship, love, and my partner of three and a half years. Thank you Michael for doing laundry and taxes with me—and also watching the Mets.

Whitney McIntosh: Thank you to the multiple people who had to listen to me process the 2023 Twins roster—including my fiancé Patrick Monahan, which was probably a nice break from me trying and failing to process the 2023 Red Sox roster. Thank you also to the Criterion Channel for giving me an unending supply of 1940s noir films to use as writing background noise.

Andrew Mearns: Ali Mearns, Koozie & Piccolo, Cindy & Clay Hansen, Nick Oristian, Kunj Shah, Tanya Anderson, Greg Kirkland, the Matts (Provenzano & Ferenchick), the ol' Cut4 family, Jake Devin, Madison Pavich, and the rest of the terrific PSA writing staff (who keep the lights on as Aaron Judge does his best to break the ones at Yankee Stadium). And to George Mearns, whose love of Thurman Munson provided the original inspiration for it all.

Dan Moore: My essay in this book would likely not exist without my editors at The Ringer, the SF Chronicle, and Oaklandside Magazine—Riley McAtee, Christina Kahrl, and Tasneem Raja, respectively—who each gave me the space to go deep in my reporting on the A's. More generally, my writing would absolutely not be possible were it not for my wife, Alex, who is as supportive as she is inspiring and strong, or my parents, Jeannie and Ken Moore, who not only encouraged my love of words, as a kid, but shuttled me to and fro an unknowable number of baseball games and tournaments, inculcating within me a lifelong love for "The Sunshine Game." I'm indebted to you all.

Leo Morgenstern: Thank you to my very first editors at The Strand, my current editors at FanGraphs and everyone who took a chance on my writing in between. Thank you to David T. for teaching me how to get my foot in the door, and thanks to the team at Baseball Prospectus for opening that door and inviting me into this wonderful book. Special thanks go out to the prospect writers here at BP, from whom I've learned so much about the Phillies system. Finally, thank you to my family for supporting my writing aspirations from the very beginning, and thank you to my partner Emma for watching countless hours of Phillies baseball with me and propping me up when the writer's block gets to be too much.

Blake Murphy: The fine deranged people of Blue Jays Twitter, and the litany of BP analysts I've brought on my show to smarten up the conversations.

Santul Nerkar: FanGraphs.com, Baseball-Reference.com.

Marc Normandin: Thanks to my friends and family for their support both this year and in others. I'd also like to curse my enemies and assume everyone knows which of these groups they belong to.

Dustin Nosler: My wife, my Dodgers Digest cohorts—Cody Bashore, Daniel Brim, Alex Campos, A.J. Gonzalez, Shane Mittleman, Chad Moriyama, Josh Thomas, Stacie Wheeler, Allan Yamashige—as well as Justin Lorber, Molly Knight, Eric Stephen and Jon Weisman.

Robert O'Connell: Thank you to the entire BP team behind this massive and splendid undertaking. A particularly grateful hat-tip to Craig Goldstein and Patrick Dubuque, whose stewardship keeps the book what it is, and my co-editors Ben Carsley and Ginny Searle, whose vast reserves of brilliance, insight and patience I drew on on a daily basis.

Robert Orr: Thank you to the fine folks at FanGraphs, Baseball-Reference, Baseball Savant, and PitchInfo for their wonderful tools; also, I feel obligated to thank my editors for putting up with my BS.

Jeffrey Paternostro: Jess and Evelyn, for making anywhere we go home. Jarrett, for finally acknowledging his home is in Central Jersey. Craig, for the gchats, never hangouts. The Prospect Team, for always picking up the slack. And all the other Slacks, discords, and Group DMs with every-changing names based on who put a typo in the chat.

Harry Pavlidis: Martín Alonso, Robert Au, Jonathan Judge, Sean O'Rourke, Shawn Brody, Amy Pircher.

Jeff Quinton: Jacqueline Arce-Quinton, Bobby Quinton, Daniel Kahneman, Amos Tversky, James McMurtry, Ben Carsley, Craig Goldstein, and Bret Sayre.

Tommy Rancel: Jamie, Alexis, Vincent, Jarek, Brooklyn, Dakota, Rebecca Basse, Carlos Alvarez, R.J. Anderson, Erik Hahmann, Craig Goldstein, Keith Law, Chris Crawford, Randy Lemery, Charles Saul, Aubrey Graham, Camron Santo, Nick Turturro, Bun from the Bayou, Joel Peralta, James Shields, Luis Diaz, Peter Rosenberg, Billy June and Roman Reigns.

David Roth: I would like to thank my wife, friends, family, co-workers at Defector, and fellow members of The Mentally Ill Mets Fans DM for being patient with me, helping me refine my thoughts about the Mets, and for helping me remain the normal man that I am.

Shaker Samman: Shoutout to Craig Goldstein, Patrick Dubuque, and Ginny Searle for once again saving me from myself, to A.J. Preller for building an exciting team in America's least exciting city, to the two dogs wailing like banshees throughout my attempts to finish writing this essay, and to Lani Kim, who did her best to corral them.

Ginny Searle: To Tori, for everything under the sun; to Ken, Rae, Nicole and Em, for strength; to Mom and Dad, for being there; to Ben Carsley, Robert O'Connell, Patrick Dubuque, Craig Goldstein, Marc Normandin, Steven Goldman and Rob Mains, for helping me stay sane through publication; to everything that roars back again in spring.

Jarrett Seidler: To Kate, who I never want to stop going to Alanis concerts with.

Ben Spanier: I would like to thank my friends and family for listening to my meandering thoughts on baseball prospects, and my bosses at the website for assigning me just enough work to get my name in the book.

Matt Sussman: To Max, Mom, Lauren, Rachel, my curling club, and my family—all for getting me through a really tough year. My divorce lawyer helped too.

Jon Tayler: Thank you to Kristin, the girls, Rachel, Barkley B. Cooltimes, the Wedding chat, and all the other people who made me smile and laugh this year. Thanks for everything, dad.

Lauren Theisen: Clete Thomas.

Ted Walker: I'm grateful for the support and inspiration of my wife, Caroline; my mom, Mary; and my friend, Adam.

Eli Walsh: Special thanks to my wife, Sam; my parents, Prov and Rory, for their boundless support; and to my BP colleagues, whose talent and creativity consistently drives me to improve my own work.

Collin Whitchurch: I would like to thank my fiancée, Jess, for accepting the fact that most of our evenings will be spent sitting on the couch watching baseball games she doesn't care about. I would like to thank my parents for buying the *Annual* every year despite probably never opening the book beyond looking for my name in it. I would like to thank Craig for not shunning me from continuing to contribute to this amazing book even when I left BP for the dark side. I would like to thank Sandy Alcantara for making me look smart by winning the NL Cy Young award.

Tony Wolfe: I'd like to thank the BP editors, whose second request to contribute to the *Annual* was as much of a pleasant shock as their first; my wife, Taylor, who was supportive when I took occasional breaks from wedding planning to contribute to this book; and Jordan Horrobin, a good friend whose Cardinals fandom finally served as a resource instead of a menace.

Index of Names

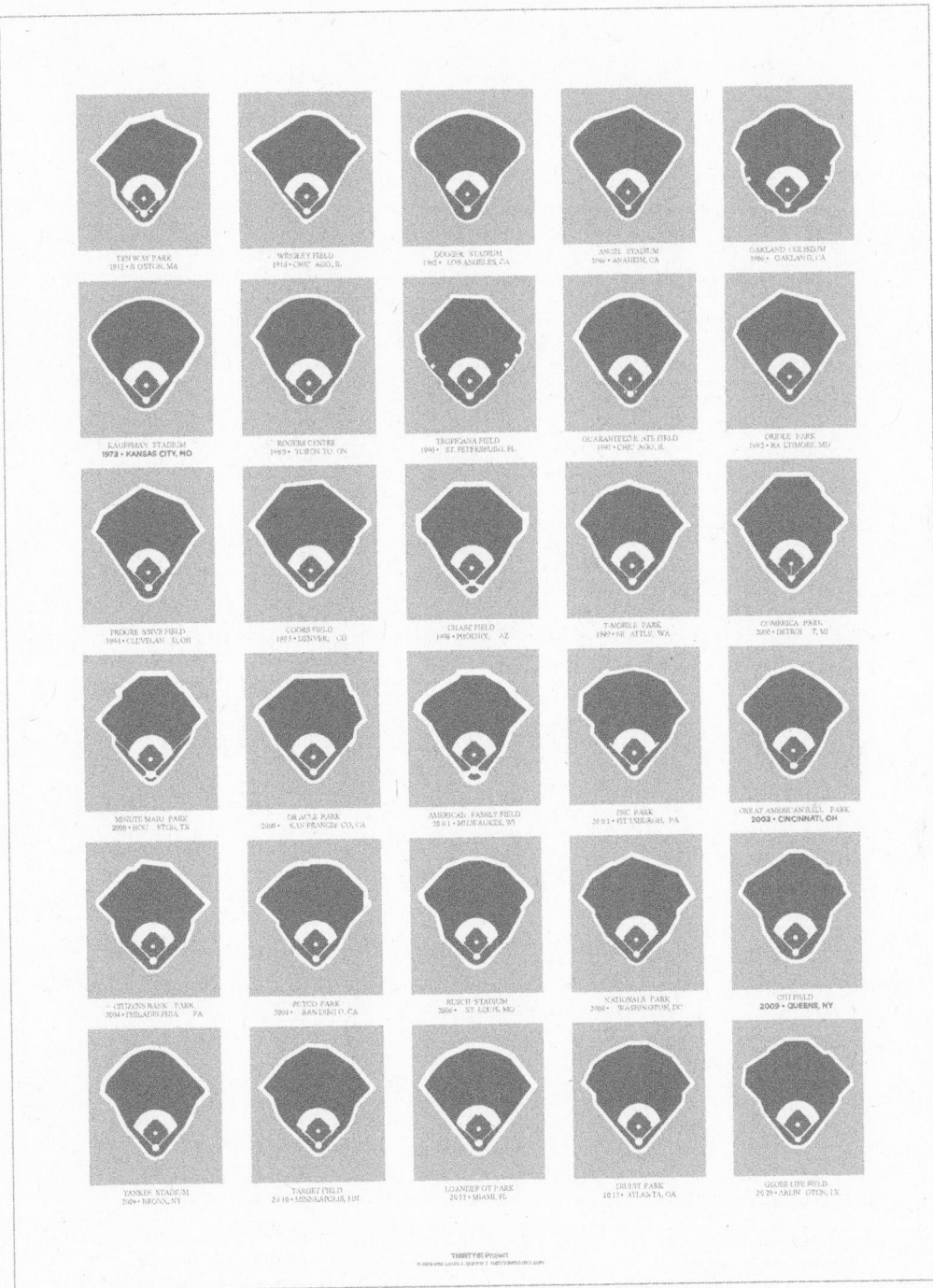